A Guide to Reviewing
Triumph of the American Nation

Complete and current, *Triumph of the American Nation* examines both the political and social history of the United States and the latest issues and events to affect the nation.

Use the list below as a convenient guide to reviewing *Triumph of the American Nation.* Page references provide examples of key features.

- **A special colorful supplement** (pages 1061–1076) with current photographs and illustrations covers the latest issues and events, including the 1988 election.
- **Eye-catching Unit Openers** (pages 442–443) include a full-page illustration, a unit outline composed of chapter and section titles, and an introduction that ties the illustration to the unit.
- **Colorful Chapter Openers** (pages 444–445) introduce main themes and provide students with a "Reading Focus."
- **Clearly numbered Sections** break the narrative into manageable daily lessons (pages 445, 451, 453, 457, 461, and 464).
- **Concise Summaries,** with time lines, conclude chapters and highlight main ideas (page 484).
- **Section Reviews** (page 448), **Chapter Reviews** (page 469), and **Unit Reviews** (page 511) reinforce learning.
- **The complete skills program** includes a skills feature in each chapter from one of six categories: Reading About History (pages 437–438); Thinking about History (pages 54–55); Writing about History (page 89); Relating Geography and History (pages 26–27); Relating Economics and History (pages 78–79); and Interpreting the Visual Record (pages 181–182).
- **Critical-thinking skills** are continually reinforced through discussion questions in the **Section Reviews** (page 180) and **Chapter Reviews** (page 187).
- **Important history terms** are boldfaced and defined in context (page 4). The **Glossary** contains an entry for each boldfaced term with page references (page 1031).
- **The comprehensive map program** builds and reinforces valuable skills and serves as the core of the essential geography-history link. Maps include both standard and metric scales (page 33), a compass rose (page 13), and well-defined keys (page 51).
- Informative special features in every chapter complement and extend the narrative:

  American Profiles present brief biographical sketches of significant individuals in American history, including Benjamin Franklin (page 50), Clara Barton (page 421), Louis Brandeis (page 621), and Coretta Scott King (page 951).

  Americana discusses artistic and cultural elements of the American heritage, such as Hornbooks and Lessons (page 86), Southern Plantations (page 335), and The Statue of Liberty (page 945).

  Decisive Moments highlight turning points in history, such as England's Rise to Power (page 22), Protection of a Free Press (page 91), and Prohibition—A Timely Reform (page 746).

  This Changing Land integrates geographic and environmental issues with historical content (pages 73, 317, and 672).

- Documentary excerpts complement the textbook narrative:

  The Declaration of Independence (pages 130–134) and *The Constitution of The United States* (pages 189–219), both fully annotated, appear in the chapters where each is discussed.

  Sources highlight excerpts from notable documents and speeches (pages 34, 369, and 419).

- **A Reference Section** (pages 990–1057) contains supplementary information, such as colorful maps and graphs, a list of important events in American history that includes portraits of the Presidents, a Glossary with page references, and a comprehensive Index.

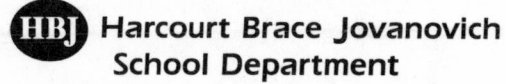

**HBJ Harcourt Brace Jovanovich
School Department**

Triumph of the American Nation

Featuring a special full-color supplement that covers the latest issues and events, including the 1988 presidential election!

Todd/Curti

Triumph of the American Nation

With 1990 Supplement

★ Comprehensive and current, **Triumph of the American Nation** examines the political and social history of the United States.

★ A functional design and logical lesson structure help students learn American history.

★ A highly practical format, with chronological and topical chapters, allows unmatched teaching flexibility.

★ A complete program of study aids assists students in reading, reviewing, and understanding content.

★ Detailed maps, charts, graphs, and special features link geography and history and help build study skills.

★ Special skills lessons in every chapter—covering six categories—develop and reinforce essential learning skills.

★ A lively narrative provides the vivid images and insights that students need to develop historical imagination.

★ High-interest special features and source readings complement the textbook and provide additional enrichment.

★ A comprehensive Reference Section reinforces content with colorful graphs, maps, and charts.

Practical organization helps students understand and master the basics of American history.

Outlines composed of chapter and section titles provide overviews of the units.

Brief introductions tie the illustrations to content.

Unit Openers feature eye-catching, full-color illustrations that spark student interest.

Clearly numbered sections break chapters into manageable daily lessons.

Chapter Openers indicate time span and the chronological or topical organization of chapters.

Chapter Introductions give students a focus for study.

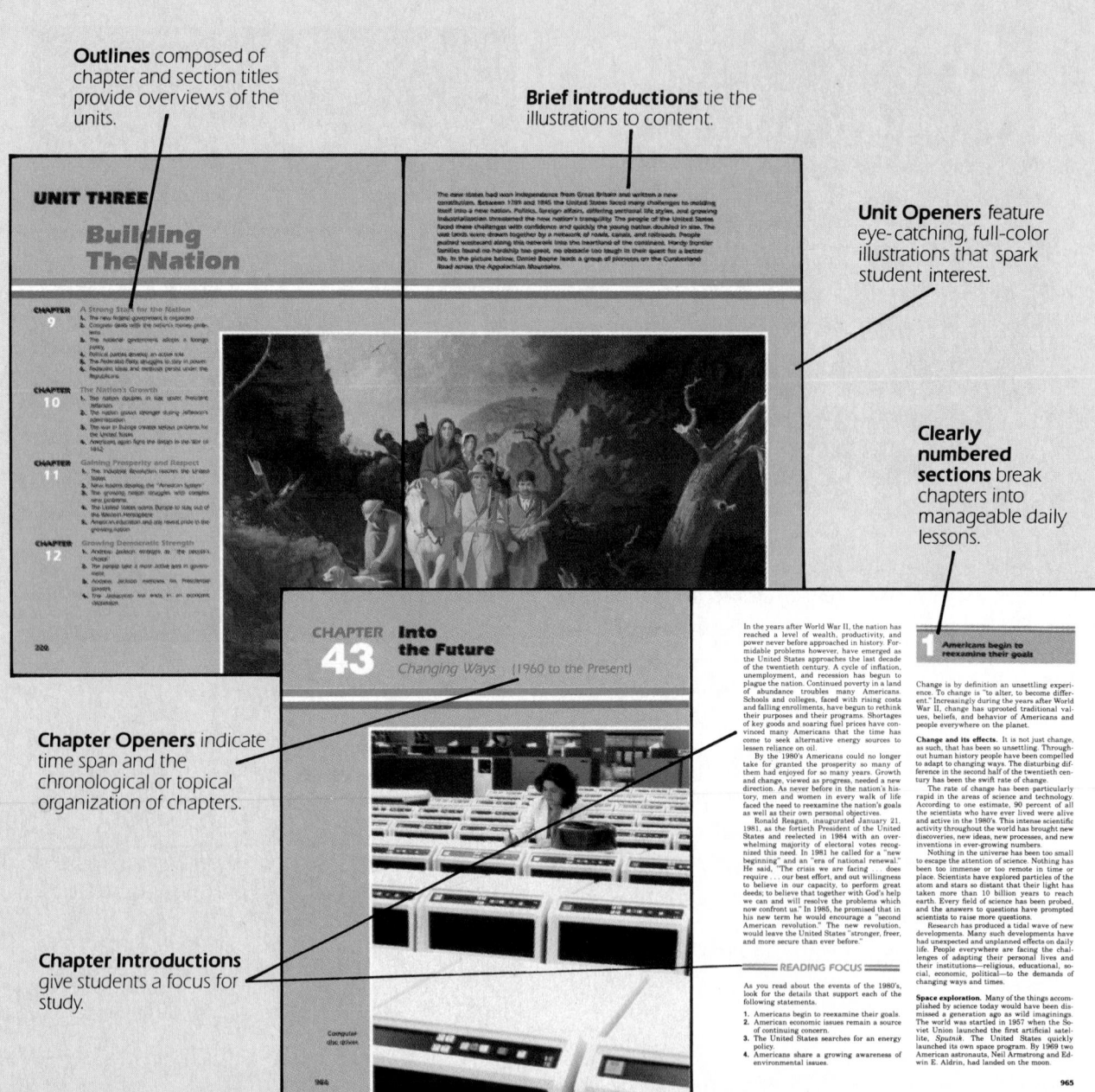

The logical lesson structure includes abundant study aids to facilitate learning and critical thinking.

troops from four Latin-American nations had arrived in Santo Domingo. Some of the United States troops were then withdrawn. In late August both sides accepted a provisional president who governed until elections were held in June 1966.

Crisis in Berlin. In Europe, too, Kennedy faced a challenge from the Soviet Union. In 1961 Soviet Premier Khrushchev renewed his threat to end the Western nations' rights of free access to West Berlin. Kennedy was not in turn that the United States would not abandon West Berlin.

In August 1961 the East German government began to erect a wall along the line between East and West Berlin. The Berlin Wall cut off the escape of East Germans into West Germany. It became a grim symbol of the conflicts between the Communist and anti-Communist nations of Europe.

The nuclear test ban. In August 1961 Premier Khrushchev also announced that the Soviet Union intended to resume nuclear testing. This news shocked people everywhere, for in 1958 the nuclear powers—the United States, Great Britain, and the Soviet Union—had agreed to suspend all testing for three years. The three-year period had not yet expired. President Kennedy warned that if the Soviets carried out their plans, the United States would be forced in the interests of its own defense to resume nuclear testing.

Nevertheless, the Soviets began a series of nuclear tests in the fall of 1961. The following spring, after the Soviet Union had turned down repeated pleas for a fully effective test ban and a general arms reduction, the United States began its own tests.

The first breaks in the long deadlock came in 1963. In June Moscow and Washington agreed on a **hot line** to provide direct teletype communication between the two capitals to help prevent nuclear war by accident.

In July American, British, and Soviet representatives agreed to ban nuclear tests in the atmosphere, under water, and in space. Underground testing would continue. The United States Senate ratified the agreement, and it went into effect in October 1963.

Communist China. The United States met its most difficult problems in Asia. There Communist China continued to threaten trouble in

much of Asia. In 1959 the Chinese Communists took over Tibet. In 1962, following a border dispute, they launched a large-scale attack on India. In response to appeals from the Indian government, the United States and Great Britain airlifted military supplies to the hard-pressed Indian troops. Then China announced a cease-fire and called for negotiations. India, shocked by what it considered unprovoked aggression, began to build up its defenses.

Conflict in Southeast Asia. In addition to China, the new countries of Southeast Asia—Laos, Cambodia, and North and South Vietnam—became major crisis areas during the troubled 1960's.

The tiny kingdom of Laos was divided into three political factions—pro-Western, Communist, and neutral. In a losing effort to secure a strong pro-Western government, the United States spent millions of dollars in Laos. Finally, in 1962, after lengthy negotiations a neutral government was agreed to in Laos.

The United States also aided Cambodia in an effort to secure a pro-Western government. As in Laos, however, the policy failed. In 1963 Cambodia asked the United States to withdraw its military and technical personnel. You will read about increasing American involvement in Cambodia and in South Vietnam in the following section.

SECTION REVIEW

Identify: Third World, Trade Expansion Act of 1962, Peace Corps, Congo crisis, Premier Khrushchev, Fidel Castro, Bay of Pigs invasion, quarantine, Berlin Wall, hot line

1. **Organizing Ideas:** (a) How did relationships among Communist nations change during the 1960's? (b) How did relationships among non-Communist nations change? (c) How did the rise of the Third World affect the foreign policy of both the United States and the Soviet Union?
2. **Summarizing Ideas:** The Cuban missile crisis brought the world to the brink of nuclear war in 1962. Explain.
3. **Comparing Ideas:** Review United States relations with Latin America in (a) the Alliance for Progress and (b) the Dominican crisis.
4. **Evaluating Ideas:** (a) What was United States policy toward Asia in the early 1960's? (b) How successful was that policy?

918

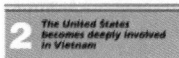

2 The United States becomes deeply involved in Vietnam

The most serious problem that the United States faced between 1960 and 1980 was a war in South Vietnam. This war had a great impact on the image of America around the world. It also influenced the way Americans perceived their own country and its role in the world.

Background to war. As you have read (page 836), when France pulled out of Vietnam in the 1950's, an international agreement divided that country into two parts. Elections that would have reunited the country, scheduled for 1956 were never held. Instead Vietnam continued to exist as two nations. North Vietnam, with its capital at Hanoi, was under a Communist government headed by Ho Chi Minh. South Vietnam, with its capital at Saigon, was a republic whose president was Ngo Dinh Diem (NOH DIN DYEM). Diem's government had strong backing from the United States.

Although the elections were not held, many Vietnamese still wanted a united country. Vietnamese guerrillas, backed by North Vietnam, fought to overthrow Diem's regime and unite the countries. In 1960 the guerrillas took the name of the National Liberation Front (NLF). Their opponents referred to them as the Viet Cong (Vietnamese Communists).

American involvement. The United States was deeply concerned over events in South Vietnam. Not long before, Communists had taken over China and had barely been beaten back in Korea. Now a Communist movement was gaining strength in South Vietnam.

President Eisenhower warned of the danger of a **domino effect** in Southeast Asia. He meant that if the government of one nation there fell to the Communists, then the government of the neighboring nation would topple in turn. According to this view, all of Southeast Asia might end up in Communist hands if one nation fell. To prevent the fall of South Vietnam to the Communists, millions of dollars in military aid and 800 United States military advisers were sent to South Vietnam during Eisenhower's administration.

Eisenhower's belief in a domino effect was shared by President Kennedy. Kennedy declared that United States foreign policy depended "in considerable measure upon a strong and free Vietnamese nation."

The formation of the NLF in 1960 was followed by increased guerrilla activity. In response, Kennedy increased the amount of military aid and the number of advisers to the threatened Diem regime.

The fall of Diem. However, Diem's administration was corrupt, and he became increasingly unpopular in South Vietnam. Diem repressed all political opponents. Also, his failure to control the NLF angered South Vietnamese military leaders. Kennedy pressured Diem to make reforms, but Diem failed to do so.

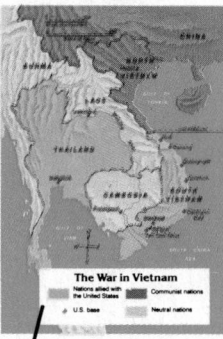

The War in Vietnam

Nations allied with the United States — Communist nations

★ U.S. base — Neutral nations

919

Important history terms are boldfaced and defined in context. The **Glossary** (not shown) contains an entry with page references for each boldfaced term.

Section Reviews develop critical thinking skills and check student recall and comprehension.

Full-color maps, charts, and graphs illustrate the narrative and build and reinforce basic history study skills.

Maps include both standard and metric scales, compass roses, and well-defined keys.

The complete program builds and reinforces essential skills.

The unique skills program provides a practical skill feature in every chapter and develops and reinforces skills in six categories:

- **Reading about History**
- **Thinking about History**
- **Writing about History**
- **Relating Geography and History**
- **Relating Economics and History**
- **Interpreting the Visual Record**

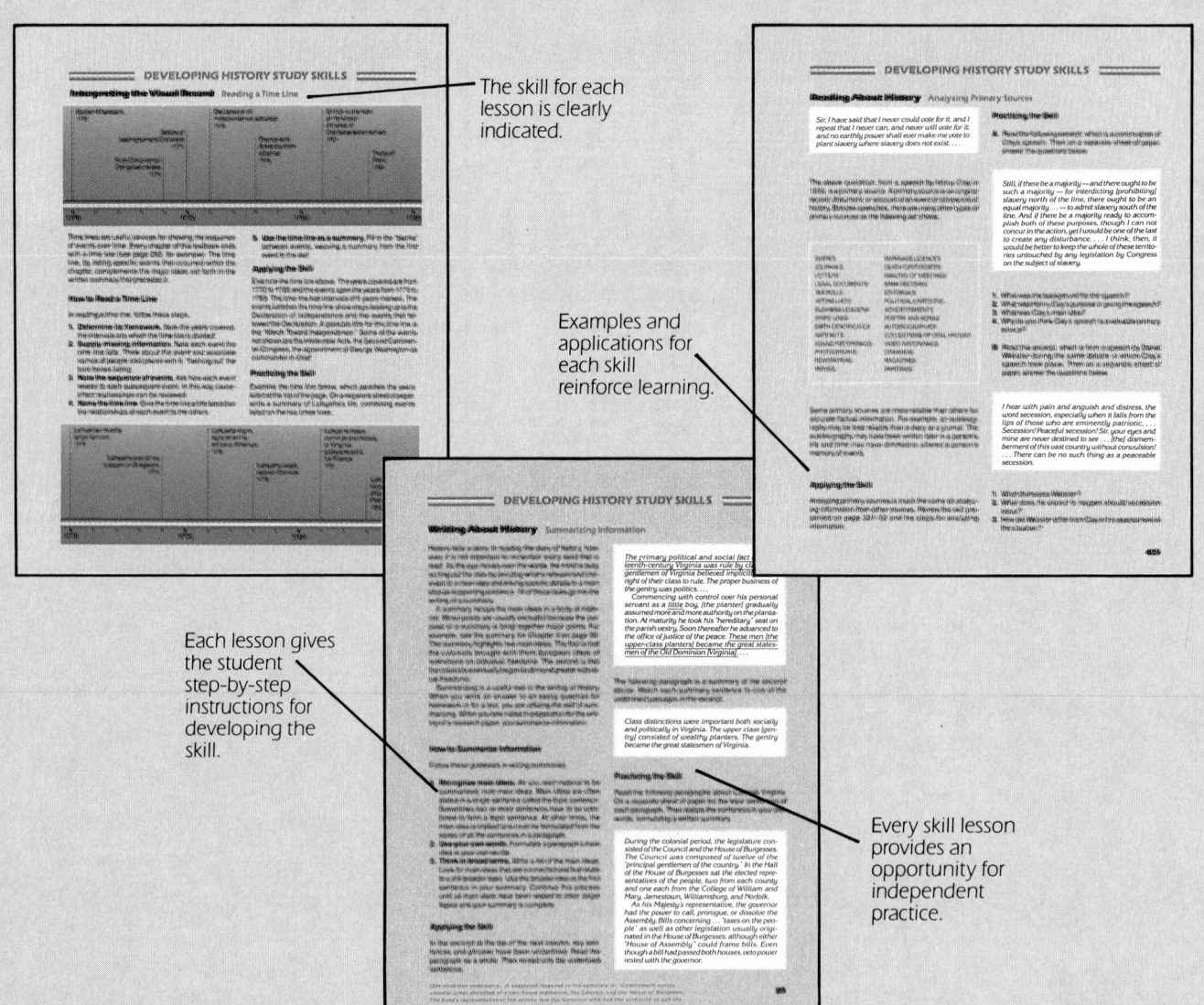

The skill for each lesson is clearly indicated.

Examples and applications for each skill reinforce learning.

Each lesson gives the student step-by-step instructions for developing the skill.

Every skill lesson provides an opportunity for independent practice.

Helpful summaries and ample review exercises provide additional reinforcement.

Practicing Critical Thinking Skills presents a variety of discussion questions. Boldfaced headings indicate the specific skill needed to answer questions.

Reviewing Important Terms asks students to apply new vocabulary in context.

Developing History Study Skills suggests additional activities to apply and practice skills.

A concise summary, complete with a time line, recaps each chapter and highlights main ideas.

Discussing Ideas reviews important information.

CHAPTER
3 SUMMARY

The settlers in the British colonies were European in language, dress, customs, and ways of thinking and acting. The settlers tried to reproduce in the New World the everyday ways of life with which they had been familiar in the Old World. Retaining their old ways of life, however, proved to be needless. Plunged, as they were, into a new and strange environment, the settlers had to change the material aspects of their lives—including houses, clothing, tools, and weapons. Slowly the ideas and practices from the Old World began to change.

The southern planters and the wealthy townspeople changed more slowly than the other colonial groups. Because their ties with England were so close, the planters and townspeople continued in some ways to be more English than they were American. The pioneer farmers and the people on the frontier changed much more rapidly. Because these people had so few ties with England, they became much more American than they were English.

Two other groups, the Native Americans and the blacks, played key roles in shaping colonial life. The contributions of the Indians, especially during the early years of settlement, were innumerable. The blacks' labor kept the southern economy going. Both these groups, however, were kept out of the mainstream of American life. Blacks were enslaved, and the Indians were treated as enemies. Thus the colonists planted the seeds of future conflicts. Only a few colonists were aware of the problems they were creating for future generations.

CONNECTING CHAPTER IDEAS

In the next chapter you will read about the influence of the emerging ideas and ideals of the colonists on the development of colonial schools, churches, and government. You will read about the beginnings of what in time was to become the American nation.

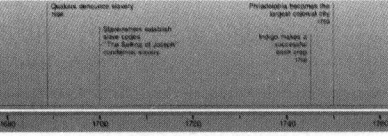

80

CHAPTER
3 REVIEW

Reviewing Important Terms

Decide whether each of the following sentences is true or false. If the sentence is false, replace the underlined term with the word or phrase that will make it true.

1. Rice was the chief cash crop in South Carolina.
2. The longhouse, a practical structure for forested country, was first built in the colonies by Swedish settlers.
3. As many as one third of the slaves sent to the New World did not survive the Middle Passage.
4. White supremacy set up strict rules for slave behavior which protected slaveowners against slave violence.
5. Most Eastern Woodland tribes were led by more than one sachem, each holding limited powers.
6. Many of the artisans who lived and worked on the plantations in the South were slaves.
7. The scarcity of tallow made the use of candles a luxury in the colonies.

Practicing Critical Thinking Skills

1. **Analyzing Ideas.** (a) Why were many of the colonial planters and merchants able to reproduce some of the familiar ways of life they had known in the Old World? (b) Why were pioneer farmers and frontiersmen unable to continue as many Old World ways as the planters and merchants?
2. **Evaluating Ideas.** The pioneers were cooperative as well as competitive. Does this statement contradict itself? Explain.
3. **Synthesizing Ideas.** Why do you think the colonists chose to establish their cities in the coastal regions? Use evidence from Chapters 1–3 to support your answer.
4. **Comparing Ideas.** Compare the experiences of black Americans and Indians in colonial America. (a) How were their experiences similar? (b) How were they different?
5. **Summarizing Ideas.** In what ways is the white settlers' treatment of blacks and Indians during the colonial period a dramatic example of the fact that America's past has shaped America's present?
6. **Relating Past to Present.** Do Americans today face the same problems that the colonists faced in learning to adapt to a new and changing environment? Explain.

Developing History Study Skills

1. **Using Economic Terms.** The pictures often provide evidence about the economic life of the colonies. Study the pictures in this chapter and then describe the differences in the lives of southern planters, townspeople, and pioneer farmers. Be sure to use such economic terms as cash crop, plantation, indigo, artisan, free enterprise, market, trading post, slave economy, and self-sufficient.
2. **Preparing a Report.** Investigate and prepare a report on an early African civilization, such as Ghana, Mali, Songhai, Ashanti, or Benin. Try to find out (a) where it was located, (c) what its accomplishments were, and (d) why it declined. In your report, include a map of Africa locating the civilization.

Relating Geography and History

Many factors contribute to the success of an enterprise such as a settlement. These factors include a favorable geographic location, natural resources, and available transportation. Another indication of the success of a settlement can be found in its population growth. Human resources are an important part of a successful community. Study the table of colonial population below and complete the following activities.

NEW ENGLAND COLONIAL POPULATION		
Colony	First Census	Fifth Census
Plymouth	102 (1620)	5,333 (1670)
Massachusetts	506 (1630)	39,752 (1680)
New Hampshire	500 (1630)	2,007 (1680)
Rhode Island	300 (1640)	4,224 (1690)
Connecticut	1,472 (1640)	21,645 (1690)

1. Make a bar graph to illustrate the information on the table. Draw the bars with different colors or patterns to represent the two figures for each colony.
2. (a) Rank the New England Colonies from the least populated to the most populated based on the results of the first census, (b) on the results of the fifth census.
3. Which New England colony experienced (a) the greatest growth? (b) the least growth?

81

Applying History Study Skills reinforces Developing History Study Skills by providing still more practice.

Relating Geography and History provides activities for applying geography skills to historical content. Most activities require use of Chapter or Reference Section maps and graphs.

Making Connections suggests additional projects and activities to enrich learning.

Reading in Depth lists books for further reading.

UNIT FIVE REVIEW

Discussing Ideas

1. Why did the Civil War happen? Give evidence to support your answer.
2. (a) What were the war aims of the North? (b) Had the North accomplished those aims by the end of the war?
3. Why did the North win the Civil War? Explain fully.
4. One result of the Civil War was the strengthening of democracy. Do you agree or disagree? Why?
5. How did the Civil War affect the lives of (a) women, (b) blacks, and (c) Indians?
6. In what ways are the American Revolution and the Civil War similar? (b) How are they different?
7. Do you think that the Civil War was another American Revolution in the sense that it was a major turning point in American history? Why or why not?

Applying History Study Skills

Analyzing Primary Sources. Just before the outbreak of war, William Howard Russell, a correspondent for the London Times, visited with Secretary of State William Seward in Washington. Read the following excerpts from Russell's diary and answer the questions below.

> Mr. Seward asserted that the Ministers of England or of France had no right to make any allusion to the civil war which appeared imminent, and that the southern commissioners who had been sent abroad could not be received by the government of any foreign power, officially or otherwise, ever to hand in a document or to make a representation, without incurring the risk of breaking off relations with the government of the United States. . . .
>
> Great Britain is in a pleasant condition. Mr. Seward is threatening us with war if we recognize the South, and the South declares that if we don't recognize their flag they will take it as an act of hostility Lord Lyons [the British minister to the United States] is pressed to give an assurance to the government at Washington that under no circumstances will Great Britain recognize the southern rebels; but at the same time Mr

> Seward refuses to give any assurance whatever that the right of neutrals will be respected in the impending struggle. . . .

(a) Why do you think the southern commissioners were sent abroad? (b) Why do you think Great Britain or France would have wished to support the Union? the Confederacy? Why might they have preferred to remain neutral? (c) What memories of the past might have caused the United States to oppose so vigorously foreign recognition of the Confederacy? (d) What did Russell mean by Britain's "pleasant condition"?

Making Connections

1. Write a newspaper account of (a) the Lincoln-Douglas debates, (b) "bleeding Kansas," or (c) the creation of the Confederate States of America.
2. Draw two political cartoons about the Dred Scott decision—one favoring the opinion and one opposing it.
3. Prepare a bulletin board display on a phase of the Civil War, including such items as pictures, maps, newspaper articles, and songs.

Reading in Depth

Catton, Bruce, Glory Road and Stillness at Appomatox (New York: Doubleday). Two of the numerous excellent histories on various aspects of the war written by this leading expert.

Commager, Henry Steele, America's Robert E. Lee (Boston: Houghton Mifflin). The story of the great Confederate general, his childhood, career at West Point, and his choice between the Union he served so well and the southern traditions he so deeply cherished.

Crane, Stephen, Red Badge of Courage (New York: Scholastic). A classic novel of the Civil War, told from the point of view of a young Union soldier.

Heidish, Macy, A Woman Called Moses: A Novel Based on the Life of Harriet Tubman (Boston: Houghton Mifflin). Marvelously moving and authentic in narration.

Pratt, Fletcher, The Civil War (Doubleday). The author explains the famous battles of the war and their significance, and also describes the colorful personalities on both sides.

441

High-interest special features complement and enrich the narrative.

American Profiles present brief biographical sketches of significant individuals in American history, including Benjamin Franklin, Clara Barton, and Coretta Scott King.

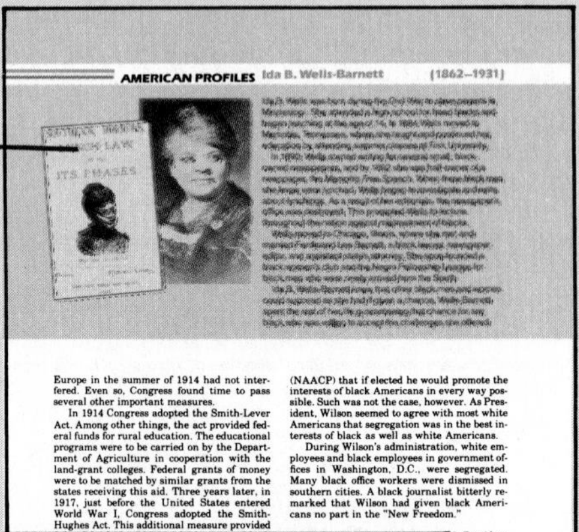

AMERICAN PROFILES Ida B. Wells-Barnett (1862–1931)

Europe in the summer of 1914 had not interfered. Even so, Congress found time to pass several other important measures.

In 1914 Congress adopted the Smith-Lever Act. Among other things, the act provided federal funds for rural education. The educational programs were to be carried on by the Department of Agriculture in cooperation with the land-grant colleges. Federal grants of money were to be matched by similar grants from the states receiving this aid. Three years later, in 1917, just before the United States entered World War I, Congress adopted the Smith-Hughes Act. This additional measure provided

(NAACP) that if elected he would promote the interests of black Americans in every way possible. Such was not the case, however. As President, Wilson seemed to agree with most white Americans that segregation was in the best interests of black as well as white Americans.

During Wilson's administration, white employees and black employees in government offices in Washington, D.C., were segregated. Many black office workers were dismissed in southern cities. A black journalist bitterly remarked that Wilson had given black Americans no part in the "New Freedom."

This Changing Land integrates in every unit geographic and environmental issues with historical content. Topics include "The Mighty Mississippi," "The Rise of Cities," and "Planet Earth and Beyond."

THIS CHANGING LAND The World's Ocean

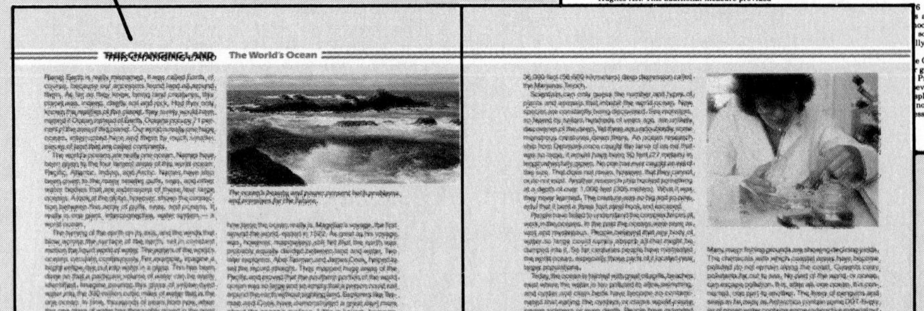

Sources provide excerpts from notable documents and speeches, including Patrick Henry's speech before the Virginia Convention, Franklin D. Roosevelt's "Four Freedoms" speech, and The Seneca Falls Declaration of Sentiments and Resolutions.

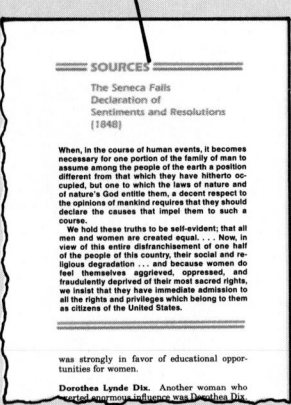

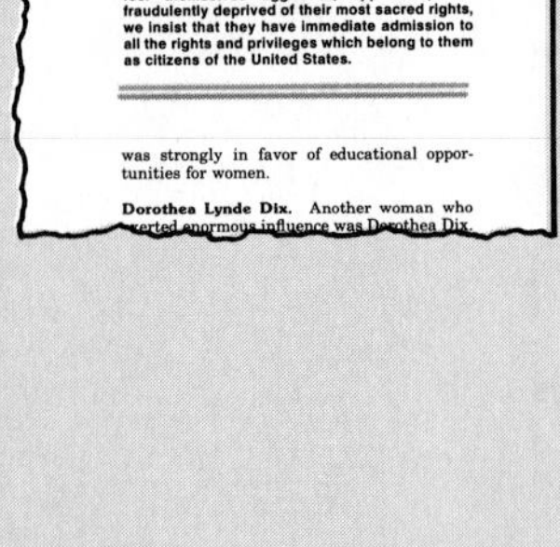

SOURCES

The Seneca Falls Declaration of Sentiments and Resolutions (1848)

When, in the course of human events, it becomes necessary for one portion of the family of man to assume among the people of the earth a position different from that which they have hitherto occupied, but one to which the laws of nature and of nature's God entitle them, a decent respect to the opinions of mankind requires that they should declare the causes that impel them to such a course.

We hold these truths to be self-evident; that all men and women are created equal. . . . Now, in view of this entire disfranchisement of one half of the people of this country, their social and religious degradation . . . and because women do feel themselves aggrieved, oppressed, and fraudulently deprived of their most sacred rights, we insist that they have immediate admission to all the rights and privileges which belong to them as citizens of the United States.

was strongly in favor of educational opportunities for women.

Dorothea Lynde Dix. Another woman who exerted enormous influence was Dorothea Dix

AMERICANA Baseball, The National Sport

dwellers in growing numbers were crowding into the ballparks to watch what would in time become one of America's favorite spectator sports.

Football, which evolved from the English game of rugby, also became increasingly popular. The first intercollegiate football contest, played between Rutgers and Princeton in 1869, had 25 players on each side. Within a few years, intercollegiate contests were being held in the West as well as in the East. Played mostly by college men, football in the early days was a rough-and-tumble game. It was so rough, in fact, that some people protested against its "brutality" and demanded its abolition. As the years passed, however, new rules of play were developed, and the game became better organized.

Basketball, which also became a typically American sport, was first played in 1892 by students at the Y.M.C.A. college in Springfield, Massachusetts. Its inventor, Dr. James Naismith, then an instructor in physical education, created the game to provide the same opportunities for recreation in the winter that baseball provided in the summer and football in the fall. Within just a few years, Naismith's game of basketball was being played all over the country.

The older rural forms of recreation—picnics, amateur baseball, horseshoe pitching—continued to enjoy popularity. Increasingly, however, the ways in which the people of the United States relaxed and amused themselves were being transformed in the new industrial age.

SECTION REVIEW

Identify: P. T. Barnum, Dr. James Naismith

1. **Analyzing Ideas:** (a) What was the Chautauqua movement? (b) Why was it important to rural dwellers?
2. **Interpreting Ideas:** How did city dwellers satisfy their growing interest in physical fitness?
3. **Summarizing Ideas:** What three major spectator sports developed in the late 1800's?

582

Americana discusses artistic and cultural elements of the American heritage, such as "Hornbooks and Lessons," "Southern Plantations," and "The Statue of Liberty."

Decisive Moments (not shown) highlights turning points in history, such as "England's Rise to Power," "Protection of a Free Press," and "Prohibition — A Timely Reform."

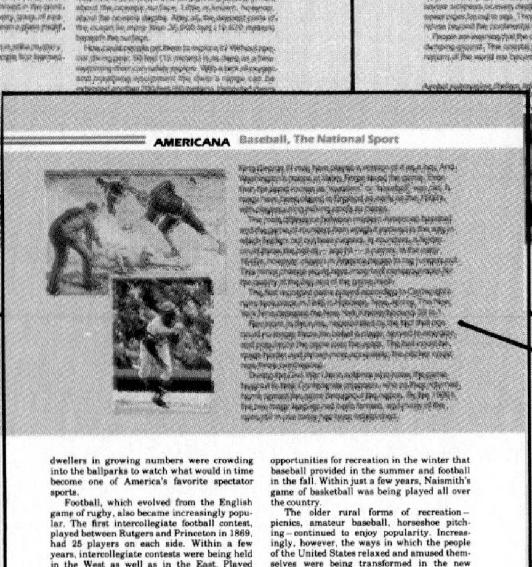

The Reference Section is packed with practical information!

Current information in the valuable **Reference Section** at the back of the textbook includes a variety of clear, full-color maps, charts, and graphs:

- Topographic, panoramic, and political maps of the United States;
- Charts detailing the United States government and the two-party system;
- Graphs illustrating population growth, family statistics, and increases in the Gross National Product.

The Reference Section also includes a **Glossary** of more than 450 history and social science terms and a comprehensive **Index.**

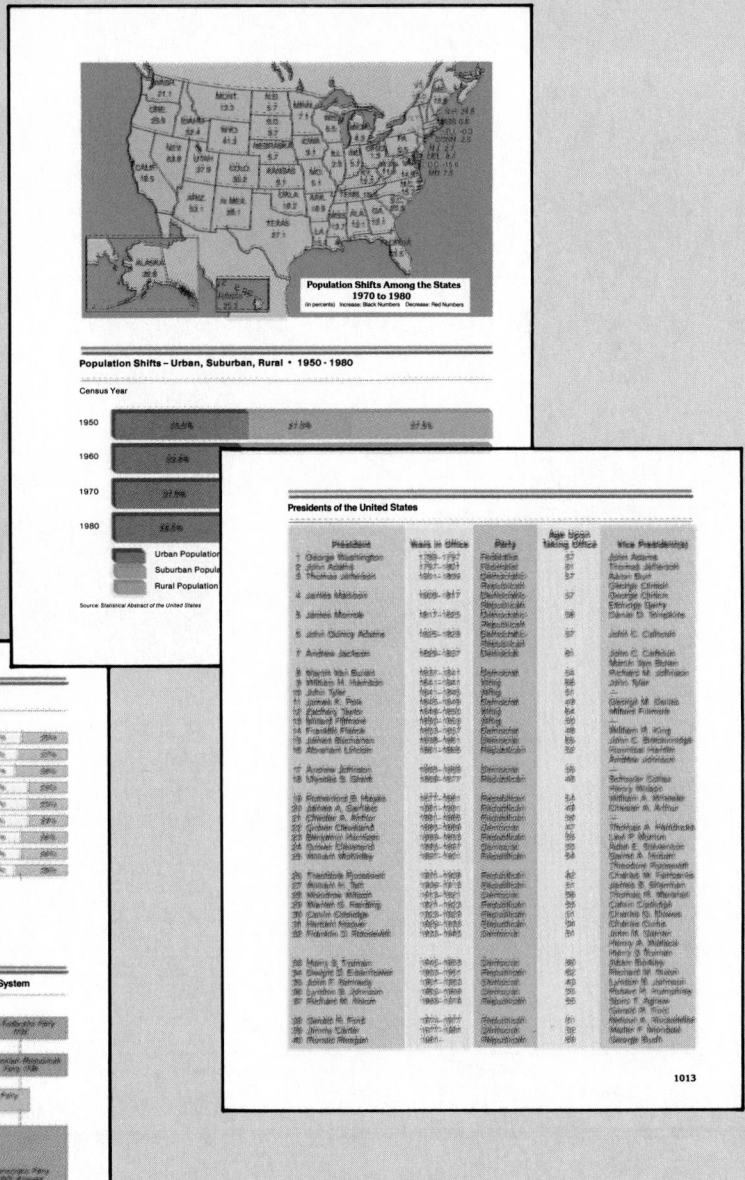

The Annotated Teacher's Edition provides answers and helpful suggestions for the busy teacher.

Underlined terms indicate new history vocabulary found in **Identify** exercises in **Section Reviews.**

Cross references to the Answer Key and Teacher's Manual indicate resources for additional information.

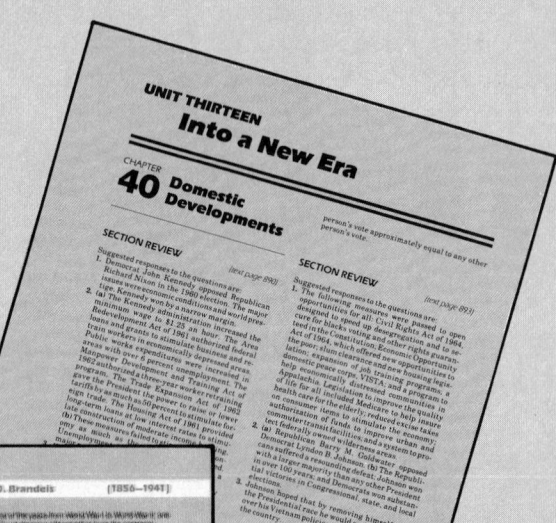

The Answer Key indicates suggested responses to all Section, Chapter, and Unit Reviews.

Annotations provide background information and suggest discussion topics, learning activities, and teaching strategies.

Coded symbols key annotations to specific points in the text.

Sample pages are reduced. Actual sizes are 8" x 10".

Additional components aid teaching, provide for testing, and offer enrichment.

Teacher's Manual and Resource Guide

The Teacher's Manual and Resource Guide contains a Teacher's Manual with appropriate learning objectives, valuable teaching suggestions, and extension activities. Also included are copying masters of 172 Enrichment Worksheets and chapter, unit, midterm, and final tests. Answers appear in an answer-key section.

Tests

The test booklet provides a two-page test for each chapter and unit and four-page midterm and final tests. All answers appear in the Answer Key of the Teacher's Manual and Resource Guide.

In addition, **The United States History Test Bank**—a breakthrough in testing—is a microcomputer software program that enables teachers to test precisely the content they want by selecting from a bank of test items. It also allows teachers to choose from hundreds of questions to create reproducible master copies of quizzes, chapter and unit tests, and midterm and final exams. A Teacher's Manual indicates the level of difficulty of each question and provides complete software instructions.

Workbook

The Workbook contains four worksheets per chapter for additional reinforcement and enrichment. A Workbook Teacher's Edition provides answers.

Sources in American History: A Book of Readings

This supplementary textbook contains 256 selected readings to extend and enrich the **Sources** features in **Triumph of the American Nation.** Selections from well-known authors and historic figures include "In Praise of American Democracy" by Alexis de Tocqueville, "A Pacifist Declares War," by Henry David Thoreau, and "Shaping the Presidency, 1984" by Theodore H. White. The fully illustrated source book provides **Reading Focus** and **Reading Review** questions for each selection. Answers to the Reading Review questions appear in the Answer Key of the Teacher's Manual and Resource Guide.

Annotated Teacher's Edition

With 1990 Supplement

TRIUMPH OF THE AMERICAN NATION

Lewis Paul Todd

Merle Curti

HBJ **Harcourt Brace Jovanovich, Publishers**
Orlando   San Diego   Chicago   Dallas

The Annotated Teacher's Edition of *TRIUMPH OF THE AMERICAN NATION* is complemented by the Teacher's Manual and Resource Guide. When used with the pupil's textbook, the ATE and TMRG provide a complete American History program.

An Annotated Teacher's Edition is not automatically included with each shipment of a classroom set of textbooks. However, an Annotated Teacher's Edition will be forwarded when requested by a teacher, an administrator, or a representative of Harcourt Brace Jovanovich, Inc.

A Teacher's Manual and Resource Guide is available for *TRIUMPH OF THE AMERICAN NATION*. For information, please contact your sales representative.

Note: Some of the material in this work previously appeared in RISE OF THE AMERICAN NATION, LIBERTY EDITION by Lewis Paul Todd and Merle Curti, copyright © 1982, 1977, 1972, 1969, 1966, 1964, 1961, copyright © 1950 by Harcourt Brace Jovanovich, Inc.; RISE OF THE AMERICAN NATION, LIBERTY EDITION, *Teacher's Manual and Resource Guide,* copyright © 1982 by Harcourt Brace Jovanovich, Inc.; and THE AMERICAN NATION—RECONSTRUCTION TO THE PRESENT *Annotated Teacher's Edition, Part I* by Lewis Paul Todd and Merle Curti, copyright © 1986 by Harcourt Brace Jovanovich, Inc.

Printed in the United States of America   ISBN 0-15-375951-8

ANSWER KEY CONTENTS

A Brief Introduction To The Annotated Teacher's Edition

OBJECTIVES OF THE TEXTBOOK

TRIUMPH OF THE AMERICAN NATION provides students and teachers with a comprehensive history of the United States. In telling this story, *TRIUMPH OF THE AMERICAN NATION* presents the past honestly and accurately. It describes the struggles and accomplishments of all Americans, including the diverse ethnic and minority groups who have made so many valuable contributions to our nation's history.

TRIUMPH OF THE AMERICAN NATION has two major goals. The first is to instruct and excite students about the nation's past. The second is to help students master those history study skills vital to a real understanding of America's historical development.

A Format That Teaches History

TRIUMPH OF THE AMERICAN NATION achieves the first goal through its clear organization and highly readable text. Believing strongly in the need to involve students in American history, the authors have written the text in a lively narrative style. To capture students' attention, each chapter begins with a short narrative that sets the scene for the chapter. (See text page 3 for an example.) This narrative leads students into the chapter itself, where anecdotes and primary source materials further enrich the text.

The authors have used a chronological approach to history. This allows students to see how ideas and events in the past have influenced ideas and events in the present. Most important, students learn how generations of Americans have struggled to realize the promises embodied in the Declaration of Independence and the Constitution of the United States. Interspersed throughout the textbook are special topical, or analytical, chapters. These chapters provide students and teachers with deeper insights into the forces influencing American history.

Finally, *TRIUMPH OF THE AMERICAN NATION* personalizes history through an emphasis on people—ordinary Americans as well as famous Americans. Throughout the text and in special features students learn about the diverse people who have come to make up our nation. They also discover how a set of common beliefs has united the American people—young and old, men and women, immigrants and minorities—for more than 200 years. Together these values and ideals form the basis of the American heritage.

Skills That Encourage Thought

The program's second goal is to help students develop and master basic history study skills. Each chapter in *TRIUMPH OF THE AMERICAN NATION* contains a one-page or two-page skill feature. These features lead students through key reading, writing, and critical thinking skills on a step-by-step basis. Each of the skills covered in the program is reinforced in the chapter and unit reviews.

ORGANIZATION OF THE PROGRAM

Special care has been taken to make the overall organization of *TRIUMPH OF THE AMERICAN NATION* consistent and easy to use for teachers and students alike. The textbook is divided into 13 chronological units. These units, in turn, are divided into chapters and sections. Study aids at the end of each unit, chapter, and section reinforce student comprehension. The Declaration of Independence, the Constitution of the United States, and a Reference Section—which includes maps, graphs, and charts—round out the student text. In addition, the textbook provides a variety of instructional aids to help teachers give their students an in-depth understanding of American history.

Unit and Chapter Organization

The text is divided in 13 units. To get students started, each unit begins with a special two-page "unit opener." This opener uses a short introduction, a dramatic picture, and a list of chapter and section titles to give students a quick preview of the unit ahead. Study aids at the end of each unit review the main ideas, reinforce history study skills, and provide opportunities for enrichment.

Within each unit, the text is divided into several chapters. A total of 43 chapters appears in *TRIUMPH OF THE AMERICAN NATION*. Each "chapter opener" includes a colorful picture, the chapter title, and chapter dates. On the opposite page is a short narrative account that sets the scene or offers a preview of the chapter contents. By examining the section titles listed under the heading entitled "Reading Focus," students become familiar with the scope of the chapter and the focus of each section.

Every chapter in *TRIUMPH OF THE AMERICAN NATION* is divided into sections. These sections are suitable as daily lessons in most American history classes. At the end of each section is a Section Review that provides a series of review questions to help students assess and interpret key facts and concepts.

Special Features

TRIUMPH OF THE AMERICAN NATION brings American history to life through the use of five types of special features—*American Profiles, Americana, This Changing Land, Decisive Moments,* and *Sources.*

Each chapter contains an *American Profiles* and an *Americana* feature. *American Profiles* are biographical sketches of ordinary as well as famous Americans. Through these sketches, students learn how people from many backgrounds have faced challenges to make outstanding contributions to American life. *Americana* features highlight cultural, technological, and social developments. These high-interest features complement the theme of the chapters in which they appear.

The student text includes 14 *This Changing Land* features and 23 *Decisive Moments* features. *This Changing Land* provides focus on geographical developments and helps students see the important relationship between geography and history. *Decisive Moments* describes pivotal events or decisions that have changed the course of American history.

Sources rounds out the extensive special features selections of *TRIUMPH OF THE AMERICAN NATION.* The 41 *Sources* are primary source excerpts that allow students to further examine certain events. These features supplement the extensive primary source material found within the text narrative and add interest, depth, and reinforcement to the narrative.

A complete listing of all the special features in *TRIUMPH OF THE AMERICAN NATION* may be found on pages xxii–xxv of the textbook.

Reference Section

Following Unit 13 is a handy Reference Section. The Reference Section is a valuable supplement to the maps, graphs, and charts in the text itself. It includes maps, charts, and graphs; a fact list on the 50 states; an illustrated history of the American flag; a chronology of key events with portraits of the nation's Presidents; a comprehensive Glossary; and a detailed Index.

Teacher Materials

Valuable teaching strategies and suggestions, as well as worksheets, tests, and teaching aids are located in the Teacher's Manual and Resource Guide — a separate component of the *TRIUMPH OF THE AMERICAN NATION* program. (For the teacher's convenience worksheets and tests are also available in a separate workbook and a test booklet.) The authors have also compiled a comprehensive selection of readings in *SOURCES IN AMERICAN HISTORY: A Book of Readings.* These readings from both primary and secondary sources are designed to enrich and extend the textbook. They have been selected with great care to offer a wide variety of materials that appeal to students.

OBJECTIVES OF THE ANNOTATED TEACHER'S EDITION

The Annotated Teacher's Edition (ATE) of *TRIUMPH OF THE AMERICAN NATION* is designed to help the teacher use the textbook more effectively. The ATE consists of two parts—an Answer Key bound into the front of the student text and blue annotations printed directly on the pupil pages.

How to Use the Answer Key

The Answer Key gives sample answers to the questions that appear in Section, Chapter, and Unit Reviews. These answers are only examples of possible student responses, and teachers should expect answers for most questions to vary according to students' perceptions of the question. The Answer Key does not always attempt to provide answers, however, to the more interpretive questions in the review exercises. Often, only brief examples of answers to these questions are given. Interpretive questions are designed to help students evaluate a topic or an idea, and student answers should be evaluated with this objective in mind. The teacher may find it useful to make selective assignments of these questions and activities, or to use them as a basis for a classroom discussion or activity.

How to Use the Annotations

The Annotated Teacher's Edition of *TRIUMPH OF THE AMERICAN NATION* contains annotations printed in blue directly on the pages of the student text. The annotations serve several functions. One such function is to provide background information for the teacher. Another function is to suggest class activities, map activities, writing activities, and discussion topics. Report topics that provide an opportunity for in-depth study of key points in the chapter are also listed.

Another function is to provide cross references to the textbook, to the Answer Key, and to the Teacher's Manual and Resource Guide (TMRG). For each section, an annotation lists the text page locations to the "Identify" items. Annotations also list the Answer Key location to the answers for the questions in each Section, Chapter, and Unit Review. Annotations are used to answer questions in captions and in the skill features. Still other annotations refer teachers to appropriate sections of the TMRG.

To help teachers match specific annotations to the text, a system of coding has been used. Whenever a symbol appears in front of an annotation, a similar symbol appears next to the student text where use of the annotation is appropriate.

TEACHER'S NOTES

ANSWER KEY

UNIT ONE

Building the Colonies

Exploring the Americas

SECTION REVIEW   *(text page 10)*

Annotations in the Teacher's Edition of the student text provide location references to the items included under "Identify."

Suggested responses to the questions are:
1. **(a)** The Mayas and Incas farmed. **(b)** The Aztecs also farmed, but they obtained much wealth from trading precious stones, cacao, gold, and silver; they were conquerors and harsh rulers.
2. **(a)** The Pueblos lived in a hot, dry environment, irrigated their lands to grow crops, and built homes with adobe. **(b)** The Plains Indians used buffalo to supply most needs; small bands hunted on the Great Plains in summer. The Plains Indians were independent, free people who chose leaders for valuable skills in the seminomadic life. **(c)** The Seed Gatherers' environment was mountainous, dry land west of the Great Plains. It was a hard environment that supplied mostly nuts, fruits, berries, and small game for food. **(d)** The Northwest Coast Indians formed permanent communities and obtained food from the sea and food, shelter, and other goods from the forests.
3. Answers will vary.

SECTION REVIEW   *(text page 14)*

Suggested responses to the questions are:
1. **(a)** Europeans wanted Asian goods they could not get elsewhere. They wanted Damascus steel for swords and armor; rugs, porcelain, and glass for their homes; and spices to flavor and preserve their foods. **(b)** New trade routes would decrease costs. The old routes were long and dangerous, and they were controlled by Italian traders who kept prices high.
2. Prince Henry established a shipyard where better ships were built as well as a school for navigators. He had maps redrawn according to the most recent information. He also promoted the use of navigational instruments such as the compass and the astrolabe.
3. The Norse voyages did not produce permanent settlements or contact with the new land. The Norse voyages were not part of an international competition for land and wealth, as were later expeditions.
4. **(a)** Dias sailed to and around the southern tip of Africa, establishing a water route to the East. **(b)** Columbus, by sailing west, proved the round-earth theory and introduced Europe to North America, greatly extending the Geographic Revolution. **(c)** Historians believe that Cabot explored the uncharted coastlines of Newfoundland, Nova Scotia, and New England. **(d)** Cartier sailed farther than earlier explorers into the interior of North America, exploring the Gulf of St. Lawrence and the St. Lawrence River.

SECTION REVIEW   *(text page 17)*

Suggested responses to the questions are:
1. They signed a treaty establishing a Line of

Demarcation west of the Cape Verde Islands. All lands explored east of the line belonged to Portugal; all lands explored to the west belonged to Spain.

2. Cortés and Pizarro, like most conquistadors, were searching for gold and other riches. They found them in abundance in the Aztec and Inca societies.

3. To protect their claims along the Atlantic coast from the French and English, the Spaniards established forts, or presidios, and Catholic missions from St. Augustine, Florida, northward to the area of South Carolina.

SECTION REVIEW   *(text page 20)*

Suggested responses to the questions are:

1. Technology, food products, language, customs, and religious beliefs of Spain were transferred and adapted to the New World, but the colonists also learned from their new environment. For example, they began to grow crops native to the Americas such as corn and tobacco. They also created a class system based on differences in the ethnic composition of the population.

2. Indian slavery was abolished by Spain in 1540 and was replaced by two varieties of forced labor — the encomienda and the repartimiento. Technically, the Indians were free, but they had to work for the right to stay on their land or for meager wages.

3. (a) The Spanish missionaries were determined to free the Indians from what they believed was the worship of false gods. (b) The Indians learned many things from the missionaries, such as carpentry, masonry, and agriculture. Often the missionaries tried to protect the Indians from the cruelty and exploitation of other colonizers. On the other hand, the missionaries helped impose on the Indians a European way of life that resulted in the destruction of Indian customs.

4. California, Arizona, New Mexico, and Texas.

SECTION REVIEW   *(text page 25)*

Suggested responses to the questions are:

1. (a) Spain sought to end British attacks on its shipping by attempting to invade and conquer the British Isles. Philip II assembled the Spanish Armada, which was the most powerful invasion force ever seen up to that time. (b) The British defeated the Armada in the English Channel in 1588. This was the beginning of the decline of Spanish power; it also signaled the rise of British power.

2. (a) Jamestown's location was very poor — swampy and infested with malaria-carrying mosquitoes. The London Company wanted the settlers to search for gold. They did so, but neglected to build good houses and to grow crops for food. Most of the settlers lacked needed survival skills. As a result, more than half the settlers died before the end of the first year. (b) John Smith became the leader of the colony and organized the men into work groups under a policy of "No work, no food." He also got some aid from the Indians. When Smith left the colony conditions became worse; in 1609, however, ships arrived from England with supplies and more skilled settlers. In 1612, John Rolfe and other colonists learned how to grow and cure tobacco, providing the colony with its most valuable product.

3. (a) The House of Burgesses was established, and the first Africans arrived in the colony. (Students might also mention that the London Company sent 60 unmarried women to the colony). (b) The establishment of the House of Burgesses was the first step toward representative government in the New World. At the same time, the arrival of Africans as bonded servants set the stage for the development of the institution of slavery in the colonies. (Students might also mention that the women married Jamestown settlers and began raising families.) (c) In 1624, James I withdrew the London Company's charter and made Virginia a royal colony. The King appointed a governor and a council to rule. The Burgesses were still elected by the settlers and continued to make laws. The laws, however, now had to be approved by the governor.

4. Slaves would not be protected by the guarantees because they were considered to be property. Also, women were not specifically mentioned.

CHAPTER 1 REVIEW   *(text page 29)*

Reviewing Important Terms

1. false, cultures
2. true
3. false, presidios
4. true
5. true
6. true
7. false, charter

Practicing Critical Thinking Skills

Suggested responses to the questions are:

1. (a) During the Renaissance, people became more aware of and curious about the world around them. One result of this interest was the desire for greater trade. (b) The desire to expand trade prompted Spain, Portugal, England, and other nations to find new routes to Asia. The expan-

sion of world trade led to the Geographic Revolution, as Europeans gained a truer idea of the lands on the earth.

2. (a) The Native Americans had developed rich and varied cultures based upon their natural surroundings. The Plains Indians had a democratic style of government in which chiefs were elected for specific purposes. The Incas and Aztecs developed complex civilizations, built great cities and religious centers, developed a calendar, had conquering armies, and maintained a clear division of classes in their society. They were ruled by a supreme authority. The Europeans also had varied cultures. They were ruled by kings, and their societies were defined by classes. (b) The Indians had a common set of beliefs. They believed it was essential for people to live in harmony with the natural world and pass on the land, unspoiled, to future generations. Their gods were nature gods. The Europeans also had a base of common beliefs. They worshipped one God. The Europeans looked upon the New World as a God-given opportunity to get rich. They did not respect the land, and so they abused it and the people they found on it. (c) The Plains Indians farmed and hunted for a living. The Aztecs and Incas farmed and traded. Although most Europeans were farmers, individual and national wealth was obtained through trade. (d) The Aztecs and Incas had a better base for understanding the Europeans than did such groups as the Plains Indians. The Aztecs and Incas had social structures similar to those existing in Europe. Indeed, the Europeans used this similarity to conquer and to transfer power from Indian to European hands. Other Indian groups differed greatly from the Europeans in both their social structures and value systems. The Europeans considered all Indians inferior, even the highly developed Aztecs and Incas. They scorned the Indians' religious beliefs and tried to change their social patterns to conform to European patterns. They enslaved the Indians or drove them from their native lands. The Indians viewed the Europeans with distrust. They feared the Europeans would destroy the natural harmony they believed essential to life, and they fought to prevent European expansion into their lands.

3. Most Londoners in 1600 were probably not aware that they were living in a revolutionary age, because they could not see the great sweep of change; they only saw what affected them. They would have needed historical perspective to realize the nature of the changes.

4. (a) Answers will vary. Students might suggest that a strong leader was needed to bring order to chaos and to force the colonists to work for their own survival. (b) Answers will vary. Students might suggest that his motive was not personal gain, but that he acted in the best interests of the colony.

5. (a) Many settled in the New World to escape the rule of a despotic government. Others saw the opportunity to live as they wished in an open land. (b) Colonizing governments were aware of the bounty of gold, silver, and other raw materials available in the New World. This bounty served as a lure to many people. (c) Each colonizing nation wished to establish its own claims in the New World and to gain the New World's wealth for itself. Rivalry flared as claims overlapped. (d) The desire to spread Christianity was a motivating force in exploring and colonizing the New World. Priests and missionaries, especially from Spain, established churches and missions in an effort to convert the Indians.

6. Troubled race relations began with the entry and conquest of New World lands. The conquistadors enslaved and killed Aztecs and Incas. The North American Indians were driven from their lands by English settlers. Africans were brought to the New World to become slaves.

Developing History Study Skills

1. Answers will vary.
2. (a) Answers will vary. (b) The Europeans knew of Europe, the southern half of Asia, the Middle East, and the northernmost part of Africa. The Norse had settled in Iceland and had seen the southeastern coast of Greenland. (c) The northern half of Asia, most of Africa, Oceania, and the lands of the Western Hemisphere had not been explored.

Relating Geography and History

1. Voyages between North America and England took between four and seven weeks.
2. (a) Answers will vary. Students might mention laws, mail, manufactured goods, people, and news. (b) Answers will vary. Students might mention raw materials, mail, and news.
3. Answers will vary. Students might mention the difficulties encountered in enforcing unpopular laws imposed from abroad; conflicts that arose because rulers misunderstood local problems; the exploitive attitudes of some rulers toward the colonies; news and mail arriving weeks after being sent; and goods delayed or lost in transit. (b) Answers will vary. Students might mention feelings of isolation due to separation; the development of new life styles as a result of the new environment; increasingly pronounced differences between home country and colonies; and the attitude of self-reliance which had become a way of life.

Expansion of British Power

SECTION REVIEW   *(text page 35)*

Suggested responses to the questions are:
1. People came from Europe to America to establish communities where they could worship as they wished, to escape wars and persecution for their religious beliefs, and to have the opportunity for a better life.
2. **(a)** The Pilgrims arrived at the onset of winter. They were few in number and poorly supplied, and they owed money to the London Company for their passage. The Puritans had more people, better skills and tools, and more financial support. **(b)** the Puritans **(c)** The Puritans had ample supplies, and many of them were skilled workers.
3. The Massachuetts Bay Company, which ran the colony, moved to the New World to escape the king's influence. Originally, all government power was held by the General Court, to which only stockholders in the company could belong. When the settlers demanded a share in the government, the leaders granted the right to vote to all Puritan men who were good church members and also allowed each town to send representatives to the General Court.
4. The Pilgrims wanted to establish a basis for self-government.

SECTION REVIEW   *(text page 39)*

Suggested responses to the questions are:
1. **(a)** Roger Williams and Anne Hutchinson were exiled from the Massachusetts Bay Colony because they disagreed with the Puritan leadership on religious beliefs and other issues. Thomas Hooker left voluntarily in search of greater opportunities on the frontier. **(b)** The reasons were very similar to those which had originally led to New World migration — religious freedom and greater economic opportunity.
2. Students should disagree. The Massachusetts charter made that colony almost self-governing; the Rhode Island charter was based on the principle of the consent of the governed;

and in Connecticut, the Fundamental Orders and then the charter allowed the citizens to govern themselves.
3. Communities were often started by people who attended the same local church. The need for defense against the Indians prompted the settlers to live close together. Not all of New England was fit for farming. Settlers concentrated where the land was good and near port cities.
4. The towns were seaports or river towns easily reached by boat. Therefore, trade, communication, and mutual assistance were easier.

SECTION REVIEW   *(text page 44)*

Suggested responses to the questions are:
1. **(a)** English settlers wanted a share of the profitable Dutch-controlled fur trade with the Iroquois Indians. Also, the Dutch were expanding east to Long Island and north to the Connecticut Valley at the same time that New England settlers were moving south into these areas. **(b)** The conflict was resolved in 1664 when an English fleet sailed into the Hudson River and took control of New Netherland.
2. The guarantee of representative government for English citizens allowed the colonial representative assemblies, which had been disbanded by the Duke of York, to regain their power.
3. New England was hilly and forested and had patches of rocky, shallow soil. It also had good harbors. Consequently, farms and communities were small and isolated. Major trading towns grew up around the harbors. The Middle Colonies had gentle, rolling hills, fertile soil, good communication along river valleys, and good harbors at the mouths of the rivers. They became the "breadbasket" of the New World because the many farms were large and produced sufficient food for the farmers as well as a surplus for sale. These colonies were famous for their iron mines, shipyards, and the manufacture of glass, paper, and textiles.
4. **(a)** New Sweden and New Netherland were in protected harbors and river valleys. **(b)** The harbors allowed for the safe anchorage of ships, thus encouraging trade. The river valleys were fertile and gave access to the interior, making a profitable fur trade possible.

SECTION REVIEW   *(text page 46)*

Suggested responses to the questions are:
1. North Carolina was settled by pioneers from Virginia who grew their own food on small farms and sold tobacco to England. South Caro-

lina was largely settled by people from overseas, many of whom built large rice plantations. Others traded in the products of the pine forests, in furs from the frontier, and in indigo.

2. Georgia was established as a place in which debtors could start a new life, and as a buffer to protect the English colonies from attacks from Spanish Florida.
3. The two chief crops were tobacco and rice. Tobacco was grown in Virginia, Maryland, and North Carolina along the rivers, on the coasts, and inland. Rice was grown in South Carolina and Georgia in the coastal lowlands.
4. (a) The Southern Colonies relied on black slaves; the Northern Colonies relied on free labor. (b) The southern plantations required many workers. With larger amounts of free land available on the frontier, settlers were unwilling to work for wages. Thus, southerners viewed slave labor as necessary and profitable. Slavery was unprofitable in the North because the smaller family farms did not require as many laborers.

SECTION REVIEW (text page 49)

Suggested responses to the questions are:
1. Furs were the most important and profitable resource of New France. This resource was the major reason for French settlements, and it provided thousands of jobs in France and the New World. The fur trade was a strength because it provided a living for many people in France and New France, and a huge profit for French merchants. On the other hand, it encouraged many colonists to move into the forests for furs rather than settle down in the farming communities. French settlements were never as strong or as well-populated as those in the British colonies.
2. (a) The British had a fine navy and well-established settlements with large populations. British settlements were closer together, covered less territory than the French settlements, and were easier to defend. (b) France was the most powerful nation in Europe in the 1750's. It had the best armies and a good navy. In New France, the French had the support of many Indian tribes and there was a single government authority that could make decisions quickly when necessary.
3. New Orleans, Quebec, and Montreal were "gateways" because they controlled access to the two major river routes into the North American interior — the Mississippi and St. Lawrence rivers.

SECTION REVIEW (text page 53)

Suggested responses to the questions are:
1. The events that led to the French and Indian War were the organization of a Virginia company to settle land in the Ohio Valley; the construction by the French of forts connecting Lake Erie with the Ohio Valley to protect the territory against the British colonists' moves; the sending of George Washington by the governor of Virginia to warn the French that the land they were fortifying belonged to the British; and the building of Fort Necessity south of the French Fort Duquesne.
2. The British colonies rejected the Albany Plan of Union because they were unwilling to give up their independence.
3. (a) 1756 (b) William Pitt became leader of the British government.
4. Louisburg was at the entry to the Gulf of St. Lawrence and the St. Lawrence River. By controlling this approach, the British navy could prevent reinforcements and supplies from reaching the French army in North America.

CHAPTER 2 REVIEW (text page 57)

Reviewing Important Terms

1. Inflation	6. patroons
2. divine right of kings	7. confederations
3. indentured servants	8. Bill of Rights
4. self-governing colony	9. militia
5. frontier	10. confederation

Practicing Critical Thinking Skills

Suggested responses to the questions are:
1. (a) Most white settlers ignored the rights of the Indians and even regarded the Indians with contempt. (b) The Indians, who had initially welcomed the Europeans, became bitter as white settlers took over their lands. (c) The Pequot War, King Philip's War, and the later Indian alliances with the French were among some of the tragic consequences.
2. Agriculture is an essential occupation for any new settlement because the production of food is necessary for survival.
3. (a) The possession of colonies could help to make a nation wealthy and therefore powerful. (b) To assure the protection of colonies and the maintenance of trade between a nation and its colonies, large armies and navies were needed.

4. By 1750, there were fewer blacks in New England and the Middle Colonies than in the Southern Colonies because slavery was uneconomical in the northern areas. The plantation system of the South required a large labor force, which was provided by the importation of black slaves; whereas the farms in the North were family farms and used little outside help.
5. North America was just one of the battlefields the Europeans used for their power struggle — they fought all around the world. Colonial areas were prizes for which each of the contending nations was ready to sacrifice blood and effort.
6. (a) Answers will vary. Students might mention instances of representative self-government but restricted suffrage; the lack of formal social class structure; and the social rankings based on prestige or wealth. (b) Answers will vary. Students might mention that even though the United States guarantees rights to all people, certain groups still face discrimination.

Developing History Study Skills

1. See the following chart. Answers will vary.

	New England Colonies	Middle Colonies	Southern Colonies
Religious Beliefs	Separatists Puritans Dissenters	Varied	Catholic Protestant Jewish
Attitudes Toward Slavery	All colonies used slaves	Slaves were legally recognized.	Slaves were an economic necessity.
Type of Government	Church-related Representative Joint-stock companies	Royal colonies Proprietary colonies	Royal colonies Proprietary colonies with representative assemblies
Reason for Settlement	Religious freedom Political freedom Economic opportunity	Economic opportunity Religious toleration Political freedom	Economic opportunity Religious freedom

2. (a) Answers will vary. Students might mention that the document set up a framework by which the settlers would establish their community in the absence of a higher authority. (b) Answers will vary. Students might mention that the primary source is the original work of the writer and that the secondary source analyzes or explains the original source. (c) Answers will vary. Students might mention that the primary source allows the reader to interpret the document for himself or herself and the secondary source helps to interpret or explain the document. In this case, the secondary source also explains the historical background.

Relating Geography and History

1. (a) Bodies of water and mountains formed protective barriers for settlers. (b) Answers will vary. Students might mention that the barriers tended to keep settlements closer together, and the people shared common problems.
2. (a) People settled along the inland waterways because there was good farming land near the rivers, and the rivers provided transportation to the port cities. Settlements began on the coasts because the original settlers landed there and because ports provided many ways to make a living. (b) The rivers provided water, fertile lands, and transportation. Some of the rivers were navigable by ocean-going ships.

CHAPTER
3 American Cultural Beginnings

SECTION REVIEW
(text page 61)

Suggested responses to the questions are:
1. Most southerners lived on small farms similar to those in New England and the Middle Colonies. Some lived on the frontier in small clearings. The wealthy planters lived on the fertile coastal plains.
2. (a) Raising a single cash crop was the best way for plantation owners to accumulate wealth. (b) The major southern cash crops were tobacco and rice. (c) Growing a single major crop was advantageous because profits were high, and the producer could concentrate on the care of this crop. (d) Reliance on a single crop could mean disaster if the crop failed or the demand for it dropped significantly.

3. **(a)** The plantations were organized like small communities. Besides the major crop, food was grown for the plantation family and workers. **(b)** Most other necessities were also provided by the plantation workers. Cloth was spun and woven by servants, and meat came from cattle and hogs raised on the plantation. Carpenters, millers, and blacksmiths also lived and worked on the plantations.

4. **(a)** Wealthy planters exchanged visits with each other. They enjoyed a good dinner, conversation, and card playing. **(b)** The richer planters owned houses in the town, where they lived a few months a year. In the towns they enjoyed music, dancing, art, theater, lectures, and sporting events.

5. **(a)** Planters sold their crops in England and received luxuries and other manufactured articles by return shipment. **(b)** Their allegiance might have followed their economic interests in a controversy between England and the other American colonies.

SECTION REVIEW   *(text page 64)*

Suggested responses to the questions are:

1. **(a)** Although the American social ladder was similar to that of England, it differed in that American class distinctions were not as rigid as those of the English. Therefore, Americans with lower social positions could move up the ladder. **(b)** In 1754, Philadelphia resembled an English town in the style of its houses and public buildings, in the speech and dress of many of its people, and in the social divisions of its society. It was different in the variety of nationalities of the inhabitants, the newness of the language called American English, and — most importantly — the abundance of opportunity available to everyone but slaves. There were plenty of jobs available in the towns and plenty of land on the frontier.

2. Wealthy colonial townspeople copied European style in their architecture; their furniture and household luxuries, which were imported from England; and their social activities, such as elaborate dinners and parties, card playing, horse racing, and theater.

3. The American dialect was influenced by the variety of people in the colonies — French, German, and Indian words became part of the vocabulary — and the physical environment, which required new words to describe new animals, products, foods, weather conditions, and places.

SECTION REVIEW   *(text page 67)*

Suggested responses to the questions are:

1. **(a)** For shelter the pioneers used caves, dug shallow pits roofed with branches covered with sod, or built log cabins. **(b)** Much of the pioneers' household equipment was homemade. It included crude heating from fireplaces and warming pans; copper or iron kettles for cooking; wooden bunks; hewn logs for tables and chairs; wooden trenchers for dishes; and gourds for drinking cups. **(c)** The pioneer diet relied on fish, game, and garden produce. **(d)** Pioneer clothing was made from homemade cloth and deerskin. **(e)** Pioneer social life centered around cooperative work that turned into social events with barbecues, sports, and dances; weddings; election-day celebrations; and sports after militia-training.

2. **(a)** The pioneers lived on the resources of the frontier. They used available wood for houses, tools, utensils, and furniture. They hunted and grew their own food; spun cloth from the wool of their own sheep and from the flax they grew in their fields; and made moccasins, shoes, and jackets from the deerskins they tanned. **(b)** Neighbors helped each other build houses, clear the land, and defend their homes and communities.

3. Self-reliant people would value freedom because they were used to making their own decisions about their lives. They would value equality because they would judge a person's worth as they would judge their own — by abilities and achievements rather than family or wealth.

4. **(a)** The frontiersmen had few personal possessions — usually a hunting knife, long rifle, powder, and shot. **(b)** Clothing consisted of buckskin. **(c)** Game, fish, nuts and berries were their common foods. **(d)** They slept under the stars, in caves, or in crude log shelters. **(e)** Once in a while the frontiersmen met to hold shooting matches, tests of strength, and to tell adventure stories.

SECTION REVIEW   *(text page 72)*

Suggested responses to the questions are:

1. **(a)** In New England and the Middle Colonies, the need for slaves was relatively limited. The small New England farms did not require large numbers of slaves, but slaves worked as household servants and in various trades. Slaves in the Middle Colonies contributed their labor and skills to commerce and industry as well as farm-

ing. In 1765, nearly seven out of eight blacks in colonial America lived in the Southern Colonies, almost all as slaves. **(b)** Slaves in New England had some legal rights. They could buy property, and they had the right to a trial by jury in the courts. Slaves could attend church if they sat in "African pews," but they could not become church members. Under British rule, all black slaves in New York were strictly separated from whites and were governed by severe disciplinary rules. In the Southern Colonies, slave codes regulated the lives of the slaves. **(c)** New England slaves worked as household servants, farm laborers, lumberjacks, carpenters, barrelmakers, blacksmiths, millers, fishers, and shipbuilders. Slaves in the Middle Colonies worked in commerce, industry, and farming, and most southern slaves labored on tobacco, rice, and indigo plantations.

2. **(a)** Slaves gained their freedom by running away, by being granted it by their masters, or by buying it. **(b)** Free blacks had few legal or social rights. In a few colonies they could vote and could own farms and businesses. However, they were forced to live in separate areas and to obey special laws enforced by white colonists. White colonists did not associate with free blacks. In every way, the blacks were treated as inferiors.

3. **(a)** Slaves would probably hate white people for the indignities they were made to suffer. **(b)** Slavery would probably reinforce a slaveowner's belief that blacks were inferior.

4. A slave buyer would probably worry about the health of the slaves. If one slave had a disease, many others could catch it, which would ruin the plantation owner's work force.

SECTION REVIEW

(text page 77)

Suggested responses to the questions are:

1. **(a)** The Eastern Woodland Indians did not have plows. The men broke the earth with hoe-like tools; the women used digging sticks to make holes into which they placed the seed. They had extremely well-kept fields. **(b)** Each tribe in the Iroquois Confederation regulated its own group, except for major concerns such as war. Major decisions were made by the governing body of the Confederation, which was made up of sachems (chiefs) from each of the tribes. The sachems of the individual tribes had to agree on a proposal before it could take effect.

2. The colonists would probably not have survived without the assistance of the Indians. They taught the colonists how to plant and cultivate; provided them with seeds; showed them how to live off the game, fish, and plants of the forests; and taught them how to travel in the wilderness.

3. **(a)** The Indians saw themselves as part of the environment and learned to live in harmony with it, without destroying it or exhausting its resources. Individuals did not own land; the tribe itself owned the land. The colonists thought natural resources were endless and used them without care or thought of the future. They wanted to change the environment to reflect their ideas of success and progress. The colonists believed property belonged to the individual and could be bought and sold. **(b)** Agreement between Indians and settlers was impossible because their views differed so much. As the settlers took over more land, the Indians had less land to use.

4. The Indians in the picture probably made their living by hunting and fishing.

CHAPTER 3 REVIEW

(text page 81)

Reviewing Important Terms

1. true
2. false, log cabin
3. true
4. false, slave codes
5. true
6. true
7. true

Practicing Critical Thinking Skills

Suggested responses to the questions are:

1. **(a)** Many of the colonial planters and merchants led settled lives; they could import many of the products and articles they had grown accustomed to in the Old World and could build in the manner of English architecture. **(b)** The pioneer farmers and the frontiersmen were unable to reproduce as many Old World ways because they were less secure financially and survival occupied most of their time. Also, many did not want to continue the Old World way of life.

2. The pioneer's individualism was necessarily both cooperative and competitive. Each pioneer family hoped to achieve a better life. Consequently, they competed among themselves in trade and for the resources of the land. They realized that they needed to help each other clear land, build homes, and protect and develop their communities if each family was to survive.

3. Colonial cities grew along the North Atlantic coast because of the good harbors and fine economic opportunities found there. Philadelphia, New York, and Boston were busy ports. Because of the many inland waterways, the coastal cities

were well situated for trade with the interior. Much of the surplus grain and meat from the Middle Colonies passed through the port cities to England and the West Indies. The Southern Colonies had fewer good harbors. The coastal plains of the South were used for plantation agriculture, thus limiting the growth of cities.

4. **(a)** The Indians and black Americans were both considered inferior by the white settlers and were treated unfairly. **(b)** However, they had different kinds of relationships with the more powerful white settlers. Because the Indians were already present, had well-established cultures, and resisted the settlers' efforts to take over their land for farms, the settlers viewed the Indians as enemies to be conquered. The black Americans were brought here by force to become a permanent labor supply as slaves. The settlers viewed slaves as valuable property and passed laws to control them and prevent their loss by escape or theft.

5. Answers will vary. Students might mention that the attitudes of the colonists toward blacks and Indians set a pattern that was difficult to alter and that there are echoes of those attitudes evident today.

6. Answers will vary. Students might mention that changes in the environment were different for the colonists than for Americans today. For example, the colonists were concerned with utilizing abundant available natural resources. Today, Americans are concerned with conserving remaining resources and with searching for alternatives. The colonists moved into their new environment; today's Americans watch their environment changing around them due to such factors as technology and population growth.

Developing History Study Skills

1. Answers will vary. Students might mention that the southern planters lived in a self-contained economic unit that survived on what it produced. Many plantations provided elegant life styles for the owners. The picture of a colonial city might suggest a life style based on busy commercial enterprise with a large population and a variety of social and economic levels. The picture showing farm life reveals a spirit of cooperation and an isolated, yet interdependent kind of life.

2. Reports should cover the points indicated in the activity.

Relating Geography and History

1. See the graph at the top of the next column. Answers will vary.

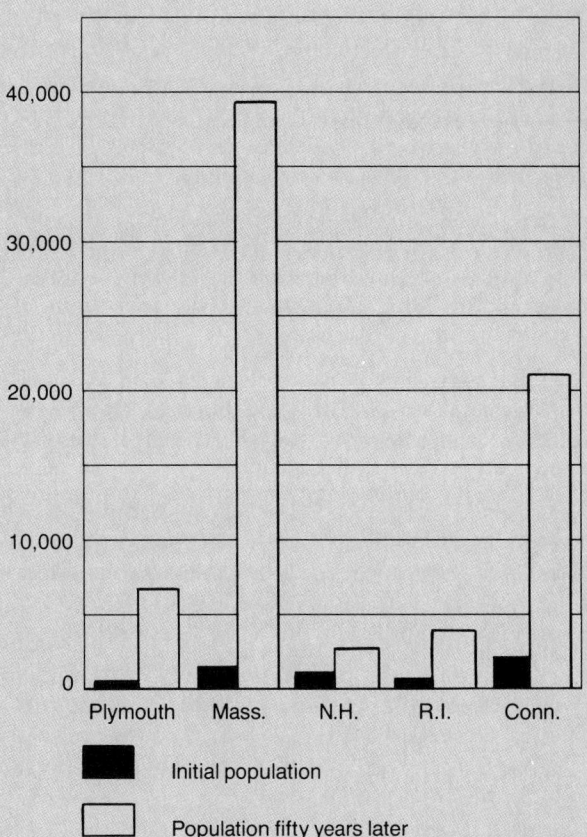

Initial population

Population fifty years later

2. **(a)** Connecticut, Massachusetts, New Hampshire, Rhode Island, and Plymouth **(b)** Massachusetts, Connecticut, Plymouth, Rhode Island, and New Hampshire

3. **(a)** Massachusetts **(b)** New Hampshire

CHAPTER

4 Democracy in Colonial America

SECTION REVIEW *(text page 85)*

Suggested responses to the questions are:

1. **(a)** An established church is a church recognized by the government of a nation and supported by taxes. **(b)** Established churches existed in much of New England, part of New York, and all of the

Southern Colonies. **(c)** The Middle Colonies had so many different religious groups that no single church was established.

2. Roger Williams advocated that no one should be taxed for the support of the church; that no laws should require people to attend church; that there should be no religious qualifications for voting; and that all people should be permitted to worship as they pleased and freely speak their minds. Lord Baltimore secured passage of the Maryland Toleration Act (1649), which guaranteed freedom to all "professing to believe in Jesus Christ." William Penn's Charter of Privileges (1701) allowed anyone who believed in God to settle in Pennsylvania, although only Christians could take part in its government.

3. **(a)** Most blacks were excluded from Christianity because slaveowners feared that Christian teaching, which emphasized the importance and dignity of every individual, would encourage blacks to rebel against slavery. **(b)** When they were allowed in church, blacks were segregated and forced to sit in "African pews."

4. Religious freedom was granted to everyone in Rhode Island; in Maryland, to those who professed a belief in Jesus Christ; and in Pennsylvania, to all who believed in One Almighty God.

SECTION REVIEW [text page 91]

Suggested responses to the questions are:
1. **(a)** In general, Europeans accepted the idea that only the sons of wealthy families needed a formal education. **(b)** The merchants and planters realized they needed schools and colleges that would teach their children more about business affairs to enable them to take over family businesses. As a result, some colonial schools began to offer courses in navigation, modern languages, accounting, and commercial law. Well-to-do colonists realized that in the rural, isolated society of the colonies, it was quite possible for their children to grow up in ignorance, no better educated than the masses of people whom they considered their inferiors. Finally, the scarcity of books in the colonies led to the establishment of library societies.

2. Students should agree. Free public education is one of the strongest roots of democracy because it makes education available to all citizens, regardless of wealth.

3. The Massachusetts education law was the first legislation in the English-speaking world that required town governments to establish schools and pay teachers.

4. *Disadvantages:* Women were considered subordinate to men. They could not vote or, if married, own property; their wages belonged to their husbands or fathers; and most women were not able to attend school beyond the elementary level. *Opportunities:* Some women were able to work in shops and small businesses. In farming areas, women helped with the work. Women who went to the frontier shared the dangers of frontier life and performed many of the customary tasks of men. Women also took an active part in settling many communities; they helped establish churches, taught children, and cared for the sick.

SECTION REVIEW [text page 95]

Suggested responses to the questions are:
1. **(a)** In the royal colonies, the king appointed the governor and his council, which held the greater share of power. The qualified voters elected an assembly to help make the laws, but the governor could veto its actions. In the proprietary colonies, the proprietor appointed the governor, and the qualified voters elected the assembly. The self-governing colonies of Connecticut and Rhode Island elected the governor and both houses of the legislature. **(b)** All colonies had a governor and an elected lower house of the legislature.

2. **(a)** There were property and religious restrictions on voting and holding office. Women and slaves were not allowed to vote. **(b)** Only white adult males who owned a specified amount of property could vote. In many colonies, men who did not belong to the established church could not vote. The property qualifications for holding office were even higher than those for voting.

3. The farmers and frontiersmen claimed that they were not adequately represented in the colonial legislature; that their taxes were high and the price of tobacco was low; and that Governor Berkeley and the wealthy planters had refused to crush an Indian uprising because they did not wish to anger the Indians, with whom many planters carried on a profitable fur trade.

4. **(a)** The usual form of government in the New England Colonies was the town meeting. In the Southern Colonies the usual form was the county. The Middle Colonies mixed both town and county forms. **(b)** The difference was based on the size of the communities. New England communities were small farming villages and towns. In the Middle and Southern Colonies, many people lived on isolated farms, and local government had to cover a much larger area.

SECTION REVIEW [text page 96]

Suggested responses to the questions are:

1. Except in the self-governing colonies of Rhode Island and Connecticut, the colonial governments had conflicting interests. The governors and their councils represented the British empire, and the assemblies represented the colonists.
2. (a) Royal governors were appointed by the Crown from among the ruling groups in Great Britain. Sometimes the king appointed his friends. (b) This process did not always produce able leaders. Many were excellent, but others lacked training and experience and were short-sighted and narrowminded. All saw their positions as a way to increase their personal wealth and power.
3. (a) The assemblies approved all grants of money to be spent by the colonial governments. (b) To some extent this made it possible for the assemblies to control whom the governors appointed to lower offices. Assemblies could demand an accounting of expenses and could withhold the salary of the governor until the end of the year.

CHAPTER 4 REVIEW   *(text page 98)*

Reviewing Important Terms

1. true	6. false, justice of
2. true	the peace
3. true	7. true
4. false, suffrage	8. true
5. true	

Practicing Critical Thinking Skills
Suggested responses to the questions are:
1. In the Old World, religion included an established church with church and state under one head. Other religions were persecuted. Education was only for the wealthy and emphasized classical subjects. The king had considerable power which was somewhat checked by Parliament. Women could not vote or own property and generally received little education. In the New World separation of church and state was favored and there was a growing spirit of tolerance. There was more educational opportunity, and the emphasis was on practical subjects. Although the colonists acknowledged the power of the king, they wanted more of a voice in local affairs and controlled governors through the power of the purse. Women were under the authority of men as in Europe, but they had a higher status because of their economic importance. Women ran small businesses, printed newspapers, and practiced trades.
2. Much of the education of the frontier settlers and pioneer farmers came from the school of experi-
ence. Faced with problems for which they had no guide, frontier settlers and pioneer farmers learned to work out their own solutions. On the farm and frontier, people had to be practical, inventive, self-sufficient, and flexible in their thinking. This was a new kind of education. Few books reached the frontier, but many pioneer farmers owned copies of the Bible and almanacs. The farmers also received some intellectual stimulation from public meetings and Sunday sermons. The ordinary townspeople had more opportunities to secure an education than did the people on the frontier. By the 1700's, in addition to the regular schools, an increasing number of private evening schools taught mathematics, accounting, modern languages, and other subjects useful to those who were interested in business. Townspeople had Bibles, almanacs, a few books, pamphlets, and a growing number of newspapers. The townspeople also picked up news and ideas from public meetings, social gatherings at the taverns, and debating societies.
3. Slaveowners did not want their slaves to become Christians because they feared that knowledge of Christianity's teachings, which emphasized the worth of each individual, might lead to slave revolts.
4. (a) America offered many economic and social opportunities to new settlers. They could easily find work in coastal towns, which had a constant need for workers. Through hard work and cleverness, they could rise to prominent positions in their communities. If they were dissatisfied, the vast frontier offered them the chance to start over on their own farms. As a result, ambition, courage, and independence became the personal characteristics most admired by the colonists. (b) Geography isolated the colonists from the king's control and fostered a sense of community among them. The colonists had to work together to build their communities, to defend themselves from Indian attacks, and to solve their local problems without advice or interference from England. (c) The colonists established democratic practices and principles such as representative assemblies, religious freedom, public education, and town meetings. As they gained self-confidence in these native institutions, their spirit of independence grew.
5. (a) Answers will vary. Students might mention representative assemblies, separation of church and state, religious freedom, public school systems, and various forms of local government. (b) Answers will vary.

Developing History Study Skills

1. Answers will vary.
2. (a) Answers will vary. Students might mention

that the poems reveal the religious frame of mind of the people; many instances of nature imagery indicate that the people were close to nature; the people did not have effective fire-fighting equipment and some of the other services we take for granted today; and women stayed home and took care of the children. **(b)** Answers will vary. Students might argue that Bradstreet's ideas were typical of the colonies because she portrays women as staying home and raising children.

Relating Geography and History

1. The citizens in New England had more opportunity to take part in the governing process because that region had more town meetings than other regions.
2. The settlements were so spread out that local government had to have jurisdiction over a wide area.
3. Officials probably had greater power in the county system of government because they were not elected officials and they were farther removed from the people.
4. The town system of government was more representative because it was made up of elected officials who met with the citizens they represented and heard them speak out on issues.

UNIT ONE REVIEW   (text page 99)

Discussing Ideas

1. **(a)** Most Indian groups felt that it was necessary to live in harmony with the natural world, had a strong sense of pride, and prized their self-reliance. **(b)** They differed in the ways that they adapted to their environment. Some groups were farmers; others were hunters; still others were Seed Gatherers. Some groups were peaceful; others were warlike. The Aztecs, Mayas, and Incas developed great civilizations.
2. The Geographic Revolution made it inevitable that an explorer would find the Americas.
3. **(a)** People came to America to search for gold, to convert Indians to Christianity, to escape religious persecution, to search for political freedom, and to find a more prosperous life. **(b)** Spanish conquistadors searched for gold; Spanish priests converted Indians; the Pilgrims and the Puritans came to escape religious persecution; political dissidents sought political freedom; and poor Europeans wanted a more prosperous life.
4. **(a)** In New Spain the colonists subjugated the Indians, used them for forced labor, and destroyed their civilizations. **(b)** The English at first coexisted with the Indians. Later, the colonists forced the Indians to abandon their lands. **(c)** The French generally had good relations with the Indians and traded extensively with them. **(d)** Answers will vary. Students might mention that the Spanish were intent on conquering the Indian civilizations and sending riches back to Spain, the English wanted to become permanent settlers and were hungry for land, and the French were primarily concerned with the fur trade.

Applying History Study Skills

Answers will vary. Students might mention that the reports discuss how settlers have become wealthy; have been granted land; and have been given clothing, tools, and weapons.

Winning Independence

5 Moving Toward Independence

SECTION REVIEW　　　　　*(text page 106)*

Suggested responses to the questions are:
1. **(a)** Colonies benefited the colonizing nation by providing a source of raw materials, markets for manufactured goods, bases from which a navy could operate, and by encouraging the development of a strong merchant fleet. **(b)** The colonizing nation benefited the colonies by providing military protection, financial backing, and a market for colonial goods and products.
2. **(a)** Under mercantilism manufacturing of goods was restricted to eliminate competition for markets. **(b)** The shipping of goods was restricted so that the colonizing nation's merchant marine would profit. **(c)** The buying and selling of goods was restricted so that the colony could buy from and sell to the colonizing nation only. Selling to the colonizing nation eliminated competition for foreign markets, and that nation could resell the colonial goods.
3. **(a)** In the 1600's and early 1700's, the New England and Middle Colonies produced many of the same products as England—among them grain, lumber, and fish. Great Britain did not want these colonial products to compete with its own. Parliament passed laws preventing the sale of these colonial products to England. The prosperity of New England and the Middle Colonies seemed threatened. **(b)** The New England and Middle Colonies soon established new markets for their goods.
4. Great Britain imported raw materials from the colonies and used them to manufacture goods which were then sold to the colonies. Sugar and molasses were imported by the colonies from the West Indies and processed into rum, which was sold in Africa. Grain, fish, meat, and lumber

from the American colonies supplied the needs of the slave laborers who produced the sugar and molasses that was sold to the colonies.

SECTION REVIEW　　　　　*(text page 108)*

Suggested responses to the questions are:
1. The British government's most pressing problem was the need for money to pay for four costly wars and to defend its worldwide empire. The British government expected its colonial subjects to help pay the war debts. It also had to find a way to govern the territories of Canada and Florida and the territory west of the Appalachian Mountains.
2. The Indians had been pushed westward by white settlers for more than 150 years. They feared that white settlers would pour over the mountains and onto their land, establishing farms and destroying their hunting grounds. Answers will vary for the second part of the question. Students might suggest that the struggle was probably unavoidable, because the needs of the Indians and those of the colonists were directly opposed. (In their answers, the students should compare the needs of each group.)
3. **(a)** The British pointed out to the colonists that they were now free of the French and Indian menace and that the British army and navy still protected them. The colonists should, therefore, help pay the cost of their own defense and that of the empire as well. **(b)** The colonists wanted to be left alone to follow their own interests. They felt that they had contributed their share to the empire during the war, and they believed that the empire's problems did not concern them.
4. **(a)** Virginia and New York **(b)** Spain

SECTION REVIEW　　　　　*(text page 112)*

Suggested responses to the questions are:
1. **(a)** Parliament wanted to develop a long-range policy for the western lands without the distraction of settler-Indian conflicts; the colonists wanted to settle the land, and fur traders

wanted free access to the area. (b) Parliament wanted the colonists to help pay for their protection and security; the colonists objected to their loss of profits. (c) Parliament wished to maintain Britain's favorable trade balance with the colonies by requiring that all taxes be paid in gold or silver rather than with paper money printed in the colonies. The currency drain made it hard for the colonists to find gold and silver to pay taxes and to conduct business activities. (d) Parliament wanted the colonists to help maintain the British army in the colonies. The colonists objected to the invasion of their privacy and to the cost.

2. The earlier taxes were indirect taxes, such as import duties. These taxes were hidden in the price of the product and were meant to regulate trade. The stamp tax was a direct tax collected within the colonies. The colonists argued that such a tax could not be levied on them because they had no elected representatives in Parliament.

3. (a) The colonists passed resolutions opposing the Stamp Act. They held a Stamp Act Congress to protest direct taxes and vowed to resist them. They signed nonimportation agreements to boycott British goods. Some groups, such as the Sons of Liberty, rioted and burned tax offices, stamps, and royal officers' homes. (b) The nonimportation agreements almost stopped British–American trade, causing British merchants to demand repeal. Some powerful Britons, such as William Pitt and Edmund Burke, sympathized with the colonists and pressured Parliament to repeal the act.

4. (a) The Declaratory Act asserted Parliament's power and authority to make and enforce laws for the colonies. It symbolized the British belief that Parliament represented all citizens of the British empire. (b) The colonists' position was that English tradition gave them the right to tax themselves through duly elected representatives, and since they had no elected representatives in Parliament, Parliament could not tax them.

SECTION REVIEW   *[text page 115]*

Suggested responses to the questions are:
1. (a) The Townshend Acts were intended to raise revenue for the empire. They levied indirect taxes — duties on goods entering seaports. Parliament believed that since the colonists had accepted indirect taxes in the past, they would accept the Townshend Acts. (b) The colonists objected to the acts because they also legalized writs of assistance.

2. (a) The writs of assistance were general search warrants permitting an official to search any home, vessel, or warehouse in the hope of finding smuggled goods. Present-day search warrants must state the exact article sought and the specific place to be searched. (b) Colonists objected to the writs of assistance because they permitted an invasion of privacy.

3. (a) Colonial courts refused to issue writs of assistance; New Yorkers refused to provide quarters for British troops; colonial legislatures sent resolutions to Parliamant declaring that only they had the right to levy taxes on the colonists; merchants signed new nonimportation agreements; and mobs took violent action against British ships, customs officials, and soldiers. (b) Parliament suspended several colonial legislatures; British soldiers were sent to protect customs officials and keep order.

4. To maintain Parliament's right to tax the colonies, the British retained a small tax on tea.

5. The burning of the *Gaspee* was significant because Great Britain retaliated by sending the accused colonists to England for trial, thus threatening Rhode Island's self-government.

SECTION REVIEW   *[text page 117]*

Suggested responses to the questions are:
1. (a) By the time the Tea Act was passed, the colonists were opposed to all taxes imposed by Parliament. In addition, this act allowed the British East India Company to undersell all competitors — even smugglers bringing in duty-free tea — and gave the company a virtual monopoly on the sale of tea in America. (b) The colonists responded by rioting, refusing to buy tea, barring tea-carrying ships from their ports, and destroying tea cargoes.

2. (a) The Intolerable Acts closed the port of Boston until the colonists paid for the tea destroyed there, revoked the Massachusetts charter and forbade town meetings in Massachusetts, required colonists to enforce the laws, and provided that British officials in Massachusetts charged with crimes committed while enforcing British law be tried in England. (b) The Intolerable Acts were intended to discourage violence and to strengthen British control over the colonies. (c) The colonists considered the Quebec Act to be another attempt to punish them. The act destroyed the claims of Massachusetts, Connecticut, and Virginia to western lands and guaranteed religious freedom for French Canadians, whose Catholicism was disliked by many colonists.

3. (a) The First Continental Congress demanded an immediate change in British policies, in

accordance with the colonists' rights as English subjects; reinstituted the nonimportation agreements and agreed not to sell goods to Great Britain; and agreed to the establishment of local "committees of safety and inspection" to provide for united action against the British government. **(b)** The delegates did not talk of independence because they still considered themselves to be English subjects.

4. **(a)** The delegates claimed the rights of life, liberty, and property; the rights of free English subjects; and the right to participate in government. **(b)** The rights were based on the laws of nature, the principles of the English Constitution, and the colonial charters.

CHAPTER 5 REVIEW   *(text page 121)*

Reviewing Important Terms

1. mercantilism
2. bounties
3. salutary neglect
4. land speculaors
5. revenue
6. direct taxes
7. writs of assistance

Practicing Critical Thinking Skills

Suggested responses to the questions are:

1. **(a)** The Navigation Acts protected British shipowners and merchants from European competition. All goods traded within the empire were to be carried in British ships. Goods from Europe and Asia went to Great Britain, where import duties were collected before the goods were shipped to the colonies. **(b)** Restrictions on colonial manufacturing were established to prevent the colonists from building industries that would compete with English industries. **(c)** The Currency Act of 1764 was passed to provide that England would get its taxes in valuable gold and silver, not in colonial paper money.

2. Wise leaders might have reconciled the gap between Great Britain and the colonies in 1776. Wise men such as Franklin, Burke, and Henry did try to reconcile the gap; but on both sides there were elements who were not interested in reconciliation. The growing economic power of the American colonies was also a strong force leading to independence.

3. Answers will vary. Students who support economic considerations might mention restrictions on manufacturing, shipping, and trading under the Navigation Acts; the decline in rum distillers' and shippers' profits due to the Sugar Act; the scarcity of gold and silver resulting from the Currency Act; the expense of housing soldiers under the Quartering Act; and the added cost to any written transaction resulting from the stamp tax. Students who support political considerations might mention the colonists' belief that their interests and those of Great Britain differed; opposition to the Stamp Act as a direct tax levied without consent of the colonists and to the writs of assistance as an invasion of privacy; and the erosion of the colonists' rights as English citizens in trials, freedom of movement (especially to the frontier), and control of local government.

4. **(a)** From 1754 to 1763, the French and Indian War brought the colonists together against a common enemy; but Franklin's Albany Plan of Union (1754), which proposed a formal defense arrangement, was rejected. After 1763, resistance to British trade regulations and taxes brought about further cooperation among the colonies. The Stamp Act Congress (1765) successfully rallied colonial resistance to the stamp tax. The Townshend Acts and writs of assistance prompted the Massachusetts legislature to adopt resolutions against them and to write letters to the other colonies urging united resistance. Maryland, South Carolina, and Georgia agreed. In 1772, Committees of Correspondence were organized to keep each colony informed of events in the other colonies. Violence by the colonists and the punitive reaction of the British resulted in the meeting of the First Continental Congress at Philadelphia in 1774, with delegates from every colony except Georgia. **(b)** The colonists became more unified as the delegates strove to find mutual solutions to their common problems. **(c)** The Congress represented a major step toward unity, but it was not a government. The colonists had no army, no general means of financing their plans, and no central leadership.

5. Answers will vary. Students might mention the conflicts between the Indians and colonial frontier settlements, the Boston Massacre, and the tea riots in the 1770's. In today's society such examples as urban-gang warfare, assassinations and assassination attempts, and vigilante-type actions might be mentioned.

6. Answers will vary. Students might mention that economic health relies to a great extent on a nation's ability to sell goods in foreign markets. Current news regarding trade relations with particular countries may be cited as examples of the importance of a favorable balance of trade. Domestic economic issues such as jobs, consumer prices, and protectionist policies might also be mentioned.

Developing History Study Skills

Answers will vary.

Relating Geography and History

1. Some people were interested in the fur trade; some wished to settle and farm the land.
2. (a) The Indians were aware that the English were more likely to make permanent settlements and to take over more of the Indians' land. (b) The Indians remembered that white settlers had pushed them off their lands on the other side of the mountains. (c) The Indians, led by Chief Pontiac, destroyed British forts and resisted white settlement of their lands. (d) The fur traders wanted to protect their livelihood and tried to discourage settlement of the western region.
3. (a) The British solution to the problems in the western lands began with the Proclamation of 1763, which reserved certain lands for the Indians, ordered settlers to leave the territory temporarily, and put the fur trade under royal control. (b) The British felt that the terms of the Proclamation of 1763 would give the government time to form a more permanent policy to deal with the western lands and to put an end to the conflict between the Indians and settlers. (c) The fur traders, the colonists who wanted to settle the lands, colonial merchants, and the land speculators all opposed the Proclamation of 1763.
4. Answers will vary. Students might mention that the vastness of the territory would make it difficult to know what was going on in all its parts; it would be difficult to enforce rules that were opposed by almost all of the people involved.

CHAPTER
6 The Struggle for Independence

SECTION REVIEW   *(text page 126)*

Suggested responses to the questions are:
1. By 1775, the Patriots had posted a watch on British troop movements in Boston and had set up a warning system for the Massachusetts countryside. They had stored arms and ammunition at Concord and other towns and had established a militia of 16,000 men ready to fight on a moment's notice.

2. The colonists resisted the British attempt to seize the powder and shot stored at Concord.
3. Most of the delegates to the Second Continental Congress recognized their historical connection to Great Britain. They considered themselves to be English and demanded their rights under English law. Unlike the radicals, who wanted independence, the conservatives assured the king that they had "not raised armies with ambitious designs of separating from Great Britain."
4. British-occupied Boston lay on a spit of land jutting into a harbor and flanked by Breed's Hill on the north and Dorchester Heights on the south. Ships entering the harbor could be easily attacked by cannons situated on these hills. Without control of both heights, the British could not supply their troops in the city or defend themselves against attack.

SECTION REVIEW   *(text page 129)*

Suggested responses to the questions are:
1. *For the break with Great Britain:* First, the British government had committed acts that many colonists believed had violated their rights as English subjects. Second, colonial blood had been shed defending these rights. Third, as citizens of an independent nation, captured Patriot soldiers could demand to be treated as prisoners of war and avoid being shot as rebels. Fourth, the Patriot government could seize the property of all Americans who remained loyal to the Crown. Fifth, the Patriots would have a better chance of winning foreign aid. The French and Spanish kings, for example, would probably favor a war that threatened to weaken the British empire. *Against the break with Great Britain:* First, the law, order, and stability maintained by the British government might be lost. Second, if the revolution failed, the colonists could be executed for treason. Third, there was a fear of revolution and anarchy within the colonies. Fourth, in merely resisting the specific acts of Parliament, the colonists had many friends and supporters in Great Britain; but they felt that they would lose British support if they attempted separation from Great Britain.
2. (a) Many Americans rejoiced at the signing of the Declaration of Independence because they supported its ideas. A substantial number were indifferent. The Loyalists, who were opposed to separation from England and were now considered traitors in their own land, feared violence at the hands of the Patriots. (b) The Declaration stated the reasons for separation from Great Britain, set forth the theory of the consent of the governed, and announced that the politi-

cal connection between the colonies and Great Britain was ended. **(c)** The Declaration of Independence was a practical document because it convincingly set forth the reasons for separation, provided the new nation with a theoretical framework upon which to establish its government, and declared that the colonies were independent states that claimed all the powers other independent countries enjoyed.

3. The theory of government presented in the Declaration held that all people are created equal and that it is the government's responsibility to see that equal opportunity and justice prevail. Furthermore, if a government proves unjust and harmful to the people, the people have the right to alter or abolish it. For the first time, government was perceived as the servant rather than the master of the governed.

SECTION REVIEW   *(text page 137)*

Suggested responses to the questions are:

1. New York City, with its central location, fine harbor, and access through the Hudson and Mohawk Valleys to the interior, was a perfect base of operations for British land and naval forces.
2. Washington's victories at Trenton and Princeton ruined British plans for a quick end to the war during the winter of 1776–77. The victories revived American spirits and resulted in an increase of volunteers for the Continental Army.
3. **(a)** St. Leger came southwest from Montreal on the St. Lawrence River, crossed Lake Ontario to Fort Oswego, and then headed east through the Mohawk Valley toward Albany. Burgoyne advanced from Canada across Lake Champlain and through the New York wilderness. Although Howe's plan called for him to go north along the Hudson River to Albany, he travelled along the coast south of New York City, up the Chesapeake Bay, through Pennsylvania to Philadelphia, and back to New York City. **(b)** Had the plan succeeded, the British would have controlled New York and would have separated New England from the rest of the states. This probably would have brought the war to a speedy conclusion.

SECTION REVIEW   *(text page 140)*

Suggested responses to the questions are:
1. **(a)** The French sent arms and supplies, troops

and officers, and used their West Indies fleet to cut off supplies to Lord Cornwallis at Yorktown. **(b)** France hoped to improve its trade with the American states; weaken its long-time rival, England; and get American help to protect its West Indian possessions. **(c)** Spain and the Netherlands supported the American cause, and volunteers from Prussia (Baron von Steuben) and Poland (Pulaski and Kosciuszko) aided the Americans.

2. The British campaign in the South failed because the Americans fought a guerrilla war which, when bolstered by the actions of the regular Continental Army, finally forced Cornwallis to retreat to the coast.
3. Clark's victorious campaigns in the Northwest cleared the western lands of British forces.
4. Yorktown is located on a peninsula at the point where the Chesapeake Bay meets the Atlantic Ocean. Washington directed the French fleet to blockade the mouth of the bay, thus cutting off British supply lines to Yorktown. Washington then moved his army south and, with the help of the French fleet, down the Chesapeake Bay to Yorktown. The two branches surrounded Cornwallis, who was forced to surrender.

SECTION REVIEW   *(text page 145)*

Suggested responses to the questions are:
1. **(a)** Black soldiers fought heroically in most of the important battles during the Revolution. **(b)** Women collected lead and helped to manufacture bullets; made uniforms for soldiers; collected and distributed hospital supplies; accompanied the troops to serve as cooks, launderers, and nurses; and occasionally acted as spies and messengers. Some women, such as Margaret Corbin, Molly Pitcher, and Deborah Sampson, fought in the ranks.
2. **(a)** See the chart at the top of page A26. Answers will vary. **(b)** The Americans' most important strength was their possession of the land. All they had to do to win was hold on to it. The Americans' most glaring weakness was their shortage of troops and inability to supply the troops. The major British strengh was its large, well-trained army. The major British weakness was having to supply the army from across the Atlantic Ocean.
3. **(a)** The United States, Great Britain, Spain, and Russia claimed territory in North America in 1783. **(b)** After the Treaty of Paris, the Western boundary of the United States was the Mississippi River.

Strengths	
American	**British**
Washington's leadership	Well-trained, well-organized, and well-fed professional army
Faith and devotion of many soldiers and citizens	Assistance from American Loyalists
Heroic actions by individual leaders	Large and professional navy
Were fighting on their own land	Resources of large empire
A professional, if small, navy	Overwhelming number of troops
Privateers	
Foreign aid from France and other nations	

Weaknesses	
American	**British**
Shortage of troops and supplies	Troops had to be supplied and reinforced from across the Atlantic
Many indifferent and selfish citizens	Never concentrated their overwhelming forces against the Americans
Weak central government	Ignorance of American land and people
Lack of money	Reliance upon Hessian troops
Substantial number of Loyalists who aided the British	Problems with European nations
	Increasing opposition at home to the war

CHAPTER 6 REVIEW   (text page 149)

Reviewing Important Terms

1. true
2. false, radical
3. false, conservatives
4. true
5. true
6. true
7. true

Practicing Critical Thinking Skills

Suggested responses to the questions are:

1. Answers will vary. Students might mention that if Great Britain had let the colonies develop freely they might not have been forced to revolt. On the other hand, the colonies might eventually have come to the point where their further development would have resulted in unacceptable competition to British commerce, agriculture, and industry; and British economic control would have become unbearably restrictive to the American colonies. War might have broken out then.
2. Students should agree. The Americans wanted to maintain both the control they had over their lives, which came partly from being 3,000 miles (4,830 kilometers) away from England, and the legal guarantees enjoyed by all British subjects.
3. (a) Answers will vary. Students who agree might suggest that a great many, if not most, colonists were either indifferent to or opposed independence, and that the colonists already had unprecedented freedom in their government and economy. Students who disagree might mention that a large percentage of the colonists wanted independence. Great Britain had committed acts that many colonists thought were intolerable and had already spilled American blood in the Boston Massacre. (b) British textbooks probably attempt to portray their nation's history in the best possible light.
4. (a) Saratoga could be called the turning point of the Revolutionary War because France recognized the United States and news of the victory bolstered American spirits. (b) The battle marked the first time colonies had successfully rebelled.
5. Answers will vary. Students might mention any of the following: Lexington and Concord were defeats for the British caused by the Americans' ability to take advantage of the terrain and fight a guerrilla action; the Battle of Bunker (Breed's) Hill was a British victory because the British simply had more bullets and supplies than the Americans; Yorktown was a victory for the Americans, resulting from masterful leadership by Washington, naval and ground help from the French, and Britain's inability to supply its armies from across the ocean or break through the French fleet blocking Chesapeake Bay.
6. French aid was certainly extremely helpful to the American cause. Before the French joined in the war, the American troops were poorly equipped and clothed. The Americans had practically no navy, and British troops outnumbered American forces. On the other hand, the Americans had dealt the British two crushing defeats (Trenton and Saratoga) before the French entered the war, and the British had sent commissioners to the Continental Congress to negotiate, indicating that they realized the war would be difficult, if not impossible, to win.
7. Answers will vary. Students might mention the following similarities and differences. *Similarities:* the use of guerrilla tactics; the use of naval blockades; and the use of propaganda to increase enthusiasm; the use of aid from other countries not directly involved in the dispute *Differences:* lack of rapid communications; lack of rail, air, and other motorized forms of transport; the smaller size of the belligerent forces in comparison to modern mass armies; and the generally primitive level of armament technology of the eighteenth century

Developing History Study Skills

(a) *Common Sense* was biased in that it was written with the direct intention of persuading the American public to break away from Great Britain and did not discuss any of the positive aspects of royal rule. (b) The Declaration of Independence is biased because it only lists the objections to royal rule. Students should support their answer with specific quotes.

Relating Geography and History

1. (a) The privateers evaded the British blockade and attacked both merchant and naval vessels. (b) The privateers were privately owned ships. Because of the blockade and other restrictions, merchant ships and fishing vessels took part in the privateering activities. The rewards were worth the risk.
2. Rhode Island's coast was unprotected.
3. (a) Individual states, except for Delaware and New Jersey, maintained their own navies. (b) Because of their greater number, and the unofficial nature of their activities, the privateers were more successful against the British sea power.

Forming a Confederation

SECTION REVIEW   *(text page 154)*

Suggested responses to the questions are:
1. The colonists had to organize new governments to replace the colonial governments that no longer functioned, and they had to prevent lawlessness and disorder in the colonies.
2. (a) The new state constitutions provided for bills of rights to protect the liberties of the citizens, guided by the principles of the Declaration of Independence. (b) The constitutions included separation of powers to prevent any individual group from becoming too powerful. (c) Separation of church and state was stipulated so that all individuals might be free to support the religion of their choice and to worship as they pleased.

3. (a) The Revolution did not end slavery. Some slaves were freed because slaveowners were troubled by the obvious contradiction between slavery and the principles of the Declaration of Independence. All slaves in Massachusetts were declared free. However, many Americans found slavery profitable, and others were unsure about the role blacks would play in American life. (b) The position of women did not change very much. They still could not vote or hold office. Married women had little control over their property or important decisions concerning their children. (c) Although slavery continued to exist, attitudes about the institution showed signs of change. Slaves were allowed to fight in the Revolution; some slaveowners freed their slaves; a few states passed laws providing for the gradual abolition of slavery; and abolitionist societies were formed. Women such as Abigail Adams began to speak out against the restrictions placed upon them and to demand a share in the nation's political life.
4. When a state tries to force someone to follow a religion in which he or she does not believe, the person will, according the the source, become hypocritical and uncooperative. Furthermore, to force a person to support a church to which he or she does not belong is sinful and unfair.

SECTION REVIEW   *(text page 159)*

Suggested responses to the questions are:
1. (a) The issue that delayed the ratification of the Articles of Confederation was the claims of several states to the lands between the Appalachian Mountains and the Mississippi River. Delegates from states without such claims believed that they would be at a disadvantage. (b) The issue was resolved by the adoption of Maryland's proposal that these lands be ceded to the central government.
2. (a) The Land Ordinance of 1785 required that each township and each section be clearly identified. Therefore, settlers who purchased land would have a clear title to the land they bought. (b) Settlements in the townships were close together, making them easier to defend in the event of attack. (c) The sale of western lands at less than a dollar per acre provided the Confederation with its major source of income. Part of the money was used to pay off war debts.
3. (a) The Northwest Ordinance provided that when any part of the Northwest Territory had 60,000 free inhabitants, the people could draft a constitution. When Congress approved the constitution, that part of the territory was admitted as a state, equal in all respects to the older states. (b) The ordinance promoted de-

mocracy by prohibiting slavery in the territory and by encouraging public education.

4. The states entered the Confederation to protect their newly won liberties, to defend themselves against foreign interference, and to cooperate for the benefit of all.

5. (a) The Northwest Territory lacked an ocean coastline. (b) Settlers would have to travel long distances overland, slowing down the rate of settlement.

SECTION REVIEW   *(text page 163)*

Suggested responses to the questions are:

1. (a) The Articles of Confederation gave the central government the power to create post offices, regulate weights and measures, borrow and coin money, declare war and make peace, and build and equip a navy. The central government could ask the states to supply men and money for an army. (b) Answers will vary. Students should include three of the following: the central government's structure was weak; it could not regulate the finances of the states, causing monetary chaos; it could not tax the states and raise money for its operations or pay war debts; it could not regulate trade to protect the nation's industry; it could not hold the states to foreign treaties; and it had no military power to back up its demands or protect the citizens.

2. (a) The merchants' chief problems were the lack of a uniform and stable currency, the loss of British trade advantages, and a depression. (b) The farmers had to deal with the currency problem, the loss of markets in the West Indies, a disproportionate tax burden, foreclosure, and, in the West, the Spanish closing of New Orleans to American goods.

3. (a) When a large number of Massachusetts farm mortgages were foreclosed, the farmers, led by Daniel Shays, banded together to stop the foreclosures by force. The rebellion was crushed by the Massachusetts militia. (b) Many Americans were alarmed because the armed revolt threatened to destroy law and order and the foundations of their society.

4. The farmers could ship their products down the rivers to New Orleans. To ship goods directly east meant crossing the mountains.

CHAPTER 7 REVIEW   *(text page 167)*

Reviewing Important Terms

1. true
2. true
3. false, ratify
4. true
5. false, section
6. false, township
7. true
8. true
9. false, confederation

Practicing Critical Thinking Skills

Suggested responses to the questions are:

1. (a) Each of the new states wrote constitutions with bills of rights guaranteeing freedom of speech, the press, religion, trial by jury, and equality of all citizens. The constitutions also included separation of governmental powers to insure that the governments would be "governments of laws, not of men." Most states separated church and state, and some passed laws providing for the gradual abolition of slavery. (b) Americans were rebelling against laws passed by the British Parliament without their consent. They wanted to make sure such events could not take place again. Their determination was inspired and supported by the ideals of the Declaration of Independence. (c) Undemocratic practices still existed. In most states, property and religious qualifications limited who could vote; women were denied any voice in government and could not control their own property; and slavery remained.

2. Rush used "revolution" here to mean a radical change in the American way of life. This change reflected the settlers' new ways of thinking. The change also referred to the constant need to adapt to new environments.

3. (a) The merchants were probably not pleased with the Confederation. The chaos in currency and trade regulations did not help business; neither did the loss of British markets in the West Indies. The merchants wanted a stronger government, with power to regulate all these things so they could go about their business. (b) Artisans, who generally served the local community, were probably satisfied with the Confederation government. They were free to sell their wares and services, their liberties were protected by state constitutions, and the tax burden fell lightly on them. (c) Many farmers were especially hard hit by the depression that followed the war. They could no longer sell to the British West Indies, and western farmers could not use the Spanish port of New Orleans, which made it impossible for them to ship their goods. The farmers probably favored a stronger central government.

4. Answers will vary. Some students might argue that the government was a success because it solved the western land question and provided a democratic policy for the new nation to get back on the road to prosperity. It provided experience in national self-government and laid a foundation for the Constitution. Other students will consider the Confederation a failure because it lacked the power to tax, support an army, defend

the borders, enforce treaties, and regulate trade; it lacked an executive and a judiciary; and the number of votes needed to pass legislation or to amend the Articles made congressional action difficult.

5. The Northwest Ordinance provided for the orderly settlement of western lands and for new areas to come into the Union as states on an equal footing with existing states. It also encouraged education and prohibited slavery.

6. Answers will vary. Students might point out that we have a tradition of a strong government and therefore the arguments would not be the same. Others might mention that many people think the federal government has too much power.

7. **(a)** Answers will vary. Students might mention that under the Articles the central government had no real authority. This situation caused so many problems that the young nation changed its form of government with the ratification of the Constitution. Later, the Civil War proved that the balance of power issue had not been resolved. Even today, some groups advocate more power for the states, while others want a more powerful central government. **(b)** Answers will vary. Students might mention that authority and liberty must be balanced in any democratic country, if the democracy is going to survive. Too much liberty can lead to confusion and anarchy, while too much authority can lead to repressive government as was the case under British rule.

Developing History Study Skills

(a) Connecticut, Virginia, and New York **(b)** Virginia, Massachusetts, and New York **(c)** Virginia, Massachusetts, and New York **(d)** approximately 110 miles **(e)** Northeast **(f)** chief pioneer routes to the Northwest Territory

Relating Geography and History

1. **(a)** *Illinois:* the Illinois, Mississippi, Wabash, and Ohio rivers; *Indiana:* the Wabash, Illinois, and Ohio rivers; *Michigan:* the Illinois River; *Ohio:* the Muskingum, Scioto, Miami, and Ohio rivers **(b)** The rivers lead to the Mississippi River, which flows to New Orleans.

2. The Spaniards would not guarantee American farmers the right to use the port of New Orleans to ship their goods to Atlantic ports or to Europe. The British refused to abandon their forts in the Northwest Territory, and some British and Spanish officers supplied weapons to the Indians and encouraged the Indians to attack settlers.

3. Answers will vary. Students might mention that the government under the Articles of Confederation was too weak to protect western set-

tlers from the Indians, the Spaniards, and the British. This weakness was the result of the lack of power under the Articles to set up an orderly system of finances; consolidate trade policies; and provide the money to establish military strength, without which the government could not enforce treaties.

8 Creating a Federal Union

SECTION REVIEW [text page 173]

Suggested responses to the questions are:

1. **(a)** The presence of Benjamin Franklin and George Washington added dignity, authority, and legitimacy to the proceedings. Franklin often helped to calm rising tempers. George Washington was unanimously chosen presiding officer of the Convention. **(b)** The Constitutional Convention was held in secret because the delegates realized that the news of what they were doing would plunge the country into heated argument and subject them to the pressures of public opinion. They knew that differences of opinion were easier to iron out in a private conference than in a public debate. They wanted to agree among themselves before presenting their proposals to the people.

2. The delegates agreed from the beginning to write an entirely new Constitution. They agreed on the need for a strong central government; on a republican form of government; and on a government in which the executive, legislative, and judicial powers would be separated. They recognized that the new government would be respected only if it had the power to tax, to raise an army, and to regulate commerce.

3. **(a)** Differences between large and small states arose over fair representation in Congress; differences arose between northern and southern states over how to count slaves for taxation and representation purposes, the central government's power to impose tariffs, and the status of the slave trade. **(b)** The large states wanted representation to be based on popula-

tion; the small states wanted each state to have equal representation. Northern states wanted to count slaves for taxation but not for representation, wanted the central government to regulate trade, and generally favored the abolition of slavery. Southern states wanted to count slaves for representation but not taxation, opposed tariffs of any kind, and wanted slavery to continue. **(c)** The Great Compromise established a two-house Congress, in which states were represented equally and by population. The three-fifths compromise stated that three fifths of the slaves would be counted for both taxation and representation. The commerce compromises gave Congress the power to levy tariffs on imports, but not on exports, and allowed the importation of slaves until 1808.

4. **(a)** At the time the Constitution was written, many Americans believed that slavery was gradually dying out in the United States and would cease to be a problem by 1808. **(b)** The antislavery forces based their assumption on conditions and trends existing in 1787. They could not foresee that the circumstances would change by 1808 and that the demand for slave labor would actually increase.

ereignty in all matters and cooperate through the agency of the central government.

2. **(a)** The delegates selected the powers given to the federal government on the basis that they were of common concern to all the states and would correct the major weaknesses of the Articles of Confederation. **(b)** Answers will vary. Students might mention the powers to levy and collect taxes; to borrow money; to coin money; to raise and support armies; to regulate commerce with foreign nations, and among the several states; and to provide and maintain a navy.

3. **(a)** The Constitution protected the states by expressly forbidding the federal government to exercise certain powers, such as the power to tax goods shipped between states. **(b)** The Tenth Amendment further specified that "the powers not delegated to the United States by the Constitution, nor prohibited by it to the states, are reserved to the states respectively, or to the people."

4. The Constitution is regarded as the "supreme law of the land." In cases of conflict, the Constitution and the laws of the federal government take precedence over the state constitutions and state laws.

SECTION REVIEW *(text page 175)*

Suggested responses to the questions are:

1. The new Constitution was to be ratified by special state conventions made up of elected delegates. It would become effective when 9 out of 13 states ratified it.

2. **(a)** Washington's influence helped to gain Virginia's approval of the Constitution. **(b)** Hamilton helped win New York with his brilliant defense of the Constitution in a series of widely read essays. **(c)** Madison played a prominent role in winning New York. **(d)** Jay also worked for ratification in New York.

3. Washington was unanimously elected President because of his reputation as a Patriot and a leader.

SECTION REVIEW *(text page 177)*

Suggested responses to the questions are:

1. In a federal union, the central government is given authority over matters of concern to the people of all states. The member states retain freedom on matters not assigned to the federal government or not expressly forbidden to the states. In a confederation, the states retain sov-

SECTION REVIEW *(text page 179)*

Suggested responses to the questions are:

1. The framers of the Constitution feared tyranny in any form, including the rule of a misguided majority.

2. **(a)** The principle of separation of powers was meant to guard against tyranny by preventing any one branch of government from becoming too strong. **(b)** The system can delay the passage of necessary laws, especially when the President belongs to one party and Congress is dominated by another. On the whole, however, the system has worked well. **(c)** Congress — the legislature — makes the laws; the chief executive — the President — carries out the laws; the judiciary — the federal court system — interprets the laws.

3. **(a)** The power of the President is checked by Congress through impeachment, ratification of treaties, confirmation of key appointments, control of taxes, and overriding the President's veto. **(b)** The President can check Congress through the veto, the annual "State of the Union" message, special sessions, special messages to Congress, and appeals to the people. The judiciary can check both the President and Congress by declaring laws unconstitutional. **(c)** Congress can check the judiciary by impeaching judges, changing the number of Su-

preme Court Justices, and refusing to confirm judicial appointments. The President can check the judiciary by appointing Supreme Court Justices and other federal judges with the consent of the Senate. The President may also grant pardons and reprieves to federal offenders. **(d)** The purpose of these checks is to prevent any one branch from becoming too powerful.

SECTION REVIEW   *(text page 180)*

Suggested responses to the questions are:
1. Because they had experienced the loss of some of their civil liberties in the period before the Revolutionary War, the framers of the Constitution were concerned with protecting these liberties. The Declaration of Independence had clearly stated that the role of government was to protect the rights and liberties of the people. The framers therefore itemized the liberties guaranteed to everyone in the Bill of Rights.
2. The Constitution and the Bill of Rights specify which liberties may not be abridged or altered without due process of law. The people may turn to the Bill of Rights for protection whenever their rights appear to be in danger.
3. **(a)** The federal courts decide what a right means and determine the limits of an individual's rights in light of current conditions. **(b)** Individual rights must be limited because they exist only in relation to the rights of others. The rights of one individual should not infringe on the rights of another.

SECTION REVIEW   *(text page 185)*

Suggested responses to the questions are:
1. **(a)** The framers of the Constitution included an amendment process because they realized that changes in society would require changes in the basic law from time to time. **(b)** They made the process slow and difficult so that amendments would be added only when they were truly needed.
2. **(a)** The elastic clause allows Congress to stretch its delegated powers to meet new situations. For example, Congress has stretched its power to regulate commerce to include improving rivers and harbors. **(b)** The judiciary has the power to decide whether or not a law passed using the elastic clause violates the Constitution.
3. **(a)** The "unwritten Constitution" includes practices essential to governmental operation that

have been established by custom and tradition, not by the Constitution. **(b)** Answers will vary. Students might mention three of the following: political parties and nominating conventions have arisen out of normal differences of opinion; cabinet meetings, regular meetings of heads of various executive departments, have arisen out of the needs of executive business; senatorial courtesy, or seeking the advice of senators of the same party, has developed into a custom to ensure greater cooperation within the party; and Congressional committees have grown into an elaborate system because of the complexity of the lawmaking process.
4. Provisions for new states were important so that the people in the rapidly growing western territories could eventually take part in their government as did the citizens of older states.
5. Students should agree. Fixed procedures such as the election process, the system of checks and balances, and the amendment process have helped maintain order, even in critical times, and have provided a framework for the growth of democracy. Furthermore, Americans have been able to adapt the Constitution successfully to meet the demands of a changing society for more than 200 years.

CHAPTER 8 REVIEW   *(text page 187)*

Reviewing Important Terms

1. true
2. true
3. true
4. false, executive power
5. false, concurrent powers
6. false, delegated powers
7. true
8. false, the elastic clause
9. false, central government
10. true
11. false, veto
12. true

Practicing Critical Thinking Skills

Suggested responses to the questions are:
1. The new Constitution reflected the fear of tyranny and the memories of royal government from before 1775; the Constitution provided checks to insure against tyrants. Students may also recall the background of English colonists. The Magna Carta and the rights of English subjects lie at the heart of the Constitution as well as at the heart of the American Revolution.
2. The Declaration of Independence states that governments are created by people to secure

their "unalienable rights of life, liberty, and the pursuit of happiness." The Preamble to the Constitution puts these ideals into action. "We, the people of the United States" have created a new government under law, the Constitution. We have formed a political union ". . . to establish justice, . . . provide for the common defense, promote the general welfare, and secure the blessings of liberty . . ."

3. The framers of the Constitution were anxious to improve the system of government, but they held different views on how to achieve this goal. Their efforts were successful only because they were willing to compromise. The Great Compromise solved the question of representation by establishing a two-house legislature. The problem of how to count slaves for representation and taxation was resolved by the three-fifths compromise.

4. (a) A republic is a system of government in which representatives elected by the people make the laws. (b) Franklin meant that in order for a republic to succeed, the people must be willing to make the effort to identify their problems and needs, to weigh the alternative courses of action, and to elect the best people to represent their wishes. (c) Provisions in the Constitution intended to help us keep our republic include the checks and balances system, fixed terms of office for government officials, frequent elections, enumerated powers, powers reserved to the people, and the guarantees of civil liberties in the Bill of Rights.

5. (a) Answers will vary. Students might mention that they come in direct contact with the government through their dealings with the post office and in obtaining a driver's license, a social security card, and a passport. Government touches the life of the student who attends a public school; and the life of everyone who travels on government-funded roads, trains, and buses, or who pays sales tax on merchandise or borrows books from public libraries. (b) Answers will vary. Students might mention taxes, money, the regulation of weights and measurements, and post offices. (c) Answers will vary. Students might mention driver's licenses, social security cards, and airline and railroad regulations. Social security, railroads, and airlines did not exist when the Constitution was written. However, Congressional regulation of such parts of American life are based on the broad interpretation of the elastic clause.

Developing History Study Skills

(a) Answers will vary. (b) The Rules Committee has the power to put one bill ahead of another or to block the procedure of any bill of which it does not approve. (c) The Conference Committee smooths out the differences between the House and Senate versions of a bill, revises the bill to try to satisfy both houses, and returns the revised bill to the House and the Senate for approval. (d) The President may sign a bill, veto a bill, or allow a bill to become law without signing it.

Relating Geography and History

1. (a) Maine, New Hampshire, Vermont, New York, Pennsylvania, Ohio, Kentucky, Tennessee, and Georgia (b) People living near the borders might have problems with Indians; disputes might arise over boundaries; or there might come a time when there would be danger of invasion. Students may think of other ideas.

2. Distant states might be faced with inconveniences as a result of being far from the seat of government. Some of these would be the long distances that their representatives to the government would have to travel; the differences in their problems and interests from those of the more populated areas; and the difficulty in getting the same quality of public services. On the other hand, when facing problems in the wilderness or foreign threats, distant areas would benefit from having a strong government to back them up and give them support — financially, militarily, and diplomatically.

UNIT TWO REVIEW   [text page 188]

Discussing Ideas

1. Great Britain's policies designed to promote the mercantilist economy were viewed by the colonists as repressive. The colonists' protests took various forms such as petitions, economic boycotts, and sometimes violence. Actions of protest, followed by reprisals and the inability of the two sides to solve their disputes, led to the outbreak of the war. Students should give specific events in their answers, such as the Tea Act, leading to the Boston Tea Party; the Stamp Act, leading to acts of protest by such groups as the Sons of Liberty, etc.

2. (a) The Americans, with the help of the French, finally wore down the British. Other reasons that might be mentioned are the fact that the Americans were fighting on their own soil; the British soldiers were not as inspired as the American forces. (b) The American army was made up of segments from assorted states that were not always in agreement; soldiers were only in service for a limited time; money and supplies were difficult to obtain because of the

weakness of the government; and they were at a disadvantage against the British navy.

3. (a) The new Constitution was written because American leaders realized that the old Articles of Confederation were not strong enough to bring order and prosperity to the country. (b) The new Constitution took care of the things that had been weaknesses in the Articles of Confederation: the establishment of a strong central government; the power to tax; the power to raise an army; and the power to regulate commerce.

4. The Constitution sets up a republican form of government in which the executive, judicial, and legislative powers are separated. In the Bill of Rights, the Constitution spells out guarantees of the individual freedoms that were not always respected by the British during the colonial period.

Applying History Study Skills

1. (a) h (b) e (c) f (d) g
2. (a) 36 square miles (93.2 square kilometers) (b) one section (c) It shows that Americans were devoted to the ideals of public education.

TEACHER'S NOTES

UNIT THREE
Building the Nation

A Strong Start for the Nation

SECTION REVIEW   *(text page 224)*

Suggested responses to the questions are:
1. **(a)** There were no federal laws, no courts, no law-enforcement officers, no navy, and a very small army. **(b)** There was no treasury and no method of collecting taxes. The American people had little money to pay the taxes that the new government would have to levy to support its operations and pay off the large Revolutionary War debt. **(c)** Difficult problems lay ahead in the area of foreign affairs. The President had to work out a foreign policy acceptable to Congress. The nation had no ambassadors and little military strength.
2. The only guidelines the newly elected officials had were the general principles of the Constitution and the experience gained from their work in the various colonial governments and in the Confederation.
3. The first Congress passed the Judiciary Act, which established the nation's courts; sent the Bill of Rights to the states to be ratified; and re-enacted the Northwest Ordinance, providing a government for the Northwest Territory. It levied a small tariff on imports to raise revenue and created three executive departments.
4. The Judiciary Act gave the Supreme Court the power of judicial review. Any state laws or decisions of state courts that violated the Constitution, or the laws and treaties made under it, were void. This helped define federal and state powers.

SECTION REVIEW   *(text pages 228–29)*

Suggested responses to the questions are:
1. **(a)** The first Congress set the precedent that, while Congress is responsible for passing laws, it relies on the Executive Department for advice and guidance. **(b)** Hamilton proposed repayment in full of the $12 million owed to France, the Netherlands, and Spain. He proposed redemption of government bonds and paper money at face value. He further suggested that the federal government pay the debts that states had contracted in waging the Revolution. He decided upon establishing a banking system in which tax officials could deposit government funds by check; the system would provide loans to the government and individuals and would guarantee a sound, uniform currency. By paying its debts and by establishing such a currency, the new government would demonstrate that it intended to meet its obligations.
2. **(a)** Both federal and state bonds were considered worthless at the end of the Revolutionary War. Many holders of bonds and Continental currency had sold their holdings to speculators for a fraction of their original worth. If the new government now redeemed these issues, the speculators would benefit, not the people. Moreover, states that had already paid their debts, or that had small debts, did not want to assume part of the debts of other states. **(b)** Hamilton convinced Congress to establish the nation's credit by paying the national and domestic debt. A compromise over state debts was reached when southerners agreed to support the Assumption Bill in exchange for a northern agreement to locate the national capital along the banks of the Potomac River on land donated by Maryland and Virginia.
3. **(a)** Hamilton argued that a national banking system would provide a convenient place to deposit tax money, a sound and uniform currency, and a reliable source for borrowing. **(b)** Jefferson opposed the bank on the grounds that it was unconstitutional and would give the rich a monopoly over the country's money. **(c)** Hamilton justified the constitutionality of the bank by referring to the elastic clause, which gave Congress the power to establish a "necessary and proper" banking system to aid in collecting taxes and borrowing money.
4. **(a)** The isolated frontier farmers had difficulty transporting their corn to eastern markets, so they turned the corn into whisky, which was much more easily transported. Whisky was the frontier farmers' major source of cash. When the federal government levied an excise tax on li-

quor, the farmers refused to pay it, thus challenging the power of the government. **(b)** The federal government demonstrated its strength by suppressing the rebellion.

SECTION REVIEW *(text page 231)*

Suggested responses to the questions are:
1. **(a)** Europeans feared that the ideas and violence of the French Revolution would spread to other countries. As a result, they went to war with the French Republic to crush the revolution. **(b)** Both Britain and France seized American ships and cargoes enroute to the enemy's ports. The British also impressed American sailors into the British navy.
2. **(a)** The Proclamation of Neutrality forbade American citizens to give any support to the warring nations, thus abandoning the treaty of alliance with France. **(b)** Jay's Treaty avoided war with Great Britain by granting the British the right to trade in American ports.
3. **(a)** Pinckney's Treaty with Spain settled the boundary between Florida and Georgia and gave westerners the right to ship their goods down the Mississippi and out through the port of New Orleans without paying duties to Spain. **(b)** The treaty gave some assurance to westerners that Spain would not close their vital trade route, the Mississippi River.
4. Washington urged the United States to have commercial relations with foreign nations but to avoid "permanent alliances with any portion of the foreign world."

SECTION REVIEW *(text page 234)*

Suggested responses to the questions are:
1. In the election of 1792, John Adams met strong opposition from George Clinton for the Vice Presidency. Adams was backed by Hamilton and his followers, who became known as the Federalists; Clinton was supported by Jefferson and his Republican followers.
2. **(a)** Differing beliefs about the role of government, the interpretation of the Constitution, and the conduct of foreign policy brought about loosely grouped alliances which became parties. **(b)** The Federalist Party included many wealthy merchants, manufacturers, lawyers, and clergy. The Republican Party was generally supported by the owners of small farms or wage earners in the towns.
3. **(a)** Hamilton had little faith in the ability of average people to govern themselves. Jefferson had great faith in the average person's ability to play an effective part in government. **(b)** Hamil-

ton wanted a loose interpretation of the Constitution; he wanted to make maximum use of the elastic clause. Jefferson believed that the Constitution gave sufficient power to the government as written. He wanted a strict interpretation of the Constitution. **(c)** Believing that people are basically good, as Jefferson did, may lead to the building of a weak federal government, a strong state government, and ironclad guarantees of individual liberties so that people may participate as much as possible in governing themselves. Believing that people are not to be trusted may lead to Hamilton's interpretation of good government — one that provides strong federal leadership.

SECTION REVIEW *(text page 237)*

Suggested responses to the questions are:
1. **(a)** America's refusal to honor the Treaty of 1778 strained relations between the United States and France. The French also resented Jay's Treaty, which they regarded as pro-British. France became increasingly hostile, the French navy seized American ships, and the French government refused to receive the American ambassador. **(b)** Adams sent three prominent Americans to Paris to try to reach an agreement with France. **(c)** Three French officials, known only as "X, Y, and Z," made three insulting demands. When Americans heard of this, they demanded war with France.
2. **(a)** In 1799, the French and the Americans agreed to end the Treaty of 1778. The United States also dropped its claims against France for illegally seizing American ships. **(b)** President Adams wanted to keep peace with France. Napoleon, the new ruler of France, wanted to begin his rule free from foreign conflicts.
3. **(a)** The Alien and Sedition Acts provided that aliens must live in the United States for 14 years before becoming naturalized citizens, the President could expel any alien he thought was dangerous to the peace and security of the nation during war or peace, and anyone who wrote or spoke against the government could be fined or imprisoned. **(b)** The acts violated the provisions of the Bill of Rights guaranteeing free speech, a free press, and due process of law to an accused person.
4. **(a)** The supporters of the Kentucky and Virginia Resolutions claimed that the Alien and Sedition Acts made the federal government too strong. Their resolutions answered by claiming the states had the power to declare a federal law null and void. **(b)** Nationwide adoption of the Resolutions would have allowed states to refuse any federal law they disagreed with, or even to withdraw from the Union if dissatisfied.

SECTION REVIEW

(text page 239)

Suggested responses to the questions are:

1. By 1800, high taxes and the very unpopular Alien and Sedition Acts had caused the Federalists' influence to decline.
2. (a) Jefferson and Burr received the same number of electoral votes. Voting in the House of Representatives did not strictly follow party lines. Finally, Jefferson was elected on the thirty-sixth ballot. (b) The Twelfth Amendment provided for separate electoral ballots for President and Vice President.
3. In *Marbury v. Madison,* Marshall clarified the principle of judicial review, or the power of the Supreme Court to determine when a law of Congress is unconstitutional. In later decisions, Marshall established that the Supreme Court could set aside laws of state legislatures when these laws were contrary to the federal Constitution and that the Supreme Court had the power to reverse the decision of a state court.

CHAPTER 9 REVIEW

(text page 243)

Reviewing Important Terms

1. false, capital stock
2. true
3. true
4. true
5. true
6. false, right of deposit
7. false, loose construction

Practicing Critical Thinking Skills

Suggested responses to the questions are:

1. (a) A Kentucky farmer would have opposed Hamilton's program. As a landowner, he would have to pay the taxes levied on Kentucky to pay the other states' war debts, although Kentucky was not admitted to the Union until after the Revolution. And, as a frontier farmer who converted his corn into whisky, he would have opposed the excise tax on liquor. (b) The Boston shipowner would have supported Hamilton's program. With the foreign debt repaid, he would have benefited in trade from the good credit of the United States. Also, a stable currency, backed by the national bank, would have made conducting business easier at home and abroad. (c) The Philadelphia merchant would have supported Hamilton's proposal. A stable currency would help stabilize trade. (d) The South Carolina plantation owner would have had mixed feelings. He would have supported a stable currency and benefited from a good credit rating. However, he would have opposed any tariff that would have interfered with importing goods from foreign nations.
2. (a) Shays' Rebellion and the Whisky Rebellion protested taxes that affected farmers' incomes. (b) The federal government did not react to Shays' Rebellion — it occurred before the Constitution was ratified — and the Massachusetts government raised a militia to fight the rebels. During the Whisky Rebellion, the federal government called out state militias to fight the rebels in Pennsylvania. (c) Both rebellions were crushed — Shays' violently, the Whisky Rebellion without bloodshed.
3. Washington established a policy of isolation. At the time, the United States could not afford to mix in foreign affairs because it was still a struggling young nation. Washington feared that foreign alliances might bind the new nation and prevent the government from acting in its own best interests.
4. *Refute:* The Sedition Act dealt only with libel and slander, which have always been considered illegal. From the time of the Zenger Case, the right to speak and print the truth was defended. *Defend:* The government could decide what was libelous or slanderous, and the intent of the act was to silence Republican opposition to Federalist policy. In fact, all ten persons fined and jailed under the act were Republicans. The First Amendment protects the right of the individual to express opinions opposing government policy.
5. Government-strengthening actions taken by the Federalists included the payment of national debts to improve the nation's credit and enable the government to borrow money; the creation of a National Bank and a standard currency; the defense of a loose interpretation of the Constitution, which extended federal authority; the order of the federal government calling out state militias to put down the Whisky Rebellion; and Supreme Court decisions by John Marshall — a federal appointee — defining the Supreme Court's right to declare state laws unconstitutional and to overturn state court decisions.
6. (a) The Kentucky and Virginia Resolutions and Marshall's decisions dealt with the issue of unconstitutional laws passed by Congress. (b) The Resolutions claimed the states had the right and power to nullify federal laws. In *Marbury v. Madison,* Marshall claimed that the right to determine unconstitutionality belonged to the Supreme Court. (c) Hamilton would have supported Marshall's decision because it strengthened the federal government and weakened the states' rights or compact theory of government proposed by the Kentucky and Virginia Resolutions.
7. Answers will vary according to the type of for-

eign policy being pursued by the government at the time of reading. However, for the post-1945 period, the trend has generally been away from the advice presented in Washington's address and toward permanent alliances (such as NATO) and engagement in "frequent controversies" in Europe and elsewhere. Students may wish to draw other examples from current events.

Developing History Study Skills

Answers will vary. Students might mention that the painting shows Daniel Boone leading a group of pioneers along the Cumberland Road across the Appalachian Mountains. The painting is probably an idealized vision. After many difficult days of wilderness trek to reach the Cumberland Gap, Boone and the pioneers would probably not have appeared in such fine clothing. The presence of women and children and the firm set of their jaws, however, is representative of the pioneer families that settled the lands beyond the Appalachians.

Relating Geography and History

1. (a) New England (b) the South
2. Adams and the Federalists were supported by the northern coastal urban manufacturing and commercial centers who appreciated the Federalist policies that favored manufacturing and trade.
3. States with frontier populations that had developed a democratic life style and an individualistic way of viewing issues, tended to respond favorably to the Jeffersonian assumption that the common person could be trusted to run the government of a republic in a responsible way. Jefferson also received support from many aristocratic southern farmers, who counted him as one of their own.

CHAPTER

10 The Nation's Growth

SECTION REVIEW   *(text page 249)*

Suggested responses to the questions are:
1. Americans feared the French would deny west-

ern farmers the right of deposit at New Orleans, thus severely limiting western trade. Also, French possession of Louisiana might prevent American expansion into the interior of the continent. France would be a powerful and aggressive nation on the western border.
2. Opponents of the Louisiana Purchase declared $15 million was too high a price for a wilderness. They also expressed fear that when the farmers filled this western territory, the eastern commercial interests in Congress would be outvoted. To strengthen their arguments, opponents insisted that the power to purchase territory from a foreign nation was not specifically granted in the Constitution.
3. (a) Lewis and Clark explored the northern Louisiana Territory, and then went beyond the Rocky Mountains into the Oregon country and to the Pacific Ocean. Pike explored the southern Louisiana Territory and then entered Spanish-held land south and west of the Lousiana Territory. (b) The Spanish and the British flanked the undefined borders of Louisiana, opening the way for border disputes. Based on the Lewis and Clark expedition, the United States joined Great Britain, Spain, and Russia in claiming the Oregon country.

SECTION REVIEW   *(text page 252)*

Suggested responses to the questions are:
1. (a) The Republicans repealed the Naturalization Act, the excise tax on whisky, and the Judiciary Act of 1801; they reduced the size of the army and navy. (b) The Republicans continued to pay installments on the public debt; they retained many Federalists in office; and they did not interfere with the Bank of the United States. Jefferson wanted to end bitterness between the Federalists and Republicans and show that he meant to unify the nation.
2. The country responded by giving Jefferson and Clinton an overwhelming victory in the election of 1804.
3. (a) The Barbary States were located on the North African coast and controlled access to the Mediterranean at the Strait of Gibraltar. Ships entering the Mediterranean had to pass very close to their lands. Furthermore, the long Mediterranean coastline with its many harbors made it easy for the Barbary pirates to attack the merchant ships of other nations. (b) New heroes, shared by people of every section of the United States, stimulated love of the nation and raised the United States in the estimation of the rest of the world.

SECTION REVIEW
(text page 256)

Suggested responses to the questions are:
1. American merchants reaped huge profits by engaging in blockade running.
2. (a) The British issued the Orders in Council, forbidding American vessels to trade in any ports controlled by France. Napoleon issued a similar set of orders and further warned that he would seize any ships entering French ports after stopping at British ports. (b) Jefferson asked Congress to pass an embargo forbidding Americans to trade with any foreign nations. (c) Merchants, farmers, and unemployed sailors were hurt economically by the embargo and angrily demanded its repeal.
3. The first action under Madison's administration was passage of the Non-Intercourse Act of 1809. This act forbade trade with France or Great Britain but allowed it with other countries. Under pressure, Congress let the law expire. In 1810, Madison signed another law in which he promised to trade only with the country — France or Great Britain — that first removed its restriction on American trade.
4. (a) Some Americans hoped to win part of Canada and Spanish Florida; war would provide an excuse for such a conquest. (b) Americans resented insults to the flag and impressment of American sailors. (c) Westerners thought that seizing Canada might end the danger of an alliance between the British and the Indians. (d) Some Americans wanted to seize Canada for its rich fur trade. (e) Great Britain and France violated the freedom of the seas. (f) Americans hoped that war would end impressment of American sailors by the British.

SECTION REVIEW
(text page 260)

Suggested responses to the questions are:
1. (a) American opinion of the War of 1812 was divided. As a result, two Republicans ran for President: Madison and anti-war De Witt Clinton. Madison won the election, but Clinton, backed by the Federalists, carried most of the New England and Middle Atlantic states. The Republicans also lost seats in Congress. (b) Merchants opposed the war because it would ruin their shipping, and they feared that the annexation of Canada and Florida would increase the power of farmers in Congress. Southerners feared that the annexation of Canada would weaken the power of the slaveholding states and increase the powers of the federal government.

2. The Treaty of Ghent ended the war, led to improved relations between the United States and Great Britain, and set up a commission to settle boundary disputes between the United States and Canada. The Rush-Bagot Agreement (1817) provided for an undefended boundary line between the United States and Canada.
3. After the War of 1812, the United States became more independent of Europe, and the European nations treated the United States with growing respect. For the next 100 years, Americans were able to concentrate on developing their own country.
4. (a) The United States' principal military aim was to capture Canada. (b) American militia were responsible for the Canadian campaign. They were poorly trained, equipped, and led. General Hull crossed into Canada, but then withdrew. A move against Montreal failed when the militia refused to leave American soil. (c) Perry defeated the British naval forces on Lake Erie. Macdonough stopped a major British invasion attempt on Lake Champlain. Jackson decisively defeated a British invasion force at New Orleans.

CHAPTER 10 REVIEW
(text page 263)

Reviewing Important Terms

1. true
2. true
3. true
4. false, freedom of the seas
5. true
6. true
7. true

Practicing Critical Thinking Skills

Suggested responses to the questions are:
1. (a) Jefferson wanted to end the rivalry between Republicans and Federalists. By his statement he meant that all Americans must work together for the good of the nation. (b) His actions were consistent with his statement. Following his Republican ideals, he urged Congress to repeal the Naturalization Act and the excise tax on whisky. He reduced the size of the army and navy to decrease the operating costs of the government. However, he kept many Federalist officeholders and continued many Federalist programs, including Hamilton's plan to pay the states' debts.
2. The Indians might have been able to hold on to their lands and prevent the white settlers from moving westward. The British might have been

able to hold on to their forts in the Northwest and thus keep a stronghold on the American continent.

3. (a) The delegates to the Hartford Convention met in secret session to propose amendments to the Constitution. Some even threatened to declare null and void any federal laws they believed were unconstitutional. The delegates ignored the prescribed methods for constitutional amendment and tried to take on the right of review constitutionally assumed by the Supreme Court. (b) Answers will vary. Students might mention that even though the delegates did not attempt to give direct aid to the enemy, the meeting undermined the war effort. In peacetime such a meeting would have been more acceptable because it would not have been harmful to the safety of the nation.

4. Answers will vary. Students might mention that from an economic point of view, the War of 1812 may be seen as a Second War of Independence. The nation began to manufacture its own goods, which led to a great degree of economic independence from England. In a political sense, it is impossible to speak of the war as a Second War for Independence. Political independence had been won in the American Revolution.

5. The first four Presidents were unable to avoid involvement in European affairs because the economy of the nation depended heavily on trade with Europe and with French and British colonies; the new nation was still weak, which encouraged European nations to make demands; and political divisions within the nation resulted in an ineffective foreign policy.

6. (a) Jefferson's statement implies that while government brings such benefits as internal order and security from threats from the outside world, the benefits of liberty and freedom of expression provided by newspapers are equally important to the quality of our lives. A government without newspapers could easily become tyrannical and undemocratic. In essence, Jefferson is relating the role of the press to the idea "Give me liberty or give me death." (b) Answers will vary. Students might mention that Jefferson's statement is applicable today to the extent that where there is a free press, such as in the United States, newspapers continue to be instrumental in checking any tendencies toward governmental abuses of liberty. Jefferson could not have foreseen, however, the extent to which newspapers have come to serve tyrannical regimes in other parts of the world. While governments may change, no nation has ever had the choice, implied in Jefferson's statement, of doing away with government altogether.

Developing History Study Skills

(a) years (b) Impressment begins Embargo Act, Madison's election, and Non-Intercourse Act. (c) Answers will vary.

Relating Geography and History

1. (a) Jefferson feared that in order to protect western interests, the United States would have to ally with the British, whose fleet would have the power to keep the port of New Orleans open. (b) Jefferson offered to buy New Orleans and West Florida from France.

2. (a) The eastern Federalists objected to the Louisiana Purchase on the grounds that a vast western territory would drain political power from eastern commercial interests. (b) The Federalists, once advocates of a loose interpretation of the Constitution, now argued for strict observance of its terms in order to block the Louisiana Purchase. Jefferson changed his views to support a loose interpretation of the Constitution in order to justify the purchase. Both sides changed their position on the Constitutional issue in order to support their position on the Louisiana issue.

3. The area between the Rocky Mountains and the northern Pacific coast was disputed territory, claimed by several countries. An American presence would strengthen the American claim.

4. The British lost an advantage in Oregon; they lost a chance for a strong alliance with the United States; and Napoleon gained resources to wage war against them.

CHAPTER

11 Gaining Prosperity and Respect

SECTION REVIEW   *(text page 267)*

Suggested responses to the questions are:

1. (a) The invention and development of power-driven machines helped bring about the Industrial Revolution. (b) The Industrial Revolution replaced hand production with machine production and shifted manufacturing from homes to factories.

2. Slater introduced water-powered machines and set up the first cotton mill in the United States.
3. (a) Capitalists used their money to build factories, install machines, buy raw materials, hire laborers, and distribute finished products. (b) The shortage of labor encouraged people to invent labor-saving machines. (c) Congress enacted a law that encouraged inventors. The law granted them exclusive rights to the profits made from their ideas.
4. Eli Whitney developed the use of interchangeable parts. James Watt produced the modern steam engine.
5. (a) Colonial towns and farms never had enough workers to develop the natural resources of the United States. (b) American workers received higher wages and better working conditions than their European counterparts. (c) The American government granted inventors and authors exclusive rights for 14 years to all profits made from their ideas.

SECTION REVIEW   *(text page 270)*

Suggested responses to the questions are:
1. (a) The phrase seemed to describe national life. The different groups in the country began to work together on common problems. The Federalist Party disappeared and the Republican Party became the only political party. Monroe's election by a large majority in 1816 and his reelection, without opposition, in 1820 were indicative of political harmony. (b) By 1817, the Republican Party had adopted many programs and beliefs of the Federalists. They now favored a loose interpretation of the Constitution, tariffs, a national bank, and an increase in the powers of the federal government at the expense of states' rights.
2. (a) The American System consisted of a national bank, a protective tariff, and a transportation system. (b) The national bank provided a uniform financial system; the protective tariff provided a wall behind which American factories could grow; and the transportation system united northeastern manufacturers and western and southern farmers to their mutual advantage.
3. When the charter for the first Bank of the United States expired, some state legislatures allowed private individuals to own and operate state banks. Some of the state banks issued paper money that had little value. The nation needed a stable and standard currency, which was best provided by a second national bank.
4. (a) During the War of 1812, British manufacturers could not sell their products in the United States. As a result, many new American factories sprang up. (b) After the war, British manufacturers sold their goods below cost in the United States in an effort to drive American manufacturers out of business. (c) The American government placed a protective tariff on manufactured goods shipped into the United States to ensure that American goods would be competitive.

SECTION REVIEW   *(text page 273)*

Suggested responses to the questions are:
1. (a) The first American canals and roads generally connected the coastal cities with the surrounding countryside. They were built by private businesses to improve trade and to make a profit. (b) The demand for improved transportation resulted in the construction of the National Road at federal expense. Begun in 1811, the road extended westward from Cumberland, Maryland, to Ohio and, by 1838, to Illinois.
2. (a) Overspeculation caused the Panic of 1819. State banks lent money too freely; southerners bought land at exorbitant prices; settlers in the West hurried to buy land; and manufacturers were building plants at an unjustified rate. The blow came when state banks could no longer meet their obligations, and the Bank of the United States began to foreclose on overdue mortgages. (b) Because the Bank of the United States foreclosed on their mortgages, many people blamed the Bank for their troubles.
3. (a) In *McCulloch v. Maryland,* Marshall stated that the federal government was supreme because it was created by the people, not by the states; that the Constitution gave Congress the power to create a national bank; and that the states did not have the right to tax the national bank or any other national institution because that right would seriously weaken the federal government. (b) In *Trustees of Dartmouth College v. Woodward,* Marshall asserted the right of the Supreme Court to declare an act by a state legislature unconstitutional. The decision also forbade state legislatures to tamper with state charters, since the charters were contracts. (c) In *Gibbons v. Ogden,* Marshall again declared a state law unconstitutional, and he expanded the interpretation of the interstate commerce clause of the Constitution. The state of New York had given Robert Fulton a monopoly over steamboat traffic on the Hudson River. Since navigation of the river involved interstate commerce, Marshall ruled that New York had no right to grant a monopoly.

SECTION REVIEW
(text page 277)

Suggested responses to the questions are:
1. When Napoleon conquered Spain in 1808, Spain's American colonies seized the opportunity to fight for their freedom and independence.
2. (a) The United States annexed West Florida over Spanish protests. Andrew Jackson's invasion of East Florida convinced Spain that the United States would not rest until it possessed this land. Spain therefore decided to sell the region. (b) The Adams-Onís Treaty of 1819, between the United States and Spain, gave the United States all of Spain's land east of the Mississippi River and any Spanish claims to the Oregon country. The United States agreed to pay $5 million in claims by American citizens against Spain and to abandon its claim to Texas.
3. (a) After 1815, Americans feared European intervention in the Western Hemisphere because France and her allies had formed an alliance to put down revolutions. Americans feared France might help Spain regain its New World colonies. Also, in 1821, Russia barred all ships of other nations from sailing along the Oregon coast. (b) President Monroe announced an American foreign policy, known as the Monroe Doctrine, to prevent intervention by European powers in the hemisphere; recognized the independence of the new Latin American states; and sent a strong protest note to Russia.
4. (a) The Western Hemisphere was no longer open to European colonization. Any attempt by a European power to gain control of any free American country would be viewed as an unfriendly act toward the United States. The United States would not interfere in the affairs of established European colonies in the hemisphere. (b) Monroe spoke for more than 10 million united people who were determined to retain their hard-won independence from Europe and to decide their own policies.

SECTION REVIEW
(text page 279)

Suggested responses to the questions are:
1. "Cultural independence" means that Americans no longer relied on European models of artistic expression. Truly American forms of language, religion, art, and literature began to develop.
2. Noah Webster wrote and published a dictionary standardizing American language. He also wrote a spelling book for elementary schools and edited a reader that contained much material on American history.

3. (a) Numerous Americans wrote books about American history. American history was included in the course of study in many elementary schools. In 1827, Massachusetts and Vermont required that American history be taught in the larger schools. (b) Jedediah Morse introduced students to United States geography. (c) Painters acquainted Americans with the leaders of the nation by painting their portraits. (d) Writers began to draw upon the American environment and experience for material for their works.

CHAPTER 11 REVIEW
(text page 283)

Reviewing Important Terms

1. true
2. true
3. true
4. false, American System
5. true
6. true
7. false, Monroe Doctrine

Practicing Critical Thinking Skills

Suggested responses to the questions are:
1. (a) The War of 1812 cut off manufactured goods from England, encouraging the growth of industry in the United States. (b) Scarcity of labor stimulated invention of labor-saving machines. (c) The government issued patents and copyrights and levied protective tariffs.
2. The development of a good transportation system was necessary to join all parts of the nation. Raw materials had to be transported to where they could be processed. The finished goods or products then had to be brought to markets to be sold.
3. (a) One policy the government could have adopted was the conquest of Indian tribes and their removal to the wilderness further west. Or the government could have protected Indian land and honored treaties defining the boundaries of Indian and white communities. (b) Arguments supporting the first policy might be that as the United States grew, the western lands were needed for agriculture and trade. Roads and canals through Indian territory were needed to unify the nation. Americans had acquired the territory by war and purchase. By legal standards of the time, the land belonged to the Americans. Arguments supporting the second policy might be that the Indians had lived on the western lands long before Europeans arrived on the continent, and they should at least be compensated for their land. As rightful owners, the Indians should decide which lands they wished to sell and which they wished to keep.

4. Answers will vary. Students who agree might mention that Supreme Court justices are appointed for life and do not have to worry about reelection when rendering a decision; interpretation of the Constitution is based on the beliefs of the interpreter; and Marshall's decisions reflected his Federalist belief in loose interpretation of the Constitution and strong federal power. Students who disagree might mention that Article 3 of the Constitution empowers the Supreme Court to hear and decide cases " . . . in law and equity arising under this Constitution (and) laws of the United States. . . . " Marshall's decisions always had a basis in the Constitution or laws of Congress. Article 4 of the Constitution states that the Constitution and the laws of Congress are the supreme law of the United States and take precedence over conflicting state laws. When Marshall declared state laws unconstitutional in the Dartmouth College case and *Gibbons v. Ogden,* he was applying Article 6 of the Constitution.

5. (a) Americans developed this system to make the United States economically independent. Congress enacted the program to build a stronger, more unified nation. (b) In *McCulloch v. Maryland,* Chief Justice Marshall ruled that the power of the federal government was supreme, that Congress had the power to create a national bank, and that no state had the power to tax the Bank of the United States. In *Trustees of Dartmouth College v. Woodward,* Marshall declared that no state had the power to interfere with a valid contract. This decision asserted the right of the Supreme Court to set aside state laws when such laws were unconstitutional and guaranteed that corporations operating under state charters would not be subjected to the whims of state legislators. In *Gibbons v. Ogden,* Marshall greatly broadened the definition of interstate commerce and paved the way for further control of interstate trade. (c) Webster's dictionary aimed at molding a national American language, distinct from English. Webster hoped his dictionary would help the United States achieve a uniform language.

6. (a) Answers will vary. Students might mention that outside influences, particularly the threat of Communist-inspired revolutions, are a concern today. (b) Answers will vary. Students might mention the concern of the United States over developments in Cuba and Nicaragua in recent years. Students might address the question of whether the relation of these countries to the Soviet Union is the same as implied by the term "colonization" in the excerpt.

Developing History Study Skills

Answers will vary.

Relating Geography and History

1. The Monroe Doctrine was written to discourage further European interference in the Western Hemisphere. This would be in the United States' best interests because it would keep strong powers from establishing themselves close to United States borders.

2. The Russians were threatening to assert their claims in the Pacific Northwest, which would involve the Oregon country.

3. It warned away European powers who might have been interested in restoring Spain's colonies. This would have posed a threat to American security. As a major foreign policy principle, it established the practice of discouraging powers from outside the hemisphere from establishing spheres of influence, thus preserving American hemispheric leadership. In the future, this policy became important as a defense tactic, especially after the Panama Canal was built.

4. (a) Great Britain had an interest in preserving their claim in Oregon as well as their commercial interests in Latin America. They were willing to support the doctrine in order to protect their interests. (b) the British navy

CHAPTER
12 Growing Democratic Strength

SECTION REVIEW *(text page 288)*

Suggested reponses to the questions are:

1. (a) The election of 1824 had four candidates, three of whom represented a section of the country: Adams, the Northeast; Crawford, the South; and Jackson, the West. No one won a majority of electoral votes, thus giving the choice to the House of Representatives. (b) Adams, who had come in second in electoral and popular votes, became President with the help of Henry Clay. Adams then appointed Clay Secretary of State. Jackson charged that Adams and Clay had made a "corrupt bargain" that cheated Jackson out of the Presidency.

2. (a) "The people" were the average white male citizens who had recently won the right to vote.

(b) Jackson's outlook and attitudes were the same as many white Americans. **(c)** Jackson had been born in poverty and had risen through his own efforts. He was identified with the hopes of those who were at the bottom and aspired to reach the top.

3. Americans differed violently in their reaction to Jackson's election. Because the votes of average people had figured decisively in an election for the first time, many wealthy and powerful Americans felt that "King Mob" had triumphed. Other Americans were jubilant, for they believed democracy had triumphed and that the ordinary people were entering a new era.

4. **(a)** The election of 1828 showed the advancing democratic forces in the United States. For the first time, ordinary citizens had elected a President. **(b)** Political power was more evenly divided between average men and the well-to-do. Jackson himself was a self-made man, not a man of wealthy background, as former leaders had been. For the first time the West was a strong force in national politics.

SECTION REVIEW   *(text page 293)*

Suggested responses to the questions are:
1. Jackson believed in political democracy; he believed that the government belonged to all the people; he believed in the Union — the United States as a whole — and in the power of the Presidency.
2. *For the spoils system:* It improves government by allowing more people to hold office, keeping government in closer touch with the citizens and giving more Americans first-hand experience in government. *Against the spoils system:* It leads to corruption because political parties may be led and supported by government officeholders whose major concern is keeping their jobs.
3. **(a)** Jackson, like many Americans of his day, believed the Indians were primitive people. Their presence on the frontier was blocking the advance of "civilization." **(b)** Jackson had made a reputation as an Indian fighter in battles with Creek and Seminole Indians. While President, he approved of the Indian resettlement program and disregarded the advice and pleas of missionaries. He ignored the decision of the Supreme Court in the case of the Cherokee removal.
4. **(a)** During Jackson's Presidency, nominating conventions came into use; restrictions on voting and holding office were removed in a number of states; people took a more active role in government; and political power was more evenly divided among Americans. **(b)** Despite these advances, democracy was still a distant goal. Women, black Americans, and Indians were denied participation in government. Criminals and the mentally ill had few rights and were harshly treated.

SECTION REVIEW   *(text page 297)*

Suggested responses to the questions are:
1. **(a)** Jackson opposed the Bank of the United States because he believed it benefited the rich at the expense of the poor and middle class. He claimed it was unconstitutional and corrupt — a tool used by rich easterners to influence Congressional legislation. **(b)** Popular slogans of the day supported Jackson by calling the Bank a monstrous monopoly. The rechartering of the Bank became the major issue in the 1832 election. Jackson won the election handily, showing the widespread support for his ideas.
2. Northern manufacturers wanted high tariffs to protect their products from competition. A protective tariff was first passed in 1816 with the agreement of Calhoun and other southerners. Tariff rates were raised in 1824 and again in 1828. This "Tariff of Abominations" threatened the trade of southern planters, whose protests led several southern states to declare the tariff null and void.
3. **(a)** The compromise tariff of 1833 satisfied the South because the tariff rates were to be reduced gradually to the level of 1816. **(b)** The North would have ten years to adjust to the lack of tariff protection. **(c)** Jackson was satisfied because he was provided with an act to enforce federal law with military power if necessary.
4. Jackson's actions supported his belief in a strong Presidency. He refused to be bound by Supreme Court decisions in the case of the Indian removals and in his insistence that the Bank of the United States was unconstitutional. He destroyed the Bank before its charter ran out by removing federal funds and depositing them in pet banks. When South Carolina threatened to secede over the tariff issue, Jackson repeated his determination to hold the Union together and privately even threatened to hang every leader.

SECTION REVIEW   *(text page 300)*

Suggested responses to the questions are:
1. The Whigs nominated several "favorite sons" to run against Van Buren in the 1836 election, hoping to throw the election into the House of Representatives and possibly get one of their candidates elected.

2. (a) Pet and wildcat banks issued bank notes far in excess of the federal funds on deposit. (b) Land speculation flooded the United States Treasury with unsound currency from the sale of public land. (c) The Specie Circular created demand for gold and silver. Banks failed, sound money disappeared, and thousands lost jobs.
3. Van Buren did not think the government could or should do anything to stop the depression.
4. (a) William Henry Harrison and President Van Buren (b) The main issue in the campaign was the depression, blamed on Van Buren and the Democrats. (c) A common person would appeal to voters, so the Whigs made Harrison into one even though he was not one. Harrison was pictured as a poor but honest man who lived in a log cabin and earned his daily bread in the hardest way.
5. (a) The cartoon shows the effect of the depression on the people. Men are sitting idle instead of working; a mother and child are begging; and people are going to a pawnbroker. The cartoon also points out that there was a shortage of gold and silver currency. (b) The cartoon is laying the blame for the depression on the money institutions. The federal customs house will accept only specie, and the local bank has issued more bank notes than it can redeem in specie.

CHAPTER 12 REVIEW (text page 304)

Reviewing Important Terms

1. true
2. false, spoils system
3. false, kitchen cabinet
4. true
5. true
6. true

Practicing Critical Thinking Skills

Suggested responses to the questions are:
1. (a) Webster-Hayne debate on the doctrine of states' rights (b) toast proposed at Jefferson Day dinner in 1830 to express Jackson's stand on nullification (c) Calhoun's reply to Jackson's toast
2. Jackson's enemies called him "King Andrew" for his belief in the power of the Presidency and his stand on the Bank of the United States and nullification. To the common people, he stood as a champion of democracy.
3. (a) Jackson believed in greater political democracy. He rotated political officeholders, supported nominating conventions, and considered himself the spokesman for all the people. He also believed in the Union, and declared that he would enforce the tariff over South Carolina's

nullification attempt. To prove his belief in the power of the Presidency, he destroyed the Bank of the United States and ignored the decisions of the Supreme Court. (b) Jackson's democratic convictions wavered most notably in his Indian policy. He did not extend the benefits of democracy to Indians or black Americans.
4. As the nation grew, the sections developed different economic patterns. The North was rapidly becoming the industrial area; the South depended heavily on cotton production and slave labor; and the West was an isolated, general farming region. Each section had special needs and demanded special legislation. The North wanted protective tariffs to aid its industry; the West wanted roads and other transportation improvements financed by the federal government; and the South wanted free international trade.

Developing History Study Skills

(a) fuel and other manufactured products (b) agricultural goods and capital goods

Relating Geography and History

(a) Both the South and New England seemed to change their views on protective tariffs. The South realized that the tariff was helping manufacturers in the North, but was not directly helping the South. Many New Englanders opposed the Tariff of 1828 when duties on raw materials were added. (b) The South reacted most vehemently to passage of the Tariff of 1828. (c) The South was forced to pay higher prices for manufactured goods. Because the South bought almost all the manufactured goods they used, the high costs were a hardship and viewed as unfair. (d) In a way, the Tariff of 1828 was beneficial to the South because the manufacturers in the North bought southern cotton. (e) South Carolina, Georgia, Mississippi, and Virginia all adopted resolutions protesting the tariff and expressing the view that a state could refuse to obey any act of Congress it considered unconstitutional. The theory of nullification was one aspect of the states' rights argument which was a threat to the Union.

UNIT THREE REVIEW (text page 305)

Discussing Ideas

1. (a) Answers will vary. Students might mention such criteria as: popularity, leadership, support of Congress, respect abroad, lack of corrup-

tion in administration, lasting benefits from the programs of administration, and historical perspective — was the President good by today's standards? **(b)** Answers will vary.

2. **(a)** In 1793 Washington's Neutrality Proclamation declared that there were no hostilities between the United States and European nations (France and Great Britain). In 1807 Jefferson recommended that Congress establish an embargo against foreign trade. **(b)** The War of 1812 established the right of American freedom of the seas and led to the Rush-Bagot agreement demilitarizing the Great Lakes. **(c)** The Doctrine established the principle that no foreign power would be allowed to establish itself in the Western Hemisphere and that the United States would not interfere in the internal affairs of European nations or take part in European wars of solely foreign interest.

3. **(a)** Jackson wanted to represent the common people. He believed that the Presidency was a powerful position, and he surrounded himself with supporters. He felt that the function of the federal government was to uphold the rights of the common people and to operate with limited powers — as long as the Union was not threatened. **(b)** Answers will vary. Students might mention that Jefferson was also a champion of the common people, although he came from the wealthy segment of society. He believed in keeping government as simple as possible, including the ways of financing it. He had faith in the wisdom of the people to govern themselves.

4. Answers will vary. Students might mention that the new, barely-organized nation relied on the proven leadership abilities of Washington to hold the country together until it had established itself. Washington chose his cabinet well. One of its members was Alexander Hamilton, who helped the country to operate successfully. His contributions included: a plan to establish international credit in order to gain the respect of the United States' trading partners in the world; protective tariffs to aid the nation's infant industries; taxes to raise revenues; and the establishment of the Bank of the United States.

5. **(a)** Answers will vary. Students might mention the election of Jefferson, the decline of the Federalist Party, the administration of Jackson, the settlement of the West, and the widespread suffrage in the new western states. In defining democracy, most students will probably express the ideas of government by the people and rule of the majority. **(b)** Answers will vary. Students might suggest that democracy was growing in this period because new states were not requiring property qualifications in order for people to be able to vote and that almost all adult males in the western states could vote. The country was growing, and people were moving farther apart geographically and gaining more experience in self-government. The common man and his interests became important to the government because the common man could vote.

6. Answers will vary. Students might mention the idealistic writings that speak of equality, as opposed to the practical applications of those writings, which were selective in interpretation.

Applying History Study Skills

(a) "But whether their theories were good or bad, they had the fault of being inapplicable, as a whole, to the society which they wished to govern, and that which occurred under the auspices of Jefferson must therefore have taken place sooner or later." **(b)** They ran the government well while it was new and unsure, giving it time to become stable. They also were responsible for writing the Constitution, which "is a lasting monument of their patriotism and their wisdom."

The Rise of Sectionalism

SECTION REVIEW   (text page 316)

Suggested responses to the questions are:
1. (a) Improved transportation helped all parts of the nation to grow. In the East, it stimulated the development of factories because eastern products could move west in greater volume. Transportation stimulated the growth of the West by bringing new settlers who could send their surplus crops to the East. As the Industrial Revolution gained momentum, new factories were built in the South, requiring new transportation to move goods. (b) The West benefited most. Pioneer settlers could move west easily, and once settled, they could send their crops to the eastern cities. Western villages began to grow into cities and eventually the Middle West developed its own thriving industries.
2. (a) American ships were larger and faster than other ships, and trade flourished. (b) This success declined after 1860 because of the superiority of British steamships and because of the Civil War.
3. (a) The Illinois and Michigan Canal connects Chicago and La Salle. The Wabash and Erie Canal connects Evansville and Toledo. The Miami and Erie Canal connects Cincinnati and Toledo. The Ohio and Erie Canal connects Cleveland and Portsmouth. The Penn State Canal connects Philadelphia and Pittsburgh. The Champlain Canal connects Lake Champlain and Albany. The Erie Canal connects Buffalo and Albany. The Chesapeake and Ohio Canal connects the Appalachian Mountains and the Chesapeake Bay. The James River and Kanawha Canal connects Richmond and the Appalachian Mountains. (b) The canals would have helped the cities become commercial centers.

SECTION REVIEW   (text page 321)

Suggested responses to the questions are:
1. (a) Until about 1830, most factory workers were native-born American women and children. (b) Workers began organizing labor unions because they were unhappy with the long hours, low wages, and harsh conditions in factories. (c) The unions wanted higher wages, a ten-hour work day, educational opportunities for children, and freedom from imprisonment for debt. (d) Many wage earners did not realize that they formed a new and important group in the nation's economic life and that they had common interests; the Americans' strong spirit of independence made it difficult for labor organizations to draw workers into unions. Wage earners were reluctant to follow rules. Cheap land was available for dissatisfied workers to farm. Labor unions were not recognized by law until 1842. The panic of 1837 made it difficult for many workers to pay union dues.
2. (a) Women workers earned less than men, but they made up most of the industrial labor force, especially in the textile and clothing industries. (b) Men and women worked long hours under poor conditions for low wages.
3. (a) White workers refused to work in the same shops and factories with black workers. Black workers had to accept lower wages if they wanted any jobs at all. Black workers were barred from membership in the trade unions. Generally, only unskilled jobs were available to blacks, and in hard times, black workers were fired and replaced by white workers. (b) Employers used black workers as strikebreakers.

SECTION REVIEW   (text page 323)

Suggested responses to the questions are:
1. (a) Irish tenant farmers were barely managing to make a living when, in 1846, the Potato Famine struck Ireland. (b) The Irish settled primarily in the slums of larger cities because that was where they disembarked upon arriving in the United States. Most were poor and did not have enough money to move to western lands.

2. Some native-born Americans resented the immigrants because they tried to settle near others from their country, would work for lower wages than American workers, and spoke and dressed differently from native-born Americans. Irish immigrants were especially resented because the majority were Roman Catholics.
3. (a) The Know-Nothing Party opposed immigration and supported only American-born Protestants for public office. (b) By the 1850's, the Know-Nothing, or American, Party was very strong. In the 1854 Massachusetts election, the party elected almost the entire state legislature. A split in the party over slavery in 1855 caused its decline.
4. Machines, factories, and the growth of urban centers were changing the traditional ways of American life.

CHAPTER 13 REVIEW   (text page 327)

Reviewing Important Terms

1. true
2. true
3. false, Waltham system
4. true
5. true
6. true

Practicing Critical Thinking Skills

Suggested responses to the questions are:
1. Answers will vary. Students might mention that the Constitution united the country politically and spiritually, but that transportation united the country physically. Better transportation was necessary for industrialization, for expansion westward, and for the growth of towns and cities.
2. As the number of factory workers increased and large numbers of workers with similar problems worked together, united demands for better wages and working conditions grew.
3. As the Industrial Revolution gained momentum, the need for labor grew. The emphasis on agriculture among Americans and the lure of cheap land in the West resulted in a chronic labor shortage. Immigrants fleeing famine and political turmoil in Europe filled the labor needs of the United States at this time. Their labor helped build the canals and railroads and produced the ever-increasing quantity of manufactured goods.
4. (a) Immigrants in both periods came to the United States hoping for a better life than they had in Europe. In colonial times, immigrants were also looking for religious freedom,

whereas in the mid-nineteenth century many immigrants (especially the Germans) were searching for a democratic state. (b) Native-born Americans blamed their problems on the immigrants because the immigrants were different and were often a direct threat to native-born Americans' jobs.
5. (a) The old ways were the ways they knew. Their ways provided security in new surroundings. (b) Native-born Americans viewed immigrants with suspicion because the immigrants seemed different. (c) Students should disagree. Most second- or third-generation children wanted to become "Americans." Children adapted more easily; they went to school in the United States and learned American ways.
6. (a) Industrialization strengthened democracy by making it possible for people to buy goods never before available to them and by raising their standards of living. It strengthened national unity by binding the nation together with a network of roads, canals, and railroads. (b) Industrialization transformed the North, creating serious differences between the North and the South.
7. The federal government is continuing efforts to improve transportation by constructing interstate highways, subsidizing passenger rail service, and providing air-traffic controllers. The United States' transportation needs are similar to those of the earlier period in the sense that all parts of the country must be connected by reliable forms of transportation. The country's needs are different, partly because many more areas are industrialized now than in the nineteenth century, making the needed system much more complex than was before necessary.

Developing History Study Skills

1. Answers will vary. Students might mention that the United States was rapidly developing economically and politically as the nation expanded in the early 1800's. In many ways, the country was also becoming more democratic.
2. (a) Answers will vary. Students should include three of the following: the Arctic Ocean, the North Atlantic, the Bering Sea, the Indian Ocean, and the South Atlantic. (b) tea and other luxuries (c) American trade had become worldwide due, in part, to the clipper ships and the expanding merchant marine.

Relating Geography and History

1. The map on page 271 in the text shows the route of the National Road. The major cities through which it passed were: Cumberland, Maryland; Wheeling, Virginia; Columbus and Springfield,

Ohio; Indianapolis and Terre Haute, Indiana; and Vandalia, Illinois.

2. (a) Before the road was completed, freight carrying overland from the West was difficult, expensive, and time-consuming. Most shipping to the East was done by river. This was expensive and sometimes perilous, because New Orleans was held by a foreign power. (b) The mountains proved to be an effective barrier to most would-be settlers of the West. With the opening of the National Road, more people, including recent immigrants seeking good farmland, were encouraged to make the move. (c) The road brought more people and more businesses to serve them. Cities along the route benefited from the steadily increasing traffic. Before the road was completed, there was little opportunity for growth, because early settlers tended to farm the land until it was worn out and then move on farther west. (d) The value of land in the West increased because demand was greater than it had been when the West was more difficult to reach.

3. Interstate 70

CHAPTER 14 Creating a Southern Economy

SECTION REVIEW   (text page 334)

Suggested responses to the questions are:

1. The South was primarily an agricultural region before 1860, but its economy was not dependent solely upon cotton. The region's climate, terrain, and soil conditions varied. This resulted in the production of many agricultural products, including tobacco, rice, and sugar cane as export staples, and wheat, corn, and cattle for domestic consumption. The towns, and a few cities, provided some industry. Trade of the South's staple products to northern and European markets was extensive. There was variety in southern society as well. Three fourths of the people were small subsistence farmers, tenants, or laborers who owned no slaves. Only a small percentage of the people controlled large plantations with many slaves.

2. Favorable climate, rich soil, slave labor, inven-

tion of the cotton gin, expanding markets, and improved transportation enabled the South to become the world's greatest cotton-producing area by 1860.

3. As slavery became firmly entrenched after 1830, free blacks were seriously discriminated against by law. They had to register with town authorities, carry identification cards to prove that they were free, and put up money or property to guarantee their good behavior. They were taxed but could not vote, could not assemble for any purpose, and in some areas were forbidden to learn to read or write. They were sometimes even prevented from attending their own churches, and they lived in constant fear of being sold into slavery for some minor infraction of the law.

4. (a) The cotton belt extended from Texas to North Carolina. (b) The Old South included Maryland, Virginia, North Carolina, South Carolina, and Georgia. (c) Cotton production moved west, south, and to a lesser extent north.

SECTION REVIEW   (text page 337)

Suggested responses to the questions are:

1. The large plantation owner might have a spacious, luxuriously furnished house, but he also had many duties. He had to supervise the work of the plantation, keep records, and provide for the needs of his family without having large cash reserves. His wife supervised a large household, looked after the health of all on the plantation, and sometimes taught the younger children.

2. Planters argued that slavery was necessary for them to have an adequate labor supply and that slaves were provided the necessities of life, had no financial worries, and received many benefits of civilization.

3. Small planters, who often wanted to become large planters, accepted slavery, as did small farmers who owned no slaves but who hoped to acquire some. Even the poor whites accepted slavery because it added to their sense of solidarity and pride in being members of the white society of the South.

SECTION REVIEW   (text page 340)

Suggested responses to the questions are:

1. Historians have used written records, work songs and religious spirituals, and interviews. Historians have also used some of the methods of sociology, anthropology, and psychology.

2. **(a)** Slaves performed a variety of jobs. Many worked in the homes of the planters. Some became skilled workers. Women learned how to spin, weave, and sew; some became cooks, maids, laundresses, dairymaids, and nurses. Men became blacksmiths, painters, shoemakers, jewelers, and silversmiths. The great majority of slaves worked as laborers on the cotton, rice, and sugar cane plantations. **(b)** Slave labor was organized either by the task system or by the gang system. **(c)** There is some evidence that slaves were more humanely treated on small farms and small plantations. On large plantations, where overseers were frequently in command, slaves were often treated harshly, if not brutally. However, because the slaves were valuable property, many planters treated their slaves reasonably well. **(d)** The northern white workers were free.

3. **(a)** Slaveowners had to teach their slaves to be obedient and accept their lot in order to maintain discipline. **(b)** This discipline encouraged many slaves to be outwardly childlike and obedient. It also encouraged deceitfulness. Many slaves were outwardly respectful and subordinate only to escape penalties or win rewards. **(c)** Slaves resisted slavery by running away, rebelling, breaking tools, setting fires, slowing down work, and by committing suicide or murdering their owners.

CHAPTER 14 REVIEW   *(text page 343)*

Reviewing Important Terms

1. staple crops
2. cotton gin
3. interstate slave trade
4. justices of the peace
5. gang system
6. task system
7. bonds
8. planters
9. justices of the peace

Practicing Critical Thinking Skills

Suggested responses to the questions are:
1. **(a)** The Industrial Revolution greatly increased the demand for cotton. Southern farmers moved westward to open up new cotton lands and profit from the growing demand. Also, cotton production tended to exhaust the soil. The western lands promised continued, bountiful crops. **(b)** Cotton planting and harvesting required a great deal of labor. Slaves became the basic laborers in the cotton fields. As cotton production increased, so did the number of slaves.
2. **(a)** The slaves would form the base of the pyramid. **(b)** The rich planters would be at the top. **(c)** Small farmers, poor whites, and even tenant farmers could move upward in the social structure. Only slaves and free blacks were denied the opportunity to better their condition.
3. Most white southerners believed they had established an orderly society that benefited all levels. The economy was based on the cotton trade, which flourished because of slave labor. Slaves were well fed, clothed, and housed. Indeed, the argument ran, they lived better than the free factory workers of the North. Without slavery, the entire society fabric would disintegrate, bringing hardship to slave and nonslave.
4. Blacks were denied freedom and the opportunity to make decisions, to develop their talents, and to improve their standard of living. Whites suffered in less obvious ways. They lived in fear of slave uprisings; they had to continually supervise slave labor because it was involuntary; they often lost money on their slaves. More importantly, the system dehumanized the slaveowners as much as it did the slaves.
5. Cotton is no longer "king." The value of cotton production ranks below that of manufactured goods, soybeans, and tobacco.

Developing History Study Skills

1. Answers will vary. Students might mention that slaves were denied property, freedom of movement, and freedom of choice about any aspect of their lives; they were reduced to the level of children by slaveowners, subject to physical coercion at the whim of their masters and overseers, and forced to conceal the resentful feelings that such treatment naturally produced.
2. **(a)** Answers will vary. Students might mention that the illustrations show the dependency of the South on slave labor and on cotton. **(b)** Answers will vary. Students who think that a realistic picture is presented might mention that the South was indeed dependent on slaves and cotton. Students who think that the picture is unrealistic might mention that the illustrations do not accurately portray the hardships of slavery.

Relating Geography and History

1. Answers will vary. Students might mention that plantations were large self-contained farms that produced one or more cash crops and depended on slave labor.
2. Answers will vary. Most students will probably choose: c, d, e, g, and j.
3. Answers will vary. Students might state: "A large landed estate using land that has been cleared of its original inhabitants, on which, through a relationship of a planter having

authority over the laborers imported to the area, a product is produced and sold on the world market."

15 Expanding The Nation's Boundaries

SECTION REVIEW   *(text page 350)*

Suggested responses to the questions are:
1. **(a)** the United States, Spain, Russia, and Great Britain **(b)** *Spain:* by agreement with Portugal; *Russia:* the explorations of Vitus Bering in 1741; *Great Britain:* the explorations of Francis Drake in 1577–80 and James Cook in 1776–78; *United States:* the explorations of Captain Gray in 1792 and Lewis and Clark in 1804–06
2. **(a)** Captain Gray reached the Columbia River in 1792. **(b)** Lewis and Clark traveled through the territory in 1804–06. **(c)** Mountain Men from the United States explored the Oregon country. **(d)** Astor built most of the American fur trade in Oregon. **(e)** Missionaries traveled to the Oregon country in the 1830's and 1840's and built missions and schools. **(f)** By the 1840's American pioneers were entering the Oregon country at the rate of a thousand a year.
3. The United States finally acquired the Oregon country by treaty with Great Britain in 1846.
4. **(a)** north of 54°40′ **(b)** 49° North

SECTION REVIEW   *(text page 354)*

Suggested responses to the questions are:
1. Missions were designed to be the centers of strong communities. On the surrounding farmlands, grapes, grain, and other crops were grown by priests and Indians. The priests taught the Indians skills such as weaving and blacksmithing and spread Spanish customs and values. The ranches were communities in themselves. The owners were often absent, thus allowing the workers, Indians, and mestizos to become skilled managers. The isolation of the missions and ranches from direct Spanish control fostered a spirit of independence.

2. When Mexico closed its doors to further settlement, the Texans revolted, reaffirmed an earlier prohibition of slavery, and canceled unoccupied land grants.
3. Since Texas wanted to permit slavery, northerners in Congress feared that its admission would increase the strength of the southern states in Congress. Others feared that to admit Texas would be to invite war with Mexico, which had not recognized Texan independence.

SECTION REVIEW   *(text page 358)*

Suggested responses to the questions are:
1. **(a)** Polk would have described the events as deliberate acts of aggression by Mexico against the United States. He would have pointed to the mistreatment of Americans by Mexican authorities, the execution of 22 Americans without a trial, the unpaid debt owed to American citizens, the refusal of the Mexican government to receive the American envoy, and the alleged violation of American territory north of the Rio Grande. **(b)** A Mexican would have pointed to American complicity in the Texas war for independence, the attack on California, the annexation of Texas, and the alleged violations of Mexican territory south of the Nueces River. Mexicans insisted that these actions were part of a United States plan to conquer the entire Southwest.
2. **(a)** The United States received title to Texas, New Mexico, and Upper California; it gave Mexico $15 million and agreed to assume debts totaling over $3 million that Mexico owed to Americans. **(b)** The southwestern boundary of the United States was extended to the Pacific, and the chief objective of "manifest destiny" was realized. **(c)** Mexico lost two fifths of its land.
3. The Gadsden Purchase of 1853 gave the United States an area south of the Gila River needed to construct a southern transcontinental railroad. With the exceptions of Alaska and Hawaii, the Gadsden Purchase rounded out the present boundaries of the United States.

SECTION REVIEW   *(text page 361)*

Suggested responses to the questions are:
1. **(a)** The Mormons were persecuted because they claimed to be a chosen people with a special revelation of the truth; because they were a prosperous and tight-knit community; and because they accepted polygamy. **(b)** They moved west to escape persecution.

2. **(a)** adventurous Americans who rushed to the gold fields of California in 1849 **(b)** They went seeking gold. **(c)** They got there by ship around Cape Horn; by ship to Central America, overland across the Isthmus of Panama, then by ship to California; and across the Great Plains and through the passes of the mountains.

3. **(a)** By means of the missions, the Spaniards broke down Indian cultural patterns and made the Indians dependent upon the missions for existence. The Mexicans took away church control of mission areas, leaving the Indians at the mercy of greedy settlers. Some Indians became virtual slaves on the large ranches. The United States government restricted the activities of the Indians and discriminated against them. Between 1848 and 1871, more than 50,000 Indians died of disease, starvation, and violence, and most of the northern tribes lost their lands to white settlers. **(b)** Answers will vary. Students might mention that cultural differences caused misunderstanding between Indians and white settlers. The Indians were also weak and unable to adequately defend themselves; their weakness was interpreted as inferiority.

CHAPTER 15 REVIEW   *(text page 365)*

Reviewing Important Terms

1. true	5. true
2. false, Oregon Trail	6. true
3. false, Santa Fe Trail	7. true
4. true	

Practicing Critical Thinking Skills

Suggested responses to the questions are:

1. **(a)** The frontier was a land of opportunity to settlers in the older parts of the country. **(b)** Manifest destiny led Americans to move westward; it brought them into conflict with neighbors to the north and south.

2. In the Pacific Northwest the pioneers were fur traders, missionaries, and farmers. In Texas, the settlers included many southerners who brought their slaves with them to cultivate cotton.

3. The Mormons migrated to Utah to escape persecution. The great migration to California in 1849 was stimulated by the lure of gold.

4. **(a)** A Mexican would have been angered by the annexation of Texas. The Americans in Texas had promised to obey Mexican laws and be responsible Mexican citizens. The Texan revolt and subsequent annexation of Texas was proof of American intentions to swallow up the Southwest. **(b)** An American living in Texas would applaud the annexation. As part of his native land, he would be defended, have open trade with other states, and have a voice in the government. **(c)** A southern planter would rejoice at a new slave state in the Union and the opportunity to move with slaves into a new American territory. **(d)** An opponent of slavery would oppose annexation because the balance of slave-nonslave states in Congress would be upset. **(e)** A frontier farmer's reaction would depend upon the farmer's views on slavery.

5. **(a)** The Spanish-speaking people and the Indians were exposed to different ways of life and ideas from the American settlers. The differences resulted in conflict and prejudice. **(b)** These people suffered discrimination and even physical deprivation and death as a result of the westward movement.

6. The American forces wanted to gain control of North Mexico (California and New Mexico) and to capture Mexico City. General Frémont organized some American settlers in California and, together with the United States Navy, occupied Upper California. Brigadier General Kearny marched from Missouri all the way through the Southwest to Los Angeles, despite stiff resistance. Two American armies invaded Mexico itself, and General Winfield Scott entered Mexico City on September 14, 1847, after a hard campaign. The war ended soon after.

7. Answers will vary according to the current aims of American foreign policy. Students might mention such general goals as promoting democracy and free enterprise, containment of communism, and securing peace with other nations.

Developing History Study Skills

1. **(a)** Kearny traveled southwest from Fort Leavenworth to Santa Fe and then to San Diego and Los Angeles. **(b)** the Santa Fe Trail and the Overland Mail

2. See the following chart. Answers will vary.

(a) Name of Territory	(b) Date of Acquisition	(c) Method of Acquisition
Louisiana Purchase	1803	Bought
Florida Cession	1819	Bought
Texas	1845	Annexation
Oregon Country	1846	Treaty
Mexican Cession	1848	Treaty
Gadsden Purchase	1853	Bought

Relating Geography and History

1. Texas, Minnesota, Oregon, Idaho, Alaska, and Hawaii
2. Oregon, Minnesota, Texas, Alaska, and Hawaii
3. Rio Grande, Columbia, Snake, Missouri, Red River, Sabine, Red River of the North, Mississippi, and Rainy
4. Answers will vary.

CHAPTER 16 Working for Reform

SECTION REVIEW *(text page 372)*

Suggested responses to the questions are:
1. **(a)** The women's movement aimed at achieving a more important role for women in American life, in the professions, in public affairs, in politics, and in the economy. **(b)** Women organized to secure their goals. At Seneca Falls, New York, the first women's rights convention declared that men and women are created equal. Other women opened schools of higher education, entered the professions, and won distinctions as authors and editors.
2. **(a)** Temperance advocates met in 1833. In 1836 several groups joined to form the American Temperance Union. In 1846 Maine adopted a prohibition law, and other states followed suit. **(b)** Although drinking did not cease, it declined. The sales of patent medicines with a high alcoholic content rose. **(c)** Congress forbade the sale of alcohol to the Indians because unscrupulous white settlers and traders sold liquor to the Indians and then defrauded them of their treaty rights while the Indians were under the influence of alcohol.
3. This was an age in which many people believed it was possible to right wrongs and improve life for the common people. The founders of the utopian communities believed a better world could be achieved by starting over and carefully planning the ideal community.
4. **(a)** Answers will vary. Students might mention that the crusade for women's rights has perhaps had the most lasting effects — women have achieved many of the aims of the original movement. Reforms in the treatment of the mentally ill have also been realized, although major prob-

lems remain. **(b)** Answers will vary. Students might mention that the temperance movement has not been too successful, especially after the repeal of Prohibition in 1933. The antiwar movement has had very mixed effects on society.

SECTION REVIEW *(text page 374)*

Suggested responses to the questions are:
1. **(a)** Horace Mann crusaded for public schools in Massachusetts, became the first secretary of the state board of education, established "normal schools", and organized a statewide system of education. **(b)** Henry Barnard was a leader in education in Connecticut and Rhode Island and became the first United States Commissioner of Education.
2. **(a)** Churches had founded religious schools; private schools objected to free, tax-supported schools; many people objected to using tax money for education; and there was some prejudice against all "book learning." **(b)** free public elementary schools in New York City in 1832; public school education in northern cities by the 1850's; beginning of public high schools in New England by 1821; and the principle of separation of church and state written into all state constitutions by the 1830's
3. Answers will vary. Students might mention that political democracy requires an educated electorate capable of rational discussions about public policy. Students answering yes should explain that only free public education insures that all people will be prepared to participate in the decision making process. Students answering no might point out that there are alternatives to tax-supported schools. Private education can also prepare citizens for their responsibilities in a political democracy and meet individual needs as well.
4. **(a)** Mann believed that education gives each person the means with which to improve life and to be independent, regardless of background. **(b)** Answers will vary. Students who agree might mention that all people ideally have the same opportunities to succeed at learning. Students who disagree might mention that schools are not always equal in quality, thus the opportunities they offer are not equal. Furthermore, other factors may cause social and economic inequalities even among educated people.

SECTION REVIEW *(text page 377)*

Suggested responses to the questions are:
1. **(a)** The colonization movement aimed to provide

a place in Africa to which free American blacks could immigrate. The movement hoped to encourage emancipation by paying slaveowners who wanted to free their slaves. **(b)** The movement failed because of lack of money and lack of black American support.

2. If black Americans were, indeed, inferior, then it was unfair to set them free to take care of themselves in a different society, and they would not be able to become equal citizens.

3. **(a)** Free blacks took legal action, petitioned Congress, formed societies for mutual aid and for improving educational and social opportunities, and held conventions to discuss their problems. **(b)** Walker advocated militant action, including violence. He felt that his people would not gain freedom otherwise. **(c)** The reaction was hostile. Northerners condemned Walker's *Appeal* as inflammatory; southerners tried to prevent its circulation.

4. The militancy of the abolitionists was seen in newspapers such as the *Liberator* and in the outspoken language of many of the abolitionists, including the Grimké sisters. Some aided runaway slaves; others, like Theodore Weld, trained new abolitionist leaders.

SECTION REVIEW   *(text page 382)*

Suggested responses to the questions are:

1. Other countries had abolished slavery by this time. The abolition movement was only a part of the general movement toward social reform.

2. **(a)** Garrison lectured on abolition and published the newspaper the *Liberator*. **(b)** Douglass was an excellent abolitionist lecturer and writer. **(c)** Stowe wrote *Uncle Tom's Cabin,* which aroused much antislavery feeling. **(d)** Garnet, a former slave, gave a fiery speech before the National Convention of Colored Citizens in 1843. **(e)** The underground railroad helped guide slaves to freedom. **(f)** The "gag rule" prevented any antislavery petition from being read in the House of Representatives.

3. Many northern wage earners feared job competition from freed blacks. Northern business people did not want anything to interfere with trade between the North and the South. Southerners feared slave violence; they also feared the loss of their economic base, which would destroy their way of life.

4. **(a)** The militant abolitionists called for defying the laws that protected slavery. Garnet even proposed wholesale rebellion. The moderates wanted to end slavery by appealing to the conscience of white America and by electing antislavery officials. **(b)** Answers will vary. Students might mention that the moderate meth-

ods might have prevented war but would have taken much longer. Others may argue that militant action was the only hope of ending slavery.

SECTION REVIEW   *(text page 384)*

Suggested responses to the questions are:

1. **(a)** Thoreau feared industrial society and national government. **(b)** Going to jail was the ultimate test of Thoreau's beliefs; he showed himself willing to accept the consequences for breaking society's law in order to demonstrate his belief.

2. **(a)** Through writing and lectures, Emerson could reach a wider audience than from a pulpit. **(b)** Emerson urged independence of thought, freedom from ignorance and prejudice, and respect for others.

3. By "pioneers," Whitman meant people who do things first; he thought Americans must march forward because "all the rest on us depend."

4. During this period, Americans became less dependent upon British models of literature. American writers such as Poe, Hawthorne, and Melville experimented with literary forms and themes. Key figures such as Thoreau, Emerson, and Whitman brought new ideas to American literature.

CHAPTER 16 REVIEW   *(text page 388)*

Reviewing Important Terms

1. true
2. true
3. false, temperance movement
4. true
5. false, normal schools
6. false, academies
7. false, American Renaissance

Practicing Critical Thinking Skills

Suggested responses to the questions are:

1. **(a)** The idea of women's rights was new. European and American societies based their view of women on religious beliefs and idealized concepts of femininity. Women were thought to be inferior to men and were intended to be their helpers but in need of their protection. The idea of equality for women needed time to grow among women as well as men. At the same time women were demanding equality, attention was being focused on a more explosive issue: slavery. **(b)** Answers will vary. Students might mention reformer Dorothea Dix, author-reformers Harriet Beecher Stowe and Margaret Fuller, Dr. Elizabeth Blackwell, and others.

2. The abolitionist movement split over methods and speed of achieving this goal. The moderates favored peaceful and gradual settlement by influencing the policies of the major political parties. The militants demanded immediate action, by violence if necessary.

3. Thoreau, Emerson, and Whitman praised freedom, democracy, the individual, and the ability of Americans to solve their problems and build a better world.

4. (a) The reform movements sought humanitarian goals by advocating prison reform, improved treatment of the mentally ill, and the end of imprisonment for debt. (b) The movement tried to make the country more democratic by advocating free public education, equality for women, and the end of slavery.

5. Reformers tried to promote the general welfare by working for women's rights, temperance, peace, and free public education. Abolitionists wanted to secure liberty and justice for slaves.

6. Answers will vary. Students who agree might mention that education is a basic need for many higher-paying jobs. Students who disagree might mention that education cannot cure immediate problems such as discrimination because of race or sex.

7. Answers will vary. Students might mention that because of advances in science and industry, people today spend much less time doing manual labor on the job and in the home than was the case 150 years ago, liberating time for educational, social, recreational, and cultural pursuits. Other students may point out that the fact that people have more time on their hands has complicated their lives considerably, since they no longer have to devote so much time to activities basic to their survival.

Developing History Study Skills

1. (a) immigration and free public education (b) 1830 to 1860 (c) Discuss means to analyze and give supporting information. (d) Answers will vary.

2. Answers will vary. Students might compare their cartoons and slogans to the publicity produced by modern-day reform movements.

Relating Geography and History

1. (a) Slaves would have taken a boat from Charleston to New York or Philadelphia, from which they would go overland to Canada. (b) From Cincinnati slaves would have gone north to Toledo and Detroit and then entered Canada. (c) From Charleston to New York it was about 1,500 miles (2,400 kilometers); from Cincinnati to Canada was about 350 miles (560 kilometers).

2. Answers will vary. Students might mention that the chance of capture was probably less at sea than traveling through slave territory.

3. (a) On the underground railroad, a slave always faced the danger of capture. A northern white might turn in the slave. The slave might also be caught by a slave catcher. (b) Some had cruel masters. Others hoped to join family members. Still others heard that they were about to be sold. Most simply had a deep desire to be free.

UNIT FOUR REVIEW *(text page 389)*

Discussing Ideas

1. (a) Planters were well educated; through the county form of local government, the planters could control the political machinery and hold most of the high political positions in the South. (b) The political leaders of the North came from the ranks of the wealthy industrialists, who controlled jobs; from old families with long-standing political influence; and from among big-city politicians who operated close to the people's daily lives. (c) Western leaders often rose from the poor side of the social structure. Westerners admired and respected achievement and would support politicians who represented their views and interests, no matter what their social class origins were.

2. (a) Manifest destiny refers to the fulfillment of the dream of continental expansion. It was the belief that the United States' expansion to the Pacific (and, for some dreamers, even beyond) was meant to be and should not or could not be discouraged. (b) The best evidence is the popular support for the Mexican War — the immediate results of which were the acquisition of vast territories. (c) Answers will vary. Students might mention that the reform movements were humanitarian and the conquering of new territories was often inconsistent with humanitarian ideals. However, except for the pacifists and maybe the abolitionists, reformers probably had little reason to quarrel with the concept of manifest destiny because they were more concerned with curing social problems.

3. (a) Improved transportation stimulated eastern industries because markets were opened up in the West as a result of better roads, new railroads, and canals. (b) Although fewer in number, southern railroads, along with better roads and steam-powered water transportation, helped southern planters ship their crops and import manufactured goods. (c) Better transportation helped the West grow. Industries were established in the Middle West and farm-

ers were able to ship more of their surplus crops to eastern cities.

4. Answers will vary. Students who believe that the war was inevitable might mention that the concept of manifest destiny was so strong that the American people would not be denied title to the Southwest. Because the territory was part of another nation, war could not be avoided. Students who believe that the war was not inevitable might mention that a compromise could have been worked out with Mexico so that some of the territories could have been purchased.

5. Answers will vary. Students might mention the following: education reformers showed their faith in democracy by pushing for an educated electorate; women's rights groups felt that, with a just cause, their fight would eventually be won. They used many of the same arguments that were stated in the struggle for American independence; the abolitionists argued that "the American people must stand each for all and all for each without respect to color and race." Many worked through political parties to present their views. Writers such as Thoreau and Emerson supported abolition of slavery and opposed other threats to individual freedom.

6. Northern industrial workers spent long hours on the job. Workers included men, women, and children. Working conditions were generally better than those in Great Britain, but many American factory workers had to live in crowded tenements and live on small wages. Slaves spent long hours on the job. Workers included men, women, and children. Working conditions varied from place to place and living conditions were poor. The major advantage for northern workers was that eventually they were able to organize unions to gain improvements in their condition. Other basic differences included: northern workers were not owned by another person; northern workers were paid wages; northern workers could leave their jobs and move West; and northern workers had more opportunities to become educated.

7. (a) Southern society was stratified by economic and social divisions. There was, however, (except for slaves) social mobility, allowing many people to better their social and economic positions. From the bottom of the social ladder to the top were slaves, free blacks, poor whites, laborers and tenant farmers, small farmers, small slave-owning farmers, and wealthy planters. (b) In the North, there were almost no slaves after 1804, and the percentage of middle-class and wealthy families was greater than in the South because of the greater number of industrialized urban areas. In the West the social structure was less formal than in the East or the South.

Applying History Study Skills

1. (a) The Oregon Trail went from Independence, Missouri, across the Great Plains and the Rocky Mountains to Fort Bridger. It then went northwest along the Snake and Columbia rivers to Oregon. The Mormon Trail went from Nauvoo, Illinois, across the Great Plains and the Rocky Mountains to the Great Salt Lake. The Pony Express went from St. Joseph, Missouri, to Salt Lake City and then to Sacramento, California. The trails followed the same route between central Nebraska and Fort Bridger. (b) south pass (c) The Overland Mail took the southerly route to avoid mountains. (d) One route went around Cape Horn and north in the Pacific Ocean to California. The other went by ship to Central America where settlers crossed the Isthmus of Panama and boarded another ship for California. (e) Answers will vary. Students might mention that the route around Cape Horn was the easiest and most comfortable because settlers did not have to contend with hostile Indians or the rugged terrain.

2. (a) The United States is the greatest nation on earth. (b) the common people (c) The excerpt shows pride in everything that is uniquely American and in the achievements of the country.

The Nation Torn Apart

CHAPTER 17 Crisis and Compromise

SECTION REVIEW *(text page 395)*

Suggested responses to the questions are:
1. **(a)** The admission of Missouri as a slave state would upset the balance of power between slave and free states in the Senate. **(b)** The Missouri Compromise resolved the crisis.
2. **(a)** Missouri was admitted as a slave state, Maine as a free state. Slavery was prohibited in the remaining parts of the Louisiana Purchase north of latitude 36°30′. The South added a slave state; the North was assured that a huge area would remain free; the balance of power was maintained in the Senate. **(b)** Compromise postponed consideration of the basic issue of slavery.
3. The major issue in the Presidential campaign of 1844 was the admission of Texas, which included the controversy over the expansion of slavery. The Whigs tried to avoid the issue, the Democrats concentrated on the westward expansion aspect, and the Liberty Party opposed slavery and the admission of Texas.
4. **(a)** Prior to 1821, there were 11 slave and 11 free states. **(b)** Louisiana and Missouri had been admitted to the Union.

SECTION REVIEW *(text page 398)*

Suggested responses to the questions are:
1. American victory raised the question of whether slavery should be permitted or prohibited in the Mexican Cession.
2. **(a)** The first proposal recommended extending the Missouri Compromise line to the Pacific, excluding slavery north of 36°30′ and permitting it south of the line. The second recommended acceptance of the Wilmot Proviso, calling for the exclusion of slavery in territories gained from Mexico. The third insisted that slaveowners had the Constitutional right to take their "property" anywhere in the territories. The fourth recommended that the people of each territory decide the issue for themselves. **(b)** President Polk and many citizens favored the first proposal. Antislavery citizens supported the Wilmot Proviso. Southern slaveowners, led by Calhoun, insisted on the third proposal. Senators Cass and Douglas proposed the popular sovereignty concept.
3. **(a)** California to be admitted as a free state; land acquired from Mexico (except California) to be organized into territories on the basis of "popular sovereignty"; Texas to receive $10 million from the United States for giving up its claim to land in New Mexico; slave trade, but not slavery itself, to be abolished in the District of Columbia; and a more effective fugitive slave law to be enacted **(b)** Answers will vary. Students might mention that this compromise relieved business groups' fears that continued controversy between the North and the South would ruin business in the country. **(c)** Henry Clay introduced and fought for the compromise. Daniel Webster sacrificed his career to support the compromise. Stephen Douglas, author of the idea of popular sovereignty, also supported the compromise. John C. Calhoun spoke for the South in opposition. Other senators, such as Thomas Hart Benton, Salmon P. Chase, and William H. Seward, opposed slavery and the compromise.
4. Compromise is sometimes called the "essence of politics" because politics must achieve a functioning government within society. Such a government can be achieved only when the members of each political party are willing to concede some of their individual ends.

SECTION REVIEW *(text page 402)*

Suggested responses to the questions are:
1. Publication of *Uncle Tom's Cabin* (1852) infuriated southerners; northern abolitionists openly defied the Fugitive Slave Law; and southern politicians wanted to seize Cuba and make it a new slave territory.

2. **(a)** The Kansas-Nebraska Act abolished the Missouri Compromise by allowing the two new territories, Kansas and Nebraska (both north of the old 36°30′ line), to decide the issue of slavery on the basis of popular sovereignty. **(b)** Two governments were set up in Kansas — one proslavery, one antislavery. Fighting broke out between the two sides.
3. Neither the Whigs nor the Democrats dared take a stand on slavery. Antislavery people in both parties formed a new party, calling themselves "Republicans."

SECTION REVIEW   *(text page 405)*

Suggested responses to the questions are:
1. **(a)** The Supreme Court ruled that residence in a free territory and a free state had not given Dred Scott his freedom. It declared that Scott was not a citizen of the United States or of the state of Missouri. Therefore, he had no right to sue in either a state or a federal court. The Court also ruled the Missouri Compromise unconstitutional according to the Fifth Amendment. **(b)** Northerners opposed the decision because now only an amendment to the Constitution would be able to keep slavery out of the territories north of the Missouri Compromise line.
2. Slavery was the basic issue of the Lincoln-Douglas debates. Lincoln held that slavery should not be extended. Douglas supported popular sovereignty in the territories. Lincoln believed the Union could not exist long half-slave, half-free; Douglas believed it could exist that way.
3. **(a)** John Brown planned to use the guns and ammunition acquired in the raid on Harpers Ferry to start a slave rebellion in Virginia. **(b)** Most southerners deplored Brown's use of force. But extreme abolitionists regarded him as a hero. Many southerners believed that Brown's action represented northern opinion, and that slavery was no longer safe from direct attack.

SECTION REVIEW   *(text page 408)*

Suggested responses to the questions are:
1. Extremists Lincoln and Breckenridge together polled 58 percent of the popular vote; moderates Bell and Douglas had 42 percent. The election demonstrated the irreconcilable differences between North and South.
2. Southerners interpreted the election of Lincoln

as proof that the North intended to use its superior strength to encroach upon the rights and interests of the South.
3. Students' charts should contain the following information. *Party* — Republican: *candidate* — Lincoln: *issues* — opposed extension of slavery; favored protective tariff, internal improvements, free land: *regions supporting party* — North, Midwest: *electoral votes* — 180. *Party* — Northern Democrat: *candidate* — Douglas: *issues* — Favored popular sovereignty: *regions supporting party* — North: *electoral votes* — 12. *Party* — Southern Democrat: *candidate* — Breckenridge: *issues* — Favored extension of slavery: *regions supporting party* — South: *electoral votes* — 72. *Party* — Constitutional Union: *candidate* — Bell: *issues* — support of the Union: *region supporting party* — South: *electoral votes* — 39.

CHAPTER 17 REVIEW   *(text page 411)*

Reviewing Important Terms

1. Tallmadge Amendment 4. Freeport Doctrine
2. Wilmot Proviso   5. Dred Scott decision
3. Ostend Manifesto

Practicing Critical Thinking Skills

Suggested responses to the questions are:
1. **(a)** The Mexican War gave Americans new land suitable for raising cotton, adding momentum to the expansion of slavery. **(b)** Garrison attacked slavery vigorously in the *Liberator*. **(c)** Stowe's novel, *Uncle Tom's Cabin,* aroused northerners against slavery and was bitterly resented in the South. **(d)** The Dred Scott decision angered northern antislavery forces. **(e)** The violence of John Brown's raid infuriated the South.
2. Lincoln was implying that Stowe's book, *Uncle Tom's Cabin,* had such an effect on public opinion that it contributed to the outbreak of war.
3. **(a)** Immigrants and unskilled laborers in the North were also prejudiced against blacks. The reluctance of northerners to allow blacks to fight in the war indicated prejudice. **(b)** Sweeping generalizations do not account for individual viewpoints. There were wide ranges of opinion on slavery in the North and the South. Many people were more moderate than the generalization suggests.
4. Answers will vary. Students might mention some of the following: *Events leading to the Civil War:* Mexican War, Wilmot Proviso, Fugitive

Slave Law, passage of the Kansas-Nebraska Act, civil war in Kansas, abolitionist activities, publication of *Uncle Tom's Cabin,* John Brown's raid, Lincoln's election, secession of seven southern states, and firing on Fort Sumter. *Issues leading to Civil War:* states' rights (including the right to secede), tariffs, expansion of slavery into the territories, balance of power in the Senate, and failure of the system of compromise. **(a)** The lists appear different. **(b)** The events illustrate the relationship between issues and action. There is no simple explanation of the causes of the war. **(c)** Answers will vary. Students might mention that war might have been avoided if the practice of compromise had continued.

5. Answers will vary. Such an occurrence is unlikely because of the American election system, which gives seats in Congress to the individual candidate who wins a plurality of votes. A new political party would be likely to replace one of the two major parties only if a proportional representation system was introduced or if some new issue arose which divided votes along different lines than those separating Democrats and Republicans.

Developing History Study Skills

1. **(a)** The Constitution guaranteed the right to own slaves. **(b)** The decision stated that the Constitution does not distinguish between slaves and other forms of property.
2. **(a)** 1854 **(b)** Slave states and territories open to slavery took up a larger area. **(c)** the Indian Reserve which has since become the state of Oklahoma

Relating Geography and History

1. **(a)** *slave states:* Alabama, Mississippi, Louisiana, Georgia, South Carolina, North Carolina, Virginia, Maryland, Delaware, Kentucky, and Tennessee; *free states:* Illinois, Indiana, Ohio, Pennsylvania, New York, New Jersey, Connecticut, Rhode Island, Massachusetts, Vermont, and New Hampshire **(b)** Missouri would be the first state entirely west of the Mississippi and one of the many new states to be carved out of the Louisiana Purchase. **(c)** Many southerners feared that if Missouri entered the Union as a free state, a precedent would be set for the rest of the new states that would be formed from the western territories.
2. **(a)** The Tallmadge Amendment was designed to prevent any more slaves from being brought into Missouri and the eventual emancipation of the children of slaves who were already there. **(b)** The amendment might have established

the right of Congress to prohibit slavery in the territories.
3. **(a)** A compromise settles a dispute between two or more sides when each side gives something up in order to reach an agreement. **(b)** The Missouri Compromise was reached when the North agreed to admit Missouri as a slave state while admitting Maine as a free state. The South agreed not to oppose the right of Congress to forbid slavery in the remaining territory north of the 36°30' line of latitude. **(c)** It did not really matter to the South whether there could be slaves north of the 36°30' line or not because cotton could not be grown profitably that far north.
4. The Missouri Compromise did not face the slavery question as a moral issue. It did help temporarily to keep the Union together, but the issue of slavery, in particular, and states' rights, in general, were destined to split the nation. In the meantime, there were years during which northern industries, population, transportation, and wealth could increase, giving the North an advantage when war came.

CHAPTER
18 A Nation Divided

SECTION REVIEW   *(text page 416)*

Suggested responses to the questions are:
1. **(a)** South Carolina, Georgia, Florida, Alabama, Mississippi, Louisiana, Texas, Virginia, Arkansas, Tennessee, and North Carolina **(b)** Delaware, Maryland, Kentucky, and Missouri
2. The South fought to win independence; proposed to fight a defensive war, holding off the North until it was war-weary and would agree to peace on southern terms; and planned to seize Washington and disrupt Union lines of communication. The North fought to restore the Union, and after 1862, to free the slaves. The northern strategy called for a blockade of the southern coastline; gaining control of the Mississippi and interior railroad lines to split the South in two; seizure of Richmond, and from there a drive southward to join the Union forces driving eastward from the Mississippi.

3. See the following chart.

	North	South
(a) **Number of States**	24	11
(b) **Population**	22,000,000	9,000,000
(c) **Industrial Development**	92% of nation's industry	8% of nation's industry
(d) **Transportation Facilities**	most of nation's railroads	few railroads
(e) **Naval Power**	large navy	almost no navy
(f) **Financial Resources**	gold	land and slaves

The North appears stronger because it had many more of the resources necessary to conduct a war.

SECTION REVIEW *(text page 422)*

Suggested responses to the questions are:
1. The blockade prevented the South from selling its cotton abroad and receiving European war materials and manufactured goods.
2. The Union hoped to keep Missouri from joining the Confederacy and to split the Confederacy in half.
3. **(a)** Sherman intended to split the Deep South and weaken southern resistance. **(b)** The "March to the Sea" left a 300-mile long, 60-mile wide path of destruction and a legacy of southern bitterness.
4. Defeat at Gettysburg put an end to Lee's attempt to invade the North. After Gettysburg, Lee never again took the offensive. The fall of Vicksburg gave Union forces control of the entire Mississippi and split the Confederacy in half.
5. Confederate soldiers and officers were allowed to return home on the promise not to take up arms again. They were permitted to take the horses and mules they owned. Lee and his officers were permitted to keep their swords and pistols.
6. Answers will vary.

SECTION REVIEW *(text page 425)*

Suggested responses to the questions are:
1. **(a)** The Civil War quickened abolitionist activities. **(b)** Abolitionists were responsible, in part, for the Emancipation Proclamation.
2. **(a)** He was afraid freeing the slaves would drive the border states to side with the Confederacy. **(b)** He changed his mind because emancipation might win support from Europe, lessening the danger of foreign intervention on the Confederate side. It would also gain support from American abolitionists.
3. The Thirteenth Amendment was passed to prohibit slavery in the United States and settle the slavery issue in a Constitutional way.
4. **(a)** Blacks at first served the northern forces as noncombatants — cooks, teamsters, nurses, scouts, spies, and steamboat pilots. In 1862, blacks in free states were organized into fighting regiments. **(b)** The war was being fought ostensibly to suppress rebellion and restore the Union. The issues of slavery and black participation in the war were thus officially downplayed. Lincoln and other northern officials feared that the use of black soldiers would antagonize the loyal border states. White northern recruits did not want to fight alongside black soldiers. Some questioned whether blacks possessed the ability or courage required of good soldiers.
5. **(a)** Black troops were less well trained than white soldiers; they received less adequate medical service; they were often assigned menial duties; only a few blacks ever received commissions; and they received lower pay than white soldiers. **(b)** The war quickened abolitionist activities. They pressured the government to issue a declaration of emancipation. Abolitionists fought on federal, state, and local levels to influence legislation and lobby for laws that would end discriminatory practices. They campaigned for the right to vote and for legal equality in the courts.

SECTION REVIEW *(text page 428)*

Suggested responses to the questions are:
1. **(a)** When the war began, the Confederacy relied entirely on volunteers. Soon, however, it turned to conscription of white males aged 18–35. As the war continued, the government first closed many exemptions, then extended the age limits to 17 and 50, and finally recruited slaves. **(b)** Some objected on the basis that the draft violated states' rights. Others complained that it exempted too many people and that it allowed the rich to avoid service.
2. **(a)** The Confederate government sold war bonds at home, borrowed abroad, taxed, and printed paper money. **(b)** As the war turned against the South, Confederate money decreased in value and prices soared. Money held by southerners bought very little.

3. **(a)** The Union blockade cut off manufactured goods and war materials from abroad that the South needed. **(b)** The South's lack of industry made it impossible to replace the lost imports. **(c)** Although the South raised adequate food crops, they could not be distributed during the war because of the deteriorating transportation system.

4. On farms and plantations, women did the work. They taught in schools and worked in mills, factories, munitions plants, ships, banks, and government offices. Northern and southern women served as full-time army nurses. Women's relief societies in the North and South staffed canteens, made bandages, and collected medicines. In the North, the women's societies raised about $15 million in war relief.

SECTION REVIEW   *(text page 431)*

Suggested responses to the questions are:
1. **(a)** The North used enlistment, draft, and a bounty system. **(b)** "Bounty jumping" developed. A man would enlist in one locality and collect his bounties, then desert and reenlist under another name in another locality and collect additional bounties. Some men also paid others to take their places in the war. **(c)** Irish immigrants objected to the draft because they felt the war would increase the number of free black workers with whom they competed for unskilled jobs.
2. The North financed the war through the tariff, war bonds, income tax, and paper money.
3. **(a)** Industry grew rapidly in the North because of the need for war supplies, the development of labor-saving machines, and tariff protection. **(b)** Technology grew as the North needed to produce goods faster for the war effort.
4. **(a)** Government aid, war orders, and the development of labor-saving machines stimulated agricultural prosperity in the North. **(b)** Congress conferred government subsidies and land grants on the railroads; it authorized two lines to construct a transcontinental railroad.

SECTION REVIEW   *(text page 436)*

Suggested responses to the questions are:
1. France and Great Britain wanted an independent South that would provide them with cotton and other raw materials, and at the same time, place no tariffs on the importation of their manufactured goods.
2. **(a)** Copperheads were northern leaders who opposed the war. **(b)** They argued that the loss of lives, money, and personal property was too great to be justified, that the South could not be beaten, and the war was therefore useless.
3. **(a)** The war and Lincoln's ability were the major issues in the election of 1864. **(b)** That an election was successfully held in wartime was a victory for representative government.

CHAPTER 18 REVIEW   *(text page 440)*

Reviewing Important Terms

1. Contrabands
2. conscription
3. writ of *habeas corpus*
4. bounty jumpers
5. greenbacks
6. homestead
7. land-grant colleges
8. subsidies

Practicing Critical Thinking Skills

Suggested responses to the questions are:
1. Answers will vary. You might suggest to the students that they refer to the campaign maps in Section 2. Students might mention any of the following: the Union blockade cut off southern trade, proved the North's superior naval strength and the South's inability to support a long war; the Mississippi River Campaign split the Confederacy in two parts and showed the North's advantage in superior numbers and a good navy; and the Battle for Richmond, 1862 — a series of resounding defeats for the Union army — showed the South's superior military leadership. Students might also describe other campaigns.
2. The Emancipation Proclamation promised freedom to slaves in Confederate states at war with the United States on January 1, 1863. The Thirteenth Amendment forbade slavery in any state or territory of the United States.
3. Lincoln believed slavery to be wrong, but he also felt that the issue of slavery must be subordinate to the main issue of saving the Union. He feared that emancipation might make the border states secede but realized the necessity of emancipation to prevent foreign intervention on the side of the Confederacy. Students might mention that Lincoln's ideas were consistent in that he placed the country before any individual who lived in it; they may also argue that Lincoln's delay in issuing the Emancipation Proclamation contradicted his belief in freedom for all.
4. **(a)** "... one nation, conceived in liberty, and dedicated to the proposition that all men are created equal," and " ... government of the people,

by the people, for the people..." (b) The common ideas are liberty, justice, equality for all people, and government by consent of the governed. Students can refer to the documents to make other comparisons.

5. (a) Women were needed on the home front to do the jobs formerly done by men. They worked in mills, factories, munitions plants, banks, and government offices. They often ran the family farms or plantations. They demonstrated their organizational skills by running relief societies, nursing organizations, and fund-raising activities. They nursed the wounded and operated hospitals. Their contributions increased their self-confidence and demonstrated to the world that women could be as useful outside the home as in it. (b) War involves the total society. With the men on the battlefields, the women must take on other jobs necessary to bring the war to a successful conclusion.

6. (a) Answers will vary. Students might distinguish between situations where the national crisis involves hostilities taking place on American soil and hostilities overseas, discuss the influence of nuclear weapons on the relevance of this question, or distinguish between what types of situations they would consider to constitute a true national crisis. (b) Answers will vary. Students might mention that this authority could lead to tyranny or that a President needs this power in order to react quickly during a national crisis. (c) Answers will vary. Students might mention that Congress would not be able to act quickly enough or that this Congressional power would avert possible tyranny.

Developing History Study Skills

(a) Clara Barton was a nurse during the Civil War. (b) She was the first woman to serve in the civil service. (c) She noted the poor conditions of first-aid on the battlefield and later founded the Red Cross. (d) 83

Relating Geography and History

1. (a) Answers will vary. Students might mention that there were fewer railroad lines in the South. When the war was in progress, two factors helped destroy many of the existing miles of track: the Union armies, and the southerners themselves who, because they lacked adequate repair and replacement facilities, broke up many branch lines to repair destroyed main lines. (b) Answers will vary. Students might mention that the limited transportation resources in the areas that had been served by ruined track caused serious shortages of food, clothing, and military supplies.

2. (a) There were not enough factories to produce weapons and other materials with which to fight the war. The South could not import enough war materials to fill the gap because of the Union blockade. (b) Answers will vary. Students might mention any three of the following items. Most battles were fought on southern soil, so the South was mainly fighting defensive battles in familiar territory, thus needing fewer troops. In order to win, the North had to conquer the South and bring it back to the Union, while the South could win its case if the war were a draw. They would still have been independent. The South was fighting for a moral cause and what were, for them, their fundamental rights. The military leaders in the South were talented and available at the start. Southerners were optimistic because they were convinced Great Britain or France would come to their aid because of "King Cotton."

UNIT FIVE REVIEW   (text page 441)

Discussing Ideas

1. Sectional tensions over a number of issues divided the North and South for many years before the Union was severed. Evidence includes: the Missouri controversy in 1820; the tariff and nullification controversy in 1832; the conflict over the annexation of Texas between 1836 and 1844; the struggle over the question of slavery in the territory acquired from Mexico, (the Wilmot Proviso in 1846 through the Compromise of 1850); the opposition of many northerners to the Fugitive Slave Act; the Kansas-Nebraska Act in 1854; the violence of bleeding Kansas; the Dred Scott decision; the Lincoln-Douglas debates; John Brown's Raid at Harpers Ferry; and the election of Lincoln. The overall divisive issue was states' rights.

2. (a) At first, northerners fought to preserve the Union. Later in the war, many also felt that freeing the slaves was just as important an aim. (b) By the end of the war, the North had defeated the South and freed the slaves. It would be several years, however, before all the former Confederate states were readmitted to the Union.

3. The North won the Civil War because they prevented the South from receiving outside help; the North was more populous, more industrialized, wealthier, militarily superior, and better motivated. Students might mention other reasons, and they might disagree with some of those given.

4. Answers will vary. Students who agree might mention that the war demonstrated that a rep-

resentative government could successfully operate during a war and even conduct an election in wartime. Students who disagree might mention that the war did not broaden suffrage to include women or the freed slaves.

5. (a) Women worked in factories, mills, shops, banks, and government offices; they worked in place of their men on farms and plantations; and they replaced men in the schools. Women improved the medical services for the fighting forces. (b) Although discriminated against, many blacks served in the military. Many northern blacks became involved with helping fugitive slaves. Slaves became free. (c) Some Indians fought in the battles of the Civil War. Indian uprisings in some of the territories and the state of Minnesota resulted in violent retaliations.

6. (a) Answers will vary. Students might mention that both wars were fought for independence on one side and for preserving a relationship on the other and that both wars were fought over sectional interests and philosophical issues. (b) Answers will vary. Students might mention that the Revolution was not a war between formerly political equals and that the Civil War did not result in the independence of one of the combatants. In the Revolutionary War, the rebels were greatly aided by a foreign power; while in the Civil War, the fact that the rebels did not receive the same kind of help was one of the factors in their defeat.

7. The Civil War was a major turning point in American history in that it resolved the controversial issues of slavery and states' rights.

Applying History Study Skills

(a) The commissioners were sent abroad in order to seek recognition from the governments of Europe. (b) Supporting the Union was safer diplomatically, since there was doubt that the Confederacy would win the war. To support the Confederacy would have indicated that there was a chance the Confederacy would win and in the case of Great Britain, a chance to continue to receive the South's cotton. This would deal a blow to the textile industry in the North, which was competing on the world market. Remaining neutral was the safest course, even though the South would be angered. (c) Memories of the effect of France's help in the Revolutionary War might have made the North determined to keep Britain or France from supporting the South. (d) He was being sarcastic because the situation was anything but pleasant. The situation was putting Britain in a position where it would be very difficult to remain neutral.

UNIT SIX
Rebuilding the Nation

19 Restoring the South to the Union

SECTION REVIEW   *(text page 448)*

Suggested responses to the questions are:
1. **(a)** Lincoln meant to bring the South back into the Union, using friendship and moderation. **(b)** He offered amnesty to all southerners who would take an oath of allegiance to the Union, except for high-ranking Confederate officers, those who had resigned from federal offices to serve the Confederacy, and Confederates who had mistreated prisoners of war. His provisions for reconstructing southern states were that a state could draw up a new constitution, elect new officials, and return to the Union when at least ten percent of the voters took an oath of allegiance.
2. **(a)** Opponents of Lincoln's reconstruction plan did not favor pardoning former Confederates or allowing them to vote and hold office. They doubted the loyalty of the Confederates to the Union and also doubted the Confederates would grant legal and political rights to blacks. **(b)** Radical Republicans wanted to punish the South and see that justice was done for former slaves. Sumner insisted on measures to guarantee equality for blacks and to educate them so that they could carry out the responsibilites of freedom. Stevens wanted to punish the South for the injustices and discriminations of slavery. He also wanted to divide up the estates of "rebel traitors" among the freed slaves. A third group wanted to preserve the Republican program by gaining voters from among the freed slaves, to whom they would grant voting rights, or by depriving former Confederate leaders of their right to vote or hold office.
3. **(a)** The Wade-Davis Bill was intended to give political power to southerners who had been loyal to the Union; to ensure that the new constitutions of the southern states would recognize the freedom of black southerners, and to ensure that southern war debts were repudi-

ated. **(b)** Lincoln believed that this bill would restrict him in rebuilding the Union. He also believed that Congress could not compel a state to abolish slavery, but that an amendment to the Constitution would be required to do so. **(c)** Radical Republicans opposed the bill because they believed it was not harsh enough.
4. **(a)** The struggle over reconstruction was at least partly about political considerations. Some Republicans were worried about the fate of their economic programs — tariffs, national banks, free land, and federal aid to railroads — should northern and southern Democrats reunite to hold their majority in Congress. These Republicans favored keeping former Confederate leaders from voting and holding office and supported voting rights for freed slaves who, they expected, would support Republican programs. **(b)** Congress felt that President Lincoln had encroached upon Congress's Constitutional powers in exercising his war powers. The legislators believed that they should determine the rules for reconstruction. Johnson's differences with Congress were greater, since his policies were much more inflexible.

SECTION REVIEW   *(text page 453)*

Suggested responses to the questions are:
1. **(a)** Many cities, homes, and farms lay in ruins. Seeds and agricultural tools were scarce. Confederate money was worthless, and United States currency was almost unavailable. Millions of men and women were uprooted and unemployed. Disease and hunger swept across the South, and thousands of people died. **(b)** Johnson was stubborn, unwilling to change his views, and unwilling to work with the moderate Republicans. As a result, control of Congress passed to the Radicals.
2. Southern laws forbade black southerners to possess firearms unless licensed to do so, to assemble without the presence of white people, to appear on roads or streets after sunset, to travel without licenses, or to start their own businesses. Some codes restricted the renting of farm land to blacks.
3. Radical Republicans had argued that white southerners could not be trusted to recognize

the complete freedom of blacks, and the black codes proved their argument. They also opposed the terms by which the southerners were allowed to re-enter the Union and wanted to dictate those terms themselves.

4. (a) Most northerners regarded the bureau as an honest effort to help rebuild the South. Most white southerners blamed the bureau for creating enmity between black and white southerners and for stirring up false hopes that all freed slaves would get farms. (b) Most of the black codes allowed former slaves to own personal property, to sue and be sued in court, and to marry legally other black people. But the codes still denied blacks their basic civil rights. (c) Lincoln and Johnson theorized that individuals had rebelled, and therefore individuals could be pardoned for the offense by the President. (d) Sumner held that southern states, seceding as complete political organizations, were no longer states, but were unorganized territories to be dealt with by Congress. (e) Stevens believed that the southern states were completely outside the Union and should be treated as if they had been conquered in war.

SECTION REVIEW [text page 457]

Suggested responses to the questions are:
1. (a) The Freedmen's Bureau was given the power to prosecute in military courts any person accused of depriving freed slaves of their civil rights. The Civil Rights Act was designed to give black Americans full citizenship and guarantee them equality. (b) Johnson contended that trial by military court violated the Fifth Amendment, and that Congress had no power to pass any laws with 11 states unrepresented. He also thought that the Civil Rights Act was a violation of states' rights. (c) The Radical Republicans passed the bills over Johnson's vetoes. The vetoes also cost him the support of moderate Republicans and strengthened the influence of Radical Republicans who demanded his impeachment.
2. Congressional reconstruction (1) divided the ten southern states that had rejected the Fourteenth Amendment into five military districts; (2) deprived most former Confederate leaders of the right to vote and to hold office; (3) gave the right to vote and to hold office to freed slaves; (4) authorized southern states to write new constitutions in which they guaranteed freed slaves the right to vote; (5) required the southern states to ratify the Fourteenth Amendment.
3. (a) The Radical Republicans were determined to remove Johnson from office because he would not support their reconstruction policies. They passed the Tenure of Office Act over Johnson's

veto, to provide grounds for his impeachment. Johnson held the law to be unconstitutional, and tested it by demanding the resignation of Secretary of War Stanton. The House then demanded impeachment for "high crimes and misdemeanors in office." (b) The evidence given at Johnson's impeachment trial indicated that he was innocent of the charges, but he was acquitted by only one vote. The trial ended Johnson's influence and made many moderate Republicans turn against the Radicals.
4. (a) Section 1 of the Fourteenth Amendment says that no state can deprive United States citizens of "life, liberty, or property, without due process of law," or deny them "the equal protection of the laws" or their civil rights. Section 2 declares that if a state denies male citizens the right to vote, the state's representation in Congress shall be reduced proportionately. Section 3 provides that any person who takes an oath of office to uphold the Constitution and then plays an active role in a rebellion against the United States shall be barred from holding any civil or military office in the United States. Section 4 makes it unconstitutional for the United States to pay any debt owed by those who rebel against the United States, or to pay compensation for slaves. (b) The Fifteenth Amendment prohibits any state from denying a citizen the right to vote because of "race, color, or previous condition of servitude." (c) Congress proposed the Fourteenth Amendment because it thought that the Supreme Court might declare the Civil Rights Act unconstitutional; it wished to add the provisions of the act to the Constitution. (d) The status of women was not changed at all by the amendment.

SECTION REVIEW [text page 461]

Suggested responses to the questions are:
1. Reconstruction governments protected homes and farms against arbitrary foreclosures; strengthened public education; spread the tax burden more evenly; reorganized local governments and judicial systems; drew up new state constitutions; abolished imprisonment for debt; and extended the legal rights of women.
2. (a) Some white southerners formed secret societies to express their resentment of the reconstruction governments. They tried to intimidate black southerners and their white sympathizers to force them out of politics. (b) Congress passed the Force Acts in 1870–71, giving the President power to use armed forces in controlling the secret societies, to suspend the writ of *habeas corpus,* and to provide for federal supervision of southern elections. The Amnesty Act of 1872, which restored political

rights to practically all former Confederates, helped virtually to end the secret societies.

3. (a) Many northerners began to lose interest in reconstruction. They became disillusioned at reports of political inexperience of black southerners and began to believe that deep conflicts in the South would continue until former southern leaders were returned to power. They thought that perhaps the freed slaves did need the supervision of white leaders. (b) Some carpetbaggers sincerely wanted to help the freed slaves exercise their rights. Some hoped to get elected to political office. Some went to make their fortunes by acquiring farm land or by starting new businesses. Some went to defraud and profit from the freed slaves.

SECTION REVIEW   *(text page 464)*

Suggested responses to the questions are:
1. (a) Tenant farming was a system in which planters rented portions of their land to farmers who supplied their own seed, mules, and provisions. In sharecropping, the sharecroppers furnished nothing but their labor, and received a percentage of the crop they produced. (b) After the Civil War, many planters could not continue to run their large farms, and freed blacks and many poor whites could not afford to buy land. Originally, tenant farming and sharecropping aided both groups and maintained production despite the desperate economic situation. (c) The tenant farmers had only small plots of land, and few could grow enough crops to accumulate enough money to buy a farm. The sharecroppers did not get paid until harvest time. To buy provisions they had to mortgage their crop shares in advance. When the crops were harvested, almost all their money went to pay their bills and interest on their mortgages. Thus, they were seldom out of debt.
2. Resentment of Radical Republican reconstruction caused white southerners to support Democratic Party candidates for both local and national offices.
3. (a) The most important agricultural progress was the development of truck farming and fruit growing. Other progress came through the use of fertilizers and modern machinery, which increased crop yields. (b) Southern industrialists and communities rebuilt and expanded the textile mills. In addition, the extension of railroads encouraged urban growth and the development of tobacco and iron and steel centers. (c) Progress in education was slow and limited. Northern philanthropists were notable contributors to the funds needed for building schools and providing teachers. The practice of segregating black and white schools added to the high costs and slow progress.

4. The graph shows that southern industry grew rapidly. The percentage of southern workers in industry almost doubled from 1870 to 1910.

SECTION REVIEW   *(text page 467)*

Suggested responses to the questions are:
1. The federal government suspended its program for helping black southerners make the transition from slavery to freedom; white Americans in both the North and the South continued to think of black Americans as inferiors; and white southerners feared that the southern way of life would be threatened if black southerners were not firmly "kept in their place."
2. (a) Many black southerners did not have the money to pay a poll tax. (b) Most blacks did not have the education to pass a literacy test. (c) The grandfather clause allowed those white southerners who could not pass the first two requirements to vote, but did not help most black southerners, since their fathers and grandfathers, as slaves, had been ineligible to vote.
3. (a) A new pattern of segregation was established through "Jim Crow" laws that divided whites and blacks by means of "separate but equal" facilities. (b) The Supreme Court's decision in *Plessy v. Ferguson* was that "separate but equal" facilities did not violate the Fourteenth Amendment.
4. (a) Washington urged black Americans to avoid protest and learn skills that would enable them to earn a living. He encouraged vocational rather than liberal arts education. (b) Du Bois believed that only continual and vigorous protests and appeals to black pride could change conditions of inequality and injustice. He demanded that blacks receive whatever kind of education they needed to achieve full equality.

CHAPTER 19 REVIEW   *(text page 469)*

Reviewing Important Terms

1. true   3. true
2. false, carpetbaggers   4. true

Practicing Critical Thinking Skills

Suggested responses to the questions are:
1. *Plessy v. Ferguson* reflected a capitulation to racial interests. It also reflected the loss of interest in the plight of blacks, and an interest in healing the wounds of the Union, even to the detriment of individuals.
2. (a) Southerners hoped that the black codes would help to restore life as they had known it before the Civil War; they expected the "Jim

Crow" laws to maintain segregation of the races. (b) The black codes denied black southerners such civil rights as the right to possess firearms and to assemble without the presence of whites. Blacks could not appear on the streets after dark or travel without permits. Blacks were also forbidden to start businesses and were forced to accept severe contracts for their labor. The "Jim Crow" laws kept southern blacks from attending the same schools or using the same public facilities as whites.

3. (a) Slavery, a major cause of the war, was ended. Another problem involved the different economic systems of the North and the South. As the South industrialized after the war, the needs of the two sections became less divergent. (b) An increase in the number of poor farmers, segregation of and discrimination against blacks, and a virtual one-party system, which tended to perpetuate sectional differences and bitterness, were directly related to the Civil War and reconstruction.

4. The New South departed from the prewar plantation system. It also involved greater crop diversification — the growing of fruits and vegetables in addition to the traditional crops; the expansion of railroads and urban centers; and the opening of new mines, mills, and factories.

5. The Congressional Civil Rights Acts of 1866 and 1875 as well as the Fourteenth and Fifteenth Amendments attempted to guarantee the citizenship and voting rights of blacks and to prevent discrimination. The federal government did little if anything to enforce these measures, however, and even effectively thwarted them in the Plessy v. Ferguson ruling. In recent decades the federal government has passed further legislation to prevent denial of civil rights and has enforced these laws to the extent of using federal troops if necessary.

6. See the following chart.

Presidential Plan	Congressional Plan
Full pardon for most southerners who took the oath of allegiance States returned to the Union when they drew up a new constitution and 10 percent of the eligible voters took the oath of allegiance	South divided into five military districts Former Confederate leaders deprived of right to vote or to hold office Freed slaves given right to hold office and to vote States must write new constitutions guaranteeing rights to freed slaves States must ratify Fourteenth Amendment

Student evaluations will vary.

7. Answers will vary. Students might suggest that northern support for the Freedmen's Bureau shows toleration while southern secret societies

show prejudice. Recent racial incidents such as school desegregation battles are not confined to southern states.

Developing History Study Skills

1. (a) President Johnson believed that the act was unconstitutional. The Radical Republicans believed the act to be a good way to find grounds to impeach Johnson. (b) The Radical Republicans stated that Johnson had ridiculed Congress and had made public threats against it.

Relating Geography and History

2. See the following chart. Answers will vary.

Raw Materials Available	Industry	Other Factors
Lumber	Paper Furniture Chemicals	Larger population meant increasing demand
Vegetables and fruits	Food processing	Development of scientific farming, new processing technology, and advertising
Iron ore	Steel	Increased industrial and commercial demand; reduced shipping costs
Petroleum	Oil, gasoline, and natural gas	Explosive growth of the auto industry; increased household cooking and heating needs
Other minerals	Chemicals	New industrial and commercial uses

CHAPTER

20 Severe Trials for Democracy

SECTION REVIEW   (text page 474)

Suggested responses to the questions are:

1. (a) Evidences of corruption in Grant's adminis-

tration include the following: in the Crédit Mobilier, a company set up to construct the Union Pacific Railroad, both the railroad and the construction company had the same directors, who awarded contracts to themselves at high profits and became rich on this graft; members of Congress voted themselves raises in salary and made the raise retroactive for two years; Secretary of the Treasury Richardson granted the right to collect overdue federal taxes to John D. Sanborn, and later evidence indicated that Sanborn had bribed politicians to use their influence to get him a contract; a group of whisky distillers avoided paying revenue taxes on distilled liquor by paying blackmail to high officials in government. (b) Many blamed Grant for his blind loyalty to his associates—for refusing to believe that many of them used him and his office for their own benefit.

2. Gould bribed the legislators of New York State to authorize sale of additional stock in the Erie Railroad. The Tweed Ring in New York City gained control of the city government by befriending immigrants in order to gain their votes, and by stuffing the ballot boxes. Tweed overloaded payrolls with friends, sold jobs, and demanded bribes from companies doing business with the city. Between 1868 and 1871, the "Ring" and its friends cost the city close to $100 million.

3. Answers will vary. Students might mention the continuation of dishonest practices carried on during the war and the rapid growth of impersonal corporations.

SECTION REVIEW (text page 478)

Suggested responses to the questions are:
1. In the spoils system, government jobs are given to political favorites. The merit system gives jobs to people who receive the highest grades in competitive examinations.
2. In the election of 1876, Tilden received 184 electoral votes, one short of the necessary majority; Hayes received 165. Four states — South Carolina, Florida, Louisiana, and Oregon — sent in two sets of returns for a total of 20 electoral votes. The vote from Oregon went to Hayes. A special Electoral Commission was created to decide which of the disputed votes would be counted. Hayes won by an 8-to-7 vote of the commission.
3. (a) Liberal Republicans urged civil service reform. (b) Stalwarts opposed reforms and reformers. (c) Half-Breeds agreed with Hayes that at least some reform was needed.
4. (a) The Pendleton Act provided for a bipartisan commission to give competitive examinations

for about 12 percent of the federal jobs; the President could broaden the list of offices requiring examination. The act forbade the party in power to ask for campaign contributions from federal officeholders. (b) Widespread government corruption, and the spoils system that fed it, were under attack by reformers. When President Garfield was shot by a disappointed office-seeker, the new President, Chester Arthur, supported the Pendleton Act.

5. "Mugwumps" left the Republican Party to vote for the Democratic candidate; Cleveland had a long record of reform activities; and Blaine did not rebuke the speaker who called the Democrats the party of "Rum, Romanism, and Rebellion."

SECTION REVIEW (text page 481)

Suggested responses to the questions are:
1. Officeholders should work in the interest of the general public who elected them to office.
2. (a) The Presidential Succession Act provided for the order of succession to the Presidency in the event of the death or disability of the President and the Vice President. (b) The Electoral Count Act was designed to prevent disputed elections such as that of 1876.
3. Tariffs were a major political issue. Big business interests fought hard for tariff protection against foreign competition while wage earners, farmers, and owners of small businesses demanded tariff reform. In the election of 1892, Cleveland promised lower tariffs. In the tariff debate, business interests succeeded in keeping high tariffs on over 600 products. The Wilson-Gorman Tariff cost the Democrats millions of votes because Americans believed they had broken their promises.
4. (a) The cartoonist appears to feel that Harrison was not a very good President. (b) The cartoonist makes Harrison look foolish next to the status of other Presidents, shows him holding papers representing scandals and broken promises, and portrays Uncle Sam as being in doubt as to whether Harrison should receive a statue.

CHAPTER 20 REVIEW (text page 485)

Reviewing Important Terms

1. true
2. false, protective tariff
3. false, graft
4. false, pension grabs
5. true
6. false, salary grab
7. true

Practicing Critical Thinking Skills

Suggested responses to the questions are:
1. The Pendleton Act established that federal jobs below the policy-making level should be filled by competitive examination, a giant step toward more honest and efficient government.
2. (a) Cleveland believed that "a public office is a public trust" and that it was the President's responsibility to make sure the public trust was carefully fulfilled. He believed in strong, courageous leadership by the President. Harrison believed the President should execute the will of the Congress, which represents the will of the people. (b) Cleveland vetoed some 200 private pension bills, kept his campaign promise by requesting a lowered tariff, advanced civil service reform, and instituted procedures for conserving natural resources. Harrison accepted the reversals of Cleveland's policies by Congress, including additional pensions and the McKinley Tariff.
3. Answers will vary. Students might suggest the following: Grant — failure; Hayes — average; Arthur — average; Cleveland — near great; Harrison — below average. Students should mention as criteria: honesty, courage, forcefulness, good judgment, and imagination.
4. (a) The Presidential Succession Act of 1886 provided for the order of succession to the Presidency in the event of the death or disability of the President and Vice President. The Act of 1967 (Amendment 25) prescribes the method of filling a vacancy in the office of the Vice President. (b) The assassination of Kennedy created a vacancy in the office of the Vice President when Johnson assumed the Presidency.
5. (a) Answers will vary. Students might mention Watergate or Abscam on the national level. (b) Answers will vary. Students might mention that reform means generally the same as it did in the post-Civil War period. (c) Answers will vary. Students might suggest outlawing lobbying or requiring full financial disclosure by all public officials.

Developing History Study Skills

1. (a) President Grant and the Republican leaders in Congress (b) The Republicans are tatooing Grant. (c) Answers will vary. Students might mention that the Congressional leaders had absolute control over Grant, and that his administration was marred by scandal.
2. (a, b, c) Answers will vary.
3. (a) The textbook implies that corrupt political machines existed because of corrupt police and courts. (b) The textbook states that machines helped immigrants. (c) The textbook states that machine politicians used their power to get rich.

Relating Geography and History

1., 2. (a, b) See the following chart.

Year	Republican	Democrat	Third Party
1876	Hayes 4,036,572 185 NE, MW, W	Tilden 4,284,020 184 S, MA	Cooper (Greenback) 81,737 0
1880	Garfield 4,453,295 214 NE, MW, W	Hancock 4,414,082 168 S	Weaver (Greenback) 308,578 0
1884	Blaine 4,850,293 182 NE, MW, W	Cleveland 4,879,507 219 S, MA	Butler (Greenback) 175,370 0
1888	Harrison 5,447,129 233 NE, MW, W	Cleveland 5,537,857 168 S	Fisk (Prohibition) 249,506 0
1892	Harrison 5,182,690 145 NE, W	Cleveland 5,555,426 277 S, MA, MW	Weaver (People's) 1,029,846 22

(c) Answers will vary.

CHAPTER

21 Settling the Last Frontier

SECTION REVIEW   *(text page 494)*

Suggested responses to the questions are:
1. (a) The revolver could be reloaded easily and several bullets could be fired in rapid succession before reloading. It caused the Indians to lose their tactical advantage. (b) The railroads brought large numbers of settlers to the West and split the buffalo herds, speeding their destruction. (c) The destruction of the buffalo eliminated the Indians' main source of food and clothing.
2. (a) The concentration policy tried to confine the Indians to a limited area. It was hoped the policy would reduce tribal warfare and provide safe

travel routes west for settlers. **(b)** As ranchers, miners, and farmers moved into the Great Plains, the government called for resettlement of Indians on defined tracts of land called reservations. The purpose was to make the best land available to, and safe for, white settlers. **(c)** When the Indians resisted the reservation policy, the government used military force to keep them on the reservations.

3. Chief Joseph and Geronimo both resisted American government policies. Chief Joseph tried to lead his people to safety in Canada, but failed and was forced to surrender. Geronimo and other Apache and Comanche leaders led raids against white settlers in the Southwest. Geronimo, too, was finally forced to surrender.

SECTION REVIEW   *(text page 496)*

Suggested responses to the questions are:

1. The list of broken promises and injustices is a long one. When the government removed Indians from their homeland between 1865 and 1890, the treaties promised aid in the form of credit and supplies. Supplies were meager, funds were cut back, and many agents of the Bureau of Indian Affairs cheated the Indians. When Indians fought back, they were pursued, captured, and punished. The Indians were treated with contempt. The Dawes Act allowed a family 160 acres of land, but speculators found ways to get most of the Indians' land, and the remainder of the land was too poor to support the people.

2. Helen Hunt Jackson, in her book *A Century of Dishonor,* provided documentary evidence that the government had broken its promises to the Indians. Sarah Winnemucca lectured across the country on the injustices to her people, the corruption of the Bureau of Indian Affairs, and the unfair distribution of land to the Indians. The National Indian Defense Organization argued that Indians should be allowed to retain their own traditions and customs.

3. Those favoring Americanization believed that Indians had to be assimilated into the American way of life to avoid continual conflict. They believed that Indians must accept Christianity, American forms of education, and individual land ownership. Those opposing Americanization pointed out that the Indians had deep-rooted cultures that could not be changed quickly or without serious problems.

SECTION REVIEW   *(text page 500)*

Suggested responses to the questions are:

1. Texans drove vast herds north to towns that

grew up along the railroads that transported the steers to urban markets.

2. (a) The cattle raisers wintered their surplus steers on the open range near the cattle towns. After fattening them during the winter, they sold them in the towns before the new cattle drives. **(b)** The arrival of sheepherders and farmers ended the open range. Sheep cropped the grass so close that none was left for the cattle. Farmers broke up the range with their farms and barbed-wire fences.

3. (a) Answers will vary. Students might mention any three of the following: Western Trail, Chisholm Trail, Shawnee Trail, Goodnight-Loving Trail. **(b)** Kansas City was a railroad junction where the Kansas-Pacific and the Atchison, Topeka, and Santa Fe railroads connected with eastern lines. It was also the northern terminus of the Shawnee Trail. **(c)** Numerous railroad lines from every direction converged at Chicago.

SECTION REVIEW   *(text page 506)*

Suggested responses to the questions are:

1. (a) The Homestead Act gave free land to the settlers. **(b)** The railroads provided transportation to the West; in order to gain the revenue that would come from settled land, the railroads advertised for settlers.

2. The farmers solved the problems of housing and fencing with sod houses and barbed wire.

3. The windmills operated pumps that drew up underground water.

4. (a) Housing was crude. This house was cut out of the hillside and was probably dark. Possessions were few; the cows, horses, cart, and plow were essential tools to earning a living. Family members probably had to rely on each other for all needs. **(b)** They used what was available for their needs. A lack of wood, for example, forced the settlers to build sod houses.

SECTION REVIEW   *(text page 508)*

Suggested responses to the questions are:

1. (a) The "Forty-Niners" were prospectors drawn to California in 1849 by the discovery of gold. The "Fifty-Niners" were those who rushed to find gold in Colorado in 1859. **(b)** These people helped to settle the West and to form the new western states.

2. (a) The mining camps at first were wild, lawless communities of tents, rough board shacks, and smoke-filled saloons. The miners made their

own laws, relying upon guns and fists to protect themselves. **(b)** Eventually schools and churches were built and local governments organized. The communities were recognized as parts of a territory, which in turn was eventually admitted to the Union as a state.
3. **(a)** The early discoveries of gold and silver attracted prospectors to the West. However, long before the end of the 1800's increasing numbers of mineral deposits were being discovered by expeditions equipped with the latest technology and knowledge of geology. The federal government sent many expeditions into the mountains, and in 1879 the United States Geological Survey was organized. Private industry also sent out carefully organized expeditions, but the individual prospector could not afford this scientific exploration. **(b)** Mining became big business with systematic exploration, new methods of extracting metal from ore, invention of powerful machinery, and growing knowledge of chemistry.

CHAPTER 21 REVIEW *(text page 510)*

Reviewing Important Terms

1. true
2. true
3. true
4. true
5. false, the open range

Practicing Critical Thinking Skills

Suggested responses to the questions are:
1. Students should agree. The first attempt to eliminate the Indians involved getting them out of the white settlers' way by forcing them onto ever-shrinking reservation lands and by ignoring their rights and their basic needs. The second attempt involved assimilating them into white American society. The Dawes Act, for example, provided for citizenship for Indians only if they abandoned their tribes and tribal customs.
2. **(a)** All three groups had to adapt to their surroundings, and only through the hardest work and much good luck could they hope to be successful. Cattle raisers faced the hazards of the long drive, scarce water, changing prices for beef, and competition from sheepherders. Farmers faced drought, grasshopper plagues, and hostile cattle raisers. Miners had only the slightest chance of finding valuable minerals. **(b)** Windmills helped ease the water problem. Barbed-wire fences eventually ended disputes over land ownership. New farming techniques aided the homesteaders; specialization aided the ranchers; and scientific surveying promoted more intensive mining. These developments

helped the settlers stay on the land. **(c)** In the long run the solutions promoted settlement, but many settlers were defeated by the harsh conditions.
3. **(a)** The federal government subsidized the building of railroads to improve transportation, passed the Homestead Act to promote settlement, managed Indian affairs to insure the settlers' safety, and established the Geological Survey to search for minerals. **(b)** Answers will vary. Students might argue that the frontier was significant to the establishment and growth of democracy. Others might contend that it established a tradition of violence and promoted anarchy. Some might see the frontier as the march of civilization, or as the conquest of civilization. Others might see it as a breeding ground for individuality, or for reckless individualism that ignores the needs of others.
4. **(a)** The Industrial Revolution provided the technology needed to develop the West. Railroads, barbed wire, windmills, mining machinery, and other inventions helped settlers survive and earn livings on the Great Plains. As the Industrial Revolution progressed, the western resources became more valuable. **(b)** Much of the new technology was devised in response to the needs of the westerners, so that they could produce more for the factories and for city dwellers.
5. **(a)** Scarcity of water is still a problem in the West. New methods of searching for, tapping, and using this scarce resource have been developed. **(b)** Railroads are still important to the economy of the West, but the development of the interstate highway system has decreased the overall importance of railroads. **(c)** Early mining centered on gold, silver, and copper. Industrial and commercial uses have made minerals like uranium and bauxite important to the mining industry. Mining is more automated and done on a much larger scale than in the period discussed in this unit.

Developing History Study Skills

1. **(a)** The main idea is the rapid settlement of the West. The second paragraph deals with the displacement of the Indians by white settlers. **(b)** Paragraph one states that by the 1890's that the Bureau of the Census declared that the frontier no longer existed. Paragraph two discusses Americanization and reservations. **(c)** Answers will vary. Students might mention "By the 1890's" in paragraph one. This phrase connects the idea of the Homestead Act initially encouraging settlement with the final results of settlement.
2. **(a)** Directly stated. "We were seldom hungry." **(b)** Implied. The phrase "the white man came

and they made little islands for us" implies that whites took away Indian lands. (c) Implied. The phrase "the islands are becoming smaller . . . " implies that Black Elk thinks his way of life is disappearing.

Relating Geography and History

1. See the following chart. Answers will vary. Students should include the chart's information on their maps.

Railroad	Indian Tribes
Great Northern	Crow, Arapaho
Northern Pacific	Dakota, Mandan, Crow
Union Pacific	Cheyenne, Pawnee, Arapaho
Atchison, Topeka and Santa Fe	Arapaho, Cheyenne
Southern Pacific	Comanche

2. (a) Answers will vary. Students might mention the disappearance of the buffalo herds and the loss of land by the Indians as more settlers arrived by rail. (b) Answers will vary.
3. Answers will vary.

UNIT SIX REVIEW
(text page 511)

Discussing Ideas

1. (a) The South was divided into five military districts, each with a military governor. Federal troops were stationed in each district to maintain law and order. The states drew up new constitutions guaranteeing the freed slaves the right to vote. Most former Confederates could neither vote nor hold office. (b) Answers will vary. Students might consider in their evaluations points such as freedom for blacks, reduction of sectional competition, the southern economic situation and modernization of southern facilities.
2. (a) Economic prospects for both were dismal. Some blacks managed to enter business or buy farms, but most worked as laborers, either in factories or fields. Indians had even less economic opportunity. Most were confined to reservations although a few became farmers and laborers. (b) The federal government developed programs to help each of these groups. On the whole, the programs were not successful. (c) Both blacks and Indians were treated as inferiors by a majority of white Americans during these years.
3. Students should answer yes. Reconstruction gave the federal government the opportunity to assert power over the states. This power continued to grow as the nation became a more integrated political, economic, and social unit. With the growth of railroads and business, the federal government was called upon to become more involved than ever in the lives of citizens.
4. The growth and importance of railroads, the passage of the McKinley Tariff, the effects of lobbies, and the growth of trusts are some examples.
5. The relationship between Congress and Andrew Johnson was antagonistic. His impeachment made Congress the dominant force in the federal government. Congress continued to dominate the federal government during the Grant administrations in spite of the numerous scandals that surfaced. Congressional power was hardly diminished by the reforms of Hayes, Garfield, or Cleveland. The era 1865–96 was one of increasing Congressional power.
6. Answers will vary. Students might mention the ending of slavery and the growth of the Populist Party as indications that the United States became more democratic. Others might cite the black codes, "Jim Crow" laws, the *Plessy v. Ferguson* ruling, and the treatment of the Indians as indications that the country had become less democratic.
7. (a) The earlier view of the Great Plains as a foreboding desert gave way to the pioneer spirit. The Great Plains became a frontier to be conquered. (b) Population pressures, the need for more farmland, the Homestead Act, and the completion of the transcontinental railroad attracted people to the Great Plains. Soon settlers were moving into this open area. (c) As Black Elk stated "they made little islands for us . . . and always these islands are becoming smaller."

Applying History Study Skills

1. The first excerpt reflects the Indian point of view. The second excerpt reflects the white government's point of view.
2. The Indians want to keep their lands. The settlers want to crush resistance.
3. The Indians are being crushed. The Indians have lost their lands.

UNIT SEVEN
The Rise of Industrialism

SECTION REVIEW   (text page 518)

Suggested responses to the questions are:
1. **(a)** The government recognized the importance of an efficient transportation system to a developing urban and industrial society. **(b)** The land-grant railroads carried government troops, mail, and military freight at reduced rates. They repaid the original loans and an additional $103 million in interest.
2. The raw materials needed for manufacturing goods flow to the city through the transportation "veins." The city (industrial heart) produces the goods, and "pumps" them out to the country through the transportation "arteries."
3. **(a)** See the following time line. Answers will vary.

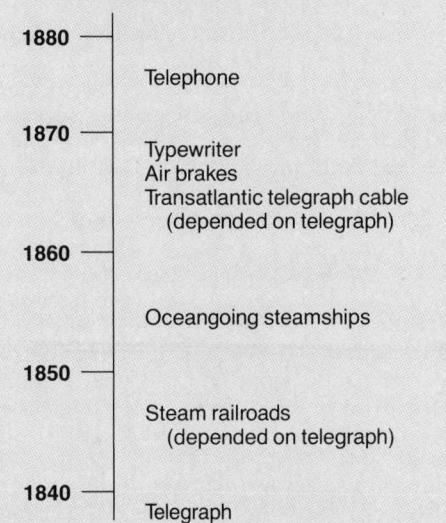

Time Line of Inventions

1880	
	Telephone
1870	Typewriter
	Air brakes
	Transatlantic telegraph cable (depended on telegraph)
1860	
	Oceangoing steamships
1850	
	Steam railroads (depended on telegraph)
1840	
	Telegraph

SECTION REVIEW   (text page 520)

Suggested responses to the questions are:
1. **(a)** Human muscle power was replaced by the power of steam, petroleum, and electricity. **(b)** Manufacturers could use machines to do work that workers were unable to do, and they could produce goods in volume.
2. **(a)** Kerosene was a cheap and efficient form of fuel for lamps to light homes, businesses, and streets. **(b)** The availability of cheap steel allowed Americans to build railroads, factories, bridges, heavy machinery, mills, and other necessities of the industrial system. In turn, the system made the country the most productive in the world and provided the people with the highest standard of living in history. **(c)** Mass production put more goods on the market at lower prices.
3. **(a)** Woolworth established chain stores, stores with branches in many cities. These stores could sell goods at lower prices because they bought their goods in large quantities at low prices. **(b)** Wanamaker established department stores, which combined many specialty shops under one roof. **(c)** Ward started a mail-order house in 1872. Mail-order houses were aimed at the rural market; customers placed, received, and paid for their orders by mail.

SECTION REVIEW   (text page 524)

Suggested responses to the questions are:
1. The corporation can gather large amounts of capital; the corporation has a perpetual life; stockholders can sell whenever they choose; and stockholders have limited liability.
2. **(a)** The Sherman Antitrust Act stated that any attempt to restrain trade was illegal. Violators of the law were subject to legal penalties. **(b)** It failed to define terms such as "trust," "combination," and "monopoly."
3. In the case of *U.S. v. E.C. Knight Company,* the Supreme Court ruled that a monopoly was not illegal except when it restrained interstate trade. This and other decisions convinced business leaders that they were free to consolidate.

4. See the following chart. Answers will vary.

Forms of Business Combination

	(a) Definition	(b) Reasons for Creation	(c) Objections	(d) Methods of Government Control
Pools	Informal organizations for agreement among corporations	To divide business among several corporations	Eliminated competition Fixed rates and prices	Declared illegal interstate commerce in 1887
Trusts	Business organizations that granted trust certificates in exchange for stock	To run several corporations as a giant business organization, to secure monopoly control	Raised prices, closed out small businesses	Sherman Antitrust Act of 1890
Holding Companies	Chartered corporations formed in order to buy controlling stock in other companies	To form great business combinations	Could also monopolize industry	Charter could be revoked under Sherman Antitrust Act
Interlocking Directorates	Groups of persons who served as directors for more than one corporation	To establish uniform policies for an entire industry	Could create monopolies	Prosecution under Sherman Antitrust Act

SECTION REVIEW

(text page 527)

Suggested responses to the questions are:
1. **(a)** These men had energy, willingness to gamble, a spirit of competition, and ability in financial affairs. **(b)** They were selfish and used unscrupulous business methods.
2. They built new industries, introduced efficient organization, and provided opportunities for investment.
3. The business leaders of the 1800's showed a belief in self-reliance by their willingness to take risks and seize opportunities. Carnegie, who knew nothing about steel manufacturing, invested money he earned from oil in the steel industry. He became one of the wealthiest men in the world and invested in every stage of steel production, from raw materials to transportation to the production of the finished products. Rockefeller also seized the opportunity to invest his money. In his lifetime he pioneered the trust form of business organization and invested in many different types of enterprises.

CHAPTER 22 REVIEW

(text page 531)

Reviewing Important Terms

1. department store
2. Iron ore and coal
3. trust
4. corporations
5. pool
6. steel
7. Industrial centers
8. financial capitalism

Practicing Critical Thinking Skills

Suggested responses to the questions are:
1. **(a)** Industrialization was made possible by improvements in transportation. Railroads and steamship lines connected industrial centers with sources of raw materials and markets for finished products. As industries grew, so did the towns and cities around them. By 1900, modern urban centers with industry and transportation networks took shape. **(b)** The nation's natural resources provided cheap raw materials for industry. Technology allowed industry to produce more and better products at lower prices. These factors contributed to profits, which were reinvested to make industry better.
2. **(a)** Answers will vary. Students might mention some of the following: Bessemer process for refining steel; telephone; and Westinghouse air brake. **(b)** Answers will vary. Students might mention that the Bessemer process provided steel for industry, the telephone improved communications essential to the conduct of business, and the Westinghouse air brake made rail transportation safer. **(c)** Steel was interdependent with several other inventions. Steel was used in almost every other heavy industry and the railroads. Railroads moved steel and the raw materials needed to make steel. Steel was used to produce the machines used to mine iron ore and coal.
3. **(a)** Morgan, the wealthiest financier in the United States, would oppose the Sherman Antitrust Act. **(b)** He might have argued that

wealth and power rightfully belong to those capable of getting them, that people have the right to use their property as they wish, and that the Sherman Antitrust Act violated that right.

4. **(a)** Each of these men was associated with an enterprise that was new to the United States. Each personally managed all aspects of the growing business with little regard for anything but profit and growth. Competitors were crushed and government officials manipulated. **(b)** Answers will vary. Students might mention that there were few laws regulating business at that time. **(c)** Answers will vary. Students might mention the rise of entrepreneurs in such fields as computer technology. Other students may feel that current laws and regulations would prevent the emergence of "robber barons."

5. **(a)** Answers will vary. Students might argue that industries should follow environmental regulations regardless of cost. **(b)** The efforts of all three are now more organized. Laws and regulations have established environmental standards that are monitored by government and private groups. **(c)** Answers will vary. Students might mention fining or requiring the offending corporation to reclaim or replace what has been lost.

Developing History Study Skills

1. **(a)** 11.5 million short tons **(b)** 60 million barrels **(c)** United States industrial production expanded rapidly between 1870 and 1900.

2. **(a)** Answers will vary. Students might mention that the development of steam-driven modes of transportation contributed to the growth of cities. **(b)** Answers will vary.

Relating Geography and History

1. **(a)** New York, Pennsylvania, New Jersey, Kentucky, West Virginia, Georgia, Maryland, Virginia, Tennessee, Alabama, Arkansas, Missouri, Michigan, Minnesota, Wisconsin, and Iowa **(b)** Answers will vary. Students might mention Pennsylvania, West Virginia, and Alabama. Deposits of iron ore and coal are near each other in these states. **(c)** It would be transported along the Great Lakes. Water transportation was less expensive for heavy materials such as iron ore.

2. **(a)** Ideally, industries are located near the raw materials they use. This reduces shipping costs and other problems created by long-distance shipping. When the supply of raw material is depleted or becomes inaccessible, the industry often moves to another location where supplies of the necessary raw materials are available.

(b) available transportation, labor supply, distance to markets, rent or land costs, and local or state regulations

3. **(a)** Steel rails were a great improvement over iron rails. Railroads carried the raw materials and finished products of the steel industry cheaply and efficiently. **(b)** As the steel industry grew, more and more workers were needed. These workers came to the towns and cities near the factories. Railroads also contributed to city growth. Towns at the end of rail lines slowly grew into urban centers as warehouses and factories moved near the railroad. Workers were needed for these auxiliary businesses and the city population grew.

SECTION REVIEW [text page 535]

Suggested responses to the questions are:

1. The large corporation-owned factories were impersonal businesses. The owners were stockholders who lived far away and who knew little about the workers or their problems. The worker could not, as in the days of small mills, appeal to the owner personally for better conditions or higher wages. As factories grew larger, individual workers ceased to be important. If workers complained they could be easily replaced.

2. As a result of mechanization, work became increasingly specialized and monotonous; machines could do the work of several wage earners, and displaced workers had to find new jobs and learn new skills.

3. **(a)** Railroads created a competitive market for goods. To sell goods at a competitive price, manufacturers often reduced wages. **(b)** When the business cycle reached depression, there were wage reductions and more unemployment. **(c)** Eastern farmers could no longer move west, so they turned to the city for work. The oversupply of workers drove wages down.

4. Industrialization more often than not produced

unsafe working conditions, low wages, and long hours for employees.

SECTION REVIEW [text page 538]

Suggested responses to the questions are:
1. Immigrants affected American workers by further crowding the slum areas of the cities, competing with established workers for jobs and driving wages down, and stimulating the economy by creating new demands for factory and farm products.
2. The Chinese Exclusion Act of 1882 was passed because workers feared that Chinese immigrants would take their jobs at lower wages.
3. (a) The Contract Labor Law of 1864 allowed American employers to recruit European labor for a specific job and time period. Workers were contracted abroad and could not leave their jobs in the United States while the contract was in force. (b) The law was repealed because of pressure from American workers who feared job competition and who argued that the law came close to setting up a slave-labor system.
4. The great influx of immigrants helped make possible rapid industrial expansion.

SECTION REVIEW [text page 541]

Suggested responses to the questions are:
1. Workers organized to solve the numerous problems of the industrial age, among them long hours and low wages.
2. (a) *Purposes:* better wages, more leisure time; formation of cooperative stores and manufacturing plants (b) *Successes:* the Knights were influential in passage of the Chinese Exclusion Act and repeal of the Contract Labor Law. They conducted a successful railroad strike in 1885. (c) *Reasons for decline:* unsuccessful railroad strike in 1886 and resulting decline in membership; discord between skilled and unskilled workers; dissatisfaction with Powderly's aims
3. (a) The A. F. of L. was a federation of separate national craft unions, each representing a group of skilled workers in a separate trade. It avoided general political reform movements and third-party political activities. (b) A craft union organizes skilled workers in a specific trade. An industrial union organizes both skilled and unskilled workers employed in a specific industry. (c) Unions such as the Electricians Union are present-day craft unions. The United Automobile Workers and the United Mine Workers are examples of industrial unions.

SECTION REVIEW [text page 545]

Suggested responses to the questions are:
1. The public believed an employer had the right to hire or fire at will; they resented the closed shop; and they blamed industrial conflict on ambitious labor leaders.
2. Many immigrants opposed union dues and rules and the insistence that no one work for less than a certain wage, seeing these as restricting their new freedom.
3. Blacks were excluded from unions because of the racial prejudice of white workers.
4. Many unions did not admit women to membership. In only a few craft unions did women play important roles; the most notable was the International Ladies' Garment Workers' Union.
5. (a) Industrial enterprises used advertisements and other publicity to win the sympathy of the public. (b) Skilled lobbyists were hired to influence legislation. (c) Corporations sometimes contributed to a political party, hoping to gain favors when the party won the election. (d) The blacklist was a list of undesirable workers whom employers in an industry would not hire. (e) Yellow-dog contracts were agreements signed by those applying for a job in which they agreed not to join unions. (f) When faced with strikes, some employers immediately locked out union workers and brought in strikebreakers. (g) Strikebreakers were nonunion workers hired to replace striking workers.

CHAPTER 23 REVIEW [text page 549]

Reviewing Important Terms

1. true
2. false, real income
3. true
4. true
5. false, black list
6. true
7. true
8. false, anarchists
9. true

Practicing Critical Thinking Skills

Suggested responses to the questions are:
1. Industrialization brought great changes in the quality of people's lives because of the conditions under which they had to work (working long hours for little pay) and live (slums). The people and the country also paid for industrialization by wasting and misusing natural resources. However, the United States became the richest, most productive country in the world, and its people enjoyed the highest standard of living.
2. (a) Answers will vary. Students might mention

that the 14–45-year-old immigrants were best able to travel and to find work in their new home. **(b)** The nation's economy gained strong, able, and eager laborers. **(c)** Many of the immigrants contributed their own customs that became incorporated in American fashion, entertainment, and social life.

3. **(a)** Grievances against employers were: blacklists, yellow-dog contracts, strikebreakers, lockouts, influence of employers on legislation through lobbyists, and contributions to political campaigns. **(b)** State governments used militia to break strikes. **(c)** The federal government used troops to break strikes and federal court injunctions as weapons against strikes.

4. Some of the leaders of the labor movement were also connected to radical movements of the period. Eugene V. Debs, a socialist leader, was also the leader of the American Railway Union. The radicals and the unions often worked toward similar goals; however, radical movements had limited influence on the labor movement.

5. **(a)** Many of the demands are the same (for example: wage demands, improved working conditions, and workers' rights). **(b)** Unions today have more viable power than the unions had between 1865 and 1900. Students might cite specific laws or bargaining successes as specific examples. **(c)** Answers will vary. Students might mention that generally, labor unions were not successful in court in the late 1800's. Unions seem to have more of a chance in court today.

Developing History Study Skills

1. **(a)** farming **(b)** Answers will vary. Students might mention that many people left the farms to find better jobs in industry. **(c)** 1890 — 5 million; 1910 — 9 million **(d)** Answers will vary. Students might mention that cities and industrial demand were growing. **(e)** Answers will vary. Students might point out that the United States was becoming a great industrial power and more workers were needed in manufacturing.

2. Answers will vary. Students might mention that the membership of the A.F. of L. grew under Gompers' leadership, indicating the workers felt he was an effective spokesperson. The union, however, was not very successful in getting its demands met by the business owners.

Relating Geography and History

1. **(a)** Great Britain, Ireland, Germany, the Netherlands, and Scandinavia **(b)** Russia (including Poland), Greece, Austria–Hungary, and Italy

2. **(a)** China — California; Italy — eastern U.S. cities; Germany — upper Midwest **(b)** Answers will vary. Students might mention the problems with the language, homesickness, and the desire to retain old customs. **(c)** Cultural exchange often took place. For example, a successful European farming technique may have been adopted by all the farmers in an area of the United States.

CHAPTER
24 Farmers Revolt Against Big Business

SECTION REVIEW *(text page 553)*

Suggested responses to the questions are:
1. **(a)** Answers will vary. Students might mention hard, primitive, independent, self-reliant, lonely, and dreary. **(b)** Answers will vary. **(c)** Answers will vary. Students might mention that hard work is not necessarily a negative aspect of life; independence and self-reliance are positive characteristics; and loneliness is a negative aspect of farm life.

2. The Saturday drive to town provided both a social opportunity for the family and an occasion to take care of necessary business.

3. **(a)** Black settlers going to Kansas in 1879 and Europeans coming to the New World both sought to begin new lives, free from discrimination. Both groups also hoped to better their lives economically. **(b)** Immigrants had to adjust to a new physical and social environment, a new language, and new customs. Blacks also faced a strange environment and an established pattern of discrimination. Although both groups were generally poor, blacks were often penniless and had to work as laborers to earn enough to start a farm.

SECTION REVIEW *(text page 557)*

Suggested responses to the questions are:
1. **(a)** Distributors bought produce from farmers at low prices and stored it until prices rose. Farmers believed that distributors got more than

their share of the wealth produced on farms and ranches. **(b)** The railroads charged differential freight rates.
2. New farmland, new farm machinery, and improved farming methods led to increased production. More food was produced than people could buy; surpluses caused farm prices to fall.
3. After the Civil War, farm production climbed sharply. But as more crops were produced, prices dropped. Therefore, even if farmers produced twice as much, they made less money.

SECTION REVIEW   *(text page 559)*

Suggested responses to the questions are:
1. **(a)** The Grange was founded to combat the isolation of farm families. Economic problems quickly changed the goal to one of cooperative economic and political action to solve farmers' problems. **(b)** It was moderately successful. Some of the cooperative marketing and purchasing activities succeeded; others failed. Political pressure met with more success, resulting in laws in several states regulating unfair railroad practices and in the Interstate Commerce Act.
2. **(a)** The Interstate Commerce Act prohibited pooling, rebates, differential freight rates, and unreasonable rates by the railroads. It established the Interstate Commerce Commission with power to investigate complaints against railroads, examine a railroad's accounts, and require railroads to follow uniform procedures. **(b)** The act did not give the commission any real power to enforce its orders. **(c)** It was the first attempt by the federal government to regulate transportation and to create a federal regulatory commission. It set a precedent for measures later adopted by Congress.
3. In the "Granger cases," including *Munn v. Illinois,* the Supreme Court upheld the right of states to regulate railroads and other businesses that affected the public. Later, the Court modified these decisions by prohibiting state regulation of interstate trade.

SECTION REVIEW   *(text pages 561–62)*

Suggested responses to the questions are:
1. **(a)** The Greenback Party's chief goal was to get more "cheap money" into circulation. **(b)** The party did not achieve its goal, but it did exert influence on legislation such as the Bland-Allison Act; it showed the farmers that power lay in united organization.
2. The Bland-Allison Act, by requiring the Treasury to buy and mint between $2 and $4 million worth of silver monthly, put more money into circulation. This was part of the goal of "cheap money" advocates.
3. **(a)** There were three factors: hard times caused by drought; increased political influence of farming and silver-mining interests when six western states entered the Union; and a deal made between Republicans supporting the McKinley Tariff and westerners supporting the Sherman Silver Purchase Act. **(b)** The Act required the Treasury to buy 4.5 million ounces of silver per month and pay for it with paper money that could be redeemed in gold or silver. **(c)** Miners hoped the price of silver would go up; farmers hoped the supply of money in circulation would increase, thus raising prices for farm products.

SECTION REVIEW   *(text page 565)*

Suggested responses to the questions are:
1. Free and unlimited coinage of silver would increase the amount of money in circulation and raise prices on farm goods; government ownership of the railroads would end railroad rate abuses; return of land held by the railroads would open up more land to farmers; a graduated income tax would lessen the farmers' tax burden; national warehouses would eliminate the distributors and allow farmers to store produce until prices rose; and the political reforms would lessen the power of big business in government and increase the political power of the farmers.
2. Conservative Democrats wanted black Southerners to vote, if they would vote for Democrats. The Populists depended upon the votes of poor whites and blacks to defeat the Democrats, but made few attempts to make an alliance between the two groups. Poor whites opposed black voting rights and the Populists because they saw a challenge to white supremacy. The result was that whites of all classes voted against the Populists, and the southern black farmer was no better off.
3. The "tight money" advocates argued that the depression was caused by a lack of confidence in the value of money. The "cheap money" advocates blame the depression on the "tight money" policies of the government.

Reviewing Important Terms

1. open-market
2. bullion
3. alliances
4. the gold standard
5. Long-haul
6. staple

Practicing Critical Thinking Skills

Suggested responses to the questions are:
1. Benefits of industrialization included the following: power-driven machines to make work easier; transportation and communication to relieve the isolation of farm life; and increased production to feed farmers and their fellow citizens better than ever before. Problems included a loss of individual control over farm decisions; a dependency upon railroads that transported farm products; banks that controlled money needed for loans; and distant markets where prices were fixed. The very advances which were beneficial were also harmful. Machinery, fertilizers, and improved seed all led to overproduction and falling farm prices, leaving the farmer in economic distress.
2. (a) The Greenback Party demanded that the government increase the supply of currency in circulation. (b) The Populist Party platform had six main planks: increase in currency, to be secured by the "free and unlimited coinage of silver at a ration of 16-1"; government ownership of railroads, telegraphs, and telephones; the return of all government land held by the railroads and other corporations; a graduated income tax; a system of national warehouses where farm produce could be stored until market conditions improved; and democratic political reforms such as direct election of United States Senators, adoption of the secret ballot, the initiative, and the referendum. (c) The basic similarity was the currency issue. The major difference was that the Populist Party did not have a one-issue platform.
3. (a) "Cheap money" would allow more people to buy farm products, raising prices; it would also let farmers pay their debts with a smaller proportion of their income. (b) The Bland-Allison Act was a partial victory; the Sherman Silver Purchase Act slightly increased the supply of currency.
4. (a) "Cheap money" would be welcomed by debtor farmers who could pay off their debts with less valuable currency. (b) Retired persons on fixed incomes would oppose "cheap money," which buys less per unit of currency. (c) Bankers would not want loans to be repaid with dollars that would buy less than the dollars that they had loaned.
5. Cooperatives helped farmers' conditions some-

what. The Grange began to exert influence on legislators, and some state laws regulating railroads were passed. The Greenback Party reached its height of power in 1878, electing members to Congress. Farmers' Alliances took the place of the Greenback Party. The Populist Party was very strong in the early 1890's.
6. (a,b,c,) Answers will vary.
7. There is more direct government support for farmers now than there was in the late 1800's. Answers will vary for the second part of the question. Students might mention the experiences of the Great Depression or foreign competition as reasons for more support today.

Developing History Study Skills

(a) It opposed demonetization. (b) It decreases the value of all forms of property as well as human labor and intentionally enriches bankers, bankrupts enterprise, and enslaves industry. (c) There would be revolution or the establishment of absolute despotism. (d) They argued that bankrupting enterprise and enslaving industry would lead to disaster. They were based on opinions. (e) No, the United States still has a democratic government.

Relating Geography and History

1. (a,b,c,d) Answers will vary. Students should focus on the fact that not all land is suitable for agriculture.
2. (a) Kansas, North Dakota, and Oklahoma (b) They are generally flat.
3. Climate and soil conditions
4. Answers will vary.

CHAPTER
25 Life Styles in the New Industrial Age

SECTION REVIEW   *(text page 575)*

Suggested responses to the questions are:
1. The city's faces included stores, offices, museums, libraries, theaters, churches, schools, freight yards, waterfronts, factories, warehouses, stockyards, wholesale markets, sum areas, tenement buildings, dirty streets, rows of

houses arranged in "blocks," and pretentious mansions. But mainly the city was people — rich, middle class, and poor.

2. **(a)** By 1890 the country was divided into three economic classes — the rich, the middle class, and the poor. The relatively small number of rich people controlled the country's wealth. The middle class consisted of professional people, smaller business owners, clerks, managers, and more successful skilled workers. On the lower rungs of the economic ladder were the very poor people, including large numbers of immigrants and almost all black Americans. **(b)** Opportunities to move from one social class to another were better in the United States than in Europe. Education was the most important means of improving one's social and economic class.

3. Industrialization provided new machines, especially the typewriter, that allowed more women to enter the labor force. Labor-saving devices allowed middle-class women to enjoy leisure time and become involved in politically minded groups. As a result, opposition to women's participation in public affairs was weakened.

4. See the following chart. Answers will vary.

Column One	Column Two
Mary Baker Eddy	Founded and oversaw the development of the Christian Science movement
Mother Frances Xavier Cabrini	Established urban hospitals, orphanages, and schools in Italian immigrant neighborhoods
Clara Barton	Advanced the nursing profession during the Civil War; founded the American Red Cross
Maria Mitchell	Discovered a new comet; became a professor at Vassar College
Josephine Ruffin, Mary Church Terrell	Established social welfare clubs and helped found two organizations to advance the status of black women
Elizabeth Cady Stanton, Susan B. Anthony, Lucy Stone, Mary A. Livermore, Julia Ward Howe, Anna Howard Shaw, Abigail Duniway, Carrie Chapman Catt	Worked for women's suffrage and other civil rights
Jane Addams	Set a model for social reform at Chicago's Hull House for slum residents; worked for world peace

SECTION REVIEW   *(text page 576)*

Suggested responses to the questions are:

1. Elementary and secondary schools' educational programs were broadened to include natural sciences and such "useful" subjects as industrial designing, drawing, business arithmetic, bookkeeping, typing, stenography, shopwork, home economics, and manual arts.

2. Colleges and universities responded with technical schools and more practical training for a wide variety of fields. They also began to enrich their courses of study with additional subjects in the natural and social sciences and modern languages. To meet individual needs, the elective system was introduced.

3. Education today does reflect the ideas of Parker and Dewey. Curriculum continues to expand to meet modern economic needs; examples are courses such as computer science and communication arts. Continued emphasis is also given to social, intellectual, and physical development.

SECTION REVIEW   *(text page 579)*

Suggested responses to the questions are:

1. Mass circulation was prompted by Americans' growing literacy and interest in the world beyond their hometowns. Inventions such as the typewriter, improved printing presses, and the linotype enabled publishers to print more newspapers and magazines at a lower cost. Businesses wished to reach many people with advertisements, so publishers printed "popular" articles to attract readers.

2. **(a)** Big business came to newspapers as leading publishers bought up smaller papers to create newspaper chains; the chains subscribed to worldwide news services such as Associated Press and United Press; and there was a trend toward standardized practices. **(b)** A greater variety and scope of news and feature stories became available. However, several newspapers run by a single publisher might well be slanted toward one point of view, depriving the public of a balanced view of events.

3. Stories by Alger and Adams glorified urban life with tales of success through hard work. Edith Wharton's novels showed the conflict between the newly rich and the older well to-do families. *The Gilded Age* by Clemens and Warner described corruption in politics and land speculation. Bellamy satirized the shortcomings of the contemporary world in *Looking Backward*. Howells realistically described middle-class urban life.

SECTION REVIEW

(text page 581)

Suggested responses to the questions are:
1. **(a)** To accommodate the new industries and businesses crowding into the business districts of the nation's cities, architects and engineers designed tall, sleek buildings. **(b)** New building materials such as steel, concrete, and plate glass were used in the new constructions.
2. Sullivan meant that the style and materials of a building should be dictated by the purpose of the building.
3. Most American artwork seemed little related to the issues of a growing urban society. Sculptors created great statues of national heroes; painters depicted the beauty of nature, the mystical, and the legendary. However, some artists were concerned with the influence of industry and the city.

SECTION REVIEW

(text page 582)

Suggested responses to the questions are:
1. **(a)** The Chautauqua movement was an educational movement that gave illustrated travel lectures, stage presentations, lectures, and religious services for summer visitors to Lake Chautauqua in upper New York State. **(b)** By 1900, imitators of the movement organized traveling tent shows that brought many rural communities a glimpse of the outside world.
2. City-dwellers joined gymnasiums and learned to ride the newly redesigned bicycle to satisfy their desire for physical fitness.
3. In the late 1800's, the three major spectator sports were football, baseball, and basketball.

CHAPTER 25 REVIEW

(text page 586)

Reviewing Important Terms

1. true
2. true
3. false, urbanization
4. false, Settlement houses
5. true
6. false, dime novels
7. true

Practicing Critical Thinking Skills

Suggested responses to the questions are:
1. **(a)** In education, there was increased school enrollment, especially in the cities; and new methods of teaching and new courses of study suitable to the industrial age, such as natural sciences, bookkeeping, typing, and stenography. **(b)** Architecture developed the skyscraper to meet the needs of expanding business and crowded cities. **(c)** Some artists showed increased interest in realistic urban and industrial scenes. **(d)** Journalism developed new techniques that promoted mass circulation, newspaper chains, and the growth of advertising.
2. **(a)** An educated people are better able to make decisions and choices for themselves. **(b)** Mass circulation of magazines and newspapers provided the information needed by an informed public in a democracy. On the other hand, newspaper chains and news services do not necessarily provide all points of view, thus inhibiting the democratic right to choose between alternatives.
3. **(a)** The concentration of wealth was a result of urbanization and made possible new social, cultural, and economic undertakings. **(b)** Settlement houses were responses to bad slum conditions resulting from rapid urbanization. **(c)** Under the elective system, college students had a choice of subjects in an expanded curriculum. **(d)** Skyscrapers resulted from dense settlement in cities and were made possible by new technological advances. **(e)** Mass circulation helped keep more people informed.
4. In an industrialized society, function is of great importance. Frills are usually eliminated; an object has a style and is made of materials best suited to its purpose. Louis H. Sullivan adopted this idea in architecture. The nature of the materials used and the flexibility they give reflect the society in which the architect lives.
5. **(a)** Today's skyscraper is larger and taller. **(b)** Answers will vary. Students might mention that the designs of today's buildings are varied and adapted to space. **(c)** More glass and lightweight metal is used in building construction today. Answers will vary for the second part of the question. Students might conclude that new building materials allow for more design flexibility.
6. **(a)** Answers will vary. Students might mention that classes in data processing and computers reflect the needs of today's society. **(b)** Answers will vary. Students might mention the need for classes in interpersonal relationships and consumer skills to better meet the needs of today's students.

Developing History Study Skills

1. Answers will vary. Students might mention that women were being granted increased opportunities.

2. See the following graphs. Answers will vary.

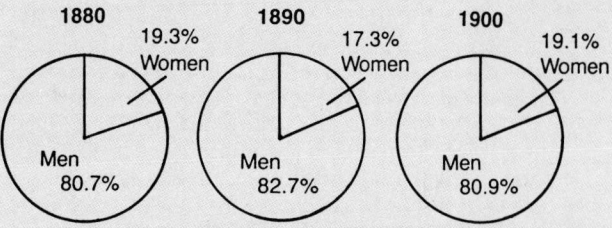

1880 — 19.3% Women; Men 80.7%
1890 — 17.3% Women; Men 82.7%
1900 — 19.1% Women; Men 80.9%

3. **(a)** Answers will vary. Students who read *The Gilded Age* might mention that it describes the excesses and abuses arising from the affluence and greed brought on by industrialization. **(b)** Answers will vary. *The Gilded Age* is generally negative although the potential for positive growth is occasionally mentioned.

Relating Geography and History

1. **(a)** Philadelphia; Newark, N.J.; Boston; Baltimore; New York City; Providence; Louisville, Ky.; Cleveland; New Orleans; Indianapolis; Chicago; St. Louis; Detroit; Milwaukee; Minneapolis; Omaha; Denver; Washington, D.C. Answers will vary for the second part of the question. Students might indicate an area of approximately 100 square miles surrounding each city.
2. Answers will vary. Students might mention the influence on fashions that city stores have and the influence on "taste" that city culture and art produces.
3. Answers will vary. Students might mention the influence on viewpoints that city newspapers have.

UNIT SEVEN REVIEW   (text page 587)

Discussing Ideas

1. Government supported the capitalistic system and followed a laissez-faire (hands off) policy of noninterference. Congress passed protective tariffs. Railroads were given government land to sell as a source of revenue. Raw materials on government, or public, land was often made available to business and industry.

2. As business became larger and new combinations were devised, it became nearly impossible for the individual to raise enough capital to compete with the corporations.
3. **(a)** Answers will vary. Students might mention that business pioneers helped build the United States economy as we know it today. **(b)** Answers will vary. Students might mention that discoveries, inventions, and innovation helped speed industrialization. **(c)** Answers will vary. Students might mention that raw materials were the building blocks of the United States' Industrial Revolution.
4. The primary attraction was job opportunity. Cities also were viewed as cultural and entertainment centers.
5. **(a)** Cities were overcrowded and tenement conditions were deplorable. Immigrants competed successfully for the available jobs. The social and educational institutions changed to accommodate the growing immigrant clientele. Prejudice and discrimination flared. **(b)** Immigrants, both as individuals and as groups, have made the United States strong.
6. **(a)** Their grievances were similar. Workers felt they were victimized by factory owners. Farmers felt they were victimized by railroad owners. The basic grievance each group had was their lack of money and their economic condition in the rapidly industrializing nation. **(b)** Both groups organized and sought changes generally through the political process. **(c)** Both felt ignored by the government.

Applying History Study Skills

1. **(a)** Answers will vary. Students might mention that farm life was isolated while city life was crowded. There were more events and diversions in city life. **(b)** Answers will vary. Students might argue that modern technology has decreased the differences.
2. **(a)** Answers will vary. Students might conclude that Jane Addams helped improve the lives of children, helped encourage others to build settlement houses, and provided a refuge for the neighborhood's children. **(b)** Answers will vary. Students might point out that the excerpt mentions the regulation of child labor, the establishment of 400 settlement houses, and the many children who came to Hull House.

UNIT EIGHT
The Arrival of Reform

26 The Square Deal and the New Freedom

SECTION REVIEW *(text page 593)*

Suggested responses to the questions are:
1. **(a)** La Follette helped to break the power of political machines in Wisconsin and restored control of the government to the people. He persuaded the legislature to levy heavier taxes on railroads and newer public utilities and to set up commissions to regulate the utilities. He also started a movement to conserve forests and waterpower sites, and he promoted good government by appointing university scholars to public positions. **(b)** His reforms closely followed the stated goals of the progressives and even went beyond them in matters such as conservation of natural resources.
2. **(a)** Florence Kelley, a leader in the National Consumers League, exposed companies that paid women less than men for equal work, allowed unhealthful working conditions, and used child labor. Under her leadership, the league organized boycotts and pressed for legislation favorable to women and children. **(b)** As president of the W.C.T.U., Frances Willard campaigned against the manufacture and sale of alcoholic beverages and for women's suffrage.
3. **(a)** Answers will vary. Students might mention any three of the following: Lincoln Steffens, Ida Tarbell, Upton Sinclair, Frank Norris, Jack London, and Ray Stannard Baker. All investigated and exposed evils and corruption in politics and business. **(b)** They all wrote for the general public in the expectation that an informed public would demand change. They were part of the progressive movement.
4. Steffens meant that demands for special privileges from the government would lead to the abuses of the privileges and to corruption.

SECTION REVIEW *(text page 595)*

Suggested responses to the questions are:
1. The Australian ballot provided a list of all candidates, which could be marked and cast in secret. Party bosses or others wielding political power could not know how any individual voted.
2. Several states, all of them west of the Mississippi, where progressivism was strong, had granted women the vote by 1914. The role of women during World War I broke down much of the remaining resistance. In 1920, at the end of the progressive era, women gained the vote nationwide when the Nineteenth Amendment was ratified.
3. The direct election of Senators by the people removed some of the power of political machines and bosses over the Senate.
4. Progressives sought to return control of the government to the people, thus making the society more democratic. They urged that the public have the power to introduce legislation (initiative), to demand a general vote on some legislation (referendum), and to remove an elected official before the next scheduled election (recall). The progressives supported direct election of Senators, and many also promoted women's suffrage.

SECTION REVIEW *(text page 600)*

Suggested responses to the questions are:
1. **(a)** Roosevelt refused to send federal troops to break the coal strike; instead he forced the owners to submit to arbitration. The government, for the first time, stepped into a labor controversy to protect the interests of all concerned. **(b)** The union did not get all its demands. Wages were increased 10 percent instead of the union demand for 20 percent. The union did not win the right to negotiate with the employers.
2. Roosevelt's failure to include black Americans in his "square deal," except when politically expedient to do so, reflected the attitudes and prejudices of most white Americans during these years, including most of the progressives.

3. Answers will vary. Students might mention that Roosevelt did instigate a successful suit against the Northern Securities Company in 1902; in 1903 Congress passed the Expedition Act and created the Department of Commerce and Labor. Roosevelt began action against other trusts — 44 during his administration. However, the trend of the times was toward larger combinations, a trend that Roosevelt could not combat.

SECTION REVIEW

Suggested responses to the questions are:
1. Roosevelt spoke in favor of conservation; he withdrew forest land and other resources from public sale; and he urged Congress to create wildlife sanctuaries and national parks.
2. The Newlands Reclamation Act provided that money from the sale of public lands in the West was to be used to build irrigation projects to reclaim wasteland; money from the sale of water was to finance additional irrigation projects. Vast acres of desert were brought under cultivation and transformed into rich farmland.
3. (a) Private interests that would be denied resources were, of course, opposed. In addition, many people did not realize the need to conserve the nation's resources, for they believed the resources were inexhaustible. (b) Roosevelt aroused the public and made a start toward national and state regulation of natural resources.

SECTION REVIEW
(text page 605)

Suggested responses to the questions are:
1. Taft's first Secretary of the Interior, Richard A. Ballinger, reserved some of Roosevelt's conservation measures and engaged in a major confrontation with conservationist Gifford Pinchot over the sale of valuable land in Alaska. Taft fired Pinchot during the controversy.
2. (a) Progressives charged that the conservative Cannon, as Speaker of the House and head of the powerful Rules Committee, used his power to block progressive legislation. (b) An amendment to the House rules deprived the Speaker of the House of the power to appoint members of the Committee on Rules (these were to be elected by members of the House), and the Speaker was barred from membership in this committee. A year later, the Speaker lost the power to make other committee appointments.

3. Roosevelt was dissatisfied with Taft and wanted to return to the White House, but he was unable to secure the Republican nomination in 1912. Consequently, he led the progressive Republicans in the formation of the Progressive Party, nicknamed the Bull Moose Party, which nominated him for the Presidency.
4. See the following chart. Answers will vary.

Election	Parties and Candidates	Platforms	Results
1908	Republican — Taft	Strengthen Interstate Commerce Act, conserve resources, improve highways, revise tariff	Taft elected
	Democratic — Bryan	Condemned "privilege" and monopoly, lower tariff, new antitrust laws, federal income tax, restrictions on court injunctions in labor disputes	
1912	Republican — Taft	See election of 1908	Wilson elected
	Democratic — Wilson	Tariff reduction, banking reform, laws favoring labor and farmers, enforcement of antitrust laws	
	Progressive — Roosevelt	Laws in favor of labor, tariff reform, initiative, referendum, recall, federal control of unfair business practices	
	Social Democratic Party — Debs	Favored gradual growth of socialism	

SECTION REVIEW
(text page 609)

Suggested responses to the questions are:
1. Wilson hoped to restore the equality of opportunity that many Americans had enjoyed when the frontier was still open to settlers.
2. (a) The Federal Reserve system consisted of 12 Federal Reserve districts, each with a Federal

A84   CHAPTER 26   UNIT EIGHT

Reserve Bank. All national banks and qualifying, interested state banks were to belong to the system. The Federal Reserve Board in Washington, D.C., was to supervise the member banks, provide financial assistance to failing banks, and regulate the amount of money in circulation. **(b)** The conservatives wanted private banking interests to control the banking industry. The progressives, arguing that the "money trust" was already too powerful, wanted the government to control the banks. The Federal Reserve system was a compromise that gave the government some control over the banking system but did not interfere with private banking corporations. **(c)** to regulate industries engaged in interstate and foreign trade

3. **(a)** The Clayton Antitrust Act prohibited: price discrimination that would help create monopolies, "tying contracts" (agreements not to do business with a competitor), and interlocking directorates in companies capitalized at $1 million or more. **(b)** Organized labor approved of the act because it exempted labor unions from prosecution as "conspiracies in restraint of trade," and it declared strikes, peaceful picketing, and boycotts legal under federal jurisdiction.

CHAPTER 26 REVIEW   (text page 613)

Reviewing Important Terms

1. muckrakers
2. referendum
3. Australian
4. city manager form of government
5. progressive

Practicing Critical Thinking Skills

Suggested responses to the questions are:
1. These Presidents faced problems created by the transformation of the United States from an agricultural country to a leading industrial power; each helped determine government's relation to industry.
2. **(a)** The goals of the "Square Deal" were to give everyone economic opportunity and fair treatment. The "New Freedom" was aimed to restore to the people equality of economic opportunity. **(b)** "Square Deal" legislation included the Elkins Act, the Hepburn Act, the Meat Inspection Act, the Pure Food and Drug Act, and the Newlands Reclamation Act. The "New Freedom" passed the Underwood Tariff, the Federal Reserve System, the Clayton Act, the Federal Trade Commission, the Smith-Lever Act, the Smith-Hughes Act, and the Federal Farm Loan Act. **(c)** Both were very influential and led the way to further reform.

3. Answers will vary. Students who support this statement might mention that 90 antitrust suits were started; the Mann-Elkins Act was passed; the Interstate Commerce Act was strengthened; the Department of Labor was created; the Children's Bureau was set up; an eight-hour day was established on projects contracted for by the federal government; jobs were added to the civil service list; the Publicity Act was adopted; and the Sixteenth Amendment, concerning a federal income tax, was ratified. Students who disagree might mention that Roosevelt's personality made him more effective in all ways.
4. The progressive movement was dedicated to reform and to creating a more democratic country. In this respect, progressivism did agree with the ideals expressed in the Declaration of Independence and the Preamble of the Constitution.
5. **(a)** Farmers would have supported Wilson because he supported banking reform much desired by the farmers. **(b)** Bankers supported Taft because conservative Republicans could be relied upon not to interfere with banking policies. **(c)** An Italian immigrant would have supported Wilson because he had shown courage and determination in fighting political machines. **(d)** A factory worker would have voted for Roosevelt who had called for legislation favorable to labor. (Wilson might be selected based on his labor record as governor of New Jersey.)
6. **(a)** The issues were the right to vote, increased occupational and educational opportunities, and increased legal power. The obstacles were tradition, lack of preparation, and legal barriers. **(b)** equal opportunities in all endeavors **(c)** They are similar.

Developing History Study Skills

1. **(a)** Wilson believed that monopolies were indefensible and intolerable. **(b)** Wilson was for big business that could make better and cheaper products, but he was against trusts.
2. **(a)** Answers will vary. Students might mention that Wilson was a strong believer in party government. **(b)** Answers will vary. Students might mention that Wilson worked through his party members in Congress.

Relating Geography and History

1. Forests were cut and depleted, rivers diverted and polluted, and wildlife habitats destroyed.
2. **(a)** Often the ecological balance was disrupted. **(b)** Forests were cut to make room for city expan-

sion and not replaced. Wildlife was pushed into smaller and smaller areas as homes and environments were destroyed.

3. Congress in 1887 established the Forest Bureau and in 1891 authorized the President to withdraw timberlands from public sale. The Newlands Reclamation Act used public monies to irrigate and reclaim wasteland. In 1907 the Inland Waterways Commission was created to study all aspects of conservation. In 1908 the White House Conservation Conference was held and the National Conservation Commission was established to study and make recommendations on the use of the nation's mineral, water, forest, and soil resources.

4. (a) Roosevelt recognized that total depletion of the nation's resources would harm the quality of life in the United States for all future generations. (b) Answers will vary.

CHAPTER
27 New Directions in American Life

SECTION REVIEW   *(text page 618)*

Suggested responses to the questions are:
1. Mass production brought the price of the automobile within reach of millions of American workers. New automobiles required other developments, such as tires, gasoline, and paved roads, that stimulated the economy and increased productivity.
2. The three-element vacuum tube, invented by Lee De Forest, made it possible to amplify electrical signals. Wireless telegraphy spread rapidly as a result.
3. (a) The purpose is to produce maximum output with minimum effort by eliminating workers' time-wasting motions. (b) An efficiency engineer might watch workers, and then show them how to operate their machines more effectively, or suggest that the machines be redesigned. (c) It results in greater economy of production, lower unit cost, and higher profits. However, workers who perform one specialized task all day feel they are merely parts of a giant machine.

4. (a) Ford realized that mass production required mass purchasing power. To increase purchasing power, he raised his workers' wages to $5 per day, vastly increasing their purchasing power. (b) The recognition of the interrelationship of wages, purchasing power, and production transformed the American economy and way of life.

SECTION REVIEW   *(text page 620)*

Suggested responses to the questions are:
1. (a) The growth of urban population increased demand for farm products. (b) Power-driven machines permitted the farmer to produce more with less labor. Trucks carried the produce to market faster and in greater quantity. Gasoline and electricity provided the power needed on the farm. (c) Fertilizers were developed and better methods of cultivation became known. The productivity of livestock and plants was improved. Blights and pests were combated, and grains and fruits that were more resistant to disease and better adapted to varying climatic conditions were developed. (d) Federal aid helped farmers increase production by assisting with research and experimentation and by disseminating information.
2. Federal aid came through the Morrill Act, which created land-grant colleges and the Department of Agriculture; the Hatch Act, which established agricultural experiment stations and farms; the Smith-Lever Act, which funded county extension agents; and the Smith-Hughes Act, which provided for public school training in agriculture.

SECTION REVIEW   *(text page 622)*

Suggested responses to the questions are:
1. (a) Scattered laws limited the workday, especially for women and children; improved working conditions; provided for compensation for accidents on the job; established minimum-wage rates; and recognized the risk of certain jobs. (b) The Supreme Court held that legislation on minimum wages and hours deprived business owners of property without due process of law, and violated workers' right to freedom of contract.
2. The federal government enacted little early social legislation because it had little power in that area.
3. (a) The loss of some major strikes, a reputation for violence, and federal prosecution resulted in the decline of the IWW after 1918. (b) More conservative unions no longer had to compete with

the IWW or suffer from its unpopular goals and methods.
4. The graph shows that conditions were improving because wages were rising rapidly.

CHAPTER 27 REVIEW   (text page 626)

Reviewing Important Terms

1. false, Social legislation
2. true
3. true
4. true
5. false, efficiency engineering
6. false, Commercial farms
7. false, self-sufficient farmers

Practicing Critical Thinking Skills

Suggested responses to the questions are:
1. (a) Answers will vary. Students might mention the increasingly productive economy that was providing more jobs and a better life for Americans, the example of poor but talented people who were able to rise and become rich and successful and provide hope to others who wanted such success, and wage earners beginning to gain better salaries and working conditions. (b) The revolution in communication enabled Americans to find out what was going on in their country. Through magazines, newspapers, and, later, radios, Americans learned of the grievances in American society. This growing awareness led to a demand for reform. Reform eventually strengthened democracy. Students may wish to apply this concept to today and discuss the role of television, newspapers, and other media in creating a demand for reform and a greater role for the citizen in government. (c) Farmers were now subject to the fluctuations of the marketplace and the business cycle. Farmers' prosperity depended upon the state of the economy.
2. (a) Older ways of life were being replaced by the new. The United States was becoming a nation of crowded cities, new sources of power, machines, and mass production. (b) There was little in past experiences to help them make this adjustment, for the Industrial Revolution was creating a world that was very different from the agrarian society they had known.
3. Answers will vary. Students might mention that Roosevelt, Taft, and Wilson reflected the progressive spirit of their times. Examples of earlier Presidents who may be cited are Andrew Jackson and Abraham Lincoln. Recent Presidents that may be named include John Kennedy and Ronald Reagan.

4. The federal government today is more involved in the formulation and regulation of social concerns than in the early 1900's. Examples of this may include federal safety regulations, antipollution standards, and the formation of the Labor Department's Wage and Hour Division.

Developing History Study Skills

1. (a) Answers will vary. Students might mention mining or ranching. (b) Answers will vary. Students might mention dairy farming or steelworking in the Northeast, tobacco or cotton farming, coal mining, or steelworking in the Southeast, coal mining, steelworking, or dairy farming in the Midwest, and ranching or coal mining in the West.
2. Answers will vary. Students might mention technological innovations affecting transportation, communication, and farm production.

Relating Geography and History

1. Answers will vary.
2. Answers will vary. Students might refer to the isolation of farm life and the overcrowding of city life.
3. (a) Answers will vary. Students might mention that child labor laws were designed to prevent the exploitation of children. Compulsory education laws were designed to improve the literacy rate in the United States. (b) Answers will vary. Students might point out that many people thought that government was interfering in their lives. (c) Answers will vary. Students might argue that both laws were aimed at children and that child labor laws helped prevent children from leaving school.

UNIT EIGHT REVIEW   (text page 627)

Discussing Ideas

1. (a) Answers will vary. Students might mention leadership, intelligence, compassion, energy, and knowledge of government. (b) Answers will vary. Students might select Theodore Roosevelt for his leadership and popularity.
2. Answers will vary. Students might feel that urbanization and industrialization have made the viewpoint expressed less practical. Students might also cite aid to farmers and social legislation as a necessary and beneficial government involvement.
3. (a) The rapidly growing population was making

greater demands on the nation's resources. **(b)** Little was done at first. The American Association for the Advancement of Science publicized the need for conservation in the 1870's, but it was not until the early 1900's that an organized effort was made to alert people to conservation. **(c)** Conservation might cause unemployment or increased prices.

4. **(a)** Industrialization provided job opportunities for large numbers of immigrants who came to the United States in the late 1800's and early 1900's. The population became more and more urban as people moved near the factories and businesses. **(b)** Answers will vary. Students might mention that products were now available to more people. **(c)** Differences among the regions were reduced to some extent.

Applying History Study Skills

1. **(a)** the triumph of a real democracy, of popular government, and of our economic system **(b)** Roosevelt wanted to work for greater equality of opportunity and for rewards for good service.
2. **(a,b,c,d,e)** Answers will vary.

UNIT NINE
Becoming a World Power

CHAPTER

28 American Expansion Overseas

SECTION REVIEW   *(text page 633)*

Suggested responses to the questions are:
1. The industrial nations needed raw materials for their factories and new markets for their goods. Bankers and business owners looked overseas for investment opportunities. Colonies would insure the materials and markets the nations needed.
2. Better transportation made worldwide markets possible, so businesses began to look overseas for markets.
3. Before the late 1800's, the United States was not interested in colonies because the western lands provided raw materials, and there were enough markets for manufactured goods within the country.
4. (a) When the frontier closed, American business people began to anticipate the time when the West would no longer be able to provide raw materials, markets for manufactured goods, and investment opportunities. (b) Growing industrialism demanded greater quantities of raw materials and expanding markets for goods. (c) The growing power that the United States had in world affairs encouraged the nation to compete against other countries for colonial possessions.

SECTION REVIEW   *(text page 637)*

Suggested responses to the questions are:
1. (a) Spanish misrule plus an economic crisis plunged Cuba into revolution. Spain exploited the Cubans, antagonizing landowners as well as landless workers. Most Cubans worked for star-

vation wages. Reform to alleviate intolerable conditions was lacking. In 1894 the United States levied a high tariff on Cuban sugar. As a result, plantations closed and thousands were without jobs. (b) Trade between Cuba and the United States was crippled by the revolution. Americans had invested more than $50 million in Cuba. The press helped to create sympathy for the revolutionaries.
2. (a) The press aroused feverish public opinion against Spain. (b) The Spanish minister to the United States, De Lôme, wrote a letter to a friend in Havana that was stolen from the mails and sold to a newspaper. In the letter, De Lôme made insulting remarks about President McKinley. (c) The sinking of the *Maine* in Havana harbor was blamed on the Spanish. (d) Americans had over $50 million invested in Cuba. The revolution was crippling American-Cuban trade.
3. (a) Fighting actually began in the Spanish colony of the Philippine Islands in the Pacific Ocean. (b) A fleet under Commodore Dewey had been making preparations for weeks. As soon as war was declared, the fleet moved on the Philippines, center of Spanish power in the Pacific.
4. With victory in the Spanish-American War, the United States became a colonial power, having acquired Puerto Rico, Guam, the Philippines, and Wake Island.
5. (a) the direction of the American fleet under Dewey in the attack on Manila (b) Opposition came from the Spanish fleet anchored just south of Manila. The red star in Manila Bay shows that there was a battle that the American fleet won.

SECTION REVIEW   *(text page 640)*

Suggested responses to the questions are:
1. Answers will vary. Students who contend that the United States violated the principle of the Declaration might mention that people have the right to live under a government of their own choice. They may agree with Carl Schurz that the United States was interested in economic expansion. Students might also contend that the United States recognized the principle by

agreeing to educate the island for self-government.
2. In 1878 the United States secured the right to use the harbor of Pago Pago as a naval base. Germany and Great Britain had similar rights. A scramble for control ensued, and a battle almost erupted. Then in 1899, Great Britain withdrew and the islands were divided between Germany and the United States.

SECTION REVIEW   *(text page 643)*

Suggested responses to the questions are:
1. **(a)** After Japan had defeated China, European nations rushed to seize Chinese territory. The United States did not want Chinese territory, but neither did it want to be squeezed out of the China trade. **(b)** The Open Door Policy insisted that "treaty ports" be open to all nations, and that equal railroad, harbor, and tariff rates apply to all.
2. **(a)** The Boxer Rebellion was an attempt by the Chinese to drive foreigners out of their country. **(b)** Western powers, including the United States, rushed troops to China to protect their citizens and property. The combined western forces crushed the Boxers. **(c)** The United States prevented the European powers from seizing additional territory as war bounty and returned about half of its share of indemnity money, which was used to educate Chinese youths in the United States. Chinese-American relations actually improved.
3. **(a)** Japan became imperialistic because, like western countries, its trade had grown to large proportions in the 1900's. Japanese leaders were convinced they should adopt the industrial techniques of western nations. The Japanese needed raw materials and markets and food for the population explosion in Japan. **(b)** Americans were concerned about Japan because of American commitments in the Pacific. Americans thought Japan might want to gain control of China, thus interfering with American trade there.

Practicing Critical Thinking Skills

Suggested responses to the questions are:
1. **(a)** American foreign policy changed at this time from isolationism to expansionism because there was a growing need for markets, for sources of raw materials, and for outlets for investments. Also, the United States' growing power in world affairs encouraged the nation to compete against other countries for colonial possessions. **(b)** One major argument used was that colonies needed the strong, "civilized" United States to look after them. Another argument — used to encourage United States' involvement in Cuba — was that American intervention was needed to enable some of the colonies to secure their own freedom.
2. The Monroe Doctrine closed the Western Hemisphere to colonization but not to trade. The Open Door Policy gave all nations access to trade in China. The Open Door Policy did not interfere with the colonizing activities of other nations.
3. **(a)** Imperialists often argued that the colonized people, who were most often members of nonwhite races, were "inferior." Acceptance of the idea of white supremacy abroad made it easier to accept at home. **(b)** Answers will vary. Students might mention that the white supremacy argument originated "at home" to begin with. They might also point out that successful colonization of nonwhite people strengthened the supremacy argument. **(c)** In the 1890's, black Americans in the United States were segregated in both the North and the South, denied voting rights by a variety of methods, and generally denied participation in the growing democracy and prosperity of the nation.
4. The nonindustrialized nations did not have the military strength to resist foreign control; also, colonies often became economically dependent on the "mother country."
5. Answers will vary. Students might argue that the press was "more involved" in foreign affairs in the late 1890's than today.
6. Answers will vary. Some students might indicate the reasons are basically the same. Others might point to such differences for involvement as the policy of containment and the United Nations.

CHAPTER 28 REVIEW   *(text page 647)*

Reviewing Important Terms

1. true
2. true
3. false, extraterritoriality
4. true
5. true
6. false, colonies
7. true

Developing History Study Skills

(a) to find new markets **(b)** Americans would go there to work and to improve life there. **(c)** No real evidence is provided. The author bases his assumption on excess products, labor, and capital in the United States.

Relating Geography and History

See the following chart. Answers will vary.

Territory	How Obtained	Present Status
Midway Is.	Annexed by U.S.	U.S. Territory
Alaska	Purchased	State
American Samoa	Annexed by U.S.	Unincorporated Territory (U.S.)
Wake Is.	Annexed by U.S.	U.S. Possession
Philippine Is.	Ceded to U.S.	Independent
Guam	Ceded to U.S.	U.S. Possession
Puerto Rico	Ceded to U.S.	U.S. Commonwealth
Hawaii	Annexed by U.S.	State
Panama Canal Zone	Jurisdiction by Treaty	Returned to Panamanian control
U.S. Virgin Is.	Purchased	Unincorporated Territory (U.S.)

1. Philippine Islands
2. **(a)** Communications were slow and defense was difficult. **(b)** Answers will vary. Students might mention that advances in communications and transportation have minimized the problems of distance.
3. Answers will vary. Students might argue that Hawaii may be considered as the most important possession because of its commercial value. The mineral resources of Alaska have made it very valuable. The cultural contributions of Puerto Rico, or the strategic positions of the Panama Canal Zone and Philippine Islands are other considerations.

CHAPTER
29 Expansion in the Caribbean

SECTION REVIEW *(text page 654)*

Suggested responses to the questions are:
1. In the Insular Cases, the Supreme Court stated that inhabitants of "incorporated" possessions such as Hawaii and Alaska, which were destined for statehood, were entitled to all Constitutional rights guaranteed to United States citizens. Inhabitants of the "unincorporated" possessions of Puerto Rico, the Philippines, and Samoa, not destined for statehood, were not entitled to *all* Constitutional rights, but were guaranteed such rights as protection of life, liberty, and property.
2. **(a)** The Foraker Act of 1900 gave Puerto Rico a governor and an executive council appointed by the United States President; the lower house was elected by Puerto Ricans. The second Jones Act (1917) made Puerto Rico a territory and gave Puerto Ricans United States citizenship. Puerto Ricans were also given the right to elect the upper and lower houses of their government. In 1950 Congress gave Puerto Ricans the power to write their own constitution. In 1952, after its ratification, Puerto Rico became a self-governing commonwealth associated with the United States. **(b)** With the Platt Amendment, the United States maintained the right to intervene in Cuban affairs to preserve Cuban independence and maintain an adequate government.
3. Such a canal would facilitate movement of naval vessels and commercial ships between the Atlantic and Pacific oceans.
4. A major reason for distrust of the "Yankee" in Latin America was the use of United States armed forces to control events in the hemisphere. Cuba was occupied for three years after the Spanish-American War and received only conditional independence in 1901. Marines entered Colombia to aid the Panamanian revolt after the Colombian government refused to act on a canal treaty. For many years, Puerto Rico's government was controlled by the United States.
5. The Caribbean Sea was once called "an American lake" because the United States controlled several important areas. Cuba was a protectorate; Puerto Rico and, later, the Virgin Islands were American territorial outposts; and the Panama Canal Zone was under American jurisdiction.

SECTION REVIEW *(text page 659)*

Suggested responses to the questions are:
1. **(a)** Intervention was necessary, Americans argued, to maintain law and order in the countries bordering the United States, in order to protect our citizens living in those countries, to prevent European countries from intervening in the Western Hemisphere, and to protect the

Panama Canal. **(b)** Answers will vary. Students might contend that the United States did indeed have to protect itself. Or they may contend that the likelihood of threat was negligible and that the United States was interested merely in investments.

2. **(a)** The Western Hemisphere was closed to further European colonization; the United States would not interfere with the existing colonies of any European power. Any attempt by European powers to intervene in the Western Hemisphere would be regarded as a threat to United States security. **(b)** France tried to seize control of Mexico. The United States protested and, after the Civil War, prepared to send an army to Mexico. Great Britain repeatedly pushed the western boundary of British Guiana onto territory claimed by Venezuela. The United States warned that it would not tolerate further interference with Venezuela. The British agreed to arbitration.

3. **(a)** The Roosevelt Corollary established the right of the United States to act as an international police officer in Latin America. **(b)** The Corollary was applied when the United States made protectorates of the Dominican Republic and Haiti. American military forces were also used to control Nicaragua and Honduras.

4. **(a)** The cartoon refers to the Venezuela debt controversy and how the United States upheld the Monroe Doctrine — the "live wire." **(b)** The cartoonist seems to approve of the strong stand of the United States against foreign intervention in Latin America. The cartoonist portrays Uncle Sam as stern and dignified and the foreigners as comical characters.

SECTION REVIEW   *(text page 661)*

Suggested responses to the questions are:
1. With encouragement from Mexico's President Diaz, American citizens had invested nearly $1 billion in Mexico by 1913. American investments included Mexican oil wells, mines, railroads, and ranches. Most of Mexico's trade was with the United States.
2. **(a)** Acts of violence, Mexican memories of the Mexican-American War, border disputes on the Rio Grande, mutual prejudice between Anglo-Americans and Mexican Americans, and American influence in Mexico's economy contributed to the hostilities between Mexico and the United States. **(b)** Dictator Diaz fled Mexico in 1910. When Madero, his successor, was assassinated by Huerta, Mexico was torn by violence and American investments were endangered. Many Americans wanted troops sent to Mexico to protect American investments and to restore

order. **(c)** Instead, Wilson urged the Latin American countries to settle the Mexican problem in their own way. He refused to recognize the Huerta government, convinced that the Mexicans would soon rid themselves of Huerta. **(d)** Huerta remained in power, American citizens were killed in Mexico, and it was rumored that Huerta might attempt to confiscate American property. When a Mexican official arrested American sailors and refused to apologize, and when a German ship arrived at Veracruz with military supplies for Huerta, Wilson ordered marines to seize Veracruz.

3. Argentina, Brazil, and Chile invited the United States, Mexico, and other nations to a conference to solve the conflict between Mexico and the United States. Conference members made recommendations, including the resignation of Huerta, which were followed.

CHAPTER 29 REVIEW   *(text page 665)*

Reviewing Important Terms

1. arbitration
2. "watchful waiting"
3. dollar diplomacy
4. territorial integrity
5. protectorate

Practicing Critical Thinking Skills

Suggested responses to the questions are:
1. **(a)** The United States needed to maintain trade, had to protect its citizens and investments abroad, and had to protect the Panama Canal. **(b)** Roosevelt's policies ignored the rights of the Latin American countries involved.
2. **(a)** Answers will vary. Students who agree might mention that the United States gained a great deal in the hemisphere through force as well as diplomacy. The United States and American business acted together to keep pro-American governments in power or to secure favorable governments through dollar diplomacy. Besides direct control, the United States exerted control through trade and investments. Students who disagree might mention that the Monroe Doctrine successfully prevented European nations from recolonizing weak nations in Latin America. **(b)** When the Panama Canal opened, the United States became committed to its defense since it was so vital to American interests. This also meant a commitment to Panama and to control of the Caribbean in order to keep the canal open.
3. **(a)** Answers will vary. Students might mention that many American business leaders viewed dollar diplomacy as a good investment and the government saw it as an opportunity to legit-

imize interference in Latin American affairs.
(b) Answers will vary. Students might point out
that some Latin Americans saw dollar diplomacy as "Yankee imperialism" while others
saw it as a source of funds for necessary improvements and modernization. (c) Answers
will vary. Students might mention that the
United States had to protect its investments
abroad. On the other hand, dollar diplomacy
gave the United States undue influence in Latin
American countries.
4. Answers will vary. Students might mention
the health, education, and social welfare programs brought to Puerto Rico by the United
States.
5. Answers will vary. Students should include the
Spanish-American War, the annexation of
Hawaii, and relations with Mexico.
6. (a) The Panama Canal treaties were part of
President Carter's effort to improve the United
States' relations with Latin America. (b)
Answers will vary. (c) Answers will vary. Students might mention the threat of a communist
takeover in Panama.

Developing History Study Skills

1. Answers will vary.
2. The United States government used the Monroe
Doctrine to justify intervention in the affairs of
Latin American nations. The situations in Mexico and Venezuela demonstrated the United
States' resolve to resist any European interference. The Drago Doctrine, the police powers of
the Roosevelt Corollary, and dollar diplomacy
further strengthened the United States position
in Latin Ameria.

Relating Geography and History

1. (a) about 2,250 miles (3,500 kilometers) (b)
about 7,000 miles (11,000 kilometers) (c) about
2,500 miles (4,000 kilometers) (d) About 2,950
miles (4,600 kilometers) (e) about 2,700 miles
(4,200 kilometers)
2. (a) American Samoa was a coaling station and
supply depot for naval and commercial ships. (b)
Midway Island was also a coaling station and
supply depot. (c) The Panama Canal linked the
two oceans, increasing the efficiency of the U.S.
Navy and reducing the distance and time necessary for commercial trade. (d) defense of the
Panama Canal and the Caribbean Sea
3. Answers will vary. For example, the United
States would establish armed space stations
along the route to protect trading vehicles. Such
a situation would be quite similar to the situation in 1898 when the United States established
naval bases at strategic points along its trade
routes.

SECTION REVIEW   *(text page 671)*

Suggested responses to the questions are:
1. The Pan-American Union aimed to substitute
arbitration for war among the American
nations.
2. The Hague Conferences set up rules for mediation and arbitration, organized the Permanent
Court of Arbitration, and drew up rules for the
conduct of war.
3. The assassination was the excuse for Austria-
Hungary to invade Serbia and, because of the
various alliances, brought the rest of Europe
into the war.
4. (a) Subjugated people in many countries longed
for independence. Countries were very proud
of themselves and eager to defend themselves
against any provocation. (b) Germany and Italy
sought to become "haves" by increasing their
empires, to match those of Great Britain,
France, and Russia. (c) Each European nation
wanted to be more powerful than its neighbors,
which led to an arms race. (d) The alliances committed European countries to defend each other
in case of attack, drawing all of Europe into a
regional conflict.

SECTION REVIEW   *(text page 677)*

Suggested responses to the questions are:
1. Naturalized Americans had friends and relatives in warring nations. There were historical
ties with Great Britain and France.
2. Britain blockaded neutral countries through
which American goods passed into Germany,
examined American mail, and ordered all neutral ships to stop at British ports to be searched.
Germany sank ships without warning, and did
not search ships before sinking them or give the
crew a chance to abandon ship.
3. (a) The first map provides an overall view of the
war from the British naval blockade in the west
to the advances on the Eastern Front. (b) The
second map gives more detailed information on
military strategies. (c) The first map shows all
of the European nations involved in the war; the
second map shows only a few nations.

SECTION REVIEW

(text page 681)

Suggested responses to the questions are:
1. (a) Wilson's reasons included fighting to stop unrestricted submarine warfare, to establish peace and justice, and to make the world safe for democracy. (b) Wilson saw the war as a crusade to make the world safe for democracy.
2. (a) The National War Labor Board and the War Labor Policies Board reduced labor disputes and established policies on hours, wages, and working conditions. (b) The War Industries Board, War Finance Corporation, Emergency Fleet Corporation, Railroad Administration, and Fuel Administration regulated necessary industries and stimulated production of war materials. (c) Citizens were urged to conserve food, and sale of some commodities was limited. The President could set prices for food and fuels, and the Fuel Administration urged people to conserve coal and oil. (d) The Committee on Public Information circulated leaflets describing United States' aims and denouncing the German government. Colleges, schools, the press, churches, lodges, women's organizations, and civic groups all cooperated with the government.
3. Answers will vary. Students might mention that it is easier to fight for a noble ideal that will take effect in another country than it is to recognize and identify problems at home.
4. (a) The poster shows women as farmers, nurses, and in civil defense. (b) Jobs such as work in steel mills, as conductors, and as engineers were new ones for women. (c) The activities of women on the home front gave visible evidence of their value as citizens and helped in the fight for women's rights.

SECTION REVIEW

(text page 685)

Suggested responses to the questions are:
1. The United States Navy helped the British Navy patrol the North Sea and bottle up the German fleet. They laid most of a mine barrier across the North Sea and convoyed merchant ships and troop transports.
2. The Germans considered the armistice terms severe. They had to evacuate France, Belgium, Luxembourg, and Alsace-Lorraine immediately; turn over enormous amounts of war material to the victors; return prisoners, money, and valuables taken from occupied lands; and renounce peace treaties with Russia and Rumania. The Allies were to occupy all German territory west of the Rhine and up to 18 miles (29 kilometers) east of the Rhine.

3. (a) Copies of the Fourteen Points, in the languages of Central Europe, were dropped by plane into enemy territory. The Fourteen Points, especially the call for self-determination, encouraged the Slavic peoples within Germany and Austria-Hungary to boycott their rulers' war efforts and thus speed their own liberation. Toward the close of the war, the people of Germany and Austria-Hungary took steps to overthrow their rulers. (b) The Fourteenth Point was the heart because it called for an association of nations "to give mutual guarantees of political independence and territorial integrity to great and small states alike." Wilson hoped that this organization could prevent future wars.
4. (a) Finland, Estonia, Latvia, Lithuania, Poland, Czechoslovakia, Austria, Hungary, and Yugoslavia were new nations. (b) Serbia and Montenegro no longer existed; Austria-Hungary was divided into two nations. (c) France, Italy, Greece, and Rumania gained territory.

SECTION REVIEW

(text page 688)

Suggested responses to the questions are:
1. (a) Wilson wanted a just peace based on his Fourteen Points. (b) Lloyd George was against generosity to Germany and "freedom of the seas." (c) Clemenceau believed the only way to defend France was to crush Germany. (d) Orlando wanted territory that Italy had been secretly promised.
2. (a) Secretariat (administrative and secretarial), Assembly (in which each nation had one vote), and Council (executive body) (b) Economic sanctions and even force might be recommended for use by League members against an aggressor. (c) The League could not insure action against aggressors (the term "aggressor" was not clearly defined; the Council could only recommend, not force, nations to act; any Council member could block the wishes of any other member because all decisions had to be unanimous); guarantee existing political boundaries (people who belonged to a different nation because the map of Europe had been redrawn had no way to secure further changes of their national boundaries); provide adequate machinery for recommending solutions to economic problems that might lead to war (trade rivalries, tariff barriers, imperialism still existed); or provide adequate measures to reduce armaments. The exclusion of Germany and the Soviet Union also hurt the League.

3. **(a)** Arguments against the League were that it was designed to enforce the unjust Treaty of Versailles; and that the guarantee of political boundaries might involve the United States in war. **(b)** The best evidence that Americans generally agreed with these arguments was the 1920 Presidential election, in which Republican Warren G. Harding, who opposed the treaty, was elected by a landslide vote.
4. The Treaty of Versailles returned Alsace and Lorraine to France; decreased the size of Germany, Russia, and Bulgaria; increased the size of Rumania, Italy, and Greece; split Austria-Hungary into Austria, Hungary, Czechoslovakia, and Yugoslavia (which included Serbia and Montenegro); and created Finland, Estonia, Latvia, Lithuania, and Poland from German, Russian, and Austro-Hungarian land.

CHAPTER 30 REVIEW   *(text page 692)*

Reviewing Important Terms

1. false, Reparations   4. false, mandate
2. true   5. true
3. true

Practicing Critical Thinking Skills

Suggested responses to the questions are:
1. **(a)** Many Americans wanted to make the world "safe for democracy." The United States had strong ties with Great Britain and France historically and economically, unrestricted submarine warfare by Germany angered Americans, and there was intense anti-German propaganda at home. **(b)** The A.E.F. took Cantigny, helped stop the Germans at Chateau-Thierry, held back the Germans at Belleau Wood, helped push the Germans back at Reims, launched an attack at St. Mihiel, and pushed forward in the Meuse-Argonne offensive. The navy patrolled the North Sea, laid a mine barrier across the North Sea, and convoyed merchant ships and troop transports.
2. The people of the world hoped that the end of the war would bring a better world, and Wilson's Fourteen Points helped raise those hopes.
3. **(a)** Nationalism — pride in country or heritage — led to international rivalry in armaments and colonies; international rivalry resulted in the forming of alliances to enhance the nation's power and maintain the balance of power in Europe and elsewhere; and imperialism increased international rivalries and the need for an arms build-up. **(b)** The Treaty of Versailles did not really diminish these factors. Only

Germany was disarmed, colonial empires remained. European countries, new and old, still competed with each other and were still afraid of each other's power and military might. **(c)** Member nations agreed to institute a cooling off period before starting a war, and nations agreed to impose economic sanctions on aggressor nations.
4. Answers will vary. Students might select a variety of themes upon which to base a patriotic poster: for example, loss of life from submarine warfare, making the world safe for democracy, and the plight of people in Belgium and elsewhere in Europe.
5. See the following chart. Answers will vary.

	Cause		Effect
(a)	Assassination of Franz Ferdinand	→	Start of World War I
(b)	Sinking of the *Lusitania*	→	Entrance of the U.S. into World War I
(c)	Arrival of fresh troops and supplies from the U.S.	→	Allied victory in World War I

6. **(a)** Civil liberties are superceded by the need to organize and to deal with the emergency at hand. **(b)** Answers will vary. Students might mention that government should never have the right to "take away" basic freedoms or that certain situations and circumstances dictate government action over individual rights.
7. **(a)** imperialism, nationalism, international rivalries, and balance-of-power systems of alliance **(b)** Answers will vary. Students might mention the United States–U.S.S.R. rivalry or the effects of terrorism.

Developing History Study Skills

(a) The excerpt gives the German point of view, and the textbook gives a more balanced account. **(b)** The steamship company carried passengers on a ship carrying explosives. **(c)** Answers will vary. Students should mention that the Germans were attempting to enforce their blockade of British ports.

Relating Geography and History

1. **(a)** the submarine **(b)** This invention resulted in the loss of thousands of civilian lives. Popular reaction against the submarine helped bring the United States into the war.
2. Answers will vary. Students might include that

tanks could roll over rugged terrain and airplanes could fly over land barriers.

3. Answers will vary. Students might include long-range artillery and bombers, chemical defoliants, and missiles.

4. Answers will vary. Students might state that a neutral nation's ships might be sunk, causing loss of life and cargo. Also, wars, which are no longer confined to the battlefield, involve many civilians.

UNIT NINE REVIEW   (text page 693)

Discussing Ideas

1. Theodore Roosevelt felt that the President's power in formulating and acting upon foreign policy was supreme. His "taking" of Panama is one example.

2. The United States intervened in both Hawaii and Cuba in part because events threatened the interests of American sugar planters.

3. Many Americans, especially the more recent immigrants, still had relatives or immediate family in Europe.

4. (a) Answers will vary. Students might argue that farmers would feel that Puerto Rico represented a new market for their produce. (b) Answers will vary. Students might mention that Nicaraguans would feel that Yankee imperialism was claiming another land for Uncle Sam. (c) Answers will vary. Students might mention that since Puerto Rico would fall under United States tariff regulations, the merchant's trade might be affected.

5. (a) Wilson's Fourteen Points were a statement of Allied war aims. They included the abolition of secret diplomacy, freedom of the seas, free trade, reduction of arms, restoration of lands, self-determination of peoples, and a general association of nations to guarantee the political independence and territorial integrity of all states. (b) Most European leaders opposed the Fourteen Points. (c) Nationalism, economic and political imperialism, and knowledge of Germany's past aggressions contributed to the reactions by Europe's leaders.

6. (a) President Theodore Roosevelt helped negotiate a peace settlement in 1905 following the Russo–Japanese War. Japanese–American relations remained friendly. United States–Chinese relations remained strong as United States businesses poured money into China. (b) They seem consistent with the policies of dollar diplomacy and economic imperialism.

7. (a) The quest for land and raw material provided the motivation for territorial infringements. (b) Military buildups and the development of new war technology may have led to the settlement of disputes by combat rather than negotiation. (c) Nations sought to increase their power and prestige and subject people sought independence. (d) Austria-Hungary's retaliation set in motion the European alliance system and involved many nations in a seemingly local dispute.

Applying History Study Skills

1. Answers will vary. Students might mention the Japanese drive to industrialize and the influence of the Open Door Policy in their essays.

2. (a) Uncle Sam (b) The cartoonist wants to show that the United States was stopping European intervention in the Western Hemisphere. (c) the 1902 crisis in Venezuela

3. Graphs will vary. (a) Export rates grew more rapidly than import rates. (b) There is no significant change in the rate of trade in 1900, the date of the Boxer Rebellion. (c) There is no change in the rate of trade.

The Golden Twenties and the New Deal

CHAPTER 31 A Decade of Prosperity Ends in a Crash

SECTION REVIEW   *(text page 701)*

Suggested responses to the questions are:
1. **(a)** War needs had created prosperity for businesses and farmers. With the war over, government contracts ended; war industries closed down or operated with a minimal work force as they retooled for peacetime; farm prices fell sharply as European markets closed, and many farmers lost their farms; many workers lost their jobs, and returning soldiers added to the unemployment. **(b)** Wages fell, but living costs rose, causing many workers to strike for higher wages.
2. **(a)** Coolidge meant that strikes by those charged with protecting the public were illegal. **(b)** Answers will vary. Students might argue that the right to strike is a basic right for wage earners, and that employers only take action when confronted with a demonstration or a strike. Other students might argue that a strike by public servants endangers the public safety.
3. **(a)** Conditions that produced the "Red scare" included the Bolshevik Revolution and violence by American radicals. **(b)** Supporters of the drive against radicals pointed to bombings and other irresponsible acts of violence. Opponents pointed out that the drive sometimes ignored the Constitutional rights of free citizens.

SECTION REVIEW   *(text page 705)*

Suggested responses to the questions are:
1. Coolidge reflected "the good old days," prosperity, and the desire of the people to withdraw from foreign commitments.

2. Attorney General Daugherty protected violators of the Prohibition amendment; Thomas W. Miller defrauded the government in the sale of alien properties; Charles R. Forbes, head of the Veterans' Bureau, could not account for $200 million spent; and Albert B. Fall, Secretary of the Interior, leased oil lands in return for bribes.
3. **(a)** The parties in 1924 were the Republicans, the Democrats, and the Progressives. There was no Progressive Party in 1928. **(b)** The 1924 candidates were Republican Calvin Coolidge, Democrat John W. Davis, and Progressive Robert M. La Follette. In 1928 Republican Herbert Hoover ran against Democrat Alfred E. Smith. **(c)** The 1924 issues were government regulation of business, assistance to farmers, social legislation, labor laws, government ownership of railroads and water-power resources, and corruption. In 1928 the issues were farm relief, regulation of public utilities, and "rugged individualism." **(d)** Coolidge won the election of 1924; Hoover won the election of 1928.
4. **(a)** The elephant represents the Republican Party; the donkey, the Democratic Party. **(b)** Senate investigations uncovered a number of scandalous and illegal activities by members of Harding's administration. The cartoonist suggests that both Republicans and Democrats were involved in the scandals.

SECTION REVIEW   *(text page 710)*

Suggested responses to the questions are:
1. **(a)** Economists refer to worldwide economic disorder, high American tariffs, excessive borrowing, lack of government control of banks and worthless stocks, inevitable business cycles, and uneven distribution of income. **(b)** Hoover instructed the Farm Board to buy agricultural surpluses to bolster farm prices, started public works like Boulder Dam to reduce unemployment, and urged Congress to create the RFC and to pass the Home Loan Bank Act to bolster key businesses financially and reduce mortgage foreclosures. **(c)** Hoover believed that the fed-

eral government should not directly extend aid to citizens but could provide assistance to business and agriculture. His program reflected this belief and the recognition that the federal government must assume certain responsibilities to help the nation out of an economic crisis.

2. Most Americans were wage earners. They were most directly affected by business failures, although farmers probably suffered just as much from falling farm prices and foreclosures. Also, while farmers might have been able to feed themselves by growing food, city people did not have this advantage.

3. The charts show the prosperity of the years 1920–1929 (rising stock prices and low unemployment), and the depression years 1929–1935 (very low stock prices and high unemployment).

CHAPTER 31 REVIEW   *(text page 713)*

Reviewing Important Terms

1. true
2. true
3. false, Communists

Practicing Critical Thinking Skills

Suggested responses to the questions are:

1. Domestic needs in the 1920's overrode interest in international relations. American workers were faced with unemployment resulting from cancellation of wartime contracts and the shutdown of factories. American farmers lost markets for their produce because European farm lands started producing normally. Americans were generally weary of involvement in Europe.

2. Coolidge meant that strikes by those charged with protecting the public were illegal. Answers for the second part of the question will vary. Students might argue that the right to strike is a basic right for wage earners in labor negotiations, and that employers take action only when confronted with a strike. Other students might argue that a strike by a public servant endangers the public safety.

3. (a) Foreign countries were unable to sell their products in the United States and therefore were unable to earn the dollars needed to purchase American products. (b) Initially, the tariffs aided American industries by restricting foreign competition. Eventually, American industries found they had few foreign markets for their increasing amount of goods. (c) Although it was originally believed the tariffs would help farmers by eliminating foreign competition in the American market, the tariffs eventually hurt farmers for the same reasons tariffs hurt industry.

4. (a) Answers will vary. People are more hesitant to spend and savings go down because there is less available money for savings accounts. (b) Buying power is reduced because it takes more dollars to buy needed goods and services. (c) People living on fixed incomes must buy less because their incomes are limited and they do not have more dollars.

5. (a) Hoover's statement was supported by the high wages and profits, and a higher standard of living that more people than ever were enjoying. (b) Some Americans felt the United States was caught in a bubble that was about to burst. They referred to unemployed workers, to farmers losing their farms, and to the slump in the coal, textile, and leather industries.

6. (a) Answers will vary. Students might argue that the foreign policies of a particular President or political party led to war. (b) Answers will vary. Students might argue that economic policies were responsible for recession or depression. (c) Answers will vary. Students might contend that Presidential policies can restore confidence in the economy.

7. (a) Nicola Sacco and Bartholomeo Vanzetti were arrested for the burglary of a shoe company and the murder of a paymaster and a guard. They were found guilty and executed. (b) They believed that government should be abolished. (c) Many people believed that the evidence was flimsy and that Sacco and Vanzetti were executed for their political beliefs. (d) Answers will vary. (e) Answers will vary. Students might argue that a jury could convict people in a similar case today.

Developing History Study Skills

1. (a) 1929 (b) Students should answer yes. The nation was recovering from the depression, and stock prices would probably rise. (c) It was a booming economy.

2. Answers will vary. For example, students may wish to know: the number of Catholic registered voters in 1960; the differing attitudes toward Catholics and immigrants in 1928 and 1960; any news stories reflecting positively or negatively on Catholics in the 1920's or 1950's.

Relating Geography and History

1. (a) They rose. (b) The United States hoped to protect industries from foreign competition. (c) They have fallen because of the Trade Agreements Act and increased dependence on foreign

raw materials and markets. **(d)** Worldwide trade has increased, but the trade deficit (the difference between the value of exports and the value of imports) has continually increased. Foreign competition has hurt certain American industries such as the auto and steel industries.

2. **(a)** The nation hoped to raise the prices of farm products. **(b)** It continued protection for farmers and raised other rates to protect industry. **(c)** Yes, they did.

3. As the tariff rate rises, United States world trade decreases.

4. **(a)** The United States exports the greatest percentage to Asia (31% — $64.8 billion). **(b)** The United States exports the least to Communist Europe (2% — $3.6 billion). **(c)** The United States imports the most from Asia (36% — $85.2 billion). **(d)** The United States imports the least from Communist Europe (0.4% — $1.1 billion).

CHAPTER

32 The Great Depression and the New Deal

SECTION REVIEW *(text page 718)*

Suggested responses to the questions are:

1. Roosevelt faced the problems of providing food, clothing, shelter, and jobs for millions of unemployed Americans.

2. Federal agencies distributed money directly to the states, allowing state and local officials to use the money as they chose.

3. Many youths could not continue school — at any level. Those who graduated could not find employment, and thousands roamed the nation in search of work. The tragedy was the waste of the nation's most important resource — its youth.

4. **(a)** There was incompetence, waste, and occasional pressure on workers at election time. **(b)** New Dealers explained that there had been no precedents for such programs and that they had been handicapped by lack of trained personnel. They argued that these programs ended hunger for millions and gave the unemployed self-respect. **(c)** Answers will vary.

SECTION REVIEW *(text page 722)*

Suggested responses to the questions are:

1. **(a)** The plan for farm recovery was to bring about higher prices for farm products. The goal was to be achieved by reducing the supply of farm products. **(b)** *For:* prices rose; farmers made more money; farmers could buy manufactured products and so stimulate industry. *Against:* taxes on food processors were passed on to consumers, who had to pay higher prices; large farmers profited more than small farmers, tenant farmers, and sharecroppers; the program was bureaucratic and inefficient; the program curtailed food production when hunger was widespread. **(c)** The Supreme Court ruled that the right to regulate agriculture belonged to the states.

2. The government made loans to modernize railroad equipment. The ICC ordered railroads to lower passenger rates and to regain lost business. Many highways and waterways were also improved.

3. **(a)** The aim of the NIRA was to revive industry by enabling employers to cooperate in a planned effort to re-employ jobless workers and to raise wages. **(b)** This aim was to be implemented by the businesses, with government supervision. Businesses were to replace competition with cooperation. Each industry was to adopt a "code of fair practices" limiting production and providing for the common control of prices and sales practices. Most codes also outlawed child labor and stipulated a 40-hour work week and minimum weekly wages. **(c)** The Supreme Court ruled that although the Constitution gave the federal government the power to regulate interstate commerce, that did not include the power to regulate every aspect of business.

SECTION REVIEW *(text page 723)*

Suggested responses to the questions are:

1. The Social Security Act of 1935 provided unemployment insurance, old-age pensions, and help to the handicapped.

2. **(a)** The purpose of the TVA was to improve the social and economic conditions of the Tennessee River Valley by developing the natural resources of the area. **(b)** TVA could benefit the nation as a model of rural development and by providing a standard for costs of producing and distributing electric power. As the living standards of the people of the Tennessee Valley rose, they became consumers of products and services from all over the country.

3. **(a)** Private power companies claimed that the TVA would not be able to charge such low prices

for electricity if it paid taxes. They claimed that the cheap electricity was a gift from the taxpayers of the entire nation to the people of one region, not the result of more efficient production; and that the TVA was an unwarranted intervention by the federal government in private industry. **(b)** Answers will vary. Students might mention that the arguments were valid for the private power companies who were trying to make profits, but had to use the new, lower standard for costs. On the other hand, improved social and economic conditions benefited not only the people of this region, but the entire nation as well.

SECTION REVIEW   *(text page 729)*

Suggested responses to the questions are:
1. **(a)** The issues in the 1936 election included continued high unemployment, a huge national debt, an unbalanced budget, and states' rights. **(b)** Democrats strongly supported the New Deal program, pointing to improved conditions they claimed resulted from the New Deal. Republicans promised to keep most New Deal programs, but to make them more efficient and less expensive, balance the budget, and restore to the states certain powers that had been taken over by the federal government.
2. **(a)** The Supreme Court had declared seven major New Deal measures unconstitutional. Roosevelt feared that the Supreme Court would block his plans for recovery. **(b)** His plan failed because Congress and the public believed that it would tamper with the system of checks and balances in the Constitution. As a result, they refused to accept the plan. **(c)** Answers will vary.
3. Brakes on the 1937 – 38 recession included the following: more than 2 million wage earners began to collect unemployment insurance; savings of depositors were protected by bank insurance; money was lent by the RFC to distressed businesses; and government agencies began new public works.

SECTION REVIEW   *(text page 733)*

Suggested responses to the questions are:
1. **(a)** The A. F. of L. did not move rapidly enough in organizing unskilled workers in mass production industries. **(b)** The A. F. of L. had always organized workers according to their trades. The CIO organized workers into industrial unions that included all workers, skilled and unskilled, in an industry.
2. **(a)** The Fair Labor Standards Act decreased the legal maximum work week; raised the minimum wage; and forbade child labor in industries producing goods for interstate commerce. **(b)** Employers contended that the act resulted in unnecessary and unwise government interference in business.
3. The Soil Conservation and Domestic Allotment Act gave benefits to farmers who withdrew land from production and made it available for soil conservation. The Bankhead-Jones Farm Tenant Act created the Farm Security Administration, which made loans to tenant farmers, sharecroppers, and farm laborers who wished to buy farms. The second Agricultural Adjustment Act provided benefits for planting soil-conserving crops; agreements with producers limiting amount of staple crops to be grown by each farmer; commodity loans on stored crops; and crop insurance against drought and flood, hail, and plant diseases.
4. Labor unions grew the most from 1940 to 1960, when approximately 8.5 million people joined unions.

SECTION REVIEW   *(text page 735)*

Suggested responses to the questions are:
1. **(a)** inflation, deficit spending, and higher taxes on individuals and corporations **(b)** Critics called attention to the failure to balance the budget and the negative effect of taxes on businesses.
2. The New Deal met with stiffer opposition and growing indifference from the public because of recovery from recession and growing concern over national defense. Congress, after 1938, had fewer New Deal supporters and ended several New Deal agencies.
3. Willkie contended that President Roosevelt's administration of the New Deal endangered basic American principles of individualism, free enterprise, and democracy. Roosevelt countered that Willkie was falsifying the facts. Willkie supported many New Deal measures, but believed that Roosevelt's administration had been too extravagant and wasteful.
4. Some students may state that Roosevelt's break with the two-term tradition may have cost him some votes.

CHAPTER 32 REVIEW   *(text page 737)*

Reviewing Important Terms

1. false, direct relief
2. true
3. false, Pump priming
4. true
5. false, parity
6. true
7. true

Practicing Critical Thinking Skills

Suggested responses to the questions are:
1. **(a)** The New Deal encouraged organization of labor, some measures seemed to favor big corporations over small businesses; the government competed with private industry; the TVA set an unfair yardstick for electric rates; deliberate scarcities were created to raise prices; and the Supreme Court ruled some measures unconstitutional. **(b)** The New Deal restored confidence and improved national morale; assisted farmers and the aged; improved the status of workers and labor unions; made notable strides in the conservation of natural resources; corrected business abuses and provided mechanisms to prevent future economic crises; and gave people jobs, income, housing, dignity, and hope. **(c)** The New Deal was wasteful, inefficient, and sometimes corrupt; allowed a huge debt to develop through deficit spending; undermined the free enterprise system and the traditional value of self-reliance; and did not solve the problems of unemployment and widespread poverty. **(d)** Answers will vary. Students might argue that it helped to bring the nation out of the depression. Others might argue that it increased the role of the federal government and took away individual initiative.
2. **(a)** Food, Drug, and Cosmetic Act and Wheeler-Lea Act **(b)** Bankhead-Jones Act, Agricultural Adjustment Acts, FSA, National Housing Act, and farm credit programs **(c)** CCC and NYA **(d)** Social Security Act **(e)** Section 7a of NIRA, Wagner Act, and Fair Labor Standards Act.
3. **(a)** The Supreme Court set aside the NRA, the AAA, and five other important New Deal measures, as well as important state laws. Roosevelt contended that the justices were not considering problems in terms of modern needs. **(b)** He proposed to appoint an additional justice for each one who did not retire at the age of 70. **(c)** Answers will vary. Students might mention the significance of a Court that follows the dictates of the President or Congress.
4. Cartoons will vary. Students might select any of the following topics: 1932 — The Depression, Prohibition, Roosevelt, or Hoover; 1936 — The New Deal, TVA, Social Security, Roosevelt, or Landon; 1940 — third-term Presidency, rising dictatorships, the New Deal, the recession of 1937 — 38, Roosevelt, or Willkie.
5. Answers will vary. Students might mention the expansion of welfare, more government jobs, and massive direct relief efforts as in keeping with the nation's reaction to the Great Depression. Students might also mention a stronger Presidency and various emergency powers assumed by federal agencies.

Developing History Study Skills

1. **(a)** direct relief **(b)** recovery **(c)** direct relief **(d)** recovery **(e)** recovery **(f)** recovery **(g)** recovery
2. **(a)** This is a statement of fact. It uses statistical information that can be checked for accuracy. **(b)** This is an opinion. Terms such as "most exciting and demanding" state the author's evaluation rather than verifiable information about Roosevelt's time.

Relating Geography and History

1. The CCC built fire trails in the forests, cleared swamps, planted trees, built small dams for flood control, and cleared land for public parks.
2. **(a)** The TVA produced electricity. **(b)** Answers will vary. Students might mention that the TVA provided much-needed flood control in many areas and cleared forests of refuse and rubble. **(c)** Answers will vary. Students might mention that the project did change the ecology of many of the rivers and opened up inaccessible land to the public. **(d)** Answers will vary. Students might argue that the project developed the area and therefore altered the ecological balance.

CHAPTER

33 Decades in Contrast

SECTION REVIEW   (text page 744)

Suggested responses to the questions are:
1. By 1920 the power-driven machine was one of the dominant symbols of the United States. There were machines on assembly lines in factories, on farms, and in the home; the number and variety of machines kept multiplying. As industries continued to grow, they tended to become more efficient. They introduced efficiency engineering, scientific management, cost accounting, and new marketing techniques.
2. **(a)** In the 1920's the passenger automobile and the truck replaced almost all horse-drawn vehicles and greatly increased mobility. By the end of the 1920's, the automobile industry had become the nation's biggest business and spurred the development and growth of numerous related businesses. **(b)** Automobiles clogged city streets and polluted the air; suburbs sprang up, connected by paved roads to the cities. **(c)** On

the farms, "Tin Lizzies," rather than horses and carriages found homes in the barns, and the isolation of the farm family was ended.

3. (a) Power-driven machines freed labor from back-breaking toil, increased productivity, and generally resulted in better wages and higher living standards for workers. (b) "Time-and-motion" studies increased efficiency of production by finding ways to lessen worker fatigue and on-the-job accidents. (c) Company unions were formed to prevent the organization of unions by employees, resulting in a decline in the strength of organized labor.

4. See the following graph. Answers will vary.

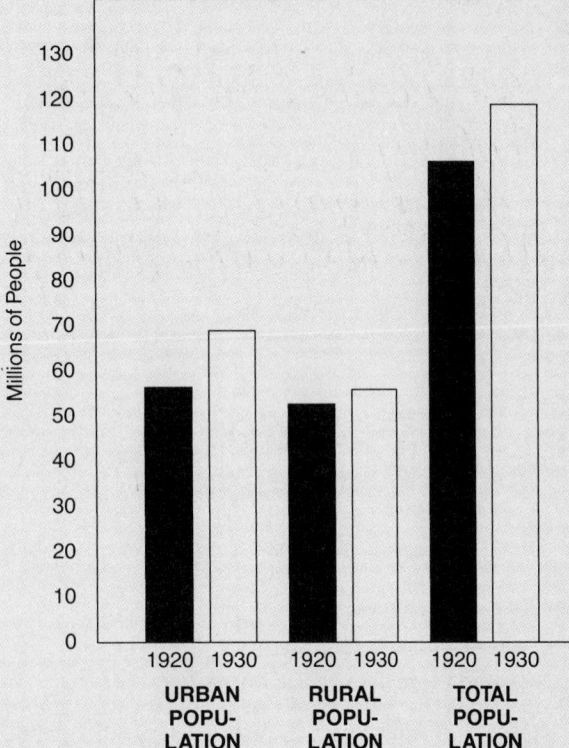

Millions of People

	1920	1930	1920	1930	1920	1930
	URBAN POPU-LATION		RURAL POPU-LATION		TOTAL POPU-LATION	

SECTION REVIEW   *(text page 748)*

Suggested responses to the questions are:
1. (a) Increased enrollment resulted from the need for a better-educated and better-trained work force, increased prosperity, growth of transportation, and growth of cities. (b) Curriculum met the demands of an industrialized society with more mathematics, engineering, science, vocational and commercial courses, and foreign languages.
2. The Nineteenth Amendment gave women the right to vote. They were freed from many household tasks by new labor-saving devices and found new opportunities for employment on assembly lines and as sales clerks, office workers, and stenographers.
3. Prohibition was never taken seriously by most Americans and was therefore unenforceable. Bootlegging was controlled by criminals, which led to lawlessness, violence, and corruption.

SECTION REVIEW   *(text page 751)*

Suggested responses to the questions are:
1. Some farmers left for the cities in search of work. Others met sheriffs carrying foreclosure notices with shotguns, clubs, and pitchforks. Some dairy farmers forced truckloads of milk to be dumped out.
2. (a) The "Bonus Army" consisted of World War I veterans who came to Washington, D.C., to demand immediate payment of the war bonus they were scheduled to receive in 1945. (b) The marchers did not succeed in getting the bonus payment. Although the Bonus Army was originally housed and fed by the army, the remnants refused to leave when ordered to do so and violence broke out.
3. Population growth slowed because few immigrants came to the United States and many young people chose not to marry and start families.
4. Answers will vary. Students might mention that the picture on text page 749 illustrates the loneliness and despair felt by the people made homeless by the depression.

SECTION REVIEW   *(text pages 754–55)*

Suggested responses to the questions are:
1. The demand for labor during World War I had encouraged many blacks to move to northern cities. The migration continued after the war. Blacks met economic and social discrimination in the North which was intensified during the 1919–1920 depression as blacks and whites competed for available jobs. Racial tension exploded into riots during the summer of 1919 when blacks fought back against some especially discriminatory acts.
2. (a) The "new Negro" was the term applied to black Americans who were proud of their heritage and who recognized that self-assertiveness was the only way to gain equality. (b) The number of businesses, banks, and insurance companies owned by blacks increased. The goal was black financial independence. Black organizations such as the NAACP worked

through the courts to obtain equal rights, elected a black Congressman, Oscar de Priest from Chicago, and slowly began to join the ranks of the Democratic Party. **(c)** The northern Democrats actively sought black support.
3. Blacks received more aid from Roosevelt's administration than from Hoover's. Consequently, blacks began shifting their allegiance to the Democratic Party.
4. **(a)** Indian policy in the 1920's was largely a continuation of the Americanization policy of the Dawes Act with the exception that all Indians received American citizenship in 1924. **(b)** The policy of Americanization was unsuccessful. Indians remained in poverty. **(c)** Mexican immigrants and many Mexican Americans worked for low wages as migrant laborers in agriculture, mining, and railroad construction in the Southwest. They were usually poor and ill-educated, and met with discrimination in jobs, housing, and education. During the depression, many immigrants returned to Mexico under the Expatriation Program. Mexican Americans joined the movement to the cities.

SECTION REVIEW   *(text page 758)*

Suggested responses to the questions are:
1. Edith Wharton, Ellen Glasgow, and Willa Cather compared the materialism of the machine age with the order and stability of earlier periods. T.S. Elliot, Theodore Dreiser, and F. Scott Fitzgerald portrayed the conflict in values created by the machine age and its potential for dehumanization. Steinbeck wrote poignantly of the poor and homeless, and Hemingway exposed the cruelties of war.
2. Traditional values were generally upheld but movies also set new standards of behavior, dress, and cultural taste.
3. **(a)** Land in industrial centers was scarce and expensive. The skyscraper, towering into the sky, used as little ground space as possible. **(b)** Built of steel, glass, and concrete and emphasizing clear-cut vertical lines, the skyscraper was an example of industrial technology and efficiency.

CHAPTER 33 REVIEW   *(text page 762)*

Reviewing Important Terms

1. Company
2. mergers
3. cost accounting
4. *mutalistas*
5. mass production

Practicing Critical Thinking Skills

Suggested responses to the questions are:
1. **(a)** Industrialization affected people on farms by providing better transportation and communication, by eliminating isolation, and by providing farm machinery and labor-saving devices. **(b)** It affected people in cities by creating larger houses and offices, more job opportunities, better transportation, the growth of suburbs, more noise and crowding, new forms of entertainment, and centers of civilization and culture. **(c)** Answers will vary. Students who define progress as "advancement in general," might argue that industrialization is progress. Students who define progress as improvement in quality of life might argue that industrialization, with its concomitant effects of loss of individual identity, pollution, and resource and power depletion is not progress. In reply, some students might point out that industry can help solve these problems.
2. **(a)** Radio, movies, and newspapers contributed to conformity because their messages reached mass audiences. For example, the syndicated editorials in chain newspapers molded the opinions of large numbers of people. These media also held up a standard of living to which many Americans aspired. **(b)** They contributed to individualism by analyzing, criticizing, and evaluating the American scene and by presenting several sides of an issue. They provided the public with various kinds of information on which to base decisions.
3. **(a)** Industrialization brought women new labor-saving devices, ready-made garments, and packaged foods, which in turn gave them leisure time to pursue their own interests. Women also entered the labor market because of rapidly multiplying jobs in mills, plants, and factories. Increased job opportunities as sales clerks, office workers, and stenographers opened up. The changing status and roles of women created the "new woman" who was economically independent, rejected many traditional female roles, refused to believe in the superiority of men, and denounced the different standards imposed on women in sexual and social relationships. **(b)** Answers will vary.
4. **(a)** All the minority groups suffered from hostility, discrimination, and poverty. **(b)** The Mexicans were an almost forgotten group, with the exception of the Expatriation Program, which attempted to send Mexican immigrants back to Mexico. The Indians remained largely separated from the mainstream, because of their concentration on reservations. Their problems were more concerned with the government and its agencies than with society at large. Black Americans, the largest minority group, were directly

involved in the problems of the period and were the most successful in uniting to improve their conditions. (c) Answers will vary. Students might mention that poverty during the Great Depression was more widespread than it is today. Poverty cut across all demographic barriers — social class, racial, geographic, occupational — to a greater extent during the depression than it does in the United States today.

5. Answers will vary. Students might feel that television, with its tremendous visual impact, has a greater effect on society today than radio did in the 1920's and 1930's.

6. (a) Answers will vary. Students might mention that people try to stretch their dollars during times of rising inflation and interest rates. (b) Answers will vary. Students might mention that people feel their money does not buy as much when inflation and interest rates are high. At these times, therefore, they may tend to spend less and to "make do with" what they have.

Developing History Study Skills

1. Answers will vary.
2. (a) There were practical reasons for not leaving the land despite drought conditions. (b) The soil was excellent. Newer methods would require less rainfall than previous methods. All the farm equipment was adapted to the specific type of farming. Somewhat favorable conditions seemed just around the corner.

Relating Geography and History

1. (a) The number of roads increased dramatically and their quality improved with new technological advances in surfacing techniques and materials. (b) People could and did live farther from work. (c) Differences between farmers and city dwellers diminished.
2. (a) The radio made it possible to communicate with many people at the same time. It also insured the "message" was the same. (b) The voices of leaders could be brought into the homes of the people.
3. Airplanes could fly over geographic barriers and travel much faster than other forms of transportation. For these reasons, news and travelers reached their destinations much more quickly, making the earth seem smaller.
4. Answers will vary. Students should realize, however, that the automobile, airplane, and radio reduced regional differences in the United States.

UNIT TEN REVIEW   *(text page 763)*

Discussing Ideas

1. (a) Harding's slogan "a return to normalcy" indicated a program changing from progressivism and the New Freedom to business and economic growth. One example of the rejection of progressive ideals was the adoption of the Emergency Tariff and passage of the Fordney-McCumber Tariff. These tariff measures reinstated higher tariffs and rejected the ideal of free trade. (b) Coolidge's statement indicates a further relaxing of the checks against big business instituted during the progressive era. (c) Hoover's belief in "rugged individualism" indicated an "every man for himself" philosophy. Government support of business was fine, but special assistance to individuals was not.
2. (a) Answers will vary. Students might include exciting, new, full of changes, carefree, uninhibited, and fads and fashions. (b) "Exciting" because the modern era had arrived and there were many things to experience. "New" because many inventions and innovations now affected everyday life. "Full of changes" because of the technological, social, and artistic changes that marked the 1920's. "Carefree" because many people adopted a "live for today, don't worry about tomorrow" attitude. "Uninhibited" because styles in clothing, music, art, etc. reflected changing moral values. "Fads and fashions" marked the era when new and different were valued for their own sake.
3. (a) There are many explanations for the causes of the Great Depression. Most economists agree that overproduction and a lack of readily available cash were partly responsible. Overinvestment and overspeculation in the stock market, inflating the value of stocks unrealistically, also contributed. (b) Answers will vary. Students might mention that runaway inflation and interest rates that cripple buying power coupled with overproduction could again cause a depression. Other students might feel that Americans are now more aware of the economic situation and that government policies could be used to avert a depression.
4. He felt direct aid would create a vast, inefficient bureaucracy and would undermine the self-respect of persons receiving it.
5. Answers will vary. Students might argue that the New Deal dramatically changed the character of the federal government. The government now became a mediator in labor disputes; a regulating agency in all walks of life; a source of welfare income for many; and an insurance company for depositors, the aged, and others. These activities have involved government in the everyday life of a citizen more than ever before.

6. (a) For minorities the depression was a catastrophe. A far higher percentage than average of minority-owned businesses and banks failed. Minorities were the "first fired and the last hired," and an estimated two thirds of the minorities in American industry lost their jobs. The New Deal did provide some jobs and relief; however, many of the programs were blatantly discriminatory. The passage of the Howard-Wheeler Act (Indian Reorganization Act) was one bright spot for minorities during the depression years. (b) Answers will vary. Students might mention that despite the fact that the depression struck across racial and social barriers, minorities were the least prepared to withstand the economic and social siege. Many had only recently been hired and so were the first to lose their jobs. The need for agricultural workers was scarce, as well. Few had savings or special skills they could rely on during the depression.

Applying History Study Skills

1. (a) 1933 (b) During the height of the New Deal, there was a decrease in the unemployment rate. (c) In 1938 the unemployment rate jumped.
2. (a) the radio's accessibility and a radio owner's ability to share in the enjoyments of the wealthy through radio programs (b) A large number of households possessing a radio would support the Lynds' contention that the radio was becoming a necessity for many families. A surprisingly low number of households with radios would indicate, perhaps, that the radio's "necessity" or acceptance was not as widespread as the Lynds' indicate, or that radios were still a "plaything" for the wealthy.

TEACHER'S NOTES

Isolationism Through World War II

34 The Nation Moves Toward Isolationism

SECTION REVIEW   (text page 769)

Suggested responses to the questions are:
1. Reasons for restricting immigration were anti-European feeling after the war; organized labor's opposition to new immigrants who were willing to work for low wages; industrialists no longer needed masses of unskilled workers; and many Americans felt that southern Europeans were hard to "Americanize."
2. (a) High American tariffs cut off European trade with the United States; Germany was not making reparations payments. Debtor countries said they had contributed more to victory in blood and sacrifice than Americans had, and war debts should be canceled. (b) Americans answered that war debts and reparations were not related; some of the loans had been made after the armistice; and some European nations were spending large sums on armaments.
3. High tariffs made it impossible for Europe to settle its debts and contributed to the Great Depression. Some countries retaliated by raising their own tariff barriers against American goods, depriving American business of foreign markets.
4. Italian, Austro-Hungarian, and Russian immigrants comprised almost half of all immigrants to the United States from 1890 to 1939.

SECTION REVIEW   (text page 771)

Suggested responses to the questions are:
1. (a) Latin Americans resented the undue interference in their internal affairs; Americans criticized the dispatching of troops as making war. (b) Marines were sent to Nicaragua to protect American lives and property as soon as disturbances broke out. Latin Americans resented this interference in their internal affairs.
2. The Mexican constitution of 1917 gave Mexicans alone the right to develop natural resources and canceled concessions made to foreigners by earlier governments. The constitution placed severe restrictions on the Catholic Church. Mexicans supported the anti-American faction in Nicaragua.
3. Morrow was sent to Mexico; Coolidge traveled to Cuba in 1928 to open a Pan-American Conference; Hoover toured South America; and the United States stopped using force in Latin American internal affairs.

SECTION REVIEW   (text page 774)

Suggested responses to the questions are:
1. (a) The naval armaments race and strained relations between Japan and the United States led to the Washington Conference. (b) It included an agreement by Great Britain, the United States, Japan, France, and Italy to bring naval strength into a 5:5:3 ratio for the United States, Great Britain, and Japan, with France and Italy having fleets of equal size with a ratio of 1.75 to the other powers. Great Britain and the United States would not further fortify any Pacific colonies except Hawaii. (c) The reason for the Four-Power Pact was the growing concern over the possibility of war in the Pacific.
2. (a) The Nine-Power Treaty guaranteed the territorial integrity of China. (b) It maintained the Open Door Policy. (c) The treaty caused Japan to partially withdraw from the Shantung Peninsula.
3. Each nation signed with the reservation that war waged in self-defense not be outlawed. Since almost all war is justified as self-defense, the pact was virtually meaningless.
4. (a) Stimson protested Japanese aggression against China, accusing Japan of violating

treaty pledges. **(b)** The League agreed with Stimson but failed to act. This failure to act may possibly be explained by the inherent weaknesses of the League.

CHAPTER 34 REVIEW   *(text page 777)*

Reviewing Important Terms

1. false, reparations
2. true
3. true
4. false, moratorium
5. true

Practicing Critical Thinking Skills

Suggested responses to the questions are:
1. Both actions reflect American isolationism after World War I. Tariffs kept foreign products out of the United States, and immigration quotas kept out foreign people.
2. The Kellogg-Briand Pact did not provide for any action to be taken against an aggressor, so it posed no threat to the Japanese invasion of Manchuria.
3. **(a)** Attitudes toward Europe were to some degree hostile because Europeans did not repay their war debts. **(b)** The United States regarded itself as the police officer of the hemisphere for most of the decade because of the large sums of American money invested in Latin American businesses and resources and because of the desire to protect the Panama Canal. By the end of the 1920's, the United States changed its attitude by renouncing this policy of intervention, and relations with Latin America improved. **(c)** The United States insisted on an Open Door Policy in China in order to safeguard American trade in that nation. The United States also recognized the importance of Japan in this region, but did not recognize Japanese claims to equal power status. Answers to the second part of the question will vary. Students might mention that the attitudes reflected a desire for isolation as well as for increased trade.
4. **(a)** The League of Nations, World Court, Washington Conference, Five-Power Treaty, Four-Power Pact, Nine-Power Treaty, and Kellogg-Briand Pact were all attempts to guarantee peace. **(b)** Answers will vary. Students might suggest a more binding permanent treaty based on the Kellogg-Briand Pact.
5. **(a)** Answers will vary. Students might mention that today's policies are generally a continuation of the 1920's policies. There are exceptions such as Cuba. **(b)** Answers will vary. Students might mention that events in El Salvador demonstrate a Good Neighbor Policy.

Developing History Study Skills

1. **(a)** 14 percent; 14 percent **(b)** 52.3 **(c)** Answers will vary. Students might point out that wars interrupt trade and therefore lower economic activity.
2. **(a)** Answers will vary. Students might mention that disillusionment after World War I, fear of overcrowding, and economic worries led to strict adherence. **(b)** Answers will vary. Students might feel it fair to allow all the passengers of the ship to enter.

Relating Geography and History

1. **(a)** Four million fewer immigrants entered the United States from 1921–30 than had from 1901–10. **(b)** Events surrounding World War I and immigration restrictions made it more difficult to enter the United States. **(c)** Answers will vary. Students might argue that this selective quota system permitted large numbers of some immigrant groups. This had obvious effects on the ethnic makeup of the United States. **(d)** Answers will vary. Students might argue that great scientists and artists may not have gotten the opportunity to display their talent because they could not enjoy the benefits available in the United States.
2. **(a)** 6.7 percent **(b)** Mexico, Ireland, and Great Britain (some students might suggest Scandinavia, which is not a country but a region comprised of several countries)

CHAPTER 35 From Isolationism to War

SECTION REVIEW   *(text page 782)*

Suggested responses to the questions are:
1. *Arguments for recognition:* the regime had been in the power for 16 years; recognition would increase trade; and there was common concern over Japanese aggression. *Arguments against:* Communists aimed at world conquest.
2. **(a)** In 1933, Congress passed an independence act for the Philippines which the Filipinos rejected because they feared the imposition of tariffs on Filipino goods and the effects of United States military presence in their coun-

try. To eliminate these fears, Congress passed the Tydings-McDuffie Act in 1934. **(b)** The act's major provision was that the Philippines would become independent 10 years after achieving commonwealth status.
3. **(a)** The Good Neighbor Policy was prompted by self-interest and a desire for friendship. The United States needed Latin American trade; the rise of dictatorships in both Europe and Asia convinced the United States that the nation must be on friendly terms with its Latin American neighbors. **(b)** The United States signed a nonintervention agreement; canceled the Platt Amendment; withdrew troops from Haiti; gave up the right to intervene in Panama's affairs; ended its control of Dominican Republic customhouses; and urged negotiations when Lázaro Cádenas announced the seizure of foreign oil companies' property in Mexico.

SECTION REVIEW   *(text page 785)*

Suggested responses to the questions are:
1. **(a)** The totalitarian dictators believed that the individual exists to serve the state and has only those rights and privileges granted by the state. The government embodies the state and has complete control over the nation and its people. **(b)** Each dictator believed his country had a superior civilization and form of government and that his country should and could conquer and control the world.
2. The roots of isolationism were disillusionment with the results of World War I and with the League of Nations; disclosure of war profiteering; belief that geographic position would protect the United States; and the continuing challenge to end the Great Depression.
3. **(a)** The neutrality acts were laws passed between 1935 and 1937 that were meant to keep the United States out of war and its citizens out of danger. **(b)** They reflected the widespread American sentiment against war in a period when conflicts were erupting in Europe, Africa, and Asia. **(c)** Many Americans believed the United States had a moral duty to uphold and protect individual rights and to aid the victims of aggression. Many also believed that unchecked aggression would one day leave the United States surrounded by enemies.
4. The events threatening peace were Italy's invasion of Ethiopia, Japan's withdrawal from the naval limitation agreement, German occupation of the Rhineland, civil war in Spain, the Italian-German military pact, the Anti-Comintern Pact, and the Japanese invasion of China.

SECTION REVIEW   *(text page 789)*

Suggested responses to the questions are:
1. Fascist leader Francisco Franco was aided by Hitler and Mussolini in the Spanish Civil War. Franco's opponents were aided by the Soviet Union and an "international brigade" of anti-Fascist volunteers from several countries, including the United States.
2. **(a)** Chamberlain believed the Munich agreement, which gave Hitler almost everything he demanded, would insure peace. **(b)** Others believed appeasement would only encourage Hitler to make further demands.
3. **(a)** The United States extended the protection of the Monroe Doctrine to Canada in 1938 and signed two agreements with Latin American nations to cooperate in opposing foreign intervention in the Western Hemisphere. **(b)** These agreements, especially the Declaration of Lima, broadened the Monroe Doctrine into a multilateral commitment to "continental defense."

SECTION REVIEW   *(text page 794)*

Suggested responses to the questions are:
1. The arms embargo helped Germany because it denied aid to France and England, which were less prepared for war than Germany.
2. In 1940, Congress passed the Smith Act to check subversive activities and the Burke-Wadsworth Act establishing a peacetime draft; Cordell Hull signed the Act of Havana to protect nonaggressors' colonial possessions in the Western Hemisphere; and Roosevelt created a Permanent Joint Board of Defense with Canada. In 1941, Congress passed the Lend-Lease Act; American troops occupied Iceland; the American navy began convoying ships; and Roosevelt drew up the Atlantic Charter with Churchill.
3. Japan invaded French Indochina in July 1941; Roosevelt froze Japanese assets in the United States and placed an embargo on strategic shipments to Japan; in November, a Japanese peace mission arrived in the United States; and on December 7, 1941, Japan attacked Pearl Harbor.
4. **(a)** Roosevelt meant that the United States had a tradition of protecting democracy. Therefore, United States business and industry would produce the materials needed to fight aggression. **(b)** First, the Neutrality Act of 1937 was amended to allow any nation to buy weapons and munitions from the United States. This helped supply the Allies. Then the Lend-Lease Act appropriated money to produce and distribute to the Allies ships, planes, tanks, and anything else needed to resist Hitler.

Reviewing Important Terms

1. false, isolationism   5. false, appeasement
2. false, dictatorship   6. false, multilateral
3. true   7. true
4. false, fascist

Practicing Critical Thinking Skills

Suggested responses to the questions are:

1. **(a)** The Great Depression hit the entire world. The Fascist dictatorships, beginning with Italy in the 1920's and continuing with Germany and Japan in the 1930's, capitalized on the fear and desperation of their citizens by promising them prosperity and power. By engaging in a large military build-up, they put people to work and took their nations out of the depression while the free nations continued to suffer from its effects. The free world, including the United States, had no desire to use its limited resources to enforce the Treaty of Versailles, the League of Nations Covenant, or the several treaties made in the 1920's. **(b)** The dictators of the 1930's appealed to their people's patriotism and promised greater glory through conquest. The Nazis believed that the Aryan race was destined to rule the world.
2. **(a)** In Munich, in 1938, the pact was signed forcing the Czechs to give most of the Sudetenland to Germany. In return, Germany promised peace and no further ambitions in Europe. **(b)** It led to war because appeasement caused aggressor nations to expect that no action would be taken against further aggression. Eventually, other nations realized that they had to stop the aggressors before they, too, were taken over.
3. **(a)** During the 1930's Americans were disillusioned with World War I and the League of Nations and with war profiteering. They believed that geographic position would protect them and that the depression should be the United States' first concern. **(b)** Some Americans began to believe that the aggressor nations were, indeed, set on world conquest. Also, they were appalled by the flagrant disregard for international law and human decency exhibited by the Axis Powers. With the fall of France, the United States' oldest ally, the American public supported Roosevelt's plea for aid to the Allies. Many Americans, however, clung to their isolationist position until the Japanese bombed Pearl Harbor.
4. **(a)** The United States recognized the Soviet Union for increased trade benefits, to deal mutually with the threat of Japan's aggression, and because the Soviet government had existed for 16 years. **(b)** Answers will vary. Students might argue that such a move would be necessary to deal with a mutual problem or common enemy.
5. Most Americans were isolationalist and did not want to become involved in European affairs.
6. Answers will vary. Students might mention that the United States no longer adheres to isolationism.

Developing History Study Skills

1. **(a)** Italy invaded Albania and Ethiopia. **(b)** 1936 **(c)** the invasion of Poland
2. Answers will vary.

Relating Geography and History

1. The Rhineland, a part of Germany, had been demilitarized by the Versailles Treaty. Czechoslovakia and Austria had German minorities. All three areas provided a buffer zone.
2. It both helped and hurt. It made communications between the two nations easier. When the tide of war turned in favor of the Allies, they had limited territory to conquer.
3. Japan's imperialistic efforts needed Manchuria's raw materials.
4. The American fleet posed the only threat to Japanese domination of its Pacific sphere of influence.

CHAPTER

36 Americans in World War II

SECTION REVIEW   *(text page 803)*

Suggested responses to the questions are:

1. Before November 1942, the Axis Powers were in control of the war. Allied successes at Guadalcanal and in North Africa and Russia in 1942 marked the beginning of continued Allied victories.
2. The Allied forces received much of their supplies from the United States through Lend-Lease. United States troops got bases, housing, and equipment from Great Britain.
3. **(a)** Without the united front that Allied cooperation made possible, both defensive and offensive

planning and fighting would have been splintered and much less effective. **(b)** All 26 of the United Nations agreed to cooperate, not to conclude a separate peace, and to endorse the war aims of the Atlantic Charter. This provided a framework for more concrete cooperation, such as joint planning by Allied military leaders. Sharing of costs through the Lend-Lease program made maximum use of financial resources.

4. **(a)** The Axis Powers in Europe were Germany and Italy. **(b)** Western Europe: Norway, Denmark, the Netherlands, Belgium, Luxembourg, and France; Eastern Europe: Finland, Estonia, Latvia, Lithuania, Poland, Czechoslovakia, Austria, Hungary, Rumania, Yugoslavia, Albania, Greece, Bulgaria, and the western U.S.S.R.; North Africa: Morocco, Algeria, Tunisia, Libya, and northwestern Egypt. **(c)** The arrows indicating Allied counterattacks are dated. Not until 1942 did the Allies begin to advance.

SECTION REVIEW *(text page 808)*

Suggested responses to the questions are:

1. **(a)** Mobilizing and allocating human resources and the nation's resources required tremendous planning. The government had to establish controls and regulations to ensure that everyone would share equally, and to prevent inflation. **(b)** Taxes were raised to draw off consumer dollars; price controls were placed on many commodities; items such as gasoline, fuel, shoes, sugar, and meat were rationed to help ensure equitable access; and rents were controlled. **(c)** Individuals were affected by higher personal income taxes, restrictions on consumer goods and food needed for the war effort, and a freeze on wages that made higher prices harder to bear.

2. **(a)** Leaders of the unions promised that workers would not strike during the war; by and large this promise was kept. **(b)** Women worked in factories, taking the place of men who had left to serve in the armed forces. Women also entered the armed forces and worked at noncombatant jobs. **(c)** Minorities fought in the war and worked in defense plants.

3. **(a)** About 8,300,000 women were in the labor force in 1920; 15,300,000 in 1950; 45,400,000 in 1980. **(b)** Women made up 20.0 percent of the work force in 1920, 29.6 percent in 1950, and 42.4 percent in 1980. **(c)** Women were needed in war-production industries to replace men. They performed many different jobs in the armed forces. As a result, prejudices about what women could do broke down.

SECTION REVIEW *(text pages 812-13)*

Suggested responses to the questions are:

1. The Italian campaign gave the Allies control of the Mediterranean. It also took the Italian army out of the war, forcing Germany to withdraw troops from the Soviet front in order to fight in Italy. From Italian bases, the Allies were able to bomb southern Germany and the German-held Balkans.

2. **(a)** The Allies had to win the Battle of the Atlantic to protect the lifeline of ships carrying soldiers and supplies necessary to fight the war. **(b)** The Allies had radar and other detection devices to warn them of plane and submarine attacks. Also, the Allies produced huge quantities of new ships and aircraft for the war.

3. The steps to the end of the war in Europe included air bombardment of Germany, the Allied crossing of the Rhine, the Russians entering Berlin, and the death of Hitler.

SECTION REVIEW *(text page 817)*

Suggested responses to the questions are:

1. The Allied strategy called for driving the Japanese out of the islands they held in the central Pacific, the Solomons, and the Philippines as air, land, and sea forces converged on Japan.

2. **(a)** Germany was to be occupied by Great Britain, the United States, France, and the Soviet Union. The "Big Three" promised to support free elections throughout Europe. In return for entering the war against Japan, the Soviet Union was to receive certain territory. **(b)** Critics charged Roosevelt "surrendered" to Soviet demands, thus paving the way for eventual Communist victory in China, aggression in Korea, and the creation of Communist governments in Eastern Europe. Defenders point out that at the time of the Yalta Conference, the Soviet Union had already conquered most of Eastern Europe. Furthermore, the Soviet Union had given assurances that they would cooperate in designing a lasting peace.

3. **(a)** Bombing and the blockade were slowly rendering Japan helpless. American victories at Iwo Jima and Okinawa broke Japanese air and sea power. On August 6, 1945, the United States dropped an atomic bomb on Hiroshima and on August 9 dropped another on Nagasaki. **(b)** Answers will vary. Students might argue that Truman made his decision to drop the bomb in order to end the war immediately and thus to save the lives of hundreds of thousands of Americans. Students might also argue the claim of

some that Japan was ready to surrender or that there can be no justification for unleasing such a force as an atomic bomb.

4. **(a)** Japan's maximum area of control extended from Manchuria and eastern China to mainland southeast Asia, to the islands of southeast Asia, including northern New Guinea; eastward to the Gilberts and northward to the islands of Kiska and Attu in the Aleutians. **(b)** The island-hopping started from Hawaii and Australia, and concentrated on certain strategic islands, bypassing other, less important islands.

CHAPTER 36 REVIEW   *(text page 820)*

Reviewing Important Terms

1. true
2. true
3. false, rationing
4. false, braceros

Practicing Critical Thinking Skills

Suggested responses to the questions are:
1. **(a)** The Allies produced more war supplies than the enemy, had better research workers and facilities, and there were more nations on the Allied side. **(b)** Science developed new instruments of war, such as radar and the atomic bomb. Technology helped the United States become the "arsenal of freedom." **(c)** Control of the skies was necessary before control of the land could be achieved. Bombers destroyed military installations, factories, and shipping, thus reducing the enemy's ability to resist invasion.
2. Answers will vary. Students who agree might mention that military necessities must take precedence over individual considerations. Students who disagree might mention that no Americans of German or Italian heritage were similarly treated or that the war was being fought to protect the rights of all individuals.
3. **(a)** Churchill became Prime Minister when Great Britain alone faced Germany. His leadership ability helped Great Britain resist Germany. **(b)** Mussolini promised Italy a return to the glories of Rome and embarked on conquest. **(c)** Hitler persuaded the Germans to fight against difficult odds and to give up their freedom for the advancement of the state. **(d)** Roosevelt had the confidence of United States citizens, who were so persuaded of his ability that they elected him to four terms.
4. **(a)** Answers will vary. Students might mention that the effects of propaganda and FDR's persuasiveness convinced many Americans to accept controls. **(b)** Answers will vary. Students

might mention wage controls because higher wages were a recent and hard-fought victory for labor.
5. **(a)** Women helped replace the men who entered the armed services and support occupations. **(b)** clerical and office jobs at first, but eventually all phases of business and industry **(c)** By war's end, women had earned far greater acceptance in all roles than before war's outbreak.
6. **(a)** Answers will vary. Students might argue that it has made peace more stable because countries fear nuclear warfare. Other students might argue that the nuclear threat has made peace more fragile. **(b)** United States defense policy today dictates that nuclear weapons be used only as a last resort.

Developing History Study Skills

(a) the fear that the Germans would develop an atomic bomb first **(b)** Truman believed that the Germans would have terrorized the world.

Relating Geography and History

1. **(a)** Moscow and Stalingrad (Leningrad) **(b)** It became more difficult to get supplies and reinforcements.
2. **(a)** approximately 550 miles (880 kilometers) **(b)** the English Channel
3. The area under Axis control gradually decreased from 1942 to 1945.
4. **(a)** Allied forces reclaimed territories from the south, west, and east in its push toward Germany. **(b)** Allied advances came from the east and southeast in the Pacific theater.
5. **(a)** About 4,000 miles (6,400 kilometers). **(b)** Burma **(c)** To retake each island would have taken too much time and too many lives.

UNIT ELEVEN REVIEW   *(text page 821)*

Discussing Ideas

1. The resentment and suspicions caused by the Treaty of Versailles resulted in Germany's attempt to reclaim lost territories and prestige. These actions led to World War II.
2. **(a)** the policy of non-involvement **(b)** Many Americans resented United States involvement in World War I and were disillusioned with peace efforts after the war. **(c)** Participation in the peace efforts and trade agreements were not strictly isolationist.
3. **(a)** By exerting total control over a nation, dictators are able to marshall all resources

toward the problems they see as most pressing. **(b)** Answers will vary. Students might mention that dictatorships arose in nations previously ruled by strong monarchs. The United States, however, had a tradition of freedom and democracy.

4. **(a)** Answers will vary. Students might argue that the attempts were similar because circumstances in Europe were quite similar. **(b)** Answers will vary. Students might argue that the United States was too powerful for either side to ignore.

5. New technology in warfare became as important as the number of men in combat and the amount of territory held.

Applying History Study Skills

(a) Stalin did not want to leave while the winter offensive was under way, and he did not feel that the issue of a second front needed discussion. **(b)** Churchill and Roosevelt did not have to personally tell Stalin that his demands would not be met.

TEACHER'S NOTES

UNIT TWELVE
Reshaping the Postwar World

CHAPTER
37 Responsibilities of World Leadership

SECTION REVIEW *(text page 826)*

Suggested responses to the questions are:
1. **(a)** the number of representatives from the Soviet republics and the question of the veto in the Security Council **(b)** The Yalta Conference agreed that two of the 16 Soviet republics would be admitted as independent nations and worked out a compromise proposal for voting in the Security Council.
2. **(a)** to promote peace, social progress, and better standards of life with greater freedom for all nations **(b)** The chief function of the Security Council is to be the police authority of the world, charged with preventing war. The chief function of the General Assembly is to provide a "town meeting" of the world in which all UN members are represented.

SECTION REVIEW *(text page 830)*

Suggested responses to the questions are:
1. **(a)** The Soviet Union's expansion during the postwar period represented, at least in part, a continuation of the expansionist ambitions of tsarist Russia. The U.S.S.R. regarded itself as the leader of a Communist revolution destined to replace the "capitalist" and "imperialist" world. The Soviets moved against those countries that they regarded as "ripe" for revolution. **(b)** The Soviets claimed that the United States might lead "capitalist nations" in an attack upon them.
2. **(a)** *United States:* control of atomic energy turned over to an international agency with "inspec-

tion rights;" "Big Five" to give up veto rights on matters involving atomic energy; *Soviet Union:* United States to destroy its atomic bombs; United States to declare atomic warfare illegal; all nations to promise not to manufacture atomic bombs **(b)** The Soviet Union did not want to abandon the veto right and would not accept international inspection.
3. **(a)** Under the Truman Doctrine, the United States lent money to Greece and Turkey to strengthen their armed forces so they could fight against Soviet influence. **(b)** The Marshall Plan provided money, supplies, and machinery to help European countries rebuild and defuse Communist influence. **(c)** The Berlin airlift prevented the U.S.S.R. from forcing Western powers out of Berlin. **(d)** NATO was a mutual defense pact of Western European countries and the United States and Canada to balance Soviet military power in Europe.

SECTION REVIEW *(text page 835)*

Suggested responses to the questions are:
1. The Soviet Union refused to remove its troops from Iran; Israel and the Arab nations went to war.
2. **(a)** The Nationalists under Chiang Kai-shek and the Communists under Mao Tse-tung had been fighting since 1927. By 1949, the Communists had defeated the Nationalist forces, which fled to Taiwan. Both the Nationalists and the Communists claimed to be the legal government of China. **(b)** The United States continued to recognize the Nationalists as the legal government of China.
3. **(a)** At the end of World War II, Korea had been "temporarily" divided at the 38th parallel into American and Soviet zones. The Soviets refused to leave until an election, which placed Communists in power, was held. South Korea held a United Nations-supervised election. Both governments claimed to be the legitimate rulers; both had well-trained armies. The North Koreans attacked. **(b)** The Great Debate began when

Chinese Communist troops entered Korea and General MacArthur proposed that the United States bomb China, blockade the Chinese coast, and help Nationalist troops invade China. Those who disagreed argued that an attack upon Communist China might bring the U.S.S.R. openly to the aid of its Communist ally and trigger a world war.

4. **(a)** The UN forces' farthest advance is shown by the black line south of the Yalu River and the Manchurian border. **(b)** UN forces counterattacked at Inchon and from the southeast. By November, the UN troops were approaching the Yalu River, near China, at which point Chinese forces poured over the border to counterattack. **(c)** China shares a common border with Korea; its nearness helped with supply and reinforcement of the North Koreans.

SECTION REVIEW   (text page 841)

Suggested responses to the questions are:
1. **(a)** Egypt seized the Suez Canal. Israel, Great Britain, and France invaded Egypt. The UN secured a cease-fire and got British, French, and Israeli troops to withdraw. **(b)** Hoping to ease a situation that might have led to widespread war, the United States voted in favor of the UN cease-fire resolution.
2. **(a)** The doctrine made clear the United States' intention to check Communist influence in the Middle East, by force if necessary. **(b)** The United States and Great Britain sent troops to Lebanon and Jordan under the doctrine to protect those nations during anti-Western agitation fostered by Egypt and Syria.
3. The summit conference never occurred because of the U-2 incident and Khrushchev's demands for an apology, an assurance to stop all such flights, and punishment of those responsible.
4. **(a)** The Vietminh tried to gain control of Indochina from the French and their Vietnamese allies. North Vietnam was recognized as a Communist state. **(b)** The Hungarian revolt against Soviet domination in 1956 was crushed by Soviet forces. **(c)** The Soviets tried to force the Western powers to withdraw from Berlin.

CHAPTER 37 REVIEW   (text page 845)

Reviewing Important Terms

1. false, containment
2. false, brinkmanship
3. true
4. true
5. true
6. true

Practicing Critical Thinking Skills

Suggested responses to the questions are:
1. **(a)** The United Nations attempts to solve international issues by debate and majority vote. **(b)** However, the organization has no enforcement arm or sovereignty. It is an organization of independent nations, not a world government. **(c)** Answers will vary. Students who believe that it was a victory might mention that the war enhanced the prestige of the United Nations and stopped Communist aggression. Students who believe that it was not a victory might mention that almost all the fighting was done by the United States and that the war merely maintained the status quo.
2. The statement is supported by the conflict over Berlin; the Soviet and American use of the veto power in the UN: the nuclear arms race; and the opposing positions of the U.S.S.R. and the United States in the Suez crisis, Korea, and Vietnam.
3. **(a)** Some United States actions successfully contained communism; others did not. China became Communist, as did North Korea and North Vietnam. Turkey and Greece remained anti-Communist, as did West Berlin, Jordan, and Lebanon. **(b)** The Truman Doctrine sought to contain communism in Turkey and Greece by providing military and economic aid to those countries. Eisenhower took the same idea and applied it to the Middle East.
4. **(a)** Many of the areas of concern in the 1950's remain the same today. Less attention today, however, is focused on Asia and more attention is focused on Latin America. **(b)** The basic policies are primarily the same as in the 1950's.

Developing History Study Skills

1. **(a)** "External" developments were international events, and "internal" developments were events inside the Soviet Union and the United States. **(b)** Students should answer no. Gaddis' analysis appears to be logical because it does not place blame and he gives evidence to support his thesis.
2. **(a)** the Soviet Union, Poland, East Germany, Hungary, Czechoslovakia, Rumania, Bulgaria, Yugoslavia, and Albania **(b)** Portugal, France, Italy, West Germany, Belgium, Great Britain, the Netherlands, Denmark, and Norway **(c)** Spain, Switzerland, Austria, Finland, and Sweden **(d)** Germany was divided. Latvia, Lithuania, and Estonia disappeared. Poland took over part of Germany.
3. **(a)** The purpose is "The revival of a working economy in the world so as to permit the emer-

gence of political and social conditions in which free institutions can exist. . ." **(b)** Answers will vary. Students might note that other history books, encyclopedias, and library reference books would be appropriate sources.

Relating Geography and History

1. The basis for NATO is mutual defense of Western Europe and opposition to Soviet aggression.
2. **(a)** Answers will vary. Students might contend that Austria may have chosen to remain neutral because of its geographic position between Western Europe and the Iron Curtain. Pressures from each side were so great and public opinion so divided that neutrality appeared the only course. **(b)** Answers will vary. Students might mention that trade agreements and other treaties among neutral nations establish these nations as a region.
3. **(a)** They refer to the relative geographic position of nations on each side. **(b)** The term "bloc" implies solidarity.

CHAPTER

38 Returning to Peace and Prosperity

SECTION REVIEW   *(text page 850)*

Suggested responses to the questions are:
1. **(a)** Postwar labor unrest led many people to believe that American unions had grown too strong and should be controlled by the federal government. **(b)** The act restricted union campaign contributions; allowed court injunctions against striking unions and an 80-day cooling-off period; prohibited the closed shop; and required employers and union leaders to sign non-Communist oaths of allegiance.
2. **(a)** The Democratic civil rights plank for 1948 supported the right of every adult (1) to vote and participate in politics, (2) to an equal opportunity to work at a job for which he or she

was qualified, (3) to have personal security, and (4) to have equal treatment in the armed forces. **(b)** These proposals split the Democratic Party. Southern delegates at the convention objected to the civil rights plank, and a number of them formed a third party with Strom Thurmond as their candidate.
3. The Fair Deal extended social security benefits; increased the federal minimum wage, authorized slum clearance and low-income housing aid, continued rent controls, adopted a new Agricultural Act, extended civil service, and expanded activities of the Reclamation Bureau.
4. The threat of worldwide Communist aggression and the indictment of Communist leaders in the United States led to increased concerns over national security.
5. See the following chart. Answers will vary.

ELECTION OF 1948

Party	Candidate	Issues	Results
Democratic	Truman	supported civil rights; favored repeal of Taft-Hartley Act; favored federal support of housing, education, and farm income, broader social security benefits	303 electoral votes
Republican	Dewey	favored Taft-Hartley and less federal spending and involvement in people's lives	189 electoral votes
States' Rights	Thurmond	opposed civil rights position of Democrats	39 electoral votes
Progressive	Wallace	opposed cold war policies of Truman; favored renewing many New Deal programs	

Suggested responses to the questions are:
1. Eisenhower believed the President should administer the programs enacted by Congress rather than lead the country. Furthermore, he expected the Cabinet departments to carry out day-to-day business and only refer the most difficult problems to him.
2. Modern Republicanism advocated a middle-of-the-road domestic policy supporting moderate extension of New Deal-Fair Deal programs, and support for the United Nations, military aid for allies, and economic aid for underdeveloped countries.
3. The Eisenhower administration abandoned wage and price controls; set up the Hoover Commission to make government more efficient and less competitive with business; gave private industry a larger opportunity to develop atomic energy; took government out of many businesses; and passed the Submerged Lands Act giving control of underwater oil deposits to the states.
4. (a) Farmers continued to face falling prices because of overproduction and increased foreign competition. (b) The soil bank program was initiated, providing for flexible farm supports and payments to farmers to take farmland out of production. The objective was to reduce production.

SECTION REVIEW *(text page 861)*

Suggested responses to the questions are:
1. (a) The act was passed to curb corruption in labor unions. (b) The act prohibited Communists and convicted felons from holding union office and outlawed secondary boycotts and picketing by persons not directly involved in a strike. The act also required full financial disclosure by unions; instructed employers to disclose any payments or loans to unions; required elections by national unions at least every five years; and guaranteed union members the right to attend meetings, nominate candidates, and vote with a secret ballot.
2. (a) Alaska was purchased from Russia for $7 million at a time when little was known about its wealth of resources. (b) Today, it is a source of timber, fish, minerals, and petroleum.
3. (a) It would be 11:00 P.M. in Fairbanks, Alaska. (b) Honolulu (c) approximately 1,350 miles (2,160 kilometers).

CHAPTER 38 REVIEW *(text page 863)*

Reviewing Important Terms

1. false, Servicemen's Readjustment Act (G.I. Bill)
2. true
3. false, internal security
4. true
5. true
6. false, soil bank program

Practicing Critical Thinking Skills

Suggested responses to the questions are:
1. Americans had to face the problem of transforming the economy from wartime production to prosperous peacetime purposes and to resume social programs of the New Deal. Also, the nation faced the problems of demobilization, aid to veterans, postwar inflation, and a housing shortage. American armed forces were quickly demobilized and within two years sharply reduced in strength. The "GI Bill of Rights" was passed to help veterans return to civilian life. Wartime controls on prices and wages were ended after about a year, but rent controls were retained.
2. (a) Eisenhower was personally popular, but Republican policies were less so. (b) In this situation, it is difficult for a President to have Congress approve legislation that the President supports and it is possible that the President will veto bills passed by Congress. As a result, few laws are passed.
3. In protecting the country against subversive elements, Congress and Presidents Truman and Eisenhower tried to restrict activities of Communists. However, it was almost impossible to do this without compromising some Constitutional rights, such as freedom of speech and assembly.
4 (a) Truman was an active and forceful leader; Eisenhower administered the laws passed by Congress, but did not wish to impose his will. (b) Truman was aggressive and controversial, but was generally admired for his courage; Eisenhower was trusted and affectionately regarded as a fatherly figure. (c) Truman presided over a reasonable transition from war to peace and enacted Fair Deal legislation; Eisenhower brought stability and prosperity.
5. (a) Answers will vary. Students might suggest that the information in the textbook is presented in a more general and analytical way than the information gathered in interviews. (b) Interviews provide insight into personal reactions. (c) Interviews often contain more opinions than facts.
6. (a) The situation is generally the same today as it was in the 1950's. Farm prices have been sta-

bilized by government subsidies and family farms are in jeopardy. **(b)** The government's relationship with farmers is similar today. Subsidies and price supports remain.

Developing History Study Skills

Answers will vary. Students might point out that Stevenson believes that McCarthy is depriving people of their basic freedoms. Eisenhower believes that McCarthy is an attention grabber.

Relating Geography and History

1. Natural gas and petroleum deposits are often found near each other.
2. Deposits of iron ore and coal are located near Birmingham, Alabama.
3. **(a)** Texas **(b)** Arizona **(c)** Utah

CHAPTER
39 Age of Advancement

SECTION REVIEW

(text page 868)

Suggested responses to the questions are:
1. The organization of research has greatly increased knowledge, has opened up new horizons in science, advanced technology, and allowed us to understand much about the forces of nature. Students might agree with the statement but should note that the advances have come so fast that they almost seem to be beyond our control.
2. Teams of scientists from around the world have conducted many fundamental studies in such areas as solar activity, gravity, and meteorology. Nations have made treaties setting aside Antarctica as a scientific preserve and governing the use of outer space.
3. **(a)** Merfson is being replaced by a machine. **(b)** Merfson's job is to push a button. The machine has a hand with a forefinger that can push the button. **(c)** Answers will vary. Students might mention that workers fear that machines and automation are eliminating the need for a human work force.

SECTION REVIEW

(text page 871)

Suggested responses to the questions are:
1. Industrial growth was spurred by abundant natural resources, an excellent transportation system, skilled workers, and advances in science and technology.
2. New industries included the aircraft, electronics, space, and atomic energy industries.
3. **(a)** The most striking effect of the transportation revolution is seen in the growth of the airline industry carrying both passengers and freight. Jet aircraft, capable of speeds up to 600 miles (960 kilometers) per hour, carried up to 360 passengers or 20 tons (18 metric tons) of freight. **(b)** The trucking industry grew rapidly. Covering the nation from coast to coast on new superhighways, trucks competed successfully with railroads. **(c)** The railroads did not share in the transportation boom. They competed less than successfully for freight with trucks and airplanes, and lost most of their passenger business to buses, planes, and the family automobile. By 1960, many railroads were bankrupt.

SECTION REVIEW

(text page 875)

Suggested responses to the questions are:
1. **(a)** Large numbers of poor people, especially from the South and Appalachia, migrated to the central cities in search of jobs. **(b)** The growing middle class of young married people migrated to the mushrooming suburbs to seek better living conditions.
2. **(a)** Leisure time encouraged television watching and taking vacations in the family car. **(b)** Growing affluence permitted many families to have two (or more) cars. **(c)** Increasing affluence permitted more people to own two or more television sets. Increased leisure time promoted television. **(d)** Advancing technology placed more jobs within the reach of women, and laborsaving devices reduced the time and labor of housework.
3. First, the shortage of workers during World War II helped break down traditional barriers against the employment of women and gave women a chance to show that they could perform various jobs and occupations as skillfully as men. Second, the rapid expansion of the postwar economy created many thousands of new jobs that did not require muscle power. Third, laborsaving devices freed many women from household chores.

4. See the following chart. Answers will vary.

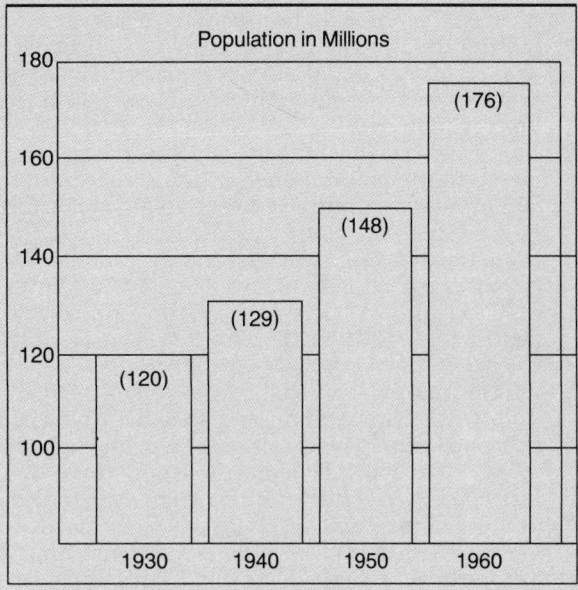

Population in Millions

The increase was so great because young people married earlier and had larger families in the prosperous 1950's.

SECTION REVIEW *(text page 878)*

Suggested responses to the questions are:
1. **(a)** Many Indian groups had already adapted to white culture and were uninterested in returning to purely Indian ways. Also, Indian ex-servicemen wanted the right to equal participation in the American mainstream they had fought to protect. **(b)** Two new policies were termination, or ending federal responsibility for Indians, and relocation of Indians to the major cities of the country. **(c)** The new policies were largely unsuccessful. States would not or could not assume responsibility for Indian affairs; relocated Indians often did not get promised jobs and found themselves in deep poverty in an alien environment.
2. **(a)** Spanish-speaking Americans include immigrants from South and Central America and the West Indies, Mexican Americans, and Puerto Ricans. **(b)** Many immigrants from South and Central America were white-collar workers. During and after World War II, hundreds of thousands of Mexicans crossed the border to seek jobs in the United States. Most became migrant farm workers. During and after the depression, many Puerto Ricans migrated to the mainland and settled in northern cities in search of jobs. **(c)** Labor unions have protested that Spanish-speaking Americans work for less than union wages; most were discriminated against in employment and housing and were forced to live in slums.
3. **(a)** In *Brown v. Board of Education of Topeka,* the Supreme Court reversed a 58-year-old decision allowing "separate but equal" facilities for the races. It declared that separate schools were inherently unequal and therefore violated the Fourteenth Amendment. **(b)** President Eisenhower sent federal troops to Arkansas to maintain the peace when several black students attempted to enroll in a white high school in accordance with the Supreme Court ruling that public schools be integrated. The action showed the federal government's commitment to school desegregation. **(c)** The act, the first since Reconstruction, attempted to secure voting rights for black Americans.

CHAPTER 39 REVIEW *(text page 882)*

Reviewing Important Terms

1. true
2. false, automation
3. true
4. false, termination
5. true
6. true
7. false, integration

Practicing Critical Thinking Skills

Suggested responses to the questions are:
1. **(a)** In the 1950's, young people seemed more concerned with a good job, security, and a house in the suburbs than with the many social and economic problems facing society. **(b)** Answers will vary.
2. The technological revolution and expanding knowledge requires trained, educated people to operate new machines, fill new jobs, and deal with new problems.
3. **(a)** Workers faced the problem of automation and learning new skills for a new age. **(b)** Black Americans left their rural homes hoping for better opportunities in expanding industry. Too often their hopes went unfulfilled as they faced discrimination in jobs and housing. **(c)** American Indians were caught between two worlds — the tribal and the new industrial. Many left the reservation only to find they lacked the skills and education required in industry. The attitudes and values of the industrial society were alien to them. **(d)** Young people became increas-

ingly mobile and indifferent to many traditional values. They appeared to be unconcerned with social problems, concentrating on their own life styles.

4. The words describe the enourmous changes in all aspects of life — work, education, family life, health, and leisure — and the growth of the economy and career opportunities.

5. (a) Answers will vary. Students might argue that pictures that represent the American Indian in traditional costumes and settings are positive. (b) Answers will vary. Students might mention that pictures depicting Indians as savages or being forcibly assimilated into white culture are judged negative. (c) Answers will vary. Students might feel American Indians would agree. Other students might mention that differences in cultural values do exist. (d) Answers will vary. Students might contend that the perceptions of young children are formed by seeing pictures and movies depicting Indians as savages.

6. (a) crime, poverty, traffic, high cost of living in cities, and pollution (b) You are close to cultural and entertainment centers. Medical, legal, and government services are also located in urban areas. (c) The problems and advantages of urban living today are generally the same as the problems and advantages of the early 1900's. (d) Answers will vary.

Developing History Study Skills

1. (a) The scientist would want to expand human knowledge but would realize that his or her work could lead to the development of weapons that might destroy the world. (b) The business person would want to increase efficiency but would not want to put people out of work. (c) The black would want a better education but might fear violence or have been conditioned to believe that he or she was inferior.

2. Answers will vary. Students might use the following classifications. *Technological changes* — automation, computers, televisions; *Social changes* — baby boom, expanding suburbs, building boom, household appliances, televisions, leisure time, working women, *Brown v. Board of Education of Topeka; Economic changes* — increasing productivity, advancing industrial technology, improved labor relations, increasingly efficient business management

Relating Geography and History

1. (a,b) Answers will vary. (c) Answers will vary. Students might mention the development of high-tech industries in the community.

2. (a,b,c,d) Answers will vary.

UNIT TWELVE REVIEW   *(text page 883)*

Discussing Ideas

1. The basic aim of the Marshall Plan, Truman Doctrine, Eisenhower Doctrine, as well as U.S. involvement in Korea and Vietnam, were to stop the spread of communism.

2. (a) The cold war was the conflict of ideologies between the United States and the Soviet Union. (b) Internal security measures caused philosophical conflicts inside the United States.

3. (a) The main goal of Truman's administration was a return to a peacetime economy. Eisenhower's goals were the completion of postwar conversion and an expansion of economic prosperity. (b) Both administrations dealt with farm and labor problems, and solidified the economy. (c) Both administrations supported the UN, helped allies and emerging nations strengthen their economies, and resisted communism. (d) Answers will vary. Students might mention that little progress was made by minorities economically or in civil rights.

4. Answers will vary. Students might mention that wage earners, young professionals, and returning G.I.s might have called the 1950's "happy days." Blacks, Indians, and Hispanics may not have considered the 1950's so happy. The difference might be caused by the fact that policies, programs, and prosperity focused on mainstream America.

5. Blacks won successes in every field. Particularly noteworthy successes were *Brown v. Board of Education of Topeka,* the Montgomery bus boycott, and Martin Luther King, Jr.'s activities. Indians did not fare as well as blacks. Termination and relocation policies were failures. Hispanics, many with only a limited knowledge of English, faced prejudice and discrimination. Hispanics remained at the bottom of the socioeconomic ladder, with few services or help from the government.

6. (a) The decision reversed the *Plessy v. Ferguson* ruling that "separate but equal" facilities were constitutional. The 1954 ruling opened the door to equal access of all public facilities for minorities. (b) The Montgomery bus boycott, formation of the SCLC, and the 1957 Civil Rights Act helped strengthen civil rights for black Americans.

7. (a) Answers will vary. Students might use the following classifications: *Developments in For-*

eign Affairs: UN charter is drafted, Berlin airlift, Eisenhower Doctrine; *Social Developments:* Armed forces return, Supreme Court outlaws "separate but equal" schools, National Defense Education Act; and *Economic Developments:* Employment Act, A.F. of L. and CIO merge, Soil bank program begins. **(b)** Answers will vary. Students might mention the Middle East crisis in 1946, the Point Four program, the widespread strikes of 1946, the establishment of the Department of Health, Education, and Welfare, the International Geophysical Year, and the 1958 launch of *Explorer I.*

Applying History Study Skills

Essays will vary.

UNIT THIRTEEN
Into a New Era

40 Domestic Developments

person's vote approximately equal to any other person's vote.

SECTION REVIEW   *(text page 893)*

Suggested responses to the questions are:
1. The following measures were passed to open opportunities for all: Civil Rights Act of 1964, designed to speed up desegregation and to secure for blacks voting and other rights guaranteed in the Constitution; Economic Opportunity Act of 1964, which offered new opportunities to the poor; slum clearance and new housing legislation; expansion of job training programs; a domestic peace corps, VISTA; and a program to help economically distressed communities in Appalachia. Legislation to improve the quality of life for all included Medicare to help insure health care for the elderly; reduced excise taxes on consumer items to stimulate the economy; authorization of funds to improve urban and commuter transit facilities; and a system to protect federally owned wilderness areas.
2. **(a)** Republican Barry M. Goldwater opposed Democrat Lyndon B. Johnson. **(b)** The Republicans suffered a resounding defeat; Johnson won with a larger majority than any other President in over 100 years; and Democrats won substantial victories in Congressional, state, and local elections.
3. Johnson hoped that by removing himself from the Presidential race he would end the division over his Vietnam policies and reduce tensions in the country.

SECTION REVIEW   *(text page 890)*

Suggested responses to the questions are:
1. Democrat John Kennedy opposed Republican Richard Nixon in the 1960 election. The major issues were economic conditions and world prestige. Kennedy won by a narrow margin.
2. **(a)** The Kennedy administration increased the minimum wage to $1.25 an hour. The Area Redevelopment Act of 1961 authorized federal loans and grants to stimulate business and retrain workers in economically depressed areas. Public works expenditures were increased in areas with over 6 percent unemployment. The Manpower Development and Training Act of 1962 authorized a three-year worker retraining program. The Trade Expansion Act of 1962 gave the President the power to raise or lower tariffs by as much as 50 percent to stimulate foreign trade. The Housing Act of 1961 provided long-term loans at low interest rates to stimulate construction of moderate income housing. **(b)** These measures failed to stimulate the economy as much as the administration hoped. Unemployment, in particular, remained a major problem.
3. Kennedy recognized the political and military potential of outer space. He hoped to make the United States dominant in outer space. At the same time, he hoped to kindle a new spirit of national pride and commitment by landing a person on the moon before any other nation did so.
4. **(a)** The Twenty-third Amendment gave residents of the District of Columbia the right to vote in Presidential elections. **(b)** The Twenty-fourth Amendment barred the poll tax as a requirement for voting in federal elections. **(c)** With the "one person, one vote" rule, the Supreme Court held that state legislatures must revise their districts to make them as equal in population as possible, making each

SECTION REVIEW   *(text page 897)*

Suggested responses to the questions are:
1. **(a)** law and order, the Vietnam War, civil liberties, poverty, racial strife, and restoration of states' rights **(b)** Wallace opposed existing welfare programs, the busing of school children, and the federal enforcement of integration. Wallace would give greater power to the police and promised to end the war in Vietnam

by negotiation, or if this failed, to achieve military victory. Nixon promised to restore law, order, and justice. He wanted to revamp the welfare program, and turn over to private enterprise the responsibility for retraining unemployed workers and rebuilding cities. Nixon claimed he would "bring an honorable end to the war," and favored a buildup of the nation's nuclear weapons. Humphrey claimed that the causes of crime — slums, unemployment, run-down schools and houses — should be eliminated. At first he defended the policies of the Johnson administration, but later he advocated a halt to the bombing of North Vietnam.

2. (a) For the first two and a half years, Nixon tried to control inflation in two ways. First, he reduced expenditures for domestic programs. Second, he allowed a policy of increased interest rates on borrowing money. In August 1971 he announced a new economic policy. It called for a 90-day wage and price freeze. Afterward, federal guidelines were placed on wages, prices, and profits. (b) Wage and price controls moderated inflation somewhat, but when controls were eased in 1973, prices rose again.

3. (a) The "new federalism" was Nixon's program for decentralizing the federal government by giving more authority to state and local governments. (b) The revenue sharing plan, which gave the states control of certain programs, was the heart of the "new federalism" program.

4. Answers will vary. Students might mention that legislative action during the Nixon administrations was a battle between the executive and legislative branches.

gal wiretapping and bugging, illegal entry, a secret White House group authorized to violate federal laws in the name of "national security," and receipt of illegal campaign funds. (b) A special Senate committee held hearings in the spring and summer of 1973 to look into possible wrongdoing by the executive branch in the Watergate affair. (c) Newspaper reporters uncovered information that pointed to possible criminal activities by members of the administration. (d) A grand jury sitting in a federal district court gathered evidence about the Watergate scandals and prepared indictments.

3. (a) As the affair dragged on, evidence mounted and numerous White House staff members were indicted and convicted. Then John Dean challenged the President's innocence, and in July 1973, it was discovered that the President had taped important conversations dealing with the affair. When he finally gave up the tapes, his part in the cover-up became known, the House Judiciary Committee approved three Articles of Impeachment, and President Nixon resigned. (b) Nixon made maximum use of his powers as President and seemed to believe he, as President, was above reproach or restraint. He sidestepped the Constitution by giving power to personal aides rather than to cabinet appointees who had to be confirmed by the Senate. He held back information from Congress and the public. He encouraged his Vice President and his staff to attack the press.

SECTION REVIEW   *(text page 900)*

Suggested responses to the questions are:
1. (a) Nixon had some limited success in controlling inflation, was pursuing a policy of withdrawal from Vietnam, and had several other foreign policy achievements to his credit. Furthermore, his opponent, George McGovern, appeared weak and lacking in judgment, and took too extreme a position on the major issues. (b) The victory was called personal because the Republicans failed to gain a significant number of seats in Congress.

2. (a) The Watergate scandals began as an attempted burglary of the Democratic National Committee offices in the Watergate building in Washington, D.C. As the months passed, a tangled web of criminal activities unfolded that appeared to reach into the highest offices of the land. These scandals included evidence of ille-

SECTION REVIEW   *(text page 902)*

Suggested responses to the questions are:
1. (a) President Ford pardoned Richard Nixon to end the bitterness over Watergate, to prevent a long and painful court procedure, and to heal the nation's wounds. (b) Critics argued that a double standard of justice was being applied; those who had taken orders from President Nixon were tried and punished, but Nixon was allowed to go unpunished.

2. (a) Ford tried to control inflation by reducing government expenditures. (b) Ford's efforts to hold inflation down caused a serious decline in industrial output.

3. (a) Ford won a narrow victory over Ronald Reagan at the Republican National Convention in 1976. The Democrats chose Jimmy Carter, whose spectacular primary campaign won him numerous supporters among young, black, and liberal delegates to the convention. (b) The election did not arouse much enthusiasm among the voters. Many remained undecided right up to Election Day.

SECTION REVIEW

(text page 909)

Suggested responses to the questions are:
1. **(a)** For unemployment, Carter called for tax cuts to encourage business investment and thus open up employment opportunities. **(b)** On inflation, Carter urged voluntary controls to curb inflation and set up wage and price guidelines. **(c)** Carter's program met with minimal success. Inflation-fighting measures resulted in a rise in unemployment. By the summer of 1980, the recession was deepening.
2. Carter's economic program failed to yield results; he appeared to vacillate in his determination; his lack of experience was visible, as was his lack of solid support in Congress, even within his own party.
3. President Carter's program called for complete government involvement through incentives and penalties. President Reagan's energy policies reduced government involvement and relied on private business to solve energy problems.
4. The 1984 issues revolved around the economy, taxes, and arms limitation. President Reagan scored an overwhelming victory over Walter Mondale. Reagan received 525 electoral and 53,428,357 popular votes while Mondale received 13 electoral and 36,930,923 popular votes.

CHAPTER 40 REVIEW

(text page 913)

Reviewing Important Terms

1. revenue sharing
2. the energy crisis
3. The deficit
4. inflation
5. pardon
6. supply-side economics

Practicing Critical Thinking Skills

Suggested responses to the questions are:
1. *Kennedy:* space program, Area Redevelopment Act, Housing Act, Trade Expansion Act, Manpower Development and Training Act, and Peace Corps; *Johnson:* Civil Rights Act, Economic Opportunity Act, VISTA, and Medicare; *Nixon:* reduced federal spending, wage and price controls, energy independence, and revenue sharing; *Ford:* reduced government spending; *Carter:* Humphrey-Hawkins Act, business tax cuts, reduced federal spending, establishment of Department of Energy, deregulation of prices of domestically produced gas and oil, and "windfall profits" tax; *Reagan:* tax cuts and reduced federal spending **(a)** The most successful President was Johnson; he understood how to get his program through Congress and had Democratic

majorities in both houses. The least successful was Ford. A Democratic Congress opposed him, and his influence was low since he had not been elected President. **(b)** Effectiveness often has little to do with public approval. Kennedy was publicly admired but had difficulty in getting his legislation through Congress. Johnson left office in a cloud of disapproval over Vietnam but had the most spectacular legislative record. In 1972, Nixon rode a crest of popularity based more on his foreign policy than on his domestic achievements.
2. Answers will vary. Students might point out that legally, at least, democracy has increased through Amendments 23, 24, and 26 to the Constitution, which expanded voting opportunities. Also Supreme Court decisions such as "one person, one vote," and civil rights legislation have increased democracy. They might also point out, however, that in some cases, practice lags behind the letter and spirit of the law.
3. *1960:* national security, international prestige, recession, and unemployment *1964:* civil rights, social legislation and Vietnam *1968:* law and order, Vietnam, civil rights, poverty, racial strife, and states' rights *1972:* Vietnam, inflation, and civil rights *1976:* inflation and unemployment *1980:* inflation, unemployment, military weakness, world image, and government spending *1984:* inflation, unemployment, military spending, the federal deficit, and relations with the Soviet Union **(a)** The problems of poverty, unemployment, and civil rights were key issues from 1964 to 1972; inflation became a continual concern beginning in 1968; Vietnam was an issue between 1964 and 1976; and unemployment was an issue in 1960, 1976, and 1980. **(b)** The economic issues and the civil rights issue were attacked in each administration but no legislative program succeeded in solving these complex problems.
4. Answers will vary. Students might argue that the President should shape government policy because the President is viewed as the government leader. Other students might see Congress as the key to shaping policy because it is the law-making, or policy-making, branch of government.
5. The style and artistry of televised campaign commercials have an important persuasive power. The up-to-the-minute coverage of voting trends and results may also have a persuasive effect. Major networks have been asked to refrain from reporting voting results and from projecting winners until polls close throughout the country.
6. **(a)** Both Presidents Carter and Reagan included tax cuts in their economic programs. Reagan's 1981 tax cut bill provided a larger tax decrease than Carter's cuts. Carter tried to fight inflation

with voluntary wage and price controls, by raising the value of the dollar, by attempting to reduce the unfavorable balance of trade, and by reducing federal spending. Reagan also planned to reduce federal spending. Reagan withdrew, however, federal controls and sanctions, saying he felt that free enterprise was the best solution to the nation's economic problems. **(b)** Answers will vary. Students might argue that President Carter's proposals met with some success. The general opinion, however, was that Carter's program did not successfully solve the complex economic problems the nation faced. **(c)** Answers will vary. Students might mention that inflation slowed under President Reagan.

Developing History Study Skills

(a) 62 percent for Reagan and 38 percent for Mondale **(b)** 11 percent for Reagan and 89 percent for Mondale **(c)** Mondale received more votes from urban areas. Reagan received more votes in suburban and rural areas. **(d)** Reagan **(e)** blue-collar workers **(f)** Blacks voted most consistently for one candidate. Mondale received 89 percent of the black vote. **(g)** Answers will vary. Students might conclude that the typical Reagan voter was a white-collar, white male who lived in the suburbs or in a rural area. **(h)** Answers will vary.

Relating Geography and History

Students' maps will vary. Student's charts should resemble the charts below.

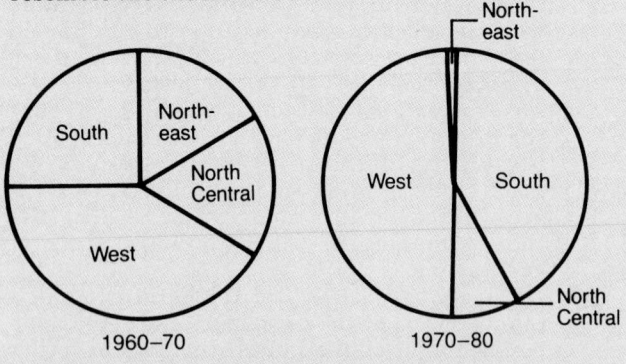

1960–70   1970–80

Answers will vary. Students might draw conclusions such as the following about population trends in the decade 1970–80.

The South and West regions will continue to gain population.
The Northeast region will begin to lose population. There will be little or no population change in the North Central region.

A New Role in World Affairs

SECTION REVIEW   *(text page 918)*

Suggested responses to the questions are:
1. **(a)** The solid front of the Communist nations began to crack, as evidenced by the Sino-Soviet dispute and split. **(b)** The non-Communist world also showed signs of strain, as some nations bridled under American leadership. France pulled out of NATO, for example. **(c)** Third World nations, now the majority in the United Nations, could apply pressure to both the United States and the Soviet Union.
2. The Soviet Union was installing missiles in Cuba. President Kennedy ordered the United States Navy to blockade, or "quarantine," Cuba. He also demanded that the Soviet Union dismantle the missile bases and withdraw Soviet missiles from Cuba. Confronted with the choice between nuclear war or meeting Kennedy's demands, Khrushchev backed down.
3. **(a)** Alliance members agreed to undertake a ten-year program to improve social and economic conditions in Latin America. Although some progress was made, the results were disappointing. Congress began to cut back America's budget for the Alliance, since much of the money did not go to the masses of poor people. **(b)** A revolution plunged the Dominican Republic into chaos. The United States sent marines and other troops to end the bloodshed. After the O.A.S. sent a small force to maintain order and a provisional president was appointed, American armed forces withdrew.
4. **(a)** The United States feared the influence of Communist China in Asia and attempted to ensure pro-Western governments by pouring millions of dollars in military aid into Laos, Cambodia, and Vietnam. **(b)** The policy failed—Laos chose a neutral government and Cambodia asked for the withdrawal of American personnel in 1963.

SECTION REVIEW   *(text page 923)*

Suggested responses to the questions are:
1. American military advisers had been in Viet-

nam since Eisenhower's administration. By the end of 1964 their number had increased to 23,000, but they were still not authorized to engage in combat. President Johnson announced on August 4, 1964, that two American destroyers had been attacked and Congress subsequently adopted the Gulf of Tonkin Resolution. Johnson ordered the bombing of North Vietnam in February 1965. In March 1965, Americans were committed to active combat; by the end of 1965 nearly 125,000 Americans had been committed. Attempts were made to negotiate with Hanoi, but, as these ended in failure, the United States responded with more bombing and more troops. By 1968 American forces numbered 540,000. In March of 1968 President Johnson limited the bombing of North Vietnam and peace talks began in Paris in May 1968.

2. **(a)** The Tet offensive was a massive military push by the Viet Cong and North Vietnamese soldiers against South Vietnam. It occurred during the lunar New Year holidays in February 1968. **(b)** The Communist forces gained control of large areas of the countryside; several cities lay in ruins; thousands of soldiers and civilians were killed; Johnson limited American bombing attacks; peace negotiations began.

3. Opponents charged that American involvement was unconstitutional because Congress had not declared war; that the war was a civil conflict in which the United States should play no part; and that the United States was destroying the nation it was seeking to save.

4. The Gulf of Tonkin Resolution justified American involvement because of the attack on American naval vessels, and North Vietnam's "systematic campaign of aggression" against its neighbors and their allies, including the United States. Therefore, the United States was justified in defending its forces and its allies.

SECTION REVIEW   *(text page 929)*

Suggested responses to the questions are:
1. **(a)** American troops were gradually withdrawn as the South Vietnamese demonstrated that they were able to defend themselves. In the spring of 1970, American and South Vietnamese troops crossed into Cambodia to destroy Viet Cong sanctuaries. American troops continued to be gradually withdrawn during President Nixon's first term, but heavy American bombing continued. Finally, a cease-fire was arranged at the Paris peace talks. **(b)** By the terms of the 1973 agreement (1) the continued military presence of North Vietnam was tacitly recognized; (2) South Vietnam was assured that it was to have a government of its own choosing;

and (3) the United States guaranteed continued economic and military aid to South Vietnam. **(c)** The conflict between North and South Vietnam ended when the North defeated the South and annexed the country.

2. President Nixon visited the communist People's Republic of China in 1972. This opened the first diplomatic exchange by the leaders of these two nations in 20 years. President Nixon visited the Soviet Union in 1972 and met with the Soviet leaders. Nixon and Brezhnev declared they had reached agreement on a number of important issues. They signed an agreement to limit nuclear armaments. With this policy the United States and the Soviet Union and Communist China began to move away from the confrontations of the cold war.

3. Ford generally followed the Nixon policies, as evidenced by his retention of Henry Kissinger as Secretary of State.

SECTION REVIEW   *(text page 933)*

Suggested responses to the questions are:
1. Carter hoped to prevent any power from imposing its social system on other nations, improve relations with allies, promote human rights throughout the world, and advance arms controls.

2. **(a)** The Panama Canal treaties returned complete control of the canal to Panama by the year 2000. **(b)** Many Americans objected to the "surrender" of national property and to the possible threat to American security posed by the loss of the canal.

3. **(a)** President Carter invited Begin and Sadat to Camp David, Maryland, for peace talks. With Carter's help, the negotiations ended in a peace treaty. **(b)** Unresolved problems included disposition of lands won by Israel in war and Palestinian self-determination in the Gaza strip and the West Bank areas.

4. Shah Pahlevi, repressive ruler of Iran but friend of the United States, was overthrown by a coalition of forces led by Ayatollah Khomeini. The Shah, seriously ill, was admitted to the United States for medical treatment. The Iranian militants seized 53 American hostages to be held until the Shah was returned for trial. The hostages were eventually released though the Shah was not turned over to the Iranians.

SECTION REVIEW   *(text page 937)*

Suggested responses to the questions are:
1. Reagan's main objective in foreign policy was to halt the expansion of communism.

2. **(a)** Reagan said it was necessary to ship missiles to Europe in order to counter the threat from the Soviet Union. **(b)** Some allies of the United States objected to their countries becoming the battleground in a dispute between the United States and the Soviet Union.
3. **(a)** Israel invaded Lebanon in an attempt to stop terrorist attacks by PLO members based in Lebanon. **(b)** The United States was among the countries that participated in an international force sent to Lebanon intended to ensure the safety of retreating members of the PLO.
4. El Salvador and the United States remained on friendly terms because both countries have an anti-communist viewpoint and a capitalist economic system. Tension arose between Nicaragua and the United States because Nicaragua's leaders expressed allegiance to Communist ideas and sought close ties with Cuba and the Soviet Union.

CHAPTER 41 REVIEW   *(text page 941)*

Reviewing Important Terms

1. true
2. true
3. true
4. false, cease-fire agreement
5. false, détente
6. true
7. true
8. false, martial law

Practicing Critical Thinking Skills

Suggested responses to the questions are:
1. **(a)** The policy of détente sought to improve relations with Communist China and the Soviet Union. Personal visits to Communist China opened a dialogue between the two nations. Personal visits to the Soviet Union sought to relax tensions, work out areas of agreement, and begin limiting nuclear armaments. This policy sought to move away from the confrontations of the cold war into an era of cooperation and relaxing tensions. **(b)** The growing hostility between the Soviet Union and China caused both of them to seek friendship with the United States. **(c)** The Arab–Israeli War threatened to bring the superpowers in on opposing sides.
2. **(a)** The United States committed itself to Southeast Asia to preserve or establish free governments, to contain the Communists' power, and to maintain its position in the world. **(b)** Kennedy sent military advisers to South Vietnam; Johnson ordered the bombing of North Vietnam following the Gulf of Tonkin Resolution; and Nixon focused on withdrawing troops and following a policy of Vietnamization, which finally ended the American involvement in the Vietnam War.
3. **(a)** Vietnamese life was dislocated by widespread devastation and human misery. **(b)** Growing numbers of Americans began to believe that American involvement in the Vietnam War was a mistake, and the public was violently divided over American involvement. Many Americans began to challenge the size of the nation's defense budgets. Inflation became a growing problem, partly as a result of enormous military expenditures.
4. **(a)** It gives the President the power to take all necessary measures to repel attack on United States forces. **(b)** attack of United States naval vessels by naval units of North Vietnam **(c)** The invasion of South Vietnam by North Vietnamese and Viet Cong soldiers was considered aggressive action against United States forces and allies. **(d)** Answers will vary. Students might feel that the President should have the power to counter any armed attack on United States forces.
5. **(a)** The newly emerging nations of Africa were fertile ground for ideological and economic competition between the superpowers. In the Angolan civil war, the Soviets trained and supplied Cuban troops to assist the pro-Communist forces there. Lack of decisive United States response encouraged the Soviets to follow a similar policy elsewhere in Africa. **(b)** The Soviets sent military and some economic aid to the Arabs in their continual conflict with Israel. The United States tried to strike a balance between economic aid to the oil-rich Arab countries and military aid to its ally, Israel. The United States and the Soviet Union have teetered on the brink of confrontation several times over the Middle East.
6. **(a)** Answers will vary. Students might mention Lebanon, El Salvador, Nicaragua, Honduras, Cuba, the Middle East, and Eastern Europe. **(b)** Answers will vary. Students might mention that much of the trouble results from the communism-democracy rivalry. Some trouble arises from the problems of newly independent nations. Both these sources can be traced to the situation of the 1960's and 1970's.

Developing History Study Skills

(a) the United Nations **(b)** The paragraphs answer the questions in the following ways: who — President Reagan; what — the proposal to begin arms limitations talks; when — today; where — in a speech at the U.N.; why — "there is no sane alternative." **(c)** Answers will vary. Students might suggest: "Reagan proposes arms talks." **(d)** Answers will vary.

Relating Geography and History

1. Students should include the following items on their lists: the Soviet-Communist Chinese split, 1964; the Congo crisis, 1960; the Bay of Pigs invasion, 1961; the Cuban missile crisis, 1962; the Dominican Republican revolution, 1965; the Berlin crisis, 1961; the Vietnam conflict, 1954 to 1973; the United States bombing of Cambodia, 1970; the Middle East conflicts, 1948 to the present; the Soviet invasion of Afghanistan, 1980; the shooting down of a Korean airliner, 1983; the situations in El Salvador, Nicaragua, and Grenada, 1980 to the present.
2. The Congo crisis, Cuban missile crisis, and Berlin crisis should be circled in red. (Some students may include the invasion of Afghanistan and the downing of the Korean jet.)
3. Answers will vary. Students might observe that confrontations between communism and democracy have happened all over the world.

CHAPTER

42 Reaching for Freedom's Promise

SECTION REVIEW   *(text page 946)*

Suggested responses to the questions are:
1. (a) The Southwest has steadily gained in population. (b) The Northeast has lost population to the Sunbelt. (c) The population of rural areas dropped sharply from 1960 to 1980. (d) Suburbs have spread out from city centers, creating huge metropolitan areas.
2. The Immigration and Nationality Act increased the number of immigrants admitted to the United States annually, especially those from other Western Hemisphere nations. In the years following its passage, a sharp increase in the number of Hispanic and Asian immigrants entering the United States occurred.
3. Urban renewal programs did not reach into old and decaying city residential areas; the middle class left the inner cities for the suburbs; many property owners ceased to maintain their inner city property; the poor and the immigrants settled in the decaying cities; and costs of running the cities and meeting human needs rose while the tax base declined.

SECTION REVIEW   *(text page 952)*

Suggested responses to the questions are:
1. The Supreme Court declared segregated schools unconstitutional in 1954; ordered an end to racially segregated schools "at once" in 1969; and ordered busing to end de facto segregation in the early 1970's. Congress passed a series of civil rights acts. The 1957, 1960, and 1965 acts protected black voting rights; the 1964 act prohibited racial discrimination in employment and public accommodations; and the 1968 act provided for open housing and extended federal protection to civil rights workers.
2. Blacks organized to take direct action in breaking down segregation through sit-ins, freedom marches, and boycotts. They registered black voters and got them to the polls. Frustration and violence led to the formation of some militant organizations, like the Black Panthers, which advocated force. Most black Americans preferred the nonviolent methods of Martin Luther King, Jr. In the 1970's, the emphasis turned from civil rights to economic opportunity, with black leaders urging programs such as affirmative action.
3. (a) Affirmative action programs are designed to make up for past discrimination that put blacks and other minorities at a disadvantage. (b) Some people oppose them because the programs do not represent the ideal of equal justice and opportunity for all. Opponents charge that affirmative action is really reverse discrimination.
4. The economic changes occurring during the Carter and Reagan administrations hit minorities especially hard. For example, while the national average for unemployment was about 12 percent, unemployment for blacks was more than 20 percent at times.
5. The two major pieces of federal legislation passed to ensure equal rights for handicapped persons were the Rehabilitation Act and the Education for All Handicapped Children Act.

SECTION REVIEW   *(text page 955)*

Suggested responses to the questions are:
1. (a) Mexican Americans have often been migrant farm laborers. They have met discrimination in housing, employment, and education. (b) Chicanos have followed the patterns set by black Americans. They have demonstrated, have worked to get Chicanos to vote, have used boycotts and sit-ins, and have sued in court for fair treatment. (c) Chicanos have made some progress in educational opportunities, bilingual programs, and political influence.

2. **(a)** The Puerto Ricans were concentrated in New York City and other cities of the Northeast, whereas the Mexican Americans were spread over a much larger area. Both faced similar problems of unemployment and discrimination. **(b)** Both groups organized politically to gain some of their demands. Some Puerto Rican groups have demanded independence for the commonwealth, but the voters in Puerto Rico have voted to reject that proposal.
3. **(a)** When Castro announced his plans to make Cuba a Communist society, many Cubans began to flee their homeland. In 1980 serious conditions in Cuba encouraged another flood of emigration, resulting in the "Freedom Flotilla." **(b)** The program provides welfare assistance, vocational training, health care, and aid in relocation to various parts of the United States.

SECTION REVIEW   *(text page 957)*

Suggested responses to the questions are:
1. **(a)** Indians have written books to educate the rest of the United States about their tragic history; have organized the fight for Indian rights; have resorted to violence on several occasions; and have relied on education and court action to gain their ends. **(b)** Each of these methods has had some success; court action and education have probably been the most effective of these methods because they provide more lasting relief for the problems the Indians face.
2. **(a)** President Nixon asked Congress to end the termination policy and substitute "self-determination." The Nixon policy provided for government assistance in housing, vocational training, and economic development. **(b)** Congress did not pass the necessary supporting legislation. The policy was only partially carried out; but the policy of termination did end.
3. Indians now make up a majority of employees in the Bureau of Indian Affairs. Their population continues to grow, and they have succeeded in getting schools and colleges to teach about the role of Indians in American history. Some tribes have also had some success in the courts and recovered some land lost to them, and many individuals have begun to share in the benefits and wealth of American society.

SECTION REVIEW   *(text page 961)*

Suggested responses to the questions are:
1. **(a)** Some of the goals of the women's rights movement include equal treatment in educational

programs, establishment of publicly financed childcare centers, repeal of state laws forbidding abortion, and passage of the Equal Rights Act of 1964 forbidding discrimination based on sex in employment and promotion practices. **(b)** By the mid-1970's women comprised 50 percent of the labor force but received wages that were only 60 percent of those received by men doing the same work. Also, few women were able to advance to high-level positions. The participation by women in the civil rights movement gave them confidence and experience to carry on their own struggle.
2. Many American women accepted their traditional roles of wives and mothers. Moreover, some feared that programs such as the ERA would result in women being drafted, in losing protection in the workplace, and in losing the right to alimony. Many feared the breakdown of traditional family bonds.

CHAPTER 42 REVIEW   *(text page 963)*

Reviewing Important Terms

1. true
2. false, white flight
3. false, Affirmative action
4. true
5. false, *de facto* segregation

Practicing Critical Thinking Skills

Suggested responses to the questions are:
1. The people of the United States live longer as a result of advances in medical science. This fact, coupled with zero population growth, is resulting in a society with a predominantly adult population. Americans also became increasingly mobile in this period. Mobility resulted in new patterns of living and a redistribution of the population. About 75 percent of the nation's population lives in urban-metropolitan areas, with the wealthy and middle class concentrated in the sprawling suburbs and the poor in the inner cities. Another major distribution trend is from the older and colder North and Northeast to the Sunbelt.
2. **(a)** These minority groups have all had to struggle to gain jobs, decent housing, educational opportunities, and political power. **(b)** While they share general problems, each has specific problems. Blacks face historical and racial discrimination; Hispanics must deal with language and cultural barriers; and Indians suffer from inconsistent and poorly managed government policies. **(c)** Answers will vary. Students might

mention that many people do not view women or handicapped persons as minorities.

3. Women face many of the discriminatory practices in education, employment, and job advancement that have plagued minority groups.

4. (a) Moderates are willing to take the slower path of court suits, legislation, and public education. (b) Militants want swift action and are more likely to use confrontation tactics. (c) Militant black groups such as the Black Panthers advised separatism and, if necessary, force. The moderates opposed these tactics, fearing they would alienate most citizens. The split resulted in a loss of power and momentum. (d) The actions of Indian militants not only caused a break in the movement's unity but resulted in a less than sympathetic implementation of the new self-determination policy of the Nixon administration.

5. (a) Many women believed that the ERA would deprive them of more than it gave them. Some women believed ERA would help to destroy the traditional bonds of the family. (b) Because of changing social patterns, more women are in the labor force and heading families and expect equality and respect. (c) Answers will vary.

6. (a) While the federal government continues to support some urban programs, much of the burden of these programs has shifted to state and local governments. (b) Employment, housing, and other activities must still meet federal guidelines, but affirmative action programs have faded since the Supreme Court decision in the Bakke case. (c) Federal guidelines for school desegregation must still be filed annually to qualify for federal funds.

Developing History Study Skills

(a) New York and Rhode Island lost population. They are in the Northeast. (b) Pennsylvania and Massachusetts had the smallest increase. They are in the Northeast. (c) New Hampshire, South Carolina, Florida, Texas, Wyoming, Colorado, New Mexico, Arizona, Hawaii, Alaska, Utah, Nevada, Idaho, Oregon, and Washington show increases of more than 20 percent. They are in the Northeast, the South, and the West. (d) Americans are moving South and West. Most southern and western states have large increases. (e) Massachusetts, Rhode Island, Connecticut, New Jersey, New York, and Pennsylvania in the Northeast (f) the Northeast (g) The major urban areas would be in the South and the West. Answers to the second part of the question will vary.

Relating Geography and History

1. (a) A Metropolitan Statistical Area (MSA) consists of a large population center and the adja-cent communities that are economically and socially connected to the population center. (b) In many cases the core city lost population. In other instances minorities and the poor replaced the people who had moved to the suburbs. (c) Retail outlets lost business and eventually reduced their size or closed completely. Many business offices went through the same process as their labor supply and clientele moved. (d) Many businesses moved to the suburbs. Retail outlets opened in suburban malls and office buildings were built outside the central city.

2. (a) New York City, Los Angeles, Chicago, Philadelphia, Detroit, Baltimore, San Diego, Dallas, Houston and San Antonio (b) San Diego and San Antonio (c) population shifts to the Sunbelt, growth of the petroleum industry, immigration from Mexico, and other economic and social factors

CHAPTER

43 Into the Future

SECTION REVIEW *(text page 970)*

Suggested responses to the questions are:

1. Dramatic advances in medical science include artificial skin, mechanical hearts, and laser-beam operations. As a result, Americans live longer. Computer technology, still in its infancy, guides automated assembly lines, helps balance the family checkbook, and provides leisure activities. The use of computers may also mean the loss of jobs for some American workers and a threat to an individual's right to privacy.

2. (a) Education was faced with lowered standardized test scores, which indicated a decline in the quality of education; overcrowded school buildings; a loss of qualified teachers; soaring costs; drug abuse; and a disrespect for authority among students. (b) In response, some states and school districts adopted tougher academic standards, increased the number of credits required for high-school graduation, and instituted stricter disciplinary codes.

3. From the New Deal on, the federal government

had grown enormously. It constantly increased its involvement and, some felt, its interference, in American lives. President Reagan believed that the size of government and its enormous expenditures were at the root of American economic problems. He called for sharp reductions in federal programs.

4. (a) Throughout the 1970's and the 1980's, Americans became more concerned with earning a living and becoming better educated. The 1980's witnessed a strong return to traditional values. (b) Many Americans feared that people were losing sight of traditional American goals and purposes.

SECTION REVIEW   *(text page 975)*

Suggested responses to the questions are:

1. Heavy government spending drives prices up and feeds inflation. When the government spends more than it earns in taxes, it must borrow the difference, causing further inflation. Government can slow down inflation by reducing its expenditures, increasing taxes to lessen consumers' purchasing power, and raising interest rates to slow borrowing.

2. Rival industrial nations such as Japan and Germany improved their technology and their efficiency. Thus they successfully competed with United States industries, gaining a sizable share of both international markets and the American domestic market.

3. (a) OPEC's sharp boosts in oil prices pushed the United States inflation rate even higher. (b) Nixon imposed mandatory wage and price freezes, but Carter called for voluntary wage and price freezes. Nixon increased interest rates to slow inflation while Carter increased federal spending and cut taxes to reduce unemployment. (c) Reagan cut federal spending in areas other than defense and reduced both personal and corporate taxes to encourage saving and investment. Increased investment in business and industry was intended to increase goods and services, stabilize prices, and create jobs.

4. An increasing budget deficit might raise interest rates and make less money available for investment.

SECTION REVIEW   *(text page 980)*

Suggested responses to the questions are:
1. The United States faced an energy crisis when

many foreign oil-producing nations formed OPEC in order to control world oil prices, when OPEC retaliated against the United States' support of Israel by placing an embargo on oil shipments to the United States, and when the Iranian revolution cut off oil shipments to the United States.

2. Presidents Carter and Reagan agreed that the United States must not depend upon foreign oil imports and that conservation methods were essential. Both supported deregulation of domestic oil prices; Carter to encourage conservation, Reagan to encourage the search for oil. President Carter urged substantial government support to help develop new energy sources, a return to greater use of coal, and research to develop synthetic fuels and solar energy. President Reagan has supported the search for new sources of conventional energy. He has not committed the government to research and development of synthetic fuels and solar energy and has favored heavy cuts in federal support for these programs.

3. (a) American industry and consumers turned to smaller, more fuel-efficient cars and took steps to make homes and home appliances more energy efficient. Americans adjusted thermostats to conserve energy used for heating and cooling. Industry also adopted more fuel-efficient methods and machines for production. (b) Coal, natural gas, nuclear power, hydroelectric power, and solar energy are being used in the United States today. (c) Coal is abundant and can be made into synthetic fuels. However, pit mining is dangerous to the lives and health of workers, strip mining adversely affects the environment, and acid rain from burned coal pollutes air and water. Natural gas may last well into the future if deep-well reserves are tapped and may be a potential substitute for gasoline. Nuclear energy is efficient but dangerous, as evidenced by the Three Mile Island accident, and generates dangerous wastes that require storing. Hydroelectricity is environmentally safe but limited in its potential. Solar energy is the best hope because it is inexhaustible and safe. However, the technology is still in the early stages of development.

SECTION REVIEW   *(text page 983)*

Suggested responses to the questions are:
1. (a) Burning and burial have been commonly used methods for disposing of waste materials. (b) Burning can release pollutants and deadly fumes into the air; wastes can seep out of burial sites to pollute the soil and the groundwater.
2. The federal government created the Environ-

mental Protection Agency and, often along with state and local governments, passed laws to regulate the use of pesticides, insecticides, and other dangerous sprays. Congress took measures to preserve and protect threatened wildlife, mandated pollution controls on motor vehicles, created an emergency fund for the cleanup of hazardous waste dumps, and set aside more wilderness preserves.

3. President Regan has decreased the federal government's involvement through cuts in the budget of the Environmental Protection Agency and has favored cutting back and simplifying environmental regulations. He has departed from earlier administrations' focus on the acquisition of more parks and wilderness areas, and has encouraged the use of federal lands for mineral exploration. In general, he has held that private industry and citizens should assume more responsibility for protecting the environment.

CHAPTER 43 REVIEW   *(text page 986)*

Reviewing Important Terms

1. false, beams of light   4. true
2. true   5. true
3. false, stagflation   6. true

Practicing Critical Thinking Skills

Suggested responses to the questions are:

1. Computers seem to dominate American life today. They are the storehouse for the knowledge explosion in science and technology. Computers guide robots on assembly lines, print our newspapers, record medical information, balance our checkbooks, and entertain us with electronic games. They are not, however, an unmixed blessing. Advances in computer technology may mean loss of jobs for some people. The use of computers to gather and store information about individuals is also a potential problem. In the wrong hands, such technology could deprive Americans of their traditional right to privacy.

2. **(a)** When Reagan became President, the most pressing problem was inflation, which had hit a high of 18 percent during the election campaign. Government spending seemed to be out of control; foreign business outproduced and undersold American business in domestic and foreign markets; and the American standard of living, once the highest in the world, had dropped to fifth. **(b)** Unemployment and inflation are being fought with the removal of sanctions and curbs to permit the free enterprise system to "work." Government spending is being limited with reduced financial support of selected programs.

3. World economics are inextricably linked through trade exchanges and currency. Dependence on fossil fuels and the inflation because of rising oil prices have affected the economies of developed and developing nations alike. The United States needs foreign resources and markets; other nations need to sell their products to America. The oil crunch of the 1970's showed clearly how events elsewhere in the world can adversely affect the nation's economy. While the United States must solve some of its domestic problems alone, it must also be aware of the broader problems affecting the world and cooperate to solve them.

4. **(a)** Oil: *advantages* — available, widespread present use, *disadvantages* — limited supply, pollution; natural gas: *advantages* — available, little pollution, *disadvantages* — expensive conversion, limited supply; coal: *advantages* — plentiful supply, relatively inexpensive, *disadvantages* — pollution, limited applications; nuclear: *advantages* — high output from small fuel supply, *disadvantages* — potential dangers, limited application at present; solar: *advantages* — plentiful supply, relatively inexpensive, clean, *disadvantages* — cost of conversion. **(b,c)** Answers will vary.

5. **(a)** The amazing economic growth of the United States has caused increasing pollution of air, water, and soil. In addition, several worldwide developments have caused a growing threat to the environment. World population has been nearly doubling every 35 years. Also, the economic systems of the industrialized nations have been based upon the assumption of continuous economic growth. Moreover, people in the underdeveloped nations need, and have begun to demand, a share of the food, clothing, shelter, and comforts of life enjoyed by the developed nations. **(b)** The United States has begun seeking new energy sources. Federal, state, and local governments have passed laws to conserve resources and to protect the environment.

6. **(a)** The goals are to explore the unknown and to insure national security. **(b)** Answers will vary. Students might contend that exploration of the unknown will lead to discoveries that will unlock earth's mysteries.

7. **(a)** The vast technological and scientific changes have improved ways of life throughout the world; yet, they have also improved our abilities to destroy the world. **(b)** Answers will vary. Students might mention that the dangers of nuclear war are so severe that we must educate people to their dangers. Others might mention that we must educate people to conserve energy or face catastrophe.

8. **(a)** Answers will vary. Students might mention that the Indians lived close to nature while European settlers cut timber, cleared land, and dammed streams with little regard to the natural habitat. **(b)** Answers will vary. Most students will agree.

Developing History Study Skills

1. the Consumer Price Index
2. 1980, 1972
3. It rose eight percent. Inflation was high.
4. It decreased 5.5 percent. Inflation was low.
5. It was smallest in 1983–1984. Inflation was low.
6. Answers will vary. Students might choose 1983 because wages were higher and inflation was low.

Relating Geography and History

1. **(a)** They went up. **(b)** Americans reduced use of oil and developed alternative sources.
2. Temperatures in the winter are higher and the need for fuel oil is small.
3. **(a)** Nevada, Florida, Texas, Hawaii, Arizona, New Mexico, Idaho, Colorado, Utah, Wyoming, Alaska, and Oregon **(b)** New York and Rhode Island **(c)** Sunbelt states have gained representatives while Snowbelt states have lost representatives in Congress. **(d)** People would not be compelled to leave.

UNIT 13 REVIEW *(text page 987)*

Discussing Ideas

1. Development and use of some alternative energy sources might harm the environment through mining and pollution.
2. Answers will vary. Students might mention the deaths of United States Marines in Lebanon to show that the nation has assumed too much world responsibility.
3. **(a)** newly independent nations aligned neither with the United States or the Soviet Union **(b)** The two superpowers competed for the allegiance of Third World nations, causing numerous confrontations.

4. **(a)** All four were based primarily on social programs. **(b)** Each plan focused on a different problem area. For example, much of the Fair Deal aimed at labor problems while the Great Society aimed at poverty.
5. See the following chart. Answers will vary.

	Blacks	Hispanics	Indians	Women
(a) Problems	Prejudice Discrimination Poverty	Prejudice Discrimination Poverty Language barrier	Prejudice Discrimination Poverty Loss of cultural identity	Discrimination
(b) Goals	Equal rights Equal economic, political, and social status	Equal rights Equal economic, political, and social status	Cultural integrity Reduced dependence on government programs	Equal rights
(c) Methods	Sit-ins Marches Demonstrations Legal action Riots	Demonstrations Political and legal action	Demonstrations Legal action Violence	Demonstrations Legal action
(d) Degree of Success	Answers will vary.	Answers will vary.	Answers will vary.	Answers will vary.

6. Answers will vary. Students might select President Reagan because he has reduced inflation and unemployment, and he has cut taxes while promoting pride in the United States.

Applying History Study Skills

(a) This is a standard news story because it presents a report of facts about its topic. **(b)** soil erosion **(c)** a report by the Worldwatch Institute **(d)** The statistics are used to illustrate the size of the problem **(e)** Answers will vary. Students might be surprised and distraught to learn that 25 billion tons of topsoil disappear annually.

Triumph
of the
American
Nation

Lewis Paul Todd

Merle Curti

Educational Consultants

Phillip Bacon
Professor of Geography
University of Houston
Houston, Texas

Gloria S. Sesso
District Social Studies Supervisor
Half Hollow Hills School District
Dix Hills, Long Island, New York

Triumph
of the
American
Nation

Lewis Paul Todd

Merle Curti

HBJ HARCOURT BRACE JOVANOVICH, PUBLISHERS

Orlando   San Diego   Chicago   Dallas

AUTHORS

Lewis Paul Todd has acquired national distinction as a writer and teacher of American history and related subjects. Dr. Todd is widely known among social studies teachers for his textbook writing and for his many articles and editorials in social studies journals, especially *Social Education,* the official journal of the National Council for the Social Studies, which Dr. Todd edited for many years.

Merle Curti is Frederick Jackson Turner Professor of American History, Emeritus, at the University of Wisconsin (Madison). He has lectured at many American colleges, at Cambridge University, and at the University of Tokyo. Professor Curti has been president of the American Historical Association, the highest honor a historian in the United States can receive. He also has been granted many awards for distinguished scholarship and historical writing, among them the Pulitzer Prize in history for *The Growth of American Thought.*

CURRICULUM CONSULTANTS

Phyllis A. Bailey
Office of Social Studies
Baltimore County Public Schools
Towson, Maryland

Brenda Clack
Teacher
Flint Schools of Choice
Flint, Michigan

Marv Elbert
Social Studies Coordinator
District U-46
Elgin, Illinois

Randall G. Felton
High School Curriculum Coordinator
Leon County District Schools
Tallahassee, Florida

Vivian Gluck
Assistant Principal
Supervision Social Studies
Stuyvesant High School
New York, New York

Sara Katz
Teacher
East High School
Denver, Colorado

William Kirtley
Teacher
Medford Senior High School
Medford, Oregon

Norma J. Peters
Supervisor of Social Studies
Roanoke County Public Schools
Salem, Virginia

Gary Smuts
Department Head of Social Studies
Cerritos High School
Cerritos, California

Note: This work is a revision of RISE OF THE AMERICAN NATION, LIBERTY EDITION by Lewis Paul Todd and Merle Curti, copyright © 1982, 1977, 1972, 1969, 1966, 1964, 1961, copyright 1950 by Harcourt Brace Jovanovich, Inc.

Some of the material in this work previously appeared in THE AMERICAN NATION: RECONSTRUCTION TO THE PRESENT by Lewis Paul Todd and Merle Curti, copyright © 1986 by Harcourt Brace Jovanovich, Inc.

PRINTED IN THE UNITED STATES OF AMERICA ISBN 0-15-375941-0

ACKNOWLEDGMENTS

For permission to reprint copyrighted material, grateful acknowledgment is made to the following sources: *The Atlantic Monthly:* From "Letters From the Dust Bowl" by Caroline A. Henderson. Copyright © 1936 by Caroline A. Henderson. Originally published in *The Atlantic Monthly. Barnes & Noble, Inc.:* From "An Account of the Province of Carolina by Samuel Wilson, 1682" (Retitled: "Carolina, 1682") from *Narratives of Early Carolina, 1650–1708,* edited by Alexander S. Salley, Jr. Published by Charles Scribner's Sons.

Continued on page 1058

CONTENTS

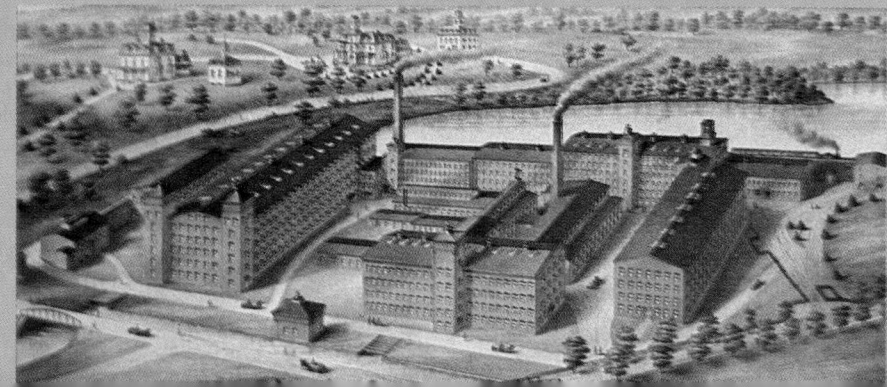

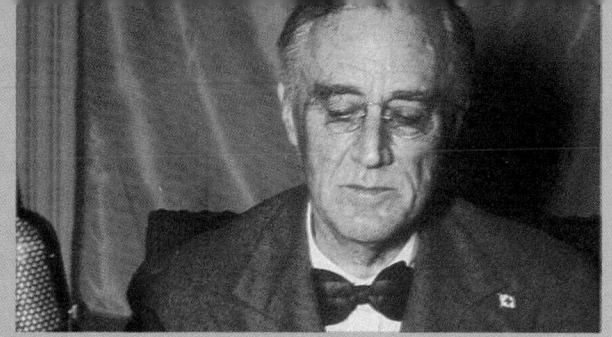

Update

Challenges of the Future   (1984 to the Present)   1061

AMERICANA

AMERICAN PROFILES

DECISIVE MOMENTS

THIS CHANGING LAND

DEVELOPING HISTORY STUDY SKILLS

SOURCES

CHARTS, TABLES, AND GRAPHS

MAPS

REFERENCE SECTION

See list of Multimedia Materials in TMRG, p.TM13.
See Making Connections, text p. 99.

UNIT ONE

Building the Colonies

The vast continents of North America and South America lie between two oceans. For many years there were no human inhabitants in the Americas. The continents were the realm of the wildlife that freely roamed the land. The Americas became inhabited more than 25,000 years ago when the first nomadic hunters came from Asia to North America. Their descendents spread throughout the American continents and populated the land. As the centuries passed, the Americas were "discovered" by other adventurers and explorers. It was not until after the defeat of the Spanish Armada in 1588, pictured below, that Great Britain, beginning its rise to world power, established an arm of its empire in the Americas. By 1763 the British had defeated their international rivals and gained control of North America.

CHAPTER 1 Exploring the Americas

(Beginnings to 1624)

A Mayan
pyramid

In this day and age *Discovery, Columbia,* and *Atlantis* shuttle astronauts into space. Satellites photograph the earth from incredible distances. With the marvels of communication that exist, it is hard to imagine that there was a time in the 1400's when people on one continent did not know that people on another continent existed. The people who lived in Europe and the people who lived in the Americas did not know that either group existed. People in Africa knew little about Europe and nothing about the Americas. Nonetheless, Europeans, Africans, and Native Americans found their lives intertwined.

By the 1400's the native peoples of the Americas had developed many varied ways of life. Some of their cultures were highly advanced. The same was true of the peoples of Africa. The people of Europe were just entering a period of rapid development. They were building powerful new nations. They were also beginning to push beyond such barriers as the Atlantic Ocean to discover, what were to them, new lands. In their search, Europeans were to act as the agents of change for both Africans and Native Americans, and for many Europeans as well.

Europeans would push into the Americas and disrupt the lives of Native Americans. Europeans would carry the practice of slavery with them to the Americas. In the process they would cause thousands of Africans to be enslaved and uprooted from their homeland. By the early 1600's thriving colonies had been established throughout the Americas.

READING FOCUS

This chapter discusses the 1400's and 1500's, characterizing the two centuries as periods of conflict and change. As you read about the dying of one age and the birth of another, look for the details that support each of the following statements.

1. The first Americans discover and settle a new world.
2. Portugal and Spain lead the way to the Americas.
3. Portuguese and Spaniards explore the New World.
4. Portugal and Spain plant their civilizations in the Americas.
5. England challenges Spain and gains a foothold in North America.

1 The first Americans discover and settle a new world

See Teaching Suggestions in TMRG, pp.TM14-15.

There was a time when the American continents lay empty of all human life. From the frozen wastes of the Arctic to the southern tip of South America, no human voice had ever echoed through the wilderness. No human foot had ever left its print upon the soil. The land belonged to the wildlife that roamed the forests and plains, soared through the air, and swam in the rivers and lakes.

The first Americans. Many historians believe that the first people to discover this immense wilderness came from Asia. The date on which those first people entered America is lost forever in the mists of history. Estimates place the date somewhere from 10,000 to more than 25,000 years ago. The widely accepted theory is that they traveled from Siberia, in Asia, to Alaska across land that now lies beneath the waters of the Bering Strait. At the time a glacier, a huge sheet of ice, covered much of what is now Canada and the northern United States. The ice locked up so much water that the level of the oceans dropped by several hundred feet. This drop in sea level exposed the land that then connected Asia and Alaska.

Through the centuries wave after wave of people wandered into Alaska from many parts of Asia. When the glacial ice melted and the sea rose again, the wanderers probably crossed the Bering Strait in small boats or, during the winter months, on foot over the ice.

These people of the dawn of American history brought little with them from Asia. They knew—or soon discovered—how to make fire. They may have brought dogs. For weapons they depended upon clubs and stone-tipped spears. The wild animals, or game, they killed provided them with food and with skins and furs for clothing.

In their never-ending search for better hunting grounds, the newcomers and their descendants moved across the great central plain of Alaska and southward along the eastern foothills of the Rocky Mountains. Over many thousands of years, these people spread out across North, Central, and South America.

Settling the land. In these new lands, the early peoples gradually increased in number. No one knows the exact size of the native population by the time Europeans first reached these shores. Estimates range from as low as 16 million to as high as 112 million. Recent estimates give a total population of 90 to 100 million, of which 10 to 12 million lived in the area that is now the United States and Canada. Today we call all of these people and their descendants Native Americans, or Indians.

The Native Americans were divided into many hundreds of different tribes speaking more than 1,000 different languages and dialects. As time passed, they invented new weapons and tools and learned to grow crops.

The Native Americans developed rich and varied **cultures,** or ways of life. Some lived by hunting, fishing, and gathering roots, nuts, and berries. Others depended mainly on farming. Still others hunted and fished to supplement the crops they grew in garden patches around their villages. Some Native Americans wandered across the land in small groups. Others settled down and lived in towns and villages. Some created **civilizations,** or highly advanced cultures, which flourished long before Europeans came to America.

The Mayas. One of the great early Indian civilizations was that of the Mayas of Yucatán and Central America (see map this page). It rivaled in richness and complexity the civilizations of Europe, Africa, and Asia. Great cities—used mainly as religious centers—contained broad plazas, massive public buildings, and magnificent temples that rose above the rain forest. Mayan artisans and artists decorated the buildings with colorful murals and striking stone carvings and sculptures. Mayan scholars developed a method of writing. Mathematicians created an accurate numbering system that included the use of the zero. Scientists worked out a calendar more precise than the one then used in Europe. Mayan astronomers made such careful observations of the stars and planets that they could predict the dates of solar eclipses.

The Mayan civilization reached its peak of brilliance more than 500 years before Columbus sailed to America. Then it began to decline, possibly because the Mayan population increased too rapidly for the available food supply. The Mayas abandoned their cities, and lush jungle growth quickly covered the Mayan ruins. Some groups of Mayas were absorbed into other tribes, while others survived until the 1540's. Their descendants still live in the same area today.

The Incas. Far to the south of the Mayas, another civilization arose, centered in what is now Peru, in South America (see map, this page). Here the Incas conquered neighboring states and organized a rich and powerful empire. Spreading out from the capital city of Cuzco, high in the Andes Mountains, a network of roads and bridges united the empire. The fortified cities of the Incas, their highway system, and their terraced fields and irrigation works were marvels of engineering.

Like the Mayas, the Incas depended upon farming for their livelihood. Two domesticated animals, the llama and the alpaca, served as beasts of burden and sources of food. Wool from these animals and from the wild vicuña provided not only everyday clothing but also material from which weavers created beautiful fabrics with intricate and colorful designs. Artisans fashioned gold and silver from the Incan

Major Indian Civilizations of the Americas

Throughout the Annotated Teacher's Edition, terms listed in the "Identify" portion of a Section Review are underscored the first time they appear. See the Teacher's Manual for each section for a listing of important vocabulary terms.

The Indians of Mexico were sophisticated scientists. The Mayas built astronomical observatories to study the stars and planets. The Aztecs developed exact calendars (inset) that guided their yearly cycle of planting and harvesting.

mines into jewelry and rich ornaments for the temples and palaces.

The Incas rigidly organized their empire in a pyramid-like structure. Every member of the society had an assigned place and task. At the base were the farmers, laborers, and artisans. Next came the noble class, composed of priests, military leaders, and government officials. At the top was the supreme ruler—The Inca, who was called the "Sun God." All power and all authority flowed from The Inca down through the nobles to the workers. So important was the Inca that when the ruler was destroyed, the entire social structure collapsed.

The Aztecs. In Mexico, far to the north of the Incas (see map, page 4), the Aztecs once lived as hunters. As they wandered, they quickly learned new ways of life from other tribes they met. They developed well-trained armies that conquered the peoples around them. In three or four hundred years, they created a mighty empire that by 1500 ruled much of Central America. Though they depended mainly on farming, the Aztecs also carried on a busy trade with distant communities. Aztecs merchants traveled far and wide throughout the Americas, dealing in precious stones, cacao beans, and gold and silver.

The Aztecs collected great wealth from the people they conquered. Part of it went toward building a beautiful capital city, called Tenochtitlán (tay·noch·tee·TLAN), on the site where Mexico City now stands. There the Aztecs raised great temples, palaces, and other public buildings.

The Aztecs who constructed this marvel were harsh rulers. The people they had conquered would need little urging to rise in rebellion against them.

▲ Report topic: How the Incas managed to govern their vast territory

5

Major Cultural Areas and Tribes of North America

The Indians of North America. The Native Americans of what are now the United States and Canada did not live as subject people in empires like those of the Incas and the Aztecs. In a few instances, several tribes did join together for mutual support or protection. Sometimes tribes traded with neighbors and staged raids against nearby enemies. As a rule, however, each of the numerous North American tribes lived a largely independent life in its own territory.

Each tribe adapted its way of life to its own environment. Usually tribes that lived near each other had similar ways of life. A region in which most of the tribes had the same sort of culture is described as a **culture area**. The different culture areas produced a rich variety of ways of life on the North American continent.

In the next few pages, we will look briefly at a few of the principal tribes in different culture areas as they were before the Europeans arrived (see map, this page). In later chapters, as we follow the advancing line of settlement across the country, we will see how these same tribes dealt with the invasion of their lands by white settlers.

Indians of the Southwest. Three major Indian groups lived in the hot, dry, semi-desert area of what is now the southwestern United States. These were the Pueblos, the Navajos, and the Apaches.

"Pueblo" is the Spanish name for "town." It is an appropriate name for a tribe that built and lived in the first "apartment houses" in America. A thousand years ago, ancestors of the Pueblos carved apartment-like dwellings out of the walls of canyons. They built other "apartments," one with 800 rooms, of stone and **adobe**, or sun-dried brick.

Nampeyo — or the "Old Lady," — was born in the small Hopi pueblo, or village, of Hano in northern Arizona. The pottery she crafted brought her widespread recognition as an important American Indian artist.

Young Hopi girls learned pottery making from their mothers, aunts, and grandmothers. They shaped and dried the clay and then painted it with dyes made by boiling wild plants. Inspired by pieces of pottery found in nearby prehistoric ruins, Nampeyo strayed from her pueblo's traditional pottery styles. The old clay pieces enabled Nampeyo to envision pots with low wide shoulders instead of the usual high narrow ones. Nampeyo experimented with new shapes, compositions, and colors. She developed new geometric and abstract designs, often with graceful curves that swept around the edges of bowls and jars.

Nampeyo was criticized for not staying with traditional Hopi forms and designs. In the 1880's, however, she found a market for her pots among the tourists whom the Santa Fe Railway brought to the Southwest. Soon her work was in great demand. Nampeyo and her husband traveled throughout the Southwest giving demonstrations of pottery making. In 1898 the Santa Fe Railway invited Nampeyo to visit the Chicago Exposition to exhibit her pottery. Today, pots made by Nampeyo are treasured objects.

The Pueblos were peaceful people. In irrigated fields they grew corn, beans, squash, and cotton. They wove textiles and created beautiful pottery. In colorful ceremonies enriched with songs, the sound of drums, and dances, they worshiped the gods and the animals, earth, and sky that the gods had created. Specially chosen and trained storytellers passed on from generation to generation the history of creation and of the human place in it.

The Navajos and the Apaches were two of the Pueblos' closest neighbors. The Navajos learned how to farm from the Pueblos. They also became skilled weavers who created wonderful designs for rugs and blankets. Unlike the Pueblos, who lived in compact towns made up of dwellings that were shared by several
▲ families, each Navajo family instead lived in its own **hogan.** This was a lodge built of adobe and logs.

The Apaches were wandering hunters who depended upon deer and buffalo for food, shelter, and clothing. They lived in **wickiups,** circular huts of brush that could be constructed in a few minutes. Neighboring tribes respected their fierceness and endurance. One of these tribes, the Pueblos, gave them the name "Apache," which means "enemy."

The Plains Indians. The Plains Indians — among them the Sioux, Pawnees, Kiowas, Dakotas, Osages, and Comanches — combined hunting and farming. For much of the year the Plains Indians lived in villages along the banks of the Missouri and the other rivers that drained into the Mississippi. There the women cultivated corn and other crops in fields around the villages.

During the summer, however, small bands of closely related families moved out onto the

Great Plains to hunt buffalo. They slept in **tepees**—cone-shaped tents of buffalo skins stretched over a frame of lodge poles. The buffalo provided the Indians with almost all of their basic needs. From the skins they made clothing, tents, ropes, and wool. With the sinews they made threads with which to sew their clothes and tents. From the bones they made tools. On the treeless plains, dried buffalo droppings served as the chief fuel.

The Plains Indians lived under a democratic form of government. Chiefs were chosen for specific purposes—to lead a hunting party or a raiding expedition. No single chief had total control for any extended length of time. Leading members of a band or of a tribe gathered in council meetings to make important decisions. Like so many other tribes of North America, the Plains Indians prized their freedom and independence.

Other Western tribes. The Shoshone, Pima, and Nez Percé (NAY per·SAY) Indians were among the tribes inhabiting the lands west of the Great Plains. This is a region of dramatic contrasts. It includes towering mountains, high rocky plateaus, deep mountain valleys, and the coastal lands of California. Much of the region is very dry, and life for the Indians there was hard. They have been called "Seed Gatherers" because they depended for food upon seeds, nuts, berries, and roots, although they also hunted small game. They were skilled in the art of basket-making. Some of their baskets were so tightly woven that they could hold water.

The Northwest Coast offered a more generous environment. From the sea and the forest, the Northwest Coast tribes secured a never-failing supply of food and materials for clothing and shelter. With the essentials of life so

The Plains Indians performed intricate dances to prepare for buffalo hunts. Before the Spaniards introduced horses to the New World in the 1500's, the Indians conducted these hunts on foot.

Noble families in Europe each had a coat of arms. So too did Indian families who lived along the Pacific Northwest Coast. Each family carved its coat of arms on a post called a totem pole. Totem poles were made of red cedar, a soft and straight-grained wood that is fairly easy to carve. Each totem pole had from one to several carved images, which took human, animal, and bird forms. Sometimes the carvings related family legends which could only be interpreted by persons familiar with the symbolic meaning of the images and with the customs of the clan.

Totem poles were carved by members of the Haida, Kwakiutl, Tlingit, and Tsimshian tribes. The main types of poles included house posts, which supported the main beams of a house; house frontal posts, which had a hole through which persons entered a house; memorial poles, which honored a dead person; mortuary poles, which contained the remains of deceased persons; grave markers, or tombstones; and welcoming figures, which were placed on the beach to greet guests arriving by canoe.

The totem pole also symbolized the wealth of its owner, for hiring an artist to carve a pole was very expensive. During the mid-nineteenth century the profitable fur trade and the introduction of better metal carving tools made the totem pole affordable to many Indian chiefs. Most totem poles stood between 10 and 60 feet (3 and 18 meters) high. They usually lasted 60 to 100 years before falling from wood decay.

plentiful, they were able to enjoy community life in large villages along the seacoast.

Indians of the Eastern Woodlands. The Eastern Woodland area reached from what is now Canada to the Gulf of Mexico and from the Atlantic seaboard to west of the Mississippi River. The people who lived in much of this area long ago were called "Mound Builders" after the huge ceremonial mounds that they built in the form of birds, bears, wolves, and other animals.

The people living in the Eastern Woodland region when the Europeans arrived were descended from the Mound Builders. Like their ancestors, the numerous tribes shared a land of plenty. Many lakes sparkled in the forest. Clear streams and rivers flowed down to the sea. The people lived in villages surrounded by the fields that they had cleared and in which they raised corn, beans, squash, tobacco, and other crops. Their hunting grounds provided them with additional food as well as skins that could be used for moccasins and furs for blankets and robes.

From the Algonquins and Iroquois in the north to the Creeks and Cherokees in the south, the Indians prized their independence. In Chapter 3 you will get a closer look at the way they lived and how they organized their tribal life. You will also see how the coming of the white settlers disrupted these age-old patterns of Indian living and, in some cases, even destroyed them.

Shared beliefs of the Indians. Despite their variety, Indians in different culture areas shared certain ways of seeing the world. They felt it was necessary to live in harmony with the natural world. This belief in a harmony with nature was at the heart of the social, economic, and religious practices of the Indians.

They worshiped the gods who had created the world, and they viewed the land as a sacred trust that they were privileged to use but were obligated to pass on unspoiled to future generations.

The Indians also shared a strong sense of pride. They were proud of their tribes and communities and of themselves as individuals. They prized their self-reliance, their individual initiative, and their independence.

The understanding that enabled the Indians to develop methods for living in harmony with the land did not prepare them for an invasion by people of another culture. This understanding was no match for the guns and other technological developments that the Europeans would bring to the Americas.

SECTION REVIEW
See underscored items, text pp. 4-7.

Identify: Native Americans, culture, civilization, Mayas, Incas, Aztecs, Pueblos, Navajos, Apaches, Plains Indians

For answers to questions, see Answer Key, p.A9.

1. **Comparing Ideas: (a)** On what did the Mayas and the Incas depend for their livelihood? **(b)** In what way did Aztec society differ from Mayan and Incan society?

2. **Organizing Ideas:** How did the cultures of each of the following groups of Native Americans reflect their environment: **(a)** the Pueblos, **(b)** the Plains Indians, **(c)** the Seed Gatherers, **(d)** the Northwest Coast Indians?

3. **Studying Maps:** Look at the map on page 6. **(a)** In what culture area is your community located? **(b)** What Indian tribes lived in this area? **(c)** Are there any traces of these Indians (place-names, reservations, or artifacts, for example) in your community today?

2 Portugal and Spain lead the way to the Americas

See Teaching Suggestions in TMRG, pp.TM15-16.

During the 1300's and 1400's Europe was stirring with new ideas. Many Europeans were filled with burning curiosity. They were living in a period called the Renaissance (ren·eh·ZAHNS), meaning a time of "new birth."

A time of energy and change. Through much of the preceding Middle Ages, Europeans had been concerned primarily with scratching out a bare living and preparing through religion for life beyond the grave. Now their interest increasingly shifted to the everyday world around them. Some turned to the sea to search for new trade routes and to explore distant lands. Others turned to art, architecture, and writing.

What started Europeans thinking new thoughts and dreaming new dreams? A series of wars called the Crusades were partly responsible. Starting in 1096 and continuing for nearly 200 years, army after army of Christians set forth from Europe on what they considered a holy mission. Their objective was to battle with Muslims for control of the Holy Land in the Middle East. Many Crusaders died in battle, while others settled down to live in the Middle East. Those who did return to Europe brought back new ideas and new products. The ideas spread, creating new ways of living and stimulating the Renaissance. The use of the new products also spread, creating new demands and stimulating more trade between Europe and Asia.

The importance of trade. Europeans wanted the products they got from Asia. They wanted the tough Damascus steel for their swords and armor. They wanted Persian rugs, Chinese porcelain, and glass to make their cold, damp castles and manor houses more livable. More than anything else, perhaps, they wanted spices. They wanted cloves, cinnamon, and nutmeg from the Spice Islands of the East Indies and, most important, pepper, or "black gold," from India. These spices gave variety and flavor to their coarse food, particularly to their meat. Spices also were used to preserve food. To pay for these products, Europeans sent woolen goods, tin, gold, and silver back along the trade routes.

The difficulty of trade. The old trade routes to Asia had always been very difficult, dangerous, and expensive. Months, sometimes years, passed before a box of spices managed to reach Europe from Asia.

Camel caravans carrying products overland from China and central Asia crossed vast wastelands and high mountain passes. Goods moving from the East Indies along the sea-land route made a long sea voyage westward across

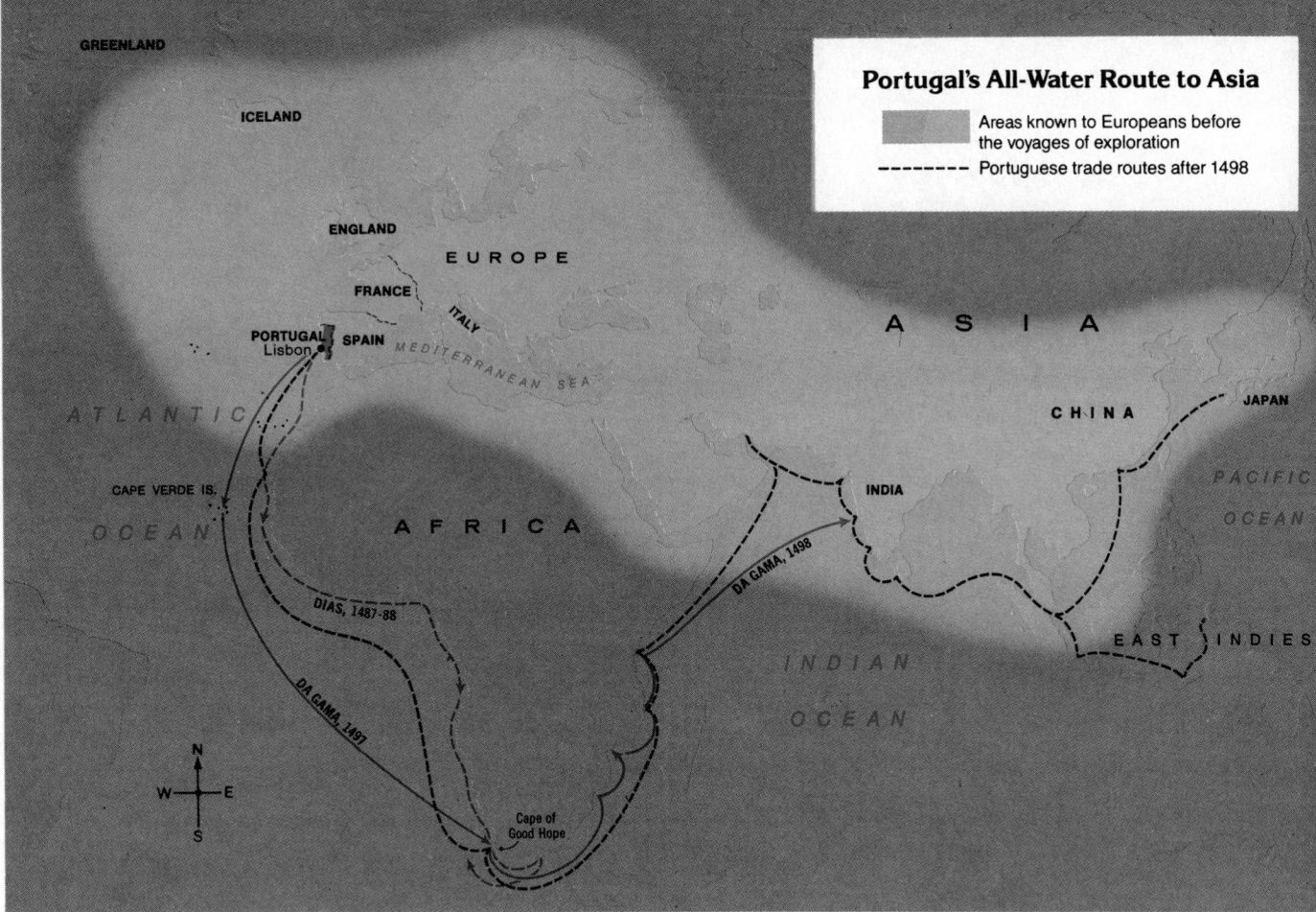

the Indian Ocean. Then the goods were carried over the burning Arabian Desert by camel caravans. Next came another sea voyage, this time across the Mediterranean Sea on ships bound for the Italian cities of Genoa or Venice. The Italian merchants of Genoa and Venice had a **monopoly**—that is, exclusive control over the supply of a product or service—on trade between the eastern Mediterranean and Europe. Finally, Asia's much-wanted products reached Europe's markets.

Many European merchants wanted to get Asian goods more cheaply and to end the control of east-west trade by the Venetians and Genoans. The Portuguese and Spaniards, and later the French, English, and Dutch, began to search for new ocean routes to Asia.

Before the search ended, European explorers had pushed back the frontiers of the world they knew. This expansion of European trade, which was linked with new forms of business and the rise of banking, has become known as the Commercial Revolution.

Portugal's sea route to Asia. Portuguese sailors led the search for an all-water route to Asia. They were financed by Prince Henry of Portugal, also known as the Navigator.

Fascinated by exploration, Prince Henry built a shipyard and a school for navigators on the coast of Portugal. There he and his followers built new types of sailing ships seaworthy enough to brave the Atlantic Ocean. They experimented with new methods of navigation and better maps. They began to use instruments, such as the compass and the astrolabe, for determining distances and direction. ▲

Prince Henry did more than experiment. He sent many expeditions south along the unexplored coast of Africa (see map, this page). After his death in 1460, Portuguese sailors continued to explore the African coast.

At small harbor settlements where they anchored their ships, the Portuguese may have learned of African kingdoms inland. They had little interest in exploring these kingdoms at that time. After trading such European goods

▲ Report topic: The astrolabe as an aid to early navigators

Columbus Reaches a "New World"

▮ Lands seen by Columbus, 1492-1504

as brass bowls, bracelets, beads, and textiles for fresh water and food, the Portuguese sailed on. Besides supplies, however, the Portuguese also took aboard African servants and slaves, carrying them back to Portugal and Spain on the return voyages. In later years some of these Africans or their descendants took part in the explorations of the Americas.

With every expedition Portuguese sailors pushed farther and farther south. In 1487 Bartholomeu Dias (DEE·ahs) and his crew rounded the southern tip of Africa (see map, page 11). Eleven years later, in 1498, Vasco da Gama followed Dias's route around the Cape of Good Hope. He continued across the Indian Ocean to India (see map, page 11).

The voyages of Dias and da Gama were enormously important to the little kingdom of Portugal and to the world. Within a few years, Portuguese vessels were sailing back and forth along the new, all-water route to India and the Spice Islands of the East Indies.

Columbus's fateful voyage. While Portuguese sailors were exploring the African coast, an Italian named Christopher Columbus set out in 1492 under the flag of Spain on the first of four great voyages. Convinced that the earth was round, a knowledge shared by many informed people of the day, Columbus believed that if he sailed far enough to the west he would reach Asia. In trying to prove his point, Columbus made a key contribution to what has

been called the Geographic Revolution, the rapid growth of European knowledge of the earth's surface.

The expedition led by Columbus included three small ships, the *Niña,* the *Pinta,* and the *Santa María.* The able crews of these ships were mainly Spaniards, but one member described as a "man of color" may have been one of the Africans brought back to Europe by the Portuguese explorers.

Finding a world unknown to Europe. Instead of reaching Asia, Columbus came upon a small island in the Bahamas (see map, this page). On the morning of October 12, 1492, Columbus and his crews went ashore and thanked God for leading them safely across the sea. Thinking that he had reached the East Indies, Columbus called the dark-skinned people on the island "Indians." Neither Columbus nor anyone in his party realized that they had, in fact, arrived at an island near the coast of North America, a continent unknown at this time to Europeans.

Columbus tried three more times to find an all-water route to the East Indies and the riches of Asia. He failed in this, but his voyages established Spain's claims in the Americas. Columbus returned from his fourth voyage a poor, lonely, broken-hearted man. He died in 1506 without knowing that his explorations would, in time, have more influence on Europe than all the riches of Asia.

An earlier European voyage. In reality, Columbus was not the first European to reach America. The Norse, or Vikings, were probably the first Europeans to land there. In the late 900's, Eric the Red and his followers built a settlement in Greenland. In the year 1000, Eric's son Leif and his crew were blown off course and landed on the northeast coast of North America. They called the country Vinland or "Wineland the Good," after the wild grapes that grew there. Other Norse followed Leif to Vinland and established settlements there, but the settlements did not last and Norse voyages to Vinland stopped suddenly. Historians still do not know why the voyages ended so abruptly.

Other Europeans may also have reached America before Columbus. If so, they left no written record.

English and French claims. Other nations also established claims to large areas of North America soon after Columbus. In 1497 John Cabot, an Italian sea captain in the pay of King Henry VII of England, sailed to North America out of the harbor of Bristol. Little is known about Cabot and even less about his famous voyage. Historians believe that on this voyage and another made the following year, he sailed along the coasts of what are now Newfoundland, Nova Scotia, and New England (see map, this page), claiming these lands for England in the name of King Henry. For this work the thrifty king presented Cabot with a gift of ten pounds and an annual pension of twenty pounds. This was a small reward indeed for the explorer who gave England its first claim to the North American continent.

French claims to a share of North America were based on the voyages of Giovanni da Verrazano (vayr·rah·TSAH·noh) and Jacques Cartier (kar·TYAY). Verrazano, an Italian sailing under the French flag, set out in 1524 to find a water route through America to Asia. He failed, but his explorations gave the French claim to new lands overseas.

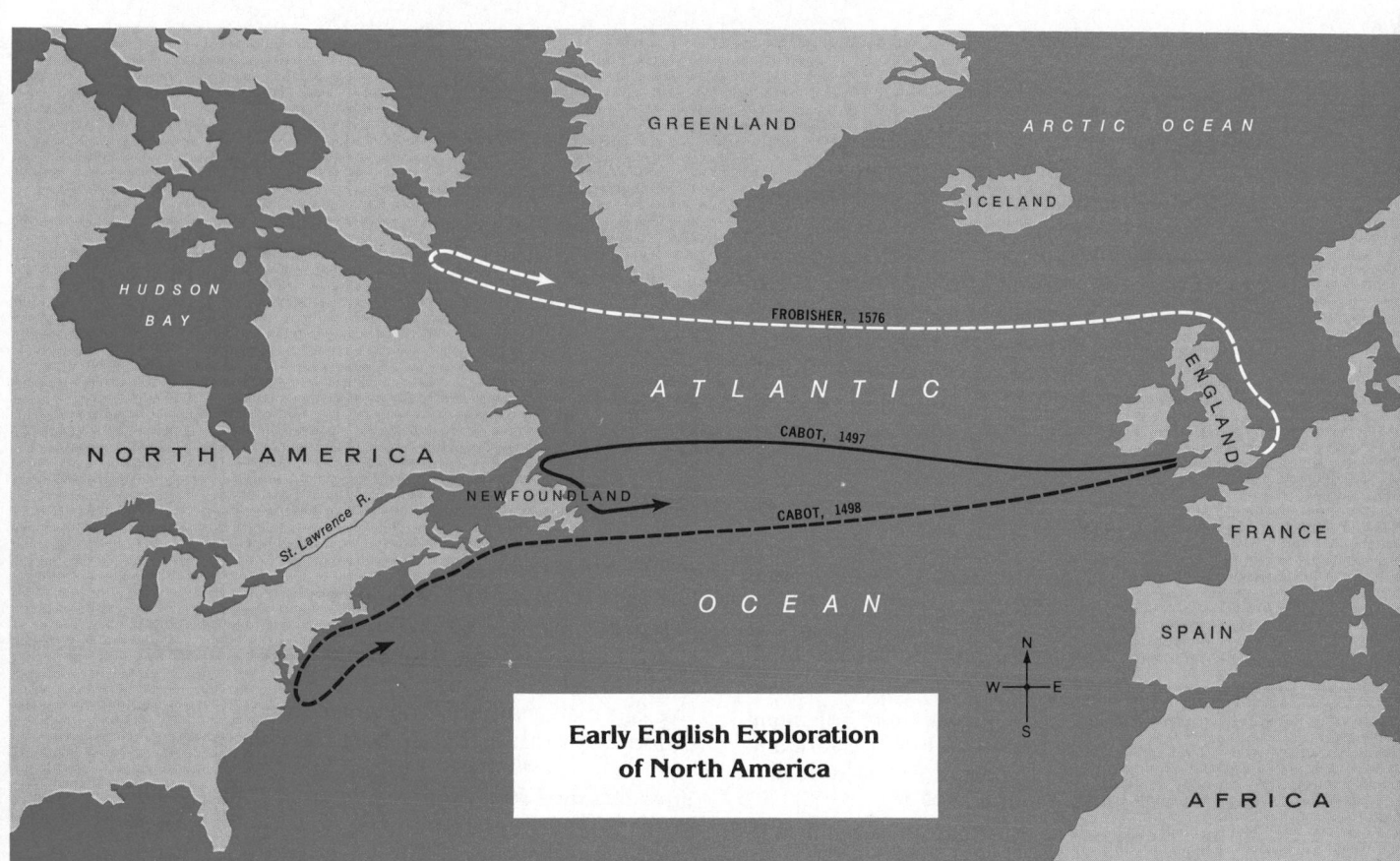

Early English Exploration of North America

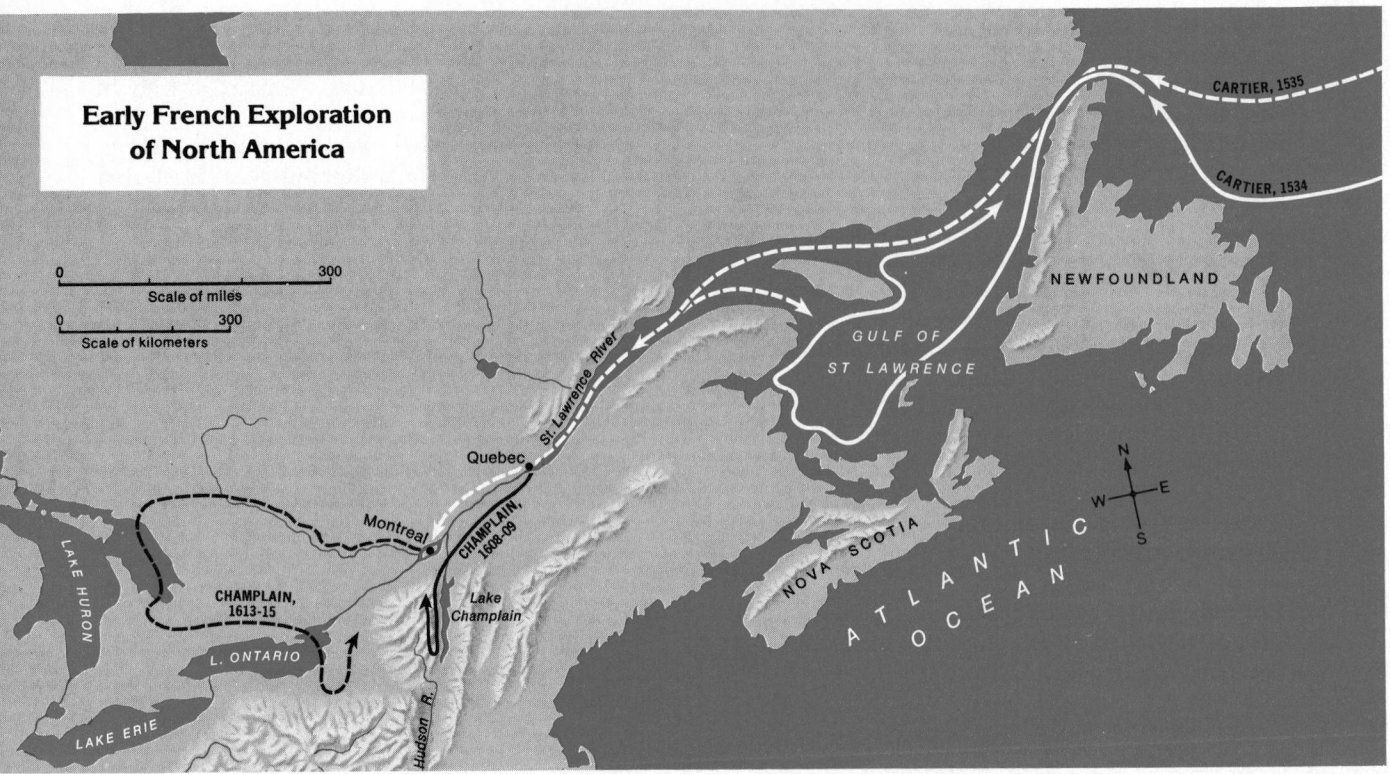

Early French Exploration of North America

0   300
Scale of miles

0   300
Scale of kilometers

CARTIER, 1535

CARTIER, 1534

NEWFOUNDLAND

GULF OF ST LAWRENCE

St. Lawrence River

Quebec

Montreal

CHAMPLAIN, 1608-09

CHAMPLAIN, 1613-15

Lake Champlain

LAKE HURON

L. ONTARIO

LAKE ERIE

Hudson R.

NOVA SCOTIA

ATLANTIC OCEAN

N W E S

Ten years later, in 1534, Cartier made the first of three voyages to the lands across the Atlantic. On the first voyage, he explored the Gulf of St. Lawrence, and on his second and third voyages, he explored the St. Lawrence River as far as the present site of Montreal. He also tried to start a settlement on a spot not far away from where Quebec now stands. The settlement was not a success, but Cartier's efforts helped to strengthen French claims to what is now Canada (see map, this page).

SECTION REVIEW

See underscored items, text pp. 10 - 13.

Identify: Renaissance, Crusades, Commercial Revolution, Prince Henry, Vasco da Gama, Christopher Columbus, Geographic Revolution, John Cabot, Giovanni da Verrazano, Jacques Cartier, 1492, 1498

For answers to questions, see Answer Key, p.A9.

1. **Analyzing Ideas:** (a) Why was there a demand in Europe for goods from Asia in the 1300's and 1400's? (b) Why did some Europeans seek new trade routes to Asia in the 1400's?

2. **Summarizing Ideas:** List four improvements in navigation that Prince Henry encouraged.

3. **Interpreting Ideas:** Why did the Norse voyages to North America have less impact on history than Columbus's voyages?

4. **Studying Maps:** Look at the maps on pages 11–14. How did each of the following explorers add to Europeans' knowledge of the world: (a) Dias, (b) Columbus, (c) Cabot, (d) Cartier?

3 Portuguese and Spaniards explore the New World

See Teaching Suggestions in TMRG, p.TM16.

Other bold adventurers soon followed the early explorers across the Atlantic. Some explored the coastline of the Americas. Others pushed into the interior. Close on their footsteps came the Spanish soldiers known as **conquistadors** (kohn·KEES·tah·dorz), that is, the conquerors.

Spanish and Portuguese claims. Spain and Portugal, both leaders in the new age of exploration and discovery, did not hesitate to claim all of the Americas. In 1494 they signed a treaty establishing a Line of Demarcation about 1,100 miles (1,760 kilometers) west of the Cape Verde Islands. According to the treaty, all new lands explored west of this line were to belong to Spain. All new lands explored to the east of the demarcation line were to belong to Portugal.

A few years later a Portuguese explorer, Pedro Álvares Cabral (cah·BRAHL), was sailing around Africa to India. His ship was blown off course, and in 1500 he landed on the shore of what is now Brazil. Cabral then claimed this territory for Portugal.

How America got its name. Amerigo Vespucci (ves·POO·chee), an Italian, sailed on at least one expedition, perhaps several, along the coast of what is now South America. His observations led him to express the bold opinion that he had seen a new continent. News of Vespucci's conclusion reached a famous geographer, who proposed calling these lands "America" in honor of Amerigo Vespucci. Thus, ironically, Columbus missed even the honor of having the lands named after him.

Discovering a "new" ocean. In 1513 a Spanish explorer, Balboa (bal·BOH·ah), started on an expedition across the Isthmus of Panama in search of gold. His expedition, like many of the expeditions that pushed into the endless wilderness of the Americas, included Africans as well as Europeans. Thirty Africans, in fact, traveled in Balboa's party.

Indian guides led Balboa's expedition through a hot, steaming rain forest. After many hardships they reached the foot of a small mountain. Balboa climbed the mountain and caught his first glimpse of a vast body of water, which he called the "South Sea." It stretched to the south and the west as far as his eyes could see. Was it another ocean? Balboa could only guess that it was.

Circling the earth. Ferdinand Magellan proved Balboa's guess correct. In 1519 he set sail from Spain on one of the greatest voyages in human history. Magellan, a Portuguese, sailed under the flag of Spain. A year after his departure, he led his small fleet through a narrow waterway, now called the Strait of Magellan, at the southern tip of South America.

For more than a month, Magellan sailed westward through the strait. At last, passing through the strait, Magellan found himself upon an immense sea—a sea so vast and calm that he named it the Pacific Ocean. Was this the mighty "South Sea" that Balboa had seen from the mountain in Panama? Magellan sailed on to find the answer.

Two years later, in September 1522, a small vessel named the *Victoria* sailed into a Spanish harbor. The 18 sailors aboard were the only survivors of the 237 who had sailed with Magellan from Spain three years earlier. These 18 men had done what no one had ever done before. They had crossed Balboa's "South Sea" and had sailed around the world. Magellan, their leader, was not among them. Killed in a battle, he lay buried in the Philippine Islands, half a world away.

Magellan's expedition proved that the lands Columbus had discovered were indeed part of a new world—continents not known to the Europeans of that day. The expedition also ▲ gave Spain its claim to the Philippine Islands. In the years that followed, Spain sent soldiers to conquer the Filipinos, missionaries to convert them to Christianity, and merchants to open up trade.

Conquest of the Aztecs and Incas. Meanwhile, other Spaniards came to the New World looking for gold. "The Spaniards are troubled with a disease of the heart for which gold is the remedy," said Hernando Cortés (kor·TAYS), a conquistador. In their search for riches, Cortés, Pizarro, and the other conquistadors destroyed the great civilizations of the Aztecs and the Incas.

Cortés landed on the coast of Mexico in the year 1519 as leader of a small army of about 550, among them some Africans. The Spanish ships seemed like "towers on the sea" to the Indians, and the guns, horses, and iron-clad men were strange and fearful sights. The Indians thought that Cortés might be the god Quetzalcoatl (ket·sal·KOAT·ul), returning as he had promised. They quickly learned he was not and began to fight back fiercely. Cortés might have perished if he had not persuaded enemies of the Aztecs to join his army. With the aid of these Indians, who greatly outnumbered his own soldiers, Cortés laid seige to Tenochtitlán, the Aztec capital. Moctezuma, the Aztec emperor, was murdered, and Cortés conquered the wealthy empire. The conquest brought glory and fortune to Cortés and enormous treasures of gold and silver to Spain.

15

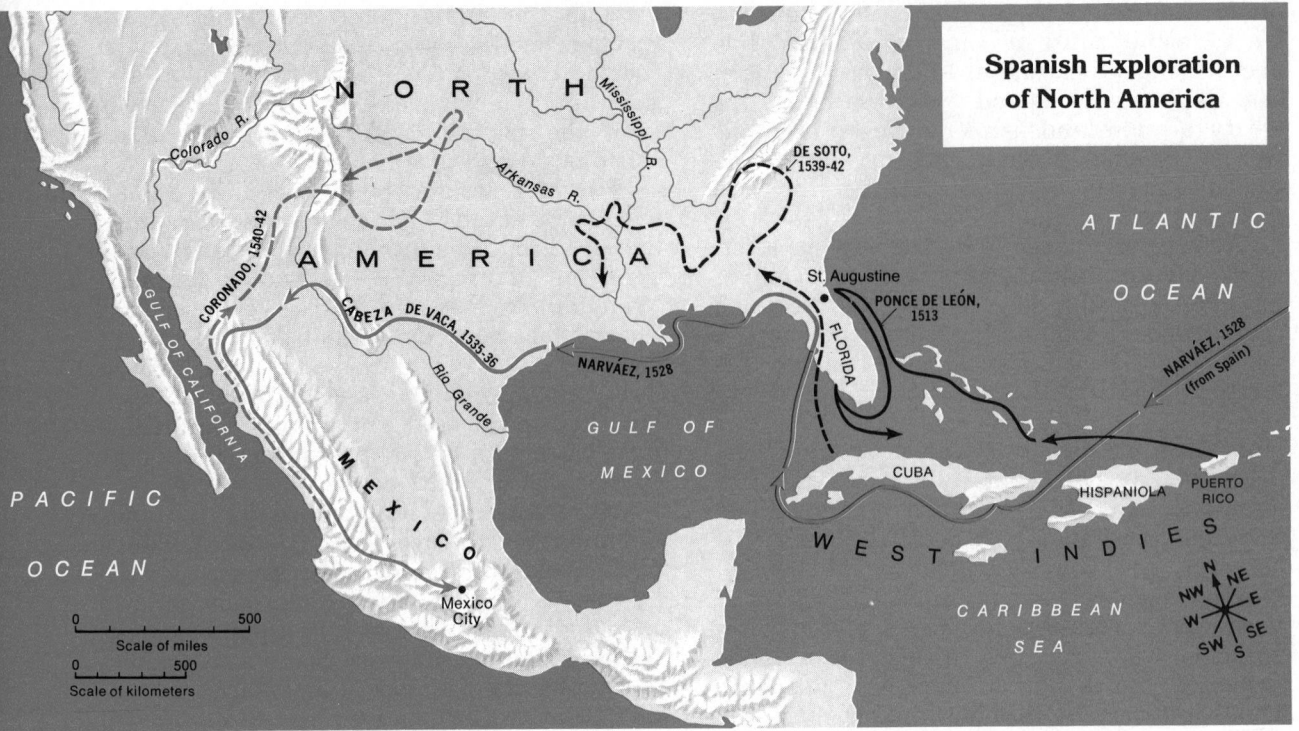

Spanish Exploration of North America

Several years later, in 1531–35, another Spaniard, Francisco Pizarro (pee·ZAHR·oh), led an even smaller army against the Incas. The Incas, frightened and divided, did not resist, and Pizarro advanced to the very heart of the Incan empire high in the Andes. There, through treachery, he kidnapped The Inca, collected a huge ransom of gold and silver, and then ruthlessly murdered his captive. The death of The Inca, their "Sun God," left the Incas without a leader, and control of the vast empire quickly passed into the hands of the Spaniards.

The search for gold. Other conquistadors pushed north and west in search of fame and fortune. In 1513 Juan Ponce de León (POHN·say day lay·OHN) first explored the land he named Florida (see map, this page). He was killed on a later expedition by the natives after looting their villages and capturing some as slaves.

In 1527 and 1528, Pánfilo de Narváez (nahr·VAH·ez) led another army into Florida (see map, this page). Years later, after wandering more than halfway across North America, only four survivors, Narváez not among them, reached Mexico City and safety. One survivor, Cabeza de Vaca (cah·BAY·sah day VAH·kuh), returned to Spain and wrote a book about the journey. Another suvivor, a black named Estevanico (es·tay·vah·NEE·koh), later led a treasure search on which he was killed.

In 1539 an expedition led by Hernando De Soto pushed into what is now the southeastern United States (see map, this page). De Soto, too, searched for riches and found none. Before he died in 1542, he reached the Mississippi River, the "Father of Waters." He was buried in the great river he discovered.

Another conquistador, Francisco Vásquez de Coronado (kor·oh·NAH·doh), led a group northward from Mexico into what is now the southwestern United States. Lured by Indian tales of seven cities with streets of gold and buildings studded with precious gems, his expedition searched for two years. Looting villages, enslaving the Indians, and killing those who fought back, Coronado and his followers reached what is now Kansas (see map, this page). They discovered the Grand Canyon but found no golden cities. Coronado returned to Mexico City without treasure.

These conquistadors failed to discover the great riches that Cortés and Pizarro had found.

The explorers did succeed, however, in giving Spain control of vital parts of North and Central America.

New settlements for Spain. During the second half of the 1500's, the Spaniards devoted serious attention to the borderlands east and north of Mexico. Disturbed by reports of French and English activities, the Spaniards built a fort at St. Augustine, Florida, in 1565 (see map, page 16). In the next few years, they established missions and **presidios** (pray·SID·ee·ohs), or forts, up the coast as far as South Carolina.

It seemed more realistic, however, to secure firm control of the land in the northern part of Mexico. In 1598 Don Juan de Oñate (oh·NYAH·tay), son of one of the richest mine owners in Mexico, set out to conquer and settle the area known as New Mexico (see map, page 19). A large and well-equipped military force and a number of Roman Catholic missionaries supported his expedition. After overcoming strong resistance by the Indians of the Acoma pueblo, Oñate claimed the land for Spain. In 1609 Santa Fe became the permanent capital of the area known as New Mexico.

Nearly a hundred years later, in 1680, the Pueblo Indians drove out the Spaniards, but the Spaniards soon reconquered the area. During the following years, the area was widely explored by Roman Catholic missionaries, including the famed Father Eusébio Francisco Kino (KEE·noh). In journals he kept of his travels, Father Kino provided an invaluable record of the land and people. These explorations (see map, page 19) and the establishment later of missions, towns, and presidios gave the Spaniards firm control of the area.

Expansion into California. During all these years, the Spaniards paid little attention to California. Even after Sebastián Vizcaíno (beth·kah·EE·noh) explored the coast in 1602 (see map, page 19), they remained indifferent. However, when both the English and the Russians began to show an interest in the Pacific coast, the Spaniards decided to expand their borders to include California. In the mid-1700's Spaniards led by Gaspar de Portolá (por·toh·LAH) and Father Junípero Serra (see map, page 19) established a chain of missions and presidios up the coast as far as San Francisco Bay. You will return to the story of these missions in Chapter 15.

SECTION REVIEW
See underscored items, text pp. 15 - 17.
Identify: Amerigo Vespucci, Balboa, Moctezuma, Francisco Pizarro, Juan Ponce de León, Hernando De Soto, Francisco Vásquez de Coronado, Juan de Oñate, Father Kino
For answers to questions, see Answer Key, p.A9.

1. **Summarizing Ideas:** How did Spain and Portugal settle the conflicting claims in the lands they wished to explore?

2. **Analyzing Ideas:** What was the chief motive for the conquests of the Aztecs and Incas?

3. **Interpreting Ideas:** How did the Spaniards try to protect their settlements in Florida and Mexico?

4 Portugal and Spain plant their civilizations in the Americas

See Teaching Suggestions in TMRG, pp.TM16-17.

Many of the soldiers who fought to conquer the Americas remained there. Together with the Native Americans and the Africans, they created a new culture in the Americas.

The colonial population. Both Portugal and Spain started colonies in the Americas. A **colony** is a land settled by people from another country that remains under the control of that country. New settlers came to these colonies in growing numbers—the Portuguese to the northeast coast of Brazil, the Spaniards to the Caribbean islands and to Mexico and Central and South America. Here in the New World, they reproduced a system of privileged classes resembling the social system they had left behind in Europe.

Spaniards born in Spain claimed the most privileged position in the colonies. Within a hundred years after Columbus's voyages, some 15,000 Spaniards were living in the Americas. Occupying a class just below them were the **Creoles**, Spaniards born in the New World. Still lower in the class structure and even more numerous were the **mestizos**, men and women born of mixed Spanish and Indian marriages. By far the most numerous of all were the Indians, most of whom continued to live in villages apart from their conquerors. There was also an increasing population of Africans, including those transported as slaves as well as many who came as free people. Finally, there were **mulattoes,** people of black and Spanish ancestry, and **zambos,** those who were of Indian and black ancestry.

Old World ways in the New World. To their American colonies the Portuguese and Spaniards brought domestic animals, plants, and seeds never before seen in the New World. In pens and crates on the decks of their ships, they transported horses, donkeys, cattle, pigs, sheep, goats, and poultry. Using barrels cut in half and filled with earth, they carried fruit and nut trees—olive, lemon, orange, lime, apple, apricot, cherry, pear, fig, almond, and walnut. In bags they brought seeds of wheat, barley, rye, rice, peas, lentils, and flax. They also transplanted sugar cane and many kinds of flowers.

In addition to these products, the Spaniards and Portuguese brought their languages and their political, economic, and social systems to the Americas. They brought their tools and their technology, as well as their religious beliefs and institutions.

In Juana Inés de la Cruz entered a convent in New Mexico and later became a great poet. She also protested the exclusion of women from university study.

The colonizers did not simply recreate European culture in the Americas. New conditions in the New World changed European ways of life. For example, the Europeans began to grow crops native to the Americas, such as corn, potatoes, pumpkins, tomatoes, tobacco, avocados, and peanuts.

The colonists prosper. By 1580, before the English or the French had won even a foothold in the Americas, Portugal and Spain had firmly established their New World colonies. The Portuguese, unlike the Spaniards, found no huge treasures of gold and silver. They had, however, developed flourishing sugar plantations in the lowlands along the northeast coast of Brazil.

The Spaniards were even more successful. In less than a hundred years after the first settlers arrived, they had built prosperous farms, ranches, and cities in the New World. They continued to secure immense fortunes in gold and silver from the old Indian mines in Mexico and in Central and South America. They operated seaports that served as centers of vigorous trade between the Old World and the New. They printed books in the New World and educated at least some of their youth in newly built colleges and universities. Mexico City and Lima in Peru compared favorably with many cities in the Old World.

Slavery in the colonies. The Europeans needed a large labor force to work the colonial mines and plantations. At first, they enslaved the Indians for these jobs, although many Indians escaped or rebelled. The systems of Indian slavery sometimes produced disastrous results. In the Caribbean islands and coastal lowlands, European cruelty and the spread of European diseases wiped out almost all of the Indian population. Faced with a severe labor shortage, the Portuguese and the Spaniards began to transport black slaves from Africa. Their numbers grew rapidly, and some historians estimate that by the mid-1500's more Africans than Europeans were living in the New World.

In the mining regions and farming lands of the interior, the Indians, many of them slaves, continued to provide the main labor source. After the Spanish government abolished Indian slavery in the 1540's, the Spaniards still used forced labor but under a different system.

Forced labor. Before the Europeans arrived,

the Indians of the Aztec and Incan empires had lived as subject peoples. The Spanish conquest simply substituted European for Indian rulers. The new rulers introduced a system of Indian labor that was only a step away from outright slavery. This system included both the **encomienda** (en·coh·mee·EN·dah) and the **repartimiento** (ray·par·tee·mee·EN·toh).

The encomienda was a grant of those Indians who lived on a specific piece of land. A new Spanish settler might receive a grant of land and the accompanying encomienda. The settler who received the grant owned neither the land nor the Indians but served as a trustee for both. In return for the use of the land and the Indians, the settler paid taxes to the Spanish Crown—to the king and queen—and, in some cases, to the Church.

A repartimiento was another system of forced Indian labor. It gave the receiver a specified number of Indians to work as forced laborers on a ranch or in a factory, mine, or monastery. From their meager wages, the Indians, including women and children, had to pay taxes to the Crown and to the Church.

The Church and the Indians. From the beginning of colonization, the Spanish king and queen, the ruling class, and the officials of the Roman Catholic Church had proclaimed that their major aim was to Christianize the Indians. A few hundred years earlier, European Crusaders had fought the Muslims to rescue the Holy Land for Christianity. Now the Spanish clergy determined to free the Indians from what the Europeans saw as false gods.

Priests and missionaries came to the colonies in large numbers. They worked tirelessly to convert the Indians. In the towns and cities, they built churches and cathedrals. In the countryside they set up missions around which they gathered the Indians. There the priests taught them the ways of European agriculture, carpentry, masonry, and other skills.

The mission system had faults. It imposed a European way of life on the natives and, in doing so, weakened or destroyed their native cultures. Nevertheless, the kindness and dedication of many of the missionaries stood in sharp contrast to the harsh exploitation practiced by other colonizers.

The most famous of the missionaries was Friar Bartolomé de Las Casas. Throughout his life he fought for freedom and justice for the

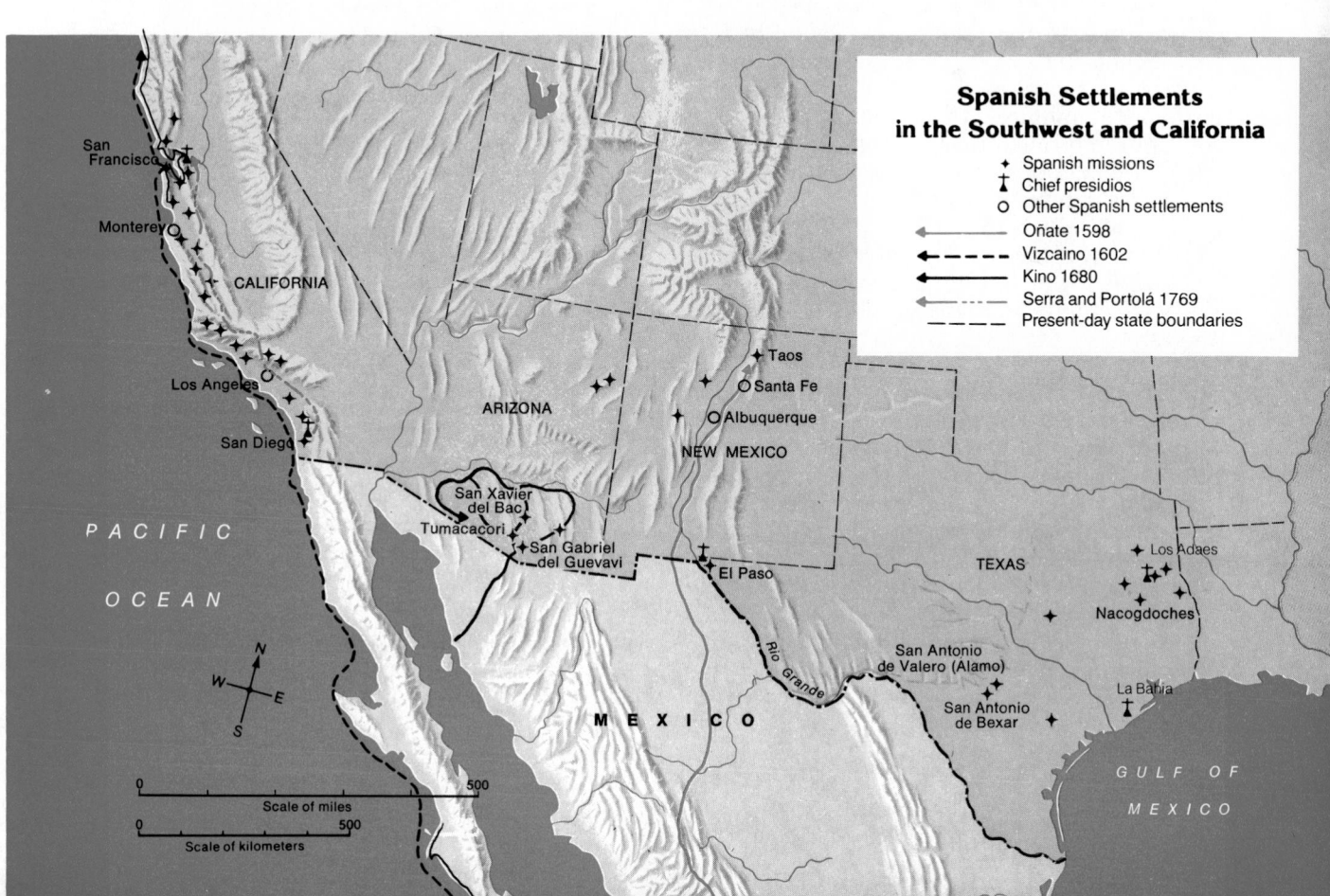

Spanish Settlements in the Southwest and California

- ✦ Spanish missions
- ✝ Chief presidios
- O Other Spanish settlements
- ← Oñate 1598
- ←--- Vizcaino 1602
- ← Kino 1680
- ←-·-·- Serra and Portolá 1769
- ---- Present-day state boundaries

Indians. He urged the Spanish Crown to forbid people from entering the New World who could not show that they were moved by love and believed in freedom. He and those who shared his faith and his convictions fought a losing battle.

Governing the Spanish colonies. At the peak of its power, Spain ruled the largest empire in the world since the time of ancient Rome. In the New World, it reached from the Atlantic to the Pacific and from California southward to the Strait of Magellan.

In law and in theory, all authority centered in the Spanish king. He ruled in the name of God and with the assistance of advisers.

In the New World, the king was represented by two **viceroys**—officials who ruled in the king's name. The viceroy located in Mexico City ruled New Spain—the Caribbean, Central America, Spanish North America, and part of South America. The viceroy located in Lima, Peru, ruled the rest of the Spanish colonies in South America. Lesser officials in descending order of rank served the viceroys. The smallest political unit in the empire was the town or village.

The system sometimes worked better in theory than in practice. Orders issued by the Crown and by the Church in Spain had to travel thousands of miles by sailing ship and then by horseback or by foot to reach the outposts of the empire. Officials at every level of the Church or government sometimes ignored the orders and laws they disliked. The system was also strained by conflicts between the high colonial officials born in Spain and the creoles, who held the lower offices. In spite of these weaknesses, the system succeeded in holding the vast empire together until well into the 1800's.

The crest of Spanish power. The gold and silver of the New World were carried to Spain in great treasure fleets. These fleets included treasure-laden galleons—huge vessels for their day, slow and clumsy, but heavily armed. Surrounding them in a great circle was a protecting convoy of smaller, swifter warships. Year after year these fleets moved the wealth of the New World to the Old.

Then, in 1580, Spain had another stroke of good fortune. King Philip II of Spain became ruler of Portugal. The two kingdoms of Spain and Portugal were united. For 60 years, until

Portugal once again became an independent country, its thriving colonies were joined to those of Spain. Portugal's rich trade with India and the Spice Islands of the East Indies brought still greater wealth to Spain. Spanish power seemed unbeatable, yet that power would soon diminish.

The new wealth helped to ruin Spain. Instead of building industries to produce goods at home, the Spaniards used gold and silver from America to buy needed products from other countries. As a result, when the flow of gold and silver decreased, Spaniards could neither pay for the goods they needed nor produce such goods themselves.

Spain paid another price for its success. It became involved in wars and rebellions all over Europe. Enemies rose up, eager to destroy its supremacy.

SECTION REVIEW
See underscored items, text pp. 17 - 20.

Identify: colony, Creoles, mestizos, mulattoes, encomienda, repartimiento, Bartolomé de Las Casas, viceroys, Philip II

For answers to questions, see Answer Key, pp.A9-10.

1. **Analyzing Ideas:** How was life in Spain's American colonies influenced by local conditions?

2. **Summarizing Ideas:** How and why did the system of Indian labor change after 1540?

3. **Interpreting Ideas:** (a) Why did Spanish missionaries try to convert the Indians to Christianity? (b) How did the Indians both benefit and suffer from these attempts?

4. **Studying Maps:** Compare the map of Spanish settlements on page 19 with a map of the United States today (see pages 992–93). What states once held Spanish settlements, missions, or presidios?

5 **England challenges Spain and gains a foothold in North America**

See Teaching Suggestions in TMRG, p.TM17.

English and Dutch sailors called "sea dogs" hastened Spain's decline by attacking the Spanish treasure ships and seizing their cargoes.

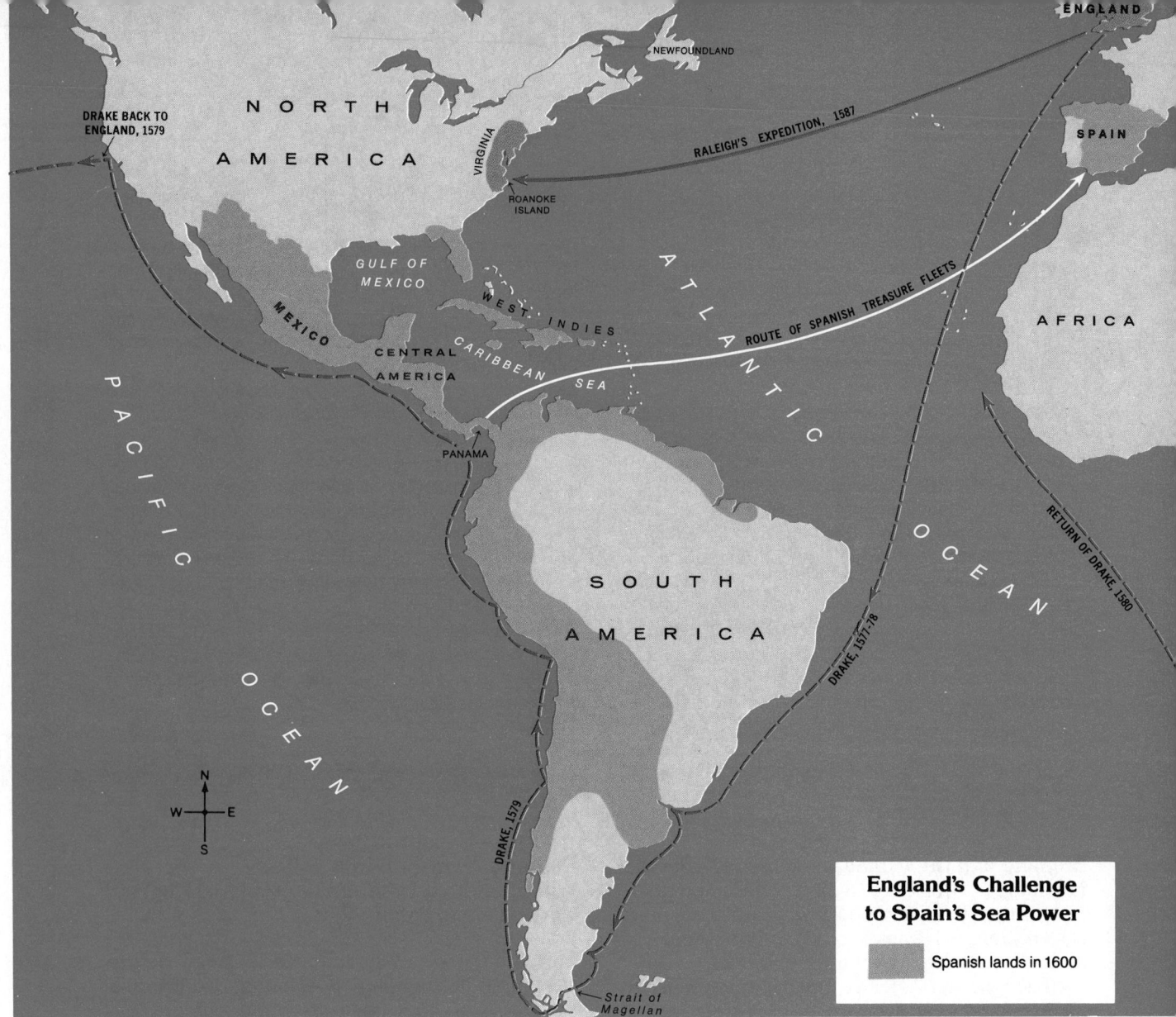

England's Challenge
to Spain's Sea Power

Spanish lands in 1600

The sea dogs. John Hawkins was the first famous English sea dog. Today he would be called a pirate—which is just what the Spaniards called him—but the English people and Queen Elizabeth I looked upon him as a hero.

Hawkins began his career in the 1560's by transporting African slaves to the Spanish islands in the Caribbean. However, he soon discovered an easier—though riskier—way to make a fortune. He began to raid Spanish seaports and attack Spanish treasure ships.

The fame and fortune enjoyed by Hawkins inspired other daring adventurers to follow his example. Among the boldest was Francis Drake. In 1577 he left England with a fleet of swift, heavily armed vessels. He headed southward, sailed through the Strait of Magellan, and then turned to the north (see map, this page). Along the western coast of South America, he attacked the unsuspecting and unprotected Spanish ships carrying gold and silver from the mines of Peru. Then, his own vessels loaded with the riches stolen from Spain, he wintered on the coast of California. The following year he returned to England by way of the Pacific and Indian oceans. Like Magellan's expedition, Drake had circumnavigated the globe. On his return to England, Queen Elizabeth I welcomed Drake as a hero and knighted him on the deck on his ship.

▲ Drake sailed around the world on his return voyage to avoid being captured by the Spaniards.

Throughout most of the sixteenth century, religious struggles often reinforced political hostilities between nations. Spain, for example, gradually became the most powerful Catholic country in Europe. At the same time England was emerging as the most powerful Protestant nation. In the summer of 1588, these two rivals met in one of the most decisive naval battles in history. This battle ultimately influenced the shaping of the American heritage.

Since the 1570's ruthless English sea dogs had been raiding and plundering Spanish treasure galleons returning home from the New World. In 1588 King Philip II of Spain retaliated by sending a mammoth fleet — the Invincible Armada — to capture England. His purpose was two-fold: to return England to Catholicism, and to break the English, who had been aiding the Protestant Dutch in their struggle for independence from Spain.

For one week in August 1588 the Spanish and English fleets fought up and down the English Channel. The Spaniards were accustomed to conventional naval warfare — pounding an enemy at close range before grappling and boarding. But the English had developed a new method of sea fighting that emphasized greater maneuverability and longer range firepower. The commanders of the clumsy Spanish galleons were thus surprised as the smaller and swifter English ships swept in and out, harrassing them with cannon fire from distances as great as 200 yards (183 meters).

The English also had a trick up their sleeves. At midnight on August 7, eight English ships, their guns loaded, their holds stuffed with anything that would burn, were set afire. Picked crews stayed with the ships long enough to be sure they were headed toward the heart of the Spanish fleet anchored in the harbor of Calais, France.

As the flaming vessels bore down on the Armada with exploding cannon fire, the Spaniards panicking, cut their anchor lines and scattered into the English Channel. There the English bombarded the Spanish ships, which began to sink or run aground. At the same time a fierce storm drove the disorganized Armada into the rough North Sea.

When the last Spanish ship limped home in the fall, half of the fleet was gone — and England was safe. Soon England would turn its attention to the planting of colonies in the New World.

England and the Armada. Queen Elizabeth's honoring of Drake was a direct challenge to the Spaniards. King Philip II was quick to meet the challenge. He assembled a mighty fleet and army to invade and conquer England.

The Spanish Armada, the most powerful invasion force ever seen up to that time, sailed against England in the year 1588. The boldness and skill of English sailors, combined with a disastrous storm, broke the back of the Armada. Most of the ships never returned to Spain.

The year 1588 was, therefore, a turning point in history. With its powerful fleet destroyed and weakened by troubles at home, Spain began to decline in power. To be sure, for many years Spain remained strong in both the Old World and the New, but it was no longer the most feared nation in Europe.

While Spain weakened, England, France, and the Netherlands grew stronger. In time, the English Royal Navy won for England the proud title of "Mistress of the Seas." By the end of the 1500's, no nation could prevent England from building colonies in the New World. By this time many people in England were eager to do just that.

The failure of early colonies. Even before the defeat of the Spanish Armada, two English adventurers had tried to build colonies in America, but both had failed, In 1583 Sir Humphrey Gilbert sailed to plant a colony in Newfoundland, but he and his companions were lost in a storm. The following year Queen Elizabeth gave Sir Walter Raleigh permission to build colonies in an area that he named Virginia (see map, page 21).

In 1587, after one expedition had ended in failure, Raleigh sent a second group of settlers. They landed on Roanoke Island off the coast of what is now North Carolina (see maps, pages 21 and 25). Unfortunately, the Spanish attempt to invade England in 1588 prevented Raleigh from sending supplies for three years. In 1590, when a relief expedition finally reached Roanoke, the settlers were gone. The fate of this "Lost Colony" remains a mystery.

The famous charter of 1606. Nearly ten years passed before anyone in England attempted to build another colony in America. Then in 1606 King James I gave a single **charter** — an official grant of certain rights, powers, or privileges — to two groups. One group, based in Plymouth, England, was known as the Plymouth Company. The other, based in London, was known as the London Company.

Both of these business ventures were organized as **joint-stock companies.** Joint-stock companies were forerunners of modern corporations. A number of people bought shares of stock in the company. The money they invested would pay the expenses of the venture — for example, the founding of a colony. Any profit the company made from trade and development of the colony would be shared by the investors. In the back of many of the investors' minds was the tantalizing picture of the vast treasures that Spain had discovered in its New World colonies!

The charter granted to the Plymouth and London companies included a very important promise by King James. All people who served either company in the English colonies would retain their rights and privileges as English subjects. Among these rights were those set forth long ago in the *Magna Carta,* the Great Charter, written in 1215. In the words of the charter of 1606, the colonists would "have and enjoy all liberties, franchises, and immunities . . . as if they had been abiding and born within this our realm of England, or any other of our said dominions."

A poor start for Jamestown. It was Christmas time, 1606, when three small ships of the London Company left England and sailed out on the wintry sea. The London Company was sending more than 100 men to start a colony in America. From the beginning almost everything seemed to go wrong. The ships took a roundabout way to America, following Columbus's route. Many of the men died on the long voyage. When the colonists finally reached Virginia in the spring of 1607, they began to build a settlement named Jamestown in honor of the king (see map, page 25). They picked the poorest possible location — a low, wooded island in a river, which they called the James, near a marsh filled with malaria-carrying mosquitoes. The men did not take time to dig wells but instead drank the river water. Because they built only the flimsiest of shel-

The defeat of the "Invincible Armada" is seen behind Queen Elizabeth. England might have been defeated by Spain without a shipbuilding program that was ordered by Elizabeth.

ters, they were drenched by rain in summer and half-frozen by cold when winter came.

The directors of the London Company back in England also made mistakes. Remembering Spain's rich discoveries, they insisted that the settlers hunt for gold. The settlers did so in vain, wasting valuable time that could have been spent in building houses and cultivating crops. To make matters worse, the settlers were not allowed to own anything, and they received, if they were fortunate, only as much food and clothing as they needed.

The worst mistake of all, perhaps, was the failure of the directors to send enough real workers to develop the resources of the settlement. The original group of settlers that sailed for Jamestown included only 12 laborers and skilled workers. The rest were "gentlemen" — in those days defined as men who had never done a day's work with their hands. Not a single settler was a farmer.

Difficult times at Jamestown. Not surprisingly, by the end of the first year, fewer than half of the settlers were still alive. They, too, might have perished had it not been for John Smith. Smith set himself up as the leader of the colony. He ordered the men to dig wells, build better shelters, clear the land, and plant corn and other crops.

John Smith was a harsh ruler. Every morning he marched the men into the fields to cultivate the crops or into the forest to cut wood. They grumbled and complained, but the rule was "No work, no food." The men worked. Thanks to John Smith and to the Indians, the colony survived. In Smith's own words, "The Indians brought us great store both of Corne and of bread ready made." Smith also raided Indian villages to get needed food.

When Smith returned to England, however, matters went from bad to worse. The winter of 1609–10 was terrible beyond belief. In later years the survivors called it "the starving time." When spring came, the half-starved colonists were prepared to abandon Jamestown. Fortunately, just at this time ships arrived from England bringing more settlers and fresh supplies, giving the colonists new hope.

In 1609 the king granted a new charter, which gave more land to the Virginia colony (see map, page 25).

Better times at Jamestown. Slowly, after 1610, the conditions began to improve. Much to everyone's surprise, tobacco saved the colony.

Europeans first learned about smoking tobacco from the Indians. By the early 1600's, the habit of smoking was spreading throughout England and the rest of Europe.

Until Jamestown was settled, the Caribbean islands supplied all the tobacco smoked by the English and other Europeans. Then around 1612 John Rolfe (who later married the Indian princess Pocahontas) learned how to grow and cure tobacco in Virginia. Within a few years, the colonists were shipping large quantities of this valuable product to England. By 1619 there were more than 1,000 colonists in Virginia, and most were raising tobacco.

Jamestown grew for other reasons, too. Among the new settlers were many skilled workers—carpenters, masons, and blacksmiths. Starting in 1618, each man who paid his own way to Jamestown was given 50 acres (20.2 hectares) of land. The colonists now were able to own their fields and sell their products.

The start of self-government. In 1619 the London Company took another big step forward by giving the colonists the right to share in their own government.

July 30, 1619, is a memorable date in American history. On that date 22 **burgesses,** or representatives, two from each of the settled districts along the James River, met in Jamestown. Each of the burgesses had been elected by the land-owning voters of the district in which he lived. The House of Burgesses, as this law-making body was called, marked the first step toward representative government in the New World.

The growth of Virginia. The date 1619 is memorable for other reasons. In that year 20 Africans arrived in the colony. These newcomers were the first of countless thousands of men and women from Africa who would work with people from many other lands in building the English colonies.

In the early years many, if not all, of the Africans were regarded as servants, bound for a period of years to the master who paid a ship captain for transporting them to America. At the end of a term of service, some of the Africans acquired land and worked it for themselves. By the 1640's, however, Africans were also being brought to the colonies as slaves.

SOURCES

MAGNA CARTA
(1215)

No freeman shall be seized, imprisoned, dispossessed, outlawed, or exiled, or in any way destroyed, nor will we proceed against or prosecute him, except by the lawful judgment of his peers or by the law of the land.

To none will we sell, to none will we deny, to none will we delay, right or justice. . . .

Wherefore our will is, and we firmly command, that the Church of England be free, and that the men in our kingdom have and hold the aforesaid liberties, rights, and concessions well and in peace, freely and quietly, fully and entirely, to them and their heirs, of us and our heirs, in all things and places forever, as is aforesaid. . . .

▲ It is ironic that tobacco saved the Jamestown colony. The colony's namesake, King James I, detested smoking, calling it in 1604, "A custom loathsome to the eye, hateful to the nose, harmful to the brain, dangerous to the lungs. . . ."

In the early years, also, there were few women in Virginia. In 1619 the directors of the London Company sent 60 unmarried women to the colony. These women quickly married Jamestown settlers.

The directors of the London Company, encouraged by Virginia's growing prosperity, sent out hundreds of new settlers. Some of them started an ironworks on the James River. Others planted olive trees and laid out vineyards, but most of the newcomers cleared a piece of land and began to grow tobacco.

Then disaster struck. Nearby Indians had become alarmed at the rapid growth of the colony. On March 22, 1622, Indians attacked the outlying farmhouses, killed 347 settlers, including John Rolfe, and burned most of the buildings. The survivors struck back at the Indians. In one episode 250 Indians who had come seeking peace died after drinking poisoned wine at a toast-drinking ceremony. Earlier efforts by the Virginians and Indians to understand and tolerate each other were largely abandoned.

Virginia becomes a royal colony. In spite of the colony's growth, King James I decided that it had been badly managed. In 1624 he withdrew the charter from the London Company and took over the management of the colony. From then on, Virginia was a **royal colony**, ruled by the king of England and his ministers. The king now appointed the governor and gave the governor power to veto, or reject, any laws. He also appointed a council, consisting of 12 members, to assist the governor.

The government of Virginia was not as restrictive as that of the Spanish colonies to the south and west, where the king of Spain and his viceroys still held absolute power. King James I did not attempt to end the House of Burgesses. The House of Burgesses continued to make the laws, subject to the approval of the governor and of the king, and the settlers continued to elect the members of the House of Burgesses.

SECTION REVIEW
See underscored items, text pp. 21-25.
Identify: John Hawkins, Francis Drake, Elizabeth I, 1588, Roanoke Island, charter, Plymouth Company, London Company, John Smith, House of Burgesses, royal colony

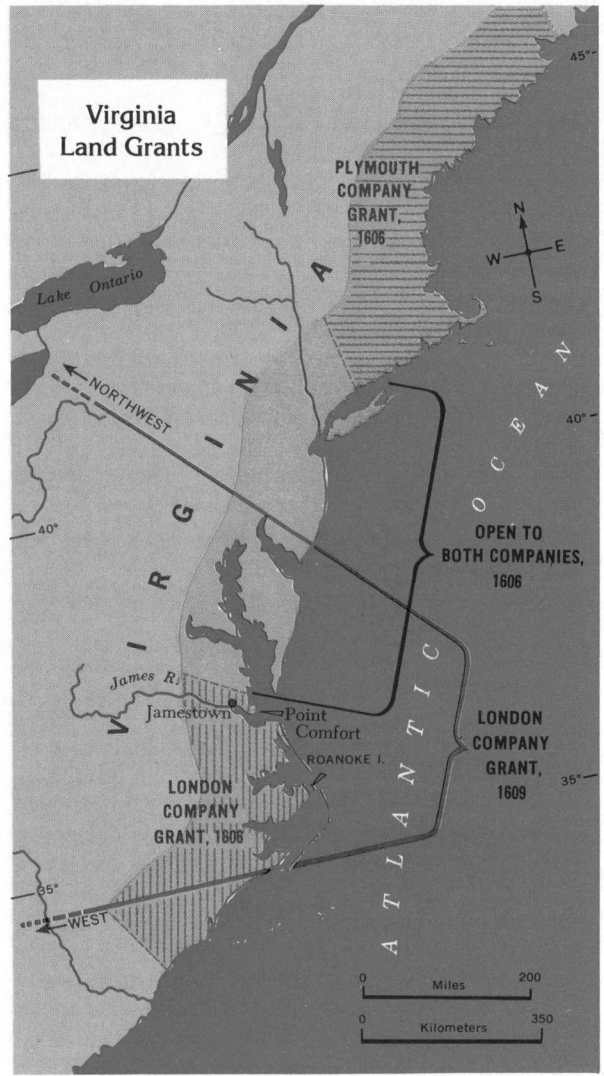

Virginia Land Grants

For answers to questions, see Answer Key, p.A10.

1. **Determining Cause and Effect:** (a) How did Spain act to stop English interference with Spain's American colonies? (b) What was the result of Spain's action?

2. **Summarizing Ideas:** (a) What problems threatened to defeat the settlement at Jamestown? (b) How were these problems solved?

3. **Analyzing Ideas:** (a) Name two important events that took place in Virginia in 1619. (b) Why were these events important? (c) How did the government of Virginia change in 1624?

4. **Studying Sources:** Read the section of the Magna Carta on page 24. Who in the Virginia colony of the 1640's would not be protected by these guarantees?

DEVELOPING HISTORY STUDY SKILLS

Thinking About History   Using Textbook Features

Within any textbook is a vast amount of information that you have to make your own. To help you understand this information, the textbook has been divided into many parts, each of which has its own function. Some parts help you preview the information you are about to study. Other parts help you study that information. Still other parts help you review what you have just studied. Using a textbook and its parts wisely is an important first move toward becoming an adept practicioner of the historian's craft.

The study of history involves the use of more than one set of tools. The history textbook itself is just one of these sets. In succeeding chapters you will read about other sets of tools that help you study history.

How to Use the Textbook

To get the most from the textbook, use these guidelines.

1. **Use the Table of Contents.** Familiarize yourself with the textbook's Table of Contents (pages v–xxvi). The Table of Contents tells how many units and chapters are in the textbook, what is included in each chapter, and the page where each unit, chapter, section, and feature can be found.
2. **Study the unit's opening pages.** Begin the study of each unit by taking time to study the unit's opening pages. For example, review the opening pages of Unit One (pages xxviii–1). Read the unit label and the unit title. Study the illustration. Ask yourself questions about the illustration and its connection with the unit title. Read the unit introduction above the illustration, becoming familiar with the unit's theme.

   Next, review the outline of the unit. Read the chapter titles. Note the contents of each chapter by reading the section titles. With this preview of the unit, you have a good idea of the unit's theme and content.
3. **Begin at the beginning of each chapter.** Each chapter begins with an illustrated page. Take time to ask yourself questions about what you see on that page: chapter label, chapter title, an illustration, and an illustration label. For example, turn to pages 2–3 for the opening pages of Chapter 1. Think about the connections between the chapter title and the illustration on page 2.

   Next, read the first column on the facing page. This column provides an introduction to the chapter. Pay particular attention to the ending section of the column, "The Reading Focus." It tells you the main parts of the chapter and gives a direction to your study of the chapter.
4. **Preview the Chapter.** Skim the chapter, noting the first section title (page 3) and the other section titles. Note the subheadings under each section title. These subheadings give you clues about the details that support each section's main idea. Note the maps, photographs, and other visuals within each section. Take time to read the captions, remembering to review them as you read and study each section. Glance at the first Section Review (page 10). Previewing gives you a framework around which to weave the fabric of history.
5. **Read the chapter carefully.** By now reading is almost as automatic as breathing. Nonetheless, use the textbook's clues to help you get the most out of your reading of a chapter. First, use the headings and subheadings as clues to main ideas and supporting details. Stay with a paragraph until you are sure you understand what it says.

   Second, pay attention to words printed in bold black type. These **boldfaced terms** are highlighted to call attention to important history terms. Most of these terms are defined in context; that is, the definition follows, or it can be determined from the sentences around it. In some instances, the term is defined in a footnote.

   Third, review the illustrations on each page before moving on to the next page. Relate the information in the illustration to the content of your reading. Finally, use the Review at the end of each section to check your reading. If you cannot remember an answer, reread the section until you find it. Then go on to the next section, repeating each of the above steps.
6. **Study the special features.** Each chapter has several special features that add to your knowledge of history. You can recognize these features easily because they appear with a color background to set them apart from the narrative of the chapter. When you read the features depends on your learning style. Some students may prefer to read each feature as a part of the previewing step. Others may prefer to read a feature as they read the page on which the feature appears. Still others may wish to read the features just before reviewing a section. When you read them is not as important as being sure you do read them.
7. **Summarize the chapter.** Each chapter ends with a Chapter Summary (page 28). The Chapter Sum-

mary helps you recap the main ideas of the chapter. It also sets the stage for the ideas to be presented in the next chapter. Through a time line, this part of the textbook also gives you a visual overview of important specific events.

8. **Review the chapter.** The textbook provides a Chapter Review page (page 29) to help you check and pinpoint the information that is important for you to remember. It does this through a variety of exercises, questions, and activities.

9. **Review the unit.** Like the Chapter Review, the Unit Review is a valuable resource that a practical student uses to determine the ideas and facts that are important enough to use in fashioning history.

10. **Use the Reference Section.** The Reference Section is your "go-with-you, use-any-time" library of information. It begins on page 990. Familiarize yourself with it now so you may utilize its valuable information at every appropriate instance.

Applying the Skill

Complete the following activities.

1. Turn to the Table of Contents. Use it to find the answers to these questions. **(a)** How many units does the text have? **(b)** How many chapters does the text have? **(c)** Who are the subjects of the feature entitled "American Profiles" in Unit Nine? **(d)** What is the subject of "This Changing Land" in Unit Four?

    If you answered the text has 13 units and 43 chapters; the Americans profiled are Pearl Buck, John Hay, and Jeanette Rankin; and the subject of "This Changing Land" is the Great Lakes, you have used the Table of Contents wisely.

2. Turn to the Glossary (page 1031) and answer these questions. **(a)** What is the first entry under "B"? **(b)** On what page of the textbook is the term *frontier* in bold-faced type? **(c)** What are the first and last entries on page 1034?

    If you discovered that the first entry under "B" is *baby boom;* that *frontier* is printed in bold-faced type on page 37; and the first and last entries on page 1034 are *embargo* and *homestead,* you have made good use of the Glossary.

Practicing the Skill

The titles, headings, and subheadings of Chapter 1 can be used to formulate a working outline of a topic. Study the sample outline on this page. Compare the outline items with the headings and subheadings of Chapter 1. On a separate sheet of paper, copy the outline, filling in the missing parts.

I. Exploring the Americas (Beginnings to 1624)

A. **The first Americans discover and settle a new world**
 1. The first Americans
 2. Settling the land
 3. The Mayas
 4. The Incas
 5. The Aztecs
 6. The Indians of North America
 7. Indians of the Southwest
 8. The Plains Indians
 9. Other Western tribes
 10. Indians of the Eastern Woodlands
 11. Shared beliefs of the Indians

B. **Portugal and Spain lead the way to the Americas**
 1. A time of energy and change
 2. The importance of trade
 3. The difficulty of trade
 4. Portugal's sea route to Asia
 5. Columbus's fateful voyage
 6. Finding a world unknown to Europe
 7. An earlier European voyage
 8. English and French claims

C. Portuguese and Spaniards explore the New World
 1. Spanish and Portuguese claims
 2. How America got its name
 3. Discovering a "new" ocean
 4. Circling the earth
 5. Conquest of the Aztecs and Incas
 6. The search for gold
 7. New settlements for Spain
 8. Expansion into California

D. **Portugal and Spain plant their civilizations in the Americas**
 1. The colonial population
 2. Old World ways in the New World
 3. The colonists prosper
 4. Slavery in the colonies
 5. Forced labor
 6. The Church and the Indians
 7. Governing the Spanish colonies
 8. The crest of Spanish power

E. England challenges Spain and gains a foothold in North America
 1. The sea dogs
 2. England and the Armada
 3. The failure of early colonies
 4. The famous charter of 1606
 5. A poor start for Jamestown
 6. Difficult times at Jamestown
 7. Better times at Jamestown
 8. The start of self-government
 9. The growth of Virginia
 10. Virginia becomes a royal colony

1 SUMMARY

The first Americans entered the New World by way of the Bering Strait so long ago that the date of their arrival probably will never be known with any certainty. Over a period of many thousands of years, the descendants of these first arrivals and the descendants of later arrivals spread throughout the American continents and firmly settled on the land. These Native Americans developed many colorful and complex ways of life as they organized themselves into groups and cultures. These groups were soon to come into contact with Europeans who were being swept during the 1300's and 1400's into a new age by developments with far-reaching consequences.

There was the Revolution called the Renaissance—an intellectual and cultural awakening of Europeans to the world around them. There was the Commercial Revolution—an economic and trade revival spurred by the discovery of new all-water routes to Asia. There was the Geographic Revolution—an age of exploration in which Europeans traced the coastlines of Africa, circumnavigated the globe, and discovered what to them was a new world across the Atlantic.

Portugal and Spain led the way in exploring and colonizing the American continents with England and other nations following. In the Americas, the people of three different continents—North America, South America, and Europe—were brought together for the first time. These people all had to learn to share the land and build a common future.

CONNECTING CHAPTER IDEAS

In the next chapter you will read about the expansion of British territory and power. From Pilgrim and Puritan beginnings to the smashing of French power in the Americas, you will trace the development of a distinctive culture that came to be called "the American way of life."

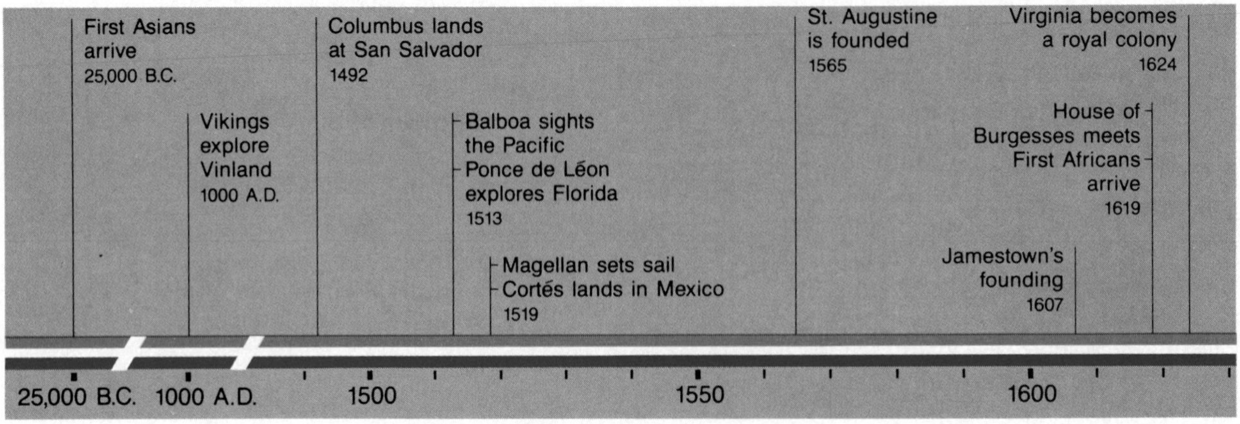

First Asians arrive 25,000 B.C.		Columbus lands at San Salvador 1492		St. Augustine is founded 1565	Virginia becomes a royal colony 1624
	Vikings explore Vinland 1000 A.D.		Balboa sights the Pacific Ponce de Léon explores Florida 1513		House of Burgesses meets First Africans arrive 1619
			Magellan sets sail Cortés lands in Mexico 1519		Jamestown's founding 1607

| 25,000 B.C. | 1000 A.D. | 1500 | 1550 | 1600 |

1 REVIEW

Reviewing Important Terms

Decide whether each of the following sentences is true or false. If the sentence is false, replace the underlined term with the word or phrase that will make it true.

1. All Native American groups had developed rich and varied underlined civilizations long before the Europeans arrived in America.
2. The Navajos built their hogans with adobe and logs.
3. In order to defend their colonial claims in North America, the Spaniards established encomiendas.
4. In the Spanish colonies, Creoles held a higher position in the social class structure than the mestizos.
5. The viceroy of Lima ruled most of the Spanish colonies in South America.
6. Both the Plymouth Company and the London Company were joint-stock companies.
7. For the first eighteen years, the Virginia colonists were ruled under the burgesses granted by King James I.

Practicing Critical Thinking Skills

1. **Interpreting Ideas.** (a) How did the spirit of the Renaissance affect the Commercial Revolution? (b) How did the Commercial Revolution promote the Geographic Revolution?
2. **Comparing Ideas.** Compare Native Americans and Europeans in 1450 in terms of their (a) cultures, (b) attitudes toward the land, and (c) ways of making a living. (d) How might these similarities and differences have affected Native Americans' and Europeans' attitudes toward one another?
3. **Interpreting Viewpoints.** Do you think that most people in London in 1600 realized that they were living in a revolutionary age? Why or why not?
4. **Using Historical Imagination.** (a) Why do you think John Smith took control of Jamestown? (b) How might he have justified the harsh measures he took?
5. **Organizing Ideas.** Explain each of the following terms in relation to European exploration and settlement of the New World: (a) freedom, (b) riches, (c) political rivalry between nations, (d) Christianity.

6. **Relating Past to Present.** The seeds of troubled race relations in America were planted early in the history of European exploration and settlement of the New World. Cite evidence in this chapter that would support this statement.

Developing History Study Skills

1. **Using Textbook Features.** Choose one of the sections in this chapter. Take each subheading in the section and turn it into a question. Find the answer to the questions, and then write a paragraph that summarizes the section, formulating the answers into statements.

2. **Using Maps.** Use reference materials in the library to find a map that shows the early trade routes between Europe and the East. Study the map and answer the following questions. (a) If you had been a trader in the Middle Ages, which of the medieval trade routes would you have used? Why? (b) Which parts of the world were known to Europeans before the voyages of exploration? (c) Which parts of the world were still unexplored?

Relating Geography and History

In today's world of instant electronic communication and supersonic flight, it is sometimes difficult to understand what it was like when wind and ocean currents were the only forms of energy to power ships across the seas. Then, time and distance had an effect on government in the colony and on trade and communications between the homeland and a colony. To understand how time and distance affected the colonists in the Americas, complete the following activities.

1. Do research to find out how long it took sailing ships to cross the Atlantic Ocean.
2. List at least three kinds of goods that the colonists depended on ships to carry (a) from the homeland to the colony, (b) from the colony to the homeland.
3. (a) In a paragraph discuss some of the problems faced by rulers and colonists because of time and distance. (b) In a second paragraph speculate on reasons why time and distance might have helped foster a sense of independence in lifestyle, trade, and government in the New World.

29

See Chapter Overview in TMRG, p.TM18.
See Chapter Objectives in TMRG, p.TM18.
See Introducing the Chapter in TMRG, p.TM18.

CHAPTER 2
Expansion of British Power
(1620–1763)

Pilgrims
setting sail

If Europe had been a happier place in the 1600's, the attractions of the New World would not have been so compelling to Europeans. Europe, however, was not a happy place for many people.

Men and women with little hope of ever making a better living in Europe looked to the Americas with new hope. Those who thought about the Americas pictured the land as rich yet thinly populated, waiting for the ax and the plow of new settlers. Ignoring the fact that the land was already occupied by the Indians, most Europeans regarded the land as theirs for the taking. Here in the New World was opportunity, almost limitless, for the men and the women who were bold enough to seize it.

So they came—to Mexico, to Quebec, to Jamestown, to New England. They came in the greatest numbers from England to settle along the Atlantic seaboard. By 1733, when Georgia was founded, British settlers had planted colonies in the West Indies and had established 13 colonies on the mainland. The boldest of the pioneers were pushing westward through the forest, clearing land, and building homes.

During these years, however, Great Britain's bitter rival France had grown stronger, not only in Europe but in all its far-flung colonies. In four different wars from 1689 to 1763, the two European powers battled for supremacy on the high seas and in Europe, Asia, and North America. Out of the final struggle, the British emerged victorious. One of Britain's grand prizes was the huge French territory in North America.

═══ READING FOCUS ═══

As you read about British expansion in North America, look for the details that support each of the following statements.

1. Pilgrims and Puritans search for a better life in North America.
2. English settlers build more colonies in New England.
3. People from several nations settle the Middle Colonies.
4. A distinctive way of life develops in the Southern Colonies.
5. New France grows and threatens the British colonies.
6. Great Britain smashes French power in North America.

1 Pilgrims and Puritans search for a better life in North America

See Teaching Suggestions in TMRG, pp.TM18-19.

Opportunity! Like a magnet, opportunity drew men and women from Europe to the New World. Even so, people would not have come in such great numbers if conditions in Europe had been better than they were.

Conflict over religion. During the 1500's and 1600's, Europe was torn by religious strife that broke out shortly after Columbus's voyages. At that time nearly everyone in Western Europe belonged to the Roman Catholic Church. The conflict began when some people began to question certain Church practices and beliefs. Martin Luther in Germany and John Calvin in Switzerland were two such people.

These religious leaders and people who shared their feelings broke away from the Roman Catholic Church and established Protestant, or "protesting," religious organizations. Roman Catholics called this movement the Protestant Revolt. Protestants called the same movement the Reformation. By whatever name, this religious conflict was not just a battle of words and ideas. Armies marched, wars were fought, and thousands of people died in battle or were burned at the stake in the name of religion.

England broke with the Roman Catholic Church in 1534. At that time King Henry VIII ▲ established the Church of England, sometimes called the Anglican Church. The king of England became the head of this Church. According to English law, all English citizens, regardless of religious beliefs, had to belong to the Anglican Church and support it.

The search for religious freedom. In spite of the law, many people in England objected to the Anglican Church. Roman Catholics insisted upon their right to worship as they always had. Among those who accepted the Protestant Reformation, some felt that the Anglican Church was too much like the Roman Catholic Church. They wanted to carry the Reformation further and to simplify or "purify" the Anglican Church. These people were known as Puritans or Dissenters.

▲ One reason for Henry VIII's breaking with the Roman Catholic Church was his desire to divorce Catherine of Aragon and marry Anne Boleyn.

One group defied the law by refusing to attend the Anglican Church or to pay taxes for its support. These people, who broke away and formed their own organizations, were called Separatists.

Life in England was grim for all of the protesting groups, Catholic and Protestant alike. They were persecuted by their neighbors, fined by the government, and sometimes sent to jail. Thousands left England, hoping to find greater religious freedom in the New World. As the years passed, other religious refugees—Catholics, Protestants, and Jews—also fled to America from many of the other European countries.

The search for political freedom. Political problems in England came to a head during the reign of James I, who ruled from 1603 to 1625. King James believed in the **divine right of kings.** That is, he insisted that a king was responsible for his actions only to God, not to any earthly power. This belief brought him into conflict with the Parliament, the lawmaking body of England.

The quarrel between king and Parliament became even more intense when Charles I became king. From 1629 to 1640, Charles I ruled without Parliament. Then in 1642 the country plunged into a civil war called the Puritan Revolution that lasted until 1649 when Charles I was beheaded. For the next eleven years, the country was ruled by a group of Puritans. Oliver Cromwell led this group until his death in 1658.

During this long period of political unrest, many people fled to the New World to escape persecution by an unsympathetic government.

Economic changes. Sweeping economic and social changes also contributed to the development of the colonies.

During the 1500's and early 1600's, Europeans faced the problem of rising prices—a situation that today we call **inflation.** One reason for rising prices was the gold and silver that poured into Spain from its American colonies. Spain's increased wealth enabled it to buy more products from other countries. The growing Spanish demand for goods whose supply was limited enabled farmers and manufacturers in England and other countries to raise their prices. Then they in turn had more money to spend. Prices rose higher and higher.

Unhappily, inflation created hardships for many thousands of English families. When the price of wool, a raw material for cloth, rose, landowners realized that they could make more money raising sheep than renting their lands to tenant farmers. Many landowners evicted these farmers from their lands.

Some of the displaced tenants were willing to risk anything to get a fresh start in life. America seemed to offer just such an opportunity. Many unemployed men and women signed contracts called **indentures.** In these contracts they promised, in return for transportation to America, to work without wages for a period ranging from two to seven years. People who signed such contracts were called **indentured servants.**

Not all English people were hurt by the economic changes that were transforming the country. Certain groups prospered, among them merchants, landowners, traders, and manufacturers. As their fortunes grew, these people began to look for profitable ways to invest their money. Many bought shares in the new joint-stock companies. The more daring financed colonies in the New World. One such group of investors, a company of London merchants, financed the first permanent settlement in New England.

The Pilgrims arrive in New England. On November 11, 1620, after two months at sea, a small, storm-battered English vessel rounded the tip of Cape Cod and dropped its anchor in the quiet harbor of what is now Provincetown, Massachusetts. Why had those on board come to the New World? Not one of the 102 passengers on the *Mayflower* could have answered for all the others.

Many were Separatists who refused to follow the practices of the Church of England. Some of the Separatists had been living in the Netherlands, where the Dutch had allowed them to worship in their own way. However, they did not want their children to grow up speaking Dutch instead of English, living more like Dutch than English subjects. These Separatists were known as the Pilgrims.

The Mayflower Compact. The London Company had given the Pilgrims a grant of land south of the Hudson River, in what was then part of Virginia, but storms blew the *Mayflower* off course. As a result, the Pilgrims found themselves on the New England coast where they had no legal right to land or to set-

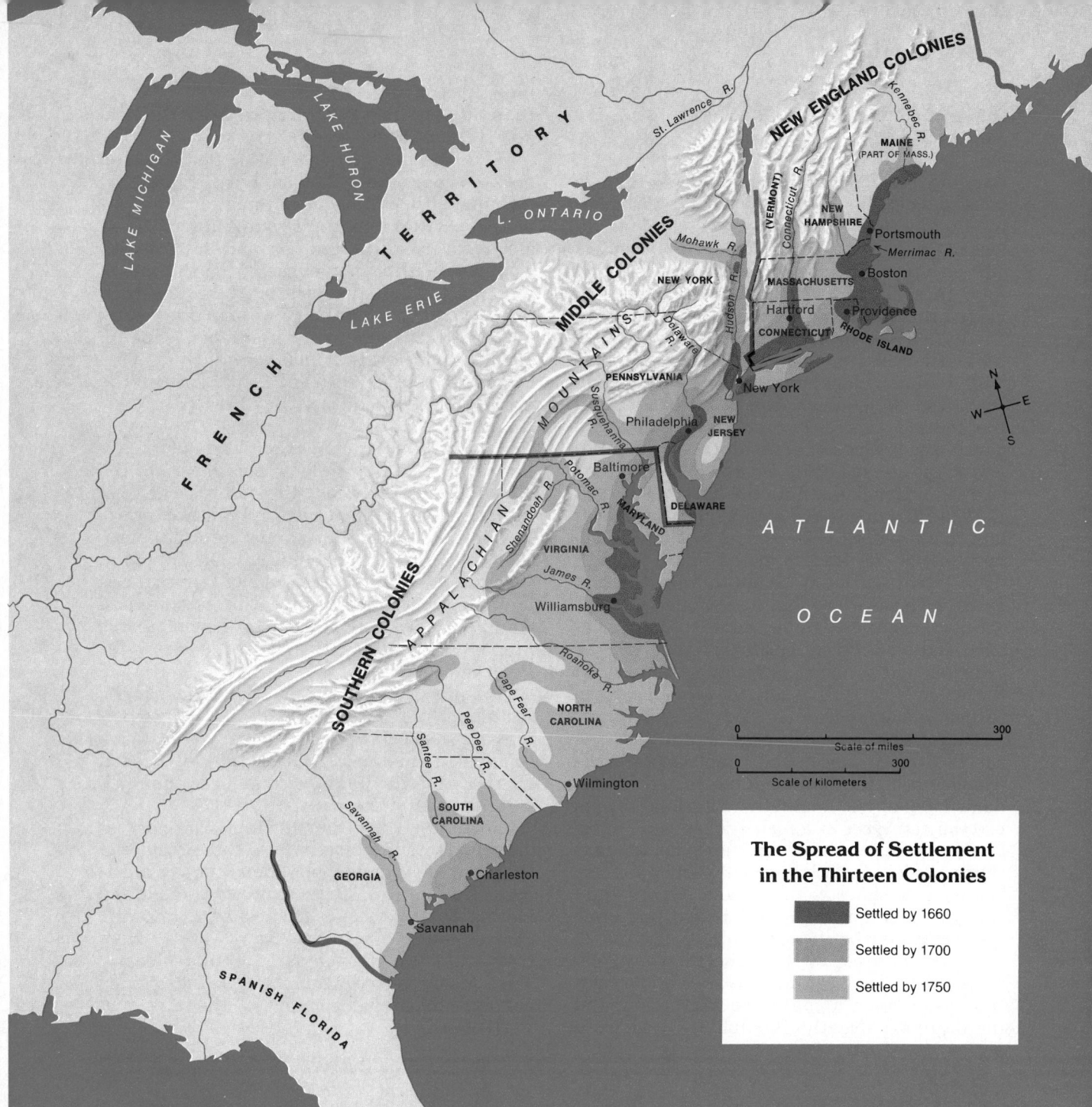

The Spread of Settlement
in the Thirteen Colonies

Settled by 1660

Settled by 1700

Settled by 1750

tle. Nor did the Pilgrims have any plans for governing the colony once they landed.

While the crew furled the sails, the Pilgrim leaders gathered in the cabin. There they wrote and signed the document that is now called the Mayflower Compact. In this compact, or agreement, they promised "all due submission and obedience" to the laws that they themselves would adopt.

The Mayflower Compact was intended to meet an emergency. It was not a plan of government. It did not pledge the Pilgrims to establish a democratic way of life. Nevertheless, this short document represented an important

See Reading 10, text pp. 525-26.

step along the road to self-government in the New World.

Landing at Plymouth. For more than a month, while the *Mayflower* swung at anchor in Provincetown harbor, a landing party looked for a place to settle. They finally chose a site on the southwestern shore of Cape Cod Bay. In earlier years English explorers had visited this place and named it Plymouth.

If the Pilgrims had arrived at Plymouth a few years earlier, they would have found a busy Indian village surrounded by farmland. As it was, an epidemic had wiped out most of the Indians. Those who survived had abandoned the village. Fortunately for the Pilgrims, the cleared fields remained, and a brook of fresh water flowed into the harbor.

The Pilgrims sailed into Plymouth harbor late in December 1620 and as William Bradford, one of the leaders, noted in his journal, "The Twenty-fifth day began to erect the first house." Those who could work toiled through the cold, cheerless winter months. Many sickened and died. Before spring arrived, half the Pilgrims had perished, but not one settler left the colony in April when the *Mayflower* returned to England.

Those who were still alive might not have survived much longer had it not been for the friendship of the Indians. One in particular, named Squanto, taught the Pilgrims how to use the resources of forest, sea, and soil effectively. Perhaps most important, he brought them seeds of native plants—Indian corn, beans, squash, pumpkins, and others—and showed them how to plant, fertilize, and grow these crops in the cleared fields.

In the autumn of 1621, the Pilgrims celebrated their first year in the New World by setting aside several days for recreation and thanksgiving. Nearly 100 Indians and more than 30 settlers newly arrived from England joined them in the celebration.

Like the Indians who had settled the land before them, the Pilgrims lived mainly by farming, although fish and game remained for many years an important source of food. They also traded with the Indians and in turn with England. With money earned from the sale of furs and lumber, they settled their debt with the London Company. However, the colony never attracted many new settlers. Finally, under a charter that was granted in 1691, Plymouth became a part of its neighbor to the north, the Massachusetts Bay Colony.

The roots of Massachusetts. The Puritans of Massachusetts Bay Colony also moved to the New World largely for religious reasons. Unlike the Pilgrims, however, the Massachusetts Bay settlers did not insist on a formal separation from the Church of England. However, they did want to change some of its practices, including Catholic-like ritual in worship and church rule by bishops. Charles I, who became king of England in 1625, refused to accept the Puritan proposals.

Finally, some prominent Puritan leaders, including John Winthrop and Sir Richard Saltonstall, decided to form a company and start a colony in America. In 1629 they secured a charter from the king and organized the Massachusetts Bay Company.

Fortunately for the Puritans, the charter did not name the place where the directors of the company would hold their annual meetings. The shrewd Puritan directors made the most of this oversight. They voted to take the charter and move to the New World, where they could run the company as they pleased. Thus Massachusetts became a **self-governing colony**, almost independent of the king and Parliament.

SOURCES

The
MAYFLOWER
COMPACT
(1620)

In the name of God, Amen. We whose names are underwritten, the loyal subjects of our dread sovereign Lord King *James*, by the grace of God, of Great Britain, France, and Ireland, King, Defender of the Faith, etc., having undertaken, for the glory of God, and advancement of the Christian faith, and honor of our king and country, a voyage to plant the first colony in the northern parts of Virginia, do by these presents solemnly and mutually in the presence of God, and one of another, covenant and combine ourselves together into a civil body politic for our better ordering and preservation and furtherance of the ends aforesaid; and by virtue hereof, to enact, constitute, and frame such just and equal laws, ordinances, acts, constitutions, and offices from time to time, as shall be thought most meet and convenient for the general good of the colony unto which we promise all due submission and obedience. . . .

▲ Writing activity: Have students pretend they are Pilgrims writing to a concerned family member in England. In their letters, students should explain why they have decided not to return to England on the April 1621 voyage of the "Mayflower."

This royal charter gave the power to rule to a few shareholders in the Massachusetts Bay Company. Once the settlers arrived, however, they too demanded a say in how the colony would be governed. Soon all male church members in good standing were given the right to vote.

The arrival of the Puritans. The Puritans began to arrive in Massachusetts during the summer of 1630—nearly 1,000 men, women, and children aboard 17 ships. Unlike the Pilgrims, the Puritan settlers had ample supplies of food, clothing, and tools. Among the colonists were skilled carpenters, masons, blacksmiths, shipbuilders, and workers trained in other trades. Several colonists were graduates of Cambridge and Oxford, England's leading universities.

One by one the ships unloaded their cargoes, and the Puritans began to build villages along the coast north of Plymouth. Like the Pilgrims, they found many cleared fields abandoned by the Indians. Some Puritans settled at Shawmut, later called Boston (see map, page 33). Others settled in small villages near Boston. A few settled at Naumkeag (NOM·keg), later called Salem, which had been a fishing and trading village since 1626.

During the next few years, shipload after shipload of passengers from England arrived to join the early settlers. By the year 1640, more than 20,000 English men, women, and children were living in Massachusetts Bay Colony.

Government in Massachusetts. Religion and government were closely tied in Massachusetts Bay Colony. The Puritan leaders wanted to establish a "Bible Commonwealth," in which the Scriptures guided every aspect of life. To make sure the settlers remained true to Puritan beliefs, the leaders required everyone to attend the Puritan version of the Church of England. Local churches were formed by mutual agreement or "covenant," and the members of each church formed a congregation. In these churches the "saints," or true believers, chose the minister. This form of congregational church organization came to be known as "the New England way."

The Puritan leaders also kept all governmental power in the General Court, which was the lawmaking body of the Massachusetts Bay Company. Only owners of stock or shares in the company—a minority of the settlers—could belong to the General Court.

From the start some settlers rebelled against the rule of the leaders. They demanded the right to share in the government. John Winthrop—the first governor—and the other leaders were soon forced to loosen their control. They granted the right to vote to all Puritan men who were good church members. They also granted each town the right to send representatives to the General Court. Thus very early in its history, Massachusetts Bay Colony, like Jamestown, possessed a representative form of government.

SECTION REVIEW
See underscored items, text pp. 31 - 32, 34 - 35.
Identify: Reformation, Puritans, Separatists, divine rights of kings, indentured servants, 1620, 1630, self-governing colony, John Winthrop
For answers to questions, see Answer Key, pp.A11-12.

1. **Summarizing Ideas:** List three reasons why people from Europe came to America in the 1500's and 1600's.
2. **Comparing Ideas: (a)** Contrast the conditions facing the Pilgrims with those facing the Puritans. **(b)** Which group was better prepared for life in the New World? **(c)** Why?
3. **Organizing Ideas:** What steps did the Puritans take to establish self-government?
4. **Studying Sources:** Read the Source on page 34. According to the Mayflower Compact, why were the Pilgrims entering into an agreement?

▲ Discussion topic: Whether the Massachusetts Bay Colony fits the definition of a theocracy--a government of officials who are seen as divinely guided

35

2 English settlers build more colonies in New England

See Teaching Suggestions in TMRG, pp.TM19-20.

Though political and economic concerns moved many Puritans to settle in the Massachusetts Bay Colony, the Puritans hoped above all to find religious freedom in the New World. Yet once settled in America, the Puritans forced the people who did not worship as they did to leave Massachusetts.

Other colonists left Massachusetts to search for new and better farmland and greater opportunities. In this way, new settlements began throughout the New England Colonies.

The founding of Rhode Island. In 1631 a deeply religious young man named Roger Williams arrived in Massachusetts Bay Colony. Before long he became pastor of a church in Salem.

The young pastor's ideas soon aroused the opposition of the leaders of the colony. Williams taught that the colonists had no right to their land unless they first bought it from the Indians. He also preached that political leaders could have no authority over religious matters. Political control or even influence over the church could only weaken or corrupt it. He also insisted that individuals had the right to worship God as their conscience directed them.

The Puritan leaders saw Williams and his ideas as threats to the Massachusetts Bay Colony. They decided to send him back to England. Williams escaped, however, fleeing for safety through the wilderness to his friends the Narragansett Indians. He lived with them for several months. Then, in 1636, with old friends from Massachusetts, he founded the village of Providence (see map, page 33) at the head of Narragansett Bay.

Another exile from Massachusetts was Anne Hutchinson, a forceful and courageous member of a prominent family and a devout student of the Bible. When she, too, challenged accepted Puritan beliefs, she was condemned as a heretic and exiled from Massachusetts. With her husband and some followers, she founded a settlement on Narragansett Bay. Other communities were also settled by men and women dissatisfied with the established order in Massachusetts Bay. ▲

In 1644 Roger Williams secured a charter for the colony of Rhode Island. Under this charter the government of Rhode Island rested upon the **consent of the governed.** In this case, it rested upon the right of all adult males to vote and have a say in their government. The settlers were also guaranteed the right to worship as they wished.

A later charter, granted in 1663, deprived more than half of the adult males of their right to vote by requiring that a man had to own a certain amount of property before he could vote. This property qualification caused much discontent. Even with this restriction on the right to vote, however, Rhode Island offered more freedom to more settlers than any other colony in New England.

Westward to Connecticut. Connecticut, like Rhode Island, sprang from the older colony of Massachusetts, but the men and women who

Anne Hutchinson had weekly religious discussions in her Massachusetts home. Finally she and her family were forced to move and settled in neighboring Rhode Island.

"I never afflicted no child, no never in my life," said gentle old Rebecca Nurse, a well-liked citizen of Salem, Massachussetts. George Burroughs, a Salem minister, was greatly admired by his congregation. Yet both Nurse and Burroughs were hanged for witchcraft in Salem during the summer of 1692. So were seventeen other men and women, as well as a number of dogs.

The witchcraft hysteria started when two young girls began suffering from fits. Sometimes they moaned or cried out that they were being pierced with pins. Sometimes they stared blankly into space. Soon other young girls began to suffer the same symptoms. The village doctor could find no physical cause. The village minister stated that the Devil had come to Massachusetts.

As winter melted into spring, the girls named three "tormentors." One was a slave known for her "voodoo" chants; the others were old women. Throughout the spring, the girls accused almost 200 people. About 50 of them confessed, named others as witches, and were freed. The rest were put in jail. The Massachusetts governor then appointed a special court to try the "witches." But the judges had no training in rules of evidence. They accepted accusations without a second witness, and they did not permit cross-examination.

Finally, in the fall of 1692, people came to their senses. The girls had begun accusing Boston clergymen, leading merchants, and even the governor's wife. It became obvious that a terrible mistake had been made. The trials were stopped and those still in prison were released. Twenty years later the Massachusetts courts annulled the convictions and awarded reparations to the relatives of those who had been executed.

Several theories have attempted to explain the Salem witch hysteria. One historian argued that the young girls had been influenced by Cotton Mather's book *Memorial Providences,* which reported a case of alleged witchcraft in Boston. According to this theory, the girls started the accusations as a prank, and then continued them both because they enjoyed the attention they received and because they were afraid of being discovered.

The dramatist Arthur Miller explored the phenomenon of hysteria itself in his 1953 play, *The Crucible.* Set in colonial Salem, the play vividly demonstrates how hysteria can easily spread, even among educated people. Many critics immediately recognized Miller's play was an analogy comparing the hysteria of Salem to the McCarthy "witch-hunts" of the 1950's. At the time the play opened, Senator Joseph McCarthy was accusing hundreds of people of being Communists or Communist sympathizers. Many innocent persons lost their jobs and were blacklisted by the government. In 1956 Miller himself was called before the House Committee on Un-American Activities. He implicated himself but refused to name any of his associates as Communist sympathizers.

In 1976 a new theory appeared, linking the Salem witch hysteria with ergot poisoning. Ergot is a fungus that grows on rye in cool, damp weather. Rye was a dietary staple in New England in the 1600's. Eating ergot, which is used to manufacture the hallucinogen LSD, leads to the kinds of symptoms observed in Salem. History proves that the years 1690, 1691, and 1692 were unusually cold and damp in Massachusetts. But 1693, the year following the trials, was warm and dry — and no "witches" were persecuted.

Whatever its causes, the Salem episode was the last recorded instance of "witch" executions in the colonies. Today, Salem still symbolizes the difficulty of making moral choices in the face of community pressures.

---

settled Connecticut were not exiles. They were sturdy pioneers who moved out to the **frontier,** the territory just beyond the line of white settlements. They moved to this territory in search of greater opportunities for themselves and their families.

In 1635 the Reverend Thomas Hooker and nearly all the members of his church in Newtown (later Cambridge), Massachusetts, decided to move farther out. In the spring of 1636, they traveled southwest through the wilderness and settled finally at Hartford, Connecticut (see map, page 33).

Other pioneers started neighboring settlements. In 1639 the settlements of Windsor and Wethersfield joined with Hartford and adopted a plan of government. This plan was called the Fundamental Orders of Connecticut.

More than 20 years later, in 1662, after 15 towns had been settled, Connecticut secured a charter from King Charles II. This charter extended the Connecticut boundaries to include settlements along Long Island Sound, the most important of which was New Haven. The charter also gave the settlers the right to govern themselves, thus making legal a practice

▲

▲   The nineteenth-century view that the Fundamental Orders marked a step toward democracy has been discredited by modern research. Under the Fundamental Orders, the needs of the community had priority over the needs of the individual.

followed from the first days at Hartford. The charter of 1662 proved so satisfactory that the citizens of Connecticut kept it as their plan of government after winning their independence in the Revolutionary War.

New Hampshire and Maine. While Connecticut was growing into a self-governing colony, pioneers were pushing northward from Massachusetts into the area that later became the states of New Hampshire and Maine.

As early as 1622, John Mason and Sir Ferdinando Gorges (GOR·jez) had been granted the right to settle this territory. In 1629 the two men divided the land between them, ignoring the Abenaki and other Indian tribes living there. Gorges took the northern territory and Mason the southern. Both men tried to build colonies, but for a number of years, their settlements remained small trading posts.

By the late 1630's, growing numbers of settlers were moving northward from Massachusetts, building settlements on the land

King Philip, also known as Metacomet, led his people in a futile attempt to drive the white settlers off their lands.

claimed by Mason and Gorges. The Puritan authorities watched this development with keen interest and decided to claim the territory for Massachusetts. By the 1650's Massachusetts had gained control over both New Hampshire and Maine. It held control over Maine until 1820, when Maine entered the Union as a separate state. New Hampshire broke away from Massachusetts in 1679, when it received a charter from Charles II and became a royal colony.

Indian resistance. By 1635 the most powerful Indians in southern New England, the Pequots (PEE·kwots), realized that the rapid expansion of white settlements threatened their way of life and even their survival. Mounting tension between the two races led to the Pequot War of 1635–37. The Puritans and the Pequots led a series of raids on each other's settlements. Then, in 1637, the Puritans set out to destroy the Pequots. They surrounded a fortified Pequot village and set fire to it. Nearly 400 Pequots — mostly women, children, and old men — burned to death or were shot as they tried to escape. Others were hunted down and killed or sold into slavery. Only a few Pequots survived the war. Smoldering hatred among the remaining Indian tribes toward the white settlers of New England was fanned by the contempt shown by most whites toward Indians. ▲

The growing hatred led in 1675 to King Philip's War. Metacomet, a proud Wampanoag chief whom the Puritans called King Philip, made an alliance with the Narragansetts and other tribes. When Metacomet decided on war, the Indians at first outmaneuvered the settlers, burning or partly destroying several villages, but the tide soon turned. The Indians, outnumbered four to one, faced starvation. The final blow came when a Christianized, or "praying," Indian murdered Metacomet. The New England authorities executed other leaders of King Philip's War and sent scores of Indian warriors into slavery in the West Indies. The Indians who survived or evaded capture were bitter. In later wars between English and French settlers, these Indians allied themselves with the French and raided New England's frontier villages.

New England in the 1750's. Although the New England Colonies had their own governments and were completely independent of one another, they all developed along much the

This picture is a detail from a drawing made in 1638 of the Puritan attack on a fortified Pequot Indian village. The Puritans and their Indian allies surrounded the walled village and set it on fire.

same lines. Most of the New England settlers shared similar origins, since the vast majority came from England and Scotland. However, black slaves could be found in all the New England Colonies.

By the 1750's towns and cities had been built around all the good harbors along the New England coast. Boston had a population of about 15,000. All of the seaport towns were busy, thriving places.

Inland the colonies were dotted with small villages. From the beginning New England farmers had settled together in small communities rather than on remote farmsteads. Religion, the Indians, and geography influenced the development of small communities in New England.

Many New England communities had been started by friends and neighbors who belonged to the same local church. Hartford, Connecticut, you will recall, began this way. These communities were carefully planned. The plan usually included a "common," or central area; land adjoining the common for houses; land for the church, or "meetinghouse"; and nearby farmland for each settler. Surplus land was held by the original settlers of a community for sale to newcomers.

Frontier communities in New England were also compact because of the need to be close to a fort or blockhouse, which the first settlers built as quickly as possible in case of conflicts with nearby Indians.

Geography also influenced the spread of small farming communities in New England. In many places the soil was shallow and filled with rocks and boulders, the land hilly and covered with forests. On such land settlers could rarely clear a large area or build a big farm. Thus New England communities remained small and compact.

SECTION REVIEW

See underscored items, text pp. 36-38.

Identify: Roger Williams, consent of the governed, Anne Hutchinson, Fundamental Orders of Connecticut, Pequot War, Metacomet, New England Colonies

For answers to questions, see Answer Key, p.A12.

1. **Analyzing Ideas:** (a) For what reason did Roger Williams, Anne Hutchinson, and Thomas Hooker each leave Massachusetts Bay Colony to found neighboring colonies? (b) How do these reasons compare with the original reasons for settling Massachusetts Bay Colony?

2. **Expressing Viewpoints:** The New England colonies practiced little self-government and relied on England to make their laws. Do you agree or disagree? Give evidence from the text.

3. **Interpreting Ideas:** Explain how religion, the Indians, and geography influenced the colonists in New England to form compact villages rather than scattered settlements.

4. **Studying Maps:** Locate the chief towns of New England on the map on page 33. How did the location of these towns make them good places for settlement?

39

3 People from several nations settle the Middle Colonies

See Teaching Suggestions in TMRG, p.TM20.

People from the Netherlands and Sweden established the first settlements in the <u>Middle Colonies</u>. In <u>1609</u> <u>Henry Hudson,</u> an English subject sailing in the service of the Dutch East India Company of the Netherlands, explored the river that ever since has carried his name.

During the next few years, Dutch traders made voyages to the Middle Atlantic coast. As a result of their favorable reports, Dutch investors secured a charter from the government of the Netherlands and organized the Dutch West India Company. The charter gave the company control over all trade and colonies in the New World. This charter conflicted with the charter granted to the London Company.

The rise of New Netherland. The Dutch West India Company acted promptly to secure the trade of the entire Middle Atlantic coast. The Dutch called the land they claimed New Netherland (see map, page 41). Around a fort that they built on the lower tip of Manhattan Island, they started the settlement of New Amsterdam, now New York City. They also established forts and trading posts on the Hudson River at the present site of Albany, on the Connecticut River near the present site of Hartford, and on the Delaware River below the present site of Philadelphia.

To attract settlers to New Netherland, the Dutch West India Company in 1629 offered huge land grants to all members who would settle at least 50 tenant farmers on their estates within four years. Some members who accepted the offer became **patroons,** or owners of large tracts of land.

Most Dutch citizens, who were free men and women, refused to go to America to live on a patroon's estate. As a result, the Dutch West India Company introduced slavery into the colony at an early date. Some of the patroons used African slaves to cultivate their estates.

In spite of attempts to attract settlers, New Netherland grew very slowly. Under the company's control, it never had more than 10,000 inhabitants. Most settlers lived in the trading center of New Amsterdam. These men and women came from many European nations as well as from Africa.

Another community outside New Amsterdam was founded and led by <u>Lady Deborah Moody,</u> a well-to-do landowner from Salem, Massachusetts. When she was warned in 1643 that her religious views did not agree with accepted Puritan beliefs, she and some followers received from Dutch officials a patent for a self-governing community on Long Island. She was an enlightened leader who paid the Indians for land, planned her community well, and maintained religious freedom.

At New Amsterdam in 1651, the crane and gallows near the wharf were used to weigh and display goods. Inside the fort were the city's largest buildings: the director's house and a stone church.

The Dutch threat to the English. From the beginning New Netherland posed a threat to the English colonies. From their base at New Amsterdam, Dutch warships could strike at English ships bound to and from New England and the Southern Colonies. From New Amsterdam the Dutch also controlled the trade of three vital river valleys—the Hudson, the Connecticut, and the Delaware. The Dutch strengthened their control even further when, in 1655, they seized Fort Christina and other Swedish settlements on the banks of the Delaware River, an area known as New Sweden (see map, this page).

Especially valuable to the Dutch was their control of the Hudson River. From a point north of Fort Orange (now Albany), the Mohawk Valley provided a route through the mountains into the Great Lakes region and the interior of the continent. The powerful league of Iroquois Indians known as the Five Nations (later the Six Nations) dominated this route. These Indians were friendly with the Dutch. They brought furs from the Great Lakes region to the Dutch posts on the Hudson River. New England settlers also wanted to share in this rich fur trade, and they were angered by Dutch control of the Hudson River.

Conflict between English and Dutch. Dutch expansion eastward into Long Island and northward in the Connecticut Valley finally brought matters to a head. This expansion plunged the Dutch into conflict with traders and settlers who were pushing southward from New England. In 1643, fearing Dutch expansion and possible Indian raids, the colonies of Massachusetts, Plymouth, Connecticut, and New Haven united their military forces in the ▲ New England Confederation. A **confederation** is a political league in which members retain most of the power of government, while a central government body takes care of common problems, such as defense.

Not only New England was threatened. Dutch expansion also threatened Maryland and Virginia to the south. The showdown between the English and the Dutch came in 1664 when an English fleet sailed into the Hudson River. Overwhelmed by superior English strength, Peter Stuyvesant, the Dutch governor, hauled down his nation's flag at New Amsterdam. Without firing a shot, the English thus ended the rival colonial power of the Dutch in North America.

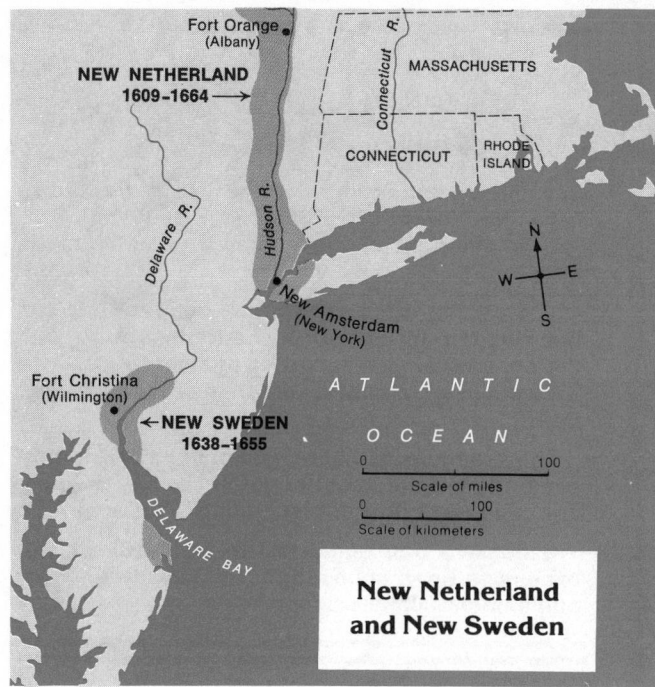

New Netherland and New Sweden

New York and New Jersey. Charles II, then king of England, presented all the territory that had once been New Netherland to his younger brother James, the Duke of York. The gift included not only the land between the Connecticut and the Delaware rivers but also Long Island, the islands of Nantucket and Martha's Vineyard, and all of Maine east of the Kennebec River. This vast territory became the property of the 30-year-old Duke of York.

James gave the name New York to part of the former Dutch colony. Then he began to hand out generous gifts of land to his friends. The largest gift, New Jersey (see map, page 33), went to Lord John Berkeley and Sir George Carteret.

In 1664 New Jersey was almost all Indian land, with only a few hundred white settlers. Dutch and Swedish colonists had earlier built several small settlements along the Delaware River. Colonists from New England had settled a few villages in the north. Berkeley and Carteret tried to attract more settlers, but they had limited success. Finally, in 1702, after these lands had changed hands many times, the king of England claimed New Jersey as a royal colony.

New York under English rule. The colony of New York had a much different history from

ENGLISH BILL OF RIGHTS (1689)

Levying of money for or to the use of the crown . . . without grant of Parliament . . . is illegal.

It is the right of the subjects to petition the king. . . .

The raising or keeping a standing army within the kingdom in time of peace, unless it be with the consent of Parliament, is against law. . . .

Elections of members of Parliament ought to be free.

The freedom of speech and debates or proceedings in Parliament ought not to be . . . questioned in any court or place out of Parliament.

Excessive bail ought not to be required, nor excessive fines imposed, nor cruel and unusual punishments inflicted. . . .

that of New Jersey. The young Duke of York took a keen interest in the former Dutch colony. As one of his first and wisest acts, he ordered his colonial officials to treat the Dutch with "humanity and gentleness." He allowed the Dutch to speak their own language and worship in their own churches.

However, in the long run the duke was a harsh ruler. He levied heavy taxes without the consent of the people, and, except for a brief two years (1683–85), he allowed them no voice in the government. Under his rule, also, many more Africans were brought as slaves to the colony. English interest in the slave trade continued to grow.

The Dominion of New England.   In 1685 the Duke of York became King James II of England. A year later, in 1686, he combined New Jersey, New York, and the New England colonies under a form of government called the Dominion of New England. He then abolished representative government in these colonies and appointed Sir Edmund Andros as governor of the Dominion.

The Dominion lasted only about two years. Citizens in England resented the harsh rule of King James as much as the colonists resented his governor, Andros. English Protestants were also disturbed by James's conversion to

Catholicism. In 1688 a revolt in England called the Glorious Revolution drove James II from the throne. In 1689 England adopted a **Bill of Rights.** This was a list of certain rights and liberties guaranteed to every citizen by the government (see Source, this page). Included in the Bill was the right to representative government. The new king and queen, William and Mary of Orange, restored the colonial charters, and the representative assemblies in the colonies regained their power.

Pennsylvania and Delaware.   One of the most remarkable of the English founders of colonies in the New World was William Penn. Penn, the son of an admiral in the Royal Navy, seemed destined for the fashionable life of the English court. Then one day in 1667, at age 22, young Penn heard a Quaker sermon on the text "There is a faith that overcometh the world." The sermon converted Penn. He became a member of the Society of Friends, often called Quakers.

Penn's father was shocked and angered by his son's conversion. The Quakers at this time were one of the most disliked religious groups in England. Penn held firm to his new faith, ▲ and his father finally forgave him and left him a large inheritance.

Part of Penn's inheritance was a debt that Charles II had owed his father. In place of the money, the king in 1681 gave Penn a charter making him **proprietor,** or full owner, of a huge grant of land in the New World. On this land Penn founded a colony, which the king named Pennsylvania. Penn's power over this **proprietary colony** was almost as great as the king's power over a royal colony.

Pennsylvania had no coastline. Penn solved this problem in 1682 by obtaining another grant of land to the south on the west bank of Delaware Bay. This new grant, long called "the lower counties," was later named Delaware (see map, page 33).

Pennsylvania, which Penn liked to call the "Holy Experiment," attracted many settlers. Penn wrote and published a pamphlet in English, French, Dutch, and German describing the colony he proposed to build. He invited honest, hardworking settlers to come, promising them religious toleration, representative government, and cheap land. Penn offered large amounts of free land, with the right to buy additional land, to settlers who established their homes in the colony.

Edward Hicks (1780–1849) was the leading American folk or primitivist painter of the first half of the nineteenth century. He was born to Anglican parents in Attleboro, Pennsylvania, but was raised a Quaker by a neighboring family. During his lifetime, he was recognized more for his preaching than for his painting.

Hicks first learned the trade of coach and sign painting. He became the head of a thriving workshop in which artisans painted clock faces, furniture, historical markers, and other practical items. Later, Hicks began making easel paintings of serene farm scenes in Pennsylvania and New York. Often he framed his pictures with moralistic verses. Hicks was afraid that art was not compatible with his religion, but he also knew that art brought meaning to life.

Hick's most persistent theme was the Biblical prophecy that the wolf would lie down with the lamb (Isaiah 11:6). He painted more than 60, and perhaps as many as 100, versions of the story, only about 25 of which survive. These paintings — all of which Hicks titled "The Peaceable Kingdom" — visualize his belief that the Quaker state of Pennsylvania was the fulfillment of Isaiah's prophecy. The paintings depict William Penn and other Quakers making a treaty with the Indians while Isaiah's beasts and a group of children play together.

Settlers poured in — Quakers from England, Wales, and Ireland; Scotch-Irish Presbyterians; Swiss and German Protestants; Catholics and Jews from many countries of Europe. Africans were also brought to the Pennsylvania colony, but the black population was never large. However, in 1700 slavery in Pennsylvania was legally recognized.

Penn kept his promises to the settlers. As for the Indians, chiefly the Delaware-Lenape, Penn treated them fairly and paid them for their land. When Penn returned to England, discontent developed. During his later years and after his death in 1718, Penn's wife Hannah helped to keep the colony intact and its people contented.

The Middle Colonies in the 1750's. By the 1750's the Middle Colonies — Pennsylvania, Delaware, New Jersey, and New York — were very prosperous. Philadelphia, on the Delaware River, was the largest, busiest seaport in America, and New York was almost as large.

From the beginning most people made their living by farming, but they did not settle in small farming villages, as in New England. Because of generally peaceful relations with the Indians, except on the western frontier, the newcomers scattered freely over the countryside. Since the soil was fertile and the land gently rolling, settlers cultivated fairly large farms. On these farms families produced not only food for their own needs but also a surplus for sale. Indeed, the Middle Colonies soon became known as the "breadbasket" of the New World. The harbors of Philadelphia and New York were always filled with ships loading flour, meat, and other foodstuffs for sale in England and the West Indies.

People in the Middle Colonies worked at a great variety of occupations. Although most were farmers, these colonists were also famous for their iron mines, their shipyards, and their manufacture of glass, paper, and textiles. From the beginning these colonies were the home of people from many different nations with many different backgrounds—much more so than any of the other colonies.

SECTION REVIEW

See underscored items, text pp. 40-42.

Identify: Middle Colonies, 1609, Henry Hudson, patroons, Lady Deborah Moody, New England Confederation, Duke of York, 1664, proprietary colony, William Penn

For answers to questions, see Answer Key, p.A12.

1. **Summarizing Ideas: (a)** Give two reasons for the conflict between the Dutch and English settlers in America. **(b)** How was the conflict resolved?

2. **Evaluating Viewpoints:** What guarantee in the English Bill of Rights was especially important to the English colonists?

3. **Comparing Ideas:** How were the Middle Colonies different from the New England Colonies geographically and economically?

4. **Studying Maps: (a)** Look at the maps on pages 33 and 41. What geographic features seem to have influenced the settlement of New Sweden and New Netherland? **(b)** How would these features have affected settlement?

---

4 A distinctive way of life develops in the Southern Colonies

See Teaching Suggestions in TMRG, pp.TM20-21.

Virginia, the first Southern Colony, started in 1607. By 1632, when Maryland was chartered, Virginia was firmly established.

The founding of Maryland. Sir George Calvert, the first Lord Baltimore, wanted to build a colony in the New World as a refuge for persecuted Catholics but with religious freedom for Protestants as well. After an unsuccessful effort in Newfoundland, he applied for a charter to more favorable land north of Virginia. He died just after the king granted a charter for Maryland. His son, the second Lord Baltimore, however, became proprietor and carried on his father's work. He remained in England but appointed able deputy governors to act for him.

The first 200 Maryland settlers, including many Catholics, sailed up Chesapeake Bay in the late winter of 1634 and settled at St. Mary's. Large plantations soon spread along the banks of Maryland's **tidewater rivers**° (see map, page 33).

The deputy governor, Leonard Calvert, died in 1647. Margaret Brent, his business manager, demanded the right to vote and as a landowner to be seated in the colonial assembly. She was permitted to vote but was denied a seat in the assembly.

As more and more Protestants arrived, some of them threatened to take over the government by force from the Calverts. Soldiers from Virginia were brought in as protection. When these soldiers threatened to mutiny because they had not been paid, Brent took bold action to solve this crisis by selling some of the proprietor's cattle to pay the troops.

To help prevent another crisis of this sort, Lord Baltimore persuaded the legislative assembly to pass the Toleration Act of 1649. This act guaranteed freedom of worship to anyone who believed in Jesus Christ. This was not complete religious freedom, since only Christians could settle in Maryland. Nevertheless, the Toleration Act marked another important step in the continuing struggle for religious freedom.

Creation of the Carolinas. In 1663 Charles II gave a charter for Carolina to eight English nobles, who were to be the proprietors of the new colony. The grant included all the territory between Virginia and Spanish Florida and westward to the "south seas."

With the aid of John Locke, a young English philosopher, the proprietors drew up a plan of government for the new colony. The plan provided a rigid system of social classes from nobles at the top to ordinary colonists at the bottom. Slaves were not even included in this system, for Locke had written that "every freeman of Carolina shall have absolute power and authority over his Negro slaves, of whatever opinion or religion soever."

The proprietor's plan was doomed to failure, since it ignored actual conditions in the New World. From the first days, the colony began to divide into two parts (see map, page 33), as determined by geography and the desire of the settlers.

°**tidewater rivers:** rivers into which, at high tide, the ocean pushes salt water some distance upstream.

Because of its excellent harbor, Baltimore, named for the Maryland colony's founder, soon became a major colonial shipping center for tobacco and grain. What means of making a living can be seen in this painting from 1752? (farming, fishing, shipping) ▲

Settling the Carolinas. The northern section, North Carolina, was settled mostly by pioneers from Virginia. They built cabins, cleared the land, grew their own food, and raised tobacco to sell in England. Many also earned their living from the pine forests, which supplied lumber and naval stores (tar, pitch, resin, turpentine) — products that were needed by England's Royal Navy and by its merchant ships.

The southern section, South Carolina, proved more attractive to settlers from overseas. Through the seaport of Charles Town (later shortened to Charleston), settlers of many different religious faiths from many different nations passed to new homes in the New World. There were Anglicans and other religious groups from England; Scots in considerable numbers; French Huguenots (HYOO·guh·nahts), who were Protestants fleeing persecution in France; Germans; Jews from various parts of Europe; emigrants from the West Indies; and, as the years passed, growing numbers of African slaves. Many settlers built large, prosperous rice plantations on the rich coastal lowlands. Others earned their living from the production of naval stores from the pine forests and from the fur trade on the frontier. After indigo (a plant used to make dye) was grown successfully by Eliza Lucas, it became another important crop.

The early colonists of North and South Carolina waged a continuing struggle for a larger voice in the government. Finally, in 1729 the proprietors sold their rights to the king. Both North Carolina and South Carolina then became royal colonies with their own representative assemblies.

The founding of Georgia. In 1732, three years after North and South Carolina became royal colonies, the king granted a charter for Georgia (see map, page 33), home of the Creek, Cherokee, and Choctaw Indians. The British° government hoped that Georgia would serve as a "buffer" against attacks from Spanish Florida, but the compelling motive for starting Georgia had little to do with politics or business. The colony was started in order to provide a place where debtors released from English prisons could start a new life.

James Oglethorpe, the leader of Georgia's founders, arrived in the colony in 1733 with the first debtors. They settled at Savannah, each person receiving 50 free acres (20.2 hectares) of land. Slavery and the sale of rum were not allowed in the colony.

Oglethorpe and the other founders tried to recruit settlers, offering liberal grants of land to all who came. Only a small number of immigrants arrived, among them New Englanders, Germans, and Scots. Some settlers de-

°**British:** In 1707 the separate countries of England and Scotland were united into a single country called Great Britain. Throughout the colonial period, however, the words "England" and "English" are often used to mean "Great Britain" and "British."

▲ Note: Answers to questions in captions appear in parentheses, as shown here. Bullets separate answers to individual questions when a caption contains more than one question.

45

On southern plantations, such as this one in South Carolina, the slave quarters were called the "street." The "street" was set up like a small village.

manded that slavery be allowed in the colony. Finally, in 1750 the founders reluctantly agreed to make slavery legal in Georgia. In 1752 the founders turned Georgia over to the king as a royal colony.

The Southern Colonies in the 1750's. By the 1750's the Southern Colonies—Maryland, Virginia, North and South Carolina, and Georgia—had all developed their own special ways of life. The great tobacco plantations in Maryland, Virginia, and North Carolina covered the rich lands along the tidewater rivers near the coast and extended inland on the Atlantic coastal plains. Farther south the luxurious homes of wealthy rice planters were scattered over the coastal lowlands. The only large towns in the Southern Colonies at this time were Charleston, with a population of 10,000, and Baltimore, with 5,000.

A distinguishing feature of the Southern Colonies was slavery. The tobacco and rice plantations required large numbers of workers. With plenty of land available on the frontier, few settlers were willing to work for wages on the plantations. As a result, the planters relied more and more upon black slave labor. By the 1750's the slavery system was firmly fixed in all the Southern Colonies.

If slaves could have been used profitably on the farms of the Middle Colonies or on the smaller farms of New England, slavery might have become more widespread in those colonies as well. In colonial times only a very small minority of people objected to slavery as such. Slavery was either profitable or unprofitable. In the Southern Colonies, it was profitable, and slaves were used in ever-increasing numbers.

Although the planters set the pattern of southern life, most southern people lived in the back country—the inland areas that lay "back" from the seacoast. These men and women—pioneers and small farmers—lived much like the people in rural New England and the Middle Colonies.

SECTION REVIEW
See underscored items, text pp. 44-46.

Identify: tidewater river, Southern Colonies, Lord Baltimore, Margaret Brent, Toleration Act of 1649, James Oglethrope.

For answers to questions, see Answer Key, pp.A12-13.

1. **Comparing Ideas:** Name three differences in the way that North Carolina and South Carolina were settled.

2. **Summarizing Ideas:** What were the two motives for establishing the colony of Georgia?

3. **Organizing Ideas:** What were the two chief crops grown in the Southern Colonies? In what regions were they grown?

4. **Contrasting Ideas:** (a) What was the most important difference between the labor force in the South and in the North? (b) What created this difference?

New France grows and threatens the British colonies

See Teaching Suggestions in TMRG, p.TM21.

The vast colonial territories claimed by Great Britain, France, Portugal, Spain, and the Netherlands spread slowly across the map of the world. These colonial areas were prizes for which each of the contending nations was ready to sacrifice blood and effort. Thus, during most of the 1600's and 1700's, the people of European nations were engaged in almost constant warfare.

Colonial rivalry in the New World. In the New World, the British flag waved proudly over islands in the Caribbean and over thirteen colonies along the Atlantic seaboard. Warships of the Royal Navy stood guard over the nearly 1,500,000 men, women, and children who lived in the seaboard colonies. The warships were needed, for Great Britain had powerful enemies.

To the south were the Spaniards. They had built a series of forts and missions that stretched from Florida to California along what is now the southern border of the United States. During the 1600's and the 1700's, however, Spain's power had been declining. By the mid-1700's the British did not think of Spain as a major threat.

To the north and west was New France, the vast territory claimed by France. This was a different story. The French had been strengthening their naval and military power in North America, and their armed forces presented a growing threat to the British colonies.

French claims in North America. French claims in North America were based on the early voyages of Verrazano and Cartier (see map, page 14). The French, like other colonizing nations, simply ignored the claims of Indians to lands on which they and their ancestors had long lived.

The first French explorer to establish settlements in the New World was Samuel de Champlain, who made his first voyage there in 1603. Before he died in 1635, he had built a settlement at Quebec, won for France the friendship of the powerful Algonquin Indians, and explored most of the St. Lawrence Valley and the area around Lake Champlain.

Other French explorers pushed up the St. Lawrence River into the Great Lakes and the heart of the vast North American wilderness. Among these daring explorers were Marquette (mar·KET), Joliet (joh·lee·ET), and La Salle.

In 1673 Father Marquette, a Jesuit missionary, and Joliet, a fur trader, crossed the Great Lakes and paddled down the Mississippi River as far as the mouth of the Arkansas River. Eight years later, in 1681–82, La Salle followed the same river route to the Gulf of Mexico. La Salle claimed the entire Mississippi Valley for France, calling it Louisiana in honor of King Louis XIV. Later, in 1718, the French built New Orleans near the mouth of the Mississippi River.

By the early 1700's, then, the French controlled the two major gateways into the heart of North America. New Orleans gave them control of the southern entrance to the entire Mississippi Valley. Quebec and Montreal gave them control of the St. Lawrence River.

Combined with the Great Lakes, the St. Lawrence River provided a natural water route. By paddling and by carrying their canoes short distances overland, French explorers and traders could bring their canoes to the Mississippi or one of the rivers flowing into it. From there they could travel to the entire region between the Appalachians and the Rockies.

French settlements. The settled area of New France consisted largely of farmhouses stretching along the banks of the St. Lawrence from Quebec to Montreal and up the Richelieu (RISH·eh·loo) River. Most of the settlers came from France, but some slaves were brought from Africa to work on the farms and to provide a labor force for New Orleans. Africans also came to New France as members of the French expeditions that explored the Great Lakes and the Mississippi Valley.

The fur trade. Beyond the settled areas of New France lay an immense wilderness inhabited by Indians with well-established patterns of hunting and farming. In this vast area, the most easily exploited resource was furs. Furs drew adventurous French pioneers into the forests. Courageous *coureurs de bois* (koo·RUR deh BWAH), or runners-of-the-woods, paddled their canoes into the interior and wintered

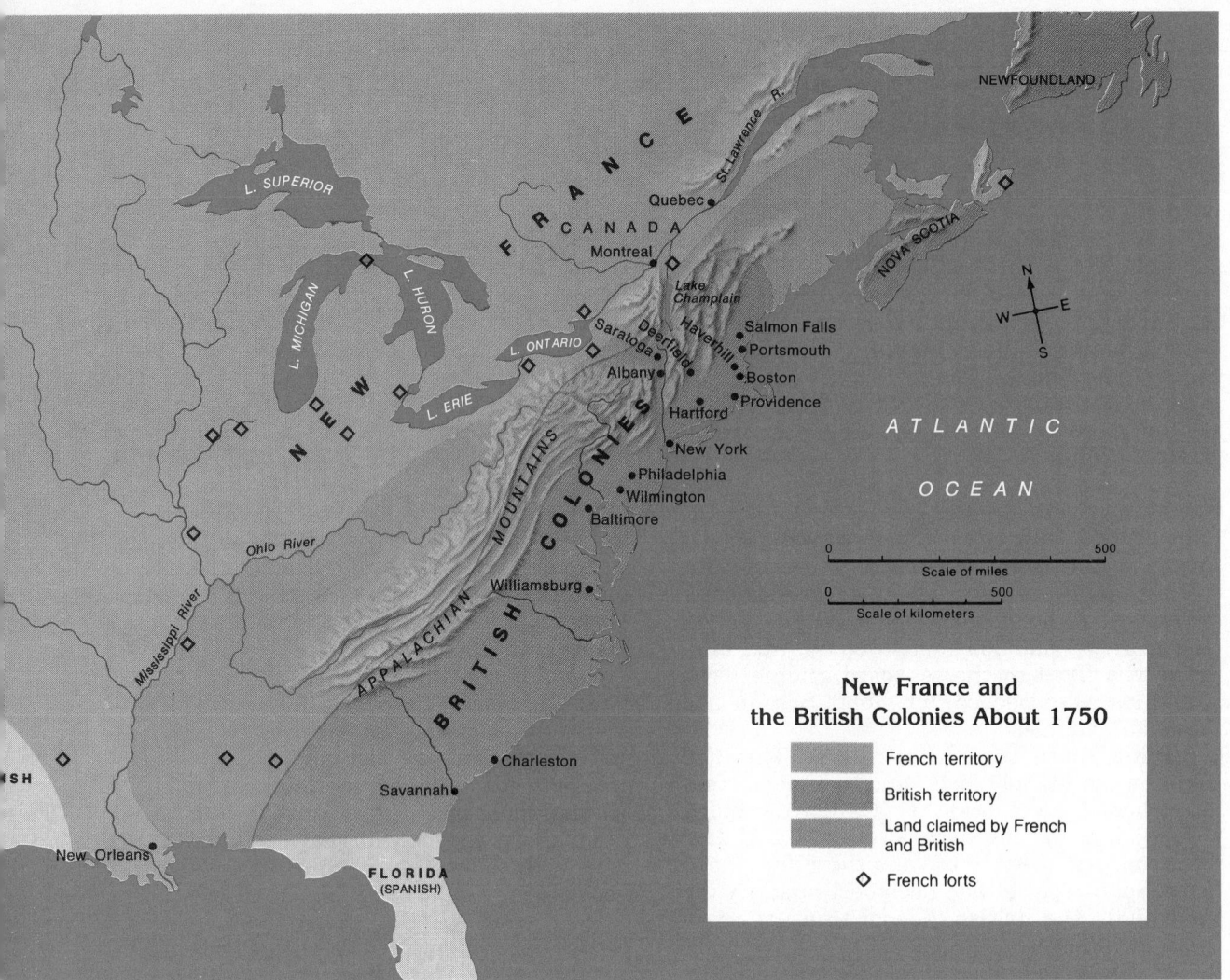

New France and the British Colonies About 1750

- French territory
- British territory
- Land claimed by French and British
- ◇ French forts

with friendly Indian tribes. Then they returned in the spring with their Indian allies to the trading center at Montreal.

For several weeks active trading took place on the river below the city. Indians exchanged their furs for European goods—blankets, cloaks, cloth, spoons, knives, hatchets, guns, powder, and liquor. When the trading finally came to an end, the Indians and the *coureurs de bois* loaded their canoes and returned to the wilderness. The French ships then began their long voyage back to Europe with the cargoes of precious furs.

The profits of the fur trade were far greater for the French than for the Indians. The fur trade also disrupted age-old patterns of Indian life. Able-bodied Indians left their villages for long periods of time to hunt, to trap, and to trade. As the years passed, the Indians depended more and more upon the fur trade for their livelihood and less upon hunting and farming. Since the different tribes also became dependent upon one or another of the rival colonial powers, they were frequently drawn into Europe's colonial wars. Moreover, competition among the Indians for the best hunting grounds became a source of friction and often led to war among the Indians themselves.

The weakness of New France. On the map New France covered an immense area, including Canada and the entire Mississippi Valley (see map, this page), but the map was misleading. Except for Quebec and Montreal, the settled areas of Canada consisted largely of farmhouses strung along the St. Lawrence like beads on a string. Beyond the settled areas, a chain of small forts and trading posts stretched in a long arc through the Great Lakes and the upper Mississippi Valley. Only the Indians and the *coureurs de bois* inhabited the vast forests of New France.

The fur trade proved to be both a strength and a weakness for New France. The fur trade provided a living for thousands—for manufacturers and workers back in France, for shipowners and merchants, and for the *coureurs de bois* and their Indian allies. However, the carefree life of the *coureur de bois* attracted the young and strong into the forests rather than to the settled areas. As a result, the French never strengthened the settled areas along the St. Lawrence River.

French and British power. By 1750 the British had certain advantages over their French rivals to the north. The British colonies were well established. British colonists outnumbered French colonists by 23 to 1. Most of the British settlements were confined to a fairly narrow belt of land along the Atlantic coast, whereas the settlements, forts, and trading posts of the French were scattered over half the continent.

▲ However, the French also enjoyed advantages. New France, united under a single government, could act quickly when action was necessary. In contrast, the separate governments of the British colonies seldom acted together even when danger threatened.

The French also had the support of a great many more Indians than did the British. French fur traders did not destroy forests and drive away game as did British settlers, who cleared the land for farming. However, members of the powerful Six Nations refused to ally themselves with the French.

Finally, France in the early 1750's was the most powerful nation in Europe. French armies were second to none. French naval forces competed with the British for control of the seas.

Between 1689 and 1748, a fierce rivalry kept France and Great Britain at war with each other off and on for a total of nearly 25 years. The two nations fought for control of the seas and possession of distant colonies. In each war North America was only one of several prizes the British and French hoped to win.

Armed forces of the two powers clashed on the seas and in Europe and Asia as well as North America, but none of the wars proved decisive.

In 1754 war clouds gathered once again. The two European nations began still another test of strength. The outcome of this struggle was to determine the destiny of the North American continent.

SECTION REVIEW

See underscored items, text p. 47.
Identify: Samuel de Champlain Marquette, Joliet, La Salle, *coureurs de bois*
For answers to questions, see Answer Key, p.A13.

1. **Interpreting Ideas:** The fur trade proved to be both a strength and a weakness for New France. Explain.

2. **Comparing Ideas:** Compare French and British power in America in 1750. **(a)** What advantages did the British colonies have? **(b)** What advantages did New France have?

3. **Studying Maps:** Locate New Orleans, Quebec, and Montreal on the map on page 48. Why can these French settlements be called "gateways" to North America?

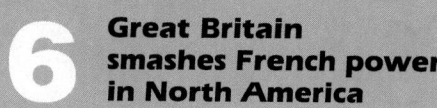

6 Great Britain smashes French power in North America

See Teaching Suggestions in TMRG, pp.TM21-22.
The decisive worldwide struggle between the British and the French broke out in 1754. In North America the expanding empires of France and Great Britain clashed in the land beyond the Appalachian Mountains. The conflict was called the French and Indian War in America, or the Seven Years' War in Europe.

The first clash in America. Wealthy Virginians caused the first of a series of events that led to the French and Indian War. These colonists formed a company and secured from the British king a huge grant of land in the upper Ohio Valley. They intended to make a profit by dividing the land into small farms and selling the farms to settlers.

The French were alarmed by the Virginians' real estate activities on territory which the French claimed as their own. In 1753 the French started constructing a chain of forts connecting Lake Erie with the Ohio River (see map, page 51).

Benjamin Franklin, the youngest son of a Boston soapmaker, was a successful printer and publisher in his early years. At the age of 42, Franklin retired from the printing business and turned his attention to science, making many discoveries and practical inventions.

Throughout his life, Franklin served in many public positions, including deputy postmaster general of the colonies and Pennsylvania delegate to the Albany Congress in 1754. Franklin's greatest public achievements, however, came when he was in his 70's and 80's. He was 70 when he helped draft the Declaration of Independence in 1776. He was 74 when, as ambassador to France, he helped gain that nation's recognition of the United States. In 1781 he was one of three American diplomats chosen to negotiate the Treaty of Paris that ended the Revolutionary War.

Franklin's last great achievement took place at the age of 81 at the Constitutional Convention. Providing both inspiration and insight throughout the convention, he helped convince delegates to settle their differences and to adopt the Great Compromise. Though he often remarked that he was too old to be a hero, the wise and respected Benjamin Franklin made many significant contributions to the new nation.

The governor of Virginia sent George Washington, a 21-year-old surveyor from Virginia, to the Ohio Valley to warn the French that the land belonged to the British. (The land had been originally granted to Virginia by the charter of 1609. See map, page 25.) The French, however, ignored Washington's warning.

The following year Washington, now a major, returned to the Ohio Valley. Leading a company of **militia**, civilians who trained as soldiers to fight in times of emergency, he built Fort Necessity a few miles south of the French Fort Duquesne (doo·KAYN). Fort Duquesne itself was situated at the strategic point where the Monongahela and Allegheny rivers join to form the Ohio River—the present site of Pittsburgh (see map, page 51). A small force of French and Indians defeated Washington and his troops in a battle fought at Fort Necessity on July 4, 1754.

Failure of the colonies to unite. The French were now entrenched along a line of scattered points from the Great Lakes south to the Ohio River, with outposts in the Allegheny Mountains. The entire northern frontier of the British colonies was open to attack from the Indian allies of the French. Moreover, the western country was closed to British traders and British settlers.

At this critical moment, delegates from seven British colonies met at Albany, New York, to discuss united action against the French and their Indian allies. They were joined by Indian representatives from the Six Nations. The Six Nations, also known as the Iroquois Confederation, occupied most of what is now central New York. Armed first by the Dutch and then by the English, they were the most powerful Indians in the eastern part of North America. They were also longstanding enemies of the French and of the Indians friendly to the French. The British colonists welcomed the Iroquois representatives to the Albany Congress.

The example of the Iroquois Confederation had an influence on Benjamin Franklin and his efforts to promote an intercolonial union. At the Albany Congress of 1754, he proposed that

▲ Report topic: Why the Mohawk, Oneida, Onondaga, Cayuga, and Seneca tribes founded the Iroquois Confederation and how the tribes governed themselves

the British colonies in America unite in a permanent union for defense. Franklin's <u>Albany Plan of Union</u> was rejected by the colonists because each colony did not want to give up its right to act independently. The colonists also turned down a somewhat similar proposal by the British government. Although rejected, these proposals forced many colonists to think about the advantages of united action.

British disasters. Only a few months after the failure of the Albany Congress, General Edward Braddock arrived from England with regiments of British regulars, or "redcoats." British redcoats and Virginia militia then advanced through the wilderness toward the French at Fort Duquesne. They were ambushed when they had almost reached their goal (see map, this page).

Braddock and most of his officers were killed. More than half his soldiers were killed, wounded, or captured. The disaster would have been even greater if George Washington and the Virginia militia had not fought back, in ways common to Indian warfare, from the cover of rocks and trees.

Braddock's disaster left the long frontier of Pennsylvania, Maryland, and Virginia open to Indian attack. Matters got even worse when British expeditions against the French forts at Niagara and Crown Point also failed and the French captured Fort Oswego and Fort William Henry (see map, this page).

British success under Pitt. Fortunately for Great Britain, <u>William Pitt</u> became the leader of the British government in the autumn of 1756. Pitt was determined to win complete vic-

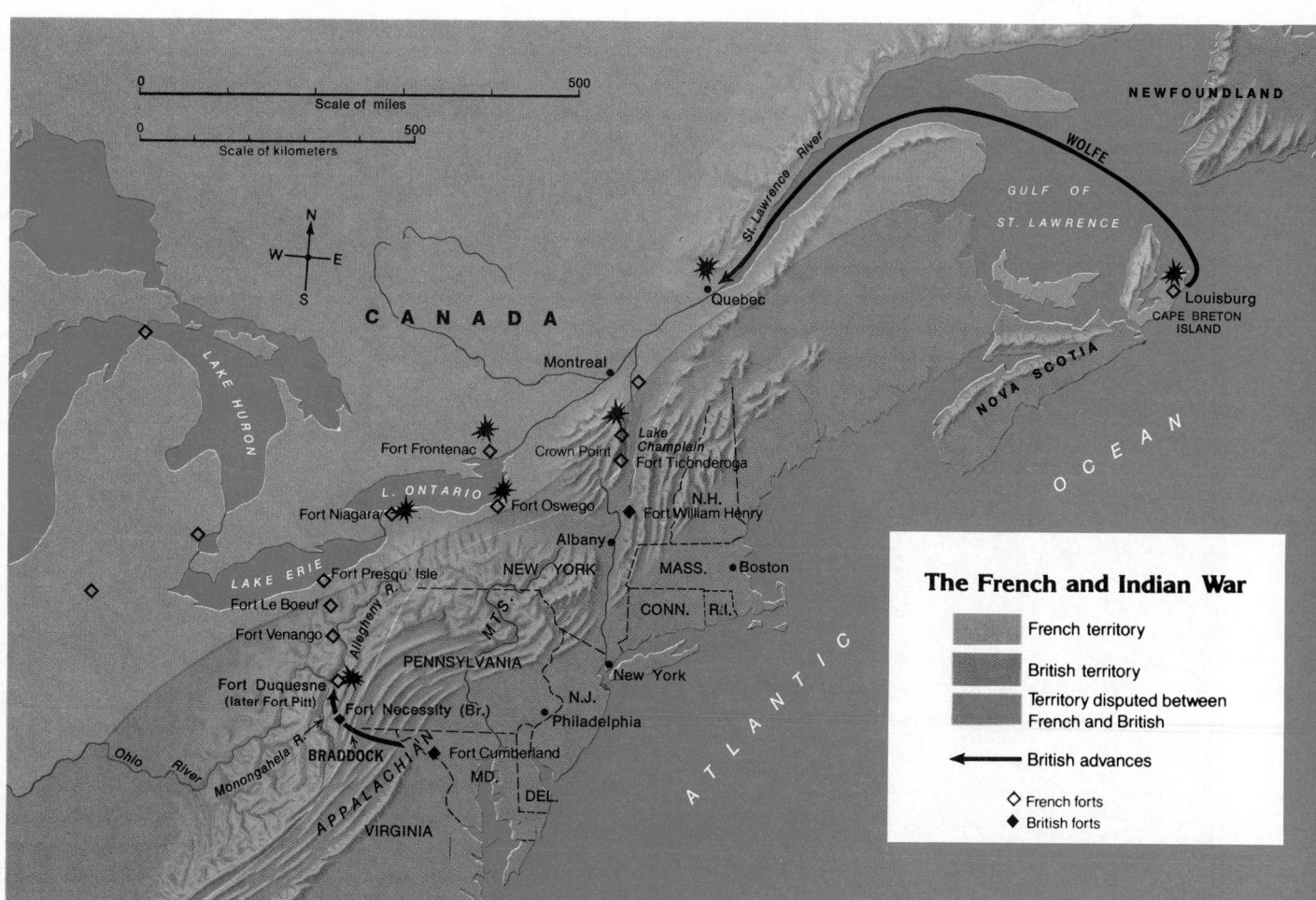

The French and Indian War

French territory

British territory

Territory disputed between French and British

⬅ British advances

◇ French forts
◆ British forts

tory for British arms. He was a strong leader, a man of enormous energy and supreme self-confidence. "I know that I can save England and that nobody else can," he reportedly said.

Under Pitt's leadership the British empire rallied. Pitt fired incompetent officials and replaced them with able leaders. He gave colonial officers rank equal to those in the king's own troops. He also strengthened the British navy and moved additional troops to America. Everywhere throughout the British empire, Pitt took the offensive, and his efforts soon met with success.

British victories. In 1758 a British naval and land force under General Jeffrey Amherst captured Louisburg, a powerfully armed French fort on Cape Breton Island (see map, page 51). The fall of Louisburg doomed New France. The victory gave the British navy a base for cutting off French reinforcements and supplies to America. During the same year, the British also captured Fort Frontenac on Lake Ontario (see map, page 51). This victory weakened French lines of communication to Fort Duquesne. The French promptly abandoned Fort Duquesne, and the British then occupied it without a struggle. They renamed it Fort Pitt, in honor of their great leader (see map, page 51).

In 1759 the British won even more sweeping victories. Amherst forced the French to retreat from their forts at Crown Point and Ticonderoga (see map, page 51). Some of Amherst's forces seized Fort Niagara (see map, page 51). This latter victory forced the French to abandon their forts in the upper Ohio Valley. In September 1759 the British captured Quebec. The battle of Quebec was a magnificent victory for the British. In the same year, Great Britain also won significant victories in Europe, in the Mediterranean, and in India.

The following year, 1760, after only slight resistance, the French surrendered Montreal

▲ Report topic: The Seven Years' War

General Braddock was unprepared for battle in the American wilderness. The French and Indians fought "Indian style," firing from behind rocks and trees. Used to fighting on the open battlefields of Europe, the British suffered a terrible defeat.

to General Amherst (see map, page 51). In 1762 Spain, fearful of British victory, entered the worldwide conflict on the side of France. Spanish aid, however, was too little and too late. The British kept winning victories all over the world. They completed their string of victories by seizing the Philippine Islands and Cuba from Spain, the West Indies sugar islands of Martinique (mar·tih·NEEK) and Guadeloupe (gwah·uh·LOOP) from France, and French territory in India.

The spoils of war. Out of this worldwide struggle, the British emerged victorious. Meeting in Paris, representatives of Great Britain, France, and Spain drew up the Treaty of Paris of 1763. Disregarding the claims and interests of native peoples of these lands, Great Britain secured most of India and all of North America to the east of the Mississippi River, except for New Orleans.

France, on the other hand, lost nearly all of its possessions in India and in America. The British allowed France to keep only four small islands in the New World. Two of these were the sugar islands of Guadeloupe and Martinique in the Caribbean.

As an ally of France, Spain was forced to give Florida to Great Britain. To make up for this loss, however, the French gave the Spaniards New Orleans and the vast territory of Louisiana west of the Mississippi River (see map, this page). The British returned Cuba and the Philippine Islands to Spain.

How war influenced the colonies. The American colonists as well as Great Britain profited from the long struggle. The colonial militias gained valuable new experience in methods of warfare. Their experience in fighting Indians was broadened by joint combat with the British against powerful French forces.

Although the colonial militias welcomed all able-bodied men, they were at first reluctant to accept black men as full fighting soldiers. Most colonists did not like the idea of supplying blacks with guns, but shortages of troops finally forced the colonists to accept black men into the militia.

The long struggle also taught the colonists that only by cooperating with one another could they hope to defend themselves. Yet colonial Americans in 1763 were still far from united.

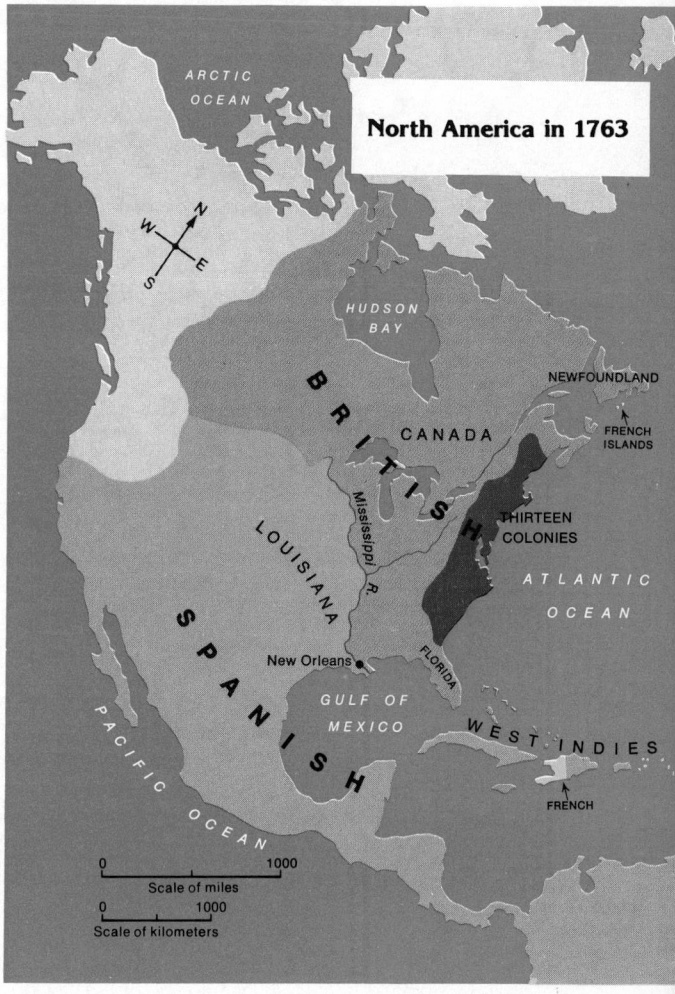

North America in 1763

SECTION REVIEW
See underscored items, text pp. 49-53.

Identify: 1754, militia, Six Nations, Albany Plan of Union, William Pitt, Jeffrey Amherst, Treaty of Paris of 1763

For answers to questions, see Answer Key, p.A13.

1. **Summarizing Ideas:** Describe the events that led to the French and Indian War.

2. **Analyzing Ideas:** Why did the British colonies reject the Albany Plan of Union?

3. **Determining Cause and Effect: (a)** In what year did success in the French and Indian War begin to shift from the French to the British side? **(b)** What event in Great Britain helped bring about this shift?

4. **Studying Maps:** Locate Louisburg on the map on page 51. Why was this fort important to both sides in the French and Indian War?

DEVELOPING HISTORY STUDY SKILLS

Thinking About History Charting Information

Organizing information into a chart or table is a common method of classifying information. To classify means to systematically organize information into categories, or groups, according to common characteristics. Classifying information into charts, tables, and other graphics highlights the common themes and relationships among seemingly unrelated pieces of data.

How to Classify Information

To classify information, follow these steps.

1. **Decide on a purpose.** Before information can be classified, a purpose for classifying must be established. The purpose for classifying can usually be turned into a title for the chart, table, or graph that is to give form to the data to be classified.

2. **Categorize the data.** Select one item in the list of items to be classified. Choose a category into which the selected item fits. Then look for other items among the data that fit into the same category. Select an item that remains uncategorized. Choose a category for it and find other items that fit the second category. Follow the same procedure for other uncategorized items until all items have been placed in a category.

3. **Formulating the chart.** Turn the purpose for classifying into a title for the chart. Use the category labels as headings for the columns or rows of the chart. Finally, place your categorized items into the appropriate rows and columns of the chart.

Applying the Skill

Look at the list below. It is an alphabetical listing of the 13 original colonies founded by English settlers.

Connecticut	New Hampshire	Rhode Island
Delaware	New Jersey	South Carolina
Georgia	New York	Virginia
Massachusetts	North Carolina	
Maryland	Pennsylvania	

Formulating a chart is one way to classify the items in the list, following the steps above. The purpose for classifying can be to organize the 13 colonies by geographic location. From reading the chapter, you know that the colonies were founded in three regions along the Atlantic seaboard.

The first item on the list is Connecticut. Your reading has told you that this colony is in the region known as New England. Examine the other items in the list to find other New England Colonies. Your list should include Massachusetts, Rhode Island, and New Hampshire.

The Thirteen Original Colonies

New England Colonies	Middle Colonies	Southern Colonies
Connecticut	Delaware	Georgia
Massachusetts	New Jersey	Maryland
New Hampshire	New York	North Carolina
Rhode Island	Pennsylvania	South Carolina
		Virginia

(1. See chart for answers. 2. Reasons for an early English settlement: to prevent [cont'd]

Select an uncategorized item. The second item on the list is Delaware. It remains uncategorized. Delaware is located in the region known as the Middle Colonies. Other Middle Colonies include New Jersey, New York, and Pennsylvania.

Returning to the list, you find that Georgia is uncategorized. It is a Southern Colony. Other Southern Colonies are Maryland, North Carolina, South Carolina, and Virginia. You are now ready to put your chart together because all items in the list are categorized.

Finally you develop your chart, using the purpose as a heading and the categories as subheadings. You then place your categorized items in the proper columns. Your chart should look like the one at the bottom of page 54.

Types of Work in the Thirteen Colonies

Type of Work	Where Found
Farming	All thirteen colonies
Fishing	All colonies except Pennsylvania
Manufacturing	Pennsylvania New Jersey Massachusetts
Mining	New York, Pennsylvania, New Jersey, Delaware, Maryland
Forestry	North Carolina South Carolina Virginia

Practicing the Skill

On a separate sheet of paper, complete the following activities.

1. Use the information in Chapter 2 to develop a chart on work and production in the colonies. Use the sample chart form to the right, and fill in the information that is missing.
2. Set up a second chart after reading the essay below written in the early 1500's. Formulate a chart on the reasons for English settlement of America. Then add to your chart two additional reasons for settlement that are presented in Chapter 2.

This enterprise may staye the Spanishe from flowing over all the face of that waste firme of America, if wee seate and plante there in time . . . her Majestie may, by the benefete of the seate, having wonne goodd and royall havens, have plentie of excellent trees for mastes, of goodly timber to builde shippes and to make greate navies, of pitche, tarr, hempe, and all things incident for a navie royall. . . . Howe easie a matter it may be to this realme, swarminge at this day with valiant youthes, rustinge and hurtfull by lack of employment, and havinge goodd makers of cable and all sortes of cordage, and the best and moste connynge shipwrights of the worlde, to be lordes of all those sees, and to spoile Phillipps Indian navye, and to deprive him of yerely passage of his treasure into Europe, and consequently to abate the pride of Spaine. . . . Wee shall by plantinge there inlarge the glory of the gospell, and from England plante sincere relligion, and provide a safe and sure place to receave people from all partes of the worlde that are forced to flee for the truthe of Gods worde.

Spaniards from settling, to obtain safe harbors, to obtain natural resources to help build a great navy, to provide jobs for the unemployed, to prevent Spain from gaining wealth, to spread the Christian religion and provide refuge for those persecuted for their beliefs; Students charts will vary.)

Other permanent settlements followed the success of Jamestown. Every good harbor along the Atlantic coast became a landing place for settlers and the beginning of a new way of life.

One of the most impressive features of the colonial world was its variety. The settlers came to America for many different reasons. In all the colonies, however, regardless of backgrounds or beliefs, the settlers had a burning desire to share in the opportunities of the New World. These early settlers were the colonial roots of the American nation. From their boundless variety and vitality developed a distinctive culture that came to be called the "American way of life." Self-government was an important feature of colonial life.

Unhappily, slavery and disregard for the rights of Native Americans were also disturbing elements in the story of colonial development. Another disturbing element was the growing rivalry between Great Britain and France. The rivalry began on the continent of Europe and spilled over into the colonies.

During more than half a century, the French threatened to conquer the British colonies and win for France control of the entire North American continent. The victory of Great Britain in the Seven Years' War, however, shattered the French dream of power in Europe. It also ended the French quest for an empire in North America. With the French threat ended, the British colonists looked to the future with thoughts of remaining loyal citizens of the British empire.

CONNECTING CHAPTER IDEAS

In the next chapter you will read about the changing ways of American life from 1607 to 1763. The mixture of people from all walks of life and of European, Native American, and African cultures produced a unique blend, making Americans distinctively different from Europeans.

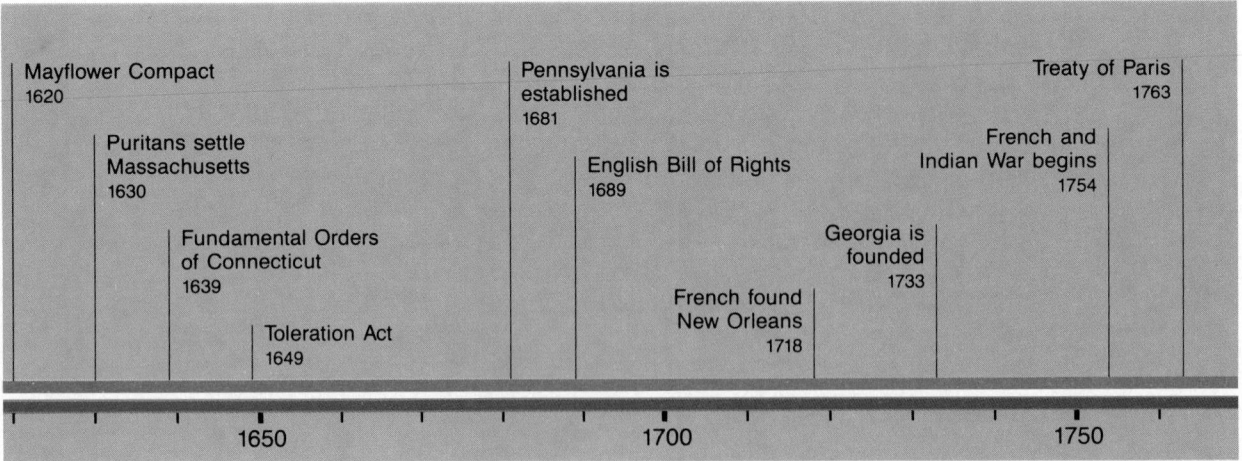

Mayflower Compact
1620

Puritans settle
Massachusetts
1630

Fundamental Orders
of Connecticut
1639

Toleration Act
1649

Pennsylvania is
established
1681

English Bill of Rights
1689

French found
New Orleans
1718

Georgia is
founded
1733

Treaty of Paris
1763

French and
Indian War begins
1754

1650   1700   1750

CHAPTER
2 REVIEW

Reviewing Important Terms

In the sentences below, the underlined terms are incorrect. On a separate sheet of paper, rewrite each sentence using the correct term.

1. Recession resulted when Spain's wealth from its American colonies helped bring about higher prices for English wool.
2. James I believed that his rule rested upon the consent of the governed.
3. In order to obtain transportation to the colonies in America, many men and women signed long-term contracts in which they agreed to become apprentices.
4. Massachusetts became a royal colony under Charles I when the Puritan directors moved their charter to the New World.
5. Sturdy pioneers moved away from the settled areas and searched for greater opportunities on the tidewater rivers.
6. Because of their failure to attract tenant farmers from among the Dutch citizens, wealthy Dutch merchants used slave labor on their estates.
7. Fear of Dutch expansion and Indian raids brought the New England colonies together in a proprietorship.
8. In 1689, England adopted a constitution that guaranteed liberties to every citizen.
9. Coureurs de bois, a group of citizens trained to fight as soldiers, were often called on to defend the British colonists.
10. A colony is a political league in which members retain most governmental power, while a central government takes care of common problems such as defense.

Practicing Critical Thinking Skills

1. **Interpreting Ideas.** (a) How did most colonists regard the Indians? (b) How did Indians who had encountered colonists regard them? (c) What were some consequences of these attitudes?
2. **Analyzing Ideas.** Why is agriculture considered an essential occupation for any new settlement of people?
3. **Determining Cause and Effect.** The two statements below follow each other in cause and effect. Explain the cause-and-effect relationship in each statement. (a) Nations desiring power (cause) needed to possess colonies (effect). (b) Nations possessing colonies (cause) needed large armies and navies (effect).

4. **Making Inferences.** Why by 1750 were there fewer blacks in New England and the Middle Colonies than in the Southern colonies?
5. **Seeing Relationships.** How did rivalry among the powerful European nations for supremacy in Europe affect their conflicts on the North American continent?
6. **Relating Past and Present.** (a) Explain how life in the colonies was characterized by undemocratic as well as democratic elements. (b) Is this true of American society today? Explain.

Developing History Study Skills

1. **Charting Information.** Prepare a chart with the headings "New England Colonies," "Middle Colonies," and "Southern Colonies." In each column, fill in information about (a) religious beliefs, (b) attitudes toward slavery, (c) type of government, and (d) reasons for settlement. Use the chart to explain whether the colonies were basically similar or different.

2. **Evaluating Primary and Secondary Sources.** Read the excerpt from the Mayflower Compact on page 34. (a) Why can this document be considered an important step toward self-government? (b) Compare this excerpt from the actual document (a primary source) with your textbook's description (a secondary source). (c) How can each source help you to understand the Mayflower Compact?

Relating Geography and History

Natural features were a major factor in the pattern of colonial settlement. Sometimes these patterns eventually resulted in social, economic, and political differences between one section and another. To understand better the connection between geographic features and settlement patterns study the maps in Chapters 1 and 2 and answer the following questions.

1. (a) What natural features formed protective barriers for the settlers? (b) How did these barriers promote a feeling of unity among the colonists?
2. (a) Explain why first settlements were located near oceans and inland waterways. (b) Describe the importance of the major rivers to the survival of the settlements established on their banks.

57

See Chapter Overview in TMRG, p.TM23.
See Chapter Objectives in TMRG, p.TM23.
See Introducing the Chapter in TMRG, pp.TM23-24.

CHAPTER 3 American Cultural Beginnings

Changing Ways (1607–1763)

A colonial plantation

Benjamin Franklin became Postmaster General of the British colonies in North America in 1753. Franklin required careful accounts from everyone handling the mails. He started new postal routes, some using horse-drawn stagecoaches instead of postriders. His ideas and suggestions provided better mail service and helped unite the colonies.

In 1763 Franklin made a trip of more than 1,600 miles (2,560 kilometers), traveling over nearly every post road. On his travels Franklin saw many colonists and learned how they were living and what they were thinking. He visited southern planters, lived with frontier townspeople, stopped overnight with farmers, and talked with frontier settlers. Franklin also saw two groups who lived in colonial America but were excluded from it—Africans, most of whom were slaves, and Indians.

For the most part, early colonists thought of themselves as loyal citizens of the European homeland from which they had come. Colonists from England thought of themselves as Britishers and looked to the Crown with loyalty. Gradually, however, a distinctive way of life began to develop in the colonies.

In this chapter you are going to study the people who lived in the colonies founded by Great Britain. You will see, as Franklin saw, that the colonists were sharply divided on many matters. Colonists began to think differently from people in England. They began to see that British interests and colonial interests did not always coincide. By the 1760's, many people began to think of themselves as colonists first and British citizens second.

═══ READING FOCUS ═══

As you read about the changing views of colonists in the British colonies, look for the details that support each of the following statements.

1. The southern planters seem more English than American.
2. The townspeople mix English with American ideas.
3. The pioneers gradually become the new Americans.
4. The Africans are denied a share in colonial life.
5. The Indians play a major role in colonial history.

1 The southern planters seem more English than American

See Teaching Suggestions in TMRG, p.TM24.

In 1763, Baltimore Maryland, founded in 1729, had only a few thousand people. Charleston, South Carolina, the largest and wealthiest southern port, had only about 10,000 people.

Southern population. By the 1760's more than 2 million people lived in the British colonies of North America. Although most of these people came from Great Britain, thousands came from other lands, including Africa. About half of the total colonial population lived in the five Southern Colonies—Maryland, Virginia, North Carolina, South Carolina, and Georgia.

In the South the proportion of country dwellers was especially high. Most southerners lived on small farms similar to those in New England and the Middle Colonies. Some lived on the frontier in small clearings cut from the forest. The wealthy planter families lived on the fertile coastal plains. A few southerners owned **plantations** several thousand acres in size. These planter families lived much like wealthy English landowners.

The plantation. The wealth of southern plantation owners came from agriculture. Food used on the plantation was grown there, but the riches of the plantation usually came from a single **cash crop,** that is, a crop raised to be sold at a profit. In Georgia and South Carolina, rice was the most important product. In Maryland, Virginia, and North Carolina, the chief cash crop was tobacco.

The large plantation was a complete economic unit. In the center stood a large house that was usually built in the popular Georgian style of architecture. Around the mansion were the simpler homes of the **overseer,** or supervisor, and the **artisans,** or skilled workers, many of whom were slaves. George Washington's estate at Mount Vernon, Virginia, for example, had cabins for carpenters, bricklayers, masons, blacksmiths, millers, and weavers.

Each plantation was almost self-sufficient, that is, it supplied almost all of its own needs. Meat was butchered from herds of cattle

▲ Writing activity: Ask students to recall films they have seen or books they have read that depict the life styles of wealthy English landowners of the 1700's. Ask students to make point-by-point comparisons with the life styles of southern plantation owners in the same period.

59

Without Eliza Lucas, the people of South Carolina would have faced serious economic troubles from 1746 to 1776. War between England and Spain had cut off the European market for the colony's staple crop of rice. In 1744 Lucas had successfully produced her first crop of indigo, a plant from which a blue dye used in printing inks and for dyeing cotton was obtained. With its rice markets closed, the colony turned to indigo, and its sales supported South Carolina's economy for three decades.

Eliza Lucas was born in the West Indies and educated in England. In 1738 her father, a British officer, settled his family in South Carolina. The following year he returned to his military post in the West Indies. Because her mother was sick, the 17-year-old Lucas became manager of the family's three South Carolina plantations.

Lucas was competent and innovative, experimenting with a variety of crops in addition to rice. Her experimentation convinced her to raise indigo, which at that time came mostly from the French colonies in the Caribbean. Obstacles, however, delayed a successful harvest. Lucas persevered and in 1744 harvested her first crop of indigo. She gave away seeds from this crop to other planters, and in 1746 South Carolina shipped 40,000 pounds of indigo to England.

Eliza Lucas's life exemplifed the strength and courage displayed by many colonists — both men and women. When Lucas died, George Washington served as a pallbearer at her funeral.

and hogs, and other foods and raw materials for clothing came from the land. The planter's wife supervised indentured servants and slaves in the spinning and weaving of cloth and other tasks. Often she took part in the work herself. The planter family needed good business ability to run a plantation.

English economic ties. Every year on the tobacco plantations, slaves rolled the large barrels of tobacco to the wharves and loaded them on vessels often owned by northern merchants. With these shipments planters often sent lists of goods that they wanted their agents in London to purchase for them. The agents sold the tobacco, rice, or indigo, then bought and shipped the articles requested to the planters.

In this way well-to-do planter families filled their homes with Old World luxuries — fine furniture, table silver, clothes, tapestries, wines, and books. Few luxuries were bought in the colonies, because even as late as the 1750's, American colonists produced few manufactured goods.

Social life. Since the plantations were more or less isolated, visits between plantation families became great social events. During two months in 1768, George and Martha Washington entertained guests at dinner 29 times and were invited out 7 times. These dinners were splendid affairs, followed by evenings of conversation or card playing. The gracious tradition of southern hospitality, which has continued to this day, grew out of the colonial custom of social visiting.

Many of the richer planter families also owned town houses where they spent several months each year. During these months they enjoyed dancing, music, art, dramatics, and lectures. The men also spent time playing cards, watching cockfights, racing horses, and hunting foxes.

English influence. The plantations of the South reminded visitors of country estates in England. They were, in a sense, part of England carried to the New World. Wealthy planter families dressed, talked, and acted much like rich English landowners. Indeed, in some ways they had more in common with well-to-do English people than with the small farmers and frontier people who lived nearby.

Yet, as you will see, when the break with England finally came, some southern planters were among the first to fight for independence. A southern planter, Thomas Jefferson, wrote most of the Declaration of Independence. Another southern planter, George Washington, led the American armies to victory.

It is also true that when the Revolution began, some wealthy southern families remained loyal to England, as did some wealthy people in the New England and Middle Colonies. Their ties with Great Britain were too strong to break.

SECTION REVIEW
See underscored items, text p. 59.
Identify: plantation, cash crop, overseer, artisan
For answers to questions, see Answer Key, p.A14.
1. **Organizing Ideas:** Describe the different social groups that lived in the Southern Colonies.
2. **Analyzing Ideas:** (a) Why did plantation owners generally rely upon a single cash crop for their profit? (b) Name the main cash crops grown in the Southern Colonies. (c) How might this plantation system be an advantage to the plantation owners? (d) How might it be a disadvantage?
3. **Summarizing Ideas:** (a) How were plantations organized to be self-sufficient? (b) List the tools and services that plantations could provide for themselves.
4. **Comparing Ideas:** (a) How did the well-to-do planter families entertain themselves in the country? (b) How did they entertain themselves in the towns?
5. **Seeing Relationships:** (a) What were the economic ties that bound the southern planters to England? (b) In what ways might these ties have had an influence on their feelings in a controversy between England and the other American colonies?

See Teaching Suggestions in TMRG, pp.TM24-25.

Wealthy townspeople in all the colonies dressed and acted like people in England. This is not surprising. Most colonial cities and towns were seaports with strong commercial ties to England. All travel and trade between the Old World and the British colonies flowed through these seaports.

By the 1750's Philadelphia, with a population of 20,000, was the largest colonial city. In one year, 1754, a total of 471 trading vessels entered and left its busy harbor. New York and Boston were a close second and third in importance. Charleston, South Carolina, and Baltimore, Maryland, were the only towns of considerable size south of Pennsylvania.

Social divisions. By the 1760's merchants were the most influential citizens in all large northern towns. This was true even in New England, where ministers had once been the leaders. The merchants together with lawyers and the families of the royal governors set the fashions for the wealthier people. The merchants drew their wealth from trade and from buying and selling land. Some owned country estates worked by tenant farmers.

Below the merchants on the social ladder were the majority of the townspeople. This group included laborers and artisans, shopkeepers, bakers, pharmacists, and printers. Women followed many of these occupations, either as partners of their husbands or as widows who carried on the enterprises. Below all these were female and male indentured servants. Far below them were male and female slaves.

Most of these classes of people resembled similar classes in England, but class distinctions in the colonies were not as rigid as in England. Through hard work and ability, artisans or even white servants could improve their positions in life. In some cases they could even join the society of the influential townspeople and southern planters. A black slave, however, could not.

Influence of the Old World. European influence could be seen in many features of town

Wealthy colonists enjoyed luxurious life styles. They copied many of the social customs of England.

life. Some wealthy families built houses similar to those seen on their visits to the Old World. Like the wealthy southern planters, wealthy town families imported furniture and household luxuries from England. The interiors of their houses as well as the exteriors reminded visitors of the Old World.

Like well-to-do people in England, wealthy town families led an active social life, with elaborate dinners and parties. Many well-to-do townspeople also enjoyed card playing, horse racing, cockfighting, and the theater. In Boston, however, strict Puritan ideas still prevailed, and such recreation was frowned upon.

Only the wealthier townspeople enjoyed this lively social life. Household servants usually lived in simply furnished rooms over the family quarters. Artisans often lived behind their small shops that fronted on the streets.

A visit to Philadelphia. Imagine that you are in colonial America, strolling through the seaport of Philadelphia in, say, 1754. In other colonial towns, the streets wind this way and that, following the early cowpaths and farm lanes. Philadelphia is different. Here William Penn's careful planning has proved worthwhile. The streets run neatly north and south, east and west. Some are paved with cobblestones; others are merely hard-pressed earth. As you walk, you pass the homes of the wealthy—red brick and white stone houses surrounded by gardens and lawns. You also pass the small shops of the artisans.

Hearing the sound of a bell, you pause to listen to the town crier. Introducing the news with "Hear ye, hear ye," he announces a sale of indentured servants who have just arrived from England.

On your way to the waterfront, you pass the market house. Throngs of housewives and servants with baskets on their arms crowd around the stalls. Farm men and women from the surrounding countryside are displaying produce for sale—butter, cheese, poultry, beef, mutton, ▲ and vegetables.

Along the waterfront. Reaching the water, you continue along Dock Street, which parallels the Delaware River. The noise of hammers and saws attracts your attention, and you see a shipyard where a small vessel is being built. Next to it fishing boats are heaving the day's catch onto the planks of the wharf. Beyond lies an English ship at anchor.

Approaching the ship, you find yourself in the midst of bustle and confusion. Men carrying boxes and bales on their shoulders push their way toward the nearby warehouse. At one side colonists, eager for the latest news from the Old World, surround a sailor and ask him many questions. On the deck of the ship are the indentured servants, waiting to be bought, some looking extremely bewildered and unhappy.

English ways of life. Walking back into town, you pass the open door of a merchant's counting house. Inside, clerks on tall stools record business transactions in their account books. Across the street is a tavern. A row of hitching posts stands in front of the tavern, and a hollow log serves as a watering trough for horses.

You have not seen the town hall or the jail or the several churches that are important parts of the city. You have seen enough to learn that life in the colonial towns is similar in many ways to life in English towns. The people dress and talk like people in England. The houses and public buildings are English in style. You see the same social divisions that exist in English towns.

A mixture of peoples. In some ways, though, the colonial towns are different from the towns of England. For one thing, people from many different nations are learning to live together in colonial America. The colonial towns as well

▲ The flavor of a plain potato was not appreciated in the 1700's. A cookbook of the period directs the cook to season boiled potatoes with nutmeg, cinnamon, pepper, dates, lemon, mace, butter, sugar, grape juice, or rosewater.

William Penn, Philadelphia's designer, had the city streets made twice as wide as usual. By the 1700's, the time of this painting, many of the lawns and orchards that Penn had planned were gone and solid walls had been built.

as the frontier and the farming areas contain settlers from many nations. German settlers fill the section of Philadelphia known as Germantown. On the streets you pass men and women from Ireland and Scotland, many on their way to western frontier lands. Listening carefully, you hear the accents of people from France, Switzerland, Sweden, and many other European countries.

This mixture of people in colonial America is producing a new American vocabulary. English visitors to the colonies hear many new, unfamiliar words. The colonists are speaking what Samuel Johnson, the famous English dictionary maker, in 1756 called the <u>American dialect</u>. The New American vocabulary has borrowed many words from other languages. From the Indians it has borrowed skunk, hickory, squash, raccoon, canoe, toboggan, moccasin, tomahawk, and wigwam. From the Dutch it has borrowed cruller, stoop, waffle, scow, boss, and cookie. From the French it has
▲ borrowed bureau, gopher, chowder, bogus, portage, and prairie. The colonists themselves have invented many new words—bullfrog, eggplant, snowplow, cold snap, trail, popcorn, shingle, and backlog.

Building the towns. The colonists are also trying to find new solutions to the many problems faced by all townspeople. Working together, they are trying to solve problems of water supply, sewage, sanitation, health, and police and fire protection. In Philadelphia, Benjamin Franklin's newspaper, the *Pennsylvania Gazette,* publishes a steady stream of articles dealing with solutions to these problems. Largely because of Franklin's efforts, Philadelphia is one of the first cities in the world to have paved streets, street lights, police and fire departments, and a public library.

A land of opportunity. The greatest difference between English and American towns can be summed up in the word "opportunity." There is plenty of work for everyone in Philadelphia, New York, Boston, and every other colonial town. Except for slaves, who usually remain slaves for life, no one need remain a servant for very long. If the town itself does not offer enough opportunity, the more venturesome of the colonists can always move west. Some stay in town only long enough to save a little money. Then they are off over the roads that lead them to a new way of life.

SECTION REVIEW
See underscored items, text p. 63.
Identify: American dialect
For answers to questions, see Answer Key, p.A15.

1. **Comparing Ideas: (a)** The social ladder in America was similar to that in England but different in one important way. Explain. **(b)** In what ways did Philadelphia in 1754 resemble an English town? In what ways was it different?

2. **Summarizing Ideas:** List three ways in which European styles of living influenced those of well-to-do townspeople in the colonies.

3. **Interpreting Ideas:** How did the American variety of spoken English reflect conditions in the New World?

3 The pioneers gradually become the new Americans

See Teaching Suggestions in TMRG, p.TM25.

In the country, the area far from the seacoast, lived more than 90 percent of all the colonists.

Farming villages. Not far from the coast, particularly in New England, New Jersey, and Pennsylvania, were many small farming villages of 50 to 100 families. Each had its own church or meetinghouse, a school, and several shops. Many villages had a cobbler to make shoes, a blacksmith to shoe horses and fix wagons, and a doctor to give medical attention. There usually was a general store to sell sugar, spices, and English cloth for dresses. Traveling barbers also came to the villages to cut hair and pull teeth.

To pay for these services, the farm families of the village and the surrounding territory hauled their surplus tobacco, grain, cattle, and hogs to the nearest seaboard or river-port town. There they sold their products.

Before returning home, farm families often stopped to make purchases in the shops displaying English luxury goods—tableware, silver and pewter vessels, and fine cloth. Thus settlers living in areas where they could market their surplus products were able to live better than more isolated colonists.

Moving inland. Many people married young in colonial America. Some newly married couples settled on land near their parents. Many more became **pioneers** who moved farther inland to unsettled areas, where land was cheaper. It was a common sight to see a couple pass through a village on their way to a new home. Behind them an ox or a horse might pull a small cart containing a few boxes with all

Scutching flax, which means beating the raw flax in order to separate the woody fiber, was a tedious task. It was pleasanter, even fun, when pioneers gathered to do it together, as in this painting, "The Scutching Bee," by Linton Park.

their belongings. Bringing up the rear, tied to the cart by a rope, might be a scrawny cow.

Pioneer shelters. At first many pioneers lived in caves along the riverbanks or in shallow pits roofed with branches and covered with sod to keep out the rain. Frequently newcomers put up three-sided log shelters with the open side facing away from prevailing winds. Sooner or later those who stayed to farm the land built a full <u>log cabin</u>. This practical structure for forested country was introduced into the colonies by Swedish settlers.

The log cabins were usually crude, drafty, one-room affairs with a dirt floor, no windows, and a door hung on leather hinges. The most important feature of most cabins was a huge fireplace where the settlers huddled for warmth and where they cooked their food. Later, if the pioneers prospered, they improved the cabin. They might buy one of the stoves invented by Benjamin Franklin to improve the heating. They might lay a wooden floor, cut windows in the walls, and cover the openings with waxed paper or glass. They often built lofts for the children to sleep in an added new rooms. If all went well, they finally nailed clapboards on the outside walls of the cabin over the rough logs.

Pioneer families rose at dawn and went to bed at dusk. There were few books, even for those who could read, and the pioneers felt little need to light the cabins at night. Usually the glow from the fireplace furnished the cabin's only light. When more light was needed, people put large splinters of pine wood into cracks in the walls, where they burned with a bright, smoky flame. Pioneer families used candles only on special occasions, for **tallow** was hard to get. Only wealthy townspeople used candles and oil lamps to any extent.

Household equipment. Pioneer families did all their cooking in the fireplace. They boiled vegetables, soups, and stews in large copper or iron kettles—which hung from a pole in the chimney. They baked in Dutch ovens beside the fireplace or in ovens in a side wall of the fireplace itself.

Early pioneer furniture and utensils were homemade and crude. Beds were little more than wooden bunks placed along the wall. Logs, hewn smooth with an ax, became chairs and benches. Smooth boards placed on trestles served as tables. Dishes were slabs of wood with a hollow place in the center to hold food. The pioneers carved spoons out of wood. They drank from gourds or from tankards that they made from wood, leather, or the horns of cattle.

Food and clothing. Once colonial Americans learned to use the abundant resources of the New World, they rarely lacked food and drink. The rivers and lakes were alive with fish, and the forests were filled with game. In the early days, settlers near the forts often saw herds of deer numbering several hundred. Turkeys were seen in all the colonies, although the settlers rapidly wiped them out. Pigeons were so plentiful from Virginia northward that they sometimes darkened the sky and broke limbs of trees in which they roosted. Wild rabbits and squirrels destroyed so many crops that payments were offered for their pelts. Pioneer women and girls tended the gardens, raised poultry, helped with the milking and butchering, and, especially in German and Dutch families, sometimes worked in the fields.

Pioneer women and girls also made the family's clothing, using spinning and weaving skills brought from the Old World. They made thread from the wool of their sheep and from the flax they grew in their fields. They spun this thread, wove it into cloth, and cut and sewed it into garments. They also tanned deerskin for ▲ moccasins, shoes, and jackets.

Life on the frontier. Some pioneers, mainly young men, chose not to settle down. They preferred to roam the frontier. Every year, in all the colonies, hundreds of adventurous youths left home to find excitement in the western forests.

Living in the wilderness, they shed many traces of European civilization. All that they owned they carried in their hands or on their backs—a hunting knife, a long rifle (see page 142), powder, and shot. Yet with this meager equipment, they managed to survive. They shed their European clothing for coonskin caps, buckskin shirts and trousers, and moccasins of deerskin. Game, fish, nuts, and berries furnished much of their food. They slept beneath the stars, in caves, or in crude log shelters.

Most of these <u>frontiersmen,</u> as they were known, preferred the lonely life of the forest to the ties of a family. Now and then they appeared at a trading post to exchange a few furs for new supplies of powder, shot, and perhaps a

▲ Writing activity: Have students keep a record of ordinary household chores they perform and compare their chores with the chores a frontier family perform.

65

Settlers on the frontier often hleped their neighbors build houses. Since these settlers lived far apart, house raisings were also great social occasions.

little corn. Many frontiersmen lived a wild and dangerous life, in which they constantly matched wits and skills against Indians and nature.

Social life and recreation. The hard life of the pioneers and frontiersmen left little time or energy for recreation. Nevertheless, they did occasionally combine work and play.

Now and then frontiersmen for miles around gathered for companionship and sport. Shooting matches were common. So were games of physical strength—foot races, wrestling matches, jumping contests, and the hurling of heavy fence rails. In the evening, before a crackling log fire, they swapped colorful tales of forest adventure and told jokes about newcomers to the wilderness.

When a pioneer family was ready to build a cabin or had cut the trees and was ready to drag them from the land to clear a field, all the neighbors came to help. House-raisings sometimes lasted several days. In the morning the men lifted the logs into place to form the cabin walls. Meanwhile, the women prepared dinner, baking great piles of cornbread and barbecuing an entire beef or deer over an open

fire. After dinner there were sports, such as wrestling, foot racing, and shooting contests. In the early evening, the settlers danced.

People who lived in areas that had been settled for some years had more opportunity to be neighborly. In these areas the farms were closer together and small villages had been built. On Sundays most settlers went to church. During the week, in appropriate seasons, they helped one another with the corn-husking, sheepshearing, sewing, and quilting. Weddings were always times of celebration. Most work also ceased on election days and on training days, when the local militia drilled in an open field in the morning and then spent the afternoon in sports and conversation.

Self-sufficiency. With a gun, an ax, a knife, a hoe, a sickle, and a kettle or two, a pioneer family could clear the land, build a house, and grow the crops. However, most pioneers lived a harsh life. They were self-sufficient not from choice but because they had to be. The great majority had no doctors, no schools, and few churches. They usually had a roof over their heads, enough to eat, and freedom from oppressive laws and heavy taxes. They paid for these advantages with lives of back-breaking labor.

New ideas among pioneers. Among these self-reliant pioneers, certain ideas began to take root and grow. The pioneers were free women and men who had created new lives in the wilderness. They were individualists, for their success depended on their own strength and skill, but they also believed in cooperation, for only by helping one another could they clear land and build houses. Even the independent frontiersmen were aware that an additional pair of strong arms and an extra rifle could sometimes mean the difference between life and death.

The pioneers considered themselves the equals of other men and women, for they saw most of their neighbors living similar lives. Finally, they were optimists, for they saw the forests yielding to their axes and homes and villages springing up in what had been wilderness land. They saw neighbors who had started with nothing raising their families in security and increasing comfort.

Along the whole length of the colonies, from New France to Spanish Florida, the pioneers lived much the same sort of life. The Germans, Scotch-Irish, and English settling the Virginia frontier had more in common with those settling the Massachusetts frontier than they had with the rich planters of their own colony or with the townspeople of the colonial seaports. Gradually their ties with European ways of life weakened, and many began to think of themselves as Americans.

SECTION REVIEW
See underscored items, text pp. 64-65.
Identify: pioneers, log cabin, frontiersmen
For answers to questions, see Answer Key, p.A15.
1. **Summarizing Ideas:** Explain how pioneer families adapted in terms of (a) shelter, (b) household equipment (c) food, (d) clothing, and (e) social life.
2. **Classifying Ideas:** (a) In what ways were pioneer families self-reliant? (b) In what ways did they benefit from the help of their neighbors?
3. **Analyzing Ideas:** Why would self-reliant people tend to value freedom and equality and tend to be optimistic?
4. **Comparing Ideas:** How did the life of frontiersmen differ from the life of pioneer farm families in terms of (a) personal possessions, (b) clothing, (c) food, (d) shelter, and (e) social life?

4 The Africans are denied a share in colonial life

See Teaching Suggestions in TMRG, pp.TM25-26.
In the 1760's about 2 million people lived in the British colonies. An estimated 300,000 to 400,000 were of African birth or background. These black colonists helped build the colonies, yet they were denied the opportunities that other colonial groups took for granted.

A class apart. For European settlers America meant freedom and an opportunity to build a better life. For black men and women it meant nothing of the kind. Unlike the vast majority of Europeans, the Africans did not come to America freely. The Africans were brought against their will, by force, literally in chains.

In the very early colonial years, the Africans were generally treated as indentured servants. However, white colonists soon came to regard the black Africans as property—a valuable kind of property, but property nonetheless. Denied their humanity, Africans became slaves, and most remained slaves for life, as did their children. Every other group in colonial society regarded black people as inferior. Even the few black people who gained their freedom were often looked down upon and denied the rights other colonists enjoyed.

Slaveowners usually taught the Africans only as much as was necessary to do their work. Thus most slaves learned the simpler skills involved in colonial farming, building, and manufacturing and enough English to obey orders.

The white colonists ignored the skills already possessed by the black arrivals. Few white colonists knew or cared that the Africans came from civilizations hundreds or even thousands of years old.

The Middle Passage. As colonial demands for slaves increased, the brutal African slave trade grew and flourished. From central and western Africa, long lines of Africans, captured by enemy tribes, were marched to west African seaports. To prevent their escape, the captives were forced to wear iron collars and were linked together by chains. The survivors of these long, cruel marches were sold to European or American sea captains. Such buyers

67

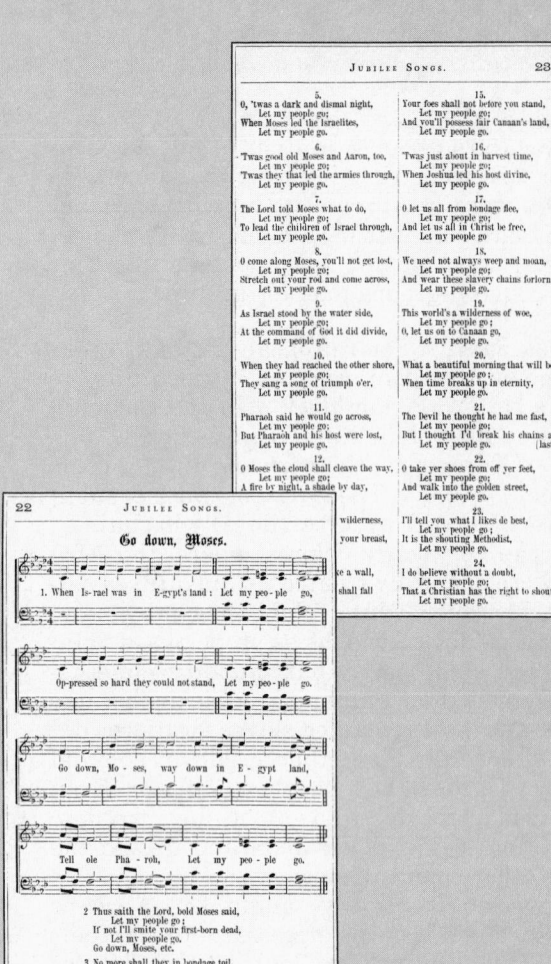

An important legacy of the slavery system of the American South was the addition of spirituals to the nation's musical culture. Spirituals were religious folk songs, usually based on stories from the Bible. Often the preacher would "call out" the first line of a hymn, and the congregation would sing the refrain.

The slaves sang spirituals not only in church but also while they worked. Spirituals kept alive the musical traditions the slaves had brought with them from Africa — clapping, choral singing, and the "ringshout" form of dance, in which the singers formed a circle and shouted at one another. The emotional anguish of many spirituals such as "Go Down Moses" reflected the slaves' dream of one day being delivered from bondage.

After the Civil War the singing of spirituals spread throughout the nation. Today spirituals remain one of the most popular and best-known forms of music in this country. They have often been called the only true American folk songs.

would select only the strongest and healthiest young Africans.

Once the slaves were selected, they were branded and packed into the slave ships. Chained together two by two, they were packed together between decks where there was not room enough for them to stand.

The weeks-long voyage to the New World, called the **Middle Passage,** was a nightmare. Some slaves killed themselves by jumping overboard or choking themselves with their chains. Many died from spoiled food. Disease, fostered by overcrowding and filthy conditions, took many more lives. Sharks trailed the slave ships and fed on the bodies of the dead that were thrown overboard. Some slaves revolted against these inhuman conditions, but these revolts seldom succeeded. Scholars estimate that from 13 to 33 percent of the slaves did not survive the horrors of the Middle Passage. This heavy loss of life did not discourage the slave traders, who made enormous profits.

Traders from several countries, including England and its colonies, usually sold the surviving Africans to planters in the West Indies. Here, before they were sent to the colonies along the Atlantic seaboard, the African newcomers were "seasoned," or broken in, by overseers. It is very likely that fewer than half the slaves survived this harsh "seasoning" period on the sugar plantations of the West Indies.

Slavery in New England. By the 1770's a relatively small number of black slaves, perhaps about 12,000, lived in New England. The small New England farms did not require the labor of large numbers of slaves. New England slaves worked as household servants for wealthy families and as farm laborers, lumberjacks, carpenters, barrelmakers, blacksmiths, millers, fishers, and shipbuilders.

Slaves in New England had some legal rights. They could buy property and had the right to trial by jury in the courts. Slaves could attend church as long as they sat in "African pews," but they could not become church members. In early New England, church membership conferred political rights, such as the right to vote and to hold office. Such political rights were denied to slaves.

Most New Englanders looked upon their slaves as wards, or adopted children, of the family. Yet these "adopted children," even in rare instances when their owners taught them to read and write, were property to be bought and sold as their owners wished.

Although slaves in New England had some rights, New England slavery still was harsh. New England slaves, like slaves everywhere, would not accept the central idea of slavery — the total and permanent ownership of human beings by other human beings. Many New England slaves fled from their masters, no matter how kind their masters might be.

Slavery in the Middle Colonies. Slaves in the Middle Colonies contributed their labor and skills to commerce, industry, and farming. As in New England, however, the number of slaves was relatively small — perhaps about 35,000.

In New Netherland, Dutch patroons and merchants, like New Englanders, often regarded their slaves as adopted children. When the British seized the area, this attitude changed. Under British rule all black slaves in

TO BE SOLD on board the Ship *Bance-Island*, on tuesday the 6th of *May* next, at *Ashley-Ferry*, a choice cargo of about 250 fine healthy **NEGROES**, just arrived from the Windward & Rice Coast. —The utmost care has already been taken, and shall be continued, to keep them free from the least danger of being infected with the SMALL-POX, no boat having been on board, and all other communication with people from *Charles-Town* prevented. *Austin, Laurens, & Appleby.*

N. B. Full one Half of the above Negroes have had the SMALL-POX in their own Country.

Henry Laurens, the slave trader named above, became president of the Continental Congress, the first government of the independent colonies.

New York except household servants were strictly separated from white colonists. Severe rules of discipline governed the slaves. Violence between white colonists and black slaves became fairly common in New York.

Attitudes toward slavery in Pennsylvania and much of New Jersey differed somewhat from those in New York. From the earliest days, at least some Quaker and German settlers in Pennsylvania and New Jersey doubted the morality of slave labor as well as its usefulness. A few of them began to speak out against the evils of slavery.

Slavery in the Southern Colonies. Of the 300,000 to 400,000 blacks in colonial America in 1765, the vast majority, or nearly seven out of eight, lived in the Southern Colonies. Almost all of these black men, women, and children were slaves.

Most southern slaves labored on tobacco, rice, and indigo plantations, but southern slaves also did many other kinds of work. Between 1732 and 1736, the *South Carolina Gazette* mentioned 28 trades that made use of slave labor. Black slaves thus made an enormous contribution to the development of the Southern Colonies.

Tobacco became one of the South's biggest cash crops. In this English advertisement for tobacco, slaves are shown packing the dried leaves in barrels and rolling them down to the docks for shipment.

In the Carolinas slavery grew rapidly, as it did in Georgia once it was allowed. The early colonists of Virginia and Maryland, however, came to depend upon black slave labor only gradually. First they tried without success to enslave the Indians. Then they tried to rely on white indentured servants, but indentured servants were hard to get and harder to keep. Black slaves provided a more dependable labor force—and a permanent one.

The status of Africans in Virginia was for some time uncertain. The first African arrivals were regarded more or less as indentured servants, but their contracts did not always insure their freedom after their term of service was completed. After 1661 the institution of slavery was clearly established in Virginia.

Throughout the late 1600's and the 1700's, slavery grew rapidly in the Southern Colonies. Planters developed new and larger plantations, requiring the labor of more and more slaves. Slave traders rushed to fill the demand.

The slave codes. As the proportion of slaves to white people increased in the Southern Colonies, white southerners became alarmed. If plantation agriculture was to expand and be profitable, the southerners needed slaves. White southerners feared that large numbers of black people would undermine **white supremacy**, control of the blacks by whites.

Slaves concentrated in large numbers might successfully revolt against their masters. Reports of occasional slave revolts in the West Indies, where black slaves far outnumbered white settlers, added to these fears.

Beginning in the 1680's, southern slaveowners tried to solve this problem by passing **slave codes.** These laws had a double purpose. First, they safeguarded slaveowners' investments in their slave property by setting up detailed regulations to prevent the theft or escape of slaves. Second, they protected slaveowners against slave violence by setting up strict rules for slave behavior.

To prevent slave revolts, the codes forbade slaves to meet together, leave the plantation, or own weapons. By law, slaves could not learn to read or write. Special guards circulated among the slaves to insure that these slave codes were obeyed.

Black resistance to slavery. In the 1600's and 1700's, punishments for all crimes were extremely cruel. Under the slave codes, however, punishments for slaves were more severe than punishments for white colonists who committed similar crimes.

For minor crimes slaves could be beaten or even have their noses split or their ears cut off. For major crimes, such as rape or murder, a slave could be hanged or burned to death.

Ralph Waldo Emerson, a leading American essayist of the 1800's, once remarked that "things are in the saddle and ride mankind." Perhaps Emerson would have cited the cotton gin as the best example of the phenomenon — technological progress — he was describing. Invented by Eli Whitney in 1793, this labor-saving device transformed the cotton industry and brought great wealth to the South. It also provided a justification for the slavery system, and thus set the North and the South on a fateful path to civil war.

Until the 1790's, the cultivation of cotton was mainly limited to the moist, semitropical coastal regions of South Carolina and Georgia. The type of cotton grown was the long-staple variety, consisting of long fibers that could easily be separated from their seeds. Because long-staple cotton could be grown only on the coast, however, the demand for it was outpacing the supply. Southern planters longed for a profitable way to grow short-staple, or upland, cotton, which could be grown in harsher climates. The difficulty with the short-staple variety was that its sticky seeds could be removed only by hand — and it took one slave a full day to clean a few pounds of cotton. As a result, cotton production in 1792 totaled only 138,000 pounds and involved fewer than 650,000 slaves.

Whitney's cotton gin changed all that. In 1794, the year after the machine was introduced, cotton production reached 1.5 million pounds, almost twelve times the 1792 level. By 1800 the South was producing 35 million pounds of cotton a year; by 1859, 350 million pounds. At the time the Civil War began, nearly four million slaves were required to support the South's rapidly growing cotton economy.

Whitney invented the cotton gin while visiting a plantation in Savannah, Georgia, shortly after his graduation from Yale. According to legend, the mechanical genius was sitting on a fence as a cat stuck its paw through the boards to catch a chicken on the other side. The chicken escaped, but not without losing some feathers. Whitney applied this cat's claw principle to his cotton-picking machine, which contained a series of wire teeth set in a wooden roller. As the roller turned, the teeth pulled the fibers through a grid. The seeds, being too large to pass through the grid, were separated from the fibers. A person using a cotton gin could clean cotton as fast as 50 persons working by hand.

Whitney later developed the concept of interchangeable parts, thus revolutionizing American industry. But he is far better known for the invention that made cotton production — and slavery — the basis of the South's pre-Civil War economy.

Slaves found many ways to harass their masters. Often they purposely slowed down their work or did it poorly. Sometimes they struck back or even killed their white masters.

Slaves sometimes succeeded in running away from their owners, but because of their skin color, they did not automatically win their freedom. In all colonies an unknown black person was immediately suspected of being a runaway slave.

Slaves could and did plot uprisings to secure their freedom. Slaveowners lived in terror of such revolts. The vaguest rumor of a slave uprising could cause panic in a white community. Whether the revolt was real or imagined, the punishment for the slaves was severe.

Vague rumors appear to have been the only evidence used against more than 100 slaves convicted of plotting a revolt in New York in 1741. Eighteen slaves were hanged, 13 burned to death, and 78 "transported," probably to the British West Indies, where the slave codes were extremely severe.

White opposition to slavery. A few white colonists condemned slavery. In 1700 Samuel Sewall of Boston, an influential judge, published a famous antislavery pamphlet called *The Selling of Joseph*. A devout Puritan, Judge Sewall gathered examples from the Bible to show that slavery was evil.

In 1688, twelve years before Judge Sewall's pamphlet appeared, the Quakers of Germantown, Pennsylvania, spoke out against slavery. These Quakers denounced the evils of owning and selling human beings as property and of separating husbands from their wives and children, which happened often when slaves were sold.

Not until the mid-1700's, however, did Quakers generally begin to oppose the brutal slave trade and, gradually, slavery itself. John Woolman, a conscientious and thoughtful Quaker tailor, journeyed through the colonies trying to persuade Quakers to free their slaves and educate them. His journal is still read and admired today.

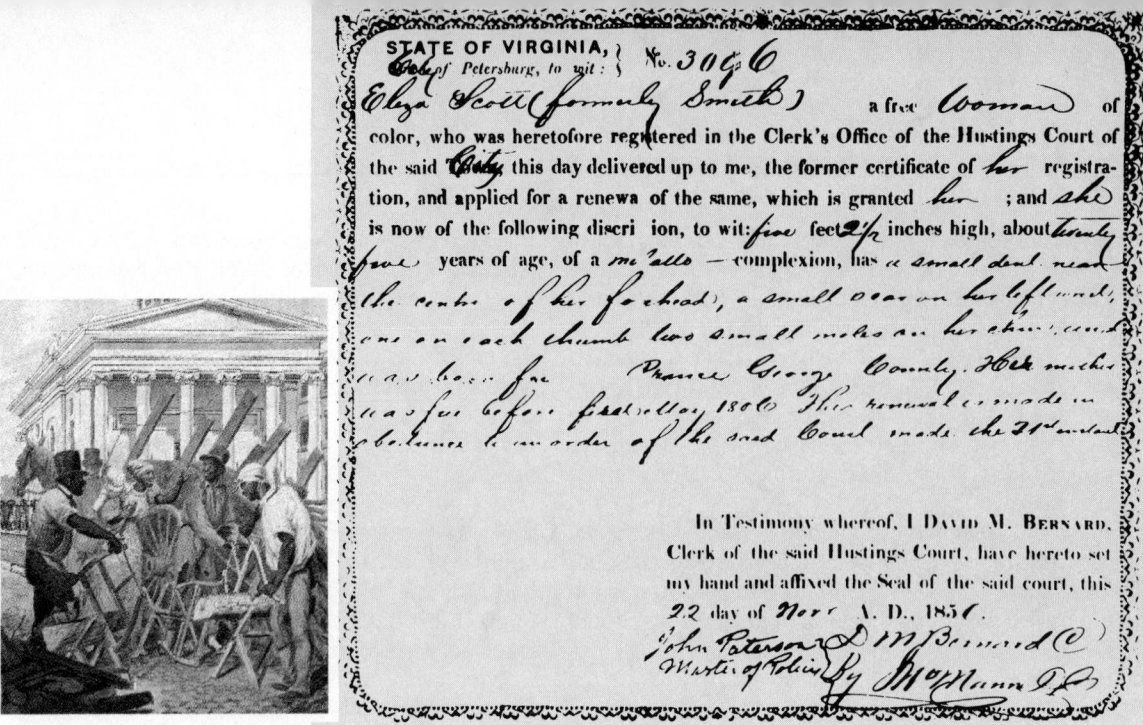

Every colony had some free blacks. Most lived in cities and earned their living as skilled workers (left): A free black's most precious possession was a registration certificate (right).

Free blacks.   A few freed slaves lived in every colony. They gained their freedom in several ways. Descendants of the early indentured Africans in Virginia inherited their freedom. Children of a white mother, regardless of the father's race, were regarded as free persons. Occasionally masters freed some or all of their slaves as a reward for faithful service or to avoid supporting them in their old age. A few slaves bought their freedom, using savings their owners allowed them to earn and keep.

Most free blacks earned their living as skilled workers. A few owned small farms or businesses. Free black men could not serve in colonial militias in peacetime, though both free black colonists and slaves were recruited into the militia in times of war. In the 1700's free blacks were not allowed to vote in any of the Southern Colonies except, for a time, in North Carolina.

White colonists seldom associated openly with free blacks except in casual, unimportant ways. A few free blacks won a respected place in their communities, but most had to endure discrimination from the white colonists.

Separate and unequal.   White colonists, especially the English, regarded blacks, whether free or slave, as a class apart—and an inferior class at that. Most were forced to live apart from white colonists and obey special laws enforced by white colonists. Even so, black men and women contributed enormously to the growth of the colonies. White colonists not only expected hard labor from blacks, they demanded it. Yet in a new land abounding with opportunity, few black men and women were permitted to work, to save, or to build better ways of life for themselves or for their families.

SECTION REVIEW

See underscored items, text pp. 68, 70-71.

Identify: Middle Passage, white supremacy, slave codes, Samuel Sewall, John Woollman

For answers to questions, see Answer Key, pp. A15-16.

1. **Organizing Ideas:** For each of the three groups of colonies, answer the following: **(a)** How great was the need for slave labor? **(b)** What legal and social rights did slaves have? **(c)** What jobs did slaves perform?

2. **Summarizing Ideas: (a)** How did some slaves gain freedom **(b)** What legal and social rights did free blacks have?

3. **Interpreting Viewpoints: (a)** How might slavery affect a slave's feelings toward white people? **(b)** How might slavery affect a slaveowner's feelings toward black people?

4. **Studying Pictures:** Look at the slave sale notice on page 69. What do you think that buyers of slaves would worry about? Why would this worry them?

The sound of the ax has rung through North American forests for centuries. Many records tell of logging long before the days of Columbus. Certainly, logging was the first commercial activity of Europeans on the North American continent.

Before European settlers arrived, forests covered approximately half of all of the land in present-day Canada and the United States — more than 3 million (7.7 million square kilometers) of the 6.1 million square miles (15.8 million square kilometers) of land was densely forested. Only cold or dryness put limitations on forest growth.

Early settlements such as Jamestown and Plymouth clung to the edge of a vast pristine forest of unknown magnitude. Yet, over the centuries before European settlement, this vast forest had been altered. The majority of Eastern Woodland Indians who made the forest home were farmers. The Indians had already begun to clear forest land before the first European settler touched foot on the shores of North America. They used fire to clear land for their corn, beans, and squash. They also burned the woods in the fall and spring to encourage the new growth which would attract deer, elk, and other browsing animals.

While the Indians made small patches of forest disappear, their patch-clearing was surpassed by the new arrivals from Europe. So determined were the Europeans to clear the forests that trees seemed almost like enemies to be destroyed. Trees had to be cut to make room for houses and fields. Houses, barns, stockades, and bridges were all built of wood, which was the only fuel used in most homes. Forest products were also used for businesses. White pine was cut for barrel staves, ship timbers, and masts. From the yellow pine forests came turpentine and rosin as well as lumber. Early iron furnaces were fueled with charcoal made from fine hardwoods. Even soapmaking depended on lye made from wood ashes.

Logging was one of the first major industries in the colonies. Large-scale logging had its origins in the deep forests of Maine with its heavy stands of pine and spruce. The logs were floated downriver to the good harbors off the Atlantic Ocean. And the long, cold winters, when little other work was done, provided an ideal environment for logging. The loggers were a tough and hardy group, and in time they simply logged out all of Maine's accessible first-growth pine and spruce.

As Maine's forests were being depleted, the center of large-scale logging gradually began to move westward. In 1840 the center of the logging industry was Maine. By 1850 it had reached New York; 1860, Pennsylvania; 1870, Michigan; and by 1880, Wisconsin. Then in 1890, as the first-growth forests of the Great Lakes neared depletion, the westward march of the logging industry divided. Part of the industry moved to the flatland pine forests of the South; part moved across the Rocky Mountains to the vast forests on the Pacific slopes.

After three centuries of deforestation, thousands of acres of forests have indeed disappeared. Today the nation has left only 10 percent of first-growth timber.

This deforestation has had far-reaching effects on the environment. Ecologists feel that the destruction of forests has had a harmful effect on flood control and soil quality. The disappearance of forests may even have effected the air humans breathe because green plants are responsible for the exchange of carbon dioxide and oxygen in the atmosphere. What is needed is more efficient management of the forest lands that remain. This is an important challenge to present as well as future generations of Americans.

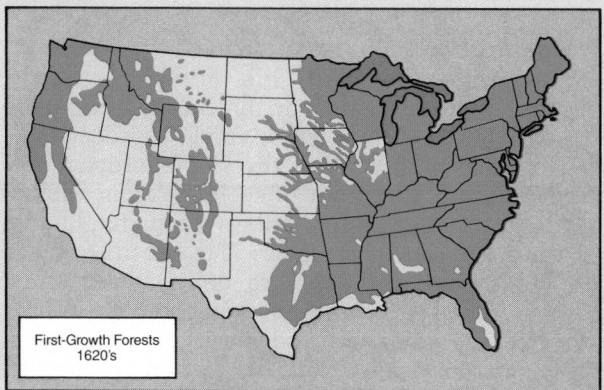

First-Growth Forests
1620's

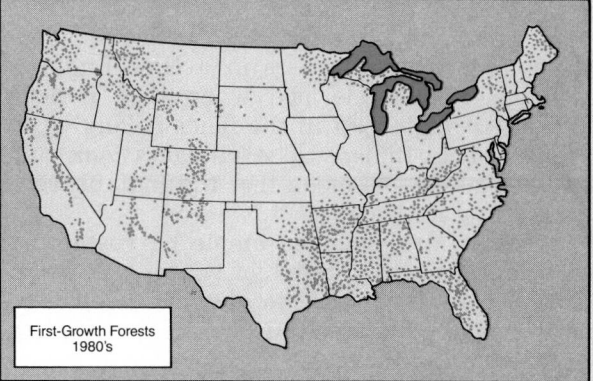

First-Growth Forests
1980's

Each dot on the map represents 25,000 acres of virgin forest.

5 The Indians play a major role in colonial history

See Teaching Suggestions in TMRG, pp.TM26-27.

From the days of the first settlements, the Indians played an important role in the development of the English colonies.

Indians of the Eastern Woodlands. Many Indian tribes lived between the Atlantic coast and the Appalachian Mountains (see map, page 6). Almost all of these Indians depended upon agriculture for their food. Among the exceptions were the Algonquin (al·GAWN·kwin) tribes of Canada. In much of their territory, the summers were too short for raising most crops, and the northern Indians, therefore, relied upon hunting for food as well as for clothing and shelter.

Tribes in the lands from Canada south to Florida used hunting only to supplement the crops they grew. Each of these tribes had its own hunting ground with clearly defined boundaries. Indians who entered a neighboring tribe's hunting ground without permission did so at their own risk.

Farming methods. The Eastern Woodland Indians had no plows, and their only domestic animal was the dog. Nevertheless, they had an effective method of farming. In the spring the men broke the sod with hoe-like tools, and the women then planted the seeds. One woman led the way down a row, using a digging stick to open shallow holes in the soil at regular intervals. Other women, following in her footsteps, dropped seed for corn, squash, or beans in the holes. Sometimes a small fish was first placed in each of the holes as fertilizer.

The care the Indians took to keep their fields free of weeds impressed the colonists. On one occasion the settlers in a New England village became alarmed when they noticed weeds springing up in the fields belonging to neighboring Indians. The villagers took this sign of neglect to mean that the Indians were preparing for war!

Indian fields yielded ample harvests, and surplus grain was stored for winter use. Often the Indians were able to give or to sell corn and beans from their surplus to the English settlers.

Social and political life. Most Eastern Woodland Indians lived in permanent villages. These communities were made up of families and groups of related families, or clans. Each village was a close-knit social unit, and all of the members participated in work, recreation, and religious ceremonies. The tribe itself included many villages spread over the tribal territory.

The Eastern Woodland Indians—and most other North American tribes—shared a more or less democratic form of government. A <u>sachem</u> (SAY·chum), or chief, seldom held absolute power. Usually there were several sachems. One might lead a hunting party; another might lead a raid against an enemy tribe; and another might lead in peacetime. Moreover, the chiefs were usually advised by a council of older men. Decisions were reached in council meetings by unanimous vote.

The Iroquois Confederation. In general, the tribes were independent of one another. There were, however, several confederations, the most powerful of which was formed during the 1500's. At that time the Seneca, Cayuga, Onondaga, Oneida, and Mohawk tribes in the land between the Hudson River and Lake Erie joined in the Iroquois Confederation.

An Indian prophet named <u>Deganawidah</u> dee·gan·ah·WEE·dah) supposedly first dreamed of the Confederation. He saw a day when the Confederation would include all Indians, war would be abolished, and peace would prevail throughout the world. His vision was passed by word of mouth from generation to generation (see Source, page 76). Some historians believe that the first appearance of white explorers may have been another reason that the five tribes united. In the 1700's, as you have read, the Confederation accepted the Tuscaroras as members and became the Six Nations.

Iroquois organization. Each tribe made its own decisions in daily life. For larger issues, such as going to war or making a treaty, the Confederation as a whole made the decisions. The governing body of the Confederation was made up of a number of sachems from each of the six tribes. Each tribe's sachems had to agree on a decision before it could take effect.

Although all the sachems were men, women had great influence in the tribes. They chose the sachems and could remove them. Women controlled the distribution of food and

The Algonquins are shown here in a village near Quebec. They were bitter enemies of the Iroquois, another Eastern Woodlands tribe, who finally succeeded in pushing them off their lands and to the west.

owned most of the property, including the **longhouses.** These were large, rectangular structures in which several families lived together, each with its own quarters.

The Iroquois Confederation grew out of a vision of peace, but the Iroquois soon became the most feared and respected Indian fighting force in North America. Iroquois warriors subdued one after another of the surrounding tribes. At the peak of its power, the Iroquois Confederation controlled tribes from the Atlantic coast to as far west as Lake Michigan and from Canada south to what is now Tennessee. In the colonial wars between the French and British, and later during the American Revolution, the opposing sides tried to outbid each other for the support of the Iroquois.

Spiritual beliefs and practices. The Eastern Woodland Indians shared with other Native Americans deeply held religious and spiritual beliefs. At the heart of their beliefs was the ▲ vision of a force that lived in every part of the universe. This spiritual force existed in the sun, moon, and stars. It existed in the wind, the rain, the running water, the forests, the growing plants, and the earth, the mother of all life.

It was present in the objects that men and women made for daily use. It was present in all living creatures—in the wildlife of the forest and the sea and in the humans who shared the earth with all other forms of life.

Among the tribes were **shamans** (SHAY·munz), or medicine men, and prophets. The shamans and prophets claimed the ability to communicate with this spiritual force. Those who possessed this ability called upon the spirit world to bring rain to thirsty crops, to grant victory in warfare, and to heal the wounded and the sick. In songs, dances, and elaborate ceremonies, the Indians worshiped this spiritual force.

The legacy from the Indians. The first British settlers along the Atlantic seaboard owed a great deal—in some cases, even life itself—to the Indians who received them with friendliness mixed with curiosity. Indian food, given freely or traded for English products, saved many of the early settlers from starvation. Many of the settlements—among them Jamestown, Plymouth, Boston, and Philadelphia—were built on the sites of former Indian villages.

Indian knowledge and skills were invaluable to the colonists. The Indians provided seeds and taught the whites how to plant and cultivate the fields. From the Indians the colonists learned how to live off the game, fish, and plants of the forest lands. Along Indian trails the whites, in time, advanced into the heart of the continent. Many of today's highways follow the routes of the old Indian trails. Hundreds of Indian words survive in our language and in place names across the land.

The whole world owes much to the Indians and their cultures. In agriculture alone the Indians' contributions have been priceless. Nearly 500 years have passed since men and women from Europe began to settle the American continents. During all that time, none of the settlers or their descendants has discovered and developed a single major agricultural product from the wild trees and plants of the New World. Yet long before the first Europeans arrived, the Indians had developed more than 50 valuable products. In addition, they had learned to use many other products of the forests and the grasslands, including a large number of medicinal plants still in use today. More than half of all the agricultural goods produced in the world today come from plants originally discovered and cultivated by American Indians.

How different our eating habits would be if we did not have corn, tomatoes, white and sweet potatoes, and the many varieties of beans! If we did not have peanuts, chestnuts, pumpkins, strawberries, blackberries, blueberries, cranberries, and crab apples! If we did not have chocolate and maple syrup! If we did not have turkeys!

Clash of cultures. These were and are impressive contributions, and the colonists gladly accepted them. Yet the colonists ignored other important lessons that the Indians could have taught them. The colonists had beliefs and values that differed from those of the Indians.

Each group found it difficult to understand and accept many of the other group's ideas.

The Native Americans had learned to live in harmony with their environment. They lived on and with the land without polluting it and without exhausting its resources. They had, as John Collier expressed it in his book *Indians of the Americas,* a "reverence and passion for the earth and its web of life."

The colonists did not understand these ideas. To them success and progress depended upon changing the natural environment. The resources of the New World appeared to have no end. They were there to be used. This was especially true in the British colonies. The French relied heavily on the fur trade, which disturbed the environment less than farming did. The French also had fewer and smaller settlements. In the British colonies, though, farming was highly important. So, heedless of the future, the colonists slashed and burned the trees, dug and planted the fields, and raised towns and cities on the former hunting grounds of the Indians.

The colonists and the Indians also had different ideas about land and property. The colonists acquired Indian lands by purchase, by treaty, and, at times, by fraud and by force. The colonists believed that property could be bought and sold by individuals. The colonists did not understand that Indian property was held collectively by the tribe. An Indian chief was actually a trustee for the tribe and had no right to give away or sell any part of the tribal lands.

Two such different ways of life could not long exist peaceably side by side. Conflict was inevitable. As the colonists pushed westward, driving the Indians from their homelands, the fighting on both sides became increasingly fierce. Finally, most colonists decided that the only solution was to exterminate the Indians.

Efforts at conversion. Not all colonists thought of the Indians as cruel, inferior beings.

SOURCES

DEGANAWIDAH'S VISION

I, Deganawidah, and the Confederated Chiefs now uproot the tallest pine tree, and into the cavity thereby made we cast all weapons of war. Into the depths of the earth, deep down into the underearth currents of water flowing to unknown regions, we cast all weapons of strife. We bury them from sight and plant again the tree. Thus shall the Great Peace be established.

▲ Discussion topic: Modern-day movements that are an echo of Deganawidah's vision (disarmament, antinuclear protests, pacifism) and the chances of these movements instituting lasting changes

Such colonists believed that it was important to draw them away from their own religious beliefs and convert them to Christianity. Roger Williams, John Eliot, Jonathan Edwards, and others tried to teach Christianity to the Indians and to deal fairly with them. Judge Samuel Sewall, who argued against slavery for black people, also criticized New Englanders for regarding the Indians as little better than animals.

Other religious groups also tried to convert the Indians to Christianity. The Quakers and Moravians especially tried to understand the Indians, to deal fairly with them, and to prove that love could overcome all barriers.

Efforts at education. A few attempts to educate the Indians in European ways of living met with little success. Eleazar Wheelock raised funds to start a college in New Hampshire where Indians could be educated and converted to Christianity, but the experiment had little success. In Virginia, at the College of William and Mary, a few Indian boys were taught in separate classes. When the boys returned to their tribes, the chiefs complained that they had been made unfit for Indian life.

Benjamin Franklin offered to supervise the education of some Indian boys. He was courteously told that Indian methods of education were better suited to the boys' development. The Indians offered instead to take some white boys and teach them Indian arts and skills. The colonists declined the offer.

Attempts at understanding. A few thoughtful colonists took genuine interest in Indian life. Roger Williams in the 1600's learned one of the Indian languages and wrote an Indian dictionary. In the 1700's Benjamin Franklin, Thomas Jefferson, and a few other scholarly colonists became interested in the customs as well as the languages of the Indians. Jefferson admired the eloquence of Indian chiefs at treaty-making ceremonies. He also appreciated the dignity and nobility they showed when facing hardship.

On the whole, however, genuine concern for the Native Americans was extremely rare in colonial America. Most colonists made no effort to understand them, distrusting and despising them instead. For their part, the Indians found little to value in the whites' way of life. Nor were the Indians able to understand why the colonists feared and hated them so intensely.

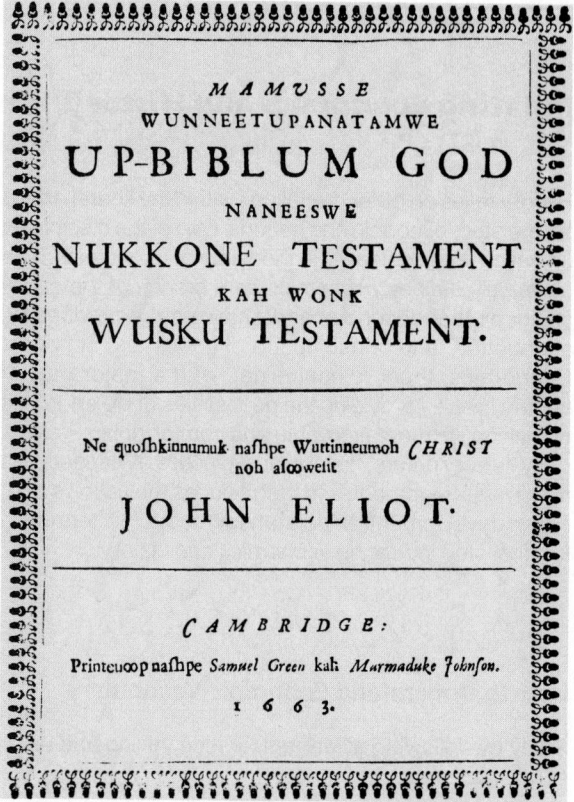

This title page comes from the first Bible printed in this country. It was translated by John Eliot, the "Apostle to the Indians."

With such deep misunderstanding on both sides, a long-lasting pattern of conflict between the Indians and the settlers was planted and nourished in colonial America.

SECTION REVIEW

See underscored items, text pp. 74-75, 77.

Identify: sachem, Deganawidah, longhouse, shaman, Eleazar Wheelock

For answers to questions, see Answer Key, p.A16.

1. **Summarizing Ideas: (a)** What methods of plowing and planting did the Indians of the Eastern Woodlands use? **(b)** Describe the political organization of the Iroquois Confederation.

2. **Interpreting Ideas:** Indians knowledge and skills were invaluable to the colonists. Explain.

3. **Comparing Viewpoints: (a)** How did the colonists' and the Indians' views of the environment and land ownership differ? **(b)** Why might such differing views lead to conflict?

4. **Studying Pictures:** How do you think the Indians pictured on page 75 might have made their living?

DEVELOPING HISTORY STUDY SKILLS

Relating Economics and History Understanding Economic Terms

History relies on other disciplines within the liberal arts to tell the story of people and nations. One of the disciplines on which it relies heavily is the study of economics. The dictionary defines economics as a branch of the social sciences that describes and analyzes the production, distribution, and consumption of goods and services. Economics, then, is concerned with a major part of human lives — providing the necessities of life and ways of making life more enjoyable and comfortable.

By its very nature, history must discuss all aspects of a nation's development, and that includes the nation's economic development. Understanding economic terms is a key first step in relating economics and history.

How to Understand Economic Vocabulary

Study the following guidelines for recognizing and using economic terms.

1. **Recognize economic terms.** Be alert to the use of economic terms. When previewing content before the study of a chapter, skim the headings and subheadings looking for terms that describe aspects of making a living. Make a mental note to pay more attention to these terms as you study the chapter.

2. **Analyze context.** Look for clues in the sentence in which the term appears or in surrounding sentences that give some understanding of the term's meaning. Consult the textbook's Glossary, or use a dictionary to expand on the term's meaning.

3. **Utilize illustrations.** Textbooks contain many illustrations. Relate the use of an economic term to an on-page illustration to see if the illustration provides an example of the term in action.

4. **Develop your own economic glossary.** Keep a list of economic terms as a part of your study materials. As you encounter an economic term, add it to your list, writing an understandable definition. Make note of the page on which you encountered the term. On the completion of a unit's study, review the list of economic terms that you have developed. Use the terms to develop a summary of the unit's economic developments.

Mercantilism

The British Empire of which George III became sovereign in 1760 was shaped largely by the principles of mercantilism. The goal of mercantilism — today it would be called economic nationalism — was the creation of a self-sufficient empire from which foreign trade and commerce were excluded. . . .

. . . By mercantilist theory, the function of colonies was to produce raw materials for the use of [homeland], to consume its manufactures and to foster its shipping. . . . This implied, as mercantilists readily admitted, that the colonies were to remain dependent agricultural regions, closely tied to the economy of an industrialized [homeland]. . . .

. . . England made clear its intention of concentrating control of the resources of [its] colonies in her own hands. It was ordered that certain commodities . . . could be sent only to England, Ireland and Wales. . . .

The commodities thus singled out for the [homeland's] monopolization were those [commodities] generally regarded as essential to the wealth and power of the state which were not produced in the British Isles themselves: sugar, tobacco, cotton, indigo, and dye woods. . . . No country could hope to attain self-sufficiency without an ample supply of these. . . .

—John C. Miller

Applying the Skill

Skim the excerpt at the top of this column, noting the words and phrases that are underlined. Each of these terms relates in some way to the production, distribution, and consumption of goods and services and to the role of economics in England's quest for colonies. Now read the excerpt carefully and thoughtfully. Use the questions at the top of the next page to help you analyze its contents.

1. What was the goal of mercantilism?

2. What was the function of colonies within a mercantilist system?

3. What did this imply that the colonies become?

4. How did England make clear its intention of keeping complete economic control?

5. What commodities were singled out for control, or monopolization, as the excerpt put it?

Now let us review the answers you got to these questions. The goal of mercantilism was the creation of a self-sufficient empire. Colonies were to produce materials for the homeland, implying that the colonies were forever to remain dependent agricultural regions. England showed its intentions of keeping complete control by determining the goods that were to be produced and the places to which the goods could be distributed. In so doing, it determined that only people in the homeland would consume those goods.

Are the meanings of the underlined terms clearer than before? If not, use the economic glossary on these pages to help you define them more clearly.

Practicing the Skill

Use Chapter 3 to complete these activities on a separate sheet of paper.

1. Find at least five economic terms in the chapter and list them.

2. Write a definition of each term. After the definition, write the page number on which you found the term.

3. Check your definition against the textbook's Glossary, or use a dictionary. Refine your definition if you need to. You know you fully understand the term if you can use it correctly in a sentence of your own. Add this sentence to your definition.

4. Use the information in Chapter 3 to compose an essay discussing various aspects of the colonial economy. Whenever possible, use economic terms from your study of this skill lesson and Chapter 3.

A Colonial Economic Vocabulary

Here are some economic words and phrases important to understanding the many quarrels between England and the colonies.

agrarian Agricultural or farm economy.

commerce *See* trade

commodity An item that can be bought and sold, such as cotton, lumber, or nails.

consumption Use of economic goods and services.

distribution Shipment of economic goods to intended destinations.

economic diversification Producing a wide variety of goods, such as cash crops and manufactured goods. In a diversified economy no one product dominates the economy.

economic nationalism Commercial policy benefiting the homeland's economy.

exports Goods sold to another country.

imports Goods bought from another country.

industrialized Having factories for manufacturing finished products. An industrialized country also has harnassed energy sources and developed transportation systems for getting raw materials to factories, and finished products to markets.

manufacture To process raw material into a finished item, often through use of machines.

mercantilism Economic system in which nations tried to export more than they imported that developed in Europe after 1500. Colonies and trade monopolies were important parts of mercantilism.

monopoly Complete control by a single company, group, or nation of a product or service in a particular market.

production The making of economic goods for consumption.

raw materials Crude resource that can be converted by processing or manufacture into an economically useful good.

resources Raw materials and other assets. Natural resources include minerals, soil, forests, water, and energy sources.

self-sufficient Able to provide all basic necessities without outside resources.

shipping *See* distribution

trade (v) To exchange, purchase, or sell goods; (n) exchange, purchase, or sale of goods.

wealth All material objects that are economically useful or valuable.

(1., 2., 3., and 4. Answers will vary. Some suggested economic terms for Chapter 3 are: free enterprise, plantation, cash crop, market, self-sufficient, overseer, and artisan.)

3 SUMMARY

The settlers in the British colonies were European in language, dress, customs, and ways of thinking and acting. The settlers tried to reproduce in the New World the everyday ways of life with which they had been familiar in the Old World. Retaining their old ways of life, however, proved to be needless. Plunged, as they were, into a new and strange environment, the settlers had to change the material aspects of their lives—including houses, clothing, tools, and weapons. Slowly the ideas and practices from the Old World began to change.

The southern planters and the wealthy townspeople changed more slowly than the other colonial groups. Because their ties with England were so close, the planters and townspeople continued in some ways to be more English than they were American. The pioneer farmers and the people on the frontier changed much more rapidly. Because these people had so few ties with England, they became much more American than they were English.

Two other groups, the Native Americans and the blacks, played key roles in shaping colonial life. The contributions of the Indians, especially during the early years of settlement, were innumerable. The blacks' labor kept the southern economy going. Both these groups, however, were kept out of the mainstream of American life. Blacks were enslaved, and the Indians were treated as enemies. Thus the colonists planted the seeds of future conflicts. Only a few colonists were aware of the problems they were creating for future generations.

CONNECTING CHAPTER IDEAS

In the next chapter you will read about the influence of the emerging ideas and ideals of the colonists on the development of colonial schools, churches, and government. You will read about the beginnings of what in time was to become the American nation.

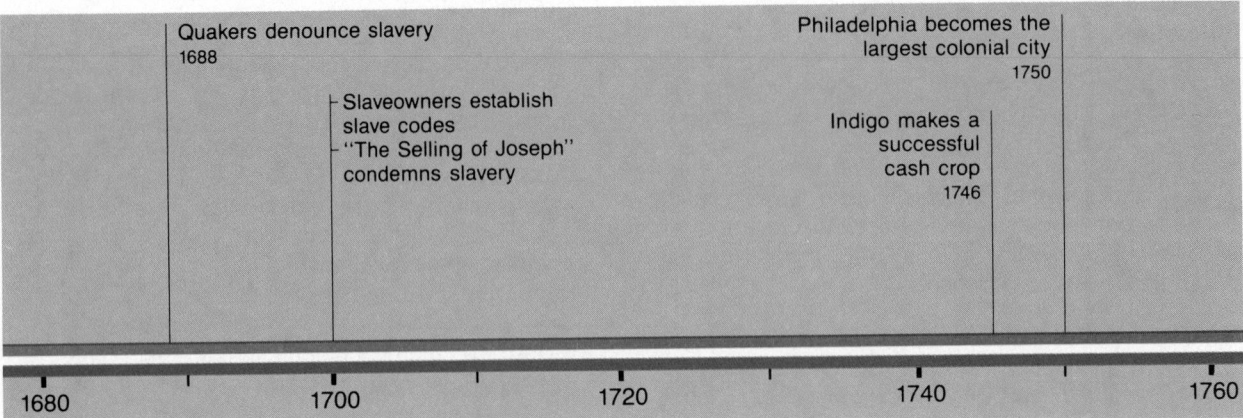

Quakers denounce slavery
1688

Slaveowners establish
slave codes
"The Selling of Joseph"
condemns slavery

Philadelphia becomes the
largest colonial city
1750

Indigo makes a
successful
cash crop
1746

1680   1700   1720   1740   1760

CHAPTER

3 REVIEW

Reviewing Important Terms

Decide whether each of the following sentences is true or false. If the sentence is false, replace the underlined term with the word or phrase that will make it true.

1. Rice was the chief cash crop in South Carolina.
2. The longhouse, a practical structure for forested country, was first built in the colonies by Swedish settlers.
3. As many as one third of the slaves sent to the New World did not survive the Middle Passage.
4. White supremacy set up strict rules for slave behavior which protected slaveowners against slave violence.
5. Most Eastern Woodland tribes were led by more than one sachem, each holding limited powers.
6. Many of the artisans who lived and worked on the plantations in the South were slaves.
7. The scarcity of tallow made the use of candles a luxury in the colonies.

Practicing Critical Thinking Skills

1. **Analyzing Ideas.** (a) Why were many of the colonial planters and merchants able to reproduce some of the familiar ways of life they had known in the Old World? (b) Why were pioneer farmers and frontiersmen unable to continue as many Old World ways as the planters and merchants.
2. **Evaluating Ideas.** The pioneers were cooperative as well as competitive. Does this statement contradict itself? Explain.
3. **Synthesizing Ideas.** Why do you think the colonists chose to establish their cities in the coastal regions? Use evidence from Chapters 1–3 to support your answers.
4. **Comparing Ideas.** Compare the experiences of black Americans and Indians in colonial America. (a) How were their experiences similar? (b) How were they different?
5. **Summarizing Ideas.** In what ways is the white settlers' treatment of blacks and Indians during the colonial period a dramatic example of the fact that America's past has shaped America's present?
6. **Relating Past to Present.** Do Americans today face the same problems that the colonists faced in learning to adapt to a new and changing environment? Explain.

Developing History Study Skills

1. **Using Economic Terms.** The pictures often provide evidence about the economic life of the colonies. Study the pictures in this chapter and then describe the differences in the lives of southern planters, townspeople, and pioneer farmers. Be sure to use such economic terms as *cash crop, plantation, indigo, artisan, free enterprise, market, trading post, slave economy, and self-sufficient.*

2. **Preparing a Report.** Investigate and prepare a report on an early African civilization, such as Ghana, Mali, Songhai, Ashanti, or Benin. Try to find out (a) when the civilization reached its height, (b) where it was located, (c) what its accomplishments were, and (d) why it declined. In your report, include a map of Africa locating the civilization.

Relating Geography and History

Many factors contribute to the success of an enterprise such as a settlement. These factors include a favorable geographic location, natural resources, and available transportation. Another indication of the success of a settlement can be found in its population growth. Human resources are an important part of a successful community. Study the table of colonial population below and complete the following activities.

NEW ENGLAND COLONIAL POPULATION		
Colony	First Census	Fifth Census
Plymouth	102 (1620)	5,333 (1670)
Massachusetts	506 (1630)	39,752 (1680)
New Hampshire	500 (1630)	2,007 (1680)
Rhode Island	300 (1640)	4,224 (1690)
Connecticut	1,472 (1640)	21,645 (1690)

1. Make a bar graph to illustrate the information on the table. Draw the bars with different colors or patterns to represent the two figures for each colony.
2. (a) Rank the New England Colonies from the least populated to the most populated based on the results of the first census, (b) on the results of the fifth census.
3. Which New England colony experienced (a) the greatest growth? (b) the least growth?

See Chapter Overview in TMRG, p.TM28.
See Chapter Objectives in TMRG, p.TM28.
See Introducing the Chapter in TMRG, p.TM28.

CHAPTER 4 Democracy in Colonial America

Changing Ways   (1607–1763)

The devout Pilgrims

Roger Williams, Puritan leader, fled to safety through the snow-covered forests of New England to live with the Narragansett Indians.

Anne Hutchinson, devout student of the Bible, founded a new settlement because she refused to submit to the authorities of Massachusetts Bay Colony.

Lord Baltimore, wealthy Roman Catholic proprietor of Maryland, argued vigorously for the passage of his famous Toleration Act.

Nathaniel Bacon, a wealthy Virginia planter, led a successful rebellion against the tyranny of the royal governor.

John Peter Zenger, editor of the *New York Weekly Journal,* a lonely figure in a cold prison cell, wrote articles for his newspaper.

Phillis Wheatley, a survivor of the Middle Passage at the age of seven, became a thoughtful writer of poems that expressed for blacks their longings for freedom.

These colonial champions of democratic ideals form a proud company. Along with other leaders, they battled for the colonists' right to be free. There were also many others whose names we do not know who struggled to advance democratic ideals. From the earliest days of settlement, despite the contradiction of slavery, a great number of colonists struggled for freedom, fought for the right to worship as they pleased, to secure an education, to speak their minds freely, and to effectively participate in government. When people have these rights and freedoms, they are said to live in a "democratic society," or in a "democracy."

In this chapter you will see how the colonists began to carry the idea of freedom into their churches, schools, and government. You will see that this idea of freedom lies at the root of what is often called "the American way of life."

═══ READING FOCUS ═══

As you read about the development of democracy in the colonies, look for the details that support each of the following statements.

1. Religious tolerance spreads through the colonies.
2. Freedom to learn and to think strike fertile soil.
3. The colonists gain valuable experience in self-government.
4. Colonial legislative assemblies gain power in America.

1 Religious tolerance spreads through the colonies

See Teaching Suggestions in TMRG, pp.TM28-29.

When settlers first left Europe to build colonies in the New World, little or no religious freedom existed in the Old World. Each European nation had an **established church,** or official church. In each nation the government collected taxes to support the established church. Everyone was required to be a member of the church and contribute to its support.

European religious practices. Naturally enough, the first settlers who came to the New World brought the idea of an established church with them. In the French, Spanish, and Portuguese colonies of the Americas, the Roman Catholic Church was the established church. In part of New York and in all of the Southern Colonies, including Maryland after 1692, the Anglican Church became the established church. The official church in the New England Colonies of Massachusetts, Connecticut, and New Hampshire was the Congregational Church. The Middle Colonies, on the other hand, had so many different religious groups that no single church was established, except for the Anglican Church in part of New York.

The early settlers also brought to the New World the bitter religious conflicts and rivalries of the Old World. Border warfare often broke out between the Protestant British colonists of New England and the Roman Catholic French colonists of New France. Although these clashes were mainly caused by economic and political differences, they were made worse by religious differences.

Even within the colonies, the various religious groups often persecuted one another. Many colonists came to the New World searching for religious freedom. However, they were thinking of freedom only for themselves. Plymouth was for Separatists. Massachusetts Bay Colony was for Puritans who had not at first completely rejected the Anglican Church. Colonists who refused to accept the official religious beliefs were often thrown into jail or driven from the colony. Once exiled, they might be put to death if they returned. Such was the fate of

THE RHODE ISLAND CHARTER
(1663)

No person within the said colony, at any time hereafter, shall be any wise molested, punished, disquieted, or called in question for any differences in opinion in matters of religion .... All and every person and persons may, from time to time, and at all times hereafter, freely and fully have and enjoy his and their own judgments and consciences in matters of religious concernments. ...

THE MARYLAND TOLERATION ACT
(1649)

Be it ... enacted ... that no person or persons ... professing to believe in Jesus Christ shall ... henceforth be any ways troubled, molested, or discountenanced ... in respect of his or her religion nor in the free exercise thereof within this province. ...

THE PENNSYLVANIA CHARTER OF PRIVILEGES
(1701)

I [William Penn] do hereby grant and declare that no person or persons inhabiting ... this province or territories who shall confess and acknowledge *One* Almighty God ... shall be in any case molested or prejudiced in his or their person or estate because of his or their conscientious persuasion or practice. ...

Mary Dyer, a Quaker, who was hanged in Boston in 1660 when she returned to protest the persecution of other Quakers.

Roger Williams and a new idea. Roger Williams, as you have read, was one colonist who dared to fight against intolerance. The colony of Rhode Island, of which he was the leading founder, became a symbol of religious freedom for America and the whole world. In Rhode Island there was no established church. Church and state—that is, the government—were separate. No one could be taxed for the support of a church. No one could be forced to attend church. No one had to belong to a church in order to vote. People could worship as they pleased and speak their minds freely.

Lord Baltimore and William Penn. In the struggle for greater religious tolerance, Lord Baltimore and William Penn also won notable victories. In both Maryland and Pennsylvania, the principle of religious <u>toleration</u> became part of the basic law.

In Maryland, as you have read, Lord Baltimore secured passage of the Toleration Act of 1649. The Toleration Act provided that all those "professing to believe in Jesus Christ" were free to practice their religion. They could not be persecuted because of their religious beliefs. The Maryland law, however, gave no protection to Jews and others who did not profess belief in Jesus Christ. Thus it did not establish the complete religious freedom that existed in Rhode Island.

In Pennsylvania religious toleration was broader than in Maryland but not as broad as in Rhode Island. Any person could settle in Pennsylvania if he or she believed that "one Almighty and Eternal God" was the "Creator, Upholder, and Ruler of the World." Only Christians, however, could take part in the government.

The growth of toleration. With Rhode Island, Maryland, and Pennsylvania leading the way, all of the colonies eventually grew more tolerant in matters of religion. As time passed, religious groups found it increasingly difficult to control the lives of all the settlers.

For practical reasons, the leaders of each colony wanted as many people as possible to settle in their colony. Increased population was likely to bring wealth to the king, the proprietors, business owners, and the people in general. Thus the colonial leaders found it almost impossible to keep people out simply because they held different religious beliefs. As people of many different religions began to settle side by side in the British colonies, religious toleration began to increase.

Restrictions upon blacks. White colonists did little to spread Christianity among black colonists, slave or free. The white colonists knew that Christianity taught the importance and dignity of each person. Slaveowners, especially in the 1600's, feared that if black people learned Christian teaching, they might rebel. Many blacks did merge some aspects of Christianity with African religious traditions. During much of the colonial period, however, the majority of black people in the colonies were in effect excluded from Christianity.

There were exceptions. Some masters taught their slaves lessons about Christianity and included them in sessions of family worship. In the early 1700's, Anglican missionary groups urged slaveowners to give Christian instruction to their slaves. The Anglicans also set up Christian schools for blacks.

The Quakers did more than any other religious group to teach Christianity to black colonists. At Philadelphia in 1700, the Quakers established a yearly religious meeting for blacks. A few other religious groups also made efforts to include black members. In 1758, for example, a Baptist congregation in Virginia accepted black members.

Blacks who were allowed to join Christian churches, however, were almost always **segregated,** or kept separate, from white church members. Anglicans in the Southern Colonies sometimes built separate chapels on their plantations where slaves could worship. Puritans reserved an "African pew" for their few black members. As late as 1787, a Methodist congregation in Philadelphia forced black members to sit in the back row. Angered by this discrimination, the black members withdrew and founded their own church—the African Methodist Episcopal Church.

Separation of church and state. Among the white colonists, the growing spirit of religious toleration weakened the foundations of the established churches. The state found it harder to collect taxes for the support of a church to which many taxpayers did not belong.

As the years passed, the established churches in the British colonies lost more and more power. Established churches continued to exist in the New England Colonies, except Rhode Island, and in the Southern Colonies until after the Revolutionary War. However, the movement toward **separation of church and state** was to destroy their privileged position as it gathered strenth.

The Great Awakening. One major force that weakened the position of the established churches was a movement known as the <u>Great Awakening</u>. In the 1730's and 1740's, a wave of religious revivals swept through the colonies. The religious awakening was led by visiting ministers from England, notably George Whitefield (WHIT·feeld) and John Wesley. They were joined by local preachers, of whom <u>Jonathan Edwards</u> of Northampton, Massachusetts, was most outstanding. Their message was clear and direct: Belonging to an established church was not enough to assure being saved. Salvation was freely available to all—men, women, or children—who of their own free will repented of their sins, believed in Christ as savior, and experienced the Holy Spirit.

The Great Awakening gave many people the experience of freedom of choice in their religious lives. This in turn helped strengthen the democratic forces in colonial life.

SECTION REVIEW
See underscored items, text pp. 83-85.

Identify: established church, toleration, separation of church and state, Great Awakening, Jonathan Edwards

For answers to questions, see Answer Key, p.A17.

1. **Summarizing Ideas: (a)** What is an established church? **(b)** Which British colonies had established churches? **(c)** Why did some colonies not have them?

2. **Analyzing Ideas:** How did Roger Williams, Lord Baltimore, and William Penn contribute to the growth of religious toleration in colonial America?

3. **Interpreting Ideas: (a)** Why were most blacks in the colonies excluded from Christianity? **(b)** In what other ways were blacks discriminated against by colonial churches?

4. **Studying Sources:** According to the Sources on page 84, who was entitled to religious freedom in Rhode Island, Maryland, and Pennsylvania?

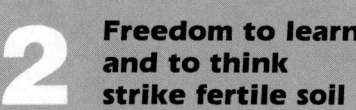

2 Freedom to learn and to think strike fertile soil

See Teaching Suggestions in TMRG, pp.TM28-29.

In addition to religious freedom, freedom to learn, to think, to speak, and to publish are among the essentials of a democratic way of life. People without these freedoms cannot vote intelligently or solve the problems that they face from day to day.

85

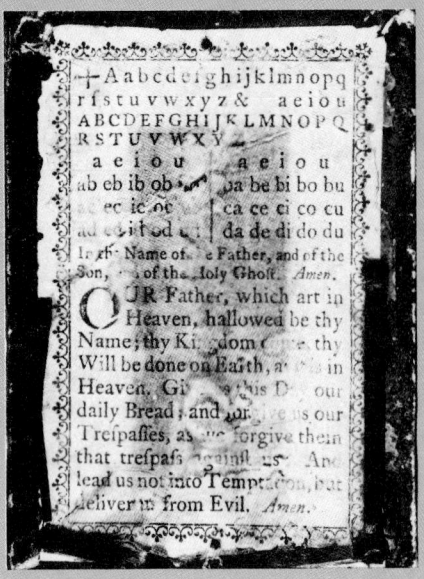

At a time when paper was scarce in the colonies, school children learned their lessons from hornbooks. Actually, hornbooks were not books at all. They were little wooden paddles on which lesson sheets were pasted. The lesson sheets were covered with thin, transparent sheets of animal horn to protect them against dust and damage. A hornbook was often hung by its handle from a child's belt.

The lesson sheets were designed to teach children how to read, and often how to count as well. A typical lesson sheet had a large cross at the top. Below was the alphabet, in both capital and small letters. Often syllables or other vowel and consonant combinations came next. Prayers were printed below. And sometimes a listing of Roman numerals followed.

Hornbooks originated in England in 1442 and were brought to the New World by the Puritans. The use of hornbooks was standard in English and American schools until about 1800, when paper — and books — became cheaper.

In the 1600's and 1700's, freedom to learn, to think, to speak, and to publish was severely limited throughout most of Europe.

Ideas about education. Europeans in general believed that only the sons of wealthy families needed a formal education. Of course, every now and then, an able boy from a middle- or lower-income home got an education and rose to prominence. A few daughters of wealthy families received some formal education from tutors. Girls in middle- and lower-income families, though, had even fewer educational opportunities than their brothers. In some Protestant families, especially Puritan families, the stress on personal knowledge of the Bible resulted in girls as well as boys learning to read.

The European settlers brought these ideas about education to the colonies. The wealthy colonial families in the towns and on large plantations hired tutors for their sons. They could also afford to buy books, pamphlets, and newspapers. Some wealthy colonists sent their sons to private schools and universities in England. Others sent their sons to one of the colonial colleges. Daughters in such families usually learned some music and literature from tutors and, in rare cases, subjects taught to their brothers. Thus, for example, Jane Colden, daughter of the lieutenant-governor of New York, became known for her work in botany.

Nine colonial colleges for male students — among them Harvard, William and Mary, Queen's College (later named Rutgers), and King's College (later named Columbia) — were started before the Revolutionary War to train ministers. They offered about the same subjects as English colleges on which they were modeled. Latin and Greek were required.

Changing ideas in education. Before long, however, the well-to-do colonists began to feel that their children needed a different kind of education. In the first place, the planters, who made their money by exporting goods to England, took an active part in business. Some of these planters became prosperous merchants who wanted their sons to know more about practical business affairs. Some colonial schools began to offer courses in navigation, geography, modern languages, accounting, and commercial law.

In the second place, the well-to-do colonists realized that they lived in a rural, isolated society. Their children could easily grow up in ignorance, no better educated than the children of poorer people were.

The young girl of seven or eight was bought off the slave ship and given the name Phillis by John Wheatley, a wealthy Boston merchant. The Wheatleys treated Phillis more as a daughter than a slave. She ate meals with the family; had a room of her own; performed only light chores; learned English from the Wheatley's twin teenagers; and studied history, geography, and the Latin classics with them.

By the time Phillis Wheatley reached her teens, she was writing classical poems that expressed her thoughts on learning, virtue, and Christianity. Although the poems were of only average literary quality, they were historically significant. Wheatley had produced what may be the first book written by a black American. Wheatley was living proof that an educated black person was as capable as an educated white person.

Phillis Wheatley was freed in 1773. She traveled to England, where her poise, wit, and charm made her popular. Unfortunately, after returning to the United States in 1778, her last few years were unhappy ones. A broken marriage and the death of her three small children disheartened Wheatley and led to her death at the age of 31. The slave girl who made history was buried in an unmarked grave.

Finally, the scarcity of books in the colonies led many merchants to organize library societies. Members of these societies paid small fees to borrow books. In a few communities, some small public and commercial libraries were also established.

Thus conditions in the New World changed the traditional ideas about education that the wealthy colonists brought with them from England.

Limitations on schooling. Most colonists — the small farmers living near the villages, the pioneers, and the shopkeepers and artisans of the towns — did not have money to buy books. Nor could they afford to hire tutors or to send their children to private schools and colleges. Most of their energy went into the hard job of earning a living. Yet many men and women in the colonies knew how to read, write, and do simple arithmetic. Even on the frontier, where neither schools nor churches existed, some children were taught to read by their parents.

▲ In the towns some children, while learning a trade as apprentices, also learned to read and write and do simple arithmetic through the kindness of their masters. In all of the colonies, there were a few elementary schools that children of poorer families could attend.

In the Middle and Southern Colonies, a few schools were maintained by the churches. South of Delaware the children of farmers and other workers had only limited opportunities to go to school.

Few children of black parents, whether slave or free, could get an education in any of the colonies. Anglican missionary societies and the Quakers offered simple schooling to a few black people. One Quaker, Anthony Benezet, opened a school for blacks in Philadelphia in 1750. Very rarely, a master or mistress taught a household slave to read and write. Phillis Wheatley, a slave child who learned in this way, studied English and Latin as well as geography, history, and astronomy. As a teenager Phillis began to write lyric poems that were later published and highly praised.

The first public schools. New England colonists could get an education more easily than people in any of the other colonies. The Puritan leaders believed that people were more likely to become God-fearing and law-abiding citizens if they could read the Bible.

For hundreds of years in Europe, the Bible had been copied mostly in Latin. During the Protestant Reformation, however, the Bible was translated and printed in German, French, English, and other European languages. The New England leaders were determined that the ability to read the English Bible should not die out in the New World.

To insure that this ability would be fostered, the Massachusetts government passed a law in 1647. This law ordered that every town having 50 householders or more should appoint a teacher of reading and writing to be paid out of town funds. The law also provided that every town having 100 householders or more must either provide a school to prepare young men for college or else pay a penalty. Families able to pay rates, or tuition, to the towns for the schooling of their children were required to do so. Tuition for children from the poorest families, however, was paid from town funds

This law was the first of its kind in the English-speaking world. It was not popular everywhere in Massachusetts. Towns sometimes neglected to provide the education ordered by the law. Nevertheless, the law was a landmark in the history of education. It expressed a new and daring idea—that education of all the people was a public responsibility.

The town schools of colonial New England, then, were one of America's greatest contributions to modern civilization. Free **public education,** paid for with public funds, remains one of the strongest roots of democracy.

The quality of schooling. The quality of education in colonial schools was not always high. Many teachers were not much better educated than the children they taught. Often, especially in New England, the teacher of the very youngest pupils was one of the mothers. She heard the children recite their lessons while she did her washing and baking. Sometimes the village preacher conducted the classes.

In many schools indentured male servants did the teaching. Although some of them were able scholars of excellent character, others were inferior in every way.

Classes were often held in a church, a town hall, or a private home. Children of all ages generally sat in the same room and were taught by the same teacher. School terms were short. Attendance was irregular, for at any time a child might have to stay at home to help plant or harvest crops or to cut wood.

Chalkboards, paper, and crayons were seldom available, and textbooks were rare. The one exception was the _New England Primer._ This little book first appeared about 1690, and more than 3 million copies were sold during the 1700's. The primer was more than a reader. It taught school children to be obedient, to be law-abiding citizens, and to worship God.

Education on farms and frontier. The education of the ordinary people in the colonies was not limited to what they could learn from their parents, in the classroom, or as apprentices. Much of the education of the frontier settlers came from experience. Faced with problems for which they had nothing to guide them, people learned to think for themselves and to work out their own solutions. People had to be practical, inventive, self-sufficient, and flexible. This was a new kind of education, and it would have great influence upon the development of American democracy.

Few books reached the frontier, but many pioneer farm families owned copies of the Bible and much-thumbed **almanacs.** The almanacs were books containing a wide variety of information. They offered advice on medicine, recipes, planting, and harvesting. They contained discussions of politics and religion and selec-

Text continues on page 90.

SOURCES

POOR
RICHARD'S
ALMANAC
(1758)

But dost thou love Life, then do not squander Time; for that's the stuff Life is made of.

Early to Bed, and early to rise, makes a Man healthy, wealthy, and wise.

At the working Man's House Hunger looks in, but dares not enter.

A Ploughman on his Legs is higher than a Gentleman on his Knees.

'Tis easier to build two Chimnies, than to keep one in Fuel.

▲ Discussion topic: Pioneers had more opportunities to think for themselves and work out their own solutions than people today.

DEVELOPING HISTORY STUDY SKILLS

Writing About History   Summarizing Information

History tells a story. In reading the story of history, however, it is not important to remember every word that is read. As the eye moves over the words, the mind is busy sorting out the data by deciding what is relevant and irrelevant to a main idea and linking specific details to a main idea as supporting evidence. All of these tasks go into the writing of a summary.

A summary recaps the main ideas in a body of material. Minor points are usually excluded because the purpose of a summary is bring together major points. For example, see the summary for Chapter 4 on page 97. The summary highlights two main ideas. The first is that the colonists brought with them European ideas of restrictions on individual freedoms. The second is that the colonists eventually began to demand greater individual freedoms.

Summarizing is a useful tool in the writing of history. When you write an answer to an essay question for homework or for a test, you are utilizing the skill of summarizing. When you take notes in preparation for the writing of a research paper, you summarize information.

How to Summarize Information

Follow these guidelines in writing summaries.

1. **Recognize main ideas.** As you read material to be summarized, note main ideas. Main ideas are often stated in a single sentence called the topic sentence. Sometimes two or more sentences have to be combined to form a topic sentence. At other times, the main idea is implied and must be formulated from the sense of all the sentences in a paragraph.
2. **Use your own words.** Formulate a paragraph's main idea in your own words.
3. **Think in broad terms.** Write a list of the main ideas. Look for main ideas that are connected and that relate to a still broader topic. Use the broader idea as the first sentence in your summary. Continue this process until all main ideas have been related to other, larger topics and your summary is complete.

Applying the Skill

In the excerpt at the top of the next column, key sentences and phrases have been underlined. Read the paragraph as a whole. Then reread only the underlined sentences.

The primary political and social fact of eighteenth-century Virginia was rule by class. The gentlemen of Virginia believed implicitly in the right of their class to rule. The proper business of the gentry was politics. . . .

Commencing with control over his personal servant as a little boy, [the planter] gradually assumed more and more authority on the plantation. At maturity he took his "hereditary" seat on the parish vestry. Soon thereafter he advanced to the office of justice of the peace. These men [the upper-class planters] became the great statesmen of the Old Dominion [Virginia]. . . .

The following paragraph is a summary of the excerpt above. Match each summary sentence to one of the underlined passages in the excerpt.

Class distinctions were important both socially and politically in Virginia. The upper class [gentry] consisted of wealthy planters. The gentry became the great statesmen of Virginia.

Practicing the Skill

Read the following paragraphs about Colonial Virginia. On a separate sheet of paper list the topic sentences of each paragraph. Then restate the sentences in your own words, formulating a written summary.

During the colonial period, the legislature consisted of the Council and the House of Burgesses. The Council was composed of twelve of the "principal gentlemen of the country." In the Hall of the House of Burgesses sat the elected representatives of the people, two from each county and one each from the College of William and Mary, Jamestown, Williamsburg, and Norfolk.

As his Majesty's representative, the governor had the power to call, prorogue, or dissolve the Assembly. Bills concerning . . . "taxes on the people" as well as other legislation usually originated in the House of Burgesses, although either "House of Assembly" could frame bills. Even though a bill had passed both houses, veto power rested with the governor.

(See solid-line underscore. A suggested response to the summary is: Government during colonial times consisted of a two-house legislature, the Council, and the House of Burgesses. The King's representative in the colony was the Governor who had the authority to call the legislature into session and adjourn it.)

This household, like most in colonial times, was an extended family. All the generations as well as the unmarried members of the family lived together. This meant more people were available to share the daily household tasks.

tions from great European writers. In many simple proverbs, they urged farmers to be content with their lives, obedient, respectful, thrifty, and industrious. The farmers also received some intellectual stimulation from public meetings and from Sunday church sermons.

Education in towns. The ordinary townspeople—owners of small shops, artisans, dock workers, and the like—had more opportunities than the farmers or pioneers for formal education. By the 1700's, in addition to the regular schools, an increasing number of private evening schools taught young men mathematics, accounting, modern languages, and other subjects useful in business.

Townspeople could also obtain reading material more easily than farmers or frontier settlers. Townspeople had Bibles, almanacs, a few books, pamphlets, and, by the 1700's, a growing number of newspapers. People who could not afford to buy the newspapers could read them or hear them read at a nearby tavern.

The papers contained news, sermons, and articles contributed by readers. People in the towns also picked up news and ideas from public meetings, gatherings at taverns, and debating societies. In these ways many colonial townspeople learned to think for themselves and to express their opinions.

Changing roles of women. The new conditions in the colonies changed the way people thought and learned. They also helped change attitudes toward women and their roles. Women played a special part in creating colonial America. Their contributions were noteworthy in the lives of colonial families and in colonial society alike.

During the 1600's and 1700's, women in the colonies, like women everywhere, were not considered equal to men. In all of the colonies, law, religion, and custom recognized men as the heads of their families. By law, men were given full authority and control over their children. Women could not vote or, if married,

During the colonial period, many leaders believed that it was dangerous to educate people or to allow them to read and speak freely. This viewpoint was expressed by William Berkeley, governor of Virginia, who once boasted that while he was governor, that state had neither free schools nor printing presses.

Many colonists, however, valued the freedom to learn, to think, and to express their opinions. One New York printer, a German immigrant named John Peter Zenger, was determined to print the truth, even at the risk of offending public officials. On November 1, 1733, the first issue of the *New York Weekly Journal* rolled off Zenger's printing press. It contained articles by Zenger's political colleagues, who were critical of New York's royal governor. For a year the *Journal* regularly printed articles that accused the governor of election fraud, bribery, and misappropriating public funds.

Under British law, Zenger was guilty of criminal libel, even if the charges printed in the *Journal* were true. Copies of the newspaper were publicly burned, and Zenger was arrested. During the ten months he spent in jail awaiting trial, his wife kept the presses running. In August 1735 Zenger was eloquently defended in court by an elderly Philadelphia lawyer, Andrew Hamilton. Hamilton compared abusive power with a great river: ". . . when it overflows its banks . . . it bears down all before it, and brings destruction and desolation wherever it comes." After describing liberty as "the only bulwark against lawless power," Hamilton challenged the jury, "While men keep within the bounds of truth, I hope they may with safety speak and write their opinions of the conduct of men in power."

The jury acquitted Zenger on the grounds that the charges printed in the *Journal* were true and therefore did not libel the governor. Although the Zenger case did not change the British libel law, it did encourage colonial newspapers to express differing political views and to be less timid in what they wrote. And it foreshadowed the First Amendment's protection of freedom of the press as a fundamental right of the American people.

own property. Any wages that women earned outside the home belonged to their husbands or, if they were unmarried, to their fathers. Most girls did not attend school beyond the elementary level unless their families were rich and hired private teachers. Thus, in America, as in Europe, women lacked the education to become ministers, lawyers, or doctors.

Despite such disadvantages, women in America had greater opportunities than women in Europe. Women were a smaller part of the colonial population than men. This fact, in many ways, favored a wider range of opportunities and greater influence for colonial women. Moreover, there was a great shortage of labor throughout the colonies. Thus some women ran shops and small businesses, printed newspapers, took up blacksmithing, and followed many other trades. On plantations the ability of women to organize and manage contributed to economic success. Those women who went to the frontier with their husbands shared the dangers of frontier life and did many of the customary tasks of men.

Women also took an active part in settling many new communities. They helped establish churches, taught the children and cared for the sick. By such contributions colonial women achieved a sense of importance despite limitations on their political rights, property rights, choice of careers, and authority within the family. As a result, women in the American colonies enjoyed higher status and more economic independence than most women in Europe.

SECTION REVIEW
See underscored items, text pp. 87-88.

Identify: Anthony Benezet, public education, *New England Primer*, almanac
For answers to questions, see Answer Key, pp.A17-18.

1. **Summarizing Ideas: (a)** What Old World ideas about education did the colonists bring with them to the New World? **(b)** In what ways did conditions in the New World help to change these ideas?

2. **Analyzing Viewpoints:** Free public education is one of the strongest roots of democracy. Do you agree or disagree? Explain your answer.

3. **Interpreting Ideas:** Why was the education law that the government of Massachusetts passed in 1647 a landmark in the history of education?

4. **Organizing Ideas:** What disadvantages did women in the colonies suffer? What opportunities did they have?

3 The colonists gain valuable experience in self-government

See Teaching Suggestions in TMRG, pp.TM30-31.

In government, religion, and education, colonists fought for freedom. During the struggle, they planted the seeds of representative government.

Virginia led the way in 1619, as you have read, by creating the House of Burgesses. The House of Burgesses gave Virginia the first representative government in America. It also provided an example for the other colonies.

Types of colonial governments. England established three types of colonies in America: (1) royal colonies administered by the English government, (2) proprietary colonies belonging to proprietors, and (3) self-governing colonies largely independent of English control. Each colony had a governor, a council, and a representative assembly.

In a royal colony—and by the 1760's eight of the thirteen colonies were royal colonies—the king appointed the governor and councilors. These men administered the laws, sat as a high court of justice, and acted as the upper house of the **legislature,** or law-making body. The lower house, or assembly, was elected by the qualified voters. Although the lower house helped to make the laws, the king or his representative could veto its actions.

In proprietary colonies—including, by the 1760's, Maryland, Pennsylvania, and Delaware—the proprietor was granted a large amount of power by the king of England. The proprietor, who usually lived in England, appointed the governor and, in the case of Maryland, the councilors who formed the upper house of the legislature. The lower house was elected by the voters, just as in the eight royal colonies. Pennsylvania's legislature had only one house—the assembly.

The two remaining colonies, Rhode Island and Connecticut, were self-governing. Each was in large part independent of England. The voters elected the governor and the representatives in both the upper and lower houses of the legislature.

The Fundamental Orders. Connecticut was the first colony to adopt a **written constitution,** or written plan of government. This constitution was known as the Fundamental Orders of Connecticut. As you have read, the Orders were adopted in 1639, only three years after Thomas Hooker and his party of settlers arrived on the banks of the Connecticut River.

The Fundamental Orders may be regarded as a written constitution even though they could be revoked or amended by a simple majority of the legislature. The "eleven orders" were a detailed guide for organizing the government and electing government officials. When disputes arose, the written law, not the opinions of the lawmakers, was to be the guide for deciding issues. This principle of government under a written constitution became a cornerstone of American government.

It is important to remember, however, that none of the colonists, including the colonists of Connecticut, were thinking of what today is called democracy. The idea of a representative assembly had already been established in England with the House of Commons, the lower house of Parliament. In organizing their representative assemblies, the colonists were simply following the British example.

Limitations on self-government. Regardless of the reason, the fact remains that many colonists had a voice in the government of the Brit-

SOURCES

FUNDAMENTAL ORDERS OF CONNECTICUT (1639)

It is ordered . . . that there shall be yearly two general assemblies or courts: . . . That first shall be called the Court of Election. . . .

It is ordered . . . that no person be chosen governor above once in two years. . . .

It is ordered . . . that to the aforesaid Court of Election the several towns shall send their deputies. . . .

The Founding of the American Colonies

	COLONIES	DATE FOUNDED–REASONS FOR FOUNDING	TYPES OF GOVERNMENT BEFORE 1776
NEW ENGLAND	Massachusetts	1620–religious freedom	Joint-stock company 1620–84; royal 1684–1776
	New Hampshire	1623–agriculture, trade, fishing	Proprietary 1623–41; joint-stock company 1641–79; royal 1679–1776
	Connecticut	1635–agriculture, trade	Self-governing 1635–62; royal 1686–89; joint-stock company 1662–87, 1689–1776
	Rhode Island	1636–religious freedom	Self-governing 1636–44; royal 1686–89; joint-stock company 1644–86, 1689–1776
MIDDLE	New York	1624–agriculture, trade	Dutch colony 1624–64; proprietary 1664–85; royal 1685–1776
	New Jersey	1629–agriculture, trade	Dutch, Swedish colonies 1629–64; proprietary 1664–1702; royal 1702–1776
	Delaware	1638–agriculture, trade	Swedish colony 1638–55; Dutch colony 1655–64; proprietary 1664–1776
	Pennsylvania	1682–religious freedom, agriculture, trade	Proprietary 1682–1776
SOUTHERN	Virginia	1607–agriculture, trade	Joint-stock company 1607–24; royal 1624–1776
	Maryland	1634–religious freedom, agriculture, trade	Proprietary 1634–91; 1715–76, royal 1691–1715
	North Carolina	1653–agriculture, trade	Self-governing 1653–63; proprietary 1663–1729; royal 1729–76
	South Carolina	1670–agriculture, trade	Proprietary 1670–1721; royal 1721–76
	Georgia	1733–refuge for debtors; buffer against Spanish Florida, agriculture	Proprietary 1733–52; royal 1752–76

ish colonies in North America. However, in the colonies, as in England at that time, the voice was still a limited one.

The right to vote, or **suffrage,** was limited in several ways. In the first place, only adult males who owned a specified amount of property could vote. To vote, a man had to prove that he owned a farm or town lot of a certain size or that he had an income and paid taxes of a certain amount. These property qualifications existed even in the self-governing colonies of Connecticut and Rhode Island.

In the second place, religious qualifications kept many people from voting. In many colonies, particularly during the 1600's, men who did not belong to the established church could not vote. Slaves were not permitted to vote in any of the colonies. Neither were women.

In addition to the people who were not permitted to vote, many who might have voted did not bother to do so. Some of these people had never enjoyed political rights in Europe. When they came to colonies, they did not concern themselves with political matters. Finally, the isolation of frontier life kept many pioneers participating in the government.

To be elected to the colonial assemblies, a man had to meet even higher qualifications than he did to vote. These qualifications varied from colony to colony. In South Carolina, for example, an assemblyman had to own 500 acres (202.4 hectares) of land and ten slaves, or other property worth a substantial sum of money. Because of these qualifications, those who were elected to colonial assemblies generally were men of wealth and influence.

The struggle over the assemblies. Many ordinary people in the colonies resented the amount of political power in the hands of the well-to-do. Their resentment sometimes led to outbreaks of violence.

Patrick Henry of Virginia (standing at right) first gained fame as a lawyer in 1763 in what was known as the case of the Parson's Cause. In this case Henry argued that a ruler who governs badly, by so doing, gives up the right to be obeyed.

This conflict between the well-to-do and the ordinary people, most of whom were farmers, is sometimes called the conflict between the seaboard and the frontier. The wealthy people on the seaboard — planters, rich town merchants, and influential lawyers — controlled the assemblies. They tended to vote for laws that protected their own interests. The ordinary people — wage earners, farmers, and frontier settlers — had only a limited voice in the assemblies. They had few legal ways to pass laws that they wanted or to protect themselves from laws that harmed their interests.

Bacon's Rebellion. In Virginia in 1676, the conflict between the well-to-do and the ordinary people finally erupted into a clash of violence. This became known as <u>Bacon's Rebellion</u>, after its leader Nathaniel Bacon.

For many years the frontier settlers and small farmers of Virginia had been dissatisfied with the rule of Governor Berkeley. These groups claimed that they, the ordinary people, were not fairly represented in the colonial legislature. They were in debt, taxes were high, and the price of tobacco was low. They further claimed that Governor Berkeley and the wealthy planters had deliberately refused to crush an Indian uprising, not wishing to anger the Indians. Many of the planters had a profitable fur trade with these Indians.

Settlers who had moved into Indian lands in the outlying regions of Virginia were eager to open up the country to white settlers. When the Susquehanna Indians resisted, the settlers demanded military action. After an Indian attack in which many colonists were killed, a wealthy young settler, Nathaniel Bacon, gathered a force of several hundred men. They marched to the frontier and wiped out the Occaneechees (awk·uh·NEE·cheez), a friendly tribe. Bacon's followers then seized Jamestown, gained control of the legislature, and passed laws favoring the ordinary people.

Bacon's Rebellion was short-lived. When Nathaniel Bacon died a few months later, Berkeley and the large planters recovered power and crushed what was left of the resistance. ▲

The need for local government. Out of their long struggle for control of the colonial legislatures, the colonists acquired practical experience in politics. It was in local government, however, especially in New England, that the colonists enjoyed the greatest opportunity to practice self-government.

From the very beginning, every colonial community, large or small, had to make rules or laws to carry on the everyday affairs of community life. In many early communities, conflicts with the Indians required defense against attack and organized force for counterattack. All communities also faced problems of fire and police protection, sanitation, and schooling. They also had to settle disputes between citizens and solve many other everyday problems.

No one questioned the need for local government. However, all the colonists had to answer one big question. Who would make and enforce the local laws?

Local government in New England. The Pilgrims thought about this question even before they set foot in New England. As you have read, in writing the Mayflower Compact, the Pilgrims drew up an agreement under which they were to live.

After they settled at Plymouth, using the Mayflower Compact as their guide, the Pilgrims established a form of local government that was later adopted by other New England communities. This new form of local government came to be called the **town meeting**.

On town-meeting days most citizens gathered in the town hall to discuss town problems, levy taxes on themselves, and elect town officers. The discussions sometimes became heated, for all citizens had the right to say what they thought.

The principal town officers usually three in number, were the <u>selectmen.</u> The selectmen administered the laws that the voters adopted in the town meeting. Only the men voted and, in the early days, the right to vote was also limited by religious and property qualifications. Nevertheless, the New England town meetings provided larger opportunities to take part in government than citizens enjoyed in either the Middle or the Southern Colonies.

Local government in other colonies. The town meeting type of government met the needs of people living in the small farming villages and towns of New England. In the Southern Colonies, most people lived on large plantations or on more or less isolated farms. Local government there had to cover a much larger area than a town. In the Southern Colonies, therefore, the people established the <u>county</u> as the unit of local government. Some southern counties covered several hundred square miles.

The chief officers of the county included the **justices of the peace.** These officers carried out the laws, acted as judges in legal disputes, and levied and collected taxes. They also provided for roads and distributed county funds to widows, orphans, and other people who could not support themselves. A county lieutenant was in charge of defending the county against Indian attacks and against serious disturbances by the colonists. These officers were usually appointed by the governor, but they were chosen from people living in the county itself.

The Middle Colonies adopted a mixture of both the town and the county type of local government. In New York the town was generally the unit of local government. In Pennsylvania the county type of local government was more important.

SECTION REVIEW
See underscored items, text pp. 92-95.
Identify: written constitution, suffrage, Bacon's Rebellion, town meeting, selectmen, county, justice of the peace
For answers to questions, see Answer Key, p.A18.
1. **Comparing Ideas: (a)** Describe the differences in the three types of colonial governments. **(b)** What features did they have in common?
2. **Summarizing Ideas: (a)** What kinds of restrictions on voting and office holding existed in the colonies? **(b)** List three examples.
3. **Analyzing Ideas:** What were the causes of Bacon's Rebellion?
4. **Interpreting Ideas: (a)** What was the usual form of local government in the New England Colonies? in the Middle and Southern Colonies? **(b)** Why did this difference arise?

4 Colonial legislative assemblies gain power in America

See Teaching Suggestions in TMRG, p.TM31.
Except in the self-governing colonies of Rhode Island and Connecticut, the colonial governments were really split into two parts. In general, the governor and the councilors usually served the interests of the British empire as a whole. The assemblies, on the other hand, represented the interests of the colonists.

▲ Report topic: How the local community government conducts its business (Students should concentrate on similarities to a town meeting, the choosing of leaders, and citizen participation.)

95

Punishments for colonial crimes were harsh. Among other punishments the convicted forger in this drawing was put on public display in the pillory for one hour.

Attitude of British officials. Because of this division, political controversy in the colonies often centered on the royal governors. Most governors were selected from the ruling group in Great Britain—politicians, lawyers, and soldiers. At times, though, the Crown appointed a favored or privileged colonist as governor.

In making appointments to the royal colonies, the Crown did not necessarily look for those with ability. Sometimes the king awarded the positions to his friends and favorites. Some royal governors were excellent administrators who tried to balance British and colonial interests. A few were narrow-minded, shortsighted, and without training or experience for the offices they held.

Whether good, bad, or indifferent, most of the governors used their positions to increase their own fortunes. Many were willing to pay handsomely to secure the jobs.

The military officers and clerks who served the royal governors were, as a rule, no better than their superiors. They were often appointed merely because they were friends of the governor. Such practices were common in Great Britain as well as in the colonies.

Even so, many able people held positions of authority in the colonies. As a result, the colonies, which enjoyed the advantage of being part of a growing British empire, owed a great deal to the Crown.

Growing power of the assemblies. As representatives of the British government, the royal officials naturally stressed the Crown's point of view. Most colonists, speaking through their representatives in the assemblies, held the opposite point of view. Why, they asked, should they pay taxes to provide high salaries to countless outsiders from Great Britain, many of whom were lazy and incompetent? What right had anybody to say that the interests of the colonists were less important than the interests of the people in Great Britain?

Fortunately for the colonists, they had one extremely powerful weapon that helped curb the authority of the royal governors. The colonists controlled the **purse strings.** That is, the colonial assemblies had the power to vote all grants of money to be spent by the colonial governments.

Suppose the governor asked for money to pay the salaries of nine new clerks he wanted to appoint. The assembly could say, "Yes, we'll grant you the money—provided you allow us to name the men you appoint." Or suppose the governor requested money to pay his official expenses. The assembly could say, "Yes, we'll grant the money—provided you first submit a statement explaining in detail how you will spend the money."

Sometimes the assemblies refused to grant funds to pay the governors' salaries until the end of each year. In this way the colonists let the governors know that they would do well to rule wisely.

The governors could not do much about these limits. They needed the money that could come only from the assemblies. Even before the Revolutionary War, the colonial assemblies were practically their own masters. They had, to a great degree, already won their freedom from British control.

SECTION REVIEW

See underscored items, text p. 96.
Identify: purse strings
For answers to questions, see Answer Key, p.A18.

1. **Interpreting Ideas:** Due to a conflict of interests, colonial governments were split into two parts. Explain.

2. **Summarizing Ideas:** (a) How were royal governors chosen? (b) What effect did this process have on the quality of their leadership?

3. **Analyzing Ideas:** (a) What power did the colonial assemblies have over the royal governors? (b) How did the assemblies use this power?

The first small seeds of democracy found root in the fertile soil of the British seaboard colonies. In Europe, the colonists had experienced restrictions on individual freedoms in religion, education, and the right to vote and hold public office. The restrictive ideas came with them to the colonies, which were supposed to be nothing more than an overseas extension of the homeland. The old restrictive ideas, however, did not fit in with the colonists' new experiences.

Discontent with these European ideas began to grow slowly during the early years of colonization. It was growing more rapidly by the mid-1700's.

Stimulated by the growth of freedom in England itself and even more by the environment of the colonies, the settlers began to demand greater freedom for themselves. During the course of their struggles to establish colonies and organize their daily lives, the settlers gained practical experience in local politics and local self-government. These early colonists laid the groundwork for the principles of religious toleration, free public education, and representative government that would later be the constitutional pillars of a new American nation.

CONNECTING CHAPTER IDEAS

In the next chapter you will read about the steps leading to separation from Great Britain. In developing their own way of life, the colonists had in some ways grown much farther away from Great Britain by 1763 than the British realized. This process of growth and the lack of understanding that accompanied it led to controversies between Great Britain and the colonies. Finally, in 1775, armed conflict erupted.

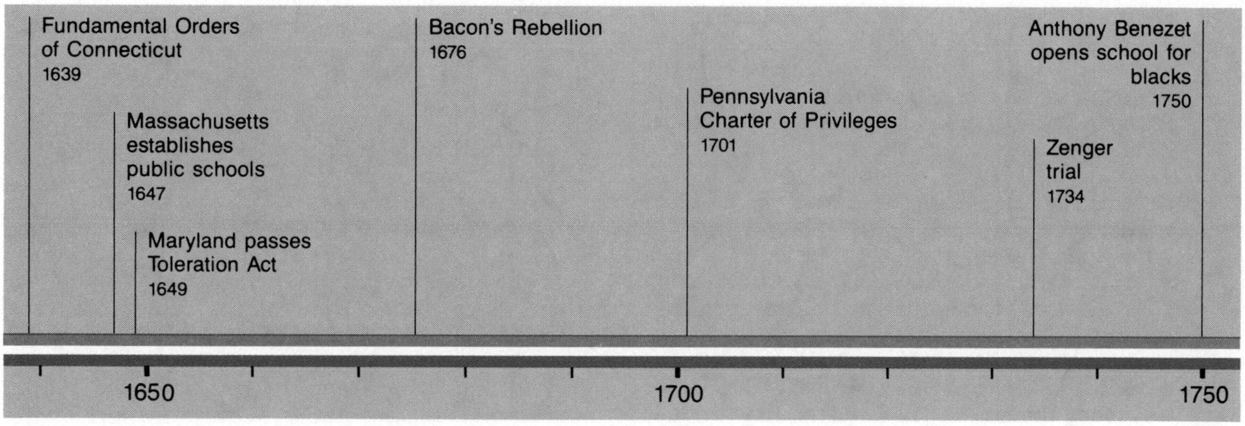

Fundamental Orders of Connecticut 1639	Bacon's Rebellion 1676		Anthony Benezet opens school for blacks 1750
Massachusetts establishes public schools 1647		Pennsylvania Charter of Privileges 1701	Zenger trial 1734
Maryland passes Toleration Act 1649			

1650	1700	1750

CHAPTER
4 REVIEW

Reviewing Important Terms

Decide whether each of the following sentences is true or false. If the sentence is false, replace the underlined term with the word or phrase that will make it true.

1. The first settlers who came to the Americas continued the European tradition of an underlined established church.
2. In Maryland, all Christians were protected against persecution under the principle of religious underlined toleration.
3. In a royal colony, the men who served as the upper house of the underlined legislature were appointed by the king.
4. Property and religious qualifications in many British colonies in North America limited underlined politics to wealthy men who belonged to the established church.
5. Because local government in the Southern colonies had to manage an area larger than a town, the underlined county was established as the unit of government.
6. The underlined county lieutenant was responsible for collecting taxes and for distributing funds to the needy.
7. One of the most powerful advantages held by the colonial assemblies was control of the underlined purse strings.
8. The growing spirit of religious toleration in the colonies led to the underlined separation of church and state.

Practicing Critical Thinking Skills

1. **Synthesizing Ideas.** The environment of the colonies gradually caused changes in the ideas and ways of life brought from the Old World. Compare and discuss Old World and New World ideas concerning religion, education, representative government, and the role of women.
2. **Comparing Ideas.** Contrast education on the colonial frontier with education in colonial towns.
3. **Analyzing Ideas.** During the colonial period, many slaves were excluded from Christianity. How did this discrimination help to maintain slavery?
4. **Summarizing Ideas.** From 1607 to 1763, the colonists developed a spirit of independence that weakened their ties with England. Explain how each of the following contributed to this growing spirit of independence: (a) opportunities in America, (b) geography, and (c) growth of colonial democracy.
5. **Relating Past to Present.** (a) Which of America's current democratic practices can be traced to ideas and institutions from its colonial past? (b) Are Americans still engaged in the process of furthering democratic ideas and practices? Give evidence to support your views.

Developing History Study Skills

1. **Summarizing Information.** Write a paragraph, using headings and subheadings from the text, that summarizes (a) the growth of religious toleration in the colonies, (b) the development of education, and (c) the struggle to establish representative government.

2. **Developing a Frame of Reference.** Read one or more poems by Anne Bradstreet. (a) What do the poems reveal about life in the colonies for the people generally? for women? (b) Do you think Bradstreet's attitudes were typical of the attitudes of colonial women? Why or why not?

Relating Geography and History

Local self-government differed in the New England, Middle, and Southern colonies partly because of settlement patterns. Each section established the kind of local government that worked best in its own particular situation. To understand better how settlement patterns influenced colonial local governments, use the information in the chapter and study the map on text page 33, then answer the following questions.

1. In which region of the colonies did the citizens have a greater opportunity to take part in the governmental process?
2. In what ways was geography responsible for the establishment of the county system of government in the Southern Colonies?
3. In which system of local government do you think the officials had greater power, town or county?
4. Which local government system do you think was more representative, town or county? Why?

UNIT ONE
REVIEW

Discussing Ideas

1. (a) What aspects of culture did most Indian groups have in common? (b) In what aspects of life did Indian groups differ?
2. Do you think that if Columbus had not "rediscovered" America, another explorer certainly would have? Why or why not?
3. (a) Name several reasons why people came to America. (b) Give examples of groups who came for each of those reasons.
4. Compare the relations between Indians and Europeans in (a) New Spain, (b) the English colonies, and (c) New France. (d) How do you account for the similarities? the differences?

Applying History Study Skills

Summarizing Information. The following excerpts are from a colonial form of public relations. These were writings designed to encourage people to settle in the British colonies. Read the excerpts, and then summarize the points that were specifically used to lure settlers.

> . . . Many persons who went to Carolina [as] servants, being industrious since they came out of their times with their masters [since their indentured service expired], . . . have gotten good stocks of cattle and servants of their own; have here also built houses and exercise their trades. And many that went thither in that condition are worth several hundreds of pounds, and live in a very plentiful condition, and their estates are still increasing.
>
> Carolina, 1682

> His majesty . . . grants to every European servant [everyone who goes to the New World as an indentured servant], whether man or woman, 50 acres of land free of all rents for ten years, which shall be distributed to them after having served their master for the time agreed on.
>
> Carolina, 1731

> The Trustees intend this year to lay out a county and build a new town in Georgia.

> They will give . . . to every man, a [warm overcoat], a musket and bayonet to those who have them not of their own, a hatchet, a hammer, a handsaw, a . . . shovel or spade, a broad hoe, a narrow hoe, a gimlet, a drawing knife, and there will be a public grindstone to each ward or village. He will also have an iron pot and a pair of pothooks, and a frying pan.
>
> Georgia, 1735

Making Connections

1. Prepare a report on the musical contributions made to American culture by the American Indians, Africans, or some other colonial group.
2. Imagine that you are a colonist in New Spain, New France, or an English colony. Write a letter to a friend "back home" about your life in America. Be sure to identify your age, where you live, and the details of your daily life.
3. Prepare a map that illustrates the diversity of settlers in the Americas before 1775. (You might do this with arrows showing routes of migration or by using colors to show how people's places of origin affected their area of settlement.)
4. Use a map of your state to locate cities, rivers, lakes, and other natural features that have names. French, Spanish, Dutch, or Indian.

Reading in Depth

Baity, Elizabeth, *Americans Before Columbus* (New York: Viking). The story of America's earliest Indian civilizations.

Cooper, James Fenimore, *The Last of the Mohicans* (New York: Scribner's). The adventures of General Munro's daughters, who escaped the massacre of Fort Henry during the French and Indian War, and Leatherstocking, the Indian scout who guided them through the wilderness to safety.

Hawthorne, Nathaniel, *The Scarlet Letter* (New York: Dutton). A classic psychological novel set in colonial New England.

History of the Thirteen Colonies (New York: American Heritage). A lavishly illustrated account of life in America from the years before the Europeans arrived until 1776.

UNIT TWO

Winning Independence

After victory in the French and Indian War in 1763, the British government began to tighten its control of the North American colonies. The new acts and regulations angered the American colonists, but their protests fell on deaf ears in England. Soon the protests turned into actions such as the Boston Tea Party, pictured below. Finally, on July 4, 1776, the American colonies declared their independence from Great Britain. After eight long years of fighting for that independence, the American colonies earned a victory that established a new nation. By 1789 the newly created states, after struggling under the Articles of Confederation, had founded a republican and federal system of government—The United States of America.

See Chapter Overview in TMRG, p.TM34.
See Chapter Objectives in TMRG, p.TM34.
See Introducing the Chapter in TMRG, p.TM34.

CHAPTER 5
Moving Toward Independence
(1763–1775)

Colonial
New York

In the year 1763, the British people shared a deep sense of pride. Victorious over all its rivals in the war just ended, Great Britain had established claims to an empire that circled the globe. Battered vessels of the British navy rode on the incoming tides, bringing the fighting men of Great Britain back to their homes and families. Still other British vessels weighed anchor and sailed out of the harbors, carrying officials to the far-flung outposts of the empire.

To the average Britisher in the homeland, the future appeared brighter than it had for many years. Thoughtful people in Great Britain and in other countries, however, realized that the British empire faced many new and troublesome problems. One place in particular that would prove troublesome was the American colonies of the New World. One of these thoughtful observers of the colonies was a French government official named Count Vergennes (vair-ZHEN).

Vergennes was mindful that France had been driven from the North American continent. He, therefore, predicted a similar speedy end to Great Britain's moment of glory. "The American colonies stand no longer in need of England's protection," he said. England, he continued, "will call on them to help contribute toward supporting the burden they have helped to bring on her, and they will answer by striking off all dependence."

Vergennes proved to be an accurate prophet of Great Britain's colonial fortunes. Just 13 years after his prediction, the British colonies along the Atlantic seaboard declared their independence from Great Britain.

═══ READING FOCUS ═══

As you read about the colonists' move toward independence, look for the details that support each of the following statements.

1. Great Britain regulates colonial industry and trade.
2. The British face new problems in governing their empire.
3. The colonists oppose taxation without representation.
4. Tensions increase between Great Britain and the colonies.
5. The gap between Great Britain and the colonies grows wider.

1 Great Britain regulates colonial industry and trade

See Teaching Suggestions in TMRG, pp. TM 34-35.

In 1763 Great Britain's steadily growing empire included 33 different colonies. Only 13 of these were located along the Atlantic seaboard. The other colonies were scattered ▲ throughout the world.

The mercantile system of trade. To understand why European leaders were so eager to build colonial empires, you must understand the policy of **mercantilism**.

Briefly, mercantilism is an economic and political policy whereby a nation tries to gain greater wealth and power than its rivals. The mercantilism of the 1600's and 1700's aimed at building a powerful, self-sufficient empire in a world divided by religious wars and bitter commercial rivalry. Under mercantilism a nation's government tried to gain greater power than its rivals by building a larger army and navy. To build greater military power, a nation needed money. To get money, a nation tried to sell to other nations more goods than it bought from them. It tried, in other words, to build a favorable **balance of trade**. A nation gains a favorable balance of trade when it **exports**, or sells abroad, more products than it **imports**, or buys from other nations.

With a highly favorable balance of trade, a nation could (1) be self-sufficient, (2) become wealthy, and (3) build a powerful army and navy. Colonies were an essential part of the plan. The British, for example, thought that colonies would strengthen Great Britain in four ways.

First, colonies would provide the raw materials essential to a small island kingdom with a growing population. Second, colonies would provide markets for goods produced in Great Britain, particularly manufactured goods. Third, colonies would encourage the growth of a strong merchant fleet, which would serve as a training school for the Royal Navy. Fourth, colonies would also provide bases from which the Royal Navy could operate.

Restrictions on manufacturing. To apply the policy of mercantilism, the British Parliament passed many laws. One series of laws re-

▲ Map activity: On a world map or a globe, have one or more students identify some of the other British colonies (there were 20 of them) in 1763. Students may then relate the location of each colony to its benefit to Britain.

103

stricted nearly all the manufacturing of the British empire to England. A 1699 law, for example, forbade the colonists to export any wool or woolen cloth—even to a neighboring colony. Later laws forbade the colonists to manufacture beaver hats or iron products for export. The British government also tried to prevent skilled workers from leaving Great Britain, fearing that they would help the colonists start their own manufacturing plants.

At first, the American colonists did not find these restrictions a burden, since they had neither the money nor the skilled labor to establish industries.

Restrictions on shipping. Beginning in 1651, another series of laws, the Navigation Acts, restricted all trade within the empire to British, including colonial, ships. Only such ships could carry goods imported from Africa, Asia, and the American colonies of Great Britain's rivals into any port of the British empire.

Encouraged by the Navigation Acts, a powerful British merchant fleet was soon sailing the seas between the colonies and Great Brit-

ain. The American colonists, as British citizens, could build and sail their own ships and thus benefited greatly from the Navigation Acts. By the early 1770's, colonial shipyards were building one third of all merchant ships sailing under the British flag. Many American colonial merchants were becoming wealthy.

Restrictions on selling and buying. The Navigation Act of 1660 listed, or "enumerated," specific colonial products that could be shipped only to England. These **enumerated goods** included such important products as tobacco, cotton, and sugar. The colonists could not sell these products to other European countries, where they might have gotten higher prices.

By the 1700's the British government was paying **bounties** on some enumerated goods. Bounties are payments made to stimulate production of certain goods. The British paid bounties on tar, resin, turpentine, and hemp to stimulate colonial production of these naval stores, needed by the merchant fleet and the ▲
Royal Navy.

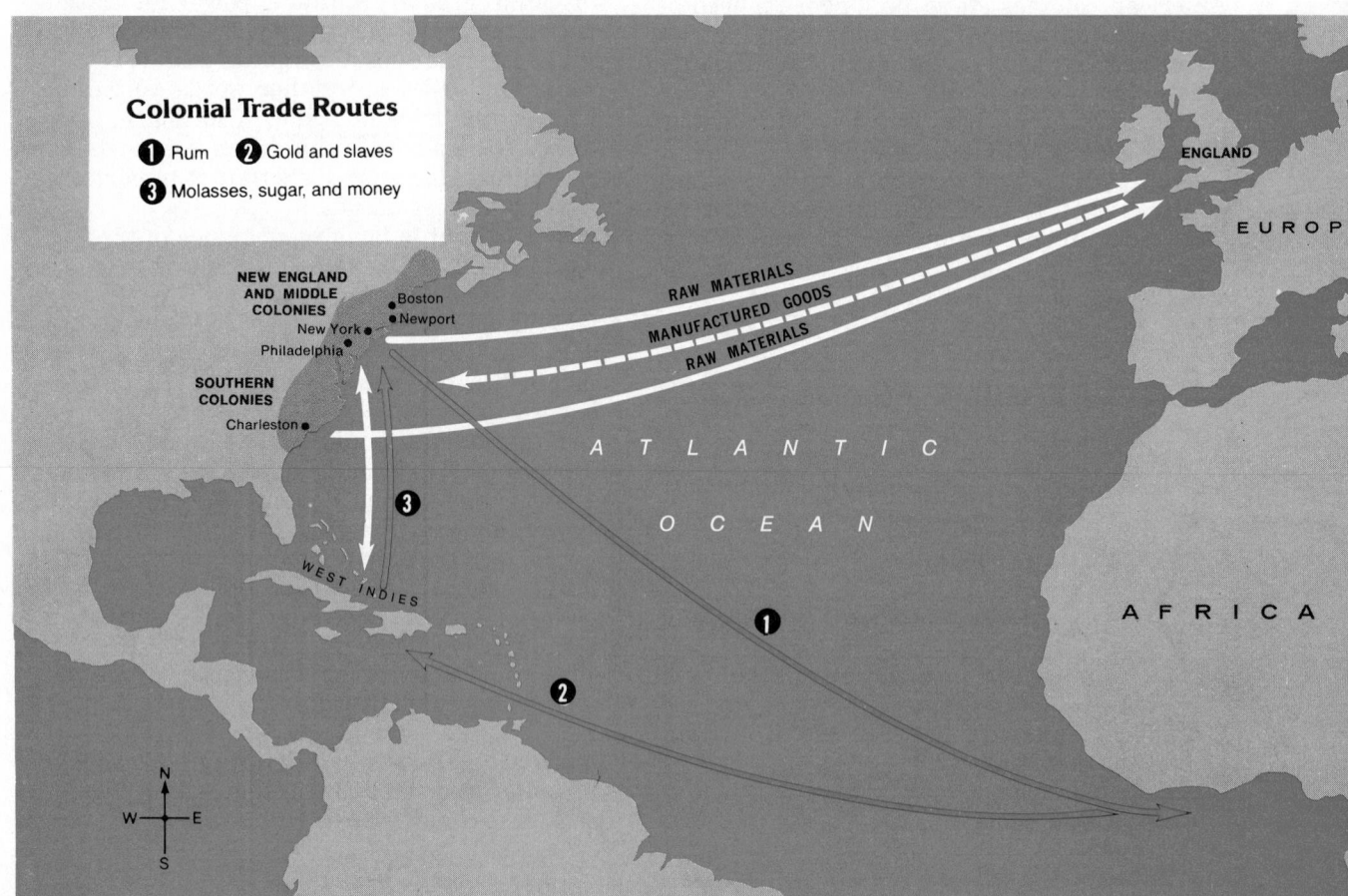

Colonial Trade Routes

❶ Rum ❷ Gold and slaves

❸ Molasses, sugar, and money

Slaves were shipped and traded as if they were cargo. This watercolor of the hold of the slave ship Albatross was painted in 1846 by a British naval officer. It is the only picture drawn from life of conditions on board a slave ship.

In 1663 Parliament passed a new Navigation Act. This act required the colonists to buy most of their manufactured goods from England. Further, all European goods headed for the colonies had to be sent first to England, where the British unloaded the goods and collected an __import duty,__ or tax, on them. Then they reloaded the products on a British vessel and sent them across the Atlantic. These requirements protected British manufacturers from the competition of their European rivals.

Friction under mercantilism. Other European nations with overseas colonies followed policies similar to Great Britain's. Thus mercantilism deepened rivalries between nations. This competition was a basic cause of the long war between Great Britain and France.

The mercantile policies also created friction within the British empire itself. They aroused jealousies even between colonial merchants. Colonial merchants with close family ties or other sources of influence in Great Britain received favors denied to other merchants.

Mercantile policies also created friction between Great Britain and some of its colonies in North America. At first, mercantilism seemed to threaten the prosperity of New England and the Middle Colonies. These colonies produced goods similar to those produced in Great Britain—grain, lumber, fish, cloth, iron, and other products. Great Britain did not want or need these colonial products. Parliament actually passed laws barring them from Great Britain.

Fortunately, the New England and Middle Colonies soon established new markets for their goods. As a result, the mercantile laws did not seriously disturb them.

Colonial trade routes. A major source of income for the colonial merchants was what has been called a __triangular trade__ involving Africa, the West Indies, and the colonies. Another busy trade route directly connected the colonies with the islands in the Caribbean Sea (see map, page 104).

Evading the mercantile laws. Most trade was perfectly legal, but some of it directly violated British mercantile laws. One of the laws most violated was the __Molasses Act of 1733.__

Planters in the British West Indies had pushed the Molasses Act through Parliament. They hoped it would force the American colonists to buy all their sugar and molasses from the British West Indies. The Molasses Act stated that the colonists could buy similar supplies from French, Dutch, or Spanish islands only by paying a very high duty. Unfortunately, the British West Indies could supply only about one eighth of the molasses needed by the colonists. The colonial merchants thus felt compelled to evade the law.

A policy of salutary neglect. If the British government had enforced the Molasses Act, many colonial merchants and businesses would have been ruined. Most rum distilleries would have been closed, and many workers would have lost their jobs.

▲ Throughout the Annotated Teacher's Edition, terms listed in the "Identify" portion of a Section Review are underscored the first time they appear. See the Teacher's Manual for each section for a listing of important vocabulary terms.

However, for a long time Great Britain did not seriously attempt to enforce the Molasses Act. Indeed, the British government did not seriously attempt to enforce most of its mercantile laws. Instead, the British followed a policy of **salutary neglect.** This means that they deliberately failed to enforce the mercantile laws.

SECTION REVIEW
See underscored items, text pp. 103-05.

Identify: balance of trade, Navigation Acts, enumerated goods, bounty, import duty, triangular trade, Molasses Act of 1733

For answers to questions, see Answer Key, p.A21.

1. **Analyzing Ideas: (a)** Under mercantilism, how did colonies benefit the colonizing nation? **(b)** How did the colonizing nation benefit its colonies?

2. **Summarizing Ideas:** Explain why it was important for a nation operating under mercantilism to place restrictions on the **(a)** manufacturing of goods, **(b)** shipping of goods, and **(c)** buying and selling of goods.

3. **Interpreting Ideas: (a)** Why were mercantile laws a potential source of tension between the New England and Middle Colonies and England? **(b)** In what ways did the colonists and the British avoid this tension?

4. **Studying Maps:** A nation's imports are sometimes directly useful in producing goods for export. Look at the map on page 104 and find three examples to support this statement.

2 The British face new problems in governing their empire

See Teaching Suggestions in TMRG, pp.TM35-36.

In 1763 Great Britain faced new problems in governing its empire. Candles burned late into the nights as British leaders wrestled with ways of dealing with the empire's rapid growth.

The need for new taxes. One problem was the need for more money. Between 1689 and 1763 the British had fought four wars, which had left their nation heavily in debt. To make matters worse, the British government now needed even more money to maintain the defenses of its expanding worldwide empire.

British leaders quite naturally expected the American colonists to help pay the war debts. After all, the British reasoned, the colonists were subjects of the king. They ought to help pay for the cost of defense, especially their own defense.

Florida and Canada. Another troublesome problem was what to do with Florida and Canada—lands acquired by the British at the end of the French and Indian War. The governments of Florida and Canada had to be completely reorganized. The Spaniards and French in these areas, long-time enemies of Great Britain, were now British subjects, but subjects in name only. How could they be made loyal subjects? What kind of government would work best in these new regions?

The western lands. Particularly confusing for the British government was the problem of the former French territory west of the Appalachian Mountains. The British themselves could not agree on what policy to apply to these lands.

One group, led by the Hudson's Bay Company, was interested solely in the fur trade. This group wanted to prohibit settlers from moving west of the mountains. A much larger group, including most of the colonists, urged the government to open the western lands to pioneer farmers and **land speculators.** Land speculators were people who bought land hoping for a quick profit from its resale. To add to the complications, several different colonies claimed that their charters had given them grants of land in this region.

Pontiac's Rebellion. In back of all the proposals and claims by the whites was the simple fact that this was Indian land. For more than 150 years, from the time the English first built settlements along the Atlantic coast, the Indians had been pushed steadily westward. In 1763 they had every reason to fear that colonial farmers would begin to pour over the mountains and drive them once again from their villages and hunting grounds.

Under the able leadership of Pontiac, an Ottawa chief, the Indians joined forces to prevent any further invasion of their lands. For nearly a year, the Indians and whites were locked in a desperate struggle. The Indians destroyed most of the British forts west of Niagara. Death and destruction raged along the length of the western frontier.

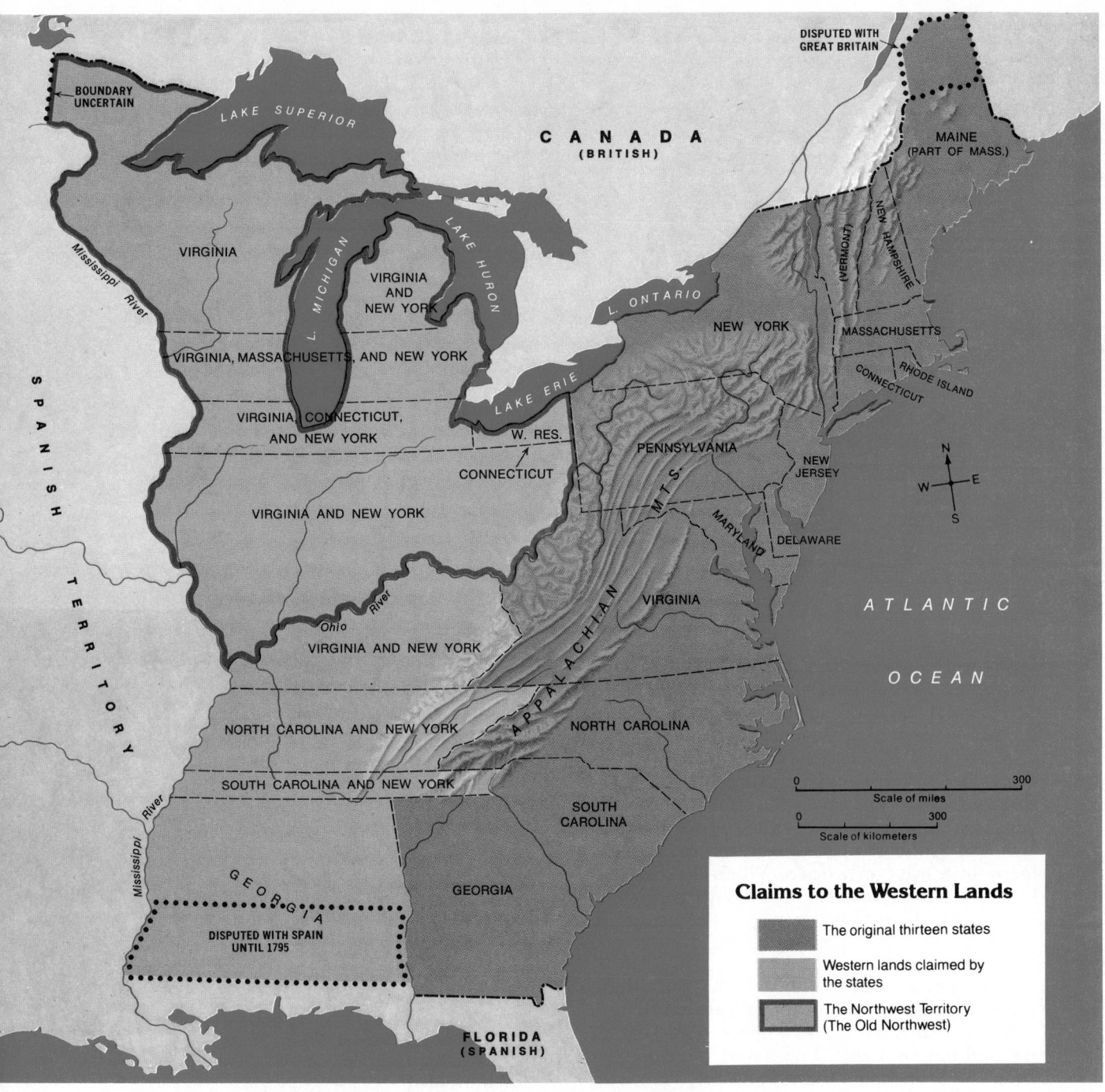

Claims to the Western Lands

The original thirteen states

Western lands claimed by the states

The Northwest Territory (The Old Northwest)

Finally, British and colonial troops recaptured the forts. The Indians accepted generous peace terms. Pontiac declared, "We shall reject everything that tends to evil, and strive with each other to see who shall be of the most service in keeping up that friendship that is so happily established between us."

Pontiac's Rebellion, the name given to the struggle, was over. Governing the western lands, however, was still a problem.

Weakness of British leaders. War debts and defense costs, the government of Florida and Canada, and the ownership of the western

Map activity: Have students point out the western lands claimed by the original states and identify the states these lands became.

107

The convening of the Stamp Act Congress, the burning of stamps and British revenue ships, and the boycotting of British goods are examples of the ways in which Americans protested the actions of the British government from 1763 to 1783. Since that time, protest movements of many kinds have been common in United States history.

Some movements, including the civil rights struggle of the 1950's and 1960's, have been peaceful. Those protesting racial segregation used such non-violent tactics as sit-ins, marches, and boycotts of public facilities. Other movements have been bloody. The Ku Klux Klan, for example, has throughout its long history used violence to protest the integration of blacks into society.

Current American protest movements include opposition to the development of nuclear weapons led by Roman Catholic bishops, demonstrations by students against South African racial policies, and protests by farmers against government agriculture policy.

lands were only a few of the serious problems facing the British government in 1763.

To solve its many problems, Great Britain needed government leaders with ideas and wisdom, who could satisfy the needs of both the colonies and Great Britain. But such officials were not in power at the time. George III, who was king from 1760 to 1820, was ineffective and stubborn. He viewed the colonies as mere overseas territories. When he became king, he surrounded himself with ministers whose first thought was always to please their ruler.

The stage set for trouble. In 1763, then, serious differences of opinion separated British officials and American colonists. The British pointed out that they had saved the colonists from the French and Indian menace. They also pointed out that the colonists were still being protected by the British army and navy. The British believed, therefore, that the colonists should help pay the cost of protecting the empire and themselves.

To this argument many colonists replied that the war was over and now they wanted to be left alone. Colonial farmers, frontier set-

tlers, merchants, and manufacturers wanted to pursue their own interests. They felt that the problems faced by the British in keeping an empire together were no concern of theirs. Settlers in all the colonies, although many were British, had begun to look upon their problems as different from those of Great Britain.

SECTION REVIEW
See underscored items, text pp. 106-08.
Identify: land speculators, Pontiac's Rebellion, 1763, George III
For answers to questions, see Answer Key, p.A21.

1. **Analyzing Ideas:** What new problems did the British government face in governing its colonies after 1763?

2. **Interpreting Ideas:** What factors led to Pontiac's Rebellion? How might this conflict have been avoided?

3. **Summarizing Ideas:** (a) What arguments did the British use in trying to persuade the colonists that they should help pay the cost of protecting the empire and themselves? (b) How did the colonists answer these arguments?

4. **Studying Maps:** Study the map on page 107. (a) What two colonies claimed the most land? (b) Which country claimed the territory to the west?

The colonists oppose taxation without representation

See Teaching Suggestions in TMRG, pp.TM36-37.

In 1763 the British began to adopt measures to put the empire on a sound footing. The person responsible for these measures was George Grenville, who became Prime Minister, or leader of the British government, in 1763. To the surprise of Grenville and other British officials, their efforts to reform colonial administration met with strong opposition from the colonists. The colonists were especially angered by laws passed by a Parliament in which they were not represented. Step by step, the gap between Great Britain and the American ▲ colonies grew wider.

The Proclamation of 1763. Pontiac's uprising prompted George III and his ministers to initiate the new colonial program. This program was intended to reduce conflict between the settlers and the Indians in the western lands formerly claimed by France that now belonged to the British. The Proclamation of 1763 ordered the settlers to withdraw temporarily from all lands west of the Appalachian Mountains. The Proclamation also reserved certain lands for the Indians, thus recognizing limited Indian rights to some of their hunting grounds. The fur trade in the western lands was brought under royal control. No trader was permitted to cross the mountains without the consent of British officials.

To the average Britisher, the measure appeared reasonable. At last, Great Britain was trying to establish a uniform policy for the Indians, the fur trade, and the disposal of western lands. This temporary stop to settlement and trade in the western lands would give the British government the time to form a policy for the colonies without the distraction of conflicts between settlers and Indians.

However, American fur traders and colonists who wanted to settle the western lands resented the Proclamation. Colonial merchants who outfitted the traders opposed it, as did land speculators.

The Sugar Act of 1764. While the colonists were still angered by the Proclamation of 1763,

Parliament landed another stinging blow by passing the Sugar Act of 1764. By this measure Parliament hoped to raise money to help pay the expenses of "protecting and securing" the colonies against attack from Indians and other nations' troops. The Sugar Act of 1764 placed a duty on molasses, sugar, and other products imported from places outside the British empire. A similar law, the Molasses Act, had been enacted in 1733. It had provided for customs officials to enforce the law. The duty set by the act of 1733 was so high, however, that the colonists openly had broken the law by smuggling. British officials had made little effort to enforce the Molasses Act and thus to prevent this smuggling. As a result, the British were spending far more to maintain the customs officials than the officials themselves were collecting under the Molasses Act.

Parliament was determined to enforce the Sugar Act of 1764 and collect the **revenue,** or income, the government needed. To make smuggling less profitable, Parliament in 1764 set the new duty on molasses at only half what it had been in 1733. In 1766 it set the duty at only one sixth of what it had been in 1733. Then British officials began to enforce the Sugar Act of 1764. British naval patrols inspected ships entering colonial harbors. Royal inspectors searched warehouses and even private homes, looking for smuggled goods. The revenue collectors also tried to enlist the aid of the colonists themselves by offering rewards to citizens who reported that their neighbors were smuggling. Special courts, having no juries and presided over by British navy officers, tried the smuggling cases and passed sentence.

Parliament hoped that the Sugar Act of 1764 would reduce taxes for citizens in Great Britain. Until now British citizens had borne almost all the defense costs of the entire empire, including the colonies in North America. Parliament also hoped that enforcement of the act would help the sugar planters of the British West Indies by preventing the smuggling of sugar from other areas of the world.

Despite the lower duty on molasses, the Sugar Act cut sharply into the business of colonial merchants, shipowners, and rum distillers. These colonists had been earning profits on duty free molasses and other goods smuggled in from French, Dutch, and Spanish islands in the Caribbean. Angry colonial merchants began to organize committees to discuss means of resistance.

▲ Time line activity: Have students begin a time line of events between 1763 and 1776. Students may add to the time line as the study of the unit progresses.

The Currency Act of 1764. Soon after the passage of the Sugar Act, Parliament passed another law forbidding the colonies to issue their own paper money. Parliament also required that in the future the colonists must pay all taxes in gold or silver coin rather than in paper money.

This regulation, called the Currency Act of 1764, antagonized many colonists, particularly colonial merchants. Money had been scarce in the colonies even before Parliament passed the new law. Since 1750 the balance of trade between Great Britain and the colonies had shifted in favor of Great Britain. Because of the shift in the balance of trade toward Great Britain, colonial merchants had to send large amounts of currency to Great Britain. These shipments of money were draining away the supply of currency in the colonies. Where, then, could the colonists find the money to carry on their business activities and pay their taxes as Great Britain demanded?

The Quartering Act of 1765. While colonial tempers were still running high, Parliament passed still another unpopular law directed toward the colonies. This law, the Quartering Act of 1765, required the colonial authorities to provide barracks and supplies for British troops stationed in America.

The Stamp Act of 1765. In the midst of the growing colonial agitation over the passage of the previous acts, Parliament adopted the Stamp Act of 1765. The Stamp Act, like the Sugar Act of 1764, attempted to raise revenue to pay for the defense of the colonies. The Stamp Act, however, was far more sweeping. It levied taxes on licenses of all kinds—college diplomas, playing cards, newspapers, advertisements, and legal documents such as deeds to land and mortgages on property. All such documents and materials had to bear a stamp showing that the tax had been paid.

Prime Minister Grenville had announced in 1764 that he wanted Parliament to impose a stamp tax. Parliament, however, did not pass the act until 1765. Thus the colonists had a full year to propose a more acceptable form of taxation. They failed to suggest an alternative. For this reason the British government was astonished when many colonists greeted the Stamp Act with angry protests. Several colonies had used such a tax themselves, and the British people had long been accustomed to it.

Also, the colonists had always paid taxes to support the empire.

The colonists, however, said that the earlier taxes had been **indirect taxes**—duties, for example, collected on goods entering colonial ports. These duties were finally paid only by those colonists who actually bought the products. Colonists often did not know that they were paying these duties because they were hidden in the price of the product. The colonists argued that the stamp tax was different. It was a **direct tax.** Unlike an indirect tax hidden in the price of the product, a direct tax was added to the price of a good. This additional money was paid directly to the British government.

The colonists were used to paying direct taxes levied by their own colonial assemblies. They regarded this power to levy their own taxes as the key to the large measure of self-government they had come to take for granted. The stamp tax, however, was a direct tax levied not by a colonial assembly but by Parliament. The American colonists had no representatives in Parliament.

The Stamp Act, then, threatened to take money directly from the colonists without their consent. Settlers buying land on the frontier would have to pay a special tax on the deed to their property. Small farmers would have to pay taxes on warehouse receipts for tobacco or grain. Artisans in the towns would be required to pay taxes for playing cards and newspapers. Planters, merchants, lawyers, and editors would be paying taxes every time they turned around. This "vicious" tax, the colonists insisted, violated their right to tax themselves. It was levied without the consent of their own representatives. Here, indeed, was "taxation without representation." Thus it violated the great British tradition, which had been won only after centuries of struggle between kings and Parliaments.

Many colonists refused to listen to the British argument that Parliament represented all British subjects, including the colonists. True, British officials admitted, colonial representatives did not sit in Parliament, but other large groups of Britishers also were not directly represented in Parliament. For example, many thousands of people living in the new, rapidly growing English cities of Manchester and Birmingham did not have the right to vote. Therefore they were not directly represented in Parliament. British officials argued that repre-

Philadelphia was a major shipping center with a lively shipbuilding trade. Many people in the city were willing to obey the Stamp Act rather than risk upsetting their profitable business. However, protesters forced the stamp distributors to leave the city, thereby making it impossible for people to pay the tax.

sentation of the American colonies in Parliament was similar to that of these British cities. It was, they said, "virtual representation." Parliament, they insisted, represented not only the citizens of Great Britain but all the people of the empire. What did the colonists mean by "no taxation without representation"? To these arguments the colonists turned deaf ears.

Opposition to the Stamp Act. After the Stamp Act of 1765 was passed, resolutions condemning the measure poured into England from the colonies. Colonial lawyers, merchants, and publishers met in protest. Colonial assemblies declared that all taxes were illegal except those levied by representatives of the people in their own legislatures.

In October 1765, delegates from nine colonies met in New York to hold a meeting known as the Stamp Act Congress. They first asserted their loyalty to the king and promised "all due subordination" to Parliament. Then the delegates vowed to resist all taxes levied without the consent of their own colonial legislatures.

Many colonial merchants, joined by other leading citizens, went a step further. They signed **nonimportation agreements,** promising not to buy or import British goods. Within a few months, products made in Great Britain almost vanished from colonial stores and warehouses.

Some colonial townspeople took even more direct action. Organized in societies called Sons of Liberty, they rioted in large towns and destroyed the offices of stamp tax collectors. They burned stamps in the streets, destroyed the houses of royal officials, and tarred and feathered citizens sympathetic to Great Britain. They justified their violent actions by claiming that they were battling for their rights as English subjects.

Repeal of the Stamp Act. The British accepted the news of colonial resistance to the Stamp Act with mixed feelings. George III exclaimed, "It is undoubtedly the most serious matter that ever came before Parliament."

British merchants were shocked. The colonial nonimportation agreements had brought British-American trade almost to a standstill. Many British merchants faced financial ruin. To prevent this, they demanded that Parliament repeal the Stamp Act. Powerful Britishers who sympathized with the colonists joined in the demand for repeal. Edmund Burke, a British leader and writer, expressed his pride in those who fought such "illegal" measures. William Pitt, who had led Great Britain to victory in the Seven Years' War, declared, "I rejoice that America has resisted."

Under such heavy pressure, Parliament repealed the Stamp Act in March 1766. News of the repeal brought wild rejoicing in the colonies and sighs of relief from British merchants and friends of the colonists. In New York City, Sons of Liberty erected a huge flagpole, called a "liberty pole." Colonists gathered around the liberty pole to celebrate the repeal. There they pledged their devotion to the cause of liberty.

The Declaratory Act of 1766. In the excitement most colonists paid little attention to another law passed by Parliament—the Declaratory Act of 1766. In the Declaratory Act, Parliament asserted that it had the "full power and authority to make laws to bind the colonies and people of America . . . in all cases whatsoever."

Thus, despite rejoicing in the colonies, the basic issue dividing the colonies from Great Britain remained unsettled. Did the British Parliament have the right to make laws for the American colonists and to tax them when the colonists had no elected representatives in Parliament? This was the basic question.

SECTION REVIEW

See underscored items, text pp. 109-11.
Identify: George Grenville, Sugar Act of 1764, Quartering Act of 1765, indirect tax, revenue, non-importation agreements, Sons of Liberty
For answers to questions, see Answer Key, pp.A21-22.
1. **Organizing Ideas:** Why did the Crown and Parliament approve the following measures and why did the colonists object to them: (a) the Proclamation of 1763, (b) the Sugar Act of 1764, (c) the Currency Act of 1764, (d) the Quartering Act of 1765?
2. **Analyzing Ideas:** Why did many colonists consider the stamp tax different from all previous taxes and duties?
3. **Summarizing Ideas:** (a) What steps did the colonists take to oppose the Stamp Act of 1765? (b) Why was the Stamp Act repealed?
4. **Interpreting Ideas:** (a) How did the Declaratory Act symbolize the British government's position on representation of the colonies in Parliament? (b) How did the British government and the colonists differ on this issue?

See Teaching Suggestions in TMRG, p.TM37.

---

4 Tensions increase between Great Britain and the colonies

In 1767, under the leadership of Charles Townshend, Parliament decided once again to try to raise revenue in America. Parliament, however, still had painful memories of how deeply the colonists resented direct taxes.

The Townshend Acts. Parliament decided, therefore, to return to the long-accepted method of collecting duties on goods entering the seaports. Since the colonists had always paid such indirect taxes, Parliament hoped the new duties would not cause any trouble.

The Townshend Acts levied import duties on articles of everyday use in America—tea, lead, glass, and colors for paint. Had Parliament stopped at this point, the colonists might not have objected, but Parliament did not stop.

Writs of assistance. In an effort to insure that the new law would be enforced, Parliament legalized **writs of assistance**, or search warrants. "Writ" is an old word meaning "written." Writs of assistance, then, were written statements giving government officials the legal right to search the colonists' businesses, their ships, and even their homes for smuggled goods.

The writs of assistance used in colonial times were quite different from present-day search warrants. Today a search warrant must state the exact article sought and the specific places to be searched. In colonial times, however, a British customs official, armed with a general search warrant, could enter any vessel or warehouse or home in America at any time. And the official could ransack the place in the mere hope of finding smuggled goods.

For many years American colonial merchants had been arguing that the writs of assistance were illegal and an invasion of their rights as English subjects. Now, in 1767, Parliament had legalized the hated writs. The colonists could not change this fact, but they could and did protest.

Arguments and resolutions. Many colonists openly expressed their resentment of the

▲ Some historians think that the American Board of Customs Commissioners, which was set up by the Townshend Acts, was a major cause of the Revolution. They cite evidence of "customs racketeering," including entrapment of American merchants and seized ships that were sold for customs violations with customs officers receiving part of the proceeds.

Townshend Acts and the writs of assistance. Many colonial courts, for example, refused to issue the writs; by 1772 almost none would.

New Yorkers refused to provide living quarters for British soldiers sent to enforce the law. Parliament promptly punished the colony by suspending its assembly, thus depriving New Yorkers of their right to representative government.

Other colonists poured out their anger in a flood of pamphlets, resolutions, and petitions. Led by Samuel Adams, the legislature of Massachusetts drafted a letter to the other colonies urging them to unite for resistance. The assemblies of Maryland, South Carolina, and Georgia promptly endorsed the letter. Parliament replied by forbidding the legislatures of these four colonies to meet.

The Virginia House of Burgesses adopted a set of resolutions summarizing the American case. The resolutions began with a statement by George Washington referring to "our lordly masters in Great Britain." The resolutions then repeated the American claim that only colonial legislatures had the right to levy taxes on the colonists.

Direct action – and violence. While many colonial leaders protested in writing, other colonists decided to act. They signed new nonimportation agreements, promising not to import or buy British goods. The earlier agreements at the time of the Stamp Act of 1765 had almost ruined British merchants and had forced Parliament to repeal the measure. Many colonists reasoned that such nonimportation agreements would work again.

Some Americans were not content with these agreements. Once again mobs poured into the streets. They boarded and smashed British ships, attacked British customs officials, and tarred and feathered anyone who informed on smugglers. British soldiers sent to protect customs officials and to keep order were sometimes attacked.

In Boston crowds taunted the soldiers, calling them "lobsters," "redcoats," and "bloody backs." Now and then a crowd hurled stones and snowballs at the soldiers. Every month friction between the citizens and the soldiers became more intense. Thoughtful colonial leaders and British commanders alike did everything possible to avoid more serious trouble, but an incident such as they dreaded finally occurred.

Samuel Adams, leader of the most extreme Patriots, was feared by British officials. Adams knew how to stir people to action with his speeches and writings.

The Boston Massacre. On March 5, 1770, a large crowd gathered in Boston around soldiers of the 29th British Regiment. The crowd yelled insults and threw snowballs. Such outbursts had occurred many times before. This time matters got out of hand. As the mob pressed closer against the soldiers, someone gave an order to fire. Three civilians were killed and two others were mortally wounded.

One of those killed was Crispus Attucks, a former slave, who had escaped 20 years earlier from his master. As a fugitive slave, he did not share the same degree of freedom as other citizens of Boston. Yet Crispus Attucks was among the first to die in the struggle over colonial freedom between Great Britain and the American colonies.

As news of the shooting spread, the people of Boston went wild with anger. A "massacre" they called the affair. They also demanded that the British withdraw all troops from their city.

Later, when passions had cooled somewhat, the British soldiers were tried for murder.

A shot rang out and the muscular black man fell, mortally wounded. Crispus Attucks was the the first person to die in the Boston Massacre. He thus played an important, if unexpected role, in the arousal of anti-British feelings in the colonies.

Little is definitely known about Attucks, a mulatto with Natick Indian ancestry. A slave of Deacon William Brown, Attucks apparently escaped in 1750 and spent the next 20 years of his life working as a whaler and dockworker around Boston.

On the evening of March 5, 1770, Crispus Attucks was in the forefront of a shouting, jeering crowd of 50 or 60 sailors, dockworkers, servants, and young apprentices. They stood at the Boston Customs House facing a group of seven British soldiers. According to an eyewitness, Attucks grabbed a soldier's bayonet and knocked the soldier down. The soldiers fired at the crowd, killing Attucks and four other civilians. The British soldiers later stood trial, but were exonerated in Attucks' death.

Attucks' name became a symbol for black and white Patriots. During the Revolutionary War, black military companies called themselves Attucks Guards, and Crispus Attucks Day was celebrated in Boston. In 1888 a monument was erected on the Boston Common to recognize Attuck's role in the Revolution.

They were defended by Josiah Quincy, Jr., and John Adams, who later became the second President of the United States. Neither of these men had any sympathy for the British, but they insisted that every person was entitled to a fair trial. All except two of the soldiers were acquitted. These two were convicted of manslaughter but were released soon after.

Repeal — and continued unrest. When Lord Frederick North became Prime Minister of Great Britain in 1770, the gap between Great Britain and the American colonies was wide indeed. The new Prime Minister urged Parliament to repeal the Townshend Acts. As Lord North pointed out, the nonimportation agreements were once again ruining the business of many British merchants. Besides, the cost of enforcing the law was proving much too heavy for Great Britain.

In 1770 Parliament repealed the Townshend Acts. Parliament also allowed the Quartering Act to expire. But in a new law, the British government was careful to retain a small import duty on tea as a symbol that Parliament had the power to tax the colonists. As George III put it, there must "always be one tax to keep up the right."

The repeal of the Townshend Acts brought a temporary end to much colonial unrest. Only an occasional act of violence reminded the British that the basic issue remained unsettled.

One such outbreak occurred in June 1772 when colonists attacked and burned the British revenue ship *Gaspee* a few miles south of Providence, Rhode Island. For the colonists the most alarming thing about the *Gaspee* affair was the British announcement that the accused colonists would be sent to England for trial. This British decision threatened to weaken the practice of self-government in Rhode Island.

No less alarming was an announcement made at this time by the royal governor of Massachusetts. From now on, Governor Thomas

Hutchinson declared, the British Crown, not the colonial assemblies, would pay the salaries of the governor and the Massachusetts judges. This action freed the governor and the judges from all dependence upon the Massachusetts legislature.

Committees of Correspondence. These new threats to colonial freedom did not go unchallenged. Led by Samuel Adams, citizens of Boston met in a special town meeting with James Otis presiding. They created a <u>Committee of Correspondence</u> consisting of 21 members to keep other colonies—and "the World"—informed about what was happening in Massachusetts. The idea worked so well that, during the next few months, other colonies organized similar committees. Many of the most prominent colonial leaders served on these committees. In Virginia, for example, the committee included Thomas Jefferson, Patrick Henry, and Richard Henry Lee.

Because the colonies had no central government where leaders of the various colonies could meet, the Committees of Correspondence performed an important service. They kept each colony informed of events and opinions in the other colonies. As it turned out, the colonists organized this new method of communication none too soon, for in 1773 Parliament adopted another measure that really started tempers boiling.

See Teaching Suggestions in TMRG, p.TM38.

The American colonies were brought to the edge of rebellion in 1773 with series of events that started with the Tea Act. Parliament passed this law to help the <u>East India Company</u>, a British trading company.

The Tea Act of 1773. The East India Company was in serious trouble. Part of its problem was the fact that many American colonists refused to buy English tea. When the Townshend Acts were repealed, the British government, you recall, insisted on retaining a duty on tea as a symbol of its power to tax the colonies. The tax was a small one, but many colonists refused to pay it. In fact, they refused to buy tea imported from England. As a result, large amounts of unsold tea were piling up in the company's warehouses in London.

Faced with possible bankruptcy, the East India Company turned to Parliament for help.

Tea was shipped in beautifully decorated wooden chests. This chest may be one of those thrown into Boston harbor during the Tea Party.

SECTION REVIEW
See underscored items, text pp. 112-15.

Identify: writs of assistance, Samuel Adams, Boston Massacre, Crispus Attucks, John Adams, Committees of Correspondence, Lord Frederick North
For answers to questions, see Answer Key, p.A22.

1. **Interpreting Ideas:** (a) How did the British justify the Townshend Acts of 1767? (b) Why did the colonists object to them?

2. **Contrasting Ideas:** (a) How did writs of assistance differ from present-day search warrants? (b) Why did the colonists object to them?

3. **Summarizing Ideas:** (a) List five actions that the colonists took to protest the Townshend Acts. (b) How did the British respond to these actions?

4. **Analyzing Ideas:** Why did the British choose to retain the tax on tea when they repealed the Townshend Acts in 1770?

5. **Determining Cause and Effect:** Why was the burning of the *Gaspee* significant?

The members of Parliament, many of whom owned stock in the British East India Company, quickly responded. They immediately lent the company a large sum of money. Then they passed a law that, in effect, gave the East India Company a monopoly of the sale of tea in America.

The new law, known as the Tea Act of 1773, permitted the East India Company to bypass British wholesalers and sell the tea directly to the American colonists through company agents. Although the American colonists would still have to pay the Townshend duty, or tax, when buying tea, the tea itself would cost less than ever before.

Violent colonial reaction. Why, given lower prices for tea, did the colonists continue their protest? For one thing, many thoughtful colonists by now opposed all taxes levied by Parliament. A more immediate issue, however, was the impact of the Tea Act upon colonial tea merchants. These merchants could no longer compete with the low prices offered by the agents of the East India Company. As a result, the colonial merchants would be driven out of business. True, the act affected only the sale of tea, but if a monopoly were granted to one British company, what was to prevent Parliament from granting monopolies to other British companies?

Faced with this threat to their businesses, the colonists reacted swiftly. Crowds rioted in the streets. The colonists also continued their boycott on British tea. The British East India Company could not sell any of its tea. In Charleston colonists stored tea in damp cellars so it would rot. In Annapolis a ship and its cargo of tea were burned. Philadelphians and New Yorkers refused to allow British ships carrying tea to enter their harbors.

In Boston, late in 1773, colonists disguised as Indians boarded ships carrying British tea and heaved the casks of tea into the water. In one wild night, the disguised colonists destroyed 342 chests of tea valued at what today would be many thousands of dollars. The Boston Tea Party, as it came to be called, drew widespread attention at home and abroad. Many colonists approved of the tea's destruction. Other American patriots were shocked at the violence.

The Intolerable Acts of 1774. British officials and merchants were furious. It had been bad enough for the colonists to refuse to pay taxes. It was far worse for them to destroy British property.

By overwhelming majorities the British Parliament passed four laws to discourage further violence and to strengthen British control over the colonists. The British called these new laws the Coercive Acts. The colonists called them the Intolerable Acts—that is, acts they could not endure.

One law closed the port of Boston to all shipping until the colonists paid for the tea that had been destroyed in Boston harbor. A second law revoked the Massachusetts charter of 1691 and forbade Massachusetts colonists to hold town meetings. A third law, a new Quartering Act, required the colonists to provide food and housing for British soldiers sent to America to enforce the new laws. A fourth law provided that British officials in Massachusetts charged with crimes committed while enforcing British laws could have their cases tried in England rather than in Massachusetts.

Great Britain was determined to enforce the Coercive Acts. General Thomas Gage, commander in chief of the British armed forces in North America, was named governor of Massachusetts. He was then given more troops to help him maintain order.

The Quebec Act of 1774. While passing what the colonists called the Intolerable Acts, Parliament also passed a fifth law, the Quebec Act. The Quebec Act was intended to establish order in Canada, which, as you recall, the British had won by treaty from the French in 1763.

The Quebec Act greatly enlarged the province of Quebec. It established the southern boundary of Canada at the Ohio River and the western boundary at the Mississippi River. It permitted French laws to continue in Canada. It also guaranteed religious freedom to French Canadians, most of whom were members of the Roman Catholic Church.

Parliament had no thought of punishing the colonists when it passed the Quebec Act. Indeed, the act was a sound piece of legislation. The Quebec Act, however, came at the same time as the hated Coercive Acts. The colonists regarded it as another attempt to punish them by destroying the claims of Massachusetts, Connecticut, and Virginia to the western lands. The Quebec Act also strengthened the Catholicism that they disliked.

▲ Discussion topic: What might have happened if Parliament had been more receptive to Edmund Burke's pleas for moderation

DECLARATION AND RESOLVES OF THE FIRST CONTINENTAL CONGRESS (1774)

The good people of the several colonies . . . declare . . . that the inhabitants of the English colonies in North America, by the immutable laws of nature, the principles of the English constitution, and the several charters or compacts, have the following rights:

Resolved,
That they are entitled to life, liberty, and property, and they have never ceded to any sovereign power whatever a right to dispose of either without their consent.

That our ancestors, who first settled these colonies, were at the time of their emigration from the mother country entitled to all the rights, liberties, and immunities of free and natural-born subjects within the realm of England. . . .

That the foundation of English liberty and of all free government is a right in the people to participate in their legislative council. . . .

Reaction to the Intolerable Acts. In spite of British actions, many colonists remained completely loyal to Great Britain. They believed that the colonists, as British citizens, should obey the laws passed by Parliament without protesting. Other colonists tried to persuade the British to work out a compromise.

By and large, however, the colonists strongly opposed the Intolerable Acts. In some cases the reaction came close to rebellion. At mass meetings colonists condemned the actions of Parliament. The colonists also began to experiment with new political organizations that would avoid or replace the royal governments. In this way they formed committees that took over many functions of government.

Many of these committees worked at the local level. In some colonies new "congresses" took on some of the tasks of the colonial assemblies. The most important step came late in the summer of 1774, when a general congress of the colonies was held.

The First Continental Congress. On September 5, 1774, delegates from all the colonies except Georgia assembled in Philadelphia at a meeting called the First Continental Congress. The Congress, pushed by delegates from Massachusetts and Virginia, adopted a number of resolutions. Denying any thought of independence, the delegates nevertheless demanded an immediate change in British policies. They solemnly asserted their rights to "life, liberty, and property"; to "all the rights, liberties, and immunities" of English subjects; to the "free and exclusive power of legislation in their own

several legislatures." They pledged each other mutual support. They revived the nonimportation agreements against British products. They further agreed not to sell goods to Great Britain or the British West Indies if, by January 1775, the British had not made compromises. Finally they resolved to create local "committees of safety and inspection" that would provide firm and uniform action against the British government.

When the First Continental Congress ended, the delegates agreed to meet again in the spring of 1775.

SECTION REVIEW
See underscored items, text pp. 115-17.
Identify: British East India Company, Boston Tea Party, General Thomas Gage, Quebec Act of 1774, First Continental Congress
For answers to questions, see Answer Key, pp.A22-23.

1. **Analyzing Viewpoints:** (a) Why did the colonists object to the Tea Act of 1773? (b) How did they express their objections?

2. **Summarizing Ideas:** (a) Describe the provisions of the Intolerable Acts. (b) What was the purpose of the Intolerable Acts? (c) Why did the colonists oppose the Quebec Act?

3. **Organizing Ideas:** (a) List three actions that the First Continental Congress took in response to the Intolerable Acts. (b) Why do you suppose that the delegates at this First Continental Congress did not talk of independence?

4. **Studying Sources:** Read the Source on page 117 (a) What rights do the delegates to the Congress claim? (b) On what grounds do they claim these rights?

DEVELOPING HISTORY STUDY SKILLS

Thinking About History   Determining Cause-Effect Relationships

Identifying and understanding cause-effect relationships is crucial to a historian. A cause is a condition, a person, or an event that makes something happen. An effect is the result or outcome of a cause. A cause may have many effects. An effect may itself produce another effect, thus making the effect into a cause in its own right. For example, because of the costs incurred in the French and Indian War, Great Britain levied taxes on the colonies to raise revenue. The taxes stirred up unrest. A visual representation of the cause-effect relationships follows:

Cause		Effect/Cause		Effect
French and Indian War	▶	New Taxes levied	▶	Colonial protests

The Cause-Effect Connection

Historians apply many techniques in investigating major events of history such as wars and revolutions. Some questions historians ask include the following.

- What is the immediate activity that triggered the event? Sometimes the question is repeated many times in a series of backward-in-time probes that eventually produce the underlying cause or causes.
- What is the background leading up to the event? An examination of the background sometimes indicates a gradual emergence of a trend that gathered momentum over time and for which the event in question was only the last result. In examining the background the historian must consider all aspects of society — the economic climate, the political institutions, religious beliefs, cultural heritage.
- Who were the people involved? The investigation into this question looks at the individuals involved — the actors and reactors, and even the bystanders. It probes their personality traits, their strengths, and their weaknesses and tries to assess the effects on the outcome. The historian also needs to examine whether any groups had a grievance, something to protect, or something of great value to gain.

For many scholars, determining cause-effect relationships is at the core of the historian's craft.

How to Determine Cause-Effect Relationships

Your task is simpler than the historian's. You read what the historian has already investigated and produced. To trace the historian's thought and recognizing the cause and effect strands that have been woven throughout a narrative, follow these guidelines.

1. **Look for cause-effect clues.** The best help is to look for cause-effect clues as you read. Some of these clues are shown here.

Cause Clues	Effect Clues
led to	upshot
brought about	outcome
spurred	outgrowth
induced	aftermath
provoked	as a consequence
instigated	gave rise to
produced	has arisen from
inspired	proceeded from
because	dependent on
as a result of	resulting in
at the root of	originating from
the origin of	gave rise to
the source of	
the reason why	

Remember, however, that historians do not always state the link between a cause and effect using the above clues. Sometimes a reader of history has to infer the cause or the effect. Sometimes, the reader even has to infer the relationship between a stated cause and a stated effect.

2. **Check for complex connections.** While looking for the superficial, or immediate, cause or effect, remember that many cause-effect relationships have complex connections. A single cause may have many effects. Likewise, a single effect may have its roots in several causes. Also an effect may itself become a cause.

Applying the Skill

The American Revolution produced a series of cause-effect relationships. On a separate sheet of paper, prepare a diagram such as the one shown on page 118. From the following list, select three statements and place them in the appropriate boxes to illustrate how an effect of one cause may itself be the cause of another effect.

1. Great Britain incurred huge debts fighting the French and Indian War.

2. The Sons of Liberty staged a tea party.

3. George III did not understand the needs of the American colonists.

4. The Intolerable Acts were designed to punish the people of Boston.

5. Parliament passed a series of revenue-producing laws, including the Tea Act.

Your completed diagram could have two possible sets of answers. If you had chosen 1, 5, and 2 in that order, you have completed the exercise correctly. The order of 5, 2, and 4 is also correct. The diagrams below illustrate these cause-effect relationships.

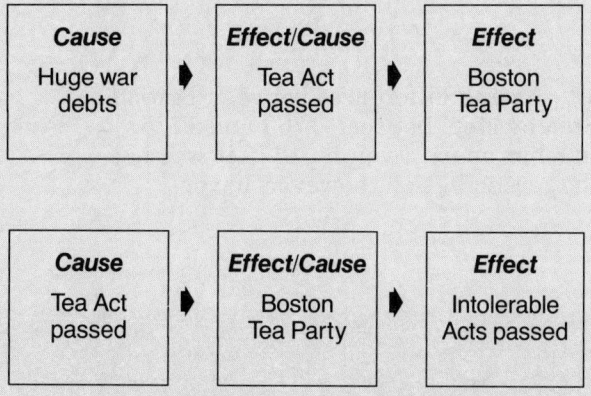

Cause	**Effect/Cause**	**Effect**
Huge war debts	Tea Act passed	Boston Tea Party

Cause	**Effect/Cause**	**Effect**
Tea Act passed	Boston Tea Party	Intolerable Acts passed

Practicing the Skill

The account in the column to the right describes the debate in the Virginia House of Burgesses in 1765 over British actions. Read the account. Then on a separate sheet of paper, answer the questions below the excerpt.

News of the passage of the Stamp Act arrived in Virginia in April. The next month Virginia's elected Assembly — or House of Burgesses, as it was called — met in Williamsburg, a little town that had been the colony's capital for nearly 70 years. . . .

In late May, as the Assembly argued about the Stamp Act, a young lawyer stood up and boldly attacked the British government. This young man was Patrick Henry. He had a number of resolutions which he hoped the members of the Assembly would agree to. One stated that nobody had the right to tax Virginians except the Virginia Assembly itself. Henry bluntly told the burgesses that if the king were allowed to tax the colonies as he pleased, it would mean the end of the colonists' freedom. When Henry compared King George to earlier tyrants in history who had been overthrown for their crimes, some of his listeners cried "Treason."

As news of the debate spread through the town, a law student, Thomas Jefferson, hurried to the House of Burgesses. Jefferson was 22 years old. The son of a tobacco grower, he had come to Williamsburg in 1760 to attend the College of William and Mary. In 1769 he would be chosen a member of the same Assembly where he now heard Patrick Henry speak.

When the debate finished, the House of Burgesses passed Henry's resolutions, and they appeared in many newspapers. Soon the country was alive with protest against the Stamp Act. Committees that called themselves the Sons of Liberty organized demonstrations. Bonfires blazed. Straw figures symbolizing the king's taxmen hung in nooses from trees. The stamp sellers got a clear message: resign your jobs or get out of town. Early in 1766 the British government gave in and repealed the Stamp Act. The colonists celebrated the good news.

1. What was the immediate cause of Patrick Henry's speech in the House of Burgesses?

2. What immediate effect did his speech have?

3. What further effect did his speech have?

4. What cause-effect relationship may be inferred between the debate in the House of Burgesses and the subsequent role of Thomas Jefferson?

5. What were the effects of the passage of Henry's resolutions by the House of Burgesses?

6. Which effect of the passage of the resolutions is inferred rather than stated directly?

for their rights   4. Thomas Jefferson was inspired by the debate in the House of Burgesses and as a result eventually became active in colonial government.   5. protests and demostrations against the Stamp Act, bonfires, and tax officials hung in effigy   6. The resolutions caused the colonists to protest against the Stamp Act.)

119

By 1763 the Seven Years' War, called in North America the French and Indian War, was finally settled. The British victory made Great Britain the leading colonial power in the world. British citizens had paid in blood and treasure to win their great empire. By 1763 the struggle was finally settled. France had been defeated, and peace had come at long last to the colonies.

Peace, however, brought new problems. During the long years of colonial warfare, the American seaboard colonies had in many ways become less dependent upon Great Britain. The settlers in each colony had learned to think of the colony as *their* land, as a place apart from England.

The American colonists had learned to love the new land that had brought most of them better lives than they or their parents had known in the Old World. By the 1760s, many colonists were beginning to think of themselves as Americans. Nearly all of the colonists, nonetheless, continued to consider themselves loyal citizens of the British empire.

A new way of life was developing in the British colonies. It was now about 150 years since the first English settlers had come to North America. As a result, the peoples of the Old World and the New World were finding it increasingly difficult to understand each other.

By 1763 the colonists along the Atlantic seaboard were beginning to think of themselves as junior partners in the expanding British empire. The British government, on the other hand, continued to regard the colonists as children to be ordered about.

CONNECTING CHAPTER IDEAS

In the next chapter you will read about growing differences between British officials and the American colonists. Step by step, between 1763 and 1775, Great Britain and its colonies moved farther apart. Even by 1775 it was not too late to reconcile the differences. The reconciliation, however, never came.

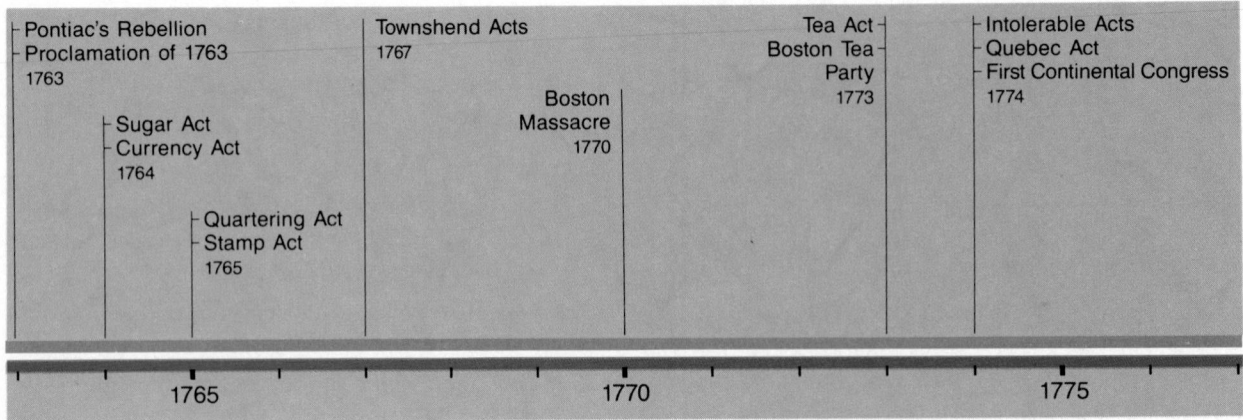

Pontiac's Rebellion
Proclamation of 1763
1763

Sugar Act
Currency Act
1764

Quartering Act
Stamp Act
1765

Townshend Acts
1767

Boston
Massacre
1770

Tea Act
Boston Tea
Party
1773

Intolerable Acts
Quebec Act
First Continental Congress
1774

1765   1770   1775

CHAPTER

5 REVIEW

Reviewing Important Terms

In the sentence below, the underlined terms are incorrect. On a separate sheet of paper, rewrite each sentence using the correct term.

1. In order to gain greater wealth and power, some European nations in the 1600's and 1700's operated under the economic and political policy of rivalry.
2. In the 1700's, the British government paid import duties on tar, resin, turpentine, and hemp to stimulate production of these materials needed by the Royal Navy.
3. When the colonists carried on trade in violation of the Molasses Act of 1733, the British government followed a policy of strict enforcement.
4. Hoping to gain a quick profit from its resale, pioneer farmers wanted to buy land in the territory west of the Appalachian Mountains.
5. Parliament passed the Sugar Act of 1764 in order to collect profits that would pay the costs of defending the colonies.
6. The Stamp Act of 1765 levied indirect taxes on such items as licenses, playing cards, newspapers, and legal documents.
7. A search warrant today is much more restrictive than the resolutions used by British customs officials in colonial America.

Practicing Critical Thinking Skills

1. **Organizing Ideas.** Explain how Great Britain applied the principles of mercantilism by means of (a) the Navigation Acts, (b) restrictions on colonial manufacturing, and (c) the Currency Act of 1764.
2. **Evaluating Ideas.** Wise leaders could have resolved the differences between Great Britain and the colonies in 1775. Do you agree? Explain.
3. **Analyzing Viewpoints.** Do you think the protests of American colonists after 1763 were based more on economic or political considerations? Use historical evidence to support your opinion.
4. **Interpreting Ideas.** (a) Trace the events from 1754 to 1775 that illustrate the increased unity of the colonists. (b) Why did the colonists become more unified as time went on? (c) In what ways did the colonists still lack unity?
5. **Synthesizing Ideas.** Does the use of violence breed more violence? Cite examples of colonial violence that indicated further violence.

6. **Relating Past to Present.** Do nations still consider a favorable balance of trade to be an important factor in their economic relations? Why or why not?

Developing History Study Skills

Determining Cause-Effect Relationships. A chain of events led to the death of several colonists during the Boston Massacre. Reread the textbook's account of the event. Then on a separate sheet of paper write a series of five descriptive statements in which each of the four statements following the first is both an effect of the event described in the preceding statement and a cause of the event described in the following statement.

Relating Geography and History

Until about 1750, the Appalachian Mountains were an effective barrier that prevented the British from any serious attempts at settlement in the lands beyond the mountains. The discovery of the Cumberland Gap and the British victory over the French gave the British clear possession of the western lands and encouraged pioneers such as Daniel Boone to open up trails that were followed by a steady stream of settlers. To understand the problems that these acquired lands and the attempts at settlement presented to the British colonists, use the information in this chapter to answer the following questions.

1. Why did settlers and frontiersmen want to move into the western lands?
2. (a) Why did the Indians resent the British victory over the French? (b) Were Indian fears justified? Why? (c) What actions did Chief Pontiac take against the British? (d) Who, besides the Indians, wanted to keep settlers out of the lands west of the Appalachians?
3. (a) What was the British solution to the problems in the western lands? (b) Why did the British believe that this policy was necessary? (c) Name four groups who opposed the measures taken by the British to stop western settlement.
4. What do you think were some of the difficulties faced by British officials in trying to enforce the Proclamation of 1763?

See Chapter Overview in TMRG, p.TM39.
See Chapter Objectives in TMRG, p.TM39.
See Introducing the Chapter in TMRG, p.TM39.

CHAPTER 6

The Struggle for Independence

(1775–1783)

Protesting
royal taxes

John Howe was a private in the army of King George III. He was also a spy. Fortunately for him, he did not look like a spy. The people Howe met as he walked along the Massachusetts roads took him for an honest Yankee artisan. His regiment had been stationed in Boston long enough for him to learn how Yankees talked. He even had learned what they were thinking about.

General Gage, British commander in Boston, had heard that the New Englanders were collecting arms and ammunition. He sent Private Howe and other spies into the surrounding countryside to learn what the colonists were doing and planning. John Howe learned fast. He discovered where powder and rifles were stored. He also learned that the Yankees were ready to fight. At a farmhouse near Lexington, he stopped to talk to an old man who was cleaning a gun. Howe asked him what he intended to shoot. "A flock of redcoats at Boston," the man replied.

Howe heard the same story everywhere he went. He saw rebellious colonists—by now called Patriots—cleaning their guns and drilling openly on village greens. In public places, he saw lists posted bearing the names of people who remained loyal to the king. He heard of Loyalists who had been tarred and feathered. He heard of Loyalists whose homes had been burned because they dared to defend the British point of view.

John Howe carried his findings back to General Gage in Boston. General Gage, who had heard the same story from other British spies, decided the time had come to teach the colonists a lesson. Gage's lesson opened the colonists' battle for independence.

═══ READING FOCUS ═══

As you read about the efforts of the Patriots to gain their independence, look for the details that support each of the following statements.

1. British-American differences break out in open war.
2. The colonists decide to fight for their independence.
3. British plans for an early victory end in disaster.
4. American Patriots defeat the British army.
5. Events off the battlefield lead to an American victory.

1 British-American differences break out in open war

See Teaching Suggestions in TMRG, pp.TM39-40.

General Gage decided to surprise the colonists and seize supplies of ammunition at Concord and several other towns. On April 18, 1775, under cover of darkness, British troops left their quarters in the sleeping city of Boston. They reached the Charles River and began to row across it.

Lexington and Concord. Patriot watchers on the west bank of the Charles River reacted quickly as two lanterns flickered in the window of the Old North Church in Boston. The signal meant that the redcoats were marching to Lexington.

Paul Revere, William Dawes, Jr., and Dr. Samuel Prescott—leaped into the saddles of their waiting horses and galloped off into the night—and into the pages of history. They rode through that fateful night shouting their cries of alarm. Behind them, as the hoofbeats of ▲ their horses faded into the distance, lamps winked on in kitchens. Women, their eyes filled with worry, hastily prepared food while the men in the family hurriedly pulled on clothes and lifted their muskets and powder horns from pegs on the wall. Then the men marched off to join others at the appointed meeting place.

British troops reached Lexington at dawn on April 19, 1775 (see map, page 125). The minutemen—militia members who had promised to be ready for action at a minute's notice—were gathered in ranks on the village green. The commander of the British patrol ordered the colonists to drop their guns and leave the green. The colonists started to leave, but held on to their guns. Then someone fired "the shot heard round the world." Immediately, without waiting for orders, the British troops fired. When the smoke cleared, eight colonists lay dead, and ten others were wounded.

The British troops went on to Concord, where they cut down a liberty pole, set fire to the courthouse, and destroyed several gun carriages. After clashing with armed Patriot forces at Concord's North Bridge, the British started back toward Boston. By now, the coun-

Text continues on page 125.

THIS CHANGING LAND   The Aging of the Nation

Inflation and the cost of living, health concerns, loneliness — a 1983 survey has identified these issues as the most serious problems faced by the nation's senior citizens.

The coming of old age brings many changes for an individual. Retirement from work, the gradual slowing of one's body, and the increased need for special services are familiar aspects of aging in the United States. Many people, however, make false assumptions about old age. The first assumption is that most people experience a sense of loss upon retirement. Though for many people retirement is at first difficult, most retirees come to enjoy the benefits they have earned over the years. The second assumption is that most older persons suffer from senility. While mental deterioration and memory loss is sometimes a part of the aging process, only a small percentage of senior citizens are thus afflicted. The final assumption is that old age is something to be dreaded. Yet many older Americans are active, productive citizens, some of whom have retired and some of whom work part-time or full-time at paying jobs.

Improved health care is enabling more people than ever to live longer, more productive lives. People age 65 and older are the fastest-growing segment of the world's population. In 1980 the United States census reported that persons 65 and older made up about 12 percent of the total population. This figure is expected to increase to 13.5 percent by the year 2000, and to 21 percent, a total of nearly 60 million citizens age 65 and older, by 2030.

The growing number of senior citizens has had a dramatic effect on families. Today nearly 5 million Americans are caring for an elderly parent in their own homes. Many other Americans rely on "long distance caretaking" services such as Aging Network Services to provide health monitoring and visitation.

A good time for all

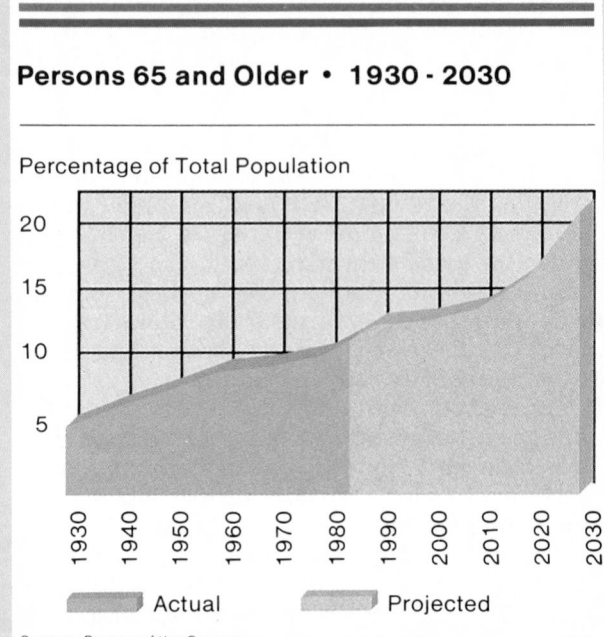

Persons 65 and Older • 1930 - 2030

Percentage of Total Population

Actual   Projected

Source: *Bureau of the Census*

The increase in the nation's older population has had a major impact on society as a whole. Many teaching hospitals have added geriatrics departments to train specialists in the health care of the elderly. Colleges and universities have added a degree in the sociology of aging to their list of degrees. The development of retirement communities reflects the demographic impact of this growing segment of the nation's population. Often located in the Sunbelt, especially Florida and the Southwest, communities such as Sun City, Arizona, with its motto "An Active Way of Life" provide recreational and health services for their residents.

Many senior citizens participate effectively as community and hospital volunteers, cooperate in beautification and crime watch programs, and organize into groups to make their political clout felt. They have influenced the election of officials who represent the interests of the elderly. These citizens have also defeated bond issues and referendums they feel do not directly benefit senior citizens.

In the 1970's a group calling itself the Gray Panthers was organized to call attention to the problems of the elderly and to fight for their rights. The Gray Panthers have done much to make the public and government officials aware of the needs and rights of senior citizens. Such social changes will continue as the increasing number of senior citizens influence United States society.

tryside was swarming with angry colonists. From behind stone walls and buildings, the colonists fired steadily as the redcoats retreated to Boston. British casualties amounted to 73 killed, 174 wounded, and 26 missing.

The redcoats reached Boston late in the day. Curious townspeople saw weary faces, bloody bandages, and men in tattered uniforms carrying their wounded comrades. When night fell, the lights of campfires, fed by many of the 16,000 minutemen, rimmed the city.

Ticonderoga and Crown Point. The days slipped by. In May came news that the "Green Mountain Boys," a small colonial force from what is now Vermont, led by Ethan Allen, had seized the British forts at Ticonderoga and Crown Point on Lake Champlain. Most welcome of all was news that powder, shot, and cannons from the captured forts were on their way to Boston.

The Second Continental Congress. Delegates to the First Continental Congress had agreed the previous year to assemble again if the British government did not meet their demands. On May 10, 1775, then, the delegates to a Second Continental Congress met. The site once again was Philadelphia.

▲ Some of these delegates, among them Samuel Adams of Massachusetts and Patrick Henry of Virginia, were **radical** in their outlook and called for extreme action. They were ready to declare independence, seize British officials, and ask France and Spain for help.

Most delegates were more **conservative**, urging more moderate action. Led by John Dickinson of Pennsylvania, they assured the king that they had "not raised armies with ambitious designs of separating from Great Britain." They made it clear, however, that they would resist tyranny with force if necessary. To

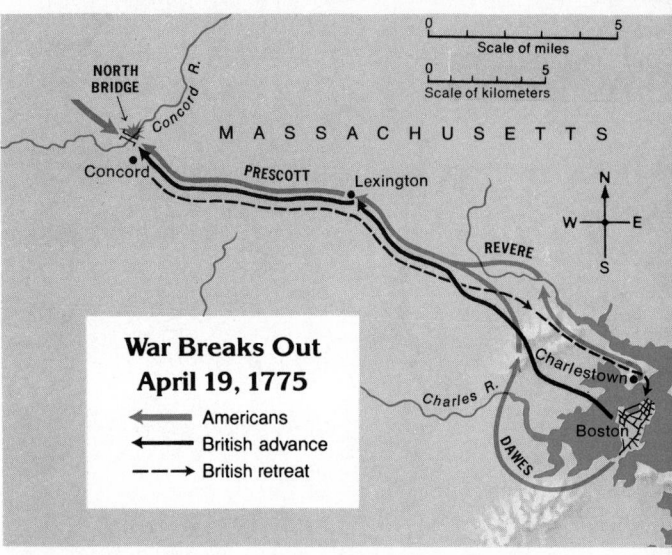

War Breaks Out April 19, 1775
⬅ Americans
← British advance
- - -→ British retreat

show that they meant business, they appointed George Washington of Virginia as commander in chief of the Continental Army.

The Battle of Breed's (Bunker) Hill. Before Washington arrived to take command of the minutemen in the Boston area, blood had again been shed. General Gage, the British commander, ordered a frontal attack on the armed New Englanders at Charlestown, overlooking Boston harbor. On June 17, 1775, in three bold assaults, the British redcoats attacked the Americans on Breed's Hill, mistakenly called Bunker Hill (see map, page 126). Both sides lost heavily. Finally, the Patriots, their ammunition exhausted, retreated with a loss of almost 450 men. However, the British left more than 1,000 men killed or wounded upon the battlefield.

Shocked at news of this disaster, George III proclaimed the colonists rebels. He ordered the Royal Navy to begin a tight naval blockade to close off all shipping to the colonies. He also hired 10,000 soldiers from the German state of

PATRICK HENRY'S SPEECH BEFORE THE VIRGINIA CONVENTION (1775)

Gentlemen may cry peace, peace. But there is no peace. The war is actually begun! The next gale that sweeps from the north will bring to our ears the clash of resounding arms! Our brethren are already in the field! Why stand we here idle? What is it that gentlemen wish? What would they have? Is life so dear, or peace so sweet, as to be purchased at the price of chains and slavery? Forbid it, Almighty God! I know not what course others may take; but as for me, give me liberty or give me death!

▲ Three of the new delegates to the Second Continental Congress were Benjamin Franklin, John Hancock, and Thomas Jefferson.

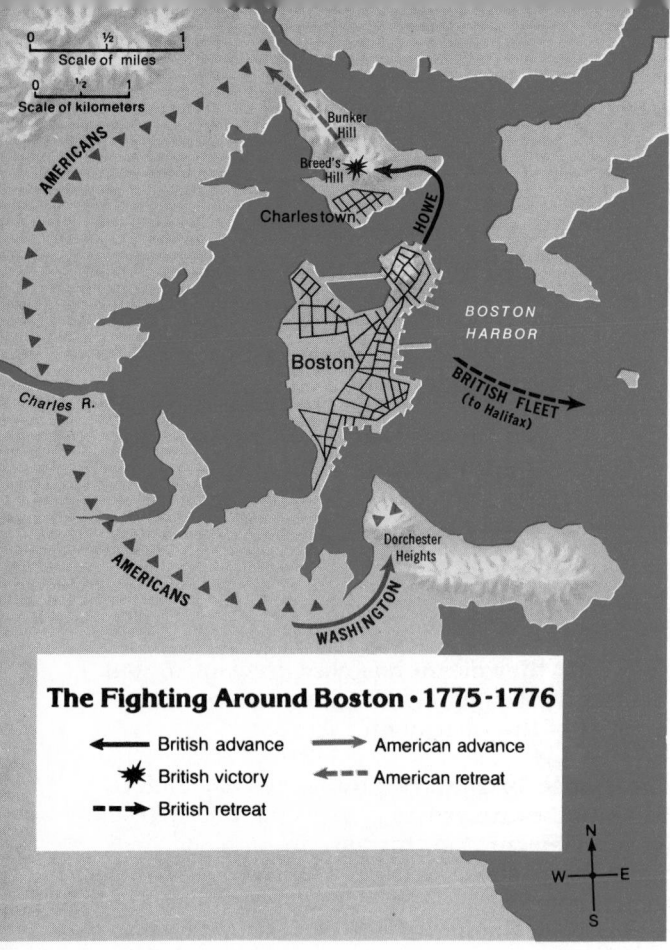

The Fighting Around Boston • 1775-1776

← British advance   → American advance
✹ British victory   ◄--- American retreat
--► British retreat

Moore's Creek Bridge. Meanwhile the Battle of Moore's Creek Bridge was fought in North Carolina. Sometimes called the "Lexington and Concord of the South," the battle ended in a decisive victory for the Patriot cause.

During 1775 Governor Martin of North Carolina had recruited nearly 2,000 Loyalists, mostly Scottish Highlanders who had come to North Carolina since 1770. These Loyalist troops were to march on Wilmington and Brunswick. There the Loyalists were to be joined by regiments of British troops and by a powerful British fleet. Operating from these bases, this combined Loyalist and British force would then control the colony.

The Patriots were fully aware of the plan. James Moore, a Patriot leader, stationed about 1,100 Patriots at Moore's Creek Bridge. The troops ripped up the planking from the bridge and greased the log supports with soap and tallow. Then they hid and waited.

The sun was just rising on February 27, 1776, when the Loyalists reached the bridge, exhausted from marching all night. Attempting to cross on the slippery logs, they were met by withering fire from the opposite bank. In a short but fierce fight, the Patriots, with only one killed and one wounded, won the battle. They took 850 prisoners, many weapons and wagons, and a large supply of gold.

When the British forces arrived in May, they found no Loyalist troops waiting to welcome them, and they sailed away. The Battle of Moore's Creek Bridge had shattered the British plan to hold North Carolina loyal to Great Britain.

Hesse, called Hessians (HESH·unz), to help fight and subdue the Americans.

British evacuation of Boston. To strengthen the colonial position, the Second Continental Congress sent diplomatic agents to request aid from France, Spain, and the Netherlands. Late in 1775 the Congress also sent a military expedition to Canada, hoping to encourage the French Canadians to rise against the British. However, the French Canadians did not show much sympathy, and the expedition failed.

In a surprise move one night early in 1776, Washington occupied Dorchester Heights, overlooking Boston and the British fleet anchored in the harbor (see map, this page). The British general, Sir William Howe, who had replaced General Gage as the commanding officer, decided that it was useless to try to hold Boston. The British fleet sailed out of the harbor on March 17, 1776. With the fleet went the entire garrison of British soldiers and about 1,000 civilian Loyalists.

SECTION REVIEW

See underscored items, text pp. 123, 125 - 26.
Identify: Paul Revere, minutemen, April 19, 1775, Ethan Allen, Hessians
For answers to questions, see Answer Key, p.A24.

1. **Summarizing Ideas:** By early 1775, what preparations had some colonists made to defend themselves from attack by the British?

2. **Analyzing Ideas:** How did General Gage's decision to "nip rebellion in the bud" lead to open war?

3. **Interpreting Ideas:** Explain why most delegates to the Second Continental Congress had a conservative, rather than a radical, view of colonial relations with Great Britain.

4. **Studying Maps:** Study the map on this page. Why were Breed's Hill and Dorchester Heights important to the British defense of Boston?

2 The colonists decide to fight for their independence

See Teaching Suggestions in TMRG, pp.TM40-41.

Until the spring of 1776, most colonists insisted they were merely resisting unjust acts of Parliament, not fighting a war.

Reasons for caution. A few Patriots, as you know, had already urged the colonists to declare their independence. Most colonists, however, were reluctant to make the final break. For one thing, the British government maintained law, order, and stability in the colonies. Some colonists feared that, without British control, they would become victims of mob rule and lawlessness. Local colonial leaders had seen mobs in action against tax collectors, British revenue officers, and Loyalists. They did not want to exchange the tyranny of Great Britain for the greater tyranny of colonial mobs.

The colonists hesitated to declare their independence for other reasons, too. First, if they revolted and failed to win, they could be executed for treason. Second, as long as the colonists were merely resisting specific acts of Parliament, they could count upon powerful support from friends in Great Britain. Such prominent Britishers as Edmund Burke, William Pitt, John Wilkes, and Isaac Barré (bah·RAY) had joined British merchants in demanding that Parliament repeal objectionable laws. However, the colonists knew that the moment they began to talk of separation from Great Britain, their British friends would turn against them and fight to preserve the British empire. Indeed many, perhaps most, men and women in the colonies remained loyal to the British empire at this time.

Reasons for independence. Two bitter facts offset these arguments against a break with Great Britain. First, the British government had committed acts that many colonists believed violated their rights as English subjects. Second, colonial blood had already been shed defending these rights.

In this explosive atmosphere, Thomas Paine's pamphlet *Common Sense* was like a spark dropped in a keg of gunpowder. Paine was a former British political writer who had come to America in 1774. His widely read pamphlet appeared in January 1776. ▲

"I offer nothing more than simple facts, plain arguments, and common sense," Paine wrote. In ringing words he pointed out that America had grown into a new and different nation with interests of its own. "The period of debate is closed. Arms, as the last resource, must decide the contest. . . . Everything that is right or reasonable pleads for separation. The blood of the slain, the weeping voice of nature cries, 'Tis Time to Part!'" Paine's stirring words helped to kindle the spirit of independence.

By declaring their independence, Paine pointed out, the colonists could gain practical advantages. First, as citizens of an indepen-

● Note: Answers to questions in captions appear in parentheses, as shown here. Bullets separate answers to individual questions when a caption contains more than one question.

In New York City, some people celebrated the Declaration of Independence by pulling down a statue of King George III. How might Loyalists have reacted to such a demonstration? (They might have considered the action as treasonous.) ●

dent nation, captured Patriot soldiers could demand to be treated as prisoners of war and avoid being shot as rebels. Second, the Patriot governments could seize the property of all Americans who remained loyal to the Crown. Third, the Patriots would have a better chance of winning foreign aid. France and Spain, for example, would probably favor and support a war that threatened to weaken the power of the British empire.

Independence declared.   Under the pressure of these arguments, colonial sentiment began to shift in favor of independence. On June 7, 1776, Richard Henry Lee of Virginia introduced a resolution in the Second Continental Congress declaring that "these United Colonies are, and of right ought to be, free and independent states." On June 11, before voting on Lee's resolution, the Congress appointed a committee of five to write a formal Declaration of Independence. These five were Thomas Jefferson, Benjamin Franklin, John Adams, Robert R. Livingston, and Roger Sherman. Jefferson was asked by the others on the committee to do the actual writing.

On June 28 the committee presented Jefferson's Declaration—with a few changes by Franklin and Adams—to the Congress. Congress did not at once discuss the Declaration itself. Instead, it debated Lee's resolution and, by adopting it on July 2, officially declared the new United States of America to be independent of Great Britain. Then the delegates turned to Jefferson's statement, which they continued to discuss on July 3.

Finally, after making some changes, Congress adopted the Declaration of Independence on July 4. In bold strokes John Hancock of Massachusetts, president of the Congress, signed the document. Then copies were rushed to the legislatures of the newly created states. On July 8, the Declaration was read and officially proclaimed in Philadelphia.

Reactions to the Declaration.   Many Americans, especially the Patriots (also known as Whigs), greeted the news of independence with wild rejoicing. Bells rang. People sang and danced around bonfires and held banquets to celebrate. The long period of indecision had finally ended.

Other Americans greeted the news with indifference. These people—and there were many in every colony—were not much concerned one way or the other.

A third group, the Loyalists (also known as Tories), refused to join in the celebrations. Some sat in silence behind closed doors and barricaded windows. For them the bonfires were omens of terror. They had seen violence during the past ten years. They knew what to expect—beatings, tar and feathers, burning houses, flights for safety to Canada or the British West Indies or England. These Tories, regarded by the Patriots as traitors in their own land, included many people of wealth and influence—merchants, lawyers, landowners, former officers of the king, church leaders.   ▲

The Declaration of Independence.   The document that declared the nation's independence has become one of history's most cherished statements. For 200 years its noble ideas and remarkable eloquence have inspired freedom-seeking people all over the world. Admiration for the Declaration, however, should not obscure the fact that it was a practical document with three major purposes.

(1) Preamble and reasons for separation.   In the first place, the Declaration was an attempt to win public support for independence. This appeal to people in Europe and America was contained in the preamble, or introduction, and in the 27 "reasons for separation" from Great Britain (see text, pages 130–133). The king was pictured as an evil ruler who intended to establish an absolute tyranny over the colonies. Each grievance pictured George III as a harsh tyrant. "He has forbidden . . . he has plundered . . . he has refused . . . he has constrained . . ." In contrast, the colonist were pictured as patient, submissive, long-suffering citizens. "We have petitioned . . . we have warned . . . we have reminded . . . we have appealed. . . ."

(2) A theory of government.   The second major purpose of the Declaration of Independence was to outline a theory of government. This inspiring theory explains why the Declaration remains today one of the most influential documents ever written.

In the opening lines of the second paragraph, Thomas Jefferson clearly and simply stated the basic principles of democracy. "All men are created equal," Jefferson wrote. ". . . They are endowed by their Creator with certain unalienable rights; . . . among these are

According to popular myth, the American Revolution was a unanimous mass movement. But in reality significant numbers of colonial Americans actually opposed independence and fought on the side of Great Britain. It is true that Loyalist strength was never sufficient to alter the outcome of the conflict. But historians now agree — based on the degree and extent of Loyalist participation — that the Revolution was a true civil war.

Loyalists probably comprised from one fifth to one third of the total colonial population. They lived in all the colonies, but they were especially numerous in New York, Georgia, and South Carolina. Although both Loyalists and Patriots came from all social classes, the Loyalists included disproportionate numbers of officeholders, professionals, wealthy landowners, and rich merchants. These persons were unwilling to sever their financially lucrative ties to Britain. Loyalism was also strong among Quakers and other pacifist groups.

Once the Revolution was underway, Patriots regarded Loyalists — in many cases their former neighbors — as traitors. Loyalists served the British as guerillas, spies, pilots, counterfeiters, and propagandists. George Washington despised the Loyalists, whom he accused of being "even higher and more insulting in their opposition than the regulars."

About 80,000 Loyalists fled persecution by going into permanent exile, leaving their property to be confiscated. About half of them went to Canada, where they founded the English-speaking provinces of New Brunswick and Ontario.

Some Loyalists managed to remain in the United States and live down their ties to Great Britain. Although a few enjoyed successful political careers, most of them were quickly forgotten — an ironic end for a group of people who had played such an important role in the *first* American civil war.

---

life, liberty, and the pursuit of happiness." **Unalienable rights** are rights that cannot be taken away from the people—not by any government, not even by the people themselves.

What is the purpose of government? Jefferson replied that governments exist "to secure these rights." Where do governments obtain this authority? They derive "their just powers from the consent of the governed." What happens when a government begins to act like a tyrant? "It is the right of the people to alter or to abolish it, and to institute new government."

The Declaration of Independence, in this passage, clearly stated the right of the American colonists to revolt against their British rulers. It stated this idea in terms familiar to many people in both Europe and America.

Thomas Jefferson was not expressing merely his own beliefs about government when he wrote the Declaration. His ideas came from two major sources. First, they came from scholars in Europe, among them <u>John Locke</u>, who during the 1600's and 1700's had been thinking about and developing new theories of government. Second, Jefferson's ideas came from the American colonists' practical experience in self-government.

The Declaration was an invitation to all peoples, in all times, to assume the right to rule themselves and to rid themselves forever of the tyranny of unwanted rulers.

(3) A formal declaration of war. The third major purpose of the Declaration, contained in the final paragraph, was to announce formally that war existed. If the Patriots failed to win independence, the leaders of the revolution could be judged guilty of treason against the British Crown and executed.

The delegates' pledge of "our lives, our fortunes, and our sacred honor" was not an idle oath. The delegates who signed the document must have done so with a deep sense of anxiety. They were pledging everything to the cause. Failure would mean ruin; it might mean death.

SECTION REVIEW
See underscored items, text pp. 127-29.

Identify: Thomas Paine, *Common Sense,* Richard Henry Lee, Thomas Jefferson, John Hancock, Whigs, Tories, unalienable rights, John Locke
For answers to questions, see Answer Key. pp.A24-25.

1. **Summarizing Ideas:** State the main arguments for and against the final break with Great Britain in 1776.

2. **Analyzing Ideas: (a)** Why were the colonists divided in their reaction to the Declaration of Independence? **(b)** What were the three major purposes of the Declaration of Independence? **(c)** Why can it be called a practical document?

3. **Interpreting Ideas:** Why was the theory of government presented in the Declaration significant?

This document explains to the world why Americans had the right to use force to change their government.

The Declaration of Independence

In Congress, July 4, 1776
The unanimous Declaration
of the thirteen united States
of America,

[PREAMBLE]

When in the Course of human events, it becomes necessary for one people to dissolve the political bands which have connected them with another, and to assume among the powers of the earth, the separate and equal station to which the Laws of Nature and of Nature's God entitle them, a decent respect to the opinions of mankind requires that they should declare the causes which impel them to the separation.

impel: force

[A NEW THEORY OF GOVERNMENT]

We hold these truths to be self-evident, that all men are created equal, that they are endowed by their Creator with certain unalienable Rights, that among these are Life, Liberty, and the pursuit of Happiness.

endowed: provided

That to secure these rights, Governments are instituted among Men, deriving their just powers from the consent of the governed,

People create governments to insure that their natural rights are protected. Governments are the servants of the people who establish them.

That whenever any Form of Government becomes destructive of these ends, it is the Right of the People to alter or to abolish it, and to institute new Government, laying its foundation on such principles and organizing its powers in such form, as to them shall seem most likely to effect their Safety and Happiness. Prudence, indeed, will dictate that Governments long established should not be changed for light and transient causes; and accordingly all experience hath shown, that mankind are more disposed to suffer, while evils are sufferable, than to right themselves by abolishing the forms to which they are accustomed. But when a long train of abuses and usurpations, pursuing invariably the same Object evinces a design to reduce them under absolute Despotism, it is their right, it is their duty, to throw off such Government, and to provide new Guards for their future security.

If a government does not serve its purpose, the people have a right to abolish it. Then the people have the right and duty to create a new government that will safeguard their security.

Despotism: unlimited power

[REASONS FOR SEPARATION]

Such has been the patient sufferance of these Colonies; and such is now the necessity which constrains them to alter their former Systems of Government. The history of the present King of Great Britain is a history of repeated injuries and usurpations, all having in direct object the establishment of an absolute Tyranny over these States. To prove this, let Facts be submitted to a candid world.

usurpations: unjust uses of power
Tyranny: absolute power
candid: impartial; fair

He has refused his Assent to Laws, the most wholesome and necessary for the public good.

He has forbidden his Governors to pass Laws of immediate and pressing importance, unless suspended in their operation till his Assent should be obtained; and when so suspended, he has utterly neglected to attend to them.

He has refused to pass other Laws for the accommodation of large districts of people, unless those people would relinquish the right of Representation in the Legislature, a right inestimable to them and formidable to tyrants only.

He has called together legislative bodies at places unusual, uncomfortable, and distant from the depository of their public Records, for the sole purpose of fatiguing them into compliance with his measures.

He has dissolved Representative Houses repeatedly, for opposing with manly firmness his invasions on the rights of the people.

He has refused for a long time, after such dissolutions, to cause others to be elected; whereby the Legislative powers, incapable of Annihilation, have returned to the People at large for their exercise; the State remaining in the mean time exposed to all the dangers of invasion from without, and convulsions within.

He has endeavored to prevent the population of these States; for that purpose obstructing the Laws for Naturalization of Foreigners; refusing to pass others to encourage their migrations hither, and raising the conditions of new Appropriations of Lands.

He has obstructed the Administration of Justice, by refusing his Assent to Laws for establishing Judiciary powers.

He has made Judges dependent on his Will alone, for the tenure of their offices, and the amount and payment of their salaries.

He has erected a multitude of New Offices, and sent hither swarms of Officers to harrass our people, and eat out their substance.

He has kept among us, in times of peace, Standing Armies without the Consent of our legislatures.

He has affected to render the Military independent of and superior to the Civil power.

He has combined with others to subject us to a jurisdiction foreign to our constitution, and unacknowledged by our laws; giving his Assent to their Acts of pretended Legislation:

For quartering large bodies of armed troops among us:

For protecting them, by a mock Trial, from punishment for any Murders which they should commit on the Inhabitants of these States:

For cutting off our Trade with all parts of the world:

For imposing Taxes on us without our Consent:

For depriving us in many cases, of the benefits of Trial by Jury:

For transporting us beyond Seas to be tried for pretended offences:

For abolishing the free System of English Laws in a neighboring Province, establishing therein an Arbitrary government, and enlarging its Boundaries so as to render it at once an example and fit instrument for introducing the same absolute rule into these Colonies:

For taking away our Charters, abolishing our most valuable Laws, and altering fundamentally the Forms of our Governments:

For suspending our own Legislatures, and declaring themselves invested with power to legislate for us in all cases whatsoever.

Twenty-six paragraphs list the supposed crimes of George III.

relinquish: give up
inestimable: priceless
formidable: causing dread

Annihilation: destruction

convulsions: violent disturbances

Naturalization of Foreigners: the process by which foreign-born persons become citizens

tenure: term

a multitude of: many

quartering: lodging

Arbitrary: not based on law
render: make

He has abdicated Government here, by declaring us out of his Protection and waging War against us.

He has plundered our seas, ravaged our Coasts, burnt our towns, and destroyed the Lives of our people.

He is at this time transporting large Armies of foreign Mercenaries to complete the works of death, desolation and tyranny, already begun with circumstances of Cruelty & perfidy scarcely paralleled in the most barbarous ages, and totally unworthy the Head of a civilized nation.

He has constrained our fellow Citizens taken Captive on the high Seas to bear Arms against their Country, to become the executioners of their friends and Brethren, or to fall themselves by their Hands.

He has excited domestic insurrections amongst us, and has endeavored to bring on the inhabitants of our frontiers, the merciless Indian Savages, whose known rule of warfare, is an undistinguished destruction of all ages, sexes and conditions.

In every stage of these Oppressions We have Petitioned for Redress in the most humble terms: Our repeated Petitions have been answered only by repeated injury. A Prince, whose character is thus marked by every act which may define a Tyrant, is unfit to be the ruler of a free people.

Nor have We been wanting in attentions to our British brethren. We have warned them from time to time of attempts by their legislature to extend an unwarrantable jurisdiction over us. We have reminded them of the circumstances of our emigration and settlement here. We have appealed to their native justice and magnanimity, and we have conjured them by the ties of our common kindred to disavow these usurpations, which, would inevitably interrupt our connections and correspondence. They too have been deaf to the voice of justice and of consanguinity. We must, therefore, acquiesce in the necessity, which denounces our Separation, and hold them, as we hold the rest of mankind, Enemies in War, in Peace Friends.

[A PROCLAMATION OF FREE, INDEPENDENT, AND UNITED STATES]

We, therefore, the Representatives of the united States of America, in General Congress, Assembled, appealing to the Supreme Judge of the world for the rectitude of our intentions, do, in the Name, and by Authority of the good People of these Colonies, solemnly publish and declare, That these United Colonies are, and of Right ought to be Free and Independent States; that they are Absolved from all Allegiance to the British Crown, and that all political connection between them and the State of Great Britain, is and ought to be totally dissolved; and that as Free and Independent States, they have full Power to levy War, conclude Peace, contract Alliances, establish Commerce, and to do all other Acts and Things which Independent States may of right do.

And for the support of this Declaration, with a firm reliance on the protection of divine Providence, we mutually pledge to each other our Lives, our Fortunes and our sacred Honor.

[SIGNERS OF THE DECLARATION]

JOHN HANCOCK
BUTTON GWINNETT
LYMAN HALL
GEORGE WALTON
WILLIAM HOOPER
JOSEPH HEWES
JOHN PENN
EDWARD RUTLEDGE
THOMAS HEYWARD, JR.
THOMAS LYNCH, JR.
ARTHUR MIDDLETON
SAMUEL CHASE
WILLIAM PACA
THOMAS STONE
CHARLES CARROLL
    OF CARROLLTON
GEORGE WYTHE
RICHARD HENRY LEE
THOMAS JEFFERSON
BENJAMIN HARRISON
THOMAS NELSON, JR.
FRANCIS LIGHTFOOT LEE
CARTER BRAXTON
ROBERT MORRIS
BENJAMIN RUSH
BENJAMIN FRANKLIN
JOHN MORTON
GEORGE CLYMER
JAMES SMITH

GEORGE TAYLOR
JAMES WILSON
GEORGE ROSS
CAESAR RODNEY
GEORGE READ
THOMAS McKEAN
WILLIAM FLOYD
PHILIP LIVINGSTON
FRANCIS LEWIS
LEWIS MORRIS
RICHARD STOCKTON
JOHN WITHERSPOON
FRANCIS HOPKINSON
JOHN HART
ABRAHAM CLARK
JOSIAH BARTLETT
WILLIAM WHIPPLE
SAMUEL ADAMS
JOHN ADAMS
ROBERT TREAT PAINE
ELBRIDGE GERRY
STEPHEN HOPKINS
WILLIAM ELLERY
ROGER SHERMAN
SAMUEL HUNTINGTON
WILLIAM WILLIAMS
OLIVER WOLCOTT
MATTHEW THORNTON

The drafting committee of the Declaration of Independence presents the document to the Second Continental Congress. From left to right are John Adams, Roger Sherman, Robert Livingston, Thomas Jefferson, and Benjamin Franklin. What did the Declaration of Independence tell the world?

(It explained the colonists' grievances against Great Britain and set forth the principles of equality, liberty, and democracy.)

3 British plans for an early victory end in disaster

See Teaching Suggestions in TMRG, p.TM41.

In the spring of 1776, while the colonists were debating independence, General Washington moved the Continental Army from Boston to New York. Washington was sure that the British would try to seize New York City and use it as a base of operations for their land and naval forces. By July Washington had nearly 30,000 troops guarding the city.

Fighting around New York City. On July 2, the same day that the Second Continental Congress voted to declare independence, General Sir William Howe sailed into New York harbor and landed British and Hessian troops on Staten Island (see map, page 135). A few days later Howe's brother, Admiral Lord Richard Howe, arrived with powerful naval reinforcements. By the end of August, British forces in the New York area exceeded 30,000, more than 8,000 of them Hessian soldiers.

Late in August General Howe landed about 20,000 troops on Long Island, where General Washington had stationed the bulk of the Continental Army. Howe's troops forced the Americans back to Brooklyn Heights.

The Americans were now caught in a trap. The British army was in front of them. The British fleet was behind them, ready to sail into the East River to cut off their only avenue of escape.

Fortunately for Washington, General Howe did not attack immediately. Under cover of fog and darkness, the Americans crossed the East River in small boats and reached the temporary safety of Manhattan Island.

With the British fleet controlling the water around Manhattan Island, Washington was unable to hold the city. After several sharp engagements, he withdrew northward to White Plains, leaving the British in command of New York City and its splendid harbor.

Retreat across New Jersey. By late October 1776, Washington's position was becoming desperate. Winter was approaching, and the Americans had suffered heavy losses in soldiers and supplies. The army was rapidly

The American General Hugh Mercer was killed in the Battle of Princeton in 1777. Ten years later the general's son, William Mercer, did this painting of the battle.

melting away as its members, faced with what seemed like certain defeat, picked up their guns and returned to their homes.

In this difficult situation, General Washington decided to retreat across New Jersey into Pennsylvania. Once in Pennsylvania, the Delaware River would separate him from the British. There he would gain time to regroup his battered forces.

During the retreat across New Jersey, soldiers continued to slip away from the army. By the time Washington reached the Delaware River, only about 3,000 troops remained. Weary and discouraged, the soldiers combed the river for small boats, which they then rowed across to the Pennsylvania side (see map, this page).

Trenton and Princeton. Confident that the war was almost won, General Howe prepared to celebrate the Christmas holidays in New York. To keep a close watch on the Americans, General Charles Cornwallis, commanding the British forces in the field, stationed 1,300 Hessians at Trenton and a second force nearby, farther south.

Howe's Christmas celebration, however, was rudely interrupted. Opening a brilliant military campaign, Washington and his troops crossed the ice-choked Delaware River on Christmas night. Early the next morning, they surprised the Hessians and took more than 1,000 prisoners.

British reinforcements under Cornwallis rushed to the Trenton area, arriving on January 2, 1777. General Cornwallis, certain that he had Washington's forces in a trap, prepared to attack in the morning. During the night the American troops slipped quietly away, leaving their campfires burning brightly to deceive the British into thinking that Washington's troops were still there.

Instead of retiring to the safety of the west bank of the Delaware River, Washington struck inland. His troops badly cut up three British regiments at Princeton, then withdrew swiftly to the hills around Morristown in northern New Jersey (see map, this page). From his camp near Morristown, Washington could raid the British lines of communication and supply to New Brunswick and Trenton. Since these cities were no longer of any particular value to the British, Howe pulled his troops out of New Jersey and back to New York.

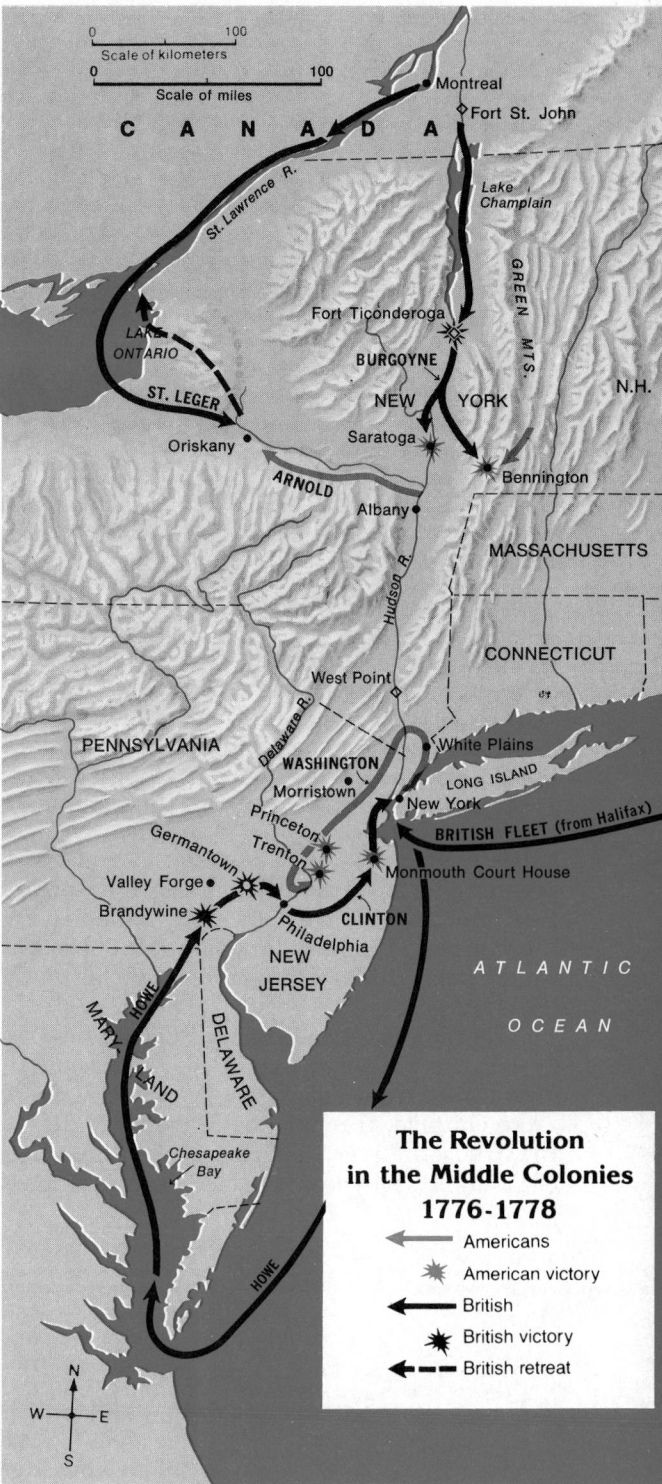

The Revolution in the Middle Colonies 1776-1778

→ Americans
✳ American victory
→ British
✳ British victory
◀--- British retreat

Washington's victories at Trenton and Princeton ruined British plans for ending the war in the winter of 1776–77. In contrast,

George Washington reviews his exhausted, nearly starving army at Valley Forge in the winter of 1777–78. The army had trouble getting supplies because few farmers or merchants would accept the Continental money.

American spirits began to revive. The Americans now believed they could win battles against British regulars. During the next few months, volunteers began to swell the ranks of the Continental Army. Washington had taken great chances, but he had won the gamble.

British disaster at Saratoga. Aroused to greater efforts by their defeats at Trenton and Princeton, the British now determined to end the war in 1777. They decided upon a plan that would separate New England from the rest of the states.

Lieutenant Colonel Barry St. Leger (SAYNT LEJ·er) was to lead an expedition, with some Indian allies, from Fort Oswego (os·WEE·goh) on Lake Ontario, through the Mohawk Valley to the Hudson River (see map, page 135). General John Burgoyne was to lead a second expedi-

tion from Canada down the Richelieu River–Lake Champlain route. General Howe was to lead a third expedition from New York up the Hudson River. These three forces were to meet at Albany and crush the American forces.

The plan looked beautifully simple to officials drawing lines on a map in the warmth and comfort of the London War Office. What they did not know, or ignored, was that these lines crossed lakes, swamps, mountains, and trackless forests swarming with militia ready to defend their homes, villages, and farms.

St. Leger reached the Mohawk Valley on schedule and laid siege to Fort Stanwix, where American forces were stationed. If the fort fell, St. Leger would have a clear road open before him to Albany. General Nicholas Herkimer of New York and a force of German-American militia tried to reach Fort Stanwix and rein-

=== SOURCES ===

THOMAS PAINE'S "THE CRISIS" (1776)

These are the times that try men's souls. The summer soldier and the sunshine patriot will, in this crisis, shrink from the service of their country; but he that stands by it now deserves the love and thanks of man and woman. Tyranny, like hell, is not easily conquered; yet we have this consolation with us, that the harder the conflict, the more glorious the triumph. What we obtain too cheap, we esteem too lightly; it is dearness only that gives everything its value. Heaven knows how to put a proper price upon its goods; and it would be strange indeed if so celestial an article as FREEDOM should not be highly rated. . . .

▲   Report Topic: The British rule of the colonies was (was not) tyrannical

force it, but a party of Tories and Indians ambushed them near the town of Oriskany (oh·RIS·kah·nee). The situation for the Americans in Fort Stanwix was desperate. Then suddenly word spread through St. Leger's forces that Benedict Arnold was approaching with a large American army. St. Leger's Indians deserted, and the British retreated to Canada.

Meanwhile, a second British force was moving southward from Canada down the difficult Richelieu River–Lake Champlain route. General Burgoyne, its leader, knew as little about the American wilderness as his superiors in London. He reached and occupied Fort Ticonderoga without serious opposition. Then his troubles began. Trying to obtain additional supplies, he sent a raiding party into what is now Vermont. There they were destroyed at Bennington by General John Stark and a force of New England militia.

Burgoyne's position was now difficult, if not impossible. His provisions were almost gone. His lines of supply were stretched to a dangerous length from Canada through the forests. The militia of New England and New York were swarming around him like angry bees.

At Bemis Heights, near Saratoga on the Hudson River, Burgoyne met the main body of the American forces in the area. Outnumbered by more than two to one and outmaneuvered by the American leaders—Philip Schuyler of New York, Horatio Gates of Virginia, Benjamin Lincoln of Massachusetts, Daniel Morgan of Virginia, and Benedict Arnold of Connecticut—Burgoyne surrendered his entire force of nearly 6,000 troops at Saratoga on October 17, 1777.

An unexplained blunder. Burgoyne might have been saved if the planned British expedition up the Hudson River had appeared in time, but it never did. Instead of marching northward from New York City, Howe embarked his troops and sailed southward. American scouts followed his progress down the coast. Much to their surprise, he passed the mouth of the Delaware River, sailed to the head of Chesapeake Bay, and disembarked. Then he marched to Philadelphia, overcoming the Patriots in the battles of Brandywine Creek on September 11 and Germantown on October 4 (see map, page 135). Once he was in Philadelphia, Howe settled down for the winter of 1777–78. Washington, meanwhile, went into winter quarters at Valley Forge.

Why Howe failed to carry through his part of the plan to split the colonies remains uncertain. Perhaps the British War Office neglected to send the orders in time. Perhaps Howe decided that Burgoyne could handle the situation without help. For whatever reason, Howe's failure contributed to the British disaster at Saratoga.

The British Parliament, sobered by the news of Burgoyne's defeat, offered to suspend the Coercive Acts and pardon the Patriots. Unfortunately for the British, their concessions came nearly two years too late.

SECTION REVIEW

See underscored items, text pp. 135 - 37.

Identify: Charles Cornwallis, Nicholas Herkimer, General Burgoyne, Benedict Arnold, Saratoga

For answers to questions, see Answer Key, p.A25.

1. **Interpreting Ideas:** Why was the capture of New York City an important part of British war plans?
2. **Analyzing Ideas:** Why were Washington's victories at Trenton and Princeton so important?
3. **Studying Maps:** Look at the map on page 135. **(a)** What routes did St. Leger, Burgoyne, and Howe plan to follow? **(b)** What would the result have been if the British plan had succeeded?

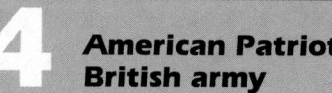

4 American Patriots defeat the British army

See Teaching Suggestions in TMRG, p.TM42.

Americans were joyous at the news of Burgoyne's defeat. The French, who sympathized with the American cause, celebrated as though they, too, had won a victory.

Aid from France. From the beginning France had been secretly providing the Americans with desperately needed arms and supplies. Benjamin Franklin, one of the American commissioners in France, began some shrewd bargaining that met with success.

On February 6, 1778, France and the United States of America signed two treaties. In the first, a commercial treaty, the two nations agreed to give each other favored treatment in matters of trade. In the other, a treaty of alliance, France agreed to recognize the independence of the United States and to wage war upon Great Britain until America was free. America promised to defend the French West Indies. Both countries promised not to make a separate peace with Great Britain.

The treaty with France came at a crucial time. Despite the victory at Saratoga, the Americans were in bad shape. Washington's army at Valley Forge was reduced to a poorly equipped, sick, hungry handful. The glad news that they now had a powerful ally filled the Patriots with new hope. Recruits began again to fill the thinned ranks of the army.

Help from abroad. France sent important aid to America in the form of gold, powder, shot, equipment, a fleet, and a considerable number of troops. Spain and the Netherlands, too, gave some support to the American cause. In addition, volunteers from a number of European countries came to America. From Prussia came Baron von Steuben, who took charge of organizing and drilling the Continental Army. From Poland came Casimir Pulaski (poo·LAS·kee) and Thaddeus Kosciusko (koz·ih·US·koh), who planned the American defenses of West Point on the Hudson River and Bemis Heights near Saratoga. From France came the German-born officer Baron de Kalb and the young Marquis de Lafayette (lah·fah·YET), who arrived in America with 12 other officers just before the Battle of Brandywine.

Changing British plans. French intervention forced the British to revise their plans for conquering their former colonies. As a first step, they replaced General Howe with Sir Henry Clinton.

Clinton had orders to strike the next blow at the southern colonies. Before doing this, however, he withdrew the British troops from Philadelphia and set out across New Jersey toward New York City. Washington pursued the British and overtook them at Monmouth Court House (see map, page 135). The battle was indecisive, with about 350 casualties on each side. After the battle the British continued their withdrawal to New York.

From then on, there were no major military activities in the North. At times, though, British raiding parties swept down on towns near New York City.

At Cowpens, Daniel Morgan used a mock retreat and this well-timed cavalry charge to destroy nearly a third of the British army in the South. Cornwallis called the defeat by the Americans a "very unexpected and severe blow."

Campaign in the Northwest. Meanwhile, Lieutenant Colonel George Rogers Clark of Virginia had been clearing the western lands of British troops. From Virginia, whose claim to this territory went back to the charter of 1609, Clark secured money and supplies for the expedition. With a small group of frontier fighters, he made his way down the Ohio River and up the Mississippi in the summer of 1778. He won Indian aid and surprised the British forts at Kaskaskia, Cahokia, and Vincennes (see map, this page). In December, however, Clark suffered a setback when the British recaptured Vincennes. In February 1779, in the dead of winter, Clark marched 170 miles (275 kilometers) eastward through the wilderness to overwhelm the British at Fort Vincennes. This bold blow cleared the entire western lands of British forces.

War in the South. In shifting the attack to the South, Great Britain hoped to profit from the aid of the Tories, who were reported to be especially numerous in the southern states.

As in the North, the British had no great trouble occupying seaports. In December 1778 they seized Savannah, Georgia. In May 1780 they forced General Benjamin Lincoln to surrender Charleston, South Carolina, and 5,000 troops. This was almost the entire American army south of the Potomac River. From these bases General Cornwallis, who now commanded the British armies in the southern states, was able to move where and when he pleased. British forces raided the countryside. They plundered and burned, trying to terrorize the Patriots and force them into submission.

But for every Tory who rallied to the British, a Patriot sprang up to oppose the British war effort. In South Carolina such southerners as Francis Marion (called "the Swamp Fox"), Andrew Pickens, and Thomas Sumter led guerrilla bands against the British forces. The **guerrillas** were hunters and farmers, not part of the regular army, who stung the British with sabotage and surprise raids. To aid these guerrilla bands, Congress sent a small army under the command of General Horatio Gates. Gates, however, was badly defeated at Camden, South Carolina, in August 1780 (see map, page 140).

The South seemed lost to the Patriot cause. Then in October 1780, a frontier militia led by Isaac Shelby, John Sevier, and others defeated a party of Tories at Kings Mountain, near the

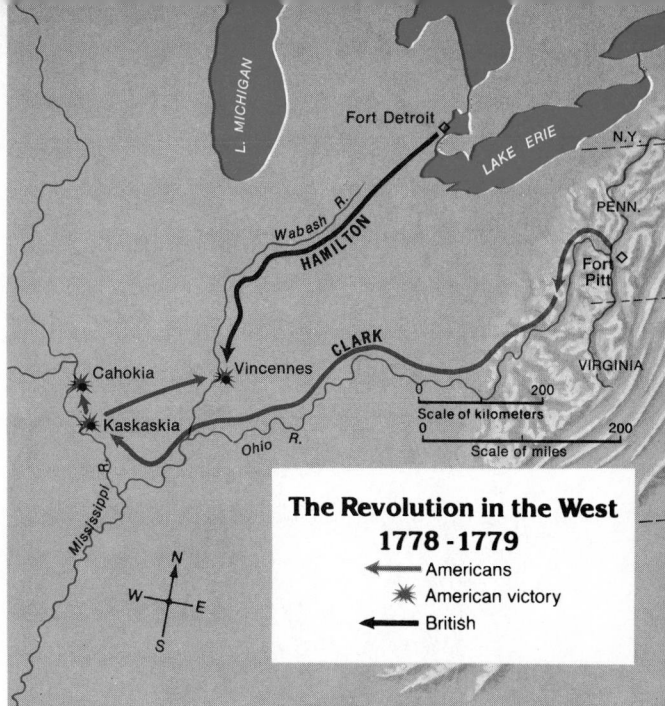

The Revolution in the West 1778-1779
→ Americans
✶ American victory
→ British

boundary between the Carolinas. At the same time, Nathanael Greene of Rhode Island replaced Gates as commander of the American forces in the South.

Although General Greene won no major battles, he and General Daniel Morgan of Virginia, supported by the guerrillas, made the British occupation of inland regions extremely costly. In January 1781 Morgan defeated a British force at Cowpens in South Carolina. Two months later, in March, the Americans struck a serious blow against Cornwallis's forces at Guilford Court House, North Carolina (see map, page 140). Although Cornwallis won, his losses were so great that he abandoned the entire campaign. He withdrew to the security of the coast, where the Royal Navy could support him. Thus, by 1781, the British were back where they had been in 1778, holding New York City and a few southern ports.

The British surrender. During the summer of 1781, the war proceeded swiftly to an end. Cornwallis moved northward into Virginia. There he based his army at Yorktown, on the peninsula between the York and James rivers (see map, page 140). He was supplied by the British fleet operating out of New York harbor. A small American army under Generals Lafayette, Von Steuben, and Anthony Wayne of Pennsylvania watched the British closely, but the American forces were too weak to attack.

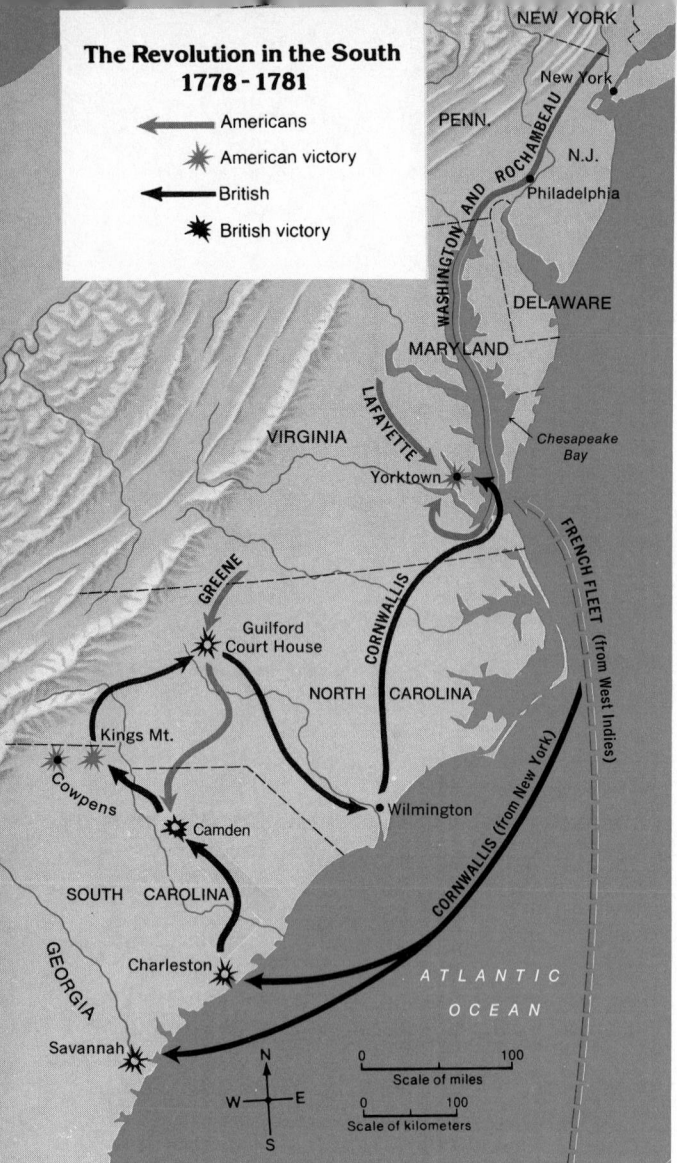

**The Revolution in the South
1778 - 1781**

⬅ Americans
✴ American victory
⬅ British
✴ British victory

NEW YORK

New York

PENN.

WASHINGTON AND ROCHAMBEAU

N.J.

Philadelphia

DELAWARE

MARYLAND

LAFAYETTE

VIRGINIA

Chesapeake Bay

Yorktown

GREENE

CORNWALLIS

Guilford Court House

NORTH CAROLINA

FRENCH FLEET (from West Indies)

Kings Mt.

Cowpens

Wilmington

Camden

CORNWALLIS (from New York)

SOUTH CAROLINA

GEORGIA

Charleston

ATLANTIC OCEAN

Savannah

N
W E
S

0   100
Scale of miles
0   100
Scale of kilometers

ing at New York, however, Washington and his army joined the French and American forces in front of <u>Yorktown</u> in Virginia (see map, this page).

Cornwallis was hopelessly trapped. Behind him was the French fleet. Before him was a greatly superior force of American troops, reinforced by 6,000 French troops. After a British squadron failed to break the French blockade, Cornwallis was ready to admit defeat. He surrendered his entire army of 7,000 soldiers on October 19, 1781. Although the formal treaty of peace was not signed until 1783, all serious fighting on the American continent ceased with the American victory at Yorktown.

SECTION REVIEW
See underscored items, text pp. 138 - 40.
Identify: Valley Forge, Casimir Pulaski, Marquis de Lafayette, Henry Clinton, Nathanael Greene, Yorktown
For answers to questions, see Answer Key, p.A25.
1. **Summarizing Ideas: (a)** List three ways in which the French aided the Americans in the Revolutionary War. **(b)** What did the French hope to gain by such aid? **(c)** Did any other European nations also support the Americans?

2. **Analyzing Ideas:** Why did the British campaign in the South fail?

3. **Interpreting Ideas:** Why was George Rogers Clark's campaign important to the Americans?

4. **Studying Maps:** Look at the map on page 140. How did the Patriots use geography in defeating the British at Yorktown?

---

5 Events off the battlefield lead to an Armerican victory

See Teaching Suggestions in TMRG, pp.TM42-43.

Both sides—the United States of America and Great Britain—faced serious problems during the eight long years of the war.

Shortage of troops and supplies. A relatively small number of colonists were willing to fight in the war. Many Americans were indifferent to the outcome of the conflict. A good number of these devoted their efforts to making the war as profitable for themselves as possible. Some merchants charged the American armies high prices for shoddy goods. Some farmers

Washington and a number of American and French soldiers remained at White Plains, New York. From there they kept an eye on the British under Clinton in New York City.

Then a messenger from Admiral de Grasse, commander of the French fleet in the West Indies, arrived at Washington's headquarters. De Grasse reported that the fleet could be spared for a few months. Where, he asked, could General Washington use it most effectively?

With skill and speed, Washington formed a brilliant plan. Following Washington's instructions, de Grasse placed his fleet across the mouth of Chesapeake Bay, cutting off Cornwallis from supplies and reinforcements. The American army in White Plains then moved toward New York, leading General Clinton to expect an attack upon the city. Instead of strik-

Victory in the final battle of the Revolutionary War was aided by the French fleet. The French fleet was in the right place at the right time because of the intelligence work of slave-turned-spy James Armistead.

In 1781 Lafayette was stationed near Richmond, Virginia. Cornwallis, the British commander, was quartered nearby in Portsmouth. James, a slave owned by Virginia planter Wiliam Armistead, sought and received permission to help Lafayette and the colonial army.

Lafayette had sent several spies into the British camp without success, but James Armistead was resourceful. Within a few months he was sending Lafayette reports on British troops, equipment, and future positions. The importance of the reports can be seen in the following statement written by Lafayette several years later. "This is to certify that the bearer by the name of James has done essential services to me while I had the honor to command in this State. Done under my hand, Richmond, November 21st, 1784. Lafayette."

In 1786 the Virginia legislature declared James Armistead a free man and awarded him an annual pension. When Lafayette visited the United States in 1824, he paid a special visit to the former slave who had helped in the fight for American independence.

---

sold their produce for the greatest profit, not caring whether it reached American or British hands. Because of this indifference and selfishness, Washington's troops starved and froze at Morristown in the winter of 1776–77 and at Valley Forge in the winter of 1777–78 while the British soldiers lived in comfort in New York and in Philadelphia.

Despite the shortage of troops, Washington at first ordered that no black soldiers, slave or free, could be recruited. Some colonial leaders feared that slaves would revolt if given arms. Some of Washington's officers believed that blacks did not make good soldiers.

Washington and other leaders changed their thinking late in 1775 when Lord Dunmore, royal governor of Virginia, offered freedom to all slaves who joined the British forces. Washington now consented to enlist free black men in the Continental armies. State militias, except in South Carolina and Georgia, enlisted slaves as well. Slaves were promised their freedom when the war ended. In most cases, however, the promise was not carried out despite the fact that black colonists had fought at Lexington, Concord, Ticonderoga, and Breed's Hill. At Breed's Hill, in fact, two black Americans, Peter Salem and Salem Poor, had been singled out for outstanding heroism.

Of some 300,000 Americans who fought in the war, about 5,000 were black. They served with courage and skill in the Continental navy and armies and in the navies and militias of the states. A French officer at Yorktown wrote: ". . . three quarters of the Rhode Island regiment consists of Negroes, and that regiment is the most neatly dressed, the best under arms, and the most precise in its maneuvers."

Weak central government. Troop shortages were not the only American problem. Another major weakness was the lack of an effective central government. The Second Continental Congress, which governed the country until 1781, had no real authority. It could only *ask* the states for troops, supplies, and money. If a state refused, the matter ended. Congress could and did borrow money from foreign coun-

141

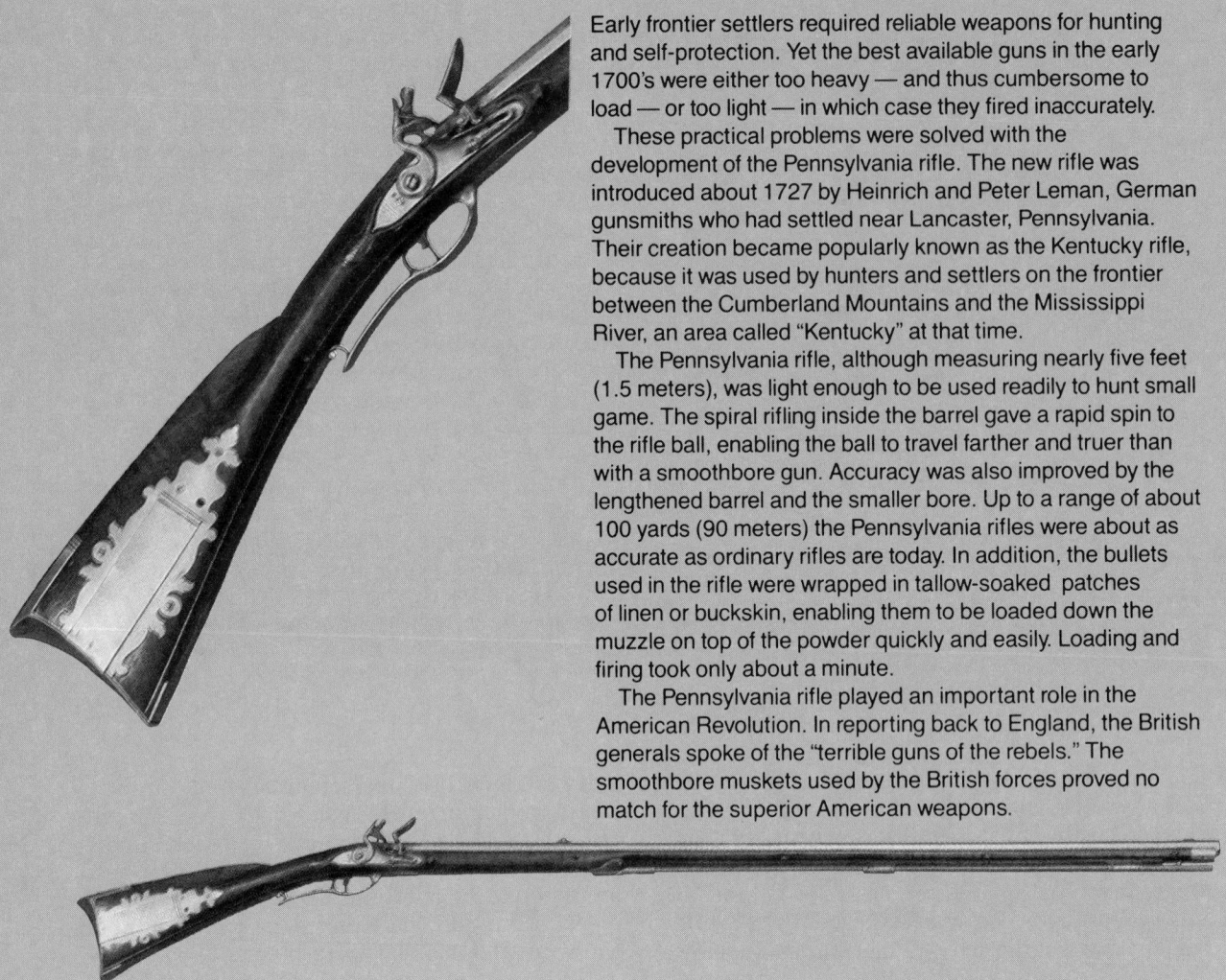

Early frontier settlers required reliable weapons for hunting and self-protection. Yet the best available guns in the early 1700's were either too heavy — and thus cumbersome to load — or too light — in which case they fired inaccurately.

These practical problems were solved with the development of the Pennsylvania rifle. The new rifle was introduced about 1727 by Heinrich and Peter Leman, German gunsmiths who had settled near Lancaster, Pennsylvania. Their creation became popularly known as the Kentucky rifle, because it was used by hunters and settlers on the frontier between the Cumberland Mountains and the Mississippi River, an area called "Kentucky" at that time.

The Pennsylvania rifle, although measuring nearly five feet (1.5 meters), was light enough to be used readily to hunt small game. The spiral rifling inside the barrel gave a rapid spin to the rifle ball, enabling the ball to travel farther and truer than with a smoothbore gun. Accuracy was also improved by the lengthened barrel and the smaller bore. Up to a range of about 100 yards (90 meters) the Pennsylvania rifles were about as accurate as ordinary rifles are today. In addition, the bullets used in the rifle were wrapped in tallow-soaked patches of linen or buckskin, enabling them to be loaded down the muzzle on top of the powder quickly and easily. Loading and firing took only about a minute.

The Pennsylvania rifle played an important role in the American Revolution. In reporting back to England, the British generals spoke of the "terrible guns of the rebels." The smoothbore muskets used by the British forces proved no match for the superior American weapons.

tries and from American citizens. However, it financed most of the war costs by issuing paper money known as "Continental currency."

These problems kept the American military effort weak and disorganized. Except for the first few weeks of the war, Washington never had more than 16,000 troops under his command at any one time. At no time was he sure how many of these he could rely on. After each victory volunteers poured in. After each defeat the army melted away. "What we need is a good army, not a large one," Washington once remarked bitterly, yet his faith and courage never faltered. It was this faith combined with the unselfish devotion of many soldiers and citizens that finally brought victory.

▲

Women in the Revolution. This faith and devotion was shared by many women Patriots. Even before 1776 women played an important part in boycotting British goods. In the struggle for independence, women found many ways to support the Revolution. Mercy Otis Warren published plays that satirized the British and Loyalists, and she started writing her *History of the American Revolution.* Many women col-

▲ Writing activity: Have students write an essay on the characteristics that Washington displayed as a military leader.

lected lead and helped manufacture bullets. Others made uniforms for the soldiers or collected and distributed medical and hospital supplies. Still others accompanied the troops, helping as cooks, doing laundry, and serving as nurses. A few performed dangerous missions as spies and messengers.

There are many legends about women who fought in the ranks, but it seems well established that Margaret Corbin and Molly Pitcher took the places of their wounded husbands. Deborah Sampson, a young Massachusetts girl, disguised herself in soldier's clothing and took part in several battles.

British problems. Fortunately for the Americans, the British, too, faced difficult problems during the Revolutionary War. One of these was the problem created by geography.

When the war started, the Americans occupied the enormous territory from Canada to Florida. The only British foothold was the seaport of Boston. To win the war, the Americans needed only to hold on to what they had. The British, on the other hand, had to regain control of this enormous territory. To regain control, they had to send troops and supplies across the Atlantic in slow sailing ships. Handicapped by the problem of supply, the British were never able to conquer and hold any sizable inland area.

British blunders. The British were also guilty of many blunders and much mismanagement. They made no great effort to concentrate an overwhelming force against the Americans.

Great Britain's major asset was its professional army. Well organized, well trained, well equipped, and well fed, the British regulars were more than a match for the Patriot troops on open, unforested land. But the British regulars were often used badly. Their superiors in England often revealed a hopeless ignorance of the land and the people of America.

One of Great Britain's major mistakes was its reliance upon the Hessian soldiers hired by George III. Many of these unfortunate Germans had been seized forcibly by their rulers, who received payment for them from George III and shipped them to America. Bewildered and homesick, they knew nothing about the war and cared less. As a result, they made poor soldiers.

The Loyalists, or Tories, who served under British colors, estimated at from 50,000 to

Disguised as a man, Deborah Sampson served well in the Continental army. She was wounded twice in battle. Dismissed upon discovery, she later received a soldier's pension.

60,000, fought bitterly and even savagely against their former neighbors, as is common in civil war. However, they too were untrained and unorganized. Often the presence of the Loyalist troops in the British ranks aroused the fighting spirit of the American Patriots opposing them.

Leaks in the blockade. The Royal Navy expected to sweep all enemy ships from the sea and by a tight blockade to cut off resources that the Americans needed to fight the war. However, America was a self-sufficient agricultural region, and the blockade was an inconvenience rather than a disaster for the Americans.

Then, too, the Americans did have a navy. During the war more than 50 ships were built and commissioned by the Continental Congress. They were commanded by such men as John Paul Jones.

Jones's most memorable victory — and perhaps the greatest naval victory of the war — took place in 1779. Jones's ship, the *Bon Homme Richard,* engaged the British ship *Serapis* in battle. With his own warship about to sink, Jones lashed the two ships together and in desperate fighting won the victory. At the height of this battle, when asked to surrender, Jones boldly declared, "I have not yet begun to fight."

143

The fledgling American navy scored some important victories against the powerful British fleet. The American also relied on state navies and privateers in their attempts to break the British blockade.

All the states except Delaware and New Jersey also built and manned their own naval vessels. Although these ships were small, the British had to spend much time in tracking them down and destroying them.

More difficult for the British to cope with were the American **privateers.** Privateers were privately owned ships whose owners were authorized by the Continental Congress or the state governments to attack enemy shipping. Slipping through the British blockade in fog or darkness, the privateers struck at naval vessels and defenseless British merchant ships. The money from the sale of captured ships and cargoes was divided among owners, captains, and crews. Since fortunes could quickly be made, this risky business attracted thousands of adventurous colonists.

Opposition to British naval policy. The British fleet interfered with the shipping of neutral nations. Angered by the interference, several nations formed the League of Armed Neutrality. Before the war ended, this league included Russia, Sweden, Denmark, Prussia, Portugal, Naples, and several other European states. In addition, France, Spain, and the Netherlands were openly at war with Great Britain. Throughout the later years of conflict, the warships of these European nations, combined with the American navy and privateers, put a drain upon Great Britain's resources.

British opposition to the war. As a result, the war became increasingly unpopular in Great Britain. In fact, many leaders in Great Britain opposed the war effort. The situation was so bad that some British politicians and officers rejoiced at the news of an American victory. Some officers actually refused to serve in America. British merchants, shipowners, and business people were losing heavily.

Great Britain could have continued to fight after Cornwallis's defeat at Yorktown in 1781. The British might have decided to concentrate overwhelming forces against the Americans. They might have finally worn the Americans down with a strict and long-continued blockade to the point where the Patriots would have asked for peace. But the price of continuing the war was heavier than most British people were willing to pay.

The peace treaty of 1783. Negotiations to end the war began soon after the surrender of Cornwallis in October 1781. The final treaty,

144 ▲ Discussion topic: Whether war justified the illegal actions of privateers

called the Treaty of Paris, was not completed until September 3, 1783.

The four American commissioners—Benjamin Franklin, John Jay, John Adams, and Henry Laurens—could hardly have won better terms. By the terms of the treaty, the Americans gained (1) independence, (2) all the land between the Appalachian Mountains and the Mississippi River from the Great Lakes south to Florida, and (3) the right to fish in the Gulf of St. Lawrence and off the coast of Newfoundland.

A very difficult problem arose when Great Britain demanded that all property and land taken from the Tories be returned to them and that all debts owed by Americans to Britishers be paid in full. Franklin and the other American commissioners insisted that this was impossible. The Tory property had been seized by the different states and had long since been sold. Large estates had been divided into many smaller pieces. The Continental Congress had no money for purchasing these properties and returning them to their former Tory owners.

Finally, after a long deadlock, the peace commissioners agreed to recommend that the new states allow persons with claims to use the American courts to recover their property.

The commissioners also agreed to recommend that private debts be handled in the same way. Actually, these recommendations were meaningless, since Congress could not force the states to open their courts to Tory claims. The British made the best of the situation and signed a preliminary treaty. Astonished at the liberal terms, the French foreign minister Vergennes declared, "The English do not make peace; they buy it."

The French were not represented in the peace talks until these decisions had been reached. They were angry as well as surprised that the United States and Great Britain had agreed upon peace terms. Franklin had to use all his arts of persuasion to smooth the ruffled feelings of the French leaders. His success in negotiating the final Treaty of Paris in 1783 proved his great skill as a diplomat.

The Americans were fortunate to be represented so ably. They were even more fortunate that the peace commissioners decided to negotiate directly with Great Britain. Spain wanted to confine the United States of America to the land between the Atlantic and the Appalachians. If the American commissioners had been forced to sit around a peace table with

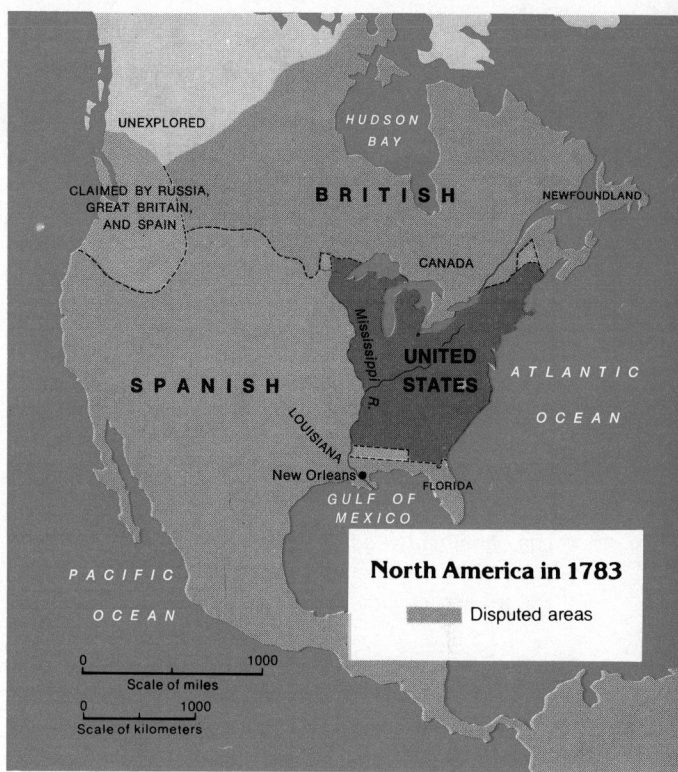

North America in 1783

Disputed areas

representatives from Spain, France, and Great Britain, the thirteen colonies would have won only their independence—nothing more. As it was, by making the most of Great Britain's desire for a quick end to the war, American peace commissioners won for their country a number of liberal concessions and a vast expanse of land west of the Appalachians.

SECTION REVIEW

See underscored items, text pp. 142 - 45.

Identify: Continental currency, John Paul Jones, privateers, League of Armed Neutrality, Treaty of Paris of 1783

For answers to questions, see Answer Key, pp. A25-26.

1. **Summarizing Ideas: (a)** What role did black soldiers play in America's struggle for independence? **(b)** What contributions did women make to the patriot cause?

2. **Organizing Ideas: (a)** Make a chart of the weaknesses and strengths of each side in the Revolution. **(b)** What was the most important strength and the most important weakness on each side? Explain.

3. **Studying Maps:** Look at the map on this page. **(a)** What nations had claims in North America in 1783? **(b)** What was the western boundary of the United States after the Treaty of Paris?

145

DEVELOPING HISTORY STUDY SKILLS

Thinking About History   Identifying Bias

Bias is a word that often conveys a negative impression because it is frequently equated with *prejudice,* an adverse leaning to something or someone that is based on ignorance or is without foundation in truth. In its simplest sense, however, *bias* is nothing more than the outlook that is present in the works of a speaker or writer. Thus to identify bias means to detect the trend or slant of a person's writing or speech. It means being aware of how words can convey negative and positive feelings and how illustrations and statistics can be used to bolster feelings in one direction or another. The following three sentences demonstrate the point.

- The general praised his troops.
- The courageous general praised his brave troops.
- The rebellious general stormed at his ragtag troops.

The first statement is a simple report of an action that shows neither favor nor disfavor. The second statement conveys a positive feeling with the words *courageous* and *brave.* In the third statement, *rebellious, stormed,* and *ragtag* call forth a critical feeling in a reader. Both the second and the third statement sway thinking by creating a feeling of emotion.

Besides words that produce a positive or negative tone, another way to pick out a person's bias is to examine the statistics and the illustrations that might be a part of the material being viewed. Statistics can be selected to bolster one viewpoint rather than another. Illustrations can be selected or devised to slant the reader's thinking in a certain direction.

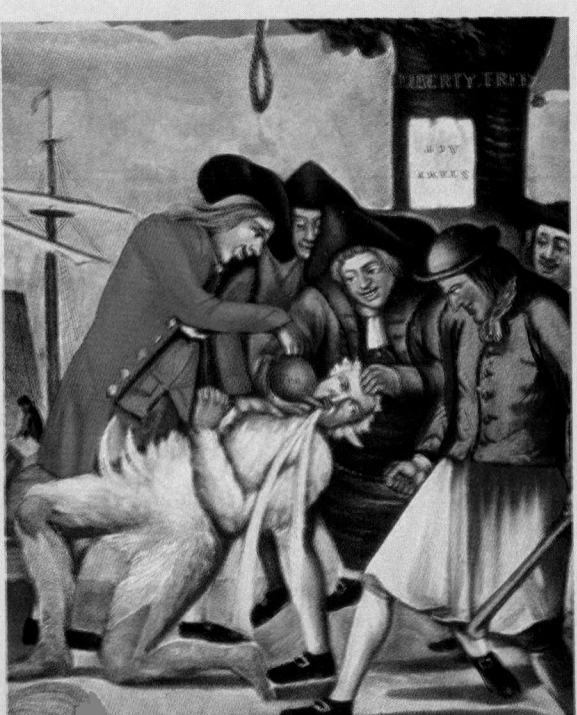

Being able to identify bias in writing and speeches and illustrations is an important skill, not just for the reader of history, but also for every reader of the daily newspaper and the weekly newsmagazine and for every television viewer and radio listener. Knowing a writer's or a speaker's purpose, knowing the writer's or speaker's viewpoint keeps you in control.

How to Identify Bias

Follow these guidelines to identify bias.

1. **Look for clues.** Check for words, phrases, statistics, or visual images that convey only one feeling or direction of thought.
2. **Assess the evidence.** Decide for yourself whether you agree or disagree with the bias on the basis of evidence presented.

Account A

At Lexington . . . a company of militia . . . mustered near the meeting house. The [British] troops came in sight of them just before sunrise; and running within a few rods of them, the Commanding Officer accosted the militia in words to this effect: "Disperse you <u>rebels</u>. . . . throw down your arms and disperse;" upon which the troops huzzaed [cheered], and immediately one or two officers discharged their pistols, which were instantaneously followed by the firing of four or five of the soldier'. . . . In Lexington, [the British] . . . <u>pillaged</u> almost every house they passed. . . . But the <u>savage barbarity</u> exercised upon the bodies of our unfortunate brethren that fell is almost incredible.

Applying the Skill

Account A (above) was written by an eyewitness at the Battle of Lexington. As you read the excerpt, see if you can tell the viewpoint from which the account was written. Note the underlined words. Decide whether *rebels, pillaged,* and *savage barbarity* convey a positive or negative tone. If you decided that the eyewitness favored the minutemen of Massachusetts you would be right because the underlined words are negative in tone toward the British.

Now study the cartoon at the left and the visual images that it contains. The colonials are pictured as mean and ugly. The tax collector, on the other hand, seems to be bravely standing up to the bully colonists. The cartoon is definitely pro-British and is intended to make the viewer feel that the colonial rebellion was the work of disrespectful rabble.

Practicing the Skill

1. Read Account B of the Battle of Lexington. On a separate sheet of paper, **(a)** list the words and phrases that indicated bias on the part of the writer and **(b)** explain what you think this bias is.
2. Study the painting of the Battle of Lexington, which is pictured below. **(a)** Which side do you think the painter favored? **(b)** What three visual elements indicate the painter's bias?
3. Write your own brief description of the Battle of Lexington. Aim for a well constructed, detailed paragraph that gives the facts without bias.

Account B

Six companies of [British] light infantry . . . at Lexington found a body of the country people under arms, on a green close to the road. And upon the King's troops marching up to them, in order to inquire the reason of their being so assembled, they [scattered] in great confusion. And several guns were fired upon the King's troops from behind a stone wall, and also from the meeting-house and other houses. . . . On the return of the troops from Concord, they [the rebels]. . . . began to fire upon them [the troops] from behind stone walls and houses. . . . And such was the barbarity and cruelty of the rebels that they scalped and cut off the ears of some of the wounded [troops]. . . .

The Battle of Lexington

From the day the first British settlers in the colonies started to adapt themselves to life in a strange environment, they began to grow away from their homeland. By 1763 the gap between Great Britain and the colonies had widened. British efforts to draw the colonies more firmly into the British empire and to get them to help pay for the cost of running the empire only antagonized the colonists. Protests and even violence against the British Crown slowly increased in the colonies. By early 1775 the situation had become exceedingly tense and uncertain.

The uncertainty ended in gunfire. With the bloodshed at Lexington and Concord on April 19, 1775, and later at Breed's Hill (Bunker Hill), hope of compromise vanished. In their Declaration of Independence, the American colonists broke their ties with Great Britain and proclaimed their message of freedom to the entire world. On the battlefields of Virginia and the surrounding area, aided by French troops and by French naval forces in the Atlantic, the Americans succeeded in wearing down the British. When Cornwallis surrendered his army at Yorktown, the colonists had, in effect, won the independence they had proclaimed earlier.

With the Treaty of Paris of 1783, the world recognized that a new nation had been born. The United States was the first nation in the modern world to break its colonial ties and to launch out as an independent country.

CONNECTING CHAPTER IDEAS

In the next chapter you will read about the problems the people of the new nation faced. The most important of these problems was how to organize an effective government around which Americans could rally with confidence and pride. The colonists move quickly to create new state governments and to establish a central government for the nation.

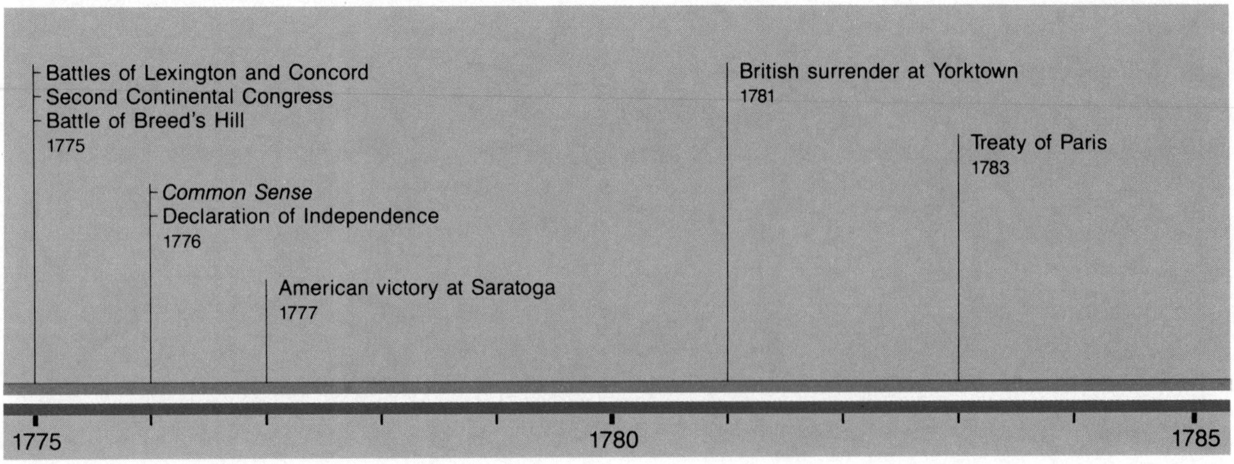

Battles of Lexington and Concord
Second Continental Congress
Battle of Breed's Hill
1775

British surrender at Yorktown
1781

Common Sense
Declaration of Independence
1776

Treaty of Paris
1783

American victory at Saratoga
1777

1775   1780   1785

CHAPTER

6 REVIEW

Reviewing Important Terms

Decide whether each of the following sentences is true or false. If the sentence is false, replace the underlined term with the word or phrase that will make it true.

1. At Lexington, British troops fired into a group of underlined minutemen who refused to drop their guns, killing 8 colonists.
2. Conservative members of the Second Continental Congress called for the immediate seizure of British officials.
3. John Dickinson led the radicals at the Second Continental Congress, urging moderate action in dealing with Great Britain.
4. The Whigs, also known as the Patriots, rejoiced at the news of the signing of the Declaration of Independence.
5. Life, liberty, and the pursuit of happiness are unalienable rights according to the Declaration of Independence.
6. Many Tories, fearing for their lives after independence was proclaimed in America, fled to Canada, the British West Indies, or Great Britain.
7. Privateers were privately owned ships used by the Americans to attack enemy shipping.

Practicing Critical Thinking Skills

1. **Making Inferences.** If, after 1763, Great Britain had maintained the same policy toward the colonies that it had followed before 1763, the Revolution might not have occurred. Comment.
2. **Analyzing Ideas.** British subjects in America fought not to obtain freedom but to confirm the freedoms they already had. Do you agree or disagree with this statement? Why?
3. **Analyzing Viewpoints.** Some British textbooks blame the American Revolution on a small group of radical agitators in America who were impatient with British leaders. (a) Do you agree or disagree with this interpretation? Explain. (b) Why do you think that British textbooks might present this interpretation of the Revolution?
4. **Evaluating Ideas.** (a) Why can the Battle of Saratoga be called the turning point of the Revolutionary War? (b) Why can it be called one of the turning points of world history?
5. **Analyzing Ideas.** Select one battle or campaign of the Revolutionary War. How did this battle or campaign illustrate the strengths and weaknesses of the Americans? the British? Use specific examples to support your answer.
6. **Evaluating Evidence.** Many historians believe that French aid was the key factor in the American victory in the Revolutionary War. Use historical evidence to support or refute this statement.
7. **Relating Past to Present.** In what ways was the American Revolution fought as wars are fought today? In what ways was the war fought differently?

Developing History Study Skills

Identifying Bias. Read the excerpt from Thomas Paine's "The Crisis" (page 136) and the Declaration of Independence (pages 130–133). Then on a separate sheet of paper, answer these questions. (a) Would you describe the writings of Thomas Paine as biased? Why or why not? (b) How is the Declaration of Independence an example of bias? Quote specific words and phrases to support your answer.

Relating Geography and History

During the Revolutionary War, more than 2,000 ships were commissioned as privateers. In 1777, marine insurance rates in London increased over 20 percent. This rate increase is an indication that the privateers were having an effect on British shipping. Rhode Island was instrumental in persuading the Continental Congress to finance a fleet of about 50 ships—the beginnings of the United States Navy. To understand how naval power helped the colonies, reread "Leaks in the blockade," pages 143–44, and answer the following questions.

1. (a) At what kinds of activity were the colonial privateers successful? (b) Who participated in privateering and why?
2. How was Rhode Island's location an important factor in the colony's particular interest in naval defense?
3. (a) In addition to the navy financed by the Continental Congress, how were other official naval vessels provided? (b) Which segment of colonial marine power was more aggressive against the British—privateers or official naval vessels? Explain.

149

CHAPTER 7

Forming a Confederation

(1775–1787)

Cradle of Liberty

"The American war is over," one of America's colonial leaders declared in 1783, "but this is far from being the case with the American Revolution." The speaker was Dr. Benjamin Rush, a prominent Philadelphia doctor and one of the signers of the Declaration of Independence. Dr. Rush knew—as did Thomas Jefferson, Benjamin Franklin, Alexander Hamilton, and many other Americans—that it was easier to outline on paper a theory of republican government than it was to build a republic that really worked.

Many problems faced the newly independent American people. One of the most serious problems was the question of unity. In 1754 the colonies had rejected the Albany Plan of Union, fearing they would lose control of their own affairs. Then, shortly after independence had been declared in 1776, the 13 colonies had formed state governments. The 13 states, for seven years had joined together in rebellion against British rule. Now that the crisis was over the question was whether the 13 states would remain united. Many observers were unsure of the answer to that question. One of the observers—David Ramsay of South Carolina—declared, "A long time, and much prudence, will be necessary to reproduce a spirit of union and . . . reverence for government."

As it turned out, the American people developed a "spirit of union" and "reverence for government" in an amazingly short time. The states had many wise leaders, who emphasized the bonds that Americans had in common rather than the differences that separated them. In 1781, all 13 states agreed to a long-term union by signing the Articles of Confederation. Nonetheless, during the early years of the Confederation the future of the union indeed looked dark. Agreeing to enter a union and acting in a unified manner became more difficult than many observers had predicted.

READING FOCUS

As you read about the creation of the league of confederation, look for the details that support each of the following statements.

1. The former colonies create new state governments
2. The states unite under the Articles of Confederation
3. The Confederation lacks the power to solve important problems.

1 The former colonies create new state governments

See Teaching Suggestions in TMRG, pp. TM44-46.

In 1775, even before the start of actual fighting, the long-established governments of the colonies began to crumble. The members of the Second Continental Congress were alarmed at this situation because they had no power to act as a government for the colonies. Thus, on May 10, 1775, the Second Continental Congress adopted a resolution urging the colonies to organize new governments.

From old governments to new. The legislatures of New Hampshire and South Carolina, both controlled by Patriots, had already written new state constitutions. During the next few months, all the colonies except Connecticut, Rhode Island, and Massachusetts adopted new state constitutions.

Connecticut and Rhode Island had always been self-governing colonies. They continued to use their colonial charters as state constitutions until well into the 1800's. In most states the legislatures prepared the constitutions without consulting the people themselves.

This method of organizing the new governments did not suit Massachusetts and New Hampshire. Both these states held constitutional conventions at which specially elected delegates drafted the constitutions. When the delegates finished their work, the voters themselves then had the chance to accept or reject the proposed constitutions.

Governments under law. The ideas in the Declaration of Independence helped shape the new state constitutions. The new state constitutions began with a bill of rights. These bills of rights contained guarantees of religious freedom, the right to free speech and a free press, the right to assemble, the right to a fair trial by jury, and equality of all citizens before the law. Under these written state constitutions, the new American states were adopting "government of laws, and not of men."

To establish a government of laws, the constitutions provided for a **separation of powers** in which the many powers of government were divided among the executive, legislative, and judicial branches. The constitution of Massa-

151

Abigail Adams, the wife of President John Adams and the mother of President John Quincy Adams, was an early champion of women's rights.

Born Abigail Smith, the daughter of a wealthy Congregationalist minister, she received no formal education. Smith, however, read many of her father's books. She also learned much from the many interesting visitors who came to the parsonage.

One of the those visitors was a young lawyer named John Adams. In 1764, five years after their first meeting, John and Abigail were married.

Abigail had confidence in her husband's abilities and supported him throughout his political career. Between 1774 and 1783, while John attended the Continental Congresses in Philadelphia and was a member of the peace mission in Paris, Abigail raised their four children and ran the family farm. During their years of separation, Abigail and John Adams wrote to each other regularly. Their correspondence shows that Abigail was quite knowledgeable about politics, and that John took his wife's counsel seriously. In fact, some of President Adams's critics claimed that Abigail Adams made many of John Adams' political decisions.

Abigail Adams' knowledge and influence are shown in the collections of letters that she wrote to her husband, to her sister, and to her son. Many of her letters also show her concern for women's rights.

chusetts provided that "in the government of this commonwealth, the legislative department shall never exercise the executive and judicial powers or either of them: the executive shall never exercise the legislative and judicial powers or either of them: the judicial shall never exercise the legislative and executive powers or either of them: to the end it may be a government of laws, and not of men." Although other state constitutions did not provide as clear a separation of powers as that of Massachusetts, all the states did limit the power of the executive department.

Separating church and state. The states also strengthened the principle of separation of church and government. When the Revolutionary War broke out, people in nine of the thirteen colonies were required by law to pay taxes to support an established church. The people had to pay these taxes even if they belonged to another church or to no church at all. By 1787, however, official churches had been abolished in all but three states—New Hampshire, Massachusetts, and Connecticut. In time, these three states also abolished their official churches.

Concern over slavery. The contradiction between the principles of the Declaration of Independence and slavery also troubled many Americans. Preachers, educators, lawyers, and public figures condemned slavery. In 1773 Patrick Henry said that slavery was "as repugnant to humanity as it is inconsistent with the Bible and destructive of liberty." Many slaveowners freed their slaves. Some did so because they were moved by the contradictions between slavery and the ideals of the Revolution. Other owners freed their slaves because the found slavery an expensive and inefficient system of labor.

Americans are free to worship as they wish. Here, early Americans attend religious services in Williamsburg, Virginia.

Thomas Jefferson was well aware that slavery contradicted the ideals set forth in the Declaration of Independence. In his writings he deplored the effects that slavery had of making slaveowners arrogant and of robbing slaves of human dignity.

Like most Americans of the time, however, Jefferson was not certain about what the exact role of blacks in American life should be. Jefferson did not want the full **abolition,** or ending, of slavery. He feared that white people and black people could not live peacefully side by side, especially in the southern states, where slaves were so numerous. Jefferson also accepted the false, but common, thinking of his time that black people lacked the capacity for self-government. He suggested, but did not advocate, the idea that slaves might be freed and established in the western lands.

Some of the new state governments were moved to action by the clash between slavery and the ideals of the war they were fighting. The Continental Congress and several states for a time prohibited the importation of slaves. During the war many of the states enlisted slaves in their armed forces and granted them their freedom. Several states adopted laws providing for the gradual freeing of slaves and the eventual abolition of slavery. In Massachusetts the Superior Court ruled that every slave within the state's borders had been freed by its constitution of 1780, which declared that "all men are born free and equal."

Antislavery sentiment stemming from the Revolutionary War also led to the formation of **abolition societies,** or groups working to end slavery. The first such society was founded by Philadelphia Quakers in 1775. By 1792 active

SOURCES

VIRGINIA STATUTE FOR RELIGIOUS FREEDOM (1786)

Well aware that Almighty God has created the mind free; that all attempts to influence it by temporal punishments . . . tend only to . . . [produce] habits of hypocrisy and meanness; . . . that to compel a man to furnish contributions of money for the propagation of opinions which he disbelieves is sinful and tyrannical; . . . that truth is great and will prevail if left to herself . . .

Be it enacted by the General Assembly that no man shall be compelled to frequent or support any religious worship . . . whatsoever; . . . all men shall be free to profess . . . their opinion in matters of religion; . . . the same shall in no wise diminish, enlarge, or affect their civil capacities. . . .

Although American women worked hard to help build the nation, they were granted few rights until the early twentieth century.

The democratic forces set in motion by the Revolutionary War did little at the time to advance the role of women. They were not permitted to vote. Married women were limited in the control of their property and in important decisions about their children. Such restrictions troubled Abigail Adams, who was successfully managing the farm and business affairs of her husband, John Adams. In a letter she urged that he and other members of the Continental Congress "remember the ladies and be more generous to them than your ancestors. Do not put such unlimited power in the hands of husbands. Remember all men would be tyrants if they could. If particular care and attention is not paid to the ladies, we are determined to foment rebellion, and will not be bound by any laws in which we have no voice or representation." Her advice was not heeded, however.

Because of these restrictions on the freedom of many Americans, the ideals set forth in the Declaration of Independence were only partially realized in the 1780's. Nevertheless, the men and women who fought the Revolutionary War had taken a long step toward the democratic way of life, and in 1783 they were about to take other steps. This is what Dr. Benjamin Rush had in mind when he wrote, "The American war is over, but this is far from being the case with the American Revolution."

abolition societies existed in all the states from Massachusetts southward to Virginia.

Moving toward democracy. During the Revolutionary War, then, Americans continued to strengthen the roots of democracy that had already been planted during the colonial period. For example, the gulf between the very rich and the ordinary narrowed somewhat due to the sale of confiscated Loyalist land. Much of this land was sold by the states to finance the military struggle, and a good deal of it sooner or later found its way into the hands of small landowners. However, the democratic way of life did not emerge full blown from the Revolutionary War. Economic differences still separated the well-to-do from the ordinary citizens. In spite of rising anti-slavery feeling, slavery still existed in much of the country. The right to vote continued to be limited by religious and property qualifications.

SECTION REVIEW
See underscored items, text pp. 151, 153.
Identify: separation of powers, abolition
For answers to questions, see Answer Key, p.A27.
1. **Analyzing Ideas:** Why was it necessary for the individual colonies to organize new governments during the Revolutionary War?

2. **Interpreting Ideas:** Why did the new state constitutions provide for **(a)** a bill of rights, **(b)** separation of powers, **(c)** separation of church and state?

3. **Organizing Ideas:** **(a)** What effects did the American Revolution have on the position of slaves in American society? **(b)** on the position of women? **(c)** What evidence is there that the contradictions between the ideals of the Declaration and the actual conditions of blacks and women troubled some people?

4. **Studying Sources:** According to the Source on page 153, what happens when a state tries to force someone to follow a religion or support it financially?

The states unite under the Articles of Confederation

See Teaching Suggestions in TMRG, pp.TM45-46.

By the summer of 1776, the former British colonies had become 13 states. Each of these states was separate and independent.

The problem of unity. The delegates to the Continental Congress agreed that the thirteen states had to unite. But in what kind of union? What kind of government should they form?

Some delegates, Benjamin Franklin among them, wanted a strong central government, stronger than any of the state governments. Most delegates, however, objected to a strong central government. They pointed out that the states were fighting a war to win their independence. Why, then, should the states deliberately create an American government that might turn out to be as tyrannical as British rule had been?

A plan for Confederation. After long debate the Continental Congress agreed that some kind of unity was needed to fight the war. Congress then appointed a committee to propose a workable plan of union.

On July 12, 1776, the committee, headed by John Dickinson of Pennsylvania, presented a report to the Continental Congress bearing the title "Articles of Confederation and Perpetual Union." After debating these Articles for more than a year, the delegates finally, on November 15, 1777, voted to adopt the Articles of Confederation.

The Articles of Confederation created a **confederation,** or league, of free and independent states known as "The United States of America." The central government of the league was to consist of a Congress having from two to seven delegates from each state. Each state delegation was to have only one vote in the Congress.

This was only the first step in forming a union. Before the Articles of Confederation could become effective, each of the thirteen states had to **ratify,** or accept, the proposal.

Adoption of the Confederation. Not until 1781 did all the states agree to enter the Confederation. Maryland was the last.

During the discussion over the Confederation, the delegates from Maryland insisted that all the states with claims to land lying between the Appalachian Mountains and the Mississippi River (see map, page 107) had to surrender their claims to the Confederation.

The Maryland delegates felt that if all the states helped to free the western lands from the British, then all the states should share the fruits of victory. They also pointed out that when the war was over, the states owning this immense western territory would have an unfair advantage over their smaller neighbors.

Maryland's stand provoked heated debates. Finally, the states with claims to western lands agreed to surrender their claims, and in 1781 Maryland ratified the Articles of Confederation. Thus the new league of states came into existence.

Land—the first problem. Control of the land west of the Appalachian Mountains gave the Confederation its first real power and a heavy

SOURCES

ARTICLES OF CONFEDERATION (1781)

Article 1. The style of this confederacy shall be "The United States of America."

Article 2. Each state retains its sovereignty, freedom, and independence, and every power, jurisdiction, and right which is not by this confederation expressly delegated to the United States in Congress assembled.

Article 3. The said states hereby severally enter into a firm league of friendship with each other for their common defense, the security of their liberties, and their mutual and general welfare, binding themselves to assist each other against all force offered to or attacks made upon them or any of them on account of religion, sovereignty, trade, or any other pretense whatever. . . .

▲ Discussion topic: Whether Maryland was justified in delaying its ratification of the Articles

The Land Ordinance of 1785: Township Land Survey

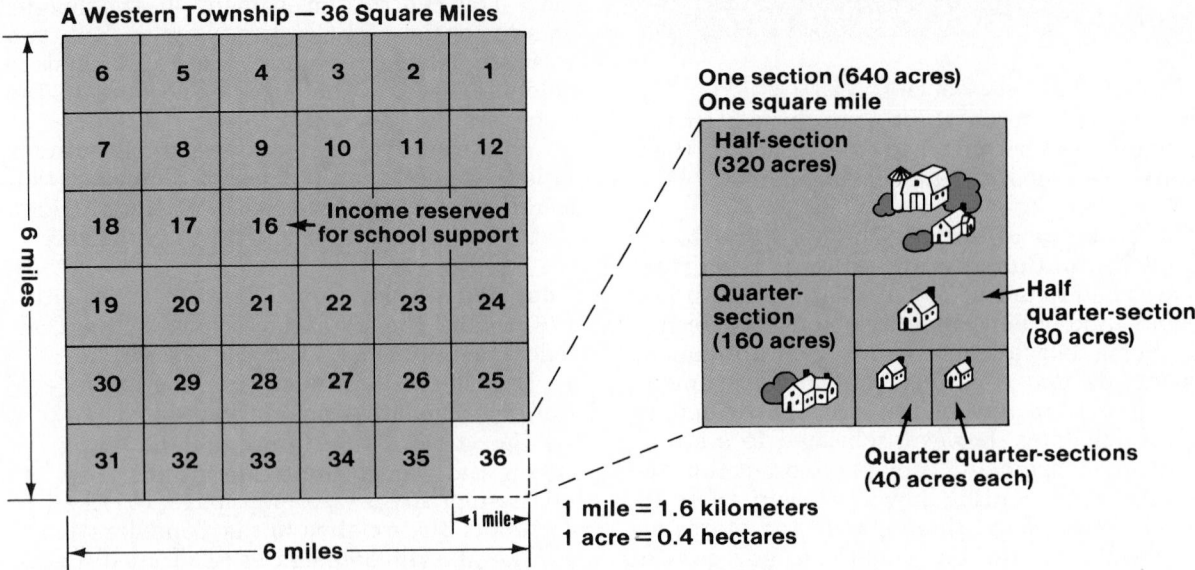

Viewed from an airplane, many parts of the United States show a neat pattern of farms and roads. This orderliness goes back to the township system of land survey first adopted in 1785. The income secured from the sale of Section 16 was to be used for school support. Four other sections in the township were reserved for government use.

responsibility. Now, in 1781, the Confederation faced many of the same problems that Great Britain and other colonial powers had faced when they first established colonies in the New World.

Settlers were already moving into the lands between the Appalachians and the Mississippi River. Nothing was more certain than that the tide of settlers would increase.

What, if anything, would be done about Indian claims to the lands on which they had lived long before Europeans arrived in America? How were the new lands to be distributed among those who "colonized" America's frontier? Who would profit from the sale of the land—a few land speculators or the settlers? Who would make laws for the towns and cities and states that would appear—the Confederation or the settlers?

Nature of the land problem. Great Britain had never developed a satisfactory land policy for the American colonies. As a result, the methods that new settlers used to secure land varied from colony to colony.

In colonial New England, a fairly orderly system had been worked out. There men and

women wishing to move west secured from the colonial assembly a grant of land that was carefully surveyed, or measured.

In other colonies, especially in Virginia, people moved to the frontier, selected whatever land appealed to them, and settled on it. This method of settlement led to frequent boundary disputes among settlers and conflict with the Indians.

The Land Ordinance of 1785. The government of the Confederation decided to work out a system by which settlers could get **titles,** or guarantees of ownership, to land beyond the Appalachian Mountains.

The Confederation's system of land settlement was written down in the Land Ordinance of 1785. It remained in effect with some changes until 1862, when it was replaced by the Homestead Act.

The Land Ordinance of 1785 provided for government survey of squares of land 6 miles long and 6 miles wide (9.7 kilometers by 9.7 kilometers), to be known as **townships.** Each township was further surveyed and divided into 36 smaller squares of 640 acres (259 hectares), or 1 square mile (2.6 square kilometers), to be known as **sections**. One section in every township, section number 16, was to be set aside for the support of public schools. Four other sections were reserved for the United States. The remaining 31 sections were to be sold by the government at a price of not less than one dollar an acre (0.4 hectare). (See chart, page 156.)

This plan had several advantages. Since settlements would be close together, they would be easier to defend if Indian conflicts arose. Also, disputes over boundaries and titles would be largely eliminated. Now government surveyors would determine the exact location of every section before settlers arrived. Finally, the sale of lands would provide the Confederation with desperately needed funds to meet current expenses and to pay off part of the Revolutionary War debt.

Government of new lands. After adopting a plan for western settlement, the Confederation turned to another problem. How should the western lands be governed?

If the Americans had followed the British example, they would have regarded the whole western area as a colony. But Americans could hardly forget their recent war. They had fought, in part, against the mercantile theory of trade, which put Great Britain's interests above the interests of the colonies. With this in mind, the Continental Congress had already adopted, in 1780, a resolution promising that new western states could come into the Confederation equal in all respects to the older states.

This decision had been hastened by other developments. Before the Revolutionary War, daring pioneers such as Daniel Boone had crossed the mountain passes and settled in what are now Kentucky and Tennessee (see map, page 107). This westward movement had been checked by the British in the Proclamation of 1763 and the Quebec Act of 1774. Both of these measures closed the western lands to settlers. Once the Revolution began, however, more and more people crossed the mountains to enter the forbidden land. For these people the problem of government had to be solved as quickly as possible.

▲ Land speculators also were eager for the Confederation to adopt a plan for governing the western lands. These speculators stood a better chance of selling the land if settlers knew that a program for orderly land development and self-government existed.

THE NORTHWEST ORDINANCE (1787)

Article 1. **No person . . . shall ever be molested on account of his mode of worship or religious sentiments. . . .**

Article 2. **The inhabitants of the said territory shall always be entitled to the benefits of the writ of habeas corpus and of the trial by jury. . . .**

Article 3. **Religion, morality, and knowledge being necessary to good government and the happiness of mankind, schools and the means of education shall forever be encouraged. The utmost good faith shall always be observed toward the Indians; their lands and property shall never be taken from them without their consent; and, in their property, rights, and liberty, they shall never be invaded or disturbed, unless in just and lawful wars authorized by Congress; but laws founded in justice and humanity shall from time to time be made for preventing wrongs being done to them, and for preserving peace and friendship with them. . . .**

Article 6. **There shall be neither slavery nor involuntary servitude in the said territory, otherwise than in punishment of crimes. . . .**

The Northwest Ordinance of 1787. In 1787 the Confederation partly fulfilled its earlier promise by passing the Northwest Ordinance. This ordinance provided for the governing of the Northwest Territory (see maps, pages 107 and 158).

In the beginning the Northwest Territory was to be ruled by a governor and three judges appointed by the Congress of the Confederation in Philadelphia. Later on, when the population included 5,000 free males of voting age, the settlers might elect a legislature to pass laws for themselves. They might also appoint a delegate to speak for them, but not to vote, in the Congress at Philadelphia. Still later, when the population of any part of the Northwest Territory reached 60,000 free inhabitants, the people could draft a constitution. Once this constitution had been approved by Congress, that part of the Northwest Territory would become a state. It would be equal in every respect to the older states. Not less than three

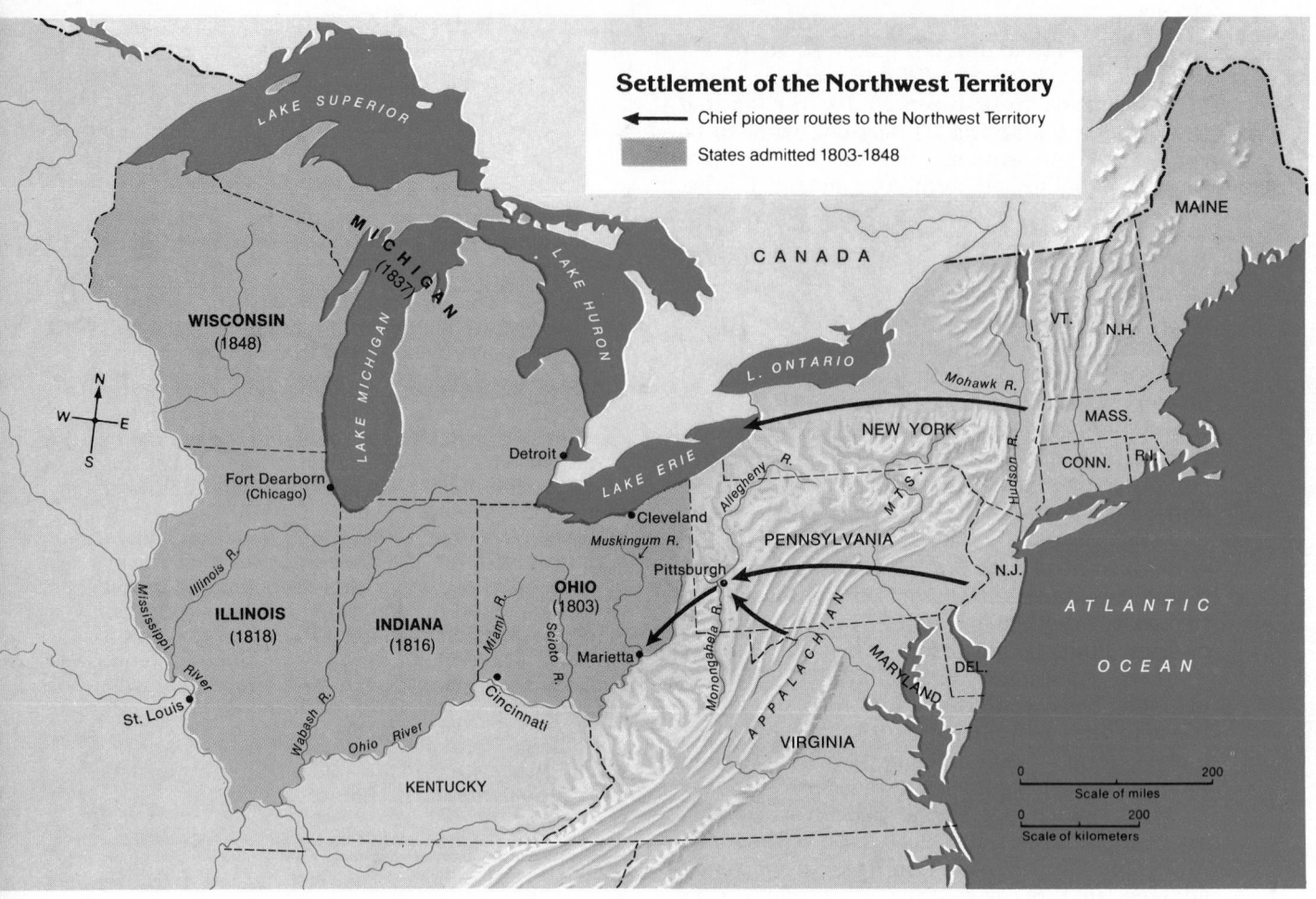

nor more than five states were to be carved out of the Northwest Territory.

Democratic achievements. Two other provisions in the Northwest Ordinance of 1787 encouraged the growth of democracy. One barred slavery from the Northwest Territory. A second encouraged public education.

The Confederation Congress believed that public education was necessary for the successful working of representative government. As a result, the Northwest Ordinance declared that "religion, morality, and knowledge being necessary to good government and the happiness of mankind, schools and the means of education shall forever be encouraged." This provision stimulated public support of schools and colleges in the territory.

The ordinance also promised that the Indians living in the territory would be treated with the "utmost good faith." This policy toward Indians was rarely followed.

Still, the overall policy developed in the ordinance was the most democratic colonial policy the modern world had known. It provided the machinery by which newer, less settled areas could eventually become equal members with parent communities. Under this general plan, almost all the new lands acquired by the United States were admitted to the Union—first as territories, later as states.

The inhabitants of the western territories sometimes had complaints against the national government. With one or two exceptions, however, no territory ever seriously considered leaving the Union, for the people knew that, sooner or later, they would be admitted as equal members. They also knew that as their population grew, their influence on government policy would become greater.

Identify: confederation, ratify, Land Ordinance of 1785, townships, sections, Northwest Ordinance of 1787

For answers to questions, see Answer Key, pp.A27-28.

1. **Summarizing Ideas: (a)** What issue delayed ratification of the Articles of Confederation? **(b)** How was this issue successfully resolved?

2. **Organizing Ideas:** How did the Land Ordinance of 1785 deal with the following problems: **(a)** property rights in the western lands, **(b)** security in the western lands, **(c)** American war debts?

3. **Interpreting Ideas: (a)** How did the Northwest Ordinance of 1787 provide for the admission of new states to the Confederation? **(b)** Explain two ways that the ordinance promoted democracy in the Northwest Territory.

4. **Studying Sources:** According to the Source on page 155 for what purpose did the states enter into a confederation?

5. **Studying Maps:** Look at the maps on pages 107 and 158. **(a)** What geographic feature that the original thirteen states share is missing from the Northwest Territory? **(b)** How might this difference have affected the rate of settlement of the Northwest Territory?

3 The Confederation lacks the power to solve important problems

See Teaching Suggestions in TMRG, pp. TM46-47.

The government created by the Articles of Confederation was able to solve some of the important problems facing the new nation. Other serious problems remained unsolved.

The problem of weakness. Many Americans insisted that the central government was too weak. On paper the Confederation appeared to have certain powers. It could regulate weights and measures. It could create post offices. It could borrow money and coin money. It could direct foreign affairs and declare war and make peace. It could build and equip a navy. It could ask the states to provide recruits and money for an army.

These powers looked sufficient on paper, but each state, jealous of its own rights, carefully guarded the use of these powers. The delegates who sat in Congress had no real authority. They were paid by the states and voted as their state legislatures directed them to vote. Each state delegation was entitled to only one vote in Congress. Rhode Island, smallest of the states, had as much influence in deciding national issues as the larger states of Virginia, New York, and Massachusetts.

No matter of importance could be settled without the consent of at least nine states. Any changes in the Articles themselves required the unanimous votes of the thirteen states. The Confederation also lacked an executive, such as a President, with power to enforce measures adopted by Congress. Finally, it had no central national court, like the Supreme Court, to protect the rights of citizens.

Lack of power to regulate finances. Money would have been a serious postwar problem even if the Articles of Confederation had created a stronger central government. As it was, the weakness of the Confederation made the money problem more difficult to solve.

To illustrate the problem, imagine a scene in a colonial store in 1783. A customer has just chosen some goods. As she counts out the money to pay the bill, she must sort through a pile of coins and paper money. There are French, Spanish, English, Dutch, German, and Portuguese coins. There are pennies coined in Vermont, Massachusetts, Connecticut, New Jersey, and Pennsylvania. There is paper money issued by the Continental Congress during the opening years of the Revolutionary War. There is also paper money issued by several of the states.

Some of the coins have been "clipped." That is, someone has stolen part of their value by scraping gold or silver from their edges. Some of the money may be counterfeit. The paper money is almost worthless—"not worth a Continental," many people grumble. Both the storekeeper and the customer would willingly exchange $1,000 worth of paper money issued by the Continental Congress for $1 worth of silver.

Obviously, only a government with power to regulate finances in all thirteen states could bring order out of such chaos. Nevertheless, the states, each fearful of losing some of its newly won authority, had not given this power to the Confederation. The Confederation could coin its own money, but it had no way of obtaining gold and silver to be coined. The Confederation had no power to force the states to contribute money for the support of the general

159

No sooner had independence been won than Yankee merchants began devising plans to break England's hold on the profitable China tea trade. A major American weapon in the trade war was the sailing ship, chief among which was the clipper.

The first clippers were small, speedy schooners built on Chesapeake Bay in the early 1800's. They were known as "Baltimore clippers." Larger ships were soon built, long and slim with radically streamlined hulls and massive sails.

The clipper's era of glory came in the first half of the 1800's. During those years clippers sailed the seven seas, outdistancing every other ship afloat. Their speed and beauty were legendary, and they made many Americans rich.

Historian Samuel Eliot Morison paid tribute to the clippers when he wrote, "Never, in these United States, has the brain of man conceived, or the hand of man fashioned, so perfect a thing as the clipper ship."

government. Less than one fourth of the money requested by Congress was ever raised.

No wonder the Confederation could not pay even the interest on the war debts. No wonder Europeans made bets as to how long the United States could survive.

Lack of power over trade. Europeans had other reasons for regarding the new nation with scorn. The colonists had rebelled against Great Britain partly because they wanted to regulate their own trade. Now, with independence won, each state proceeded to make trade regulations to benefit its own citizens. The resulting confusion led many Americans to think that perhaps the British had been right in insisting that only a central authority could best regulate trade.

Trade with foreign countries as well as trade between the states suffered from the Confederation's lack of power to impose any regulations. The trade advantages that colonial merchants had formerly enjoyed with the British West Indies and Great Britain were now denied to them. The British, regarding the Americans as a foreign people, no longer gave them bounties and favored treatment in British ports.

Manufacturers and the workers in manufacturing industries also suffered from the lack of controls over trade. During the Revolutionary War, when the British naval blockade made it difficult for Americans to import goods, Americans developed their own industries. As soon as the war ended, though, British merchants flooded American markets with cheaper British manufactured goods.

American manufacturers began to talk about a central government with power to levy import duties on manufactured goods from Great Britain and other countries. Such duties, added to the costs of imported goods, would make the prices of foreign goods and of American goods more nearly equal.

Lack of power to enforce treaties. To add to the confusion, the Confederation did not have the power to enforce its own treaties. When John Adams tried to negotiate a commercial treaty with Great Britain in 1785, the British only smiled. Of what value was a treaty, they politely asked Adams, when any one of the thirteen states could ignore it? No, the British said, under the American system of government, not one but thirteen treaties would be needed. ▲

The British were right, of course. American leaders like John Jay admitted that the peace treaty of 1783 was constantly being "violated ... by one or other of the states." Britishers found it impossible to collect the debts owed them by Americans. Tories found it impossible to secure compensation for the property seized from them during the Revolution.

Britishers grew increasingly angry at the failure of the Americans to pay the Tories. Using this failure as an excuse, the British refused to withdraw from the forts and trading posts in the Northwest Territory, as they had agreed to do in the Treaty of Paris in 1783.

Lack of military power. The refusal of the British to leave the western forts, which protected their fur trade, aroused the anger of the Americans living west of the Appalachians. The westerners wanted a display of military power, but the Confederation was unable to meet their demands.

Also as a result of its lack of military strength, the Confederation was powerless to solve the problems between the settlers and the Indians. The Indians continued to resist the advance of the settlers, who continued to cut down forests and farm the land on which the Indians depended for their livelihood.

To make matters worse, reckless Spanish and British officers in North America sometimes urged the Indians to attack western settlers. From their forts in the Northwest Territory, the British supplied the Indians with guns and ammunition. The Spaniards, who controlled Florida and Louisiana, including all of the land west of the Mississippi River, also supplied the Indians with weapons and encouraged their use against the settlers.

John Adams negotiated with the British to get them to give up their forts in the Northwest Territory. Meanwhile, other Americans tried to get the Spaniards to make concessions. Both efforts failed.

Americans also failed to get the Spaniards to give them the right to use the port of New Orleans (see map, page 162). This port was important to settlers living in the Ohio Valley and in the land east of the Mississippi River. These settlers had no roads over which they could carry their products across the mountains to the eastern markets and seaports. The only way they could sell their products was to float them down the Mississippi River to New Orleans. There they could load them on sea-

going vessels and ship them to the Atlantic ports or to Europe. Unfortunately for the western settlers, the Spaniards who controlled New Orleans refused to guarantee Americans the right to use this seaport. The American government was not strong enough to force Spain to grant this right.

The threat of civil war. Following the Revolution, the country went into an economic **depression** – a sharp decline in business activity and jobs.

The farmers of Massachusetts were especially hard hit. Before the Revolutionary War, much of their cash income had come from the sale of their farm produce and forest products to the British West Indies. After the break with Great Britain, this market was closed to them. Thus they found it increasingly difficult to get money to pay their taxes and the interest on their mortgages. To make matters worse, merchants and owners of businesses, mostly from Boston, controlled the Massachusetts legislature. This group passed new laws that shifted the burden of taxation onto the farmers. Among these taxes was a heavy tax on land.

During the summer of 1786, farmers gathered in hastily assembled meetings to demand relief, but the Massachusetts legislature refused to act. Farm after farm was lost to **foreclosure,** or seizure for nonpayment of taxes or interest on the mortgage. Finally, some Massachusetts farmers banded together and took matters into their own hands.

Shays' Rebellion. Led by Daniel Shays, the Massachusetts farmers demanded that the state legislature end the foreclosure of farms and give farmers a larger representation in the legislature. A group under Shays also tried unsuccessfully to seize the arsenal at Springfield in an effort to secure guns.

Frightened by this defiance of the law, citizens of Boston raised funds to equip a militia to put down Shays' Rebellion. The troops hunted Shays and his men through the snowy woods. They killed many and drove some across the state boundary into what is now Vermont. Some of the rebels were caught and put on trial. A few were hanged. Shays himself was later pardoned. His rebellion was thoroughly crushed.

Nevertheless, many Americans were deeply alarmed by Shays' Rebellion. These people

▲ After Shays' Rebellion had been suppressed, the Massachusetts legislature enacted many of the reforms sought by Shays' rebels.

161

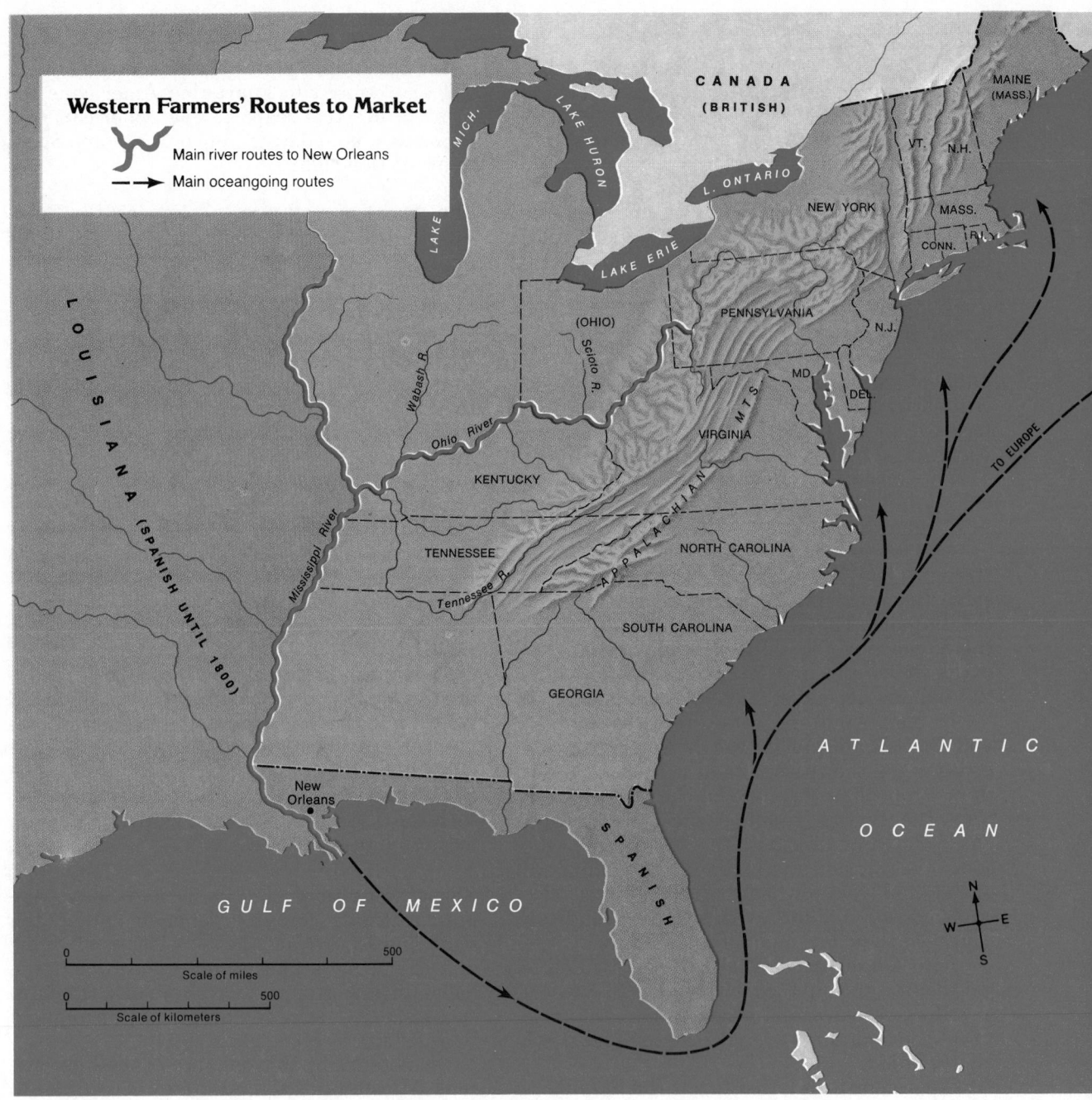

Western Farmers' Routes to Market

〰️ Main river routes to New Orleans

- - -► Main oceangoing routes

thought that the armed revolt would undermine law and order and might even destroy the new nation. George Washington said of the troubles, "Good God! who but a tory could have foreseen or a Briton predicted them!"

Signs of returning prosperity. Not all of the problems facing the country in the 1780's could be blamed on the weaknesses of the Articles of Confederation. Hard times would have followed the war even if the government had been stronger. After all, property had been destroyed by the war. Trade connections with Great Britain and other nations had been broken. Within the United States, commerce and business had been seriously disturbed.

▲ Report topics: The roles that one of the following played in Shays' Rebellion: George Washington, John Hancock, and Moses Sash (a black man)

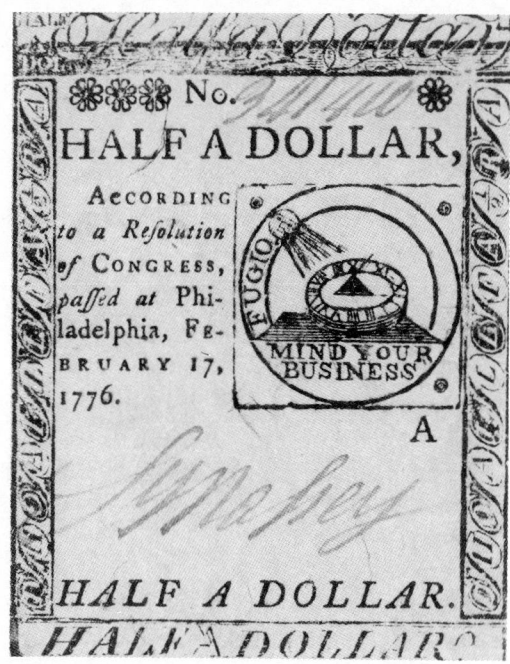

Bills like these "Continentals," issued by the Continental Congress in 1776, were still in circulation at the time the Articles of Confederation were in effect.

Even as early as 1785, only two years after the war ended, there were signs of better times ahead. By then American ships were once again busily trading with countries outside the British empire. Sailors, shipowners, merchants, farmers, and manufacturers were sharing in the profits of this growing trade. Many of the trade barriers between states were not enforced. As a result, American products continued to cross state lines in considerable quantities.

By 1785 some Americans were satisfied with the system of government under the Articles of Confederation. They were pleased with the signs of returning prosperity. They were satisfied with the wise policy that the Confederation was developing for the western lands.

A need for change. Despite these improvements, the central government still was too weak to solve many of the problems facing the new country. It was not strong enough to establish a sound financial system, to regulate trade, to enforce treaties, or to use military force when force was needed.

These government weaknesses disturbed groups of Americans—merchants and manufacturers, workers in the cities, and western-ers, who needed a strong central government to protect them from the Indians, the Spaniards, and the British.

A meeting to discuss the Articles of Confederation had been planned for Philadelphia in the spring of 1787. News of Shays' Rebellion spread rapidly and helped convince delegates to the meeting that major changes were needed in the Articles.

SECTION REVIEW

See underscored items, text p. 161.

Identify: depression, foreclosure

For answers to questions, see Answer Key, p.A28.

1. **Summarizing Ideas: (a)** What powers did the Articles of Confederation give to the central government? **(b)** What were three major weaknesses of the central government under the Articles of Confederation?

2. **Using Historical Imagination:** What would have been your chief problems in the 1780's if you had been **(a)** a merchant or **(b)** a farmer?

3. **Determining Cause and Effect: (a)** What were the causes of Shays' Rebellion? **(b)** Why did this rebellion alarm many Americans?

4. **Studying Maps:** Study the map on page 162. Why was it easier for farmers to send goods through New Orleans than directly east?

DEVELOPING HISTORY STUDY SKILLS

Relating Geography and History   Reviewing Map Basics

- What river forms the boundary between Georgia, and South Carolina?

- Approximately how far is New York from Boston?

- Is Kentucky or West Virginia farther south?

Such geographic questions can be answered by consulting maps. Certain questions relating to history can also be answered by consulting maps.

- Which were the original 13 colonies?

- Which states comprised the Northwest Territory?

- Which nation first claimed Florida?

A map is an illustration drawn to scale of all or a part of earth's surface. On a map, colors, shadings, lines, symbols, and labels are used to convey information. Reading and interpreting the information on maps means understanding the language and symbols of maps.

How to Read a Map

To effectively gather information from a map, follow these guidelines.

1. **Study the map's title.** The title may also give information about the time period reflected by the map.

2. **Study the map key, or legend.** The legend contains information that explains any special symbols used on the map. Then study the map to see what standard symbols are used. Standard symbols include dots and dashes for boundary lines, dots for cities, stars and stars within circles for capitals, and color. On the maps in this textbook, blue is always used for water areas and a blue line for rivers. Gray is used to show areas that are not an essential part of the map's subject matter. A political map uses color to distinguish one political unit from another.

3. **Note differences in the labels.** On maps in this textbook, labels printed in italic type designate natural features such as oceans, rivers, mountains, and lakes. Features placed on the earth by humans are shown on maps in.Roman, or regular type. Review the labels on the map on page 158. Note that cities are labeled in upper and lower case letters. States and countries are labeled in upper case letters. The size and weight of the type used usually indicates the importance of the label to the map's main topic.

4. **Check the map's directions.** Most maps in this textbook have a compass rose, or a direction indicator. For a map without a compass rose, it is always assumed that north is at the top.

5. **Study the distance scales.** Maps in this textbook have both a scale of miles and a scale of kilometers. The scale of miles for the map on page 158 of this textbook indicates that the space between two tick marks equals 100 miles. A scale is best used to determine the straight-line distance between two places.

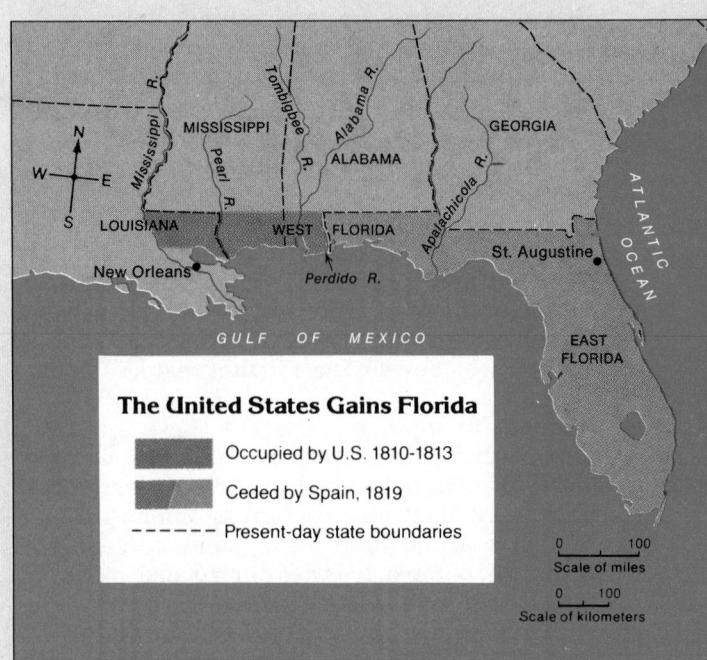

The United States Gains Florida

- Occupied by U.S. 1810-1813
- Ceded by Spain, 1819
- - - - - Present-day state boundaries

0   100
Scale of miles

0   100
Scale of kilometers

Applying Your Skills

Study the map on this page. Note the title. The subject is
the United States acquisition of Florida. Study the key.
The key tells you the time period reflected on the map. It
shows the special color that indicates when the United
States occupied the area in 1810–1813. It shows a second color to indicate the area that became the state of
Florida after the territory had been ceded by Spain in
1819.

Note the compass rose and the scale of miles. With the
aid of the compass rose and the scale of miles, you can
tell that New Orleans, Louisiana, lies slightly southwest
and about 500 miles (800 kilometers) from St. Augustine,
Florida.

Practicing Your Skills

Study the map on this page. It indicates the point around
which the population of the United States has been
equally distributed at different time periods in history.
Then on a separate sheet of paper, answer the following
questions.

1. What is the title of the map?

2. **(a)** How is center of population defined? **(b)** Where is
this definition found on the map?

3. What symbol is used to illustrate the subject of the
map?

4. What symbol is used to represent present-day state
boundaries?

5. How can you distinguish a natural feature from a
human-made feature?

6. **(a)** In what state was the center of United States population in 1790? **(b)** in 1850? **(c)** in 1980?

7. **(a)** What was the direction of movement up to 1840?
(b) between 1840 and 1860? **(c)** after 1900?

8. Approximately how far did the center of population
move between 1790 and 1980?

9. How is the geographical relationship between the
area of the map and the United States as a whole
illustrated?

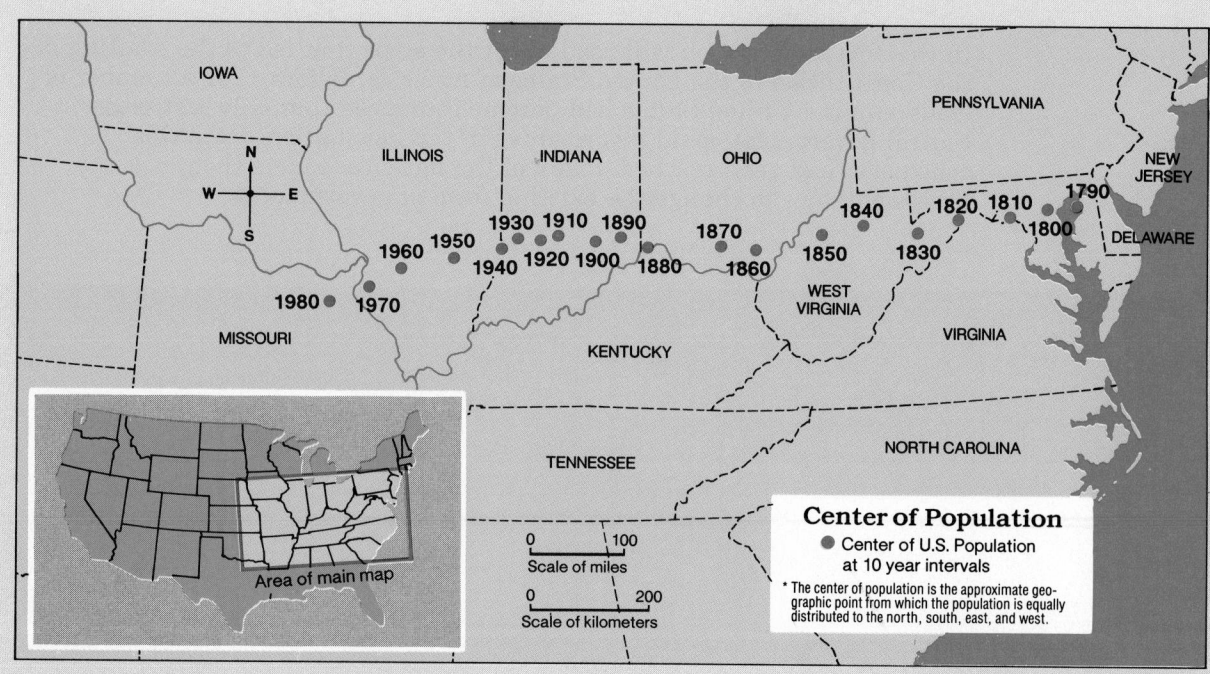

4. a broken line   5. natural features are in italic type and human-made features are in regular
type   6. (a) Maryland;   (b) West Virginia;   (c) Missouri   7. (a) west   (b) west   (c) southwest
8. 800 miles (1280 kilometers)   9. an inset

165

Early in 1775, more than a year before the colonists declared their independence, the old colonial governments began to crumble. British officials left the colonies. Tories, loyal to the British king and Parliament, fled to Canada, the British West Indies, and Great Britain. By 1776 the Americans faced the problem of creating new state governments and a new central government.

The state constitutions that Americans wrote during the Revolutionary War reflected the people's deep-seated desire for a voice in their own government. All of the new governments were based upon written constitutions. All of the new constitutions contained bills of rights guaranteeing freedom to every citizen.

During the Revolutionary War, Americans also tackled the problem of building a central government. In their first effort to govern themselves at the national level, the leaders of the 13 free states wrote the Articles of Confederation. This experiment with a league of more or less independent states was only partly successful.

There were two basic problems in creating a truly unified league of states. First, there was the problem of dividing powers between the states and the central government. The Confederation had given no solution to this problem. Second, the Confederation could not establish laws binding upon all the states and the people of the states.

CONNECTING CHAPTER IDEAS

In the next chapter you will read about the steps that led to the drafting of the Constitution of the United States of America. Before 1787 a number of leaders in the United States had become convinced that only a stronger central government could secure order in the new nation. Once this conclusion had been reached, many of the nation's leaders then took the necessary steps to change the existing form of government.

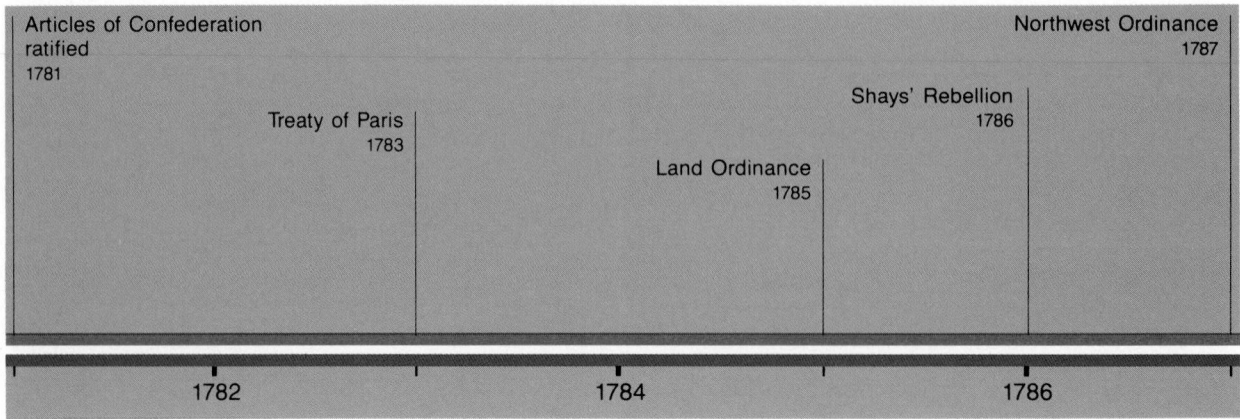

Articles of Confederation ratified 1781 — Treaty of Paris 1783 — Land Ordinance 1785 — Shays' Rebellion 1786 — Northwest Ordinance 1787

1782   1784   1786

Reviewing Important Terms

Decide whether each of the following sentences is true or false. If the sentence is false, replace the underlined term with the word or phrase that will make it true.

1. By dividing the powers of government among the executive, legislative, and judicial branches, the state constitutions provided for a separation of powers.
2. The first abolition society was founded by Philadelphia Quakers in 1775.
3. Each of the thirteen states had to abrogate the Articles of Confederation before they went into effect.
4. The Land Ordinance of 1785 set up a system by which settlers could get titles to land beyond the Appalachian Mountains.
5. Each township under the 1785 land ordinance was limited to 640 acres.
6. Each section under the Land Ordinance of 1785 was subdivided in 36 squares of 259 hectares.
7. The depression that followed the Revolution brought a sharp decline in business activity.
8. Massachusetts farmers rebelled in 1786 against foreclosure by banks on a number of mortgages.
9. The Articles of Confederation created a union of free and independent states known as "The United States of America."

Practicing Critical Thinking Skills

1. **Analyzing Ideas.** (a) During the Revolutionary War, in what ways did democracy increase in America? (b) Why do you think America became more democratic during this period? (c) What undemocratic practices still existed?
2. **Expressing Viewpoints.** Benjamin Rush, a signer of the Declaration of Independence from Pennsylvania, once said, "The American war is over, but this is far from being the case with the American Revolution." Explain what he meant.
3. **Contrasting Viewpoints.** What attitude was generally held toward the Articles of Confederation by (a) merchants, (b) artisans, (c) farmers, and (d) westerners?
4. **Interpreting Ideas.** Was the government under the Articles of Confederation a success or a failure? Use historical evidence to support your opinion.

5. **Summarizing Ideas.** Explain how the Northwest Ordinance of 1787 produced lasting benefits to the United States.
6. **Evaluating Ideas.** Do the arguments presented in 1785 against a strong central government apply today? Explain.
7. **Relating Past to Present.** Starting with the Articles of Confederation, American government has been faced with the problems of finding (a) a balance between the power of the states and the power of the central government and (b) a balance between liberty and authority. Explain each statement.

Developing History Study Skills

Reviewing Map Basics. Compare the map on page 107 with the map on page 158. Then on a separate sheet of paper, answer these questions. (a) What original states once had claims to Indiana? (b) to Michigan? (c) to Wisconsin? (d) What is the distance in miles between Pittsburgh, Pennsylvania, and Marietta, Ohio? (e) What direction from Marietta is Pittsburgh? (f) What is the meaning of the arrows on the map on page 158?

Relating Geography and History

The economic survival of the western farmers depended on their ability to ship their goods to eastern markets and Europe. Overland shipment to the Atlantic coast was impossible because there were no roads. In order to understand the problems faced by farmers in the West, study the maps on page 158 and 162. Use the information and the maps in this chapter to complete the following activities.

1. (a) In the absence of overland shipping routes, list the waterways that could be used by farmers in Illinois, Indiana, Michigan, and Ohio to ship their goods to eastern markets. (b) Where did these waterways lead?
2. In what ways did the Spaniards and the British create problems for the western farmers?
3. Write a paragraph explaining how problems in the western regions helped convince government planners that the country needed a stronger central government.

See Chapter Overview in TMRG, p.TM48.
See Chapter Objectives in TMRG, p.TM48.
See Introducing the Chapter in TMRG, p.TM48.

CHAPTER 8

Creating a Federal Union

(1787–1789)

The people celebrate

168

In the spring of 1787, a number of the most distinguished leaders in America traveled toward Philadelphia. The leaders came from all the states except Rhode Island. Some arrived on sailing vessels. Some came in carriages. Some rode in on horseback with their extra clothing packed in saddlebags. These leaders were official delegates to a meeting called the Constitutional Convention.

The Congress of the Confederation decided to hold this convention because of a meeting at Annapolis, Maryland, in 1786. The Annapolis meeting had been called to discuss uniform trade regulations for all of the states.

Only five states, however, were represented at Annapolis. The delegates decided that they could accomplish nothing with such a slim representation. Instead, they petitioned Congress to call another meeting of all the states. At this meeting delegates would not only discuss commercial problems, but they would also study the weaknesses of the Confederation. Congress, however, was slow to act on this proposal. Finally, it called the meeting for "the sole and express purpose of revising the Articles of Confederation."

The delegates to the Convention soon decided to do more than merely strengthen the Articles of Confederation through a revision. They decided to write a new Constitution. Between May and September of 1787, the delegates drafted a Constitution that remains the foundation of government in the United States. That Constitution has also become a model for representative government throughout the world.

═══ READING FOCUS ═══

As you read about the important work of forming a new government, look for the details that support each of the following statements.

1. A spirit of compromise prevails at the Constitutional Convention.
2. The states ratify the Constitution only after heated debate.
3. The Constitution establishes a workable form of government.
4. The Constitution separates and balances the powers of government.
5. The Constitution seeks to safeguard individual liberty.
6. The Constitution is a flexible, living document.

1 A spirit of compromise prevails at the Constitutional Convention

See Teaching Suggestions in TMRG, p.TM49.

On the morning of May 14, 1787, the date set for the start of the Constitutional Convention, only the delegations from Pennsylvania and Virginia appeared. By May 25, however, delegates from seven states—a majority—were present at Philadelphia's Independence Hall, and the most famous convention in American history began.

The delegates. The 55 delegates to the Constitutional Convention were a remarkable cross section of American leadership. Most of them had played active parts in forming their state governments. Many were learned in history and political philosophy. More than half had been members of the Second Continental Congress or the Congress of the Confederation. Eight had signed the Declaration of Independence. Nearly all had taken part in the American Revolution. Several had been diplomatic representatives from the United States to the governments of Europe. These men understood the problems their country faced.

Benjamin Franklin, now 81 years old, was the oldest member of the Convention. Deeply respected by the other delegates, Franklin often helped to calm rising tempers. Most of the delegates, however, were relatively young. George Washington, unanimously chosen presiding officer, and John Dickinson were among the older members at 55. James Madison of Virginia was 36, James Wilson of Pennsylvania was 45, and Alexander Hamilton of New York was only 32.

Several important leaders who had helped win the struggle for independence were not present at the Convention. Patrick Henry of Virginia refused to attend, saying that he "smelled a rat." He feared that the Convention would take away too much of the power that he believed should belong to the states. Samuel Adams of Massachusetts had not been chosen as a delegate. Thomas Jefferson, John Adams, and Thomas Paine were in Europe.

Meeting in secrecy. The Convention was held in secret. Guards stood watch at every

Edmund Randolph of Virginia (left) refused to sign the Constitution, although he later supported its adoption. Alexander Hamilton (right) was one of the most persuasive backers of a strong federal government.

door. Each delegate agreed not to discuss Convention business with outsiders.

Why all this secrecy? The delegates feared that news of what they were doing would plunge the country into argument. They also knew that it would be easier to iron out differences in a private conference room than in a public debate. They felt that they must first agree among themselves before presenting proposals to the public.

Official notes of the proceedings were kept, but they were not released until 1818. James Madison kept an unofficial record. He jotted down notes during the meetings and then labored far into the night writing them out with a quill pen. Madison's notes, which were far more complete than the official record, were kept secret until after his death in 1836.

Areas of agreement. The delegates to the Constitutional Convention represented different sections of the country with different interests. Yet from the beginning, they agreed on a number of important matters.

Most of the delegates agreed that the country needed a strong central government. They recognized that the new government would be respected only if it had the power to

tax, to raise an army, and to regulate commerce. They had learned this from their experience with the Articles of Confederation.

However, none of the delegates favored a government with unlimited power. They agreed that they must build a **republican form of government.** In such a government, the supreme power rests in the voters, who elect representative officials to run the government for them. The delegates also agreed that they wanted a government in which no single section of the country or group of people could dominate the rest.

There were many other issues on which the delegates did not agree. Sectional issues and economic problems divided them. If the delegates had refused to compromise, the writing of the Constitution would have been impossible. Fortunately for later generations, most of the delegates at Philadelphia arrived at compromises time and again.

The Great Compromise. One of the most serious conflicts of the Convention was a struggle between the large and small states over representation in Congress. Governor Edmund Randolph of Virginia, a large state, presented one plan. It provided that the population of

170

each state would determine the number of representatives that it could send to Congress. William Paterson of New Jersey, speaking for the small states, proposed that each state would have equal representation in Congress. Paterson firmly opposed Randolph's Virginia Plan. "New Jersey will never confederate on the plan before the committee," he declared. "She would be swallowed up."

Speaking for the larger states, James Wilson of Pennsylvania threw back a challenging question: "Are not the citizens of Pennsylvania equal to those of New Jersey? Does it require 150 of the former to balance 50 of the latter? No," Wilson warned, "if the small states will not confederate on this plan, Pennsylvania . . . would not confederate on any other."

After a month of debate, the delegates finally adopted what is known as the Great Compromise. It was first proposed by Roger Sherman of Connecticut. By a narrow margin, the Convention voted for a Congress of two houses—a Senate and a House of Representatives. Each state, large or small, would be represented by two Senators, thereby giving each state equal power in the Senate. In the House, however, representatives would be based upon population.

The three-fifths compromise. Equally complicated differences arose between delegates from the northern and the southern states. These differences arose from a conflict between the economic interests of northern merchants and southern planters.

One dispute arose over the counting of slaves. Southerners wanted slaves to be counted when figuring the number of representatives to be elected to the House of Representatives. However, they did not want slaves to be counted when determining the amount of taxes to be paid. Northerners, on the other hand, thought that slaves should be counted when figuring taxes, but not when figuring representatives.

As a compromise northerners and southerners agreed to count three fifths of the slaves for purposes of establishing both represen-

Pennsylvania's State House was not only where the Constitution was written, but also where the Declaration of Independence was signed. From here, too, the famed Liberty Bell rang out to announce that signing.

For the people of Philadelphia, the summer of 1787 was remarkable for two reasons. One was the Constitutional Convention, which met there from May to September. The other was the presence on the Delaware River of a strange looking boat built by a cantankerous inventor named John Fitch.

John Fitch had learned about European experiments with steamboats and had decided to make a boat of his own. His first boat contained two sets of paddles, one on each side of the boat. Steam power drove the paddles through the water. The boat's average speed was eight miles (13 kilometers) per hour against the current.

Curious onlookers watched the boat's trial runs on the Delaware River, with a few even venturing on the boat for short trips. Among the many convention delegates who took a ride was William Samuel Johnson, who wrote: "The exhibition yesterday gave the gentlemen present much satisfaction." Nevertheless, both Washington and Franklin turned down Fitch's request for financial backing.

In 1790, Fitch built a bigger boat, which began carrying passengers regularly up and down the Delaware. But Fitch's nickname of "poor John Fitch" turned out to be true. The boat lost money, partly because of competition from excellent coach lines, and partly because the engine was so large that it left little room for paying passengers. In 1791 a storm grounded the boat, and Fitch could not afford to salvage it. Fitch died in 1798 poor and embittered by his failures.

Less than ten years after Fitch's death, Robert Fulton demonstrated the *Clermont* on the Hudson River. Fulton had better luck commercially, and travel by steamboat became an accepted form of transportation. Though he considered himself a failure, John Fitch had helped start the Transportation Revolution.

tatives and taxes. For example, if a state's population included 100,000 free persons and 100,000 slaves, the state would be assigned a population figure of 160,000 for determining the amount of taxes to be paid and the number of representatives to be elected.

The commerce compromises. Other clashes between the economic interests of the South and the North arose over the control of commerce and the regulation of the slave trade.

Northern merchants wanted the central government to regulate commerce with foreign nations as well as among the states. Southern planters opposed this proposal. They feared that the government might pass laws unfavorable to southern interests. For example, southern planters earned much of their income by exporting tobacco to Europe and the northern states. In turn, they imported either from

Europe or the northern states many finished goods, such as household furnishings and farm equipment. If Congress imposed **tariffs,** or duties, on exports, overseas buyers would have to pay a higher price for southern tobacco. The planters feared that this rise in price would make them lose customers. Tariffs on imported goods, on the other hand, would raise the prices of products purchased by the planters. Under the circumstances, the southern delegates were opposed to all tariffs. They therefore opposed giving Congress unlimited power to regulate trade.

The delegates finally reached a compromise acceptable to both the North and the South. This compromise gave Congress the power "to regulate commerce with foreign nations, and among the several states," including the power to levy tariffs on imports. However, Congress was denied the power to levy tariffs on exports of any kind.

The southern planters were troubled by still another problem. Since Congress now had the power to regulate commerce and to tax imports, would it not be possible for Congress to outlaw the slave trade or to levy taxes on slaves imported into the country?

After a vigorous discussion, the Convention agreed that until 1808 the states could continue to import slaves. But after 1808 Congress would have the right to decide whether to regulate or prohibit the further importation of slaves.

The slave trade compromise was probably necessary for the Constitution to gain needed support in the South, but it was a setback for the antislavery forces. At the time the Constitution was written, many Americans believed that slavery was gradually dying out in the United States. They felt it would no longer be a problem in 1808. That was a fateful mistake. More than half a century would pass before a tragic war would bring an end to slavery in the United States.

Completing the Constitution. Finally, as the summer months of 1787 passed and as agreements were reached, the Constitution was completed. Time and again the Convention seemed near failure. Time and again angry members threatened to leave unless they got what they wanted. In the end, wise judgment prevailed. The delegates always found a way to compromise the differences that ▲ threatened to divide the country.

SECTION REVIEW

See underscored items, text pp. 169-73.

Identify: James Madison, Edmund Randolph, William Paterson, Great Compromise, Roger Sherman, tariffs

For answers to questions, see Answer Key, pp.A29-30.

1. **Interpreting Ideas: (a)** How do you think the presence of Benjamin Franklin and George Washington helped the proceedings of the Constitutional Convention? **(b)** Why do you think the delegates to the Constitutional Convention felt that it was important to meet in secret?

2. **Summarizing Ideas:** On what ideas for a central government did the delegates agree at the beginning of the Constitutional Convention?

3. **Organizing Ideas:** The delegates reached compromises to settle their differences on four important issues. **(a)** Describe each of the issues. **(b)** Present the different points of view on each issue. **(c)** What compromises did the delegates finally arrive at?

4. **Analyzing Ideas: (a)** What assumption did many antislavery Americans make when they agreed to the provisions on the slave trade that were written into the Constitution? **(b)** Why was this assumption incorrect?

---

2 The states ratify the Constitution only after heated debate

See Teaching Suggestions in TMRG, pp.TM49-50.

On September 17, 1787, 39 delegates signed the document prepared over the long, hot summer. Afterwards, the framers of the Constitution met for a farewell dinner. The next day they began to leave Philadelphia. Each delegation was in a hurry to return to its state, for the decisive struggle was yet to be waged. The decision to ratify, or approve, the Constitution would be made in special conventions held in each of the states. The Constitution would not become "the surpreme law of the land" until conventions in nine of the thirteen states had ratified it.

Differing opinions. Most of the delegates who left Philadelphia in September were prepared to lead the struggle for ratification. A few who had refused to sign the Constitution hurried home to lead the fight against it.

In general, the American people divided into two groups in their thinking about the

● As the delegates were leaving, two black ministers--the Reverend Richard Allen and the Reverend Absalom Jones-- held a "kneel-in" to protest the segregation in the churches of the day.

173

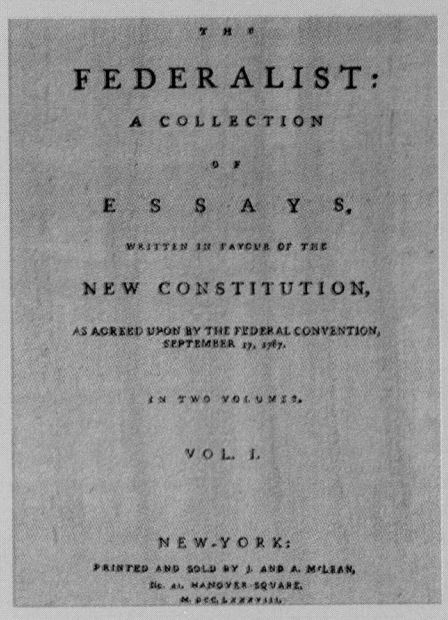

During 1787 and 1788 the effort to ratify the Constitution received significant help from a series of 85 articles that appeared in New York newspapers over the signature "Publius." The eloquent Publius was in reality three persons — James Madison, John Jay, and Alexander Hamilton. Their essays were later collected and published in book form as *The Federalist*.

The Federalist authors based their case for the Constitution on the weaknesses of the Articles of Confederation and on the superiority of the proposed new governmental system. The essays analyzed and discussed many government functions, from the power to tax to the conduct of foreign affairs. They persuaded many New York readers that the Constitution represented the best governmental compromise that could be reached.

Today *The Federalist* remains the classic defense and analysis of the Constitution. One historian has said that ". . .*The Federalist* stands third only to the Declaration of Independence and the Constitution itself among all the sacred writings of American political history."

Constitution. One group, the <u>Federalists</u>, wanted a strong **federal government**. The other group, the <u>Anti-Federalists</u>, just as strongly opposed strengthening the powers of the central government. The Anti-Federalists preferred to protect the rights and the powers of the individual states.

Objections to the Constitution. Concern over surrendering too much power to the federal government was only one of the issues troubling those who opposed the Constitution. Many opponents believed that the new Constitution did not give the voters enough control over the officials who would run the new federal government. The Constitution permitted the states to retain the right to decide who could vote and who could not vote. As you know, most states had property restrictions on voting, and several states still had religious restrictions. These restrictions prevented many men from voting. Neither the Constitution nor the states granted suffrage to women. Slaves, most free blacks, and even Indians living in settled areas surrounded by white settlements were not included in discussions regarding the right to vote. In brief, the <u>franchise</u>, or the

right to vote, was limited to a minority of the population.

To be sure, the Constitution did create a republican, or representative, form of government. However, the Constitution sharply limited the influence of even that select group of male citizens who were allowed to vote. The President and the Vice President were to be chosen by **electors.** The electors were to be selected not by the voters but "in such manner" as each state legislature should direct. Senators were to be chosen not by the voters but by the state legislatures. Only the members of the House of Representatives were to be elected directly by the voters.

Another serious objection to the Constitution was the lack of a bill of rights. Without a bill of rights, many Americans feared that the new federal government could take away their hard-won rights.

Struggles for ratification. In December 1787 Delaware became the first state to ratify the Constitution. Before the year's end, New Jersey and Pennsylvania followed Delaware's example. Georgia and Connecticut ratified early in 1788.

In February 1788 Massachusetts, one of the larger, crucial states, ratified the Constitution by the margin of 19 votes. Next came Maryland, South Carolina, and finally New Hampshire. Now the count stood at nine states, the number needed.

Meantime, however, Americans directed their attention to the ratification struggles going on in Virginia and New York. The new government could hardly hope to succeed without these large and important states.

The battles in Virginia and New York were fought with much feeling on both sides. The final victory in favor of the Constitution was very close. A change of only eleven votes in Virginia and of three votes in New York would have defeated ratification in these states. The victory in Virginia was largely due to the enormous influence of George Washington. The victory in New York was to some extent a personal triumph for Alexander Hamilton, James Madison, and John Jay. These three men defended the Constitution in a series of brilliant essays that were printed in the newspapers and widely read. Later the essays were published as a famous volume, *The Federalist.*

Time for celebration. When Virginia and New York ratified the Constitution, eleven states made up the Union. The new government could be started with some degree of confidence. Now only two states remained outside the Union. North Carolina did not enter until November 1789, and Rhode Island delayed ratifying the Constitution until the spring of 1790.

The fight over ratification had been a bitter one, and the margin of victory was close. Nevertheless, it was a victory, and during the summer and fall of 1788 the country celebrated it. The old government was ended. The new government was ready to start.

The first election. When all the states except North Carolina and Rhode Island had accepted the Constitution, elections were held. George Washington was unanimously elected President, and John Adams Vice President. Elections for the new Congress of the United States did not arouse much enthusiasm. In general, those elected to Congress had favored the Constitution either in the Convention or during the struggle for ratification, or both.

Traveling over the bad roads, the new Senators and Representatives slowly gathered in New York, the temporary capital of the nation. They awaited the coming of President-elect Washington and the inauguration of the new government.

SECTION REVIEW

See underscored items, text p. 174.
Identify: federal government, Federalists, Anti-Federalists, franchise, electors

For answers to questions, see Answer Key, p.A30.
1. **Summarizing Ideas:** How was the Constitution to be ratified?
2. **Organizing Ideas:** What roles did (a) Washington, (b) Hamilton, (c) Jay, and (d) Madison play in the Constitution's ratification?
3. **Interpreting Ideas:** Why do you think that Washington was unanimously elected the first President of the United States?

3 The Constitution establishes a workable form of government

See Teaching Suggestions in TMRG, pp.TM50-51.
The form of government created under the United States Constitution is based upon the principles of **federalism,** or the division of powers between the national, or federal, government and the state governments.

Creating a federal union. Under the Articles of Confederation, the relations between the central government and the state governments had been a thorny problem. The Confederation left most power in the hands of thirteen free and equal states. The central government held no real authority over the states or over the people themselves. The delegates to the Constitutional Convention wanted to correct the weaknesses of this form of government.

Most delegates agreed that only a **federal union** would be strong enough to establish an orderly society. In a federal union, each state delegates some of its power to the national government. The framers of the Constitution corrected most of the weaknesses of the Articles of Confederation by creating such a union.

Individuals and the law. Having agreed to organize a federal union, the delegates faced

The delegates to the Constitutional Convention met here, in the East Room of the Pennsylvania State House during the hot summer of 1787. The raised table between the fireplaces is where the Convention's president, George Washington, sat throughout the four months of debate over the new Constitution.

another troublesome problem. How could the federal, or national, government enforce its laws? Suppose, for example, that a citizen of New Jersey refused to obey a federal law. Should the federal government ask New Jersey to punish the offender? Suppose New Jersey refused to comply. Would not the federal government need to have the power to maintain its authority?

The longer the delegates debated this matter, the more convinced they became of the answer. To avoid trouble between the states and the federal government, all laws passed by the federal government had to apply equally to every individual within the union. To insure obedience to these laws, the delegates decided that the federal government had to have the power to reach into the states themselves to punish violators.

Because of this decision, Americans have always lived under two governments and two systems of law—federal and state. They have two citizenships. That is, they are citizens both of the United States and of the state in which they live.

Delegated powers. The decision to give the federal government power to enforce its laws led to another difficult problem. What laws should the federal government be allowed to pass? In other words, what powers should the states delegate, or surrender, to the federal government?

After long debate the delegates decided to give certain specific powers to the Congress of the United States. All of these powers, known as **delegated powers,** are listed in the Constitution. They include the powers "to lay and collect taxes . . . to borrow money . . . to coin money . . . to regulate commerce with foreign nations, and among the several states . . . to raise and support armies . . . to provide and maintain a navy."

From this listing it is clear that the delegates gave the federal government authority only over matters of common concern to the people of all the states. It is also clear that in selecting these delegated powers, the framers of the Constitution tried to correct major weaknesses of the Articles of Confederation— lack of financial power, lack of power to regulate commerce, and lack of military power.

Reserved powers. In a federal union, the member states still retain freedom to act on matters not delegated to the federal government or expressly forbidden to the states. To guarantee the states' independence of action,

▲ Class activity: Have students use the list of weaknesses of the Articles of Confederation formulated earlier to find an article, section, or clause of the Constitution that addresses a specific weakness.

the delegates listed several powers that could not be exercised by the federal authorities. For example, the federal government is forbidden to levy any "tax or duty . . . on articles exported from any state."

By implication all powers not specifically granted to the federal government, nor denied to the states, were kept by the states. But to avoid any misunderstanding, the Ninth and Tenth Amendments were adopted in 1791. The Tenth Amendment leaves no room for doubt: "The powers not delegated to the United States by the Constitution, nor prohibited by it to the states, are reserved to the states respectively, or to the people." Those powers retained by the states are known as **reserved powers.** They include control over transportation within the state, marriage, divorce, and public education.°

Shared powers. Every government must possess certain powers simply to exist and function effectively. All governments, for example, must have the power to raise money and to enforce law and order. Both the federal government and state governments use the same methods to raise money—taxation and borrowing. Both levels of government also have police forces to maintain order. In addition, both governments have court systems for trying people who violate laws.

Powers shared by the federal government and the states are called **concurrent powers.** They exist concurrently with, or at the same time as, powers delegated to the federal government on the one hand and powers reserved for the states on the other.

The supreme law of the land. The framers of the Constitution realized that conflicts might arise between federal and state laws. To settle such conflicts, they inserted this clear statement in the Constitution: "This Constitution, and the laws of the United States which shall be made in pursuance thereof, and all treaties made, or which shall be made, under the authority of the United States, shall be the supreme law of the land." By including this statement, they proclaimed that in cases of conflict the Constitution and the laws of the federal government should rank higher than state constitutions and state laws.

°In recent years the federal government has secured a great deal of control over public education by means of financial support, Supreme Court decisions, and the creation of a Department of Education.

4 The Constitution separates and balances the powers of government

See Teaching Suggestions in TMRG, pp.TM51-52.

Another fundamental principle of American government is the separation of powers, which includes a system of **checks and balances** on these powers.

Protection against tyranny. The framers of the Constitution firmly believed in government under law. They wanted to protect the country from tyranny in any form. They believed that a misguided majority might be as dangerous to good government under law as a privileged minority or a power-mad dictator.

When they wrote the Constitution, therefore, the framers tried to guard against what one of them called an "excess of democracy." At no time did they seriously consider including a guarantee of the right to vote in the Constitution. Instead, they left it to the states to decide who could vote and who could not.

The framers were equally careful to guard against seizure of the government by a military dictator. They had not forgotten the troubled years before the Revolutionary War. Even closer to them were recent attempts to establish a military dictatorship over the thirteen states. In 1782, for example, army officers had offered the title of king to General Washington. If Washington had wanted to be a dictator, the history of the United States might have been different.

Separation of powers. To help guard against tyranny in any form and to keep any one branch of the government from becoming too strong, the delegates agreed that the legislative, executive, and judicial powers of the government must be kept separate.

With this idea in mind, the delegates set up three separate branches of the government, each having certain powers. To Congress they gave the <u>legislative power</u> (Article 1). To the chief executive, or President, they granted the <u>executive power</u> to carry out the laws (Article 2). To the federal courts, the delegates gave the <u>judicial power</u> to interpret the laws (Article 3).

In addition to separating the powers of the federal government, the delegates wrote a system of checks and balances into the Constitution. Each branch was given certain powers that could restrain or balance the powers of the other branches if either of the other branches tried to abuse or exceed its powers.

Checks on the President. A President who is thought to be guilty of "treason, bribery, or other high crimes and misdemeanors" can be <u>impeached.</u> That is, the President can be accused by the House of Representatives of acting unlawfully or misusing power and then be tried by the Senate. If found guilty, the President can be removed from office. A President can make a treaty, but a two-thirds vote of the Senate is necessary to ratify it. A President can appoint important officers, but the Senate must confirm these appointments by a majority vote. Since Congress has control over taxes and spending, it can interfere with any Presidential policy that requires the spending of money. Finally, a two-thirds vote of Congress can overrule the President's **veto**, or rejection, of laws proposed by Congress.

Checks on Congress. The President, in turn, can check and balance the powers of Congress. Perhaps the President's most important check is the power to <u>veto</u> Congressional legislation. Congress needs a two-thirds majority to override a veto, and this is difficult to obtain. The President can also influence the thinking of Congress through annual State of the Union messages and special messages to Congress. The Chief Executive can also bring pressure on Congress by calling a special session and asking for the passage of specific laws.

The President also can exert influence by directing public attention to specific issues. As the office of the Chief Executive developed, press conferences and speeches directly to the people became more important. If a press conference or a public address results in a barrage of letters and telegrams to Congress, it may be more willing to accept the President's point of view.

Checks by and on the judiciary. The federal judiciary—the Supreme Court and the lower federal courts—interprets the laws. The federal judiciary has the power to declare that a law passed by Congress and approved by the President is <u>unconstitutional.</u>

However, the powers of the Supreme Court and of other federal courts can be checked in several ways. Congress can impeach federal judges. Congress also determines by law the number of justices on the Supreme Court. At different times laws have set the number of justices at as few as five and as many as ten.

The President, in turn, appoints all federal judges, with the consent of the Senate. The President's desire for a certain interpretation of the Constitution may sometimes conflict either with Congress or the Supreme Court. If the President appoints justices to the Supreme Court who are friendly to the administration's viewpoint, and if the Senate approves these appointments, the President is checking or balancing the power of Congress, of the judiciary, or of both. A further check on the judiciary is the President's power to pardon or reprieve persons who have been convicted of crimes in the federal courts.

Pros and cons of checks and balances. The separation of powers with checks and balances in the federal government has sometimes been criticized for slowing down the workings of government. Important laws may be needed, but a President belonging to one party and a Congress dominated by another party may not be able to agree on a law. As a general rule, however, the system has worked well.

In time of war or other crisis, Congress usually declares a national emergency and grants all the special powers the President may need in order to act quickly. When the emergency is over, the special powers can be withdrawn.

The principle of the separation of powers with checks and balances was written into the Constitution as a safeguard for the future. It was meant to protect the liberties of the people.

Identify: legislative power, executive power, judicial power, checks and balances, impeach, veto, unconstitutional

For answers to questions, see Answer Key

1. **Analyzing Ideas:** Why did the framers of the Constitution fear "an excess of democracy"?

2. **Summarizing Ideas: (a)** What is the purpose of the separation of powers in government? **(b)** What are some disadvantages of this separation of powers? **(c)** What are the chief responsibilities of the three branches of the federal government?

3. **Organizing Ideas:** List the principal checks on the power of **(a)** the President, **(b)** the Congress, and **(c)** the federal judiciary. **(d)** What is the purpose of these checks?

5 The Constitution seeks to safeguard individual liberty

See Teaching Suggestions in TMRG, pp.TM52-53.

Still another fundamental principle of the American Constitution is protection of the liberties of individuals.

American colonists had always insisted upon protection of their civil liberties—their rights as individuals against the powers of government. Some civil liberty protections appear in the Constitution itself, for example, the separation of powers with checks and balances. Others were written into the first ten amendments—the Bill of Rights. Still others have been added in later amendments.

Guarantees in the Constitution. The Constitution itself provides important guarantees of civil liberties. For example, it prohibits both *ex post facto* laws and bills of attainder.

An *ex post facto* law is a law passed "after the deed." Such a law sets a penalty for an act that was not illegal when it was committed.

A bill of attainder is a law that punishes a person by fine, imprisonment, or seizure of property without a court trial. If Congress had the power to adopt bills of attainder, the lawmakers could punish any American, and that person could do nothing to appeal the sentence. Instead, the Constitution provides that only the courts can impose punishment for unlawful

acts, and then only by following the duly established law. To prevent arbitrary convictions by judges, the Constitution also provides that "the trial of all crimes . . . shall be by jury."

The Constitution also protects the citizen's right to the writ of *habeas corpus.* The writ of *habeas corpus* is a legal document that forces a jailer to release a person from prison unless the person has been formally charged with, or convicted of, a crime. The Constitution states that "the privilege of the writ of *habeas corpus* shall not be suspended, unless when in cases of rebellion or invasion the public safety may require it."

The Constitution also gives special protection to people accused of treason. The framers of the Constitution knew that the charge of treason was an old device used by tyrants to get rid of persons they did not like. Such rulers might bring the charge of treason against persons who merely criticized the government, not just against those involved in an armed uprising against the government. To prevent such use of this charge, the Constitution carefully defines treason: "Treason against the United States shall consist only in levying war against them, or in adhering to their enemies, giving them aid and comfort. No person shall be convicted of treason unless on the testimony of two witnesses to the same overt act, or on confession in open court."

The Constitution also protects the innocent relatives of a person accused of treason. Only the convicted person can be punished. No penalty can be imposed upon that person's family.

These are only a few of the guarantees of personal rights that were written into the Constitution. They are important examples of the way that the Constitution establishes a common standard of law for every American citizen, old and young, rich and poor alike.

The Bill of Rights. Despite the safeguards written into the Constitution, some states at first refused to ratify it because it did not offer greater protection to the rights of individuals. They finally agreed to ratification after they had been promised that a bill of rights would be added to the Constitution by amendment when Congress met.

In 1789–90 the first Congress of the United States wrote the ideals of the Declaration of Independence into the Bill of Rights, the first ten amendments to the Constitution. The Bill of Rights protects individuals against any ac-

Here the Convention delegates assemble in Independence Hall. Benjamin Franklin said of the product of their labors, "It astonishes me . . . to find this system approaching so near perfection as it does. . . ."

tion by the federal government that may deprive them of life, liberty, or property without "due process of law."

Among the guarantees of liberty in the Bill of Rights, several are especially important. The First Amendment guarantees freedom of religion, speech, press, assembly, and petition. The Fourth Amendment forbids unreasonable searches and seizures of any person's home. The Fifth, Sixth, and Eighth Amendments protect individuals from arbitrary arrest and punishment by the federal government.

The Bill of Rights was ratified by the states in 1791. It has remained one of the best-known features of the Constitution. The American people have turned to it for support whenever their rights as individuals have seemed to be in danger. No document in American history, except, perhaps, the Declaration of Independence, has been cherished more deeply.

▲ **Interpreting individual rights.** Although the Constitution, Bill of Rights, and later amendments guarantee certain rights equally to all Americans, individual rights are not absolute. The rights of an individual exist in relation to

the rights of others. In guaranteeing freedom of speech and of the press, for example, the Bill of Rights does not grant individuals the right to say or print anything they like at any time. For example, laws forbid individuals to say or print anything that may defame an innocent person's character. Freedom of speech and of the press as well as all the other rights guaranteed by the first ten amendments must be interpreted by the courts if they are to have any real meaning.

SECTION REVIEW

See underscored items, text pp. 179.

Identify: civil liberties, Bill of Rights, *ex post facto* law, bill of attainder, writ of *habeas corpus,* treason

For answers to questions, see Answer Key, p.A31.

1. **Analyzing Ideas:** Why were the framers of the Constitution especially interested in protecting civil liberties?

2. **Interpreting Ideas:** How do the civil liberties guaranteed in the Constitution help to prevent abuses of power?

3. **Summarizing Ideas: (a)** Which branch of the federal government makes decisions on the limits to an individual's rights? **(b)** Why is it that the rights of individuals are not unlimited?

DEVELOPING HISTORY STUDY SKILLS

Interpreting the Visual Record   Reading Charts

Interpreting information in different kinds of charts enables the student of history to discover important relationships. The most frequently used charts include tables, multicolumn tables, organization charts, and flow charts.

A table is a simple one-column chart. A multi-column charts combines several tables to present several sets, or categories, of information. An organization chart shows the structure of an organization by indicating the ranking of the parts of an organization and the relationships between parts. A flow chart illustrates a sequence of events or the steps in a process. Often arrows are used to indicate the sequence.

How to Read a Chart

Follow these guidelines when reading a chart.

1. **Define the chart's purpose.** Identify the type of information presented on the chart. Note the chart's title and subtitle. Note all other labels.
2. **Study the chart's parts.** Identify the specific information given under each element of the chart such as a column, row, box, or circle.
3. **Analyze the information.** When reading quantities, note increases or decreases in amounts. When reading dates, note intervals of time. When tracing steps in a process or reading an organization chart, note directional lines or arrows.
4. **Put the data to use.** Formulate generalizations or draw conclusions from the data.

Applying the Skill

Study the chart on this page, which gives information about the amendments to the Constitution and lists the date of enactment and the rights or issues covered by each. The tabulation of the information in this form enables a reader to draw several conclusions from the data. One conclusion is that the first ten amendments were all enacted in the same year, 1791. In the years from 1798 through 1870, only five amendments were ratified. Only four amendments were ratified in the nineteenth century. The longest interval (61 years) between the passage of amendments took place between 1804 and 1865. It took only 74 years to add the first 13 amendments, while it took 103 years to add the next 13. Finally, only eight amendments deal with matters of government. The other 18 deal with personal freedoms.

Amendments to the Constitution

Amendment	Year Enacted	Subject
1st	1791	Personal freedoms
2nd	1791	Right to keep weapons
3rd	1791	Quartering of troops
4th	1791	Search and seizure; search warrants
5th	1791	Rights of accused persons
6th	1791	Speedy trial
7th	1791	Jury trial
8th	1791	Bails, fines, punishments
9th	1791	Rights of the people
10th	1791	Powers of the states
11th	1798	Suits against states
12th	1804	Election of President and Vice President
13th	1865	Abolition of slavery
14th	1868	Rights of citizens; privileges and immunities, due process, and equal protection
15th	1870	Extension of suffrage to black males.
16th	1913	Income tax
17th	1913	Direct election of senators
18th	1919	Prohibition on liquor
19th	1920	Women's suffrage
20th	1933	Change in dates for Presidential and Congressional terms of office
21st	1933	Repeal of prohibition
22nd	1951	Two-term limit on Presidential tenure
23rd	1961	Right to vote in Presidential elections for residents of the District of Columbia
24th	1964	Poll tax banned in federal elections
25th	1967	Presidential disability and succession
26th	1971	Voting age lowered to 18

181

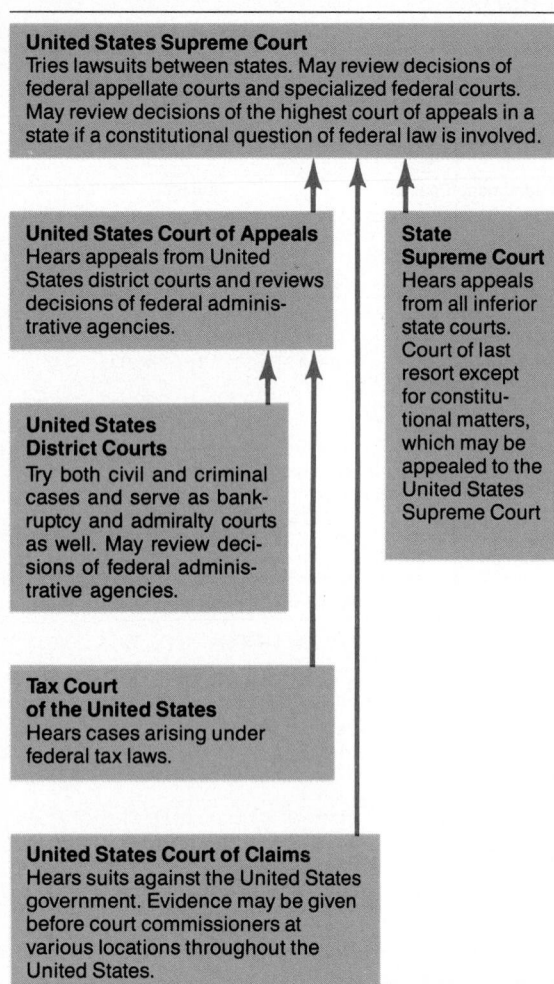

The Federal Court System

United States Supreme Court
Tries lawsuits between states. May review decisions of federal appellate courts and specialized federal courts. May review decisions of the highest court of appeals in a state if a constitutional question of federal law is involved.

United States Court of Appeals
Hears appeals from United States district courts and reviews decisions of federal administrative agencies.

State Supreme Court
Hears appeals from all inferior state courts. Court of last resort except for constitutional matters, which may be appealed to the United States Supreme Court

United States District Courts
Try both civil and criminal cases and serve as bankruptcy and admiralty courts as well. May review decisions of federal administrative agencies.

Tax Court of the United States
Hears cases arising under federal tax laws.

United States Court of Claims
Hears suits against the United States government. Evidence may be given before court commissioners at various locations throughout the United States.

The Making of United States Foreign Policy

Congress
Implements War Powers Act provisions
Allocates government funds
Approves treaties and nominations (Senate)
House Foreign Affairs Committee and Senate Foreign Relations Committee

State Department
Secretary advises the President and serves as nation's chief diplomat
Implements policy decisions
Supervises administration of foreign affairs and foreign aid

Defense Department
Secretary and Joint Chiefs of Staff advise President
Implements policy decisions
Manages armed forces

President
Commander in chief of the armed forces
Makes foreign policy decisions
Makes executive agreements
Makes nominations for diplomatic staff

Central Intelligence Agency
Director advises President
Gathers and analyzes information

The People
Influence actions of legislative and executive branches through voting patterns, lobbying, the media, and public opinion

Other Executive Branch Agencies Involved in Foreign Policy
Treasury
Commerce
International Communications Agency
Peace Corps
Agriculture

The organization chart above concerns the federal court system. The placement of the boxes and the direction of the arrows indicates the structure of the system and the relationship of the lower courts in the federal system and the state courts to the Supreme Court.

Practicing the Skill

Study the chart at the top of the next column. Then on a separate sheet of paper, answer the following questions.

1. The chart is **(a)** a multicolumn chart, **(b)** a table, **(c)** a flow chart.

2. The chart is about **(a)** making foreign policy, **(b)** Presidential-Congressional relations, **(c)** the importance of democracy.

3. The chief diplomat of the United States is **(a)** Congress, **(b)** the President, **(c)** the head of the Central Intelligence Agency.

4. A conclusion that can be drawn from the chart is **(a)** the President receives no input from other agencies of government in making foreign policy, **(b)** the President relies only on the people in making foreign policy, **(c)** the President makes foreign policy, using input from many executive agencies as well as the people.

6 The Constitution is a flexible, living document

A final fundamental principle of American government is the adaptability of the Constitution to changing times and the changing circumstances of the nation.

The Constitution has successfully survived the years for two main reasons. First, it lays down rules of procedure that must be followed even in critical times. Second, it is a "living" document. Americans have been able to adapt the Constitution to changing ways and changing times. In general, the Constitution works as well today for an industrialized nation of 50 states and a population of over 236 million people as it once worked for an agricultural nation of 13 states and 4 million people.

Provision for amendment. The framers of the Constitution were as wise in what they did *not* write as in what they did write. They wrote down only the fundamental laws for the nation. They left it to Congress to pass additional laws as they might be needed. Each time Congress meets, it passes such laws.

Even so, the framers knew that changes in the fundamental law might have to be made from time to time. Accordingly, they wrote Article 5, which carefully specifies the procedure by which the Constitution may be amended (see chart, page 1010).

Because the amending process is slow and difficult, it is seldom used unless the need for change appears great. Some people think the process is too slow and difficult. Others think it wise that no changes can be made in the "supreme law of the land" until the pros and cons have been thoroughly debated. In any event, only 26 amendments have been adopted since 1789, including the first ten amendments—the Bill of Rights.

The elastic clause. The framers provided still greater flexibility to the Constitution by inserting what is known as the **elastic clause**. To the specific powers granted to Congress, this clause adds the power "to make all laws which shall be necessary and proper for carrying into execution the foregoing powers."

James Madison (left) and Benjamin Franklin (right) were influential members of the Constitutional Convention. Franklin worked at compromise, cooling hot tempers. Madison's notes remain the major source of information about the Convention's secret deliberations.

When John Marshall was appointed Chief Justice of the United States in 1801, the nation's system of constitutional law had not yet been clearly defined. Nor had the present relationship between the executive, legislative, and judicial branches of government been established. The Supreme Court was perceived as having little power, with almost no influence over the other two branches.

Chief Justice Marshall changed all that. In a series of brilliant decisions handed down between 1801 and 1835, Marshall almost single-handedly gave structural form to the Constitution. His opinion in *Marbury v. Madison* (1803) is universally regarded as the classic justification of judicial review and thus the fundamental premise on which United States constitutional doctrine rests.

It was a petty political squabble that gave Marshall the historic opportunity to assert the Court's right of judicial review. Following the election of 1800, the outgoing Federalist administration sought to preserve its power by creating several new judgeships. One of the so-called "midnight judges" (see page 238) who did not receive his appointment on time was William Marbury. Marbury appealed to the Supreme Court for a writ of mandamus to compel James Madison, the new secretary of state, to deliver the commission.

In deciding the case, Marshall agreed with Marbury's claim. The Supreme Court, however, had no right to compel Madison to deliver Marbury's commission. Marshall held unconstitutional that portion of the Judiciary Act of 1789 that had expanded the original jurisdiction of the Supreme Court to include the right of issuing writs of mandamus.

For the first time in history, the Supreme Court had annulled an act of Congress. Henceforth the Constitution would be the supreme law of the land — and the Court would be its final interpreter.

The elastic clause allows Congress to stretch its powers and to pass laws not specifically authorized in the Constitution. Congress, for example, has the delegated power to regulate commerce. It has stretched this power to improve rivers and harbors and to require the payment of minimum wages to workers employed by industries engaged in interstate commerce.

Whenever Congress has stretched its powers in this way, a question has arisen over whether such actions are "necessary and proper." The Constitution does not clearly state how this question should be answered. In 1803, however, Chief Justice John Marshall established the tradition that the power to answer such questions rests in the Supreme Court.

The Supreme Court as referee. The power of the Supreme Court to decide whether or not a law or a treaty violates the Constitution is known as the power of **judicial review**. This means that the Supreme Court has the power to review, or examine, an act of Congress and to determine whether or not the Constitution permits such an act. When the Supreme Court exercises this power of judicial review, it acts as a referee for the nation.

When the Supreme Court acts, its word is final, but the Supreme Court can — and sometimes does — reverse an earlier decision. Also, the people of the United States can, by the process of amendment, alter the Constitution.

The "unwritten Constitution." The Constitution, then, has proved to be a flexible, enduring plan of government. Amendments have altered certain provisions of the Constitution and added others. Court decisions and acts of Congress, especially under the elastic clause, have given new meanings to certain provisions of the Constitution.

Other changes in American government have come about through custom. For example, the Constitution says nothing about political parties, which Washington and others distrusted as likely to cause quarrels. Neither does the Constitution provide for regular meetings of the heads of the executive departments concerned with defense, foreign affairs, finances, and other matters. Such meetings, nevertheless, take place and have become an important part of the executive system.

Custom has established other important practices in the operation of the federal government. For example, before a federal official is

We the People

of the United States, in order to form a more perfect Union, establish Justice, insure domestic Tranquility, provide for the common defence, promote the general Welfare, and secure the Blessings of Liberty to ourselves and our Posterity, do ordain and establish this Constitution for the United States of America.

Article I.

Section. 1. All legislative Powers herein granted shall be vested in a Congress of the United States, which shall consist of a Senate and House of Representatives.

Section. 2. The House of Representatives shall be composed of Members chosen every second Year by the People of the several States, and the Electors in each State shall have the Qualifications requisite for Electors of the most numerous Branch of the State Legislature.

No Person shall be a Representative who shall not have attained to the Age of twenty five Years, and been seven Years a Citizen of the United States, and who shall not, when elected, be an Inhabitant of that State in which he shall be chosen.

Representatives and direct Taxes shall be apportioned among the several States which may be included within this Union, according to their respective Numbers, which shall be determined by adding to the whole Number of free Persons, including those bound to Service for a Term of Years, and excluding Indians not taxed, three fifths of all other Persons. The actual Enumeration shall be made within three Years after the first Meeting of the Congress of the United States, and within every subsequent Term of ten Years, in such Manner as they shall by Law direct. The Number of Representatives shall not exceed one for every thirty Thousand, but each State shall have at Least one Representative; and until such enumeration shall be made, the State of New Hampshire shall be entitled to chuse three, Massachusetts eight, Rhode Island and Providence Plantations one, Connecticut five, New York six, New Jersey four, Pennsylvania eight, Delaware one, Maryland six, Virginia ten, North Carolina five, South Carolina five, and Georgia three.

When vacancies happen in the Representation from any State, the Executive Authority thereof shall issue Writs of Election to fill such Vacancies.

The House of Representatives shall chuse their Speaker and other Officers; and shall have the sole Power of Impeachment.

Section. 3. The Senate of the United States shall be composed of two Senators from each State, chosen by the Legislature thereof for six Years; and each Senator shall have one Vote.

Immediately after they shall be assembled in Consequence of the first Election, they shall be divided as equally as may be into three Classes. The Seats of the Senators of the first Class shall be vacated at the Expiration of the second Year, of the second Class at the Expiration of the fourth Year, and of the third Class at the Expiration of the sixth Year, so that one third may be chosen every second Year; and if Vacancies happen by Resignation, or otherwise, during the Recess of the Legislature of any State, the Executive thereof may make temporary Appointments until the next Meeting of the Legislature, which shall then fill such Vacancies.

No Person shall be a Senator who shall not have attained to the Age of thirty Years, and been nine Years a Citizen of the United States, and who shall not, when elected, be an Inhabitant of that State for which he shall be chosen.

The Vice President of the United States shall be President of the Senate, but shall have no Vote, unless they be equally divided.

The Senate shall chuse their other Officers, and also a President pro tempore, in the Absence of the Vice President, or when he shall exercise the Office of President of the United States.

Much of the wording of the Constitution was the work of Gouverneur Morris, a delegate from Pennsylvania. The opening passages of the original document are shown here.

appointed to work in a state, the President usually seeks the advice of the Senators of that state, provided that they belong to the same political party. This custom is called **senatorial courtesy**. Custom and the pressure of work have also led Congress to use an elaborate system of committees in making laws.

Practices such as these, growing out of custom and tradition, are sometimes called the **unwritten Constitution**. The Constitution does not refer to them, but they are so firmly established that they can be thought of as unwritten laws.

Admitting new states. The delegates, as you have seen, had drawn up a Constitution in which power was distributed between the states and the federal government. By making it possible for new states to enter the Union with minimum difficulty, they added more flexibility and strength to the government.

Since it was clear that the population of the western lands would grow rapidly, it was important to provide in advance for the admission of new states. So long as a western area remained a territory, Congress was responsible for its government. When the population grew large enough, the territory could apply for admission as a state. In general, the laws Congress passed to govern the admission of new states followed the Northwest Ordinance (see pages 157–158).

SECTION REVIEW

See underscored items, text pp. 183 - 85.

Identify: elastic clause, judicial review, senatorial courtesy

For answers to questions, see Answer Key, p.A31.

1. **Analyzing Ideas: (a)** Why did the framers of the Constitution provide for an amendment process? **(b)** Why did they make this amendment process a difficult one?

2. **Summarizing Ideas: (a)** How does the elastic clause of the Constitution broaden the powers specifically granted to Congress? **(b)** How are these powers limited by the federal judiciary?

3. **Evaluating Ideas: (a)** What is the "unwritten Constitution"? **(b)** Give three examples of this "unwritten Constitution" and explain why each arose.

4. **Interpreting Ideas:** Why was it important for the framers of the Constitution to include provisions for new states to enter the Union?

5. **Expressing Viewpoints:** The Constitution's success results from its combination of fixed procedure and adaptability. Do you agree or disagree with this statement? Explain your answer.

By the mid-1780's increasing numbers of Americans believed that the Articles of Confederation were not providing an effective government. Difficulties with trade and difficulties with foreign nations were two major problems that the Confederation government could not seem to handle. Shays' Rebellion in 1786 convinced most Americans that serious changes would have to be made.

The delegates who met in the spring of 1787 to revise the Articles of Confederation included many of the ablest leaders in the United States. Convinced that the Confederation was not strong enough to bring order and prosperity to their country, they abandoned all thought of revising the Articles of Confederation. Instead, they proceeded to draw up a completely new Constitution. Patrick Henry called this action "a revolution as radical as that which separated us from Great Britain." Out of their long political experience, their keen intelligence, and their great learning, the framers of the Constitution fashioned a blueprint for a truly united nation—the United States of America.

An observer once referred to the Constitution as "the most wonderful work ever struck off at a given time by the brain and purpose of man." Revised, modified, and amended, the Constitution has served the American people since 1787. It will continue to stand as a lasting tribute to the wisdom and foresight of its creators as long as it endures.

CONNECTING CHAPTER IDEAS

The Constitution created a republican form of government. It did not, however, create the nation. In the next chapter you will see how men and women from many walks of life began to work at unifying their country and establishing it as a respected member of the family of nations.

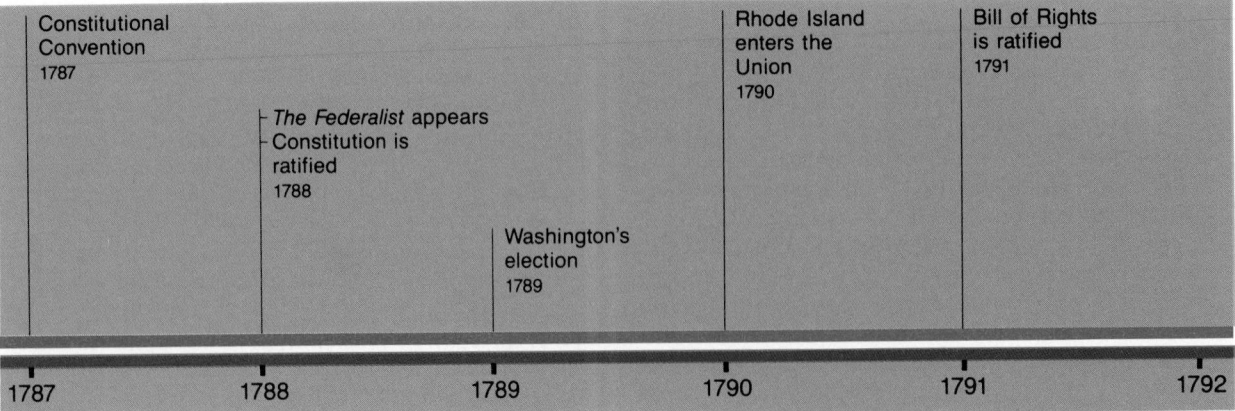

Constitutional Convention 1787

The Federalist appears
Constitution is ratified 1788

Washington's election 1789

Rhode Island enters the Union 1790

Bill of Rights is ratified 1791

1787   1788   1789   1790   1791   1792

Reviewing Important Terms

Decide whether each of the following sentences is true or false. If the sentence is false, replace the underlined term with the word or phrase that will make it true.

1. In a <u>republican</u> government supreme power rests in the voters who elect representative officials.
2. Under the Constitution, Congress cannot levy <u>tariffs</u> on goods exported from the United States.
3. Until it was amended in the twentieth century, the Constitution limited the <u>franchise</u> to a minority of the adult population.
4. The <u>delegated powers</u> listed in the Constitution give specific powers to the President.
5. The <u>reserved powers</u> listed in the Constitution are shared by the federal government and the states.
6. The <u>concurrent powers</u> listed in the Constitution give specific powers to Congress.
7. Congress is forbidden to punish any individual by passing a <u>bill of attainder</u>.
8. <u>Judicial review</u> allows Congress to pass laws not specifically authorized in the Constitution.
9. The Federalists, who were opposed by the Anti-Federalists, wanted strong <u>state governments</u>.
10. In a <u>federal union</u>, each state delegates some of its power to the national government.
11. The President may <u>impeach</u> a bill to stop its passage.
12. An individual's rights against the powers of the government are called <u>civil liberties</u>.

Practicing Critical Thinking Skills

1. **Analyzing Primary Sources.** How did the new Constitution reflect the political experiences of the colonists before 1775?
2. **Interpreting Ideas.** Describe the connections between the Preamble to the Constitution and the theory of government that is described in the Declaration of Independence.
3. **Analyzing Ideas.** The Constitution is fundamentally a document of compromises. Explain this statement, using specific examples.
4. **Interpreting Viewpoints.** Benjamin Franklin was once asked what sort of government was set up in the Constitution. He answered, "A republic, if you can keep it." **(a)** What is a republic? **(b)** What did Franklin mean by his statement? **(c)** What provisions in the Constitution were intended to help us keep our republic?

5. **Relating Past to Present. (a)** Name five ways in which government touches your life directly. **(b)** Which of these areas is specifically provided for in the Constitution? **(c)** Which has arisen as a result of the flexibility of the Constitution? Explain.

Developing History Study Skills

Reading Charts.   Study the chart on page 1011. Then on a separate sheet of paper, answer these questions. **(a)** In your opinion, which step in the passage of a bill is the most important? Why? **(b)** How does the Rules Committe play a key role in the passage of a bill? **(c)** What is the purpose of the Conference Committee? **(d)** Name the three courses of action that a President can follow when he receives a bill.

Relating Geography and History

In *The Federalist,* Alexander Hamilton, John Jay, and James Madison defended the Constitution against such objections as the "error which limits republican government to a narrow district." Madison refuted the argument that the new nation was too large to be run by a republican-type government. To understand the argument presented by Madison on this point, study the map on page 162, read the following excerpt, then answer the questions below.

"*. . . As almost every State will on one side or other be a frontier, . . . so the States which be at the greatest distance from the heart of the Union, and which, of course, may partake least of . . . its benefits, will be at the same time immediately contiguous to [bordering on] foreign nations, and will consequently stand, on particular occasions, in greatest need of its strength and resources.*"

1. **(a)** Which states were the greatest distance from the "heart of the Union" and bordered on foreign nations? **(b)** What problems might face the states with frontier borders?
2. James Madison argued that if the outlying states "should derive less benefit . . . from the Union in some respects than the less distant States, they will derive greater benefit from it in other respects. . . ." Explain what you think he meant.

UNIT TWO
REVIEW

Discussing Ideas

1. Why did the American Revolution occur? Give specific evidence to support your answer.
2. **(a)** Why were the Americans able to win the Revolution? **(b)** What handicaps did they face in their effort to win the war?
3. **(a)** Why did American leaders decide to write the Constitution? **(b)** How did the Constitution solve the problems that arose during the Confederation period?
4. In what ways does the Constitution reflect the reasons that Americans fought the Revolutionary War?
5. **(a)** What was Alexander Hamilton's view of the average person's basic nature? **(b)** How did this view influence Hamilton's political beliefs?

Applying History Study Skills

1. **Determining Cause-Effect Relationships.** Match each of the following causes with the correct effects below. Explain your answers.

Causes

a. Parliament passes the Intolerable Acts.
b. The British win the French and Indian War.
c. General Gage secretly plans to capture colonial war materials.
d. British traders deal dishonestly with the Indians in the Ohio Valley.

Effects

e. France gives up land in North America.
f. Paul Revere sets out to warn the people of Lexington and Concord.
g. Pontiac's army destroys British forts and settlements along the western frontier.
h. Colonists begin to organize units of citizen-soldiers called minutemen.

2. **Reading Charts.** Study the chart on page 156. Then on a separate sheet of paper, answer the following questions. **(a)** How large was each western township to be? **(b)** What portion of a township was reserved for school support? **(c)** What does this chart show about American attitudes toward education in the western lands?

Making Connections

1. Make a series of army recruiting posters that might have been used during the Revolution to encourage Americans to join the army.
2. Write a skit dramatizing the meeting of the Stamp Act Congress. Be sure to present all of the viewpoints that would have been expressed at the Congress. You might want to act out the skit with some of your classmates.
3. Suppose you were a European political cartoonist in the 1780's. Create a series of cartoons to illustrate your attitude toward the newly formed United States.
4. Investigate the early history of your state and prepare on oral report that explains **(a)** how it was first organized—as a colony or a territory of the United States, **(b)** under what circumstances it became a state, and **(c)** who were some of the important people who helped in the early development of the state.
5. Develop a time line for Unit Two. Include entries for at least 10 events. Then answer these questions. **(a)** What is the theme of your time line? **(b)** Does that theme represent a significant number of ideas about the period before, during, and after the Revolutionary War? Explain.

Reading in Depth

Book of the Revolution (New York: American Heritage). A general account of the Revolution, with lavish illustrations.

Bristow, Gwen, *Celia Garth* (New York: Crowell). An exciting novel about a young seamstress in Charleston who serves the war effort by becoming a spy for the Continental army.

Davis, Burke, *Three for Revolution* (San Diego: Harcourt Brace Jovanovich). Description of events that prepared Patrick Henry, George Washington, and Thomas Jefferson to lead the Revolution.

Franklin, Benjamin, *Autobiography* (New York: Dodd, Mead). The life story of this outstanding American.

McDowell, Bart, *The Revolutionary War: America's Fight for Freedom* (Washington, D.C.: National Geographic Society). Source materials are used to trace the background of the Revolution, from Braddock's unlucky expedition 1775 through years of growing colonial unrest.

THE CONSTITUTION
OF THE UNITED STATES OF AMERICA

[The text of the Constitution is printed on the white background, the commentary on the blue background. Portions of the text printed in brackets and ruled with blue have gone out of date or have been changed by amendment.]

PREAMBLE

We, the people of the United States, in order to form a more perfect Union, establish justice, insure domestic tranquility, provide for the common defense, promote the general welfare, and secure the blessings of liberty to ourselves and our posterity, do ordain and establish this CONSTITUTION for the United States of America.

The Preamble states the purposes of the Constitution, and makes it clear that the government is established by consent of the governed. We, the people, have supreme power in establishing the government of the United States of America.

ARTICLE 1
LEGISLATIVE DEPARTMENT

By separating the functions of government among branches concerned with lawmaking (Article 1), law executing (Article 2), and law interpreting (Article 3), the Framers were applying the principle of separation of powers and developing a system of checks and balances as a defense against tyranny.

Section 1. Congress

All legislative powers herein granted shall be vested in a Congress of the United States, which shall consist of a Senate and House of Representatives.

Practice has modified the provision that all lawmaking powers granted in the Constitution are vested in Congress. For example, such administrative agencies as the Interstate Commerce Commission can issue regulations that in some ways have the force of laws.

Section 2. House of Representatives

1. Election and Term of Members The House of Representatives shall be composed of members chosen every second year by the people of the several States, and the electors in each state shall have the qualifications requisite for electors of the most numerous branch of the state legislature.

Clause 1. The members of the House of Representatives are elected every two years by the "electors" (voters) of the states. Except for the provisions of Amendments 15, 19, 24, and 26, the individual states decide who may or may not vote.

2. Qualifications No person shall be a representative who shall not have attained to the age of twenty-five years, and been seven years a citizen of the United States, and who shall not, when elected, be an inhabitant of that state in which he shall be chosen.

Clause 2. This clause specifies that a member of the House of Representatives must be (1) at least 25 years of age, (2) a United States citizen for at least 7 years, and (3) a resident of the state in which elected. Custom has added the requirement of residency in the Congressional district from which a representative is elected. Each state is divided into Congressional districts for the purpose of electing representatives; each district elects one. TERM OF OFFICE: 2 years.

Clause 3. The portion of this clause beginning on line 5 forms what came to be called the Three-Fifths Compromise. Amendment 13 and Section 2 of Amendment 14 overruled this provision in the case of black Americans but not for Native Americans. However, since 1940 Native Americans have been included in the population census. Originally each state was entitled to one Representative for every 30,000 people. Later, membership was limited by law to a total of 435. A census of the United States is taken every ten years to determine the number of Representatives to which each state is entitled. Regardless of its population, however, each state is entitled to at least one representative in the House.

Clause 4. The *executive authority* refers to the governor of the state; a *writ of election* is an order for a special election to fill the vacant seat.

Clause 5. In actual practice it is the majority party—the political party having the largest number of members in the House—that chooses the Speaker of the House and other House officials (clerk, doorkeeper, sergeant-at-arms, postmaster, and chaplain). The Speaker is the only official chosen from among the members of the House. The House, by a majority vote, can impeach (accuse) an Executive Department officer or a federal judge. The trial of the impeached official takes place in the Senate. (See Section 3, Clause 6.)

Clause 1. Under the provisions of Amendment 17, the 100 senators are now elected directly by the voters of the states in the same manner as the representatives. The method of electing senators provided here, by which the state legislatures chose senators, came to be considered undemocratic and was therefore changed.

Clause 2. One third of the Senate comes up for election every two years. This procedure was established in the first Senate, whose senators were divided into three groups. One group was to serve for two years, the second for four years, and the third for six years. As a result, the terms of senators today overlap, making the Senate a "continuing" body, in which two thirds of the members are "carried over" through every election. In contrast, every member of the House of Representatives is elected every two years. Under Amendment 17, if a senator resigns or dies, the state governor can call a spe-

3. Apportionment of Representatives and Direct Taxes Representatives and direct taxes shall be apportioned among the several states which may be included within this Union, according to their respective numbers [which shall be determined by adding to the whole number of free persons, including those bound to service for a term of years, and excluding Indians not taxed, three fifths of all other persons]. The actual enumeration shall be made within three years after the first meeting of the Congress of the United States, and within every subsequent term of ten years, in such manner as they shall by law direct. The number of Representatives shall not exceed one for every 30,000, but each state shall have at least 1 Representative; [and until such enumeration shall be made, the state of New Hampshire shall be entitled to choose 3; Massachusetts, 8; Rhode Island and Providence Plantations, 1; Connecticut, 5; New York, 6; New Jersey, 4; Pennsylvania, 8; Delaware, 1; Maryland, 6; Virginia, 10; North Carolina, 5; South Carolina, 5; and Georgia, 3.]

4. Filling Vacancies When vacancies happen in the representation from any state, the executive authority thereof shall issue writs of election to fill such vacancies.

5. Officers; Impeachment The House of Representatives shall choose their Speaker and other officers; and shall have the sole power of impeachment.

Section 3. Senate

1. Composition and Term The Senate of the United States shall be composed of two Senators from each state [chosen by the legislature thereof], for six years; and each Senator shall have one vote.

2. Classification; Filling Vacancies [Immediately after they shall be assembled in consequence of the first election, they shall be divided as equally as may be into three classes. The seats of the Senators of the first class shall be vacated at the expiration of the second year, of the second class at the expiration of the fourth year, and of the third class at the expiration of the sixth year, so that one third may be chosen every second year; and if vacancies happen by resignation, or otherwise, during the recess of the legislature of any state, the executive thereof may make temporary appointments until the next meeting of the legislature, which shall then fill such vacancies.]

cial election to fill the vacancy. The state legislature, however, may empower the governor to name a temporary senator.

3. Qualifications
No person shall be a Senator who shall not have attained to the age of thirty years, and been nine years a citizen of the United States, and who shall not, when elected, be an inhabitant of that state for which he shall be chosen.

Clause 3. This clause specifies that a senator must be (1) at least 30 years of age, (2) a United States citizen for at least 9 years, and (3) a resident of the state in which elected. TERM OF OFFICE: 6 years.

4. President of the Senate
The Vice President of the United States shall be President of the Senate, but shall have no vote, unless they be equally divided.

Clause 4. To serve as president of the Senate and vote only in case of a tie is the sole duty the Constitution assigns to the Vice President. In recent years the Vice President has assumed additional duties at the President's request, such as attending cabinet meetings, traveling abroad on good-will tours, and carrying out such ceremonial duties as entertaining leading officials from abroad and representing the government at important events.

5. Other Officers
The Senate shall choose their other officers, and also a president *pro tempore,* in the absence of the Vice President, or when he shall exercise the office of President of the United States.

Clause 5. "Other officers" include a secretary, chaplain, and sergeant-at-arms. These officers are not members of the Senate. *Pro tempore* is a Latin expression meaning "for the time being," or "temporarily."

6. Trial of Impeachments
The Senate shall have the sole power to try all impeachments. When sitting for that purpose, they shall be on oath or affirmation. When the President of the United States is tried, the Chief Justice shall preside; and no person shall be convicted without the concurrence of two thirds of the members present.

Clause 6. Only the President, Vice President, cabinet officials, and federal judges are subject to impeachment and removal from office. Members of the House and Senate cannot be impeached, but they can be censured and even removed from office by the members of their respective houses. Officials may be impeached only for committing "treason, bribery, or other high crimes and misdemeanors" (see Article 2, Section 4). The Chief Justice of the Supreme Court presides at the impeachment trial of a President. The Vice President presides over all other impeachment trials. The Senate can find an impeached official guilty only if two thirds of the senators present agree on the verdict. The only President ever impeached was Andrew Johnson, in 1867; he was saved from conviction by one vote. In 1974 Richard M. Nixon resigned as President after the Judiciary Committee of the House of Representatives recommended to the House that he be impeached.

7. Penalty for Conviction
Judgment in cases of impeachment shall not extend further than to removal from office, and disqualification to hold and enjoy any office of honor, trust, or profit under the United States; but the party convicted shall nevertheless be liable and subject to indictment, trial, judgment and punishment, according to Law.

Clause 7. The punishment for conviction in impeachment cases can consist only of removal from office and disqualification from holding any other federal office. However, the convicted person may also be tried in a regular court of law for this same offense. Although not impeached, President Nixon was granted a Presidential pardon, which spared him a possible criminal court trial.

Clause 1. Under this provision Congress has passed a law stating that, unless the constitution of a state provides otherwise, Congressional elections must be held on the Tuesday following the first Monday in November of even-numbered years. (Until 1960 Maine held elections in September.) Congress has also ruled that representatives must be elected by districts, rather than by the state as a whole, and that secret ballots (or voting machines, where required by state law) must be used.

Clause 2. Under Amendment 20 Congress now meets on January 3, unless it sets another day by law.

Clause 1. Until 1969 Congress used this clause to disqualify elected candidates who had broken the law or who were charged with gross misconduct and prevent them from taking office. In 1969, the Supreme Court ruled that Congress had to seat all senators and representatives who met the requirements of Article 1, Section 2, Clause 2. A *quorum* is the minimum number of persons required to be present to transact business; a majority of the House or Senate constitutes a quorum. In practice, business is often transacted with less than a quorum present and may go on as long as no member objects to the lack of a quorum.

Clause 2. Each house has extensive rules of procedure. Each house can censure, punish, or expel a member. Expulsion requires a two-thirds vote.

Clause 3. Each house is required to keep a journal of its activities. These journals, called the *House Journal* and the *Senate Journal,* are published at the end of each session of Congress. A third journal, called the *Congressional Record,* is published every day that Congress is in session, and furnishes a daily account of what representatives and senators do and say. If one fifth of those present insist on a roll call of the members' votes, each member's vote must be recorded in the proper house journal.

Clause 4. Both houses must remain in session for the same period of time and in the same place.

Section 4. Elections and Meetings

1. Holding Elections The times, places and manner of holding elections for Senators and Representatives shall be prescribed in each state by the legislature thereof; but the Congress may at any time by law make or alter such regulations, except as to the places of choosing senators.

2. Meetings The Congress shall assemble at least once in every year, [and such meeting shall be on the first Monday in December,] unless they shall by law appoint a different day.

Section 5. Rules of Procedure

1. Organization Each house shall be the judge of the elections, returns and qualifications of its own members, and a majority of each shall constitute a quorum to do business; but a smaller number may adjourn from day to day, and may be authorized to compel the attendance of absent members, in such manner, and under such penalties as each house may provide.

2. Proceedings Each house may determine the rules of its proceedings, punish its members for disorderly behavior, and, with the concurrence of two thirds, expel a member.

3. Journal Each house shall keep a journal of its proceedings, and from time to time publish the same, excepting such parts as may in their judgment require secrecy; and the yeas and nays of the members of either house on any question shall, at the desire of one fifth of those present, be entered on the journal.

4. Adjournment Neither house, during the session of Congress, shall, without the consent of the other, adjourn for more than three days, nor to any other place than that in which the two houses shall be sitting.

Section 6. Privileges and Restrictions

1. Pay and Privileges The Senators and Representatives shall receive a compensation for their services, to be ascertained by law, and paid out of the Treasury of the United States. They shall in all cases, except treason, felony and breach of the peace, be privileged from arrest during their attendance at the session of their respective houses, and in going to and returning from the same; and for any speech or debate in either house, they shall not be questioned in any other place.

Clause 1. The provision concerning privilege from arrest establishes the principle of "Congressional immunity." According to this principle, members cannot be arrested or brought into court for what they say in speeches and debates in Congress. The aim of this provision is to enable members of Congress to speak freely. They are subject to arrest, however, if they commit a crime, and, under the laws governing slander and libel, are liable for any false or defamatory statements they may make outside Congress.

2. Restrictions No Senator or Representative shall, during the time for which he was elected, be appointed to any civil office under the authority of the United States, which shall have been created, or the emoluments whereof shall have been increased during such time; and no person holding any office under the United States, shall be a member of either house during his continuance in office.

Clause 2. This clause emphasizes the separation of powers in the federal government. Legislators cannot, while they are members of Congress, hold positions also in the executive or judicial departments. Nor can legislators resign and then accept positions that were created during their term of office. Thus members of Congress cannot set up jobs for themselves in the executive or judicial branches of the government. Furthermore, if a member resigns and is appointed to an existing executive or judicial position, he or she cannot profit from any increase in pay in this position that was voted during the member's term in Congress.

Section 7. Method of Passing Laws

1. Revenue Bills All bills for raising revenue shall originate in the House of Representatives; but the Senate may propose or concur with amendments as on other bills.

Clause 1. All revenue, or money-raising, bills must be introduced in the House of Representatives. This provision grew out of a demand that the popularly elected branch of the legislature should have the "power of the purse." (Until Amendment 17 was ratified, the House was the only popularly elected branch.) It was also felt that the voters had more control over representatives, who are elected for two-year terms, than over senators, who are elected for six-year terms. Thus representatives would be more careful than senators in considering revenue bills. Since the Senate has the power to amend any bill, however, it can amend a revenue bill in such a way as actually to introduce a revenue bill of its own.

2. How a Bill Becomes Law Every bill which shall have passed the House of Representatives and the Senate, shall, before it become a law, be presented to the President of the United States; if he approve he shall sign it, but if not he shall return it, with his objections to that house in which it shall have originated, who shall enter the objections at large on their journal, and proceed to reconsider it. If after such reconsideration two thirds of that house shall agree to pass the bill, it shall be sent, together with the objections, to the other house, by which it shall likewise be reconsidered, and, if approved by two thirds of that house, it shall become a law. But in all

Clause 2. When both houses of Congress pass a law, it is then sent to the President. If the President does not approve of a bill, one of several things may occur. The President may (1) veto, or refuse to sign, the bill; (2) permit the bill to become a law without signing it by holding it for ten days (not counting Sundays) while Congress is in session; (3) hold the bill near the end of a session in the hope that Congress will adjourn within ten days. In that case, the bill fails to become a law, just as though the President had formally vetoed it. This type of veto is called a "pocket veto." A bill vetoed by the President can become a law, however, if two thirds or more of both houses vote for the bill a second time. When this happens, Congress is said to have "overridden the Presidential veto."

such cases the votes of both houses shall be determined by yeas and nays, and the names of the persons voting for and against the bill shall be entered on the journal of each house respectively. If any bill shall not be returned by the President within ten days (Sundays excepted) after it shall have been presented to him, the same shall be a law, in like manner as if he had signed it, unless the Congress by their adjournment prevent its return, in which case it shall not be a law.

Clause 3. A *joint resolution* results from declarations passed by both houses of Congress on the same subject. It becomes a law in the same manner as a bill. A Congressional declaration of war takes the form of a joint resolution. A *concurrent resolution* represents only an expression of opinion on the part of either house of Congress. It does not have the force of law and, therefore, does not require Presidential approval. The process of amending the Constitution may start this way. A vote censuring a representative or senator, or an expression of sympathy, takes the form of a concurrent resolution.

3. Presidential Approval or Veto Every order, resolution, or vote to which the concurrence of the Senate and House of Representatives may be necessary (except on a question of adjournment) shall be presented to the President of the United States; and before the same shall take effect, shall be approved by him, or being disapproved by him, shall be repassed by two thirds of the Senate and House of Representatives, according to the rules and limitations prescribed in the case of a bill.

Section 8 places important powers in the hands of Congress, indicating that the Framers were aware of the weaknesses of the Congress under the Articles of Confederation. This section lists 18 powers granted to Congress—the *delegated* or *enumerated powers*. The first 17 are expressed powers because they clearly designate specific areas in which Congress may exercise its authority. The eighteenth power is contained in the famous elastic clause, from which has come the doctrine of implied powers. The elastic clause permits the stretching of the other 17 powers.

Section 8. Powers Delegated to Congress

The Congress shall have power

Clause 1. This clause gives Congress the power to levy and collect taxes, duties, or tariffs (taxes on imported goods collected at customhouses), and excises (taxes on goods produced, sold, or consumed within the country). The term *imposts* includes duties and excise taxes. Notice that these taxes must be uniform throughout the United States. According to this clause, the power to tax may be used only (1) to pay the government's debts and (2) to provide for the common defense and general welfare. The Social Security tax on payrolls is a present-day use of the power to tax.

1. To lay and collect taxes, duties, imposts and excises, to pay the debts and provide for the common defense and general welfare of the United States; but all duties, imposts and excises shall be uniform throughout the United States;

Clause 2. The power granted in Clause 2 enables the government to borrow money by issuing bonds for sale, on which the government pays interest. This clause, extended by Clause 18, has also given Congress the power to establish national banks and the Federal Reserve System.

2. To borrow money on the credit of the United States;

3. To regulate commerce with foreign nations, and among the several states, [and with the Indian tribes];

Clause 3. Congress is given direct control over interstate and foreign commerce. This provision has been extended, by the use of Clause 18, to give Congress control over transportation, communication, and navigation. In order to exercise this broad power, Congress has set up administrative agencies, such as the Interstate Commerce Commission and the Federal Communications Commission.

4. To establish an uniform rule of naturalization, and uniform laws on the subject of bankruptcies throughout the United States;

Clause 4. This clause provides the power to regulate the methods by which aliens become citizens of the United States and to form rules regarding bankruptcy.

5. To coin money, regulate the value thereof, and of foreign coin, and fix the standard of weights and measures;

Clause 5. Congress is permitted to coin money, to determine the gold and silver content of money, and to order the printing of paper money. It also permits Congress to set up uniform standards for measuring weights and distances.

6. To provide for the punishment of counterfeiting the securities and current coin of the United States;

Clause 6. Under this clause Congress authorizes the Treasury Department to investigate counterfeiting of money or of government bonds.

7. To establish post offices and post roads;

Clause 7. In 1970 Congress transferred authority over the postal system to the executive branch in the Postal Reorganization Act. The Post Office Department was replaced by an independent agency, the United States Postal Service.

8. To promote the progress of science and useful arts by securing for limited times to authors and inventors the exclusive right to their respective writings and discoveries;

Clause 8. This clause shows that the Framers were eager to promote the progress of science and the arts. Under this power Congress has passed laws providing that inventors be granted *patents* (exclusive rights to manufacture and sell their inventions for 17 years) and that authors and composers be granted *copyrights* (exclusive rights to control the publication or performance of their works for their lifetimes plus 50 years).

9. To constitute tribunals inferior to the Supreme Court;

Clause 9. Congress is granted the power to establish the federal district courts, the Courts of Appeals, and special courts.

10. To define and punish piracies and felonies committed on the high seas, and offenses against the law of nations;

Clause 10. Congress protects and controls citizens and ships of the United States when they are out of the country. It may also punish counterfeiting in the United States of bonds and notes of a foreign government.

Clause 11. Congress is given the power to declare war. Although Congress alone has this power, several Presidents have taken military action without prior consent of Congress. In 1846 President Polk sent troops into an area claimed by both the United States and Mexico. In 1950 President Truman ordered American troops into Korea. And in the mid-1960's, through executive order, American troops became involved in the conflict in Vietnam without a formal declaration of war. The 1973 War Powers Resolution requires the President to report to Congress within 48 hours any new commitment of American troops to a foreign war. Unless Congress declares war, the President must end hostilities within 60 days and withdraw the troops within 90 days. Congress can require earlier withdrawal by passing a joint resolution, which the President cannot veto. Letters of marque and reprisal were licenses issued by the government to privateers (armed ships, privately owned), allowing them to attack enemy ships during wartime. In the War of 1812, the government of the United States issued many of the licenses to American privateers, who did extensive damage to British trade. Today, the issuing of such licenses is outlawed by international agreement.

Clause 12. The two-year limit in Clause 12 on money appropriations for the army was included to keep the major military power under strict civilian control.

Clause 13. Notice that appropriations for the navy were not limited. An air force, of course, was not dreamed of when the Constitution was written.

Clause 14. Under the power granted in this clause, Congress has established rules and regulations governing military discipline and the procedure of courts-martial.

Clause 15. The term *militia* now refers to the National Guard units of the states. These units may now be called up by the President to keep law and order. They can become part of the United States Army in emergencies.

Clause 16. Congress is authorized to help states support their militia.

Clause 17. This clause enables Congress to exercise exclusive control over the government of the District of Columbia. In 1973 Congress relinquished some of its control by allowing the District to choose local officials. By this clause Congress also controls all installations owned and operated by the federal government in the various states.

11. To declare war, [grant letters of marque and reprisal,] and make rules concerning captures on land and water;

12. To raise and support armies, but no appropriation of money to that use shall be for a longer term than two years;

13. To provide and maintain a navy;

14. To make rules for the government and regulation of the land and naval forces;

15. To provide for calling forth the militia to execute the laws of the Union, suppress insurrections and repel invasions;

16. To provide for organizing, arming, and disciplining the militia, and for governing such part of them as may be employed in the service of the United States, reserving to the states respectively, the appointment of the officers, and the authority of training the militia according to the discipline prescribed by Congress.

17. To exercise exclusive legislation in all cases whatsoever, over such district (not exceeding ten miles square) as may, by cession of particular states, and the acceptance of Congress, become the seat of the government of the United States, and to exercise like authority over all places purchased by the consent of the legislature of the state in which the same shall be, for the erection of forts, magazines, arsenals, dock-yards, and other needful buildings;—and

18. To make all laws which shall be necessary and proper for carrying into execution the foregoing powers, and all other powers vested by this Constitution in the government of the United States, or in any department or officer thereof.

Clause 18. "Necessary and proper" are the key words in the so-called *elastic clause*. Only by combining the power granted in this clause with one of the other 17 powers can Congress use the implied powers granted to it in the Constitution. Laws based on this clause are, of course, subject to review by the judicial branch.

Section 9. Powers Denied to the Federal Government

Section 9 limits the powers of Congress.

1. [The migration or importation of such persons as any of the states now existing shall think proper to admit, shall not be prohibited by the Congress prior to the year 1808; but a tax or duty may be imposed on such importation, not exceeding $10 for each person.]

Clause 1. Such persons refers to slaves. This provision grew out of the commerce compromise at the Constitutional Convention held in Philadelphia in 1787. It was agreed that Congress would not prohibit the importation of slaves prior to 1808, and that it would not impose an import tax of more than $10 per slave. The importation of slaves into the United States became illegal in 1808.

2. The privilege of the writ of *habeas corpus* shall not be suspended, unless when in cases of rebellion or invasion the public safety may require it.

Clause 2. The guarantee of the *writ of habeas corpus* (meaning "you may have the body, or person") protects a person against being held in jail on insufficient evidence or no evidence at all. The lawyer of a person arrested can obtain a writ, or court order, that requires the arrested person to be brought before a judge who must determine whether there are sufficient grounds to hold the person in jail. If there are no such grounds, the person must be freed.

3. No bill of attainder or *ex post facto* law shall be passed.

Clause 3. A "bill of attainder" is a legislative measure that condemns and punishes a person without a jury trial. Under the Constitution Congress cannot by law single out certain persons and inflict punishment on them. The power to punish belongs to the judiciary. An *ex post facto law* is a law that punishes a person for doing something that was legal before the law was passed, or that increases the penalty for earlier actions. Because of this clause, the Lindbergh kidnaping law of 1932, for example, could not be applied to persons who committed the crime of kidnaping before that year.

4. No capitation or other direct tax shall be laid, unless in proportion to the census herein before directed to be taken.

Clause 4. A capitation tax is a direct tax imposed on each person, such as the poll tax on persons voting. This provision was inserted to prevent Congress from taxing slaves per poll, or per person, for the purpose of abolishing slavery. Amendment 16 makes the income tax an exception to this clause. Amendment 24 outlaws federal poll taxes.

5. No tax or duty shall be laid on articles exported from any state.

Clause 5. The southern states wanted to make sure that Congress could not use its taxing power to impose taxes on southern exports, such as cotton and tobacco.

6. No preference shall be given by any regulation of commerce or revenue to the ports of one state over those of another; nor shall vessels bound to, or from, one state, be obliged to enter, clear, or pay duties in another.

Clause 6. This clause declares that the United States is an open market in which all states have equal trading and commercial opportunities.

Clause 7. This clause concerns the all-important power of the purse. Since Congress controls expenditures, it can limit the powers of the President by limiting the amount of money the Chief Executive may spend to run the government. This clause is perhaps the single most important curb on Presidential power in the Constitution. Furthermore, the requirement to account for money spent and received helps to protect against misuse of funds.

Clause 8. This clause prohibits the establishment of a nobility. It also discourages bribery of American officials by foreign governments.

According to Section 10, states cannot (1) make treaties, (2) coin money, (3) pass either bills of attainder or *ex post facto* laws, (4) impair obligations of contract, (5) grant titles of nobility, (6) tax imports or exports without the consent of Congress, (7) keep troops or warships in time of peace. (8) deal with another state or foreign power without the consent of Congress, and (9) engage in war unless invaded.

Clause 1. Because Shays's Rebellion was still fresh in the minds of the delegates to the Constitutional Convention, and since several of the states at that time were being urged to pass legislation relieving debtors from the payment of their debts, the delegates decided to protect creditors once and for all by denying states the right to pass laws that would impair obligations of contract. During the Great Depression, which began in 1929, and the New Deal period (1933–45), the Supreme Court upheld state laws relieving debtors or mortgagees from paying their debts on the due dates, but payments were simply postponed, not canceled.

Clause 2. Forbidden to the states in this clause is the power to vote for taxes on goods sent in or out of a state, unless Congress agrees.

Clause 3. This clause forbids the states to keep troops or warships in peacetime or enter into an agreement with another state or a foreign nation, unless Congress agrees.

7. No money shall be drawn from the Treasury, but in consequence of appropriations made by law; and a regular statement and account of the receipts and expenditures of all public money shall be published from time to time.

8. No title of nobility shall be granted by the United States; and no person holding any office of profit or trust under them, shall, without the consent of the Congress, accept of any present, emolument, office, or title, of any kind whatever, from any king, prince or foreign state.

Section 10. Powers Denied to the States

1. No state shall enter into any treaty, alliance, or confederation; grant letters of marque and reprisal; coin money; emit bills of credit; make any thing but gold and silver coin a tender in payment of debts; pass any bill of attainder, *ex post facto* law, or law impairing the obligation of contracts, or grant any title of nobility.

2. No state shall, without the consent of the Congress, lay any imposts or duties on imports or exports, except what may be absolutely necessary for executing its inspection laws; and the net produce of all duties and imposts, laid by any state on imports or exports, shall be for the use of the Treasury of the United States; and all such laws shall be subject to the revision and control of the Congress.

3. No state shall, without the consent of Congress, lay any duty of tonnage, keep troops, or ships of war in time of peace, enter into any agreement or compact with another state, or with a foreign power, or engage in war, unless actually invaded, or in such imminent danger as will not admit of delay.

ARTICLE 2
EXECUTIVE DEPARTMENT

Section 1. President and Vice President

1. Term of Office The executive power shall be vested in a President of the United States of America. He shall hold his office during the term of four years, and, together with the Vice President, chosen for the same term, be elected, as follows:

2. Electoral System Each state shall appoint, in such manner as the legislature thereof may direct, a number of electors, equal to the whole number of Senators and Representatives to which the state may be entitled in the Congress; but no Senator or Representative, or person holding an office of trust or profit under the United States, shall be appointed an elector.

3. Former Electoral Method [The electors shall meet in their respective states, and vote by ballot for two persons, of whom one at least shall not be an inhabitant of the same state with themselves. And they shall make a list of all the persons voted for, and of the number of votes for each; which list they shall sign and certify, and transmit sealed to the seat of the government of the United States, directed to the president of the Senate. The president of the Senate shall, in the presence of the Senate and House of Representatives, open all the certificates, and the votes shall then be counted. The person having the greatest number of votes shall be the President, if such number be a majority of the whole number of electors appointed; and if there be more than one who have such majority, and have an equal number of votes, then the House of Representatives shall immediately choose by ballot one of them for President; and if no person have a majority, then from the five highest on the list the said House shall in like manner choose the President. But in choosing the President, the votes shall be taken by states, the representation from each state having one vote. A quorum for this purpose shall consist of a member or members from two thirds of the states, and a majority of all the states shall be necessary to a choice. In every case, after the choice of the President, the person having the greatest number of votes of the electors shall be the Vice President. But if there should remain two or more who have equal votes, the Senate shall choose from them by ballot the Vice President.]

Clause 1. This provision gives the executive power to the President. The President may use all of the means available to carry out the laws or refrain from using some of these means. Of course, the power and prestige of the Presidency depend to some extent on the personality of the person who holds the office.

Clauses 2, 3. These clauses established the electoral system, but very little that the Framers decided about electing a President has survived in the form they intended. The delegates to the Constitutional Convention, still fearful of popular rule, decided that the President and Vice President ought to be elected by a small group of persons called "electors" chosen according to a method determined by each state legislature. Until Andrew Jackson's Presidency, electors were chosen by state legislatures. Since then the people have voted directly for the electors. Some changes in the method of electing a President have been made by formal amendment, as in Amendment 12; other changes have resulted from political practice.

Clause 4. Today Presidential elections are held on the Tuesday after the first Monday in November. Electoral votes are cast on the Monday after the second Wednesday in December.

Clause 5. This clause specifies that the President must be (1) a native-born citizen of the United States, (2) at least 35 years of age, and (3) a resident of the United States for at least 14 years. TERM OF OFFICE: 4 years.

Clause 6. If a President dies or is removed from office, the Vice President succeeds to the office. John Tyler, in 1841, was the first Vice President to succeed to the Presidency. By assuming the office of President, not simply serving as an acting President, Tyler established a precedent that has since been followed. Under the Presidential Succession Act of 1947, if both the President and the Vice President die or are removed from office, the order of succession is as follows: (1) Speaker of the House, (2) President *pro tempore* of the Senate, and (3) the cabinet members in the order in which their offices were created. Amendment 25, adopted in 1967, clarifies the procedure to be followed in case the President or Vice President is unable to serve or resigns.

Clause 7. Today the President's salary is $200,000 a year, plus a $50,000 expense account and a nontaxable fund for travel and official entertainment limited to $112,000. The Vice President's salary is $94,200 a year plus a $10,000 expense allowance.

Clause 8. The President assumes office officially only after taking the oath of office, which is administered by the Chief Justice of the United States.

4. Time of Elections The Congress may determine the time of choosing the electors, and the day on which they shall give their votes; which day shall be the same throughout the United States.

5. Qualifications No person except a natural-born citizen, [or a citizen of the United States, at the time of the adoption of this Constitution] shall be eligible to the office of President; neither shall any person be eligible to that office who shall not have attained to the age of thirty-five years, and been fourteen years a resident within the United States.

6. Filling Vacancies In case of the removal of the President from office, or of his death, resignation, or inability to discharge the powers and duties of the said office, the same shall devolve on the Vice President, and the Congress may by law provide for the case of removal, death, resignation or inability, both of the President and Vice President, declaring what officer shall then act as President, and such officer shall act accordingly, until the disability be removed, or a President shall be elected.

7. Salary The President shall, at stated times, receive for his services, a compensation, which shall neither be increased nor diminished during the period for which he shall have been elected, and he shall not receive within that period any other emolument from the United States, or any of them.

8. Oath of Office Before he enter on the execution of his office, he shall take the following oath or affirmation:—"I do solemnly swear (or affirm) that I will faithfully execute the office of President of the United States, and will to the best of my ability, preserve, protect and defend the Constitution of the United States."

Section 2. Powers of the President

1. Military Powers The President shall be Commander in Chief of the Army and Navy of the United States, and of the militia of the several states, when called into the actual service of the United States; he may require the opinion, in writing, of the principal officer in each of the executive departments, upon any subject relating to the duties of their respective offices, and he shall have power to grant reprieves and pardons for offences against the United States, except in cases of impeachment.

Clause 1. The important point in this provision is that it places the armed forces under civilian control. The President is a civilian but is superior in military power to any military officer. The words *principal officer in each of the executive departments* are the basis for the creation of the President's cabinet. Each cabinet member is the head of one of the executive departments. The President chooses the cabinet members, with the consent of the Senate, and can remove any cabinet official without asking Senate approval.

2. Treaties and Appointments He shall have power, by and with the advice and consent of the Senate, to make treaties, provided two thirds of the Senators present concur; and he shall nominate, and by and with the advice and consent of the Senate, shall appoint ambassadors, other public ministers and consuls, judges of the Supreme Court, and all other officers of the United States, whose appointments are not herein otherwise provided for, and which shall be established by law; but the Congress may by law vest the appointment of such inferior officers, as they think proper, in the President alone, in the courts of law, or in the heads of departments.

Clause 2. The President makes treaties with the advice and consent of two thirds of the Senate. A treaty ratified by the Senate becomes the supreme law of the land. The President can also enter into executive agreements with foreign governments that have the same force as treaties but do not require Senate approval. With the consent of the Senate, the President can appoint ambassadors, public ministers, consuls, and other diplomatic officials, as well as federal judges, military officers, and members of administrative agencies. "Inferior officers" are those subordinate to the cabinet members or to federal judges. At the present time, a majority of federal government positions are filled by men and women who have passed examinations given by the United States Civil Service Commission.

3. Filling Vacancies The President shall have power to fill up all vacancies that may happen during the recess of the Senate, by granting commissions which shall expire at the end of their next session.

Clause 3. If a vacancy in an important position occurs when Congress is not in session, the President has the power to fill such a vacancy with an interim appointment. When Congress meets again, this appointment or a new appointment must be submitted to the Senate so that it may be approved.

Section 3. Duties of the President

He shall from time to time give to the Congress information of the state of the Union, and recommend to their consideration such measures as he shall judge necessary and expedient; he may, on extraordinary occasions, convene both houses, or either of them, and in case of disagreement between them, with respect to the time of adjournment, he may adjourn them to such time as he shall think proper; he shall receive ambassadors and other public ministers; he shall take care that the laws be faithfully executed, and shall commission all the officers of the United States.

The President's duties include the following: (1) *Legislative duties:* delivering annual and special messages to Congress; calling special sessions of Congress; approving or vetoing bills (see Article 1, Section 7). (2) *Diplomatic duties:* receiving (or refusing to receive) ambassadors or ministers of foreign countries to indicate that the United States recognizes (or refuses to recognize) the government of these countries. The President can also send home the ambassador of a foreign country as a sign that the United States is breaking off diplomatic relations with that country. (3) *Executive duties:* executing all the laws. In actual fact the administration and enforcement of the laws are in the hands of the various government departments, commissions, and administrative agencies; but the President is responsible for seeing that they are carried out. (4) *Military duties:* commissioning of United States armed forces officers.

(See annotation of Article 1, Section 3, Clauses 6–7.)

By authorizing the establishment of a system of federal courts, Article 3 creates the judicial power—the power to hear and decide cases. Under the judicial powers granted by the Constitution or developed through Supreme Court decisions, the courts have declared unconstitutional certain laws of Congress, acts of the President, laws of the state legislatures, and decisions of the state courts.

Only the Supreme Court is established by the Constitution itself, but the Constitution gives Congress the authority to establish the lower courts that exist today. Since the Constitution does not state the number of justices to be appointed to the Supreme Court, Congress decides the number by law. Today the Supreme Court has nine justices. Congress has created two types of lower courts. One type includes federal district courts and Courts of Appeals, which review cases sent up by the district courts. District courts and Courts of Appeals are called "constitutional courts" because they are general courts deriving their power directly from the Constitution. The second type of court deals with cases of a specialized nature. The Court of Claims, the Tax Court, and the Court of Customs and Patent Appeals are included in this second group. The Framers of the Constitution wanted to make sure that federal judges would be independent of political influence. Accordingly federal judges are appointed for life, subject to good behavior, and their pay cannot be reduced by law during their term of office.

Clause 1. Here the words *law* and *equity* have special meanings. *Law* means the common law—the laws that originated in England and that have been based on centuries of judicial decisions. *Equity* refers to principles of justice also developed in England to remedy wrongs in situations in which the common law was inadequate. Today, in the United States, law and equity are applied by the same judges in the same courts. The power of the federal courts extends to two types of cases: (1) those involving the interpretation of the Constitution, federal laws, treaties, and laws relating to ships on the high seas and navigable waters; and (2) those involving the United States government itself, foreign diplomatic officials, two or more state governments, citizens of different states when the sum involved is more than $10,000, and a state or its citizens versus foreign countries or citizens of foreign countries.

Section 4. Impeachment

The President, Vice President and all civil officers of the United States, shall be removed from office on impeachment for, and conviction of, treason, bribery, or other high crimes and misdemeanors.

ARTICLE 3
JUDICIAL DEPARTMENT

Section 1. Federal Courts

The judicial power of the United States, shall be vested in one Supreme Court, and in such inferior courts as the Congress may from time to time ordain and establish. The judges, both of the supreme and inferior courts, shall hold their offices during good behaviour, and shall, at stated times, receive for their services, a compensation, which shall not be diminished during their continuance in office.

Section 2. Jurisdiction of Federal Courts

1. General Jurisdiction The judicial power shall extend to all cases, in law and equity, arising under this Constitution, the laws of the United States, and treaties made, or which shall be made, under their authority; to all cases affecting ambassadors, other public ministers and consuls; to all cases of admiralty and maritime jurisdiction; to controversies to which the United States shall be a party; to controversies between two or more states; [between a state and citizens of another state;] between citizens of the same state claiming lands under grants of different states, and between a state or the citizens thereof, and foreign states, citizens or subjects.

2. Supreme Court In all cases affecting ambassadors, other public ministers and consuls, and those in which a state shall be party, the Supreme Court shall have original jurisdiction. In all the other cases before mentioned, the Supreme Court shall have appellate jurisdiction, both as to law and fact, with such exceptions, and under such regulations as the Congress shall make.

3. Conduct of Trials The trial of all crimes, except in cases of impeachment, shall be by jury; and such trial shall be held in the state where the said crimes shall have been committed; but when not committed within any state, the trial shall be at such place or places as the Congress may by law have directed.

Section 3. Treason

1. Definition Treason against the United States, shall consist only in levying war against them, or in adhering to their enemies, giving them aid and comfort. No person shall be convicted of treason unless on the testimony of two witnesses to the same overt act, or on confession in open court.

2. Punishment The Congress shall have power to declare the punishment of treason, but no attainder of treason shall work corruption of blood, or forfeiture except during the life of the person attainted.

ARTICLE 4
RELATIONS AMONG THE STATES

Section 1. Official Acts

Full faith and credit shall be given in each state to the public acts, records, and judicial proceedings of every other state. And the Congress may by general Laws prescribe the manner in which such acts, records and proceedings shall be proved, and the effect thereof.

Section 2. Privileges of Citizens

1. Privileges The citizens of each state shall be entitled to all privileges and immunities of citizens in the several states.

Clause 2. Original jurisdiction means the right to try a case before any other court may hear it. *Appellate jurisdiction* means the right of a court to try cases appealed from lower courts. Most of the cases tried by the Supreme Court are cases appealed from lower federal and state courts. Cases involving foreign diplomats and any state of the United States may be started directly in the Supreme Court.

Clause 3. Every person accused of a federal crime is guaranteed a jury trial near the scene of the crime. But accused persons may give up this privilege, if they wish. Amendments 5, 6, and 7 expand the provisions of this clause.

Clause 1. Treason is the only crime specifically defined in the Constitution. To be found guilty of treason, a person must be shown to have helped wage war against the United States, or to have given aid and comfort to its enemies. A person cannot be convicted without the testimony of two witnesses to the same act unless the person confesses in open court.

Clause 2. The punishment for treason, as determined by Congress, is death or a fine of $10,000 and imprisonment for not less than five years. This clause further states that the punishment for treason cannot be extended to the children of a traitor. In 1953, Julius and Ethel Rosenberg became the first American citizens who were convicted and executed for treason in peacetime.

The purpose of this provision is to make sure that the official records of one state are respected in all the other states. Official records of this kind include birth certificates, marriage licenses, death certificates, corporation charters, wills, and court decisions. This provision also protects a citizen's right to collect money that has been awarded by a court decision in one state, even if the person who owes the money moves to another state.

Clause 1. The terms *privileges* and *immunities* simply mean the rights of citizens. Thus a state cannot discriminate against citizens of other states in favor of its own citizens, except in certain very special areas—such as voting, for example. A state can impose residence requirements for voting, so that citizens of another state must reside in the state for a specified period before they can vote as citizens of their new state.

Clause 2. This provision prevents a prisoner or a person charged with a crime from escaping justice by fleeing across a state line. It provides that a criminal be returned by the state where captured to the state where the crime was committed— a process known as extradition. A governor of a state cannot be forced to extradite, or return, a prisoner, however, if the governor feels that such action will result in injustice to the accused person.

Clause 3. Since the ratification of Amendment 13 in 1865 brought an end to slavery in this country, the clause is now of historical interest only.

Clause 1. The Northwest Ordinance of 1787 provided that new states be admitted to the Union on completely equal footing with the original thirteen states. Although the Constitution declares here that new states may not be created within the territory of any other state without its consent, an exception did occur in 1863, when West Virginia was formed from the western part of the state of Virginia. This exception occurred during the Civil War, and West Virginia received permission from the loyal, rather than the secessionist, government of Virginia.

Clause 2. Under this provision Congress has the power to control all property belonging to the federal government. It can set up governments for territories and colonies of the United States. It can grant independence to a colony, as it did to the Philippines in 1946. It can set aside land for national parks and build dams for flood control.

If public property is being destroyed and public safety endangered in a state, the President may decide to send troops into that state without having been requested to do so by local authorities. The President may even proclaim martial law in a state. This section also guarantees that states can govern only by consent of the governed.

2. Extradition A person charged in any state with treason, felony, or other crime, who shall flee from justice, and be found in another state, shall on demand of the executive authority of the state from which he fled, be delivered up, to be removed to the state having jurisdiction of the crime.

3. Fugitive Slaves [No person held in service or labor in one state, under the laws thereof, escaping into another, shall, in consequence of any law or regulation therein, be discharged from such service or labor, but shall be delivered up on claim of the party to whom such service or labor may be due.]

Section 3. New States and Territories

1. Admission of New States New states may be admitted by the Congress into this Union; but no new state shall be formed or erected within the jurisdiction of any other state; nor any state be formed by the junction of two or more states, or parts of states, without the consent of the legislatures of the states concerned as well as of the Congress.

2. Powers of Congress The Congress shall have power to dispose of and make all needful rules and regulations respecting the territory or other property belonging to the United States; and nothing in this Constitution shall be so construed as to prejudice any claims of the United States, or of any particular state.

Section 4. Guarantees to the States

The United States shall guarantee to every state in this Union a republican form of government, and shall protect each of them against invasion; and on application of the legislature, or of the executive (when the legislature cannot be convened) against domestic violence.

ARTICLE 5
METHODS OF AMENDMENT

The Congress, whenever two thirds of both houses shall deem it necessary, shall propose amendments to this Constitution, or, on the application of legislatures of two thirds of the several states, shall call a convention for proposing amendments, which, in either case, shall be valid to all intents and purposes, as part of this Constitution, when ratified by the legislatures of three fourths of the several states, or by conventions in three fourths thereof, as the one or the other mode of ratification may be proposed by the Congress; provided that [no amendment which may be made prior to the year 1808 shall in any manner affect the first and fourth clauses in the Ninth Section of the First Article; and that] no state, without its consent, shall be deprived of its equal suffrage in the Senate.

ARTICLE 6
GENERAL PROVISIONS

1. Public Debts All debts contracted and engagements entered into, before the adoption of this Constitution, shall be as valid against the United States under this Constitution, as under the Confederation.

2. The Supreme Law This Constitution, and the laws of the United States which shall be made in pursuance thereof; and all treaties made, or which shall be made, under the authority of the United States, shall be the supreme law of the land; and the judges in every state shall be bound thereby, anything in the constitution or laws of any state to the contrary notwithstanding.

3. Oaths of Office The Senators and Representatives before mentioned, and the members of the several state legislatures, and all executive and judicial officers, both of the United States and of the several states, shall be bound by oath or affirmation, to support this Constitution; but no religious test shall ever be required as a qualification to any office or public trust under the United States.

One of the most important features of the Constitution is that it can be amended, or changed. An amendment must first be *proposed* and then *ratified*. So far, all amendments have been proposed by Congress and ratified by state legislatures except Amendment 21, which was ratified by the convention method. The fact that only 26 amendments have been adopted since 1789—and only 16 since 1791—indicates that it is not easy to change the Constitution, and that changing it is a serious matter, requiring much thought and discussion in Congress, in the state legislatures, and among the people. Notice that there are two areas in which the Constitution cannot be amended under any circumstances. The first exception is obsolete because it is a reference to the period that preceded 1808. The second exception is still very important because it guarantees that every state shall have equal representation in the Senate.

Clause 1. This provision was important because it announced to all that the new government would assume and pay back all debts of the government under the Articles of Confederation. It was one of several actions favored by Alexander Hamilton and undertaken by Congress in order to establish the credit of the new government.

Clause 2. This is the famous "supremacy clause" of the Constitution. It declares that the "supreme law of the land" is (1) the Constitution, (2) the laws of the United States passed under this Constitution, and (3) the treaties made under the authority of the United States. According to the supremacy clause, the power of the national government is superior to the power of the state governments, provided that the actions of the national government are in accordance with the Constitution. The Supreme Court determines whether the actions of the President and Congress are constitutional.

Clause 3. No religious qualification shall ever be required as a condition for holding public office. This provision results from the fact that in the United States there is separation of church and state. This means that a person's religion is supposed to remain a private matter, with no bearing on consideration for public office.

The Constitutional Convention was summoned by the Congress of the Confederation to amend the Articles of Confederation. Under the Articles amendments had to be approved by all thirteen states. Instead of amending the Articles, however, the delegates to the Constitutional Convention drafted an entirely new plan of government. Realizing that it would be difficult to get the approval of all the states—Rhode Island, for example, had not even sent delegates to Philadelphia—the Framers provided that the Constitution would go into effect after ratification by only nine states, not thirteen. As a result opponents of the Constitution said it had been adopted by revolutionary means.

ARTICLE 7
RATIFICATION

The ratification of the conventions of nine states, shall be sufficient for the establishment of this Constitution between the states so ratifying the same.

DONE in Convention by the unanimous consent of the States present the seventeenth day of September in the year of our Lord one thousand seven hundred and eighty seven and of the independence of the United States of America the twelfth. IN WITNESS whereof We have hereunto subscribed our names.

GEORGE WASHINGTON—
President and deputy from Virginia

New Hampshire

JOHN LANGDON
NICHOLAS GILMAN

Massachusetts

NATHANIEL GORHAM
RUFUS KING

Connecticut

WILLIAM SAMUEL JOHNSON
ROGER SHERMAN

New York

ALEXANDER HAMILTON

New Jersey

WILLIAM LIVINGSTON
DAVID BREARLEY
WILLIAM PATERSON
JONATHAN DAYTON

Pennsylvania

BENJAMIN FRANKLIN
THOMAS MIFFLIN
ROBERT MORRIS
GEORGE CLYMER
THOMAS FITZSIMONS
JARED INGERSOLL
JAMES WILSON
GOUVERNEUR MORRIS

Delaware

GEORGE READ
GUNNING BEDFORD
JOHN DICKINSON
RICHARD BASSETT
JACOB BROOM

Maryland

JAMES McHENRY
DANIEL OF ST. THOMAS JENIFER
DANIEL CARROLL

Virginia

JOHN BLAIR
JAMES MADISON

North Carolina

WILLIAM BLOUNT
RICHARD DOBBS SPAIGHT
HUGH WILLIAMSON

South Carolina

JOHN RUTLEDGE
CHARLES COTESWORTH PINCKNEY
CHARLES PINCKNEY
PIERCE BUTLER

Georgia

WILLIAM FEW
ABRAHAM BALDWIN

THE AMENDMENTS TO THE CONSTITUTION

[The first ten amendments to the Constitution are called the Bill of Rights. The Bill of Rights limits the powers of the federal government but not the powers of the states. The Supreme Court has ruled, however, that the "due process" clause of Amendment 14 protects individuals against denial by the states of certain rights included in the Bill of Rights. For example, the Supreme Court has decided that neither the federal government nor the states can deprive any individual of freedom of religion, speech, press, petition, assembly, or of several other rights that pertain to the fair treatment of an accused person.]

AMENDMENT 1
FREEDOM OF RELIGION, SPEECH, PRESS, ASSEMBLY, AND PETITION (1791)

Congress shall make no law respecting an establishment of religion, or prohibiting the free exercise thereof; or abridging the freedom of speech, or of the press; or the right of the people peaceably to assemble, and to petition the government for a redress of grievances.

Amendment 1 protects five great civil liberties: (1) Freedom of religion means that Congress cannot interfere with the right to worship as one sees fit. The Supreme Court, however, has ruled that Congress can require "conscientious objectors" to bear arms during wartime. Congress has, however, made special provisions to permit conscientious objectors to participate in war work without bearing arms. In interpreting the phrase *establishment of religion,* the Supreme Court has decided that this phrase erects a wall of separation between church and state. The Supreme Court has prohibited state and local school authorities from requiring prayers or a devotional reading of the Bible in public schools. (2) Freedom of speech means the right to speak out privately and publicly. However, this right does not permit anyone to slander people (make false and malicious remarks about them). Furthermore, the Supreme Court has declared that freedom of speech can be limited by the federal government if there is a "clear and present" danger that what is said may injure the general welfare. (3) Freedom of the press gives newspapers, television, and magazines the right to express ideas and opinions provided they do not libel people (publish false and malicious remarks about them) or incite the violent overthrow of the government. Also, the use of the United States mails may be denied to those publications that spread obscenity and fraudulent ideas. (4) Freedom to assemble is the right to attend meetings and join clubs. (5) The right to petition for redress of grievances means the opportunity to express complaints to any official of the federal government.

AMENDMENT 2
RIGHT TO KEEP ARMS (1791)

A well regulated militia, being necessary to the security of a free state, the right of the people to keep and bear arms, shall not be infringed.

The purpose of this amendment was to prevent Congress from denying states the right to have a militia (or National Guard) of armed citizens. It also protected Americans' right to keep weapons in order to resist a tyrannical government. However, Congress and many states have regulated the ownership and use of weapons by citizens through gun control legislation.

Amendments 3 and 4 guarantee all citizens the right to privacy and security in their own homes. Amendment 3 was designed to prevent the national government from requiring citizens to house and feed military personnel in their homes. The quartering of troops in the colonists' homes by the British government had been a source of friction between the American colonists and the British before the American Revolution.

AMENDMENT 3
QUARTERING OF TROOPS (1791)

No soldier shall, in time of peace, be quartered in any house, without the consent of the owner, nor in time of war, but in a manner to be prescribed by law.

The supporters of this amendment aimed to limit issuance of search warrants to the following conditions: (1) The warrant must be issued by a judge. (2) There must be a good reason for its use. (3) The officer who asks for a search warrant must take an oath affirming reasons for demanding the warrant. (4) The warrant must describe the place to be searched and the persons or things to be seized. The Supreme Court has decided that evidence illegally seized cannot be used in either federal or state courts. Under this amendment the federal government prohibits wiretapping unless a court permit is obtained showing a reasonable certainty that one of a certain list of crimes is being committed. In 1967 the Supreme Court held that eavesdropping and bugging by electronic means are permissible but only within certain limits; for example, police may use eavesdropping devices if they secure a warrant in advance by showing probable cause. In 1968 the Supreme Court forbade the use of criminal evidence obtained by police listening in on a party line, but evidence derived from wiretapping is permitted in federal courts in some crimes.

AMENDMENT 4
SEARCH AND SEIZURE;
WARRANTS (1791)

The right of the people to be secure in their persons, houses, papers, and effects, against unreasonable searches and seizures, shall not be violated, and no warrants shall issue, but upon probable cause, supported by oath or affirmation, and particularly describing the place to be searched, and the persons or things to be seized.

This amendment lists the rights of an accused person: (1) A person accused of a capital crime or any other serious crime must first be accused by a grand jury (a jury of 12 to 23 persons) before being brought to trial. An indictment or presentment by a grand jury is merely a formal accusation. (2) A person cannot be tried twice for the same crime. (3) A person cannot be required to give incriminating testimony in a courtroom or before a grand jury or Congressional committee. However, under the Immunity Act of 1954, a witness can be required to testify in certain cases if the evidence he or she may provide cannot be used in any trial of that person. (4) A person cannot be deprived of life, liberty, or property without due process of law—or according to the law of the land. (5) Congress cannot take private property for public use without paying a fair price for it. This provision, an important protection of property rights, establishes the principle of eminent domain. Members of the armed forces are tried by military courts and commissions and are not subject to the provision calling for indictment by a grand jury.

AMENDMENT 5
RIGHTS OF ACCUSED PERSONS (1791)

No person shall be held to answer for a capital, or otherwise infamous crime, unless on a presentment or indictment of a grand jury, except in cases arising in the land or naval forces, or in the militia, when in actual service in time of war or public danger; nor shall any person be subject for the same offense to be twice put in jeopardy of life or limb; nor shall be compelled in any criminal case to be a witness against himself, nor be deprived of life, liberty, or property, without due process of law; nor shall private property be taken for public use, without just compensation.

AMENDMENT 6
RIGHT TO SPEEDY TRIAL (1791)

In all criminal prosecutions, the accused shall enjoy the right to a speedy and public trial, by an impartial jury of the state and district wherein the crime shall have been committed, which district shall have been previously ascertained by law, and to be informed of the nature and cause of the accusation; to be confronted with the witnesses against him; to have compulsory process for obtaining witnesses in his favor, and to have the assistance of counsel for his defense.

This amendment continues the rights of an accused person. Notice that all witnesses against an accused person must appear on the witness stand, and that the government must help the accused to produce favorable witnesses. If an accused person cannot afford to hire a lawyer, the judge will assign one, and the government will pay the lawyer's fee. These provisions under Amendment 6 apply to federal courts. However, under the "due process" clause of Amendment 14, the Supreme Court has decided that state courts must also assign a lawyer to defend an accused person who cannot afford one.

AMENDMENT 7
JURY TRIAL IN CIVIL CASES (1791)

In Suits at common law, where the value in controversy shall exceed $20, the right of trial by jury shall be preserved, and no fact tried by a jury shall be otherwise re-examined in any court of the United States than according to the rules of the common law.

This amendment provides for a jury trial in federal civil cases (trials where one person sues another) in which more than $20 is involved. By custom, however, civil cases are not tried before federal courts unless they involve much larger sums of money.

AMENDMENT 8
BAILS, FINES, PUNISHMENTS (1791)

Excessive bail shall not be required, nor excessive fines imposed, nor cruel and unusual punishments inflicted.

Persons accused of a crime and awaiting trial may be permitted to leave jail if they or someone else posts bail—a sum of money serving as a guarantee that the accused will appear for trial. The courts determine the amount of bail asked for. Cruel and unusual punishments, such as torture and beheading, are prohibited. In a series of rulings, the Supreme Court declared invalid convictions of accused persons based on confessions secured by torture or other "third degree" methods.

AMENDMENT 9
POWERS RESERVED TO THE PEOPLE (1791)

The enumeration in the Constitution, of certain rights, shall not be construed to deny or disparage others retained by the people.

The Constitution does not describe specifically all the rights to be retained by the people. This amendment was added in order to guarantee that those fundamental rights not enumerated must be respected by the national government at all times.

AMENDMENT 10
POWERS RESERVED TO THE STATES (1791)

The powers not delegated to the United States by the Constitution, nor prohibited by it to the states, are reserved to the states respectively, or to the people.

This is known as the reserved power amendment. Powers delegated to the national government are listed in Article 1, Section 8. Powers prohibited to the states are found in Article 1, Section 10. Amendment 10 makes it clear that all other powers—the so-called reserved powers—are left to the states or to the people.

This is the first amendment to the Constitution that was prompted by an unpopular Supreme Court decision. In the case of *Chisholm* v. *Georgia* (1793), the Supreme Court ruled that two citizens of South Carolina could sue Georgia in a federal court for property that Georgia had confiscated. The states objected, arguing that since the states were sovereign, it was undignified to permit a state to be sued by a citizen of another state in a federal court. As a result of this amendment, a citizen of the United States or of a foreign nation who wishes to bring suit against any state is required to introduce the case in the courts of the state that is being sued.

This amendment alters Article 2, Section 1, Clause 3. Before this amendment the electors voted for two persons, without designating which was to be President and which Vice President. As a result in 1796 the people elected a Federalist President (John Adams) and a Republican Vice President (Jefferson). In 1800 the electors of the victorious Republican Party each cast one vote for Jefferson, whom they wanted to be President, and one vote for Burr, whom they wanted to be Vice President. The result, of course, was a tie. Amendment 12, which instructs electors to cast separate ballots for President and Vice President, prevents such situations. (See also Amendment 23, which makes provision for choosing electors of President and Vice President by the District of Columbia.)

AMENDMENT 11
SUITS AGAINST STATES (1798)

The judicial power of the United States shall not be construed to extend to any suit in law or equity, commenced or prosecuted against one of the United States, by citizens of another state, or by citizens or subjects of any foreign state.

AMENDMENT 12
ELECTION OF PRESIDENT
AND VICE PRESIDENT (1804)

The electors shall meet in their respective states and vote by ballot for President and Vice President, one of whom, at least, shall not be an inhabitant of the same state with themselves; they shall name in their ballots the person voted for as President, and in distinct ballots the person voted for as Vice President, and they shall make distinct lists of all persons voted for as President, and of all persons voted for as Vice President, and of the number of votes for each, which lists they shall sign and certify, and transmit sealed, to the seat of the government of the United States, directed to the President of the Senate; the President of the Senate shall, in the presence of the Senate and House of Representatives, open all the certificates and the votes shall then be counted; the person having the greatest number of votes for President, shall be the President, if such number be a majority of the whole number of electors appointed; and if no person have such majority, then from the persons having the highest numbers not exceeding three on the list of those voted for as President, the House of Representatives shall choose immediately, by ballot, the President. But in choosing the President, the votes shall be taken by states, the representation from each state having one vote; a quorum for this purpose shall consist of a member or members from two thirds of the states, and a majority of all the states shall be necessary to a choice. [And if the House of Representatives shall not choose a President whenever the right of choice shall devolve upon them, before the fourth day of March next following, then the Vice President shall act as President, as in the case of the death or other constitutional disability of the President.] The person having the greatest number of votes as Vice President, shall be the Vice President, if such number be a majority of the whole number of electors appointed, and if no person have a majority, then from the two highest numbers on the list, the Senate shall choose the Vice President; a quorum for the purpose shall consist of two thirds of the whole number of Senators, and a majority of the whole number shall be necessary to a choice. But no person constitutionally ineligible to the office of President shall be eligible to that of Vice President of the United States.

AMENDMENT 13
SLAVERY ABOLISHED (1865)

Section 1. Neither slavery nor involuntary servitude, except as a punishment for crime whereof the party shall have been duly convicted, shall exist within the United States, or any place subject to their jurisdiction.

Section 2. Congress shall have power to enforce this article by appropriate legislation.

Amendments 13, 14, and 15 resulted from the Civil War. Amendment 13 freed the slaves, Amendment 14 made blacks citizens, and Amendment 15 forbade the states to deny black Americans the right to vote. Amendment 13 forbids slavery, and under Section 2, Congress has the power to enforce this order.

AMENDMENT 14
RIGHTS OF CITIZENS (1868)

Section 1. Citizenship Defined All persons born or naturalized in the United States, and subject to the jurisdiction thereof, are citizens of the United States and of the state wherein they reside. No state shall make or enforce any law which shall abridge the privileges or immunities of citizens of the United States; nor shall any state deprive any person of life, liberty, or property, without due process of law; nor deny to any person within its jurisdiction the equal protection of the laws.

This section contains a number of important provisions. By the definition of citizenship given here, black Americans were granted citizenship. The second sentence, forbidding states to abridge the privileges and immunities—the rights—of citizens, meant that the states could not interfere with the right of black Americans and other citizens to live a peaceful, useful life or to travel. This amendment, like Amendment 5, contains a "due process of law" clause. Amendment 5 denies to Congress and Amendment 14 denies to the states the power to deprive any person of life, liberty, or property without due process of law. This amendment, originally intended to protect black citizenship, has been broadly interpreted by the courts as a protection for corporations. Corporations, under this interpretation, are considered as persons. Their property cannot be taken away except by fair, legal methods. Thus, for example, the Interstate Commerce Commission can fix railroad rates only after giving railroad corporations an opportunity to present their side of the case. The "due process" clause also protects individuals from unfair actions by their state governments. It protects their rights of freedom of religion, speech, press, petition, and peaceful assembly and the rights of persons accused of crimes against state abuses. It prevents a state, in the exercise of its police power (the power to protect its people), from depriving anyone of civil liberties, except during a national emergency. The last provision of Section 1 prevents a state from denying equal protection of the laws. In 1954, in the case of *Brown* v. *Board of Education of Topeka,* the Supreme Court interpreted this provision to mean that segregation in public schools is unconstitutional. Also, in *Baker* v. *Carr* (1962) the Supreme Court ruled that unfair apportionment of representation in state legislatures violates the "equal protection" clause of this amendment.

This section was never implemented, but later civil rights law and Amendment 24 guaranteed the vote to black Americans. Amendment 19 gave women the right to vote. The Dawes Act and the 1924 citizenship law enfranchised Native Americans. And Amendment 26 changed the voting age from 21 to 18. This section dealing with apportionment of Representatives is sometimes called the "dead letter clause" of Amendment 14 since its provisions were never carried out.

This section aimed to punish the leaders of the Confederacy for having broken their oath to support the Constitution of the United States. All officials who had taken this oath and who later joined the Confederacy in the Civil War were disqualified from holding federal or state offices. Although many southern leaders were excluded under this section from holding office after the war, by 1872 most of them were permitted to return to political life. In 1898 all of the others were pardoned.

This section makes three important points: (1) The public debt of the United States incurred in fighting the Civil War was valid and could never be questioned by southerners. (2) The Confederate debt was void. It was illegal for the federal government or the states to pay any money on Confederate debts. This provision was meant to serve as a harsh lesson to all who had invested money in Confederate bonds. (3) No payment was to be made for the loss of former slaves.

Section 2. Apportioning Representatives Representatives shall be apportioned among the several states according to their respective numbers, counting the whole number of persons in each state [excluding Indians not taxed]. But when the right to vote at any election for the choice of electors for President and Vice President of the United States, Representatives in Congress, the executive and judicial officers of a state, or the members of the legislature thereof, is denied to any of the [male] inhabitants of such state, [being twenty-one years of age] and citizens of the United States, or in any way abridged, except for participation in rebellion, or other crime, the basis of representation therein shall be reduced in the proportion which the number of such [male] citizens shall bear to the whole number of male citizens [twenty-one years of age] in such state.

Section 3. Disability for Insurrection No person shall be a Senator or Representative in Congress, or elector of President and Vice President, or hold any office, civil or military, under the United States, or under any state, who, having previously taken an oath, as a member of Congress, or as an officer of the United States, or as a member of any state legislature, or as an executive or judicial officer of any state, to support the Constitution of the United States, shall have engaged in insurrection or rebellion against the same, or given aid or comfort to the enemies thereof. But Congress may by vote of two thirds of each house, remove such disability.

Section 4. Public Debt The validity of the public debt of the United States, authorized by law, including debts incurred for payment of pensions and bounties for services in suppressing insurrection or rebellion, shall not be questioned. But neither the United States nor any state shall assume or pay any debt or obligation incurred in aid of insurrection or rebellion against the United States, [or any claim for the loss or emancipation of any slave]; but all such debts, obligations and claims shall be held illegal and void.

Section 5. Enforcement The Congress shall have power to enforce, by appropriate legislation, the provisions of this article.

AMENDMENT 15
RIGHT OF SUFFRAGE (1870)

Section 1. The right of citizens of the United States to vote shall not be denied or abridged by the United States or by any state on account of race, color, or previous condition of servitude.

Section 2. The Congress shall have power to enforce this article by appropriate legislation.

The purpose of this amendment was to extend the *franchise,* or the right to vote, to blacks. Thus, according to this amendment, any person who can meet all of the qualifications for suffrage in a particular state cannot be deprived of the right to vote simply because of race or color.

AMENDMENT 16
INCOME TAX (1913)

The Congress shall have power to lay and collect taxes on incomes, from whatever source derived, without apportionment among the several states, and without regard to any census or enumeration.

In 1894 Congress passed an income tax law. The following year the Supreme Court declared this tax law unconstitutional. The Court stated that the income tax was a direct tax and, therefore, according to the Constitution (Article 1, Section 2, Clause 3; Article 1, Section 9, Clause 4) should have been apportioned among the states according to their population. This decision was unpopular because it prevented the government from taxing people on the basis of their incomes in order to pay for government expenses, which were already large and growing larger. Amendment 16 is a response to the Supreme Court decision. It gave Congress the power to tax incomes from any source and without apportionment among the states according to population. Today income taxes are the federal government's major source of income.

AMENDMENT 17
ELECTION OF SENATORS (1913)

Section 1. Method of Election The Senate of the United States shall be composed of two Senators from each state, elected by the people thereof, for six years; and each Senator shall have one vote. The electors in each state shall have the qualifications requisite for electors of the most numerous branch of the state legislatures.

Section 2. Filling Vacancies When vacancies happen in the representation of any state in the Senate, the executive authority of such state shall issue writs of election to fill such vacancies: *Provided* that the legislature of any state may empower the executive thereof to make temporary appointments until the people fill the vacancies by election as the legislature may direct.

[**Section 3. Not Retroactive** This amendment shall not be so construed as to affect the election or term of any Senator chosen before it becomes valid as part of the Constitution.]

Before the passage of this amendment, senators were chosen by the state legislatures (see Article 1, Section 3, Clause 1). There was a great deal of dissatisfaction with this method because it gave the voters little control over the Senate. Amendment 17 provides for the direct election of senators by the voters of each state, thus making senators more responsive to the will of the voters who put them in office.

This amendment outlawed the making, sale, or transportation of alcoholic beverages in the United States except for special purposes. This amendment was later repealed by Amendment 21.

This amendment, extending the right to vote to all qualified women, marked the greatest single step in extending the suffrage in the United States. Women's struggle to win this basic right began many years before Amendment 19 was finally ratified.

When the Constitution was written, transportation and communication were so slow that a new President and new members of Congress elected in November could not reach the capital to take office until March 4. However, since sessions of Congress began in December, a session including newly elected members could not be held until 13 months after their election. Thus, even if a member running for reelection was defeated in November, he or she would serve in the session of Congress that began the month after this election and continue to serve several more months. Since defeated candidates had been rejected by the voters, they were called "lame ducks," suggesting that their political wings had been clipped. One purpose of Amendment 20 was to limit the term and power of lame duck members.

AMENDMENT 18
NATIONAL PROHIBITION (1919)

[**Section 1.** After one year from the ratification of this article the manufacture, sale, or transportation of intoxicating liquors within, the importation thereof into, or the exportation thereof from the United States and all territory subject to the jurisdiction thereof for beverage purposes is hereby prohibited.

Section 2. The Congress and the several states shall have concurrent power to enforce this article by appropriate legislation.

Section 3. This article shall be inoperative unless it shall have been ratified as an amendment to the Constitution by the legislatures of the several states, as provided in the Constitution, within seven years from the date of the submission hereof to the states by the Congress.]

AMENDMENT 19
WOMEN'S SUFFRAGE (1920)

Section 1. The right of citizens of the United States to vote shall not be denied or abridged by the United States or by any state on account of sex.

Section 2. Congress shall have power to enforce this article by appropriate legislation.

AMENDMENT 20
"LAME DUCK" AMENDMENT (1933)

Section 1. Beginning of Terms The terms of the President and Vice President shall end at noon on the 20th day of January, and the terms of Senators and Representatives at noon on the 3rd day of January, of the years in which such terms would have ended if this article had not been ratified; and the terms of their successors shall then begin.

Section 2. Congressional Term The Congress shall assemble at least once in every year, and such meeting shall begin at noon on the 3rd day of January, unless they shall by law appoint a different day.

Section 3. Presidential Succession If, at the time fixed for the beginning of the term of the President, the President-elect shall have died, the Vice President-elect shall become President. If a President shall not have been chosen before the time fixed for the beginning of his term, or if the President-elect shall have failed to qualify, then the Vice President-elect shall act as President until a President shall have qualified; and the Congress may by law provide for the case wherein neither a President-elect nor a Vice President-elect shall have qualified, declaring who shall then act as President, or the manner in which one who is to act shall be selected, and such person shall act accordingly until a President or Vice President shall have qualified.

Section 4. Filling Presidential Vacancy The Congress may by law provide for the case of the death of any of the persons from whom the House of Representatives may choose a President whenever the right of choice shall have devolved upon them, and for the case of the death of any of the persons from whom the Senate may choose a Vice President whenever the right of choice shall have devolved upon them.

[**Section 5. Effective Date** Sections 1 and 2 shall take effect on the 15th day of October following the ratification of this article.]

[**Section 6. Time Limit for Ratification** This article shall be inoperative unless it shall have been ratified as an amendment to the Constitution by the legislatures of three fourths of the several states within seven years from the date of its submission.]

AMENDMENT 21
REPEAL OF PROHIBITION (1933)

Section 1. The eighteenth article of amendment to the Constitution of the United States is hereby repealed.

Section 2. The transportation or importation into any state, territory, or possession of the United States for delivery or use therein of intoxicating liquors, in violation of the laws thereof, is hereby prohibited.

[**Section 3.** This article shall be inoperative unless it shall have been ratified as an amendment to the Constitution by conventions in the several states, as provided in the Constitution, within seven years from the date of the submission hereof to the States by the Congress.]

This amendment, which repealed Amendment 18, was the only amendment ratified by special state conventions instead of state legislatures. Congress felt that a popular referendum (vote) would give the people a better chance to voice their opinions on prohibition. As in Amendments 18 and 20, Congress included a provision that the amendment, to become law, have a seven-year limit for ratification by the states.

The original Constitution placed no limit on the number of terms a President could be elected to office. Washington and Jefferson, however, set a two-term precedent. In 1940 this tradition was broken when Franklin D. Roosevelt was elected for a third term, and in 1944, when he won a fourth term. The purpose of this amendment was to write the two-term precedent into law. The bracket portion was included so that the amendment would not apply to President Truman, who was in office at the time the amendment was ratified. Note that anyone who succeeds to the Presidency and completes less than two years of another person's term may be elected for two more terms.

AMENDMENT 22
TWO-TERM LIMIT
FOR PRESIDENTS (1951)

Section 1. No person shall be elected to the office of the President more than twice, and no person who has held the office of President, or acted as President, for more than two years of a term to which some other person was elected President shall be elected to the office of the President more than once. [But this Article shall not apply to any person holding the office of President when this Article was proposed by the Congress, and shall not prevent any person who may be holding the office of President, or acting as President, during the term within which this Article becomes operative from holding the office of President or acting as President during the remainder of such term.]

[**Section 2.** This Article shall be inoperative unless it shall have been ratified as an amendment to the Constitution by the legislatures of three fourths of the several states within seven years from the date of its submission to the states by the Congress.]

Amendment 23 enabled residents of the District of Columbia to vote for President and Vice President. In effect, it gave the capital city three members in the Electoral College, the same number elected by each of the least populous states.

AMENDMENT 23
PRESIDENTIAL ELECTORS FOR
DISTRICT OF COLUMBIA (1961)

Section 1. The District constituting the seat of Government of the United States shall appoint in such manner as the Congress may direct:

A number of electors of President and Vice President equal to the whole number of Senators and Representatives in Congress to which the District would be entitled if it were a State, but in no event more than the least populous state; they shall be in addition to those appointed by the States, but they shall be considered, for the purposes of the election of President and Vice President, to be electors appointed by a State; and they shall meet in the District and perform such duties as provided by the twelfth article of amendment.

Section 2. The Congress shall have power to enforce this article by appropriate legislation.

AMENDMENT 24
POLL TAX BANNED IN NATIONAL ELECTIONS (1964)

Section 1. The right of citizens of the United States to vote in any primary or other election for President or Vice President, for electors for President or Vice President, or for Senator or Representative in Congress, shall not be denied or abridged by the United States or any state by reason of failure to pay any poll tax or other tax.

Section 2. The Congress shall have power to enforce this article by appropriate legislation.

This amendment forbade the collection of poll taxes—taxes persons had to pay before they were able to vote—as a requirement for voting in federal elections (in 1964 five southern states still had poll taxes). In 1966 the Supreme Court ruled that poll taxes were illegal as a requirement for voting in state and local elections as well.

AMENDMENT 25
PRESIDENTIAL DISABILITY AND SUCCESSION (1967)

Section 1. In case of the removal of the President from office or his death or resignation, the Vice President shall become President.

Section 2. Whenever there is a vacancy in the office of the Vice President, the President shall nominate a Vice President who shall take office upon confirmation by a majority vote of both houses of Congress.

Section 3. Whenever the President transmits to the President *pro tempore* of the Senate and the Speaker of the House of Representatives his written declaration that he is unable to discharge the powers and duties of his office, and until he transmits to them a written declaration to the contrary, such powers and duties shall be discharged by the Vice President as Acting President.

Section 4. Whenever the Vice President and a majority of either the principal officers of the executive departments or of such other body as Congress may by law provide, transmit to the President *pro tempore* of the Senate and the Speaker of the House of Representatives their written declaration that the President is unable to discharge the powers and duties of his office, the Vice President shall immediately assume the powers and duties of the office as Acting President.

Thereafter, when the President transmits to the President *pro tempore* of the Senate and the Speaker of the House of Representatives his written declaration that no inability exists, he shall resume the

This amendment was intended to clarify Article 2, Section 1, Clause 6, particularly in the case of the temporary disability of a President. The problem of disability in office existed during the last part of President Wilson's term and occurred again when President Eisenhower was disabled by a heart attack. This amendment provided two ways (see sections 3 and 4) the Vice President could assume the duties of the office of the President, as well as a procedure by which the President could again perform the duties of office when the disability ended.

However, the first use of this amendment did not involve Presidential disability. It involved a Presidential resignation. In 1974 Richard M. Nixon became the first President in American history to resign from office. And Vice President Gerald R. Ford, who succeeded as President, became the first person to become President without being first elected to that office or to the Vice Presidency. This unique situation occurred in the following way. In 1973 Vice President Spiro T. Agnew had resigned, and President Nixon had filled the vacancy according to the provisions of Section 2 of this amendment. Gerald R. Ford, a member of the House of Representatives, had been named Vice President with the approval of Congress. Therefore when Nixon resigned as President during the Watergate scandal, Ford took over the Presidency. A vacancy then existed in the Vice Presidency (see Section 2). President Ford named Nelson A. Rockefeller as Vice President, and this nomination was also approved by a majority vote of both houses of Congress.

powers and duties of his office unless the Vice President and a majority of either the principal officers of the executive department or of such other body as Congress may by law provide, transmit within four days to the President *pro tempore* of the Senate and the Speaker of the House of Representatives their written declaration that the President is unable to discharge the powers and duties of his office. Thereupon Congress shall decide the issue, assembling within 48 hours for that purpose if not in session. If the Congress, within 21 days after receipt of the latter written declaration, or, if Congress is not in session, within 21 days after Congress is required to assemble, determines by two-thirds vote of both houses that the President is unable to discharge the powers and duties of his office, the Vice President shall continue to discharge the same as Acting President; otherwise, the President shall resume the powers and duties of his office.

Congress, in the Voting Rights Act of 1970, had lowered the minimum voting age from 21 to 18, but the Supreme Court ruled that this law applied only to federal elections. Amendment 26 specified that 18 was the legal voting age in state, local, and federal elections.

AMENDMENT 26
VOTING AGE LOWERED TO 18 (1971)

Section 1. The right of citizens of the United States, who are 18 years of age or older, to vote shall not be denied or abridged by the United States or by any State on account of age.

Section 2. The Congress shall have power to enforce this article by appropriate legislation.

BICENTENNIAL OF THE CONSTITUTION

On September 17, 1987, the United States commemorates the bicentennial of the signing of the Constitution with a re-creation of the Grand Federal Procession in Philadelphia. The original Procession, or parade, was held in Philadelphia on July 4, 1788, to celebrate the ratification of the Constitution. At that time, people rejoiced that the United States was establishing a new form of government. Today, Americans are celebrating the triumph of that government, which has become a model for the world.

The 1987 Grand Federal Procession is only one of many festivities commemorating the bicentennial of the Constitution. These bicentennial celebrations are entitled "We the People — 200" and are being held throughout the country. The events are designed to foster a greater awareness of the Constitution and to celebrate the American way of life. Programs include music and dance festivals, symposia on the nation's ethnic and cultural diversity, and workshops and programs to make citizens, including students, more aware of the continuing evolution of the Constitution.

Above all, We the People — 200 is a celebration of the continuity of the American government. For 200 years this government has derived its strength and endurance from the Constitution, which has lasted longer than any other written constitution.

UNIT THREE

Building the Nation

The new states had won independence from Great Britain and written a new constitution. Between 1789 and 1845 the United States faced many challenges to molding itself into a new nation. Politics, foreign affairs, differing sectional life styles, and growing industrialization threatened the new nation's tranquility. The people of the United States faced these challenges with confidence and quickly the young nation doubled in size. The vast lands were drawn together by a network of roads, canals, and railroads. People pushed westward along this network into the heartland of the continent. Hardy frontier families found no hardship too great, no obstacle too tough in their quest for a better life. In the picture below, Daniel Boone leads a group of pioneers on the Cumberland Road across the Appalachian Mountains.

CHAPTER 9

A Strong Start for the Nation

(1789–1801)

The oath
of office

It is April 30, 1789. At New York City, the temporary capital of the nation, a crowd has gathered in Wall Street to witness the inauguration of the first President of the United States. It is a solemn occasion. Above the crowd, on the balcony of Federal Hall, stands George Washington, unanimously chosen by the Electoral College. Robert R. Livingston, Chancellor of the State of New York, administers the Presidential oath of office to him. For a moment there is silence, then a burst of cheers breaks from the crowd below.

Many thoughts must have passed through Washington's mind as he gazed down on the sea of faces and as the waves of sound rose around him. Perhaps Washington weighed in his mind the chances for the new government's success. He knew that most people still thought of themselves as citizens of individual states—of New York, or Delaware, or Virginia—rather than as citizens of the United States. The people would now hail him as President of the United States. Washington was fully aware, however, that the United States was not yet a nation.

Indeed, Washington was not alone in his worries. Many of his close associates also worried about the future of the new nation. John Adams, newly elected Vice President, feared that the Republic might not last beyond his own lifetime. On one occasion, Alexander Hamiliton had felt that the Constitution was "frail and worthless." The new President himself thought of the United States as an "experiment entrusted to the hands of the American people." Washington knew that it was his responsibility to give direction to this great American experiment.

READING FOCUS

As you read about the nation's start under the new Constitution, look for the details that support each of the following statements.

1. The new federal government is organized.
2. Congress deals with the nation's money problems.
3. The national government adopts a foreign policy.
4. Political parties develop an active role.
5. The Federalist Party struggles to stay in power.
6. Federalist ideas and methods persist under the Republicans.

1 The new federal government is organized

See Teaching Suggestions in TMRG, pp.TM56-57.

Washington's trip from Mount Vernon, his home in Virginia, to New York City was a triumph. All along his route crowds gathered to cheer him. His welcome in New York was overwhelming.

Now the celebrations were over. President Washington and the other elected officials—Vice President John Adams; the Senators, two from each state; and the 59 Representatives—had taken the oath to uphold the Constitution. They had the task of organizing the new government and of making it work.

Basic problems. To guide them, the newly elected federal officials had only the Constitution and their experience in the various colonial governments and in the Confederation. They had no federal laws, no courts, no law-enforcement officers. Each act they took established a **precedent**, or model, for future action.

The new leaders also faced serious financial problems, but there was no federal treasury and no method for collecting taxes. Worse still, there was little money in the country with which the people could pay the taxes that the new government would have to levy. Finally, the new government owed a large debt from the Revolutionary War and from the government under the Confederation.

Difficult problems also lay ahead for the new nation in its relations with other nations. The President had to work out a foreign policy acceptable to Congress. He had to appoint diplomatic officials and instruct them in their duties. If trouble should arise, the nation had little military strength. The navy had been disbanded. The army numbered only some 600 officers and enlisted soldiers.

The Constitution gave the new government the power to deal with these and other problems. Dealing with them successfully would call for strong leadership.

Congress goes to work. One of the first and most important measures Congress adopted was the Judiciary Act of 1789. The act established the basic structure of the federal court system. It provided for a Chief Justice

▲ Throughout the Annotated Teacher's Edition, terms listed in the "Identify" portion of a Section Review are underscored the first time they appear. See the Teacher's Manual for each section for a listing of important vocabulary terms.

223

and five Associate Justices of the Supreme Court. The first Chief Justice appointed by the President and approved by the Senate was John Jay. The Judiciary Act also established thirteen district courts and three circuit courts.

The Judiciary Act gave the Supreme Court the power to declare void, or without force, state laws and decisions of state courts that violated the federal Constitution or laws and treaties made under it. If this power—the power of judicial review—had not been granted to the Supreme Court, each state would have been free to interpret federal laws in its own way. The United States would have been a league of **sovereign,** or independent, states, not a federal union. For this reason, the Judiciary Act was essential to building the federal system. Important though it was, the Judiciary Act did not definitely settle the question of state or federal sovereignty. As you will see, the issue remained to trouble the nation until it was finally decided by the tragedy of the Civil War.

The first Congress also took other important steps. It sent the Bill of Rights to the states to be ratified. It re-enacted, or passed for a second time, the Northwest Ordinance providing a government for the Northwest Territory. Mainly to raise revenue, it levied a small tariff on imports.

Creating a cabinet. Congress also created three executive departments to help President Washington with his work. The Department of State was created to help the President handle foreign and other affairs. The Department of the Treasury was set up to deal with financial problems, and the Department of War to manage military matters.

The heads of these departments came to be known as the President's **cabinet,** or advisers. However, the cabinet as it exists today was not officially recognized in law until 1907. The heads of these departments, called Secretaries, met with the President in informal meetings. The Secretaries, however, could only advise the President. Then, as now, the responsibility for making final decisions in the Executive Department rested with the President alone.

President Washington's first cabinet included Thomas Jefferson as Secretary of State, Alexander Hamilton as Secretary of the Treasury, and Henry Knox as Secretary of War. Washington also appointed Edmund Randolph as Attorney General. Randolph's responsibility

was to advise the President on matters of law. This was at first a part-time job. The Department of Justice was not created until 1870. Samuel Osgood received the appointment of Postmaster General.

SECTION REVIEW
See underscored items, text pp. 223 - 24.

Identify: Judiciary Act of 1789, cabinet
For answers to questions, see Answer Key, p.A35.

1. **Organizing Ideas:** List the basic problems faced by the young republic in 1789 in (**a**) maintaining order, (**b**) regulating finances, and (**c**) developing a foreign policy.

2. **Interpreting Ideas:** What guidelines did the newly elected officials have for organizing the new government?

3. **Summarizing Ideas:** Describe the measures adopted by the first Congress in its efforts to solve the republic's problems.

4. **Analyzing Ideas:** How did the Judiciary Act help prevent conflicts between federal and state governments?

2 Congress deals with the nation's money problems

See Teaching Suggestions in TMRG, pp.TM57-58.
Among the many problems faced by the new federal government, the most urgent was that of raising money. During the first year or two, the task was exceptionally difficult.

The problem of finances. As one of its first acts, Congress adopted a small tariff on articles imported into the United States. Congress realized that the revenue from this tariff would not even begin to pay the expenses of running the new government. More money, much more, would have to come from other taxes. But what kind of taxes?

There was another big question. Where would the American people get the gold and silver coin or the paper money to pay their taxes? In 1789 there was very little currency in the United States. The Constitution gave Congress the power "to coin money," but where were the gold and silver to come from?

To find solutions to these and other financial problems, Congress turned to the new Secretary of the Treasury, Alexander Hamilton, for help. In turning to the Secretary of the Treasury, the first Congress set an important precedent. While Congress is responsible for passing laws, it has always relied heavily on the Executive Department both for advice and for guidance.

Repaying the war debt. Hamilton devised a program that would put the nation's finances on a sound basis. First, he asked Congress to establish the nation's credit by paying its debts. Hamilton knew that a nation, like an individual, must pay its debts or lose the trust of its neighbors and find it impossible to borrow in the future.

The United States and the separate states owed a combined war debt of over $80 million —a staggering sum for those days. Hamilton proposed to repay all of this debt.

Everybody agreed that the United States should pay $12 million owed to France, the Netherlands, and Spain. The United States therefore arranged to repay with interest, over a fixed period, the money that these countries had lent.

The domestic debt was another matter. Many members of Congress objected to Hamilton's proposal to repay $44 million borrowed from Americans during the course of the Revolutionary War.

The Continental Congress had borrowed this money by issuing paper money and selling <u>government bonds</u>. Government bonds are certificates issued by a government in exchange for a loan of money. Each certificate is a promise that the loan, plus interest, will in time be repaid. But, as you know, the government's credit during and after the war was so low that its paper money was "not worth a Continental." Government bonds were equally low in value. Many people who had originally held the bonds and paper money had sold them to speculators for a fraction of their original, or face, value.

Hamilton now proposed that the bonds and paper money be paid off at their original value. Hamilton's opponents objected. Why should the entire country pay out its hard-earned money to benefit a few speculators? However, Hamilton convinced Congress that if the nation's credit was to be established all debts must be paid.

The remainder of the total debt, about $25 million, was owed by several states to Ameri-

A 1787 United States coin was called the Brasher doubloon (top). Coins with the Liberty profile came later.

225

The Washington, D.C., of the early 1800's was a rustic place. Here is a view of the Senate section of the Capitol. It would be several years before the great central dome would be built, joining it to the House of Representatives.

can citizens. Hamilton wanted the federal government to take over, or assume, this debt and pay back every penny the states owed. This proposal started a violent argument. States with small debts and states that had paid their war debts argued that it was unfair to force them to assume their neighbors' burdens. Southerners protested that most state bonds, too, were in the hands of speculators, who would profit at the expense of the people.

Defeat seemed certain, but at the last moment a compromise was arranged. In the Assumption Bill, southerners, led by Jefferson, agreed that the national government should assume the state debts. Northerners, led by Hamilton, agreed to vote for a bill to locate the new national capital on the banks of the Potomac River on land donated by Virginia and Maryland. The government was moved to the new capital, Washington, D.C., in 1800.

Hamilton's bank proposal. The second part of Hamilton's program called for Congress to pass a bill creating a **national bank,** to be called the Bank of the United States. By a national bank Hamilton did not mean just one bank, but a banking system. The system would consist of a large central bank with branch banks in major American cities.

Hamilton carefully pointed out the advantages of a national banking system. The branch banks would provide safe places for tax officials to deposit money collected from the people. When the government wanted to transfer money from one place to another, the branch banks could do this by sending checks. This would avoid the risk of actually shipping gold and silver. Moreover, when the central bank did not have as much money to lend as the government wanted to borrow, it could always turn to its branch banks for help.

Finally, the Bank of the United States would provide what Hamilton called "a sound, uniform currency." Currency would have the same value all over the country. People would have faith in paper money, or **bank notes,** bear-

x

ing the name of the Bank of the United States. People would prefer these bank notes to the paper money printed by small local or state banks. As a result, Hamilton predicted, small, shaky banks would close down. Other banks would work hard to win the public's confidence. All this would be good for business—and for the country as a whole.

Adoption of the bank proposal. Hamilton's arguments in favor of a Bank of the United States were sound. His opponents, led by Jefferson, also had sound arguments.

First, according to Hamilton's proposal, the Bank of the United States would sell 25,000 shares of stock at $400 each. This amounted to a total **capital stock,** or money value, of $10 million. The government would buy one fifth of all the shares. The other four fifths would be bought by private investors, who would, of course, be wealthy Americans. Jefferson argued that this would give wealthy people control over the country's money power.

Jefferson also argued that a national bank would have an unfair advantage over local or state banks. Again he was right. All government funds would be deposited in the Bank of the United States and its branches. These funds could be loaned to individuals and businesses at a profit to the national bank. Private banks would thus have no opportunity to earn profits on the deposit and loan of government funds.

Finally, Jefferson claimed that the bank would be unconstitutional. The Constitution did not give the federal government power to create a bank. In reply, Hamilton pointed to the elastic clause of the Constitution. This clause gave Congress the right "to make all laws which shall be necessary and proper for carrying into execution the foregoing powers," including the power "to lay and collect taxes" and "to borrow money on the credit of the United States." Hamilton said that it was "necessary and proper" to create a bank that would help Congress collect taxes and borrow money.

Thus the arguments ran for and against Hamilton's proposal. In spite of heated debate in the cabinet, Washington leaned toward Hamilton's side. In 1791 Congress passed a bill granting a charter to the Bank of the United States despite strong opposition.

Hamilton's tariff proposal. The third part of Hamilton's financial program called on Congress to pass another tariff law. Congress earlier had levied a small tariff on imported goods, mainly to raise revenue. Now Hamilton proposed a new kind of tariff—what is now called a "protective" tariff.

The difference between a tariff to raise revenue and a protective tariff is one of purpose and therefore of rates. For example, Congress might place a low tariff, or duty, on a blanket manufactured in Great Britain. British manufacturers could pay the duty and still compete with American manufacturers for American trade. This would be a **revenue tariff.** Now imagine that Congress placed a very high tariff on each British-made blanket, perhaps as high as 100 percent of its value. Then the British-made blanket would have to be sold in the United States for at least twice what it cost the British manufacturer to make it. The British manufacturer could not sell blankets in America that would compete with those of American manufacturers. A tariff of this kind would not raise revenue for the government, since the British manufacturer would have to abandon the American market. However, it would protect American manufacturers from competition and thus be a **protective tariff.**

Congress did not even consider Hamilton's proposal for a protective tariff. Nevertheless, the proposal shows how Hamilton wanted to bind wealthy Americans—in this case, manufacturers—to the government by ties of self-interest. This proposal also reveals how well Hamilton understood the young nation's needs. He saw that the United States could not become truly independent until it could produce most of the goods that it needed.

The Whisky Rebellion. In a fourth proposal, Hamilton urged Congress to levy an **excise tax** on distilled liquors. All distillers would have to pay this tax on every gallon (3.8 liters) of liquor they produced and sold.

Congress passed the tax. For reasons that become clear when you picture the country as it was in the 1790's, the tax fell most heavily on the people living on the frontier.

In the 1790's the frontier was almost totally isolated from the settled areas along the Atlantic coast. Only the roughest of trails—for the most part the old Indian trails—connected the frontier with the eastern seaboard. As a result, frontier farmers could not transport their corn to markets in the settled areas. This was a major problem, for corn was the most impor-

George Caleb Bingham (1811–1879) was born in Virginia but moved west to Missouri with his family in 1819. He was mainly a self-taught artist who drew and painted the life he saw around him in Missouri and other parts of the West.

Bingham was drawn to politicians and frontier notables, riverboats, and local scenery. His portraits and landscapes were in the Romantic tradition. They were technically proficient, showing the life of the frontier in clearly organized compositions crowded with people and depicting specific moments.

Bingham became well known for his sweeping views of the Missouri and Mississippi rivers. *The Jolly Boatmen* shows the crew of a flatboat, which may have been bound for New Orleans, taking time out for relaxation as they float downriver. A country fiddler, like the one on the right, was the mainstay of much frontier entertainment.

tant crop of the frontier farmers. Fortunately, there was an easy solution to the problem. The farmers built stills and converted the corn into whisky. Then they loaded the jugs and kegs of whisky on the backs of mules and drove the mules eastward to the markets. Whisky was the major source of cash for the frontier farmers, and it was whisky that was now being taxed by the federal government.

The freedom-loving frontier settlers refused to pay the tax. In 1794 federal marshalls tried to enforce the law, but armed groups of farmers drove them away. The governor of Pennsylvania at first refused to call out the militia to crush the uprising. In this so-called "Whisky Rebellion," frontier farmers challenged the power of the federal government.

At Hamilton's urging, President Washington called out the militia from neighboring states. The rebellion melted away when 15,000 militiamen were sent to the scene. No lives were lost, but the federal government had demonstrated its strength.

Success for Hamilton's program. Hamilton's financial program proved a great success. By paying off its debts, the new government showed that it was powerful enough to meet its obligations. The national banking system provided a sound, uniform currency. The excise

tax brought a small amount of much-needed revenue. More important, it extended the influence of the government to the frontier.

To be sure, Hamilton's financial program put money into the pockets of the well-to-do. Americans who owned government bonds, who invested in the Bank of the United States, and who needed a sound, uniform currency were delighted. They became supporters of the new government.

Hamilton's financial program benefited not just the wealthy, but all Americans. It gave the United States a workable money system and a credit reputation that few of the older nations of Europe enjoyed.

SECTION REVIEW
See underscored items, text pp. 225 - 228.

Identify: government bonds, Assumption Bill, revenue tariff, protective tariff, Whisky Rebellion, excise tax

For answers to questions, see Answer Key, pp. A35-36.

1. **Summarizing Ideas: (a)** What precedent did the first Congress set when it asked Hamilton for advice on its financial problems? **(b)** What policies did Hamilton propose to solve these problems?

2. **Interpreting Ideas: (a)** Why did some Americans object to having Congress repay both national and state war debts to American citizens? **(b)** How were these issues resolved?

3. **Comparing Viewpoints: (a)** What were Hamilton's arguments for a national bank? **(b)** Why did Jefferson oppose the national bank? **(c)** How did Hamilton justify the constitutionality of the bank?

4. **Determining Cause and Effect: (a)** What were the causes of the Whisky Rebellion? **(b)** Of what significance was the role taken by the federal government in dealing with the rebellion?

3 The national government adopts a foreign policy

See Teaching Suggestions in TMRG, p.TM58.

The United States was born in a world torn by revolution and warfare. The world situation greatly complicated the problems of the new government.

The French Revolution. In the spring of 1789, a revolution broke out in France. The revolutionists were inspired by some of the ideas expressed in the American Declaration of Independence. They stated their goals in the ringing cry "liberty, equality, fraternity."

Unhappily, the revolution soon became a bloodbath. The revolutionists mobbed and beheaded thousands of people in the upper classes and nobility, including King Louis XVI and Queen Marie Antoinette. Thousands of other upper-class French men and women escaped to England and other neighboring countries. There, safe from the sharp blade of the guillotine, they laid their plans to regain control of France.

It was impossible for people in neighboring countries to remain indifferent. Many, particularly the ruling classes, were filled with horror. They feared that the example set by the French revolutionists might spread to their own countries. As a result, they were eager to see the revolution crushed. By 1793, in response to this widely expressed concern, the governments of Great Britain and other European countries were at war with what was now the Republic of France.

American reactions. American citizens did not remain untouched by the fires of revolution and warfare raging in Europe and on the seas. The French seized American ships carrying goods to Great Britain and its possessions. The British seized American ships carrying goods to France or its colonies. They also **impressed,** or kidnaped, American sailors to serve in the British navy.

American citizens took sides. Hamilton and his followers favored Great Britain, while Jefferson and his followers favored France.

What policy should the United States adopt? According to a treaty made with France in 1778, the United States was obliged to defend the French West Indies, but if the United States aided France, it would soon find itself at war with Great Britain. Such a war would be suicidal. The new nation was not prepared for armed conflict on either land or sea.

It was a grave situation that President Washington faced in April 1793 when the minister from France, Edmond Genêt (zheh·NAY), arrived in the United States. Genêt reminded Americans of the Treaty of 1778. He did not insist that America defend the French West Indies. He did, however, demand that the United States open its seaports to French naval vessels and privateers.

If the United States agreed to do as Genêt demanded, the American nation would be at war with Great Britain. Nevertheless, many Americans welcomed Genêt with enthusiasm. They urged President Washington to honor America's obligations to France. Other Americans, friendly to Great Britain, urged Washington to break all relations with France—an act that would invite war with our former ally.

President Washington ignored the pressures from both groups and chose the wiser course of **neutrality.** Backed unanimously by his cabinet, he issued a Proclamation of Neutrality on April 22, 1793. The proclamation forbade American citizens to give active support on land or at sea to any of the warring nations. Congress supported President Washington by passing a neutrality act.

War with Great Britain avoided. In spite of the neutrality act, the United States remained on the brink of war. Indeed, in 1793, conflict with Great Britain seemed certain.

To save its West Indian colonies from starvation, France for the first time permitted Americans to trade with the French West Indies. The British then seized American ships, claiming that trade not permitted in peacetime could not be carried on in wartime.

As American ships were seized and American sailors were impressed into the British navy, many Americans became increasingly angry. They began to drill on village greens, to fortify harbor entrances, and to build warships. In the midst of these war preparations, Congress closed all American ports and talked of forbidding Americans to buy British products.

In an effort to prevent war, President Washington sent Chief Justice of the Supreme Court John Jay to try to settle the outstanding differences between Great Britain and the United States. Jay was only partly successful. "Jay's Treaty," as the settlement was called, greatly disappointed many Americans.

In the treaty the British won the right to trade freely in all American ports. In return, they promised to withdraw their troops by 1796 from certain forts they continued to occupy on the northwestern frontier. They continued to insist upon the right of British fur traders to carry on their business in American territory. The important issue of impressment remained unsettled.

The more hot-headed Americans claimed that Jay had sold out to the British. Mobs burned Jay in effigy, but Jay had accomplished his major purpose. The treaty had prevented war with Great Britain. At the same time, it had prodded the Spaniards into actions that proved extremely helpful to the United States.

The end of differences with Spain. News of Jay's Treaty came as a blow to Spain. The Spaniards had just signed an agreement with the French Republic. Because of this agreement, the Spaniards faced a probable war with Great Britain. When the United States and Great Britain settled their differences, Spain acted to insure American neutrality in the war that Spain and France were now waging against Great Britain.

In 1795, in a treaty negotiated by Thomas Pinckney, the Spaniards granted everything that Americans had been demanding since 1783. The treaty settled the dispute between the United States and Spain over boundaries between Florida and Georgia. Spain also agreed to curb Indian attacks upon settlements in Georgia and in the western lands. Even more important, Spain gave Americans the right to navigate the Mississippi River freely. This right allowed Americans to transfer goods at the port city of New Orleans from river boats to oceangoing ships without paying duties to Spain.

This right—the **right of deposit**—was especially important to western farmers. They floated their heavy products on rafts down the Ohio and the Mississippi to New Orleans. There they sold the products to ships bound for Europe or the Atlantic coast ports. After completing the sale, they broke up their rafts and sold the lumber.

Although this was a clumsy method of carrying on trade, it was cheaper than sending bulky goods by pack train directly to eastern markets. Pinckney's Treaty seemed to assure westerners that Spain would no longer threaten to close their vital trade route, the Mississippi River.

Washington's Farewell Address. In 1796 President Washington, refusing to serve a third term, prepared to return to Mount Vernon. During his two terms, he had helped to set the new nation on a solid foundation. His ad- ▲

SOURCES

WASHINGTON'S FAREWELL ADDRESS (1796)

The great rule of conduct for us in regard to foreign nations is in extending our commercial relations to have with them as little political connection as possible. So far as we have already formed engagements, let them be fulfilled with perfect good faith. . . .

Europe has a set of primary interests which to us have none or a very remote relation. Hence she must be engaged in frequent controversies, the causes of which are essentially foreign to our concerns. . . .

It is our true policy to steer clear of permanent alliances with any portion of the foreign world, so far, I mean, as we are now at liberty to do it. . . .

It was late August 1794. Along the rapids of the Maumee River — near present-day Toledo, Ohio — more than 2,000 Indians were hiding behind a natural stockade of fallen oak trees. The Indians included Little Turtle and his Miami warriors; Black Wolf and the Shawnee; Blue Jacket and the Ottawa, Chippewa, and Potawatomi; and several warriors from the Iroquis, Sauk, and Fox tribes. About 70 Canadian rangers were waiting with them.

The Indians and Canadians were well armed. They had been given muskets, ammunition, blankets, and other provisions by the lieutenant governor of Upper Canada. Twice before they had defeated American armies in the Northwest Territory. Now, with bright red warpaint covering their faces, they waited to ambush the approaching troops of Major General "Mad Anthony" Wayne.

Wayne's hot temper and reckless courage had won him his nickname and made him famous. On the battlefield, however, Wayne was a cool, thoughtful, and careful leader. For a year he had been drilling his troops in methods of Indian fighting. In addition, he had reinforced his 2,000 regulars with several hundred mounted Kentucky riflemen. These tough veterans of the frontier had long experience in Indian warfare.

On August 20, 1794, Wayne's troops came upon the Indians' natural fortress. A squadron of mounted American soldiers swiftly charged the Indians' left flank.

Although the Indians shot two captains, a lieutenant immediately took command and continued the charge over the timbers. Then infantry and riflemen fired a volley and charged with their bayonets before the Indians could reload. In about 40 minutes the battle was over. Fifty Indians were dead, and their comrades had scattered. They sought — but were denied — refuge in the British-held Fort Miami. The Indians were more surprised by the failure of the British to come to their assistance than by their own defeat. Wayne ended the campaign by destroying the Indians' villages, fruit trees, and cornfields.

The Battle of Fallen Timbers, as it has since been called, brought an end to almost 20 years of warfare between the Indians and the settlers in the Northwest Territory. When Wayne summoned them to negotiate a peace the following August, they were ready to cede their claims to much of Ohio and southeastern Indiana.

Under the terms of this peace, known as the Treaty of Greeneville, the Indians surrendered title to their southern holdings in exchange for about $20,000 worth of goods. For the first time since the Revolutionary War, peace had come to the frontier. The vast region beyond the Appalachians was open to settlement. White settlers and Indians in the Northwest would not fight each other again until the War of 1812.

The place at which the Battle of Fallen Timbers was fought is now a state historical park.

---

ministration had organized the machinery of government. It had avoided war with Great Britain and France and had settled the long-standing argument with Spain. These were solid accomplishments.

Nevertheless, Washington was troubled. Disliking political factions, he was troubled by the sharp, often bitter arguments between Hamilton and his followers and Jefferson and his followers. Washington was also troubled about the relations of the United States with other countries.

In his Farewell Address to Congress, Washington urged the American people to avoid the formation of political parties. He also warned them to avoid "permanent alliances" with "any portion of the foreign world." Washington feared that such foreign alliances might prevent the United States government from acting in its own best interests.

SECTION REVIEW

See underscored items, text pp. 229 - 30.

Identify: impress, neutrality, Jay's Treaty, Thomas Pinckney, right of deposit

For answers to questions, see Answer Key, p.A36.

1. **Determining Cause and Effect: (a)** How did the French Revolution affect the political situation in Europe in the early 1790's? **(b)** How did this situation in turn affect the policies of Great Britain and France toward the United States?

2. **Interpreting Ideas:** How were United States relations toward France and Great Britain redefined by **(a)** the Treaty of Neutrality and **(b)** Jay's Treaty?

3. **Summarizing Ideas: (a)** State the provisions of Pinckney's Treaty. **(b)** Why was the treaty important?

4. **Studying Sources:** According to the Source on page 230, what economic and political policy did Washington urge in dealings with foreign nations?

4 Political parties develop an active role

See Teaching Suggestions in TMRG, pp.TM58-59.

The Constitution said nothing about political parties. As early as the Presidential election of 1792, however, something resembling two major parties appeared in American politics. These parties centered around Alexander Hamilton and Thomas Jefferson.

Rise of the two-party system. In the election of 1792, Washington was re-elected by unanimous vote. Vice President John Adams was also re-elected but against strong opposition. He was opposed by George Clinton of New York, a candidate backed by Thomas Jefferson and his followers.

Hamilton's followers came to be called Federalists. The Federalist Party was strongest in New England and along the Atlantic seaboard. It included many wealthy merchants, manufacturers, lawyers, and church leaders. John Adams, himself a Federalist, said that Federalists represented "the rich, the well-born, and the able."

The opposition party was led by Thomas Jefferson. Its members called themselves Republicans. Although some wealthy people were Republicans, most of Jefferson's supporters were the owners of small farms or wage earners in the growing towns.

Party differences. Jefferson's beliefs were quite different from Hamilton's. Hamilton had little faith in the ability of average people to govern themselves. Jefferson, on the other hand, had great faith in the average person's ability to play an effective part in government. Jefferson had expressed this faith in the Declaration of Independence when he wrote that all governments should secure their power from "the consent of the governed."

Hamilton, distrusting average people, wanted to give power to wealthy people. He wanted to create a strong federal government under their control. He knew that a **strict,** or literal, **interpretation** of the Constitution would not permit a sufficiently strong federal government. Thus Hamilton chose to read his own meaning into the Constitution by a **loose,** or elastic, **interpretation.**

Jefferson wanted the people, particularly the small farmers who made up 90 percent of the total population, to have controlling power in the country. He favored a limited federal government, strong state governments, and ironclad guarantees of individual liberties. He believed that the Constitution *as written* gave sufficient power to the government. When a question arose as to the meaning of the Consti-

▲ *In this cartoon the spirit of George Washington looks down upon two men who symbolize opposing political views. They are pulling at the pillars that support the nation. "Should you remove one," he warns, "you destroy the whole."*

tution, Jefferson chose a strict interpretation. For example, as you have read, Jefferson argued against a national bank on the ground that the Constitution did not mention a bank or banking. Hamilton, interpreting the Constitution loosely, argued that the Constitution gave the government power to regulate money. Since a bank was needed to carry out this regulation, Congress could create such a bank.

By 1794 most voters had chosen the political party they preferred. From that day to this, American political life has revolved around the **two-party system.** In 1794, however, political parties were not like political parties today. They were loosely grouped alliances centering around leaders of different political beliefs. Later, third parties also developed from time to time to press for policies they felt the two major parties were neglecting.

Nominating candidates. On March 4, 1797, President John Adams, a Federalist, took the oath of office. A few minutes later, Thomas Jefferson, a Republican, was sworn in as Vice President.

A Federalist President, a Republican Vice President. How did such a curious situation develop? The answer lies in the election of 1796. This election also provides an example of how custom helped to shape American political institutions.

Both the Federalists and the Republicans entered the election year determined to win. President Washington had announced that he intended to retire. The Presidency and the Vice Presidency now were wide open.

The Constitution gave no directions for nominating candidates for the Presidency and Vice Presidency. The leaders of the two parties decided to keep political power in their own hands by holding Congressional conferences, ▲ later called **caucuses.** In these caucuses the leaders would choose the candidates. The voters at large would have no part in choosing those who were nominated.

Months before election day, the Federalists in Congress held their caucus. They chose John Adams and Thomas Pinckney as the Federalist candidates for President and Vice President. Republican members of Congress, in a similar party meeting, chose as their candidates Thomas Jefferson and Aaron Burr. Thus the leaders of the political parties selected the candidates that they, the leaders, wanted to run.

The artist John Krimmel captured the excitement and holiday spirit of an early election day in Philadelphia. The building in the center later became known as Independence Hall.

Role of the electors. On election day voters all over the country traveled to polling places and voted for officials in local, state, and federal governments. The voters did *not,* however, vote directly for the President and Vice President. Instead, they voted for electors who had already been chosen. Each state selected its electors in any way it chose—by popular vote, by the choice of the state legislature, or by a combination of both methods.

These chosen electors in each state then voted, as the Constitution provided, "by ballot for two persons." That is, they cast electoral votes for President and Vice President. The candidate receiving the largest vote, provided it was a majority, was declared President. The candidate with the second largest vote was declared Vice President.

According to the Constitution, the electors could vote for anyone they wished. This small, select group was supposed to be better informed, and therefore able to choose more wisely, than the American voters at large.

▲ Caucuses are still important groupings in Congress. Have a student volunteer look up the names of some of the caucuses that are organized on a permanent basis in Congress.

233

The framers of the Constitution had not known that the country would divide into two political parties. They had not foreseen that the electors might choose a President from one political party and a Vice President from another. In 1796, however, this happened.

The election of 1796. When the electors gathered to vote for the President and the Vice President, they had before them four names—the Federalist candidates, John Adams and Thomas Pinckney, and the Republican candidates, Thomas Jefferson and Aaron Burr. It was expected that the electors would choose either *both* Federalist candidates or *both* Republican candidates.

Some leading Federalists did not like John Adams, however, and they worked out a plan to make Pinckney President and Adams Vice President. Their plan backfired. John Adams received the largest number of votes, Thomas Jefferson the next largest. As a result, the United States had a Federalist President and ▲ a Republican Vice President.

Custom and the Constitution. Custom, rather than law, prevented a similar situation from happening again. After 1796, electors began to understand that they were expected to vote only for the previously nominated candidates. The Federalist electors, for example, understood that they should vote for the Federalist candidates. Likewise, the Republican electors understood that they were to cast their votes for the Republican candidates. This custom became a part of the "unwritten Constitution."

SECTION REVIEW
See underscored items, text p. 233.
Identify: two-party system, caucus
For answers to questions, see Answer Key, p. A36.
1. **Analyzing Ideas:** How did Presidential politics in 1792 indicate the rise of political parties?
2. **Summarizing Ideas: (a)** Why were the Federalist Party and the Republican Party formed? **(b)** Who belonged to each?
3. **Comparing Viewpoints: (a)** What did Jefferson and Hamilton believe about the average person? **(b)** What did they believe about the proper interpretation of the Constitution? **(c)** How did these beliefs reflect the kind of government each wanted for the nation?

See Teaching Suggestions in TMRG, p. TM60.
President John Adams was not pleased at having a Republican Vice President. He had little time to worry about it, however, because war threatened the nation.

On the verge of war. American relations with France had grown steadily worse since 1793. The French resented America's refusal to aid France as it was obliged to do by the Treaty of 1778. The French also resented Jay's Treaty, which France regarded as pro-British.

As a result, France had become increasingly hostile during Washington's second administration. The French navy had seized American ships and had kept them from reaching British ports. The French government had refused to receive the diplomatic representative sent by President Washington to Paris. Nevertheless, President Adams decided to try once more to make peace with France.

The XYZ affair. Early in 1797 President Adams sent three prominent Americans to Paris to try to reach an agreement with France. The Americans were visited privately by three French officials. The French officials, later identified only as "X, Y, and Z," made three insulting demands.

First, the American government must apologize publicly to France for remarks made by President Adams in a speech to Congress. Second, the United States must grant a loan to France. Third, the American envoys must pay a bribe of $250,000.

When news of this insult reached America, many Americans demanded war. Rallying around the slogan "Millions for defense, but not one cent for tribute," Americans began war preparations. In 1798 the government created the Navy Department, built warships, fortified harbors, and strengthened the army. The United States was actually at war, although no formal declaration had been made. Within a few months, American warships captured more than 80 vessels flying the French flag.

War avoided. President Adams then performed one of the most courageous acts of his

▲ Class activity: Have one or more students gather news articles about the activities of the
234   Vice President of the United States. In a follow-up discussion, students might discuss the
ways these activities might be impaired with a Vice President who represents a different
party from that of the President.

John Jay's name is often missing from lists of famous colonial leaders. Jay contributed much, however, to the start of the new nation. He was first widely honored for his work on the peace commission at the end of the Revolutionary War. The resulting Treaty of Paris, due largely to Jay's negotiations, was favorable to the United States. In 1784 Congress appointed Jay Secretary of Foreign Affairs. He soon became convinced, however, that the United States needed a stronger central government. For this reason, he contributed five papers on foreign affairs to *The Federalist*.

After the new government was formed under the Constitution, George Washington appointed Jay the first Chief Justice of the Supreme Court. In 1794 Jay was sent on a diplomatic mission to Britain to avert war. While the treaty, now called Jay's Treaty, succeeded in averting war, its concessions — especially on freedom of the seas — caused angry American mobs to denounce Jay and burn him in effigy. Demoralized and realizing his chances of succeeding Washington as President were ruined, Jay resigned as Chief Justice. Jay's contributions, however, will always be recognized by students of American history.

career. Although many members of his own party were demanding war, Adams tried once again to secure peace. In 1799 he sent another group of commissioners to Paris.

By the time the Americans arrived, Napoleon had overthrown the government and made himself dictator of France. Napoleon wanted to begin his rule free from conflicts with foreign nations. Thus he was eager to reach a settlement with the United States.

The Americans and the French agreed to abandon the old treaty of 1778. The United States agreed to drop its claims against France for illegally seizing American ships. Nevertheless, the French continued to seize American ships that attempted to trade with the British.

In spite of the agreement's shortcomings, President Adams had avoided full-scale war with France. Like Washington before him, Adams believed that the infant nation could survive only if it avoided European conflicts. In avoiding war, President Adams sacrificed any popularity that he might have enjoyed with his own party.

The Alien and Sedition Acts. In 1798, while anti-French feeling was running high, the Federalist majority in Congress passed a series of laws designed, they said, to unite the country. It was generally understood, however, that these new laws would also weaken the Republican Party.

These measures, often called the Alien and Sedition Acts, included four different laws. Congress passed these laws against the advice of President Adams and other party leaders.

The Naturalization Act stated that **aliens,** or foreigners, must reside in the United States for 14 years before they could become **naturalized citizens.** Up to that time, only 5 years of United States residence had been required. Congress said that this act would protect the country from enemy aliens in wartime. However, since most newcomers joined the Republican Party as soon as they became citizens, the real reason for the law was clear. The Federalist Party wanted to remain in office.

The Alien Act authorized the President to expel "all such aliens as he shall judge dangerous to the peace and safety of the United States" or those involved in plots against the government. The Alien Enemies Act authorized the President, in time of war or invasion, to imprison or banish any foreigners the Pres-

Gilbert Stuart painted this portrait of John Adams in 1815. Both Adams and his sometime political rival Thomas Jefferson died on July 4, 1826—the fiftieth anniversary of the republic.

ident considered a danger to public security. The Federalists said that these two laws were necessary war precautions. It was clear, though, that they could also be used to silence anti-Federalist opinion. After all, a Federalist President would be able to decide which aliens were "dangerous" to American security.

The Sedition Act was intended to silence American citizens themselves. **Sedition** means, among other things, the use of language to stir up discontent or rebellion against a government. Under the Sedition Act, fines and imprisonment could silence anybody who wrote, said, or printed anything "false, scandalous, and malicious" against the government, the Congress, or the President "with intent to defame."

If these laws had been fully enforced, they would have ended all opposition to the Federalist Party. The Naturalization Act went into ef-

fect at once. The Alien Act and the Alien Enemies Act were not enforced, but the mere threat of them drove many French aliens from the country. Likewise, fear of punishment under the Sedition Act undoubtedly kept many Americans silent.

Twenty-five persons were prosecuted under the Sedition Act. Ten—all Republicans and most of them newspaper publishers—were fined and jailed. The Sedition Act thus interfered with freedom of the press and freedom of speech, two principles protected by the First Amendment and deeply cherished by Americans then and now. Many Americans believed that the Alien and Sedition Acts were unjust attempts by the government to interfere with the rights of individuals—aliens and citizens alike.

Virginia and Kentucky Resolutions. The Republicans were furious. They claimed that these measures destroyed free speech and greatly increased the power of the federal government, particularly the power of the President. They voiced their protest in the Kentucky and Virginia Resolutions.

The Kentucky Resolutions, prepared by Thomas Jefferson, were adopted by the legislature of the new state of Kentucky in 1798 and 1799. The Virginia Resolutions, prepared by James Madison, were adopted by the legislature of Virginia in 1798. Together, these resolutions outlined the **states' rights,** or **compact, theory** of the Constitution. This theory included the following ideas: (1) The federal government had been created by the states. (2) The federal government was merely an agent for the states, operating under a compact, or agreement, that had delegated to the federal government certain specific powers and no more. (3) The federal government, or its agent, could be criticized by its creators, the states, if it committed unauthorized acts. Who would determine when an act was unauthorized, or unconstitutional? Why, the states, of course.

Carried to an extreme, the states' rights, or compact, theory would give the states the power to declare **null and void,** or not lawful and binding, any act of Congress that the states felt was unconstitutional. The theory could lead to **secession,** or withdrawal, of one or more states from the Union. Of course, Hamilton and the Federalists completely opposed this interpretation of the Constitution.

The Federalists claimed that the government had been created by the people, not by the states. They also said that the Supreme Court was the sole judge of whether or not an act of Congress was unconstitutional.

The Kentucky and Virginia Resolutions were sent to the other state legislatures. To the disappointment of Jefferson and Madison, the Resolutions did not receive favorable action. The Federalists controlled most of the state governments, and they opposed the Resolutions. Nevertheless, the Resolutions proved to be effective political weapons. They offered the voters a choice between a strong federal government and a weaker union in which the power of the states would be greater than the power of the federal union.

SECTION REVIEW

See underscored items, text pp. 235 - 36.
Identify: naturalized citizen, alien, sedition, compact theory, null and void, secession
For answers to questions, see Answer Key, p.A36.
1. **Analyzing Ideas:** (a) Why were relations between France and the United States strained between 1793 and 1797? (b) How did President Adams attempt to repair relations with France in 1797? (c) Why did his attempt fail?

2. **Summarizing Ideas:** (a) Describe the agreement that France and the United States reached in 1799. (b) What was the main goal of each country in reaching an agreement?

3. **Organizing Ideas:** (a) List the main provisions of the Alien and Sedition Acts. (b) How did they violate the Bill of Rights?

4. **Using Historical Imagination:** (a) In what way were the Kentucky and Virginia Resolutions an answer to the Alien and Sedition Acts? (b) How would nationwide adoption of the Resolutions have changed American government?

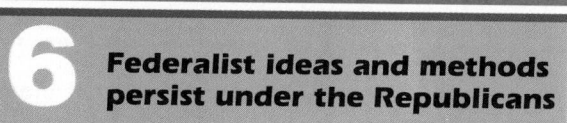

6 Federalist ideas and methods persist under the Republicans

See Teaching Suggestions in TMRG, p.TM61.
By 1800, the Federalists had lost much of their earlier influence. Many Americans, including Federalists, disliked the high taxes levied to prepare for war. Most damaging to the Federalists, however, was the public's anger at the Alien and Sedition Acts.

Courts in early rural America generally were informal places. In this scene the jury hears a lawyer plead his case while small boys play in the hayloft of the barn that serves as a court.

The election of 1800. In the election year 1800, members of both parties in Congress met in caucuses to select candidates, as they had done in 1796. The Federalists chose President John Adams to run for a second term, with Charles C. Pinckney as his running mate for Vice President. The Republicans again chose Thomas Jefferson for President and Aaron Burr for Vice President. Burr was a brilliant New York lawyer and a top-ranking leader of the Republican Party.

The Republicans won the election, gaining control of the Presidency and of both houses of Congress. Despite their victory, however, the Republicans and the country faced an extremely serious situation. There were even rumors of civil war.

The problem was that Jefferson and Burr had both received the same number of electoral votes. The candidate with the largest number of electoral votes was to be President. The candidate with the second-largest number was to be Vice President. Now there was a tie.

At first glance, this problem seemed easy to solve. The Constitution clearly stated that in case of a tie, the House of Representatives would make the final decision, with the total representation from each state having a single vote. Ordinarily, the House would have given the Presidency to Jefferson since the Republican caucus had nominated him for this position. Some Federalists in the House, however, preferred Aaron Burr. Burr was a Republican but was not as strong a supporter of Republican principles as Jefferson. Hamilton distrusted Burr and supported Jefferson as the lesser of two evils.

The Federalists did not have enough voting strength to win the office for Burr. They could and did prevent Jefferson from winning a majority of the votes on 35 successive ballots. Finally with Inaugural Day little more than two weeks away, the deadlock broke. Jefferson won on the thirty-sixth ballot.

Because of the confusion in the election of 1800, Congress drew up the Twelfth Amendment. Ratified in 1804, the amendment stated that electors must vote on separate ballots for President and for Vice President.

The midnight appointments. Having lost control of the executive and legislative branches, the Federalists strengthened their hold on the judicial branch. During the four months between Election Day and Jefferson's inauguration on March 4, 1801, the Federalist majority in the old Congress passed a new Judiciary Act. This act of 1801 increased the number of judges in the federal courts by 16.

President Adams appointed Federalists to these positions, working until late in the evening of his last day in office signing the commissions of the new judges. These last appointees were given the name of **midnight judges.**

Chief Justice John Marshall. The most significant appointment made by Adams—though not one of his midnight appointments—was that of John Marshall of Virginia as Chief Justice of the Supreme Court. Probably no single act of President Adams's administration had more far-reaching results.

John Marshall remains one of the most highly regarded of America's Chief Justices. A firm Federalist, he largely dominated the other justices on the Supreme Court during the 34 years he served, from 1801 to 1835. In more than 500 opinions, Chief Justice Marshall helped to mold the political and economic structure of the new nation.

Basic principles under Marshall. During his long term as Chief Justice, John Marshall established three basic principles of American law. These principles became foundation stones of the federal union.

Marshall stated (1) that the Supreme Court had the power to determine when a law of Congress was unconstitutional. This principle —the power of judicial review—had been included in the Judiciary Act of 1789. However, it was not made clear until John Marshall handed down in 1803 a famous decision in the case of *Marbury v. Madison* (see page 184). In this decision Marshall declared that part of the Judiciary Act passed by Congress in 1789 was unconstitutional. "It is emphatically the province and duty of the judicial department to say what the law is," Marshall stated. Jefferson and others were shocked at this interpretation of the Constitution. As Jefferson expressed it, Marshall had turned the Constitution into "a mere thing of wax in the hands of the judiciary,

SOURCES

MARBURY v. MADISON (1803)

The powers of the legislature are defined and limited; and that those limits may not be mistaken, or forgotten, the Constitution is written. To what purpose are powers limited, and to what purpose is that limitation committed to writing, if these limits may, at any time, be passed by those intended to be restrained? . . . It is a proposition too plain to be contested that the Constitution controls any legislative act repugnant to it. . . . A legislative act contrary to the Constitution is not law. . . . It is emphatically the province and duty of the judicial department to say what the law is. . . .

Samuel F. B. Morse, an artist and the inventor of the telegraph, painted this picture entitled "The Old House of Representatives." In the painting the members of the Supreme Court, including Chief Justice John Marshall (second from the right, top row), meet with the members of Congress.

which . . . [they] may twist and shape into any form they please."

In later decisions Marshall established two other basic principles. He declared (2) that the Supreme Court had the power to set aside laws of state legislatures when these laws were contrary to the federal Constitution. He also stated (3) that the Supreme Court had the power to reverse the decision of a state court.

Significance of Marshall's work. Marshall strengthened the federal government at the expense of the states by weakening the legal basis for the states' rights, or compact, theory of government. He helped to shape the loose collection of states into a *national* union.

As the years passed and as the Supreme Court handed down its decisions, Jefferson's alarm increased. From his home at Monticello, Virginia, the former President wrote, "The great object of my fear is the federal judiciary. That body . . . ever acting, with noiseless foot . . . gaining ground step by step, and holding what it gains, is engulfing insidiously the special [state] governments."

Despite his fears, Jefferson could not alter the course of events. In decision after decision, the Supreme Court broadened the meaning of the Constitution. Owing largely to John Marshall's efforts, the federal government became increasingly powerful. When he later became President, Jefferson himself would help to strengthen the federal government.

SECTION REVIEW
See underscored items, text p. 238.

Identify: Judiciary Act of 1801, midnight judges, John Marshall, *Marbury v. Madison*
For answers to questions, see Answer Key, p.A37.

1. **Analyzing Ideas:** Why had the Federalist cause become unpopular by 1800?

2. **Interpreting Ideas:** (a) How did the election of 1800 become deadlocked? (b) How were similar difficulties prevented in the future?

3. **Summarizing Ideas:** Discuss how each of three decisions by Chief Justice John Marshall established basic principles that strengthen the federal government.

239

DEVELOPING HISTORY STUDY SKILLS

Interpreting the Visual Record Analyzing a Painting

Most American history textbooks, as this one does, contain many reproductions of paintings that have historical events as subject matter. The paintings may or may not be actual eyewitnesses of the events shown. The paintings, however, help readers of history to visualize events in ways that are often superior to the written word.

Take the painting on page 233, for example. Painted by John Lewis Krimmel, it depicts an election day in Philadelphia about 1800. The painting shows some things about the architecture of the day, how people dressed, and common modes of transportation. How authentic this information is depends on when the artist painted the work. Before relying on a painting as a document of past events, it is important to do some research on the artist's life. Many artists have chosen historical events as the subjects of their paintings. Many of the artists, however, were not eyewitnesses. Some may have painted from an eyewitness' memory, which may have become distorted over time, or painted from a description found in a book or other source. Other artists have relied completely on imagination.

How to Analyze a Painting

To analyze a painting effectively, follow these steps.

1. **Determine the subject of the painting.** Note the people it portrays and any objects surrounding them. Most paintings have been given titles by their artists. Check the painting to see if it has a title. Also check the caption accompanying the painting, if it has one.
2. **Examine the details.** Study the details of the painting, including the nature of the background. The visual evidence the painting contains may add to your understanding of a historical event or period.
3. **Determine the artist's viewpoint.** Note whether the events are portrayed favorably or unfavorably.
4. **Use its information cautiously.** Determine whether the painting is an accurate description of the actual events. Otherwise, treat the painting as an item of interest but not as an authentic source of information.

Applying the Skill

Examine the painting below. It is called the "Scutching Bee." The artist is Linton Park who was born in 1826. The painting shows a group of people, probably neighbors, who gathered to scutch flax, a crop from which the pioneers made a coarse linen cloth. The pioneers got together to beat the flax in order to separate its fibers.

The painting is useful for its revealing details of pioneer life. The people are dressed quite nicely for such an outdoor activity, with the women seemingly garbed in their Sunday best and some of the men wearing fancy hats. A pile of cut timbers awaits construction into a barn or

Linton Park was a farmer and lumberjack in western Pennsylvania. In the 1840's he began to paint scenes of frontier life. This painting, "Flax Scutching Bee," was completed in the 1860's.

house. Children are playing on the logs and seem about to be scolded by a watchful mother. Some couples seem to be paying more attention to each other than to scutching flax. A valid generalization that can be drawn from the painting is that pioneers knew how to combine work and fun.

Practicing the Skill

Study the painting "George Washington's Resignation" on this page. Then on a separate sheet of paper, answer the questions in the next column.

1. In this painting George Washington is turning in his sword to Lady Liberty. What fire is she tending?

2. **(a)** Where is Washington's sword? **(b)** How has he handed it over?

3. For what do the eagle and the cornucopia stand?

4. How does the author show his feelings of respect for Washington?

5. What do Mount Vernon and the plow in the painting's background symbolize?

John James Barralet was born in Ireland in 1747 and died in Philadelphia in 1815. Barralet's most renowned works of art were portraits of early American leaders. He completed "George Washington's Resignation" in 1799, three years after Washington had left the Presidency.

nation and the cornucopia symbolizes the abundant resources of the new nation   4. by using positive symbols of the United States and showing Washington peacefully turning over the symbols of leadership to Lady Liberty   5. Washington's return to Mt. Vernon and life as a gentleman planter)

241

Between 1789 and 1800, the nation's leaders breathed life into the Constitution. During these years they organized a new government and welded the more or less independent states into a union.

Under President Washington and President John Adams, the Federalists set the machinery of government into motion. They also successfully launched the United States ship of state into the hazardous waters of world affairs.

These early years were full of peril for the young nation, which had to prove itself worthy to take its place among the family of nations. More than once a false move would have tossed the ship of state upon rocks that would have torn holes in the "frail fabric" of the new republic. Despite the danger, by the time President Adams and most of the Federalist Congressmen left office, Americans could look with pride upon a growing nation. They could see that peoples of all races and ethnic backgrounds were slowly being knit together to form a nation.

Americans were still unsure of themselves and of their future. Though united in a national will and purpose, Americans were divided on many issues. The division increasingly expressed itself through national political parties. State boundaries were gradually becoming less and less important. At the same time, the national government was steadily gaining in strength.

CONNECTING CHAPTER IDEAS

In the next chapter, you will read about the vast territory beyond the Mississippi River that was acquired by the new nation. The nation had survived the strain of war. It was now ready to grow in strength and unity of purpose.

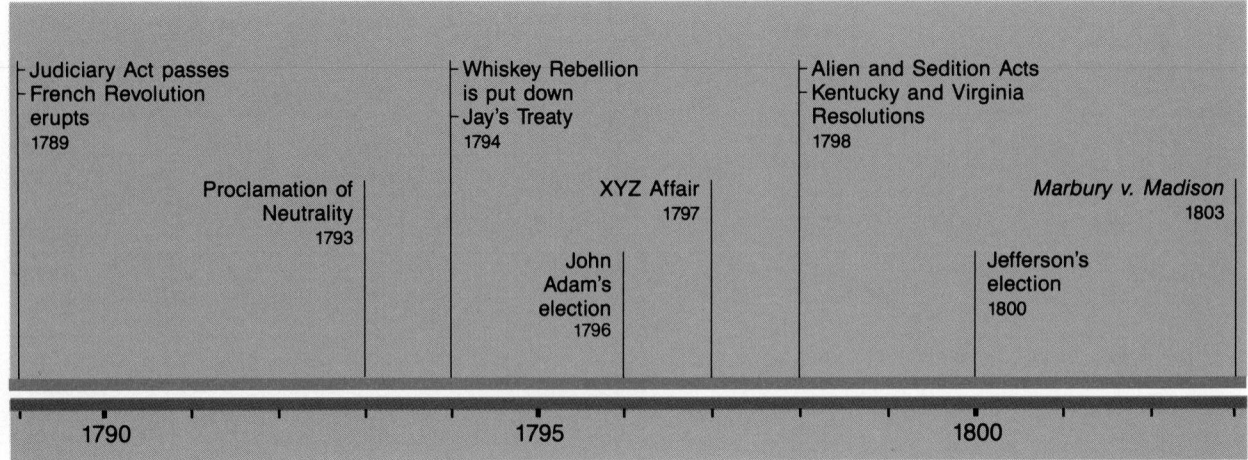

Judiciary Act passes
French Revolution erupts
1789

Proclamation of Neutrality
1793

Whiskey Rebellion is put down
Jay's Treaty
1794

John Adam's election
1796

XYZ Affair
1797

Alien and Sedition Acts
Kentucky and Virginia Resolutions
1798

Jefferson's election
1800

Marbury v. Madison
1803

1790   1795   1800

CHAPTER

9 REVIEW

Reviewing Important Terms

Decide whether each of the following sentences is true or false. If the sentence is false, replace the underlined term with the word or phrase that will make it true.

1. Hamilton proposed that the Bank of the United States should be founded with a total <u>revenue tariff</u> of $10 million.
2. The <u>protective tariff</u> proposed by Hamilton would have bound the wealthy to the government by ties of self-interest.
3. Congress passed an <u>excise tax</u> on liquor, which was paid by the distillers.
4. Originally, Presidential candidates were chosen by party <u>caucuses</u> in Congress.
5. One idea of the <u>compact theory</u> of the Constitution was that the federal government was merely an agent for the states.
6. Because of the <i>ex post facto</i> law, western farmers were able to transfer goods to larger vessels at New Orleans without paying duty to Spain.
7. Hamilton's desire for a strong central government led him to advocate a <u>strict interpretation</u> of the Constitution.

Practicing Critical Thinking Skills

1. **Analyzing Viewpoints.** How would each of these people have felt about Hamilton's economic program: (a) a farmer from Kentucky, (b) a shipowner from Boston, (c) a merchant in Philadelphia, and (d) a plantation owner from South Carolina?
2. **Determining Cause and Effect.** Compare Shays' Rebellion with the Whisky Rebellion in terms of (a) their causes, (b) the reactions of the federal government to each rebellion, and (c) their outcomes.
3. **Summarizing Ideas.** Describe President Washington's policy toward foreign nations. Why did he favor this policy?
4. **Evaluating Ideas.** Refute or defend the claim that the Sedition Act violated the First Amendment to the Constitution.
5. **Analyzing Ideas.** Find historical evidence to support or refute the following statement: A belief in a strong central government was the basis of many actions taken by the Federalists while in office.
6. **Comparing Ideas.** (a) What issue do the Kentucky and Virginia Resolutions have in common

with Justice Marshall's decision in <i>Marbury v. Madison?</i> (b) What opinion do the Resolutions and the court decision express about this issue? (c) With which document would Alexander Hamilton have agreed? Why?
7. **Relating Past to Present.** Can the foreign-policy advice in Washington's Farewell Address be applied to the United States today? Why or why not?

Developing History Study Skills

Analyzing a Painting. Review the painting on pages 220–21. Then on a separate sheet of paper, complete the following activity. Describe the painting in your own words. Use information from the textbook to add to your description. Decide whether the painting is a realistic or an idealized version of the actual happening and explain your reasoning.

Relating Geography and History

The election of 1800 was significant for a number of reasons. One of these was the peaceful change in leadership after a particularly bitter partisan battle. To understand how the partisan nature of the electorate was also, to a large degree, geographic, study the map on page 259 and the following table. Then answer the questions below.

STATES CARRIED BY CANDIDATES IN THE ELECTION OF 1800

Adams	Jefferson	Divided
Vermont	New York	Pennsylvania
New Hampshire	Virginia	North Carolina
Massachusetts	Kentucky	Maryland
Rhode Island	Tennessee	
Connecticut	Georgia	
New Jersey	South	
Delaware	Carolina	

1. In what region were most of the states that voted (a) for Adams? (b) for Jefferson?
2. Explain the significance of the location of the states that voted for Adams.
3. Explain the geographic and economic factors that led to the support Jefferson received.

243

See Chapter Overview in TMRG, p.TM62.
See Chapter Objectives in TMRG, p.TM62.
See Introducing the Chapter in TMRG, p.TM62.

CHAPTER 10 The Nation's Growth

(1801–1817)

Settling the
frontier

On March 4, 1801, John Adams, the outgoing President, left the "President's House" a worried, troubled man. He did not attend the inaugural ceremony for his successor, Thomas Jefferson. A firm Federalist, Adams feared that the victory of Jefferson and the Republican Party might mean the end of the new nation. Another Federalist politician, perhaps sensing that the Federalists would never again regain the Presidency, felt that Jefferson's election showed the way "to anarchy and ruin."

While Adams's carriage was jolting over the rough road leading out of Washington, D.C., a still unfinished city, Jefferson was reading his Inaugural Address. Jefferson himself referred to the election and the party changeover as "the Revolution of 1800." Nevertheless, in his address Jefferson tried to quiet the fears of many Federalists.

Jefferson pledged himself to "the honest payment of our debts." He promised to preserve "the general government in its whole constitutional vigor." He also promised "a jealous care of the right of election by the people." His speech was a moderate one designed to reassure the Federalists.

Jefferson's speech succeeded in calming the fears of many people. Alexander Hamilton, a strong Federalist, accepted Jefferson's speech as "a pledge . . . that the new President will not lend himself to dangerous innovations, but in essential points will tread in the steps of his predecessor."

The inauguration of Thomas Jefferson marked the beginning of a long period of Republican control in the United States. During these years, the United States more than doubled in territorial size. It also fought a second war with Great Britain to protect its rights, emerging from the war stronger than ever.

READING FOCUS

As you read about the nation's growth in the years following 1800, look for the details that support each of the following statements.

1. The nation doubles in size under President Jefferson.
2. The nation grows stronger during Jefferson's administration.
3. The war in Europe creates serious problems for the United States.
4. Americans again fight the British in the War of 1812.

1 The nation doubles in size under President Jefferson

See Teaching Suggestions in TMRG, pp.TM62-63.

Thomas Jefferson's pledge that Republicans would act with moderation did not prevent him from taking vigorous leadership as President. When the opportunity came to double the size of the United States, Jefferson acted quickly, even without Constitutional authority.

A rising threat. In 1800 Napoleon, then the ruler of France, resecured Louisiana from Spain. France had ceded this territory to Spain in 1762. Louisiana covered an enormous but vaguely defined area. It stretched westward from the Mississippi River to the Rocky Mountains and northward to Canada (see map, page 248). Although Spain and France attempted to keep the news a secret, rumors of this huge deal reached the United States government.

The rumors alarmed Jefferson and other Americans. French control of the Gulf of Mexico and the mouth of the Mississippi could deprive westerners of the right of deposit at New Orleans and severely limit their trade. French possession of Louisiana would check American expansion westward. It would also place France, a powerful and aggressive nation, upon the western border of the United States.

Unlike many Federalists, who were concerned with eastern shipping and finance, the Republican Jefferson believed that strengthening western lands was necessary. He believed that the westerners would remain loyal citizens only if the federal government insured a free outlet for their goods into the Gulf of Mexico. "The day that France takes New Orleans," President Jefferson warned Americans, "we must marry ourselves to the British fleet and nation."

Jefferson urged the American minister to Paris, Robert R. Livingston, to offer Napoleon as much as $10 million for New Orleans and for West Florida—an area east of New Orleans. This would guarantee American control of the Mississippi River and an outlet for western farm products. To aid Livingston, Jefferson sent James Monroe to Paris.

The sale of Louisiana. When the American commissioners made their offer to Napoleon's

The Mississippi is truly one of the world's great rivers. Only Africa's Nile and South America's Amazon are longer than the Mississippi River. Among these three great world-class rivers, the Mississippi is unique. It is entirely a one nation river, a United States river, beginning in Minnesota and ending some 2,348 miles (3,779 kilometers) south in Louisiana.

The Mississippi and its tributaries drain almost the entire plains area that lies between the Appalachian Mountains on the east and the Rocky Mountains on the west. This vast drainage area touches 30 states and covers 1,247,300 square miles (3,230,507 square kilometers).

The Mississippi River begins as a small, clear stream flowing out of Lake Itasca in northwestern Minnesota. Near Grand Rapids, Minnesota, the Mississippi finally turns to the south on its long journey toward the Gulf of Mexico. Along its southward path, "Old Man River" picks up a series of tributaries. At Cairo, Illinois, the now muddy waters of the Mississippi are joined by the Ohio River, doubling the volume of water carried by the mighty Mississippi. This juncture also marks the division between the upper Mississippi and the lower Mississippi.

South of Cairo the floodplain becomes a broad, flat, fertile valley, in places more than 50 miles (80 kilometers) in width. The velocity of the river slows, and the river winds back and forth across the valley in great sweeping loops called meanders. The huge sweeping meanders triple the river's length. The distance by riverboat down the lower Mississippi to the Gulf of Mexico is 1,700 miles (2,720 kilometers). The distance by air is just 600 miles (960 kilometers).

Sometimes, especially when in flood, the river changes its course, cutting off loops to form horseshoe-shaped water bodies called oxbow lakes. In the lower Mississippi the velocity of the river is very slow and the downward gradient, or slope, toward the Gulf is amazingly slight. As a result, the river deposits silt along its edges creating embankments that are called natural levees.

During times of flood, the Mississippi drainage basin has special problems. The meandering course and the slight gradient conspire to slow down the flow of flood waters. Consequently the river tops its natural levees, spreading a broad sheet of floodwater that stretches for miles over the level land.

The answer to this flooding problem seemed obvious enough to early settlers. All that was needed, they reasoned, was to construct their own levees on top of the natural levees. By 1850, there was a continuous line of contructed levees upstream from New Orleans to Memphis, Tennessee. As the levees were made higher, however, the confined river grew higher. And, during times of flood, the river often broke through one of its confining walls, sending torrents of water to flood the land for miles. In the spring of 1927, for example, the Mississippi went on a real rampage, reaching the highest flood crest on record. Some 18 million acres (7,300,000 hectares) of land were flooded and thousands of people were evacuated from their homes. More than 300 people lost their lives, and damages exceeded $300 million.

As the Mississippi approaches the Gulf of Mexico, many smaller channels, or distributaries, break off from the main channel. The river deposits its huge load of silt in these stream channels, forming a triangularly shaped landform called a delta. Over thousands of years the delta of the Mississippi has extended slowly southward into the Gulf of Mexico. Today the true delta lies south of New Orleans where the mighty Mississippi River pours its waters into the Gulf of Mexico.

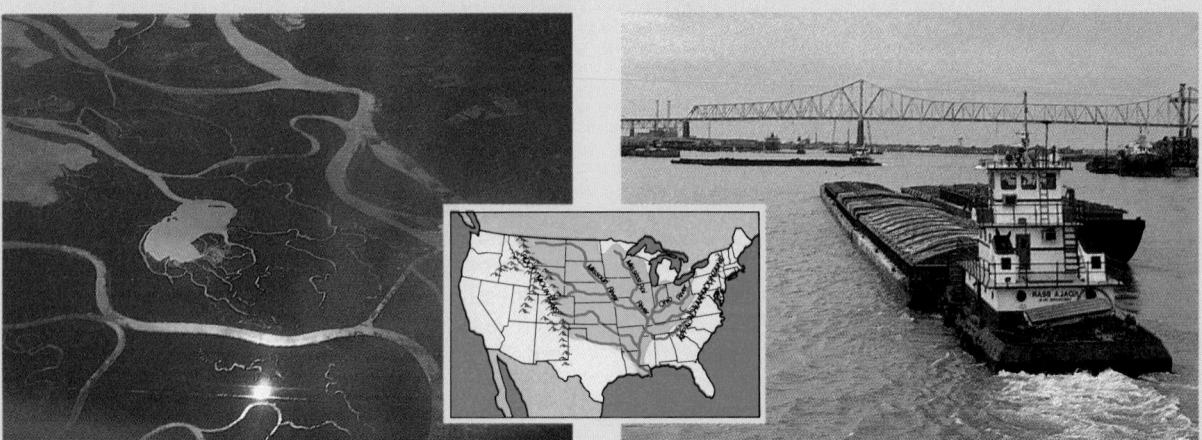

representative, there was a moment of silence. Then the representative smiled. How much would they pay for *all* of Louisiana, he asked. The Americans tried to conceal their astonishment. After some discussion they agreed that the United States would pay the equivalent of about $15 million for the entire area. This land sale, probably the largest in history, was negotiated early in 1803.

Why did Napoleon sell this valuable French territory? The answer lay in the Caribbean Sea. Before France could control Louisiana, it had to have a strong naval base in the West Indies. One possible base was the island of Santo Domingo, site of the former French colony of Haiti.

In 1791, during the French Revolution, the black people of Haiti, most of them slaves, had risen in revolt against the French. Under the leadership of Toussaint L'Ouverture (too·SAN loo·vair·TYUR), they had won independence. In 1800 Napoleon had tried to reconquer the entire island of Santo Domingo but had failed.

Without control of Santo Domingo, France had little use for Louisiana. Moreover, by 1802 Napoleon was planning to conquer all of Europe, which would mean a renewal of war with Great Britain. Napoleon knew that the British navy could easily seize his overseas possessions, including those in America. Therefore he decided to save what he could, and $15 million was better than nothing.

Purchase despite questions. Napoleon's offer to sell Louisiana pleased Jefferson but also troubled him. Jefferson, as you know, had always opposed giving the federal government any powers not specifically granted by the Constitution. The Constitution said nothing about the government's right to buy territory from a

Thomas Jefferson wanted Americans to inform themselves about their government. "If a nation expects to be ignorant and free," Jefferson said, "it expects what never was and never will be."

foreign nation. Jefferson felt that an amendment to the Constitution would be necessary before the purchase could be made. However, his advisers warned him that Napoleon might change his mind while the amendment was being adopted. Jefferson therefore sent the treaty of purchase to the Senate for approval. He later admitted that he had "done an act beyond the Constitution."

In the Senate, Jefferson's political enemies, including some Federalists, strongly objected to the treaty. They declared that $15 million was too high a price for a wilderness. They frankly expressed their fear that when farmers filled this vast western territory, the eastern commercial interests in Congress would be outvoted.

Most Federalists insisted that the Constitu-

SOURCES

JEFFERSON'S FIRST INAUGURAL ADDRESS (1801)

It is proper you should understand what I deem the essential principles of our government: . . . equal and exact justice to all men, of whatever state or persuasion, religious or political; peace, commerce, and honest friendship with all nations, entangling alliances with none; the support of the state governments in all their rights, as the most competent administrations for our domestic concerns and the surest bulwarks against anti-republican tendencies; the preservation of the general government in its whole constitutional vigor, as the sheet anchor of our peace at home and safety abroad; a jealous care of the right of election by the people. . . .

▲ Class activity: Have one or more students restate in appropriate words what Jefferson considered to be the role of government in using power. Students may then discuss whether Jefferson's purchase of Louisiana contradicted his principles.

247

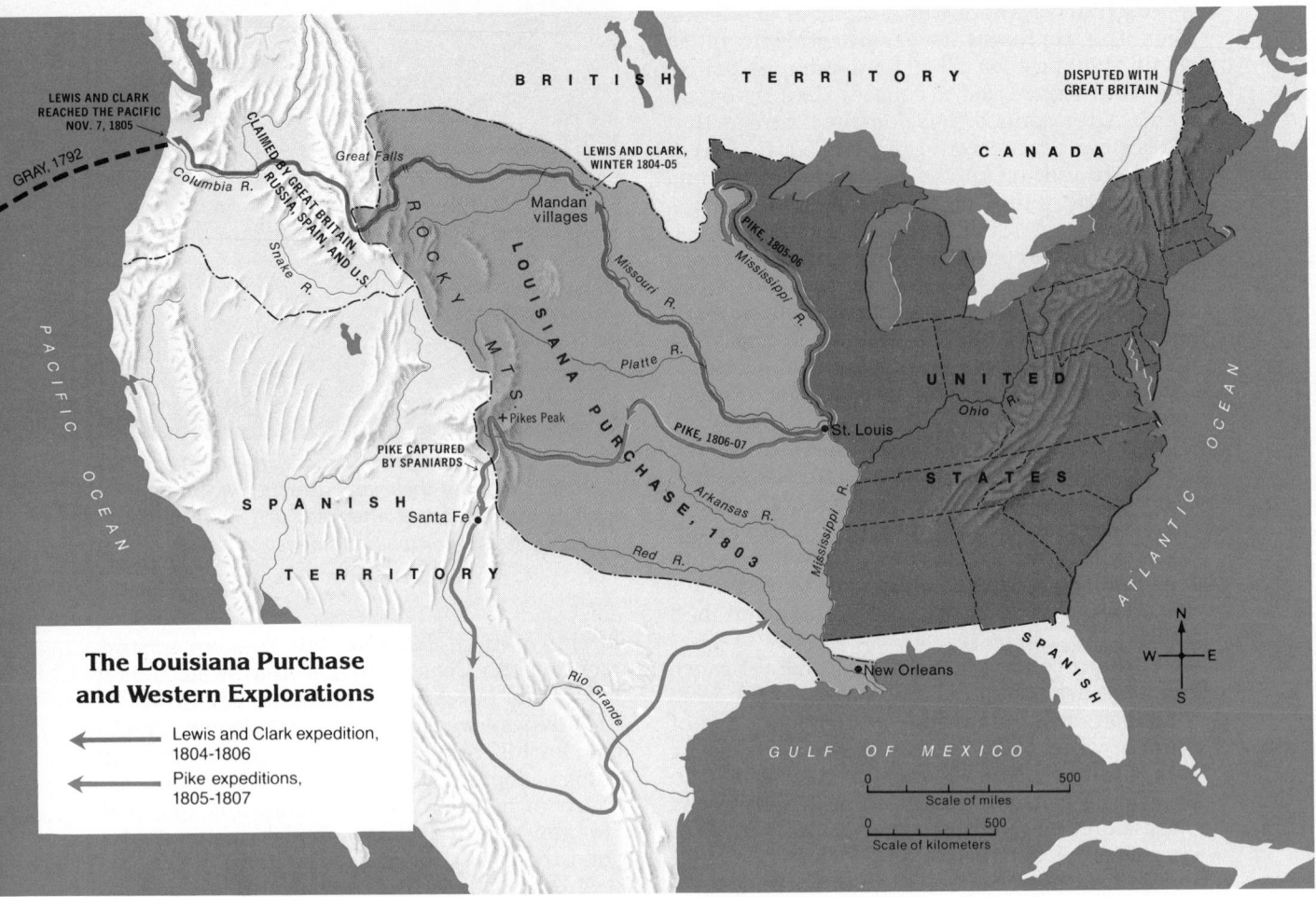

The Louisiana Purchase and Western Explorations

← Lewis and Clark expedition, 1804-1806

← Pike expeditions, 1805-1807

LEWIS AND CLARK REACHED THE PACIFIC NOV. 7, 1805

GRAY, 1792

Columbia R.

Great Falls

CLAIMED BY GREAT BRITAIN, RUSSIA, SPAIN, AND U.S.

Snake R.

ROCKY MTS.

Mandan villages

LEWIS AND CLARK, WINTER 1804-05

LOUISIANA PURCHASE, 1803

Missouri R.

Platte R.

+Pikes Peak

PIKE CAPTURED BY SPANIARDS

PIKE, 1806-07

Arkansas R.

Red R.

SPANISH

Santa Fe

TERRITORY

Rio Grande

PACIFIC OCEAN

BRITISH TERRITORY

CANADA

DISPUTED WITH GREAT BRITAIN

PIKE 1805-06

MISSISSIPPI R.

St. Louis

UNITED

Ohio R.

STATES

Mississippi R.

New Orleans

SPANISH

ATLANTIC OCEAN

GULF OF MEXICO

0   500
Scale of miles

0   500
Scale of kilometers

N
W—E
S

tion did not give the federal government power to buy territory. The Federalists' position was as inconsistent as Jefferson's. The Federalists had long claimed that the Constitution should be broadly interpreted and that it gave the federal government all powers not specifically denied to it.

The stands taken by Jefferson and the Federalists on this issue illustrate how ideas change as interests and situations change. Despite Federalist objections, the treaty of purchase was approved. In 1803 Louisiana, or the Louisiana Purchase, became part of the United States.

During the transfer of ownership, apparently no one considered the claims of Indian tribes to the lands across the Mississippi River that they and their ancestors had regarded as their own. Jefferson had once hoped to see the eastern tribes adopt an agricultural way of life and the white settlers' culture. Now he favored

the removal of these Indians to lands across the Mississippi already occupied by western tribes.

The Lewis and Clark expedition. Nobody knew the boundaries of Louisiana, although a few white trappers and many Indian tribes had some idea of what lay within the territory. Jefferson decided to explore the vast region that the nation had bought. He assigned the task to a United States army expedition led by Meriwether Lewis and William Clark (see map, this page). ▲

The expedition of about 45 men left the Mississippi at St. Louis on May 14, 1804, and traveled up the Missouri River to its headwaters. There they hired Indian guides and horses and journeyed over perilous mountain trails to the headwaters of the Clearwater River. Then they built canoes and made their way down the Clearwater and the Columbia Rivers to the Pacific Ocean.

In this mural in Oregon's capitol building, Lewis and Clark (center) are shown at Celilo Falls on their journey toward the Pacific. They reached this point in 1805 with the help of their Indian guide, Sacajawea (right).

The expedition enjoyed good luck, good planning, and the friendliness of several Indian tribes, notably the Mandans and the Shoshones. During the first winter, Lewis and Clark hired a French-Canadian fur trader and his Indian wife, Sacajawea (sak·uh·juh·WEE·uh), to serve as guides and interpreters. Their aid in understanding Indian ways of life was vital.

The expedition's relations with the Indians were further aided by York, Clark's black slave, whom Clark freed at the end of the expedition. His dark skin made York seem less strange to the Indians than the whites did.

On September 23, 1806, the Lewis and Clark expedition returned to St. Louis. They brought back maps, journals, specimens of plants and insects, the bones and pelts of animals, and boxes of soil and stones.

Meanwhile, other bold explorers, including Zebulon Pike, were pushing into Spanish lands to the west. These early expeditions gave Americans their first real knowledge of the lands beyond the Mississippi.

Louisiana, with its immense area and rich resources, was an important addition to the nation. As Robert R. Livingston, minister to France, observed, "From this day the United States take their place among the powers of the first rank."

SECTION REVIEW

See underscored items, text pp. 247 - 49.

Identify: Toussaint L'Ouverture, Louisiana Purchase, Lewis and Clark, Sacajawea, Zebulon Pike

For answers to questions, see Answer Key, p.A38.

1. **Analyzing Ideas:** Why were Americans uneasy about France's takeover of Louisiana from Spain in 1800?

2. **Summarizing Ideas:** What objections were made to the Louisiana Purchase?

3. **Studying Maps:** Trace the expeditions of Lewis and Clark and of Pike on the map on page 248. **(a)** What areas within the Louisiana Purchase, and beyond it, did these expeditions visit? **(b)** What evidence can you find on the map that might foreshadow disagreements with other nations as a result of the Louisiana Purchase?

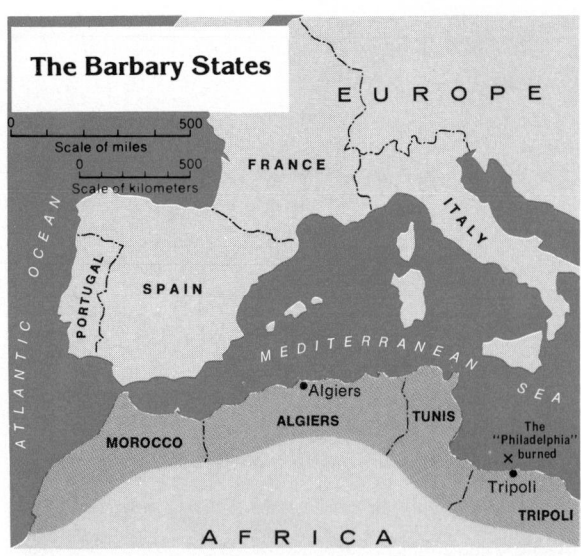

The Barbary States

EUROPE

FRANCE

ITALY

ATLANTIC OCEAN

PORTUGAL

SPAIN

MEDITERRANEAN SEA

MOROCCO

•Algiers

ALGIERS

TUNIS

The "Philadelphia" × burned

•Tripoli

TRIPOLI

AFRICA

Scale of miles 0 500
Scale of kilometers 0 500

2 The nation grows stronger during Jefferson's administration

See Teaching Suggestions in TMRG, pp. TM63-64.

Thomas Jefferson's prompt action in the purchase of Louisiana was only one of several vigorous steps he took as President. He urged Congress to repeal a number of Federalist laws that he felt were harmful to the nation's best interests. He also did not hesitate to use military force to protect American rights.

Federalist laws repealed. The Alien and Sedition Acts of 1798, which Jefferson strongly opposed, had expired before he became President. The Naturalization Act, also passed in 1798, was still in effect, and at Jefferson's urging Congress promptly repealed it. Congress also repealed the excise tax on whisky, which Jefferson regarded as unconstitutional. Congress likewise repealed the Judiciary Act of 1801. Thus the "midnight judges" appointed on the eve of Jefferson's inauguration could not assume office.

Jefferson then turned his attention to the army and the navy. He persuaded Congress to cut funds for them and reduce them in size. Jefferson opposed a strong military establishment because it would greatly strengthen the federal government. Moreover, by reducing the armed forces, Jefferson could operate the government more economically.

Federalist programs continued. The Republicans, however, did not wipe out all the work of the Federalists. Jefferson acted with moderation. During his administration he continued many Federalist programs and kept many Federalists in office.

Hoping to end the bitterness between the Federalists and the Republicans, Jefferson said in his Inaugural Address, "We are all Republicans; we are all Federalists." Then Jefferson showed through his actions that he meant to bring unity to the nation.

Although Jefferson had argued that the Bank of the United States was unconstitutional, he could do nothing to disturb it, for its charter ran until 1811. While Secretary of State in Washington's administration, Jefferson had also opposed Hamilton's plan to have the federal government assume the state debts. Nevertheless, Jefferson saw to it that Secretary of the Treasury Albert Gallatin paid off installments on the public debt as rapidly as possible.

Defending American rights. In a war with the pirates of North Africa, Jefferson actually pushed forward the Federalist ideal of a strong federal government.

The Muslim rulers of the Barbary States of North Africa—Morocco, Algiers, Tunis, and Tripoli—had long been seizing the ships of Christian nations and holding their crews for ransom. Instead of declaring war on the pirates, the European governments had decided that it was cheaper to make the yearly payments of tribute, or bribes. Since 1783 the United States, whose merchants traded with the Mediterranean countries, had also been paying this tribute. However, when the rulers of Tripoli made exorbitant demands upon the United States, Jefferson met the challenge. He sent a squadron of naval ships to attack the harbor of Tripoli in the Mediterranean (see map, this page).

This did not end the trouble, however. In 1805 the ruler of Tripoli finally signed a peace treaty, but the piracy of other Barbary States continued until 1815. In that year an American fleet under Captain Stephen Decatur, reinforced by European warships, finally ended all payment of American tribute to the pirates along the Barbary coast.

American ships could now sail the Mediterranean freely. Europeans regarded the United States with new respect and admiration. More-

In the years following the Revolutionary War, not all foreign countries respected the new nation called the United States of America. This was true not only of Great Britain but also of the tiny Barbary States along the northern coast of Africa (see map, page 250). For two centuries the Barbary States had demanded money tribute from European countries that traded along the Mediterranean. They saw no reason to exempt American merchants from the tribute system.

At first the United States had complied with the tribute system. But in 1801 Thomas Jefferson became President. He was a frugal chief executive who deeply resented the fact that the United States was spending almost one fifth of its annual revenue to ransom prisoners captured by the Barbary States and to ensure the safety of American merchant ships on the Mediterranean.

When Tripoli decided to raise the cost of protection, Jefferson refused the new terms. Tripoli then declared war on the United States. Jefferson responded by sending a squadron of seven ships, led by the frigates *Constitution* and *Philadelphia* against Tripoli.

Misfortune struck when the *Philadelphia* ran aground and was captured by Barbary pirates. The entire expedition might have met disaster, but a new and daring hero, Stephen Decatur, entered the picture. Decatur, then 25 years old, seized a pirate schooner, which he renamed the *Intrepid.* On the night of February 16, 1804, he and a crew of 80 Marines sailed the *Intrepid* into Tripoli harbor. Decatur's men boarded the *Philadelphia.* Fighting with cutlasses, swords, and pistols, they defeated the enemy sailors in only 20 minutes. Only one Marine was wounded. Decatur then set the *Philadelphia* ablaze.

Decatur's raid changed the course of relations between the United States and the Barbary States. Tripoli gave up its demand for protection payments. Lord Nelson, England's greatest naval hero, called the raid "the most bold and daring act of the age."

Decatur was honored by Congress. After proving himself again a hero in the War of 1812, he sailed against Barbary pirates once more. As a result of his efforts, all the Barbary States agreed in 1815 to end their acts of piracy against American vessels.

over, American naval forces gained valuable experience during the war. The American people took great pride in the heroic exploits of Decatur and other naval commanders. These new heroes, honored by people in every section of the United States, stimulated pride in the growing nation.

The election of 1804. The Republicans entered the Presidential election of 1804 confident of victory. For their Presidential candidate they turned again to Thomas Jefferson. Instead of Aaron Burr, who had served as Vice-President during Jefferson's first term, they chose George Clinton of New York as Jefferson's running mate. Jefferson and Clinton won a sweeping victory, carrying all the states except Delaware and Connecticut.

Hamilton and Burr. In the meantime, Burr had accepted Federalist support in his campaign for governor of New York in the spring of 1804. Alexander Hamilton, who did not trust Burr, urged the Federalists to vote against him. Burr lost the election. Blaming Hamilton

for his defeat, Burr demanded an apology for an uncomplimentary remark that Hamilton had supposedly made during the election campaign. When Hamilton refused to apologize, Burr challenged him to a duel.

The two men met in the early morning of July 11. At the signal to fire, Burr raised his pistol, took careful aim, and shot. Hamilton, who had not tried to fire, fell mortally wounded and died shortly afterward.

Aaron Burr's next adventure puzzled Americans at the time and has puzzled historians ever since. In 1805 and 1806, he involved several prominent Americans in vague schemes. He might have wanted to persuade westerners to leave the Union and set up a separate republic or wanted to conquer Mexico and set up an independent empire. Whatever the facts were, Burr was arrested and charged with treason.

Chief Justice John Marshall, who presided at the trial, followed the strict definition of treason given in the Constitution. Burr was acquitted and chose to live in Europe in exile. Later he returned to New York, where he lived and died under the shadow of disapproval.

Identify: tribute, Barbary States, Stephen Decatur, Aaron Burr

1. **Analyzing Ideas: (a)** What important changes did the Jefferson administration make in the Federalist program? **(b)** Which Federalist policies did the administration continue and why?

2. **Interpreting Ideas:** How did the country respond to Jefferson's blend of Federalism and Republicanism in the election of 1804?

3. **Studying Maps:** Look at the map on page 250. **(a)** How did the location of the Barbary States enable them to interfere with American trade in the Mediterranean? **(b)** How did the war with the Barbary pirates strengthen the federal government?

3 The war in Europe creates serious problems for the United States

See Teaching Suggestions in TMRG, pp.TM64-65.

In 1803 Napoleon began his conquest of Europe. By 1807 Napoleon had almost reached his goal, but he still faced problems. To the east stood Russia. To the west, across the English Channel, stood Great Britain. British troops had been driven from the European mainland, but the British navy was powerful at sea. Napoleon also knew that Great Britain might soon put its troops back in Europe.

Wartime profits. One of Napoleon's desperate problems was that of supply. The British navy controlled the seas across which France had to bring needed products.

America was an important source of supply for both France and Great Britain, but especially France. Great Britain could send its merchant fleet to any part of the world to obtain imports. France had few ships and therefore relied upon American merchant vessels. American merchants made handsome profits from the European war. From 1789 to 1805 the tonnage, or carrying capacity, of the American merchant marine increased enormously.

Interference with America's trade. Great Britain was determined to destroy America's trade with France. In 1807 the British adopted a series of measures called Orders in Council.

These Orders forbade American vessels to enter any ports under Napoleon's control in Europe, the West Indies, or India.

While Great Britain was trying to shut off all trade with France, Napoleon attempted to **blockade,** or seal off, the British Isles. In a series of Orders, he forbade all nations, including the United States, to trade with the British. He further warned that he would seize every ship that entered French ports after stopping at Great Britain or any British colony. Moreover, he threatened to seize every ship that submitted to inspection by British cruisers or that paid duties to the British government.

The British Orders in Council and Napoleon's Orders both violated the principle of **freedom of the seas.** This principle soon became, and has remained, an important pillar of American foreign policy.

For many months American merchants matched wits with the French and British navies by engaging in the dangerous but highly profitable practice of blockade running. The profits attracted so many merchants and shippers that in 1807 United States foreign trade soared to the highest level in the nation's history. This risky trade involved the United States in constant conflict with both the British and the French.

Another source of conflict between the United States and Great Britain was continuing British **impressment,** or seizure, of American sailors.

In the summer of 1807, the British ship *Leopard* demanded the right to search the American frigate *Chesapeake* for deserters from the British navy. The commander of the *Chesapeake* refused, whereupon the *Leopard* opened fire. Three Americans were killed and 18 wounded. Four *Chesapeake* sailors were seized and taken aboard the *Leopard.* Many outraged Americans demanded war.

The Embargo Act of 1807. Jefferson did not want war. However, he did want to end the continuing American conflict with Great Britain and France. He decided that the only answer short of war was to remove American ships from the high seas.

With this in mind and with his cabinet's approval, Jefferson urged Congress to pass an **embargo.** This was a law forbidding Americans to trade with any foreign nation, including, of course, Great Britain and France. Late in December 1807, Congress passed the Embargo Act, which forbade American vessels to leave for foreign ports. With the Embargo Act the United States temporarily abandoned the principle of freedom of the seas in the hope of avoiding war.

From the outset the Embargo Act could not be fully enforced. Americans smuggled goods across the border to Canada. Some merchants kept their vessels abroad. There, sailing under British or French licenses, they continued to earn large profits. Nevertheless, American trade suffered badly.

New England merchants were the first to feel the pinch. They angrily demanded repeal of the Embargo Act, claiming that Jefferson was deliberately trying to ruin them. Farmers, unable to sell their crops to foreign buyers, and unemployed sailors joined the merchants in demanding repeal.

Reluctantly Jefferson gave in to the growing pressure. On March 1, 1809, three days before he left office, Congress, with his support, repealed the Embargo Act.

Drifting toward war. Following the precedent started by George Washington, Jefferson refused to run for a third term. In the Presidential election of 1808, James Madison of Virginia, a Republican, won the office by a substantial vote.

Madison was a quiet, scholarly man. For eight years before becoming President, he had served as Jefferson's Secretary of State. Madison shared Jefferson's views. He was determined to gain respect for American rights on the high seas, but by peaceful means. However, during his first administration, the country moved toward war.

Madison's diplomacy. In place of the Embargo Act, Congress in 1809 passed the Non-Intercourse Act. This law forbade American merchants to do business with Great Britain or France, although trade with other nations was allowed. Yet trade with Great Britain and France was precisely what Americans were demanding. Because of continued pressure from merchants, Congress in 1810 allowed the Non-Intercourse Act to expire. American shipowners and captains once again turned to the dangerous business of running the blockade.

Still searching for a way to avoid war, President Madison on May 1, 1810, signed a new

According to this cartoon, in order to maintain peace, President Jefferson (center) had to suffer the insults of both King George III of Great Britain (left) and Napoleon, Emperor of France (right).

law. This law urged Great Britain and France to remove their restrictions on American shipping. It also promised that when either nation did this, the United States would refuse to trade with the other nation.

Failure of Madison's policy. The keen-witted Napoleon quickly seized the chance to force the United States to take sides against Great Britain. In August 1810 he announced that France would no longer interfere with American shipping. As the United States later learned, Napoleon had no intention of keeping his word. Nevertheless, President Madison had no choice but to forbid all trade with Great Britain. From the British point of view, the United States had chosen to become an enemy. Madison's policy had failed.

Declaration of war. Instead of declaring war on the United States, however, the British decided to remove *their* restrictions on American shipping. On June 16, 1812, Parliament suspended the Orders in Council that had

▲ Writing activity: Have students write a letter to the editor of a Boston newspaper from either of two viewpoints--a farmer's or a New England merchant's--protesting the Embargo Act of 1807.

253

interfered with American trade. Unhappily, there was no trans-Atlantic cable, telephone, or radio to carry this news to the American people. So, unaware of the British action, only two days later, on June 18, Congress declared war on Great Britain. Why?

Most historians agree that the War of 1812 was fought mainly over freedom of the seas and the impressment of American sailors, but there were other reasons as well. Members of Congress from eastern states with a strong interest in trade were divided in their feelings about the war. However, the great majority of members from the agricultural southern and western states favored the war. How can this be explained?

Land hunger. Western land hunger was an old story. Pioneer farmers quickly exhausted the fertility of their soil. Then they moved westward to new land, which they cleared, planted—and eventually wore out. By 1812 the pioneers had almost reached the end of the forested areas.

The northwestern farmers did not want to move onto the treeless prairies of the United States, where there was no timber to build houses and fences. Some farmers mistakenly believed that the prairie soil was poor. To them the rich wooded land of southern Canada lying just across the border looked much more attractive.

Farmers living in Tennessee, western Georgia, and what is now northern Alabama longed for the lands of Spanish Florida bordering the Gulf of Mexico (see map, page 259). They wanted this land not only for farming, but also because it served as a safe hiding place for runaway slaves and as a base for Indians who kept attacking American frontier settlements. People from this section of the country clamored for the conquest of Florida. War with Great Britain would provide an excuse for conquest, because Spain had been Britain's ally ever since Napoleon had invaded Spain.

National pride. The rising spirit of pride in the new nation also led to the War of 1812. Americans resented impressment of American sailors and insults to the flag. Many Americans now believed that the United States was destined to expand until the American flag flew over the Western Hemisphere from the North Pole to the Strait of Magellan. At the very least, they said, Canada, Mexico, and the land as far as the Pacific Ocean should belong to the United States.

Indian relations. Troubled relations with the Indians also led westerners to demand war. Many Indians in the northwestern areas had been reluctantly persuaded, bribed, or forced to give up more and more of their land to the advancing white settlers. Time after time, they had been promised that this was the last land they would be forced to give up. Every time the promise had been broken.

A great leader of the Shawnee tribe, Tecumseh, decided to make a final stand against expansion by whites. Encouraged by Canadian officials and fur traders, he formed a defensive confederation of Indian tribes in the Ohio country.

In the early 1800's Tecumseh and his brother, the Prophet, kindled a religious revival among the Indians of the Northwest. Indian warrior and Indian priest, they traveled far and wide among the scattered tribes, urging them to preserve their traditions and not to sell any more land to white settlers. "Sell a country!" Tecumseh cried. "Why not sell the air, the clouds, and the great sea? . . . Did not the Great Spirit make them all for the use of his children?"

Tecumseh had no wish to start a war. He asked only that white settlers leave the Indians alone and stop taking their lands. Although Tecumseh opposed war, he gathered warriors at Tippecanoe on the Wabash River. Even this show of readiness to resist by the Indian tribes could not stop the westward movement of white settlers.

Demands of the "War Hawks." As the influence of Tecumseh and his brother spread along the frontier, westerners became alarmed. Most of them believed that British fur traders in Canada were supplying the Indians with arms. Why not seize Canada, the westerners asked, and put an end, once and for all, to the dangers of an alliance between the British and the Indians?

In the Congressional elections of 1810, the citizens of the frontier regions elected several young men to Congress. Among them were Henry Clay of Kentucky, John C. Calhoun of South Carolina, Felix Grundy of Tennessee, and Peter B. Porter of western New York. Known as "War Hawks," these youthful members helped to whip up a war spirit in

His worst enemy described him as "one of those uncommon geniuses, which spring up occasionally to produce revolutions and overturn the established order of things." His fellow Shawnees revered Tecumseh as the leader who would stop the westward push of white settlers onto Indian lands. By the time he reached adulthood, Tecumseh was a highly respected warrior whose word was accepted without question by Indians and whites alike.

In 1808 Tecumseh and other Shawnees were forced to move westward into the Indiana Territory. There Tecumseh started a political crusade urging his fellow Shawnees to take up farming on a full-time basis. He also spoke to other Indian groups throughout the Midwest and Southeast.

In his speeches, Tecumseh described how many once-powerful Indian tribes had "vanished before the avarice and the oppression of the White Man, as snow before a summer sun." He reminded his listeners that the sale or cession of land to whites was illegal without the consent of all Indian tribes together. Tecumseh explained that he hoped to create a nation where Indians could maintain their traditions while gradually adapting to Western civilization.

Unfortunately, Tecumseh's dream never became a reality. While Tecumseh was traveling in the South, his brother was maneuvered into the Battle of Tippecanoe. The Indians escaped outright defeat, but their casualties were high and most of their weapons and supplies were destroyed. The outbreak of war in 1812 left Tecumseh little time to put matters right. Tecumseh joined the British army, hoping a defeat of the Americans would bring the peace the Indians sought. When Tecumseh was killed at the Battle of the Thames, the dreams of an Indian confederation existing peacefully with the United States died with him.

Congress. "We shall drive the British from our continent," declared Felix Grundy. "They will no longer have an opportunity of intriguing with our Indian neighbors. . . . That nation [Britain] will lose her Canadian trade, and by having no resting place in this country, her means of annoying us will be diminished."

Because of western demands, in the late fall of 1811, General William Henry Harrison led American troops into what is now Indiana. The Indians had gathered at the point where the Tippecanoe River flows into the Wabash River (see map, page 259). Tecumseh, at the time, was away seeking the support of southern Indians—the Creeks, Choctaws, and Cherokees.

The Prophet sprang a surprise attack against the American troops, but the Indians were forced back. They fought bravely, and Harrison lost many soldiers. When Harrison left the battlefield, he was not sure of the outcome, but the Indians, who had also suffered badly, fled northward. Although the Battle of Tippecanoe was not a decisive victory for Harrison, it helped make him a frontier military hero.

In 1813 Harrison defeated the British and their Indian allies at the Battle of the Thames in Canada. Tecumseh was killed, and the confederation that he and his brother had organized fell apart. British hopes of regaining power in the area were destroyed.

Identify: blockade, freedom of the seas, *Leopard*, *Chesapeake*, Embargo Act of 1807, James Madison, Tecumseh, War Hawks, 1812
For answers to questions, see Answer Key, p.A39.

1. **Interpreting Ideas:** How did American merchants profit from the Napoleonic Wars?

2. **Analyzing Ideas:** (a) How did France and Great Britain attempt to hinder each other's trade with the United States? (b) What response did President Jefferson make to these attempts? (c) How did the country respond to Jefferson's action?

3. **Summarizing Ideas:** Describe two measures that President Madison took to try to prevent European interference with American trade.

4. **Organizing Ideas:** Explain how each of the following led to the War of 1812: (a) land hunger, (b) national pride, (c) settler-Indian conflict, (d) fur trade, (e) desire for freedom of the seas, (f) impressment of American sailors.

4 Americans again fight the British in the War of 1812

See Teaching Suggestions in TMRG, pp.TM65-66.

When Congress declared war against Great Britain on June 18, 1812, many Americans expected a swift victory. Henry Clay, among others, believed that the Kentucky militia could conquer Canada in three weeks. As it turned out, the war dragged on for two years.

The election of 1812. In May, only a few weeks before war was declared, Republican leaders nominated Madison for a second term. The Federalists, most of whom opposed the war, supported De Witt Clinton of New York, whom anti-war Republicans had nominated. Although Madison won the election by a comfortable margin, Clinton carried all the New England and Middle Atlantic states except Vermont and Pennsylvania. Moreover, the Federalists made heavy gains in Congress. The election clearly revealed that many Americans, especially New Englanders, strongly opposed the war.

A divided country. Even after the conflict started, many Federalists continued to feel that it was unnecessary. Merchants realized that war would ruin what was left of their ship-

ping. Furthermore, they objected to proposals to annex Canada and Florida to the United States. They saw clearly that additional land would greatly increase the power of the farmers. Why, the Federalist merchants asked, should they fight a war that would weaken their influence in the federal government?

Even some Republicans had misgivings about the war. John Randolph of Virginia raised an issue that would haunt the halls of Congress for many years. He declared that annexing Canada would increase the strength of that part of the United States that did not have slavery and weaken the power of the southern states. Randolph also feared that a war would so increase the powers of the federal government that the traditional rights of the states would be endangered.

Handicaps to the war effort. The opposition of most Federalists and some Republicans weakened the war effort in other ways as well. Governors of New England states would not permit their state militias to invade Canada. When Congress debated a compulsory draft law to raise troops for the army, the New England Federalists denounced the measure.

Daniel Webster, a gifted young orator from Massachusetts, declared that **compulsory military service** was unconstitutional. "Where is it written in the Constitution?" Webster cried. "In what article is it contained that you may take children from their parents and parents from their children and compel them to fight the battles of any war in which the folly or the wickedness of the government may engage it?" New Englanders in general and Federalists in particular referred to the War of 1812 with contempt as "Mr. Madison's War."

When the war dragged on without success and American ships were swept from the seas, New England Federalists became increasingly bitter. Finally, on December 15, 1814, a group met in secret session at Hartford, Connecticut, in what was known as the Hartford Convention. The delegates proposed several amendments to the Constitution increasing the power and influence of the commercial sections of the country. A desperate minority even threatened to declare null and void any federal laws they believed to be unconstitutional. However, the Hartford Convention met too late to have any effect upon the war.

Although most southerners and westerners favored the war, they too were divided. South-

The White House, the executive mansion of the President of the United States, is the oldest public building in Washington, D.C. It was designed by an Irish immigrant, James Hoban, who modeled the original mansion in the classical Georgian style of the 1700's.

In 1800 President John Adams became the first chief executive to live in the mansion, then unfinished. During the War of 1812 British troops burned part of the building. The mansion then came to be called the White House because of the white paint used to cover its smoke-damaged walls. President Theodore Roosevelt made the name official by having it stamped on his stationery.

Throughout its history, the White House has survived numerous alterations and restorations, including a total reconstruction of its interior in the early 1950's.

erners wanted to conquer Florida. Westerners were just as eager to conquer Canada. As a result, the American military leaders found it difficult to make plans that would please even those who supported the war.

Lack of preparation. The country was not prepared for war. The navy's fleet of a dozen ships was helpless before the more than 800 warships of the British Royal Navy. The army had fewer than 7,000 troops at the outbreak of the war. Many of its commanders were well-meaning but elderly Revolutionary War veterans. They proved no match for superior British commanders.

Another weakness was the American failure to appoint a single commander to direct the entire war effort. Moreover, the militia on which the Americans chiefly depended was poorly equipped and trained.

Black soldiers and sailors. Little effort was made to recruit blacks, except in New York. There the legislature passed a special act for raising two regiments of black troops. Yet many black men, slave and free, took part in the war. Fugitive slaves, hoping to win their freedom, fought both on the American side and on the British side.

Black soldiers fighting on the American side made many contributions. After British forces seized Washington, D.C., American leaders in Philadelphia, also fearing seizure, appealed to local blacks to help secure the city's defenses. About 2,500 responded.

In Louisiana, General Andrew Jackson ignored the fear of many white officers that it would be dangerous to arm black troops. Instead, he called on "the free men of color" to fight the British. He promised them the same pay as white soldiers and the same bonuses in cash and land that white soldiers would receive after the war. When the war was over, Jackson addressed his black troops: "I expected much from you, but you have surpassed my hopes."

Naval officers also testified to the bravery of black sailors under fire. Captain Oliver H. Perry had at first been disturbed when he was sent "blacks, soldiers, and boys" as naval reinforcements. He later wrote that the blacks in his crew "seemed absolutely insensible to danger."

Despite their contributions and bravery, not many of the slaves who fought in the war were granted their freedom.

Ending in stalemate. The chief military goal of the Americans in the War of 1812 was the conquest of Canada. Despite several attempts, the Americans failed to achieve this goal.

On the other hand, by gaining control of Lake Erie, the Americans succeeded in keeping a Canadian force from occupying American territory for any length of time. Lake Erie was secured in 1813 through the victory of Captain Oliver H. Perry and his small naval force. His report of the victory—"We have met the enemy and they are ours"—is still an honored part of American naval tradition. Equally important was the victory of Captain Thomas Macdonough on Lake Champlain, near Plattsburg, New York, in 1814. Macdonough's victory prevented a British invasion of the United States from Canada.

The one outstanding American military victory of the War of 1812 was that of General Andrew Jackson at New Orleans. Jackson, born near the border between North and South Carolina, had already won fame as an Indian fighter in Tennessee. When he heard of British operations near New Orleans, he rushed to Louisiana. In a large-scale encounter with British forces, Jackson won. This victory helped promote the future political fortunes of General Jackson. It also gave the people of the United States the impression that they had won the War of 1812.

Actually, the victory at New Orleans had no effect upon the war's outcome. Negotiations for a peace treaty between the Americans and the British at Ghent in Belgium had been under way for some time. The Americans and the British had reached an agreement before the battle of New Orleans was fought. Lack of modern means of communication kept this news from reaching New Orleans in time to stop the battle.

The Treaty of Ghent. The Treaty of Ghent, signed on Christmas Eve, 1814, had limited direct results. It said nothing about the impressment of American sailors or about neutral rights on the high seas. The treaty did arrange for the release of all prisoners of war and for the restoration of all occupied territory. It also provided for a commission to settle boundary disputes between the United States and Canada. Most important, it restored peace and led eventually to greatly improved relations between the United States and Great Britain.

Settling disputes peaceably. Shortly after the war ended, the United States and Great Britain created a number of other commissions. These tackled the long-standing problems of trade, furs, and fishing rights along the North Atlantic coast.

These commissions produced worthwhile

Text continues on page 260.

The War of 1812

A slow start for the United States
1812

JULY	British capture Detroit; wipe out Fort Dearborn (Chicago)
NOV.	United States drive on Montreal fails.
AUG.–DEC.	U.S. naval vessels *Constitution, Wasp,* and *United States* defeat British in key sea battles.

The situation improves for the United States
1813

APRIL	U.S. forces raid York (Toronto), burning the public buildings.
SEPT. 10	U.S. Navy under Admiral Perry defeats British in Battle of Lake Erie; British evacuate Detroit.
OCT. 5	U.S. troops under General William Henry Harrison defeat British and Indian forces in Battle of the Thames; Tecumseh dies in battle, and Indians abandon British cause.
NOV.– JAN. 1814	Tennessee militia under Jackson and Coffee subdue Creek uprising.

United States gains: the tide turns
1814

JULY 5	U.S. troops under Generals Scott and Brown defeat British at Battle of Chippewa.
JULY 25	Battle of Lundy's Lane, the war's most sharply contested land engagement, ends in a draw.
SEPT. 11	Capt. Thomas Macdonough leads U.S. to victory in Battle of Lake Champlain, giving U.S. undisputed control of the lake.
AUG. 24	British troops defeat U.S. sailors and civilians at Bladensburg and march on to Washington, D.C.
AUG. 24–25	British capture Washington, D.C., and burn the Capitol, the White House, and other public buildings in retaliation for U.S. raid on York.
SEPT. 12–14	U.S. forces withstand British attempts to capture Fort McHenry and Baltimore; Francis Scott Key writes verses to the "Star–Spangled Banner;" British withdraw from Chesapeake Bay.
DEC. 24	Treaty of Ghent signed, ending the War of 1812.
1815	
JAN. 8	U.S. forces, led by Andrew Jackson, defeat British in Battle of New Orleans; battle is actually fought 2 weeks after the war's end.

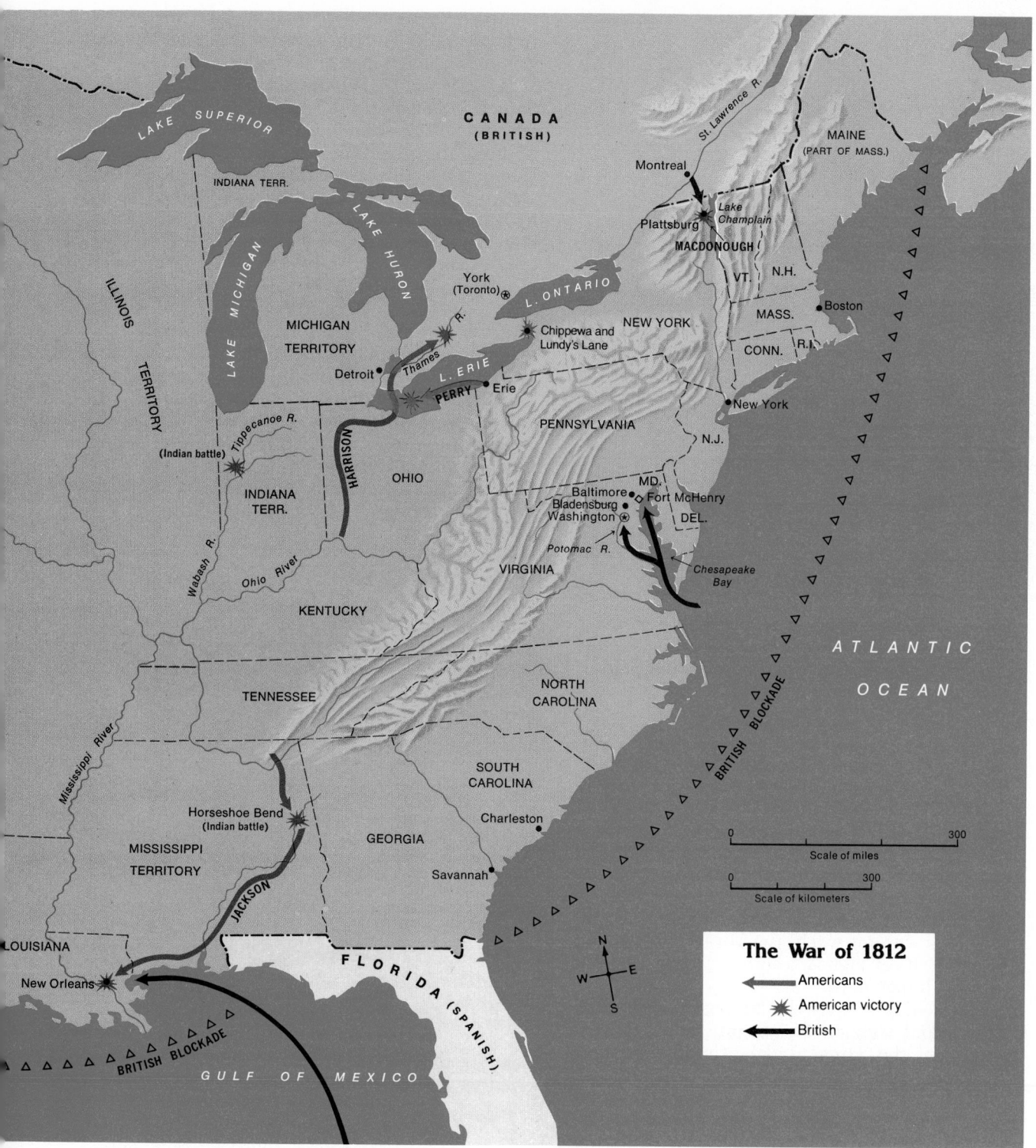

The War of 1812

Americans
American victory
British

Land surveying was a popular occupation for the adventuresome. Here a group of surveyors seek to determine where the border between Maine and Canada actually lay.

results. One commission did away with trade discriminations and allowed American ships to sail to all British ports except those in the West Indies. Another commission gave Americans the right to fish along the Canadian coast and to dry their fish on Canadian shores.

The Rush-Bagot Agreement. While the commissions were at work, the United States and Great Britain signed another treaty of even greater importance.

Immediately after the war, both the United States and Canada had begun to build warships on the Great Lakes to defend their frontiers. American, Canadian, and British leaders agreed that this was a needless expense and an invitation to future trouble. The Rush-Bagot Agreement, signed in Washington in 1817, provided that the United States and Canada would maintain only a few small vessels for police purposes on Lake Champlain and the Great Lakes. Years later the agree-

ment was extended to include land fortifications as well. Thus the agreement was one of the lasting outcomes of the War of 1812.

In 1818 another commission established the boundary between the United States and Canada extending from Lake of the Woods, west of Lake Superior, to the Rocky Mountains. The northeastern boundary from the Atlantic Ocean to Lake of the Woods was later settled by the Webster-Ashburton Treaty of 1842. The boundary from the Rocky Mountains to the Pacific Ocean was fixed by treaty in 1846 (see map, pages 996–97).

The war as a turning point. The War of 1812 also marked a turning point in American history. From 1789 to 1815, events in Europe had helped to shape United States policies, especially foreign policies. After the Treaty of Ghent, the United States became much more independent of Europe. Equally important, the nations of Europe treated with growing respect the young country that had not hesitated to go to war with the greatest naval power in the world.

During the next 100 years, moreover, the United States was not directly involved in European wars. Americans concentrated upon the job of developing their own country. After 1815 the American people as a whole turned their backs on Europe and began the exciting task of occupying the western lands.

SECTION REVIEW
See underscored items, text pp. 256, 260.
Identify: compulsory military service, Daniel Webster, "Mr. Madison's War," Hartford Convention, Rush-Bagot Agreement
For answers to questions, see Answer Key, p.A39.
1. **Summarizing Ideas: (a)** How did the election of 1812 reflect popular feelings about the approaching war with Britain? **(b)** Why did some Americans oppose the war?
2. **Analyzing Ideas:** How did the Treaty of Ghent and the Rush-Bagot Agreement settle the main differences between the United States and Great Britain?
3. **Interpreting Ideas:** In what way was the War of 1812 a turning point in American history?
4. **Studying Maps:** Look at the map on page 259. **(a)** What was the United States' principal military aim in the war? **(b)** Why did it fail to achieve this aim? **(c)** How did Oliver H. Perry, Thomas Macdonough, and Andrew Jackson contribute to the American cause?

DEVELOPING HISTORY STUDY SKILLS

Interpreting the Visual Record Reading a Time Line

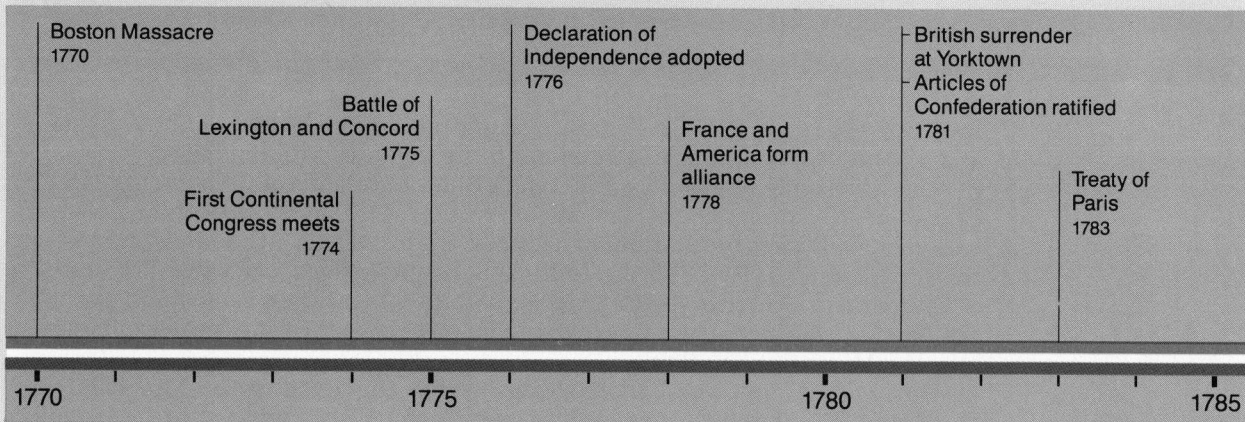

Time lines are useful devices for showing the sequence of events over time. Every chapter of this textbook ends with a time line (see page 262, for example). The time line, by listing specific events that occurred within the chapter, complements the major ideas set forth in the written summary that precedes it.

How to Read a Time Line

In reading a time line, follow these steps.

1. **Determine its framework.** Note the years covered and the intervals into which the time line is divided.
2. **Supply missing information.** Note each event the time line lists. Think about the event and associate names of people and places with it, "fleshing out" the bare bones listing.
3. **Note the sequence of events.** Ask how each event relates to each subsequent event. In this way cause-effect relationships can be reviewed.
4. **Name the time line.** Give the time line a title based on the relationships of each event to the others.

5. **Use the time line as a summary.** Fill in the "blanks" between events, weaving a summary from the first event to the last.

Applying the Skill

Examine the time line above. The years covered are from 1770 to 1785 and the events span the years from 1770 to 1783. The time line has intervals of 5 years marked. The events listed on the time line show steps leading up to the Declaration of Independence and the events that followed the Declaration. A possible title for this time line is the "March Toward Independence." Some of the events not shown are the Intolerable Acts, the Second Continental Congress, the appointment of George Washington as commander in chief.

Practicing the Skill

Examine the time line below, which parallels the years listed at the top of the page. On a separate sheet of paper, write a summary of Lafayette's life, combining events listed on the two times lines.

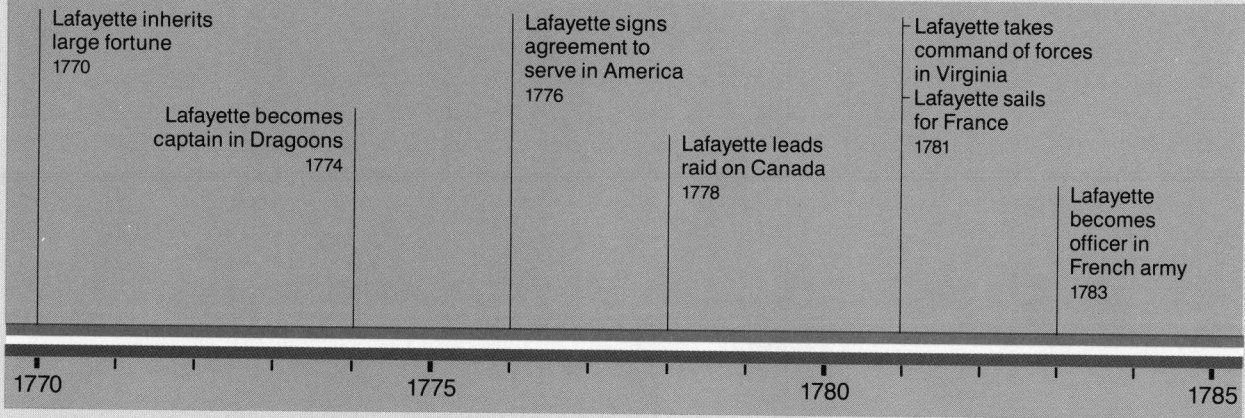

261

Between 1801 and 1815 the young, struggling United States doubled in size, adding the vast territory of Louisiana to its domain. The Louisiana Purchase was one of Thomas Jefferson's outstanding accomplishments as President. Not to his credit, or to that of other Americans, was the treatment afforded the Indians who made their homes in the lands west of the Appalachians. By 1815 the Indians had been driven from the new state of Ohio and the territory of Michigan, both of which had been carved out of the Northwest Territory. The way was now open for the advance of pioneers into the Mississippi Valley.

During this time, the United States became involved in the Napoleonic Wars, which plunged Europe and the rest of the Western world into turmoil between 1796 and 1815. The United States failed to maintain for itself freedom of the seas, and it failed to stay out of war. Nevertheless, it emerged from the conflict without the loss of territory or of national strength. The War of 1812 also marked a turning point in the relations between Canada and the United States. Despite bitterness between the two nations stirred up by the war, the way was paved for the peaceable settlement of disputes in the future.

Finally, the troubles that Americans faced in this period of turmoil helped to draw them together into a united nation. The American people emerged from the War of 1812 with a strong feeling of unity and of national pride.

CONNECTING CHAPTER IDEAS

In the next chapter you will read about the rapid growth of the United States. The new nation undertook to become economically, politically, and culturally independent of Europe. It did this through the development of the American System, the establishment of the Monroe Doctrine, and a surge of pride in American cultural endeavors.

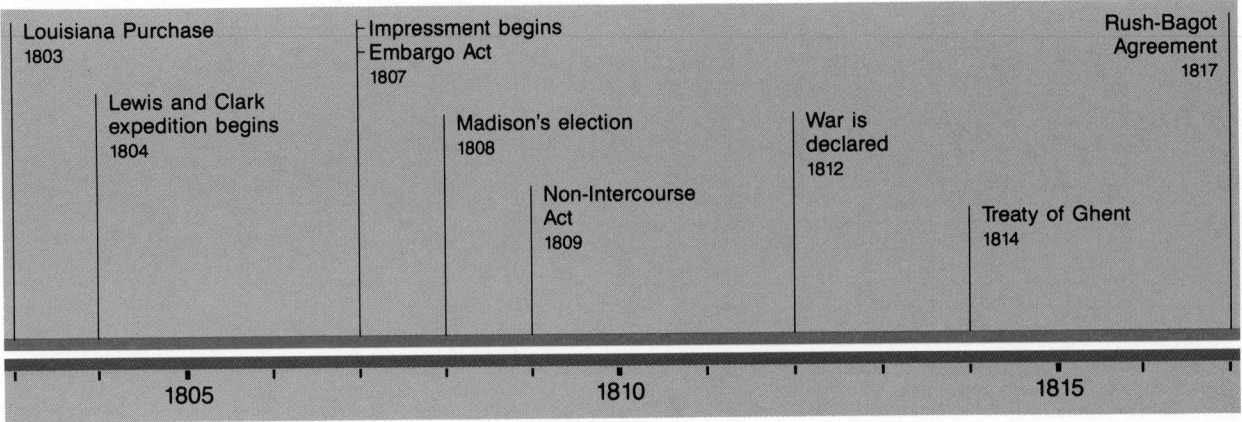

Louisiana Purchase
1803

Lewis and Clark
expedition begins
1804

Impressment begins
Embargo Act
1807

Madison's election
1808

Non-Intercourse
Act
1809

War is
declared
1812

Treaty of Ghent
1814

Rush-Bagot
Agreement
1817

1805   1810   1815

For answers to questions, see Answer Key, pp. A39-40.

Reviewing Important Terms

Decide whether each of the following sentences is true or false. If the sentence is false, replace the underlined term with the word or phrase that will make it true.

1. Up until 1815, the United States was forced to pay a yearly <u>tribute</u> to the rulers of the Barbary States.
2. Aaron Burr's activities in 1805 and 1806 led to his arrest on charges of <u>treason</u>.
3. Napoleon imposed a <u>blockade</u> in an attempt to cut off Great Britain from overseas trade.
4. The British Orders in Council and Napoleon's Orders both violated the principle of <u>writ of assistance</u>.
5. British <u>impressment</u> of American sailors was a major factor leading to war between the United States and Great Britain.
6. The trade <u>embargo</u> imposed in 1807 forbade American vessels to sail for and Americans to trade with any foreign nation.
7. During the War of 1812, New England Federalists denounced <u>compulsory military service</u> as unconstitutional.

Practicing Critical Thinking Skills

1. **Interpreting Ideas.** In his Inaugural Address, Jefferson said, "We are all Republicans, we are all Federalists." **(a)** What did he mean by this statement? **(b)** Were his actions as President consistent with this statement? Give specific examples to support your opinion.
2. **Summarizing Ideas.** In the early 1800's many Americans, especially those on the frontier, feared an alliance between the Indians and the British. How would such an alliance have benefited the Indians? the British?
3. **Evaluating Information.** The delegates to the Hartford Convention of 1814 were accused of treason by some of their opponents. **(a)** What did they do to bring on the accusation? **(b)** Evaluate the accusation in the light of the Constitutional definition of treason (Article 3, Section 3, on page 203) and the fact that the United States was at war.
4. **Evaluating Viewpoints.** Some historians believe that the War of 1812 was really the Second War of Independence. Do you agree or disagree? Explain your reasoning.

5. **Synthesizing Ideas.** Why do you think that, despite their intentions, the first four Presidents of the United States were unable to avoid involvement in European affairs?
6. **Relating Past to Present.** Thomas Jefferson made this statement: "Were it left to me to decide whether we should have a government without newspapers or newspapers without a government, I should not hesitate a moment to prefer the latter." **(a)** What did he mean? **(b)** Do you think his statement applies today? Explain.

Developing History Study Skills

Reading a Time Line. Study the time line on the opposite page. Then answer these questions. **(a)** Into what intervals of time is the time line divided? **(b)** Which three events shown on the time line had a direct influence on United States participation in the War of 1812? **(c)** Use the events shown on the time line to write a three-paragraph summary of Chapter 10.

Relating Geography and History

The Louisiana Territory was explored soon after its purchase by Meriwether Lewis and William Clark in 1804–06 and Zebulon M. Pike in 1805–07. In addition to almost doubling the size of the United States and adding a vast treasure of land and natural resources, there were many important political considerations before, during, and after the sale. In order to understand how the Louisiana Purchase affected American policies and status, study the map on page 248, reread Section 1 (pages 245–49), and answer the following questions.

1. **(a)** What kind of alliance did Jefferson wish to avoid if France remained in possession of Louisiana? **(b)** What action did Jefferson initiate in order to avoid the unwanted alliance?
2. **(a)** How did sectional interests arise in the objections to the Louisiana Purchase? **(b)** How did the Purchase reverse the Constitutional philosophies of both Jefferson and the Federalists?
3. What do you think was the motive behind Jefferson's sending the Lewis and Clark Expedition all the way to the Pacific?
4. State two reasons why the British might have been unhappy about the Louisiana Purchase.

See Chapter Overview in TMRG, p.TM67.
See Chapter Objectives in TMRG, p.TM67.
See Introducing the Chapter in TMRG, p.TM67.

CHAPTER 11   Gaining Prosperity and Respect

(1817–1825)

An early factory

The War of 1812 could, by no means, be considered a victory for either side. The war, however, marked a turning point in American affairs because it freed Americans from involvement in the affairs of Europe. Americans in 1815 could now turn their full attention to developing the resources of their own nation.

The war itself had greatly stimulated a feeling of patriotism and national pride in the hearts of most Americans. It had helped unite Americans in their determination to strengthen the growing nation. So strong was this feeling of patriotism and pride that the period from about 1817 to 1825 came to be known as the "Era of Good Feelings."

The term "Era of Good Feelings," however, did not mean that the nation was united in other ways. The nation was still divided into major regions, each of which had different characteristics and resources. The Industrial Revolution was reshaping the Northeast, particularly New England. The South, mainly an agricultural region, was devoting more of its efforts to the growing of cotton becoming more dependent on slavery. The West—the land between the Appalachian Mountains and the Mississippi River—was attracting growing numbers of pioneer settlers, its interests different from the North and South.

Individually, members of Congress looked out for the special interests of their states and their own sections of the country. Collectively, Congress, along with the President, had to weld the Northeast, the South, and the West into a unified whole. The nation's leaders solved this problem of **sectionalism** versus unity, at least temporarily, by means of a program that was called the "American System."

═══ READING FOCUS ═══

As you read about the nation's new found prosperity, look for the details that support each of the following statements.

1. The Industrial Revolution reaches the United States.
2. New leaders develop the "American System."
3. The growing nation struggles with new and complex problems.
4. The United States warns Europe to stay out of the Western Hemisphere.
5. American education and arts reveal pride in the growing nation.

1 The Industrial Revolution reaches the United States

See Teaching Suggestions in TMRG, pp.TM67-68.

In the 1700's the invention and development of power-driven machines changed the way many products were made. More manufacturing was done in factories and less in the homes and small shops of workers.

The arrival of Samuel Slater. The shift to factories and machines has become known as the Industrial Revolution. Samuel Slater, who landed in New York in 1789, was one of many skilled workers in this revolution.

Although only 21 years old when he left England, Slater was already a highly skilled mechanic. He had worked in a cotton textile mill and knew a great deal about the new spinning and weaving machines built by British inventors. What is more, he knew that British industrialists wanted to keep the secrets of these new machines from other countries. For this reason, the British government had forbidden the machines to be sold. It had also forbidden textile workers to leave the country.

Slater nevertheless slipped away. He arrived in New York with empty hands and almost empty pockets, but in his head were plans for power-driven clothmaking machines.

Samuel Slater went to Rhode Island. There, with the financial aid of Moses Brown, a Quaker merchant, Slater reproduced from memory the machines he had used in England. Indeed, he even improved them. Soon Slater was operating a successful cotton factory, or mill, using water-powered machinery.

The growth of the factory system. Soon other Americans began to operate mills at water-power sites in New England and the Middle Atlantic states. At first the new mills did nothing more than spin thread with power-driven machines. The mill owners then distributed the thread to homes scattered over the surrounding countryside. Working at hand looms in their own homes, women wove the thread into cloth, which they then returned to the mill owners. Within a few years, however, mills began to weave the cloth as well as spin the yarn. This development came to be known as the **factory system**. During the early 1800's,

▲ Discussion topic: Slater's activities are an early example of what today is often called industrial espionage. Have students discuss industrial espionage, its causes and effects.

265

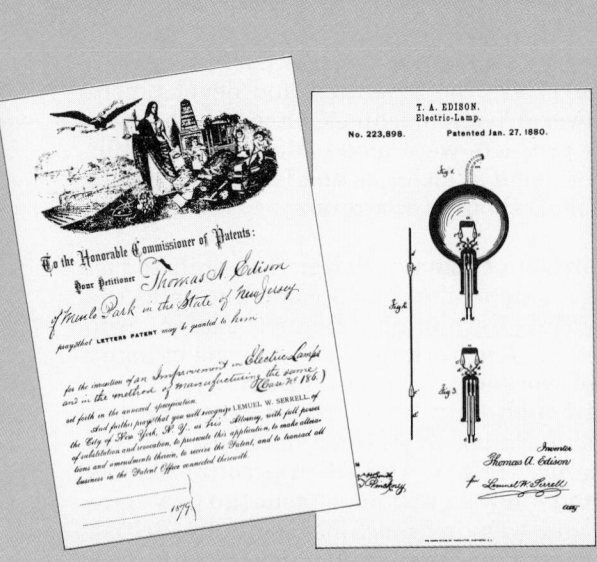

Article 1, Section 8, of the Constitution directs Congress "To promote the progress of science and useful arts . . ." Accordingly, Congress established the U.S. Patent Office in 1790. Under the first patent law, inventors sent an explanation of their device to the Secretary of State, who convened a committee of cabinet members to accredit the invention. This procedure was very impractical, because members of the patent committee had other full-time jobs. Nor did they have any method for determining whether a device already existed. Nevertheless, the system worked for a time because patent applications numbered less than a thousand a year.

Today the patent system is administered by the Patent and Trademark Office of the Department of Commerce, which processes more than 100,000 patent applications per year. Inventors submit plans and a working model of their device. Skilled examiners study the invention to determine whether it is indeed new and useful. Inventors who are granted patents (about 70,000 per year) have exclusive rights to their creative efforts for 17 years.

The patent system encourages Americans to invent, to conduct research, to commercialize new technology, and to make public their inventions. Throughout the world, patent systems are important contracts between inventors and society.

---

more and more work was done by this factory system.

The power-driven machines and the buildings to house them were very expensive to build and maintain. Individual workers could not afford them. Thus **capitalists°** like Moses Brown built the factories, installed the machinery, purchased raw materials, hired workers, and distributed the finished products. After starting in the textile industry, the Industrial Revolution spread rapidly to the manufacturing of many other products, among them firearms, clocks, and watches.

The Industrial Revolution would have come to America in time even without Samuel Slater. As it turned out, however, Slater pioneered in developing America's factory system.

° The property, equipment, and money used to produce goods or provide services are known as **capital**. A **capitalist** is a person who invests capital in a business with the hope of earning profits.

The search for labor-saving machines. From the earliest days of settlement, the colonial towns and villages never had enough workers to develop America's seemingly limitless natural resources. Slowly but steadily, pioneer men and women pushed westward. With so much land available, they preferred to own their own farms rather than work as hired hands. Faced with this labor shortage, American farmers put their numerous sons and daughters to work at an early age.

The growing towns also had more work to be done than they had people to do it. This shortage of labor stimulated colonial manufacturers to invent labor-saving machines for factories and farms and to provide better working conditions and higher wages than were common in Europe.

Encouraging inventors. Because of these conditions, the American government took steps to encourage inventors. In 1790 Congress enacted a law granting inventors as well as authors exclusive rights for 14 years to all profits made from their ideas. This law meant that the new tools or the new books belonged to their inventors or authors and could be produced and sold only with their permission for a period of 14 years.

New sources of power. Another important part of the Industrial Revolution was the discovery and use of new sources of power to run machinery. The textile machinery first used in Great Britain was driven by water power. In 1769, however, James Watt, a Scottish inventor, took out an English patent for a steam engine. By the 1790's steam power was rapidly replacing water power in British mills.

Although Americans in the 1790's knew about steam engines and were even building some of their own, steam power did not come quickly to the United States. By 1812 there were only ten steam-powered mills in the new nation. Americans were not uninterested in steam as a power source, but their rivers and streams, especially in New England, provided an ample supply of water to power the nation's first factories.

Interchangeable parts. Meanwhile Eli Whitney, a Connecticut resident, hit upon a new idea for building machines, an idea that French inventors also developed. Whitney's idea grew out of his work with guns. Before the early 1800's, all guns were manufactured by gunsmiths, who hammered out each part separately and assembled the parts by hand. When any gun part was damaged, a new part had to be made by hand to replace it.

In 1798 Eli Whitney decided that he could manufacture guns using a new principle of production. He wrote to the Secretary of the Treasury requesting a contract. "I should like," he wrote, "to undertake the manufacture of 10,000 or 15,000 stand of arms. I am persuaded that machinery moved by water, adapted to this business, would greatly diminish the labor and facilitate the manufacture of this article. Machines for forging, rolling, floating, boring, grinding, polishing, etc., may all be made use of to advantage."

Although Whitney's request was unusual, he got his contract from the government. When more than two years had passed, though, people began to think Whitney's project had failed.

Then the young inventor made a trip to Washington. Before a group of skeptical officials, he unpacked a box containing the parts of ten identical guns. At Whitney's request an official selected one part from each of the piles scattered about the table. The first gun was then assembled. This process was repeated until all ten guns had been assembled from these **interchangeable parts** and fired. Those present witnessed what was actually the beginning of **mass production** in America.

A look ahead. Not even the most far-sighted Americans ever dreamed that the developments taking place around them were destined to change life everywhere.

In years to come, the Industrial Revolution would help to unite the American people. It would help solve problems of transportation by binding the nation together with a web of steel rails. It would provide Americans with unheard-of labor-saving devices. It would profoundly affect the roles and status of both women and men in American life. It would help Americans conquer the wilderness and make use of what were then considered the inexhaustible resources of forest and sea and soil. It would in time transform the United States into the wealthiest nation on earth.

SECTION REVIEW
See underscored items, text pp. 265-67.

Identify: sectionalism, Industrial Revolution, factory system, capitalist, interchangeable parts, mass production

For answers to questions, see Answer Key, pp. A40-41.

1. **Analyzing Ideas: (a)** What technological advance helped to bring about the Industrial Revolution? **(b)** How did the Industrial Revolution change the system of manufacturing in Great Britain and the United States?

2. **Evaluating Ideas:** What role did Samuel Slater play in the development of the American factory system?

3. **Summarizing Ideas:** How was the American factory system aided by **(a)** capitalists, **(b)** the shortage of labor in American towns, and **(c)** laws governing inventions?

4. **Interpreting Ideas:** How did Eli Whitney and James Watt contribute to the Industrial Revolution in the United States?

5. **Organizing Ideas: (a)** What colonial American conditions prompted the search for labor-saving machines? **(b)** How were these conditions different from conditions in Europe? **(c)** How did the American government encourage inventors?

2 New leaders develop the "American System"

See Teaching Suggestions in TMRG, pp.TM68-69.

Most of those who tackled the job of running the new nation after the War of 1812 were new on the national scene. The older leaders of the opening years of the nation's history were passing from the scene.

The famous three. Three of the new leaders were particularly outstanding. They were destined to play prominent roles in the nation's history for the next 35 years. Each came from a different section of the country.

Henry Clay, a Republican from Kentucky, ▲ entered Congress in 1811. Clay, as you know, was one of the "War Hawks" who had clamored for war with Great Britain in 1812. Trained in the law and striking in appearance, Henry Clay was an impressive orator. He became the acknowledged representative of the western parts of the country.

John C. Calhoun of South Carolina also entered Congress in 1811. He, too, was a lawyer, a persuasive speaker, and a Republican. Like Clay, he had also favored the War of 1812. With his keen mind and his devotion to politics, Calhoun soon became the major representative of the southern states and of the doctrine of states' rights.

Daniel Webster, a Federalist from Massachusetts, entered Congress in 1813. He was born on a farm in New Hampshire. Like Clay and Calhoun, Webster became a lawyer, practicing first in New Hampshire and later in Boston, Massachusetts. Like Clay and Calhoun, Webster was a powerful speaker. In Congress he quickly became the outstanding representative of the northeastern part of the country. At first Webster favored low tariffs. Then, as industrial interests in the Northeast replaced shipping interests, he became a defender of high protective tariffs.

Daniel Webster (top) used moving oratory to gain legislation that favored the industrial Northeast. John C. Calhoun (middle) strove equally hard to protect the very different interests of the agricultural South. Henry Clay (bottom) worked tirelessly to balance these sections' conflicting needs and to further the interests of the West.

The elections of 1816 and 1820. It was an older leader, however, who won the Presidential election of 1816. James Monroe, a Republican who had served as Secretary of State under President Madison, easily defeated the Federalist candidate, Rufus King. King, a brilliant and able Senator from New York, represented

▲ Class activity: Ask the students whether any present-day leader is as representative of an entire region as were Calhoun, Clay, and Webster. Ask students to name present-day political leaders and the major interest groups each seems to represent.

a dying party. By 1816 the Federalists were so weakened that they won only three states.

In 1817 even a Boston publication that had opposed Monroe in the election said that the times ahead would prove to be an "Era of Good Feelings." This phrase pleased the new President, and as the years passed it did seem to describe national life. The different groups in the country began to work together on common problems. The Federalist Party as such disappeared. For more than ten years, the Republican Party, originally founded by Thomas Jefferson, was the only political party in the United States.

By 1820 political harmony was so widespread, at least on the surface, that President Monroe ran for re-election without opposition. He won all of the electoral votes but one and was re-elected President.

The American System. In 1816, even before President Monroe was elected for the first time, the Republicans took steps to strengthen the growing nation. In so doing, they increased the powers of the federal government at the expense of states' rights. To justify their actions, they used a loose interpretation of the Constitution, like the one favored earlier by Alexander Hamilton and the Federalists. This was one reason that the Federalist Party disappeared. By 1816 the Republicans were doing many things the Federalists had favored doing for years.

National-minded leaders like Henry Clay of Kentucky insisted that the nation needed a sound economic program that would enable the United States to become independent of the rest of the world. The economic program that the Republicans adopted in 1816 came to be called the **American System,** a term later used by Henry Clay in a speech in Congress.

The American System developed by the Republicans rested on three major foundations. (1) A national bank would provide a sound, uniform financial system. (2) A protective tariff would provide a wall behind which American factories could grow and prosper. (3) A transportation system would ease trade between the northeastern manufacturers and the western and southern farmers.

The second Bank of the United States. In 1816 a national bank was badly needed. Five years earlier, in 1811, the charter of the first Bank of the United States had expired. When this happened, a number of state legislatures, especially in the West, promptly began to grant bank charters to private individuals. These state charters permitted individual investors to organize and operate their own banks.

Between 1811 and 1816, the number of state banks nearly tripled. Many of the new banks were poorly regulated. As a result, some of them began to issue more and more of their own paper money. Much of the new paper money declined in value, and some of it soon became worthless.

This unhealthy financial situation could not be tolerated. It was clear that a national bank was essential to the nation's well-being. Thus in 1816, Congress granted a charter creating the second Bank of the United States.

The protective tariff of 1816. In 1816 the Republicans enacted a protective tariff. In doing so, they adopted another of Hamilton's basic ideas and made it part of the American System. During the early 1800's and especially during the war years from 1812 to 1815, Americans had found it difficult to get manufactured goods from Europe. As a result, new factories had sprung up on American soil. When the War of 1812 ended, British manufacturers naturally wanted to drive their American competitors out of business.

The ink was hardly dry on the Treaty of Ghent in 1815 before British ships began to deliver factory-made goods to American ports. The British manufacturers were dumping goods. That is, they were selling large quantities of their goods below cost to drive rival manufacturers out of business. Once American factories closed, the British manufacturers would raise the prices of their products. They could then recover their earlier losses, knowing that they faced little competition from the ruined Americans.

American factory owners had no intention of being driven out of business. They demanded government protection against their British rivals. Thus Congress adopted the Tariff Act of 1816, which levied what seemed to be high duties on manufactured goods shipped into the United States.

In 1816 most Americans favored the protective tariff. Even Thomas Jefferson, who had earlier opposed the protective tariff recommended by Hamilton, now approved the Tariff Act of 1816. John C. Calhoun of South Carolina, who later became a strong foe of tariffs, supported the Tariff Act of 1816, assuming that the South would develop industries of its own. In protecting its infant industries, the young nation was looking forward to becoming self-sufficient and economically independent.

SECTION REVIEW

See underscored items, text pp. 268 - 69.
Identify: Henry Clay, John C. Calhoun, Daniel Webster, James Monroe, American System, Tariff Act of 1816

For answers to questions, see Answer Key, p.A41.

1. **Analyzing Ideas: (a)** Why was the period from about 1817 to 1825 known as the "Era of Good Feelings"? **(b)** How did the Republican Party of this period differ from the earlier Republican Party?

2. **Organizing Ideas: (a)** What were the three major foundations of the American System? **(b)** How did each of these promote national unity?

3. **Interpreting Ideas:** Why had a second national bank become necessary by 1816?

4. **Summarizing Ideas: (a)** How did the War of 1812 affect American and British manufacturing? **(b)** What action did British manufacturers take after the war? **(c)** How did the American government respond?

3 The growing nation struggles with new and complex problems

See Teaching Suggestions in TMRG, pp.TM69-70.
Soon after the Constitution went into effect, four new states were added to the original thirteen—Vermont (1791), Kentucky (1792), Tennessee (1796), and Ohio (1803). Between 1810 and 1820, the population west of the mountains doubled to more than 2 million. Five new states entered the Union—Louisiana (1812), Indiana (1816), Mississippi (1817), Illinois (1818), and Alabama (1819).

Demand for better transportation. Until shortly after the War of 1812, the western settlers depended almost entirely upon the rivers or upon very poor roads for transportation. Flatboats and rafts could float products downriver, but westerners could not use them to transport manufactured goods upriver. Keelboats, invented for this purpose, were laborious and slow. As a result, most manufactured products from the eastern areas reached the western lands by means of rough roads across the mountains. Transporting goods by wagon over these roads was costly and time-consuming.

A good transportation system was as essential to the new nation as a good Constitution and a strong federal government. Farmers in the new western states needed roads and canals to carry their products to eastern markets. Northeastern manufacturers needed roads and canals to move their manufactured goods into the sparsely settled areas of the country. Southerners were also interested in improving transportation. As John C. Calhoun of South Carolina put it, "We are greatly and rapidly—I was about to say fearfully—growing. This is our pride and our danger, our weakness and our strength. . . . Let us, then, bind the republic together with a perfect system of roads and canals."

First steps by private enterprise. During the 1790's and early 1800's, owners of businesses throughout the country organized private companies to build roads and canals. By 1811, private companies had built more than 1,400 miles (2,250 kilometers) of improved toll roads in New York State alone. These were private roads that charged a fee, or toll, to those who used them.

Nearly all of the new roads and canals built by the early 1800's reached out from the coastal cities into the surrounding country. These roads and canals did not run into sparsely settled regions or through the Appalachian Mountains.

Improvements at public expense. A growing number of citizens demanded that the federal government finance and build the needed highways and canals. During President Jefferson's administration, Albert Gallatin, Secretary of the Treasury, proposed that the federal government build a network of highways covering the entire United States. Congress did not adopt Gallatin's ambitious proposal. It did, however, vote money in 1806 for building a road from Cumberland, Maryland, across the mountains into what is now West Virginia.

Construction of the road began in 1811. Within a few years this road, called the Cumberland Road or the National Road, was pushed westward from Cumberland, Mary-

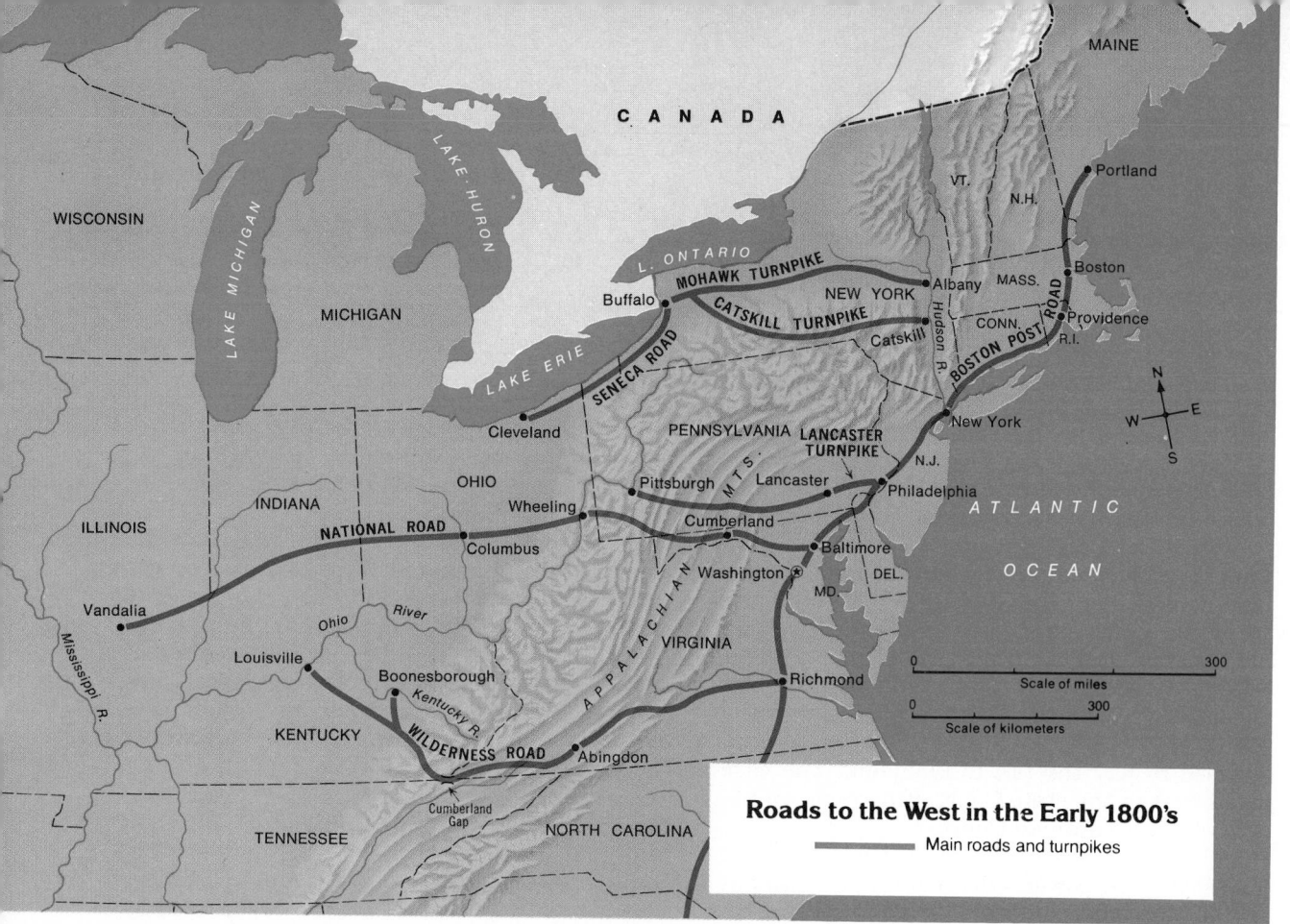

Roads to the West in the Early 1800's

━━━━━━ Main roads and turnpikes

land, as far as Ohio. Between 1822 and 1838, with additional grants of money from Congress, the National Road was extended across Ohio and Indiana to Vandalia, Illinois (see map, this page). As each section was finished, the federal government turned it over to the states through which it ran. Thousands of settlers poured into the western country over the National Road after the War of 1812.

In 1816, with the National Road progressing westward, Congress approved a bill calling for "internal improvements" at government expense. President Madison vetoed the bill because he felt that the Constitution did not give Congress the power to spend money in this way. President Monroe shared Madison's convictions. Then Congress abandoned its plans for further internal improvements at the public expense.

Even so, the economic program adopted by Congress during Madison's administration had accomplished a great deal. It had set up a national bank that provided Americans with a reasonably sound currency. It had given the manufacturers a protective tariff. It had helped

to open up the western areas by pushing the National Road farther westward. In general, it had strengthened the different sections and had drawn them closer together.

The Panic of 1819. By 1818 all sections of the United States were enjoying prosperity. Conditions were so prosperous, in fact, that various groups had begun to indulge in **overspeculation.** This was excessive, risky investment in land, stock, or commodities in the hope of making large profits. Southerners, tempted by rising prices for cotton, bought land at inflated prices. Western settlers, tempted by rising prices for grain and meat, also scrambled to buy land. Manufacturers in the Northeast, eager to take advantage of the general prosperity, bought land and built new mills and factories.

All of these groups borrowed money to finance their enterprises. Many banks encouraged the frenzy of speculation by lending money too freely on the flimsiest security.

Then came the crash. Late in 1818 the directors of the Bank of the United States or-

271

dered all their branch banks not to renew any personal mortgages. The directors also ordered the branch banks to present all state bank notes to the state banks for immediate payment in gold or silver or in national bank notes. State banks could not make their payments and closed their doors. Farmers and manufacturers could not renew their mortgages, and many lost their property.

By mid-1819, because of numerous foreclosures, the Bank of the United States had acquired huge areas of land in the South and Middle West and many businesses in the East. People ruined by foreclosure blamed the bank for their troubles and called it "the Monster."

Increased federal power. In the midst of the financial panic, Chief Justice Marshall of the Supreme Court handed down one of his most important decisions in the case of *McCulloch v. Maryland.* The Maryland state legislature had attempted to tax the Baltimore branch of the Bank of the United States. When the bank refused to pay the tax to Maryland, the case went first to the state Court of Appeals and finally to the Supreme Court.

Three major issues were involved. (1) Who has sovereign power—the federal government or the state governments? (2) Does the Constitution give Congress power to create a national bank? (3) If Congress does have this power, do the states then have the right to tax the bank?

In 1819 Marshall decided all these issues in favor of the federal government. Referring to the first point, he declared that "the government of the Union, then, . . . is emphatically and truly a government of the people." Thus, concluded Marshall, since the federal government was created by the people, not by the states, the power of the federal government was supreme.

Referring to the second point, Marshall admitted that the Constitution did not specifically give Congress the power to create a bank. He went on to say that the Constitution *did* give Congress the right to do whatever was "necessary and proper" to carry out any of its specific powers. Thus, reasoned Marshall, since Congress had the power to levy and collect taxes and to borrow money, it also had the right to create a national bank to carry out these financial powers.

Referring to the third point, Marshall declared that "the power to tax involves the power to destroy." If a state had the power to tax a national institution such as the Bank of the United States, it could severely weaken or destroy federal power. Therefore, Marshall stated, neither Maryland nor any other state had the right or the power to tax the Bank of the United States.

Marshall's continuing influence. In 1819 Marshall wrote another far-reaching decision. In the case of *Trustees of Dartmouth College v. Woodward,* Marshall set aside a law passed by the state legislature of New Hampshire. This law changed the charter of Dartmouth College, a private institution. The college's trustees claimed that the new law was unconstitutional. When the case came before the Supreme Court, John Marshall supported the trustees. Marshall pointed out that a charter was a valid contract guaranteed by the Constitution. Thus

=== **SOURCES** ===

McCULLOCH v. MARYLAND (1819)

The power to tax involves the power to destroy. . . . If the states may tax one instrument, employed by the [federal] government in the execution of its powers, they may tax any and every other instrument. They may tax the mail; they may tax the mint; they may tax patent rights; they may tax the papers of the customhouse; they may tax judicial process; they may tax all the means employed by the government, to an excess which would defeat all the ends of government. This was not intended by the American people. They did not design to make their government dependent on the states. . . .

The question is, in truth, a question of supremacy; and if the right of the states to tax the means employed by the general government be conceded, the declaration that the Constitution, and the laws made in pursuance thereof, shall be the supreme law of the land, is empty and unmeaning declamation. . . .

The Mississippi River was another pathway for Americans on the move. In 1832 artist Leon Pomarede captured this "View of St. Louis." The early steamboats shown would soon be replaced by giant "paddle wheelers."

no state had the power to interfere with such a contract.

This decision was important for two reasons. First, it asserted the right of the Supreme Court to set aside state laws when such laws were unconstitutional. Second, it guaranteed that corporations operating under state charters would not be subject to the whims of state legislators.

Five years later, in 1824, in *Gibbons v. Ogden,* Marshall declared another state law unconstitutional. The New York legislature had attempted to give Robert Fulton and his business associates a monopoly on steamboat traffic on the Hudson River. Marshall argued that the Constitution had given the federal government the power to regulate interstate commerce. Since navigation on the Hudson River involved **interstate commerce,** the state had no right to grant a monopoly. The monopoly granted by the state legislature was therefore unconstitutional.

Marshall's argument greatly broadened the definition of interstate commerce. His decision thus paved the way for later federal control of such interstate commerce as telegraph, telephone, radio, and television, as well as kid-

naping and car theft if the criminals were to cross state lines.

John Marshall's decisions did much to strengthen the powers of the federal government. While Congress, through the American System, was seeking to build a stronger, more unified nation, Marshall on the Supreme Court bench was moving toward the same goal.

SECTION REVIEW
See underscored items, text pp. 270 - 71, 273.
Identify: toll roads, National Road, overspeculation, interstate commerce
For answers to questions, see Answer Key, p.A41.
1. **Organizing Ideas: (a)** Where and by whom were the first American canals and roads built? **(b)** What action did the federal government take to improve transportation?

2. **Interpreting Ideas: (a)** What caused the Panic of 1819? **(b)** Why did many people blame the Bank of the United States for their troubles?

3. **Summarizing Ideas:** What principles concerning the power of federal and state governments were decided in the following Supreme Court cases: **(a)** *McCulloch v. Maryland,* **(b)** *Trustees of Dartmouth College v. Woodward,* **(c)** *Gibbons v. Ogden?*

The United States warns Europe to stay out of the Western Hemisphere

See Teaching Suggestions in TMRG, p.TM70.

The growing spirit of national pride and the increase in federal power strongly influenced developments within the United States. These new feelings of pride and strength also influenced American foreign policy.

At this time the people of Latin America were struggling to win their independence from Spain and Portugal. Americans were deeply interested in the revolutions that were taking place south of the United States.

Revolutions in Latin America. In the early 1800's, as you know, Napoleon was trying to control all of Europe. In 1808 he conquered Spain. This was the signal for Latin Americans to rise in revolt.

The enormous South American continent is broken by mighty mountain barriers, such as the Andes, and by dense rain forests, such as those of the Amazon River Valley. As a result, the Latin-American struggle for independence took place in a number of separate revolutions (see map, page 275). These separate struggles were fought for essentially the same objectives: freedom and independence.

By 1822 the American continents were not yet free of foreign control. Russia still claimed the vast unexplored territory of Alaska. Great Britain still ruled Canada, British Honduras, British Guiana (gee·AHN·ah), and a number of West Indian islands. Spain still ruled Cuba and Puerto Rico. France and the Netherlands still ruled French and Dutch Guiana and several of the islands in the Caribbean. However, Europeans were on their way out. The growing forces of democracy and the drive toward national independence were remaking the map. These independence movements also struck a blow at slavery. Soon slavery persisted only in Cuba and Brazil.

American control of Florida. The United States was neutral in the conflicts between Spain and Portugal and their colonies. However, between 1810 and 1813, the United States annexed the territory known as West Florida from a powerless Spain.

Spanish authorities in East Florida at this time were unwilling to return fugitive slaves to their American owners or to those who claimed to own them. Nor did the Spanish authorities restrain the Seminole Indians of East Florida from launching raids into southern Georgia and Alabama.

In 1816 the United States government ordered Andrew Jackson to move troops up to the Spanish forts in East Florida. He proposed instead to the government that American troops conquer all of East Florida. Receiving no reply, Jackson seized two Spanish forts and executed two British fur traders accused of giving arms to Indians. The Spaniards, deeply involved with troubles in Latin America, could only protest. Jackson's invasion of East Florida, called the First Seminole War, convinced Spain that the United States would not rest until the Stars and Stripes flew over all of Florida. Thus Spain decided to sell Florida while it still held claim to the area.

In 1819 the two countries signed the Adams-Onís Treaty. It gave the United States all the land east of the Mississippi River, together with any claims that Spain might have to the Oregon country. In return, the United States agreed to assume $5 million in claims that American citizens held against Spain for damages to American shipping during the Napoleonic Wars. More important, the United States agreed to abandon its claim to Texas as part of the Louisiana Purchase.

British interest in Latin America. As a colonial power, Great Britain did not sympathize with the revolutions in Latin America. Nevertheless, like many United States citizens, the British looked forward to an increasingly profitable trade with the former colonies of Spain and Portugal. The British wanted to retain the trade of Latin America, which, since the start of the revolutions, had been carried largely in British ships. If the Spanish colonies were restored to Spain, British merchants would lose the profitable trade.

European interference. Until 1815 and Napoleon's final defeat, the European nations were too busy with their own problems to take an active part in Latin-American affairs. After the fall of Napoleon, however, a number of European nations joined in an alliance to put down revolutions. Americans became alarmed at rumors that France, encouraged by the European alliance, might help Spain recover its New World colonies.

To add to American alarm, in 1821 the tsar of Russia warned the ships of other nations to avoid the Pacific coast from Alaska southward to the 51st parallel. This order barred American vessels from the Oregon coast, which the United States claimed jointly with Great Britain. The Oregon country had already become a useful port of call for Yankee traders, who traded cloth and other manufactured goods to the Indians in exchange for furs. Russia was

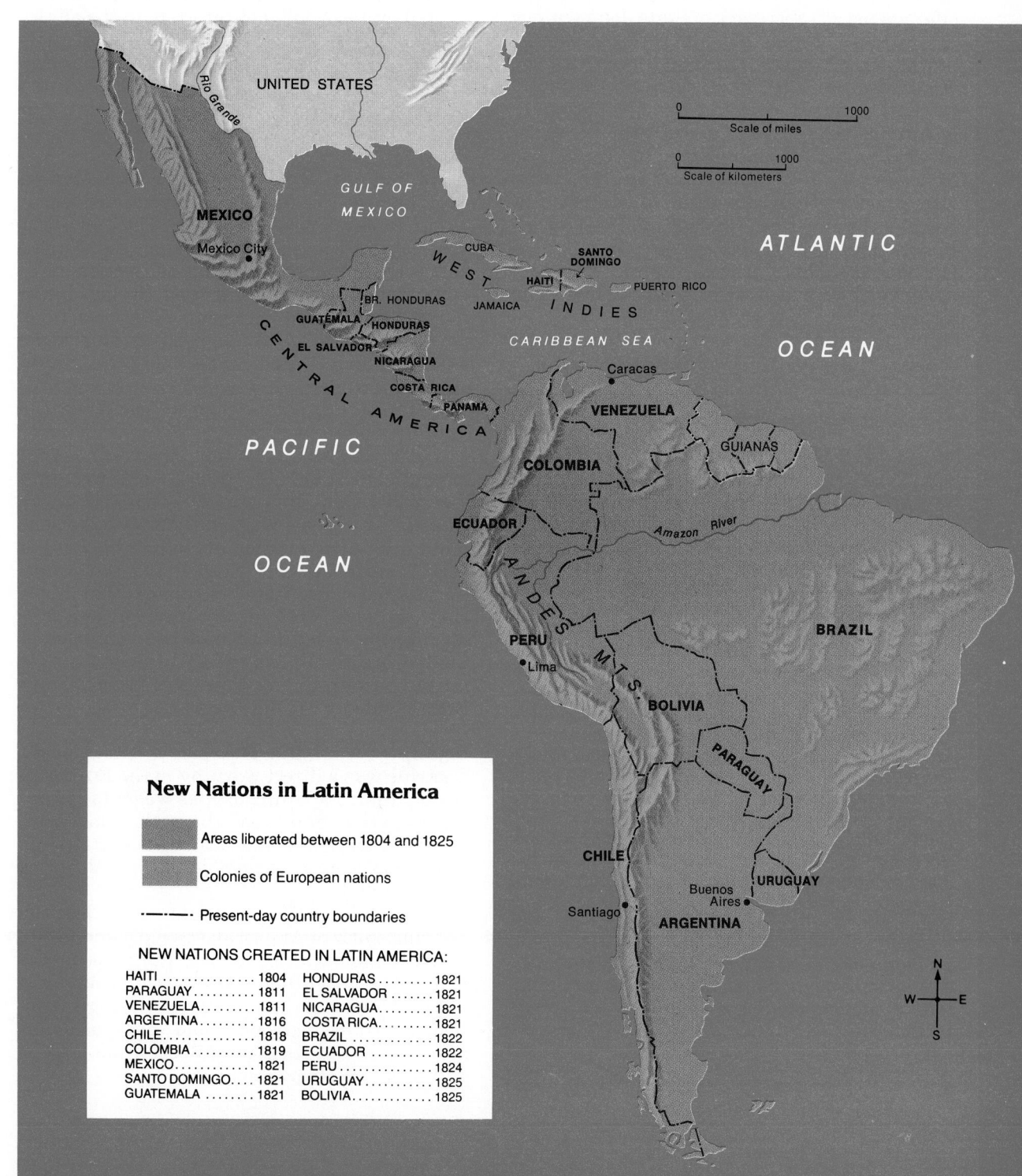

New Nations in Latin America

Areas liberated between 1804 and 1825

Colonies of European nations

– · – · – Present-day country boundaries

NEW NATIONS CREATED IN LATIN AMERICA:

HAITI 1804	HONDURAS 1821
PARAGUAY 1811	EL SALVADOR 1821
VENEZUELA 1811	NICARAGUA 1821
ARGENTINA 1816	COSTA RICA 1821
CHILE 1818	BRAZIL 1822
COLOMBIA 1819	ECUADOR 1822
MEXICO 1821	PERU 1824
SANTO DOMINGO 1821	URUGUAY 1825
GUATEMALA 1821	BOLIVIA 1825

also establishing trading posts along the coast of northern California. For these reasons, the American government did not permit the tsar's order to go unchallenged.

The Monroe Doctrine. The United States met the Russian threat and possible European intervention in Latin America with three specific actions. (1) Secretary of State John Quincy Adams sent a strong note of protest to Russia, bluntly asserting American rights to sail the Pacific waters. (2) The United States recognized the independence of the revolutionary governments of Latin America. (3) President Monroe, in his annual message to Congress on December 2, 1823, announced an American foreign policy that later came to be known as the Monroe Doctrine. The Monroe Doctrine actually extended the policy that Washington had stated in his Farewell Address and that Jefferson had added to in his statements on foreign policy.

═══ SOURCES ═══

THE MONROE DOCTRINE (1823)

The American continents . . . are henceforth not to be considered as subjects for future colonization by any European powers. . . . We owe it, therefore, to candor and to the amicable relations existing between the United States and those powers [Quadruple Alliance] to declare that we should consider any attempt on their part to extend their system to any portion of this hemisphere as dangerous to our peace and safety. With the existing colonies or dependencies of any European power, we have not interfered and shall not interfere. But with the governments who have declared their independence and maintained it, and whose independence we have . . . acknowledged, we could not view any interposition for the purpose of oppressing them, or controlling in any other manner their destiny, by any European power in any other light than as the manifestation of an unfriendly disposition toward the United States. . . .

Our policy in regard to Europe, which was adopted at an early stage of the wars which have so long agitated that quarter of the globe, nevertheless remains the same, which is, not to interfere in the internal concerns of any of its powers. . . .

In this famous message, President Monroe made four clear declarations. (1) The Western Hemisphere was no longer open to colonization by European powers. (2) Any attempt by any European country to establish colonies in the New World or to gain political control of any American country would be viewed as an unfriendly act toward the United States. (3) The United States would not interfere in the affairs of European nations or in the affairs of their colonies already established in the Americas. (4) In return, Europe must not in any way disturb the political status of any free country in the Western Hemisphere.

Enforcing the Doctrine. With the Monroe Doctrine, the United States proclaimed a policy of "America for Americans." The important question, of course, was whether the United States could enforce the Monroe Doctrine.

Fortunately for the United States, Latin Americans resisted European intervention, as did Great Britain. Although Latin Americans knew that the United States was acting in its own self-interest, they welcomed its commitment to the independence of all the Americas from Europe.

Great Britain gave the Doctrine its real strength. In 1823 and, in fact, until well into the 1900's, the British navy controlled the Atlantic sea lanes. Only with British consent could ships of any nation, including the United States, move between Europe and the Americas. Americans were fortunate that British merchants were keenly interested in preserving the independence of the countries of Central and South America. At the first hint of interference from any European power, Great Britain sided with the Americas.

Significance of the Doctrine. The Monroe Doctrine was a direct warning to the European powers that the United States was vitally concerned in the affairs of all the nations in North, Central, and South America. The Doctrine was to become a major principle of United States foreign policy.

The Monroe Doctrine also revealed the growing spirit of American strength and unity. President Monroe spoke for a united people of more than 10 million citizens. He spoke for a nation that was becoming increasingly conscious of its own strength and that was determined to retain its independence from Europe and to decide its own policies.

Identify: First Seminole War, Monroe Doctrine
For answers to questions, see Answer Key, p.A42.

1. **Determining Cause and Effect:** What effect did Napoleon's conquest of Spain have on Spain's colonies in North and South America?

2. **Summarizing Ideas:** (a) Describe how the United States acquired East and West Florida. (b) State the terms of the Adams-Onís Treaty.

3. **Interpreting Ideas:** (a) Why were Americans fearful of European intervention in the Western Hemisphere after 1815? (b) What actions did President Monroe take to prevent intervention?

4. **Studying Sources:** (a) According to the Source on page 276, what were three main provisions of the Monroe Doctrine? (b) How did the Doctrine reflect growing feelings of American pride and strength?

Noah Webster categorized differences between American English and British English.

5 American education and arts reveal pride in the growing nation

See Teaching Suggestions in TMRG, p.TM71.

The American System made Americans *economically* independent of Europe. With the Monroe Doctrine, the United States declared itself *politically* independent from Europe. With development of truly American education, art, and literature, the United States began to become less dependent on Europe *culturally.*

After the American Revolution, American Protestant churches cut their close ties with church authorities in Europe. Many, though not all, educators, artists, and writers of this period revealed in their work the growing spirit of **nationalism,** or national pride. They helped to unite the nation perhaps as much as the business and political leaders who were at the same time working for economic and political independence.

A national university proposed. Pride in their new nation prompted some Americans to favor a national university to train people for public service and provide the nation with educated citizens. George Washington had wanted such an institution. So had John Quincy Adams, who became President in 1826. Other patriotic Americans favored the idea of a national university. In spite of this strong support, the proposal never became a reality.

Noah Webster — author and educator. An illustration of the growing spirit of independence was Noah Webster's project for molding an American language, distinct from English. "America," Webster had declared in 1783, "must be as independent in *literature* as she is in *politics,* as famous for *arts* as for *arms.*" With this in mind, Webster labored at the tremendous task of publishing a dictionary — *An American Dictionary of the English Language.* In it the British spelling of many words was simplified. When his dictionary was finally published in 1828, Webster hoped that it would help Americans to achieve a uniform language.

Webster also prepared a spelling book. Published as early as 1783, it was used in nearly every elementary school in America. By the time Webster died in 1843, more than 15 million copies had been sold, and nearly 100 million copies were sold before the book went out of general use. Like Webster's dictionary, his spelling book helped Americans develop a uniform national language.

American history and geography. In addition to his work on the dictionary and the spelling book, Webster edited a famous school reader, *An American Selection of Lessons in Reading and Speaking.* Hoping to arouse a spirit of national pride as well as a reverence for American heroes, Webster devoted more than half of his school reader to material from American history. He later wrote complete books about American history.

Meanwhile Jedidiah Morse, a minister and scholar, was introducing American youth to the geography of their country. His geographies were also largely devoted to the story of American life.

A number of other authors wrote American history books. Among them was Hannah Adams of Massachusetts, probably the first American woman to support herself by writing. Before the Era of Good Feelings ended, American history had become an accepted part of the course of study in many American elementary schools. One indication of growing national pride was legislation passed in 1827 by Massachusetts and Vermont. This legislation required all the larger schools in these states to teach American history.

The arts. During the early years of the nation's growth, the spirit of nationalism also influenced a number of artists.

There were, for instance, the architects who first designed the nation's capital, Washington, D.C., among them the French engineer, Pierre L'Enfant (lon·FON). There was Benjamin Banneker, a free black from Maryland, who helped to survey the site of the city. Many others also played a large part in the design and construction of the city. Thomas Jefferson, for example, proposed the locations of the Capitol building and the White House. As the city of Washington grew, it helped give American citizens a feeling of permanence, a conviction that the new nation was destined to endure.　　　▲

During this same period, such painters as Charles Willson Peale, Gilbert Stuart, and John Trumbull painted many portraits of the

Samuel F. B. Morse captured the new spirit of American art early in his life. He was just 19 when he painted this watercolor of his family. He is at the left of his father, who was a minister and the author of schoolbooks about geography.

Few people who saw young Benjamin Banneker working in his father's tobacco fields could have imagined that he would teach himself mathematics, astronomy, and history. No one could have imagined that at the age of 60 he would serve as scientific assistant in the surveying of the District of Columbia. Why? Because Benjamin Banneker was black.

Banneker was a natural mathematician and as a young man taught himself astronomy. He later taught himself how to use various surveying instruments. In 1791 Major Andrew Ellicott was appointed by President Washington to survey a projected site for the new national capital. Ellicott was unable to find an assistant who knew enough about scientific apparatus. While visiting his cousin in North Carolina, Major Ellicott learned about Banneker's self-taught skills and asked Banneker to help him in the survey. For three months, Banneker surveyed and recorded data needed for the project.

Many of Banneker's journals and other possessions were destroyed in a fire that took place on the day of his funeral. But enough of his writings remain to testify to his extraordinary scientific abilities. In 1970 Banneker Circle in Washington, D.C., was named in his honor.

---

nation's leaders. Although these painters lacked the originality and skill of the greatest artists, their portraits helped make the nation's founders known to many Americans.

Writers. During the early 1800's, some writers began to draw upon the American scene for the material in their stories. Mason Locke Weems (better known as Parson Weems) published a biography of George Washington, written in glowing terms. Washington Irving turned chiefly to the Dutch society of the Hudson Valley for his material. He produced such works as "The Legend of Sleepy Hollow," "Rip Van Winkle," and the *Knickerbocker History of New York.* James Fenimore Cooper's *Leatherstocking Tales,* a series of novels, had as its hero a white frontier scout skilled in forest crafts and versed in Indian lore. The tales stereotyped Indians as either "fine" and "noble" or "treacherous" and "savage."

A new feeling of unity. Nationalism was one of the forces that helped to shape American life during the first 30 or more years of the nation's

history. This national pride influenced rich and poor alike in all sections of the country. It influenced the lives of pioneers clearing the forests, the owners of businesses in the growing cities, and the political leaders in Washington. It stimulated educators, artists, and writers as well as the men, women, and children who listened to their ideas and read their books and looked at their paintings. Thus the new nation became stronger and more unified as the years went by.

SECTION REVIEW

See underscored items, text pp. 277 - 79.
Identify: nationalism, Hannah Adams, Benjamin Banneker, John Trumbull, Washington Irving
For answers to questions, see Answer Key, p.A42.

1. **Summarizing Ideas:** What does the term "cultural independence" mean?

2. **Organizing Ideas:** What contributions did Noah Webster make to American education?

3. **Interpreting Ideas:** How did Americans in the early 1800's express their spirit of nationalism in the following areas: **(a)** history, **(b)** geography, **(c)** painting, **(d)** literature?

DEVELOPING HISTORY STUDY SKILLS

Relating Economics and History   Applying Economic Terms

Many important changes that took place in the early 1800's in the United States had to do with the economy. Two profound influences were the development of a factory system and the opening of the lands west of the Appalachian Mountains to further settlement. In recounting the history of this period, historians necessarily use many economic terms.

You have already been introduced to the skill of understanding economic vocabulary (see pages 78–79 in Chapter 3). Refresh your memory on the terms included in the Glossary on page 79. Then review the steps listed on page 78.

Applying the Skill

The following sentences are restatements of information presented in Chapter 11, sections 1–3. Read the statements. Then use the glossary on this page to reformulate the statements in your own words, substituting your definition of the term for the underlined term.

1. Henry Clay advocated the protective tariff as a means of helping infant industries.

2. Toll roads are excellent examples of private enterprise in action.

3. The factory system relied on mass production and the use of interchangeable parts for its success.

4. It is possible that overspeculation led to the financial panic of 1819.

5. Many homeowners and industrialists lost their property through foreclosure.

An Era of Good Feelings Economic Glossary

capital   Property, equipment, and money used to produce goods or provide services.

capitalist   One who provides or makes use of capital with the intention of making a profit.

competition   Rivalry between two parties for the business of a third party.

dumping   Selling large quantities of goods below cost to drive rivals out of business.

factory system   Procedure by which goods are produced in factories rather than in the homes of workers.

financial panic   Economic depression caused by widespread fright; usually brought on by loss of confidence in paper money or by overspeculation. *See* overspeculation.

foreclosure   Legal proceeding by which mortgaged property is taken over by the loan holder, usually a bank.

industrialist   *See* capitalist.

infant industry   Factory not yet strong enough to withstand foreign competition.

interchangeable part   Manufactured item, made in quantities, each of which can be substituted for another.

mass production   Manufacture of large numbers of a product, each exactly alike.

mortgage   Granting property as security in exchange for a loan.

overspeculation   Risky investments in land, commodities, and stocks, made with the intention of earning a profit.

private enterprise   Private business freely organized and operating for profit without the undue interference of government. Also called **free enterprise.**

protective tariff   Tax on imports designed to prevent foreign competition.

Practicing the Skill

A. Read the excerpt below by Carl Degler. Then on a separate sheet of paper, tell which of the following statements are accurate restatements of the information in the excerpt.

1. In Georgia, the legislature issued paper money to finance internal improvements.

2. Private capital was used to finance the Erie Canal.

3. Both private and public capital invested in mixed enterprise corporations and helped to finance transportation systems.

4. Toll roads, railroads, and canals were among the internal improvements funded by public expense alone.

Internal Improvements

A measure of the importance the American people attached to canals and railroads was the support which their governments gave to such enterprises.... Financial assistance from government was often crucial in the building of lines of transport. The best-known example, of course, was the Erie Canal, which was entirely [government]-built.... Two other ventures in which the state assumed full responsibility ... were the Blue Ridge Railroad of Virginia and the Western and Atlantic of Georgia.

But the commonest mode of public assistance to internal improvement was the so-called mixed enterprise, in which public and private funds were pooled. For some 40 years before the Civil War, Virginia employed the mixed corporation in the building of internal improvements. Three fifths of the capital in such corporations was contributed by private [enterprise] and two fifths by the state [government]....

Carl Degler

B. Read the excerpt from a speech by Henry Clay at the top of the next column. Then on a separate sheet of paper answer the questions below the excerpt.

The Need for a Home Market

The creation of a home market is not only necessary to procure for our agriculture a just reward of its labors, but it is indispensable to obtain a supply of our necessary wants. If we cannot sell, we cannot buy. That portion of our population (and we have seen that it is not less than four fifths) which makes comparatively nothing that foreigners will buy, has nothing to make purchases with from foreigners. It is in vain that we are told of the amount of our exports supplied by the planting interests [southern plantation owners who exported cotton and other crops]. They [the exports] may enable the planting interest to supply all its wants; but they [the exports] bring no ability to the nonplanting interests....

The superiority of the home market results, first from its steadiness and comparative certainty at all times; second, from the creation of reciprocal interest; third, from its greater security; and lastly, from an ultimate and not distant augmentation [increase] of consumption, and consequently, of comfort from increased quantity and reduced prices.

But this home market, highly desirable as it is, can only be created and cherished by the PROTECTION of our own legislation against the inevitable prostration [collapse] of our industry, which must ensure from the action of foreign policy and legislation.... This is only to be accomplished by the establishment of a tariff....

Henry Clay

1. What two reasons does Clay give for the creation of a home market?

2. What are the four characteristics, which according to Clay, give the home market its superiority?

3. What does Clay say is the relationship of the protective tariff to foreign policy?

4. Is the planting interest four fifths or one fifth of the population?

5. Did Clay believe the protective tariff would reduce competition or capital? Explain.

reduced prices 3. Once protective tariffs are enacted, foreign policy must support them. 4. one fifth of the population 5. Clay thought the protective tariff would reduce competition because the tariff would increase the price of imports.)

281

During the decade following the War of 1812, the desire for independence and for national unity reached a peak in the United States. The period from about 1817 to 1825 was called the "Era of Good Feelings."

During the Era of Good Feelings, Americans from all walks of life worked at the task of making their nation strong and independent of the rest of the world. Congress, supported by many in business and farming, adopted the American System. The purpose of the system was to make the United States economically independent and self-sufficient. The system consisted of three elements. (1) A national bank provided a sound financial base. (2) A high tariff protected Ameican industry. (3) A national transportation system connected the East and the West.

Meanwhile, President Monroe and his advisors took steps to keep the nation politically independent of Europe. The means they used for this purpose was a policy that came to be known as the Monroe Doctrine.

During these same years, educators, artists, and writers devoted their efforts to American themes and heroes. Their efforts helped make the United States culturally, as well as politically, independent of Europe.

Beneath the surface during the Era of Good Feelings, divisive forces were at work. As a result, sectional controversy soon split the new nation. In time the controversy would plunge the country into four terrible years of warfare.

CONNECTING CHAPTER IDEAS

In the next chapter you will read about the strengthening of the American spirit and the extension of voting rights to more Americans. The democracy practiced in the Jacksonian era marked a step forward in the long struggle to extend full voting rights to all Americans.

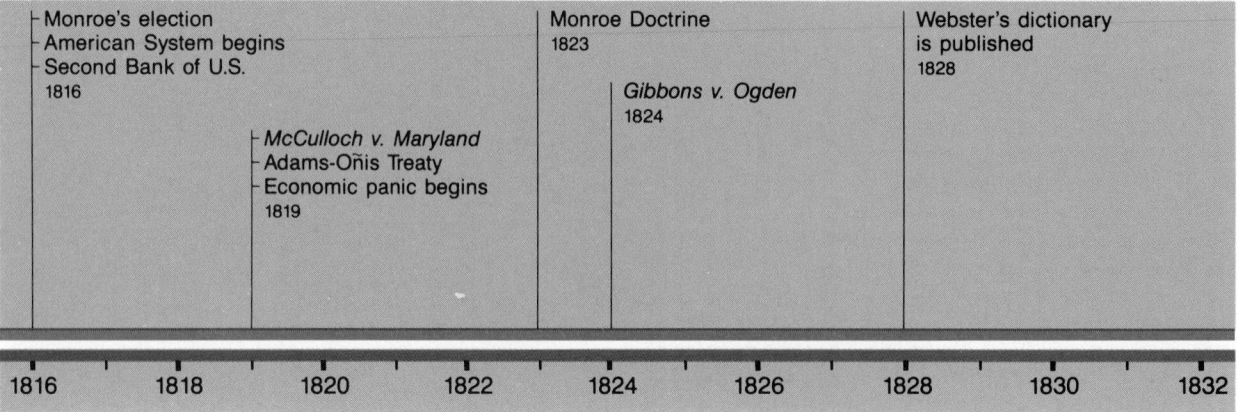

Monroe's election
American System begins
Second Bank of U.S.
1816

McCulloch v. Maryland
Adams-Oñis Treaty
Economic panic begins
1819

Monroe Doctrine
1823

Gibbons v. Ogden
1824

Webster's dictionary
is published
1828

| 1816 | 1818 | 1820 | 1822 | 1824 | 1826 | 1828 | 1830 | 1832 |

For answers to questions, see Answer Key, pp.A42-43.

CHAPTER
11 REVIEW

Reviewing Important Terms

Decide whether each of the following sentences is true or false. If the sentence is false, replace the underlined term with the word or phrase that will make it true.

1. The factory system came into being as mills began to weave cloth as well as spin yarn.
2. Capitalists built factories, installed machinery, hired workers, and sold the finished products.
3. The invention of guns made from interchangeable parts proved that many goods could be manufactured in larger quantities than ever before.
4. As part of the Monroe Doctrine, a protective tariff was instituted to make American factories grow and prosper.
5. People in all sections of the United States contributed to overspeculation with excessive, risky investments in land, stocks, and commodities.
6. An 1824 case involving Robert Fulton led to a Supreme Court decision broadening the definition of interstate commerce.
7. The American System was an expression of the United States' concern with the affairs of all the nations in North, Central, and South America.

Practicing Critical Thinking Skills

1. **Summarizing Ideas.** Explain the role that each of the following contributed to the growth of industry in the young nation: (a) the War of 1812, (b) the shortage of labor in the United States, and (c) the policies of the government.
2. **Interpreting Ideas.** Why was the growth of the nation's transportation system so important to the development of the nation?
3. **Using Historical Imagination.** The program of road building and other internal improvements begun after the War of 1812 ignored the Indians who lived in the area. (a) Suggest two policies that the federal government might have adopted concerning the Indian population of these lands. (b) What arguments might have been made in support of each policy?
4. **Comparing Viewpoints.** Thomas Jefferson said that John Marshall made the Constitution "a mere thing of wax ... [the justices of the Supreme Court] may twist and shape into any form they please." Do you agree of disagree with Jefferson's feelings about Marshall's decisions? Give evidence to support your opinion.

5. **Synthesizing Ideas.** Explain how each of the following revealed the growing spirit of nationalism: (a) the American System, (b) the decisions of the Supreme Court, and (c) Webster's *American Dictionary of the English Language*.
6. **Relating Past to Present.** Study the excerpt from the Monroe Doctrine on page 276. Then answer the following questions. (a) Which of the ideas it contains are still important today? (b) Name some recent world events that have caused the United States to apply ideas expressed in the Monroe Doctrine.

Developing History Study Skills

Applying Economic Terms. Write a paragraph describing the Industrial Revolution in the United States in the 1800's, using as many as the following terms as possible: *factory system, capital, capitalist, raw materials, interchangeable parts, mass production, the American System, protective tariff, private enterprise, overspeculation,* and *interstate commerce.*

Relating Geography and History

Between 1804 and 1825, eighteen new nations were established in Latin America. During that time, the United States became increasingly interested in maintaining its own independence and in acquiring more land. When certain European monarchies showed an interest in recolonizing the weak new Latin American countries, American leaders felt it necessary to warn them away. To understand how the policies of self-interest and self-defense were expressed in the Monroe Doctrine, reread Section 4 (pages 274–76), study the maps on pages 275 and 994–95, and then answer the following questions.

1. Why was it in the United States' best interests to keep European powers out of the Caribbean and other Latin American regions?
2. Against what specific menace was the Monroe Doctrine written?
3. How did the Monroe Doctrine establish a policy of "America for Americans," as well as a major foreign policy principle?
4. (a) Why was Great Britain willing to support the Monroe Doctrine? (b) What power made the Monroe Doctrine enforceable?

See Chapter Overview in TMRG, p.TM72.
See Chapter Objectives in TMRG, p.TM72.
See Introducing the Chapter in TMRG, p.TM72.

CHAPTER 12 Growing Democratic Strength
(1825–1845)

The people's choice

What is democracy? Abraham Lincoln partly defined it when he referred to "government of the people, by the people, for the people." The right of all qualified persons to vote and hold office—to participate in their own government—is the *political* side of democracy.

There is more than the political side to democracy. Democracy also has a social side and an economic side. In an *economic* and a *social* democracy, the people have an equal opportunity to gain an education. They may choose the careers they want. They are free to achieve individual economic independence and to be equal in the eyes of the law.

This larger idea of democracy began to develop roots in the early years of United States history. For most Americans, however, social democracy remained sharply limited. The noble ideal of the Declaration of Independence that all persons are created equal by no means applied to blacks, to Indians, to other minorities, or to women.

Political democracy was also limited in the early years. When the Constitution was adopted, the states, in varying degrees, restricted the right to vote and hold public office. Many states, for example, required that citizens own a certain amount of real estate or property as a qualification for voting.

During the early years of the nation's history, however, political democracy made increasing gains. The constitutions of the new western states allowed all white male taxpayers the right to vote. Gradually the eastern states relaxed their voting requirements. By the late 1820's many of the voting restrictions were gone. Voting, however, was still the exclusive preserve of white males. Political democracy also scored a victory in 1828 with the election of Andrew Jackson as President.

═══ READING FOCUS ═══

As you read about the nation's growing democratic strength, look for the details that will support each of the following statements.

1. Andrew Jackson emerges as "the people's choice."
2. The people take a more active part in government.
3. Andrew Jackson exercises his Presidential powers.
4. The Jacksonian era ends in an economic depression.

Andrew Jackson emerges as "the people's choice"

See Teaching Suggestions in TMRG, pp.TM72-73.

By 1824 the Era of Good Feelings was drawing to a close. The growing power of the ordinary people as well as the rivalry among the major sections of the country were clearly revealed in the political struggles from 1824 to 1828. During these years the Democratic Party—the same party that bears that name today—began to take shape.

The election of 1824. In 1824 four men ran for the Presidency, and all four called themselves Republicans. At least three of them were **favorite son**° candidates, nominated to represent different sections of the country. John Quincy Adams of Massachusetts—the son of John Adams, the second President—represented the northeastern states. William H. Crawford of Georgia represented the southern states. Andrew Jackson of Tennessee represented the western states. Henry Clay saw himself a national leader, although he came from Kentucky, a western state.

Of the four candidates, Henry Clay had the most definite program. Clay urged support for the American System that he had done so much to develop. In the American System, as you have read, Clay and other leaders in Congress tried to serve as well as balance the interests of the different sections of the country. In these years Clay began to establish himself as the Great Compromiser—a role he was to play many times in the years ahead. Crawford and Jackson hedged on most specific issues, including the tariff and the development of roads.

When the electoral votes were counted, Jackson had 99, Adams had 84, Crawford had 41, and Clay had only 37. No candidate had the majority (131 votes) needed for election. In such a situation, according to the Twelfth Amendment to the Constitution, the House of Representatives had to choose the President from the top three candidates. As the fourth candidate, Clay was automatically eliminated.

°**favorite son:** The term usually refers to a candidate placed in nomination on the first ballot by a state delegation as an honor—but with little hope of being nominated.

Andrew Jackson — seventh President, military hero, and Indian fighter — was the first chief executive to hail from west of the Appalachian Mountains. He was aware that his native Tennessee was widely regarded as a frontier area, barely civilized. After his victory at the Battle of New Orleans, he wanted a house that would equal the mansions of Virginia and Massachusetts.

Jackson owned some 800 acres (324 hectares) of land not far from Nashville, where in 1819 he built a great plantation house. Jackson called his Tennessee home the Hermitage. It was made of bricks produced on the estate. Six fluted columns graced the front of the rectangular house, which was surrounded by fine formal gardens.

Jackson made the Hermitage a prosperous cotton plantation, and he gained a new reputation as a successful country gentleman and slaveowner. But tragedy came to the Hermitage. Rachel Jackson died unexpectedly just before Jackson's first inauguration. And in 1835 much of the building was destroyed by a fire. Jackson had the Hermitage rebuilt. It survived the Civil War intact and today is a major tourist attraction. Jackson and his wife are buried there.

He persuaded his followers in the House to vote for Adams and Adams won. John C. Calhoun of South Carolina became Vice President.

Jackson against Adams.   The new President, John Quincy Adams, appointed Henry Clay as his Secretary of State. Jackson and his followers claimed that this was part of a "corrupt bargain." They maintained that Clay had supported Adams in exchange for the top post in the cabinet.

The charge of a "corrupt bargain" was false. Both Clay and Adams had done what they thought was best for the country. Jackson, however, believed that the charge was true. He was especially bitter because he had won the largest number of electoral votes.

Jackson was so angry that he resigned from the Senate in 1825 and launched a vigorous campaign to become President in 1828. During this three-year battle, both Adams and Jackson called themselves Republicans. Adams, however, referred to himself as a National-Republican, while Jackson called himself a Democratic-Republican.

By the 1830's, however, Jackson's party was officially calling itself the Democratic Party. Jackson's opponents organized the Whig Party in 1834, taking their name from the old Whig Party in England, which had opposed the tyranny of George III. For the next 20 years, the Democrats and Whigs were the two major political parties in the country.

The election of 1828.   By 1828 most white adult male citizens had won the right to vote. Many of these new voters considered Jackson to be their leader. They were proud that he had been born in a log cabin and had achieved success by his own efforts.

In the election of 1828, Jackson won a sweeping victory over Adams. Jackson won every state west of the Appalachian Mountains and south of the Potomac River and also won in Pennsylvania and New York. John C. Calhoun was re-elected as Vice President.

Jackson's first inauguration.   On March 4, 1829, political democracy celebrated its greatest victory up to that time. Everywhere ordinary Americans rejoiced at Jackson's election. The nation's tiny capital on the banks of the Potomac was jammed with 10,000 visitors. "A monstrous crowd of people is in the city," Daniel Webster wrote. "I never saw anything like it before. Persons have come five hundred miles to see General Jackson, and they really seem to think that the country is rescued from some dreadful danger."

The inaugural celebration was itself a symbol of a new era. After his Inaugural Address, the new President held open house in the Executive Mansion—the White House. Jackson's followers jammed in to greet him. Men with muddy boots climbed on chairs and tables to get a better view. Furniture was broken, trays of food were knocked over, and fights broke out.

The President himself narrowly escaped injury from the excited crowd and had to flee from the mansion. Dignified citizens watching the scene with horror feared that "King Mob" had replaced law and order in America.

Jackson, the man. What was he like, this man who aroused such conflicting emotions?

Born on the Carolina frontier in 1767, Jackson was the son of immigrant parents from northern Ireland. He grew up without formal schooling. Like many other Americans, he moved westward with the advancing line of settlement.

Jackson's opponents made fun of him. They claimed that he could not spell, that he told rough stories, chewed tobacco, and wore strange-looking "backwoods" clothes. Whether or not these claims were ever true, they certainly did not apply to Jackson's later life. When he became a wealthy planter and a famous American hero, Jackson took on the manners of a gentleman. Tall and slender with thick, white hair, he looked very distinguished. His followers called him "Old Hickory."

Jackson's outlook and attitudes seem to have been the same as those of many white Americans. This was especially true of his attitude toward blacks. Although his attitude was often contradictory, Jackson apparently was not aware of the contradictions. During the War of 1812, as you recall, he praised "free men of color" for their courage, patriotism, and valor. Yet later, as a slaveowner and national leader, he wrote letters expressing different, very unfavorable opinions about slaves. However, on at least one occasion he instructed that "my Negroes shall be treated humanely."

Jackson's attitude toward the Indians was also contradictory. Before becoming President, he had won a reputation as an Indian fighter. In ruthless, hard fighting, Jackson had de-

By the time Andrew Jackson became President at the age of 62 (top), he had been a lawyer, cotton planter, land speculator, frontier fighter, army officer, Congressman, Senator, and judge. Following his two terms as President, he retired in ill health to his home, the Hermitage, near Nashville, Tennessee. The bottom photo, taken in 1845, was the first ever of an American President.

Washington, D.C., had never seen anything quite like Jackson's inaugural celebration. His happy supporters overran the White House, tracking mud and damaging furniture. After several hours, tubs of punch were placed on the lawn to draw them out and get them on their way.

feated the Creek Indians in Mississippi and Alabama and the Seminoles in Florida. Jackson respected the Indian military leaders and honored them in defeat. Still, like most white Americans, he regarded the Indians as primitive people who were inefficient and incapable of "improvement."

Significance of the 1828 election. Jackson's triumph in the election of 1828 was largely the result of advancing democratic forces in America. Great changes had clearly taken place since the days of President Washington and the Federalists. For one thing, political power was now more evenly divided between well-to-do people and average people. The average people no longer stood in awe of leaders who, it had been supposed, were especially qualified by birth and education to lead the nation. Before the inauguration of 1829, all the Presidents were men from wealthy backgrounds. Andrew Jackson, in contrast, had been born into poverty and had risen through his own efforts.

Jackson's election also indicated that the western section of the country was a new force to be reckoned with in national politics. Andrew Jackson was from Tennessee. He was the first President from a state that did not border on the Atlantic.

Not all of Jackson's followers were westerners. Of course, many western settlers had voted for him because they felt that he would under-

stand their problems, but many small farmers everywhere voted for him for the same reason. Many southern planters voted for him because, as a planter and slaveowner himself, he would understand their point of view. Some city workers as well as owners of small businesses voted for him because they believed he would help them to get the laws they wanted. Many owners of small businesses, fearful of the growth of big business, wanted the opportunity to expand their own enterprises. They believed that Andrew Jackson, a self-made man, would help them. Thus with the support of a majority of ordinary white Americans, Andrew Jackson became President.

SECTION REVIEW
See underscored items, text pp. 285, 287.

Identify: political democracy, favorite son, John Quincy Adams, "King Mob"
For answers to questions, see Answer Key, pp. A43-44.

1. **Interpreting Ideas:** (a) What was unusual about the election of 1824? (b) Why did Jackson think a "corrupt bargain" had been made?

2. **Summarizing Ideas:** Jackson was a representative of "the people." (a) Who were "the people"? (b) In what ways did Jackson represent their interests? (c) In what ways was he one of them?

3. **Analyzing Ideas:** Explain the different reactions to Jackson's election in 1828.

4. **Evaluating Ideas:** (a) Why was the election of 1828 significant? (b) Why can it be called the "Revolution of 1828"?

2 The people take a more active part in government

See Teaching Suggestions in TMRG, pp.TM73-74.

Andrew Jackson, the new President, had no carefully developed political program. Despite this lack, Jackson held three firm convictions.

First, he believed in greater political democracy. He believed that the government belonged to all of the people who could vote, and he was determined that the majority must rule. Second, although Jackson believed that the federal government's powers should be limited, he also believed in the Union—that is, the United States as a whole. Thus he believed the young nation had to be preserved at any cost. Third, Jackson believed in the power of the Presidency.

Extending the spoils system. As one of his first steps, the President removed many of his political opponents from public (government) office and replaced them with his supporters. Under the **spoils system,** as it came to be called, a victorious political party could fill public offices with party supporters. It often did so without regard for their abilities or qualifications. The name "spoils system" came from the popular expression "to the victor belong the spoils." The spoils system had already become common in some northern and western states. It had also been used to some extent in the federal government. Jackson applied it more vigorously then ever.

In general, Jackson removed those officeholders he suspected of having supported his political opponents. All these officeholders were men. Women were denied government jobs as well as the vote. Although Jackson replaced only about one fifth of all federal officeholders, he set a precedent that later Presidents often followed with drastic results.

Defending the spoils system. Jackson maintained that the spoils system actually improved the government. He claimed that any person was as good as any other. "The duties of all public officers are, or at least admit of being made, so plain and simple that men of intelligence may readily qualify themselves for their performance," Jackson stated.

Jackson also believed that it was sound policy to keep changing officeholders. He felt that government workers who remained too long in office became indifferent to the public welfare and forgot that they were, in fact, servants of the people.

Above all, Jackson believed that as many Americans as possible should learn by experience how the government worked. He felt it was good democratic practice to rotate the offices among as many people as possible. He believed that the more people who held office, the more able the government would be to meet the changing needs of the people.

Jackson's policies brought politics into the range of the ordinary white male citizen. Even a poor man could risk devoting his time to political activities if he could hope for a job as a reward for faithful service.

Defects of the spoils system. Because of Jackson's policies, however, political parties came to be led and supported by officeholders who were paid by the government. These officeholders also contributed a certain percentage of their salaries to their political organizations. The spoils system also encouraged many people to use the public payroll for their own gain, enriching themselves at the taxpayers' expense. Jackson was not entirely responsible for these political abuses, but extending the spoils system helped such abuses to spread through national politics.

Nominating conventions. During Jackson's administration, the use of nominating conventions to choose candidates for federal office increased. Until this time candidates for federal office had been selected by legislators gathered in closed meetings, or caucuses. The voters at large had little if any voice in the nominating process. In the meantime, however, a different practice had been developing at the local level. Groups of voters, meeting in their own communities, chose delegates for county conventions. These conventions in turn nominated officials for county offices.

This practice gradually spread upward into state politics and eventually into national politics. By 1832 the present practice of nominating the President and Vice President in nominating conventions had been established.

The "kitchen cabinet." Hoping to bring the government and the people closer together, Andrew Jackson surrounded himself with a

He was usually barefoot, wearing ragged trousers and a flour sack for a shirt. The isolated farm family, eager for news and companionship, offered him a meal and a place to sleep. In return, he entertained them with stories of his wilderness adventures. Sooner or later he pulled a pamphlet from his shirt and would speak earnestly of God, for he was a missionary for the Swedenborgian Church.

His real name was John Chapman, but everyone called him Johnny Appleseed. For more than 40 years, Chapman wandered through Pennsylvania, Ohio, and Indiana, planting apple seeds wherever he went. Later, he would retrace his steps and prune the trees he had planted.

Chapman began his wanderings at about the age of 25. The trees he planted made apples and apple by-products — cider, apple butter, and vinegar—a staple frontier food. Indians regarded him as a medicine man. In later years, many folktales were told about Johnny Appleseed, none more dramatic than a true story about the War of 1812. Chapman, the story goes, ran 30 miles (48 kilometers) to call American troops to Mansfield, Ohio, to help prevent an Indian raid.

Chapman died at age 71 and was buried near Fort Wayne, Indiana. A city park there is named in his honor. Perhaps the best summary of the man we call Johnny Appleseed appears on one of the many memorials to him: "He planted seeds so that others may enjoy the fruit."

group of unofficial advisers. Jackson's political enemies called these advisers the **kitchen cabinet.** The term implied that these advisers entered the White House by a back door and met with the President in secret.

Some of the members of the kitchen cabinet were newspaper editors. Recognizing the importance of friendly relations with the press, President Jackson placed a number of well-known editors in public office. In return, they helped Jackson to mold public opinion, to gain good publicity, and to win support for the policies he favored.

Speaking for "the people." On most issues, Jackson believed that only the President could speak for the nation as a whole. He felt that members of Congress and state officials spoke for their own section of the country. Of course, not all the people in each section of the country shared the same interests or agreed on all issues. Still, by 1830 the views of the three sections of the nation were becoming more defined.

Each section had its outstanding champion. Daniel Webster of Massachusetts represented the most powerful interests of the Northeast — the merchants, manufacturers, bankers, and property owners in general. John C. Calhoun of South Carolina represented the planters of the South. Thomas Hart Benton of Missouri became the advocate of the West, especially of western farmers and land speculators who wanted cheap, or free, public land. Henry Clay of Kentucky, the Great Compromiser, tried to balance the interests of the sections and, in the process, to become President.

Andrew Jackson claimed to speak for most ordinary white Americans everywhere. He placed himself, as he said, at the head of "the humbler members of society — the farmers, mechanics, and laborers" who had "neither the time nor the means" to secure the things that they wanted from government.

Jackson's Indian policy. As an old Indian fighter and frontiersman, Jackson shared with other westerners a belief that Indians were primitive people who were blocking the westward movement of "civilization." Thus it was easy for Jackson to conclude, along with Jefferson, Monroe, and other national leaders, that Indians would be happier and better off in lands west of the Mississippi River, far from white neighbors. In these areas, Jackson felt, the Indians might keep their own ways of life or gradually accept the practices of the whites.

The process of uprooting the Indians had been going on for a long time. Many tribes had been persuaded, often by bribery or trickery, to give up their claims to ancestral lands and move into lands set aside for them by Congress. Indian resettlement was often marked by dishonesty and brutality on the part of government officials. Sometimes Indian removal took place at gunpoint.

With President Jackson's encouragement, Congress passed the Indian Resettlement Act of 1830. This act provided for the removal of Indian tribes to lands west of the Mississippi in the area of the Red River and the Arkansas River. Four years later Congress established this area as a special Indian territory. During Jackson's two terms, 94 treaties were negotiated with Indian tribes. These treaties ended Indian titles to lands in the existing states and provided for removals to Indian territory.

Many Indians resisted these policies and practices. The Sauk and Fox Indians of southern Wisconsin and northern Illinois had been forced to move into Iowa Territory across the Mississippi River. Discontented, they reoccupied the homelands they had given up. White forces moved against them in 1832 in what was called the Black Hawk War. The Indian leader Black Hawk and his followers fought bravely and skillfully, but the Sauks and Foxes were overwhelmed.

In Georgia, Florida, Alabama, and Mississippi, the once powerful Creeks, Choctaws, Chickasaws, Cherokees, and Seminoles had adopted many of the white settlers' ways of life. They came to be known as the Five Civilized Tribes. By the end of 1833, the Creeks, Choctaws, and Chickasaws had signed removal

In 1800 a Cherokee silversmith named Sequoyah created a written language for his people. Combining English, Hebrew, and Greek letters with other symbols, he developed a Cherokee alphabet. By 1828 his people could publish their own newspaper, **The Cherokee Phoenix.**

▲

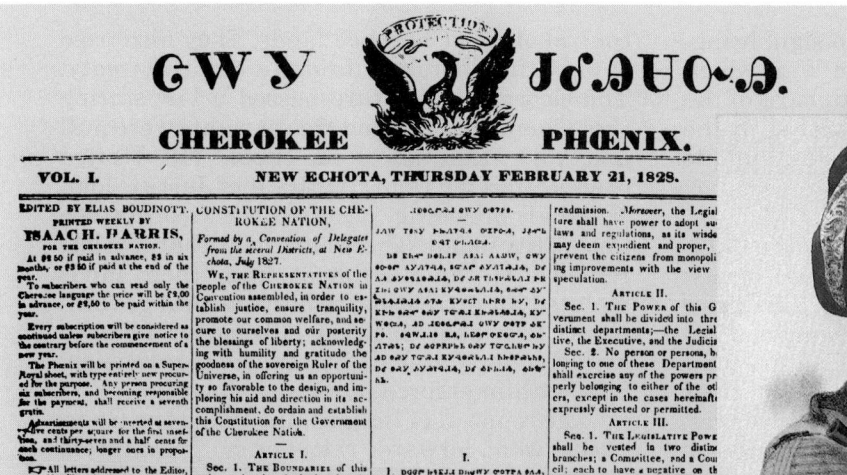

"I loved my towns, my cornfields, and the home of my people," said the feeble, wrinkled man who was guest of honor at a Fourth of July celebration at Fort Madison in the Iowa Territory. "I was once a great warrior. Now I am poor. . . . Now I am old."

The speaker was Black Hawk, chief of the Sauk and Fox Indians, who in 1832 led his people in battle against the whites who had invaded his homeland. The brief but tragic struggle, which marked the end of Indian-held lands in the Illinois and Wisconsin territories, has come to be known as the Black Hawk War.

In 1804, five Sauk and Fox chiefs signed a treaty with Governor William Henry Harrison of the Indiana Territory, in which they surrendered 51 million acres (21 million hectares) east of the Mississippi River. Black Hawk refused to recognize the treaty, maintaining that the chiefs had been bribed with liquor and fancy clothes before signing the document.

At first, Black Hawk demonstrated his resistance to the United States government by joining with the British in the War of 1812. Soon after the war ended, white squatters appeared in the Rock River Valley, the homeland of the Sauk and the Fox. The white settlers took over the Indians' lodges, fenced in cornfields, and destroyed the Indians' boats. In 1828 the federal government ordered the Indians to vacate the valley and to relocate to a reservation in the Iowa Territory.

Black Hawk chose to defy the resettlement order. In the summers of 1829, 1830, and 1831 — as had been customary for over a hundred years — the Sauk and Fox attempted to return to the Rock River Valley to plant their crops. But each time they were driven back across the Mississippi River by volunteers called out by the Illinois governor.

In 1832 Black Hawk, believing that other tribes would assist his people in the struggle for their land, defiantly crossed the Mississippi once more. After an initial surprise victory over the whites, the Indians' strength faded. Aid from other tribes never materialized, and Black Hawk's food supplies were quickly exhausted. Black Hawk was forced from the battlefield without victory.

In the final battle, at the Bad Axe River in Wisconsin, nearly 1,000 Indians — including women and children — were slaughtered by artillery mounted on the steamboat *Warrior.* Black Hawk put on a white deerskin and surrendered. The brutality of the Black Hawk War broke the will of many Indians to resist white encroachment on their lands. Within a few years most of the tribes had fled the Old Northwest Territory to the Far West, thus abandoning those lands to white settlers.

treaties. The Seminoles refused to sign, bringing on the costly Second Seminole War, which lasted until 1842. Finally defeated, most of the Seminoles moved westward. A few hid in the Florida Everglades, where their descendants remain today.

The fate of the Cherokees.   Most of the Cherokees, too, refused to sign a removal treaty. With the aid of missionary teachers, the Cherokees had developed a written language. They published a widely read newspaper in their own language and supported schools for their children. Some owned plantations and slaves. The Cherokees governed themselves under a written constitution that provided for a legislature, a judicial system, and a law-enforcing militia. They were proud of their advanced agriculture, arts, and crafts.

White settlers and land speculators in Georgia were determined to crush the Cherokees, especially after gold was discovered. Using legal and illegal means, they gained control of rich Cherokee lands. They also tried to force the Cherokees to sign a removal treaty. The Georgia legislature passed a law stating that Cherokee laws and treaty rights were null and void — that is, of no effect. The United States Supreme Court, with Chief Justice John Marshall presiding, declared the Georgia law unconstitutional. The Court held that forcible removal of the Cherokees from their lands violated their treaties with the federal government. President Jackson is reported to have said, "John Marshall has made his decision; now let him enforce it."

The removal of Indians, including the Cherokees, went forward. Little or no preparation was made for their resettlement. Tragic stories are told of how Indians, especially the Cherokees, were driven from their homes during the bitter cold of winter to follow what became known as the "Trail of Tears." Thinly dressed, without moccasins, sometimes in chains, often without food, the Indians were forced by federal troops into what was for them a strange and barren wilderness to the west of the Mississippi River.

Although Jackson showed some personal concern for the plight of the Indians, in his role as President he was responsible for the removal of a great many. His official position remained one of uncompromising support for Indian resettlement. He refused to listen to missionary groups who wanted to help the Indians achieve orderly, settled lives. He ignored not only the Supreme Court but also political critics, including Henry Clay, who opposed his Indian policy. When Jackson left the White House, the first major Indian removals had been largely carried out.

A product of his times. In the 1820's and 1830's, most white Americans shared Andrew Jackson's attitudes toward Indians. Although American ideas of equality and justice had been stated, they were not yet widely practiced. They did not apply to Indians or to black Americans, either slave or free. They did not apply to women, who more than 50 years after the Declaration of Independence were still treated as inferiors both in law and by custom. Moreover, criminals and mentally ill persons had few rights and were badly mistreated; few Americans saw anything wrong with this. Employers, too, often treated their workers harshly and unjustly.

Andrew Jackson, by the standards of the times, took important strides toward fuller political democracy for average white male Americans. Important as these steps were, the democratic ideal of equal opportunity for each citizen remained a distant goal.

SECTION REVIEW

See underscored items, text pp. 289 - 29.
Identify: spoils system, nominating convention, kitchen cabinet, Indian resettlement
For answers to questions, see Answer Key, p.A44.

1. **Organizing Ideas:** What three convictions underlay Jackson's actions as President?

2. **Summarizing Ideas:** Describe the arguments for and against the spoils system.

3. **Evaluating Viewpoints:** (a) What was Jackson's attitude toward American Indians? (b) How do his actions before and during his Presidency reflect these attitudes?

4. **Interpreting Ideas:** (a) In what ways was democracy strengthened during Jackson's term as President? (b) In what ways was the nation still undemocratic?

3 Andrew Jackson exercises his Presidential powers

See Teaching Suggestions in TMRG, pp.TM74-75.
President Jackson, in his first message to Congress early in 1829, opened his attack against the second Bank of the United States.

Opposing the Bank. Jackson disliked banks and failed to understand banking. He saw the Bank of the United States as a "money power"—a monopoly that "the rich and powerful" used to their own advantage. He pointed out most shares of Bank stock were owned by wealthy investors in seaboard states. Only a handful of Americans living west of the Appalachians owned stock.

Why, the President asked, should the government continue to grant control of the Bank to a few wealthy people, most of them easterners? "Many of our rich men," he declared, ". . . have besought us to make them richer by acts of Congress. By attempting to gratify their desires, we have in the results of our legislation arrayed section against section, interest against interest, and man against man, in a fearful commotion which threatens to shake the foundations of our Union."

To his charge that the Bank was a tool of rich easterners Jackson added the serious charge that it engaged in questionable political activities. He charged, for example, that by granting loans to members of Congress, the Bank was able to influence legislation. There is little doubt that it did, at least after Jackson made his accusation—an accusation that many people considered unfair. Once its directors were convinced that the President intended to destroy their Bank, they fought back with every weapon at their command.

Jackson also claimed that the mere existence of the Bank was unconstitutional. In so doing, he expressed his belief in the limited powers of the federal government. He also ignored the Supreme Court decision of 1819 in *McCulloch v. Maryland* that the Bank was acceptable under the Constitution. Jackson, however, indicated that he did not intend to be bound by verdicts of the Supreme Court.

Many Americans joined Jackson in opposing the Bank. Farmers and wage earners who wanted easy credit opposed the Bank's lending policies. They were angry because the Bank refused to lend them money without adequate security in land or goods as a pledge of repayment. From a banker's point of view, this was sound practice.

Some business owners also resented the sound banking policies of the second Bank of the United States. Being refused easy credit by the national Bank, they turned to private and state banks. Powerful banking interests centering in New York City also resented the special privileges enjoyed by the Bank of the United States. Popular slogans of the day denounced the Bank as a monstrous monopoly.

The Bank as an election issue. Angered at the opposition, the supporters of the Bank, including Henry Clay, decided to force a showdown. They persuaded Bank president Nicholas Biddle to apply for a renewal of the Bank's charter. The bill passed both houses of Congress in the summer of 1832, four years before the charter was due to expire.

Henry Clay and the National-Republicans deliberately raised the issue at this time. They hoped that Jackson would veto the bill. If he did, the National-Republicans could make the Bank a major issue in the election of 1832. President Jackson did as they wished. In forceful terms he vetoed the bill to recharter the Bank of the United States.

Late in 1832 the National-Republicans nominated Henry Clay for the Presidency. Clay and his followers campaigned in favor of rechartering the Bank. Andrew Jackson, running for re-election as the Democratic candidate, continued his vigorous opposition. The Bank became the major campaign issue.

Jackson won the election, with Martin Van Buren of New York as his Vice President. Clay and the National-Republicans suffered a crushing defeat. Under these circumstances, everyone understood that the Bank charter would not be renewed in 1836.

Destroying the Bank. Not content to wait for the Bank to die a natural death in 1836, Jackson set out to destroy it by gradually withdrawing all federal deposits. Federal funds were now deposited in certain state banks. These so-called **pet banks** were selected, Jackson's enemies claimed, on the basis of their loyalty to President Jackson and to his party. The Bank of the United States, now deprived of federal deposits, was badly crippled. Nevertheless, it survived until its charter expired in 1836.

Andrew Jackson and his supporters felt that they had won a great victory over a government-approved monopoly of the money power by wealthy easterners. In their opinion, this was another triumph for democracy. It was also a reflection of Jackson's concern with the need for easy credit for the people in the rising middle class.

Jackson's support of the Union. In his fight with the Bank of the United States, Andrew Jackson flatly stated that he, as President, did not intend to be restricted by the Supreme Court. This statement did not indicate any lack of respect for the federal Union set up by the Constitution. Indeed, beginning in 1830, Jackson fought so strongly in support of the Union that southern champions of **states' rights,** who had supported Jackson, were completely con-

---

SOURCES

JACKSON
VETOES
THE BANK BILL
(1832)

Distinctions in society will always exist under every just government. Equality of talents, of education, or of wealth cannot be produced by human institutions. In the full enjoyment of the gifts of Heaven and the fruits of superior industry, economy, and virtue, every man is equally entitled to protection by law; but when the laws undertake to add to these natural and just advantages artificial distinctions, to grant titles, gratuities, and exclusive privileges, to make the rich richer and the potent powerful, the humble members of society—the farmers, mechanics, and laborers—who have neither the time nor the means of securing like favors to themselves, have a right to complain of the injustice of their government. There are no necessary evils in government. Its evils exist only in its abuses. . . .

▲ After the Bank of the United States lost its federal charter, it reopened as the Bank of the United States of Pennsylvania under a state charter.

In this newspaper cartoon, Andrew Jackson is shown triumphing over the downfall of the second Bank of the United States. The fleeing figure with horns is Nicholas Biddle, the president of the Bank. What do you suppose the newspaper's opinion of the event was? (The newspaper seems to have favored Jackson's policies.) ▲

fused. The issue that forced Jackson into his firm position was a revolt of South Carolina planters against a high protective tariff.

Southern reaction to rising tariffs. As you have read (page 269), Congress passed the tariff of 1816 to protect America's new and growing manufacturing industries from foreign competition. The tariff rates were raised in 1824 and again in 1828.

Because of its high rates, the Tariff Act of 1828 was called the "Tariff of Abominations" by its enemies. The tariff was passed by such a large majority in Congress that southern planters became alarmed. Reflecting their alarm, Vice President John C. Calhoun wrote —but did not sign—a statement expressing his views about the tariff and the larger issue of states' rights. Calhoun argued that each state had the right to **nullify,** or refuse to obey, any act of Congress that it considered unconstitutional. This was a restatement of the compact theory of government earlier set forth in the Kentucky and Virginia Resolutions.

The legislature of South Carolina adopted Calhoun's statement, which came to be known as the "South Carolina Exposition and Protest." It also passed a set of resolutions calling the tariff unconstitutional and unjust. Georgia, Mississippi, and Virginia adopted their own similar resolutions.

Webster's defense of the Union. Calhoun's doctrine of states' rights set off bitter debate in Congress. A widely held southern view was clearly expressed by Senator Robert Y. Hayne of South Carolina. Hayne argued that in opposing the tariff, southerners were simply resisting "unauthorized taxation." Hayne also restated Calhoun's views that the states could nullify unconstitutional acts of Congress.

A different viewpoint was widely held in the North. Daniel Webster of Massachusetts eloquently expressed it in one of the most famous speeches ever given in the Senate. Webster declared that the United States was not a mere league, or compact, of states. He argued that it was "the people's government,

▲ Note: Answers to questions in captions appear in parentheses, as shown here. Bullets separate answers to individual questions when a caption contains more than one question.

295

made for the people, made by the people, and answerable to the people." No state had the power to declare an act of Congress unconstitutional, Webster insisted. If each state could obey only those laws it chose to accept, Webster declared, the Union would become a "mere rope of sand."

Webster maintained that only one agency had the power to decide whether acts of Congress were unconstitutional. That agency, he said, was the Supreme Court. In thunderous words he flung out his challenge to Calhoun and Hayne and all who accepted the doctrine of states' rights and nullification: "Liberty *and* Union, now and forever, one and inseparable!"

Jackson's defense of the Union.
Which side would the President support? The answer was not long in coming.

At a dinner in April 1830, President Jackson rose from his chair, fixed his eyes upon Vice President Calhoun, held his glass in the air, and proposed a toast: "Our Federal Union —it must and shall be preserved."

A long moment of silence followed. Then the fiery Calhoun, voice of the southern planters, rose and threw back a defiant challenge: "The Union—next to our liberty, the most dear! May we always remember that it can only be preserved by respecting the rights of the states."

The battle was on. The leaders of both sides were able fighters who were reluctant to compromise when principles were at stake.

The conflict smoldered for two years. Then, in 1832, Congress adopted a new tariff measure with somewhat lower rates than the "Tariff of Abominations." The new act was still a protective tariff, and southerners therefore felt that it was no better than the old tariff. Convinced that the supporters of a protective tariff controlled Congress, South Carolina decided to take action.

South Carolina's threat to secede.
In November 1832 South Carolina adopted the Ordinance of Nullification. It declared the tariff acts of 1828 and 1832 "null, void, and no law," and not "binding upon this state, its officers, or citizens." The ordinance was a clear defiance of the United States government. It closed with a solemn warning. If the federal authorities tried to enforce the tariff law after February 1, 1833, South Carolina would secede from the Union.

The President's reaction.
President Jackson now moved into the spotlight. As Chief Executive of the United States, he was charged with enforcing the laws. He acted promptly. In off-the-record statements he lived up to his reputation as a fighting man. He warned that he was prepared to "hang every leader . . . irrespective of his name or political or social position. . . . Tell them," he said to a member of Congress, "that they can talk and write resolutions and print threats to their hearts' content. But if one drop of blood be shed there in defiance of the laws of the United States, I will hang the first man of them I can get my hands on to the first tree I can find."

For the public record, Jackson was more moderate. A carefully worded statement repeated his belief in the Union and his determination to uphold it. Nevertheless, he left the way open for a peaceable solution.

Calhoun was out on a limb. The other southern states had refused to follow South Carolina along the road to secession. Calhoun and his followers stood alone against the full might of the United States. With possible violence facing the country, political leaders proposed to end the crisis by compromise.

SOURCES

WEBSTER'S REPLY TO HAYNE (1830)

When my eyes shall be turned to behold, for the last time, the sun in heaven, may I not see him shining on the broken and dishonored fragments of a once glorious Union; . . . Let their last feeble and lingering glance, rather, behold the gorgeous ensign of the republic . . . bearing for its motto no such miserable interrogatory as, *What is all this worth?* Nor those other words of delusion and folly, *Liberty first, and Union afterwards:* but everywhere, spread all over the land, and in every wind under the whole heavens, that other sentiment, dear to every true American heart—Liberty *and* Union, now and forever, one and inseparable!

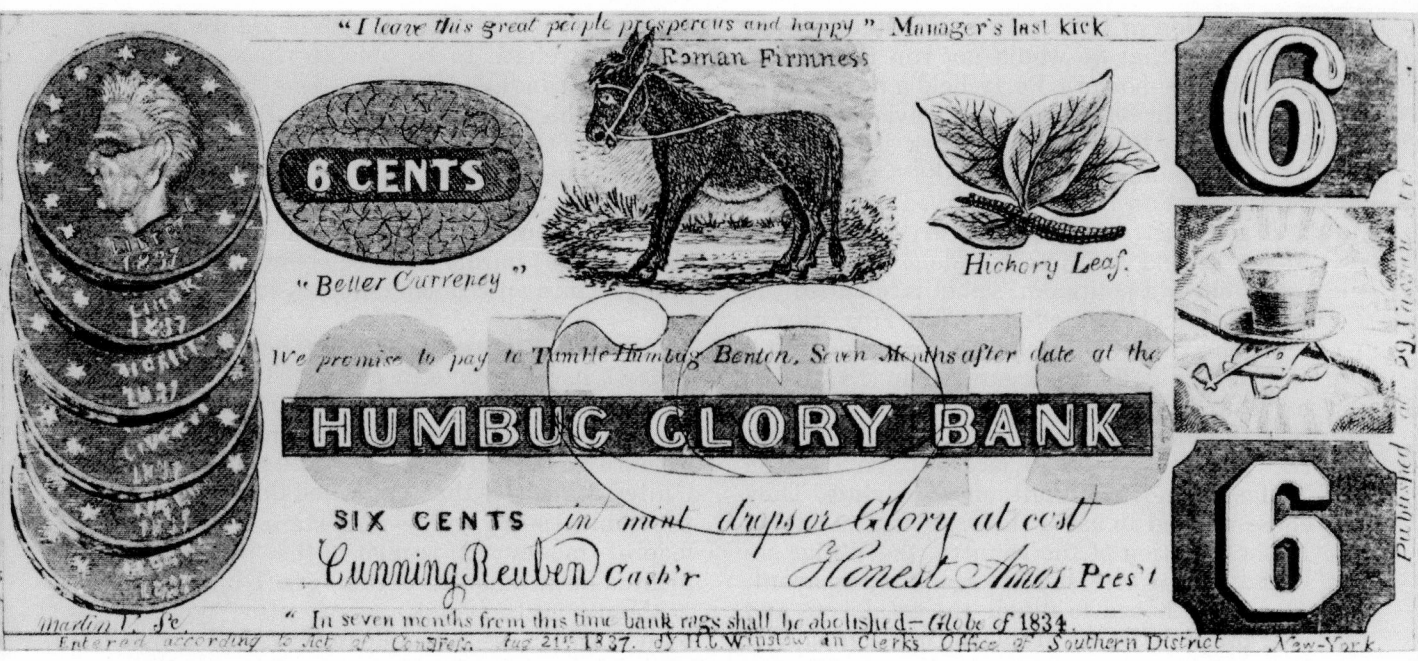

Jackson's destruction of the Bank and establishment of pet banks brought him ridicule in many forms, including this joke currency.

A compromise tariff. Under the leadership of Henry Clay, the Great Compromiser, Congress adopted a compromise measure, the Tariff Act of 1833. Under this act, tariff rates were to be reduced gradually to the level of 1816, which Calhoun had once supported. This reduction was part of what many southern leaders demanded, but the reductions in the rates were to take place over ten years. In this way manufacturers would be better able to adjust to the lack of high-tariff protection.

Along with the compromise tariff act, Congress in 1833 also adopted the <u>Force Act</u>. This act gave the President the power to enforce federal tariff laws, by military force if necessary.

Secession had been avoided. "Old Hickory" became a symbol of a strong, united nation.

SECTION REVIEW

See underscored items, text pp. 294 - 95, 297.

Identify: Nicholas Biddle, pet banks, "Tariff of Abominations," nullify, states' rights, Force Act

For answers to questions, see Answer Key, p.A44.

1. **Analyzing Ideas: (a)** Why did Jackson oppose the Bank of the United States? **(b)** What evidence is there that many Americans agreed with him?

2. **Contrasting Ideas:** Describe the disagreement over tariffs that reached its peak in 1828.

3. **Evaluating Ideas:** How did Clay's compromise tariff of 1833 satisfy **(a)** the South **(b)** the North, and **(c)** Jackson?

4. **Organizing Ideas:** Jackson believed in a strong Presidency. Give examples to support this statement.

4 The Jacksonian era ends in an economic depression

See Teaching Suggestions in TMRG, pp.TM75-76.

In March 1835 Andrew Jackson passed the midpoint of his second term as President. From Jackson's point of view, his administration had been a great success. He had won every major battle with his political opponents. His supporters were devoted to him. One of them expressed a widely held opinion that "General Jackson may be President for life if he wishes." Despite such support Jackson made it clear that he was ready to retire.

The election of 1836. In 1835, after Jackson announced that he would not run for a third term, the Democratic Party held a nominating convention in Baltimore. The convention chose Martin Van Buren of New York as its Presidential candidate.

Martin Van Buren had served in Jackson's first administration as Secretary of State and in his second as Vice President. Van Buren was a shrewd politician, sometimes called the "Little Magician" or even the "Sly Fox." He entered the race with Jackson's strong support.

The Whig Party, organized in 1834, was made up of various groups united chiefly by their dislike of "King Andrew" Jackson and the policies of the Democratic Party. The Whigs did not nominate one candidate. They chose instead to use a "favorite son" strategy. In each section of the country, the Whigs selected a "favorite son" to run for President. They thus hoped to divide the total vote and prevent Van Buren from getting a majority, throwing the election into the House of Representatives. There the Whigs hoped to have enough strength to be able to choose one of their own candidates.

The Whig strategy failed. Van Buren won a majority of the electoral votes. In his Inaugural Address on March 4, 1837, Van Buren announced that he would follow in Jackson's footsteps. He soon discovered that this was impossible. He was hardly in office before the nation plunged into an economic depression.

The roots of the depression. The depression of 1837 had its roots in events that occurred largely during Jackson's administration. After his election in 1832, Jackson had gradually withdrawn federal funds from the Bank of the United States. He then deposited this money in pet banks, many in western states. With the federal money as security, the pet banks printed large amounts of their own bank notes.

Many pet banks were also **wildcat banks,** which issued bank notes far in excess of the federal funds on deposit. Because they

The panic of 1837 left workers idle and forced some women and children to beg. The signs on the buildings in this cartoon illustrate the problem. The federal government demanded to be paid in specie. However, people could not obtain specie because banks were no longer redeeming bank notes with it.

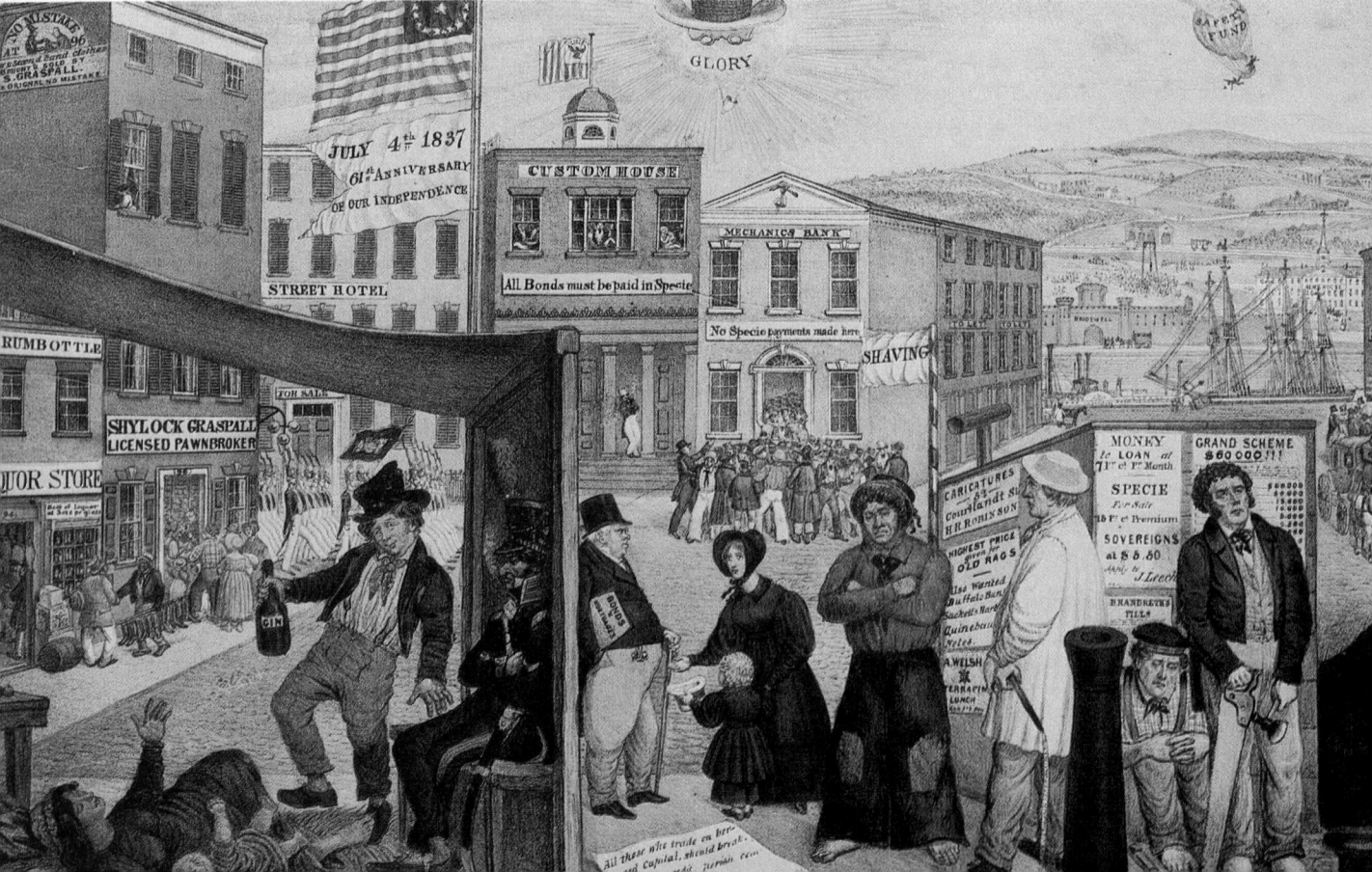

were so plentiful and had so little real value, these bank notes were easy to borrow. People borrowed this "easy money," often with a minimum of security, to buy land and to invest in the nation's growing transportation system. For a time it seemed as though almost everyone was speculating with borrowed money.

Land speculators were especially active. Between 1830 and 1836, yearly federal income from the sale of public land rose from about $2 million to about $24 million. Much of this money was in the form of "wildcat" bank notes. The United States Treasury was flooded with this unsound currency.

In July 1836 President Jackson acted to check the wave of speculation sweeping across the country by issuing the Specie Circular. This Executive Order forbade the Treasury to accept as payment for public land anything except gold and silver, known as **specie,** or bank notes backed by specie.

The panic of 1837. Shortly after Jackson issued his order, the trouble began. The sale of public land dropped off sharply because few people had gold or silver coins to pay for the land. Persons holding bank notes began to ask the banks to exchange the bank notes for the gold or silver itself. Many banks could not redeem their own bank notes. As a result, banks began to fail. By the end of May 1837, soon after President Van Buren took office, every bank in the United States had suspended specie payment. Before the panic ended, hundreds of banks had gone out of business.

As the banks failed and sound money disappeared from circulation, business suffered. Factories closed. Construction work ended on buildings and roads. Thousands of workers lost their jobs. Hungry people rioted in the streets of New York and Philadelphia.

President Van Buren and other leaders of the time did not think that the government could or should do anything to try to stop the depression. Van Buren declared that "the less government interferes with private pursuits, the better for the general prosperity." Thus he could only sit back and wait for the depression to run its course.

The depression was only one problem President Van Buren faced. More than anything else, though, it cost him re-election.

The election of 1840. In December 1839 the Whig Party held a nominating convention

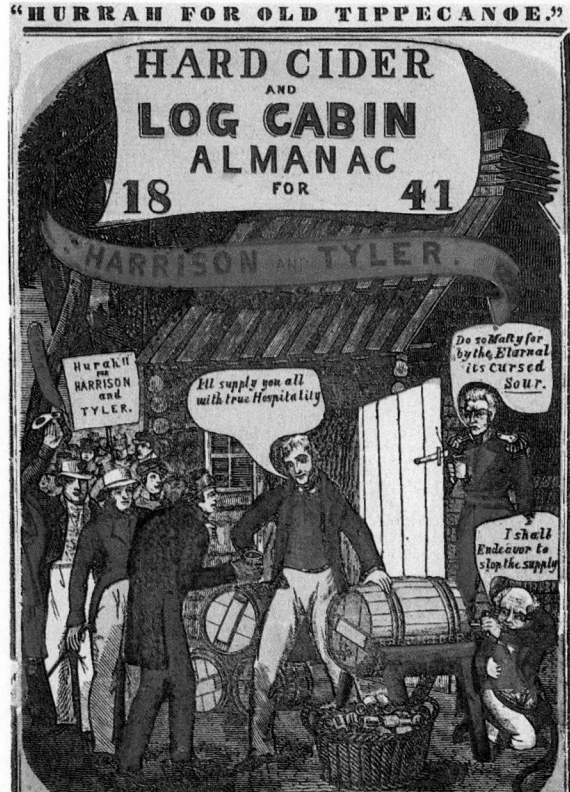

In the campaign of 1840, hard cider became a symbol of Harrison's's homeyness. Here he uses cider to entertain his supporters while his opponent, Martin Van Buren, attempts to stop him.

at Harrisburg, Pennsylvania. The delegates sniffed victory in the air. They did not attempt to publish a **platform**, or statement of the party's political policies. Instead, they chose to fight the campaign entirely on the issue of the depression, which they of course blamed on Van Buren and the Democrats. To lead the fight, they nominated a hero of the War of 1812, General William Henry Harrison of Ohio, with John Tyler of Virginia as his running mate.

The campaign of 1840 was one of the most boisterous in American history. Although Harrison owned a large, prosperous farm, he was pictured as a poor but honest man who lived in a log cabin and earned his daily bread by hard labor. The Whigs built log cabins for headquarters. They entertained the crowds at political rallies with barrels of hard cider. Recalling General Harrison's battle with the Indians at the Tippecanoe River in 1811, the

The adoption of a party platform is an important part of a national nominating convention. Have student volunteers obtain copies of the most recent party platforms and report on the issues each contains. In a follow-up activity students may compare and contrast approaches to the issues.

299

Harrison supporters also used the log cabin to present their candidate as a simple man of the people, as this hand-sewn emblem shows. Actually, Harrison's home was a stately white mansion, containing 22 rooms.

Whigs aroused enthusiasm for their candidates by shouting, "Tippecanoe, and Tyler, too." To ridicule their opposition, the Whigs shouted, "Van, Van is a used-up man."

The Whigs won an overwhelming victory, but General Harrison did not live to enjoy his triumph for long. He died shortly after he took office. Vice President John Tyler, a states' rights Democrat who intensely opposed Jackson, succeeded to the Presidency.

A look ahead. During President Tyler's administration and that of his Democratic successor, James K. Polk, who was inaugurated in 1845, the boundaries of the nation were extended to the Pacific Ocean. During these same years, the differences between the North and South became increasingly serious. As you will see in Unit Four, these differences produced severe tensions that finally ended in the outbreak of a tragic war.

SECTION REVIEW

See underscored items, text pp. 298 - 99.

Identify: wildcat banks, specie, Specie Circular, Martin Van Buren, platform, William Henry Harrison, John Tyler

For answers to questions, see Answer Key, pp. A44-45.

1. **Summarizing Ideas:** What strategy did the Whig Party follow in the election of 1836?

2. **Determining Cause and Effect:** How did (a) pet banks and wildcat banks, (b) land speculation, and (c) the Specie Circular help cause the depression of 1837?

3. **Evaluating Ideas:** What did Van Buren think the federal government should do during the 1837 depression?

4. **Organizing Ideas:** (a) Who were the candidates in the election of 1840? (b) What were the campaign issues? (c) Why and how was Harrison pictured as a "common man"?

5. **Studying Graphics:** Study the political cartoon on page 298. (a) What aspects of a depression are pictured? (b) What point of view is expressed?

DEVELOPING HISTORY STUDY SKILLS

Thinking About History   Analyzing Information

Significance of the 1828 election

[ANDREW] Jackson's triumph in the election of 1828 was largely the result of advancing demo-cratic forces in America. Great changes had clearly taken place since the days of President Washington and the Federalists. For one thing, political power was now more evenly divided between well-to-do people and average people. The average people no longer stood in awe of leaders, who, it had been supposed, were especially qualified by birth and education to lead the nation. Before the inauguration of 1829, all the Presidents were men from wealthy back-grounds. Andrew Jackson, in contrast, had been born into poverty and had risen through his own efforts.

Jackson's election also indicated that the west-ern section of the country was a new force to be reckoned with in national politics. Andrew Jack-son was from Tennessee. He was the first Presi-dent from a state that did not border on the Atlantic.

Not all of Jackson's followers were westerners. Of course, many western settlers had voted for him because they felt that he would understand their problems, but many small farmers every-where voted for him for the same reason. Many southern planters voted for him because, as a planter and a slaveowner himself, he would understand their point of view. Some city work-ers as well as owners of small businesses voted for him because they believed he would help them to get the laws they wanted. Many owners of small businesses, fearful of the growth of big business, wanted the opportunity to expand their own enterprises. They believed that Andrew Jackson, a self-made man, would help them. Thus with the support of a majority of ordinary white Americans, Andrew Jackson became Pres-ident.

These statements, taken from the textbook, are an exam-ple of one kind of information historians provide in their writings. The information is usually obtained through their own analysis of the events of the period. A reader of history must also be able to analyze information, both in the writings of historians and in primary sources.

To analyze information means to break it apart into bits and pieces, such as facts and opinions, causes and effects, before and after time-relationships. Like the pieces of a jigsaw puzzle, however, the pieces that result from analysis must be put back together. Like the histo-rian you put the pieces back together in ways that reveal the relationships of the pieces, each to the other and each to the whole.

How to Analyze Information

1. **Read the material carefully.** Before beginning any analysis of material, you must first understand what you are reading. The best way to do this is to look for main ideas in the material and for the details that sup-port the main ideas. After a careful reading of the whole you are then ready to begin your analysis.

2. **Ask yourself questions.** Ask *who* or *what* is involved. Ask who did what to whom. Ask *when* and *where* the action is taking place. Ask *how* if it's appro-priate, and always ask *why.*

3. **Separate fact from opinion.** Facts are provable and observable. They usually can be checked in more than one source. Opinions are beliefs that may or may not be observable or proved true. Separating opinion from fact helps you recognize the historian's analysis. Certain words or phrases often precede opinions in most historical writing. Some examples of these phrases include *It is believed, It would appear, The evi-dence seems to warrant.*

4. **Search for bias.** Facts can be selectively used to present a one-sided view. Be alert to words, phrases, or facts that support a single viewpoint when it seems evident that more than one viewpoint is possible.

5. **Check for cause-effect relationships.** Look for the clue words that indicate that part of a sentence states a cause and another part states an effect. Also re-member that a cause may be stated separately from its effect and that an effect may itself be a cause.

6. **Come to a conclusion.** After assembling the bits and pieces, do something with them. Draw a conclusion, form a generalization, consider a hypothesis for future reading.

301

Applying the Skill

Reread the excerpt from the textbook on page 301. An analysis of the paragraph reveals the following bits and pieces. The *who* of the paragraph is Andrew Jackson. The *what* is the great changes in democracy that have taken place since the days of Washington and the Federalists. The *when* is the period up to the inauguration of 1829. The *where* is the United States.

Other questions still need to be asked. What is the connection between Jackson's triumph and the advancing democratic forces. One is a *cause* (advancing democratic forces), the other is the *effect* (Jackson's triumph). Do the authors prove the assertion that great changes had clearly taken place? They talk about the division of power being equalized and the change in the ways the average person viewed the nation's leaders. They mention that before Jackson, all Presidents had been from wealthy backgrounds, but Jackson had been born in poverty.

Remember that paintings, tables, charts, and maps also present information for analysis. The painting at the bottom of the page of Jackson's inauguration adds information on the attitudes and events surrounding the 1828 election.

Practicing the Skill

Read the following excerpt, which is from the *Age of Jackson* by Arthur Schlesinger, Jr., a Harvard Professor and winner of the Pulitzer Prize. Then on a separate sheet of paper, answer the questions below.

1. What is the main idea of the first paragraph?
2. What details are provided in support of the main idea?
3. What is the main idea of the second paragraph?
4. What details are provided in support of the main idea?
5. What cause-effect relationship is stated in the second paragraph?
6. What conclusion or generalization did the author make?
7. Did you detect any bias? Explain.

Jackson was hardly the uncouth, semiliterate backwoodsman of legend. He was actually an urbane and dignified gentleman with distinguished manners and bearing. But although a country squire himself, he had no sense of commitment to the old ruling aristocracy; he had a commanding eye and a gift for decision; and there surged through him a sense that the people had made him their trustee in the use of the powers of government. . . .

Jackson's first spectacular act as President expressed his sense of devotion to the people. This was the redistribution of federal jobs, which Jackson and his supporters regarded as a reform measure and called "rotation in office" and which his opponents decried as the "spoils system." Whatever the results of this practice — and some results were certainly deplorable — Jackson's intent was clear enough. It was to destroy what seemed to him a monopoly of officeholding by a certain class. . . . This measure was only the first of a series designed to serve the political, social, and economic aspirations of the common man.

Inauguration Day, 1829

social, and economic aspirations of the common man. 4. See broken-line underscore.
5. Jackson's "rotation in office" system would end control of government bureaucracy by the upper class. 6. Jackson's intent was to bring the common man into government.
7. Answers will vary.)

302

During most of the years between 1824 and 1841, Andrew Jackson occupied the center of the national stage. During these years, Jackson stood as a symbol of democracy and national unity.

Jackson was far more than a symbol of national unity. He firmly believed that the President should assume an active role as the nation's leader. He thought that the people should share in the task of government. He firmly believed that the Union established by the Constitution was a national Union. In the eight years of his administration, Andrew Jackson did much to make the government more democratic. He brought the people into closer touch with the government. During the controversy surrounding the enactment of a high protective tariff, he fought the battle to maintain national unity and to ease the divisions caused by sectionalism.

The depression that started in 1837 and continued through the administration of Jackson's successor, the Democrat Martin Van Buren, gave the Whigs a chance to win control of the government. The Whigs made the most of their opportunity. In the campaign of 1840, they sent General William Henry Harrison to the White House. With the Whig victory and the inauguration of Harrison, the colorful Jacksonian era ended.

CONNECTING CHAPTER IDEAS

In the next chapter you will read about the building of new industries in the United States. The building of roads and canals, the development of steamboats, and the construction of railroads improved transportation. Wage earners began seeking improved working conditions. Immigrations swelled the ranks of wage earners, giving the nation an immense labor supply.

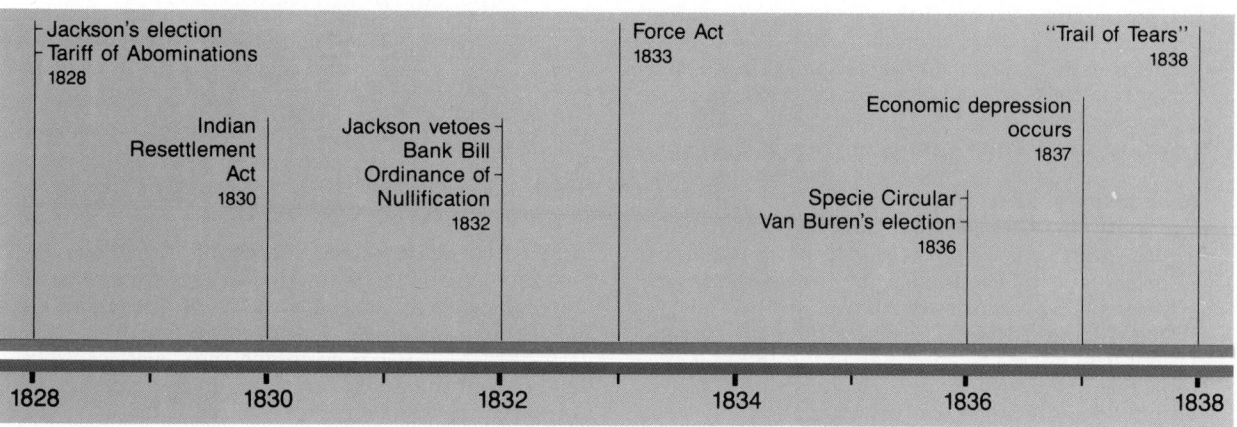

Jackson's election
Tariff of Abominations
1828

Indian Resettlement Act
1830

Jackson vetoes Bank Bill
Ordinance of Nullification
1832

Force Act
1833

Specie Circular
Van Buren's election
1836

Economic depression occurs
1837

"Trail of Tears"
1838

| 1828 | 1830 | 1832 | 1834 | 1836 | 1838 |

CHAPTER

12 REVIEW

Reviewing Important Terms

Decide whether each of the following sentences is true or false. If the sentence is false, replace the underlined term with the word or phrase that will make it true.

1. John Quincy Adams, William H. Crawford, Andrew Jackson, and Henry Clay have been called favorite son candidates, since they each represented specific areas of the country.
2. Unqualified party supporters were often given public offices under the American System.
3. Andrew Jackson's circle of unofficial advisers came to be known as the midnight judges, since they were accused of meeting him in secret.
4. Indian resettlement was the government policy used to relocate the tribes on lands west of the Mississippi River.
5. President Jackson had federal funds deposited in the so-called pet banks as a way of crippling the Bank of United States.
6. To discourage speculation, Jackson ordered the treasury to accept only specie or bank notes backed by specie as payment for public lands.

Practicing Critical Thinking Skills

1. **Analyzing Ideas.** Describe the circumstances under which the following statements were made: (a) "Liberty *and* Union, now and forever, one and inseparable!" (Webster), (b) "Our Federal Union—it must and shall be preserved." (Jackson), and (c) "The Union—next to our liberty, the most dear!" (Calhoun).
2. **Comparing Viewpoints.** Jackson's enemies called him "King Andrew" while his friends called him "a man of the people." How could Andrew Jackson's policies produce such opposite reactions?
3. **Analyzing Viewpoints.** Study again the three convictions Jackson held when he became President (page 289). Then complete the following activity. (a) Cite specific examples which indicate that Jackson held these convictions throughout his Presidency. (b) On which convictions was he inconsistent? Explain.
4. **Organizing Ideas.** Trace the increase in sectionalism during the first half of the 1800's. Give specific examples of events indicating that sectional disagreement was growing.

Developing History Study Skills

Analyzing Information. The following table indicates recent import-export patterns for the United States. Study the table; then answer the questions below.

Commodity	Exports	Imports
Agricultural goods	20%	9%
Nonagricultural Raw Materials	5%	5%
Fuel	3%	27%
Capital goods	34%	11%
Other manufactured products	38%	48%

(a) For which groups of commodities does the United States import more than it exports? (b) For which group of commodities does the United States export more than its imports?

Relating Geography and History

The first protectionist tariff was passed in 1816. Partisan support for the tariff took on a regional character. In 1828, the "Tariff of Abominations" raised duties and added certain raw materials to the list of dutiable goods. Again, the voting was based on regional interests. To understand how each region viewed the tariff, study the following table, and answer the questions below.

HOUSE OF REPRESENTATIVES				
	Tariff of 1816		Tariff of 1828	
Regions	For	Against	For	Against
New England	17	10	16	23
Mid-Atlantic	44	10	57	11
West	4	0	17	1
South	23	34	15	58

(a) Which region seemed to change its views on protective tariffs? Explain. (b) Which region reacted most vehemently to the passage of the Tariff of 1828? (c) How did the South see the Tariff of 1828 as a hardship? (d) How might the Tariff of 1828 have helped the South? (e) How did the passage of the Tariff of 1828 promote sectional politics?

UNIT THREE
REVIEW

Discussing Ideas

1. **(a)** How would you decide whether a person had been a good President or not? **(b)** Use those standards to decide who you think was the best President between 1789 and 1841.
2. By 1830, what principles of American foreign policy had been established by **(a)** Presidential proclamations, **(b)** the War of 1812, and **(c)** the Monroe Doctrine?
3. **(a)** What was Jackson's concept of the Presidency? of the function of the federal government? **(b)** Compare his views to Jefferson's.
4. The character of George Washington strengthened the new government and the brilliance of Hamilton enabled it to function successfully. Comment.
5. **(a)** Trace the growth of democracy from 1787 to 1840. Be sure to define democracy as you give examples of its growth. **(b)** Why was democracy growing in this period?
6. How do you explain the difference between what was said and what was done concerning minority groups in America between 1789 and 1845?

Applying History Study Skills

Analyzing Information. The following excerpt is from *Democracy in America*, by Alexis de Tocqueville. Having come to the United States on business for the French government, de Tocqueville wrote about his observations of democracy at work. Read the excerpt and then answer the questions below.

> The accession of the Federalists to power was, in my opinion, one of the most fortunate incidents that accompanied the formation of the great American Union; they resisted the inevitable propensities [natural inclinations] of their country and their age. But whether their theories were good or bad, they had the fault of being inapplicable, as a whole, to the society which they wished to govern, and that which occurred under the auspices of Jefferson must therefore have taken place sooner or later. But their government at least gave the new republic time to acquire a certain stability, and afterwards to support without inconvenience the rapid growth of the very political creed of their opponents; and the Federal Constitution, which subsists at the present day, is a lasting monument of their patriotism and their wisdom.

(a) Quote the sentence that reveals de Tocqueville's opinion that the aristocratic Federalists could not have avoided being defeated as the country grew. **(b)** How was the Federalist era a "most fortunate incident," according to de Tocqueville?

Making Connections

1. Make a chart showing the advantages and disadvantages of Great Britain and the United States at the beginning of the War of 1812.
2. Make a map of the United States as it appeared in 1841. The map should show important land features, such as rivers and mountains, as well as the chief transportations routes, such as the National Road and the Erie Canal.
3. Write an article about Jefferson that might have appeared after his inauguration in the *National Intelligencer and Washington Advertizer,* a newspaper friendly to him.
4. Write a skit dramatizing an argument over the tariff question between a South Carolina planter and a northern cotton cloth manufacturer.

Reading in Depth

Akers, Charles W., *Abigail Adams: An American Woman* (New York: Little Brown). Biography of one of America's "founding mothers."

Cunliffe, Marcus, *The Nation Takes Shape: 1789–1837* (Chicago: University of Chicago Press). A standard history of this formative period in American history.

DeVoto, Bernard, *Journals of Lewis and Clark* (Boston: Houghton Mifflin).

Hale, Edward Everett, *A Man Without a Country* (Darby, Pennsylvania: Folcroft). The classic novel of a young officer involved in the Burr conspiracy.

Remini, Robert G., *The Revolutionary Age of Andrew Jackson* (New York: Harper and Row). A dramatic account of the times of Andrew Jackson.

St. George, Judith, *The Amazing Voyage of the New Orleans* (New York: G. P. Putnam's). An account of Nicholas Roosevelt's steamboat voyage down the Ohio and Mississippi River in 1811.

See list of Multimedia Materials in TMRG, p.TM79.
See Making Connections, text p. 389.

UNIT FOUR

The Rise of Sectionalism

The four decades between 1820 and 1860 were a time of tremendous growth in the United States. The frontier was pushed westward across the Great Plains and Rocky Mountains until it reached the Pacific Coast. Vast new tracts of land became United States territory as manifest destiny and land-hungry pioneers brought expanded national boundaries. Lines of Conestoga wagons (below, bottom) carried settlers, all their household belongings clattering in the back, across the continent to a new life. Roads, canals, and railroads (below, top), formed a transportation network that linked the growing nation. Along this transportation network flowed the raw materials and finished products of a strengthening economy as the Industrial Revolution rapidly transformed the United States.

CHAPTER 13 Building New Northern Industries

Changing Ways (1820's–1860's)

Trading
at the fair

By the 1840's the Industrial Revolution was moving steadily ahead in the United States. "I visited the . . . factory . . . at Waltham, within a few miles of Boston," Harriet Martineau, an English traveler, wrote of a trip she made in 1834–35. "Five hundred persons were employed at the time of my visit."

The Waltham textile plant was one of the largest in the country at the time. There were also many other factories, most of them only a few years old. The mills and factories were simple structures of wood, stone, or brick. They stood on the banks of rivers and streams and used the swiftly flowing water to provide power for their machines. Surrounding the factories were the small houses of the workers and the larger houses of the owners.

Particularly in the northeastern states, factories and the towns springing up around them were becoming an increasingly important part of American life by the 1840's. The growth of manufacturing towns was a clear sign that changes were beginning to alter life in the Northeast. These changes would, in time, affect the entire nation.

In Harriet Martineau's travels, she also saw other signs of change. She saw new roads connecting the towns with one another. She saw the building of new canals connecting river with river, lake with river, and lake with lake. She saw new railroads connecting the growing towns with one another, with the surrounding countryside, and with sea ports along the Atlantic coast. This growing transportation system reached across the Appalachian Mountains to the farms and towns in the western regions. The rapidly developing transportation system and the new mills and factories were part of the Industrial Revolution that was beginning to transform the United States from an agricultural to an industrial nation.

=== READING FOCUS ===

As you read about the changing ways that industrialism was bringing to the Northern States, look for the details that support each of the following statements.

1. Improved transportation unites the nation and stimulates business.
2. Wage earners help create the early industrial system.
3. Immigration swells the nation's rapidly growing population.

Improved transportation unites the nation and stimulates business

See Teaching Suggestions in TMRG, pp.TM80-81.

Without a good system of transportation, the United States could never have expanded westward to the Pacific coast. Just as the Constitution gave the American people a strong federal union of states, so roads, canals, and railways enabled Americans to work together to build their nation.

Roads and highways. The development of better roads and highways was well under way by the 1820's. Especially in the East, private companies had built hundreds of miles of good roads and turnpikes. To open up the western region, several state legislatures had financed the building of state-owned roads leading into the interior.

The most important road project was the National Road, started in 1811. Financed by the federal government, the National Road cut across state boundaries and progressed slowly westward. By 1853 it had reached almost to the Mississippi River (see map, page 271), and the federal government then turned the road over to the states.

By 1860, Americans could look with pride at the roads and highways that crisscrossed the eastern half of the nation. In 1790, according to estimates of the Bureau of the Census, there had not been a single important stretch of hard-surfaced road in the entire United States. By 1860 more than 88,000 miles (141,000 kilometers) of surfaced roads had been completed in the nation.

Effects of the roads. The developing network of roads changed the lives of many thousands of Americans. Farmers in the outlying parts of the eastern states and in the lands west of the Appalachian Mountains could at last buy and sell products in the city markets of the East. The roads were usually crowded with freight wagons and other traffic.

Although moving produce by wagon cost less than carrying it on the backs of horses or mules, wagon transportation still was quite expensive. In 1817, for instance, it cost $13 to transport a barrel of flour some 275 miles (440

▲ Throughout the Annotated Teacher's Edition, terms listed in the "Identify" portion of a Section Review are underscored the first time they appear. See the Teacher's Manual for each section for a listing of important vocabulary terms.

309

kilometers) from Pittsburgh to Philadelphia over one of the nation's best highways.

The Erie Canal. Canals were one answer to the demand for cheaper transportation. As early as the 1780's, leaders of New York State had urged that a canal be built between Albany and Buffalo to provide inexpensive water transportation from New York City to the Great Lakes.

Demand for the canal grew stronger when the National Road was started. New Yorkers saw that Baltimore would be connected to areas to the west by the only highway through the mountains. Baltimore might thus become the leading Atlantic port. Thoroughly alarmed, the New York legislature, acting under the leadership of Governor De Witt Clinton, authorized the building of the Erie Canal.

In 1817 the dirt began to fly in one of the major engineering feats in American history. When the canal was finished in 1825, a new waterway, 42 feet (12.8 meters) wide and at least 4 feet (1.2 meters) deep, stretched all the way westward from the Hudson River at Troy to Lake Erie at Buffalo (see map, this page).

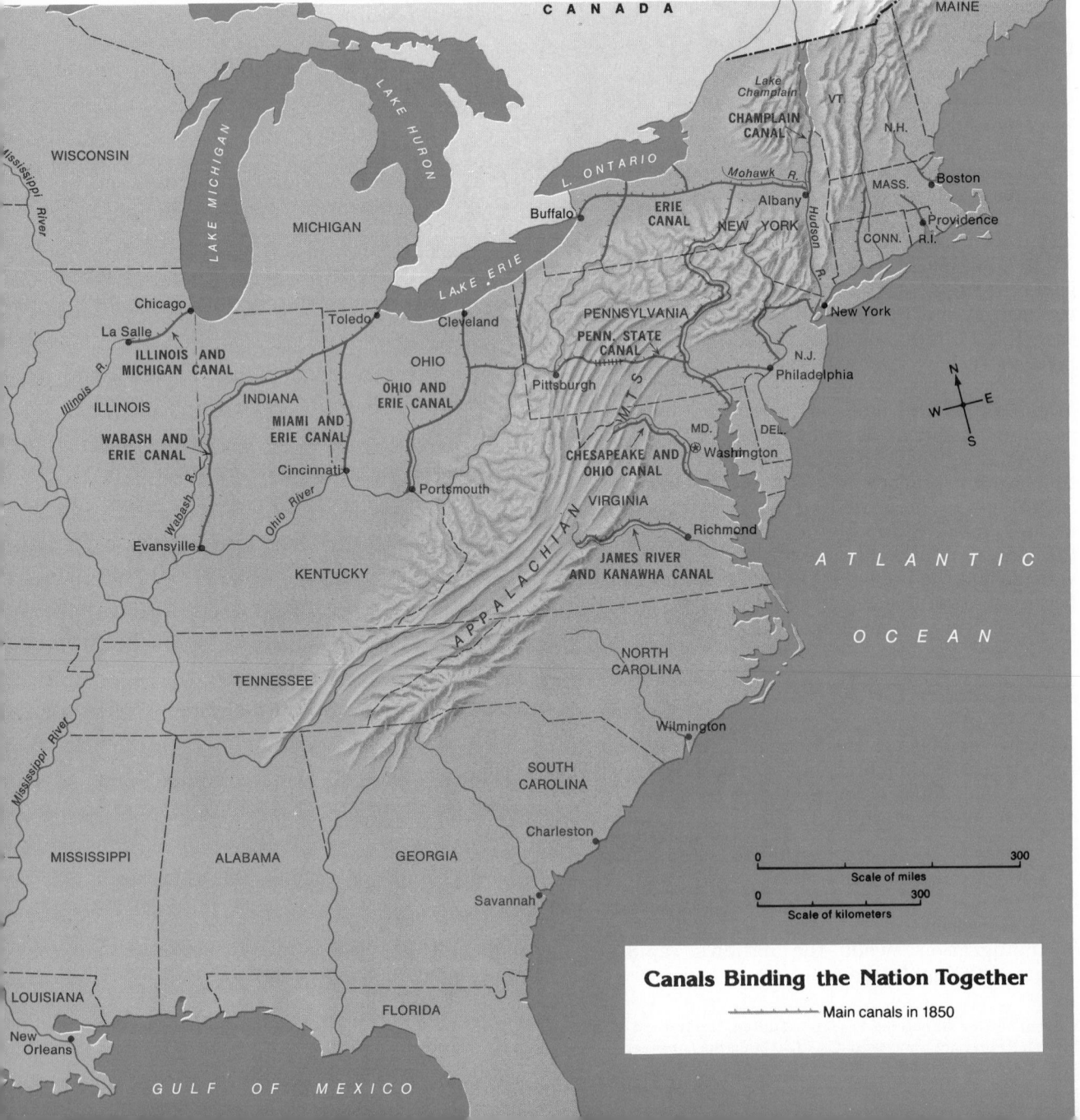

Canals Binding the Nation Together
—⊦—⊦—⊦— Main canals in 1850

By the 1850's railroad stations like this one at Stratford, Connecticut, were bustling with freight loading and passengers. Watching the trains come and go was an exciting pastime, especially for children (left).

The Erie Canal was an immediate success. Heavy barges were drawn through the water by ropes tied to horses and mules plodding along a towpath bordering the canal. Passengers rode in luxury barges with gaily colored curtains at the windows.

Cities began to grow along the canal route, among them Utica, Syracuse, and Rochester. New York City became the "gateway to the West" and the nation's leading commercial port. Its population doubled within ten years after the canal's opening. Cheap water transportation had done all this. Before the canal was built, transporting a ton of goods by road from Buffalo to New York cost more than $100. Now the same ton of goods could be carried through the canal and down the Hudson River for $5 to $10.

The canal-building era. As New York City investors made huge profits, business people in other commercial cities, such as Philadelphia and Baltimore, also began to build canals. By the 1830's canals were being dug throughout the country. When the depression of 1837 hit, more than 3,000 miles (4,800 kilometers) of canals had been built, most of them in the northern states. With the depression, however, the enthusiasm for canal building ended abruptly. This was partly because railroads were becoming important and partly because the states now were unable or unwilling to invest in canals. Several states failed to repay money that people had invested in canal bonds. Some states sold the state-owned canals to private companies. Others continued to operate the canals they had built, but for some

time, state development of transportation facilities ended.

River steamboats. Another essential link in the new transportation system was the steamboat, or steamer. Before 1800, inventors in both Europe and America had built steam-driven boats. In 1787, for example, a steamboat invented and built by John Fitch had made a successful trial run on the Delaware River. However, it was Robert Fulton's demonstration of the *Clermont* on the Hudson River in 1807 that first drew widespread attention.

Fulton and his business partners realized that huge profits could be earned in the western areas. Up to this time, as you know, riverboats could not navigate economically upstream. In 1811 Fulton and his partners built a steamboat at Pittsburgh and took it down the Ohio River to the Mississippi. Called the *New Orleans,* it ran successfully up and down the Mississippi until July 1814, when it ripped its hull on a snag near Baton Rouge, Louisiana, and sank. By this time, other enterprising people were building and operating steamboats. During the next 50 years, river steamers handled most of the traffic in the Mississippi Valley. Steamers threaded their way east and west to the growing villages and towns on the rivers flowing into the Mississippi. Other steamboats appeared on the Great Lakes.

Building railroads. Like the early roads and canals, the railroads grew out of commercial rivalry among the eastern cities. Baltimore led the way. Construction of the first section of the Baltimore and Ohio Railroad began on July 4,

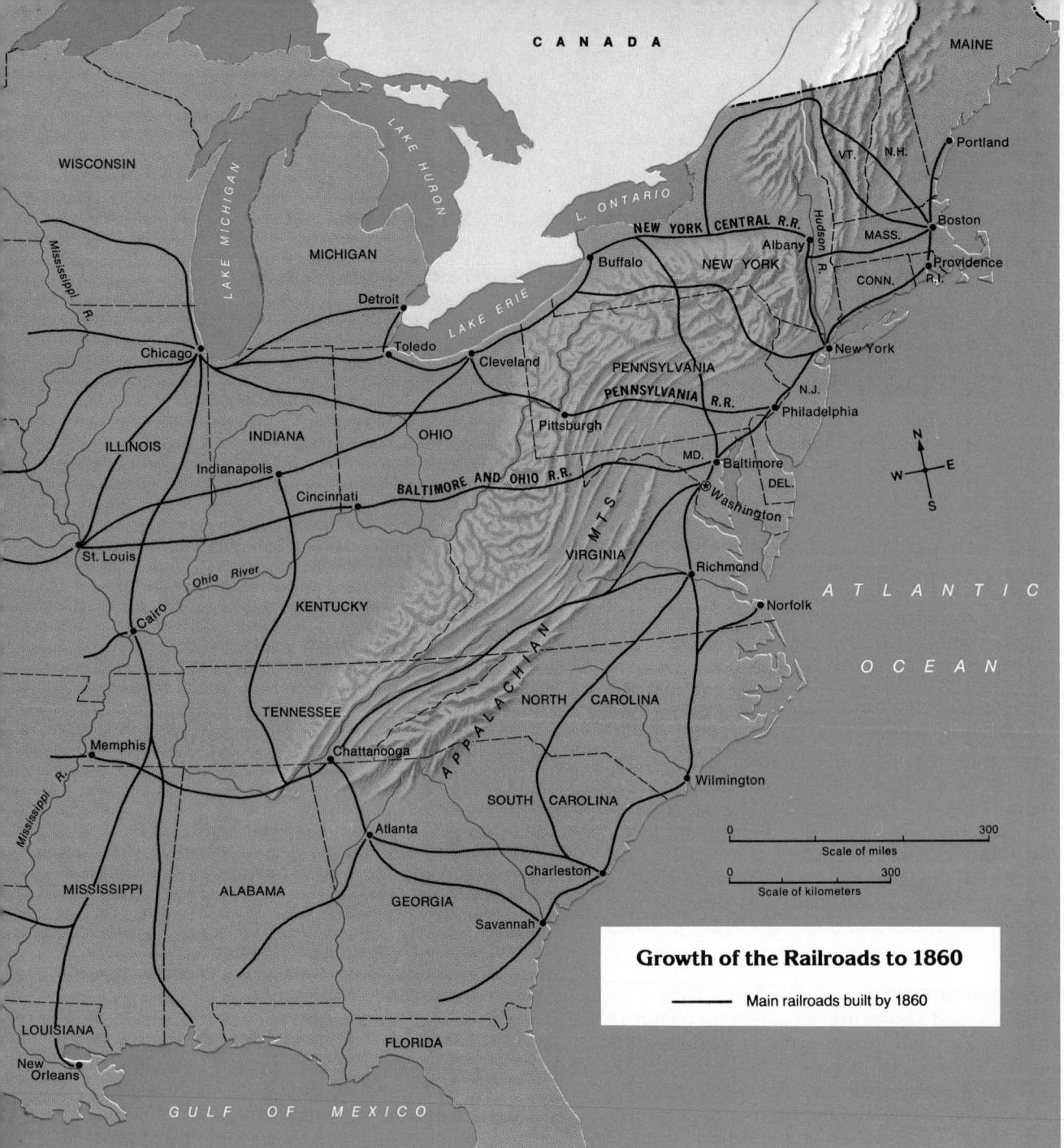

Growth of the Railroads to 1860

——— Main railroads built by 1860

1828, but there were few signs of the railroads' future success at that time.

The first locomotive on the Baltimore and Ohio—the *Tom Thumb*, built by Peter Cooper of New York—was a crude, undependable contraption. The rails were wooden timbers with thin strips of metal along the top. With much clanging of metal, the *Tom Thumb's* top speed was about 10 miles (16 kilometers) an hour.

Railroads soon made rapid progress despite violent opposition from the stagecoach lines. Seaports built rail lines into the interior. By 1833, merchants of Charleston, South Carolina, had financed a 136-mile (219-kilometer) railroad (see map, this page). At the time it was the longest railway line in the world under a single management. Boston, New York, and Philadelphia followed suit. By 1840, iron rails had replaced the early wooden rails, and greatly improved locomotives were operating over a network of nearly 3,000 miles (4,800 kilometers) of track. By 1860 some 30,000 miles (48,000 kilometers) of track linked the older eastern seaboard states with the western region as far as the Mississippi River (see map, page 312).

Effects of improved transportation. As each new stage of the transportation system was completed, new western areas were linked with the eastern seaboard. Eastern products moved west in ever-growing volume, stimulating the development of eastern industries.

The new means of transportation also spurred the development of the western regions. Pioneer settlers could now travel to these lands more easily than ever. Once settled, the pioneers could send their surplus crops to the eastern cities. The improved system of transportation brought the western farms and eastern factories closer together.

At the same time, western villages began growing into large towns and even cities. At first these communities served mainly as centers of trade between western farms and eastern factories. By 1860 the towns and cities in what is now called the Middle West were developing thriving industries of their own.

As the Industrial Revolution gained momentum, Americans built more and more mills and factories. Some were built in the South, and growing numbers sprang up in the Middle West, but most were located in New England and the Middle Atlantic states.

A growing nation. A protective tariff shielded the developing industries from foreign competition. They also benefited from an ever-expanding market area and from a rapidly growing population.

In 1790 the nation consisted of only 13 states, all located along the Atlantic seaboard. By 1860 the nation consisted of 33 states, eight of them west of the Mississippi River, including California and Oregon on the Pacific coast.

Over this same 70-year period, the population had grown from about 4 million to more than 31 million. The overwhelming majority of these people, like their parents and grandparents before them, earned their livelihood by farming. In 1840 nearly nine out of every ten Americans lived in rural areas.

The towns, however, were growing in number and in size. In 1790 there had been 24 towns and cities with more than 2,500 people. By 1860 there were 392 such towns and cities.

Investment of capital. Where did the money, or capital, invested in the new mills and factories come from?

Some of the necessary capital came from European investors, but much came from well-to-do Americans—especially merchants. During the years of the Embargo Act (1807–09) and the War of 1812, many Americans had money to invest. By 1820 about $50 million had been invested in manufacturing in the United States. The amount had risen by 1850 to $500 million. By 1860 it totaled more than $1 billion.

This money was used mainly to build small, individually owned factories or mills. The owner was often the manager, who hired and directed the workers and worked side by side with them. Sometimes larger businesses were organized as **partnerships**. In these, two or more persons shared ownership and operation of the business.

The merchant marine. While industry was growing, American ships were carrying American goods to all parts of the world. Even before 1800, Yankee sailing vessels had been familiar sights in the ports of China, Java, Sumatra, Siam (now Thailand), India, and the Philippines. The ships left their home ports with cargoes of beads, knives, gunpowder, cotton goods, pottery, and rum. Stopping at harbors in the Pacific Northwest, the captains traded these goods with the Indians for furs. The furs were then carried to China and sold. The returning vessels brought tea and other luxuries to the United States.

From the 1820's to the 1860's, ever larger and faster sailing ships were added to the American **merchant marine**, or commercial fleet. Americans carried on a flourishing trade with China and other Asian countries. By 1860, Americans had secured more than half of all the commerce to and from the great Chinese port of Shanghai and were trading along the Yangtze (YANG·tsee) River in China. American whalers were likely to appear for water and provisions in almost any port of the world (see map, pages 314–15).

Yankee traders were equally successful on the Atlantic. As early as 1824, they carried most of the traffic in passengers and freight

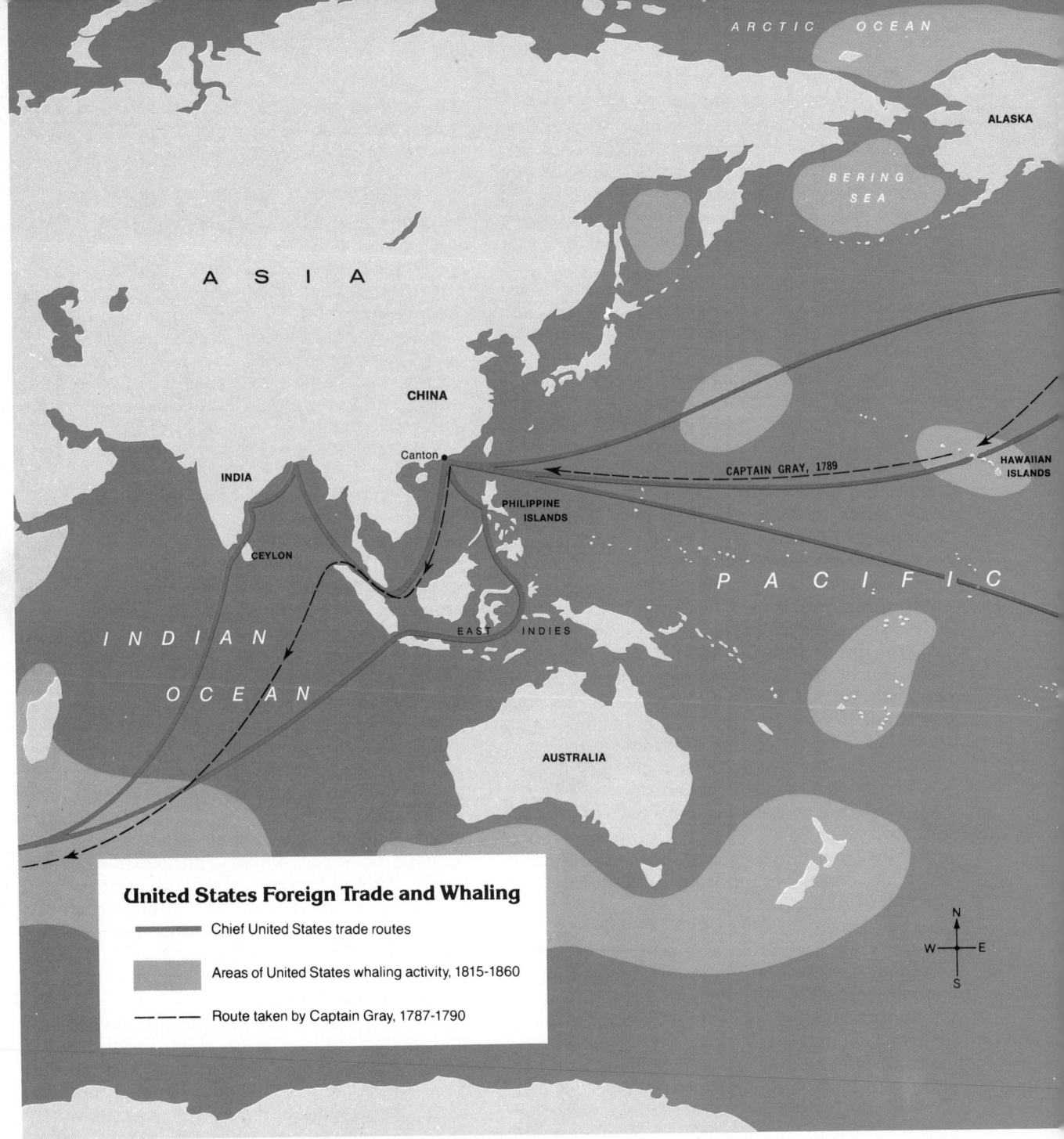

United States Foreign Trade and Whaling

— Chief United States trade routes

⬜ Areas of United States whaling activity, 1815-1860

- - - Route taken by Captain Gray, 1787-1790

between England and the eastern ports.

Clipper ships. During the 1840's and 1850's, the sailing ships of American merchants became world-famous. The celebrated <u>clipper</u> <u>ships</u> were the pride and glory of the seas, outdistancing every other ship afloat. The clippers made the run from China to New York in as little as 75 days. They captured the rich trade of the Orient from slower vessels that required

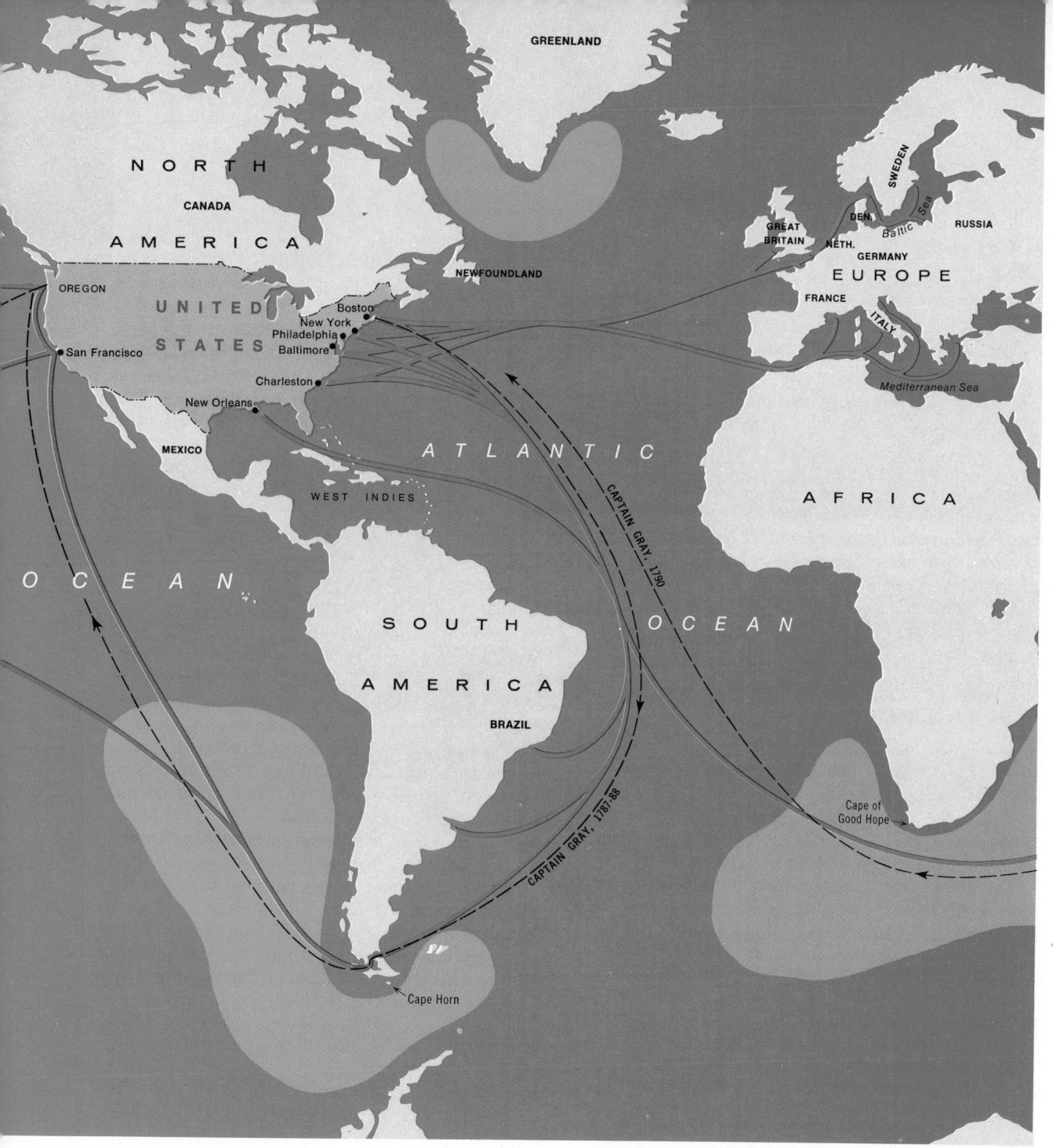

nearly a year to make the same journey. The activities of the merchant fleet kept American shipyards busy. The fortunes from commerce helped to pay for America's growing industries.

At this same time, the British, who had been outdistanced by the Yankee sailors and shipbuilders for 50 years, were busily building ocean-going steamships. By 1860, steamships had shown their superiority over sailing vessels. During the Civil War, American ship-

New England was the base for most American whaling expeditions. As shown in this painting, the whalers faced extreme danger in their quest for valuable whale oil.

owners lost much of their already dwindling business. Thereafter, the United States merchant marine declined until the 1900's.

SECTION REVIEW

See underscored items, text pp. 309 - 314.

Identify: National Road, Erie Canal, *Clermont, Tom Thumb*, partnership, clipper ship

For answers to questions, see Answer Key, p.A47.

1. **Summarizing Ideas:** (a) How did improved transportation affect the various regions of the nation? (b) Which section of the country do you think benefited the most from improvements in transportation? Explain.

2. **Organizing Ideas:** (a) What factors helped make the American merchant marine so successful between 1820 and 1860? (b) Why did it decline after 1860?

3. **Studying Maps:** Study the map on page 310. (a) List the canals shown on the map and the two points each canal connects. (b) What effects did the canal have on the cities at either end?

2 Wage earners help create the early industrial system

See Teaching Suggestions in TMRG, pp.81-82.

Manufacturers had to find workers to run the machines and do other work in the new factories. Where did they find these workers?

Early labor supply. Until about 1830 most wage earners were native-born American women and children. In 1816 there were 100,000 industrial workers; two out of three were women or girls. By 1822, women worked in over 100 industrial occupations. In 1831, children under 12 years of age made up about 40 percent of all the wage earners in the cotton textile mills of Rhode Island.

Why did so many women take jobs in industry? In New York and New England, one reason was the need of many farm families for greater income. Another reason was the desire of some women to escape the drudgery of farm work. As for the children, it was commonly believed that hard work, even hard industrial work, was good for children.

During the early 1800's, factory owners often contracted for the labor of an entire family. Advertisements similar to the following were frequently printed in the newspapers of the industrial towns: "Families Wanted—Ten or twelve good respectable families, consisting of four or five children each, from 9 to 16 years of age, are wanted to work in a cotton mill in the vicinity of Providence [Rhode Island]." Of course, employers also hired individual men and women to work in their factories.

Conditions of labor. The family system of labor seems harsh today, but it had certain ad-

Text continues on page 318.

 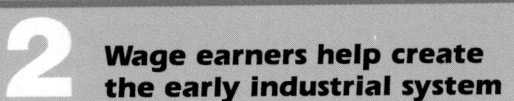 Report topic: Child labor laws in the state

On the morning of August 27, 1818, a momentous event occurred at the frontier town of Detroit. On that August morning, the very first steamboat to ply the waters of the Great Lakes puffed through the strait between Lakes St. Clair and Erie. The steamboat's name was *Walk in the Water,* and its home port was Buffalo, New York. On its voyage from Buffalo to Detroit, the new steamboat had maintained an average speed of 8 miles (13 kilometers) an hour. The arrival of the *Walk in the Water* was heralded as the beginning of a new era.

The Great Lakes — Superior, Michigan, Huron, Erie, and Ontario — are the largest group of freshwater lakes in the world. Together they have comprised the most important inland waterway in North America. They are the chief route used by the early explorers and settlers of the Northwest Territory. And as steamboats became increasingly efficient, the cheap transportation they offered turned the Great Lakes region into one of the most productive industrial areas of the nation.

The development of the Erie Canal (pages 310–11) dramatically improved commerce and quickly opened the Great Lakes country to pioneer settlement. Travelers on the canal boats probably complained of overcrowding, of poor food, and swarming mosquitoes, but they traveled westward cheaply and they carried their household goods with them. This new water route quickly became the most important route to the West. By the 1830's there were 75 new lake steamers. Competition had reduced the cost of deck passage from Buffalo to Detroit to just three dollars. A cheap, all-water route could take immigrants to the heartland of the continent.

The Great Lakes also provided a wonderful opportunity for farmers to get their crops to the populous eastern markets. By 1845 the total cost of shipping a bushel of wheat from Chicago to New York was just 25 cents. In that year nearly one million bushels (352,400 hectoliters) of wheat passed through the port of Buffalo. Many farmers in New England and the Middle States, working worn out land, joined the stream of immigrants headed for the Lake Plains.

The role of the Great Lakes in trade and transportation has certainly not been limited just to the opening of the Plain's rich farmlands. Ships sail from Great Lakes ports, more than 1,000 (1,600 kilometers) miles inland, to any other port in the world. This development has been made possible by a series of canals and locks built by both Canada and the United States. These canals and locks have corrected the differences in water levels among the lakes. For example, Lake Superior at the western end of the Great Lakes lies 600 feet (182 kilometers) above sea level. Lake Ontario at the eastern end is just 245 feet (75

Seaway locks

kilometers) above sea level. The Saint Lawrence Seaway, the name given to the route, opened in June, 1959. The Seaway allows ocean-going ships to sail all of the way from the Atlantic Ocean to Lake Superior.

The Great Lakes continue to offer the cheapest means for shipping the huge wheat crops of western Canada and the northern United States to flour mills in eastern Canada and Buffalo; the cargoes of iron ore to steel mills of northern Indiana, Ohio, and Pennsylvania; and a variety of raw materials and manufactured goods to markets throughout the United States and Canada. Those who proclaimed the arrival of *Walk in the Water* nearly 200 years ago as heralding a new era were prophetic beyond anyone's wildest dreams.

Buffalo, New York

vantages for the workers. The family was kept together instead of being split up to work in different towns. The work was not always difficult. Machinery ran much more slowly than it does today, and the children did the lighter tasks. In a textile mill, for example, children might mend broken threads or carry boxes containing bobbins, or spools. The hours were long —12 to 14 hours a day six days a week. Even so, the workdays were no longer than those on the farms during the seasons of planting and harvesting.

Conditions in Great Britain. Conditions in the factories of America at this time were generally better than in those of Great Britain, where the Industrial Revolution had advanced further. During the early 1800's, young children in Great Britain were taken from orphanages and poorhouses to do hard work in factories, mills, and mines. As late as 1830, a Parliamentary investigating committee reported that children only 8 and 9 years old were working from dawn to dusk under harsh, unhealthy conditions.

This report led Parliament in 1833 to pass a factory act, placing limits on the working hours of children. Over the years other laws helped to eliminate the worst evils of the British factory system.

One reason that conditions were better for American workers was that labor was more scarce in the United States than it was in Great Britain. Thus a ruthless employer would have difficulty hiring and keeping workers. Also, American workers could be lured from the factories by the vision of cheap, abundant land to the west. As a result, some employers honestly tried to provide good working conditions and decent treatment for their workers in order to keep them.

The Waltham system. A notable but short-lived experiment was begun at Waltham, Massachusetts, in 1813. Only persons of good character were employed in the Waltham textile plant. The women and girls lived in company-owned boarding houses, with matrons in charge to see that certain rules were observed. Employees were fired for lying, profanity, and laziness. All employees were required to attend church. Educational programs, lectures, debates, and social gatherings were organized for and by the workers. The factories at Waltham were clean and cheerful. There were flower boxes mounted at the windows and pictures hung above the looms.

The Waltham system spread to several other factories. For a while it worked well. Women and girls as well as men welcomed a chance to leave home and get at least a little "book learning," often unavailable on the farm. By 1840, however, the system began to break down. Many workers resented the supervision of almost every detail of their lives. Others objected to unduly long hours for low pay. As factories grew in size, employers began to hire immigrants, who had begun to stream into the country during the 1830's. The immigrants could usually be hired for lower wages.

Rising discontent. Although working conditions in American factories were generally better than those in Great Britain, by the 1830's and 1840's many American workers labored under extremely harsh conditions. Some workers were forced to toil as many as 16 hours a day in the dirty, crowded tenement areas of such cities as Boston, New York, and Philadelphia. Conditions were particularly depressing in the clothing industries. Its workers, mostly women and children, labored in lofts—the dark, dirty upper stories of buildings. Other women and children did sewing in their slum lodgings, receiving a tiny payment for each garment that they completed.

As time passed, the argument that hard work was good for children began to break down. More people, including some workers, demanded educational opportunities for children. They agreed that democracy could not work among illiterate people and that the chance to improve oneself required schooling. To meet these demands, some manufacturers opened Sunday schools and evening schools for the boys and girls, but such efforts were unsuccessful. Children who had worked long hours six days a week were in no condition to attend classes in their few hours of free time.

Early labor organizations. The wage earners felt a rising discontent with many features of the new industrial economy. Some skilled workers, especially bootmakers and printers, reacted by forming local workers' organizations. These organizations—the earliest American labor unions—tried to get higher wages and better working conditions for their members. Thus the growth of the labor movement accompanied the growth of industry.

"For the last last half a century, it has been deemed a violation of women's sphere to appear before the public as a speaker; but when our rights are trampled upon and we appeal in vain to legislators, what shall we do but appeal to the people?" Sarah G. Bagley's speech was typical of both her concerns and her tactics.

Sarah worked in a cotton mill and at first enjoyed her work. In 1840 she even wrote about the "Pleasures of Factory Life" for the *Lowell Offering,* a magazine put out by the female mill workers. When the mill owners began to speed up machine operations without either increasing wages or decreasing the 75-hour workweek, Sarah urged the women to form a union.

The Female Labor Reform Association was organized in 1845, and Bagley was elected president. A fiery and energetic speaker, she organized a petitition drive urging the Massachusetts legislature to pass a 10-hour workday. The legislature's failure to act, however, convinced Sarah Bagley that the time for a female labor organizer and political activist had not yet come. Taking a job as the first woman telegraph operator in the United States, she soon disappeared from public view.

The labor movement was especially active during the late 1820's and the early 1830's. By 1834, when representatives of labor met in their first national convention, there may have been as many as 300,000 organized workers in the United States. Also in 1834 a group of workers organized the National Trades Union. The National Trades Union never became powerful. Nevertheless it did represent a significant beginning for labor organizations and for labor philosophy.

The workers' demands. The workers' organizations made a number of demands, including higher wages and a ten-hour workday. The workers won partial success in 1840 when President Martin Van Buren established the ten-hour day for all government workers.

Most wage earners had other important goals in addition to shorter hours. Many workers wanted equality of educational opportunity. They also demanded an end to the common practice of putting persons who were not able to pay their debts into prison. By the early 1840's, nearly all of the states had ended this practice.

By the 1830's and 1840's, organized labor had become a new force in American life. Workers had begun to develop the idea of unions and of **collective bargaining**. This is bargaining between union representatives and employers over wages, hours, and working conditions. Unions had begun to develop other methods of trying to win their points as well. They used the **strike,** or the union members' refusal to work until their employers met their demands. They also used the **picket line,** or a group of union members marching outside a factory during a strike to persuade other workers not to take their jobs.

Problems of women workers. In 1824 more than 100 women mill workers joined in a strike of men workers in Rhode Island. Ten years later some of the young women in the mills at Lowell, Massachusetts, left their jobs to protest what they regarded as unfair treatment. In 1844 Sarah Bagley, a Lowell mill worker, organized the Lowell Female Labor Reform Organization. This group gathered signatures for a petition to the state legislature demanding a ten-hour day. The group also published a paper and organized branches in other mill towns.

The location of Lowell, Massachusetts, where two rivers, the Merrimack and the Concord, met made it a prime site for textile mills. Following the building of the first mill there, Lowell became one of the great textile centers in the country. This view shows several factories along the Merrimack.

Such efforts met with little success. When large-scale Irish immigration got under way in the 1840's, penniless Irish men and women had to take whatever wages they could get. Often factory owners paid barely enough for workers to survive on. Both immigrants and native-born women, whether working in mills and factories or doing piecework at home for the clothing industry, received lower wages than men. Often the wages they were paid were just above starvation levels.

Problems of black workers. The aims of the early labor unions did not include better working conditions for black workers. Since competition for jobs was often fierce, white workers resented the fact that blacks, to get jobs at all, often accepted lower wages.

White workers refused to work in the same shops and factories with blacks. Black workers were barred from membership in the trade unions. Excluded from the unions, black workers often served as <u>strikebreakers</u>. On rare occasions when white workers and black workers did agree to organize, the white workers insisted on separate unions.

Things were no better for black workers in the unskilled trades. During hard times blacks working at unskilled jobs in canal construction and railroad building were often fired and replaced by white workers.

Because of these conditions, resentment and bitterness on both sides led to labor riots in Philadelphia, New York, and other cities. In 1855, for example, violence erupted when black wage earners took the jobs of white dock workers on the New York City waterfront.

Weakness of organized labor. In these early years, the American labor movement was not yet strong enough to win many of the workers' demands. There were several reasons for this weakness.

In the first place, many wage earners did not realize that they formed a new and important group in the nation's economy and that they had interests in common. This was partly the result of tradition. Most Americans had been farmers, and the early factories and mills drew most of their labor supply from the farms. The Americans' strong spirit of independence and individualism made it hard to draw workers into labor unions. Wage earners continued to think of themselves as individuals who could look after their own interests.

In the second place, cheap land was always available. This cheap land did not actually attract many dissatisfied workers. Nevertheless, cheap land did draw westward thousands of farmers who might otherwise have turned to the cities for jobs.

In the third place, until 1842 labor unions

▲   Discussion topic: The effectiveness of labor unions today were not recognized by law. In that year the supreme court of Massachusetts decided in one case that labor unions had a legal right to exist in Massachusetts. This decision set a precedent, though not a strong one. Wage earners had to struggle in one state after another for the right to organize.

In the fourth place, the depression of 1837 threw thousands of men and women out of work. These unemployed workers could not afford to pay union dues. They usually had to accept any job they could get, regardless of what the job paid.

Finally, during the 1830's immigrants began to come to the United States in large numbers. Many of them were willing to work for low wages. Immigration, therefore, forced down the wages of many native-born American workers and almost brought the labor movement to a halt.

SECTION REVIEW

See underscored items, text pp. 318-20.

Identify: Waltham system, collective bargaining, strike, picket line, Sarah Bagley, strikebreaker

For answers to questions, see Answer Key, p.A47.

1. **Organizing Ideas: (a)** What groups made up most of the factory labor force during the early 1800's? **(b)** Why did workers begin organizing labor unions during the 1820's and 1830's? **(c)** What did these unions want? **(d)** Why were the early attempts to organize unions only partially successful?

2. **Comparing Ideas: (a)** In what ways was the situation of women workers different from that of men workers? **(b)** In what ways was it similar?

3. **Analyzing Ideas: (a)** How were black workers discriminated against in jobs and unions? **(b)** How were they used by employers to weaken the labor movement?

3 Immigration swells the nation's rapidly growing population

See Teaching Suggestions in TMRG, pp.TM82-83.

Between 1790 and 1830, the population of the United States increased from about 4 million to nearly 13 million. Nearly all of this growth resulted from births in the United States itself. During these years fewer than 400,000 immigrants entered the country.

In the 1830's, however, the small stream of immigration swelled to a great flood. From 1830 to 1840, more than half a million immigrants poured into the United States. Forty-four percent came from Ireland, 30 percent from Germany, 15 percent from Great Britain, and the remainder from other European countries. Between 1840 and 1850, a million and a half immigrants arrived in the United States, 49 percent of them from Ireland.

Irish immigrants. The Irish came to escape terrible conditions in their homeland. In Ireland during those years, many people worked as tenant farmers on the estates of landowners who lived in England. The landowners did little or nothing to improve the conditions of their tenants, who barely managed to make a living. Then, in 1846, a terrible famine struck Ireland. Thousands died during the "Potato Famine," as it was called. Other thousands fled across the Atlantic to America.

The people who left Ireland were attracted to the United States for several reasons. They liked what they had heard about American democracy. They were thrilled at the reports of plenty in the United States. Moreover, American contractors encouraged them to come and work on the roads, canals, and railroads. American manufacturers attracted them into the new mills and factories.

Hardships of immigration. The immigrants endured terrible hardships in reaching the United States. The following news item from the *Edinburgh Review* of July 1854 gives an idea of their sufferings: "Liverpool was crowded with emigrants. . . . The poor creatures were packed in dense masses in ill-ventilated and unseaworthy vessels, under charge of improper masters, and the natural result followed. Pestilence [disease] chased the fugitive to complete the work of famine. Fifteen thousand out of ninety thousand emigrants . . . in British bottoms [ships] in 1847 died on the passage or soon after arrival. The American vessels, owing to a stringent [strict] passenger law, were better managed; but the hospitals of New York and Boston were nevertheless crowded with patients from Irish estates."

Poor, unable to move to the western lands, many Irish immigrants found homes in the slums of such growing cities as New York, Boston, Albany, Baltimore, St. Louis, Cincinnati,

▲ The "Potato Famine" had its roots in Ireland's dependence on the potato for food. The 1845 - 46 famine was caused by a disease that destroyed the potato crop.

321

revolutions failed. Other Germans came to escape military service. Above all, they came to earn a better living.

Most German immigrants settled in the middle western states—Ohio, Indiana, Illinois, Wisconsin, Iowa, and Missouri. Able, thrifty farmers, they built prosperous farms. Many also settled in the cities. By the 1860's they formed large communities in such cities as Buffalo, Detroit, Cleveland, Cincinnati, Chicago, and St. Louis.

Immigrants resented. Most immigrants quickly became American citizens. Because many had come to the United States in search of political freedom, they helped to strengthen political democracy. Because they were eager to work, they contributed to the wealth of the growing nation. Despite these contributions, many native-born Americans resented the immigrants. They feared that large numbers of "foreigners" would change the older ways of living in America.

Some Germans, for instance, aroused suspicion because they organized their own clubs, gathered in social halls to talk and sing, established their own churches and schools, published their own newspapers, and continued to speak German. Many native-born Americans viewed these activities with misgivings.

The Irish became the chief targets of American resentment. Like many newcomers to a strange land, they tried to settle near their friends from the Old Country. As a result, growing numbers of Irish people settled in the cities. Many dressed as they had in Ireland. Their accent sounded strange to other Americans. Many native-born Protestants disliked the Irish immigrants simply because most of them were Roman Catholics. Because the Irish were "different" in these and other ways, some Americans at first looked upon the newcomers with suspicion. Suspicion of this kind unfortunately has been the fate of every large immigrant group.

Resentment against the immigrants often led to friction and violence. Riots broke out in several cities. As more immigrants arrived, resentment against them increased. In 1845 a national organization of native-born Americans was started. A year later, this society was reorganized as a secret order called the Supreme Order of the Star-Spangled Banner or the Sons of the Sires of '76. Members solemnly promised to oppose foreigners and to support

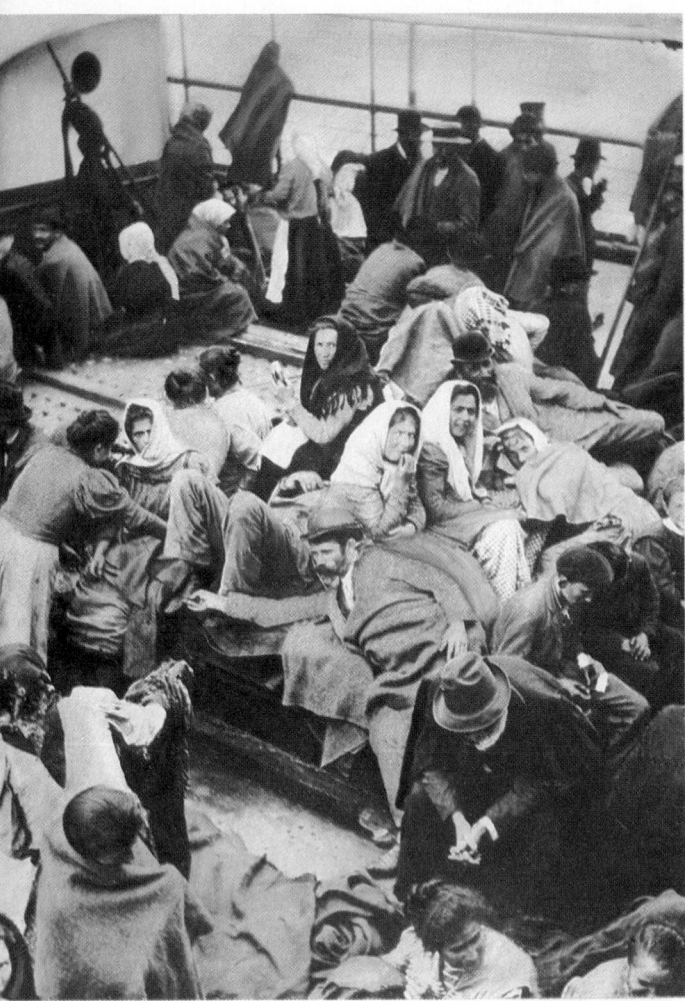

Millions of immigrants came to America in search of a better life. Many of these immigrants faced overcrowded and unsanitary conditions on the voyage from Europe.

and New Orleans. Many Irish men went to work as unskilled laborers on roads, canals, and railroads. Many Irish women took jobs in factories, where they displaced native-born American wage earners.

German immigrants. Germans formed the second largest group of immigrants. Between 1845 and 1860, more than 1.3 million Germans landed in the United States.

Many Germans came because, after 1815, Europe (and the German states in particular) was controlled by rulers who opposed democracy. Thousands of Germans who rebelled against political oppression fled when their

For more than 16 million immigrants who entered the United States between 1892 and 1943, Ellis Island was their first glimpse of America. As the nation's chief immigration station for half a century, the tiny island in New York Harbor was viewed by many immigrants with both fear and exultation. They nicknamed it the "island of tears," and with good reason. For every ten persons who landed at Ellis Island, two were refused admission to the United States.

All immigrants were required to pass a medical examination, and many persons were turned away because they were too old or too ill. Those who passed the examination were then questioned by immigration inspectors. Immigrants who had prison records were immediately disqualified, as were persons who had no money or sponsors in the United States. The unfortunate persons who did not meet medical and immigration standards were put on ships to be transported back to their own countries.

From 1943 to 1954, Ellis Island served as a detention station for aliens and deportees. In 1965 it became part of the Statue of Liberty National Monument. Today both are being restored. Together with the Statue of Liberty, Ellis Island continues to symbolize the pain and joy of the American immigrant experience.

only American-born Protestants for public office. When asked about the society, members would answer, "I know nothing." Because of such answers, the organization came to be known as the Know-Nothing Party.

During the early 1850's, the Know-Nothing Party, by now officially called the American Party, was very strong in American political life. In the election of 1854, it polled one fourth of the total vote of New York and two fifths of Pennsylvania's vote. In Massachusetts it elected every state officer and nearly the entire legislature. However, the election of 1854 was the high tide of the movement. In the national convention of the Know-Nothing Party in 1855, southern members and northern members split over the question of slavery. As a result of this split, the Know-Nothing Party gradually lost its strength.

Changing ways of life. From the 1830's to the 1860's, familiar, traditional ways of American life were replaced by new and unfamiliar ways. Most older Americans did not realize that machines, factories, and an **urban**, or city,

way of life were causing the revolution taking place around them. Immigrants were only one of many new elements in the changing pattern of American society. However, many native-born Americans blamed all their troubles, both real and imaginary, on the flood of new immigrants.

SECTION REVIEW

See underscored items, text pp. 321, 323.

Identify: Potato Famine, Know-Nothing Party, urban

For answers to questions, see Answer Key, pp.A47-48.

1. **Synthesizing Ideas: (a)** What conditions led the Irish to immigrate to the United States? **(b)** Where did they settle? Why?

2. **Analyzing Ideas:** Why did some native-born Americans resent the immigrants?

3. **Summarizing Ideas: (a)** What was the major aim of the Know-Nothing Party? **(b)** How successful was it in achieving this aim?

4. **Organizing Ideas:** What were some things that were causing changing ways of life from the 1830's to the 1860's?

DEVELOPING HISTORY STUDY SKILLS

Writing About History Formulating a Thesis Statement

Section 1 of this chapter begins in this fashion.

> "Without a good system of transportation, the United States could never have expanded westward to the Pacific coast."

This statement expresses the main idea of the section. As such it is called a thesis statement. It serves the same function as the topic sentence of a paragraph, expressing as it does the main idea of the section.

Many times in the course of your studies you are called upon to express your thoughts in writing. Most of the time you have questions for which you express answers. Or the teacher has prepared a list of thesis statements ahead of time from which you make a choice. But the time will arise, if it has not already risen, when you are required to write an essay about any topic of your choice. Then before you can write your essay, you must formulate a thesis statement.

How to Formulate a Thesis Statement

Follow these steps as you formulate a thesis statement.

1. **Choose a topic of interest.** Begin to collect facts about the general topic, keeping good notes.

2. **Begin to narrow the topic.** Look for related facts. Make a generalization based on the related facts. The narrowing of the topic may take place in stages as you gather more facts and acquire more information about your area of interest.

3. **Organize the collected facts.** Discard those facts that have no bearing on the general statement or narrow the statement even further to include the facts.

4. **Formulate the thesis statement.** Refine the generalization, turning it into a thesis statement that can be fully proven by the collected facts.

Applying the Skill

Read the following facts about the Presidency of Andrew Jackson. As you read, think about a general statement that might be made about Jackson's Presidency based on these facts.

- During Jackson's administration, the right to vote was extended to more Americans.

- Nominating conventions brought more and more people into the electoral process.

- Women, however, still had no direct political role in government during Jackson's Presidency.

- Blacks, too, had no political power.

- Indians were not citizens of the nation.

- The Cherokee Indians were removed from their homeland against their wills during Jackson's administration.

The facts all relate to democracy and citizenship during Jackson's Presidency. The first two statements indicate extensions of democracy, but the last four statements refer to gaps in the extension of democracy. Based on these facts one could say that the Jackson administration helped to promote the growth of democracy in the United States. One cannot say, however, that democracy had become a reality for all Americans. Thus a possible general statement relating all these facts might be: Though there were limits to Jacksonian Democracy, the period helped to advance democracy in the United States. Another way of formulating this general statement, thus turning it into a thesis statement is: During the Jacksonian Period, democracy advanced for white males but not for women, blacks, and Indians.

Practicing the Skill

Review the general development of industry in the 1840's in the United States and the role that the Lowell factory model played. Also read the two excerpts on page 325. After collecting your facts, draw up a general, or thesis, statement on the Lowell factory model. Write the statement on a separate sheet of paper.

Regulations of the Manufacturing Company

Every overseer is required to be punctual himself, and to see that those employed under him are so.

*****

The overseers may, at their discretion, grant leave of absence to those employed under them, when there are sufficient spare hands in the room to supply their place; but when there are not sufficient spare hands, they are not allowed to grant leave of absence unless in cases of absolute necessity.

*****

All persons are required to board in one of the boardinghouses belonging to the company, and conform to the regulations of the house in which they board.

*****

All persons are required to be constant in attendance on public worship, at one of the regular places of worship in this place.

*****

Persons who do not comply with the above regulations will not be employed by the company.

*****

Persons entering the employment of the company are considered as engaging to work one year.

*****

All persons intending to leave the employment of the company are required to give notice of the same to their overseer, at least two weeks previous to the time of leaving.

*****

Anyone who shall take from the mills, or the yard, any yarn, cloth, or other article belonging to the company will be considered guilty of stealing, and prosecuted accordingly.

*****

The above regulations are considered part of the contract with all persons entering the employment of the Manufacturing Company. All persons who shall have complied with them, on leaving the employment of the company, shall be entitled to an honorable discharge, which will serve as a recommendation to any of the factories in Lowell. No one who shall not have complied with them will be entitled to such a discharge.

Memories of a Factory Girl, 1898

I had been to school constantly until I was about ten years of age, when my mother, feeling obliged to have help in her work besides what I could give, and also needing the money which I could earn, allowed me, at my urgent request (for I wanted to earn money like the other little girls), to go to work in the mill. I worked first in the spinning-room as a "doffer." The doffers were the very youngest girls, whose work was to doff, or take off, the full bobbins, and replace them with the empty ones.

I can see myself now, racing down the alley, between the spinning-frames, carrying in front of me a bobbin-box bigger than I was. These mites had to be very swift in their movements, so as not to keep the spinning frames stopped long, and they worked only about fifteen minutes in every hour. The rest of the time was their own, and when the overseer was kind they were allowed to read, knit, or even to go outside the mill-yard to play.

Some of us learned to embroider in crewels, and I still have a lamb worked on cloth, a relic of those early days, when I was first taught to improve my time in the good old New England fashion. When not doffing, we were often allowed to go home, for a time, and thus we were able to help our mothers in their housework. We were paid two dollars a week; and how proud I was when my turn came to stand up on the bobbin-box, and write my name in the paymaster's book, and how indignant I was when he asked me if I could write. "Of course I can," said I, and he smiled as he looked down on me.

The working hours of all the girls extended from five o'clock in the morning to seven in the evening, with one-half hour for breakfast and for dinner. Even the doffers were forced to be on duty nearly fourteen hours a day, and this was the greatest hardship in the lives of these children. For it was not until 1842 that the hours of labor for children under twelve years of age were limited to ten per day; but the "ten-hour law" itself was not passed until long after some of these little doffers were old enough to appear before the legislative committee on the subject, and plead, by their presence, for a reduction of the hours of labor.

The Industrial Revolution gained momentum throughout the United States during the early 1800's. Textile mills, ironmaking plants, and other industrial establishments appeared in the South. The major industrial developments, however, took place in New England, New York, Pennsylvania, and the growing cities of the Middle West. The new industries in the North and the Middle West attracted many immigrants, who found jobs in railroad building, industry, and farming.

Industrial towns and cities with their factories, their whirring machines, and their manufacturers, financiers, and wage earners became a major influence in America. Industrialism strengthened democracy in several ways. First, it provided people with new and different ways of earning a living. Second, it put money in people's pockets, enabling them to buy goods never before available to them and raising their standards of living. Third, it produced a greater array of goods than ever before and produced them more efficiently and more cheaply. Finally, it strengthened national unity by binding the nation together with a network of roads, canals, and railroads.

Industrialism also created new problems. Wage earners, more and more dependent for their pay upon forces beyond their individual control, began to join together in labor unions. Conflict between workers and owners became increasingly common. Finally, industrialism transformed the North into a new and distinct section of the country. In the process, serious differences between the North and the South were created.

CONNECTING CHAPTER IDEAS

In the next chapter you will read about the development of the South's economy. Cotton became King in the South. Planters kept their positions of power. They insisted on retaining slavery, recognizing that slaves played leading roles in the maintenance of the South's economy.

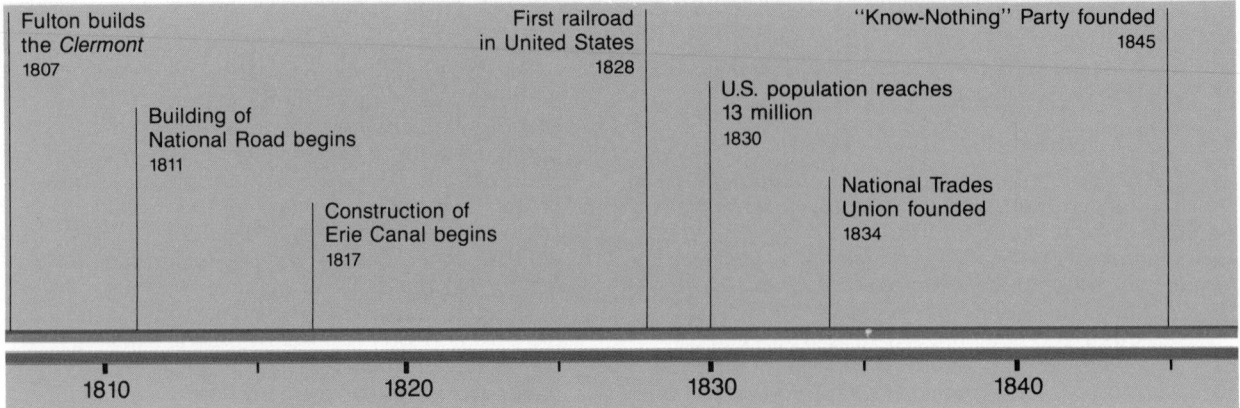

Fulton builds
the *Clermont*
1807

Building of
National Road begins
1811

Construction of
Erie Canal begins
1817

First railroad
in United States
1828

U.S. population reaches
13 million
1830

National Trades
Union founded
1834

"Know-Nothing" Party founded
1845

1810   1820   1830   1840

CHAPTER

13 REVIEW

Reviewing Important Terms

Decide whether each of the following sentences is true or false. If the sentence is false, replace the underlined term with the word or phrase that will make it true.

1. During the 1840's and 1850's American clipper ships were able to sail from China to New York in as little as 75 days.
2. With the development of steamships and the coming of the Civil War, the United States merchant marine declined until the 1900's.
3. The factory system began to break down by 1840, in part because workers resented the supervision of almost every detail of their lives.
4. Collective bargaining between union representatives and employers emerged as an idea by the 1830's and 1840's.
5. Striking workers used picket lines outside factories to persuade other workers not to take their jobs.
6. A new urban way of life contributed to a revolution in the way Americans lived from the 1830's to the 1860's.

Practicing Critical Thinking Skills

1. **Analyzing Ideas.** The development of better methods of transportation was as important in uniting the country as the Constitution itself. Do you agree or disagree with this statement? Explain your answer.
2. **Synthesizing Ideas.** The growth of labor unions paralleled the growth of industry. Explain this statement.
3. **Seeing Relationships.** Explain the connection between immigration and industrialization during the period from the 1820's to the 1860's.
4. **Comparing Ideas. (a)** Compare the reasons for immigration during colonial times with the reasons for immigration during the period 1830–50. **(b)** Why did native-born Americans blame immigrants for many of their troubles?
5. **Interpreting Ideas. (a)** Why would immigrants tend at first to keep their old ways of life? **(b)** Why would preserving old ways of life lead to resentment against immigrants? **(c)** Would the children and grandchildren of immigrants be as likely to follow the old ways? Why or why not?

6. **Determining Cause and Effect. (a)** In what ways did industrialization strengthen democracy and unite the nation? **(b)** In what ways did it promote sectionalism?
7. **Relating Past to Present.** How is the federal government today continuing to improve transportation begun in the early 1800's? Compare the nation's transportation needs today with those of the earlier period.

Developing History Study Skills

1. **Formulating a Thesis Statement.** Turn to pages 220–21. Review the outline for Unit Three, noting the unit title, the titles for each chapter in the unit, the illustrations, and the introduction. Formulate a thesis statement for an essay covering the topics of Unit Three.
2. **Using Maps.** Look closely at the map on pages 314–15. **(a)** Locate three areas where American sailors hunted for whales during the 1800's. **(b)** What products did the United States buy from China in exchange for furs? **(c)** Using the colonial trade map on page 104, explain ways in which American trade had changed since colonial times. Also explain why it had changed.

Relating Geography and History

The economy of the West was given a boost when the National Road was completed. The road, also called the Cumberland Road, was begun in Cumberland, Maryland in 1811. By 1853, the road had almost reached the Mississippi River—a distance of 591 miles (947 kilometers). In order to understand the significance of the National Road, complete the following activities.

1. Draw a map showing the National Road and the cities through which it passed.
2. On a separate sheet of paper, write a brief statement showing how each of the following was an improvement over conditions that existed before the National Road was completed. **(a)** Freight carrying became easier and cheaper, **(b)** more European immigrants moved to the West, **(c)** cities grew larger, **(d)** and land values increased.
3. Use a present-day road map to discover which of today's highways follows most nearly the path of the National Road.

327

See Chapter Overview in TMRG, p.TM84.
See Chapter Objectives in TMRG, p.TM84.
See Introducing the Chapter in TMRG, p.TM84.

CHAPTER 14

Creating a Southern Economy

Changing Ways (1820's–1860's)

Inspecting cotton

"Cotton is king" was an expression heard often in the South during the 1840's and 1850's. The expression indicated the importance attached to cotton by a great majority of the people living in the southern states. Indeed, by the 1850's the cotton grown, shipped, and sold by southerners was worth more than all the rest of the nation's exports put together.

In attaching importance to "King Cotton," southerners were not thinking of themselves alone. They knew that countless other people—in the northern states, in Europe, and around the world—depended upon southern cotton for a living. Merchants who traded and shipped cotton and sailors who manned the ships depended on cotton. Owners of cotton textile factories and the workers in them gained a living from cotton. Storekeepers and traders who sold cotton goods wherever they could find buyers—in the United States, in Europe, in Africa, in India—were dependent on cotton for a living.

Southerners could ask in the 1840's and 1850's, "What other product grown on the land and fashioned into finished articles affects so many people in so many different parts of the world?" The answer was "None."

Great changes had taken place in the southern states since the 1790's. When the Constitution was adopted, tobacco, not cotton, had been the most important southern crop. At that time, also many people in the South as well as in the North had thought that slavery would eventually disappear in the United States.

In the 1850's with King Cotton holding sway over the southern economy, nearly 4 million black slaves lived and worked in the South. The South, with its system of slave labor and its dependence on cotton as a cash crop, was becoming increasingly different from the industrial North.

READING FOCUS

As you read about the changing ways of the South's Cotton Kingdom, look for the details that support each of the following statements.

1. The southern states develop into the Cotton Kingdom.
2. The planters control the positions of power.
3. The slaves play leading roles in the development of the South

1 The southern states develop into the Cotton Kingdom

See Teaching Suggestions in TMRG, pp. TM84-85.

The southern states, by the 1840's and 1850's, covered a vast area stretching southward from Maryland and the Ohio River to the Gulf of Mexico. Louisiana, Arkansas, and Texas were also part of this great region.

The farm lands. Travelers in the South at this time were most impressed by the endless cotton fields, but they also saw many other **staple crops,** including tobacco, rice, and sugar cane. In Virginia, North Carolina, Kentucky, Tennessee, and Missouri, where the climate and soil were most favorable for tobacco growing, the fields were green with broad, flat tobacco leaves. Rice fields flourished in the swampy coastal areas of South Carolina and Georgia. To the west, in the delta of the Mississippi River, sugar cane ripened in the warm winds that swept in from the Gulf of Mexico. Travelers in Virginia might see large fields of wheat and corn. In Texas they could see herds of long-horned cattle.

Southerners received much of their cash income from their staple crops—mainly cotton, tobacco, rice, and sugar cane. Most of these staple crops were grown on plantations. However, travelers in the South in the 1850's also saw many small **subsistence farms,** much like those in the Northeast and Middle West. On these farms families raised corn and other food crops and livestock largely for their own use.

Towns and industries. Since the southern economy depended mainly on agriculture, industries and towns grew more slowly in the South than in the North. But the southern states had many towns and a few important cities, among them Richmond, Virginia; Charleston, South Carolina; and New Orleans, Louisiana.

The southern towns and cities had their shopkeepers, skilled workers, and professional people—doctors, lawyers, ministers, and teachers. Along the wharves and on the streets, visitors could see sawmills, paper mills, brickyards, leather tanneries, foundries, turpentine and whisky distilleries, and cotton mills.

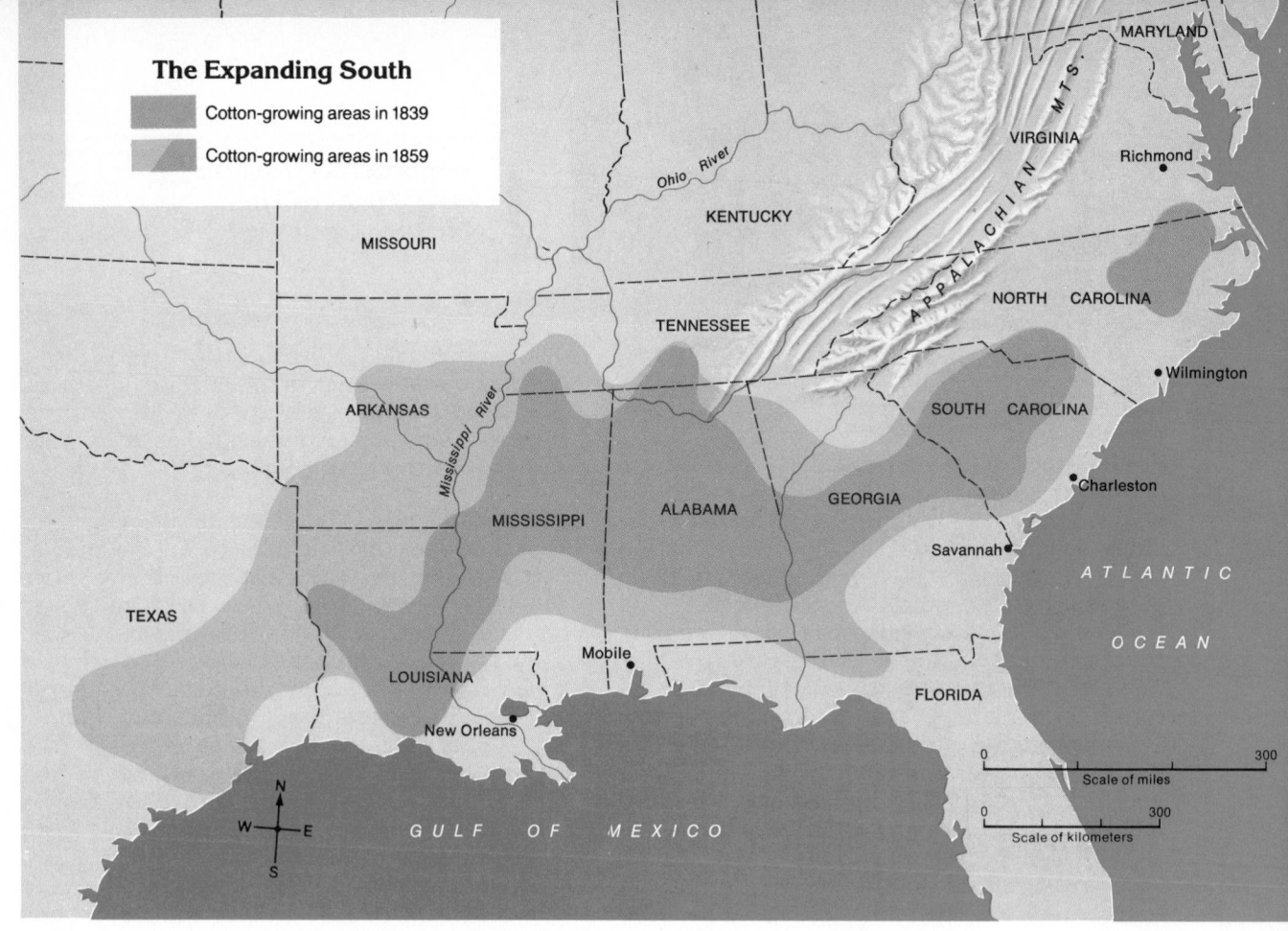

By 1860 about 10,000 miles (16,000 kilometers) of railroad tracks had been laid throughout the southern states. Along the rivers and coastlines, hundreds of steamboats carried the South's staple crops to northern and European markets. On return trips they brought manufactured goods to the South.

By the 1850's some leading southerners were urging further development of southern industry and commerce. The southern economy, in short, was varied and complex, but southerners never lost sight of the reality that "cotton is king."

The growing cotton economy. In the late 1700's, as you know, British investors developed power-driven machinery for spinning thread and weaving cloth. Before long, textile mills were operating in the New England and the Middle Atlantic states. The new mills consumed ever larger amounts of raw cotton fiber. To meet the growing demand, Southern farmers and plantation owners raised more cotton. This brought them face to face with a problem

that threatened to slow the further development of the cotton economy.

The problem centered in the cotton plant itself. The heart of the plant, called the boll, is a tangle of fibers and seeds. These had to be separated before the cotton could be used. When done by hand, this was a slow and therefore expensive process, even with slave labor.

Eli Whitney, who also invented interchangeable gun parts, solved the problem. In 1793 he invented the **cotton gin,** a machine that separated the seeds from the cotton fiber. Before this invention, a man or woman working a full day could at best separate by hand only a few pounds of fiber. Whitney's cotton gin, when operated by power, could separate more than 1,000 pounds (450 kilograms) a day!

More and more southern farmers now began to raise and sell cotton, first in Georgia and South Carolina and later in the rich soils of the Gulf Coast states and the Mississippi Valley (see map, this page). Big 500-pound (226.8-kilogram) bales of raw cotton fiber were shipped in ever greater quantities to the textile

Humorless, logical, and sincere, John C. Calhoun was extremely intelligent and a powerful debater. In all, he served the people of the United States for almost 40 years. He began his career as a nationalist. He ended his career as a sectionalist and a key leader of the South's cause before the Civil War.

Calhoun began his career in 1810 as a member of the House of Representatives. He served as Secretary of War under James Monroe, and was elected Vice President under John Quincy Adams in 1824 and again under Andrew Jackson in 1828.

By 1828, Calhoun had shifted from his nationalist position to a states' rights position. The imposition of the high tariff of 1828 on manufactured goods had hurt South Carolina and other southern agricultural states. To justify a state's resistance to the law, Calhoun worked out a theory — *The South Carolina Exposition and Protest.* The theory was put into practice in 1832 when South Carolina nullified the tariffs of 1828 and 1832.

Calhoun's stand on states' rights — as well as several personal disputes with Jackson — made it impossible for him to remain as Vice President. He resigned in 1832 after winning election to the United States Senate.

In 1850 Calhoun took part in the Senate debate on the issue of slavery in the territories. Calhoun opposed Henry Clay's compromise, fearing the consequences for the South if slavery in the territories was forbidden. Exhausted and ill, he had his speech read by another senator. In his speech, he urged the Senate to adopt "such measures as will satisfy the States belonging to the Southern section, that they can remain in the Union consistently with their honor and their safety." John C. Calhoun did not live to see the outcome of the debate or the war that followed the South's secession from the Union.

mills of New England, the Middle Atlantic states, and Great Britain.

The cloth woven on the looms of the American and British mills went to clothing manufacturers. Soon ready-made dresses, shirts, and trousers were being sold in worldwide markets.

In 1791 total American production of cotton fiber had been only 4,000 bales. By 1830 it had jumped to 732,000 bales. In 1860 the figure stood at more than 4 million bales, two thirds of the world's total production of cotton. Cotton alone represented about two thirds of the value of the entire nation's exports in the year 1860.

The cotton-growing area expands. From 1800 to 1860, southern prosperity increasingly depended on cotton. Textile manufacturers paid high prices for the supply that was often too small to meet their needs.

As the demand for cotton increased, the rich soils of the Gulf Coast states and the Mississippi Valley attracted cotton growers. Many southerners moved west, cleared the soil, and started cotton plantations. Thus, by 1845, the states of Louisiana, Mississippi, Alabama, Arkansas, Florida, and Texas were added to the original southern states.

Cotton Production • 1800 - 1860

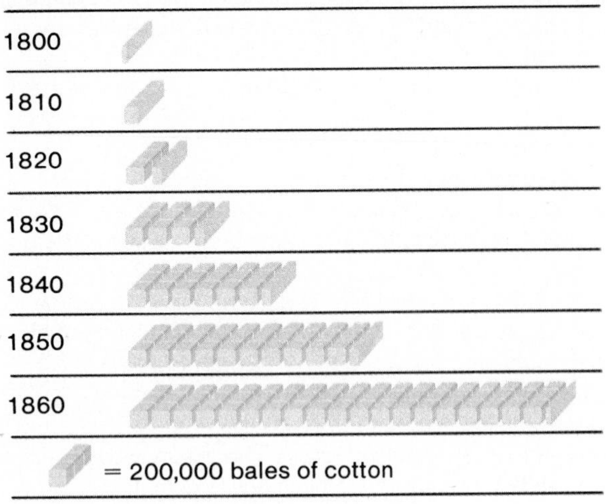

Year	
1800	
1810	
1820	
1830	
1840	
1850	
1860	

= 200,000 bales of cotton

Slave Population • 1800 - 1860

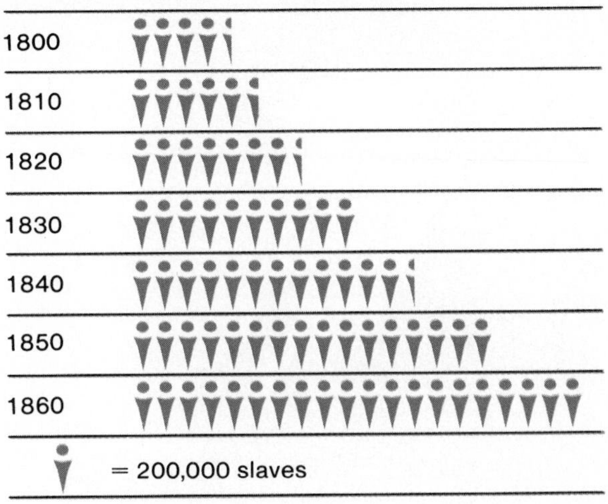

Year	
1800	
1810	
1820	
1830	
1840	
1850	
1860	

= 200,000 slaves

By the late 1850's, the cotton economy had reached the height of its power. The cotton lands, or cotton belt, stretched in a long crescent from North Carolina in the east to Texas in the west (see map, page 330). Travelers journeying in the fall along the dusty roads throughout the region saw the major wealth of the South in every field. Ripe cotton bolls shone white in the hot sunlight, ready to be picked, cleaned of seed, packed in bales, and shipped to mills in New England and Great Britain.

Growth of population. During the first half of the 1800's, the Cotton Kingdom grew in population as well as in area. By 1860 the population of the South had risen to approximately 12 million. About 4 million were black slaves. The rest were, for the most part, descendants of pre-Revolutionary settlers. They were mostly of English and Scotch-Irish ancestry, although many people of French origin lived in the coastal plains of the Carolinas and around New Orleans. Also, groups of Germans had started settlements in Texas.

On the whole, though, European immigrants were not attracted to the South. Up to this time, most of the immigrants to the United States had come from countries of northern Europe, like Ireland and Germany. The climate and ways of living in the northern states were more familiar to them than were the warmer climate and ways of living in the South. Of the more than 4 million immigrants living in the United States by 1860, only 13.5 percent lived in the southern states.

Southern social groups. In the South, as in other parts of the country, the population was divided into a number of social and economic groups. Except for the slaves, who had no opportunity to better their lot, energetic and ambitious people continually moved from lower to higher economic groups. In the words of one southern historian, a family could mount "from log cabin to plantation mansion on a stairway of cotton bales."

Who were the men and women who built the Cotton Kingdom? What were the major social and economic groups to be found in the South in 1860?

The slaves. From the day they first arrived in the New World, the slaves were at the bottom of the social and economic ladder. In 1790, when the new nation was in its first year under the Constitution, there were about 700,000 slaves and 60,000 free blacks in the original thirteen states. Their numbers increased rapidly. By 1820 the slave population had more than doubled. By 1840 more than half of the men, women, and children in Mississippi were slaves. In that year the proportion of slaves to free people was almost as high in Alabama and Louisiana.

By 1860 the total slave population had reached roughly 4 million. Of this total population, about 500,000 lived and worked in towns and cities. The rest, about 3.5 million, worked on farms and plantations.

As white planters moved from the older southern states into the rich new cotton areas of the Gulf Coast states, some of them took their slaves with them. Others sold their slaves before leaving and bought new ones on arrival. The increasing demand for slaves in the Gulf Coast states led to a flourishing **interstate slave trade**. Professional slave traders bought slaves in the border states and transported them to slave auction centers in New Orleans and Natchez, Mississippi. There the slaves were driven to auction blocks and sold to the highest bidders.

Free blacks. Not all the blacks in the South were slaves. By 1860 about 250,000 free blacks lived in the South, most of them in towns and cities. Some of them had been freed by their owners. However, as slavery became more firmly established, masters became more and more reluctant to free their slaves. To do so meant large financial loss and the disapproval of neighbors.

Free blacks in the South enjoyed less and less freedom in the early 1800's. After 1830 the legislatures of all the southern states passed laws severely restricting the movements of free black people. Free blacks had to register with town authorities and carry a pass to show that they were not runaway slaves. Often they had to post bonds—money or a pledge of property—to guarantee their good behavior. Their property was taxed, but they could not vote. Nor could they testify in court against white citizens or slaves, although slaves as well as white citizens could testify against them.

There were many other discriminations. Free black southerners could not assemble freely for any purpose. In many places they were forbidden to attend churches, even all-black churches, unless a white person was present. Laws in some areas forbade them to learn how to read and write.

Although these severe laws and regulations were not always enforced, free black southerners lived under the constant threat that they might be. In addition, free blacks never knew when some new law or discrimination might be

Slaves lived with the constant fear that they would be auctioned off to new owners. Family members were sold separately and often never saw each other again.

imposed. They never knew when they might be punished or even sold into slavery for some minor violation.

The poor whites. Poor whites, about 10 or 12 percent of the southern white population, formed another distinct social and economic group in the South. Other white southerners looked down on the poor whites, calling them "hillbillies," "crackers," or "piney woods folks."

Most poor whites were frontier families, many of whom lived in rough log cabins. They lived on the poorer soils, called "pine barrens," or along the rugged Appalachian mountainsides and other hilly areas that were hard to farm. Partly for this reason, their standard of living was low. These people often suffered from poor health, but they had pride and a fierce independence.

Laborers and tenants. White farm laborers and **tenant farmers** formed another large

▲ It has been estimated that the market value of slaves just before the Civil War was $2 billion.

333

southern group. The farm laborers were hired to work for wages during the harvest season or to do work regarded as too dangerous for slaves, who were expensive to buy and keep. The tenant farmers rented and tilled fields that were usually worn out from overuse. These tenant farmers generally lived hard lives and were in debt to the landowners.

Small farmers. Many independent farmers in the South owned small plots of productive land and lived much like small farmers in other parts of the country. They built simple but reasonably comfortable frame houses, considerably better than the log cabins of the poor whites. Each year the small farmers sold a bale or two of cotton as a cash crop. Their food came largely from the corn, potato, and vegetable patches around their houses. They were almost self-sufficient and also had a small cash income of about $100 a year.

The slaveowners. None of the white groups mentioned so far owned slaves. These groups made up about three fourths of the white southern families. The remaining fourth, fewer than 305,000 families, owned the roughly 4 million slaves in the South. These slaveowners can be divided into two groups—the small slaveowners and the **planters**.

Some small southern farmers who prospered bought a slave or two, or perhaps a slave family. A prosperous small farmer might have eight or ten slaves.

When small farmers acquired a few slaves, their scale of living usually did not change. They often continued to work in the fields, alongside their newly purchased slaves. Although the farmers' cash income might increase to perhaps several hundred dollars a year, they remained separated from the rich planters on the one hand and the poor whites on the other. Some small farmers lived in the cotton belt, with only a fence separating them from the plantations. However, most of them lived to the north of the cotton belt and in the fertile valleys of the Appalachian Mountains.

The most influential people in the South—the planters—were also the fewest in number. According to the Bureau of the Census, a planter was a person engaged in agriculture who owned 20 slaves or more. In 1860 the Bureau of the Census reported that there were only about 50,000 planters in the South.

Identify: "King Cotton," staple crop, cotton gin, subsistence farm, interstate slave trade, tenant farmer, planter

For answers to questions, see Answer Key, p.A49.

1. **Interpreting Ideas:** The southern economy before 1860 was varied and complex. Explain.

2. **Analyzing Ideas:** Why was the South able to become the world's greatest cotton-producing area by 1860?

3. **Summarizing Ideas:** In what ways were free blacks discriminated against in the South after 1830?

4. **Studying Maps:** Look at the map on page 330. **(a)** Locate the cotton belt. **(b)** Where is the Old South? **(c)** In what directions did cotton production expand between 1839 and 1859?

2 The planters control the positions of power

See Teaching Suggestions in TMRG, pp.TM85-86.

The planters held most of the important political positions in the South. They were usually chosen by the voters in the southern states as their Senators and Representatives in the Congress of the United States.

Who were the planters? Many southern planters were descendants of the wealthy colonial planters of the eastern seaboard states. Others worked their way up the economic and social ladder. For example, Joseph Emory Davis, a brother of Jefferson Davis, produced 3,000 bales of cotton each year on Mississippi land he had carved out of frontier wilderness. Southerners who started life as small farmers and rose to high positions included John C. Calhoun of South Carolina and Andrew Jackson of Tennessee.

Educational leadership. For the most part, the wealthy planters and their families received excellent educations. This in itself helps to explain their strong influence. Believing firmly in the importance of education, they hired private tutors for their children or sent the boys to private schools. While few girls were sent to college, a high proportion of boys went to college. Most young southern men attended William and Mary College, the University of Virginia, or some other southern col-

The plantation was the chief economic unit of the South from the colonial period until slavery was abolished in 1863. It was a self-sufficient community in which everyone earned a living from a single product grown for export — cotton, tobacco, rice, or indigo — and in which everyone's living conditions were determined by the plantation owner.

Plantations first developed in the Virginia colony, where wealthy investors used indentured servants to grow tobacco. But the development of a widespread plantation economy in the South depended upon and was intimately connected with the institution of slavery.

On the eve of the Civil War, the Southern planter aristocracy (usually defined as owning more than 50 slaves) only numbered about 10 thousand families. But the way of life of the planters and their slaves gave a special identity to the Old South and left a permanent mark on American civilization.

lege. Many others went north to Yale, Harvard, Princeton, West Point, and Annapolis. Hundreds of these young graduates of southern and northern colleges became leaders in the South.

Political leadership. The county form of local government found throughout the South had been introduced into Virginia by the first English settlers. It later spread throughout the southern states. This form of local government enabled the planters to control the machinery of southern government and to hold most of the leading political offices in the South.

The **county** was the most important southern political unit, and the most important county officers were the **justices of the peace**. These officers — varying in numbers up to 35 for each county — were appointed by the governor of each state, who was usually a wealthy planter. The justices had broad powers. They levied taxes. They provided for the building of roads, bridges, and schoolhouses. They appointed sheriffs to enforce the law.

Once a month the justices of each county met as a judicial body to try cases. The justices also met informally and unofficially to choose candidates for election to their state legislature and to Congress. Without their approval it

was difficult if not impossible for any southerner to win an election for county, state, or national office.

The plantation home. Travelers who journeyed through the counties of the South in the 1850's occasionally passed imposing mansions set well back from the road, with close-clipped lawns sweeping down to the fields or a river. The houses were shaded by tall trees and surrounded by formal gardens. They looked cool and inviting with wide verandas and white Grecian pillars supporting the roof.

Many of these mansions, often having 12 or 15 luxuriously furnished rooms, were places of great beauty. These were the homes of the wealthy planter families who owned 100 to 500 slaves or more. However, even as late as 1860, fewer than 2,500 planters could afford such luxury.

The planter family that owned from 20 to 100 slaves lived well, but more modestly. Their home might have as many as eight or ten rooms, with wide halls and deep verandas, or porches, surrounded by spacious, shaded grounds. The furnishings inside the house were usually comfortable but not luxurious, for most of the family's wealth was tied up in land and slaves. They could not afford expensive

335

A slave-auctioning firm in New Orleans circulated this poster advertising a sale in 1835. The firm offers a variety of slaves—cooks, housekeepers, coachmen—aged 7 to 45.

household goods or lavish entertainment. In fact, such planter families often lived lonely, isolated lives.

The planter's duties. The owner, or master, of a plantation, regardless of its size, had to attend to an endless number of details. In addition to supervising the work on the plantation itself, the planter had to keep records of his business transactions. Letters and orders had to be written to shipowners and bankers and to the agents who sold the cotton to the textile mills.

The day-by-day management of the plantation was very time-consuming. Each morning the planter or an overseer assigned jobs to the slaves, such as tending the cotton, hoeing corn, cultivating other food crops, cutting wood, carrying water, feeding livestock, and doing household jobs. There was always much work to be done, for a cotton grower also raised most of the food eaten by the family and the slaves.

In terms of money in the bank, the planter was not usually rich. The planter shipped cotton through an agent in the North Atlantic states or in Great Britain. The agent sold the cotton and shipped back whatever agricultural tools, clothing, books, and household furnishings the planter wanted. Frequently, after the cotton was sold and the purchases were made, the planter ended up in debt to the agent who handled the business.

The mistress of the plantation has often been romanticized as a frail and lovely person of leisure. In fact, she usually had her hands full as the supervisor of a large household. The many activities for which she was responsible might include spinning and weaving as well as preparing and storing food. The mistress also looked after the health of everyone who lived and worked on the plantation. Often she taught the younger children when it was hard to find a tutor.

Economics of slavery. It is impossible to say whether or not slave labor was really profitable for the southern planters. Many planters and most small farmers did not keep accurate accounts. Thus they did not know from one year to the next just how much they had earned or lost.

Before 1840 some southerners believed that slave labor was becoming less profitable than hired labor. In 1837 George Tucker, a professor at the University of Virginia, argued in a book entitled *The Law of Wages, Profits, and Rents* that slavery was an inefficient system of labor. To support this argument, Tucker and others pointed to the high cost of buying slaves; to the fact that unwilling workers were usually poor workers; to the expensive supervision that was required to keep slaves at work; to the cost of food, clothing, and shelter; and to the economic losses caused by a slave's illness or death.

After 1840 such arguments were heard less often. Many southerners had come to feel that slavery was not only necessary for the South, but that it was also profitable. Thus southerners were angered when, in 1857, a farmer from North Carolina published a book that tried to prove that the South was economically inferior to the North because of the inefficiency of slavery. The author, Hinton Rowan Helper, called his book *The Impending Crisis*. Feeling in the South ran so high against Helper that he found it wise to move to the North.

Actually, most historians today would not agree with Helper. There is evidence that the large rice, sugar, and cotton plantations were often profitable to their owners, depending partly upon weather conditions and market prices and depending especially on managerial skill. On the other hand, some planters were regularly in debt, and many were barely able to break even.

The proslavery argument. Whether or not slavery was a profitable labor system, by 1860 it had become firmly established on all southern plantations and many small southern farms. As slavery grew and spread, it became the subject of increasingly bitter controversy between southerners and northerners. In defending their way of life, southerners developed what has come to be called "the proslavery argument."

The proslavery argument declared, in part, that slavery was necessary because without it southern planters would not have an adequate labor supply. The argument held further that the institution of slavery was not only necessary but was of positive value to the slaves themselves. It gave them shelter, clothing, and food. It took care of them in sickness and old age. In short, it provided them with a secure and stable existence.

The champions of slavery often contrasted the secure life of the slave with the uncertain lot of wage earners in the mills, factories, and mines of the North and of Europe. These white workers, it was argued, were exploited mercilessly by employers who had no concern for their well-being. Their employers paid them barely enough to live on, fired them when there was no work to do, and discarded them when they were too ill or too old to work.

The proslavery arguments were popularized throughout the South by leaders at rallies, by newspaper editors, by novelists and short-story writers, and by preachers. The arguments were mainly advanced by, or on behalf of, the large plantation owners. The small planters, who often wanted to become large planters, also accepted the argument, as did small farmers who owned no slaves but who hoped in time to buy some. Even the poor whites accepted the proslavery argument. It added to their sense of solidarity and pride in being members of the white society of the South.

Most white southerners, then, accepted the arguments in defense of slavery and opposed the arguments against slavery. White southerners largely accepted the leadership of the great plantation owners and the institution of slavery itself. They identified slavery with the southern way of life. They saw any criticism of slavery, or any efforts to restrict it, as a threat to their homes, their land, and their way of life.

SECTION REVIEW

See underscored items, text pp. 335-36.

Identify: county, justice of the peace, Hinton R. Helper

For answers to questions, see Answer Key, p.A49.

1. **Evaluating Ideas:** The life of a plantation owner was comfortable, but not easy. Support or refute this statement using specific examples.

2. **Summarizing Ideas:** State the main points of the proslavery argument.

3. **Analyzing Viewpoints:** Why did the average non-slave-holding white southerner accept the institution of slavery?

3 The slaves play leading roles in the development of the South

See Teaching Suggestions in TMRG, pp.TM86-87.

Historians have had to use a variety of sources and methods in attempting to picture slave life in the southern states in the years before 1860.

The study of slavery. On the basis of documents and records alone, no historian can accurately reconstruct what it was like to be a slave. There are many records, but most of them were written by white southerners or by white travelers from the North or from Europe.

A few slaves who could write left short accounts of their lives. A larger number who escaped to the North or to Canada wrote more detailed autobiographies. Long after slavery ended, scholars interviewed former slaves and recorded their memories.

In addition to written records, historians have examined the surviving work songs and religious songs in which the slaves expressed some of their feelings. Historians have also used some of the scholarly methods of sociology, anthropology, and psychology. What, then, are some things that can be said about slavery as the slaves actually lived it?

Posters like that on page 336 drew buyers to scenes like this one in St. Louis. The slave auctioneer (center) announces the strengths and skills of the slaves to the audience. At such a sale, a child might be bought for only $200 or $300. However, a strong field hand in the group might sell for $1,500.

The work the slaves did. By 1860 the nearly 4 million slaves in the South performed a wide variety of jobs. Many worked in the homes of the planters, merchants, lawyers, and doctors, cooking the meals, doing the housekeeping, and tending the children.

Some of the slaves became skilled workers. Women learned to spin, weave, and sew. Some became cooks, maids, and nursemaids. Men became blacksmiths, painters, shoemakers, jewelers, and silversmiths. Others learned carpentry, bricklaying, and other tasks required to build a house. Some could not only build the house but also could make necessary plans, draw up contracts, and complete the entire structure.

Some slaves were hired out by their owners to work in tobacco factories, in sugar and flour mills, and in iron works. A great many did hard, unskilled work in building canals, roads, and railroads and in draining swamps. Large numbers were used as dock workers, lifting and carrying heavy loads on and off ships.

The great majority of the slaves on the cotton, rice, and sugar-cane plantations did the hard work of the fields. These men and women planted the crops in the spring and cultivated them through the summer. In the fall they picked cotton, cut sugar cane, harvested rice and grain, and slaughtered livestock. In the winter the slaves mended fences and cleared new land.

How slave labor was organized. On farms and small plantations, the slaves were usually supervised by their owners. On small farms owners sometimes worked alongside their slaves.

On large plantations work was organized either by the task system or by the gang system. Under the **task system,** each slave was given a particular job to do each day and could stop working when the job was finished. At such times some slaves earned wages by working for someone else. Under the more widely used **gang system,** an overseer assigned groups of slaves to work under drivers. A white overseer often was used, but black overseers were common. The drivers usually were slaves. The gang worked as long and as hard as the overseer or driver saw fit. The purpose of the gang system was to get as much work as possible out of the slave labor force.

How slaves were treated. On some plantations, especially those with overseers, slaves were often treated harshly, if not brutally. However, many slaveowners treated their slaves reasonably well because the slaves were valuable property. For example, suppose a planter owned 50 slaves. At a cost of from $1,000 to $1,500 for each slave (an average price in the 1850's), the planter's investment in slaves was from $50,000 to $75,000. The death of a single slave meant a serious financial loss. Even the illness of a slave meant a setback. Any illness or injury resulting from ill-treatment was against the planters' interests. To protect their investment, therefore, they were apt to keep their slaves adequately fed, clothed, and housed.

Much of the proslavery argument was based on these grounds. Advocates of slavery argued that the living conditions of the slaves — their workday, food, clothing, and shelter — were better and more secure than those of workers in the mills and factories of the North.

That argument left out much. Industrial workers of the North could quit their jobs and look for other work. If they had some cash, they could move to the relatively cheap farmland of the western regions. Most important, they were free persons. Slaves, by contrast, were property. They had no voice in deciding the conditions of their work or even of their own lives. Free workers, to be sure, had to submit to the discipline and rules of the mill or factory where they worked, but that discipline differed sharply from slave discipline.

Slave discipline. Slaveowners had to teach their slaves to be slaves — that is, to be obedient and accept their lot. Slaveowners did this partly by persuasion. They taught their slaves that it was their religious duty to obey their master, mistress, or overseer. Slaves were taught to believe that any white person was superior by nature to any black person.

These efforts were conscious and deliberate. Plantation owners bought handbooks on how to manage slaves. Some handbooks contained question-and-answer lessons, which the slaves had to memorize. These lessons were meant to teach them always to obey and respect white people, never to argue with them, and to accept their own condition as slaves.

Under these psychological pressures and dependent as they were upon their masters for food, clothing, and shelter, some slaves came to regard themselves as children. Many masters encouraged this attitude by giving small gifts or special privileges to obedient slaves, as is often done with children.

When persuasion failed, masters and overseers could and often did resort to brutal-

ity. If slaves showed signs of disobedience, stubbornness, or independence, they might be flogged or whipped. If this did not work, slaves might suffer even more painful and degrading punishments. They might be branded or have their noses slit. The worst threat that the slaves faced was that they might be sold and thus deprived of the few cherished family ties they had developed.

This discipline did encourage many slaves to be outwardly childlike and obedient toward white people. However, it also forced them to be deceitful. Many slaves showed outward respect and obedience to escape penalties or win rewards. Such outward behavior sometimes concealed bitter resentment and hatred toward white people.

How slaves resisted. Despite all the efforts to control them, many slaves found ways of resisting slavery. No one knows how many slaves escaped from the plantations. Some fled to join relatives from whom they had been separated while others sought freedom in the North or in Canada. The number of fugitives probably ran into thousands each year. Many, however, were captured by professional slave catchers, who used bloodhounds to hunt down runaways.

Beginning in colonial times, slaves had plotted uprisings to gain their freedom. These rebellions continued into the 1800's.

In 1791 the slaves of Haiti carried out a successful revolt against their French masters. In Henrico County, Virginia, a slave named Gabriel Prosser heard of this revolt and was inspired by it. He secretly organized a group of slaves, forged weapons, and set a date for an uprising in 1800. Gabriel Prosser's plot was betrayed by two fellow slaves. Pursued by a Virginia militia, the group disbanded but was caught and punished.

An uprising was said to have been organized in Charleston, South Carolina, in 1822 by Denmark Vesey, a former slave. Reports of this plot may have rested largely on unfounded fears among white southerners, since no actual act of rebellion took place. Whatever the facts may have been, 37 blacks were put to death and others were severely punished.

In 1831 a slave named Nat Turner led a slave uprising in Southampton County, Virginia. Outwardly obedient, Nat Turner had learned to read the Bible and was deeply religious. Believing that God had chosen him to

▲ John C. Calhoun tried to argue that free blacks had a higher percentage of blindness, deafness, and mental disorders than slaves did. Calhoun's defense of slavery on these grounds only served to infuriate abolitionists and freesoilers.

339

Nat Turner (center) was convinced that God meant him to lead the slaves to freedom. Turner persuaded 60 others to join him in his rebellion. After his capture, he freely admitted what he had done but pleaded "not guilty" to the charges. When asked why, he replied, "Because I don't feel guilty."

slaughter white people and free the slaves, Nat Turner began his rebellion. Before troops suppressed it, 60 white people and more than 100 slaves were killed. Turner was captured, brought to trial, and hanged. After this rebellion all southern states tightened their control over black people, free as well as slave.

Most slaves, of course, took no part in rebellions. Most never tried to run away. Yet despite the discipline and restrictions of slavery, black men and women were not wholly robbed of their personality. They found ways of expressing their thoughts and feelings within the family and in the distinctive life of the slave quarters. These expressions combined survivals of their African heritage with some traits of white southern culture.

Slaves often expressed joy in songs and dances, and humor in folk tales and jokes. They also found outlets for their unhappiness and misery under bondage in haunting religious songs called **spirituals**. These hymns, rich in Biblical lore, were modeled in part on the "gospel hymns" sung by white Christians, but they were also strongly influenced by traditional African musical forms. Nearly all these spirituals movingly expressed the slaves' deep longing for freedom.

The heritage of slavery. The slaves made enormously valuable contributions to the wealth of their owners, of the southern economy, and of the nation. They also made valuable contributions to the culture of the South. However, these contributions were made at enormous costs to the slaves. While slavery existed in the United States, black people were deprived of the opportunities and freedoms enjoyed by most other Americans.

SECTION REVIEW
See underscored items, text pp. 338-40.

Identify: task system, gang system, Gabriel Prosser, Denmark Vesey, Nat Turner, spirituals

For answers to questions, see Answer Key, pp.A49-50.

1. **Interpreting Ideas:** What resources have historians used to develop an understanding of southern slave life?

2. **Summarizing Ideas:** (a) What work did slaves do? (b) How was their work organized? (c) How were they treated? (d) What was the basic difference between southern slaves and northern white workers?

3. **Analyzing Ideas:** (a) Why was it necessary to teach slaves how to be slaves? (b) How did the methods of disciplining slaves affect the way slaves behaved? (c) How did slaves attempt to resist slavery?

DEVELOPING HISTORY STUDY SKILLS

Reading About History   Developing a Structured Overview

A student of history is required to read and to remember a great deal of information. One way to remember what has been read is to develop a structured overview of the information. A structured overview is a kind of diagrammatic outline.

How to Develop a Structured Overview

Follow these steps to develop a structured overview.

1. **Identify the major ideas.** Read the information, observing, or supplying, headings for each major idea or main topic.

2. **Identify the supporting details.** Reread the material, this time observing, or supplying, subheadings to correspond to supporting details.

3. **Structure the headings.** Form an overview by structuring the headings and subheadings in the same manner as the sample below.

Applying the Skill

Skim Section 3 of this chapter about the roles of the slaves in the development of the South. Note that the section covers three main topics: (1) the work slaves did, (2) the conditions under which slaves lived and worked, and (3) methods of slave resistance. To make a structured overview of Section 3, then, these headings would indicate the main topics: work, conditions, resistance.

What are the subtopics? Read through the section again. Note that under the category of work, two topics are discussed: the type of work done by slaves and how slave labor was organized. The subtopics, then, become: types of work and organization of work. Can these subtopics be broken down further? What subtopics belong in the remaining main topics? Check the structured overview for Section 3 below.

Practicing the Skill

Read Section 1 of this chapter. Then, on a separate sheet of paper, develop a structured overview of the reading.

Slavery and the Development of the South

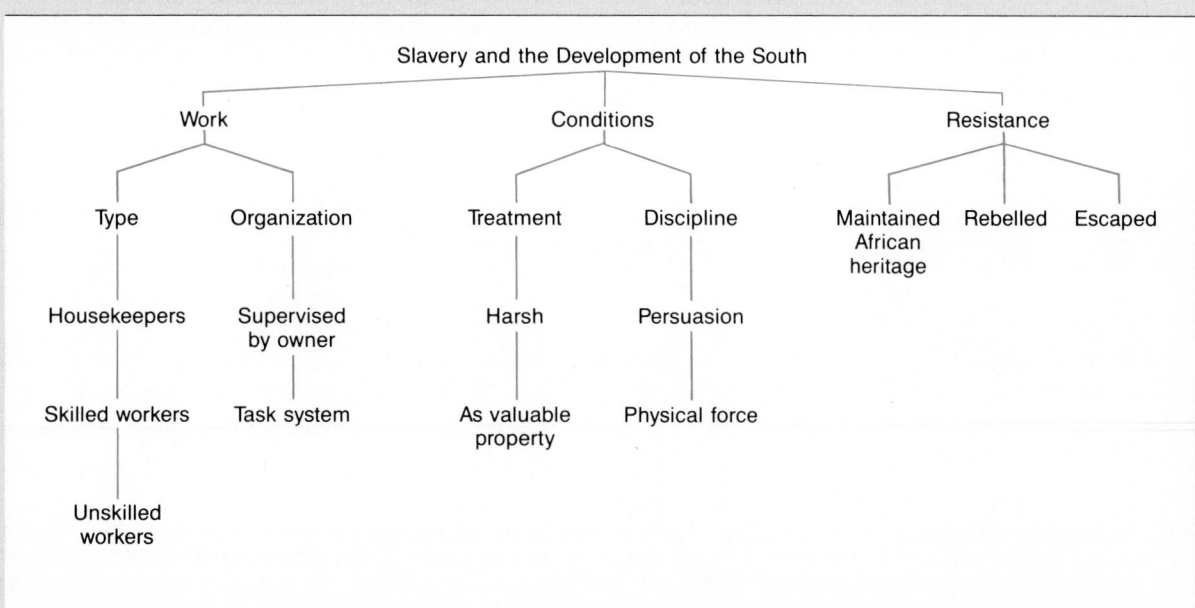

(TITLE: Development of the Cotton Kingdom MAJOR IDEAS: Economy, Population, Social and Economic Groups SUPPORTING DETAILS: [Economy] agriculture--staple crops, subsistence farming; industry--cities, factories, transportation, cotton-growing expansion [Population] whites, blacks, immigrants [Groups] slaves, free blacks, poor whites, laborers and tenants, small farmers, slaveowners)

The South, like the Northeast, was greatly influenced by the Industrial Revolution. The invention of the cotton gin gave planters an effective machine for cleaning the seeds from cotton. The invention of power-driven machines for spinning and weaving yarn created a growing demand for cotton fiber. Inventions such as the railroad and the steamboat and the development of an improved system of canals and roads also helped the South's booming economy. These transportation advances made it possible for planters to ship their cotton to the new factories in the Northeast. Planters also continued to ship their cotton to Great Britain.

Except for the cotton gin, however, machines were little used on farmlands in the South. Slaves cleared the land, plowed the fields, planted the seeds, and harvested the highly profitable crop of cotton. As the years passed and larger areas of the South were planted in cotton, slaves became more numerous and valuable to the planters.

Only a small percentage of the southerners owned slaves. The slaveowners were, in general, the wealthiest, the best educated, and the most influential people in the South. They were the political leaders who ran the governments in the southern states and who represented the South in the Congress of the United States. These southern leaders—and their families—helped create a way of living different from that in any other section of the country.

CONNECTING CHAPTER IDEAS

In the next chapter you will read that distinctive ways of living and working also developed in the West. During the first half of the 1800's hunters and fur traders were followed by farmers, ranchers, and other settlers looking for new oppotunities. The West developed rapidly with the onrush of new settlers into Oregon, Texas, other parts of the Southwest, and California.

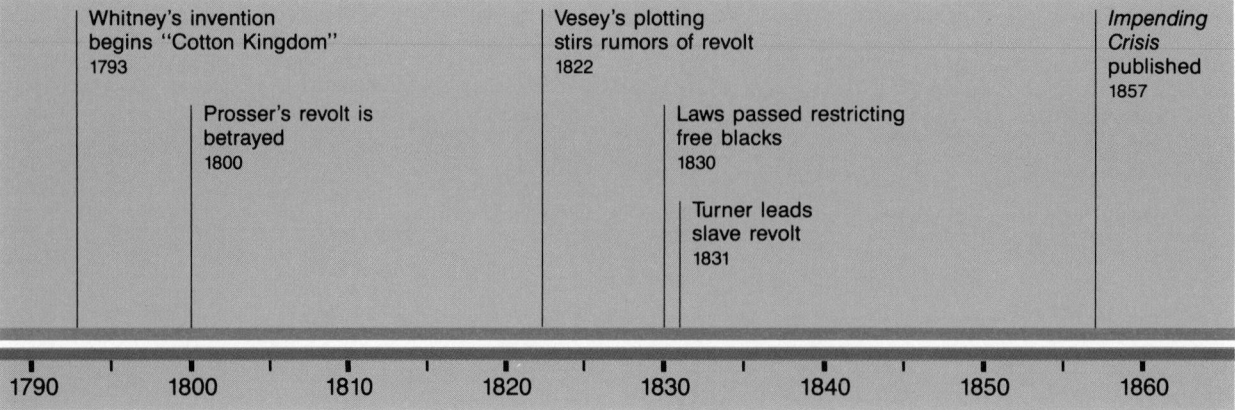

Whitney's invention begins "Cotton Kingdom" 1793	Vesey's plotting stirs rumors of revolt 1822	*Impending Crisis* published 1857
Prosser's revolt is betrayed 1800	Laws passed restricting free blacks 1830	
	Turner leads slave revolt 1831	

1790   1800   1810   1820   1830   1840   1850   1860

CHAPTER

14 REVIEW

Reviewing Important Terms

In the sentences below, the underlined terms are incorrect. On a separate sheet of paper, rewrite each sentence using the correct term.

1. Southerners received much of their cash income from food crops most of which were grown on large plantations.
2. Eli Whitney's automatic thresher could separate more than 1,000 pounds of fiber a day.
3. New Orleans, Louisiana, and Natchez, Mississippi, were important markets in the intrastate slave trade.
4. In the South, sheriffs levied taxes and provided for the building of schools, roads, and bridges.
5. The purpose of the task system, which involved overseers and drivers, was to get as much work as possible out of the slave labor force.
6. Under the gang system, slaves sometimes earned wages by working for someone other than their owner.
7. Free blacks were often forced to post bail to guarantee their good behavior.
8. The smallest social group in the South, the slaveowners, numbered only 50,000 in 1860.
9. The most important officials in the southern counties were the governors.

Practicing Critical Thinking Skills

1. **Seeing Relationships.** Explain the relationship (a) between cotton production and westward expansion and (b) between cotton production and slavery.
2. **Using Historical Imagination.** Imagine that southern society could be described as a pyramid, with the lowest economic groups at the bottom and the highest at the top. (a) Which group would form the base of the pyramid? (b) Which group would be at the top? (c) Was it possible for people in southern society to move up to a higher level on the pyramid? Explain.
3. **Analyzing Viewpoints.** Why did most white southerners see slavery as an essential part of the distinctive southern way of life?
4. **Summarizing Ideas.** List the ways in which both blacks and whites suffered from the institution of slavery.
5. **Relating Past to Present.** In a recent year the South's cotton crop was valued at about $1.3 billion. Compare it to the value of other crops in the South, such as soybeans ($2.3 billion) and tobacco ($2.4 billion). Manufactured goods produced in the South were valued at more than $250 billion. Is cotton still "king" in the South? Why or why not?

Developing History Study Skills

1. **Developing a Structured Overview.** You are about to write a newspaper editorial in which you disagree with the proslavery argument. Prepare a structured overview from which you would write the editoral.

2. **Forming Hypotheses.** Study the illustrations in this chapter. (a) What conclusions can you draw about life in the South before the Civil War? (b) Do you think that these illustrations present a realistic picture of life at that time? Why or why not?

Relating Geography and History

Before the Civil War, the economy of the South depended on plantation agriculture. Even though the textbook has described the general characteristics of a southern plantation, the term is difficult to define. To define the term fully, complete the following activities.

1. Write a brief definition of *plantation* as the word applies to the American South before the Civil War.
2. List the letter of each of the following phrases that fits your definition of "plantation."
   (a) wheat farm in Kansas
   (b) centrally managed vegetable farm complex in Maryland
   (c) large landed estate
   (d) one racial or social group exerting authority over another
   (e) crops raised on land that had been cleared of original inhabitants.
   (f) orange grove in Florida
   (g) produces a cash crop.
   (h) any large farm in a hot climate
   (i) cattle ranch in Wyoming
   (j) located in land-rich, but labor-poor area
3. Rewrite your definition using the items you selected from *2,* and other items you wish to add.

343

See Chapter Overview in TMRG, p.TM88.
See Chapter Objectives in TMRG, p.TM88.
See Introducing the Chapter in TMRG, p.TM88.

CHAPTER 15

Expanding the Nation's Boundaries

Changing Ways (1820's–1860's)

Indian guide

344

Since the early 1800's, the Indians of the United States were being persuaded, bribed, or forced to move across the Mississippi River. At the same time, restless white settlers were moving across the Mississippi and casting eager eyes even farther westward. In 1821 Missouri became the first state west of the Mississippi to be admitted to the Union. More pioneers subdued the Iowas and other tribes farther north and formed Iowa Territory in 1838.

To the west of Missouri and Iowa lay the Great Plains. Then known to the pioneers as the Great American Desert, the area did not attract settlers until later. As a grassland, the Great Plains provided food for buffalo herds and hunting grounds for such tribes as the Dakotas, Arapahos, Osages, and Poncas.

Just west of the Great Plains, in the Rocky Mountain region, were the homelands of the Crows, Shoshones, Flatheads, Coeur d'Alenes, Nez Percés, Utes, and other tribes. The forests, fertile valleys, and dry areas of the Oregon Territory were the homelands of the Cayuses, Yakimas, Chinooks, and other tribes.

South and southwest of the northern Great Plains lay Texas, New Mexico, and Arizona. These territories were settled by Spaniards, Mexicans, Wichitas, Kiowas, Apaches, Comanches, Navajos, Hopis, Zuñis, Pueblos, Papagos, Yumas, and Mohaves. Still farther west, in California, were other small groups of Indians.

From the 1820's to the 1860's, the Industrial Revolution created a distinctive way of life in the North. Cotton created a vastly different way of life in the South. During these same years, the "West," as it is known today, was added to the nation.

READING FOCUS

As you read about the changing ways that expansion to the Pacific brought to the nation, look for the details that support each of the following statements.

1. Fur traders and settlers expand into the Oregon country.
2. American settlers create the Lone Star Republic of Texas.
3. War with Mexico adds the entire Southwest to the nation.
4. A surge of migration brings California into the Union.

1 Fur traders and settlers expand into the Oregon country

See Teaching Suggestions in TMRG, pp.TM88-89.
Beyond the Rocky Mountains, lay an enormous area of towering mountains, magnificent forests, and fertile valleys drained by rivers teeming with fish. This area is now called the Pacific Northwest. In the 1800's it was known as the Oregon country or simply as Oregon. It stretched northward from the 42nd parallel, the northern border of California, to the parallel of 54°40', the southern boundary of Alaska (see map, page 360). Until the early 1820's, the Oregon country was simultaneously claimed by four nations—Spain, Russia, Great Britain, and the United States.

Conflicting claims. The Spanish claim to the Oregon country dated back to an agreement between Spain and Portugal in 1494. Spain gave up its claim in 1819 under the same treaty in which it ceded Florida to the United States (page 274).

Russia based its claims to the Oregon country on the explorations of Vitus Bering, a Dane who had explored the area for Russia in 1741. After Bering's explorations, the Russians had established missions and trading posts in Alaska and in the Pacific Northwest.

Increasing Russian pressure along the Pacific coast after 1815, you recall, was one reason why in 1823 President Monroe had warned Russia and other European nations not to colonize the Western Hemisphere. In 1824 the Russians withdrew their claims to all land south of the 54th parallel.

Great Britain based its claim to the Oregon country on voyages made to the Pacific by Francis Drake in 1577–80 and by Captain James Cook in 1776–78. The government of Great Britain encouraged a profitable British fur trade with the Indians of the Pacific Northwest.

The United States had established its first claim to the Oregon country in 1792. In that year Captain Robert Gray, a merchant sea captain from Boston, discovered the Columbia River. Gray promptly began trading for furs with the Indians there. The claim was
Text continues on page 348.

Report topics: The explorations of Bering, Drake, Cook, and Gray.

345

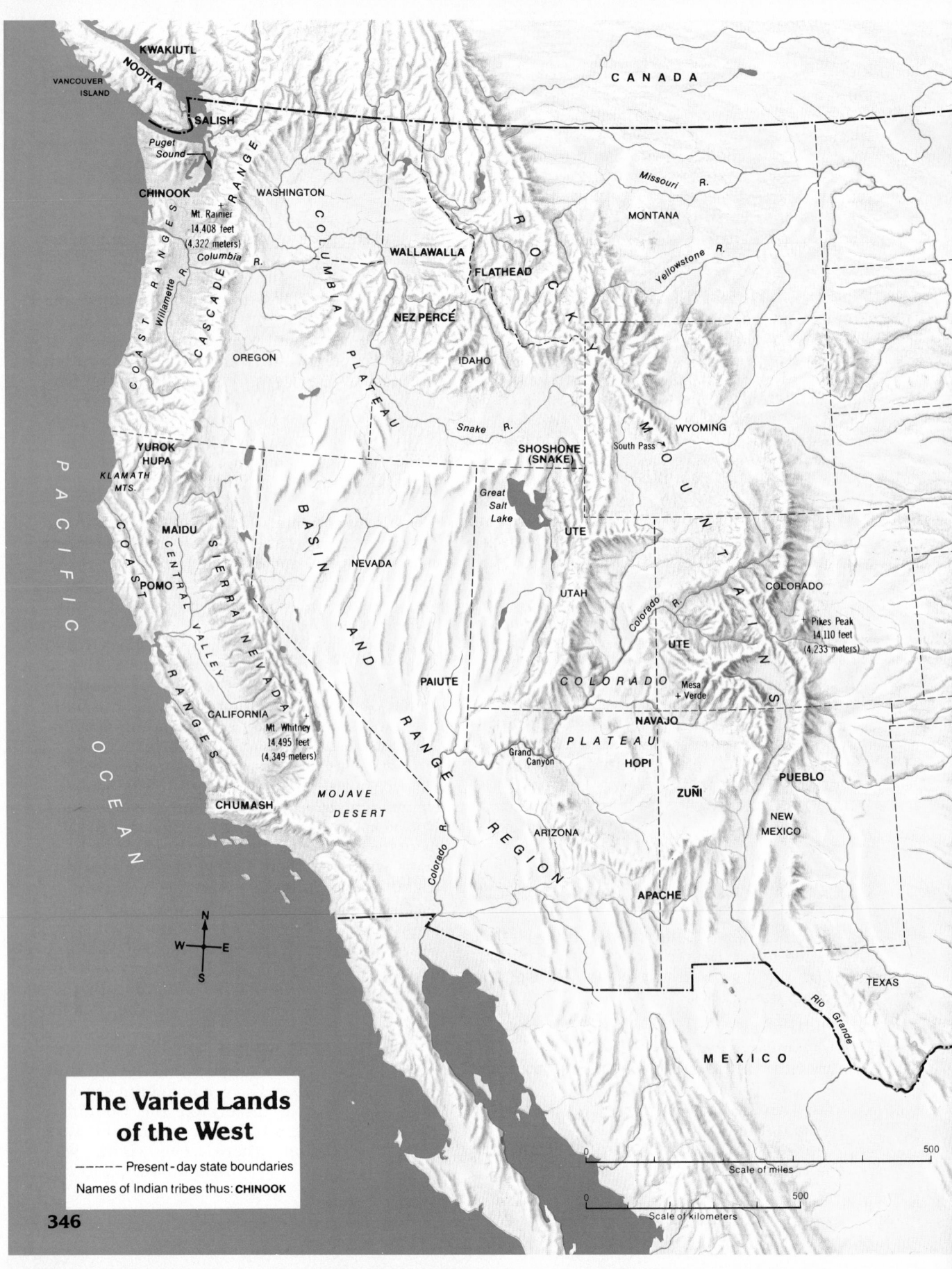

KWAKIUTL

NOOTKA

VANCOUVER
ISLAND

SALISH

Puget
Sound

CHINOOK

Mt. Rainier
14,408 feet
(4,322 meters)

Columbia R.

WASHINGTON

COAST RANGES

WILLAMETTE R.

CASCADE RANGE

COLUMBIA

WALLAWALLA

FLATHEAD

NEZ PERCÉ

OREGON

IDAHO

Snake R.

PLATEAU

CANADA

Missouri R.

MONTANA

Yellowstone R.

ROCKY

WYOMING

South Pass

MOUNTAINS

YUROK
HUPA

KLAMATH
MTS.

MAIDU

POMO

COAST RANGES

CENTRAL VALLEY

SIERRA NEVADA

CALIFORNIA

Mt. Whitney
14,495 feet
(4,349 meters)

CHUMASH

MOJAVE
DESERT

BASIN

NEVADA

AND

PAIUTE

RANGE

Great
Salt
Lake

UTE

UTAH

Colorado R.

REGION

Colorado R.

SHOSHONE
(SNAKE)

COLORADO

UTE

Grand
Canyon

PLATEAU

HOPI

ZUÑI

ARIZONA

APACHE

NAVAJO

Mesa
Verde

Pikes Peak
14,110 feet
(4,233 meters)

COLORADO

PUEBLO

NEW
MEXICO

PACIFIC

OCEAN

N
W   E
S

MEXICO

TEXAS

Rio Grande

The Varied Lands
of the West

— — — Present-day state boundaries

Names of Indian tribes thus: **CHINOOK**

0   500
Scale of miles

0   500
Scale of kilometers

During the first half of the nineteenth century, hardy pioneers, looking ever westward, ventured beyond the Mississippi into an entirely new frontier. The West was an enormous land of many regions — grass-covered but treeless plains, parched deserts, and towering snow-capped mountains. Each region was different in climate, landforms, soil, and vegetation from anything the pioneers had previously experienced east of the Mississippi. The regions of the West presented a whole new geography. They were lands whose mysteries had to be probed and tested before permanent settlements could be fully undertaken.

The first in the series of new geographic regions begins just beyond the western boundary of Missouri and continues to the Rocky Mountains. This great grass-covered region became known as the Great Plains. The Plains are a level to rolling region with few trees. It is a dry region with too little rainfall to support forests, but enough to support a carpet of low-growing grass.

The explanations for this vast grassland lies in the nature of the western landscape. In the United States the prevailing wind blows from west to east. As moisture-laden air flows onto the North American continent from the Pacific Ocean, it runs headlong into the towering Cascade and Sierra Nevada mountain ranges. The mountain ranges force the air to rise. As the air rises, it cools; and as air cools, it drops its moisture as snow or rain. Thus, rain or snow falls frequently on the western slopes of the Cascades and Sierra Nevadas. The air then slides down the eastern slopes of these mountains. With its downward rush, the air warms, snatching whatever moisture it can from the desert country between the Pacific Ranges and the Rocky Mountains. The air on the eastern slopes thus becomes a drying body of air until it reaches the Rockies. Then the air is once again forced to rise, cool, and lose its moisture on the Rockies' western slopes. The air then slides down the eastern slopes of the Rockies, becoming the warm winds that make the Great Plains a region of decreasing moisture from east to west.

Along the western edge of the plains the great mountain masses of the Rockies rise. This mountain range stretches from Alaska into Texas. Precipitation, available from the air that was forced to rise over the mountain peaks, provides the Rockies with abundant moisture to feed the dense forests of pine, fir, and spruce covering the mountainsides. Most precipitation, however, occurs as snow during the late winter and early spring. Depths of 25 feet (7.6 meters) or more are usual. For the early pioneer, the Rocky Mountain region seemed to be a land more suited to trappers and miners than farmers. Later pioneers found areas well suited to farming and other commercial ventures.

A vast, dry area fills the entire country between the Pacific Ranges and the Rockies. It is hardly a landscape that the early pioneers saw as hospitable, especially the farmers accustomed to the lush green of the land east of the Mississippi. Miners and prospectors, however, found this region a valuable treasury of minerals.

On the western edge of the continent lay many fertile valleys. In the northwest, sheltered from winter blasts by the Cascade Mountains, the fertile valleys are watered by broad rivers and streams. To the south, in California, between the Sierra Nevada and the Coastal Ranges the great valleys are rich with good soil and abundant water for irrigation. The westernmost edge of the United States is a land of great variety and abundance, as many pioneers, their descendants, and other newcomers have discovered.

Oregon's Sweetwater River flows west from the Rocky Mountains.

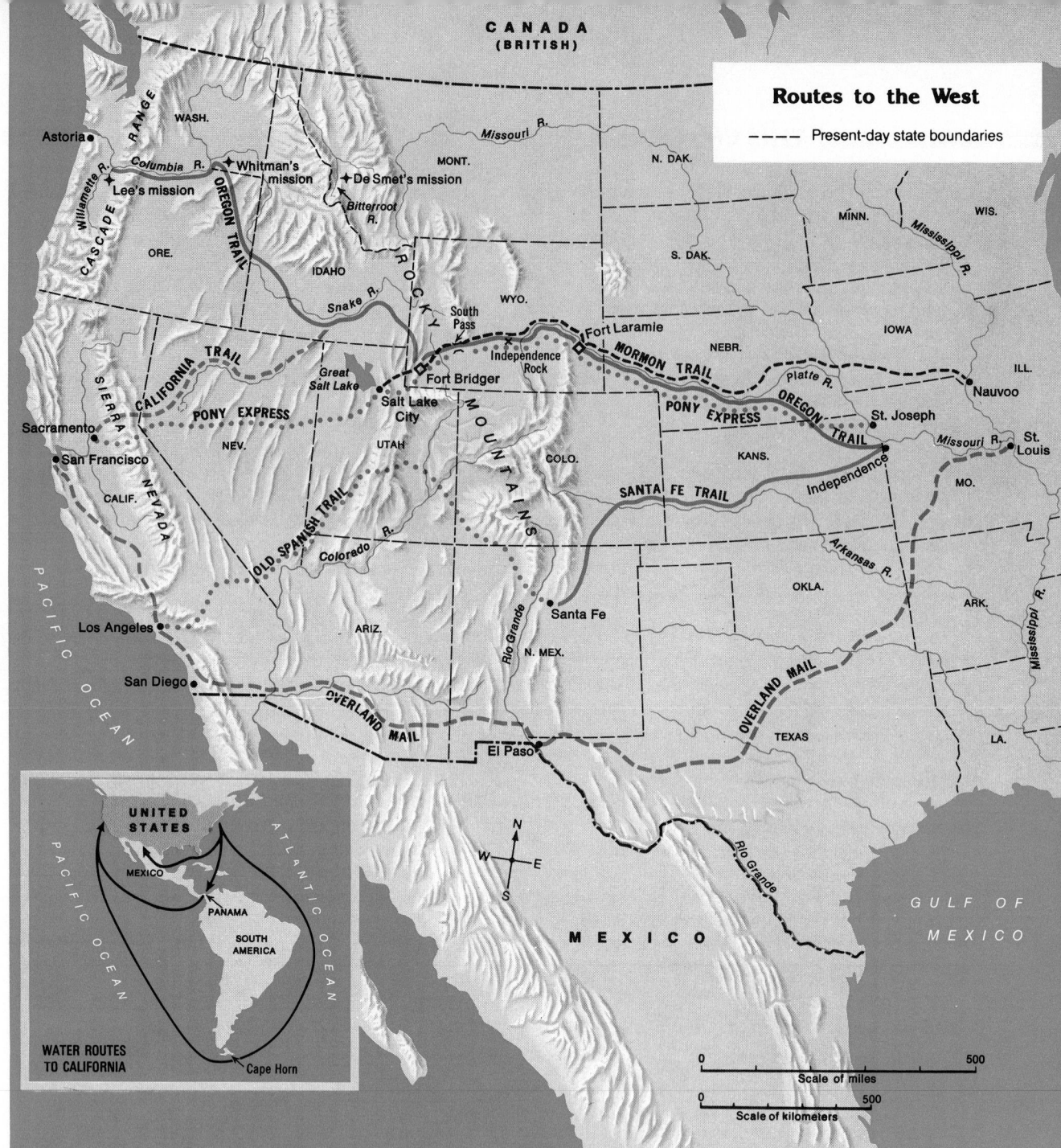

Routes to the West

– – – – Present-day state boundaries

WATER ROUTES TO CALIFORNIA

strengthened when American fur traders began traveling overland to the Oregon country in the early 1800's.

In 1818 Great Britain and the United States agreed to occupy the Oregon country jointly for ten years. Ten years later, after Spain and Russia had given up their claims, Great Britain and the United States renewed ▲ their agreement.

American fur traders. The American interest in the far western fur trade began in earnest after the Lewis and Clark expedition of 1804–06 (page 248). Centering in St. Louis, the western trade was gradually organized by enterprising business concerns such as the Rocky Mountain Fur Company. This company outfitted rugged "Mountain Men" who roamed the West searching for animal skins, or pelts.

▲ The "Convention of 1818" under which joint occupation was established also set the northern boundary of the Louisiana Purchase at the 49th parallel and renewed a commercial treaty between Great Britain and the United States that had been signed in 1815.

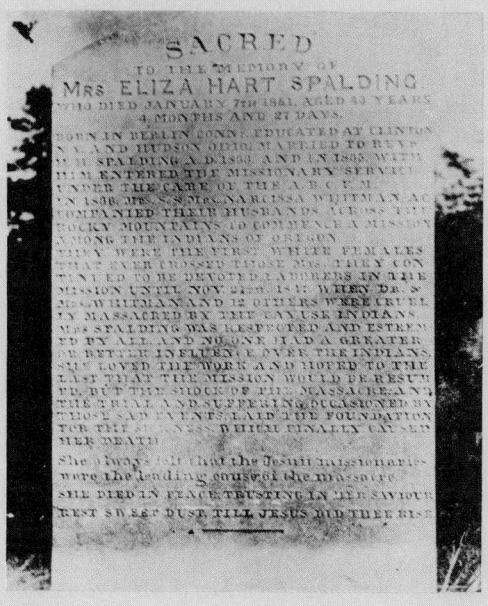

For the last 15 years of her life, Elizabeth Hart Spalding worked as a pioneer missionary among the Nez Percé Indians. Elizabeth Hart was born in Connecticut and educated in New York, where she taught school. In 1830 she began a correspondence with Henry Harman Spalding, and three years later they were married.

The Spaldings were deeply religious. While Henry studied theology, Elizabeth attended theological lectures. In 1835 the Spaldings met Dr. Marcus Whitman, who invited them to join him and his wife as missionaries in the Oregon country.

Reaching Idaho in 1836, the Spaldings set up a mission among the Nez Percés. Elizabeth Spalding learned the Nez Percé language and began teaching the Indian women to sew, spin, and weave. She also drew Biblical scenes to illustrate her husband's sermons. At first, the Spaldings' mission and school were very successful. As more white settlers moved in, however, the Indians grew increasingly hostile. It soon became obvious that there was no future in Idaho, so in 1847 the Spaldings moved to Oregon.

Four years later Elizabeth Spalding died of tuberculosis. In 1913 her body was reburied near the old mission house at the Nez Percé National Historical Park in Idaho.

Mountain Men like Jedediah Smith and James Beckwourth were as rough-and-ready a group as one could find in America at this time.

In their explorations of the Far West, the Mountain Men followed Indian trails across the Rockies and through passes that were later used by settlers moving west. One of these, South Pass in what is now Wyoming, led to a trail that crossed the Continental Divide and cut through the Snake and Columbia river valleys to the Pacific Ocean. This route came, in time, to be known as the Oregon Trail (see map, page 348).

Rivalry for furs. Another successful western business venture was the American Fur Company. It was formed in 1808 in New York by John Jacob Astor, a German immigrant. By the 1820's it controlled most of the American trade in the Upper Mississippi Valley, in the Rockies, and in the Oregon country. Astor soon had sales offices in St. Louis, New York, England, France, Austria, and China. In 1832 the company sold 25,000 beaver skins, nearly 50,000 buffalo hides, about 30,000 deerskins, and many other pelts.

Rivalry among the fur trade companies and greed for profits often led to dishonest trading with the Indians. The government tried to solve these problems by setting fixed prices for animal pelts. Largely because of pressure from the private trading companies, the government gave up its effort in 1823.

Missionaries in Oregon. The fur trade led in the 1830's and 1840's to the settlement of the Oregon country south of the Columbia River. The surge of settlement was set off mainly by missionaries and by New England business groups interested in trade and fishing.

The first missionaries traveled to the Oregon country with fur traders. Jason Lee, a Methodist, built a mission and a school for Indian children in the fertile Willamette Valley in 1834. Samuel Parker, a Presbyterian minister, followed a year later. In 1836 four Presbyterian missionaries—Dr. Marcus Whitman, Narcissa Prentice Whitman, Henry Spalding, and Elizabeth Hart Spalding—made the long, hard trip across the Rocky Mountains. In 1840 Father Pierre De Smet, a Jesuit priest, arrived in the Oregon country.

▲ By 1846 nearly 5,000 Americans has settled in the area south of the Columbia River, which was controlled by the United States. In comparison only 700 British subjects settled in the area controlled by Great Britain, which was north of the Columbia.

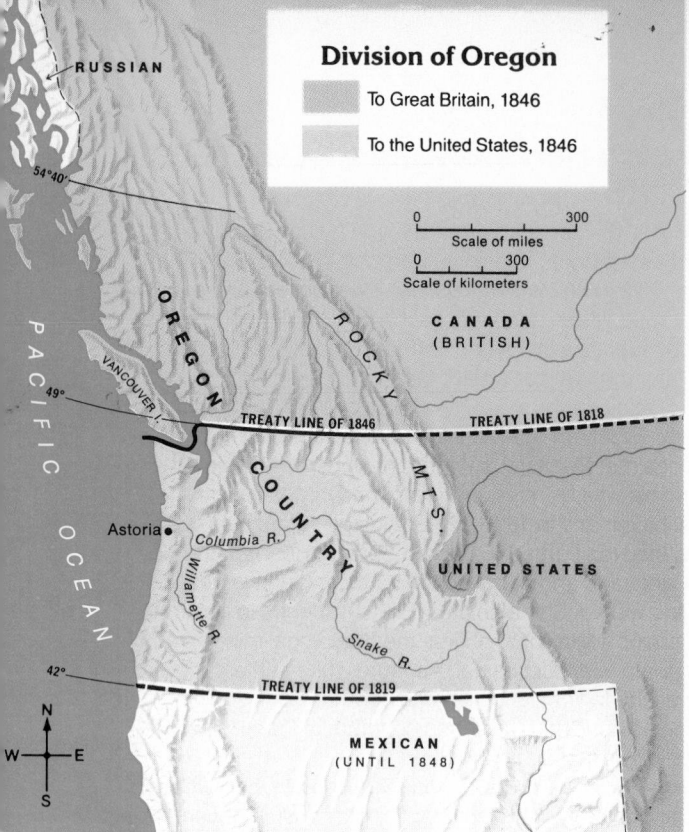

Division of Oregon

To Great Britain, 1846

To the United States, 1846

RUSSIAN

54°40'

PACIFIC OCEAN

OREGON COUNTRY

VANCOUVER I.

49°

TREATY LINE OF 1846

TREATY LINE OF 1818

ROCKY MTS.

CANADA (BRITISH)

Astoria

Columbia R.

Willamette R.

UNITED STATES

Snake R.

42°

TREATY LINE OF 1819

MEXICAN (UNTIL 1848)

0   300
Scale of miles
0   300
Scale of kilometers

N W E S

made western expansion the main issue of their campaign.

Although some Americans spoke with bitter and even warlike words about this issue, calmer minds won out. Great Britain agreed in the Treaty of 1846 to give up its claims to the Oregon country south of the 49th parallel (see map, this page). Thus by 1846 a boundary existed between the United States and Canada from the Atlantic to the Pacific Ocean. At first this boundary was marked by a few small fortifications. Since then it has been completely unfortified.

In 1848 that part of the Oregon country that now clearly belonged to the United States was organized as Oregon Territory.

SECTION REVIEW

See underscored items, text pp. 348-50.

Identify: Mountain Men, Oregon Trail, John Jacob Astor, the Whitmans, Treaty of 1846

For answers to questions, see Answer Key, p.A51.

1. **Summarizing Ideas:** (a) Which countries claimed the Oregon country? (b) What was the basis of their claims?

2. **Organizing Ideas:** How did each of the following help to lay the basis for American claims to the Oregon country: (a) Captain Gray, (b) Lewis and Clark, (c) Mountain Men, (d) Astor, (e) missionaries, (f) settlers?

3. **Interpreting Ideas:** How did the United States finally acquire the Oregon country?

4. **Studying Maps:** Look at the map on this page. (a) Locate the boundaries of the Russian claims. (b) Locate the United States–Canada boundary established in 1846.

The early settlers. During these same years, some white settlers brought black slaves with them. However, most of the settlers opposed slavery, and in 1845 it was prohibited by law in the Oregon country. The same law set up severe discriminations against free black settlers, ordering them to leave the country within two years.

From the beginning the settlers in the Oregon country felt a need for government. In 1843 nine settlers drew up a resolution, which said in part, "We the people of Oregon territory, for the purposes of mutual protection and to secure peace and prosperity among ourselves, agree to adopt . . . laws and regulations, until such time as the United States of America extend their jurisdiction over us."

Settling British-American claims. According to the agreement reached in 1818 and later renewed, Great Britain and the United States were to occupy the Oregon country jointly. By 1840 a new solution was needed to settle rival British-American claims.

Many Americans were demanding that the British withdraw all claims to the land south of the line 54° 40'. This demand became a major issue in the Presidential election of 1844. The Democrats, led by James K. Polk of Tennessee,

2 American settlers create the Lone Star Republic of Texas

See Teaching Suggestions in TMRG, pp.TM89-90.

In the early 1820's American traders and settlers were beginning to drift southwestward into Indian and Mexican lands. Their arrival began a chain of events that led the United States to acquire the vast area that is now Texas, New Mexico, Arizona, California, Nevada, and Utah as well as parts of Colorado and Wyoming.

▲ The feelings of this period are reflected in some of the campaign slogans of 1844--"Fifty-four Forty or Fight," "Reoccupation of Oregon," "All of Oregon or None."

Early Spanish settlement. As you have read (pages 6–7), many Indian tribes lived in this immense area long before the Spaniards arrived in the Americas. The Spaniards ignored the Indians and immediately claimed the land for the Spanish Crown and called it New Spain. The Spaniards based their claim on the early explorations of Coronado and others and on later Spanish settlements throughout the area.

During the 1600's and 1700's, the Spaniards spread northward from Mexico City—the heart of their New World empire. As early as 1609, they established Santa Fe in what is now New Mexico. From Santa Fe, their chief northern outpost, the Spaniards kept a firm hold on the region for many years, with only a temporary setback in a Pueblo revolt that broke out in 1680. In the 1700's, fearing French and British expansion, the Spaniards strengthened their colonizing efforts. They established presidios (or forts), missions, villages, towns, and large ranches throughout the present states of Texas, New Mexico, Arizona, and California.

The missions. The center of each mission was the church, often a beautiful structure built of stone or adobe. Surrounding the church were living quarters for the priests and workshops in which the Indians learned weaving, silver working, blacksmithing, and other crafts. Generally the main buildings were enclosed within an adobe or stone wall. Around the mission buildings were farming areas where the priests and Indians grew grain, grapes, and other crops and at times raised cattle. Indians who had won the confidence of the priests sometimes had farms of their own near the missions.

Most of the missions were set up by Franciscan priests. The priests tried to win the Indians to Christianity, to teach them some of the Spanish ways of life, and to make them loyal Spanish subjects. The priests, however, were only partly successful. In their zeal they tried to suppress Indian religions and customs, thinking that this was in the best interests of the Indians. They often treated the Indians as children and punished them for breaking mission rules. Indians often resented the labor that was forced on them and were unhappy with the suppression of their own culture. Many of them fled from the missions.

The Spaniards hoped strong communities would develop around the missions, with each mission as the center of community life. Although this goal was only partly realized, the missions did play a major role in shaping the life of the northern areas of New Spain.

Ways of life in New Spain. The Spanish ranches also played a key role. These huge estates, some with thousands of sheep or cattle, were widely scattered over the vast northern part of New Spain. Usually far from missions and presidios, the ranches were complete communities in themselves. Here lived a few Spaniards, a larger number of creoles, and a much larger number of mestizos and Indians. The owners often lived in town houses in Mexico City or in Spain. They visited their estates only occasionally. Thus many of the workers became very capable in the management and supervision of the estates. Other workers developed great skills as riders. They became models for the American cowboys, who would later work on the plains.

From California to Texas, the ruling groups shared certain values and beliefs. They were Roman Catholics. They had a deep pride in Spanish culture. They were also fiercely independent—a trait encouraged by their remoteness from the centers of government in Santa Fe and Mexico City. Coupled with this spirit of independence was a suspicion of outsiders—whether explorers, military scouts, or traders. The Spaniards tried to protect themselves from intruders by forbidding all trade with Americans. At times, they seized and imprisoned American explorers and traders who entered their lands.

Throughout the region, as indeed throughout Latin America, attitudes toward the lower classes, especially the Indians, varied greatly. On the one hand, mission priests often treated the lower classes as children. On the other hand, the owners of mines, ranches, and businesses often mistreated and abused the workers. In time, the smoldering unrest and resentment of the lower classes burst into revolution.

The Mexican Revolution. The Spanish and Portuguese colonies in the Americas could not remain untouched by the revolutions and wars that swept across Europe in the early 1800's. In 1810 a Mexican priest, Father Miguel Hidalgo y Costilla (ee·DAHL·goh ee koh·STEE·yah), led an uprising of the oppressed people of New Spain. He was joined by another priest, Father José Maria Morelos y Pavón (moh·RAY·lohs ee

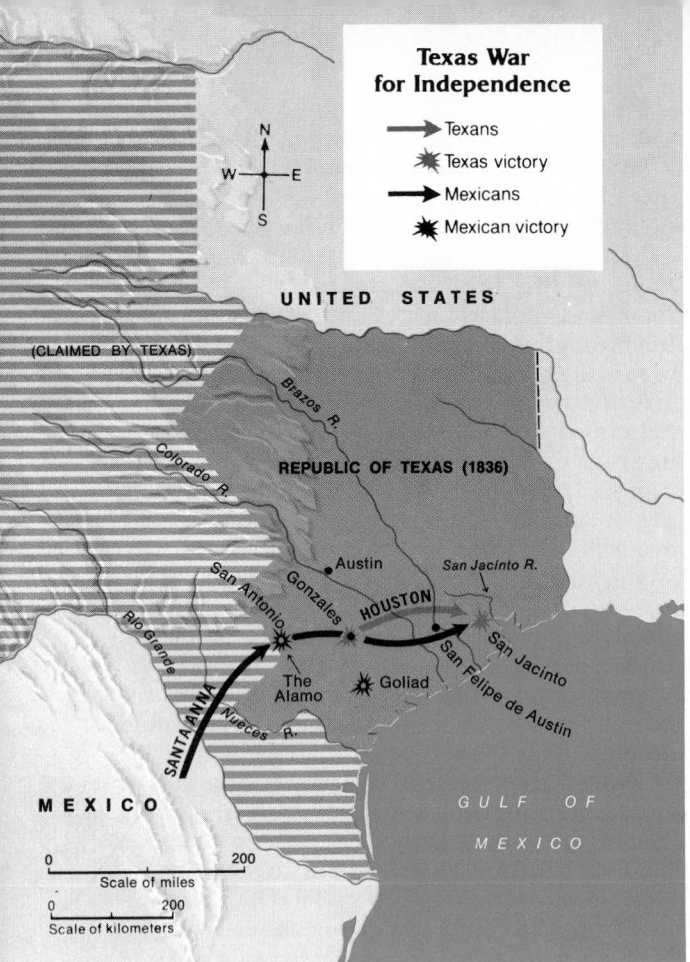

Texas War for Independence

→ Texans
✺ Texas victory
→ Mexicans
✦ Mexican victory

UNITED STATES

(CLAIMED BY TEXAS)

Brazos R.

Colorado R.

REPUBLIC OF TEXAS (1836)

Rio Grande

San Antonio

Gonzales

Austin

HOUSTON

San Jacinto R.

San Jacinto

San Felipe de Austin

The Alamo

Goliad

SANTA ANNA

Nueces R.

MEXICO

GULF OF MEXICO

0   200
Scale of miles

0   200
Scale of kilometers

pah·VOHN). The revolution at first had some success. Soon, however, control passed into the hands of ambitious military leaders. Their chief interest was in winning independence from Spain. In this they were successful. In 1821 the former colony of New Spain became the independent Republic of Mexico. In the meantime, Fathers Hidalgo and Morelos, who had been largely responsible for starting the revolution, suffered the fate of martyrs. The oppression of the Indians and the workers remained largely untouched by the revolution.

A change in policy. Even before Mexico won its independence, the Spanish authorities began to relax their attitude toward outsiders. In 1820, Moses Austin, a Connecticut-born pioneer, received permission to start a colony of a few hundred families in what is now the state of Texas. In return, he promised that the settlers would become loyal Spanish subjects.

Moses Austin died in 1821 before he could establish his colony. By then, however, the new government of Mexico had adopted a more liberal attitude toward American traders. Soon a

thriving trade developed over what came to be called the Santa Fe Trail (see map, page 348). Wagons loaded with household goods, tools, and other products lumbered west from St. Louis, Missouri. They followed the rugged trail to Santa Fe, the distributing center for much of northern Mexico. On their return trip, the wagons carried valuable loads of silver, gold, and hides. The journey was always dangerous. The traders were often attacked by Indians— especially the Comanches—whose lands they crossed. The traders sometimes attacked, or counterattacked, the Indians. Bitterness and resentment on both sides deepened.

Settlers in Texas. Some Mexican leaders were opposed to American settlement. Others thought that a relatively small number of American settlers would soon become Mexican citizens. As such, they would serve as a buffer against a rush of Americans into Texas and the seizure of the region by the United States. At the time, the Mexican population of Texas, largely concentrated in four small towns, numbered between 4,000 and 8,000. The pro-settlement side won the debate.

In 1821 the Mexican government gave Stephen F. Austin a renewal of the grant of land that his father Moses had received. That same year Stephen Austin and the "Old Three Hundred," his hand-picked settlers, began to build a vigorous American colony in Texas.

Other settlers soon followed. By 1830 more than 20,000 Americans, many of them southerners, had entered Texas. By that time, slavery had been outlawed in Mexico. Thus it was technically illegal for southerners to bring slaves into Texas. However, since the Mexican authorities did little to enforce this law, many southerners brought their slaves anyway.

Convinced that too many independence-minded Americans were entering, the Mexican government in 1830 passed a law to restrict further settlement in the Mexican states bordering the United States. Land grants not already taken up were canceled. The Mexicans also restated that slavery on Mexican lands was forbidden. To enforce their laws, the Mexicans strengthened their army posts throughout Texas.

The fight for independence. The American settlers in Texas protested vigorously against what they said were restrictions on their rights. The Mexican leaders would not recon-

The Battle of San Jacinto was the final and decisive battle of the Texas Revolution. The battle, one of the strangest ever fought, took place on April 21, 1836, along the banks of the San Jacinto River (see map, page 362) north of present-day Houston.

Neither of the opposing forces in this engagement was what military experts would have considered a model army. The Texas troops were a combination of settlers determined to secure their independence from Mexico, frontiersmen seeking excitement, and adventurers attracted by offers of land bounties. Most of the Mexican soldiers were public employees or hacienda laborers. The hacienda owners had contracted with the Mexican government to sign their employees into the Mexican army in exchange for land.

The two opposing generals, in contrast to their troops, had extensive military experience. Antonio Lopez de Santa Anna, a wealthy landowner, had served as a commander in the Mexican army for many years. Sam Houston, leader of the Texas troops, had fought under Andrew Jackson in the Indian wars.

In 1835 the Mexican government had dispatched an army of 6,000 men under Santa Anna to put down the Texas rebellion. Following the slaughter of Americans at the Alamo and at Goliad in March 1836, Santa Anna's troops moved eastward in four divisions. Sam Houston, now commander of the Texas army, pursued them. Santa Anna led himself and about 1,500 of his men into a trap by camping on a peninsula near Harrisburg, at Buffalo Bayou.

The Texans confronted the Mexicans there in a brief skirmish on April 20, but then withdrew. The next day, the Mexican troops were taking their customary afternoon rest. A group of fresh reinforcements had just arrived and were tired from their march. Officers, soldiers, and sentries were sleeping soundly. Then cries of "Remember the Alamo! Remember Goliad!" rang out as the Texans attacked without warning. In less than 30 minutes the battle was over. Nearly every Mexican was killed or captured, and Santa Anna was taken prisoner. Among Houston's 800 men, fewer than a dozen were killed; about 30 Texans were wounded, including Houston who was shot in the ankle.

The overwhelming victory and the capture of Santa Anna ended Mexican resistance to the Texas rebellion. Texas had won its independence.

---

sider, because in their eyes the settlers had broken their promises to obey Mexican laws. After several clashes with Mexican officials, fighting broke out. One of the most memorable battles took place in San Antonio.

Infuriated by an earlier defeat, General Santa Anna, the dictator President of Mexico, led a large army into Texas. The Mexican army besieged a force of almost 200 settlers in the Alamo, a fortified former mission at San Antonio (see map, page 352). The defenders, including James Bowie and William B. Travis, the joint commanders, and newcomer Davy Crockett, refused to surrender despite overwhelming odds. When Santa Anna stormed the fort on March 6, 1836, the defenders all were killed. On March 27 another force was put to death by the Mexicans at Goliad (goh·lee·AHD) after it had surrendered and laid down its arms. "Remember the Alamo!" became a rallying cry for Texans.

Independence for Texas. In March, while the defenders of the Alamo were still holding off the Mexicans, a group of Texans assembled at Washington-on-the-Brazos (BRAZ·us), declared their independence on March 2, 1836. The group, made up mostly of American settlers, also drafted a constitution for a new Republic of Texas, often called the Lone Star Republic. Sam Houston, a former governor of Tennessee, became the first elected president of the Republic of Texas, and Lorenzo de Zavala (day sah·VAH·lah) the first vice president.

Annexation delayed. During the revolution American sympathy was with the Texans. American volunteers crossed into Texas and fought against Santa Anna. When the new republic petitioned to join the United States, strong opposition developed. Since Texas wanted to permit slavery, northerners in

▲ Between 1838 and 1845, Texas conducted its own foreign policy and was recognized by Britain and France as an independent country.

353

Congress feared that its admission would increase southern influence in Congress. Others feared that to admit Texas would be to invite war with Mexico, which had not recognized Texas' independence. Thus the admission of Texas was delayed until 1845.

Free blacks and Indians in Texas. Texas wanted to allow slavery, but it did not want free black settlers within its borders. In 1840 the new Lone Star Republic ordered them to leave Texas or be sold into slavery. The free black settlers, many of whom had fought for Texas' independence, protested. The Texans then decided that they could remain — but only if they made a special appeal to the Congress of the Lone Star Republic.

In some southeastern counties of Texas, free blacks formed a sizable minority. The Ashworth family, for example, had come to Texas in the early 1830's to take up land granted to them by the Mexican government. The Ashworths as well as other free black settlers in Texas owned land, cattle, and even slaves. For a time the free blacks got along fairly well with their white neighbors, but as the war between North and South approached, tensions and even feuds arose.

The American newcomers found various Indian tribes in possession of great stretches of the plains and highlands. Raids by the Comanches of west Texas and New Mexico cost the Americans cattle, horses, and some lives. As time passed, the Americans sought to push many of these tribes northward into Indian Territory, into Mexico, or onto reservations.

SECTION REVIEW

See underscored items, text pp. 351-54.
Identify: Father Hidalgo, Father Morelos, Moses Austin, Santa Fe Trail, Stephen Austin, Santa Anna, Alamo, Sam Houston, Lone Star Republic, Ashworth family

For answers to questions, see Answer Key, p.A51.
1. **Summarizing Ideas:** Describe the importance of missions and ranches to the development of New Spain.

2. **Analyzing Ideas:** Why did the Texans fight to gain their independence from Mexico?

3. **Interpreting Ideas:** Why did the United States delay the annexation of Texas?

---

3 War with Mexico adds the entire Southwest to the nation

See Teaching Suggestions in TMRG, pp.TM90-91.

The annexation of Texas in 1845 moved the United States one step closer to war with Mexico, which broke out in 1846.

Sources of friction. A major factor in the conflict was the difference in the two ways of life that met and clashed in the vast region west of Texas. This region included the Mexican area known as Upper California, now the state of California. Mexico inherited this entire area from the Spaniards, who claimed it as early as 1494. This was more than a hundred years before the first English settlement on the Atlantic coast. Spanish language, law, architecture, and customs prevailed except in those areas where the original Indian cultures had been untouched by the missions.

Against this frontier of Spanish culture pressed a tide of energetic, land-hungry Americans. These Americans believed firmly that it was the **manifest destiny** — the historic duty — of their nation to expand to the Pacific Ocean.

In the 1830's and early 1840's, ill feeling between Mexico and the United States steadily mounted. During most of these years, the Republic of Mexico was torn by revolutions. Its government was often powerless to control local affairs. The Mexican government tried, but failed, to keep Americans from settling on Mexican soil.

Americans often violated Mexican laws and were thrown into jail. Frequently they were mistreated. In one incident 22 Americans suspected of plotting a revolution were executed by the Mexicans in 1835.

Debts owed by the impoverished Mexican government to United States citizens also contributed to the ill feeling. During Mexico's revolutions, the property of many Americans living in Mexico had been damaged or destroyed. In 1839 an international commission examined American claims and awarded United States citizens about $2 million. By 1845 Mexico had paid only three installments on this debt. The Americans chose to ignore the fact that at this time they themselves were far behind in payments of some $200 million to Great Britain.

The Mexicans also had many grievances against the United States. They were bitter about American expansion into Texas and the violations of Mexican laws by American settlers. They were bitter, too, about the Texas revolution of 1836, which they blamed on the United States. They feared that events in Texas were only the beginning of an American attempt to win control of the entire Southwest.

Rising war fever. American naval and military commanders in the Pacific area had orders to seize Upper California if war broke out. In 1842 Commodore Thomas A. C. Jones, hearing a false rumor that war had been declared, sailed swiftly to Upper California and seized the capital at Monterey. He hauled down the Mexican flag and raised the Stars and Stripes. The next day, learning that he had made a mistake, Jones apologized profusely and withdrew in haste.

In the Presidential election of 1844, the Democrats demanded that Texas as well as Oregon be annexed to the nation. When the Democrats won by a very narrow popular majority, the government took steps to admit Texas to the Union without delay. To the Mexicans, who had never officially recognized the Republic of Texas, this was the final blow. The Mexican government broke off diplomatic relations with the United States.

Texas was finally admitted to the Union in December 1845. Meanwhile, the new President, James K. Polk, had more ambitious plans. He wanted the United States to acquire the whole vast area stretching from Texas to the Pacific Ocean, but he hoped to do so by peaceful means. In November 1845 he sent Ambassador John Slidell to the Mexican government with an offer to buy Upper California and New Mexico. The Mexican government refused to receive Slidell, and he returned empty-handed.

Outbreak of war. President Polk was now sure that Mexico would never give up New Mexico and Upper California or its claim to Texas. However, he still wanted this area to belong to the United States and was ready to declare war to get it. Several members of his cabinet urged him to delay, saying that Mexico would probably soon commit some act that would justify war.

In January 1846, however, Polk ordered troops under General Zachary Taylor to move

Chapultepec Castle, just outside Mexico City, became the traditional home of Mexican rulers. It was the scene of heavy fighting during the war.

southward from the Nueces (noo·AY·ses) River to the north bank of the Rio Grande (see map, page 357). Ever since Texas had declared its independence from Mexico, the Texans had claimed that their territory reached southward to the Rio Grande. The Mexicans, for their part, rightly insisted that it ended farther north at the Nueces River.

Both American and European maps had accepted the Nueces River as the southern boundary of Texas. This was the boundary Spain had fixed in 1816, three years before the United States gave up all claims to Texas in the treaty by which Florida was purchased from Spain. Now, however, when he sent troops into this area, Polk claimed that he was acting defensively. The Mexicans insisted that the United States was acting aggressively.

Months passed, and President Polk's impatience grew daily. Finally, on May 9, the President notified his cabinet that he intended to recommend war with Mexico within a few days. That very night he received the news he had long been wanting. Mexican troops had crossed the Rio Grande and had fought with American forces.

Convinced that the American people would approve his action, Polk sent his war message to Congress on May 11. He declared, "Mexico has passed the boundary of the United States, has invaded our territory and shed American blood upon American soil. . . . War exists, and notwithstanding all our efforts to avoid it, exists by the act of Mexico herself." On May 13, Congress declared war.

Opposition to the war. Although Congress declared war, many of its members questioned American actions. One of these was Abraham Lincoln, a young Illinois lawyer then serving his only term in Congress. In 1847 he introduced in Congress his famous Spot Resolutions. In them he questioned whether the "spot" on the north bank of the Rio Grande where American blood had been shed was really United States soil. As you have just read, there was good reason to believe that the land between the Rio Grande and the Nueces River was not a part of Texas.

Others in Congress shared Lincoln's concern. In addition, many American citizens, especially in the North and East, voiced their opposition to the war. They felt that Polk had deliberately provoked the war, a view that most historians share today. They believed that the true cause of the war was Polk's determination to have New Mexico and California for the United States. Despite this opposition, however, the Congress and the American people generally supported the war once it began.

The war in the West. Armed forces of the United States operated in three different areas (see map, page 357). The American forces had the easiest time in California and New Mexico, which included present-day Arizona. For one thing, the Mexicans had not kept strong forces in the presidios in these regions. Equally important, in both California and New Mexico, many wealthy Spanish families had political, economic, and even marriage ties with the newly arrived American settlers. As a result, many Mexicans did not resist the invading ▲ American armies.

In the summer of 1846, an expedition under Brigadier General Kearny left Fort Leavenworth on the Missouri River, took Santa Fe, and won control of New Mexico. Kearny then went on to southern California. Despite stiff resistance near San Diego, with a Mexican victory at the Battle of San Pascual, Kearny

managed to get the upper hand. Other Mexican victories at Los Angeles, Santa Barbara, and Chino Rancho failed to halt American advances.

Even before news of the war reached Upper California, a few dozen Americans led by William B. Ide had begun to plot against Mexican rule. They carried on their discussions in the camp of Captain John C. Frémont, a famous explorer who had arrived in California the previous autumn. At Sonoma on June 14, 1846, Ide and a band of American settlers proclaimed the Republic of California, or the Bear Flag Republic. They hoisted a flag with a bear and a star painted on it as a symbol of independence.

On July 7 Commodore J. D. Sloat of the United States Navy, hearing of the outbreak of war, landed naval forces at Monterey on the California coast. There he raised the American flag and proclaimed California a part of the United States. Frémont then organized most of the Americans, including the Bear Flaggers, into a "California battalion." With Commodore Robert F. Stockton, Frémont's forces moved south and captured Los Angeles.

The war in Mexico. Fighting was fierce in the region south of the Rio Grande. An expedition under General Zachary Taylor won victories at Palo Alto and Resaca de la Palma (ray·SAH·kah day lah PAHL·mah) on May 8 and 9, 1846, before war was actually declared. Taylor then went on to capture Monterrey, Mexico, in September 1846 and to check the Mexican forces under Santa Anna at Buena Vista (BWAY·nah VEES·tah) in February 1847.

Despite these defeats the Mexicans continued to fight. Polk ordered an expedition to advance against Mexico City, the capital of Mexico, over the route once traveled by Cortés. Led by General Winfield Scott, an expeditionary force including marines landed near Veracruz on the Gulf of Mexico. Nearly every step of the long, mountainous road to the "Halls of Montezuma" was bitterly contested. Hard battles were fought at several places, but on September 14, 1847, American troops entered Mexico City as victors.

End of the war. By 1848 Upper California, New Mexico, and all of northern Mexico were in American hands. General Taylor's troops held northern Mexico, and General Scott's forces walked the streets of the Mexican capital. The defeated Mexicans had to end the

▲ Report topic: In May 1846 the Mexican government seriously considered handing California over to Great Britain as security for a loan. Ask one or more students to research why the deal did not go through and why the Mexican government proposed the deal in the first place.

war on the Americans' terms. These were written down in the Treaty of Guadalupe Hidalgo (gwah·dah·LOO·pay ee·DAHL·goh) in 1848.

From the Mexican point of view, these terms were severe indeed. Mexico was forced to give up Texas, New Mexico, and Upper California—two fifths of Mexico's land. In return for this huge area, called the Mexican Cession (see map, page 360), the United States gave Mexico $15 million. The United States also agreed to pay debts totaling over $3 million that Mexicans owed to Americans. It further promised to respect the religious preferences and the civil and property rights of Mexicans in the newly acquired territory.

The dreams of Americans who had believed in their nation's "manifest destiny" had come true. The southwestern boundary of the United States reached to the Pacific.

Finally, in 1853, Congress approved a payment to Mexico of $10 million for the Gadsden Purchase (see map, page 360). This was an area of land south of the Gila River needed to construct a southern transcontinental railroad. It was named for James Gadsden of South Carolina, who, as minister to Mexico, negotiated the purchase. ▲

Culture conflicts. Two fifths of Mexico's territory and about 75,000 Spanish-speaking people passed into United States hands as a result of the war. Differences in the cultures of the Americans and the new Spanish-speaking citizens created serious problems.

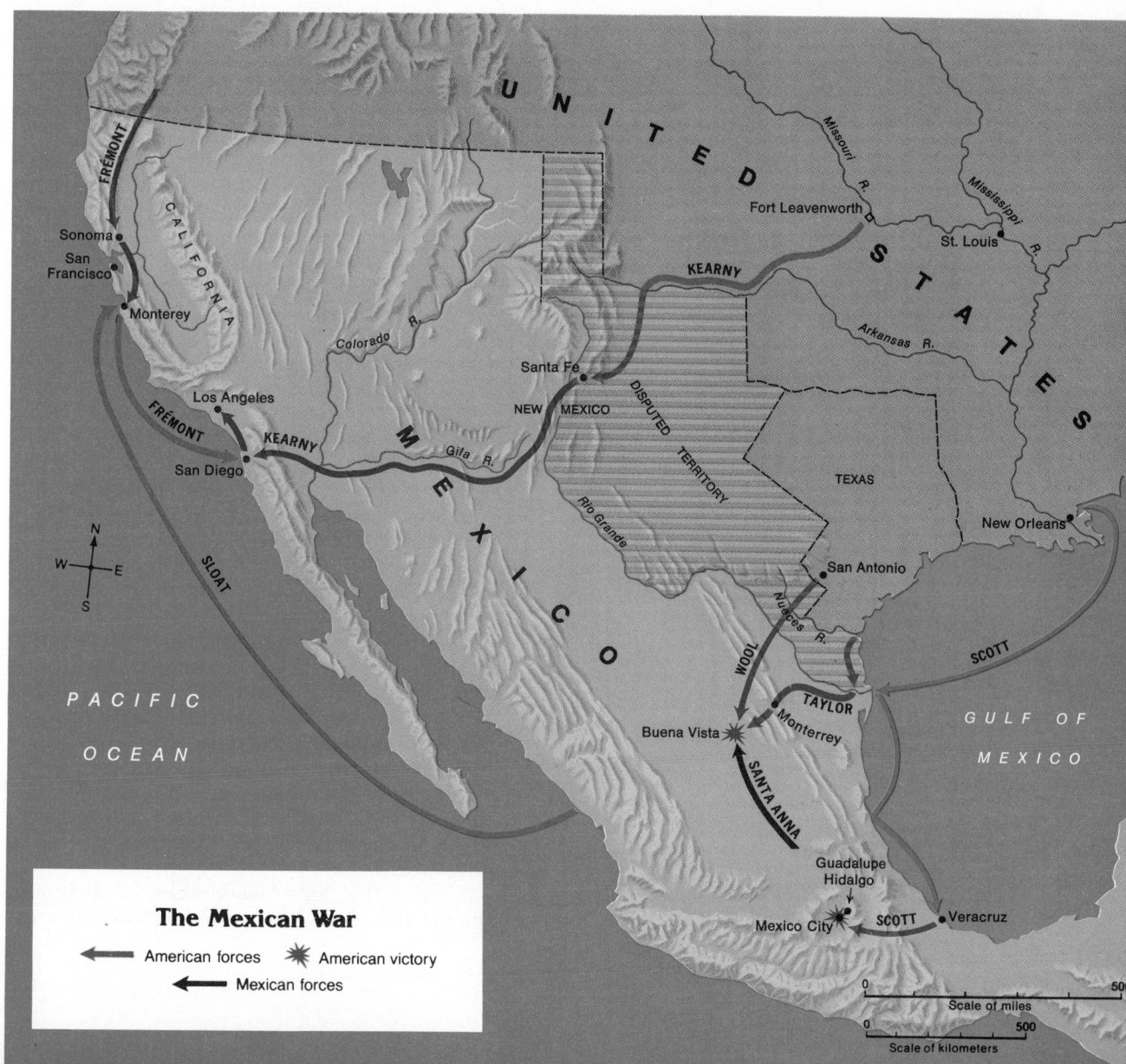

The Mexican War

⟵ American forces ✳ American victory
⟵ Mexican forces

For the well-to-do Spanish families with ties to the Americans, adjustments were usually easy. Other Spanish-speaking people did not fare so well. Some lost part or all of their property. Also, Americans challenged land titles that had come down from Spanish or Mexican authorities by starting costly legal battles. Even when American courts upheld the original land titles, long-lasting bitterness remained.

Under the treaty of 1848, Spanish-speaking citizens were granted all the rights of American citizenship. All to often, these were only "paper" rights. Their culture blended Spanish, Mexican, and Indian ways of life. It was regarded by many Americans as inferior to their own. This prejudice helped spark rebellions in Santa Barbara, Los Angeles, and Taos, New Mexico.

Poor Mexican-Americans suffered even more. After the American takeover, many of them worked for low wages on American ranches, mines, and railroads. They found their own traditions of family loyalty, personal honor, and devout Catholicism less respected than in the past. During the turbulent early years of the American Southwest, Mexican-American bandits sometimes raided American settlements. These raids, in part, were protests against injustices suffered by the **peons.** In response, local American vigilante committees and Texas and New Mexico Rangers were organized to enforce law and order. Often, though, they resorted to harassment, beatings, and lynchings.

SECTION REVIEW

See underscored items, text pp. 354-58.
Identify: manifest destiny, James K. Polk, Zachary Taylor, Spot Resolutions, Bear Flag Republic, Winfield Scott, Mexican Cession, peons
For answers to questions, see Answer Key, p.A51.
1. **Comparing Viewpoints: (a)** How would President Polk have described the events leading to the Mexican War? **(b)** How would a Mexican have described the same events?

2. **Summarizing Ideas: (a)** What were the terms of the Treaty of Guadalupe Hidalgo? **(b)** What was the significance of this treaty in American history? **(c)** Why did the Mexicans think the treaty terms were harsh?

3. **Interpreting Ideas:** Why was the Gadsden Purchase important?

4 A surge of migration brings California into the Union

See Teaching Suggestions in TMRG, pp.TM91-92.
As early as the 1820's and 1830's a stream of settlers had pushed west. They crossed the Great Plains and threaded their way through the Rocky Mountains to Oregon and beyond. When the war with Mexico ended, this stream of settlers to the West would become a flood.

The Mormons and Utah. One of the largest groups was the Mormons. The Mormon Church, or the Church of Jesus Christ of Latter-Day Saints, was founded in western New York in 1830 by young Joseph Smith. Smith announced that he had found golden plates on which sacred scriptures were engraved. When translated, these became known as the *Book of Mormon.* Thousands of converts joined the new religious faith.

In Kirtland, Ohio, in Independence, Missouri, and in Nauvoo, Illinois, Mormons attempted to build an ideal society where they could live and worship in their own way. In each place they were driven away by hostile neighbors. These neighbors did not understand them and disliked the Mormon idea that they were a chosen people with a special revelation of truth. Many people further disapproved of the Mormons because they openly accepted polygamy—the practice of a husband having more than one wife at the same time. In Missouri people who favored slavery disliked the Mormons simply because most Mormons came from the Northeast. They feared that these Mormons would oppose slavery. It made little difference to the proslavery Missourians that Joseph Smith and other Mormon leaders opposed the abolition of slavery.

The Nauvoo community in Illinois prospered more than the other two. By 1844 it had become a thriving town of 15,000 persons, but trouble was brewing. Some Mormons opposed polygamy and disliked Smith. Finally people in nearby towns, fearing and resenting the prosperity of the Mormons, attacked Nauvoo. Joseph Smith and his brother Hyrum were killed. Once again the Mormons were forced to move west.

Under the able leadership of Brigham Young, the Mormons moved out of Nauvoo.

When Mormon leader Brigham Young first set eyes on the valley of the Great Salt Lake in 1847, he proclaimed, "This is the place!" Young regarded the site as the fulfillment of God's promise to Joseph Smith that the Mormons would find a homeland in the wilderness.

The Mormons had to endure many physical hardships in their new environment, including drought and locusts. But they survived, and they decided to build a temple to God for delivering them from their long quest.

The many-spired Mormon Temple, built in stages from 1853 to 1893, is one of the largest religious structures in the world. Today three and one half million members of the major Mormon sect, the Church of Jesus Christ of the Latter-Day Saints, consider this temple the center of their "kingdom of Zion." Only worthy Mormons are permitted to enter the temple.

Their loaded wagons moved westward across the plains and through the towering Rockies, finally stopping in 1847 on the eastern shore of Great Salt Lake (see map, page 348). There the Mormons plowed and irrigated the fields, learning many lessons about desert farming that they passed on to later western settlers. They laid out Salt Lake City on the Jordan River and erected a temple that would become famous throughout the world. The Mormons also sent missionaries to other parts of the world and brought converts to their new communities. Finally, in 1896, Utah entered the Union as the 45th state.

Spanish influence in California.   Beyond the shore of Great Salt Lake, hidden by the towering Sierra Nevada mountains, lay Upper California. Neither Spain nor Mexico had ever been strong enough to develop this rich land into a thriving region. By the early 1800's, the Spaniards had completed the chain of missions begun by Gaspar de Portola and Father Junípero Serra. They had also built a few presidios and several small towns, among them San Diego, Los Angeles, Monterey, and Yerba Buena (YAIR·bah BWAY·nah), where San Francisco now stands (see map, page 19). Also, scattered over this immense territory were the estates, small communities in themselves, of powerful Spanish landowners. The Mexican Revolution of 1821 caused few changes in this vast region.

Life in this land of rare beauty, vast distances, and unbelievable contrasts of climate and topography moved at an easy, leisurely pace. As late as 1846, when the Mexican War broke out, only about 4,000 Mexicans lived in California. Fewer than 500 of them were soldiers in a half dozen or so forts.

Although Spanish, and later Mexican, control was never strong, the influence of Spanish culture can be seen to the present day throughout California. Towns, rivers, and mountains bear Spanish names. Spanish laws, customs, and architecture continue to enrich life in California to this day.

American settlers in California.   A region so rich and beautiful naturally attracted restless Americans pressing westward. In 1841 a party of men, women, and children led by John Bidwell, "the prince of California pioneers," set out from Missouri. Their trip across the plains and mountains, as revealed in the journal of their leader, is a tribute to human courage. "We knew only," Bidwell wrote, "that California lay to the west."

The Bidwell pioneers were followed by many others, and by 1848 several hundred Americans had settled in California. Among those who set out for California were members

359

The Nation's Growth to 1853

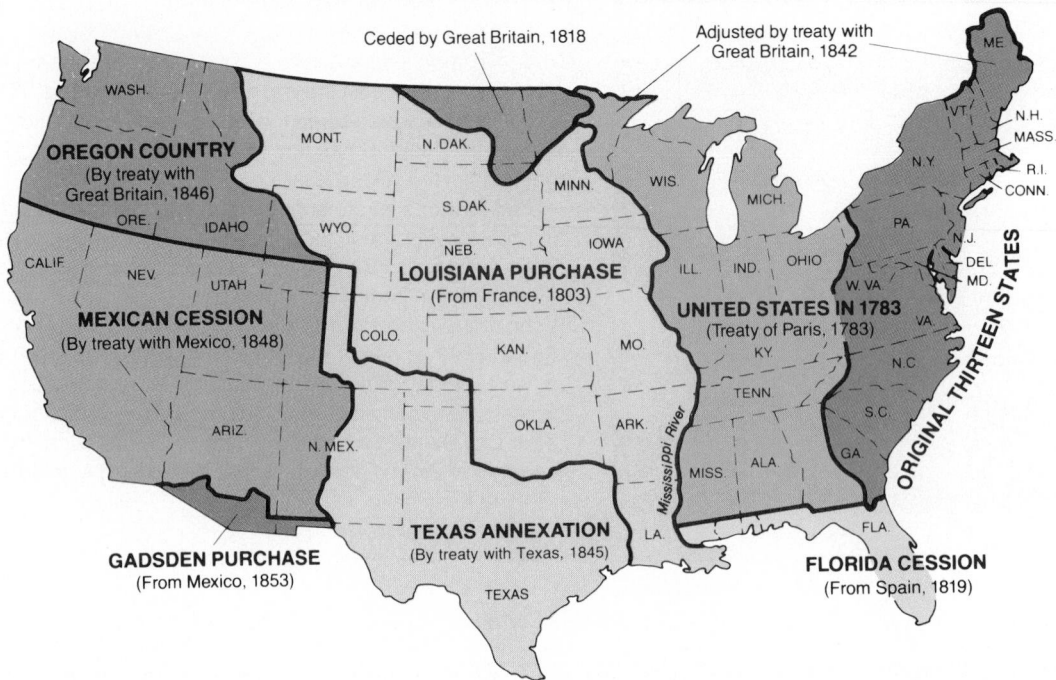

The Nation's Growth to 1853

Ceded by Great Britain, 1818

Adjusted by treaty with Great Britain, 1842

OREGON COUNTRY
(By treaty with Great Britain, 1846)

MEXICAN CESSION
(By treaty with Mexico, 1848)

LOUISIANA PURCHASE
(From France, 1803)

UNITED STATES IN 1783
(Treaty of Paris, 1783)

ORIGINAL THIRTEEN STATES

GADSDEN PURCHASE
(From Mexico, 1853)

TEXAS ANNEXATION
(By treaty with Texas, 1845)

FLORIDA CESSION
(From Spain, 1819)

of the ill-fated Donner party. Caught in 1846 by the icy grip of an early winter in the Sierra Nevada, the Donner party built crude shelters and struggled to survive. Soup made of boiled leather and powdered bones became a luxury. Of the 79 persons who started out in the Donner party, 34 died before an expedition out of California rescued the survivors.

Gold in California.   Among the early settlers in California was John A. Sutter from Switzerland. His sawmill and fort at Sacramento were the center of bustling activity. On the morning of January 24, 1848, one of his employees, James W. Marshall, detected flakes of yellow metal at the bottom of a stream where a new mill was being built. The shining metal was gold. Despite Sutter's desire to keep the discovery secret until the new mill was built, the news spread like wildfire.

Stories of huge fortunes made overnight spread throughout the nation. Some stories were true; most were false. True or false, the stories stirred everyone's imagination. In 1849, a year after the discovery of gold, thousands of adventurous Americans sold all they owned and joined the westward rush to the gold fields of California.

The gold rush.   Adventurers from Europe and the eastern United States reached California by three routes (see map, page 348). The longest route was the safest and most comfortable, as comfort went in those days. This route was by ship around Cape Horn.

The quickest, most crowded, and most expensive route was by ship to Central America. From there travelers went by land across the Isthmus of Panama and by another ship from there to San Francisco. Every old ship that could float was pressed into service. Crowds of men in bright shirts and slouch hats, armed with bowie knives and pistols, raced to cross the isthmus and board one of the few ships sailing between Panama and California.

A third route was fit only for the rugged and the brave. It led across the Great Plains and through the mountain passes—the route of the Bidwell and Donner parties. Many of the wagon trains of the "Forty-Niners" took as long as five months to make the trip from the eastern seaboard. Many trails along the route were lined with household goods thrown away to lighten the load, with dead bodies of animals, and with the graves of those struck down by Indians, disease, hunger, thirst, cold, or heat.

The first wave of "Forty-Niners" jammed into lawless mining camps. Some found riches beyond their wildest dreams; most found only disappointment. As the months went by, two streams of travelers passed each other on the trails and roads leading from San Francisco to the mining regions. Going were newcomers eager for fortunes. On the way back were the disappointed gold seekers who had given up the search.

Included in the wave of "Forty-Niners" were black people, slave and free. Some worked as servants. Others searched for gold in crews under the direction of a slaveowner. A few became independent miners. Moses Rodgers, for example, born a slave in Missouri, became a mining authority whose advice was often sought by other gold seekers.

Statehood for California. Gradually the uproar subsided, and some newcomers began to build houses, hotels, stores, and shops in the rapidly growing towns and cities. Some settled on the land and began to farm. Settlers built schools and churches. A government that was partly military and partly civilian was formed.

Late in 1849 a convention met and drafted a state constitution, which was accepted by the people. The constitution outlawed slavery in California but included restrictions and discriminations against Indians. In 1850 Congress approved the constitution, and California entered the Union as a free state.

The fate of the Indians. The Indians of California suffered an unhappy fate under both Spanish and Mexican rule. In 1834 the Mexican government responded to complaints of ill treatment of the mission Indians. Eager to seize mission lands and wealth, it removed the missions from control of the Catholic Church. The mission Indians were not adequately prepared to get along on their own in the white settlers' society. Deprived of much of their own culture, they were easy prey for settlers. Some of the Indians became virtual slaves on the great ranches.

The Indians suffered even more cruelly when American settlers moved in and California became part of the United States. From 1848 to 1871, more than 50,000 California Indians died of disease, starvation, and violence. In northern California the Karok, Yurok, Shasta, and Hupa tribes, after bitter struggles, gave up their lands to white newcomers.

The Treaty of Fort Laramie. The Indians who lived on the western plains and in the mountains along the newly opened routes to the Far West also faced a grim future. An endless stream of covered wagons and herds of cattle moved westward across Indian territory. Ancient hunting grounds were disturbed and age-old traditions and ways of life were disrupted. Faced with this threat, the Indians resorted to attacking the wagon trains and their night encampments.

In an effort to solve the problem, the United States government invited the Indians to a great conference to be held at Fort Laramie in what is now the state of Wyoming. The conference opened in the autumn of 1851. Large delegations of Indians arrived and set up colorful camps around the fort. Led by their chiefs, they included the Sioux, Assiniboins, Arikaris, Crows, Gros Ventres, Shoshones, Arapahos, and Cheyennes. The American delegation included government officials and army detachments. Father De Smet arrived from Oregon. Jim Bridger, leader of the Mountain Men, acted as interpreter. For several days there were games, celebrations, and speeches.

Out of the meeting came the Treaty of Fort Laramie. In it the federal government agreed to pay $50,000 to the Indians each year for 50 years in return for the safety of the settlers moving west. The treaty also gave the government the right to build forts along the western trails. The Senate did not ratify the treaty, but the government made the annual payments for 15 years. The Indians generally kept the agreement until after the Civil War. Then they became increasingly disturbed by new waves of settlers. ▲

SECTION REVIEW

See underscored items, text pp. 358-61.

Identify: Joseph Smith, Brigham Young, John Bidwell, Donner expedition, John Sutter, Treaty of Fort Laramie

For answers to questions, see Answer Key, pp.A51-52.

1. **Interpreting Ideas: (a)** Why were the Mormons persecuted? **(b)** How did the Mormons respond to persecution?

2. **Summarizing Ideas: (a)** Who were the "Forty-Niners"? **(b)** Why did they go to California? **(c)** How did they get there?

3. **Analyzing Ideas: (a)** How were the Indians treated by the Spanish, Mexican, and United States governments? **(b)** Why do you suppose they received such treatment?

Relating Geography and History Reading a Historical Map

A historical map is a kind of special purpose map that focuses on an event such as a battle or a journey. Historical maps make use of specific symbols and labels so the legend of a historical map is usually very important to an understanding of the map. Historical maps help students of history to visualize spatial relationships, routes across land and water, and the impact of topography on troop movements and settlement patterns.

How to Read a Historical Map

Follow these steps to use historical maps effectively.

1. **Use map basics.** Review the basic map-reading guidelines presented on page 164–65 of Chapter 7. Consult the title of the map, if it has one, to determine its purpose. Consult the map key, or legend, to identify special symbols that may be used on the map. Refer to the compass rose to determine the location of north and the other directions. Note the scale of miles and the scale of kilometers for future reference.

2. **Read the map labels.** Historical maps often give most of their information through the use of labels or short captions within the map. Sort out the information that is geographical from that which is historical.

3. **Relate map and textbook content.** More often than not, maps in a textbook are placed in proximity to the content they illustrate. Skim the map at the same time you are skimming the material for study. When reading the material that corresponds to the subject of the map, take time to study the map and relate the map to the content. Make comparisons and draw conclusions. Note any special relationships (time, cause-effect) illustrated by the map. The map should help you visualize how an event took place and why it unfolded as it did.

Applying the Skill

Study the two historical maps at the bottom of the page. Note the title of the map to the left. The title connects the map with a historical topic — the Defense of the Alamo. It

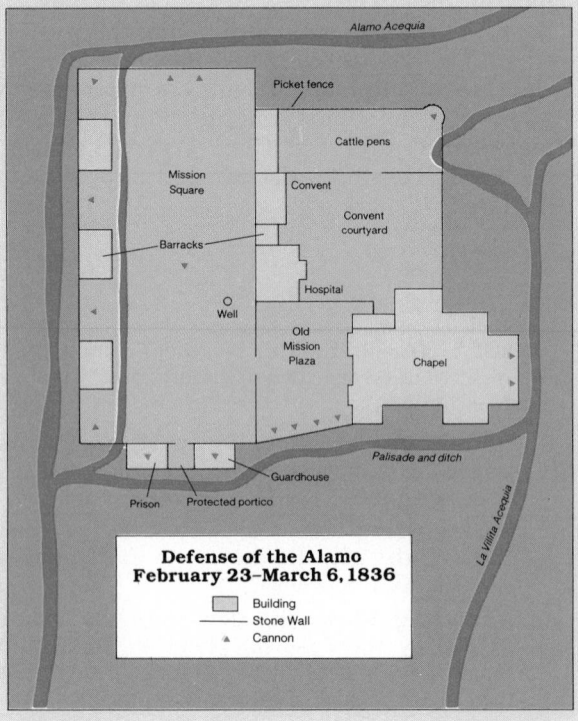

Defense of the Alamo
February 23–March 6, 1836

☐ Building
— Stone Wall
▲ Cannon

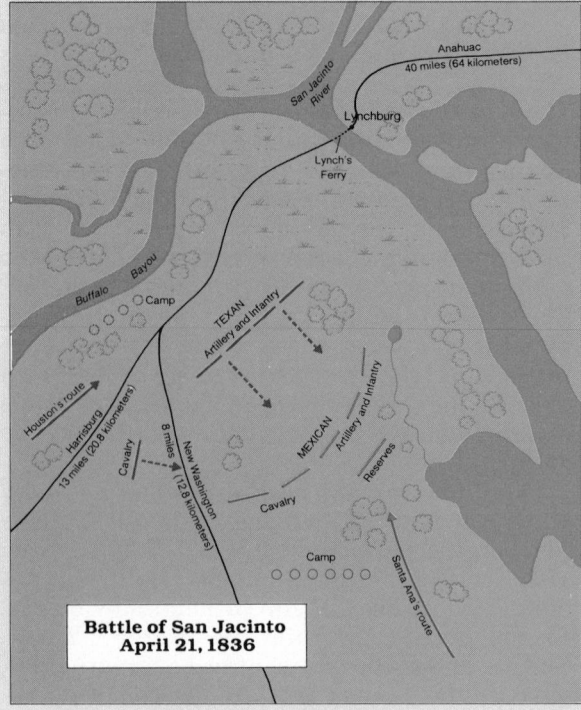

Battle of San Jacinto
April 21, 1836

also provides a time frame so that you know the defense of the Alamo took place over a period of two weeks. The map is a diagram of the interior and immediate exterior of the Alamo. The legend provides you with information about certain symbols: the buildings, stone wall, and cannon. From the diagram you can tell that the Alamo compound consisted of a number of buildings surrounded by a stone wall and that as many as 16 cannons were stationed at strategic spots. A map such as this enables a reader to see how it was possible for the Mexicans to surround the building and lay siege to it for an extended time and eventually to slaughter most of its defenders.

The map at the bottom right of page 362 also concerns the fight for Texas independence. From the title you see the name of the battle that the map depicts and the date on which the battle took place. You see many labels, most of which are imparting historical information. It is necessary to read the labels to see how the opposing forces lined up against each other. The map also provides information regarding distances and the geographic setting of the battle.

Practicing the Skill

Study the map below carefully. Then on a separate sheet of paper, answer the following questions.

1. **(a)** What is the title of the map? **(b)** What is the subject of the map? **(c)** What special function does the * serve?

2. What area of Texas was settled before 1800? How does the map illustrate that?

3. A number of dates are found within the boundaries of Texas. What do these dates indicate?

4. In what general direction did the settlement of Texas move?

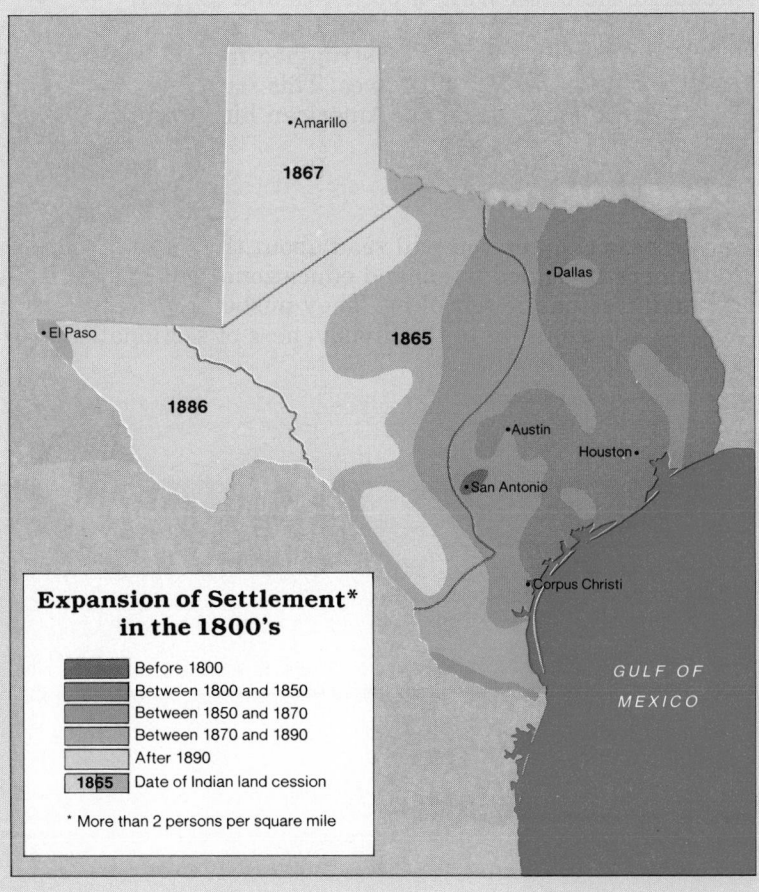

Expansion of Settlement* in the 1800's

- Before 1800
- Between 1800 and 1850
- Between 1850 and 1870
- Between 1870 and 1890
- After 1890
- 1865 Date of Indian land cession

* More than 2 persons per square mile

(1. (a) Expansion of Settlement in the 1800's (b) the expansion of settlements on the Texas frontier (c) to provide additional information which is necessary to understanding the map 2. (a) San Antonio and the surrounding areas (b) by coloring in the land area with a specific color which is identified on the legend 3. the dates of Indian land cessions 4. West)

The westward movement really began with the first settlers along the eastern seaboard of North America. By the early 1800's, the white settlers had advanced beyond the Mississippi River. By the 1840's bold pioneers had survived the long trek across the continent and were building new homes in the Oregon country. Other settlers were moving into Texas, Utah, California, and other parts of the West that were held by Mexico.

The Mexican authorities failed to control the tide of American settlers moving into the Southwest. Finally, the United States, eager to acquire territory all the way to the Pacific coast, declared war on Mexico. As a result of the Mexican War, the United States won the territory that now includes the present-day states of Texas, New Mexico, Arizona, Utah, Nevada, and California. Manifest destiny—the belief that the United States was fated to own the land from sea to sea—had been fulfilled.

The lands newly acquired had been settled by Spanish-speaking people who followed their own life styles and held ideas different from those of the American newcomers. These differences in language and ideas sometimes produced the bitter fruit of prejudice and conflict.

Both the North and the South struggled for control of the West. Northerners and southerners struggled in the halls of Congress as well as on the western lands themselves. This struggle over the West is one of the keys to an understanding of American history during the generation before the Civil War.

CONNECTING CHAPTER IDEAS

In the next chapter you will read about the national concern with reform. Reformers struggled to expand educational opportunities for all Americans through free public schooling. They pushed especially for the abolition of slavery, contributing to the divisiveness of sectionalism.

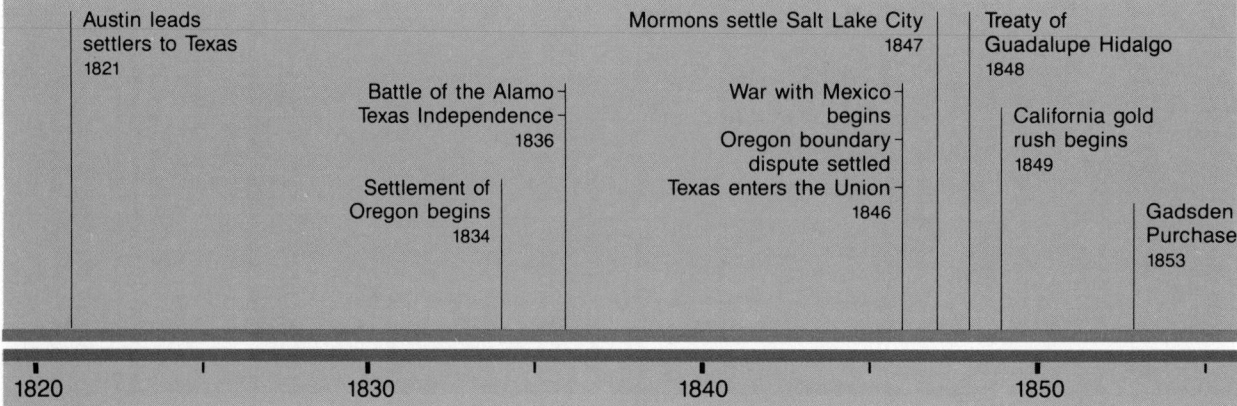

Austin leads
settlers to Texas
1821

Battle of the Alamo
Texas Independence
1836

Settlement of
Oregon begins
1834

Mormons settle Salt Lake City
1847

War with Mexico
begins
Oregon boundary
dispute settled
Texas enters the Union
1846

Treaty of
Guadalupe Hidalgo
1848

California gold
rush begins
1849

Gadsden
Purchase
1853

1820   1830   1840   1850

CHAPTER
15 REVIEW

Reviewing Important Terms

Decide whether each of the following sentences is true or false. If the sentence is false, replace the underlined term with the word or phrase that will make it true.

1. Jedediah Smith and James Beckwourth were among the <u>mountain men</u> who roamed the West searching for pelts.
2. The <u>Santa Fe Trail</u> crossed the Snake and Columbia river valleys to the Pacific Ocean.
3. The <u>Oregon Trail</u> cut through what is now Kansas and Colorado before connecting with the Old Spanish Trail.
4. In 1836 the <u>Lone Star Republic</u>, the Republic of Texas, declared its independence from Mexico.
5. Many American colonizers of Texas viewed the <u>peons</u>, who were of mixed Spanish and Indian ancestry, as inferior people.
6. Friction arose between Mexico and the United States, partly because of the idea that it was the <u>manifest destiny</u> of the United States to expand to the Pacific Ocean.
7. The $10 million <u>Gadsden Purchase</u> of 1853 allowed the construction of a southern transcontinental railroad.

Practicing Critical Thinking Skills

1. **Analyzing Ideas.** Explain why the following ideas played an important part in the history of the United States (a) the idea of the frontier and (b) the idea of manifest destiny.
2. **Comparing Viewpoints.** Compare the motives of the Americans who pioneered in the Pacific Northwest with the motives of the Americans who pioneered in Texas.
3. **Evaluating Viewpoints.** What motives led Americans to settle Utah and California?
4. **Using Historical Imagination.** How would you have felt about the American annexation of Texas if you had been (a) a Mexican living in Texas, (b) an American living in Texas, (c) a southern slave owner, (d) an opponent of slavery, or (e) a farmer living on the American frontier?
5. **Determining Cause and Effect.** (a) What effect did the expansion of American boundaries after 1820 have on the Spanish-speaking people who lived in these areas? (b) What effect did this expansion have on the Indians who lived there?

6. **Summarizing Ideas.** What was the general strategy of American forces in the Mexican War? How did they carry out this strategy? Use the map on page 357 to help you.
7. **Relating Past to Present.** In the period covered in this chapter, the foreign policy of the United States was based on the idea of manifest destiny. What do you believe is the main goal of American foreign policy today?

Developing History Study Skills

1. **Reading a Historical Map.** Examine the map on page 357 of the textbook. (a) Describe the journey made by Kearny that is shown on the map. (b) Over what two historic trails did much of Kearny's travels take place?

2. **Classifying Information.** Use the information in this chapter and the map on page 360 to classify the United States acquisition of land during the 1800's by (a) name of the territory acquired, (b) the date of acquisition, and (c) method of acquisition.

Relating Geography and History

The issue of settling boundaries is more easily accomplished when a generally recognized feature is used, such as a parallel line or body of water. This method was particularly important in the New World where claims were made in broad, general terms meant to encompass vast areas of land, much of which had not yet been explored. The United States, in its drive to span the continent, was involved in a number of disputes over boundary lines to the north and south, as well as territorial divisions in the interior. To understand how the United States determined its state and national borders use the maps on pages 992–93 and 996–97, to complete the following.

1. Name the states west of the Mississippi River whose northern boundaries were not settled, for the most part, on a parallel line or lines.
2. Of the states you named in 1, which are bordered on the north by a body of water?
3. Name the rivers that form United States or state boundaries west of the Mississippi River.
4. Do research to find out how the borders of your state were settled.

See Chapter Overview in TMRG, p.TM93.
See Chapter Objectives in TMRG, p.TM93.
See Introducing the Chapter in TMRG, p.TM93.

CHAPTER 16   Working for Reform

Changing Ways   (1820's–1860's)

Women's
strike, 1860

366

The term "to ferment" means "to be inwardly active, agitated, or excited, to seethe mentally or emotionally." It would be difficult to find a more accurate term than "ferment" to describe the activities of the American people in the years from the 1820's to the 1860's.

The United States was indeed in ferment during these years. Changes in the United States were taking place with bewildering speed. The very appearance of the nation was changing. Industrialization was transforming the North into a region of factories and busy towns. Cotton growing was bringing prosperity to plantation owners and others dependent on cotton in large areas of the South. Land-hungry pioneers were pushing across the Great Plains, through the Rocky Mountains, and into the fertile valleys of the Pacific Northwest and sunny California.

The ideas of the people were also changing. By the time Andrew Jackson became President in 1829, nearly all white male adults had won the right to vote. The growth of political democracy brought new hope to the freedom-loving people of the nation. Those who had the right to vote, and those who hoped to win it, expected to use their newly won power to make the ideals of democracy work more effectively in everyday affairs.

During the period from the 1820's to the 1860's, reformers were seeking to improve almost every aspect of society. "We are all a little wild here with numberless projects of social reform," Ralph Waldo Emerson, the New England writer and philosopher, wrote to a friend in England. The story of this period of reform, this age of change, is told in this chapter.

═══ READING FOCUS ═══

As you read about the changing ways that reformers brought about, look for the details that support each of the following statements.

1. Reformers struggle to improve American life.
2. Free public education makes a promising start.
3. A strong movement develops to abolish slavery.
4. The antislavery movement begins to divide the nation.
5. Writers preach faith in democracy and the individual.

1 Reformers struggle to improve American life

See Teaching Suggestions in TMRG, pp.TM93-95.

One of the many reforms Americans were working for in the period from the 1820's to the 1860's was a more important place for women in American life.

The status of women. From the earliest days, women worked together with men to build America. They shared the hard work and the danger. They helped transform the wilderness into a land of prosperous farms and thriving towns and expanding cities.

But women were regarded almost everywhere as inferior by nature to men, mentally as well as physically. Tradition, religious ideas, and the law contributed to this attitude. If a marriage was unhappy, divorce laws made it almost impossible for a woman to end the marriage. As late as the 1860's, married women in many states had no control over property they inherited or over wages they earned. Nor did they have legal control over their children. In practice, however, men seldom used their full legal rights over their wives and children.

Some of the changes in the America of the early 1800's also affected women unfairly. For example, the increasing importance given to high school and college education and to specialized training—from which women were excluded—restricted some occupations to men. Among these were medicine and midwife service. In earlier years, American women had worked in such jobs.

The Industrial Revolution also undermined the economic self-sufficiency of most American families. In doing so, it reduced the very difficult and important economic role that women had played in earlier family life. Moreover, it created a new and exploited class of women workers. The Industrial Revolution also led to an expanding middle class. This middle class held an ideal of the "lady." "Ladies" practiced only "genteel" activities in the home, such as needlework and the entertainment of guests. It was considered "unladylike" for a woman to take any active part either in public meetings or in politics.

Throughout the eighteenth century, home and church played the central roles in women's education. A few privileged women were allowed to sit in on their brothers' lessons with private tutors or to read in family libraries. If a woman became classically educated, it was because she was self-motivated or had a father who cared about her intellectual growth. Thomas Jefferson was such a father. Yet even he held the conventional view that women needed to learn mainly domestic and fine arts. His definition of public education was limited primarily to free white males.

In the early nineteenth century, women were still educated mainly at home or in local schools that taught the rudiments of reading, writing, and arithmetic. Since women could not vote, many males objected to the education of women at public expense.

Thomas Mann, a leading proponent of public education, believed that girls as well as boys should be educated in the common schools. He did not, however, view education as the means by which women could develop careers of their own: "The leaders of our country need knowledge. . . . But the mothers need it more, for they determine, to a great extent, the very capacity of the rulers' minds to acquire knowledge and apply it." In other words, education for women was only useful insofar as it continued to reinforce woman's traditional place — in the home.

As late as 1820 no seminary or college in the United States admitted women. Some women began working to change that situation. Prominent among them was Emma Willard, who realized that educational barriers against women were having a detrimental effect on women's total position in society. Willard's Female Seminary at Troy, New York, was designed to educate teachers as well as homemakers. The curriculum included subjects traditionally reserved for males. It also included gymnastics and physiology — two subjects that shocked many school visitors.

Women had learned early that they could not expect men to lead the movement for women's education. The continued success of the movement depended in large part on the initiative of women who had themselves already benefitted from education. The founder of the first women's college in the United States — Mount Holyoke — was Mary Lyon, a teacher who had worked her own way through school.

Many fine colleges for women were soon established. But equal education for men and women required equal access to resources and research facilities. The nation's first coeducational college, the Oberlin Collegiate Institute in Ohio, permitted women to choose between the courses offered to men and a special "ladies' curriculum." Oberlin's first four women graduates received their Bachelor of Arts degrees in 1841.

By 1890 American colleges and universities were graduating 2,500 women annually. And by 1900 the proportion of coeducational institutions of higher education had reached 70 percent.

The improvements in women's education did not automatically lead to professional jobs and careers for many women. Yet a most important battle had been won. The pioneers of women's education had at last put to death the myth that women were intellectually unfit for a life outside the home.

Declaring women's rights. In the 1820's and 1830's, a few women began to protest their exclusion from high school and college education, the professions, and participation in public affairs. A few leaders of the **women's rights movement** came from Europe, where a similar struggle was under way. For example, Ernestine L. Rose of Poland and Frances Wright of Scotland crossed the Atlantic to help American women in their struggle for equal rights.

American women bore the brunt of the struggle. One of the American leaders was Lucretia Mott, a Philadelphia Quaker. Another was Elizabeth Cady Stanton who, as a girl, had been troubled by legal discriminations against the women clients of her father, an upstate New York lawyer. These two were largely responsible for organizing the first women's rights convention. It was held at Seneca Falls, New York, in July 1848. The women delegates adopted a Declaration of Sentiments, which said, "All men and women are created equal," and went on to list demands for political, social, and economic equality with men. In spite of these early demands, decisive gains in these fields did not come until after 1850. Early victories came mainly in the field of education.

Education for women. By the 1820's education for girls and women was getting under way. Emma Hart Willard opened the Troy Female Seminary at Troy, New York, in 1821 and began to teach mathematics, science, history, and other subjects. During the next few years, Catharine Esther Beecher, Mary Lyon, and other dedicated women opened schools for girls. In 1837 Mount Holyoke Female Seminary opened in Massachusetts. Later known as Mount Holyoke College, it was the first women's college in the United States.

The coeducation movement made some headway in the Middle West. The first male college to open its doors to women was Oberlin Collegiate Institute in Ohio. Against bitter protests, Oberlin admitted women four years after it was founded in 1833. A few colleges in the Middle West followed Oberlin's example. In 1855 the University of Iowa became the first state university to admit women.

Early achievements. Slowly and against strong opposition, women began to win places in what had been considered a "man's world." Dr. Elizabeth Blackwell became the first woman to win a medical diploma in the United States. She began to practice medicine in New York City in 1850 and later founded the first school of nursing in the United States. In 1875 Blackwell became a professor in the London School of Medicine for Women. Her sister-in-law, Antoinette Louisa Blackwell, became the first fully ordained female minister in the United States.

Other women won distinction as writers and editors. Louisa May Alcott wrote a number of children's books, among them *Little Women,* which was translated into several languages. Harriet Beecher Stowe wrote *Uncle Tom's Cabin* (pages 380–81). Margaret Fuller's *Woman in the Nineteenth Century* is a classic in the history of feminism. It defied the customs that restricted women to conventional roles and urged the full development of women's potentials. Fuller's brilliant literary criticism was published in *The Dial* and in the *New York Tribune.* Jane Swisshelm edited several papers in which she advocated property rights, women, and opposed slavery.

The most influential woman in journalism was Sarah Josepha Hale, editor of *Godey's Lady's Book.* In this widely read magazine, she supported many of the traditional ideals of the "lady." Hale opposed women's suffrage but

was strongly in favor of educational opportunities for women.

Dorothea Lynde Dix. Another woman who exerted enormous influence was Dorothea Dix. In 1841 she was horrified by the cold, bare, filthy conditions of a jail she inspected near Boston. She laid the facts she discovered before the Massachusetts legislature, but the lawmakers did nothing.

Goaded to further action, Dorothea Dix visited every jail and poorhouse in Massachusetts and gathered overwhelming evidence. She packed notebook after notebook with horrors almost beyond belief. In all of the jails and poorhouses, she found old men, young girls, the poor, and the mentally ill thrown together in cold, dirty prisons. Some were chained to walls, beds, or floors. Some wore iron collars or straitjackets. Some had been kept in cages for years.

Finally, Dorothea Dix returned to the Massachusetts legislature with her evidence. This time the legislators listened. They began to pass laws to improve conditions in jails and poorhouses and to establish a public institution for the mentally ill. During the next few years, she repeated her reform work in other states. Moreover, her efforts helped to improve conditions in European jails and institutions for the poor and mentally ill.

By the 1850's, largely because of Dorothea Dix and others who shared her views, important reforms had been made in the United States. The death penalty for some crimes had been abolished. A growing number of people were demanding the abolition of capital punishment. Most states had outlawed the whipping of prisoners. Imprisonment for debt had been ended. Men and women were kept in separate sections of prisons. The mentally ill were separated from other prisoners. More attention was given to the individual criminal, and more effort was made to reform than to punish.

Dorothea Dix died in 1887 at the age of 85. A famous English doctor said of her, "Thus has died and been laid to rest . . . the most useful and distinguished woman that America has ever produced."

The crusade against alcohol. A struggle against the use of alcoholic beverages enlisted men and women who saw drunkenness as a

threat both to religion and to family life. This battle was known as the **temperance movement**. It got under way on a national scale in 1833 when advocates of temperance held a convention in Philadelphia. The delegates included not only religious leaders but also physicians and business people who believed that drinking was physically harmful. They also felt it decreased the efficiency of workers, caused accidents, and added to the tax bills for maintaining public order.

The temperance movement grew rapidly. In 1836 several groups united to form the American Temperance Union. Politicians, hoping to attract votes, took up the cause. Some reformers, insisting that any drinking was harmful and sinful, demanded state laws prohibiting both the manufacture and the sale of all alcoholic drinks.

The widespread agitation soon produced results. In 1834, only a year after the national movement got under way, Congress passed a law forbidding the sale of alcoholic beverages to Indians. Quakers, missionaries, and some Indian leaders had long been trying to stop the sale of rum and whisky to Indians. They believed that unscrupulous white traders defrauded the Indians of their treaty rights

The women shown here were among the most prominent reformers in the United States during the mid-1800's. They are (from left to right) Frances Wright, Dorothea Dix, Margaret Fuller, and Elizabeth Cady Stanton.

"I was a rebel at the age of five," Ernestine Rose once said. In her youth she argued with her father, the rabbi of a Russian-Polish town, who often responded to her questions by saying, "Little girls must not ask questions."

By the age of 16, Rose had become a very independent young woman. She left home, going first to Berlin, then to Paris, and London. In England, Ernestine met a young jeweler named William Rose. They were married in 1836 and soon afterward sailed for the United States.

In the United States, Ernestine Rose continued to ask probing questions. Why couldn't women vote? Why were black people enslaved? Why were factory workers paid so little? Battling injustice as an eloquent speaker, she became known as "Queen of the Platform."

Rose devoted most of the next 30 years to the cause of women's rights. She attended the national conventions and addressed hundreds of private groups and more than 20 state legislatures. By 1869 her efforts had left her almost crippled by neuralgia and rheumatism. The Roses then moved back to England, where Ernestine Rose died at the age of 82.

while the Indians were under the influence of liquor. These people welcomed the 1834 law, but as it turned out, the law banning the sale of liquor was generally ignored.

State laws prohibiting the use of alcoholic beverages were more effective. In 1846 Maine became the first state to pass a prohibition act. Other states soon followed.

Many people, especially brewers and distillers, opposed these laws. Other citizens protested that the states had no power to decide what anyone should or should not drink.

One unexpected result of the **prohibition** laws was a sharp rise in sales of patent medicines with a high alcohol content. However, the reformers did produce some results, and drinking among most classes decreased. In many communities a drunken man became an object of curiosity or even of contempt.

Efforts to end war. From about 1820 to 1860, many Americans as well as Europeans devoted their efforts to the peace movement. Quakers in the United States had always opposed the use of force, except when necessary for police purposes. However, an organized antiwar movement did not develop in America until after the War of 1812. In 1828 many local peace societies joined together to form the American Peace Society. The members of the society insisted that war was anti-Christian, inhumane, and uneconomical.

One leader of the peace movement was Elihu Burritt, a self-educated Connecticut blacksmith. He developed a pledge card against war that was signed by more than 40,000 persons in America and England. Influenced by William Ladd, a Maine sea captain and farmer known as "the apostle of peace," Burritt urged the nations of the world to form an international organization and a world court for the purpose of settling international disputes.

Efforts to build ideal communities. Not all the people who longed for a better world tried to change existing institutions of daily life. Some men and women chose to follow the example of religiously inspired groups. They chose to withdraw from the world around them to build ideal communities, which they called **utopian** (yoo·TOH·pee·un), **communities.**

Robert Owen, a wealthy British manufacturer, started a utopian community in 1825 at New Harmony in Indiana. It failed, but its failure did not discourage other utopian experiments. Two well-known but short-lived experiments were Brook Farm, near Boston, and the Oneida (oh·NI·dah) Community in central New York State.

SECTION REVIEW

See underscored items, text pp. 367-68, 370-71.

Identify: reformer, women's rights movement, temperance movement, prohibition, American Peace Society, utopian communities
For answers to questions, see Answer Key, p. A53.

1. **Organizing Ideas: (a)** What were the goals of the women's rights movement during the 1840's and 1850's? **(b)** How did the movement's supporters try to reach these goals?

2. **Summarizing Ideas: (a)** Describe the growth of the temperance movement. **(b)** What were its results? **(c)** Why did Congress forbid the sale of liquor to Indians?

3. **Interpreting Ideas:** In what way did utopian communities reflect the spirit of this period in American history?

4. **Analyzing Ideas: (a)** Which of the reform movements had the most lasting effects on American society? **(b)** Which had the least? Explain.

2 Free public education makes a promising start

See Teaching Suggestions in TMRG, p. TM95.

Of the many reform programs none was more closely related to the growth of democracy than the movement for **free public schools.**

The problem of education. In colonial times New England towns were required by law to provide elementary schools. These New England schools were not entirely free. Parents who could afford to do so paid tuition fees for their children. The towns paid only for the children of poor parents.

By the early 1800's, however, these so-called "common" schools of New England had reached a very low level. Buildings were inadequate, and the quality of teaching was generally poor. Conditions were even worse in the Middle Atlantic and southern states, where people lived farther apart. Indeed, in many areas schools run by churches provided almost the only chance children had to get an elementary education.

By the 1820's and the 1830's, this situation was changing. Many people were demanding public, tax-supported schools. Reformers insisted that public education was necessary both to insure that voters were intelligently informed and to prevent the spread of crime and social disorder.

Leaders in the movement. Among the outstanding leaders of the struggle for free and improved public education were Horace Mann and Henry Barnard. Horace Mann turned from a brilliant legal and political career to become a crusader for public schools in Massachusetts. When the Massachusetts legislature created a state Board of Education in 1837, Mann became its first secretary. He used his growing power to establish **normal schools** for training teachers. He also began to organize the local school districts into a statewide system of education.

Henry Barnard did for Connecticut and Rhode Island what Horace Mann was doing for Massachusetts. His efforts won national recognition. In 1867 Barnard became the first United States Commissioner of Education.

The work of these and other leaders, among them Calvin E. Stowe of Ohio, Caleb Mills of

SOURCES

HORACE MANN ON EDUCATION (1848)

Education, they, beyond all other devices of human origin, is a great equalizer of the conditions of men—the balance-wheel of the social machinery. I do not here mean that it so elevates the moral nature as to make men disdain and abhor the oppression of their fellow men. . . . But I mean that it gives each man the independence and the means by which he can resist the selfishness of other men. It does better than to disarm the poor of their hostility toward the rich: it prevents being poor. . . .

By the 1860's when E. L. Henry painted this picture of a country schoolroom, all the states had agreed that they should provide tax-supported elementary schools. However, state and local funds were often short and public schools often were roughly furnished and lacked adequate supplies.

Indiana, John Swett of California, and Emma Hart Willard of Connecticut and New York, was of great importance. It helped to set the pattern of free public education throughout the United States.

Objections to public education. The struggle for free, tax-supported elementary schools was not won easily. Churches that had already set up religious schools, or that hoped to do so, objected strongly. Private schools, both religious and secular, voiced their opposition. Many taxpayers, including some wage earners and farmers, objected to using tax money to pay for schools.

Many Americans also had strong prejudices against "book larnin'." A pioneer in Illinois said that he "didn't think folks was any better off for reading, an' books cost a heap and took a power of time. 'Twant so bad for men to read," he admitted, "for there was a heap of time when they couldn't work out and could jest set by the fire; and if a man had books and keered to read he mought; but women had no business to hurtle away their time."

Early victories. In spite of such opposition, the movement for tax-supported elementary schools gained strength. In 1832 New York City established a system of free public elementary schools. Four years later, in 1836,

Philadelphia followed suit. By the 1850's nearly all white children, at least in the northern cities, could obtain a free elementary school education.

Meanwhile, New England led the way in efforts to provide free high school education. The first public high school in America, the English High School of Boston, opened in 1821. In 1827, Massachusetts adopted the first state law requiring towns with 500 or more families to provide a high school education for town youths at public expense.

The movement grew slowly. By 1850 the nation had only 55 public high schools, although there were more than 6,000 private high schools, or **academies,** as they were called. A high school education was still beyond the reach of most American youths.

The educational ladder. The democratic system of free public education in the United States has been called "a great educational ladder." By the 1860's the "ladder" was beginning to be erected. Most white children could expect to receive an elementary school education. In some larger towns, those who did not have to go to work could attend free public high schools.

A growing number of states established public universities. North Carolina pioneered by providing in 1776 in its constitution for a

▲ Report topics: "National Issues in Education," "The Role of the Federal Government in Determining School Policy," "The Establishment of a Nationwide High School Curriculum."

373

state university. The University of North Carolina graduated its first class in 1798. Other states followed North Carolina's example. By the late 1850's, 16 states had universities supported in part by public funds.

Alongside this system of free public schools and universities was the older system of private elementary schools, academies, and more than 100 church-supported colleges. Most of these colleges were small, with 100 to 300 male students and 6 to 12 professors.

It was significant that the principle of the separation of church and state was being written into all of the state constitutions. By the 1830's no person could be compelled to pay taxes to support any church or any school that taught particular religious doctrines.

Black students in college. In the period from the 1820's to the 1860's, the doors of higher education began to be opened – but only slightly – to qualified black students. In 1823 Alexander Twilight received a degree from Middlebury College. A few years later, the first blacks graduated from Amherst, Bowdoin, and Ohio universities.

Three colleges for black students were established in this period – Avery College and Lincoln College in Pennsylvania and Wilberforce College in Ohio. However, the only truly co-racial as well as coeducational college was Oberlin in Ohio. Oberlin was founded in 1833 by people who believed in abolition. Out of 8,800 young men and women who attended Oberlin between 1833 and 1861, 245 were black. Some were fugitive slaves or the sons and daughters of fugitives.

Most of the black women at Oberlin were enrolled in a Preparatory Department or in a special Ladies' Course. Mary Jane Patterson became, in 1862, the first black American woman to receive a college degree. After graduation, she taught school in Philadelphia for several years. Then, in 1871, she became the first black principal of a newly established high school for blacks in Washington, D.C.

SECTION REVIEW
See underscored items, text pp. 372-74.
Identify: free public school, normal school, academy, Oberlin, Mary Jane Patterson

For answers to questions, see Answer Key, p.A53.
1. **Summarizing Ideas:** Describe the contributions made to American education by (**a**) Horace Mann and (**b**) Henry Barnard.

2. **Organizing Ideas:** (**a**) Why was there opposition to free public schools? (**b**) List four achievements of the supporters of free public schools.

3. **Analyzing Ideas:** Does political democracy depend on free public schools? Explain.

4. **Studying Sources:** Read the Source on page 372. (**a**) What does Mann mean by calling education "a great equalizer"? (**b**) Do you agree or disagree with him? Explain your answer.

3 A strong movement develops to abolish slavery

See Teaching Suggestions in TMRG, pp.TM95-96.
The most vigorous reform movement between the 1820's and the 1860's was the antislavery, or abolition, crusade. No other single movement did as much to drive a wedge between the North and the South.

Background of abolition. A few Americans in colonial days objected to slavery, as you have read (page 71). After the Revolutionary War, this antislavery sentiment grew. By the 1780's and 1790's, several antislavery societies had been organized in the North.

In the nation's early years, some thoughtful southerners as well as northerners believed that slavery was morally wrong. These southerners found support among some planters who believed that slavery was no longer profitable. Tobacco growing used up the fertility of the soil and decreased the value of both land and crops. At the same time, the cost of feeding, clothing, and housing slaves either remained the same or increased.

A few planters, as you know, freed their slaves. But the problem was complex. Some southern slaveowners, even though they believed that slavery was wrong or unprofitable, hesitated to free their slaves. They worried that their slaves would be unable to take care of themselves in a difficult and even hostile society. They also worried about the effects of a freed black population on southern society. Their views were strengthened by the common belief that black people were inferior.

Slavery and cotton. The conflict in southerners' minds over whether or not to free their slaves was largely erased after Eli Whitney's invention of the cotton gin in 1793. Because of the cotton gin, the demand for slaves grew by leaps and bounds. Moral and political questions about slavery were raised less and less as the Cotton Kingdom became prosperous.

The renewed value of slaves to the economy did not wholly stop the antislavery movement, even in the South. As late as 1830, several Virginians publicly opposed slavery. Some also proposed measures for doing away with it gradually.

In the early 1820's, Benjamin Lundy, a mild-mannered but persistent Quaker, published a weekly antislavery newspaper, *The Genius of Universal Emancipation,* in Baltimore. Like most antislavery advocates in the 1820's, Lundy was moderate in his approach. He had hopes of bringing about the gradual **emancipation,** or freeing, of the slaves by appealing to the public's moral instincts.

Attempts at colonization. Lundy, like many others who opposed slavery, supported the American Colonization Society. This society was founded in 1817 to colonize free black people and to buy slaves to be returned to freedom in Africa. There they set up the West African country of Liberia. They modeled it after Sierra Leone, which was a nearby British refuge for freed slaves.

Lundy sincerely hoped to encourage emancipation by giving financial help to owners who wanted to free their slaves. However, the most influential members of the society — planters in Kentucky, Virginia, and Maryland — were not opposed to slavery. These planters wanted to rid the nation of free blacks. They believed that the presence of free blacks encouraged slaves in their desire to be free. The planters thought that colonization offered the best solution to the "race problem."

Faults in colonization. The colonization experiment was not very successful. By 1831 only 1,420 black Americans had been settled in Liberia. In part, the problem was lack of money. It was also true that most American blacks opposed the colonization movement. There were exceptions, of course. Paul Cuffe, a successful black merchant, had sent 38 black Americans to West Africa at his own expense even before the American Colonization Society was formed.

The growing opposition to colonization among blacks was strengthened by discourag-

FIFTH ANNIVERSARY
OF THE
MASSACHUSETTS ANTI-SLAVERY SOCIETY,
WEDNESDAY, JANUARY 25, 1837.

[☞ The public meetings, during the day, will be held in the SPACIOUS LOFT, OVER THE STABLE OF THE MARLBOROUGH HOTEL, and in the evening, in the REPRESENTATIVES' HALL.]

HOURS OF THE MEETINGS.

Meeting for Delegates at 9 o'clock in the morning, at 46, Washington Street.

First public meeting at 10 o'clock A. M., in the LOFT OVER THE STABLE OF THE MARLBOROUGH HOTEL.

Second public meeting at 1-2 past 2 o'clock, P. M. same place.

Evening meeting at 1-2 past 6 o'clock, in the REPRESENTATIVES' HALL.

☞ The Committee of Arrangements respectfully inform the ladies that ample accommodations have been prepared for them. The loft is spacious, clean, well warmed, and will accommodate, with ease and perfect safety, at least 1000 persons.

☞ AMOS DRESSER, a citizen of this State, who was 'Lynched' at Nashville, for the crime of being an Abolitionist, will be present, and during the meetings in the afternoon and evening, will give a history of that affair.

Abolitionist groups flooded the South with antislavery pamphlets and the House of Representatives with petitions to outlaw slavery.

ing reports of hardships in Liberia. To most black Americans, Africa was a strange, far-off place. Despite their grim lot, most black Americans had come to think of the United States as their home.

Early efforts by black people. In addition to condemning colonization, free blacks took steps early in the nation's history to improve their own lot, and, if possible, that of the slaves. They formed their own Afro-American churches. They organized societies for mutual aid and for improving opportunities in education and social life for black people.

Free blacks also took legal action to improve their circumstances. In 1794, free blacks asked Congress in a formal petition to take steps for "the relief of our people." In 1800, free black Americans of Philadelphia petitioned Congress to correct injustices in a law requiring fugitive slaves to be returned to their owners or to persons who might claim to be their owners. The same petition also asked Congress to provide for gradual emancipation of all slaves.

The first of a new, more vigorous series of

Slaves were sometimes forced to wear tags like these. Such tags registered the slaves by location, number, and occupation.

conventions held by black Americans met in Philadelphia in 1830. The delegates suggested that some black Americans might like to move to Canada. Those who did not choose to emigrate were urged to use every legal means to improve their lives in the United States.

David Walker's *Appeal*. These moderate activities were overshadowed in 1829 by the publication of *Appeal*, an essay by David Walker. Walker, a black American, began his *Appeal* by describing black slaves as "the most degraded, wretched, and abject set of beings that ever lived since the world began."

Walker's essay was a powerful call for bold and vigorous action by black Americans. Southern blacks, slave and free, must strike for their freedom—violently, if necessary. If white Americans wanted to prevent racial war, insisted Walker, they had to recognize at once the rights and humanity of black Americans.

Northerners, including white antislavery forces, condemned Walker's book as inflammatory and dangerous. Southerners put a price on Walker's head and tried to halt circulation of his *Appeal*.

A new mood. David Walker's *Appeal* was one example of growing militancy, or aggressiveness, in the abolition movement. William Lloyd Garrison's newspaper, the *Liberator*, was another example of this mood.

In his very first issue of the *Liberator*, published in Boston in 1831, Garrison, a white abolitionist, wrote, "I shall strenuously contend for the immediate enfranchisement [freeing] of our slave population. . . . I am in earnest—I will not equivocate—I will not excuse—AND I WILL BE HEARD."

Slavery, Garrison insisted, contradicted the Bible and the Declaration of Independence. It was both a sin and a crime. It had to be abolished at once.

Garrison condemned southern slaveowners, but he also condemned northerners who apologized for slavery or kept silent about it. Equal rights for blacks in the North was a leading object of Garrison's crusade.

Garrison's outspoken language offended many moderate white Americans who were against slavery. However, his religious and moral fervor and that of his New England followers was shared by rising abolitionist leaders elsewhere. In New York, Arthur and Lewis Tappan, deeply religious men and wealthy merchants, fought for abolition, as did Isaac Hooper, a Quaker who aided runaway slaves. Many people became abolitionists at religious revivals led by Charles G. Finney. In fact, revivalism was an important factor in the development of the abolition movement.

The most important abolitionist leader outside the East was Theodore Weld. He trained 70 young men who carried abolitionism into hundreds of communities in Ohio, western Pennsylvania, and upstate New York.

The abolitionist movement was mainly confined to the Northeast and the West, where people had no investment in slaves. A few southerners did free their slaves and move north, where they worked for abolition. James G. Birney of Alabama was an example.

Angelina and Sarah Grimké, daughters of a prominent South Carolina slaveholder, left their home in Charleston in protest against slavery. As writers and speakers, the Grimké sisters were doubly impressive since they testified from firsthand experience with slavery. Barred from many lecture platforms because of the prejudice against women in public affairs, the sisters became champions of the rights of women as well as of slaves.

Identify: abolition movement, Benjamin Lundy, emancipation, American Colonization Society, David Walker's *Appeal,* William Lloyd Garrison, *Liberator,* Theodore Weld, Angelina and Sarah Grimké

For answers to questions, see Answer Key, pp. A53-54.

1. **Evaluating Ideas: (a)** What were the goals of the colonization movement? **(b)** Why did attempts at colonization fail?

2. **Interpreting Ideas:** How was the belief that blacks were inferior used to justify not setting them free?

3. **Analyzing Ideas: (a)** How did free blacks try to improve their own situation and that of the slaves? **(b)** What was Walker's position on how to achieve equality? **(c)** What do you suppose was the reaction to his *Appeal?*

4. **Summarizing Ideas:** In what ways did the abolition movement become more militant?

4 The antislavery movement begins to divide the nation

See Teaching Suggestions in TMRG, pp. TM96-97.

In 1833 the abolition movement gained strength when the British Antislavery Society forced Parliament to end slavery in the British empire. Also in 1833 American abolitionists formed the American Anti-Slavery Society, modeled on the British society.

The American Anti-Slavery Society, a national organization, had many affiliated groups on the local and regional level. These groups quickly multiplied. By the mid-1830's there were more than 1,000 of them in the United States, with about 150,000 members.

The American Anti-Slavery Society tried to influence public opinion by appealing to the conscience of white America. It circulated pamphlets and poured petitions into Congress and into state legislatures. The society also supported many lecturers, including Theodore Weld and the young men he had trained.

Frederick Douglass. Probably the most effective lecturer of the American Anti-Slavery Society was Frederick Douglass, a self-educated former slave. Douglass told northern and midwestern audiences of his cruel treatment as a young slave in Maryland. He spoke of how his master had tried to prevent him

Frederick Douglass once said, "No man can put a chain about the ankle of his fellow man without at last finding the other end fastened about his own neck." What do you think Douglass meant?

from learning how to read. He told how a professional slave-breaker had overworked, beaten, and nearly starved him. He told how, finally, he had attacked and beaten the slave-breaker. Of this experience Douglass said, "I was a changed being from that night. I was nothing before, I was a man now ... with a renewed determination to be a free man."

Douglass condemned slavery and demanded its immediate abolition. He also insisted that it was time for the American people to listen to his message. "The lesson which they must learn, or neglect to do so at their own peril, is that Equal Manhood means Equal Rights, and further, that the American people must stand each for all and all for each without respect to color or race."

Split in the movement. The American Anti-Slavery Society was soon split by differences among its members. In particular, the militant position of William Lloyd Garrison alienated more moderate members. Garrison insisted on the right of women to hold leading offices in the

American Anti-Slavery Society and to speak publicly to mixed audiences. He stood firm even when, in 1838, an angry mob tried to break up a meeting in Philadelphia at which Angelina Grimké and other women spoke. The mob burned the hall itself the next day. Garrison's abolitionist foes insisted that the struggle for women's rights should be kept separate from the antislavery movement.

Garrison antagonized members of the society in other ways. He denounced the churches and the federal government for compromising with slavery. Claiming that the Constitution itself protected slavery, he insisted that antislavery people should refuse to vote or to hold public office.

Other leaders of the American Anti-Slavery Society deplored Garrison's militant views and actions. Thus in 1840 the society split apart.

Garrison controlled the original organization, while a new society promoted the more moderate program of his opponents.

Moderate programs. In their first major attempt at political action, moderates formed the Liberty Party. In 1840 they nominated James G. Birney, a former Alabama slaveowner, as their Presidential candidate. In the election of that year, Birney polled only 7,000 votes. In the election of 1844, the Liberty Party won more votes, but only 62,000 of the 2.5 million votes cast. Nevertheless, the political abolitionists were not discouraged. They kept working to influence politicians of the major parties.

Militant programs. Some abolitionists demanded more vigorous action. In their eyes the laws protecting slavery were immoral and

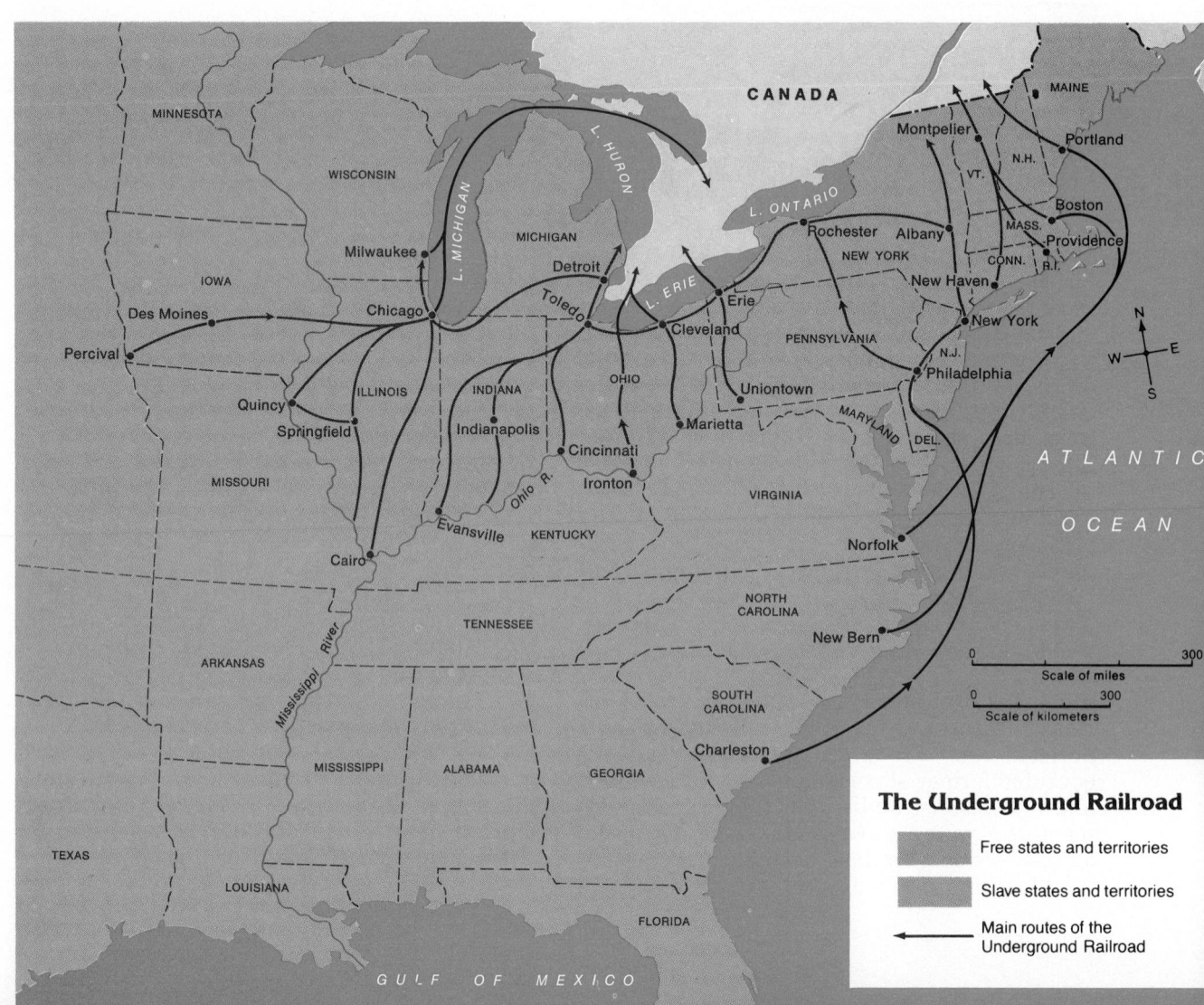

The Underground Railroad

Free states and territories

Slave states and territories

Main routes of the
Underground Railroad

The underground railroad was a secret system used between 1830 and 1860 to help southern slaves escape to freedom. It was neither underground nor a railroad, but was so called because its activities were carried out in darkness and disguise and because it used railroad terms as code words. Hiding places such as secret rooms and tunnels (shown here) were called "stations," routes were "lines," sympathetic persons who helped the slaves escape were "conductors," and the fugitives themselves were "freight."

The work of the railroad involved hiding runaway slaves and giving them food, clothing, and directions to the next station. Northern abolitionists and free blacks, as well as many southern slaves who themselves were unable to escape, participated in the system. The most daring conductor was Harriet Tubman, a former slave who had escaped via the railroad. Tubman was called the "Moses of her people" for helping more than 300 slaves escape. She later worked as a spy for the Union during the Civil War.

It is estimated that the underground railroad helped between 40,000 and 100,000 slaves reach freedom. The railroad's existence aroused northern sympathies and southern anger, and thus contributed to the ill-will that resulted in the Civil War.

should be defied. The most outspoken of these abolitionists was Henry Highland Garnet, a former slave from Maryland.

Garnet made a fiery speech before the National Convention of Colored Citizens in Buffalo in 1843. He proclaimed, "Brethren, arise, arise! Let every slave throughout the land do this, and the days of slavery are numbered. You cannot be more oppressed than you have been; you cannot suffer greater cruelties than you have already. Rather die like free men than live as slaves." By a majority of one, the convention voted to suppress Garnet's speech. Several years later, however, it was published.

The underground railroad. Some antislavery Americans took more direct action in the abolition movement by helping runaway slaves escape. They formed what came to be known as the "underground railroad." Slaves who learned about the railroad might hide until pursuit died down and then flee north across the Ohio River or the Mason-Dixon line.

Fleeing north, however, did not bring the slaves their freedom because of a Fugitive Slave Law passed by Congress in 1793. Owners of runaway slaves could recover the slaves simply by appearing before a magistrate and declaring that the captured slaves belonged to them. Thus fugitive slaves were not safe until they reached Canada.

Once across the Mason-Dixon line or the Ohio River, however, runaway slaves hoped to contact an agent on the underground railroad. The agent would arrange their escape. Hiding in attics and haylofts by day and taken to the next "station" by night, the slaves slowly made the long trip northward. In time, with good luck, they completed the dangerous journey and found freedom in Canada.

Black Americans as well as whites were active in the underground movement. Some of these black Americans were well-to-do, such as James Forten, a Philadelphia sailmaker, and Robert Purvis, a free black born in Charleston, South Carolina, and educated at Amherst Col-

379

lege. Purvis's zeal in helping slaves to freedom won him the title of "president" of the underground railroad.

Other black Americans active in the underground movement were themselves escaped slaves. Frederick Douglass was one. Another was William Wells Brown, the first black American novelist. Harriet Tubman, a fugitive slave, returned to the South time and time again. At great personal risk, she led many slaves to freedom by way of the underground.

Uncle Tom's Cabin. The perils of escaping from slavery were vividly portrayed in the famous novel, *Uncle Tom's Cabin,* written by Harriet Beecher Stowe, a northern white woman, and published in 1852.

In *Uncle Tom's Cabin,* Stowe described the inhumanity of the slave system and efforts to escape from slavery as she had heard about them from fugitives. The book was often moralistic in tone, as was common in the writing style of the times, but the characters came

Harriet Beecher Stowe's book, Uncle Tom's Cabin, *made northerners more aware of the evils of slavery. Southerners regarded the book as yet another attempt to interfere with their way of life.*

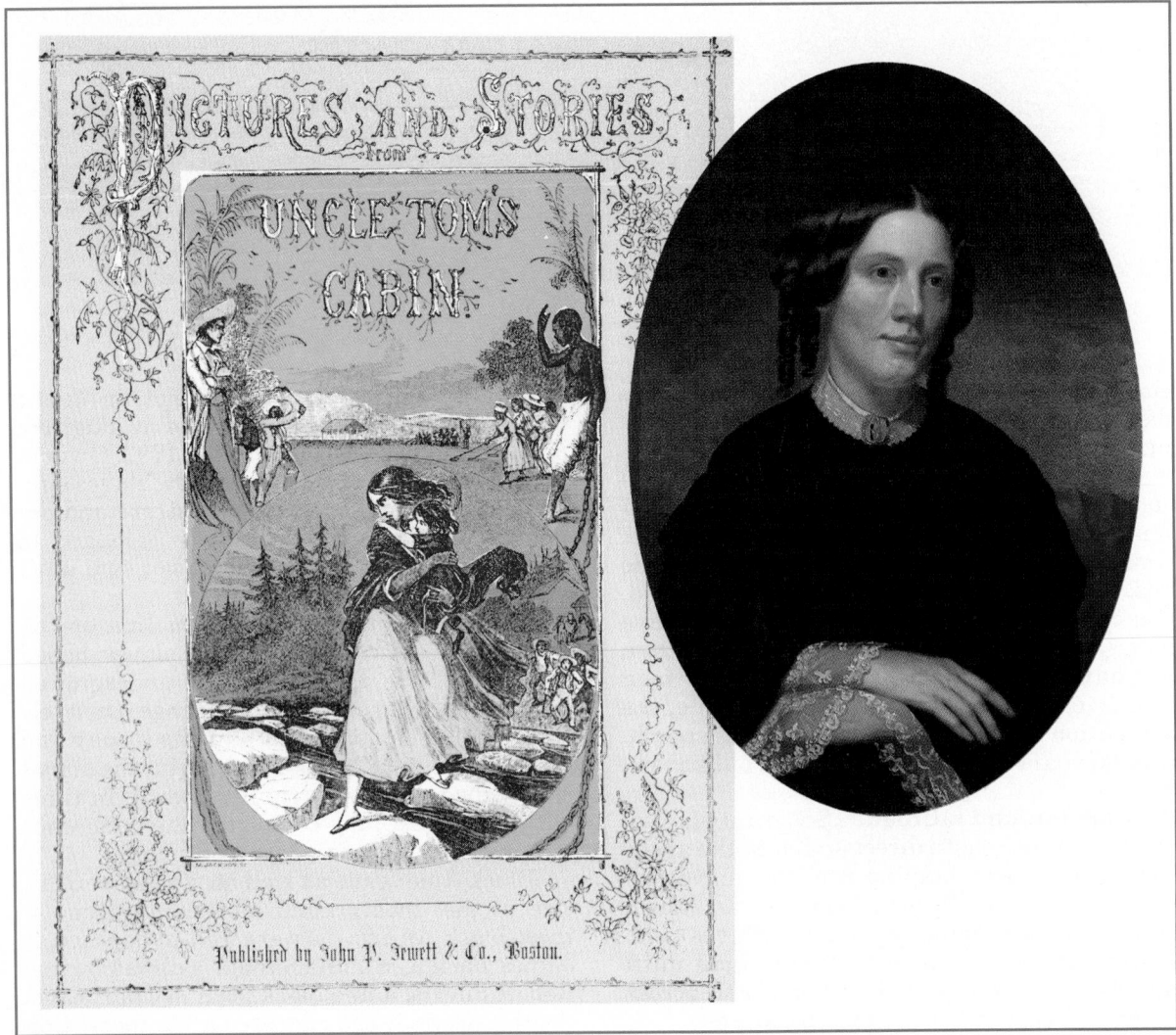

Harriet Tubman is shown here at the left with a group of former slaves whom she led to freedom. Tubman said later, "I started with this idea in my head: 'There's two things I've got a right to . . . death or liberty.'"

alive in a way readers never forgot. *Uncle Tom's Cabin* was made into a play, which became one of the most popular in American theater history.

In the South *Uncle Tom's Cabin* was bitterly denounced for presenting a false and distorted picture of slavery. Southerners were angered in spite of the fact that the book gave examples of masters' kindnesses toward slaves and of loyalty and affection on the part of slaves toward masters. Southerners were especially furious because Stowe's book encouraged support for the activities of the underground railroad.

Northern resistance. The abolitionists aroused widespread opposition in the North as well as in the South. William Lloyd Garrison once remarked that he found "contempt more bitter, opposition more stubborn, and apathy more frozen" in the New England states than in the South.

Garrison's remark was an overstatement, but not by much. Abolitionist preachers in the North were sometimes forced to quit by their churches. Leading citizens such as Wendell Phillips of Boston, a gifted writer and speaker, were barred from clubs and social gatherings because of their antislavery activities. William Lloyd Garrison was once forced to flee for safety to a Boston jail. More than once Theodore Weld and his students were attacked by

angry audiences. Elijah P. Lovejoy, an abolitionist editor who lived in Alton, Illinois, was murdered as he tried to prevent a hostile mob from destroying his printing press.

Citizens at Canterbury, Connecticut, became angry when Prudence Crandall turned her boarding school into a teacher-training institution for black girls. They polluted her water supply, tried to burn her house, and otherwise harassed her. Only after a mob assault in 1834 did she end her courageous but losing struggle. Sojourner Truth, a former slave, was attacked by mobs that were determined to break up meetings in which she denounced both slavery and the unequal treatment of women.

Many wage earners and business people opposed the abolition movement. Northern wage earners feared the job competition of free black workers and often broke up antislavery meetings. Most northern trade union leaders were either indifferent to the antislavery movement or actively opposed to it. They feared that abolition of slavery would flood northern cities with low-paid, competitive black workers. Most northern business groups frowned upon the abolitionists. The groups believed that such activities would hamper trade between the North and South.

Some northerners feared that the abolitionists' activities might lead the South to leave the Union. In fact, this was exactly what Garrison and many of his militant followers hoped would happen.

Southern reactions. Southerners, understandably, were most embittered by the antislavery movement. Nat Turner's rebellion of 1831 (page 339) came at the very time that the new, militant abolition movement was beginning. Many southerners dreaded the thought of widespread slave revolts. They angrily blamed abolitionists in general and William Lloyd Garrison in particular.

As losses from runaway slaves grew, slaveowners became furious. Trying to prevent further rebellion and to stop the flight of slaves, southern legislatures tightened the slave codes. Free blacks as well as slaves were placed under strict supervision.

Even federal officials resisted the abolitionists. When southern postmasters refused to deliver abolitionist literature, the United States Post Office Department supported them. In 1836, southerners in the House of Representatives pushed through the so-called "gag rule." This forbade any member to read an antislavery petition in the House.

Such actions by federal officials violated freedom of speech and of the press—basic civil liberties guaranteed by the Constitution. The "gag rule" was finally repealed, mainly through the efforts of former President John Quincy Adams, who had been elected a Representative to Congress from Massachusetts. However, the struggle for civil liberties was just beginning, and the North and South drew further apart.

SECTION REVIEW

See underscored items, text pp. 377-80.

Identify: American Anti-Slavery Society, Frederick Douglass, Liberty Party, underground railroad, Harriet Tubman, *Uncle Tom's Cabin*

For answers to questions, see Answer Key, p.A54.

1. **Interpreting Ideas:** How was the antislavery movement in step with the times both inside and outside the United States?

2. **Summarizing Ideas:** Explain the role each played in the abolition movement: **(a)** Garrison, **(b)** Douglass, **(c)** Stowe, **(d)** Garnet, **(e)** underground railroad, **(f)** "gag rule".

3. **Analyzing Ideas:** What were the reasons for opposition to the abolition movement?

4. **Organizing Ideas: (a)** What methods did militant and moderate abolitionists use? **(b)** Which methods do you think were most effective? Why?

5 Writers preach faith in democracy and the individual

See Teaching Suggestions in TMRG, p.TM97.

Michel Chevalier, a French visitor to the United States in the year 1834, was impressed by the young nation's vigor. "All is here . . . boiling agitation," he commented. "Experiment follows experiment. . . . Men change their houses, their climate, their trade, their condition, their sect; states change their laws, their officers, their constitutions." All this vigor was reflected in the work of writers and scholars.

The "American Renaissance." The experiments in writing between the 1820's and 1860's produced a new American literature. Many earlier American writers had felt inferior to British writers. Some, like Washington Irving, imitated British styles, even when dealing with American subjects. Others, like Noah Webster, wanted an independent American literature. Such writers vigorously rejected British models.

By the 1840's the question of whether to follow or reject models of British literature seemed less important. American writers seemed surer of their nation and themselves. They felt freer to treat the subjects that concerned them.

The result was a flowering of American literature. Edgar Allan Poe broke new ground in writing criticism, poetry, and short stories. Nathaniel Hawthorne, in his novels *The Scarlet Letter* (1850) and *The House of the Seven Gables* (1851), dealt with themes of sin and guilt. Herman Melville explored the struggle between good and evil in *Moby Dick* (1851), which has been called one of the world's great novels.

These writers and many others brought fresh voices and ideas to American literature. This fruitful period is sometimes referred to as the "American Renaissance." Three key figures in it were Henry David Thoreau, Ralph Waldo Emerson, and Walt Whitman.

Henry David Thoreau (1817–1862). Henry David Thoreau hated the industrial society that he saw rising in the United States. To Thoreau machines were unnecessary gadgets

The American artist Asher Durand painted this majestic picture, "Kindred Spirits." In it he shows members of the "American Renaissance"—the painter Thomas Cole and the writer William Cullen Bryant.

that complicated life. "Nature is sufficient," Thoreau declared. To prove his point, he lived alone for about two years in a cabin that he built on the banks of Walden Pond near Concord, Massachusetts. There, free from the machines and the institutions that he believed imprisoned the human spirit, he wrote the classic book <u>Walden</u> in 1854.

Thoreau distrusted the power of the national government as much as he feared the new industrial society. Thoreau objected strongly to a government that allowed slavery to exist. He wrote, "I cannot for an instant recognize that political organization as *my* government which is the *slave's* government also."

Thoreau did not limit his distrust to verbal or written criticism. In 1846, believing that war with Mexico was an unjust attack and an attempt to extend slavery, he refused to pay his poll tax to the government. Thoreau was jailed but released the next day when a member of his family paid the tax without his knowledge.

Thoreau argued that people had a duty to disobey unjust laws, even at the cost of imprisonment, if their consciences told them that the laws were unjust. He explained these ideas in an essay published in 1849, which has become famous as "<u>Civil Disobedience</u>." Its ideas later influenced Leo Tolstoy in Russia, Mohandas Gandhi in India, and Martin Luther King, Jr., in the United States. ▲

Thoreau foresaw two grave dangers to human liberty. He feared industrialism, with its concern for the material things of life and its disregard for the individual. He also distrusted the national state, with its indifference to the individual and its glorification of power.

Ralph Waldo Emerson (1803–1882). Henry David Thoreau and Ralph Waldo Emerson were close friends. Both lived in Concord, Massachusetts. Both believed in the supreme importance of individual freedom.

Emerson started his career as a Unitarian minister. He left his church in 1832, at age 29, to become a "preacher to the world." For most of the next 50 years, Emerson wrote and lectured. He traveled widely, and wherever he went he urged people to stand on their own feet, to free themselves from ignorance and prejudice, to think for themselves, and to respect others. Democracy with its free institutions would not work, he said, if the individuals in a democratic society were not free.

Emerson had a deep faith in America, in democracy, and in the ability of men and women

▲ Class activity: Have students relate the activities of Tolstoy, Gandhi, and King to Thoreau's ideas on civil disobedience.

383

SOURCES

Whitman's Preface
To *Leaves of Grass*
(1855)

The Americans of all nations at any time upon the earth have probably the fullest poetical nature. The United States themselves are essentially the greatest poem. In the history of the earth hitherto the largest and most stirring appear tame and orderly to their ampler largeness and stir. Here at last is something in the doings of man that corresponds with the broadcast doings of the day and night. Here is not merely a nation but a teeming nation of nations. . . .

Other states indicate themselves in their deputies . . . but the genius of the United States is not best or most in its executives or legislatures, nor in its ambassadors or authors or colleges or churches or parlors, nor even in its newspapers or inventors . . . but always most in the common people. . . . It awaits the gigantic and generous treatment worthy of it.

to solve their problems and build a better world. Emerson was critical of the growing emphasis on material things and the growing power of the national government. However, Emerson did not share Thoreau's fear of industrialism.

Nor was Emerson troubled, as many Americans were, by the swelling tide of immigration. Welcome the immigrants, he urged, "The energy of Irish, Germans, Swedes, Poles, and Cossacks, and all the European tribes—and of the Africans, and of the Polynesians—will construct a new race, a new religion, a new state, a new literature, which will be as vigorous as the new Europe which came out of the smelting-pot of the Dark Ages."

Walt Whitman (1819–1892). One day in 1855, Emerson received a copy of a newly published volume of poems entitled *Leaves of Grass*. Emerson was greatly impressed by the originality of the book. He wrote the author, Walt Whitman, "I greet you at the beginning of a great career."

In *Leaves of Grass,* Whitman sang the praises of the growing nation. Even more than Emerson, he believed deeply in democracy. He believed in the ability of the American people

to build an ever better way of life for themselves and their children. "The old and moth-eaten systems of Europe have had their day," he wrote. "Here [in America], we have planted the standard of freedom, and here we will test the capacities of men for self-government."

Whitman, like Emerson, did not share Thoreau's fear of industrialism. On the contrary, he hailed science and industry as liberating forces that would end the age-old burdens of superstition and toil. In his "Carol of Occupations," he glorified workers and the machines they operated. In "Pioneers! O Pioneers!" he challenged Americans to share his faith in the future. "We must march" he wrote,

We the youthful sinewy races,
all the rest on us depend,
Pioneers! O Pioneers!

The larger meaning. Emerson, Thoreau, Whitman, and many others raised powerful voices in praise of freedom and democracy. This faith in the individual and in democracy lay at the roots of the reform movements you have read about in this chapter.

Years earlier, in 1776, Thomas Jefferson had expressed the same faith in the words "We hold these truths to be self-evident: that all men are created equal, that they are endowed by their Creator with certain unalienable rights, that among these are life, liberty, and the pursuit of happiness." Emerson, Thoreau, Whitman, the reformers you have been reading about, and many other people were trying to apply the principles of the Declaration of Independence to their everyday lives.

SECTION REVIEW
See underscored items, text pp. 382-84.
Identify: "American Renaissance," *Walden,* "Civil Disobedience," *Leaves of Grass*
For answers to questions, see Answer Key, p.A54.

1. **Interpreting Ideas: (a)** What two major developments did Henry David Thoreau fear as threats to human liberty? **(b)** Why is it significant that Thoreau went to jail for his beliefs?

2. **Summarizing Ideas: (a)** Why did Ralph Waldo Emerson think of himself as a "preacher to the world"? **(b)** What are the main ideas of Emerson's "message"?

3. **Synthesizing Ideas:** Explain Walt Whitman's idea that Americans are pioneers who must march forward.

4. **Analyzing Ideas:** Why could this period be called an "American Renaissance"?

DEVELOPING HISTORY STUDY SKILLS

Writing About History   Composing an Essay

You have already learned about two preliminary steps to the composing of an essay: formulating a thesis statement (Chapter 13, pages 324–25) and developing a structured overview (Chapter 14, page 341). The next step is the actual writing of the essay.

An essay is a short composition written on a specific topic. You compose an essay when you write a report. You compose an essay when you answer a thought question or follow a set of directions that call for a response in your own words. Here is an example of a directive that demands an essay response.

ESSAY: Show the key role that women played in aiding the success of the abolitionist movement, 1830–1865, by discussing the purpose of the abolitionist movement (3 points); identifying two women involved in the abolitionist movement and describing their roles (6 points); and explaining two results of the abolitionist movement (6 points).

Refer to this essay directive as you read how to determine the information for which the essay directive calls.

How to Compose an Essay

Follow these steps in reading an essay directive and composing an essay.

1. **Look for informational terms.** As you read the essay directive, look for informational terms that give clues to the content of the essay. In the example above, informational terms include *key role, women, success, abolitionist movement, purpose, two women,* and *two results.*

2. **Determine the essay's scope.** Note whether the directive asks you to address one main idea or several main ideas. Note whether the directive contains a time frame.

3. **Note the performance terms.** Performance terms are the words in the essay directive that indicate just what you are to do. For a list of common performance terms and their meanings see the following.

- **Discuss:** tell in some detail; assess fully the historical significance

- **Identify:** name; place at a point in time and in association with a group

- **Describe:** create a full-bodied word picture of actions and events

- **Explain:** show a cause-effect relationship

- **State:** make a complete, formal statement consisting of several sentences on the assigned subject

- **Show:** give a detailed cause-effect relationship with examples

- **Compare (contrast):** indicate similarities and differences (or differences alone)

4. **Make mental notes:** Gathering mental notes for a response to each part helps to formulate the response in your own words. Another helpful device is to complete a structured overview using the main parts and the informational terms plus additional data.

Applying the Skill

You have already examined the informational terms of the essay directive above. You need to provide information about the key roles of women in the abolitionist movement between 1830 and 1865 that contributed to the movement's success. To do this you are going to discuss the purpose of the movement, identify two women who were participants in it and tell how they aided its success. You are also going to explain two results of the movement.

The essay directive has three parts. To be completely answered, each part must be addressed in its own paragraph. Keep to the time frame, naming no one before 1830 nor any reformer after 1865.

Pay attention to the weight you should give to each part. The number of points assigned to each part is the best clue. The part with the most points is the part that should have the most detail.

385

In making your mental notes, all you need to do is to refer to the instructional terms section and review the performance terms. The next step is composing the essay in your own words. Here is a sample answer to the essay directive given on page 385.

The purpose of the abolitionist movement was to end slavery. Two women who were instrumental in ending slavery were Harriet Beecher Stowe and Sojourner Truth.

Harriet Beecher Stowe wrote Uncle Tom's Cabin, a novel that portrayed the evils of slavery and vividly recounted the perils faced by slaves who tried to escape. The novel spurred renewed northern demands for slavery's end.

Sojourner Truth, a former slave, joined the abolitionist movement as an outspoken critic of slavery. Her dignity in the face of pro-slavery demonstrations added greatly to the respect northerners felt for the abolitionists.

The abolitionist movement had several results. One result was the widening rift between the North and the South. Southerners feared widespread slave revolts, which they claimed were being promoted by abolitionists. As the number of runaway slaves increased, southerners tightened slave codes and demanded strict adherence to the Fugitive Slave Law, angering northerners. Another result was the development of the underground railroad. This system, supported and staffed by abolitionists, helped escaping slaves reach freedom in the North and in Canada.

Practicing the Skill

Write your answers on a separate sheet of paper.

1. Read the essay directive below. Following the steps for formulating an essay, restate the directive in your own words, telling what each part of the essay must show and what should be included in each paragraph.

2. Using the work you did for the first question, write a three-part essay. Refer to the textbook or to any other materials to find facts with which to make your essay complete and accurate.

ESSAY: Compare reforms in the Civil War period by identifying three reform movements (3 points); stating the goals of each (6 points); and discussing the similarity of their goals (6 points).

(1. Answers will vary. 2. Answers will vary.)

16 SUMMARY

From the 1820's to the 1860's, reforms and other developments transformed the United States with bewildering speed. Factories and factory towns sprang up in the northern states. Slavery became increasingly important in the cotton-growing areas of the South. New means of transportation stimulated trade and sped the westward movement of land-hungry pioneers. Immigrants in steadily mounting numbers poured into the nation's growing cities and spread out upon the farms of the American heartland.

The American people plunged enthusiastically into the job of building the nation, spurred by new ideas and by the desire to make democracy work. This faith in democracy stimulated wave after wave of reform movements. Among them were the movements for women's rights, for more humane treatment of criminals and the mentally ill, for ending the sale of alcoholic beverages, and for equality of educational opportunity.

One other reform movement played a leading role in the political events of this period—the movement for the abolition of slavery. Abolitionism quickly took on a militant and uncompromising tone. The abolition movement helped widen the gap between people disturbed by the evils of slavery and people whose way of life was built around an economy based on slavery.

CONNECTING CHAPTER IDEAS

As reform movements continued throughout the 1830's, 1840's, and 1850's, the problem of slavery became increasingly severe. In the next chapter you will read about the failure of compromise in solving the crisis over slavery. The controversy reached a bitter climax in armed conflict between North and South.

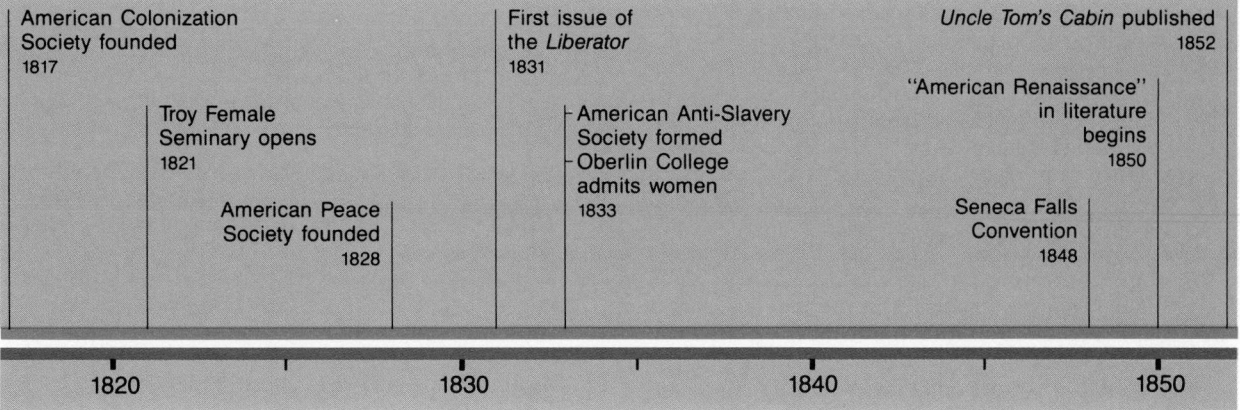

American Colonization Society founded
1817

Troy Female Seminary opens
1821

American Peace Society founded
1828

First issue of the *Liberator*
1831

American Anti-Slavery Society formed
Oberlin College admits women
1833

Uncle Tom's Cabin published
1852

"American Renaissance" in literature begins
1850

Seneca Falls Convention
1848

1820　　1830　　1840　　1850

CHAPTER
16 REVIEW

Reviewing Important Terms

Decide whether each of the following sentences is true or false. If the sentence is false, replace the underlined term with the word or phrase that will make it true.

1. Among the goals of the women's rights movement of the 1820's and 1830's was protesting the exclusion of women from higher education and the professions.
2. Emma Hart Willard and Mary Lyon were at the forefront of the coeducation movement that led to the founding of such schools as Mount Holyoke College.
3. Work accidents and inefficiency were among the concerns of activists in the peace movement.
4. In 1846, Maine passed the first state prohibition act, banning the use of alcoholic beverages.
5. Horace Mann was influential in establishing common schools for teachers in Massachusetts.
6. By 1850, there were 6,000 private high schools, known as normal schools, but only 55 public high schools.
7. Walt Whitman, Henry David Thoreau, and Ralph Waldo Emerson were prominent figures in the period known as the Era of Good Feelings.

Practicing Critical Thinking Skills

1. **Interpreting Ideas.** (a) Why do you think that the movement for women's rights failed to gain strength before the Civil War? (b) Which women of the period who were reformers do you think made the most significant contribution to American life? Explain.
2. **Summarizing Ideas.** Why did a split develop in the abolition movement between the militants and the moderates?
3. **Evaluating Ideas.** Thoreau, Emerson, and Whitman represented the American spirit at this time. Cite information from the textbook to support this statement.
4. **Organizing Ideas.** In what ways did this reform era (a) seek humanitarian goals and (b) try to make the nation more democratic?
5. **Analyzing Ideas.** Reread the Preamble to the Constitution of the United States (page 189). What steps toward fulfilling the ideals stated in the Preamble were taken during the period covered in Chapter 16? Cite specific examples from the text, relating each to a phrase from the Preamble.

6. **Analyzing Viewpoints.** In general, do you agree with Horace Mann that education "prevents being poor"? Did any social conditions other than lack of education cause poverty in Mann's time?
7. **Relating Past to Present.** In your view, has Walt Whitman's faith in science and industry as liberating forces proved sound? Has Henry David Thoreau's fear that science and industry would complicate people's lives come true? Use specific examples to support your answers.

Developing History Study Skills

1. **Analyzing on Essay Question.** Read this essay topic: *Discuss how the flood of immigrants between 1830 and 1860 helped the cause for free public education.* Answer on a separate sheet of paper, the following questions: (a) What two topics does the essay statement mention? (b) What period of history does the essay cover? (c) What does *discuss* mean? (d) Restate the essay topic in your own words.

2. **Illustrating Viewpoints.** Slogans and cartoons have often been used to call attention to a needed reform. Devise a slogan or a cartoon that might have been used in one of the reform movements of the 1800's. Then on a separate sheet of paper, explain why your slogan or cartoon is persuasive? Indicate to which group it is meant to be persuasive. Explain what action it suggests.

Relating Geography and History

Because of the great distance to Canada and the dangers of the Underground Railroad, runaway slaves faced many hardships. To understand the plight of runaway slaves, use the information on pages 379–80 and the map on page 378 to answer the following questions.

1. (a) Describe a route that a runaway slave might have taken from Charleston to Canada, (b) from Cincinnati to Canada. (c) About how long were these routes?
2. Why do you suppose that most of the Southern routes began on the Atlantic coast rather than inland?
3. (a) What dangers did slaves face on the Underground Railroad? (b) Why did many slaves risk these dangers?

388

UNIT FOUR
REVIEW

Discussing Ideas

1. **(a)** Why did the planters become the political leaders in the South? **(b)** Who were the political leaders in the North? Why? **(c)** Who might have been the political leaders in the West? Explain.
2. **(a)** What is manifest destiny? **(b)** what evidence is there that many Americans believed in manifest destiny by the mid-1800's? **(c)** Is the idea of manifest destiny consistent with the reform impulse felt by many Americans during the same period?
3. How was improved transportation important to the development of the **(a)** North, **(b)** South, and **(c)** West?
4. Do you think the Mexican War was inevitable? Why or why not?
5. How did the various reform movements that arose in the early and mid-1800's reflect faith in democracy?
6. Compare the lives of northern industrial workers with the lives of slaves on southern plantations.
7. **(a)** How would you characterize southern society before the Civil War? Explain how the various economic groups fit into the southern social structure. **(b)** How did southern society differ from society in the North? the West?

Making Connections

1. **(a)** Make a drawing to illustrate southern society before the Civil War, showing the various economic groups and their standing in the society. **(b)** How would your drawing be different if it represented northern society? **(c)** How would your drawing be different if it represented western society?
2. Read some poems by Emerson, Longfellow, Thoreau, or Whitman. **(a)** How did the poet seem to feel about America? **(b)** Do his poems seem characteristic of the period in which they were written? Explain.
3. Write a speech that might have been given at a meeting in support of women's rights, temperance, or peace.
4. Conduct research on high school education in the mid-1800's. How did it compare with your education in terms of **(a)** subjects studied, **(b)** size of classes, and **(c)** extracurricular activities?
5. Prepare an oral report on one of the following people: Daniel Webster, John C. Calhoun, Sarah Bagley, or Harriet Tubman. A possible source of information is the *Dictionary of American Biography*.

Applying History Study Skills

1. **Reading a Historical Map.** Examine the map on page 348 of the textbook. **(a)** Describe the routes of the Oregon Trail, the Mormon Trail, and the Pony Express. What did each of these trails have in common? **(b)** Locate the pass through the Rocky Mountains that enabled travelers to use these routes. **(c)** Why do you think the Overland Mail took the long southern route to San Francisco? **(d)** Describe the two water routes to California. **(e)** Contrast the water routes to California with the overland routes. Which way do you think is the least difficult? Why?

2. **Using Primary Sources.** Read the excerpt from Walt Whitman's Preface to *Leaves of Grass* on page 384 of the textbook. **(a)** What do you think Whitman means when he calls the United States a "nation of nations"? **(b)** what is the "genius" of America? **(c)** How does this excerpt express a new national pride?

Reading in Depth

Blassingame, John W., *The Slave Community* (New York: Oxford University Press). An account of the life and culture of slaves in the United States.

Clarke, Mary S., *Bloomers and Ballots* (Viking). A well-documented life of Elizabeth Cady Stanton, one of the first fighters for women's suffrage and rights.

Morrison, John and Zabrisky, Charlotte, *American Mosaic* (New York: New American Library). The immigrant experience in the words of those who lived it.

Petry, Ann, *Harriet Tubman: Conductor on the Underground Railroad* (Archway). An exciting biography of this former slave, called the "Moses of her people."

Poe, Edgar Allan, *Tales* (New York: Dodd, Mead). A collection of short stories by this American master of suspense.

Tyler, Alice Felt, *Freedom's Ferment* (New York: Harper and Row). Excellent summary of the major reform movements of the 1820's–1850's.

UNIT FIVE

The Nation Torn Apart

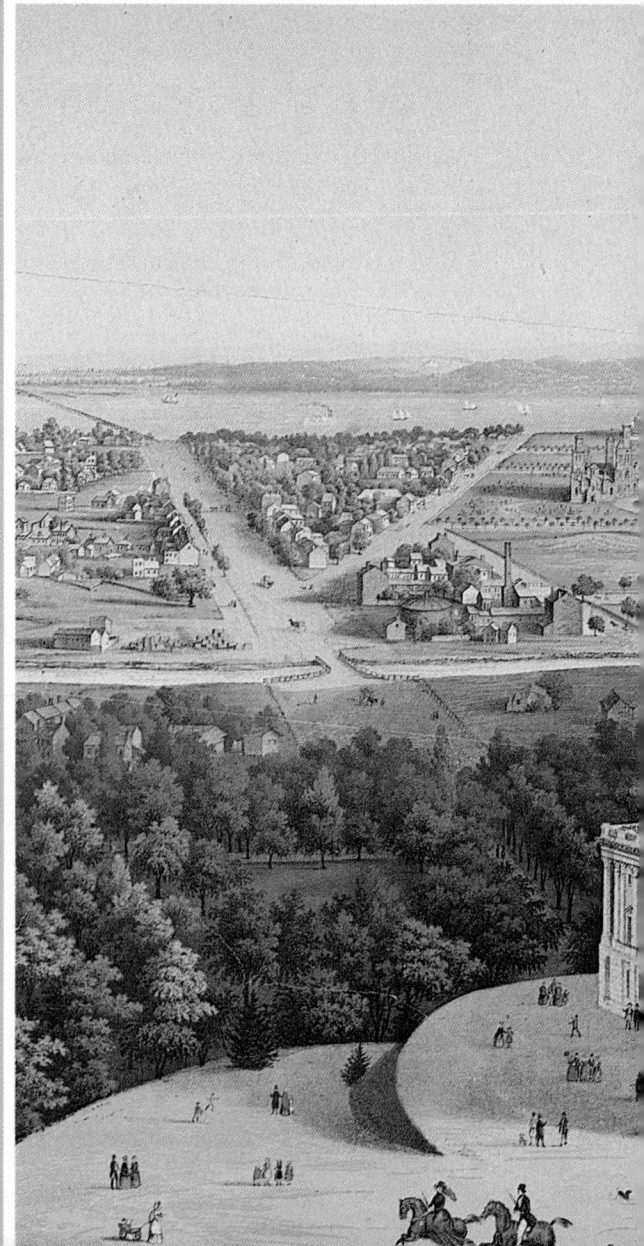

The Constitution of the United States created a federal union, a partnership between the states and the national government. Washington, D.C. (pictured below), the nation's capital, stands as a symbol of that federal union. The location of the city itself between the North and the South symbolizes the spirit of compromise that guided the young nation through its early years. By 1860, however, compromise no longer solved the increasing sectional differences that threatened the very existence of the Union. In 1861 those differences erupted in a bloody civil war. The Confederate states renounced the Constitution and withdrew from the Union. Four long years of fighting ended in a northern victory and the preservation of the Union. As a result, Washington, D.C., the city and the symbol, continues to stand for one nation—The United States of America.

See Chapter Overview in TMRG, p.TM100.
See Chapter Objectives in TMRG, p.TM100.
See Introducing the Chapter in TMRG, p.TM100.

CHAPTER 17 Crisis and Compromise

(1845–1861)

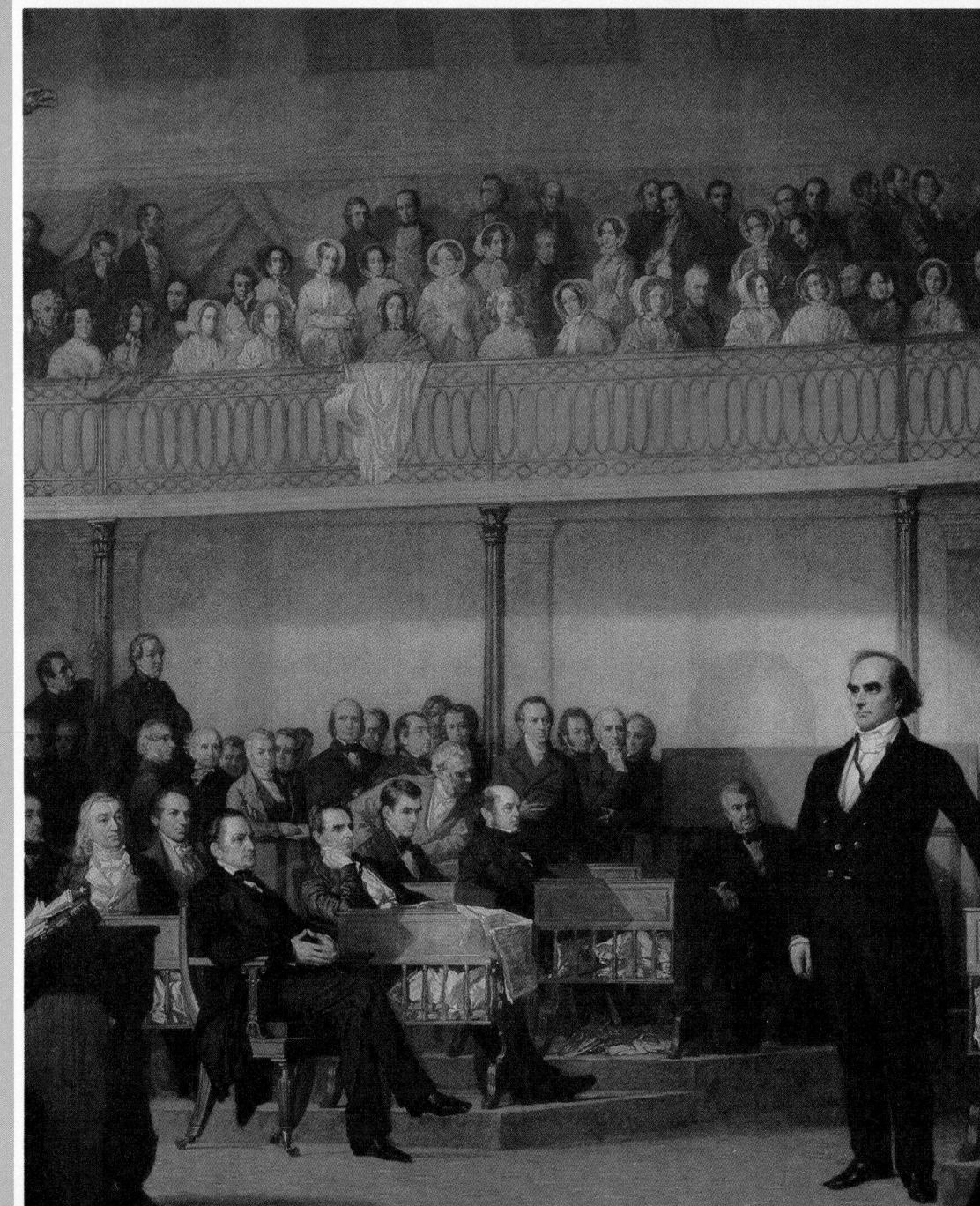

The Union's champion

The growing conflict among the nation's three sections—North, South, and West—forms the most tragic of themes in United States history. The story that unfolds during this unhappy period is one of compromise, of breakdowns of compromise, of growing conflict, and of ever more desperate attempts to restore harmony.

The basic problem leading to the civil conflict was that the North, the South, and the West had developed along very different lines. To be sure, many people in the three sections shared common political and democratic institutions. They shared a common heritage of beliefs and traditions. It is also true that each section had developed its own characteristic way of life. The differences within each section began to be more important than the many common and shared elements. The people in each of the three sections held radically different views about such issues as internal improvements at federal expense, banking and currency, tariff, and slavery.

The industrial North was intent on increasing its productivity and its profits. Large areas of the agricultural South remained largely dependent upon the single crop of cotton. The West, as the last frontier, was filled with growing towns and with restless pioneers.

This chapter reviews the tensions that were rising among the three sections of the country from 1845 to 1861. It discusses attempts at compromise over the balancing of free states with slave states. It shows the reluctance of the South to consider any alternative to slavery. It discusses the growing southern unrest over the issue of states' rights. Finally it describes the breakdown in unity that led to the Civil War, or the War Between the States.

═══ READING FOCUS ═══

As you read about the time of crisis and compromise, look for the details that support each of the following statements.

1. The North and South maintain an uneasy political balance.
2. The Compromise of 1850 eases mounting tension.
3. The long period of compromise finally comes to an end.
4. The North and South move steadily toward war.
5. Southern states withdraw from the Union and war begins.

1 The North and South maintain an uneasy political balance

See Teaching Suggestions in TMRG, pp.TM100-01.

The first serious clash between the North and the South over the issue of slavery had arisen in 1819–20. It involved the question of admitting Missouri to the Union. At times the controversy had become so heated that some politicians talked boldly of "disunion" and "civil war." Former President Thomas Jefferson followed the debates from his hilltop home. He wrote that "this momentous question, like a fire bell in the night, awakened and filled me with terror. I considered it at once as the knell of the Union."

Dispute over Missouri. To understand Jefferson's grave concern, you have to turn back to 1819, when the United States was composed of 11 free states and 10 slave states. At that time Alabama was about to be admitted to the Union as the eleventh slave state. With Alabama's admission, the North and the South would each then have 22 votes in the Senate.

Then the Territory of Missouri, in which slavery already existed, asked to be admitted to the Union. If Missouri entered as a slave state, the South would have 24 Senate votes and the North would have only 22.

Tallmadge's explosive proposal. On February 13, 1819, before Alabama was admitted, Representative James Tallmadge of New York offered an amendment to Missouri's application. The Tallmadge Amendment proposed to ▲ outlaw the further introduction of slaves into Missouri. It also proposed to free, on their twenty-fifth birthday, all children born into slavery in Missouri after it became a state.

Tallmadge and his supporters argued that Congress had the power to prohibit slavery in any territory of the United States. He pointed out that Congress had already used this power when it created the Northwest Ordinance (see page 157).

The Missouri Compromise. The House of Representatives, where the North held a majority, adopted the Tallmadge Amendment, but the Senate rejected it. ●

▲ Throughout the Annotated Teacher's Edition, terms listed in the "Identify" portion of a Section Review are underscored the first time they appear. See the Teacher's Manual for each section for a listing of important vocabulary terms.

393

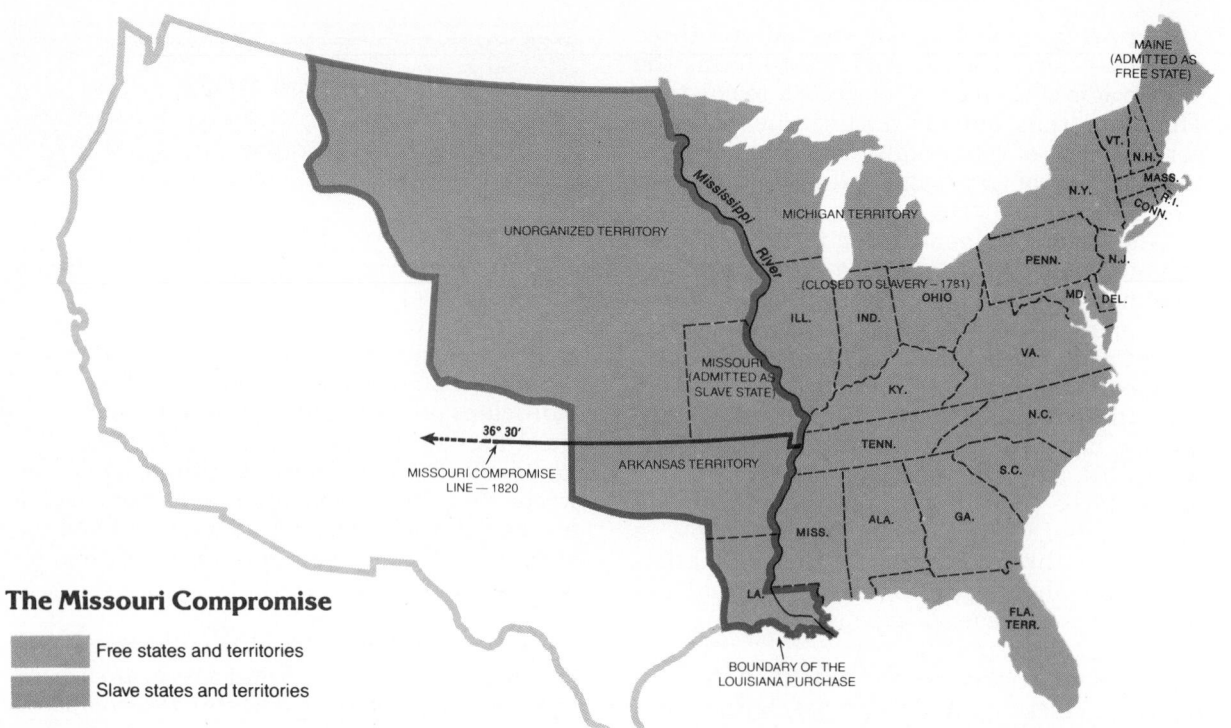

The Missouri Compromise

▨ Free states and territories

▨ Slave states and territories

MAINE (ADMITTED AS FREE STATE)

UNORGANIZED TERRITORY

Mississippi River

MICHIGAN TERRITORY

(CLOSED TO SLAVERY — 1781)

MISSOURI (ADMITTED AS SLAVE STATE)

36° 30′

MISSOURI COMPROMISE LINE — 1820

ARKANSAS TERRITORY

BOUNDARY OF THE LOUISIANA PURCHASE

VT. N.H. MASS. R.I. CONN. N.Y. PENN. N.J. OHIO MD. DEL. ILL. IND. VA. KY. N.C. TENN. S.C. MISS. ALA. GA. LA. FLA. TERR.

Why, with 11 free states and only 10 slave states represented in the Senate at this time, was the South able to win this victory? The answer is that certain northern Senators voted with the southern **bloc,** or solid group of legislators, to defeat the amendment.

Congress was now deadlocked. The House favored the amendment, while the Senate opposed it. The deadlock was broken, however, through mutual concessions known as the Missouri Compromise.

At this time, Maine was also petitioning Congress to enter the Union — as a free state. To keep an even balance of free and slave states, the Senate agreed to combine the admission of Maine with that of Missouri. Senator Jesse Thomas of Illinois introduced an amendment that received strong support from Henry Clay of Kentucky. This amendment proposed that Missouri be admitted as a slave state. It also proposed that slavery be prohibited in the rest of the Louisiana Purchase, north of latitude 36° 30′ (see map, this page). Southern members of Congress were willing to accept this restriction because cotton could not be grown profitably on the land to the north of the 36° 30′ line.

The crisis seemed to have passed, but in 1820 the antislavery forces in Congress threatened to exclude Missouri from the Union. They objected to Missouri's constitution, which discriminated against free blacks. Henry Clay then proposed the so-called second Missouri Compromise. Clay argued that the proposed constitution of Missouri could not deny citizens of Missouri the privileges and protections they were entitled to under the Constitution of the United States. When this proposal was accepted, Missouri was admitted as a slave state.

Thus the crisis of 1819–20 passed, but thoughtful Americans realized that danger lay ahead for the young nation. "This is a reprieve only, not a final sentence," Jefferson declared. John Quincy Adams wrote in his diary that the conflict over Missouri was a "mere preamble — a title page to a great, tragic volume."

Other divisive issues. As you have read (pages 295–97), during the years from 1828 to 1832 conflicting views over the tariff brought the United States perilously close to disunion. Indeed, South Carolina had threatened to secede. Although this crisis passed, the growing antislavery movement continued to inflame emotions and divide the nation (pages 375–82).

The deadlock over Texas. The slavery issue grew larger and more ominous. As it did, the struggle for control of the western areas became more intense. Every time a territory applied for admission to the Union as a state, northern and southern members of Congress came into conflict.

In 1836 and 1837, Congress admitted Arkansas and Michigan into the Union without dispute, for one was slave and the other free. Trouble arose when the newly organized Republic of Texas (pages 350–54) applied for admission. Since slavery already existed in Texas, Congress would have to admit Texas as a slave state. Doing so would upset the balance between the North and the South.

President Van Buren and many Congressional leaders were eager at this time to keep the slavery issue out of politics, but Texans could not afford to let the matter rest. Only 50,000 free people lived in the Lone Star Republic. If Mexico, with its population of 6 to 7 million, decided to reconquer its former territory, Texas would be in serious trouble. Texans needed a powerful ally to protect them against Mexico. Faced with this situation, Texas began to negotiate treaties of friendship and trade with France, Belgium, the Netherlands, and Great Britain.

For several years the issue of Texas hung in the balance. Mexico refused to recognize Texas' independence. Great Britain and France, on the other hand, continued to support an independent Texas. American opinion remained divided over whether or not to admit Texas to the Union.

The election of 1844. This was the situation in the United States in the election year of 1844. Henry Clay, the Whig candidate, tried to avoid the issue. James G. Birney, again the candidate of the antislavery Liberty Party, firmly opposed the admission of Texas. James K. Polk of Tennessee, the Democratic candidate, came out for "the re-annexation of Texas and re-occupation of Oregon!"

The Democratic Party's 1844 slogan was clever politics. It implied that the United States had always owned Texas and Oregon. This was not true, but the slogan shifted the focus from the troublesome issue of slavery to the popular issue of expansion. Northerners and southerners alike wanted their country to expand westward.

Polk won the election. In February 1845, shortly before he took office, Congress voted to admit Texas into the Union. The provisions for admission included the following points. (1) With the consent of Texas, a total of five states could be carved out of the territory. (2) If Texas did divide, any land north of the 36° 30′ line would be closed to slavery. (3) The United States would take over the boundary dispute with Mexico. (4) Texas would retain its lands and pay its debts.

Texas accepted these terms and entered the Union in December 1845. Thus the balance between North and South swung by two states in favor of the South. (It had already swung in favor of the South when Florida entered the Union in March 1845.) The balance was restored by the admission of Iowa in 1846 and Wisconsin in 1848, both free states.

Thus, for more than 25 years, from the Missouri Compromise of 1820 to the year 1846, Congress had walked a tightrope. By a series of compromises, the North and the South had managed to resolve the troublesome problems that had threatened to split them apart. This was the situation in 1846 when the United States went to war with Mexico.

SECTION REVIEW
See underscored items, text pp. 393-95.
Identify: Tallmadge Amendment, Henry Clay, "the re-annexation of Texas and re-occupation of Oregon!", James G. Birney

For answers to questions, see Answer Key, p.A57.

1. **Analyzing Ideas: (a)** Why did Missouri's application for admission to the Union create a crisis? **(b)** How was the crisis settled?

2. **Interpreting Ideas: (a)** What did the North and South each gain by the Missouri Compromise? **(b)** Why did Jefferson call the Compromise "a reprieve only, not a final sentence"?

3. **Synthesizing Ideas:** How did the election of 1844 reflect the issues of the time?

4. **Studying Maps:** Look at the map on page 394. **(a)** How many slave states were there at this time? How many free states? **(b)** By 1821, which states from the Louisiana Purchase had been admitted to the Union?

The Compromise of 1850 eases mounting tensions

See Teaching Suggestions in TMRG, pp.TM101-02.

In February 1848, the United States signed a treaty that ended the war with Mexico. In it Mexico ceded its northern territory, a huge area of land called the Mexican Cession. Would slavery now be permitted or prohibited in the states that were to be carved out of this huge new area?

Division over the Mexican Cession. In general, Americans held four different views as to what should be done with this new area — land now regarded as the nation's Southwest.

First, President Polk and many citizens felt that the problem could best be solved by building upon the Missouri Compromise of 1820. The Missouri Compromise, you recall, outlawed slavery in all remaining areas of the Louisiana Purchase north of latitude 36° 30' (see map, page 394). President Polk now proposed to extend this line to the Pacific, prohibiting slavery north of the line and allowing slavery south of the line.

Second, citizens strongly opposed to slavery accepted the Wilmot Proviso. In August 1846, shortly after the Mexican War started, David Wilmot, a Democratic representative from Pennsylvania, presented a resolution to Congress. The Wilmot Proviso flatly declared that "neither slavery nor involuntary servitude shall ever exist" in the lands acquired from Mexico. All but one of the northern states adopted resolutions that approved of the Wilmot Proviso.

Southerners took a third point of view. John C. Calhoun, probably the most influential southern voice, insisted that Congress had no right to prohibit slavery in the Southwest. Indeed, he insisted, Congress had a duty to protect the rights of slaveowners to their "property," the slaves, in *all* the territories. Calhoun based his argument on the Fifth Amendment to the Constitution. This amendment guarantees that no person shall "be deprived of life, liberty, or property, without due process of law."

A fourth group was led by Senator Lewis Cass of Michigan and Senator Stephen A. Douglas of Illinois. This group argued that the people of each territory should decide whether or not to permit slavery in their territory. The solution proposed by Cass and Douglas came to be known as **popular sovereignty** or "squatter sovereignty."

Straddling the issue. The problem of slavery in the territories was the burning issue in the Presidential election of 1848. However, both major parties, the Democrats and the Whigs, refused to take a stand on this issue. Both parties included southerners as well as northerners, and any strong stand would have split either party.

President Polk, exhausted by four years in office, refused in 1848 to run for reelection on the Democratic ticket. The Democrats then turned to Lewis Cass of Michigan, one of the authors of popular sovereignty.

The Whigs nominated General Zachary Taylor, who had earned the title "Old Rough and Ready" as a fighter in the Mexican War. General Taylor was a southerner, but he had never been seriously involved in politics. His political views were not widely known.

Effects of a third party. The efforts of the Whigs and Democrats to straddle the slavery question drove many northerners to a newly formed third party — the Free-Soil Party. The Free-Soilers opposed any further extension of slavery into the territories. Using the slogan "Free Soil, Free Speech, Free Labor, and Free Men," they nominated former President Martin Van Buren of New York.

Van Buren and the Free-Soilers had great influence on the election, even though they failed to carry a single state. By capturing Democratic votes, especially in New York State, Van Buren unintentionally helped to throw the election to the Whig candidate, General Zachary Taylor. More important, the Free-Soilers won 12 seats in the House of Representatives. Otherwise, the House was almost evenly divided between Whigs and Democrats. The Free-Soil Party therefore held the balance of power in the lower house. It is important to note, however, that in many cases, especially in New York, religious and ethnic considerations were at least as influential as the slavery issue in determining how people voted.

Another crisis. The Congress that assembled in December 1849 was torn by dissension. In fact, tempers were so much on edge that members of the House of Representatives had to vote 63 times before electing a Speaker of the House and getting down to business.

One issue facing Congress was California's application to enter the Union as a free state. Southerners refused to consider the application. If California entered the Union as a free state, the existing balance of 15 slave and 15 free states would be upset in favor of the North.

Another issue before Congress was the controversy between the state of Texas and the

▲   Report topic: Why Martin Van Buren was willing to be a candidate for the Free-Soilers

newly acquired but as yet unorganized territory of New Mexico. Texas, where slavery was permitted, claimed that its boundary extended westward into country that the federal government had decided belonged to New Mexico. The antislavery members of Congress naturally tried to confine Texas to the smallest possible limits. Southerners just as naturally resented northern attempts to limit the area of Texas.

Arguments over other issues echoed through the halls of Congress. Southerners strongly resisted a proposal to abolish slavery in the District of Columbia. They also resisted a proposal to organize New Mexico and Utah into territories, since the proposal made no reference to slavery. Southerners wanted the proposal to state clearly their right to own slaves in New Mexico and Utah during the territorial period.

Many northerners, on the other hand, were just as strongly opposed to a southern proposal for a new and more effective fugitive slave law. The original Fugitive Slave Law of 1793 made state and local officials responsible for capturing runaway slaves and returning them to their owners. In 1842, however, the Supreme Court had ruled that state officials did not have to help federal officials in the capture and return of runaway slaves. Southerners now wanted a new law that would require state officials to assist in capturing runaway slaves.

All of these issues were loaded with political dynamite. Any one could lead to a break between the North and the South. In the opening months of 1850, many people felt that the United States stood on the brink of disunion, if not on the brink of war.

Clay's compromise. Henry Clay of Kentucky, whose earlier compromises had saved the Union from disasters, was known and respected as the "Great Compromiser." Now, in 1850, ill and weary from years of devoted effort to the Union, he stood before the Senate to plead once more for reason and moderation.

Clay's proposed compromise included several parts: (1) The admission of California as a free state. (2) The organization of the land acquired from Mexico (except California) into territories on the basis of "popular sovereignty." Thus the settlers might decide for themselves whether or not they wanted slavery in their territory. (3) A payment of $10 million to Texas by the United States, if Texas abandoned all claims to New Mexico east of the Rio Grande. (4) The abolition of the slave trade—that is, of the buying and selling of slaves—but not of slavery itself in the District of Columbia. (5) A more effective fugitive slave law, one that would compel state and local law enforcement officials to aid federal officials in the capture and return of runaway slaves.

The Great Debate. For more than six months, Clay's proposals provoked one of the most critical debates in American history.

The Great Debate of 1850 was the great effort of three political leaders. Clay (center) asks for compromise as Webster (head on hand at the left) and Calhoun (standing third from right) listen. Within two years, all three were dead.

Daniel Webster—like Clay, a veteran Whig leader—supported Clay's compromise. He argued that slavery was not likely to prosper in the newly acquired lands. For this reason, Webster declared, it would be unnecessary and unwise for the North to insist on excluding slavery from this area. Many northerners opposed Webster and accused him of betraying the cause of freedom. Stephen A. Douglas of Illinois, who had argued for popular sovereignty, supported Webster and Clay.

John C. Calhoun of South Carolina spoke for the South. He opposed popular sovereignty and all other compromises on the question of slavery. Calhoun was an old man. Like Webster and Clay, he had served his country in Congress for almost 40 years. He was so weak that he had to be carried into the Senate, where a colleague read his speech condemning the compromise. Calhoun insisted, as he had always done, that slaveowners had the right to take their property anywhere in any of the territories and that Congress had the duty to protect this right. Most southern Senators supported Calhoun.

Other Senators, Whigs and Democrats alike, strongly opposed Calhoun. Among this group were Thomas Hart Benton of Missouri, Salmon P. Chase of Ohio, and William H. Seward of New York. These men sternly denied that the Constitution protected slavery. They opposed the proposed fugitive slave law and urged Congress to exclude slavery from the territories. Many of them agreed with Seward that there is a "higher law than the Constitution." They felt that "all legislative compromises are radically wrong and essentially vicious."

Victory for compromise. As it turned out, most Americans in both the North and the South favored compromise at this time. In September 1850 both houses of Congress adopted all of Clay's compromise measures by large majorities.

John C. Calhoun did not live to see the outcome of the Great Debate. He died in March, leaving a great gap in the ranks of southern leaders. Nor did President Taylor live to see the outcome. He died in July, and his successor, President Millard Fillmore of New York, signed the compromise bills.

Thus compromise, sometimes called "the essence of politics," once again saved the day. Throughout the nation Americans hailed the work of Clay and his colleagues as a great triumph for national unity. Business groups supported it, expressing their fear that continued controversy between the North and the South would ruin business everywhere.

Would the compromise endure? This was the major question on the lips of many Americans in the fall of 1850.

SECTION REVIEW
See underscored items, text pp. 396-98.
Identify: Wilmot Proviso, popular sovereignty, Stephen A. Douglas, Zachary Taylor. Henry Clay, Daniel Webster
For answers to questions, see Answer Key, p.A57.
1. **Analyzing Ideas:** How did American victory over Mexico in 1848 aggravate the slavery issue?

2. **Organizing Ideas: (a)** Describe the four proposals for handling the slavery issue in the lands of the Mexican Cession. **(b)** What groups supported each proposal?

3. **Summarizing Ideas: (a)** State the terms of Clay's compromise of 1850. **(b)** Which section of the country profited most from the compromise? **(c)** Who were the main figures involved in the Great Debate and what position did each take?

4. **Interpreting Ideas:** Why is compromise sometimes called the "essence of politics"?

3 **The long period of compromise finally comes to an end**

See Teaching Suggestions in TMRG, pp.TM102-03.
The Compromise of 1850 lasted about four years. These four years proved to be the lull before the storm.

Prosperity and growth. Prosperity and growth—these were two of the striking characteristics of the United States during the early 1850's. The South prospered as the price of cotton rose and the annual production of cotton more than doubled. The Northeast prospered as new factories were built to meet a growing demand for manufactured products. The factories provided plenty of jobs for large numbers of people, including many European immigrants. The Middle West prospered and expanded as railroads opened up the fertile prairie lands. The railroads enabled the farmers to transport and sell their products, often at

A dramatized version of Harriet Beecher Stowe's Uncle Tom's Cabin *played to packed houses both in the United States and abroad. This poster shows the heroine, Eliza, racing across an icy river as fierce bloodhounds pursue her.*

greatly increased prices. The railroads also increased the price of farmland and encouraged the growth of new towns.

The railroads were becoming a vital part of the nation's growing economy. Between 1847 and 1861, railroad mileage in the United States increased from about 9,000 miles (14,500 kilometers) to more than 30,000 miles (48,300 kilometers). Most of the new railway lines reached from the Northeast into the Middle West, helping to bind these two areas together (see map, page 312). As a result, when war did come in 1861, the South faced a much more powerful combination than it would have faced had war broken out in 1850 or earlier.

The attention of most Americans in both the North and the South had for the moment shifted from the problem of slavery to prosperity and growth. As a result, the election of 1852 was uneventful. Both major parties condemned further argument over slavery and accepted the Compromise of 1850 as final. When the votes were counted, the Democratic candidate, Franklin Pierce of New Hampshire, had won 27 states. His rival, the Whig candidate, General Winfield Scott, a hero in the Mexico War, had won only 4 states.

Ominous undercurrents. In his Inaugural Address, President Pierce urged the American people to work for national harmony. However, that hoped-for harmony was being ruined by dissension.

The publication of Harriet Beecher Stowe's *Uncle Tom's Cabin* in 1852 infuriated southerners. They insisted that her picture of slavery was a vicious falsehood. Many northerners,

on the other hand, accepted the picture as absolute truth, and their attitudes against slavery hardened.

The Fugitive Slave Law of 1850, which was part of the Compromise of 1850, also helped to keep the issue of slavery before the people. The writer Ralph Waldo Emerson expressed the feelings of most militant abolitionists about the Fugitive Slave Law when he wrote, "This filthy enactment was made in the nineteenth century by people who could read and write. I will not obey it."

Several northern states responded to the pressure of abolitionists. These states openly defied the Fugitive Slave Law by passing "personal liberty laws." Such laws forbade local officials to help in the capture and return of fugitive slaves.

Many northerners defied the Fugitive Slave Law. Meanwhile, some southerners talked of increasing their power in Congress by acquiring new slave territory. The Spanish colony of Cuba seemed especially attractive. In fact, many advocates of manifest destiny, or expansionism, had long hoped to gain control over that island.

The Ostend Manifesto. In 1848 President Polk had tried to buy Cuba for $100 million. Spain had refused to consider the offer, but some southerners continued to cast longing eyes at Cuba. Finally, in 1854, the American ministers to Great Britain, France, and Spain met in Ostend, Belgium. They issued a statement now known as the "Ostend Manifesto."

The ministers declared that if Spain refused to sell Cuba to the United States, the

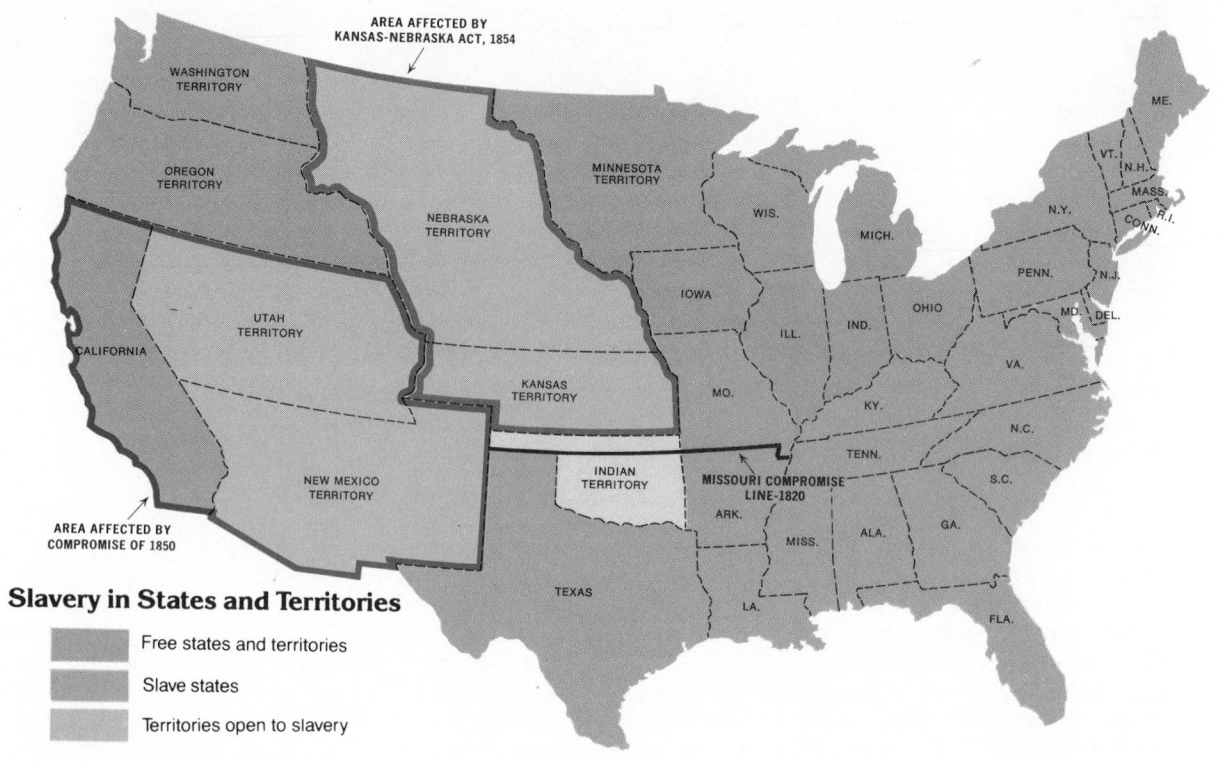

AREA AFFECTED BY
KANSAS-NEBRASKA ACT, 1854

WASHINGTON
TERRITORY

OREGON
TERRITORY

MINNESOTA
TERRITORY

ME.

VT.
N.H.
MASS.
N.Y. R.I.
CONN.

NEBRASKA
TERRITORY

WIS.

MICH.

IOWA

PENN.
N.J.
OHIO MD. DEL.

UTAH
TERRITORY

ILL. IND.

VA.

CALIFORNIA

KANSAS
TERRITORY

MO.

KY.

N.C.

NEW MEXICO
TERRITORY

INDIAN
TERRITORY

MISSOURI COMPROMISE
LINE–1820

TENN.

S.C.

AREA AFFECTED BY
COMPROMISE OF 1850

ARK.

MISS. ALA.

GA.

TEXAS

LA.

FLA.

Slavery in States and Territories

Free states and territories

Slave states

Territories open to slavery

United States would have the right to seize it by force. President Pierce disavowed this statement, but northern abolitionists were furious. They pointed out that southerners were ready to plunge the nation into war in order to add slave territory to the Union.

The Kansas-Nebraska Act. Thus, in 1854, undercurrents like these were eroding national unity. Senator Stephen A. Douglas of Illinois then increased the tensions without meaning to do so. Douglas wanted federal support for building a transcontinental railroad westward from Chicago. He felt that if the land west of the Missouri River were cleared of Indians and organized as a territory, it would be settled faster and its need for a railroad would be increased. To achieve these ends, Douglas sponsored and carried through Congress the Kansas-Nebraska Act. This act had the effect of repealing the Missouri Compromise.

The Missouri Compromise of 1820, as you know, had established the 36° 30′ parallel of latitude from the Mississippi River to the Rocky Mountains as the boundary between slave and free territory. Missouri was the only exception. The Kansas-Nebraska Act created two new organized territories in the West—Kansas and Nebraska (see map, this page). Both these territories were north of the old 36° 30′ line and, therefore, closed to slavery. However, the Kansas-Nebraska Act of 1854 abolished the Missouri Compromise dividing line. It stated that the territories were now "perfectly free to form and regulate their domestic institutions in their own way."

Northern reaction. Both major political parties were split by the Kansas-Nebraska Act. Most southern Democrats and southern Whigs voted for the bill. Many northern Democrats joined northern Whigs in opposing it. From 1854 until 1861, when war broke out, neither party was able to reunite its northern and southern wings.

Indeed, the Kansas-Nebraska Act plunged the entire nation into violent controversy over the slavery question. In Illinois an obscure lawyer, Abraham Lincoln, protested against opening the new territories to slavery. In Boston, the day after the Kansas-Nebraska Act was passed, armed forces were needed to enforce the Fugitive Slave Law. A battalion of United States artillery, four platoons of marines, and a sheriff's posse were called out to escort a runaway slave from the courthouse to the ship that was waiting to carry him back to the South.

Everywhere throughout the North, people once again talked about slavery. The Fugitive Slave Law became increasingly difficult to enforce. "Anti-Nebraska" meetings were held, at which Douglas was denounced for reopening the slavery dispute.

The race for Kansas. Senator Charles Sumner of Massachusetts was one of many militant abolitionists who believed that the Kansas-Nebraska Act would plunge the country into serious trouble. "It puts freedom and slavery face to face and bids them grapple." And grapple they did on the plains of the new territory of Kansas.

The ink was hardly dry on the Kansas-Nebraska Act before eager pioneers and land speculators from both the North and the South rushed into the new territory. Competition over the choicest land and the most promising town sites quickly led to bitter disputes.

The confusion worsened when northern and southern extremists on the slavery issue began a race to control the new territory. Northerners formed an "Emigrant Aid Company" to encourage antislavery settlers to move into Kansas. The northern settlers founded Lawrence, Topeka, and other new settlements. Meanwhile, proslavery settlers from Missouri crossed over the border into Kansas and started the proslavery towns of Atchison, Leavenworth, and Lecompton. In the mad scramble for land and for control of the territory, the land claims of the Indians were brushed aside or ignored.

The time soon came for the settlers in Kansas to draw up a constitution and organize a territorial government. This brought them face to face with the crucial question: Was slavery to be allowed in Kansas or not? The proslavery forces rushed voters into the territory and elected a proslavery legislature, which promptly passed laws favoring slaveowners. The antislavery forces then drafted a constitution forbidding slavery and elected an antislavery legislature. By the end of 1855, the territory of Kansas had two different constitutions and two different governments—one proslavery, one antislavery.

Dilemma in Washington. Back in Washington, members of Congress watched the struggle with dismay—and no one with greater dismay than the author of the Kansas-Nebraska Act, Stephen A. Douglas. When Douglas had argued for popular sovereignty, he had hoped to remove the bitter issue of slavery from the heated politics of Congress and to allow the settlers in the territories themselves to decide the issue.

Obviously, Douglas's intentions had backfired. Congress was now forced to take sides and, hopelessly divided, it was not able to reach a decision.

Bleeding Kansas. While Congress argued, violence raged in what people called "Bleeding Kansas." Northerners and southerners alike rushed weapons into the territory. An armed proslavery group burned part of the town of Lawrence, a center of the antislavery settlers. In revenge, a fanatical white abolitionist, John Brown, gathered an armed group, including his own sons, and murdered five unarmed proslavery men. The fighting over slavery and over disputed land claims took the lives of more than 200 men and women before federal troops moved in to restore order.

The Republican Party. One immediate result of the struggle over Kansas was the formation of a new political party. Neither of the two major parties, the Whigs and the Democrats, dared take a stand on Kansas or any other issue involving slavery. Each party needed the support of its members in the Middle West, where the Kansas-Nebraska Act was popular. For this reason, antislavery members in both parties decided that the time had come to organize a new party pledging to prevent the further expansion of slavery in the territories.

Many towns and cities in the Middle West claim to be the birthplace of the Republican Party. However, it was at a convention in Jackson, Michigan, on July 6, 1854, that the delegates chose a name. They took the old label of Thomas Jefferson's party for their new organization and called themselves "Republicans."

The election of 1856. The election returns in the Presidential contest of 1856 showed that sectional lines were rapidly stiffening in the

John C. Frémont, "The Pathfinder," was always on the move. Born in Georgia, he moved throughout the South while his father made a living teaching French and dancing.

In 1841 Frémont eloped with 16-year-old Jennie Benton, daughter of the powerful Senator Thomas Hart Benton. Benton, impressed with his adventurous son-in-law, persuaded Congress to authorize expeditions for Frémont to explore the Rocky Mountains, the Oregon country, and northern California. Frémont's vivid descriptions heightened American interest in acquiring these territories.

Frémont, captivated by California's wealth and scenic beauty, hoped to gain the region for the United States. The Mexican authorities, sensing his plans, ordered him to leave. Instead, in the summer of 1846, Frémont led a group of American settlers in a revolt that set up the Bear Flag Republic. Frémont purchased land in California, amassing a fortune from the gold found there. When California gained statehood in 1850, he became its first United States senator. Frémont was also chosen as the first Republican Presidential candidate in 1856, but he lost to James Buchanan.

At the start of the Civil War, Frémont was made a major general in the Union Army and placed in charge of the Western Department. President Lincoln had him transferred after he had disputes with slaveholders. Frémont, however, resigned from the army.

After the war, Frémont invested in several western railroads. When one of the lines went bankrupt in 1870, he lost his fortune. The man who had helped blaze trails westward slowly faded from public view.

nation. The Whigs, who had tried to dodge the slavery issue, came in a poor third, with only 8 electoral votes. The Democrats nominated James Buchanan of Pennsylvania. They supported the Compromise of 1850 and the Kansas-Nebraska Act "as the only sound and safe solution of the slavery question." They came in first with 174 electoral votes (14 slave and 5 free states).

It was the Republican Party, however, that showed most clearly the danger facing the Union. The Republicans, who nominated John C. Frémont, the explorer of the Great West, came out squarely against any further expansion of slavery. Under the slogan "Free Soil, Free Speech, Free Men, and Frémont," the new Republican Party received 114 electoral votes —all of them from 11 free states. The Republican Party was plainly a purely sectional politi-

cal organization, drawing all its support from the North. It seemed almost certain that the long period of compromise had come to an end.

SECTION REVIEW
See underscored items, text pp. 399, 401.

Identify: Franklin Pierce, Fugitive Slave Law of 1850, Ostend Manifesto, John Brown

For answers to questions, see Answer Key, pp.A57-58.

1. **Summarizing Ideas:** How did the issue of slavery continue to cause trouble from 1850 to 1854?

2. **Determining Cause and Effect: (a)** What were the provisions of the Kansas-Nebraska Act? **(b)** Describe the consequences of the act's passage.

3. **Analyzing Ideas:** Explain the conditions that led to the formation of the Republican Party in 1854.

4 The North and South move steadily toward war

See Teaching Suggestions in TMRG, p.TM103.

By 1857 the hope of compromise seemed remote. From 1857 to 1861, the nation drifted toward disunion.

The Dred Scott decision. On March 6, 1857, two days after President Buchanan took the oath of office, the Supreme Court handed down the Dred Scott decision. The decision was named after the slave Dred Scott.

Dred Scott's owner had taken him from Missouri, a slave state, into Illinois, a free state, and into Wisconsin Territory, which was free under the terms of the Missouri Compromise. His owner then took him back into Missouri. Befriended by members of a family that had once owned him, Dred Scott was eager to prove in court that he was a free man because he had lived in a free state and a free territory. One lower court decided for Scott, another Court against him. Finally the case reached the Supreme Court.

The Supreme Court ruled that residence in a free territory and free state had not given Dred Scott his right to freedom. It decided that Scott (and therefore all slaves) was not a citizen of the United States or of the state of Missouri. Therefore, he had no right to sue in either a state or a federal court.

Had the Supreme Court stopped at this point, the Dred Scott case might have gone almost unnoticed by the general public. However, the Supreme Court went on to rule that the Missouri Compromise was unconstitutional because Congress had no power to exclude slavery from the territories. The Court based this decision on the Fifth Amendment, which prohibited Congress from depriving any person of "property, without due process of law." The only other time that the Court had declared an act of Congress unconstitutional was in the case of *Marbury v. Madison* in 1803.

The abolitionist forces in the North were severely jolted by the Dred Scott decision. Now, because of the Supreme Court decision, only an amendment to the Constitution could keep slavery out of the territories. Such an amendment would have to be ratified by three fourths of all the states. In view of southern opposition, such a majority was out of the question. The antislavery forces now determined to gain strength and win the election of 1860.

A new leader. The contest for the office of United States Senator from Illinois in 1858 turned out to be a prelude to the general election of 1860. Stephen A. Douglas was running for reelection as a Democrat. He knew that if he won the Senate race in 1858, he had a good chance of winning the Democratic nomination for the Presidency in 1860.

To oppose Douglas, the Illinois Republicans put up Abraham Lincoln. Born in a log cabin in Kentucky, Lincoln was a self-made man. Gifted with a down-to-earth sense of humor and with much political shrewdness, Lincoln was a match for Douglas in wit, in logical argument, and in general ability.

Lincoln was not an abolitionist. However, he believed that slavery was morally wrong. He accepted the basic principle of the new Republican Party that slavery must not be ex-

---

══ SOURCES ══

DRED SCOTT v. SANFORD (1857)

The right of property in a slave is distinctly and expressly affirmed in the Constitution. The right to traffic in it, like an ordinary article of merchandise and property, was guaranteed to the citizens of the United States, in every state that might desire it, for twenty years. And the government in express terms is pledged to protect it in all future time, if the slave escapes from his owner. . . . And no word can be found in the Constitution which gives Congress a greater power over slave property, or which entitles property of that kind to less protection than property of any other description. The only power conferred is the power coupled with the duty of guarding and protecting the owner in his rights. . . .

Harpers Ferry was founded in 1747 in what is now West Virginia by a millwright named Robert Harper. Harper set up a ferry and a grist mill at the place where the Shenandoah and Potomac rivers meet. It was a beautiful scenic spot, surrounded by high bluffs.

In 1796 the United States government erected an arsenal at Harpers Ferry. By the mid-1800's, the town was a manufacturing center for guns and ammunition, as well as a storage center for military supplies. Later, the construction of the Chesapeake & Ohio Canal and tracks for the Baltimore & Ohio Railroad made it a major transportation link between the lands east of the Appalachians and the Ohio valley.

John Brown's seizures of the arsenal in 1859 brought the town to national prominence. During the Civil War, the arsenal changed hands a number of times as Union and Confederate troops fought back and forth through the area. Each time one side retreated, it destroyed part of the town's industrial plant, so that by the end of the war little was left.

Today Harpers Ferry is primarily a tourist attraction. The Harpers Ferry National Historical Park, which was established there in 1963, includes the John Brown Museum and the fire engine house in which Brown was taken prisoner.

tended any further. In accepting his nomination as Senator, he declared, "A house divided against itself cannot stand. I believe this government cannot endure permanently half slave and half free. I do not expect the Union to be dissolved—I do not expect the house to fall—but I do expect it will cease to be divided. Either the opponents of slavery will arrest the further spread of it, and place it where the public mind shall rest in the belief that it is in the course of ultimate extinction, or its advocates will push it forward till it shall become alike lawful in all the states, old as well as new North as well as South."

The Lincoln-Douglas debates. Confident of his position and of his ability to defend it, Lincoln challenged Douglas to a series of debates. Throngs of people came to seven Illinois towns to hear Lincoln and Douglas vigorously debate the issues of the day. Newspapers in every section of the land reported the debates. Lincoln greatly impressed those who heard him and many who read what he said.

In the debates Lincoln asked Douglas how he could reconcile his principle of popular sovereignty with the Dred Scott decision. This put Douglas in a tight spot. In the Dred Scott decision, the Supreme Court had ruled that no one had the right to outlaw slavery in any territory. Douglas, on the other hand, had argued for popular sovereignty, allowing the people in each territory to make their own decision about slavery. If Douglas replied that he believed in the Dred Scott decision, he would win the support of southerners but lose much northern support. If he continued to argue for popular sovereignty, he would lose southern support but win many northern votes. With his eye on the Presidency in 1860, what could Douglas say to please both sides?

Douglas was a skillful politician. His answer to Lincoln became known as the Freeport Doctrine, after the Illinois town where the debate took place. Douglas cleverly replied that the legislature of a territory could refuse to pass a law supporting slavery and in effect could exclude slavery from the territory.

Douglas's statement met with enough approval in Illinois to elect him Senator. Nevertheless, the Freeport Doctrine weakened Douglas in the South. By doing so, it also cost him the nomination for the Presidency in 1860 by a united Democratic Party. Southerners began to realize that Douglas's popular sovereignty did not mean that he favored the expansion of slavery.

John Brown's raid. In the fall of 1859, John Brown tried to start a slave rebellion in Virginia. With money obtained from abolitionists, he armed a party of about 18 men. On October 16 he seized the federal arsenal at the town of Harpers Ferry, in what is now West Virginia. He planned to seize the guns stored in the arsenal, give them to nearby slaves, and lead the slaves in what he hoped would be a widespread rebellion.

It was a bold idea, but almost certain to fail. Brown and his followers were captured by Colonel Robert E. Lee of the United States Army in command of a unit of marines. After a trial that Brown admitted was more fair than he had reason to expect, he was hanged for "murder, criminal conspiracy, and treason against the Commonwealth of Virginia."

Many northerners were shocked at John Brown's raid and quickly condemned it. Many northern abolitionists, however, hailed Brown as a hero and a martyr. Lydia Maria Child, a prominent writer and abolitionist, offered her help to Brown in prison. Frederick Douglass, who had refused to join Brown's scheme because he felt that it was doomed to fail, applauded Brown's courage. Southern newspapers quoted the opinions of such abolitionists as typical of what the whole North was thinking. To southerners, John Brown's raid was convincing evidence that the North was determined to abolish slavery.

SECTION REVIEW
See underscored items, text pp. 403–04.
Identify: Dred Scott decision, Abraham Lincoln, Freeport Doctrine
For answers to questions, see Answer Key, p.A58.
1. **Analyzing Ideas: (a)** What was the Supreme Court decision in the Dred Scott case? **(b)** Why did this decision arouse widespread opposition?
2. **Summarizing Ideas:** Explain the main issues in the Lincoln-Douglas debates.
3. **Interpreting Ideas: (a)** What was the purpose of John Brown's raid? **(b)** Describe the reaction of both sides to the raid.

Many abolitionists praised John Brown as the hero of the oppressed slaves. After Brown's execution, these abolitionists called him a martyr.

5 Southern states withdraw from the Union and war begins

See Teaching Suggestions in TMRG, pp.TM104-05.
By 1860 the disappearing ties between the two sections was reflected in the tensions dividing the political parties. The widening split became clear in 1860, when the national parties met to draw up platforms and to nominate candidates for the Presidency.

The parties take their stands. The Whig Party was greatly weakened by 1856, when many southern Whigs voted for the Democrats. In 1860 what was left of the old Whig Party nominated John Bell of Tennessee for the Presidency and changed its name to the Constitutional Union Party. The party adopted a platform that called upon all citizens to recognize "no political principles other than the Constitution of the country, the Union of the states, and the enforcement of the law."

The Democratic Party split wide open in 1860. One group, consisting mostly of south-

HONEST ABE TAKING THEM ON THE HALF SHELL..

A cartoonist shows Abraham Lincoln devouring the Washington political establishment in the election of 1860.

erners, took a strong proslavery position. This group nominated John C. Breckinridge of Kentucky for the Presidency and demanded federal protection for slavery in the territories. The other group, mostly northern Democrats, nominated Stephen A. Douglas for the Presidency. It took the position that popular sovereignty should decide the slavery question in the territories.

The Republicans, meeting in Chicago, determined to make the most of the split in the Democratic Party. They abandoned one strongly antislavery candidate, Governor William H. Seward of New York, partly because he seemed to be identified with eastern "money interests." The Republicans also believed that a candidate from the Middle West was more likely to win the election. The convention then went on to name Abraham Lincoln as its candidate.

The Republican platform was a purely sectional platform. It was designed to win the support of northern industrialists and wage earners and of farmers, particularly in the Middle West. The platform opposed the extension of slavery into the new territories.

Thus four political parties entered the Presidential race in 1860. The Republicans, with Lincoln at their head, were supported by many northern industrialists and midwestern farmers who opposed any further extension of slavery. Aligned against the Republicans in the North were Democrats led by Douglas. The Douglas Democrats wanted to keep things much as they were. Douglas urged the people to vote for him on the ground that, if Lincoln were elected, the South would then secede from the Union.

In the South the contest was between the moderate Constitutional Unionists, led by Bell, and the southern Democrats, led by Breckinridge. The southern Democrats made it clear that they would regard the election of Lincoln as proof that the North was using its superior strength to encroach upon the rights and interests of the South.

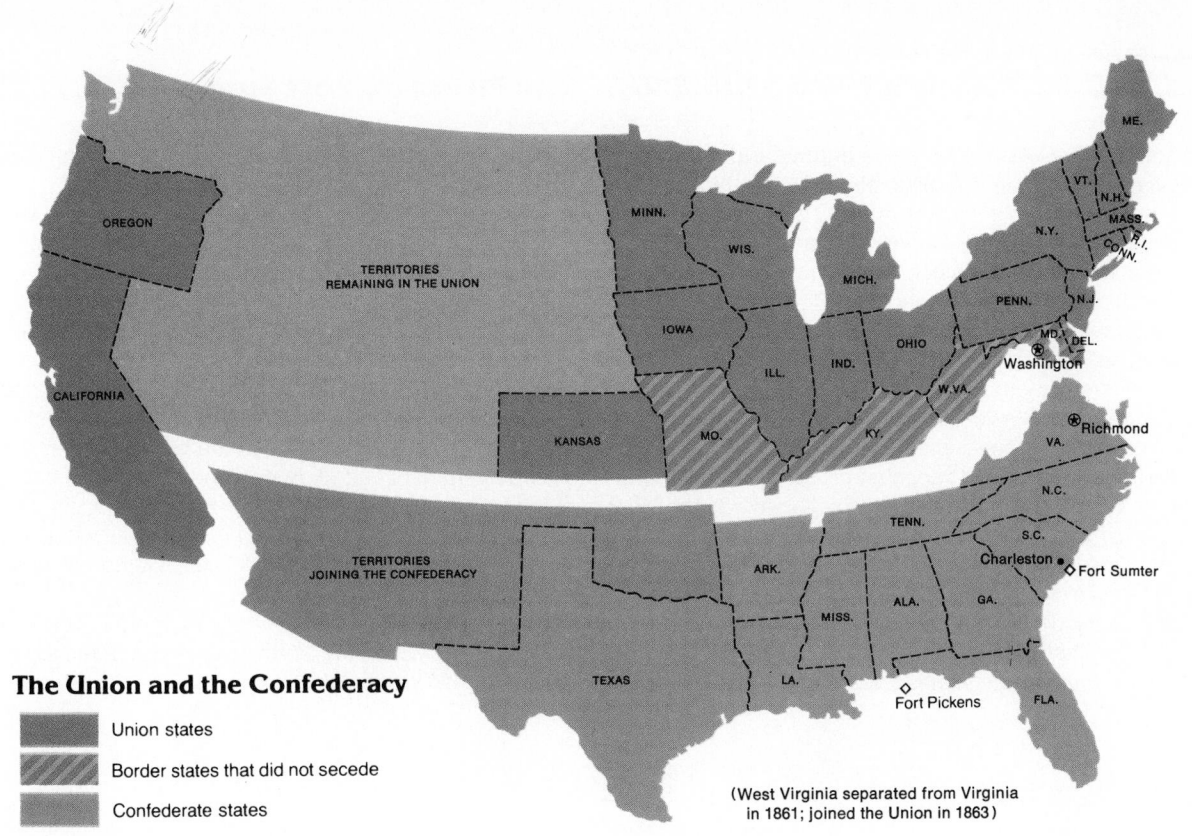

The Union and the Confederacy

- ■ Union states
- ▨ Border states that did not secede
- ▨ Confederate states

(West Virginia separated from Virginia
in 1861; joined the Union in 1863)

Results of the election. Lincoln won the election, receiving 180 electoral votes, all from the northern free states. Breckinridge mustered 72 electoral votes, all from the southern slave states. Douglas drew 12 electoral votes, while Bell received 39.

The count of the popular vote showed that Lincoln had polled 40 percent, Douglas 29 percent, Breckinridge 18 percent, and Bell nearly 13 percent. Lincoln was elected President, but by a minority of the popular vote.

In both the North and the South, Lincoln and Breckinridge, who opposed any compromise on the issue of slavery in the territories, won more electoral votes than the moderates, Douglas and Bell. Thoughtful observers noted this development with alarm. Did it mean that the southern states would carry out their threat to **secede**, or withdraw, from the Union.

Secession from the Union. The fateful answer came quickly. Shortly after the November election, the legislature of South Carolina called a special convention to consider secession. The delegates unanimously voted that

South Carolina was no longer a state of the Union. Other southern states, not without some opposition, followed South Carolina's example. Mississippi, Florida, Alabama, Georgia, Louisiana, and Texas soon passed acts of secession.

Early in 1861, delegates from six of the seven seceding states met at Montgomery, Alabama. There they drafted a constitution for the Confederate States of America. Although the Confederate Constitution resembled the Constitution of the United States, there were some major differences. The Confederate Constitution stressed "the sovereign and independent character" of each state. It also guaranteed the right to own slaves.

The Montgomery convention elected as President of the Confederacy Jefferson Davis, a Mississippi planter who had formerly served as United States Senator and Secretary of War. The delegates also elected Alexander H. Stephens of Georgia as Vice President.

Buchanan's inaction. While southern states were seceding from the Union, what did Pres-

Fort Sumter was the only one of three federal forts in Charleston, South Carolina, still in Union hands at the time of Lincoln's inauguration. The commander of Sumter, Major Robert Anderson, and his eighty men were virtually under siege within the fort. Realizing he was in no position to hold off a Confederate attack, Anderson sent Lincoln a letter asking for additional supplies and troop reinforcements.

Anderson's letter posed a major problem for President Lincoln. The President hoped to delay the outbreak of hostilities while seeking a peaceful compromise. Sending fresh supplies and troops to Fort Sumter might be perceived by the Confederacy as an act of war. On the other hand, if Lincoln failed to honor Anderson's request, the fort would pass into Confederate hands. Finally, against the advice of a majority of his cabinet, Lincoln decided to steer a middle course. He notified the governor of South Carolina that he was sending a relief expedition to Fort Sumter, but that it contained provisions only.

In the meantime, the food supply in Fort Sumter was running dangerously low. Unaware that the relief expedition was on its way, Major Anderson finally offered to surrender the fort in two days' time. But General Pierre Beauregard, Confederate commander of the Charleston district, was unwilling to wait.

At 4:30 on the morning of April 12, 1861, the Confederate guns around the harbor opened up on Fort Sumter. Major Anderson promptly returned the fire. The shooting continued for 34 hours, as the citizens of Charleston crowded the waterfront to watch the battle. By the time the bombardment ended, Anderson's forces were out of ammunition, and the fort had been reduced to ruins. The next day, April 14, Anderson led his troops out of the fort and surrendered to the Confederates. Remarkably, no one had been killed on either side.

News of the fall of Fort Sumter ended all hopes of compromise. Men in the North and the South rushed to join the armed forces. War had begun.

---

ident Buchanan do? The answer was, almost nothing. He did announce that no state in the Union had the right to secede, but he also stated that the federal government had no power to hold any state in the Union against its will. Thus, for four months, from Lincoln's election until the inauguration, the only efforts to meet the crisis were several half-hearted proposals for compromise. All these proposals were quickly rejected by leaders in both the North and the South.

In fairness to Buchanan, it should be said that his policy did prevent war for several months. It also gave compromise proposals a chance to be heard. Since he had only four months more in the White House, Buchanan may have concluded that the incoming President should be allowed to settle the problem in his own way.

Outbreak of war. During this time Confederate troops occupied—without resistance—all but two of the forts and navy yards in the states that had seceded. By the time Lincoln was inaugurated on March 4, 1861, only Fort Pickens at Pensacola, Florida, and Fort Sumter at Charleston, South Carolina (see map, page 407), remained in the hands of the federal government. Southerners—or at least those southerners who held the most extreme point of view—claimed that these forts belonged to the Confederate States of America, not to the United States of America.

SECTION REVIEW
See underscored items, text pp. 405-07.
Identify: Constitutional Union Party, John C. Breckinridge, secede, Confederacy, Jefferson Davis
For answers to questions, see Answer Key, p.A58.
1. **Interpreting Ideas:** In the election of 1860, those "who opposed any compromise on the issue of slavery . . . won more electoral votes than the moderates." Comment on this statement.

2. **Determining Cause and Effect:** How did Lincoln's election in 1860 help bring on the Civil War?

3. **Studying Charts:** Make a chart with four columns—each column headed by the name of a political party in 1860. In each column, fill in (a) the name of the Presidential candidate, (b) his position on the main issues, (c) the regions of the country supporting his party, and (d) the number of electoral votes he received.

DEVELOPING HISTORY STUDY SKILLS

Reading About History Analyzing Primary Sources

Sir, I have said that I never could vote for it, and I repeat that I never can, and never will vote for it; and no earthly power shall ever make me vote to plant slavery where slavery does not exist. . . .

The above quotation, from a speech by Henry Clay in 1850, is a primary source. A primary source is an original record, document, or account of an event or of a period of history. Besides speeches, there are many other types of primary sources as the following list shows:

DIARIES	MARRIAGE LICENCES
JOURNALS	DEATH CERTIFICATES
LETTERS	MINUTES OF MEETINGS
LEGAL DOCUMENTS	BANK RECORDS
TAX ROLLS	EDITORIALS
VOTING LISTS	POLITICAL CARTOONS
BUSINESS LEDGERS	ADVERTISEMENTS
SHIPS' LOGS	POETRY AND SONGS
BIRTH CERTIFICATES	AUTOBIOGRAPHIES
ARTIFACTS	COLLECTIONS OF ORAL HISTORY
SOUND RECORDINGS	VIDEO RECORDINGS
PHOTOGRAPHS	DRAWINGS
NEWSPAPERS	MAGAZINES
MOVIES	PAINTINGS

Some primary sources are more reliable than others for accurate factual information. For example, an autobiography may be less reliable than a diary or a journal. The autobiography may have been written later in a person's life and time may have dimmed or altered a person's memory of events.

Applying the Skill

Analyzing primary sources is much the same as analyzing information from other sources. Review the skill presented on pages 301–02 and the steps for analyzing information.

Practicing the Skill

A. Read the following excerpt, which is a continuation of Clay's speech. Then on a separate sheet of paper, answer the questions below.

Still, if there be a majority — and there ought to be such a majority — for interdicting [prohibiting] slavery north of the line, there ought to be an equal majority . . . — to admit slavery south of the line. And if there be a majority ready to accomplish both of these purposes, though I can not concur in the action, yet I would be one of the last to create any disturbance. . . . I think, then, it would be better to keep the whole of these territories untouched by any legislation by Congress on the subject of slavery.

1. What was the background for the speech?
2. What was Henry Clay's purpose in giving the speech?
3. What was Clay's main idea?
4. Why do you think Clay's speech is a valuable primary source?

B. Read this excerpt, which is from a speech by Daniel Webster during the same debate in which Clay's speech took place. Then on a separate sheet of paper, answer the questions below.

I hear with pain and anguish and distress, the word secession, especially when it falls from the lips of those who are eminently patriotic, . . . Secession! Peaceful secession! Sir, your eyes and mine are never destined to see . . . [the] dismemberment of this vast country without convulsion! . . . There can be no such thing as a peaceable secession.

1. What distresses Webster?
2. What does he expect to happen should secession occur?
3. How did Webster differ from Clay in his assessment of the situation?

Why did the North and South go to war in 1861? What was the immediate cause of the tragic conflict? There is no easy way to answer these two questions. Historians have studied the issues for years and still reach different conclusions.

Some historians have stressed the basic economic and social differences of the North and the South. Other historians have pointed to disagreements over tariffs, internal improvements at public expense, money and banking, the disposal of public lands, and slavery. Still other historians have emphasized the issue of states' rights.

Thoughtful historians have not attempted to give short and simple explanations of the war between the North and South. All they have done is try to explain why northern extremists and southern extremists, a minority in each section, felt and acted as they did. The historians have pointed out only that the great majority in the North held similar views. Most northerners felt that the benefits of the Union were too important and that patriotism was too precious to permit the Union to be destroyed. The historians have indicated only that many in the South who loved the Union and would have preferred to stay in it had equally compelling reasons for supporting the Confederacy. Some supported the Confederacy out of loyalty to the principle of states' rights. Others were determined to protect their homes and property. Still others gave their support out of consideration for the position taken by kinfolk, neighbors, and friends.

CONNECTING CHAPTER IDEAS

In the next chapter you will read about the struggle that pitted brother against brother, parents against their sons and daughters, and relative against relative. The Civil War lasted four years. At its end, the reunited nation faced important changes.

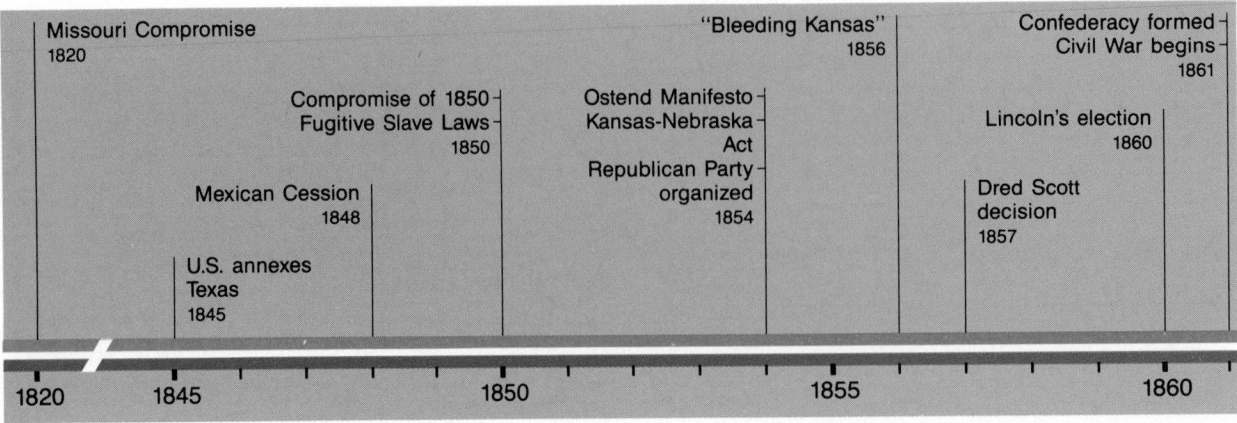

17 REVIEW

Reviewing Important Terms

In the sentences below, the underlined terms are incorrect. On a separate sheet of paper, rewrite each sentence using the correct term.

1. The Wilmot Proviso, proposed in 1819, would have freed all children born into slavery in Missouri, after it became a state, on their twenty-fifth birthday.
2. The Ostend Manifesto declared that slavery would not exist in lands acquired from Mexico.
3. The Tallmadge Amendment asserted the United States' right to seize Cuba by force if Spain refused to sell the territory.
4. According to the Dred Scott decision, the legislature of a territory could refuse to pass a law supporting slavery and in effect could exclude slavery from the territory.
5. The Freeport Doctrine jolted abolitionists, since it declared that the Missouri Compromise was unconstitutional.

Practicing Critical Thinking Skills

1. **Summarizing Ideas.** How did each of the following events and people increase sectional bitterness: (a) the Mexican War, (b) William Lloyd Garrison, (c) Harriet Beecher Stowe, (d) the Dred Scott decision, and (e) John Brown's raid?
2. **Analyzing Sources.** When President Lincoln met Harriet Beecher Stowe, he said, "Well, so you're the little lady who started this great war!" What did Lincoln mean by this remark?
3. **Evaluating Viewpoints. (a)** Do you believe that white southerners were the only Americans who regarded blacks as inferior during the period before the Civil War? Give evidence to support your opinion. **(b)** Why would it be unfair to make the generalization that all southerners were proslavery and all northerners were antislavery?
4. **Determining Cause and Effect.** Make a list of events leading to the Civil War. Then make a second list of the issues that caused the war. **(a)** Are the lists different? the same? **(b)** What can you conclude from your answers in part **(a)** of this question? **(c)** Do you think the war could have been avoided if any of these events had not taken place? Why or why not?
5. **Relating Past to Present.** Between 1854 and 1860, the Republican Party replaced the Whig Party as the second major political party. Would it be possible today for a new political party to replace one of the two major parties? If so, under what conditions? Would such a change be likely? Why or why not?

Developing History Study Skills

1. **Analyzing Primary Sources.** Read the excerpt from the Dred Scott decision on page 403. **(a)** How did the Supreme Court justify its opinion that slaves were property? **(b)** According to the decision, should slaves have been treated differently from other types of property? Explain.

2. **Interpreting Maps.** Study the map on page 400. **(a)** When did Kansas become a territory? **(b)** In terms of geographical area, was a larger part of the country made up of free states or of slaves states and areas open to slavery? **(c)** Which area on the map is neither a free state, a slave state, nor open to slavery?

Relating Geography and History

Missouri's application for statehood revealed how serious the sectional division was between the North and South over slavery. If Missouri entered the Union as a free state it would destroy the balance between free states and slave states in the Senate. It would further imperil the political power of the South, whose representatives were already outnumbered in the House. To further analyze the significance of the Missouri situation, answer the following questions.

1. **(a)** List the eleven slave states and eleven free states before 1820. **(b)** What was geographically significant about Missouri? **(c)** What impact might Missouri's location have on future territories who wished to join the Union?
2. **(a)** What was the purpose of the Tallmadge amendment? **(b)** What pattern might the amendment have set for the future?
3. **(a)** What is a compromise? **(b)** For what reasons can the Missouri solution be rightly called a compromise? **(c)** In what way was it not a real compromise?
4. The Missouri Compromise only postponed what sooner or later would "burst on us as a tornado." Comment.

See Chapter Overview in TMRG, p.TM106.
See Chapter Objectives in TMRG, p.TM106.
See Introducing the Chapter in TMRG, p.TM106.

CHAPTER 18   A Nation Divided

(1861–1865)

The tragedy
of war.

On April 15, 1861, the day after Fort Sumter fell, President Abraham Lincoln declared that the government of the United States faced an armed revolt against its authority.

In the northern states, recruits enthusiastically answered Lincoln's call to arms. From many walks of life, they came—Republicans and Democrats, native-born Americans, and newly arrived immigrants.

The poet Walt Whitman captured in verse the feeling of unity that gripped northerners in those trying days:

Beat! beat! drums!—blow! bugles! blow!
Through the windows—through the
    doors—burst like a ruthless force,
Into the solemn church, and scatter the
    congregation;
Into the school where the scholar is
    studying;
Leave not the bridegroom quiet—no
    happiness must he have now with his
    bride;
Nor the peaceful farmer any peace,
    ploughing his field or gathering his
    grain;
So fierce you whirr and pound, you
    drums—so shrill you bugles blow.

In the South, the call to arms by the Confederate leaders was also answered with a sense of dedication to a cause. The period from the firing on Fort Sumter in 1861 to the surrender at Appomattox Court House in 1865, however, was the most tragic in the nation's history.

═══ READING FOCUS ═══

As you read about the awful struggle to preserve the Union, look for the details that support each of the following statements.

1. The North and South develop their war strategies.
2. The North and South struggle through four years of conflict.
3. Freeing the slaves becomes a goal for the Union.
4. The war brings severe hardship and suffering to the South.
5. Life behind Union lines undergoes important changes.
6. The Union faces political problems at home and abroad.

1 The North and South develop their war strategies

See Teaching Suggestions in TMRG, pp.TM106-07.

When President Lincoln called for Union volunteers, there were only seven states in the Confederate States of America, or the Confederacy—South Carolina, Georgia, Florida, Alabama, Mississippi, Louisiana, and Texas. The call to arms meant every state had to choose.

Choosing sides. Virginia, on April 17, 1861, became the eighth state to join the Confederacy. When Virginia left the Union, the United States Army lost several of its ablest officers. The most famous Virginian to take up arms for the South was Robert E. Lee, to whom President Lincoln had offered command of the Union forces. Arkansas, Tennessee, and North Carolina soon followed Virginia into the Confederacy. By May 20, eleven states had seceded from the Union to join the Confederacy (see map, page 407).

The mountainous counties in northwestern Virginia did not follow the rest of the state into the Confederacy. In 1863 these counties were admitted to the Union as the state of West Virginia. Control of this area, part of which lay on the Ohio River, was important to the North. It helped to keep open the lines of communication between the states of the Northeast and the Mississippi River.

The **border states**—Delaware, Maryland, Kentucky, and Missouri—were also important to the Union. For a time, it remained uncertain which side some of them would join.

Maryland was especially important. If it joined the Confederacy, the Union capital at Washington, D.C., would be cut off from the northern states. Many Marylanders sympathized with the Confederacy, and for a time the state hung in the balance. On April 19 a mob of angry citizens attacked the Sixth Massachusetts Regiment as it passed through Baltimore. To prevent the passage of Union troops and to avoid further bloodshed, Maryland authorities burned the railroad bridges connecting Baltimore with Philadelphia and Harrisburg. Lincoln was determined to keep Maryland in the Union. He sent federal troops into the state and arrested the leading Confederate sympathizers. Pro-Union leaders soon

▲ Map activity: Have the students point out key waterways in the border states. Then have the students explain why the border states's decision not to secede was strategically important to the Union.

413

won power, and Maryland then remained in the Union.

The other border states—Delaware, Kentucky, and Missouri—also decided in favor of the Union. Delaware never hesitated. Kentucky at first ignored Lincoln's call for volunteers and tried to remain neutral. However, when the Confederate army invaded Kentucky in September, the state declared for the Union. Missouri's government was controlled by southern sympathizers. After several battles had been fought, however, Missouri officially lined up with the North.

The "North" also included the Pacific coast states of California and Oregon. In 1863, after West Virginia joined the Union, a total of 24 states were fighting on the northern side.

In many states, especially in the border states, families were torn apart as some members enlisted with the Confederacy, others with the Union. Three of Mrs. Lincoln's brothers fought and died for the South. Robert E. Lee's nephew commanded Union naval forces on the James River in Virginia while his famous uncle was fighting Union army forces not many miles away. These divisions within families and the breakup of lifelong friendships were among the many tragic results of the war.

Northern advantages. The North had tremendous material advantages over the South. It was greatly superior in population, in manufacturing, in agricultural and natural resources, in finances, and in transportation facilities. The strength of the North had recently been increased by the admission of three new states to the Union—Minnesota (1858), Oregon (1859), and Kansas (1861).

The population of the 24 northern, western, and border states totaled 22 million, plus about 800,000 immigrants who entered during the war years. About 400,000 foreign-born men served in the Union armies.

Varied economic resources gave the North a huge advantage over the chiefly agricultural South. When the war began, the North had 92 percent of the nation's industries and almost all the known supplies of coal, iron, copper, and other metals. The North also owned most of the nation's gold. Confederate wealth was largely in land and slaves.

Northern transportation facilities were also far superior to those of the South. Most of the nation's railroad lines were located in the North and the Middle West. Thus the North could move troops and supplies almost at will. It could easily transport food from midwestern farms to workers in the eastern cities and to armies in the field. Moreover, with control of the navy and most of the merchant marine, the North could continue to carry on trade with nations overseas.

Southern advantages. The 11 states of the Confederacy had a combined population of only about 9 million. This figure included more than 3.5 million slaves. Northerners therefore outnumbered white southerners by more than four to one.

Nevertheless, southerners felt confident because to win, they had only to fight a defensive war. The South needed only to protect its territory until the North tired of the struggle. The North, on the other hand, had to conquer an area almost as large as Western Europe.

The Confederacy also had the advantage that many of its ablest officers were West Point graduates with long years of army experience. Also, southerners were used to outdoor living. They were generally more familiar with firearms and horses than many soldiers from the Northeast, who had been raised in cities.

Another reason for southern optimism was the belief that cotton was "king." Southerners believed that the textile mills of Great Britain and France were so dependent on raw cotton that these countries would have to come to the aid of the Confederacy.

War aims. Another advantage that southerners had over northerners was the fact that southerners were fighting for more clearly defined goals. The major aim of the Confederacy never varied. Southerners fought to win their independence—the right to govern themselves as they saw fit. Also, once northern armies invaded the Confederacy, southerners fought to defend the things that people cherish most—their homes and families. In addition, many southerners—both slaveholders and nonslaveholders alike—were fighting to preserve slavery. By this time, as you know, slavery had become firmly established in the South. Most white southerners had come to identify with its way of life.

In contrast, northerners who supported the war were fighting for less tangible goals, no matter how deeply felt. At the start of the war, most northerners believed with President Lin-

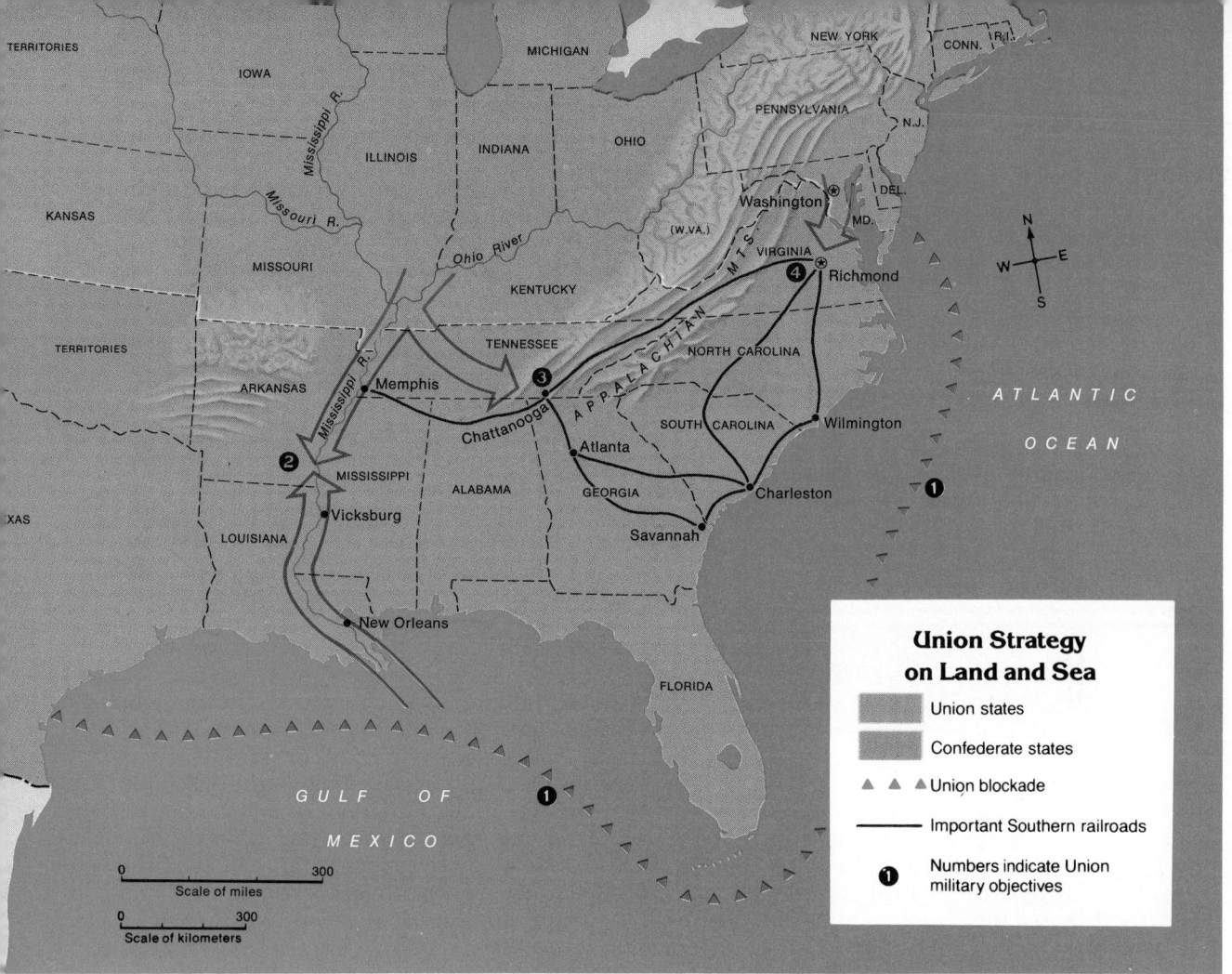

Union Strategy on Land and Sea

- Union states
- Confederate states
- ▲ ▲ ▲ Union blockade
- —— Important Southern railroads
- ❶ Numbers indicate Union military objectives

Scale of miles 0 — 300

Scale of kilometers 0 — 300

coln that they were fighting for one major aim—to preserve the Union. Only a few extreme abolitionists saw the war as a means to end slavery. As the war dragged on, more and more northerners came to believe that freeing the slaves was as important as restoring the Union—that the two aims, indeed, were inseparable.

War strategies. The overall strategy of the South was as clear and simple as its war aims. Southerners proposed to fight a defensive war. They would try to hold the North at arm's length until northerners grew war-weary and agreed to peace on southern terms. There was one exception to this defensive strategy. It was a plan to seize Washington, D.C., and strike northward through the Shenandoah Valley into Maryland and Pennsylvania. By this plan the South hoped to drive a wedge between the Northeast and the Middle West and disrupt

Union communications. This would bring the war to a speedy end.

Overall northern strategy (see map, this page) included four different plans of attack. (1) The North would try to strangle the South by blockading the Confederate coastline. (2) Northern armies would try to split the Confederacy in two by seizing control of the Mississippi River. (3) They would seize control of interior railroad lines leading to seaports along the Atlantic. (4) A northern army would try to seize Richmond, Virginia, which had become the Confederate capital in May 1861. It would then drive southward and finally link up with other Union forces driving eastward from the Mississippi Valley.

Such were the war aims and plans of the Confederacy and the United States. In the spring of 1861, as the northern "Boys in Blue" and the southern "Boys in Gray" trudged to their first battlefield, no one knew that four long, cruel years of fighting lay ahead.

▲ Map activity: Have students trace the Union strategies on a wall map.

Identify: Robert E. Lee, border states, "Boys in Blue," "Boys in Gray"
For answers to questions, see Answer Key, pp.A59-60.

1. **Organizing Ideas: (a)** Name the states that joined the Confederacy. **(b)** Name the border states.

2. **Comparing Viewpoints:** Compare the war aims and strategies of the North and South.

3. **Studying Charts:** Make a chart comparing the North and the South with respect to **(a)** number of states, **(b)** population, **(c)** industrial development, **(d)** transportation facilities, **(e)** financial resources, and **(f)** naval power. Based on your chart, which side appears to have been the stronger? Why?

2 The North and South struggle through four years of conflict

See Teaching Suggestions in TMRG.

The first important battle of the Civil War was fought on July 21, 1861, near a stream called Bull Run in northern Virginia. In this engagement, the First Battle of Bull Run, the Confederates defeated the Union recruits, who fled to Washington, D.C.

Northerners were stunned. If the Confederate commanders had taken advantage of their victory, they could easily have captured Washington, D.C. However, the Confederate troops, elated by victory, scattered to celebrate instead of pursuing the Union army.

The Union blockade. Meanwhile, Union warships and other vessels hastily converted into naval service had begun to blockade the Confederate coastline (see map, page 417). As time passed, the blockade became increasingly effective. Daring Confederate sea captains kept trying to run the blockade, but as the years wore on fewer and fewer ships slipped through.

The blockade was a severe handicap to Confederate plans. The South had counted on exporting cotton, tobacco, sugar, and other products to Europe for sale there. The profits would then go to buy European military equipment and manufactured goods. As the blockade tightened, European products vanished from southern stores. Southern manufacturers could not make up the deficiencies.

As products became increasingly scarce, the prices of southern goods shot skyward. Patriotic southern women began to make substitutes. Using looms and spinning wheels brought down from dusty attics, they spun and wove fabrics for clothing and uniforms. Before the war ended, southerners were melting church bells to make cannons.

War at sea. Although the Confederacy failed to break the Union blockade, daring Confederate ships made the sea lanes dangerous for northern shipping. Between Lincoln's election and the fall of Fort Sumter, the South seized a number of United States vessels then in southern harbors. During the war southerners also purchased in England the *Alabama*, the *Florida*, and 17 other warships. Although these few vessels posed no serious threat to the United States Navy, they did sink more than 250 merchant ships before the war ended.

More important to the war's outcome was the ever-present possibility of Union naval actions. These could be attacks on southern harbors or the landing of a Union army behind Confederate lines. Fortunately for the South, all of its important harbors had been heavily fortified long before the war. Early in 1861 the Confederacy seized these fortifications and held them throughout the war. Nevertheless, Union forces managed to capture New Orleans and several forts on the Atlantic coast.

The Union on the offensive. The Appalachian Mountains divided land operations into two major theaters of war — the eastern theater and the western theater.

Shortly after the Union disaster at the First Battle of Bull Run, President Lincoln gave 34-year-old General George B. McClellan, a West Point graduate, command of the eastern theater of war. A superb organizer and popular with his troops, McClellan quickly turned a mob of untrained volunteers into the Army of the Potomac. In November 1861 Lincoln elevated McClellan to General-in-Chief of all the Union armies. But McClellan was overly cautious. The saying "All quiet along the Potomac" became a public joke. Lincoln finally commented, "If General McClellan does not want to use the army, I would like to *borrow* it."

While the Army of the Potomac marked time in the East, Union forces in the western theater fought small skirmishes in Missouri.

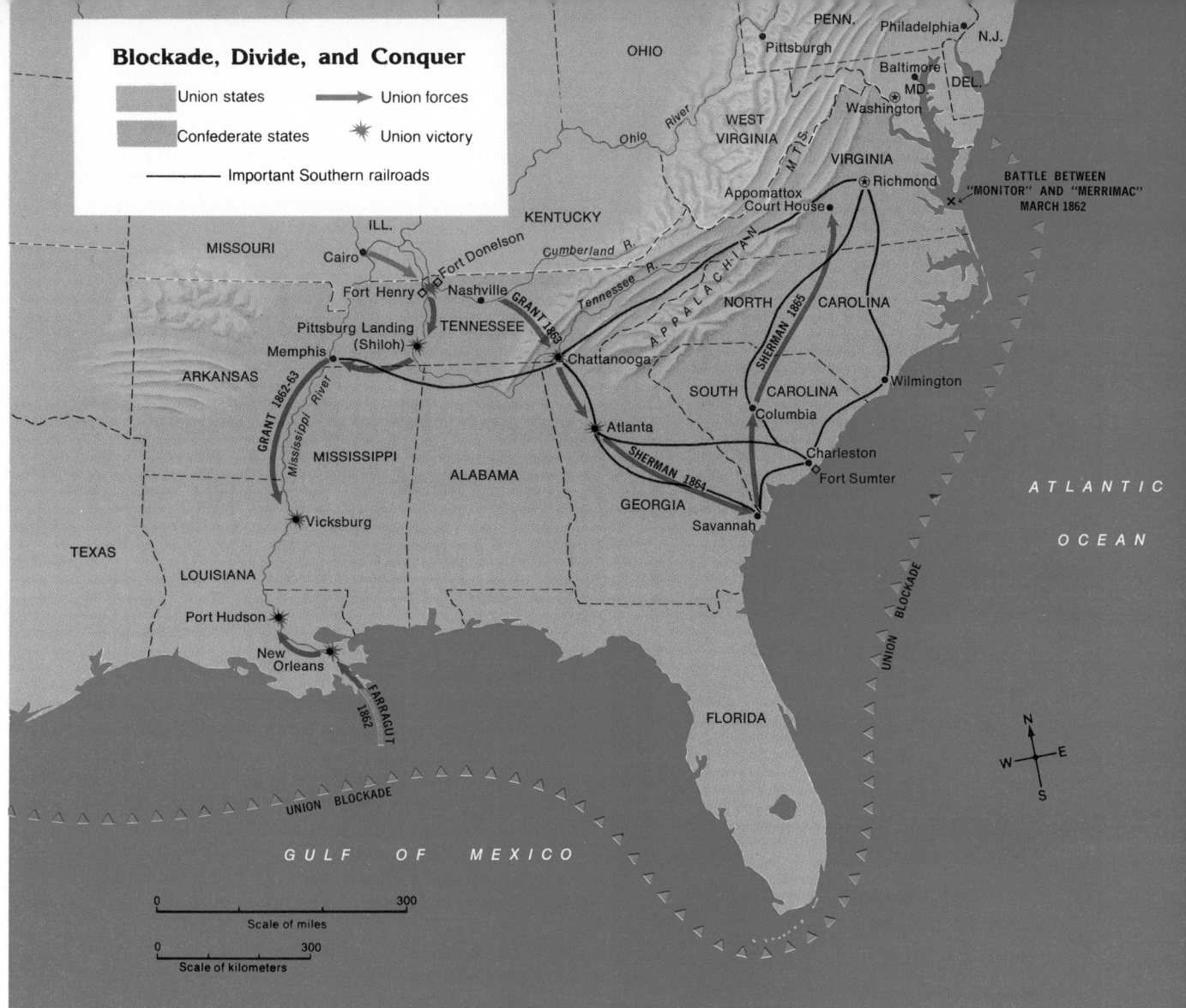

Blockade, Divide, and Conquer

Union states

Confederate states

Union forces

Union victory

Important Southern railroads

The goal was to prevent that state from joining the Confederacy. By 1862 Missouri had been made secure, and General <u>Henry W. Halleck</u>, commander of the western theater, opened a drive into Tennessee.

War in the West. The Union drive began in western Kentucky where the Tennessee River empties into the Ohio River. From here an infantry unit commanded by General Ulysses S. Grant—one of General Halleck's subordinate officers—moved southward. On February 6, 1862, Grant captured Fort Henry on the upper Tennessee River. On February 16 he captured Fort Donelson on the Cumberland River (see map, this page). These victories opened the way for an invasion of the Deep South by way of the Tennessee and Cumberland rivers.

General <u>Nathan Bedford Forrest</u>, one of the South's best generals, managed to escape capture. Forrest would prove to be so dangerous that Union General William T. Sherman later ordered his troops to hunt Forrest down "if it costs ten thousand lives and bankrupts the federal treasury."

In the operations along the Tennessee, the Union infantry was assisted by gunboats. These small warships were capable of steaming along the shallow river waters. Indeed, in both this campaign and the Mississippi River campaign, gunboats proved extremely useful to both sides.

With Fort Donelson in Union hands, Grant continued southward along the Tennessee River to Pittsburg Landing, sometimes called Shiloh (SHY·loh), in Tennessee. Here General

417

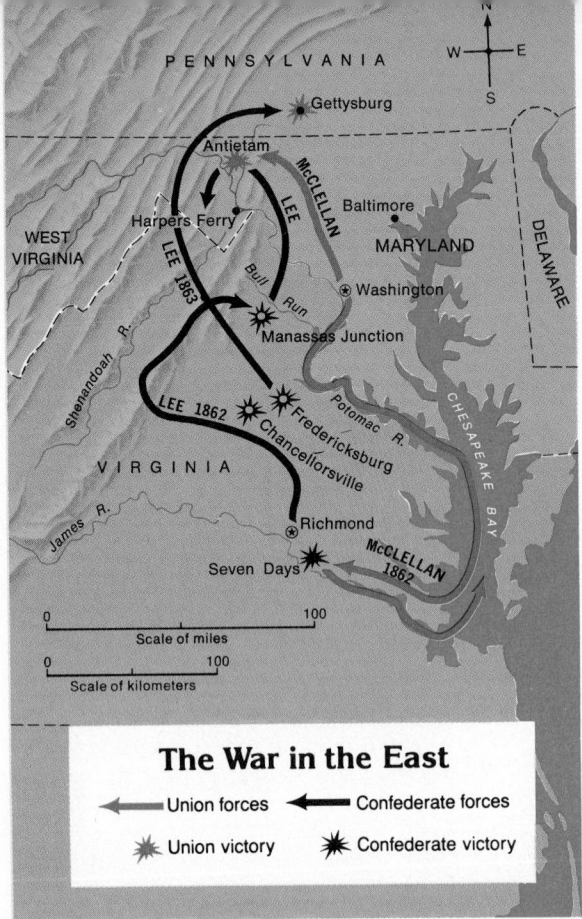

The War in the East

← Union forces   ← Confederate forces

✳ Union victory   ✳ Confederate victory

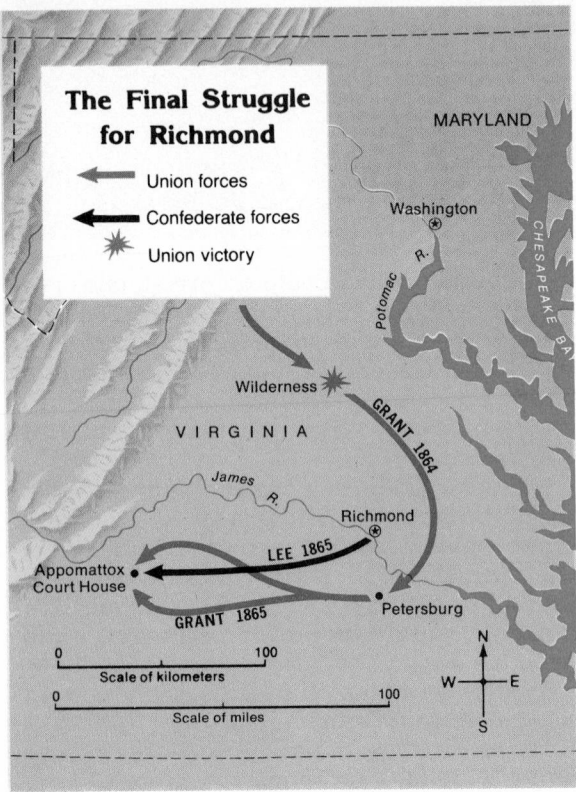

The Final Struggle for Richmond

← Union forces

← Confederate forces

✳ Union victory

Albert S. Johnston of Texas, Confederate commander in the West, surprised and completely defeated him. However, Johnston died and his death, coupled with the arrival of Union reinforcements, allowed Grant to take the offensive. After desperate fighting, Grant finally drove the Confederate army from the field. At the end of May, Union forces occupied Corinth, in northern Mississippi.

At the same time, other Union forces were fighting to the south and north to gain control of the Mississippi River. On the night of April 23, Union Flag Officer (later Admiral) David G. Farragut of Tennessee ran his gunboats past the forts guarding New Orleans and captured the city. Meanwhile, a combined Union naval and land expedition under Commodore A. H. Foote and General John Pope was moving southward down the Mississippi. In June this expedition seized Memphis, Tennessee. It then continued as far south as Vicksburg, Mississippi (see map, page 417).

Thus, by the summer of 1862, Union forces in the western theater had almost split the Confederacy in two along the Mississippi. Casualties had been enormous on both sides. Confederate armies made the Union troops pay dearly for their gains. Nevertheless, Union armies had driven the Confederates out of Kentucky and western Tennessee. Only a short length of the Mississippi and Port Hudson, Louisiana, remained in Confederate hands.

War in the East. Union victories in the West during 1862 were more than balanced by major Confederate victories in the East.

In April 1862 General McClellan finally started the long-awaited offensive against the Confederate capital at Richmond, Virginia. Leaving General Irving McDowell with 40,000 troops to guard Washington, D.C., McClellan transported more than 100,000 troops down the Potomac River. After he seized Yorktown, Virginia, McClellan began a slow, cautious advance up the peninsula between the York and the James rivers (see top map, this page). By mid-May McClellan's troops were within a few miles of Richmond. Here McClellan paused to wait for reinforcements.

Because of the actions of the brilliant Confederate officer General Thomas J. ("Stonewall") Jackson, McClellan's reinforcements never arrived. In May and June, with only 18,000 soldiers, Jackson fought a series of engagements in the Shenandoah Valley where

▲ Although never actually defeated, General McClellan was called "Mac the Unready" and "Tardy George" by his critics.

he defeated Union forces three times larger. Jackson presented a constant threat to Washington, D.C., and kept badly needed reinforcements from reaching McClellan.

In June Confederate troops defending Richmond launched furious counterattacks, known as the Seven Days' Battles, against McClellan's army. Led by General Robert E. Lee, General "Stonewall" Jackson, and the dashing cavalry officer General James E. B. ("Jeb") Stuart, the Confederate troops forced McClellan to drop back to the James River.

On August 29–30, the Confederates won another victory at the Second Battle of Bull Run (see top map, page 418). Union General John Pope, overconfident because of his victories in the western theater, launched a new drive toward Richmond, but Lee and Jackson caught Pope at Bull Run and defeated him.

Encouraged by these successes, the Confederacy decided to stage three powerful offensives. Their goals were (1) to regain control of the Mississippi, (2) to recover the ground lost in Tennessee and Kentucky, and (3) to invade Maryland and draw that state into the Confederacy. All three offensives failed.

On September 4 General Lee crossed the Potomac into Maryland with 40,000 picked troops, confident of victory. On September 17, at Sharpsburg near Antietam Creek (see top map, page 418), Lee engaged General McClellan's force of 70,000 troops and was stopped. The Battle of Antietam was the bloodiest single day of the war. Both sides were so exhausted that McClellan did not try to pursue ▲ the Confederates and win a decisive victory.

The Battle of Gettysburg. The year 1863 opened with both sides discouraged. The southern offensive in the fall of 1862 had failed, and the South had begun to despair of winning support from Great Britain and France. The North, although victorious in the western theater, had suffered defeats in the East. The capture of Richmond by the Union seemed extremely remote.

Such was the situation when in June 1863 General Lee again struck into the North. He still hoped to drive a wedge into the Union and deal a fatal blow to the northern war effort. By the end of the month, his army, 75,000 strong, was moving northward across Maryland into Pennsylvania. On June 30, advance patrols of the Confederate and Union armies met at Gettysburg, Pennsylvania (see top map, page 418).

═══ **SOURCES** ═══

LINCOLN'S GETTYSBURG ADDRESS (1863)

Four score and seven years ago our fathers brought forth on this continent a new nation, conceived in liberty, and dedicated to the proposition that all men are created equal.

Now we are engaged in a great civil war, testing whether that nation, or any nation so conceived and so dedicated, can long endure. We are met on a great battlefield of that war. We have come to dedicate a portion of that field as a final resting place for those who here gave their lives that that nation might live. It is altogether fitting and proper that we should do this.

But, in a larger sense, we cannot dedicate—we cannot consecrate—we cannot hallow—this ground. The brave men, living and dead, who struggled here, have consecrated it far above our poor power to add or detract. The world will little note nor long remember what we say here, but it can never forget what they did here. It is for us, the living, rather, to be dedicated here to the unfinished work which they who fought here have thus far so nobly advanced. It is rather for us to be here dedicated to the great task remaining before us—that from these honored dead we take increased devotion to that cause for which they gave the last full measure of devotion; that we here highly resolve that these dead shall not have died in vain; that this nation, under God, shall have a new birth of freedom; and that government of the people, by the people, for the people, shall not perish from the earth.

For two days the main armies fought desperately on the hills around the town.

On July 3 Lee staked the fate of his army and, as it turned out, of the Confederacy itself on a bid for victory. Led by General George E. Pickett, 15,000 of Lee's finest troops charged up Cemetery Ridge through the devastating fire of Union troops commanded by George G. Meade. For a brief moment, the Confederate battle flag floated on the crest of the ridge. However, the Union forces proved to be too strong, and the broken remnants of Pickett's force had to fall back.

The next day, July 4, Lee started his sorrowful but skillful retreat back to Virginia. To Lincoln's disappointment, the overcautious

▲ The strength shown by the Union forces at Antietam discouraged intervention by Great Britain and France on the side of the Confederacy, thus shifting the tide of victory toward the Union.

During the first three years of the Civil War, the Union forces suffered from a lack of coordinated military leadership. As commander in chief, President Lincoln realized he had to defeat the Confederates on their own territory in order to preserve the Union. He lacked a military adviser, however, with an overall vision of how best to divide and conquer the South.

The President turned to a succession of reputable military leaders to command the eastern Union forces — the Army of the Potomac. Each of these generals — George B. McClellan, Ambrose E. Burnside, Joseph Hooker, and George B. Meade — ultimately proved an unsatisfactory choice. Lincoln fared no better in his selection of commanders on the western front, where he was disappointed in turn by Henry W. Halleck, Don Carlos Buell, and William Rosencrans. But eventually four great generals emerged on the battlefields to bring Union victory. They were Ulysses S. Grant, George H. Thomas, Philip H. Sheridan, and William T. Sherman. The greatest of these was Grant.

When the Civil War began, Ulysses Grant was working as a clerk in his father's leather store. As a volunteer with an Illinois regiment, he soon proved himself an aggressive, fearless, and imaginative soldier. Grant led several spectacular Union campaigns, notably the siege of Vicksburg, Mississippi (May-July 1863). He was promoted after each of his victories, and in March 1864 was appointed supreme commander of all Union forces.

Grant immediately rose to the challenge of giving strategic direction to Lincoln's broad objectives. In April 1865 he accomplished what all other Union generals had failed to do — capture Richmond, the Confederate capital. With General Robert E. Lee's surrender to Grant on April 9, the Civil War was over.

Lincoln's choice of Grant was truly a decisive moment for both the Union and the Confederacy.

Meade did not pursue the Confederate forces. "Our army held the war in the hollow of their hand," Lincoln said, "and they would not close it. Still, I am very grateful to Meade for the great service he did at Gettysburg."

The battle for Vicksburg. On July 4, 1863, the Union won another victory with the fall of Vicksburg, Mississippi. Starting in March 1863, General Ulysses S. Grant marched his army southward from Memphis and rapidly overcame Confederate opposition in five battles. On May 22 he laid siege to Vicksburg, the stronghold of Confederate forces on the Mississippi River.

For six weeks Vicksburg held out, suffering terrible punishment from Grant's cannons and from Union gunboats in the river. Finally, on July 4, reduced to starvation, the Confederate defenders surrendered. Five days later Port Hudson, Louisiana, fell into Union hands. Within a week a Union steamboat from St. Louis arrived in New Orleans, which had been held by Union forces for more than a year.

With Union control of the Mississippi River, the Confederacy was finally split in two along the Mississippi. Another of the North's major objectives had been accomplished. The time was approaching for the final drive to end the war.

A Union breakthrough. On September 9, 1863, a Union army under General William S. Rosecrans occupied Chattanooga, Tennessee, a key railway center and gateway to the Deep South. Rosecrans then set out after the Confederates, commanded by General Braxton Bragg. Bragg turned on Rosecrans at Chickamauga Creek and defeated him, driving him back into Chattanooga. If troops under General George H. Thomas had not held back the Confederates long enough to allow Rosecrans to retreat, the battle would have ended in utter disaster for the North. For his part in the battle, General Thomas won the title "Rock of Chickamauga." General Thomas then replaced General Rosecrans as commander of the Union army at Chattanooga.

The Union army stayed in Chattanooga until late November. Then, reinforced with fresh troops, the army, under the command of General Grant himself, opened an offensive. In the bitter battles of Lookout Mountain and Missionary Ridge, the Union troops broke through Confederate defenses and opened the way into the Deep South.

Clara Barton is best known for her nursing activities during the Civil War and for founding the American Red Cross.

She began her career, however, as a teacher and served a clerkship in the Patent Office. It is believed that this position made her the first woman to be appointed as a civil servant. At the beginning of the Civil War, Barton and friends witnessed the Battle of Bull Run. Disturbed by the poor quality of the battlefield's first-aid facilities, Barton began collecting bandages, medicine, and food for distribution to army hospitals and camps. Barton nursed the wounded and dying on the battlefields of Second Bull Run, Antietam, and Fredericksburg. She quickly won respect and soon became known as the "Angel of the Battlefield."

Barton kept meticulous records on the wounded and the imprisoned, helping families trace hundreds of missing soldiers. Through her later efforts, the American Association of the Red Cross was organized in 1881.

After serving as president of the American Red Cross for 23 years, Barton resigned in 1904. A lifelong feminist, she spent her last years speaking for women's rights.

Beginning of the end. On March 9, 1864, General Grant became supreme commander of all Union armies. Two months later, on Grant's orders, General William T. Sherman set out from Chattanooga with 100,000 troops to invade Georgia. The greatly outnumbered Confederate army under General Joseph E. Johnston fell back, fighting heroically and destroying railroads and bridges as it retreated. Sherman pushed on relentlessly, and on September 2 he entered Atlanta. Two months later, with some 60,000 troops, he left Atlanta and started toward Savannah, Georgia (see map, page 417). On December 22 Sherman wired President Lincoln, "I beg to present you as a Christmas gift the city of Savannah."

Behind him on his "March to the Sea," Sherman left a path of destruction 300 miles (480 kilometers) long and 60 miles (96 kilometers) wide. Railroad tracks, heated red-hot in giant bonfires, were twisted around trees and telegraph poles. Bridges lay in tumbled ruins. Crops were uprooted, livestock slaughtered, and farmhouses burned to ashes. Sherman intended to weaken southern resistance, but he also left a legacy of southern bitterness.

By the spring of 1865, Sherman's army was moving northward through the Carolinas.

General Joseph E. Johnston's weary army was trying to slow him down.

Meanwhile, in May 1864, General Grant had been hammering away at Richmond, Virginia, pushing through difficult terrain against fierce Confederate resistance (see bottom map, page 418). Despite enormous losses in this Wilderness Campaign, Grant fought on. "I propose to fight it out along this line if it takes all summer," he wrote.

Appomattox Court House. In the spring of 1865, Sherman's army continued to move northward, and Grant's troops were hammering at the doors of Richmond. On April 2 Lee withdrew from the city.

From Richmond, Lee moved swiftly westward toward Lynchburg, Virginia, with Grant close on his heels (see bottom map, page 418). Lee thought that he might escape with his army into North Carolina and there join forces with General Johnston, who was as yet undefeated. However, Lee's position was hopeless, and on April 9 he surrendered.

The two generals, Lee and Grant, met in a house in the small village of Appomattox Court House in Virginia. Lee was in full dress uniform with a jewel-studded sword at his side.

Grant wore a private's shirt, unbuttoned at the neck. Aided by his military secretary, Lieutenant Colonel Ely Samuel Parker—a Seneca Indian and a civil engineer—Grant drafted the terms of surrender.

Grant offered Lee generous terms. He allowed the officers and soldiers to return to their homes after their promise that they would not again take up arms against the Union. The troops had to surrender their weapons, but Grant permitted Lee's officers to keep their pistols and swords. When Lee mentioned the distressing condition of southern agriculture, Grant said, "Let all the men who claim to own a horse or mule take the animals home with them to work their little farms. This," he said, "will do much toward conciliating our people."

The meeting ended, Lee mounted his horse and rode off. Union troops started to cheer. Grant ordered them to be silent. "The war is over; the rebels are our countrymen again," he said.

Thus the long, bitter conflict ended.

SECTION REVIEW

See underscored items, text pp. 416 - 19.

Identify: First Battle of Bull Run, George McClellan, Army of the Potomac, Henry Halleck, Nathan Forrest, Albert S. Johnston, David Farragut, "Stonewall" Jackson, "Jeb" Stuart, George Pickett, George Meade

For answers to questions, see Answer Key, p.A60.

1. **Interpreting Ideas:** It has been said that the Union blockade was as effective in overpowering the South as were the armies of Grant and Sherman. Explain.

2. **Evaluating Ideas:** Why were Union campaigns in Missouri and in the West important to the success of Union strategy?

3. **Determining Cause and Effect: (a)** What was the purpose of Sherman's "March to the Sea"? **(b)** What were its consequences?

4. **Analyzing Ideas:** Explain the significance of the battles at Gettysburg and Vicksburg.

5. **Summarizing Ideas:** What were the terms of surrender that Grant offered Lee?

6. **Studying Maps:** Select one of the maps appearing on pages 415, 417, and 418. Study the map. Then describe a battle or campaign shown on the map in a few paragraphs.

See Teaching Suggestions in TMRG, pp.TM108-09.

The soldiers dying for the Confederacy and for the Union were not the only Americans willing to sacrifice everything for their beliefs. A small but growing number of northern abolitionists began to speak out more loudly about the cause to which they were dedicated. These abolitionists were determined at all costs to link the freeing of the slaves to the saving of the Union.

Growing abolitionist activity. The war quickened abolitionist activities. Frederick Douglass expressed the view of all abolitionists when he declared that the Union could not be preserved unless the slaves were emancipated, or given their freedom.

The abolitionists added practical reasons to their moral and humane arguments for freeing the slaves. Emancipating the slaves, they said, would encourage slaves to flee the South. This would strike a heavy blow at the southern wartime economy, which depended on slave labor. Moreover, freeing the slaves would rally strong antislavery sentiment elsewhere in the world to the Union side. Soon after the war started, the abolitionists pressured the national government to issue an immediate declaration of emancipation.

Lincoln's early opposition. President Lincoln had long believed slavery to be wrong. However, he now insisted that the issue of slavery had to be subordinated to the main issue of saving the Union. Lincoln feared the emancipation of the slaves would force the border states—Missouri, Kentucky, and Maryland—to leave the Union.

As late as August 1862, Lincoln expressed his reluctance to turn the war into a crusade to free the slaves. "My paramount object in the struggle," he declared, "is to save the Union, and it is not either to save or to destroy slavery. If I could save the Union without freeing any slave, I would do it, and if I could save it by freeing all the slaves, I would do it. And if I could save it by freeing some and leaving others alone, I would do that. What I do about

Fleeing to what they hoped was freedom, slaves crossed the Rappahannock River in Virginia to Union lines in 1862. Earlier in the war, not knowing what to do with such slaves, the Union sometimes returned them to their masters.

slavery and the colored race I do because I believe it helps to save this Union."

Abolitionist gains. Deeply disappointed, the antislavery forces in Congress challenged the President's position. In April 1862 Congress abolished slavery in the District of Columbia, paying owners for the loss of their slaves. In July of the same year, Congress confiscated the property, including slaves, of all persons who were in rebellion against the Union. A short time later, Congress abolished slavery in United States territories. Congress also supported a plan for giving financial aid to states that would adopt a program for setting slaves free over a period of years. To committed abolitionists, however, these moves by Congress were far from enough.

The Emancipation Proclamation. By September 1862 Lincoln had reluctantly decided that a war fought at least partly to free the slaves would win European support and lessen the danger of foreign intervention on the side of the Confederacy. It would also strike a blow at the Confederacy and win wholehearted support for the Union from growing numbers of American abolitionists.

Lincoln prepared an Emancipation Proclamation but kept it secret, waiting for news of a northern victory to add to its impact. On September 22, 1862, five days after Union forces stopped Lee's troops at the bloody Battle of Antietam, Lincoln issued a preliminary Proclamation of Emancipation. In it he declared that all slaves in states or parts of states still fighting against the United States on January 1, 1863, would from that time on be forever emancipated—free, that is, wherever Union armies could liberate them or they could escape to the North.

On January 1, 1863, Lincoln issued his final Emancipation Proclamation. Abolitionists, although pleased, were still skeptical of Lincoln's intentions. For one thing, the Emancipation Proclamation did not free slaves in the border states or in certain parts of Virginia and Louisiana that were under Union control. Lincoln made these exceptions because he was still worried about driving the border states out of the Union. He was also uncertain that the Constitution gave him the authority to free any slaves anywhere.

Despite these criticisms most people in the United States and overseas now concluded that Lincoln had at last clearly stated a second vital issue of the war.

The Thirteenth Amendment. When President Lincoln issued his Emancipation Proclamation, he based it upon his constitutional authority as commander in chief of United States military forces. Whether this authority gave him the right to free the slaves—whether, that is, his Proclamation had the force of law—was an unanswered question.

To settle the slavery question once and for all, Congress early in 1865 approved an amendment to the Constitution. This Thirteenth Amendment freed slaves everywhere in the United States and its territories. The amendment was finally ratified by the necessary three fourths of the states eight months after the end of the war.

Continuing discrimination. The Emancipation Proclamation had little effect on the pattern of racial discrimination in the North. Thus black and white abolitionists continued their campaign on federal, state, and local levels of government. As a result of these pressures, Congress repealed a law forbidding black Americans to be employed as mail carriers. Congress in 1865 also passed a law that required horse-drawn streetcars in Washington, D.C., to carry black passengers without discrimination. Sojourner Truth boldly defied conductors and passengers to test this law and was successful.

The Department of State and the Department of Justice ruled in individual cases that black men were citizens. The Supreme Court of the United States for the first time permitted a black lawyer to argue a case before the Court. Because of these actions by branches of the federal government, the Dred Scott decision of 1857 was in effect overturned. That decision, you recall, had denied that a black person could be a citizen (page 403).

With the help of white abolitionists, blacks campaigned in several states for the right to vote and to receive legal equality in courts. In California, Illinois, and Indiana, laws forbidding black Americans to enter these states were challenged. Blacks vigorously attacked segregated public schools. Where they were not able to bring about school desegregation, they demanded improvements in the inferior all-black schools their children attended—when they were able to attend any school at all.

Not all of these campaigns for civil rights succeeded during the war or for a long time thereafter. However, they did start to break down barriers that had set black Americans apart as less than equal citizens.

Aid to fugitives. Northern blacks also took part in efforts to bring relief to fugitive slaves, or **contrabands,** as they were called. During the war years, these people were held in federal camps. Often they faced conditions of gross neglect in these camps.

Church groups and black and white abolitionists organized volunteer aid societies that sent clothing and medical supplies to the con-trabands. These societies also prodded the federal government into organizing work and relief opportunities as well as schools for the contrabands. Teachers in these schools were dedicated young abolitionists from the North, black and white. Nevertheless, the efforts made on behalf of the contrabands were small compared with the need.

Black noncombatants in the war. While abolitionists kept up their pressure on the government, black Americans made important contributions to northern victory.

Early in the war, some runaway slaves who reached the Union lines in search of freedom were sent back to Confederate lines. In 1862 Congress finally forbade these practices. In so doing, Congress supported such Union officers as Benjamin Butler and John C. Frémont. These officers had welcomed the fugitives and put them to work at important noncombatant tasks. At that time, northern commanders were forbidden to use blacks, either slave or free, as fighters.

Before the war ended, about 200,000 blacks served the northern fighting forces as noncombatants. Among them were cooks, teamsters, nurses, scouts, spies, and steamboat pilots.

Exclusion from military service. There were several reasons why black Americans, slave and free, were at first forbidden to fight in the war. First, official northern policy stated that the war was being fought to suppress rebellion and restore the Union. Thus the issues of slavery and of black participation in the war were officially downgraded, although they could not be ignored. Second, President Lincoln and other northern officials feared that the use of black soldiers would antagonize the loyal border states. Third, many white northern recruits made it clear that they did not want to serve with black soldiers.

Abolitionists, white and black, denounced the policy of excluding blacks from the Union forces. They declared that it was unfair to prevent black men from fighting for the emancipation of their own people.

The heavy demands of war eventually caused the North to accept black soldiers in the Union army. When it proved harder and harder to recruit white northern soldiers, the rejection of black volunteers could no longer be justified. Several Union generals in the conquered areas of the South asked permission to

In July 1863, almost 90 courageous men of the all black 54th Massachusetts Regiment died trying to capture South Carolina's Fort Wagner.

use black troops and to test their fighting ability. In Louisiana, Union commanders wanted to use free blacks who had organized their own regiment and were eager to fight.

Blacks in military service. These increasing pressures led at last to a change in northern military policy. In the summer of 1862, the War Department authorized the raising of five regiments of black troops in the Sea Islands off the coast of South Carolina, occupied by Union forces. In Massachusetts and other northern states, free blacks were organized into regiments. Before the war ended, about 186,000 black Americans served in northern armed forces, including 29,000 in the navy.

The reluctant admission of blacks into the Union forces did not mean that they lived and fought on equal terms with white soldiers. Black soldiers were less well trained than white soldiers and received less adequate medical services. They frequently were assigned the menial, nonmilitary chores around camp. Although blacks served as noncommissioned officers, only a very small number actually received commissions.

Black soldiers were often badly treated, not only by white soldiers but also by northern white civilians. Through most of the war, black soldiers received less pay than white soldiers. Some black troops refused to accept any pay at all until this injustice was ended. Finally,

Congress in 1864 provided that black soldiers were to receive the same pay as white soldiers.

Despite the discriminations against them, after 1862, black soldiers and sailors fought bravely in almost all battles of the war. Their courage and ability often astounded their officers and foes. For unusual valor in the Civil War, 21 black Americans received the Congressional Medal of Honor.

SECTION REVIEW
See underscored items, text pp. 423-24.
Identify: Emancipation Proclamation, Thirteenth Amendment, contrabands, Sojourner Truth
For answers to questions, see Answer Key, p.A60.

1. **Determining Cause and Effect: (a)** How did the Civil War affect abolitionist activities? **(b)** How did abolitionist activities affect the war?

2. **Interpreting Ideas: (a)** Why did Lincoln at first oppose freeing the slaves? **(b)** Why did he change his mind and issue the Emancipation Proclamation?

3. **Analyzing Ideas:** Why was the Thirteenth Amendment passed?

4. **Summarizing Ideas: (a)** In what ways did blacks contribute to the war effort? **(b)** Why were blacks at first excluded from military service?

5. **Organizing Ideas: (a)** How were black troops discriminated against? **(b)** How did abolitionists fight racial discrimination on the home front?

4 The war brings severe hardship and suffering to the South

See Teaching Suggestions in TMRG, p.TM109.

The appearance of former slaves in the northern armies was dramatic proof that the War Between the States was transforming the lives of people in the Confederacy.

During the first few weeks of the war, there was excitement—and confidence—in the air. Southern men and boys left for the battlefields, filled with high-spirited notions of adventure. After a few months, casualty lists grew and food and supplies became scarce. The war then became a grim reality, relieved only occasionally by news of a Confederate victory. From 1861 to 1865, the South was a nation in arms.

General Robert E. Lee witnessed many grim scenes of war. After surveying one group of dying soldiers, he said, "It is well that war is so terrible, or we should grow too fond of it."

Raising an army. During the war, by volunteer enlistments and the draft, the Confederacy raised an army of about 400,000 soldiers. In the first year of the war, the Confederacy relied entirely on volunteer enlistments. In April 1862, however, it turned to **conscription,** or the draft. The draft made every white male citizen between 18 and 35 liable for military service.

The draft was unpopular, and many southerners claimed that it was unfair. The original conscription law exempted workers in many occupations. It also permitted a drafted man to hire a substitute. This "substitute" provision favored wealthy people, who could afford to hire substitutes. Poorer people grumbled that the conflict was "a rich man's war and a poor man's fight." Late in 1863 the Confederate government stopped the privilege of hiring substitutes. In 1864 it reduced exemptions and increased draft limits to include all white males between 17 and 50. In the last months of the war, the Confederacy's need for troops grew so desperate that it reluctantly decided to recruit slaves. It promised to set them free if they remained loyal to the end of the war.

States' rights. Many southerners insisted that conscription was contrary to the Confederate constitution. Believing strongly in states' rights, they therefore denied that the Confederate government had the authority to force the citizens of a state into military service. The state authorities in North Carolina refused to enforce the conscription law.

Southerners also objected to other policies of the central government at Richmond on the ground that states' rights were violated. When President Davis suspended the **writ of *habeas corpus,*** the state courts promptly denied his right to do so. Many southerners applauded the decision of the courts and South Carolinians even talked about seceding from the Confederacy itself.

Southern finances. Raising money was a far more difficult problem for the Confederacy than raising an army, for most southern wealth was in land and slaves. The Union blockade, which cut off most southern trade, also prevented the Confederacy from raising money from customs duties.

Early in the war, patriotic southerners lent $100 million to the Confederacy in return for war bonds, but this source of income was soon

The impact of war is clear in this photo, taken in Richmond, Virginia, the once-proud capital of the Confederacy. During the war it was the target of Union attack, though it held out bravely until April 1865, when Lee evacuated the city.

exhausted. The government borrowed another $15 million from abroad and raised about $100 million from taxation. All this income was far from adequate, and the Confederacy had to rely mainly on paper money.

Before the war ended, the government had printed more than $1 billion in Confederate bank notes. The Confederate government promised to exchange these notes for gold or silver "after the ratification of a treaty of peace between the Confederate States and the United States of America." As southern victory became increasingly remote, the Confederate currency steadily declined in value while prices skyrocketed. By 1865 each dollar bill was worth only 1.6 cents in gold. With northern victory the Confederate war bonds and bank notes became worthless.

Southern industry. Paper money was only one reason for skyrocketing prices. Another was the shortage of goods. The Union blockade of southern ports cut off almost all luxuries, such as tea and coffee, as well as many essentials—clothing, hardware, medicines, and soap. As one historian put it, "The blockade was the real destroyer of the South."

Despite heroic efforts, mills and factories in the Confederacy could not supply the needs of either the army or the civilian population. Confederate soldiers often marched without shoes, slept without blankets, and lived in ragged clothing. Fortunately for the Confederates, they managed to capture large supplies of food, clothing, and munitions.

Agriculture and transportation. Civilians felt the pinch of hard times even more than the soldiers. City families especially suffered from the shortage of goods and the soaring prices. By 1863 many southerners were facing near-starvation.

This tragic situation was not caused by lack of food, for the South was an agricultural region. Despite the flight of slaves to the Union lines, there was still enough labor, slave and free, to work the farms and plantations. The serious problem was lack of transportation.

When the war started, the Confederacy had only about 9,000 miles (14,500 kilometers) of railroads out of a total of more than 30,000 miles (48,000 kilometers) for the entire country. Southern planters had depended largely on the rivers to send their cotton to the seaports. As the war continued, the Confederacy had difficulty keeping even its limited railroad mileage in operation. Southerners tore up branch lines and used branch line engines, cars, and rails to keep main lines in operation. The southern transportation problem grew increasingly severe. Before the war ended, people in Richmond rioted for food while barns in the Shenandoah Valley were filled with wheat.

During the last few months of the war, the food shortage became so desperate that many Confederate soldiers deserted to get back home and help feed their families. The war brought sorrow and suffering to rich and poor alike.

SECTION REVIEW

See underscored items, text p. 426.
Identify: conscription, writ of *habeas corpus*
For answers to questions, see Answer Key, pp.A60-61.
1. **Interpreting Ideas: (a)** Describe the changes in the way the South raised troops during the war. **(b)** Why did many southerners object to military conscription?
2. **Analyzing Ideas: (a)** What methods did the Confederate government use to raise money for the war? **(b)** Why was issuing huge amounts of paper money harmful to the South?
3. **Organizing Ideas:** How did each of the following help to defeat the South: **(a)** the Union blockade, **(b)** lack of industry, **(c)** lack of transportation?

5 Life behind Union lines undergoes important changes

See Teaching Suggestions in TMRG, pp.TM109-10.
Northerners never experienced the hardship and suffering endured by most southerners. Nevertheless, the war created problems and brought many changes in northern life.

Raising an army. During the war more than 2 million soldiers, including 186,000 blacks, served in the Union forces. The North, like the South, at first recruited its troops by volunteer enlistments. In March 1863, however, Congress passed a conscription law making all able-bodied male citizens between 20 and 45 liable for military service. As in the South, the law allowed a drafted man to hire a substitute.

The federal law also permitted a drafted man to buy exemption from military service by paying $300 to the government.

The Conscription Act aroused violent opposition, especially among recent immigrants from Ireland. The Irish newcomers did not want to be forced to fight a war that was likely to increase the number of free black workers, with whom they competed for unskilled jobs. Moreover, black workers, unable to get jobs, at times broke strikes organized by Irish dockworkers and other laborers. Racial tensions then reached the boiling point.

Riots, combining opposition to the draft with opposition to blacks, broke out in a number of cities. The most serious riot, beginning on July 13, 1863 in New York City, lasted for four terror-filled days. Mobs of whites burned an orphan asylum for black children. They demolished shops and houses of black Americans as well as those of white abolitionists. Seventy-six people were killed.

The bounty system. The draft provided only a small fraction of the Union troops. Much more effective as a means of raising troops was the **bounty** system. To attract volunteers, federal, state, and local governments each paid a bounty to all who volunteered for service. When the bounties were totaled, a man might receive as much as $1,000 for enlisting.

While the bounty system was an effective recruitment device, it did give rise to the dishonest practice of "bounty jumping." A volunteer would enlist in one locality and collect bounties. Then he would desert and re-enlist under another name in another locality and collect additional bounties. Some **bounty jumpers** enlisted and deserted as many as 20 or 30 times before they were caught.

Northern finances. To raise money for the war, the North relied on four sources of revenue: the tariff, war bonds, an income tax, and issuance of paper money.

From 1832 to 1861, southern planters and many western farmers had opposed high tariffs. In 1861, however, with several southern states out of the Union, the Republicans in Congress promptly passed the Morrill Tariff Act. This raised import duties to an average of 25 percent of the value of the imported goods. The Morrill Tariff Act protected American manufacturers from the competition of European rivals. After war broke out, Congress

The Union navy underwent a major buildup during the Civil War. It was especially important in cutting off shipping into and out of southern ports. This is the crew of the U.S.S. Hunchback *during a brief lull in the action.*

raised the rates until by 1864 they reached an average of 47 percent, the highest rates up to that time.

Southern planters and midwestern farmers had also favored a decentralized banking system. In such a system, state and local banks could issue their own bank notes and make loans with little if any federal control. After 1861, however, the Republican Congress adopted a law that did away with state bank notes and established a system of national banks.

▲ In 1863 Congress passed the National Banking Act. The new law permitted five or more individuals with a capital of $50,000 to organize a national bank. The bank directors were required to invest at least one third of the bank's capital in United States bonds. When the bank had deposited these bonds with the Secretary of the Treasury, it was allowed to issue national bank notes up to 90 percent of the value of the bonds. This provision had two important effects. First, it encouraged banks to buy government bonds (that is, to lend the government money). Second, it provided a sound and uniform currency for the entire country.

Neither the tariff nor the sale of government bonds, however, provided enough money to pay northern war costs. Therefore, Congress passed an income tax. By the war's end, incomes between $600 and $5,000 were being taxed 5 percent. Incomes of $5,000 or more were being taxed 10 percent.

Congress also issued paper money, known as **greenbacks** because the back of the money was usually printed in green. The value of the greenbacks, like the value of the Confederate paper money, depended upon the government's ability to redeem them in gold or silver at some future date. Thus their value rose with every northern victory and fell with every northern defeat. At one point the greenback dollar was worth only 35 cents in gold, but by the war's end it was worth 78 cents. Paper money helped to drive prices upward, but inflation never got out of hand as it did in the South.

Booming northern industry. Inflation did not get out of hand in the North partly because northern industry could produce all the materials needed by the armed services and the civilian population. With the tariff to protect them from foreign competition and huge war orders to meet, manufacturers built new factories during the war years. Thus the war continued a development that was well under way before 1861.

The war also stimulated the development and use of laborsaving machines. Elias Howe's sewing machine, first patented in 1846, enabled clothing manufacturers to produce uniforms more rapidly for the Union armies. An

In March 1862 a dramatic Civil War battle was fought between two ironclad ships near Newport News, Virginia. The Union's *Monitor* was a low-lying gunboat designed for shallow-water use. It was much faster and more maneuverable than the larger *Merrimack,* originally a wooden Union frigate that had been salvaged by the Confederacy. During the battle, iron armor on both ships served as protection and prevented a decisive victory for either side.

Neither ship was to fight again. The *Merrimack* was later intentionally destroyed; the *Monitor* sank in a storm off Cape Hatteras, North Carolina. The Battle of the *Monitor* and *Merrimack* had no effect on the outcome of the war, but it demonstrated to the world the importance of steam-powered, armor-plated warships.

improved version of a shoe-making machine patented by Gordon McKay in 1862 made it possible to mass-produce shoes.

There was a great deal of **profiteering** during the war as greedy businesses took unfair profits at a time of national crisis. Even worse, there were cases of outright fraud. Some manufacturers sold the government blankets and uniforms of such poor quality that they fell apart in the first heavy rains.

Agricultural expansion. Northeastern and midwestern agriculture also boomed during the war. It was stimulated by government aid, war orders, and the development of laborsaving machines.

The Republican Party, as you have read, represented a combination of midwestern farmers and northeastern business groups. It is not surprising, therefore, that the Republican Congress passed laws favorable to farmers.

The Homestead Act of 1862 gave 160 acres (64.8 hectares) of land to anyone who paid a small registration fee and lived on the land as a **homestead** for five years. Under this act, between 1862 and 1865 the United States government gave about 2.5 million acres (over 1 million hectares) of land in the **public domain** —government land—to some 15,000 settlers. Much of this land now available for homesteads had been owned by Indians who ceded their rights in Texas and Kansas and much of Nebraska to the government.

In 1862 the government also adopted two other measures to aid agriculture as well as industry. (1) It created the United States Department of Agriculture. (2) With the Morrill Act of 1862, it launched the United States upon a huge program of agricultural and industrial education. The Morrill Act gave each state 30,000 acres (12,140 hectares) of land for each Senator and Representative it had in Congress under the 1860 census. The income from the sale or rental of this land was to be used to support at least one college in which agriculture and the mechanic arts, such as engineering,

SOURCES

HOMESTEAD
ACT
(1862)

Any person who is the head of a family, or who has arrived at the age of twenty-one years, and is a citizen of the United States . . . shall . . . be entitled to one quarter-section or a less quantity of . . . public lands, upon which said person may have filed a . . . claim.

Northern industry gave the Union army giant mortars such as this that could fire at cities and armies from great distances. Because of such weapons and other advances in transportation and communication used by the armies, the Civil War is sometimes considered to be the first modern war.

were to be emphasized. These colleges came to be called **land-grant colleges**.

Farmers of the northeastern and midwestern states prospered with rising prices and a ready market for all they could produce. With money in their pockets, thousands of farmers were able to buy such laborsaving machinery as mechanical reapers, which had been invented by Obed Hussey and Cyrus H. McCormick in the early 1830's. The reaper, improved plows, and other farm machinery helped to speed a revolution in agriculture.

Growth of the railroads.   Railroads also prospered during the war. For example, the value of Erie Railroad stock increased sevenfold in three years. New lines were built, many with the help of government **subsidies**, or financial aids, and land grants. These railroad lines helped to unite the states of the Northeast and the Middle West.

During the war the Republican Congress decided to build a transcontinental railroad, which people had been talking about for a long time. In 1862 Congress granted a charter to the Union Pacific Railroad, and California granted one to the Central Pacific Railroad. The charter authorized them to build a railway between Omaha, in Nebraska Territory, and California. Congress also promised the railroads liberal cash subsidies and generous gifts of land along the right of way. The actual construction did not begin until after the war had ended. However, the subsidies and land grants approved by Congress and the President showed how far the new Republican government was prepared to go in providing federal aid for business and industry.

SECTION REVIEW

See underscored items, text pp.428-31.

Identify: bounty, bounty jumpers, National Banking Act, greenbacks, Elias Howe, profiteering, Homestead Act of 1862, homestead, public domain, land-grant college, Cyrus McCormick, subsidies

For answers to questions, see Answer Key, p.A61.

1. **Determining Cause and Effect: (a)** What methods did the North use to raise an army? **(b)** What abuses developed in this process? **(c)** Why did some recent Irish immigrants object to the draft?

2. **Summarizing Ideas:** Describe the methods used by the North to finance the war.

3. **Analyzing Ideas: (a)** Why was there an industrial boom in the North during the war? **(b)** How did the war affect the growth of technology?

4. **Interpreting Ideas: (a)** What conditions promoted agricultural prosperity during the war? **(b)** What steps did Congress take during the war to encourage the building of railroads?

THIS CHANGING LAND   Regulating Water Rights

In any arid or semi-arid region there is no resource more precious or more jealously guarded than water. In the eastern United States, however, where precipitation is usually abundant, there seems to be plenty of water for every possible purpose. Laws governing the use of water, however, had come with the European settlers to the colonies along the Atlantic coast.

This law is called the Law of Riparian Rights. The term *riparian* comes from the Latin word *ripa*, meaning "riverbank." The basic legal idea of the Law of Riparian Rights is that the owner of property that borders a stream or river has a right to the undiminished flow of water in the stream and the right to use the water reasonably. The permission of the owner, or owners, of all riparian land is required for any increase or decrease in the flow, any

Early uses of water such as powering a water wheel did little to damage water or diminish its flow.

change in the direction of the flow, or any action that might pollute the water. In the past the traditional practices of farming and other uses of water in the eastern United States did little to alter the flow of a stream or to damage the water.

The Law of Riparian Rights, however, has drawbacks in an arid landscape where water is scarce. This reality probably struck with greatest impact in July 1847 when the Mormon settlers shattered their wooden plows on the sunbaked soil of the Great Salt Lake desert. These farmers quickly dammed one stream flowing down the western slopes of the Wasatch Mountain Range and flooded a few acres of land until the ground was moist enough to plant their first crops.

This practice was the beginning of western irrigation, and it raised questions about the practicality of the Law of Riparian Rights in the western United States. The Law of Riparian Rights does not allow for the permanent removal of water from a stream because such removal would reduce the flow of water. Yet removal of water from a stream is absolutely imperative for irrigation. Thus, in the dry West the law and the requirements for survival conflict.

A new law dealing with the realities of the West had its origins in the Mormon settlement of the Great Salt Lake area. As land was laid out for farming purposes, Brigham Young, the Mormon leader, insisted that every field adjoin an irrigation ditch that was connected to a stream from the Wasatch Mountains. The main ditches were planned by a church committee and dug jointly by everyone who would be using the water. Controls over water usage were rigidly enforced. Each main irrigation ditch was supervised by a church committee whose responsibility was to see that each farmer received only enough water for efficient farming. Within just two years of their arrival in the Salt Lake Valley, the Mormon's irrigation system was working smoothly.

Brigham Young saw clearly that while irrigation was basic to survival, it also defied the law. Consequently, he began developing a new legal concept that would allow for irrigation. He called his new concept the Law of Prior Appropriation.

The basic theme of this law is, "First in time, first in right." In other words, this new law gives the legal right to water-use to the first person to use it. The law also states that water-use has to be for a beneficial purpose such as farming, mining, or manufacturing. Finally, the Law of Prior Appropriation says that the good of the community shall override the good of any individual. Thus, a limited resource such as water is to be divided in such a way that as many people as possible can share its bounty.

feature is placed in Unit Five to demonstrate to students that agreement and cooperation did exist among the sections and to contrast to the divisiveness of sectionalism. The feature also highlights the West's emergence as a region with its own interests and problems.

In time, this new legal concept has become the basic water law for all 17 western states. It is now very much part of the nation's legal system. In fact, some states in the eastern regions of our nation are looking at it carefully for it seems to fit modern conditions better than the Law of Riparian Rights. Water today is used for purposes never dreamed of by the authors of that earlier law. Laws, to fulfill their purposes, need to reflect the changing needs of society, and the pioneers in the nineteenth century West furnished us with an excellent example of keeping laws current.

Irrigation ditches carry water from the western mountains to crop fields miles away.

6 The Union faces political problems at home and abroad

See Teaching Suggestions in TMRG, pp.TM110-11.

The war thrust an almost unbearable burden on President Lincoln. Even while he was occupied with the fighting itself, he had to deal with foreign affairs.

Great Britain and France. During the first two years of war, the governments of Great Britain and France were friendly to the Confederate States of America. There were reasons why many Europeans wanted the South to win. European manufacturers, particularly the British, looked forward to the creation of a new nation. They thought the Confederacy would provide them with cotton and other raw materials and, at the same time, place no tariffs on the importation of their manufactured goods. European shipowners looked forward to the weakening of their business competitors in New England and the Middle Atlantic states that a Confederate victory might bring.

To be sure, millions of Europeans hoped for the end of slavery in the South. However, Lincoln at first discouraged these people when he made it clear that he was fighting the war not to free the slaves but to preserve the Union.

Strained relations. Only a few months after the war started, one incident nearly led to a disastrous break between the United States and Great Britain. A Union warship commanded by Captain Charles Wilkes stopped a British steamer, the *Trent*, and seized two Confederate commissioners to Great Britain and France — James M. Mason and John Slidell. The British, furious at this violation of their rights as a neutral, talked of war with the United States and actually sent troops to Canada. President Lincoln managed to avoid trouble by releasing the two Confederate agents and admitting that Wilkes had been wrong.

Even more serious was the problem of Confederate warships built in British shipyards. Some of these warships, among them the *Florida* and the *Alabama*, left Great Britain in the summer of 1862 and began to destroy Union merchant vessels. Great Britain stopped the construction of other such Confederate warships when the American minister to Great

433

A cartoonist shows three snakes bearing the face of Copperhead leader Clement Vallandigham attacking the Union.

Britain warned the British foreign minister that "this is war."

Northern victories on the battlefield and the Emancipation Proclamation issued by President Lincoln finally ended the threat of foreign intervention in the war in favor of the Confederacy.

The Copperheads. Foreign intervention was not the only danger that the Union faced. In the North — as well as in the South — there was from the beginning active opposition to the war. Leaders of the opposition in the North were called "Copperheads" by Union sympathizers, after the poisonous snake of that name. The Copperheads argued that the war's costs in lives, money, and loss of personal liberty were too great to be justified. They also argued that the South could not be defeated and that the war was therefore useless. Finally, they insisted that even if the North should win, a Union based on compulsion was a denial of the Constitution and of democracy.

The strength of the Copperheads, most of whom were members of the Democratic Party, varied from place to place and from month to month. The more extreme Copperheads organized secret societies called the Knights of the Golden Circle and the Sons of Liberty. They discouraged enlistment and encouraged northern soldiers to desert from the Union army. They also helped Confederate prisoners held in northern prisons to escape and smuggled war materials into the Confederacy.

The most influential Copperhead leader was Clement L. Vallandigham, a member of Congress from Ohio. He was finally arrested in 1863 and convicted of opposing the war effort. Lincoln banished him to the Confederacy, but Vallandigham promptly moved to Canada.

The election of 1864. Dissatisfaction over the war split the Democratic Party. In the election of 1864, many Democrats joined the Republicans to form the Union Party. This party chose Lincoln for the Presidency and Andrew Johnson of Tennessee, a former Democratic member of Congress but an opponent of the Confederacy, for the Vice Presidency. The Democratic Party responded by naming General George B. McClellan as its candidate for the Presidency.

Antiwar feeling was running so high in 1864 that President Lincoln fully expected to be defeated. "We are now on the brink of destruction," he wrote to a friend. "It appears to

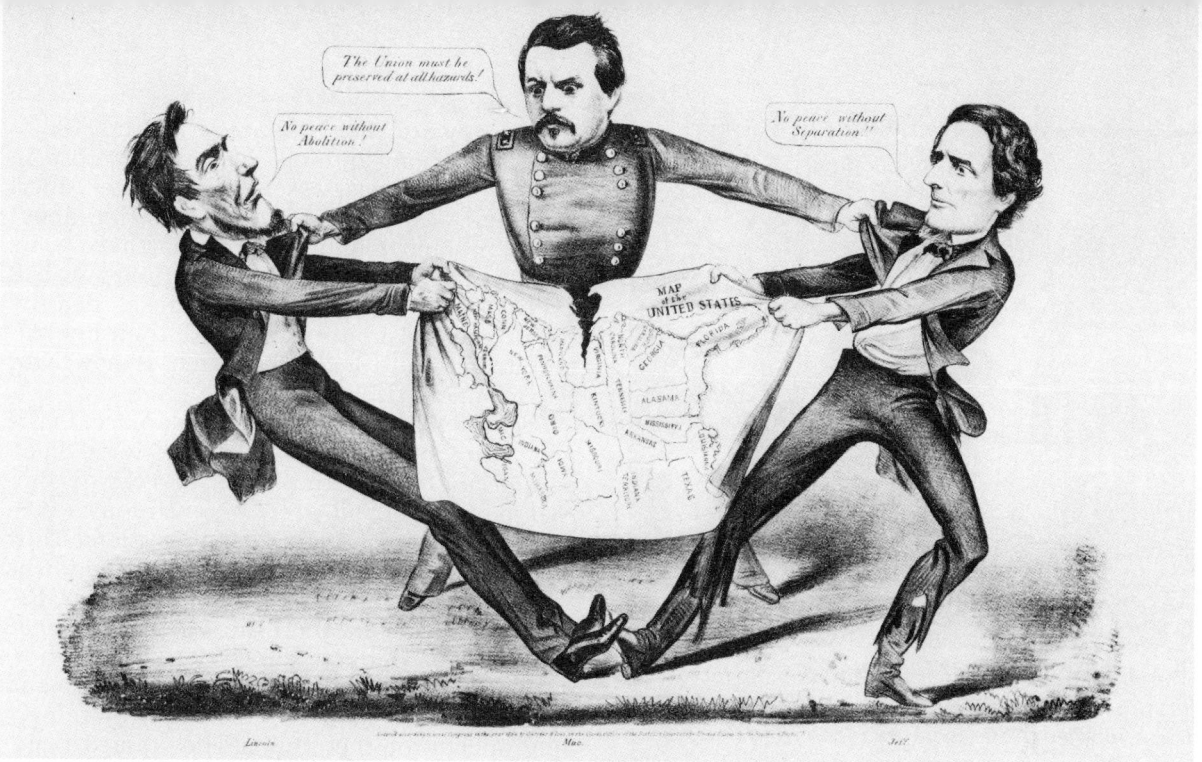

This cartoon from the 1864 election seems to favor McClellan, who tries to keep his opponent, Lincoln, and Jefferson Davis from pulling the Union apart. But the voters gave Lincoln 212 electoral votes to McClellan's 21.

me that the Almighty is against me, and I can hardly see a ray of hope."

The tide of the war turned in favor of the North shortly before the election. Sherman's capture of Atlanta convinced many voters that the end of the war was near. Moreover, Lincoln's opponent, General McClellan, refused to support the platform of his own Democratic Party, which declared that the war was a failure and ought to be stopped immediately. As a result, Lincoln won an overwhelming victory, receiving 212 electoral votes to 21 for the Democratic candidate. That a Presidential election was successfully held in wartime was in itself a victory for representative government.

Expanding roles for women. The continuing strength of representative government during the war did not bring any broadening of the **suffrage** to include women. In fact, leaders in the women's rights movement largely suspended their activities to work for other causes. Several, including a 20-year-old newcomer to the movement, Anna E. Dickinson, spoke publicly for the Union cause.

Elizabeth Cady Stanton (page 368) organized the National Woman's Loyal League. The League supported the abolitionist effort to convert the war into one for the emancipation of the slaves. Her friend and associate Susan B. Anthony provided leadership in the collection of 400,000 petitions in support of the Thirteenth Amendment. Lucy Stone, an Oberlin graduate and an effective speaker and worker, also supported the National Woman's Loyal League. After the war, she helped organize the American Equal Rights Association, which sought voting rights for blacks and women.

While the cause of women's rights made little progress during the war, other important developments were taking place. Women on both sides of the conflict demonstrated their organizational skill and the capacity for hard work in activities for which they had little or no experience. Their important contributions to the war effort in both North and South gave them greater self-confidence and opened new possibilities to them. On farms and plantations, they did the work of their husbands, fathers, and brothers. They taught in schools, replacing men who were now soldiers. As never before, their efforts were needed in mills, factories, munitions plants, shops, banks, and government offices.

Women had long been employed in textile factories, but the war sent them into other factories as well. These women are at work in a factory making bullets for northern guns.

At the start of the war, army medical services scarcely existed in the Confederacy and were woefully inadequate in the North. Before the war was over, at least 3,200 northern and southern women had served as full-time army nurses. Dorothea Dix (page 369–70) served as Superintendent of Nurses in the Union armies. She brought some order and efficiency into hastily improvised hospitals, despite army prejudice against the presence of women. Clara Barton, with no official position, collected medical supplies and food and managed, against great odds, to get them to battlefields where they were most needed. "Mother" Ann Bickerdyke—colorful, brusque, and completely devoted to her "soldier boys"—defied army red tape and introduced sanitation, proper food, and medical supplies into many Union army hospitals. In the Confederacy, Phoebe Pember, Ella Newsom, and Kate Cummings were outstanding among hundreds of women who cared for the sick and wounded in army hospitals.

At the outbreak of the Civil War, 20,000 women's relief societies were organized in the North and South. These societies staffed canteens, sewed uniforms, made bandages, and collected medicines. Lacking an overall organization, southern women in these societies nevertheless carried out desperately needed relief work. In the North, the women's societies raised about $15 million for war relief.

Policy toward the Indians. In the 1860's most American Indians had no interest in fighting what was, essentially, white America's civil war. Still, it is estimated that about 3,000 Indians fought on the northern side. Meanwhile, the southerners recruited four brigades from the Five Civilized Tribes, then living in Indian Territory, and with their help attempted to control the area that is now New Mexico and Arizona.

Some ominous events also took place. In the new state of Minnesota, the Eastern Sioux became angry when they failed to receive promised payments and grew resentful at injustices by government agents and settlers. They burned and looted Minnesota farms and towns and killed about 500 settlers and soldiers. Retaliation was swift and brutal. At Mankato 38 Indians were publicly hanged.

In the Colorado Territory, Arapahos and Cheyennes resented the intrusion of miners and ranchers on their lands. They raided stagecoach stations and ranches and murdered a white family. In reprisal, Colonel J. M. Chivington, a preacher commanding a unit of militia, surprised a larger group of Indians at Sand Creek and killed 500 of them, including women and children. Mutilation of the Indian bodies by the militia matched in brutality practices long condemned in Indian fighting. General Nelson A. Miles of the United States Army later called the Sand Creek massacre "the foulest and most unjustifiable crime in the annals of America."

The violence in Minnesota and Colorado were omens of the conflict between Indians and whites that was to break out when the Civil War ended.

SECTION REVIEW

See underscored items, text pp. 433-36.

Identify: *Trent* affair, Clement L. Vallandigham, suffrage, Elizabeth Cady Stanton, Lucy Stone, Clara Barton, Sand Creek massacre

For answers to questions, see Answer Key, p.A61.

1. **Analyzing Ideas:** Why did some European governments sympathize with the Confederacy?
2. **Summarizing Ideas:** (a) Who were the Copperheads? (b) What were their opinions on the war?
3. **Interpreting Ideas:** (a) What were the issues in the election of 1864? (b) Why was this election a victory for representative government?
4. **Comparing Ideas:** How did women contribute to the war effort in the North and South?

DEVELOPING HISTORY STUDY SKILLS

Reading About History   Understanding Biographical Accounts

History is not just the recounting of events or the study of issues and questions. It is also the story of people and the roles they have played in shaping events and influencing issues. Many individuals have helped to shape American history. How can a student of history learn about these people? One way is through biography — an account of a person's life.

A biography is a secondary source which is based on primary sources and other secondary sources. It helps to explain a person's place and significance in history. Included in a biography are the events that shape a person's life and a recounting of the person's accomplishments. A biography also includes specific information about the person's personality, attitudes, values, and motivations. Each chapter of this text includes a short biographical sketch of a person or group that has had some impact on American history.

How to Read a Biographical Account

In order to get the most from a biographical account, follow these steps.

1. **Trace major events.** Ask yourself what were the major events of the person's life.

2. **Determine personal influences.** Look for the events that most influenced the person's life. Decide what impact these influences had. Also determine how the person influenced historical events. Discover what attitudes and values the person held. Identify the personality traits that are revealed through the account, and discover what motivated the person to act as he or she did.

3. **Assess significance.** Look for the person's accomplishments and decide his or her significance in history.

Applying the Skill

In the next column is Robert E. Lee's General Order Number 9, often considered his Farewell Address. It is the kind of primary document often included in a biography. Read the document. Note that the document gives the following important facts about Lee's life.

Lee was the commander of the Army of Northern Virginia. His troops had been engaged in a hard battle for four years and had suffered many casualties. Lee surrendered because to continue the battle would have meant many more losses, losses which Lee could no longer justify. Lee considered his men courageous, steadfast, and devoted. He had a deep affection for them and they for him.

Reread the sentence beginning, "But feeling that valor and devotion could accomplish nothing . . . " This sentence tells you about Lee's attitudes toward war and the loss of human lives. The order also indicates the respect that Lee felt for the men that served under him.

---

10 April, 1865

General Order
Number 9

After four years of arduous service marked by unsurpassed courage and fortitude, the Army of Northern Virginia has been compelled to yield to overwhelming numbers and resources.

I need not tell the survivors of so many hard fought battles, who have remained steadfast to the last, that I have consented to this result from no distrust of them.

But feeling that valor and devotion could accomplish nothing that could compensate for the loss that would have attended the continuance of the contest, I determined to avoid the useless sacrifice of those whose past services have endeared them to their countrymen.

By the terms of the agreement, officers and men can return to their homes, and remain until exchanged. You will take with you the satisfaction that proceeds from the consciousness of duty faithfully performed, and I earnestly pray that a merciful God will extend to you his blessing and protection.

With an unceasing admiration of your constancy and devotion to your country, and a grateful remembrance of your kind and generous consideration for myself, I bid you an affectionate farewell.

R. E. Lee

437

Practicing the Skill

Below are two letters written by General Lee. One is to his sister; one is to John Letcher, Governor of Virginia. Read each letter and then on a separate sheet of paper, answer the questions that follow each excerpt.

April 20, 1861.

My Dear Sister: I am grieved at my inability to see you. . . . I have been waiting for a 'more convenient season,' which has brought to many before me deep and lasting regret. Now we are in a state of war which will yield to nothing. The whole South is in a state of revolution, into which Virginia, after a long struggle, has been drawn; and though I recognize no necessity for this state of things, and would have forborne and pleaded to the end for redress of grievances, real or supposed, yet in my own person I had to meet the question whether I should take part against my native State.

"With all my devotion to the Union and the feeling of loyalty and duty of an American citizen, I have not been able to make up my mind to raise my hand against my relatives, my children, my home. I have therefore resigned my commission in the Army, and save in defense of my native State, with the sincere hope that my services may never be needed, I hope I may never be called on to draw my sword. I know you will blame me; but you must think as kindly of me as you can, and believe that I have endeavoured to do what I thought right.

"To show you the feeling and struggle it has cost me, I send you a copy of my letter of resignation. I have no time for more. May God guard and protect you and yours, and shower upon you everlasting blessings, is the prayer of your devoted brother,

R. E. Lee

---

28 August, 1865

Hon. John Letcher

My dear Sir:
I was much pleased to . . . learn . . . of the kindness and consideration with which you were treated during your arrest and of the sympathy extended to you by your former Congressional associates and friends in Washington. The conciliatory manner in which President Johnson spoke of the South must have been particularly agreeable to one who has the interests of its people so much at heart as yourself. I wish that spirit could become more general. It would go far to promote confidence and to calm feelings which have too long existed. The questions which for years were in dispute between the State and Genl. Govts., and which unhappily were not decided by the dictates of reason, but referred to the decision of war, having been decided against us, it is the part of wisdom to acquiesce in the result, and of candor to recognize the fact.

The interests of the State are therefore the same as those of the U[nited] States. Its prosperity will rise or fall with the welfare of the country. The duty of its citizens then appear to me too plain to admit of doubt. All should unite in honest efforts to obliterate the effects of war, and to restore the blessings of peace. They should remain if possible in the country; promote harmony and good feeling; qualify themselves to vote; and elect to the State and General Legislatures wise and patriotic men, who will devote their abilities to the interests of the country, and the healing of all dissensions. I have invariably recommended this course since the cessation of hostilities, and have endeavored to practice it myself. . . .

R. E. Lee

---

1. When was the letter to Lee's sister written? What historical event was in progress at the time?

2. Why did Lee resign his commission in the Army?

3. What did he expect would be his sister's reaction to this news?

4. What information does the letter to his sister reveal about Lee's attitude toward war?

5. What information does the letter reveal about Lee's relationship to his sister? Explain.

6. **(a)** When was the letter to Letcher written? **(b)** What event had just occurred?

7. What advice did Lee have for Virginians? Why?

8. What information does the Letcher letter reveal about Lee's attitude about the Union?

9. Based on this attitude, which of these words apply to Lee — conciliatory, patriotic, commonsensical, dogmatic, strong, emotional, rational, dictatorial, Napoleonic? Explain.

10. Using information from each document, how would you summarize Lee's attitude about war? about the Union?

In 1865 the terrrible trial by fire and sword that was the Civil War came to an end. The sorrowing nation estimated its losses. The war cost the southern states more than a billion dollars. The northern states spent several times that amount. After all pensions and other costs of the war were paid, the war probably cost the American people a total of $10 billion—an equivalent in today's dollars of many, many times that amount.

The conflict was also terribly costly in lives. Not counting those permanently injured and maimed, the North lost about 369,000 soldiers. The South lost about 258,000 soldiers. There were also the uncounted losses of civilians from hunger, starvation, and disease.

The war had many far-reaching results. It ended the institution of slavery. It settled once and for all the doctrine of secession. It strengthened the Union by increasing the power of the federal government at the expense of the states. It strengthened democracy by showing that a representative form of government could operate successfully in wartime. Finally, the four-year ordeal helped speed the development of American industry.

In the spring of 1865, the people of the United States could look only into the immediate future. And the big problem they faced, northerners and southerners alike, was "to bind the nation's wounds" and join hands as a reunited people. Unknown to them, however, a new era was about to begin—one with new opportunities and new dreams.

CONNECTING CHAPTER IDEAS

In the next chapter you will read about efforts to reconstruct the Union and to ease the war's legacy of bitterness. Lincoln's assassination cut short a lenient treatment of white southerners and opened the way for a reconstruction along radical lines.

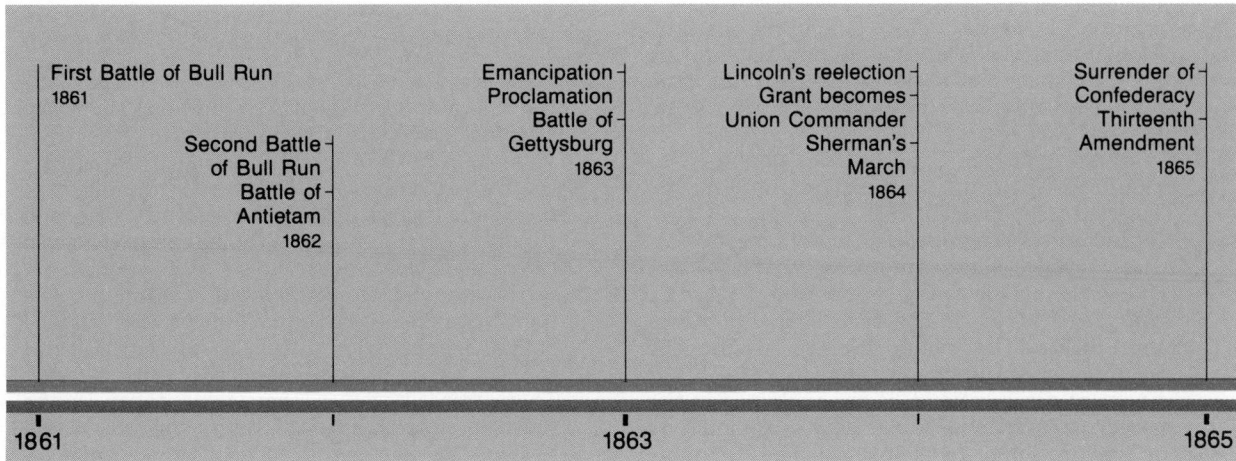

First Battle of Bull Run
1861

Second Battle of Bull Run
Battle of Antietam
1862

Emancipation Proclamation
Battle of Gettysburg
1863

Lincoln's reelection
Grant becomes Union Commander
Sherman's March
1864

Surrender of Confederacy
Thirteenth Amendment
1865

| 1861 | 1863 | 1865 |

CHAPTER
18 REVIEW

Reviewing Important Terms

In the sentences below, the underlined terms are incorrect. On a separate sheet of paper, rewrite each sentence using the correct term.

1. Bounty jumpers held in federal camps during the Civil War often faced conditions of gross neglect.
2. After April 1862, the Confederacy used voluntary enlistment to increase the size of its army.
3. South Carolinians threatened to withdraw from the Confederacy itself after President Davis suspended the Articles of Confederation.
4. The contrabands volunteering for the Union army would enlist, desert, and reenlist in order to collect repeatedly the premium paid to new volunteers.
5. The value of Confederate currency rose with every northern victory and was worth 78 cents in gold by the end of the Civil War.
6. An 1862 law entitled anyone who lived on government land as a plantation for five years to receive 160 acres free of charge.
7. The academies supported by the income from the sale or rental of government land emphasized areas such as agriculture and engineering in their curricula.
8. Railroad lines connecting the Northeast and the Middle West were built with the help of government suffrage.

Practicing Critical Thinking Skills

1. **Organizing Ideas.** Select one battle or campaign of the Civil War. Explain how the fighting and the outcome of the selected battle or campaign illustrated the strengths and the weaknesses of each side.
2. **Comparing Ideas.** Explain the differences between the Emancipation Proclamation and the Thirteenth Amendment.
3. **Evaluating Viewpoints.** Discuss Lincoln's attitude toward black Americans. Explain how some of his beliefs changed over time.
4. **Analyzing Ideas.** It has been said that Abraham Lincoln's Gettysburg Address contains one of the great definitions of democracy. **(a)** What important democratic ideas are explained in the speech? **(b)** Which ideas are held in common by the Declaration of Independence, The Preamble to the Constitution, and the Gettysburg Address?

5. **Determining Cause and Effect.** The Civil War caused changes in the roles of women. **(a)** What kinds of situations and jobs did the war open up to them? **(b)** Do you think that wars have generally had an effect on the roles of women in American society? Why or why not?
6. **Relating Past to Present.** Lincoln suspended the writ of *habeas corpus* and suppressed freedom of speech and freedom of the press during the war. **(a)** Does a national crisis justify suspension of civil liberties? **(b)** Should the President have this power? **(c)** Should Congress have this power? Explain your answers.

Developing History Study Skills

Understanding Biographical Accounts. Review the American Profile of Clara Barton on page 421 of the textbook. Then answer the following questions. **(a)** For what is Clara Barton best known? **(b)** What is significant about her work as a civil servant? **(c)** How did her work on the battlefield lead to the founding of the American Association of the Red Cross? **(d)** How old was Barton when she resigned her office as president of the American Red Cross?

Relating Geography and History

In addition to the tremendous pressures applied from outside by a strong enemy, internal failures were responsible to some extent for the defeat of the Confederacy. In order to understand what some of these failures were, complete the following activities.

1. Use the map on page 417 to find out about the railroad system in the South during the Civil War. **(a)** Write a brief paragraph explaining why the railroads were inadequate for the needs of the Confederacy. **(b)** Write a second paragraph summing up the results of the failure of southern railroads to move goods.
2. **(a)** How do you think the South's economic system was a disadvantage in time of war? **(b)** The South has been described as an agricultural country trying to fight a modern, industrial war. There were, however, some advantages on the southern side that explain why the war lasted so long. Make a list of at least three points favorable to the South's military outlook.

UNIT FIVE
REVIEW

Discussing Ideas

1. Why did the Civil War happen? Give evidence to support your answer.
2. (a) What were the war aims of the North? (b) Had the North accomplished those aims by the end of the war?
3. Why did the North win the Civil War? Explain fully.
4. One result of the Civil War was the strengthening of democracy. Do you agree or disagree? Why?
5. How did the Civil War affect the lives of (a) women, (b) blacks, and (c) Indians?
6. (a) In what ways are the American Revolution and the Civil War similar? (b) In what ways are they different?
7. Do you think that the Civil War was another American Revolution in the sense that it was a major turning point in American history? Why or why not?

Applying History Study Skills

Analyzing Primary Sources. Just before the outbreak of war, William Howard Russell, a correspondent for the London *Times,* visited with Secretary of State William Seward in Washington. Read the following excerpts from Russell's diary and answer the questions below.

> Mr. Seward asserted that the Ministers of England or of France had no right to make any allusion to the civil war which appeared imminent, and that the southern commissioners who had been sent abroad could not be received by the government of any foreign power, officially or otherwise, ever to hand in a document or to make a representation, without incurring the risk of breaking off relations with the government of the United States. . . .
> Great Britain is in a pleasant condition. Mr. Seward is threatening us with war if we recognize the South, and the South declares that if we don't recognize their flag they will take it as an act of hostility. Lord Lyons [the British minister to the United States] is pressed to give an assurance to the government at Washington that under no circumstances will Great Britain recognize the southern rebels; but at the same time Mr.

> Seward refuses to give any assurance whatever that the right of neutrals will be respected in the impending struggle. . . .

(a) Why do you think the southern commissioners were sent abroad? (b) Why do you think Great Britain or France would have wished to support the Union? the Confederacy? Why might they have preferred to remain neutral? (c) What memories of the past might have caused the United States to oppose so vigorously foreign recognition of the Confederacy? (d) What did Russell mean by Britain's "pleasant condition"?

Making Connections

1. Write a newspaper account of (a) the Lincoln-Douglas debates, (b) "bleeding Kansas," or (c) the creation of the Confederate States of America.
2. Draw two political cartoons about the Dred Scott decision—one favoring the opinion and one opposing it.
3. Prepare a bulletin board display on a phase of the Civil War, including such items as pictures, maps, newspaper articles, and songs.

Reading in Depth

Catton, Bruce, *Glory Road* and *Stillness at Appomatox* (New York: Doubleday). Two of the numerous excellent histories on various aspects of the war written by this leading expert.

Commager, Henry Steele, *America's Robert E. Lee* (Boston: Houghton Mifflin). The story of the great Confederate general, his childhood, career at West Point, and his choice between the Union he served so well and the southern traditions he so deeply cherished.

Crane, Stephen, *Red Badge of Courage* (New York: Scholastic). A classic novel of the Civil War, told from the point of view of a young Union soldier.

Heidish, Macy, *A Woman Called Moses: A Novel Based on the Life of Harriet Tubman* (Boston: Houghton Mifflin). Marvelously moving and authentic in narration.

Pratt, Fletcher, *The Civil War* (Doubleday). The author explains the famous battles of the war and their significance, and also describes the colorful personalities on both sides.

441

UNIT SIX

Rebuilding the Nation

Before the Civil War the United States had experienced unprecedented growth. The war, however, had interrupted that growth. From the ashes of war arose the question of whether the nation would be able to recapture its earlier vitality. In 1865, to be sure, the first task that lay before the United States was reconstruction. Much of that task meant the rebuilding and expansion of the transportation and communication networks that linked the nation. The completion in 1869 of the first transcontinental railroad, pictured below, was a symbol of the nation's determination to overcome all obstacles and continue on its course to greatness. By 1900, ideas as well as raw materials and manufactured products flowed smoothly across rail and wire from one section of the nation to another.

See Chapter Overview in TMRG, p.TM114.
See Chapter Objectives in TMRG, p.TM114.
See Introducing the Chapter in TMRG, p.TM114.

CHAPTER 19
Restoring the South to the Union
(1865–1900)

The South's heavy burden

Bitterness between the North and the South continued for many years after the Civil War ended. This bitterness was inevitable because many people on each side of the conflict believed that their cause was right and just. When the war ended, southerners were willing to reenter the Union. Nonetheless, they did not think that they should be treated as a conquered people. Many northerners, on the other hand, felt that secessionists should earn their return to the Union.

The bitterness increased during the decade that followed the war as the struggle to rebuild the Union aroused further resentment. Rebuilding meant solving difficult political and constitutional problems. It meant restoring economic vigor to the South's devastated industries. It meant reopening normal trade relations among the states. Finally it meant solving the problem of bringing black Americans into the mainstream of national life.

Solutions to these problems had to be found at a time when a breakdown of public morality occurred in both the North and the South. Corruption reached into every level of government. This breakdown of public morality stemmed partially from the war, which had dislocated life in every section of the country. It also stemmed from the many changes that took place during the latter half of the 1800's. Chief among these changes were the rapid development of industry, technological advances in farming, a flood of immigrants, and the booming growth of cities.

══ READING FOCUS ══

As you read about the efforts of both northerners and southerners to restore the Union, look for the details that support each of the following statements.

1. President Lincoln strives for lenient reconstruction.
2. The nation struggles to restore order to the South.
3. The Radical Republicans enact a program of reconstruction.
4. White southerners regain control of their state governments.
5. The New South advances in agriculture, industry, and education.
6. Black southerners struggle for a place in the New South.

1 President Lincoln strives for lenient reconstruction

See Teaching Suggestions in TMRG, pp.TM114-15.

At the time of his Second Inaugural Address, President Lincoln issued a stirring call for a lenient reconstruction policy. He said in part:

"With malice toward none, with charity for all, with firmness in the right, as God gives us to see the right, let us strive on to finish the work we are in, to bind up the nation's wounds, to care for him who shall have borne the battle, and for his widow, and his orphan—to do all which may achieve and cherish a just and lasting peace among ourselves and with all nations."

Lincoln's program. As early as December 8, 1863, Lincoln began to develop a program of **reconstruction** based upon "charity for all." ▲ The practical, flexible program rested on Lincoln's theory that the Confederate states had never left the Union.

First, Lincoln offered **amnesty,** a full pardon, to all southerners who would take an oath of allegiance to the Union and who would promise to accept federal laws and proclamations dealing with slavery. Several groups of southerners were excluded from Lincoln's offer of amnesty. Those who had resigned positions in the federal government to serve in similar positions in the Confederacy were excluded. Members of the Confederate government, high-ranking officers in the Confederate military forces, and Confederates who had mistreated prisoners of war were also excluded.

Second, Lincoln set the conditions for a state's return to the Union. He declared that a state could return to the Union on a basis of full equality with all other states when at least 10 percent of those who had voted in the election of 1860 had taken the oath of allegiance to the Union. Each person taking the oath also had to have been a qualified voter in the state before its secession from the Union.

In 1863 the program applied only to areas already conquered by Union armies. Lincoln intended to apply the program to all other Confederate areas as soon as they were in Union hands. Lincoln agreed that Congress must give final approval to admitting members of Congress from the reconstructed states. More-

▲ Throughout the Annotated Teacher's Edition, terms listed in the "Identify" Portion of a Section Review are underscored the first time they appear. See the Teacher's Manual for each section for a listing of important vocabulary terms.

445

over, as time passed, Lincoln revealed flexibility in his own thinking. For example, in a letter written in 1864, he stated that the restoration of the southern states to the Union "must rest upon the principle of civil and political equality of both races; and it must be sealed by a general amnesty." In his last public address, delivered on April 11, 1865, only four days before his death, he declared that he favored giving the vote to those blacks who had fought for the Union and to those with some educational qualifications.

Opposition to Lincoln's program. Not all Republican leaders agreed with Lincoln's ideas on reconstruction. Many opposed the idea of pardoning former Confederates and allowing them to vote and hold office. These Republican leaders doubted the loyalty of former Confederates. They also doubted whether, if given political power, the former Confederates would permit blacks to enjoy legal and political rights.

The Republicans who were most opposed to Lincoln's reconstruction policy were called Radicals. The Radical Republicans were by no means a well-defined group. Different Radicals took different positions on political and economic issues and on methods of readmitting the former Confederate states. The two most outspoken Radicals were Senator Charles Sumner of Massachusetts and Representative Thaddeus Stevens of Pennsylvania.

Senator Sumner insisted on measures to guarantee the political and legal equality of black Americans and to educate them for the responsibilities of freedom. Representative Stevens wanted to punish the South for all the injustices and **discriminations** that black southerners had suffered under white rule. Stevens also wanted to do everything possible to make sure that in the future the freed slaves would be treated justly. Stevens also believed that political and legal rights for former slaves would be meaningless if the blacks did not have economic independence. He urged that the estates of "rebel traitors" be divided up and given to the freed slaves. Few Radical Republicans accepted so extreme a policy.

During the war and in the months following Confederate surrender, a majority of Republican leaders, more moderate in their views, lined up with Lincoln's reconstruction policies. However, many moderates agreed with the Radicals that Lincoln, in exercising his war powers, had encroached upon the constitutional powers of the legislative branch. They all felt that Congress, not the President, should lay down the rules for restoring the southern states to the Union.

Some Republicans frankly admitted that their thinking about reconstruction was influenced by practical politics. They believed that, when the war ended, white southerners would reject the wartime Republican Party and flock to the Democratic Party. Southern Democrats returning to Congress would probably support northern Democrats, thus making the Republicans a minority party. Such a combination might endanger measures supported by many Republicans—a high tariff, national banks, free land, and federal aid to railroads.

The Republicans could keep the Democrats from gaining majority power in state as well as federal governments in two ways. First, they could give voting rights to the former slaves. These new voters would support the Republicans at the polls in gratitude for emancipation. Second, they could keep former Confederate leaders from voting and holding public office.

Such political considerations played some part in shaping the attitudes of many Republicans toward reconstruction. Historians disagree as to how large a part. However, many Republican members of Congress approached the difficult problems of reconstruction with a genuine desire to help the freed slaves and to guarantee them fair treatment in American life.

The Wade-Davis Bill. Opposition to President Lincoln's plan for reconstruction found expression in the Wade-Davis Bill. Some Radical Republican members of Congress thought the bill was too mild. However, enough moderate Republicans supported it to allow the bill to be passed by a slender majority in early July 1864.

The Wade-Davis Bill provided for readmitting the southern states into the Union under harsher conditions than those favored by Lincoln. The bill was intended to give political power to southerners who had remained loyal to the Union. It was also intended to insure that the new constitutions of the southern states would recognize the freedom of black southerners. Finally, the bill was intended to insure that Confederate war debts were **repudiated,** or not paid.

President Lincoln refused to sign the Wade-Davis Bill. He felt that its rigid provisions

The Lincoln Memorial honors the greatness of Abraham Lincoln, the nation's sixteenth President. The Memorial is 188 feet (57 meters) long and 118 feet (36 meters) wide. The building stands on the 164 acres (66 hectares) of Potomac Park in the nation's capital.

A national Lincoln memorial had been considered since 1867, but not until 1911 did Congress appoint a Lincoln Memorial Commission. The Memorial's cornerstone was laid on Lincoln's birthday, February 12, 1915, and completed 7 years later.

The building itself was designed by Henry Bacon, a renowned architect of the times. Bacon styled the Memorial after a Greek temple, ringing it with 36 stately Doric columns — one for each state in the Union at the time of Lincoln's assassination.

The larger-than-life statue is the creation of sculptor Daniel Chester French. He shows Lincoln sitting in solitude, perhaps brooding over the fate of the southern states. Viewers of the statue, however, receive a sense of the courage and the tragedy that surrounded Lincoln in life. The Memorial brings to mind the words Secretary of War Edwin Stanton spoke on hearing of Lincoln's death: "Now he belongs to the ages."

would restrict him when the time came to rebuild the Union. He also believed that Congress did not have the constitutional authority to compel a state to abolish slavery. Abolition of slavery, he believed, would require an amendment to the Constitution.

Lincoln's assassination. Whether or not Lincoln could have won acceptance of his policy must remain unanswered. On the evening of April 14, 1865, President and Mrs. Lincoln arranged to go to Ford's Theater in Washington, D.C., with friends. The long war was finally over, and the weary President was to attend a performance of the popular comedy *Our American Cousin.* As Lincoln watched the play, ▲ John Wilkes Booth slipped quietly into the President's special box and shot him. Booth, a former actor, then leaped to the stage shouting "*Sic semper tyranis!* (Thus always to tyrants!)

The South is avenged!"

Lincoln was carried to a house across the street from the theater, too badly wounded to be taken to a hospital or back to the White House. The President lingered through the night, never regaining consciousness. At seven o'clock in the morning President Lincoln breathed his last.

Sorrow and anger gripped the nation — South as well as North, black as well as white. White southerners had despised Lincoln during the war. Yet many had come to feel that he was a wise, compassionate leader who offered the best program of reconstruction. Flags flew at half-mast, bells tolled, and weeping crowds filed through the funeral train as it stopped in cities between Washington, D.C., and Lincoln's burial place in Springfield, Illinois. Meanwhile, Vice President Andrew Johnson became President.

▲ Report topic: John Wilkes Booth

President Johnson. <u>Andrew Johnson</u> was a self-educated man. Without any formal schooling, he had spent his boyhood as a tailor's apprentice. Later his devoted wife had helped him to improve his meager writing ability. While still a young man, he was elected mayor of his community, a small mountain village in eastern Tennessee. This was the beginning of a political career in the Democratic Party that took him to the Senate of the United States in 1857. Although he owned a few slaves, Johnson disliked the large planters who were so influential in the South. He had resisted the secession of Tennessee in 1861.

Johnson's service for the Union during the war won him an appointment as military governor of Tennessee. He was responsible for controlling those areas of his state occupied by Union troops. When the Republicans, including Lincoln himself, feared that they might lose the Presidential election in 1864, Johnson, a Democrat, was placed on the "Union" ticket. The hope of the Republicans was that he would draw votes for Lincoln.

Andrew Johnson had many admirable qualities. He possessed a stubborn fighting spirit and the moral courage to act according to his convictions. Unfortunately, he was not a flexible man. Whereas Lincoln always tried to understand the positions of his political opponents, Johnson tended to insist upon the rightness of his own views. Johnson lacked sufficient patience, tact, and political skill to be the effective leader that the nation needed at this critical time in its history.

Johnson and reconstruction. One of Johnson's first decisions as President was to offer rewards for the arrest of Jefferson Davis and other former Confederate leaders. Most Radical Republicans were pleased with Johnson's action. The Radicals believed that he would help them carry out their harsher program of reconstruction.

▲ President Johnson soon disappointed the Radicals. He adopted a more conciliatory attitude toward the South and claimed that he intended to follow Lincoln's program. For a time he seemed to be doing so. He officially recognized the reconstructed governments of Tennessee, Arkansas, Louisiana, and Virginia. Johnson also kept all of the members of Lincoln's cabinet.

In several ways, however, Johnson did not follow Lincoln's program, either in details or in general approach. Lincoln had kept an open mind about the best method of reconstructing the Union. Johnson refused to consider any plan but his own. His stubbornness antagonized the Radical Republicans, as did his policy of pardoning former Confederates. When the Radicals objected to his policies, Johnson answered their arguments with name-calling and personal abuse.

Johnson managed to antagonize even the moderate Republicans. Most moderates shared with the Radicals the belief that any program of reconstruction must provide civil and political equality for both races. Johnson opposed this viewpoint.

End of Presidential reconstruction. Nevertheless, the reconstruction program proceeded for a time along the lines laid down by Lincoln and modified by Johnson. Within a few months, all the former Confederate states except Texas had adopted new constitutions and organized new governments.

When Congress assembled on December 4, 1865, Senators and Representatives from the southern states, most of whom had been leaders in the Confederacy, were waiting outside the doors to take their seats in the national legislature. To many observers it looked as though the long and dreadful war was finally ended and the restored nation was about to start anew.

SECTION REVIEW
See underscored items, text pp. 445-48.

Identify: reconstruction, amnesty, Charles Sumner, Thaddeus Stevens, discrimination, Wade-Davis Bill, John Wilkes Booth, Andrew Johnson
For answers to questions, see Answer Key, p.A64.

1. **Analyzing Ideas: (a)** What did President Lincoln mean when he said, "With malice toward none, with charity for all"? **(b)** What were the main terms of Lincoln's reconstruction plan?

2. **Summarizing Ideas: (a)** What were the main arguments against Lincoln's reconstruction plan? **(b)** Explain the reasoning of Lincoln's opponents.

3. **Evaluating Viewpoints: (a)** What were the provisions of the Wade-Davis Bill? Why did **(b)** Lincoln and **(c)** some Radical Republicans object to the bill?

4. **Organizing Ideas:** To what extent was reconstruction policy **(a)** a struggle between the two major political parties and **(b)** a struggle between two branches of the federal government?

▲ Johnson's southern origins also tended to make members of Congress suspicious that the President was being too easy on the South, even though he had opposed his state's (Tennessee) secession and had supported the Union.

DEVELOPING HISTORY STUDY SKILLS

Thinking About History   Analyzing Viewpoints

Issues in history are often complex, allowing for no easy solutions. One of these complex issues was how to treat the rebellious South after the Civil War. Most people agreed that the South must be restored to the Union. A number of influential people, however, held different viewpoints on how the restoration, or reconstruction, of the Union, should be accomplished.

The complexity of such issues can be understood mainly by analyzing each viewpoint or set of viewpoints and evaluating the similarities or differences among the viewpoints.

How to Analyze Viewpoints

The effectively analyze viewpoints, follow these steps.

1. **Identify the main idea.** The person's main idea, or premise, must be identified and separated from supporting details.

2. **Determine the main idea's support.** The main idea of the viewpoint can be supported by facts or by opinions or by a combination of fact and opinion. In general, a viewpoint's strongest support comes from facts. Not all viewpoints, however, are based on fact. Determine whether the main idea is supported by fact or opinion.

3. **Consider how the details are used.** Decide if the supporting details are used logically. Check whether the person has the proper experience and background to speak or write with authority on the subject. See if the person is being objective or is expressing a bias.

Applying the Skill

Abraham Lincoln and Thaddeus Stevens each held viewpoints on how the South should be treated after the Civil War. Read and analyze Lincoln's statement at the top of the next column. Then compare it with the viewpoint held by Stevens.

> *With malice toward none, with charity for all, with firmness in the right as God gives us to see the right, let us strive to finish the work we are in, to bind up the nation's wounds, to care for him who has borne the battle and for his widow and orphan, to do all which may achieve and cherish a lasting peace among ourselves.*
>
> Abraham Lincoln

> *Nobody, I believe, pretends that with their old Constitutions and frames of government, they can be permitted to claim their old rights under the Constitution. They have torn their Constitutional States into atoms, and built on their foundations fabrics of a totally different character. Dead men cannot raise themselves. Dead states cannot restore their existence as it was. Whose especial duty is to do it? In whom does the Constitution place the power? ... The future condition of a conquered power depends on the will of the Conqueror. They [the conquered states] must come in as new states or remain as conquered provinces. ...*
>
> Thaddeus Stevens

Lincoln's main idea is that the South is still part of the Union. Reconstruction is to be a healing process — a binding of the nation's wounds. The key words then are *nation, peace,* and *binding.* In this excerpt, no facts are presented. Lincoln's opinions, however, seem reasonable and logical.

Stevens, on the other hand, held the viewpoint that the South was a conquered province that should be made to reapply for readmission to the Union. Key terms in identifying Steven's viewpoint are *claim old rights, torn fabric,* and *conquered provinces.* Stevens argues that dead men cannot raise themselves nor can dead states restore their own existence. He further states that the future of a conquered power rests with the North.

Stevens considered the bonds with the Union completely severed when the southern states seceded. Lincoln, however, considered the bonds to be merely "wounded."

449

Practicing the Skill

The following two viewpoints are on the reconstruction governments in the South. Study these viewpoints. Then on a separate sheet of paper, answer the questions below the two excerpts.

Historian A

Northern "carpetbaggers," working with southern "scalawags," came to the South after the Civil War to take advantage of the terrible situation there. The carpetbaggers wanted to make money and seize political power for the Republican Party. The scalawags wanted power and money for themselves.

Under the radical governments of the carpetbaggers and scalawags, blacks could vote, but many wealthy whites (plantation owners) could not. As a result, elections in the South were a farce.

The Northern Radicals were lying when they said they wanted Negroes to vote and hold office in the name of justice. This is shown when one notices that few of the Northern states allowed the Negroes to vote and none ever promoted a Negro into any office.

The South was now plunged by this misgovernment into corruption and plundering beyond belief. Radical Republican legislatures, supported by military power, piled up expenses against their poor states to fantastic heights. In Florida the cost of printing in 1869 was more than the entire cost of the state government in 1860. In Arkansas a Negro was given $9,000 for repairing a bridge which had originally cost $500. In South Carolina the legislature voted extra pay of $1,000 on a horse race.

A Congressional Committee reported that one of the leading carpetbag governors made over $100,000 during his first year though his salary was $8,000. Another carpetbag governor was charged with stealing and selling the food of the Freedmen's Bureau for the relief of helpless and ragged ex-slaves.

Historian B

Other historians have exaggerated the reckless spending of the Radical Republican governments in the South after the Civil War. When one looks at who benefited from this spending he notices that only a few of the Negro and white radical leaders profited personally. . . .

As a matter of fact, taxes, government spending, and public debts were bound to increase in the southern states after the war no matter who controlled them. For there was no way to escape the cost of physical reconstruction — the repair of building, etc. And much of this physical reconstruction took place while radicals were in office. They expanded the state railroad systems, increased public services, and provided public school systems — in some states for the first time. Since schools and other public services provided for Negroes as well as for whites, a considerable increase in the cost of state government could hardly have been avoided. In Florida, between

1869 and 1873, the number of children in public school tripled, while in South Carolina the number quadrupled.

Thus radical rule, in spite of its shortcomings, made substantial achievements, too many to simply equate it with incompetence and corruption. In Mississippi the radicals had a remarkably good record. They had two honest and able governors, and according to Vernon L. Wharton, achieved a system of public education better than any the state had known before, among other achievements. Finally, granting mistakes, the radical governments were by far the most democratic the South had ever known. They were the only governments in southern history to extend to Negroes complete civil and political equality. When the Southern whites took over again, the Negroes lost these rights for another century.

1. What is Historian A's premise?
2. What are the key words that give you a clue to the premise of Historian A?
3. Name one supporting detail Historian A used in supporting his premise.
4. What bias, if any, does Historian A display?

5. What is Historian B's premise?
6. What key words give you clues to the main premise of Historian B?
7. Name one supporting detail Historian B used to support his premise.
8. What, if any, bias does Historian B display?

4. shows an unbalanced account with a one-sided story against northerners; HISTORIAN B: 5. Radical rule had its shortcomings, but it also had substantial achievements. 6. See solid-line underscore. 7. See broken-line underscore. 8. provides a balanced account with a two-sided story.)

2 The nation struggles to restore order to the South

See Teaching Suggestions in TMRG, pp.TM115-16.

A new chapter in United States history opened when Congress met on December 4, 1865. It was, however, a different chapter from that outlined by either Lincoln or Johnson. The new chapter proved to be one of the most troubled in the nation's history.

Economic chaos in the South. The scene in the South at the end of the war was one of utter poverty. Crumbling chimneys rose from the ashes of once lovely mansions. Bridges lay in ruins, and railroads were destroyed.

The devastation in the cities was especially grim. A visitor reported that Columbia, South Carolina, was "a wilderness of crumbling walls, naked chimneys, and trees killed by flames." Rubble covered the business section of Richmond, Virginia, one of the great southern manufacturing centers. The scene in Atlanta, Georgia, was one of devastation. City and countryside alike, wherever armies had fought, were largely in ruins.

Social chaos. The southern economy as well as southern property had been torn apart by the war. A citizen of Mississippi wrote in April 1865 that "our fields everywhere lie untilled. Naked chimneys and charred ruins all over the land mark the spots where happy homes . . . once stood. Their former inhabitants wander in poverty and exile, wherever chance or charity affords them shelter or food. Childless, old age widows, and helpless orphans beggared and hopeless, are everywhere." Conditions were not as bad as this everywhere, but they were bad enough.

The plight of some 3.5 million freed slaves was far worse. The former slaves were at last free, at least in name, but free to do what? Most of them had never been given an opportunity to learn how to read and write. None had owned land. Few knew what it was like to work for their own wages. Nor could most of their former owners pay them wages, for Confederate money was worthless and United States currency was scarcely to be found in the South. The land itself remained, but seeds and farm tools had almost disappeared.

After the war many schools in the South were set up to educate the freed slaves, young as well as old. One observer noted the eagerness of the new learners: "I have seen three generations sitting on the same bench, spelling the same lesson."

Disease, always the companion of hunger and lack of sanitation, swept across the South. It was especially serious in the cities and their outskirts, where uprooted people struggled to survive in makeshift shelters. Thousands died during the summer and winter of 1865–66. In some crowded urban areas, as much as one quarter to one third of the black population died of disease. The death rate among the white population was almost as grim.

Relief efforts for freed slaves. Even during the war, some abolitionists tried to aid the freed slaves who had fled into areas controlled by Union forces. When white planters abandoned their plantations on islands off the coast of South Carolina, black people there were left helpless and destitute. Idealistic men and women, white and black, helped the freed slaves to operate these plantations and to set up schools there. Outstanding among the volunteers was Laura Towne of Massachusetts. She looked after the health of former slaves, helped them with legal problems, and established the Penn School. This school later became a teacher-training institution with vocational as well as academic programs.

451

Elsewhere, relief societies financed by northern religious and charitable groups tried to fill the needs of freed slaves for food, shelter, jobs, and schooling. Josephine Griffing, an Ohio abolitionist and women's rights leader, set up one such program in Washington, D.C., that provided food, clothing, shelter, and job training for freed blacks. She also urged Congress to undertake a program to find places to live in the North and West for homeless black people and to help them become self-supporting citizens. She herself helped thousands find homes and jobs in many localities.

The Freedmen's Bureau. During the war, the United States Army provided food and clothing for impoverished southerners, black and white, in areas under its control. Once the war was over, it was clear that neither the army nor the voluntary relief societies could meet the pressing needs of southerners, especially the freed slaves. At the urging of Josephine Griffing and others, Congress in 1865 created the Freedman's Bureau to look after "refugees, freedmen°, and abandoned lands." This was the first important example in the nation's history of federal support for needy and underprivledged people. The Freedmen's Bureau was headed by General Oliver Otis Howard of Maine. In 1867 General Howard also founded Howard University in Washington, D.C., which offered higher education to the freed slaves.

Northerners and southerners differed in their attitude toward the Freedmen's Bureau. Most northerners regarded it as an honest effort to help the South bring order out of chaos. Most white southerners, on the other hand, resented the bureau. They charged that many bureau agents encouraged the freed slaves to look upon their former owners as enemies and, by doing so, created racial friction.

White southerners also charged the bureau with raising false hopes among the freed slaves, thereby making readjustment increasingly difficult. One of these false hopes was the former slaves' belief that they would all receive farms. During the summer and fall of 1865, the rumor spread that every former slave would get "forty acres and a mule" as a Christmas gift from the federal government. This rumor was based on a statement in the Freed-

°**freedmen** was the term used in these years to refer to former slaves—women and children as well as men.

men's Bureau bill that abandoned land or land for which taxes had not been paid could be distributed among the former slaves. Many freed slaves accepted the rumor as truth. Overjoyed at the prospect of soon owning farms and understandably linking freedom with the right to choose where and how they worked, some freed slaves decided not to work for white southerners.

Restrictions on freed slaves. In this situation southern leaders began to take steps to restore life as they had known it. One step was the adoption of laws to regulate the conduct of the freed slaves.

Laws of this kind, known as "slave codes," had existed before the war. The new **black codes**, which varied from state to state, contained many of the same provisions as the old slaves codes. As white southerners pointed out, however, they also included certain improvements in **civil rights** for the former slaves. Under the new codes, former slaves were permitted to own personal property, to sue and be sued in court, to act in court cases involving one or more black persons, and legally to marry members of their own race.

However, in general the codes denied blacks their basic civil rights. Mississippi, for example, using its old code, merely substituted the word "Negro" for "slave." Black southerners were forbidden to possess firearms unless licensed to do so. They were forbidden to assemble unless white southerners were present. Nor could blacks appear on the streets after sunset or travel without permits. Above all, the codes established white control over black labor. They prohibited black southerners from starting businesses. They provided for strict labor contracts, including severe apprenticeship regulations and stern punishments if contracts were broken. Some codes also restricted black southerners from renting or leasing farmland. The black codes indicated that white southerners had the intention of confining the freed slaves to a clearly defined, subordinate way of life.

Such was the situation in December 1865 when the newly elected Senators and Representatives from all the former Confederate states except Texas appeared in Washington to take their seats in Congress. The former Confederate states had taken some, but not all, of the steps required by both President Lincoln and President Johnson for readmission to the

Union. The new Senators and Representatives fully expected to take their seats in Congress and to share with northern members the task of rebuilding the Union.

Congress, however, refused to admit the southern Senators and Representatives. What motives prompted Congress to reject the South's newly elected representatives? Why did Congress refuse to accept Lincoln's and Johnson's programs for restoring the South to the Union?

Reasons behind rejection. From the time Lincoln's program began to take shape, Radical Republicans had argued that southern leaders could not be trusted. Now, in December 1865, the Radicals pointed to the black codes as evidence that white southerners were unwilling to recognize the complete freedom of black Americans.

The Radical Republicans also opposed the Lincoln and Johnson theory about the nature of the war. Both Lincoln and Johnson had argued that the conflict was a **rebellion of individuals.** This being so, they believed that the President could use the pardoning power granted him by the Constitution to restore the South to the Union.

Senator Charles Sumner opposed Lincoln's theory with the **state suicide** argument. According to Sumner, the southern states, as complete political organizations, had committed "state suicide" when they seceded from the Union. Now, with the war over, they were like any other unorganized territory of the United States. This being the case, Congress alone had the constitutional right to establish the terms for admitting them to the Union.

Representative Thaddeus Stevens held an even more drastic point of view. According to Stevens, the former Confederate states did not exist even as territories. In Stevens's opinion they were **conquered provinces** and should be treated as such.

Historians cannot be sure of the motives that led Radical Republicans to take the positions they did. Some Radicals were influenced by economic and political considerations. However, a good many Radical and moderate Republicans had a sincere feeling of obligation to the freed slaves. They genuinely wanted to make sure that white southerners did not deprive black southerners of their freedom or take steps to reduce them to a permanently inferior way of life.

Many moderate Republicans shared Lincoln's attitude toward the South. If Johnson had been less insistent upon having his own way, if he had been willing to work with the moderate Republicans, they and the Democratic members of the House and Senate might have carried through a reconstruction program acceptable to white southern leaders. However, President Johnson would not change his views, and control of Congress passed into the hands of the Radicals.

SECTION REVIEW
See underscored items, text p. 452.
Identify: Josephine Griffing, General Oliver Otis Howard, black codes
For answers to questions, see Answer Key, pp.A64-65.
1. **Evaluating Ideas: (a)** Describe the most pressing problems facing the South in 1865. **(b)** How did Andrew Johnson contribute to the problems of reconstruction?

2. **Summarizing Ideas:** Name the main restrictions placed on black southerners by white southern leaders.

3. **Analyzing Ideas:** Why did Congress reject the new southern members of Congress?

4. **Comparing Ideas: (a)** Contrast northern and southern opinions about the Freedmen's Bureau. **(b)** How did the new black codes differ from the old slaves codes? **(c)** Compare the theories about the nature of the Civil War held by Lincoln and Johnson with those held by **(d)** Sumner, and **(e)** Stevens.

3 The Radical Republicans enact a program of reconstruction

See Teaching Suggestions in TMRG, p.TM116.
By their refusal in December 1865 to seat the southern members of Congress, the Radical Republicans gained control of both houses of Congress. Within a few months, they restored military rule in the South and sowed long-lasting seeds of bitterness.

The first steps. Congress immediately appointed a joint committee of six Senators and nine Representatives to study the entire question of reconstruction. While Congress waited for the committee's report, it passed a bill enlarging the powers of the Freedmen's Bureau. The new law gave the bureau power to

▲ Charles Sumner stated such strong antislavery views that a southern senator once beat him severely in the Senate chamber. Thaddeus Stevens believed so strongly in equality that he asked to be buried in a cemetery for blacks.

prosecute in military courts, rather than in civil courts, any person accused of depriving freed slaves of their civil rights. President Johnson promptly vetoed the bill. He argued (1) that trial by military courts violated the Fifth Amendment of the Constitution and (2) that Congress had no power to pass *any* laws with 11 states unrepresented. Johnson's veto infuriated the Radical Republicans, who finally gathered enough votes to pass the bill over the President's veto.

In the meantime, Congress passed a civil rights bill. It was the first in a series of federal acts designed to give black Americans full citizenship and guarantee them complete equality of treatment. Johnson also vetoed this bill on the ground that it was an unconstitutional invasion of states' rights. Enough moderate Republicans joined the Radicals to pass the Civil Rights Act over Johnson's veto.

Johnson's vetoes cost him the support of moderate Republicans who, without any desire to punish white southerners, believed that Congress should protect the rights of former slaves. The vetoes also strengthened the influence of Thaddeus Stevens and the other Radical Republicans.

The Fourteenth Amendment. Congress feared that the Supreme Court might declare the Civil Rights Act unconstitutional. It decided to write the provisions of the act into the Constitution by amendment. This amendment, the Fourteenth, was the outcome of compromise between moderate and Radical Republicans. Some Radicals had hoped to outlaw all forms of racial segregation and discrimination. That objective does not seem to have been shared by the moderates, nor even by all Radicals who shaped the Amendment.

The Fourteenth Amendment (pages 211–12) made black Americans citizens of the United States and of the states in which they lived. It forbade states to deprive citizens of the rights of life, liberty, and property without **due process of law** or to deny any citizen the **equal protection of the laws.** It went further and excluded former Confederate leaders from holding public office, state or federal. It provided for reduction of Congressional representation of states that deprived black Americans of their rights as citizens. The amendment also forbade southern states to repay Confederate war debts or to pay former slaveowners for the loss of their slaves.

Congressional elections of 1866. Tennessee ratified the Fourteenth Amendment in July 1866 and was immediately readmitted to the Union. On the advice of President Johnson, all of the other southern states rejected the amendment by overwhelming votes.

What would Congress do next? The answer depended in part on the Congressional elections in the fall of 1866. If the Democrats won control of Congress, they might return to Lincoln's and Johnson's programs or modify them. If the Republicans won, they might fight for further restrictions on the political role of the former Confederates and for stronger guarantees of the rights of blacks.

Several events helped to swing voters toward the Republicans. Violent race riots were especially influential in shaping public opinion. In Memphis, Tennessee, 46 blacks were killed and 12 black schools and 4 black churches were burned. In a riot at New Orleans, about 200 people, mostly black, were killed or wounded. Many northerners, shocked by such violence, began to feel that perhaps the Radical Republicans were right to demand further federal protection for the freed slaves.

In the late summer of 1866, President Johnson made a trip to Chicago, stopping along the way to make election speeches. When opponents heckled him, Johnson's answers often seemed to reflect a lack of understanding of the election issues, as well as bitter hatred of Radical Republicans. His language, often blunt and crude, antagonized many voters.

More important, however, as a reason for Republican strength was the memory of the war itself. During the terrible conflict, both sides had suffered immense casualties. Voters, fearful of losing the fruits of hard-won military victory, voted for Republican candidates.

In the election the Republicans increased their hold on both houses of Congress. With more than a two-thirds majority in both the Senate and the House, the Republicans, if they held together, could now override Johnson's Presidential vetoes.

Reconstructing the South. In March 1867 a combination of Radical and moderate Republicans passed, over Johnson's vetoes, a complete program for reconstruction. The new program contained five major provisions.

First, Congress divided the ten southern states that had rejected the Fourteenth Amendment into five military districts. Each

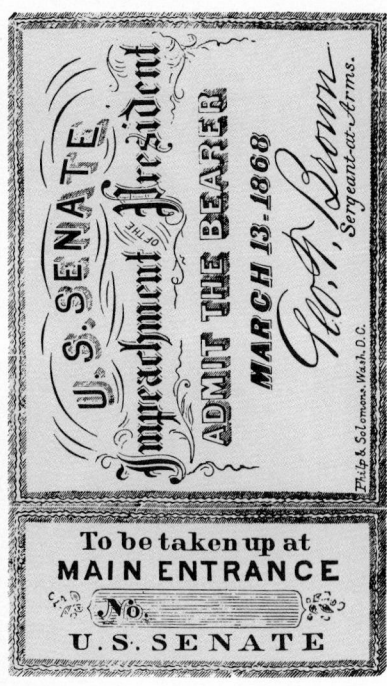

In February 1868 this House committee, led by an old, ill, and unforgiving Thaddeus Stevens (standing), drafted the articles of impeachment against President Johnson. Tickets for the trial that followed were in great demand.

district was under a military governor, with federal troops to maintain law and order while the states drafted new constitutions and organized new governments.

Second, Congress deprived most former Confederate leaders of the right to vote and hold office. The restrictions were the same as those that had already been written into the Fourteenth Amendment.

Third, Congress gave the freed slaves the right to vote and hold office.

Fourth, Congress authorized the states to write new constitutions that guaranteed freed slaves the right to vote.

Fifth, Congress required the states to ratify the Fourteenth Amendment.

The white southern governments that had been formed under the Presidential plan of reconstruction now had no choice but to accept the new program. One by one, the states held conventions and drafted new constitutions. They then organized their new governments and entered the Union under the terms that were laid down by Congress.

Johnson's impeachment and trial. By the summer of 1868, all but three southern states had returned to the Union on the terms laid down by Congress. (Mississippi, Texas, and Virginia finally accepted the terms and were readmitted in 1870.) Meanwhile, the Radical Republicans determined to remove their hated enemy, President Johnson, from office.

Several things led the Radical Republicans to this decision. They certainly were affected by the emotional hatreds and tensions of the times. More important, the Radicals knew that the success of their reconstruction program depended heavily on its enforcement. They were convinced that Johnson would not enforce Congressional policy. He confirmed their suspicions when, by executive order, he restricted the power of military commanders in the South and removed commanders known to be sympathetic to Radical programs.

To find grounds for **impeachment** and to reduce the President's power, Congress in 1867 adopted the Tenure of Office° Act over Johnson's veto. Under this law the President could not dismiss important civil officers without the Senate's consent. Believing the law unconsti-

°tenure of office: the period during which an individual has the right to continue in office.

"Let Us Have Peace" was Ulysses S. Grant's campaign slogan in the 1868 Presidential election. This campaign poster plays up Grant's war record, which was the source of his great popularity.

tutional, Johnson decided to put it to a test. In February 1868 he demanded the resignation of Secretary of War Edwin M. Stanton. Stanton had consistently cooperated with Johnson's political enemies.

The House immediately adopted a resolution that "Andrew Johnson, President of the United States, be impeached of high crimes and misdemeanors in office." The Radicals also charged that Johnson "did attempt to bring into disgrace, ridicule, contempt, and reproach the Congress of the United States." The Radicals cited occasions when the President publicly made "with a loud voice certain intemperate, inflammatory, and scandalous harangues" against Congress "and did therein utter loud threats and bitter menaces."

Under the Constitution a President may be impeached on grounds of "treason, bribery, or other high crimes and misdemeanors" (pages 191 and 202). Although the charges brought by the House against President Johnson were of doubtful legality, he was nevertheless impeached.

Johnson's trial before the Senate, presided over by Chief Justice Salmon P. Chase, lasted about two months. After prolonged debate it became clear that Johnson was not guilty of any offense for which he could legally be removed from office. Nevertheless, when the Senate vote was counted, it stood 35 to 19 against Johnson, just one vote short of the necessary two-thirds majority required for removal from office. Johnson continued to serve as President for almost a year, until his term expired, but his influence was at an end.

Decline of Radical power. It soon became apparent, however, that the Radical Republicans had overreached themselves. When they tried to remove the President from office, they lost the support of many moderate Republicans. Moreover, public opinion finally began to turn against them.

As the election of 1868 approached, the Republicans realized they were in trouble. In hopes of winning the election, they unanimously nominated Ulysses S. Grant for the Presidency. Grant had no political experience. He did not share the moral conviction of many Radical Republicans of the need to protect the freed slaves. Nevertheless, he was popular as a war hero.

The Democrats chose as their Presidential candidate Horatio Seymour, a wealthy New Yorker and former governor of his state. The Democratic platform denounced the Radical Republican program of reconstruction, declaring it unconstitutional. It also condemned the Radicals for their attempt to remove Johnson from office.

Economic issues were also important in the election of 1868. The platform of the Democratic Party, for example, favored a **cheap money policy**. During the war the federal government had issued $450 million in paper money known as "greenbacks." After the war, in 1866, the Republican Congress had provided for the gradual withdrawal of the greenbacks from circulation. By 1868 nearly $100 million had been withdrawn. In their 1868 platform the Democrats promised, if elected, to reverse this policy and reissue the paper money. The Democrats knew that this "cheap money" plank would antagonize wealthy bondholders.

▲   Class activity: Ask students to define the meanings of "treason," "bribery," "high crime," and "misdemeanor." Have the students consult a dictionary if necessary. Then have students compare the Constitutional grounds for impeachment with the charges brought against President Johnson.

Those bondholders fully expected that the money they had lent the government would be repaid in gold. The Democrats also knew that the proposal would appeal to many less well-to-do voters, particularly those who owed money. With more currency in circulation, debtors could more easily pay off their debts.

Republican candidate Ulysses S. Grant barely squeaked through to victory. Although he won by an electoral vote of 214 to 80, capturing 24 of the 36 states, his popular majority was only 309,000 out of almost 6 million votes.

The Radical Republicans studied the election returns with growing concern. They realized that many voters had turned against the Republicans because of their **hard money policy.** They also realized that the black vote had made possible their thin majority of the popular vote.

The Fifteenth Amendment. With this disturbing conclusion in mind, the Radicals drew up the Fifteenth Amendment and submitted it to the states for ratification. The Fifteenth Amendment was short and to the point: "The right of citizens of the United States to vote shall not be denied or abridged by the United States or any state on account of race, color, or previous condition of servitude."

The Fifteenth Amendment was ratified by the necessary three fourths of the states and became part of the Constitution in 1870. Mississippi, Texas, and Virginia—the last three southern states to return to the Union—were required to ratify the amendment as a condition for readmission.

Women, you recall, made many contributions to Union victory in the Civil War. Leaders of the women's rights movement expected, in return, that women would now receive the same legal protections and voting rights as blacks. Despite their protests, women were included in neither the Fourteenth nor the Fifteenth Amendments.

SECTION REVIEW
See underscored items, text pp. 454-56.
Identify: Civil Rights Act, impeachment, Tenure of Office Act, Ulysses S. Grant, cheap money policy
For answers to questions, see Answer Key, p.A65.
1. **Interpreting Ideas: (a)** Explain how the new Freedmen's Bureau law and the Civil Rights Act aimed at protecting the freed slaves. **(b)** Why did Johnson veto both laws? **(c)** What were some of the results of Johnson's vetoes?

2. **Organizing Ideas:** Describe the five major provisions of the Congressional reconstruction plan.

3. **Determining Cause and Effect: (a)** Why was Johnson impeached? **(b)** What were the consequences of his impeachment?

4. **Analyzing Sources:** Read **(a)** the Fourteenth Amendment and **(b)** the Fifteenth Amendment on pages 211–13 and summarize the main ideas of each. **(c)** Why did Congress propose the Fourteenth Amendment? **(d)** What did the Fifteenth Amendment do for the status of women?

4 White southerners regain control of their state governments

See Teaching Suggestions in TMRG, p.TM117.

The program of the Radical Republicans for reconstruction brought far-reaching changes to the South, but only for a short time. For varying periods—as long as ten years in only three states—Radical Republicans and their allies controlled the former Confederate states.

Help from the North. In the ten years after the surrender of the Confederacy, the main concern of the federal government was the restoration of the Union. Providing aid to the war-ravaged South and to needy southerners took second place. The Freedmen's Bureau was severely limited by lack of funds and by opposition from most southerners and many northerners. Its work was supplemented, however, by teachers and missionaries, black as well as white. Most of the northern volunteers were moved by humanitarian and democratic ideals. Many won the confidence of the men, women, and children whom they had come to help. Others, equally well-meaning but unfamiliar with southern ways of life and perhaps less tactful, antagonized the people with whom they tried to work.

Carpetbaggers and scalawags. White southerners especially resented the arrival in the South of northerners whom they jeeringly called <u>carpetbaggers</u>. This nickname implied, wrongly, that the newcomers were all fly-by-night adventurers who carried everything they owned in suitcases made of carpeting material, which were common at the time.

▲ Under reconstruction, 700,000 blacks registered to vote in the occupied southern states. The number of whites registered to vote was 620,000.

457

In 1870, the Mississippi legislature chose Hiram Revels to serve in the United States Senate. The significance of that act: Hiram Revels became the first black person to serve in United States Congress.

Revels was ordained a minister in the African Methodist Church in 1845 and served several congregations in the Midwest. He finally settled in Baltimore, where he became pastor of a church and principal of a school for blacks. During the Civil War, Revels organized two regiments of black soldiers and served as a chaplain in the Union Army. In 1863, he went to St. Louis to establish a school for blacks.

After the war Revels helped the Freedmen's Bureau set up schools throughout Mississippi. Hoping to give direction to Mississippi's reconstruction, he entered politics in 1868, serving as an alderman and as a state senator.

Then came Revels' historic appointment to the United States Senate to complete Jefferson Davis' term. Revels served with dignity in the Senate, displaying intelligence and integrity.

The carpetbaggers came for many different reasons. Some sincerely wanted to help the freed slaves exercise their newly acquired rights. Some hoped to get themselves elected to political office. Some came to make their fortunes by acquiring farmland or by starting new businesses. However, some came for reasons of pure greed or fraud. Horace Greeley, the editor of the *New York Tribune,* wrote that such carpetbaggers were "stealing and plundering, many of them with both arms around the Negroes, and their hands in their rear pockets, seeing if they cannot pick a paltry dollar out of them."

Most white southerners and some northerners scorned the northern carpetbaggers who moved into the South. Especially strong scorn and abuse were directed toward those native-born southerners who had chosen to cooperate with the northern authorities.

Some of these native-born southerners had the best of motives. Having opposed slavery and secession, they had sympathized with the Union during the war. Now they believed that the best way to restore peace and prosperity to the South and to the nation was to forgive and forget. However, others were selfish and ambitious individuals who seized any opportunity to advance their own fortunes at the expense of their neighbors.

Whatever the motives of these native-born southerners, most were held in contempt by other white southerners. They were often referred to as **scalawags,** which was a word used to describe scoundrels.

Reconstruction governments. Such were the individuals who largely controlled southern state governments during part of the Radical reconstruction period. Northerners held most of the important political offices, at least during the early years. They were able to get themselves elected partly because they persuaded the freed slaves to vote for them. Also, many white southerners were deprived of the right to vote and others refused to take part in political activities.

The enormous influence of northerners in southern politics can be seen by examining the election results in the seven southern states readmitted to the Union by 1868. As a result of the first postwar elections held in these states, 4 of the 7 governors, 10 of the 14 United States Senators, and 20 of the 35 United States Representatives were carpetbaggers. In general, southern scalawags and freed slaves had to be

▲   Only southerners who had opposed the Confederacy could vote or hold office. These people were among those who were called "scalawags."

content with the less important state and federal offices.

Black southerners in public life. Blacks were elected to the southern reconstruction governments, and they played an important role in some of them. However, the black's role in these governments has often been exaggerated. Only one black American served briefly as a southern governor. In only one southern state—South Carolina—did black members for a time hold a majority in the state legislature. Only Mississippi sent black Senators, two of them, to Washington. One was Hiram Revels, a native of North Carolina who, after studying at Knox College in Illinois, had been a teacher and minister. The other was Blanche K. Bruce, who had escaped from slavery in Virginia and who had also been a teacher.

Many other blacks in reconstruction politics showed independence and political skill. Among them were Robert Brown Elliott of South Carolina, a brilliant lawyer and scholar, and P. B. S. Pinchback of Louisiana, son of a Mississippi planter and a black mother.

The blacks in public life during reconstruction did not demand revenge upon white southerners. In fact, most black leaders favored returning the right to vote to their former white masters. The records of those elected to the United States Congress compared well with the records of many of their white colleagues.

Reconstruction governments at work. The southern reconstruction legislatures started many needed and long overdue public improvements. The new legislatures, for example, strengthened public education and, for the first time, made it available to large numbers of black children.

The reconstruction governments also pushed forward other constructive programs. They spread the tax burden more equitably. They introduced overdue reforms in local government and the judicial system. They abolished imprisonment for debt. They extended the legal rights of women. They passed laws to protect homes and farms against illegal foreclosures—that is, against unjustified seizure by dishonest officials. Most of the southern state constitutions drafted during the period of reconstruction continued in effect for many years.

Such programs greatly increased the debts of the southern states. In addition, the reconstruction governments misspent huge amounts of money.

White southerners who had once dominated public life deplored large expenditures for needless luxuries authorized by legislators, white and black, in some reconstruction governments. They also denounced some reconstruction legislators for outright corruption.

Some of the new legislators were all too willing to enrich themselves while granting favorable railroad and corporation charters to business groups, often northern, who wanted to develop southern enterprises. However, southern Democrats who briefly controlled southern legislatures in the first years after the war had followed some of the same corrupt practices. As you will read, public morality in all sections of the United States sank to an extremely low level during the years following the Civil War.

Secret societies. Whatever the merits and demerits of the reconstruction governments may have been, most white southerners resented them. Since many former Confederate leaders were denied the vote and since others chose to boycott politics, some white southerners expressed their opposition by defying the law through intimidation and violence. By 1867 some white southerners were attacking carpetbaggers, scalawags, and politically active black southerners through a number of secret societies. The best known were the Knights of the White Camellia and the Ku Klux Klan.

These secret organizations tried to frighten black southerners and their white sympathizers into staying out of politics. Bands of hooded members clad in ghostly white costumes rode through the countryside at night, stopping now and then at a house to issue warnings. When warnings failed, cabins and churches were burned and some freed slaves were beaten or killed. White sympathizers and friends of blacks sometimes received the same treatment. Moderate white southerners, disgusted with the brutality and fearful of northern reaction, disapproved of these actions. However, for a time they were unable to prevent them.

Congress tried to end the lawlessness by passing a series of Military Enforcement Acts, sometimes called the Force Acts (1870–71). These acts gave the President power to use federal military forces to control the secret societies, to call upon the state militias when neces-

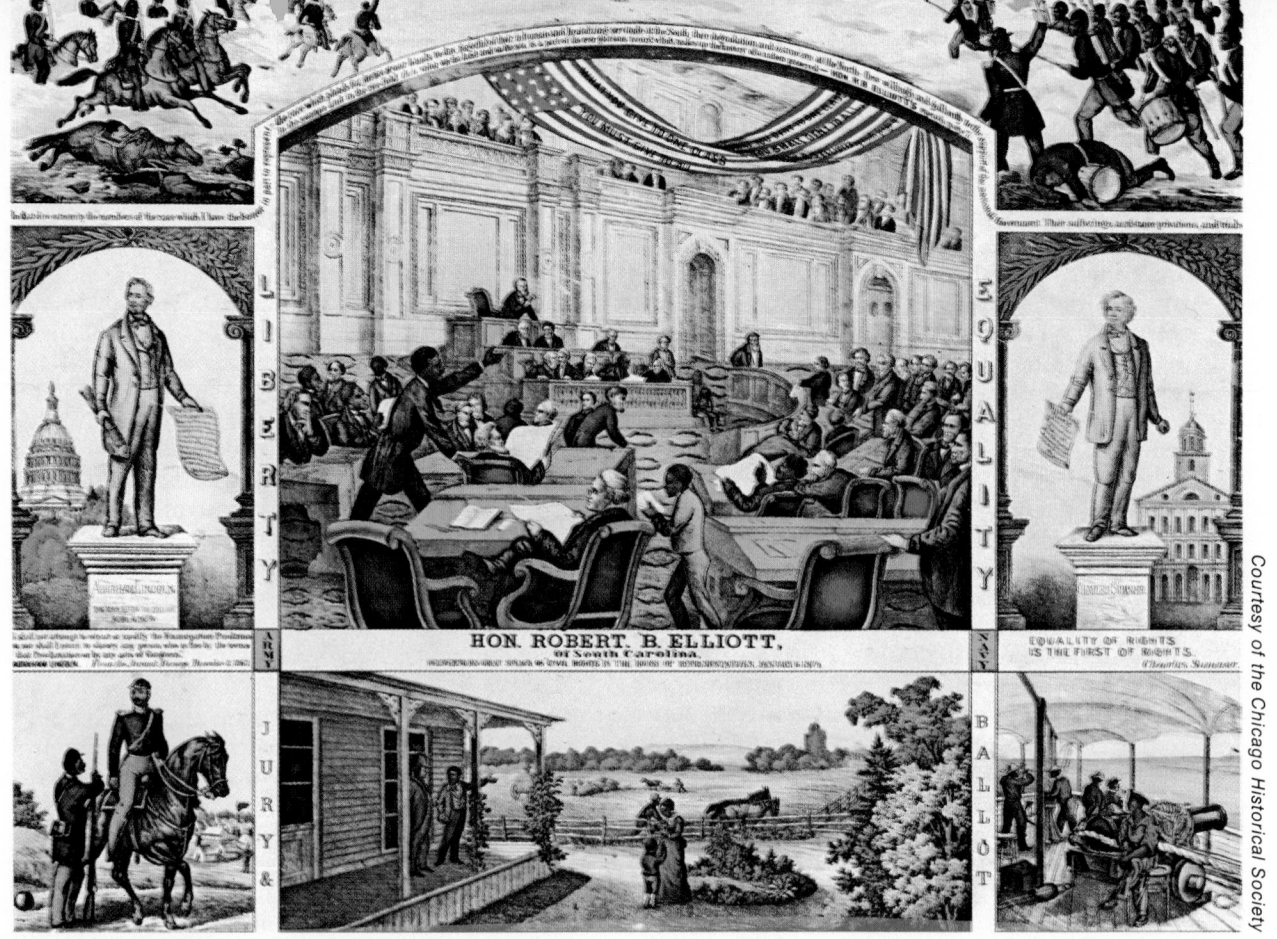

HON. ROBERT. B. ELLIOTT,
of South Carolina

This magazine illustration features Representative Robert Brown Elliott speaking to Congress in 1874. The words at the top are his: "What you give to one class, you must give to all. What you deny to one class, you shall deny to all."

sary, and to suspend the writ of *habeas corpus*. They also provided for federal supervision of southern elections.

To many white southerners, the Force Acts seemed unduly harsh. Yet compared with the treatment of the losers in civil wars elsewhere, the former Confederates were not severely punished. There were never more than 25,000 federal troops in the occupied states after the war. No political leader was executed, few were imprisoned, and President Johnson made liberal use of his pardoning power. Jefferson Davis, for example, was released from prison within two years. Except for the loss of slaves, property was seldom seized by the federal government as punishment for what many northerners regarded as treason.

Further leniency prevailed in 1872, when Congress passed the <u>Amnesty Act</u>. This act restored political rights, including the right to vote, to about 160,000 former Confederates.

After 1872 only about 500 white southerners were still barred from political activity.

The Force Acts, the withdrawal of many southerners from the secret societies, and finally the Amnesty Act virtually ended the power of the Ku Klux Klan and other such groups at that time. Most white southerners began to vote again, and white southern leadership reemerged. The reconstruction governments in several states were thus replaced by governments representing traditional white southern rule.

The end of reconstruction. During the early 1870's, northerners began to lose interest in the problems of southern reconstruction. Radical Republican power and leadership was diminished by the death of Thaddeus Stevens in 1868 and of Charles Sumner in 1874.

At first many northerners had championed the cause of the freed slaves. Now they became

▲ Discussion topic: The amnesty granted Civil War participants compared with the amnesty granted Vietnam War draft evaders. (Note: All Vietnam War draft evaders were threatened with prison sentences before amnesty was granted; only leaders of the Confederacy were threatened with prison.)

disillusioned at reports, often exaggerated, of the political ineptness of black southerners. Some northerners seemed to ignore the fact that the former slaves had little, if any, education and no political experience. Other northerners grew weary of the problems of black southerners and less willing to press for an effective program to help them learn their new roles as citizens.

Many northerners began to say that perhaps the freed slaves *did* need the supervision of white southern leaders. Perhaps it would be better, they now said, to let southerners work out their own problems of government and race relations. Northerners justified their retreat by referring to the Constitution, which left many powers in the hands of the states. No doubt many northerners, sincere enough earlier in demanding equal rights for the freed slaves, were increasingly and uncomfortably aware that blacks were not treated as equal citizens in most northern states. Thus many northerners now found it easier to concentrate on strengthening national unity and to give less attention to the rights of black Americans. This attitude was shared by a growing number of northern businesses. It was clear that a disorganized, poverty-stricken South was not good for business on either side of the Mason-Dixon line.

In 1877 the last of the federal troops of occupation were withdrawn from the southern states, ending the reconstruction era. Reconstruction left many major problems unsolved and created new and equally urgent problems. This was true even though many forces in the North and the South continued working to reconcile the two sections.

SECTION REVIEW

See underscored items, text pp. 457-60.
Identify: carpetbagger, scalawag, Hiram Revels, Knights of the White Camelia, Force Acts, Amnesty Act
For answers to questions, see Answer Key, pp.A65-66.
1. **Evaluating Ideas:** How successful were the reconstruction governments?
2. **Determining Cause and Effect:** (a) Why did some white southerners form secret societies such as the Ku Klux Klan during reconstruction? (b) How did the federal government react to the secret societies?
3. **Analyzing Viewpoints:** (a) How did racial prejudice in the North influence the attitudes of some northerners toward reconstruction? (b) For what reasons did the carpetbaggers go to the South?

The New South advances in agriculture, industry, and education

See Teaching Suggestions in TMRG, pp.TM117-18.

During the 1880's many southerners started to speak of the "New South." Those who used this term urged southerners to abandon the system of **one-crop agriculture**, developing instead, all the resources of a rich land. Above all, those who shared these beliefs urged southerners to build up the region's manufacturing industries.

Breakup of plantations. One characteristic of the postwar South was the breakup of many, though by no means all, of the large plantations. This process started in 1865, immediately after the war ended. Planters, who had little if any cash to hire farm laborers, sold portions of their plantations to the more prosperous independent farmers. Between 1865 and 1880, the number of small farms more than doubled, while the size of the average southern farm decreased.

Some black southerners, who had emerged from slavery without education, without land, and almost without clothes, also benefited from the breakup of the large plantations. As the years passed, a small but growing number of former slaves acquired small farms.

Tenant farming and sharecropping. While some poor white southerners and a few black southerners became owners of small farms, many others became **tenant farmers.** Under this system, a planter usually rented portions of the plantation to several tenants, who supplied their own seed, mules, and provisions. The owner managed the scattered tenant holdings much as if these made up the old-time plantation. Thus some advantages of large-scale production were retained. Many tenants remained tenants all their lives. Others saved enough to buy land and become small landowners.

Less fortunate was the **sharecropper.** This farm worker furnished nothing but labor, getting a cabin, seed, tools, a mule, and a plot of land from the owner. In return for farming this land, the sharecropper received a percentage of the crop. Since sharecroppers did not get paid until harvesttime, they had to buy provisions

461

Savannah, Georgia, had been badly damaged during Union General William T. Sherman's "March to the Sea" in 1864. After the war Savannah was rebuilt. The city soon became an important cotton port on the Savannah River.

for their families on credit. To obtain credit, they had to give a lien, or mortgage, on the crops they expected to plant and harvest. The debts they could not pay at harvesttime were added to the bill to be paid a year later.

When the crops were harvested, almost all of the sharecroppers' share of the money usually went to pay their bills. Because they also had to pay interest on this debt, sharecroppers found it very difficult to get out of debt. As long as they were in debt, they were practically bound to the soil, since the law forbade them to leave the state until their bills were paid. Frequently the owner of the land also owned the store where the sharecroppers could buy their supplies on credit. Since the sharecroppers were seldom free from debt and almost never had any cash, they had to buy at the owner's store and go deeper into debt.

Many sharecroppers raised only cotton or tobacco since the landowner insisted on cultivating these crops exclusively. The owner argued that the sharecroppers did not know anything about other crops and that cotton and tobacco were the only dependable cash crops.

Although tenant farming and sharecropping existed in other parts of the country, these practices were especially widespread in the South. Indeed, tenant farming and sharecropping provided a workable solution to the frequently desperate economic situation of the postwar years. At the same time, they also made it difficult for the South to abandon its traditional one-crop system and to develop a diversified farming economy.

Agricultural progress. Despite the problems facing southern farmers, the South made considerable progress during the postwar years. Southerners, like farmers elsewhere in the nation, benefited from new developments in science and technology. During the 1870's and 1880's, improved machines for sowing, cultivating, fertilizing, and reaping were introduced. In 1872 both Alabama and Virginia established agricultural colleges. By 1900 all the other southern states had followed their example.

Cotton continued to be the most important single crop. Indeed, by 1871 the South was growing more cotton than it had in 1860. The older states increased their yield per acre by using commercial fertilizers and improved farming methods. Much of the total increase, however, came from the opening of new cotton lands in the Southwest. By 1900 Texas alone was planting and harvesting one third of all the nation's cotton.

Improved farming methods led to greatly increased production of tobacco, rice, sugar, corn, and other traditional crops. However, the most important change in southern agricultural life was the development of truck farming and fruit growing. Because of the growth of railroads and the invention of the refrigerator car, fresh vegetables and fruit could be shipped to northern cities. The long growing season in the South and an abundance of cheap labor also stimulated truck farming. As early as 1900, thousands of refrigerator cars were rolling northward with welcome cargoes of vegetables, watermelons, strawberries, oranges, apples, and peaches.

Industrial progress. An even more remarkable development in the New South was the growth of industry. In industry as in agriculture, the South responded to forces that were transforming economic life in other regions of the United States and, for that matter, in most of Europe.

Southern industrial development actually started before the outbreak of the Civil War. By 1860 about 10 percent of the manufactured wealth of the United States came from southern textile mills, ironworks, lumber projects, and sugar refineries. The war and reconstruction ruined many southern industries, and for nearly 20 years the South made little industrial progress.

By the late 1870's, more and more southerners felt that southern progress depended upon industrialization. The development of industry would enable the South to make better use of its rich natural resources.

Money to build factories, mines, steel mills, railroads, and other industries came in part from northern investors and in still larger part from the South itself. Profits from expanding agriculture were poured into new industrial ventures. In community after community, the people themselves gathered in mass assemblies to plan a factory, often a textile mill, and to raise the necessary capital. By 1900 more than 400 cotton textile mills had been built. Throughout the South farming villages were transformed into mill towns within a few short years. Poor whites provided most of the labor for the new factories. Black laborers were almost entirely excluded from the new industrial development.

Southern Workers Employed in Manufacturing • 1870-1910

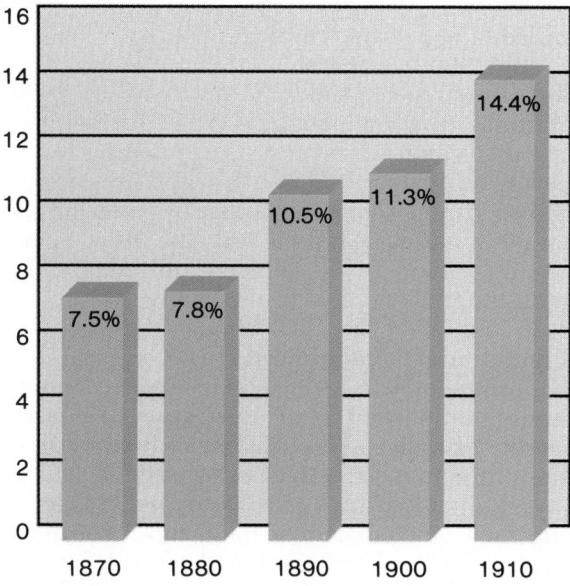

Percentage of Total Work Force

Source: *Regions, Resources & Economic Growth*

Many early mills were controlled by a single family or a small group of persons. They owned the houses in which the workers lived, the stores where they bought their goods, and the other town buildings. The men and women who worked in these mills depended on the owners for their jobs and had to spend their wages to rent company-owned dwellings and to buy supplies from company-owned stores. As a result, the labor organizations that were rapidly growing in the North during these years made little headway in the South.

The growth of southern industry also depended on improvements and extensions of southern railroads. The war left southern railroads in terrible condition, but old railroads were quickly rebuilt, and new lines constructed. By 1890 the southern railroad system was twice as large as in 1860.

Industrial development in the New South led to the growth of cities. Between 1870 and 1890 Durham, North Carolina, developed from a small village to a flourishing tobacco center.

Richmond, Virginia, and Nashville, Tennessee, became leading urban centers. The population of Atlanta, Georgia, increased from 37,000 to 65,000 between 1880 and 1890. Birmingham, Alabama, founded in 1871 on the site of a former cotton field, within a few years became a bustling iron and steel center, often called "the Pittsburgh of the South."

By 1900, southern manufactured products were worth four times as much as in 1860. With its growing industrial cities, its factories and mills and mines, and its developing transportation system, the South was beginning to be more and more like other regions of the United States. Nevertheless, the New South had a long way to go to catch up industrially with other sections of the country.

Educational developments. During the closing years of the 1800's, able and far-seeing leaders urged southerners to improve their educational system and thus make better use of their human resources. Southern education did improve, but every forward step was taken in the face of tremendous handicaps. Southern leaders had to deal with widespread poverty despite improving economic conditions. There was also a traditional reluctance to support public education with tax money. Maintaining separate schools for white and black children added to the cost of education.

Among the outstanding contributions to southern education were the gifts of northern **philanthropists.** Especially noteworthy were the gifts of George Peabody and John F. Slater, both northern millionaires. The Peabody Fund was created in 1867, the Slater Fund in 1882. Money from these funds helped to provide educational opportunities for white and black southerners alike in the postwar years.

The money from private sources, however, was only a fraction of what was needed. Most of the burden of rebuilding schools and opening up educational opportunities for whites as well as blacks had to be shouldered by the southern states. Slowly, as the economic situation improved, the South provided more opportunities.

The "Solid South." Most southerners belonged to the Democratic Party. There were southern Republicans, to be sure, but they were completely outnumbered in local, state, and national elections. For example, when the Presidential elections rolled around, the former Confederate states cast all their electoral votes for the Democratic candidates. Thus people began to refer to the southern states as the "Solid South."

The "Solid South" was born during reconstruction days, when Radical Republican governments controlled the southern states. In their determination to rid themselves of Republican rule, white southerners poured into the Democratic Party. After 1877, when the last federal troops were withdrawn from the South, most white southerners continued to support the Democratic Party.

SECTION REVIEW
See underscored items, text pp. 461, 464.
Identify: New South, one-crop agriculture, the Pittsburgh of the South, philanthropist, George Peabody, John Slater, Solid South
For answers to questions, see Answer Key, p.A66.
1. **Analyzing Ideas: (a)** Define tenant farming and sharecropping. **(b)** Explain why they were common in the postwar South. **(c)** Why was it hard for a tenant farmer or sharecropper to become a farm owner?
2. **Determining Cause and Effect:** Why did the South generally support the Democratic Party after the Civil War?
3. **Organizing Ideas:** Outline the progress made in the South in the areas of **(a)** agriculture, **(b)** industry, and **(c)** education.
4. **Studying Graphics:** Look at the graph on page 463. What does the graph tell you about the growth of industry in the South after the Civil War?

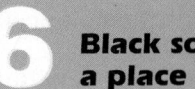

6 Black southerners struggle for a place in the New South

See Teaching Suggestions in TMRG, p.TM118.
Many black southerners had hoped to share in the progress of the New South and in the nation's ideals of freedom and equality. They did not for several reasons. First, the federal government suspended its programs for helping black southerners make the transition from slavery to freedom. Second, whites in both the North and South continued to think of blacks not as equals but as inferiors. Third, white southerners feared that the white southern way of life would be threatened if blacks were not firmly "kept in their place."

▲ Class activity: Have students draw conclusions about the relationship between the South's growing industry and its education system. (Note: The South needed trained workers; money from industry could help improve education.)

Cartoonist Thomas Nast depicted a black man casting his vote in an election shortly after the Civil War. Who do you think the figures on the left represent?

Preventing blacks from voting. For more than ten years after white southern Democrats regained control of southern governments in 1877, many blacks continued to vote. A few even held public office.

Early in the 1890's, however, the new Populist Party threatened the power of both the Democratic and Republican parties (see Chapter 20). In the South, Populist organizers had their greatest success among poor white people, but some also worked hard to win the support of black voters. Southern Democrats, alarmed by this development, attempted to prevent blacks from voting.

Beginning with Mississippi in 1890, the southern states adopted laws and framed new constitutions that in effect kept most blacks from voting on grounds other than "race, color, or previous condition of servitude." By the early 1900's, the guarantees of civil rights in the Fourteenth and Fifteenth Amendments had become largely ineffective in the South. In most areas, few blacks voted and fewer still held public office, even in minor positions.

A number of states adopted a **poll tax**—a fixed tax imposed on every voter—and also a **literacy test**—and examination to determine whether a person can read or write. Since many black southerners had little money and

little, if any, education, these laws kept large numbers from voting.

The poll tax and the literacy test also deprived many poor whites of the vote. To remedy this situation, several states, starting with Louisiana in 1898, added a **grandfather clause** to their constitutions. This clause declared that even if a man could not pay the poll tax or pass the literacy test, he could still vote if he had been eligible to do so on January 1, 1867, or if he were the son or the grandson of a man who had been eligible to vote on January 1, 1867. The grandfather clause was declared unconstitutional by the Supreme Court in 1915. While it was in force, it kept many black southerners from voting.

Segregating the races. Meanwhile, a pattern of <u>segregation</u>, or separation, of white and black southerners was taking shape.

Except in a few instances, the Radical Republicans had not tried to bring white and black children together in southern public schools. However, black and white southerners used the same transportation facilities and other public services. The Civil Rights Act of 1875 had declared that "all persons within the jurisdiction of the United States shall be entitled to the full and equal enjoyment of the ac-

▲ Note: Answers to questions in captions appear in parentheses, as shown here. Bullets separate answers to individual questions when a caption contains more than one question.

465

The Jim Crow system of racial segregation in the South would not have been nearly so effective had it not been sanctioned by a series of Supreme Court decisions in the late 1800's. The most important and far-reaching of these decisions was rendered in *Plessy v. Ferguson* (1896), in which the Court upheld a Louisiana law requiring railroads "to provide equal but separate accommodations for the white and colored races."

The case began when a group of black citizens in New Orleans decided to test the constitutionality of the segregation law, which they believed to be in violation of the Fourteenth Amendment. They recruited a volunteer — Homer Plessy — to buy a railroad ticket and sit in the "whites only" section of the train. Plessy did so and was arrested.

Ruling on the case four years later, the Supreme Court declared that the Fourteenth Amendment "could not have been intended to abolish distinctions based upon color, or to enforce social, as distinguished from political equality . . ."

In upholding the constitutionality of separate-but-equal facilities, the Supreme Court opened the door for widespread racial repression in the South. As one historian wrote, "The South's adoption of extreme racism was due not so much to a conversion as it was to a relaxation of the opposition." The Supreme Court's attitude stated in the *Plessy v. Ferguson* decision signaled the end of legal opposition to segregation. A half-century of legally-justified discrimination had begun.

commodations, advantages, facilities, and privileges of inns, public conveyances on land or water, theaters and other places of public amusement; subject only to the conditions and limitations established by law and applicable alike to citizens of every race and color, regardless of any previous condition of servitude."

Even after white southern rule was restored in 1877, southerners of both races often used the same transportation facilities and other public services. Then in 1883 the Supreme Court ruled against the Civil Rights Act of 1875 on the ground that the Fourteenth Amendment forbade only states, not individuals or corporations (such as railroads), from discriminating against black citizens. In spite of their decision, black and white southerners in many places continued to use the same public accommodations.

In 1881 Tennessee passed the first of the so-called "Jim Crow" laws. Under this law, white southerners and black southerners were required to ride in separate railway cars. Other states followed Tennessee's example. By the 1890's all southern states required such separation, not only in schools but in streetcars, railroads, and railroad stations. Within a few years, this pattern of segregation spread to parks, playgrounds, and other public facilities.

In 1896 the Supreme Court added legal support to segregation. In the case of *Plessy v. Ferguson*, the Court ruled that it was not a violation of the Fourteenth Amendment to provide **separate but equal** facilities for blacks. This 1896 ruling by the Supreme Court was a serious blow to the efforts of black Americans to improve their lives.

Black southerners' reactions.   Confronted by segregation and denied their political and civil rights, some black southerners migrated to other nearby states, such as Oklahoma and Kansas, or moved to the growing northern cities. Most, however, stayed in the South and worked to develop their own black communities. Black southerners strengthened their own churches, lodges, and mutual aid societies, developed their own businesses, and, against handicaps, tried to secure an education. Their efforts began to produce results. In 1865 only about 5 percent of all black adults could read and write. By 1900 more than 50 percent possessed these basic skills.

Southern black leaders also protested the growing pattern of segregation and discrimination and the denial of civil rights guaranteed by the Fourteenth Amendment. On the lecture platform, in churches, in the press, and in conventions, they demanded their constitutional rights. In 1889 the former black abolitionist Frederick Douglass, now an old man, asked whether "American justice, American liberty, American civilization, American law, and American Christianity could be made to include and protect alike and forever all American citizens in the rights which have been

▲   Ironically, the term "Jim Crow" derived from the stage name of a popular white performer in the 1800's, Thomas D. Rice, who performed in blackface.

guaranteed to them by the organic and fundamental laws of the land."

In Baltimore, E. J. Waring, a black lawyer, urged blacks to fight discrimination by lawsuits against officials and citizens guilty of violating their rights. In Memphis, Ida Wells Barnett, teacher and publisher, was dismissed from teaching for denouncing the inferior segregated schools for black children. She then launched a single-handed crusade against black lynchings—that is, the murder of black people by white mobs. Even after a mob broke into her newspaper office and threatened her life, she persisted in exposing the evils of "lynch law."

Booker T. Washington. The leading black voice from 1890 to 1915 was that of Booker T. Washington. The son of a slave mother and a white father, Washington received a vocational education at Hampton Institute in Virginia. He then founded and built Tuskegee Institute in Alabama. Washington was convinced that vocational education, not classical or liberal arts education, was necessary to provide black people with the skills they needed to earn a living. He felt that such education would prepare blacks for jobs in the skilled trades, small businesses, farming, and household work.

Washington also spoke out against lynching and illegal discrimination, especially in the years just before his death in 1915. Generally, Washington remained convinced that black southerners would make greater progress by avoiding protests and emphasizing vocational training and by owning farms, homes, and small businesses.

W. E. B. Du Bois. Booker T. Washington's views met a strong challenge from a younger black, W. E. B. Du Bois (doo·BOYCE). Born and reared in western Massachusetts, Du Bois studied in German universities and earned his Ph.D. at Harvard. At first he felt that if white Americans came to understand past black achievements and present black conditions, their attitudes toward black Americans would in time improve.

Gradually, however, Du Bois came to believe that only vigorous and continuous protests against inequalities and injustices, and effective appeals to black pride, could change existing conditions. In *The Souls of Black Folk,* a book of eloquent essays, Du Bois criticized

Booker T. Washington's emphasis on vocational training. He urged broader educational opportunities, including liberal arts education, for blacks. Du Bois urged blacks to demand their rights to have whatever kind of education they needed to achieve full equality and opportunity in American life. Along with a few like-minded black leaders, he organized a meeting in 1905 at Niagara Falls that demanded an end to all unequal treatment based on race and color.

The appeals and demands of the Niagara Movement aroused many Americans, white as well as black. One outcome was the formation of the National Association for the Advancement of Colored People (NAACP). The NAACP worked through the courts to end restrictions on voting and other civil injustices. In time it succeeded in winning Supreme Court decisions that declared unconstitutional the grandfather clause in southern state constitutions, jury trials conducted under mob pressure, and segregation by local law of housing for black people. The Urban League, likewise organized by both blacks and whites, fought for equal job opportunities for black workers and against discrimination in urban housing.

The work of the NAACP and the Urban League brought some progress for black citizens in the North and West. These national organizations were also represented in the southern states, but they made less progress there. Most black southerners continued to experience discrimination, segregation, and denial of equal rights.

SECTION REVIEW

See underscored items, text pp. 465-67.

Identify: segregation, "Jim Crow" laws, *Plessy v. Ferguson,* Ida Wells Barnett, Booker T. Washington, W. E. B. Du Bois, NAACP, Urban League

For answers to questions, see Answer Key, p. A66.

1. **Interpreting Ideas:** Why did black southerners not share in the progress of the New South?
2. **Analyzing Ideas:** Explain how each of the following affected the right of black southerners to vote: (a) poll tax, (b) literacy test, (c) grandfather clause.
3. **Determining Cause and Effect:** (a) How was a new pattern of segregation established in the South? (b) How did the Supreme Court contribute to the separation of races?
4. **Comparing Viewpoints:** Describe the disagreement between (a) Booker T. Washington and (b) W. E. B. Du Bois over what blacks should do to improve their situation.

President Johnson's efforts to apply Lincoln's lenient reconstruction policy were effectively blocked by the Radical Republicans, who controlled Congress. For various reasons, the Radical Republicans were determined to impose their reconstruction plans upon the South.

Southern blacks were faced with the challenges of freedom—finding gainful employment, setting up households, going to school, and taking part in the political process. On the other hand, white southerners used every means to defeat the northern program of imposed reconstruction.

Eventually northerners went on to other interests and stopped trying to impose their will upon the South. In 1877 the last federal troops were withdrawn from the South.

During the 1880's and 1890's, the outline of a New South began to emerge. With the slow but steady development of a more varied agriculture, truck farmers shipped their fruits and vegetables to markets in the North. Southern mines supplied increasing amounts of ore to southern blast furnaces. As textile mills and other factories were constructed, quiet southern villages were transformed into thriving towns.

In 1900 the South, still basically an agricultural region, continued struggling to recover economically from the disasters of the war. Nonetheless, southerners were beginning to reap some of the same industrial gains made by northerners and westerners and were making great strides forward into the future. Blacks, however, still struggled to find a place for themselves in the New South.

CONNECTING CHAPTER IDEAS

In the next chapter you will read how widespread graft and corruption during the postwar years threatened the American political process. You will also read about reform groups and their efforts to eliminate dishonesty in government.

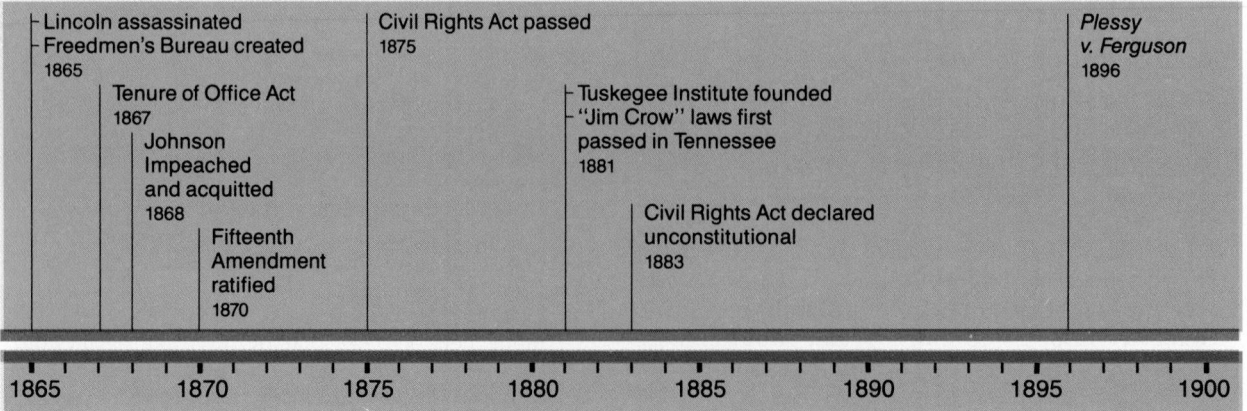

Lincoln assassinated
Freedmen's Bureau created
1865

Tenure of Office Act
1867

Johnson
Impeached
and acquitted
1868

Fifteenth
Amendment
ratified
1870

Civil Rights Act passed
1875

Tuskegee Institute founded
"Jim Crow" laws first
passed in Tennessee
1881

Civil Rights Act declared
unconstitutional
1883

*Plessy
v. Ferguson*
1896

1865   1870   1875   1880   1885   1890   1895   1900

CHAPTER
19 REVIEW

Reviewing Important Terms

Decide whether each of the following sentences is true or false. If the sentence is false, replace the underlined term with the word or phrase that will make it true.

1. During the Civil War, President Lincoln proposed a lenient policy of underline{reconstruction}, based on his theory that the Confederate states had never left the Union.
2. Northerners who held political office in the South after the Civil War were called underline{scalawags} by white southerners.
3. The underline{black codes} passed by state governments in the South, restricted the rights of southern black Americans.
4. The House of Representatives has the Constitutional power to initiate proceedings of underline{impeachment} against the President.

Practicing Critical Thinking Skills

1. **Interpreting Ideas.** How did the Supreme Court decision in *Plessy v. Ferguson* reflect the spirit of the times?
2. **Organizing Ideas.** (a) Why did the southern states pass the black codes and Jim Crow laws? (b) What restrictions were placed on black southerners by these statutes?
3. **Summarizing Ideas.** (a) What problems that caused the Civil War were solved by the war and reconstruction? (b) What new problems were caused by the war and reconstruction?
4. **Contrasting Ideas.** How was the New South that emerged during the 1880's and 1890's different from the prewar South?
5. **Comparing Ideas.** How did the federal government's attitude and actions toward minorities during reconstruction compare with the government's attitude and actions toward minorities today? Explain the reasons for the similarities and differences that you find.
6. **Analyzing Ideas.** Make a chart with two columns. In column one list the provisions of the Presidential plan for reconstruction. In column two list the provisions of the Congressional plan for reconstruction. Use your chart to write an essay that explains the differences between the two plans. Conclude your essay with a paragraph in which you indicate which plan you think would have been best for the United States.

7. **Relating Past to Present.** During reconstruction many northerners sincerely felt that only southerners were prejudiced against black Americans. Today there seems to be little difference among the various sections of the United States regarding racial prejudice. Write an essay in which you either agree or disagree with the above statements. Use specific examples to support your answer.

Developing History Study Skills

1. **Analyzing Viewpoints.** Reread "Johnson's impeachment and trial" on pages 455–56. (a) How did President Johnson's interpretation of the Tenure of Office Act differ from that of the Radical Republicans? (b) According to the Radical Republicans, what grounds were there to impeach President Johnson?
2. **Using Historical Imagination.** Read *Freedom Road* by Howard Fast, a novel about reconstruction. (a) Write an essay discussing how reconstruction changed the lives of the people Fast portrays. (b) Compare the novel's presentation of the period with the account in your textbook, discussing how it is similar and how it is different. (c) Account for the similarities and differences you discover.

Relating Geography and History

The New South grew out of the devastation of the Civil War and the changes of reconstruction. By the 1880's southern agriculture was producing a variety of new crops as well as a greater quantity of the traditional ones. Southern industry also had made great progress. To gain a better understanding of industrial development in the New South, complete the following activities.

1. Reread "The New South advances in agriculture, industry, and education" on pages 461–64.
2. Make a chart with three columns. In the first column name the raw materials available in the South in the late 1880's. In the second column name the industry or industries that each raw material might support. In the third column list the other factors that might contribute to the growth of each southern industry listed.

469

See Chapter Overview in TMRG, p.TM119.
See Chapter Objectives in TMRG, p.TM119.
See Introducing the Chapter in TMRG, p.TM119.

CHAPTER 20

Severe Trials for Democracy

(1865–1897)

A period of
scandals

Change is often disturbing, and in no period of American history was change more disturbing than in the decades following the Civil War. White and black southerners struggled to adjust their lives to the drastic changes that took place during the reconstruction period. Equally striking changes were occurring in the Northeast, the Middle West, and the West during these years of turmoil.

The major cause of these changes was the rapid growth of industry after the war. New power-driven machinery was invented and installed in large factories. Giant corporations were organized. Trusts, holding companies, and other methods evolved to consolidate businesses. New methods of mass production were adopted. These exciting developments made many new products and services available to more and more Americans and helped to raise their standard of living.

There were dark shadows, however, in this bright picture. As industries grew in the United States, American cities also grew and became overcrowded. Other problems arose with increasing industrialization and the growth of the cities—problems of sanitation, disease, fire, and transportation.

In order to understand this dramatic and disturbing period of American history clearly, it is necessary to look at it from several points of view. In this chapter you will see how graft and corruption plagued American political life during the postwar years. This graft and corruption posed a major threat to the workings of the American political system. In this chapter you will also learn how repeated efforts were made to root out this dishonesty in government. In later chapters you will see how increasing industrialization created many complex problems, not only for the owners of large and small businesses, but also for farmers, miners, and wage earners.

═══ READING FOCUS ═══

As you read about democracy's severe trials, look for the details that support each of the following statements.

1. Graft and corruption spread in the postwar years.
2. A start is made toward restoring honest government.
3. Efforts at political reform move forward.

1 Graft and corruption spread in the postwar years

See Teaching Suggestions in TMRG, pp.TM119-20.

As industry expanded after the Civil War, huge fortunes were made. Many Americans seemed to approve financial success no matter how it was achieved. Operators of businesses often asked politicians for favors or to return favors with cash or other rewards. As a result, **graft** and corruption infected every level of American government. It was Ulysses S. Grant's unhappy fate to occupy the White House at this disturbing time.

President Grant. In 1868, when he won the Presidency on the Republican ticket, Grant enjoyed the respect of millions of Americans. His well-earned reputation rested upon his success as commander of the Union armies during the latter years of the Civil War. Had he never served as President, Grant would have lived and died a popular hero. Unfortunately, his lack of political experience was a serious handicap. Grant's eight-year administration would prove to be one of the darker pages in the history of the Presidency.

Grant himself was honest and upright. His great weakness—which could have been a virtue if tempered by reason—was his total loyalty to friends. Being honest himself, he could not believe that his associates were any less honest. He stubbornly refused to admit that some of his friends used him to advance their own fortunes.

The Crédit Mobilier scandal. Even before Grant took office, the federal government was involved in an unsavory scandal. In 1861 California chartered the Central Pacific Railroad. A year later Congress chartered the Union Pacific Railroad. The Central Pacific was to build eastward from Sacramento, California, and the Union Pacific was to build westward from Omaha, in Nebraska Territory. When the two lines met, the East and West coasts at last would be joined by the nation's first transcontinental railroad.

Building such a railroad was extremely expensive and risky. Since the completed railroad would be important to national development, the federal government gave generous

With the settlement of California came the need to find the best overland mail route to the West. During the 1850's, a circuitous southern route was promoted, but Senator William Gwin of California favored a more direct path. He persuaded the freight firm of Russell, Majors, and Waddell to demonstrate a mail delivery system using continuous horse-rider relays along a route that followed the Oregon Trail.

The experiment, known as the Pony Express, operated between April 1860 and October 1861. To cover its 1,800 mile (2,897 kilometer) route, which began at St. Joseph, Missouri, and ended at Sacramento, California, required about 10 days. Riders changed horses six to eight times per run as they stopped to exchange mail at stations spaced about 10 to 15 miles (16 to 24 kilometers) apart. They rode night and day, galloping across dangerous terrain at speeds up to 25 miles (40 kilometers) per hour.

The Pony Express ceased operation with the completion of the transcontinental telegraph system, and its promoters were ruined financially. But its daring riders earned a place in United States history as colorful heroes of the western frontier.

---

subsidies to the railroad companies. Among these subsidies were loans in the form of government bonds. The companies would receive $16,000 in bonds for every mile of track completed on the level plains, $32,000 for every mile through hilly country, and $48,000 for every mile in the mountains.

The small group of stockholders who controlled the Union Pacific Railroad saw a chance to make enormous profits from the construction of the railroad. They organized a construction company called the Crédit Mobilier (kray·DEE moh·bee·LYAY). Their control of the Union Pacific enabled them to award construction contracts to their own company, the Crédit Mobilier. These contracts were paid for by other stockholders of the Union Pacific at several times the actual cost. As a result, much of the money invested by stockholders in the Union Pacific as well as a large share of the government subsidies went to this small group of greedy men.

When Congressional committees finally investigated, they discovered that some members of Congress had owned stock in the Crédit Mobilier. The company owners had given these members stock or had sold it to them at half price in an effort to bribe them and to block investigations.

The salary grab and tax scandals. In 1873, while the Crédit Mobilier scandal was occupying Congress, the Senators and Representatives voted themselves a 50 percent increase in salaries—from $5,000 to $7,500 per year. Moreover, each member of Congress would receive two years' back pay, or $5,000. The public was so outraged at this **salary grab** that Congress hastily repealed the act at the opening of its next session.

Public resentment had hardly died when another scandal made headlines. Secretary of the Treasury William A. Richardson signed a contract with John D. Sanborn. The contract gave Sanborn authority to collect overdue federal taxes, with the right to keep half of all he could collect. By various devious methods, Sanborn collected $427,000.

When asked to explain the affair, Sanborn swore that he had kept only a small part of the "commission," having been forced to give $156,000 to his "assistants"! The "assistants" were politicians who had used their influence to swing the tax-collection contract to Sanborn. However, the contract was legal, and the "commission" was paid in full. A new law prevented the situation from recurring, however, and Richardson resigned.

The new Secretary of the Treasury, Benjamin H. Bristow, an honest official, discovered that taxes were not being collected on nearly 90 percent of the liquor distilled in the United States. Further investigation revealed that high public officials were guilty of blackmail and fraud.

According to the tax law, a distiller who failed to pay revenue taxes on distilled liquor had to pay a double tax if caught. Any informer who revealed to the government that a company had failed to pay its taxes received 10 percent of the tax penalty as a reward. Informers soon saw, however, that they could collect more by blackmailing the tax-evading company than by reporting the evasion. The Secretary of the Treasury discovered that a ring, or group, of whisky distillers and blackmailers had been defrauding the federal government of at least a million dollars a year.

Graft in the federal government. Meanwhile, yet another scandal was unearthed. It was discovered that Secretary of War William W. Belknap had accepted $24,500 in bribes from a trader at Fort Sill in what is now Oklahoma. Belknap had decided to give the profitable trading rights with the Indians to a New York friend, but the trader who had the contract was making a huge profit from the Indians around Fort Sill. Therefore, the trader agreed to pay Belknap and his friend each $6,000 a year if he were allowed to keep his trading rights.

When evidence of this bribery was presented in 1876, the House of Representatives voted unanimously to impeach Belknap, who hastily resigned. Despite all the evidence, the Senate's impeachment trial failed to convict him. The Senators who voted "not guilty" claimed that because Belknap had resigned he was no longer subject to trial by the Senate.

There were still other evidences of graft in the federal government. The Secretary of the Navy "sold" business to builders and suppliers of ships. The Secretary of the Interior was involved with land speculators. President Grant himself had no part in these illegal activities. Nevertheless many people felt that Grant was at fault for allowing his friends to hide behind his good name.

Other scandals. Corruption was as bad, if not worse, in the state governments. In 1868 the Erie Railroad, which was controlled by Daniel Drew, James ("Jim") Fisk, Jr., and Jay Gould, wanted to sell $10 million worth of additional stock. Gould, to smooth the way, went to the New York State capital at Albany with a trunk full of money to bribe lawmakers to legalize the stock sale. Evidence suggested that the governor of New York sold his influence for $20,000 and that state senators got $15,000.

Perhaps worst of all was the corruption in municipal, or city, government. William M. Tweed, an uneducated chairmaker, rose in 15 years to be a multimillionaire "dictator" of New York City in the 1860's and 1870's. "Boss" Tweed controlled the city government through Tammany Hall, New York's Democratic party structure. Tammany Hall, was a **political machine**—a party organization based on political patronage.

Tweed gained control very simply. He or some of his followers met immigrant families when they landed, fed them, found them jobs and housing, and left them baskets of food at Thanksgiving and Christmas. After they secured the right to vote, the newcomers returned Tweed's "friendship" by voting for can-

This Thomas Nast cartoon focuses on "Boss" Tweed's ability to escape from charges brought against him by corruption-fighting officials. Tweed eventually went to jail, where he died in 1878.

473

didates he favored. Moreover, when election outcomes seemed doubtful, the ballot boxes were stuffed with votes in favor of Tweed's candidates. That is, Tammany supporters voted several times, using different names and addresses each time.

How did Tweed use his power? He gave city jobs to many of his friends. He demanded kickbacks from people who wanted city jobs. He demanded bribes from companies that wanted to provide city services. A courthouse, started in 1868, was to cost $250,000. Three years later, still uncompleted, it had cost $8 million. In three years Tweed and his crooked ring stole an estimated $20 million from New York City. It is estimated that between 1868 and 1871 "Boss" Tweed's ring and his business friends cost the city close to $100 million.

Reasons for corruption. Why was public morality at such a low level in the years following the Civil War?

The war itself was partly responsible. In the crisis of wartime, the all-important consideration is to get things done quickly. Cost is secondary to what is considered national survival, and money flows freely into war industries. During the war years, with business booming, unscrupulous business interests and legislators had a rare opportunity to engage in dishonest practices. These practices were continued in the postwar years.

A related and equally significant explanation of the postwar graft was the rapid growth of large-scale industry, about which you will read in Chapter 22. In earlier times, when factories and businesses were small, their owners were well known in their own communities. If their practices were dishonest, they were likely to lose their neighbors' good will.

The new large corporations were impersonal. The people who controlled them were hardly known even by many of their own stockholders. Within the corporations, it was easier for dishonest individuals to get away with questionable practices.

SECTION REVIEW
See underscored items, text pp. 471-74.

Identify: graft, Crédit Mobilier, salary grab, William Belknap, Tammany Hall, political machine, Tweed Ring
For answers to questions, see Answer Key, pp.A67-68.

1. **Interpreting Ideas:** Ulysses S. Grant's administration was a dark page in the history of the American Presidency. **(a)** What evidence in this section supports this conclusion? **(b)** Why did people blame Grant for the scandals that occurred during his administration?

2. **Summarizing Ideas:** Give examples of graft and corruption on the state and local levels during the postwar years.

3. **Analyzing Ideas:** Why was public corruption so widespread during the postwar years?

2 A start is made toward restoring honest government

See Teaching Suggestions in TMRG, pp.TM120-21.

Newspapers in the late 1860's and the early 1870's were filled with stories and political cartoons attacking government graft and corruption among federal, state, and local officials.

These revelations of corruption stirred a widespread demand for reform. No reform movement aroused greater interest than the proposal to appoint persons to government jobs on the basis of merit. Under the spoils system, which Andrew Jackson had helped to extend, government jobs were given to political favorites. Under the proposed merit system, those who received the highest grades in competitive examinations would get the jobs. It would not matter whether they were Republicans or Democrats. All these public jobs in the federal, state, and local governments would be called civil service jobs.

Growth of the reform movement. In 1871, in response to the demand for reforms, Congress set up a Civil Service Commission to study the problem and to make recommendations. Although President Grant appointed able men to the commission, he gave it little support. In 1875 the chairman resigned in disgust and the commission was discontinued.

Meanwhile, in 1872, a group of reform-minded Republicans had started the Liberal Republican Party, nominating Horace Greeley, the editor of the *New York Tribune,* as their Presidential candidate to run against the regular Republican candidate, President Grant. The Democrats also nominated Greeley, hop-

Thomas Nast, a political cartoonist, originated and popularized many symbols in use today. He created the Republican elephant, the Tammany tiger, and the Democratic donkey. He is also credited with creating the present-day image of Santa Claus.

Nast and his mother moved to the United States from Bavaria when Nast was 6 years old. Early showing an artistic flair, he studied at the Academy of Design in New York City. When Nast was 15, he showed some of his drawings to Frank Leslie and was hired as an illustrator for *Frank Leslie's Illustrated Newspaper.*

In 1861 Nast became a staff artist for *Harper's Weekly.* His most famous cartoons were done for *Harper's* during the Civil War and the decade following. His war illustrations helped influence Northern opinion in favor of the Union cause. President Lincoln even called Nast the North's "best recruiting sergeant." Nast's later cartoons helped break up the Tweed Ring and defeat Horace Greeley in the 1872 Presidential election. Nast summed up his goal: "I try to hit the enemy between the eyes and knock him down!"

Nast did over 3,000 drawings during his 25-year career. Though best remembered for his political cartoons, Nast was an excellent artist. Museums and galleries around the United States display many of his sketches.

---

ing by this means to benefit from the split in the Republican Party.

The Liberal Republican platform included a pledge to fight corruption in public life and a specific plank, or section, urging civil service reform. Nevertheless, Grant was reelected President easily.

The defeat at the polls in 1872 was a disheartening blow to the reformers. Within a year, however, they began to gather strength. For one thing, new public scandals drove more Americans into the reform movement. Also, growing dissatisfaction with Grant's Republican administration enabled the Democrats to win control of the House of Representatives in the Congressional elections of 1874.

The election of 1876. The Democrats, heartened by the growing demand for reform, approached the 1876 elections confident of a victory. They chose as their Presidential candidate Governor Samuel J. Tilden of New York. Governor Tilden had won national atten-

tion by helping to break up the Tweed Ring in New York. The Democratic platform demanded civil service reform and an end to graft in public life.

The Republicans, who were running scared, nominated a man well known as a reformer, Governor Rutherford B. Hayes of Ohio. Hayes promised to work for civil service reform in the federal government. He also promised to end the troubled period of reconstruction.

Both Tilden and Hayes were wealthy. Both were closely associated with industrialists and business groups. Tilden's one big asset was the fact that he was running against a party that was identified with scandal.

The election gave Tilden 250,000 more popular votes than Hayes received. The first count of the electoral votes also gave Tilden an advantage over Hayes—184 to 165. Most newspapers at first reported Tilden had won.

However, the papers had jumped to the wrong conclusion. Tilden with his 184 electoral votes was one short of the necessary majority.

▲ Class activity: In current magazines and newspapers, have students find examples of cartoons that comment on the behavior of political figures. As a follow-up activity, have students write a paragraph, interpreting the cartoons they selected.

475

Ordinarily, when no Presidential candidate has a clear majority of the electoral vote, the House of Representatives chooses the President, but this was no ordinary election. Four states—South Carolina, Florida, Louisiana, and Oregon—had each sent in *two* different sets of returns. In all, 20 electoral votes from these four states were claimed by both the Republicans and the Democrats. Tilden needed only one of these disputed votes to win. Hayes, however, needed all 20.

The single disputed vote from Oregon was quickly settled in favor of Hayes. The 19 votes from the three southern states remained a problem. The Republicans claimed all three states for Hayes. The Democrats insisted that since these states were still under reconstruction governments, the will of the majority had not been expressed. For a time the controversy threatened to plunge the nation into violence.

Settling the dispute. Unfortunately, the Constitution provided no clear procedures for solving this situation. According to the Constitution, the votes had to be counted. But by whom? If the Republican-controlled Senate counted the votes, the Senators would throw out the Democratic returns and give the election to Hayes. If the Democratic-controlled House counted the votes, the Representatives would throw out the Republican returns and give the election to Tilden.

In order to break the deadlock, Congress created an Electoral Commission of 15 members. On it were five Senators, five Representatives, and five Supreme Court Justices. By previous arrangement the Senate chose three Republicans and two Democrats. The House chose two Republicans and three Democrats. Four Justices—two Republicans and two Democrats—were to name a fifth member of the commission—an independent voter without ties to either party.

It was generally understood that the independent member of the Electoral Commission would be Justice David Davis. At the last minute, however, Davis resigned from the Supreme Court because of his election to the Senate. His place on the Electoral Commission went to a Republican. It was not surprising, therefore, that when the disputed votes were counted, they went to the Republicans by a straight party vote of eight Republicans as opposed to the seven Democrats on the Electoral Commission.

Thus it was that Hayes, who had received a minority of the popular votes, entered the White House as President. The controversial election of 1876–77 did, however, represent a victory for compromise and for the process of orderly government.

Difficulties for Hayes. President Hayes had four difficult years in the White House. Throughout his administration the Democrats controlled the House and for two years, from 1879 to 1881, the Senate as well. Although the Democrats did not try to upset the decision of the Electoral Commission, they called Hayes "His Fraudulency" and "Old Eight to Seven" to remind him that they questioned his right to the Presidency.

Hayes also faced opposition from his own party. The election of 1876 split the Republicans into two groups—the Stalwarts and the Half-Breeds. The Stalwarts, sometimes called "Old Guard" Republicans, were against reform and reformers. They also opposed the President himself, whom they called "Granny Hayes." The Half-Breeds, led by James G. Blaine of Maine and John Sherman of Ohio, agreed with Hayes that at least some steps toward reform were needed.

To fulfill his promise of ending reconstruction, President Hayes named a former Confederate leader to his cabinet and withdrew the last federal occupation troops from the South. As the remaining reconstruction governments lost power, southern Democrats were free to manage state affairs in their own way. Southern Democrats elected to Congress from the "Solid South" now allied with northern Democrats to break the power of the Radical Republicans, who had controlled Congress during the period of reconstruction.

Hayes's battle for reform. In spite of strong opposition, Hayes was the first President to take serious steps to reform the civil service. He refused to follow the practice of many earlier Presidents of discharging thousands of officeholders and replacing them with political favorites. He also insisted that all persons recommended by members of Congress for jobs should be carefully investigated. He courageously removed a prominent Republican, Chester A. Arthur, from his job as Collector of Customs in New York because of Arthur's questionable political activities. One of his own cabinet members, Carl Schurz, a German-born

▲ Hayes' election was part of a secret bargain between Democrats and Republicans. Hayes promised southern Democrats that if elected he would remove federal troops from the South, help pay for new railroads, and appoint a southerner to the cabinet. The Democrats agreed and Hayes kept his word as President.

Republican, introduced the merit system into the Department of the Interior.

The election of 1880. Well before the nominating conventions for the 1880 elections, President Hayes announced that he would not run for reelection. The Stalwart wing of the Republican Party, fed up with talk of reform and eager to return to the "good old days," tried to win the nomination for former President Ulysses S. Grant. The Half-Breed wing of the party managed to block this attempt, and the Republican convention finally nominated a war veteran, General James A. Garfield of Ohio. To win the support of the Stalwarts, the convention nominated for Vice President Chester A. Arthur, a leading Stalwart.

The Democrats also pinned their hopes for the Presidency on a war veteran, General Winfield S. Hancock of Pennsylvania.

During the campaign, neither the Democrats nor the Republicans faced up to basic problems of the new industrial age—labor legislation, regulation of railroads and other big business, the money issue, and an income tax. Thus it was a third party, the Greenback-Labor Party, as you will read, that squarely faced the controversial issues of the time.

Garfield won the election with an electoral vote of 214 to Hancock's 155. However, the popular vote was close—4,449,053 for the Republicans, 4,442,035 for the Democrats.

Civil service reform. On July 2, 1881, President Garfield was shot by a disappointed—and mentally unbalanced—government job seeker. Garfield died in September.

The President's tragic death shocked the nation into an awareness of the evils of the old spoils system. Chester A. Arthur, the new President, responded to the widespread demand for reform and supported the Pendleton Civil Service Act.

The Pendleton Act, which became law in 1883, set up a commission to give competitive examinations for those seeking government jobs. The first examinations were to include only about 12 percent of federal jobs, but the President was given authority to broaden the list. The Pendleton Act also forbade the party in power to ask for campaign contributions from federal officeholders. President Arthur appointed an able leader for the new commission and extended the list of jobs for which civil service examinations had to be taken.

Thus, after years of agitation, reformers at last managed to write into law the principle that federal jobs below the policy-making level should be filled by merit. A long step had been taken toward making government more honest and efficient.

The election of 1884. When the election year of 1884 rolled around, Chester A. Arthur made it clear that he wanted to run for the Presidency. However, his Republican Stalwart supporters had lost faith in him because of the reform activities he had supported. Instead of Arthur, the leader of the Half-Breed wing of the Republican Party, James G. Blaine, won the nomination.

Blaine was a handsome, colorful, and persuasive candidate, but during his long political career, he had made many enemies. These

In an attempt to save President Garfield after he was shot, his doctors used a device invented by Alexander Graham Bell. It found the exact location of the bullet near his spine, but blood poisoning set in and eventually killed Garfield.

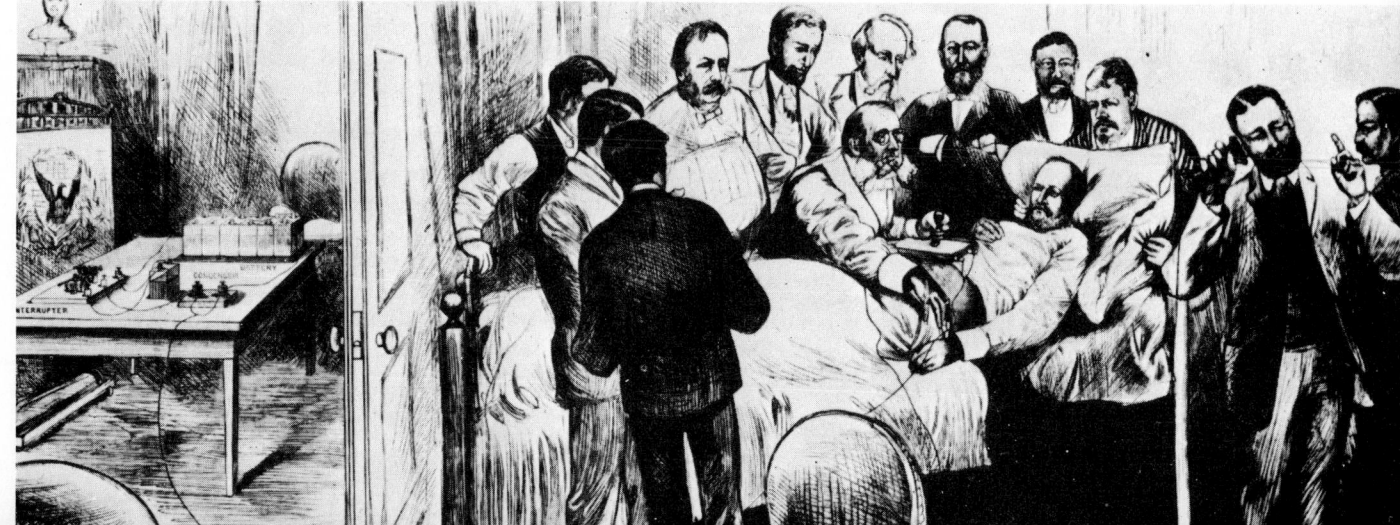

enemies now accused Blaine of having used his political influence to secure favors for big business—at a generous profit for himself. Unhappy with Blaine's nomination, a large group of Republicans, nicknamed "Mugwumps," bolted from the party and chose to support the Democratic candidate.

The Democrats made the most of Blaine's reputation as "a tool of the special interests." They chose a reformer as their Presidential nominee, Grover Cleveland, who had been governor of New York. Cleveland was known to be honest, courageous, independent—and stubborn when fighting for a principle.

In the campaign the big issues of the day were almost forgotten as the politicians heaped abuse upon the rival candidates. Each party raked over the personal life of the opposition candidate.

Throughout the campaign the two candidates, Blaine and Cleveland, ran neck and neck. Then, on the very eve of the election, at a reception given for Blaine by a group of Protestant clergy, a speaker called the Democrats the party of "Rum, Romanism, and Rebellion."

The speaker's use of the word "rum" was a deliberate attempt to smear the Democrats. His use of the word "rebellion" referred to the alliance between northern Democrats and the "Solid South" Democrats. Both references were bad enough, but the speaker's reference to "Romanism"—the Roman Catholic religion— was fatal. It was generally agreed that Blaine's failure to rebuke the speaker for this insult to Roman Catholic voters cost him the election. Grover Cleveland thus won the Presidency, squeaking through with 219 electoral votes to Blaine's 182.

The election of 1884 was the first Presidential victory for the Democrats in 28 years. It was one sign that memories of the Civil War were beginning to fade.

SECTION REVIEW

See underscored items, text pp. 474-76, 477-78.
Identify: civil service, Horace Greeley, Samuel Tilden, Rutherford Hayes, James Blaine, James Garfield, Chester Arthur, "Mugwumps"
For answers to questions, see Answer Key, p.A68.

1. **Contrasting Ideas:** How is the spoils system different from the merit system of appointing people to government jobs?
2. **Interpreting Ideas:** In what ways was the election of 1876 one of the most unusual in American history?
3. **Organizing Ideas:** What position did each of the following take concerning reform: **(a)** Liberal Republicans, **(b)** Stalwarts, **(c)** Half-Breeds?
4. **Analyzing Ideas: (a)** Explain the provisions of the Pendleton Act. **(b)** Why was it enacted?
5. **Summarizing Ideas:** What factors led to Cleveland's election in 1884?

3 Efforts at political reform move forward

See Teaching Suggestions in TMRG, p.TM121.
When President Cleveland entered the White House in 1885, the movement for political reform entered a new phase.

Cleveland's firm stand. President Cleveland believed that "a public office is a public trust." He took a firm stand on important issues, even though he risked antagonizing his own party.

He supported civil service reform by doubling the number of federal jobs on the classified list. He took a step toward conserving the nation's natural resources by recovering vast areas of public land illegally held by railroads, lumber companies, and cattle interests. He signed a bill in 1887 creating a federal Division of Forestry.

One of his most courageous acts was his attempt to block **pension grabs** by veterans of the Union army. For many years the Pension Bureau had been very generous in handing out pensions. Now and then, however, requests for pensions were based on such flimsy grounds that even the bureau rejected them. Often, when this happened, the disappointed pension seeker asked his representative in Congress to get the pension for him by pushing a special bill through Congress. Cleveland vetoed more than 200 of these bills. He thus angered many ex-soldiers, who were united in the politically powerful veterans' organization the Grand Army of the Republic, known as the G.A.R.

Important laws. In addition to Cleveland's personal accomplishments, Congress adopted several important laws during the years from 1885 to 1889.

The Presidential Succession Act of 1886 provided that if both the President and the Vice President died or were disabled, the cabinet officers would succeed to the Presidency in the order in which their offices had been created.

The Electoral Count Act of 1887 was designed to prevent another disputed election similar to the election of 1876. The act provided that if a state sent in more than one set of electoral returns, Congress had to accept the returns approved by the governor of the state.

In 1887 Congress tried to quiet the clamor of small business people and farmers against unfair business practices by the railroads. It passed the Interstate Commerce Act, about which you will read in Chapter 24. Congress refused, however, to accept President Cleveland's strong recommendation that tariff rates be lowered.

The election of 1888. President Cleveland's reform activities and especially his campaign for lower tariffs antagonized political leaders in his own party. Nevertheless, in 1888 the Democrats nominated him for a second term.

Although Cleveland won nearly 100,000 more popular votes than his opponent, <u>Benjamin Harrison</u>, he lost by an electoral count of 233 to 168. The Republicans won the Presidency and control of both houses of Congress.

Cleveland's policies reversed. Benjamin Harrison was a successful lawyer, a veteran of the Union army, and the grandson of former President William Henry Harrison. He was not, however, a strong President. In his opinion, his duty as Chief Executive was to follow the wishes of the Senators and Representatives, who in turn had the responsibility of carrying out the wishes of the people.

During President Harrison's administration, the Republicans reversed many of President Cleveland's policies. Instead of supporting the civil service system, they replaced Democratic officeholders (except those on the classified list) with Republicans. Congress passed an act that almost doubled the number of pensioners and their dependents. Congress also adopted the highest protective tariff the country had had up to that time, the <u>McKinley Tariff of 1890</u>.

The "Old Guard" Republicans did not have everything their way. In an effort to appeal to farmers, laborers, miners, small business people, and the American public in general, Congress passed two important laws in 1890. The Sherman Silver Purchase Act was in-

According to this cartoon, Uncle Sam had little reason to be pleased with Benjamin Harrison's Presidency. What failings does the cartoonist lay at Harrison's door?

(Poor appointments, broken promises, Tanner scandal)

tended to appeal to western mining interests. ▲ The act was also meant to increase the amount of money in circulation as a benefit to farmers, wage earners, and small business interests. The Sherman Antitrust Act was intended to protect the public from monopoly practices and other abuses of free enterprise that had arisen with the growth of industry. You will read about these two laws in the next unit.

Growing dissatisfaction. Neither the Sherman Silver Purchase Act nor the Sherman Antitrust Act stopped the growing dissatisfaction with President Harrison's Republican administration. Wage earners had no reason to hope their demands would be met by Republicans. Many farmers, abandoning hope of help from either party, began to join labor organizations in efforts to win control of the government and bring about reforms. Many Americans, struggling to make ends meet at a time of rising prices, blamed their troubles on the Republican-sponsored McKinley Tariff.

Two widely read books expressed the growing dissatisfaction with the concentration of wealth in the hands of a few. Henry George's *Progress and Poverty*, first published in 1879, contrasted the wealth of the privileged few

▲ Western mining interests were rapidly growing. In Harrison's term 6 western states entered the Union. They were Washington, Montana, North Dakota, Wyoming, and Idaho. Colorado entered in 1876 during Grant's administration.

479

with the poverty of many people. George blamed this inequality on the fact that a few persons had monopoly control over the nation's choicest land sites and other natural resources. George proposed a new system of taxing land. He thought that this system would abolish great fortunes and provide a good standard of living for everyone.

In 1894 the book *Wealth Against Commonwealth* by Henry Demarest Lloyd was published. The author concluded that the giant new corporations and business enterprises were running the new industrial economy for their own gain.

Lloyd's book expressed the deep discontent of millions of Americans. What concerned many Americans was that the new industrialism had created extremes of poverty and wealth. Expanding industries brought vast wealth to a few owners, while the majority of workers lived in poverty. For a solution to this problem, many Americans turned to government—whether controlled by Republicans or Democrats.

By 1892 the demand for government action could not be ignored. Owners of small businesses, wage earners in every section of the country, and especially the western farmers were calling for reform.

The election of 1892. Increasing discontent turned the election of 1892 into a spirited three-way contest. Both the Republicans and the Democrats realized that they had to do something about reform. They were prodded into action by the strength of a new party, the Populist Party, which had been created in 1891. The Populist Party, which you will read about later, was organized by farmers, but it also attracted wage earners and other discontented voters.

The Republicans were on the defensive. President Harrison and the Republican Party received widespread criticism. Nevertheless, the Republicans decided to stand on their record. The party nominated President Harrison for a second term.

The Democrats were eager to take advantage of the demands for reform from both workers and farmers. They nominated Grover Cleveland, who was already known as a champion of honest politics.

The Democrats won, with Cleveland gathering 277 electoral votes to Harrison's 145. The Democrats also won control of Congress, but the new Populist Party—an out-and-out reform party—made a remarkable showing. Although the Populist candidate, James B. Weaver, collected only 22 electoral votes, his popular vote totaled more than 1 million. The Populist Party also elected three governors and numerous representatives to state legislatures and to Congress.

The Wilson-Gorman Tariff. From the beginning President Cleveland was in trouble. His election had stemmed in part from his promise to lower the McKinley Tariff. A tariff bill that he supported was introduced in the House in December 1893. By the time the bill had gone through the House and Senate, over 600 amendments had been tacked on to it raising tariff rates for particular products.

The Wilson-Gorman bill, as the amended bill was called, did provide overall lower average tariff rates than the McKinley Tariff. However, it was still a high **protective tariff,** and President Cleveland was furious. He refused to endorse it by signing it, preferring instead to leave it on his desk for ten days. After that time it automatically became law without his signature.

During the tariff debates in the Senate, powerful **lobbies,** or pressure groups, tried in every way possible to influence the votes of doubtful Senators. Producers of iron, steel, wool, glass, and hundreds of other products demanded tariff protection.

One of the most active lobbies was the American Sugar Refining Company, usually called "the sugar trust."° The original House bill had completely removed the tariff on raw and refined sugar. The sugar trust, determined to get the tariff restored, immediately went to work on the Senate. In the end, the trust won, and the tariff on sugar was restored.

The Wilson-Gorman Tariff cost the Democrats the support of millions of Americans who were convinced that the Democrats had broken their campaign promise to do away with a high protective tariff.

Decision against an income tax. The original tariff bill favored by President Cleveland would have sharply lowered the tariff rates. Expecting a loss in government revenue because of the lower rates, the House added a

°**trust:** a group of companies centrally controlled to regulate production, reduce production costs, and eliminate competition.

▲ Grover Cleveland, elected in 1884 and 1892, is the only President who has served a second term that did not directly follow the first.

Panic hit the floor of the New York Stock Exchange as investors raced to sell their stocks in May 1893. Plunging stock prices set off a crippling depression that would last five years and cause hardship for millions across the nation.

clause to the tariff bill providing for a 2 percent tax on all incomes of more than $4,000.

The income tax clause provoked violent debate, but it finally became law. Opponents of the income tax immediately tested the new measure in the courts. In 1895 the Supreme Court declared it unconstitutional. The Supreme Court ruled against the income tax because it was a direct tax not apportioned among the states according to population, as required by the Constitution (page 197).

The Democratic administration could not be held responsible for the Supreme Court's negative decision on the income tax. Nevertheless, millions of Americans considered the Court's decision as merely one more example of how the government favored big business. Thus the Supreme Court's rejection of the income tax helped to fan the flame of protest sweeping the country.

Financial panic. On May 5, 1893, only two months after Cleveland took office, a financial panic began as the value of stocks on the New York Stock Exchange suddenly plunged. As the weeks passed, the situation rapidly became worse. Thousands of businesses failed. Facto-

ries closed their doors. Perhaps as many as 4 million workers were unemployed. The prices of farm produce dropped so low that farmers could not afford the cost of shipping it. By the end of the year, the American nation was in the grip of one of the worst depressions in its history.

SECTION REVIEW

See underscored items, text pp. 478-80.

Identify: pension grab, Benjamin Harrison, McKinley Tariff of 1890, Populist Party. Wilson-Gorman Tariff, lobbies, sugar trust

For answers to questions, see Answer Key, p.A68.

1. **Interpreting Viewpoints:** What did Grover Cleveland mean when he said that "a public office is a public trust"?

2. **Analyzing Ideas:** Explain how each of the following laws helped to prevent a potential national problem: **(a)** Presidential Succession Act of 1886, **(b)** Electoral Count Act of 1887.

3. **Summarizing Ideas:** How did the issue of tariffs play a part in politics during the 1880's and 1890's?

4. **Studying Graphics:** Study the cartoon on page 479. **(a)** What is the cartoonist's attitude toward Harrison? **(b)** How does the cartoonist express this attitude?

DEVELOPING HISTORY STUDY SKILLS

Interpreting the Visual Record   Analyzing Political Cartoons

Throughout America's history, political cartoons have been used to influence public opinion. A political cartoon is a drawing that presents a point of view. Political cartoons often appear in the editorial sections of newspapers and news magazines.

Some cartoons express a positive point of view. More often, cartoons are critical of an event, person, or group. Cartoons are a powerful means of communication because they often present their message in a simple, direct, and often humorous manner.

To get across their message, cartoonists employ two major techniques: caricature and symbolism. A caricature is an exaggeration or distortion of the physical features of someone or something. The cartoon to the left below is a caricature of four presidents. Note exagger-

ated features such as President Nixon's nose, President Kennedy's hair and teeth, and Presidents Eisenhower's and Johnson's ears.

Symbolism is the use of one device to stand for another. The elephant as a symbol of the Republican party was the invention of Thomas Nast and first appeared in the 1874 cartoon at the right below. Other symbols common in political cartoons are Uncle Sam to represent the United States and the donkey to represent the Democratic party.

Cartoonists also use labels and captions to get across their message. Cartoon labels help identify important symbols, caricatures, and ideas. Cartoon captions often hint at the main idea of a cartoon, or may represent the words of a character in the cartoon.

Caricatures of (from left to right) Presidents Eisenhower, Kennedy, Johnson, and Nixon.

Note the many animals used as symbols in this 1874 Nast cartoon.

How to Read a Political Cartoon

To read a political cartoon, follow these steps.

1. **Identify the caricatures.** Identify each figure and object being characterized. Note what parts of the figures and objects, if any, are exaggerated or distorted. Determine whether the figures are presented in a positive or negative light.

2. **Identify the symbols used.** Decide what each symbol represents.

3. **Read all labels.** Reading labels helps you understand the story on the viewpoint of the political cartoon.

4. **Read the caption.** Note the caption's relation to the cartoon. Decide whose viewpoint is being expressed — a cartoon figure or some unknown person.

Applying the Skill

Study the Nast cartoon at the bottom left. Note that it is dated October 21, 1871, the date the legendary "Boss" Tweed took over Tammany Hall in New York City. The pot-bellied figure is a caricature of Tweed. The size of Tweed's belly is exaggerated to denote his greed. Read the title and note that Tweed has a bag of money in place of brains. Nast is again suggesting Tweed's greed through the use of this symbolism. Now read the caption. It seems to be coming from Boss Tweed himself who expected a just "reward" for any favors he did for people. The political cartoonist is saying that Tweed was also arrogant.

Practicing the Skill

Study the political cartoon at the bottom right. Then, on a separate sheet of paper, answer the following questions.

1. **(a)** Who is the central figure in the political cartoon? **(b)** How do you know?
2. How does the cartoonist depict this figure?
3. What technique is the cartoonist employing?
4. What is the figure doing?
5. To what does the title "Tweedledee and Sweedledum" refer?
6. **(a)** What is the caption? **(b)** Who is saying it? **(c)** What does the caption mean?
7. **(a)** Where is the action taking place? **(b)** How do you know?
8. How would you explain the message of the cartoon?
9. What is the cartoonist's viewpoint?

THE BRAINS OF THE TAMMANY RING. (*Harper's Weekly*, October 21st, 1871.)

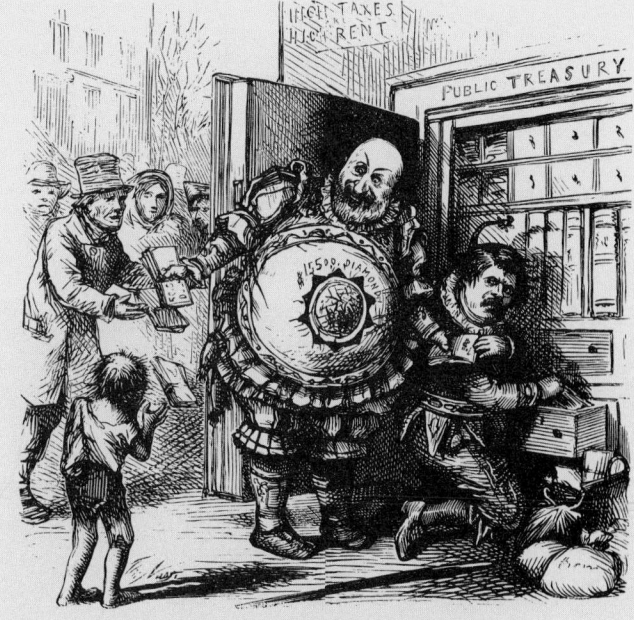

TWEEDLEDEE AND SWEEDLEDUM.
(*A New Christmas Pantomime at the Tammany Hall.*)
CLOWN (*to* PANTALOON). "Let's Blind them with *this*, and then take *some more*."

Unrest, changing ways of living, and new problems were characteristics of every section of the United States from 1865 to 1900. The Civil War's four long years had disrupted the nation and shaken long-established ways of living. To an even greater extent, however, the new problems were the result of the transformation of the United States from an agricultural nation into a great industrial power.

Industrialization and its changes brought serious problems as well as excitement and drama to the American scene. Morality in public life sank to an all-time low as a "get-rich-quick" spirit and greed for power infected many Americans. Wealth and power became concentrated in the hands of a relatively few pioneers of the new industrial age. Through their control of the railroads, mines, factories, banks, and giant corporations, the new industrial and financial leaders exerted a powerful influence over government at every level. The control exercised by this small group threatened the working of the democratic process. Americans, however, recognized the threat and began to take steps to correct the situation.

CONNECTING CHAPTER IDEAS

In the next chapter you will read how the last frontier was conquered and how the lands once inhabited by Native Americans were claimed by white settlers. You will read how farmers, ranchers, and miners contributed to the settlement of the West.

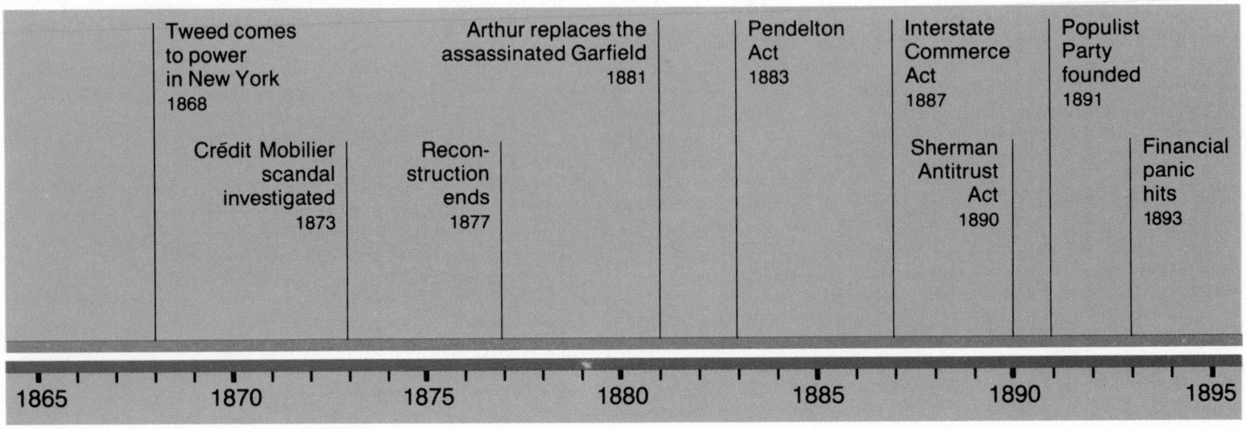

Tweed comes to power in New York 1868	Arthur replaces the assassinated Garfield 1881	Pendelton Act 1883	Interstate Commerce Act 1887	Populist Party founded 1891	
Crédit Mobilier scandal investigated 1873	Recon-struction ends 1877		Sherman Antitrust Act 1890		Financial panic hits 1893

1865	1870	1875	1880	1885	1890	1895

CHAPTER
20 REVIEW

Reviewing Important Terms

Decide whether each of the following sentences is true or false. If the sentence is false, replace the underlined term with the word or phrase that will make it true.

1. Powerful lobbies attempted to influence the votes of lawmakers.
2. Business interests in the United States favored a high tax on imports known as an excise tax.
3. The years of President Grant's administration were characterized by corruption and cash rewards called scandal.
4. President Cleveland attempted to block large salary grabs by Civil War veterans.
5. Some public employees in federal, state, and local government held civil service jobs.
6. When Congress voted itself a large raise in 1873, critics termed it the pension grab.
7. A political machine was a party organization based on patronage.

Practicing Critical Thinking Skills

1. **Interpreting Ideas.** Explain how the Pendleton Act made a significant contribution to the development of democracy in the United States.
2. **Comparing Viewpoints. (a)** Compare the views held by Grover Cleveland and Benjamin Harrison on the proper role of the President. **(b)** In what ways did their views affect their actions as President? Support your answer.
3. **Organizing Ideas.** Historians have rated American Presidents by the following categories: great, near great, average, below average, and failure. Make a list of the Presidents elected between 1865 and 1896 and rank them according to these categories. Explain factors you considered in making your judgments.
4. **Comparing Ideas.** Compare the Presidential Succession Act of 1967 (see Amendment 25, pages 217–18) with the one enacted in 1886. **(a)** How are the two acts different? **(b)** What circumstances prompted the passage of the 1967 act?
5. **Relating Past to Present. (a)** Cite recent examples of graft and corruption in local, state, and federal governments. **(b)** Does the word "reform" seem to mean the same today as it did in the time period just studied? Explain. **(c)** What reforms are needed on the local, state, and federal levels to guard against corruption in government?

Developing History Study Skills

1. **Analyzing a Political Cartoon.** Study the political cartoon on page 470 of the textbook. **(a)** Who do the two characters in the cartoon represent? **(b)** What action is taking place? **(c)** Write a paragraph that summarizes the idea the artist meant to convey with this cartoon.
2. **Using Your Textbook.** For each of the pictures in this chapter, complete the following activities. **(a)** Develop a title for the picture. **(b)** List three adjectives that come to mind as you view each picture. **(c)** Write a brief paragraph in which you describe the main idea of each picture.
3. **Making Inferences.** Reread "Graft and corruption spread in the postwar years", on text pages 471–74. Then read each of the following statements and determine if the statement was implied or stated in the textbook. **(a)** Corrupt political machines existed because some police and courts were also corrupt. **(b)** Political machines provided some assistance to immigrants. **(c)** Machine politicians used their power to get rich.

Relating Geography and History

Presidential elections often have been influenced by geographic factors. Regional voting preferences in Presidential elections highlight the importance of regional goals and beliefs. To better understand the influence of regional voting patterns on Presidential elections, complete the following activities.

1. Make a four-column chart. In column one list the years 1876, 1880, 1884, 1888, and 1892. In column two list the Republican candidates and their popular and electoral vote for the elections named in column one. In column three list the popular and electoral vote for the Democratic candidate in each election. In column four list the vote totals for any major third party candidates.
2. Find maps illustrating the distribution of electoral votes in the elections listed on your chart. **(a)** Indicate on your chart which candidate, if any, carried the largest number of states in the following regions: New England, Middle Atlantic, South, Midwest, and Far West. **(b)** Describe any regional voting patterns you discover. **(c)** Use the information in your textbook to analyze each election. Identify any issues that may have contributed to the voting patterns in each election.

485

See Chapter Overview in TMRG, p.TM122.
See Chapter Objectives in TMRG, p.TM122.
See Introducing the Chapter in TMRG, p.TM122.

CHAPTER 21 Settling the Last Frontier

(1865–1900)

Plains Indian
village

Chief Joseph, leader of the Nez Percé Indians, surrendered to his conquerors sorrowfully, but with dignity. "I am tired of fighting," he said. "Our chiefs are killed. . . . It is cold and we have no blankets. The little children are freezing to death. . . . My heart is sick and sad. From where the sun now stands I will fight no more, forever." The year was 1877. The place was the plains of Montana, only a few miles from the Canadian border.

For years beyond memory, the Nez Percés had lived peacefully in the region where the present states of Oregon, Washington, and Idaho meet. By the mid-1860's, however, land-hungry pioneers moving into the Pacific Northwest began looking greedily at the fertile valleys and hunting grounds of the Nez Percés. In 1877 the federal government ordered the Nez Percés to resettle in a remote region. During the move, trouble broke out, and a small band of Nez Percés murdered 19 white soldiers and settlers.

Chief Joseph decided his people should flee to a new homeland in Canada. The group of 200 warriors and 600 women and children traveled more than 1,300 miles (2,100 kilometers) through unbelievably rugged terrain, outwitting the pursuing troops for two months. Finally, the Nez Percé Indians were surrounded by United States troops and forced to surrender, just short of the Canada—United States border.

Thus, in 1877, Chief Joseph faced his conquerors on the last frontier of the West, the Great Plains. This vast area had belonged to the Indians from earliest times. Now it was being claimed by white settlers.

READING FOCUS

As you read about the settlement of the West, look for the details that support each of the following statements.

1. The Indians make their last stand on the Great Plains.
2. The government tries to "Americanize" the Indians.
3. Ranchers build a cattle kingdom on the plains.
4. Farmers plow the tough sod of the last frontier.
5. Miners find new treasures in the western mountains.

1 The Indians make their last stand on the Great Plains

See Teaching Suggestions in TMRG, pp.TM122-23.

No sharp line separates the prairies of the Midwest from the Great Plains. The 100th meridian, however, is usually accepted as the dividing line. From the 100th meridian toward the Rocky Mountains the annual rainfall gradually decreases, and the grass gets shorter (see map, page 500).

The Great American Desert. The westward advance of the settlers halted along the line of the 100th meridian for at least a generation during the early 1800's. Earlier explorers, accustomed to wooded country with abundant rainfall, reported that the Great Plains were arid and uninhabitable. Maps of the times called the plains the "Great American Desert."

As long as the whites believed the plains to be barren desert, they were content to leave the region to the Indians. In fact, the federal government had moved many tribes to the plains from east of the Mississippi and promised to keep white settlers out. By the 1850's, however, the mistaken notion of the plains as desert was being dispelled. Traders and pioneers who crossed the plains on their way to California and the Pacific Northwest reported that much of the plains country was good for farming and cattle raising. White settlers gradually began to move onto the plains.

Bows and arrows against guns. The Plains Indians were determined to defend their hunting grounds and their way of life. They had learned what later white settlers would have to learn—how to adapt to the plains environment. Herds of wild horses, descendants of those of the Spanish conquistadors, now roamed the plains. The Indians had mastered these horses and had become expert riders. On horseback they could hunt the buffalo which provided them with food, clothing, and shelter.

The Indians were powerful adversaries. They rode superbly. Before they secured rifles, they fought with spears and with short bows, from which they could drive their arrows with amazing rapidity and penetrating force. To protect themselves they used shields made of

Text continues on page 490.

487

Among the geographic regions of the United States, none is a more unified physical entity than the Great Plains. The western edges of this vast area lie at the foot of the Rocky Mountains. The meeting point of plains and mountains creates so distinctive a line that there is no difficulty recognizing the western boundary of the Great Plains.

The eastern boundary of the Great Plains is not quite so sharply defined, formed as it is by a combination of three physical phenomena. The first useful measure of the eastern boundary is the 100th meridian, 100° West Longitude. The second useful measure is the 2,000-foot (610 meter) contour line. The High Plains of the west meet the Central Lowlands to the east at 2,000 feet (610 meters) above sea level. The third useful measure is the 20-inch (51-centimeter) rainfall line — the dividing point between forest and grassland. The differences east and west of these lines are clearly discernible.

The land of the Great Plains slopes gently eastward from the Rocky Mountains, which serves as a continental divide. From the divide's crest, rivers and streams flow either eastward or westward. The rivers and streams of the Great Plains flow eastward from the Rocky Mountains, forming a vast drainage basin with the Missouri and Mississippi as the principal rivers. Streams swollen by melting snow rush down the mountain slopes, transporting huge volumes of soil. When the streams reach level land, the water suddenly slows and silt is deposited in the streambed. Over thousands of years, deposits of silt have made the western edges of the Great Plains several thousands of feet higher in elevation than the eastern side.

Of all of the unifying factors of the Great Plains region by far the most important is climate. The climate of the great Plains is characterized by a number of extremes.

One extreme is the variation in rainfall from year to year, making the region very dry — so dry that the region was once called the Great American Desert. Droughts on the plains can be frequent and devastating. Temperatures present another extreme. During wintertime on the northern plains, temperatures are among the lowest recorded anywhere on the North American continent. Temperatures may drop to −50° F (−45° C). In the summer, on the other hand, temperatures on the plains frequently soar above 100°F (37° C).

Tornadoes, hail, and blizzard weather are extremes that plains dwellers experience. The central and southern portions of the Great Plains suffer more hailstorms and tornadoes than any other area in the country. Even though storms may not occur frequently in any one place, a single storm can easily wipe out an entire year's crop. Wind also plagues the people of the plains. On this open, treeless landscape, winds sweep across the land with greater force than in any other part of our country, often carrying fertile topsoil with them.

As one plain's settler put it, the real "Grizzly of the Plains" is the blizzard. Almost every winter, cold-air masses move out from Canada, traveling southeastward along the foot of the Rockies, then swinging out into the central Great Plains, and dropping snow. The winds whip up the snow into drifts, which are often so deep that livestock can neither reach food, nor can ranchers get food to them.

The Great Plains are no different today than they were to new settlers first braving the strange new environment. These new settlers learned new techniques, challenging this treeless, dry, grassland. That the Great Plains, the last frontier to be settled, is an inhabited, richly productive region demonstrates the success with which the settlers met the challenge.

The Colorado plains

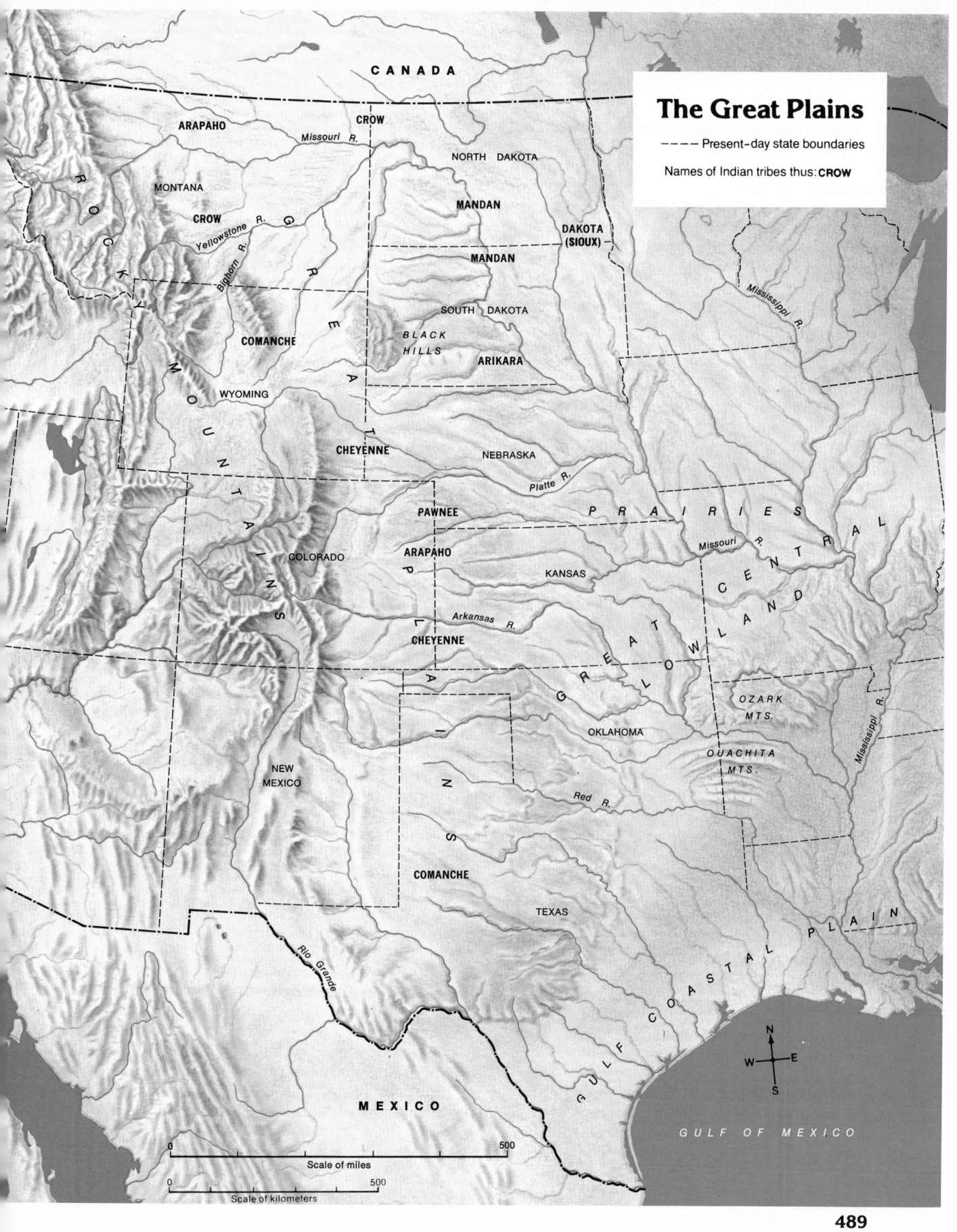

The Great Plains

- - - - - Present-day state boundaries

Names of Indian tribes thus: **CROW**

CANADA

ARAPAHO

CROW

Missouri R.

NORTH DAKOTA

MONTANA

CROW

Yellowstone R.

MANDAN

DAKOTA
(SIOUX)

Bighorn R.

MANDAN

COMANCHE

SOUTH DAKOTA

Mississippi R.

BLACK
HILLS

ARIKARA

WYOMING

CHEYENNE

NEBRASKA

Platte R.

P   R   A   I   R   I   E   S

PAWNEE

Missouri   R.

COLORADO

ARAPAHO

KANSAS

C   E   N   T   R   A   L

CHEYENNE

Arkansas   R.

G   R   E   A   T

L   O   W   L   A   N   D

OZARK
MTS.

Mississippi R.

OKLAHOMA

OUACHITA
MTS.

NEW
MEXICO

Red R.

COMANCHE

TEXAS

C   O   A   S   T   A   L   P   L   A   I   N

Rio Grande

G   U   L   F

N

W   E

S

MEXICO

GULF   OF   MEXICO

0   500
Scale of miles

0   500
Scale of kilometers

ROCKY

MOUNTAINS

GREAT

PLAINS

On the eve of the Civil War, the United States had about 30,000 miles (48,000 kilometers) of railroad track. About 28 million acres (11 million hectares) of federal lands had been granted to states for railroad construction. The feverish growth of the railroad as an economic and social phenomenon led the noted essayist Ralph Waldo Emerson to observe, "the Americans take to this little contrivance, the railroad, as if it were the cradle in which they were born."

Yet in 1860 no railroad extended into the undeveloped territories west of the Mississippi River. Although the need for a federally-subsidized transcontinental railroad had been obvious for some time, northerners and southerners could not agree on a location for the route.

Then in 1862 the federal government intervened. It commissioned two companies to build a railway stretching along the 42nd parallel between Omaha, Nebraska, and Sacramento, California. The Union Pacific Railroad company was to lay track westward from Omaha, while the Central Pacific Railroad company was to build eastward from Sacramento. Each company would receive generous loans and 6,400 (2,590 hectares) acres of free land for each mile of track laid.

Work was begun on the railroad in 1863. The proposed route covered towering mountain ranges and long stretches of desert. Supplies had to be transported great distances over this rugged and dangerous terrain. Neither section of the railroad could have been completed without the cheap labor of immigrant gang workers. The Union Pacific hired many thousands of European immigrants, mainly from Ireland, and the Central Pacific relied on Chinese workers. Indeed, one fourth of all Chinese immigrants in America in 1868 were building the transcontinental railroad.

The railroad companies worked toward each other. By late 1868 the construction had turned into a race to see which company could lay the most track in the shortest time and thus collect the largest federal subsidy. Finally the two lines met on May 10, 1869, at Promontory Point in northern Utah. A silver sledgehammer was used to drive in the last spike, which was made of gold especially for the occasion. The Union Pacific won the race, having completed 1,089 miles (1,753 kilometers) of track; the Central Pacific, which had more difficult terrain to cover, completed 689 miles (1,109 kilometers). And the nation now had its first transcontinental railroad.

---

buffalo hide. These they coated with glue made from horses' hooves and hardened over the fire to an almost iron-like consistency. A favorite Indian tactic was to gallop around the enemy, hiding behind their horses and shields and deliberately drawing enemy fire. When the enemy's ammunition was exhausted, the Indians darted in to strike with arrows and long spears.

Faced with these weapons and tactics, white intruders at first were at a disadvantage. Their long rifles could be reloaded and fired from the back of a galloping horse only with great difficulty.

The invention of the revolver in the late 1830's ended the Indians' temporary superiority in weapons. The revolver could be reloaded easily at full gallop. Several bullets could be fired in rapid succession without reloading. Armed with this new weapon, settlers in the 1850's could move out onto the plains with more confidence.

A new Indian policy. This new movement of white settlers brought about a change in government policy toward the Indians. In 1849 the Bureau of Indian Affairs became part of the Department of the Interior. The bureau had responsibility for carrying out the federal government's Indian policies. One early policy was **concentration**. This was the attempt to confine the Indian tribes to certain limited areas of the West. In these areas the tribes would be free to carry on their own affairs and continue their lives as hunters. It was hoped the policy would reduce warfare among the tribes and would clear routes for white settlers heading for California and Oregon.

More settlers on the plains. An individual traveling on foot across the Great Plains was in grave danger of dying from thirst, sunstroke, or cold. Thus the early pioneers who crossed the plains depended upon horses and oxen for transportation. A rider on horseback, however, could not transport goods in bulk. To fill this need, caravans of covered wagons set out upon the plains, forming circles around campfires at night for protection against Indian attack. As time passed, stagecoach lines offered a speedier form of transportation.

After the Civil War, the Great Plains attracted increasing numbers of land speculators, ranchers, miners, engineers, and farmers. These newcomers were determined to possess the land and its resources for themselves.

Government policy toward the Indians changed again, now calling for their resettlement on **reservations**. These were sharply defined tracts of land set aside by the government for the Indians. Most reservations were too small to support the hunting way of life. Therefore, the Indians were supposed to get food through government agents on the reservation and to farm, although reservations were located on the poorest land.

Railroads cross the plains. Construction of the first transcontinental railroad began in 1866. Chinese workers were imported to do most of the physical labor on the Central Pacific. Most of the workers on the Union Pacific, building from Omaha, in Nebraska Territory, were recent Irish immigrants. All work was done under the watchful eyes of scouts, who protected the railroad builders from hostile Indians.

The first **transcontinental railroad** contributed enormously to the nation's economic growth. It brought the Atlantic and the Pacific seaboards within a week's journey of each other and opened a speedy route to the rich resources of the West, a route followed by northerners and southerners alike.

The railroad also split the vast buffalo herds of the plains. The herds were split again and again as other rail lines were built across the grasslands. Finally the completion of the Northern Pacific Railway in 1883 sealed the fate of the last, northernmost buffalo herd (see map, page 498).

Destruction of the buffalo. The Plains Indians depended mainly on the buffalo for their living. Government agents and army officers, knowing this, sometimes encouraged the destruction of the great herds as a means of keeping the Indians on reservations. Parties of hunters debarked from trains with horses and equipment, killed the buffalo at will, and loaded the hides on trains bound for eastern markets. It has been estimated that between

The meeting of the "iron horse" and the buffalo signaled the end of a way of life. Soon huge buffalo herds, such as the one shown here, disappeared from the Plains. So too did the culture of the Indians whose lives depended upon the buffalos.

▲ Class activity: Have students compare the importance of railroads today with their importance in the mid-1800's. (Note: Railroads have lost their importance in the communication area. Air travel diminishes their importance for speed. Trucks travel where railroads do not. Railroads remain a basic means of transport for bulk shipments.)

491

White Bird, a Cheyenne who had fought against General Custer's troops as a boy, painted this picture of the Battle of Little Bighorn. News of Custer's defeat in the West by Sioux and Cheyenne Indians reached the East just as the nation began celebrating its 100th birthday on July 4, 1876.

1871 and 1874, hunters killed nearly 3 million buffalo each year. By 1875, buffalo hides were selling from 65 cents to $1.15 apiece. The waste was frightful. Buffalo carcasses were abandoned, and for every hide taken, four were left on the plains.

The disappearance of the buffalo doomed the Plains Indians. The Indians saw the dwindling herds and the increasing number of white settlers. They saw the treaties, by which they agreed to give up land or to move to reservations, broken again and again by whites. They learned that the agents who ran the reservations were often corrupt. The Indians also came to resent the restrictions of the reservations and the attempts by the federal government to change their way of life.

Many Indians decided to resist the whites. They left the reservations and tried to resume their lives as hunters on the plains. This brought another change in government policy toward the Indians, one in which the United States Army played a key role. The army's mis-sion was to keep the Indians on the reservations and to force the return of those who fled.

The Indian wars. Despite their advantages over the Plains Indians, white settlers and the army had to fight long and hard to drive them from their hunting grounds. Between 1865 and 1886, the United States conducted a costly and brutal campaign against the Plains Indians. In all the engagements of this campaign, former soldiers who had fought for the South or the North in the Civil War now fought together against the Indians.

In 1866 Congress decided to recruit four all-black regiments—the 24th and 25th Infantries and the 9th and 10th Cavalries—to fight in the Indian wars. One fifth of the army's soldiers on horseback in the western campaigns were enrolled in the 9th and 10th Cavalries.

During the 30-odd years of the Indian wars, the Indians fought back against white and black military forces in an effort to hold on to their lands and to keep their distinctive ways

▲ "Buffalo Bill" Cody boasted of killing 4,280 buffalo in 18 months. By 1889 there were only about 550 buffalo left on the plains. Today there are more than 15,000 buffalo because of conservation efforts.

of life. As in earlier conflicts with settlers, the Indians were not always united in their struggle. Traditional tribal rivalries explain in part why the federal regiments were often able to enlist Indians as highly useful scouts.

Still, Indian resistance was remarkable. The smaller the area into which the Indians were driven, the more desperately they fought back. There was brutality on both sides, and army leaders fought not only with guns but also with broken promises. In 1877, the same year in which Chief Joseph made his heroic attempt to lead his people to freedom in Canada, President Hayes admitted, "Many, if not most, of our Indian wars have their origin in broken promises and acts of injustice on our part."

Custer's last stand. Just the year before, one broken promise had brought disaster. The Sioux had been promised as a permanent home the Black Hills in what are now South Dakota and Wyoming, which they considered sacred. However, after gold was discovered in the Black Hills, the 7th Cavalry, in 1876, was ordered to remove the Indians to a less desirable area. The removal operation was under the command of General George Custer, an experienced Indian fighter. Several years earlier, Custer had attacked a peaceful Indian village on the Washita River in Oklahoma. In the attack unarmed women and children as well as warriors were killed.

In June of 1876, General Custer attacked a large camp of Sioux and Cheyenne near the Little Bighorn River in Montana. The Sioux and Cheyenne warriors had two outstanding leaders. One was Sitting Bull, able, honest, and idealistic. The other was Crazy Horse, uncompromising, reckless, a military genius, and the most honored hero of the Sioux.

In fierce fighting along the Little Bighorn, Custer and his whole detachment of 264 troops were killed and some bodies mutilated. General Custer's last stand provoked long controversy, but none could deny that it was a major humiliation for the United States government. Still, the action at the Little Bighorn for a time marked the end of major fighting on the northern Great Plains. Troops pursued and harried the Sioux and Cheyenne until Crazy Horse and Sitting Bull were defeated and the Indians forced onto reservations.

Resistance ends in the Southwest. To the south and west, meanwhile, the Apaches continued their three centuries of almost uninterrupted war against the whites. First there had been the Spaniards, then the Mexicans, and finally the North Americans. From time to time, bands of Apaches and Comanches led by Cochise, Victorio, Geronimo, and others rode out of their reservations and spread terror along the Mexican–United States border. Finally, in 1886, Geronimo surrendered. With his surrender, organized resistance came to an end on the southern plains and in the rugged mountains of the Southwest.

The end of the fighting. It was on the northern plains, however, that the United States cavalry wrote the final bloody chapter in the long and tragic history of Indian-white warfare.

The events leading up to this final tragedy had their roots in 1889 with a religious revival that swept through the Indian tribes. The revival was celebrated in what the whites called the "Ghost Dance." It was based on the belief that an Indian Messiah was about to appear. With his arrival dead Indians would rise from their graves to join the living, the buffalo would again roam the plains, and the white intruders would vanish from the Indian lands like mist under the morning sun.

The Ghost Dance was not a call to war. It was, on the contrary, the celebration of a vision —the restoration of the old and treasured Indian way of life. As such, it awakened new hope in the hearts of a broken, despairing people. The Ghost Dance cult quickly gained followers, including many Sioux on the northern plains. White miners and settlers, alarmed at what they feared might be another outbreak of warfare, demanded that the army put an end to the activity.

At Wounded Knee in South Dakota in December 1890, a unit of the 7th Cavalry responded to this demand. The cavalry arrested a band of Sioux men, women, and children who were traveling to the Pine Ridge Reservation in search of food and protection. The troops surrounded the Indians and disarmed them. During the process a disturbance broke out, and someone fired a shot. Immediately, without warning, the troops opened fire with rifles and with Gatling guns, the earliest type of machine guns. They poured a deadly hail of lead into the band of unprotected Sioux, killing or mortally wounding 90 men and 200 women and children.

▲

▲ Report topic: Dee Brown's book, "Bury My Heart at Wounded Knee."

493

Many Americans expressed their horror at such brutality. Others rejoiced that at last General Custer had been "avenged." The brutal massacre at Wounded Knee brought an end to all organized armed resistance from Indians.

SECTION REVIEW

See underscored items, text pp. 487, 490-93.

Identify: Great American Desert, Bureau of Indian Affairs, concentration, reservations, transcontinental railroad, Chief Joseph, George Custer, Geronimo, Ghost Dance, Wounded Knee

For answers to questions, see Answer Key, pp. A69-70.

1. **Analyzing Ideas:** How did the following contribute to the defeat of the Indians: (a) the revolver, (b) the railroads, (c) the destruction of the buffalo?

2. **Organizing Ideas:** Describe and explain the purpose behind each of these United States policies toward the Indians: (a) concentration, (b) reservations, (c) military force.

3. **Comparing Ideas:** Contrast the actions of Chief Joseph and Geronimo in response to United States policy toward the Indians.

2 The government tries to "Americanize" the Indians

See Teaching Suggestions in TMRG, pp. TM123-24.

The Indians had once claimed all the North American continent as their own. By 1890 their conquerors had stripped them of most of their land and confined them to reservations.

The reservations. On the reservations, far ▲ removed from their original tribal lands, the Indians confronted the problem of adapting their ways of life to unfamiliar climates and terrains. When they tried to escape, they were pursued, captured, punished, and sent back to the reservation. To make matters worse, just when some of the Indians were beginning to adjust to their new environments, the government would move them to different reservations.

Legally, the reservation Indians were **wards** of the government, like minor children without parents. In return for the lands they had given up, they were supposed to receive certain supplies, such as blankets, seed corn, and basic food. These supplies were often poor in quality and quantity and slow in reaching the Indians. Some agents in charge of the reservations were honest, but many agents profited from corrupt deals with traders and with those who provided the supplies. The Indians were commonly treated with contempt or, at best, as children might be treated.

Americanizing the Indians. Even with the Indians confined to the reservations, there was still a serious "Indian problem" in the view of most white Americans. Most white Americans believed that the Indians had to undergo **Americanization**. This meant that the Indians had to be assimilated into the white

This photograph shows the Pine Ridge Indian Reservation in southwestern South Dakota. It was the final, government-run home of the Sioux, who had tried to stop the spread of settlement onto their lands but had been unable to do so.

Thoc-me-tony, "Shell-Flower," was the daughter of a Paiute chief. Her Anglicized name became Sarah Winnemucca.

While she was still a child, Winnemucca's grandfather took her to work in the San Joaquin Valley in California. There she displayed an excellent facility for languages, learning English, Spanish, and two more Indian languages in addition to Paiute.

Difficulties between the Paiutes and white settlers erupted in the 1860's. Indian agents on the Paiute reservation stole money and supplies. When the Paiutes stole some cattle in retaliation, soldiers from a nearby army post attacked the Indian camp. The soldiers killed many women and children and burned the Paiutes' belongings.

In 1872 the Malheur Reservation was established for the Paiutes in Oregon. Samuel Parrish, an Indian agent who had won the respect of the Paiutes, was appointed to run it. Winnemucca became his interpreter and taught at the agency school. When war broke out between the Bannock Indians and the United States Army, Winnemucca offered her services as an intermediary to General Oliver Otis Howard.

Winnemucca also spent much time pleading the cause of her people. Her speeches drew so much attention that she was invited to come to Washington, D.C., to talk with President Grant. In 1883 she published *Life Among the Paiutes*, a vivid and honest book about the Indian's need for lands of their own. She then opened a school for Paiute children in Nevada.

Sarah Winnemucca spent her life helping Indians and whites understand each other. When she died at 47, many promises of land had been made to the Indians but few had been fulfilled.

American way of life and forced to accept the culture of the dominant majority. To the Indians—reduced in numbers to between 200,000 and 300,000 at that time—this idea meant giving up many of their deeply held values and customs. These included the collective or tribal ownership and use of land; a belief that work was only a means of providing food and shelter, not an end in itself; marriage traditions, including having more than one wife; many religious beliefs; and even clothing styles and adornments. Indian men, for example, resented efforts to make them cut their long, braided hair. Nor did Indian men and boys accept the idea that they were supposed to plant and cultivate the soil; that had always been women's work.

The vast majority of white Americans neither understood nor appreciated the Indian cultures. They were unaware of the importance of these cultures to the Indians' sense of identity and self-respect.

Reform activities. Some Americans, however, were deeply troubled by the long history of the white settlers' injustice to the Indians. Helen Hunt Jackson, in her book *A Century of Dishonor* (1881), provided documentary evidence of the government's broken promises. The reformers were also deeply disturbed by the corruption, inefficiency, and lack of leadership in the Bureau of Indian Affairs.

One reform group, the National Indian Defense Organization, argued that the deep-rooted cultures of the Indians could not be rapidly changed without grave consequences. Members of this group argued that the Indians should be allowed to retain their own tradi-

▲ Helen Hunt Jackson later wrote a book--"Ramona"--that investigated conditions among the Mission Indians of California. To further the cause of the Indians, Jackson gave a complimentary copy of "Ramona" to every member of Congress.

495

tions and customs. Most other reform organizations, however, believed that the Indians could and should be speedily Americanized. They felt that the Indians must adopt Christianity, white American forms of education, and individual land ownership.

Reformers who urged individual land ownership for the Indians actually strengthened, without intending to, the more selfish interests of land speculators, miners, ranchers, and farmers who were already occupying the unsettled areas of the West. These groups, who wanted the more valuable parts of Indian reservations, supported the reformers' policy of individual Indian ownership. Since individuals could more easily be persuaded or bribed to sell their land, such a policy would open remaining reservation lands to white occupation.

Writing the policy into law. The federal government in the Dawes Act of 1887 made a general policy of what it had been trying to do in a piecemeal fashion. With the Dawes Act, Congress hoped to hasten the time when the Indians living on reservations would be successfully Americanized.

The Dawes Act provided that each male head of an Indian family could, if he wished, claim 160 acres (64.8 hectares) of reservation land as his own. Bachelors, women, and children were to be entitled to lesser amounts. Legal ownership of the property was to be held in trust by the federal government for 25 years. During this period the Indians could neither sell their land nor use it as security for a mortgage. This restriction was intended to protect the Indians from unscrupulous land speculators. The Burke Act of 1906 modified this provision. It gave the Secretary of the Interior authority to reduce the 25-year trust period in those cases where the Secretary was persuaded that the Indians were capable of handling their own affairs.

The Dawes Act and the Burke Act also provided that Indians who accepted the land and abandoned their tribal way of life were to be given citizenship, including the right to vote. Meanwhile, Congress voted larger but still inadequate funds for the education of Indian children. Regular day schools or boarding schools far from their homes were set up. In these schools the children were taught, often by poorly trained and unsympathetic teachers, to look down on Indian ways of life as inferior and degraded.

Failure of the policy. The new laws persuaded and enabled some Indians to adopt the way of life of the white majority and to become American citizens. Even so, Indians who left the reservations to live in American towns and cities often met with discrimination in jobs and unfair treatment. Most Indians remained on the reservations, clinging as best they could to their tribal customs and living as wards of the federal government. The government policy of encouraging individual land ownership and individual farming among the Indians largely failed when land speculators found loopholes in the Dawes Act. Between 1887 and the 1920's, much of the reservation land was, in one way or another, taken from the Indians. The land that remained was generally eroded and inferior. Moreover, provisions for safeguarding the health of the Indians were neglected. Malnutrition and disease were widespread.

The late 1800's and early 1900's were in many ways the Indians' darkest period. Yet many kept their vitality and spirit, insisting that they be treated as separate peoples with worthy views of life.

SECTION REVIEW

See underscored items, text pp. 494-96.

Identify: ward, Americanization, Helen Hunt Jackson, Dawes Act of 1887, Burke Act
For answers to questions, see Answer Key, p.A70.

1. **Analyzing Ideas:** It has been said that much of United States policy toward Indians during the 1800's consisted of broken promises and acts of injustice. Give examples to support this view.

2. **Summarizing Ideas:** Describe the efforts by reformers to improve conditions for Indians during the late 1800's.

3. **Comparing Ideas:** What arguments were made for and against Americanizing the Indians?

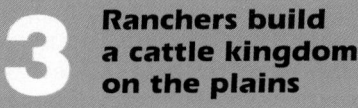

3 Ranchers build a cattle kingdom on the plains

See Teaching Suggestions in TMRG, p.TM124.

Cattle ranchers began to move out onto the Great Plains in the 1860's, long before the Indians were conquered. By the 1890's the cattle industry had become big business. Its prod-

Between 1883 and 1938 Wild West shows designed to glorify the American cowboy toured the United States. Similar in format to circuses, the shows usually reenacted a dramatic Indian attack on settlers' wagon trains heading west. The attack was followed by a last-minute rescue by the U.S. Cavalry. Other featured events included bronco-busting, rough-riding, roping, Indian ceremonials, and sharp-shooting.

The first Wild West show was organized by William F. "Buffalo Bill" Cody. In his youth Buffalo Bill had been a Pony Express rider, buffalo hunter, Union scout, and Indian fighter.

Along with the western novel, the Wild West show personified the cowboy as the gallant defender of a mythic civilization. Many of the stereotypes used in Wild West shows — the strong hero, the warlike Indian, the dastardly villain, and the beautiful woman in distress — were later popularized by western films. These stereotypes gave a false but enduring impression of the American West.

---

ucts passed from the western ranges through the stockyards, slaughterhouses, and packing plants to become major items of domestic and world trade.

Rise of the <u>Cattle Kingdom</u>. Many of the animals for the cattle industry came from the ranches in southeastern Texas formerly operated by Spaniards and Mexicans. These ranches were occupied by the Texans, who also took over the huge herds of wild cattle, called <u>longhorns,</u> estimated in 1865 to number about 5 million head. The wild herds sprang from the cattle that were lost by the Spaniards and by the American wagon trains crossing the plains in earlier days.

It was no easy task for the first Texans to learn how to handle the cattle, wild or tame. A writer in the 1870's warned that "the wild cattle of Texas, . . . animals miscalled tame, are fifty times more dangerous. . . than the fiercest buffalo."

In learning how to handle cattle, the Texans owed a great deal to Mexican **vaqueros** (vah·KAY·rohs), or cowboys, and to Indians. Many slaves also learned the dangerous business of handling cattle. After emancipation freed slaves comprised perhaps one third of those working in cattle raising. With the aid of the horse, the saddle, the rope, and the revolver, white and black cowboys learned how to handle the longhorns on the open grasslands. Mexican Americans, who made up a large part of the cowboy population, continued to play an important role in cattle ranching. It became a profitable occupation and a distinctive way of life.

The long drive. People in the nation's growing cities needed enormous quantities of beef. The problem was to find a means of getting the steers to urban markets. The solution was transportation provided by the railroads, which in the 1860's began to push out upon the Great Plains.

As the steel rails moved westward, enormous herds of steers were driven from Texas north on **long drives** to towns that grew up along the railroads. By 1870, Kansas cattle towns like Abilene, Ellsworth, and Ellis, all on the Kansas Pacific Railroad, and Dodge City and Wichita on the Atchison, Topeka, and Santa Fe Railway had become roaring, riotous, lawless communities (see map, page 498).

During the early years of the long drives, nearly all the steers driven from Texas were

---

▲ Several black cowhands became well known for their skills. Nat Love, known as "Deadwood Dick," was famous for winning a shooting contest in Deadwood, South Dakota. Bill Pickett gained fame by discovering how to bulldog, or to control a steer by grasping its horns. About one in every seven cowhands was black.

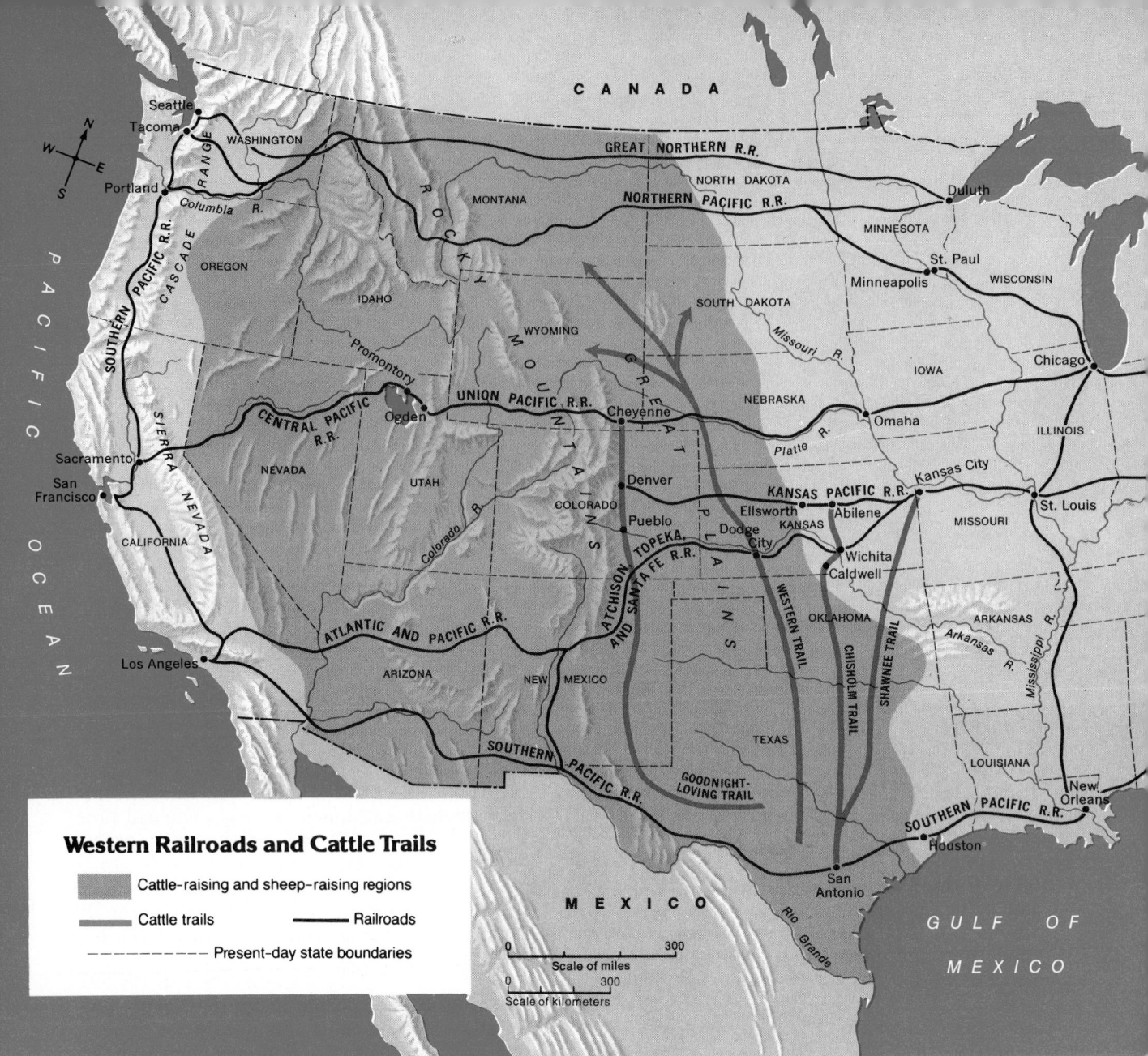

Western Railroads and Cattle Trails

- Cattle-raising and sheep-raising regions
- Cattle trails
- Railroads
- Present-day state boundaries

0 — 300
Scale of miles

0 — 300
Scale of kilometers

sold in the cattle towns at good prices. In time, however, the number of cattle began to exceed the demand. Texans who arrived in late fall were either unable to sell their steers or had to sell them at a loss.

The open range. At this point, enterprising cattle raisers began to winter their surplus ▲ steers on the **open range**, or unfenced grazing lands, near the cattle towns. After fattening

them during the winter, they sold them at high prices in the towns before the new cattle drives from Texas arrived to glut the market.

This was not the first time that cattle had been pastured on the short grass of the Great Plains. Many wagon trains had wintered on the plains, and the pioneers had discovered that their horses and cattle grew fat on the short and thin, but nutritious, grass. The open-range cattle industry did not develop, however,

▲   Class activity: Have students compare the use of the open range with the Indian's concept of land use and ownership.

until the railroads provided access to markets and the Texans provided the cattle.

News that quick money could be made in the open-range cattle business soon reached the eastern seaboard and spread to Europe. The cattle rush that followed was similar to the gold rush that had populated California in 1849–50. Prices for land and steers soared as newcomers on the Great Plains staked out their claims.

People rushed to the cattle country to make their fortunes. They built dugouts, sod huts, or simple ranch houses and pastured their herds on the open grasslands. Some, though by no means all, did become wealthy.

Until the 1880's the cattle ranchers ruled the Great Plains. This was the period of the long drive, the open range, the roundup, and the picturesque roving cowboy.

End of the open range. The open-range cattle industry ended, however, almost as quickly as it had started. As the supply of steers rapidly increased, beef prices fell disastrously low. In 1885 a severe drought burned up the grasses on the overstocked range, and cattle starved by the thousands.

Even more disastrous for the cattle ranchers was the development of the sheep industry and farming. To be sure, Mexican Americans had been grazing sheep in New Mexico for a long time. However, the arrival in the 1880's of large numbers of sheepherders and farmers from the older areas of the United States doomed the open range. Sheep cropped the grass so close that little was left for the cattle. Farmers broke up the open range with their farms and barbed-wire fences. The cattle ranchers fought desperately to keep the range open, but it was a hopeless battle. By the late 1880's, the open, unfenced range was fast becoming a thing of the past.

By the 1890's the western cattle industry centered in the high plains running through eastern Montana, Wyoming, Colorado, the New Mexico Territory, and western Texas. Most ranchers by now owned their grazing land and fenced it in with barbed wire.

<u>Ranches</u> varied in size from about 2,000 to 100,000 acres (about 800 to 40,000 hectares). Western ranches had to be large since each steer required a grazing area of 15 to 75 acres (or about 6 to 30 hectares). The size of the area depended upon the amount of rainfall.

(Railroads were used to ship cattle to market in St. Louis and Chicago.)

Complete with a "tonsorial parlor," or barber shop, Dodge City in 1878 was a typical cattle town. Note the railroad tracks at the bottom of the photograph. Why were such tracks a common sight in every Western cattle town?

Rainfall of the United States

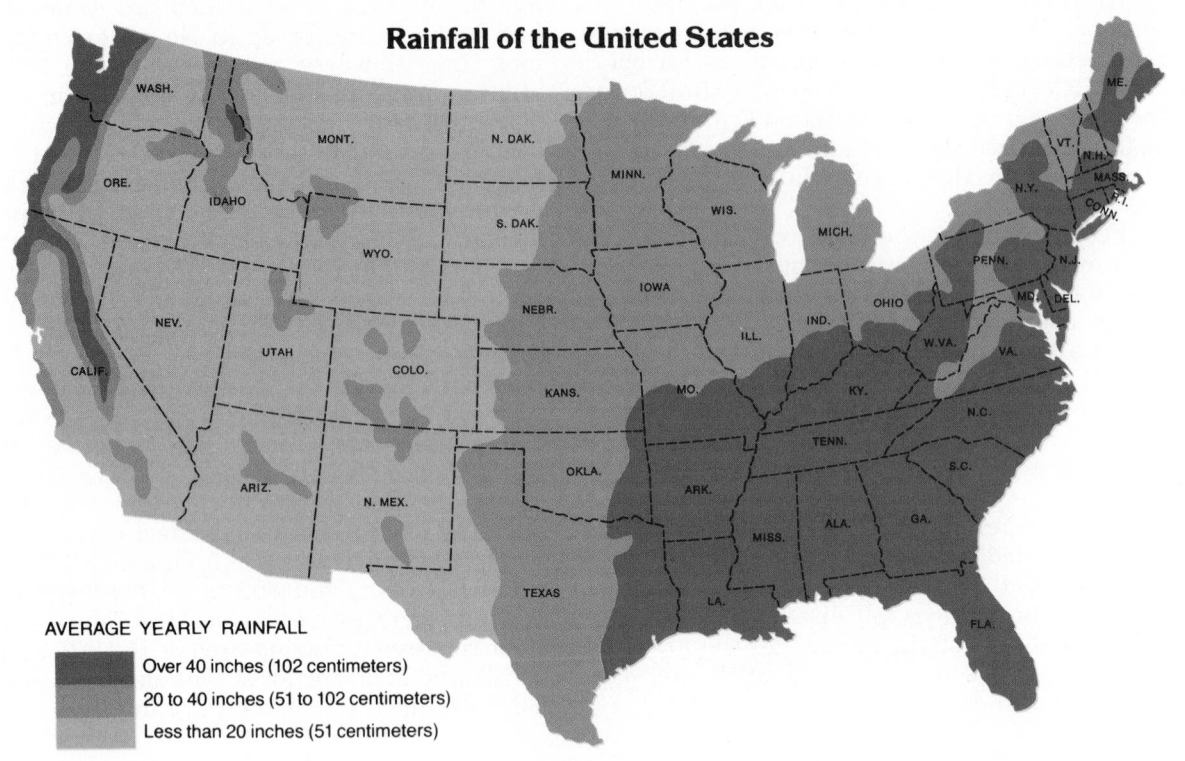

AVERAGE YEARLY RAINFALL

Over 40 inches (102 centimeters)

20 to 40 inches (51 to 102 centimeters)

Less than 20 inches (51 centimeters)

With the invention of better instruments for drilling into the ground and the improvement of windmills for pumping water, many cattle raisers watered their herds from wells scattered over their ranches. In years of abundant rainfall, cattle ranchers might prosper, since their herds could fatten on the natural grasses. In years of drought, they had to feed their cattle hay or cottonseed cake, a costly practice that could wipe out their profits.

Growth and specialization. The cattle industry tended to become more and more specialized. Many ranchers on the plains began to concentrate on breeding and raising cattle. The steers were then sold to farmers in the rich corn and pasture lands of the prairies. After being fattened for market, the cattle were shipped to nearby stockyards in Omaha, Kansas City, St. Louis, Sioux City, St. Paul-Minneapolis, and Chicago (see map, page 498). There they were slaughtered and transported in refrigerator cars to eastern cities and sometimes from there to Europe.

Ranchers used the prairies, the semiarid plains, the high plateaus, and the mountain valleys of the West for cattle grazing lands. On these lands they produced a substantial portion of the nation's meat and wool. By the 1890's the western livestock industry had become an organized, specialized business, closely tied to the nation's economic life.

SECTION REVIEW
See underscored items, text pp. 497-99.

Identify: Cattle Kingdom, longhorns, vaqueros, long drive, open range, ranch

For answers to questions, see Answer Key, p.A70.

1. **Seeing Relationships:** What was the relationship between the railroads and the long drive?

2. **Analyzing Ideas: (a)** Why was the open range important to the cattle industry? **(b)** Why did it disappear?

3. **Studying Maps:** Look at the map on page 498. **(a)** Locate three cattle trails and name them. **(b)** Why was Kansas City important to the cattle industry? **(c)** Why did Chicago become an important trading center in 1890?

DEVELOPING HISTORY STUDY SKILLS

Writing About History   Connecting Ideas in Paragraphs

Compare the following paragraphs to see which is clearer and more readable.

> The Indian in California in the 1860's could not vote. He could not attend a school for whites. He was not permitted to testify in court. He could not even claim damages for injury. He had no civil rights whatever.

> The Indian in California in the 1860's could not vote. He could not attend a school for whites. He was not permitted to testify in court. He could not even claim damages for injury. In short, he had no civil rights whatever.

The difference between the two paragraphs is one phrase, "In short." This phrase links the main idea of the paragraph, the fact that the Indian in California in the 1860's had no civil rights, to a list of facts supporting the main idea. Without the transitional phrase it is unclear that the last sentence in the paragraph contains the main idea.

Good writing depends on clarity. One way to write clearly is to make sure all ideas are connected. Continuity in writing is strengthened by the use of transitional words and phrases, bridges that carry the reader from one sentence to the next or from one paragraph to the next. A transitional word or phrase can indicate sequence and chronology, consequence, addition, contrast and comparison, summation, emphasis, or relationship. In the next column is a list of transitional words and phrases. Used properly, they can help make the organization of sentences and paragraphs clear.

How to Establish Continuity in Writing

To establish continuity in writing, follow these guidelines.

1. **Be logical.** Organize sentences in a paragraph so that one sentence naturally and logically follows another. In paragraphs with a topic sentence, every sentence should support the main idea expressed in the topic sentence.

2. **Show relationships.** Use transitional words and phrases to show how ideas are related to each other and to make smooth connections between successive paragraphs. Study the list of transitional words and phrases below. Note the many different transitional words and phrases and the relationship each word or phrase conveys.

Transitional Words and Phrases

- **Sequence and chronology:** first, second, finally, later, meanwhile, after, now, soon, formerly, then

- **Consequence:** as a result, therefore, consequently, accordingly, for that reason, hence

- **Addition:** furthermore, in addition, also, plus, moreover, as well as

- **Contrast and comparison:** on the other hand, however, yet, nevertheless, on the contrary, similarly, in the same way, likewise

- **Summation:** in general, in summary, in conclusion, in short

- **Emphasis:** indeed, especially, in fact

- **Spatial Relationship:** outside, inside, near, behind, ahead, above

Applying the Skill

In the paragraph in the first column on page 502, one idea logically follows another but no transitional words or phrases make clear the relationship between ideas. Read the paragraph. Think of ways to better connect the ideas.

Indian Resettlement

The great vacant areas west of the Mississippi River seemed to provide sufficient raw land for full Indian resettlement. It was recognized that the new occupants would have to be given help if they were to become established and support themselves under the American economic and agricultural system. The Indians were to be supplied with tools, with seed, and with building materials. Agents and other staff were charged with maintaining proper standards of public health and law enforcement as well as for instructing the tenants in the intricacies of American rural life. On paper, the system probably was as good as could have been devised under the existing conditions. As applied to California, and as there administered, it was a complete failure.

Indian Resettlement

The great vacant areas west of the Mississippi River seemed to provide sufficient raw land for full resettlement. **However,** *it was recognized that the new occupants would have to be given help if they were to become established and support themselves under the American economic and agricultural system.* **Hence,** *they were to be supplied with tools, with seed, and with building materials. Agents and other staff were charged with maintaining proper standards of public health and law enforcement as well as for instructing the tenants in the intricacies of American rural life. On paper, the system probably was as good as could have been devised under the existing conditions.* **Nevertheless,** *as applied to California, and as there administered, it was a complete failure.*

At the top of the next column is the same paragraph with some transitional words and phrases. Note that with the use of the word *however,* it is clear that the second sentence is in contrast to the first. The use of the word *hence* in the third sentence shows that the Indians were given tools as a result of the recognition that they needed help. The use of the word *nevertheless* in the last sentence establishes another contrast. Note that other transitional words or phrases could be substituted for those used in the paragraph.

Practicing the Skill

The excerpt below continues the discussion of the Indian reservation system in California. Read the excerpt. Then on a separate sheet of paper list the transitional words and phrases used and explain what ideas they connect and how. Refer to the list on page 501 to help you identify the words and phrases used and for clues to the ideas they connect.

The Indians of California

California was unique in the United States with respect to the structure of its indigenous society. While, to the east, one found substantial tribes or confederacies such as the Iroquois, Sioux, or Apache, along the Pacific Coast were scattered dozens of little units, often no more than single villages. . . . There was no superior controlling class. . . . nor any significant intergroup coordination. Each unit was confined to its own clearly recognized home, with an adjacent territory for foraging of not more than a few miles in extent. To tear out such a tribelet, in toto, and transport it to a far place and strange surroundings, inflicted a profound emotional injury. Moreover, it was customary for the army and the Indian Service to gather together the scraps and remnants of a dozen different linguistic stocks and throw them together in a confused mass on an undeveloped, unprepared reservation. . . .

Furthermore, once established upon the reservations, the Indians found it very difficult to develop any settled economy or social organization because of incessant attacks and harassment by the neighboring white population. These people bitterly resented the removal of good land for the use of the Indians. Repeated instances are on record of outright invasion and appropriation of sizeable tracts for farming, as well as of unrestrained trespass for the ranging of livestock.

(See solid-line underscores for transitional terms and broken-line underscores for ideas connected by the transitional terms.)

In 1888 these settlers in Custer County, Nebraska, used the side of a hill as the basis for their home. The house is part dugout and part sod walls.

4 Farmers plow the tough sod of the last frontier

See Teaching Suggestions in TMRG, pp.TM124-25.

Farm families, single men, and some single women followed the cattle ranchers onto the prairies and plains. From 1870 to 1900, American pioneers settled more land than had all previous generations combined.

In the 263 years from the first tiny settlement at Jamestown in 1607 until 1870, white settlers claimed and occupied nearly 408 million acres (165 million hectares) of what had once been Indian land. This pace was almost leisurely compared to the speed with which later settlers conquered the prairies and the plains. In the 30 years between 1870 and 1900, pioneers settled an additional 430 million acres (174 million hectares). This was an area roughly equal to the combined areas of Norway, Sweden, Denmark, the Netherlands, Belgium, Germany, and France.

What was happening in America at this time to make possible such rapid settlement?

Free land. One attraction of the West was free land. In 1862 Congress enacted the Homestead Act, which granted 160 acres (64.8 hectares) to any individual who wished to settle a farm, or, as it was called, a **homestead.**

Farmers as well as land speculators rushed to accept the offer. Thousands were ex-soldiers who sought new homes in the West. Thousands of others came from worn-out farms in the East, particularly from New England, in the hope of finding more fertile land. Still other thousands came from Europe. In many areas of the Middle West, more than half of the pioneer settlers were immigrants—Germans, Norwegians, Swedes, Danes, Czechs, Finns, and Russians.

Railroads and settlement. Without the railroad, however, the free land in the West, no matter how attractive, would have remained unpopulated. During the 1870's and the 1880's, four great transcontinental railroads crossed the prairies and the plains. These railroads along with their branch lines opened up the western country for settlement.

The rail lines into and through the wild western country were built only at enormous cost. Moreover, the investment was extremely risky. Investors did not know when, if ever, the new railroads would begin to make a profit and reward them for their risks. Thus the government, which was eager to have the railroads built, encouraged the pioneer railroad companies with cash subsidies and grants of land.

At the time the grants were made to the railroads, the land itself was almost worthless. Before the railroad companies could profit from their grants, they had to persuade people to move into the unsettled areas. Because the land was close to the railroads and therefore would be valuable, the railroad companies could hope to sell it, even though free land was available in more remote areas. More important was the fact that once the land was settled, the railroads would gain revenue from passengers and freight. In addition, any land that the railroads could not sell immediately would rise in value as settlers built farms, villages, and towns along the right of way.

With such things in mind, the railroads started extensive advertising campaigns. They sent literature and agents all over the United States and even into Europe. Life on the plains was pictured in glowing colors. As an added lure, prospective purchasers were sometimes

● Class activity: Refer students to the immigration graph on page 1001 of the Reference Section of the textbook. Have students compare the immigration figures for the years between 1860 and 1890 with those for the years before the Civil War.

503

offered free railroad transportation to any land they might buy. The transatlantic steamship lines were always eager to obtain passengers and freight. They also began advertising campaigns in Europe.

The problems of houses and fences. Despite such efforts, settlers did not at first pour into the plains. For one thing, many still believed the old myth of the Great American Desert. An even more important factor slowing settlement was the scarcity of wood.

Pioneer families solved the problem of housing, as people have always done, by making use of whatever building material was available. On the plains this was sod. Cut out of the soil, bricklike chunks of sod formed the walls of shelters called **sod houses**. With a few precious pieces of wood the settlers framed the roof, finishing it with a layer of sod to keep out wind and rain and snow.

Fencing presented an even more difficult problem. Pioneer families could not farm without fences to protect their crops, and on the plains there was no material for fences. The first pioneers tried everything, even mud

Finding fencing materials on the Great Plains was a problem that was solved by the invention of barbed wire. Several types of barbed wire were invented. The one that proved most popular was invented by Joseph Glidden.

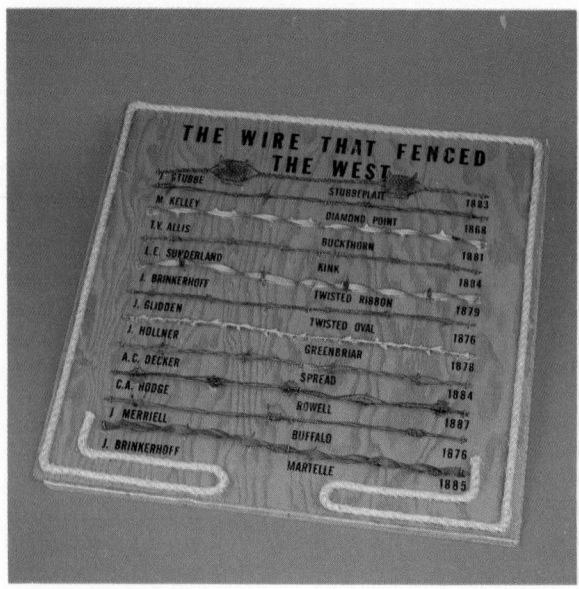

walls, but without success. Ordinary wire strung between a few precious wooden posts was not effective. Cattle could get their heads through the smooth strands of wire and gradually work an opening in the fence.

The problem of fencing was finally solved by Joseph Glidden with his invention of barbed wire. Glidden took out his patent in 1874. Barbed-wire fences proved effective as a barrier to cattle, and within 10 years the open range was criss-crossed by a network of barbed-wire fences.

The problem of water. Scarcity of water, like scarcity of wood, was a problem that pioneer farm families had never had to face in the eastern part of the United States. Eastern farmers took their water from springs bubbling to the surface or from shallow wells. On the Great Plains, where the water was much deeper underground, machinery was needed to drill deeper wells. Once the well shafts had reached the water, the farmers then needed mechanical pumps to draw the water to the surface.

In a search for oil during the 1860's, petroleum companies developed new drilling machinery capable of penetrating farther beneath the surface than ever before. This machinery speedily found its way to the Great Plains. Farmers and ranchers used it to tap water supplies deep underground.

Meanwhile, other inventors were developing windmills capable of operating pumps to draw water to the surface. Daniel Halladay of Connecticut developed the self-governing windmill. This device automatically adjusted itself to wind pressure and thus operated at a uniform speed.

Windmills were first used on the Great Plains to provide water for steam locomotives crossing the plains and for herds of cattle. The windmill really came into its own when farmers began to settle on the semiarid lands. Factories producing windmills were soon doing a thriving business.

Other problems. Railroads, barbed wire, factory-made windmills—all products of the new industrial age—helped farmers conquer the Great Plains. So, too, did the development of **dry farming**. Dry farming involved deep plowing and careful cultivation to keep the surface of the soil pulverized and thus conserve as much precious moisture as possible.

The pioneer farm families had other prob-

George Catlin's painting captures a moment in a Plains Indian buffalo hunt. The Indians who hunted with bows and arrows or with spears did not threaten to wipe out the buffalo population, but the white newcomers with rifles did.

lems to solve, problems for which inventors, manufacturers, and agricultural experts had no ready answers. For one thing, the cattle ranchers resented the settlers who broke up the open range with their fences. Bitter fights raged in the early days between ranchers and farmers, and many unmarked graves soon dotted the plains. However, it was an unequal struggle, and by sheer force of numbers the farmers eventually won.

Nature also contributed to the settlers' difficulties. Until men and women learned how to deal with the plains environment, life was sometimes extremely harsh. The unrelieved round of daily labor impressed writers who tried to describe the life of the farmers on the Great Plains. O. E. Rölvaag (ROHL·vahg), author of *Giants in the Earth* and *Peder Victorious,* was one such writer. His novels provide a picture of empty plains and lives spent beneath a burning sun, of grasshopper plagues, of drought, of ruined crops, of bitter cold, and of blinding blizzards. Many pioneers gave up the difficult struggle and moved back east, but others remained.

Farm families in the 1880's and 1890's also encountered many new problems created by in-dustrialism. In the new industrial age, as you will read, farmers became increasingly concerned with freight and shipping charges, prices fixed in distant markets, the cost of farm machinery, interest rates on mortgages, and many other factors they could not control.

The Oklahoma Sooners. After the Civil War, many Plains Indians were moved to western portions of Indian Territory. This left a large area of unoccupied land in the central part of present-day Oklahoma. Several treaties had reserved these lands for the Five Civilized tribes—the Cherokees, Creeks, Chickasaws, Choctaws, and Seminoles. When white intruders moved onto this land, federal troops at first drove them off. In 1885, however, the government negotiated with the Creeks and Seminoles to open this part of Indian territory to white settlement.

In March 1889 President Benjamin Harrison issued a proclamation that set in motion a wild rush to the District of Oklahoma. The President announced that free homesteads of 160 acres (64.8 hectares) would be available "at and after the hour of twelve o'clock noon, on the twenty-second day of April." The army immediately set up patrols along the district boundaries to guard against premature entry and waited for the rush to begin.

It was a short wait. By April 22 almost 100,000 land-hungry pioneers—some in wagons, others on horseback—were packed solidly along the boundary line. Exactly at noon the officer in charge fired a shot, and the wild stampede began.

Even the swiftest riders discovered that they were not there soon enough. Many Sooners had evaded the patrols, slipped across the boundary, and staked out claims before the area was officially opened.

Within a few hours of the deadline, every inch of Oklahoma District was occupied. Thousands of disappointed landseekers started back along the roads they had eagerly traveled a short time earlier.

More land was soon available—again at the expense of the Indians. In 1889 land previously reserved for the Sauk, Fox, Potawatomi, Cheyenne, and Arapaho Indians was thrown open to white settlement. In the years that followed, the huge Cherokee Strip and reservations assigned to the Kickapoo, Iowa, Comanche, Apache, and Wichita Indians were also opened to settlement. All told, the Indians lost more than 11 million acres (nearly 4.5 million hectares) of land to white settlers.

The last frontier. The roll call of states entering the Union in the half-century after 1865 is an impressive one. Nebraska entered in 1867; Colorado in 1876; North Dakota, South Dakota, Montana, and Washington all in 1889; Idaho and Wyoming in 1890; Utah in 1896; Oklahoma in 1907; and New Mexico and Arizona in 1912.

In 1890 the Superintendent of the Census Bureau made a significant statement: "Up to and including 1880," he declared, "the country had a frontier of settlement, but at present the unsettled area has been so broken into by isolated bodies of settlement that there can hardly be said to be a frontier line."

SECTION REVIEW
See underscored items, text pp. 504-05.

Identify: homestead, sod houses, Joseph Glidden, Daniel Haladay, dry farming, Oklahoma Sooners
For answers to questions, see Answer Key, p.A70.
1. **Determining Cause and Effect:** How was western settlement speeded by **(a)** the Homestead Act and **(b)** the railroads?

2. **Summarizing Ideas:** How did plains farmers solve the problems of housing and fencing?
3. **Analyzing Ideas:** Why was the windmill important to the Great Plains farmers?
4. **Studying Graphics:** Look at the picture on page 503. **(a)** What does it indicate about life for farm families on the plains? **(b)** How did the natural environment affect farmers' lives?

5 Miners find new treasure in the western mountains

See Teaching Suggestions in TMRG, p.TM125.

Developments of the new industrial age made it possible for the farmer to conquer the last western frontiers. The West, in turn, helped to speed the Industrial Revolution. From western farms came unending food supplies for the growing city populations. From western mines came an apparently limitless supply of gold and silver to provide capital to build industries. From other western mines came a steadily swelling volume of metals.

"Forty-Niners" and "Fifty-Niners." The discovery of gold in California drew fortune hunters by the tens of thousands to the Pacific coast in 1849–50. Some of the "Forty-Niners" made fortunes, but most were disappointed. Refusing to admit defeat, prospectors began to explore the valleys and slopes of the mountainous regions between the Pacific Ocean and the Great Plains. The development of mining communities again put pressure on the government to force Indians onto reservations.

In 1859, prospectors discovered gold near Pikes Peak in the unorganized territory of Colorado. More than 100,000 "Fifty-Niners" rushed to the scene to stake their claims. Caravans of covered wagons lumbered across the plains with the slogan "Pikes Peak or bust" lettered on the white canvas. Some prospectors shouldered packs and crossed the plains on foot. Others pulled handcarts behind them. Perhaps half of the fortune hunters returned the way they had come, with their slogan changed to "Busted, by gosh!" Nevertheless, enough settlers remained to organize the Territory of Colorado in 1861.

Even more valuable than the Colorado deposits were the discoveries of silver in 1859 in

▲ Central City, Colorado, once a rough and tumble mining town, is now preserved as a popular tourist attraction.

Taylor, Nevada, was one of many mining towns that boomed for a while, then faded away. Here it is in its heyday in 1881. Note the American flag flying at half-mast in honor of the recently assassinated President Garfield.

the western part of the Territory of Utah. Within a decade nearly $150 million worth of silver and gold had been extracted from the famous Comstock Lode located in what is now the state of Nevada. By 1890 the total had reached $340 million. Enough of the early prospectors stayed after the stampede of 1859 to organize the Territory of Nevada, which became a state in 1864.

Gold in the Black Hills. In 1874, as you have read, prospectors found gold in the Black Hills of South Dakota. Like the discovery of gold in California, another gold rush followed. This area was Indian territory, the Sioux Reservation, which the federal government was supposed to preserve for the Indians. However, the government made only half-hearted efforts to keep prospectors out of the region. The lure of gold was too strong, and the government soon completely abandoned its efforts to protect the Indians. In 1877 the government opened the entire area to white settlers.

Early mining communities. During and after the Civil War, mining communities sprang up in many areas of the West. Life in these mining camps has been described vividly in *The Luck of Roaring Camp* by Bret Harte and in *Roughing It* by Mark Twain. These and other contemporary accounts present a picture of wild, lawless communities of tents, rough board shacks, and smoke-filled saloons strung along a muddy street.

Each mining camp passed through several stages of development. At first, people made their own laws, relying for safety upon fists or guns to protect themselves and their families. Then some citizens began to organize as private police forces, often called **vigilantes** (vij·ih·LAN·teez), in an effort to maintain order. Soon men and women built schools and churches—crude shacks, but important steps toward civilized living. With the schools and churches came organized local government. Then came the appeal to Congress for recognition as a United States territory. Eventually

▲

As many as 1,000 black prospectors may have come to California during the Gold Rush. The miner in this 1852 photograph is using a device to wash gold out of gravel.

government sent many expeditions into the mountains, and in 1879 the <u>United States Geological Survey</u> was organized. Private industry also sent out carefully organized expeditions. The picturesque prospector with pack horse and hand tools continued to roam the mountains. Long before the end of the 1800's, however, an increasing number of the mineral deposits were discovered by expeditions equipped with the latest technological devices and knowledge of geology.

The development of the nation's industries brought a growing demand for metals of all kinds. Copper, needed when the electrical industry developed, was found in enormous quantities around Butte, Montana; Bingham, Utah; and in Nevada and Arizona. Lead and zinc were discovered in the same area. These and other metals have helped the United States to become the leading industrial nation in the world.

Mining as big business. Other developments brought about great changes in mining. New methods of extracting the metal from the ore were discovered. Colleges of mining engineering were opened, powerful machinery was invented, great corporations were organized, and armies of skilled technicians and engineers moved into the mining regions. New equipment and the growing knowledge of chemistry and metallurgy enabled companies to work low-grade ores with profit.

By the 1890's mining had become big business. Engineers, equipped with the latest tools of science and technology, were converting the West into a region of enormous value to the industrial development of the nation.

the territory would adopt a constitution and be admitted to the Union as a state.

Today the mountain regions, the valleys, and the high plateaus of the West are dotted with abandoned mining communities—**ghost towns**. The gaping mine shafts and the sagging, windowless cabins stand as mute testimony to the fact that prospectors and miners once pioneered on this vast frontier.

Systematic exploration. The early discoveries of gold and silver acted like magnets, drawing adventuresome prospectors into the unexplored regions of the West. Before long, however, exploration was conducted on a more systematic basis, partly because of federal efforts. Between 1865 and 1879, the federal

SECTION REVIEW

See underscored items, text pp. 506-08.

Identify: "Pikes Peak or bust," Comstock Lode, Bret Harte, Mark Twain, vigilantes, ghost towns, United States Geological Survey

For answers to questions, see Answer Key, pp.A70-71.

1. **Summarizing Ideas: (a)** Who were the "Forty-Niners"? the "Fifty-Niners"? **(b)** What impact did these people have on settlement of the West?

2. **Organizing Ideas: (a)** Describe life in the early mining communities. **(b)** What stages of development did the communities go through?

3. **Analyzing Ideas: (a)** How and why was the individual prospector replaced by organized mining expeditions? **(b)** What circumstances helped mining to become big business by the 1890's?

The conquest of the Plains Indians and the settlement of the land west of the Mississippi River took place, for the most part, during and immediately after the Civil War. Settlers poured into the prairies and plains in great numbers after the passage of the Homestead Act in 1862. By the 1890's they had settled so much of the West that the Superintendent of the Census Bureau announced that the frontier no longer existed.

The vast region of the West, almost half of the total area of the present United States, had from time immemorial belonged to the original inhabitants, the Indians. The white government and the onrush of settlers drove the Indians from their lands and forced them to live on reservations. Efforts to "Americanize" the original Americans ended in failure. The West that the whites had settled was not one region, but many regions, each basically different from the others. The group of settlers—cattle ranchers, farmers, and miners—learned to adapt themselves to their environment. They learned to make use of the most easily developed natural resources—the grasslands, the fertile soil, and the precious metals.

CONNECTING CHAPTER IDEAS

In the next chapter you will read about the transformation of the nation from a mainly agricultural country to one of the great industrial giants of the modern world. You will also read how transportation and communication systems helped link the nation together and gave new directions to American life.

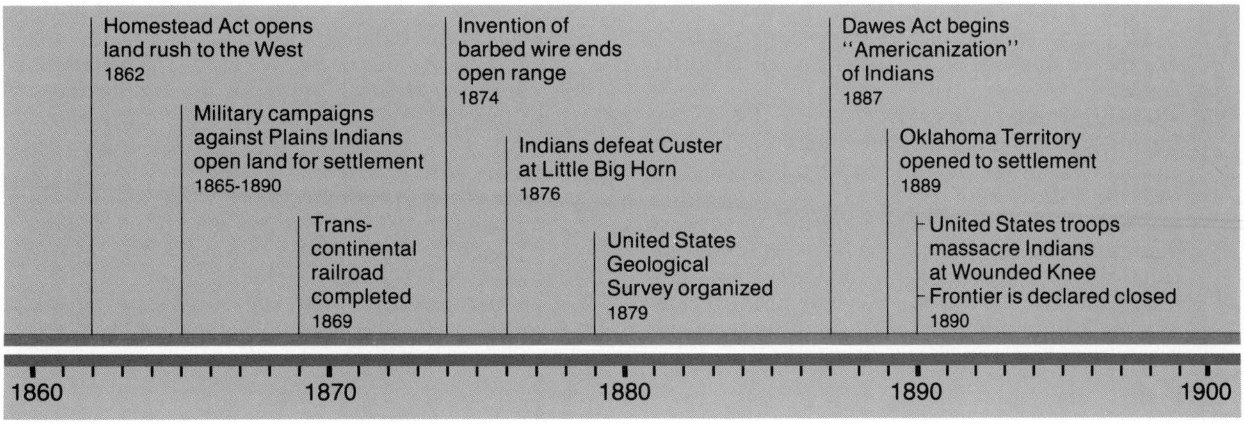

Homestead Act opens land rush to the West 1862	Invention of barbed wire ends open range 1874	Dawes Act begins "Americanization" of Indians 1887
Military campaigns against Plains Indians open land for settlement 1865-1890	Indians defeat Custer at Little Big Horn 1876	Oklahoma Territory opened to settlement 1889
Transcontinental railroad completed 1869	United States Geological Survey organized 1879	United States troops massacre Indians at Wounded Knee Frontier is declared closed 1890

| 1860 | 1870 | 1880 | 1890 | 1900 |

CHAPTER
21 REVIEW

Reviewing Important Terms

Decide whether each of the following sentences is true or false. If the sentence is false, replace the underlined term with the word or phrase that will make it true.

1. The invention of underlined barbed wire helped make fenced ranches possible.
2. The movement of cattle from Texas to rail centers in the North was called the long drive.
3. Mexican cowhands were called vaqueros.
4. Reservations were areas of land set aside for the use of Indians.
5. Unfenced grazing lands, often located near cattle towns, were called ranches.

Practicing Critical Thinking Skills

1. **Evaluating Ideas.** It has been said that the United States tried to solve the "Indian problem" by eliminating the Indians. Do you agree or disagree with this statement? Give evidence to support your answer.
2. **Comparing Ideas.** (a) Compare the problems that miners, cattle raisers, and farmers faced in settling the land west of the Mississippi River. (b) What solutions did each group find for their problems? (c) How effective were these solutions?
3. **Interpreting Ideas.** The last frontier disappeared by 1890. (a) What actions did the federal government take to encourage settlement and development of the West? (b) What is the significance of the frontier in American history?
4. **Analyzing Ideas.** (a) What effect did the Industrial Revolution in America have on the development of the American West? (b) What effect did the development of the American West have on the Industrial Revolution in the United States?
5. **Relating Past to Present.** Answer the following questions comparing some important aspects in the West in the late 1800's with the situation existing today. (a) Is the scarcity of water still a problem in the West? Give evidence to support your answer. (b) Do railroads today play the same role in the economy of the West that they did in the late 1800's? Why or why not? (c) How has the mining industry changed in terms of the major minerals mined and the methods used?

Developing History Study Skills

1. **Connecting Ideas in Paragraphs.** Reread page 509 of the textbook. (a) What is the main idea in the first paragraph? the second paragraph? (b) What evidence supports the main ideas in paragraphs one and two? (c) List the transitional words and phrases used and explain what ideas they connect and how?
2. **Making Inferences.** Read the following passage. Then study the statements below. Which one expresses an idea that is stated directly in the passage and which one expresses an idea implied by the passage? Explain your choices.

Once we were happy in our own country and we were seldom hungry, for then the two-leggeds and the four-leggeds lived together like relatives, and there was plenty for them and for us. But the white men came, and they made little islands for us and other little islands for the four-leggeds, and always these islands are becoming smaller. . . .
— Black Elk, Sioux Indian

(a) Before the arrival of settlers, the Indians were seldom hungry. (b) The white settlers took away the Indians' lands. (c) Black Elk's way of life is disappearing.

Relating Geography and History

The settlers who poured onto the Great Plains between 1870 and 1900 brought many changes. To understand the impact of these changes, complete the following activities.

1. Draw or trace the map on page 498, including the railroads, towns, and cattle trails. Fill in the names of the Indian tribes from the map on page 489. Under the name of each railroad that crossed the Great Plains, list the Indian tribes through whose tribal land the railroad passed.
2. Write a paragraph assessing the impact of change on the Great Plains. In the paragraph answer these questions: (a) In what ways did the coming of the railroads affect the Plains Indians' way of life? (b) In what ways did the Indians have an effect on the settlers?
3. Conduct research and report on the role of women or the importance of blacks in the development of the West.

UNIT SIX
REVIEW

Discussing Ideas

1. **(a)** Describe reconstruction as it was finally carried out under the Radical Republican Congress. **(b)** Do you think reconstruction was successful? Explain.
2. Compare the situation of blacks and western Indians from 1865 to 1900. Consider **(a)** economic status, **(b)** relations with the federal government, and **(c)** treatment by whites.
3. Did the federal government become more powerful in the years after the Civil War? Give evidence to support your answer.
4. What evidence is there that industrialization was increasingly affecting the nation's development after the Civil War? Give specific examples.
5. Trace the relationship between Congress and the President from 1865 to 1900.
6. Did the United States become more or less democratic during the years 1865–1900? Give reasons for your answer.
7. **(a)** How did the attitudes of white settlers toward the Great Plains change during the 1800's? **(b)** Why did this change take place? **(c)** How did this new way of thinking affect the Indians who had been living on the Great Plains?

Applying History Study Skills

Analyzing Viewpoints. The Plains Indians and the white settlers had very different views of the struggle that took place between them. Read the following two quotations, one from a speech given by Chief Sitting Bull and one from a report filed by a commissioner of Indian affairs. Then answer the questions below.

What treaty that the whites ever made with us have they kept? Not one. When I was a boy, the Sioux owned the world. The sun rose and set in their lands. They sent 10,000 horsemen to battle. Where are the warriors today? Who killed them? Where are their lands?

If they—the Indians—stand up against the progress of civilization and industry, they must be relentlessly crushed. The westward course of population is neither to be denied nor delayed for the sake of all the Indians that ever called this country their home. They must yield or perish.

1. What point of view is expressed by the writer of each passage?
2. What is the main area of disagreement between the writers?
3. On what points do the two writers agree?

Making Connections

1. Imagine you are a journalist in the South just after the Civil War. Write a feature story describing the conditions that you observe in the cities and the countryside.
2. Develop a skit about the impeachment of Andrew Johnson. Have some of your classmates join you in acting out the skit for the class.
3. Prepare a list of the major events in U.S.-Indian relations from 1865 to 1900. Include such items as **(a)** battles, **(b)** signing of treaties, **(c)** establishment of reservations.
4. Conduct research and prepare an oral or written report on the roles of women on the "last frontier." Include their political status, as well as their roles in daily life.
5. Develop a time line for Unit Six. Include entries for at least 10 events. **(a)** What is the theme of your time line? **(b)** Does that theme represent a significant aspect of life in the United States during this period? Explain.

Reading in Depth

Brown, Dee, *Bury My Heart at Wounded Knee* (New York: Holt, Rinehart and Winston). A dramatic account of the "last frontier" from the Indian point of view.

Holt, Rackham, *George Washington Carver* (Garden City, NY: Doubleday). The biography of the son of a slave whose determination enabled him to become a distinguished scientist.

Joseph, Alvin, *The Patriot Chiefs* (New York: Viking). Biographies of the great Indian leaders, such as Crazy Horse and Chief Joseph.

Rölvaag, Ole Edvart, *Giants in the Earth* (New York: Harper and Row). Moving novel of the difficult life of pioneers in North Dakota.

Swarthout, Glendon, *The Shootist* (Garden City, NY: Doubleday). Excellent novel of the "wild west."

511

UNIT SEVEN

The Rise of Industrialism

CHAPTER 22

The Growth of American Industry

1. Transportation and communication systems bind the nation together
2. Expanding business creates more products for more people
3. New forms of business organization appear as industry expands
4. Business pioneers give new directions to American life

CHAPTER 23

The Struggle to Organize Workers

1. Industrialism creates new problems for wage earners
2. Immigration adds strength and variety to American society
3. Wage earners organize to overcome their grievances
4. Organized labor faces opposition as it seeks reforms

CHAPTER 24

Farmers Revolt Against Big Business

1. Farm life remains laborious, but simple
2. Farmers face complex new problems in the industrial age
3. Farm organizations join efforts to regulate the railroads
4. Farm organizations put increasing pressure on government
5. The farmers fail to win control of the national government

CHAPTER 25

Life Styles in the New Industrial Age

1. Cities grow and change under the impact of industrialism
2. Education responds to the changing patterns of American life
3. American writing reflects the new industrial age
4. Architecture and other fine arts respond to a changing society
5. New forms of recreation enrich American life

512

During the second half of the nineteenth century, from 1865 to 1900, the United States underwent the change from an agricultural to an industrial nation. New machines were put to use in larger, more modern factories such as the Assabet Manufacturing Company (below). Enterprising business leaders developed new techniques to raise the money needed for growth. Farmers produced larger harvests to feed an ever-increasing population. Cities grew as industrialization increased and waves of immigrants poured through the golden door into the United States. By 1900 the United States had become the world's leading manufacturing nation. Accompanying industrialization, however, were a host of problems. The nation's leaders found solutions to these problems in the democratic traditions of the United States.

See Chapter Overview in TMRG, p.TM128.
See Chapter Objectives in TMRG, p.TM128.
See Introducing the Chapter in TMRG, p.TM128.

CHAPTER 22

The Growth of American Industry

Changing Ways   (1860's–1890's)

The Corliss
Engine, 1876

In the 1870's a majority of Americans lived in rural villages and towns with a population of less than 2,500. It was a time of dirt roads; of horse-drawn carriages and wagons; and of covered bridges, their wooden sides plastered with circus posters and notices of county fairs. It was a time of oil lamps, woodstoves, the hand pump, and the open well. It was also a time of the Saturday-evening bath in a washtub in the center of the kitchen floor.

This was the time of quilting and sewing circles, of spelling bees and of the one-room schoolhouse. It was the time of the country store with its tubs of butter and pickles and its cracker barrel. Yard goods and ready-made clothing were displayed, household articles hung from the ceiling, and groceries spilled over the shelves.

A symbol of town life was the small family-owned factory. A symbol of the countryside was the village blacksmith shop. Located at the crossroads, the shop had its charcoal fire, its huge bellows, its iron forge, and its burly smith in a grimy leather apron shaping and fitting a new set of shoes to a neighbor's horse.

But a new industrial age with rapidly growing cities was coming into being. Large factories with smoke pouring from their towering stacks filled the cities. Long lines of railroad cars rumbled across the countryside. A growing number of farm machines and advanced techniques in agriculture increased the output of America's farms. In brief, life in the new industrial age was being transformed in many ways. The blacksmith shop, once a symbol of rural America, began to disappear. This, then, is the story of how America began to change from a rural, agricultural economy to an urban, industrial way of life.

READING FOCUS

As you read about the changing ways of an industrial age, look for the details that support each of the following statements.

1. Transportation and communications systems bind the nation together.
2. Expanding business creates more products for more people.
3. New forms of business organization appear as industry expands.
4. Business pioneers give new directions to American life.

1 Transportation and communication systems bind the nation together

See Teaching Suggestions in TMRG, pp.TM128-29.

The heart of an industrial society is the city, where factories and workers are concentrated and most raw materials are fashioned into finished products. It is also the city where most goods and services are exchanged.

If the city is the heart of an industrial society, the routes of transportation are the veins and arteries. Into the city flow the vital resources gathered from farm and mine and forest and sea. Out of the city flow the unending supplies of manufactured articles. These move day and night over a vast transportation network to every corner of the land and overseas.

Just as the human body cannot function without heart and veins and arteries, so an industrial economy cannot function without its urban manufacturing centers and an efficient system of transportation and communications.

The growth of cities. During the years between 1865 and 1900, the modern city with its busy railroad yards, its smoking factories, its wage earners, and its office workers took shape. During these years, scores of American cities grew from sprawling towns to huge **urban centers.** In 1870 about 75 percent of the people lived in the country or communities of fewer than 2,500 inhabitants. By 1900 only about 60 percent of all Americans lived on farms or in small rural communities. The urban population had skyrocketed. In 1870 only about 10 million of the nation's total population of 40 million were urban dwellers. By 1900 more than 30 million of America's 76 million people lived in urban areas.

Many revolutionary developments aided the growth of cities. Among them were the discovery of new sources of power, the application of hundreds of new inventions and new processes, and the expansion of the nation's transportation and communications network.

The growth of railroads. Between 1870 and 1900, railway mileage in the United States increased from 53,000 miles (85,000 kilometers) to more than 190,000 miles (306,000 kilometers). During these same bustling years,

▲ On the chalkboard have a student construct a simple bar graph illustrating the population percentage figures described in this paragraph. Then have the class form conclusions about the growth of cities.

515

A busy dock scene in Chicago in 1899 provides evidence of the city's growth as a center of transportation.

the railroads improved in speed, comfort, and safety. Double sets of tracks replaced single sets, allowing traffic to flow in two directions at once. Iron rails, which had shattered beneath heavy loads, were replaced by steel rails. Bridges of iron and later of steel replaced wooden bridges. Coal, a more efficient fuel, replaced wood in locomotives. In 1869 George Westinghouse patented the air brake. George M. Pullman's sleeping cars increased the comfort of passengers. Dining and parlor cars also appeared.

By 1893 a half-dozen **trunk lines**, or major railroads, crossed the plains to the Far West. All over the United States feeder, or branch, lines linked the trunk lines with surrounding areas. Soon a network of steel rails served every part of the country.

Financing railroad construction. The construction of railroads into the still unsettled West was enormously expensive. To encourage the building of new lines, the government provided grants of land and loans of money.

The original land grants set aside large areas of land within which the railroad could claim a specified amount. Until the railroads exercised their claim, none of the land could be sold to the public. Some railroads ran into construction or other difficulties and did not exercise their choice for ten years or more. Others never exercised the right at all, and the government took title to the land. In round

figures, the national government turned over 131 million acres (53 million hectares) of land to the railroads. At the time, this land was worth a total of approximately $123 million. The government also made loans of close to $65 million to the railroads.

In return, the land-grant railroads and their competitors carried government troops, military freight, and United States mail for less than the standard rates. In 1945 a Congressional committee reported that railroads had already "contributed over $900 million in payment of the lands which were transferred to them under the Land Grant Act." The railroads also paid an additional $103 million in interest.

Other transportation. While land transportation improved, traffic on the sea lanes and inland waterways also developed. After 1850, sailing ships on the oceans and on the Great Lakes were replaced by steam-driven, steel-hulled freighters and sleek passenger liners. These ocean-going vessels carried millions of emigrants from Europe to the rest of the world, mostly to the United States. They also carried raw materials and manufactured goods to and from the expanding world markets.

Meanwhile, in the growing urban areas, new methods of transportation enabled people to move quickly within the crowded cities. By the late 1800's, electric trolleys were rapidly replacing horse-drawn cars. Steam-driven and, later, electric-powered elevated trains rumbled along above crowded city streets. By the early 1900's, subway trains carried passengers below the streets of New York and Boston.

As steel-framed skyscrapers climbed higher into the air, elevators, powered first by steam and then by electricity, carried passengers and freight from story to story. Without the elevator, skyscrapers could not have been used.

From telegraph to telephone. Equally important developments came in the field of communications.

The **telegraph** had been first developed in the United States by Samuel F. B. Morse and in England by Charles Wheatstone during the late 1830's and the early 1840's—just as the new steam railroads began to appear. The telegraph moved across the country with the railroads. Indeed, without a telegraph system the nation's railroads could not have operated safely.

An international communications revolution was begun in 1844 with Samuel Morse's demonstration of the telegraph. By the 1850's, the American landscape was changing to accommodate wire-carrying telegraph poles. The first telegraph wires followed the route of the railroads, which used the telegraph to keep trains on schedule and to warn engineers of safety hazards on the tracks. The telegraph wires were also used to transmit business orders, price quotations, news, and other vital information.

Many people began to see the need for a worldwide telegraph system, and they wondered if messages could be sent under water as well as over land. First, however, a waterproof shield to protect the wires had to be devised. After numerous unsuccessful attempts, the usefulness of gutta-perche — a soft, waterproof substance that comes from a Malaysian tree — was discovered and a waterproof sheath for telegraph wire was perfected.

In 1851 two English brothers, Jacob and John Brett, succeeded in laying a cable insulated with gutta-perche under the English Channel between France and England. The next step was to lay a similar cable across the Atlantic Ocean.

United States navy engineers had determined that the ocean floor between Newfoundland and Ireland consisted of soft, fairly level mud — an ideal bed for a transatlantic cable. In 1856 Cyrus West Field, an American financier, organized the Atlantic Telegraph Company and began to plan an undersea cable to stretch between those two locations.

Field failed in his first two attempts to lay a cable. While his third try was successful, the transmitted signals were extremely weak and distorted. This problem was solved with Lord Kelvin's invention of the reflecting galvonometer, a device that proved vital to the reception of telegraph messages.

Then in 1865 Field rented the largest ship afloat, the British steamer *Great Eastern,* to make a fourth attempt at laying a cable. One cable broke and was lost before success finally came on July 27, 1866, linking Valencia, Ireland, with Heart's Content, Newfoundland.

Soon a network of undersea cables was laid around the world. By the 1960's new technology made it possible to send 2,500 words per minute. It had become possible to send a message anywhere and receive an answer in a few minutes.

In 1866, about 25 years after Morse's invention, Cyrus W. Field succeeded in laying a transatlantic telegraph cable. During the next few years, additional underwater cables connected North America with other continents. Americans now had almost instantaneous communication with the rest of the world.

In 1876 Alexander Graham Bell, a teacher of the deaf in Boston, applied for a patent on a telephone he had invented. Bell's telephone quickly captured the public's imagination, and in 1885 the American Telephone and Telegraph Company was organized to put the new invention into widespread use.

Other inventions. The telegraph, the underwater cable, and the telephone were landmarks in the history of communications, but other important inventions and developments also reshaped American life. In the 1860's Christopher Sholes of Wisconsin developed the typewriter, which later became an essential part of all business operations. An improved postal system, without which modern business could not function, was also developed.

New machines for making cheap paper from wood pulp and for printing newspapers, books, and magazines also contributed to more effective communication. There was also the camera, which later provided new forms of recreation as well as new techniques for industry and research.

By 1900, improvements in transportation and communications were binding all parts of the United States into a single complex economic unit. The National Banking Act of 1863 had established a sound, uniform currency for the entire country. Specialized business enterprises, both agricultural and industrial, sprang up in all parts of the land, each playing its part in the ever-expanding, interlocking economic system.

517

SECTION REVIEW
See underscored items, text pp. 515-17.

Identify: urban center, George M. Pullman, trunk lines, telegraph, Cyrus W. Field, Alexander Graham Bell

For answers to questions, see Answer Key, p.A73.

1. **Interpreting Ideas: (a)** Why did the federal government help finance the building of the railroads? **(b)** How did the railroads repay the government for federal aid granted them?

2. **Analyzing Ideas:** Explain this statement: If the city is the heart of an industrial society, the routes of transportation are the veins and arteries.

3. **Studying Graphics: (a)** Prepare a time line of the inventions mentioned on pages 516–17. Include at least one invention that depended for its development on an earlier invention.

---

2 Expanding business creates more products for more people

See Teaching Suggestions in TMRG, pp.TM129-30.

● The industrialization of the United States was the result of developments in many different fields. These developments, which took place more or less at the same time, included new sources of energy, new machines, new and bigger industries, and new methods of distributing and selling products and services.

New sources of energy. In the late 1700's, people learned how to convert the energy of wood and coal into steam and to use the steam as a source of power in tasks that had been done for centuries by human, animal, or water power. For more than a hundred years, the steam engine remained the most important "mechanical slave" ever developed up to that time. Then, in the late 1800's, two new sources of power—oil and electricity—were harnessed.

From earliest times people had known about the dark, thick substance that oozed from the earth in certain places and that is now called "petroleum," or "oil." In the early 1850's, kerosene, an efficient and inexpensive fuel for lamps, was first refined from petroleum. The growing demand for kerosene prompted Edwin L. Drake, a retired railroad conductor, to try to drill an oil well near Titusville, Pennsylvania, in 1859. While he was drilling, people thought he was crazy. When the oil began to flow, however, people quickly began sinking wells of their own.

Kerosene rapidly replaced whale oil as an efficient fuel for lamps. In every American city, peddlers carted kerosene through the streets, selling it from door to door. As the years passed, oil was also increasingly used as a lubricant for the nation's many new machines.

The development of the internal combustion engine, which burned gasoline or diesel fuel—both refined from oil—finally turned oil into one of the nation's major sources of power. In Chapter 27 you will read how oil as a source of power had a revolutionary effect on American life.

Power from electricity. Electricity, like oil, was known long before it was put to practical use. The work of two Italians, Galvani and Volta, led in the late 1700's and early 1800's to the invention of the storage battery. The storage battery supplied small amounts of electric current at low voltages and greatly aided those who were experimenting with the uses of electricity. The discoveries of the principles governing the electric motor and the dynamo had even greater effects. Although many persons contributed to these discoveries, a major share of the credit belongs to England's Michael Faraday and America's Joseph Henry.

Thousands of Americans first learned about the dynamo at the Centennial Exhibition at Philadelphia in 1876, where they saw one in operation converting mechanical energy into electrical energy. In 1882 Thomas Edison built in New York City the first large central power plant in the United States for generating electricity. Edison drove his dynamos with steam engines. Other steam-powered electric generating plants soon appeared in other cities. Another giant stride forward came in 1895 with the opening at Niagara Falls of the first large hydroelectric plant for producing electricity from water power. In spite of these developments, by 1900 only about 2 percent of America's manufacturing industries were powered by electricity.

Steel for new industries. Behind the story of new sources of power lies still another story—the discovery of new ways of producing steel. Steel, a mixture of iron, carbon, and other elements, was not a new material. People had made it for centuries and fashioned it into weapons, tools, and utensils. Until the mid-

● Industry's environmental impact was already the concern of a few. Divide the class into small groups. Have the groups report on George Parkins Marsh's 1864 classic study, "Man and Nature."

1800's no one knew how to produce steel cheaply and in large quantities.

The United States had an abundance of the raw materials vital to the new industrial age—iron ore and coal. Immense deposits of iron ore lay near the western shores of Lake Superior. Nearly one half of the world's known coal deposits were waiting to be tapped.

In the 1850's Henry Bessemer in England and William Kelly in the United States independently discovered a new process for making large quantities of steel cheaply by burning out impurities in molten iron with a blast of air. During the next few years, even more effective processes were developed.

The annual production of steel in the United States soared. In 1870, for example, the United States produced only about 68,000 tons (about 62,000 metric tons) of steel. By 1918 production had increased to 44 million tons (40 million metric tons).

The growth of mass production. Much of the growing steel production at this time went into the construction of railroads, bridges, heavy machinery, factories, mills, and other industrial enterprises. American businesses were laying the foundations of an industrial system that eventually would make the United States the most productive country in the world. The system would also provide Americans with the highest national standard of living in history.

As businesses expanded and factories grew larger, their owners and managers developed more and more efficient methods of production. During the first half of the 1800's, Eli Whitney and others had developed interchangeable parts. This development in turn called for a **division of labor**. For instance, a shoemaker no longer made an entire shoe. Instead, in large shoe factories, one worker might run a machine that cut only heels. Another worker might run a machine that shaped soles. All the different parts were then brought together at a central location and assembled by other workers into a shoe. In this way, vast quantities of shoes could be made quickly and cheaply. This division of labor was soon adopted by most American industries. It made possible the **mass production** of products of every kind.

New ways of selling products. The small general store as well as the small family-owned factory became less important in

After 1859 the sound of an oil gusher was welcome to most Americans. Such wells soon made the United States a major oil producer, adding greatly to its industrial growth.

America during the late 1800's. New types of stores arose to handle the ever-growing quantities of products from the nation's factories.

The **specialty store** concentrated upon a single line of goods—hardware, clothing, groceries, shoes, and so forth.

The **department store** combined many specialty stores under one roof. John C. Wanamaker opened one of the first department stores in the United States in Philadelphia in 1876. Marshall Field opened another in Chicago in 1881. Other department stores soon opened in other cities.

<u>Chain stores</u>—stores with branches in many cities—also began to appear. Pioneers in this field of selling were the Great Atlantic and Pacific Tea Company (A & P), founded in 1859, and the chain of stores started by Frank Woolworth in 1879. **Chain stores,** like department stores, bought goods in large quantities at low prices. They then passed on these low prices to their customers. Since women were commonly paid less than men, managers gladly hired women as clerks.

Large-scale professional advertising began to appear in the 1880's. Such advertising introduced new products, promoted mass purchasing, and helped create large national markets for the streams of new manufactured products that were now available.

Specialty stores, department stores, and chain stores were all part of the urban scene. In 1872, however, Aaron Montgomery Ward started in Chicago a mail-order business aimed

United States farmers ordered supplies from catalogs such as this one. Catalog products soon earned a reputation for quality and were delivered to even the most remote farming village.

at the rural market. A few years later, the Sears, Roebuck mail-order business was started. Montgomery Ward and Sears, Roebuck used the same business methods. Customers placed orders and paid for them by mail; their goods were shipped to them by mail or railway express. Catalogs from these two mail-order houses became prized possessions in rural households and in the bunkhouses and camps of cattle ranchers and sheepherders. They helped to bring the outside world to isolated farms and speeded the transformation of farm life.

SECTION REVIEW

See underscored items, text pp. 518-20.

Identify: Edwin L. Drake, Michael Faraday, Joseph Henry, Thomas Edison, division of labor, mass production, Marshall Field, chain store

For answers to questions, see Answer Key, p.A73.

1. **Summarizing Ideas:** In what ways did the revolution in power affect (a) workers and (b) manufacturers?

2. **Analyzing Ideas:** How did each of the following developments help transform the lives of average Americans in the late 1800's: (a) availability of kerosene, (b) cheap steel, (c) mass production?

3. **Organizing Ideas:** What basic premise or idea did the following people have regarding the selling of goods: (a) Frank Woolworth, (b) John Wanamaker, (c) Montgomery Ward?

3 New forms of business organization appear as industry expands

See Teaching Suggestions in TMRG, pp.TM130-31.

Most American factories and stores in the 1860's and 1870's were **individual proprietorships**—small enterprises owned by individuals or families. The individual or the families knew all the workers, often by their first names. Most wage earners in the 1860's lived in small towns, worked in small factories, and often took part in community activities with their employers.

During the next 30 years, much of this small-town, personal relationship disappeared. It was crowded out by the huge industrial plant located in or on the outskirts of a large city and employing hundreds, even thousands, of wage

Small family businesses have played an important role in the social and economic growth of the United States. First on the frontier and then in towns and cities, energetic families created their own business establishments and worked from sunup to sundown in order to maintain them.

Mom-and-pop stores — as these small businesses came to be affectionately called — were often located in small communities or city neighborhoods. They offered a limited range of goods, such as groceries or hardware, from their location in the middle of the block or on a back street. They cultivated a small but faithful clientele who appreciated the special attention and returned again and again. The typical mom-and-pop store was frequently the central neighborhood meeting place. Friends and relatives gathered there to exchange news and gossip while they shopped.

Mom-and-pop stores are still a vital part of the American landscape. Many of the proprietors of these businesses today represent minority groups. Unfortunately, small businesses now account for a smaller percentage of the nation's economic activity than at any time in history. Most new small businesses opening today fail within five years.

earners, who were often strangers to one another and even more remote from the owners.

Partnerships. As businesses grew in size, the owners had to find ways of sharing expanding costs and responsibilities. The **partnership** as a form of business organization became more and more common.

A partnership of two or more persons offers greater capital and skill than a single person can usually provide, but partnerships do have one major weakness. Each partner is completely liable, or responsible, for anything that happens to the business.

Corporations. As industries grew, another form of organization, the **corporation,** became more common. It gradually replaced individual proprietorships and partnerships as the leading form of business organization.

To start a corporation, three or more persons apply to a state agency for a **charter,** or license, to start a specific business en-

terprise. This charter allows the interested persons to organize a corporation and sell shares of **stock,** or certificates of ownership, to raise the capital needed to carry on the enterprise. The **stockholders** or **shareholders** — those who invest money in the enterprise — may periodically receive **dividends,** that is, a share of the corporation's profits. Legally, a corporation is regarded as an individual — an "artificial person" entirely separate from its owners. It possesses certain rights, such as the right to make contracts, to buy and sell property, and to sue and be sued in court.

The corporation has important advantages over the individual proprietorship and the partnership. First, the corporation can draw ▲ upon very large supplies of capital because it can sell shares of stock to many people. Second, the charter gives the corporation perpetual life; that is, the corporation is not ended by the death or resignation of one or several of its owners. Third, stockholders can sell all or part of their stock whenever they choose. Finally,

▲ Many of the new industries such as mining, iron, and steel were ill-suited to small-scale operations. These industries required heavy equipment and a large labor force. They also required sufficient financial reserves to withstand periodic hard times and fluctuating demands for products.

Production of Raw Steel 1870 - 1900

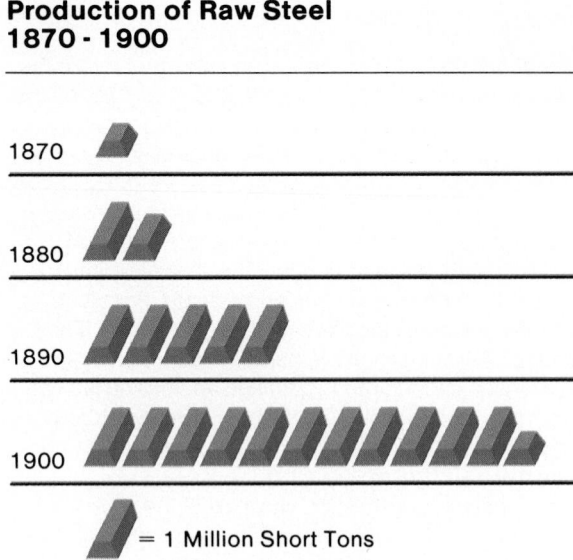

= 1 Million Short Tons

Source: *Historical Statistics of the United States*

Production of Crude Petroleum 1870 - 1900

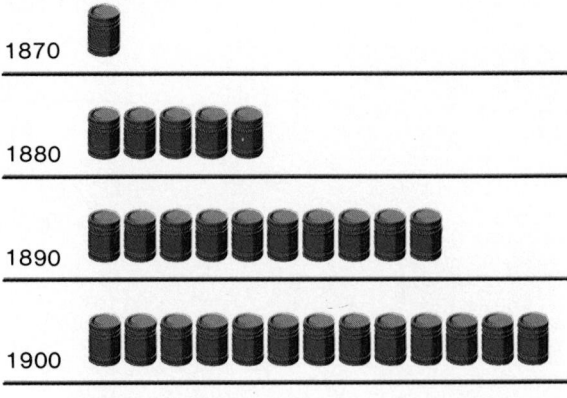

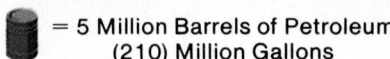 = 5 Million Barrels of Petroleum (210) Million Gallons

Source: *Historical Statistics of the United States.*

investors have only limited liability. That is, if the corporation fails, the stockholders lose only the money they have invested in its stocks. The stockholders cannot be made to pay any debts owed by the bankrupt corporation.

During the first half of the 1800's, only a few large American industries were organized as corporations. These corporations were usually owned by only a handful of persons. By the 1860's, however, business owners needed increasing amounts of capital to build, equip, and operate the new enterprises that were exploiting the vast resources of America's forests, soils, mines, and waters. Forming corporations became a favored method of gathering large amounts of capital. After 1860, corporations became very common.

Business consolidation. During the latter half of the 1800's, there was also a growing trend toward business **combination**, or consolidation. Corporations in the same type of business would frequently join together to create large combinations.

Economists have pointed out many advantages in these combinations. Several corporations, when banded together, could save some of the costs of production and distribution. Through consolidation a business could eliminate competing salespeople and advertising. A consolidated company could purchase larger quantities of raw materials at lower prices and make better use of byproducts. It could arrange better bargains with banks, transportation companies, and workers. In short, through consolidation a business could substitute cooperation for competition and thus reduce waste, costs, and risky losses.

These large commercial enterprises sometimes presented dangers to important principles of freedom in the American economic system. Through consolidation a group of corporations might gain a **monopoly,** or complete control, over a particular field of business. Monopolistic control could lead to restraint of free trade. That is, it could reduce competition, the heart of a free enterprise economy. ▲

For example, a business combination might have so much power that it could undercut prices until its competitors failed. Then the combination could raise prices to make up its losses. Or if a consolidated enterprise gained monopoly control of an entire business field, it could charge excessive prices for its products or services. In such cases, consumers lost the right to shop around for the best bargains. These and other economic practices stemming from monopoly created problems for everyone.

Corporation pools. One of the earliest ways in which corporations combined was by organizing **pools.** To form a pool, several corporations simply agreed to divide all their business opportunities among themselves. For example, several railroads serving the same city might agree on what percentage of local business each would handle. Or they might agree to charge uniform freight rates so that none would gain a price advantage. Or a group of manufacturing corporations might agree to divide the country into several market areas, each reserved for the sales force of one of the corporations in the pool and off limits to all the others.

Unlike the corporation, which operated under a legal charter, a pooling agreement had no legal standing. For that reason, courts refused to judge cases in which a member of a pool violated such an agreement with the other members. However, in 1887, pools were declared illegal in interstate commerce and practically disappeared.

Powerful trusts. Meanwhile, other business owners developed a second form of business consolidation, called the **trust.** Business owners who wanted to organize a trust first had to reach an agreement with the major stockholders in the several corporations involved. The promise of greater profits from a larger organization was often all that was needed to persuade stockholders to enter a trust.

Under the trust agreement, the promoters of the trust, called the "trustees," gained control of the stock in all the corporations and thus of the corporations themselves. In exchange, the trustees gave the stockholders of the corporations trust certificates on which dividends were paid out of the profits of the trust.

With control of the stock in their hands, the trustees could run several corporations as a single giant business enterprise. If the trustees could get control of enough corporations, they could secure monopoly control of an entire business. They could then control prices. They could, for example, lower prices temporarily in one area to drive a competitor out of business, while raising prices everywhere else.

During the 1870's and the 1880's, giant trusts swallowed up corporations in many of the nation's largest industries, including oil, steel, sugar refining, and whisky distilling. When a trust did get control of enough corporations to secure a monopoly and end competition, it often raised prices on the products it controlled. The consumers and smaller competing businesses complained bitterly as the trust closed in on them.

Magazines and newspapers of the time were filled with articles, letters, and editorials pointing out the evils of the "all-powerful monopolies" and pleading with the government to step in and restore freedom of enterprise. However, local, state, and federal governments had passed no laws that said trusts and monopolies were illegal, although under the **common law,**° which courts might or might not enforce, "conspiracies in restraint of trade" were forbidden.

The Sherman Antitrust Act. Finally, in 1890, during the administration of President Benjamin Harrison, Congress passed the Sherman Antitrust Act. The public assumed that the act was intended to restore a larger measure of free competition by breaking up giant "trusts"—a term that had come to mean any monopoly or near-monopoly of an industry. This also seemed to be what Congress intended, for Section 1 of the act declared, "Every contract, combination in the form of trust or otherwise, or conspiracy, in restraint of trade or commerce among the several states or with foreign nations is hereby declared to be illegal." The act further stated that individuals and corporations found guilty of violating the law would be liable to legal penalties.

Actually, few Americans, including lawyers and members of Congress, understood what the new law did and did not prohibit. The act failed to define such words as "trust," "combination," "conspiracy," and "monopoly." Because of such loose wording, the Sherman Antitrust Act was difficult to enforce. The government lost seven out of the first eight cases that it brought against giant business combinations, or trusts.

In 1895 the Supreme Court handed down a decision in the case of *U.S. v. E. C. Knight Company* that made the antitrust law almost meaningless. The Court ruled that the company, which had control of 98 percent of the sugar-refining business, was not guilty of violating the antitrust law because its control of the

°**common law:** a system of law based upon custom, tradition, and precedents established by courts of law.

▲ Ironically, labor first felt the brunt of the Sherman Act. Beginning in 1894, employers routinely obtained court injunctions against strikes, claiming that refusal to work was a conspiracy in restraint of trade and therefore a violation of the Sherman Act.

523

refining process alone did not involve restraint of interstate trade. A monopoly itself was not illegal, the Court stated. It became illegal only when it served to restrain interstate trade.

This and other decisions by the Supreme Court convinced businesses that they were free to consolidate. Thus the movement to form business consolidations actually speeded up in the years after the Sherman Antitrust Act was passed. Some historians see in this development evidence that the act was not really a reform measure. Such historians instead regard the act as an effort by big business to combat the growth of organized labor.

Despite its glaring weakness, the Sherman Antitrust Act was an attempt by the federal government to make rules for the conduct of big business. It established an important precedent for later and more effective laws.

Holding companies.   After 1890 some of the nation's business leaders abandoned the trust for another form of business consolidation – the **holding company.** To form a holding company, it was necessary to get a charter from one of the states. The directors of the holding company then issued stock in the holding company itself. With the money raised by selling this stock, the directors bought controlling shares of stock in two or more corporations that were actually engaged in producing goods or services, such as manufacturing companies or transportation companies. The holding company did not itself produce either goods or services, but the company did control all the corporations whose stock it held.

After the 1890's the holding company became very popular. It was legal. It was responsible for its actions because, unlike the trust, it operated under a charter that could be revoked if the terms were violated.

Other ways to consolidate.   Another form of consolidation was an **interlocking directorate.** In an interlocking directorate, some or all of the directors of one company served as directors of several other companies. Thus they could develop a uniform policy for the entire industry.

There were, of course, other ways to establish a uniform policy. Directors of different companies could simply meet and make secret agreements on prices and other matters.

Business leaders who tried to establish uniform policies for an entire industry – either through interlocking directorates or through secret understandings – were subject to prosecution under the Sherman Antitrust Act. However, it was difficult to prove that a monopoly existed. It was especially difficult when the monopoly had been created by means of interlocking directorates and secret agreements.

SECTION REVIEW
See underscored items, text pp. 521-22.
Identify: individual proprietorship, partnership, corporation, stock, dividend, combination, monopoly, Sherman Antitrust Act
For answers to questions, see Answer Key, pp.A73-74.
1. **Interpreting Ideas:** What advantages does the corporation have over the partnership as a method of business organization?
2. **Summarizing Ideas: (a)** What are the provisions of the Sherman Antitrust Act of 1890? **(b)** Why was this law difficult to enforce?
3. **Analyzing Ideas:** How did the Supreme Court decisions in the late 1800's aid big business?
4. **Studying Graphics:** Make a chart entitled "Forms of Business Combinations" with four columns headed Pools, Trusts, Holding Companies, and Interlocking Directorates. Below each heading **(a)** define this form of business consolidation, **(b)** give reasons for its creation, **(c)** name objections to it, and **(d)** name methods used to control its abuses.

Business pioneers give new directions to American life

See Teaching Suggestions in TMRG, p.TM131.
The people who presided over the new world of throbbing machines, noisy factories, and crowded cities were the business leaders and the financiers. Their influence was reflected in local, state, and national politics.

Influence of business leaders.   Between 1789 and 1860, thirteen Presidents had been elected – seven from the South, six from the North. Between 1860 and 1900, each of the seven Presidents elected was from the industrial regions of the Northeast or the Middle West. On nearly all essential issues, moreover, most of the major differences between the Republicans and Democrats diminished.

The business leaders of this period were not all of a single type. They varied greatly in per-

▲   The Clayton Act (1914) eventually remedied some of the Sherman Act's loopholes by declaring that unions were not "illegal combinations in restraint of trade under the anti-trust laws" because "the labor of a human being is not a commodity or article of commerce."

sonalities, abilities, and methods of doing business. They were pioneers, with the virtues as well as the shortcomings of pioneers. Some were rough, some were refined. All were eager to seize the unlimited opportunities of the new industrial world emerging around them. Some were fabulously successful. Others, the small business owners, never amassed fortunes or won great power. All of them—big-business leaders and small-business owners alike—shared the ideal of self-reliant individualism. This ideal was also shared by the few women who were permitted to take an active part in business. Among these women were Nettie Fowler McCormick in farm machinery, Lydia Pinkham in patent medicines, and Kate Gleason in machine tools.

Cornelius Vanderbilt. "Commodore" Cornelius Vanderbilt was born in 1794, when George Washington was President of the United States. By 1865 Vanderbilt, who had started life as a poor boy, had accumulated great wealth and owned a fleet of steamships worth $10 million. When he died in 1877 at age 82, he was worth $105 million.

Even in his seventies, "Commodore" Vanderbilt was an energetic man with a defiant bearing. He could hardly write, his spelling was impossible, and his temper earned him many enemies. He seemed to act on impulse, following his own hunches. He even consulted astrologers or fortunetellers about how to manage his business affairs.

What did Vanderbilt contribute to American life? For one thing, he consolidated the railroad companies that provided service between New York and Chicago. Before he took control of the different lines, passengers and freight had to be transferred 17 times between the two cities during a 50-hour trip. When he had completed the consolidation, one train made the entire trip in about 24 hours. He replaced iron rails and wooden bridges with steel rails and steel bridges. He built double tracks to make two-way traffic safe and speedy. He constructed new locomotives and terminals. Achievements such as these helped to make possible the rapid development of America's industrial economy.

Andrew Carnegie. Andrew Carnegie was another fabulous business leader during the early decades of industrialism. Born in 1835 in Scotland, Carnegie came to America at age 12 and

At age 16 Cornelius Vanderbilt founded his own business. With borrowed money, he bought a boat and used it to ferry passengers and freight across New York Harbor.

Andrew Carnegie's philanthropy in his later years grew out of his personal philosophy, expressed in 1889: "The man who dies . . . rich dies disgraced."

Horatio Alger, Jr., was the son of a Massachusetts minister. Alger, Jr., attended Harvard College and Divinity School because his father wanted him to become a minister. Alger, Jr., however, ran off to Paris, but soon returned to be ordained a minister in a Massachusetts church. In 1866 he moved to New York City where he became the chaplain of a shelter for orphaned youth.

Alger dreamed of producing serious novels for adults. He failed in this, but he did write. His books for boys made him one of the most widely read authors of the 1800's.

Ragged Dick, published in 1868, was Alger's eighth book and the one that set him on the road to fame. The book's hero is Ragged Dick, a New York City shoeshine boy. He saved the life of little Johnny Rockwell, who had carelessly fallen off a ferry boat. The act earned Dick the gratitude of the boy's father and a job in Mr. Rockwell's business. From there, Ragged Dick moved on to fame and fortune.

Horatio Alger, Jr., wrote 119 fast-paced adventure stories. Almost all of them followed the poor-boy-works-hard-and-makes-good formula. Alger's world, however, was a fantasy world in which melodramatic events were common. His heroes succeeded mainly through luck. The stories may have been simple tales, but his readers loved them, buying an estimated 20 million copies of his books.

settled with his parents in Allegheny, now a part of Pittsburgh. At 14 he was working 12 hours a day as a bobbin boy in a cotton mill for $1.20 a week. He studied hard and at 16 was a telegraph clerk earning about $4.00 a week—a fair salary in those days. At 17 Carnegie became private secretary to the president of the Pennsylvania Railroad.

In 1850 Carnegie bought an oil well, and he made money in the new oil industry, but he soon turned to the steel industry. In it he spent the rest of his business life.

Carnegie frankly admitted that he knew nothing about steel manufacturing. His success lay in his ability as a seller and promoter. He knew how to gather around him people who were specialists. He was a relentless driver, never satisfied with himself or with others. One day he received a telegram from one of his plant superintendents: "We broke all records for making steel last week." Carnegie sent

back another telegram: "Congratulations. Why not do it every week?"

Carnegie, however, also recognized the achievements of others. People he liked rose rapidly up the ladder to financial success. Charles M. Schwab, for instance, entered one of Carnegie's plants as a stake driver at a dollar a day. He became president of the Carnegie Steel Company at age 34. Schwab's share of profits in 1896 was $1.3 million. Similar stories are told of Carnegie's friendship for Henry Phipps, Henry C. Frick, and others.

By 1900 Andrew Carnegie, who began as a poor immigrant boy, was said to be the second richest man in the world. He owned all the types of property and equipment necessary for the mass production of steel, including deposits of iron ore, limestone, and coal; ships and railways to carry the raw material to smelters and mills; and huge steel plants from which the finished products poured forth.

Carnegie sold his steel property in 1901 for nearly $500 million. This tremendous financial deal was negotiated by J. P. Morgan, the most famous investment banker of the time. Out of the negotiations, in which 11 steel companies were merged, was born the mighty United States Steel Corporation, then the largest corporation in the world. Many economic historians have regarded this event as a critical point in the development of American capitalism. It marked a shift from **industrial capitalism**, in which corporations were controlled by their industrial owners, to **financial capitalism**, in which whole industries were dominated by bankers.

Carnegie retired in 1901. He spent much of the rest of his life giving away his money for education and other causes. "I started life as a poor man," he once said, "and I wish to end it that way." Before his death he had disposed of more than $350 million. Many public libraries stand today as monuments to Carnegie's generosity. Foundations created by his money still support causes such as education, world peace, and medical research.

John D. Rockefeller. Even richer than Carnegie was John D. Rockefeller, born in 1839, who during his lifetime accumulated the world's greatest fortune. One of five children, Rockefeller left high school after one year to work as a clerk for about $3 a week. In 1858, at age 19, he went into the wholesale food business. The Civil War brought large profits to the new company, and Rockefeller promptly invested his money in oil refineries. From this point on, oil became his major interest. He pioneered in developing the trust as a form of big business organization. Although he was ruthless in forcing his competitors to choose between joining him or going down to ruin, Rockefeller is given major credit for introducing order and efficiency into the highly chaotic and wasteful oil industry.

By 1900, Rockefeller's interests had broadened. He owned controlling stock in the gigantic Standard Oil Company, in railway lines, in steamship lines, in iron ore deposits in Colorado and in the Lake Superior region, in steel mills, and in many other enterprises. When the United States Steel Corporation was being organized by J. P. Morgan, Rockefeller sold to the newly formed corporation his iron ore deposits and Great Lakes steamers, receiving $80 million for the iron ore deposits alone.

Like Carnegie, Rockefeller later gave away many millions, and the foundations created with his money today continue to foster research and promote the welfare of the American people.

Pioneers of industrialism. These were only a few of the many pioneers of the new industrial society. Like other pioneers—cattle raisers, prospectors, frontier farmers, and wage earners—they helped to develop the resources of a new land. They were endowed with great energy and rare ability. They were gamblers, willing to take chances in the hope of gain. They were highly competitive people in a highly competitive society at a time when few laws had been passed to bring order into the mad rush of business enterprise. They were absorbed in the excitement of building a new industrial world, of creating huge fortunes, of securing power.

These business leaders have often been condemned as **robber barons** for their selfishness and ruthless business methods, for exploiting their workers and forcing their rivals out of business. At the same time, their critics have acknowledged that they also benefited the nation. They were responsible for building new industries, introducing more efficient organizational methods, and providing opportunities that enabled many people to invest their savings profitably in the new industries springing up all over the nation. However they are viewed today, these business leaders played an important part in an important period of the nation's development. They helped to give new directions to American life.

SECTION REVIEW

See underscored items, text pp. 425, 427.
Identify: Nettie Fowler McCormick, J. P. Morgan, industrial capitalism, financial capitalism, Standard Oil Company

For answers to questions, see Answer Key, p.A74.

1. **Interpreting Ideas: (a)** In what ways could Vanderbilt, Carnegie, and Rockefeller be consider "pioneers of industrial society"? **(b)** In what ways could they be considered robber barons?

2. **Organizing Ideas:** What important contributions did the business pioneers of the late 1800's make to American economic life?

3. **Analyzing Ideas:** Find evidence to support the following statement: The most successful business leaders of the late 1800's generally believed in the ideal of self-reliant individualism.

● Class activity: Have pairs of students prepare in-depth mock interviews with industrial leaders of the period. Each presentation should highlight the subject's major accomplishments and personal philosophy.

527

DEVELOPING HISTORY STUDY SKILLS

Relating Economics and History   Interpreting Economic Statistics

Statistics are numerical data. A chart is a useful tool for organizing large amounts of data in a small space. A statistical chart makes it possible to analyze numerical data easily, to see relationships, and to make comparisons. Knowing how to read statistical tables is an important skill for any student of history.

How to Read a Statistical Table

Reading a statistical table in a multicolumn chart involves scanning groups of numbers up and down the columns and across the rows. To read statistical tables, follow these guidelines.

1. **Identify the type of data.** Note the chart's title and subtitle, if any. Note any other titles, headings, subheadings, and labels.

2. **Examine the components.** Note the specific statistics given under each title or heading. Read across each row and down each column.

3. **Relate numbers and values.** Notice in what quantities each category of statistics is recorded. Values may vary from column to column or from row to row and may be misread if not carefully studied. For instance, in the chart to the right, track is recorded in miles while capital invested is recorded in millions of dollars. Often, as in this chart, a note in parentheses will indicate whether the data is to be read in thousands, millions, billions, tons, dollars, or other units.

4. **Look for relationships.** Observe the statistics presented, noting both the differences and the similarities in what happened in any given year and over a period of years.

5. **Read footnotes.** Deviations in the presentation of data are sometimes explained in footnotes. A footnote may also indicate that changes in recording procedures have taken place that make it difficult to compare information within the same category. A blank space usually indicates that no figures were available or that no activity took place.

Applying the Skill

Study the statistical chart below. Note that the title and subtitle indicate that the subject of the chart is the railroad industry between 1870 and 1900. To find out the specific information that the chart gives, read the column titles and the row titles. These titles indicate that for each five-years in the 30-year period the table includes information on the miles of railroad built, the capital investment in railroads, and the total railroad income.

Note the values of the numbers in each column. The figures in Column 2 are recorded in miles. How many miles of railroad were operating in the United States in 1880? The answer is 93,262 miles. Studying the other statistics in Column 2 reveals further information about the railroad industry. What is one interpretation of these statistics?

Railroads • 1870–1900

Year	Miles of Track	Capital Invested (Millions)	Total Income (Millions)
1870	52,922	$ 2,476	NA
1875	74,096	$ 4,658	$ 503
1880	93,262	$ 5,402	$ 613
1885	128,320	$ 7,842	$ 772
1890	166,703	$10,122	$1,092
1895	180,657	$11,007	$1,425
1900	193,346	$12,814	$2,013

Source: *Historical Statistics of the United States*
NA = Not Available

Study the chart further, comparing the statistics across each row and down each column. One relationship among the statistics in this chart is the increase from 1870 to 1900 of the numbers in each column. One interpretation of this fact might be that the railroad industry was growing rapidly between 1870 and 1900.

Note the NA on the table. As the footnote indicates, this information was not available.

Practicing the Skill

Study the table below. Then, on a separate sheet of paper, answer the following questions.

1. What is the subject of the data on the table?
2. What specific information is given?
3. For what years is the information given?
4. In what value is the information recorded?
5. In general, between 1879 and 1899 did the amount of capital invested in manufacturing increase or decrease?
6. Was there any specific industry in which the opposite occurred?
7. **(a)** In 1899 was more capital invested in textiles and textile products or in leather products? **(b)** In 1879 how did these two capital amounts compare?
8. How does the footnote aid your interpretation?

Capital Invested in Manufacturing* • 1878–1980

Industry	1879	1889	1899
Food and Kindred Products	897,000,000	1,839,000,000	3,760,000,000
Textiles and Textile Products	998,000,000	2,024,000,000	3,145,000,000
Leather Products	328,000,000	640,000,000	891,000,000
Rubber Products	10,000,000	36,000,000	74,000,000
Wood and Forest Products	847,000,000	1,950,000,000	2,868,000,000
Paper Products	90,000,000	200,000,000	455,000,000
Printing, Publishing and Allied Industries	144,000,000	466,000,000	801,000,000
Chemical Products	206,000,000	478,000,000	871,000,000
Petroleum Refining	37,000,000	151,000,000	195,000,000
Stone, Clay, and Glass Products	156,000,000	408,000,000	741,000,000
Iron and Steel Products	472,000,000	1,143,000,000	1,581,000,000
Other Metal Products	116,000,000	276,000,000	646,000,000
Machinery, Excluding Transportation Equipment	414,000,000	1,160,000,000	1,917,000,000
Transportation Equipment	17,000,000	156,000,000	337,000,000
Miscellaneous Manufacturing	89,000,000	230,000,000	344,000,000
Total	4,821,000,000	11,157,000,000	18,626,000,000

Source: *Historical Statistics of the United States*
*In 1929 Dollars

(1. money invested in manufacturing 2. the amount of capital invested in major United States industries in the late 1800's 3. 1879, 1889, and 1899 4. in 1929 dollars 5. increase 6. no 7. (a) textiles and textile products; Textile products investment was triple that of leather products. 8. The footnote indicates the year at which the dollar is valued.)

By the opening years of the 1900's, the United States had become the leading industrial nation in the world. Smoking factory chimneys, rumbling machinery, and long trains of freight cars pulling into and out of congested urban centers symbolized the industrial world.

In the Northeast and Middle West and to a lesser extent elsewhere in the nation, industrialism was transforming the lives of the people. Raw materials from America's vast reservoir of natural resources poured into the mills and factories. Finished products in ever-growing quantities flowed from the factories into the marketplace and into people's homes.

Mass production led to specialization. Financiers raised the capital to build the railroads and the factories. Manufacturers developed more efficient methods of producing goods. Merchants developed new methods of advertising and selling. Many workers—clerks, stenographers, managers, factory workers, and others—staffed the new industrial plants. New methods of business organization were developed and employed. Great corporations and combinations of corporations were increasingly replacing the individual or family-owned enterprises that had been the most common form of business organization.

Throughout America a new spirit of fierce competition drove people at a faster and faster pace. It was an exciting and a productive period in the nation's history, but some of the changes created problems for many people.

CONNECTING CHAPTER IDEAS

Much of the nation's history since 1865 is concerned with the efforts of Americans to adjust their ways of life to the new forces of growing industrialism. In the next chapter you will read how wage earners attempted to solve their problems by organizing labor unions.

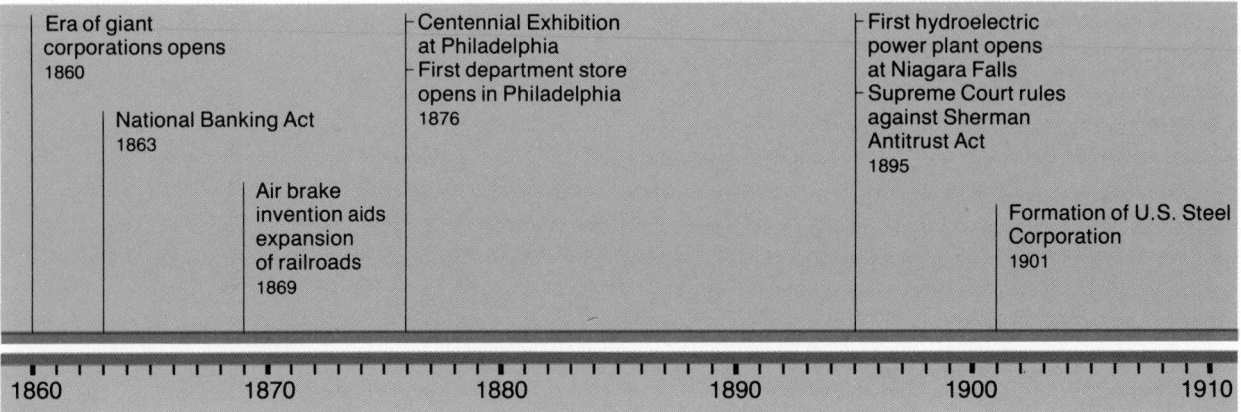

Era of giant corporations opens
1860

National Banking Act
1863

Air brake invention aids expansion of railroads
1869

Centennial Exhibition at Philadelphia
First department store opens in Philadelphia
1876

First hydroelectric power plant opens at Niagara Falls
Supreme Court rules against Sherman Antitrust Act
1895

Formation of U.S. Steel Corporation
1901

1860   1870   1880   1890   1900   1910

22 REVIEW

Reviewing Important Terms

In the sentences below, the underlined terms are incorrect. On a separate sheet of paper, rewrite each sentence using the correct term.

1. The specialty store sold a variety of different products under one roof.
2. Zinc and lead are the raw materials needed to produce steel.
3. A monopoly is an organization that owns all of the stock in many companies.
4. To raise capital to carry on business, individual proprietorships sold stock.
5. To form a charter, several corporations agree to divide business opportunities among themselves.
6. The Bessemer process was important to the production of high quality kerosene.
7. Rural centers have the following characteristics: factories, efficient transportation and communication, and a population greater than 2,500.
8. The merger of 11 steel companies to form the United States Steel Corporation marked the beginning of industrial capitalism.

Practicing Critical Thinking Skills

1. **Interpreting Ideas. (a)** How were industrialization, transportation, and the growth of cities in America interrelated? **(b)** How did the abundance of natural resources and the development of advanced technology in America help contribute to its rapid growth as an industrial power?
2. **Organizing Ideas. (a)** List the discoveries or inventions between 1865 and 1900 that you think did the most to encourage America's industrial growth. **(b)** How did each affect the growth of industry? **(c)** Were any of them interdependent? Explain.
3. **Analyzing Viewpoints. (a)** How do you suppose J. P. Morgan felt about the passage of the Sherman Antitrust Act? **(b)** What arguments might he have made to support his position?
4. **Evaluating Ideas. (a)** Describe how Vanderbilt, Carnegie, or Rockefeller rose "from rags to riches." **(b)** Were their methods legal? Acceptable? Explain. **(c)** Is it likely that a person today could rise "from rags to riches" as the industrialists did in the late 1800's? Why or why not?
5. **Relating Past to Present. (a)** Should industries in the United States bear responsibility for what happens to the environment as a result of their activities? Why or why not? **(b)** How do the environmental efforts of government, business, and private groups today compare with those of the late 1800's? **(c)** How would you penalize those corporations who carelessly disregard environmental concerns?

Developing History Study Skills

1. **Interpreting Economic Statistics.** Review the charts on page 522 of the textbook. **(a)** How much raw steel was produced in 1900? **(b)** How much more crude petroleum was produced in 1900 than in 1870? **(c)** Based on these charts, what inferences can you make about United States industrial production from 1870 to 1900?

2. **Making Inferences.** Look at the pictures in this chapter that show scenes of nineteenth century life and industry. **(a)** Use the information in these illustrations to formulate at least five inferences about transportation, building materials, and sources of energy in the late nineteenth century. **(b)** Compare your inferences with what you have read. Cite evidence to evaluate your inferences as accurate, inaccurate, or incomplete.

Relating Geography and History

The United States had the many natural resources necessary to industrialize. Industrial expansion and improvements in transportation changed the nation. To better understand the connection between natural resources and the growth of industry, study the map of mineral resources on pages 1020–21 and answer the following questions.

1. **(a)** In which states east of the Great Plains was iron ore discovered? **(b)** In which states east of the Great Plains would you expect the steel industry to develop? Why? **(c)** Iron ore from the Mesabi Range in Minnesota was used in the Pittsburgh steel mills. Along what route would the ore be most easily transported? Why?
2. **(a)** Explain the importance of the location and accessibility of raw materials in determining the location of an industry. **(b)** What are some other factors to be considered in locating a factory?
3. The steel industry and railroads depended on each other for many things. **(a)** How did the two industries help each other? **(b)** How did each affect the growth of cities?

See Chapter Overview in TMRG, p.TM132.
See Chapter Objectives in TMRG, p.TM132.
See Introducing the Chapter in TMRG, p.TM132.

CHAPTER 23

The Struggle to Organize Workers

Changing Ways   (1860's–1890's)

A company
town

On April 14, 1865, when President Lincoln was shot in Ford's Theater in the nation's capital, the United States was chiefly an agricultural country. By 1900 it had undergone a period of unprecedented industrial development. By utilizing its vast resources, the United States had become the leading industrial and manufacturing nation in the world.

The amazing industrial growth of the United States was made possible by a number of advances. The development of power-driven machines and the construction of giant factories greatly expanded the production of manufactured goods. Improvements in the transportation system allowed raw materials and finished products to reach their destinations quickly and cheaply. The organization of businesses into larger corporations and the co-operation of government in furthering the economy added to the efficiency of industrialization. Finally, the new machines were operated by growing numbers of workers.

Many of the new industrial workers came from America's farms and rural areas. They also came from Europe in a mighty and yearly flood of immigration.

Both the older Americans and the immigrants entered a new and unfamiliar world when they moved from the farms and rural villages into the growing industrial communities of the United States. In the early days of power-driven machines and mass production, the new industrial workers were pioneers as much as were the settlers who had earlier pushed America's frontiers westward to the Pacific. Like the pioneers who helped conquer the West, wage earners in the late 1800's faced many complex problems.

READING FOCUS

As you read about the new problems caused by industrialization and urbanization, look for the details that support each of the following statements.

1. Industrialism creates new problems for wage earners.
2. Immigration adds strength and variety to American society.
3. Wage earners organize to overcome their grievances.
4. Organized labor faces opposition as it seeks reform.

1 Industrialism creates new problems for wage earners

See Teaching Suggestions in TMRG, pp. TM132-33.

The amazing industrial developments that swiftly transformed the United States between 1865 and 1900 created new problems as well as new opportunities for wage earners. Like all other Americans, wage earners had to adapt themselves to rapid changes.

New owner-worker relations. For one thing, large corporations began hiring thousands of workers. The growth in the size of corporations changed the old-time relations between owners and employees. In earlier days when factories were small, the owner knew the workers and sometimes took a personal interest in their welfare and the welfare of their families. In the huge factories, however, workers seldom saw the owners. In the new business combinations, most of the owners were stockholders living in widely separated parts of the country.

Nor did many owners know at first hand what working conditions were like in their factories and mines. They bought shares of stock as an investment and hired managers to run the plants for them. As the factories grew larger, the owners lost sight of the workers as individuals, looking on them as mere objects. If a worker objected to the way a factory was run, he or she could easily be replaced.

Workers in so-called company towns faced the greatest disadvantages. There were mining districts in Pennsylvania and West Virginia and textile-mill regions in the South where companies owned entire towns—all the houses, stores, and other buildings. The companies employed the teachers and the doctors. The local magistrates and the police owed their jobs to the company. In these towns workers did not dare to protest the rent they paid for their company-owned houses or the prices they paid in the company-owned store. Frequently, the workers did not receive all of their wages in cash. Part of their wages were given in credit to be used at the company store.

Individual workers in the new industrial society could not hope to improve their working conditions. Nor could they reasonably hope to become an owner beyond, perhaps, buying a few shares of stock. To be sure, some workers

● "Scrip," as this form of credit was called, could be spent only at the company stores, where employers charged what they wanted. Many state courts defeated attempts to outlaw scrip. For example, a Pennsylvania court labeled one anti-scrip law "an insulting attempt" to put workers under state authority.

did become supervisors of other workers and department managers. A few workers eventually rose to positions of wealth and power. In general, though, as factories grew larger and management was more impersonal, it became harder for individual workers or groups of workers to bargain with employers over increasing their wages and improving their working conditions.

Effects of mechanization. The use of power-driven machines in factories also created new problems for wage earners. Factory work became increasingly specialized and increasingly monotonous. Often machines were geared to high rates of output, and workers ended the day exhausted from the pressures of keeping up with the machinery's high rate of speed. Moreover, the new machinery often produced much more with fewer workers. Thus the installation of the new machines could cause **technological unemployment** by throwing workers out of jobs. Sometimes new jobs were created because workers were needed to build and repair the machines. Also, the higher output of the machines increased the nationwide production of goods. The increased production thereby created new jobs of many kinds. However, displaced workers often found it difficult to learn new skills and get new jobs.

Machines were also physically dangerous. Until about 1910 employers did little to safeguard workers from accidents. When an accident occurred, the owner usually blamed the worker. If disabled, the worker received no compensation to pay the costs of doctors and hospitalization. When a worker was killed, the worker's family was usually left without an income, for employers did not insure the lives of workers.

Industrial hazards from machines and unsafe and unhealthy working conditions were a major problem. Between 1900 and 1910, for example, 3 percent of all employed workers in the United States were killed or injured annually in industrial accidents. In 1911 a fire in the unsafe Triangle Building in New York City brought death to 146 women textile workers. In a strike just the year before, the women had protested against their unsafe working conditions. The owners, however, paid no heed to their protests.

Effects of the railroads. Before the nationwide network of railroads was built, American manufacturers usually sold their products only in nearby markets. With the railroad network, however, a competitive national market for goods was created. A manufacturer could use the railroads to sell products anywhere in the country, provided the manufacturer's prices were as low as those elsewhere.

This creation of a competitive national market for goods also created a competitive national market for labor. For example, if cotton goods were being made cheaper in southern mills because of lower wages, then New England manufacturers of cotton goods were inclined to lower wages to compete with the lower-priced output of the southern mills.

Business cycles and the frontier. Like other citizens, workers were greatly influenced by what economists call the **business cycle.** This was the expansion of business and industry during periods of prosperity and their contraction during periods of depression. Workers lived in constant dread of being laid off or having their wages sharply reduced whenever business conditions took a downturn. Even when business was good, unemployment per-

The Business Cycle

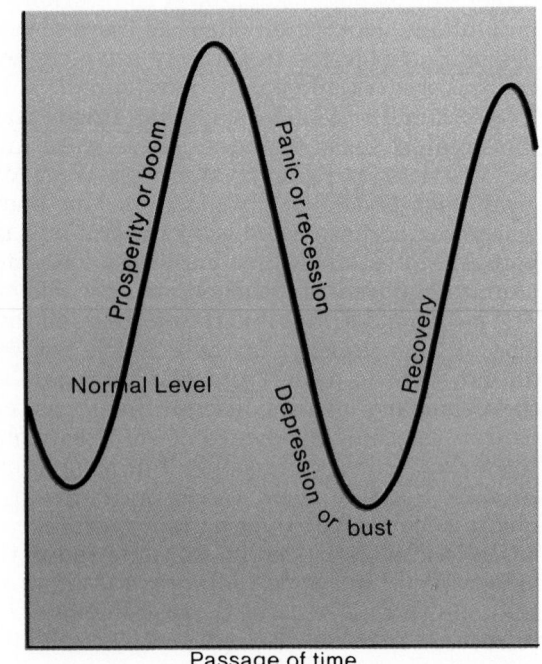

Economic activity

Prosperity or boom

Panic or recession

Recovery

Normal Level

Depression or bust

Passage of time

▲ Discussion topic: The American writer Henry David Thoreau perceived very early some of the issues of the new age. Ask students to explain what might have prompted him to write in Walden (1854), "But lo! men have become the tools of their tools."

sisted and brought misery to many industrial workers.

Between 1870 and 1900, hundreds of thousands of jobless persons searched for work. In 1889, a fairly typical year, about 19 percent of the workers in manufacturing and transportation were jobless.

As long as the frontier remained open, farmers on worn-out eastern land could choose between migration to the frontier or migration to the city. Many chose to continue farming and moved west. After about 1900, however, eastern farm families had fewer and fewer opportunities to find good, cheap western land. They turned in larger numbers to the cities for work, swelling the work force of the cities and driving down industrial wages.

Low wages and long hours. During the last quarter of the 1800's, many wage earners complained bitterly about their low wages. Unskilled male workers might earn no more than $10 a week. Skilled male workers—those whose jobs required a certain amount of training and education—might earn no more than $20 a week. In both skilled and unskilled jobs, the wage scale for women workers was even lower. In 1903, for example, a woman might receive $2.16 for a 62-hour workweek in a cap factory. Still, industrial expansion brought higher **real wages**° to workers as a whole. Nevertheless, large numbers of workers, like many farmers, believed that they were not receiving a fair share of the profits from the country's industrial growth.

Wages tended to be low for several reasons: the increasing power of employers over employees, the competitive national labor market, depressions, and the flood of immigrant workers into the labor market.

Wage earners also complained about their long working hours. After 1865 an 11-hour day was common in American industry. Yet even in the 1880's, many textile workers worked from 12 to 14 hours daily, and the 12-hour day was common in the steel industry.

It was indeed a new and rapidly changing world with which the American wage earner wrestled in the late 1800's. The problems of wage earners were complex, and the workers, the owners of the industries, and Americans in general lacked ready answers.

°**real wages:** wages measured in terms of actual purchasing power, or what the money will buy.

SECTION REVIEW

See underscored items, text pp.533-34.

Identify: company town, technological unemployment, Triangle Building fire, business cycle

For answers to questions, see Answer Key, pp.A75-76.

1. **Seeing Relationships:** How did the move toward huge, corporation-owned factories change relations between owners and workers?
2. **Summarizing Ideas:** Discuss the problems faced by wage earners as a result of increasing mechanization.
3. **Analyzing Ideas:** How did each of the following affect workers: (a) railroads, (b) the business cycle, (c) the end of the frontier?
4. **Drawing Conclusions:** What evidence do you find to show that industrialization could bring problems as well as benefits?

2 Immigration adds strength and variety to American society

See Teaching Suggestions in TMRG, pp.TM133-34.

Between 1865 and 1900, immigrants came seeking jobs and new opportunities. In trying to find places for themselves in their new homeland and in the industrial age, the immigrants were often greeted with suspicion.

The immigrants. Part of the difficulty was the overwhelming number of immigrants who poured into the country. From 1870 to 1899, more than 11 million women, men, and children entered the United States.

The changing character of **immigration** as well as the swelling tide alarmed many Americans. Until the early 1880's, most immigrants came from northwestern Europe—Great Britain, Ireland, Scandinavia, Germany, and the Netherlands. After 1890 an increasingly large number came from southern and eastern Europe—Russia (including Poland), Greece, Austria-Hungary, and Italy. The languages, customs, and ways of living of these immigrants were quite different from those of immigrants from northwestern Europe.

Effects of immigration on labor. The immigrants had an enormous influence on American life. Although some settled on farms, the great majority moved to the densely crowded slum areas of the cities. Here tenement owners

In 1869 Joseph Becker painted this picture of cheering Chinese "gandy dancers," or railroad workers. Gandy dancers took their name from the Gandy Manufacturing Company, which made tools used in railroad construction. Chinese immigrants supplied much of the labor that built the western railroads.

profited in higher rents from the competition for housing between native-born Americans and newcomers from Europe.

Most immediate of all, however, was the immigrants' effect upon established workers. Immigrants competed for jobs, thereby lowering wages. To be sure, immigrants helped to stimulate the economy by creating new demands for factory and farm products. Most wage earners, however, were more disturbed by the job competition of the immigrants than they were impressed with the stimulating effects of immigration.

▲ **Tensions on the Pacific Coast.** Chinese workers on the Pacific Coast, particularly in California, were early victims of the rising distrust of all immigrants. By the terms of the Burlingame Treaty of 1868, Chinese people had the right to immigrate to the United States. For some years Chinese laborers had been welcome additions to the labor supply. They had been forced to accept the hardest and least desirable jobs for very low wages. They were the backbone of the construction gangs that built the western section of the first trans-

continental railroad. By 1870, 75,000 Chinese had settled in California, where they made up 20 percent of the labor force.

Then in 1873 a depression hit the country. As unemployment mounted, California workers worried that the Chinese would take their jobs at low wages. Fear and insecurity were intensified because the Chinese, for reasons not always of their own choosing, lived entirely to themselves. Thus they did not have an opportunity to learn and adapt to the ways of living accepted by most Californians.

Restricting Chinese immigration. Ill feeling was fanned into violence by crowds of unemployed California workers who gathered on street corners and sand lots. The **sand lotters** soon attacked the Chinese, killing some and burning the property of others.

In cooperation with distressed farmers, California workers were able to influence the writing of a new state constitution in 1879. California's new constitution discriminated against the Chinese by prohibiting them from owning property or working at certain jobs.

Text continues on page 538.

▲ To help students understand what many immigrants faced, you may wish to read to the class Mark Twain's penetrating indictment of Chinese immigrant treatment in America. The article, entitled "Disgraceful Persecution of a Boy," was published in the "New York Galaxy" in 1864.

No nation in the history of the world has ever received as many immigrants as the United States.

Immigration is the movement of people to a foreign land to live. The reasons lying behind immigration are as varied as people themselves. New lands to farm and better jobs; escape from religious or political persecution, starvation, or war; and a desire to satisfy simple curiosity are all reasons for immigration. Whatever the reasons, the truth remains — the United States is a land of immigrants.

Thousands of years ago the first trickle of immigrants began arriving. Their route of travel led out of Asia, across a great land bridge connecting Siberia and Alaska. During colonial times about one million immigrants came to the 13 colonies. At that time, the majority of immigrants came from England. Large numbers of Dutch, French, Germans, and Scotch-Irish also arrived in the colonies during this period. Beginning in 1619, thousands of blacks came from Africa to the colonies as slaves. The immigrants brought with them their languages and the values and traditions that have formed the basic patterns of the American way of life.

In the 1830's the number of immigrants began to increase rapidly. More than half a million arrived in that decade alone, followed by 1,700,000 in the 1840's, and 2,600,000 in the 1850's. Most of these new arrivals came from northwestern Europe. The table at the bottom of the page shows rather dramatically the role of this region of Europe as a source of immigrants during these decades.

The great wave of immigration continued to sweep across the United States from 1860 to 1890. More than 10 million immigrants arrived on the nation's shores during those 30 years. Most came from northern and western Europe. A shift, however, was beginning to appear as more immigrants arrived from southern and eastern European nations.

The years from 1890 to 1930 were the greatest era of immigration known in history. Nearly 22 million immigrants poured into the United States during that 40-year period, a number that exceeded the immigration total from colonial times until 1890, But the source of these numbers shifted notably from earlier periods. Most of the new arrivals came from southern and eastern Europe. The table below will help you see these new immigration patterns.

In 1924 Congress passed a law to begin in 1929 limiting the number of immigrants to 150,000 per year. This restrictive legislation sharply reduced the number of immigrants. Also, the Great Depression tarnished for many immigrants the dream of a better life in the United States. Indeed, in 1933, in the heart of the depression, total arrivals numbered only 23,068 and after departures, the actual number of immigrants for the year was just 12,383.

Another dramatic shift has taken place in immigration patterns in the last decade. Changes in immigration laws have allowed more immigrants from India and the Far East. The war in Vietnam, the take-over of Cuba by Castro, and low employment and poverty in Mexico and the Caribbean Islands have also contributed to this shift. The chart provides a graphic illustration of the most recent immigration patterns.

Sources of Immigration, Selected Years • 1840 - 1980

	1840	1850	1890	1910	1940	1970	1980
Northwestern Europe	50,228	228,168	143,279	170,815	16,000	42,000	33,200
Central and Eastern Europe	29,710	78,947	196,020	502,099	27,239	30,800	21,200
Southern Europe	188	1,228	55,963	253,277	6,215	41,500	10,200
Asia	2	7	4,448	23,553	1,913	94,900	236,100
Africa	6	0	112	1,072	202	8,100	14,000
Australia, New Zealand, and Pacific Islands	0	0	1,167	998	228	2,800	1,700
North, Central, and South America, and the Caribbean	3,815	15,768	3,833	89,534	17,822	151,100	204,500
Other Countries	118	45,882	62	43	137	400	1,200
Total	84,066	369,980	455,302	1,041,570	70,756	373,300	530,600

Source: *Historical Statistics of the United States*
   Statistical Abstract of the United States

The opponents of Chinese immigration also succeeded in getting Congress to pass an exclusion bill in 1879. This bill prohibited all but a few Chinese from settling in the United States in any year. Because this bill violated the Burlingame Treaty of 1868, President Hayes vetoed it. Under pressure, however, the Chinese government agreed not to object if the United States regulated immigration. In 1882 Congress enacted a new Chinese Exclusion Act, which, with several extensions, continued in effect until World War II. The Chinese Exclusion Act forbade the immigration of Chinese laborers and denied American citizenship to Chinese born in China. Only students and a few other groups of Chinese could enter the United States.

Other restrictions. The Chinese Exclusion Act of 1882 was the first of a long series of restrictions on immigration, enacted mainly because of pressure from worker groups. Another was the repeal of the Contract Labor Law.

The Contract Labor Law had been adopted by Congress in 1864, when booming wartime industries desperately needed workers. This law permitted American employers to recruit laborers in Europe. Under the law it was legal for employers to have workers abroad sign contracts agreeing to come to the United States to work for a specified employer for specified wages for a specified time. It was illegal for the workers to leave their jobs while the contract was in force. American workers objected to the law because (1) it came dangerously close to setting up a slave-labor system and (2) it subjected American workers to the unfair competition of cheap foreign labor.

Following the repeal of the Contract Labor Law in 1885, American wage earners pressured Congress for other restrictive measures. One bill that kept coming up for 30 years would have forbidden entry to any immigrant who could not read and write. Congress actually did pass this law on several occasions, but each time the President then in office vetoed the bill. In 1917, however, Congress passed a literacy test bill over President Woodrow Wilson's veto, and the door to immigration was shut a little further.

The role of immigrants. Except for the Chinese Exclusion Act, the restrictions placed on immigration from 1865 to 1900 were relatively minor. Without the more than 11 million immigrants who poured into the United States between 1870 and 1900, profits to owners of industry would have been much smaller. As it was, employers could keep wages of immigrants lower than those of established Americans. Without immigrants America's industrial progress also would have been much slower. Immigrant muscles and brains helped to transform the United States from a predominantly agricultural country into a giant industrial power.

SECTION REVIEW

See underscored items, text pp. 535-36.
Identify: immigration, sand lotters
For answers to questions, see Answer Key, p.A76.
1. **Summarizing Ideas:** Discuss three ways in which immigration affected American workers.
2. **Determining Cause and Effect:** Why did Congress pass the Chinese Exclusion Act of 1882?
3. **Interpreting Ideas: (a)** Explain the provisions of the Contract Labor Law of 1864. **(b)** Why was it repealed?
4. **Analyzing Ideas:** Immigrants have helped to transform the United States. Give evidence to support this statement.

3 Wage earners organize to overcome their grievances

See Teaching Suggestions in TMRG, pp.TM134-35.

Faced with the problems of the new industrial age, wage earners in cities looked to organization as a solution to their problems. ▲

The National Labor Union. Labor organizations were not new. During the war years 1861–65, however, as industry boomed and the cost of living soared, the **labor movement** gained new momentum.

In 1866 the National Labor Union was launched under the leadership of William Sylvis, an experienced and able organizer of iron molders. In 1868 the National Labor Union helped push through Congress a law setting an 8-hour workday for laborers and mechanics employed by or in behalf of the federal government. After unsuccessfully supporting a third-party movement in the election of 1872, this union faded away.

▲   Among workers' problems were periodic wage reductions from fluctuations in the business cycle. For example, after the 1873 Panic (from problems with over-speculation), skilled workers earning $3.50 to $5.00 per day had their wages cut to $1.50 to $2.00 per day.

Thomas Anshutz (1851–1916) was a painter best known for his stark, realistic canvases of everyday, working-class life in the United States. He began his formal training at the National Academy of Design in New York, but in 1875 he went to Philadelphia. There he enrolled in the Pennsylvania Academy of Fine Arts, where he spent most of his professional career.

At the Pennsylvania Academy of Fine Arts Anshutz became an apprentice to Thomas Eakins, the painter and sculptor renowned for his mastery of human anatomy. Anshutz learned from his mentor the art of letting the human body speak for itself. Like Eakins, Anshutz rejected conventional beauty in his paintings. He insisted on portraying people in real-life situations. *Noontime at the Mill,* which depicts steelworkers taking a lunch break, is typical of Anshutz's factual, objective style. Many people regarded Anshutz's choice of subject matter — which often included black workers — as inappropriate. His paintings were unusual in an era when idealized portraits and idyllic scenes were popular.

Later, as head of the Pennsylvania Academy, Anshutz was known as a "maker of painters." He believed in discovering and developing the natural creative tendencies of each student. He carried on the legacy of Thomas Eakins, however, by providing the students with a foundation of essential skills. Many young artists who studied under Anshutz have become famous in their own right.

The Knights of Labor. Far more important than the National Labor Union was the Knights of Labor, founded in 1869 in Philadelphia by Uriah S. Stephens, a tailor. The Knights of Labor tried to unite all American workers into one great union—foreign-born and native-born, blacks and whites, skilled and unskilled, women and men. Several women headed local units or "assemblies" and a few became national leaders. The Knights aimed "to secure to the toilers a proper share of the wealth that they create; more of the leisure that rightfully belongs to them." Among other things, they favored an 8-hour workday.

The Knights of Labor also tried to organize and run cooperative stores and manufacturing plants, as some farmers already had done. They hoped to save for themselves the profits that normally went to manufacturers and distributors and at the same time to produce lower-priced goods. However, most of their co-operative enterprises failed, largely because they did not have enough money to buy good machinery and to hire qualified managers.

In some of their efforts the Knights of Labor were more successful. They were influential, for example, in causing Congress to pass the Chinese Exclusion Act in 1882 and to repeal the Contract Labor Law in 1885.

The Knights of Labor officially frowned on **strikes,** preferring to settle disputes between management and laborers through industrial **arbitration.°** However, a successful railroad strike in 1885 did much to boost the group's membership. For the first time in American labor history, railroad operators met strike leaders on equal terms and agreed to labor's

°**arbitration:** the judging of a dispute between two sides by an impartial person whose decision they agree in advance to accept.

▲ The union movement also represented an attempt to restore the social status and pride of the artisan at a time when the machine and commerce were more highly valued. Pride in skilled craftwork was often the casualty of the subdivision of labor into small, boring tasks.

chief demands. When the railroad strike occurred, the Knights numbered about 500,000 members. By 1886 their membership had reached 700,000. This growth also owed much to the idealism and enthusiasm of Terence V. Powderly, who succeeded Uriah S. Stephens as leader of the Knights of Labor.

The Haymarket Affair. On May 4, 1886, while the Knights were at the peak of their power, a large group of workers gathered in Haymarket Square in Chicago. They were there to protest an attack on strikers on May 3 in which one striker had been killed and a number of others wounded.

The meeting was orderly and the crowd was just beginning to leave when nearly 200 police officers appeared. Suddenly, without warning, a bomb burst in the midst of the police. Seven people were killed and many others wounded.

No one ever identified the bomb thrower. Nevertheless, eight "radicals," who on earlier occasions had advocated violence, were arrested. Seven were sentenced to death, the eighth to 15 years in prison.

No evidence was ever produced to indicate that organized labor was responsible for the Haymarket Affair. Yet no other event during the 1880's did more to turn public opinion against organized labor.

Decline of the Knights of Labor. The Knights, as the leading labor organization, suffered most of all. The decline of the organization was almost as rapid as its rise. From 1886 to 1888, its membership dropped from the high of 700,000 to only 260,000, and by 1890 only about 100,000 members were enrolled.

There were several reasons for this decline in membership. For one thing, the Knights lost an important railroad strike in 1886. This strike angered the public because of violence accompanying it and because of shortages of food and coal resulting from it. In the second place, the Knights included too many opposing groups to develop real strength. Skilled workers especially disliked the Knights' policy of taking in unskilled workers, with whom they felt they had little in common.

Finally, Terence V. Powderly's aims came to be too general to satisfy numerous workers. Many wage earners were now convinced that a strong labor movement had to avoid political crusades and concentrate on improving conditions for specific groups of workers.

Other organizations rose to take the place of the Knights. Some, like the American Railway Union and the United Mine Workers, had specialized goals. The most important labor organization was the American Federation of Labor (A. F. of L.).

The A. F. of L. Started in 1881 under another name and reorganized in 1886, the A. F. of L. quickly replaced the Knights of Labor as the leading American labor organization.

Unlike the Knights of Labor, the A. F. of L. was a federation of separate national **craft unions.** Each craft union represented a group of skilled workers in a separate trade, or craft, such as carpentry, welding, or typography. The A. F. of L. sought to organize all skilled workers by their craft rather than by the industry in which they worked. However, the A. F. of L. did include a few **industrial unions** that tried to organize all workers, unskilled as well as skilled, in a single industry.

Each A. F. of L. union was free to bargain collectively for all its members, to call strikes, and to manage its own affairs. The A. F. of L. also differed from the Knights of Labor in keeping itself aloof from general reform movements and from independent or third-party political activities. The A. F. of L. was an economic organization of workers emphasizing craft unionism—"pure and simple unionism."

The A. F. of L. program called for an 8-hour workday and a 6-day workweek. It backed legislation protecting workers on dangerous jobs and compensating them and their families in case of injury or death. It also demanded higher wages and better working conditions. The A. F. of L. threw its weight in political contests to whichever party or candidate came closest to representing its aims.

The A. F. of L. accepted the capitalist free-enterprise system. Its leaders in general discouraged strikes and favored bargaining with management. The A. F. of L. did insist, however, on controlling the skilled labor market, on getting a larger share of the output of industry through higher wages and shorter hours, and on improving labor conditions.

With the exception of a single year, the president of the A. F. of L. from 1886 to 1924 was its principal founder, Samuel Gompers. Under Gompers's leadership the A. F. of L. grew rapidly. In 1890 it had only 100,000 members, but by 1900 membership had climbed to 500,000.

Identify: National Labor Union, Uriah Stephens, strike, arbitration, Terence Powderly, Haymarket Affair, Samuel Gompers
For answers to questions, see Answer Key, p.A76.

1. **Analyzing Ideas:** Why did some workers organize unions during the mid-1800's?

2. **Organizing Ideas:** Describe the **(a)** purpose, **(b)** successes, and **(c)** reasons for the decline of the Knights of Labor.

3. **Comparing Ideas: (a)** How did the American Federation of Labor differ from the Knights of Labor? **(b)** What is the difference between a craft union and an industrial union? **(c)** Give examples of each today.

---

4 Organized labor faces opposition as it seeks reforms

See Teaching Suggestions in TMRG, p.TM135.

During the late 1880's, the workers attempts to form unions and to seek recognition of their unions' right to bargain for them met strong and widespread opposition.

▲ **Public opposition.** During the late 1880's, Americans in general as well as the government usually supported employers in conflicts between employers and unions or between employers and workers striking for union recognition. This opposition to unions is not hard to understand. Most Americans had grown up in the older, rural America. Individual workers then had more control over their fates than they now had in the giant corporations. Most Americans also believed that employers had the right to hire and fire their employees as they pleased.

Many Americans resented union demands for the **closed shop**. The businesses that had such agreements with a union could hire only union members. Employers resented this restriction on what they considered their right to hire anyone they pleased. Many workers also resented these closed-shop agreements, which forced them to join a union.

Moreover, many Americans believed that most workers were quite content with their lot. The fact that as late as 1914 only about one worker out of ten belonged to a labor organiza-tion seemed to support this belief. Many Americans held that the best workers could still rise to become managers and even owners. Most Americans blamed the entire labor problem as well as industrial conflict itself on "power-hungry" labor leaders interested in their own personal advancement.

Immigrants and labor unions. Many union leaders were of foreign birth. In several labor organizations, especially in the textile and coal-mining industries, immigrant workers were a source of strength. Immigrant workers took leading parts in the strikes of New York garment workers as well as in the textile workers' strike in Lawrence, Massachusetts.

However, a great many immigrants opposed labor unions. Coming from rural backgrounds in Europe, most immigrants had no previous experience with labor organizations. Bewildered by their new environment, they often did not feel a need to join with native-born American workers in an effort to promote common interests.

Many immigrants had left Europe partly to be as free as possible from all sorts of restrictions. Thus they did not like labor unions, with their dues, their rules, and their insistence that no one work for less than a certain wage. Many immigrants felt that however bad working conditions in the United States might be, they were better than working conditions back in Europe.

Most immigrants, also, were unskilled workers. Thus the A. F. of L. made little or no effort to admit them to the craft unions. Finally, there was widespread prejudice among native-born American workers toward immigrant workers. This prejudice deepened when foreign-born workers were recruited by business managers to break strikes.

Women and unions. Many unions did not admit women to membership, but in a few craft unions women played important roles. Most notable was the International Ladies Garment Workers Union, in which Rose Schneiderman and Leona O'Reilly were leaders. The A. F. of L. expressed interest in organizing women but did not vigorously pursue this aim.

In 1903 the National Women's Trade Union League was founded, largely by middle-class women. It assisted women workers in several ways, especially by providing financial support during strikes. The league stressed

---

▲ The unions also earned public distrust because of some violent incidents that occurred before unions became strong. (e.g., the terrorizing of the Molly Maguires - - a secret miners' organization; the 1877 railroad strike into which federal troops were called; the Haymarket Square bombing)

541

voting rights for women as a means for advancing their economic equality and promoted minimum, or "living," wages for women.

Blacks and unions. Because of the racial prejudice of many white workers, blacks were excluded from most labor organizations. A notable exception was the Knights of Labor, which enrolled black workers without discrimination, at least until the organization's later years.

At first the leaders of the A. F. of L. favored including skilled black workers in their craft unions. They believed that if this were not done, black workers might undermine the purposes of the federation by accepting lower wages. When the machinists' union and others refused to admit blacks, Samuel Gompers, by then the dominant power in the A. F. of L., backed down. He insisted that union constitutions should not specifically exclude black members but admitted that in practice the unions might do so. The United Mine Workers and a few other A. F. of L. unions admitted black members on equal terms with white members. Most of the other unions insisted, however, that any black workers admitted to A. F. of L. membership had to be organized in separate unions.

Most northern blacks were unskilled workers. Thus after the decline of the Knights of Labor, the A. F. of L. policy of organizing only skilled workers in effect excluded black wage earners from northern labor organizations. In the South, where there were many skilled black workers, the labor market in the skilled trades was controlled by all-white A. F. of L. unions. As a result, many skilled southern black workers were forced to take jobs as unskilled laborers.

By 1902 in both the North and the South, 43 national labor unions had not a single black member, and 27 others had only a handful. Gompers argued that blacks had only themselves to blame for their exclusion because few were skilled workers and fewer still were willing to accept the self-discipline and cooperation necessary in trade unionism. Booker T. Washington, however, declared that the union movement itself was holding back the economic progress of black workers by refusing to admit them as apprentices and by making no effort to organize them.

The virtual exclusion of blacks from the American labor movement closed off to the great mass of black Americans an important opportunity to be included in the mainstream of American life. It also weakened the effectiveness of the labor movement itself.

Division in the ranks of labor. The mechanization of industrial plants also weakened the power of wage earners to unite. When factories were small, skilled workers could see that the work of unskilled workers, however minor, was an essential part of the production process. When factories grew large and workers became strangers, skilled workers came to look down on unskilled workers.

Thus the wage earners themselves divided into two groups: (1) a small number of skilled workers who gained more and more bargaining power with employers, and (2) a large number of unskilled, unorganized laborers whose voices and interests counted for very little.

Industry against the unions. With most Americans generally distrustful of unions, huge industrial enterprises did not find it difficult to influence public opinion and government in their own favor. They hired lawyers to fight their battles in the courts. They spent money on advertising and publicity to win public sympathy. They paid skillful lobbyists to get favorable laws passed or to defeat bills that employers did not like. Some corporations contributed to the political party they thought most likely to win an election, hoping to secure government favors.

To discourage workers from joining unions, employers also developed more direct methods. For example, employers' associations, made up of several manufacturers, compiled **black lists.** These were lists of workers considered as undesirable—sometimes because the workers were incompetent, sometimes because they were labor organizers, sometimes merely because they belonged to a union. A black list was circulated throughout an entire industry all over the country. Any person whose name appeared on a black list was barred from getting a job in that industry, at least under her or his own name.

Many employers also required workers applying for a job to sign a written agreement not to join a union. The workers called these agreements **yellow-dog contracts.** A worker who violated such a contract was fired.

Employers used still other methods to prevent workers from organizing. Sometimes pri-

▲   Class activity: Have small groups of students role-play union leaders. Ask each "union" to
develop workable plans and policies to remedy problems discussed in the textbook.

The cartoonist who drew this picture in 1883 obviously saw the battle between management and labor as a very uneven one. What advantages does the cartoonist think that one side enjoyed over the other in the struggle?

(Management is armed with support from a corrupt legislature and an industry-subsidized press; its advantages are big money from monopolies. Labor's sole weapon is the strike; its biggest disadvantage is poverty.)

vate detectives, posing as workers, joined unions and reported strike plans and names of union leaders to employers. Sometimes when strikes broke out, employers actually paid agents to commit acts of violence, which were then blamed on labor. At other times, the workers themselves resorted to violence. In either case, such violence gave employers a good excuse for calling in the local police, the state militia, or even federal troops to restore order and break the strike.

Sometimes employers fought strikes with another weapon—the **lockout.** They closed their plants, thus locking out the workers. Then they brought in **strikebreakers**— nonunion workers hired to do the work of those on strike—and the plant was reopened despite the angry strikers picketing outside its gates. At other times, owners simply locked their plants and waited until the hungry, impoverished strikers were willing to return to work on any terms.

Government support of industry. With public opinion on their side, employers counted on government aid in conflicts with workers. Despite some exceptions they generally got such aid.

In most serious labor disputes, governors sent the state militia to the scene, which was to the employers' advantage. Whenever they sent the militia, the governors argued that the troops were needed to protect property, prevent violence, and maintain order. Since the governors were sworn to uphold law and order, this seemed reasonable. On the other hand, the arrival of the state militia often made it impossible for the workers to continue to strike.

In the last quarter of the 1800's, the Presidents of the United States in general followed the example of the state governors in ordering troops to a scene of trouble. Thus during a series of railroad strikes in Pennsylvania and Maryland in 1877, when state troops could not restore order, President Hayes sent federal

543

Jacob Coxey was a model citizen. Born in Pennsylvania, he attended public schools and then worked in a steel mill. He later moved to Massillon, Ohio, where he ran a stone quarry. By 1893 Coxey was a wealthy and respectable businessman.

Coxey, however, held uncommon political beliefs. He was a member of the Populist Party and had developed his own economic theories. When a depression hit the nation in 1893, throwing thousands out of work, Coxey burned to see his economic theories put into practice.

Coxey had a sympathetic Congressman introduce bills based on his ideas. These bills provided for government-sponsored road-building projects, which would furnish work for the unemployed. While the bills were in Congress, Coxey organized a march on Washington to win support for them.

Only about 100 men marched out of Massillon on Easter Sunday 1894. Additional recruits, however, joined the group as it traveled east. The growing size of the group began to alarm some government officials and editorial writers who feared the march might turn into a rebellion.

About 500 marchers entered Washington on May 1. A crowd lined Pennsylvania Avenue to watch Coxey's "army" troop toward the Capitol. At the Capitol, however, police kept the marchers back and prevented Coxey from speaking.

Coxey's army became the topic of many jokes. But Jacob Coxey had the last laugh. In 1944, at the age of 90, he at last got to make his speech on the Capitol steps. By that time Congress had enacted the kinds of laws Coxey had called for fifty years earlier.

---

soldiers to keep the trains running. The strikes collapsed.

Federal troops also stepped in near Chicago in 1894 when a strike was called against the Pullman Palace Car Company by the American Railway Union led by Eugene V. Debs. The strike was supported by railway workers around Chicago and elsewhere, who refused to handle trains that included Pullman cars. When Governor Altgeld of Illinois refused to call out the state militia or ask for federal help, President Cleveland sent federal troops anyway. Cleveland declared that such action was justified in order to guarantee mail delivery, although mail trains were in fact running and

the mails were being delivered. Organized labor resented such use of federal troops.

The courts support industry. In the late 1800's, the courts generally sided with management. For example, during the Pullman strike the railroad owners asked a federal court in Chicago to issue an **injunction,** or court order, forbidding Debs and other labor leaders to continue the strike. The court issued the injunction. It claimed that the strikers had entered into "a conspiracy in restraint of trade" and were therefore violating the Sherman Antitrust Act of 1890, which declared such conspiracies illegal.

Debs defied the court order. He was promptly arrested and sentenced to six months in jail for refusing to obey the injunction. Labor denounced this conviction as "government by injunction," but the Supreme Court upheld the ruling. Debs was jailed, and the Pullman strike was broken.

After 1895, employers often secured injunctions to prevent or break up strikes. Labor leaders complained bitterly, but their only possible relief was (1) that the Supreme Court would reverse its decision in the Debs case, or (2) that Congress would modify the Sherman Antitrust Act so that it could not be used against labor unions.

Radical movements. After the Haymarket Affair of 1886, many Americans began to identify the labor movement with radicalism. However, most Americans in the 1880's and 1890's did not distinguish among the goals and methods of the three major radical movements — **anarchism**, **communism**, and **socialism**.

The anarchists believed that people could work and live happily together in voluntary associations if they could be freed from the restraints of government. They believed that their ideal society could be gained only by the violent overthrow of the government and of **capitalism**—the economic system under which industry is owned and controlled by private individuals. Although the anarchists were few in number, their reputation for violence deeply alarmed the nation.

The best-known anarchist was Emma Goldman, an immigrant from Russia. Though feared and hated generally by the middle class and disliked by many workers, Goldman was appreciated in radical circles. She was a tough, fighting champion of working people, of free speech, and of complete freedom for women. Emma Goldman was also an uncompromising foe of militarism and the use of police force in what she regarded as the exploitation of ordinary people.

The followers of Karl Marx believed that wage earners would always be exploited under capitalism. They argued that capitalism had to be replaced by an economic system in which the workers could own and control the means of production.

In time, the followers of Marx developed into two separate groups. One group, known as communists, insisted that the only way to build the new society of workers envisioned by Marx was by means of revolution and the violent seizure of power.

The other group, known as socialists, generally did not advocate revolution. The socialists believed that the workers, organized in unions committed to socialism and in a political party, could vote themselves into power and by democratic means could reconstruct the economic and social foundations of society. Socialist leaders included Daniel De Leon, Morris Hillquit, Kate Richards O'Hare, Eugene V. Debs, and Victor Berger.

The influence of the radical movements upon American labor organizations was never as strong as it became in some parts of Europe. Union members by and large continued to support Republicans, Democrats, or third-party candidates and policies according to the union members' personal judgment of issues and of their own best interests.

Influence of organized labor. In the face of strong opposition from management, government, and the middle class, organized labor made solid gains. For example, in 1896 there were 5,462 strikes. Of these, 3,913 achieved full or partial success for the workers. In 1903 there were 12,660 strikes that succeeded in whole or in part. By the early 1900's, the lot of most American workers was beginning to improve.

SECTION REVIEW
See underscored items, text pp. 541, 544-45.

Identify: closed shop, National Women's Trade Union League, Eugene V. Debs, Pullman strike, anarchism, communism, socialism, capitalism, Emma Goldman

For answers to questions, see Answer Key, p.A76.

1. **Interpreting Ideas:** Why did public opinion in the late 1800's usually support employers rather than workers?

2. **Analyzing Ideas:** Why did many immigrants oppose the labor movement?

3. **Evaluating Ideas:** Why were black workers excluded from the labor movement?

4. **Summarizing Ideas:** How were women workers treated by the labor movement?

5. **Organizing Ideas:** How did employers use each of the following against organized labor: (a) publicity, (b) lobbyists, (c) political contributions, (d) black lists, (e) yellow-dog contracts, (f) lockouts, (g) strikebreakers?

▲ Class activity: Divide the class into small groups. Have each group prepare a simple chart comparing the goals of anarchism, communism, and socialism as outlined on this page.

Relating Economics and History   Understanding Economic Reports

How has the United States changed economically since 1790? Historians answer this question by examining statistical reports. Particularly useful is data collected and recorded by the Bureau of the Census. This data is presented in two volumes entitled *The Historical Statistics of the United States.* The volumes include information on such topics as population, manufacturing, employment, transportation, education, and agriculture. The statistics are organized into tables and charts. By analyzing and comparing data, historians are able to note trends and to draw conclusions about economic, social, and political changes over time.

You, too, can use these volumes in your study of history. When using the *Historical Statistics* consult the index to locate tables appropriate to your inquiry. Often, the needed statistics appear on separate tables. Follow the guidelines for reading statistical tables presented in Chapter 22. Concentrate on finding relationships between the numbers in the tables. Look for patterns of change. Then draw conclusions based on your analysis of the statistics.

Labor Force by Age and Sex* • 1900–1980

Year	Male			Female		
	Total	16 to 19 Years**	20 Yrs. and Older	Total	16 to 19 Years**	20 Yrs. and Older
1980	57,186	4,085	53,101	42,117	2,625	38,491
1960	47,013	2,634	44,379	22,222	1,703	20,518
1940	39,959	2,565	37,395	13,007	1,396	11,612
1920	32,053	2,947	29,106	8,229	1,640	6,589
1900	22,641	2,834	19,807	4,999	1,230	3,769

Source: *Historical Statistics of The United States*
*In Thousands of Persons
**Prior to 1947, 14 to 19 Years

Applying the Skill

The charts on this page were adapted from tables presented in *The Historical Statistics of the United States.* They contain the kinds of data that historians use to determine how the labor force has changed over the years.

Study the chart at the top of the next column, which covers the period from 1900 to 1980 and which gives statistics on the age and sex of the labor force at 20-year intervals. A comparison of the number of women in the labor force in 1900 with the number of men in the labor force in the same year shows that in 1900 male workers outnumbered female workers more than 5 to 1. In 1980, 57,186 thousand men and 42,117 thousand women were in the labor force. The ratio of male to female workers had dropped to less than 2 to 1. One can conclude from this information that the role of women in American society has changed dramatically since 1900. The statistics in the other columns reveal further relationships among data about workers in the United States during this 80-year period.

Now study the chart below which provides information for the years 1870–1890, in 10-year intervals. New information (new years, different interval, new age groupings) about the history of labor can be learned from this chart.

Labor Force by Age and Sex* • 1870–1890

Year	Total Labor Force	Sex		Age	
		Male	Female	10 to 15 Years	16 and over
1890	23,318	19,313	4,006	1,504	21,814
1880	17,392	14,745	2,647	1,118	16,274
1870	12,925	11,008	1,917	765	12,160

Source: *Historical Statistics of the United States*
*In Thousands of Persons

Labor Force by Industry* • 1860–1890

Year	Total Labor Force	Agri-culture	Fishing	Mining	Construc-tion	Manu-facturing	Trade	Trans-portation	Teachers	Domestics
1890	23,320	9,960	60	440	1,510	4,390	2,960	870	350	1,580
1880	17,390	8,920	41	280	900	3,290	1,930	541	230	1,130
1870	12,930	6,790	28	180	780	2,470	1,310	295	170	1,000
1860	11,110	5,880	31	176	520	1,530	890	225	115	600

Source: *Historical Statistics of the United States*
*In Thousands of Persons 10 Years Old and Over

Practicing the Skill

On this page are two additional charts adapted from tables in *The Historical Statistics*. Study the charts, keeping in mind the charts on page 546. Then on a separate sheet of paper, answer the following questions.

1. (a) What is the subject of the chart at the top of this page? (b) How does the data overlap with the chart at the bottom of page 546? (c) Was the percentage of people employed in agriculture 50 percent, less than 50 percent, or more than 50 percent of the total labor force? (d) Next to agriculture, what industry employed the largest number of workers?

2. Examine the statistics for sex and age and by industry and note any differences. (a) Is there an explanation for the differences? (b) Are the differences significant enough to be important? Explain.

3. (a) What is the subject of the data on the chart at the bottom of this page? (b) How did union membership change between 1900 and 1930?

4. Compare the chart on the bottom of this page to the chart at the top of page 546. (a) What was the total labor force in 1900? (b) How many people were in unions at this time? (c) What was the total work force in 1920? (d) How many people were in unions at that time? (e) What conclusions about union membership can be made based on the information in these two charts?

Labor Union Membership in Selected Industries* • 1900–1930

Year	Total Union Membership	Building Construction	Textiles	Chemicals, Glass, and Stone	Communication and Transportation	Trade	Theater and Music
1930	3,393	904	35	35	882	10	134
1925	3,519	837	36	42	893	10	110
1920	5,048	888	149	52	1,256	21	99
1915	2,583	533	22	53	576	15	90
1910	2,140	459	21	60	480	15	60
1905	2,022	373	14	51	446	50	38
1900	868	153	8	48	189	20	9

Source: *Historical Statistics of the United States*
*In Thousands of Persons

Varying methods of statistical calculation may result in slightly different figures.

late 1800's (c) less than 50 percent (d) manufacturing 2. totals are different (a) Yes, in the age and sex chart totals are rounded. (b) No, differences are relatively small. 3. (a) labor union membership (b) Membership increased from 1900 to 1920 and decreased from 1920 to 1930. 4. (a) 27,640,000 (b) 868,000 (c) 40,282,000 (d) 5,048,000 (e) Answers will vary. Responses should focus on the data for the years between 1900 and 1920.)

The rapid development of large-scale industry between 1865 and 1900 created new problems for wage earners who attempted to solve their problems by organizing labor unions. Through the labor movement, Samuel Gompers and other labor leaders outlined and pushed for a program of economic freedom that differed in many respects from the traditional political ideas on which the democratic spirit of free enterprise was based.

The growth of great corporations made it increasingly difficult for the individual worker to meet and solve his or her own problems. As a result, some workers organized unions through which they could act as a united group. They began to demand government protection in the form of laws providing maximum hours of work, minimum wages, and accident compensation.

By 1900, labor organizations were beginning to exert considerable influence upon government at both the state and the federal levels. They began supporting those candidates in the major political parties who were most friendly to the progress of the workers. They also began to insist that it was their democratic right to organize, to bargain as a group, and to strike if necessary to protect their rights.

In their demands and in their actions, wage earners were reacting to the new industrial society that was transforming the United States. Like all other Americans, they were seeking to adjust to the industrial age.

CONNECTING CHAPTER IDEAS

Despite the benefits industrialism brought to farmers, increasing industrialization also created many new problems: overproduction, falling prices, high production costs, the scarcity of money, and unfair railroad practices. In the next chapter you will read how farmers across the United States responded to the complex problems presented by the new industrial era.

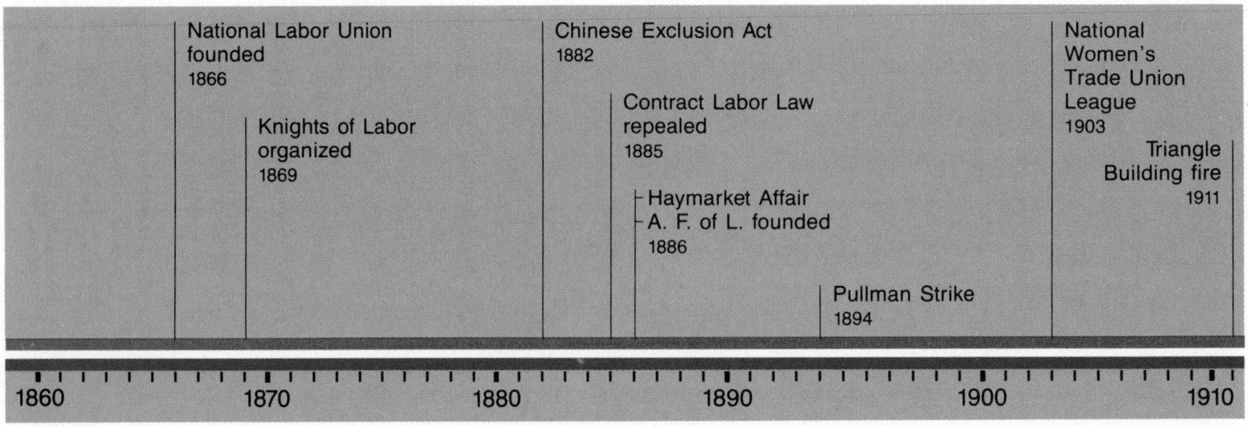

National Labor Union founded
1866

Knights of Labor organized
1869

Chinese Exclusion Act
1882

Contract Labor Law repealed
1885

Haymarket Affair
A. F. of L. founded
1886

Pullman Strike
1894

National Women's Trade Union League
1903

Triangle Building fire
1911

1860　　1870　　1880　　1890　　1900　　1910

CHAPTER

23 REVIEW

Reviewing Important Terms

Decide whether each of the following sentences is true or false. If the sentence is false, replace the underlined term with the word or phrase that will make it true.

1. An injunction is a court order to end a strike.
2. Pay measured in terms of actual purchasing power is known as net income.
3. One method of settling a dispute between labor and management is arbitration.
4. A labor union is an organization of wage earners.
5. A person whose name appears on a yellow-dog contract can not get a job in a particular industry.
6. The business cycle is the natural movement of the economy between periods of prosperity and decline.
7. Labor unions helped protect the common interests of members.
8. People who want to end all government are known as socialists.
9. A lockout takes place when striking workers are not allowed to enter the factory where they work.

Practicing Critical Thinking Skills

1. **Analyzing Ideas.** In human terms, what did the United States lose in becoming an industrialized nation? What advantages did it gain?
2. **Synthesizing Ideas.** The majority of immigrants coming to the United States during the late 1800's were between the ages of 14 and 45. (a) Why do you think this was the case? (b) How might this fact have been significant for the nation's economy? (c) What effect might it have had on fashions, entertainment, and social life?
3. **Organizing Ideas.** In the period 1870–1900, what were the major grievances of working people against (a) employers, (b) state governments, and (c) the federal government?
4. **Interpreting Ideas.** In what ways were the radical movements and the labor movement connected during the late 1800's?
5. **Relating Past to Present.** (a) Compare the demands that labor unions make today with the demands they made during the late 1800's (b) How does the power that labor unions held during the period 1865–1900 compare to the power that they hold today? Give specific examples to support your answers. (c) In general, do the courts treat unions differently today? Explain.

Developing History Study Skills

1. **Understanding Economic Reports.** Study the bar graph entitled "Changes in Occupations • 1890–1980," on page 1015 of the textbook. (a) What occupation decreased in the number of workers from 1890 to 1980? (b) Speculate as to why this decrease took place. (c) How many workers were engaged in manufacturing occupations in 1890? in 1910? (d) Speculate as to why this increase took place. (e) Based on the information you have read in the textbook and this graph, write a brief paragraph about the shift of occupations from 1890 to 1910.

2. **Drawing Conclusions.** Consider the following conclusions about working people at the end of the nineteenth century. Use information from your textbook to decide whether or not the evidence presented supports each conclusion. Then write a paragraph in which you include specific examples from the textbook that either support or refute each conclusion.

   ● Samuel Gompers became an effective spokesman for American workers.
   ● If it had not been for government support of industry, most workers would have been union members.

Relating Geography and History

When they arrived in the United States, many immigrants began living a way of life that was far different from the way of life that they had left behind. Others, however, were able to establish a way of life similar to that in their homeland. To understand the impact that these two different situations had on settlement patterns, answer the following questions.

1. Reread the section "Immigration adds strength and variety to American society" on pages 534–38. (a) From what countries did the most immigrants come before 1890? (b) after 1890?
2. Find a map of the settlement of immigrants in the United States in your school or local library. (a) In what parts of the United States did large numbers of immigrants from China, Italy, and Germany settle? (b) Why did immigrants from the same homeland often settle and live together in the communities of the United States? (c) What are some of the effects that the settlement of a large number of immigrants from the same country had on an area?

549

See Chapter Overview in TMRG, p.TM136.
See Chapter Objectives in TMRG, p.TM136.
See Introducing the Chapter in TMRG, p.TM136.

CHAPTER 24

Farmers Revolt Against Big Business

Changing Ways (1860's–1890's)

An alliance of farmers

After the Civil War, American farmers took up the challenge of feeding the nation. Neither the farmers nor the great majority of other Americans, however, were aware of the developments that were to transform life in the United States and throughout the world.

By 1870 the symbols of the new industrial age were beginning to appear and to change farmers' lives. Steel rails stretched across the prairies and through remote mountain valleys. The chugging engines that traveled along these rails brought new settlers. The result was an opening up of new land to settlement and farming and the bringing of older farmland into closer touch with the cities.

The development of steel plowshares and harrows aided in cultivating the tough sod of the prairies. Still other kinds of farm machines had begun to appear on some of the nation's more prosperous farms. With these machines farmers were able to produce more goods with less labor and with fewer workers. The increased agricultural output was needed to feed the populations of the rapidly growing industrial cities with their ever-larger markets.

These technologically related developments gave the farmers every reason to believe that better times lay ahead for them and their families. Better times were 30 years away. In this 30-year period, American farmers were forced to confront overproduction, falling farm prices, high production costs, the scarcity of money, and unfair railroad practices. As farmers struggled to remain an important part of the expanding industrial economy, they began to make their voices heard through national farm organizations and political rallies.

READING FOCUS

As you read about farmers' problems and the actions farmers took to solve them, look for the details that support each of the following statements.

1. Farm life remains laborious, but simple.
2. Farmers face complex new problems in the industrial age.
3. Farm organizations join efforts to regulate the railroads.
4. Farm organizations put increasing pressure on government.
5. The farmers fail to win control of the national government.

1 Farm life remains laborious, but simple

See Teaching Suggestions in TMRG, pp.TM136-37.

Every ten years, as required in the Constitution, a **federal census** has been taken. The collected information has been recorded and published by the government. The returns from the 1870 census showed that the nation's urban population was growing more rapidly than the rural population. In 1860 about 80 percent of all Americans lived in rural areas. By 1870 only about 75 percent lived on farms or in small towns and villages. Even so, the United States was still for the most part a farming country.

The 2.7 million farms that the census takers visited in 1870 varied greatly. Some farms were large, others small. Some farmers were prosperous; others just managed to earn a living. Regardless of their size or their degree of prosperity, the American farms of 1870 shared certain characteristics.

The day of hand tools. Manual labor and a few simple hand tools characterized work on most farms in 1870. It is easier, perhaps, to visualize life on the typical farm of 1870 by starting with things that the farm family did not yet have.

No farmers, for instance, had gasoline-driven machines or machines powered by electricity. Farmers pumped water by hand, lifted it in buckets from open wells, or, if they were fortunate, ran a pipe from a hilltop spring and allowed the water to flow to the barn and the farmhouse. There were no electric or gas stoves. Farm women usually cooked on iron, wood-burning stoves; only a few had the new kerosene stoves. There were no gas or electric lights; for lighting, farmers used smoky kerosene lamps and lanterns. There was no central heating; there were only stoves and, in the milder South, open fireplaces. In 1870 there was no free delivery of mail. Also there were no mail-order catalogs from which farm families could order their ready-made clothing, tools, or equipment.

On some of the nation's large and more prosperous farms, machines were becoming increasingly important. Steel plows were in general use. More horse-drawn corn planters, mowers, hayrakes, and reapers as well as

▲ Discussion topic: Encourage students to describe images they may have formulated about American farm and rural life during this period. Have them point out the sources of their ideas (e.g., books and textbooks, movies, television).

551

Homer settled in Prouts Neck on the coast of Maine. There he developed his watercolor techniques and painted his favorite subjects — the sea and New England rural life. He learned to apply "washes" to his works to instill feeling and dramatic lighting qualities. Homer's seascapes and landscapes are noted both for their grandeur and intensity of feeling. The people in Homer's paintings are often symbolic — for example, the courageous sea captain or the hard-working farmer. *Snap the Whip* shows New England farm children at play in the realistic style typical of Winslow Homer's works.

steam-powered threshers were being manufactured and put to use in the fields.

In 1870 the average farmers depended almost entirely upon hand tools—axes, saws, spades, pitchforks, sickles, scythes, and rakes. For power they relied mainly on their muscles and on horses, mules, or oxen.

The self-reliant farm family. Farming was not an easy way of life. The family rose at daybreak—or even earlier in winter—to milk the cows, bring in firewood, feed the pigs and chickens, and fill the water trough for the livestock. When the night fell, the family was still busy with its unending chores. A self-reliant farm family had an independence that few wage earners enjoyed.

All American farmers in 1870 were not independent. Nearly one fourth of the farm families were either tenants or sharecroppers. Sharecropping was especially common among black farmers in the South.

Social life. Except for farmers who lived close to a growing city or a large town, opportunities for social activities in 1870 were limited. Most farm families had only three centers of social activity—the nearest town, the church, and the school.

The Saturday drive to town in a wagon or buggy was a big weekly event. Even a 10-mile (16- kilometer) trip meant about four hours on the road. As for the "town," it might be nothing more than a country store at the crossroads, with a blacksmith shop on the opposite corner. On the other hand, it might be a sizable village or even a county seat with a courthouse, a railroad station, several stores, a bank, a doctor's office, a lawyer's office, and a cluster of houses.

These Saturday trips combined business with pleasure. While the farm women shopped and while the farmers arranged for the sale of their cash crops or settled accounts at the bank or the store, the children played with their

552

friends. The shopping and the business gave families an opportunity to chat with neighbors, to catch up on the latest news, and perhaps to watch some horse trading in front of the blacksmith shop.

The Sunday trip to church was another bright spot in the week. The entire family, freshly scrubbed and dressed in their best clothes, drove to church in the wagon or buggy. There they worshiped, sang hymns, listened to the sermon, and afterward gathered in front of the church for leisurely talk before driving home once again.

The local school. On weekdays the children attended a one-room elementary school. To reach it, some of the boys and girls walked several miles along the country roads. School terms were short, for the children had to help with spring planting and fall harvesting. The teacher, usually a young woman, taught all grades. The emphasis in 1870, as in earlier times, was on "readin', 'ritin', and 'rithmetic." During the school term, the teacher often lived in the homes of the pupils, staying a month in one home, then a month in another, and so on throughout the term.

The school was also a community center. Graduation day was a big occasion, and now and then there were spelling bees and other events in which parents as well as their children could take part.

Loneliness of farm life. For most farm families, however, farming in 1870 was a hard, lonely way of life. It was especially hard and lonely on the prairies and plains.

Hamlin Garland, who spent his boyhood on farms in Wisconsin, Iowa, and the Dakotas, pictured in his writing the dreary loneliness in isolated farming communities. In his famous collection of tales, *Main-Traveled Roads*, Garland wrote:

"The main-traveled road in the West (as everywhere) is hot and dusty in summer, and desolate and drear with mud in fall and spring, and in winter the winds sweep the snow across it; but it does sometimes cross a rich meadow where the songs of the larks and bobolinks and blackbirds are tangled. . . .

"Mainly it is long and wearyful, and has a dull little town at one end and a home of toil at the other. Like the main-traveled road of life, it is traversed by many classes of people, but the poor and the weary predominate."

Immigrant farmers from Europe, who by 1870 were moving out onto the western prairies and plains, faced special difficulties. These immigrant pioneers had to adjust not only to a strange physical environment but also to a strange and bewildering social environment. Churches were different; schools were different; life in nearly every way was different from what they had known in the Old World. At first neither they nor their American-born neighbors understood each other's language and customs.

Hardest of all, perhaps, were the lives of black settlers who ventured onto the prairies and plains. One great exodus of about 15,000 blacks from the southern states arrived in Kansas in 1879, where they hoped to start new lives free from discrimination. These black newcomers—penniless, weary, and often ill from their long journey—took up homesteads in the unfamiliar lands. To buy a calf, a pig, a few chickens, or a plow, the men worked for wages on nearby farms, on railroads, or in mines. Despite these hardships, many of the black settlers managed to carve out homes for their families in Kansas. Smaller groups of blacks settled in other parts of the West. Most of them endured some form of discrimination from their white neighbors.

New problems. Most American farmers of the 1870's were not unhappy with their lot. They expected to work hard, and they expected to live more or less apart from their neighbors. The hardships that troubled them most were new ones growing out of the new industrial economy.

SECTION REVIEW

See underscored items, text p. 551.
Identify: federal census
For answers to questions, see Answer Key, p.A77.

1. **Summarizing Ideas:** (a) List three adjectives that describe farm life in 1870. (b) Explain why you selected each adjective. (c) Do any of the adjectives seem to be negative? Are any of them positive? Explain.

2. **Analyzing Ideas:** Why was the Saturday drive to town such an important part of farm life?

3. **Comparing Ideas:** (a) Compare the reasons for the movement of blacks to Kansas in 1879 to the reasons for the immigration of Europeans to America. (b) Compare the problems these blacks may have faced adjusting to their new homes to the problems the immigrants faced.

2 Farmers face complex new problems in the industrial age

See Teaching Suggestions in TMRG, pp.TM137-38.
For American farmers in general, the last 25 or 30 years of the 1800's brought many new problems. Most of the nation's farmers found themselves in serious trouble. What were some of the new problems that farm families faced?

Overproduction and falling prices. The fundamental causes of agricultural discontent—overproduction and falling prices—were rarely understood by farmers.

From 1865 to about 1900, farmers produced more food than people could afford to buy. This increase of food in the American markets was the result of (1) the rapid opening of new farmland on the prairies and plains and (2) the development of new farm machinery and improved methods of farming.

Why did American farmers not sell their surplus products to other countries? They did, but competing agricultural countries such as Russia, Canada, Argentina, and Australia were also seeking customers and often had the same products that American farmers wanted to export. Thus there was an increased amount of certain kinds of food on the world market as well as in the United States.

In an **open-market economy,** whenever the supply of any commodity is greater than the demand for that commodity, prices fall. Starting in the 1930's, the federal government tried to support farm prices in the United States, but in the late 1800's, only a few farmers even suggested such a possibility. Thus farm prices kept falling.

Wheat, which had sold for $2.50 a bushel (35.2 liters) in 1868, dropped to about 78 cents a bushel in the late 1880's. Because of high transportation costs and other factors, however, the farmers actually often got only 30 cents a bushel. Corn fell to 15 cents a bushel and, being cheaper than coal, was often used for fuel. Cotton, which in the late 1860's had sold for 65 cents a pound (0.45 kilogram),

This cartoon depicts the farmer of the late 1800's as a thin, tattered figure in contrast to the well-fed, well-dressed industrialists who were helped by tariffs passed by Congress and President McKinley (shown dressed as the waiter).

dropped to 5 cents a pound in 1895. Thus growers of these important **staple crops** were often farming at a loss.

High farm costs. To add to their difficulties, farm families had to pay high prices for their shoes, clothing, kerosene, furniture, farm machinery, household equipment, and other goods. In many instances, prices were high because cheaply made European goods had been kept out of American markets by the high tariffs put on imports to protect American manufacturers. In some instances, prices were high because they had been artificially raised by monopolies.

To make matters worse, farm families almost always owed money. Many had borrowed money in the form of mortgages to pay for their land, homes, and barns. They had added to this burden of debt by borrowing money to pay for fences, livestock, seed, and machinery. As prices for farm products fell, the farmers could not pay their debts. To head off disaster, they increased their mortgages by borrowing more money, thus adding to their debt.

The 1880's were often called "the decade of mortgages." Of the total number of farms in the country, 43 percent were mortgaged. In Kansas the number reached 60 percent. Of course, these mortgages often were necessary. By means of mortgages, families with little or no money could borrow the capital they needed to buy a farm, purchase farm machinery, or make improvements on existing farms. It was not so much mortgages themselves but rather the hard times and the high interest rates that troubled the farmers.

During the late 1800's, interest rates on western farm loans ran from 8 to 20 percent. These rates were higher than interest rates charged to industrial and commercial enterprises. Bankers and other money lenders justified the higher rates on farm loans on the ground that farming was a riskier business than industry or commerce. In addition to the high rates, money brokers charged a commission for arranging farm loans. In several farm states, loan brokers starting with nothing became millionaires within a few years.

The problem of money. The farmers blamed their troubles on the shortage of money, which was only part of the problem, but an important part. To understand the farmers' point of view, it is necessary to see how money affected their everyday lives.

The first thing to remember is that money is a **medium of exchange**—that is, something of value given in exchange for goods or services. Its value is determined by the goods or services it will buy. A flour miller might say, "One dollar will buy one bushel of wheat." A farmer might say, "One bushel of wheat will buy one dollar." The miller and the farmer are saying the same thing; both of them are stating the value of a dollar *and* the value of a bushel of wheat.

The second thing to remember is that there are two ways to change the value of a dollar *and* the value of a bushel of wheat. All other things being equal, if you *increase the amount of wheat*—for example, double it—then "one dollar will buy two bushels of wheat" or "two bushels of wheat will buy one dollar." If you *decrease the number of dollars in circulation*— say, by one half—you can accomplish the same result. For example, one half as many dollars will now buy just as much wheat. That is, "50 cents will buy one bushel of wheat" and "one dollar will buy two bushels of wheat," or again, "two bushels of wheat will buy one dollar." In practice, the problem of money value is not this simple, but the illustration may help to clarify the problem of western farmers.

Falling farm prices. Between 1870 and 1900, the price, or value, of farm products fell lower and lower. In other words, the value of money rose higher and higher. Consider a specific example. In 1868 Olaf Erickson sold 1,000 bushels (35,238 liters) of wheat at $2.50 a bushel. In 1868, then, his wheat brought him $2,500. Since his interest payments amounted to $250 that year, Olaf could pay this interest with the income from 100 bushels (3,524 liters) of wheat, or one tenth of his income. Each year from 1868 on, Olaf continued to grow and sell 1,000 bushels of wheat. But by 1890 wheat was bringing only 75 cents a bushel. Olaf's income in 1890, therefore, was only $750. Since his interest payments still amounted to $250, he now had to pay his debt with the income from 334 bushels (11,769 liters) of wheat, or one third of his total income.

As far as Olaf could tell, he had done nothing to cause this. Yet his income had dropped from $2,500 to $750 a year. Something was wrong. Olaf and his family were working as hard and raising as much wheat as ever.

Output and Price of Wheat • 1867 - 1900

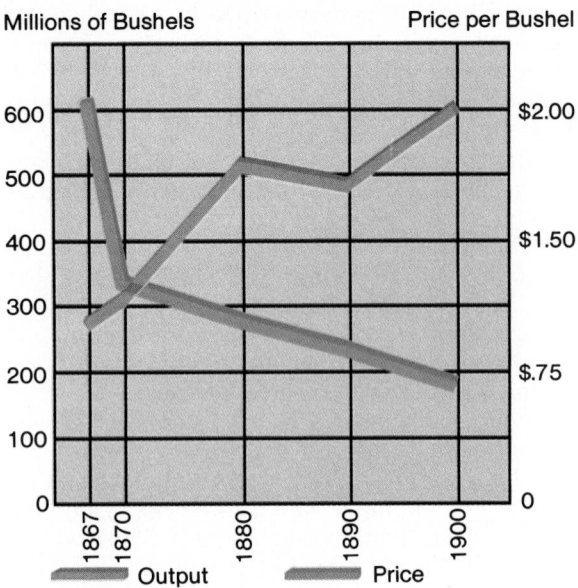

Millions of Bushels   Price per Bushel

Source: *Historical Statistics of the United States*

Clearly, Olaf reasoned, the *value of money* had changed. Money was harder to get; money was scarce or "tight." It had gone up in value. That was why, Olaf thought, the same amount of wheat brought him fewer dollars each year.

Olaf forgot that there were many more farmers in 1890, both in the United States and in other countries, than there had been in 1868. These farmers were producing far more wheat than they had produced in 1868.

Although Olaf did not understand the whole problem, he did have his finger upon one key to his difficulties. The supply of money in the United States was not expanding rapidly enough during the late 1800's to meet the needs of the new industrial economy. The answer, as Olaf saw it, was simple enough: Let the government increase the amount of money in circulation. This would "cheapen" the dollar and raise the price of farm products. Olaf could then pay his debts and buy the goods that his family needed.

The distributors. Farmers also blamed many of their difficulties on the distributors who bought from the farmers and sold to whole-salers and retailers. The services performed by these brokers, produce buyers, grain-elevator operators, and stockyard owners were important in the distribution of farm products. However, the farmers believed that the distributors were taking too large a share of the wealth produced on farms and ranches.

Many distributors no doubt did take advantage of the farmers. Farmers, having little cash and credit and needing money to pay their debts, had to sell their goods at harvest time even if prices were low. The distributors, backed by considerable capital, could afford to store what they bought from the farmers until prices went up. Of course, prices did not always go up, and distributors were sometimes ruined when prices fell.

The railroads. Farmers, especially on the prairies and plains, reserved their chief hatred, however, for the railroads. Like other Americans, including small business owners, farmers had at first welcomed the railroad with enthusiasm. They believed that it would open distant markets to them and increase the value of their farmland by bringing more farmers into the community. Farmers who could afford to do so often bought a few shares of railroad stock. The governments of small farming communities often invested money in railroad stocks and bonds in return for the railroad's promise to build a branch line to the community.

Unfortunately, events did not always turn out as the farmers expected. In the first place, the railroad stock that farmers owned represented only a small part of all the stock sold. Therefore the farmers had little voice in determining railroad policies.

In the second place, the farmers expected that competition among the railroads would keep freight rates low. In this hope they were also disappointed. For example, competing railroads bid against each other for **long-haul shipments** between two distant cities served by two or more lines, sometimes cutting their rates so low that they operated at actual losses. Railroads made up these losses, however, by charging much higher rates for **short-haul shipments** to those communities that were served by only one railroad.

Farmers and other small shippers protested, of course, against this so-called "long-haul, short-haul abuse" on the part of the railroads. However, it was very difficult for them to do anything about the situation.

Many of the hardships that farmers faced in the late 1800's were new, strange, and complicated. Most farmers did not at first understand the complexities of overproduction, falling prices, "tight money," high interest rates, distributors, and high shipping costs. Like all other Americans, the farmers had to grope their way into the industrial age.

SECTION REVIEW

See underscored items, text pp. 555-56.

Identify: medium of exchange, staple crops, long-haul shipments, short-haul shipments

For answers to questions, see Answer Key, p.A77-78.

1. **Organizing Ideas:** What were the farmers' grievances against the **(a)** distributors and **(b)** railroads?
2. **Seeing Relationships:** How were the new problems that farmers faced in the late 1800's related to industrialization?
3. **Studying Graphics:** Look at the graph on page 556. How does it illustrate a major problem American farmers faced in the period following the Civil War?

3 Farm organizations join efforts to regulate the railroads

See Teaching Suggestions in TMRG, p.TM138.

Many farmers soon learned that only through cooperative action could they hope to share the numerous advantages that were emerging from the new industrial economy.

The Grange. The first national farm organization started in 1867 was called the Grange, or the Patrons of Husbandry. Its founder, Oliver Hudson Kelley, wanted to establish in every farm community a national organization with a local chapter where farm families could meet to learn better ways of farming.

At first Kelley fought an uphill battle in organizing the Grange. By 1872, however, farm prices were falling rapidly, and the farmers, bewildered and disturbed, joined the Grange in growing numbers. By 1875 some 1.5 million farmers, most of them in the Middle West, were Grange members.

Farmers' cooperatives. Kelley had started the Grange primarily to combat social isolation

and lack of educational opportunity. The farmers who joined in the 1870's, however, were more interested in solving economic problems and carrying out their slogans — "Cooperation" and "Down with monopoly."

Working together in the Grange and in other local farm organizations, many farmers set up cooperative associations, usually called **cooperatives.** Cooperatives owned and managed by the farmers themselves could bypass distributors. The cooperative could (1) sell the produce of a group of farmers directly to big-city markets and (2) buy farm machines, clothing, and household goods in large quantities at wholesale prices. Before long, farmers set up not only cooperative stores but also cooperative grain storage elevators, creameries, and even factories to manufacture their own farm machines and equipment.

Some of these early cooperative ventures were successful. However, most of them failed, partly because farmers often lacked business experience, partly because farmers did not have enough capital to compete successfully with established businesses. Despite failures the farmers did not give up, for they still had the possibility of political action.

Opposing unfair railroad practices. As early as 1870, farmers, the owners of small businesses, and lawyers persuaded the Illinois state legislature to investigate unfair practices by the railroads. In 1871 the Illinois legislature created a commission to fix maximum freight rates and made it illegal for a railroad to charge differential freight rates. The legislatures of Minnesota and Iowa passed similar laws, as did the legislature of Wisconsin, where the Grangers were the chief backers of railroad regulation.

The railroads opposed these laws and sometimes refused to obey them. In 1876 and 1877, the Supreme Court heard a series of cases known as the "Granger cases," of which the most far-reaching was *Munn v. Illinois.* The Court ruled that state legislatures had the right to regulate businesses that affected the public, including grain elevators and railroads.

Unfortunately for the farmers, the railroads either evaded the laws or exerted enough pressure on the legislators to get the laws repealed. The most serious blow for the farmers, however, came in 1886, when the Supreme Court qualified its decision in the "Granger cases." It now ruled that state legis-

▲ Writing activity: Have the students write a brief paragraph explaining whether participating in a cooperative may serve an individual's interest.

557

Alexander Graham Bell is best known for inventing the telephone. Bell, however, felt his major contributions where in teaching deaf persons and in teaching them to speak.

Bell, born and educated in Scotland, worked with his father, a speech professor who had invented a system called Visible Speech. This system consisted of symbols that showed the position of the vocal organs during speech. Bell worked to adapt Visible Speech for the deaf. The method he developed remains the basis today for teaching the deaf to speak. In 1871 Bell moved to the United States and soon began training teachers of the deaf at Boston University.

Bell's interest in sound, hearing, and speech led him to read extensively about the conversion of sound into electricity. In 1875, almost by accident, Bell discovered the conditions needed to transmit the human voice over a telephone wire. By 1877 commercial development of the telephone had begun and the Bell Telephone Company was founded.

During his last 25 years, Bell continued to experiment seeking ways to overcome the physical disabilities that often hindered the accomplishments of the handicapped.

latures had no power to regulate traffic that moved across state boundaries. The Court held that only the federal government could regulate the interstate activities of railroads.

The Interstate Commerce Act. The 1886 Supreme Court decision led Congress to pass the Interstate Commerce Act of 1887 to correct a number of the railroads' practices.

Pooling arrangements by the railroads were one of the practices opposed by farmers, many business people, and the public. Several railroads operating in the same area and across state borders would join to form a pool. All members of the pool then agreed not to compete, but instead to charge certain agreed-upon rates. As a result, farmers and others using the railroads often had to pay exorbitant rates.

Another practice the public wanted corrected was the granting of special favors. In order to get business, competing railroads often gave large corporations especially low rates. Sometimes, instead of actually lowering the rates, the railroads agreed to grant **rebates,** that is, to refund part of the shipping charges.

Farmers, small businesses, and the public also complained, as you know, that railroads sometimes charged more for a short haul than for a long haul. It sometimes cost more to send goods a few miles than to send the same goods from, say, Chicago to New York.

SOURCES

MUNN v. ILLINOIS (1877)

Property does become clothed with a public interest when used in a manner to make it of public consequence, and affect the community at large. When, therefore, one devotes his property to a use in which the public has an interest, he, in effect, grants to the public an interest in that use, and must submit to be controlled by the public for the common good, to the extent of the interest he has thus created. He may withdraw his grant by discontinuing the use; but, so long as he maintains the use, he must submit to the control. . . .

Provisions of the act. The Interstate Commerce Act applied to all railroads passing through more than one state. The act made it illegal for such railroads to (1) make pooling arrangements, (2) give special favors in the form of lower rates or rebates, (3) charge more for a short haul than for a long haul over the same line, or (4) charge unjust or unreasonable rates. The act also required the railroads to print and display their rates and to give a minimum of ten days' public notice before they changed those rates.

Finally, the Interstate Commerce Act created an Interstate Commerce Commission (ICC) of five members appointed by the President and confirmed by the Senate. The commission had authority to (1) investigate complaints against the railroads, (2) summon witnesses, (3) examine a railroad's accounts and correspondence, and (4) require railroads to file annual reports about their operations and finances and to adopt a uniform system of accounting.

The commission, however, had no real authority to fix rates and to enforce its orders. If a railroad refused to accept the commission's proposals, the commission had to appeal to the courts for an order compelling the railroads to obey. In some instances, the courts refused to grant the commission's requests for such orders. In other instances, the courts reversed the commission's decision.

The Interstate Commerce Act was the first important attempt by the federal government to regulate transportation and to create a federal regulatory commission. Because the act set a precedent for more sweeping measures later adopted by Congress, it marked a turning point in the history of the relations between the federal government and business.

SECTION REVIEW

See underscored items, text pp. 557-58.

Identify: the Grange, Oliver Kelley, cooperatives, *Munn v. Illinois,* rebates

For answers to questions, see Answer Key, p.A78.

1. **Summarizing Ideas:** (a) What were the goals of the Grange? (b) How successful was the Grange in achieving these goals?

2. **Interpreting Ideas:** (a) What were the provisions of the Interstate Commerce Act of 1887? (b) What were its limitations? (c) Why was the act significant?

3. **Analyzing Ideas:** What role did the Supreme Court play in the effort to regulate the railroads?

See Teaching Suggestions in TMRG, pp.TM138-39.

4 Farm organizations put increasing pressure on government

While struggling with the effects of railroad legislation, farmers also turned to a more serious problem—falling prices for farm produce. Ignoring the facts of overproduction and competition from farmers overseas, they blamed low farm prices solely on the scarcity of money.

Politics and paper money. During the late 1860's and the 1870's, money was becoming increasingly scarce. In 1865, for example, the amount of currency, or money of all kinds, in circulation in the United States averaged $31.18 per person. By 1878 the average had dropped to $17.08.

Faced with growing hardship, farmers demanded that the government increase the supply of currency in circulation. When neither the Republicans nor the Democrats promised to help them, farmers began to join the Greenback-Labor Party, commonly called the Greenback Party.

The Greenback Party took its name from the paper money, known as **greenbacks,** issued by the government during the Civil War. After the war the government began to withdraw the greenbacks from circulation. Farmers and other "cheap money" advocates protested. They wanted *more,* not fewer, greenbacks in circulation.

The "cheap money" people did not get what they wanted. Instead, Congress adopted the Resumption Act in 1875. This act ordered the Secretary of the Treasury to redeem *in gold* all greenbacks presented to the Treasury on or after January 1, 1879. As a result of this compromise, by January 1, 1879, greenbacks were worth their full, or face, value in gold. Under these circumstances, owners of greenbacks did not bother to redeem them. Congress decided to allow 346 million greenbacks to remain in circulation as part of United States currency.

In 1875, dismayed by Congress's decision to redeem the greenbacks in gold, the "cheap money" advocates decided to take their case to the people at the polls. Although the newly organized Greenback Party did not win a significant number of votes in the 1876 election,

This cartoonist obviously had little respect for those who favored greenbacks. What devices does he use to make fun of these people? What kind of people does he show them to be?

the Greenbackers continued their battle for "cheap money."

The silver issue. Rutherford B. Hayes, who became President in 1877, successfully opposed the pressure of the Greenbackers to get more paper money into circulation. However, he was unable to block another move by the "cheap money" people to increase the volume of currency in the economy.

Back in 1834 the government had adopted a law providing for the coinage of both gold and silver, at a ratio of about 16 to 1. That is, the government offered to buy 16 ounces (453.6 grams) of silver for the same price it paid for one ounce (28.3 grams) of gold. At the time, silver was relatively scarce, and silver producers could sell 16 ounces of silver to private buyers for *more than* one ounce of gold. As a result, they did not take silver to the United States Mint to be coined into silver dollars.

In the 1870's, however, this situation changed. With the discovery of huge silver deposits in parts of Colorado and Nevada, the supply of silver increased tremendously. The value of silver **bullion,** or uncoined metal,

began to fall. In 1874, for the first time in more than 30 years, 16 ounces of silver bullion were sold on the open market for *less than* one ounce of gold.

Faced with falling prices, silver producers remembered the government's offer to buy silver at the ratio of 16 to 1. They now tried to sell their silver bullion to the Treasury Department but discovered that in 1873 Congress had passed a law removing silver dollars from the list of standard coins. Furious at the loss of a profitable market for their bullion, silver producers denounced Congress for what they called the "Crime of '73."

The "Crime of '73" became a rallying cry for those who demanded that the government buy silver. This demand came mostly from westerners, but it was also supported by other Americans, including farmers, who wanted more currency in circulation.

The Bland-Allison Act. In 1877 Representative Richard P. Bland of Missouri introduced a bill calling for free and unlimited coinage of silver dollars at a ratio of 16 silver dollars to 1 gold dollar. When this bill reached the Senate, it was modified by Senator William B. Allison of Iowa to become the Bland-Allison bill.

The Bland-Allison bill authorized the Treasury Department to buy and to mint not less than $2 million and not more than $4 million worth of silver each month. President Hayes vetoed the bill, but Congress passed it over his veto in 1878. The new law was a partial victory for the silver interests, the Greenbackers, and other "cheap money" people.

Failure of the Greenbackers. The Greenback Party reached its greatest power in 1878, when it polled 1 million votes and elected 14 members to Congress. This was a shock to the two major parties, but the triumph was short-lived. Two years later the Greenback Presidential candidate, James B. Weaver, received only 300,000 votes.

Although it failed to achieve its goal, the Greenback movement, like the Grange movement, taught the farmers several valuable lessons. The farmers learned from their experience with the Grange that they could, if united, gain influence in state legislatures. They learned from the Greenback movement that their influence might be felt even in Congress. Above all, they learned that the secret of power lay in organization.

▲ (symbolic associations: the donkey as a symbol for stubborness and stupidity; the dancing as the idea of blind worship without understanding; the farmers as foolish yokels)

Farmers' alliances. Even before the Greenback Party began to break up, farmers were forming organizations called **alliances.** During the early 1880's, the different state alliances in the North and Northwest set up a loose federation called the Northern, or Northwestern, Farmers' Alliance. The southern groups joined in a much more tightly knit organization known as the Southern Alliance.

Like the Grange, the alliances experimented with cooperative buying and selling organizations. They were prepared to take action to protect the farmers from the exploitation they were subjected to by manufacturers, railroads, and distributors.

Hard times in the late 1880's transformed the alliances into influential political organizations. By 1890, for example, the Southern Alliance had 3 million white members, while 1 million southern black farmers were enrolled in an affiliated Colored Alliance. A proposal to merge the Southern Alliance and the Northwestern Farmers' Alliance failed, however, because southerners insisted upon separate white and black lodges in the merged alliance. The Northern alliance leaders refused to accept this arrangement.

Desperate conditions. Starting in 1886, a 10-year series of droughts on the Great Plains turned farmland into arid desert. Driven to desperation, thousands of farmers finally gave up and moved back east. Others remained and continued to fight the land and those they held responsible for much of their trouble—the owners of railroads and factories, the directors of banks and insurance companies that held farm mortgages, and the distributors who bought and sold farm produce. The farmers also continued their pressure, along with other "cheap money" interests, to get the government to put more money into circulation.

Sherman Silver Purchase Act. In 1889 and 1890, six new states entered the Union—North Dakota, South Dakota, Montana, Washington, Idaho, and Wyoming. These states, all in the West, greatly increased the political strength of the farmers and the silver-mining interests in Congress. Members of Congress representing farming and silver-mining areas agreed to make a deal with the Republicans, who wanted to increase tariff rates. They agreed to vote for the McKinley Tariff Act if the high-tariff members voted for a "cheap money" bill.

As a result of this deal, the Sherman Silver Purchase Act became law in 1890. This act required the United States Treasury to purchase 4.5 million ounces (127.6 million grams) of silver each month at the market price and to pay for this silver with paper money that could be redeemed in gold or silver.

Silver miners hoped that the law would raise the price of silver, and farmers hoped that, by increasing the supply of money, it would raise the prices of farm produce. These expectations were not realized. The purchased silver was not coined, and the money in circulation did not greatly increase.

New farm leaders. Leaders of the Farmers' Alliances who supported the Sherman Silver Purchase Act and other legislation favorable to farmers became national figures. Among them was Ignatius Donnelly of Minnesota, a spellbinder on the platform and a pamphleteer with a biting literary style. In Kansas there was "Sockless Jerry" Simpson, who denounced the rich eastern monopolists. Kansas produced two other influential leaders—Mary Elizabeth Lease, a colorful and dynamic orator, and Annie Diggs, an editor and an effective behind-the-scenes political worker. One of the most effective of the speakers and writers was Sara Elizabeth Emery of Michigan. Her widely read book *Seven Financial Conspiracies,* which was published in 1888, called on farmers and workers to unite and break the "conspiratorial money power."

In the South a new group of political leaders representing the poorer farmers arose to challenge the leaders of the Democratic Party. Among them were Governor James Hogg of Texas, Tom Watson of Georgia, and "Pitchfork Ben" Tillman of South Carolina.

Thanks to such leaders, the voices of farmers would be heard more clearly in the nation. The needs and concerns of the farmers that these leaders addressed would become increasingly important in national politics.

SECTION REVIEW

See underscored items, text pp. 559-61.

Identify: greenback, Greenback Party, "Crime of '73," Farmers' Alliances, Sherman Silver Purchase Act of 1890, Sara Elizabeth Emery

For answers to questions, see Answer Key, p.A78.

1. **Summarizing Ideas: (a)** What were the goals of the Greenback Party? **(b)** How successful was it in achieving these goals?

▲ For example, in the four years following the 1887 drought, one-half of the people who had migrated to Kansas went back east again. Their wagons displayed slogans such as "In God we trusted; in Kansas we busted."

561

2. **Analyzing Ideas:** Why was the Bland-Allison Act a partial victory for the "cheap money" advocates?

3. **Organizing Ideas: (a)** What factors led to the passage of the Sherman Silver Purchase Act? **(b)** What were its provisions? **(c)** What did the act's supporters hope it would accomplish?

5 The farmers fail to win control of the national government

See Teaching Suggestions in TMRG, pp.TM139-40.

By 1890, the American farmers debated forming a third party. This was the issue that farmers discussed in schoolhouses and Grange halls in the summer of that year. Many northern farmers favored a third party. Because of a split in southern Democratic ranks, most southern farmers opposed it.

The Populist Party. The Congressional elections in the fall of 1890 drew farm men and women into what seemed to be a fiery crusade. Speakers such as Mary Elizabeth Lease bluntly stated the farmers' grievances. In a powerful speech, she proclaimed, "Wall Street° owns the country. It is no longer a government of the people, by the people, and for the people, but a government of Wall Street, by Wall Street, and for Wall Street. The great common people of this country are slaves, and monopoly is the master. The West and South are bound and prostrate before the manufacturing East. . . . We want money, land, and transportation. . . . The people are at bay. Let the bloodhounds of money who have dogged us thus far beware."

Fired by this new militant spirit, farmers decided in 1891 to forget their political differences and form a third party. A meeting made up chiefly of Farmers' Alliance leaders from the West and Middle West launched the People's Party, or the Populist Party, at Cincinnati, Ohio, in 1891. In Omaha, Nebraska, the following year, the Populists drew up a platform and nominated James B. Weaver of Iowa for President of the United States.

°**Wall Street:** a street in New York City's financial district, the nation's principal financial center; often used as a symbol of large banking and business interests.

The Populist platform. On July 4, 1892, the Populists adopted their platform, demanding far-reaching reforms. In part, it stated, "We meet in the midst of a nation brought to the verge of moral, political, and material ruin. . . . The people are demoralized. . . . We have witnessed for more than a quarter of a century the struggles of the two great political parties for power and plunder, while grievous wrongs have been inflicted upon the suffering people. We charge that the controlling influences dominating both these parties have permitted the existing dreadful conditions to develop without serious effort to prevent or restrain them. Neither do they now promise us any substantial reform."

The Populist platform then listed the specific demands of the farmers: (1) an increase in the currency, to be secured by the "free and unlimited coinage of silver at a ratio of 16 to 1"; (2) government ownership of railroads, telegraphs, and telephones; (3) the return to the government of all land held by railroads and other corporations in excess of their needs; (4) a graduated income tax, requiring people with higher incomes to pay a proportionally higher tax; (5) a system of national warehouses where farm produce could be stored until market conditions improved, with the government providing loans on each deposit by a farmer; (6) democratic political reforms, including the direct election of United States Senators and the adoption of the secret ballot, the initiative, and the referendum.

The Populist Party had some support from industrial wage earners. Its platform demanded shorter working hours and restrictions on immigration, which many workers held responsible for unemployment and low wages.

The election of 1892. In the campaign of 1892, great crowds of farmers in the Middle West gathered at outdoor meetings and picnics to listen to eloquent Populist speakers. Weaver, the Populist Presidential candidate, traveled widely and spoke to enthusiastic audiences in the Middle West.

In the South, however, the story was different because of the racial situation. Conservative Democrats and Populists alike were willing to let black southerners vote — but only if it seemed certain that they could control the black vote. Populist leaders, however, urged poor farmers, white and black, to vote together against their "exploiters," the well-to-do plant-

▲ Discussion topic: Have students analyze the excerpt from Mary Elizabeth Lease's speech. What does Lease see as the problems of the people? According to Lease, who controls the government? What do the people want?

ers and business people of the Democratic Party. This angered many white southerners, rich and poor alike, who feared that the Populist bid for black support might endanger white supremacy. Populist speakers in the South were greeted with howls and jeers.

The Populist bid for southern black votes was not very successful. The Populists did not attempt to build a strong or lasting alliance between poor white and black southerners. They did not work for federal supervision of elections, which would have guaranteed the right of black southerners to vote. Nor did the Populists support other efforts of southern blacks to overcome their grievances. Thus Populist candidates in the election of 1892 were generally defeated in the South.

President Benjamin Harrison, running for reelection on the Republican ticket, was defeated by the Democratic candidate, Grover Cleveland. The Democratic victory was a sweeping one, but the Populists made an impressive showing in the nation, despite their weakness in the South. They polled more than 1 million popular votes, won 22 electoral votes for their Presidential candidate, and gained seats in state legislatures and in Congress. Democrats and Republicans alike realized that the Populist movement was much more than ▲ the protest of a few discontented Americans.

Depression and discontent. For the two older political parties, however, the Populist movement was only the beginning of their difficulties. In 1893 the country sank into a serious economic depression. Farm prices plunged. Factories closed, and thousands of unemployed workers walked the streets trying to find jobs.

President Cleveland blamed the crisis on the Sherman Silver Purchase Act of 1890. He believed that it was not "tight money" that had led to the depression but rather uncertainty over the value of money. Cleveland insisted that the only way to end the depression was to accept gold as the single standard of value for the nation's currency. This was an oversimplified explanation, for the depression was worldwide, but there was some truth in the President's view.

Farmers and wage earners, on the other hand, blamed the depression on "tight money." They felt that the Sherman Silver Purchase Act had not gone far enough. They demanded that the government increase the amount of

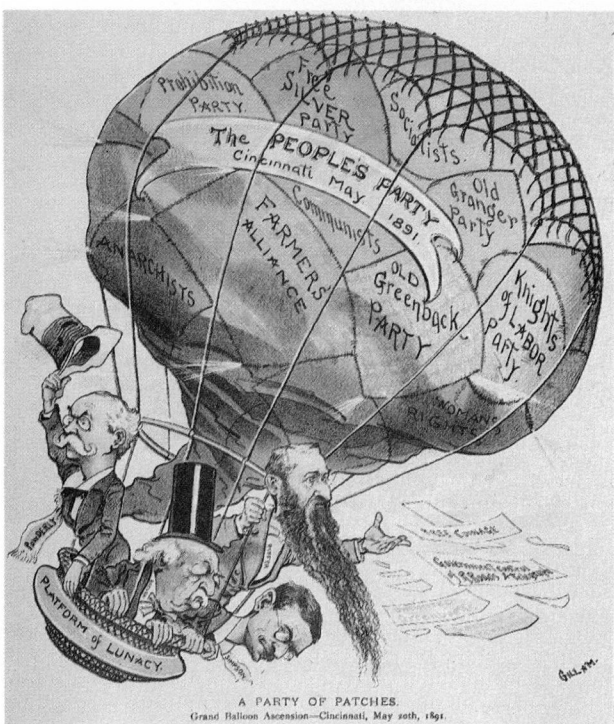

A PARTY OF PATCHES.
Grand Balloon Ascension—Cincinnati, May 20th, 1891.

The Populist Party is likened to a balloon made up of a patchwork of special-interest groups. Who are the riders? (Populist candidates)

currency in circulation by the "free and unlimited coinage of silver at a ratio of 16 to 1." They believed that the resulting increase in "cheap money" would end the depression.

Shrinking gold reserves. By 1893, however, the policy of __bimetallism__ had become a matter of deep concern for the Treasury Department. This policy meant that two metals, gold and silver, furnished the security for all the nation's currency. The value of silver had fallen until the actual silver in a silver dollar was worth only 60 cents. Since silver as well as gold provided the backing, or security, for the nation's currency, more Americans began to grow uneasy about this situation. As a result, many people began to exchange their silver bank notes for gold coins rather than for silver coins. By March 1893 the gold reserves had shrunk to only a little more than $100 million.

The shrinkage in gold reserves created a serious government crisis. If the **gold reserves** completely disappeared, the government would not be able to keep its promise to exchange gold coins for paper money. It would, instead, have

▲ Class activity: Have each student create a print ad for one of the three 1892 Presidential candidates. Each ad should reflect the candidate's appeal to voting groups.

563

In 1892 a Republican and a Democrat in Chicago bet on an election. The one whose candidate lost would have to pull a wagon through the streets of the city carrying the one whose candidate won. Joseph Kir painted the triumphant Democrat and the "workhorse" Republican in his picture "The Last Bet."

to pay with silver. Since by midsummer of 1893 the value of a silver dollar had fallen to 49 cents, prices would soar and the nation would head toward economic disaster.

Stopping the run on gold. President Cleveland called a special session of Congress to repeal the Sherman Silver Purchase Act. Representatives of silver mines, farmers, and "cheap money" people in general refused to consider repeal. By late fall, however, the administration finally had enough votes to push the repeal bill through Congress.

Repeal of the Sherman Silver Purchase Act stopped the flow of silver into the Treasury, but gold reserves continued to shrink. There were still many millions of silver bank notes in circulation, and the Treasury kept on redeeming them in gold. By 1895 the gold reserves had dropped to only $41 million. It seemed to be only a question of time before the United States would go off the **gold standard**—stop redeeming its paper currency with gold—and runaway inflation would start.

At this critical point, President Cleveland accepted the offer of a group of bankers headed by J. P. Morgan to lend gold to the government in return for government bonds as security. The arrangement worked. With leading bankers behind the government, confidence returned and the run on the gold reserves ended. Many Americans, those with "sound money" views, felt that President Cleveland and the bankers had acted wisely and had saved the nation from disaster. "Cheap money" Americans were furious and pointed out that the bankers had charged a generous commission for their services. They insisted that the President had made a deal with Wall Street.

Choosing candidates. By the time of the Presidential election of 1896, both major parties were split between the "sound money," gold-standard people and the "cheap money," silver people.

The Republicans chose as their Presidential candidate William McKinley of Ohio. Although McKinley tried to straddle the money issue, he came to be regarded as the leader of those people who favored the gold standard.

The Democratic convention opened with a bitter struggle between the "sound money" wing of the party and the "silver" wing. The "sound money" delegates were soon howled down, and "cheap money" delegates adopted a platform demanding "free and unlimited coinage of both gold and silver." The battle lines were drawn, with the Republicans on the "sound money" side and the majority of Democrats on the "cheap money" side. But the Democratic delegates had not yet selected a Presidential candidate.

William Jennings Bryan. The field was wide open when a handsome young lawyer stepped forward to address the convention. Only 36 years old, William Jennings Bryan of Nebraska had served in the House of Representatives for four years. This was his only political experience in the national capital. Nevertheless, his striking appearance and his compelling speech captured the attention of his audience.

"You come to us and tell us that the great cities are in favor of the gold standard," Bryan cried. "We reply that the great cities rest upon our broad and fertile prairies. Burn down your cities and leave our farms, and your cities will spring up again as if by magic; but destroy our farms and the grass will grow in the streets of every city in the country. . . .

"Having behind us the producing masses of this nation and the world, supported by the commercial interests, the laboring interests, and the toilers everywhere, we will answer their demand for a gold standard by saying to them, 'You shall not press down upon the brow of labor this crown of thorns, you shall not
▲ crucify mankind upon a cross of gold!'"

With the closing words of Bryan's "Cross of Gold" speech, wild tumult broke out at the convention. Here was the Democratic candidate!

The Democratic nomination of Bryan and the adoption of a platform demanding free and unlimited coinage of silver left the Populists in an awkward position. The Democrats had stolen their thunder. When they met in convention, the Populists decided to support Bryan as their Presidential candidate. To preserve their party identity, they nominated Tom Watson of Georgia for the Vice-Presidency rather than Arthur Sewall of Maine, who was the Democratic nominee.

Bryan's crusade. Bryan turned the election campaign into a crusade. In 14 exhausting weeks, during which he traveled vast distances by railroad, Bryan made 600 speeches to 5 million people in 27 states. Bryan's speeches succeeded in rousing his supporters to frenzies of enthusiasm.

The "sound money" people threw all their energy and resources into defeating Bryan. Under the leadership of Mark Hanna of Ohio, McKinley's campaign manager and a wealthy business leader, the Republicans raised at least $3.5 million to offset Bryan's $300,000 campaign fund. Some of this campaign fund was used to bring trainloads of people to McKinley's hometown to hear him read disarming speeches from his front porch. Nearly every influential newspaper in the country backed the Republicans. Many factories paid their workers on the Saturday before election with the warning that they would have no jobs if Bryan won the election.

McKinley's victory. Bryan lost with 176 electoral votes to McKinley's 271. The popular vote was much closer—7 million for the Republicans, 6.5 million for the Democrats. Although the country had decided in favor of the gold standard, the farmers and other "cheap money" advocates had come close to winning the Presidency and control of Congress.

Defeat in the 1896 election and the arrival of better times for the farmers ended the power of the Populist Party. As you will read, however, during the early 1900's, a new third party, the Progressive Party, as well as progressive Democrats and Republicans won many of the same reforms that the Populists had demanded.

SECTION REVIEW
See underscored items, text pp. 562-65.

Identify: Mary Elizabeth Lease, James Weaver, bimetallism, gold standard, William McKinley, William Jennings Bryan, "Cross of Gold" speech, Mark Hanna
For answers to questions, see Answer Key, p.A78.

1. **Evaluating Ideas:** Explain how the Populist Party Platform would have helped farmers.

2. **Interpreting Ideas:** In the political struggle in the South, black southerners were caught in the middle. Comment.

3. **Comparing Ideas:** How did the "tight money" and "cheap money" people each explain the cause of the depression of 1893?

▲ Discussion topic: Have the class analyze the excerpt from Bryan's "Cross of Gold" speech. Upon what evidence was each statement based? What devices did he use?

565

DEVELOPING HISTORY STUDY SKILLS

Thinking About History   Identifying Assumptions

The study of history involves the evaluation of viewpoints as well as the analysis of facts. To evaluate viewpoints the student of history must be able to identify the assumptions that underlie many viewpoints. An assumption is a belief that something is true without actually knowing it is true. Often in a viewpoint an assumption is unstated and must be inferred, or figured out, from the context of the statement.

Here, for example, are two assumptions held by many Americans:

- Democracy is the most desirable form of government.

- Education is important to today's citizen of the United States.

Few people in the United States would question the validity of either of these statements. The statements are assumed to be true and are often used as the basis for arguments about foreign affairs, government, or education.

The excerpt below about McCuffey's readers — a popular reading book in the nineteenth century — is based on this unstated assumption: Education should reflect the changes in society.

> McCuffey's emphasis pleased an agrarian age. His environmental picture squared with the physical facts, and people knew just enough of the outside world to share his doubts about the cities. His readers thus gained strength by applying the eternal verities [truths] to a simple culture, uncomplicated by urban and industrial problems. This very strength, however, became a source of weakness as village and farm gave way to city and factory.

Generally when a viewpoint is based on an assumption, no evidence is given to support the basic assumption. It is assumed that the reader or listener will agree with the underlying assumption and therefore accept the reasoning that is developed from it. The conclusion about McCuffey's readers is that the reading books were a source of weakness in the new industrial age. Note that no supporting data is provided to support the conclusion.

How to Identify an Assumption

To identify an assumption underlying a viewpoint, follow these guidelines.

1. **Identify the conclusion.** As you read or listen to a stated view, look for clues that point to a concluding statement. Some examples of these clues are *in summary, thus, however,* and *therefore*.
2. **Assess the evidence.** Examine the facts and arguments used to support the conclusion. Determine whether the evidence is based on fact or opinion.

Applying the Skill

Read the following excerpt, which lists some 1872 rules for school teachers. Then answer the questions at the top of page 567.

Rules for Teachers

- Teachers each day will fill lamps, clean chimneys.
- Each teacher will bring a bucket of water and a scuttle of coal for the day's session.
- Make your pens carefully. You may whittle nibs to the individual tastes of the pupils.
- Men teachers may take one evening each week for courting purposes, or two evenings a week if they go to church regularly.
- After ten hours in school, the teachers may spend the remaining time reading the Bible or other good books.
- Women teachers who marry or engage in unseemly conduct will be dismissed.
- Every teacher should lay aside from each pay a goodly sum of his earnings for his benefit during his declining years so that he will not become a burden on society.
- Any teacher who smokes, uses liquor in any form, frequents pool or public halls, or gets shaved in a barber shop will give good reason to suspect his worth, intention, integrity, and honesty.
- The teacher who performs his labor faithfully and without fault for five years will be given an increase of 25 cents per week in his pay, providing the Board of Education agrees.

1. What is the conclusion of these rules?
2. What assumption underlies the rule allowing men who attend church regularly to "court" an extra night each week?
3. What assumption underlies the rule that women who marry will be dismissed?
4. What is the underlying assumption of the entire list of rules?

Now let us consider your answers. The conclusion is that a teacher who follows these rules for 5 years will be eligible for a small raise. It is assumed that men who attend church regularly will be better behaved than men who do not, therefore they can be trusted to court two evenings a week rather than one. Women who marry will be dismissed because, it is assumed, they will have less time to devote to teaching. The assumption that underlies the entire list of rules is that a teacher who faithfully follows the rules will be a better teacher than a teacher who does not follow them.

Practicing the Skill

Read the excerpt below about the effect of industrialization on women and society. Then on a separate sheet of paper, answer the following questions.

1. What is the author's conclusion?
2. What facts or arguments are used to support this conclusion.
3. **(a)** What assumption is made by the author about the division of labor between the sexes? **(b)** What is assumed about men's work? women's work? **(c)** Are these assumptions proved in the excerpt?
4. What does the author mean by "the doctrine of separate spheres of labor"?
5. **(a)** Do you agree with the author that "industrialization . . . created the material conditions under which the doctrine of separate spheres could take root"? Explain. **(b)** What other explanations might there be for the "separate spheres" of labor?

Industrialization and the Role of Women

Small wonder, then, that so many people commented on the exhaustion and ill-health of American women during the 19th century. Industrialization had introduced many novelties into their homes . . . but they still had a great deal of hard work to do. These improvements had not, however, lifted the burden of women's domestic cares, in spite of radical changes in the patterns of daily work at home. _The process of housework had changed in such a way that adult males and small children of both sexes were no longer needed to do domestic labor: wood did not have to be chopped, nor water carried, nor grain hauled to the mill._ Men and children could be spared, to the schools, to the factories, to the offices of the burgeoning industrial economy. _Adult women and their grown daughters, on the other hand, could not be spared: meals still had to be cooked; sick children had to be tended; infants to be nursed; clothes had to be made, mended, and laundered and industrialization had done nothing at all to ease the burden of those particular chores._

Industrialization, at least in these its earliest phases, had in fact created the material conditions under which the doctrine of separate spheres could take root and flourish. Merchant flour, cast-iron stoves, municipal water, and manufactured boots had made it possible for men to work at wage labor without endangering (indeed, with some chance of improving) the standard of living of their families. As time wore on, the need to pay cash for flour, or for coal, or for any of the other commodities that were so swiftly appearing on the market, ensured that, once having entered the market for wage labor, men would stay there. Once that had happened, they ceased to train their sons in the multitudinous crafts that had been the heritage of men's work at home — preparing fuel, mending ironware, working in leather, building fireplaces, making cider, butchering pigs — and then the process was complete. A new generation of men came into adulthood having learned the skills needed to work for wages, not the skills needed to work at home.

For women the transition to the industrial order was different. Merchant flour, cast-iron stoves, municipal water, and manufactured boots _did not free them from their labors._ Insofar as these commodities allowed men and boys to leave their homes, and insofar as these commodities also created new jobs that only women could perform, _women were tied even more strongly than they had been before to their cast-iron hearth._

Increasing industrialization created many new problems after 1870 for farmers as well as for all other Americans. Most farmers lost the individual freedom they had possessed when they were more self-sufficient, producing a good part of what they needed on their own land. Overproduction brought falling prices. Increasingly, farmers became dependent upon forces that they could not control. They depended upon the railroads that carried their goods to market and upon prices fixed in distant markets. They were affected by tariffs that sometimes raised the cost of the manufactured goods they needed to buy. They were also affected by the supply of money made available by the federal government.

Faced with these new problems, farmers either organized new political parties or increased their role in the old parties in an effort to influence state and federal governments. They hoped to secure laws that would regulate the railroads, the industries, and the other parts of the economic system and thus make life easier for themselves.

Industrialism brought benefits as well as problems. Power-driven machines increased production and made life immeasurably easier. Developments in transportation and communications broke down the isolation of farm life and brought farm families into touch with the life of the world beyond the borders of the farm.

It was difficult for farmers, as it was for all other Americans, to adjust to the all too real problems of the new industrial age. By the 1900's, however, the farmers began to see that their best hope of realizing the bright promise of the new age was in learning to work together.

CONNECTING CHAPTER IDEAS

Throughout the last half of the nineteenth century, growing numbers of Americans migrated to cities. In the next chapter you will read how cities exerted a powerful influence upon all aspects of American life including education, literature, art, architecture, and recreation.

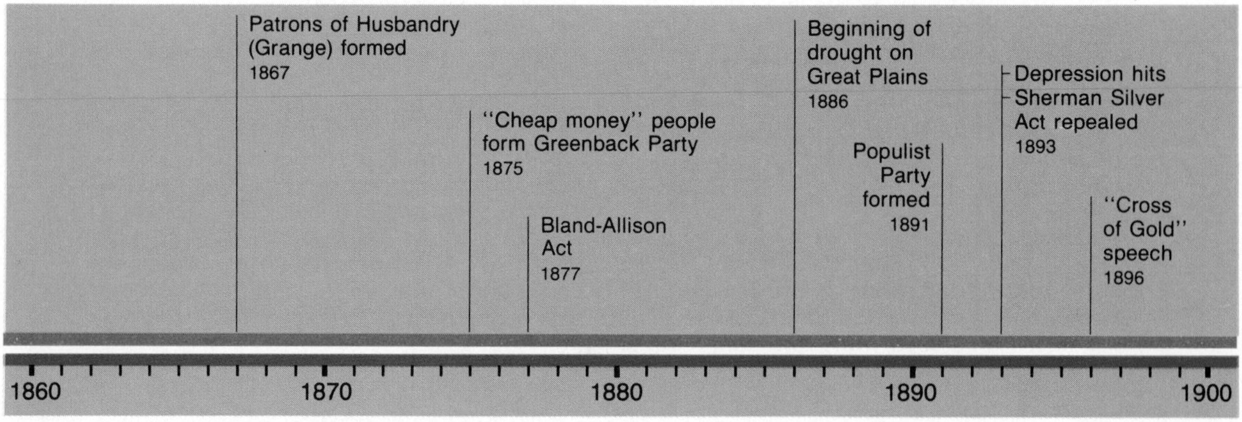

Patrons of Husbandry
(Grange) formed
1867

"Cheap money" people
form Greenback Party
1875

Bland-Allison
Act
1877

Beginning of
drought on
Great Plains
1886

Populist
Party
formed
1891

Depression hits
Sherman Silver
Act repealed
1893

"Cross
of Gold"
speech
1896

1860   1870   1880   1890   1900

CHAPTER
24 REVIEW

Reviewing Important Terms

In the sentences below the underlined terms are incorrect. On a separate sheet of paper, rewrite each sentence using the correct term.

1. In a medium of exchange economy, prices fall whenever supply exceeds demand for a commodity.
2. Unminted gold or silver is called greenbacks.
3. Farmers organized holding companies for cooperative buying and political action.
4. The monetary policy of the United States which backs paper money in gold is called bimetallism.
5. Short-haul shipments were cargoes carried by railroads to cities served by more than one rail company.
6. Major agricultural products grown in large quantities are called cash crops.

Practicing Critical Thinking Skills

1. **Comparing Ideas.** How did industrialization both benefit and hurt farmers during the late 1800's?
2. **Summarizing Ideas.** Summarize the platform of the (a) Greenback Party and (b) Populist Party. (c) Describe the similarities and differences you discover.
3. **Analyzing Ideas.** (a) Why did farmers favor "cheap money" (greenbacks) and the free and unlimited coinage of silver? (b) To what extent were farmers successful in obtaining these things?
4. **Comparing Viewpoints.** Explain why you would have felt as you did about "cheap money" vs. "sound money" if you had been a (a) debtor farmer, (b) retired person living on a fixed income, or (c) banker.
5. **Evaluating Ideas.** During the late 1800's, farmers learned that one way to gain power was through organization. Cite examples from the textbook to support this statement.
6. **Synthesizing Ideas.** Imagine that you live on a farm in Kansas in 1880. Prepare at least three journal entries describing some typical activities, such as a (a) trip to town, (b) day at school, (c) meeting of the local chapter of the Grange.
7. **Relating Past to Present.** How does the relationship between the government and the farmers today compare with their relationship during the late 1800's? Account for the similarities or differences you discover in your comparison.

Developing History Study Skills

Identifying Assumptions. Read the following excerpt from the Populist Party Platform adopted on July 4, 1892. Then answer the questions below.

> *Silver, which has been accepted as coin since the dawn of history, has been demonetized [deprived of its standard value as money] to add to the purchasing power of gold by decreasing the value of all forms of property as well as human labor, and the supply of currency is purposely abridged to fatten usurers [moneylenders], bankrupt enterprise, and enslave industry. A vast conspiracy against mankind has been organized on two continents, and it is rapidly taking possession of the world. If not met and overthrown at once, it forebodes terrible social convulsions, the destruction of civilization, or the establishment of an absolute despotism.*

(a) What was the Populist Party's position on demonetizing silver? (b) What assumptions did the Populists make about silver as a currency? (c) What did the Populists claim would be the results if this happened? (d) What arguments did the Populists use to support their conclusions? Were these based on facts or opinions? (e) Is this assumption proven? Explain.

Relating Geography and History

Agricultural land use is determined by a variety of factors. Topography, rainfall, length of growing season, and many other variables influence which crops are produced in a particular area. To better understand the influence of various factors on agriculture, study the map on pages 1016–17. Then answer the following questions.

1. Give a reason why some land in each of the following states has no agricultural use: (a) Alaska, (b) Florida, (c) Arizona, (d) Maine.
2. (a) Which three states have the most land in wheat production? (b) How are those states geographically similar?
3. What factors have made Florida and California major fruit-producing states?
4. Research the major agricultural items produced in your state. Then design a map legend (key) to be used with a map of your state. Your legend should illustrate the chief agricultural products in recognizable symbols.

See Chapter Overview in TMRG, p.TM141.
See Chapter Objectives in TMRG, p.TM141.
See Introducing the Chapter in TMRG, p.TM141.

CHAPTER 25

Life Styles in the New Industrial Age

Changing Ways (1860's–1890's)

Promoting a labor union

"We cannot all live in cities," Horace Greeley once remarked, "yet nearly all seem determined to do so." Greeley, a famous newspaper editor of the times, was speaking of a change in the way Americans lived. From 1865 to 1900, people were moving away from the rural areas and into the great urban centers, a movement known as **urbanization.**

What was the compelling attraction of the growing cities? The answer was opportunity—for education, for adventure, and to win fame and fortune. The city offered both men and women jobs in offices and factories. It offered work in the building trades as new homes, offices, and skyscrapers were constructed. It was a center of employment for both skilled and unskilled workers. The city offered the really adventuresome and hard-working the chance to carve out a successful career in any of hundreds of enterprises. Many people, especially youth, were eager to share in the excitement of the new industrial age and the opportunities the cities offered. They found the many attractions of urban life irresistible.

New forms of journalism and literature flourished. Colleges and universities responded to the challenge of educating people for the new industrial age. Architects responded with new designs to suit the new age. Even forms of recreation changed to accomodate the new life styles of this era.

For a number of years, ways of life in the city and the countryside drew far apart, and terms such as "city slicker" and "country hick" were often heard. As the years after 1900 passed, however, differences between rural and urban areas became less marked.

═══ READING FOCUS ═══

As you read about the new urban ways of life, look for the details that support each of the following statements.

1. Cities grow and change under the impact of industrialism.
2. Education responds to the changing patterns of American life.
3. American writing reflects the new industrial age.
4. Architecture and other fine arts respond to a changing society.
5. New forms of recreation enrich American life.

1 Cities grow and change under the impact of industrialism

See Teaching Suggestions in TMRG, pp.TM141-42.

The city had many faces. It was stores and banks and offices, museums and libraries and theaters, churches and schools. It was freight yards—and, in seaports, waterfronts—ringed by factories, warehouses, stockyards, and wholesale markets. It was drab tenement buildings and alleys littered with rubbish. It was row after row of houses arranged, in newer cities, in a neat pattern of blocks or squares. It was the costly show places of the self-appointed leaders of "society." Mainly the city was people—rich people, people with modest incomes, poor people. All were affected by the new industrial way of life.

Concentration of wealth. In this new industrial age, wealth was concentrated in the hands of relatively few people. To be sure, some Americans had always been rich while others had been poor. However, the gap between the richest and the poorest had never been greater.

Many of the new millionaires built huge mansions filled with expensive and gaudy furnishings. They bought race horses, yachts, and summer estates. They traveled abroad. Sometimes they gave expensive parties.

As time went on, however, the newly rich, and especially their college-educated children, smoothed off the rougher edges. Many business leaders accepted the responsibility for using their money to improve their communities. They gave money to build and support churches, colleges, art galleries, and libraries.

For example, during his lifetime Andrew Carnegie gave $60 million to help towns and cities establish free public libraries. Men of enormous wealth, such as Ezra Cornell, Leland Stanford, John D. Rockefeller, Sr., Jonas Clark, Matthew Vassar, and Cornelius Vanderbilt, founded or gave endowments to colleges and universities. J. P. Morgan, Henry C. Frick, Andrew W. Mellon, and dozens of others built up costly and valuable art collections, many of which were in time opened to the public. Others, including women, gave financial support to American symphony orchestras, social welfare, and the arts.

▲ Writing activity: Have students write short, informal essays on life in a big city versus life in a rural area. Which would they prefer? Why?

571

Women's colleges such as Fontbonne College in St. Louis and coeducational universities provided women with new educational opportunities in the first decades of the 1900's.

The middle-income group. Lower down on the economic ladder were the professional people, the smaller business people, the clerks, the managers, and the more successful skilled workers. These people raised their standard of living and enjoyed "modern conveniences," such as gas and electric lighting, modern plumbing, and new household appliances. They went to the theater, used libraries, and bought magazines and books. Many of them sent their children not only through high school but also to college.

Women in religion and welfare. In activities such as religion and social welfare, several women achieved international reputations. Mary Baker Eddy founded Christian Science and contributed to its growth with her inspirational leadership and administrative ability. Other women were active in church missionary work abroad, establishing training schools, colleges, and hospitals in Turkey, Japan, India, and other countries. A number of Catholic women founded religious orders. The most famous was Mother Francis Xavier Cabrini. After emigrating from Italy in 1889, she established hospitals, orphanages, and schools in

the Italian-American communities of New York, Chicago, and other cities. Mother Cabrini was the first American citizen to become a saint in the Roman Catholic Church.

The tireless and competent Clara Barton, after her contributions to nursing in the Civil War, established the American Red Cross. Despite opposition and indifference, she broadened its purposes to include not only aid to soldiers in wartime but also help to civilians in such disasters as floods, earthquakes, major fires, and epidemics.

Opportunities for women. New coeducational universities in the Middle West and the West and such women's colleges as Mount Holyoke, Wellesley, Vassar, and Smith in the East meant that more young women could obtain an education equal to that once enjoyed only by young men. Many people at first doubted that girls had the physical and mental ability to do college work, but the experiment proved successful. Women college graduates became increasingly active in civic affairs. Some became business executives, and others entered the professions. By 1900 there were 1,000 women lawyers, 3,000 women ministers, and

▲ Writing activity: Have students write brief paragraphs pointing out how the expanded educational opportunities for women contributed to the changing lifestyles in the United States.

Joseph Mitchell lived on Nantucket Island, off the coast of Massachusetts. He was a schoolteacher with an absorbing interest in astronomy. He watched the stars and made careful records of his observations. The area's sea captains and the federal government's Coast Survey recognized his skills and consulted with him on questions of navigation.

Joseph Mitchell passed along his interest in the stars to Maria, one of his ten children. From an early age, Maria spent many nights "sweeping the skies" with her father. She later explained that understanding the movements of the heavenly bodies helped her feel a part of an orderly universe. Through the years Maria and her father never stopped recording their observations of the skies.

On the night of October 1, 1847, Maria went alone to the roof of the house and into a shed that served as an observatory. As she peered through the telescope, she saw something that changed her life. Her father wrote the event into his notebook: "This evening at half past ten Maria discovered a telescopic comet."

Word spread throughout the scientific community: a young woman, an amateur, had discovered a new comet before all the other astronomers in the world. Honors began to pour in. King Frederic VII of Denmark sent a gold medal. The American Academy of Arts and Sciences made her a member, as did the Association for the Advancement of Science. Mitchell was the first woman admitted to both these organizations.

Mitchell's fame also led to the offer of a teaching job at the newly opened Vassar Female College in New York. In 1865 she accepted the offer and became professor of astronomy. She demanded much of the women who were her students. At the same time, she helped encourage in them the "free thought and free inquiry" that she said were "the very first steps on the path of science." Mitchell also fought for the equality of women in all fields. She stated firmly, "I believe in women more than I do in astronomy."

7,500 women doctors in the United States. Maria Mitchell, an astronomer on the faculty of Vassar College, had discovered a comet that was named for her.

Non-college women who wanted careers or who were compelled by circumstances to work outside the home found new opportunities in business. The development of the typewriter meant more jobs as stenographers and clerks in offices and banks and workers in industrial plants. Tradition and prejudice, however, blocked opportunities to most of these women to advance into supervisory and management positions.

A great many women of the white middle class joined the women's clubs that rapidly multiplied after the Civil War. These clubs at first concentrated mainly on discussions of literary and cultural topics. By 1900 they were also fighting for an end to political corruption,

As a wealthy young woman, Jane Addams had complained, "I am filled with shame that with all my apparent leisure, I do nothing at all." But her efforts at the Hull House aided thousands of the needy.

for better health and recreational conditions, and for women's suffrage.

Black women also established clubs, which concentrated on social welfare. Active in this movement were Josephine Ruffin and Mary Church Terrell, who also were leaders in the founding of the National Federation of Afro-American Women and the National Association of Colored Women.

Toward women's suffrage. After the Civil War, you recall, women did not receive voting rights and other rights under the Fourteenth and Fifteenth Amendments. Differences over the stand to be taken on this issue split the women's rights movement. Elizabeth Cady Stanton and Susan B. Anthony refused to support the amendments. In 1869 they organized the National Woman Suffrage Association, which excluded men from membership. The Association adopted as its goal a women's suffrage amendment to the Constitution. Lucy Stone, her husband Henry Blackwell, Mary A. Livermore, and Julia Ward Howe launched the

more conservative American Woman Suffrage Association. It worked for woman suffrage amendments to state constitutions. In 1890, after many years of rivalry, the two organizations merged as the National American Woman Suffrage Association.

Veterans of the women's rights movement were reinforced by younger leaders. Abigail Duniway of Oregon, a strong opponent of women's legal disabilities, became an effective speaker and lobbyist. Anna Howard Shaw, a graduate of Boston University in both theology and medicine, was a forceful speaker and untiring campaigner. Carrie Chapman Catt of Iowa, a pacifist as well as a women's-rights advocate, proved herself a brilliant orator and skilled administrator.

Despite the efforts of such leaders, progress toward women's suffrage was slow. The women suffragists were ridiculed and denounced by many women as well as men, by professional politicians, and by some religious groups. They also were opposed by the liquor industry, which feared that voting women might succeed in outlawing the manufacture and sale of alcoholic drinks.

Although by 1900 only a few western states had given women the right to vote, in the next 15 years the number grew. Meanwhile, in states that gave them limited suffrage, women took part increasingly in school-board elections and local politics.

Jane Addams. Jane Addams (1860–1935) was one of America's most influential women — a social reformer, humanitarian, and crusader for peace. Horrified by the suffering she saw in sprawling city slums, Addams decided to dedicate her life to helping the poor. In 1889 she opened Hull House in the slums of Chicago. She provided kindergartens for the children of working mothers, classes in child care, and recreational facilities for youth and adults. She also insisted on the collection of garbage from slum streets and fought incompetent and corrupt politicians and city officials.

For a time many business and political leaders opposed her as a dangerous meddler. Eventually, however, even her most bitter critics admitted that she was performing a great service. Social workers from all parts of the United States and from foreign countries visited Hull House. They then returned to their own communities to apply the new ideas that they had learned.

Jane Addams also helped secure child-labor laws and funds for public parks. In 1931 she received the Nobel Peace Prize for her active work in the cause of world peace. Her most enduring memorial was the growing recognition by people in all walks of life that they shared a responsibility for helping to reduce poverty.

The lower-income groups. On the lower rungs of the economic ladder in American life were the very poor people, including large numbers of immigrants and almost all Mexican Americans, Indians, and blacks. These lower-income groups enjoyed only a few of the advantages of the new urban culture. They could not afford to send their children to school beyond the elementary grades. In fact, children from poor families often had to take jobs in factories even before they finished elementary school. Nor could most of the poorer people afford to go to doctors or hospitals when they were sick.

Yet improvements in urban living affected at least a few of the poor. In the late 1880's, high-minded men and women founded social settlement houses similar to Chicago's Hull House in some of the worst slum areas of the major cities. These centers for recreation, education, and decent living gave hope to many immigrant youths and lightened the hardship of many elderly men and women. In addition, the Salvation Army, a religious group founded in England, provided food and shelter to many of the most poverty-stricken urban citizens. By 1900 some cities were building a few playgrounds in the poorest areas.

Opportunities to climb the economic ladder did exist, even for the poor. These opportunities far surpassed those in the Old World. They drew immigrants to the American cities in an ever-swelling volume. Finally, these economic opportunities encouraged many poorer people to struggle for an education and to rise above the environment into which they had been born.

SECTION REVIEW
See underscored items, text pp. 572-75.

Identify: Mary Baker Eddy, Mother Cabrini, Clara Barton, Maria Mitchell, Mary Church Terrell, National American Woman Suffrage Association, Jane Addams, settlement house, Salvation Army.
For answers to questions, see Answer Key, pp. A79-80.
1. **Interpreting Ideas:** Explain what is meant by this statement: The city had many faces.

2. **Analyzing Ideas: (a)** What social-class divisions existed in the United States by 1890? **(b)** To what extent could a person move from one social class to another?
3. **Seeing Relationships:** What is the relationship between the nation's industrialization and the women's rights movement?
4. **Organizing Ideas:** List the names of each woman mentioned in this chapter in one column. In a second column after each name, state that person's contribution to American life.

---

2 **Education responds to the changing patterns of American life**

See Teaching Suggestions in TMRG, p.TM142.
In 1870 about 7 million children were enrolled in American schools, most of them in the lower grades. Only 30 years later, in 1900, the number had more than doubled. During this same period, the number of high schools multiplied 10 times. This growth reflected not only the increasing throngs of children in America's cities but also the increasing wealth that could be taxed to support education.

From old ways to new. The character of the schools—including courses of study and methods of teaching—was also changing.

Pupils in the earlier rural classrooms were all too familiar with the sharp sting of the hickory stick, wielded by teachers on the theory "Spare the rod and spoil the child." Children learned reading, writing, and arithmetic and memorized a few more or less related facts about geography and history. The few students who went to high school or to a private academy spent much time learning Latin, Greek, and mathematics. Most educators believed that these subjects provided mental training and therefore fully equipped students for later life.

Some reformers began to demand a new program of education better suited to the industrial age. A few educational pioneers, such as Colonel Francis W. Parker of Chicago, stressed the idea that education is not just the memorization of facts but also the broadening of a child's experience. Education, Parker insisted, must prepare children to live in an ex-

Before 1860 women were admitted into only a few colleges. But by 1901, 128 women's colleges had been founded, several previously all-male colleges had admitted women, and women made up one fourth of all undergraduates.

panding and complex world of science and industry.

John Dewey also stressed the idea that education is not something apart from the rest of life but an essential part of life itself. By the 1890's Dewey's experimental school in Chicago was attracting attention for its program of "learning by doing" and for its emphasis upon making children physically sound, intellectually competent, and socially well-adjusted. Ella Flagg Young, the head of the Chicago school system, worked closely with both Parker and Dewey. This able educator was the first woman to serve as head of a major school system in the nation.

Most schools, it is true, continued along more traditional lines. Nevertheless, Parker, Dewey, and other pioneers proved to have a great influence on the course of American education.

Influences of industrialism. The needs of the new industrial society were also reflected in the schools. By 1900, educational programs included the natural sciences and such "practical" and "useful" subjects as industrial designing, business arithmetic, bookkeeping, typing, stenography, shopwork, home economics, and manual arts. Superintendents and principals also became more businesslike in emphasizing efficiency and organization.

Colleges and universities. The colleges and universities also responded to the needs of the new age. New technical schools, such as the Columbia University School of Mines, the Massachusetts Institute of Technology, and the Case School of Applied Science, turned out more and more graduates prepared to take important jobs in railroad building, in mining, and in other engineering projects. The state universities and land-grant colleges emphasized practical training for a variety of fields.

Even the older colleges, which emphasized the classics, often added more scientific and "practical" subjects to their traditional courses of study. Under the influence of leaders like Charles W. Eliot of Harvard and Andrew D. White of Cornell, the colleges modified the old, rigid curriculum in which students studied mainly Latin, Greek, and mathematics.

Colleges and universities also enriched their educational programs by adding courses in the social sciences and modern languages as well as in the natural sciences. It was no longer possible for every student to take all the subjects in the curriculum. To meet individual needs, the elective system was introduced.

At the same time, marked progress was made in the professional studies of medicine and law. In these and other ways, education responded to the changing patterns of everyday life.

SECTION REVIEW
See underscored items, text pp. 575-76.

Identify: Colonel Francis W. Parker, John Dewey, Ella Flagg Young
For answers to questions, see Answer Key, p.A80.

1. **Interpreting Ideas:** What changes were made in the courses of study in public schools to meet the needs of the new industrial society?

2. **Summarizing Ideas:** Describe how colleges and universities responded to the needs of the new age.

3. **Analyzing Ideas:** Does education today reflect any of the ideas favored by Parker and Dewey? Explain.

▲ Discussion topic: Have students discuss whether they favor education for its own sake (a general, well-rounded background) or education toward a specific career goal. Have them cite reasons for their answers.

3 American writing reflects the new industrial age

See Teaching Suggestions in TMRG, p.TM143.

The most obvious influence on the new urban industrial age was an enormous increase in circulation of printed material.

Newspapers and magazines. Between 1870 and 1900, the number of daily newspapers in the country increased from 600 to nearly 2,500. Their circulation multiplied six times—a jump far greater than the growth in population. This huge expansion reflected gains in the reading ability of many Americans and a growing interest in the events of the world.

Several mechanical inventions enabled publishers to print more newspapers, magazines, and books at lower costs. Most important of these inventions were the typewriter, improved printing presses, and the linotype, a fast and efficient typesetting machine.

Mass circulation was also stimulated by the rapidly developing art of advertising. Businesses were ready to advertise, but only in newspapers and magazines that reached large audiences. The desire to secure advertising stimulated publishers to print more and more "popular" articles written in a catchy style to attract the largest possible numbers of readers.

"Titans of the press." Three of the outstanding leaders of the new trend in journalism were Charles A. Dana, Joseph Pulitzer, and William Randolph Hearst.

Dana, publisher of the New York *Sun,* dug up sensational news and gave it prominent space on the front pages of his paper. Pulitzer, publisher of the New York *World,* followed much the same technique. His paper appealed to the general reader because of its human-interest stories and many articles on the scandalous activities of the rich and the tragedies of the poor. Stories by Elizabeth Seaman, who defied the prejudice against women reporters, were especially popular. Under the name Nelly Bly, she reported what she found when she worked in a factory, entered a mental institution by pretending to be insane, or got herself jailed. Pulitzer also developed the comic strip, the sports page, and a section with columnists, puzzles, and advice to readers.

Hearst, Pulitzer's chief rival, outdid Pulitzer at his own game. Hearst bought the New York *Journal* in 1895 and raised its circulation beyond that of any other paper. By denouncing the irresponsibility and selfishness of some of the well-to-do, Hearst appealed to the masses of people. His special success rested on his ability to hire gifted feature writers, able sports reporters, and popular comic artists. He also was able to get the most sensational news before anyone else and to play it up for all it was worth—frequently far more than it was worth.

Journalism as big business. Well before 1900 journalism adopted the methods of other big business enterprises. Leading publishers bought up small papers and organized great newspaper chains. Large chains could use the same feature articles, the same comic strips, and even the same editorials. This was especially true as the different parts of the nation and the world became increasingly interdependent and public interest reached out beyond the local community to national and world affairs. The newspaper chains also subscribed to great news-reporting services, or **syndicates,** such as the Associated Press (AP) and the United Press (UP), which collected news items from every corner of the earth. Even independent newspapers were influenced by the trend toward standardized practices in journalism.

By 1900 there also were numerous foreign-language newspapers for immigrants and about 150 newspapers for black Americans. Although these publications had limited resources, they served important functions. They gave their readers a sense of identity with other people of the same national origin or racial background. Most of these newspapers also were uncompromising in their opposition to discrimination.

Mass-circulation magazines. Like the newspapers, magazines adapted themselves to the changing times. Some of the older magazines, such as the *Atlantic Monthly, Harper's,* and *Scribner's,* continued to appeal to the better educated. Even before the Civil War, however, a new type of low-priced, popular magazine had appeared, which contained material aimed at mass circulation among "average" readers. The *Ladies' Home Journal,* established in 1883, was one of the most successful, providing reading material that interested millions of

Started as a weekly in 1850, Harper's *magazine remained popular into the 1900's. It published political cartoons and works of important writers, including Charles Dickens.*

women. It further built up its circulation by setting its price at 10 cents. Under the editorship of a Dutch immigrant, Edward Bok, the *Ladies' Home Journal* sponsored many crusades to raise standards of living and improve community life.

Literature about urban life. American literature, too, reflected the growing influence of urban industrialism. The success stories for boys that Horatio Alger, Jr., and W. T. Adams (under the name of Oliver Optic) turned out by the dozens were extremely popular. These stories in a sense glorified an urban society in which a hard-working boy from humble beginnings could climb to the top by sheer pluck — and luck.

William Sydney Porter (O. Henry) struck a very different note with short stories that presented realistic pictures of American life, both urban and rural. Different again were the novels of Edith Wharton, which focused on the conflicts between the newly rich and older

well-to-do families of New York in the 1880's. Henry James's novels explored the tensions felt by the members of America's leisure class who chose to live in the sophisticated urban centers of Europe.

One of the best-known novels of the period was *The Gilded Age,* written by Samuel L. Clemens (Mark Twain) and Charles Dudley Warner. In a humorous but biting manner, the writers described the corrupt activities of politicians and land speculators in the nation's capital. Edward Bellamy's *Looking Backward: 2000–1887* contrasted an ugly urban America with an imaginary socialist America of the future. In Bellamy's future America, poverty and corruption have been eliminated and people live cooperatively in freedom and dignity. Among the ablest writers of his time was William Dean Howells. In *A Hazard of New Fortunes* and other realistic stories, he provided a faithful picture of middle-class life, chiefly in urban America.

Notable exceptions. There were, of course, many authors whose writing was not influenced by the changing ways of life. Emily Dickinson, for example, created short, thought-provoking poems that have since been recognized as gems of beauty and originality.

The growing reading public also enjoyed highly romantic and sentimental novels as well as colorful Wild West adventure stories that enterprising publishers put out in paper covers for only 10 cents. Many of these famous **dime novels** had the unfortunate side effect of reinforcing the stereotypes of Mexicans and Indians as villains.

Local-color writers. Some writers reacted against the more or less standardized ways of city life. They concentrated upon describing those regions of the United States that still largely followed the older, rural ways of living. One of these **local-color writers,** Edward Eggleston, touched a "folksy" note in describing life in rural Indiana in his book *The Hoosier Schoolmaster.*

The greatest of the local-color writers was Samuel L. Clemens (Mark Twain), the first important writer from west of the Atlantic seaboard states. His *Life on the Mississippi* dramatized the crude, vigorous, racy aspects of the American steamboat era. *The Adventures of Tom Sawyer* and *The Adventures of Huckleberry Finn* were landmarks in the representation of the adolescent American boy. At the same time, these books satirized the middle-class values and racial prejudices of a rural community in Missouri. Twain's *Roughing It* vividly portrayed the raw life of western mining camps.

The colorful and heroic verses of Joaquin (hwah·KEEN) Miller and the realistic stories of mining camps written by Bret Harte brought the Far West into the nation's literature. Helen Hunt Jackson also did much to increase the awareness of the Far West with her stories of Spanish missions and of Indian life in old California. Hamlin Garland, in *Main-Traveled Roads* and other books, wrote of the harsh conditions endured by many of the pioneers on the northern prairies.

The South, too, had its share of local-color writers. George Washington Cable, Kate Chopin, and Grace King presented life among the French-speaking Creoles of Louisiana. Thomas Nelson Page popularized a romantic image of master-slave relations on Virginia plantations before the Civil War. Joel Chandler Harris of Georgia won fame for his "Uncle Remus" tales, based on stories brought from Africa by slaves.

The writings of black authors also partly reflected the influence of the local-color school of writing. Local color distinguished *My Southern Home,* the last book of the pioneer black novelist William Wells Brown. Another important black writer, Paul L. Dunbar, was hailed as the first black American writer "to feel the Negro life esthetically and express it lyrically." Some of the novels and tales of Charles W. Chesnutt, a black writer of North Carolina, also reflected the local-color school of writing.

New England, like other regions, excited the imaginations of local-color authors, among them Mary E. Wilkins Freeman and Sarah Orne Jewett. These writers pictured the changes in rural life in New England as young people abandoned the unproductive family
▲ farms to seek their fortunes in the cities.

SECTION REVIEW
See underscored items, text pp. 577-79.
Identify: journalism, Elizabeth Seaman, Horatio Alger, Jr., Edith Wharton, Emily Dickinson, dime novels, local-color writer, Mark Twain, William Wells Brown, Paul L. Dunbar, Sarah Orne Jewett
For answers to questions, see Answer Key, p.A80.
1. **Summarizing Ideas:** What factors made possible the mass circulation of newspapers and magazines?

2. **Seeing Relationships:** (a) Give evidence to show that newspaper publishing became big business. (b) How might this have affected the reading public?
3. **Analyzing Viewpoints:** Explain how some novels of the late 1800's reflected the growing influence of urban industrialism in American life.

4 Architecture and other fine arts respond to a changing society

See Teaching Suggestions in TMRG, p.TM143.
Architecture and art, no less than journalism and literature, revealed the influence of urban life and the growth of industry in the years after 1865.

Decline and revival. For a number of years after the Civil War, American architecture reached what many have regarded as a low level. During the 1870's and 1880's, many successful business leaders and financiers poured fortunes into huge, gaudy mansions. These overdone showplaces as well as many equally tasteless public buildings and smaller houses were a far cry from the beautiful structures that Americans had designed and built along simple, classical lines during the late 1700's and the early 1800's.

Toward the end of the 1800's, however, a number of architects, notably Henry Hobson Richardson and Richard Morris Hunt, began to design more pleasing, practical houses and public buildings in a more dignified and restrained style.

The World's Columbian Exposition, or World's Fair, held in Chicago in 1893, helped to quicken public interest in good architecture. Many of the buildings that housed the exhibits were designed in the simple classical style. Thousands of visitors carried back to their home communities memories of beautiful structures with noble pillars and clean, direct lines that they had seen.

New trends in architecture. One structure at the Chicago World's Fair, the Transportation Building, heralded a new day in architecture. Its architect, Louis H. Sullivan, taught that "form follows function," meaning that the best-

▲ Writing activity: Encourage student volunteers to write a local-color piece (play, story, poem, or travel diary) about life in their region of the nation.

579

The 21-story Flatiron Building, New York City's first skyscraper, still stands as a landmark in the series of developments that helped make modern American cities possible.

designed building is one that has a style and uses materials perfectly suited to the purposes of the building. Gradually this idea was adopted by more and more architects, among them Frank Lloyd Wright. Wright started to practice his profession in Chicago in 1893 and became one of the world's foremost architects.

The availability of such new building materials as steel, concrete, and plate glass plus the necessities of urban life did much to stimulate a new type of business structure.

Skyscrapers. As city business districts became more crowded and as real-estate values soared, architects tried to solve the problem by building upward. How could they erect taller buildings? Ingenious architects constructed huge steel frames and filled the spaces with stone, brick, concrete, and glass. The Home Insurance Building, built in Chicago in 1884, set the example for these towering structures.

During the next few years, in both Chicago and New York, builders found ways to erect taller and taller skyscrapers.

The new towering buildings turned the narrow streets below into dark, gloomy canyons. To solve this problem, New York City adopted an ordinance requiring architects to set back the higher stories of all tall buildings so that more light would reach the streets. This ordinance accomplished its purpose. It also relieved the rectangular lines of the box-like skyscraper and accounted for the magically beautiful character of the New York skyline. Like many other activities of American life, architecture revealed more and more the influence of new times and new ways of living.

Painting and sculpture. The new industrial age had less influence on painters and sculptors than it did on architects. Between 1865 and 1900, the most important development in the fine arts was the increasing skill of American artists who had studied in European art centers. The improving standards in American art also rested in part on the ability and the willingness of wealthy Americans to collect masterpieces, to establish art schools, and to buy the works of American artists.

The themes that painters and sculptors chose often seemed to have little to do with the growing urban industrial society. Gifted sculptors created great statues of Lincoln and other national heroes. One outstanding creation was the Adams Monument in Rock Creek Cemetery in Washington, D.C., made by Augustus Saint-Gaudens (saint·GAW·dunz). This brooding, hooded figure, sometimes referred to as "The Peace of God," suggests the mystery of life and death.

A number of painters did equally outstanding work. George Inness captured on canvas the beauties of woodland scenes. Winslow Homer's brilliantly colored seascapes suggested the strength and primitive force of the sea. Mary Cassatt, influenced by the new French Impressionist style and by Japanese art, painted portraits of women and children notable for lively charm and for exquisite tone and color.

The work of a number of artists, however, did reveal the influence of industrial and urban America. Thomas Eakins, for example, painted famous and wealthy Americans with such frank realism that they would not buy his works. Eakins, however, refused to change his

▲ Report topic: Have interested students visit the library to find picture books showing architectural styles. In reports to the class the students should show the ways in which the changes reflected the new industrial age.

style for the sake of immediate popularity and profit and continued to paint life as he saw it. In a painting designed to reveal the surgeon's scientific skill, *The Surgical Clinic of Professor Gross,* Eakins suggested very concretely the new scientific trend of the age.

SECTION REVIEW

See underscored items, text p. 580.

Identify: Frank Lloyd Wright, Augustus Saint-Gaudens, Winslow Homer, Mary Cassatt, Thomas Eakins

For answers to questions, see Answer Key, p.A81.

1. **Analyzing Ideas:** How did architecture in the late 1800's **(a)** meet the requirements of the urban industrial age and **(b)** take advantage of the new materials made available by the age?

2. **Interpreting Ideas:** What did Louis Sullivan mean by "form follows functions"?

3. **Summarizing Ideas:** Describe the themes that inspired the noted American sculptors and painters of this period.

5 New forms of recreation enrich American life

See Teaching Suggestions in TMRG, pp.TM143-44.

Recreation was also transformed by the new urban industrial age. The well-to-do, having time and money, were the first to enjoy such new sports as tennis and golf. Gradually, however, the middle-income groups also began to enjoy these new forms of recreation.

New types of recreation. For many thousands of American children and their parents in the late 1800's, one of the most memorable events of the year was the arrival of the circus. P. T. Barnum's tent circus, which he started in Brooklyn in 1871, was called "the greatest show on earth."

Equally awaited was the summertime Chautauqua (shuh·TAW·kwuh). The **Chautauqua movement** was an educational enterprise started in 1874 on the shores of Chautauqua Lake in upper New York State. Each year several thousand Americans from all over the United States traveled to Chautauqua Lake to enjoy a summer vacation and to benefit intellectually and spiritually from the lectures and sermons provided for them. Study groups using Chautauqua publications were organized in many towns and villages. As the years passed, the program at Chautauqua Lake became increasingly varied. Illustrated travel talks, stage presentations, and humorous acts were added to the more serious lectures and religious services. Other enterprising leaders also organized traveling tent programs similar to those earlier developed at Chautauqua Lake. By the early 1900's, the traveling Chautauquas were bringing a glimpse of the outside world into many rural communities.

The theater gained in popularity during the 1800's, particularly for middle-income groups. At its best the theater offered admirable plays performed by great actors, American and foreign-born. Some of the most appealing programs, however, were the melodramas that reminded city dwellers of their own rural background. Such plays as *Way Down East* and *The Old Homestead* attracted large audiences. There was also an equally popular series of melodramas on significant urban themes, such as *Bertha, the Sewing-Machine Girl.* Vaudeville shows, providing a variety of singing, dancing, and gymnastic acts, also attracted large audiences.

By 1900, amusement parks were attracting crowds of city people and making fortunes for their owners. In many cases trolley-car companies built amusement parks just outside the city, thereby reaping profits from the parks as well as from trolley fares.

Physical exercise and sports. During the last quarter of the 1800's, an increasing number of middle-class city dwellers became aware of the need for physical exercise, especially for youth. One answer was gymnasiums, which appeared in growing numbers in cities and towns as well as in schools and colleges.

In these years the bicycle changed from a clumsy, high-wheeled, dangerous contraption into something like the machine we know today. As a result, bicycling became a popular fad as well as a means of getting to and from work for many people.

These same years also saw the rapid development of three major spectator sports—baseball, football, and basketball.

Baseball in various forms had been played long before the first professional team, the Cincinnati Red Stockings, was formed in 1869. Seven years later, in 1876, the National League was organized. In 1900 the American League was formed. Well before 1900, urban

King George III may have played a version of it as a boy. And Washington's troops at Valley Forge loved the game. Even then the sport known as "rounders" or "baseball" was old. It many have been played in England as early as the 1500's, with players using milking stools as bases.

The main difference between modern American baseball and the game of rounders from which it evolved is the way in which fielders put out base runners. In rounders, a fielder could throw the ball at—and hit—a runner. In the early 1840's, however, players in America began to tag runners out. This minor change would have important consequences for the quality of the ball and of the game itself.

The first recorded game played according to Cartwright's rules took place in 1846 in Hoboken, New Jersey. The New York Nine defeated the New York Knickerbockers 23 to 1.

Revisions in the rules, necessitated by the fact that one could no longer throw the ball at a player, served to energize and popularize the game over the years. The ball could be made harder and thrown more accurately; the pitcher could now throw overhanded.

During the Civil War Union soldiers who knew the game taught it to their Confederate prisoners, who as they returned home spread the game throughout the nation. By the 1900's the two major leagues had been formed, and many of the rules still in use today had been established.

dwellers in growing numbers were crowding into the ballparks to watch what would in time become one of America's favorite spectator sports.

Football, which evolved from the English game of rugby, also became increasingly popular. The first intercollegiate football contest, played between Rutgers and Princeton in 1869, had 25 players on each side. Within a few years, intercollegiate contests were being held in the West as well as in the East. Played mostly by college men, football in the early days was a rough-and-tumble game. It was so rough, in fact, that some people protested against its "brutality" and demanded its abolition. As the years passed, however, new rules of play were developed, and the game became better organized.

Basketball, which also became a typically American sport, was first played in 1892 by students at the Y.M.C.A. college in Springfield, Massachusetts. Its inventor, Dr. James Naismith, then an instructor in physical education, created the game to provide the same opportunities for recreation in the winter that baseball provided in the summer and football in the fall. Within just a few years, Naismith's game of basketball was being played all over the country.

The older rural forms of recreation—picnics, amateur baseball, horseshoe pitching—continued to enjoy popularity. Increasingly, however, the ways in which the people of the United States relaxed and amused themselves were being transformed in the new industrial age.

SECTION REVIEW

See underscored items, text pp. 581-82.

Identify: P. T. Barnum, Dr. James Naismith

For answers to questions, see Answer Key, p.A81.

1. **Analyzing Ideas: (a)** What was the Chautauqua movement? **(b)** Why was it important to rural dwellers?

2. **Interpreting Ideas:** How did city dwellers satisfy their growing interest in physical fitness?

3. **Summarizing Ideas:** What three major spectator sports developed in the late 1800's?

Class activity: Ask each student to create a feature entitled "Art in American Life" or "Recreation in American Life." Students may choose any appropirate subject and use the feature on this page as a model for format and style. Display the features.

DEVELOPING HISTORY STUDY SKILLS

Interpreting the Visual Record   Using a Photograph as a Documentary Source

- What was urban life in the nineteenth century like for poor people?
- Where and at what jobs did immigrant families work?
- How was the life style of poor people different than the life style of wealthy people in the late 1800's?

Information for answering questions such as these can be gained by studying photographs. Photographers have documented much of the nation's history and their work has become an important part of the historical record. This textbook, as most American history textbooks do, contains many reproductions of historical photographs. Photographs, like paintings, help readers to visualize the events described in written form.

A photograph can be an important source of information. A photograph can tell a story, express a mood, or depict important details. The photograph on page 576, for example, was taken in the early 1900's. It depicts female students in a laboratory class. Information about schools, how people dressed, and the state of science at the time the photograph was taken is contained in the photograph.

A photograph, however, can be misleading. A photograph captures a moment in time. The events preceding and following that moment are not presented. Taken out of historical context, a photograph can distort perception of an event or a mood. A photograph can also be misleading because it often captures only what the photographer wishes to record. The photographer may pose, or frame, the subject to present a point of view. It is important, therefore, when using a photograph as a source of information to analyze it carefully.

You have already been introduced to the skill of analyzing a painting (see text pages 240–41). Review the steps listed on page 240. To effectively analyze a photograph, follow these same steps.

Applying the Skill

The following photograph was taken in the late 1880's by Jacob Riis. Riis was a journalist who investigated the living conditions in the tenements in lower New York City. Study the photograph and read the caption. Note that the caption indicates that this is a rear tenement on Roosevelt Street in New York City. Study the details of the photograph. The photograph show rows of laundry-draped and dilapidated porches that emphasize the cramped living conditions of the tenements in this part of New York City. Much of Riis' investigation focused on the crowded, squalid condition of these tenement buildings.

The photograph is useful for its revelations of the conditions in which tenement families lived. The picture also establishes a melancholy mood, even a mood of depression. A valid generalization drawn from this photograph is that the New York City tenements were crowded and depressing.

This photograph taken by Jacob Riis in the late 1880s shows a rear tenement on Roosevelt Street in lower New York City.

Practicing the Skill

Below is another photograph taken in the late 1880s by Jacob Riis. Study the photograph and read the caption. Then on a separate sheet of paper, answer these questions.

1. What is the subject of the photograph?

2. What location is shown in the photograph?

3. What are the people in the photograph doing?

4. **(a)** What details in the photograph give you information on the crowded conditions in the tenements? **(b)** What details indicate the people in the photograph are poor?

5. What generalization can you draw from this photograph about the conditions of the urban poor in New York City?

6. **(a)** What is the photographer's point of view? **(b)** How can you tell?

7. Why were tenements sweatshops used for such work instead of factories?

Jacob Riis documented all aspects of urban life with his photographs. Here workers are making neckties in a Division Street tenement in New York City. Tenement sweatshops were often used for such work rather than factories because there were no laws regulating sweatshop labor conditions.

(1. workers in a sweatshop 2. a tenement 3. making neckties 4.(a) Answers will vary. (b) their occupation and dress 5. Answers will vary. 6.(a) the photographer deplores tenement sweatshop conditions (b) his choice of subjects and its presentation 7. There were were no laws regulating sweatshop labor conditions.)

Growing numbers of people poured into the great urban centers during the late 1800's. Each year the cities exerted a more and more powerful influence upon all aspects of American life, including education, journalism, literature, architecture, art, and recreation.

What had made the cities so attractive and such a powerful influence to so many people? The cities were the centers of industry with their factories and mass production. The factories, and mass production, depended upon power-driven machines. The power-driven machines—and the almost countless numbers of inventions and discoveries that made the new machines possible—were the results of new applications of science and technology to industry. Scientists, engineers, manufacturers, and business leaders were the people who applied the new technology. Without the advances in science and technology, there would have been no thriving factories and no large industrial cities.

The world of the late 1800's was changing with bewildering speed. New leaders were appearing, and new ways of living and working were transforming American society. The American people, rich and poor, city dwellers and country folk—had to adjust their lives to the new conditions of the industrial age that was transforming the United States so rapidly.

CONNECTING CHAPTER IDEAS

The new age was full of promise for a richer and fuller life for all people everywhere. Before the promise could be realized, however, many problems still had to be solved. In the next chapter you will read about some of these problems and the ways in which American people tried to solve them.

First intercollegiate football game held
1869

P.T. Barnum starts "the greatest show on earth"
1871

Chautauqua movement begins
1874

Baseball's National League forms
1876

Mary Baker Eddy founds Christian Science
1879

Clara Barton establishes the American Red Cross
1881

Ladies Home Journal established
1883

Hull House opened by Jane Addams
1889

Frank Lloyd Wright begins career as architect
1893

| 1870 | 1875 | 1880 | 1885 | 1890 |

585

CHAPTER
25 REVIEW

Reviewing Important Terms

Decide whether each of the following sentences is true or false. If the sentence is false, replace the underlined term with the word or phrase that will make it true.

1. Dana, Pulitzer, and Hearst were the leaders of new trends in journalism.
2. Newspaper syndicates such as the Associated Press provided materials for publication in a number of newspapers at the same time.
3. The movement of people from rural areas to cities is called industrialization.
4. Tenement houses were centers for education and recreation, usually located in a poor area of a major city.
5. The Chautauqua movement was an educational enterprise started in upper New York State.
6. Adventure stories and romantic sagas put out in paper covers were called local-color novels.
7. The mass circulation of newspapers and magazines was stimulated by the development of advertising.

Practicing Critical Thinking Skills

1. **Organizing Ideas.** How did industrialization and urbanization affect (a) education, (b) architecture, (c) art, (d) journalism?
2. **Interpreting Ideas.** How might American democracy have been affected by the (a) increase in educational opportunity and (b) mass circulation of newspapers and magazines?
3. **Synthesizing Ideas.** Explain how each of the following terms reflects the changing ways of American life during the late 1800's: (a) concentration of wealth, (b) settlement house, (c) elective system, (d) skyscrapers, (e) mass-circulation newspapers and magazines.
4. **Evaluating Ideas.** What might be the relationship between functionalism in architecture and an industrialized society?
5. **Comparing Ideas.** Compare a skyscraper built in the late 1890's with one built recently in terms of (a) size, (b) design, (c) materials used. What can you conclude from the differences you find?
6. **Relating Past to Present.** (a) Does education today reflect the needs of modern society? Explain. (b) Describe the changes you would make in the educational system so that it would better meet society's needs.

Developing History Study Skills

1. **Using a Photograph as a Documentary Source.** Use the photographs on pages 572 and 576 and the information in Chapter 25 to write a brief paragraph about educational opportunities for women from 1860 to 1890.
2. **Using Charts and Graphs.** Data are often presented in tabular form. To make sense out of this data, it can be helpful to present the information in another form. Consider the table below. Convert the data into circle (pie) graphs that show the percentages of men and women graduates for each of the three years listed.

Date	1880	1890	1900
Total receiving college degrees	12,896	15,539	27,410
Women receiving college degrees	2,485	2,682	5,237

3. **Using Historical Imagination.** Read one of the novels discussed on pages 578–79. Then write an essay in which you discuss the following aspects of the novel: (a) the novel's relationship to industrialization or urban life, and (b) the opinions expressed in the novel about the vast changes taking place in society at that time.

Relating Geography and History

The remarkable growth of cities and the development of syndicated newspaper chains after the Civil War greatly influenced the spread of ideas. To understand the impact that cities and newspapers had on the American life style, reread page 577 and then complete the following activities.

1. Turn to page 1004 and study the chart at the top of the page. Locate the column headed "City population in 1890." On an outline map of the United States (a) name and locate all the cities on the chart that had a population over 100,000 in 1890. Indicate the surrounding areas that you think were directly influenced by each city.
2. Write a paragraph that summarizes how large cities influence the areas around them.
3. Conclude your paragraph with one or more statements that assesses the ways in which a big city newspaper might affect the people in areas outside that city.

UNIT SEVEN
REVIEW

Discussing Ideas

1. After 1865 in what ways did the government encourage business and industry?
2. Why did it become more difficult for individuals to start their own businesses after the Civil War?
3. Briefly describe how important each of these was in the industrialization of the United States: (a) individual business people, (b) discoveries and inventions, (c) abundant natural resources.
4. Why was city life so attractive to many people during the late 1800's?
5. What effects did large-scale immigration have on American society (a) during the late 1800's, (b) in the long run?
6. Compare the situation of farmers and industrial workers in the late 1800's in terms of (a) grievances, (b) methods of seeking improvement in their situation, (c) relationship with the federal government.

Applying History Study Skills

1. **Using a Photograph as a Documentary Source.** Choose two pictures in this unit, one showing farm life and the other showing city life in the United States during the late 1800's or the early 1900's. (a) How did farm life differ from city life? (b) How would the scenes in these pictures compare to scenes of life today?
2. **Drawing Conclusions.** Read the following statements and complete the activity below.

   - In 1888 Jane Addams and Ellen Starr rented the old Hull Mansion in a run-down section of Chicago populated by immigrants.
   - Before long, other young people . . . came to live at Hull House. They became increasingly interested in the personal histories of the neighbors who came to the House each week. They began to find out about the little children sewing all day long in the garment trade.
   - The regulation of child labor was one political issue in which Hull House residents became involved because of their knowledge of the lives of the neighbors.
   - By 1910 more than 400 settlement houses had been established in the United States.

   (a) List three conclusions you can draw about the influence and achievements of Jane Addams.
   (b) Explain how you reached each conclusion.

Making Connections

1. Prepare a bulletin board display about a city in your region that became important during the industrial age (1865–1900). Include pictures, charts, graphs, maps, cartoons, and short descriptions of the important historical events and facts in the development of the city.
2. Prepare a line or bar graph showing the growth of (a) coal production, (b) iron production, (c) oil production, or (d) railroad lines between 1860 and 1900. Beneath the graph, write a paragraph explaining what is shown on the graph and why it is important.
3. Research the natural resources in your state—especially the raw materials and energy sources—that have contributed to the industrial growth of your state or the nation. Write a report analyzing your findings.
4. Imagine that you are preparing a museum exhibit on paintings of the industrial age (1865–1900). It will consist of five paintings of your choice. Research and select the five paintings. Then write a catalog for the viewers of the exhibit. The catalog should give some facts about, as well as your comments on, each painting in the exhibit.

Reading in Depth

Jones, Maldwyn A., *Destination America* (New York: Holt, Rinehart and Winston). Study of immigrants who came to the United States between 1814 and 1914.

Josephson, Matthew, *The Robber Barons* (San Diego: Harcourt Brace Jovanovich). The story of the men who compiled huge fortunes as the United States industrialized.

Selvin, David, *Champions of Labor* (New York: Abelard-Schuman). Biographies of the early American labor leaders.

Wharton, Edith, *The Age of Innocence* (New York: Scribners). A classic novel about high society in New York in the 1870's.

Wise, Winifred, E., *Jane Addams of Hull House* (San Diego: Harcourt Brace Jovanovich). Story of Jane Addams' career as a reformer and founder of Hull House.

UNIT EIGHT

The Arrival of Reform

In the early 1900's the spirit of reform swept the United States. Attempts to reform politics, economics, and society gained renewed strength from a new group of reformers called progressives. Writers, government officials, and business leaders joined the ranks of the progressives. These reformers sought to improve all aspects of life in the United States. The right of women in all states to vote in national elections was one important change sought by the progressives. Demonstrations, such as the one shown below, were successful in winning suffrage for women. In 1920 the Nineteenth Amendment extended to women in all states the right to vote in all elections. In time most of the reforms sought by the progressives were enacted into law.

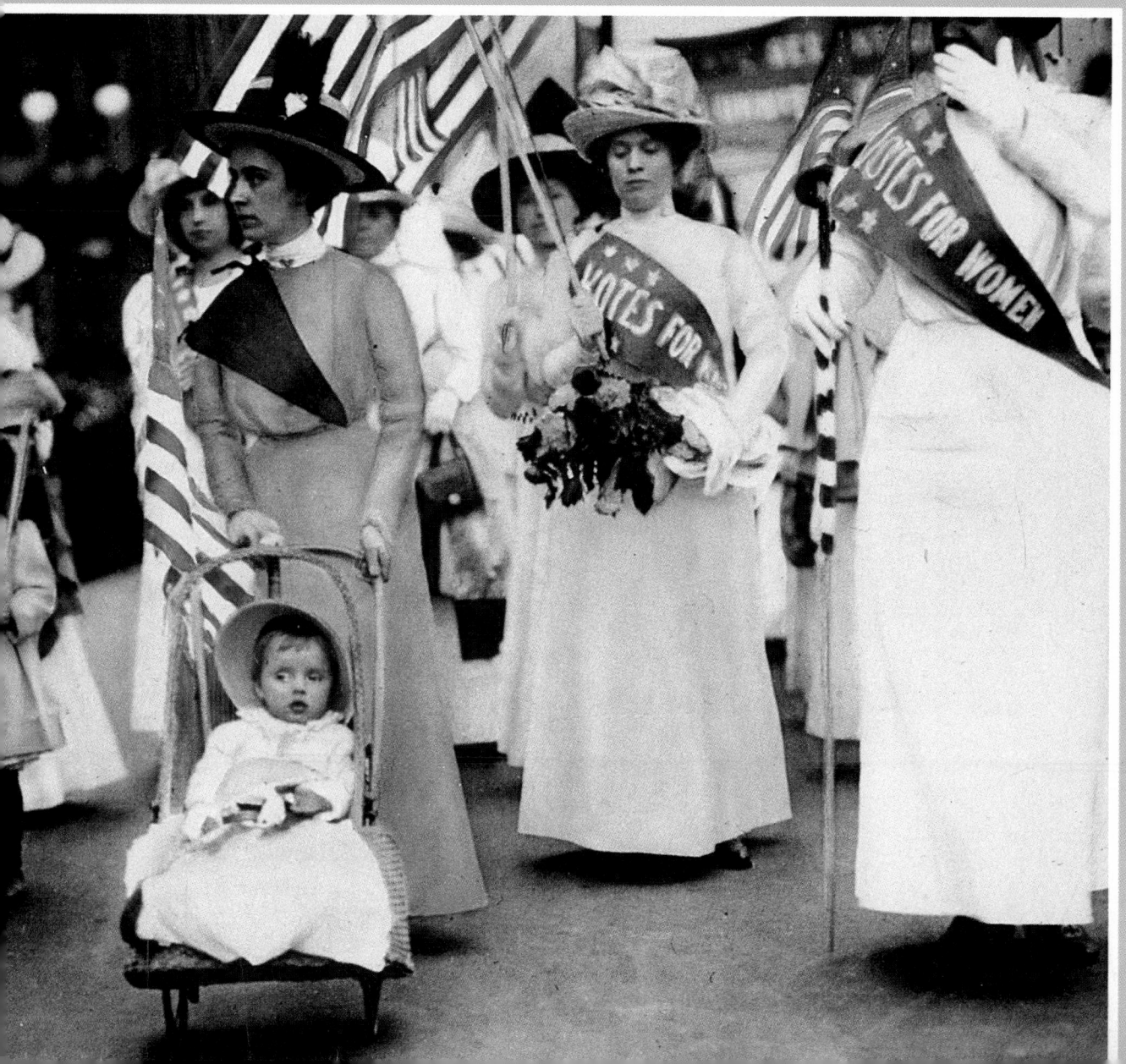

See Chapter Overview in TMRG, p.TM148.
See Chapter Objectives in TMRG, p.TM148.
See Introducing the Chapter in TMRG, p.TM148.

CHAPTER 26

The Square Deal and the New Freedom

(1897–1920)

Time of
the trusts

The election of William McKinley as President in 1896 marked the end of the Populist Party. Many Americans feared that McKinley's election also marked the end of the reform movement. Within six years, however, a new reform movement, the progressive movement, would sweep the country. It would span the terms of three Presidents, each of whom would contribute to the progressive movement.

The first of the three, Theodore Roosevelt, succeeded to the Presidency on the death of McKinley in 1901. Roosevelt was then elected in his own right in 1904, serving until 1909. Colorful and dynamic, he promised to give Americans a "Square Deal." He interceded on the side of labor in a coal miner's strike and earned the name of "trust buster" for his efforts to regulate big business. He also spurred conservation efforts by urging the creation of wildlife sanctuaries and national parks.

From 1909 to 1913, William Howard Taft served as President. A huge man, highly intelligent and thoroughly competent, he advanced the reform movement in the areas of business, labor, and conservation. Taft, however, failed to capture the public's imagination.

From 1913 to 1921, Woodrow Wilson served as President. A scholar and idealist, he promised Americans a "New Freedom" and took important steps toward achieving this goal. Under his leadership, tariffs were reduced, a new banking system was established, educational funding programs were enacted, and antitrust laws were strengthened.

═══ READING FOCUS ═══

As you read about the styles of Presidential leadership, look for the details that support each of the following statements.

1. The progressives open the door to reforms in America.
2. The progressives promote more democratic forms of government.
3. Theodore Roosevelt promises Americans a "Square Deal."
4. Roosevelt acts to conserve America's natural resources.
5. The progressive movement gains and loses under Taft.
6. Wilson's "New Freedom" expands opportunities for Americans.

1 The progressives open the door to reforms in America

See Teaching Suggestions in TMRG, p.TM149.

In 1897 McKinley and the conservative Republicans seemed to have a clear road before them. Having just defeated William Jennings Bryan in his bid for the White House, Republicans now passed the Dingley Tariff of 1897, ▲ which raised average tariff rates to a new high of 57 percent. In the meantime, the depression of 1893–96 gave way to prosperity.

Surrounded by prosperity, many Americans in the late 1890's had forgotten the Populists. Yet by 1900 a new reform known as the **progressive movement** was underway.

Aims of the progressives. The progressive movement cut across party lines. It included people from the Democratic Party as well as discontented Republicans. Leaders of the progressive movement had specific aims. (1) They wanted to restore control of the government to the people. (2) They wanted to correct the abuses that had crept into American life. (3) They wanted to restore greater equality of opportunity by drawing up new rules for the conduct of business. The progressives believed that these reforms would create a more prosperous and a more democratic country.

Robert M. La Follette. Robert M. "Fighting Bob" La Follette of Wisconsin was one of the outstanding leaders of the progressive movement. He won victories over the Republican political machine that dominated Wisconsin. In doing so, he won a reputation for fearless honesty. The farmers and working people elected him to the governorship of Wisconsin in 1900.

As governor, La Follette helped to break the power of the political machine that had been running the state. He persuaded legislators to levy heavier taxes on the railroads and on the newer **public utilities**—the gas, electric, and streetcar companies. He persuaded the legislators to create commissions to regulate companies with a public interest. He also started a movement for the conservation of Wisconsin's forests and waterpower sites. Many of these sites had come under the control of big industrial corporations.

In December 1873 bands of women spontaneously entered saloons in several Ohio and New York towns. After singing hymns and praying aloud, the women convinced the owners to close the saloons. Within six months the women's temperance crusade had spread throughout 23 states, resulting in the closing of some 3,000 saloons.

The following year delegates from 17 states founded the Woman's Christian Temperance Union (WCTU). The organization dedicated itself to the supression of the manufacture, sale, and consumption of alcoholic beverages. The WCTU stressed the physical, psychological, and social dangers of alcohol. But it also took an increasing interest in other issues, such as labor reform, prison reform, tobacco and narcotics abuse, and especially women's suffrage.

The broadened scope of the WCTU was due primarily to Frances Willard, who served as its president from 1879 to 1898. As president of the Illinois WCTU, Willard had conceived the idea of a statewide petition requesting women's suffrage on the issue of prohibition. She collected more than 100,000 signatures and lobbied vigorously at the state capital. Although the petition died in committee, most Illinois towns voted for local option in deciding on prohibition. The Illinois campaign became a model for similar campaigns in other states.

Frances Willard thought of the WCTU "as a school to interest women in life beyond the family circle." To encourage this interest, she stressed the closeness between the home and the WCTU. She coined the organization's slogan, "For God and Home and Native Land." The WCTU's badge — a bow of white ribbon — symbolized the purity of the home.

In 1883 Willard founded the World's Woman's Christian Temperance Union (WWCTU), the first women's international organization. Today the WWCTU includes about 1 million members in 72 countries.

The national WCTU reached a pinnacle of success with the ratification of the Eighteenth Amendment to the Constitution (1919), which prohibited the manufacture, export, import, and sale of alcoholic beverages. Although the Twenty-first amendment repealed Prohibition in 1933 (see pages 746 – 47), the WCTU did not die.

Indeed, the efforts of Frances Willard had awakened the political interests of thousands of women, making it easier for other reform groups to bring about change. A notable example of a successful contemporary reform group is Mothers Against Drunk Drivers (MADD). Founded in 1980 by the mother of a teenager killed by a drunk driver, MADD encourages citizen participation in the reform of the drunk-driving problem. MADD has successfully lobbied state legislatures to tighten drunk-driving laws. In 1984, in direct response to MADD efforts, Congress passed a law reducing federal highway subsidies to states that fail to raise the drinking age to 21 by October 1987.

The La Follette administration promoted good government in Wisconsin by using university scholars to help legislators find needed facts and draft laws that the courts could not easily set aside. He also appointed scholars to serve on the new state regulatory commissions. The "Wisconsin Idea," as the movement started by La Follette was called, soon attracted nationwide attention.

Encouraged by La Follette's example, other public officials attacked corrupt government and powerful corporations. Joseph W. Folk became governor of Missouri in 1906 largely as a result of his success in prosecuting a ring of corrupt politicians in St. Louis. Charles Evans Hughes became governor of New York in 1907 chiefly because of his success in uncovering questionable business practices of certain insurance companies. Hiram Johnson became governor of California in 1910 after fighting the political bosses and powerful railroads that had great influence in the state.

Women reformers. Even though most women still lacked the vote, some of them took part in groups whose purpose was to influence public opinion and government. The National Consumers League, in which Florence Kelley was a leader, brought unfavorable publicity to stores and companies that paid women less than men for equal work and that maintained unhealthful working conditions. The league urged the public to boycott consumer goods produced by child labor and by women who were unfairly treated. With the cooperation of the National Child Labor Committee, the

592 ▲ As a result of LaFollette's example, other states passed laws to protect their citizens' welfare, including laws on child labor, minimum wage, and workers' compensation.

league also secured legislation in the interests of women and children.

Many women also took part in the work of the Anti-Saloon League, which supported political candidates who pledged opposition to the liquor interests and opposed those who did not.

The muckrakers. The progressive movement also included many social workers, scholars, journalists, preachers, and novelists. Theodore Roosevelt applied the name **muckrakers** to the writers who exposed the evils and corruption in politics and the business world. Although Roosevelt used the term in an unfavorable sense, the writers accepted it with pride, and it came into popular use.

The muckracking movement is usually dated from an article, "Tweed Days in St. Louis," written by Lincoln Steffens and Claude H. Wetmore for the October 1902 issue of *McClure's Magazine.* The following month *McClure's* began to publish Ida M. Tarbell's critical *History of the Standard Oil Company.* Many other magazines also began publishing attacks on abuses in American life.

The muckraking novelists included Upton Sinclair, whose sensational novel *The Jungle* exposed unsanitary practices in the meat-packing plants. The book, incidentally, turned many of his readers into vegetarians. Frank Norris's novel *The Octopus* exposed the railroads' control over the political and economic life of the farmers. Jack London in *The War of the Classes, The Iron Heel,* and *Revolution* warned of a revolution that could wipe out private capitalism.

A few of the muckrakers called attention to the plight of American blacks. The most impressive work was *Following the Color Line* by Ray Stannard Baker, a series of magazine articles published as a book in 1908. This was a competent and honest report of segregation and racial discrimination in a nationwide context.

The root of the problem. The muckrakers brought to light many abuses in American life. Lincoln Steffens, however, pinpointed the basic problem in a series of articles later published as a book entitled *The Shame of the Cities.* Years later, in his *Autobiography,* Steffens summarized his conclusions. The basic problem facing Americans was not the development of industrialism or of business, large or small. The source of the evil was "privilege" — the

The Christmas 1903 edition of McClure's Magazine featured Ida Tarbell's exposé of John D. Rockefeller, the founder of Standard Oil.

demand for special privileges from government. This had to be controlled, according to Steffens, or abuses and corruption were sure to be the results.

SECTION REVIEW

See underscored items, text pp. 591-92.

Identify: Dingley Tariff of 1897, progressive movement, Charles Evans Hughes, Hiram Johnson, National Consumers League

For answers to questions, see Answer Key, p.A83.

1. **Organizing Ideas:** (a) How did La Follette reform government in Wisconsin? (b) To what degree did his reforms reflect the goals of the progressive movement listed on page 591?

2. **Summarizing Ideas:** Describe the reform activities promoted by (a) Florence Kelley and (b) Frances Willard.

3. **Comparing Ideas:** (a) Name three muckrakers and explain why they can be described as muckrakers (b) What do their muckraking activities have in common?

4. **Analyzing Ideas:** What did Lincoln Steffens mean when he identified the basic problem and greatest evil in American life as "privilege"?

2 The progressives promote more democratic forms of governments

See Teaching Suggestions in TMRG, pp.TM149-50.

Americans in all walks of life in the early 1900's shared the view that special privileges handed out by government were the source of corruption. They also agreed that one way to combat the evils of special privileges was to restore the control of government to the people.

The Australian ballot. A major step toward more democratic government was the adoption of the **Australian ballot,** or secret vote. Until about 1890 each political party printed its own ballots in a distinctive color. Thus when a person cast a ballot—in open view of anybody who cared to watch—it was easy to determine how the person had voted. The secret ballot, developed in Australia and adopted in the United States, eliminated this open voting. Ballots listing the names of all candidates on a single sheet of paper were printed at public expense. The voters could then mark and cast their ballots in secrecy.

The initiative, referendum, and recall. In trying to secure a more democratic government, the progressives supported the use of the initiative, referendum, and recall. All of these reform measures had been advocated by the Populists in the 1890's.

The **initiative** enables voters in a state to initiate, or introduce, legislation at any time. Suppose, for instance, that a group of citizens wanted to increase the amount of state money spent for public schools. They would draw up a bill and attach to it a petition containing the signatures of a certain percentage of the voters in the state (usually from 5 to 15 percent, depending upon state law). When the petition was presented to the state legislature, the representatives were required by law to debate the bill openly.

The **referendum** was a companion to the initiative. By securing a specified number of signatures to a petition, voters could compel the legislature to place a bill before *all* the state's voters for approval or disapproval.

The **recall** enabled voters to remove an elected government official before the official's term expired. When a specified number of voters, usually 25 percent, presented a petition, a special election had to be held. In this election all of the voters would have the opportunity to vote for or against allowing the official to continue in office.

South Dakota, in 1898, was the first state to adopt the initiative and the referendum. Eventually 20 states adopted initiative and referendum procedures. A total of 12 states adopted the recall.

The direct primary. In trying to make government more responsive to the people's wishes, the progressives also advocated the **direct primary**.

Traditionally, candidates for government offices were nominated in political conventions. These were easily controlled by professional politicians. The direct primary remedied this situation by providing "a nominating election" well in advance of the regular election. Individuals who wanted to run for office would first get a specified number of signatures on a petition. Then they could have their names printed on the primary ballot of any one of the political parties. On the day of the primary election, the registered voters of each party then marked their ballots for the candidate of their choice. First adopted by Wisconsin in 1903, the direct primary soon spread to almost every state.

Women's suffrage. Although the progressives did little if anything to secure the vote for blacks, many promoted women's suffrage. By 1900 four states—Wyoming, Utah, Colorado, and Idaho—had granted full voting rights to women. Vigorous campaigns by woman suffragists between 1910 and 1914 led seven other states, all west of the Mississippi, to give women the right to vote.

Throughout the early 1900's, strong opposition existed even within progressive circles to a Constitutional amendment granting women the vote. Woodrow Wilson, the progressive Democrat who was elected President in 1912, opposed such an amendment on the ground that states alone had the power to fix suffrage requirements. In response, a group of militants led by the courageous and persistent Alice Paul, organized a demonstration against Wilson on his inauguration day that ended in a near riot. Other demonstrations bordered on violence when opposition to them mounted. Activist leaders were jailed and fined. Meantime the militants increased pressure on Congress to grant women the right to vote.

Despite conservative disapproval of militant tactics, the vigorous participation of women in the war effort in World War I broke down much opposition to women's suffrage. Finally, in 1920, with the ratification of the Nineteenth Amendment by the required number of states, the right of women to vote throughout the United States was written into the Constitution.

▲ Today the secret ballot is standard in all elections in all 50 states. Discuss with students the polling places, types of ballots, voting machines, and other election procedures practiced in their communities.

Direct election of Senators. Another reform advocated by the progressives was the direct election of United States Senators. According to the Constitution, Senators were chosen by state legislatures. During the early 1900's, however, progressives in the House of Representatives urged the adoption of an amendment that would allow the people to vote directly for Senators. The Senate, which was often criticized as a "rich man's club" and which included many politicians who owed their jobs to political bosses and political machines, blocked this amendment.

In the end, however, the rising power of the progressives proved too much for the machine politicians. In 1913, in the Seventeenth Amendment, the right to choose Senators was given to the voters at large.

Reform of city government. While winning victories at the state and federal level, the progressives were also trying to reform corrupt city governments. Most municipal governments consisted of a mayor and a large city council, elected by the voters and given complete responsibility for running city affairs. Under this system a well-organized political machine, using corrupt election procedures, could easily win control of city governments.

Galveston, Texas, led the way to a new type of government in 1900 after a hurricane and tidal wave killed one sixth of the city's people and destroyed a third of its property. To meet the emergency, Galveston gave a commission of five persons extraordinary power to run the city. The **commission form of government** soon spread to other cities. By 1912 more than 200 American communities had adopted it. Supporters argued that it was simpler, more efficient, and less expensive than older types of city government.

In 1908 Staunton, Virginia, developed the **city manager form of government**. The city manager, an expert in municipal administration without political connections, is appointed by an elected city council or board of commissioners to run the city as efficiently as possible. City manager government soon spread to many cities.

The progressives were, indeed, a powerful force in American life in the early 1900's. In addition to bringing about these changes in government, they also sought to bring about changes in the relations between business and government.

SECTION REVIEW
See underscored items, text pp. 594-95.

Identify: Australian ballot, initiative, referendum, recall, direct primary, Seventeenth Amendment, city manager form of government
For answers to questions, see Answer Key, p.A83.
1. **Interpreting Ideas:** How did the Australian ballot help prevent abuses in elections?
2. **Evaluating Ideas:** How successful were women suffragists in reaching their goal during the progressive era?
3. **Summarizing Ideas:** How did the Seventeenth Amendment make the American political system more democratic?
4. **Analyzing Ideas:** Use specific examples to support or refute this statement: Progressives sought to make America more democratic.

3 Theodore Roosevelt promises Americans a "Square Deal"

See Teaching Suggestions in TMRG, pp.TM150-51.

President McKinley entered the elections of 1900 confident of victory. The Democrats, who had again nominated William Jennings Bryan, tried to make free silver a major campaign issue. Americans in general, including most farmers, however, were enjoying prosperity. They returned McKinley to the White House with an electoral vote of 292 to 155.

On September 6, 1901, McKinley was shot by a half-crazed assassin. He died a few days later. To the dismay of conservative Republicans, Vice President Theodore Roosevelt became the nation's Chief Executive.

Roosevelt's background. Theodore Roosevelt was born in 1858 into a well-to-do New York family. He studied at Harvard, where he acquired a taste for history and politics. After graduation he served a two-year term, from 1882 to 1884, in the New York state legislature. For part of the next two years, he lived on a cattle ranch in Dakota Territory. Returning home in 1886, he unsuccessfully ran for mayor of New York City, then devoted the following three years to the study and writing of history.

During the next few years, Roosevelt served on the federal Civil Service Commission, as president of the New York City Police Commission, and as Assistant Secretary of the Navy.

PART ONE

A SCHOOL HISTORY

OF THE

Negro Race in America

FROM 1619 TO 1890

COMBINED WITH THE HISTORY OF THE
NEGRO SOLDIERS IN THE SPANISH-AMERICAN
WAR, ALSO A SHORT SKETCH OF LIBERIA

BY

EDWARD A. JOHNSON, LL.B.

Author of "Light Ahead for the Negro" and "The Negro Almanac and Statistics"

REVISED EDITION, 1911

ISAAC GOLDMANN CO., Printers, 200-204 William Street, New York

Edward A. Johnson, a black textbook author, is shown here with a page from his School History of the Negro Race in America, *an important study on black Americans.*

When war with Spain broke out in 1898, he resigned his Navy post to organize, with Leonard Wood, a volunteer cavalry regiment known as the "Rough Riders." After the war he became the Republican governor of New York. In that post his independent actions so alarmed the Republican political bosses that in 1900 they decided to get him out of active politics by "kicking him upstairs" into the Vice-Presidency.

This was the man who at age 42 became the youngest President the United States had ever had—and, as the conservative Republicans had correctly feared, one of the most independent. ▲

Roosevelt was a good politician, ready to compromise when necessary. He did not start the progressive movement. Nor did he go as far as many progressives felt he could and should go, but he gave the progressive movement dramatic national leadership. His general popularity, his enthusiasm, his ability as a speaker, and his position enabled him to promote a number of reforms. One notable exception was government policy toward Indians, whose needs and rights were largely ignored.

Settling a coal strike. Less than a year after succeeding McKinley as President, Roosevelt took bold action in a struggle involving organized labor. In the spring of 1902, a strike broke out in Pennsylvania in the coal mines owned largely by railroad companies serving the region. The miners worked long hours, lived in company towns, and bought from company stores. Because of low wages, they found it hard to make ends meet. Organized as part of the United Mine Workers union, they had asked for a 9-hour day, a 20-percent wage increase, improved working conditions, and recognition of their right to bargain as a union. The mineowners refused to negotiate with the union, whereupon the miners went on strike.

By autumn the country faced a coalless winter with factories closed and homes without heat. The mineowners demanded that the President send federal troops into the area to break the strike. Roosevelt refused. Instead, he summoned representatives of the owners and of the union to meet at the White House.

At the meeting the mineowners refused to listen to a proposal for impartial arbitration. Furious at this lack of cooperation, Roosevelt let it be known that he might send the army to take over the mines in the name of the government. Faced with this prospect, the mine-

▲ Show the film **The Life and Times of Teddy Roosevelt** (CBS TV) or filmstrip **The Age of Theodore Roosevelt** (GA) to give students an overview of the life and times of this colorful historical figure.

owners agreed to accept the decision of a board of arbitration.

After four months of study, the board gave the miners a 9-hour day and a 10-percent wage increase. However, the board did not grant the miners the right to negotiate as a union.

Although the miners won only part of their demands, the case was a landmark in the history of organized labor. For the first time, the federal government had stepped into a labor controversy to protect the interests of all concerned—wage earners, owners, and the public.

The Danbury Hatters' case. Organized labor was not pleased, however, with the outcome of another labor dispute. In 1902 the hatters' union started a nationwide effort to boycott, or to halt the purchase of, the hats produced by a manufacturer in Danbury, Connecticut. The hat company claimed that the boycott restrained trade and was therefore illegal under the Sherman Antitrust Act. After a long delay, the Supreme Court decided in favor of the hat manufacturer in 1908. As a result, the members of the hatters' union were held liable for three times the damages that the hat manufacturer had suffered.

Theodore Roosevelt was in no way responsible for the Supreme Court ruling. Nevertheless, organized labor, thoroughly alarmed at the outcome of the Danbury Hatters' case, held the government responsible for failing to draft laws that provided reasonable protection for labor unions.

Roosevelt and blacks. Some progressives fought the exploitation of black workers, established settlement houses for blacks, and organized national societies to protect the legal rights of black citizens. However, the progressives on the whole neglected the plight of black Americans. Many progressive leaders, to be sure, spoke out against racial injustice, but most of them believed that this problem could, at that time, be dealt with realistically only at state and local levels.

Theodore Roosevelt, too, did little to help the blacks. He did become involved in southern politics, where questions of segregation and black leadership were important issues. Thus, against the opposition of segregated southern Republican organizations, Roosevelt sometimes supported the claims of black politicians to federal office and to participation as delegates at Republican national conventions.

In such matters Roosevelt often used Booker T. Washington as his adviser. Once, after a conference with Washington, Roosevelt invited the black leader to lunch with him at the White House. When the episode became known, a storm of criticism swept the South. Roosevelt did not repeat the invitation.

In general, Roosevelt's neglect of blacks reflected the attitudes and prejudices of most white Americans, including most of the progressives, during these years.

Roosevelt as "trust buster." Under pressure from both reformers and business leaders, the federal government during Roosevelt's administration took steps toward regulating business practices in the interest of the public welfare. Before this time, as you recall, the federal government, with few exceptions, had not become greatly involved in business affairs.

Early in his first term, Roosevelt directed his Attorney General to bring suit under the Sherman Antitrust Act against the Northern Securities Company. This was a holding company that controlled the three leading

═══ **SOURCES** ═══

THEODORE
ROOSEVELT'S
"NEW
NATIONALISM"
SPEECH
(1910)

Our country—this great republic—means nothing unless it means the triumph of a real democracy, the triumph of popular government, and, in the long run, of an economic system under which each man shall be guaranteed the opportunity to show the best that there is in him. . . .

I stand for the square deal. But when I say that I am for the square deal, I mean not merely that I stand for fair play under the present rules of the game, but that I stand for having those rules changed so as to work for a more substantial equality of opportunity and of reward for equally good service. . . .

*Americans had long worried about the influence of trusts, as this 1880's cartoon,
"Bosses of the Senate," shows. What symbols does the artist, Joseph J. Keppler, use to
demonstrate how powerful these trusts had become?*

(trust interests depicted as enormous bags of money surrounding members of Congress,
who are unaware, unconcerned, or cooperating with trust influences)

railroads serving the country between Lake
Michigan and the Pacific Northwest. "We do
not wish to destroy corporations," Roosevelt
announced, "but we do wish to make them sub-
serve the public good." In 1904 the Supreme
Court held that the Northern Securities Company did restrain trade and was illegal under
the Sherman Antitrust Act.

Early in 1903, while the Northern Securities Company case was still pending in the
courts, Congress passed the Expedition Act to
speed up antitrust cases by giving them a priority over the other cases in federal courts. Another measure created the Department of Commerce and Labor, with a Secretary in the
President's cabinet. The new department included a Bureau of Corporations authorized to
investigate and report on corporate activities.

The election of 1904. Roosevelt's progressive ideas antagonized many Republican politi-

cal leaders. When election year 1904 rolled
around, the Republican political leaders would
have abandoned him in favor of a more conservative candidate had they dared. However, by
this time Teddy Roosevelt enjoyed widespread
popularity. No other Republican candidate
had a chance of taking the nomination from
him.

During the campaign, Roosevelt had announced that he was "unhampered by any
pledge, promise, or understanding of any kind,
save my promise, made openly to the American
people, that so far as my power lies I shall see
to it that every man has a square deal, no less
and no more." This promise carried weight
because Roosevelt had convinced voters that he
meant what he said.

Roosevelt went on to win a resounding victory at the polls – 336 electoral votes to 140 for
his Democratic opponent, Judge Alton B.
Parker of New York.

▲ Refer students to the cartoon on textbook page 590. What national symbol is shown wrapped
in trusts? How are the people and the nation symbolized by the cartoonist? Have students use
the cartoon on page 590 and the one on this page to name specific industries involved in
trust activities.

Renewed efforts at regulation. After 1904, encouraged by the Supreme Court decision in the Northern Securities Company case and by his reelection, Roosevelt started action against a number of other trusts. Altogether, 44 suits against trusts were started during his administration.

Even when the Supreme Court ordered a trust to dissolve, the business executives who had controlled the various corporations in the trust often continued to meet informally and share in the decisions of the separate corporations. By secret arrangements of this kind—often called "communities of interest"—the corporations continued to do informally what they had previously done as a trust. The advantages of large-scale operations for consumers and sometimes for the corporations were very great. Moreover, big business was so tied together that any attempt to break up a monopoly was like trying to unscramble the eggs in an omelet. The trend of the times was toward larger and larger business combinations. Neither Roosevelt nor anyone else could reverse this trend.

"Good" and "bad" combinations. Before leaving office in 1909, Roosevelt concluded that the problem of trusts was not simply one of size. What really mattered was whether a business combination, regardless of size, was "good" or "bad" for the public as a whole. He asked Congress to pass laws defining "good" and "bad" practices, but Congress refused.

In 1911, two years after Roosevelt left office, the Supreme Court adopted his point of view. The Court ruled that the Sherman Antitrust Act's prohibition of "all combinations in restraint of trade" should mean "all *unreasonable* combinations." The Supreme Court from then on decided whether a large business combination was "reasonable" or "unreasonable" by looking not merely at its size but also at its effect upon the public.

Important railroad legislation. The Roosevelt administration had more success in regulating railroads than in breaking up trusts. On the President's recommendations, Congress adopted two laws that put teeth into the Interstate Commerce Act of 1887 and strengthened the Interstate Commerce Commission.

The Elkins Act of 1903 made it illegal for a shipper to accept a rebate, just as the Interstate Commerce Act had made it illegal for

Cartoonist Clifford Berryman pokes fun at the idea of "good" and "bad" trusts. Bear-hunter "Teddy" has slain the "bad trusts." How does the cartoonist picture him dealing with the "good" ones?
(by placing them under federal regulation)

railroads to give one. Many railroads approved of this act, for it freed them from giving special privileges to large shippers.

The Hepburn Act of 1906 gave the Interstate Commerce Commission authority (1) to regulate express and sleeping-car companies, oil pipelines, bridges, railroad terminals, and ferries doing business across state lines; (2) to fix "just and reasonable" rates, subject to approval by the federal courts; (3) to restrict the granting of free passes; and (4) to require that railroads use uniform methods of accounting.

Laws protecting public health. President Roosevelt also gave leadership to a movement to protect public health.

Government chemists had long known that the products of some distilleries, drug companies, and meat-packing plants were endangering public health. Patent medicines often contained harmful habit-forming drugs or ingredients that could not possibly relieve any ailments. Many canned foods were spoiled or were treated with poisonous preservatives. As Upton Sinclair had pointed out in his book *The Jungle,* meats in the packing houses were often from diseased animals.

Against the powerful opposition of the meat-packing interests, Roosevelt and the progressives in Congress secured passage in 1906 of the Meat Inspection Act. The act required government approval of all meat shipped from one state to another. Also under pressure from reform groups, including a women's letter-writing campaign, Congress passed the Pure Food and Drug Act of 1906. The act forbade the manufacture, sale, or transportation of impure food and patent medicines containing harmful ingredients. It also required patent-medicine containers to carry labels listing their exact contents. Five years later, in 1911, Congress supplemented this law by making it illegal to use false or misleading labels.

These acts helped to strengthen the developing theory that the federal government was responsible for protecting the public welfare.

SECTION REVIEW

See underscored items, text pp.597-600.
Identify: Danbury Hatters' case, Northern Securities Company case, Department of Commerce and Labor, square deal, Elkins Act of 1903, Hepburn Act of 1906, Pure Food and Drug Act of 1906
For answers to questions, see Answer Key, pp.A83-84.
1. **Analyzing Ideas: (a)** Why was organized labor pleased with Roosevelt's handling of the 1902 coal strike? **(b)** Was this a clear-cut victory for labor? Explain.

2. **Interpreting Ideas:** How did Roosevelt's attitude toward black Americans reflect the attitudes and prejudices of most white Americans?

3. **Evaluating Viewpoints:** Roosevelt claimed to be a "trust buster." Do the facts support his claim? Why or why not?

4 Roosevelt acts to conserve America's natural resources

See Teaching Suggestions in TMRG, p.TM151.
"The first work I took up when I became President," Roosevelt wrote in his *Autobiography,* "was the work of **reclamation**." This job of reclaiming the nation's **natural resources** proved to be one of his greatest contributions.

Wasted natural resources. Before Theodore Roosevelt became President, almost nothing had been done to safeguard the nation's resources. Indeed, Americans had always used their natural resources without regard for the future. Pioneer farmers had cut and burned their way westward, transforming forest land into farm land. The federal and state governments had carelessly encouraged waste, especially during the latter half of the 1800's. They handed over to private individuals and to corporations priceless natural resources—agricultural and grazing lands, forest regions, mineral deposits, oil fields, and water-power sites.

By 1900 only 200 million acres (81 million hectares) of the nation's original 800 million acres (324 million hectares) of virgin forest were still standing. Four fifths of this timber was privately owned. The executives who ran the nation's corporations cared no more about waste than the pioneer settlers had. Lumber companies destroyed forests without regard for wildlife, flood control, fire protection, replanting, or the preservation of young trees. Cattle raisers and sheepherders overgrazed semiarid lands, stripping them of their protective covering of grass. Often they helped turn these lands into dust bowls.

Coal companies worked only the richest and most accessible veins, leaving the bulk of the coal buried in abandoned mines. Oil companies allowed natural gas to escape unused into the air. The growing cities polluted rivers and streams with sewage and industrial wastes, destroying fish and creating a menace to public health. The American people were simply unused to thinking that their natural resources were exhaustible.

Early conservation efforts. By the late 1800's, a rapidly growing population was making heavier and heavier demands upon the nation's resources. The growing industries were devouring raw materials in ever larger quantities. A few thoughtful Americans realized that the nation's resources could not last forever.

As early as 1873, the American Association for the Advancement of Science had demanded some action to prevent the waste of natural resources. Because of these efforts and the efforts of other farsighted people, Congress in 1887 established the Forest Bureau in the Department of Agriculture. In 1891 Congress authorized the President to withdraw timberlands from public sale. Acting under this

▲ Discussion topic: Ask the students what role the government plays in protecting the public from unsafe products. Are there any products currently under testing to determine if they contain harmful substances--food preservatives, coloring, or other additives? Have the students give examples of warnings on product labels.

Thomas Moran (1837–1926), an English-born immigrant to the United States, was a self-taught painter who helped acquaint Americans with the beauty of their own country and with the need for national parks.

Moran's love for the landscapes of the western United States inspired such paintings as "The Grand Canyon of the Yellowstone," which hangs in the United States Capitol in Washington, D.C.

Moran made his first trip to the West in 1871, traveling with territorial surveyors in what is now Yellowstone National Park. The surveyors nicknamed him "Yellowstone" Moran because of his evident affection for the area's natural wonders. Moran's vivid, expansive paintings of the region reinforced the nation's growing conservation movement. In 1872 Congress established Yellowstone National Park, beginning the National Park System.

law, President Harrison set aside a national forest reserve of 17 million acres (7 million hectares), and Presidents Cleveland and McKinley more than doubled this area.

A small beginning toward the **conservation** of natural resources had been made. However, the public had not yet learned to think of the need for conservation as a serious national problem.

Roosevelt's leadership. President Roosevelt awakened public interest to the need for conservation, aroused Congress to action, and managed to get the federal and state governments to adopt new policies. In 1901 he warned Americans that "the forest and water problems are perhaps the most vital internal problems of the United States." In a special message to Congress, he reminded the legislators that "the mineral wealth of this country, the coal, iron, oil, gas, and the like, does not reproduce itself. . . . If we waste our resources today," he went on to say "our descendants will feel that exhaustion a generation or two before they otherwise would."

Roosevelt was never content with mere talk. During his administration he withdrew from public sale 150 million acres (60.7 million hectares) of forest land—an area much larger than France. He also withdrew millions of acres of coal and phosphate lands and potential water-power sites. In response to his urging, Congress created wildlife sanctuaries and national parks. In these activities, Roosevelt met opposition from private interests.

The Newlands Reclamation Act. One of the most important acts of his administration, however, received considerable support, especially from western members of Congress. Early in his Presidency, Roosevelt supported the Newlands Reclamation Act. This act provided that money from the sale of public lands in 16 western states and territories was to be used to build irrigation projects that would reclaim wasteland—that is, make it suitable for farming. Money from the sale of water to the farmers who settled on the reclaimed land was to go into a fund used to finance other irrigation projects.

Reclamation work started at once. Within four years 28 different irrigation projects were under way. By 1911 the Shoshone (shoh·SHOH·nee) Dam in Wyoming and the Roosevelt Dam in Arizona were in operation. Water from the enormous reservoir created by the Roosevelt Dam flowed through irrigation canals and ditches to transform 200,000 acres (80,940 hectares) of desert into rich farmland. As other projects were completed, additional thousands of acres of wasteland were brought under cultivation.

▲ Under Roosevelt, between 1901 and 1909 the number of national parks doubled, and Roosevelt personally announced the creation of more than 50 wildlife preserves.

601

In 1903 Theodore Roosevelt (third from left) spent several days at Yosemite Park in California discussing conservation with the great naturalist ▲ John Muir (far right) and other concerned men.

The White House Conference. In 1907 Roosevelt created the Inland Waterways Commission. After studying nearly every aspect of the conservation program, the commission urged the President to hold a national conference to publicize the need for conservation.

This meeting, the White House Conservation Conference of 1908, was a great success. One result was the appointment of a 50-member National Conservation Commission made up of nearly equal numbers of scientists, business executives, and political leaders. This commission went to work at once on a study of the country's mineral, water, forest, and soil resources. Another important outgrowth of the White House Conference was the appointment of state conservation agencies in 41 of the states by governors who were convinced of the need for them.

Thus Theodore Roosevelt helped to arouse public opinion to the need for conservation. Equally important, he established the foundations of a solid conservation program that would have far-reaching effects.

SECTION REVIEW
See underscored items, text pp. 600 - 01.

Identify: conservation, reclamation, natural resources, Shoshone Dam

For answers to questions, see Answer Key, p.A84.

1. **Summarizing Ideas:** What actions did Theodore Roosevelt take to arouse the nation to the need for conservation?
2. **Analyzing Ideas:** What was the significance of the Newlands Reclamation Act of 1902?
3. **Organizing Ideas: (a)** Why did some people oppose the idea of conserving natural resources? **(b)** In what ways did Roosevelt establish the foundations of a solid conservation program?

5 The progressive movement gains and loses under Taft

See Teaching Suggestions in TMRG, pp.TM151-52.

A financial panic and depression hit the nation in 1907. Despite it, President Roosevelt's popularity was at its peak. It was clear that the Republican nomination was his for the asking, but Roosevelt would not run again.

The election of 1908. At the Republican convention, Roosevelt supported his close friend and associate William Howard Taft of Ohio, who won the nomination on the first ballot. The Republican platform called for strengthening the Interstate Commerce Act of 1887 and the Sherman Antitrust Act of 1890, conserving the nation's resources, improving the highway system, and revising the tariff.

The Democrats again chose William Jennings Bryan as their Presidential candidate. The Democratic platform condemned the Republican Party as the party of "privileges and private monopolies." It called for a lower tariff, new antitrust laws, a federal income tax, and restrictions on the use of court injunctions in labor disputes.

One unusual feature of the election campaign was the action taken by the American Federation of Labor. In 1908 the A. F. of L. abandoned its traditional policy of supporting friends of organized labor in both political parties and came out for Bryan and the entire Democratic ticket.

Despite the support of organized labor, the Democrats lost by a considerable margin, with Taft receiving 321 electoral votes to Bryan's

▲ Muir, almost blinded in an accident in his youth, spent the rest of his life traveling throughout America to enjoy its beauties. He influenced Roosevelt to protect wilderness areas.

162. The Republicans also retained control of both houses of Congress.

Reforms under Taft.   William Howard Taft, a Cincinnati lawyer and judge, had served the Roosevelt administration in the Philippines and in the War Department. Taft was a cautious man. His training as a lawyer and his temperament led him to stress the legalistic restrictions on his Presidential power. As one commentator put it, the change from Roosevelt to Taft was like changing from an automobile to a horse-drawn carriage. Despite his conservative nature, however, Taft recognized the force of the progressive movement and supported a number of important reforms.

Taft's administration chalked up an impressive list of accomplishments that progressives had favored. Taft's Attorney General started 90 antitrust suits against big corporations compared with 44 suits started under President Roosevelt. Following Taft's recommendation, Congress strengthened the Interstate Commerce Act by passing the Mann-Elkins Act of 1910. This new legislation placed telephone, telegraph, cable, and wireless companies under the jurisdiction of the Interstate Commerce Commission. Congress also created a new department with cabinet rank—the Department of Labor. In response to the growing attack upon the use of child labor, Congress established a Children's Bureau in the Department of Labor. It also established an 8-hour day for all workers on projects contracted for by the federal government.

The Taft administration also took steps to create a healthier political climate. President Taft himself added a considerable number of federal jobs to the civil service list. Congress adopted the Publicity Act requiring political parties to make public sources and sums of money spent in political campaigns.

Taft's administration was partly responsible for the adoption of a constitutional amendment to make possible a federal income tax. The Sixteenth Amendment, which had been proposed in 1909, was ratified in 1913.

Progressive opposition.   In spite of these reforms, President Taft began to lose the support of the progressives in the Republican Party. As a result, he relied more and more on conservatives in the party.

The split between President Taft and the progressives appeared as early as April 1909,

when Congress adopted the Payne-Aldrich Tariff. The progressives had worked for lower tariff rates, and at first Taft had supported their position. Then he switched to the high-tariff point of view and swung his influence behind the Payne-Aldrich measure. In the new act, some reductions were in fact made, but rates on many thousands of items were actually increased.

In the midst of the tariff battle, Taft was also violently attacked for his stand on conservation. Indeed, some of his most bitter critics charged that he had undermined Roosevelt's conservation program. Although this was an unfair charge, it is true that the conservation movement suffered a setback during the opening months of Taft's administration.

Taft's Secretary of the Interior, Richard A. Ballinger, was a cautious lawyer. Ballinger concluded that the President's authority to withdraw land from sale extended only to timberland. He therefore restored to public sale valuable water-power sites that President Roosevelt had previously withdrawn. Gifford Pinchot, head of the Forest Service under both Roosevelt and Taft, promptly protested. Taft sided with Pinchot, and the lands in question were returned to the forest reserve. However, Pinchot, an ardent conservationist, was convinced that Ballinger favored private interests and was opposed to the conservation program.

Pinchot's fears were strengthened when Ballinger allowed extensive coal lands and timberland in Alaska to pass into private hands. This action aroused a storm of controversy throughout the country. In the midst of the storm, Taft removed Pinchot from office.

Although Ballinger resigned in 1911 and the new Secretary of the Interior restored the Alaskan lands to the federal forest reserve, the damage had been done. Taft's stand on the Ballinger controversy cost the Republicans many votes in the Congressional elections of 1910. For the first time in 16 years, the Republicans lost control of the House of Representatives.

Actually, Taft did a great deal to advance the conservation program. With authorization from Congress, he withdrew almost 59 million acres (24 million hectares) of coal lands from public sale. He also signed the Appalachian Forest Reserve Act, which added large tracts of land in the southern Appalachians and in the White Mountains of New Hampshire to the federal reserves.

▲   Report topic: Ask interested students to find out what their state's child labor laws are -- minimum age, wage, and hours. The students should report their findings to the class in an oral report.

603

Roosevelt's spirited campaign captured the imaginations of cartoonists as far away as Germany. "I'm feeling like a bull moose," Roosevelt told a reporter, and thus was he depicted.

A victory for progressives. Early in 1910 the progressives of the Republican Party launched an attack upon the Speaker of the House. Since 1903 Speaker Joseph "Uncle Joe" Cannon of Illinois had been one of the most powerful officers in the government. As Speaker, he appointed all House committees and selected their leaders. He appointed himself head of the powerful Committee on Rules, which determined the order of business in the House. In this capacity, he could prevent any bill to which he objected from reaching the floor of the House for debate. Moreover, as presiding officer of the House he could determine who should speak during debate by recognizing or refusing to recognize anyone he pleased. As a result of these powers, "Uncle Joe" ruled the House with an iron hand.

The progressives charged that Cannon, a conservative, had used his great power to block progressive legislation. They planned to put an end to Cannon's control. In March 1910 Representative George W. Norris of Nebraska proposed an amendment to the House rules. He moved that in the future the Committee on Rules be elected by the members of the House and that the Speaker be excluded from membership on the Rules Committee.

Speaker Cannon, with solid support from the conservatives, fought desperately to maintain his power. After heated debate, about 40 progressive Republicans voted with the Democrats in favor of Norris's motion and stripped the Speaker of his traditional powers over the Committee on Rules. A year later the House deprived the Speaker of the power to appoint members of the remaining committees. The Speaker remained an extremely influential figure, but the Speaker's power was diminished.

Split in the Republican Party. By 1912 the Republican Party was split wide open, with the "old guard" on one side and the progressives on the other. Theodore Roosevelt, by now dissatisfied with Taft's leadership, decided to run again for the Presidency. To do so, Roosevelt had to brush aside the obvious candidate of the progressive forces, Robert M. La Follette of Wisconsin. Roosevelt also had to line up enough delegates to the nominating convention to insure his own nomination.

President Taft held the advantage that a President always has at a political convention. The Roosevelt supporters claimed that many of their delegates to the convention were refused seats by the Taft forces. Not surprisingly, the convention named Taft as its candidate. Angered by this, Roosevelt's supporters called another convention, which nominated him for the Presidency. Thus a new third party was launched—the Progressive Party, sometimes called the "Bull Moose" Party.°

The Bull-Moose Republicans with Teddy Roosevelt at their head adopted a platform calling for numerous reforms. The platform favored legislation in the interest of labor and advocated tariff reform. It endorsed the initiative, referendum, and recall, and it declared that it stood for government control over unfair business practices. In a spirited campaign, Roosevelt popularized his "New Nationalism" program. "New Nationalism," to Roosevelt, meant extending the powers of the federal government to make it an effective instrument in the battle for progressive measures and social reform.

°The party adopted as its emblem the powerful bull moose as a tribute to Roosevelt, who often used the term to describe a person's strength and vigor.

Wilson as the Democratic candidate. The Democrats were confident that the split in the Republican Party would insure their own victory. Their platform called for tariff reduction, banking reform, laws favoring workers and farmers, and the enforcement of stronger antitrust laws. As their candidate they chose Governor Woodrow Wilson of New Jersey.

Wilson, the son of a Presbyterian minister, had been president of Princeton University before he became governor of New Jersey in 1910. As governor, he fought the political machine bosses of his party, showing remarkable independence. He also took the lead in pushing through the legislature laws designed to reform the weak corporation laws of the state. As he showed more and more interest in other progressive measures, Wilson became the logical choice of the progressives in the Democratic Party.

An idealist and a man of convictions, Wilson was determined, courageous, and independent. He sensed the popular discontent in the country. His neatly turned phrases about establishing a "New Freedom" for ordinary Americans greatly appealed to those who were convinced that special privilege menaced the welfare of the nation.

The election of 1912. Still another party was involved in the election of 1912. The Social Democratic Party or Socialist Party had been organized in 1901. It had shown increasing strength in cities. In 1912, for example, 79 Socialist mayors were elected in 24 states. The Socialist Party candidate for President in 1912 ▲ was Eugene V. Debs.

The election proved to be a clear-cut victory for the progressives, a defeat for the conservatives. Wilson received 435 electoral votes and Roosevelt 88, whereas Taft received only 8.

Debs won no electoral votes but received almost a million popular votes.

Despite his overwhelming electoral vote, Wilson was a "minority" President. He received only 6 million popular votes out of a total of more than 15 million. Nevertheless, he could count upon widespread public support.

SECTION REVIEW
See underscored items, text pp. 603-04.
Identify: Mann-Elkins Act of 1910, Publicity Act, Sixteenth Amendment, Gifford Pinchot, Joseph Cannon, "New Nationalism"
For answers to questions, see Answer Key, p. 84.
1. **Analyzing Ideas:** Why did Taft's opponents consider him to be against conservation?
2. **Summarizing Ideas:** (a) What were the reasons for the revolt against "Uncle Joe" Cannon? (b) What were the results?
3. **Interpreting Ideas:** Why did Roosevelt form the Bull Moose Party?
4. **Studying Graphics:** Make a chart comparing the parties, candidates, platforms, and results of the elections of 1908 and 1912.

6 Wilson's "New Freedom" expands opportunities for Americans

See Teaching Suggestions in TMRG, p.TM152.
President Wilson hoped to restore the equality of opportunity that many Americans enjoyed when the frontier was still open to settlers. He believed that this equality had been largely destroyed by the closing of the frontier, by great corporations, and by the often corrupt alliance of government and business.

SOURCES

WILSON'S "NEW FREEDOM" SPEECH (1912)

I take my stand absolutely, where every progressive ought to take his stand, on the proposition that private monopoly is indefensible and intolerable. And there I will fight my battle.

. . . I am for big business, and I am against trusts. Any man who can survive by his brains, any man who can put the others out of the business by making the thing cheaper to the consumer at the same time that he is increasing its intrinsic value and quality, I take off my hat to, and I say: "You are the man who can build up the United States, and I wish there were more of you." . . .

▲ Labor organizer Eugene Debs was twice jailed--once for continuing a railroad strike which the Supreme Court had ruled "in restraint of trade" and once for violating the Espionage Act by giving an inflammatory speech which was deemed "inciting to riot."

605

President Wilson at once recommended to Congress a positive program to promote the public welfare. Opposed by pressure groups and lobbies representing special business interests, Wilson used all his skills as a speaker to win popular support for his program.

Tariff reform. Like most Democrats, Wilson believed that high protective tariffs benefited the trusts by excluding from the country products that foreign manufacturers could make and market more cheaply. It was also true, of course, that tariffs protected jobs and helped workers maintain higher wages than foreign workers received.

To check the trend toward monopoly and reduce the cost of living, the Wilson administration pushed through Congress the Underwood Tariff Act of 1913. This act did not establish **free trade**,° but it reduced tariffs more than any tariff act had in the previous 50 years. It lowered duties on almost a thousand items, including cotton and woolen goods, iron, steel, coal, wood, agricultural tools, and many agricultural products. The average of all duties was reduced from 41 to 29 percent. The Underwood Tariff Act also included a section providing for a **graduated income tax**. The new law provided for a tax ranging from 1 to 6 percent on incomes over $3,000 per year.

The Underwood Tariff was passed against strong opposition, but it did answer the widespread cry for tariff reform. Moreover, its graduated income tax provision laid down the principle that those with more income had to bear a heavier share of the expenses of government. This rule is sometimes called the "ability-to-pay" principle of taxation.

°**free trade:** the exchange of goods between countries unhampered by regulations or protective tariffs aimed to keep out foreign goods.

The Federal Reserve System. The second important achievement of Wilson's "New Freedom" program was in the field of money and banking. Almost everyone was dissatisfied with the existing banking system, but people disagreed on how to reform it.

In general, the more conservative business groups wanted greater private control over the existing banking system. They argued that this control would enable the stronger banks to help the less-favored banks in times of financial crisis.

On the other side were the Bryan Democrats and the progressive Republicans. They believed that the existing banking system was already dominated by the "money trust"—the great private investment banking firms like J. Pierpont Morgan and Company, which often controlled big business consolidations. The reformers wanted the government, not private bankers, to control the banking system. This control, they argued, would enable the government to regulate the amount of currency in circulation and thus help to stabilize prices.

The Federal Reserve Act of 1913 was a ▲ compromise between these two sides. It provided for the establishment of 12 Federal Reserve districts, each with a Federal Reserve Bank. The operations of these district banks were to be supervised and coordinated by a Federal Reserve Board in Washington, D.C. All national banks were to be members of a Federal Reserve Bank. All state banks that met certain requirements were invited to join.

The Federal Reserve Banks were strictly "bankers' banks." They provided services only for member banks, not for business concerns or private citizens. In times of crisis, when weak banks were on the point of failing, the Federal Reserve Banks could transfer money reserves and thus help prevent failure and the loss of people's savings.

▲ The Federal Reserve is still in operation today. It is supervised by a Federal Reserve Board, whose members are appointed by the President with the consent of the Senate. In addition to controlling the amount of money in circulation, it regulates prime interest rates, which influence the total economy.

The Federal Reserve System also made it possible to put more money into circulation or to withdraw some from circulation according to the needs of the time. It thus provided a more elastic currency by controlling the amount of lending that member banks could do.

Antitrust laws strengthened. The third major achievement of Wilson's "New Freedom" program was its effort to strengthen the antitrust laws. The Clayton Antitrust Act of 1914 helped to put teeth in the older Sherman Antitrust Act.

The Clayton Act was aimed at business practices that until then had not been illegal. (1) It prohibited business organizations from selling at lower prices to certain favored purchasers *if* such price discrimination helped to create a monopoly. (2) It prohibited "tying contracts"—that is, contracts requiring a purchaser to agree not to buy or sell the products of a competitor. (3) It declared interlocking directorates illegal in companies with capital investments of $1 million or more. (4) It prohibited corporations from acquiring the stock of another company *if* the purchase tended to create a monopoly.

The Clayton Act also attempted to protect farmers and wage earners. The Sherman Antitrust Act of 1890 had been used on a number of occasions against labor unions. The Clayton Act, on the other hand, declared that labor unions and farm organizations had a legal right to exist. It said that they could not "be held or construed to be illegal combinations or conspiracies in restraint of trade, under the antitrust laws."

The Clayton Act also prohibited the granting of an injunction in a labor dispute *unless* the court decided that an injunction was necessary "to prevent irreparable injury to property." This act also declared that strikes, peaceful picketing, and boycotts were legal under federal jurisdiction.

Organized labor hailed the Clayton Act as a great victory. However, as you will read, the courts interpreted the act in such a way that the injunction continued to be used as a weapon against strikes.

The Federal Trade Commission. The Federal Trade Commission, created by Congress in 1914, was also part of President Wilson's "New Freedom" program. The commission was authorized to advise and regulate industries

Woodrow Wilson, shown here on a 1912 election campaign poster, believed that the duty of progressivism was, "to cleanse, to reconsider, to restore . . . every process of our common life."

engaged in interstate and foreign trade. The commission was to be a bipartisan body of five members.

The commission was authorized to (1) require annual and special reports from corporations, (2) investigate the business activities of persons and most corporations, (3) publish reports on its findings, and (4) order corporations to stop unfair methods of competition. Among the unfair practices investigated by the commission were mislabeling, adulteration of products, and false claims to patents. If a corporation refused to obey an order to "cease and desist" from such practices, the commission could ask the courts to enforce its ruling. The law protected the corporation by providing that it could appeal to the courts if it considered the "cease-and-desist" order to be unfair.

The Federal Trade Commission was intended to prevent the growth of monopolies and to help bring about a better understanding between big business and the government.

Other "New Freedom" measures. The tariff, money and banking, regulation of trusts— these were the major problems tackled by Congress during Wilson's first administration. Much more reform legislation might have been adopted if the outbreak of World War I in

▲ Discussion topic: Ask the students how the FTC helps protect consumers, even though its purpose is to stop unfair practice in competition. (Some unfair practices include mislabelling and adulteration of products. This directly affects consumers of the products.)

607

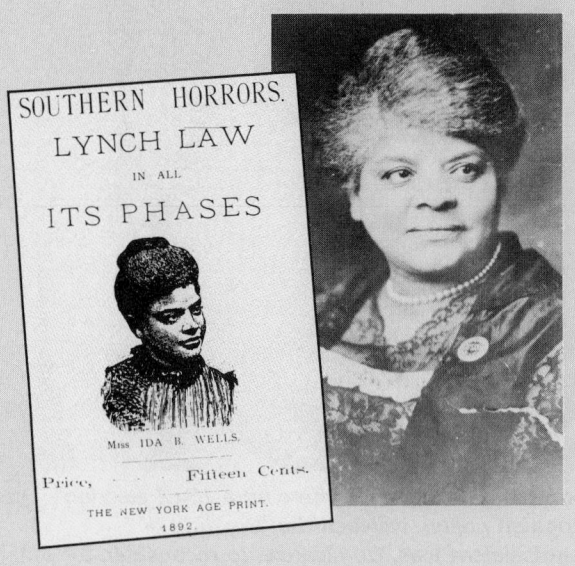

Ida B. Wells was born during the Civil War to slave parents in Mississippi. She attended a high school for freed blacks and began teaching at the age of 14. In 1884 Wells moved to Memphis, Tennessee, where she taught and continued her education by attending summer classes at Fisk University.

In 1890, Wells started writing for several small, black-owned newspapers, and by 1892 she was half-owner of a newspaper, the *Memphis Free Speech*. When three black men she knew were lynched, Wells began to investigate and write about lynchings. As a result of her editorials, the newspaper's office was destroyed. This prompted Wells to lecture throughout the nation against mistreatment of blacks.

Wells moved to Chicago, Illinois, where she met and married Ferdinand Lee Barnett, a black lawyer, newspaper editor, and assistant state's attorney. She soon founded a black women's club and the Negro Fellowship League for black men who were newly arrived from the South.

Ida B. Wells-Barnett knew that other black men and women could succeed as she had if given a chance. Wells-Barnett spent the rest of her life guaranteeing that chance for any black who was willing to accept the challenges she offered.

Europe in the summer of 1914 had not interfered. Even so, Congress found time to pass several other important measures.

In 1914 Congress adopted the Smith-Lever Act. Among other things, the act provided federal funds for rural education. The educational programs were to be carried on by the Department of Agriculture in cooperation with the land-grant colleges. Federal grants of money were to be matched by similar grants from the states receiving this aid. Three years later, in 1917, just before the United States entered World War I, Congress adopted the Smith-Hughes Act. This additional measure provided federal funds for vocational education in both rural and urban areas of the country.

The Federal Farm Loan Act of 1916 made it easier for farmers to borrow money. This act divided the country into 12 agricultural districts. It established a Farm Loan Bank for each district where farmers could get low mortgage rates.

Blacks and the "New Freedom." During the election campaign of 1912, Woodrow Wilson promised an officer of the National Association for the Advancement of Colored People (NAACP) that if elected he would promote the interests of black Americans in every way possible. Such was not the case, however. As President, Wilson seemed to agree with most white Americans that segregation was in the best interests of black as well as white Americans.

During Wilson's administration, white employees and black employees in government offices in Washington, D.C., were segregated. Many black office workers were dismissed in southern cities. A black journalist bitterly remarked that Wilson had given black Americans no part in the "New Freedom."

The election of 1916. By 1916 President Wilson had established himself as a vigorous leader. The delegates to the Democratic convention pointed with pride to his solid list of achievements and enthusiastically renominated him for a second term.

The Republicans chose Supreme Court Justice Charles Evans Hughes, former governor of New York, as their candidate. The Progressive Party nominated Theodore Roosevelt. However, Roosevelt was unwilling to split the Republican vote again, refused the nomination, and supported Hughes. The Progressive Party,

Progressive goals of the early 1900's included the elimination of child labor from the workplace. Photos such as this one — of young waterboys at a Pennsylvania steel mill — aroused public sympathy in favor of protective legislation.

deprived of Roosevelt, decided not to nominate another candidate. As a result the Republicans, once more united, entered the campaign hopeful of victory.

The campaign of 1916 centered not only upon Wilson's record of domestic issues but also upon America's relation to the war that had broken out in Europe in 1914. Hughes toured the country, criticizing the Democrats for the Underwood Tariff and for their handling of foreign affairs. Wilson, on the other hand, contented himself with delivering speeches from the front porch of his summer home in New Jersey. Speakers for the Democratic Party adopted the slogan "He kept us out of war."

The election itself turned out to be one of the closest in American history. The final electoral vote was 277 for Wilson, 254 for Hughes. California proved to be the decisive state — the Democrats won in California by a margin of only 3,773 popular votes! Despite the closeness of the vote, Wilson had won against a united Republican Party, as had not been true in the election of 1912. Even more reassuring, he had collected nearly 600,000 more popular votes than Hughes.

Woodrow Wilson seemed to feel that his first term in office had accomplished his goals,

though many progressives believed much remained to be done. In any event, it was not "New Freedom" measures that occupied the President during his second administration. Within a month of Wilson's second inauguration on March 4, 1917, the United States entered World War I.

SECTION REVIEW
See underscored items, text pp. 606-08.
Identify: "New Freedom," Underwood Tariff, free trade, graduated income tax, Smith-Lever Act, Federal Farm Loan Act

For answers to questions, see Answer Key, pp.A84-85.

1. **Analyzing Ideas:** For what reason did Wilson start the "New Freedom" program?

2. **Summarizing Ideas: (a)** Describe the Federal Reserve System. **(b)** In what ways was it a compromise between the views of the conservatives and those of the progressives? **(c)** What was the function of the Federal Trade Commission?

3. **Interpreting Ideas: (a)** How did the Clayton Antitrust Act of 1914 put teeth in the older Sherman Antitrust Act? **(b)** Why did organized labor praise the Clayton Act?

Class activity: Have students draw their own political cartoons to highlight some aspect of the Presidency of Roosevelt, Taft, or Wilson. (Possible topics: Roosevelt—Bull Moose Party, "Square Deal," reclamation; Taft—relationship with Roosevelt, "Uncle Joe" Cannon; Wilson—"New Freedom," blacks)

609

DEVELOPING HISTORY STUDY SKILLS

Writing About History   Expressing Viewpoints

Being informed about and able to express a view on important issues is an important skill for today's citizen. United States citizens today, for example, are concerned with and may wish to express their viewpoints on issues such as the following.

- Should the government do more to regulate big business?

- Should federal income tax laws be reformed?

- Is the proliferation of nuclear arms really a deterrent to war?

Students are often called on to express their viewpoint on a topic. You may be asked to express your view on a selected topic from a list prepared by the teacher or on an issue of your own choice. The following guidelines should help you express your viewpoint.

How to Express a Viewpoint

To effectively express a viewpoint in an essay, follow these steps.

1. **Research the issue.** Find out what the opposing viewpoints are.

2. **Determine your position on the issue.** Collect data to support your position.

3. **State your position.** Write an opening paragraph that identifies the issue and states your viewpoint.

4. **Support your position.** Compose additional paragraphs that provide data to support your viewpoint. Conclude with a paragraph in which you summarize your position and clearly restate your reasonings.

Why Women Should Vote

This paper is an attempt to show that many women today are failing to discharge their duties to their own household properly because they do not perceive that as society grows more complicated it is necessary for women to extend their responsibility to many things outside of [their homes] if [they are] to continue to preserve the home. . . . One could illustrate it in many ways. A woman's simplest duty is to keep her home clean and wholesome and to feed her children properly. Yet if she lives in a tenement house . . . she cannot fulfill these simple obligations by her own efforts because she is utterly dependent upon the city administration for the conditions which render decent living possible. Her basement will not be dry, her stairways will not be fireproof, her house will not be provided with windows to give light and air . . . unless the Public Works Department sends inspectors who constantly insist that these elementary decencies be provided. . . .

The second is a responsibility for the education of children . . . that they may be provided with good schools; . . . be kept from vicious influences on the streets; . . . that when working they may be protected by adequate child-labor legislation.

In a complex community like the modern city all points of view need to be represented; the resultants of diverse experience need to be pooled if the community would have sane and balanced progress. If it would meet fairly each problem as it arises . . . It must not ignore the judgments of its entire adult population.

In closing, may I recapitulate that if a woman would fulfill her traditional responsibility to her own children; if she would educate and protect from danger factory children who must find their recreation on the street; if she would bring the cultural forces to bear upon our materialistic civilization . . . then she must bring herself to the use of the ballot — that latest implement for self-government. May we not fairly say that American women need this to preserve the home?

Jane Addams

610

Applying the Skill

Read the excerpt on page 610 by Jane Addams. Note that the title indicates that the issue is women's suffrage. The first paragraph offers a clue to the writer's viewpoint. Addams indicates that society has changed and that it is time for women to accept new responsibilities outside the home. Her position is then restated clearly and precisely in the concluding paragraph, ". . . then she must bring herself to the use of the ballot — that latest implement for self government."

The arguments Addams uses to support her viewpoint are stated in paragraphs two, three, and four, and then restated in her concluding paragraph. Addams argued that in a modern, complex community "all points of view need to be represented" and by all she meant both male and female.

Practicing Your Skill

Read the statement below written in 1910 by Mrs. Gilbert E. Jones. Then on a separate sheet of paper, answer the questions and complete the activity.

1. What issue is the writer addressing?
2. What is the writer's position?
3. What major arguments does the writer use to support her position?
4. Does the writer make a strong case for her viewpoint? Explain.
5. Choose a current issue. Use the guidelines on the preceding page to prepare a paper expressing your viewpoint on the subject.

The Question of Women Suffrage

A great many states have granted to women school suffrage, but only a partisan or sectarian issue will bring out the woman's vote. In Massachusetts women have voted on school boards, and after thirty years' training, only 2 or 3 percent of the women register to vote. This hardly can be pronounced "success," or worthwhile. . . .

A very conscientious investigation by this League cannot find that the ballot will help the wage-earning woman. Women must resort to organization, association, and trade unions, and then they can command and maintain a standard wage. Supply and demand will do the rest. Women are not well trained and often very deficient and unskilled in most of their occupations. They are generally only supplementary workers and drop their work when they marry. When married, and home and children are to be cared for, they are handicapped way beyond their strength. Married women should be kept out of industry, rather than urged into it, as scientists, physicians, and sociologists all state that as women enter into competitive industrial life with men, just so does the death rate of little children increase and the birth rate decrease.

The question of woman suffrage should be summed up in this way: Has granting the ballot to women in the two suffrage states where they have had it for forty years brought about any great reforms or great results? No — Wyoming has many more men than women, so the results cannot be measured. . . .

Have the saloons been abolished in any of the suffrage states? No.

Do men still drink and gamble? Yes, without a doubt.

Have the slums been done away with? Indeed no.

Are the streets better cleaned in the states where women vote? No, there are quite as bad as in New York City and elsewhere. . . .

Have women purified politics? No, not in the least.

Have women voted voluntarily? Some do; but thousands are carried to the polls in autos and carriages; otherwise they would not vote.

Has pure food and pure milk been established by the women's vote? Not at all.

Have women's wages been increased because women vote? No, indeed.

Have women equal pay for equal work? Not any more than in New York City.

Are there laws on the statute books that would give women equal pay for equal work? No, and never will be.

Are women treated with more respect in the four suffrage states than elsewheree? Not at all. . . .

Mrs. Gilbert E. Jones

(1. the need for women to organize 2. Women must better organize to deal with social problems. 3. lists problems that have not been solved by women gaining the right to vote 4. Answers will vary. 5. Answers will vary.)

The victory of the Republicans in the election of 1896 broke the strength and momentum of the Populist movement. With the triumph of the Republicans and with the return of prosperity, many people concluded that the reform movement started by the Populists had lost its force.

The reform movement, however, was not dead. On the contrary, in the early 1900's it gained new life in the progressive movement. Guided by the progressives, including President Theodore Roosevelt, the relationship of government and business began to change. In earlier times, the government's role had been, in general, that of a referee who stood on the sidelines and stepped in only when it seemed that one of the players had disobeyed the rules. Now, in the twentieth century, the government was beginning to take a more active part, to accept more responsibility for regulating the activities of business in the interest of the public welfare. Both Republicans and Democrats were responsible for this changing view of the role of government in the new industrial age.

The reforms started under President Roosevelt were continued by President Taft and, to an even greater degree, during the Democratic administration of President Wilson. As you will read, the efforts were interrupted by the outbreak of World War I in 1914.

CONNECTING CHAPTER IDEAS

The transformation of the United States from a mainly agrarian economy to an industrial economy was completed between the years 1900 to 1920. In the next chapter you will read how new inventions and new ideas revolutionzed the average American's way of thinking and standard of living.

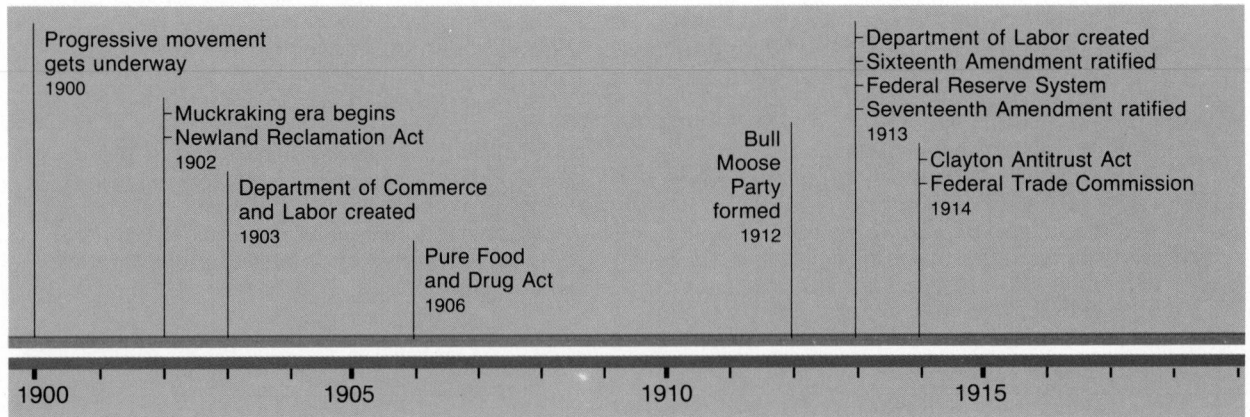

Progressive movement
gets underway
1900

Muckraking era begins
Newland Reclamation Act
1902

Department of Commerce
and Labor created
1903

Pure Food
and Drug Act
1906

Bull
Moose
Party
formed
1912

Department of Labor created
Sixteenth Amendment ratified
Federal Reserve System
Seventeenth Amendment ratified
1913

Clayton Antitrust Act
Federal Trade Commission
1914

1900   1905   1910   1915

CHAPTER
26 REVIEW

Reviewing Important Terms

In the sentences below, the underlined terms are incorrect. On a separate sheet of paper, rewrite each sentence using the correct term.

1. The <u>trust busters</u> wrote articles that exposed corruption and scandal in public life.
2. <u>Initiative</u> is a procedure under which a proposed law is submitted to the voters for approval or rejection.
3. The <u>Wisconsin</u> ballot lists all candidates, and people cast their votes in secret.
4. The organization of city government by which a city employs an appointed administrator to direct the operation of the city is called a <u>commission form of government</u>.
5. The <u>muckraker</u> movement was an organized effort begun in the early 1900's to correct abuses and injustices, to restore greater equality of economic opportunity, and to return government control to the people.

Practicing Critical Thinking Skills

1. **Interpreting Ideas.** The basic issue with which Presidents Roosevelt, Taft, and Wilson had to deal was the role of government in the new industrial age. Explain.
2. **Organizing Ideas.** Compare Roosevelt's "Square Deal" and Wilson's "New Freedom" in terms of (a) goals, (b) legislative accomplishments, and (c) long-range effects.
3. **Evaluating Ideas.** Present evidence to support or refute this statement: Despite his apparent weakness, President Taft was actually a more effective progressive President than Roosevelt.
4. **Comparing Viewpoints.** Explain how the ideals of progressivism agree with the ideals expressed in the Declaration of Independence and the Preamble to the Constitution.
5. **Synthesizing Ideas.** How might you have voted in the election of 1912 if you had been: (a) a farmer, (b) a banker, (c) an Italian immigrant, and (d) a factory worker? Give reasons for your answers.
6. **Relating Past to Present.** Use primary and secondary sources to find out more about the women's movement between 1865 and 1900. (a) What were the key issues and obstacles? (b) What issues for which they fought remain issues today? (c) How do the methods used during that time period compare with the methods today?

Developing History Study Skills

1. **Expressing Viewpoints.** Reread "Wilson's New Freedom Speech", 1912, on page 605 of the textbook. Use the information in Chapter 26 and the excerpt from Wilson's speech to answer the following questions. (a) How did Wilson feel about monopolists? (b) What distinction did Wilson make between big business and trusts?
2. **Finding Main Ideas.** Read the following excerpt and answer the questions below.

Wilson' strengthening and extension of the presidential powers constituted perhaps his most lasting contribution to American political practice. A strong believer in party government, he decided to work through and with his party in Congress, rather than to govern by a coalition of progressives, as he might have done. Moreover, he conceived of himself as the responsible leader of his party, as the only leader who could speak for it and the country. Therefore, he felt himself personally charged with the introduction and sponsorship of important legislation. . . .

(a) What is the main idea of the paragraph? (b) What are the supporting ideas?

Relating Geography and History

By the early 1900's Americans began to be more aware of the environment. They began to realize that the nation's natural resources might not last forever, and that some were being ruined by exploitation and pollution. Actions were taken to protect and conserve the environment. To recognize the effect that industrial development had on the nation's environment, answer the following questions.

1. How did the rapid use of raw materials by industry affect the nation's forests, rivers, and wildlife?
2. (a) How did the growth of cities affect rivers and lakes? (b) How did city growth affect the forests and wildlife?
3. What steps did federal and state governments take to protect the environment?
4. Reread President Theodore Roosevelt's statements in the subsection "Roosevelt's leadership" on page 601. (a) What did Roosevelt mean by his remarks? (b) Do his words still apply today? Explain.

613

See Chapter Overview in TMRG, p.TM153.
See Chapter Objectives in TMRG, p.TM153.
See Introducing the Chapter in TMRG, p.TM153.

CHAPTER 27 New Directions in American Life

Changing Ways   (1900–1920)

Everyday life, 1910

614

As the United States approached the middle of the twentieth century, Frederick Lewis Allen wrote a book reviewing and interpreting 50 years of American history. He called this book *The Big Change* and gave it the subtitle *America Transforms Itself, 1900–1950*.

The transformation, as Allen saw it, was "in the character and quality of American life by reason of what might be called the democratization of our economic system, or the adjustment of capitalism to democratic ends." It was, he went on to say, "the way in which an incredible expansion of industrial and business activity, combined with a varied series of political, social, and economic forces, has altered the American standard of living and with it the average American's way of thinking and his status as a citizen."

During the years from 1900 to 1920, the United States was in full process of passing from a predominantly agrarian economy to a predominantly industrial economy. New inventions aided the transformation. Automobiles meant changing country roads into paved highways. New methods of production made it easier to feed an urban nation.

A growing number of Americans, including business owners and managers, became increasingly aware of the need to modify some of the attitudes and practices carried over from the early days of the Industrial Revolution. The courts, for example, responded with decisions that improved working conditions.

In 1920 there were still many large and difficult problems that remained unsolved. Workers still had to struggle for recognition of their rights to safe and humane working conditions. But "the big change" from the rural to the urban way of life was already beginning to have an important influence on the direction of American life.

READING FOCUS

As you read about the years from 1900 to 1920, look for the details that support each of the following statements.

1. New inventions and new ideas revolutionize American industry.
2. The lives of farmers improve in the early 1900's.
3. Conditions improve for industrial workers in the United States.

1 New inventions and new ideas revolutionize American industry

See Teaching Suggestions in TMRG, pp.TM153-54.

In 1900 America was still in the horse-and-buggy age, but that age would not last much longer. Great changes were transforming the nation, but even greater changes were to come.

Signs of change. In 1900, Americans still rode in horse-drawn streetcars. Hitching posts and watering troughs were common sights. Livery stables and blacksmith shops were centers of activity in every town. When night fell, the lamplighter turned on the gas lamps that still lighted the streets in most American cities and towns. And the streets were more likely to be dusty lanes that turned to sloppy messes whenever it rained.

It is easier, perhaps, to picture the America of 1900 by listing the things that people did not have and did not know. High school educations were more for the few and the fortunate. Most young people went to work right after eighth grade. There were no rock groups, no concerts that attracted thousands of frenzied youths, and no tape recorders. There were no supermarkets, where one-stop shopping took place. No income taxes reduced a wage earner's take-home pay. No one had heard of vitamins, penicillin, or other antibiotics. Women could vote in only four states—Wyoming, Colorado, Utah, and Idaho. Motion pictures, radios, television, and airplanes did not exist. In those days automobiles were still curiosities that attracted crowds of onlookers. People often called automobiles "horseless carriages."

Yet, in 1900, Americans had already entered a new way of life. By 1900, railroad builders had laid down 192,566 miles (309,896 kilometers) of track. All the great trunk lines had been built across the continent. Day and night, long lines of freight cars rumbled across the countryside loaded with the products of America's fertile farmlands, the tonnage from its mines, steel from its mills, and manufactured goods from its factories. New railroad lines were still being built. By 1920 railroad mileage reached its high mark of 260,000 miles (418,500 kilometers) of track.

Automobiles and highways. While this network of steel rails expanded, inventors in Europe and America were experimenting with a new source of power. This was the internal combustion engine, in which fuel, usually gasoline, was converted into a vapor and exploded within the engine walls. Among the American experimenters were Charles E. Duryea, George B. Selden, Elwood Haynes, Alexander Winton, and Henry Ford. These inventors and others developed the gasoline engine.

By 1900, "horseless carriages" were appearing on the roads. At first the automobile was an expensive toy for wealthy people. Mass production soon lowered costs, however, bringing the automobile within reach of people with modest incomes. Whereas in 1900 there were only 8,000 automobiles in the United States, by 1920 there were 8 million passenger cars and 1 million trucks.

Development of the automobile depended, of course, upon other inventions and developments. One was the discovery by Charles Goodyear of the process for vulcanizing, or hardening, rubber, for which he obtained his first patent in 1844. Other inventions led to improvements in refining petroleum into gasoline and in developing batteries, generators, and other electrical devices.

The development of the automobile also depended upon—and helped to stimulate—the construction of paved roads. In 1904 nearly all rural roads were little better than dirt lanes, although some were surfaced with gravel, clay, or crushed oyster shells. By 1924, however, 472,000 miles (760,000 kilometers) of rural highways had paved surfaces. By 1924, older roads were being widened, graded, and paved at the rate of about 40,000 miles (64,000 kilometers) a year, at an annual cost of approximately $1 billion.

The airplane. By 1900, Europeans and Americans, among them Samuel P. Langley, were experimenting with another new method of transportation—powered flight. Orville and Wilbur Wright, on December 17, 1903, became the first to put such a machine into the air. Their first flight went only about 120 feet (37 meters) and did not attract much attention. Within a few years, however, the first crude flying machines were being replaced by more effective planes, and air pioneers were making longer and longer flights. In 1919 a Navy seaplane crossed the Atlantic by way of the Azores. That

same year two Englishmen, John Alcock and A. W. Brown, flew nonstop from Newfoundland to Ireland.

Developments in communications. Equally revolutionary were developments in communications. People were barely getting used to the idea of the telephone when in 1895, an Italian inventor, Guglielmo (goo·LYEL·moh) Marconi, first demonstrated wireless telegraphy. Eight years later, from a station at Cape Cod, Massachusetts, he transmitted a message across the ocean to England and received a reply.

One of the most significant inventions in the field of communications was the three-element vacuum tube, invented by Lee De Forest in 1906. This invention made it possible to amplify even weak electrical impulses, or signals. Within a few years, wireless equipment had been installed on all large vessels. Wireless messages in the dots and dashes of Morse code were being sent over land and sea by powerful transmitters. Meanwhile, scientists and engineers were experimenting with transmitting the spoken word through the air. However, commercial radio broadcasting did not become a reality until the 1920's.

The motion picture. Several inventors, American, British, and French, contributed to the development of the motion picture. In 1895 two Americans, Thomas Armat and Woodville Latham, successfully used their projector in public showings.

In the early days, films ran only a few minutes. Then, in 1903, a pioneer "picture story" called *The Great Train Robbery* demonstrated the possibilities of the motion picture. Soon directors and producers were proving to ever larger audiences that the motion picture could do a great deal that was impossible on the stage. One early director, D. W. Griffith, won fame in 1914 for his film *The Birth of a Nation*. Night after night people crowded into the early movie theaters to watch such popular stars as Mary Pickford, Douglas Fairbanks, and Charlie Chaplin.

New methods of production. The new world that was coming into being in the early 1900's depended upon new power sources—oil and electricity. Between 1900 and 1920, oil production in the United States jumped from 63 million to about 443 million barrels a year. By 1914 nearly one third of the nation's factory

▲ Discussion topic: Ask students to discuss how various industries and businesses depend upon automobile manufacturing and travel. (steel, service stations, motels, etc.)

machines were driven by electricity, and the use of electric power was rapidly increasing. High-voltage transmission lines carried the pulsing energy of dynamos—steam-driven or water-driven—to widely scattered cities. Smaller transmission lines carried electricity to towns and villages throughout the country and even to some isolated farms.

Productivity of America's factories was greatly increased not only by new sources of power but also by the **assembly line**. On an assembly line, workers stood at stations beside a slowly moving track, or conveyor belt. At each station, workers added a new part to the product on the track. Finally, a steady succession of finished products came off the end of the assembly line. Improved in the early 1900's by Henry Ford for use in the manufacture of automobiles, the assembly line soon became an essential part of America's developing industrial economy.

Increasing efficiency. The use of **efficiency engineering** also increased the productivity of factories. Frederick W. Taylor was a major contributor to this idea. Taylor wanted greater efficiency from machines and from the workers operating the machines. To get it, he developed "time-and-motion" studies of plant operation. Using a stop watch, Taylor timed the workers operating machines and counted the number of motions each worker made to complete a particular operation. Then he worked out ways to reduce the number of movements of the workers' hands and feet. Sometimes workers were trained to use their hands and feet more effectively. Sometimes the machine was redesigned and its controls placed in more convenient locations.

Taylor's methods made great economies possible in every stage of mass production. Each process in the mechanized industrial plant was simplified and speeded up along the assembly line. Each worker performed a highly specialized task, working with the least possible effort to produce the maximum output. However, some workers complained that such methods made them, more than ever, like parts in a great machine.

The "Ford idea." Henry Ford had made a major contribution to American industry in developing the assembly line. Even more important was his new and revolutionary theory of increasing employee wages.

THE PIERCE-ARROW CAR

Our idea is that the car should go "there and back" in the shortest possible time, with the least trouble to both owner and driver, with the greatest comfort to the owner in transit, at the least expense, weight of car and equipment considered, and without interruption of the trip by reason of or the fault of the car, and that it should do this not only now and then, but always. That is the service that the Pierce-Arrow Car is planned to perform.

The Pierce-Arrow Motor Car Company, Buffalo, N. Y.

The Pierce Arrow was for years the height of luxury in American cars. What clues indicate that this car was intended for a wealthy owner?
(chauffeur; mansion in background; "both owner and driver")

On January 5, 1914, Ford announced that he was nearly doubling the wages of the workers in his plants. Beginning immediately, he said, his 13,000 employees would receive a minimum wage of $5 for an 8-hour day. This announcement swept almost all other news off the front pages of America's newspapers. The New York *Herald* called it "an epoch in the world's industrial history."

Why was Ford's action considered so important? In taking this step, Ford had recognized an important fact about the American economic system. Rising wages gave American workers greater purchasing power to buy more and more of the products of America's expanding industry.

Ford was both warmly applauded and sharply criticized for his action. However, the criticism did not prevent the "Ford idea" from spreading to other industries. As the years passed, more people came to understand that mass production and mass purchasing power are interdependent. This understanding was

Report topic: The auto industry has pioneered other worker-oriented programs. Ask interested students to investigate the industry's role in setting up group-health insurance plans. The students should present oral reports of their findings to the class.

617

The first barns in the United States were functional structures built to house animals and store crops. Early settlers brought barn designs from their native lands, but they had to change those plans to accommodate America's soil and climate.

American barns, much bigger than their European counterparts, were built of logs, lumber, or stone, and were usually rectangular in shape. Wooden frames were laid out on the ground and raised with the help of neighbors. The owner and the barn-raising helpers then added the sides and the roof. Round barns were often built by religious sects, such as the Shakers, who claimed that the round barn kept "the devil from hiding in the corner."

American barns had pitched 45-degree roofs. European thatched roofs did not provide adequate insulation in the harsh climates of New England and the Midwest. Moreover, they were dangerous because fireplace sparks and lightning could ignite the thatch. As a result, seasoned wooded shingles or shakes soon became standard roof material.

The first barns were unpainted. Later, Virginia settlers used stain-like paints in grayish pastels, red, and ochre. Northern farmers mixed red oxide with skim milk and lime to make a plastic-like coating that lasted for years. This was the famous American-barn-red, which was used until 1850, when linseed oil paints came into use.

---

an essential part of what Frederick Lewis Allen called "the big change" transforming America in the opening years of the twentieth century.

SECTION REVIEW

See underscored items, text pp. 616-17.

Identify: Charles Goodyear, Samuel Langley, Wright brothers, Guglielmo Marconi, *The Great Train Robbery,* assembly line, Frederick Taylor

For answers to questions, see Answer Key, p.A86.

1. **Interpreting Ideas:** How did mass production of the automobile help to transform American life?

2. **Analyzing Ideas:** Why was the three-element vacuum tube an important invention?

3. **Organizing Ideas:** (a) What is the purpose of efficiency engineering? (b) What are its advantages? (c) its disadvantages?

4. **Summarizing Ideas:** (a) What was the "Ford idea"? (b) Why was it important to the American economy?

2 The lives of farmers improve in the early 1900's

See Teaching Suggestions in TMRG, p.TM154.

By the early 1900's, the farmer had become an important part of the nation's industrial economy. On thousands of small farms tucked away in mountain valleys and in other remote areas, farm families lived much as farmers had lived 100 years earlier. These more or less **self-sufficient farmers** were exceptions. Most of the nation's farm produce was raised by farmers who, whether they liked it or not, had in many ways become owners of a business.

Growing demand for farm products. One factor that helped turn farms into businesses was the startling growth of America's city population. Between 1900 and 1920, the urban population increased by about 24 million. Urban dwellers increased from about 40 percent of the total population to more than 50 percent. The swelling urban population was made up in part of farm youths leaving home to seek their fortunes in the cities. It was made up in much larger part of the more than 14 million immigrants who poured into the United States between 1900 and 1920. Regardless of the source, however, the growing urban population meant more mouths to feed and a growing demand for farm products. The commercial farmers struggled to meet this demand.

Commercial farms. Some farmers specialized in one, two, or three crops, or in raising dairy cattle or other livestock. Such **commercial farmers** needed money, or capital, to buy machinery and to hire labor. They had to keep careful accounts and to pay careful attention to market conditions. They were, in brief, one part of an abstract thing known as the "nation's economy." When the economy prospered, farmers likewise could hope to prosper. When the economy went into a depression, farmers were certain to suffer accordingly.

The rapidly growing demand for farm products enabled farmers to receive higher prices. Between 1900 and 1920, farm prices increased threefold. In the same period, the average value of farmland quadrupled. As prosperity spread, more and more farmers began to buy agricultural machinery.

Farmers had been using labor-saving machinery long before the turn of the century. Not until after 1900, however, did the shift from hand tools to power-driven machines begin to transform the farming industry. According to census records, in 1870 the total value of all farm implements and machinery in the United States amounted to $271 million. By 1900 the figure had risen to $750 million, by 1920 to $3.6 billion. One revealing measure of the machine age was the use of tractors. In 1910 there were only 1,000 tractors on American farms; by 1920 there were 246,000.

Gasoline and electricity revolutionized rural as well as urban life in the early 1900's. Power-driven machinery—pumps, plows, seeders, harvesters, milking machines, trucks, and tractors—eased the farmers' burden of labor, enabling them to produce far more products with much less toil. However, human sweat and muscle were still necessary on the commercial farms. The need for farm laborers to work on the commercial farms was met in part by an increase in immigration from Mexico and the Philippines, and, for a short time, from Japan.

Growth of scientific agriculture. Scientific knowledge as well as power-driven machinery helped to revolutionize farming. Chemists discovered new fertilizers and better methods of cultivation to stop soil exhaustion and replenish worn-out land. Biologists improved the life span and the productivity of livestock, plants, grains, and fruits. Bacteriologists discovered ways to check blights and diseases in both plants and animals. Scientists also developed new grains and fruits resistant to disease and better adapted to varying climatic conditions.

Federal aid to farmers. Much of the new research and experimentation was carried on by the Department of Agriculture and by the land-grant colleges that were created by the Morrill Act of 1862.

Work by scientists such as this Department of Agriculture chemist greatly improved crop yields.

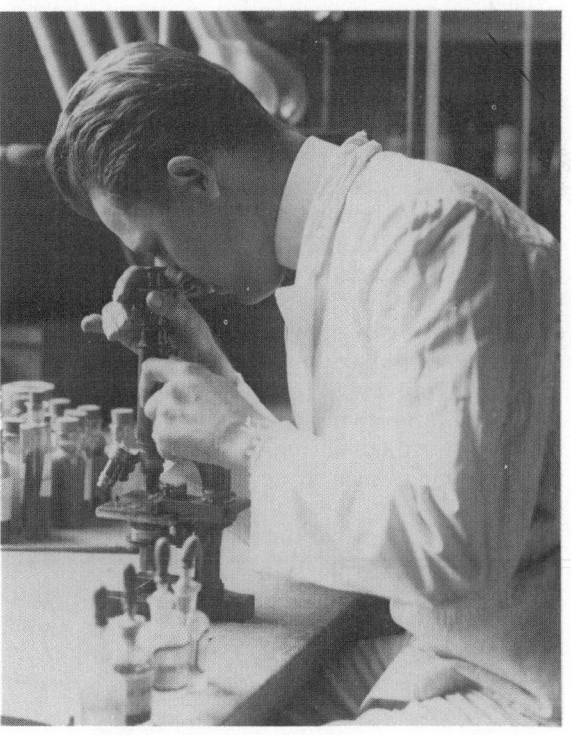

▲ Urban demands for food and rising farm production were accompanied by the growth of a new industry, namely food processing. Many varieties of canned, packaged, and eventually frozen foods appeared in grocery stores.

619

Tractors of the early 1900's were powered by a kerosene engine mounted directly on the frame of the machine.

In later years the federal government greatly expanded this program of aid to farmers. The Hatch Act of 1887, for example, provided money for agricultural experiment stations and farms in each state. The Smith-Lever Act of 1914 provided additional money for the employment of **county extension agents** who carried "practical information on subjects relating to agriculture and home economics" to the farmers of each county. The Smith-Hughes Act of 1917 provided money for the support of vocational education in public schools, including education in agriculture, industries, trade, home economics, and teacher training.

Changing ways of living. The new industrial age altered the everyday lives of farm families, too. By 1920 loneliness and social isolation were becoming memories to many of the nation's farmers. The slender threads of humming telephone wires were spinning a net of communications across the countryside. The automobile—notably Henry Ford's "Tin Lizzie"—was bringing the farm closer to the town and the city. Once a five-mile (eight-kilometer) drive to town had meant a one- or two-hour trip behind "Old Dobbin." By 1920 the same trip could be made in the family car in half an hour or less. This meant more trips to town, often for an evening at the movies.

With increased prosperity, farm families could provide better education for their children. The one-room school continued to dominate the rural educational scene, but more and more farm children came from miles around to enjoy the advantages of consolidated schools, which served several towns or school districts. Many children were able to continue their education at the state university. For farm children, no less than for their parents, life "down on the farm" in the early 1900's was far more comfortable and interesting than it had ever been before.

SECTION REVIEW
See underscored items, text pp. 618-20.

Identify: self-sufficient farmers, commercial farmers, county extension agent

For answers to questions, see Answer Key, p.A86.

1. **Determining Cause and Effect:** How did each of the following affect and change farm life in the years from 1900 to 1920: **(a)** urbanization, **(b)** mechanization, **(c)** scientific agriculture, **(d)** federal aid?

2. **Summarizing Ideas:** What kinds of federal aid were provided to farmers?

3 Conditions improve for industrial workers in the United States

See Teaching Suggestions in TMRG, pp.TM154-55.

Conditions for the industrial worker as well as for the farmer improved considerably during the early 1900's. First, wage earners benefited from the fast-increasing productivity of the American economic system. Second, through organization, wage earners were beginning to exert their influence on state legislatures and on Congress. Third, many Americans were beginning to realize that industrialization had raised serious problems that had to be solved if democracy itself was to survive. Fourth, through articles in magazines and newspapers, the public was becoming aware of the wage earners' grievances.

Early social legislation. To improve the conditions of wage earners, legislators began to pass **social legislation,** as these laws were often referred to. These laws mainly were passed by the northern and western states. The South did little during this period to promote the welfare of workers through state laws.

In general, the first state laws improved working conditions and limited hours of work. As early as 1879, a Massachusetts law prohibited women and children from working more than 60 hours a week. Oregon enacted a similar law in 1903, and other states followed suit. Meanwhile, New York State passed a series of laws protecting workers as well as consumers.

The recognition that certain types of work involved special risk led Utah in 1896 to pass a law limiting the workday of miners to eight hours. In 1902 Maryland passed the first law to compensate workers for on-the-job accidents.

▲ In 1900 Pauline Feldman helped organize the ILGWU (International Ladies Garmet Workers Union). After the terrible fire at the Triangle Shirtwaist Company in New York killed more than 100 workers, she helped pressure the New York legislature to enact work-safety codes.

During most of the years from World War I to World War II, one Supreme Court decision after another bore the comment, "Holmes and Brandeis dissenting." Today many of these dissents have become the law of the land.

After graduating from Harvard Law School, where he achieved its highest academic record, Brandeis spent considerable time doing *pro bono* work—work without pay for public causes. He soon became known as "the people's attorney."

Perhaps Brandeis' most famous legal contribution was the "Brandeis Brief" in *Muller v. Oregon.* In it, Brandeis backed up his legal arguments with statistics to show that long hours damaged women's health. Since then, the use of supporting statistics has become commonplace in the courts.

In 1916 Brandeis became the first Jewish justice appointed to the Supreme Court. In general, he displayed a liberal outlook on social issues. He strongly believed, however, that the power of the federal government should be shared with the states. Brandeis retired from the Supreme Court in 1939.

This law was declared unconstitutional, but New York passed a successful compensation law in 1910, as did Wisconsin in 1911.

In 1912 Massachusetts set a precedent by passing the first minimum wage law. The Massachusetts law established a **minimum wage—** employers could not ask a wage earner to work below this rate.

Supreme Court objections. These early laws represented a new approach to the problems of wage earners in the emerging industrial society. Much of this early social legislation was declared unconstitutional by the Supreme Court. The Court ruled that limiting owners' control over their businesses deprived the owners of part of their property without the "due process of law" guaranteed in the Fifth and Fourteenth Amendments.

The Supreme Court also held that social legislation violated people's rights to **freedom of contract**. According to the Supreme Court, when workers accepted employment and an employer agreed to pay them, a contract had been made even though the terms were not written down. Following this freedom-of-contract line of reasoning, the Supreme Court declared unconstitutional in 1905 a New York law that had fixed a maximum workday of 10 hours for bakers.

Changing court attitudes. Many people argued that it was unrealistic to assume that the individual worker could actually bargain with a corporation that employed thousands of people. They insisted that in reality the Supreme Court was depriving all workers of freedom to bargain with their employers.

Supreme Court justices gradually changed their attitude toward social legislation. Like other citizens, they were influenced by the progressive temper of the times. The justices found other clauses in the Constitution that enabled states to limit people's right to do as they pleased with their property. The Court increasingly held that the Constitution had reserved to each state the power to enact laws necessary to protect the health and well-being of all of its citizens. On these grounds the Supreme Court upheld an Oregon law that provided a 10-hour day for women. This set a precedent for the Court's approval of other social legislation.

Federal labor laws. The states rather than the federal government enacted most of the early social legislation. However, the state laws were ignored, and certain states, especially in the South, lagged behind others. This situation prompted organized labor to seek relief through federal laws.

▲ This is a good opportunity to point out the flexibility of the Constitution and Supreme Court's
interpretation of it. Note that the Court first hampered social legislation on the basis of the
Fifth Amendment. Later it altered its position, finding other clauses that allowed state
regulation of private business operations.

621

Average Annual Wages of Workers 1898 - 1920

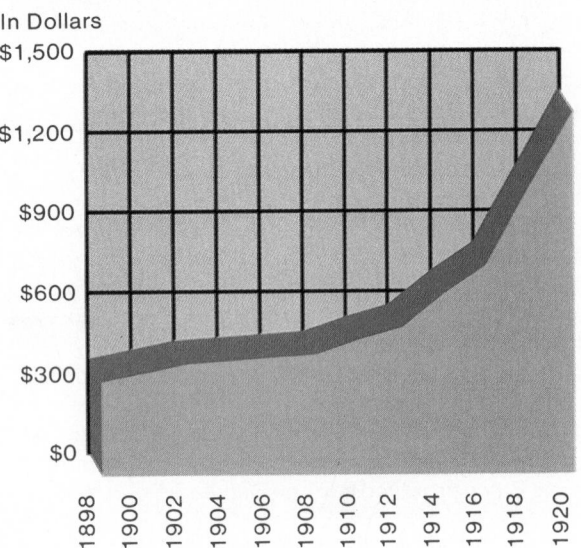

In Dollars

Source: *Historical Statistics of the United States*

Except for its constitutional power "to promote the general welfare" and "to regulate interstate commerce," the federal government had little power to control labor relations. To be sure, the federal government did have the power to control working conditions for its own employees. In 1868, you recall, Congress established an 8-hour day for laborers and mechanics employed by or on behalf of the United States government. In 1892 all federal-government employees were given an 8-hour day.

▲ Later, in 1906, acting under its power "to regulate interstate commerce," Congress passed an Employers' Liability Act. This act protected railroad workers from bearing all the costs of accidents that occurred on the job. Although this law was ruled unconstitutional, later legislation met the Court's objections.

In 1916, when the railroad workers' unions threatened to strike for an 8-hour day, Congress passed the Adamson Act. This act gave railroad workers the same pay for an 8-hour day that they had been getting for a 10-hour day.

During President Wilson's administration, Congress also granted labor's request that it be exempt from the charge of conspiring "to restrain trade." As you have read, the Clayton Antitrust Act of 1914 helped to modify some of the clauses in the Sherman Antitrust Act of 1890 to which labor had objected.

The IWW.   Despite the progress in social legislation, many workers still felt the need to organize to win better working conditions. One union that appeared in the early 1900's was the Industrial Workers of the World (IWW). The IWW was set up as a radical union of skilled and unskilled workers. It demanded the overthrow of the capitalist system by general strikes, boycotts, and sabotage.

The IWW, or "Wobblies" as they were known, won some strikes in western mining and labor camps and in the textile mills of Lawrence, Massachusetts. It lost a textile strike in Paterson, New Jersey. Weakened in the years after by its reputation for violence and by federal prosecution, the IWW after 1918 ceased to be a challenge to more conservative trade unions.

Advances for organized labor.   By the time World War I broke out in Europe in 1914, labor still had many grievances, and it was still far from its goals. Trade-union activities and political methods for achieving the goals had met only partial success. Nevertheless, organized labor could look back upon a number of reforms gained through 50 years of struggle. Perhaps most important, organized labor enjoyed a small but growing measure of public support.

SECTION REVIEW
See underscored items, text pp. 620-22.

Identify: social legislation, minimum wage, freedom of contract, Employers' Liability Act, IWW

For answers to questions, see Answer Key, pp.A86-87.

1. **Summarizing Ideas: (a)** Describe the social legislation passed by the states to aid workers. **(b)** On what grounds did the Supreme Court declare this legislation unconstitutional?

2. **Interpreting Ideas:** Why was it that for many years the federal government did not enact social legislation?

3. **Analyzing Ideas: (a)** Why did the IWW become less important after 1918? **(b)** What did its decline mean for the labor movement?

4. **Studying Graphics:** Look at the graph on this page. Does the evidence it gives indicate that conditions for workers were getting better or worse in the early 1900's? Explain.

▲   Class activity: Ask several students to interview working people to learn about "fringe benefits" now available in the job market. Discuss their findings in class. (health and retirement insurance plans, education, paid vacations and sick days, discounts from certain stores and catalogs, etc.)

Almost from the beginning of colonization, cities have played an important role in United States history. From Charleston in the South to Boston in the North, urban centers developed, producing life styles that often contrasted sharply with the ways of life of farm, plantation, and frontier families. Cities quickly became the centers of colonial life. The colonial urban centers — Boston, New York, Philadelphia, Baltimore, and Charleston — were port cities. As such, they carried on the colonial trade and manufacturing. Urban centers provided workers and large markets for finished goods.

In the newly settled regions across the Appalachians, cities also developed rapidly. By 1830, Cincinnati, Louisville, Pittsburgh and St. Louis formed a wedge of urbanism in an otherwise rural frontier. Rural areas supplied the cities with raw material for their factories, mills, and packing houses. The cities, in turn, provided the goods and services needed by farmers. Detroit, Cleveland, and Buffalo, while founded early, experienced their real growth with the development of canals and lake transportation. Chicago and Milwaukee flourished in the 1850's and 1860's as the West filled with settlers. In the South, urban growth was confined largely to port cities such as New Orleans, Mobile, Savannah, Charleston, Richmond, and Louisville. These ports exported agricultural products to other regions and, like cities everywhere, supplied their trade areas with imports. Even the West produced urban areas. Galveston, Houston, Austin, and San Antonio were all important cities 30 years before the Civil War. Farther west, San Francisco, Denver, Portland and Seattle were important urban settlements on the eve of the Civil War.

When geographers study cities, two terms, site and situation, are used over and over. Site refers to the actual physical qualities of the place occupied by a city. Before the coming of the railroad virtually all important cities were located on navigable water. Railroad networks, and later automobiles, made the intersections of railroad trunk lines and highways attractive new sites for urban growth.

United States Urbanization • 1800 - 1980

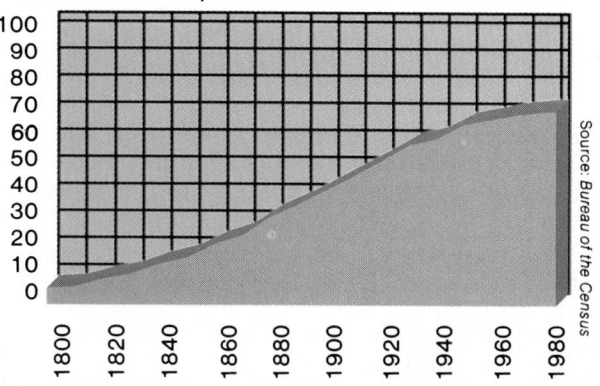

Percent of Total Population

Source: Bureau of the Census

Of even greater importance for urban growth, is situation. Situation refers to the city's geographic relationship to the surrounding area. This area is the city's trade area. The key to this relationship is the accessibility of the trade area. If connections between the city and the trade area are excellent, the city has an ideal situation and will grow and prosper even without the most desirable of sites.

So dominant has the city become in the United States that in 1980, nearly 75 percent of the people lived in places with a population of 2,500 or more. In the older parts of the country, where urban places first developed, a new phenomenon is visible. The northeastern seaboard has become an almost continuous stretch of urban and suburban land. As the French geographer, Jean Gottman, who calls this area "megalopolis" (a city-state) puts it, this region has developed "a kind of supremacy, in politics, in economics, and possibly even in cultural activities, seldom before attained by an area this size." In modern times, the city has become the dominant element of the American landscape.

San Francisco, 1890's (left) and 1980's (right)

═══ DEVELOPING HISTORY STUDY SKILLS ═══

Relating Economics and History   Interpreting a Map for Economic Purposes

- What major resources had been developed in the United States by 1900, and how were they distributed?
- Where were the major manufacturing centers of the period?

A good source for finding such economic information as that listed above is a special purpose map. An economic map is a special purpose map that provides information about the distribution of resources, information on manufacturing, agriculture, trade, transportation, communication, and other economic topics. An economic map is useful in relating geography, history, and economics.

How to Interpret a Map for Economic Purposes

To effectively interpret a map for economic purposes, follow these guidelines.

1. **Read the map.** Follow the guidelines listed on page 164. Pay special attention to the economic information noted in the map key.
2. **Note relationships.** Study the data on the map. Draw conclusions about economic activities.
3. **Use the map's information.** Form hypotheses and draw conclusions about economic activities from the information on the map.

Applying the Skill

Study the map below. Note that the title indicates that it provides information on the distribution of economic activities and natural resources within the United States in 1900.

A check of the key shows that the locations of deposits of the following natural resources are shown on the map: iron ore, petroleum, natural gas, copper, silver, and gold. By closely studying the map, the locations of these deposits can be determined. For example, major deposits of silver and gold are located in the West, copper in the Southwest and Great Lakes region, and iron ore in the Northeast. Note the locations of other resources and the relationships of those locations.

Practicing Your Skill

Again study the map below. Then on a separate sheet of paper, answer these questions.

1. In addition to the location of natural resources, what economic information is presented on the map?
2. According to the map, what economic activity is located in Alabama? West Virginia? Pennsylvania?
3. What conclusions about the location of iron ore and the steel industry in 1900 can be drawn from this map?
4. In what regions of the United States were petroleum deposits found? gold and silver deposits?
5. What conclusions about the abundance of natural resources and the development of industrial areas can be drawn from this map?

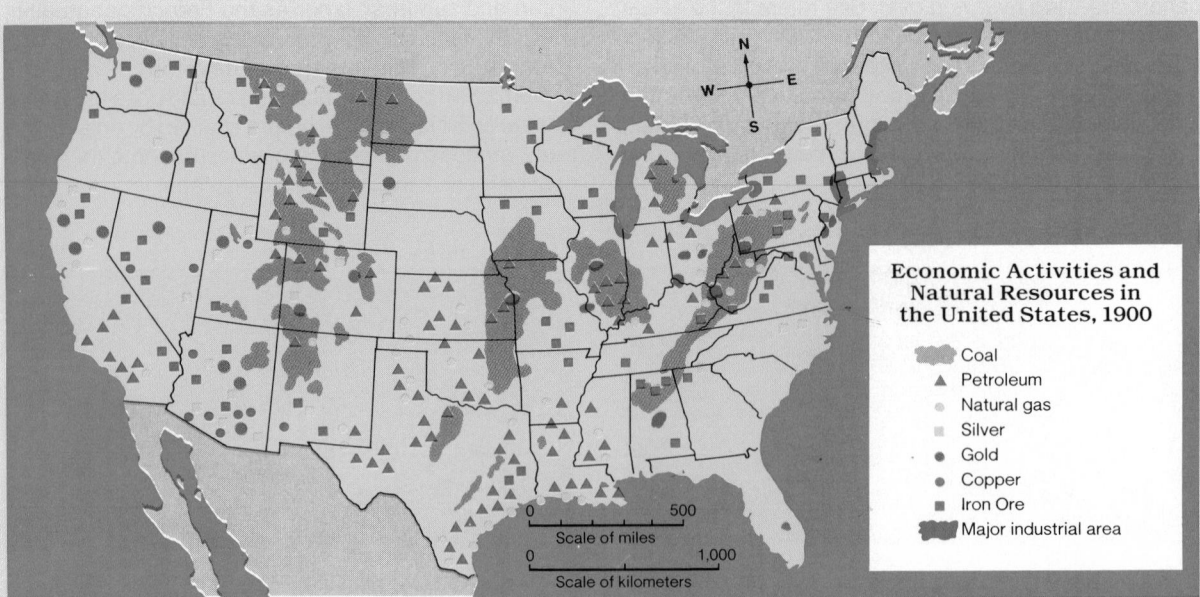

Economic Activities and Natural Resources in the United States, 1900

- Coal
- ▲ Petroleum
- Natural gas
- ■ Silver
- ● Gold
- ● Copper
- ■ Iron Ore
- Major industrial area

located near iron ore deposits.   4.(a) Southwest, Rocky Mountains, Far West
(b) Southwest, Rocky Mountains   5. Nearness to natural resources has been
important to the development of major industrial areas.)

During the years between 1900 and 1920, the United States completed the process of passing from a mainly agricultural economy to a mainly industrial economy. By 1920 the United States had become the most productive industrial nation on the face of the earth.

In 1900, Americans were still living in the horse-and-buggy age. It was, however, a dying age. Old ways were rapidly giving way to new. People living during the years between 1900 and 1920 saw the emergence of automobiles, airplanes, radios, motion pictures, and assembly lines. These and many other developments greatly transformed the ways Americans were living.

The nation's rapidly increasing productivity and its steadily rising standard of living were only the most obvious signs of the new United States. Less obvious, but equally important, were the changes that were beginning to take place in the thinking of great numbers of Americans.

More and more people were altering some of the attitudes and practices that they had carried over from the early days of the Industrial Revolution. More and more people were realizing that organized labor had an important role to play in the new industrial economy. Slowly but surely, Americans were taking the first halting steps toward what Frederick Lewis Allen called "the adjustment of capitalism to democratic ends."

CONNECTING CHAPTER IDEAS

During the years between 1865 and 1890 Americans devoted most of their time and energy to the settlement of the West and the development of a nationwide industrial economy. After 1890, however, Americans came to realize that is was beneficial to become involved in world affairs. In the next chapter you will read how the United States became involved in the Spanish–American War, emerging as a leader in the race for empire with vast holdings in the Pacific.

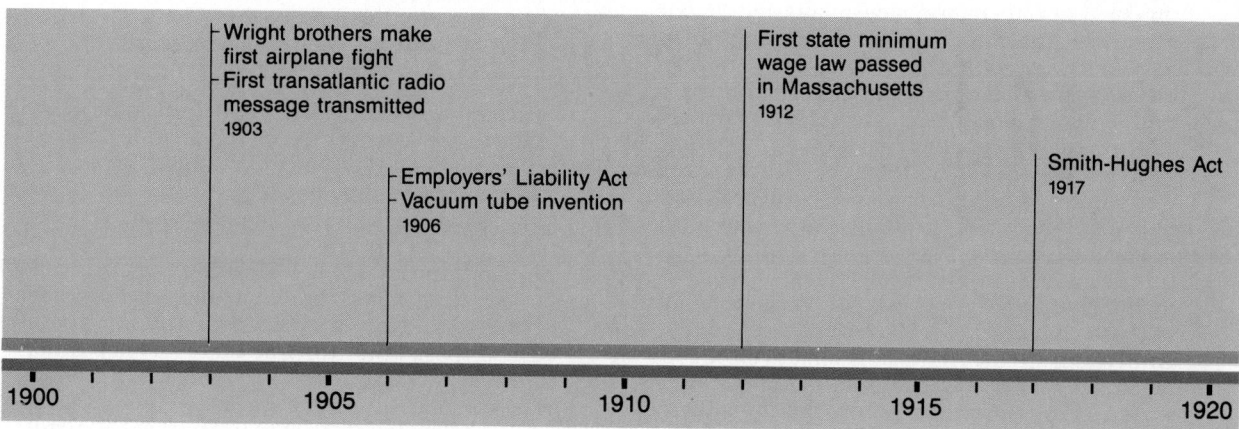

Wright brothers make first airplane fight
First transatlantic radio message transmitted
1903

First state minimum wage law passed in Massachusetts
1912

Employers' Liability Act
Vacuum tube invention
1906

Smith-Hughes Act
1917

1900   1905   1910   1915   1920

CHAPTER
27 REVIEW

Reviewing Important Terms

Decide whether each of the following sentences is true or false. If the sentence is false, replace the underlined word or phrase that will make it true.

1. Tax-reform legislation, passed mainly in northern and western states, helped to improve conditions for workers.
2. In the early 1900's, the Supreme Court held that social legislation violated people's rights to freedom of contract.
3. The use of efficiency engineering increased the productivity of factories.
4. County extension agents were hired through the 1914 Smith-Lever Act to provide information on agriculture and home economics to farmers and their families.
5. By reducing the number of movements of the workers' hands and feet, mass production simplified each production step on the assembly line.
6. Scientific agriculture specialized in a few cash crops and adopted many business techniques from the industry.
7. In the early 1900's many farmers, known as commercial farmers, lived in mountain valleys and other remote areas in much the same manner as farmers and their families had lived 100 years earlier.

Practicing Critical Thinking Skills

1. **Interpreting Ideas. (a)** In what ways did industrialization strengthen the belief that the United States was the land of opportunity? **(b)** In what ways did the revolution in communication help initiate reform movements and contribute to the growth of political democracy? **(c)** By having a national, rather than a local, transportation system, farmers had wider markets as well as more competition. How might this have affected their economic freedom?
2. **Evaluating Ideas.** In 1900 the United States was rapidly passing from an agricultural to an industrial economy. **(a)** What were some of the important changes taking place as a result of this revolution in American industry? **(b)** Why might it have been difficult for people to adjust to these changes?
3. **Analyzing Ideas.** Americans tend to elect Presidents who reflect the spirit of the times. Gather evidence to support or refute this hypothesis, using Theodore Roosevelt, William Howard Taft, or Woodrow Wilson as an example. Can you think of earlier Presidents who reflected the spirit of their times? Explain. Can this be said of any of our most recent Presidents? Explain.
4. **Relating Past to Present.** Compare the attitude of the federal government today toward social legislation with its attitude during the early 1900's. Give specific examples to support your conclusions.

Developing History Study Skills

1. **Interpreting Maps for Economic Purposes.** Study the two maps, Agriculture in the United States (pages 1016–17) and Mineral Resources in the United States (pages 1020–21.) Use the information on these maps to answer the following questions. **(a)** What is the major economic activity of the Southwestern United States? **(b)** What type of occupations would you expect to find in the Northeast? the Southeast? the Midwest? and the West?
2. **Classifying Information.** Use the information in this chapter to classify technological changes between 1900 and 1920. Then write an essay in which you evaluate the three most important changes. (Be sure to explain how you classified the changes you found in the chapter.)

Relating Geography and History

As industrialization grew and urbanization spread, the differences between life in the city and life on the farm increased. Review the major aspects of farm life and city life discussed in Units Seven and Eight. After finishing your review, complete the following activities.

1. Write an essay in which you describe one of the following: a teenager's life on a farm in 1900, or a teenager's life in the city in 1900.
2. After completing your essay, answer this question. What were the major differences between farm life and city life for a teenager in 1900?
3. Research the following legislation from this time period: child labor laws and compulsory school attendance laws. **(a)** What was the purpose of each of these laws? **(b)** Was there any opposition to either of these laws? If so, on what grounds was the opposition based? **(c)** Were these two pieces of legislation related in any way? Explain.

626

UNIT EIGHT
REVIEW

Discussing Ideas

1. (a) What characteristics do you think are necessary for a good President? (b) According to your list, who was the best President—Taft, Roosevelt, or Wilson? Support your answer.

2. Thomas Jefferson and Andrew Jackson both believed with Thoreau that the "government is best which governs least." Do you think this viewpoint became less practical by the early 1900's? Explain your answer by referring to specific events described in Unit Three.

3. (a) Why was there a need for the conservation of natural resources during the late 1800's and early 1900's? (b) What was done to make people aware of the problem? (c) Why might some people have opposed conservation?

4. How did industrialization affect (a) the make-up and location of the nation's population, (b) the daily lives of Americans, (c) differences among the regions of the nation?

Applying History Study Skills

1. **Expressing Viewpoints.** Reread the excerpt from Theodore Roosevelt's "New Nationalism" Speech on page 597 of the textbook and answer the following questions. (a) According to Roosevelt what elements constitute the triumph of "this great republic"? (b) What did Roosevelt mean by a "square deal"?

2. **Interpreting a Political Cartoon.** Analyze the political cartoons found in Unit Eight and complete the following activities for one of the cartoons. (a) Identify the subject of the cartoon. (b) List the symbols used by the cartoonist and explain what each symbol represents. (c) Decide if the cartoonist's view of the subject is positive or negative. What gives you that impression? (d) Refer to the information in this chapter (and reference books, if necessary) to discover the historical events that prompted the cartoonist to create each illustration. Write a paragraph that could be used to replace the cartoon. (e) Select any topic in Unit Three for which no political cartoon appears and develop one. On the back of your cartoon, explain the reasons for selecting the symbols and techniques you used to convey your idea (see page 611).

Making Connections

1. Prepare a report on a national park located in your region. (a) Why was it founded? Under what circumstances? (b) How large is it? (c) What are its main features? If possible, include a map and pictures of the park in your report.

2. Interview an officer of a local bank to learn about the workings of the Federal Reserve System. Prepare a diagram or chart to illustrate how the system operates.

3. Read an article or a book by a muckraker, such as Ida Tarbell's *History of the Standard Oil Company* or Lincoln Steffens' *The Shame of the Cities*. Then write an essay summarizing the main point of the book or article in which you answer the following questions. (a) What arguments does the author use to prove the main point? (b) Do you find the book or article persuasive? Why or why not?

4. Make a list of the political reforms discussed on pages 593–95. (a) How did each reform on your list make politics or government more democratic? (b) What, if any, are the negative aspects of each reform?

Reading in Depth

Cook, Fred J., *Muckrakers: Crusading Journalists Who Changed America* (Garden City, NY: Doubleday). Account of the lives and works of the leading muckrakers.

Hofstadter, Richard, *The Age of Reform: From Bryan to F.D.R.* (New York: Knopf). A classic history of reform and the people involved.

Riis, Jacob, *How the Other Half Lives* (Darby, PA: Darby Press). Written in 1890, this book is a famous exposé of slum conditions.

Sinclair, Upton, *The Jungle* (Cambridge, MA: Bentley). Famous novel of conditions in the meat-packing industry that had a great impact on President Roosevelt.

Washington, Booker T., *Up from Slavery* (Garden City, NY: Doubleday). The autobiography of an ex-slave, who became one of the foremost black leaders in the United States.

UNIT NINE

Becoming a World Power

Between 1898 and 1914 the United States, now an industrial nation, began to look beyond its territorial limits for land and markets. This search for expanded markets meant many changes for the United States. Chief among these changes was a growing involvement in world affairs. One of the nation's first international ventures was the Spanish–American War in which the United States overwhelmed the decaying Spanish empire. In a battle scene from that war shown below, black United States soldiers rescue the Rough Riders from a Cuban fort. Not all battles and not all international ventures, however, were as successful as the one pictured here. By 1920 the United States, disillusioned with war and world affairs, rejected the Treaty of Versailles and returned to more limited involvement in world affairs.

See Chapter Overview in TMRG, p.TM158.
See Chapter Objectives in TMRG, p.TM158.
See Introducing the Chapter in TMRG, p.TM158.

CHAPTER 28 American Expansion Overseas

(1898–1914)

The Great
White Fleet

During much of the nineteenth century, Americans devoted most of their energies to the settlement and development of the continental United States. To be sure, Americans traveled to Europe, and Europeans traveled to America. There was also vigorous trade between the two continents. Nonetheless, after 1865, it was the settlement of the West and the development of a nationwide industrial economy that occupied the American people. There was little attention paid to the affairs of other nations in the world.

By the 1890's, however, a change was taking place in American interests. Americans began to realize there was some benefit to be secured by an interest in world affairs. As the Middle West became a major industrial area, American farmers and business owners became interested in securing new markets where they could sell the surplus products of farms and factories. Some Americans even became interested in acquiring or controlling lands beyond the continental boundaries of the United States because they saw these overseas lands as new markets for American products and as a potential source of unlimited quantities of raw materials.

In this chapter you will learn how Americans acquired a new interest in world affairs. You will learn, too, how they emerged from a brief war in 1898 with Spain, which possessed the Philippine Islands and other islands in the Pacific Ocean. You will learn how this growing Spanish empire in the Pacific created new problems for the United States. You will also discover how United States leaders were forced to develop new policies for dealing with the nations of East Asia in order to protect their growing interests in the Pacific.

═══ READING FOCUS ═══

As you read about American interest in Asia and other overseas lands, look for the details that support each of the following statements.

1. American interest in expansion abroad increases.
2. The war with Spain turns the United States into a colonial power.
3. The United States takes over the Philippines, Hawaii, and Samoa.
4. The United States plays a larger role in East Asia.

1 American interest in expansion abroad increases

See Teaching Suggestions in TMRG, pp.TM158-59.

Great Britain, France, Spain, the Netherlands, and Portugal—these were the old colonial powers. Back in the 1400's and 1500's, they had started their policies of **imperialism**—of establishing colonies and building empires for economic gain, prestige, and missionary purposes. Now, in the mid-1800's, these powers owned and controlled a large portion of the world, but huge areas of it still remained unclaimed.

The new imperialism. During the latter half of the 1800's, there was a mad rush to gain ownership or control of the remaining uncolonized lands. Nations previously little interested in expansion joined the race—among them Belgium, Germany, Italy, Japan, and Russia. Within a few years, the rival colonial powers seized control over almost all of Africa and sliced off large portions of China and other areas in East Asia. By the early 1900's, most of the underdeveloped regions of the world had been divided among the rival colonial empires.

The Industrial Revolution was largely responsible for the mounting interest in colonies. Factories needed raw materials in ever-growing quantities. Manufacturers, to keep their factories operating, had to find new markets for their finished products. Improvements in transportation, especially in the steamship, enabled businesses to buy and sell in a truly worldwide market. As trade increased and profits accumulated, business executives and bankers looked overseas for opportunities to invest savings.

It is not surprising that Great Britain, the world's leading industrial power before 1900, built the largest empire. Right behind Great Britain were France, Belgium, the Netherlands, and Germany. Industrialization in each of these countries was in full swing by the late 1800's.

There were still other reasons for the growth of worldwide imperialism in the late 1800's and the early 1900's. One was the invention of new instruments of warfare, notably repeating rifles and machine guns. By 1900 these new weapons were becoming standard army equipment. With them small bands of

▲ Throughout the Annotated Teacher's Edition, terms listed in the "Identify" portion of a Section Review are underscored the first time they appear. See the Teacher's Manual for each section for a listing of important vocabulary terms.

631

professional soldiers could conquer and control people in underdeveloped regions who did not have similar weapons.

Another reason for the growth of imperialism was the attitude of people in the colonial powers. There were objectors in every country, but, in general, ordinary people were as eager for empire as were leaders of government and business. English factory workers, French shopkeepers, German farmers—these and other solid citizens of the colonial powers were all proud of their country's empire. With this support the governments of the colonial powers were able to spend the huge sums of money needed for armies to occupy the colonial territories and for navies to guard the sea lanes to and from the colonies.

A changing American attitude. Americans, with some exceptions, had never been interested in acquiring colonies. Indeed, Americans had cast off their own colonial status in the American Revolution. Thus American sympathies were with colonial peoples, not with the colonizing powers.

America's lack of interest in acquiring colonies is easy to understand. For 300 years the undeveloped American West was, in a sense, an American colony. Even as late as 1867, when Secretary of State Seward bought Alaska from Russia for just over $7 million, Americans referred to Alaska as "Seward's folly" and "Seward's icebox." It was not until 30 years later, in 1897, when gold was discovered in Alaska, that Americans began to realize what a great bargain they had made.

During the late 1800's, the United States became the world's leading exporter of agricultural products. By 1890, however, it was feeling the competition of agricultural nations such as Canada and Argentina. American growers and processors of grain, livestock, and cotton as well as the manufacturers of agricultural machinery were eager to sell their products abroad. It was not surprising, therefore, that America's agricultural interests in general supported government efforts to open up new markets overseas.

Although by 1890 the United States was rapidly becoming one of the world's leading industrial nations, there was a big difference between American and European businesses. European nations lacked sufficient raw materials and markets at home. They needed firm control of new sources of raw materials and new markets. American businesses, operating in a young and only partly developed country, were not under the same pressure. The country as a whole, and especially the great American West, still offered large supplies of vital raw materials. There were almost limitless opportunities for the sale of manufactured goods and the investment of surplus money within the United States.

However, some American business leaders realized that this situation would not last forever. For this reason, by 1890 American business and agricultural interests were increasingly pleased to have the United States seek overseas for economic opportunities, if not for actual colonies.

American expansionists. Until 1898, at least, American interest in colonies was stimulated not so much by the leaders of big business as by preachers, scholars, politicians, and military leaders.

One advocate of American expansion was Josiah Strong, a Congregational minister and social reformer. His widely read book *Our Country,* written in 1885, argued that the American branch of the "Anglo-Saxon race" was destined to extend its "civilizing" influence to the peoples in Latin America, Asia, and Africa.

An even more influential book was written by Captain Alfred Mahan in 1890 under the title *The Influence of Sea Power upon History, 1660-1783.* Mahan's book attempted to show that the world's greatest nations had risen largely because of their sea power and that greatness depended upon sea power. Therefore, he argued, the United States had to strengthen its navy and also had to secure the control of colonies overseas.

Mahan claimed that colonies were needed as naval bases and as refueling stations, or "coaling stations." He also pointed out that colonies would provide raw materials and markets. Colonies would thereby strengthen the industrial organization on which a modern sea power is forced to rely.

Strengthening the navy. Even before Mahan's book appeared, Congress had taken steps to strengthen the navy. These steps were needed. In 1880, for example, the United States had fewer than 100 "seagoing vessels." Many were "seagoing" in name only, with rusty boilers and rotted planking.

▲ Discussion topic: Mahan's theories were applicable in the days before air power and missile arsenals. Have students consider whether sea power is important today. (Students should consider the priorities placed by modern nations on nuclear-powered navies.)

The situation began to change in 1882, however, when Congress authorized the construction of "two steam-cruising vessels of war." Three years later the Navy Department created the Naval War College at Newport, Rhode Island. About this time the Bethlehem Steel Corporation began to manufacture armor plate—tough steel sheets to protect the hulls and superstructures of warships. By 1895 the "White Squadron," sometimes called the "Great White Fleet," was under construction.

Ready for a new role. By 1895 some American business leaders were beginning to worry that their European competitors might gain control of the markets of underdeveloped areas. A new navy, small but modern and efficient, was ready for action. For these reasons, Americans felt that the United States was destined to play a leading role in world affairs.

SECTION REVIEW

See underscored items, text pp. 631-32.
Identify: imperialism, "Seward's folly," Josiah Strong, Alfred Mahan
For answers to questions, see Answer Key, p.A89.

1. **Organizing Ideas:** How did the Industrial Revolution contribute to the mounting interest among the newly industrialized nations in acquiring colonies?

2. **Interpreting Ideas:** How did the transportation revolution encourage the search for colonies?

3. **Analyzing Ideas:** Why was the United States at first not interested in acquiring colonies?

4. **Comparing Ideas:** Explain how each of the following affected American interest in colonies: (a) closing of the frontier, (b) industrial development, (c) growing power in world affairs.

2 The war with Spain turns the United States into a colonial power

See Teaching Suggestions in TMRG, pp.TM159-60.
The war with Spain, which lasted only a few weeks in the spring and the summer of 1898, marked a turning point in American history. Before the war, the only lands the United States owned beyond its immediate boundaries were Alaska and the Midway Islands. The United States had acquired the Midway Islands in the central Pacific in 1867. Within a few years after the war ended, however, the American flag flew over several islands in the Pacific. The United States was now deeply involved in East Asia, and American influence was strongly felt in the lands bordering the Caribbean Sea.

Trouble in Cuba. Cuba and Puerto Rico, both in the Caribbean, were the last remnants of Spain's once mighty empire in the New World. Spaniards had once called Cuba "the Ever Faithful Isle." In 1868, however, when a violent revolution broke out, the Cubans proved to be something less than faithful to their Spanish rulers. It took Spain ten years to crush this uprising. Spain did so only with a promise of long-awaited reforms, but discontent continued to smolder.

The trouble was that most Cubans worked at starvation wages for extremely wealthy landowners. To make matters worse, the Spanish government's policies, directed from Madrid, managed to anger the wealthier Cuban landowners as well as the landless workers.

Spanish misrule and an economic crisis finally plunged Cuba into another revolution. The United States was partly responsible for the economic crisis. In 1890, you recall, Congress adopted the McKinley Tariff Act. This act allowed Cuban sugar, the major crop of the island, to enter the United States free of duty. As a result, trade between the United States and Cuba prospered, reaching a total of more than $100 million a year. However, in 1894 the United States adopted the Wilson-Gorman Tariff Act. This act placed a 40-percent duty on all raw sugar imported into the United States. When the 1894 tariff went into effect, sugar piled up in Cuban warehouses, plantations closed, and thousands of Cubans lost their jobs.

Revolution in Cuba. Angered by the economic crisis and by Spain's failure to provide the long-promised reforms, the Cubans again revolted in 1895. Bands of revolutionists roamed through the countryside, killing, burning, and plundering.

The Spaniards, led by General Valeriano Weyler, nicknamed "The Butcher," responded savagely. General Weyler ordered all people living in territory controlled by the revolutionists into concentration camps run by the

Spaniards. Spanish soldiers then marched through the abandoned countryside, destroying buildings and putting to death all persons found in the area without permission. What the revolutionists had not destroyed during earlier raids, the Spaniards did. Large areas of Cuba were reduced to utter ruin. Starvation and disease plagued the land.

Growing American sympathy. Legally, the revolution in Cuba was no concern of the United States. Spain was a sovereign, independent nation, free to do as it pleased with its own colonies. This was freely admitted by the American government, which officially adopted a policy of neutrality.

However, the effects of the revolution were not confined to Cuba. The revolutionists themselves did everything possible to win American sympathy and support. They waged a vigorous propaganda campaign in America. José Martí, one of Hispanic America's greatest prose writers, aroused sympathy for Cuba by his persuasive articles. The revolutionists also bought quantities of American arms and ammunition, which they smuggled into Cuba.

The revolution also affected some American pocketbooks. Before the uprising began, Americans had invested more than $50 million in Cuban plantations, transportation projects, and businesses. These investments were in danger. Moreover, trade between Cuba and the United States was crippled by the revolution.

As months passed, more and more Americans expressed their sympathy for the revolutionists. They recalled their own struggle for freedom during the American Revolution.

American newspapers helped to inflame public opinion. Two New York papers— William Randolph Hearst's New York *Journal* and Joseph Pulitzer's New York *World*—were especially active in supporting the revolutionists. These publishers quickly discovered that sales skyrocketed when they printed sensational stories and pictures of the Spanish atrocities in Cuba.

Newspapers in other towns and cities quickly copied the financially successful methods of Hearst and Pulitzer. Before long, many Americans, feeding on the sensational stories and pictures, clamored for intervention. By 1898 even the more conservative newspapers, including weekly religious journals, insisted that the United States had the moral responsibility of restoring order in Cuba.

McKinley's attempts to avoid war. When President William McKinley was inaugurated on March 4, 1897, he strongly opposed war. The United States was just emerging from the depression that had started in 1893. The President, many of his advisers, and business leaders in general feared that war, or even the threat of war, would throw the country back into a depression. For nearly a year, the President held to an official policy of neutrality, but early in 1898 several events forced his hand.

On February 9, 1898, American newspapers headlined a letter written by the Spanish minister to the United States. In the letter, Dupuy De Lôme (LOH·may) described President McKinley as "weak and a bidder for the admiration of the crowd" and as a "would-be politician." The Spanish minister had written the letter to a friend in Havana. It was not meant for publication. Indeed, it had been stolen from the mails and sold to the press, but the harm was done. Unthinking Americans concluded that the uncomplimentary remark reflected the attitude of all Spaniards.

On February 16, Americans read even more startling news in their papers. The night before, the United States battleship *Maine,* which had been sent to Cuba in January to protect American lives and property, had sunk in Havana harbor with the loss of more than 250 American lives. Its captain stated that there had been an explosion of unknown origin and urged that "public opinion should be suspended until further report." In Havana flags flew at half-mast, theaters and places of business were closed, and expressions of sympathy were sent to Washington. All of this was brushed aside by the public. People jumped to the conclusion that the Spaniards had destroyed the ship. "Remember the *Maine!*" quickly became a national slogan.

Despite these incidents, President McKinley refused to declare war. Assistant Secretary of the Navy Theodore Roosevelt declared that the President "has no more backbone than a chocolate éclair." However, McKinley still hoped for a peaceable solution.

Spanish concessions. Late in March, with the President's approval, the Department of State sent an **ultimatum°** to Spain. In the ul-

°**ultimatum:** in diplomatic language, a final statement of terms whose rejection may lead to the breaking off of diplomatic relations or to war.

timatum the United States demanded that Spain (1) immediately cease all fighting and grant an armistice to the revolutionists, (2) negotiate with the Cubans for self-government or independence, and (3) abolish the concentration camps.

On April 9 the Spanish government accepted the ultimatum. The Spaniards hedged on the issue of independence, but the American minister in Madrid felt that with patience independence for Cuba could be achieved. In cabling the good news to President McKinley, he added, "I hope that nothing will now be done to humiliate Spain."

War declared. Despite the Spanish concession, on April 11, 1898, President McKinley asked Congress to intervene in Cuba. It seemed that the war spirit had proved too strong for the President to resist.

On April 19 Congress by large majorities voted to use the land and naval forces of the United States to secure full independence for Cuba. Congress also adopted the Teller Resolution. This resolution stated that the United States claimed no "sovereignty, jurisdiction, or control" over Cuba. The United States wanted only to **pacify,** or bring peace to, the besieged Caribbean island. The resolution promised that once Cuba was free the United States would "leave the government and control of the island to its people."

Victory in the Pacific. Curiously enough, American fighting in the "war for Cuban liberty" started not in Cuba but in the Pacific. For weeks before Congress declared war, Theodore Roosevelt, the Assistant Secretary of the Navy, had been preparing for any developments. Roosevelt had sent orders to Commodore George Dewey, in command of a fleet anchored at Hong Kong, to prepare for action. When Dewey learned that war had been declared, he promptly headed for the Philippine Islands, the center of Spanish power in the Pacific.

On the night of April 30, 1898, Dewey's six ships slipped past the fortress of Corregidor and into the harbor of Manila, capital of the Philippines (see map, this page). At daybreak on May 1, the American warships opened fire. Their guns outranged those of the Spanish vessels, and by noon the one-sided battle was over. The Spaniards lost nearly 170 men and all their vessels. The Americans lost one man—who died of heatstroke.

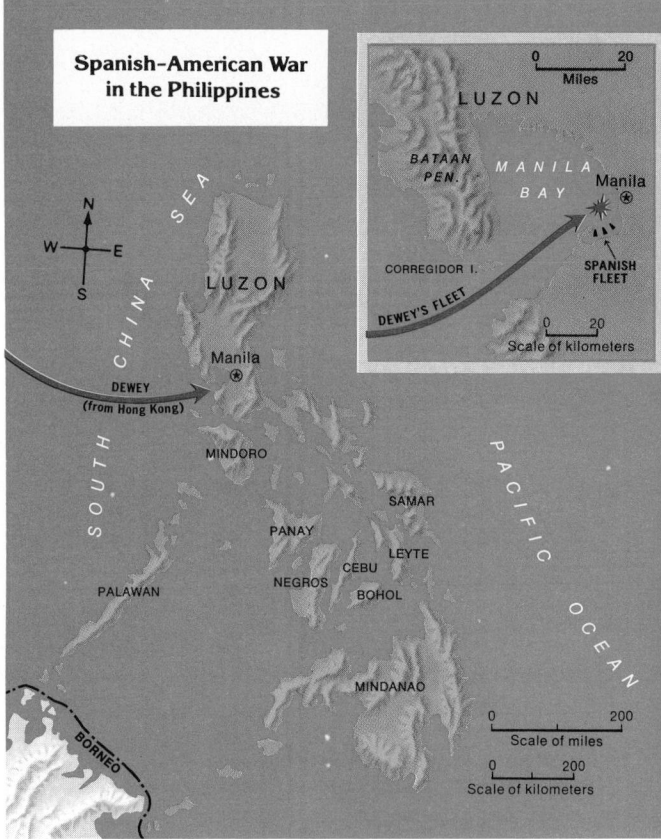

Spanish–American War in the Philippines

Although Commodore Dewey controlled Manila harbor, he did not have the forces to seize the city. While he waited for the force to arrive from the United States, he sent weapons to a band of Filipinos led by Emilio Aguinaldo (ah·gwee·NAHL·doh). The Filipinos, eager to throw off Spanish rule and win their independence, prepared to attack Manila.

Two months passed. Then, early in August, American transports arrived with a strong landing party. The Spanish position was hopeless. Cut off by Dewey's warships, surrounded by Filipino revolutionists, and faced with an attack by an American army, Manila surrendered on August 13, 1898.

Victory in the Caribbean. Meanwhile, on April 29, Spain's Atlantic fleet under Admiral Cervera (sair·VAIR·ah) had sailed westward from the Cape Verde Islands for Cuba (see map, page 636). The Spaniards slipped into the harbor at Santiago, Cuba, for refueling. Here they were bottled up by an American squadron commanded by Admiral William T. Sampson and Commodore W. S. Schley.

▲ McKinley was caught in a web of events and opinions—widespread American tendencies to blame Spain for the "Maine" (evidence pointed to a mine that could well have been planted by Cuban rebels), Spanish pride that would not permit surrender, and the Cuban rebels' unwillingness to give Spain any diplomatic maneuvering opportunity.

635

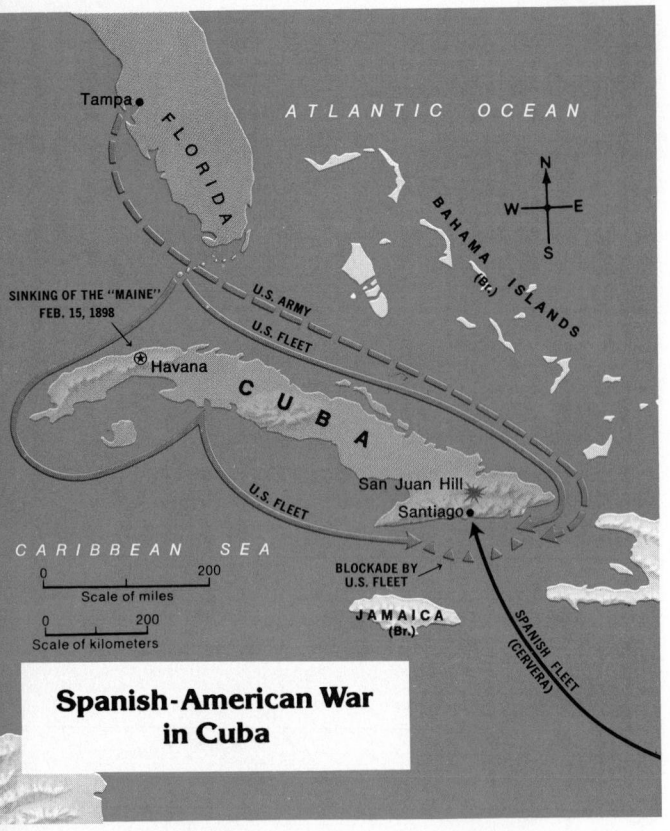

Spanish-American War in Cuba

sonal direction of Clara Barton, provided such aid as it could.

On June 24 the two armies clashed. Slowly, fighting hard, the Americans under General William Shafter pushed the Spaniards back through the fortified village of El Caney and across San Juan Hill (see map, this page). By July 2, American forces had advanced to within a short distance of Santiago. It was this fact that led Admiral Cervera to make his desperate attempt to escape with the Spanish fleet. The destruction of the Spanish navy was the final blow. The Spanish commander at Santiago surrendered his forces on July 17, just 15 days after Cervera's defeat.

Black soldiers, who had not been allowed to mix with white troops on the ships carrying them to Cuba, fought well in several engagements. Frank Knox, later to be Secretary of the Navy, wrote home that he had never seen "braver men anywhere." He added, "Some of those who rushed up the hill will live in my memory forever."

Many Cuban patriots also fought and gave their lives for the freedom of their country. Among them was Cuba's great leader, José Martí, who was one of the first to die in the Battle of Dos Rios.

Meanwhile another American army, under General Nelson A. Miles, landed on the Spanish island of Puerto Rico, east of Cuba. The Americans encountered almost no opposition and by the end of July were in control of the island.

The rewards of victory. The United States entered the war claiming that it was fighting merely to free the oppressed Cubans. It ended the war with an empire on its hands.

American and Spanish commissioners met in Paris in October 1898 to negotiate a peace treaty. By the terms of the treaty, Spain surrendered all claim to Cuba. In addition, Spain ceded to the United States the following territories: Puerto Rico; the Pacific island of Guam; and the Philippines—in exchange for which the United States agreed to pay Spain $20 million. The United States also acquired Wake Island in the Pacific. American armed forces had landed on Wake on July 4, 1898. Congress later annexed Wake.

The Cuban and Puerto Rican people did not share fully in the fruits of victory. As you will read, their hopes and expectations of freedom and independence were only partly realized.

On Sunday morning July 3, 1898, Cervera's fleet left Santiago and made a dash through the American blockade for the open sea. The fleet was met by murderous fire and not a single Spanish vessel managed to escape.

Fighting in Cuba. The War Department was quite unprepared for fighting on land. When the war began, the regular army numbered fewer than 30,000 officers and troops, including four regiments of black soldiers. It was scattered in small contingents all across the country.

More than 200,000 Americans immediately volunteered for war service, including four more units of black soldiers and Theodore Roosevelt. Roosevelt resigned as Assistant Secretary of the Navy to lead the "Rough Riders."

The first American troops to arrive in Cuba were improperly trained and equipped. The food was poor, and the army was without adequate hospital and sanitary facilities. Hundreds of American soldiers died needlessly from dysentery, typhoid, malaria, and yellow fever. The American Red Cross, under the per-

Joseph Pulitzer (1847–1911), Hungarian-born publisher of the New York *World,* left in his will a $500,000 fund to endow annual prizes for distinguished achievement in American journalism and letters. The bequest was part of a $2 million gift to establish a school of journalism at Columbia University, which would administer the awards.

The Pulitzer Prizes have been awarded each May since 1917 in accordance with the founder's wishes. Columbia, however, has expanded the scope and variety of the awards. Prizes are now awarded in several categories of newspaper work, ranging from local reporting to editorial cartoons. The prizes in letters are awarded to works of fiction, nonfiction, poetry, drama, history, biography, and autobiography. A prize for musical composition is also awarded annually. The monetary value of each award is $1,000; its prestige, however, is immeasurable.

Until 1898, except for the Midway Islands, the United States owned no overseas possessions. When the Senate ratified the peace treaty, however, the United States became a colonial power.

▲ The expansionists—the followers of Alfred Mahan, Theodore Roosevelt, and others—were delighted. Many other Americans were deeply troubled. Was it wise and proper, they asked, for the United States to join the European powers in the race for empire?

SECTION REVIEW
See underscored items, text pp. 634-36.

Identify: José Martí, William Randolph Hearst, Joseph Pulitzer, ultimatum, Teller Resolution, Commodore Dewey, Emilio Aguinaldo, Admiral Cervera, "Rough Riders"

For answers to questions, see Answer Key, p.A89.

1. **Determing Cause and Effect: (a)** What were the causes of the Cuban revolt against Spain? **(b)** Why did this revolt affect the United States?

2. **Organizing Ideas:** How did each of the following help bring about the war with Spain: **(a)** sensational press coverage, **(b)** the De Lôme letter, **(c)** destruction of the *Maine*, **(d)** American investments and trade with Cuba?

3. **Analyzing Ideas: (a)** Where did the war over Cuban independence actually begin? **(b)** Why?

4. **Seeing Relationships:** The war with Spain marked a turning point in American history. Explain.

5. **Studying Maps:** Study the map on page 635. **(a)** What does the red arrow indicate? **(b)** On the large map, locate the area illustrated by the inset map. When Dewey captured Manila, did he have any opposition? How can you tell from the map?

3 The United States takes over the Philippines, Hawaii, and Samoa

See Teaching Suggestions in TMRG, p.TM160.

The Philippine Islands presented the American nation with a difficult problem: Should the United States set the islands free, just as it intended to set Cuba free? Or should it force the Filipinos to accept American rule?

American dilemma. President McKinley wrestled with this problem. Finally he decided to establish American rule in the Philippine Islands. As he later explained, the United States could not return the Philippines to Spain, for "that would be cowardly and dishonorable." It could not give them to France, Germany, or Great Britain, for "that would be bad business and discreditable." It could not turn them over to the Filipinos, for they were "unfit

▲ Business and popular opinion were also fervently expansionist. The minority, anti-expansionist opinion, argued that expansion violated the spirit of the Declaration of Independence. Included in this group were Andrew Carnegie, Samuel Gompers, Mark Twain, and Jane Addams.

for self-government." McKinley concluded, "There is nothing left for us to do but to take them all, and to educate the Filipinos, and uplift and civilize and Christianize them."

President McKinley's motives were better than his knowledge of the facts. His reference to "Christianizing" the Filipinos ignored the fact that many had long since been converted to Catholicism. A major exception was the Moros, a group of people who were Muslims.

Divided public opinion. Many Americans agreed with McKinley that it was America's duty to "educate" and "uplift and civilize and Christianize" the Filipinos. Others hoped to profit economically by following the path of world empire. Still others believed that America needed the islands as naval and military bases.

Opponents of imperialism viewed the decision with serious misgivings. They argued that in taking the Philippines the United States was violating its own Declaration of Independence and the principle that people had the right to live under a government of their own choice. "It will be only the old tale of a free people seduced by false ambitions and running headlong after riches and luxuries and military glory," warned Carl Schurz, a prominent Republican. A few opponents, including some blacks, argued that imperialism was based in

part on the false assumption of white racial superiority. They argued that American expansion abroad could only work to the disadvantage of blacks seeking to improve their lives in the United States.

Conquest and early rule. The conquest of the Philippines turned out to be more difficult than the defeat of Spain. The Filipinos, led by Emilio Aguinaldo, fought as fiercely against American rule as they had against Spanish rule. For three years 70,000 American troops fought in the islands at a cost of $175 million and with a casualty list as high as that of the war with Spain. By 1902, however, the American forces were finally victorious.

Despite this unhappy beginning, the United States tried to live up to McKinley's promise "not to exploit, but to develop; to civilize, to educate, to train in the science of self-government." In the Philippine Government Act of 1902, Congress set up a government for the islands. The act provided for an appointed governor, a small elected assembly, and an appointed upper house. The United States Congress could veto all legislation. The plan did not go into effect until 1907. Meanwhile, William Howard Taft, the first governor, ruled wisely. He cooperated closely with the Filipinos and included many Filipinos in the new government.

(The cartoonist treats it lightly. • as mischievous children • by the Uncle Sam figure • a belt • gives Aguinaldo a "whipping") /

Many Americans did not take the Filipino fight for independence seriously. What was the cartoonist's view? How are the Filipinos represented here? How is the United States
▲ *represented? What is Uncle Sam holding? What does he intend to do?*

Filipino dissatisfaction. Many Filipinos wanted full self-government—nothing less. Their dissatisfaction became apparent in 1907 when the elected lower house met for the first time. Three quarters of the representatives were pledged to work for independence. Their hopes rose in 1913 when Woodrow Wilson became President of the United States. Leading Democrats had opposed the conquest of the Philippines, and the Democratic Party had pledged itself to grant independence at the earliest possible date.

These hopes, however, were soon dashed. The Jones Act of 1916 did give the Filipinos the right to elect the members of both houses of the legislature. However, Congress did not grant independence but merely promised it "as soon as a stable government can be established."

Meanwhile conditions in the islands improved. Highways, railroads, and telegraph and telephone lines were built. Education reduced illiteracy from 85 percent in 1898 to 37 percent in 1921. Disease was greatly reduced and Filipino health steadily improved. Exports and imports swelled in volume as American tariffs on products from the Philippines were reduced and finally removed. Most important of all, the United States eventually kept its promise to set the islands free.

Early relations with Hawaii. Before 1865 the United States relations with the Hawaiian Islands were through traders and missionaries (see map, page 640). After 1865 American businesses began to develop the resources of Hawaii—chiefly sugar cane and pineapples. In 1875 Hawaii signed a treaty with the United States. In return for the right to sell sugar in the United States without payment of any duty, the Hawaiians promised not to sell or lease territory to any foreign power. In 1887, when this treaty was renewed, the United States leased Pearl Harbor as a naval base.

Native Hawaiians became increasingly alarmed as the wealth and power of the islands passed into foreign hands. Finally, led by Queen Liliuokalani (leh·LEE·woh·kah LAH·nee), they announced their intentions to end foreign influence.

Revolution and annexation. The American businesses in Hawaii, aided by influential Hawaiians, met this challenge by starting a revolution on January 16, 1893. The American minister to Hawaii quickly intervened. Claim-

Queen Liliuokalani, the last monarch of Hawaii, wanted to reduce the influence of American business groups and missionaries over the affairs of the native Hawaiians.

ing that he was acting only to protect American lives and property, he requested the aid of marines conveniently at hand on a nearby warship. The Hawaiian soldiers, concluding that the marines had come to help the revolutionists, refused to fight. The new government, controlled by the foreign business interests and the missionaries, asked to be annexed to the United States. The American minister promptly raised the Stars and Stripes, and on February 1, 1893, marines began to patrol the islands.

When news of these events reached the United States, furious protests poured into Congress. Many Americans did not want island territory. They were indignant at the manner in which American marines had been used in Hawaii. They were also afraid that overseas expansion would lead to heavy military expenditures.

President Cleveland sent a commission to Hawaii to investigate. The commission ordered the American flag hauled down and heard evidence from both sides. The commission found that the revolution had been started largely by

▲ By 1820, the Hawaiian Islands were already recognized as an important way station en route to China. There had been a movement to annex the Islands in 1854, but Hawaiian insistence on statehood killed the resolution.

639

American business groups, aided by the American minister and the marines, and that the Hawaiians had no desire to be annexed.

After studying the report, Cleveland concluded that Queen Liliuokalani should be returned to her throne. To do this would require the exercise of American force against the new government. By now Congress was fed up with the whole affair, and in 1894 it adopted a resolution refusing to interfere further in Hawaii.

Then came the war with Spain, which generated a new spirit in America. The question of Hawaii once again was brought up on the floor of Congress. This time, in 1898, by an overwhelming vote the islands were annexed to the United States and given territorial status.

American control of Samoa. As in Hawaii, American interests in the Samoan Islands were of long standing. In 1878 the United States secured from a Samoan chief the right to use the harbor of Pago Pago (PAHN·goh PAHN·goh) on the island of Tutuila (too·too·EE·lah) as a naval base. The Samoans granted similar privileges to Germany and Great Britain.

The three countries—Great Britain, Germany, and the United States—then scrambled to control the islands. At one point, in 1889, a naval clash among the three powers was narrowly avoided, largely because a typhoon blew the rival squadrons out to sea.

Finally, in 1899, the British withdrew and the islands were divided between Germany and the United States. Germany later lost control of its share of the islands when it was defeated in World War I. Tutuila, with its excellent harbor of Pago Pago, remained in the hands of the United States and became a major naval base in the Pacific.

SECTION REVIEW

See underscored items, text pp. 638-39.

Identify: William Howard Taft, Jones Act, Queen Liliuokalani

For answers to questions, see Answer Key, pp. A89-90.

1. **Drawing Conclusions:** Did the United States violate the Declaration of Independence when it took the Philippines?

2. **Interpreting Ideas:** The scramble for the Samoan Islands demonstrated the rivalry among nations to acquire colonies. Explain.

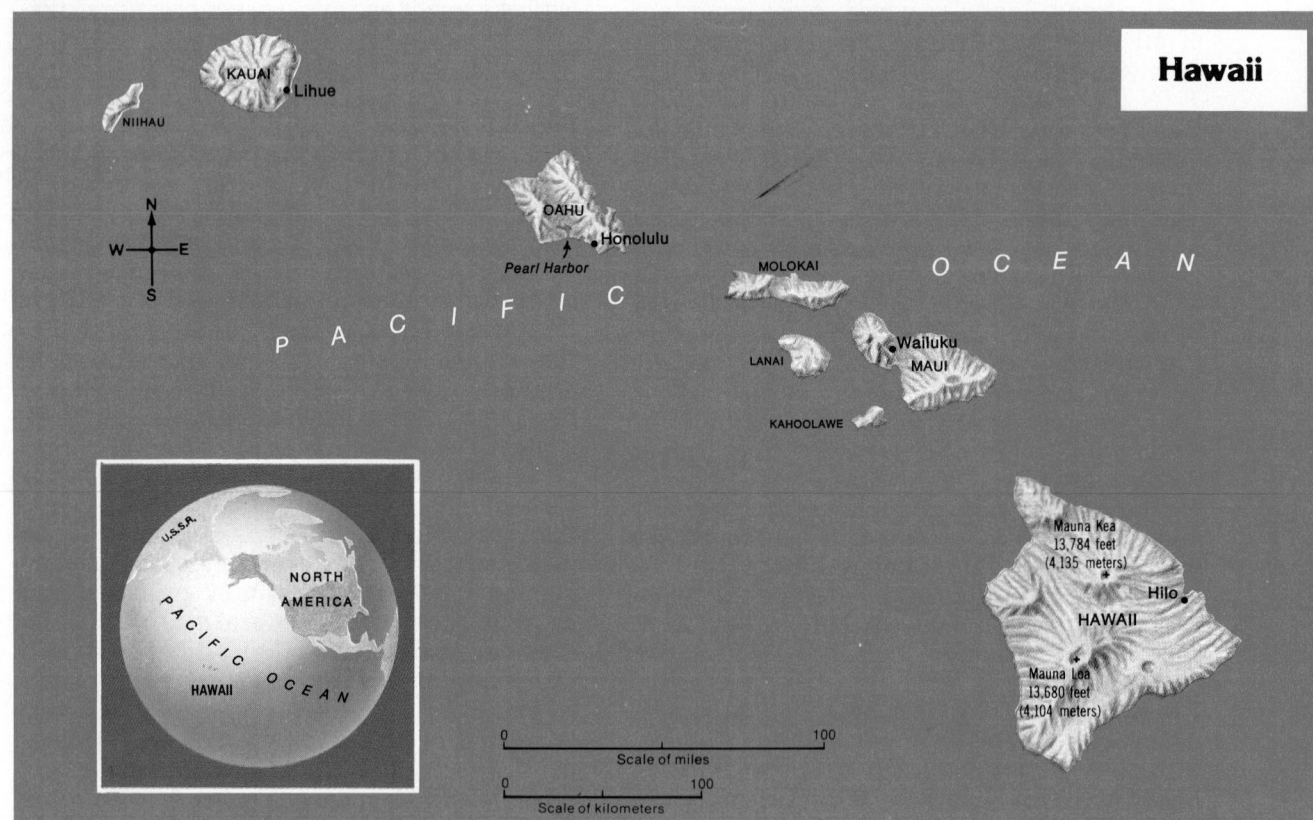

4 The United States plays a larger role in East Asia

See Teaching Suggestions in TMRG, pp.TM160-61.

In 1900 United States territory in the Pacific included Hawaii, Midway, Guam, Wake, the Philippine Islands, and part of Samoa. With this new territory the American people assumed heavy responsibilities. These new responsibilities led to a change in the United States' relations with China.

Early relations with China. America's interest in China began in the 1780's with profitable trade between the two countries. By the early 1800's, the China trade had become a flourishing business. Ships from Philadelphia, New York, and New England ports made the long, hazardous voyage around South America and up the West Coast to the Pacific Northwest. There they traded with the Indians, exchanging blankets, axes, guns, and other goods for furs. When they had a full cargo of furs, they sailed for China. There they traded the furs for tea, silk, porcelain, jade, and other valuable goods. Many merchants and shipowners in the United States and many European countries made fortunes from the China trade.

As time passed, China's rulers grew disturbed at the influence of foreigners on their country. When China placed restrictions on British traders, however, Great Britain waged a successful war (1839–42) and forced the Chinese to open certain **treaty ports** to British trade.

Americans demanded and secured similar trading privileges. The American envoy to China, Caleb Cushing, negotiated a treaty that gave the United States all the trading privileges granted by China to other nations. In addition the treaty gave Americans the right of **extraterritoriality.** This meant that Americans in China who were charged with violations of Chinese laws had the right to be tried in American courts in China. Other foreign nations also secured similar privileges.

Crisis in China. These concessions from China encouraged foreign traders to settle there. As time passed, outsiders, including missionaries from the United States and other countries, exercised growing influence. Many of the imperialistic powers were interested in East Asia. The United States seemed least eager of all to grab Chinese territory. As a result, relations remained friendly throughout the 1800's.

In the 1890's, however, a major crisis developed. Japan entered the race for colonies with an attack upon China in the Sino-Japanese War of 1894–95. In this war Japan won the large island of Formosa, territory on the Shantung Peninsula, and control of Korea.

Germany, Russia, Great Britain, and France rushed in to seize their share of China. It appeared that China would soon be carved up and divided by European powers.

The Open Door Policy. The crisis in China posed a problem for the United States. John Hay, who became Secretary of State in 1898, had a solution for the problem. He sent a note to all the powers concerned seeking two assurances. Hay asked (1) that they would keep open all "treaty ports" and (2) that they would guarantee to all nations engaged in trade with China equal railroad, harbor, and tariff rates.

In short, Hay asked for an Open Door Policy. Such a policy would insure American businesses the opportunity to compete on equal terms with other traders in China. Although the response to his note was not encouraging, Hay announced on March 20, 1900, that the Open Door Policy was in effect.

The Boxer Rebellion. Understandably, the Chinese resented the efforts of others to control their country. On the rising tide of resentment, the Chinese launched a movement to drive all "foreign devils" from their country. The movement was led by a Chinese secret society that westerners called "the Boxers."°

In the spring of 1900, the Boxers suddenly attacked. They killed about 300 foreigners in north China, surrounded the foreign area in Tientsin (TIN·TSIN), and besieged the foreign legations in Peking, where men and women from many nations gathered for protection.

The foreign powers promptly rushed troops to relieve the besieged people. The force included 2,500 American troops from the Philippines as well as military units from Japan and several European nations. By August 14 the

°**the Boxers:** the Chinese name for this society literally meant "righteous harmonious band." Westerners wrongly translated the Chinese name to "righteous harmonious *fists*" and hence called the society "the Boxers."

● Though it was a bold step away from the isolationism of the time, the Open Door Policy could probably never have been backed by military force. This diplomacy worked for about 10 years because imperialist nations tried to avoid a major war among themselves.

641

In March 1932 *The Good Earth* was published in the United States. The novel, set in China, told the story of a poor peasant named Wang and his rise to prominence. The book was a best-seller for 21 months, won the Pulitzer Prize for literature, and was translated into more than 50 languages. The American Academy of Arts and Letters later cited it as "the most distinguished work of American fiction" published in the years 1930–35.

The author of this remarkable work was Pearl Buck, an American woman with a deep understanding of Chinese society. Buck, whose parents were Presbyterian missionaries, grew up in a Chinese community, speaking Chinese before English. When she was 17, Buck returned to the United States to attend college. After graduation, she went back to China to teach. There she met and married John Buck, a missionary. The couple lived in a small village like the one described in *The Good Earth*.

Pearl Buck began writing fiction in the mid-1920's. *The Good Earth* was her second published novel. In the next five years she produced two more novels about the Wang family, biographies of her mother and her father, and several other books. In 1938 Buck was awarded the Nobel Prize for literature, the first American woman to receive this honor.

Before her death, Buck published over 60 books, many of them with Asian backgrounds. She also became deeply concerned with the problems of the displaced, orphaned, and abandoned children of the world and founded several organizations to care for such children.

force had relieved the foreigners in Tientsin and Peking, but not before 65 of the besieged had been killed.

The Boxer Rebellion provided an excellent excuse to seize additional Chinese territory, but John Hay took a firm stand in opposition. On July 3, even while the expeditionary force was fighting its way inland to Peking, he announced that the United States wanted to "preserve Chinese territorial and administrative entity . . . and safeguard for the world the principle of equal and impartial trade with all parts of the Chinese Empire."

Largely because of American influence, China did not lose any territory as a result of the Boxer Rebellion. China did, however, have to pay the foreign powers $333 million as compensation for loss, damage, and injury. The

American share amounted to about $24 million. Half of this sum the United States government turned over to American citizens to compensate them for losses of personal property in China. The American government returned the rest of the money to China.

Grateful for this American action, the Chinese government used the money to send Chinese students to the United States. This fund enabled thousands of China's ablest youth to study in American colleges and universities. These students helped to build closer understanding between the two countries.

The Open Door Policy in China had other far-reaching results. It immediately involved the United States in the affairs of Russia and Japan, both of whom were expanding their influence in East Asia.

The opening of Japan. Before 1853 the Japanese had lived in almost complete isolation from the rest of the world. Japan's rulers forbade foreigners to enter Japan. Only the Dutch had won the right to carry on a limited amount of trade through one small Japanese port. In 1853, however, Japan's isolation was shattered when Commodore Matthew C. Perry arrived in Japanese waters with a squadron of American naval vessels. Perry demanded an audience with the Japanese rulers.

The presents that the Americans and Japanese exchanged during a conference in 1854 symbolized the difference between the two countries. The United States received gifts of silk, brocades, lacquerware, and other fine handmade articles. The Japanese received tokens of the new industrial world—a telegraph set, guns, and model railroad trains.

As a result of this conference and a later one, the United States and Japan signed the Treaty of Kanagawa. With this treaty both countries expressed a desire for peace, friendship, and developing trade. Japan also agreed to open two ports to United States trading vessels. Later, Japan opened other ports.

Japan's search for empire. Few events in modern history have had such far-reaching effects as the opening of Japanese ports. Two major developments followed at once. First, American and other traders started a lively commerce with Japan that grew to large proportions in the 1900's. Second, Japanese leaders were convinced that they should adopt the industrial techniques of the western nations.

By the late 1800's, Japan was a transformed country. However, the "new" Japan faced new problems. Knowledge of science, medicine, and sanitation had reduced the death rate, and the lower death rate meant a larger population. This created difficulties, for Japan was small, without enough farmland to feed its people adequately. The Japanese also needed raw materials for their new factories and markets for their products.

Faced with these problems, Japan started upon a program of imperialism similar to that being followed by other industrial nations. Japan needed colonies to secure food for its surplus population and to provide raw materials and markets for its growing industries. Thus Japan entered the race for empire and became one of the contestants in the struggle for control of East Asia.

As you have seen, Japan started its career as an imperial power with an attack upon China in the Sino-Japanese War of 1894–95. Ten years later Japan plunged into another war, this time with Russia.

The United States in the Pacific. Although the Russo-Japanese War of 1904–05 took place nearly half a world away from the United States, Americans were immediately concerned. Their new commitments in the Pacific had given Americans a direct interest in the affairs of East Asia. The war between Russia and Japan, fought on Chinese soil and in Pacific waters, threatened to interfere with American trading and missionary interests in China. It also threatened to weaken, if not destroy, the Open Door Policy.

Acting on his own authority, President Theodore Roosevelt warned Germany and France that if they aided Russia the United States would side with Japan. With Roosevelt acting as mediator, representatives from Russia and Japan met at Portsmouth, New Hampshire, during the summer of 1905. There they worked out terms for settling the conflict. In 1906 Roosevelt received the Nobel Peace Prize for his efforts.

The Treaty of Portsmouth transferred Russia's interest in Korea and Manchuria to Japan. It also gave Japan the southern half of Sakhalin Island.

Roosevelt was delighted with the results of his efforts to end the Russo-Japanese War. The Treaty of Portsmouth left the Open Door Policy intact. It maintained for a time the balance of power in East Asia. None of the colonial powers, including Japan and Russia, had a dominant position in China. The doors of China remained open to American business and trade.

SECTION REVIEW
See underscored items, text pp. 641, 643.

Identify: extraterritoriality, John Hay, Commodore Perry, Treaty of Portsmouth
For answers to questions, see Answer Key, p.A90.

1. **Summarizing Ideas: (a)** Describe the circumstances that led to the Open Door Policy. **(b)** What were the provisions of this policy?

2. **Organizing Ideas: (a)** What was the Boxer Rebellion? **(b)** How did it end? **(c)** What were its effects on United States–China relations?

3. **Analyzing Ideas: (a)** Why did Japan become imperialistic? **(b)** Why were Americans concerned about growing Japanese imperialism?

▲ Writing activity: Have students write letters or stories from the viewpoint of Japanese people seeing Westerners for the first time. You may wish to provide some additional insights or sources of information about Japanese culture at the time of Perry's arrival.

DEVELOPING HISTORY STUDY SKILLS

Thinking About History   Determining Fallacies in Reasoning

Students of history must often analyze and evaluate statements and viewpoints. To do so it is necessary to recognize fallacies in reasoning. A fallacy in reasoning is either an unsound and unsupported argument or an erroneous conclusion. Each of the following statements contains a fallacy.

> *Everyone knows that if the United States does not take the Philippines, another great power will do so.*

> *The sinking of the* Maine *caused the Spanish-American War.*

> *President Carter lost the 1980 Presidential election because of the Iranian hostage crisis.*

In the first statement the argument that the United States had to take the Philippines or another country would is an example of an unsound and unsupported argument. In the second statement the conclusion that the sinking of the *Maine* caused the Spanish-American War is an example of an erroneous conclusion. The third statement indicates that a previous event caused a later event.

There are many different types of fallacies. In his book *Historian's Fallacies,* David H. Fischer mentions more than two dozen kinds of fallacies. He groups them into 11 categories. Two of these broad groups are fallacies of cause and effect and fallacies of proof.

Fischer cites the following example of a common fallacy in thinking. One historian charged that John D. Rockefeller had bribed public officials and engaged in acts of fraud. In rebuttal, a second historian said that Rockefeller was a "hard-working, home-loving, religious" man who founded the University of Chicago, and that "his house was filled with social workers." The second historian's statements do not relate to the charges made by the first historian. Thus, they are irrelevant.

How to Recognize Fallacies in Reasoning

To recognize fallacies in reasoning, follow these guidelines.

1. **Read the statement carefully.** Look for the main idea and identify the conclusion.

2. **Identify fallacies in reasoning.** Ask how each conclusion was reached. Refer to the following list of fallacies.

CAUSE-AND-EFFECT FALLACIES

Some errors of reasoning occur in determining cause and effect relationships. The following list describes the most common cause-effect fallacies.

- Single Cause — identifying only one cause for a major event. For example, the statement "the De Lôme letter caused the Spanish-American War" contains a single-cause fallacy. Many different events, people, and issues combined to create the war. The single-cause fallacy should not be confused with accurate statements about the main causes of historical events. A historian who writes about "a major cause," or the "main cause" is quite properly ranking causes by importance.

- Correlation as Cause — identifying an event that occurs at the same time as another as the cause of the event. The following statements illustrate correlation as cause fallacy: "The U.S. had periods of prosperity under the administrations of Harding, Eisenhower, and Reagan. Therefore, Republicans cause prosperity." The fact that prosperity occurred during the administrations of these Republican Presidents does not mean that Republicans cause prosperity.

- Previous Event as Cause — identifying an event that occurred before another as the cause of the second event. The reasoning is that if Event Z happened after Event Y, then Y caused Z. An example of this fallacy is the statement, "Great Britain withdrew its interest in the Panama Canal, thus enabling the United States to build the canal." In fact, many factors besides Great Britain's withdrawal enabled the U.S. to build the canal.

644

PROOF FALLACIES

An error of reasoning that occurs when a conclusion is erroneously drawn from the evidence presented is called a fallacy of proof. Fischer offers these guidelines: ". . . every fact in history is an answer to a question, and . . . evidence which is useful and true and sufficient in answer to question B may be false and useless in answer to question A. A historian must not merely get the facts right. He must get the right facts right. . . . Historical evidence must be a direct answer to the question asked and not to some other answer."

- Irrelevant Evidence — using irrelevant information to prove a major thesis. For example, if a historian is trying to prove that economic considerations caused the Spanish-American War, it is beside the point to criticize the personalities of Spanish leaders. (You may wish to review pages 301–02 to refresh your memory on how to distinguish between relevant and irrelevant information.)

- Majority View — arguing that because "everyone" says something is so, it must be true.

3. **Evaluate the statement.** Determine the validity of the statement based on the errors in reasoning and the evidence presented.

Applying the Skill

Read the following selection on the cause of the Spanish–American War. Then identify the fallacies it contains:

> In the opinion of this writer, the Spanish–American War would not have occurred had not the appearance of Hearst in New York journalism precipitated a bitter battle for newspaper circulation. The Cuban insurrection and its attendant horrors furnished a unique opportunity to the proprietors of the sensational press to . . . provide the type of news that sold papers.
>
> Joseph Wisan

This selection contains a single-cause fallacy. The author contends that sensational newspaper accounts alone set off the Spanish–American War.

Practicing the Skill

Read the following statements and determine the fallacy or fallacies that each statement contains. Then on a separate sheet of paper, list the fallacies that you have identified.

Statement A

In retrospect, many Americans agreed that the United States had fulfilled its duty to "educate, uplift, civilize, and Christianize" the Filipinos. After all, highways, railroads, and telephone lines had been built, disease had been reduced, and the economy had improved. All was due to United States help.

Statement B

These people [individuals who had been involved in the Hawaiian revolution and in the Provisional Government] were the cause of the revolution . . . in 1887. There will never be any peace while they are here.

Queen Liliuokalani

Statement C

Whole Country Thrills with the War Fever yet the President Says "It Was an Accident"

Headline in the New York Journal

Statement D

On the fatal night of the [Andrea] Doria's collision with the Swedish ship Gripsholm, off Nantucket . . . the lady retired to her cabin and flicked a light switch. Suddenly there was a great crash, and a grinding metal, and passengers and crew ran screaming through the passageways. The lady burst forth from her cabin and explained to the first person in sight that she must have set the ship's emergency brake!

Alvin Moscow in *Collison Course*

(1.(a) See solid-line underscore; single cause. (b) See solid-line underscore; single cause.
(c) See solid-line underscore; majority view. (d) See solid-line underscore; correlation as cause.)

28 SUMMARY

During the latter half of the 1800's, the major colonial powers of Europe engaged in a lively race for empire. The United States, however, was not especially interested in entering the race. To be sure, in 1867 Secretary of State Seward persuaded Congress to annex the Midway Islands and to purchase Alaska. Congress made the purchase reluctantly, however, because Americans on the whole were indifferent to building an empire.

Toward the end of the 1800's, American sentiment about expansion began to change. It was the Spanish-American War that finally started the United States down the road of colonialism.

The war with Spain in 1898 began in protest against Spanish policy in Cuba. It ended with a treaty in which Spain agreed to give up its claim to Cuba and in which the United States gained the Philippine Islands as well as Guam and Puerto Rico. In addition to the Philippines and Guam, the United States acquired other territories in the Pacific area. Hawaii was annexed in 1898, and a portion of Samoa was acquired in 1899.

To protect its growing interests in the Pacific, the United States insisted upon an equal opportunity to share in the business and trade of East Asia. This Open Door Policy involved Americans in the troubled affairs of East Asia and committed the United States to a role of power politics in the Pacific.

CONNECTING CHAPTER IDEAS

America's interest in colonies was not confined to the Pacific area. As you will read in the next chapter the Caribbean offered even larger and more inviting opportunities for the development of American interests.

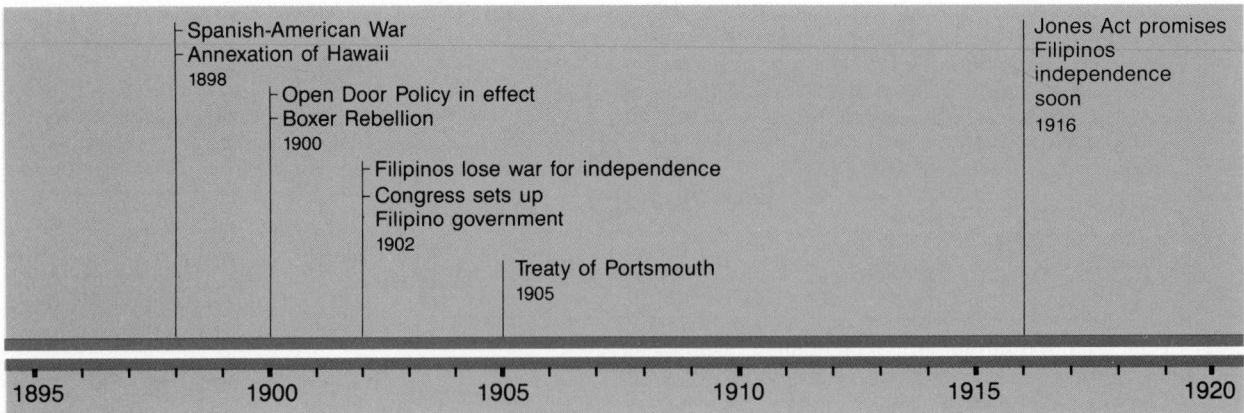

Spanish-American War
Annexation of Hawaii
1898

Open Door Policy in effect
Boxer Rebellion
1900

Filipinos lose war for independence
Congress sets up
Filipino government
1902

Treaty of Portsmouth
1905

Jones Act promises Filipinos independence soon
1916

1895   1900   1905   1910   1915   1920

CHAPTER
28 REVIEW

Reviewing Important Terms

Decide whether each of the following sentences is true or false. If the sentence is false, replace the underlined term with the word or phrase that will make it true.

1. Imperialism, the policy of establishing colonies, became strong again in the late 1800's as nations sought raw materials and markets.
2. Chinese cities opened to foreign trade were called treaty ports.
3. The right of nationality meant that Americans in China who were charged with violations of Chinese laws had the right to be tried in American courts in China.
4. The Teller Resolution stated that the United States claimed no sovereignty or control over Cuba, but only wanted to pacify the island.
5. The United States issued an ultimatum to Spain in March 1898.
6. In the late 1800's, American expansionists wanted the United States government to acquire tariffs, or overseas settlements, to strengthen the nation's industrial organization.
7. During the troubles between Spain and Cuba, President McKinley tried to preserve the nation's neutrality.

Practicing Critical Thinking Skills

1. **Analyzing Ideas. (a)** Why did the foreign policy of the United States change from one of isolationism to one of expansionism? **(b)** What arguments did the expansionists use to defend their position?
2. **Comparing Ideas.** Was there a contradiction in the United States favoring the Open Door Policy for China and the policy of the Monroe Doctrine for the Western Hemisphere? Explain.
3. **Interpreting Ideas.** Some anti-imperialists argued that American imperialist policy worked to the disadvantage of black Americans at home. **(a)** How might this have been true? **(b)** Do you agree or disagree with the argument? Why? **(c)** What was the situation of black Americans at home in the 1890's? (See pages 464–67.)
4. **Evaluating Ideas.** Explain why industrial nations were able to dominate the nonindustrialized areas of the world.
5. **Comparing Ideas.** Compare the role of the press in foreign affairs today with the role of the press of the late 1890's.

6. **Relating Past to Present.** Is the United States involved overseas today for the same reasons it was involved during the period covered in this chapter? Explain.

Developing History Study Skills

Determining Fallacies in Reasoning. Read the following excerpt. Then answer the questions below.

Today we are raising more than we can consume. . . . Therefore, we must find new markets for our produce, new [use] for our [money], new work for our labor. . . . Think of the tens of thousands of Americans who will invade mine and field and forest in the Philippines when a liberal government . . . shall establish order and [fairness] there! Think of the hundreds of thousands of Americans who will build . . . a civilization of energy and industry in Cuba . . . when a government of law replaces the double reign of anarchy and tyranny!

(a) What is the solution for Americans raising more than they can consume? **(b)** What would be the results of having a "liberal government in the Philippines? a "government of law" in Cuba? **(c)** What evidence is provided to support these conclusions?

Relating Geography and History

Less than 20 years after the 1898 war with Spain, the American flag flew over many new lands. To recognize the extent of United States expansion, make a chart with three columns. In the first column list all the lands that came into United States possession between 1865 and 1918. In the second column describe how each of these lands was obtained. In the third column describe the present status of each land listed in the first column. Now answer the following questions.

1. Which possession was the farthest from the continental United States?
2. **(a)** What problems did the vast distances between possessions cause in the early 1900's? **(b)** Does geographic distance present the same problems today? Explain.
3. Which of these possessions seemed the most important or valuable to the United States in the early 1900's? Why?

647

See Chapter Overview in TMRG, p.TM162.
See Chapter Objectives in TMRG, p.TM162.
See Introducing the Chapter in TMRG, p.TM162.

CHAPTER 29

Expansion
in the Caribbean

(1898–1914)

Spreading
U.S. control

On December 10, 1898, the Spaniards signed the Treaty of Paris that formally brought the Spanish-American War to an end. By the terms of the treaty, Spain agreed (1) to leave Cuba, (2) to cede Puerto Rico and Guam to the United States, and (3) to cede the Philippine Islands to the United States in exchange for a payment of $20,000,000.

For the United States, Spain, Cuba, and Puerto Rico, the end of the war proved to be a major turning point. The signing of the Treaty of Paris was a sad day for the Spanish nation. The Spaniards had a good reason for their sorrow. The war that they had fought and lost struck the final blow to the once mighty Spanish empire.

It was also a disappointing day for the Cubans. They had hoped that peace would bring the freedom for which they had struggled so long. The United States, however, attached strings to Cuban independence that effectively delayed it until 1934. Puerto Ricans had also hoped for freedom and independence. But Puerto Rico became a territory of the United States and eventually became a self-governing commonwealth.

For the American people, however, the war marked a crucial step forward on the path of imperialism and world power. After 1898 and the signing of the war-ending treaty, the United States rapidly became a major power in the Pacific and in East Asia. Between 1898 and 1914, the United States also gained power and influence among the nations in the Caribbean and the nations of South America. United States interest in events close to home turned the Caribbean Sea into what was sometimes called "an American lake." The United States also modified the Monroe Doctrine and changed its foreign policy in the Western Hemisphere.

═══ READING FOCUS ═══

As you read about the growth of United States power and influence in the Western Hemisphere, look for the details that support each of the following statements.

1. Americans begin to build an empire in the Caribbean.
2. The United States modifies and strengthens the Monroe Doctrine.
3. Conflict breaks out between the United States and Mexico.

1 Americans begin to build an empire in the Caribbean

See Teaching Suggestions in TMRG, pp.TM162-63.

Less than 20 years after the war with Spain, the American flag was flying over Puerto Rico, the Panama Canal Zone, and the Virgin Islands. The United States revised their foreign policy, sending American advisers to the countries in the Caribbean.

Several important questions faced the nation. How would the United States respond to the desires of Cubans and Puerto Ricans for total independence? Were the people in the newly acquired territories entitled to all the rights guaranteed to citizens of the United States? As the question was often stated, "Does the Constitution follow the flag?"

The Insular Cases. In the Insular Cases of 1901, the Supreme Court settled the issue of constitutional rights. It ruled that there were two kinds of possessions—incorporated and unincorporated. The incorporated possessions—Hawaii and Alaska—were destined for statehood. The citizens of these possessions were therefore entitled to all the constitutional rights guaranteed to United States citizens. The unincorporated possessions—Puerto Rico, the Philippines, Samoa, and others—were not destined for statehood. The people of these areas were *not,* therefore, entitled to all constitutional guarantees. The people of the unincorporated possessions could not, however, be deprived of life, liberty, or property without the due process of law.

The Insular Cases and several similar Supreme Court decisions between 1901 and 1922 helped to develop an American colonial policy. However, it was Congress that passed the laws ruling America's growing colonial empire.

A government for Puerto Rico. In 1900, Congress passed the Foraker Act, which provided a new government for Puerto Rico (see map, page 650). It would consist of a governor and an executive council appointed by the President of the United States and a lower house elected by the Puerto Ricans.

Discontented Puerto Ricans demanded a larger voice in their own government. In 1917, shortly after the Filipinos won their citizenship in the Jones Act of 1916, the United

▲ Discussion topic: One anti-imperialist argument claimed that taking over territories without consent of their local populations was unconstitutional. Explore with students how historical precedents—questions involving Native Americans, Louisiana Territory settlers, and Alaskans—had been handled.

649

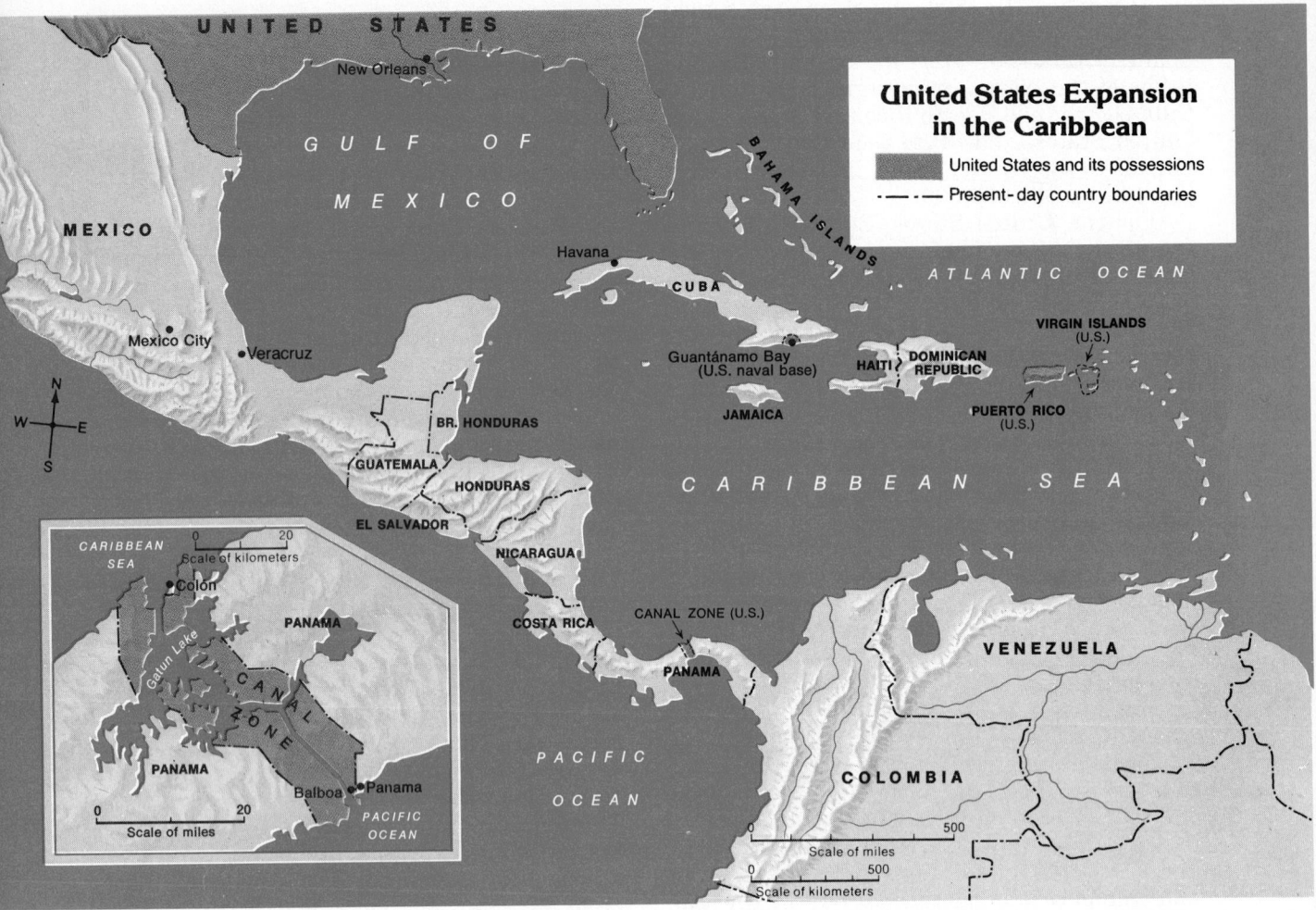

United States Expansion in the Caribbean

☐ United States and its possessions
·—·—· Present-day country boundaries

States adopted a second Jones Act. This act made Puerto Rico a United States territory and made the Puerto Ricans American citizens. In addition Puerto Ricans were also granted the right to elect members of both houses of their legislature.

In 1950 Congress gave Puerto Ricans the power to write their own constitution. In 1952, after the constitution had been ratified by popular vote, Puerto Rico became a self-governing commonwealth. It makes its own laws and controls its own finances. The United States, however, provides for the island's defense and includes Puerto Rico within its tariff system. It places no restrictions on immigration from Puerto Rico to the United States.

Strings on Cuban independence. Although Cuba was never considered an American colony, American influence over Cuban affairs remained strong after the war (see map, this page). The Teller Resolution, which Congress adopted in 1898, had pledged that the Cubans would be given their independence. Nevertheless, for three years after the war, Cuba was ruled by an American army of occupation under the command of General Leonard Wood.

In 1901 Congress finally turned Cuba over to the Cuban people, but with four conditions. These conditions were incorporated into the Army Act of 1901 as the Platt Amendment. (1) The Cuban government must never enter into any foreign agreements that might endanger Cuban independence. (2) The Cuban government must never incur debts that it could not repay in a reasonable time. (3) The Cuban government must give the United States "the right to intervene for the preservation of Cuban independence [and] the maintenance of a government adequate for the protection of life, property, and individual liberty." (4) The Cuban government must place naval bases at the disposal of the United States. Congress also announced that the United States would not withdraw its military forces until the Platt Amendment had been written into the new Cuban constitution.

This was not the "independence" Cubans had expected, yet they had to agree to American demands. Therefore, they accepted the Platt Amendment, and in 1902 the American forces were withdrawn.

An American protectorate. Actually, Cuba became a **protectorate** of the United States. That is, the United States, a strong nation, tried to supervise Cuba, a weaker nation, by keeping partial control over Cuban affairs. Cubans, who had fought for independence, resented this relationship.

Between 1906 and 1920, American troops landed in Cuba three times to maintain order and to protect American business and property. Moreover, American diplomatic pressure frequently forced the Cubans to accept policies favored by the United States. In 1934, as you will see, Congress abolished the Platt Amendment, thus ending America's role as "protector" of Cuba.

Growing interest in a canal. In 1898, when the Spanish-American War began, the U.S. battleship *Oregon* was in California waters. It immediately started to sail around South America in an effort to join the Atlantic fleet. Public imagination was stirred, and for six weeks daily reports of the ship's progress appeared in every newspaper. The *Oregon's* lengthy voyage convinced many Americans that a canal between the Atlantic and the Pacific was needed.

In the years after the war, the United States followed along a path of empire. As the empire grew, people began to insist that the United States needed two navies—one in the Pacific, the other to safeguard the Atlantic and the Caribbean. The alternative to a two-ocean navy was a canal connecting the two oceans.

The best site for a canal was that narrow part of Colombia known as the Isthmus of Panama. Indeed, a French company in the 1880's had tried but had failed to build a canal there. Another possible canal route was through Nicaragua (see inset map, page 650). A canal in either place would enable a fleet to

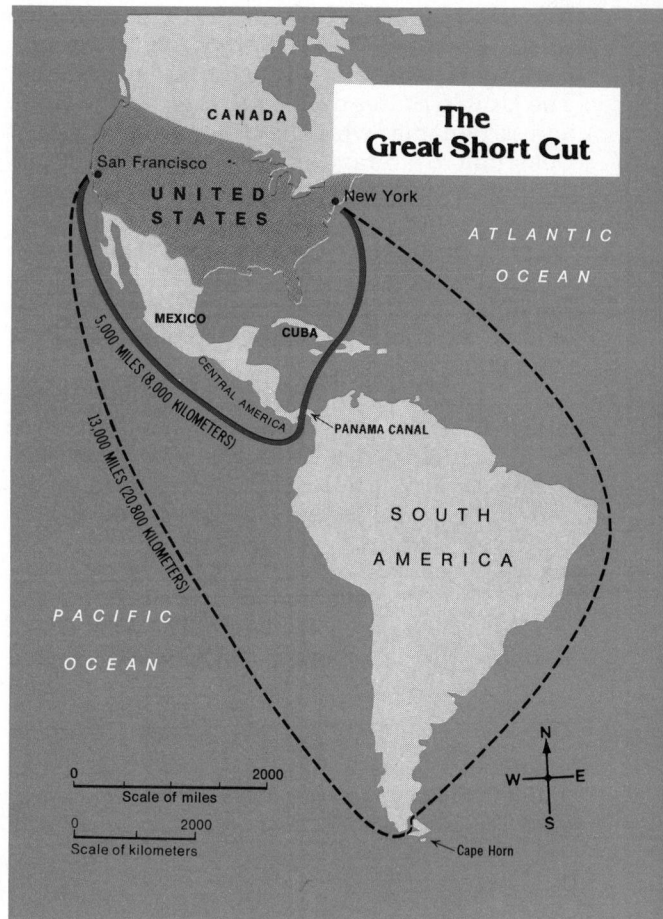

The Great Short Cut

pass easily and quickly from one ocean to the other. The map on this page shows the benefit in time and distance that the canal would provide.

The United States had considered building a canal through the Isthmus of Panama for many years. As early as 1850, the United States and Great Britain had agreed on terms for a canal in the Clayton-Bulwer Treaty. If a canal were built, both nations would together control it and guarantee that it be unfortified and open to all other nations, even in wartime.

By 1898, however, Americans had concluded that the canal was so vital to their national interests that the United States had to have exclusive control over it. In 1901 Great Britain agreed to give up all rights to share in the building and control of the canal. The United States was now free to build and operate the canal, but it was understood that the canal would be open to all nations, even in time of war.

▲ Class activity: Have a small group of students report—in the form of a panel presentation--from the abolition of the Platt Amendment in 1934 to the present.

651

Negotiations with Colombia. The next step was to secure a right of way either through Nicaragua or across the Isthmus of Panama. The United States decided in favor of the route across Panama, which was then a province of Colombia. Secretary of State John Hay immediately opened negotiations with the Colombian government, and a treaty was soon ready for ratification. In return for a 99-year lease to a 16-mile (26-kilometer) strip of land across Panama, the United States agreed to pay Colombia $10 million and a yearly rental of $250,000.

▲ At this point Colombia's legislators adjourned without taking action, hoping to win better terms. Many Americans, including President Theodore Roosevelt, were furious because Colombia's delay blocked the entire canal project.

Revolution in Panama. Fortunately for the United States, many leaders in the province of Panama also were angry at Colombia's delay.

In Panama a group secretly organized a revolution. They were encouraged by representatives of the French company that had earlier tried to build a canal and now wanted to recover as much as possible of its investment.

One Panamanian leader secretly traveled to Washington and asked the American government for assistance. Although open aid was refused, the Panamanian left Washington convinced that the United States would not interfere once the revolution began.

According to rumors, the revolution was to begin on November 4, 1903. On November 2 an American gunboat, the *Nashville,* arrived at Colón (see inset map, page 650). Hardly had it landed when a Colombian ship arrived with Colombian soldiers. The Colombian generals commanding the expedition immediately proceeded to the city of Panama, leaving orders for the troops to follow. Shortly after they reached Panama, however, the Colombian generals were seized and jailed. The arrest of the Colombian generals was a signal for the outbreak of

In this 1904 cartoon President Theodore Roosevelt is depicted as a police officer. Do you think this view is a flattering or a critical one? Why? (Answers will vary.)

John Milton Hay was both a writer and a diplomat. This unique combination permitted Hay to influence the nation's ideas and its actions in world affairs.

After graduating from Brown University, Hay studied law with an uncle in Springfield, Illinois. There he met Abraham Lincoln, who called him to Washington as his assistant private secretary. Hay spent five years in Europe in various minor diplomatic posts and then became an editorial writer for the *New York Tribune.* Hay also wrote and published books on travel, poetry, and socioeconomic issues.

In 1897 Hay was named ambassador to Great Britain, and the following year he became the United States Secretary of State. An active Secretary of State, Hay was instrumental in the acquisition of the Philippines and in favorably settling of Alaska's boundary with Canada. John Hay's major diplomatic achievement was the "Open Door" policy, which emphasized equal economic opportunity in China for American and European merchants and protected the Chinese people from the colonial rivalries seen elsewhere around the globe.

the revolution, and the city of Panama quickly fell under the control of the revolutionists.

Meanwhile, during a dispute that broke out in Colón, Colombian soldiers and naval officers threatened to kill every American in the city. At this point United States Marines landed. Colombian authorities demanded to know what right the Americans had to interfere. The Americans said that a treaty between the United States and Colombia signed in 1846 had guaranteed the United States free passage through the isthmus. The United States government also added that no Colombian troops would be permitted to land within 50 miles (80 kilometers) of Panama.

Right of way through Panama. Largely because of American aid, the revolution in Panama was a success. On November 4, 1903, the new government took control in Panama, and two days later the United States recognized Panama's independence. On November 13 the United States formally received the first Panamanian minister to Washington, Philippe Bunau-Varilla (boo·NOH vah·REE·yah). On November 18, only two weeks after the revolution had broken out, Panama granted the United States the right of way across the isthmus for the canal.

In the Hay–Bunau-Varilla Treaty, Panama

gave the United States a perpetual lease to a 10-mile (16-kilometer) strip of land between the Atlantic and the Pacific oceans. In return for this land, the United States agreed to pay Panama $10 million outright and a yearly rental of $250,000.

President Theodore Roosevelt once boasted, "I took Panama." At other times, he denied that the United States had in any way helped to carry out the revolution. One fact is certain—the revolution worked to the advantage of the United States.

Colombia was furious, of course, and the affair added to the fear and distrust of the "Yankee" that was already strong in Latin America. In 1921 the United States tried to pacify Colombia by giving it $25 million as partial compensation for the loss of Panama.

Building the canal. Meanwhile, work on the canal progressed under the supervision of the United States Army Corps of Engineers. One of the first and most difficult tasks was to conquer malaria, yellow fever, and other tropical diseases that made working difficult.

Dr. Walter Reed and his colleagues working in Cuba discovered that yellow fever was transmitted by a certain mosquito, the *Stegomyia.* Using this and other medical dis-

653

Walter Reed checked the time. It was 11:50 on the night of December 31, 1900. At his desk in an American army barracks in northern Cuba, he turned back to the letter he was writing his wife in the United States.

"Only ten minutes of the old century remain," he wrote. "The prayer that has been mine for twenty years, that I might be permitted in some way or at some time to do something to alleviate human suffering, has been granted. A thousand Happy New Years!"

It was Reed's role in the conquest of yellow fever that fulfilled his desire to alleviate human suffering. In 1900 a yellow fever epidemic had broken out among American troops stationed in Havana, Cuba. The United States government promptly sent a team of physicians led by Reed to investigate. The symptoms of the dreaded tropical disease included high fever, a yellowing of the skin, vomiting, and internal bleeding. Yellow fever had killed countless victims over the centuries, but no one knew what caused it or how to prevent it.

Reed's team was familiar with the work of the Cuban physician Carlos Finlay, who had theorized that yellow fever was transmitted by a mosquito. Reed decided that the only way to test this theory was to conduct experiments on human beings. Several volunteers, including James Carroll, a member of the commission, allowed themselves to be bitten by infected mosquitoes. Carroll and the other volunteers were treated and survived.

This experiment, which proved at last what before had only been suspected, had far-reaching implications. William C. Gorgas, chief surgeon of the American forces in Cuba, began to enforce strict mosquito-control measures. Within three months Havana was freed from the disease that had plagued it for 300 years.

Walter Reed returned to Washington, where he died in 1902 from appendicitis. But Reed's work — and his desire to alleviate human suffering — was carried on by Gorgas, who eradicated yellow fever in Panama so that the digging of the Panama Canal could proceed.

coveries, Dr. William C. Gorgas, the surgeon in charge of the American health program in Panama, was able to turn a deadly tropical jungle into a relatively healthful region.

By 1914 the canal was completed (see inset map, page 650) at the cost of approximately $400 million. Its completion was a major triumph of engineering and a personal triumph for the engineer in charge, Colonel George W. Goethals (GOH·thulz). The first traffic moved through the canal just as World War I broke out in Europe. Since then the canal has added immeasurably to the naval strength of the United States. The canal's value in peacetime for trade has been almost incalculable.

SECTION REVIEW
See underscored items, text pp. 649, 651, 653-54.

Identify: Insular Cases, protectorate, Hay–Bunau-Varilla Treaty, Walter Reed, George Goethals
For answers to questions, see Answer Key, p.A91.

1. **Analyzing Viewpoints:** How did the Supreme Court answer the question, "Does the Constitution follow the flag"?
2. **Organizing Ideas: (a)** What provisions did Congress make for the government of Puerto Rico? **(b)** Why can it be said that the Platt Amendment made Cuba an American protectorate?

3. **Interpreting Ideas:** Why was the United States interested in a canal through Central America?
4. **Analyzing Ideas:** American policies in Latin America contributed to the growing distrust of the "Yankee" there. Explain.
5. **Studying Maps:** Using the map on page 650, explain why the Caribbean Sea was once called "an American lake."

---

2 **The United States modifies and strengthens the Monroe Doctrine**

See Teaching Suggestions in TMRG, p.TM163.

During the early 1900's, the United States intervened in the internal affairs of the smaller countries in the Caribbean area. How did the United States justify such interference?

Reasons for interference. Intervention was necessary, Americans argued, to maintain law and order in countries bordering on the United States. In the first place, the United States government had a duty to protect the lives and properties of its own citizens living in other countries. Second, the United States was determined as a matter of self-interest and self-defense to prevent European nations from intervening in the political affairs of the Western Hemisphere. There would be less chance for such intervention if law and order prevailed. Third, the United States was concerned about the defense of the canal it was then building across the Isthmus of Panama.

The Monroe Doctrine of 1823. Americans developed the argument of self-defense into a well-defined foreign policy. As you recall, the original Monroe Doctrine of 1823 warned the European powers (1) not to attempt any further colonization in the Americas and (2) not to interfere with independent nations in the Western Hemisphere.

When this warning was issued and for many years after, the United States did not have the naval strength to enforce it. However, as long as American and British interests did not clash in Latin America, the British Navy could be counted on to support Monroe's words. Moreover, the Latin American countries themselves made several efforts to cooperate in the

organization of their own defense. In fact, Mexico, Argentina, and Chile did successfully resist European attempts to interfere.

The first test. The first major test of the Monroe Doctrine came during the 1860's, when Emperor Napoleon III of France tried to establish a French-dominated empire in Mexico. Napoleon III, together with Great Britain and Spain, sent an expedition to Mexico, supposedly to force Mexico to repay its debts. After Mexico repaid its debts, Great Britain and Spain withdrew, but Napoleon III refused to pull out his troops. Instead, aided by Mexicans who opposed the President, Benito Juárez (HWAH·res), the French troops installed Maximilian of Austria as emperor of Mexico. President Juárez fled to El Paso del Norte near the United States border.

The United States immediately protested that French occupation of Mexico was a clear violation of the Monroe Doctrine. However, the United States was fighting the Civil War and until 1865 was unable to take firm action. Then, with the war ended, the United States prepared to send an American army to the Mexican border—farther, if necessary.

The building of the Panama Canal was an enormous undertaking. In this photograph the 70-foot (21-meter) deep Miraflores Lower Locks stand near completion.

Secretary of State Elihu Root in 1905 summed up American Caribbean policy: "The key to our attitude toward these countries can be put in three sentences. We do not want to take them for ourselves. We do not want foreign nations to take them for themselves. We want to help them."

The American army was not needed. Napoleon, faced with the danger of war in Europe and convinced that he could not hold Mexico, withdrew his forces. Juárez and his followers destroyed Maximilian's army and executed Maximilian in 1867.

Thus ended a difficult situation. However, the American government had shown its firm resolve to resist European interference in Latin America.

A second test. A second major test of the Monroe Doctrine came in 1895. The immediate issue was a boundary dispute between Venezuela and British Guiana.

Great Britain had acquired British Guiana in 1814. Time and again Great Britain had pushed the western boundary of British Guiana onto territory claimed by Venezuela. Finally, in 1882, Venezuela had had enough. It demanded that Great Britain submit the controversy to **arbitration,** meaning that the British would have to agree in advance to accept the decision of a neutral party.

The British refused, and in 1895 Venezuela asked the United States to intervene. President Cleveland decided to act. In an extremely strong message, Secretary of State Richard Olney warned Great Britain that the United States would not tolerate any further interference with Venezuela and demanded an immediate settlement of the problem by arbitration.

Great Britain angrily rejected Olney's demands. In the first place, the British retorted, the Monroe Doctrine had not been violated. Second, the Monroe Doctrine was not a recognized part of international law. Third, the United States had no business interfering.

President Cleveland refused to accept this explanation. When the British refusal to arbitrate reached him, he appointed an American commission to investigate the controversy and reach a decision. This was a direct challenge to British imperial power.

Realizing that war between Great Britain and the United States was a real possibility, responsible leaders in both countries urged moderation. Partly because of their efforts and partly because of British difficulties in South Africa at the time, the British government suddenly reversed its position. It agreed to arbitrate the boundary dispute and even offered to help the American commission's investigation.

The Monroe Doctrine had been successfully upheld. On this occasion the United States could claim that it had used its foreign policy to protect a weak nation against a great power. Even more important, perhaps, was the fact that the British, desiring American friendship, now in effect recognized that the United States had special interests in the Caribbean area.

A third test. In 1902, seven years later, Venezuela found itself unable to repay debts owed to Great Britain, Germany, and Italy. After their demands for repayment produced no results, the three countries took joint action. They withdrew their diplomatic representatives, blockaded the Venezuelan coast, and seized several small gunboats.

At this point President Theodore Roosevelt warned the European powers that any attempt to seize territory in the Western Hemisphere would violate the Monroe Doctrine. Then he urged the countries involved to submit the dispute to arbitration. They did, and the matter was settled.

The Drago Doctrine. By the early 1900's, growing numbers of Americans were investing money in the Caribbean countries and other parts of Latin America. Latin American leaders watched with concern the growth of American investments and the growing influence of the United States. In 1902 one of these leaders, Luis M. Drago, Argentine Minister of Foreign Affairs, expressed this concern in a policy for Latin America that came to be known as the Drago Doctrine.

Drago rejected the claim that any foreign nation had the right to use force to collect debts from a Latin American nation. He argued that when individuals or nations lent money, they did so at their own risk.

Nearly all of Latin America's leaders as well as many United States citizens agreed with Drago. However, in 1904 President Roosevelt announced a policy that exempted the United States from the principle that foreign debts concerned only the debtor country and foreign investors.

The Roosevelt Corollary. The Dominican Republic was the reason for Roosevelt's announcement (see map, page 650). It owed long-overdue debts to several European countries as well as to American investors. When the European countries threatened to use armed force to collect the money, President Roosevelt at once intervened.

This cartoon refers to the Venezuelan crisis of 1902. "That's a live wire, gentlemen" says Uncle Sam. Whom is he warning? What is the live wire that he is pointing to? What does he imply would happen if they step on the live wire?

(European powers symbolized by Great Britain and Germany · the principles of the Monroe Doctrine · They will touch off confrontation with the United States.)

Roosevelt announced in 1904 that if it became necessary for any nation to interfere in the affairs of a Latin American country, the United States had to carry out the task, not a European government.

The policy announced in 1904 came to be known as the Roosevelt Corollary to the Monroe Doctrine. With this policy the United States assumed the role of "international police officer" in the Western Hemisphere. On several occasions during the next two decades, the United States used the Roosevelt Corollary to justify its intervention in the affairs of several Latin American nations.

There were, of course, two ways of looking at the Roosevelt Corollary. From the United States' point of view, the North Americans were protecting their weaker neighbors from European intervention. On the other hand, Latin Americans were well aware that the policy could be used against them and that it was basically an insult to their national pride.

Dominican Republic as protectorate. The United States first exercised its "international police power" by intervening in the affairs of the Dominican Republic. As part of an agreement with the Dominican government in 1905, President Roosevelt promised to guarantee the Republic's **territorial integrity**. That is, he promised to use American armed forces, if necessary, to prevent any European country from seizing Dominican territory. In exchange for this guarantee, the Dominican government agreed to allow an American agent to collect its customs duties. In addition it agreed to turn over 45 percent of the duties to the Dominican government and to use the rest of the money to pay foreign creditors.

Although customs duties doubled under American supervision and the financial position of the Dominican Republic improved, the Dominican people resented United States control. Finally, in 1916, during President Wilson's administration, the Dominican government announced it intended to end the protectorate.

The United States answered this challenge by landing marines and suspending the Dominican legislature. For eight years, until

The U.S. Government Printing Office (GPO) is probably the largest printing establishment in the world. Located almost entirely in Washington, D.C., it currently has 16,000 titles in print, ranging from "The Life of the Fruit Fly" to the *Congressional Record.*

In addition to printing and distributing government publications, the Government Printing Office reprints documents for sale to the public. It also designates certain libraries throughout the country as depositories for government documents.

Because of the thousands of pages it must process annually, the Government Printing Office has adopted the fastest computerized printing technology available. For example, the GPO has a machine that can print the 22,000 characters of a phone book page in 20 seconds.

From the earliest days of this nation, Congress and other governmental agencies had substantial printing requirements. At first the work was contracted out to private shops. But despite the vigilance of Congress, the contracting process created scandal and corruption. The Printing Act of 1860 was passed to correct this situation. It established the GPO, an independent bureau, to carry out the printing and binding of publications for the executive and legislative branches.

In 1895 a second Printing Act gave the Public Printer, the head of the GPO, authority over all federal government printing.

1924, the Dominican Republic was ruled by a Dominican military dictatorship under the American government. The United States withdrew its military forces in 1924 but did not end its role of "protector" until 1940.

Protectorate in Haiti. The same general methods used to secure control of the Dominican Republic were applied to Haiti (see map, page 650) in 1914. During Wilson's administration revolutions shook the debt-ridden Haitian republic, and the United States landed marines there.

The Haitians were then asked to ratify a treaty prepared by the United States Department of State. This treaty gave the United States the right to (1) supervise Haiti's finances, (2) intervene to maintain order, and (3) control the Haitian police force. After considerable American pressure, Haiti ratified the treaty, which went into effect early in 1916.

Neither the treaty nor the continued presence of American troops restored order completely. During the next four or five years, nearly 2,000 Haitians were killed in riots and other outbreaks of violence.

Nevertheless, some improvements did come to Haiti during the years of United States control. Some Americans, however, agreed with those Haitians who argued that better sanitation, health, and education and increased prosperity were not worth the loss of freedom.

Interference in Central America. Twice between 1900 and 1920, American military forces were used in Nicaragua and Honduras to gain a large measure of control over these republics. In addition, the United States had great influence over the governments of Colombia, Costa Rica, and Guatemala (see map, page 650). This influence was secured by a policy labeled **dollar diplomacy** by its critics.

Under the so-called dollar diplomacy, American bankers, sometimes by invitation of the Department of State, lent money to Caribbean governments. When the debtors failed to repay their debts or the interest on their loans, the United States government intervened to protect American investments. This intervention took various forms, including the landing of marines, the supervision of elections, and support to the political group that favored the United States.

The Virgin Islands. Back in 1868 Secretary of State Seward had tried to get Congress to buy three of the Virgin Islands (see map, page 650) from Denmark. Congress had refused; it refused again in 1902.

In 1917, however, with World War I raging in Europe, the United States feared that Germany might secure control of these strategic bases. It renewed the offer to buy the islands, and this time negotiations were completed. With the payment of $25 million to Denmark, the islands became outposts of America's Caribbean empire.

As the map on page 650 shows, the Virgin Islands lie at the eastern edge of the West Indies. United States naval bases on the islands, in Puerto Rico, and at Guantánamo Bay in Cuba help to guarantee American control over the Caribbean Sea and the approaches to the Panama Canal.

SECTION REVIEW

See underscored items, text pp. 655-58.

Identify: Napoleon III, Benito Juárez, arbitration, Richard Olney, Drago Doctrine, territorial integrity, dollar diplomacy

For answers to questions, see Answer Key, pp.A91-92.

1. **Interpreting Ideas: (a)** How did the United States justify its intervention in Latin American affairs? **(b)** Do you agree that this intervention was justified? Why or why not?

2. **Organizing Ideas: (a)** What were the provisions of the original Monroe Doctrine of 1823? **(b)** Describe two occasions on which the Monroe Doctrine was tested and upheld.

3. **Analyzing Ideas: (a)** In what way did the Roosevelt Corollary modify the original Monroe Doctrine? **(b)** Give examples of cases in which the Roosevelt Corollary was applied.

4. **Studying Graphics: (a)** What is the subject of the cartoon on page 657? **(b)** What attitude does the cartoonist seem to have toward this situation? How can you tell?

3 Conflict breaks out between the United States and Mexico

See Teaching Suggestions in TMRG, pp.TM163-64.

Beginning with the early 1800's and particularly after the Mexican-American War in 1848, the United States and Mexico had been uneasy, if not hostile, neighbors.

Unreconciled differences. Relations between the two countries had been troubled by repeated acts of violence. The Mexican people could not forget that through the Mexican-American War they had lost one third of their country to their powerful northern neighbor.

Moreover, in the years following the war, the borderlands between Mexico and the United States remained a source of tension. During the 1870's and 1880's, American troops often pursued bands of Indians across the border into Mexican territory. There were long-standing disputes involving the water rights to the Rio Grande and the Colorado River. Banditry, smuggling, and cattle rustling were common along the border. Underlying all of these conflicts was the deep-seated and mutually shared prejudice of Anglo-Americans and Mexican Americans in the borderlands.

It was American investments south of the Rio Grande that eventually involved the United States in outright conflict with Mexico. By the time Woodrow Wilson became President in 1913, American citizens had invested nearly $1 billion in Mexican oil wells, mines, railroads, and ranches. Most of Mexico's trade was with the United States.

Dictatorship and revolution. Mexico was closely tied to the United States, and Mexico's President, Porfirio Diaz, was largely responsible for this. Diaz, although called "President," was actually a dictator. With the exception of three years from 1881 to 1884, he had ruled Mexico since 1877. During his long rule, he had brought peace and order to Mexico and had helped to develop the country's resources.

To develop Mexico's resources, Diaz had encouraged foreign investors to finance and operate mines, factories, and other industries by offering them special privileges. With this encouragement, foreign capital, much of it

▲ Diaz's government catered to the interests of a small class of wealthy land owners, military officials, and privileged clerics at the expense and exploitation of the common people and the country's resources.

● *This painting, "Impassioned Democracy," is part of a giant mural that decorates Mexico's Palacio Nacional. The mural was done by artist Diego Rivera in the 1930's as a visual record of Mexico's leading historical figures and issues.*

from American investors, had poured into Mexico. Thus foreign investors and the privileged friends of dictator Diaz enjoyed most of the benefits of Mexico's developing economy.

In 1910 the Mexicans staged a successful revolution and restored constitutional government to their country. Diaz resigned and left ▲ for Europe. Francisco Madero then became President, but only for a short time. Early in 1913 Madero was assassinated by <u>Victoriano Huerta</u> (HWAIR·tah), who then seized control of the government.

Huerta had many enemies, including friends of the late President Madero. His enemies also included many Mexicans who demanded drastic social and economic reform. The struggle against Huerta, led by <u>Venus-</u>

<u>tiano Carranza</u>, plunged Mexico more deeply into bitter fighting and bloodshed.

Wilson's "watchful waiting." Many Americans were deeply troubled by this situation. Many were dismayed because Huerta had risen to power as the result of a cold-blooded murder. Others with investments in Mexico were disturbed by attacks on their property. President Wilson was urged to send military forces into Mexico to protect American investments and to restore law and order.

The President chose instead to follow a policy that he hoped would preserve the independence of the Mexican people. He outlined his policy in a speech shortly after his election. "The United States will never again seek one

● Class activity: Have students examine the mural shown on this page. Ask them to suggest a title that illustrates the Mexican viewpoint. Questions to consider: Is there a suggestion of hostilities? What is in the background? Who owns the oil wells? What do the peoples' faces and actions reveal?

additional foot of territory by conquest," he declared. "We have seen material interests threaten constitutional freedom in the United States," he went on to say. "Therefore we will now know how to sympathize with those in the rest of America who have to contend with such powers, not only within their borders but from outside their borders also." He then urged the Latin American countries to settle the Mexican problem in their own way.

Although some European countries promptly recognized the Huerta government, Wilson refused to do so. He was convinced that the Mexicans themselves would soon get rid of Huerta. Meanwhile, the United States would follow a policy of "watchful waiting."

Wilson's refusal to intervene pleased most Latin Americans. However, many Americans criticized the President as they saw American lives and property destroyed in Mexico.

American intervention. As the months passed, even President Wilson began to lose patience. Hundreds of small revolutionary groups roamed Mexico, but they were not organized and Huerta remained in power. American citizens in Mexico were killed, and there were rumors that Huerta might try to confiscate, or seize, American property.

The final crisis came in April 1914, when a Mexican official arrested several American sailors near Tampico, Mexico, which was under martial law. The sailors were soon released, but Huerta refused to apologize for the incident. To make matters worse, a German ship arrived at Veracruz with machine guns and other military supplies for Huerta. President Wilson then ordered United States marines to occupy Veracruz. This action united Mexican public opinion against the United States.

The ABC mediation. At this critical stage, Argentina, Brazil, and Chile—sometimes called the "ABC powers"—invited President Wilson to send representatives to meet with Mexican leaders and those of other nations to try to reach a solution. Wilson accepted the invitation, and the conference was held at Niagara Falls, Canada. Among its other recommendations, the conference urged Huerta to retire. Huerta did retire, faced with the fact that his forces were being beaten by those of his rival, Carranza.

Carranza then established himself in power in Mexico, and American forces withdrew from Veracruz. In 1915 Carranza guaranteed that Mexico would respect foreign lives and property, and the United States recognized him as leader of the Mexican government.

American troops in Mexico. Carranza's reforms divided his followers, who began to quarrel among themselves. One of those who turned against Carranza was Francisco "Pancho" Villa (VEE·yah). Villa was angry at the United States for helping Carranza. Hoping to force American troops to intervene in Mexico, Villa and his followers in 1916 seized 18 Americans in northern Mexico and put them to death. Later, Villa crossed the border and raided Columbus, New Mexico, killing 17 Americans.

President Wilson announced he would send an expedition into Mexico to capture Villa "dead or alive." Carranza reluctantly agreed, and General John J. Pershing led some 5,000 troops across the border. The deeper Pershing pushed into Mexican territory, the more hostile the Mexicans became. For a time the threat of war hung over both countries. Finally, in January 1917, American troops withdrew from Mexico without having captured the elusive Villa.

Mexican immigration. One major result of the years of unrest in Mexico was the increased immigration of Mexicans into the United States. Many came as political exiles. Others came to escape from the uncertainties of life in a country torn by revolution. Still others came, in search of a better life in a more prosperous country.

SECTION REVIEW

See underscored items, text pp. 659-61.

Identify: Porfirio Diaz, Victoriano Huerta, Venustiano Carranza, ABC powers, "Pancho" Villa, John Pershing

For answers to questions, see Answer Key, p.A92.

1. **Organizing Ideas:** Give examples to show how the economic interests of the United States and Mexico were closely interwoven.

2. **Interpreting Ideas: (a)** What differences and events contributed to the growing hostilities with Mexico? **(b)** Describe the circumstances that led to Wilson's policy of "watchful waiting." **(c)** Explain the policy. **(d)** Why did Wilson abandon "watchful waiting"?

3. **Analyzing Ideas:** How did the ABC powers help solve the conflict between the United States and Mexico?

DEVELOPING HISTORY STUDY SKILLS

Writing About History   Composing an Expository Essay

In Chapter 16 (pages 385–86) you learned how to compose an essay. Now you will learn how to write a special type of essay called an expository essay. An expository essay explains a body of facts or ideas. Often the student of history is required to write an expository essay to respond to a directive beginning with such words as *discuss, identify, state,* or *explain.*

How to Compose an Essay

Follow these steps in reading an essay directive and composing an essay.

1. **Look for informational terms.** As you read the essay directive, look for informational terms that give clues to the content of the essay. Informational terms may include such terms as *key role, women, success, political events, purpose,* and *results.*

2. **Determine the essay's scope.** Note whether the directive asks you to address one main idea or several main ideas. Note whether the directive contains a time frame.

3. **Note the performance terms.** Performance terms are the words in the essay directive that indicate just what you are to do. Common performance terms and their meanings are listed here.

- **Discuss:** tell in some detail; assess fully the historical significance

- **Identify:** name; place at a point in time and in association with a group

- **Describe:** create a full-bodied word picture of actions and events

- **Explain:** show a cause-effect relationship

- **State:** make a complete, formal statement consisting of several sentences on the assigned subject

- **Show:** give a detailed cause-effect relationship with examples

- **Compare (contrast):** indicate similarities and differences (or differences alone)

4. **Make mental notes:** Gathering mental notes for a response to each part helps to formulate the response in your own words. Another helpful device is to complete a structured overview using the main parts and the informational terms plus additional data.

Applying the Skill

Read the essay directive that follows.

Describe three ways in which the United States intervened in Cuban affairs between 1898 and 1934, and explain the reasons for its actions.

Note that the directive has two parts. You need to provide a description of ways in which the United States intervened in Cuba *and* an explanation of the reasons for these actions. To properly respond to this directive, then, the essay must both describe and explain United States intervention in Cuba. Preparation for a proper response might include this outline:

I. Introduction

II. Three ways the United States intervened in Cuba

    A. Platt Amendment

    B. Military occupation

    C. Diplomatic pressures

III. Reasons for intervention

IV. Conclusion

Notes indicating the ways the U.S. intervened might be organized and added to the outline under II. See the completed example at the top of page 663.

II. Three ways the United States intervened in Cuba

    A. Platt Amendment

    B. Military occupation

        1. Army occupied island three times

        2. Maintained naval bases

    C. Diplomatic pressure

        1. Regulated foreign policy

        2. Influenced economic decisions

Notes indicating the reasons for U.S. intervention might be organized and added to the outline under III.

III. Reasons for intervention

    A. Self-interest

        1. To protect United States business interests

        2. To prevent European interference

        3. To expand United States influence in the Western Hemisphere

    B. Self-defense

        1. To maintain law and order in nations near the United States

        2. To keep European interest out of Western Hemisphere

At the top of the next column is an expository essay which answers the directive posed in column two on page 662. Note the thesis statement: Between 1898 and 1934 the United States intervened in Cuban affairs out of concern for its own national security and its own self-interest. Note as well the organization of the essay shown in the next column. The first two paragraphs describe three ways in which the United States intervened in Cuba. Then, in a third paragraph, reasons for this intervention are given.

Note also that the conclusion of the essay is not merely a summary. The conclusion brings the reader back to the directive and the thesis statement.

Introduction

Between 1898 and 1934 the United States intervened in Cuban affairs militarily, economically, and diplomatically. It did so out of concern for its own national security and its own self-interest.

Body of Essay

Although Cuba was promised its independence under the Teller Amendment of 1898, this independence was not immediately realized. For three years after the Spanish–American War, the island remained under American military control. Then, in 1901, under the Platt Amendment, Cuba was granted its independence, but even this was not the independence Cubans dreamed of. So many conditions were attached to its self-rule that in reality the Platt Amendment made Cuba a United States protectorate, not a fully independent nation.

Under the terms of the Platt Amendment, the United States maintained naval bases on the island, kept watch over Cuba's foreign and economic affairs, and actually occupied the island three times to maintain order and to protect United States business and property there. Moreover, United States diplomatic pressure frequently forced the Cubans to accept policies favored by the United States.

Continuing intervention in Cuban affairs was necessary, Americans argued, for the same reasons it was necessary elsewhere in the Caribbean area — to protect American self-interest and national security. They wanted to prevent Europeans from interfering in the political and economic affairs of the Western Hemisphere. And they wanted to protect American business and property.

Conclusion

In short, the United States was determined as a matter of self-interest and self-defense to prevent European nations from involvement in the Western Hemisphere. This meant intervening in the affairs of Cuba.

Practicing Your Skill

Read the essay directive below. On a separate sheet of paper, prepare an outline to organize your response. Then compose your essay, referring to your textbook and other materials to make your essay complete

Describe two major problems associated with building the Panama Canal, and explain how the canal eventually was completed.

The Spanish-American War of 1898 marked a turning point in America's position in the world. After the war the United States embarked upon a program of imperialism similar in many ways to that being followed by the major powers of the Western world, as well as Japan.

The influence of the United States was particularly strong in the countries bordering the Caribbean Sea. The Panama Canal provided a connecting link between the various parts of the United States' rapidly growing empire. To protect that vital artery of trade, the United States took steps to bring other Caribbean countries under its influence. Each new step the United States government took, each new commitment it assumed, led to still further steps and still further commitments.

The United States had long before expressed its special interest in the Caribbean and the rest of Latin America by issuing the Monroe Doctrine. In 1904 the United States added the Roosevelt Corollary to the Monroe Doctrine.

The corollary stated that the United States could intervene in the domestic affairs of Latin American countries, including Mexico. The United States justified this intervention on the ground that it was acting as the friendly police officer for the Western Hemisphere. To Latin Americans in general, however, the United States appeared more like a bully.

CONNECTING CHAPTER IDEAS

In the next chapter you will read why and how the United States was drawn into World War I and how the nation emerged from that conflict as a great world power.

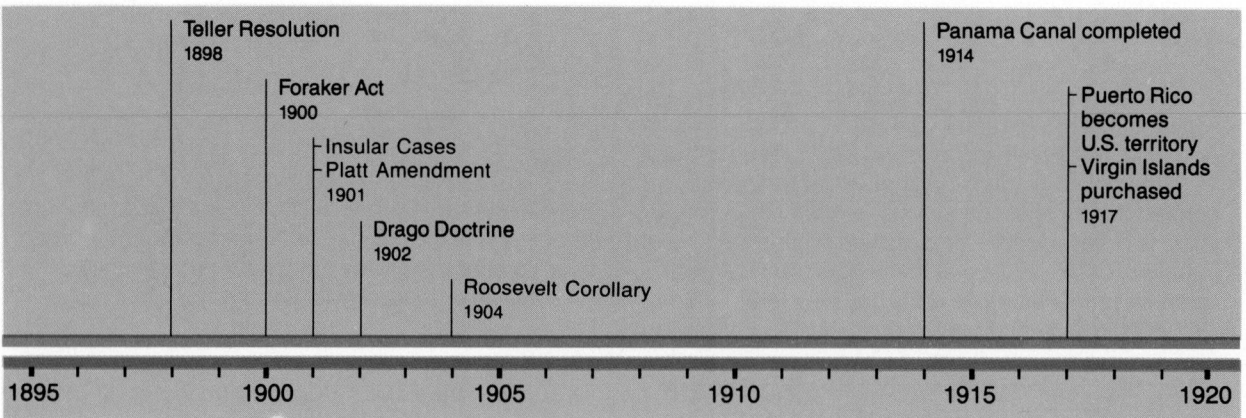

Teller Resolution
1898

Foraker Act
1900

Insular Cases
Platt Amendment
1901

Drago Doctrine
1902

Roosevelt Corollary
1904

Panama Canal completed
1914

Puerto Rico becomes U.S. territory
Virgin Islands purchased
1917

1895   1900   1905   1910   1915   1920

CHAPTER
29 REVIEW

Reviewing Important Terms

In the sentences below, the underlined terms are incorrect. On a separate sheet of paper, rewrite each sentence using the correct term.

1. The United States intervened in a dispute between Great Britain and Venezuela after Great Britain refused to submit to territorial integrity.
2. President Wilson's decision not to interfere in Mexican affairs was called dollar diplomacy.
3. Influence secured through money loaned to Latin American governments was labeled watchful waiting by critics of the policy.
4. In 1905, President Roosevelt promised to use American forces to protect the Dominican Republic's arbitration.
5. A weak nation whose affairs are supervised by a more powerful nation is a territory.

Practicing Critical Thinking Skills

1. **Evaluating Ideas.** (a) How would you justify Theodore Roosevelt's policies in the Caribbean? (b) How would you criticize them?
2. **Analyzing Ideas.** (a) It has been said that the Monroe Doctrine protected Latin America from Europe but not from the United States. Do you agree or disagree? Explain the reasons for your answer. (b) The Panama Canal created new commitments for the United States. Explain.
3. **Summarizing Ideas.** (a) Discuss dollar diplomacy from the point of view of United States business and government. (b) Discuss dollar diplomacy from the Latin American point of view. (c) Which view most closely parallels your view of dollar diplomacy? Explain.
4. **Interpreting Ideas.** Has Puerto Rico benefited from its relationship with the United States? Explain.
5. **Organizing Ideas.** Make a time line of foreign affairs for the years 1898 to 1914. Be sure to include events from Chapter 28 and Chapter 29. Use pictures or drawings to illustrate at least three major events in the United States' new role as a world power.
6. **Relating Past to Present.** In the 1970's the United States and Panama signed a treaty giving Panama greater influence and control over the Panama Canal. (a) Why was the United States willing to relinquish control? (b) Should the United States have agreed to such a treaty?

Why or why not? (c) What circumstances might lead the United States to attempt to regain control of the Panama Canal?

Developing History Study Skills

1. **Composing an Expository Essay.** Write an expository essay to answer the question below. Prepare an outline to organize your essay before writing and be sure to include an introduction and conclusion.

   Essay: How did the United States try to improve relations with its Latin American neighbors? Explain why these efforts were largely unsuccessful.

2. **Reading with a Purpose.** Reread Section 2 on pages 654-59 in order to answer this question: How did the United States use the Monroe Doctrine to strengthen its position in Latin America?

Relating Geography and History

The development of a modern navy was a key to United States expansion. The United States acquired the needed naval bases and coaling stations around the globe. As further colonies were acquired, the navy became necessary for colonial administration and territorial defenses. To better understand the tasks faced by the United States in the defense and administration of its new possessions, answer the following questions.

1. Using the scales of miles and kilometers in an atlas or other reference map, measure and record these distances: (a) San Francisco to Honolulu (b) San Francisco to Manila, (c) Honolulu to Pago Pago (American Samoa), (d) San Francisco to Midway Island, (e) Midway Island to Tokyo.
2. Explain the importance to the military, to trade, or to both in the early 1900's of each of the following: (a) American Samoa, (b) Midway Island, (c) the Panama Canal, (d) the Virgin Islands.
3. If United States space exploration leads to the discovery of needed raw materials on the moon or the planets, how would the United States protect that trade? Do you see any similarities between this situation and the one faced by the United States in the late 1800's and early 1900's? Explain.

665

CHAPTER 30
Involvement in World War I
(1914–1920)

Off to the
"Great War"

On the morning of July 29, 1914, New Yorkers and other Americans across the nation opened their newspapers with shocked surprise. Screaming headlines announced the beginning of war in Europe. The New York *Tribune* reported, "AUSTRIA DECLARES WAR, RUSHES VAST ARMY INTO SERBIA; RUSSIA MASSES 80,000 MEN ON BORDER." Other papers across the country carried a variation of the same news.

In general, the reaction of the American public was one of stunned disbelief. For many years governmental and business leaders had devoted much effort to develop international understanding and to promote peace.

Now, in the summer of 1914, all of these efforts had suddenly been turned aside by the Europeans. The American people reacted by withdrawing their interest in international affairs. As events unfolded across the Atlantic Ocean, the United States tried to steer a neutral course among the warring nations.

With the passing months, however, it became clear that the United States could not remain neutral. Step by step, the events of war pushed the nation closer to involvement. Finally, in the spring of 1917, the United States entered the war on the side of the Allies, a group composed of Great Britain, France, Russia, Italy, and several other nations.

The conflict that started in 1914 was the world's first total war. Few people anywhere remained unaffected by it. Before the war ended four years later, 30 nations on six continents would be involved. More than 8 million soldiers and sailors and an equal number of civilians would lose their lives in this devastating world war.

═══ READING FOCUS ═══

As you read about the world's first total war, look for the details that support each of the following statements.

1. Peacekeeping efforts fail and World War I breaks out.
2. The United States attempts to remain neutral.
3. The United States declares war and mobilizes its strength.
4. American troops and ideals help the Allies win the war.
5. The United States refuses to join the League of Nations.

1 Peacekeeping efforts fail and World War I breaks out

See Teaching Suggestions in TMRG, p.TM166.

During the late 1800's and the early 1900's, the leading nations of the world had taken important steps toward international cooperation. By 1914 many Europeans and Americans were convinced that major wars would never again occur.

Growing interdependence. For nearly 100 years, a movement for international peace had been steadily gaining strength. During the early 1900's, antiwar societies in both Europe and America published pamphlets insisting that war failed to solve any problems—and that even the victors paid too high a price.

Industrial technology was rapidly bringing the people of the earth closer together. Railway trains rumbled across national boundaries. Passenger ships, freighters, the telegraph, the telephone, and underwater cables linked people in all parts of the world.

The number, variety, and importance of activities that people of different nations could and did carry on together increased greatly. Many businesses now bought and sold in worldwide markets and built industries in different countries. Humanitarian associations, including the Red Cross, organized on an international basis. Professional groups—scientists, engineers, doctors, and scholars—formed international societies and pooled their knowledge for the benefit of all peoples.

Governments as well as individual citizens also engaged in a growing number of activities requiring international cooperation. By 1914 at least 30 international agencies of government were dealing with problems shared by many nations. Among them were transportation, communication, disease and sanitation, postal regulations, and maritime rules.

The Pan-American Union. Meanwhile the governments of the leading nations of the world had been making new efforts to prevent war. On several occasions during the late 1800's and the early 1900's, delegates from many different nations met to discuss the issues of war and peace. In 1889–90, delegates from the Latin American countries and the

▲ Discussion topic: Have students read the opening paragraph and discuss the meaning of "International cooperation." What are recent examples of its success or failure?

667

United States met in Washington, D.C., and organized the International Union of American Republics. The union aimed to abolish war and to substitute for it arbitration between the American republics.

In 1910 the name of the International Union of American Republics was changed to the Pan-American Union. Under that name it held periodic meetings to discuss common problems. (Later, in 1948, the members of the Pan-American Union created the Organization of American States, known as the O.A.S.)

In the early 1900's, United States expansion and interference in the Caribbean area angered many Latin Americans and thus weakened the influence of the Pan-American Union. Nevertheless, throughout the Americas the Pan-American Union was the symbol of hope for a new, more peaceful world.

The Hague Conference. Millions of people in both Europe and the Americas had also taken hope from two conferences held in Europe.

The First Hague Conference, called by the tsar of Russia, met at The Hague in the Netherlands in 1899. Twenty-six nations sent delegates. The delegates strongly urged nations to try to settle disputes through **mediation** or arbitration. In cases involving mediation, two or more nations engaged in a dispute would ask a disinterested third party or nation to recommend a solution. In cases involving arbitration, two or more nations engaged in a dispute would agree in advance to accept the decision of a neutral party. To encourage arbitration, the First Hague Conference organized the Permanent Court of Arbitration with headquarters at The Hague. The conference also tried to lessen the horrors of warfare by outlawing certain weapons and by drawing up rules for the conduct of war.

The Second Hague Conference, called by the tsar of Russia and President Theodore Roosevelt, met at The Hague in 1907. This time 44 nations sent delegates. The conference drafted additional rules for the conduct of war and adopted the Drago Doctrine. As you remember, this doctrine stated that no nation should use force to collect debts "unless the debtor country refused arbitration, or having accepted arbitration, failed to submit to the award."

The first two Hague Conferences encouraged those who were working to promote peace. A third conference was being planned when war broke out in Europe.

Other efforts to promote peace. Although President Roosevelt believed that some wars were necessary, he played a leading role in the peace movement. He was responsible for the 1905 peace conference at Portsmouth, New Hampshire. There Japan and Russia reached an agreement ending the Russo-Japanese War. President Roosevelt and his successor, President Taft, also played active parts in other international negotiations.

President Wilson, who took office in 1913, was an even stronger champion of international understanding. He supported his Secretary of State, William Jennings Bryan, who negotiated antiwar treaties with 21 nations in 1913 and 1914. These treaties declared that every dispute had to be submitted to a joint commission for investigation and recommendation. The nations signing the treaties promised not to go to war until the commissions had made their reports.

By 1914 such efforts had built what seemed to be a solid and enduring structure of peace. Why, then, did war break out?

The spark that led to war. In spite of the many efforts made to preserve peace in the early 1900's, the European nations during these years were standing on a powder keg. When a spark was struck to the powder, the hopes and plans for peace of peoples everywhere exploded.

The spark was struck in the Balkan Peninsula of Europe (see map, page 669) in the early summer of 1914. There Serbian nationalists had pledged to free all Slavs° living under the rule of the Austro-Hungarian empire. The Serbian nationalists assassinated the Archduke Franz Ferdinand, heir to the throne of Austria-Hungary, and his wife Sophie as they rode through the streets of Sarajevo (SAH·rah·yeh·voh), the capital of the province of Bosnia. Bosnia had only recently become part of the Austro-Hungarian empire.

The Serbian conspirators were caught and brought to trial, but Franz Joseph, emperor of Austria-Hungary, and his advisers decided to use this opportunity to destroy Serbia's power completely. Thus Austria-Hungary made certain harsh demands against Serbia, which Serbia refused to meet.

°**Slavs:** a people widely spread over central, eastern, and southeastern Europe whose languages come from the same basic root. The Slavs under Austro-Hungarian rule were called South Slavs.

▲ The assassin was Gavril Princip, a member of the Black Hand, a Serbian terrorist organization. Princip was sent to prison, where he died in 1918 of tuberculosis.

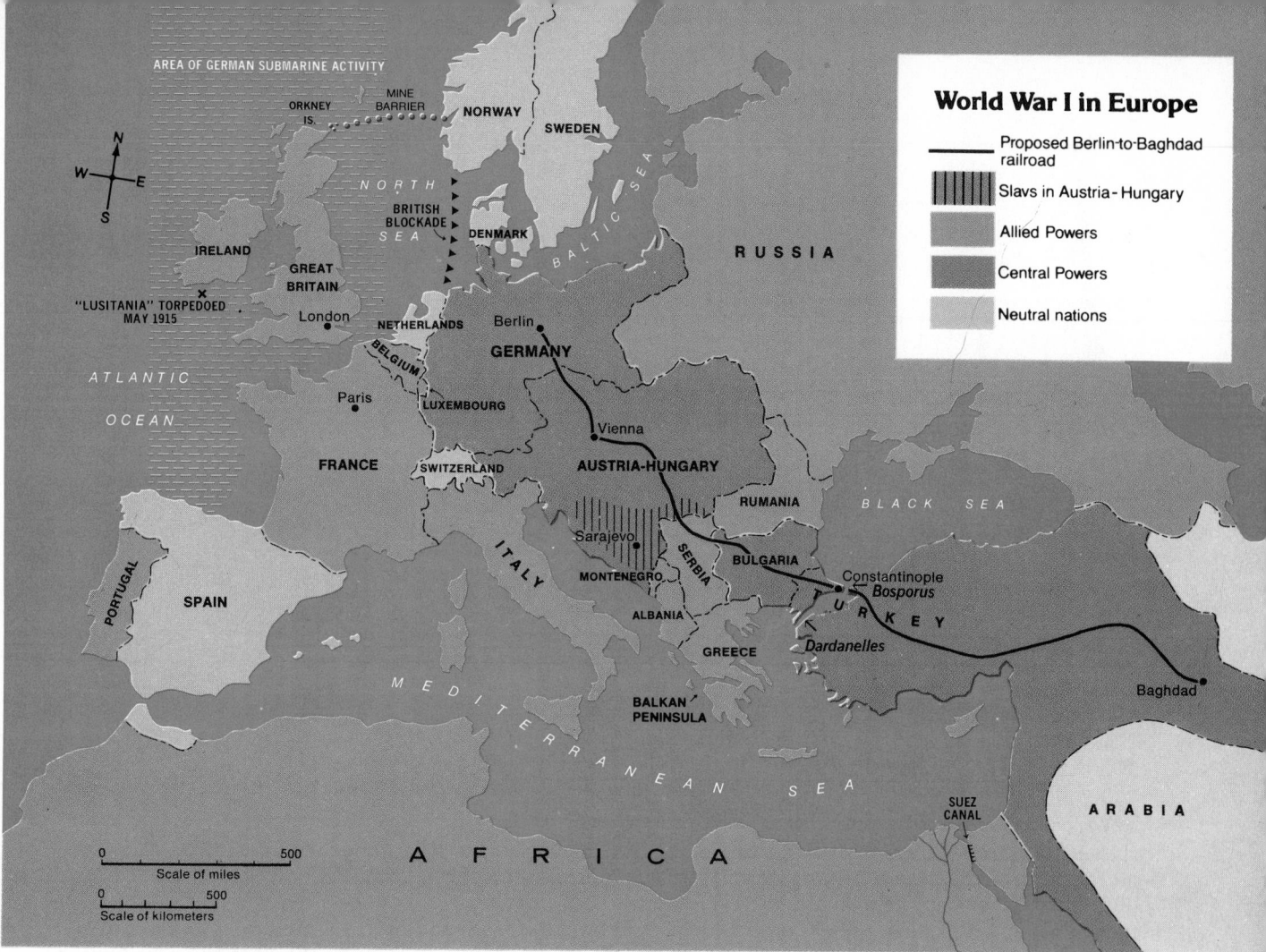

AREA OF GERMAN SUBMARINE ACTIVITY

World War I in Europe

Proposed Berlin-to-Baghdad railroad

Slavs in Austria-Hungary

Allied Powers

Central Powers

Neutral nations

As tension grew, European diplomats struggled to solve the differences between Austria-Hungary and Serbia. The efforts failed and, with the support of Germany, its main ally, Austria-Hungary declared war on Serbia on July 28, 1914.

The movement of Austrian armies across the border into Serbia triggered a chain reaction. Within a week Austria-Hungary and Germany were at war with Russia, France, and Great Britain. Before the conflict ended, it had engulfed 30 nations on six continents. The nations siding with Austria-Hungary and Germany were known as the Central Powers. Those allying themselves with Russia, France, and Great Britain were referred to as the Allied Powers, or simply as the Allies.

Did the tragic incident at Sarajevo really start World War I? Yes and no. It was the immediate cause, the spark that touched off the explosion. However, there were deep, underlying causes that help to explain why the war came and spread so rapidly and widely.

Nationalism as a cause. An intense spirit of nationalism was one of the underlying sources of tension. The term **nationalism** often refers to the strong feeling people have for their own country. It may also refer to the desire of people ruled by others to throw off this foreign rule and create their own nation.

It was the desire to free certain Slavs from Austro-Hungarian rule that led the Serbian conspirators to assassinate the heir to the

669

During World War I, the Central and Allied forces engaged in bloody trench warfare along the German-French border. Here troops carefully make their way through the barren "no-man's land" — the war zone — in an attempt to capture an enemy trench.

throne of Austria-Hungary. Austria-Hungary declared war on Serbia in order to crush this rising spirit of nationalism among the Slavic people. This spirit of nationalism was not confined to the Balkan Peninsula. In almost every country of Europe as well as in the colonies overseas, people ruled by other nations longed for independence.

Imperialism as a cause. Another source of tension was imperialism — the struggle for colonies. As you recall, during the late 1800's and the early 1900's the major powers of the world were engaged in a race for empire. By 1914, so far as colonies were concerned, the nations of Europe could be grouped into two classes: the "have" nations and the "have-not" nations.

Great Britain and France, each with huge colonial empires, were among the "have" powers. Although Russia owned no colonies, it possessed immense areas of underdeveloped land and thus was also a "have" nation.

Germany, on the other hand, was a "have-not" nation. It owned colonies in Africa and in the Pacific, but its colonial empire was relatively small, and Germany wanted additional territory. Italy was in a similar situation. One of the reasons that finally brought Italy into the war on the Allied side was a promise of colonies when the war ended.

International rivalries. Rivalry among nations was not, however, confined to the race for colonies. Austria-Hungary attacked Serbia partly to strengthen its hold on the Slavic peoples and partly to increase its influence in the Balkan Peninsula. Russia, on the other hand, came to Serbia's aid to prevent Austria-Hungary from increasing its influence.

France supported Russia not only because it was Russia's ally but also because it wanted to recover Alsace-Lorraine, a former French area that the Germans had conquered in 1871. Italy desired nearby territories within the Austro-Hungarian empire. Every Balkan country looked greedily at territory belonging to its neighbors. Russia longed for ice-free harbors in the Baltic Sea and for an outlet through the Dardanelles and the Bosporus into the Mediterranean Sea (see map, page 669). Germany, the major Baltic Sea power, and Turkey, which controlled the Dardanelles, feared and distrusted Russia.

Systems of alliance. The mounting tensions with their accompanying plots and intrigues

On January 10, 1918, Jeannette Rankin, the first woman to be elected as a representative in Congress, introduced into the House the women's suffrage amendment. The roll call for passage was close — 274 in favor, 136 against. The vote was exactly one more than the required two-thirds for passage.

Rankin also believed strongly in the quest for world peace. In 1917 Rankin, along with 55 other members of Congress, had voted against America's entry into World War I.

In 1940, Rankin was again elected to the House of Representatives. In Congress, she opposed the draft and military expenditures, and cast the only vote against United States entry into World War II. That vote cost her any chance for reelection in 1942.

After the World War II, Rankin studied different methods of promoting pacifism, particularly Ghandi's passive resistance. Rankin remained an outspoken pacifist throughout the rest of her life. She opposed American cold war policies and the nation's involvement in Korea. In January 1968, at the age of 88, she led the Jeannette Rankin Brigade in a march on Washington, D.C., to protest the war in Vietnam.

led to an armaments race, or race for military power. Long before 1914 the relative sizes of their navies and armies occupied a major part of the attention of all of the governments in Europe.

Besides building up their military forces, European nations tried to gain security with the **balance-of-power system.** This meant that every nation tried to increase its own strength by securing as many allies as possible. Thus Germany, Austria-Hungary, and Italy joined in what became known as the Triple Alliance. To maintain a balance of power, Great Britain, France, and Russia joined in what became known as the Triple Entente (ahn·TAHNT). Both of these rival alliances had been completed by 1907.

Austria's declaration of war on Serbia set the whole system of alliances into motion. Of all the nations, only Italy failed to live up to its treaty obligations, which pledged Italy to support Austria-Hungary and Germany. Waiting to see which side would promise the most, Italy did not enter the war until 1915, and then it fought on the Allied side.

Peace or war? During the early 1900's, as you may recall, strong forces pulled peoples and nations in two directions at the same time. With one hand, governments tried to strengthen the bonds between nations and build a solid structure of peace. With the other hand, governments plotted and schemed against one another and desperately planned for war or for the protection of their national interests in case war broke out.

SECTION REVIEW
See underscored items, text pp. 667-71.
Identify: interdependence, mediation, Slavs, Central Powers, Allied Powers, nationalism, imperialism, balance-of-power system, Triple Alliance, Triple Entente
For answers to questions, see Answer Key, p.A93.
1. **Organizing Ideas:** What was the purpose of the Pan-American Union?
2. **Analyzing Ideas:** Why did the first two Hague Conferences greatly encourage those who were working to promote peace among nations?
3. **Interpreting Ideas:** Why is the incident at Sarajevo considered the spark that set off World War I?
4. **Determining Cause and Effect:** How did the following help cause World War I and encourage its rapid spread: (a) nationalism, (b) imperialism, (c) international rivalries, (d) the balance-of-power system?

Planet Earth is really misnamed. It was called Earth, of course, because our ancestors found land all around them. As far as they knew, being land creatures, this planet was, indeed, chiefly soil and rock. Had they only known the realities of this planet, they surely would have named it Ocean instead of Earth. Oceans occupy 71 percent of the area of this planet. Our world is really one huge ocean, interrupted here and there by much smaller pieces of land that are called continents.

The world's oceans are really one ocean. Names have been given to the four largest areas of this world ocean: Pacific, Atlantic, Indian, and Arctic. Names have also been given to the many smaller gulfs, seas, and other water bodies that are extensions of these four large oceans. A look at the globe, however, shows the connection between this array of gulfs, seas, and oceans. It really is one giant, interconnective, water system — a world ocean.

The turning of the earth on its axis, and the winds that blow across the surface of the earth, set in constant motion the liquid world of water. The waters of the world's oceans circulate continuously. For example, imagine a bright yellow dye put into water in a glass. This has been done so that a particular volume of water can be easily identified. Imagine pouring this glass of yellow-dyed water into the 330 million cubic miles of water that is the one ocean. In time, thousands of years from now, when this one glass of water has thoroughly mixed in the giant connected system of ocean water, every glass of sea water, no matter where in the world's ocean a glass might be dipped, would contain yellow dye.

Much about the geography of oceans is still a mystery. It was less than 500 years ago that people first learned

The ocean's beauty and power present both problems and promises for the future.

how large the ocean really is. Magellan's voyage, the first around the world, ended in 1522. As great as his voyage was, however, mapmakers still felt that the earth was probably equally divided between land and water. Two later explorers, Abel Tasman and James Cook, helped to set the record straight. They mapped huge areas of the Pacific and proved that the southern portion of the world ocean was so large and so empty that a person could sail around the earth without sighting land. Explorers like Tasman and Cook have demonstrated a great deal more about the ocean's surface. Little is known, however, about the ocean's depths. After all, the deepest parts of the ocean lie more then 35,000 feet (10,670 meters) beneath the surface.

How could people get there to explore it? Without special diving gear, 50 feet (15 meters) is as deep as a free-swimming diver can safely explore. With a tank of oxygen and breathing equipment the diver's range can be extended another 200 feet (60 meters). Helmeted divers can work at 600 feet (185 meters) if they breathe a special mixture of gases. Modern submarines can operate at 2,000 feet (610 meters), and some new, small, special research and rescue vessels can descend to 15,000 feet (4600 meters). Most of what scientists have learned about the ocean floor, however, has been learned by sending instruments into depths that people cannot yet safely explore.

Some interesting things have been learned about the ocean's geography. Ocean floors consist of much heavier rock than that found on continents. Another surprise is that the earth's crust, the thin outermost layer, is much thinner under the ocean than on land. Also discovered are a 40,000-mile (64,000 kilometers) long submarine mountain range called the Mid-Ocean Ridge, and a

A specially designed research ship

36,000-foot (58,600 kilometers) deep depression called the Marianas Trench.

Scientists can only guess the number and types of plants and animals that inhabit the world ocean. New species are constantly being discovered. Sea monsters, so feared by sailors hundreds of years ago, are unlikely discoveries of the deep. Yet there are undoubtedly some monstrous creatures down there. An ocean research ship from Denmark once caught the larva of an eel that was so large, it would have been 90 feet (27 meters) in length when fully grown. No one has ever caught an eel of this size. That does not mean, however, that they cannot or do not exist. Another research ship hooked something at a depth of over 1,000 feet (305 meters). What it was they never learned. The creature was so big and so powerful that it bent a three foot steel hook and escaped.

People have failed to understand the complex forces at work in the oceans. In the past the oceans were seen as vast and mysterious. People believed that any body of water so large could surely absorb all that might be dumped into it. So for centuries people have mistreated the world ocean, especially those parts of it located near larger populations.

Today, the ocean is tainted with great oil spills, beaches exist where the water is too polluted to allow swimming, and oyster and clam beds have become so contaminated that eating the oysters or clams would cause severe sickness or even death. People have extended sewer pipes far out to sea. They have dumped poisonous refuse beyond the continental shelf.

People are learning that the ocean cannot be used as a dumping ground. The coastal waters of all the industrial nations of the world are becoming increasingly polluted.

Many major fishing grounds are showing declining yields. The chemicals with which coastal areas have become polluted do not remain along the coast. Currents carry pollutants far out to sea. No part of the world, or ocean, can escape pollution. It is, after all, one ocean. It is connected, one part to another. The livers of penguins and seals as far away as Antarctica contain some DDT. Every jar of ocean water contains some radioactive material put into the ocean by people. Right now, neither DDT nor radioactive wastes are present in quantities that might directly affect people. But the message is clear. The great world ocean has limits. It must be used intelligently to keep its resources available for all.

A robot submarine (below, left) collects data from the ocean's depths. A researcher (above) investigates marine life. The ocean's resources must be protected without destroying its beauty (below, right).

Discussion topic: Have students consider the possible conflicts between complete freedom of the seas (one of Wilson's Fourteen Points) and the responsibility to protect the ocean environment. What can be done about vessels from other nations that are damaging the ocean's ecosystem?

673

2 The United States attempts to remain neutral

See Teaching Suggestions in TMRG, pp.TM167-68.

America's first reaction to the outbreak of the war in Europe was one of shocked surprise and withdrawal. The war seemed unreal, a nightmare that surely would not last long.

American neutrality. Nevertheless, the war was real, and President Wilson urged Americans to be "neutral in fact as well as in name" and "impartial in thought as well as in action." From the beginning, however, Americans were torn between the desire to avoid war and their sympathy for one side or the other.

Millions of recently naturalized Americans had friends and relatives in Europe. Men and women of German origin — or of Austrian or Turkish origin — wanted the Central Powers to

In 1914 heavy bombing nearly leveled the city of Reims in northeastern France and destroyed the interior of the historic Reims Cathedral, including its irreplaceable stained-glass windows.

win. Most Americans, however, were sympathetic to the Allied Powers. The ties of language, similar democratic governments, and deep-rooted traditions bound Americans to Great Britain. The ties with France were also strong. After all, the French back in 1778 had come to the aid of Americans fighting for their independence. As World War I went on, this sympathy for the Allies led thousands of young Americans to enlist in the British, Canadian, and French armed forces. A special unit of volunteer American fliers, called the Lafayette Escadrille, was created as part of the new French flying force.

Although in 1914 American sympathies were divided, most Americans supported the President's policy of neutrality and prayed for an early end to the war.

The German plan of attack. The Central Powers, under the leadership of the German High Command, had every intention of ending the war quickly. They wanted to conquer France before the Russians could fully mobilize. With France at their mercy, they could then turn against Russia.

Long before the war the French, fearful of German attack, had built strong fortifications along the entire Franco-German frontier. However, the French had not fortified the border between France and Belgium. The French counted on an international agreement, which the Germans had signed, that in the event of war Belgium would be respected as a neutral nation.

The German Chancellor, however, declared that the international agreement respecting Belgium's neutrality was merely "a scrap of paper." The German High Command launched an attack against neutral Belgium and Luxembourg. Seven German armies were to reach the borders of France in six days and strike in a great wheeling action at northern France (see map, page 675).

Failure of the plan. The German plan failed, largely because Belgium resisted. Because of gallant resistance by the small Belgian army, the Germans took 18 days to cross Belgium, not the six called for in the German timetable. This delay gave General Joffre, commander of the French armies, time to rush troops to the Belgian border. In addition it gave the British time to transport an army of about 90,000 to northern France.

The French and the British arrived too late to save Belgium. Nor were they able to stop the Germans at the Belgian frontier. Crushed by the superior might of the Germans, the French and British retreated to the Marne River, where General Joffre hastily prepared his main defense.

Fighting against seemingly hopeless odds, the French and British stopped the Germans early in September 1914 at the Marne River in the First Battle of the Marne. The Germans then fell back to the Aisne (AYN) River, where they dug a line of trenches and checked an Allied counteroffensive.

The First Battle of the Marne was one of the decisive battles of the war. If the Germans had won, they might have crushed all remaining French and British resistance in a few weeks.

Stalemate on the Western Front. By 1915 the war in Western Europe had reached a **stalemate.** Both sides were dug in along a 600-mile (965-kilometer) line reaching from the Swiss border to the English Channel. During the next three years, both the Germans and the Allies, with only a thin strip of land called **no-man's land** separating their trenches, fought desperately along the Western Front. Neither side was able to break through the enemy line or to end the **trench warfare.** Thousands died in this bloody struggle, but until the spring of 1918 neither side made a significant gain.

There were other fronts—and on all of them troops were fighting and dying. The Central Powers and Russia were locked in combat along the entire Eastern Front. Turkish troops defended a precarious line that reached southward through Palestine as far as Medina, in Arabia, against the British and French and their allies. The fighting forces of Austria-Hungary and Italy faced each other north of the Adriatic Sea.

The British blockade. The prospect of a long war was bad news indeed for Americans who hoped to remain neutral. It meant, among other things, that warfare on the high seas would grow fiercer as Great Britain and Germany tried to prevent supplies from reaching the other side.

The British fleet controlled the seas, at least during the opening months of the war. It blockaded the German coast (see map, page 669) and laid explosive mines in the North Sea. To the angry astonishment of Americans, the

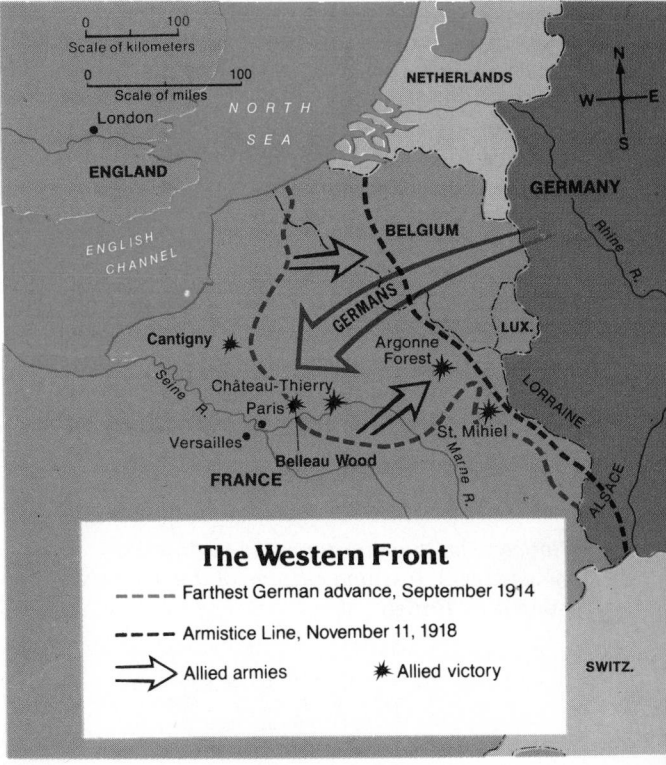

The Western Front

- - - - Farthest German advance, September 1914

- - - - Armistice Line, November 11, 1918

➡ Allied armies   ✴ Allied victory

British navy also blockaded neutral countries, such as Norway, Sweden, Denmark, and the Netherlands, through which American goods flowed into Germany. American anger increased when the British began to examine American mail bound for Europe and ordered all neutral ships to stop at British ports, where their cargoes were searched. The United States protested that Great Britain's actions violated neutrality.

Submarine warfare. American anger at Great Britain subsided, however, in the face of German submarine warfare. According to international law, naval vessels of countries at war had the right to stop and search a neutral ship for weapons, munitions, and other materials useful in war, known as **contraband.** The naval vessel had the right to seize a neutral ship carrying contraband and take it into port as a prize of war. If it were impossible to take the neutral vessel into port, the warship was required to take its passengers and crew to a safe place before sinking the prize.

Submarines were not armed to defend themselves against enemy warships while on the surface. Thus they could not take seized vessels into port. Nor could submarines take

▲ American reporter Richard Harding Davis saw the Germans pass through Belgium to France. Davis described the army: "...not men marching but a force of nature like a tidal wave, an avalanche...a gray army has rumbled by with the mystery of fog and the pertinacity of a steam roller."

675

the passengers and crew of a large vessel on board. Least of all could they surface and search neutral ships, for the moment they rose to the surface they were "sitting ducks" for even one well-aimed shot from a naval gun. Submarines were designed to lurk in the ocean depths, to strike suddenly without warning at an enemy ship, and to slip away quickly before a counterattack.

The German surface fleet, although powerful, was still no match for the British navy. The Germans, therefore, had concentrated on building submarines, called U-boats. Early in the war, the Germans notified President Wilson that they intended to turn their subma-

Notices like this one appeared in American newspapers, warning citizens of the dangers of sailing on British ships.

NOTICE!

TRAVELLERS intending to embark on the Atlantic voyage are reminded that a state of war exists between Germany and her allies and Great Britain and her allies; that the zone of war includes the waters adjacent to the British Isles; that, in accordance with formal notice given by the Imperial German Government, vessels flying the flag of Great Britain, or of any of her allies, are liable to destruction in those waters and that travellers sailing in the war zone on ships of Great Britain or her allies do so at their own risk.

IMPERIAL GERMAN EMBASSY
WASHINGTON, D. C., APRIL 22, 1915.

rines loose in the Atlantic. President Wilson promptly replied that the United States would hold Germany responsible for any acts that endangered American property and lives on the high seas.

The *Lusitania.* The Germans were convinced that their submarine blockade would ruin Great Britain. They therefore ignored President Wilson's warning and ordered their U-boats to patrol the Atlantic shipping lanes. On March 28, 1915, a British steamer was torpedoed and sunk near Ireland, carrying to their deaths more than 100 persons, including an American.

This and other incidents led to the sinking of the British liner *Lusitania* off the southern coast of Ireland on May 7, 1915, with the loss of 1,198 lives, including 128 Americans. Since the *Lusitania* was carrying war materials bound for England, the Germans believed that their action was justified.

In three strongly worded messages to the German government in Berlin, the American State Department protested against the sinking of the *Lusitania*. The messages warned that any repetition of such action would have serious consequences. American anger at the *Lusitania* affair was still at the boiling point when on August 9, 1915, another U-boat sank the *Arabic,* a British liner, with the loss of two American lives.

Alarmed at the American reaction, Germany on September 1 gave a written promise that in the future "liners will not be sunk by our submarines without warning . . . provided that the liners do not try to escape or offer resistance." Americans had to be content with this promise.

The sinking of the *Lusitania* marked a turning point in American feeling about the war. Increasing numbers of Americans began to realize that the conflict in Europe was not far off but close at hand. They began to understand that neutrality might become impossible. Nevertheless, in 1915 most still hoped that the United States could avoid war.

More sinkings, more promises. In March 1916 the Germans broke their promise and attacked a French passenger vessel, the *Sussex.* Lives were lost and several Americans were injured. President Wilson threatened to break off diplomatic relations with Germany unless it agreed to abandon submarine warfare.

In what became known as the "*Sussex* pledge*," Germany renewed its earlier promise not to sink liners without warning and without providing for the safety of the passengers. However, the Germans added an important reservation. They would keep the promise on condition that the United States would persuade the Allies to modify the food blockade of Germany, which, according to Berlin, was inflicting hunger and even starvation on the German people. The United States replied that the British blockade had nothing to do with German violation of American neutral rights on the high seas.

A rising war spirit. American opinion was divided over Wilson's efforts to enforce neutrality. Some people, including former President Theodore Roosevelt, felt that the United States was not firm enough. Others believed that the American government was unwisely going too far in its threatening demands on Berlin. Secretary of State Bryan, for example, resigned during the *Lusitania* crisis. In Bryan's opinion, the United States should forbid American citizens to travel on British and French ships. Bryan also believed that Congress should stop Americans from selling war materials to nations at war.

President Wilson refused to follow the advice of those who shared Bryan's views. Instead, Wilson supported a program for strengthening the army and navy. The National Defense Act, passed in June 1916, increased America's regular army from 106,000 to 175,000 soldiers and provided for officers' training camps. A three-year naval program was started in 1916. In 1916 the government also created the Council of National Defense and the United States Shipping Board. These agencies planned the mobilization of the country's resources in case of war and began a huge shipbuilding program.

▲ The war preparations did not mean that either Wilson or the public had abandoned all hope of remaining neutral. Indeed, many Americans voted for the reelection of Wilson in November 1916 on the ground that "he kept us out of war."

Six months later, under the leadership of President Wilson and Congress, the American people entered the conflict, millions of them with considerable enthusiasm. What happened to lead the administration to abandon neutrality and take this step?

Identify: trench warfare, contraband, U-boats, *Lusitania,* "*Sussex* pledge"

For answers to questions, see Answer Key, p.A93.

1. **Interpreting Ideas:** President Wilson stated that the United States had to be "neutral in fact as well as in name" and "impartial in thought as well as in action." Why did many Americans find it difficult to maintain such impartiality?

2. **Analyzing Ideas:** America's neutral rights were violated by both Great Britain and Germany. Explain.

3. **Studying Maps:** Examine the maps on pages 669 and 675. **(a)** Locate the area in the first map that is shown enlarged in the second map. Which map would be more useful in gaining an overall impression of the war? **(b)** in gaining information on military strategies? **(c)** in naming the countries on each side? Explain your answers.

3 The United States declares war and mobilizes its strength

See Teaching Suggestions in TMRG, pp.TM167-68.

During the winter of 1916–17, all American hope of remaining neutral finally vanished. The German leaders themselves were largely responsible for this development.

Diplomatic relations broken. On February 1, 1917, Germany decided to renew unrestricted submarine warfare, thus going back on the "*Sussex* pledge." A German proposal to permit only one American passenger ship to sail to England each week added insult to injury.

The German High Command made this decision fully aware that it would almost certainly bring the United States into the war. The High Command took the risk that submarines could destroy Great Britain's power before the United States could provide help.

Wilson met the new challenge promptly. On February 3 he broke off diplomatic relations with the German government.

Moving toward war. On February 24, British naval intelligence agents revealed a German message they had intercepted and decoded. The message had been sent from Germany by Foreign Secretary Arthur Zimmerman to the German minister in Mexico. It contained in-

▲ Writing activity: Have the students write a paragraph supporting or refuting this statement: Wilson's war preparations increased the likelihood of United States entry into World War I.

677

structions about what to do in case war broke out between Germany and the United States. In this event, the German minister was to offer Mexico an alliance with Germany. With German support Mexico was to attack the United States and "reconquer the lost territory in New Mexico, Texas, and Arizona." When Wilson released the Zimmermann note to the Associated Press on March 1, Americans were shocked and angry.

On March 12 President Wilson, through the State Department, announced that all American merchant vessels sailing through war zones would be armed for defense against German submarines. The public received this announcement with mixed reactions but in general approved.

Still other and deeper forces moved American sympathies toward the Allies and toward war with Germany. For one thing, American ties with Great Britain and France were traditionally closer than those with Germany. Not least important, American shipments of munitions to the Allied Powers had risen from $6 million in 1914 to nearly $500 million in 1916. By April 1917, American bankers had loaned about $2 billion to the Allies. Naturally, these American investors wanted an Allied victory. However, historians have found no evidence to show that economic interests consciously influenced Wilson's conduct in the critical weeks before the United States entered the war.

The President's "War Message." As the weeks passed, President Wilson reluctantly concluded that America's entrance into the war was inevitable. Supported by his entire cabinet, the President called for a special session of Congress. On April 2, 1917, a solemn and hushed group of Senators, Representatives, and distinguished guests gathered to hear President Wilson present his impassioned "War Message."

The President condemned Germany's submarine warfare as "the wanton and wholesale destruction of the lives of noncombatants, men, women, and children, engaged in pursuits which have always, even in the darkest periods of modern history, been deemed innocent and legitimate. Property can be paid for; the lives of peaceful and innocent people cannot be. . . . The challenge is to all mankind," the President declared. "The wrongs against which we now array ourselves are no common wrongs; they cut to the very roots of human life."

Wilson was too great an idealist to rest his case upon the evils of unrestricted submarine warfare alone. He also summoned the American people to rise in a crusade for a better world: "We are glad to fight thus for the ultimate peace of the world and for the liberation of its peoples, the German people included; for the rights of nations great and small and the privilege of men everywhere to choose their way of life and of obedience. The world must be made safe for democracy. Its peace must be planted upon the tested foundations of political liberty. We have no selfish ends to serve. We desire no conquest, no dominion. We seek no indemnities for ourselves."

Congress promptly declared war. The Senate approved a war declaration on April 4, the House on April 6, 1917. America's entry into the conflict had an immediate effect upon other neutral countries. Between April 1917 and July 1918, a number of Latin American states declared war. Most of the other American countries, although unwilling to enter the war, severed diplomatic relations with Germany.

Raising an army. As soon as war was declared, the United States began to mobilize its work force, its industries, and its natural resources. On May 18 Congress adopted the Selective Service Act, which required the registration of all men between the ages of 21 and 30. The act was amended on August 31, 1918, to include all men between 18 and 45. During the war more than 24 million Americans were registered by their local draft boards, and 2.8 million of this group were drafted into the army. Before the war ended, more than 4.7 million Americans served in the armed forces.

About 371,000 black Americans served in World War I, but, as in earlier wars, they often met prejudice and discrimination. They were restricted to separate units, recreation centers, and living accommodations. Most of the 200,000 black troops sent to Europe served in noncombatant battalions, though many of them requested combat duty. All of the 10,000 blacks who served in the navy were assigned to noncombat duties.

As the war progressed, the bravery and courage of black units under fire were plain to see. The first Allied unit to drive through to the Rhine River was the 369th, a black regiment attached to the Ninety-third Division. For outstanding courage in battle, Henry Johnson and Needham Roberts of the 369th became the first

Every hour around the clock, an armed sentry begins patrol of the Tomb of the Unknown Soldiers — commonly called the Tomb of the Unknowns — in Arlington National Cemetery near Washington, D.C. The sentry guards the last resting place of four unidentified veterans who fought and died for the United States.

After World War I, the Allied governments were not able to identify many of their war dead. Each government chose a symbolic unknown soldier and built a monument in his honor. The marble-topped crypt in which the American unknown soldier is buried carries the inscription, "Here lies in honored glory an American soldier known only to God."

In 1958 Congress decreed that one unknown soldier from World War II and one from the Korean War be buried beside the remains of the unknown soldier from World War I. In the 1970's a fourth crypt was added, containing the remains of an unknown soldier from the Vietnam War.

Each Memorial Day the President of the United States visits the Tomb of the Unknown Soldiers, paying tribute to all Americans who have died in the service of their country.

black Americans to be awarded the *Croix de Guerre,* or Cross of War, a coveted French military honor.

Financing the war. To finance the war, the government borrowed money by selling war bonds. The government also boosted income-tax rates and levied excise taxes on railroad tickets, telegraph and telephone messages, alcoholic beverages, tobacco, and amusements.

▲ **Mobilizing industry.** To stimulate production and prevent waste, Congress gave President Wilson sweeping wartime powers.

The President was authorized to set prices on many commodities, including such essentials as food and fuels. He was also authorized to regulate, or even to take possession of, factories, mines, meat-packing houses, food-processing plants, and all transportation and communication facilities. The President exercised these vast powers through a number of wartime agencies, or boards.

The War Industries Board, established in 1917, became the virtual dictator of manufacturing. By the war's end the Board had regulated the production of 30,000 commodities.

The War Finance Corporation loaned public funds to businesses manufacturing war materials. The Emergency Fleet Corporation built ships faster than German submarines could destroy them. The Railroad Administration operated the railroads, reorganized the lines, and controlled rates and wages. The Fuel Administration urged a larger production of coal and oil and encouraged greater economies in their use.

Mobilizing labor. Successful mobilization depended upon the full cooperation of labor. To deal with labor disputes, President Wilson in April 1918 appointed the National War Labor Board. This board arbitrated disputes between workers and employers. The War Labor Policies Board established general policies affecting wages, hours, and working conditions. These measures and the cooperation of organized labor and business management reduced labor disputes to a minimum during the war years.

Conserving food. The problem of food was equally critical. Late in 1917 Congress adopted and submitted to the states an amendment to

▲ Discussion topic: The United States had to orchestrate a massive, rapid mobilization because it was
scarcely prepared for a full-scale war. Have students consider whether the United States has
greater "war-readiness" today. Ask the students what developments have influenced today's situation?

679

SERVICE

FALL IN!

NATIONAL LEAGUE FoR WOMANS SERVICE

Schools, churches, the press, fraternal lodges, women's and civic groups all cooperated with the government's campaign "to sell the war to the American people."

the Constitution prohibiting the manufacture, sale, or transportation of alcoholic liquors. The amendment was passed, in part, to help conserve grain, which is used in making alcohol. This Eighteenth Amendment was ratified by the necessary three fourths of the states in 1919 and went into effect on January 16, 1920.

The government also made other moves to guarantee food for the American people and their allies. Herbert Hoover, who had successfully managed food relief in war-stricken Belgium, was placed in charge of the Food Administration. Hoover brought about a vast expansion of agriculture and reduced the hoarding and waste of food. He encouraged people to plant "victory gardens" and urged them to observe "wheatless" and "meatless" days. The sale of sugar and other commodities was limited. All this took place without rationing. In-

stead the Food Administration, with the crucial help of women's groups, used persuasion to get people to cooperate.

Public opinion and dissent. The government also undertook to gain the cooperation of all Americans in the war effort. The Committee on Public Information circulated millions of leaflets describing in glowing language America's official war aims and denouncing the German government. Colleges, schools, the press, churches, fraternal lodges, women's organizations, and civic groups all cooperated with the government's campaign "to sell the war to the American people." In all sorts of public gatherings, well-known people gave brief speeches publicizing the nation's war aims and philosophy.

From the beginning most Americans enthusiastically supported the war. There were, however, some dissenters, who, in greater or lesser measure, were not in sympathy with the government's war effort.

To deal with those people, Congress in June 1917 adopted the Espionage Act. This act was aimed at treasonable and disloyal activities. In May 1918 Congress strengthened the Espionage Act by an amendment, often called the Sedition Act. This act provided penalties of up to $10,000 in fines and 20 years' imprisonment, or both, for anyone found guilty of interfering with the sale of war bonds, attempting to curtail production, or using "disloyal, profane, scurrilous, or abusive language" about the American form of government or about any of its agencies.

Under these laws, the Department of Justice arrested at least 1,597 persons. Of these, 41 received prison sentences of from 10 to 20 years. In addition, newspapers and periodicals found guilty of criticizing the government's conduct of the war were deprived of their mailing privileges.

Many loyal Americans, themselves thoroughly in sympathy with the war effort, objected to the Espionage Act and Sedition Act. They held that the constitutional rights of citizens should not be interfered with, even in wartime.

For the most part, however, Americans did not need arguments or laws to secure their loyalty. Americans entered the war on a great wave of enthusiasm. They were convinced, as Wilson had put it, that this was indeed a crusade "to make the world safe for democracy."

Identify: Zimmermann note, unrestricted submarine warfare, Selective Service Act, Henry Johnson, Espionage Act

For answers to questions, see Answer Key, p.A94.

1. **Analyzing Ideas:** In his "War Message," President Wilson asked Congress to declare war on Germany. **(a)** What reasons did he give? **(b)** Why did he view the war as a crusade?

2. **Organizing Ideas:** How did the United States mobilize **(a)** workers, **(b)** industries, **(c)** natural resources, and **(d)** public opinion?

3. **Interpreting Ideas:** In the crusade "to make the world safe for democracy," black members of the American armed forces often faced discrimination. Comment on this contradiction.

4. **Studying Graphics:** Examine the poster on page 680. **(a)** What roles does it show for women? **(b)** Were any of these roles new for women? **(c)** What effects do you think World War I may have had on the movement for women's rights?

4 American troops and ideals help the Allies win the war

See Teaching Suggestions in TMRG, p.TM168.

America's declaration of war came none too soon. In the spring of 1917, the Allies were facing a grim situation, and by the end of the year their position was desperate.

The military situation in 1917. By early 1917 the Allies had suffered enormous losses. In March they were further disturbed by news that the tsar of Russia had been deposed and a new revolutionary government established. America's entry into the conflict in April was a bright spot in a year during which Allied fortunes sank lower and lower.

In the fall Germany threw a number of crack divisions into the Austrian campaign, and on October 24 the Austrians and Germans crashed through the Italian lines at Caporetto. French and British troops, rushed from the Western Front, helped to stop the rout and saved Italy from collapse.

Most serious of all, however, was the news from Russia. On November 7 the Bolsheviks, a party of radical Communists, seized power. A month later the Bolsheviks signed an armistice with Germany. Almost three months later, in March 1918, they concluded the peace treaty of Brest-Litovsk (BREST lih·TOFSK). Meanwhile Rumania, unable to stand alone against the Central Powers in eastern Europe, in 1918 signed a peace treaty at Bucharest.

Thus, by the end of 1917, the Germans were free to concentrate most of their forces on the Western Front. General Ludendorff, commander of the German armies, prepared for an offensive intended to end the war before American troops could play an important role.

American naval forces. Meanwhile the United States Navy, which had been rapidly building its strength since 1916, went into action. Before the war ended, the United States had established 45 naval bases, which were located as far north as Murmansk, in Russia, and as far south as Greece.

In cooperation with the British Navy, American naval forces patrolled the North Sea and effectively bottled up the German fleet. They also laid most of a 230-mile (370-kilometer) barrier of mines that stretched across the North Sea from Norway to the Orkney Islands (see map, page 669). This barrier greatly increased the hazards for German submarines seeking to reach the open waters of the Atlantic Ocean or to return to their bases in Germany.

Meanwhile other naval vessels helped to convoy merchant ships and troop transports through the submarine-infested waters of the Atlantic Ocean. The convoy system was so effective that 2 million American soldiers or more were transported across the Atlantic with the loss of only a few hundred lives. It was a remarkable tribute to naval efficiency and a severe blow to the Germans.

The A.E.F. in France. While the United States Navy was busy on the high seas, American land forces were being organized. President Wilson appointed General John J. Pershing as Commander of the American Expeditionary Forces (the A.E.F.). Pershing had served in Cuba, in the Philippines, and as commander of the expedition sent into Mexico to capture Pancho Villa.

Pershing landed in France early in June 1917. By the end of June, the first regiments of the First Division arrived. On July 4 several thousand "Yanks" marched through Paris amid the heartfelt cheers of the French people.

American troops arrived in ever-swelling numbers. By the fall of 1918, more than 2 million had landed in France. To supply and maintain this huge army, the Americans built huge docks and railroads as well as networks of telephone and telegraph lines in Europe. They landed 17,000 freight cars and more than 40,000 trucks. The Americans also built training camps, hospitals, storage houses, and ammunition dumps.

Germany's last bid for victory.   On March 21, 1918, the Western Front exploded into violent action once more. The Germans, reinforced by seasoned troops released from the Russian front, launched a powerful campaign, or "peace offensive," to end the war. At the end of two weeks, the Germans had gained a large area of land and inflicted 160,000 casualties. By the end of May, they were at the Marne River, only 37 miles (59 kilometers) from Paris.

Pershing's original plans had called for a period of training behind the lines before his troops went into action. He had also insisted that American troops fight as a separate army under their own top command. However, in the spring of 1918, he consented to putting every available soldier into the lines immediately. French, British, and American troops fought together under a unified Allied command directed by the French military leader Marshal Foch (FOSH).

Under the command of General John J. Pershing, the American Expeditionary Force distinguished itself during the Allied victory drive. Here, in July 1918, American troops perform bravely at the front near Méry, to the east of Paris.

Europe After World War I

- ·—·—· Post-war boundaries
- New independent nations

Scale of miles — 0 ... 500
Scale of kilometers — 0 ... 500

NORWAY
SWEDEN
FINLAND
ESTONIA
LATVIA
LITHUANIA
DENMARK
GERMANY
RUSSIA (U.S.S.R. AFTER 1922)
IRELAND
GREAT BRITAIN
NETHERLANDS
BELGIUM
LUXEMBOURG
GERMANY
POLAND
Versailles
LORRAINE
CZECHOSLOVAKIA
ALSACE
FRANCE
SWITZERLAND
AUSTRIA
HUNGARY
RUMANIA
PORTUGAL
SPAIN
ITALY
YUGOSLAVIA
BULGARIA
ALBANIA
GREECE
TURKEY

NORTH SEA
BALTIC SEA
ATLANTIC OCEAN
BLACK SEA
MEDITERRANEAN SEA

Stopping the German advance. Fighting desperately, French, British, Belgian, and American troops finally stopped the Germans. On May 28 the First Division of the United States Army took Cantigny (kahn·teen·YEE). Three days later the Third Division, in a last ditch defense of Paris, only 40 miles (64 kilometers) away, helped the French hold the Germans at Château-Thierry (shah·TOH teh·REE). At Belleau (BEL·loh) Wood the Second Division, strengthened by the 4th Marine Brigade, held back the Germans in six days of fighting (see map, page 675).

Then, on July 15, the Germans threw everything they could into one final, ferocious assault around Reims (REEMZ). In this action, the beginning of the Second Battle of the Marne, the Allied lines held. On July 18 Marshal Foch ordered a counterattack spearheaded by the First and Second American Divisions and the First French Morocco Division. The Germans began to fall back. The tide at last had turned.

The Allied victory drive. The Allies now took the initiative. In July, Foch launched a terrific offensive along the entire length of the line. The Germans were driven back.

The Americans fought as a separate army under General Pershing's command. The American troops, 500,000 strong and supported by French troops and British planes, launched a powerful attack on the area around St. Mihiel (SAN mee·YEL) in September 1918. After three days of savage fighting, this key section of the southern front was safely under American control.

683

Then, against heavy artillery and machine-gun fire, the Americans drove toward Sedan, the highly fortified position that the Germans had held since 1914. For 47 days the United States troops pushed toward their objective. The fighting in this tremendous Meuse-Argonne (MYOOZ ahr·GUN) offensive involved 1.2 million combatants. The Americans suffered 120,000 casualties, but they pushed the German line back and captured 28,000 prisoners and large supplies of war materials.

Important though they were, the American victories were only part of the offensive against the crumbling German lines. Belgians, British, and French, confident of victory, were fighting fiercely against the enemy.

Under such hammer blows, the German morale began to sag, and Germany's allies lost heart. In September the Turkish armies in Palestine and Arabia suffered crushing blows, and Bulgaria surrendered unconditionally. On November 3 the crews of the German ships at Kiel, a German naval base, mutinied rather than go to sea. Army units also mutinied, and riots broke out in a number of German cities. On November 3 Austria signed an **armistice** with the Italians.

Convinced at last that the war was lost, Kaiser Wilhelm II, ruler of Germany, fled to the Netherlands, leaving the country in the hands of revolutionists. Germany finally signed an armistice with the Allies on November 11, 1918.

The armistice terms. The armistice was signed in a railroad car in the forest of Compiègne (kon·PYEN·yuh) in France on the eleventh hour of the eleventh day of the eleventh month of 1918. The Germans signed grimly, for the terms were severe.

The Germans agreed to evacuate France, Belgium, Luxembourg, and Alsace-Lorraine without delay. They agreed to surrender to the Allies an enormous amount of war materials, including most of Germany's naval vessels, and to return prisoners, money, and all valuables which they had taken from the occupied countries. They agreed to renounce the Treaty of Brest-Litovsk with Russia and the Treaty of Bucharest with Rumania.

In addition, the Allies reserved the right to occupy all German territory west of the Rhine as well as a strip of territory about 18 miles (29 kilometers) wide along the east bank of the Rhine.

Wilson's Fourteen Points. An American expression of idealism as well as American fighting strength played a large part in breaking the Central Powers' will to fight. As you recall, in November 1917 the Bolsheviks seized control of Russia and shortly thereafter signed a peace treaty with Germany. At this time the Bolsheviks published a number of secret treaties that the Allies had drawn up at the beginning of the war. These secret treaties outlined in great detail how the Allies planned to divide the spoils of war if they defeated the Central Powers.

President Wilson chose this opportunity to lay before the world what he firmly believed was "the only possible program for world peace." Wilson's program, which he presented to Congress on January 8, 1918, included fourteen points, or principles.

The first group of points aimed to end the causes of modern war, as Wilson understood these causes. Specifically, he called for open, instead of secret, diplomacy; for freedom of the seas instead of their control by the strong naval powers; for removal of tariffs and other economic barriers between nations; for reduction of land weapons; and for temporary international control of colonies in place of the existing imperialism.

President Wilson also called for the liberation of peoples whose lands had long been ruled by Russia, Austria-Hungary, Germany, and Turkey. Among these peoples were the Poles, Czechs, Slovaks, and South Slavs. Wilson's proposal also included the people living in the German-held region of Alsace-Lorraine. These and other groups were to have the right of **self-determination**. That is, they were to decide for themselves the country in which they wished to live.

The Fourteenth Point was the heart of President Wilson's program. In it Wilson urged the creation of a "general association of nations" to give "mutual guarantees of political independence and territorial integrity to great and small states alike."

Influence of Wilson's program. The Fourteen Points and statements explaining them were printed during the war in the languages of the peoples of central Europe. They were dropped by plane into the heart of enemy country. All this publicity encouraged the Slavic peoples within Germany and Austria-Hungary to boycott the war efforts of their

▲ Discussion topic: Wilson wrote, "There must not be a balance of power, but a community of power; not organized rivalries, but an organized common peace." Have students analyze how Wilson's Fourteen Points attempted to improve on the balance-of-power international system.

rulers and to speed up their own liberation. Even the German people read the Fourteen Points and found in them hope for a just and lasting peace.

As defeat pressed upon them, the German and Austrian peoples saw in the Fourteen Points an escape from the harsh penalties that the Allies would impose. Thus when the German military offensives failed in the summer of 1918, and when President Wilson made it clear that he would negotiate only with a German authority that was representative of the people, the people of Germany and Austria-Hungary took steps to overthrow their rulers.

SECTION REVIEW

See underscored items, text pp. 681-82, 84.

Identify: Bolsheviks, convoy, General Pershing, peace offensive, Marshal Foch, armistice, Fourteen Points, self-determination

For answers to questions, see Answer Key, p.A94.

1. **Summarizing Ideas:** What contributions did the United States Navy make to winning the war?
2. **Interpreting Ideas:** Who considered the armistice terms of 1918 severe? Why?
3. **Analyzing Ideas:** (a) How did Wilson's Fourteen Points help win the war? (b) Why was the Fourteenth Point the heart of Wilson's program?
4. **Studying Maps:** Examine the map on page 683. Compare this map with the map on page 669. (a) Name some of the new independent nations. (b) Which nations no longer existed after World War I? (c) Which nations gained territory as a result of the war?

5 The United States refuses to join the League of Nations

See Teaching Suggestions in TMRG, pp.TM168-69.

On November 11, 1918, almost everyone in America took the day off from work. Factories, offices, stores, and schools closed their doors. Americans, old and young, poured into the streets of every city and town and village across the land to celebrate the armistice that ended World War I. In a joyful statement to the press, President Wilson announced, "Everything for which America fought has been accomplished." So it seemed to him, and so it seemed to Americans in general on November 11, 1918.

Three weeks later, on December 4, 1918, the army transport *George Washington* steamed out of New York harbor for Europe. Its most distinguished passenger was President Woodrow Wilson, bound for the peace conference at Paris.

Wilson hoped to persuade the other representatives at the conference to adopt the Fourteen Points that he had earlier outlined as "the only possible program for world peace."

The "Big Four." The peace conference, which opened on January 18, 1919, had much of the tension of a melodrama. The stage, however, was the world. The principal characters were the chief officials of the four leading powers— Great Britain, France, Italy, and the United States. The outcome of the drama would affect millions of people.

Wilson arrived at the conference after a triumphal journey through Great Britain, Italy, and France. Masses of people had turned out to greet the man who symbolized their hope for a better world. Encouraged by this reception, Wilson felt that he could use his great popularity to bring about a just peace based on his Fourteen Points. However, the three other leading delegates at Paris, supported by powerful interests in their homelands, had very different aims.

David Lloyd George, the British Prime Minister, had just won a general election by using such slogans as "Hang the Kaiser" and "Make Germany Pay." He had no intention of becoming unpopular with the British voters by showing generosity toward the Germans. He had no wish to give up England's naval supremacy and accept Wilson's idea of "freedom of the seas."

The "Tiger" of French politics, Premier Georges Clemenceau (ZHORZH klay·mahn·SOH), believed that the only way to defend France was to crush Germany. Italy's Vittorio Orlando wanted to acquire territory that had been secretly promised to Italy when it joined the Allies in 1915.

Secret treaties. The united opposition of Lloyd George, Clemenceau, and Orlando was not the only problem President Wilson faced. There was also the problem of secret treaties. In 1917 the Russian Bolsheviks published secret treaties that the Allies had made before

▲ Wilson had a genuine sympathy for the broken, defeated peoples. He had grown up in the Reconstruction South, where southerners were treated as defeated aliens.

685

Most historians agree that the Senate's rejection of the Treaty of Versailles was as much the fault of President Wilson as that of any of the treaty's opponents. From the moment the war ended, Wilson's efforts to negotiate a just peace were hampered by his own self-defeating behavior. The primary example of this was his choice of delegates to the Versailles Peace Conference.

Wilson chose to lead the very important diplomatic mission himself, and he did not seem to care about the "advice and consent" of the Senate. If anything, Wilson did his best to make the negotiation of the peace a partisan issue. In the 1918 Congressional elections Wilson had made a blanket endorsement of Democratic candidates and called on the American people to make the election a referendum on his foreign policy. The people responded by returning control of both houses of Congress to the Republicans. Wilson was now in a dangerous position, for whatever treaty he might negotiate at Versailles would have to be submitted to a hostile Senate for ratification.

Under these circumstances Wilson might have courted the Senate's favor by naming some Republican senators to the peace delegation, but he did not. He instead chose Colonel Edward House, his closest political adviser; Robert Lansing, Secretary of State; General Tasker H. Bliss, Army Chief of Staff; and Henry White, an unknown career diplomat. Even these men were excluded from any meaningful input; Wilson insisted on personally carrying on the negotiations.

Returning triumphant from Europe with the treaty in hand, Wilson was now ready for a fight with the Senate. As Colonel House later wrote, ". . . [he] finds great difficulty in conferring with men against whom, for some reason, he has a prejudice and in whom he can find nothing good."

The result was that the Senate could not accept the treaty without amending it, and Wilson could not compromise with the Senate. The conflict led to the collapse of Wilson's greatest dream — United States leadership in a League of Nations.

---

the United States entered the war. The new Communist rulers of Russia hoped to discredit the Allies by exposing these treaties as "imperialist diplomacy."

Under these treaties the Allies agreed to divide the spoils of victory. Great Britain was to take over Germany's colonies, except for certain territories in the Pacific Ocean that were to go to Japan. (Japan had declared war on Germany in 1914.) France, Russia, Serbia, and Italy were to enlarge their national boundaries at the expense of Germany and Austria-Hungary. Finally, Germany was to make huge payments, called **reparations**, to the Allies to compensate for damages resulting from the war. These secret treaties contradicted several of Wilson's Fourteen Points, such as open diplomacy, national self-determination, and the end of colonialism.

Wilson's dilemma. Faced with these secret treaties and with the opposition of Lloyd George, Clemenceau, and Orlando, Wilson could either compromise or walk out of the Paris Peace Conference. Indeed, at one point he almost did walk out, but he realized that such a step might be regarded as a confession of failure. He was also afraid that communism might

spread from Russia into central Europe if a peace treaty were delayed and conditions remained unstable. His strongest reason for staying, however, was his faith in a League of Nations. Such a League, he was convinced, would in time remedy any injustices that the peace treaty might contain.

The Treaty of Versailles. The final peace treaty, called the Treaty of Versailles, was completed and signed late in June 1919. The treaty showed the results of bargaining between Wilson on one side and Lloyd George, Clemenceau, and Orlando on the other.

The Treaty of Versailles and related treaties made important changes in the map of the world. Germany's colonies were given to the Allied victors, but under a **mandate system**. This system required the new owners to account for their colonial administration to the League of Nations.

Certain border areas of pre-war Germany were lopped off. One important area, Alsace-Lorraine, was returned to France. Other areas were included in a new country, Czechoslovakia, and in a re-created Poland. To satisfy the nationalist desires of various peoples in eastern Europe, several other independent states were created. These included Finland, Estonia, Latvia, Lithuania, and Yugoslavia. Certain border changes were made for Italy, Greece, Rumania, and Belgium (see map, page 683).

Under the Treaty of Versailles, the German government had to accept full responsibility for starting the war and had to agree to remain disarmed. Germany also agreed to pay large reparations for war damage.

Wilson realized that vengeance and greed were weak foundations for a lasting peace, and he successfully opposed some of the more unreasonable Allied demands. Moreover, he had the great personal satisfaction of seeing the Covenant of the League of Nations written into the Treaty of Versailles.

The League of Nations. The League of Nations, with headquarters at Geneva, Switzerland, provided international machinery to make war less likely. The machinery consisted of (1) a permanent Secretariat, or administrative and secretarial staff; (2) an Assembly, in which each member nation had one vote; and (3) a Council, the all-important executive body. The Council had five permanent members—the five great powers of France, Great Britain, Italy, Japan, and the United States. Other na-

tions were also represented by means of rotating membership. Germany and the Soviet Union (Russia) were excluded from League membership. Closely related to the League were the Permanent Court of International Justice and other agencies. They dealt with such issues as reducing armaments and improving conditions of health and labor throughout the world.

The League Covenant did not outlaw war. However, each League member agreed, before going to war, to make every effort to solve its difficulties in a friendly way and even then to wait during a **cooling off period** before striking a blow. If any member failed to do this, the other members might then decide, through the Council, to apply **economic sanctions**. This meant that they would refuse to trade with the offender. Moreover, the Council might go further and recommend the use of force against the aggressor nation. To forestall efforts to change the new map of the world by force, each League member was to guarantee the territorial integrity and political independence of every other member.

Weaknesses of the League. The League of Nations had several serious weaknesses. For

Representatives from 27 Allied Powers met in the mirrored Palace of Versailles, just outside Paris, to draw up the 1919 peace treaty. Woodrow Wilson, Georges Clemenceau, and David Lloyd George appear in the center of this painting.

one thing, taking action against an **aggressor** was almost impossible for several reasons. First, the term "aggressor" was not clearly defined. Second, the Council could only recommend that nations take action, but could not force them to act. Third, any Council member could block the wishes of the other members, because all important Council decisions had to be unanimous.

Another basic weakness of the League was its guarantee of existing political boundaries. When the map of Europe was redrawn, some peoples found that they were now part of a different nation—one that they did not want to belong to. These peoples had no way to secure further changes in their national boundaries.

A third weakness was the League's failure to provide adequate machinery for recommending solutions to economic problems that might lead to war. Trade rivalries, tariff barriers, and imperialism still existed, yet the League could not do much more than study such problems. Another weakness was exclusion of the Soviet Union and Germany from membership. Finally, the League was unable to tackle the problem of reducing armaments.

Despite its shortcomings, the League of Nations was a promising beginning in the difficult task of creating a new world order, dedicated to international peace and justice. In the 1930's about 60 nations belonged to the League. The League was bringing an important new ingredient into international affairs —the organized moral judgment of a majority of the nations of the world.

The Senate rejects the League. Early in July 1919, President Wilson returned from Paris to ask the Senate to approve the Treaty of Versailles and thus bring the United States into the League. The Senate shattered his hopes by rejecting the treaty. Senator <u>Henry Cabot Lodge</u> of Massachusetts, head of the Committee on Foreign Relations, and other ▲ Republican Senators opposed the League.

Many Americans thought that the Treaty of Versailles was unjust. They were unwilling to have the United States join a League that pledged its members to carry out the provisions of the treaty. Many Americans pointed with alarm to the article of the Covenant that pledged each member to guarantee the existing political boundaries of the other members. Americans argued that such a pledge might involve the United States in war.

Despite the opposition to the League of Nations, the Senate might have voted for it if Wilson had been willing to accept amendments proposed by Senator Lodge and his supporters. These amendments were designed to safeguard American interests and to prevent the United States from being drawn into European wars. Wilson believed, however, that these amendments would so weaken the League that it would become ineffective. He refused to compromise.

To win public support, Wilson traveled across the country making speeches in defense of the League. Finally, exhausted by the long strain, in the fall of 1919 he collapsed and for seven months lived in seclusion. His one remaining hope was that the public would support his cause by electing a Democratic President in the 1920 election. As you will read, the Republican landslide of that year and the election of President Harding seemed to indicate that Americans wanted to forget the League and world problems in general. They ignored Wilson when he warned, "Arrangements of the present peace cannot stand a generation unless they are guaranteed by the united forces of the civilized world."

The rise of Japanese, Italian, and German expansionism in the 1930's proved the accuracy of Woodrow Wilson's prophecy. For by that time, as you will read, the League of Nations had become too weak to prevent the outbreak of another world war.

SECTION REVIEW

See underscored items, text pp. 685-88.

Identify: "Big Four," reparations, Treaty of Versailles, mandate system, economic sanctions, Henry Cabot Lodge

For answers to questions, see Answer Key, pp.A94-95.

1. **Comparing Ideas:** Compare the views of (a) Wilson, (b) Lloyd George, (c) Clemenceau, and (d) Orlando concerning the treaty of peace.

2. **Summarizing Ideas:** (a) Describe the structure of the League of Nations. (b) What machinery did the League set up for the prevention of war? (c) Describe some of the major weaknesses of the League.

3. **Analyzing Ideas:** (a) List two arguments presented by people who opposed the League. (b) What evidence is there that Americans generally agreed with these arguments?

4. **Studying Maps:** Using the maps on pages 669 and 683, identify four ways in which the Treaty of Versailles changed the map of the world.

▲ Rational opposition held that to keep peace, the League must have exclusive control of armed forces and an enforceable world law. Emotional arguments claimed that the United States was being tricked by foreign diplomats and that Germany and Italy had been betrayed.

DEVELOPING HISTORY STUDY SKILLS

Reading About History   Comparing Historical Accounts

Historians use many sources to reconstruct and interpret historical events and periods. You have already been introduced to the skill of analyzing primary sources (Chapter 17, page 409). Historians also use secondary sources in their investigation of history. Biographies, reference books, and textbooks are examples of secondary sources.

Secondary sources differ from primary sources. A primary source, as you recall, is an original account of an event. A secondary source is an account based on one or more primary sources. Students of history are often called on to compare a primary and secondary account of a historical event.

How to Compare Historical Accounts

To effectively compare historical accounts, follow these guidelines.

1. **Determine the nature of the source.** Note when and by whom each of the historical accounts was written. Identify the type of document from which each source came. Determine whether the account being examined is a primary or a secondary source. Research information about the author of the source if needed.

2. **Read each source carefully.** Identify the main idea as well as all of the supporting details contained in each source.

3. **Identify the similarities and differences.** As you read the sources, note the similarities and differences between them. Identify any bias in either account. Determine the sources used in the secondary account.

Applying the Skill

Read the two excerpts in the next column. Then follow the guidelines listed above to compare the two sources.

We have no quarrel with the German people, only with their government. With militaristic forces rampant, there can be no assured security for the democratic governments of the world. Hence, the world must be made safe for democracy. War is terrible. But the right is more precious than peace, and we shall fight for the things which we have always carried nearest our hearts — for democracy, for the right of those who submit to authority to have a voice in their own governments, for the rights and liberties of small nations, for a universal dominion of right by such a concert of free peoples as shall bring peace and safety to all nations and make the world itself at last free.

Woodrow Wilson

Still other and deeper forces moved American sympathies toward the Allies and toward war with Germany. For one thing, American ties with Great Britain and France were traditionally closer than those with Germany. Not least important, American shipments of munitions to the Allied Powers had risen from $6 million in 1914 to nearly $500 million in 1916. By April 1917, American bankers had loaned about $2 billion to the Allies. Naturally, these American investors wanted an Allied victory. However, historians have found no evidence to show that economic interests consciously influenced Wilson's conduct in the critical weeks before the United States entered the war.

The first excerpt is from a speech made by Wilson before Congress; the second is from your textbook. Wilson's speech is a primary source. Wilson was a participant at the time of the event. The textbook account of the event is a secondary source. It is a retelling of the event by another person. Wilson condemns Germany for terrible deeds and sees war as a way to right those wrongs. The textbook presents other possible reasons, traditional and economic, for the declaration of war.

689

Practicing the Skill

In the following excerpt, two historians reconstruct the period just before the United States entered World War I. They offer their interpretations of President Wilson's ideas and the reasons for United States entry into the war. Read the excerpts. Then on a separate sheet of paper answer these questions.

1. Is the Peterson excerpt a primary source? the Barnes excerpt?

2. **(a)** How are these sources similar? **(b)** How are they different?
3. What primary sources and other sources does each historian cite in his interpretation?
4. **(a)** What conclusions does Peterson reach? **(b)** Barnes? **(c)** Compare the conclusions of these two historians.
5. **(a)** Based on Wilson's speech, the excerpt from the textbook, and these two historical interpretations, what conclusions can you draw about the United States' entry into World War II? **(b)** Support the conclusions you have drawn.

Propaganda in Its Broadest Meaning

The British campaign to induce the United States to come to their assistance affected every phase of American life; it was propaganda in its broadest meaning. News, money, and political pressure each played its part and the battle itself was fought not only in London, New York, and Washington, D.C., but also in the American classrooms and pulpits, factories, and offices. It was a campaign to create a pro-British attitude of mind among Americans, to get American sympathies and interests so deeply involved in the European war that it would be impossible for this country to remain neutral.

The New York Times, which perhaps gave more serious attention to European events than any other American newspaper, had an Englishman, Mr. Ernest Marshall, as the head of its London bureau, and his subordinates were largely Britishers. . . . The New York World's London correspondent was an Irishman [and] . . . his staff, like Mr. Marshall's, was largely composed of British

newspapermen. So was that of the Sun. . . . The result was "that the American view of Europe was normally and unavoidably colored very deeply by the British attitude." . . .

The most important of the reasons for the American action in 1917 was the product of British propaganda. People under the influence of the propaganda came to look upon the struggle of 1914–1918 as a simple conflict between the forces of good and evil; they felt that all that was wrong was that certain malevolent individuals had gained control of an autocratic government and were attempting to dictate to the rest of the world. In the minds of American leaders there was developed a blind hatred of everything German. After this hatred had distorted American neutrality, it created a willingness to sacrifice American youth in an attempt to punish the hated nation.

H. C. Peterson

The Anglo-Saxon Myth

First and foremost, we must take into account the fact that Wilson's intellectual perspective was predominantly Anglo-Saxon. He [Wilson] had little knowledge of, or sympathy with, continental European culture and institutions. His great intellectual heroes were such English writers as John Milton, John Locke, Adam Smith and Walter Bagehot. He did his graduate work in the Johns Hopkins University Seminar under Herbert Baxter Adams, where the "Anglo-Saxon Myth" reigned supreme. Wilson was a persistent student and admirer of the English constitution and frankly regarded the British system of government as superior to our own. . . . Wilson was

also profoundly moved by the British propaganda relative to German atrocities and territorial ambitions. This was particularly true after Lord Bryce lent his name to the prestige and veracity of the propaganda stories as to German savagery. Of all living Englishmen, Bryce was probably the man whom Wilson most admired and trusted. When Bryce sponsored the propaganda lies, Wilson came to believe that they must have a substantial basis in fact. This helped on his rationalization that England was fighting the battle of human civilization against wild beasts. . . .

Harry Elmer Barnes

Barnes focuses on Wilson's admiration for "things" British as well as the influence of British propaganda. 3. Neither cites primary sources; Peterson generalized from the staff makeup of two American newspapers. Barnes cites no sources. 4. (a) See solid-line underscore. (b) See broken-line underscore. (c) Both cite British influences for the US entry into World War I, but both differ as to source of the influence. 5. (a) Answers will vary. (b) Answers will vary.)

The outbreak of World War I in the summer of 1914 came as a blow to millions of Americans and other peoples throughout the world. During the opening years of the 1900's, great strides had been made toward international cooperation. In 1914, however, all hopes for peace were shattered under the blows of fierce national rivalries.

Despite the United States' desire to remain neutral, it became increasingly clear that the American nation, as a major power, could not remain apart in a conflict involving the other great powers. Step by step the United States moved toward war and, in 1917, entered the conflict that had turned most of Europe into a battleground.

The war had far-reaching consequences for the American people. As a "total" war, it directly and deeply involved every part of life and every man, woman, and child in the country. The total participation demanded by the war led to the creation of a vast government bureaucracy to manage and control agriculture, labor, transportation, and the naval and military effort. The government directed and to a large extent controlled public opinion. Constitutional guarantees of freedom of speech and of the press were sometimes ruthlessly disregarded by the government in the name of "national security" and "Americanism."

War-weary people hailed the armistice of November 11, 1918, as a turning point in history. Hundreds of millions of people looked to the United States for leadership in the effort "to make the world safe for democracy."

CONNECTING CHAPTER IDEAS

Despite President Wilson's plea for involvement in the League of Nations, Americans turned their backs on world affairs. In the next chapter you will read about the prosperity the nation enjoyed under the leadership of three Republican Presidents. This prosperity, however, was shattered in 1929 by a stunning economic collapse.

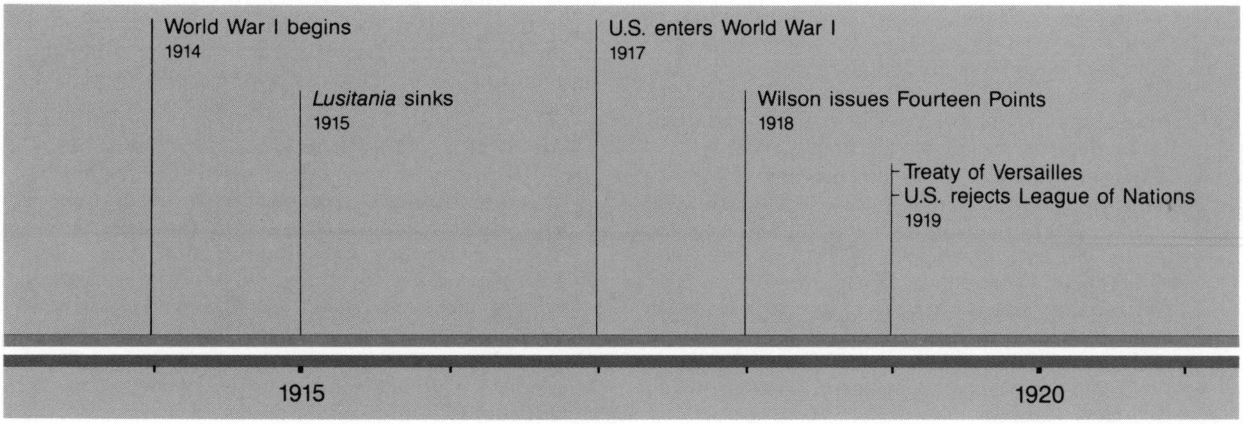

World War I begins
1914

U.S. enters World War I
1917

Lusitania sinks
1915

Wilson issues Fourteen Points
1918

Treaty of Versailles
U.S. rejects League of Nations
1919

1915

1920

CHAPTER

30 REVIEW

Reviewing Important Terms

Decide whether each of the following sentences is true or false. If the sentence is false, replace the underlined term with the word or phrase that will make it true.

1. Mandates are payments that a defeated nation is required to make to pay for the cost of a war.
2. Neutral ships were forbidden to carry contraband, or supplies of weapons to warring nations.
3. During the 1930's most European nations maintained a balance-of-power system by securing as many allies as possible.
4. The League of Nations adopted a reparation system which required sovereign nations to account for the treatment of their colonies.
5. In 1915 the war in Western Europe had reached a stalemate, which lasted until 1918.

Practicing Critical Thinking Skills

1. **Analyzing Ideas. (a)** Why did the United States enter World War I? **(b)** What part did American troops play in the victory of the Allies?
2. **Summarizing Ideas.** The end of World War I brought with it a spirit of high idealism and hope to people throughout the world. Explain.
3. **Organizing Ideas. (a)** How were the factors that led to World War I—nationalism, imperialism, international rivalries, and the balance-of-power system—related? **(b)** Did the Treaty of Versailles diminish any of these factors as a future cause of war? Explain. **(c)** How did the League of Nations propose to protect world peace?
4. **Synthesizing Ideas.** One method used to encourage support for the war was the displaying of patriotic posters, such as the one on page 680 (also see pages 784 and 798). Create one or more posters that would have aroused Americans to serve their nation during World War I either in the armed services or on the home front.
5. **Illustrating Ideas.** Draw a cause-and-effect diagram (see pages 118–19) for one of the following topics: **(a)** why World War I started, **(b)** why the United States entered World War I, **(c)** why the Allies were victorious in World War I.
6. **Evaluating Ideas. (a)** Why are civil liberties often restricted in times of crisis or war? **(b)** In such times of emergency should the government have complete control to suspend a citizen's civil liberties? Explain.

7. **Relating Past to Present. (a)** What were the major obstacles to world peace in the early 1900's? **(b)** Are today's obstacles to world peace similar or different? Explain.

Developing History Study Skills

Comparing Historical Accounts. Reread the section on the sinking of the *Lusitania* on text page 676 and the following excerpt from the official German statement about the sinking of the *Lusitania*. Then answer the questions below.

> *The English steamship company must have been aware of the dangers to which passengers on board the* Lusitania *were exposed. In taking them on board in spite of this, the company quite deliberately tried to use the lives of American citizens as protection for the ammunition being carried. The company also violated the clear provisions of American laws, which expressly prohibit the carrying of passengers on ships that have explosives on board. The company thereby recklessly caused the deaths of American passengers on the* Lusitania.

(a) How do the two accounts differ? **(b)** According to the official German statement, how did the English steamship company violate American laws? **(c)** Based on the two accounts presented, write a brief paragraph explaining why the Germans sank the *Lusitania*.

Relating Geography and History

New weapons used in World War I changed how wars were fought. To understand how advances in technology helped shape modern warfare, study the map on page 669. Then answer the following questions.

1. **(a)** What new weapon enabled Germany to break through British naval defenses? **(b)** How did this weapon affect the conduct of war?
2. How did airplanes and tanks reduce the importance of certain geographic barriers?
3. List some of the technological advances in weaponry made since World War I and explain how each has further reduced the importance of geographic barriers in warfare.
4. Modern weapons made the policy of neutrality difficult to follow. Explain.

UNIT NINE
REVIEW

Discussing Ideas

1. How did Theodore Roosevelt interpret the power of the President in the area of foreign policy?
2. How did the presence of American sugar planters in Hawaii and Cuba influence the political events of each of those nations?
3. Why was it difficult for many Americans to remain neutral during World War I?
4. How might you have felt about the control of Puerto Rico by the United States if you had been (a) an American farmer, (b) a citizen of Nicaragua, (c) a British merchant?
5. (a) Describe Wilson's Fourteen Points. (b) What was the reaction of Europe's leaders to them? (c) What factors might account for their reactions?
6. (a) Describe the United States' relations with Asia in the years 1898 to 1920. (b) Do they seem to be consistent with United States foreign policy in other parts of the world? Explain.
7. How did each of the following contribute to the outbreak of World War I: (a) imperialism, (b) the armaments race, (c) the growth of nationalism, (d) the assassination of Austria's Archduke.

Applying History Study Skills

1. **Composing an Expository Essay.** Using the information in this chapter, write an expository essay to answer this question: Why did European powers not try to divide up Japan?

2. **Interpreting a Political Cartoon.** Examine the cartoon on page 657. (a) By what symbol is the United States represented? (b) What is the point of this cartoon? (c) What historical events prompted the cartoonist to draw this cartoon?

3. **Using Charts and Graphs.** Use these statistics to make a graph and then answer the questions that follow: United States Exports to China, 1890, $3 million; 1895, $4 million; 1900, $29 million; 1905, $53 million. United States Imports from China, 1890, $16 million; 1895, $21 million; 1900, $27 million; 1905, $28 million. (a) What differences exist between the growth rate of imports and exports? (b) Did the Boxer Rebellion have a negative impact on U.S. trade with China? Explain. (c) Does it appear that the Open Door policy had an effect on U.S. trade with China? Explain.

Making Connections

1. Read *All Quiet on the Western Front,* the well-known novel of World War I. (a) What seems to be the author's attitude toward war? How can you tell? (b) How reliable is the novel as a source of information about World War I? Explain. (c) In what way is a novel a valuable source of information about an event or period in history?
2. Select one event in the United States' relationship with Latin America from 1898 to 1920. Write an account of the event as it might appear in a Latin American textbook for high school students.
3. Conduct research on one of these World War I topics: (a) the role of blacks, (b) the role of women, (c) songs, (d) George Creel and the Committee of Public Information, (e) military technology.
4. Draw a map showing the battles and other major events of World War I that will illustrate why the war could be called a *world* war.
5. Define imperialism and then answer the following questions: (a) How do political imperialism and economic imperialism differ? (b) Why might some people consider dollar diplomacy a form of imperialism?

Reading in Depth

Beisner, Robert, *From Old Diplomacy to the New, 1856–1900* (New York: Crowell). Study of the ideas, traditions, and events that shaped United States foreign policy from 1865 to 1900.

Ellis, E.R., *Echoes of Distant Thunder: Life in the United States 1914–1918* (New York: Coward, McCann and Geoghagen). Investigation of attitudes and behavior in the United States while war raged "over there."

Reynolds, Quentin, *They Fought for the Sky* (New York: Holt, Rinehart and Winston). Story of the first air war in history.

Tuchmann, Barbara, *The Guns of August* (New York: Macmillan). An award-winning history of the early days of World War I that reads like a novel.

Werstein, Irving, *1898: The Spanish–American War* (Totowa, NJ: Cooper Square). Study of the role of journalists, weaponry, and the United States presence in the Philippines and the Caribbean.

693

UNIT TEN

The Golden Twenties and the New Deal

The 1920's were a dazzling yet a troubled time. Advances in technology resulted in rapidly changing life styles. Confidence in the economy was high; but labor strikes, intolerance, and problems caused by prohibition also marked the Twenties. Women and blacks and other minorities continued to seek equality. This quest seemed to many to be a minor disturbance amid the glitter of the decade. The 1920's, however, ended with the stock market crash. Dazzle gave way to depression. Unemployment, low wages, and low farm prices were widespread and caused national despair. The faces of the unemployed workers shown in the painting reflect that despair. The New Deal, started in 1933, eventually ended the hard times. It also redefined the government's role and responsibilities in the lives of American citizens.

See Chapter Overview in TMRG, p.TM172.
See Chapter Objectives in TMRG, p.TM172.
See Introducing the Chapter in TMRG, pp.TM172-73.

CHAPTER 31

A Decade of Prosperity Ends in a Crash

(1920–1932)

Broadway's 1920's dazzle

The signing of the armistice between the Allies and the Central Powers on November 11, 1918, brought an end to the fighting that marked World War I. The end of the war also marked the high point in Woodrow Wilson's Presidential career. To many Americans, democracy had triumphed.

The President's triumph, however, was to be short-lived. During the next two years, Wilson bore the heavy burden of frustration, shattered dreams, and broken health. Even before the armistice, in the Congressional elections on November 5, 1918, American voters had returned Republican majorities to both the House and the Senate, revealing their dissatisfaction with Wilson's leadership. Two years later, in the elections of 1920, the voters of the country turned their backs completely on Wilson and the Democratic Party. Instead, they selected a Republican President, Warren G. Harding, to lead the nation.

During the 1920's three Republican Presidents—Harding, Calvin Coolidge, and Herbert Hoover—presided over a country that, on the whole, enjoyed a period of such prosperity that it was labeled the "Golden Twenties." To be sure, there were hard times for many. Farmers suffered as operating costs soared and prices for their goods dipped. Workers still sought improved working conditions. Minorities continued to experience discrimination in their efforts to gain equality. Women had received the vote, but still had a way to go before attaining equal rights in many areas of life. Nevertheless, the nation's growing wealth was widely shared. By 1928, real wages were one third higher than they had been in 1914. Two out of three families owned automobiles. But this era of the "Golden Twenties" ended with a stunning economic collapse. The next decade began with the most shattering depression in American history.

READING FOCUS

As you read about the Golden Twenties and the Great Depression, look for the details that support each of the following statements.

1. The Democrats lose popularity and face growing unrest.
2. Republicans assume responsibility for governing the country.
3. The Great Depression shatters the prosperity of the 1920's.

See Teaching Suggestions in TMRG, p.TM173.

Before America's entry into the war, President Wilson had concentrated on his program of domestic reform. His first administration, from 1913 to 1917, reduced tariffs, strengthened the antitrust laws, and established the Federal Reserve System. In these and other ways, Wilson tried to restore competition in American business and to protect consumers.

Even before the war, however, Wilson felt that his program had achieved its goals. After the war he became deeply involved in organizing world peace. As a result, he had little time left for domestic affairs. Such problems included a postwar business slump, a decline in farm prices, and unemployment.

Losing support at home. The American people, however, were tired of international issues. They were more interested in domestic affairs than in a peace treaty or a League of Nations. The Congressional elections of 1918, held just before the armistice, showed this. President Wilson appealed to the voters for a Democratic Congress. Instead, the voters elected a Republican majority in both the House and Senate.

When Wilson returned from the Versailles Conference in the summer of 1919, he found many Senators critical of the Covenant, or constitution, of the League of Nations. However, the President refused to compromise on the covenant's basic points and instead tried to win the public to his point of view.

Late in the summer of 1919, after three weeks of a grueling nationwide speaking tour, Wilson suffered a stroke. It left him partially paralyzed, and he remained an invalid until his death in 1924.

The postwar depression. Wilson's illness came at a time when the country was suffering from a severe postwar **depression**. With the signing of the armistice, the government began to cancel its wartime contracts. Wartime industries suddenly faced the problem of converting to peacetime production. New machinery had to be installed and new customers found.

▲ Throughout the Annotated Teacher's Edition, terms listed in the "Identify" portion of a Section Review are underscored the first time they appear. See the Teacher's Manual for each section for a listing of important vocabulary terms.

697

Note: Answers to questions in captions appear in parentheses, as shown here. Bullets separate answers to individual questions when a caption contains more than one question.

Strikers stand united as they strike for better working conditions. What economic problems caused so many workers to strike after World War I?

(end of wartime contracts and industrial reconversion caused unemployment)

During the conversion, factories closed down or operated with greatly reduced labor forces.

Farmers also suffered during the transition from war to peace. As European farmland returned to normal production, the American farmers' wartime markets in Europe disappeared. Farm prices, which had soared during the war, dropped as competition increased. Wheat, for example, which had sold for as high as $2.26 a bushel (35.2 liters), dropped to less than $1 a bushel in 1922. Almost half a million American farmers, unable to pay their debts, lost their farms during this troubled period.

Wage earners also suffered. Many who had worked in government wartime agencies lost their jobs when the war ended. Other wage earners were thrown out of work when factories closed down or cut back operations. And many of the 4.5 million returning veterans could not find work.

As the depression deepened, as wages fell, and as more people lost their jobs, discontent swelled. To make things worse, the high cost of living rose even higher. In 1919 it climbed 77 percent above prewar levels. In 1920 it rose an additional 28 percent. Under such conditions, many workers resorted to strikes. During 1919 more than 4 million workers were at one time or another out on strike. Three strikes were especially serious.

The Boston police strike. On September 9 the Boston police force went on strike for higher wages and improved conditions, leaving the city without police protection. When rioting and looting broke out, the state guard was called in. The police force, realizing that the strike was lost, announced that they would return to their posts.

At this point, however, the Boston police commissioner refused to allow them to return to their jobs. He announced that he intended to hire a new police force. Governor Calvin Coolidge supported the commissioner. "There is no right," Coolidge flatly stated, "to strike against the public safety by anybody, anywhere, any time." Coolidge's statement was widely applauded. It brought him to public attention and helped him win the Republican Vice-Presidential nomination in 1920.

The coal strike. Less than two months after this police strike, on November 1, 1919, the United Mine Workers (U.M.W.) went out on

Expand on the theme presented here of transition from wartime to peacetime production. Make sure that students understand that in the case of the production of goods and farm products, the end of the war meant the cancelling out of many overseas markets as well as less demand at home.

strike. Led by their colorful and combative president John L. Lewis, they demanded higher wages and a shorter workweek. On November 9 United States Attorney General A. Mitchell Palmer secured an injunction ordering the officers of the U.M.W. to stop all activities tending to encourage the strikers.

However, the coal miners refused to return to work. Finally, on President Wilson's suggestion, the problem was submitted to a board of arbitration. The board of arbitration gave the miners a 27-percent wage increase. The board, however, refused to consider a reduction in the weekly hours of work.

The steel strike. Discontent in the steel industry led to a strike involving more than 300,000 workers. The steelworkers had long been dissatisfied with their working conditions. In some plants they worked as long as 12 hours a day, 7 days a week. Moreover, they had not been able to form a union to bargain for them. During the summer of 1919, however, an A. F. of L. committee launched a vigorous organizing campaign in the steel towns. The strike started on September 22, 1919, after management refused to recognize the committee's right to speak for all steelworkers.

As the weeks passed, violence erupted around some of the steel mills. At Gary, Indiana, martial law was declared, and federal troops moved in to keep order. Finally, with public opinion running against the steelworkers, the strikers returned to their jobs in January 1920. Three years later, however, the steel companies agreed to the steelworkers' demand for an 8-hour day.

Labor's declining strength. By early 1920 American export trade was soaring as orders for goods poured in from the war-devastated countries. The value of American exports rose to three times the 1913 level.

As economic conditions improved and jobs became more plentiful, many workers lost interest in unions. Membership in the A. F. of L., which had reached a peak of more than 4 million early in 1920, began to decline.

There were, of course, other reasons for the decline of the labor movement. The failure of the steel strike and of other strikes during 1919 discouraged workers. The use of the injunction, as in the strike of the United Mine Workers, was another discouraging factor. Also, Supreme Court decisions broadened the base for use of the injunction, restricted labor organizing activities, and ruled that legislation intended to improve working conditions was unconstitutional. Industrial management, moreover, launched a widely publicized campaign against the "union shop." In it labor unions were identified with socialism and communism. A "Red scare" that swept the country in 1919–20 caused many Americans, including many workers, to turn against organized labor.

Text continues on page 701.

Many immigrants suspected of Communist sympathies were deported from Ellis Island during the "Red scare" of the immediate postwar period. Attorney General A. Mitchell Palmer (inset) played a controversial role in the government's attack on alleged radicals during the "Red scare."

Ben Shahn (1898–1969), a painter and graphic artist renowned for his themes of social protest, was born in Lithuania. His family emigrated to the United States when he was eight years old, and in 1918 Shahn became an American citizen. Having suffered the poverty and degradation of a ghetto life both in Lithuania and in his new country, Shahn was forever outraged by any form of injustice. He dedicated his chosen profession — art — to the creation of a more just society.

Shahn first apprenticed himself to a lithographer. He then attended New York University, the City College of New York, and the National Institute of Design. In 1925 he embarked on a lengthy tour of Europe, during which he painted and studied the work of the artists he most admired.

Shahn returned to the United States four years later. He became deeply interested in the controversy surrounding the 1927 execution of Niccola Sacco and Bartolomeo Vanzetti. These Italian anarchists had been arrested during the height of the Red Scare for murder and armed robbery. Many people believed that the jury in the case — inflamed by the widespread hysteria of the times — had judged Sacco and Vanzetti on the basis of their political beliefs rather than on the basis of the evidence.

In the view of Ben Shahn, the execution of Sacco and Vanzetti had been a political crucifixion. The case moved him to create an unforgettable series of 23 provocative, cartoonlike paintings. *The Passion of Sacco and Vanzetti,* one painting in the series, depicts the corpses of the two men in their coffins. Standing over the coffins are the judge and two of the prosecution's key witnesses.

The Sacco-Vanzetti series made Shahn famous. His style became immediately recognizable for its unique combination of realism and abstraction. Shahn later learned the art of fresco painting from the eminent Mexican artist Diego Rivera, and he painted several well-known murals. In these works, as well as in his paintings, Shahn continued to explore controversial subjects, including labor movements, race relations, and atomic warfare. Throughout his career Shahn was committed to expressing the values and aspirations of ordinary Americans.

Shahn's last years were devoted to book illustration and to commercial art, but he never abandoned the credo that had gained him fame: "A work of art in which powerful compassion is innate . . . will serve ultimately to dignify that society in which it exists."

The "Red scare." During the postwar years, federal and state governments conducted a vigorous drive against anarchists, Communists, and socialists. The Espionage Act, passed in wartime to punish treasonable or disloyal activities, remained in effect after the war. Under this law revolutionists and suspected revolutionists were arrested and fined. Some who were aliens were deported to the countries from which they had come.

One important reason for the postwar concern with radicals was the Russian Bolshevik Revolution of 1917. This event frightened many Americans who feared that **radicals** in the United States might try to follow the Bolshevik example. Rumors of revolutionary plots circulated widely from 1917 through 1920.

There was more than rumor to arouse alarm, even though radical leaders disapproved of acts of irresponsible violence. During the spring and summer of 1919, more than 30 bombs were discovered by postal authorities in packages addressed to prominent citizens. In New York City on September 16, 1920, a bomb exploded in crowded Wall Street at noontime, killing 38 persons and injuring hundreds.

Meanwhile, in the fall of 1919, Attorney General Palmer instructed agents in the Department of Justice to arrest radicals throughout the country. Among those arrested were several hundred aliens who were deported.

Many Americans, both Democrats and Republicans, criticized this drive against radicals, pointing out that many of the raids were conducted without search warrants. They argued that Attorney General Palmer's actions sometimes ignored the constitution.

The critics also directed their fire against state governments. During this postwar period, about one third of the states had passed laws to punish advocates of revolutionary change. By 1920 many Americans who had no sympathy with radicals were growing alarmed at the widespread violation of civil liberties. Leaders from both major political parties agreed with President Wilson that Americans could not solve their problems by trying to suppress unpopular political views.

SECTION REVIEW

See underscored items, text pp. 697, 699 - 700.

Identify: depression, John L. Lewis, Bolshevik Revolution

For answers to questions, see Answer Key, p.A97.

1. **Summarizing Ideas: (a)** Describe the causes and nature of the depression that followed World War I. **(b)** How was the depression related to the many strikes that occurred in 1919?
2. **Analyzing viewpoints:** During the Boston police strike, Governor Coolidge made this statement: "There is no right to strike against the public safety by anybody, anywhere, any time." **(a)** What did he mean? **(b)** Do you agree with his viewpoint? Why or why not?
3. **Comparing Ideas: (a)** What conditions produced the "Red scare"? **(b)** Explain the arguments for and against the drive against radicals.

2 Republicans assume responsibility for governing the country

See Teaching Suggestions in TMRG, pp.TM173-74.

In the Presidential election of 1920, the country's unsettled condition gave the Republican candidate, Senator Warren G. Harding of Ohio, a clear advantage over his Democratic opponent, Governor James M. Cox of Ohio. Many voters blamed the administration in office for the troubled times. The Republicans' plea for a return to "normalcy" had great appeal. Many Americans were tired of Europe and its wars and tired of Wilson's attempts to "make the world safe for democracy." Business people were worried about the 1919 depression. Workers and farmers suffered from unemployment and failing prices.

The election of 1920. Warren G. Harding, the Republican candidate, was a genial Ohio newspaper owner who had climbed to the top of the political ladder in his own state. He had served as a United States Senator. Handsome and distinguished, with a warm, easygoing manner—much too easygoing, as it turned out—he had many friends in every walk of life.

Harding won the election with 16 million votes to Cox's 9 million. The electoral vote was even more sweeping, giving Harding 404 to Cox's 127. Eugene V. Debs, the Socialist candidate, who was in prison for violating the Espionage Act, received nearly 1 million votes.

Farm relief and financial reform. Harding did not take over an easy job when he entered the White House. Late in 1920 a second postwar depression had hit the country. Farmers,

Discussion topic: President Harding declared, "Present need is not heroics but healing; not nostrums but normalcy; not revolution but restoration, ...not surgery, but serenity." Have students consider which aspects of American life needed healing. What attitudes were revealed by Harding's statement?

701

AMERICAN PROFILES Amelia Earhart   (1898–1937)

As a young girl growing up in Kansas, Amelia Earhart was strong willed and independent. These qualities helped her become a famous pilot in the 1930's.

During World War I, Earhart left school to become a nurse. After the war she did not return to school. Instead, she moved to California and became fascinated with airplanes, spending all her free time at airports. In 1920 she made her first solo flight.

Just two years later, Earhart bought her first airplane. In it, she climbed to 14,000 feet, setting a new altitude record for women. By 1928 Earhart's reputation as a flyer had grown. In that year she became the first woman to fly across the Atlantic. Her successful crossing made her an instant celebrity.

Still, Earhart was not satisfied because she had not made the trip alone. She continued to study navigation and sharpen her flying skills. In 1932 she took off from Newfoundland and landed in Ireland 15 hours and 39 minutes later. Earhart had become the first woman to fly twice across the Atlantic and the first to fly it alone.

Earhart was now truly famous. She added to her fame with other long-distance flights and speed records. Her example encouraged women to travel by air, both as pilots and as passengers.

In 1937 Amelia Earhart and a navigator set out from Florida to fly around the world. For 32 days newspaper and radio reports tracked the flight. Then the plane vanished somewhere over the Pacific Ocean. A huge search proved unsuccessful. To this day the mystery of what happened to Amelia Earhart has not been solved.

wage earners, business leaders, and the public in general were clamoring for government action and for President Harding's promised return to "normalcy."

● Responding to widespread demands for help, Congress adopted the Emergency Tariff on May 27, 1921. This measure raised rates on some farm products but failed to raise farm prices generally. Congress also adopted the ▲ Budget and Accounting Act. This law was designed to reduce excessive spending and waste in government and to provide a more efficient method of handling government expenditures. It also created a Bureau of the Budget in the Treasury Department, with a director appointed by the President.

Up to this time, Congress had made annual appropriations on a piecemeal basis. No great concern was given to balancing the budget. Under the new system, all government agencies and departments had to submit annual requests for funds to the Director of the Budget. The director then drew up a detailed budget. Estimated income and expenditures for the coming **fiscal year**° were listed on this budget. The President submitted the budget to Congress. Congress could then raise or lower the estimates, if it so desired.

°**fiscal year:** the 12-month period considered as a year for general accounting and budgeting purposes. The fiscal year of the United States government begins on July 1.

▲ Point out that the tarriffs were one concrete sign of America's re-emerging isolationist instinct. The tariffs compounded the problems foreign nations had in repaying their World War I debts to the U.S. because the tariffs made the sale of goods in the American market impossible.

Charles G. Dawes, the first Director of the Budget, was an extremely capable administrator. Under his leadership and that of the Secretary of the Treasury, Andrew W. Mellon, the government used surplus revenues to reduce the national debt. At the end of World War I, the debt totaled more than $25 billion. During the 1920's it was cut by about one third.

▲ Some critics held that Mellon's financial measures reduced the taxes of the wealthy and placed too heavy a burden on the average wage earner, while checking a needed expansion of social services for the poor. However, most Americans approved of economy in government spending and of the reduction of the national debt.

War veterans. Congress also tackled the problem of the war veterans. Many war veterans as well as many other Americans felt that the government should provide "adjusted compensation" for veterans. These people pointed out that during the war members of the armed forces had risked their lives for low pay while workers at home earned high wartime wages in more or less safe jobs.

In 1921 Congress created the Veterans' Bureau. Harding then appointed Charles R. Forbes as its first director. The Veterans' Bureau handled veterans' claims for compensation and hospitalization, provided medical care for sick veterans, and administered the veterans' insurance program.

The Veterans' Bureau was only a partial answer to the demands of veterans. The American Legion, the Veterans of Foreign Wars, and other veterans' organizations continued to press for adjusted compensation. Congress responded in 1922 with a bonus bill. Harding vetoed the bill because it did not include any provision for raising the money to be spent.

The Fordney-McCumber Tariff. In 1922
● Harding signed the Fordney-McCumber Act into law. The new tariff wiped out the reductions made in the Underwood Tariff of 1913 and set considerably higher rates on hundreds of manufactured products. It also continued the limited protection for farmers provided by the Emergency Tariff of 1921.

The Fordney-McCumber Tariff also authorized the President, under certain circumstances, to raise or lower any tariff rate by as much as 50 percent. As it turned out, most of the adjustments made were upward.

● This tariff protected many newer industries such as china, toys, rayon, and chemicals.

Public scandals. Despite some solid accomplishments, the Harding administration left a long, sorry record of corruption. Harding was not himself involved in the corruption. His mistake was in appointing certain undeserving men to office. His cabinet did contain such able and respected men as Charles Evans Hughes, the Secretary of State; Andrew W. Mellon, who headed the Treasury Department; and Herbert Hoover, the Secretary of Commerce. However, Harding's administration also contained dishonest politicians who disgraced his administration.

Self-seeking politicians known as the "Ohio Gang" placed one of their members, Harry M. Daugherty, in the cabinet as Attorney General. Daugherty used his position to protect persons who violated the Prohibition amendment. Another Harding official, Thomas W. Miller, defrauded the government in the sale of alien properties—that is, foreign-owned properties that were seized by the American government during World War I. Charles R. Forbes, the head of the Veterans' Bureau, could not satisfactorily account for $200 million spent by his organization.

The most famous scandal took its name from the naval oil reserve lands at Teapot

(The Senate carried out the investigation.)
This cartoon shows the Senate washing out the "dirty linen" of the Harding administration. Why is the Senate shown washing out the dirty linen?

▲ *"The chief business of the American people is business," President Calvin Coolidge stated in 1925. Coolidge firmly believed that government should leave business to itself.*

Dome in Wyoming. Secretary of the Interior Albert B. Fall persuaded the Secretary of the Navy, Edwin C. Denby, to transfer the Teapot Dome reserve and another oil reserve at Elk Hills, California, to Fall's jurisdiction. In return for bribes, Fall leased the oil reserves to private oil speculators.

Some hint of this corruption reached Harding early in 1923. However, the scandals did not become public until later, when Fall, Forbes, and Miller were prosecuted and imprisoned. Meanwhile, Harding's health broke under the strain, and he died in the summer of 1923 of a heart attack.

On Harding's death, Calvin Coolidge, the Vice President, became President. Coolidge, a man of unquestioned honesty, helped to restore public confidence in the Republican Party.

The election of 1924. In the decade following their defeat in 1920, the Democrats gener-

ally failed to work out a clear-cut program to challenge the Republicans. They turned away from the spirit of reform that had marked Wilson's first administration. More and more the Democrats accepted the same conservative principles followed by the Republicans. As the years passed, it became difficult to distinguish between the two parties.

Only once during the 1920's did the Republican program face any serious opposition. Curiously enough, the opposition came in part from within Republican ranks.

The revolt broke out in 1924 when the Republicans nominated the staunchly conservative Calvin Coolidge for the Presidency. Coolidge believed that government should encourage, but not regulate, business. He also disapproved of special legislation to help workers or farmers.

Resisting these conservative policies, a group of progressive Republicans broke away and formed a new Progressive Party. They nominated Senator Robert M. La Follette of Wisconsin as their standard bearer. The Progressive Party received the backing of farmers, organized labor, and the socialists. The party called for federal credit and other assistance for farmers, and social legislation and additional laws to protect the rights of labor. In addition it advocated government ownership of railroads and water-power resources.

La Follette received almost 5 million votes, the largest number any third party had ever mustered. La Follette died shortly after the campaign, however, and the Progressive Party lost its strength and faded into insignificance.

The Democrats in 1924 nominated John W. Davis, a conservative corporation lawyer. During his campaign Davis concentrated on the scandals of the Harding era. The Republicans met this challenge by claiming credit for the prevailing prosperity, and this claim proved effective. Despite the Progressive revolt, which split the Republicans into two factions, Coolidge won the election by a landslide. He piled up 382 electoral votes to 136 for Davis and just 13 for La Follette.

Thrift in government. In a period of extravagance and "big money," Coolidge became a symbol of the thrifty, old-fashioned, simple country American. He emphasized thrift in government.

In 1924 Congress passed a bonus bill that provided adjusted compensation for all veter-

● Among the factors in this prosperity were a confident business community, low interest rates regulated by the Federal Reserve Board, mechanization and improvement of manufacturing efficiency, the ability of advertising to stimulate consumerism, and the development of new products.

ans except those with ranks above captain. The payments were not to be given in cash but in the form of a paid-up 20-year life insurance policy. Veterans who held the policy for 20 years would receive full compensation. In the name of economy, Coolidge vetoed the bonus bill, but Congress passed this bill over his veto.

Coolidge also vetoed a bill to stabilize farm prices by allowing the government to buy up farm surpluses and sell them abroad.

▲ In other matters, too, Congress and the President disagreed, but the President remained popular. "Keep Cool with Coolidge" was a slogan of the day. He probably could have been re-elected in 1928, but a year before the election he announced that he did not choose to run.

The election of 1928. The Republicans then nominated Herbert C. Hoover of California. Hoover was a successful mining engineer with a notable record as administrator of food relief in Europe during and after the war and as Secretary of Commerce after 1921.

The Democrats nominated New York's governor Alfred E. Smith. Smith advocated a federal farm-relief program and also urged stricter regulation of public utilities. These planks in the Democratic platform had strong appeal for many Americans. However, Smith had political handicaps that cost him support within his own party. He was opposed to Prohibition, he was a Roman Catholic, and he had ties with the Tammany political machine in New York City. All these things made him unpopular with large groups of voters, especially in the South and West.

Hoover received 444 electoral votes to Smith's 87. Smith lost his own state of New York. In addition he lost several traditionally Democratic states in the South that for the first time since the Civil War gave their votes to a Republican.

Herbert C. Hoover. President Hoover expressed his political beliefs in the phrase "rugged individualism." His general point of view was very close to Harding's idea of "normalcy" and to Coolidge's belief that government should encourage business but not give special assistance to individuals. Hoover, however, displayed greater imagination than his Republican predecessors. He believed that experts in fields other than government could make important contributions to government.

He also believed that the government should take some part in planning for the social and economic development of the nation.

When Hoover took office, he looked forward to a long period of increasing prosperity. He believed that Americans now expected more than the necessities of life. "The slogan of progress," he declared, "is changing from the full dinner pail to the full garage." For about six months, booming business and heavy consumer buying seemed to bear out Hoover's optimistic prediction.

SECTION REVIEW
See underscored items, text pp. 703 - 05.

Identify: "Ohio Gang," Teapot Dome scandal, Robert La Follette, Alfred E. Smith
For answers to questions, see Answer Key, p.A97.

1. **Interpreting Ideas:** How did Coolidge's election to the Presidency in 1924 reflect the temper of the times?

2. **Organizing Ideas:** Despite some solid accomplishments, the Harding administration left a long, sorry record of corruption. Explain.

3. **Comparing Ideas:** Discuss the elections of 1924 and 1928 in terms of (a) parties, (b) candidates, (c) issues, and (d) results.

4. **Studying Graphics:** Look closely at the cartoon on page 703. (a) What do the elephant and donkey represent? (b) In a sentence or two, explain the meaning of the cartoon.

3 The Great Depression shatters the prosperity of the 1920's

See Teaching Suggestions in TMRG, pp.TM174-75.

Flourishing business conditions and a rising standard of living contributed to the political success of the Republican Party during the 1920's. Between 1922 and 1929, jobs were plentiful. Americans on the whole were better fed, clothed, and housed than ever before.

"Easy money." During the prosperity of the "Golden Twenties," many Americans made and spent money with ease. Millions of workers received high wages and many businesses earned large profits. An ever-growing number of stockholders received substantial dividends.

As Americans bought more consumer goods, the retail trade recorded rapidly

▲ Writing activity: Have students write a brief essay comparing Coolidge's views and policies on government business regulation with President Reagan's views and policies.

705

increasing sales. Some of the business profits supported expansion and new product research. Some paid for workers' recreational facilities, some for company programs providing insurance and pensions for employees. Large sums flowed into medical research, education, and the welfare of the poor.

As surplus income piled higher and higher, more and more Americans were tempted to invest their savings or their profits in the stock market, hoping for big returns.

Not all Americans shared in the prosperity of the "Golden Twenties." This was notably true of Indians, Spanish-speaking Americans, and most blacks. Many workers lost their jobs when new machines were installed in factories. Some, such as blacksmiths and harness makers, whose skills were no longer needed, found it difficult to adapt to the monotonous work on assembly lines. Furthermore, some industries —such as coal, textiles, and leather—never fully recovered from the postwar slump of the early 1920's.

Falling farm income. Finally, many farmers did not share in the general prosperity. One of their problems was a shrinking market for farm products. After 1918, as you recall, American farmers lost many of their wartime European markets. Moreover, during the 1920's Congress passed laws that almost ended immigration into the United States. As a result of these laws, American farmers lost a traditional source of new customers. Although the markets were shrinking, farm production—aided by new machines and techniques—rose by more than 20 percent between 1919 and 1929.

With fewer people able or willing to buy food and with more food available, farm prices dropped. While the farm prices were falling, the prices of industrial goods that the farmers needed rose higher and higher. Many farmers found it increasingly hard to meet their mortgage payments or the payments on their farm machines. Thus during the industrial prosperity of the 1920's, many farmers sank deeper and deeper into debt, and many lost their farms. The situation of sharecroppers and tenants, white and black alike, was even worse than that of the small farmers.

Effort to aid farmers. By the end of the 1920's, the nation's farm economy had deteriorated to the point that the government could no longer afford to ignore it. President Hoover gave his support to the Agricultural Marketing Act, which was adopted in the summer of 1929. This act created a Federal Farm Board with power to lend up to $500 million to cooperative farm groups to help them store crops during years when a surplus of farm products brought falling prices. The theory was that the farmers could sell their stored products later when prices went back up. Unfortunately, surpluses continued year after year and prices continued to fall. In the end the Farm Board used up its financial resources without bolstering farm income.

Prosperity ends in the crash. In spite of the failing agricultural economy, few Americans other than the farmers and those at the bottom of the economic ladder were concerned about the nation's economic health. Most Americans believed, with Herbert Hoover, that "we in America are nearer to the final triumph over poverty than ever before in the history of any land." Given this widely shared belief, the depression that started late in 1929 came as a stunning blow to most Americans.

SOURCES

HERBERT HOOVER'S "RUGGED INDIVIDUALISM" SPEECH (1928)

During one hundred and fifty years we have built up a form of self-government and a social system which is peculiarly our own. It differs essentially from all others in the world. It is the American system. It is just as definite and positive a political and social system as has ever been developed on earth. It is founded upon a particular conception of self-government in which decentralized local responsibility is the very base. Further than this, it is founded upon the conception that only through ordered liberty, freedom, and equal opportunity to the individual will his initiative and enterprise spur on the march of progress. And in our insistence upon equality of opportunity has our system advanced beyond all the world. . . .

Discussion topic: Ask students to compare the situation of farmers in the 1920's with that of farmers today. (Consider number of farmers, farm income, and government programs.)

The New York Times.

Copyright, 1929, by The New York Times Company.

THE WEATHER

Rain today and probably tomorrow; somewhat colder tomorrow.

NEW YORK, TUESDAY, OCTOBER 29, 1929.

TWO CENTS

SENATORS RENEW DEMAND ON HOOVER

Roosevelt's Memory Honored In Navy Day Fete on Ships

EUROPE IS DISTURBED

STOCK PRICES SLUMP $14,000,000,000 IN NATION-WIDE STAMPEDE TO UNLOAD; BANKERS TO SUPPORT MARKET TODAY

Sixteen Leading Issues Down $2,893,520,108; Tel. & Tel. and Steel Among Heaviest Losers

A shrinkage of $2,893,520,108 in the open market value of the shares of sixteen representative companies resulted from yesterday's sweeping decline on the New York Stock Exchange.

American Telephone and Telegraph was the heaviest loser, $448,905,162 having been lopped off of its total value. United States Steel common, traditional bellwether of the stock market, made its greatest nose-dive in recent years by falling from a high of 202½ to a low of 185. In a feeble last-minute rally it snapped back to 186, at which it closed, showing a net loss of 17½ points. This represented for the 8,131,055 shares of common stock outstanding a total loss in value of $142,293,446.

In the following table are shown the day's net depreciation in the outstanding shares of the sixteen companies referred to:

Issues.	Shares Listed.	Losses in Points.	Depreciation.
American Radiator	10,096,289	10⅝	$104,748,997
American Tel. & Tel.	13,203,093	34	448,905,162
Commonwealth & Southern	30,764,468	3¼	96,138,962
Columbia Gas & Electric	8,477,307	22	186,500,754
Consolidated Gas	11,451,188	20	229,023,760
DuPont E. I.	10,322,481	18¾	190,030,628
Eastman Kodak	2,229,703	41⅞	93,368,813
General Electric	7,211,484	47½	342,545,490
General Motors	43,500,000	6¾	293,625,000
International Nickel	13,777,408	7⅞	108,497,088
New York Central	4,637,086	22⅝	104,914,071
Standard Oil of New Jersey	24,843,643	8	198,749,144
Union Carbide & Carbon	8,730,173	20	174,615,460

PREMIER ISSUES HARD HIT

Unexpected Torrent of Liquidation Again Rocks Markets.

DAY'S SALES 9,212,800

Nearly 3,000,000 Shares Are Traded In Final Hour—The Tickers Lag 167 Minutes.

NEW RALLY SOON BROKEN

Selling by Europeans and "Mob Psychology" Big Factors in Second Big Break.

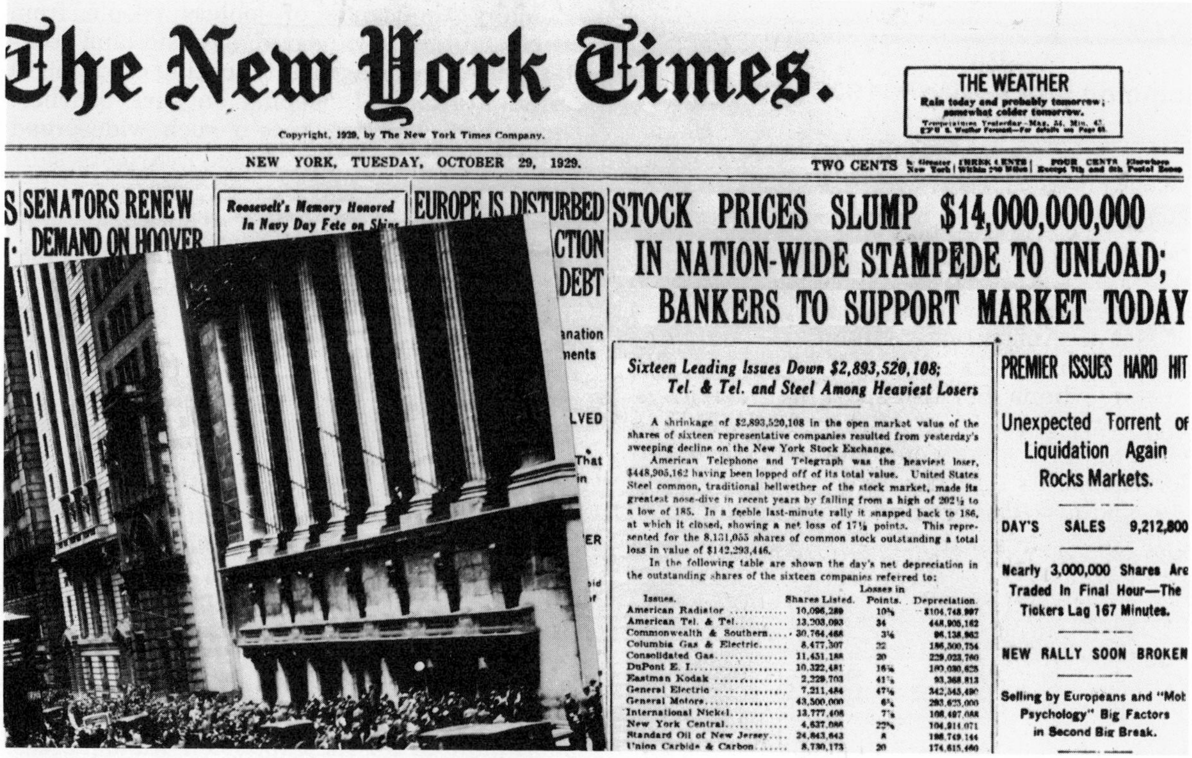

Newspapers across the country chronicled the stock market crash of 1929. The superimposed picture shows the sad crowds that clustered around the Stock Exchange, vainly hoping to salvage some of their investments.

For years the prices of stocks had been moving upward. After Hoover's election in November 1928, moreover, a frenzy of speculation gripped the country. Convinced that they were entering "four more years of prosperity," investors bought feverishly. Despite repeated warnings that stock prices were too high, Americans, rich and middle class alike, invested in stocks, often on credit. During most of 1929, stock prices soared to ever higher levels.

The stock market crash. Then the bubble burst. On October 24, 1929, a panic of selling hit the New York Stock Exchange as frantic orders to sell stock came pouring in. The causes of this panic were chiefly overproduction and overspeculation. More goods had been produced than could be profitably sold. A great many stocks were either worthless or wildly inflated. That is, either the businesses behind such stocks existed on paper only, or the actual value of the stocks was far less than their market value.

Overproduction and overspeculation had caught up with the American people. The inflated prices of stocks tumbled downward. On October 29, prices sank to a shattering new low when over 16 million shares of stock were dumped on the market. By mid-November the average value of leading stocks had been cut in half, and stockholders had lost $30 billion. With this crash of the stock market, the Great Depression started.

At first, business and government leaders tried to reassure the American people. "Business is fundamentally sound," announced Secretary of the Treasury Mellon. Such words, no matter how reassuring, could not stem the tide of economic disaster sweeping the country.

The Great Depression. Before 1929 ended, banks all over the nation were closing their doors. Businesses everywhere cut back production, and many concerns, finding themselves without customers, were forced out of business. Factories and mines were shut down. Empty railroad cars piled up on the sidings. By 1930 between 6 and 7 million Americans were un-

Report topic: Have interested students report on the operation of the stock market. The presentation should include how stock is bought and sold. The students should present their findings to the class in oral reports.

Common Stock Price • 1920 - 1935

Average Price Per Share (1926 = 100)

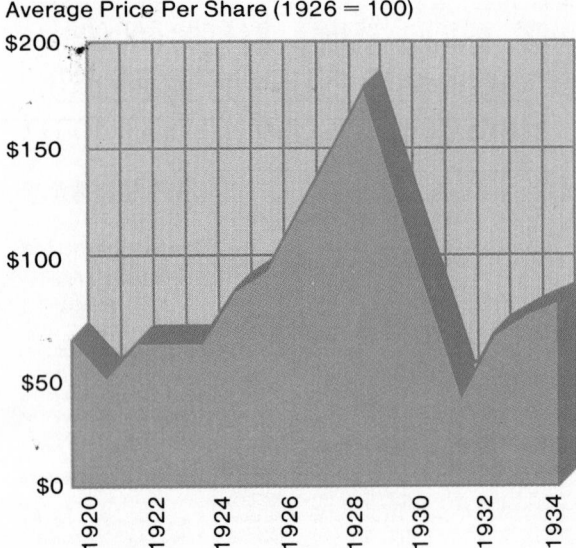

Source: *Historical Statistics of the United States*

employed. The result was a chain reaction. Unemployment meant fewer customers; a decrease in customers caused further cutbacks in production; these cutbacks, in turn, resulted in more unemployment. By 1932 nearly 12 million Americans were out of work.

The depression struck at all classes. Many well-to-do Americans helplessly watched their fortunes, invested in stocks or businesses, disappear. The industrial workers and the farmers suffered most. Most wage earners had no savings to tide them over a period of unemployment. In every city thousands of unfortunate men and women stood in lines to get free meals of bread and soup. Families forced out of their homes moved to makeshift huts that they built on unused land at the edges of the city. Such huts were often made of scrap lumber, packing boxes, and corrugated iron.

For the farmers the depression came as a final blow. Between 1929 and 1932, farm prices fell lower and lower, and more and more farmers lost their farms to their creditors. In some midwestern states, desperate farmers used force to prevent sheriffs from foreclosing mortgages on their farms.

Many thousands of jobless people from cities and farms wandered over the land seeking jobs at any wages, hitchhiking or riding in freight trains and sleeping on park benches. Never had America known such widespread suffering.

Causes of the depression. There is no simple way to explain the Great Depression. President Hoover insisted that the major cause was the worldwide economic disorder that followed World War I. Many economists agreed. They pointed to the vast destruction of property during the war and the worldwide dislocation of trade during and after the war.

Other economists argued that America's high tariff policies helped to stifle world trade and hurt American business. High tariffs, they claimed, prevented other countries from selling their goods in the United States. This in turn prevented them from securing the dollars that they needed to buy American products.

Still other economists blamed the depression on the excessive borrowing of money—for stocks, for comforts purchased on the installment plan, or for the expansion of businesses. These critics also claimed that the federal government failed to control bank loans and to protect the public against the sale of stocks that had no value.

Some economists have argued that depressions are an inevitable part of the American economic system. According to this view, business expands during periods of prosperity in order to obtain the largest possible profits. When factories produce more goods than consumers can buy, the factories have to cut down on production, at least until their surpluses are consumed. For this reason, these economists have argued, prosperity and depression are inevitable parts of the business cycle.

Finally, some economists have traced the Great Depression to uneven distribution of income. These economists have argued that if farmers had received better prices for their products and if workers had received higher wages, the American people would have been able to buy a larger proportion of the surplus goods. Had this happened, these economists claim, the factories would have kept busy and the depression could have been avoided.

Hoover and the depression. The depression confronted the Hoover administration with two emergencies. First, there was the widespread

Class activity: Have volunteers find various examples of newspaper articles from the period of the stock market crash. After students have shared the examples with the class, discuss the differences in coverage and points of view among the articles.

misery of people without jobs or farms, without money to buy enough food or clothing, and increasingly without hope. Some Americans urged the federal government to extend direct relief to those in need. Hoover, however, believed that direct aid was a responsibility of local communities. Direct federal relief, he said, would create a vast, inefficient bureaucracy and undermine the self-respect of the persons receiving it. Unfortunately, local communities did not have the resources to cope with the ever-rising tide of human misery.

To the second emergency, the collapse of business and agriculture, Hoover responded more actively. He instructed the Farm Board to buy up agricultural surpluses in an effort to raise falling farm prices. With the support of Congress, he started several public works programs, among them Boulder Dam (later called Hoover Dam) on the Colorado River. These projects were intended to stimulate business and provide employment for jobless workers.

Also at Hoover's urging, Congress created the Reconstruction Finance Corporation (RFC) in February 1932. The RFC could lend large sums of money to banks, life insurance companies, railroads, farm mortgage associations, and other enterprises. Hoover hoped that federal loans would strengthen these key businesses and thus provide jobs for millions of workers. Although the RFC advanced nearly $2 billion in loans to American business before the end of the Hoover administration, the depression grew worse.

In response to a recommendation by Hoover, Congress also passed the Home Loan Bank Act in July 1932. This act created a series of special banks designed to provide financial assistance to savings banks, building and loan associations, and insurance companies—all of which lent money on mortgages. By providing financial aid to such institutions, Hoover hoped to reduce foreclosures on homes and farms as well as to stimulate the construction of residential buildings.

In adopting these measures, the President and Congress were accepting, for the first time, the idea that the government had to assume certain responsibilities when the nation's economy suffered a serious setback. Unfortunately, the measures adopted did not stop the downward trend.

The election campaign of 1932. In the summer of 1932, the Republicans renominated

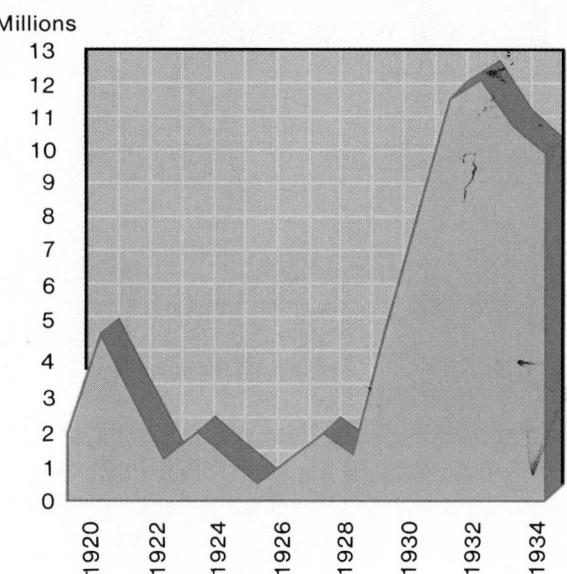

Unemployment • 1920 - 1935

Millions

Source: *Historical Statistics of the United States*

Herbert Hoover for President. As their candidate the Democrats chose Franklin Delano Roosevelt of New York.

Roosevelt had extensive political experience. He had served as a state senator in New York and as Assistant Secretary of the Navy. In 1920 he had been the Democratic nominee for Vice President. In 1921 Roosevelt had been stricken with polio. Paralyzed from the waist down, he fought back to regain partial use of his legs. Roosevelt then regained the attention of the nation while serving as governor of New York.

There was really only one important issue in the campaign—the depression. Hoover continued to blame the depression on international conditions. He declared that his policies were beginning to bring recovery and that Roosevelt's would destroy the American system.

Both of these claims were rejected by Roosevelt. He maintained that Republican policies, not international conditions, were to blame for the depression. He argued that the federal government should help provide direct relief to the needy and direct aid to farmers. He called for a

Refer the students to the chart, Immigration to the U.S., 1821 - 1980, on page 1000.
Ask the students why immigration may have declined in the 1920's and 1930's.

709

Auto license tags in the 1932 Presidential election campaign showed the Democratic candidates favoring repeal of the Eighteenth Amendment.

broad program of public works. He also demanded that safeguards be set up to prevent wild speculation and fraudulent issues of stock. To accomplish this he proposed laws to protect the bank depositor, the purchaser of stocks, and the homeowner. Referring to the unemployed workers, the desperate farmers, and others, Roosevelt stated that these "forgotten" Americans "at the bottom of the economic pyramid" had to have a "new deal."

Roosevelt's victory. Roosevelt and his running mate, John Nance Garner of Texas, won a sweeping victory in 1932, with Roosevelt winning 23 million popular votes to Hoover's 16 million. Roosevelt carried 42 states and piled up 472 electoral votes to Hoover's 59.

Moreover, the Democrats secured decisive majorities in both houses of Congress. These Democratic victories meant that Roosevelt's programs would have strong support in Congress.

A majority of voters throughout the 1920's had given the Republicans credit for the prosperity of those years. Now a great many Americans seemed to be saying that the Republicans would have to take the blame for the depression. Many of those who voted for the Democrats were really voting against Hoover rather than for Roosevelt. Many more saw in Roose-

velt the kind of dynamic personality that they believed was needed to lead the country out of its troubles.

Roosevelt had promised the American people a "new deal." During the four months between Election Day and Inauguration Day—March 4, 1933—workers, farmers, and even many business leaders waited hopefully to see how the new President would carry out his campaign pledge.

SECTION REVIEW
See underscored items, text pp. 707, 709.
Identify: stock market crash, RFC, Home Loan Bank Act, Franklin D. Roosevelt
For answers to questions, see Answer Key, pp.A97-98.
1. **Analyzing Ideas:** (a) How do economists explain the major causes of the Great Depression? (b) What measures did Hoover take to combat the depression? (c) How did these measures reflect his philosophy of government and the role it should take in economic affairs?

2. **Synthesizing Ideas:** According to the 1920 census, more Americans were living in cities than on farms. How does this fact relate to the hardships experienced by wage earners and their families with the coming of the depression?

3. **Studying Graphics:** Look at the graphs on pages 708 and 709. How do they illustrate the events that are described in this section?

Class activity: Divide the class into small groups. Have each group give a report on the effects of the '29 crash and the Depression in the U.S.—a major world power—on other major nations at this time.

DEVELOPING HISTORY STUDY SKILLS

Relating Economics and History   Reading Economic Graphs

Much important economic data is presented on graphs. Interpreting graphs enables the student of history to recognize the relationships between economic trends and historical events. The most frequently used graphs include bar graphs, circle graphs, and line graphs. The graphs on this page are line graphs. Line graphs are especially useful in illustrating economic trends involving quantities or amounts over a period of time.

You have already been introduced to the skill of reading charts. The steps for reading a graph are basically the same as those listed on page 181. In step 2, however, the parts of a line graph are the vertical axis and the horizontal axis.

Applying the Skill

Study the graph below. The title indicates that the subject of the graph is the Consumer Price Index (CPI). The Consumer Price Index is a statistical measure of the change in prices over a period of time based on a sampling of urban family purchases. Economists consider the CPI one measure of the rate of inflation. The title of the graph also indicates that the time frame for this data is 1920 to 1940.

Study the vertical axis. Note that the price index amounts appear along this axis. The label at the top of

the axis indicates that these values are based on the 1923 Consumer Price Index of 100. Next study the horizontal index. This lists the years between 1920 and 1940 in increments of 2 years. Trace the rise and fall of the Consumer Price Index along the graph. Refer to the dates along the horizontal axis to find the CPI in any specific year. Note the slope of the line from year to year to discover the trend in the CPI as it rises and falls.

Practicing the Skill

Study the graph below. Then on a separate sheet of paper, answer these questions.

1. What is the subject of this graph?

2. What do the numbers on the vertical axis measure?

3. What data is given on the horizontal axis?

4. In what year between 1929 and 1943 was unemployment at its highest? at its lowest?

5. Refer to your textbook to identify the key events of the period from 1929–1943. **(a)** What seems to be the connection between economic depression and unemployment? between war and unemployment? **(b)** Does it appear that the New Deal helped reduce unemployment?

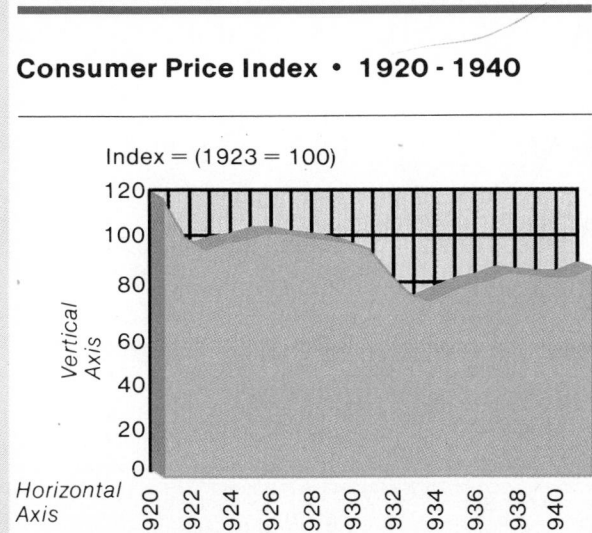

Consumer Price Index • 1920 - 1940

Index = (1923 = 100)

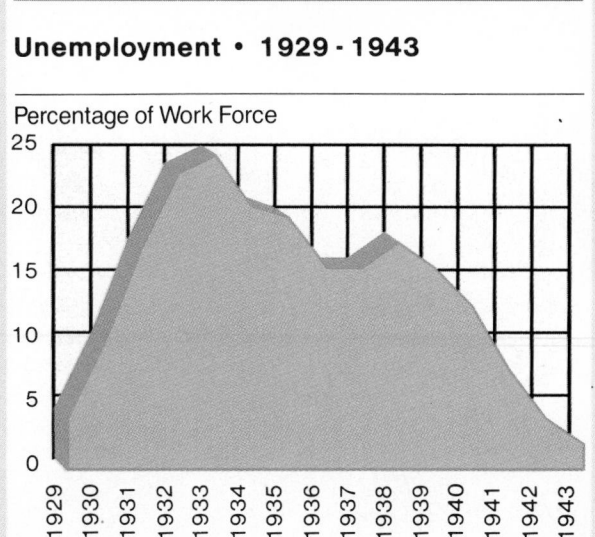

Unemployment • 1929 - 1943

Percentage of Work Force

The joyous celebrations of victory that followed the signing of the armistice on November 11, 1918, soon came to an end. In 1919 and 1920, the United States was troubled by two short but severe postwar depressions, serious labor unrest, and feverish concern over what was termed a "radical" threat to the country. During this period America's minorities suffered from renewed prejudice and discrimination.

By 1921, however, Americans were beginning to enjoy a decade of unparalleled prosperity. During the Golden Twenties, as the decade was called, business activity reached an all-time high and relatively few Americans were unemployed.

Here and there warning voices called attention to the difficulties faced by farmers and to other weaknesses of the economic system. For the most part, however, Americans were willing to believe that prosperity had come to stay.

Then, toward the end of 1929, the great industrial machine that the United States had built up began to grind to a halt. At first people refused to believe that the situation was serious. As the months passed, however, increasing numbers of businesses failed. Millions of Americans lost their jobs, farms, homes, and their life's savings. It became clear that the nation was confronted with a crisis of major proportions.

What was wrong? Americans did not agree on all the answers to this very important question. They did agree that something had to be done to save the country from complete economic collapse.

CONNECTING CHAPTER IDEAS

In such an atmosphere, the election campaign of 1932 was fought. In the next chapter you will read about the victory of Franklin Delano Roosevelt and the Democratic Party. You will also read about a series of experiments that came to be referred to as the "New Deal."

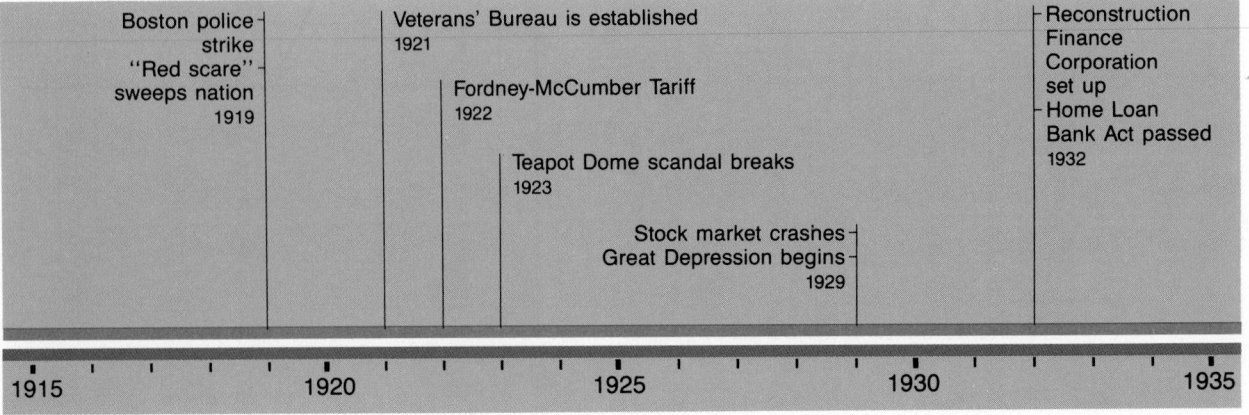

Boston police strike
"Red scare" sweeps nation
1919

Veterans' Bureau is established
1921

Fordney-McCumber Tariff
1922

Teapot Dome scandal breaks
1923

Stock market crashes
Great Depression begins
1929

Reconstruction Finance Corporation set up
Home Loan Bank Act passed
1932

1915   1920   1925   1930   1935

CHAPTER
31 REVIEW

Reviewing Important Terms

Decide whether each of the following sentences is true or false. If the sentence is false, replace the underlined term with the word or phrase that will make it true.

1. A recession is a period of sharply decreased economic activity and high unemployment.
2. The fiscal year for the United States government begins on July 1.
3. During the "Red scare" many Americans were concerned that pacifists would try to follow the example set by the Bolshevik Revolution and overthrow the United States government.

Practicing Critical Thinking Skills

1. **Interpreting Ideas.** Why were Americans more interested in domestic affairs than in international relations in the year 1920?
2. **Analyzing Viewpoints.** During the Boston police strike, Governor Coolidge made the following statement: "There is no right to strike against the public safety by anybody, anywhere, any time." What did he mean? Do you agree or disagree with this viewpoint? Why?
3. **Organizing Ideas.** The Fordney-McCumber Tariff of 1922 established high tariff rates. (a) How did this tariff affect foreign countries? (b) How did it affect American industries? (c) How did it affect American farmers?
4. **Seeing Relationships.** When the cost of living goes up, how does it affect (a) attitudes about spending and saving, (b) buying power, and (c) people living on fixed incomes?
5. **Synthesizing Ideas.** Speaking in the 1920's, Herbert Hoover said, "We in America are nearer to the final triumph over poverty than ever before in the history of any land." (a) What facts supported his opinion? (b) Why were some Americans critical of his view?
6. **Evaluating Ideas.** Is it fair to blame or praise a President or a political party for (a) a war, (b) a depression, or (c) national prosperity? Explain your position.
7. **Relating Past to Present.** Find out more about the Sacco-Vanzetti trial, which finally led to the execution of the two anarchists. (a) What were the main circumstances surrounding the case? (b) Sacco and Vanzetti were political anarchists. What were their political beliefs? (c) Why do some people feel that the men were innocent and unjustly executed? (d) What is your position on the guilt or innocence of Sacco and Vanzetti? (e) Could the Sacco-Vanzetti case take place in the United States today? Explain.

Developing History Study Skills

1. **Reading Economic Graphs.** Study the two graphs, "Common Stock Prices, 1920–1935" (page 708) and "Unemployment, 1920–1935" (page 709). Then answer the following questions. (a) In what year did the average price of a share of common stock reach its highest value? (b) Would you expect the trend begun in 1933 to continue? Explain you answer. (c) Based on these two graphs, what conclusions can you draw about the United States economy from 1920 to 1929?
2. **Developing a Frame of Reference.** One reason given for the defeat of Presidential candidate Alfred E. Smith in 1928 was that he was a Roman Catholic. Yet in 1960 Americans elected as President a Roman Catholic, John F. Kennedy. What information would be helpful in forming a frame of reference to explain this apparent change in attitude of the American electorate?

Relating Geography and History

The United States enjoys an advantageous position in world trade. Political considerations such as tariffs have often had an effect on the economy and world trade. To recognize the extent of United States world trade and the influences of tariffs, study the chart and map on page 1019. Then answer the following questions.

1. (a) Did tariffs rise or fall between 1920 and 1930? (b) Why was this policy followed? (c) Have they risen or fallen since 1933? Why? (d) What have been the effects of this policy?
2. (a) What did Congress hope to accomplish by the Emergency Tariff of 1921? (b) the Fordney-McCumber Tariff? (c) Did these tariffs accomplish their goal?
3. In general, how does the tariff rate affect United States world trade?
4. (a) To what region does the United States export the greatest percentage of its trade? (b) the least? (c) From what region does the United States import the greatest percentage? (d) the least?

See Chapter Overview in TMRG, p.TM176.
See Chapter Objectives in TMRG, p.TM176.
See Introducing the Chapter in TMRG, p.TM176.

CHAPTER 32

The Great Depression and the New Deal

(1933–1941)

A 1930's street scene

President Franklin Delano Roosevelt took office on March 4, 1933, at the height of the Great Depression. He began his administration with a ringing call to the American people to face the future with courage and faith. "The only thing we have to fear is fear itself," he confidently stated. His calm words helped to lift the American people from their despair and to rally them behind his new administration.

The President outlined his program, which was called the New Deal, in a forceful and dramatic Inaugural Address. He then presented his proposals to Congress, with recommendations for immediate action.

The New Deal had three general aims—relief, recovery, and reform. Relief was aimed at those who were in economic distress. Recovery was timed to spur the economy to action. Reform was intended to prevent the ills that had caused the Depression.

Putting the 3 R's into law, however, was not entirely successful. The American people's clamor for action often resulted in the mixing of the three aims together in a single legislative act of Congress. Sometimes a measure adopted to realize one of the aims interfered with another measure designed to achieve the other two aims. Slowly, however, the legislative program brought improvements.

The New Deal was interrupted by the United States' entry into World War II. But for eight years, from 1933 to 1941, a steady stream of New Deal measures poured out of Washington, D.C. Each measure was meant in some way to contribute to the restoration of the nation's social, economic, and political health.

READING FOCUS

As you read about the New Deal reforms, look for the details that support each of the following statements.

1. New Deal measures provide relief and speed recovery.
2. Recovery measures stimulate agriculture and industry.
3. The New Deal carries out reform measures.
4. Opposition increases toward New Deal policies and programs.
5. New Deal reforms continue despite growing criticism.
6. The New Deal's great experiment comes to an end.

1 New Deal measures provide relief and speed recovery

See Teaching Suggestions in TMRG, pp. TM176-78.

By 1933 Americans had endured two full years of the depression. Each year, each month, each week, each day the situation had become increasingly desperate. "I am afraid," Charles M. Schwab, chairman of the Bethlehem Steel Corporation said, "Every man is afraid."

Rich and poor alike, Americans lived in growing fear. Despair was widespread. "We are at the end of our rope," President Hoover declared on his last day in office.

Restoring confidence. Fortunately, the incoming President, Franklin D. Roosevelt, did not share this fear. In his Inaugural Address, he challenged Americans to rise above their fear. Speaking in a strong, calm, confident voice, he promised "action, and action now."

Roosevelt's confidence was contagious. He had been in the White House only two months when Will Rogers, one of America's most popular humorists, expressed the feeling generally held throughout the nation. "The whole country is with him, just so he does something," Rogers declared. "If he burned down the Capitol, we would cheer and say, 'Well, we at least got a fire started anyhow.'"

President Roosevelt did indeed "get a fire started." On March 5, 1933, his first full day in the White House, he began the "New Deal" for "the forgotten man." One of his first acts was to call a special session of Congress. During the next hundred days, he sent fifteen messages to the Congress, which responded by adopting fifteen relief and recovery measures.

Restoring the banking system. On March 4, when Roosevelt took office, the nation's economic system was paralyzed. For months people had been selling stocks and rushing to the banks to withdraw their money before the banks failed. Throughout the country people were hiding their money in mattresses, under carpets, and in other places they considered safe. As a result of this run on the banks, many banks failed. Others closed their doors in an effort to avoid failure. With so many banks closed, the everyday business life of the nation ground to a halt. People could not pay their

---

▲ Discussion topic: Sir Kenneth Clark, in his book Civilisation [sic] stated that "...it is lack of confidence, more than anything else, that kills a civilisation [sic] We can destroy ourselves by cynicism and disillusion, just as effectively as by bombs." Discuss this statement with students.

715

══ SOURCES ══

FRANKLIN D. ROOSEVELT'S FIRST INAUGURAL ADDRESS (1933)

● **So, first of all, let me assert my firm belief that the only thing we have to fear is fear itself— nameless, unreasoning, unjustified terror which paralyzes needed efforts to convert retreat into advance. . . .**

Our greatest primary task is to put people to work. This is no unsolvable problem if we face it wisely and courageously.

It can be accomplished in part by direct recruiting by the government itself, treating the task as we would treat the emergency of a war, but at the same time, through this employment, accomplishing greatly needed projects to stimulate and reorganize the use of our natural resources.

Hand in hand with this, we must frankly recognize the overbalance of population in our industrial centers and, by engaging on a national scale in a redistribution, endeavor to provide a better use of the land for those best fitted for the land. . . .

In the field of world policy I would dedicate this nation to the policy of the good neighbor—the neighbor who resolutely respects himself and, because he does so, respects the rights of others—the neighbor who respects his obligations and respects the sanctity of his agreements in and with a world of neighbors. . . .

═══════════

bills by checks. There was not enough currency in circulation to meet the everyday needs of even a depressed economy.

On March 5 President Roosevelt issued a proclamation closing every bank in the nation for an indefinite period. The newly convened Congress then rushed through emergency banking laws forbidding any bank to reopen until it could prove its ability to carry on business without endangering its customers' deposits. Most banks were able to satisfy the financial authorities in the Treasury Department and quickly reopened.

In order to make sure people would never again lose their bank savings, Congress in June created the Federal Deposit Insurance Corporation (FDIC). The FDIC insured individual bank deposits up to $2,500. (The amount insured by the FDIC has been increased through the years to the present figure of $100,000.)

Cheaper dollars. Congress also authorized the Secretary of the Treasury to call in all gold coins and gold certificates then in circulation. With this action Congress abandoned the gold standard, which in the past had meant that all paper currency was redeemable in gold. In so doing Congress devalued the dollar. The administration hoped that cheaper dollars would help the farmers by forcing agricultural prices upward. In this respect, however, the measure was a disappointment.

Pump priming. In its efforts to revive the nation's economy, the New Deal followed a procedure called **pump priming**. When the pump in a well does not draw water, it is sometimes necessary to prime the pump by pouring a little water down the well shaft. This water seals the crack around a washer in the shaft and thus helps to create a vacuum into which the well water rises so that it can be pumped up.

Roosevelt's administration planned to pump money into the nation's economy through federal loans and spending. The hope was that such action would stimulate the flow of more money.

One of the major pump-priming agencies was the Reconstruction Finance Corporation. The RFC had been started in Hoover's administration (see page 709). Under Roosevelt it continued to pour huge sums into the nation's economy. It did this in the form of loans totaling $11 billion to railroads, banks, insurance firms, and industrial enterprises. Much of this money was quickly repaid.

Direct relief for the unemployed. In addition to emergency measures to reopen the banks and to get more money into circulation, the New Deal provided **direct relief** to jobless, hungry Americans.

By 1933 nearly 14 million men and women ▲ were out of work. In response, the Roosevelt administration immediately launched what seemed at the time to be a colossal program of direct relief. In two years federal agencies distributed $3 billion to the states. Local authorities were allowed to use the money as they chose—to provide direct relief or jobs. At one time nearly 8 million families were on direct relief. However, few Americans liked this

He would amble onto the stage wearing cowboy gear, usually doing a few rope tricks. But the important part of any appearance by Will Rogers was his humorous comments on current events. "Well, all I know is what I read in the papers," he announced to his audience, and then stirred his listeners to laughter with keen observations.

Rogers was born in Oklahoma. Leaving school at 18, he became a cowboy and an expert roper. In fact, his roping skills won him jobs in Wild West shows. Rogers moved on to vaudeville, crisscrossing the nation with his lariat and his jokes. Rogers became a Broadway star, a movie actor, a radio commentator, and a newspaper columnist. Through it all he remained the cowboy-philosopher who spoke a common sense that appealed to all Americans.

It was politics that brought out the best in Rogers' humor. "This President business," he wrote, "is a pretty thankless job. Washington, or Lincoln either, didn't get a statue until everybody was sure they were dead." And: "All I can say about the United States Senate is that it opens with a prayer and closes with an investigation."

At the height of his popularity, Will Rogers died in an Alaskan plane crash. His death saddened the many Americans who had laughed at his jibes and understood that there was no malice behind them.

---

kind of help. What the unemployed wanted were jobs, and plans were made to replace direct relief with programs to provide work.

Work relief. The federal government attacked this problem in several ways. For instance, during 1933–34 it paid nearly $1 billion in wages to men and women on relief lists who were given jobs on "make-work" projects. Many of these projects—raking leaves and picking up litter in parks—had relatively little value. Critics of the New Deal called this kind of work "boondoggling."

President Roosevelt and other New Dealers knew that federal charity and "make-work" projects were at best necessary evils. What Americans needed and what the New Dealers wanted to provide was socially useful work. To this end, a new agency, the Works Progress Administration (WPA) was created in 1935, with Harry L. Hopkins as its head. The WPA cooperated with state and local governments, which shared in both the cost and the administration of the work relief program.

The WPA helped people in many different ways. By 1936 more than 6,000 schoolhouses had been constructed or repaired; new sewage plants had been built in 5,000 communities; about 128,000 miles (206,000 kilometers) of secondary roads had been constructed or improved. Many other public improvements had been made as well. Unemployed actors, musicians, and writers enriched American life by providing plays, concerts, guidebooks, and other forms of recreation. At the peak of its activity, in March 1936, nearly 4 million Americans were working for the WPA.

Work for youth. Perhaps the greatest tragedy of the depression was its effect upon millions of young Americans. Many were forced to leave school or college because they lacked food and clothing or were homeless. Those who graduated during the depression years faced unemployment. Thousands of jobless young Americans roamed across the nation in search of work.

Two agencies were created to bring immediate work relief to the nation's youths. In 1933 the Civilian Conservation Corps (CCC) was organized. At times as many as 500,000 young men between 18 and 25 were enrolled in the CCC. Nearly all of them were unmarried; most came from poverty-stricken families. These youths lived in work camps scattered across the land in which they received food, clothing, and shelter. They were also paid wages, which they were expected to share with their families. In the CCC they had opportunities for recreation and education.

The young Americans in the CCC did socially useful work. They built fire trails in the forests, cleared swamps, planted trees, built small dams for flood control, cleared land for public parks, and in other ways helped to conserve the nation's natural resources.

A second New Deal work relief measure aided young people who were still in school. The National Youth Administration (NYA), created in 1935, distributed federal money to needy students willing to work. These students were paid regular wages for performing useful tasks in and around their school. During its first year, the NYA gave jobs to more than 400,000 students.

The New Deal youth programs saved hundreds of thousands of youths from idleness, helped them to maintain their self-respect, and enabled many to get an education. It also kept many young Americans out of the overcrowded job market in business and industry.

Evaluating the relief program. The New Deal relief projects aroused much criticism. It is true that many mistakes were made; there was bad management; there was waste.

Some New Dealers admitted the truth of these criticisms. They explained, however, that there had been no successful past examples to follow in the gigantic tasks they had undertaken. They also pointed out that they had been handicapped by lack of trained personnel to carry out some of their programs.

Despite admitted weaknesses in the work relief program, New Dealers claimed that it had justified itself. Work provided by the federal government, they insisted, had saved millions of Americans from hunger and allowed them to retain some measure of self-respect.

SECTION REVIEW
See underscored items, text pp. 715 - 18.

Identify: New Deal, pump priming, direct relief, WPA, CCC, NYA

For answers to questions, see Answer Key, p.A99.

1. **Organizing Ideas:** What immediate problems faced Roosevelt when he took office in 1933?

2. **Interpreting Ideas:** How did the New Deal respect the rights of states in distributing funds for relief purposes?

3. **Analyzing Ideas:** Why can it be said that the greatest tragedy of the depression was its effect on millions of young people?

4. **Expressing Viewpoints:** (a) What criticisms were leveled against the New Deal relief program? (b) How did the New Dealers answer these criticisms? (c) In your opinion were the New Deal measures well conceived? Explain.

2 Recovery measures stimulate agriculture and industry

See Teaching Suggestions in TMRG, p.TM178.

The New Deal measures to provide direct relief and work relief were intended to meet the urgent needs of millions of suffering Americans. At the same time, the New Deal administration launched a recovery program designed to restore the nation's economic health.

Saving the farmers' homes. When Roosevelt became President, two out of every five farms were mortgaged. Moreover, farmers faced mounting debts—back taxes, interest payments, and payments on the principal of their loans. Unable to pay their debts, many lost their farms to banks, insurance companies, and private mortgage holders. Some families then rented as tenants the land they had once owned. Others were left homeless and jobless.

To relieve this situation, the federal government made available a huge sum of money that farmers could borrow at low interest rates. Some farmers borrowed to buy seed, fertilizer, and equipment. Others borrowed to buy back their farms or to pay their taxes.

Still others borrowed money from the government to refinance loans that they could not afford to repay at the time. Under the new government program, a farmer could borrow $5,000 from the Federal Land Banks to pay off the debt to a mortgage holder. The new loan

Despite the growing importance of big cities in American life, many artists found their subject matter in rural, small-town settings. During the years of the Great Depression, a group of Midwestern artists painted the farm, the farm community, and its traditional values. These artists included Grant Wood, Thomas Hart Benton, and John Steuart Curry.

This painting by Grant Wood is called *American Gothic*. It has become famous as a vivid study of determined, hardworking farm people and their entire way of life. The details in the painting provide you with information about life on the farm. Artists such as Wood became interested in the American farmer during the Great Depression, a time when national attention was often focused on farmers and their concerns. Through their paintings, Wood and other artists of farm life introduced a generation of urban Americans to life on the farm.

from the government could run as long as 50 years, with interest at 2 1/4 percent.

This system enabled hundreds of thousands of families to protect their farms and homes. The programs were administered by the Farm Credit Administration (FCA), created in 1933.

Higher income for farmers. The New Dealers also tried to increase the farmers' income. The first step was to raise the prices of farm products. The government set out to increase farm prices by using the principle of supply and demand. Consider the example of a grocery store that has bought more oranges than it can sell. The surplus oranges are about to rot. The store reduces the price of the oranges. Next time, the store will order fewer oranges. By reducing the supply it can sell all the oranges at a good price. This is essentially the policy that the New Deal applied to farm goods in the Agricultural Adjustment Act of 1933.

Limiting farm production. The government reduced the supply of farm products by several methods. Under the Agricultural Adjustment Administration (AAA), farmers who agreed not to use one quarter to one half of their land were paid a certain sum of money for each acre that they took out of production. The money for these **subsidies**, or benefit payments, came from taxes levied on the food processors—the meat packers, the canners, the flour millers, and the others who prepared or processed farm products.

Under this program large amounts of farmland were taken out of production. In 1933 a million cotton planters planted about 10 million acres (4 million hectares) less. As a result the 1933 cotton crop was reduced by about 4 million bales and the price of cotton almost doubled. The cotton planters received almost $200 million in federal subsidies. Producers of wheat, corn, hogs, rice, tobacco, dairy products, cattle, rye, barley, peanuts, flax, grain, sorghum, and sugar signed similar agreements to limit their production.

Evaluating the farm program. New Dealers were pleased with their agricultural recovery program. They pointed out that the prices of

The problems faced by farmers were Roosevelt's deepest concern. He felt that the nation needed to balance out what he saw as an overcommittment to industry.

719

farm products had risen and farmers were earning more money. They also pointed out that farmers were now spending more money and thus helping to get industry rolling again. These favorable results, the New Dealers said, were the outcome of sound federal planning.

However, there was also severe criticism of the New Deal farm program. Critics pointed out that the money for subsidies came from taxes on the food processors. These taxes were passed along to consumers in the form of higher prices. Thus money was being taken from consumers and given to the farmers. While farmers were getting more money, city dwellers were experiencing a decline in purchasing power.

Also, the owners of large farms benefited far more from the program than did the owners of small farms. Poorer farmers felt that the benefit payments that finally filtered down to them were inadequate for their needs.

Many critics felt that the program resulted in red tape, confusion, and inefficiency. They believed that it concentrated too much power in too many government agencies.

Finally, millions of Americans condemned a program that deliberately decreased food supplies when hunger was widespread.

The AAA declared unconstitutional. The Supreme Court brought the Agricultural Adjustment Act of 1933 to an end. In a 1936 decision in the case of *United States v. Butler*, the Court stated that Congress had no constitutional right to regulate agricultural production. The Court ruled that this power belonged to the states and that the federal government had no authority to interfere.

▲ **Construction of public works.** New Deal programs also attempted to revive the building industry. The New Dealers recognized that the building industry is one of the keys to a nation's economic health. The industry uses large quantities of materials from many sources. As a result, when construction work is going on, workers are busy in forests, mines, and factories throughout the country.

The building program of the New Deal started in June 1933. At that time, the Public Works Administration (PWA) began to contract with private firms for the construction of public works, such as bridges, government buildings, power plants, conservation projects, and dams. The federal government also encouraged states and municipalities to carry on their own building programs, offering them loans and gifts.

By the summer of 1936, public works projects included about 70 municipal power plants, several hundred schools and hospitals, nearly 1,500 waterworks, and many federal, state, county, and municipal buildings.

Repair and building of homes. The New Dealers also sought to revive the building industry by stimulating the construction of homes. Like so many New Deal measures, this program was double-barreled; it had as a second goal the relief of homeowners.

When President Roosevelt took office, an average of 1,000 American homes were being foreclosed and sold at public auction every day. In June 1933 Congress tried to end this situation by creating the Home Owners Loan Corporation (HOLC). With money borrowed at low interest rates from this government agency, many homeowners could pay off their old mortgages. At the same time, they arranged with the HOLC to pay off their new mortgages over a long period with much smaller monthly payments. Between 1933 and 1936, the homes of more than 1 million American families were thus saved.

To provide further aid to the owners of homes and businesses and the building industry, the Federal Housing Administration (FHA) was established in 1934. The FHA encouraged banks to lend money to individuals for repairing and building homes and business properties. It did this by insuring the banks against losses on such loans. Yet so desperate was the financial position of most Americans that relatively few people were able to take advantage of the FHA loans.

A federal housing program to provide homes for the very poor was no more successful. Although the PWA lent and gave money to some 27 cities for clearing slums and building low-cost apartment houses, the results were disappointing. For one thing, rents for the finished apartments were usually more than poor families could afford.

Aid to transportation. No less important than the building industry to a nation's economic life is its transportation system. The depression hit the railroads a stunning blow. Between 1929 and 1933, almost one third of all the railroad companies in the United States went bankrupt. Others were saved from complete collapse only by loans from the RFC.

To recover lost business, some western railroads lowered their passenger rates from 3.2 cents to 2 cents per mile. The experiment proved so successful that the Interstate Commerce Commission ordered all lines to adopt the same rate. Government loans also enabled the railroads to install modern equipment, such as diesel engines and streamlined trains.

All of these measures helped the railroads. However, at the same time, the government also spent huge sums of money to improve the nation's highways and waterways, thereby giving a boost to the railroads' competitors.

The NIRA. All these New Deal recovery measures were more or less indirect methods of reviving the nation's industrial machine. With the National Industrial Recovery Act (NIRA), the New Deal tackled the problem head on.

The NIRA went into effect in June 1933 as a two-year emergency measure. It was intended to aid industry, consumers, and labor. Under the act employers would cooperate in stabilizing prices, finding employment for jobless workers, and raising wages. Cooperation was to replace competition as one of the major driving forces of American industry. Antitrust legislation, such as the Sherman and Clayton antitrust acts, was disregarded.

The NIRA provided that each industry should, with the aid of the National Recovery Administration (NRA), adopt a "code of fair practices." Once these codes had been approved by the President, they became binding upon the entire industry.

Some 95 percent of American industries adopted fair-practices codes within a few months. In general, the codes limited production and provided for the common control of prices and sales practices. Most codes also outlawed child labor and required that adults not work more than 40 hours a week and that wages not be less than $12 to $15 a week.

Perhaps the most important—and certainly the most controversial—provisions in the NIRA were contained in the famous Section 7a. This section guaranteed workers the right to bargain collectively with their employers.

Criticisms of the NIRA. Critics of the NIRA were many and outspoken. Owners of small businesses charged that the NRA codes of fair practices had mostly been made by and for large corporations. They insisted that the minimum-wage provisions in the codes favored the highly mechanized factories that could afford to pay higher wages. Other critics charged that it was difficult to enforce the codes. Also, the courts usually refused to enforce the fair-practices provisions of the codes. Finally, while the NRA was supposed to aid recovery by increasing the purchasing power of consumers, many manufacturers defeated this purpose by raising prices to cover increases in wages.

The main objection to the NIRA for many businesses was that it stimulated unionization and collective bargaining. Moreover, certain provisions in Section 7a of the act were not clear. For instance, did company unions, under the influence of managers and owners, have the right to engage in collective bargaining? Labor said that company unions could not honestly represent the workers and should be outlawed. Management disagreed.

The National Labor Board. To settle the confused points of the law, Congress established an agency that later became the National Labor Relations Board (NLRB). The board could conduct elections in plants and determine which labor organization had the right to bargain for all the workers in that particular plant. It also served as a board of arbitration to settle labor disputes.

The board was unpopular with business managers and owners. They claimed that it usually settled disputes in favor of labor. As a result, business began to oppose the entire NRA program. When management refused to grant union demands, a wave of strikes broke out. Despite these problems the National Labor Board, before the summer of 1935, settled more than four fifths of the 3,755 disputes referred to it and avoided nearly 500 strikes.

The NIRA declared unconstitutional. In May 1935, in the case of *Schechter v. United States*, the Supreme Court declared the NIRA unconstitutional. The Court held that in giving the federal government the right to regulate interstate commerce, the Constitution did not give the government the power to regulate every aspect of business.

The Wagner Act. One important idea in the ▲ NIRA was quickly reborn. In 1935 Congress passed the famous National Labor Relations Act. This measure was often called the Wagner

▲ Several important Supreme Court decisions did finally uphold the Wagner Act in 1937. The majority decision ruled that the right to organize for bargaining was "a fundamental right" and "an essential condition of industrial peace."

721

Act after one of its sponsors, Senator Robert F. Wagner of New York.

The Wagner Act, like Section 7a of the NIRA, guaranteed to labor the right to organize, to bargain collectively for better wages and working conditions, and to engage in "concerted activities . . . for other mutual aid." The Wagner Act condemned as unfair to labor such practices as discriminating against or discharging a worker for belonging to a union. It also declared that the majority of the workers in any plant or industry could select representatives to bargain with management.

Under the Wagner Act, the organization of labor proceeded rapidly. While the Wagner Act was in a sense a reform measure, it was also intended to promote industrial recovery. It aimed to do this by guaranteeing to organized labor a better chance of raising workers' wages and thus increasing their purchasing power. No single measure of the New Deal aroused more controversy than the Wagner Act.

SECTION REVIEW

See underscored items, text pp. 719 - 22.
Identify: AAA, subsidy, *United States v. Butler,* HOLC, Section 7a, NLRB, *Schechter v. United States,* Wagner Act.

For answers to questions, see Answer Key, p.A99.
1. **Summarizing Ideas: (a)** Explain the basic New Deal plan to aid farmers. **(b)** What were the major arguments for and against the New Deal farm recovery program? **(c)** Why did the Supreme Court declare the Agricultural Adjustment Act of 1933 unconstitutional?

2. **Organizing Ideas:** What steps were taken during the New Deal to help the transportation industry?

3. **Analyzing Ideas: (a)** What was the aim of the NIRA? **(b)** How was the aim to be carried out? **(c)** Why did the Supreme Court declare the NIRA unconstitutional?

3 The New Deal carries out reform measures

See Teaching Suggestions in TMRG, pp.TM178-79.
Although relief and recovery measures were urgently needed in the early 1930's, only fundamental reforms could protect the nation against another depression. Such reforms became increasingly important goals of the New Deal in 1935 and thereafter.

Protection for investors. New Deal reforms strengthened banks in several ways. For example, the power of the Federal Reserve System was increased by placing commercial and savings banks under its supervision. The Federal Reserve Board was given additional power to regulate credit as a check upon reckless speculation.

Another series of laws was designed to protect the public against worthless stocks. Any bank, brokerage house, or salesperson that failed to give full and honest information about the true value of stocks and bonds offered for sale was subject to a severe penalty. In 1934 the Securities and Exchange Commission (SEC) was created to administer these laws and to regulate the stock exchanges.

Social security for the people. One key reform measure of the New Deal, the Social Security Act of 1935, tackled the problem of individual security. The act had three major goals.

First, it provided unemployment insurance for individuals who lost their jobs. The money to be used for this purpose was raised by a payroll tax on businesses employing more than eight workers.

A second goal of the Social Security Act was to provide old-age pensions ranging from $10 to $85 a month for persons over 65. The money for this purpose was raised by a payroll tax on employers and a social security tax on the wages of employees.

A third goal of the Social Security Act was to help the handicapped—the blind, the aged, the disabled—as well as dependent children. Federal pensions up to $20 a month were available for needy persons over 65, provided that the states paid an equal amount. Federal funds were also available for those states that sought to protect the welfare of the handicapped.

President Roosevelt called the Social Security Act "a cornerstone in a structure which is being built." It was admittedly only a beginning, for it did not include all workers. Nevertheless, by 1937 nearly 21 million workers were entitled to unemployment benefits, and 36 million retired workers to old-age pensions. ▲

Electricity for homes. Another reform movement sought to bring electricity to more Americans. Despite widespread development of electric power up to the 1930's, only one third of America's homes had electricity. In rural areas only 15 out of every 100 houses were wired.

▲ Roosevelt's answer to opponents of employee contributions was that these funds gave the contributors "a legal, moral, and political right to collect their pensions and unemployment benefits." He also felt that the contributions guaranteed that the act would not be scrapped by some future politician.

To solve this problem, the President in 1935 created the Rural Electrification Administration (REA). The REA had the responsibility of developing a program for generating and distributing electricity to isolated rural areas.

Regulating utility companies. In 1935 also, Congress passed the Public Utility Holding Company Act, also called the Wheeler-Rayburn Act. This measure gave the Federal Power Commission authority to regulate the interstate production, transmission, and sale of electricity. It gave the Federal Trade Commission similar authority over gas. It gave the Securities and Exchange Commission authority to regulate the financial practices of public utility holding companies.

By regulating the financial operations of the public utility holding companies, the New Deal hoped to end a trend toward monopoly in public utilities. The measure was designed to prevent any holding company from controlling more than a "single integrated public utility system" operating in a single area of the country. Under the law utility companies were forbidden to engage in any business other than the production and distribution of gas or electric power. They were also forbidden to issue new stocks and bonds without the approval of the Securities and Exchange Commission.

Finally, in a "death-sentence" clause, the Public Utility Holding Company Act gave the public utility holding companies five years to readjust their financial affairs. At the end of five years, any company that could not prove that it was actually distributing gas or electricity in a given area would be dissolved.

The TVA. With the creation of the Tennessee Valley Authority (TVA), Congress in 1933 launched the United States upon an experiment that had no parallel in American history. The scene of this monumental experiment included parts of seven states in the region drained by the Tennessee River and its tributaries (see map, page 725).

The TVA moved into this region with a plan that was to improve economic and social conditions for the benefit of the people who lived in the valley. It would also benefit all Americans.

▲

Over the next ten years, the TVA constructed 21 large dams on the Tennessee River and its major tributaries and thousands of smaller dams on creeks and brooks. Power plants were erected to convert the "white coal" of the river into vast quantities of electricity. Whereas in 1935 only 1 in every 100 homes in Mississippi had electricity, by 1945 about 20 homes out of 100 were wired. The per capita consumption of electric power in the TVA region was 50 percent higher than the average per capita consumption for the entire United States. Moreover, rates for electric power had been cut by about one third.

The TVA dams were also planned as part of a program to control floods, to prevent soil erosion, and to restore the fertility of the land. Under the TVA, fertilizer plants were opened, river and road transportation improved, and public parks, schools, and hospitals were constructed. Vast changes have come to the region because of TVA programs.

Criticisms of the TVA. There is another side to the TVA story. Privately owned power companies, representing a $12 billion industry, bitterly fought the TVA. They declared that the TVA was an unnecessary intervention by the federal government into the affairs of private industry. The owners of privately owned companies insisted that the lower TVA rates for electric power were not the result of more efficient production. If the TVA paid taxes as all private industries did, critics insisted, the power agency would have to charge much higher rates for its electricity.

Advocates of the TVA believed that its rates should be used as a standard to govern the rates charged by private power producers. The private power companies insisted that use of the TVA rates as a standard was unfair. Critics of the TVA charged that the less expensive electricity it generated was a gift from the taxpayers of the entire nation to the people of one region.

SECTION REVIEW

See underscored items, pp. 722 - 23.

Identify: SEC, social security, REA, public utilities, TVA

For answers to questions, see Answer Key, pp.A99-100.

1. **Summarizing Ideas:** What were the three main purposes of the Social Security Act of 1935?

2. **Interpreting Ideas:** (a) What was the purpose of the Tennessee Valley Authority? (b) Although the TVA was located in a single region, how might it be seen as a benefit to the whole nation?

3. **Comparing Ideas:** (a) What arguments have been used against the TVA? (b) Do you think these are valid arguments? Explain.

▲ Other important public projects of the New Deal years were the Bonneville and Grand Coulee dams in the Pacific Northwest.

723

In 1933, during the darkest days of the Great Depression, President Franklin D. Roosevelt presented a plan to Congress to improve the economic conditions of one of the regions of the nation hardest hit by the depression. The region was the valley of the Tennessee River.

The Tennessee River, the largest tributary of the Ohio River, flows southwest through Tennessee and Alabama, then turns northward, reenters Tennessee, and finally flows northwest across Kentucky and enters the Ohio River at Paducah, Kentucky. The Tennessee River, 650 miles (1,040 kilometers) in length, drains an area of 40,910 square miles (108,547 kilometers).

In 1933, Congress granted Roosevelt's request and passed the legislation that created the Tennessee Valley Authority, usually referred to as the TVA. Congress set for the TVA the goals of conserving the valley's resources and of speeding the region's economic development.

The Tennessee Valley in 1933 epitomized the serious problems caused by poor farming practices. Much of the land in the Tennessee Valley slopes steeply. The original forest cover had helped protect these slopes from soil erosion. The valley's forests, however, had been stripped away. With the trees cut and the stumps and root systems removed, erosion reached frightening proportions. During rainy periods, water would run rapidly off slopes, carrying the rich topsoil with it. The Tennessee River and its tributaries began to fill with silt. This presented a flood danger to the low-lying farms and cities along the Tennessee River and beyond to the Ohio and Mississippi river systems. In addition, so much soil was being carried by

the Tennessee River that the river had become almost useless for navigation.

Against this background President Roosevelt decided to create the TVA. There was, however, a constitutional question as to how far the federal government could go in improving the quality of life in this, or any, region. The President did have the power to establish an authority to control the often rampaging waters of the Tennessee River on the grounds that it would be removing barriers to interstate commerce. The President's use of this power created the TVA with the dual purposes of controlling flooding in the Tennessee River Valley and improving navigation.

Today a nine-foot (2.7–meter) channel is maintained which allows barge traffic to move safely all of the way upstream to Knoxville. This directly fulfills one of the TVA's specific purposes. In a sense, most of today's other activities of the TVA are a logical extension of the nine-foot channel. Navigation development, for example, required the construction or purchase of a series of dams so that stream flow and water depth could be regulated. With the availability of dams it seemed only natural to produce and sell hydro-electric power as part of the operation of the dams.

The TVA controls 31 dams, most of which have power-generating facilities. Thus, the TVA became the supplier of electricity to a broad area centering on the river. In time, as the power needs of the region grew, the demand for power out-stripped the capacity of the water-powered facilities. So, the TVA began building other power

Construction of the Norris Dam

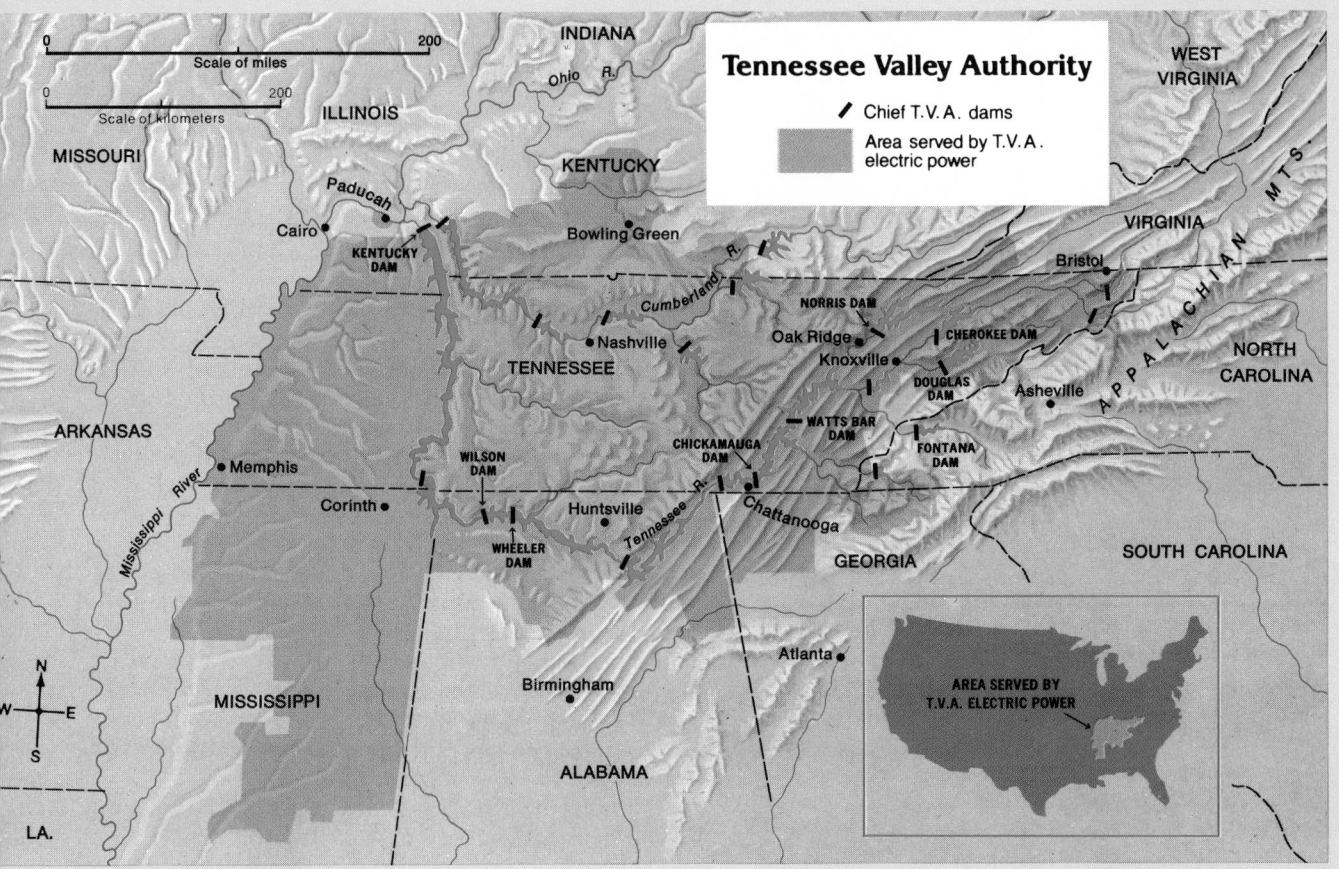

Tennessee Valley Authority

/ Chief T.V.A. dams

Area served by T.V.A. electric power

AREA SERVED BY
T.V.A. ELECTRIC POWER

sources. Today, about 80 percent of the electricity produced in the valley comes from thermal plants rather than water power. Ten of these plants burn coal and several are nuclear-powered facilities. Originally, TVA power was among the cheapest in the nation. This cheap power attracted several industries that are heavy power users, such as the huge aluminum plant at Alcoa, south of Knoxville. Partly because of the availability of large quantities of power, one of the nation's first atomic research centers was located at Oak Ridge, west of Knoxville. The TVA also became a large developer and producer of artificial fertilizer whose production requires enormous amounts of power.

From its beginnings, it was clear that if the TVA was to truly control the Tennessee River, it would require more than just dams on the river itself. It was imperative that the headwaters of the river be studied and controlled if they were to rectify the conditions that caused flooding downstream. In this way the sphere of TVA activities began to broaden. With the help of the Soil Conservation Service, an erosion control program was put into effect

on the region's farms. Trees were planted on the eroded hillsides. Soil studies were conducted to determine the best use of the valley's farms. Detailed mapping of the region was completed by the U.S. Geological Survey. Finally, where dams had been built and reservoirs created, the shores of the reservoirs were landscaped to create parks. These new parks encouraged the development of a tourist industry and, indeed, the new lakes have become one of the nation's finest inland water recreation regions.

It is important to note in this context, however, that other southern areas, such as the Piedmont from North Carolina to Alabama, as well as the lower Mississippi River Valley, have also experienced considerable prosperity in the last 40 years. There has been injection of both capital and initiative in the Tennessee Valley. Manufacturing has increased rather dramatically in this region as well as in the Tennessee Valley. Perhaps TVA's success has resulted in a new appreciation of what could be made of the resources of the entire South if a region's resources were managed with wisdom.

Unemployment • 1929–1939

Year	Number of Unemployed	Percentage of Work Force Unemployed
1929	1,600,000	3.2%
1930	4,300,000	8.7%
1931	8,000,000	15.9%
1932	12,100,000	23.6%
1933	12,800,000	24.9%
1934	11,300,000	21.7%
1935	10,600,000	20.1%
1936	9,000,000	16.9%
1937	7,700,000	14.3%
1938	10,400,000	19.0%
1939	9,500,000	17.2%

4 Opposition increases toward New Deal policies and programs

See Teaching Suggestions in TMRG, pp.TM179-80.

By 1936 the United States had made considerable progress in its battle against the depression. National income had risen sharply since 1932, having jumped from a low of less than $47 billion to almost $70 billion. Industrial production was double that of 1932.

In 1936, however, as many as 3.5 million people were on relief projects. Nine million workers were still unemployed. Many factories and mines were still closed or were working at far less than full capacity.

Roosevelt's supporters. In June 1936 the Democrats enthusiastically renominated Roosevelt for a second term. Lined up behind the President were not only most Democrats but also countless rank-and-file Republicans. Most of the progressive Republican leaders who had supported him in 1932 continued to do so. Labor was overwhelmingly for the President, as were many farmers who remembered the New Deal benefits they had recently received. Many on relief also supported Roosevelt. And finally, black voters in the North almost solidly rejected their traditional Republican ties and supported the Democratic party.

Roosevelt's critics. Roosevelt's Republican critics included most big business leaders, many small business people who had suffered under the NRA, bankers, private power companies, newspapers, and many professional people.

Opponents of President Roosevelt sometimes claimed that he was undermining the Constitution. They pointed out that the Supreme Court had declared unconstitutional seven out of nine important New Deal measures. Critics insisted that the American way of life—individualism, free enterprise, and private property—was being abandoned for socialism and government control. They denied that the New Deal had restored prosperity. They pointed to the nation's continued unemployment. They stressed the fact that the administration had piled up a huge national debt of over $33 billion and had failed to balance the budget.

Republican promises. The Republicans in 1936 nominated friendly, thrifty Alfred M. Landon, Governor of Kansas, for President. Landon, a liberal Republican, had the support of many farmers who trusted his judgment. In a period when most states and the federal government had piled up huge debts, Governor Landon had balanced the Kansas budget.

The Republican platform promised to continue most New Deal measures, which, they claimed, they could carry out more effectively than the Democrats. The Republicans also promised to balance the budget and to restore to the states powers that the federal government had seized to carry out the New Deal program. Thus the Republicans adopted what had been the Democratic states' rights position.

Roosevelt's victory. The election campaign was filled with angry charges and countercharges. More than 45 million Americans voted, reflecting keen popular interest. Roosevelt swept the country with an electoral

Text continues on page 728.

DEVELOPING HISTORY STUDY SKILLS

Relating Economics to History Classifying Economic Policies

- How could the Great Depression be ended?
- Should the government assume a larger role in regulating the economy?
- Should the government become responsible for the aid and welfare of workers and farmers?

Economic questions such as these were of great concern to Americans in the 1930's. How these and other economic questions would be answered depended on the economic philosophies of the nation's leaders. Students of history are often called on to classify the economic philosophies and policies of government leaders.

American economic philosophies and programs fall into three categories: conservative, progressive, or somewhere in between. Conservative economic philosophy calls for little government intervention in the economy. Progressive economic philosophy is highlighted by increased government interaction with the economy.

To analyze and evaluate economic philosophies and policies it is first necessary to classify them. You have already been introduced to the skill of classifying information. Review pages 54–55 to refresh your memory.

Applying the Skill

Read the following excerpt and classify the economic philosophy of each President mentioned in the excerpt. Refer to your textbook for further information on the policies mentioned in the excerpt.

> *Throughout the first half of the 20th century politicans argued over what to do about economic problems. Each leader seemed to have his own ideas and philosophies.*
>
> *Wilson pressed to reduce the tariff, strengthen antitrust laws, promote competition in American business, and protect consumers.*
>
> *Coolidge said that government should encourage, but not regulate, business.*
>
> *In various New Deal programs Franklin Roosevelt called for direct aid to farmers and wage earners, government regulation of farm surpluses and prices, and income [social] security.*

Wilson's economic programs have often been called progressive. Stronger antitrust laws, consumer protection, and government promotion of business competition call for government involvement in the economy. Coolidge's stated philosophy falls somewhere between conservative and progressive. His belief that "government should encourage, but not regulate, business" implies some government intervention in the economy. Franklin Roosevelt's economic philosophy is clearly progressive. Programs such as direct aid to farmers and wage earners, government regulation of prices, and social security require much government involvement in the workings of the economy.

Practicing the Skill

Read the following list of economic acts, events, programs, and policies. Then on a separate sheet of paper, classify each as conservative or progressive and state a reason for your classification.

Federal Reserve System

Emergency Tariff Act of 1921

Budget and Accounting Act

Fordney-McCumber Tariff

Bonus Bill

Agricultural Marketing Act

Works Progress Administration projects

Agricultural Adjustment Act of 1938

Reconstruction Finance Corporation

Home Loan Bank Act

Federal Deposit Insurance Corporation

Civilian Conservation Corps

National Youth Administration

Federal Land Banks

Bank Holiday

National Industrial Recovery Act

Federal Housing Administration

Employers' Liability Act

Underwood Tariff Act

(All these measures can be classified as progressive measures. Only the Budget and Accounting Act and the Underwood Tariff Act reduced in any way government involvement in the economy. Students reasons will vary.)

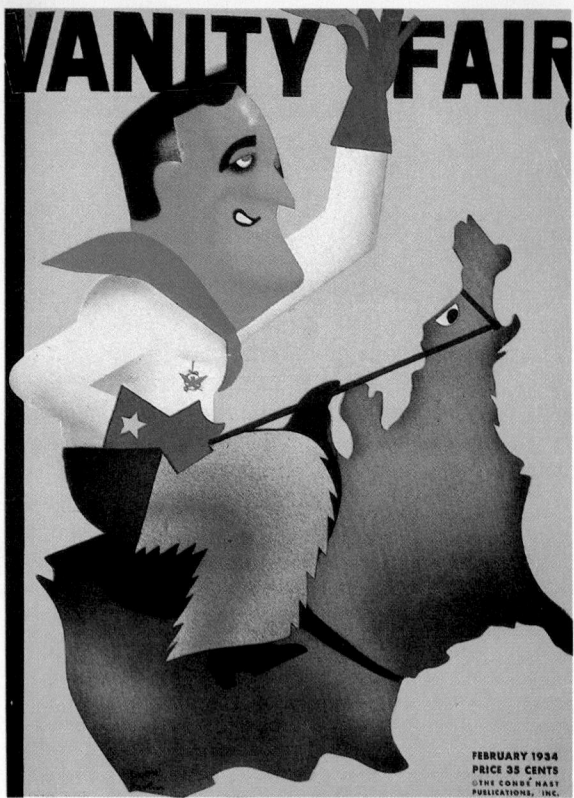

FEBRUARY 1934
PRICE 35 CENTS
©THE CONDÉ NAST
PUBLICATIONS, INC.

This 1934 cover of the magazine Vanity Fair
*reflected the thinking of those Americans who
believed that Roosevelt had assumed too much
power in the first year of his Presidency.*

vote of 523 to 8. Roosevelt's popular vote
was also impressive—27,476,673 to Landon's
16,679,583. Moreover, the Democrats won or
kept control of all but six governorships and
maintained their leadership of both houses of
Congress. Not since the reelection of President
Monroe in 1820 had a Presidential candidate
won such strong backing.

Roosevelt and the Supreme Court. Early in
his second term, Roosevelt opened an attack
on the Supreme Court. Roosevelt was upset
because the Court had set aside as unconstitutional seven important New Deal laws. He was
also disturbed because the Court had declared
unconstitutional a New York State measure
providing minimum wages for women and children. Moreover, the federal courts had used the
injunction to block federal agencies from carrying out New Deal measures.

Roosevelt declared that all too often certain
Supreme Court justices thought in terms of the
"horse-and-buggy" era. "A dead hand was
being laid upon this whole program of prog-

ress," the President later declared. It was, he
said, the hand of the Supreme Court.

President Roosevelt asked Congress for
power to appoint an extra justice to the Supreme Court for each existing justice who did
not retire upon reaching age 70. At the time,
six of the nine justices were 70 or older. Roosevelt's proposal, therefore, would have enabled
him to appoint six new justices more favorable
to the New Deal.

Changes in the Supreme Court. Although
the President fought vigorously for his "reform" proposal, he lost. Members of Congress
in his own party refused to support him, and
public opinion ran against him. In general,
people did not want to tamper with the delicate
balance of legislative, executive, and judicial
powers written into the Constitution.

Although Roosevelt lost the battle for Court
"reform," he gained most of the things he
wanted. The Court began to approve important
New Deal measures. The National Labor Relations Act and the Social Security Act were
tested and found constitutional. Moreover, the
Court approved an act passed by the state of
Washington establishing minimum pay for
women and children. This act was almost identical to the New York State law that the Court
had earlier declared unconstitutional.

Had the Court suddenly realized that it
might be well to approve certain popular legislation to prevent a drastic reform of the Court
itself? Many Americans believed this to be
true. In any case, Roosevelt was able to replace, because of death or retirement, all but
two of the original justices with members who
appeared to be more sympathetic to New Deal
legislation.

Business slump in 1937–38. Early in 1937,
while the issue of the Supreme Court was
being argued across the land, the nation's industrial machinery once again slowed down.
By the autumn of 1937, factories were closing
and unemployment was rising.

The Democrats spoke of what was taking
place as a **recession**, that is, a business slump
less severe than a depression. The Republicans, on the other hand, called it the "Roosevelt depression." Roosevelt's opponents blamed
the Democrats and the New Deal for the present business slump in just the same way that
the Democrats in 1931 had blamed the Republicans for the Great Depression.

Politics aside, there was fairly widespread agreement on the major cause of the slump. Instead of balancing the budget as he had promised to do back in 1932, Roosevelt had piled up the largest national debt in history. The Republicans had made the most of this fact in the 1936 election campaign. However, many Democrats and friends of the New Deal had also become increasingly uneasy about the mounting debt.

Mindful of the growing criticism, by 1936 Roosevelt had begun to cut spending for relief and public works. Unfortunately, private industry was not yet strong enough to give jobs to the men and women who were dropped from relief projects because of the cutbacks. Once again, therefore, the nation's economic system started on a downward spiral.

New pump priming. Fortunately, measures adopted to fight the Great Depression acted as brakes against the 1937–38 recession. More than 2 million wage earners in 25 states, protected by the Social Security Act, began to collect unemployment insurance. The new banking laws protected the savings of depositors. Many government agencies were ready to lend money to business and to construct public works, thus creating new jobs.

Roosevelt and Congress began once again to prime the economic pump by increasing government lending and spending. The Reconstruction Finance Corporation again came to the rescue of businesses in trouble. The WPA doubled the number of workers on its payroll from 1.5 million to 3 million.

By the end of 1938, the nation's economic machinery was once again picking up speed. The Democrats were quick to claim another victory for the New Deal. The Republicans, on the other hand, insisted again that recovery had come in spite of the New Deal. Many Americans, Democrats and Republicans alike, continued to express alarm at the ever-growing national debt.

SECTION REVIEW

See underscored items, text pp. 726, 728.
Identify: Alfred M. Landon, recession
For answers to questions, see Answer Key, p.A100.

1. **Summarizing Ideas: (a)** On what major issues did the election of 1936 focus? **(b)** What positions did each party take on these issues?
2. **Expressing Viewpoints (a)** Why did Roosevelt try to reform the Supreme Court? **(b)** Why did

his plan fail? **(c)** What position would you have taken on the issue? Give arguments to support your opinion.
3. **Analyzing Ideas:** How did the measures adopted to fight the Great Depression act as brakes against the recession of 1937–38?

---

5 New Deal reforms continue despite growing criticism

See Teaching Suggestions in TMRG, pp.TM180-81.

During the 1936 campaign, President Roosevelt had promised that, if reelected, he would continue the New Deal. Neither the business recession of 1937–38 nor the mounting criticism of his policies prevented Roosevelt from continuing his program.

The A. F. of L. and the CIO. The Wagner Act of 1935 guaranteed to workers the right of collective bargaining and forbade employers to discriminate against organized labor. Under the protection of this law, the American Federation of Labor began to organize unskilled workers in the mass production industries—steel, automobiles, aluminum, aircraft, utilities. However, the A. F. of L. did not move rapidly enough to please many labor leaders.

Growing impatience with the A. F. of L. led John L. Lewis, powerful head of the United Mine Workers, and a group of like-minded labor leaders to organize in 1935 the Committee for Industrial Organization (CIO). The CIO immediately launched a drive to organize workers in the automobile, steel, rubber, oil, radio, and other industries into industrial unions. The new industrial unions included all workers, skilled and unskilled, in an industry. The United Automobile Workers (UAW), for example, represented all workers in automotive plants. In earlier times workers in the automobile industry had negotiated contracts through many separate unions—electrical, welding, metalworking, and the like. Now they negotiated as a single powerful organization. The CIO also encouraged the inclusion of black workers in the new industrial unions.

Disturbed by the growing influence of the CIO, the leaders of the A. F. of L. ordered it to disband. When CIO leaders refused to obey this order, the A. F. of L. expelled them. However, the CIO continued to operate, and in May 1938

▲ Discussion topic: Have students review text pages 716 - 29 then analyze and discuss other ways New Deal measures might have softened the blow of the 1937 - 38 recession.

729

Here, auto workers in a General Motors factory stage a sit-down strike in 1936. It was through this 44-day sit-down strike at Flint, Michigan, that the GM workers won the right to be represented by the United Auto Workers.

it reorganized as a separate body, the Congress of Industrial Organizations (still called CIO), with John L. Lewis as its first president. By 1940 the CIO could boast of having 3.6 million members, roughly equal to the membership of the older A. F. of L.

The sit-down strike. Meanwhile, forceful organizing campaigns by both the A. F. of L. and the CIO resulted in a wave of strikes.

In November 1936 several hundred workers in the General Motors plant at Flint, Michigan, staged a **sit-down strike**. Instead of leaving the plant and organizing picket lines, the striking workers simply sat down at their machines and refused to work. They then announced that they would not leave until management granted their demands.

The sit-down strike, which made it impossible for management to bring in strikebreakers, proved extremely effective. Within a few months, this relatively new labor weapon spread to many other plants, involving more than half a million workers. All of the leading automobile manufacturers except Ford now

recognized the United Automobile Workers, the powerful new CIO union, as the bargaining agent for the automobile industry. The United States Steel Corporation, long a foe of labor unions, finally accepted the CIO steelworkers' union as the bargaining agent of the steelworkers. The CIO also organized the workers in many other industries.

In 1939 the Supreme Court ruled that sit-down strikes were illegal. Nevertheless the CIO—as well as the A. F. of L.—continued to forge ahead. In general, the Wagner Act of 1935, with its guarantee of collective bargaining, had given organized labor its great opportunity for growth.

Jurisdictional strikes. Much of the labor unrest of the late 1930's sprang from bitter rivalry between the A. F. of L. and the CIO. Disputes arose over which had **jurisdiction**, or the right, to enroll a particular group of workers. Sometimes these disputes led to jurisdictional strikes. In such cases management found it hard to know which side to recognize or to bargain with, and the government stepped

▲   Strikers felt government intervention would be unlikely because of the tolerant attitude of the Roosevelt administration. Employers often gave in quickly to workers' demands because they feared efforts to clear their plants of sit-down strikers might result in destruction of factory property.

in to settle the issue. The great wave of strikes that reached its peak in 1937 and 1938 diminished in the following years as both labor and management reluctantly came to accept government intervention.

Fair Labor Standards Act. The New Deal labor program did not merely encourage and support organized workers. It also aimed at reforming labor conditions in the United States. To this end, President Roosevelt in 1937 proposed the Fair Labor Standards Act, sometimes called the Wages and Hours Law. This law provided a minimum wage scale and a maximum workweek for many workers.

Strong opposition quickly developed to the Fair Labor Standards Act. Many employers claimed that it encouraged unneeded and unwise government interference and control over industry. However, the law went into effect in October 1938.

The Fair Labor Standards Act provided that a legal maximum workweek of 44 hours in 1938 be decreased to 40 hours by 1940, with time-and-a-half pay for overtime. It also provided that minimum wages of 25 cents an hour in 1938 be increased to 40 cents an hour by 1945. It prohibited the employment of children under 16 in industries producing goods for interstate commerce. The Department of Labor was responsible for enforcing the act.

Although the Fair Labor Standards Act affected only workers employed in interstate industries, by 1940 about 13 million men and women were benefiting from the law. Roosevelt hailed the new law as being, after the Social Security Act, "the most farsighted program for the benefit of workers ever adopted in this or in any other country."

Important though the Fair Labor Standards Act was, it did not insure freedom from racial discrimination in employment. In 1941 A. Philip Randolph, a powerful and militant black labor leader, threatened to march on the national capital with 10,000 blacks to demand equal employment opportunities. Responding to this pressure, Roosevelt established the Fair Employment Practices Committee (FEPC). The FEPC worked to counteract racial discrimination in industries that had contracts with the federal government.

Helping the farmers. Other far-reaching New Deal measures were meant to improve the economic position of the nation's farmers. In 1936, when the Supreme Court ruled against the Agricultural Adjustment Act of 1933, Congress passed another law.

The Soil Conservation and Domestic Allotment Act of 1936 set up a soil conservation program. Farmers who took part in the program leased part of their lands to the government. Under the supervision of state farm agencies, the farmers worked to restore the fertility of the leased land by practicing conservation measures, by using fertilizers, and by sowing soil-restoring plants, such as clover. In return, the farmers received a certain sum of money for every acre they withdrew from production.

By this means the government hoped to develop nationwide knowledge of sound conservation practices. Equally important, by limiting production the government hoped to raise the prices of farm products.

The Bankhead-Jones Act. With the Bankhead-Jones Farm Tenant Act of 1937, the New Deal undertook to help tenant farmers, sharecroppers, and migratory farm workers, who moved from place to place in search of jobs. The new law created the Farm Security Administration (FSA) to lend money at low interest to tenant farmers, sharecroppers, and farm laborers wishing to buy farms. Those who received the loans had 40 years to repay.

Agricultural Adjustment Act of 1938. The heart of the New Deal agricultural reform program was the second Agricultural Adjustment Act, passed in 1938. This act contained a number of important provisions:

(1) It provided payments to farmers in proportion to the number of acres that they withdrew from production and planted in soil-conserving crops.

(2) The government was authorized to decide the amount of various staple crops that could be marketed each year. With the approval of two thirds of the producers of these commodities in each locality, the government then assigned a certain allotment to each farmer. Farmers who exceeded this allotment had to pay a fine when they sold such crops during a time of surplus.

(3) When harvests were large, the surpluses were stored by the government for later use in lean years. However, farmers did not lose their income from the surplus crops. The government gave them commodity loans on all stored crops.

▲ The Soil Conservation Service taught farmers soil-saving techniques to remedy some of the problems that had caused the Dust Bowl.

731

Labor Union Membership • 1900 - 1980

Year	Number of Union Members	Percentage of Labor Force Composed of Union Members
1900	500,000	2.8%
1920	5,000,000	11.7%
1940	8,500,000	15.5%
1960	17,000,000	23.6%
1980	22,500,000	25.2%

Source: *Historical Statistics of the United States*
Statistical Abstract of the United States

The amount of these loans was fixed at slightly below **parity**. Parity was a figure based on average prices of each of the commodities for the base period from August 1909 to July 1914, a relatively prosperous period for farmers. When the market price of a commodity rose to the parity level, farmers were to sell their stored crops and repay the loans. If the market price remained below parity, the farmers kept the money and the government kept their crops. By this method the government hoped to keep the price of agricultural products at a steady level and benefit both farmers and consumers.

(4) The act also authorized the government to insure wheat crops against drought, flood, hail, and plant diseases.

Evaluating the farm program. In 1932, in the depths of the Great Depression, farm income had sunk to less than $5 billion. By 1938 it had risen to more than $8 billion. By 1940 it totaled more than $9 billion.

Critics reminded the country that the increased income came from higher prices paid by consumers and from subsidies paid by the government—with taxpayers' money. These critics charged that money had been "taken from Peter to pay Paul."

Critics, including many farmers, also resented increasing government controls over farm production. They feared that subsidies would destroy farmers' independence. Moreover, critics charged that the government's price support program was causing America's agricultural products to lose out in the highly competitive foreign markets.

Such criticisms ended, at least temporarily, in 1941 when the United States was plunged into World War II. Then, as New Deal supporters were quick to point out, the country owed much to the farm legislation of the 1930's. This legislation had improved the economic condition of many Americans, had increased the fertility of millions of acres of land, and had enabled the United States to feed a large portion of the war-devastated world.

Housing for low-income groups. During his second term, Roosevelt also continued his efforts to ease the housing problem. The National Housing Act of 1937, usually called the Wagner-Steagall Act, had two aims: (1) to stimulate business by government spending for the construction of houses and (2) to "remedy the unsafe and unsatisfactory housing conditions and the acute shortage of decent, safe, and sanitary dwellings for families of low income in rural and urban communities."

The National Housing Act created the United States Housing Authority (USHA), which began an ambitious program of housing construction. By 1941 the USHA had lent $750 million for the construction of more than 160,000 housing units.

Other New Deal reforms. In 1938 Congress passed the Food, Drug, and Cosmetic Act, which replaced the earlier Pure Food and Drug Act of 1906. The 1938 act required adequate testing of new drugs before they were offered for sale. It also required manufacturers to list the exact ingredients of their products on their labels. In addition, the Wheeler-Lea Act, also passed in 1938, prohibited manufacturers from making false or misleading claims about their products in their advertising.

In 1939 Congress tackled the problem of improper political practices. The Hatch Act placed restrictions upon federal officeholders below the policy-making level in the executive branch of the government. Such officeholders

▲ Discussion topic: Have students analyze the graph to answer questions such as these:
What is the subject of the graph? How many workers belonged to labor unions in 1900?
in 1920? What percentage of the labor force was unionized in both years?

were prohibited (1) from taking an active part in political campaigns, (2) from soliciting or accepting political contributions from workers on relief, and (3) from using their official positions to try to influence Presidential or Congressional elections. In 1940 the Hatch Act was amended to include state and local government employees whose pay came completely or partially from federal funds. The 1940 amendment also limited the amount of money a political party could spend in any one year. A maximum of $3 million was established. The amount any individual could contribute was $5,000 a year. This law was not effective because both parties soon found ways legally to avoid these limits.

SECTION REVIEW

See underscored items, text pp. 729 - 32.

Identify: John L. Lewis, CIO, industrial union, sit-down strike, minimum wage, A. Philip Randolph, FEPC, parity, Hatch Act.

For answers to questions, see Answer Key, p.A100.

1. **Summarizing Ideas: (a)** Why was the CIO organized? **(b)** How did the CIO differ from the A. F. of L.?

2. **Analyzing Ideas: (a)** How did the Fair Labor Standards Act benefit workers in the United States? **(b)** Why did some people oppose it?

3. **Organizing Ideas:** What measures were taken from 1935 to 1938 to help improve the economic conditions of farmers?

4. **Studying Graphics:** Look at the graph on page 732. According to the graph, during what period did labor unions achieve their greatest growth?

6 The New Deal's great experiment comes to an end

See Teaching Suggestions in TMRG, p.TM181.

By the middle of his second term, President Roosevelt's influence was beginning to decline. In 1937, as you have read, he had suffered a major defeat when he failed to push through Congress his bill for reorganizing the Supreme Court. In the Congressional elections of 1938, he suffered an even more serious defeat.

Congressional elections of 1938. As the elections approached, Roosevelt decided to liberalize the Democratic Party. Singling out those conservative Democrats who had voted against his reform program, he urged voters to defeat them at the polls.

Roosevelt's effort to liberalize the Democratic Party failed. With only one exception, all the members of Congress whom Roosevelt had opposed were reelected. Moreover, the voters chose a great many new Democratic members who were foes of the New Deal. Adding to Roosevelt's dismay, the Republicans won additional seats in Congress. Nevertheless, the Democrats continued to hold a sizable majority in both the House and the Senate.

New Deal activities suspended. President Roosevelt, a shrewd politician, was quick to see the meaning of the 1938 elections. Realizing that public opinion was turning against him, he began to suspend earlier New Deal activities. By 1939 Congress was cutting appropriations for many New Deal agencies.

As a result of the threatening world situation, the PWA and the WPA shifted their attention from public works to projects involving national defense, such as the building of airports and military highways. Other New Deal agencies, such as the Civilian Conservation Corps and the National Youth Administration, ended operations when Congress cut off further appropriations. Although the TVA weathered attacks both in and out of Congress, the President's recommendation for similar projects in six other areas of the country received little support.

The driving impulse of the New Deal had spent itself. Those who maintained that the reform objectives of the New Deal were still far from being realized faced stiffer opposition and growing public indifference.

Opposition to New Deal finances. Much of the opposition to the New Deal came from people who believed that Roosevelt's financial policies were undermining the nation's economic system. In general, three different methods were used for financing New Deal relief, recovery, and reform programs.

One method was inflation. Although Congress authorized President Roosevelt to print paper money, he never did so. He did, however, take the nation off the gold standard. This cheapened the value of the dollar.

A second method was **deficit spending.** This meant that the government spent more than it received in taxes, leaving the budget unbalanced, or showing a deficit. In the 1930's the

733

President Roosevelt frequently used the radio to defend his policies. The highly persuasive "Fireside Chats" reassured the nation.

__national debt__ increased from about $16 billion to more than $40 billion. Men and women in both parties, but business leaders in particular, lost confidence in an administration that piled up a larger and larger national debt.

The third method by which the New Deal had financed the operation of new programs was by raising taxes. Despite strong opposition, Congress passed the Revenue Act of 1935, often called the Wealth Tax Act. With this measure Congress increased the income tax for individuals and large corporations and levied taxes on gifts and estates. In spite of these measures, the new revenue did not balance the budget, and the national debt continued to grow.

In the Revenue Act of 1936, Congress laid a steeply graduated tax on those corporate profits that were not distributed to stockholders. Business bitterly complained that the new tax would discourage business expansion and prevent the accumulation of surpluses for use in depression years.

In 1938, however, as a result of growing opposition to the New Deal, Congress began to reverse the taxation policy of earlier years. The Revenue Act of 1938 sharply reduced corporation taxes. In 1939 Congress abolished the tax on undistributed profits. At the same time, it raised the corporation income tax to a maximum of 19 percent. In addition, for the first time in history, Congress required employees of cities and states to pay taxes to the federal government.

A third term. Despite the fact that his influence was weakening, and despite the fact that the two-term tradition for Presidents was widely accepted as part of the unwritten Constitution, Roosevelt decided to run for a third ▲ term. The President did not at first announce his decision to the public, although he hinted that the critical world situation might compel him to be a candidate. However, behind the scenes he arranged matters so that it would have been almost impossible for any Democrat to run against Roosevelt without obtaining his consent.

The Democratic convention chose Roosevelt on the first ballot at Chicago in July 1940. It also, without general enthusiasm, accepted Henry A. Wallace of Iowa as his running mate. Wallace, a former Republican, had been Roosevelt's Secretary of Agriculture.

The Democratic platform promised to extend social security, to stress the low-cost housing program, and to advance government ownership of public utilities. The platform also promised to keep the United States out of the war that had broken out in Europe and to send no American armies abroad unless the nation were attacked.

Wendell Willkie. The Republicans chose as their candidate Wendell L. Willkie of New York, a utilities company president with Democratic leanings and a long progressive record. Willkie favored many of the principles of the New Deal. On the other hand, he felt that the New Deal was extravagant. He also believed it had been administered in such a way as to endanger individualism, free enterprise, and democracy. Warmhearted and engaging, Willkie developed a strong following and became a formidable candidate.

▲ Discussion topic: The appropriateness of a third term for President Roosevelt was major 1940 election issue. Have students consider what circumstances might necessitate or justify more than two terms. Are there any dangers in allowing an unlimited number of terms for a President? Explain.

The Republican platform condemned the New Deal for its "shifting, contradictory, and overlapping administrations and policies." It promised to revise the tax system to stimulate private enterprise and to promote prosperity. It also promised to keep the major New Deal reforms but to administer the laws governing these reforms with greater efficiency and less waste. The Republicans also demanded a constitutional amendment that would limit Presidents to a maximum of two terms in office. Like the Democrats, the Republicans promised to keep America out of war unless the nation were attacked.

The campaign of 1940. The threat of a second World War hung over the election campaign of 1940. Indeed, in the fall of 1940, while the American people were preparing to vote in the Presidential election, Great Britain was fighting desperately for survival.

Both Roosevelt and Willkie advocated a strong program of national defense. Both urged all aid to Great Britain short of war. In general, there was no important difference in their attitudes toward the terrible conflict that was raging abroad.

On domestic issues, however, they differed sharply. Willkie attacked Roosevelt for irresponsibility and Roosevelt attacked Willkie for "unwitting falsifications of fact." Willkie traveled thousands of miles through 34 states in a whirlwind campaign. Roosevelt limited himself to a few speeches.

Roosevelt won a sweeping victory in an election in which more Americans voted than in any previous contest in American history. But the returns clearly showed that the President had lost some of his earlier popularity. Roosevelt's 60 percent popular majority in the election of 1936 was reduced to just under 55 percent. In round numbers this meant that 27 million Americans voted for Roosevelt, and 22 million for Willkie. The popular vote was therefore much closer than indicated by the electoral vote of 449 for Roosevelt and 82 for Willkie. Although the Democrats retained control of Congress, the Republicans increased their strength in both Congress and the state legislatures.

During Roosevelt's third term, the New Deal domestic programs received less attention as foreign problems and war itself absorbed American energies. Thus a great period of reform in American history came to an end.

In August 1940, Wendell Wilkie returned to his hometown of Elwood, Indiana, on his way to accept the Presidential nomination of the Republican Party.

Whether this suspension of reform activities was the result of war or whether the reform impulse had spent itself remains unanswered.

SECTION REVIEW

See underscored items, text pp. 733 - 34.
Identify: deficit spending, national debt, Henry Wallace, Wendell Willkie.
For answers to questions, see Answer Key, p.A100.

1. **Summarizing Ideas:** (a) Describe the three methods used by New Dealers to raise money. (b) Why were these methods criticized?

2. **Organizing Ideas:** Present evidence to support the view that Roosevelt's influence was decreasing by 1940.

3. **Comparing Ideas:** In what ways did Roosevelt and Willkie disagree on domestic issues?

4. **Analyzing Viewpoints:** Do you think the fact that Roosevelt was running for a third term as President had any influence on the way people voted? Explain.

Class activity: Divide the class into small groups. Have each group research the New Deal programs still in existence and how these programs benefit people today. The groups should present oral reports to the class.

735

32 SUMMARY

When Franklin D. Roosevelt became President of the United States in 1933, the nation was in the depths of the worst depression it had ever experienced. President Roosevelt, a person of great energy and overwhelming enthusiasm, inspired the people with his own confidence and faith in the future.

Surrounding himself with men and women who shared his views about the nation's problems, Roosevelt immediately opened a three-pronged attack upon the depression. First, in a series of relief measures, Congress, led by the administration, provided food, clothing, and shelter for the millions of unemployed and needy Americans. Second, in a series of recovery measures, Congress attempted to revive the nation's agriculture and industry and place the economy on a solid foundation. Third, in a series of reform measures, Congress developed a program designed to protect future generations from the catastrophe of economic depression.

By 1936 the New Deal program faced a large and growing body of opposition, some from within the Democratic Party itself. Many critics felt that the government was interfering too much with the free enterprise system, and, in so doing, was threatening individualism and democracy.

By the end of 1938, the opposition had become so strong that President Roosevelt decided to postpone other far-reaching reforms that he had been considering. Indeed, during 1939, 1940, and 1941, the administration suspended the activities of several of the agencies created by the New Deal.

CONNECTING CHAPTER IDEAS

The decades of the 1920's and the 1930's—the one characterized by widespread prosperity, the other by poverty and unemployment—left distinctive marks upon the American scene. In the next chapter you will read how every aspect of life—including education, literature, and the arts—was influenced by the changing ways and times.

Beginning of New Deal Civilian Conservation Corps Tennessee Valley Authority 1933	National Labor Relations (Wagner) Act Social Security Act CIO is organized 1935	National Housing Act 1937			Roosevelt wins third term 1940	
	United States v. Butler 1936		Fair Labor Standards Act 1938	Hatch Act 1939		Fair Employment Practices Committee 1941

1935	1940

CHAPTER
32 REVIEW

Reviewing Important Terms

Decide whether each of the following sentences is true or false. If the sentence is false, replace the underlined term with the word or phrase that will make it true.

1. Immediate help for hungry and unemployed Americans was termed <u>pump priming</u>.
2. Under the terms of the Agricultural Adjustment Act the government gave <u>subsidies</u> to farmers.
3. <u>Parity</u> was the government's attempt to stimulate the economy through loans and spending.
4. Work stoppages during which employees refused to leave their machines were called <u>sit-down strikes</u>.
5. Government policies guaranteeing farm prices at previous prosperous levels, or <u>direct relief</u>, are often criticized.
6. In spite of attempts to curb government spending and borrowing, the <u>national debt</u> continues to grow annually.
7. Most of the labor unrest of the 1930's was the result of strikes concerning the <u>jurisdiction</u> of competing unions.

Practicing Critical Thinking Skills

1. **Comparing Ideas.** (a) Why was the New Deal controversial? (b) What were the major arguments in favor of the New Deal? (c) What were the major arguments against it? (d) What is your evaluation of the New Deal? Give specific examples to support your position.
2. **Summarizing Ideas.** Summarize the various ways in which the New Deal tried to help one of the following: (a) the consumer, (b) low-income families on farms and in cities, (c) young people, (d) the aged, or (e) workers.
3. **Interpreting Ideas.** (a) Why did Roosevelt say that certain members of the Supreme Court thought in terms of the "horse-and-buggy" era? (b) How did he propose to remedy this situation? (c) How would his proposal have affected the balance of powers among the branches of the federal government?
4. **Synthesizing Ideas.** Draw a political cartoon that might have appeared in a newspaper or magazine during the Presidential election campaign of 1932, 1936, or 1940. Be sure that the cartoon clearly presents a point of view about an issue or candidate of the campaign. Give your completed cartoon a pertinent title.

5. **Relating Past to Present.** Using the New Deal as a basis for comparison, how do you think the United States would react to a severe economic crisis such as the depression today?

Developing History Study Skills

1. **Classifying Economic Policies.** Classify the following list of New Deal legislation on the basis of whether it was a direct relief program or a recovery measure.

   a. Civilian Conservation Corps
   b. Tennessee Valley Authority
   c. Works Progress Administration
   d. National Housing Act
   e. Wagner Act
   f. Agricultural Adjustment Act
   g. National Industrial Recovery Act

2. **Identifying Fact and Opinion.** The statements below have been written by scholars. Identify whether each is a statement of fact or of opinion. Explain your answers.

   a. Before TVA one out of every 100 farms in Mississippi had electricity, 1 out of 36 in Georgia, 1 out of 25 in Tennessee and Alabama.
   b. Franklin D. Roosevelt's times may well be judged to have been the most exciting and demanding in the history of the republic, as uncertain as the first fluid years under Washington, as hazardous as the first dark years under Lincoln.

Relating Geography and History

Several New Deal programs were aimed at improving land use and conserving resources. To understand the relationship between land use and the New Deal, do the following activities.

1. Reread the section "Work for youth" on pages 717–18. What did the CCC do to help conserve the nation's natural resources?
2. Reread pages 723–25. (a) What type of power was produced by the TVA? (b) Was it produced in an environmentally safe way? Explain. (c) Why might some people argue that the TVA projects harmed the environment more than they helped it? (d) Do you feel that the TVA was a benefit or a harm to the environment? Support your position.

737

See Chapter Overview in TMRG, p.TM182.
See Chapter Objectives in TMRG, p.TM182.
See Introducing the Chapter in TMRG, p.TM182.

CHAPTER 33
Decades in Contrast
Changing Ways   (1920–1939)

Changing
life styles

Writers and historians have pinned many different labels on the decade of the 1920's. Among these labels are the Golden Twenties, Roaring Twenties, Decade of Wonderful Nonsense, the Jazz Age, Ballyhoo Years, and the Age of Disillusionment.

▲ The labels suggest the diverse characteristics of the 1920's. These years were marked by widespread prosperity, by a sharp increase in the productivity of American industry, and by disillusionment with the outcomes of World War I. They were also marked by an emphasis on the material aspects of life, by the urge to get rich quick, and by the desire to have a good time. On the other hand, levels of education increased, and schools became more effective. New educational and employment opportunities for women also arose.

The decade of the 1930's was a very different story. The labels for the 1920's become a mockery when applied to the grim years of the Great Depression. The 1930's opened with the collapse of the nation's economy. Many banks failed, and people throughout the nation lost the savings of a lifetime. Millions of Americans lost their jobs, and millions were homeless, hungry, and destitute.

By the mid-1930's, however, hope began to replace despair. Inspired by President Franklin D. Roosevelt and aided by the 3 R's of the New Deal, Americans began to face the future with renewed faith and confidence. Even so, progress was limited, and millions of men and woman were still looking for work, Moreover, as the 1930's drew to a close, growing problems in Europe and Asia cast longer and darker shadows across the land.

═══ READING FOCUS ═══

As you read about the characteristics of the 1920's and the 1930's, look for the details that support each of the following statements.

1. Machines continue to transform countryside, town, and city.
2. Industrialization speeds up changes in American society.
3. The depression drastically alters people's lives.
4. America's minorities struggle against hard times and discrimination.
5. Literature and the arts reflect changing ways and times.

1 Machines continue to transform countryside, town, and city

See Teaching Suggestions in TMRG, pp.TM182-83.

By 1920 the power-driven machine had become one of the dominant symbols of America. There were machines in factories, on farms, and in the home—and still the number and variety of machines kept multiplying. These machines helped transform America from a rural to an urban nation. They also affected the daily lives of Americans both in the city and on the farm.

Energy and efficiency. American industry in the 1920's could draw on vast reserves of energy to power its machines. There were enormous deposits of coal, huge underground pockets of oil and natural gas, water-power sites, and the know-how to generate large amounts of electrical power.

Use of the "new" sources of power, oil and electricity, soared during the 1920's. Between 1920 and 1930, petroleum production doubled. In the same years, production of electricity went from 50 billion kilowatt-hours annually to 114 billion.

Manufacturers and engineers tackled the problem of using this abundance of energy most efficiently. Older machines were improved, and new machines were developed for factory, farm, and home. However, it was the organization of machines on a conveyor-belt **assembly line** that provided one of the striking characteristics of the 1920's.

As you have read, **mass production** was an essential element of American industry long before the 1920's. Manufacturers had been using standardized interchangeable parts ever since Eli Whitney and European inventors had developed them more than a century earlier. The conveyor belt greatly increased the efficiency of the manufacturing process. First used on a large scale in automobile production by Henry Ford in 1914, the assembly line was soon adopted by other industries.

Efforts to increase efficiency were applied to workers as well as to machines. During the 1920's "time-and-motion" studies of machines and their operators were generally undertaken before a new machine or process was installed in an industrial plant.

▲ Class activity: Have the class assemble a newsmagazine highlighting the United States in the 1920's and 1930's. Small groups might prepare sections on world and domestic events, the arts, sports, science, and people. Time and Newsweek (both of which first appeared in the 1920's) may serve as models.

739

In his 1928 painting Boomtown, *Thomas Hart Benton presented a view of America's spreading industrialization. Cars and the oil production on which they depend explain the boom experienced in this Western town.*

Business executives also applied this efficiency engineering, or scientific management, to business planning and bookkeeping. This new approach to industrial efficiency was called <u>cost accounting</u>. Cost accountants found out the cost of each item of machinery, material, and labor that went into the total cost of producing or selling a product. They were then in a position to show business concerns how to cut costs and at the same time gain greater production at lower prices.

Bigger and bigger industries. Mass production could be carried on only by large, highly organized industrial concerns. During the Golden Twenties, there was plenty of surplus capital to finance industrial development. As a result, older industries grew by leaps and bounds, while new industries in many different areas of the economy climbed into the ranks of the corporate giants.

Most of the growth of industry was the result of <u>mergers</u>—that is, the combining of two or more independent companies into one larger. company. Between 1919 and 1929, for example, more than 1,000 mergers took place in manufacturing and mining. By 1930 only 200 corporations owned nearly half of the country's corporate wealth and one fifth of the total national wealth.

The attitude of government also encouraged the growth of large-scale industry. In the 1920's the government did not make any great effort to enforce the Sherman and the Clayton Antitrust Acts. Business and government were more interested in efficiency than in competition.

Advertising and marketing. Marketing techniques also became more effective during the 1920's. Advertising firms studied public psychology to discover how to appeal to consumers most effectively. Advertising firms also encouraged Americans to abandon the deeply rooted American ideal of thrift. In an age of abundance, they said, continued prosperity depended upon spending, not saving.

Mail-order houses, department stores, and chain stores continued to grow in number and size. The companies that had pioneered new methods of marketing during the late 1800's— Montgomery Ward, the Great Atlantic and Pacific Tea Company, F. W. Woolworth, Marshall Field, and Sears, Roebuck—were still among the leaders in their fields. These companies and many new ones were getting a big portion of the nation's retail business.

Two new developments that would contribute to a future revolution in the packaging of goods emerged in the 1920's. In 1923 Clarence Birdseye developed a method of quick-freezing for preserving perishable foods. In the same year, the Du Pont company bought the American patent rights to cellophane, a transparent wrapping material. By the late 1920's, frozen foods were being sold in stores, and cellophane was attracting attention.

The "automobile revolution." Even more important to the story of America's economic expansion in the 1920's was the development of the automobile and the expanding automobile industry. In 1920 about 8 million passenger cars and about 1 million trucks were registered in the United States. By 1930 about 23 million cars—an average of one car for every six citizens—and 3.5 million trucks were traveling the nation's roads.

This "automobile revolution" had far-reaching consequences. By 1930, cars, trucks, and buses had almost completely replaced horse-drawn vehicles. Even railroads and trolley cars were beginning to suffer from the competition of the gasoline-driven vehicles.

By the 1930's, the automobile was already revolutionizing the American way of life. This "revolution" gave the American people more mobility and helped to make even the remotest regions of the nation accessible.

"The history of every country begins in the heart of a man or a woman," wrote Willa Cather. Although she would spend 40 years in New York City, the history in her heart was begun in Nebraska, her childhood home.

Cather was ten when her family moved to Nebraska, making their home in the small town of Red Cloud. The broad plains around the town and the area's Norwegian and Bohemian immigrants made a lasting impression on Willa Cather.

At the University of Nebraska, Cather made up her mind to be a writer. After graduation, she moved to Pittsburgh, where she held jobs as a writer, editor, and teacher. She also began to write short stories, many of which were printed in popular magazines.

In 1906 Cather moved to New York City to write and edit for *McClure's*, a famous muckraking magazine. Her distance from Red Cloud seemed to help her see the town with a sharper eye. Increasingly her stories explored the people and places she had loved as a child.

Cather quit her job with *McClure's* in 1912 to devote herself to writing. The next year her novel *O Pioneers!* was published. The well-received book dealt with the lives of immigrant settlers on the Great Plains. Willa Cather had now found her style. Her novels, among them *My Ántonia, A Lost Lady,* and *Death Comes for the Archbishop,* won Cather popularity and awards. She continued writing until her death at age 74.

By the end of the 1920's, the automobile industry had become the nation's biggest business, with an annual product valued at $3.5 billion in 1929. This new industrial giant used huge quantities of steel, glass, rubber, and other materials in manufacturing automobiles. It also created a rising demand for materials to build paved roads, garages, and service stations. It is estimated that 5 million persons, or one of every nine American workers, were employed in the automobile industry or a related business by 1930.

New industries. Many other new industries emerged during the 1920's. The increasing availability of electricity stimulated production of many labor-saving devices for the homemaker. Among them were refrigerators, vacuum cleaners, toasters, electric fans, and electric stoves.

The chemical industry became one of America's most rapidly growing enterprises in the 1920's. By 1929 several American chemical companies were larger than any European competitors. In 1930 Du Pont, the giant among chemical companies, was producing 1,100 different products in 80 different factories in the United States. Among the products pouring out of the chemical plants were rayon, synthetic resins, and a growing variety of plastics.

Despite all the benefits, there was a negative side to the nation's rapid industrialization. Chemicals, gasoline, and other technical innovations began to pollute America's rivers and lakes—and even the air. In the cities, traffic and air pollution became problems. In the 1920's, however, few Americans paid much attention to these disadvantages. Most were content to enjoy the advantages of the machine age's quickening tempo.

Workers' gains and losses. The nation's growing industrialization greatly affected the lives of wage earners. The ever more rapid development of power-driven machines continued to free workers from backbreaking toil. Increases in productivity brought generally higher wages and an improved standard of living for the workers.

Wage earners at times benefited from the "time-and-motion" studies. Such studies could discover ways of lessening fatigue and eliminating accidents on the job. These studies showed that workers were happier and produced more when employers showed an interest in them. Applying this lesson, some employers introduced profit sharing and retirement plans and provided cafeterias, game rooms, and ballparks for employees.

Although employers as a whole showed increasing interest in working conditions, they opposed labor unions even more vigorously than before the war. A growing number of corporations in the 1920's started **company unions.** These were unions organized by the employers or their representatives rather than by the workers. Company unions as well as the higher standard of living contributed to the decline in strength of organized labor during the 1920's.

Urbanization. The growing industrialization also affected where Americans lived. It encouraged the movement of people from the countryside to cities and industrial centers. This is the process known as **urbanization.**

According to the 1920 census, the population of the United States was almost 106 million. For the first time in American history, those living in cities and towns outnumbered farm and country dwellers. The urban population then totaled 54 million, the rural population 51 million. By 1930 almost 69 million people lived in urban areas; the rural population, on the other hand, had reached only about 54 million. Moreover, a large percentage of the rural population lived in small towns and villages, not on farms.

Towns and cities were undergoing spectacular growth. Between 1920 and 1930, the rapidly growing population pushed 25 of America's older cities above the 100,000 figure. By 1930 as many as 93 cities had populations of 100,000 or more. Some of these urban areas more than doubled their population during this decade.

Changes in urban life. The very appearance of urban centers began to change. Huge new apartment houses appeared on what had been vacant lots or the sites of one-family houses. New skyscrapers pierced the skyline as builders tried to provide office space for the cities' growing industries. On the darker side, crowded housing conditions spurred the growth of slums in many cities.

Streets built in earlier times for horse-drawn vehicles and for a more leisurely way of life became increasingly crowded and noisy as automobiles and trucks multiplied. During the 1920's a new method of transportation, the bus, began to compete with the older electric trolleys. Although not a single bus was registered in the United States in 1920, about 40,500 were registered by 1930.

Perhaps most spectacular of all was the development of suburban areas. Streetcar lines and paved roads pushed out from the cities into the surrounding countryside. Farms in outlying areas were divided into building lots, and row after row of houses appeared in developments with such fanciful names as "Sunset Acres," "Grand View," and "American Venice."

Changes on the farms. By the 1920's developments in technology were breaking down the isolation and loneliness of farm life. Paved roads were reaching deeper into the countryside. Telephone and electric wires stretched along roads and across fields to farmhouses. Radio sets, a product of the 1920's, brought music, news, and entertainment into remote areas. Henry Ford's "Tin Lizzies" were parked beside barns and houses.

Machines also helped to ease farmers' burdens. Where electricity was available, it was used for lighting, for pumping water, and for refrigeration. Milking machines could now be found on many dairy farms. Trucks, tractors, and power-driven farm implements were being used by growing numbers of farmers. At the same time, more efficient farming methods and better plants and breeds of livestock were increasing farm productivity.

Farm problems. Increased productivity also created problems. A surplus of farm products drove farm prices downward. To be sure, not all farmers were hit equally hard by rising surpluses and falling prices. Dairy and truck farmers profited from the shift in American eating habits away from cereals toward more

Class activity: Have small groups research the development of their city or community during the 1920's and 1930's. Students might present a report or arrange a bulletin board display illustrating their findings.

743

milk, butter, vegetables, and fruit. The citrus-fruit industries of California, Texas, and Florida also experienced development. Tobacco growers enjoyed a seller's market as cigarette smoking became more popular. The large, mechanized farms continued to prosper, because they could afford the best equipment and could market their products economically.

While the large, mechanized farms prospered, many of the small, family-owned farms were hard-hit. Handicapped by lack of money to buy expensive equipment, the farmers found it increasingly difficult to make a living.

These economic problems, coupled with the lure of the cities, led to a drop in farm population. Between 1920 and 1930, the number of people actually living on farms decreased from 31.6 million to 30.4 million. Young people in growing numbers were leaving farms to seek new opportunities in the booming cities.

SECTION REVIEW
See underscored items, text pp. 739 - 41, 743.

Identify: assembly line, mass production, cost accounting, merger, Clarence Birdseye, company union, urbanization
For answers to questions, see Answer Key, pp.A101-02.

1. **Summarizing Ideas:** Explain the viewpoint that the machine and the word "efficiency" characterized America in the 1920's.

2. **Analyzing Ideas (a)** What was the "automobile revolution"? **(b)** In what ways did the automobile change life in the cities? **(c)** in the country?

3. **Organizing Ideas:** How were workers affected by **(a)** power-driven machines, **(b)** "time-and-motion" studies, and **(c)** company unions?

4. **Studying Graphics:** Reread this section, making note of all the population statistics given. Then make a line or bar graph showing the urban population, rural population, and total population from 1920 to 1930.

2 Industrialization speeds up changes in American society

See Teaching Suggestions in TMRG, pp.TM183-84.

The urbanization and the industrialization of the 1920's altered the structure of American society. They led to changes in how people lived, learned, and amused themselves.

Growth of school enrollment. After World War I, it became increasingly clear that Americans needed a far more extensive education than that which had once been considered adequate. This fact, linked with the growth in urban population and improvements in transportation, led to an increased enrollment in the nation's schools.

In 1900 total high school enrollment had been under 700,000. By 1920, it had risen to about 2.5 million. The enrollment soared to 4.8 million by 1930 and continued to increase even during the heart of the depression.

The colleges showed similar gains. By the end of the 1930's, nearly 1.5 million students, or one out of every six or seven of college age, were enrolled in colleges and universities.

Minority groups made significant, though limited, gains in education. For example, a growing number of blacks in the North and South received a high school education, and more attended colleges and universities. By 1930 about 15,000 black Americans held academic degrees. Yet many blacks as well as Indians and Spanish-speaking Americans found that even an adequate elementary education was impossible to obtain. Because of prejudice and neglect, the doors of opportunity all too often remained closed to them.

Changes in the schools. To meet the needs of the enormously increased student body, American states and communities had to spend huge sums for new school buildings, textbooks, equipment, and teachers' salaries. The wealth created by the growing industrialization provided taxes that paid for these changes.

Some of the larger cities began to build high schools for as many as 5,000 to 10,000 students. In rural areas cars and buses permitted students from widely scattered areas to attend centrally located consolidated schools.

America's schools had to make other changes as well. Industrial society, with its emphasis upon highly specialized skills, called for men and women trained in mathematics, engineering, science, and the skilled trades. To meet the new needs, educators enlarged the curriculum to include more work in vocational training, home economics, commercial courses, health, physical education, foreign languages, and civic education. Special trade schools, technical schools, and commercial schools were built throughout the country in an effort to keep up with the machine age.

▲ Report topic: Have interested students research and report on the ways in which each of these academic or vocational disciplines was taught in the 1920's and '30's and how it is taught today. The students should include reasons for changes in the teaching of each discipline.

By the 1930's great strides were also being made in adult education. Radio stations began to give reports and commentaries on the news of the day. By 1936 at least 350 forums provided the chance to hear discussions of public issues. At the same time, vocational training for adults was also becoming more common.

Toward more effective education. During these years students of education were reaching new conclusions about how people actually learn and about the process of education. Educators, following the lead of psychologists William James and G. Stanley Hall, were proving that a child's mind can be molded—within limits. Other scholars, among them John Dewey, continued to teach that life itself is an education. They felt that the way to produce effective citizens is to give boys and girls actual experience in democratic living. Still other scholars, led by psychologists such as Edward L. Thorndike, worked out tests useful in measuring intelligence and evaluating the educational process.

▲ **New opportunities for women.** During the 1920's the role of women underwent changes as striking as those in education. These changes brought new freedom and opportunity to women in American society.

An important step toward this new freedom was the adoption of the Nineteenth Amendment in 1920. This amendment gave women the right to vote in national elections. This right was a landmark in the struggle to win equality with men. The new League of Women Voters and other groups encouraged women to take an active part in political life.

Industrialization brought other changes in women's roles. The rapidly multiplying machines in mills, plants, and factories created new jobs on assembly lines for women. This was especially true in the textile and tobacco factories springing up in the South. Moreover, women were finding increasing opportunities to work as sales clerks, office workers, stenographers, and secretaries.

Equally important, the burden of housework was eased by new labor-saving devices—washing machines, irons, new types of stoves, vacuum cleaners, and refrigerators. Ready-made clothing and inexpensive sewing machines also relieved women of much of their labor. Packaged foods and canned goods helped to lighten the task of preparing family meals.

Middle-class women now had more time to read, to attend art exhibits, to hear lectures. Others now had time to work for civic improvements, to take part in political affairs, and to influence public opinion through such organizations as the League of Women Voters. Still others took active parts in parent-teacher associations. Never before had so many women found time and opportunity to develop interests outside the home.

The "new woman." The changing status and roles of women brought various expressions of a new sense of freedom. The "new woman," often a career woman, was more or less independent economically. She openly challenged what Charlotte Perkins Gilman, a leader of the new feminism, called "this man-made world." The new woman rejected the traditional female roles and refused to believe in the superior competence of men. She also denounced the different standards that were imposed on women in economic, sexual, and social relationships.

Alice Paul, leader of the Woman's Party, salutes the passage of the Nineteenth Amendment. The Woman's Party continued to fight for complete equality of the sexes.

▲ Class activity: Have interested students give profiles of these prominent women: union leader Rose Schneiderman; reformers Margaret Sanger and Crystal Eastman; journalist Martha Gellhorn, Freda Kirchway, and Dorothy Thompson; entrepreneurs Helena Rubenstein, and Elizabeth Arden.

745

The ratification of the Eighteenth Amendment in 1919 culminated a grass-roots temperance drive that had begun a century earlier. About 1800 many rural, native-born Americans were becoming alarmed at the high rates of crime and disease among immigrant workers in urban slums. They attributed the "sinful" nature of city life to alcohol abuse.

Unaware of the complex psychological and social causes of alcohol abuse, the temperance advocates first called for voluntary abstinence from alcoholic beverages. When that campaign failed, they lobbied to legally ban the manufacture and sale of liquor.

By 1846 Maine had passed the first state prohibition law; by 1855, 12 other states had done so. But in spite of the efforts of the Woman's Christian Temperance Union and the Anti-Saloon League, most states had rescinded statewide prohibition by the 1890's. They instead passed local-option laws, permitting each county to vote itself "wet" or "dry."

United States entry into World War I provided a convenient argument for the prohibitionists. They pointed out that German-Americans dominated the brewing industry. They asked: What could be more patriotic than prohibition, which would lessen the economic influence of persons whose loyalty was in question? And prohibition would free large quantities of grain, thus increasing the food supply for the armed forces. This argument converted many "wets" to "drys," thus clearing the way for the passage of the Eighteenth Amendment and national prohibition.

This defiance of conventional conduct among women was, in part, symbolized by the flappers. These young women, wearing above-the-knee dresses, bobbed hair, and lipstick, shocked older Americans as well as many people their own age. They took advantage of the freedom and mobility of the automobile, discussed sex openly and frankly, and smoked cigarettes. Flappers also defied the national Prohibition law by drinking in illegal bars called "speakeasies."

To some militant feminists, such indications of social freedom and equality did not go far enough. The Woman's Party challenged remaining legal discriminations against women. It demanded full equality in politics, business, the professions, sports, and the arts. In particular, the Woman's Party set as its goal an equal rights amendment that would outlaw all discrimination based on sex.

Influence of the automobile. Other changes in American society were a result of the nation's increasing prosperity.

By the 1920's the automobile was no longer the exclusive possession of the well-to-do. When working-class families were interviewed in a typical midwestern city in 1923, nearly half of them owned cars. The automobile was a major source of American recreation, as entire families piled into the car for an evening's ride or a weekend trip.

Although the automobile made travel comfortable and private, it also created new problems. Traffic accidents and deaths kept rising. Young people asserted their independence by driving off in the family car, free from parental supervision. Many Americans believed that the automobile was disrupting the family and destroying the nation's moral code.

The automobile also increased the difficulties of law enforcement by providing a convenient means of escape. It played a major role in the breakdown of Prohibition by providing a means for transporting illegal liquor.

Prohibition problems. In January 1919 the Eighteenth Amendment was ratified (see page 214). This amendment gave the federal government power to prohibit "the manufacture, sale, or transportation of intoxicating liquors."

In October 1919 Congress passed the Prohibition Enforcement Act, usually called the Volstead Act, over President Wilson's veto. This act defined as "intoxicating liquor" any beverage containing more than one half of one percent of alcohol, thereby making even beer and wine illegal.

The Prohibition experiment created serious problems in American life. Long coastlines in the east and west and unguarded frontiers to the north and south made it impossible to stop the flow of illegal liquor into the country.

Bootlegging became big business controlled by criminal elements in the large cities. The gangster Al Capone, who ruled Chicago's underworld, commanded a small army of gangsters equipped with revolvers, sawed-off shotguns, and submachine guns. Gang wars and other violence became common in many American cities during the "Roaring Twenties." Moreover, the gangs branched out to seize control of gambling establishments and dance halls. By the end of the decade, they had begun to develop the so-called "rackets." The racketeers collected "protection" money from businesses, threatening violence if their victims failed to pay.

The people themselves were partly to blame for this widespread violation of the law. Many Americans who were otherwise law-abiding refused to take Prohibition seriously. Finally, in 1933, the Prohibition era ended with the adoption of the Twenty-first Amendment, which repealed the Eighteenth Amendment. It returned the power to control the sale of intoxicating drinks to the states themselves.

Radio. Meanwhile another new development—radio—was helping to transform the lives of millions of Americans, both young and old alike.

KDKA, the first commercial broadcasting station, began to operate in Pittsburgh on November 2, 1920. Radio immediately became a craze. By 1929, sales of radio sets and parts amounted to almost $400 million. More than 600 broadcasting stations had been licensed, and one third of all American homes owned radio receivers.

Radio brought an enormous variety of information and entertainment directly to American families in their homes. The most popular programs featured "crooners," jazz musicians, comedians, sports announcers, and newscasters. However, many Americans felt that radio was not fulfilling its great promise as an instrument of education and culture. They criticized the dominant role of advertisers, who paid the broadcasting companies and entertainers and often determined what programs would be presented.

Despite the trivial content of many programs, however, radio served the nation in a variety of ways. By providing common experi-

Thousands of law officers like this one in Philadelphia tried to stop the flow of illegal liquor and beer during Prohibition in the 1920's. But as fast as government officials destroyed a supply of liquor, more was produced to replace it.

ences for all Americans, it increased the feeling of national unity. Radio also helped to overcome the isolation of rural life. It encouraged popular interest in current events, including sports, and offered useful information on health, home economics, and farming techniques. It made serious music available to more Americans than ever before. Finally, radio provided greater safety for airplanes and ships.

Sports. During the 1920's public interest in sports grew markedly. Baseball remained the most popular professional game, with between 9 and 10 million people attending major league games annually. Babe Ruth, who replaced Ty Cobb as the idol of fans, in 1927 astounded the baseball world with a record 60 home runs.

College football drew some 30 million spectators in the same year. Red Grange, a halfback for the University of Illinois, became a national hero. Jim Thorpe, with a Sauk, Fox, Potawatomi, and Irish heritage, also became a national hero. After playing football at Carlisle, an Indian college in Pennsylvania, he won medals in several events at the Olympic Games in Stockholm, Sweden, in 1912. Later, as an outstanding player in big league baseball and professional football, Thorpe was acclaimed as "the outstanding athlete of the half century." In boxing, fans in 1927 spent over $2.6 million to see the famous Dempsey-Tunney match. Amateur as well as professional interest also increased in such sports as golf, tennis, swimming, skating, and bowling.

Feats and fads. Americans in the 1920's were unusually responsive to new fads and fashions and dramatic public events. This period has been called the "Jazz Age" with some justice, for the rhythmic music of jazz was perhaps the most consistently popular of the new fashions. Other fads shifted rapidly from year to year: from the Chinese-originated game of mah-jongg, to crossword puzzles, to dances like the Charleston, to eccentric activities like flagpole sitting.

Some of the nation's enthusiasm was directed to individual accomplishments. The first glorified hero of the time was Charles A. Lindbergh, who in May 1927 made the first nonstop flight from New York to Paris in his plane *The Spirit of St. Louis*. Another fearless voyager was Commander (later Admiral) Richard E. Byrd. Byrd made the first flights to both the North and the South Pole. Other Americans who followed the example of Lindbergh and Byrd proved that the postwar period was an age of daring and feats as well as fads.

SECTION REVIEW
See underscored items, text pp. 745-46, 748.
Identify: John Dewey, Edward Thorndike, Nineteenth Amendment, Charlotte Perkins Gilman, flappers, Woman's Party, Babe Ruth, Red Grange, Jim Thorpe, Charles A. Lindbergh, Richard E. Byrd
For answers to questions, see Answer Key, p.A102.
1. **Interpreting Ideas:** (a) Why did school enrollment increase during the 1920's? (b) How did school curriculums change?
2. **Summarizing Ideas:** How did women's lives begin to change during the 1920's?
3. **Analyzing Ideas:** What problems arose as a result of Prohibition?

3 The depression drastically alters people's lives

See Teaching Suggestions in TMRG, p.TM184.

It can't be true! That was the initial reaction of Americans everywhere to the collapse of the nation's economy.

Unhappily, it was true. In a few months during the winter of 1929–30, the prosperity of the "Golden Twenties" had been replaced by unemployment, poverty, and desperation.

What was it like? By 1932 industrial output had been reduced to half the 1929 figure. Wages had been cut by 60 percent, and one fourth of the nation's work force was jobless. The best estimates place the number of unemployed at about 12 million.

A white-collar worker opened his pay envelope. It contained a pink slip informing him that his services were no longer needed. He had worked for the same company, one of the nation's largest corporations, for 40 years. He was 56 years old. He joined the millions of other jobless men and women.

No one really knew the number of people looking for work, and those seeking work were the breadwinners. Some 30 million others depended on them for food, clothing, and shelter.

These were the statistics. They translated into hunger, into the sad eyes of starving chil-

Much art in the 1930's depicted the plight of the down-and-out. In his painting titled "How Long Since You Wrote to Mother?" Raphael Soyer captured the loneliness of hungry men who came to missions for bread and coffee.

dren, into long lines of haggard men and women waiting for handouts of thin soup and dry bread provided by private and public charities. The men and women in the bread lines came from all walks of life and all social classes. There were former middle-income people and people from poor backgrounds. There were wage earners, business executives, and professional people. Hunger played no favorites.

Hunger was everywhere. "We saw a crowd of some 50 men fighting over a barrel of garbage which had been set outside the back door of a restaurant," one observer reported. This was not an isolated incident. Across the country men and women followed garbage trucks to the city dumps. Four hospitals in New York City reported 95 deaths from starvation in 1931. How many went unreported was never known.

Death came from self-inflicted causes as well. The Metropolitan Life Insurance Company reported that 20,000 Americans committed suicide in 1931.

Uprooted people. More than a million men and some women, many of them teen-agers, roamed the country looking for work. They rode the freight trains, thumbed rides on the roads, and did odd jobs where they could find them. They begged or stole food and slept wherever they could find shelter, on park benches or in shantytowns.

Every city had its shantytowns. Homeless people built them on vacant lots or on the city dumps out of packing boxes and scrap metal. "Hoovervilles" they were sometimes called, mocking the Hoover administration's failure to provide direct relief. There were also "Hoover blankets"—old newspapers used for warmth on park benches.

Many city people moved into the country hoping to find shelter and to raise their own food. Many farmers moved into the cities hoping to find work. People who had lost their homes or could no longer afford to pay rent moved in with relatives or friends. It was common to find several families crowded together in four or five rooms.

Rebellion on the farm. By 1932, farmers in some areas of the country were burning their corn to keep warm. Others armed with clubs, pitchforks, and shotguns confronted sheriffs who were trying to deliver foreclosure notices.

Other farmers, also armed, formed roadblocks and forced trucks loaded with milk to dump it on the road. With milk selling at 10 cents a quart in the stores, dairy farmers could not afford to operate. "They say blockading the highway's illegal," an Iowa farmer said. "Seems to me there was a Tea Party in Boston that was illegal, too."

The "Bonus Army." Farmers were not the only demonstrators. The "Bonus Army," 17,000 strong, arrived in Washington, D.C., in June 1932. They were veterans of World War I and they called themselves the "Bonus Expeditionary Force." Many arrived with their families. They traveled in freight cars, trucks, and wagons and on foot. They were in Washington to plead for a war bonus owed them. The money was not due until 1945, but they wanted it in advance.

They were allowed to live in empty government buildings and to camp on a swampy area across the Potomac River. The army provided them with tents, cots, field kitchens, and food. When the Senate refused to grant the bonus payment, most of them gave up and returned home with money provided by the government.

Some 2,000 of the veterans, many of whom had no place to go, decided to stay. They were ordered to leave. In a clash with the police, several veterans and police officers were killed. Army troops then moved in with machine guns, tanks, and tear gas. The troops drove the veterans from the buildings and broke up their encampment across the river, burning the shacks as they did so.

Slowing population growth. By the mid-1930's the New Deal had relieved much of the worst suffering and had restored a measure of hope. Nevertheless, grinding poverty continued to crush the dreams of millions of men, women, and children across the country. "I see one third of the nation ill-housed, ill-clad, ill-nourished," President Roosevelt said in 1937.

The Statue of Liberty still stood in New York harbor to welcome the poor, the homeless, the oppressed from other countries. However, the United States was no longer the "land of promise." Immigration had almost ceased. During the 1930's more people left America than entered it.

The number of marriages and the number of births also slowed. Many young people could not afford to marry and start families. In the decade of the 1930's, the population increased only about half as much as it had during the prosperous years of the 1920's.

More subdued living. Many of the rich and the well-to-do continued to live much as they had during the 1920's. For most Americans, however, even those who managed to hold onto their jobs, everyday life was much more subdued than it had been during the years of the "Golden Twenties."

Fewer people bought houses, household appliances, and new clothes. The sale of newspapers and magazines declined. At the same time, however, people read more, borrowing books from the public libraries.

People also tried to make things last. They kept their automobiles longer. This was possible, in part, because the number of service stations and repair shops doubled during the depression years.

Recreational activities reflected the slower pace of everyday life in the depression years. Not surprisingly, free recreation received the most attention. Hobbies, such as stamp collecting, became increasingly popular. So, too, did games that could be played at home, including cards, particularly bridge.

The radio. Radio, already popular in the 1920's, was the most common and the most influential form of entertainment in the 1930's. E. B. White, one of the keenest observers of the American scene, commented on the impact of the radio on rural folk. When they speak of "The Radio," White wrote, they have in mind "a pervading and somewhat godlike presence which has come into their lives and homes."

The growing popularity and influence of the radio, not only in rural areas but throughout the nation, was understandable. It provided something for just about everyone—news; music, including symphonies and operas; quiz programs and comedians; soap operas; church services; and adventure stories. All of these entered American homes through the mere turning of a dial.

President Roosevelt understood how effective radio could be in reaching people and broadcast a series of "Fireside Chats." These brought the people close to their government and added comfort and hope to the lives of millions. The "Fireside Chats" also helped Roosevelt gain and hold his popularity and win four successive Presidential elections!

▲

▲ Class activity: Encourage interested students to prepare readings of several of the "Fireside Chats." Have the class skim this unit to review the issues and measures Roosevelt addressed in each chat. Then discuss how the chats may have reassured the public.

Identify: Fireside Chat, "Hoovervilles"

For answers to questions see Answer Key, p.A102.

1. **Summarizing Ideas:** How did some farmers react to the depression?

2. **Analyzing Ideas:** (a) What was the "Bonus Army"? (b) Was its stay in Washington, D.C., successful? Explain.

3. **Determining Cause and Effect:** What effects did the depression have on population growth in the United States? Why?

4. **Studying Graphics:** Study the pictures in this section. Based on them, write a description of life during the depression.

4 America's minorities struggle against hard times and discrimination

See Teaching Suggestions in TMRG, pp.TM184-85.

The 1920's and 1930's were difficult times for **minorities** in the United States. Minorities did not share in the prosperity of the "Golden Twenties."

▲ **Black migration to the North.** Before World War I, many black families had moved from the South to the growing northern industrial centers. There they had hoped to escape poverty and discrimination and to find jobs, housing, and better education for their children.

World War I, with its heavy demand for industrial workers, had increased this migration. During the war about half a million southern blacks had found jobs in such places as the coal mines of West Virginia and Illinois, the steel mills of Pittsburgh, and the automobile factories of Detroit.

The movement into urban areas continued after the war. Between 1910 and 1930, the black population of the northern states rose from a little over 1 million to nearly 2.5 million. In the same years, the number of black wage earners in American industries grew from about 600,000 to nearly 1 million.

Black families did not find in the North all the opportunities they sought. Blacks got the hardest jobs and the lowest pay. Northern white wage earners sometimes staged protest strikes against the hiring of blacks. Housing shortages, brought on by wartime building re-strictions, also led to tensions when blacks tried to move into white neighborhoods in search of places to live.

Disappointed hopes. World War I, the war "to make the world safe for democracy," had naturally aroused the hopes of black Americans. Black soldiers returning from Europe, where they had been treated as equals, looked forward to new and greater freedom at home. They were angry and disappointed to find conditions in America little changed.

They were especially discouraged to find a new Ku Klux Klan operating in the North as well as in the South. The new Klan harassed Jews, Catholics, foreign-born citizens, and anyone else it chose to call "dangerous" and "un-American." However, blacks were the special object of Klan violence.

There were other reasons for black bitterness as well. In 1919–20 the nation's economy went into a postwar depression. This heightened the competition for jobs between blacks and whites and led to increased racial tension.

The riots of 1919. The rising tensions burst out in violence during the summer of 1919. Riots in more than 20 cities, northern and southern, brought death and injury to hundreds of men and women and destroyed thousands of tenements in city slum areas.

The riots generally began when blacks fought back against some especially discriminatory act. Frightened whites, convinced that black Americans were trying to threaten them and gain control, responded with more violence. Police forces, ill-equipped to deal with riots, usually sided with whites, causing blacks to take even more desperate actions.

The riots solved no problems. Nor did they spur local or national officials to try to remedy even the more obvious causes of the trouble. As a result, black Americans were now more ready to follow leaders who insisted that blacks had a lawful right to defend themselves when the law itself failed to do so.

Black pride. In the 1920's many blacks felt a growing sense of racial identity and pride along with an increasing interest in their African backgrounds. These feelings were strongly expressed by Marcus Garvey, a black immigrant from Jamaica in the West Indies.

Garvey became convinced that blacks could never win true freedom and equality in the

▲ Point out other difficulties blacks faced in the migration to the North: the hostile city atmosphere which often provoked violence between blacks; harsh northern winters for which blacks were not always physically prepared; the lack of the closeness there had been in many rural southern communities.

751

Jacob Lawrence is one of the best-known artists in America today. He grew up in Harlem and got his start as a painter through the New Deal's WPA. During the late 1930's, Lawrence's portraits of Frederick Douglass, Harriet Tubman, John Brown, and Toussaint L'Ouverture attracted widespread attention from the art world. These works were followed by his famous series *Migration of the Negro*.

Describing his choice of subject matter, Lawrence wrote: "In the Harlem community . . . there was a great interest in Negro history. . . . We had Negro history sessions at the YMCA and I became fascinated. . . . I guess it was part of my search for an image. . . ."

Lawrence has continued to explore all aspects of the black experience in America. The recent painting on this page shows a black university. Lawrence shows us the energy and excitement of college life.

United States. He popularized a form of black nationalism that encouraged a "back-to-Africa" movement. He eloquently described the achievements of black Africans and urged his listeners to return "home," where they might enjoy opportunities they could never find in white-dominated America.

None of Marcus Garvey's half-million black followers ever moved to Africa as he suggested. Nonetheless, Garvey's program did help to awaken in many blacks a new sense of racial pride.

Most black leaders of the 1920's opposed Garvey's movement as unrealistic and escapist. They insisted that blacks, having long been Americans, could and had to win the rights and opportunities that other Americans enjoyed. However, these leaders also encouraged American blacks to become interested in the achievements and hopes of black people in Africa and other parts of the world. Racial solidarity, they urged, should replace the narrow outlook that separated black Americans from blacks in other lands and that divided black Americans into different economic and social groups.

The "new Negro." Growing black pride was also stimulated by new achievements in arts and literature. One work was *The New Negro* ▲ by Alain Locke, a professor at Howard University. This important book both reflected and encouraged the changes taking place in black communities.

The new black leaders insisted that the "new Negro" had to be proud of the black heritage. They insisted that black Americans stop being defensive and apologetic to white Americans. The "new Negro" had to realize that self-assertiveness, not accommodation, was the only effective way to gain full equality.

As part of this assertion of identity, many blacks came to believe that it was necessary to develop a separate black economy within the American economy. Businesses owned and operated by blacks would serve the black communities. The profits from these businesses would flow to blacks and further stimulate financial independence.

By 1929, blacks ran some 25,700 stores. Many factories, banks, and insurance companies were owned and operated by blacks as well.

▲   Report topic: Have a volunteer outline for the class the basic ideas in The New Negro, by Alain Locke. Then, conduct a class discussion concerning these ideas in light of the black experience in the United States today. Do the ideas still apply?

Gains in civil rights. The growing sense of pride and self-assertiveness led blacks in both the North and the South to make headway in their struggle for equal justice under the law. Black leaders denounced lynching, white terrorism, and discrimination in housing and in the courts. In these areas the efforts of the NAACP to bring lawsuits designed to bring about the enforcement of equal rights for blacks began to show important progress.

The major political parties did little to further the struggles of blacks in the 1920's. The Republican Party was trying to build strong political organizations in the South. As a result, the Republican administrations hesitated to meet the demands of southern blacks for federal protection of their voting rights or for a fair share of federally appointed jobs. Nevertheless, Oscar de Priest of Chicago ran as a Republican and in 1928 became the first black elected to Congress in 28 years.

The Democratic Party held power in the South and continued efforts to exclude black voters. In spite of this, Democrats in northern cities began to seek black support, and blacks slowly began to join the Democratic Party.

Blacks and the depression. For blacks the coming of the depression was a catastrophe. Many businesses and banks owned by blacks went bankrupt. Black workers lived with the bleak knowledge that they were "the first fired and the last hired." During the worst years of the depression, an estimated two thirds of the blacks in American industry lost their jobs.

The New Deal provided black Americans with relief and employment in the Works Progress Administration, the Civilian Conservation Corps, and the National Youth Administration. By 1936, one sixth of those on relief were blacks. One black newspaper writer explained the meaning of one New Deal program to blacks: "The really important thing about the WPA is that it is a guarantee of a living wage." Blacks also had a share of new low-cost housing, and black farmers and sharecroppers received benefits from New Deal agricultural agencies. However, blacks suffered some degree of discrimination in almost all New Deal programs. A smaller percentage of blacks were employed in the work programs, and the housing and agricultural programs were particularly unfair to blacks.

Nevertheless, blacks did receive more aid under the New Deal than they had under Hoover's administration. In addition, at the urging of Eleanor Roosevelt, the President's wife, blacks were appointed to important federal positions. Among them were Mary McLeod Bethune, Ralph Bunche, and Robert C. Weaver. These and other leaders made up an informal group of advisers often called the "black cabinet."

Such New Deal actions revolutionized the voting habits of black Americans. By 1936, black voters were shifting to the Democratic Party. By the end of the decade, the Democrats had firmly secured the black vote.

The depression and the new opportunities provided by the New Deal increased the determination of blacks to win their legal and constitutional rights. In many northern cities, black leaders organized "don't-buy-where-you-can't-work" campaigns. In the rural areas, tenant farmers, black and white, often joined together against wealthy landlords. The National Negro Congress united black and interracial organizations from all across the nation in the struggle for black rights.

Despite these advances and the progress stimulated by New Deal programs, much remained to be done. For the vast majority of blacks, the elimination of prejudice and full acceptance into the mainstream of American life remained an unfulfilled dream.

Indian policy. Other racial and ethnic problems in the nation were becoming critical in the 1920's. The policy of "Americanizing" the Indians under the Dawes Act (page 496) had failed. Individual farm ownership was contrary to Indian traditions. Many tribes had never engaged in farming. Indians who did try to learn modern methods of farming often had to struggle with worn-out, nonfertile land. As for education, the government-sponsored boarding schools and day schools deprived Indian children of their tribal identity but gave them no identity that they could find meaningful.

In 1924 the Indian population as a whole received United States citizenship, partly in recognition of the young Indian men who had fought in World War I. Citizenship did not lessen the harsh fact that Indian poverty was greater than that of any other group in the United States. The discovery of oil on some Indian lands brought unexpected wealth to a few Indians, but for most life was grim. Still, earlier predictions that the Indians were a vanishing race proved incorrect. The Indian popula-

▲ Roosevelt abandoned the practice of segregation in federal offices. He initiated racial integration of the armed forces; he also appointed one or more black advisers on race relations for almost every new bureau or commission.

753

tion increased from about 243,000 in 1863 to about 350,000 in 1924.

Indians and the New Deal. In 1928 a report by the Institute for Government Research described the destructive conditions on Indian reservations. The report and other criticisms led Congress in 1934 to pass the Howard-Wheeler Act, or the Indian Reorganization Act.

The new law halted the breaking up of reservations by granting lands to individual Indians. It tried to restore to tribal ownership parts of reservations that had not yet become individual homesteads. The act also emphasized local control. It permitted tribes to choose whether or not they wished to practice local self-government. It allowed them to strengthen community life by reestablishing traditional beliefs, customs, and crafts. Under the act, Indians were allowed to engage in any business of their choice, to make contracts, and to sue or be sued in court.

The Howard-Wheeler Act also tried to teach Indians to use their land more effectively. Soil-conservation practices and improved methods of raising and marketing crops and livestock were taught. The new educational programs included adults and children and made the school a center of community life.

Many problems remained in spite of the change in policy. Some tribes that had been more or less successfully "Americanized" disliked the new policy. They believed it would keep them inferior in American society. Efforts to improve unused Indian lands met with little success. Thus although the new policy brought greater freedom and recognition to the Indians, its aim of raising Indian standards of living was not realized.

Mexican Americans. As you may recall, many former citizens of Mexico became citizens of the United States at the close of the Mexican War in 1848. In the 1890's increasing numbers of Mexicans migrated into the United States looking for jobs. The need for labor during World War I and the desire of many Mexicans to escape the troubled economic and political conditions in Mexico increased the flow across the border. During the 1920's about half a million new Mexican immigrants arrived.

Most of these immigrants were poor families from rural areas. They were forced to work for low wages as migrant laborers in agriculture, in mining, and in railroad construction throughout the Southwest and, increasingly, the Middle West. They entered the United States speaking a different language and practicing different customs. For the most part poor and ill-educated, they met with prejudice and discrimination in jobs, housing, and schools.

Established labor groups resented them because they lowered wage scales by accepting, out of necessity, almost any rate of pay. White resentment also grew because these new immigrants could cross and recross the border as economic conditions in Mexico improved or worsened.

Despite these burdens, Mexican Americans became active in the organized labor movement. They shared problems and developed a sense of cooperation through *mutalistas*, or self-aid societies. Particularly in New Mexico, Mexican Americans made their influence felt politically.

The United States and Mexico jointly developed a program to deal with immigration from Mexico. The Expatriation Program, as it was called, was designed to persuade Mexican immigrants to return to their own country. From the Mexican point of view, the purpose of the program was to revitalize the Mexican economy by making use of the skills the Mexicans had learned while in the United States. Some 500,000 men and women did return to Mexico. Only too often, however, they were disappointed with their decision. Conditions in their native land were bleak and they were ready, whatever the obstacles, to try once again to improve their lives in the United States.

The depression added to the burdens of the Mexican Americans. Jobs in agriculture and on railroads became scarce. Increasingly, the Mexican Americans moved from rural areas into the cities, where there was at least some hope, however slim, of finding work. At least in the cities, if jobs were not available, New Deal relief programs were.

SECTION REVIEW

See underscored items, text pp. 751 - 54.

Identify: Marcus Garvey, *The New Negro,* Oscar de Priest, National Negro Congress, Indian Reorganization Act, *mutalistas,* Expatriation Program

For answers to questions, see Answer Key, pp.A102-03.

1. **Summarizing Ideas:** What factors helped cause the race riots of 1919?

2. **Interpreting Ideas: (a)** What does the term "new Negro" mean? **(b)** How did the growing black pride affect business **(c)** How did it affect politics?

▲   Report topic: Have interested students present reports on Mexican-American political advancement in the southwestern United States.

3. **Analyzing Ideas:** Why did blacks increasingly vote for candidates from the Democratic Party?

4. **Evaluating Ideas: (a)** What was American policy toward Indians during the 1920's? **(b)** How successful was it? **(c)** What was the situation of Mexican Americans during the 1920's and 1930's?

5 Literature and the arts reflect changing ways and times

See Teaching Suggestions in TMRG, p.TM185.

During the 1920's and 1930's, writers and artists struggled to deal with issues raised by changes in society. The struggle was with changing standards and values brought on by prosperity during the 1920's and depression during the 1930's. At other times, the struggle was to find new forms of expression that seemed appropriate to the machine age.

Concern for a vanishing past. Although American literature reflected the changing ways of life, one group of writers revealed their concern for a vanishing past. Edith Wharton and Ellen Glasgow contrasted the order and stability of bygone New York and Virginia with the restless materialism of the newly rich. In her writings Willa Cather recaptured the vitality and heroism of pioneer life in Nebraska and compared it to the empty lives of those whose major goal was material success.

Reactions to life in the 1920's. Many writers, however, focused directly on the conflicts and confusions of the emerging industrial world. T. S. Eliot in his poem *The Waste Land* (1922) pictured society in the machine age as grim, barren, standardized, cheap, and vulgar.

Several writers revealed the tragedy of equating success with money and the things money could buy. Theodore Dreiser's *An American Tragedy* (1925) unraveled the sordid story of a youth who deliberately let his girlfriend drown in order to pursue what in the end proved to be a futile goal. F. Scott Fitzgerald in his first novel, *This Side of Paradise* (1920), vividly pictured the confusion of the college "jazz set," bored with the futility of fast living and hard drinking. Later, in *The Great Gatsby* (1925), Fitzgerald portrayed the emptiness of life devoted primarily to a frenzied struggle to make money. Sinclair Lewis wrote a number of books highlighting the deadening conformity and hypocrisy of middle-class life in America, among them *Main Street* (1920), *Babbitt* (1922), and *Elmer Gantry* (1927). In 1930 he received the Nobel Prize in literature, the first American writer to be so honored.

Literature of the 1930's. Several writers reacted forcefully to the crushing impact of the depression. The most gripping picture of those years was John Steinbeck's novel *The Grapes of Wrath* (1939). The story follows the sad fortunes of a poor but self-respecting Oklahoma family. Driven from their home in the dust bowl, they sought survival in California. Unhappily, life in California proved lonely and harsh. Sad though the story is, it ends on a glimmer of hope for the homeless, downtrodden wanderers.

Sinclair Lewis viewed the depression from a different angle. In a sobering novel, *It Can't Happen Here* (1935), Lewis contended that American society in the 1930's was ripe soil from which a dictatorship might arise.

Ernest Hemingway was another writer who came to grips with basic issues confronting America and the world. In *A Farewell to Arms* (1929), he stripped the romance and glamor from World War I. In *For Whom the Bell Tolls* (1939), he presented a graphic picture of the violence and brutality of the Spanish Civil War and in so doing provided a preview of World War II.

The Harlem Renaissance. Black writers and artists, inspired by the image of the "new Negro," produced important works that led to a cultural renaissance or rebirth. Their works aroused the interest of many white Americans while strengthening the growing pride of black Americans. This cultural rebirth of the 1920's centered in New York City's black community of Harlem. It has been called the "Harlem Renaissance," but its rich expressions were not confined to Harlem.

These new cultural contributions were marked by originality, freshness of style, and vigor. Jazz music, with its exciting and spontaneous rhythms, and the blues, reflecting the joy, laughter, sadness, and pain of black Americans, found outstanding composers and performers in the 1920's and 1930's. Among these

Class activity: Carl Sandburg's poem "They Have Yarns" (from the longer work "The People Yes") affirms the poet's belief in American common sense and good humor, even in the face of the changes wrought by industrialization. Have a group prepare a reader's theater presentation of this poem.

One of the great painters who captured the look of America in the 1920's and 1930's was Edward Hooper. There is a quality of starkness and loneliness that can be found in many of his scenes such as this one, Early Sunday Morning.

were W. C. Handy, Jelly Roll Morton, Louis Armstrong, and Duke Ellington. Black spirituals became part of the repertory of Marian Anderson, who in the 1920's was just beginning her career as one of the world's greatest singers of classical as well as folk music. Also during the 1920's, Paul Robeson began his brilliant career as an actor, concert singer, and civil rights activist.

The literature of the Harlem Renaissance reflected the racial pride of the "new Negro." Langston Hughes, Claude McKay, and Countee Cullen wrote verse marked by haunting bitterness and defiance but also by joy and hope. This many-sided emotional richness among black writers was exemplified by Jean Toomer's *Cane*. This work portrayed black environments in the rural South, in Washington, D. C., and in New York City. It starkly revealed its characters' intense emotions while also portraying their beauty and dignity.

Among the black writers of the 1930's, Richard Wright was a towering figure. In the four short novels that make up *Uncle Tom's Children* (1938), he explored southern racial problems. His most famous novel, *Native Son,* is a harsh picture of life in the slums of Chicago. His autobiography, *Black Boy,* is a powerful portrayal of his family's experiences during his childhood years.

Journalism. Newspapers and magazines also reflected the influence of the machine age. By the 1920's journalism had become big business. *Reader's Digest,* started in 1922 by Dewitt Wallace, won nationwide circulation with its collection of condensed articles from other journals. *Time,* the brainchild of Henry R. Luce, was widely read for its concise reporting of current events. The enormous success of *Time* led to the founding of competitors, chief among them *Newsweek,* started in 1933 during the depth of the depression. Luce, who had made a fortune out of *Time,* bought the humorous magazine *Life* in 1936. He transformed it into the first American publication devoted to photojournalism, in which articles are developed largely through the use of photographs. It, too, soon attracted competitors, the most successful of which was *Look.*

Class activity: Have interested students report on aspects of jazz, gospel, and folk music—history, techniques, personalities. The students should present their findings in oral reports to the class.

Meanwhile, many of the individually owned newspapers were being bought by large newspaper chains. Chain newspapers ran the same syndicated columns and editorials, the same comics, sports news, and advertisements. They subscribed to the same news services—the Associated Press, the United Press, and the International News Service. Like the magazines, the newspapers reflected the problems of industrial America.

Painting and design. In painting and design, Americans were more and more influenced by such European artists as Cézanne, Manet, Monet, Degas, Matisse, and Picasso. Some modernists boldly experimented with geometric designs that often resembled machines in their emphasis on hard angles, masses, and abstract form. Many American artists continued to paint the more conventional themes, but they painted them in new ways. Others tried to reveal the meaning of the machine age in their paintings of factories, warehouses, slums, railroads, and other scenes of urban life.

New art forms. The machine age also opened up entirely new forms of art. In the hands of artists, the camera captured the spirit and meaning of the new age. New methods of art reproduction enabled people to own inexpensive yet excellent copies of the world's outstanding works of art. When these reproduction techniques were adopted by the mass-circulation magazines, millions of Americans were able to see the work of the world's greatest photographers, illustrators, and artists.

Aided by commercial artists and industrial designers, manufacturers began to produce telephones, furniture, fabrics, clothing, typewriters, glassware, refrigerators, stoves, automobiles, and many other articles that showed that machines and machine products might be beautiful in design and structure.

The movies. Motion pictures, the movies, were one new product of the machine age. They were a fascinating combination of new technology, big business, and art.

The movies rapidly became an important part of American life. In the 1920's huge and lavish motion picture palaces were built in large cities throughout the country. By the end of the decade, the motion picture industry had become the fourth largest one in the nation. Even during the hard times of the depression, movies remained popular. In 1938, movie audiences numbered more than 80 million a week. In that same year, more than 500 American movies were produced.

The movies both reflected and shaped American society. Traditional values—the home, hard work, thrift—were usually upheld in movie stories. However, the movies often popularized less traditional values. The world of the "jazz set" and the flappers, when portrayed on the screen, looked glamorous. People began to copy the styles and manners of the movies.

Artistically, movies made great advances. Storytelling in the silent films of the 1920's was much more polished and sophisticated than in most prewar films. Directors also explored more demanding themes. Erich von Stroheim's *Greed* described with great power how greed for money warped the character and finally destroyed the lives of a working-class couple. Robert Flaherty's *Nanook of the North,* a documentary, captured the grandeur of nature and the difficulty of life in the Arctic. Great comics like Charlie Chaplin and Buster Keaton left audiences rocking with laughter— and furthered the art of silent-movie making.

In 1927 Warner Brothers released the first successful "talkie," *The Jazz Singer*. For a time, as moviemakers adapted to using sound, motion pictures became more stiff and stagy. Soon, however, sound techniques were mastered, and movies became more exciting and popular than ever.

In the 1930's Fred Astaire and Ginger Rogers sang and danced through a series of films that took people's minds off the problems of the depression. Directors like Howard Hawks, in *His Girl Friday,* and Frank Capra, in *Meet John Doe* and *Mr. Smith Goes to Washington,* studied manners and morals in contemporary society. John Ford, in *Stagecoach, Young Mr. Lincoln,* and *The Grapes of Wrath,* produced works that questioned and celebrated American history.

Architecture. Inspired by such outstanding architects as Louis Sullivan and Frank Lloyd Wright, other architects began to promote the idea that a building ought to use the materials and follow the forms most suitable to the purposes for which it was to be used.

For many people the skyscraper became a symbol of the influence of the machine upon architecture. Built of steel, glass, and concrete, it towered into the sky in order to use as little

▲ Class activity: Have a group of volunteers set up a library display of books and art prints
that illustrate the art, architecture, literature, and cinema of the 1920's and 1930's. Then
lead a class discussion comparing the styles and techniques of the 1920's and 1930's with those
of today.

757

Jazz, with its syncopated rhythms, was a distinctly American form of music. King Oliver's Jazz Band, featuring Louis Armstrong (standing third from right), was one of Jazz's most popular pioneers.

expensive ground space as possible. Upper stories were set back to prevent the streets from being darkened. In the emphasis upon clear-cut vertical lines and the massing of windows, the skyscraper was an excellent example of how purpose and materials dictated design.

Music and dancing. Music, too, showed the influence of the industrial age. Many people believed that jazz expressed the rhythms and the accelerated speed and energy of the machine. Music also became increasingly available through the radio, the phonograph, and musical instruments manufactured at lower and lower costs. Moreover, wealth created by the new industrial age supported symphony orchestras and opera companies.

Social dancing was transformed by jazz, while the dance as an art form was revolutionized by Isadora Duncan, Ruth St. Denis, Katherine Dunham, Ted Shawn, and Martha

Graham. These dancers emphasized free and ▲ expressive movements in contrast to the traditional, formal patterns of the ballet.

SECTION REVIEW
See underscored items, text pp. 755 - 58.

Identify: Edith Wharton, Ellen Glasgow, Willa Cather, *The Waste Land, An American Tragedy,* F. Scott Fitzgerald, Sinclair Lewis, *The Grapes of Wrath,* Ernest Hemingway, Harlem Renaissance, *Cane,* Richard Wright, Charlie Chaplin, *The Jazz Singer,* Frank Lloyd Wright, Isadora Duncan
For answers to questions, see Answer Key, p.A103.

1. **Interpreting Ideas:** How did some writers show their disillusionment with the United States of the 1920's?

2. **Synthesizing Ideas:** How did the movies both reflect and shape American society?

3. **Organizing Ideas:** How did the skyscraper symbolize the influence upon architecture of (**a**) land values and (**b**) industrialization?

▲ Class activity: Have students interested in dance present profiles of these and other influential dancers of the 1920's and 1930's.

DEVELOPING HISTORY STUDY SKILLS

Writing About History Investigating Oral History

To bring a period alive, historians often seek out personal accounts of the events and attitudes of the time. They interview participants and eyewitnesses, then record the interview either in writing or with a tape recorder. Such interviews are called oral histories, and they add much to a historian's treasury of information. Such oral histories can be considered primary sources. For this reason, the time lapse between the events occurrence and the interview may be an important consideration.

Students of history are often called on to conduct and interpret interviews. The process of conducting an interview requires planning and research. Only by applying proper techniques of questioning can useful information be gained from an oral history.

How to Prepare an Oral History

There are three parts to effective interviewing: preparation, interviewing, and post-interview analysis and reporting. To prepare an oral history, follow these guidelines.

1. **Identify the topic.** Determine the information needed and from whom the information can be obtained.

2. **Research the topic.** Gather available information on the topic on which to base your questions.

3. **Set up an interview.** Identify yourself and state clearly the purpose of the interview. Arrange a time when the interview can be conveniently scheduled.

4. **Prepare questions.** Formulate questions that will elicit the information you need. Group the questions into categories. Determine a direction for the interview so that one question leads logically to the next.

5. **Conduct the interview.** Explain again the purpose of the interview. Be an active listener, paying close attention to the responses and interacting when appropriate. Be sure to record the responses accurately. This can be done most easily through the use of a tape recorder.

6. **Write the oral history.** Accurately transcribe the information collected in the recorded interview.

7. **Analyzing the interview.** Apply the skill you have developed to analyze the information gathered in the interview. Then prepare a summary of the information.

Applying the Skill

Studs Terkel wrote an oral history of the Great Depression which he titled *Hard Times.* Read the following excerpt. Then determine what questions Terkel might have asked to elicit the responses contained in the excerpt.

> *I knew the Depression had really hit when the electric lights went out. My parents could no longer pay the $1 electric bill. The kerosene lamps went up in the home. And in the business. My father had a restaurant. This did something to me, because it let me know that my father was not the greatest cat in the world. I always thought he was. . . .*
>
> *I remember that kerosene lamp, because for Christmas, '30, around in there, I got a little book that pictured Lindbergh's flight. My mother was telling me how great Lindberg was. She told me I would fly a plane like that. But she didn't tell me about my chances of flying. That was the point, you see. 'Cause they were trying to shield me. . . .*
>
> *One time, my father and I tore a wall down to enlarge the business. I must have been around eight or nine. I could see blood coming from his hands, from using the crowbar, and I kissed his hand.*
>
> *The restaurant was in the black community. But we made as much money off white people as we did off blacks. White people wanted to come in and get fried chicken. He had them fooled that there was something mystical about the batter he used.*
>
> Robin Langston

Terkel asked Langston questions such as "When did the reality of the depression strike you?" and "How did the depression affect you and your family?" Langston responded to the first question by recalling that his family could not even pay the $1 electric bill so the electricity was turned off. He also recalled his father's restaurant closing. Langston's response to the second question recounts his parents trying to shield him from the realities of the depression. Terkel, of course, asked many other questions to gather information for his oral history.

759

Practicing the Skill

Read the excerpts from *Hard Times* below. Then on a separate sheet of paper, list the questions that Terkel asked Mary Owsley and her daughter, Peggy Terry. Then list the questions you would ask to obtain further information.

There was thousands of people out of work in Oklahoma City. They set up a soup line, and the food was clean and it was delicious. Many, many people, colored and white, I didn't see any difference, 'cause there was just as many white people out of work than were colored. Lost everything they had accumulated from their young days. And these were facts. I remember several families had to leave in covered wagons. To Californy, I guess. . . .

I knew one family there in Oklahoma City, a man and a woman and seven children lived in a hole in the ground. You'd be surprised how nice it was, how nice they kept it. They had chairs and tables and beds back in that hole. And they had the dirt all braced up there, just like a cave.

Oh, the dust storms, they were terrible. You could wash and hang clothes on a line, and if you happened to be away from the house and couldn't get those clothes in before that storm got there, you'd never wash that out. Oil was in that sand. It'd color them the most awful color you ever saw. It just ruined them. . . . I had to use 'em, understand, but they wasn't very presentable. . . .

The majority of people were hit and hit hard. They were mentally disturbed you're bound to know, 'cause they didn't know when the end of all this was coming. There was a lot of suicides that I know of. From nothin' else but just they couldn't see any hope for a better tomorrow. . . . Part of 'em were farmers and part of 'em were businessmen, even. . . .

A lot of times one family would have some food. They would divide. And everyone would share. Even the people that were quite well to do, they was ashamed. 'Cause they was eatin', and other people wasn't. . . .

My husband was very bitter. That's just puttin' it mild. . . . He couldn't see why as wealthy a country as this is, that there was any sense in so many people starving to death. . . .

My husband went to Washington. To march with that group that went to Washington . . . the bonus boys."

Mary Owsley

I first noticed the difference when we'd come home from school in the evening. My mother'd send us to the soup line. And we were never allowed to cuss. If you happened to be one of the first ones in line, you didn't get anything but water that was on top. So we'd ask the guy that was ladling out the soup into the buckets — everybody had to bring their own bucket to the get the soup — he'd dip the greasy watery stuff off the top. So we'd ask him to please dip down to get some meat and potatoes from the bottom of the kettle. But he wouldn't do it. . . .

Then we'd go across the street. One place had bread, large loaves of bread. Down the road just a little piece was a big shed, and they gave milk. My sister and me would take two buckets each. And that's what we lived off for the longest time.

I can remember one time, the only thing in the house to eat was mustard. My sister and I put so much mustard on biscuits that we got sick. And we can't stand mustard till today.

There was only one family around that ate good. Mr. Barr worked at the ice plant. Whenever Mrs. Barr could, she'd feed the kids. But she couldn't feed 'em all. They had a big tree that had fruit on it. She'd let us pick those. Sometimes we'd pick and eat 'em until we were sick.

Her two daughters got to go to Norman for their college. When they'd talk about all the good things they had at the college, she'd kind of hush 'em up because there was always poor kids that didn't have anything to eat. I remember she always felt bad because people in the neighborhood were hungry. But there was a feeling of together. . . .

When they had food to give to people, you'd get a notice and you'd go down. So Daddy went down that day and he took my sister and me. They were giving away potatoes and things like that. But they had a truck of oranges parked in the alley. Somebody asked them who the oranges were for, and they wouldn't tell 'em. So they said, well, we're gonna take those oranges. And they did. My dad was one of the ones that got up on the truck. They called the police, and the police chased us all away. But we got the oranges. . . .

Peggy Terry

(Answers will vary. Examples include: What kinds of people went through the soup line? What happened to people who lost their homes? How bad were the dust storms? Did you ever have to go hungry?)

During the 1920's the process of industrialization rapidly gathered momentum. Machines replaced or lightened human labor on the farm, in the factory, and in America's homes. The developing technology created a higher standard of living. At the same time, it began to give new directions to people's goals and to transform their daily lives.

Many critics of American life claimed that modern technology was standardizing life. These critics were disturbed that the machine was being used largely to make money and to provide meaningless recreation.

Other students of American society defended the new technology. They pointed to the obvious fact that it relieved people of backbreaking toil and that it made possible more leisure, more consumer goods, more comforts, and more time for education and for pleasure. All of these advantages, they argued, provided a greater measure of freedom for the individual American.

As the 1920's drew to a close, however, the arguments over the advantages and disadvantages of modern technology were suddenly buried beneath the crushing impact of the Great Depression. For several desperate years, life for many Americans, and especially for the minorities, became a grim struggle for survival. The New Deal, born with the inauguration of President Franklin D. Roosevelt in March 1933, brought new hope to suffering Americans. In the following years, it brought growing relief from the heaviest burdens of unemployment and poverty.

CONNECTING CHAPTER IDEAS

During the decades of the 1920's and 1930's American society experienced a great deal of change. The United States relations with foreign nations went through equally complex changes in these two decades. In the next chapter you will trace the development of American foreign policy and learn how the United States policy of isolationism slowly evolved into one of cooperation with other nations to prevent war.

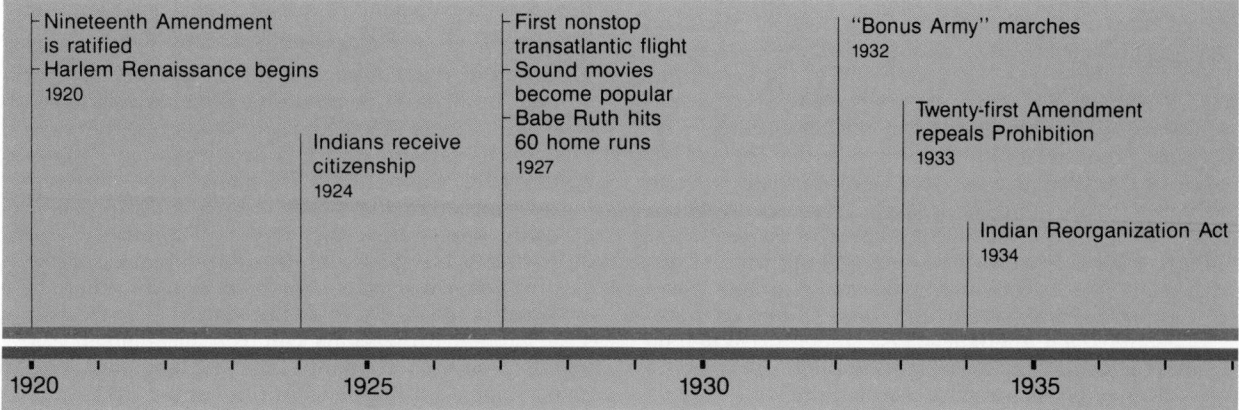

- Nineteenth Amendment is ratified
- Harlem Renaissance begins
1920

Indians receive citizenship
1924

- First nonstop transatlantic flight
- Sound movies become popular
- Babe Ruth hits 60 home runs
1927

"Bonus Army" marches
1932

Twenty-first Amendment repeals Prohibition
1933

Indian Reorganization Act
1934

1920   1925   1930   1935

CHAPTER
33 REVIEW

Reviewing Important Terms

In the sentences below, the underlined terms are incorrect. On a separate sheet of paper, rewrite each sentence using the correct term.

1. <u>Labor</u> unions are labor associations organized by employers rather than by the workers.
2. Industries grew substantially during the 1920's primarily as a result of <u>alliances</u>, or the combination of two or more independent companies into one larger company.
3. Business executives applied the principle of <u>product accounting</u> to determine the total cost of every item of production and marketing.
4. Mexican Americans became involved in the labor organization movement by establishing <u>braceros</u>, or self-aid societies to cooperatively solve their problems.
5. Two elements of <u>small-scale production</u> are the assembly line and interchangeable parts.

Practicing Critical Thinking Skills

1. **Synthesizing Ideas.** How did industrialization affect the lives of people (a) on farms and (b) in cities? (c) Does industrialization always mean progress? Explain.
2. **Interpreting Ideas.** (a) How did the radio, movies, and newspaper chains contribute to conformity? (b) How did they contribute to individualism?
3. **Analyzing Ideas.** (a) What are the relationships between industrialization and the role of women? (b) Was the effect of industrialization on the role of women positive or negative? Explain.
4. **Comparing Ideas.** (a) In what ways were the situations of blacks, Indians, and Mexicans similar during the 1920's and 1930's? (b) How were they different? (c) Compare the poverty that existed during the Great Depression with the poverty that exists in the United States today.
5. **Evaluating Ideas.** Does television today have more, the same, or less effect on society than radio did in the 1920's and 1930's? Explain.
6. **Relating Past to Present.** During the depression, people were making special efforts to make their dollars stretch and such things as automobiles and appliances last longer. (a) When do people today try to stretch their dollars? (b) Why do they try to stretch their dollars?

Developing History Study Skills

1. **Investigating Oral History.** Preparing an oral history of the Great Depression means using good questions. Prepare a series of five questions to ask in an interview. Your questions may ask about age, place of residence, place of work, and how their life was affected by the Depression.
2. **Finding Main Ideas.** Read the following excerpt written by a woman living through the drought in Oklahoma. Then answer the questions below.

   Naturally you will wonder why we stay where conditions are so disheartening. . . . There are . . . practical considerations that serve to hold us here, for the present. Our soil is excellent. We need only a little rain—less than in most places—to make it productive. . . . The newer methods of farming suggest possibilities of better control of moisture in the future. Our entire equipment is adapted to the type of farming suitable for this country and would have to be replaced at great expense with the tools needed in some other locality. We have spent so much in trying to keep our land from blowing away that it looks foolish to walk off and leave it, when somewhat more favorable conditions seem now to "cast their shadows before [us]."

   (a) What is the main idea of the excerpt? (b) What details support the main idea?

Relating Geography and History

During the 1920's and 1930's, the automobile, the airplane, and the radio came of age. To understand how these inventions reshaped Americans' sense of geography, answer the following questions.

1. How did the automobile affect (a) the number and quality of roads, (b) distances between where people lived and worked, (c) differences between farmers and city dwellers?
2. (a) What advantages did radio have over the telegraph and the telephone? (b) How did radio bring Americans closer to their leaders?
3. It has been said that the development of the airplane caused the earth to become smaller. What is meant by this statement?
4. What generalizations can you form about the effects of the automobile, the airplane, and radio on regional differences in the United States?

UNIT TEN
REVIEW

Discussing Ideas

1. Explain how each of the following demonstrates a rejection of both progressivism and the ideals of the New Freedom: **(a)** Harding's slogan, "a return to normalcy," **(b)** Coolidge's statement, "the business of America is business," **(c)** Hoover's belief in "rugged individualism."
2. **(a)** Make a list of five words or phrases that describe American life during the 1920's. **(b)** Explain each of your choices.
3. **(a)** Why did the Great Depression happen? **(b)** Could such an economic collapse ever happen again? Why or why not?
4. Why did President Hoover oppose direct relief by the federal government?
5. Do you think the New Deal changed the basic character of the federal government? Explain.
6. **(a)** How did the depression affect the lives of minorities? **(b)** Why did it affect them that way?

Applying History Study Skills

1. **Reading Economic Graphs.** Study the economic chart, "Unemployment, 1929–1939" (page 726). Then answer the following questions. **(a)** In what year was unemployment the highest? **(b)** How might you use this chart to prove that the New Deal had eased the depression? **(c)** How might you use the chart to prove the opposite?
2. **Developing a Frame of Reference.** The following passage is from a book entitled *Middletown*. This study of American life in the 1920's was written by Robert and Helen Lynd. Read the passage, and then answer the questions below.

   The radio is rapidly crowding its way in among the necessities in the family standards of living. A remarkable feature of this new invention is its accessibility. Here skill and ingenuity can in part offset money as a way to share in the enjoyments of the wealthy. With but little equipment one can call in the life of the rest of the world from the air.

   (a) What did the Lynds find remarkable about radio? **(b)** How would knowing the number of families with radios in 1920 and 1930 help you develop a frame of reference for the Lynds' statement?

Making Connections

1. In your community, try to locate buildings, roads, or bridges that were built during the New Deal. Prepare a map of your community that indicates their location.
2. Make a list of items in your home or school that were not yet invented or in use during the 1920's and 1930's. Write an essay about daily life without those items.
3. Create a bulletin board display entitled, "Heroes of the Golden Twenties and Thirties." Include in the display pictures, short biographies, or newspaper headlines to feature people such as Charles Lindbergh, Amelia Earhart, Babe Ruth, Joe Louis, Jesse Owens, Gertrude Ederle, Bobby Jones, Helen Wills Moody, and Bill Tilden.
4. Draw a series of political cartoons on the New Deal. Be sure to keep the cartoons simple and to make clear the point of view expressed in each.
5. Make a bar or line graph on one aspect of the 1920's and 1930's, such as **(a)** government spending, **(b)** average family income, **(c)** cost of living, **(d)** number of bank failures.
6. Use the information on pages 755–58 to write an essay titled "Literature and the Arts Reflect Changing Ways and Times."

Reading in Depth

Allen, Frederick Lewis, *Only Yesterday* (New York: Harper and Row). A popular history that documents the fads and fashions of the 1920's.

Burke, John, *Winged Legend: The Story of Amelia Earhart* (New York: Berkley). A biography of America's outstanding woman aviator, whose plane disappeared over the Pacific in 1937.

Lewis, Sinclair, *Babbitt* (San Diego: Harcourt Brace Jovanovich). A satirical novel about middle-class life in the 1920's.

Shannon, David, *The Great Depression* (Englewood Cliffs, NJ: Prentice-Hall). Eyewitness accounts of life during the depression, including discussions of farming, education, and relief efforts.

Wright, Richard, *Black Boy* (New York: Harper and Row). The story of the early life of a major American writer.

See list of Multimedia Materials in TMRG, p.TM187.
See Making Connections, text p. 821.

UNIT ELEVEN

Isolationism Through World War II

The years between 1920 and 1941 were difficult ones. The United States and the nations of Europe had been rocked by World War I. As these nations attempted to recover, they were plunged into a deep economic depression. In Europe several nations turned to strong leaders to solve their postwar problems. These leaders ended democratic government and stirred nationalism to dangerous levels. In the United States disillusionment with the results of World War I led the nation to avoid international involvement and to adopt a policy of isolationism. That isolation, however, was shattered in 1941 by the attack on Pearl Harbor, The U.S.S. Arizona Memorial (below) symbolizes the end of United States isolation and the nation's assumption of world leadership.

See Chapter Overview in TMRG, p.TM188.
See Chapter Objectives in TMRG, p.TM188.
See Introducing the Chapter in TMRG, p.TM188.

CHAPTER 34

The Nation Moves Toward Isolationism

(1920–1932)

A nation's
reaction

During the 1920's and 1930's, Americans had faced rapidly changing conditions at home. The economy had moved from a postwar depression to a boom to almost complete collapse in the Great Depression.

Relations with foreign nations went through equally complex changes during the decades of the 1920's and the 1930's. The end of World War I in 1918 had released in people emotions they had long held in check. Millions of people on every continent mourned for loved ones killed in the war. Mixed with the sorrow, however, was wild joy that the war to end all wars was over. Millions of people offered prayers of thanksgiving and prayers for the fulfillment of President Wilson's vision of a world rebuilt on a foundation of lasting peace.

Wilson realized, as millions of Americans did not, that it is easier to win a victory on a battlefield than it is to build a lasting peace. He warned Americans that great problems remained to be solved and challenged them to take up the responsibility of world leadership. The United States, however, refused the challenge by rejecting the Versailles Treaty.

Unhappily, Wilson's plea for world leadership went unheeded. As a result, the idealism that imbued Americans at the end of the war soon faded. Americans were tired of wartime restrictions and were eager to return to the everyday business of living. Also, as their European Allies began to quarrel over the spoils of war, many Americans became increasingly disillusioned.

During the 1920's, the American people and their representatives in Congress restricted immigration and raised tariffs. They rejected Wilson's policies, both domestic and foreign. They refused to join the League of Nations. In the following years, Americans turned their backs on Europe and on the challenge of world leadership.

READING FOCUS

As you read about the growing isolationism of the postwar years, look for the details that support each of the following statements.

1. America closes its doors to Europe's people and goods.
2. The United States moves toward the Good Neighbor Policy.
3. Americans cooperate with other nations in efforts to prevent war.

See Teaching Suggestions in TMRG, pp.TM188-89.

After World War I, the United States drew back from involvement in world affairs. The United States refused, for example, to join the League of Nations, in part, to avoid becoming entangled in Europe's troubles and quarrels.

The United States also tried, with considerable success, to keep out the people and products of Europe and Asia. The immigration and tariff laws passed during this period were the most restrictive in United States history.

Closing the doors. By almost completely halting immigration during the 1920's the United States reversed one of its oldest traditions. Earlier laws and international agreements had excluded the Chinese, the Japanese, and other Asians. Despite these exceptions, few questioned the historic role of the United States as· a place of opportunity for immigrants. Indeed, during the decade before World War I, more Europeans settled in the United States than in any previous decade.

Why did a nation of immigrants suddenly close its doors? One reason was an anti-European feeling that arose. However, certain Americans had reasons of their own.

Organized labor, for example, argued that new immigrants were willing to work for lower wages than American workers and thus pulled down the standard of living. Industrialists had formerly favored immigration as a source of cheap, unskilled labor. By 1920, with the railroads built and basic industries such as steel well developed, they no longer needed masses of unskilled workers. Finally, many established Americans felt that the more recent immigrants, mainly from eastern and southern European nations, did not easily become "Americanized."

The immigration laws. Congress passed three laws in the 1920's that progressively restricted immigration from Europe. The Emergency Quota Act of 1921 introduced a **quota system**. ▲ This limited the number of Europeans and others who could be admitted to 3 percent of the total number of persons of their nationality

▲ Throughout the Annotated Teacher's Edition, terms listed in the "Identify" portion of a Section Review are underscored the first time they appear. See the Teacher's Manual for each section for a listing of important vocabulary terms.

767

Immigration to the United States 1890 - 1939

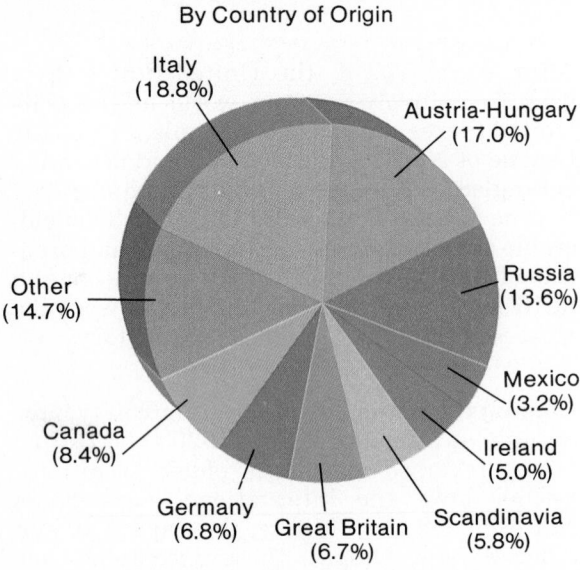

By Country of Origin

Italy (18.8%)
Austria-Hungary (17.0%)
Russia (13.6%)
Mexico (3.2%)
Ireland (5.0%)
Scandinavia (5.8%)
Great Britain (6.7%)
Germany (6.8%)
Canada (8.4%)
Other (14.7%)

Source: *Statistical Abstract of the United States.*

residing in the United States in the year 1910. The act also set a total yearly limit of about 350,000 immigrants.

In 1924 an even more restrictive law reduced the yearly quota from 3 to 2 percent. It also changed the base year from 1910 to 1890. This change discriminated against Italians, Austrians, Russians, and other eastern and southern Europeans who had immigrated to America mainly after 1890.

Finally, the National Origins Act of 1929 shifted the base year of immigration to 1920. However, it counterbalanced this more liberal provision by reducing the yearly limit on im-
▲ migrants to 150,000.

The new immigration policies aroused a great deal of bitterness, especially among eastern and southern Europeans. The Japanese were also aroused because the immigration act of 1924 ended the Gentlemen's Agreement of 1907. Japan had faithfully observed the agreement and resented the policies which closed the doors to Japanese immigrants.

The war of tariffs. While closing its doors to immigrants, the United States also raised tariff barriers to keep out foreign products. In fact,

the ink was hardly dry on the peace treaties before the nations of the world were engaged in another war—a trade war fought with tariffs. As you have read, the Fordney-McCumber Tariff of 1922 increased import duties on hundreds of items.

In 1930 Congress passed the Hawley-Smoot Tariff Act, providing for the highest tariff in American history. President Hoover felt that some of the rates were too high. He also pondered a petition signed by 1,000 leading economists who argued that such high tariffs would raise prices, create hardships for American consumers, and seriously interfere with world trade. Nevertheless, believing that protective tariffs encouraged business prosperity, Hoover signed the bill.

America's high-tariff policy proved a cruel blow to many countries in Latin America and in Europe. When America's high tariffs deprived these countries of their best markets in the United States, their economic strength declined. Factories closed, people were thrown out of work, and the surplus of farm products mounted steadily.

Some countries struck back by raising their own tariff barriers against American goods. Thus the high tariffs that Congress hoped would aid American industry in the end deprived many American businesses and farms of the foreign markets they badly needed.

War debts and high tariffs. America's high-tariff policy created still another problem. How could European countries pay their war debts to the United States if they could not sell their goods in this country?

The war had changed America's relation to Europe from debtor to creditor. Before the war American business leaders had borrowed money from Europeans to finance new industries. During the period before the United States entered the war in 1917, however, Europeans began to sell their American stocks and bonds to buy war goods. As the war progressed, the American government also loaned huge sums to the warring countries. As a result, by 1918 nearly all the European countries owed money to the United States. The total amounted to about $10 billion.

The American government reduced the interest rates on the loans. It also arranged for the debtor nations to repay the money over a long period of time. Despite the generous terms, the bankrupt European countries emerged from the war not knowing how they could repay their debts.

President Wilson reminded Congress of one possible solution to Europe's problems. He declared that if the United States wished Europe to repay its debts, Americans had to buy European products. However, this became impossible when the United States adopted a high-tariff policy.

War debts and reparations. The only other solution open to the European Allies was to collect war damages, or **reparations**, from Germany. They could then use this money to repay their war debts to the United States. In 1921 a Reparations Commission fixed the total of German reparations at $33 billion. Germany, however, was in the midst of a severe economic crisis and completely unable to pay such a huge sum. In an effort to secure the money, Germany borrowed from bankers in the United States and Europe.

There was a limit to the amount that the German government could borrow, and, as the years passed, the reparations had to be reduced. In spite of this relief, however, Germany's economic situation grew steadily worse. By 1930 the Germans could make no further payments.

▲ **A legacy of bitterness.** Faced with this situation, the debtor countries notified the United States that they could no longer meet their payments on the war debts. They argued that they had contributed far more to victory in blood and sacrifice than had America. It would be only fair of the United States, they said, to cancel all war debts.

The American government refused to admit such a claim. It insisted that the war debts to the United States and German reparation payments to the Allies were two entirely separate matters. Americans pointed out that some of the loans—perhaps as much as a third of the total—had, in fact, been made after the armistice. Americans also reminded the European countries that they were not too poor to spend large sums for armaments.

In 1931 the debtors, with the exception of Finland, refused to make even a token payment. President Hoover then declared a year's halt, or **moratorium**, on the payment of war debts and reparations. However, Germany did not make any more payments, and the whole question was left unsolved.

In the end, most of the war debts and most of Germany's reparations remained unpaid. Nevertheless, America's unsuccessful attempt to collect the war debts increased Europe's resentment against the United States. Also, the European victors' unsuccessful attempt to collect reparations from Germany created a feeling of bitterness among the German people. This bitterness, as you will see, contributed to the rise of Adolf Hitler in the early 1930's.

SECTION REVIEW
See underscored items, text pp. 767 - 69.
Identify: quota system, Hawley-Smooth Tariff, reparations, moratorium
For answers to questions, see Answer Key, p.A107.
1. **Summarizing Ideas:** List four reasons why various Americans favored restricting immigration after World War I.
2. **Organizing Ideas: (a)** What reasons did the European Allies give for stopping payments on their war debts? **(b)** How did Americans answer these arguments?
3. **Interpreting Ideas:** In what ways did America's high-tariff policies backfire?
4. **Studying Graphics:** Look at the graph on page 768. According to the graph, from what countries did the largest percentage of immigrants come?

2 The United States moves toward the Good Neighbor Policy

See Teaching Suggestions in TMRG, pp.TM189-90.

During the early 1900's Presidents Theodore Roosevelt, William Howard Taft, and Woodrow Wilson all intervened in Latin-American affairs. They claimed intervention was necessary (1) to safeguard the Panama Canal, (2) to prevent European countries from extending their influence in the Caribbean, and (3) to protect American citizens and property.

This Caribbean policy was continued by Presidents Harding and Coolidge. Critics of the policy referred to it as "dollar diplomacy." Many Latin Americans called it "Yankee imperialism."

Investments and intervention. The prosperity of the "Golden Twenties" provided many Americans with money to invest. The underdeveloped countries of Latin America offered

● To prepare the class for this section, you might begin with a review of the Monroe Doctrine and U.S. relations with Latin America in the 1800's and early 1900's. Suggested topics for review: Panama canal, Roosevelt Corollary, Roosevelt's "Big Stick" policy, the Drago Doctrine, Dollar Diplomacy.

769

President Coolidge (center) came to Cuba to open the seventh Pan-American Conference. He hoped his trip would show that the United States wanted to work together with Latin America.

many inviting opportunities for investment. American dollars financed the building of factories, railroads, mines, and ranches in the lands to the south. Whereas in 1913 United States investments in Latin America totaled $1.3 billion, by 1928 these investments totaled more than $5 billion.

American interest in Latin America grew in proportion to the amount of American money invested there. President Coolidge frankly declared that the United States government would protect the property and lives of American citizens wherever they went.

During these years many Latin American countries were undergoing social and economic revolutions. Frequently two groups in a country struggled to gain control. Each group claimed that it alone represented the people and was the legal government. When this happened, the United States tended to recognize the group most friendly to American interests.

In some instances, the United States played an active role in the struggle for power. On oc-casion it forbade the sale of arms to the group it disliked and armed the group it supported. Worst of all from the Latin American point of view, the United States sometimes sent armed forces to protect American lives and property. ▲

Relations with Nicaragua. American policy toward Nicaragua offers an example of the kind of intervention that Latin Americans fiercely resented. The United States was particularly interested in Nicaragua because of large American investments there. Moreover, Nicaragua was close to the vital Panama Canal. Finally, there was the prospect that a new canal might eventually be built through Nicaragua itself. President Taft had sent marines into the country during an internal conflict to protect American investments and the nearby Panama Canal. President Coolidge withdrew the marines in 1925 but sent them back in 1926 when new disturbances broke out.

This policy was unpopular throughout Latin America. It was also unpopular with many Americans who claimed that the United States was really making war. President Coolidge denied this and spoke of the American occupation as a police duty. However, criticism was so strong that the administration took measures to solve the problem by more peaceful means.

In 1927 President Coolidge withdrew most of the marines, leaving only enough to protect American property if violence again broke out. This relieved some of the tension, but the Nicaraguans demanded the withdrawal of *all* marines and the end of American interference. In 1933 President Hoover finally withdrew all United States troops.

Relations with Mexico. Relations with Mexico also reflected the determination of the United States to protect American interests south of the Rio Grande. During Wilson's administration a sweeping social revolution in Mexico had raised new problems in the uneasy relations between the two countries. American lives and property suffered in the upheaval. Far more threatening to Americans who had invested in Mexican property was a new policy established in the Mexican constitution of 1917.

Article 27 of the Mexican constitution declared that "only Mexicans . . . have the right to acquire ownership [of, or] . . . to develop, mines, waters, or mineral fuels in the Republic

▲ Discussion topic: Have the students compare U.S. relations with Latin America in the 1920's with relations today. Have students give reasons for their answers.

of Mexico. The nation may grant the same right to foreigners, provided that they agree to be considered Mexicans in respect of such property, and accordingly not to involve the protection of their government in respect of the same." This article also canceled concessions made to foreigners by earlier governments. Foreign investors were quick to protest.

During 1917 and 1918, the United States was too involved in the European war to take any action in regard to Mexico. Moreover, not all of the provisions of the constitution were at once applied. However, after the armistice in 1918, oil investors and other American owners of property in Mexico clamored for intervention. These business interests were joined by many American Catholics who were disturbed by anti-Catholic provisions in the Mexican constitution and the anticlerical policies of the Mexican government. The situation grew worse when the Mexicans supported the anti-American faction in Nicaragua. By 1927, American-Mexican relations were close to the breaking point.

In 1927 the United States began slowly to modify its policy. President Coolidge took the first step by sending Dwight W. Morrow, a successful banker, as ambassador to Mexico. Instead of threatening Mexico with United States power, Morrow tried to understand the Mexican point of view. His sincerity, intelligence, and charm quickly won him many friends in Mexico. The skillful work of Morrow and other American "ambassadors of good will" repaired much of the damage done in the past. The Mexicans agreed to recognize American titles to subsoil minerals, such as petroleum, that had been in effect before the constitution of 1917.

New relations with Latin America. The Morrow mission marked a turning point in American relations with Mexico and with other Latin American countries. From 1927 on, both Coolidge and his successor, Herbert Hoover, worked hard to develop friendlier relations with the Caribbean republics and with the South American nations. Coolidge went to Havana, Cuba, in 1928 and personally opened a Pan-American Conference. Hoover toured South America in the months before his inauguration.

Latin Americans were pleased by the friendly attention of an American President and a President-elect. They were also pleased when the United States stopped using the 1904 Roosevelt Corollary to the Monroe Doctrine. The Corollary stated that the United States had the right to act as police officer of the Western Hemisphere.

In 1930 the State Department declared that the Monroe Doctrine would no longer be used to justify United States intervention in Latin-American domestic affairs.

Thus by the early 1930's, relations with Latin America had been considerably improved. The governments of these nations now encouraged American investments and gave them greater protection than in the past.

SECTION REVIEW
See underscored items, text pp. 769 - 71.
Identify: "Yankee imperialism," Nicaragua, Dwight W. Morrow
For answers to questions, see Answer Key, p.A107.
1. **Interpreting Ideas: (a)** Why did United States Caribbean policy during the early 1900's arouse resentment in Latin America and criticism in the United States? **(b)** Why did many Latin Americans resent United States policy toward Nicaragua?
2. **Summarizing Ideas:** What were the reasons for American hostility toward Mexico from 1917 to 1927?
3. **Organizing Ideas:** What steps did the United States take from 1927 to 1930 to improve its relations with Latin America? 4 tonight 2peife)

3 Americans cooperate with other nations in efforts to prevent war

See Teaching Suggestions in TMRG, p.TM190.
While the United States was improving its relations with Latin America, it also took steps to move toward international cooperation.

America and the League of Nations. As time passed, American experts in international law, public health, and finance became important advisers in activities of the League of Nations. During Harding's administration the United States began to send observers to Switzerland to take unofficial parts in League committee work dealing with epidemics, slavery, and the narcotics trade. By 1924, American delegates were attending League conferences.

▲ Point out to students that the nation's isolationist stance actually improved relations with
Latin American nations because it helped convince them that the U.S. had no aggressive
political intentions south of the Rio Grande. Also, Hoover's policies put these nations on a more
equal diplomatic footing.

771

The League of Nations held its first informal meeting in Geneva, Switzerland, in 1920. No official American delegates attended the League's meetings at the start, though some Americans later served the League as advisers.

Both Harding and Coolidge recommended that the United States join the Permanent Court of International Justice, popularly known as the World Court, created in 1920 to arbitrate international disputes. However, the Senate, guarding its right to make treaties and influenced by Americans who feared "entangling alliances," agreed to join only on its own terms. The nations already belonging to the World Court refused to accept the Senate's terms, and the matter was dropped.

▲ **The armaments race.** The government was more successful in its efforts to stop the naval armaments race in which it was engaged with Great Britain and Japan. Relations with Japan were particularly strained after World War I. Americans resented the Japanese occupation of the Shantung Peninsula in China. This occupation, begun in 1914, violated America's Open Door Policy, which was designed to keep China's territory intact and to prevent any single power from dominating China. Americans were concerned because Japan was allied with Great Britain.

As a result of the tension created by this situation, each of the three powers was rapidly building up its naval strength. Many people in all three countries feared that the naval armaments race might lead to war.

The Washington Conference. Against this disturbing background, nine powers with interests in Asia met in the American capital during 1921 and 1922. Secretary of State Charles Evans Hughes opened the Washington Naval Conference by boldly proposing a 10-year **naval holiday** during which no new warships were to be built. He suggested that the United States, Great Britain, and Japan each scrap enough of its own warships to bring the naval strength of the three great sea powers into a ratio of 5:5:3. These limitations applied only to capital ships, that is, to battleships and heavy cruisers. According to this plan, Great Britain and the United States would be equal in naval strength while Japan would have three fifths as much tonnage as each of the other two countries. France and Italy were to have fleets of equal size, with a ratio of 1.75 to the other powers.

At first, Japan refused to accept the plan. Finally, eager to make economies at home, the Japanese accepted the proposal on the condition that Great Britain and the United States would not further fortify any Pacific colonies, except Hawaii. These agreements were included in the Five-Power Treaty.

Other agreements. The Five-Power Treaty was only one of the agreements reached at the conference. Among others were the Four-Power Pact and the Nine-Power Treaty.

In the Four-Power Pact, Japan, Great Britain, France, and the United States agreed to respect one another's rights in the Pacific and to consult with one another in the event of any act of aggression in the Pacific area.

▲ Discussion topic: Have students discuss whether the U.S. follows one or several policies in dealing with the nations of the world today. Include in the discussion any elements of foreign diplomacy that may have changed between World War II and the present. (Consider the roles of terrorism, covert activity, and the media.)

Bernard M. Baruch was a man of many accomplishments, not the least of which was his status as a millionaire by age 30. His meteoric rise on Wall Street began with a position in a brokerage house at $5 a week.

With the profits from astute stock investments, he bought a seat on the New York Stock Exchange. He then set up his own office, which soon made him even more successful.

In 1916, as the United States approached involvement in World War I, President Wilson appointed Baruch to the Council of National Defense — an advisory commission. After the United States entered the war, Baruch served as chairman of the War Industries Board. Under his leadership, the nation increased its industrial output by nearly 20 percent.

Throughout World War II Baruch served as a special adviser to the Office of War Mobilization. In 1946, Baruch was appointed as United States representative to the United Nations Atomic Energy Commission. There he presented the Baruch Plan, a series of proposals for the international control of atomic energy. Throughout his public service Baruch displayed a foresight equal to that which he applied to his own financial success.

In the Nine-Power Treaty, the nations represented at the Washington Conference guaranteed the territorial integrity of China. They promised to uphold the Open Door Policy by promoting trade and relations "between China and the other powers upon the basis of equality of opportunity."

Events in Asia following the Washington Conference seemed to justify the belief that a major step toward peace had been taken. Japan withdrew, at least partially, from the Shantung Peninsula. Japan also withdrew troops that had occupied parts of Siberia during the Russian Revolution. At a London Naval Conference in 1930, Japan agreed to extend the holiday. The agreement to extend the naval holiday marked the high point of Japanese cooperation with the Western powers.

The attempt to outlaw war. The United States also tried to prevent war by what has been called a policy of "wishful thinking." In 1928 Secretary of State Frank B. Kellogg joined with the French foreign minister, Aristide Briand (ah·rees·TEED bree·AHN), in asking all nations to sign a pledge outlawing war "as an instrument of foreign policy." The signers were also to agree to settle all disputes by peaceful methods.

Eventually 62 nations accepted the document. However, the Kellogg-Briand Pact, or the Pact of Paris as it was called, proved to be little more than a statement of good intentions. In signing, each nation added its own reservations. Not one was willing to outlaw war waged in self-defense. Since nearly every nation going to war pleads self-defense, this reservation destroyed the pact's effectiveness.

Finally, the document said nothing about enforcement. Those who signed it were not even bound to consult with one another in case some government acted aggressively.

The crumbling peace structure. The opening act in the tragedy that later engulfed the entire world began in 1931. Without warning, the Japanese army rolled across the frontiers of Manchuria (see map, page 816). China, large but helpless, could do little to defend its great northern province. Within a few months, the Japanese had torn the province away from the Chinese. A Japanese program to sweep

▲ Remind students that Americans at this time were grappling with the distressing effects of the depression. An editorial in the Philadelphia Record declared, "The American people don't give a hoot in a rain barrel who controls North China." Ask students whether such an attitude would be possible today?

773

Call students' attention to the contrast in colors between the lower and upper portions of
the Washington Monument. The contrasting colors mark the resumption of construction
after almost 30 years.

AMERICANA The Washington Monument

One of the nation's most treasured memorials rises 555 feet (169 meters) above the Mall in Washington, D.C. Built in honor of the first President of the United States, the Washington Monument is the tallest structure in the nation's capital. At the time of its dedication in 1885, it was also the tallest building in the world.

Construction was begun in 1848 with private funds raised by the Washington National Monument Society. Work on the memorial was interrupted during the Civil War and reconstruction, but resumed at government expense in August 1880. The monument was completed in December, 1884.

The monument, which weighs 80,000 tons, is built of masonry covered with white Maryland marble. Its interior is hollow, except for a circular 898-step stairwell and an elevator shaft. The inner walls are inlaid with 189 memorial stones donated by individuals, cities, states, and other nations. Today, the monument is maintained by the National Park Service.

"foreign" influence out of the Far East and to build an Asia for Asians had begun.

Japan's aggression violated the Covenant of the League of Nations. It was an outright challenge to the Open Door Policy of the United States. Japan was bluntly reminded of these facts by Secretary of State Henry L. Stimson. In a formal note issued in 1932, Stimson protested Japan's flagrant violation of the Nine-Power Treaty and of the Kellogg-Briand Pact, both of which Japan had signed. President Hoover and Congress, however, were unwilling to use force or even economic sanctions to enforce the Stimson declaration.

Meanwhile, the League of Nations met to consider what action, if any, should be taken. President Hoover sent an American representative to this meeting. The League sent a commission to Manchuria to investigate, but beyond a statement of its agreement with Stimson's declaration, the League failed to act. Confident that the nations of the world would not act together to preserve peace, Japan withdrew from the League of Nations. It then made preparations to invade and conquer China and Southeast Asia.

The structure of peace had begun to crumble. As you will see, Fascist Italy and, after 1933, the rising Nazi regime in Germany realized that they too could safely embark upon programs of aggression. The world powers might have reinforced the crumbling structure of world peace by collective action, but they were unwilling and unable to act together.

SECTION REVIEW
For answers to questions, see Answer Key, pp.A107-08.
Identify: World Court, armaments race, Charles Evans Hughes, naval holiday, Frank B. Kellogg, Henry L. Stimson
See underscored items, text pp. 772 - 74.

1. **Organizing Ideas: (a)** What conditions led to the Washington Naval Conference of 1921–22? **(b)** What were the major provisions of the Five-Power Treaty? **(c)** What was the reason for the Four-Power Pact?

2. **Interpreting Ideas:** Why was the Nine-Power Treaty significant for **(a)** China, **(b)** the United States, and **(c)** Japan?

3. **Synthesizing Ideas:** Why was the Kellogg-Briand Pact of 1928 little more than a statement of intentions?

4. **Analyzing Ideas: (a)** How did the United States react to the Japanese invasion of Manchuria? **(b)** What was the reaction of the League of Nations? Why?

774

DEVELOPING HISTORY STUDY SKILLS

Relating Geography and History   Reading a Special Purpose Map

Historians use many different types of special purpose maps. A look at page xxvii of the Table of Contents, for example, shows that there are 7 special purpose maps in the Reference Section of this textbook. Other special purpose maps are included throughout the textbook.

A special purpose map relates data to the geographic setting shown on the map. You have already reviewed the basic steps in reading a map (Chapter 7, pages 164–65). You have also been introduced to two types of special purpose maps: a historical map (Chapter 15, pages 362–63) and an economic map (Chapter 27, page 624).

Applying the Skill

Study the map of the League of Nations below. The map's title is "The League of Nations." The map shows the original members of the League; nations admitted as members after January 10, 1920; nations that were not members of the League; and the dates that certain nations withdrew from the League.

Practicing the Skill

Study again the map below. Then on a separate sheet of paper, answer these questions.
1. Which nations withdrew from the League of Nations?
2. **(a)** Which nation was expelled from the League? **(b)** In what year was it expelled?
3. Which two African nations were admitted to the League after January 10, 1920?
4. Which Latin American nations remained in the League until the outbreak of World War II?

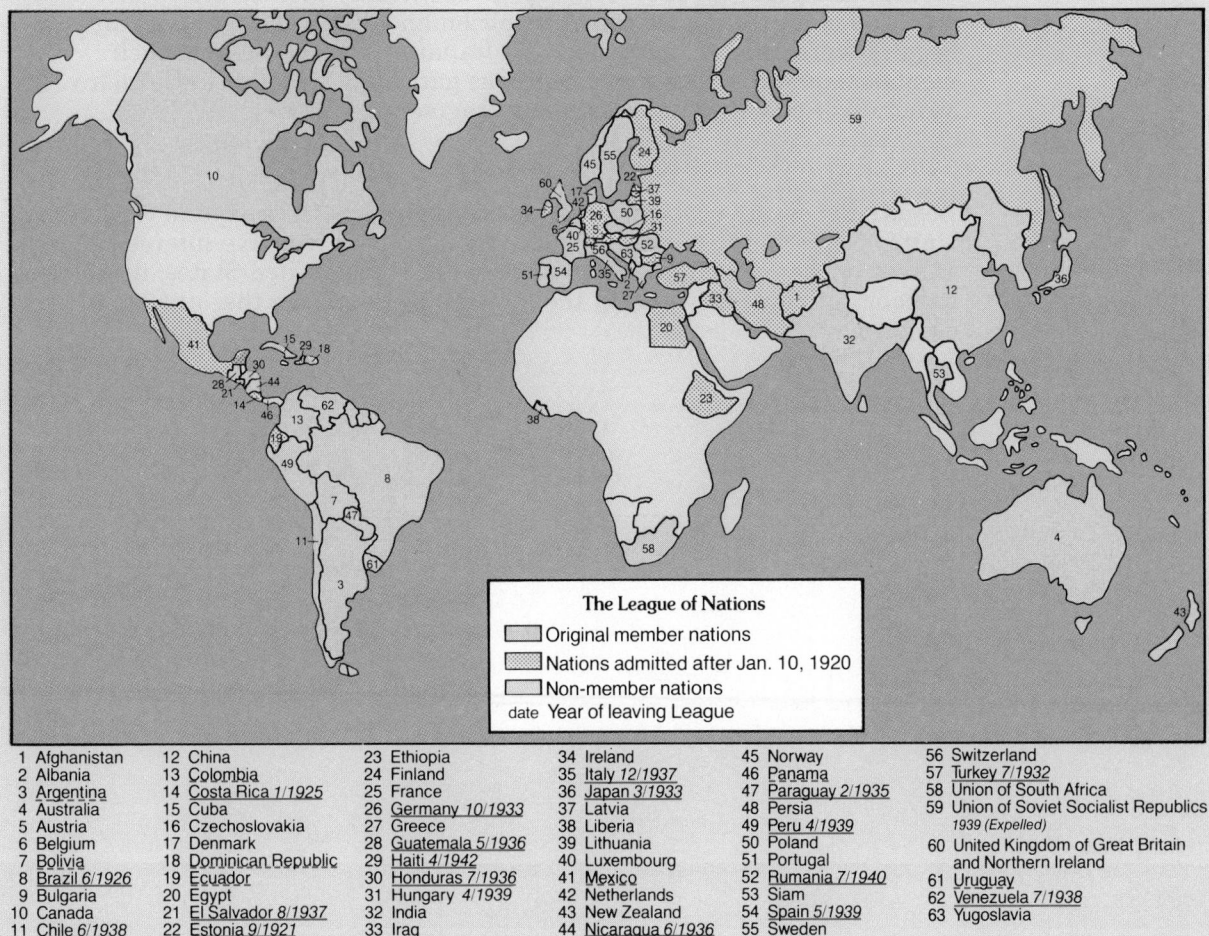

The League of Nations

- Original member nations
- Nations admitted after Jan. 10, 1920
- Non-member nations
- date Year of leaving League

1 Afghanistan	12 China	23 Ethiopia
2 Albania	13 Colombia	24 Finland
3 Argentina	14 Costa Rica 1/1925	25 France
4 Australia	15 Cuba	26 Germany 10/1933
5 Austria	16 Czechoslovakia	27 Greece
6 Belgium	17 Denmark	28 Guatemala 5/1936
7 Bolivia	18 Dominican Republic	29 Haiti 4/1942
8 Brazil 6/1926	19 Ecuador	30 Honduras 7/1936
9 Bulgaria	20 Egypt	31 Hungary 4/1939
10 Canada	21 El Salvador 8/1937	32 India
11 Chile 6/1938	22 Estonia 9/1921	33 Iraq

34 Ireland	45 Norway	56 Switzerland
35 Italy 12/1937	46 Panama	57 Turkey 7/1932
36 Japan 3/1933	47 Paraguay 2/1935	58 Union of South Africa
37 Latvia	48 Persia	59 Union of Soviet Socialist Republics
38 Liberia	49 Peru 4/1939	1939 (Expelled)
39 Lithuania	50 Poland	60 United Kingdom of Great Britain
40 Luxembourg	51 Portugal	and Northern Ireland
41 Mexico	52 Rumania 7/1940	61 Uruguay
42 Netherlands	53 Siam	62 Venezuela 7/1938
43 New Zealand	54 Spain 5/1939	63 Yugoslavia
44 Nicaragua 6/1936	55 Sweden	

(1. (a) See solid-line underscore.   (b) They are all Latin American nations.   2. (a) Union of Soviet Socialist Republics   (b) 1939   3. Egypt, Ethiopia   4. See broken-line underscore.)

34 SUMMARY

During the 1920's the American people as a whole rejected President Wilson's call to assume world leadership. To be sure, during the immediate postwar years, the United States did help Europe by supplying food, clothing, medical supplies, and huge loans of money. During the 1920's the United States worked closely with the League of Nations in efforts to reduce international friction. The United States called for a naval holiday in an effort to slow the arms race. It negotiated several treaties in an effort to prevent aggression in the Pacific. Finally, the nation called for a pact to outlaw war. The United States also took steps to establish better relations with Latin America. Nevertheless, the United States' refusal to join the League of Nations, its harsher immigration policies, and its higher tariff barriers did not win friends for America.

By 1932 the faith and goodwill that had been so widespread throughout the world in 1918 were rapidly evaporating. In place of the prosperity of the 1920's, the world was faced with a deepening economic depression. In place of faith and goodwill, the world was confronted by intense international rivalry and a growing feeling of suspicion and distrust. Japan had already begun its program of aggression, the Italians were threatening their neighbors, and the Nazi movement was gathering strength in Germany. The structure of peace was breaking into fragments.

CONNECTING CHAPTER IDEAS

Despite the severe economic depression Americans were experiencing, the United States was beginning to take an increasingly active interest in world affairs. In the next chapter you will read how the United States abandoned its policy of neutrality during the late 1930's to become the "arsenal of democracy."

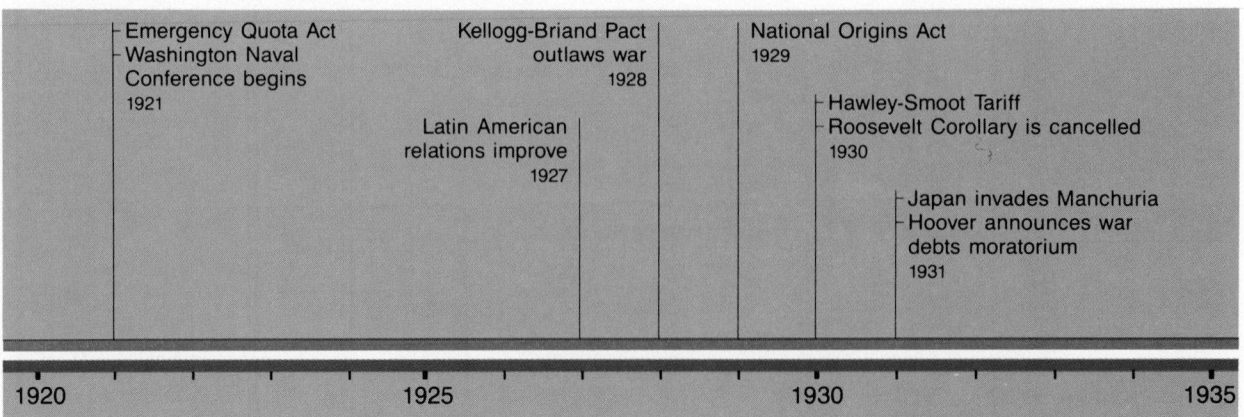

| Emergency Quota Act
Washington Naval
Conference begins
1921 | Kellogg-Briand Pact
outlaws war
1928

Latin American
relations improve
1927 | National Origins Act
1929

Hawley-Smoot Tariff
Roosevelt Corollary is cancelled
1930

Japan invades Manchuria
Hoover announces war
debts moratorium
1931 |

| 1920 | 1925 | 1930 | 1935 |

CHAPTER
34 REVIEW

Reviewing Important Terms

Decide whether each sentence is true or false. If the sentence is false, replace the underlined term with the word or phrase that will make it true.

1. Most of Germany's war damages, or morato-riums were never paid.
2. In 1924 the change in the quota system caused resentment among eastern and southern Euro-peans because it discriminated against them.
3. The 10 year naval holiday was an attempt to slow the armaments race.
4. In 1931 when all the nations, except Finland refused to pay their war debts, President Hoover declared a reparation, or temporary halt on the repayment of war debts.
5. In 1921 and 1922 leaders at the Washington Con-ference attempted to stop the armaments race, or the intense competition among countries to build up strength in military weapons.

Practicing Critical Thinking Skills

1. **Analyzing Ideas.** During the decade after World War I, the United States shut its doors to many immigrants and placed high tariffs on for-eign goods. How are these two actions related?
2. **Interpreting Ideas.** The Kellogg-Briand Pact did not survive the challenges posed by the Jap-anese invasion of Manchuria. Why?
3. **Summarizing Viewpoints.** How would you characterize American attitudes toward (a) Eu-rope, (b) Latin America, and (c) Asia during the 1920's? How do you account for those attitudes?
4. **Evaluating Ideas.** In the period just studied, world peace was crumbling in part because the world powers could not act collectively to coun-teract aggression. (a) What attempts were made to guarantee peace? (b) What further steps could have been taken to ensure world peace?
5. **Relating Past to Present.** (a) Compare United States relations with the Latin American na-tions in the 1920's and today. (b) Could you call the current United States policy a "Good Neigh-bor Policy?" Why or why not?

Developing History Study Skills

1. **Reading Special Purpose Maps.** Study the map, United States Imports and Exports on text

page 1019. Then answer the following questions. (a) What percentage of the United States' im-ports came from Latin America? exports? (b) How many billions of dollars in trade did the United States spend in imports from Western Europe? (c) Based on the information on this map and in the chapter, how would international wars affect the economy of the United States?

2. **Identifying Fact and Opinion.** Read the fol-lowing excerpt about immigration quotas. After you have read the excerpt, identify statements of fact and statements of opinion. Explain the reasons for your choices. Then answer the ques-tions below.

> *One steamship from Constantinople arrived at Ellis Island just before midnight on August 31. She brought nearly 700 steerage passen-gers, out of which only about 125 were allowed to land because the August quota had been exhausted. These poor people, who, through no fault of their own, had arrived four minutes only before midnight brought in the September quota. All appeals were in vain. Henry H. Curran, the Commissioner of Immigration, said he could do nothing but abide by the ruling. . . .*

(a) Why were the quotas so strictly adhered to?
(b) What would you do to remedy the situation described in the excerpt above?

Relating Geography and History

Many factors influence the movement of people from one land to another. To examine United States im-migration patterns, answer the following questions.

1. Using the graph on immigration on page 1000, (a) compare immigration to the United States from 1901–10 to immigration from 1921–30. (b) How do you explain this change? (c) What effect did this have on the makeup of the United States? (d) What other effects might this change have had on United States history? (Consider the contributions that immigrants have made to the United States throughout its history.)
2. Using the chart on immigration on text page 768, answer the following questions. (a) What percentage of immigrants came to the United States from Great Britain? (b) From what three countries did the smallest percentage of immi-grants come?

777

See Chapter Overview in TMRG, p.TM191.
See Chapter Objectives in TMRG, p.TM191.
See Introducing the Chapter in TMRG, p.TM191.

CHAPTER 35

From Isolationism to War

(1932–1941)

The heat
of battle

In 1933, when Franklin Delano Roosevelt was inaugurated as President for the first time, it was clear that few Presidents had entered office under such unfavorable circumstances.

The Great Depression, the most severe economic collapse the country had ever experienced, was becoming worse week by week, not only in the United States but throughout the world.

Equally disturbing was the emergence of warlike dictatorships in Japan, Italy, Germany, and Russia. Americans first became deeply troubled in 1931 as the Japanese war machine seized the province of Manchuria from the defenseless Chinese.

At that time, however, there was no way for Roosevelt or anyone else to foresee the deeper trouble that was to come. In 1933 Adolf Hitler rose from obscurity to win control of Germany. No one could foresee that by 1936 a powerful German army would move into the Rhineland, violating the Versailles Treaty. Nor could anyone then know that by 1940 Hitler's Nazis, Mussolini's Fascists, and the Japanese warlords would have plunged the world into the most devastating conflict in its entire history.

During the 1930's the United States moved away from isolationism to take an increasingly active interest in foreign affairs. It recognized the Soviet Union, opening diplomatic relations in 1933. It made provisions to grant independence to the Filipinos in 1946. It expanded the Good Neighbor Policy and renounced the use of armed intervention in inter-American affairs. Although the United States tried to remain neutral in a war-torn world, by the end of 1941 the American people found themselves playing a leading role in the struggle against the dictatorships that had arisen.

═══ READING FOCUS ═══

As you read about the events leading to World War II, look for the details that support each of the following statements.

1. The United States broadens its relations with other countries.
2. Americans try to follow a policy of isolationism.
3. The nation finds isolationism difficult to maintain.
4. The United States becomes involved in World War II.

1 The United States broadens its relations with other countries

See Teaching Suggestions in TMRG, pp.TM191-92.

American foreign policy in the 1930's was influenced by two basic considerations: (1) the Great Depression at home and abroad and (2) the rise of underlined dictatorships in Europe and Asia.

The Soviet Union. In 1933 the United States recognized the Soviet Union. Those favoring this move argued that it was realistic to recognize a regime that had been in power for 16 years. They pointed out that increased trade between the two countries would be helpful to the United States. Finally, they insisted that the two countries shared a concern about the threat of Japanese aggression.

In reply to these arguments, the opponents of recognition pointed out that the Communists made no secret of their goal of world conquest. This objection was met when the Soviet Union promised to stop all propaganda activities in the United States. As it turned out, this promise was not kept. Moreover, recognition of the Soviet Union did not greatly increase trade between the two countries.

Toward Philippine independence. In the Jones Act of 1916, as you may recall, the United States promised to give the Filipinos their independence. During the 1920's this action was postponed on the ground that the Filipinos were not yet ready for independence. In 1933, however, late in Hoover's administration, Congress passed an independence act for the Philippines over the President's veto.

The Philippine legislature rejected this measure. Many Filipinos feared that one of the act's provisions, giving the United States the right to keep military and naval bases, would enable Americans to continue their control in the Philippines anyway. Other Filipinos argued that once they were free, the United States would then raise its tariff barriers against Philippine products.

Trying to overcome these fears, Congress in 1934 passed the Tydings-McDuffie Act. This measure was more acceptable to the Filipinos. It provided for the establishment of a Philippine Commonwealth and outlined a gradual

Class activity: The interval between the two world wars has sometimes been called the "twenty years' truce." Some scholars point out that historians may someday consider the two wars as one war. Have students write position papers that explore why the 1919 peace was followed by a second great war.

779

ATLANTIC OCEAN

San Juan ★

PUERTO RICO

Ponce •

0   30
Kilometers

0   20
Statute Miles

CARIBBEAN SEA

Among all the peoples of Latin America, Puerto Ricans have most directly experienced the positive and negative aspects of United States foreign policy. Today the Commonwealth of Puerto Rico, a politically autonomous entity, enjoys a voluntary association with the United States. But the relationship has not been an easy one.

Spain ceded Puerto Rico — an island in the West Indies — to the United States after the Spanish-American War. The "unincorporated territory" of Puerto Rico became a United States colony, ruled by Congress through a Presidentially appointed governor.

Puerto Ricans today are citizens of the United States, self-governing in their internal affairs under the terms of a constitution ratified by popular vote in 1952. But they cannot vote for President, and their elected commissioner in Congress has no vote. Puerto Ricans are subject to federal laws and to United States military service but are exempt from federal income taxes.

10-year tariff increase on Philippine goods imported into the United States. This would give the Filipinos an opportunity to adjust to an independent economy.

Ten years after the establishment of a commonwealth the Philippines were to become entirely independent. The United States would retain its naval bases in the area, however.

The Good Neighbor Policy. During the 1930's the United States also redoubled earlier efforts to improve relations with Latin America. The policy started by Coolidge and Hoover was expanded by Roosevelt.

Self-interest as well as a genuine desire for friendship motivated the Good Neighbor Policy. During the 1920's many Americans began to realize that the United States could not afford to continue antagonizing its Latin American neighbors. When the Great Depression came, this realization hardened into firm conviction. The United States needed Latin-American trade. The rise of dictatorships in both Europe and Asia further strengthened the conviction among Americans that the United States had to establish friendlier relations with Latin America and other nations around ▲ the world.

SOURCES

PROCLAMATION
OF PHILIPPINE
INDEPENDENCE
(1946)

Whereas it had been the repeated declaration of the . . . government of the United States of America that full independence would be granted the Philippines as soon as the people of the Philippines were prepared to assume this obligation; and

Whereas the people of the Philippines have clearly demonstrated their capacity for self-government; . . .

Now, therefore, I, Harry S Truman, . . . do hereby recognize the independence of the Philippines as a separate and self-governing nation. . . .

▲ Partly as a result of this cooperation, the United States would later be able to rely on Latin American resources during World War II, and Brazil would become actively involved in the Alliance. Argentina would eventually declare war on Germany and Japan toward the war's end.

In 1933 President Roosevelt declared, "In the field of foreign policy, I would dedicate this nation to the policy of the good neighbor—the neighbor who resolutely respects himself and, because he does so, respects the rights of others." Later that year, in a conference held in Montevideo, Uruguay, the United States joined the other American countries in a pledge not to interfere in the affairs of their neighbors. "No state," the pledge declared, "has the right to intervene in the internal or external affairs of another state."

The Montevideo Pact marked a turning point in United States relations with Latin America. As President Roosevelt put it, "The definite policy of the United States from now on is one opposed to armed intervention."

The policy in action. Nor were these mere words. In 1934 the United States canceled the Platt Amendment, under which it had claimed the right to intervene in Cuban affairs. That same year the remainder of American troops were finally withdrawn from Haiti. In 1936 the United States gave up its right to intervene in Panama's affairs. Also the United States gradually ended its control over the customhouses of the Dominican Republic—a control exercised since 1905.

The Good Neighbor Policy was put to a severe test in 1938. In that year President Lázaro Cárdenas (LAH·sah·roh KAHR·day·nahs) of Mexico confiscated the properties of all foreign oil companies. Foreign investors, including Americans, protested and demanded action from their governments. President Roosevelt refused to intervene on behalf of American investors. Instead, he urged the American oil companies to negotiate directly with Mexico. As a result of these negotiations, the Mexican government agreed to pay a small part of what the American companies had claimed.

The Good Neighbor Policy inspired this song, set to a Latin American beat. The writers wanted to promote a spirit of friendliness throughout the nations of the Americas.

International trade agreements. The United States also tried to promote an international revival of trade. The Roosevelt administration offered to negotiate with any country special trade agreements that would provide for lowering tariffs.

In the Trade Agreements Act of 1934, Congress authorized the President to raise or lower existing tariffs by as much as 50 percent without Senate approval. As a result, the Roosevelt administration could bargain, or reciprocate, with other countries. A nation that lowered its tariffs on United States goods would, in turn, receive more favorable tariffs on the goods that it sent to the United States. By 1940 Secretary of State Cordell Hull had signed 22 such **reciprocal trade agreements.**

Equally important was the provision of the Trade Agreements Act known as the **most-favored-nation clause.** This clause offered any country the opportunity to be treated as well as the nation seemingly "most favored" in any tariff agreement. This act therefore helped to end tariff discriminations against the United States. The Trade Agreements Act also stimulated American business by improving trade relations with other nations.

New tariff agreements worked out with Canada and Great Britain under the Trade Agreements Act were especially important. They led to a great increase of trade between these countries and the United States. They also provided an economic foundation for the political cooperation that became so important in World War II.

SECTION REVIEW
See underscored items, text pp. 779 - 82.

Identify: dictatorship, Good Neighbor Policy, Montevideo Pact, Lázaro Cárdenas, Cordell Hull, reciprocal trade agreements, most-favored-nation clause

For answers to questions, see Answer Key, pp.A108-09.
1. **Comparing Ideas:** What were the arguments for and against recognition of the Soviet Union in 1933?
2. **Summarizing Ideas: (a)** What conditions led to the passage of the Tydings-McDuffie Act? **(b)** What was the major provision of the act?
3. **Organizing Ideas: (a)** What were the conditions that prompted the Good Neighbor Policy? **(b)** Give examples of the policy in action.

2 Americans try to follow a policy of isolationism

See Teaching Suggestions in TMRG, pp.192-93.
In the early 1930's the militaristic leaders of Japan, Italy, and Germany started building up their armies and weapons arsenals in Asia and Europe. Their leaders seemed determined to prepare for **aggression.**

The rise of dictatorships. As the years passed, the Roosevelt administration had to deal with a growing number of **totalitarian°** rulers. In 1922 Benito Mussolini seized power in Italy as the leader of **fascism.** Fascism was a system of government concentrating all political, economic, and cultural power in the state. It was dedicated to aggressive expansionism. Mussolini, a swaggering, domineering ruler, dreamed of controlling the Mediterranean and the Middle East.

The Japanese warlords who seized control of Japan in the late 1920's also had dreams of expansion and military glory. Their seizure of Manchuria in 1931 was only one step in a program designed to win complete control of East Asia and the Pacific.

Adolf Hitler, the Austrian-born, Jew-hating fanatic who climbed to power in Germany in 1933, was a ruthless dictator who also longed for conquest. Josef Stalin, who in the 1920's succeeded V. I. Lenin as the leader of the Soviet Union, openly intended to spread communism throughout the entire world.

There were other dictators, including General Francisco Franco, who came to power in Spain in 1939 after a bloody civil war. However, the **dictatorships** of Japan, Italy, and Germany proved to be the most aggressive.

Hitler, Mussolini, and the Japanese warlords expressed their contempt for democracy. It was, in Mussolini's words, "a rotting corpse" that had to be replaced by "efficient" government and a "superior" way of life.

All of the dictatorships scorned the democratic rights of free speech and a free press. In totalitarian systems individuals existed to serve the state and had no rights except those that the state chose to give them.

All of the dictatorships glorified force. Compelling the people to work for "bullets rather than butter," they converted their industries to war production. Their major efforts were devoted to building powerful military machines.

Mounting tension. By the mid-1930's the dictators were ready to move. In 1935 Mussolini's blackshirted Fascists attacked the African nation of Ethiopia. In their attack they used bombers and poison gas against a practically defenseless people.

°**totalitarian:** This term refers to a dictatorship that exercises total control over a nation and suppresses individual freedom.

▲ Discussion topic: Have students consider the elements that made totalitarianism possible. (i.e. mass control facilitated by tightly linked transportation and communication systems; desparate economic conditions created by World War I settlements)

In 1934 and 1935, the Japanese broke the pledges made at the Washington Naval Conferences of 1921–22 and in later treaties. They began a rapid build-up of their navy.

Then in March 1936, German troops moved into the Rhineland (see map, page 786), clearly violating the Treaty of Versailles. In July civil war broke out in Spain. In October Germany and Italy signed a military alliance and began to call themselves the **Axis° Powers**. In November 1936 Germany, Italy, and Japan joined in an Anti-Comintern† Pact, thus hiding their aggressive designs under the pretense of resisting communism.

On July 7, 1937, Japanese and Chinese troops clashed on the Chinese-Manchurian border. This border incident developed into a full-scale war. In time, historians referred to it as the start of World War II in East Asia.

Roots of isolationism. Despite the growing threat to peace, most Americans remained determined to practice **isolationism**. They believed that the United States could and should isolate itself from other people's wars. Why did Americans feel this way?

In the first place, most Americans were disillusioned about the results of World War I. The war had not brought peace, disarmament, and democracy across the earth. Instead, it had been followed by constant quarreling among the European powers, by tariff wars, and by failures to reduce armaments.

Most important, the League of Nations had not become an effective instrument for peace. American isolationists refused to believe that the League might have been more successful had the United States joined. They argued that the League's weakness was the best possible evidence that the United States had been wise *not* to join. This widespread disillusionment became increasingly intense when the League failed to check the aggressions of Italy, Germany, and Japan in 1935–37.

American disillusionment about the war grew more intense in 1934 when the Senate started to investigate war profits. Figures re-

"Worker," this German poster of 1932 urges, "Elect the Front-line Soldier, Hitler!" Why did Hitler and the Nazi Party appeal to the German people?
(They promised to restore German pride.)

leased by the Senate suggested that many American bankers and munitions makers had reaped rich profits from World War I. Many people concluded that America's loans to the Allies were largely responsible for drawing the nation into war. This conclusion has since been rejected by most historians. In the 1930's, however, it fed the spirit of disillusionment.

Disillusionment about World War I was not the only basis for American isolationism. Most Americans believed that the Atlantic and Pacific oceans would protect the United States from attack even if the dictators succeeded in crushing all opposition in Europe and Asia. Many also argued that the improved relations with Latin America gave the nation another safeguard against attack.

°**Axis:** a name made up by Mussolini, who said that the line from Rome to Berlin formed the "axis" on which the world would turn thereafter. Eventually Japan was included among the Axis Powers. The nations who fought the Axis Powers were known as the Allies.

†**Comintern:** an international organization, dominated by the Russian Communist Party, whose aim was to spread communism throughout the world.

▲ Note: Answers to questions in captions appear in parentheses, as shown here. Bullets separate answers to individual questions when a caption contains more than one question.

783

Most Americans disapproved of acts of aggression by the Axis Powers. Even so, many were firm isolationists who supported a policy of neutrality for the United States, as this poster shows.

The isolationists were strengthened by two other groups. Many Americans believed that the government's first responsibility was to combat the depression. Many others, deeply convinced **pacifists,** believed that all wars were unjustifiable and that the United States had to avoid being drawn into another conflict. Pacifism was strong, especially among young people, in both the United States and Great Britain during the 1930's.

Isolationism in practice.   In 1934, American isolationists won a victory when Congress passed the Johnson Debt Default Act. This act forbade the American government and private citizens to lend money to any country that had **defaulted,** or failed to repay, its war debts.

The Johnson Debt Default Act underscored Americans' annoyance at the failure of all European nations except Finland to repay their war debts. Americans were especially annoyed because some of the defaulting nations were pouring money into weapons. Americans did not intend to provide them any more money for weapons or to risk becoming involved in another war because of entangling investments.

Between 1935 and 1937, the isolationists won other victories in a series of neutrality acts passed by Congress. These acts, which reflected widespread public sentiment against war, were prompted by Mussolini's attack upon Ethiopia, by the civil war in Spain, and by the aggressive actions of Germany and Japan.

In general, the neutrality laws did three things. (1) They prohibited the shipment of munitions to **belligerents,** or warring nations. (2) They authorized the President to list commodities other than munitions that could be sold to belligerents only on a "cash-and-carry" basis. (3) They made it unlawful for Americans to travel on the vessels of belligerent nations.

The neutrality laws were intended to keep Americans out of war and to prevent the involvement of American citizens in such disasters as the sinking of the *Lusitania* in 1915. With these laws the United States abandoned its long-established doctrine of freedom of the seas and withdrew the traditional rights of citizens to travel where and how they wished.

Dissatisfaction with neutrality.   Isolationism by no means represented the thinking of all Americans. Many Americans were dismayed by totalitarian governments and their abandonment of individual rights that earlier generations had fought so hard to establish.

Still other Americans regretted that the neutrality laws made it difficult for the United States to help the victims of aggression. In their view, if the United States allowed aggressors to crush weaker neighbors, the United States might one day find itself surrounded by powerful enemies.

Finally, many citizens argued that the United States had a moral duty to aid the victims of unprovoked aggression. This attitude cut across party lines. There were internationalists as well as isolationists in both the Democratic and Republican parties.

Changes in policy.   Between 1933 and 1937, President Roosevelt did not take a firm stand on America's responsibility in a troubled world. At times he sided with the isolationists, at other times with the internationalists.

By 1937, however, Roosevelt had become more deeply impressed with the seriousness of the world situation. He felt that the United States should take a positive stand against aggression. In a speech on October 5, 1937, the President said, "If we are to have a world in which we can breathe freely and live in amity without fear—the peace-loving nations must make a concerted effort to uphold laws and principles on which alone peace can rest secure. . . .

"When an epidemic of physical disease starts to spread, the community approves and joins in a quarantine of the patients in order to protect the health of the community against the spread of the disease."

Continuing isolationism. In the "quarantine" speech, Roosevelt expressed views that most Americans were not yet ready to accept. Proof of this came with the _Panay_ incident. On December 12, 1937, Japanese planes bombed and strafed a United States gunboat, the _Panay_, and three American oil tankers on the Yangtze River in China. Several Americans were killed and many were wounded in the incident.

Secretary of State Hull immediately sent a sharp note to the Japanese government. He demanded full apologies, compensation, and a promise that no such incident would recur. The Japanese agreed to all of Hull's demands.

During this incident, the American public revealed its strong feelings. A public opinion poll at the time showed that 54 percent of Americans felt that the United States should withdraw from China.

By the end of 1937, the tide of aggression was rising rapidly in Asia as well as in Europe. Many Americans, including President Roosevelt, were becoming increasingly alarmed. Nevertheless, most Americans believed that the United States could remain isolated.

SECTION REVIEW
See underscored items, text pp. 782 - 85.
Identify: totalitarian, Benito Mussolini, Adolf Hitler, Josef Stalin, Francisco Franco, Axis Powers, isolationism, pacifists, belligerents, _Panay_ incident
For answers to questions, see Answer Key, p.A109.
1. **Comparing Ideas:** What were the philosophies of the totalitarian dictators in terms of (a) the role of the individual and the role of government and (b) the role of their nation in the world?
2. **Synthesizing Ideas:** What were the roots of the widespread isolationism of the 1920's and early 1930's?
3. **Interpreting Ideas:** (a) What were the neutrality acts of 1935–37? (b) Why were they passed? (c) Why were they opposed by some Americans?
4. **Organizing Ideas:** What were the major events from 1935 to 1937 that threatened peace?

3 The nation finds isolationism difficult to maintain

See Teaching Suggestions in TMRG, p.TM193.
By 1938 the dictators of the Axis Powers were becoming more ruthless. During 1938 and 1939, headlines of new aggressions crowded the front pages of America's newspapers.

The spread of warfare. In 1938, Japanese forces were attacking along the length of the Chinese coast and pushing inland up the river valleys. Meanwhile, in Europe the Spanish Civil War was bringing misery to hundreds of thousands of other people.

Spain had become an international battleground. Hitler and Mussolini were helping Franco. This provided them the opportunity to test their latest military equipment and to give picked "volunteers" actual battle experience. Soviet "volunteers" were fighting against Franco and his Nazi and Fascist allies. Among Franco's foes in the "International Brigade" were volunteers from many other countries, including the United States.

The United States reacted to this threat to world peace by joining France and Great Britain in a program of nonintervention. With President Roosevelt's approval, Congress in January 1937 barred all shipments of war materials to either side in the civil war in Spain.

New aggressions—and Munich. Another crisis developed when, on March 11, 1938, Hitler's powerful army moved into Austria (see map, page 786). Two days later Hitler announced the union of Austria and Germany.

With Austria under his control, Hitler turned greedy eyes toward western Czechoslovakia. This area, known as the Sudetenland (soo·DAY·tuhn·land), contained a large proportion of German-speaking people. Hitler demanded that Czechoslovakia turn over the region to Germany. Czechoslovakia, with one of the best-trained armies in Europe and with the sympathy of other democratic nations overwhelmingly on its side, refused to bow to Hitler's demands.

Tension was at the breaking point when Hitler and Mussolini met with the prime ministers of Great Britain and France at Munich.

Aggressions Leading to World War II

■ Axis Powers
■ Axis-controlled lands before September 1, 1939

GERMAN INVASION OF POLAND
STARTS WAR SEPT. 1, 1939

NORWAY
SWEDEN
FINLAND
ESTONIA
LATVIA
LITHUANIA
Moscow
DENMARK
BALTIC SEA
SOVIET UNION
NORTH SEA
EIRE
GREAT BRITAIN
London
NETHERLANDS
Berlin
GERMANY
Warsaw
POLAND
BELGIUM
LUX.
RHINELAND
1936
1938
1939
1938
CZECHOSLOVAKIA
ATLANTIC
OCEAN
Paris
Munich
AUSTRIA
HUNGARY
RUMANIA
FRANCE
SWITZERLAND
BLACK SEA
PORTUGAL
CIVIL WAR 1936-1939
SPAIN
ITALY
Rome
YUGOSLAVIA
BULGARIA
TURKEY
1939
ALBANIA
GREECE
TO ETHIOPIA 1935
MEDITERRANEAN SEA

0   500
Scale of miles
0   500
Scale of kilometers

There on September 30, 1938, the four leaders signed a pact that gave Hitler almost all he demanded. The Czechs, forsaken by their friends, had no choice but to turn over most of the disputed region to Germany.

Neville Chamberlain, Prime Minister of Great Britain, returned to England blindly confident. He expressed the certainty that the Munich agreement had ended the threat of aggression in Europe. "I believe," he said, "it is peace for our time."

Other leaders did not share Chamberlain's confidence. They believed that his policy of ▲ **appeasement** would only lead Hitler to make further demands. Throughout Europe nations began to speed up rearamament.

Growing American concern. President Roosevelt, as early as January 28, in a special message to Congress, coupled a promise to work for peace with a warning that it was time for the United States to build up its defenses. Congress increased appropriations for the armed forces and, in May, authorized more than $1 billion for a "two-ocean navy."

Roosevelt privately referred to the aggressions of Japan, Italy, and Germany as "armed banditry." Officially, however, the President sent personal notes to foreign rulers, including Hitler and Mussolini, urging them to settle their differences by negotiation and international cooperation. Since the United States was openly committed to a hands-off, isolationist policy, no one paid much attention to the President's words of caution.

Defending the Western Hemisphere. As the Czech crisis worsened, Roosevelt did make one commitment. In August 1938, in a speech to Canadians, he extended the protection of the Monroe Doctrine to Canada. He promised that "the people of the United States will not stand idly by if domination of Canadian soil is threatened by any other Empire."

Roosevelt's promise to Canada was only one of several steps the United States was taking to develop a defense policy for the nations of North and South America. Earlier, at the Buenos Aires Conference of 1936, the United States and the 20 other members of the Pan-American Union had agreed to regard a threat to any American country as a threat to the security of all. The 21 members also agreed to consult together if such a threat developed.

In December 1938, with the clouds of war rapidly gathering, the Pan-American Union met again in Lima, Peru. The delegates repeated their pledge to oppose foreign intervention in the Western Hemisphere.

Roosevelt's promise to Canada and the Declaration of Lima demonstrated that the Monroe Doctrine had become a **multilateral**, or many-sided, policy rather than a **unilateral**, or one-sided policy. By 1938 it was clear, as Roosevelt said, that "national defense has now become a problem of continental defense."

New crises lead to World War II. On January 4, 1939, in his annual message to Congress, President Roosevelt warned that the world situation had become extremely grave. He urged Congress to reconsider the neutrality legislation adopted during 1935–37 and to increase appropriations for the armed services.

The President's worst fears were soon confirmed. On March 15, 1939, Hitler's armies moved into the rest of Czechoslovakia. On April 7, Mussolini's troops invaded Albania (see map, page 786).

Awakening at long last to their common peril, Great Britain and France decided to stand firm. They announced that an attack upon Poland would mean war.

Great Britain and France also tried to get the Soviet Union to join with them in resisting, by force if necessary, any further aggression by either Hitler or Mussolini. It was with shock, therefore, that the democratic nations learned on August 23, 1939, that the Soviet Union had just signed a **nonaggression pact** with its warring neighbor, Germany.

Seemingly freed by the Soviet pact from the danger of a two-front war, Hitler struck swiftly. On September 1, without warning, German bombers and powerful armored divisions crossed the border into Poland (see map page 786). On September 3, 1939, Great Britain and France declared war on Germany.

While Great Britain and France were busy mobilizing their armies, Soviet troops invaded Poland from the east. By the end of September, all organized Polish resistance had been crushed, and Germany and the Soviet Union divided Poland between them.

Text continues on page 789.

SOURCES

FRANKLIN D. ROOSEVELT'S "FOUR FREEDOMS" SPEECH (1941)

In the future days, which we seek to make secure, we look forward to a world founded upon four essential human freedoms.

The first is freedom of speech and expression—everywhere in the world.

The second is freedom of every person to worship God in his own way—everywhere in the world.

The third is freedom from want—which, translated into world terms, means economic understanding which will secure to every nation a healthy peacetime life for its inhabitants—everywhere in the world.

The fourth is freedom from fear—which, translated into world terms, means a worldwide reduction of armaments to such a point and in such a thorough fashion that no nation will be in a position to commit an act of physical aggression against any neighbor—anywhere in the world. . . .

Throughout history people have searched for ways of bringing life-giving water to their farmlands. As early as 5000 B.C. the Egyptians cultivated land made fertile by the flood waters of the Nile. By 3000 B.C. they had developed an elaborate system of canals that diverted water from the Nile to their fields. At this same time great irrigation systems were in operation in China, India, and Southeast Asia. When the Spaniards arrived in Mexico and Peru, they found that the Aztecs and Incas were also skilled irrigation farmers.

Irrigation systems in the United States came later than it did in these other civilizations. Early settlement was in the eastern half of the nation where there was ample precipitation and water for agriculture. In the 1840's Mormon settlers built irrigation canals in the Salt Lake Valley. These were the first major irrigation projects begun in the United States.

Today approximately one out of every eleven acres, over 40 million total acres (16 million hectares), of United States cropland is irrigated. In the 11 western states, in fact, one acre out of every three acres is irrigated. And in the United States, irrigation accounts for more than 40 percent of all the water used.

The amount of water required for irrigation depends upon the crop being grown, the nature of the soil on which the crop is grown, and the rate of water evaporation. Rice, for example, requires more water than cotton. If the soil is porous or sandy, water will run through it rapidly.

Furrow irrigation (below, left) and "walking" sprinklers are common in western states.

More irrigation water is needed for porous soil than would be needed for a more densely compacted soil. Wheat grown in a hot dry area will need more water than wheat grown in a cool area because much of the water is lost to evaporation.

Approximately 80 percent of the irrigation in the United States is surface irrigation. There are two chief methods of surface irrigation: (1) flood irrigation and (2) furrow irrigation. In flood irrigation the entire surface of the soil is covered with water. On many farms, small walls of soil, called dikes or levees, divide the field into sections. Dikes help hold the water on the field, and they also allow the farmer to flood each of the sections of the field separately. Flood irrigation, to work effectively, requires a level field and ample supplies of water. In addition, the soil must be deep and it must be able to hold large quantities of water. Typical crops grown by flood irrigation in the United States are rice, wheat, and oats.

Furrows are narrow ditches that are dug across a field. The farmer plants seeds in the ridges between the furrows. As water flows down the furrows it seeps into the ridges bringing life-giving nourishment to the plants. Furrow irrigation works well with a great variety of soils and crops. In the United States, corn, cotton, and potatoes are often irrigated by furrows, since all are crops grown in rows.

Rapidly growing in importance in the United States is sprinkler irrigation. In this system, water flows through

pipes that either lie on the ground or are mounted on wheels that can travel across a field above the ground. The recent popularity of sprinkler irrigation is due largely to its cost and efficiency. Sprinkler irrigation is the least expensive form of irrigation. It works on sloping as well as level land which greatly reduces the cost of preparing the land for irrigation. Sprinkler irrigation also is much less costly to maintain. Plastic and metal piping are much cheaper than the cost of keeping a field level or keeping dikes and furrows in repair.

Irrigation has become increasingly important in the United States even in the more humid areas. It has allowed farmers to supplement rainfall exactly when crops need the moisture. Irrigation has greatly increased crop yields in all regions of the United States.

A portable broadcast sprinkler

The Soviets then demanded and won the right to establish military and naval bases in Estonia, Latvia, and Lithuania, all independent republics at the time (see map, page 786). The Soviet Union also demanded the right to establish military bases in Finland. On November 30, after Finland refused to grant Soviet demands, the U.S.S.R. attacked its small neighbor. The Soviet government claimed that its actions were necessary to protect the Russian homeland from invasion.

Thus World War II started and began to spread across Europe.

SECTION REVIEW

See underscored items, text pp. 786 - 87.
Identify: Neville Chamberlain, Munich agreement, appeasement, Declaration of Lima, multilateral, unilateral, nonaggression pact
For answers to questions, see Answer Key, p.A109.
1. **Summarizing Ideas:** How did the Spanish Civil War become an international event as well as an internal conflict?
2. **Analyzing Viewpoints:** (a) How did Neville Chamberlain view the Munich agreement? (b) Why did others have a different view?
3. **Analyzing Ideas:** (a) What actions did the United States take to prepare for the defense of North America? (b) How did these actions broaden the Monroe Doctrine?

4 The United States becomes involved in World War II

In 1939 most Americans were in favor of the Allies. They were, however, determined to stay out of war. President Roosevelt voiced a widely shared feeling in a "fireside chat" over radio on September 3. He announced, "As long as it remains in my power to prevent, there will be no blackout of peace in the United States."

Neutrality laws amended. On September 21, 1939, however, Roosevelt again urged Congress to amend the Neutrality Act of 1937. "I regret that Congress passed the Act. I regret equally that I signed the Act," he declared. Roosevelt pointed out that the existing embargo on the export of munitions actually favored Germany. If it were not for the embargo, Great Britain and France could use their control of the seas to secure from the United States the arms that they desperately needed. Adolf Hitler did not need military equipment, for he had been preparing Nazi Germany for war for many years.

▲ Roosevelt had not remained passive. He maintained diplomatic relations with the exiled governments and froze the American assets of the conquered nations so that the Germans could not use them. He also channeled funds for a top-secret atomic energy program to beat the Germans to the atomic bomb.

Many lives that might have become American biographies ended in Europe during the 1930's and 1940's when Hitler waged his war against the Jews. Hitler drew on the deeply rooted anti-Semitism, or hatred of Jews, of many Europeans. In 1933 the Nazis began a systematic program to settle the "Jewish problem" in Germany. Jews were deprived of their citizenship, forbidden to use public facilities, and excluded from almost every type of work. Thousands of Jews fled Germany: some for other European nations, some for the United States.

When World War II broke out, some 8 million Jews were trapped in Europe. In 1941 the Nazis began what they called the "final solution" — extermination of the Jews. At special camps, such as Auschwitz and Treblinka, hundreds of thousands were killed in gas chambers, cremated, or buried in mass graves. Six million Jews died in what has come to be remembered as the Holocaust. Another 6 million people — Gypsies, political prisoners, and prisoners of war — also perished in these camps.

Tattooed numbers on arms mark the survivors of the concentration camps. These survivors, however, have even deeper marks in their hearts and minds. They have struggled to recover from their horrifying experiences and to reunite with their shattered families. Many have moved to the United States, where they have started new lives. Others emigrated to the Middle East to develop what has become the nation of Israel. To all lovers of freedom and liberty, the memory of the Holocaust, however, serves as a grim warning of the great inhumanity that underlies prejudice.

After a six-week debate, Congress finally agreed on a compromise proposal. The new law abolished the arms embargo and allowed any country to buy weapons or munitions from the United States, provided that the goods were transported to that country on foreign ships. This new neutrality law, which went into effect on November 4, 1939, greatly helped the Allied nations resisting Hitler.

Declaration of Panama. While Congress debated the problem of neutrality, the delegates to the Pan-American Union issued a declaration. It warned all belligerent war vessels to stay out of a "safety zone" around the Americas roughly 300 to 1,000 miles (480 to 1,600 kilometers) wide. Germany, Great Britain, and France challenged this declaration. They claimed that no nation or group of nations had the right to close any part of the high seas to their ships. The declaration was nevertheless an important indication of cooperation among the nations of the Western Hemisphere.

The fall of France. While Hitler carried on his blitzkrieg, or "lightning war," against Poland in 1939, the French mobilized. They prepared for an attack against the Maginot (mah·zhee·NOH) Line—the chain of forts along the eastern frontier. But Hitler did not attack. People joked about the "phony war," calling it a "sitzkrieg," or sitting war.

Great Britain and France declared war on Germany after Hitler invaded Poland in 1939. Here, German soldiers fire at snipers in the Polish capital of Warsaw. Scenes like this became common all across Europe in the next five years.

On April 9, 1940, the joking ceased as Hitler demonstrated the true meaning of "blitzkrieg." In the following weeks, his powerful armored divisions, supported by fighter planes and bombers, rapidly overran Denmark, Norway, the Netherlands, Belgium, Luxembourg, and northern France (see map, page 802). On May 26 the British began a heroic evacuation of their troops from the beaches of Dunkirk, a seaport in northern France. Although the British were forced to leave much of their equipment, they succeeded in saving most of the troops. On June 10 Italy, sensing that France was doomed, declared war on France and Great Britain.

Hitler's blitzkrieg did not halt until June 22, 1940, when France signed an armistice with Germany. In London the French National Committee pledged continued resistance by the Free French under General Charles de Gaulle. The French nationalists began to rally parts of the French colonial empire against the Nazis. Meanwhile, Marshal Pétain (pay·TAN) became the leader of a German-controlled French government. Headquarters for the occupation government was at Vichy (vee·SHEE) in central France.

The Battle of Britain. With the fall of France, Great Britain stood alone and almost defenseless. On May 10, 1940, Winston Churchill replaced Neville Chamberlain as Prime Minister of Great Britain. With a rare gift for leadership, Churchill rallied the British people, strengthening their hopes and their will to fight. Churchill promised that the British would never surrender. If by chance Great Britain itself were to fall, he declared, "then our Empire beyond the seas, armed and guarded by the British fleet, would carry on the struggle until, in God's good time, the New World, with all its power and might, steps forth to the rescue and liberation of the Old."

By the end of June, with France under Nazi control, Churchill prepared his people for the coming Battle of Britain. "Hitler knows that he will have to break us in this island or lose the war," Churchill said. "If we can stand up to him, all Europe may be free and the life of the world may move forward into broad, sunlit uplands. But if we fail, then the whole world, including the United States, including all that we have known and cared for, will sink into the abyss of a new Dark Age. . . . Let us therefore brace ourselves to our duties, and so bear our-

"We shall defend our island, whatever the cost may be . . .; we shall never surrender."
This was Prime Minister Winston Churchill's pledge to the people of Great Britain. Here,
in 1940, Churchill gives his famous "V for victory" sign.

selves that, if the British Empire and its Commonwealth last for a thousand years, men will still say, 'This was their finest hour.' "

The supreme test for the British came in the late summer of 1940. In August Hitler unleashed his fighters and bombers against Great Britain. The Royal Navy fought back furiously. The Royal Air Force, though almost hopelessly outnumbered, flew day and night, sometimes shooting down as many as 100 Nazi bombers in a single 24-hour period. In October, advised by his military chiefs that an attempt to invade Great Britain would be suicidal, Hitler postponed his invasion plan.

"Never in the field of human conflict," Churchill declared "was so much owed by so many to so few." The proud leader was re-
▲ ferring, of course, to the Royal Air Force.

American defense measures. During the summer and fall of 1940, the United States was strengthening its own defenses.

Many Americans feared the possibility of subversive activities. To guard against such activities, Congress passed the Alien Registration Act, commonly known as the Smith Act. This law reinforced legislation controlling aliens and made it illegal for any person in the United States to advocate the overthrow of the government by force or violence or to belong to an organization that advocated the violent overthrow of the government.

In July Secretary of State Hull and the foreign ministers of the other American nations gathered in Havana, Cuba. They drew up plans for preventing Germany from seizing the Western Hemisphere colonies of the countries it had conquered. The Act of Havana stated that the moment any colony was in danger, the American republics, acting singly or collectively, would take control of the colony. From then until the end of the war, the colony would be governed by a group of trustees from the American republics.

▲ Although Britain had fewer fighter planes than Germany, the British planes were of superior quality. The combination of these high quality planes and the ingenious new invention of radar enabled the British to stave off two years of relentless German air attacks.

Two weeks later President Roosevelt met with Prime Minister Mackenzie King of Canada. At this meeting the two leaders created a Permanent Joint Board of Defense to plan for the "defense of the north half of the Western Hemisphere."

In 1940 Congress furiously debated the pros and cons of the first peacetime draft in American history. The Burke-Wadsworth Act was finally passed and signed by President Roosevelt on September 16, 1940. The law required all men between 21 and 35 to register for the draft. It also made them liable for one year of military training.

Roosevelt's Lend-Lease proposal. By the end of 1940, American supplies were flowing to Great Britain and America's defense program was gathering momentum. Still, Roosevelt was worried that the British could not afford much longer to pay cash for needed war materials. In his annual message to Congress, Roosevelt declared, "Our country is going to be what our people have proclaimed it to be—the arsenal of democracy." Roosevelt proposed that the United States increase greatly its production of military equipment so that it could lend or lease to the British and to the other Allies any materials needed to carry on the fight.

Roosevelt's Lend-Lease proposal provoked a storm of controversy. Many people agreed with the President that the Lend-Lease proposal offered the best hope of avoiding full-fledged participation in the war. Others, including the isolationists, were sure that Lend-Lease would involve America in a shooting war.

Congress finally passed the Lend-Lease Act in March 1941. It appropriated an initial sum of $7 billion for ships, planes, tanks, and anything else that the Allies needed. When on June 22, 1941, Hitler's armies invaded the Soviet Union despite the German-Russian nonaggression pact, the United States made Lend-Lease materials available to the U.S.S.R.

The Battle of the Atlantic. The Lend-Lease arrangement inevitably drew the United States closer to war. By the spring of 1941, German and Italian submarines were turning the North Atlantic into a graveyard of ships. In April American naval vessels began to trail enemy submarines, radioing their location to British warships. In July American troops occupied Iceland to prevent its occupation by Germany's troops.

In September Roosevelt issued "shoot-on-sight" orders to American warships operating in the "safety zone" established back in 1939. American warships also began to accompany and protect, or **convoy**, merchant vessels as far as Iceland. In November Congress voted to allow American merchant vessels to enter combat areas. Roosevelt armed the merchant vessels and provided them with gun crews.

The Atlantic Charter. In 1941 the United States was moving rapidly toward undeclared war with Germany. That August, Roosevelt and Churchill met to discuss the larger issues involved in the conflict. At this meeting the two leaders drew up a broad statement of war aims that came to be called the Atlantic Charter.

Like Woodrow Wilson's Fourteen Points, the Atlantic Charter listed a number of common principles for building a lasting peace and a better world. In the Atlantic Charter, Roosevelt and Churchill pledged themselves to work for a world free of aggression, a world in which every nation, large or small, would have the right to adopt its own form of government. Once the aggressors were crushed, the Charter declared, all nations had to work together to free all people everywhere from the burden of fear and want.

Growing threat from Japan. While war raged in Europe, Japan was adding to its conquests in the Far East. In July 1941, Japanese troops occupied French Indochina (see map, page 816). Thoroughly alarmed, President Roosevelt immediately froze all Japanese assets in the United States. He also placed an embargo on the shipment of gasoline, machine tools, scrap iron, and steel to Japan. Japan promptly retaliated by freezing all American assets in areas under its control. As a result, trade between the United States and Japan practically ended. Then in August the United States sent a Lend-Lease mission to China.

The Japanese were convinced that American resistance was stiffening. They began to make plans for an attack upon the United States. Even as its war leaders made the final preparations, however, the Japanese government sent a "peace" mission to Washington. On November 20, 1941, this mission demanded that the United States (1) unfreeze Japanese assets, (2) supply Japan with as much gasoline as it needed, and (3) cease all aid to China. The

---

▲ To help Great Britain fight the German sea efforts, Roosevelt also made a "destroyers-for-bases" deal. He traded Britain 50 old but usable destroyers for six naval bases in the Caribbean. Britain also leased to the U.S. bases in Bermuda and Newfoundland. In by-passing direct loan or sale, Roosevelt was able to adhere to neutrality laws.

The Japanese bombed the base at Pearl Harbor on the morning of December 7, 1941. The attack ended America's long period of isolationism and thrust the surprised nation headlong into the war that now spanned the entire globe.

United States refused to meet these demands but offered several counterproposals.

Pearl Harbor and war. On December 7, 1941, the Japanese mission announced that further negotiations were useless. The Japanese said that the United States had failed "to display in the slightest degree a spirit of conciliation."

That morning, even before Japan's reply had been delivered to the American government, Japanese planes attacked without warning the United States fleet anchored in the huge American naval and air base at Pearl Harbor, in Hawaii (see map, page 816). The Americans lost almost all of their planes and eight battleships and suffered the partial destruction of several other naval units. More than 2,000 soldiers, sailors, and civilians were

▲ killed, and almost 2,000 more were wounded. The same day the Japanese also attacked Wake, Midway, Guam, the Philippine Islands, and other American bases.

Shocked and angered, Americans almost unanimously supported President Roosevelt the next day when he asked Congress for a declaration of war against Japan. The Senate declared war unanimously, the House with only one dissenting vote. Great Britain and the government leaders who had fled from Hitler's armies and were now in exile also immediately declared war against Japan. Three days later, on December 11, Germany and Italy declared that a state of war with the United States existed, whereupon Congress declared war upon those two countries.

SECTION REVIEW
See underscored items, text pp. 790 - 94.

Identify: Declaration of Panama, blitzkrieg, Charles de Gaulle, Marshal Pétain, Winston Churchill, Smith Act, Act of Havana, Lend-Lease, convoy, Atlantic Charter, Pearl Harbor
For answers to questions, see Answer Key, p.A109.

1. **Interpreting Ideas:** How did the United States arms embargo aid the aggressor nations?

2. **Summarizing Ideas:** What actions did the United States take to prepare for the possibility of war?

3. **Determining Cause and Effect:** Trace the events that led to the Japanese attack on Pearl Harbor.

4. **Interpreting Viewpoints: (a)** What did Roosevelt mean when he called the United States "the arsenal of democracy"? **(b)** How did Roosevelt plan to make the nation the "arsenal of democracy"?

▲ Class activity: Have volunteers find examples of U.S. and foreign news accounts about the bombing of Pearl Harbor. "As Others See Us," edited by Ralph E. Weber, is an excellent source of articles from the foreign press. Use the examples as a basis for a discussion of propaganda techniques.

DEVELOPING HISTORY STUDY SKILLS

Relating Geography and History Using a Map as a Documentary Source

Students of history are often called on to use a map as a documentary source. You may be asked, for example, to interpret the influence of the geographic setting in the sequence of historical events.

You have already been introduced to the skills involved in reading a map (Chapter 7, pages 164–65). You have also been introduced to the skills of using a photograph as a documentary source (Chapter 25, page 583–84). Refresh your memory on the skills contained on those pages to prepare you to use a map as a documentary source.

Applying the Skill

Study the map below. Then answer these questions.

1. What is the title of the map?
2. **(a)** What forces were involved in the invasion of Normandy? **(b)** Which group landed at Utah Beach?
3. Read the account of the Normandy invasion on text page 810 and answer these questions. **(a)** What was the purpose of the invasion? **(b)** In what ways does the map illustrate the information about which you just read?

Review the answers you got for these questions. The map's title is "The Invasion of Normandy." The U.S. First Army, the 21st Army Group, and the British Second Army were involved in the invasion. The U.S. First Army landed at Utah Beach. The purpose of the invasion was to force the German army to fight on both a western and eastern front. The map illustrates the geographic setting of the invasion and the military deployment of troops at Normandy.

Practicing the Skill

Study the following maps. Then on a separate sheet of paper, answer these questions.

1. Study the map on page 786. **(a)** What is the subject of the map? **(b)** What color represents the Axis Powers? **(c)** In what year did Germany invade the Rhineland? Poland? **(d)** Hitler claimed he invaded the Rhineland and Poland to resecure former German lands. How might this be supported by the map?
2. Study the map on text page 802. **(a)** What is the subject of the map? **(b)** From which three points did the Allies advance into Germany? **(c)** Why did the Allied advance take these routes?

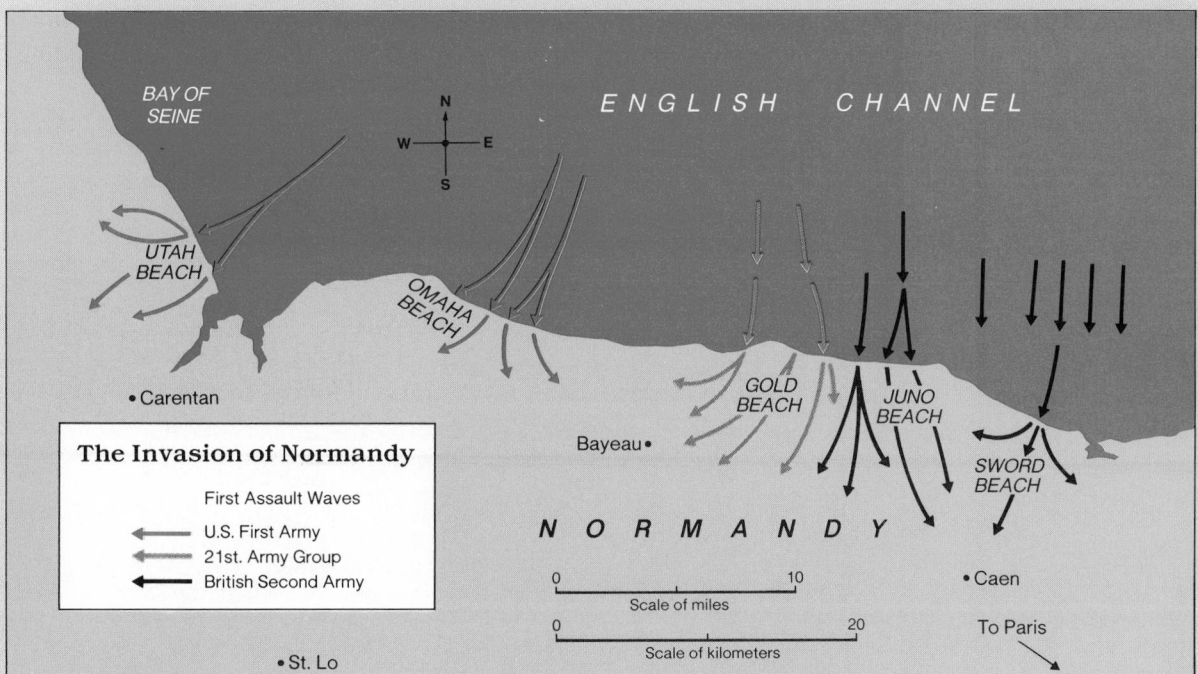

(1.(a) German and Italian aggressions that led to World War II (b) Red; (c) 1936; 1939; (d) The map illustrates that these lands border Germany. 2.(a) Allied victory in Europe during World War II. (b) from Paris, southern France, and Poland; (c) The northern routes led to Berlin, the southern routes to Vienna.)

During the 1930's one of the greatest tragedies of the modern world began to unfold. The tragedy started with the Great Depression, which plunged millions of people all over the world into unemployment, confusion, and unrest. Then, in the middle 1930's, the armies of Japan, Italy, and Germany began to march into weaker countries, leaving death and destruction behind. Before 1941 drew to a close, most of the nations of the world were involved in World War II.

The overwhelming majority of the American people were at first determined to remain out of the war. They supported Congress when it enacted neutrality legislation in 1935, 1936, and 1937. As the dictators of Japan, Italy, and Germany crushed their weaker neighbors, however, Americans realized that the democratic way of life and the fate of free people everywhere were in danger. More and more, Americans saw that by helping other nations to resist aggression, the United States would strengthen democracy and protect itself.

By 1939, when World War II broke out in Europe, the United States had begun to reverse its policy of isolationism. During the next two years, neutrality was abandoned as the United States became "the arsenal of democracy." American ships carried cargoes of war materials to Great Britain, the Soviet Union, and China. America's navy, air force, and army were strengthened with feverish speed. Then, on December 7, 1941, the Japanese struck at Pearl Harbor. The United States was at war.

CONNECTING CHAPTER IDEAS

In the next chapter you will read about the United States participation in the devastating global conflict known as World War II. You will also read of the terrible lasting effects this war had on the world.

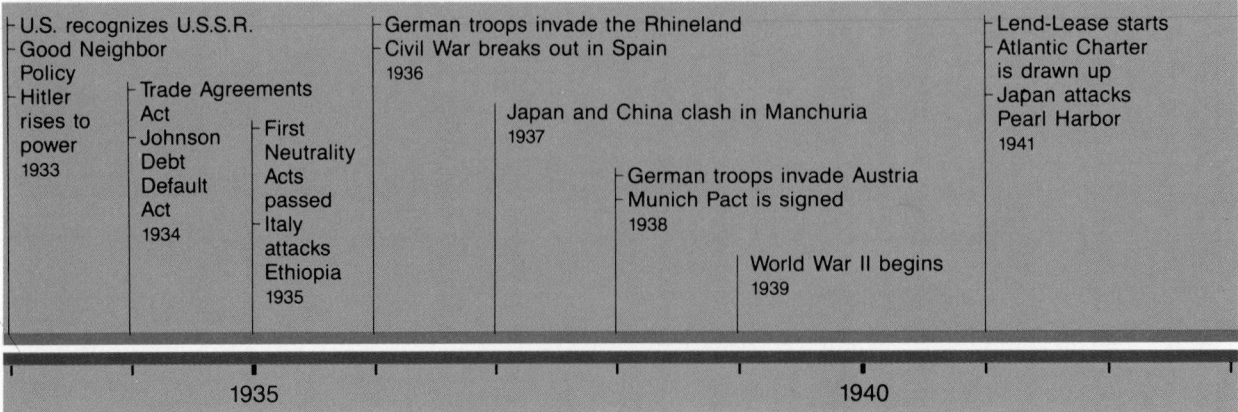

U.S. recognizes U.S.S.R.
Good Neighbor Policy
Hitler rises to power
1933

Trade Agreements Act
Johnson Debt Default Act
1934

First Neutrality Acts passed
Italy attacks Ethiopia
1935

German troops invade the Rhineland
Civil War breaks out in Spain
1936

Japan and China clash in Manchuria
1937

German troops invade Austria
Munich Pact is signed
1938

World War II begins
1939

Lend-Lease starts
Atlantic Charter is drawn up
Japan attacks Pearl Harbor
1941

1935   1940

CHAPTER
35 REVIEW

Reviewing Important Terms

Decide whether each of the following sentences is true or false. If the sentence is false, replace the underlined term with the word or phrase that will make it true.

1. The United States maintained a policy of containment throughout the 1930's.
2. A form of government in which one person or a small group of people completely controls the government and the people of a nation is called a monarchy.
3. Hitler began his blitzkrieg, or "lightning war," against Poland in 1939.
4. In 1922 Benito Mussolini seized power in Italy and established a communist government.
5. Neville Chamberlain, Prime Minister of Great Britain, advocated a policy of nonaggression towards the German government.
6. In 1938 President Roosevelt demonstrated that the Monroe Doctrine was a unilateral policy.
7. The Allied Powers used a system of convoys to insure that commercial vessels reached their destination safely.

Practicing Critical Thinking Skills

1. **Seeing Relationships. (a)** How was the depression related to the rise of dictatorships during the 1930's? **(b)** How were nationalism, imperialism, and belief in racial superiority related to the causes of World War II?
2. **Interpreting Ideas.** Munich has become a symbol of the policy of appeasement. **(a)** What does this statement mean? **(b)** How did appeasement help lead to World War II?
3. **Analyzing Viewpoints. (a)** Why did many Americans believe in isolationism during the 1930's? **(b)** Why did that attitude start to change by the late 1930's?
4. **Analyzing Ideas. (a)** Why did the United States recognize the government of the Soviet Union? **(b)** Why might it be necessary to recognize a country's government even if the United States does not approve of that government's policies?
5. **Interpreting Viewpoints.** What was the reaction of most Americans to totalitarian aggression during the early and middle 1930's?
6. **Relating Past to Present.** Are United States dealings with other nations today affected in any way by what was learned from the events leading to World War II? Explain.

Developing History Study Skills

1. **Using a Map as a Documentary Source.** Study the map, "Aggressions Leading to World War II" on page 786. Then answer the following questions. **(a)** What two aggressions did Italy commit in the 1930's? **(b)** When did Germany occupy the Rhineland? **(c)** What aggressions marked the beginning of World War II?
2. **Using Primary and Secondary Sources.** Read the following excerpts from an eyewitness account of the bombing of Pearl Harbor. Then use this account as well as the information in your textbook to write your own secondary account of the Japanese attack on Pearl Harbor.

   The sky was full of planes bearing the Rising Sun emblem of Japan. . . . Some sixty enemy planes were diving at our ships. . . .

   At about 8:00 A.M., a terrific explosion in the Arizona, *astern of us, fairly lifted us in the water. She blew up in an enormous flame and a cloud of black smoke when her forward magazine exploded after a Japanese bomb had literally dropped down her funnel. . . . It was a scene which cannot easily be forgotten—the* Arizona *was a mass of fire from bow to foremast, on deck and between decks, and the surface of the water for a large distance round was a mass of flaming oil from millions of gallons of fuel oil. Over a thousand dead men lay in her twisted wreck.*

Relating Geography and History

Factors such as geographic location and the presence of natural resources played an important role in the outbreak of World War II. To understand how these factors influenced the start of the war, use the information in this chapter to answer the following questions.

1. Why did Germany take control of the Rhineland, Czechoslovakia, and Austria?
2. Did the geographical closeness of Germany and Italy help or hurt the Axis war effort? Explain.
3. Why did Japan invade Manchuria?
4. What geographic reason did Japan have for bombing the American base in Pearl harbor?

797

See Chapter Overview in TMRG, p.TM195.
See Chapter Objectives in TMRG, p.TM195.
See Introducing the Chapter in TMRG, p.TM195.

CHAPTER 36
Americans in World War II
(1941–1945)

The nation
unites

It was December 7, 1941, when Japan's savage blow at Pearl Harbor plunged the United States into World War II. The conflict had been under way a little more than two years.

The enemies of the United States had the great advantage of what military leaders call "interior lines of supply and communication." Germany and Italy in Europe and Japan in Asia were so situated geographically within their spheres of influence that the supply lines from their farms and factories to the fighting fronts were relatively short. The United States, on the other hand, had to establish and protect supply lines that stretched thousands of miles across the Atlantic to Europe. It also had to establish supply lines across sea and land to fighting forces in the Pacific.

The enemies of the United States had another great advantage. They had been preparing for war, some in secret for many years. During these years of preparation, they had raised and trained huge armies. They had converted their factories to the production of war materials. They had built up vast supplies of rifles, machine guns, tanks, planes, and other instruments of modern warfare.

The United States, on the other hand, had not begun to prepare for war until the summer of 1940 when it abandoned all pretense of neutrality. Even then preparations were limited to supplying the Allies with aid. Indeed, it was this lack of preparation that led Hitler, Mussolini, and the Japanese war leaders to believe that they could win the war even with the United States as a declared enemy. They thought they would emerge victorious before the United States could mobilize its enormous resources. Overwhelming odds or not, the American people grimly entered the worldwide conflict.

READING FOCUS

As you read about the events of World War II, look for the details that support each of the following statements.

1. The Allies overcome early disasters and begin an offensive.
2. Americans accept controls and win the "battle of production."
3. The Allies gradually fight their way to victory in Europe.
4. Allied victories in the Pacific bring an end to World War II.

1 The Allies overcome early disasters and begin an offensive

See Teaching Suggestions in TMRG, p.TM196.

Throughout most of 1942, while Americans were desperately trying to convert to a wartime economy, the United States and its allies suffered a series of almost unrelieved disasters in every theater of the war.

Disaster in the Pacific. The scene at Pearl Harbor on the evening of December 7, 1941, was one of nearly total destruction. America's offensive power in the Pacific had been wiped out by the Japanese surprise attack.

By the end of December, Japan had seized the American islands of Guam and Wake and captured the British colony of Hong Kong. They had also launched attacks upon the American-controlled Philippine and Midway Islands, Thailand, and British Malaya (see map, page 816).

The new year brought a mounting fury of destruction. Japanese conquests covered a widening area of the Pacific and Far East (see map, page 816). On January 2, 1942, Japanese troops poured into Manila, the capital of the Philippines. On January 11 the Japanese invaded Borneo and Celebes (SEL·eh·beez) in the Netherlands Indies. On February 15 the advancing tide of Japanese troops overran the British naval base at Singapore. Later in the month, in the Battle of the Java Sea, a Japanese naval force delivered a crushing blow to a fleet of American, British, Dutch, and Australian warships.

By the end of March, the Japanese had conquered most of the Netherlands Indies with its rich supplies of oil, tin, rubber, quinine, and other vital war materials. They had also seized Rangoon, Burma, and were driving British, Indian, and Chinese troops out of Burma.

In the Philippines, a small force of Americans and Filipinos under General Douglas MacArthur continued their heroic but hopeless resistance against the Japanese. In January 1942 Manila surrendered, and MacArthur's forces retired to the Bataan Peninsula. In March MacArthur himself was ordered to Australia to take command of the Allied forces in the South Pacific. Fighting against over-

● Three powerful U.S. fleet aircraft carriers, the Enterprise, Lexington, and Saratoga, were at sea and escaped the destruction at Pearl Harbor.

799

whelming odds, the hungry, sick, exhausted survivors on Bataan were captured on April 9. On May 6 the outnumbered and starving troops on the fortress of Corregidor guarding Manila Bay surrendered. The Japanese also cut the Burma Road, destroying the last land route to China.

Thus by the end of May 1942, less than six months after their attack on Pearl Harbor, the Japanese had overcome almost all opposition. They were poised to strike west at India, south at Australia, and east through Hawaii at the Pacific coast of the United States.

American gains in the Pacific. Despite some opposition at home, the United States accepted the British argument that the defeat of Hitler in Europe had to be the first Allied objective. However, the war in the Pacific proved to be more than a mere holding operation.

Two impressive naval victories began to turn the tide of war in the Pacific in United States favor. In May 1942, carrier-based planes from a British-American naval force caught a Japanese fleet moving southward in the Coral Sea, off the northeastern coast of Australia. The planes sank or severely damaged more than 30 Japanese warships. The Battle of the Coral Sea halted a major advance toward Australia. The Allied victory in the Coral Sea battle was the first serious reversal of Japanese plans since Pearl Harbor.

Japanese forces received another setback early in June 1942 when they launched a two-pronged seaborne attack on the Aleutian Islands and Hawaii. The ultimate Japanese objective was an invasion of the United States. American forces stopped the northern campaign, but only after Japanese troops had occupied the Aleutian islands of Attu and Kiska (see map, page 816). American naval forces were able to block the southern campaign by defeating the Japanese in a major battle off the island of Midway. The Battle of Midway stopped a Japanese drive toward Hawaii.

▲ **Turning the tide in the Pacific.** There are several reasons why the United States began to stem the Japanese tide. First, early in 1942 the United States and Great Britain had pooled their resources to create a unified Pacific command. Second, the American people were beginning to win the important "battle of production" at home. The products of the nation's farms and factories were pouring into

Pacific supply depots and forward bases. Finally, time had been gained by the courageous resistance of Americans and Filipinos on Bataan and Corregidor.

On August 7, 1942, the United States undertook its first major offensive action when marines stormed ashore at Guadalcanal in the Solomon Islands (see map, page 816). For four desperate months, American marines and army troops clung to a toehold around Guadalcanal's airport. They repelled savage attacks from the air, from the sea, and from the surrounding jungle.

In November the Japanese made a desperate effort to regain their former bases in the Solomons, which they needed to carry out their planned invasion of Australia. Admiral William F. Halsey intercepted the huge Japanese fleet and in a furious battle on November 12–15 completely routed the Japanese. The island of Guadalcanal was at last secure. The tide of battle in the Pacific had turned in the Allies' favor.

Disaster in Europe. The situation in the Atlantic and in Europe during most of 1942 was grave. German and Italian submarines in the Atlantic sank ships more rapidly than the United States and Great Britain could build new ones. Great Britain was now an isolated fortress in the Atlantic. The valiant people of Great Britain could not hold out much longer unless reinforcements and supplies arrived and unless the devastating Nazi bombings were stopped.

On the continent of Europe, the tide of Axis conquest was rolling with terrifying speed. Yugoslavia fell to the Axis powers. The Greeks had been reduced to near starvation. The Soviet Union had lost its rich grainfields in the Ukraine region, and many Soviet industrial centers had been ruined. Part of the destruction was done by the Soviet people themselves. As they retreated before the Germans, they applied a **scorched-earth policy** to their land, destroying everything that they could not carry with them.

Despite Soviet resistance, the Nazi divisions rolled on in the summer offensive of 1942. The Germans overran the oil fields of the Caucasus and rumbled into the outskirts of Stalingrad on the Volga River (see map, page 802). Beyond lay the Ural Mountains, where the Soviet people were feverishly building new industries to help in the war effort.

▲ One of Japan's mistakes, which helped turn the tide in favor of the Allies, was characterized by a Japanese admiral as "victory fever." Rather than consolidating and organizing its conquests, Japan had over-extended itself toward still greater conquests.

The Allies were able to turn the tables on the Axis forces in part because of the injection of U. S. manpower and materials into the war effort. Here, guarded by U. S. warships, a huge convoy moves toward an Allied battlefront.

In the Mediterranean the Axis forces were triumphant everywhere. German and Italian aircraft with bases in Italy, Greece, the Greek island of Crete, and North Africa all but forced British naval craft out of the Mediterranean. They thus denied the British the use of the Suez Canal route to the Indian Ocean. Great Britain was compelled to send its ships thousands of miles around Africa to reach Egypt, the Middle East, and India. By the autumn of 1942, the German *Afrika Korps* under General Erwin Rommel had advanced to the frontiers of Egypt. There the well-trained corps stood poised for a final thrust at the Suez Canal and the oil fields of the Middle East.

Allied victories. November 1942 marked a turning point of the war. In the Pacific, as you have read, the three-day naval battle of Guadalcanal started the Allies on their long drive toward Tokyo. In North Africa British General Bernard L. Montgomery caught Rommel by surprise late in October at El Alamein in Egypt and drove him back across the desert into Libya toward eventual defeat.

On November 8 a mighty invasion fleet led by General Dwight D. Eisenhower landed thousands of British, Canadian, and American troops on the northern coast of Africa (see map, page 802). On November 19 the Soviet troops began to encircle the German forces at Stalingrad. Within several weeks the Soviet troops overwhelmed the Germans at Stalingrad and forced them to surrender.

"This is not the end," Winston Churchill said in November 1942. "It is not even the beginning of the end. But it is, perhaps, the end of the beginning." Subsequent events justified Churchill's reassuring words. Before 1942 was over, the Allies held the initiative in Europe, as in the Pacific.

Wartime cooperation. How had the Allies been able to survive the earlier disasters? Why were they able in November 1942 to begin to seize the initiative? One answer is that the tremendous combination of America's human resources and war materials was beginning to have its effect. Another answer is that in their struggle the Allies were working as a team. ▲

On January 1, 1942, the 26 Allied nations, calling themselves the **United Nations**°, issued a joint declaration. The countries (1) promised full cooperation in the war effort, (2) agreed not to make a separate peace, and (3) endorsed the war aims outlined in the Atlantic Charter by Churchill and Roosevelt (page 793).

Early in 1941, as you recall, even before the United States had entered the war, Congress laid the basis for cooperation among the Allies with the Lend-Lease program (page 793). After the attack on Pearl Harbor, the aid program went into high gear. The United States shipped immense quantities of war materials across the submarine-infested sea routes to its allies in the Pacific and to Great Britain, the U.S.S.R., and the British armies in Egypt and the Middle East. Before the war ended, Lend-Lease aid reached more than $50 billion. Of this total 69 percent went to Great Britain, about 25 percent to the U.S.S.R., and small quantities to other Allies.

Text continues on page 803.

°**United Nations:** The wartime Allies called themselves the United Nations. When in 1945 they formed a permanent organization, they continued to use this same name for that organization.

▲ During the summer of 1942, the Allies, mostly at the urging of British strategists, had begun air raids of German cities to knock out German industry. The attacks set back production and communication and brought the realities of the war to the German people.

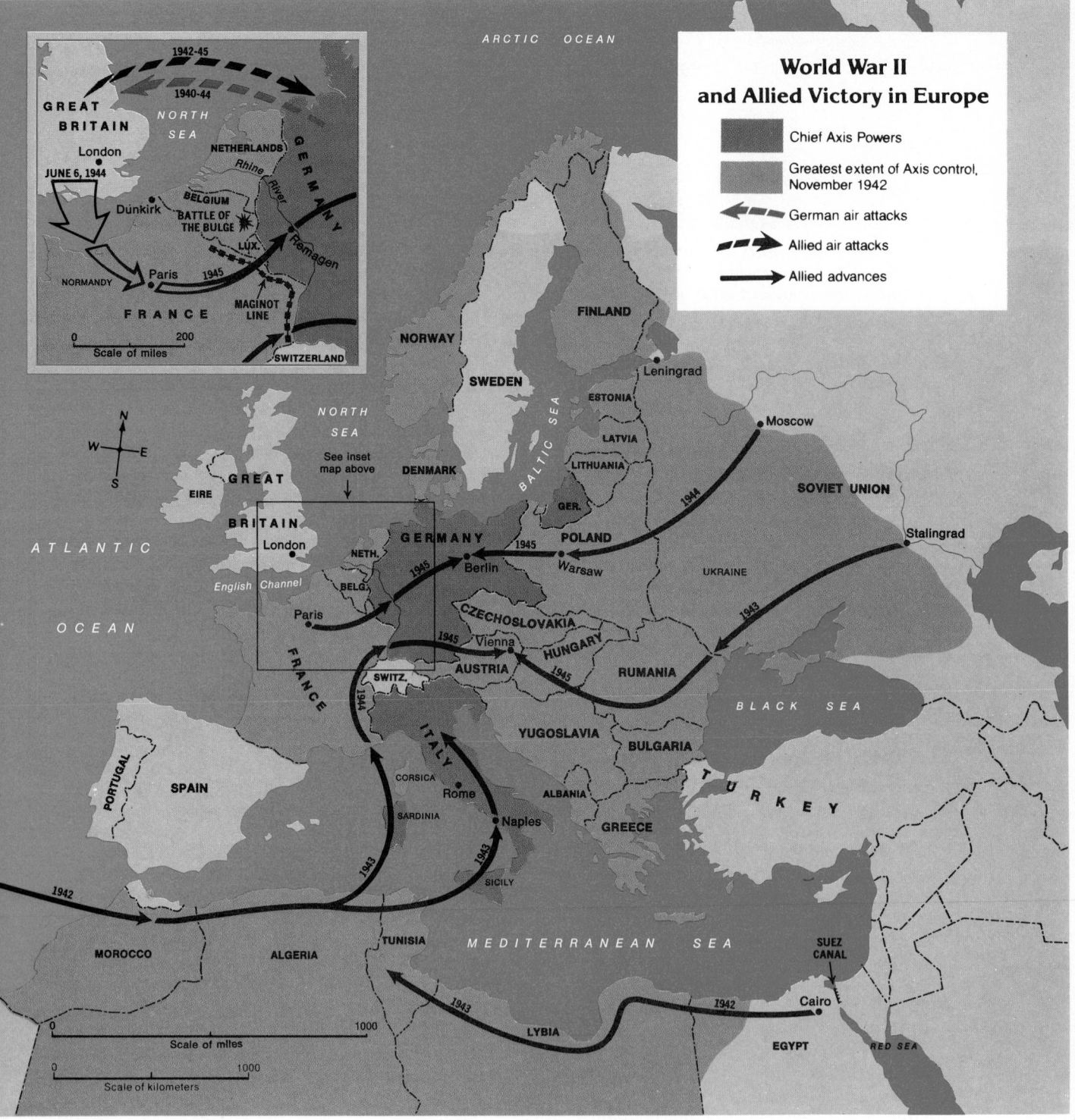

World War II and Allied Victory in Europe

Chief Axis Powers

Greatest extent of Axis control, November 1942

German air attacks

Allied air attacks

Allied advances

Inset Map

1942–45

1940–44

GREAT BRITAIN

London

JUNE 6, 1944

Dunkirk

NETHERLANDS

Rhine River

GERMANY

BELGIUM

BATTLE OF THE BULGE

LUX.

Remagen

NORMANDY

Paris

1945

MAGINOT LINE

FRANCE

SWITZERLAND

NORTH SEA

Scale of miles
0   200

Main Map

ARCTIC OCEAN

NORTH SEA

FINLAND

NORWAY

SWEDEN

Leningrad

ESTONIA

LATVIA

LITHUANIA

GER.

Moscow

SOVIET UNION

BALTIC SEA

DENMARK

See inset map above

GREAT BRITAIN

London

English Channel

NETH.

GERMANY

Berlin

POLAND

Warsaw

1945

1944

Stalingrad

UKRAINE

1943

ATLANTIC OCEAN

EIRE

BELG.

Paris

1945

FRANCE

CZECHOSLOVAKIA

Vienna

HUNGARY

1945

RUMANIA

BLACK SEA

SWITZ.

AUSTRIA

1944

1945

PORTUGAL

SPAIN

ITALY

CORSICA

Rome

SARDINIA

YUGOSLAVIA

BULGARIA

TURKEY

ALBANIA

Naples

1943

GREECE

SICILY

1943

1942

MOROCCO

ALGERIA

TUNISIA

MEDITERRANEAN SEA

SUEZ CANAL

1943

1942

Cairo

LYBIA

EGYPT

RED SEA

Scale of miles
0   1000

Scale of kilometers
0   1000

N W E S

World War II in Europe

Dark days for the Allies

1939

SEPT.–OCT.	German invasion and conquest of Poland.

1940

APR.–JUNE	German invasion of Denmark, Norway, Luxembourg, Belgium, Netherlands, France.
MAY	British evacuation from Dunkirk.
JUNE–JULY	Fall of France; establishment of Vichy government.
AUG.–OCT.	Battle of Britain (German air attacks).
OCT.	Axis aggressions in Balkans.
NOV.–FEB. 1941	British offensive in Mediterranean and North Africa.

1941

FEB.–MAY	Battle of the Atlantic begins.
MAR.–APR.	Axis counteroffensive in North Africa.
APR.–JUNE	German invasion of Greece, Yugoslavia, Crete.
JUNE	German invasion of U.S.S.R. begins.

Allied gains: the tide turns

1942

MAY–AUG.	Allied air attacks on Germany begin.
OCT.–NOV.	Allied counteroffensive in North Africa begins.
NOV.–MAR. 1943	Russian counteroffensives in U.S.S.R.; German surrender of Stalingrad.

1943

MAY	Allied victory in North Africa; end of African campaign.
JULY–AUG.	Allied invasion of Sicily.
JULY–JAN. 1944	Russians drive Germans back in U.S.S.R. and enter Poland.
SEPT.	Allies begin Italian campaigns.
SEPT. 8	Italy surrenders.

1944

JUNE 6	Allied invasion along Normandy coast (Operation Overlord).
AUG.	Allied forces land in southern France.
AUG. 25	Allies liberate Paris.
SEPT.	Allies liberate Belgium, Luxembourg.
SEPT.	Battle for Germany begins.
SEPT.–DEC.	Russians conquer Yugoslavia and Hungary.
DEC.	Battle of the Bulge (last German counteroffensive).

Allied victory in the Pacific

1945

FEB.–APR.	Allied invasion of Germany.
MAY 7	Germany surrenders
MAY 8	V-E Day

Lend-Lease was not a one-way arrangement. During the war the United States received in exchange goods and services valued at nearly $8 billion, most of which came from Great Britain. For example, when the American air forces began to arrive in England, the British provided bases, housing, and equipment. The Lend-Lease program was an outstanding example of Allied cooperation.

Cooperative planning. Joint planning of strategy was an even more decisive Allied effort. Shortly after the attack on Pearl Harbor, Prime Minister Churchill and a group of military, naval, and technical aides met in Washington, D.C., with General George C. Marshall, Chief of Staff of the Army, and the commanders of America's air, land, and sea forces. This meeting was the first of a series held by the Allied military leaders.

These conferences required a tremendous give-and-take. Final decisions were not always popular with all concerned. For example, the Soviets urged their Allies to relieve the pressure on the Soviet Union in Eastern Europe by opening a second front in Western Europe. Roosevelt finally agreed with Churchill that the Allies were not sufficiently prepared to do this. They decided instead to land troops in North Africa, where they could strike at southern Europe. Despite such differences among the Allies, the high degree of cooperation achieved was indispensable to the final victory. ●

SECTION REVIEW

See underscored items, text pp. 799 - 801.

Identify: Douglas MacArthur, William Halsey, scorched-earth policy, *Afrika Korps,* Erwin Rommel, Bernard Montgomery, Dwight D. Eisenhower, United Nations

For answers to questions, see Answer Key, pp. A110-11.

1. **Interpreting Ideas:** November 1942 marked a turning point of the war. Why?
2. **Synthesizing Ideas:** How did the Lend-Lease program help both the United States and its allies?
3. **Analyzing Ideas:** (a) Why was Allied cooperation so important in winning the war? (b) In what specific ways did the Allies cooperate?
4. **Studying Maps:** Study the map on page 802. (a) Locate the Axis countries. (b) In November 1942, which countries were under Axis control? (c) How does the map illustrate the fact that 1941 to mid-1942 were dark days for the Allies?

● The Anglo-American cooperative effort was particularly strong. The Combined Chiefs of Staff planned closely with both British and U.S. officials. In all military efforts, an American in command always had a British officer as a second in command and vice versa.

2 Americans accept controls and win the "battle of production"

See Teaching Suggestions in TMRG, pp.TM196-97.

The Allied victories were won on the farms and in the factories of the Allied nations as well as on the fighting fronts. By the end of 1942, the United States had made itself "the arsenal of democracy."

Hitler's errors. When Hitler declared war upon the United States, he had already made three mistakes. First, he failed to conquer Great Britain. He may have succeeded if he had launched an invasion after the British lost their equipment at Dunkirk. Second, his surprise attack upon the U.S.S.R. in June 1941 and his failure to take Moscow led to disaster at Stalingrad. Third, on December 11, 1941, Hitler declared war upon the United States. He failed to realize how swiftly conversion to war production would take place.

America's soaring production. One of the amazing demonstrations of America's productivity took place on the nation's farms. Despite the fact that 2 million agricultural workers served in the armed forces, farmers managed to raise record-breaking crops. They raised enough food to supply the American people as well as their Allies.

The output of America's mines and factories was equally impressive. For example, between July 1940 and July 1945, United States manufacturing plants produced 296,601 military planes, including about 97,000 bombers; 86,388 tanks; 88,077 scout cars and carriers; 16,438 armored cars; 2.4 million trucks; 991,299 light vehicles, such as jeeps; 123,707 tractors; 17.4 million rifles and side arms; 2.7 million machine guns; 315,000 pieces of artillery; and 41.4 billion rounds of ammunition. ▲

In addition, America's shipbuilders created the greatest navy and merchant marine the world had ever seen. By 1943 five ocean-going vessels were being launched every 24 hours.

All in all, production during the war years was 75 percent greater than in peacetime. According to Donald M. Nelson, first chief of the

Shipyards such as this one in Baltimore were busy around the clock, producing military and merchant marine vessels.

▲ Class activity: Have interested students report on some of the innovations that greatly aided the Allied effort: the Jeep, the PT boat, radar, the Liberty ships, dehydrated food, the development of sulfa drugs and penicillin. The students should present oral reports of their findings to the class.

Both Allied and Axis powers in World War II used radio as an effective tool of psychological warfare. Radio broadcasts could be manipulated to build confidence in one's own forces or to demoralize the enemy.

The Allied propaganda effort was led by the British Ministry of Information and the United States Office of War Information (OWI). The OWI operated radio stations throughout Europe and the Pacific, from which it effectively attacked enemy morale. The broadcasts convinced many people in occupied countries and in countries threatened with Axis takeover of the ultimate victory of the Allies.

The Allies also used radio broadcasts to transmit classified military information. To avert the possibility of broken codes, English was not used. Instead, Navajo Indian radio operators who accompanied the Allied soldiers into battle transmitted the classified information in their own language. The Navajo code completely baffled the Axis powers, and the code was never broken. The Navajo operators and their native language helped to bring about Allied victory, not only in the wider war but in the psychological one as well.

War Production Board, created in January 1942, "American industry turned out more goods for war than we ever produced for our peacetime needs—yet had enough power left over to keep civilian standards of living astonishingly high."

Financing the war. Where did the money come from to finance the war? A little more than one third came from taxes, which were raised to the highest level in American history. The government borrowed the remainder, chiefly by selling huge issues of bonds. Because of this borrowing, the national debt shot upward from about $49 billion in 1941 to nearly $259 billion by the spring of 1945.

The dollar cost of the war was staggering. By 1945, military expenditures totaled $400 billion. This was twice the sum that the federal government had spent for all of its activities, including all wars, between 1789 and 1940!

Government agencies. In its efforts to organize the war effort and to mobilize the nation's resources, the federal government created a complex network of agencies.

At the top there was a policy-making board called the Office of War Mobilization (OWM). Its job was to unify the activities of the many war agencies.

Just below the OWM was the War Production Board (WPB). This board affected the daily lives of nearly every man, woman, and child in the United States. The WPB controlled the allocations of raw materials to industrial plants. It searched the country for scrap iron and the nation's kitchens for fats, tin, and aluminum. It directed the conversion of factories from peacetime to wartime production and stimulated the construction of new plants.

In addition, the WPB restricted the production of all consumer goods that required materials necessary to the war effort. It rationed

▲ Though their effects were comparatively mild, rationing and conservation measures affected every part of American life. Tin and aluminum cans were collected and reprocessed. Non-essential vehicles were allowed three gallons of gas a week. To save cloth, hemlines were shortened and lapels became narrower.

Women in the Labor Force • 1890–1980

Year	Number of Women Employed Outside the Home	Percentage of the Labor Force Composed of Women
1890	3,600,000	16.8%
1900	5,000,000	17.0%
1910	7,700,000	19.5%
1920	8,300,000	20.0%
1930	10,600,000	20.4%
1940	13,800,000	27.1%
1950	18,300,000	29.6%
1960	23,200,000	33.4%
1970	32,500,000	38.1%
1980	45,400,000	42.4%

Source: *Historical Statistics of the United States*

gasoline to conserve oil and rubber. It even controlled clothing styles to save wool, cotton, rayon, and other vital materials.

To prevent transportation shortages and bottlenecks, the federal government also created the War Shipping Administration and the Office of Defense Transportation. These agencies supervised the railroads, express services, and shipping. The result was that supplies and troops moved efficiently over land and sea.

Mobilizing human resources. The Office of War Information bolstered the morale of the armed forces and of civilians by publicizing the achievements of war production. It also gained support for Allied war aims by broadcasting them in dozens of languages to people all over the world.

The War Manpower Commission (WMC) discouraged men and women from working in nonessential occupations. By 1945 it had channeled nearly 30 million wage earners into the war production effort, including 12 million black American workers and 50,000 Indian workers. By 1943 the labor force included 2 million women working in war plants, replac-

ing men who had left to serve in the nation's armed services.

The WMC also operated the Selective Service System. By the end of the war, the Selective Service had drafted nearly 10 million out of the more than 15 million Americans who served in the armed forces. Included were more than 350,000 Mexican Americans and 1 million black Americans, among them both volunteers and draftees. Despite black protests, official military policy required blacks to serve in segregated units, as in previous wars. In 1944–45, however, some white and black troops in Europe were integrated to meet an emergency situation.

Also included in the armed forces were about 25,000 Indian volunteers. Among tribes with warrior traditions, the rate of enlistment was high. In general, the Indian volunteers enjoyed the respect of their white and black fellow soldiers. Indian soldiers who returned to the reservations after the war took back with them new ideas to their families and their tribal communities.

For the first time the American armed forces, which had previously used women only as nurses, accepted women in uniform to replace men in noncombatant jobs. More than 250,000 women entered the army (the WAC), the Coast Guard (the SPAR), the Navy (the WAVES), and the Marine Corps. As full-fledged military personnel, women worked as machinists, storekeepers, office workers, radio operators, and drivers of jeeps and trucks. The performance of women in the armed forces and in the nation's war plants did much to break down prejudices about what women could and could not do.

Government price control. One of the ways in which the government most closely regulated the lives of civilians was through price controls. In World War I, the shortage of consumer goods and the increased purchasing power of industrial and agricultural workers had driven prices skyward. This brought on inflation and caused suffering, especially among the poor.

The government was determined to prevent inflation in World War II. As a first step, the government raised income taxes. This drained off dollars that would otherwise have been spent on goods in the stores. As a second step, the government encouraged Americans to buy war bonds, arguing that such purchases were

Discussion topic: Despite deeply rooted beliefs in individualism and free enterprise, Americans accepted government controls during this period. Have students discuss the reasons for this. Ask: Are there any circumstances under which Americans might accept such controls today?

both a patriotic duty and a sound investment. However, these measures alone could not prevent inflation.

In 1942, following the example of European governments, Congress created the Office of Price Administration (OPA). The OPA established ceilings, or top limits, on prices and set up a system of **rationing**. The OPA issued ration books containing coupons that purchasers had to use in addition to money to buy gasoline, fuel, shoes, coffee, sugar, fats and oils, meat, butter, and canned goods. The OPA also established rent controls.

Despite these efforts, the prices of consumer goods rose, especially food prices. By 1944 the cost of living had risen 30 percent above 1941 prewar levels. Some Americans violated the price control and rationing system by paying exorbitant prices to obtain more than their share of rationed products. Most Americans, however, accepted **price controls** and rationing as wartime necessities.

Control of wages and profits. Shortly after the attack on Pearl Harbor, the leaders of organized labor promised President Roosevelt that American workers would not strike during the war. At the same time, they insisted that the government had to ensure that workers would be fairly treated. By the spring of 1942, however, the cost of living had risen, and workers were becoming restless.

In July 1942 the National War Labor Board (NWLB) tried to work out a compromise. It granted a 15-percent wage increase to meet the rises in living costs. Several months later Congress and President Roosevelt authorized the NWLB to freeze the wages and salaries of all workers at the newly established levels.

For a time there was relatively little trouble. However, as prices continued to rise, labor again became restless, and here and there strikes broke out. In such instances the government usually stepped in and for the most part settled the disputes quickly.

The government also tried to regulate profits—mainly by means of taxation. Personal income taxes were greatly increased for people in the higher income brackets. The most drastic means of controlling profits was the excess profits tax, levied in 1940. This tax obliged corporations to pay to the government as much as 90 percent of all excess profits. Americans did not like government controls. Nevertheless, they accepted them with the understanding that they would be removed when the emergency was over.

The Japanese Americans. The upheaval in everyday life resulting from these controls and from the whole vast war effort revealed the extraordinary willingness of the American people to make sacrifices for the national emergency. Despite discomforts and sacrifices,

Hastily built tarpaper barracks were the new homes for Japanese Americans in 1942 when they were forced to leave their former homes and relocate in detention camps. This camp was set up in the desert near Manzanar, California.

the people maintained a remarkably high level of morale.

Americans also suffered deep anxieties and fears. However, these fears did not lead to the widespread repressions of minority groups that occurred in World War I. The tragic exception to this overall tolerance was the forced relocation of some 100,000 Americans of Japanese birth or parentage.

After the Japanese attack on Pearl Harbor, many Americans were genuinely fearful of a Japanese attack on the United States. This fear was soon turned against the **Nisei**—native-born Americans whose ancestors came from Japan. As a result, most Japanese Americans—the great majority of whom lived in California—were forced to leave their homes and were taken to detention camps in other states, where they were imprisoned until the end of the war. Most of the Nisei lost their homes and businesses. Yet there had never been any real proof that these Japanese Americans had been disloyal. Indeed, nearly all of the Nisei remained loyal, patriotic American citizens despite their harsh, unfair treatment. Many of those allowed to serve in the armed forces distinguished themselves for bravery.

After the war Americans regretted their unjustified actions against the Nisei. In 1945 the Nisei were permitted to leave the detention camps and settle wherever they wished. In 1948 Congress passed an act to help the Nisei recover a part of their losses.

Minorities in wartime. American minorities contributed not only to the fighting but to efforts on the home front as well. In 1941 President Roosevelt directed that a Fair Employment Practices Committee be set up to end discriminatory hiring policies in defense industries. As a result, the doors of the defense industries opened to minority workers.

Less was accomplished, however, in promoting equal housing opportunities in the overcrowded cities. Discrimination on the part of white Americans led to outbursts of violence and even riots in several cities. In Detroit in 1943, for example, federal troops restored order after 25 blacks and 9 whites died in a riot.

In 1942 the United States and Mexico signed a treaty. Under its terms thousands of Mexicans known as **braceros** entered the United States on a temporary basis as farm workers. Their efforts helped keep vital food production high during the war.

Prejudice and discrimination against Mexican Americans in jobs, housing, and recreation facilities also aroused bitter resentment. This resentment erupted in a riot in Los Angeles between United States servicemen and Mexican Americans.

Aware of their contributions to the war effort, blacks and other minorities became increasingly restless. As they listened to patriotic speeches about freedom for all, they became more determined to make these ideals meaningful for themselves.

▲

SECTION REVIEW

See underscored items, text pp. 805 - 08.
Identify: OWM, WPB, WMC, Selective Service System, price controls, rationing, Nisei
For answers to questions, see Answer Key, p.A111.

1. **Analyzing Ideas: (a)** Why did the federal government establish controls and regulations over many aspects of American life during the war? **(b)** What were some of these controls? **(c)** How did they affect individuals?

2. **Organizing Ideas:** How did the following contribute to the war effort: **(a)** unions, **(b)** women, **(c)** minorities.

3. **Studying Graphics:** Examine the graph on page 806. **(a)** About how many women were in the labor force in 1920? in 1950? in 1980? **(b)** What percentage of the labor force did women represent in 1920? in 1950? in 1980? **(c)** What may have contributed to the changes?

3 The Allies gradually fight their way to victory in Europe

See Teaching Suggestions in TMRG, p.TM197.

In the summer of 1942 President Roosevelt and Prime Minister Churchill decided to strike at what Churchill called the "soft underbelly" of the Axis.

Victory in North Africa. The opening blow, as you recall, fell late in October 1942, when the British broke through Rommel's lines at El Alamein and began to drive the Germans back into Libya. Meanwhile, on November 8, a force of 500 troop transports and 350 warships under General Eisenhower's command landed thousands of Allied troops in French Morocco and Algeria. The African offensive was the greatest combination of land, sea, and air forces brought together up to that time.

The loss of French areas in North Africa was a serious blow to the Germans. Although they continued to fight with great skill, their efforts were hopeless. Allied planes and ships cut their supply lines from Italy. General Montgomery's British Eighth Army drove steadily westward, while American forces moved eastward. Outnumbered and caught between the jaws of two enemy forces in Tunisia (see map, page 802), the Germans and Italians surrendered early in May 1943.

In the victory in North Africa, the Allies captured more than 250,000 Axis troops. Far more important, the Allied nations now had control of the Mediterranean, their warships protected by planes based at airfields along the North African coast. The Allies could ship supplies to India through the Suez Canal and to the Soviet Union by way of Iran.

Invasion of Italy. From their newly won North African bases, the Allies subjected Sicily and Italy to merciless bombing. Then, early in July 1943, British, Canadian, and American troops landed in Sicily. The Sicilians offered little resistance, and the crack German troops were greatly outnumbered by the invaders, who swiftly overran the island.

Americans and other Allied peoples were thrilled at the rapid conquest of Sicily and by other good news during the summer of 1943. Late in July the Italians ended Mussolini's dictatorial rule and organized a new government. Before dawn on September 3, the British Eighth Army landed on the southern coast of the Italian mainland. On September 8 the Italian government surrendered unconditionally, and the following day an Allied invasion force landed at Salerno.

Despite these great successes the campaign for Italy was one of the longest and most difficult of the war. German troops were rushed in to fill the gaps left by the Italians. Difficult mountain terrain and bad weather helped the Germans. On October 1 Naples fell to an American army under General Mark W. Clark, but for several months the Allies were unable to advance beyond Cassino south of Rome. In an effort to outflank the German lines, Allied troops landed on the Anzio beaches southeast of Rome on January 22, 1944, but the Nazis fought desperately. It was not until June 4, 1944, that the Allied armies entered Rome.

General Dwight D. Eisenhower talks to a battle-weary American soldier along the front lines five months after the invasion of France on D-Day in 1944. One month later, the Germans staged their last offensive against the Allies.

From Rome they moved north. Progress was slow, and every inch of soil was won at great cost by the Allies—Americans, British, Canadians, Indians, New Zealanders, South Africans, French, Moroccans, Algerians, Senegalese, Poles, Greeks, Arabs, Brazilians, and a Jewish brigade from Palestine.

Importance of the Italian campaign. The victories of 1943–44 in Italy were immensely important. Through them the Allies strengthened their control of the Mediterranean. The loss of Italy deprived Germany of desperately needed troops. Moreover, from Italian bases Allied fliers were able to bomb southern Germany and the German-held Balkans, including the rich oil fields in Rumania.

Finally, in their efforts to check the Allies in North Africa and Italy, the Germans had been forced to withdraw troops from the Soviet front. This had helped the Soviet Union to regain great stretches of valuable farmland in the Ukraine. Despite the Italian campaign,

▲ Mussolini had previously been deposed. In April 1944, he had been captured and executed by a group of Italian partisans.

809

however, the Nazis continued to concentrate most of their military forces against the Soviet Union, and the Soviets continued to call for a second front in Western Europe.

Victory in the Atlantic. The victories in Italy were possible only because the Allies had won control of the Atlantic Ocean. During the early months of the war, German submarines waged a mighty battle against ships carrying supplies to Europe. The Allies suffered staggering losses of ships, vital war materials, and lives.

Gradually, however, the Allies gained the upper hand. Radar and other devices for detecting planes and submarines were developed. New warships, including small aircraft carriers, were built by American and British shipyards. In 1942 the Axis sank 585 Allied and neutral vessels in the Atlantic. In 1943 the Axis sank only 110 ships. By the end of 1943, the Battle of the Atlantic was won.

Over the sea lanes, great convoys carried urgently needed military supplies to the Mediterranean war fronts and to Great Britain, which by 1943 had been converted into a vast base for the invasion of Western Europe.

Victory in the air. While the Allied navies were winning the Battle of the Atlantic, Allied planes began their offensive against Germany and German-occupied Europe. By early 1943 the Anglo-American air assault had become a major factor in the struggle. During the last year of the war, fleets of as many as 2,000 heavy bombers were dropping tons of bombs on a single target area.

The constant blows against German transportation centers, industrial plants, and military installations weakened German morale. The Allied air raids brought relief to Great Britain, which had suffered tremendous damage from German air attacks. They also helped Soviet armies who were seeking to drive the Nazis from Soviet soil.

Liberation of Western Europe. The terrific air assault on Germany was part of a larger strategy—the invasion and conquest of Germany. By June 1944 General Eisenhower, who had been named Supreme Commander of the Allied invasion armies in Western Europe, was satisfied that it was time to launch the attack.

Operation Overlord, as the invasion was called, began before dawn on the morning of June 6, 1944 (D-Day). More than 11,000 planes roared into the air. Some dropped airborne troops at key points a few miles inland from the German-occupied French coast. Others bombed roads, bridges, railway junctions, and German troop concentrations. Still others formed a mighty umbrella under which a huge invasion fleet of nearly 4,000 troop transports, landing craft, and warships moved across the English Channel to the Normandy beaches (see map, page 802).

The Germans had worked for years to make these beaches unconquerable. Heavy artillery and machine guns were located in reinforced concrete pillboxes. Barbed wire and tank traps lined the shores. Other tangles of barbed wire were strung on steel and concrete piles and sunk just below the water's surface for hundreds of feet offshore.

Despite the years of preparation, the Germans were powerless to stop the invasion. The Nazis resisted fiercely, but they were outplanned, outnumbered, and outfought. Allied tank forces ripped through the German defenses and fanned out behind the lines. Aided by the French resistance, or underground movement, they quickly overran the countryside. On August 25, 1944, Paris fell. By this time the Allies had landed more than 2 million troops and millions of tons of munitions and supplies.

Meanwhile, early in August, the United States Seventh Army landed on the southern coast of France. It pushed rapidly up the Rhone Valley to join the Allied troops pouring in from Normandy. Within six months after D-Day, France had been liberated and the Allies had swept into the outer defenses of Germany's famous Siegfried Line, which paralleled the Maginot Line. Here the attack at last ground to a halt. The Allied armies paused while new ports were opened, supplies were brought up, and military units were regrouped.

The election of 1944. The preparations for the final drive into Germany did not interfere with the regular November elections in the United States. The Republican candidate for the Presidency was Thomas E. Dewey, governor of New York. He had attracted national attention when, as a district attorney, he had successfully prosecuted racketeers in New York. The Republicans considered Dewey a strong candidate. However, the war was going well, and the Democrats argued that it would be unwise to replace experienced leaders. The argument proved convincing. Roosevelt, run-

During the days of the Roman Empire, the Elbe River marked the northernmost boundary of the Roman advance into what are now the two German republics. Since World War II, however, the Elbe has come to symbolize the easternmost boundary of Western influence in Europe.

It was on April 25, 1945, that Soviet and American forces joyfully greeted each other on the banks of the Elbe, uniting the eastern and western fronts. This historic meeting split Hitler's army and signaled the collapse of Nazi Germany. An immediate controversy ensued, however, over the American decision to halt its penetration of Germany at the Elbe because the Soviet military occupation of eastern Germany soon acquired ominous political overtones. By 1949 the postwar fate of Europe was sealed into two separate spheres of influence — one Soviet, one American.

The decision to halt the eastward drive of American troops at the Elbe had both political and military origins. By mid-March of 1945 the Soviets, who had already encircled the bulk of the German army, were entrenched along the Oder River within striking distance of Berlin. Meanwhile American armies were advancing southeast in pursuit of the last remaining German forces.

On April 9 American troops under Lieutenant General William Simpson established a bridgehead on the Elbe River within 55 miles (89 kilometers) of Berlin. Simpson was planning to advance on the German capital when he received word from Lieutenant General Omar Bradley, "You have to stop right where you are. You can't go any farther. You must pull back across the Elbe . . . I just got it from Ike."

Ike, of course, was Supreme Allied Commander Dwight Eisenhower. Simpson was incensed at being denied the opportunity to race the Soviets to Berlin. The nearest Soviet troops were 100 miles (161 kilometers) away. It would take the Soviets several days to reach the Elbe and then march to Berlin.

What prompted Eisenhower's decision about the direction the Allied armies would take? Eisenhower reasoned that the nationality of the troops who conquered Berlin would be meaningless in the context of political agreements that had already been made concerning the postwar division of Germany into four zones of occupation — Soviet, American, British, and French. Even if the Americans were to capture Berlin first, they would have to surrender most of it — and all the surrounding area — to the Soviets.

Furthermore, Eisenhower's overriding concern remained what it always had been — the defeat of Hitler's Germany. Like Churchill and Roosevelt, he had no crystal-ball insight into Soviet postwar behavior. His immediate problem was a military one. Little did he realize at the time that half a century later people would continue to debate the implications of his decision on the postwar history of Europe.

---

ning for a fourth term, won with an electoral vote of 432 to Dewey's 99. The new Vice President was Harry S Truman of Missouri.

Germany's last counterattack. While the Allies were regrouping, the Germans were preparing a counterattack. On December 16 some 24 German divisions struck at a weakly held
▲ point in the Allied lines. German armored forces broke through, creating a dangerous bulge in the Allied lines. Christmas 1944 found the Allies fighting desperately in the Battle of the Bulge (see map, page 802), trying to prevent the Germans from plunging onward to the sea. Reinforcements were rushed up. The German divisions were shattered and thrown back behind the Siegfried Line.

Their defeat cost the Germans dearly. Even more important, as Eisenhower pointed out, was "the widespread disillusionment within the German army and Germany itself."

Invasion of Germany. By February 1945, Allied preparations had been completed for the invasion of Germany. The air forces continued to blast industrial areas, military bases, and transportation lines. Then, in March, the Allies crossed the Rhine, encircled Nazi troop concentrations, and plunged toward the heart of Germany (see map, page 802).

Meanwhile, the Soviets had been driving the Germans out of the Ukraine. They had conquered Nazi-held Rumania and Hungary and were closing in upon the Nazis from the south and east. Churchill had grown concerned over the Soviet Union's postwar intentions. He was alarmed at the deep penetration of the Soviet armies into Europe and argued that the Allies should race the Soviets to Berlin and Prague. This vital political problem might have been decided by the leaders of the Allied governments including, of course, President Roosevelt. Instead, the civilian leaders left the

▲ The Germans had hoped to split Allied forces in two by breaking through to the port of Antwerp. The plan was foolhardy, therefore not expected by the Allies. It cost the Allies 77,000 casualties and delayed until late January the re-establishment of the old line.

Crowds fill Times Square in New York City, celebrating the German surrender on V-E Day, May 8, 1945.

decision to General Eisenhower. He, as Supreme Commander, concluded that his first objective should be the immediate and total destruction of the German armies. It would be "militarily unsound," he declared, to depart from this objective for political considerations. As a result of this decision, American forces under Eisenhower advanced only as far as the Elbe River. There on April 25 American troops joined the Soviet forces at Torgau.

▲ **Victory in Germany.** Events that ended the war in Europe then followed in rapid order. On May 1 Hitler reportly took his own life in the burning ruins of Berlin. On May 2 the Soviet troops hammered their way into the last Nazi strongholds of the city, and nearly 1 million German soldiers in Italy and Austria surrendered. Germany was in chaos. Within a week the Nazi forces in the Netherlands, Denmark, and Germany stopped fighting. Early on the morning of May 7, the German High Command surrendered unconditionally. The surrender was announced the next day. Thus May 8, 1945 marked the formal end of the war in Europe.

In Churchill's words, the victory over Germany was "the signal for the greatest outburst of joy in the history of mankind." As for himself, he wrote, his joy was tempered by "an aching heart and a mind oppressed by forebodings." He was weighed down by the awful tragedy of the war and concerned over the postwar intentions of the U.S.S.R.

Revelations of Nazi horrors. The first outbursts of joy at the end of the war in Europe were soon dulled by shocking news coming out of Germany. During the war the few refugees that managed to escape Nazi control had brought reports of terrible persecution and massacres of Jews. When the Allied armies entered and occupied the conquered country, the full extent of Nazi horrors came to light.

The world now heard in detail the bloodcurdling crimes the Nazis had committed in their <u>concentration camps</u>. In one of the most terrible displays of brutality in human history, the Nazis had created these camps, or "death factories," to destroy their "political enemies" and to exterminate the entire Jewish population (see page 790).

The horrified world labeled this program of extermination the <u>Holocaust</u>. In it nearly 12 million men, women, and children, about half of them Jews, had been slaughtered after suffering indescribable anxieties, agonies, indignities, and tortures.

Roosevelt's death. President Roosevelt did not live to see the end of the war or to share in the world's horror over the Nazi atrocities. Worn out by his vast responsibilities, he died suddenly on April 12, 1945, in the "Little White House" at Warm Springs, Georgia. People all over the world were stunned at the news of his death. For three days American radio stations canceled programs to devote time to his memory. Vice President Harry S Truman, who now became President, declared, "His fellow countrymen will sorely miss his fortitude and faith and courage in the time to come. The peoples of the earth who love the ways of freedom and hope will mourn for him."

SECTION REVIEW

See underscored items, text pp. 810 - 12.

Identify: Operation Overlord, D-Day, Siegfried Line, Battle of the Bulge, concentration camps, Holocaust

For answers to questions, see Answer Key, p.A111.

1. **Evaluating Ideas:** Why was the Allies' Italian campaign important?

In 1944, Truman had been nominated, and elected, Vice President, replacing Henry A. Wallace, who had been considered too radical.

2. **Analyzing Ideas: (a)** Why was it vital for the Allies to win the Battle of the Atlantic? **(b)** Why were the Allies able to win this battle?

3. **Summarizing Ideas:** Describe the events of 1945 that led to the fall of Germany and to the end of the war in Europe.

4 Allied victories in the Pacific bring an end to World War II

See Teaching Suggestions in TMRG, p.TM198.

President Roosevelt's death in April 1945 came only a month before the Allied victory in Europe and only four months before the defeat of the Japanese ended World War II.

By 1943 the United States and its Allies were taking the offensive in the Pacific. The overall strategy, directed by Admiral Chester W. Nimitz, had three parts. (1) Air, land, and naval forces would strike westward at the Japanese-held islands in the Central Pacific. (2) A fleet under Admiral Halsey would drive the Japanese from the Solomon Islands. (3) General MacArthur would advance with troops along the New Guinea coast and on to the Philippine Islands. The ultimate objective was Japan.

Early victories. During 1943, American, Australian, and New Zealand troops pushed forward through the jungles and across the Central and South Pacific. The struggle was grim, for the Japanese clung to every foot of land. Few prisoners were taken.

Driving the Japanese from their position before Port Moresby, American and Australian troops fought their way up the New Guinea coast. Before the end of 1943, much of New Guinea had been recovered. American and New Zealand forces also won victories in the Solomon Islands.

Meanwhile, in the Central Pacific, Admiral Nimitz's powerful fleet moved into the Gilbert Islands, and American marines seized Tarawa and Makin (see map, page 816). Far to the north, Japan's troops were dislodged from the Aleutian strongholds of Attu and Kiska. The threat to Alaska was now ended.

Despite these successes, won at extreme cost in lives after ferocious fighting, the major Japanese positions remained untouched.

Island hopping. By 1944 a growing volume of troops and supplies was arriving in the Pacific. Powerful new warships and aircraft carriers, grouped into swift task forces, swept through the outer screen of protecting islands blasting Japanese installations and shipping routes. Carrier planes were raining explosives on the Japanese-held islands prior to invasion.

Suddenly, on January 31, 1944, the Allies struck again, this time against the Marshall Islands (see map, page 816). Three days later they seized Kwajalein (KWOJ·ah·lin), one of the keys to Japanese control of the Marshalls. Kwajalein was the first Japanese possession occupied by the Allies. Three weeks later Eniwetok (en·ih·WEE·tok) was stormed successfully. From these two bases, strong fleets of B-24 bombers began to blast Truk, a major stronghold in the Carolines and the key to Japanese control of the Southwest and Central Pacific. Meanwhile General MacArthur, continuing his advance up the New Guinea coast, seized Hollandia. By July all of New Guinea was in MacArthur's hands, with only bypassed pockets of Japanese troops left to surrender or to starve.

A month earlier, in June 1944, task-force raids and swift strikes by carrier-based planes pinned down Japanese air and naval forces and hammered the defenses of Saipan and Guam in the Mariana Islands (see map, page 816). Then under cover of intense air and naval bombardment, landing craft swept in upon the beaches. From fleets near the Philippines, the Japanese sent out swarms of planes, only to lose more than 400 in a few hours. The following day hundreds of American planes roared from the decks of carriers to strike a severe blow at the retreating Japanese fleet.

Though shocked and saddened by the appalling loss of life, the American people were thrilled at the victories on Guam and Saipan. They had long dreaded the thought of a slow, bloody, island-by-island advance to Japan. Now Americans realized that the nation's tremendous sea and air power enabled it to seize key positions in the Pacific, leaving Japanese forces isolated and helpless on numerous islands far behind the line of battle.

Victory in the Philippines. Probably the most gratifying news from the Pacific in 1944 was the reconquest of the Philippines. In October vast naval forces moved up from the New Guinea–Solomons theater of war and in from

● In this "leap-frogging" strategy, Allied forces bypassed major Japanese strongholds by sealing off all air and sea routes and leaving them without supplies while the Allies built new strike bases in less strongly defended spots nearer Japan.

813

General Douglas MacArthur (left) wades ashore in the Philippines in 1944, keeping the promise to return that he had made two years earlier.

Saipan and Guam. The converging forces poured upon the beaches of Leyte (LAY·teh) in the central Philippines (see map, page 816). and eventually captured the island. Meanwhile, in the Battle of Leyte Gulf, American naval forces shattered Japan's remaining sea power.

Overcoming bitter land resistance, the conquering troops then spread over the Philippines. Early in February 1945, Manila fell to the Americans. "I shall return," MacArthur had promised when, following orders, he had left Corregidor in 1942. "I'm a little late, but we finally came," he said in Manila in 1945 as the American and Filipino flags were raised above the city.

The Yalta Conference. Long before the Allied victories in 1945, leaders of the great powers had met at a series of conferences to develop a common strategy and to form plans for a lasting peace. Early in February 1945, President Roosevelt, Prime Minister Churchill, and Premier Stalin met at Yalta in the southern part of the Soviet Union. At the Yalta Conference, they made far-reaching decisions concerning the postwar world.

One group of decisions involved the creation of a new world organization. The three heads of state agreed to call a conference to meet in San Francisco on April 25, 1945. The purpose would be to draw up a charter for a new international organization.

In another group of decisions, Roosevelt, Churchill, and Stalin made plans for the occupation of postwar Germany and the future of Poland and the other liberated nations in Eastern and Central Europe. They agreed to divide Germany into four military zones to be occupied and controlled by the United States, Great Britain, the Soviet Union, and France. They also agreed that the "Big Three"—the United States, Great Britain, and the Soviet Union—would support free elections in Poland and throughout Europe. This would guarantee the right of Europeans to choose their own governments. These and other agreements were announced to the public.

Secret agreements. The "Big Three" also reached several secret agreements. In one of these, Stalin promised that the Soviet Union would enter the war against Japan within three months after the war in Europe ended. In exchange for this promise, Roosevelt and Churchill, upon recommendation of top military leaders, agreed to two points. (1) They would recognize the Mongolian People's Republic, which had once been part of China but now claimed its independence under Soviet protection. (2) They would allow the Soviet Union to have the Kurile Islands, the southern half of Sakhalin Island, an occupation zone in Korea, and certain rights in Manchuria (see map, page 816). Several of these territories and privileges had been held by Russia before it lost them in the Russo-Japanese War of 1904–05.

Details of the Yalta Conference did not become public until long after Roosevelt's death. Down through the years, critics have severely condemned Roosevelt for what they called his "surrender" to Soviet demands. The critics charged that as a result of his "surrender," Roosevelt gave the Soviet Union control of Manchuria, paved the way for the Chinese Communists' victory over Chiang Kai-shek (CHAHNG KI·SHEK), the Chinese Nationalist leader, and opened the door to Communist

One of America's greatest victories during World War II was the capture of Iwo Jima by United States Marines. A newspaper photographer, Joe Rosenthal of the Associated Press, who was at Iwo Jima took a photograph of several Marines as they raised the American flag there. The photograph won the Pulitzer Prize and became one of the most famous pictures from World War II.

After the war the photograph was used as a model for the United States Marine Corps War Memorial shown here. Atop a black marble base is a sculptured reproduction of Rosenthal's photograph. Around the base is an engraved listing of United States wars. Battles in which the United States Marines distinguished themselves are also listed. An inscription on the base, dedicated to all American veterans, reads "Uncommon valor was a common virtue." The memorial stands outside the Arlington National Cemetery, near Washington, D.C. The statue honors the many brave Americans who have fought to defend our nation in past wars.

aggression in Korea. They also held him responsible for Soviet occupation of East Berlin and East Germany and the creation of Communist governments in Eastern Europe. These governments were created without the free elections that Stalin had promised.

Roosevelt's defenders have replied to these charges by reminding the critics of the military situation at the time of the Yalta Conference. Soviet armies had already conquered most of Eastern Europe, including Poland. American troops, on the other hand, had not yet crossed the Rhine and were still fighting the Japanese in the Philippines. Moreover, Allied military leaders had warned that the invasion of Japan, scheduled for the spring of 1946, might cost the United States as many as 1 million troops.

Also, Roosevelt's defenders insisted, Stalin had given Churchill and Roosevelt reason to believe that the Soviet Union would cooperate in building a new world organization designed to establish the foundations of a lasting peace. As Churchill himself later wrote, "Our hopeful assumptions were soon to be falsified. Still, they were the only ones possible at the time."

The road to victory. On February 19, 1945, United States Marines landed on the beaches of Iwo Jima (EE·woh JEE·mah). Nearly 20,000 American marines were killed or wounded in the successful effort to gain control of this barren volcanic island, only 750 miles (1,200 kilometers) from Tokyo (see map, page 816). Among the marines who helped raise a flag of victory over Iwo Jima was Ira Hayes, an Indian. Hayes later received the Congressional Medal of Honor.

A few weeks later, the largest landing force in Pacific history invaded Okinawa (oh·kih·NAH·wah), a Japanese island some 300 miles (480 kilometers) from the Japanese homeland. Okinawa fell in June 1945.

Japan still had many well-trained and well-equipped soldiers. It still controlled large areas of China. Badly needed American supplies were being flown across the eastern Hi-

Text continues on page 817.

815

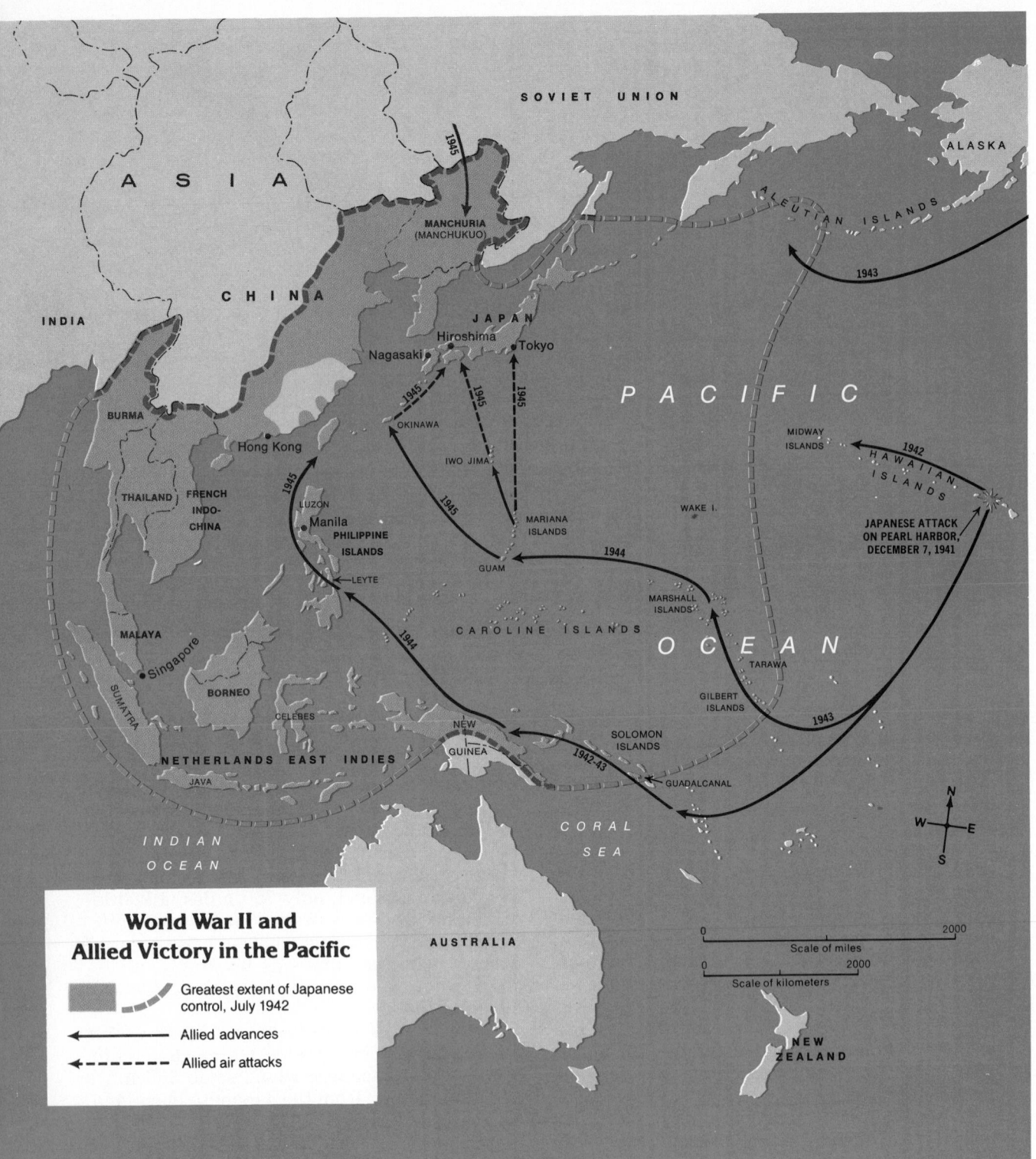

World War II and Allied Victory in the Pacific

Greatest extent of Japanese control, July 1942

⟶ Allied advances

- - -➤ Allied air attacks

SOVIET UNION

ALASKA

ASIA

ALEUTIAN ISLANDS

MANCHURIA
(MANCHUKUO)

CHINA

1945

JAPAN

1943

PACIFIC

INDIA

Hiroshima

Tokyo

Nagasaki

BURMA

OKINAWA

1945

1945

1945

MIDWAY
ISLANDS

1942

HAWAIIAN
ISLANDS

Hong Kong

IWO JIMA

THAILAND

FRENCH
INDO-
CHINA

LUZON

Manila

PHILIPPINE
ISLANDS

1945

1945

MARIANA
ISLANDS

GUAM

WAKE I.

1944

JAPANESE ATTACK
ON PEARL HARBOR,
DECEMBER 7, 1941

LEYTE

MALAYA

Singapore

BORNEO

CELEBES

1944

CAROLINE ISLANDS

MARSHALL
ISLANDS

OCEAN

TARAWA

SUMATRA

NETHERLANDS EAST INDIES

JAVA

NEW
GUINEA

SOLOMON
ISLANDS

1942-43

GUADALCANAL

GILBERT
ISLANDS

1943

INDIAN
OCEAN

CORAL
SEA

N
W E
S

AUSTRALIA

0   2000
Scale of miles

0   2000
Scale of kilometers

NEW
ZEALAND

World War II in the Pacific

Dark days for the Allies

1941

JULY	Japan invades French Indochina.
DEC. 7	Japanese attack Pearl Harbor.
DEC. 8–11	United States declares war against the Axis.
DEC.	Japanese invasion of Thailand and Br. Malaya; capture of Wake, Guam, Hong Kong; invasion of Philippines, Midway.

1942

JAN.	Fall of Manila.
JAN.–MAY	Japanese occupy Netherlands Indies and Burma.
FEB.	Singapore surrenders to Japanese.
FEB.–MAR.	Battle of the Java Sea.
APR.–MAY	Fall of Bataan and Corregidor.
MAY	Battle of the Coral Sea.
JUNE	Battle of Midway.
JUNE	Japanese occupy Attu and Kiska in Aleutians.

Allied gains: the tide turns

AUG.	U.S. marines land on Guadalcanal.
NOV.	Allied victory in naval battle of Guadalcanal.

1943

JAN.–SEPT.	Allied gains in New Guinea.
MAR.–AUG.	Allies force Japanese from Aleutians.
JUNE–DEC.	Allied offensive in South Pacific: Solomon Is.
NOV.–FEB. 1944	Allied offensive in Central Pacific: Gilbert Is., Marshall Is., Kwajalein, Eniwetok.

1944

APR.–JULY	Allies seize Hollandia and regain New Guinea.
JUNE–AUG.	Allies capture Saipan and Guam in Mariana Is.
OCT.	Allied campaign to reconquer Philippines begins.

1945

FEB.	Allies liberate Manila; end of Philippines campaign.
FEB.–MAR.	U.S. marines conquer Iwo Jima.
APR.–JUNE	U.S. marines conquer Okinawa.
MAY–AUG.	Allied air offensive against Japanese home islands.

Allied victory in the Pacific

AUG. 6	Atomic bomb dropped on Hiroshima.
AUG. 9	Atomic bomb dropped on Nagasaki.
AUG. 10	Japan asks for peace.
AUG. 15	V-J Day
SEPT. 2	Japan signs formal surrender.

malayas and trucked over the newly opened Stilwell Road to embattled Chinese troops. These supplies were only a fraction of what China needed, and Chinese troops were in no position to undertake a major offensive. Moreover, the inner defenses on the Japanese homeland were strong. On the other hand, Japan was blockaded, and, after the war in Europe ended in the spring of 1945, the full weight of the Allies was available for the final struggle in the Pacific. By the early summer of 1945, the blockade and the relentless bombings were destroying Japan's power to resist.

The end of World War II. With Roosevelt's death in April 1945, the responsibility for defeating Japan fell upon his successor, President Truman. In July Truman met with Stalin and Clement Attlee, the new British Prime Minister, at Potsdam, Germany. At this meeting the three Allied leaders discussed plans for the control and occupation of Germany. They also issued an ultimatum to Japan, calling for its unconditional surrender. Japan rejected the ultimatum on July 29.

Events then moved quickly. First the United States dropped the atomic bomb on Hiroshima. Two days later, the United States dropped a second atomic bomb on Nagasaki. On August 10 the Japanese government asked for peace.

On August 14, 1945, President Truman announced by radio that Japan had accepted the Allied peace terms. He then proclaimed August 15, 1945, as V-J Day. The formal surrender was signed on September 2, 1945. World War II had come to an end.

SECTION REVIEW

See underscored items, text pp. 813, 815 - 16.

Identify: Chester Nimitz, Ira Hayes, Potsdam, Hiroshima

For answers to questions, see Answer Key, pp. A111-12.

1. **Organizing Ideas:** What was the Allied strategy for winning the war in the Pacific?

2. **Summarizing Ideas:** (a) Discuss the agreements reached at the Yalta Conference of 1945. (b) Explain the arguments made by some Americans for and against these agreements.

3. **Analyzing Ideas:** (a) Why did the Japanese finally surrender? (b) Was the dropping of the atomic bomb necessary to end the war? Explain.

4. **Studying Maps:** Examine the map on page 816. (a) Trace the area of maximum Japanese control during the war. (b) With the help of the map, explain the island-hopping strategy.

▲ Truman faced a difficult decision in choosing to use the bomb. But the alternative—a full-scale invasion of Japan—entailed extending the war at least another year, facing forces of perhaps 5,000,000 suicide aircraft, and losing 2,000,000 American lives.

817

DEVELOPING HISTORY STUDY SKILLS

Thinking About History   Evaluating Decisions

In February, 1945, leaders of the United States, Great Britain, and the Soviet Union met at the Black Sea resort of Yalta. Their goal was to hammer out a plan for the post-World War II world. The decisions these leaders reached have been debated endlessly ever since that fateful meeting. Students of history, like historians themselves, must be able to evaluate decisions.

How to Evaluate Decisions

To evaluate a decision, follow these steps.

1. **Determine the nature of the decision or decisions that had to be made.** Take into account the conditions that existed at the time the decision was made.

2. **Identify the alternatives available.** Note the possible options the decision maker had.

3. **List the risks and benefits of each alternative.** Note that many alternatives have both short-term and long-range effects that must not be overlooked.

4. **Evaluate the alternatives by weighing risks against gains.** Once again, do not overlook the long-range impact of an alternative.

5. **Analyze the results of the decision.** Determine if, all things considered, the decision was a good one or a bad one. Realize as well that long-range effects may not have been evident at the time a decision was made.

Applying the Skill

The Allied leaders thought it necessary that the Soviet Union join with the Allied forces to defeat Japan. Read the excerpt below.

> The Soviet Union demanded certain concessions in order to join the Allies in the final battle against Japan. The Soviet Union wanted parts of eastern Poland ceded to the Soviet Union, and they wanted some control of Polish elections and internal affairs. The Soviets also wanted territory formerly held by Japan. They also sought ports in Manchuria and control of the Manchurian railroad.

Now evaluate the Allied leaders' decision.

The Big Three at Yalta made the following concessions to the Soviet Union in exchange for entering the war against Japan. The Soviet Union received Southern Sakhalin Island, Central Kurile Island, ports in Manchuria, and joint control of the Manchurian railroad. In addition, the Polish border was redrawn to give parts of eastern Poland to the Soviets. Though free elections were guaranteed elsewhere in Eastern Europe, the Soviet Union was given control of Polish elections. This series of decisions has been harshly criticized since the end of World War II.

What alternatives did the Allies have? The leaders of the United States and Great Britain could have refused Soviet demands and walked out of the meeting. The leaders, however, felt that Soviet military strength was needed to defeat the Japanese and bring an end to the war in the Pacific. At this time, it was not certain that the Manhattan Project to develop the atomic bomb would be successful. The Allied leaders envisioned an island-hopping struggle costing thousands of lives.

Another alternative was to negotiate smaller concessions. In this case the Soviets would not part from their original demands. Therefore, the leaders of the United States and Great Britain thought it worthwhile to acquiesce to Soviet demands in order to enlist their support in the fight against Japan.

Practicing the Skill

Read the following situation. Then on a separate sheet of paper, evaluate the decision.

> After Roosevelt's death, President Truman faced the challenge of ending the war. Germany had already been defeated. The prospects of defeating Japan quickly, however, seemed remote. Truman had two alternatives. (1) Send more American troops to the Pacific theater. Advisers warned Truman that the war would last another year and a half and cost as many as one million American lives. (2) Use the atomic bomb on Japan. The bomb was untested. Advisers also warned against possible international outrage at the use of the weapon. Truman chose the latter alternative.

([Decision] defeat the Japanese quickly; [Alternatives] See solid line underscore; [Risks] Alternative 1 -- loss of American lives; Alternative 2--untested nature of bomb's effects; public outrage; [Benefits] Alternative 1--none; Alternative 2--shorten war; save lives; [Results Analysis] Answers will vary.)

The cost of World War II in human lives, money, and property was enormous. In the United States alone, the federal government spent more money on the war than it had during the entire period from 1789 to 1940, including the cost of all earlier wars. Property worth billions of dollars was destroyed throughout Europe, the islands of the Pacific, China, and Japan. Farms, factories, and parts of many of the world's major cities were reduced to rubble.

The loss of human life was staggering. According to General Marshall's final report, 201,367 Americans had been killed by the end of June 1945. About 600,000 had been wounded, and 57,000 were missing. Other nations lost much more heavily. It has been estimated that more than 3,000,000 Germans, more than 3,100,000 Russians, more than 1,500,000 Japanese, and more than 375,000 British troops were killed in battle. Civilian deaths resulting from bombings, starvation, disease, and imprisonment in concentration camps ran into countless millions. The exact number of dead will never be known with any certainty, for vast numbers of people simply disappeared. Many more millions of people were uprooted and left homeless. These were only some of the immediate and terrible effects of the most devastating war the world had ever seen.

CONNECTING CHAPTER IDEAS

The United States emerged from World War II with a new role in world affairs. In the next chapter you will read how the United States sought to carry the heavy burden of responsibility which accompanies world leadership.

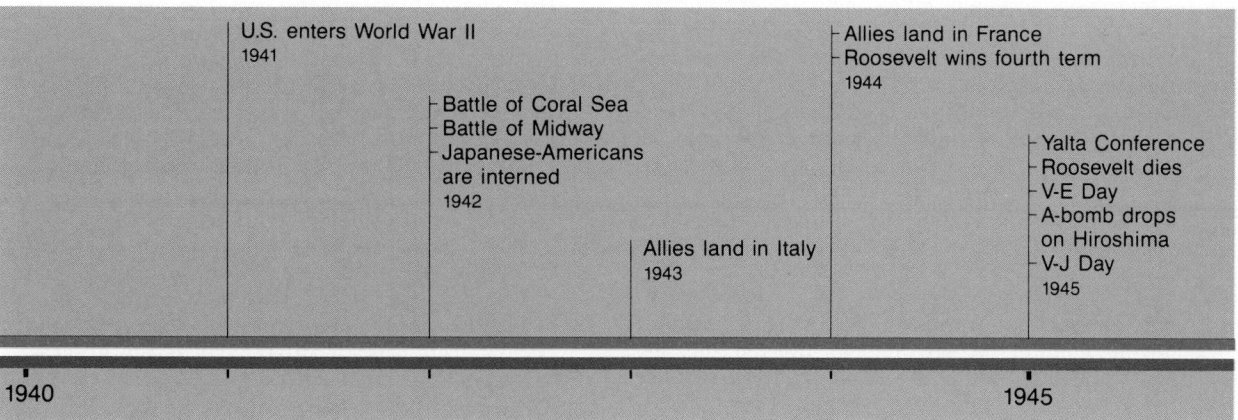

U.S. enters World War II
1941

├ Battle of Coral Sea
├ Battle of Midway
├ Japanese-Americans
  are interned
1942

Allies land in Italy
1943

├ Allies land in France
├ Roosevelt wins fourth term
1944

├ Yalta Conference
├ Roosevelt dies
├ V-E Day
├ A-bomb drops
  on Hiroshima
├ V-J Day
1945

1940   1945

CHAPTER

36 REVIEW

Reviewing Important Terms

Decide whether each of the following sentences is true or false. If the sentence is false, replace the underlined term with the word or phrase that will make it true.

1. After the Japanese attack on Pearl Harbor, many Americans became fearful of the Nisei.
2. As the Soviet people retreated from the German invasion troops, they applied a scorched-earth policy to their land.
3. During World War II, the United States government issued coupons to establish price controls.
4. In 1942 the United States and Mexico signed a treaty which allowed thousands of Mexicans known as mutalistas to enter the United States.

Practicing Critical Thinking Skills

1. **Organizing Ideas. (a)** What were the most important reasons for the Allied victory in Europe? **(b)** What role did science and technology play in winning the war? **(c)** What role did air power play in both the European and Pacific theaters?
2. **Evaluating Ideas.** United States action against the Nisei was justified because the Constitutional rights of all citizens are suspended in wartime. Do you agree or disagree? Why?
3. **Interpreting Ideas.** At certain times in a country's history, the power of a single personality becomes an extremely important force. Apply this idea to **(a)** Churchill, **(b)** Mussolini, **(c)** Hitler, or **(d)** Roosevelt.
4. **Analyzing Ideas.** Despite their deeply rooted belief in individualism and free enterprise, Americans accepted many new governmental controls during World War II. **(a)** Why? **(b)** Which controls do you think met the greatest resistance? Explain.
5. **Seeing Relationships.** Use primary and secondary sources to find out more of the role of women during World War II. **(a)** Why did women enter the work force? **(b)** At what kinds of jobs did they work? **(c)** What effects did the war have on the role of women in American society? Explain.
6. **Relating Past to Present.** The atomic bomb was used to end World War II. **(a)** How has the development of nuclear weapons affected the stability of peace and the threat of world war today? **(b)** What role do nuclear weapons play in the United States' defense today?

Developing History Study Skills

Evaluating Decisions. Read the following excerpt from a radio address President Harry S Truman made on August 9, 1945, the day the second atomic bomb was dropped on Japan. Then answer the questions below.

I realized the tragic significance of the atomic bomb. Its production and its use were not lightly undertaken by this Government. . . . We know now how close [our enemies] were to finding it. And we know the disaster which would come . . . to all peaceful nations, . . . if they had found if first.

That is why we [undertook] the long and uncertain and costly labor of discovery and production.

We won the race of discovery against the Germans.

(a) According to President Truman, what was the main reason for producing the atomic bomb? **(b)** What did President Truman feel would be the result if the Germans had developed the atomic bomb first?

Relating Geography and History

The conflict that began in September 1939 was called a world war because many nations were involved and fighting raged in many countries. Tremendous distances and other geographic factors helped determine the outcome of the war. To better understand the effect of geography on strategy and warfare, answer the following questions.

1. Study the map on page 802. **(a)** German armies pushed to the vicinity of what two Russian cities? **(b)** What effects did the distance between Germany and the German armies have?
2. The map inset illustrates German air attacks on Great Britain. **(a)** How far is London from Berlin? **(b)** What geographic factor made Great Britain especially difficult for Germany to conquer?
3. Describe how the area of Axis control changed from 1942 to 1945.
4. **(a)** Use the information on the map on page 802 to describe Allied advances and victory in Europe. **(b)** Use the information on the map on page 817 to describe Allied advances in the Pacific.
5. Study the map on page 817. **(a)** How far is Pearl Harbor from Tokyo? **(b)** What was the greatest extent of Japanese control to the west? **(c)** For what geographic reason did the Allies employ the strategy of island hopping in the Pacific?

820

UNIT ELEVEN
REVIEW

Discussing Ideas

1. In what ways did the "peace" ending World War I lead to World War II?
2. **(a)** What is isolationism? **(b)** Why was the United States basically isolationist after World War I? **(c)** In what ways was the United States *not* isolationist in that period?
3. During the 1930's, some nations resorted to dictatorships in order to resolve problems caused by the worldwide depression. **(a)** How might a dictatorship be able to solve such problems? **(b)** Why do you think the United States did not become a dictatorship during this period?
4. Compare the attempts of the United States to remain neutral before World War I and World War II. **(a)** Account for the similarities you discover. **(b)** Why did each of these attempts fail?
5. World War II was as much a battle of the scientists and engineers as a battle of the foot soldiers. Explain.

Applying History Study Skills

Evaluating Decisions. The following excerpts come from a book by W. Averell Harriman, Roosevelt's special envoy to Churchill and Stalin during World War II. Read the excerpts and then answer the questions below.

1. Stalin, however, was unwilling to leave the Soviet Union [to attend the Casablanca Conference] with his winter offensive under way.
2. "I must say that things are now so hot that it is impossible for me to absent myself for even a single day," he wrote.
3. Stalin also made it plain that for him the paramount question was still the Second Front in the west—and that required no further talk, only action.
4. Stalin's refusal to attend, in effect, spared Roosevelt and Churchill the embarrassment of having to rebuff his demands face to face.
5. The Casablanca decisions to invade Sicily and step up the bomber offensive against Germany came as a bitter disappointment to Stalin and his generals.

(a) On what two reasons did Stalin base his decision to be absent from the Casablanca Conference? **(b)** What was the result of Stalin's refusal to attend the conference?

Making Connections

1. Interview relatives or acquaintances who lived in your area during World War II. Ask them to comment on aspects of the war effort that directly affected their lives. You might ask them about such subjects as food and gas rationing, civil defense activities, and changes in local factory output.
2. Investigate the Supreme Court cases, such as *Korematsu v. U.S.,* that arose from the internment of Japanese Americans. **(a)** What were the major questions raised by the cases? **(b)** How did the Court resolve the questions?
3. Make a tape recording (from records or your own performing) of songs that were popular during World War II. Play the tape for the class. Then lead a discussion on what can be learned about this (or any) time period from its popular songs.
4. Develop a time line for Unit Eleven. Include entries for at least ten events. Then answer the following questions. **(a)** What is the theme of your time line? **(b)** Does that theme fairly represent the major events in United States history during that time period?
5. Read *Hiroshima* by John Hersey or *Baba Yar* by A. Kuznestov. Then write an essay describing your reaction to the information presented by the book you read.
6. Research and prepare a report on the Manhattan Project and the development of the atomic bomb.

Reading in Depth

Frank, Anne, *Diary of a Young Girl* (Garden City, NY: Doubleday). A vivid account of a Jewish girl and her family as they hide from the Nazis.

Hichiya, M., *Hiroshima Diary* (Chapel Hill, NC: University of North Carolina Press). Eyewitness accounts of the devastation caused by the first atomic bomb used in war.

Merrian, Eve, *Growing Up Female in America* (Garden City, NY: Doubleday). Using primary sources such as letters and diaries, this book tells what life was like for American women during various historical periods since the Civil War.

Westheimer, David, *Von Ryan's Express* (Garden City, NY: Doubleday). An action-packed novel of American and British prisoners of war who make a daring escape in the last days of World War II.

821

UNIT TWELVE

Reshaping the Postwar World

Growth and change have always been major forces in United States history. The years following World War II, 1945 to 1960, were no different. Now a world leader, the United States helped war-torn nations rebuild and kept a wary eye on the Soviet Union. At home the pace of life quickened as the population boomed. The economy surged as new ideas and technology spurred growth. Nowhere were growth and change more evident than the nation's cities, such as Philadelphia (below). Minorities, seeking their share of freedom and opportunity, and farm families poured into urban centers seeking a better life. Suburbs blossomed as newly affluent Americans sought to escape urban problems. New cities were built and older ones revitalized. The nation's culture had truly become urbanized.

See Chapter Overview in TMRG, p.TM202.
See Chapter Objectives in TMRG, p.TM202.
See Introducing the Chapter in TMRG, p.TM202.

CHAPTER 37

Responsibilities of World Leadership

(1945–1960)

UN General
Assembly

The end of World War II in 1945 brought rejoicing in all the victorious countries. But the joy and gaiety were restrained. The dominant feeling was one of immense relief. The mood of the American people was summed up by the reporter who wrote that "everybody talked of the 'end of the war,' not of 'victory.'"

It was all so different from the aftermath of World War I. In 1918, Americans had been content to let the world take care of itself. In 1945 they felt they knew better.

In the 1930's, Senator Arthur H. Vandenberg of Michigan had been a leading isolationist. In 1944 he echoed the thoughts of millions of Americans when he experienced a German rocket attack in London. "How can there be immunity or isolation," he asked, "when man can devise weapons like that?"

Later, in an important Senate speech, Vandenberg renounced his isolationism. He urged American cooperation in building a new world order. "I want a new dignity and a new authority for international law," he announced. "I think American self-interest requires it."

In 1945 the American people were rapidly becoming aware that, like it or not, the United States was destined to play a new role in the world. Not even the most farsighted among them, however, realized the heavy burden of responsibility that world leadership would force the United States to carry in the troubled years ahead.

The United States participated in the founding of the United Nations, attempted to contain an ever-expanding Communist influence in the **cold war,** and sought to reduce the spread of arms. It assisted in the recovery of war-torn Europe, gave aid to developing nations, and prepared to participate in the space race.

═══ READING FOCUS ═══

As you read about the United States' new world role, look for the details that support each of the following statements.

1. The United States helps to organize the United Nations.
2. The United States and the U.S.S.R. engage in a cold war.
3. Growing nationalism and Communist aggression lead to war in Asia.
4. The United States continues to meet the challenges of communism.

1 The United States helps to organize the United Nations

See Teaching Suggestions in TMRG, pp.TM202-03.

During the war the Allies—or United Nations, as they called themselves—joined together to defeat Italy, Germany, and Japan (page 801). Allied leaders—among them Roosevelt, Churchill, and Stalin—converted the wartime alliance into a permanent organization for peace.

Americans pledged to support an international organization of nations. Democrats and Republicans alike agreed to back a program of international cooperation. American officials were among the leaders in this effort.

Planning the United Nations. Delegates from the United States, Great Britain, the U.S.S.R., and China met in 1944 at Dumbarton Oaks, an estate in Washington, D.C. There they began planning for a postwar United Nations organization. Quick agreement was reached on most questions of procedure. Some questions created problems, however, that were more difficult to solve.

What, for instance, should they do about the U.S.S.R.'s demand that it be represented in the United Nations not by one delegation but by 16—one for each of the 16 Soviet republics? What should they do about the Security Council, the body that was charged with keeping peace in the world?

At Yalta in February 1945 (page 814), Roosevelt, Churchill, and Stalin reached agreement on several issues that had deadlocked the Dumbarton Oaks Conference. They agreed ▲ that two of the Soviet Union's 16 republics would be admitted to the United Nations as though they were independent nations. The leaders also worked out a compromise on voting procedure in the Security Council. Finally, they agreed to call a conference in San Francisco on April 25, 1945, to draw up the official Charter of the United Nations.

Delegates from 50 nations, representing three fourths of the peoples of the earth, took part in the San Francisco Conference. Despite their differences, the delegates all worked for one objective—to form a world peace organization. In just eight weeks, the Dumbarton Oaks and the Yalta proposals were reshaped into the

▲ Throughout the Annotated Teacher's Edition, terms listed in the "Identify" portion of a Section Review are underscored the first time they appear. See the Teacher's Manual for each section for a listing of important vocabulary terms.

825

United Nations Charter. On October 24 — now celebrated as United Nations Day — the United Nations (UN) came into official existence.

Purposes and organization. The purposes of the UN are clearly stated in the Preamble to the Charter. "We the peoples of the United Nations, determined to save succeeding generations from the scourge of war, . . . to promote social progress and better standards of life in larger freedom, . . . have resolved to combine our efforts to accomplish these aims."

In general, the UN seeks to maintain peace, to provide security, to promote justice, to increase the general welfare, and to establish human rights. Six major organs and many related agencies were created to carry out the work of the UN.

(1) The Security Council was to be the police authority of the world, charged with preventing war. It was to consist of 11 members.° Five of these, the so-called "Big Five" powers — the United States, China, France, the Soviet Union, and Great Britain — were to hold permanent seats. The six nonpermanent members were to be elected for two-year terms. The Security Council was to have at its command an international military force to check aggression. On matters of peace and security, any one of the five permanent members could prevent action by its negative vote, or veto.

(2) The General Assembly was to be the "town meeting" of the world, in which all UN members were to be equally represented. It was to make recommendations for the peaceful settlement of disputes. It was to elect all the nonpermanent members of the Security Council and members of other agencies.

(3) The Economic and Social Council, composed of 18 members (now 57), was to study world economic, social, cultural, and health problems. It was to make recommendations on these problems to the General Assembly or to individual member countries.

(4) The International Court of Justice, modeled after the World Court, was to decide legal questions referred to it by disputing nations. It was to give advisory opinions when asked to do so, but it could not enforce its decisions.

(5) The Secretariat was to handle the administrative work of the UN.

°It later was increased to 15 members — five permanent members plus ten nonpermanent members.

(6) The Trusteeship Council was to look after the welfare of peoples living in colonial areas of the world.

Early years of the UN. Early critics of the UN insisted that it was doomed to fail because the member nations had not given up any of their national sovereignty. Other people, however, shared the opinion expressed by President Truman in 1945. "This charter," he stated, "points down the only road to enduring peace. There is no other."

As crises broke out in many parts of the world, Truman's statement took on new meaning. By 1948 the world situation had become so tense that Trygve Lie (TRIG·vuh LEE), the first Secretary-General of the UN, issued a warning. "The trouble," he declared, "lies in the intense conflict over the settlement of the last war . . . between the two most powerful single nations in the world today — the United States and the Soviet Union."

SECTION REVIEW
See underscored items, text pp. 825 - 26.
Identify: Dumbarton Oaks Conference, San Francisco Conference, "Big Five," Trygve Lie
For answers to questions, see Answer Key, p.A115.
1. **Synthesizing Ideas: (a)** What problems were left unsolved at the Dumbarton Oaks Conference? **(b)** How were these issues resolved later at Yalta?
2. **Summarizing Ideas: (a)** Summarize the purposes of the United Nations. **(b)** What are the major functions of the Security Council and the General Assembly?

2 The United States and the U.S.S.R. engage in a cold war

See Teaching Suggestions in TMRG, pp.TM203-04.
At the end of World War II, millions of people suffered from lack of food, clothing, shelter, and medical care. The United States responded generously to this worldwide need for help.

America's new role. The United States played an active role in creating three important UN agencies: (1) the United Nations Relief and Rehabilitation Administration (UNRRA), (2) the International Bank for Reconstruction and Development, and (3) the International Monetary Fund. These agencies supplied food, clothing, shelter, and medical care to millions of people in war-damaged nations and provided money to rebuild ruined industries. A large part of the money for these activities came from the United States.

After the war ended, American dollars and supplies flowed directly to the war-devastated areas. Major contributions came from private American organizations—churches, schools, fraternal societies, and civic groups. An even larger contribution came from the United States government in the form of supplies, equipment, loans, and the assistance of specialists and experts.

Expanding Soviet influence. America's new role of world leadership brought it into conflict with the Soviet Union, which also emerged from the war as a major power. The postwar policies of the Soviet Union in some ways continued the expansionist policies of tsarist Russia. However, the U.S.S.R. now regarded itself as the leader of a Communist revolution destined to replace the "capitalist" and "imperialist" world—a world in which the United States was the principal power.

Even before World War II ended, the Soviets had begun to move aggressively against their weaker neighbors. In 1940 Latvia, Lithuania, and Estonia—countries to which the Russians had some historical claims—were incorporated into the Soviet Union. As a result of World War II, the U.S.S.R. also acquired large parts of Poland and Rumania. Through Communist governments that they helped to set up, the Soviets by 1948 had gained control of the "free" governments of Poland, Rumania, Hungary, Czechoslovakia, and the eastern part of Germany. Moreover, Soviet influence reached beyond Eastern Europe into the Mediterranean area. Moscow-trained Communists were especially active in Greece and Italy.

The U.S.S.R. was deeply entrenched in East Asia, as well as in Europe. As a result of the Yalta agreements and because of its last-minute entry into the war against Japan, the Soviet Union gained control of large areas that had been Chinese and Japanese territory.

Mounting tensions. The Communist leaders defended their actions on grounds of self-defense. They pointed out that in 1918–19 during the Bolshevik Revolution, the Allies, including American troops, had occupied north-ern Russia and Russian Siberia. Believing that war between communism and capitalism was inevitable, they feared that the United States would lead the capitalist nations in a new attack against the U.S.S.R. They reminded the world that the Nazi invasion of their country had cost them 21 million lives and the destruction of hundreds of their towns and cities. In view of these facts, the Soviets insisted on maintaining powerful military forces and on controlling bordering areas from which new attacks might be launched.

The United States objected bitterly to the Soviet Union's domination of its weaker neighbors. The United States, which had demobilized most of its own troops, resented the Soviet policy of maintaining huge military forces. Moreover, Americans loathed the ruthless methods used by the Soviet Union to crush all opposition. Most Americans regarded the Soviet Union as the world's newest aggressor.

As friction increased, the Soviet press and radio, rigidly controlled by the government, became increasingly anti-American. The Soviet government refused to join the United Nations Educational, Scientific, and Cultural Organization (UNESCO), which had been established to promote understanding among the peoples of the world. It permitted only a very few Americans to visit the U.S.S.R. or its **satellite nations**—those nations dominated by the U.S.S.R.

Deadlock over atomic energy. Inability to reach agreement on international control of the atomic bomb greatly added to the mounting tension between the United States and the U.S.S.R. Early in 1946, acting on American initiative, the UN created an International Atomic Energy Commission. At the Commission's first meeting, the United States representative, Bernard M. Baruch (buh·ROOK), presented America's proposal for international control.

Baruch proposed that complete control of atomic energy be turned over to an international agency responsible to the UN. This agency would have full authority to enter any country to inspect atomic energy installations. The United States—at that time the only nation that had atomic bombs—was ready, Baruch announced, to give up its secrets to the new world authority. However, he warned, the United States would not reveal any secrets until the UN provided for "immediate, swift,

▲ The U.S.S.R. also took over Bulgaria, Yugoslavia, and Albania. Even these countries were called republics (in which representatives of the people make the laws), they took orders from the U.S.S.R.

827

and sure punishment for those who violate the agreements that are reached by the nations." Baruch insisted that each of the "Big Five" on the Security Council give up its right to the veto on all matters involving atomic energy.

When the United States proposal reached the Security Council, the Soviet Union killed it by a veto. The Soviet Union then offered its own proposal. It opposed any system of international inspection and control. Instead, it insisted that the United States destroy its atomic bombs, that the UN declare atomic warfare illegal, and that all nations promise not to manufacture atomic bombs. However, the Soviet Union flatly refused to give up its veto right in the Security Council. This meant that if any nation, including the U.S.S.R., violated its promise not to make atomic bombs, the Soviet Union or any other permanent Security Council member could block all UN action by a single veto.

The Truman Doctrine. Wary of Communist aggression, the United States formulated a policy of **containment**. This policy aimed to contain, or restrict, Soviet expansion and to check the spread of communism. The new policy was first applied to Greece and Turkey.

In 1947, Greek Communists supported by the Soviets were about to seize control of the conservative Greek government. At the same time, the Soviet Union was trying to force Turkey to give up control of the Dardanelles, the strait between European and Asiatic Turkey. Soviet control of Greece and the Dardanelles would enable the U.S.S.R. to dominate the northeastern Mediterranean and the Suez Canal.

This situation prompted President Truman in 1947 to announce the Truman Doctrine. This doctrine stated that the United States had to "help free people to maintain their free institutions and their national integrity." He then asked Congress for authority to help the Greeks and Turks strengthen their armed forces to check the spread of communism. Congress responded with an initial appropriation of $400 million. In 1948 the United States also established and later increased its naval forces in the eastern Mediterranean.

The Marshall Plan. Aid to Greece and Turkey, however, was not enough to prevent the spread of communism. All of war-torn Europe was in economic difficulty. Throughout Europe Communists were winning converts among hungry, disillusioned people.

Early in June 1947, Secretary of State George C. Marshall suggested a solution to Europe's economic problems. The "Marshall Plan," as this program came to be called, proposed to help European countries to get their farms, factories, and transportation systems operating efficiently again. The United States would provide money, plus supplies and ma-

=== SOURCES ===

THE
MARSHALL
PLAN
(1947)

It is logical that the United States should do whatever it is able to do to assist in the return of normal economic health in the world, without which there can be no political stability and no assured peace.

Our policy is directed not against any country or doctrine but against hunger, poverty, desperation, and chaos. Its purpose should be the revival of a working economy in the world so as to permit the emergence of political and social conditions in which free institutions can exist. . . .

Any government that is willing to assist in the task of recovery will find full cooperation, I am sure, on the part of the United States government. Any government which maneuvers to block the recovery of other countries cannot expect help from us. Furthermore, governments, political parties, or groups which seek to perpetuate human misery in order to profit therefrom, politically or otherwise, will encounter the opposition of the United States. . . .

chinery, to any nation that would take part in the program. The Soviet Union and its satellites were included in the offer.

The Marshall Plan provoked heated Congressional debate. Those who favored the proposal insisted that the best way to block communism was to restore Europe's economic health. Opponents of the program declared that the United States could not afford to "carry Europe on its back." In the spring of 1948, however, Congress approved the Marshall Plan, officially known as the European Recovery Program.

The Soviet Union and its satellites denounced the plan as "Yankee imperialism." Nevertheless, the Marshall Plan was an outstanding success. Slowly but steadily Europe began to recover from the war.

The Berlin airlift. Meanwhile tension had mounted in Germany. In 1945 the great powers had agreed to a joint occupation of Germany (see map, this page). Berlin, within the Soviet-controlled zone, was also divided into four sections, each controlled by one of the four powers.

On June 24, 1948, the Soviets suddenly blocked all roads, canals, and railways connecting Berlin and the Western Zone of Germany. By this move they apparently hoped to force the three Western powers out of Berlin.

The British-American answer to the Soviet challenge was the Berlin airlift. Starting in the summer of 1948 and continuing for more than a year, British and American planes transported over 2 million tons of food and supplies to Berlin. This crisis in relations between the East and the West was finally resolved in 1949 with the aid of the UN.

NATO. The Soviet blockade of Berlin and Communist efforts to wreck the Marshall Plan aroused growing alarm in Western Europe. In April 1949 nine Western European nations° joined the United States, Canada, and Iceland in an alliance known as the North Atlantic Treaty Organization (NATO).

In the Atlantic Pact—the treaty proposing the NATO alliance—each member nation agreed that "an armed attack against one or more of them in Europe or North America
● shall be considered an attack against them

°Great Britain, France, Belgium, the Netherlands, Luxembourg, Italy, Denmark, Norway, and Portugal. West Germany, Turkey, and Greece joined later.

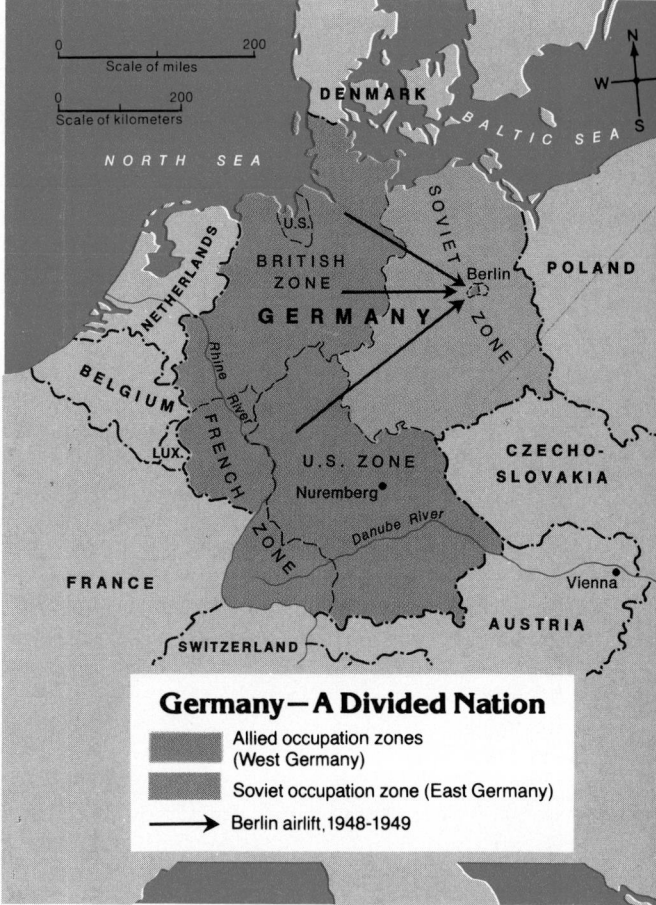

Germany—A Divided Nation

▮ Allied occupation zones (West Germany)

▮ Soviet occupation zone (East Germany)

→ Berlin airlift, 1948-1949

all." They also agreed to resist such an attack with armed force, if necessary.

Since the Atlantic Pact was a treaty, it had to be approved by the United States Senate. Senate debate focused on whether or not the Atlantic Pact would compel the United States to go to war to assist a member nation without an act of Congress. This, you may remember, was the main issue that had kept the United States out of the League of Nations in 1919. However, in July 1949 the Senate did ratify the agreement. Eventually General Eisenhower was named Supreme Commander of the NATO forces.

Thus by the end of 1949 an American policy of containment had taken shape, at least in regard to Europe. NATO strengthened the military defenses of Western Europe. The Marshall Plan strengthened the economy of Western Europe, thus reducing the discontent that so often helped the spread of communism.

Meanwhile, however, trouble was brewing in the Middle East and in Asia.

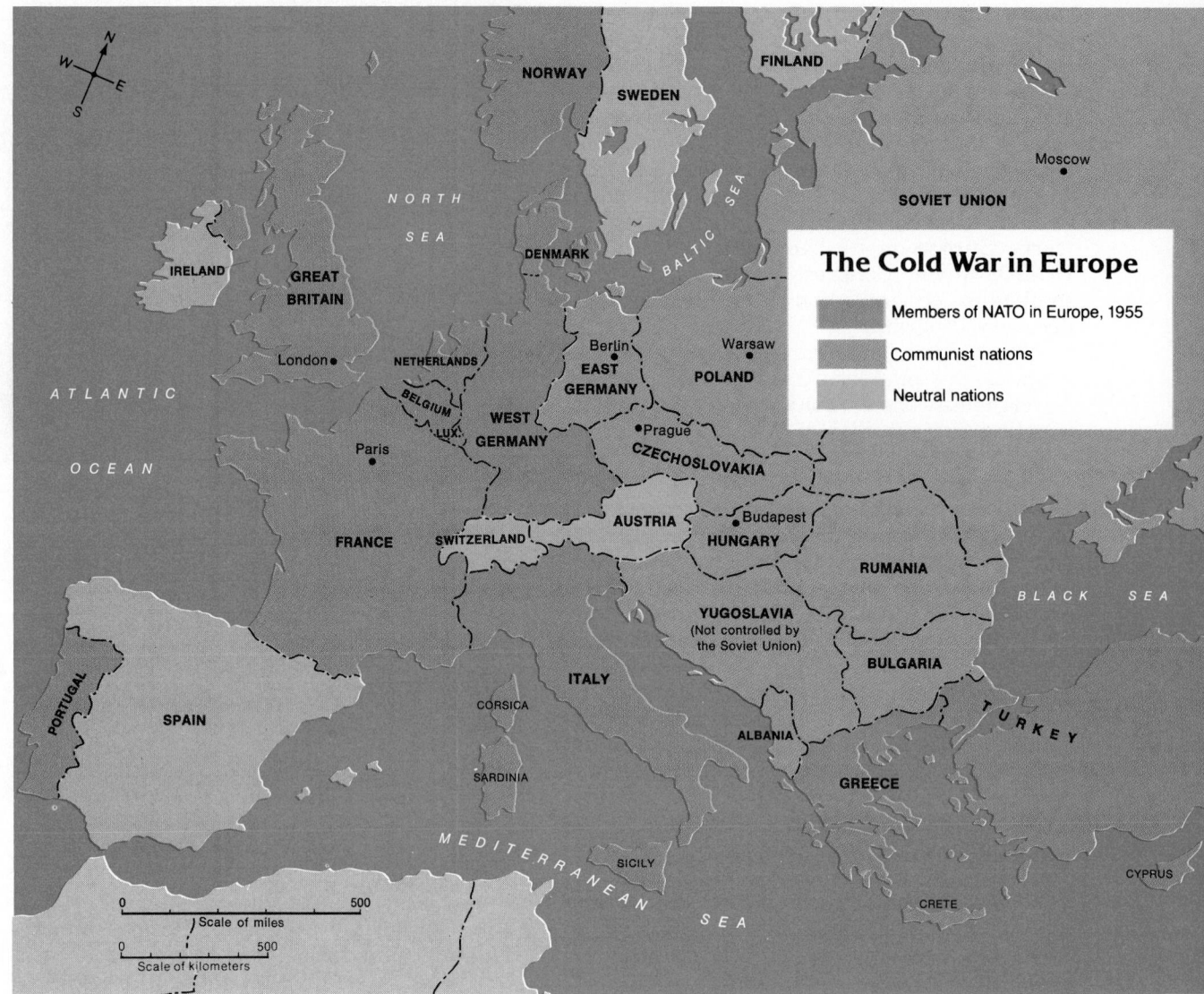

The Cold War in Europe

- Members of NATO in Europe, 1955
- Communist nations
- Neutral nations

NORWAY

SWEDEN

FINLAND

Moscow

SOVIET UNION

NORTH SEA

BALTIC SEA

DENMARK

IRELAND

GREAT BRITAIN

London ●

Berlin ●

Warsaw ●

NETHERLANDS

EAST GERMANY

POLAND

BELGIUM

WEST GERMANY

LUX.

Prague ●

CZECHOSLOVAKIA

ATLANTIC

OCEAN

Paris ●

Budapest ●

AUSTRIA

HUNGARY

RUMANIA

BLACK SEA

SWITZERLAND

FRANCE

YUGOSLAVIA
(Not controlled by
the Soviet Union)

BULGARIA

PORTUGAL

SPAIN

ITALY

CORSICA

ALBANIA

TURKEY

SARDINIA

GREECE

MEDITERRANEAN SEA

SICILY

CRETE

CYPRUS

Scale of miles
0   500

Scale of kilometers
0   500

SECTION REVIEW

See underscored items, text pp. 827 - 28.

Identify: UNESCO, satellite nations, Bernard Baruch, containment, George Marshall

For answers to questions, see Answer Key, p.A115.

1. **Interpreting Ideas:** (a) Why did the Soviet Union try to expand its influence during the postwar period? (b) How did the Soviets justify their actions?

2. **Comparing Ideas:** (a) Compare the Soviet and the American plans for control of atomic energy. (b) Why did efforts at control end in deadlock?

3. **Organizing Ideas:** How did each of the following help to contain communism: (a) the Truman Doctrine, (b) the Marshall Plan, (c) the Berlin airlift, (d) NATO?

3 Growing nationalism and Communist aggression lead to war in Asia

See Teaching Suggestions in TMRG, p.TM204.

Postwar troubles were not confined to Europe. During President Truman's administration, growing tensions between Jews and Arabs threatened the peace in Palestine. Communists gained control of China, forcing Chiang Kai-shek to Taiwan. Other troubles erupted in Korea.

Middle East tensions. Iran soon became a trouble spot. During World War II, both American and Soviet troops were stationed in Iran. After the war the United States pulled out its troops. However, the Soviets were eager to control the oil-rich land adjoining their border to the south and did not remove their troops. Tension mounted. Finally, after the UN intervened in 1946, the Soviets withdrew their military forces from Iran.

Meanwhile trouble broke out in Palestine, at the eastern end of the Mediterranean Sea. Since World War I, Great Britain had ruled Palestine under a mandate from the League of Nations. On May 14, 1948, Great Britain voluntarily gave up this mandate. The Jews in
▲ Palestine then proclaimed the independence of the new state of Israel.

This action angered Arabs and plunged Israel into war with Egypt, Transjordan (later renamed Jordan), Lebanon, Syria, Iraq, and Saudi Arabia. The UN at once took steps to end the fighting. Finally a UN mission under the leadership of a black American, Dr. Ralph J. Bunche, managed to get both sides to agree to an armistice. As a result of his efforts, Dr. Bunche received the Nobel Peace Prize.

Communist victory in China. While an uneasy peace was being restored in the Middle East, Chinese Communists were rapidly winning control of China. The struggle for control of China had begun long before World War II.

In 1927, four years before the Japanese moved into Manchuria, Chiang Kai-shek, leader of the Chinese Nationalist forces, opened war on the Chinese Communists. For a time China was torn by civil conflict. But after Japan attacked China, both of the opposing Chinese factions fought against the Japanese. During World War II, the United States encouraged such cooperation. Chinese troops heroically resisted the invading armies of Japan. In 1945, in recognition of these valiant efforts, China was admitted to the United Nations as one of the "Big Five."

With the end of World War II, the struggle between Chiang's Nationalist forces and the Chinese Communists once again erupted. The Soviet Union gave limited support to the Chinese Communists, led by Mao Tse-tung (MAU TSAY·TOONG). The United States at first provided military assistance to Chiang's Nationalists, but the Nationalists were weakened by internal conflicts and corruption. As the outlook

Ralph Bunche (right) took the job of peacemaker in Palestine with the knowledge that a predecessor had been assassinated for his efforts.

for Nationalist victory grew dim, the United States withdrew its support. By 1949 the Communists had conquered most of China. Chiang and the Nationalist government retreated to the island of Formosa, or Taiwan.

The United States continued to recognize the Nationalists as the legal government of China. Also, the Nationalists continued to represent China in the UN Security Council.°

The division of Korea. Meanwhile trouble was brewing in Korea. Between 1910 and 1945, the Koreans had been ruled by Japan. During the closing days of World War II, however, Soviet and American troops swept the Japanese out of Korea. After the war General Douglas MacArthur was appointed Supreme Commander of the Allied Powers and placed in charge of the occupation forces in Japan.† His responsibilities also included the southern portion of Korea.

Text continues on page 833.

°The People's Republic of China replaced Nationalist China in the Security Council in 1972.

†During the occupation period, relations between Japan and the Western powers were restored to a friendly basis. In 1951 Japan received independence in a treaty signed at San Francisco.

● Taiwan is about 100 miles (160 kilometers) from the Chinese mainland.

831

Enormous changes have taken place in where Americans live and in what they do to earn a living. In the 1700's and early 1800's the typical American family lived on a farm. The entire family worked together to raise a few cattle, hogs, and chickens. Farm families grew corn and garden vegetables, or perhaps a little wheat. Most of these family farms would have been classified as subsistence farms — farms designed to produce enough food to meet each family's basic needs. Surpluses, if there were any, were sold to bring in a few dollars to purchase those things the family could not produce at home.

This situation began to change during the latter half of the 19th century. Scientific agriculture made American farms increasingly productive. The development of new strains of seed and new fertilizers doubled and even

A nineteenth-century farm

tripled the yields of a number of crops. Studies in animal husbandry — the breeding and care of livestock — also greatly increased meat production. Along with these changes, the invention of the tractor and other farm machinery greatly reduced the need for human labor on the American farm. Accompanying these changes has been a shift in the very reason for farming. A commercial role — the growing of crops and the raising of livestock for profit — has replaced the traditional subsistence role of farming. In a sense, farming changed from a way of life to a business.

The United States has shifted from a rural to an urban society. Most people now work and live in urban areas. In 1850, when the United States was still largely a rural nation, each farmer, on the average, produced only enough food to feed four persons. The graphs on page 1018 of the Reference Section illustrate the increase in farm production. Today, each farmer, on the average, produces enough food to feed 80 persons. Yet, today, only four percent of all Americans live on farms. In fact the

nation's farms produce more food than the people of the United States can consume, even though the number of persons earning a living as farmers is sharply reduced. These surpluses have enabled the United States to become one of the world's great food exporters. About one sixth of all the food exports in the entire world come from United States farms.

The amount of land that one family can manage has also changed. As the chart "Average Size of Farms" on page 1018 shows, the "family farm" — 160 acres (64.8 hectares) — has become a thing of the past. Machinery has made the difference. Interestingly, though, as late as 1935 the average-sized farm in the United States was exactly 160 acres. Today, however, it is over 400 acres (160 hectares).

All of the changes in agriculture have led to a change in the idea of farm ownership. In recent years, tenancy — working land belonging to someone else — has been rapidly increasing, especially in the Corn Belt. The reason for the increase in tenancy is that the only way expensive farm machinery can be used efficiently is to have large acreages. It has, therefore, become common practice to enlarge the farm by renting additional land. In Iowa and Illinois, for example, at least one quarter of all farm land is operated under some sort of tenant-farming arrangement.

The decline in the United States of the traditional family farm is directly associated with the demands of commercial agriculture. Today the cost advantages of large-scale farming have become of primary significance. The ability to purchase, operate, and maintain expensive farm equipment has shifted the control of farm efficiency away from the family farm. The family farm, it seems, is being transformed by progress.

One less farm

At the end of the war, a line drawn across the Korean peninsula at the 38th parallel (see map, page 835) separated American occupation forces in the south from Soviet occupation forces in the north. Americans and most other concerned peoples considered this a temporary arrangement.

Despite UN efforts to unite the country, Korea remained divided, and Soviet and American troops were not withdrawn. Then in 1948 North Korea and South Korea set up separate governments, each claiming authority to rule the entire country. The North Korean government, controlled by Communists and supported by the Soviets, called itself the "People's Republic of Korea." The South Korean government, of which Syngman Rhee (SING·man REE) had been chosen president in an election sponsored by the UN, called itself the "Republic of Korea." The United States and 30 UN members (but not the Soviet Union) recognized the Republic of Korea as the country's lawful government.

Finally the United States and the Soviet Union withdrew their troops. Each left behind a Korean army it had helped to train. These two Korean armies now faced each other across the 38th parallel.

U.S. soldiers move cautiously through a South Korean town as UN forces push North Korean and Communist Chinese troops back toward the 38th parallel.

The Korean challenge. On June 25, 1950, the North Korean army suddenly launched a full-scale invasion of South Korea. In an emergency session, the UN Security Council adopted a resolution ordering an immediate cease-fire. Had the Soviet delegate been present, he would undoubtedly have vetoed this action. However, the Soviet government was boycotting the Security Council because of its refusal to admit Communist China to the United Nations.

Meanwhile President Truman was busy conferring with the heads of the State and Defense departments. On June 27, 1950, the President pledged American aid to South Korea. That same evening the Security Council adopted a second resolution. It termed North Korea an "aggressor" and called on UN members to furnish all possible assistance to the South Koreans.

War in Korea. The UN itself had no troops to throw into action. Soviet vetoes in the Security Council had blocked every effort to create a UN military force. Although 19 UN members finally contributed assistance, the major burden of defending South Korea against the North fell upon the United States.

In response to the UN's call, President Truman ordered the United States Seventh Fleet into action. It was charged with preventing any attack upon Formosa and blockading the Korean coast. Truman also ordered United States air and ground forces into Korea.

For a time it looked as though the North Koreans would overrun all of Korea. The South Koreans were hopelessly outnumbered. Neither they nor the first American troops rushed to the scene could stand up against the heavily armored, Soviet-made tanks of the North Korean army. By early August the South Korean and UN troops under General MacArthur were desperately defending a small area around Pusan in southeast Korea (see map, page 835).

Then the tide suddenly turned. On September 15, 1950, MacArthur staged a seaborne attack against Inchon and then swept eastward, recapturing Seoul (SOHL), the capital of South Korea. At the same time, a strongly reinforced UN army, now well equipped and powerfully supported from the air, attacked from southeastern Korea. The North Korean

"In war there is no substitute for victory," said General Douglas MacArthur (seated next to driver), commander of UN forces in Korea. Here he inspects troop positions along the front lines early in the Korean war.

forces, caught in a huge trap, began to break up. Thousands surrendered. The rest fled northward across the 38th parallel. Mac-Arthur's troops followed in hot pursuit. By November the UN forces were at the Yalu River, the boundary between North Korea and Communist China.

Then suddenly the tide turned again. Late in November hundreds of thousands of Chinese Communist "volunteers" swarmed across the Yalu River to reinforce the North Korean troops. The UN troops, their lines extended, were outnumbered in many cases by hundreds to one. Finally, after weeks of desperate fighting, MacArthur's forces managed to set up their defense line near the 38th parallel.

The Great Debate. The entry of Chinese Communist troops completely changed the nature of the war. President Truman faced new, serious questions. Should he heed MacArthur's request and allow him to blockade the China
▲ coast and bomb the Chinese mainland? Should he also help Chiang Kai-shek's Nationalist forces to launch an invasion of China?

MacArthur's proposal provoked heated debate. His supporters argued that quick, decisive action would bring a speedy end to the Korean conflict. Those who disagreed argued that an attack upon Communist China might cause the U.S.S.R. to support its Communist ally openly. This would certainly start another world war.

MacArthur's opponents also pointed to another danger. If the United States committed its military forces to a major war in Asia, the Soviet Union would be free to do as it pleased in Europe.

Stalemate in Korea. By January 1951 President Truman had reached his decision. He ordered General MacArthur to establish the strongest possible defense line near the 38th parallel. However, he forbade blockading the China coast, bombing China, and using Chiang's troops to invade China. The war in Korea was to remain strictly a "police action" to protect South Korea. In 1951, therefore, the Korean War reached a stalemate.

MacArthur refused to accept Truman's decision as final and tried to appeal to Congress over the President's authority. In April 1951 President Truman removed MacArthur from his post. "I could do nothing else and still be President," Truman explained. General Matthew B. Ridgway replaced MacArthur as commander of the UN forces.

American policy and Point Four. During 1951 and 1952, the United States continued the rapid buildup of its land, sea, and air forces. This military buildup was only part of America's response to the challenge of communism around the world. With economic aid and technical assistance, the United States helped less fortunate areas of the world to raise their

Discussion topic: Have the students compare these statements. MacArthur: "If we lose the war in Asia the fall of Europe is enevitable;. . ." Truman: "we must try to limit the war to Korea . . . to prevent a third world war."

▲ standards of living. The Marshall Plan was intended primarily for Europe. A new plan, the Point Four program, was intended to help developing areas anywhere in the world. The Point Four program consisted of bringing many scattered activities for providing scientific and industrial aid into a carefully planned, coordinated program.

The Point Four program got off to a slow start. The Korean War, however, convinced even the most hesitant Americans that the world was facing a grave crisis from the attempts by the U.S.S.R. to expand Communist influence throughout the world. By 1952 most Americans believed that the United States policy should include provisions for foreign aid and the strengthening of military defenses throughout the non-Communist world.

SECTION REVIEW

See underscored items, text pp. 831, 833, 835.
Identify: Ralph Bunche, Chiang Kai-shek, Mao Tse-tung, Taiwan, Douglas MacArthur, 38th parallel, Syngman Rhee, Point Four program
For answers to questions, see Answer Key, pp.A115-16.

1. **Summarizing Ideas:** Describe the postwar events that created tension in the Middle East.

2. **Interpreting Ideas: (a)** How did China come to have two governments by 1949? **(b)** What was the American position concerning China?

3. **Determining Cause and Effect: (a)** What were the causes of the Korean conflict? **(b)** What issues provoked the Great Debate during that conflict?

4. **Studying Maps:** Examine the map on this page. **(a)** Locate the line of farthest advance by UN forces. **(b)** Describe the events of the war from September to November 1950. **(c)** What geographic advantage did China have when it sought to aid North Korea that the United States did not have?

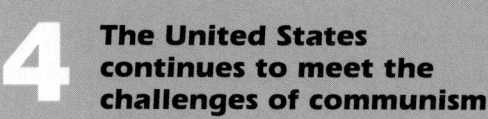

4 The United States continues to meet the challenges of communism

See Teaching Suggestions in TMRG, pp.TM204-05.
Dwight D. Eisenhower was elected President in November 1952. When he took office, he and his Secretary of State, John Foster Dulles, continued the bipartisan foreign policy that had been followed since America's entry into World War II.

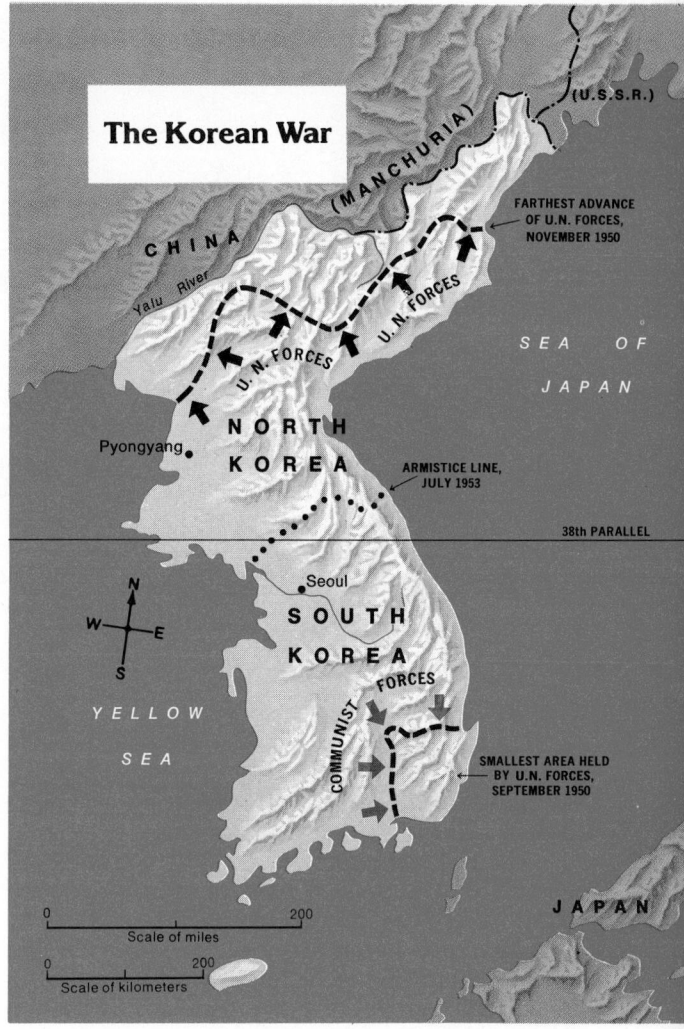

The Korean War

(U.S.S.R.)

(MANCHURIA)

CHINA

Yalu River

FARTHEST ADVANCE OF U.N. FORCES, NOVEMBER 1950

U.N. FORCES

U.N. FORCES

SEA OF JAPAN

Pyongyang

NORTH KOREA

ARMISTICE LINE, JULY 1953

38th PARALLEL

Seoul

SOUTH KOREA

N W E S

COMMUNIST FORCES

YELLOW SEA

SMALLEST AREA HELD BY U.N. FORCES, SEPTEMBER 1950

JAPAN

0   200
Scale of miles

0   200
Scale of kilometers

Ending the Korean War. During the 1952 election campaign, Dwight Eisenhower had promised to do everything within his power to end the Korean War (see map, this page). In December 1952, before his inauguration as President, he visited the battle area for talks with political and military leaders. Peace talks were being carried on at this time in Panmunjom (PAN·MUHN·JUM) in Korea. Finally, on July 27, 1953, North Korea and the UN signed an armistice agreement. This agreement recognized the division of Korea into two countries—North Korea and the Republic of South Korea.

In a formal treaty, the United States promised to defend South Korea against any future attack. The United States also undertook to

835

One of the nation's most powerful and controversial secretaries of state, John Foster Dulles was an expert in the field of international law. He served on the War Trade Board in World War I and later helped negotiate reparations from Germany and other Central Powers. After World War II, he served for 4 years as a United States delegate to the United Nations General Assembly.

President Eisenhower named Dulles as Secretary of State in 1953. Dulles pursued a dynamic policy to counteract communism, which he considered a moral evil. He encouraged the development of nuclear weapons for "massive retaliation" and criticized Third World nations that wanted to follow a neutral policy in the cold war. Dulles supported anticommunist, reactionary leaders in Southeast Asia and Latin America. His greatest achievement, he felt, was the Southeast Asia Treaty Organization (SEATO), which he believed had saved South Vietnam and other nations in Southeast Asia from early takeover by Communist forces.

Dulles resigned from office in 1959. His policies, however, continued to influence the postwar world for many years.

help the South Koreans improve their economic and social conditions.

The Korean War had lasted three years and cost 33,629 American lives (and an estimated 1.5 million Communist casualties). The war had been unpopular at home. It did not change the dictatorship that ruled South Korea. It did, however, increase the prestige of the United Nations. It also showed that the prompt use of force could, at least in some cases, check Communist aggression.

Developments in Indochina. Only a few months after the Korean armistice, world peace was threatened by another crisis in East Asia. Ever since the end of World War II, Indochina, a French colony, had been torn by armed conflict. A group of revolutionary nationalists, the Vietminh (VYET·MEEN), who were mainly Communists, had been fighting to win control of the entire country from the French and their anti-Communist Vietnamese allies. When it became clear that Communist China was actively aiding the Vietminh, the United States during President Truman's administration began to send military equipment and economic help to the Vietnamese and French armies.

Early in 1954 the Vietminh, supported by the Chinese, launched a powerful drive against the French and their Vietnamese supporters. In May 1954 the key French fortress of Dienbienphu (dyen·byen·FOO) fell to the Vietminh and Chinese forces.

In July 1954 a conference was held in Geneva, Switzerland, to discuss the fate of Indochina. Although the United States had helped finance the French cost of the war, it preferred to play the role of observer at Geneva. The delegates from France, Indochina, Communist China, the Soviet Union, and Great Britain recognized the independence of Cambodia, Laos, and Vietnam. The area of Vietnam to the north of the 17th parallel became the Communist state of Vietminh, later known as North Vietnam. The portion of Vietnam to the south of the 17th parallel became known as South Vietnam (see map, page 919).

Changes in American foreign policy. Under President Eisenhower and Secretary of State Dulles, American foreign policy underwent several changes. Dulles announced a firmer American policy toward the Communist world. Instead of containment, Dulles spoke of a "rollback" of the Soviets in Eastern Europe.

▲ Nor did it change the boundary between North and South Korea, which remained at the 38th parallel.

Dulles also developed a policy that some ▲ people called **brinksmanship.** Dulles believed that the Communists only understood force. Therefore, he felt that in order to maintain peace the United States had to be ready to go to the brink of war. "The ability to get to the verge of war without getting into war is the necessary art," Dulles claimed.

Such a policy was increasingly frightening in the mid-1950's. By that time, both the Soviet Union and the United States had developed hydrogen bombs. These weapons were vastly more powerful than the atomic bombs dropped at the end of World War II.

Soon the United States and the Soviet Union were engaged in an arms race. Each side built up a stockpile of nuclear weapons. The reason for stockpiling was to threaten the other side. Each side was demonstrating its willingness to destroy the other if attacked. This policy was known as **massive retaliation.**

The United States also continued its efforts to strengthen Western Europe. In October 1954 the United States and its European allies agreed to give the Federal Republic of Germany (West Germany) full sovereign powers. They also agreed to admit West Germany to NATO and to allow it to build an army of 500,000 troops to serve under the NATO command. The United States, Great Britain, and France also agreed to regard an attack upon West Germany as an attack upon themselves.

Changes in Communist policy. In February 1956 startling news came out of the So-viet Union. Communist Party leader <u>Nikita Khrushchev</u> publicly attacked his predecessor, Josef Stalin, calling him a cruel tyrant. Stalin had died in 1953.

What was behind this attack? Was Khrushchev about to adopt a friendlier attitude toward the "free world"? Was he about to loosen the U.S.S.R.'s tight grip on its satellites in Eastern Europe? Would he be willing to end the arms race? Hope began to stir, and in the satellite countries people began to demand greater freedom from Soviet control.

In October 1956 the leaders of the Communist Party in Poland elected the Polish nationalist Wladyslaw Gomulka (VLAH·dee·slaf goh·MUL·kah) as first secretary of the party. Although a long-time Communist, Gomulka promised the Poles freedom of speech, press, and religion. Encouraged by Gomulka's stand, Poles staged anti-Soviet demonstrations in the streets. On several occasions they exchanged shots with Soviet troops.

The Polish revolt attracted worldwide attention. What would Khrushchev do? Instead of crushing the revolt, Khrushchev surprised the world and granted concessions. He withdrew some Soviet troops from Poland and granted some freedom to the Poles.

Revolt in Hungary. Inspired by the example of the Poles, the Hungarians also rebelled against the Soviets. On October 23, 1956, Hungarian students and workers rioted in the streets of Budapest, demanding greater freedom.

Hungarian freedom fighters rebelled against the Soviets in October 1956. At first they appeared victorious and pushed the Soviets out of Budapest. However, Soviet troops later returned to ruthlessly crush all Hungarian resistance.

Following Egypt's nationalization of the Suez Canal in 1956, Great Britain and France attempted to restore international control over the waterway by launching an air attack against Egypt. Many Egyptian vessels were destroyed during the week-long bombing.

The next morning Soviet tanks, guns, and armored cars, supported by jet planes, moved into Budapest. Violent fighting broke out as units of the Hungarian army joined the "freedom fighters." After four days of fighting, the U.S.S.R. agreed to pull its troops out.

Even while the Hungarians were celebrating, Soviet forces began a massive attack upon Budapest. "All Budapest is under fire," the Budapest radio reported.

Within a few days, the Hungarian fight for freedom came to a tragic end. With all organized resistance ruthlessly crushed, a new Hungarian government, a puppet of the U.S.S.R., began to round up the rebels and imprison them or deport them to the Soviet Union. Refugees by the thousands fled into Austria.

Egypt and the Suez Canal. In the same week that the Hungarians rebelled, another crisis developed, this time over the Suez Canal in Egypt. For a few tense days, the world hovered on the brink of another war.

The Suez Canal, connecting the Mediterranean and the Red seas, ran entirely through Egyptian territory. Owned and operated by an international company, the canal was open on equal terms to ships of all nations. By arrangement with Egypt, British troops were stationed at the Canal Zone to safeguard it and protect British interests.

After World War II, the Egyptians became increasingly dissatisfied with British military occupation of the Canal Zone. Finally, in June 1956 the last British troops withdrew.

▲   The UN voted to condemn the Soviet Union, but was unable to stop the brutal attack on Hungary.

In the meantime, in 1954, Colonel Gamal Abdel Nasser led a successful revolution and became President of the Republic of Egypt. Nasser was determined to modernize the country and extend Egyptian influence throughout the Middle East. One of Nasser's major plans involved building a large irrigation dam and electric generating plant at Aswan on the Nile River. Furious when the Soviets, Americans, and British failed to finance the project, Nasser announced that Egypt was going to seize the canal and operate it.° The Western powers tried in vain to persuade Nasser to agree to international control by the 18 nations that regularly used the canal. Great Britain and France in particular saw Nasser's **nationalization** of the Suez Canal as a threat to the free flow of oil from the Middle East to Western Europe.

The Suez crisis. On October 29, 1956, the Israeli army moved rapidly westward through the Sinai Peninsula toward the Suez Canal. The Israeli government announced that its troops had invaded Egyptian territory to forestall a planned attack upon Israel by Egypt.

On October 30 the British and French issued a 12-hour ultimatum. They demanded that Egypt and Israel cease fighting and allow French and British troops temporarily to occupy key points in the Canal Zone. When Egypt refused, the British and French bombed Egyptian airfields and moved troops into the northern part of the Canal Zone.

In response the Soviet Union denounced Israel, France, and Great Britain as aggressors. It threatened to intervene with force if the three nations did not immediately withdraw.

The United States now found itself in an embarrassing position. Great Britain and France, its allies in NATO, had ignored both Washington and the UN. They had created a situation that could easily lead to a general war. Moreover, the United States was unwilling to permit the Soviet Union to claim that it was the only champion of Egypt and other small nations against "Western imperialism." Reluctantly the United States voted in favor of a UN General Assembly resolution calling for an immediate cease-fire and the withdrawal of British, French, and Israeli troops. Great Britain, France, and Israel accepted these terms.

°In 1959 the Soviet Union agreed to provide money and engineers to build the dam. Construction began in 1960 and was completed in 1969.

The Eisenhower Doctrine. One result of the Suez crisis was that the United States adopted what came to be known as the Eisenhower Doctrine. In January 1957 President Eisenhower asked Congress to authorize him to use military force if this were requested by any Middle Eastern nation to check Communist aggression. He also asked Congress to set aside $200 million to help those Middle Eastern countries that desired such aid from the United States. Congress granted both requests. The United States thus indicated its intention of checking Communist influence in the Middle East.

The Eisenhower Doctrine was soon tested. Early in 1958 Egypt and Syria, linked in a temporary union, urged the other Arab nations to join them in opposing Western influence.

During the next few months, the Arab world was torn by intrigue. Rebellion broke out against the pro-Western government in Lebanon. In Iraq army officers killed the pro-Western leaders and seized control of the government. The leaders of Lebanon and Jordan, now convinced that their pro-Western governments would soon be overthrown, too, appealed to the United States and Great Britain for help. President Eisenhower immediately sent American marines to Lebanon. At the same time, Great Britain flew paratroopers into Jordan.

For several weeks American and British forces remained ready for any emergency. Late in September, after the Secretary-General of the UN reported that the situation was improving, Great Britain and the United States withdrew their troops.

The race into space. The crisis in the Middle East was not the major development of 1957–58. The most startling news, which broke on October 4, 1957, was compressed into a single word: *Sputnik.* The Russians had succeeded in orbiting an artificial satellite around the earth.

The American public, long convinced that no nation was superior to the United States in science and technology, was shocked. Recognizing the Soviet feat, President Eisenhower assured the American people that the United States had its own rocket and missile program. On January 31, 1958, the United States launched a small satellite, *Explorer I,* into orbit, and the space race was under way.

Rockets powerful enough to carry satellites into space could also be used to launch atomic and hydrogen bombs. By 1960 both the Soviet Union and the United States were building

Soviet Premier Nikita Khrushchev visited the United States at the request of President Eisenhower in September 1959. Khrushchev's 12-day, cross-country tour included a stop at an Iowa farm (above) and a speech before the United Nations.

stockpiles of intercontinental ballistic missiles (ICBM's). Each of the missiles was equipped with a nuclear warhead. Push-button war that could destroy millions of lives in an instant had become a dreadful possibility.

Tension over Berlin. Meanwhile, in November 1958, the Soviet Premier issued an ultimatum on Berlin. Khrushchev gave the Western powers six months to agree to withdraw from Berlin and make it a free, demilitarized city. If the Western powers did not agree, the Soviet Union would turn over to Communist East Germany complete control of all lines of communication to West Berlin. If the Western powers then tried to gain access to West Berlin without the permission of the East German government, the Soviet Union would help the East Germans to meet force with force. The United States, Great Britain, and France replied by repeating firmly that they would remain in West Berlin.

During 1959, however, the situation began to improve. The Soviet Union met with the Western leaders in a "Big Four" foreign ministers' conference. Although the conference failed to reach any important agreements, it did open the door to further negotiations.

Premier Khrushchev himself seemed to be opening the door a bit wider when, in September, he visited the United States. At the end of his visit, he and Eisenhower issued a joint declaration, stating that the most serious issue facing the world was disarmament. They also agreed that the problem of Berlin and "all outstanding international questions should be settled, not by the application of force, but by peaceful means through negotiation."

SOURCES

DWIGHT D. EISENHOWER'S DISARMAMENT PROPOSALS (1955)

I should address myself for a moment principally to the delegates ▲ from the Soviet Union, because our two great countries admittedly possess new and terrible weapons in quantities which do give rise in other parts of the world, or reciprocally, to the fear and danger of surprise attack.

I propose, therefore, that we take a practical step, that we begin an arrangement very quickly; as between ourselves—immediately. These steps would include:

To give each other a complete blueprint of our military establishments . . .

Next, to provide within our countries facilities for aerial photography to the other country. . . .

▲ Discussion topic: Why the Soviet Union chose not to accept Eisenhower's disarmament proposals.

The National Air and Space Museum, a part of the Smithsonian Institution in Washington, D.C., is one of the United States' favorite tourist attractions. Nearly nine million visitors a year view the museum's display of 270 aircraft, 100 spacecraft, and 50 rockets.

The museum's exhibits tell the story of the American adventure in flight. They include the Wright brothers' plane; Charles Lindbergh's *Spirit of St. Louis;* fighter planes from the two world wars; X-1 and X-15 rockets; a model of *Spacelab;* and space capsules from the Mercury, Gemini, and Apollo missions. Visitors can touch a rock from the surface of the moon. They can also view the solar system in the museum's gigantic planetarium.

Congress created the first National Air Museum in 1946. By 1966 so many advances had been made in flight and space technology that the name of the museum had to be changed. The collections of the National Air and Space Museum were housed in temporary quarters until the permanent building on the Mall opened in 1976.

Encouraged by Khrushchev's apparent willingness to negotiate, the Western powers agreed to meet with the Soviet Premier at a summit conference.

Summit conference abandoned. The summit conference was never held. Early in May 1960, shortly before the conference was scheduled to open in Paris, Premier Khrushchev charged the United States with "aggression." He announced that on May 1 the Soviets had detected and shot down a United States plane flying over Soviet territory.

American officials at first insisted that the U-2, as the plane was called, was engaged in weather research and had strayed off its course. Later the United States admitted that the U-2 had been engaged in aerial reconnaissance over the U.S.S.R.

Premier Khrushchev was furious. He refused to take part in the summit conference unless Eisenhower agreed to stop all such future flights over his country, apologize for past acts of "aggression," and punish those responsible for the flights.

Hoping that the meeting could still be held, President Eisenhower announced that the U-2 flights had been stopped and would not be resumed. He refused, however, to apologize. Khrushchev, refusing to accept anything less than an apology, left for home. During the remaining months of his second term, President Eisenhower continued to seek ways of reducing world tensions. His efforts were fruitless. Khrushchev refused to have anything to do with a summit conference.

SECTION REVIEW

See underscored items, text pp. 835, 837, 839 - 40.
Identify: Dwight David Eisenhower, John Foster Dulles, brinksmanship, arms race, massive retaliation, Nikita Khrushchev, Gamal Abdel Nasser, nationalization, Aswan Dam, *Sputnik,* ICBM

For answers to questions, see Answer Key, p.A116.

1. **Determining Cause and Effect: (a)** What were the causes and results of the Suez crisis in 1956? **(b)** Explain the United States position.

2. **Summarizing Ideas: (a)** What was the Eisenhower Doctrine? **(b)** How was it tested by events in the Middle East?

3. **Analyzing Ideas:** Why was the summit conference scheduled for May 1960 not held?

4. **Organizing Ideas:** How did each of the following reveal the continuing challenge of communism: **(a)** developments in Indochina, **(b)** revolt in Hungary, **(c)** tension over Berlin?

DEVELOPING HISTORY STUDY SKILLS

Thinking About History   Evaluating Historical Interpretations

How did the cold war begin? Interpretations of how the cold war began are many and varied. A historical interpretation is a judgment, or explanation, by a historian of why an event or series of events happened as it did. Historians often emphasize different cause or different effects or actually disagree in their interpretations of the causes and effects. This difference in emphasis or disagreement occurs, in part, because different historians bring to their interpretations different points of view and frames of reference. To effectively interpret historical accounts, a student of history must be able to analyze historical interpretations and evaluate the differences in interpretations by weighing supporting evidence.

How to Evaluate Historical Interpretations

To effectively evaluate historical interpretations, follow these steps.

1. **Identify the central points of the interpretation.** Determine the author's main thesis and conclusions. Note the events, issues, and people the author cites as cause of an event.

2. **Determine the author's point of view** (Chapter 19, pages 449–50). Identify circumstances that might have influenced the author's interpretation. Note whether the author was a participant or an observer of the event. Note when the interpretation was written.

3. **Assess the evidence.** Study the information the author provides to support the interpretation.

4. **Check the author's reasoning.** Identify any fallacies in reasoning (Chapter 28, pages 644–45). Note any assumptions made by the author (Chapter 24, pages 566–67).

5. **Compare the interpretation with other interpretations of the same or similar events.** Note the similarities and differences in the interpretations. Analyze the reasons for any differences you discover.

6. **Evaluate the interpretation.** Based on your analysis, accept or reject the interpretation.

Applying the Skill

Read the following excerpt from an article written in 1947 by George Kennan, at that time Counsellor of the United States Embassy in Moscow. Then answer this question: How does Kennan explain the differences that led to the cold war between the United States and the Soviet Union?

The Kremlin's Conduct of Foreign Policy

Of the original [Soviet] ideology, nothing has been officially junked. Belief is maintained in the basic badness of capitalism, in the inevitability of its destruction, and in the obligation of the [workingman] to assist in that destruction and take power into his own hands . . .

[The Soviet regime believes that there is an] innate antagonism between capitalism and socialism. . . . It has profound implications for Russia's conduct as a member of international society. It means that there can never be on Moscow's side any sincere assumption of a community of aims between the Soviet Union and powers which are regarded as capitalist. It must invariably be assumed in Moscow that the aims of the capitalist world are antagonistic to the Soviet regime, and therefore to the interests of the people it controls. If the Soviet Government occasionally sets it signature to documents that would indicate the contrary, this is to be regarded as a tactical maneuver permissable in dealing with the enemy (who is without honor) and should be taken in the spirit of caveat emptor *[let the buyer beware]. Basically, the antagonism remains. . . . And from it flow many of the phenomena which we find disturbing in the Kremlin's conduct of foreign policy: the secretiveness, the lack of frankness, the duplicity, the wary suspiciousness and the basic unfriendliness of purpose. . . .*

This means that we are going to continue for a long time to find the Russians difficult to deal with.

George F. Kennan

842

Kennan states that the cold war resulted from inflexible communist antagonism toward capitalism. He argues that the Soviet Union will not deal in good faith with capitalist nations because Soviet ideology sees capitalism as its enemy. He concludes that for a long time the Russians will be difficult to deal with.

An analysis of Kennan's statement reveals the following supporting facts.

SOVIET BELIEFS

1. Basic badness of capitalism

2. Inevitability of capitalism's destruction

3. Antagonism between capitalism and socialism

IMPLICATIONS

1. No recognition of a community of aims

2. Capitalists are without honor

3. Socialist trickery is permissable

RESULTS

1. Secretive conduct of Soviet foreign policy

2. Lack of frankness

3. Duplicity

4. Wary suspiciousness

5. Basic unfriendliness

To evaluate Kennan's interpretation, it is important to consider his frame of reference. At the time this article was published, Kennan was a high-ranking official of the United States embassy in the Soviet Union. Thus, he was considered an authority on U.S.-Soviet relations.

To further evaluate Kennan's comments, each point should be weighed against other interpretations of the beginnings of the cold war. In this case, interpretations vary widely. While some historians agree with Kennan's interpretation, many offer other explanations.

The evaluation of Kennan's interpretation, therefore, rests on his credibility and the persuasiveness of his arguments.

Practicing the Skill

The excerpt in the next column from Michael Parenti's *The Holy Crusade: Some Myths of Origin* (1969) is an interpretation of the beginning of the cold war that differs from Kennan's interpretation. Read the excerpt. Then on a separate sheet of paper answer these questions.

1. What is Parenti's main thesis?
2. **(a)** How long after the beginning of the cold war did Parenti write this article? **(b)** What effect might this time span have on his interpretation of the events that started the cold war?
3. **(a)** What supporting facts does Parenti present to support his interpretation? **(b)** Are these facts well-documented?
4. **(a)** Compare Parenti's interpretation of the beginnings of the cold war with Kennan's. **(b)** In your opinion, which interpretation is more persuasive? Why?

"Getting Tough" with the Kremlin

It was Harry Truman who succeeded to the Presidency before the war's end, and no reading of his opinions and actions would uphold the view that the United States was motivated by a sincere intention to extend friendly cooperation, only to be taken by surprise by Russian aggressiveness. If Truman brought anything to the White House it was an urgency shared by Harriman, Vandenberg, Byrnes, and others "to get tough" with the Kremlin. "Unless Russia is faced with an iron fist and strong language, another war is in the making," he concluded as early as 1945. Soon after taking office, he asserted to one visitor "that the Russians would soon be put in their places" and that the United States would then "take the lead in running the world in the way that the world ought to be run . . ." On the eve of the first atomic test — before Potsdam and long before the alleged "Soviet betrayals" Truman's first thoughts were of the Russians, not the Japanese: "If it explodes, as I think it will, I'll certainly have a hammer on those boys." His Secretary of State James Byrnes, told one scientist that the bomb was needed to "make Russia more manageable in Europe" . . . What is overlooked is the probability that Truman's own belligerent, uncompromising, and ungracious approach was a major factor in actualizing the struggle and in preventing the kind of accommodation between the United States and the Soviet Union that is just beginning to emerge today."

Michael Parenti

---

and therefore, equally to blame for the cold war. 2. 25 years (reference to detente in last paragraph) ; (b) Answers will vary. 3. (a) See underscore. (b) yes 4. (a) Parenti concluded that the cold war was caused by both sides; Kennan places the blame on the Soviet Union. (b) Answers will vary.

843

World War II transformed America's relations with the rest of the world. Any hopes that the United States could return to a position of isolationism vanished in the smoke and flames of the conflict. As the richest and most powerful nation on earth, the United States had to accept the responsibilities of world leadership. During the postwar years, these responsibilities proved far heavier than anyone could have foreseen as the war ended in 1945.

The immediate problem was the worldwide challenge of communism. During the Truman administration, the United States developed a foreign policy that sought to contain the Soviet Union and to check the spread of communism. The United States offered military aid to friendly as well as to nonaligned nations. It also formed collective defense arrangements, notably the North Atlantic Treaty Organization, with other nations to build a shield of military might around the non-Communist world.

The United States also sought in a number of ways to remove the threat of war and to strengthen the foundations of peace. Under Democratic and Republican presidents alike, the United States continued to support the United Nations, to work for disarmament, and to help less fortunate countries achieve a richer and more rewarding way of life. The United States developed the Marshall Plan and other programs of economic and technical assistance. Through such programs the United States brought new hope, first to the war-ravaged countries of Europe, later to the emerging nations of the underdeveloped world.

CONNECTING CHAPTER IDEAS

As the United States tried to strengthen the foundations of worldwide peace, American society was readjusting to a postwar society. In the next chapter you will read how, under the leadership of Presidents Truman and Eisenhower, Americans meet this challenge.

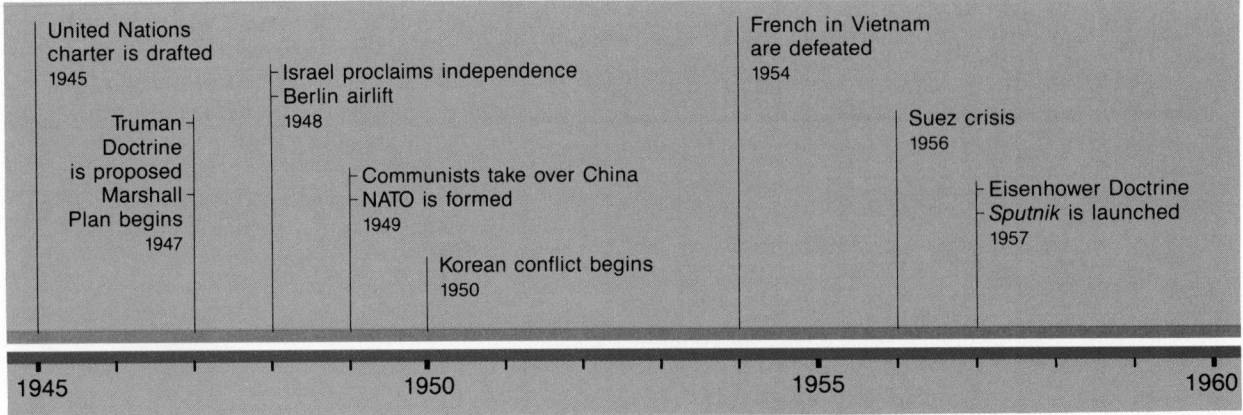

United Nations charter is drafted
1945

Truman Doctrine is proposed
Marshall Plan begins
1947

Israel proclaims independence
Berlin airlift
1948

Communists take over China
NATO is formed
1949

Korean conflict begins
1950

French in Vietnam are defeated
1954

Suez crisis
1956

Eisenhower Doctrine
Sputnik is launched
1957

1945   1950   1955   1960

CHAPTER
37 REVIEW

Reviewing Important Terms

Decide whether each of the following sentences is true or false. If the sentence is false, replace the underlined term with the word or phrase that will make it true.

1. The policy of underline appeasement was aimed at restricting Soviet expansion.
2. Being prepared to go to the verge of war is the policy of massive retaliation.
3. The Korean War was officially termed a police action since Congress did not issue a formal declaration of war.
4. Egypt's nationalization of the Suez Canal added to the crisis brewing in the Middle East.
5. After World War II the United States and the Soviet Union clashed over several issues which began the cold war between the two major world powers which lasted for two decades.
6. The Soviet Union's policy of aggression towards many of the eastern European countries after the war resulted in the creation of satellite nations.

Practicing Critical Thinking Skills

1. **Interpreting Ideas.** (a) In what ways is the United Nations a world government? (b) In what ways is it not? (c) Was the Korean War a victory for the United Nations and the United States? Why or why not?
2. **Analyzing Ideas.** In 1948 a world leader said "The trouble lies in the intense conflict . . . between the two most powerful single nations in the world today—the United States and the Soviet Union." Give evidence to support this statement. Is this statement still true today? Use specific examples to support your answer.
3. **Evaluating Ideas.** (a) How effective were the Marshall Plan and other actions taken by the United States during the years 1945–60 in meeting the challenge of communism? (b) The Eisenhower Doctrine was an extension of the containment policy developed during the Truman administration. Discuss.
4. **Relating Past to Present.** (a) How do the major areas of concern in foreign policy in the 1950's compare with those of today? (b) How does present United States policy toward these areas of concern compare with the foreign policy of the United States in the 1950's?

Developing History Study Skills

1. **Developing Historical Interpretations.** Read the following passage by historian John Lewis Gaddis on the origins of the Cold War. Then answer the questions below.

   The cold war grew out of a complicated interaction of external and internal developments inside both the United States and the Soviet Union. The external situation—circumstances beyond the control of either power—left Americans and Russians facing one another across a helpless Europe at the end of World War II.

   (a) What did Gaddis mean when he referred to "external" and "internal" developments? (b) Would you say Gaddis' analysis was slanted? Why or why not?

2. **Using a Map as a Documentary Source.** Study the map, "The Cold War in Europe" (page 830). (a) Locate and name the communist nations of Europe. (b) Which nations belonged to NATO in 1955? (c) Which nations remained neutral? (d) Compare this map with the map on text page 683, "Europe After World War I." Describe how boundary lines changed as a result of World War II.

3. **Using Primary and Secondary Sources.** (a) According to the document on page 828, what was the purpose of the Marshall Plan? (b) What other sources might you investigate to learn more about the Marshall Plan?

Relating Geography and History

Geographers often study the earth by dividing it into regions that share similar features, including common political goals. To understand the relationships among nations, study the map on page 830. Then answer the following questions.

1. What is the basis for the NATO alliance?
2. (a) Select a neutral nation shown on the map and explain why it may have chosen to remain neutral. (b) In what sense might the neutral nations be considered a region?
3. (a) Nations aligned with the Soviet Union are known as the East. Those that oppose the Soviet Union are called the West. Why are these terms used? (b) Nations aligned with the Soviet Union are also called the Soviet Bloc. What does this term imply?

See Chapter Overview in TMRG, p.TM206.
See Chapter Objectives in TMRG, p.TM206.
See Introducing the Chapter in TMRG, p.TM206.

CHAPTER 38 Returning to Peace and Prosperity

(1945–1960)

Returning home, 1945

846

After World War II, problems at home became as complex as international problems. The nation had faced a decade of depression and almost four years of bitter warfare. Americans were now eager to return to the business of daily life in peacetime. The return, however, was not easy as many had anticipated.

The task of leading the nation through this troublesome postwar period fell to Harry S Truman, who had become President upon Roosevelt's untimely death in April 1945. Truman was almost 61 years old, gray-haired, plain in appearance, and folksy in manner. He had a winning grin that showed his liking for people.

Born and raised on a Missouri farm, Truman had served overseas in World War I. After a successful career in local politics, he had been elected to the United States Senate. In the Senate he had faithfully supported New Deal programs. He had also attracted the attention of the Democratic Party leaders as head of a committee that investigated the national defense program. When Roosevelt needed a new running mate in his bid for a fourth term, he selected Truman. In 1945, after having served only a few months of his fourth term, Roosevelt died. Truman was suddenly elevated to the highest office in the land.

As the nation's new President, Truman had to handle the problems and challenges of the postwar period. Truman recognized the enormity of the task he faced. He expressed it simply when he said: "I felt like the moon, the stars, and all the planets had fallen on me."

Truman, however, proved to be equal to the tremendous challenges he faced. He successfully directed the emergence of the United States as a recognized world power and stood up to Communist expansion. Both Truman and his successor, Dwight D. Eisenhower, would struggle with the huge burden of guiding the nation toward peace and prosperity.

READING FOCUS

As you read about the decade following World War II, look for the details that support each of the following statements.

1. President Truman promotes a Fair Deal program.
2. President Eisenhower encourages modern Republicanism.
3. The nation admits two states and prospers during Eisenhower's Presidency.

1 President Truman promotes a Fair Deal program

See Teaching Suggestions in TMRG, pp.TM206-07.

After World War II ended, the American people had two major concerns. (1) They wanted to transform the economy from wartime production to peacetime purposes. (2) Most Americans also wanted to resume and extend the New Deal social programs, many of which had been suspended during World War II.

Return of the armed forces. After Japan surrendered, Americans were eager to return to peacetime conditions. They wanted their sons and daughters, brothers and sisters, husbands and friends, home again. Men and women in the armed forces were just as eager to return to their homes in the states.

The nation's military leaders, involved in the postwar occupation of defeated enemy nations, reluctantly gave in to public pressure. Within two years, the military forces had sharply reduced their strength.

After World War II, the government did far more to help veterans return to civilian life than had ever been done before. Government help came through the Servicemen's Readjustment Act of 1944. This "GI Bill of Rights," as it was called, provided for (1) government loans to help veterans set up businesses or farms, (2) government loans to buy homes, (3) pensions and hospital care, and (4) educational opportunities. Under the GI Bill, hundreds of thousands of veterans received money for tuition, books, and part of their living expenses while they attended school or college.

The Employment Act of 1946. The federal government also, for the first time, assumed responsibility for maintaining a high level of employment. Although the Employment Act of 1946 did not guarantee "full employment," it did commit the federal government to maintain a strong economy and high employment through federal spending. The act's effectiveness was marred by the decision of Congress, against Truman's wishes, to abolish the Fair Employment Practices Committee. During the war this committee had helped to enlarge job and other opportunities for blacks and other minorities.

Other postwar legislation. In August 1946 President Truman signed the Atomic Energy Act. This act established a government monopoly over the production of all fissionable materials. It placed the control of nuclear research and production in a newly created Atomic Energy Commission (AEC).

The National Security Act of 1947 centralized the responsibility for military research and planning. It created a new executive department, the Department of Defense, headed by a civilian Secretary of Defense. The act provided the new Secretary with three assistants, the Secretaries of the Army, Navy, and Air Force. The act also created the Central Intelligence Agency (CIA) to gather intelligence data abroad.

In 1947 Congress also proposed the Twenty-second Amendment (page 216), which became part of the Constitution in 1951. This amendment limited a President's length of service to two terms. The Twenty-second Amendment reflected the widely shared opinion that executive power might get out of hand if a President were not limited to eight years in office.

Postwar inflation. Some Americans had feared a postwar recession in the economy as industry shifted from wartime to peacetime production. However, there was no serious unemployment as veterans returned to civilian life. Most Americans—with important exceptions—had jobs and enjoyed a high degree of prosperity.

Prosperity did bring its own problems, including inflation. For more than a year after the war ended, President Truman kept wartime price controls (pages 806–07). However, demands for ending these controls grew stronger. When Republicans, who opposed controls, gained a majority in Congress in 1946, Truman ended all controls on prices and wages, though not on rents.

Prices at once started to rise. High wartime wages, saved during the war years when most consumer goods had been scarce, had created an enormous reserve of purchasing power. With money to spend and an ever-increasing demand for goods of all kinds, American consumers created a seller's market for American business.

President Truman retained rent controls because of a severe housing shortage that would have caused rents to skyrocket. Few houses had been built during the Great Depression and almost none during the war, even though the population was increasing. Truman tried to provide government subsidies for new housing but failed. By 1947, however, the housing industry was moving into high gear. The housing situation, while still serious, began to improve.

Labor unrest. Rising prices led to demands for higher wages. In many cases industry met the demands—but raised prices to cover the increased costs of production. The rise in prices, in turn, spurred labor to demand even higher wages. Thus inflation continued its upward spiral, with workers blaming industry, industry blaming workers, and consumers caught in the middle.

Labor unrest led to strikes. In 1946 almost 4.6 million workers went out on strike at one time or another. Two of the most serious ● strikes involved the railroads and the coal-mining industry. President Truman, who was generally sympathetic to organized labor, ended the railroad strike by threatening to draft the strikers into the army. The federal government also ended the coal miners' strike by seizing the mines and issuing an injunction ordering the miners to return to work.

The Taft-Hartley Act. The postwar labor unrest and strikes led to public demand for stronger federal controls over organized labor. When the Republicans won control of Congress in 1946, they felt that their victory in part reflected a rising demand for new labor legislation. In June 1947 Congress passed the Labor-Management Relations Act, better known as the Taft-Hartley Act. President Truman vetoed the act, which he called "a clear threat to the successful working of our democratic society." Nevertheless, Congress passed the Taft-Hartley Act over his veto.

In general, the new law aimed to reduce the power that organized labor had won during the New Deal. The Taft-Hartley Act restricted the contributions of unions to political campaigns. It permitted management to seek injunctions to end strikes and to sue union officials for violations of contracts or for engaging in certain strikes. The law forbade closed-shop agreements requiring workers to belong to a union before they could be hired. It also gave the President power to require an 80-day cooling-off period when a strike threatened to affect the national health and safety. The law

▲ Make sure students understand the basic idea of supply and demand. When demand (consumers with money) exceeds supply, prices rise. When supply exceeds demand, prices fall.

also required employers and union leaders to sign non-Communist oaths of allegiance.

Another provision of the Taft-Hartley Act allowed states to ban union-shop agreements within their borders. Such union-shop agreements require workers to join a union within a specified period after they are hired. By 1950, twelve states had passed legislation, known as **right-to-work laws,** barring such agreements.

The Taft-Hartley Act proved highly controversial. Supporters argued that it merely corrected the unfair advantages granted to labor in the Wagner Act of 1935 (page 721–22). Organized labor, on the other hand, protested that the new law deprived workers of many benefits won over a long period.

Gains for organized labor. During the postwar years, however, organized labor did make notable gains. Workers in general won substantial wage increases.

One labor agreement set an important precedent. In 1948, General Motors and the United Automobile Workers (UAW) signed a contract with an escalator clause. This clause tied wage increases to the cost of living. Other unions soon adopted similar contracts. Some union contracts linked pay increases to formulas based on increases in the cost of living as well as rising productivity. Union contracts often included welfare provisions, among them provisions for retirement pensions and health insurance.

The election of 1948. By 1948 the nation was enjoying a high level of prosperity. Under such favorable conditions, the Democrats met to choose their Presidential candidate.

The Democratic convention nominated President Truman on the first ballot. Largely at Truman's insistence and that of Mayor Hubert H. Humphrey of Minneapolis, the delegates included a strong civil rights plank, or section, in their platform. This plank urged Congress to guarantee the right of every adult (1) to vote and take part in politics, (2) to have an equal opportunity to work at any job for which he or she was qualified, (3) to receive personal security, and (4) to enjoy equal treatment in the armed services. The Democratic platform also favored repeal of the Taft-Hartley Act, federal support of housing, education, and farm income, and broader social security benefits.

The Democratic platform split the party. Southern delegates vigorously opposed the civil rights plank. A number of southern Democrats formed a separate States' Rights Party and nominated Governor J. Strom Thurmond of South Carolina for President.

Former Vice President Henry A. Wallace also left the Democrats to head a new third

In the 1948 campaign, Harry S Truman promised, "There will be a Democrat in the White House—and you're looking at him." Few believed him, including this newspaper, which headlined his defeat before the returns were in.

party. Wallace's Progressive Party attacked Truman's foreign policy for being too anti-Communist. The party warned that Truman's policies might lead to war with the Soviet Union. The Progressive Party also sought the support of labor and liberals by promising to renew and extend many New Deal measures.

With the Democrats divided, public opinion polls and most newspapers predicted that the Republican candidate, Governor Thomas Dewey of New York, would win. But President Truman launched a shrewd election campaign. He asked a special session of the Republican-controlled Congress to live up to its 1946 campaign promises and do something to halt rising prices and solve the housing crisis. When Congress adjourned without acting on these measures, Truman toured the country and denounced the legislators for failing to meet their responsibilities.

The election result was an astonishing victory for President Truman. He polled 49.4 percent of the popular vote to Dewey's 45 percent. Truman won 303 electoral votes, Dewey 189, and Thurmond 39. Wallace won no electoral votes at all. The Democrats also regained control of Congress and won many important state and city elections.

The Fair Deal. Heartened by his victory, President Truman decided to launch a broad program of reform. He urged Congress to adopt a Fair Deal program and extend some of the New Deal reforms. Many observers doubted that the President could win support for his program from the various groups in his own party. Time after time during Truman's second term, many southern and some northern Democrats did join the Republicans to block Fair Deal measures.

President Truman did, however, have some success with the Fair Deal program. Between 1949 and 1952, Congress did the following: (1) It extended social security benefits to include 10 million more persons. (2) The minimum wage for workers in interstate industries was raised from 40 to 75 cents an hour. (3) Congress authorized the federal government to clear slums and to build 810,000 low-income housing units over a six-year period. (4) Rent controls were continued to 1951. (5) A new Agricultural Act established farm price supports at 90 percent of parity through 1950 and thereafter on a sliding scale of 75 to 90 percent. (6) More federal employees were brought under civil ser-vice. (7) The work of the Reclamation Bureau in flood control, hydroelectric plants, and irrigation projects was expanded.

On the other hand, President Truman failed to persuade Congress to repeal the Taft-Hartley Act, to broaden support for education, to enact health insurance, and to secure all of the civil rights proposals he favored.

Concern over internal security. In 1947 President Truman asked the Federal Bureau of Investigation (FBI) and the Civil Service Commission to investigate the loyalty of all federal employees. By the end of 1951, more than 3 million employees had been investigated and cleared, 2,000 had resigned, and 212 had been fired as "security risks."

Meanwhile, in 1948 the FBI and the Department of Justice began an intensive investigation of Communist activity in the United States. Before the year ended, 11 Communist leaders had been indicted, tried, and sentenced to prison.

Finally, Congress passed the Internal Security Act of 1950. This law required all Communist organizations in the United States to file their membership lists as well as statements of their financial operations with the Attorney General's office. Concern over internal security weakened efforts to promote the Fair Deal program. The issue also played a major role in the Presidential election of 1952.

SECTION REVIEW
See underscored items, text pp. 847 - 50.
Identify: GI Bill, Twenty-second Amendment, right-to-work laws, Hubert H. Humphrey, J. Strom Thurmond, Henry Wallace, Internal Security Act of 1950
For answers to questions, see Answer Key, p.A117.

1. **Analyzing Ideas: (a)** Why was the Taft-Hartley Act passed? **(b)** What were its provisions?

2. **Interpreting Ideas: (a)** What were the provisions of the civil rights plank of 1948? **(b)** Why did these provisions cause controversy?

3. **Summarizing Ideas:** Describe some important achievements of Truman's Fair Deal program.

4. **Organizing Ideas:** What postwar national and international conditions led to an increased concern over national security in the United States?

5. **Using Graphics:** Make a chart comparing the parties, candidates, issues, and results of the election of 1948.

Discussion topic: Ask students which parts of Truman's Fair Deal are being carried out today. (minimum wage raised periodically, low-income housing in cities, farm-price supports) Ask which parts he failed to enact, but which are now being carried out. (civil rights)

DEVELOPING HISTORY STUDY SKILLS

Writing About History   Composing a Comparative Essay

You have already been introduced to the skill of composing an essay (Chapter 16, pages 385–86). You have also been introduced to the skill of composing an expository essay (Chapter 29, pages 662–63). The student of history is often called on to compose another type of essay: a comparative essay. You compose a comparative essay when you follow a set of directions that instruct you to compare things. To compare means to identify the similarities and differences. Here are some examples of directives that demand a comparative essay response.

- Compare the causes of World War I and the causes of World War II.
- Describe the similarities and differences between today's feminist movement and the women's movement of the 1840's.
- Compare and contrast the Populists and the Progressives.

Each of these directives requires you to compose a comparative essay in response.

Applying the Skill

Read and respond to the following directive.

- Compare Franklin Roosevelt's New Deal program with Harry Truman's Fair Deal.

Prepare and compose a comparative essay for this directive. First make a chart or develop a structured overview with these categories: economic philosophy, legislation, success in dealing with national problems, historical context. Next fill in data in the appropriate category. Under legislation, for example, it might be noted that both Roosevelt and Truman promoted legislation to protect business, to benefit workers, and to aid farmers. Specific information can be added in this category. For example, workers benefitted from the National Labor Relations Act in the New Deal and from minimum wage increases in the Fair Deal. Continue to fill in the informational chart, which should resemble the one below.

The New Deal and the Fair Deal

	New Deal	Fair Deal
Economic Philosophy	Government should be involved in balancing competing economic interests.	Similar philosophy
Legislation	To protect private enterprise, worker, and farmer. Developed price supports; fuel the economy.	Similar legislation
Success Rate	Success rate considered high by historians and economists.	Less successful than Roosevelt. Repeal of Taft-Hartley failed. Labor unrest and economic instability after war.
Historical Context	Emergency situation: Great Depression followed by World War II	Peacetime but period of economic fluctuation; Depression, war over but problems of reconversion and inflation plague economy.

After completing the chart, use the information to complete an outline such as the one below. Organize your outline in the order your essay will take.

I. Introduction

II. Similarities

    A. Economic philosophy

    B. Goals

    C. Legislation

III. Differences

    A. Success rate

    B. Historical context

IV. Conclusion

Once the outline has been completed, you can begin to compose your essay. The comparative essay on the next page is one reponse to the directive: Compare Franklin Roosevelt's New Deal and Harry Truman's Fair Deal. Note that the first paragraph includes a topic sentence that states the points to be compared.

The next paragraphs list the similarities and differences between the New Deal and Fair Deal. Note the transitional phrases (Chapter 21, pages 501–02) used to connect ideas in these paragraphs. The final pararaph restates the main ideas and emphasizes the comparisons that have been made in the essay.

Practicing the Skill

Read the following directive. Then on a separate sheet of paper, compose a comparative essay.

- Compare the Eisenhower Administration's concern for internal security with the Truman Administration's concern.

Sample Essay

INTRODUCTION

Harry S. Truman was a devoted follower of Franklin D. Roosevelt. To a large extent, his Fair Deal was an extension of Roosevelt's New Deal.

PARAGRAPH LISTING SIMILARITIES

Like Franklin D. Roosevelt, Truman believed that the government should aid in balancing competing economic interests. Like Roosevelt, he desired to protect the working man and the farmer as well as business. Thus, Truman attempted to bring to fruition many domestic goals begun during Roosevelt's administration. These goals included full employment for all Americans, a comprehensive Social Security system, and federal support for housing and education. Franklin D. Roosevelt, for instance, promoted the National Labor Relations Act, while Truman extended and raised the minimum wage laws. In addition, Franklin D. Roosevelt developed price supports in the AAA Act of 1938 while Truman continued price supports at 90 percent through 1950.

PARAGRAPHS CITING DIFFERENCES

The two Presidents had differing success rates, however, in part due to the differing political and economic climates under which they were operating. Truman was operating under peacetime conditions which in the main were prosperous. Roosevelt was operating in an emergency situation. First, the country was depressed economically. Later, the country was at war.

During the Truman administration there was much labor unrest. Truman failed to get a repeal of the Taft–Hartley Law which placed restrictions on labor. Roosevelt, on the other hand, was able to dominate Congress and get the type of legislation he desired. In the main, FDR had the people solidly behind him.

CONCLUSION

In conclusion, Truman's Fair Deal was an attempt to continue the program of Franklin D. Roosevelt. Truman had some success in this effort, but changing times limited his success.

(Essays will vary. Students should recognize that internal security was a problem for both administrations. In general, security measures established during the Truman years were continued or increased by the Eisenhower administration.)

2 President Eisenhower encourages modern Republicanism

See Teaching Suggestions in TMRG, pp.TM207-08.

In the 1952 Presidential campaign, the Republicans adopted the slogan "It's time for a change." However, they did not agree among themselves as to the nature of the change they wanted. Like the Democrats, they split into a conservative wing and a liberal wing.

The election of 1952. Confident of a victory, each wing of the Republican Party fought to control the nominating convention. The conservatives failed to gain the nomination for Senator Robert A. Taft of Ohio. The liberals won, nominating General Dwight D. Eisenhower for the Presidency and Richard M. Nixon of California for the Vice Presidency.

In 1952 President Truman chose not to run for reelection. Consequently the Democrats then entered their 1952 nominating convention as a divided party. In general, conserva-

tive Democrats had little liking for the New Deal and the Fair Deal. Moreover, southern Democrats differed sharply with many of their colleagues on the issue of civil rights. Faced with this party split, the Democrats finally chose Governor Adlai E. Stevenson of Illinois for their Presidential candidate and Senator John Sparkman of Alabama as their Vice-Presidential nominee.

Both parties waged hard-fought campaigns. The Republicans charged the Democrats with "political corruption" and promised to "clean up the mess in Washington." The Republicans condemned their opponents for steadily enlarging the powers of the federal government over the states. Further, Eisenhower charged the Truman administration with "bungling" in the Korean War.

Stevenson was an effective campaigner. He defended the Fair Deal and the foreign policies of the Truman administration. He insisted that there was no easy road to the "peace, prosperity, and progress" that the Republicans were promising the voters.

On November 4, 1952, voters in record numbers cast their ballots. Eisenhower won 57 percent of the popular vote and an overwhelm-

"I like Ike!" people chanted whenever Dwight D. Eisenhower appeared. When Eisenhower returned from service in Europe, he was one of the most popular persons in America—a fact that led to his landslide election as President.

Appeals to give blood are common today. Not long ago, however, the techniques that made blood drives and blood banks possible had not been developed. That blood drives and blood banks are common is due, in large part, to the efforts of Charles Richard Drew.

Drew was an excellent student and athlete. His athletic skills won him a scholarship to Amherst College. There he developed an interest in biology and began to dream of becoming a doctor. He attended McGill University Medical School in Canada. After receiving his degree, Dr. Drew returned to Washington and taught at Howard University.

In 1938 Drew was granted a fellowship at Columbia-Presbyterian Medical Center in New York. There Drew did the research that made today's blood banks possible. When World War II broke out, Drew was asked to help develop programs for storing and supplying blood to the Allied armies.

It was soon clear that America would be entering the war and would need a blood program of its own. Drew was named director of the effort in 1941. The Army's announcement that it would not accept blood from blacks raised a storm of protest. When the Army then announced that it would accept blood from blacks, but would use it only for blacks, Drew resigned.

Drew returned to Howard University and his teaching career. He continued to win honors and awards until his death in an automobile accident.

---

ing majority of 442 to 89 in the electoral count. He carried even the traditionally Democratic states of Virginia, Tennessee, Florida, and Texas. Nevertheless, the Republicans won only bare majorities in both houses.

Eisenhower's background. Dwight D. Eisenhower had been born in Texas in 1890 and raised in Kansas. After graduating from West Point in 1911, he served in Texas, Kansas, France, and the Philippines. As World War II drew nearer, Eisenhower advanced rapidly in rank and finally was named Supreme Commander of the Allied Forces in Europe.

By the end of the war, Eisenhower was one of the country's most popular heroes. Both the Democrats and the Republicans urged him to accept nomination for the Presidency in 1948, although his political preferences were not

known. Despite the pressure, Eisenhower at that time refused to get involved in politics. He left the Army to become President of Columbia University in 1948. In 1950, he returned to military service as the military commander of the NATO forces. Eisenhower held this position until he decided to run for the Republican nomination in 1952.

Eisenhower's administration. Eisenhower's style of Presidential leadership was a sharp change from the styles of Roosevelt and Truman. They had been active, vigorous leaders who had pressed Congress to pass their programs. Eisenhower believed that a President should not do too much leading. Instead, he felt that Congress should shape its own programs and that the President should carry them out. In carrying out these programs, Eisenhower expected his Cabinet members and his various appointees to handle the daily business of government. Only the most difficult problems were to be referred to him.

Economy in government and a balanced budget were "the first order of business" in Eisenhower's administration. Appropriations for defense and foreign aid were reduced significantly in spite of arguments from some Democrats that the administration was weakening national security. In 1956, for the first time in eight years, the government ended its fiscal year with a surplus.

Despite concern for a balanced budget, the Eisenhower administration did not attempt to repeal the basic social and economic legislation of the New Deal–Fair Deal era. President Eisenhower was personally in sympathy with much of this legislation. He supported a moderate extension of some of the New Deal–Fair Deal programs. This middle-of-the-road policy in domestic affairs—together with support for the United Nations, military aid for American allies, and economic and military help for underdeveloped countries—came to be called "modern Republicanism."

Social legislation.   Early in April 1953, President Eisenhower signed a joint resolution of Congress, transforming the Federal Security Agency into the Department of Health, Education, and Welfare (HEW). Oveta Culp Hobby, who had commanded the Women's Army Corps, became HEW's first Secretary. In January 1954, in his State of the Union message, Eisenhower urged Congress to expand the social security program and consider ways of providing additional federal aid for housing, education, and health.

Congress responded by extending social security to an additional 10.5 million persons and by increasing benefits. By 1955 about 90 percent of the nation's workers were covered by social security.

Congress also set aside additional money for the construction of hospitals and for medical research. In 1955 it authorized $500 million for slum clearance and urban redevelopment.

However, Congress refused to appropriate money to build schools and raise teachers' salaries. Many members of both political parties feared that federal support of education might lead to federal control. In 1958, however, after the Russians had successfully launched several earth satellites, Congress adopted legislation providing loans for able students, chiefly for students of science.

The farm problem.   While dealing successfully with a number of domestic problems, the Eisenhower administration grappled with others for which there appeared to be no ready solutions. One such problem was the state of the nation's farms.

During the Eisenhower years, surplus crops from the nation's farms continued to be a problem. In an effort to discourage farmers from overproducing, Congress in 1954 replaced its fixed price support system with a flexible one.

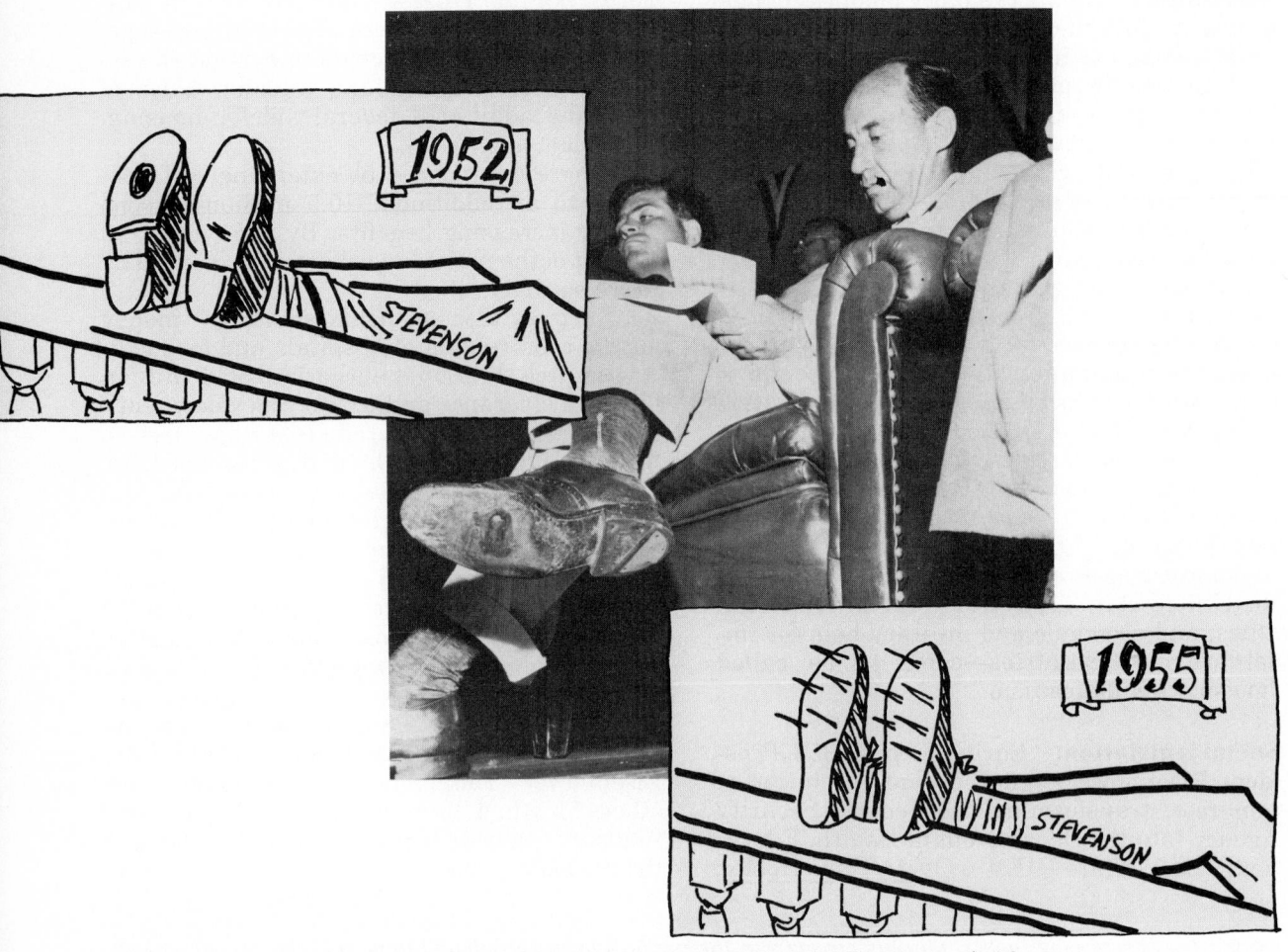

During the 1952 Presidential campaign, Democratic candidate Adlai Stevenson (with hole in shoe) presented himself as an ordinary American citizen. A cartoonist later parodied the contrast between Stevenson's strategies for the elections of 1952 and 1956. By 1955 Stevenson was literally ready to "run" for the Democratic nomination — and the Presidency.

Between 1952 and 1956, farm income dropped 26 percent. There were a number of reasons for this situation, including the loss of foreign markets and growing competition from farmers in other countries. Basically, however, the problem was an old one—overproduction in relation to the nation's needs. Since the early 1930's, farm productivity had almost doubled, largely because of advances in science and technology.

From 1942 to 1954, the government tried to guarantee farmers a fixed price support of 90 percent of parity. When prices dropped below this 90-percent level, the government bought surplus crops at the fixed price. Under this policy, grain elevators, warehouses, and storage facilities were overflowing. Storage charges alone were costing the government nearly a million dollars a day. Surpluses continued to pile up, and prices continued to fall.

In an effort to prevent these huge surpluses, Secretary of Agriculture Ezra Taft Benson persuaded the Eisenhower administration to end fixed price supports. In their place Congress adopted a flexible scale of price supports. This new policy aimed at discouraging farmers from growing crops that were flooding the market.

In 1956 the government made a major

Refer the students to the chart, Farm Acres Harvested and Farm Production, on page 1018. Ask the students what relationship exists between the number of acres harvested and the production index today.

change in the farm program. The **soil bank program,** as it was called, was designed to encourage the use of more land for providing forage, for growing trees, and for creating reservoirs. Farmers were to be paid for withdrawing land from commercial cultivation. By the end of 1958, the soil bank had paid $1.6 billion to farmers for withdrawing land previously used for growing crops.

Encouraging private business. The Eisenhower administration generally tried to reduce government interference with the states and with private business. For many years there had been controversy over whether Florida, Louisiana, Texas, and California owned the oil fields off their coasts. With the approval of the Eisenhower administration, Congress settled this controversy with the Submerged Lands Act of 1953, which gave the states control of the underwater oil deposits.

The Tennessee Valley Authority also became an issue in 1954 when the Atomic Energy Commission required additional electricity. ▲ Opposing a TVA proposal to build steam plants to generate electricity for the AEC, the administration awarded the contract to a group of private utility companies. However, the contract aroused such a storm of controversy that it was canceled.

The Eisenhower administration made other efforts to encourage private enterprise. (1) It abandoned the wage and price controls im- posed during the Korean War. (2) It set up a new commission to recommend ways of securing greater efficiency in government and removing government competition with private business. (3) In 1954 Congress amended the Atomic Energy Act, giving private industry a larger opportunity to develop atomic energy for peaceful uses. (4) The federal government also reduced or completely ended its participation in certain business activities.

Internal security. President Eisenhower faced the continuing problem of internal security during his administration. As you have read in Chapter 37, concern over the spread of communism became widespread after World War II. Revelations that American atomic secrets had been passed on to the Soviet Union, the victory of the Communists in China, and the outbreak of the war in Korea increased this concern.

During the Truman administration, Senator Joseph McCarthy of Wisconsin began to charge high government officials of sympathy with communism. In 1951 he even attacked General George C. Marshall, accusing him of conspiracy against the government. By the time Eisenhower became President, McCarthy, as head of a Senate subcommittee, was investigating the State Department and other government agencies. In his relentless hunt for Communists, he was joined by large numbers of private citizens. Actors, writers, educators,

Senator Joseph McCarthy (center) aired charges of communism against the U.S. Army during the 1954 Senate hearings. As millions of Americans watched the proceedings broadcast live on television, McCarthy's popularity plummeted.

and other individuals and organizations were investigated and accused of communism or sympathy toward it.

Many Americans praised McCarthy for his patriotic zeal. Others criticized him for recklessness and disregard of constitutional rights. By the end of 1953, a national poll indicated that Americans who supported his activities outnumbered his critics by almost two to one.

The Senator was at the peak of his power and influence when he began to look for spies and Communists in the Army. The Army counterattacked with the revelation that McCarthy had attempted to use his influence to get the Army to give preferential treatment to one of the young men on his staff. McCarthy, claiming that the Army was trying to blackmail him in an effort to stop his investigation, demanded a public hearing.

The hearing, begun in April 1954 in full view of television cameras, continued into June. Huge numbers of Americans, sometimes numbering 20 million, watched the event daily. Before it was over, Senator McCarthy was a discredited man. He had destroyed himself by his sarcasm, his endless interruptions, and his reckless and unsupported accusations. By the end of the year, the Senate censured him. The vote was 67 to 21.

SECTION REVIEW

See underscored items, text pp. 853, 855, 857.

Identify: Adlai Stevenson, Oveta Culp Hobby, soil bank program, Joseph McCarthy

For answers to questions, see Answer Key, p.A118.

1. **Interpreting Ideas:** What did Eisenhower think was the proper role of the President?
2. **Analyzing Ideas:** What was meant by modern Republicanism?
3. **Synthesizing Ideas:** How did the Eisenhower administration encourage private enterprise?
4. **Organizing Ideas:** (a) What problem faced farmers during the 1950's? (b) What attempts were made to solve this problem?

3 The nation admits two states and prospers during Eisenhower's Presidency

See Teaching Suggestions in TMRG, p.TM208.

Toward the end of his first term, Eisenhower's popularity as President seemed undiminished.

However, this popularity did not carry over to the Republican Party as a whole. In the 1954 Congressional elections, the Republicans had lost control of Congress. As the months passed, it became increasingly clear that Republican chances for victory in the 1956 elections depended upon Eisenhower's willingness to run for a second term.

The election of 1956. In September 1955 the nation was shocked to learn that President Eisenhower had suffered a heart attack. Even after his recovery was certain, the public wondered whether he would run for reelection. Eisenhower himself answered that question in February 1956 with the declaration that he was willing to be a candidate.

Both of the major parties held nominating conventions in August. The Republicans enthusiastically renominated Eisenhower and Nixon. The Democrats renominated Adlai Stevenson and chose as his running mate Senator Estes Kefauver of Tennessee.

In the campaign the Republicans reminded voters that the country was enjoying the highest standard of living in American history. The Democrats blamed the Republicans for the continuing high cost of living and for falling farm prices. They also charged that the Republicans had failed to develop an effective foreign policy.

Eisenhower's popularity returned him to the White House with a popular vote of more than 35 million to Stevenson's nearly 26 million and an electoral vote of 457 to 73. Nevertheless, the voters returned a Democratic majority to Congress, increasing the lead that the Democratic Party had won in 1954.

In the 1958 Congressional elections, the Democrats won by a landslide, piling up large majorities in both houses. Thus, for his last six years in office, Eisenhower had to work with a Congress controlled by the Democrats.

The Labor Act of 1959. During Eisenhower's second term, there were problems with organized labor. In 1957–58 a Congressional committee headed by Senator John L. McClellan revealed corrupt leadership in certain unions, notably in the powerful Teamsters Union. Several labor officials were brought into court and given jail sentences. The leaders of the AFL-CIO insisted that the corrupt practices were confined to only a small segment of organized labor. They took steps, however, to put their own house in order.

▲ Discussion topic: Discuss the power of the media, especially television. Would newspaper stories have had the same effect on McCarthy's popularity? Ask the students what other events were made widely known by television (for example, presidential debates, Watergate).

In the meantime, Congress adopted the Labor-Management Reporting and Disclosure Act of 1959. This law contained a number of important and far-reaching provisions: (1) It prohibited Communists or persons convicted of felonies within the five previous years from serving as officials or employees of labor unions. (2) It prohibited **secondary boycotts°** and the picketing of parties other than those directly involved in the strike. (3) It required labor unions to file with the Secretary of Labor annual reports giving complete information about their financial activities and other matters. (4) It required employers to report any loans or payments made to unions as well as any payments made to labor relations consultants. (5) It required national labor organizations to hold elections at least every five years. (6) It provided a bill of rights guaranteeing members of labor unions the right to attend meetings, nominate candidates for office, and vote in elections using secret ballots.

The new labor legislation went into effect in September of that year. In the meantime, President Eisenhower and Congress faced another labor-management problem.

The steel strike of 1959. In 1959 the contract between the steel industry and the United Steel Workers of America came up for renegotiation. The workers asked for a wage increase and other benefits. They claimed that the steel industry could afford to meet these requests without raising the price of steel. The industry refused to discuss a wage increase unless the union would agree to changes in work rules.

In July the union called a strike involving 500,000 steelworkers and plants that produced 85 percent of the nation's steel. Negotiations dragged on for weeks. Finally, President Eisenhower invoked the Taft-Hartley Act, asking for an 80-day anti-strike injunction. The injunction went into effect in November, and the workers returned to their jobs.

The injunction did not, of course, settle any of the issues. It was not until January 1960 that the union and the industry reached an agreement providing for step-by-step wage increases over a period of 30 months. In the dispute over work rules, the union maintained the right to place its own workers.

°**secondary boycott:** the support of a boycott by other unions and other parties not directly involved in the dispute.

A noteworthy event of the Eisenhower years was the opening of the Saint Lawrence Seaway, which linked the Atlantic Ocean with the Great Lakes.

Gains for organized labor. During Eisenhower's administration organized labor won several notable advances. Congress raised the hourly minimum wage under the Fair Labor Standards Act from 75 cents to $1. In June 1955 the Ford Motor Company and the General Motors Corporation signed contracts that moved the United Automobile Workers toward a guaranteed annual wage. The new contracts provided, among other things, for the companies to pay unemployment benefits to the workers.

During the 1950's a growing number of unions set up welfare funds to aid unemployed, disabled, and retired workers. Some of the unions used surplus capital to buy stocks, bonds, and real estate.

In 1955 the A. F. of L. and the CIO voted to combine. The new organization, called the AFL-CIO, with George Meany as president and Walter Reuther as vice-president, had 15 million members.

Alaska and Hawaii. In 1959, during President Eisenhower's second term, Alaska and Hawaii were admitted as the 49th and 50th states of the Union. They were the first states that did not share a common border with any of the other states. Alaska, now the largest state in the Union, adjoins northwestern Canada, far to the north of the state of Washington. Hawaii, a group of islands in the Pacific Ocean, is located about 2,400 miles (3,860 kilometers) west of California.

Alaska, as you have read, was purchased from Russia in 1867 by Secretary of State William Seward at a time when several nations were competing for its fur trade. So little was known then of its riches that for years Americans called Alaska "Seward's Folly." In the 1900's, however, Alaska became an important American source of timber and fish and of gold and other minerals. Later, in the early 1970's, a massive pipeline was built to transport enormous supplies of crude oil from the far north to the southern shore of Alaska for shipment in tankers.

Alaska's population today exceeds 479,000. About one fifth are Native Americans—Eskimos of the north, Aleuts of the southwest and the Aleutian Islands, and various Indian tribes, mainly from along the southeastern coast of the state. Adult members of these minority groups became American citizens when Alaska became a state.

The first known inhabitants of the Hawaiian Islands were Polynesians. They were expert seafarers who probably sailed there in ocean-going canoes from other Pacific islands hundreds of years ago. Beginning in the late 1700's, European and American ships stopped in the islands for fresh water and food. American missionaries arrived in the 1820's. In the late 1800's, American planters, as you may recall, developed prosperous sugar and pineapple plantations and gained control of the islands. The United States annexed the islands in 1898, and Hawaii became a territory.

Many immigrants from Japan and other parts of East Asia came to the Hawaiian Islands to work on the plantations. They remained to become farmers, factory and service workers, and business people. Out of a population of more than one million, about 60 percent are of Japanese, Chinese, Filipino, Korean, or Polynesian ancestry or of mixed descent.

In 1959 the citizens of Anchorage, Alaska, celebrated their new statehood. Some of them added a 49th star to the American flag, which would soon be redesigned. Alaska adopted as its state motto "North to the Future."

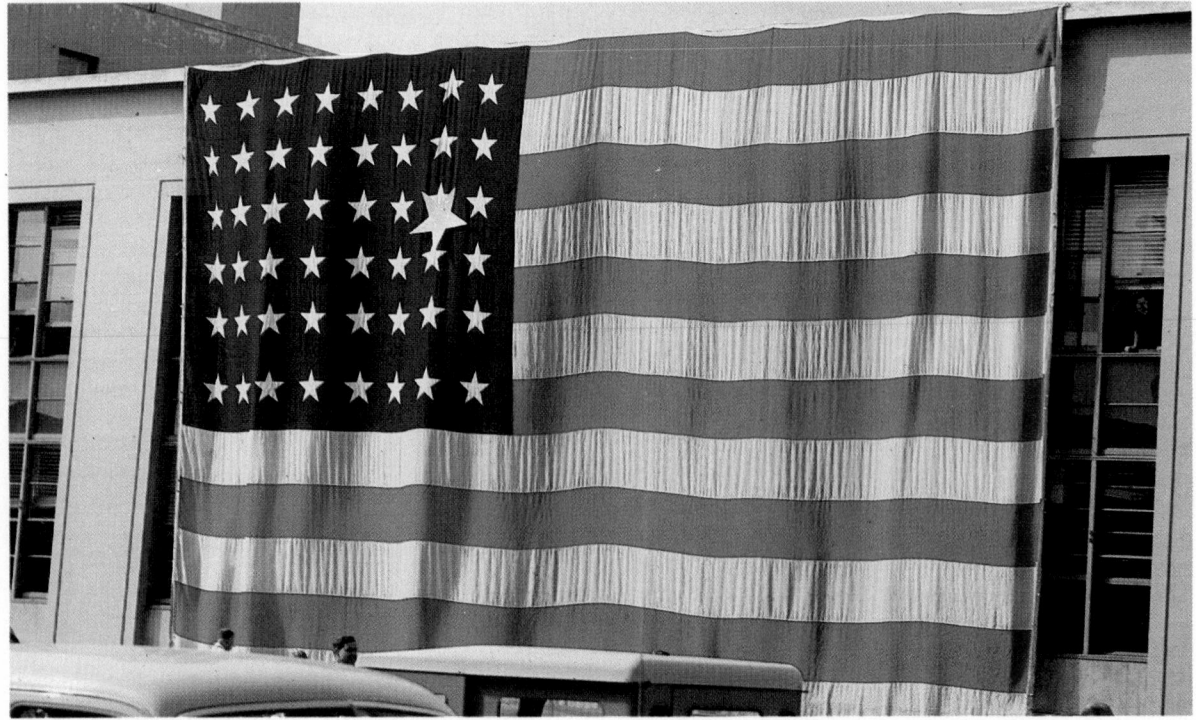

After World War II, an art movement in New York City began to attract worldwide attention. There a group of young artists were experimenting with a new type of painting known as Abstract Expressionism.

The Abstract Expressionists painted in many different styles. Yet they shared certain beliefs about painting. For instance, they did not think the subject of a painting had to be a person, place, or event in history. Instead, a painting could be an abstract arrangement of colors and shapes that expressed a feeling.

One of the most famous of these artists was Jackson Pollock. In 1947 Pollock began to make "drip paintings," such as this one. First he would roll out a large canvas on the floor. Then he splattered paint onto the surface. Pollock's movements as he painted determined what the painting would look like.

Continuing prosperity. By 1960, Americans still faced stubborn domestic and international problems. Nevertheless, they continued to enjoy a rising standard of living. To be sure, during the 1950's economic progress had been slowed down twice by recessions—the first in 1953–54, the second in 1957–58. The 1957–58 recession was the more severe of the two. Unemployment climbed to more than 5.5 million, the stock market slumped, and many Americans feared the country was entering another depression. However, by 1959 unemployed workers were returning to their jobs. The stock market had reached record high levels, business was booming, and a spirit of optimism prevailed throughout the land.

In 1950 the **gross national product°** (GNP) had been 264.7 billion dollars. By 1960 it had risen to about 510 billion dollars. Never before in the nation's history had so many Americans

---

° **gross national product (GNP):** the total money value of all goods and services produced in the nation annually.

enjoyed such prosperity. The enjoyment of "Eisenhower prosperity" was tempered, however, by the struggle with communism throughout the world.

SECTION REVIEW

See underscored items, text pp. 858 - 59, 861.
Identify: AFL-CIO, George Meany, Walter Reuther, gross national product
For answers to questions, see Answer Key, p.A118.

1. **Summarizing Ideas: (a)** Why was the Labor-Management Reporting and Disclosure Act of 1959 passed? **(b)** What were its provisions?

2. **Analyzing Ideas: (a)** Why was Alaska called "Seward's Folly" during the 1800's? **(b)** Why would it be unlikely to be called a "folly" today?

3. **Studying Maps:** Turn to the map on pages 992–93 and answer these questions: **(a)** If it is 1:00 A.M. in Denver, Colorado, what time is it in Fairbanks, Alaska? **(b)** What is the capital of Hawaii? **(c)** How far is it from Ketchikan, Alaska, to Barrow, Alaska?

38 SUMMARY

In 1945 the immediate problem facing the nation was that of converting from a wartime to a peacetime economy. During the postwar years, Americans met this problem squarely, made the necessary adjustments, and entered the 1950's on a wave of unprecedented prosperity. Harry S Truman, a devoted follower of President Roosevelt, had some success in continuing the New Deal reforms with his Fair Deal program. Nevertheless, the Republican Party made political gains.

With the election of Dwight D. Eisenhower in 1952, twenty years of government by the Democrats came to an end. President Eisenhower promised to reform the federal government by reducing spending, taxes, and regulations. He also wanted to transfer many federal programs to the state and local governments. The Republicans discovered that this was easier said than done. In 1960, when the Eisenhower administration drew to a close, the size of the federal bureaucracy remained about the same as it had been in 1952.

For a few years in the early 1950's, the search for Communists in government and in private life had seriously crippled the everyday life of the nation. Even so, the majority of Americans enjoyed eight years of relative calm and prosperity during the Eisenhower administration. There were, however, serious domestic problems calling for solutions.

CONNECTING CHAPTER IDEAS

During the years from 1945 to 1965 American society witnessed phenomenal technological growth. In the next chapter you will read how revolutionary changes in science and technology helped build a national economy of abundance.

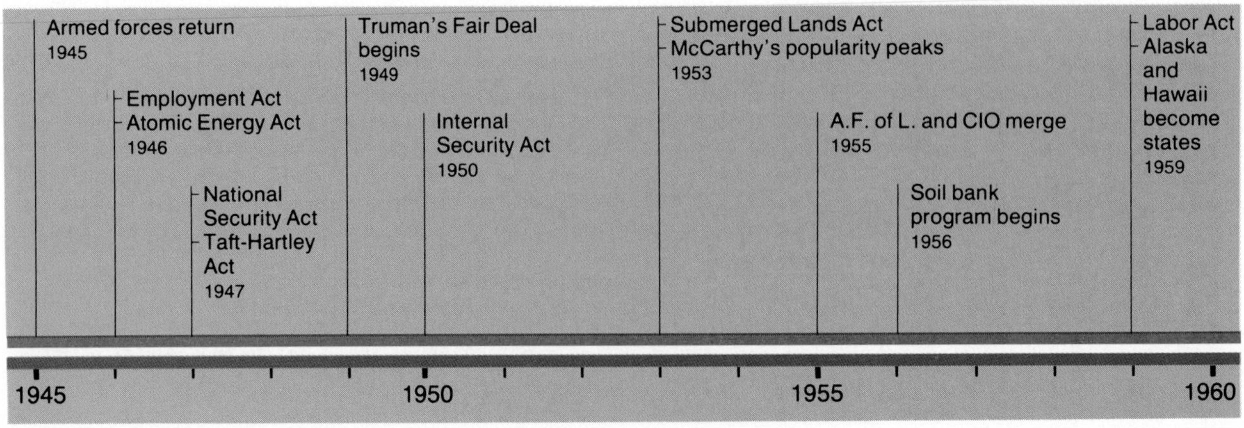

Armed forces return
1945

Employment Act
Atomic Energy Act
1946

National
Security Act
Taft-Hartley
Act
1947

Truman's Fair Deal
begins
1949

Internal
Security Act
1950

Submerged Lands Act
McCarthy's popularity peaks
1953

A.F. of L. and CIO merge
1955

Soil bank
program begins
1956

Labor Act
Alaska
and
Hawaii
become
states
1959

1945   1950   1955   1960

CHAPTER
38 REVIEW

Reviewing Important Terms

Decide whether each of the following sentences is true or false. If the sentence is false, replace the underlined term with the word or phrase that will make it true.

1. The Taft-Hartley Act provided for government loans, pensions, hospital care, and educational opportunities for veterans.
2. The gross national product is defined as the total money value of all goods and services annually produced in a nation.
3. The concern over social security led to rise of McCarthyism.
4. By 1950, right-to-work laws which prohibited closed or union shops were passed by twelve states.
5. The Labor-Management Reporting and Disclosure Act of 1959 prohibited picketing and other secondary boycotts.
6. The parity program, which began in 1956 was designed to encourage the use of more land for providing forage, for growing trees, and for creating reservoirs.

Practicing Critical Thinking Skills

1. **Organizing Ideas.** Describe United States demobilization and conversion to peacetime after World War II. What problems did the nation face? What steps did it take to solve them?
2. **Interpreting Ideas.** From 1954 to 1960, the government operated with a Republican President and a Congress controlled by Democrats. **(a)** What does this tell you about national politics at this time? **(b)** Why might this situation make it difficult for the federal government to get things done?
3. **Summarizing Ideas.** Describe the tension between internal security and Constitutional rights that arose during the 1950's.
4. **Comparing Ideas.** Compare the Presidencies of Truman and Eisenhower in terms of **(a)** their attitudes toward the job, **(b)** the support they received from the American people, and **(c)** their accomplishments while they held office.
5. **Interviewing Eyewitnesses.** Interview someone who was an adult during the 1950's. Ask him or her to share impressions of the political or economic events of that decade. Then answer the following questions. **(a)** How does the information gathered in your interview compare with the information presented in your textbook? **(b)** What are the advantages of using an interview to learn about events of a historical period? **(c)** What are the disadvantages?
6. **Relating Past to Present.** **(a)** How does the situation of farmers today compare with their situation during the 1950's? **(b)** How does the government's relationship to farmers today compare with that of the 1950's?

Developing History Study Skills

Composing a Comparative Essay. Read the following excerpts, then write a comparative essay to answer the question: How did Adlai Stevenson and Dwight Eisenhower view Senator Joseph McCarthy and his anticommunist crusade?

> Adlai Stevenson: *Because we believe in a free mind we are also fighting those who, in the name of anti-communism, would assail the community of freedom itself. . . . The pillorying of the innocent has caused the wise to stammer and the timid to retreat.*

> Dwight Eisenhower: *Senator McCarthy is, of course, so anxious for the headlines that he is prepared to go to any extremes. . . . I really believe that nothing will be so effective in combating his particular kind of troublemaking as to ignore him.*

Relating Geography and History

The needs of World War II and continuing technological advances strengthened American business and industry. One reason for the continuing strength of American industry was the abundance of mineral resources. To recognize the importance of mineral resources to modern industry, study the map on pages 1020–21 and answer the following questions.

1. What other important energy source is often found near petroleum deposits?
2. Why has the steel industry developed around Birmingham, Alabama?
3. **(a)** Which state has the most numerous petroleum and natural gas deposits? **(b)** precious metal deposits? **(c)** uranium deposits?

See Chapter Overview in TMRG, p.TM209.
See Chapter Objectives in TMRG, p.TM209.
See Introducing the Chapter in TMRG, p.TM209.

CHAPTER 39

Age of Advancement

Changing Ways (1945–1960)

An atomic test, 1951

Change and *growth* are the words that best describe American society in the years following World War II. Change and growth have been central features of American life from the day the first European settlers landed on the shores of the New World. Through the course of the centuries that followed the nation's founding, Americans had lived with change. They had lived with change as they settled the nation and as they built the United States into one of the world's most prosperous nations. They also lived with change as they entered a new technological age.

The new and overriding fact of change in the postwar years, however, was the startling increase in the rate with which change was taking place. Never before in human history had so many changes taken place in such a brief span of time. One observer, writing in the early 1960's, declared that the changes were "so wide-sweeping that they are taking us from one epoch of human history into another."

During the 1940's, not even the most far-sighted observers could foresee the amazing scientific and technological developments that would, in the years immediately ahead, profoundly alter older ways of living in the United States and throughout the world. In 1945 the opportunities and challenges of the new age had not yet been fully revealed.

By 1960 Americans had profited from many of the opportunities of this new age and had accepted its challenges. The United States was the richest, most productive nation in the world. The nation's wealth, however, was not shared equally among all Americans. Minorities still bore the burdens of poverty and prejudice. But they had taken major steps toward achieving the full equality so neatly stated in the Declaration of Independence.

READING FOCUS

As you read about the amazing changes of the postwar years, look for the details that support each of the following statements.

1. Science and technology make revolutionary advances.
2. The nation builds an economy of abundance.
3. Most Americans enjoy the advantages of a booming economy.
4. Poverty in a land of abundance haunts the nation's minorities.

1 Science and technology make revolutionary advances

See Teaching Suggestions in TMRG, p.TM210.

Before World War II, major advances had been made in science in both Europe and America. Breakthroughs had been made by scientists working by themselves or with a few colleagues in the laboratories of prominent universities or private industry. During and after the war, however, scientific research and development became increasingly a carefully organized team effort.

Organizing human intelligence. The distinguished scholar Alfred North Whitehead observed that when human beings began to organize research, they invented "the art of inventing." This "invention," he concluded, was one of humanity's greatest achievements. The first demonstration of what scientists and engineers could accomplish by such large-scale cooperation had occurred during World War II.

Late in 1939 the federal government committed its first funds for the exploration and development of atomic energy. This exploration and development effort soon became an all-out, top-secret effort to produce an atomic bomb for the United States. Thousands of the nation's leading scientists, engineers, and construction workers devoted their time and talents to the Manhattan Project.

Never before had so much money ($2 billion), so much intelligence, and so much effort been channeled into a single undertaking. The atomic bombs that leveled Hiroshima and Nagasaki in August 1945 provided the necessary evidence, terrible though it was in this case, of the effectiveness of organized research. The effectiveness of organized research was to be demonstrated again during the 1960's with another massive project. This was the *Apollo* program—the successful effort conducted over nearly 10 years to land American astronauts on the moon.

The growth of organized research. The successes of wartime efforts like the Manhattan Project and the development of radar prompted government and private industry in the postwar years to devote more and more money to

▲

▲ The Manhattan Project was carried out at a uranium refinery in Oak Ridge, Tennessee; a plutonium refinery at Hanford, Washington; and at a laboratory at Los Alamos, New Mexico.

When she was 14, Eleanor Roosevelt wrote, "It seems to me that we should leave some mark upon the world and not just live and pass away." Eleanor Roosevelt left her mark upon the world. In the process, she became one of the most popular and widely recognized persons in the world.

Born to a prominent family (President Theodore Roosevelt was her uncle), she married a distant cousin, Franklin Delano Roosevelt. In the early years of the marriage, Eleanor concentrated on making a home and raising five children. But as Franklin's political career advanced, Eleanor became increasingly involved with politics.

In 1921 Franklin Roosevelt was stricken with polio. While he recovered, Eleanor became his "legs and eyes." She attended meetings, made tours, organized voters, and reported back to him.

After Franklin's inauguration as President in 1933, Eleanor made countless trips to see for herself the conditions of the needy. She fought for more and better positions for women in government and investigated charges of discrimination against blacks. To further these interest, she wrote newspaper and magazine columns and made radio broadcasts. During World War II, she flew thousands of miles on goodwill missions to Allied troops.

After Franklin's death, Eleanor's public life continued. President Truman made her a member of the first United States delegation to the United Nations. There she helped to settle the questions of wartime refugees and to draft that organization's Declaration of Human Rights.

Eleanor Roosevelt remained active until her death at age 72. One writer summed up her contributions this way: "Mrs. Roosevelt has done more good deeds on a bigger scale for a longer time than any other woman who ever appeared on our public scene."

scientific research and development, both in the public and private sectors of the nation. In 1930 only $166 million was spent for organized research and development. By 1960 the amount spent on organized research and development had risen to more than $12 billion, approximately two thirds of which came from the federal government. However, most of the work itself was carried on in the laboratories of private industry, universities, and independent research institutes.

As a result of organized scientific activity, knowledge began to accumulate at a staggering rate. The amount of information available to the human race, it was estimated, was doubling every 10 years. People began to speak of the **knowledge explosion.** Even more significant, each advance opened up new horizons for science and made possible further progress in technology. As you will see, new industries were created and thousands of new products became available. Most important, scientists made fantastic progress in understanding the basic forces of nature.

Each fresh discovery also created new problems. With the invention of the art of inventing, changes were occurring so rapidly that the world could never be the same again.

International scientific research. As the years passed, international scientific research came to be carried on by teams of scientists from many countries. For example, during the period from July 1, 1957, to December 31, 1958 — known as the International Geophysical Year — scientists of 66 nations worked together. They conducted worldwide studies of gravity, geomagnetism, meteorology, oceanography, solar activity, cosmic rays, and other fundamental subjects.

In 1959 the United States and 11 other nations, including the Soviet Union, signed a treaty governing the use of Antarctica. They agreed not to exercise any territorial claim over the vast, ice-covered continent. They also set the continent aside as a scientific preserve open to the scientists of all nations.

Looking ahead, in 1967 a similar treaty relating to outer space was signed by 62 countries. The treaty (1) prohibits the orbiting of nuclear weapons and (2) prohibits any nation from claiming sovereignty over the moon or any planet. President Johnson called the treaty "the first firm step toward keeping outer space free forever from the implements of war."

The computer revolution. The electronic computer was one of the most significant postwar products of the technological revolution. The first modern computers were developed shortly after World War II. By 1960 there were about 5,000 computers in use in the United States. Nevertheless, what was to become a computerized society was still in its infancy. Eventually, thousands of computers would be installed in laboratories, business offices, government agencies, hospitals, schools, banks, scores of other organizations, and increasingly in private homes.

In a fraction of a second, computers can perform calculations that even the most efficient individual could not complete in a lifetime. Computers available by the 1960's could perform in one second 357,000 additions or subtractions or 178,000 multiplications or 102,000 divisions. They were being used in laboratories to provide instant analysis of complex tech-

LOOK   JOHN DEMPSEY

"Merfson, I'm afraid I have some rather unpleasant news for you."

Automation was a topic of concern to many Americans in the 1950's. In this cartoon a lighter view of one problem produced by automation is presented.

nical problems that could not be studied in any other way. They were being used in businesses and banks for accounting, bookkeeping, and billing. They were being used by governments to check income tax returns and to record data on births, marriages, public health, car registrations, and criminal records. They were being used in industry to forecast economic trends and control assembly lines in automated factories.

In brief, machines were doing much of certain kinds of mental work once performed by men and women. In fact, any data that could be measured or counted could be handled more efficiently by computers than by human beings.

Business and industry automate. Other equipment performed still other operations far more swiftly and efficiently than individuals could hope to do. For example, the Bell Telephone Company reported that if it had not installed automatic switchboards, by 1962 a work force equal to the total of all the women in the nation between the ages of 18 and 30 would have been required to handle the 90 billion telephone calls made in the United States in that year alone.

Robot welders such as this one at an automated iron-casting plant are examples of advancing technology in industry. What problems has automation caused?

The automated machines used in many industries performed a whole series of operations. Some adjusted themselves to correct their own errors. Automated factories could turn raw materials into finished products with only a handful of technicians on the job to plan and control the process.

Americans watched the rapid increase in **automation** with mixed feelings. Some hailed it as a triumph of human ingenuity that would lead the nation to higher and ever higher standards of living. Others shared the deep concern of Walter Reuther, president of the United Automobile Workers, who was worried about jobs. He toured a plant in which automatic machines had reduced the number of workers from 800 to 15. Reuther agreed that the plant was indeed efficient. "But," he pointedly asked, "are these machines going to buy cars?"

The leaders of organized labor were not opposed to automation as such. Instead they criticized "irresponsibly introduced" automatic machines that could "result in unprecedented unemployment." They made it clear that they expected wage earners to receive a fair share of the prosperity that would come from increasingly efficient production.

SECTION REVIEW
See underscored items, text pp. 865 - 68.

Identify: Manhattan Project, knowledge explosion, International Geophysical Year, automation
For answers to questions, see Answer Key, p.A119.

1. **Analyzing Ideas:** Why can it be said that the organizing of research is one of humanity's greatest achievements? Do you agree? Why or why not?

2. **Summarizing Ideas:** In what ways have the United States and other nations cooperated in scientific research since World War II?

3. **Studying Graphics:** Examine the cartoon on page 867. **(a)** What is the unpleasant news for Merfson? **(b)** How can you tell? **(c)** What is the cartoonist saying about the effect of automation and computers on business?

2 The nation builds an economy of abundance

See Teaching Suggestions in TMRG, pp.TM210-11.

The most obvious impact of the revolution in science and technology was upon the nation's economy. After World War II ended, the United States entered a period of unprecedented prosperity. This prosperity was built on what economists called an **economy of abundance.** This term applied to an economic system that was capable of producing more goods and services than Americans as a whole could consume.

Growing productivity. In the 1950's a group of distinguished economists stated that "America today has the strongest, most productive economic system in human history. . . . The United States, with little more than 6 percent of the world's population and less than 7 percent of the land area, now produces and consumes well over one third of the world's goods and services and turns out nearly one half of the world's factory-produced goods."

During the 75 years preceding World War II, the United States had doubled its output of goods about once every 24 years. After World War II, the rate of growth climbed sharply. If it continued, the United States would double its production every 18 years.

The roots of prosperity. There were many reasons for America's remarkable economic growth. Among them were an abundance of natural resources, an excellent transportation

▲ Discussion topic: Ask students to compare the workers' fears about automation in the 1800's (machines rather than hand tools) with automation in the 1950's (no people needed to operate machines).

system, and great numbers of skilled workers. Growth was spurred, too, by steadily improving labor-management relations, highly organized and efficiently managed industries, efficient methods of distribution, and an economic system that rewarded both individual effort and teamwork. The role of advertising in stimulating the desire of consumers for more goods and services also played a part in economic growth.

Above all, advances in science and technology sent the economy spiraling upward. Power-driven machinery and increasingly complex equipment were now common in nearly every field of human activity. They were found on farms and in mines, in factories and laboratories, in offices and homes. Out of America's industrial plants using new machines and new processes poured an endless variety of products in ever-increasing quantities.

American farm production was also setting new records. Advances in agricultural science and technology, in farm management, and in marketing helped make Americans on the whole among the best-fed people in the world. Each year the nation's farms produced huge amounts of food to feed Americans and to export to other nations.

New and expanding industries. New industries joined older ones in providing products, services, and opportunities for more and more Americans.

The aircraft industry, still in its infancy in the 1920's, grew in the years following World War II to a multibillion-dollar enterprise. Commercial airlines directly employed thousands of men and women. Many other thousands of workers were employed in the plants producing aircraft for the airlines and for private individuals, business firms, and the armed services.

The electronics industry had been small in the early 1920's. It boomed during World War II with the production of radio transmitters, radar, and other military equipment. During the postwar years, it grew still more rapidly with the production of television sets, computers, automation controls, radios, phonographs, and countless complex items for homes and businesses. In the late 1950's, the electronics industry received another big boost. It joined with the aircraft industry and hundreds of other enterprises in an entirely new undertaking—the space program.

Another completely new industry, atomic energy, also expanded greatly during the postwar years. Although military uses continued to dominate, peaceful applications of atomic energy were growing more numerous. For example, the first commercial nuclear-powered plant for generating electricity began operations near Pittsburgh in 1957. By 1960 three more plants were operating, and several others were nearing completion. Moreover, radioisotopes produced by nuclear reactors were being ▲ used for research in many fields, including

America's space program was, literally, getting off the ground in 1958 when this Jupiter-C Explorer II rocket was launched. Though it was a sign of things to come, few people then could have predicted the extent of today's space achievements.

▲ Class activity: Ask students to find out how many nuclear-powered electric generating plants are in operation now and where they are located (Source: the Atomic Energy Commission). Then discuss why some people are for them and others are against them.

869

medicine, where they were also used in the treatment of patients. By 1960 the United States and the world had crossed the threshold of the nuclear age. As you will read, the new age presented problems as well as promise.

While new industries grew, older industries modernized their plants and expanded their operations by mergers and by continuing to develop new products. Among the postwar industrial giants were the steel, automotive, petroleum, chemical, pharmaceutical, and business-machine industries. The giant of industrial giants was Exxon Oil Company, which was by 1982 the largest corporation in the world.

The revolution in transportation. The nation's advance into an economy of abundance would not have been possible without revolutionary developments in transportation.

In 1945, commercial airlines were still operating out of small airports. They carried only about 3 million passengers annually, most of them in two-engine, propeller-driven planes that could hold only 20 to 40 passengers. By the 1960's they operated out of huge, sometimes overcrowded airports. They used jet aircraft and carried more than 60 million passengers annually as well as ever-growing amounts of freight.

Speed as well as size and versatility became a major factor in aircraft design during the postwar years. By the late 1950's, jet aircraft had been designed for use on commercial air routes that could fly at 600 miles (965 kilometers) an hour, close to the speed of sound.

During the postwar years, traffic problems on the nation's streets and highways became an engineer's nightmare. Between 1945 and 1960, the number of automobiles, buses, and trucks more than doubled, from 31 million to nearly 74 million. The Federal Aid Highway Act, adopted by Congress in 1956, provided for the construction of 42,500 new miles (68,400 kilometers) of superhighways. Almost as soon ▲ as the act was passed, traffic experts began to talk of the need for an even more ambitious highway construction program.

As the number of cars on American roads multiplied, the federal government started a $75-billion interstate highway program to accommodate them. Cloverleaf designs like this soon appeared across the landscape.

The railroads, once the main carriers of the nation's passengers and freight, did not share in the transportation boom. Although they still carried more than half the nation's freight, the railroads met stiff competition from the trucking industry. Moreover, they lost most of their passenger business to private automobiles, buses, and planes.

Some daily trains carrying workers to and from their city jobs were still crowded, but with few exceptions even the commuter railroads operated at a loss. Rising taxes and increasing operating costs added to the gloomy picture. Railroad managers argued that if commuter services were to continue in full force, federal, state, and local governments would have to subsidize train service. During the 1950's their pleas for help fell for the most part on deaf ears. By 1960 many railroads were in bankruptcy or nearing it. As a whole the American economy, however, had never been more prosperous.

SECTION REVIEW

See underscored items, text pp. 868, 870.

Identify: economy of abundance, Federal Aid Highway Act

For answers to questions, see Answer Key, p.A119.

1. **Determining Cause and Effect:** What were the causes of America's dramatic economic growth after World War II?
2. **Summarizing Ideas:** What new industries developed rapidly after World War II?
3. **Analyzing Ideas:** What was the connection between the transportation revolution and (a) the airline industry, (b) the trucking industry, and (c) the railroads?

3 Most Americans enjoy the advantages of a booming economy

See Teaching Suggestions in TMRG, pp.TM211-12.

The rapidly rising standard of living in the late 1940's and the 1950's sprang from phenomenal advances in almost every field of science and technology. There were, however, other contributing factors. For one thing, during the depression and the war—a period of more than 15 years—millions of Americans had not been able to buy the things they wanted and, in many cases, badly needed. Equally important, there was a postwar population explosion, called by some the **baby boom**. It created millions of new citizens who required food, clothing, housing, education, and entertainment.

The population explosion. During the war and the prosperous postwar years, young people married earlier and had larger families. The resulting growth in population was spectacular. Where during the depression years of the 1930's the population increased by only 9 million, during the 1940's it rose by 19 million. In the 1950's it exploded with an increase of 28 million. In that single ten-year period, the increase was about equal to the total population of the country on the eve of the Civil War.

The nation's growing prosperity also attracted immigrants. Between 1951 and 1960, more than 2.5 million men and women arrived to swell the nation's population.

America's population was not only growing. It was also moving in a great human tide across the face of the land. Two major migrations of people—one into the central cities, the other out of them—were producing dramatic changes in American life.

Changes in the central cities. The migration into the central cities consisted for the most part of impoverished men, women, and children from the rural areas. Many of these came from the South and from Appalachia, the area around the Appalachian Mountains in the eastern United States. Growing numbers also poured into the cities from Puerto Rico and Mexico and increasingly as the years passed from other Spanish-speaking countries.

The hearts of the cities—the business and financial centers—were being completely rebuilt. **Urban renewal** programs were started during Truman's administration and continued under President Eisenhower. Under such programs, older sections of cities were torn down. Old, decaying structures were replaced by new housing and buildings. In city after city, blocks of gleaming new office buildings and apartment houses towered as visible symbols of the nation's wealth and vitality.

At times, however, urban renewal programs destroyed good, low-cost housing. Such programs could disrupt established neighborhoods and force low-income families into poorer housing. At times the wealth and vital-

Class activity: Have each student ask someone born in the 1940's to recall crowded conditions as a result of the baby boom. (For example, by the 1950's, schools had to double up in classrooms, etc.) Have the students share these recollections with the class.

871

The shift from city to suburb is one of the most remarkable phenomena in United States history. It is estimated that by the end of this century, 80 percent of Americans will be suburbanites.

An early pioneer of this new American life style was William J. Levitt, who bought a potato field on Long Island in 1949 and used mass production techniques to construct private homes. One historian described the process this way: "Convoys of trucks moved over the hardened pavements, tossing out prefabricated sidings at 8 A.M., toilets at 9:30, sinks and tubs at 10, sheetrock at 10:45, flooring at 11." Hundreds of houses were built in this manner at affordable prices.

The growth of suburbia was dependent upon the automobile. Many suburban families bought two cars because of the long distances between home, work, school, and shopping areas.

The similarity of life styles in suburbia and the pressure to conform there has inspired many books critical of the phenomenon. Among them are John Keats's *Crack in the Picture Window,* Herbert Gans's *Levittowners,* and John Cheever's *Wapshot Chronicle.*

ity of the business centers of cities stood in grim contrast to the decay in many surrounding residential areas. As you will see in Chapter 42, even while the nation as a whole was enjoying the economic boom of the postwar years, the central cities and the millions of newcomers to the cities faced increasingly critical problems.

The expanding suburbs. In the meantime, many young married couples were moving out of the cities to seek better living conditions for raising families. This movement strengthened the trend toward more widespread ownership of homes. By 1960 more than 60 percent of all American homes were occupied by people who owned them. One of America's oldest dreams was being realized.

All over the nation, families who could afford to do so were moving out of the older cities into the **suburbs**. The countryside around the cities was being leveled by bulldozers at a rate, according to one estimate, of some 3,000 acres (1,200 hectares) every day. Huge suburban housing developments were springing up almost overnight. Department stores and banks were opening branches in the new suburban shopping centers. Many industries were also following the people out of the central cities. The new suburban communities had to create new schools, police departments, fire departments, water and sewage systems, churches, libraries, hospitals, parks, and scores of other public services almost from scratch. These expanding metropolitan areas were being tied together by the ever-growing network of highways and superhighways.

Rural America was rapidly being replaced by a new and very different way of life. By 1960 almost 85 percent of the total increase in population was taking place around urban centers. These changes were creating new problems.

As the suburbs spread in an unplanned sprawl, the housing developments, shopping centers, highways, and roads ate up irreplaceable farmland at an alarming rate. The lack of planning contributed to the deterioration of the environment and of the quality of life itself.

The building boom. The changes in American life were also creating new opportunities. The movement into the suburbs stimulated a building boom. New jobs were available for millions of workers in housing, lumbering. and related industries. During the war years, almost no new houses had been built. After the war the pent-up demand for much-needed housing suddenly exploded.

● Between 1950 and 1960, nearly a million new houses and apartments went up each year. In several of these years, the number even passed the million mark. The housing boom was accompanied by a similar boom in the construction of schools, hospitals, offices, factories, and government buildings. The need for highways to connect the suburbs with the central cities further stimulated the building boom.

More goods for more people. With jobs available and money to spend, Americans went on a buying spree. During the 1950's they bought nearly 50 million new automobiles. By ▲ 1960 about three fourths of all American families owned at least one car, and one out of every seven was a two-car family.

The sales of household appliances and other products also soared as the nation's young families furnished their new homes and older families began to enjoy the fruits of prosperity. Washing machines, dishwashers, toasters, vacuum cleaners, refrigerators, freezers, radios, and—newest of all—television sets poured from the factories into America's homes.

Television, invented and developed before World War II, appeared on the market in the late 1940's. By 1950 some 3 million Americans owned sets. By 1960 the number had risen to 50 million. More homes had television sets than had running water or indoor toilets.

A changing labor force. The labor force that produced these goods and services was different from that of only a generation earlier. It contained a much larger proportion of women. In 1940 one out of every four employed workers had been a woman. By 1960 the proportion had risen to one out of three.

The rapid rise in the number of women workers was the result of several developments. In the first place, the demand for workers during World War II broke down prejudices and gave women a chance to show that they could do as well as men in many different jobs. Even more significant, the rapidly expanding economy in the postwar years created thousands of new jobs. Many of these new jobs called for brainpower and manual dexterity

rather than sheer muscle. Moreover, the growing use of labor-saving appliances freed women from many of the burdens of housework.

Another striking change in the labor force was the growth in the number of white-collar workers—teachers, lawyers, doctors, computer operators, clerks, office workers, and so on. In 1956, for the first time, men and women in white-collar occupations, including the rapidly growing service industries, outnumbered blue-collar workers. By 1960 almost one in every seven Americans worked for the local, state, or federal government.

Leisure time. Shorter workweeks and paid vacations gave most Americans more leisure time than they had even dreamed of a generation before. Between 1940 and 1960, the average workweek dropped from 44 to 40 hours. In some of the skilled trades it was down to 35 hours. During this same period, the average paid vacation increased from one to two weeks.

With more free time and more money, Americans piled into their cars for vacations in the mountains, in the country, or at the seashore. Motels, fast-food chains, and service stations multiplied along the highways. Golf courses were crowded. Sailboats and power launches appeared in growing numbers on lakes and small harbors along all of the nation's coastline.

At home the major source of entertainment was the television set. In the average home, according to one estimate, the TV was turned on at least five hours every day. More than any other single development, television began to weaken regional differences and to shape a uniform culture for the entire country.

Television did not, however, devour all of America's newly acquired leisure time. The sale of books, magazines, records, and tapes soared into the millions during the years following the war.

Need for better education. The changes transforming American life in the postwar years placed a heavy burden on the nation's educational system. The growth of population was in itself a problem. Between 1950 and the early 1960's, the number of students enrolled in America's schools and colleges increased from about 31 million to more than 50 million. This flood of students severely taxed the already overcrowded classrooms. And even

▲ In the 1950's Americans bought over 6½ million cars a year, almost 18,000 cars each day.

873

larger numbers were certain to follow in the immediate future.

The number of students was not the only problem facing the schools. When the Soviet Union launched *Sputnik* in 1957, American confidence was shaken. Was the Soviet success due to a better educational system?

Critics in increasing numbers began to question the quality of American education. They charged that school standards were far too low. Schools, they said, were failing to prepare students for life in the rapidly changing postwar world. Such critics called for more demanding courses in mathematics, the sciences, English, and foreign languages.

In response to such criticism, Congress passed the National Defense Education Act in 1958. The act granted federal money to schools and colleges for teaching science and foreign languages. It also provided funds for loans to college students.

An uncommitted generation. Another issue troubled many older Americans. This was the indifference of young people as a whole to many of the traditional values of American life. The young men and women coming of age in the late 1940's and the 1950's were sometimes labeled as "the uncommitted generation." Their goals in life appeared to be a good job, a house in the suburbs, and a retirement program that would provide them with security in their old age. They were, it seemed, unconcerned about politics and reluctant to be bothered about the larger issues confronting the nation and the world.

This tendency to conform, to avoid controversy, was not confined to youth. It was widely shared among all age groups, women and men alike. During the 1950's America seemed on the verge of becoming a homogenized society. One historian referred to the decade of the 1950's as "the years of repose."

Books of the period. A number of the more serious books mirrored the attitudes and the problems of the times. Two of the best-selling books dealing with the war years were James Jones's *From Here to Eternity* and Norman Mailer's *The Naked and the Dead*. Among the

As television technology grew more sophisticated, a new teaching tool entered the classroom—educational television. Broadcast by the National Educational Television network, these televised classes had mixed success.

novels reflecting the deadening effect of conformity were Sloan Wilson's *The Man in the Gray Flannel Suit* and W. H. Whyte, Jr.'s, *The Organization Man.* J. D. Salinger's widely read *The Catcher in the Rye* vividly captured the life of an adolescent boy coming of age in the postwar years. Ralph Ellison's novel *Invisible Man* dealt with the attempt by a black to find his place in a hostile white society.

One of the most influential books of the 1950's was *The Affluent Society* by the Harvard economist John Kenneth Galbraith. Galbraith reminded privileged Americans that in their pursuit of wealth they were neglecting the nation's poor, permitting the cities to decay, and causing the environment to deteriorate.

SECTION REVIEW

See underscored items, text pp. 871 - 72, 874 - 75.

Identify: baby boom, urban renewal, suburb, National Defense Education Act of 1958, John Kenneth Galbraith

For answers to questions, see Answer Key, pp.A119-20.

1. **Organizing Ideas:** During the 1950's America's population was moving in a great human tide across the face of the land. Explain this statement in terms of (a) the growth of central cities and (b) the growth of suburbs.

2. **Analyzing Ideas:** How were the following related to one another: (a) increased leisure time, (b) the two-car family, (c) the rising popularity of television, (d) more women in the labor force?

3. **Interpreting Ideas:** Why were more women entering the labor force in the 1950's?

4. **Using Graphics:** In 1930 the population of the United States was about 120 million. Make a chart or graph reflecting population growth in the years that followed: 1930's—increase of 9 million people; 1940's—increase of 19 million; 1950's—increase of 28 million. Why was the increase so great during the 1950's?

4 **Poverty in a land of abundance haunts the nation's minorities**

See Teaching Suggestions in TMRG, p.TM212.

Millions of Americans did not share in the prosperity of the postwar years. The poor came from all races and all national backgrounds. They lived in rural areas and in the cities. However, it was the nation's minorities—particularly Indians, Hispanic Americans, and blacks—that bore the heaviest burdens of poverty. In their struggle to overcome prejudice and discrimination, America's minorities battled for freedom, justice, and dignity as well as for a share of the nation's material goods.

The first Americans. In this struggle no minority in the country faced more obstacles than the American Indians. In addition to discrimination, severe unemployment, and widespread poverty, the Indians have had to cope with numerous federal regulations and controls. Their problems have been compounded by shifting federal policies and programs.

The efforts to overcome these handicaps have been carried on by Indians from all walks of life—doctors, lawyers, scientists, writers, teachers, singers, athletes, and others. Theirs has been a long, difficult, and at times disheartening struggle.

Failure of the Reorganization Act. As you have read (pages 753–54), Congress had reversed a long-standing policy when it adopted the Indian Reorganization Act in 1934. This act was intended to encourage Indians to practice self-government and to strengthen tribal customs and tribal life. The promises of the act were seldom fulfilled. Some tribes that had already managed fairly well in adapting to the white culture rejected the new policy. They claimed that it would keep them in an inferior status in relation to the white majority.

Also, many of the 25,000 young Indians who had served in the armed forces during World War II were reluctant to return to tribal ways of life. These Indian veterans felt that the country for which they had fought and for which many had died owed them the full rights and opportunities of American citizenship. They believed that the complete recognition of these rights was more important than preserving tribal ways of life.

The termination policy. During the 1950's the federal government once again adopted a new Indian policy. In this policy it reversed much of the 1934 program and established entirely new goals. One of the new goals was known as **termination**.

The termination program was intended to end all federal ties with the Indians. Responsibility was to be transferred to those states with large Indian populations. Acting under this policy, the government terminated federal ser-

▲ Report topic: Have each student find out about life for one Indian tribe, especially in relation to "termination" policies. The students should present their findings in oral reports to the class.

875

Puerto Ricans were often at the bottom of the economic ladder, but many had a fierce pride in their cultural heritage. This pride is evident here in their annual parade in New York City.

vices for a number of tribes, including the Menominees of Wisconsin and the Klamaths of Oregon. The policy was a disaster for the Indians because states were unwilling or unable to provide needed services.

The second goal of the new Indian policy was to assimilate the Indians into the majority culture. This called for relocating as many Indians as possible in cities. The Bureau of Indian Affairs attracted thousands of Indians to cities with promises of job training and job placement. In many cases these promises were not kept. Some Indians managed to overcome great odds and achieve success. Many others, facing discrimination and without the support of tribal life, lived in loneliness and poverty in the cities, which remained for them a strange environment. Some, embittered by the experience, returned to the reservations. For most Indians, <u>relocation</u>, like termination, proved to be a failure.

Immigration from Mexico. People from Mexico also faced hardships during the postwar years. As you have read (**page 808**), the *bracero* program encouraged the entry of Mexican farm workers during World War II. The

policy of importing contract labor was continued after the war. From the Mexican point of view, it provided work for otherwise unemployed workers. It also provided relief through the money sent home by the *braceros* to impoverished Mexican families. However, opposition to the program was building up on both sides of the border. The Catholic Church opposed it on the ground that it broke up families. The Mexican government began to object because the Mexican economy was expanding and labor was needed in Mexico itself. The program also met growing opposition from organized labor in the United States. The newly formed farm labor unions pointed out that it was competitively unfair to American workers.

Before the program was abandoned in 1962, more than 4.5 million Mexican workers had been imported as contract laborers into the United States. This number does not include the unknown number of illegal migrants, or undocumented immigrants.

Spanish-speaking immigrants. The *braceros* who came as farm laborers were required to return to Mexico after their contracts ended. During the 1950's, however, more than 360,000 Mexican immigrants entered the United States to become American citizens. They were joined by another 450,000 Spanish-speaking immigrants from countries in Central and South America and the West Indies. These newcomers came from all walks of life. A large percentage were highly educated professionals and white-collar workers.

Puerto Ricans. By the 1950's Puerto Ricans made up one of the largest Spanish-speaking groups in the United States. Unlike other immigrants, who had to be naturalized to become American citizens, Puerto Ricans were American citizens at birth. As you recall, Puerto Rico became an unincorporated territory of the United States in 1898 and then, after 1952, a commonwealth. Since 1917, Puerto Ricans have been legally entitled to the rights and privileges of American citizenship.

Even before the depression of the 1930's brought severe hardships to their island, many Puerto Ricans had migrated to New York City in search of jobs. During and after the depression, they came in ever-increasing numbers. Between 1945 and 1960, migration to the United States varied between 30,000 and 45,000 annually.

Puerto Ricans who moved to New York City, Newark, Chicago, and other northern cities faced many problems. Most came from rural villages. They lacked the skills necessary to compete for jobs in a highly complex urban environment. Many had only a limited knowledge of the English language, which handicapped them both in the labor market and in the schools. Perhaps most serious, they were victims of prejudice and discrimination.

Because of these handicaps, most of the newcomers were able to get only unskilled jobs that paid the lowest wages. Puerto Rican families were crowded into such tenement districts as Spanish Harlem in New York City.

In some ways the experience of Puerto Ricans in the United States resembled that of earlier immigrants. As you will see (page 955), many gradually moved up the economic ladder and found places in small businesses, semi-skilled trades, the professions, and the arts. In the 1950's, however, progress of this kind remained beyond the grasp of most Puerto Ricans.

A major victory for black Americans. Black Americans returning from World War II, like other minority veterans, often faced bitter disappointments. In spite of their war service, they continued to be treated in many ways as second-class citizens. To be sure, by the 1940's blacks had won substantial successes in every field of activity—science, medicine, the professions, business, music and art, entertainment, and sports. At best, however, only a very small minority of American blacks had achieved such success. For most blacks, the doors of opportunity remained closed or at best only slightly open.

During the years after the war, the movement to end discrimination in government, business, education, and sports speeded up. President Truman urged Congress to adopt legislation strengthening civil rights laws and their enforcement. When Congress failed to act, Truman used his executive powers to order an end to segregation in the armed forces and in the government.

The Supreme Court rules. The most important development, however, was the Supreme Court decision of 1954 during Eisenhower's administration. In *Brown v. Board of Education of Topeka*, the Court reversed the 58-year-old *Plessy v. Ferguson* ruling (see page 466) that

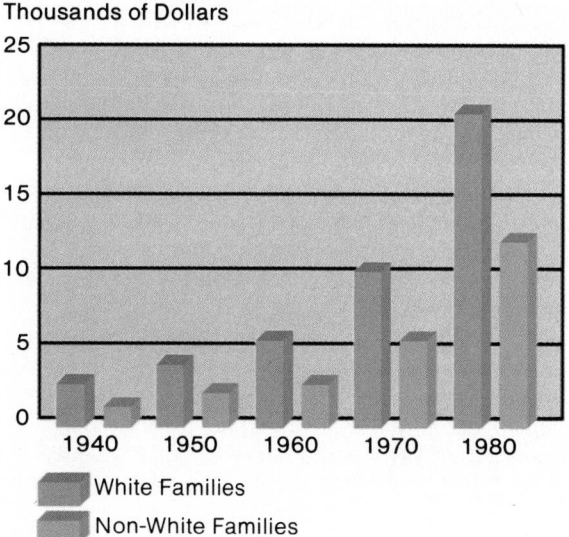

Median Family Income • 1940-1980

Thousands of Dollars

White Families
Non-White Families

Sources: *Historical Statistics of the United States*
Statistical Abstract of the United States

"separate but equal" facilities were constitutional. The Court unanimously ruled that state or local laws requiring black citizens to send their children to separate schools violated the Fourteenth Amendment.

Several months after the 1954 decision, the Supreme Court required local school authorities to work out plans for gradually ending segregation in public school systems. The Supreme Court also instructed federal district courts to require local school authorities to "make a prompt and reasonable start toward full compliance" and to move "with all deliberate speed in carrying out the law."

Direct action. Encouraged by the Supreme Court ruling, civil rights supporters redoubled their efforts to break down discrimination. Dissatisfied with the slow response in a number of states to the Supreme Court's rulings, blacks turned to direct action.

Early in December 1955 <u>Rosa Parks</u>, a 40-year-old seamstress in Montgomery, Alabama, took a courageous step. Her action led to a nationwide protest movement. On her way home from work, Rosa Parks boarded a bus and took

▲ Many southerners believed that the Supreme Court had taken away the rights of individual states, and there was a great deal of resistance to the Supreme Court ruling.

877

"It was just the times. I think people needed some event to start getting something accomplished. That's it."

The event was the refusal of the speaker — a black woman named Rosa Parks — to give up her seat on a Montgomery, Alabama, bus to a white passenger. The date was December 1, 1955. And the something that eventually got accomplished was the elimination of racial segregation in public transportation.

According to a Montgomery ordinance, blacks were prohibited from sitting in the front, or "white," section of public buses. The ordinance further required blacks — a row at a time — to give up their seats to whites if the white section were filled.

Parks later stated: "I don't care what your color or race is, we both paid the same fare so I shouldn't have had to move." Parks' refusal to yield her seat to the white man led to her arrest. An interviewer at the scene later reported, "When I asked her what had happened, she said she did not move . . . she had made up her mind

never to move again."

A spontaneous protest against Parks' arrest quickly spread throughout the black community. Several black leaders, including the Reverend Martin Luther King, Jr., organized a boycott of the city's bus lines. During the year that followed, blacks rode in carpools and held weekly meetings on the philosophy of nonviolent resistance. Finally in December 1956, as a result of the Supreme Court's intervention against segregation in public transportation, blacks and whites rode together on unsegregated buses for the first time in Montgomery's history. Parks' courage and the Montgomery bus boycott showed blacks everywhere that they could act effectively as a mass movement.

Today at 72 years of age, Rosa Parks continues to work for civil rights. For her, the 1955 incident marked the beginning of an ongoing struggle: "I did not decide that December 1st was to be any different than any other day. History made that decision for us."

---

a seat in the front section reserved for whites. The driver ordered her to move to the back. She refused and was arrested.

The next day, led by a 26-year-old minister, Martin Luther King, Jr., 50,000 blacks joined in a boycott of Montgomery's bus system. It was a peaceful protest, and it worked. When the bus system began to drift toward bankruptcy, King and other black leaders were arrested. Finally, almost a year after Rosa Parks's initial action, the Supreme Court declared that the Alabama segregation law was unconstitutional.

Inspired by the victory in Alabama, Martin Luther King called a conference of southern black leaders. Early in 1957 these leaders organized the Southern Christian Leadership Conference (SCLC). The organization announced to the nation that it intended to attack discrimination everywhere in the country by nonviolent means.

Congress finally acts. Efforts by both whites and blacks to avoid violence were only partially successful. Attempts at school integration as the Supreme Court had directed in 1954 led to violence in a number of communities. In 1957 President Eisenhower sent federal troops to Little Rock, Arkansas, to maintain order

when several black students tried to enter the all-white high school.

Responding to the growing unrest and violence, Congress in 1957 adopted a Civil Rights Act designed to secure voting rights for black citizens. This was the first civil rights act since Reconstruction.

The struggle by blacks and other minorities for freedom and justice continued into the 1960's and beyond. You will read about this struggle in Chapter 42.

SECTION REVIEW

See underscored items, text pp. 875 - 78.
Identify: termination, relocation, Rosa Parks, boycott, SCLC, integration
For answers to questions, see Answer Key, p.A120.

1. **Analyzing Ideas:** (a) Why did the Indian Reorganization Act fail? (b) What new Indian policy was set up in the 1950's? (c) How successful was the new policy?

2. **Comparing Ideas:** (a) Identify several groups of Spanish-speaking Americans. (b) How are their backgrounds different from one another? (c) How has their treatment in the United States been similar?

3. **Synthesizing Ideas:** Why is each important to the black civil rights movement: (a) *Brown v. Board of Education of Topeka,* (b) Eisenhower's action in Little Rock, Arkansas, in 1957, (c) Civil Rights Act of 1957?

DEVELOPING HISTORY STUDY SKILLS

Thinking About History   Determining a Frame of Reference

A value is an idea or belief that guides the actions of a person, group, or nation. Values give a person, group, or nation a frame of reference upon which to base actions, decisions, and judgments. Honesty, patriotism, freedom, and good sportsmanship are among the values held by many Americans. The laws of a nation often reflect the values that a majority of its people hold. The direct aid programs during the depression reflected a belief held by many people in the United States in aiding those in need.

People may hold different sets of values or they may assign different priorities to the same values. In either case, arguments may arise when people's frames of reference do not agree. Many times these conflicts can be resolved only through legal action. The *Brown v. Board of Education of Topeka* Supreme Court decision in 1954 was the result of conflicting frames of reference. The Browns, a black family, believed in equal opportunity in education. They attempted to enroll their daughter in a nearby school. The school board refused her admission because the school was for whites only. The school board believed in segregation in schools. For a further discussion of this landmark case, refer to text page 877.

When examining conflicts, it is important to determine each side's frame of reference in the conflict. Only when the differing frames of reference are identified can the conflict be fully understood. Students are often called on to determine values and to identify the underlying frames of reference held by the people or groups involved in the conflict.

How to Identify Frames of Reference

To identify the values in a conflict, follow these guidelines.

1. **Analyze the conflict.** Determine the source or sources of the conflict.

2. **Examine the arguments.** Note what each side is saying. Assess any evidence given in support of the arguments.

3. **Identify the frames of reference.** Analyze each position in the conflict to determine the values motivating each side.

Applying the Skill

The excerpt below is from a speech made by Senator Joseph McCarthy. On page 880 is an excerpt from a speech made by Senator Margaret Chase Smith. Both speeches were made in 1950. Read the excerpts and identify the frames of reference of Senator McCarthy and Senator Smith.

At issue was the national security of the United States. Senator McCarthy argued the State Department was "infested" with Communists and that this was weakening the United States. McCarthy claimed to value patriotism and unquestioning loyalty to the United States. He regarded criticism of his "crusade" as treasonous. He valued national security and freedom from communism over personal freedom.

Senator Smith believed that McCarthy's investigative techniques were a greater threat to the United States than the threat of communism. She believed in preserving personal freedom over national security.

The reason why we find ourselves in a position of impotency [powerlessness] is not because our only powerful potential enemy has sent men to invade our shores, but rather because of the traitorous actions of those who have been treated so well by this nation. It has not been the less fortunate or members of minority groups who have been selling this nation out, but rather those who have had all the benefits that the wealthiest nation on earth has had to offer — the finest homes, the finest college education, and the finest jobs in government we can give.

This is glaringly true in the State Department. There the bright young men who are born with silver spoons in their mouths are the ones who have been the worst. . . . In my opinion the State Department, which is one of the most important government departments, is thoroughly infested with Communists.

I have in my hand 57 cases of individuals who would appear to be either card carrying members or certainly loyal to the Communist Party, but who nevertheless are still helping to shape our foreign policy. . . .

Senator Joseph McCarthy

879

Those of us who shout the loudest about Americanism in making character assassinations are all too frequently those who, by our own words and acts, ignore some of the basic principles of Americanism —

The right to criticize.
The right to hold unpopular beliefs.
The right to protest.
The right of independent thought.

The exercise of these rights should not cost one single American citizen his reputation or his right to a livelihood nor should he be in danger of losing his reputation or livelihood merely because he happens to know someone who holds unpopular beliefs. . . .

The American people are sick and tired of being afraid to speak their minds lest they be politically smeared as Communists or Fascists by their opponents. Freedom of speech is not what it used to be in America. It has been so abused by some that it is not exercised by others. . . .

As an American, I condemn a Republican Fascist just as much as I condemn a Democrat Communist. I condemn a Democrat Fascist just as much as I condemn a Republican Communist. They are equally dangerous to you and me and to our country. As an American, I want to see our nation recapture the strength and unity it once had when we fought the enemy instead of ourselves.

Senator Margaret Chase Smith

Practicing the Skill

Read the excerpt below. It describes Rosa Parks experience on the bus in Montgomery, Alabama, in 1955. Then on a separate sheet of paper, answer the following questions.

1. What is the nature of the conflict?

2. **(a)** What arguments did Rosa Parks use to support her actions? **(b)** What was her frame of reference?

3. **(a)** What arguments did the bus driver use to support his actions? **(b)** What was his frame of reference?

4. What, then, were the values in conflict in this situation?

As I got up on the bus and walked to the seat, I saw there was only one vacancy that was just back of where it was considered the white section. So this was the seat that I took, next to the aisle, and a man was sitting next to me. Across the aisle there were two women, and there were a few seats at this point in the very front of the bus that was called the white section. . . . The third stop is when all the front seats were taken, and this one man was standing and when the driver looked around and saw he was standing, he asked the four of us, the man in the seat with me and the two women across the aisle, to let him have those front seats.

At his first request, didn't any of us move. . . . When the driver saw that I was still sitting there,

he asked if I was going to stand up. I told him, no, I wasn't. He said, "Well, if you don't stand up, I'm going to have you arrested." I told him to go on and have me arrested.

He got off the bus and came back shortly. A few minutes later, two policemen got on the bus, and they approached me and asked if the driver had asked me to stand up, and I said yes, and they wanted to know why I didn't. I told them I didn't think I should have to stand up. After I had paid my fare and occupied a seat, I didn't think I should have to give it up. They placed me under arrest then and had me to get in the police car, and I was taken to jail and booked on suspicion, I believe.

Rosa Parks

(1. the unequal treatment of blacks on public buses in Montgomery, Alabama. 2.(a) See solid-line underscore. (b) She felt that segregation was unjust. 3. (a) See broken-line underscore. (b) As a public servent, he probably felt it was his duty to uphold the laws of the city. 4. equality versus segregation)

During the years following World War II, the United States entered a period of rapid growth and spectacular change. Revolutionary developments in science and technology brought the nation to a position of unprecedented wealth and power.

No one in 1945 could have predicted the amazing developments that took place during the 1950's. Between 1945 and the early 1960's, an almost limitless variety of new products and services became available to a growing number of Americans. Young married couples could buy a new home for a down payment of only a few hundred dollars and have 30 years in which to pay the balance. Millions of cars rolled off the assembly lines. Labor-saving equipment for homes and farms poured out of the nation's factories in an unending stream. Medical science produced thousands of new medical products, including the priceless gift of anti-polio vaccine. Never before in history had so many people enjoyed so much prosperity.

There was, unhappily, a major flaw in the emerging economy of abundance. Millions of people shared only slightly, if at all, in the nation's new prosperity. In a land of abundance, poverty continued to haunt large numbers among the nation's minorities.

CONNECTING CHAPTER IDEAS

During the time from 1960 to the 1980's the United States moved through a turbulent period in domestic affairs. In the next chapter you will trace the development of domestic policies of six Presidents and learn how each responded to the growing needs of the American society.

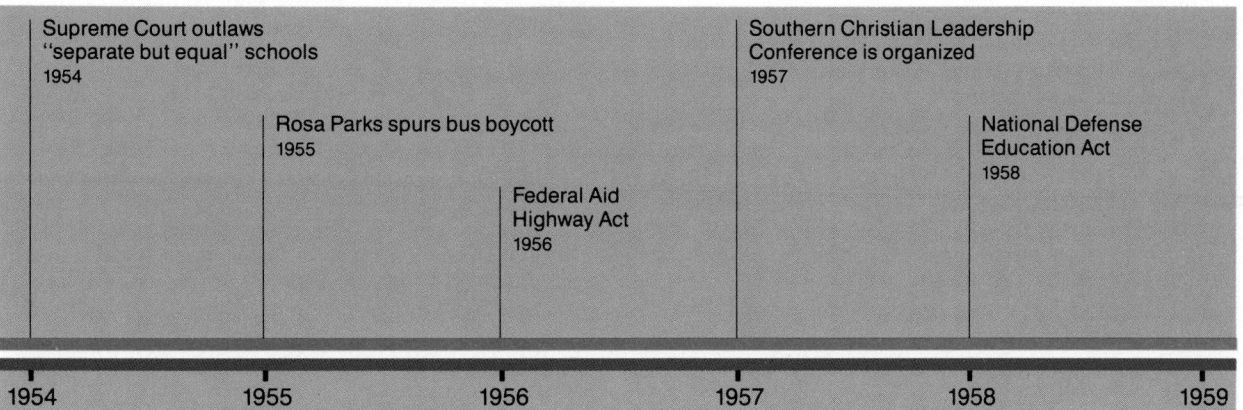

Supreme Court outlaws "separate but equal" schools
1954

Rosa Parks spurs bus boycott
1955

Federal Aid Highway Act
1956

Southern Christian Leadership Conference is organized
1957

National Defense Education Act
1958

| 1954 | 1955 | 1956 | 1957 | 1958 | 1959 |

CHAPTER
39 REVIEW

Reviewing Important Terms

Decide whether each of the following sentences is true or false. If the sentence is false, replace the underlined term with the word or phrase that will make it true.

1. After World War II the United States entered a period of unprecedented prosperity which was built on what economists called an economy of abundance.
2. The replacement of workers with machines is termed the knowledge explosion.
3. Under urban renewal programs, older sections of cities were torn down and replaced with new buildings and houses.
4. In the 1950's, the federal government reversed its policy toward American Indians and adopted a policy of reorganization.
5. After World War II, industry in the United States increasingly relied on automation to perform a whole series of manufacturing operations to enhance productivity.
6. The boycott of Montgomery's bus system organized by Dr. Martin Luther King., Jr., to protest segregation was successful.
7. The Supreme Court orders in the early 1950's for school segregation were met with violence in many communities.

Practicing Critical Thinking Skills

1. **Interpreting Ideas.** (a) Why were the young people of the 1950's called the "uncommitted generation"? (b) If the young people of the 1950's were called the "uncommitted generation," what might be a good term for the present generation? Explain your choice.
2. **Analyzing Ideas.** Why has it become more and more important since World War II for American citizens to be educated?
3. **Organizing Ideas.** What was the effect of the transformation of the United States from a rural to an industrial society on (a) workers, (b) black Americans, (c) Indians, and (d) young people?
4. **Evaluating Ideas.** Explain why *change* and *growth* are good words to use in describing American society after World War II.
5. **Interpreting Viewpoints.** Gather examples of pictures and drawings of American Indians from magazines, package labels, book jackets, sports team logos, and other sources. (a) Which of these images are positive? Why? (b) Negative? Why?

(c) Would American Indians agree with your assessment? Explain. (d) How might people's attitudes be affected by such images?
6. **Relating Past to Present.** (a) What are some of the problems of living in today's urban society? (b) What are some of the advantages? (c) How do these advantages and problems compare with the advantages and problems of urban living in the early 1900's? (d) What is the most serious problem for today's urban society to solve?

Developing History Study Skills

1. **Determining a Frame of Reference.** Use the information in this chapter to explain what value conflicts individuals faced in each of the following circumstances: (a) a scientist working on the Manhattan Project, (b) a businessperson deciding to automate a factory, (c) a black person attending the first integrated high school.

2. **Classifying Information.** Use the information in this chapter to classify technological, social, and economic changes that occurred in the United States during the decades of the 1950's and 1960's. Select a change from any category and write an essay describing the effect that change has had on society. Conclude your essay with a paragraph in which you evaluate the effects of the change on American society.

Relating Geography and History

Demographic trends made 1945 to 1960 a period of great change. Many communities in the United States were affected in the 1950's by the changes that shaped them into their present form. To recognize the trends that shaped your community, complete the following activities.

1. Visit your local or school library or historical society to research the growth and development of your community. (a) What was the population in 1950? (b) What is the current population? (c) What factors explain any population changes?
2. Obtain maps of your community from 1950 and today and answer the following questions. (a) What major highways have been built since 1950? (b) What businesses or industries have located in your community since 1950? Why did they locate in your community? (c) What other changes on the map did you notice? (d) Which of these changes can be traced to the events and trends discussed in this chapter? Explain.

UNIT TWELVE REVIEW

Discussing Ideas

1. Give evidence to support or refute this statement: After World War II, the United States' foreign policy goals were to maintain the military defenses of the non-Communist world and to strengthen its economic foundations.
2. (a) What was the cold war? (b) In what ways was it a domestic as well as a foreign war?
3. Compare the administrations of Truman and Eisenhower in terms of (a) goals, (b) domestic achievements, (c) foreign achievements, and (d) weaknesses.
4. Looking back, who might consider the 1950's the "good old days" or "happy days"? Who might not consider the 1950's to have been so good and happy? What might cause this difference in point of view?
5. Compare the situation of blacks, Hispanics, and Indians during the 1950's.
6. (a) What was the importance of the Supreme Court decision in *Brown v. Board of Education of Topeka?* (b) What other actions were taken in the 1950's to strengthen the civil rights of black Americans?
7. Study the time lines on pages 844, 862, and 881. Then complete the following activities. (a) Classify the entries on the three time lines according to the topic of each entry. (b) Are there any important events mentioned in this unit that are not included on the three time lines? If so, list each of the events.

Applying History Study Skills

Writing a Comparative Essay. Compile a list of questions about issues or events of the 1950's. You might want to include McCarthyism, the U-2 incident, *Sputnik,* or the elections of 1952 and 1956. Use the questions to interview two adults old enough to remember the 1950's. When you conduct each interview, ask not only what the person *remembered* about an event or issue, but also what the person *felt* and why or how the feelings arose. Sample questions might include:

● "How did you feel about that?"
● "Why did you think that way?"

When you have completed your interviews, write a comparative essay in which you discuss the similarities and differences of the points of view of the people you interviewed.

Making Connections

1. Interview your principal or a teacher in your school who taught in the school or elsewhere during the 1950's. Try to find out how school curriculum and procedures were affected by such world events as the launching of *Sputnik* and the McCarthy hearings.
2. Imagine that you were a newspaper reporter for TASS, the official Soviet news agency. Write an article on one confrontation between the United States and the Soviet Union or on the general topic of the cold war.
3. Watch a movie of the 1950's, such as *The Wild One* or *Rebel Without a Cause*. Write a short report discussing how the movie reflects the spirit of the 1950's.
4. Prepare a pictorial time line showing advances in transportation from 1900 to 1960. If possible, also include a short quotation showing how people reacted to each innovation.
5. Research one or more Indian tribes presently living in or originally from your region. Prepare a report on how the tribe has been affected by the policies of the federal government, such as relocation and termination.

Reading in Depth

Harrington, Michael, *The Other America: Poverty in the United States* (New York: Macmillan). The influential book that alerted an affluent United States to the plight of the poor.

Keenan, George, *Realities of American Foreign Policy* (New York: W. W. Norton). A noted diplomat explores the nature and goals of American foreign policy in the years after World War II.

Knebel, Fletcher, *Seven Days in May* (New York: Harper and Row). A suspense-filled novel of intrigue at the highest levels of government.

Michener, James, *The Bridges at Toko-ri* (New York: Random House). An exciting novel about the Korean War.

Miller, Merle, *Plain Speaking: An Oral Biography of Harry S Truman* (New York: Berkley). A candid look at Truman, the man and the President.

Schlesinger, Arthur M., *Dynamics of World Power* (New York: Chelsea House). An investigation of the United States' role in the postwar world.

See list of Multimedia Materials in TMRG, p.TM215.
See Making Connections, text p. 987.

UNIT THIRTEEN

Into a New Era

The United States has faced many international and domestic challenges since 1960. Attempts to contain communism have led to a long, controversial war in Vietnam. Events in Cuba and the Caribbean have threatened national security. Within the United States revelations of Presidential wrongdoing have shocked the nation. Unsettling confrontations have arisen as many groups continue efforts to secure equal rights. Unemployment and inflation continually have plagued the economy. The future remains bright, however, as Americans continue to work together to solve their problems. Just as scientists and citizens have developed alternative energy sources, such as the solar panels below, so each generation of Americans has willingly taken up the challenge of helping the United States retain its world leadership and maintain its democratic ideals.

See Chapter Overview in TMRG, p.TM216.
See Chapter Objectives in TMRG, p.TM216.
See Introducing the Chapter in TMRG, p.TM216.

CHAPTER 40

Domestic Developments
(1960 to the Present)

A successful
launch, 1963

"Things are in the saddle, and ride mankind." The words are those of Ralph Waldo Emerson, a keen observer of the human scene, who lived in Massachusetts more than a century ago. His observation could be accurately applied to the United States and the rest of the world during the years from 1960 through the 1980's.

During these years six different Presidents—John Kennedy, Lyndon Johnson, Richard Nixon, Gerald Ford, Jimmy Carter, and Ronald Reagan—occupied the White House. These Presidents watched over the fortunes of the United States during one of the most turbulent periods in the nation's history.

Johnson responded to the nation's cities, troubled by poverty and decay, and exploding in riots, with his Great Society. During Nixon's administration, the nation celebrated one of its proudest achievements when the first Americans landed on the moon. Each of the Presidents tinkered with the nation's economy. The American economy would prosper for a time only to be followed by a sharp slump. Each President also directed the nation's course in world affairs.

To what extent did these six Presidents lead the nation and shape the course of events? To what extent were they themselves shaped and driven by forces beyond their control? Did they make policies, or were the policies forced upon them by events over which they had little if any control? Such questions resist easy answers. Nevertheless, the questions themselves, even without answers, may help to illuminate the lives and the fates of the six Presidents who served the nation during these years.

═══ READING FOCUS ═══

As you read about this turbulent and rapidly changing period, look for the details that support each of the following statements.

1. Kennedy calls the nation to a "New Frontier."
2. Johnson urges Americans to build the "Great Society."
3. Nixon promises "to bring America together."
4. The Watergate scandals force Nixon to resign.
5. President Ford completes Nixon's second term.
6. Presidents Carter and Reagan face critical domestic problems.

1 Kennedy calls the nation to a "New Frontier"

See Teaching Suggestions in TMRG, pp.TM216-17.

The nation's unresolved problems at home and abroad were brought strongly to the attention of American voters in the Presidential campaign and election of 1960.

The election of 1960. Both parties nominated young, energetic candidates for the Presidency. The Republican nominee, Richard M. Nixon of California, had served in both houses of Congress. Since 1953 he had been Vice President under Eisenhower. The Democratic nominee, John F. Kennedy of Massachusetts, had also served in both houses of Congress.

During the election campaign, the Presidential candidates made use of television to bring their messages to the attention of the voters. Of particular significance was a series of television debates in which the two candidates faced each other. Key issues were the nation's defenses and the economy, which had been in a recession since 1958. Kennedy called for a "supreme national effort" to reverse what he called the downward trend of the nation's fortunes at home and abroad. He promised, if elected, "to get America moving again" by leading the nation to a <u>New Frontier</u>."

Nixon insisted that the United States was stronger in relation to the Communist world than it ever had been before. Nixon charged Kennedy with favoring "wild experimentation." Nixon promised, if elected, to build a more secure nation on the foundations of Eisenhower's policies.

Voters turned out in record numbers in the November election. Out of about 68 million votes cast, Kennedy squeezed through by a slim margin of 118,000 votes. In the electoral college, however, Kennedy won 303 electoral votes to Nixon's 219. Lyndon B. Johnson of Texas, who had been Democratic leader in the Senate since 1954, was elected Vice President.

At 43 Kennedy was the first Roman Catholic and the youngest man ever elected President. He was acutely aware of the problems he faced. Barely half of the voters had shown a willingness to follow the new administration toward a New Frontier. Moreover, conservative Democrats in Congress, mostly from the ▲

● Throughout the Annotated Teacher's Edition, terms listed in the "Identify" portion of a Section Review are underscored the first time they appear. See the Teacher's Manual for each section for a listing of important vocabulary terms.

887

South, had in the past voted with conservative Republicans to defeat measures similar to those Kennedy now wanted.

Economic problems. Once in office, Kennedy prepared to attack the related problems of unemployment and sluggish economic growth. The immediate problem was unemployment. In January 1961 more than 5 million Americans—nearly 8 percent of the total labor force—were unemployed. The unemployment rate among black Americans was double the rate for the nation as a whole.

The problem of unemployment had its roots in the nation's rapidly changing economic life. Some economists stressed that the American economy was not growing as rapidly as it should. Industries were not modernizing or building new factories as rapidly as many of them had done in the past.

Coupled with slow economic growth was the problem of underline{automation}, or the use of machines to do the work formerly done by men and women. Also, the increasingly complex American economy called for new skills on the part of workers. As a result, there were far fewer opportunities for the untrained and the poorly educated.

Encouraging employment and housing. In line with Kennedy's proposals, Congress took steps to increase spending power and retrain workers. Minimum wages were raised to $1.25 an hour, and 4 million more workers were included under wage-hour protection. The Area Redevelopment Act of 1961 authorized the federal government to make loans and grants to stimulate business and retrain workers in depressed areas. Congress also set aside $900 million for building public works in areas where more than 6 percent of the labor force was unemployed. In 1962, it passed the Manpower Development and Training Act providing for a three-year worker retraining program. Yet even with these and other measures, unemployment remained a major problem.

The Housing Act of 1961 tried to strengthen the nation's economic and social fabric. This act provided long-term loans at low interest rates to stimulate the construction of moderate-income housing. It included funds to provide hospitals and housing for the elderly. The largest authorization was for urban renewal, including the planning and improvement of mass transportation facilities. Congress also voted nearly $1.5 billion to aid in the construction of buildings for medical and dental schools and to assist colleges in building classrooms, libraries, and laboratories.

The Trade Expansion Act. In 1962 Congress took a major step to stimulate America's foreign trade. This step was prompted in part by the creation of the Common Market, a large trading area composed of six European nations. To improve trade among themselves, the Common Market nations gradually lowered the tariffs that had limited trade. By 1962 the Common Market nations were enjoying increasing prosperity. Recognizing that the Common Market could greatly affect the United States, Congress passed the Trade Expansion Act of 1962.

This act allowed the President, over a five-year period, to cut tariff rates 50 percent below the 1962 level or raise them 50 percent above the 1934 level. The President could also remove *all* tariffs on products for which the

═══ **SOURCES** ═══

JOHN F.
KENNEDY'S
INAUGURAL
ADDRESS
(1961)

We dare not forget today that we are the heirs of that first revolution. Let the word go forth from this time and place, to friend and foe alike, that the torch has been passed to a new generation of Americans— born in this century, tempered by war, disciplined by a hard and bitter peace, proud of our ancient heritage—and unwilling to witness or permit the slow undoing of those human rights to which this nation has always been committed, and to which we are committed today at home and around the world.

Let every nation know, whether it wishes us well or ill, that we shall pay any price, bear any burden, meet any hardship, support any friend, oppose any foe to assure the survival and the success of liberty. . . .

▲ Class activity: Read the excerpt from Kennedy's Inaugural Address aloud or play one of the many recordings of the speech. Then discuss why it was so moving (dynamic, eloquent), and who the "new generation" was (people born in this century).

United States and the Common Market countries together accounted for 80 percent of all world trade.

The act contained an "escape clause" that allowed the President to retain or reimpose tariffs to protect industries hurt by tariff reduction. Endangered industries and workers in them could also receive loans and other government aid.

Congress passed several measures designed to aid the nation's farmers. These acts at best had limited success. By the end of 1963, the nation's farmers continued to struggle with surplus products and declining incomes.

The space program.   In April 1961 the Soviet Union, which had launched the first satellite, made another advance into space. It sent the first astronaut, Yuri Gagarin, into orbit around the earth.

A month later Alan Shepard became the first American to make a rocket flight. Nevertheless Shepard did not orbit the earth as the Soviet had. Not until February 1962 was an American, Lieutenant Colonel John Glenn, launched into orbit.

President Kennedy, meanwhile, had become concerned that the United States might lose the race into space to the Soviets. He committed the United States to a program to make the United States first in space exploration. The United States, he declared, would land a man on the moon by 1970.

The space program also proved to be a source of new jobs for American workers. Soon some 9,000 firms were participating in the research and development of space-related products. By 1964 more than 30,000 scientists and specialists were working for the National Aeronautics and Space Administration (NASA), the agency in charge of the program. Estimates of the total number of Americans engaged in some phase of the space program ranged from 3 to 5 million. Moreover, by 1964 the program had created some 3,200 different products, many of which found their way into daily use.

The space program and the other parts of Kennedy's economic program seemed to be successful. By late 1961 the economy had begun to pull out of the recession. It then entered a time of growth that would last until 1970.

Changes in suffrage.   During the Kennedy administration, several major changes took place in voting rights. The Twenty-third Amendment to the Constitution, adopted in 1961 (see page 216), enabled residents of the District of Columbia to vote in Presidential elections. The Twenty-fourth Amendment, adopted in 1964 (see page 217), forbade the poll tax as a requirement for voting in federal elections. Poll taxes had been used in many areas to prevent poor blacks from voting.

Other citizens fought for fairer representation in national, state, and local legislatures. Election districts in many states had remained unchanged for many years. However, the population in these states had generally shifted from rural to urban and suburban areas. This meant that rural districts were often over-represented in the legislatures.

Between 1962 and 1964, the Supreme Court handed down several decisions relating to representation. The most far-reaching was the Court's "one person, one vote" ruling. According to this decision, election districts for state legislatures as well as for the House of Representatives must be as nearly equal in population as practicable. The Supreme Court thus set in motion a political revolution intended to make each citizen's vote have approximately equal value. This was meant to provide genuine representative government at both state and federal levels.

Unfinished business.   During his time in office, Kennedy took important steps to insure equal justice for blacks (see Chapter 42). In June 1963, for example, Kennedy sent a civil rights bill to Congress. Despite his support, the chances of the bill's passage were uncertain. Kennedy also had plans for mass transit, medical care, and aid-to-education programs. By late 1963 he had not been able to get any of these programs through Congress.

Kennedy was reluctant to put too much pressure on Congress to pass these bills. The next year, 1964, was an election year. Kennedy, who had won so narrowly in 1960, knew he would need broad political support if he wished to be reelected.

One area of the nation where Kennedy's political support seemed weakest was the South. To build up enthusiasm for himself and his programs, Kennedy planned a trip to Texas in November 1963.

At 12:30 in the afternoon on Friday, November 22, 1963, while riding in a motorcade through Dallas, Texas, President Kennedy was

▲   One important result of the space race was the introduction of communications satellites, which made possible instant telephone and television transmission from around the world.

killed by an assassin. Vice President Johnson, who also was in the motorcade, immediately drove under close guard to the Presidential plane. There, in the cabin of the plane at 2:38 P.M., Lyndon B. Johnson was sworn in as the thirty-sixth President of the United States.

The tragic weekend. Americans reacted to the tragic news with shocked disbelief, then with deeply felt anger and grief. For three days, while the body of John F. Kennedy lay in state in the Capitol, radio and television stations suspended regular programming. All but the most essential businesses closed their doors. Messages of sorrow and sympathy poured in from all over the world. The leaders of many nations flew to Washington to pay their respects to the late President.

In the meantime, within an hour and a half of the fatal shooting, the Dallas police had seized a suspect, Lee Harvey Oswald. Oswald was placed under heavy guard in a Dallas jail. Two days later, while being moved from one jail to another, he was shot and killed in full view of millions of Americans who were watching the event on television. His murderer, Jack Ruby, pushed through a group of police officers to shoot Oswald at close range.

Americans were deeply troubled by this new act of brutality. With Oswald gone, grave questions remained unanswered. Was Lee Harvey Oswald truly the assassin? If so, had he acted alone? Or was he part of a conspiracy to assassinate President Kennedy? Was Jack Ruby part of that conspiracy, and did he kill Oswald to keep him from talking?

The Warren Commission. To answer these questions and to put an end to wild rumors and speculation, President Johnson appointed a commission to investigate the case. The commission was headed by Earl Warren, Chief Justice of the Supreme Court.

In September 1964 the Warren Commission released its report. After carefully examining the available evidence and the testimony of 532 witnesses, the commission unanimously concluded that (1) Lee Harvey Oswald had assassinated President Kennedy, (2) he had acted alone, (3) Jack Ruby also had acted alone, and (4) there was no evidence of a conspiracy.

The report did not, however, end the questions and speculations. Critics continued to question the procedures used by the commission as well as its conclusions. In 1979, a committee of the House of Representatives conducted its own investigation of the assassination. It heard from witnesses whom the Warren Commission had not called. It found experts who used new methods to study tapes made at the time of the shooting. Using these methods the committee found evidence that more than one gun had been fired at Kennedy. However, the committee could not say who had fired the other gun or guns, or who else might have been involved in a conspiracy.

SECTION REVIEW

See underscored items, text pp. 887 - 90.

Identify: New Frontier, automation, Common Market, John Glenn, NASA, Lee Harvey Oswald, Warren Commission

For answers to questions, see Answer Key, p.A123.

1. **Summarizing Ideas:** What were the parties, candidates, issues, and results of the election of 1960?

2. **Organizing Ideas:** (a) What actions did the Kennedy administration take in the areas of unemployment, housing, and foreign trade? (b) How effective were these actions?

3. **Interpreting Ideas:** Why did Kennedy believe it was important for the United States to land an astronaut on the moon by 1970?

4. **Analyzing Ideas:** What was the significance for democratic government of the (a) Twenty-third Amendment, (b) Twenty-fourth Amendment, and (c) "one person, one vote" ruling?

2 Johnson urges Americans to build the "Great Society"

See Teaching Suggestions in TMRG, p.TM217.

Five days after the assassination of President Kennedy, Lyndon B. Johnson, in his first Presidential address to Congress, dedicated himself to the "ideas and the ideals" that John F. Kennedy had "so nobly represented." President Johnson gave top priority to three items—a civil rights law, a tax cut, and an "unconditional war on poverty." He declared, "All this and more can and must be done." Thus the new President invited Americans to build what he would later call the "Great Society."

Johnson had served long years in both the House and the Senate. He knew how the lawmakers thought and worked and how to get legislation through Congress.

An impressive record. Congress responded to President Johnson's leadership. Before adjourning in October 1964, Congress chalked up one of the most impressive legislative records in the nation's history. Most far-reaching was the Civil Rights Act of 1964 (see Chapter 42), but there were other important measures.

The Revenue Act of 1964 cut personal and corporate income taxes by $11.5 billion. By leaving more money in the hands of consumers and businesses, the new law greatly stimulated the economy.

The Economic Opportunity Act of 1964 marked an important attempt to "break the cycle of poverty." It created an Office of Economic Opportunity (OEO) and authorized $1 billion to begin the war against poverty. The new agency was to work with state and local governments to increase employment and expand training programs, especially for the nation's needy young people.

Congress also passed several other measures. For example, it authorized $375 million to help cities improve urban and commuter transit facilities. It also established a system to preserve federally owned wilderness areas. However, several measures strongly supported by President Johnson were still being considered when Congress adjourned to begin the 1964 election campaign.

The election of 1964. The Republicans nominated Barry M. Goldwater, a conservative Senator from Arizona, for the Presidency and Representative William E. Miller of New York as his running mate. The Democrats nominated Lyndon B. Johnson and his choice for Vice President, Senator Hubert H. Humphrey of Minnesota.

From the start of the race, both parties were divided. Goldwater was a firm conservative. He favored a sharply limited role for the federal government. Many moderate Republicans refused to support him. The Republicans also lost the support of most black voters. Goldwater was one of only six Republican Senators who had voted against the Civil Rights Act of 1964.

The Democrats, too, lost many loyal voters. Many white southern Democrats felt that President Johnson, a Texan, had betrayed them by leading the battle for the Civil Rights Act. They supported Goldwater because of his vote against the act and his support of states' rights.

In November nearly 70 million voters turned out. They elected President Johnson by an overwhelming electoral vote of 486 to 52. The popular vote was 42 million to 26 million. The Democrats also won substantial victories in state and local elections and in Congress.

Toward the "Great Society." Encouraged by his sweeping victory, President Johnson challenged Americans to join him in building the "Great Society." He argued that Americans, now more prosperous than ever, could help build a new world, not just a new nation. Americans had three major tasks: "To keep our economy growing. To open for all Americans the opportunities now enjoyed by most Americans. To improve the quality of life for all."

By the time Congress adjourned in the fall of 1965, it had adopted laws dealing with all of the President's major recommendations. In one of the most far-reaching laws, the legislators provided a comprehensive program of aid to education (see Chapter 43). Congress also established Medicare, a national program of health insurance for persons over 65. Medicare provided basic health coverage, with social security paying the larger part of the costs of hospital treatment or home nursing care, the patient paying the rest. Medicare also included

After July 1, 1965, millions of the nation's senior citizens became eligible for Medicare. This program helped them to pay for the ever-increasing cost of their hospital, doctor, and other medical bills.

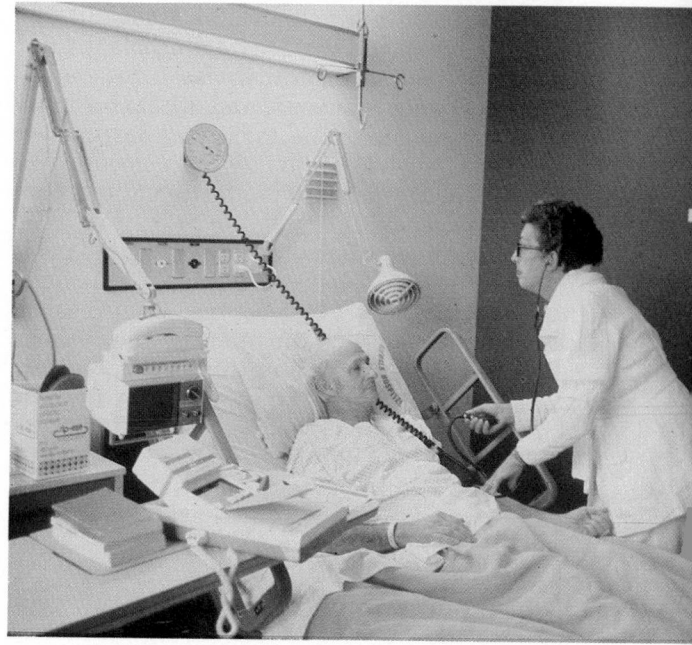

Shanks in The Buffalo Evening News

"Hope I know where we're goin'."

More than any President in modern history, Lyndon Johnson had control of Congress. To what does the cartoonist compare Johnson's persuasiveness? How is Congress portrayed?

▲ (A tidal wave • as being helplessly carried along with the LBJ program)

voluntary supplementary coverage, enabling individuals covered by social security to buy low-cost health insurance to cover doctors' bills and other health services. The Medicare bill also provided for federal grants to states that wished to start health care programs for the needy. Such care was known as Medicaid.

Responding to President Johnson's urging, Congress reduced federal excise taxes on automobiles, television sets, and other consumer items. The cut in excise taxes was designed to encourage Americans to buy more goods. This in turn would stimulate production and reduce unemployment.

In still other efforts to raise the standard of living of impoverished Americans, the legislators adopted several measures. Congress increased to $1.5 billion the funds for the Office of Economic Opportunity's anti-poverty program. Congress also voted $1 billion to help develop the depressed economy of the 11-state Appalachian region. In addition, Congress authorized $7.5 billion to improve the nation's housing. Much of this money was intended to help those who lived in low-income areas.

Loss of momentum. As it turned out, 1965 marked the peak of Johnson's program and

his popularity. Continued racial unrest in the nation damaged Democratic programs. Also, more people began to question increasing federal spending and government involvement in their daily lives. Most important, by 1966 the war in Vietnam, as you will read in Chapter 41, was absorbing more and more of the nation's resources and the administration's time and energy. As the war intensified, the President became the target of increasing criticism from Congress, from newspapers, and even from the pulpits of churches. Antiwar demonstrations disrupted the President's speeches at public ceremonies. Gradually, Johnson became more cut off from the American people. He was less able to get Congress to carry out his programs.

McCarthy's challenge. Eugene J. McCarthy, Democratic Senator from Minnesota, first revealed the extent of the dissatisfaction with Johnson. In November 1967 Senator McCarthy declared that he intended to campaign for the Presidency against Johnson. His purpose was to give voters a chance to show that they opposed the administration's Vietnam policy.

In the nation's first 1968 Presidential primary, held in New Hampshire in March, McCarthy made a surprisingly strong showing. In part his success was due to the thousands of young volunteers from all over the country who poured into the state to work for him. They campaigned hard for McCarthy because he inspired them with hopeful idealism.

Political developments. The New Hampshire primary triggered a series of political developments. A few days after the primary, Senator Robert F. Kennedy of New York announced that he, too, would seek the Democratic nomination for President. Senator Kennedy, a brother of the late President Kennedy, was an outspoken critic of President Johnson's Vietnam policy.

A second political development, one that stunned the nation, was President Johnson's declaration in March that he would not run for reelection. As Johnson later explained, he hoped that removing himself from the Presidential race would end the growing division among the American people over his conduct of the Vietnam War. Even some of Johnson's political enemies praised his decision.

President Johnson's withdrawal opened the door to the candidacy of Vice President Hubert

▲ Note: Answers to questions in captions appear in parentheses, as shown here. Bullets separate answers to individual questions when a caption contains more than one question.

Humphrey. He soon joined Senators McCarthy and Kennedy in the heated race for the Democratic nomination.

Two assassinations. Early in April 1968, the nation mourned the death of the great civil rights leader Martin Luther King, Jr. (see Chapter 42). In June the nation again grieved. this time for Senator Robert F. Kennedy, killed by an assassin's bullet just after he had won a close victory over Senator McCarthy in the California primary.

The assassinations of President John F. Kennedy, <u>Martin Luther King, Jr.</u>, and Robert F. Kennedy led many people at home and abroad to wonder if violence was an ingrained part of American society. What, people asked, was happening to the nation? There was no easy answer, but President Johnson did appoint a commission to study the question of violence. Also, Congress, over strong opposition, passed a gun-control law, although critics called the new law a "halfway measure."

The end of a dream. Back in 1963 President Johnson had dedicated himself to building a Great Society—free from poverty, discrimination, and injustice. During his first two years in office, he made substantial progress toward that goal. Then, as the Vietnam War began to absorb the administration's attention, domestic programs suffered. Thus, Lyndon Johnson's ▲ dream of a Great Society became marred by the war abroad and by continuing unrest and violence at home.

SECTION REVIEW
See underscored items, text pp. 890 - 93.

Identify: "Great Society," Barry Goldwater, Medicare, Medicaid, Eugene McCarthy, Robert Kennedy, Dr. Martin Luther King, Jr.
For answers to questions, see Answer Key, p.A123.

1. **Analyzing Ideas:** President Johnson believed that two goals of the United States were "to open for all Americans the opportunities now enjoyed by most Americans" and "to improve the quality of life for all." What legislation did he promote to achieve each of these goals?

2. **Organizing Ideas:** With reference to the election of 1964, discuss (a) the candidates and parties and (b) the results for the parties and the nation.

3. **Summarizing Ideas:** What did President Johnson hope to accomplish by refusing to run for reelection in 1968?

3
Nixon promises "to bring America together"

See Teaching Suggestions in TMRG, p.TM218.

It was a restless, disturbed nation that in August 1968 watched the Presidential nominating conventions on television.

Choosing candidates. The Republicans, meeting first, gathered at Miami Beach. Richard M. Nixon, who represented the middle ground as well as the "establishment" of the Republican Party, was nominated on the first ballot. He chose <u>Spiro T. Agnew</u>, Governor of Maryland, as his running mate.

The Democratic convention, held in Chicago, was one of the most tumultuous in history. To Americans watching on television, the convention hall was a disorderly arena. There McCarthy and Kennedy supporters contended against "establishment" Democrats represented by Hubert H. Humphrey.

The bitter fight in the convention hall was reflected in the city's streets. Thousands of young people had gathered in Chicago to demonstrate against the Vietnam War and for candidates favoring peace. Claiming that the demonstrations had gotten out of hand, the Chicago police moved in. The violent confrontations that followed, resulting in numerous injuries, were also witnessed by millions of television viewers.

In the convention hall, the "establishment" won. Humphrey was picked on the first ballot ● and chose Senator Edmund S. Muskie of Maine as his Vice-Presidential candidate.

The campaign of 1968. The three main issues of the campaign were violence and disorder, Vietnam, and racial strife. Public opinion polls showed that seven out of every ten Americans were convinced that "law and order had broken down in the country." Two out of every three felt that the war in Vietnam was being badly managed. The overwhelming majority of white citizens believed that the civil rights struggle was going "too fast." An equally large majority of black citizens were convinced that the movement was "not going fast enough."

During the campaign neither Nixon nor Humphrey aroused great enthusiasm among voters. The emergence of a third-party can-

● Reverend Channing E. Phillips of Washington, D.C., was also put on the ballot. He was the first black to be nominated for President at a national convention.

893

During the 1968 Democratic convention in Chicago, National Guardsmen were ordered to keep demonstrators away from the hotel where party leaders were meeting.

didate, George C. Wallace of Alabama, founder of the American Independent Party, further complicated matters.

George C. Wallace. From the beginning, third-party candidate Wallace hammered at the issue of law and order. Wallace also expressed opposition to existing welfare programs, forced busing of school children, and the federal enforcement of integration. He pledged, if elected, to repeal open housing legislation, to give the police greater power to deal with demonstrations and civil disorders, and to restore to the states and local communities control over welfare programs and the schools. As to Vietnam, he promised to end the war by negotiation, if possible, but to achieve a military victory if negotiations failed.

Richard M. Nixon. Nixon stressed the nation's need for new leadership. He declared that the Democrats had brought the United States close to disaster and that it was "time for a change." Like Wallace, he promised to restore law and order but added the word "justice" to his pledge.

Nixon insisted that the Democratic programs of massive federal spending to combat poverty had failed. He promised to review the entire welfare program and to turn over to private businesses the primary responsibility for retraining unemployed workers and rebuilding the cities.

Nixon also promised the nation that he would "bring an honorable end to the war" in Vietnam. He did not say how he would end the war, explaining that he did not wish to upset the delicate peace talks then going on in Paris.

Nixon was more specific, however, in his ideas about military policy and national defense. He favored a buildup of nuclear capability to insure that the United States held superiority over all potential enemies. His recommendations included the development of an anti-ballistic missile system (ABM).

Hubert H. Humphrey. During most of the campaign, Humphrey found himself in difficulty. His party was badly divided. Millions of people associated the violence in Chicago with the Democrats.

Humphrey was convinced that force, no matter how strongly applied, would not end the unrest and violence afflicting the nation. "We can only cut crime," he declared, "by getting at its causes: slums, unemployment, run-down schools and houses. This is where crime begins and that is where it must end." He cautioned that the attack against crime "must not jeopardize hard-won liberties of our citizens."

To meet the crippling problems of poverty and of urban decay, Humphrey called for "a Marshall Plan for the cities based upon self-help, local initiative, coordinated planning, and private capital."

Vietnam caused Humphrey the most trouble. At the start of his campaign, he lost much support by defending the unpopular administration policy. However, at the end of September he called for a halt to the bombing of North Vietnam, and his chances began to improve. They improved still further when, less than a week before the election, President Johnson announced that he had ordered a halt to all bombing north of the DMZ (Demilitarized Zone) that divided Vietnam, offering hope for an earlier end to the war.

The election results. The 1968 Presidential election was indeed a close one. Out of more than 71 million popular votes cast, Nixon's

▲ Point out that Hubert Humphrey had enjoyed a long and distinguishing career as a leader in his home state of Minnesota and in the Senate. However, as Johnson's Vice President he was at a disadvantage because he felt bound to support Johnson's unpopular war policies.

margin of victory over Humphrey was only 260,000 votes. The electoral vote of 302 for Nixon, 191 for Humphrey, and 45 for Wallace did not, however, reflect this closeness. The Democrats kept control of Congress.

Keenly aware of his narrow victory, President-elect Nixon pledged that his "great objective" would be to unite the country. Convinced that the "silent majority" of the American people stood midway between extreme conservatism and extreme liberalism, Nixon sought to hold to a "center" line.

To the moon. President Nixon was inaugurated on January 20, 1969. Just six months later, on July 20, 1969, American astronauts landed on the moon. The promise that President Kennedy had made back in 1961 to land a man on the moon before the end of the decade had been kept.

The costs were high. Three astronauts had died in a sudden flash fire. About $24 billion had been spent on the moon shot. Some critics argued that such money could have been better spent on solving problems at home.

Nevertheless, Americans stayed near television sets or radios for news when Neil Armstrong, Michael Collins, and Edwin E. Aldrin, Jr., lifted off in *Apollo 11* for the moon. Millions of Americans watched in fascination four days later when the lunar lander named *Eagle* settled down on the moon's surface. Many felt a great pride when Armstrong stepped out of the spacecraft and onto the moon saying, "That's one small step for a man, one giant leap for mankind."

Difficulties with Congress. The Nixon administration, handicapped by a Democratic majority in Congress, had more trouble implementing its policies. In an effort to commit the Supreme Court to his own view of a strict interpretation of the Constitution, the President filled the vacancy created by Earl Warren's retirement by appointing Warren E. Burger as Chief Justice. However, Nixon was unable to secure Senate approval for two other nominees to fill a Supreme Court vacancy. Finally, the Senate approved Nixon's choice of Harry Blackmun, a respected moderate judge.

Differences between the administration and Congress also led to other compromises and stalemates. The President insisted on cutting down federal spending, contending that such spending was excessive and that many pro-

President Nixon tried to get many programs passed into law, but the Democratic Congress often foiled his efforts. According to this cartoon, what were some of the programs?

(Welfare reform, revenue sharing, government reorganization, foreign aid)

grams were unwise and poorly administered. But critics in Congress insisted that cuts in spending for social welfare, education, and other domestic programs were not justified. They also objected to the administration's reluctance to make substantial cuts in the military budget.

Difficulties at home. Nixon had inherited the Vietnam War from President Johnson. He also inherited the anger of antiwar protesters. Huge demonstrations were held in Washington, New York, and other cities calling for an end to the war. Nixon had announced that he had a plan to end the war, but for many of the demonstrators he was not moving fast enough.

Then in May 1970, the nation learned that President Nixon had ordered the invasion of Cambodia. Antiwar activists were outraged by this action. A wave of new protests swept across the nation.

At Kent State University, the protest turned violent. The National Guard was called out. On May 4, trying to break up a gathering of students, the Guard opened fire. Four students were killed.

▲ Armstrong's voice crackled across 240,000 miles (384,000 kilometers) of space to be heard by millions of Americans.

The biographies of over 58,000 Americans share the same last line: Killed or missing in action in Southeast Asia, 1959–1975. The names of these Americans are carved onto the black granite walls of the Vietnam Veterans Memorial in Washington, D.C. For most Americans, this monument represents a long-overdue public recognition.

Almost from the beginning, the nation's commitment to the Vietnam war was not as intense as for previous wars. Public opinion of United States participation in Vietnam was sharply, often bitterly, divided. Many of those who fought in the conflict also came to question the reasons for United States involvement.

In earlier conflicts, war veterans were welcomed home with joyous celebrations. Vietnam veterans, however, returned to an indifference that at times bordered on hostility. Many veterans learned to keep silent about their experiences in a war the nation wanted to forget.

Although some veterans had trouble readjusting after the stress of combat, many others found the return to civilian life smooth going. They raised families and held jobs. A fair number ran for elective offices. As time passed, many veterans began to insist on public acknowledgment of their efforts for the nation. The dedication of the monument was a step forward in that battle for recognition.

The nation was shocked and sobered. Nixon's campaign promise to "bring America together" now seemed to ring hollow. The war in Vietnam still appeared to be tearing America apart.

Inflation and the energy crisis. Among the other serious problems facing President Nixon when he took office was **inflation**. The rising rate of inflation was partly a result of vast spending for the Vietnam War. It was also a result of basic problems in the American economy and society, and partly a result of international events. Nixon's attempts to handle inflation met with mixed success.

The skyrocketing cost of oil was a major contributor to inflation in the United States and throughout the world. The major oil-exporting nations had in 1960 formed the Organization of Petroleum Exporting Countries (OPEC). OPEC wanted to get higher prices for its oil from importing countries. Then, in the fall of 1973, the Arab oil-producing nations sharply increased the price of oil and, in the midst of a new Arab-Israeli war, cut off all shipments to the United States and other industrial nations that had been supporting Israel. A few months later, the Arabs lifted their embargo, but OPEC kept oil prices high.

High oil prices and the embargo caused critical problems for Western Europe and Japan, which depended almost entirely on Arab oil. The United States, which depended upon Arab oil for only about 6 percent of its total requirements, also faced a serious situation.

For several years there had been a growing scarcity of energy in the United States. The 6-percent cutoff of oil coupled with soaring prices brought a serious **energy crisis** during the winter of 1973–74. The cost of gasoline, heating oil, and electricity rose drastically. In some parts of the country, shortages caused real hardships. As a result, Nixon announced a program to make the United States independent

▲ Discussion topic: How the "energy crisis" changed the living habits of many Americans. (conservation, 55 miles-per-hour speed limit, car pools, compact cars, lowered thermostats, more insulation, etc.)

of all foreign countries for its energy requirements by the early 1980's.

Other important developments. In March 1971 Congress adopted the Twenty-sixth Amendment (page 218), lowering the voting age to 18 in both federal and state elections. The Census Bureau estimated that 25 million additional young people were now eligible to vote in the next Presidential election.

Before the end of President Nixon's first term, he signed a $30.2 billion bill for **revenue sharing.** This act gave federal revenue to states and local communities for public programs. Nixon regarded this "new federalism" as an essential part of his program for decentralizing the power of the national government.

SECTION REVIEW

See underscored items, text pp. 893 - 97.

Identify: Spiro Agnew, George Wallace, Neil Armstrong, Warren Burger, inflation, energy crisis, Twenty-sixth Amendment, revenue sharing

For answers to questions, see Answer Key, pp.A123-24.

1. **Organizing Ideas: (a)** What were the basic issues of the 1968 Presidential election? **(b)** What position did each candidate take on these issues?

2. **Analyzing Ideas:** How did President Nixon respond to the energy crisis of the early 1970's?

3. **Summarizing Ideas: (a)** What was the "new federalism"? **(b)** What actions did Nixon take to promote the "new federalism"?

4. **Studying Graphics:** Examine the political cartoon on page 895. Then write a short paragraph explaining its meaning.

4 The Watergate scandals force Nixon to resign

See Teaching Suggestions in TMRG, pp.TM218-19.

Nixon's second term in office began with the triumph of a sweeping reelection victory. It ended less than two years later with a disgraced administration and with the President's resignation from office.

The election of 1972. At their 1972 convention, the Republicans again nominated Richard M. Nixon and Spiro T. Agnew. The Democrats nominated Senator George M. McGovern of South Dakota, a liberal, as their Presidential candidate. Governor George C. Wallace of Alabama, an early contender for the Democratic nomination, had been wounded by a would-be assassin and did not take an active part in the 1972 campaign.

The Democratic convention included among its delegates an unusually large number of black Americans, young people, other minorities, and women. Older party regulars believed that the newcomers were moving the Democrats too far to the left, beyond the majority views of the nation. They bitterly opposed McGovern's nomination.

From the start McGovern was in trouble. He chose Senator Thomas Eagleton of Missouri as his running mate. Then it was revealed that Eagleton had at one time been hospitalized for emotional illness. McGovern first announced his continued support of Eagleton. Then he changed his mind and asked Eagleton to step down. The Democratic National Committee then chose Sargent Shriver, former head of the Peace Corps, to replace Eagleton.

The incident called McGovern's judgment into question and cost him votes. In addition, many traditional Democratic voters opposed him, and others were lukewarm toward his candidacy. Nevertheless, McGovern campaigned tirelessly. He hit hard at inflation, corruption, what he called the Nixon administration's "indifference" to civil rights, and above all against United States participation in the Vietnam War.

Nixon was confident of victory. He could count on most of the 12 million to 15 million votes that might have gone to Governor Wallace if he had run. Moreover, Nixon's achievements in foreign affairs were widely praised by Democrats and Republicans alike. He had sharply reduced America's military role in South Vietnam and had improved relations with both Communist China and the Soviet Union. President Nixon also encouraged his supporters to spend heavily on whatever steps they thought were necessary to insure his reelection.

Nixon won one of the greatest victories in American history, winning about 47 million votes to McGovern's 29 million. The electoral vote was 521 to 17. Nixon's victory was largely personal, and Republicans failed to make significant gains in the House and Senate, which were controlled by the Democrats.

897

Nixon's social policies. President Nixon saw his landslide victory as a mandate, or command by the voters, to carry out his foreign policies and his domestic policies. These domestic policies called for a reduced role for the federal government.

Nixon believed that the expansion of federally funded social programs had worsened the conditions they were supposed to correct. He opposed large federal spending for job training for the handicapped, special education for the disadvantaged, and the use of school buses to speed up racial integration. He called for a halt to federal support for low-cost housing and urban renewal on grounds that neither had succeeded. He criticized publicly financed day care support for children of working mothers. He urged tighter controls over expenditures for Medicare and Medicaid, declaring his preference for private health insurance plans.

In January 1973 Nixon called for cutbacks or terminations in more than 100 federal programs in the next budget. To get his program through, he relied partly upon his Republican followers in Congress but also upon continuing support from conservative Democrats, chiefly from southern states.

Executive power. Although Nixon in general favored a reduced role for the federal government, his powers as President had grown. Ever since the 1930's, foreign and domestic problems had encouraged, if not required, increased executive power. During this time Congress had allowed a growth in power under both Democratic and Republican Presidents.

However, in Nixon's second term, critics began to worry about his use of executive power. At times Nixon seemed to believe that he as President was, or should be, above criticism or restraint. He had turned over much of the authority of Cabinet officers, where appointment required Senate approval, to his personally appointed White House staff. Nixon also held back vital information from Congress and the public. Members of the administration, especially Vice President Agnew, attacked newspaper and television reporting as irresponsible and unfair. These events and others fed a growing uneasiness that Nixon's use of the Presidency threatened the constitutional balance of powers.

The Watergate affair. The threat to the balance of powers became clearer as a series of scandals emerged during Nixon's second term. The disastrous Watergate affair, as the scandals were called, began in June 1972 with an attempted burglary of the Democratic National Committee offices in Washington's Watergate Apartments complex. Five men were caught in the building. At first they gave false names, but they were soon correctly identified. The trail then led to the organization for which they had been working, the Committee to Re-elect the President.

The White House tried to dismiss the episode as a "third-rate burglary," but news reporters refused to believe this. As the months passed, news reports began to unravel a tangled web of criminal activities that appeared to reach into the highest offices in the land. As a result, by 1973 both the legislative and the judicial branches of government had become actively involved in the Watergate investigations. A special Senate committee, chaired by Senator Sam Ervin of North Carolina, held televised hearings during the spring and summer of 1973. The Attorney General appointed a Special Prosecutor, who organized a staff and began to sift the evidence. A grand jury sitting in a federal district court headed by <u>Judge John Sirica</u> began to gather evidence and prepare indictments.

The resignation of Agnew. Meanwhile, the Justice Department had been investigating the financial affairs of Vice President Agnew. By the fall of 1973, government investigators were prepared to indict Agnew for crimes, including bribery and extortion, committed while he was Governor of Maryland and Vice President of the United States.

For a time Agnew angrily proclaimed his innocence of the alleged wrongdoings. However, in the late fall he decided to throw himself on the mercy of the court and plea-bargain for a light sentence.

Agnew's part of the bargain included his immediate resignation as Vice President and a *nolo contendere* ("no contest") plea to a single count of tax evasion ($29,500 of undeclared income in 1967). In return, the Court agreed not to sentence Agnew to jail for the tax evasion and not to prosecute him for other criminal activities he allegedly committed.

The extremely lenient sentence—a $10,000 fine and unsupervised probation for three years—was widely criticized. Nevertheless, Attorney General Elliot Richardson defended it on grounds that a long trial "would have been likely to inflict upon the nation serious and permanent scars."

In accordance with the Twenty-fifth Amendment to the Constitution, President Nixon nominated a new Vice President. He chose Gerald Ford, the Republican leader of the House of Representatives. The Senate confirmed the nomination.

Mounting evidence. Meanwhile, the Watergate investigations continued. The grand jury charged that members of the administration, if not the President himself, had approved the Watergate burglary and had then attempted to cover up the administration's part in the affair. The grand jury also charged that members of the administration, if not the President himself, had approved of the illegal entry into the offices of a psychiatrist. This break-in was undertaken in an effort to secure damaging personal evidence against one of the psychiatrist's patients, Daniel Ellsberg. Ellsberg had earlier released classified material relating to the government's plans and actions during the Vietnam War.

Investigators also uncovered evidence of the illegal use by the administration of wiretapping and bugging. There was also a plan to set up a secret White House group known as the "plumbers" authorized to break federal laws in the name of "national security." Investigators also claimed that the White House had tried to involve the CIA and the FBI in some of its illegal activities. They further claimed that during the 1972 election campaign huge sums of money had been collected from corporations with the understanding that the administration would do special favors for such contributors. As the months passed, additional evidence of wrongdoing steadily accumulated. Numerous officials of the White House staff were indicted. Some pleaded guilty and went to jail. Others went to trial; most of them were convicted and sentenced.

The White House tapes. From the beginning President Nixon protested that he was innocent of any wrongdoing. However, White House lawyer John W. Dean, who had already confessed to his own participation in the scandals, challenged him. Although the growing volume of evidence seemed to support Dean, it was his word against the word of the President. The issue remained unresolved.

In July 1973, however, the Senate committee investigating Watergate suddenly learned that for the past two years Nixon had been secretly taping everything said in his offices and over most of his White House telephones. This evidence could prove or disprove the President's claim of innocence of the charge of obstructing justice.

The Senate Watergate Committee and the Special Prosecutor immediately issued subpoenas. They requested President Nixon to turn over those tapes that contained discussions relating to the Watergate affair and the alleged cover-up. Nixon refused to surrender them on grounds of **executive privilege** and "national security."

The courts then ruled that the President had to release those portions of the relevant tapes that did not relate to national security. After considerable delay Nixon released some, but not all, of the tapes. A growing conviction that he was withholding damaging evidence became even more widespread when it was discovered that important parts of certain tapes had been erased. Finally, in August 1974, the Supreme Court ordered Nixon to release the requested tapes.

The Supreme Court ruling was the final blow to the President's efforts to conceal his part in the illegal White House activities during his administration. The tapes Nixon reluctantly turned over to the Special Prosecutor revealed that his repeated claims of innocence had been false. From the beginning he had been involved in efforts to cover up the Watergate affair.

Nixon's resignation. The revelation of Nixon's betrayal of the public's trust came as the House of Representatives was preparing to vote on the issue of Presidential impeachment. After a three-month investigation, the House Judiciary Committee had approved three Articles of Impeachment.

The three articles that the Judiciary Committee sent to the House charged the President with violating his oath of office by (1) obstruction of justice, (2) abuse of power, and (3) willful disobedience of subpoenas issued by the House of Representatives.

Faced with probable impeachment by the House and conviction by the Senate, President Nixon chose to resign. He submitted his resignation on August 8, 1974. He denied any guilt, however, and admitted only to having made

Two years after Nixon had accepted renomination, he announced his resignation from the Presidency. Standing by Nixon in this photograph are his daughter and son-in-law.

some "mistakes" and to having lost his "power base" in Congress.

Nixon was the first President in the nation's history to resign from office. His departure brought an end to a grave constitutional crisis that had threatened to weaken, if not destroy, the democratic process. At issue had been the preservation of the system of checks and balances, the principle of the separation of powers, and the rule of law itself.

SECTION REVIEW

See underscored items, text pp. 897 - 99.

Identify: George McGovern, Senate Watergate Committee, Judge John Sirica, Gerald Ford, Articles of Impeachment

For answers to questions, see Answer Key, p.A124.

1. **Interpreting Ideas: (a)** Why did Nixon win the 1972 election by a landslide? **(b)** Why was it called a "personal" victory?

2. **Summarizing Ideas: (a)** What was the "Watergate affair"? **(b)** What role did Congress have in investigating the affair? **(c)** What part did news reporters play? **(d)** What role did the courts have?

3. **Determining Cause and Effect: (a)** What were the events that led to President Nixon's resignation? **(b)** Why did some people think that Nixon's administration posed a threat to the principle of the separation of powers?

---

5 | President Ford completes Nixon's second term

See Teaching Suggestions in TMRG, p.TM219.

On August 9 the Vice President, Gerald Ford, was sworn in as the 38th President of the United States. Following the procedure set forth in the Twenty-fifth Amendment, he nominated Governor Nelson A. Rockefeller of New York for Vice President and Congress confirmed the nomination. Thus, for the first time since the Constitution was adopted, both the President and the Vice President held their high offices by appointment, rather than through election by the voters.

Gerald Ford. Gerald Ford was a man gifted with the common touch. Before Nixon appointed him to the Vice Presidency he had represented his home state of Michigan in Congress for a quarter of a century. As leader of the Republicans in the House, Ford had won the respect of his colleagues in both political parties. He was liked for his honesty and unassuming manner. "I am a Ford, not a Lincoln," he declared upon becoming Vice President. When he was sworn in as the nation's Chief Executive, he won respect for his candid assessment of his position. "I am acutely aware," he said, "that you have not elected me as your President by your ballots."

The Nixon pardon. A month after he took office, Ford lost much of the early confidence he had won. At that time he granted Nixon an unconditional pardon for all the federal crimes he "committed or may have committed or taken part in" while serving as President. Nixon accepted the pardon, which legally was an admission of guilt.

Ford's critics charged that by granting the pardon he had prevented the American people from ever learning the full truth about the Nixon administration. The critics pointed to the double standard of justice that gave Nixon a full pardon while his fellow conspirators were punished for following their leader's wishes. Some of the critics questioned whether the pardon had not been agreed upon in advance in exchange for Nixon's resignation.

President Ford insisted that these charges were not true. He defended the pardon on the

▲ Discussion topic: What Ford meant by saying, "I am a Ford, not a Lincoln".
(Reference is to average car--Ford--versus high-priced car--Lincoln. He was telling Americans that he was one of them, an average person, and not above them.)

ground that a public trial would have only prolonged the bitterness and the division produced by Watergate. He had acted, he said, because he wanted to heal the nation's wounds.

Ford's amnesty program. A week after he broke the news of the Nixon pardon, Ford dropped another bombshell with the announcement of an **amnesty** for the Vietnam draft evaders and military deserters. This, too, became a highly controversial issue and further lessened the President's initial popularity.

During the Vietnam War, thousands of young men had crossed the border into Canada or had gone to European countries to escape the draft. A smaller but still substantial number already in the armed services had deserted and fled the country. Both groups felt that the war was morally wrong and that for this reason they could not, in conscience, support it.

Ford declared that he could not condone the draft evasion and desertion. However, he added, it is time to "heal the scars of divisiveness." He then offered a conditional pardon. Those who wanted it would have to reaffirm their allegiance to the United States and agree to spend up to two years of alternative service working for the public. This service might be in hospitals, rehabilitation centers, conservation efforts, or similar activities.

Only a handful of the more than 200,000 resisters and deserters accepted the President's offer. They compared the conditional pardon they were offered with the full pardon granted Nixon. In their view, President Ford measured mercy and justice by a double standard.

Presidential leadership. In spite of his long and close ties with Congress, Ford found himself in repeated conflicts with it during the two years of his administration. In the Congressional elections of 1974, held only three months after Ford became President, the Democrats in both houses were able to greatly increase their already large majorities. Ford, a moderate conservative Republican, could not accept many Democratic proposals for social welfare programs.

Since Republicans in Congress could not defeat the bills, Ford used his Presidential veto to kill them. During his term in office, he vetoed more bills than any President had ever ▲ vetoed in such a short time. In most cases, Congress was unable to pass the bills over Ford's veto.

President Gerald Ford announced his WIN program—Whip Inflation Now. Ford's program urged Americans to counteract rising costs by voluntarily curbing wage and price demands.

Economic problems. President Ford's frequent use of the veto was the result in part of his attempt to combat the problem of inflation. He had inherited this problem from Nixon, just as Nixon had inherited it from the years of the Vietnam War.

Ford, like Nixon, was convinced that excessive government spending was a major cause of the worst inflation the country had experienced since 1947. In 1973 inflation was driving up the cost of living at an annual rate of 9 percent. During 1974 the rate soared above 12 percent. People living on fixed incomes, principally the nation's elderly, were hardest hit.

Ford attempted to reduce federal spending and slow down the economy, but these efforts led to a sharp business slump. To add to the confusion, Ford and Congress disagreed over the best way to handle the still soaring cost of oil and gasoline and the threatening shortage of energy.

The election of 1976. With the election of 1976 approaching, Ford announced that he intended to run for the office that he had been occupying by appointment. His critics, including members of his own party, faulted him for lack

▲ Ford used the veto more than 50 times in two and one-half years.

901

of vigorous leadership. His supporters, although not all were enthusiastic about his candidacy, pointed out that he had helped to restore confidence in the Presidency.

Ford won a narrow victory at the nominating convention over Ronald Reagan of California, who represented the conservative wing of the Republican Party. The convention balanced the ticket with the choice of a Reagan conservative, Robert Dole of Kansas, as the Vice-Presidential candidate.

The Democratic convention again had a large representation of young delegates, women, blacks, and liberals. It chose Jimmy Carter of Georgia on the first ballot with Senator Walter F. Mondale of Minnesota as his running mate.

Carter had been almost unknown on the national stage when he first began to run for the nomination. His spectacular campaign in the state primaries attracted wide attention and led to his nomination.

Carter had attended Annapolis. After a successful career as a naval officer, he had returned to his home state of Georgia. There he had built up the family peanut business and later served as governor of the state.

The key issues in the election campaign were inflation and unemployment. Carter and Ford met in televised debates, the first since the Kennedy-Nixon debates of 1960. Neither candidate, however, aroused much enthusiasm. Political pollsters said the election was "too close to call."

▲ Jimmy Carter won, but by the narrowest of margins—297 electoral votes to Ford's 241. The Democrats once again swept the Congressional contests.

SECTION REVIEW
See underscored items, text pp. 900 - 02.

Identify: Nelson Rockefeller, amnesty, Jimmy Carter
For answers to questions, see Answer Key, p.A124.

1. **Analyzing Ideas: (a)** Why did President Ford pardon Richard Nixon? **(b)** Why did some people criticize the pardon?

2. **Evaluating Ideas: (a)** How did President Ford attempt to fight inflation? **(b)** What were the results?

3. **Summarizing Ideas: (a)** Describe the events that led up to the nominations of Gerald Ford and Jimmy Carter for President in 1976. **(b)** Why was the general election too close to call?

See Teaching Suggestions in TMRG, pp.TM219-20.

On January 20, 1977, Jimmy Carter was sworn in as the 39th President of the United States. Following the inaugural ceremony, he and his wife, Rosalynn, walked down Pennsylvania Avenue to the White House.

During the campaign Carter had promised, if elected, to stay in touch with the people. The walk—rather than the usual ride in a limousine surrounded by Secret Service men—was a symbol of his intention to keep the promise.

Beginning "an open administration." The next day, as one of his first Presidential acts, Carter granted an unconditional pardon to the draft evaders of the Vietnam War. The pardon, which President Ford had refused to grant, did not include deserters, whose cases were to be treated individually.

In his first report to the nation, President Carter pledged, among other things, that government regulations would be written in "plain English." He said he would hold "town hall meetings" to keep in touch with the people. He also planned "call-in" sessions on the radio and TV networks to answer questions. He held the first of these "call-in" sessions early in March, and for two hours took phone calls directly from the people. A few days later, he made a trip to New England where he attended an old-fashioned New England town meeting and answered questions directed to him from the audience.

Before long, however, President Carter discovered that his executive duties left him little time for direct communication with even a sampling of ordinary citizens. Problems both at home and abroad confined him closer and closer to the White House. Within a few months, critics were complaining that he was too heavily preoccupied with foreign affairs. They claimed that he was neglecting the increasingly serious domestic problems, particularly unemployment, inflation, and energy.

Combating unemployment. Through the fall and winter of 1976–77, the nation seemed to be slowly but steadily recovering from the recession of 1972–75. Unemployment remained high, however, especially among blacks and Hispanics in the cities. For the country as a whole it averaged about 7 percent. This meant that approximately 7 million men and women were out of work.

Shortly after Carter took office, he sent Congress a plan designed to stimulate the economy and provide jobs. The plan called for a $50 rebate on 1976 taxes for every American citizen. It also called for tax cuts to encourage business to increase capital investments, which in turn would open new employment opportunities. Congress adopted the plan but, with Carter's approval, eliminated the rebates.

The efforts to reduce unemployment met only limited success. In the fall of 1978, almost two years after Carter became President, more than 6 million Americans remained jobless. Congress tried again to remedy the situation with a tax cut. The bill called for $18.7 billion of tax relief, mainly for upper-middle-class and wealthy Americans. Senator Edward M. Kennedy, speaking for large numbers of critics, urged the President to veto the bill. He claimed that it "unfairly ignored the needs of the average taxpayer for tax relief." Despite the widespread protests, Carter signed the bill.

At the same time, Congress adopted and the President approved the Humphrey-Hawkins "full employment" bill. The bill set as a national goal the reducing of unemployment to 4 percent by 1983. It also set as a goal the reducing of inflation to 3 percent by 1983 and to zero by 1988. The law did not say how the President and Congress would achieve these goals. It did, however, state that any programs used to combat inflation must not be permitted to interfere with efforts to reduce unemployment.

Other economic issues. During 1977 and 1978, while the Carter administration was struggling to combat unemployment, the cost of living rose sharply. By the fall of 1978, it was growing at the rate of 10 percent a year. Carter then tried to fight inflation with a voluntary system of wage and price controls.

The President's anti-inflation program was received with mixed reactions. Business, in general, favored it. Organized labor protested that it was unfair. Why, labor asked, had the President failed to include guidelines for interest rates, dividends, and profits?

President Carter also tried to raise the shrunken value of the dollar in the interna-

Following his inauguration in January 1977, President Jimmy Carter broke tradition and walked back to the White House from the Capitol Building, a surprise to the cheering crowds.

tional markets. At the same time, he attempted to reduce the nation's unfavorable balance of trade. This imbalance was especially marked in regard to Japan. The Japanese were successfully competing in the American market with automobiles, electronic equipment, agricultural and industrial machinery, and other products. The value of Japanese imports into the United States now far outweighed American sales to Japan.

Finally, in a further effort to control inflation, the President proposed to reduce federal spending. His "lean budget" reduced expenditures for social services while increasing military spending by 3 percent. It was severely criticized by farmers, minorities, and liberals in general.

The anti-inflationary measures also had an undesirable side effect. They increased unemployment. By the summer of 1980, America was moving deeper and deeper into a recession. With the Presidential elections approaching in the fall, this was worrisome news indeed for Jimmy Carter.

Discussion topic: Compare actions of Nixon, Ford, and Carter to help the economy. (Nixon: revenue sharing, programs cut, higher interest rates, wage/price freeze. Ford: federal spending cuts, vetoed social programs. Carter: federal spending cuts, voluntary wage/price controls, tax relief, change balance of trade.)

903

The energy problem. The energy problem remained the most urgent of all the long-term domestic problems facing the nation. Energy costs also contributed greatly to the soaring rate of inflation.

Four months after he took office, Carter sent his energy program to Congress. It emphasized the need for underlined conservation. Speaking over the television networks, the President warned of a possible "national catastrophe" unless Congress and the people as a whole united behind the conservation effort.

Carter's program was called a "carrot-and-stick" approach. It mixed incentives to conserve energy with penalties to discourage wasteful practices. It proposed to increase the cost of domestically produced oil and gas by gradually deregulating prices of these fuels. The plan called for Presidential authority to impose additional taxes on gasoline to discourage its use. It stressed the development of other sources of energy, especially coal, nuclear power, and solar energy.

Not until the fall of 1978 did Congress pass an energy bill. The bill was a much watered-down version of Carter's original proposal. It provided some new taxes and tax credits and did begin to deregulate fuel prices. Congress also set aside $54 billion for highway improvement and the development of mass transit systems.

In the meantime Congress had created the Department of Energy (DOE). The DOE was given the major responsibility for improving older energy systems and developing alternative energy sources.

An energy crisis. Events overseas contributed to energy problems in the United States. A revolution in Iran (see page 932), stopped oil shipments from that country. This disturbed the flow of oil to nations around the world.

Americans felt the impact by the spring of 1979. Gas shipments to filling stations were reduced or cut off. Many stations cut back their business hours or closed altogether. Lines of cars waiting for gas soon jammed city streets. Waits of an hour or more were common. Several states adopted systems to restrict the days on which gas could be bought. To add to the crisis, oil exporting nations soon raised their oil prices, which sent the cost of gas and oil products soaring.

By the summer of 1979, Americans had cut back somewhat on their use of gas. The gas shortage eased, but the danger of another crisis

Signs of the worsening energy situation in the late 1970's were the seemingly endless lines of cars stretching from gas stations along jammed city streets in some parts of the nation. People often waited an hour or more to get gas.

Each year thousands of people visit Presidential libraries throughout the United States. Some visitors are scholars who have made appointments to study the documentary and other research collections. Others are tourists and interested viewers of the general public.

Franklin D. Roosevelt was the first President to plan his library while still in office. The arrangements FDR made provided the basis for the Presidential Libraries Act of 1955. Since the act's passage, six other Presidential libraries have been constructed, dedicated, and opened to the public.

The Truman Library (1957) is located at Independence, Missouri. Among other memorabilia, it includes a mural of important events that took place during Truman's Presidency. It also contains a replica of the Oval Office of the White House.

The Lyndon Baines Johnson Library (1971), together with the LBJ School of Public Affairs is located on the campus of the University of Texas at Austin. The Eisenhower Center (1972) in Abilene, Kansas, consists of a museum and a library.

The Herbert H. Hoover Library (1972), was erected in Hoover's birthplace of West Branch, Iowa. The John Fitzgerald Kennedy Library (1979) is in Boston, while the Gerald R. Ford Library (1981) is in Ann Arbor on the campus of the University of Michigan.

Pictured to the left are an exterior view (top) and two displays (center, bottom) from the John Fitzgerald Kennedy Library.

still existed. In July, Carter set forth another energy plan, calling for a massive program to develop synthetic fuels. The long-range goal of the plan was to cut importation of oil in half.

Obstacles to Carter's success. By the summer of 1980, a public opinion poll revealed that only 21 percent of the American people approved of President Carter's performance in office. This was the lowest figure for a President since the 1930's, when the poll was first taken. It was even lower than the figure for President Nixon at the height of the Watergate affair. Why was Carter's rating so low?

Part of the answer lay in Carter's inexperience. When running for office he had stressed his independence from Washington's political establishment. This helped him in the campaign but hurt him in office. He often had trouble enlisting support for his programs, even among members of his own party.

Part of the problem was the programs themselves. They were hard to define. He proclaimed his first energy program as "the moral equivalent of war" but failed to press Congress to pass the bill. He seemed changeable, almost fickle at times. In 1979 he changed five of his Cabinet members, among them the Secretary of HEW, whom he had just praised for doing an excellent job.

Part of the trouble lay in the nature of the problems Carter faced. Energy, inflation, un-

Ronald Reagan and George Bush proved to be a formidable team for the Republican Party. They won the 1980 election by a wide margin, foiling the bid by Democrats Jimmy Carter and Walter Mondale for reelection.

employment, foreign affairs—they were all complicated. They had no easy solutions, and at times it seemed that Carter offered no solutions at all.

Choosing candidates. The campaign for the Presidential nominations in 1980 was a long one. Critics, in fact, began to ask whether the United States needed a system as lengthy, costly, and complex to nominate candidates.

Ronald Reagan was again a leading contender for the Republican nomination. He held off challenges from a variety of opponents and easily won the nomination at Detroit. He picked George Bush, one of those former opponents, as his running mate.

Jimmy Carter wanted to run for reelection. Usually a President in office has little trouble in securing his party's nomination. By early 1980, however, Carter's popularity was low. Many Democrats feared that if Carter ran again it would mean defeat for the Democratic nomination. As the incumbent, Carter had the edge and in the end won renomination from his party. Walter Mondale again was the candidate for Vice President.

Many people were unhappy with the choice between Carter and Reagan. Representative John Anderson of Illinois recognized this dissatisfaction. Originally, he had tried for the Republican nomination but had lost to Reagan. Now he decided to run as an independent candidate who would appeal to such people.

The election of 1980. The election campaign of 1980 was hard fought. Reagan warned of the nation's military weakness. He also stressed Carter's failure to solve the nation's economic problems. He reminded voters of the ever-rising rates of inflation and unemployment and spoke of the current recession as the "Carter depression." If elected, Reagan promised, he would cut spending in government, cut taxes, and stimulate business.

Carter tried to remind people of his foreign policy achievements. For the first time since Herbert Hoover was President, he claimed, no American soldier had died in battle. He spoke of improved relations with China and the Egyptian-Israeli peace treaty. Carter pointed out the number of times in the past when Reagan had favored military intervention.

Carter reminded voters that in a nuclear age a President had to show restraint.

Once again political pollsters said the election was too close to call. Thus, for many, the morning after election day was a surprise. Reagan had won a sweeping victory with 42,797,153 popular votes compared with Carter's 34,434,100. The electoral vote was 489 to ▲ 49. Anderson received no electoral votes.

Analyzing the results. More surprising than the size of Reagan's victory was the outcome in Congressional races. The Republicans won control of the Senate for the first time since 1952. The Democrats kept control of the House, but Republicans made gains there as well.

Many people asked if the Republican victory represented a new movement in politics. Were Americans becoming more conservative? Were they tired of massive federal programs that raised their taxes and complicated their lives as Reagan charged? Or had they simply rejected Carter for failing to handle the large problems adequately?

The Republicans take control. President Reagan entered office with widespread support. His warm, winning, relaxed nature and his reputation for managing personal differences added to the "honeymoon" initially enjoyed by new administrations.

Reagan's popularity, high from the beginning, soared to new heights when, 70 days after he became President, he survived an assassination attempt. His courage and grace when he was shot, seriously wounded, and hospitalized won him the sympathy, good will, and respect of the American people.

Reagan's economic program. Reagan outlined his economic program during the election campaign. Once in office, he began immediately to try to win support for it and move it through Congress.

The first priority was victory over inflation. In order to win this victory, the government would have to balance the budget—that is, to reduce expenditures to match the amount of money available from taxes.

At the same time, however, Reagan proposed to reduce taxes. He called for 25 percent tax cuts for all Americans over three years. Reagan argued that such cuts would stimulate the economy. People would have more money

Nancy Reagan has served as an invaluable assistant and adviser to her husband, the President of the United States. As First Lady Mrs. Reagan has performed a substantive, as well as ceremonial, role in the Reagan administration.

to save, and this money would be available to invest in business. If people did not save, they would have more money to spend, leading to increase production and more jobs. These polices were examples of <u>supply-side economics</u> and quickly became known as "Reagonomics."

The Reagan program aroused a storm of controversy. Many critics charged that the proposed tax cuts favored the wealthy and corporations. They also claimed that spending cuts would damage programs that aided the needy, protected the environment, and supported public education. Critics also insisted that tax cuts could not be combined with huge military spending. They warned that such a policy would only increase inflation.

"Reaganomics" in action. Reagan launched a strong effort to ensure adoption of his program. He worked closely with members of the Congress. He also spoke directly to the American people, asking them to write their Senators and Representatives in support of his policies.

Reagan's efforts were successful. Congress approved the tax cuts. It also made heavy cuts

● Refer the students to page 1011. Ask the students to explain why the passage of Reagan's far-reaching tax-cut bill was a significant victory.

In the early 1980's many Americans found themselves among the ranks of the unemployed. State and local employment agencies were faced with increased numbers of persons seeking jobs and unemployment compensation.

in domestic spending. At the same time it increased the military budget. But would the program work? All through 1981 and 1982 the economy declined. Inflation did come down; in two years it dropped from 18 percent to about 4.5 percent. But unemployment grew. In December 1982 the jobless rate hit 10.8 percent, the highest since 1941. Industrial output dropped. Businesses failed at the highest rate since 1932. One economist said, "The economy is probably in the worst shape it has been in for nearly half a century."

December 1982 marked the low point. After that the jobless rate began a slow but steady decline. Industrial output surged. The inflation rate remained low. Increasing numbers of Americans began to buy new houses and cars.

One dark spot remained, though, and was growing larger. The balanced budget that Reagan had promised never appeared. Instead the federal **deficit**, the amount by which expenses exceed income, was greater than ever. Many Americans felt that such huge deficits were a threat to the future of full economic recovery (see Chapter 43).

Reagan and energy. The energy crisis had reached its peak by the time Reagan took office. Conservation measures had cut the amount of oil that the nation used. The economic recession also helped ease the energy crisis because the demand for energy dropped sharply with so much industry idle.

Reagan believed that private investment could handle the nation's energy needs. He wanted to disband the Department of Energy, calling it an example of too much government. He gave little support to government efforts to develop synthetic fuels.

Reagan also favored opening federal lands for energy exploration. His Secretary of the Interior James Watt leased huge areas of the sea floor to private companies so that they could search for oil and gas. He also leased parts of national forests and other federal lands to coal companies. Often the granting of these leases was bitterly opposed by environmental groups.

The election of 1984. Despite the often harsh attacks on his domestic and foreign policies

Refer the students to the chart, Political Party Identification, on page 1007. Ask the students to what groups the Republican party appealed in order to win the Presidency in 1980 and 1984. Ask them to cite data from the chart to substantiate their answers.

(see Chapter 41), Reagan's personal popularity remained high. Early in 1984, Reagan announced that he would seek a second term with George Bush again as his Vice-Presidential running mate.

In the campaign, Reagan took credit for leading the economic recovery. He also stated that the spirit and outlook of the American people had recovered as well. "America is back," he announced, and this slogan became the theme of his campaign.

Several candidates waged a spirited battle for the Democratic nomination. Former Vice President Walter Mondale, the early favorite, had to hold off challenges by Senator Gary Hart of Colorado and the Reverend Jesse Jackson before his nomination was assured in the primaries.

Mondale's announcement of his choice for a Vice-Presidential running mate caused a burst of excitement when he picked Representative Geraldine Ferraro of New York. Ferraro was the first woman to be a major party candidate for such high office.

Mondale and Ferraro started far behind Reagan and Bush in the polls. To close the gap, Mondale attacked "Reaganomics." Reagan's tax cuts, he charged, favored the rich, while his budget cuts hurt the poor. Mondale also claimed that economic disaster lay ahead unless the huge deficits were reduced. To cut the deficit, Mondale wanted tax increases, but increases that were fairly spread out among rich and poor. He claimed that Reagan had "secret plans" to raise taxes and cut Social Security if he were reelected. In foreign affairs, Mondale charged that Reagan had refused to negotiate with the Soviets on arms limitation, thus increasing the chances for an arms race and nuclear war.

Reagan denied all of Mondale's charges. He said that Mondale stood for the failed policies of the past that had brought on the nation's economic ills. Reagan promised no tax increases and no cuts in Social Security and promised to cut the deficit. In foreign affairs, Reagan said that his firm stands with the Soviet Union and his decisive actions as in Grenada (see Chapter 41) had restored the world's respect for the United States.

As the race heated up, Reagan remained far ahead in the polls. Less than a month before the election, one poll showed him leading comfortably in 48 states. Election results mirrored the poll's data. Reagan swept all the elec-

Analysis of Voting Patterns • 1984

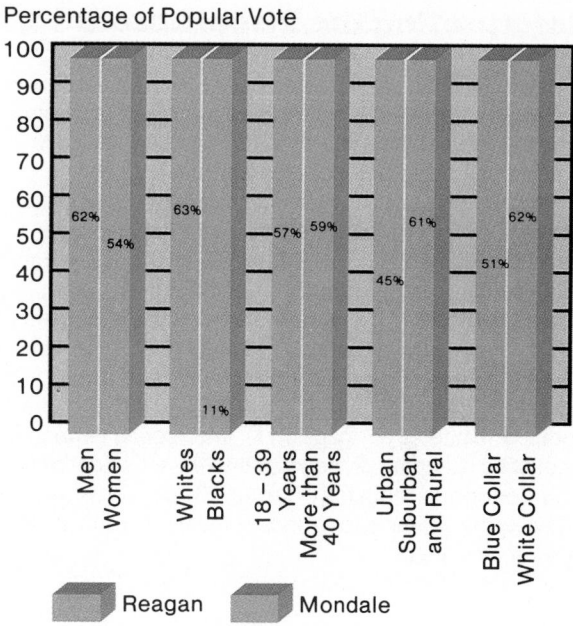

Percentage of Popular Vote

Source: A compilation from media exit-poll interviews

toral votes except those of Minnesota and the District of Columbia, 525 to 13. Reagan received 53,428,357 popular votes compared to 36,930,923 for Mondale.

SECTION REVIEW

See underscored items, text pp. 904, 907 - 09.

Identify: energy conservation, Department of Energy, supply-side economics, deficit, Geraldine Ferraro

For answers to questions, see Answer Key, p.A125.

1. **Organizing Ideas:** What programs did President Carter support to **(a)** fight unemployment and **(b)** reduce inflation? **(c)** How effective were his efforts in each area?

2. **Summarizing Ideas:** What factors contributed to President Carter's unpopularity as President?

3. **Comparing Ideas:** How did the energy policies of Presidents Carter and Reagan differ?

4. **Analyzing Ideas:** Describe the issues and the results of the Presidential election of 1984.

Interpreting the Visual Record   Generalizing from the Visual Record

The student of history is often called on to research and report on a specific topic. An assignment of this nature usually requires the interpretation of large amounts of data. Much of the information will be presented on tables, charts, and graphs. To effectively use this data, you must be able to form generalizations and draw conclusions from the information on the tables, charts, or graphs. Generalizing and drawing a conclusion are the processes of deriving a general statement from information.

You have already been introduced to the preliminary steps in generalizing from the visual record: reading charts (Chapter 8, pages 182–83), reading economic graphs (Chapter 31, page 711), interpreting economic statistics (Chapter 22, pages 528–29), and understanding economic reports (Chapter 23, pages 546–47). Review the skills in each of these presentations to refresh your memory.

How to Form Generalizations

To form generalizations from data, follow these guidelines.

1. **Collect data.** Research the topic and gather information in forms useful for analysis.
2. **Identify relationships among the data.** Note the features that are common to the data. Determine all cause-effect relationships among the data. To spot generalizations as you read, look for one of the following clue words or phrases.
   - many
   - most
   - often
   - as a rule
   - generally
   - usually
3. **Form the generalization.** Make a general statement from the information. Keep in mind that your generalization must account for all the facts. Also, the generalization must not go beyond the facts at hand.
4. **Refine the generalization.** As you gather more information on the topic, refine your generalization. In some cases you may reject your first generalization in light of the new information. Then repeat the above steps.

Apply the Skill

Study the chart at the bottom of this column, which covers the period from 1950 to 1980 and which gives statistics on conditions of the poor. A comparison of the poverty rate in 1950 with the poverty rate in 1960 show a decrease of 8 percent. Comparison of the poverty rates in 1950, 1960, and 1970 illustrates a continued decrease in percentages. This trend, however, does not continue to 1980. The poverty rate in 1980 is 13 percent, the same as it was in 1970. From these statistics you can state the following generalization: some conditions for the poor improved between 1950 and 1970. Note that other general conclusions can be drawn from these statistics.

Now study the next row on the chart. It gives statistics on infant mortality rates. Note that the rates are given as a percentage of the live births. Mortality rates for the white

Condition of the Poor • 1950–1980

	1950	1960	1970	1980
Poverty Rate (Percentage)	30	22	13	13
Infant Mortality as a percentage of live births				
White	2.7	2.3	1.8	1.1
Black	4.4	4.4	3.3	2.2
Difference	1.7	2.1	1.5	1.1
Life Expectancy in years				
White	69.1	70.6	71.7	74.4
Nonwhite	60.8	63.9	65.3	69.5
Difference	8.3	6.7	6.4	4.9
Median Family Income (in 1980 dollars)	$10,500	$14,000	$19,200	$21,000

Source: *The New York Review*

population and the black population are presented. The difference between the mortality rate for black infants and white infants is also shown. Note that for both whites and blacks the infant mortality rate has declined. A stated generalization from these figures might be: infant health care has improved since 1950. Again, other generalizations can be stated about the infant mortality rate.

The third row of the chart provides information about life expectancy. Note that statistics are given for both the white and the nonwhite populations. The difference in life expectancy for these two populations is also given. Study the figures. One generalization that can be derived from this data is that people are living longer now than they did in 1950. Once again note several other general statements can be made about the data.

Now study the final row of the chart: median family income. First you must define the term "median family income." The median family income is that income which falls in the middle of the total range of all family incomes. Or in other words, half of the family incomes are above the median and half are below it. Note that these statistics are given in 1980 dollars. The figures show that the median family income has risen between 1950 and 1980. The following is a generalization about the median family income: income has increased since 1980.

Practicing the Skill

Study the chart on the Presidential elections from 1960 to 1984 on this page. Then on a separate sheet of paper, answer these questions.

1. **(a)** Who won the election of 1960? **(b)** What general statement can you make about the popular vote in the 1960 election?

2. **(a)** Who won the election of 1964? **(b)** What generalization can you make about the popular vote in this election? **(c)** What conclusion can you draw about the candidates and the issues in the 1964 election from the statistics given on the chart?

3. **(a)** Compare the popular and electoral vote received by Richard M. Nixon in 1968 and 1972. **(b)** What conclusions can you draw from these statistics?

4. **(a)** Compare Ronald Reagan's vote totals in the elections of 1980 and 1984. **(b)** State a generalization from the statistics on those two elections.

5. What generalization can you make about the independent or third-party candidates listed in the footnotes at the bottom of the chart?

Presidential Elections • 1960–1980

Year	Republican Candidate	Popular Vote	Electoral Vote	Democratic Candidate	Popular Vote	Electoral Vote
1960[1]	Richard M. Nixon	34,108,546	219	John F. Kennedy	34,227,096	303
1964	Barry M. Goldwater	27,176,799	52	Lyndon B. Johnson	43,126,506	486
1968[2]	Richard M. Nixon	31,785,480	301	Hubert H. Humphrey	31,275,166	191
1972[3]	Richard M. Nixon	47,165,234	520	George S. McGovern	29,170,774	17
1976[4]	Gerald R. Ford	39,148,940	240	Jimmy Carter	40,828,929	297
1980[5]	Ronald Reagan	43,899,248	489	Jimmy Carter	35,481,435	49
1984	Ronald Reagan	52,609,797	525	Walter Mondale	36,450,613	13

1 – Sen. Henry F. Byrd (D) received 15 electoral votes.
2 – George C. Wallace received 46 electoral votes.
3 – John Hospers and Theodora Nathan each received an electoral vote.
4 – Ronald Reagan received one electoral vote.
5 – John B. Anderson received 5,719,437 popular votes but no electoral votes.

Source: *World Almanac, 1985*

40 SUMMARY

John F. Kennedy's prediction in 1960 that the United States was entering one of the most critical periods in its history proved all too true. From the 1960's to the 1980's, the American people moved through an often bewildering variety of problems. The nation's economy boomed in the early 1960's, but faltered throughout the 1970's. By the early 1980's the economy was in its worst shape since the Depression.

In these hectic years, six Presidents held office. The assassination of one and the resignation of another shocked Americans and provided tests of how well our system of government works.

The Presidents you have read about in this chapter also faced serious difficulties abroad. Warm relations with old allies cooled and old enemies became new friends. New nations in Asia and Africa began to play an increasingly important part in world affairs. The United States' foreign policies, of which you will read in Chapter 41, influenced and interacted with its domestic policies. Indeed, at times it was difficult to untangle the two.

CONNECTING CHAPTER IDEAS

Despite the complex problems the United States faced on the domestic scene from 1960 through the 1980's, Americans found out that the responsibilities of world leadership could prove to be a heavy burden for the nation. In the next chapter you will read how the United States became involved in international conflicts and responded to global problems.

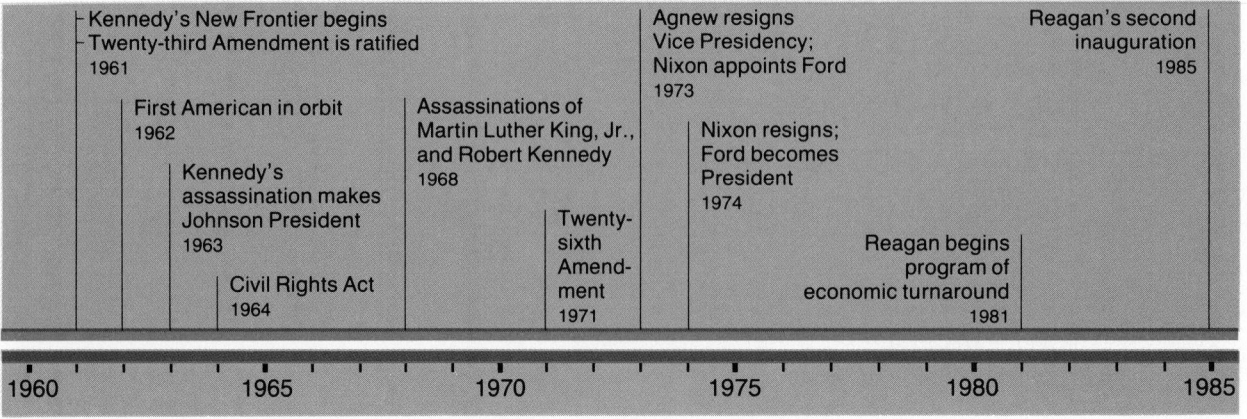

Kennedy's New Frontier begins Twenty-third Amendment is ratified 1961		Agnew resigns Vice Presidency; Nixon appoints Ford 1973		Reagan's second inauguration 1985
First American in orbit 1962	Assassinations of Martin Luther King, Jr., and Robert Kennedy 1968	Nixon resigns; Ford becomes President 1974		
Kennedy's assassination makes Johnson President 1963	Twenty- sixth Amend- ment 1971	Reagan begins program of economic turnaround 1981		
Civil Rights Act 1964				

| 1960 | 1965 | 1970 | 1975 | 1980 | 1985 |

CHAPTER
40 REVIEW

Reviewing Important Terms

In the sentences below, the underlined terms are incorrect. On a separate sheet of paper, rewrite each sentence using the correct term.

1. President Nixon authorized a program of taxation that gave federal revenues to states and local communities for public programs.
2. The cutoff of oil coupled with rising prices in the early 1970's was called inflation.
3. Supply-side economics is the amount by which government expenses exceed government income.
4. Two domestic problems that President Nixon faced in this first administration were the energy crisis and deflation.
5. President Gerald Ford granted Richard Nixon an unconditional amnesty.
6. Early in his first administration, President Reagan proposed that Congress pass legislation implementing a program based on revenue sharing.

Practicing Critical Thinking Skills

1. **Organizing Ideas.** Make a list of the major legislation passed during the administrations of Presidents Kennedy, Johnson, Nixon, Ford, Carter, and Reagan. (a) Which Presidents were most successful in getting legislation passed? Why? (b) Which Presidents were generally considered effective? How do their reputations compare with their legislative records?
2. **Interpreting Ideas.** It has been said that the United States has become more democratic in recent years. Do you agree or disagree? Give specific examples to support your answer.
3. **Summarizing Ideas.** List the key issues in the Presidential elections since 1960. (a) In which campaigns were the issues similar? (b) Why do you think these issues kept reappearing?
4. **Expressing Viewpoints.** Should Congress or the President have the leading role in shaping government policies? Why? (Use examples from the Presidential administrations described in this chapter to support your opinion.)
5. **Analyzing Ideas.** In recent years television has become an important force in American politics. How does television affect elections during the campaigns and on election day?
6. **Relating Past to Present.** (a) Compare President Reagan's program for fighting inflation with President Carter's program. (b) Carter was unsuccessful in his attempt to deal with the problem. Do you agree? Explain. (c) Based on the information in your textbook and your knowledge of current events, has President Reagan's program been successful? Explain.

Developing History Study Skills

Generalizing from the Visual Record.   Refer to the bar graph on text page 909 to answer the following questions.

(a) About what percentage of men cast their ballots for Ronald Reagan? for Walter Mondale? (b) About what percentage of black voters cast their ballots for Reagan? for Mondale? (c) Which Presidential candidate received the greater percentage of votes among urban voters? among suburban and rural voters? (d) Which Presidential candidate had the greater support among white-collar workers? (e) In which category of voters was support for the candidates divided almost equally? (f) Which group shown on the chart voted most consistently for one candidate? What evidence supports your answer? (g) Using data from the bar graph, write a brief paragraph that profiles the typical Reagan voter. (h) Suppose you were the Democratic Presidential candidate in the 1988 election. Write a paragraph that briefly outlines a campaign strategy designed to help you increase your support. Include the groups that you would target in your campaign.

Relating Geography and History

Geography specialists who study population patterns are called demographers. The United States census provides demographers with a wealth of information. One use demographers have for the information is the prediction of population trends. Plot the sets of data below on maps or construct two pie graphs. Then, using the plotted information, draw at least three conclusions or predictions about population trends in the decade 1980–1990.

Region of the United States	Percent Change	
	1960–1970	1970–1980
Northeast	9.8	0.2
North Central	9.6	4.0
South	14.3	20.0
West	24.2	23.9

Source: Statistical Abstract, 1984

See Chapter Overview in TMRG, p.TM221.
See Chapter Objectives in TMRG, p.TM221.
See Introducing the Chapter in TMRG, p.TM221.

CHAPTER 41

A New Role in World Affairs

(1960 to the Present)

The signing of
SALT II

From the 1960's through the 1980's, Americans faced a complex, and sometimes troubling, domestic scene. First President Kennedy and later Presidents Johnson, Nixon, Ford, Carter, and Reagan all tried to cope with domestic problems. Often however, a number of events overseas held the attention of each President.

After World War II, the United States had taken on the responsibilities of world leadership. Americans were now learning that such responsibility could be a heavy burden and could have serious effects on their lives at home. Worldwide problems—pollution of the environment, nuclear disarmament, feeding of the rapidly growing population—demanded attention. Trying to solve such problems required international cooperation, a sense of national purpose, and large sums of money. The American people were called on to supply each of these as solutions were sought.

The nation's growing involvement in Vietnam proved enormously costly. It also deeply troubled many Americans and has continued to haunt the nation.

In one sense, Vietnam was part of a larger issue confronting Americans: Had the United States assumed more responsibilities around the world than it could possibly meet, even with all its wealth and power? This issue has continued to trouble Americans whenever an opportunity has arisen for the United States to enter the arena of world politics. The issue arose with the Cuban missile crisis. It stirred angry emotions during the entire Vietnam conflict. It has colored United States actions in the Middle East and in Central America.

══ READING FOCUS ══

As you read about the foreign problems and global relationships of the last several decades, look for the details that support each of the following statements.

1. The United States assumes global responsibilities.
2. The United States becomes deeply involved in Vietnam.
3. World tensions are relaxed during the Nixon and Ford administrations.
4. President Carter's foreign policy produces mixed results.
5. World tensions increase during President Reagan's administration.

1 The United States assumes global responsibilities

See Teaching Suggestions in TMRG, p.TM222.

During the 1960's and 1970's, the dangers of nuclear war and Communist aggression continued to haunt Americans.

A changing world. One major development in world affairs was the growing competition American business faced from Japan, the Soviet Union, and the Common Market countries of Western Europe. Another revolutionary development was the entry of a large number of newly independent nations into the world community. By 1986 UN membership had grown to more than 159 nations. Most of these new nations had emerged from former colonies in the nonindustrial areas of Asia and Africa.

Shifting relationships. A third major development was the changing balance of world power. The newly independent nations of Asia and Africa, together with developing countries in Latin America, refused to align themselves with either the Soviet Union or the United States, forming a group called the **Third World.**

The solid front of communism had broken up by the late 1960's when the split between Communist China and the Soviet Union was complete. In 1966 France pulled out of the NATO alliance, showing that the solid front among anti-Communist nations was also becoming strained.

By the 1960's all of the powerful nations—both Communist and non-Communist—were competing for the resources and the markets as well as the political support of the Third World nations. Thus many of the world crises facing the United States grew out of the problems of Africa, Latin America, and Asia.

Kennedy's foreign policy. In this rapidly changing world, President Kennedy and, later, President Johnson generally followed the basic foreign policy developed under Truman and Eisenhower. However, there were new steps in foreign policy during the early 1960's. The Trade Expansion Act of 1962 was passed to increase world trade as well as to meet the growing competition of the Common Market countries. Kennedy and Johnson also sponsored programs to strengthen international cultural relations by sending outstanding American musicians, theater groups, writers, and artists to visit friendly, neutral, and Communist countries.

The Peace Corps. The most imaginative new program was the Peace Corps. This was a government-supported organization of Americans who volunteered to live among the people of underdeveloped lands and to help them with day-to-day problems. In September 1961 the first American volunteers arrived in the African nation of Ghana to serve as teachers.

From the beginning the Peace Corps was a notable success. By 1970, Americans, mostly young men and women, were serving overseas in 59 different countries. The Peace Corps symbolized America's desire to provide humane assistance as well as economic and military leadership in the non-Communist world.

Trouble in Africa. President Kennedy had to deal with the problems of America's relations with the emerging African nations. The most serious crisis developed in the Congo (now the Republic of Zaïre).

The Congo, a former Belgian colony, became independent in June 1960. Many rival groups—among them pro-Communist and pro-Western groups—battled for control of the government. The problem grew worse when the mineral-rich Katanga province seceded from the newly formed nation.

In response to an appeal by the Congo government, the UN sent troops from African and Asian nations to police the troubled country.

The UN force prevented a full-scale civil war, but it was not at first able to end the bloodshed. A new crisis developed in 1961 when Patrice Lumumba, leader of the pro-Communist faction, was assassinated. Soviet Premier Khrushchev demanded withdrawal of all UN troops and threatened to intervene. President Kennedy warned that the United States would defend the UN operation.

With firm American backing, the UN continued its difficult peacemaking operation in the Congo. By 1965 the fighting ended and Katanga province rejoined the nation. By the late 1960's, most scars of the civil war seemed healed. The Congo (Zaïre) became one of the most prosperous African nations.

Cuba and the Bay of Pigs. President Kennedy faced a very serious problem in Cuba. Early in 1959, guerrilla forces led by Fidel Castro overthrew the government of Cuban dictator Fulgencio Batista (bah·TEES·tah). At first the United States welcomed Castro's rise to power. However, American sympathy rapidly faded when Castro began to act like a ruthless dictator. He put to death hundreds of political enemies, jailed thousands, and took control of foreign-owned property. In addition, he lashed out against "Yankees" and accepted a Soviet offer of military aid if the United States interfered in Cuba.

By the summer of 1960, the United States had placed an embargo on the purchase of Cuban sugar. It had also urged the Organization of American States (O.A.S.) to condemn Cuba's actions.

Kennedy had inherited a plan developed under Eisenhower to overthrow the Castro government. During 1960 a force of anti-Castro Cubans had been trained in Central America with the active support of the United States Central Intelligence Agency (CIA). The plan called for this force to invade Cuba. According to the plan, the Cuban underground would rise, join the invaders, and overthrow the Castro government. President Kennedy decided to allow the plan to be carried out. ▲

On April 17, 1961, the invasion force landed on the beaches of the Bahía de Cochinos, or the Bay of Pigs. The invasion was a total failure. The Cuban underground never joined the battle. Most of the invading "Freedom Fighters" were killed or captured. In reply to a storm of criticism, President Kennedy admitted that the invasion attempt had been a mistake and assumed full responsibility for it.

The Alliance for Progress. To deal with the Communist presence in Cuba, Kennedy proposed a program called the Alliance for Progress. The United States and 19 Latin American countries (all but Cuba) had joined the Alliance by 1961.

The Alliance members agreed to a 10-year program to improve social and economic conditions in Latin America. Finances for the program were to come from private and government sources in Latin America and the United States plus Japan, Western Europe, and international agencies such as the World Bank.

During the first four years, the United States contributed $4.5 billion to the program,

▲ More than 1,400 anticommunist Cubans comprised the invasion force. President Kennedy allowed them to carry out their plan on the condition that no United States troops be involved.

MISSILE SHELTER TENT

MISSILE ERECTOR

CABLE

TRACKED PRIME MOVERS

OXIDIZER TANK TRAILERS

FUEL TANK TRAILERS

Photographs like this, taken on October 23, 1962, by an American U-2 spy plane, supplied President Kennedy with evidence of a Soviet-constructed missile launch base in Cuba. Such evidence triggered the Cuban missile crisis.

the Latin American countries $22 billion. Some progress was made, but the results were disappointing. Much of the money was used to help business interests and military forces in Latin America rather than the masses of poor people. Congress, increasingly impatient, began to reduce the budgets for the Alliance.

The missile crisis. Meanwhile, relations with Cuba worsened. The United States cut off all trade with Cuba. The O.A.S. did not go that far, but it did vote Cuba out of the organization in 1962. Castro announced his commitment to communism, and the Soviet Union stepped up shipments of military equipment to Cuba. This led to a frightening crisis in the fall of 1962.

In mid-October American intelligence sources reported that the Soviet Union was equipping Cuba with long-range jet bombers and offensive missiles that could deliver nuclear bombs to most of the eastern United States. On October 22 President Kennedy ordered the Navy to establish a blockade—or **quarantine**—against any further shipment of offensive weapons to Cuba. He also demanded that the Soviet Union immediately dismantle the Cuban missile bases and withdraw Soviet missiles and bombers from Cuba.

▲ The world waited tensely for Khrushchev's reaction. Faced with the choice between nu-

clear war or meeting Kennedy's demands, Khrushchev backed down. During the next few weeks, the Soviets began to dismantle the missile bases and remove the missiles and bombers. Nonetheless, a Communist nation supported by the Soviet Union was now established only 90 miles (144 kilometers) from the United States.

The Dominican issue. Another Latin American crisis arose in the spring of 1965. A revolution plunged the Dominican Republic into chaos. Calling the situation "grave," President Johnson ordered 400 marines into the Dominican capital, Santo Domingo. His aim was to protect the lives of Americans there. This was the first time since 1926 that the marines had been ordered into a Latin American country. During the next two weeks, 22,000 additional American troops landed, and 10,000 more stood by in navy vessels offshore.

President Johnson justified his action on the grounds that it was necessary to prevent a possible Communist takeover and to enable the people to hold free elections. He made it clear that the American forces would be withdrawn as soon as the O.A.S. took responsibility for maintaining order.

Representatives of the O.A.S. accepted the responsibility. By midsummer a small force of

▲ The United States was put on full military alert. For six days, tensions mounted throughout the world. Then Khrushchev replied that the missiles would be removed and the bases destroyed. Said Secretary of State Dean Rusk: "We're eyeball to eyeball, and I think the other fellow just blinked".

917

troops from four Latin American nations had arrived in Santo Domingo. Some of the United States troops were then withdrawn. In late August both sides accepted a provisional president who governed until elections were held in June 1966.

Crisis in Berlin. In Europe, too, Kennedy faced a challenge from the Soviet Union. In 1961 Soviet Premier Khrushchev renewed his threat to end the Western nations' rights of free access to West Berlin. Kennedy warned in turn that the United States would not abandon West Berlin.

In August 1961 the East German government began to erect a wall along the line between East and West Berlin. The Berlin Wall cut off the escape of East Germans into West Germany. It became a grim symbol of the conflicts between the Communist and anti-Communist nations of Europe.

The nuclear test ban. In August 1961 Premier Khrushchev also announced that the Soviet Union intended to resume nuclear testing. This news shocked people everywhere, for in 1958 the nuclear powers—the United States, Great Britain, and the Soviet Union—had agreed to suspend all testing for three years. The three-year period had not yet expired. President Kennedy warned that if the Soviets carried out their plans, the United States would be forced in the interests of its own defense to resume nuclear testing.

Nevertheless, the Soviets began a series of nuclear tests in the fall of 1961. The following spring, after the Soviet Union had turned down repeated pleas for a fully effective test ban and a general arms reduction, the United States began its own tests.

The first breaks in the long deadlock came in 1963. In June, Moscow and Washington agreed on a **hot line** to provide direct teletype communications between the two capitals to help prevent nuclear war by accident.

In July, American, British, and Soviet representatives agreed to ban nuclear tests in the atmosphere, under water, and in space. Underground testing would continue. The United States Senate ratified the agreement, and it went into effect in October 1963.

Communist China. The United States met its most difficult problems in Asia. There Communist China continued to threaten trouble in much of Asia. In 1959 the Chinese Communists took over Tibet. In 1962, following a border dispute, they launched a large-scale attack on India. In response to appeals from the Indian government, the United States and Great Britain airlifted military supplies to the hard-pressed Indian troops. Then China announced a cease-fire and called for negotiations. India, shocked by what it considered unprovoked aggression, began to build up its defenses.

Conflict in Southeast Asia. In addition to China, the new countries of Southeast Asia—Laos, Cambodia, and North and South Vietnam—became major crisis areas during the troubled 1960's.

The tiny kingdom of Laos was divided into three political factions—pro-Western, Communist, and neutral. In a losing effort to secure a strong pro-Western government, the United States spent millions of dollars in Laos. Finally, in 1962, after lengthy negotiations a neutral government was agreed to in Laos.

The United States also aided Cambodia in an effort to secure a pro-Western government. As in Laos, however, the policy failed. In 1963 Cambodia asked the United States to withdraw its military and technical personnel. You will read about increasing American involvement in Cambodia and in South Vietnam in the following section.

SECTION REVIEW

See underscored items, text pp. 915 - 18.

Identify: Third World, Trade Expansion Act of 1962, Peace Corps, Congo crisis, Premier Khrushchev, Fidel Castro, Bay of Pigs invasion, quarantine, Berlin Wall, hot line

For answers to questions, see Answer Key, p.A126.

1. **Organizing Ideas: (a)** How did relationships among Communist nations change during the 1960's? **(b)** How did relationships among non-Communist nations change? **(c)** How did the rise of the Third World affect the foreign policy of both the United States and the Soviet Union?

2. **Summarizing Ideas:** The Cuban missile crisis brought the world to the brink of nuclear war in 1962. Explain.

3. **Comparing Ideas:** Review United States relations with Latin America in **(a)** the Alliance for Progress and **(b)** the Dominican crisis.

4. **Evaluating Ideas: (a)** What was United States policy toward Asia in the early 1960's? **(b)** How successful was that policy?

Discussion topic: How Kennedy's foreign policy compared with Truman's containment and Eisenhower's brinksmanship.

2 The United States becomes deeply involved in Vietnam

See Teaching Suggestions in TMRG, pp.TM222-23.

The most serious problem that the United States faced between 1960 and 1980 was a war in South Vietnam. This war had a great impact on the image of America around the world. It also influenced the way Americans perceived their own country and its role in the world.

Background to war. As you have read (page 836), when France pulled out of Vietnam in the 1950's, an international agreement divided that country into two parts. Elections that would have reunited the country, scheduled for 1956 were never held. Instead Vietnam continued to exist as two nations. North Vietnam, with its capital at Hanoi, was under a Communist government headed by Ho Chi Minh. South Vietnam, with its capital at Saigon, was a republic whose president was Ngo Dinh Diem (NOH DIN DYEM). Diem's government had strong backing from the United States.

Although the elections were not held, many Vietnamese still wanted a united country. Vietnamese guerrillas, backed by North Vietnam, fought to overthrow Diem's regime and unite the countries. In 1960 the guerrillas took the name of the National Liberation Front (NLF). Their opponents referred to them as the Viet Cong (Vietnamese Communists).

American involvement. The United States was deeply concerned over events in South Vietnam. Not long before, Communists had taken over China and had barely been beaten back in Korea. Now a Communist movement was gaining strength in South Vietnam.

President Eisenhower warned of the danger of a **domino effect** in Southeast Asia. He meant that if the government of one nation there fell to the Communists, then the government of the neighboring nation would topple in turn. According to this view, all of Southeast Asia might end up in Communist hands if one nation fell. To prevent the fall of South Vietnam to the Communists, millions of dollars in military aid and 800 United States military advisers were sent to South Vietnam during Eisenhower's administration.

Eisenhower's belief in a domino effect was shared by President Kennedy. Kennedy declared that United States foreign policy depended "in considerable measure upon a strong and free Vietnamese nation."

The formation of the NLF in 1960 was followed by increased guerrilla activity. In response, Kennedy increased the amount of military aid and the number of advisers to the threatened Diem regime.

The fall of Diem. However, Diem's administration was corrupt, and he became increasingly unpopular in South Vietnam. Diem repressed all political opponents. Also, his failure to control the NLF angered South Vietnamese military leaders. Kennedy pressured Diem to make reforms, but Diem failed to do so.

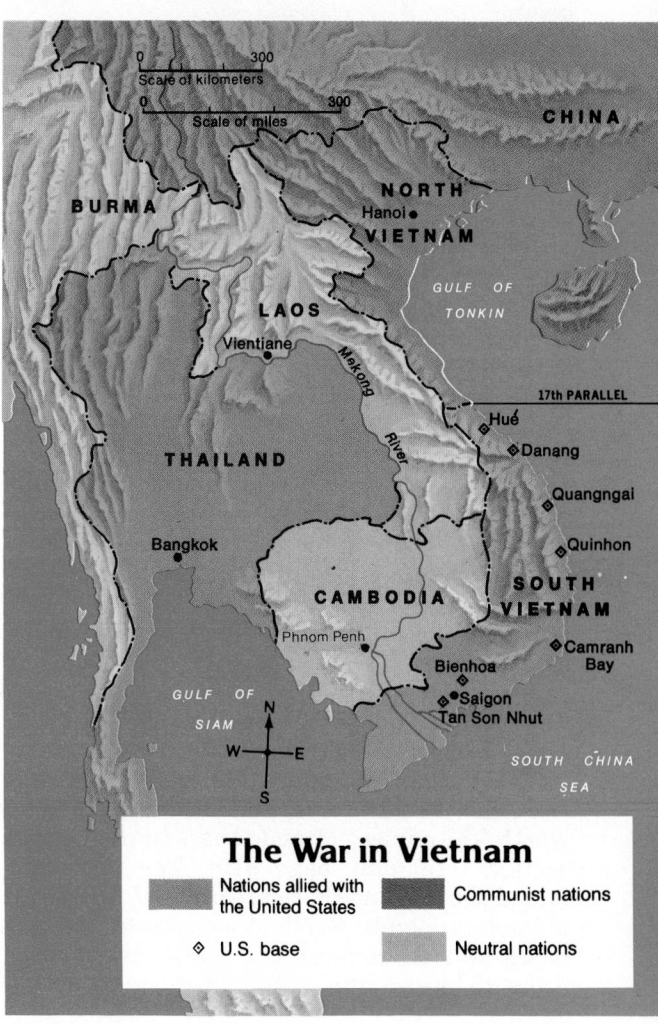

The War in Vietnam

Nations allied with the United States

Communist nations

◇ U.S. base

Neutral nations

919

"Ike made a promise," President Lyndon Johnson often said, "and I have to keep it." Here, on a trip to South Vietnam, he visits some of the hundreds of thousands of American troops sent to that nation to try to keep the promise.

Finally, the United States government learned that South Vietnamese military leaders were planning to seize power from Diem. Kennedy made no effort to stop them or to inform Diem. In 1963, the military took over, and Diem was assassinated.

The new government fared no better than Diem's in the struggle against the NLF. The United States nevertheless remained committed to South Vietnam. After Kennedy's death, President Johnson stated, "I am not going to be the President who saw Vietnam go the way China went." He expanded American aid programs. By late 1964 there were 23,000 American advisers in South Vietnam.

The Gulf of Tonkin Resolution. On August 4, 1964, President Johnson appeared on television with shocking news. He announced that two American destroyers had been attacked by North Vietnamese torpedo boats in the Gulf of Tonkin (see map, page 919). The President stated that he had therefore ordered American planes to bomb North Vietnamese torpedo bases and oil refineries. He also asked Congress to grant him authority to take action against North Vietnam.

The President did not tell the nation that the American ships had been assisting South Vietnamese gunboats that were making raids on North Vietnam's coast. He also did not inform the nation that there was some doubt whether there had been any attack on the American ships at all.

Three days later Congress granted the President's request. It adopted what became known as the Gulf of Tonkin Resolution. This gave the President power "to take all necessary measures to repel any armed attack against the forces of the United States and to prevent further aggression."

The House voted unanimously for the measure. The Senate passed it by a vote of 88 to 2. Senator Wayne Morse of Oregon, who voted against it, warned that "we are in effect giving the President warmaking powers in the absence of a declaration of war. I believe that to be a historic mistake."

A turning point. As late as October 1964, President Johnson still stated that he did not intend to commit American troops to a war in Asia. "We are not," he declared, "about to send American boys nine or ten thousand miles

▲ Discussion topic: Ask students to explain how the Gulf of Tonkin Resolution amounted to giving the President warmaking powers. ("... all necessary measures..." may include combat attacks.) Who is supposed to have the power to declare war? (Congress, the representatives of the people).

away from home to do what Asian boys ought to be doing for themselves." Nevertheless, the Gulf of Tonkin Resolution changed the situation in South Vietnam and marked a turning point in United States participation there.

Viet Cong attacks in South Vietnam continued, and American responses grew stronger. In February 1965 President Johnson ordered American planes to bomb targets in North Vietnam. The bombing of North Vietnam would continue, with occasional pauses, until March 1968.

President Johnson ordered more United States ground forces to South Vietnam as well. In March 1965 the first marines landed there. By early 1966 there were 190,000 United States troops in South Vietnam. By mid-1966 the number was 265,000. By the end of 1967 it had risen to 500,000.

A widening war. As American aid increased, North Vietnam increased its support of the Viet Cong. Supplies flowed from North to South Vietnam over a network of routes that became known as the Ho Chi Minh Trail. As the war went on, troops from North Vietnam also moved south along the trail to join the Viet Cong in the fighting.

The United States tried in several ways to end the fighting. President Johnson halted bombing raids for brief periods. He also offered $1 billion in economic aid to Southeast Asia. Nevertheless, the North Vietnamese continued to insist that the United States had to get out of Vietnam before peace talks could begin. This the United States refused to do.

Differing strategies. Unlike the Communists, the Americans and the South Vietnamese relied heavily on air power in fighting the war. The Air Force poured bombs, napalm, rockets, and machine-gun fire on Viet Cong villages, hideouts, and supply routes in South Vietnam. In North Vietnam air raids were aimed at supply depots, industrial plants, and strategic roads and bridges. By the end of 1968, Americans had dropped more bombs on North Vietnam than they had used during all of World War II.

With support from the air, South Vietnamese and American ground forces carried out **search-and-destroy missions** against the Viet Cong. In areas they could not hold or defend, they moved the people to refugee centers and burned the villages.

The Viet Cong and the North Vietnamese, who lacked extensive air power, usually avoided large-scale fighting. Instead they used guerrilla tactics and terrorism. They planted bombs in a country marketplace or on a street in a busy city. They tortured or assassinated unfriendly village leaders. They practiced "hit-and-run" warfare, striking swiftly, then melting back into the jungle.

Effects of the war. The war had a shattering impact on all participants. In South Vietnam, a country about the size of the state of Washington, more than 1.6 million troops were fighting by 1968.° By that time American casualties totaled more than 27,000 killed and 92,000 seriously wounded.

Vietnamese civilians bore the heaviest burden of suffering. Though air strikes were aimed at military targets, civilians were often the victims. By the end of 1967, civilian casualties were totaling between 100,000 and 150,000 a year. By 1968 at least 2 million of the 16 million people of South Vietnam were displaced and had become refugees.

Elections in South Vietnam. The United States knew that the people of South Vietnam would have to have faith in their government if the war was to be won. For this to happen, the Vietnamese people would have to believe that their government was genuinely concerned about their welfare.

Unfortunately graft and corruption had continued under the rule of the military leaders who overthrew Diem. The United States urged these leaders to end corruption and move toward a more democratic form of government.

South Vietnam held elections in the fall of 1967. Defying the Viet Cong, who tried to sabotage the elections, an estimated 51 percent of those eligible voted. The South Vietnamese elected General Nguyen Van Thieu (nuh·WIN van TYOO) as President.

Some American observers saw the election as a positive step toward a stable, democratic South Vietnamese government. At the same time, American military leaders were issuing optimistic reports on the progress of the fight-

---

°By the end of 1968, troops in the war numbered as follows: on the allied side about 750,000 South Vietnamese, 540,000 Americans, 45,000 South Koreans, and 15,000 Australians, New Zealanders, Thais, and Filipinos. There were an estimated 300,000 Viet Cong and North Vietnamese regulars.

Map activity: Ask the students to find Vietnam on a world physical map. Then ask: What is Vietnam's topography? What problems would this present to soldiers with modern equipment? How far is Vietnam from the equator? How does this affect climate? How would Vietnam's monsoons affect soldiers?

921

THE GULF OF TONKIN RESOLUTION (1964)

Whereas naval units of the Communist regime in Vietman, in violation of the principles of the Charter of the United Nations and of international law, have deliberately and repeatedly attacked United States naval vessels lawfully present in international waters, and have thereby created a serious threat to international peace; and

Whereas these attacks are part of a deliberate and systematic campaign of aggression that the Communist regime in North Vietman has been waging against its neighbors and the nations joined with them in the collective defense of their freedom; . . . Now therefore, be it

Resolved by the Senate and House of Representatives of the United States of America in Congress assembled, That the Congress approves and supports the determination of the President, as Commander in Chief, to take all necessary measures to repel any armed attack against the forces of the United States and to prevent further aggression.

ing. The war, they claimed, would be over soon. Victory was in sight.

The Tet offensive. In February 1968 came startling evidence that victory was not near. The Viet Cong and the North Vietnamese launched surprise attacks all across South Vietnam during Tet, the lunar New Year holidays. They seized partial control of or terrorized 26 of the provisional capitals of South Vietnam.

The South Vietnamese and Americans soon beat back this Tet offensive. Nevertheless, the cost of victory was high. Large sections of several cities were blasted into rubble. Thousands of soldiers and civilians were killed. Also, the Viet Cong gained firm control of large areas of the countryside.

Aftereffects of Tet. The Tet offensive dealt a staggering blow to predictions that the enemy was being defeated. It also demonstrated that the "other war"—the effort of the Saigon government to win the loyalty of the Vietnamese people—was still far from won.

At the end of March 1968, with the Tet offensive still a raw memory, President Johnson declared that the United States would limit its bombing to invasion routes and to the area immediately north of the Demilitarized Zone (DMZ). This was a supposedly neutral strip of land separating North and South Vietnam.

The Hanoi government responded to Johnson's steps with the long-awaited offer to begin peace talks. In May 1968 the United States and North Vietnam began these talks in Paris.

Criticism of the war. The Tet offensive contributed to the mounting criticism of the war in the United States. By the fall of 1968, the Vietnam conflict had become the second longest war in American history and the third largest in terms of lives lost and money spent. Only the Revolutionary War had lasted longer, and only World War I and World War II had cost more in money, resources, and lives.

Growing numbers of Americans were convinced that the Vietnam War was a grave mistake. They felt that the conflict was basically a civil war in which the United States should have no part. Moreover, they added, the United States was destroying South Vietnam in the process of "saving it" from communism. These critics urged an immediate end to the bombing and a rapid end to the war.

A constitutional question. Congress criticized the war as well. In March 1968 the Senate Foreign Relations Committee held a televised hearing on the conduct of the war.

At the heart of Congress's concern was an issue of constitutional powers. The Constitution makes the President the commander in chief of the nation's armed forces. It also gives him extensive powers over the conduct of foreign affairs. Nevertheless, the Constitution reserves to Congress the power to declare war. Now in Vietnam the United States was engaged in an undeclared war over which Congress had little control.

Most Americans agreed that at times the President had to make major decisions without waiting for Congress to act. Did this mean, however, that in matters of war and peace the role of Congress was no longer relevant? No one, it seemed, had a conclusive answer.

The costs of commitment. Members of Congress and many Americans were also concerned with the larger issue of American

Registration Acknowledgment			Selective Service System		
Selective Service Number	Date of Birth	Social Security Number	Phone	Sex	Date of Record
60-0000212-7	05-16-60	431-35-6054	501-423-2684	M	01-08-82

Name and Current Address	Permanent Address
LINDSAY CALVIN JOHNSON RT 1 FALL BRANCH RD BLOUNTVILLE, TN 37617	RT 1 FALL BRANCH RD BLOUNTVILLE, TN 37617

Thomas K. Turnage Director	Registrant's Signature	SSS Form 3A

During the Vietnam War many people objected to the Selective Service System — the method by which about 1,700,000 American men were drafted into military service. Many of the Vietnam draftees were poor, came from working-class backgrounds, or belonged to minority groups. Critics charged that the system enabled wealthier, white Americans to avoid military service by attending college and obtaining student deferments. Some draft resisters burned their draft cards and refused to be inducted.

The first national draft was instituted in 1917, although draftees had served both the Union and the Confederacy during the Civil War. The World War I system supplied almost 3 million soldiers without much opposition. The World War II draft inducted more than 10 million men; the Korean draft, about 2 million.

In 1973 the draft was abolished in favor of a volunteer army and a registration system for a standby draft. Today all men are required to register with the Selective Service System by their eighteenth birthday.

foreign policy in general. The American commitment to stop the spread of communism had become enormous. By 1969 the United States was providing some form of aid to 70 nations. It had formal commitments to defend 42 nations against any form of aggression, Communist or otherwise. To back up these commitments, the United States had 3.5 million men and women in the armed forces. Another 1.2 million civilian employees supported these troops. As of January 1968, total military expenses amounted to $87.6 billion a year, or a total expenditure of $439 for each American.

Critics pointed out that Congress voted only $24 billion for health, education, and welfare in that same year. They claimed that huge foreign commitments drained resources that could be spent at home. Critics also claimed that military expenses were contributing to inflation. This would raise prices, making it more difficult to sell American products abroad.

President Johnson's decision. Such criticisms of the war continued to mount. Debate over the course of the war spilled out onto the streets. Huge demonstrations were held to protest the war. At times, prowar and antiwar demonstrators clashed. Many people feared that the country was being torn apart.

President Johnson was eligible to run for reelection in 1968. Nevertheless, growing criticism of the war and strengthening political opposition meant his victory would be doubtful. In March 1968, when he announced the bombing limits, he also announced that he would not seek reelection.

SECTION REVIEW
See underscored items, text pp. 919 - 22.

Identify: Ho Chi Minh, NLF, Viet Cong, domino effect, Gulf of Tonkin Resolution, Ho Chi Minh Trail, search-and-destroy missions, DMZ
For answers to questions, see Answer Key, pp.A126-27.

1. **Summarizing Ideas:** Trace the steps of American involvement in South Vietnam starting in 1962.

2. **Determining Cause and Effect:** (a) What was the Tet offensive? (b) What were some of its consequences?

3. **Comparing Ideas:** What were some of the arguments presented by opponents of the Vietnam War?

4. **Studying Sources:** According to the Source on page 922, why was the United States justified in taking action in South Vietnam?

American military involvement in Southeast Asia ended with the fall of Saigon in 1975. The American departure from the capital of South Vietnam triggered a massive exodus of the native population, as thousands of South Vietnamese fled the invading North Vietnamese army. Many of the refugees later resettled in other countries, including the United States.

3 World tensions are relaxed during the Nixon and Ford administrations

See Teaching Suggestions in TMRG, p.TM223.

The war in Vietnam remained the most serious problem confronting the nation when Richard M. Nixon became its next President in January 1969.

Nixon's plan for Vietnam. During the election campaign, Nixon had declared that if elected he would "bring an honorable end to the war." Nixon's plan called for the gradual withdrawal of American troops as soon as the South Vietnamese showed that they were able to defend themselves. The plan also replaced the search-and-destroy policy with a <u>protective-reaction policy</u>. Under this new policy, American troops would engage the enemy only when attacked or threatened by attack. Nixon hoped that the new tactics would both reduce American casualties and help quiet the fierce opposition to the war.

The invasion of Cambodia. The Nixon plan disappointed those Americans who wanted a quick end to the nation's military involvement in Vietnam. They were further disheartened in the spring of 1970 by Nixon's startling announcement that South Vietnamese and American troops were crossing the border into "neutral" Cambodia. The objective of the invasion, Nixon said, was to destroy North Vietnamese and Viet Cong supply centers and camps along the eastern border of Cambodia. As soon as these centers from which the Viet Cong had been launching their attacks against South Vietnam had been wiped out, the troops would be withdrawn. Nixon promised that all American forces would be out of Cambodia by the end of June.

President Nixon kept his promise. In the meantime, however, the American invasion of Cambodia had triggered widespread antiwar demonstrations in the United States. Further, it intensified a long-standing conflict between Communist and non-Communist forces in that Southeast Asian nation.

The cease-fire agreement. The protective-reaction policy and the withdrawal of some American ground troops from South Vietnam

▲ The bombings of Cambodia had been kept secret from the American people. Antiwar demonstrations in response included the infamous shootings of unarmed protesters at Kent State and Jackson State.

during Nixon's first term in office did reduce American casualties. However, there was no reduction in the fury of the air war. American air power destroyed large areas in South Vietnam that were controlled by the Viet Cong and the North Vietnamese. American planes also mined the harbors of North Vietnam and rained bombs upon North Vietnamese supply routes and ammunition centers in Laos and Cambodia.

Meanwhile the negotiations in Paris continued. Nixon's foreign policy adviser, Henry Kissinger, patiently tried to break the deadlock. Just before the Presidential election of 1972, Kissinger announced that "peace is at hand," but the welcomed announcement was premature. The United States continued military operations for two months, including massive bombing of Hanoi during December. Early in January 1973, a **cease-fire agreement** finally was reached.

There were three key terms in the agreement. (1) The continued presence of North Vietnamese military forces in South Vietnam was tacitly agreed to. (2) South Vietnam was assured that it was to have a government of its own choosing. (3) The United States guaranteed continued economic and military aid to South Vietnam. President Nixon then withdrew the remaining American troops from South Vietnam. As a result of continuing pressure, most American prisoners of war were later released by North Vietnam.

The costs of war. American participation in this longest and most unpopular war in the nation's history had been enormously costly. By the spring of 1973, when the last troops left Vietnam, direct expenditures totaled $137 billion. Some 45,729 Americans had been killed in action and more than 300,000 wounded. As for the people of Southeast Asia, estimates put South Vietnamese deaths at 160,903 and those of the Viet Cong and North Vietnamese at 922,295. In addition, more than 6 million people called **refugees** were uprooted and made homeless. Large areas of Vietnam, Laos, and Cambodia had been devastated.

The Vietnam War left feelings of anger and division in American society. The sharp disagreement over what to do about thousands of American draft resisters and deserters who had fled to Canada, Sweden, and elsewhere was but one example of this lingering bitterness (see Chapter 40).

Most Americans agreed that there had to be "no more Vietnams." One element that had contributed to involvement in Vietnam was the President's war-making power (see page 920). Once the war in Vietnam had started, Congress could at any time have ended America's involvement by cutting off funds for further military operations. However, Congress was reluctant to take this step while American troops were actually fighting in the conflict.

After the war's end, in November 1973, Congress passed the War Powers Resolution over Nixon's veto. The law provided that the President could not send troops into combat for a period longer than 60 days unless Congress approved. The resolution also provided that Congress could, by a joint resolution, order the immediate removal of troops from an area of combat.

Later events in Southeast Asia. The peace in Southeast Asia did not last long. Communist forces there took the offensive in 1973 and 1974. In Cambodia, during 1974 and 1975, Communist troops captured much of the country and surrounded the capital of Phnom Penh. In April 1975 the remaining Americans were evacuated by helicopters and the Communist armies took control of Cambodia.

Meanwhile in South Vietnam, resistance to the Communists also was crumbling. By March 1975, South Vietnamese troops were in retreat before the advancing North Vietnamese and Viet Cong. In a last desperate effort to prevent a complete collapse of South Vietnam, President Ford asked Congress to vote $722 million in emergency military aid. Congress, certain that the South Vietnamese cause was hopeless and fearing a renewal of America's involvement, refused to support him.

By the end of April, Saigon was surrounded. American helicopters and ships lying off the coast withdrew the remaining Americans as well as 100,000 South Vietnamese. The Vietnamese refugees, for the most part destitute, were temporarily housed on American military bases until they could be relocated in the United States. Thus, with the Communist takeover of South Vietnam, three decades of fighting in Vietnam came to an end.

Nixon's foreign policies. Apart from the unpopular Vietnam War, Nixon's foreign policies won widespread approval. His success in im-

Text continues on page 927.

Nixon's opponent, George McGovern of South Dakota, had waged a strong antiwar campaign. Suddenly, Nixon could claim to be the real candidate of peace. Shortly after he won the election, the cease-fire fell through and Nixon ordered the bombing of Hanoi.

THIS CHANGING LAND   Planet Earth And Beyond

Many scientists have used the analogy of Earth as a spaceship and its inhabitants as the passengers aboard. Earth fits the analogy amazingly well. Earth travels far out into space. Each year, Earth engages in an almost unbelievable space trip as it makes its annual voyage around the sun. The total trip logs 595 million miles (952 million kilometers) a year. In addition, Earth, along with our sun and the other planets in our solar system, is part of the Milky Way Galaxy. The Milky Way Galaxy turns like a giant ferris wheel in space, traveling more than 376 million miles (602 million kilometers) through space each year.

There are about five billion passengers cruising through space on this very special spaceship, Earth. But where are the passengers going? What makes up the universe through which spaceship earth is traveling?

On a clear night with the naked eye an observer can see about 3,000 stars. With a three lens telescope it is possible to see 600,000 of them. There are, in fact, more than 200 billion, billion stars in the universe.

One star system is the Milky Way Galaxy, a glowing band of starlight that comes from its more than 100 billion stars. The Milky Way is special because one of those stars is the sun. Earth and the other plants — Mercury, Venus, Mars, Jupiter, Saturn, Uranus, Neptune, Pluto, and their moons — are part of the enormous Milky Way Galaxy. Yet the Milky Way Galaxy is but one of many of galaxies in the Universe.

Daily, as science and technology advance, scientists are learning more about the mysteries beyond planet Earth. Passengers have already entered the space age. People from Earth have walked on the moon. Space flight is a proven success with the many missions of the space shuttles. Satellites have been launched, recaptured, and repaired far out in the vastness of space. Plans for space stations are far advanced, and the time is rapidly approaching when people will be working and living beyond the confines of Earth's atmosphere.

These scientific achievements are already part of the reality of life today. What about tomorrow? Think about earth's chief star — that rather small yellowish dwarf star that is called "sun". The sun has nine planets associated with it. One of these planets is Earth. Scientists are continually learning about the unique properties of earth and the solar system's other eight planets. Voyager and other space probes are sending back data that will unlock the mystery of what lies beyond the Milky Way, in the vastness of the universe with its 200 billion, billion stars.

An artist's renditions of the solar system (left) and the Milky Way (right)

proving relations with Communist China and the Soviet Union was impressive.

Nixon, like other recent Presidents, insisted upon maintaining a military force strong enough to meet any challenge to the nation's interests and security. He demonstrated his opposition to communism by insisting upon the continued exclusion of Cuba from the O.A.S. This opposition was also apparent in his approval of the secret use of funds by the CIA to try to prevent a Socialist-Communist election victory in Chile. The CIA later made it difficult for the Marxist government elected by those parties to govern. Like earlier Presidents, Nixon largely ignored the denial of human rights in anti-Communist countries that received American military and economic assistance in exchange for military bases. These countries included Spain, Greece, South Korea, South Vietnam, and Iran.

Nixon's foreign policy stressed skillful, realistic, and flexible diplomacy that would recognize changing conditions in the world. Nixon's chief adviser on foreign policy was Henry Kissinger. Kissinger was a refugee from Nazi Germany who had become a professor of political science at Harvard University.

Without conferring much with the Department of State, Nixon and Kissinger planned the broad outlines of American foreign policy. Their "personal diplomacy" involved an unprecedented number of conferences with leaders in other countries. President Nixon himself traveled to Western Europe, the Soviet Union, China, Canada, Iceland, and the Middle East for talks with other heads of state. Shortly after his reelection in 1972, he appointed Kissinger Secretary of State.

A new policy toward China. In one of his most dramatic moves, Nixon visited the People's Republic of China in February 1972. With this visit, the door that had been shut and barred between the two countries for more than 20 years began to swing open. Each government promised not to seek dominance in the Asian Pacific region, to cooperate in preventing other powers from doing so, and to avoid international war. Both governments agreed to develop trade, improve cultural and scientific relations, and work to restore full diplomatic relations. As for the major obstacle to improved relations, President Nixon promised eventual withdrawal of United States military forces from Taiwan and Indochina. In what was regarded as proof of America's desire to cooperate, the Nixon administration used its influence to support China's ally, Pakistan, when war broke out between Pakistan and India over the independence of East Pakistan (renamed Bangladesh).

Détente with the Soviet Union. In May 1972, three months after Nixon had visited Peking, he met for talks with Soviet leaders in Moscow. Nixon and Communist Party Secretary Leonid Brezhnev (BRESH·nev) agreed to cooperate in efforts to improve trade and to tackle world problems involving space, health, and the environment.

Early in 1972 the world was surprised to learn that a secret arrangement had been made for President Nixon to visit China. Just months earlier, the idea of an American President strolling in Peking would have been unthinkable.

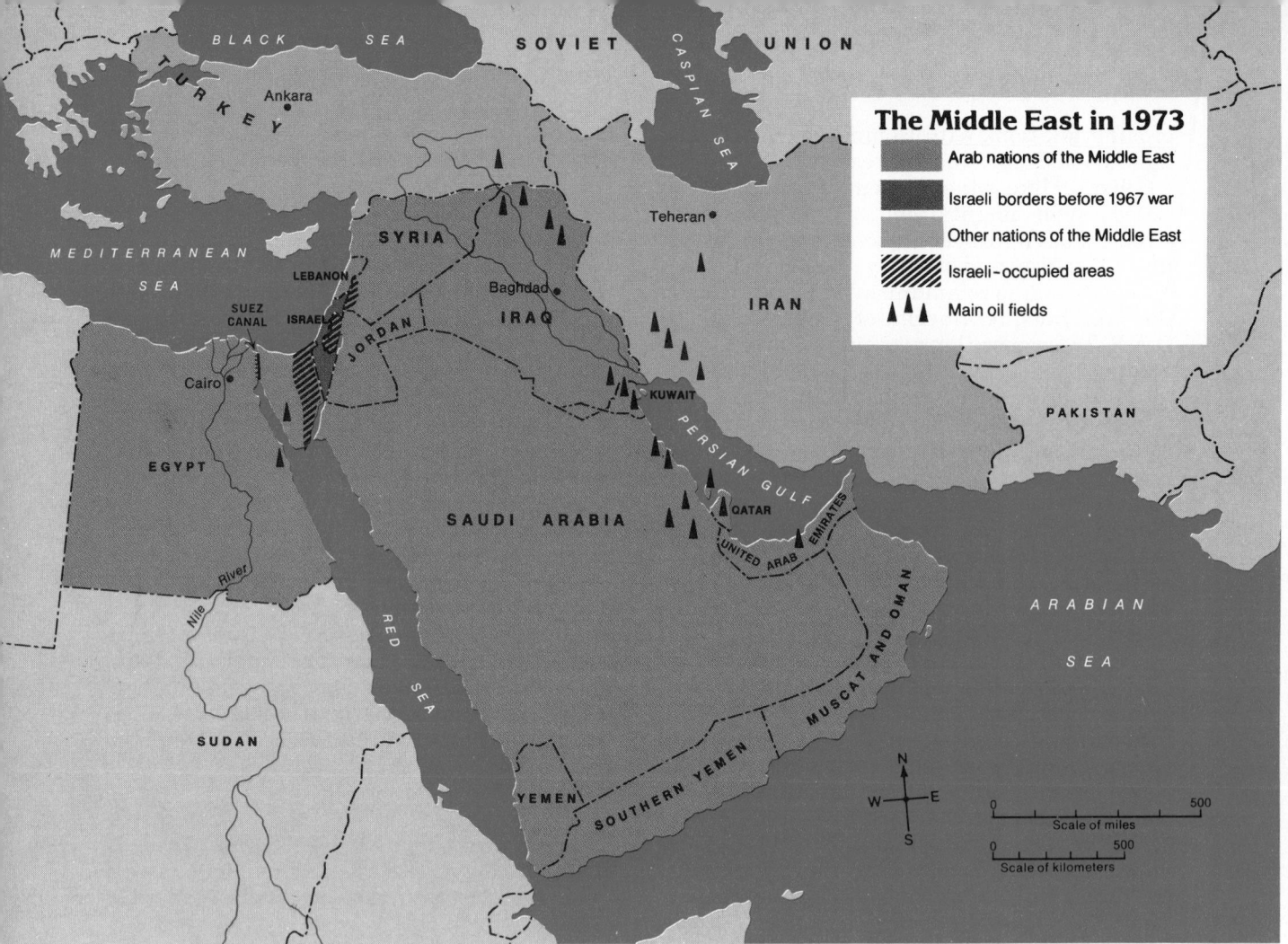

The Middle East in 1973

- Arab nations of the Middle East
- Israeli borders before 1967 war
- Other nations of the Middle East
- Israeli-occupied areas
- Main oil fields

Nixon and Brezhnev also signed two documents intended to limit nuclear armaments. These documents were based upon earlier negotiations known as the Strategic Arms Limitation Talks (SALT). One of the documents, an executive agreement, froze offensive missiles at near existing levels for a five-year period. The other document, a treaty requiring Senate approval, limited each nation to two antiballistic missile sites in its territory. It also placed a limit on the size of American and Soviet land-based and submarine-based missile forces. The Senate ratified this treaty in August 1973. The two countries seemed to be entering a period of détente, or the relaxation and reduction of tensions between them.

Arab-Israeli conflict. One area of the globe that posed a threat to détente was the Middle East. In 1967 the Israelis believed that the Arab nations were massing large military forces to destroy Israel. In June, powerful Is-raeli forces struck at Egypt, Jordan, and Syria, defeating them in a war lasting only six days. After the war Israel kept large areas of land that had belonged to these three Arab states. The Arab nations, bitter at their defeat, sent trained guerrillas into Israel. The Israelis continued to strike back.

For many years the Soviet Union sent aid of various kinds, including military aid, to the Arab nations but not to Israel. The United States tried to help the Arab nations overcome their poverty, and it gave military aid to those nations resisting communism. It also gave military aid to Israel.

The Yom Kippur War. Another Arab-Israeli war erupted in October 1973. Egypt and Syria, seeking to recover territories lost in the 1967 war, suddenly launched an attack upon Israel. The Israelis at that time were observing Yom Kippur, a day holy to Jews. They were caught by surprise and suffered heavy casualties.

By the second week of the war, however, Israeli troops were driving back Syrian tanks in the north and had crossed the Suez Canal in the south. Soon Israeli forces were within 60 miles (96 kilometers) of Cairo.

In the meantime the United Nations had called for a cease-fire, but the fighting continued. The Egyptians, faced with almost certain defeat, called upon the Soviet Union for help. The Soviets threatened to send their own troops to help end the fighting. President Nixon immediately ordered a "precautionary alert" for all American forces around the world. A major military confrontation seemed possible.

Fortunately, the two great powers persuaded the Arabs and the Israelis to accept the cease-fire and to prepare for negotiations. Détente had survived its first critical trial.

However, many Israelis were bitter at being forced to end the fighting just as a final victory was within their grasp. Also, the Arabs were angered by American support of the Israelis. Several Arab nations cut off all shipments of oil to the United States and other countries that were friendly to Israel. Although the immediate crisis was over, the cease-fire had brought only an uneasy peace.

President Ford's foreign policy. On August 9, 1974, Gerald R. Ford replaced Nixon as President. Ford followed Nixon's foreign policies.

Early in 1975, Ford urged Congress to provide $222 million in military aid to Cambodia, Congress refused because it was determined to close the door on further military adventures by the United States.

A few months later, however, Congress joined in the praise of Ford's action in the _Mayaguez_ incident. In May, the _Mayaguez,_ an unarmed American cargo ship, was seized by Cambodian Communists. Ford promptly sent air, sea, and ground forces to free the vessel and its crew of 39 men. In the action 15 American servicemen were killed, 50 wounded, and 3 missing. The President was sharply criticized for what many considered an unnecessary and ill-timed venture. Others applauded him for acting decisively.

Changes in détente. When Ford became President, he had taken over negotiations on a trade agreement between the United States and the Soviet Union. Senator Henry Jackson of Washington was one of many critics of the proposed agreement. Jackson insisted that trade between the two nations should not be freer until the Soviet Union relaxed its restrictions on the emigration of its citizens, including political dissenters and Jews who wanted to move to Israel.

In the fall of 1974, the Soviet Union apparently accepted the "Jackson amendment." They agreed at that time to increase the number of exit visas for Jewish citizens. A few months later, however, the Soviets rejected the trade agreement. Moscow declared that it could not allow the United States to interfere with Soviet emigration policy.

The Soviet rejection was a setback for the policy of détente. As you will see, during the Carter administration this rift in the policy became noticeably wider.

SECTION REVIEW

See underscored items, text pp. 924 - 25, 927 - 29.

Identify: protective-reaction policy, Henry Kissinger, cease-fire, refugee, War Powers Resolution, Phnom Penh, Leonid Brezhnev, SALT, détente, Yom Kippur War, _Mayaguez_ incident, Senator Henry Jackson

For answers to questions, see Answer Key, p.A127.

1. **Synthesizing Ideas: (a)** How did the United States wind down its involvement in the Vietnam War? **(b)** What were the terms of the 1973 cease-fire? **(c)** How was the conflict between North and South Vietnam finally resolved?

2. **Organizing Ideas:** Describe President Nixon's policy of détente toward China and the Soviet Union.

3. **Comparing Ideas:** How did President Ford's foreign policy compare with Nixon's?

4 President Carter's foreign policy produces mixed results

See Teaching Suggestions in TMRG, pp.TM223-24.

President Carter made some important foreign policy decisions during his administration. A hostage crisis in the nation of Iran, however, damaged his popularity with the people.

President Carter's goals. Several months after his inauguration in January 1977, President Carter outlined the goals of his administration in a speech delivered at Notre Dame University. "We are now free," he declared, "of that inordinate fear of communism which once led us to embrace any dictator who joined in that fear. We fought fire with fire, never thinking that fire is better fought with water."

Carter then went on to express the hope that the great powers would resolve not to try to impose their social systems on other countries. During his administration, he said, he intended to work to improve America's relations with its allies, to advance human rights everywhere in the world, and to make genuine progress in arms control.

Carter's inexperience hindered his efforts to carry out this program. In addition, he at times had to resolve the conflicting views of the men and women he had chosen to advise him on foreign affairs. His Secretary of State, Cyrus R. Vance, was an experienced diplomat who preferred to handle problems through patient negotiations. Vance often clashed with the President's tough-minded National Security Adviser, Zbigniew Brzezinski (zuh·BIG·nee·ehv bruh·ZHIN·skee), a Columbia University professor of political science. Brzezinski was more inclined to take a hard line, particularly on issues involving the Soviet Union.

The Panama Canal treaties. The first major test of the President's program developed over the Panama Canal treaties. As soon as the treaties were ratified, Panama would begin to exercise almost total control over the operation of the canal itself. By the year 2000, Panama would gain complete control of the canal.

The treaties caused a storm of controversy in Congress and throughout the country. Critics argued that the United States was surrendering national property and endangering the nation's security. Supporters, including the President, insisted that the United States had never possessed sovereignty over the Canal Zone. They also pointed out that the terms of the treaties prevented any hostile country from ever securing control.

After an extended and often bitter debate, the Senate finally ratified the treaties by a close vote in the spring of 1978.

The issue of human rights. In August 1975 the leaders of 33 European nations plus the United States and Canada had gathered in Helsinki, Finland. There the leaders signed a statement outlining the basic goals of "peace, security, justice, and cooperation." High on the list of commitments was the pledge to support **human rights.**

Carter, as President, also placed the issue of human rights high on the list of priorities for his administration. Nevertheless, Carter's commitment to freedom and justice for all people everywhere met with mixed reactions both at home and abroad.

Not surprisingly, strong opposition came from countries ruled by military dictatorships. Many leaders from such countries often ignored the rights of their subjects. At the same time, however, many diplomats both in the United States and among its allies felt that by insisting upon worldwide observance of human rights the President was interfering in the domestic affairs of other countries. These critics reminded Carter that the United States would resent any effort by other nations to interfere in the nation's domestic affairs. They argued that the President's emphasis upon this issue did not help to relax international tensions or to promote world peace.

Africa. African affairs were another source of trouble for Carter. The huge continent had vast natural resources, a population of nearly half a billion, and a growing number of newly independent states. As a result, it was the scene of competition between the United States and the Soviet Union. Both powers as well as the other industrial nations attempted to establish their influence and their social and political systems in the African nations.

In 1975, during President Ford's administration, Portugal had withdrawn from Angola, and this last remaining colony in Africa won its independence. Angola was then torn by a civil war. Cuban troops trained and equipped by the Soviets soon moved in to support the Communist-inspired leaders.

Henry Kissinger, then Ford's Secretary of State, warned that the United States could not remain indifferent to Soviet interference in Africa. Yet Americans were reluctant to become involved in another Vietnam-type military venture. Thus, there was little the United States could do. As it developed, the Soviet success in Angola led to similar Cuban-Soviet intervention in other African countries, notably Ethiopia.

During Carter's administration the United States tried to counteract Communist intervention in Africa. The United States encouraged the African states to deal with their own problems and to solve them in their own way. Andrew Young, a black civil rights activist who had supported Carter's election campaign, served the President as Ambassador to the United Nations. Ambassador Young was an outspoken critic of white imperialism in Africa. He sharply criticized the Republic of South Africa's racial policies and practices. He also strongly supported black majority rule in Rhodesia (now Zimbabwe).

Young's interest in and concern for Africa and the developing countries made him an influential figure in the United Nations. His followers were dismayed, therefore, when in August 1979 he resigned his post as Ambassador. Young's unauthorized meeting with a representative of the Palestine Liberation Organization (PLO) embarrassed the administration and forced him to submit his resignation. President Carter accepted the resignation with "deep regret."

The Middle East. The troubled Middle East provided the President with a major foreign policy achievement. The renewal of war between Egypt and Israel was a danger when Carter became President. The first really hopeful development came at the end of 1977 when President Sadat of Egypt accepted Premier Begin's invitation to visit Israel. A few weeks later, Begin returned the visit and the door was opened to the first peace negotiations since the Arab-Israeli War of 1973. During the next nine months, Secretary of State Vance worked with the Egyptians and the Israelis in an effort to hammer out an agreement. These discussions ended in a stalemate.

At this point, President Carter invited Begin and Sadat to meet with him in Washington and they accepted. At the end of 13 days of secret discussions at Camp David, the President's mountain retreat in nearby Maryland, they reached a tentative framework for a peace settlement.

In April 1979, gathered on the White House lawn, the three men signed a formal peace treaty. The treaty ended 30 years of war between Egypt and Israel. After the signing, in an emotion-filled moment, the three embraced. Each of them quoted the prophet Isaiah: "And they shall beat their swords into plowshares and their spears into pruning hooks."

Working out the details of the treaty proved a harder task. What should be done with the

This was the moment for which the Camp David meetings on Middle East peace were aiming—the signing of a framework for peace by Carter (center), Begin (right), and Sadat (left) at the White House.

lands Israel had occupied during the wars? How should Palestinian demands for a homeland on the Israeli-controlled West Bank of the Jordan River and on the Gaza Strip be handled? Israel did, among other things, return the Sinai to Egypt. Nevertheless, little progress was made on the remaining problems. The possibility of renewed war in the Middle East remained a constant threat.

President Carter's personal efforts to solve the Arab-Israeli conflict did not meet with unqualified approval. The Arabs were furious at what they called Sadat's "betrayal." Also they criticized Carter for bringing Egypt and Israel together into even an uncertain relationship. But many American critics felt that the President had tilted his influence toward the Egyptian-Palestinian side in order to maintain the good will of the Arab oil-exporting nations, particularly Saudi Arabia.

Iran. For many years Iran, across the Persian Gulf from Saudi Arabia's rich oil fields, had been a key to United States defense arrangements in the Middle East. Back in 1953 the United States had helped overthrow what it considered a pro-Communist government in Iran. With American backing the Shah Mohammed Reza Pahlevi had been restored to his throne. During the 1970's the Shah received about $8 billion worth of American military

▲ Sadat was assassinated by extremists in his country in 1981. Leaders from all over the world traveled to Egypt to mourn his death and show their respect.

931

equipment. The Shah harshly repressed political opponents. His secret police, some of whom had been trained by Americans, were accused of torturing and murdering such opponents.

Anger against the Shah flared up in a revolution in 1979, and the Shah fled the country. His government was overthrown by a militant religious leader, the Ayatollah Khomeini (ah·yah·TOL·ah ko·MAY·nee) and his followers. The new leaders blamed the United States for the sufferings the Iranian people had endured under the Shah. They bitterly resented President Carter's decision to admit the Shah into the United States for medical reasons at the very time the Iranian leaders were demanding his return for trial.

American hostages in Iran. In an attempt to force the United States to return the Shah to Iran, on November 4, 1979, a group of Iranian militants seized 53 American hostages in the American Embassy and in the Foreign Office in Teheran.

President Carter reacted by freezing some $8 billion of Iranian assets held by the United States and warned Iran of possible boycotts.

He urged America's allies to add their pressure in defense of international law.

After almost six months, the Iranian leaders had either refused or were unable to secure the release of the hostages. A daring military rescue mission ended in disaster due to mechanical failures in the desert some 200 miles (320 kilometers) from Teheran with the loss of 8 Americans.

The hostages remained in Iran, and it seemed that little progress was being made toward their release. American naval and air forces in the Indian Ocean and the Persian Gulf area continued the buildup in strength that had been started several months earlier.

The situation grew still more dangerous when a border dispute led to war between Iran and Iraq in September. Iran accused the United States of pushing Iraq to go to war to punish Iran for holding the hostages.

Finally, the Algerian government helped to negotiate an agreement between Iran and the United States. On January 20, 1981, just as Ronald Reagan took his oath as President, the hostages were freed. After 444 days of captivity, they returned to the United States.

The American hostages who had been held for more than a year in Teheran, Iran, returned to the United States as popular heroes. Their release from captivity was a cause of celebration for many Americans.

A cartoon satirizes President Carter's attempts to build a united front against Communism. The cartoon on the wall is a parody of a colonial cartoon urging American colonists to unite against Great Britain.

The Carter Doctrine. Early in January 1980, the Soviets invaded Afghanistan, a Muslim country on the eastern border of Iran. They intended to replace the existing pro-Communist head of government with another leader whom the Soviets considered more receptive to Soviet influence. The Soviet invasion of Afghanistan brought Communist troops to the Persian Gulf, the lifeline to vital oil supplies.

President Carter labeled the Soviet move a serious threat to world peace. He then warned the Soviet Union to withdraw from Afghanistan. When the Soviets showed no intention of withdrawing, the United States made several countermoves. Carter ordered a cut in sales of electronic equipment and grain to the Soviet Union. The United States withdrew from the 1980 summer Olympics in Moscow, and urged other countries to follow suit. Congress made it clear that a key arms limitation treaty between the Soviet Union and the United States would be postponed indefinitely. The treaty's rejection would mean that a new arms race costing both countries vast sums was almost certain.

Finally, the President announced what was called the <u>Carter Doctrine</u>. He declared that any use of military force by the Soviet Union in the Persian Gulf would be met with a major military response by the United States. The United States thus seemed to be stating that its national interest included the defense not only of Japan and Western Europe, but also of the Middle East and the Persian Gulf.

SECTION REVIEW

See underscored items, text pp. 930 - 33.

Identify: Cyrus Vance, Zbigniew Brzezinski, Angola civil war, Andrew Young, President Sadat, Premier Begin, Shah Mohammed Reza Pahlevi, Ayatollah Khomeini, Carter Doctrine

For answers to questions, see Answer Key, p.A127.

1. **Summarizing Ideas:** Describe President Carter's foreign policy goals.

2. **Determining Cause and Effect: (a)** What were the terms of the Panama Canal treaties? **(b)** Why did they cause controversy?

3. **Analyzing Ideas: (a)** How did President Carter move Israel and Egypt closer to peace? **(b)** What problems remained?

4. **Sequencing Ideas:** Describe the events that led to the taking of American hostages in Iran in 1979.

Discussion topic: Compare the foreign policy goals of Presidents Kennedy, Johnson, Nixon, Ford, Carter, and Reagan.

933

See Teaching Suggestions in TMRG, pp.TM224-25.

President Reagan's first term was marked by outbreaks of trouble in Central America and the Middle East. Relations between the United States and the Soviet Union also reached their coolest level since the early 1960's.

Relations with the Soviet Union. Reagan was a longtime foe of communism. He had opposed President Nixon's policy of détente. He also believed that President Carter's emphasis on human rights directed attention away from a great danger—the buildup of Soviet power.

President Reagan made it clear that his administration would oppose Soviet expansion everywhere, even at the risk of confrontation. To carry out this policy, Reagan called for large increases in military spending. He wanted new weapons systems for the military and an increased American presence in such areas as the Indian Ocean and the Persian Gulf.

Poland. Economic conditions in Poland, a satellite of the Soviet Union, had been growing steadily worse through the late 1970's. Many basic products were in short supply, and the prices of goods soared.

In 1980 a Polish labor union called Solidarity was formed. Its members demanded greater freedoms and economic reforms in the nation. The union won concessions from the communist government on a number of points. These victories led Solidarity to demand more reforms.

By December 1981 tensions were high. In a lightning move, the Polish government declared **martial law**, or rule by the military. The government sent troops to shut down key Solidarity centers and to arrest union leaders.

Many Americans believed that the Soviet Union, fearing a possible democratic revolt on its borders, had pressured the Polish government to take action. Soviet troops lined the Polish border, ready to "restore order" as they had in Hungary in 1956 and in Czechoslovakia in 1968.

President Reagan warned the Soviet Union not to take action. To back up his words, he called for new trade restrictions against the Soviets, mainly in the area of computers and other types of electronic equipment. He also asked United States allies to support the trade restrictions.

The Soviet Union stayed out of Poland, but martial law remained in effect until 1983. Solidarity had been broken, and United States-Soviet relations worsened.

The people of Poland rallied behind the banners of Solidarity in 1980 and 1981. Tragically, the government cut short the Poles' brief experiment in freedom with the declaration of martial law in December 1981.

In the early 1980's, South Africa's apartheid policy came under increasing criticism from individuals and governments throughout the world. In July 1985, the United States Congress passed a bill limiting American trade with South Africa until the South African government modified its racial policies.

Missiles and arms control. Arms control proved another source of East-West friction. As part of the arms buildup, Reagan wanted American military installations in Europe to have more up-to-date nuclear missiles.

Many people in the European countries where the missiles would be located opposed such a move. They feared that Europe might become the battleground on which a nuclear war between the United States and the Soviet Union would be fought. Some European nations had already expressed reluctance at being drawn into disputes between the superpowers. For example, several European allies of the United States had refused to support Reagan's call for trade restrictions against the Soviet Union. Now, millions of Europeans joined in demonstrations against the installation of new missiles. Leaders of these countries urged President Reagan to reach arms control agreements with the Soviet Union.

For a time there seemed to be progress toward a resumption of meaningful talks. Yuri Andropov became the new leader of the Soviet Union late in 1982. At that time Reagan offered to work with Andropov on arms control. But serious talks concerning strategic arms limitations were delayed because of a series of events which occurred over the next three years.

In August 1983 the Soviets shot down a Korean passenger airliner that had entered their territory. All 269 passengers, including several Americans, were killed. Despite condemnations from leaders around the world and President Reagan, the Soviets refused to apologize for the incident, claiming the plane had been on a spying mission. Later that year, the deployment of American missiles in Europe provoked the Soviets to walk out of the arms control talks. Finally, in 1984 the Soviet Union boycotted the Olympic Games in Los Angeles, California.

United States–Soviet relations were also hampered by the death of both Andropov and his successor, Konstantin Chernenko, within two years. In an effort to improve relations, President Reagan and the new Soviet leader, Michail Gorbachev, held a summit meeting in Geneva in November 1985. Although the two leaders made little progress on the substantive issues, people around the world were relieved that the superpowers were talking again.

Events in the Middle East. The Middle East remained a hot spot. The war between Iran and Iraq dragged on, with neither side able to gain the upper hand. As long as it continued, serious dangers for the rest of the world would persist. Oil supplies to other nations might be cut off, causing another severe shortage. Or the war might spread throughout the Middle East.

Egypt, which had become a major American ally in the Middle East, faced a crisis of its own. President Anwar Sadat was assassinated in October 1981. His successor, Hosni Mubarak, pledged to continue Sadat's policies, but by 1984 Egypt's relations with Israel had cooled. Arab countries that had broken with Egypt after the Camp David treaty began to resume relations.

Conflict in Lebanon. One of the toughest problems in the Middle East involved the Palestinians who had left their lands after the founding of Israel in 1948. Many still lived as refugees. Many still wanted to reclaim their lands from Israel.

By the 1970's many former Palestinians had settled in Lebanon, to the north of Israel. The best-known and strongest Palestinian group, the Palestine Liberation Organization (PLO) was centered there.

In the summer of 1982, Israel launched massive attacks against Palestinian positions in Lebanon. Israel was seeking to wipe out bases from which the PLO could make raids and to destroy its effectiveness.

The United States protested the Israeli action, fearing it could lead to wider war. In spite of this, Israel pressed its attacks and forced the PLO out of Lebanon.

To ensure the safety of the PLO as it pulled out, an international force entered Lebanon. American Marines were a part of that group. The peacekeeping force did its job, but had to return to Lebanon when fighting increased between Christian and Islamic groups there.

As marines became targets in the civil unrest and American deaths increased, many in the United States public and in Congress feared that the nation was getting too deeply involved in Lebanon. President Reagan said that a pullout of the marines would damage both hopes for peace and American prestige. The President and Congress compromised. The marines would stay, but with an 18-month time limit.

Within weeks of that agreement, a terrorist bomb killed 241 marines at their base in Lebanon. In a similar attack, 56 members of the French peacekeeping force died. By early 1984 the United States and other nations of the force were pulling their troops out of Lebanon.

Israel also pulled its troops back to southern Lebanon. Still, peace did not come. Fighting for control of the government continued. And in September, 12 people were killed in another terror bombing at the American Embassy in Beirut.

Nicaragua and El Salvador. President Reagan ▲ faced his most serious crisis in Central America, in the nations of Nicaragua and El Salvador. In both nations a small, very rich group controlled the government, usually with the support of the military. The large majority of people in both countries were poor, with little voice in government and little hope of any reform. Political dissent in both countries was harshly repressed.

In 1979 Nicaraguan rebels known as Sandinistas overthrew the dictatorship of Anastasio Somoza Debayle, whose family had ruled, with strong United States backing, since the 1930's. The Carter administration quickly recognized the new five-member junta, or ruling group, and sent Nicaragua $83 million in economic aid. The junta, however, also accepted aid and advisers from Cuba and delayed the free elections it had promised.

When Reagan took office, he cut aid to Nicaragua. He charged that the Sandinistas were exporting unrest to other nations in Central America by shipping Cuban and Soviet weapons to rebels in those nations. As an example, Reagan pointed to El Salvador.

El Salvador had experienced revolution in 1979. A military group, promising reforms, seized power at that time. But the new military government proved more repressive than the old. Soon fierce fighting broke out between the government forces and guerrillas. These guerrillas were Communists, Reagan charged, backed by the Sandinistas.

A search for solutions. Reagan's plan to control the Communist threat in Central America had a number of parts. He favored sending aid to the Nicaraguans known as contras, who were waging their own guerrilla war against the Sandinistas. He also wanted massive military and economic aid for the government of El Salvador. Reagan felt that, with United States support, democratic reforms could be made there, if the government could hold off a communist takeover.

Reagan sent American advisers to train El Salvador's troops. Congress also voted for aid

▲   Discussion topic: The relationship of Central American governments to the security of the United States.

"There's a freedom train a comin', but you've got to register to ride." This was the message of a recent voter registration drive directed by the Reverend Jesse Jackson.

While in college, Jackson took part in the civil rights march from Selma to Montgomery, Alabama, with Dr. Martin Luther King, Jr. In Chicago in1971, Jackson formed Operation PUSH (People United to Save Humanity) to instill pride in the city's blacks. The program's success won Jackson national attention.

In the early 1980's Jackson became influential in political circles. In 1983, his voter registration drive among blacks in Chicago helped Harold Washington become that city's first black mayor. In November 1983, Jackson declared his candidacy for the 1984 Democratic Presidential nomination. He urged the formation of a "rainbow coalition" of the poor, minorities, and women — people he identified as "the desperate, the disinherited, and the despised." Jackson's primary campaign earned him 458 1/2 votes at the Democratic nominating convention.

to El Salvador. Congress was not as quick to support the contras, especially when it learned that the American CIA was helping them mine Nicaraguan ports.

Reagan also demonstrated his willingness to use force to stop the spread of communism. The government of <u>Grenada</u>, a tiny Caribbean island, had been overthrown. Reagan said that the overthrow was part of a Soviet-Cuban move to make the island a center for the export of revolution. In October 1983 he sent American troops to Grenada. Order and a government more favorable to the United States were quickly restored.

Reagan's move in Grenada worried many Americans. Was it a rehearsal for a similar move in Central America? Debate over America's role in the region increased in Congress. Was it right to support the contras? Did the presence of American military advisers mean that the United States was risking a Vietnam-like war in El Salvador? If the guerrillas won in El Salvador, would Communist revolution spread?

New events raised new questions and some hopes. In 1984 El Salvador held free elections. Its new president, <u>José Napoleon Duarte</u>, offered to meet with the guerrillas and discuss ways to reach peace. In Nicaragua the junta promised to hold free elections in November 1984, though Reagan warned that such elections might be a fraud.

Other Latin-American countries tried to solve the region's problems. Mexico, Panama, Venezuela, and Colombia—countries known as the <u>Contadora group</u>—proposed a treaty. The treaty would limit military forces and guarantee political reforms. Hopes that the Central American nations would accept the treaty were high.

SECTION REVIEW
See underscored items, text pp. 934 - 37.

Identify: Solidarity, martial law, Konstantin Chernenko, Palestine Liberation Organization, junta, Sandinistas, Grenada, José Napoleon Duarte, Contadora group

For answers to questions, see Answer Key, pp.A127-28.

1. **Summarizing Ideas:** What was President Reagan's main foreign policy objective?

2. **Analyzing Viewpoints: (a)** Why did President Reagan want to ship missiles to Europe? **(b)** Why did some of the United States' allies object to this?

3. **Determining Cause and Effect: (a)** Why did Israel invade Lebanon in 1982? **(b)** How did the United States become involved?

4. **Comparing Ideas:** Explain briefly how similar events in Nicaragua and El Salvador led to different results in those nations' relations with the United States.

DEVELOPING HISTORY STUDY SKILLS

Reading About History   Interpreting News Stories

Newspapers and newsmagazines can be important sources of historical information. Through their articles newspapers chronicle the major events of the day. Unlike an editorial which states an opinion, a news story should be objective. It should supply information and let the reader make the judgment.

A standard news story usually follows this format. First a headline briefly states the main idea of the article. This is followed by a dateline that indicates where and sometimes when the story was written, if the writing did not take place in the newspaper's office. A byline indicating the author of the article sometimes precedes the article. In the standard format the lead or first paragraph contains all the essential information about the subject. It usually tells *who, what, when,* and *where.* If the first paragraph does not answer *how* or *why,* the next paragraph may. Often the rest of the article gives details to explain *how* and *why.*

Students of history are often called on to interpret and draw conclusions from news stories. You have already been introduced to the skills necessary to interpret a news story: analyzing information (Chapter 12, pages 301–02), analyzing viewpoints (Chapter 19, pages 449–50), identifying bias (Chapter 6, pages 146–47), and identifying assumptions (Chapter 20, pages 556–67). You might wish to review the skills on those pages before interpreting a news story.

How to Interpret a News Story

To effectively interpret a news story, follow these steps.

1. **Read the headline.** Determine the story's main idea.

2. **Check for a dateline and byline.** If present, note when the story was written, where, and by whom.

3. **Read the first paragraph.** Note the answers to the questions *who, what, where,* and *when.*

4. **Read the rest of the story.** Determine, if possible, the answers to *how* and *why.* Identify the historical content of the story. Evaluate the reliability of the story.

5. **Identify bias.** Look for words that may slant the story. Analyze the facts that are presented to evaluate the objectivity of the article.

6. **Analyze the story.** Use the information to draw conclusions and form generalizations.

Applying the Skill

Read the news story on page 939. Look for the main idea of the story, when it was written, where it was written, and by whom. Look also for supporting details.

Now review your findings. The headline indicates that the story is about peace talks between U.S. Secretary of States George P. Shultz and King Hussein of Jordan. The story was written in Washington, on May 31, by Bernard Gwertzman. The first paragraphs provide these answers.

- What — Talks with King Hussein over the prospects for Middle East peace had advanced significantly but difficulties remained.
- Who — Secretary of State Shultz and King Hussein
- When — May 31
- Where — a news conference in Washington, D.C.

Though the how and why questions are not directly answered, the article gives background information on the current difficulties in the peace negotiations.

The story appears objective. Note that nowhere is the writer's view apparent. Also, no emotional words are used by the reporter to slant the story. The opinions of both sides seem fairly stated as well. This story is a factual, objective report of a news conference held by Secretary Shultz on May 31.

Practicing the Skill

Select and read a news story from the front page of a recent newspaper or the lead story in a recent newsmagazine. Then on a separate sheet of paper, answer these questions.

1. What is the headline of the article?

2. Where was the story written? **(b)** When was it written?

3. **(a)** Does the story include a byline? **(b)** If so, who wrote the article?

4. How do the first paragraphs answer these questions: **(a)** Who? **(b)** What? **(c)** Where? **(d)** When?

5. **(a)** Are the how and why questions answered? **(b)** If, so, what answer for each is given?

6. Is the story you selected objective? Explain.

SHULTZ LISTS GAINS FOR MIDEAST PEACE FROM HUSSEIN VISIT

But Key Differences Remain on Organizing Talks With Israel and Palestinians

BY BERNARD GWERTZMAN

Special to *The New York Times*

WASHINGTON, May 31 — Secretary of State George P. Shultz said today that talks with King Hussein of Jordan during his visit here this week had advanced the prospects for Middle East peace "in a very significant way."

But he said the differences remained on the key question of how to organize negotiations between Israel and a Jordanian-Palestinian delegation.

In a news conference summing up the Reagan Administration's view of the four days of talks that ended tonight, Mr. Shultz said, "There are obstacles between here and the time when King Hussein and his delegation can sit down with Israel, but there is motion today."

Impetus to Peacemaking

"The King's visit has given impetus to the process of peacemaking," Mr. Shultz said. "I think what the King has done is move the process in a very significant way."

Mr. Shultz said there had been active discussions with King Hussein on the next step advocated by the Jordanian leader: a meeting between the United States and a Jordan-Palestinian delegation to prepare the way for negotiations with Israel.

In explaining why the Reagan Administration judged King Hussein's mission here to have been so positive, even though some of what he said was not greatly different from previous Jordanian positions, Mr. Shultz mentioned several statements by the Jordanian leader.

He noted that King Hussein had said on Wednesday that Jordan and the Palestine Liberation Organization were committed to negotiating with Israel and to start these talks by the end of the year if possible. Differences persist, however, over the Jordan-P.L.O. insistence on holding the talks under the "umbrella" of an international conference, an idea opposed by the United States and Israel.

Mr. Shultz cited the apparent P.L.O. willingness now to abide by key Security Council resolutions, as stated by King Hussein. And he said approvingly that King Hussein had said negotiations with Israel should proceed "in a nonbelligerent environment," which would suggest that there was no place for terrorist acts while the talks went on.

But beyond these specifics, the Reagan Administration seemed to share King Hussein's view that the situation for the Middle East peace efforts seemed more right than it had for some time.

Reflection on Lebanon

King Hussein, in a speech this morning, said "the Lebanese tragedy has caused both Israelis and Palestinians to reassess the validity of their previous policies."

"Each is considering the need for negotiated peace," he said. "Each is skeptical. The Palestinians need hope, the Israelis need trust. It is important for all of us to provide the hope and the trust they need."

On the issue of the makeup of a Palestinian negotiating team, Mr. Shultz said there had been "a little headway" on finding Palestinians who would be acceptable to the United States. The Administration has said it will meet with a joint group if it will lead to negotiations with Israel and if the Palestinians are not members of the Palestine Liberation Organization — in absence of the P.L.O. openly agreeing to American conditions for recognizing the organization.

Mr. Shultz said he would not object to delegates who were members of the Palestine National Council and not P.L.O. members if they were "people of good will, who are thoughtful, responsible and truly dedicated to nonviolent, negotiated solutions and are truly ready to strive for peace with Israel."

The council is a 400-member group that includes both P.L.O. and non-P.L.O. members and serves as the quasi-parliament for the liberation group. Israeli officials have said they regard national council membership as tantamount to P.L.O. affiliation because the P.L.O. choose the P.N.C.

The Israelis assert that both Palestinian groups are dedicated to destroying Israel. King Hussein, who has insisted throughout this visit that the P.L.O. leadership had given him the authority to speak for it here, told a dozen members of Congress on Thursday that Yasir Arafat, the P.L.O. leader, had agreed to name non-P.L.O. members to a joint delegation, but wanted at least some P.N.C. members chosen.

The new development during King Hussein's visit was his public declaration, repeated in a long speech today, that the P.L.O. had authorized him to say that it had finally agreed to negotiate with Israel on the basis of two key United Nations Security Council Resolutions, No. 242 of 1967, and No. 338 of 1973. He made the speech before the American Enterprise Institute, a Washington-based public policy research group.

The United States has said it will not deal with the Palestinian Liberation Organization until the group recognizes both Israel's right to exist and those two resolutions.

When John F. Kennedy became President in January 1961, the United States and the Soviet Union were locked in the cold war. The Soviet attempt to install long-range missiles in Cuba brought the two great powers to the brink of a nuclear war. Fortunately, reason prevailed and the Soviet Union withdrew the offensive weapons.

Under President Johnson the United States became involved in what turned out to be the longest and most costly war in the nation's history. The Vietnam conflict was costly in lives, in money and resources, and in its divisive effect upon the American people.

During the Nixon-Ford years, the United States withdrew from Vietnam, reopened its ties with China, and began to establish improved relations with the Soviet Union. Détente with the Soviet Union offered visions of improved international relations and even a lasting peace. As President Carter's term drew to a close and President Reagan's term began, the period of détente seemed to fade. President Reagan made it clear that he would oppose Soviet expansion everywhere, even at the risk of confrontation.

There were few heartening developments in America's foreign affairs. A highlight during the Carter years was the peace treaty between Egypt and Israel negotiated with Carter's personal help. However, by 1980 no decisions had been reached on the basic issues dividing the Arabs and the Israelis. An area of growing concern during the 1980's was continued United States involvement in Central American and Caribbean affairs.

CONNECTING CHAPTER IDEAS

While the United States sought to assume a role as world leader, women and minority groups were fighting for their share of the "American dream." In the next chapter you will read about the progress made by women and minorities. You will also read how the new patterns of population growth and distribution drastically altered the way Americans lived.

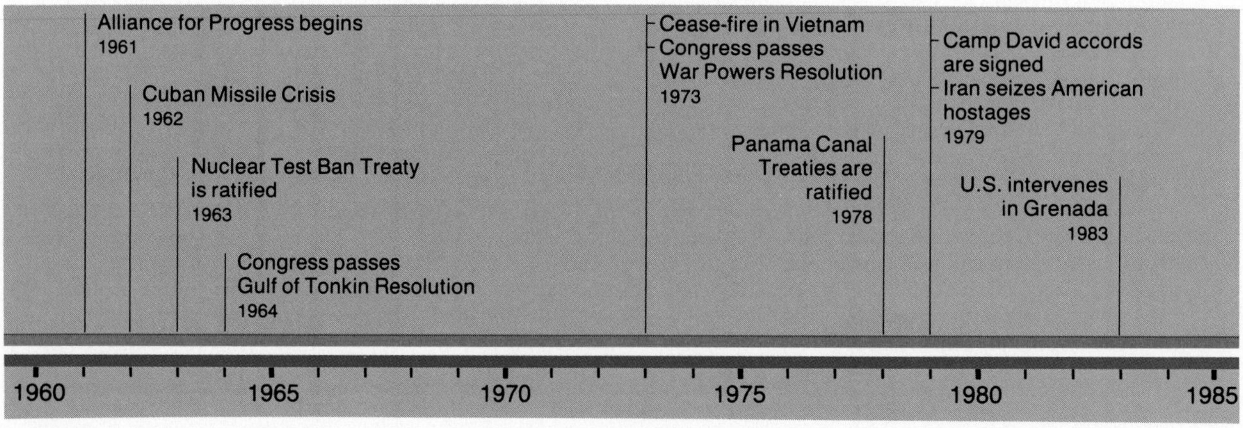

Alliance for Progress begins
1961

Cuban Missile Crisis
1962

Nuclear Test Ban Treaty
is ratified
1963

Congress passes
Gulf of Tonkin Resolution
1964

Cease-fire in Vietnam
Congress passes
War Powers Resolution
1973

Panama Canal
Treaties are
ratified
1978

Camp David accords
are signed
Iran seizes American
hostages
1979

U.S. intervenes
in Grenada
1983

1960   1965   1970   1975   1980   1985

CHAPTER 41 REVIEW

Reviewing Important Terms

Decide whether each of the following sentences is true or false. If the sentence is false, replace the underlined term with the word or phrase that will make it true.

1. The newly independent nations of Asia and Africa that refuse to align themselves with either the Soviet Union or the United States are sometimes called the Third World.
2. During the Cuban Missile Crisis, President Kennedy ordered the Navy to establish a quarantine around Cuba.
3. In Vietnam, search-and-destroy missions were part of the American military strategy in the late 1960's.
4. In January 1973, a treaty ended United States participation in the Vietnam War.
5. The relaxation of tensions between the United States and the Soviet Union in the early 1970's was called disarmament.
6. President Carter emphasized human rights as an important element of foreign policy in his administration.
7. President Eisenhower had warned that the spread of communism in Southeast Asia would have a domino effect.
8. President Reagan called for new trade restrictions against the Soviet Union after the Communist government in Poland declared a junta.

Practicing Critical Thinking Skills

1. **Summarizing Ideas.** (a) What was the policy of détente worked out by Nixon and Kissinger? (b) What major changes among Communist nations made this new policy possible? (c) How did the Arab–Israeli War of 1973 test détente?
2. **Organizing Ideas.** (a) Why did the United States commit itself to opposing Communist expansion in Southeast Asia? (b) Describe the actions taken by the Kennedy, Johnson and Nixon administrations with regard to Vietnam.
3. **Interpreting Ideas.** Describe the impact of the Vietnam War on (a) Vietnam and (b) the United States.
4. **Analyzing Sources.** Study the excerpt from the Gulf of Tonkin Resolution on page 922. (a) What power does it give the President? (b) According to the document, what events led Congress to pass the resolution? (c) How was this resolution used to justify sending American troops to Viet-

nam? (d) Should the president have the power given to him by this resolution? Explain.
5. **Seeing Relationships.** How has competition between the United States and the Soviet Union affected events in (a) Africa and (b) the Middle East since the 1960's?
6. **Relating Past to Present.** (a) What are the trouble spots in the world today? (b) How are events occurring in those trouble spots today influenced by events that occurred during the 1960's and 1970's?

Developing History Study Skills

Interpreting a News Story. Read the following news story and then answer the questions below.

By Barry Schweid, Associated Press

> UNITED NATIONS—President Reagan, declaring he is ready for "constructive negotiations" with the Soviet Union, today proposed regular meetings between senior experts from the two sides to reduce tensions and the threat of war.
> "We recognize that there is no sane alternative to negotiations on arms control and other issues between our two nations," Reagan said in a prepared speech to the U.N. General Assembly.

(a) Where was this news story written? (b) How do the first two paragraphs answer the questions *who, what, when, where,* and *why*? (c) What would be a good headline for this story? (d) Write an editorial on the subject matter of this article.

Relating Geography and History

Since 1960, the rivalry between the United States and the Soviet Union has created numerous trouble spots, the realignment of alliances has caused friction, and the emergence of new nations has resulted in conflict. To recognize the global scope of the United States' role in world affairs, complete the following activities.

1. Prepare a list of the areas of conflict or tension mentioned in this chapter. Be sure to include the date(s) of the incident(s) on your list.
2. Circle in red all the incidents on your list involving the United States and the Soviet Union.
3. Based on the information in your textbook, form two generalizations about the confrontation between communism and democracy.

See Chapter Overview in TMRG, p.TM226.
See Chapter Objectives in TMRG, p.TM226.
See Introducing the Chapter in TMRG, p.TM226.

CHAPTER 42

Reaching for Freedom's Promise

Changing Ways   (1960 to the Present)

Becoming a
U.S. citizen

From colonial days to the present, more than 50 million immigrants have come to the United States. Many immigrants have come seeking greater opportunities than they could have hoped for in the lands of their birth. The majority of immigrants during the past one hundred years entered through New York harbor. Their first glimpse of the New World was the Statue of Liberty, the symbol of freedom and justice.

In recent years, however, the ports of entry for the immigrants and the countries of their origin have changed dramatically. Many of the newcomers entered through Florida, or crossed the border from Mexico, or passed through the ports along the Pacific coast. Today men, women, and children from Asia, the Middle East, Mexico, Central and South America, and the West Indies far outnumber immigrants from Europe.

These new immigrants have joined the nation's other minorities, including blacks and Indians, who had long carried a burden of prejudice and discrimination. Now minorities throughout the nation are demanding that the United States truly become a nation of equal opportunity for all.

In the 1960's the nation entered a time of unprecedented upheaval that was to last through the 1970's. In the 1980's, a time of consolidation has taken place. The number of farms has declined, but the size of farms has increased. New suburbs have developed where farms once stood. The values the American people traditionally have lived by have stood the test of time and will continue to influence new generations of Americans.

READING FOCUS

As you read about the struggles of women and minorities for equal rights, look for the details that support each of the following statements.

1. New patterns of population growth and distribution alter ways of life.
2. Black Americans demand equal rights and opportunities.
3. Hispanics share the struggle for freedom and justice.
4. Indians refuse to accept the role of "vanishing Americans."
5. Women redouble efforts to win equal rights and opportunities.

1 New patterns of population growth and distribution alter ways of life

See Teaching Suggestions in TMRG, pp.TM226-27.

During the years after 1960, America's population continued to grow and shift. The movement from rural to urban areas continued. This led to a severe crisis for American cities.

Growth of population. By 1980 there were 47 million more people living in the United States than there had been in 1960. The increase in that 20-year period alone—from 179 million in 1960 to more than 226 million in 1980—almost equaled the total population of the country a century earlier.

One reason for this growth was the remarkable advances made by medical science. Antibiotics and many other drugs created in the postwar years made important contributions. So, too, did new methods and improved instruments for diagnosis and treatment. As a result, doctors reduced the nation's death rate, especially among children.

In the years following World War II, the birth rate soared to an average level of 3.5 births per woman. By the 1970's, however, the birth rate was slowing down. In December 1972 the Census Bureau reported that it had dropped to about 2 births per woman. This is the level of Zero Population Growth (ZPG). This birth rate replaces the existing population but does not increase it.

The birth rate reached its lowest point in the nation's history in 1976. Although it rose slightly during the remaining years of the 1970's, it seemed having two children was the popular goal for many American families.

The redistribution of people. The growing ▲ mobility of Americans also had far-reaching effects, particularly after 1960. Americans were increasingly able and willing to move from place to place. In earlier times many people had lived their whole lives in the areas in which they were born. However, by the 1960's and 1970's, this pattern was changing. One out of every five Americans was moving to a new residence each year.

These population movements affected different sections of the country in different ways.

▲ Refer the students to the map on page 1005. Ask the students for evidence from the map that shows the redistribution of people. Have the students cite examples.

943

The West and the South, particularly the Sunbelt areas, became the fastest-growing sections of the nation. In 1964 California passed New York to become the most populous state. During the 1970's about 40 percent of the nation's total population growth occurred in the Sunbelt states of Florida, Texas, and California.

Meanwhile, the states of the Northeast were losing population in relation to the rest of the country. By 1980 the high cost of home heating during the cold winters was convincing more and more people to move to the warmer southern states.

Change in rural population. Another dramatic change in American life was the sharp decline in farm population. Between 1940 and 1980, the number of people living on farms dropped from more than 30 million to around 6 million. In some years more than 1 million men and women left the farms to seek better opportunities elsewhere.

By the 1970's each farm worker was producing enough food for more than 50 people. American farms were producing more than enough food to feed Americans. From the 1960's through the 1980's, farm products were a substantial part of the nation's total exports.

Better strains of plants, greater use of fertilizer, and improved breeds of livestock made such productivity possible. These new developments combined to raise the average yield of some farm crops by as much as 50 percent. At the same time, worker productivity increased twice as fast on the farm as it did in industry.

Although the farm population was shrinking, rural areas and their small towns were growing faster than metropolitan areas. Between 1970 and 1980, nonmetropolitan areas grew by 15.4 percent. Metropolitan areas grew only by 9.1 percent.

Improved transportation and communication systems allowed many businesses to move out of urban centers. Also the rural areas did not suffer from many of the problems that troubled the nation's older urban areas.

Urban areas. Many of those who left farms moved to urban areas. These urban areas included central cities and the suburbs around them. These cities and their suburbs were

The 1970's and 1980's witnessed the rapid urbanization of rural areas. This photo shows the construction of a modern office complex in a rural area. Such new construction is often followed by more construction.

A gift from France to the United States, the Statue of Liberty rises 302 feet (92 meters) above Liberty Island in New York Harbor. Officially called *Liberty Enlightening the World,* the statue has come to represent a new way of life for millions of immigrants to the United States.

The statue was first proposed in 1865 by the French historian Edouard de Laboulaye. Construction of the monument began in France under the direction of sculptor Frederic-Auguste Bartholdi and was financed by contributions from the French people. Engineer Gustave Eiffel, who later built the Eiffel Tower in Paris, designed the statue's gigantic interior steel supports. Laborers pounded out by hand the thin copper sheets that were assembled over Eiffel's framework.

In 1884 the completed statue was disassembled and shipped to New York City in 214 packing crates. The statue was dedicated in 1886 and became a national monument in 1924. Private contributions from both France and the United States sponsored a complete restoration of *Liberty* in honor of the statue's centennial in 1986.

closely related. Originally the cities were the work-places and the suburbs were the living areas. Gradually the boundaries between the cities and the suburbs became harder to draw.

These city-suburbs combinations were given the name of Metropolitan Statistical Areas (MSA's). By 1980 there were over 280 MSA's in the nation. Over 72 percent of the nation's population lived in such areas.

New immigrants. These MSA's received a swelling tide of men and women from other lands. During the 1960's and 1970's, immigration increased sharply. Patterns of immigration also changed dramatically.

The Immigration and Nationality Act of 1965 abolished the old national origins acts of the 1920's (see page 768). It also changed the ethnic character of the nation's population. The new law provided for the annual admission of 120,000 immigrants from the Western Hemisphere and 170,000 from all other nations. No more than 20,000 could come from any single country. Preference was to be given to members of families of American citizens and to people with specialized skills.

One result of the law was a sharp increase in the number of Asians and Hispanics entering the country. By the mid-1970's more than 300,000 were arriving each year. In 1977, for example, some 150,000 Asians and more than 200,000 Hispanics entered.

Most of the newcomers, although by no means all, were poor. Most settled in the cities. There they moved into the homes and apartments left by the white middle class who had moved to the suburbs or back to rural areas. As immigrants and minorities moved into the cities, increasing numbers of whites moved out. This **white flight** contributed greatly to the decay of the cities.

The urban crisis. In the 1960's and 1970's, conditions in America's cities became desperate. Urban renewal programs had helped rebuild the business and financial areas of many cities. However, the older residential areas had often become heavily overcrowded. Many had deteriorated into slums. Property owners, discouraged by the flight of the middle class to the suburbs, refused to spend money to repair their buildings. The core areas of the cities were so

Discussion topic: Ask students to name specific problems in large cities they have lived in or visited. Then, lead a class discussion concerning possible solutions to these problems.

945

By the mid–1980's more than 25 million Americans — more than 10 percent of the population — were aged 65 or older. As the percentage of elderly persons in the population continued to rise, government-sponsored assistance for the aged became an increasingly complex issue.

badly run down that they needed to be entirely rebuilt. This would take years and require the investment of billions of dollars.

Meanwhile, people living in the slums needed more and better services — health, education, sanitation, recreation, and police and fire protection. They also needed jobs and job-training programs. However, the cities did not have the finances to do the work that had to be done. The people most able to pay the taxes needed to support such programs were leaving. Those least able to pay and most in need were becoming more numerous. City after city faced the prospect of bankruptcy.

"Social dynamite."   The urban crisis was in fact a national crisis. In 1961 James B. Conant of Harvard issued a report titled *Slums and Suburbs* that attracted nationwide attention. The report pointed out the alarming contrast between the poverty of life in the decaying cores of the cities and the growing wealth of the suburbs.

Nevertheless, during the next two decades, conditions grew steadily worse. "We are allowing social dynamite to accumulate in our large cities," Conant warned.

SECTION REVIEW

See underscored items, text pp. 943 - 46.
Identify: Zero Population Growth, Sunbelt, MSA, Immigration and Nationality Act of 1965, white flight, *Slums and Suburbs*

For answers to questions, see Answer Key, p.A129.

1. **Organizing Ideas:** How was each of these areas affected by population movements between 1960 and 1980: **(a)** Southwest, **(b)** Northeast, **(c)** rural areas, **(d)** suburbs?

2. **Analyzing Ideas:** How did changes in the Immigration and Nationality Act of 1965 change the ethnic character of the nation's population?

3. **Synthesizing Ideas:** What factors contributed to the urban crisis of the 1960's and 1970's?

---

2 Black Americans demand equal rights and opportunities

See Teaching Suggestions in TMRG, p.TM227.

The "social dynamite" that Conant had warned about exploded in city after city during the 1960's. Meanwhile, black Americans had grown frustrated with their slow progress toward full equality of opportunity. They became increasingly insistent upon "freedom now."

The civil rights movement. During the 1950's blacks at long last began to receive support from both the Supreme Court and Congress. As you have read (page 877), in 1954 the Supreme Court ruled that state and local laws requiring blacks to send their children to separate school systems violated the Fourteenth Amendment. Three years later Congress adopted the Civil Rights Act of 1957. This law, strengthened by a related act in 1960, authorized the Department of Justice to sue local officials who tried to prevent qualified blacks from voting.

These developments were immensely encouraging. More immediately important, however, was action taken by the blacks themselves. Under leaders such as the Reverend Martin Luther King, Jr., they began to use nonviolent methods, such as boycotts and peaceful demonstrations, to win their rights.

The **civil rights movement** that got under way in the late 1950's and early 1960's was a heroic struggle led and sustained by blacks. However, it also drew the active support of whites—particularly ministers, rabbis, nuns, priests, lawyers, writers, and students. The mass media also helped to stir the conscience of white America by bringing the details of the struggle into millions of homes.

Direct action. The movement developed a number of tactics to speed the integration of all public facilities. In addition to the boycott, which had been effective in Montgomery, Alabama (see page 878), the **sit-in** became a useful device. In February 1960 four black students in Greensboro, North Carolina, refused to leave a "whites-only" lunch counter at a department store until they were served. Day after day they returned. Meanwhile demonstrations in their support were staged across the nation. In July the Greensboro lunch counter was finally integrated. Similar sit-ins spread rapidly over the South to press for the integration of movie theaters, libraries, parks, and other public gathering places.

"Freedom rides" and "freedom marches" by whites and blacks also dramatized the struggle for civil rights. In 1963 A. Philip Randolph, a veteran black trade union leader, organized a march on Washington. More than 250,000

In 1967 President Johnson appointed Thurgood Marshall to the Supreme Court. Marshall is the first black American to serve on the nation's highest court.

men, women, and youths gathered in the nation's capital to support passage of a civil rights bill. The highlight of the event was Martin Luther King's "I have a dream" speech.

Other demonstrations followed, including the 1965 march for voting rights by more than 3,000 blacks and whites from Selma to Montgomery, Alabama. Thousands of walkers, blacks and whites, were led by Martin Luther King and protected by the National Guard along the 54-mile (86-kilometer) route.

Achievements. Congress responded to the protest movement with the Civil Rights Act of 1964 and the Voting Rights Act of 1965. The 1964 measure outlawed racial discrimination in employment and in public accommodations. The 1965 act authorized federal supervision of registration in districts where fewer than half of those of voting age were registered.

By the mid-1960's race barriers had been largely broken down in hotels and restaurants, in buses and trains and airlines, and in other public places. Impressive gains had also been made in voter registration. In 1965, for example, only 6 percent of the black citizens of Mississippi were registered to vote. By 1967 more than 33 percent had been registered.

In March 1965, Reverend Martin Luther King, Jr., (center) led a march from Selma, Alabama, to the state capital at Montgomery to demand voting rights for blacks. Such marches effectively drew attention to the need for federal civil rights legislation.

The gains in school desegregation in the South were slower. By 1967 token desegregation was a fact throughout the South. Nevertheless, only 16 percent of black southern students attended integrated schools.

In the fall of 1969, the Supreme Court, in its toughest ruling to date, ordered an end to all racially segregated school systems "at once." By the early 1970's, many southern school districts were integrated, and the movement continued throughout the decade.

By the 1970's, in fact, school segregation was more widespread in northern cities than in the South. The courts then began to rule against this **de facto segregation**° in the northern schools. Often they ordered the busing of students from one school to another to achieve a desired balance of races. Opposition to such busing was often fierce. Demonstrations, at times violent, erupted over busing in Boston, Chicago, and other cities.

A shifting emphasis. In spite of the gains, by the mid-1960's many blacks were frustrated. Essential though civil rights were, they did not

°**de facto segregation:** segregation that exists not by law, but because of neighborhood residence patterns.

provide adequate housing either in rural areas or in overcrowded city slums. They did not provide the training or education that allowed disadvantaged people to build a better way of life. It was also becoming clear that integrated schools were not necessarily better schools in terms of the quality of education they provided.

By the mid-1960's the goals of the movement had shifted from civil rights to economic and social issues—jobs, housing, and discrimination by businesses and by organized labor in hiring practices. But as the war in Vietnam absorbed more and more of the nation's resources, black Americans felt that their problems were being neglected. Their goal of equal opportunity seemed as remote as ever.

Violence in the inner city. The depth of ▲ black frustration was starkly revealed in riots that broke out in the community of Watts in Los Angeles, California, in the summer of 1965. The National Guard was finally called in to restore order. In the riots 4,000 persons were arrested, hundreds were injured, 34 were killed, and the damage from burning and looting totaled $35 million.

This urban violence shocked the nation. It especially alarmed those Americans, black and white alike, who had believed that the civil rights movement was making progress and that race relations were improving. Any lingering optimism in that regard was swept away during the next two years when rioting broke out in cities across the nation. Among the hardest hit were Detroit, Cleveland, Newark, Baltimore, and the nation's capital, Washington, D.C.

Many Americans, black as well as white, blamed the violence on a group of new militant black leaders, but this was by no means the whole truth. The rate of unemployment among black workers the country over was double that of white workers. Among black teenagers in the inner cities the jobless rate was much higher. As the riots demonstrated, poverty from which there seems to be no escape is a fertile breeding ground for violence.

New leaders and "black power." One of the best known of the new black leaders was Elijah Muhammad, who headed the Black Muslims, the largest and economically most powerful black group. Another was Malcolm X, formerly a Muslim minister, who preached that the black and white races could exist only if they

▲ Sadly and ironically, the most damage during the riots was done to the black communities themselves.

were completely separated from each other. Before his death, however, Malcolm X gave up his rigid racist position, referring to it as "sickness and madness." In 1965 he was assassinated by black radicals he had antagonized.

Among the other new leaders were Floyd McKissick and Stokely Carmichael, who had been active in militant civil rights organizations. Also included were the founders of the Black Panther Party—Huey P. Newton, Bobby Seale, and Eldridge Cleaver. The Black Panthers advocated immediate confrontation with "the white power structure" and the use of force, if necessary, to protect black Americans against aggressive "white racism."

Black extremists demanded **black power.** In economics, black power seemed to mean the growth of independent black businesses. In education it meant local community control of largely black schools. In politics it meant the growth of political power either by the formation of a black political party or by control of politics in black neighborhoods through bloc voting. Socially it meant black self-reliance, self-respect, and racial pride.

Moderate black leaders shared many of the objectives of the black power movement, but they rejected its tactics. Among these leaders were Roy Wilkins of the NAACP and Dr. Martin Luther King, Jr., head of the Southern Christian Leadership Conference (SCLC). King, the most influential of the black leaders and a devoted advocate of nonviolence, denounced the appeal to black racism and the threatened use of force. Those who rejected integration, he believed, did a cruel disservice to black people.

Signs of progress. By the mid-1960's the black power movement was making gains. Politically these gains were revealed in the election of black Americans to public office—for example, Edward W. Brooke of Massachusetts to the United States Senate; Carl B. Stokes and Richard Hatcher as mayors of Cleveland, Ohio, and Gary, Indiana, respectively; Julian Bond to the Georgia legislature. In addition, the Supreme Court also had its first black member, Justice Thurgood Marshall.

In the spring of 1968, Congress adopted a new civil rights act. The new act extended federal protection to civil rights workers and also included a guarantee of open housing. The open-housing provision barred discrimination in the sale or rental of all housing with the exception of owner-occupied-home sales.

The Kerner Commission. In the summer of 1967, President Johnson appointed a National Advisory Commission on Civil Disorders headed by Governor Kerner of Illinois to investigate inner city riots and violence. The Kerner Commission's report in 1968 was the most thorough federal study of the race problem.

The report acknowledged that gains had been made in civil rights laws and desegregation. However, it warned that little or nothing had been accomplished in those basic areas that mattered most to a majority of America's black people—housing, jobs, and economic security, educational opportunities, and living conditions in the inner cities. "Our nation," the Kerner Commission reported, "is moving toward two societies, one black, one white—separate and unequal."

SOURCES

MARTIN LUTHER KING, JR.'S "I HAVE A DREAM" SPEECH (1963)

. . . I say to you today, my friends, that in spite of the difficulties and frustrations of the moment I still have a dream. It is a dream deeply rooted in the American dream.

I have a dream that one day this nation will rise up and live out the true meaning of its creed: "We hold these truths to be self-evident; that all men are created equal."

I have a dream that one day on the red hills of Georgia the sons of former slaves and the sons of former slaveowners will be able to sit down together at the table of brotherhood. . . .

I have a dream that my four little children will one day live in a nation where they will not be judged by the color of their skin but by the content of their character.

I have a dream today. . . .

The commission warned of continued disorder and the destruction of democratic values unless improvements were made at once in those basic areas. This could be done, it said, only by "commitment to national action — compassionate, massive, and sustained."

The death of Martin Luther King, Jr. The assassination of Martin Luther King, Jr., Nobel Peace Prize winner and most respected of black leaders, on April 4, 1968, fell with stunning force on all Americans, white and black alike. Dr. King was in Memphis, Tennessee, to lead a nonviolent demonstration when he was killed by an assassin's bullets. In the last speech he made before his death, Dr. King said, "It is no longer a question of violence or nonviolence. It is nonviolence or nonexistence."

Dr. King's death was a grim reminder of the importance of the Kerner Commission's warnings. While the nation mourned the loss of Dr. King, riots broke out in Chicago and Washington. In 1983, Congress approved a federal holiday (the third Monday in January) to recognize Dr. King's accomplishments.

Political advances. The massive effort called for by the Kerner report did not develop. Yet neither its worst predictions nor the revolution threatened by radical black nationalists had taken place either.

In 1975 the Civil Rights Commission reported that many black citizens, as well as members of other minorities, were still prevented from voting by various unfair means. Even so, black citizens were making important political gains. By the end of the 1970's, 4,503 black Americans were serving in elected public offices. This number was only 10 percent of all such offices, but it was an improvement over earlier years. By the mid-1980's there were 17 black members of the House of Representatives. There were black mayors in such cities as Los Angeles, Atlanta, Chicago, Detroit, Gary, Newark, and Washington, D.C.

Andrew Young, a civil rights leader, served during part of Carter's administration as the outspoken United States Ambassador to the United Nations. Carter also appointed the first black woman to a Cabinet post. This was Patricia Harris, Secretary of Housing and Urban Development and, later, Secretary of Health, Education, and Welfare.

New black leaders were gaining greater political power. They were learning how to get out the black vote, an important factor in the election of President Carter in 1976. They were forming political alliances and making effective use of lobbying tactics.

An uncertain outlook. The Equal Rights Commission brought lawsuits against corporations and labor unions to end unfair employment practices. In a number of schools and businesses, **affirmative action** programs were begun. This meant that blacks and members of other minorities were at times given preference when applying to schools or for jobs. They were given preference even when their qualifications were no better than those of other applicants. The idea behind such programs was to make up for past discrimination, which had left blacks and minorities at a disadvantage. Nevertheless, many Americans objected. Such programs, they said, did not represent the ideal of "equal justice for all." They were instead, critics claimed, reverse discrimination.

The Supreme Court ruled on an affirmative action case in 1978. Allan Bakke, a white, had been turned down by a medical school when he tried to enroll. Bakke claimed that his qualifications were equal to or better than those of blacks who had been admitted under a quota system. (A quota system sets aside a fixed number of places for certain categories of people, in this case, blacks.) Bakke was, he said, a victim of reverse discrimination. The Court agreed with Bakke and ordered the school to admit him.

The Reagan administration and blacks. In his first term President Reagan took several stands that were unpopular with many blacks. Reagan was on record as opposing affirmative action programs. He also favored giving tax breaks to segregated private schools, but the measure never passed. Reagan also fought unsuccessfully against an extension of the Voting Rights Act of 1965 that would help blacks register to vote. Many blacks felt Reagan's actions on the two bills showed he was not concerned with black needs.

Blacks and the economy. Reagan's domestic policies also disturbed blacks. The budget cuts that Reagan called for (see Chapter 40) affected federal jobs programs, welfare payments, Medicaid, Medicare, and food stamps. Many blacks relied on the help that these programs provided.

Dr. Martin Luther King, Jr., the Nobel-Prize-winning civil rights leader, was assassinated in Memphis, Tennessee, on April 4, 1968. As people across the nation mourned, his widow, Coretta Scott King, bore her grief and made plans to go on with his work. Within a short time, Mrs. King gained recognition in her own right as a major civil rights leader.

Coretta Scott was born in Alabama. From an early age, she loved music. Coretta won a scholarship to Antioch College in Ohio, majoring in education and music. After graduation, she continued her studies at the New England Conservatory of Music in Boston.

It was in Boston that Coretta Scott met a young minister from Atlanta who was studying at Boston University. She and Martin Luther King, Jr., were married in 1953. The couple returned to the South, to Montgomery, Alabama. Just a year later Dr. King attracted national attention as the leader of a bus boycott. In the years that followed, both the Kings became deeply involved with the civil rights movement. Mrs. King also found time to bring up four children, to teach music, and to perform "freedom concerts" to raise funds for various civil rights causes.

Since her husband's death, Mrs. King has continued the nonviolent struggle against what she called the "three great evils . . . racism, poverty, and war." She has been named director of several organizations dedicated to seeking peace and ending racial injustice. She also has set out to build the Martin Luther King, Jr., Center for Social Change in Atlanta as a "living monument" to her husband.

In addition the recessions that hit the nation during the Carter and Reagan administrations hurt blacks more than whites. During Carter's term in office, black unemployment averaged 12.4 percent. During Reagan's first term the figure jumped to 16.2 percent. From 1970 to 1982, the median income of black families slipped from 61 percent to 55 percent of the median for white families. The poverty rate for blacks in the Reagan years rose from 32.7 to 35.7 percent. This meant that over a span of just four years, 1.3 million blacks had moved below the official poverty line.

Reagan had promised that his programs would turn the economy around and that they would provide a "safety net" for those in need. But by 1984, many blacks believed that economic recovery had not reached them and that too many blacks had slipped through holes in the "safety net."

The outlook. Large numbers of blacks turned out to vote for Jesse Jackson, a black minister, in the Democratic Presidential primaries of 1984. Jackson finished third in the delegate count, but his quest for nomination stirred blacks, and many whites as well. Jackson had first worked with Martin Luther King, Jr., (whose birthday became a national holiday in 1986) in the civil rights movement back in 1966. Jackson's try for the Presidency was evidence that King's dream of a nation in which people of all races and creeds would be united in peace and justice was still alive.

▲ **Gains for another minority.** The successes that blacks achieved in their demands for equal rights inspired other minorities to undertake similar campaigns. Their efforts will be discussed in the following sections of this chapter.

However, one minority was in a special category. It contained members of all the other minorities and whites as well. This group was the handicapped.

Organizations of handicapped citizens began to lobby for their rights. Why, they asked legislators, should their tax money go to constructing public buildings that were inaccessible to people in wheelchairs? Gradually the handicapped made their points. Laws were passed requiring wheelchair ramps and special parking spaces at public facilities. Signs in raised letters or Braille were put up for the blind, and visual signs posted for the deaf.

Federal laws were passed that affected the handicapped in other ways. The Rehabilitation Act of 1973 forbade discrimination in jobs, education, and housing because of physical handicaps. The Education for All Handicapped Children Act of 1975 required public schools to provide free education to children with physical and mental handicaps. Other federal and state laws helped the handicapped to enter the mainstream of American life.

SECTION REVIEW

See underscored items, text pp. 947 - 50.

Identify: Martin Luther King, Jr., sit-in, A. Philip Randolph, de facto segregation, Malcolm X, black power, Thurgood Marshall, affirmative action

For answers to questions, see Answer Key, p.A129.

1. **Organizing Ideas:** What were some actions taken by Congress and the Supreme Court since 1954 to guarantee the civil rights of all Americans?

2. **Classifying Ideas:** What types of actions did civil rights groups take during the 1960's and 1970's in their effort to end discrimination?

3. **Analyzing Ideas:** (a) What is the purpose of affirmative action programs? (b) Why do some people oppose them?

4. **Determining Cause and Effect:** Describe how blacks were affected by changes in the nation's economy during the administrations of Carter and Reagan.

5. **Summarizing Ideas:** What federal laws were passed to help ensure equal rights for handicapped Americans?

---

3 Hispanics share the struggle for freedom and justice

See Teaching Suggestions in TMRG, pp.TM227-28.

The discrimination suffered by blacks was also experienced by other ethnic groups. The Hispanics, 15 million according to the 1980 census, were second only to blacks in terms of numbers. There are some estimates that Hispanics will overtake the blacks and become the nation's largest minority during the 1980's.

The Hispanics. The Hispanics are people from a number of different Spanish-speaking countries and their offspring. They include large numbers of Mexicans, Puerto Ricans, Cubans, Filipinos, Dominicans, and recent immigrants from other South American countries and the West Indies. All of these people share a common Spanish-influenced heritage. In addition to the Spanish language and Spanish cultural traits, they often share the ties of the Roman Catholic religion.

Despite their common heritage, the Hispanics are a varied group. These immigrants represent a wide range of jobs, from farm workers to lawyers. In fact, more than 30 percent of the immigrants from South America have been highly educated professionals and white-collar workers. The most numerous of the Hispanics are the Mexican Americans. Among them are the descendants of Mexicans living in California, New Mexico, Arizona, and Texas when these lands belonged to Mexico. These people often call themselves Hispanos.

Migrant farm workers. Most of the recent Hispanic immigrants, including the undocumented or illegal migrants, came from poor rural areas to seek a better life in the United States. The great majority worked for the large commercial farms. Most were illiterate, at least in English, and insecure in their jobs. As migrant workers these men, women, and children labored for low pay in lettuce and asparagus fields, citrus groves, and apple orchards. They moved as the crops matured to Oregon, Washington, Nebraska, and the Great Lake states, living in substandard shacks or mobile trailers. They received little benefit from the social legislation that was intended to protect workers. "We were jailed, beaten, even killed," wrote the historian Dr. Julian Navo.

From the early 1900's on, some efforts had been made to organize the migrant workers. These early efforts met only limited success. In the 1960's, however, Cesar Chavez made headway in organizing the workers in the California vineyards and lettuce fields. Sympathetic priests, civic groups, and idealistic students aided in his efforts. In 1965 he launched a strike that led to a nationwide boycott of produce not bearing the label of the United Farm Workers. In 1970, the strikers finally won. Although the gulf between Mexican Americans and other farm workers was still wide, it had begun to narrow.

Mexican Americans in cities. In time, large Mexican-American communities or *barrios* grew up in such cities as El Paso, Los Angeles, Denver, Seattle, Minneapolis, and Chicago. The residents of the *barrios* met with prejudice and discrimination in employment, in courts of law, in relations with the police, and in schools where English was often an unknown language to them.

Despite obstacles, an increasing number of Mexican Americans went to high school and college, acquiring vocational and professional skills. Loyal to family and to their Mexican-American culture, the city dwellers contributed to the economic development of the country as well as to the arts. During the Vietnam War, the death rate for Mexican-American servicemen was higher than that for any other group. This was due largely to the fact that many fought in high-risk branches of the service, such as the Marines.

The Chicano movement. Inspired in part by the struggles of blacks for their rights, Mexican Americans in the 1960's took increasing pride in their Hispanic background. They, too, struggled to win their civil rights. They also fought to overcome the prejudice that many "Anglos," as they called other Americans, held against them.

Referring to themselves as "Chicanos," leaders of the movement used boycotts, sit-ins, demonstrations, political organizations, and the courts to secure their rights. In New Mexico, Reies López Tijerina formed an organization to regain land that, he claimed, Anglos had taken illegally. In Denver, the boxer, newspaper editor, and poet Rodolfo "Corky" Gon-

Mexican Americans have had success in winning political power, especially in southwestern states. Henry Cisneros was elected mayor of San Antonio, the third largest city in Texas.

zales won recognition for his work in the Democratic Party. He organized demonstrations and became one of the leaders of the Chicano movement. In Los Angeles Vilma Martinez, like a growing number of Mexican-American women, took an active part in defending the rights of her people.

Many new militant organizations sprang up. One of them, *La Raza Unida,* sought to register Mexican Americans and to see that they voted. Youth organizations also demanded Mexican-American studies and the use of Spanish in high schools and colleges.

Mexican-American studies soon were recognized in many schools and colleges. Able Mexican-American historians, social scientists, and humanists were professors at leading universities. *El Grito del Norte* and other newspapers and periodicals were further evidence of the vitality of the Chicano movement.

The Puerto Ricans. Puerto Ricans made up the second largest Spanish-speaking group in the United States. As you recall, Puerto Rico has long had a special commonwealth relationship with the United States. The inhabitants of the island are legally American citizens.

Many Puerto Ricans have left their homeland in search of jobs in the United States. By 1975 more than 5 million Puerto Ricans, including mainland-born descendants, were living in the United States.

The Puerto Ricans were concentrated in New York. There, by the mid-1970's, they made up 10 percent of the city's population. Large numbers also lived in Newark, Philadelphia, Cleveland, Chicago, Boston, and other cities. In these urban areas they faced problems of unemployment, poor housing, prejudice, and discrimination.

The lives of young Puerto Ricans were especially difficult. Making up 33 percent of New York's school population, they were handicapped because they did not speak English. The dropout rate was very high. Street gangs, friction with the police, and high unemployment added to their problems. Yet many realized that education was a road to a better life. Evidence of this was the fact that in 1975 more than 17,000 young Puerto Ricans were enrolled in colleges and universities.

Despite difficulties and discrimination, many Puerto Ricans moved up the economic ladder. Some found places in small businesses, in semi-skilled trades, and in offices. By the late 1970's, about 10 percent of employed Puerto Rican males held professional or technical jobs. More and more were able to leave the crowded slums for better living conditions in the cities or in the suburbs. In the field of the arts, entertainment, and sports, José Feliciano, Rita Moreno, and Roberto Clemente became well known.

Puerto Ricans realized that political methods could improve their position and as a result they set up political organizations. Other politicians soon became aware of their bloc-voting power. In 1970 Herman Badillo of New York City became the first Puerto Rican member of Congress.

Many Puerto Ricans, on the other hand, rejected the "establishment." They emphasized forceful demands and revolutionary tactics to win greater opportunity. Frustration and pride led some to support Puerto Rican independence. Nevertheless, in a number of elections Puerto Ricans have rejected both statehood and independence, preferring instead to remain a commonwealth.

The Cubans. In 1959, as you have read (page 916), Fidel Castro overthrew the government of the reactionary dictator, Fulgencio Batista. When it soon became clear that Castro wished to create a Communist state, refugees began to escape to the United States. Many crossed the 90-mile stretch of water in small fishing boats. From 1961 to 1970, more than 208,000 arrived. During the 1970's the number landing on these shores each year increased steadily. In 1977 alone more than 66,000 Cuban refugees entered the United States. Most of them settled in the Miami area.

In an effort to relieve the strain on the city, county, and state, the federal government set up the Cuban Refugee Program. With an annual budget of $40 million, it provided welfare assistance, health services, and vocational training. The refugees, largely middle class, used their assets, skills, and initiative to set up businesses and other enterprises. As a result of their efforts, they soon became an important part of the Miami area's economy.

Efforts by the refugee program to promote settlement in other parts of the country were effective. By the mid-1970's half of the Cubans were living in New York, Chicago, Los Angeles, and other cities. In 1979 the Census Bureau estimated that the Cuban population in the United States had reached 700,000.

Then, in the spring of 1980, a flood of refugees began to pour into Florida. The "Freedom Flotilla," an improvised fleet of privately owned boats, ferried them from Cuba to southern Florida. It was a dangerous, haphazard operation. Some of the boats, estimated to number more than 2,000, were capable of carrying only five or ten people.

At first President Carter welcomed the refugees with "open heart and open arms," but he soon was forced to change his position. By the end of May, more than 60,000 refugees had entered and several thousand more were arriving each day. Increasing numbers of American citizens objected to the arrival of the Cubans. They claimed that the nation was in a recession and that unemployment was high. They feared that the newcomers would take already scarce jobs.

Opposition to the uncontrolled flood of people approached the stage of violence. Finally the Carter administration announced that the "Freedom Flotilla" would be shut down. By that time, more than 125,000 Cubans had entered the United States.

Legal gains for Hispanics. The civil rights legislation of the 1960's and 1970's already discussed helped the nation's Hispanic population. There were two other laws, however, that had special importance for Hispanics.

One of these was the Voting Rights Act of 1975. It required governments to print materials in other languages as well as English in areas with many non-English-speaking voters.

The other law was the Bilingual Education Act. It ordered public schools to provide instruction to students in their native languages while they learned English. By the early 1980's, however, opposition to bilingual education was rising. Critics claimed it was not an effective teaching tool and that it slowed the rate at which students learned English.

Immigration and Hispanics. Changes in legal immigration to the United States were discussed earlier in this chapter. By the 1970's and 1980's, the problem of illegal immigration had become a major concern.

Estimates of the number entering the country each year ranged from 100,000 to 500,000. Possibly half of the illegal aliens crossed the border from Mexico.

Many Americans believed that illegal aliens, by their willingness to work for lower wages, took jobs away from citizens. Many Americans feared the aliens would enter the welfare roles and raise taxes for all Americans. Still other Americans were concerned for the aliens themselves. They were unlikely to turn to the authorities for help. Thus illegal aliens were good targets for exploitation and abuse.

President Reagan said, "The simple truth is that we've lost control of our own borders, and no nation can do that and survive." His administration led a fight for a bill to curb illegal immigration. One version would have granted amnesty for aliens who had been in the United States for a certain number of years. It would have also provided penalties for employers who hired illegal aliens.

Many Hispanic leaders opposed the passage of such a bill. They worried that it might lead to increased job discrimination and other civil rights abuses against all Hispanics. Some people felt that in order to enforce such a bill, a national identification system would have to be set up, and they opposed such a step. Opponents of the bill joined forces and kept the measure from becoming law.

The outlook. Despite impressive gains in recent years, Hispanics in the United States

Each year, uncounted thousands of aliens pour into the United States. These newcomers were among the more than 100,000 Cubans who sailed here from their homeland in 1980.

still face many problems. Median income for Hispanic families in the early 1980's was $16,228 compared to the white median of $24,950. Hispanics must also still contend with prejudice and discrimination.

SECTION REVIEW

See underscored items, text pp. 952 - 54.

Identify: Hispanos, migrant farm workers, Cesar Chavez, *barrio*, "Anglos," Chicanos, Rodolfo "Corky" Gonzales, Vilma Martinez, Herman Badillo, "Freedom Flotilla"

For answers to questions, see Answer Key, pp.A129-30.

1. **Evaluating Ideas; (a)** In general, how have Mexican Americans been treated by other Americans? **(b)** What actions have members of the Chicano movement taken? **(c)** How successful has the Chicano movement been?

2. **Comparing Ideas:** Compare the situation of Puerto Ricans with that of Mexican Americans in terms of **(a)** problems and **(b)** attempts to solve the problems.

3. **Analyzing Ideas: (a)** Why have many Cubans come to the United States since 1959? **(b)** How has the Cuban Refugee Program tried to help them adjust to their new life?

Indians refuse to accept the role of "vanishing Americans"

See Teaching Suggestions in TMRG, p.TM228.
From the day the Europeans invaded their land, the American Indians battled for survival. A century ago they made their last stand against the United States Army on the Great Plains. By 1892 the wars were over and the Indians had been subdued. Events would demonstrate that they had not been defeated.

Years of frustration. For the next 75 years, government policies toward the Indians changed repeatedly. In some cases they even reversed themselves. Such policy shifts left the Indians confused and frustrated. They also helped to keep the Indians the poorest of the poor among the nation's minorities.

Yet the American Indians refused to fulfill some earlier predictions and vanish. Against great odds they not only survived but also increased in numbers. According to the Bureau of the Census, in 1980 there were about 1,400,000 Indians living in the United States. More than 500,000 of these are in urban centers, the rest in rural areas.

Growing awareness. In the 1950's the government had adopted a policy designed to "terminate" its responsibilities to the Indians and to relocate them in cities. The policy, as you have read, proved to be a disaster.

Following the example of the blacks, Indian activists in the 1960's began to form organizations to promote Indian interests. They fought to overcome the damage caused by such policies as termination.

One of the oldest of the organizations was the National Congress of American Indians (NCAI). Founded during World War II, the NCAI became increasingly active during the 1960's. Other organizations, among them the National Indian Youth Council and the Native American Movement, joined in the battle for Indian rights.

Books, several written by Indians, attracted public attention to the problems of the Native Americans. The books and the publicity they received helped to stir the consciences of growing numbers of American citizens.

The New Indians by Saul Steiner alerted readers to a new "uprising" led by Indian intellectuals who wanted to develop "red power." In 1969 Vine Deloria, Jr., a Standing Rock Sioux and a former director of NCAI, published one of the most influential books, *Custer Died for Your Sins*. In it Deloria outlined the tragic history of broken white promises, set forth the goals Indians were struggling to achieve, and provided a glimpse of what white Americans could learn from the First Americans. A year later Deloria continued his indictment of white America and his plea for understanding with another book, *We Talk, You Listen*. The following year Dee Brown's *Bury My Heart at Wounded Knee* appeared and became one of the most widely read of the recent books.

People began to pay attention to Indian problems. President Johnson was one of them. In 1968 he asked for, and Congress passed, a program of more than $500 million in aid to the Indians.

Violence. The growing awareness of Indian problems was quickened by militant Indian action. One group of Indians took over Alcatraz Island, a former Federal prison in California, to dramatize their demands.

The American Indian Movement (AIM) was launched by young urban Indian leaders in the late 1960's. In the fall of 1972, some 500 members of AIM banded together, calling themselves "The Trail of Broken Treaties." They marched on Washington, D.C., occupied the Bureau of Indian Affairs, and did some $2 million in damage. They finally received official promises that the government would pay attention to their complaints.

In February 1973, members of AIM seized the trading post and church at the Sioux Pine Reservation in Wounded Knee, South Dakota. This was the village where in 1890 United States cavalry units had brutally massacred more than 200 Indians. For 71 days heavily armed Indians and United States marshals grimly confronted each other over the barricades that separated them. In the end, after the government promised to consider their demands, the Indians surrendered.

The end of termination. Meanwhile the federal government had once again reversed itself. In 1970 President Nixon asked Congress to repeal the termination policy of 1953. He then announced a policy of "self-determination

In 1963, the national unemployment rate was 7 percent, but among Indian groups it ranged from 43.4 percent to 89.6 percent. The average Indian yearly income ranged from almost zero to $1,000 (national average was $5,000). The average Indian death age was 42 (62 for the general population).

without termination." From now on, Nixon declared, the Indians would be encouraged to develop their own tribal life on their reservations. In supporting them the government would provide assistance for housing, vocational training, and economic development.

Although Indians welcomed the new policy, they could not forget the repeated reversals in the past. They continued to fear that termination would be renewed.

As it turned out, Congress failed to pass the necessary laws to make the proposed policy effective. Moreover, the tactics employed by AIM angered the Nixon administration. As a result the reform movement begun by the federal government was only partially carried out. However, the federal government did lay to rest the policy of termination.

Moving forward. Although AIM's violent tactics lost some support for the Indians, other Indian leaders continued to move toward their goal of running their own lives in their own way. These leaders increasingly relied on educational activities and on court action to gain their ends.

The Indians made gradual progress. By 1975, for the first time in history, Indian men and women made up a majority of the employees of the Bureau of Indian Affairs. At the same time, more and more schools and colleges had developed programs of Indian studies that informed students of the Indians' part in the nation's life.

The Indians won other victories as well. For example, the Indians of the Taos Pueblo in New Mexico recovered 48,000 acres (19,400 hectares) of land, including the sacred Blue Lake, that had been made part of a national park. Indians in Maine, who claimed that more than half of the state had been illegally taken from them, took their case to the courts. Congress awarded them $81.5 million and the right to purchase up to 300,000 acres (120,000 hectares) of land.

The Indian today. Today, as in the past, generalizations about the Native Americans must be made carefully. The Indians of the United States are now divided into more than 450 tribes or communities and speak more than 100 different languages. Although most continue to battle poverty, many have become well-to-do and some have become wealthy. Many are highly educated and highly skilled.

Here, in northern New Mexico, is Blue Lake, for centuries held sacred by the Indians of the Taos Pueblo. The lake had been made part of a national park in the 1970's, but the federal government finally returned Blue Lake to its traditional Indian owners.

There are Indian doctors, lawyers, scientists, and engineers. A large number have become completely "Americanized." However, many refuse to abandon traditional ways and continue to live apart from the mainstream of American culture.

For the most part, Native Americans remain intensely proud of their heritage. They have contributed richly to American life. They also have much more to contribute.

SECTION REVIEW

See underscored items, text p. 956.
Identify: NCAI, Vine Deloria, Jr., AIM
For answers to questions, see Answer Key, p.A130.

1. **Evaluating Ideas: (a)** What methods have Indians used to dramatize their needs and problems **(b)** Which have been most effective? Explain.

2. **Analyzing Ideas: (a)** What was President Nixon's Indian policy? **(b)** How effective was it?

3. **Summarizing Ideas:** Describe the progress made by Indians in recent years.

DEVELOPING HISTORY STUDY SKILLS

Interpreting the Visual Record   Comparing Maps

- How have national boundaries in the Middle East changed since 1920?

Answers to questions such as this one can be found by comparing maps. Students of history are often called on to analyze the information contained on a series of maps.

You have already been introduced to skills that will help you compare the information on maps. Refresh your memory about map basics (Chapter 7, pages 164–65) and composing a comparative essay (Chapter 38, pages 851–52). Use the skills developed in these exercises to help you compare maps.

Applying the Skill

The maps at the bottom of the page show the Middle East at four different times. Study the maps of the Middle East in 1920 and 1948. Then answer these questions.

1. **(a)** In 1920 what nation controlled Palestine? **(b)** What nation controlled Syria?

2. **(a)** In 1948, what nation controlled Palestine? **(b)** What nation controlled Syria?

3. **(a)** What nation appears on the 1948 map that was not on the 1920 map? **(b)** Where did the territory for this new nation come from?

Review the answers you got for the questions. From the 1920 map it can be ascertained that Palestine was under British control and Syria was under French control. In 1948 neither Palestine nor Syria were under the control of another nation. The 1948 map includes Israel, a nation that was not on the 1920 map. The territory for the creation of Israel came from Palestine. You may also note that the 1948 map contains information on a 1947 U.N. proposal to settle Middle East boundary conflicts.

Practicing the Skill

Continue to study the maps at the bottom of the page, this time focusing on the 1967 and 1984 maps. Then on a separate sheet of paper, answer these questions.

1. **(a)** In 1967 what nation controlled the Sinai Peninsula? **(b)** In 1984 what nation controlled the Sinai Peninsula?

2. **(a)** In 1967 what nation controlled the Golan Heights? **(b)** In 1984 what nation controlled the Golan Heights?

3. Study all the maps and answer these questions. **(a)** To what nation did the Sinai Peninsula originally belong? **(b)** To what nation did the Golan Heights originally belong?

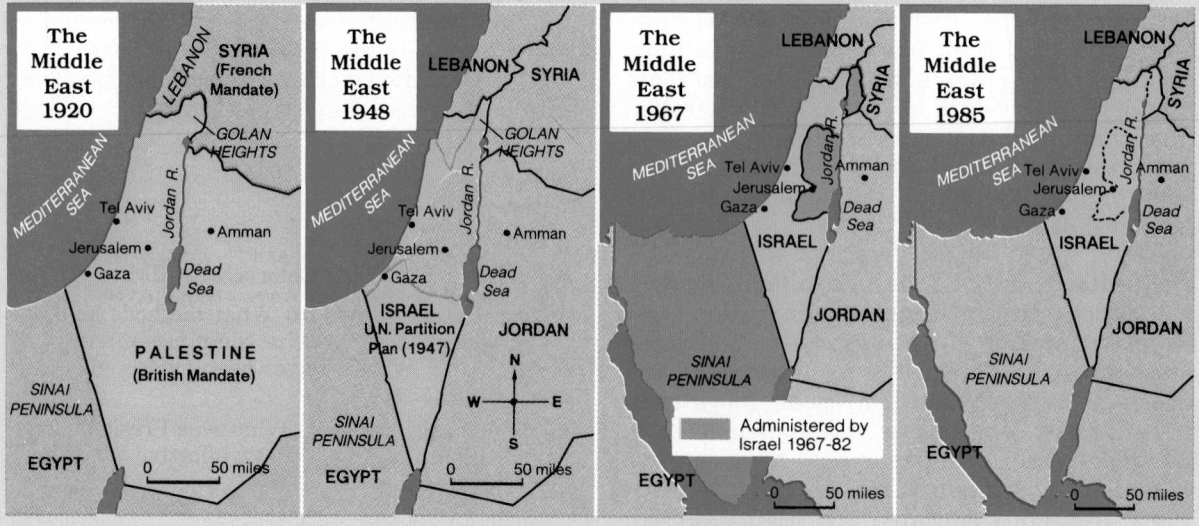

Women redouble efforts to win equal rights and opportunities

See Teaching Suggestions in TMRG, pp.TM228-29.

American women make up 53 percent of the population. They are the largest group struggling against discrimination. During the 1960's the struggle came to be known as women's liberation or the women's rights movement.

Reasons for early successes. In part the movement gained strength because of the growing number of American women who were now employed. By the mid-1970's women made up about 50 percent of the nation's labor force. Their average wages, however, were only 60 percent of those paid to men doing comparable work. Even more revealing, only a small percentage of women held higher-paying and more responsible positions. Among the directors of large corporations, for example, only 3 percent were women.

Another factor in the rise of the women's rights movement was the civil rights movement. Many women had been actively involved in the civil rights movement and had gained ability and confidence for their own struggle.

Their struggle was also aided by a clause in the Civil Rights Act of 1964. This clause outlawed discrimination based on sex in employment. Using this clause, women battled to secure equal treatment in business, education, and the other professions.

Growing numbers of women agreed with movement leaders that sex discrimination kept many women from realizing their full potential. According to public opinion polls, a majority of American women did not feel that taking care of a home and rearing children were restrictive or frustrating roles. By the mid-1970's, however, a majority of American women did approve of equal opportunities for their sex in all areas of life.

Women's rights organizations. One of the first and most prominent groups within the women's rights movement was the National Organization for Women (NOW). NOW and other feminist groups shared a number of goals. They demanded equal treatment of women in educational programs, including faculty appointments in universities. They worked for publicly financed day-care centers for children. They attempted to get state laws forbidding abortion repealed. They strongly opposed the treatment of women as sex objects. Some of the groups also insisted that men should share in the tasks of homemaking and childrearing.

The ERA. Most of the women's rights organizations pressed for a Constitutional amendment to guarantee women equal rights. By 1978 the Equal Rights Amendment (ERA) that had been passed by Congress in 1972 had been ratified by 35 of the required 38 states. By 1980, however, no additional states had ratified the amendment.

The ERA failed because many American women believed that the ERA would deprive them of more than it gave them. Some feared it might make them subject to the military draft. Others feared it would end alimony payments to women. Still others thought it would put an end to laws protecting women in the workplace. Many women also believed that the ERA would help to destroy the traditional bonds of the family.

Opponents of ERA organized their own counter-movement. They put pressure on state legislatures and succeeded in preventing ratification in key states. By the early 1980's, the hope for passage of any Equal Rights Amendment was dead.

New freedoms for women. Despite the failure of the ERA, steps were being made toward meeting some goals of the women's rights movement. Legal suits were filed against businesses, colleges, and other institutions. Such suits charged the institutions with sex discrimination in hiring, pay, and promotion practices.

Women also entered careers in fields formerly dominated by men. Women enlisted in the armed forces in growing numbers. Women became police officers and ministers. Sally Ride became the first female astronaut, and Kathryn Sullivan was the first woman to walk in space. Women won new recognition in such sports as tennis and golf. Dress and social customs were less strictly categorized as masculine and feminine.

The question of abortion became a major issue in the 1984 Presidential race. Ronald Reagan firmly opposed abortion and backed a

▲ Phyllis Schlafly was the woman organizing the anti-ERA movement. She traveled across the country making personal and television appearances to argue against the Equal Rights Amendment.

959

Constitutional ban on abortion. His opponent, Walter Mondale, felt that abortion was a personal and religious matter.

Political gains. In political affairs women were still underrepresented. However, change was in the air.

Several women in Congress became nationally known. Among them were Bella Abzug, Shirley Chisholm, Barbara Jordan, Elizabeth Holtzman, and Nancy Kassebaum. With the start of the new Congress in 1985 there were 24 women serving in Congress, 22 in the House of Representatives and 2 in the Senate.

Perhaps the most impressive gains for women in politics came at the state and local levels. In 1974 no women served as governors, 519 were state representatives, and 91 were state senators. Ten years later 816 women were representatives and 177 were senators. Martha Layne Collins of Kentucky and Madeleine Kunin of Vermont were the only women serving as governor. Also in 1984, 86 cities with populations greater than 30,000 had women as mayors. Dianne Feinstein of San Francisco was the most widely known.

Other women in government included Carla Hills, Secretary of Housing and Urban Development under President Ford. In 1980 President Carter appointed two women. Juanita Kreps and Patricia Harris, to his Cabinet. President Reagan named Elizabeth Dole as Secretary of Transportation and Margaret Heckler as Secretary of Health and Human Services. He also chose Jeanne Kirkpatrick as United States Ambassador to the United Nations. (Shortly after Reagan's 1984 election, Kirkpatrick announced she would resign in 1985.) His most widely noted appointment, however, was that of Sandra Day O'Connor to a seat on the Supreme Court.

Walter Mondale, Democratic candidate for President in 1984, made history when he selected Geraldine Ferraro as his Vice-Presidential running mate. Ferraro had served three terms in the U.S. House of Representatives. A mother of three children, Ferraro had earned a law degree in night school. She later served as a prosecutor for the District Attorney in New York City. The selection of Ferraro marked the first time a major party had chosen a woman as a candidate for the Vice Presidency.

This 1985 portrait of the Supreme Court justices illustrates the move toward equal rights for all Americans. The first black justice, Thurgood Marshall (lower left), was appointed by President Johnson in 1967. The first female justice, Sandra Day O'Connor (upper right), was appointed by President Reagan in 1981.

In 1984 the Democratic party made political history with the nomination of New York Congresswoman Geraldine Ferraro for Vice President.

The balance sheet. The list of advances that women have made in the struggle for equal rights is an impressive one. Yet some women feared that further movement toward equality would be harder to achieve as the 1980's neared an end.

The failure to win ratification of the ERA and the growing opposition to legal abortions were just two of the more obvious signs of resistance to the women's rights movement. President Reagan had appointed a task force to wipe out state and federal laws that discriminate against women. After two years the task force had found many such laws, but had taken no action to have them repealed. President Reagan's opposition to affirmative action programs affected women as well as minority groups, cutting chances for jobs and promotions. Reagan's budget cuts also hurt women in such areas as welfare, day care, family planning, and legal aid.

Economic issues remained a vital concern to women in the 1980's. They still earned, on the average, only 60 percent of what men did for comparable work. This figure had not changed significantly for 30 years.

The economic slump was another source of pain for some women. In the mid-1980's, one of every seven families was headed by a woman; almost 40 percent of those families had incomes below the poverty line.

What was the outlook for women? Transportation Secretary Dole may have summed it up when she said, "Women have not reached the golden age as far as opportunities go, but we've made a lot of progress."

SECTION REVIEW

See underscored items, text pp. 959 - 60.

Identify: NOW, Equal Rights Amendment, Sally Ride, Nancy Kassebaum, Sandra Day O'Connor

For answers to questions, see Answer Key, p.A130.

1. **Summarizing Ideas: (a)** What are some of the goals of the women's rights movement? **(b)** Why did the women's rights movement gain strength by the mid-1970's?

2. **Analyzing Viewpoints:** Why did some people object to the women's rights movement?

Discussion topic: Ask these questions. How many teachers are in the school? How many are women? men? What subjects are mostly taught by women? by men? Why? How many administrators are in the school district? How many are women? men? Why? How many secretaries are women? men? Why?

961

42 SUMMARY

More than two hundred years ago, the American nation was founded on the principle that "all men are created equal." By the 1980's the promise of 1776 remained only partially fulfilled.

Even so, during the years after World War II, and particularly during the past two decades, the movement toward freedom and justice for all Americans made steady progress.

Despite progress, problems still remained. The cities, in which so many of the poor and the minorities were concentrated, continued to decay. Also, from the mid-1970's on, the nation's economic health was poor. Soaring prices and scarce jobs damaged the chances of many minority members to better their lives.

In spite of these obstacles, however, blacks, Hispanics, Indians, and women were demanding and winning a share of "the American dream." Women and minorities had moved a great deal closer to full equality. A black man had sought a major party's nomination for President, making a strong showing. A white woman won the nomination for Vice President on a major-party ticket. Women, blacks, and other minorities, still had a great distance to travel to reach the full equality of the American dream.

CONNECTING CHAPTER IDEAS

Despite the growing economic prosperity the United States achieved in the years after World War II, Americans realized that they could no longer take prosperity for granted. In the next chapter you will read how the United States, under the leadership of President Reagan, sought to resolve the continuing economic, environmental, and energy problems the nation faced.

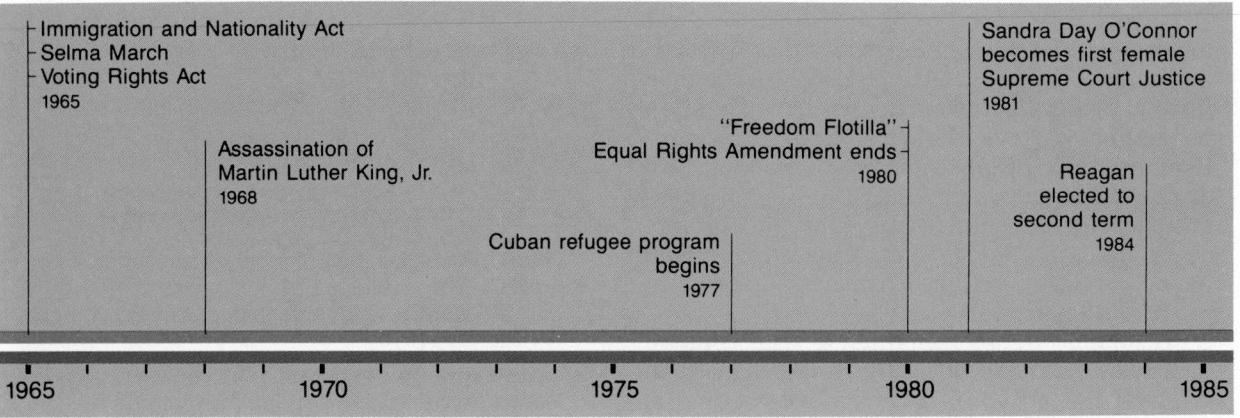

Immigration and Nationality Act
Selma March
Voting Rights Act
1965

Assassination of
Martin Luther King, Jr.
1968

Cuban refugee program
begins
1977

"Freedom Flotilla"
Equal Rights Amendment ends
1980

Sandra Day O'Connor
becomes first female
Supreme Court Justice
1981

Reagan
elected to
second term
1984

1965   1970   1975   1980   1985

CHAPTER

42 REVIEW

Reviewing Important Terms

Decide whether each of the following sentences is true or false. If the sentence is false, replace the underlined term with the word or phrase that will make it true.

1. The civil rights movement of the 1950's and early 1960's attracted support from many whites—particularly clergy, lawyers, and students.
2. The increasing number of whites fleeing to the suburbs as immigrants and minorities moved to the cities has been termed urban migration.
3. Reverse discrimination programs sought to make up for past discrimination when minorities applied to schools or for jobs.
4. Mexican-American communities in large cities are sometimes called barrios.
5. In the 1970's, the courts began to rule against de jure segregation that existed in the North.

Practicing Critical Thinking Skills

1. **Summarizing Ideas.** Describe the major changes that have occurred in the population of the United States in the years since 1960.
2. **Comparing Ideas.** (a) How are the problems of Hispanics, blacks, and Indians similar? (b) How are they different? (c) How are the situations of these groups different from that of both women and the handicapped?
3. **Expressing Viewpoints.** Today women make up more than 50 percent of the population of the United States. Nevertheless, they are often considered a minority. Why do you think this is so?
4. **Interpreting Ideas.** Equal rights movements often suffer from conflicts between moderates and militants. (a) What sort of tactics might be favored by moderates? (b) by militants? (c) How did such conflicts affect the black civil rights movement? (d) How did similar conflicts affect the movement for Indian rights?
5. **Evaluating Ideas.** (a) What were some of the major arguments made against the Equal Rights Amendment? (b) What were the major arguments supporting it? (c) Based on your research, take a stand on the ERA and defend your position in a paper or speech.
6. **Relating Past to Present.** What is the present federal policy toward (a) urban problems, (b) affirmative action, and (c) school desegregation? How does it compare with the federal policies discussed in this chapter?

Developing History Study Skills

Evaluating Data from Maps. Refer to the map on page 1005 to answer the following questions.

(a) List the states in which the population shows a decrease. In what region of the nation are these two states located? (b) What two states have the smallest percentage of population increase? In what region of the nation are these two states located? (c) List the states in which the population shows an increase of more than 20 percent. In what regions of the nation are these states located? (d) Based on the map's data, what trend in population in the United States is shown? Cite data from the map to support your answer.

Now refer to the map on page 1002, "Population Distribution in the United States."

(e) In what states are most of the areas of dense population located? In what region of the nation are these states located? (f) In what region of the nation are most major metropolitan areas located? (g) Carefully compare the data shown on the two maps. If the trend in the population shift shown on the map on text page 1005 were to continue for the next 20 years, in what way would the map on text page 1002 most likely change? Using data from the maps, write a paragraph explaining your answer.

Relating Geography and History

Urban geographers study living and working patterns in cities, urban growth patterns, and how people respond to the urban environment. To understand the work of urban geographers, use the information in this chapter to answer the following questions.

1. (a) What is a Metropolitan Statistical Area (MSA)? (b) How did the population of the core city change when large numbers of people moved to the suburbs? (c) How did the movement to the suburbs affect businesses in the city? (d) How did the businesses adapt?
2. (a) Find the ten largest United States cities in an almanac or other reference book and list them on your paper. (b) Which cities have been added to the list in the last decade? (c) What factors have influenced the recent growth of the cities newly added to the list?

963

See Chapter Overview in TMRG, p.TM230.
See Chapter Objectives in TMRG, p.TM230.
See Introducing the Chapter in TMRG, p.TM230.

CHAPTER 43

Into the Future
Changing Ways   (1960 to the Present)

Computer disc drives

964

In the years after World War II, the nation has reached a level of wealth, productivity, and power never before approached in history. Formidable problems however, have emerged as the United States approaches the last decade of the twentieth century. A cycle of inflation, unemployment, and recession has begun to plague the nation. Continued poverty in a land of abundance troubles many Americans. Schools and colleges, faced with rising costs and falling enrollments, have begun to rethink their purposes and their programs. Shortages of key goods and soaring fuel prices have convinced many Americans that the time has come to seek alternative energy sources to lessen reliance on oil.

By the 1980's Americans could no longer take for granted the prosperity so many of them had enjoyed for so many years. Growth and change, viewed as progress, needed a new direction. As never before in the nation's history, men and women in every walk of life faced the need to reexamine the nation's goals as well as their own personal objectives.

Ronald Reagan, inaugurated January 20, 1981, as the fortieth President of the United States and reelected in 1984 with an overwhelming majority of electoral votes, recognized this need. In 1981 he called for a "new beginning" and an "era of national renewal." He said, "The crisis we are facing ... does require ... our best effort, and our willingness to believe in our capacity to perform great deeds; to believe that together with God's help we can and will resolve the problems which now confront us." In 1985, he promised that in his new term he would encourage a "second American revolution." The new revolution, would leave the United States "stronger, freer, and more secure than ever before."

===== READING FOCUS =====

As you read about the events of the 1980's, look for the details that support each of the following statements.

1. Americans begin to reexamine their goals.
2. American economic issues remain a source of continuing concern.
3. The United States searches for an energy policy.
4. Americans share a growing awareness of environmental issues.

1 Americans begin to reexamine their goals

See Teaching Suggestions in TMRG, pp.TM230-31.

Change is by definition an unsettling experience. To change is "to alter, to become different." Increasingly during the years after World War II, change has uprooted traditional values, beliefs, and behavior of Americans and people everywhere on the planet.

Change and its effects. It is not just change, as such, that has been so unsettling. Throughout human history people have been compelled to adapt to changing ways. The disturbing difference in the second half of the twentieth century has been the swift rate of change.

The rate of change has been particularly rapid in the areas of science and technology. According to one estimate, 90 percent of all the scientists who have ever lived were alive and active in the 1980's. This intense scientific activity throughout the world has brought new discoveries, new ideas, new processes, and new inventions in ever-growing numbers.

Nothing in the universe has been too small to escape the attention of science. Nothing has been too immense or too remote in time or place. Scientists have explored particles of the atom and stars so distant that their light has taken more than 10 billion years to reach earth. Every field of science has been probed, and the answers to questions have prompted scientists to raise more questions.

Research has produced a tidal wave of new developments. Many such developments have had unexpected and unplanned effects on daily life. People everywhere are facing the challenges of adapting their personal lives and their institutions—religious, educational, social, economic, political—to the demands of changing ways and times.

Space exploration. Many of the things accomplished by science today would have been dismissed a generation ago as wild imaginings. The world was startled in 1957 when the Soviet Union launched the first artificial satellite, *Sputnik*. The United States quickly launched its own space program. By 1969 two American astronauts, Neil Armstrong and Edwin E. Aldrin, had landed on the moon.

Today hundreds of satellites orbit the earth. They serve numerous purposes. Some relay television, radio, and telephone messages across continents and the seas. Some survey military activities, search the earth for oil and other resources, and provide data on the weather. Others enable ships at sea to determine their exact location within a matter of seconds. Still other space craft have flown to Jupiter, Saturn, and beyond the solar system, sending scientific data and photographs back to earth. In 1981 the United States successfully launched the space shuttle *Columbia*—the first reusable space vehicle. Within a few years, it has been joined by several other space-shuttle ships.

Shuttle flights have accomplished many tasks. Crews of men and women have performed scientific experiments, launched new satellites and recovered old satellites, and have studied the possibilities of manufacturing medicines and industrial parts in the gravity-free environment of space. In 1985 crew members of the shuttle *Discovery* even carried out a highly secret mission for the United States military. The shuttle program received a tragic setback in 1986, however, when *Challenger* exploded moments into its flight.

Today, space flight has also become big business. NASA, the agency that runs America's space program, launches satellites for a variety of businesses.

Advances in health care. The exploration of outer space has been paralleled by equally dramatic discoveries on earth. Medical science has made major advances in the cure and control of disease. New technologies have been quickly adapted to medicine. For example, the laser, an amplified beam of light often used in communications and industry, has become a major medical tool. Doctors use it, for example, to perform delicate eye surgery.

New drugs and new methods of treatment have been perfected. Illnesses and diseases that once were common have been dramatically reduced. For example, mumps has been reduced by almost 98 percent and measles by more than 99 percent. Polio has been almost wiped out. The number of deaths from heart attacks and strokes also has fallen sharply. Heart attacks and strokes, however, remain among the leading causes of death in the United States.

Operations to transplant organs have become common. About 100 Americans each year receive new hearts, and 5,000 get new kidneys. Research has also produced artificial replacements for such parts of the body as hip joints, skin, and blood. In one remarkable procedure, patients have been fitted with mechanical hearts.

The new medical advances have raised some serious concerns. In 1960 health care costs for the United States were $27 billion.

Scientists and engineers have changed the nature of many medical tasks. Here doctors use sophisticated microscopes and a ray of light produced by a laser to perform surgery.

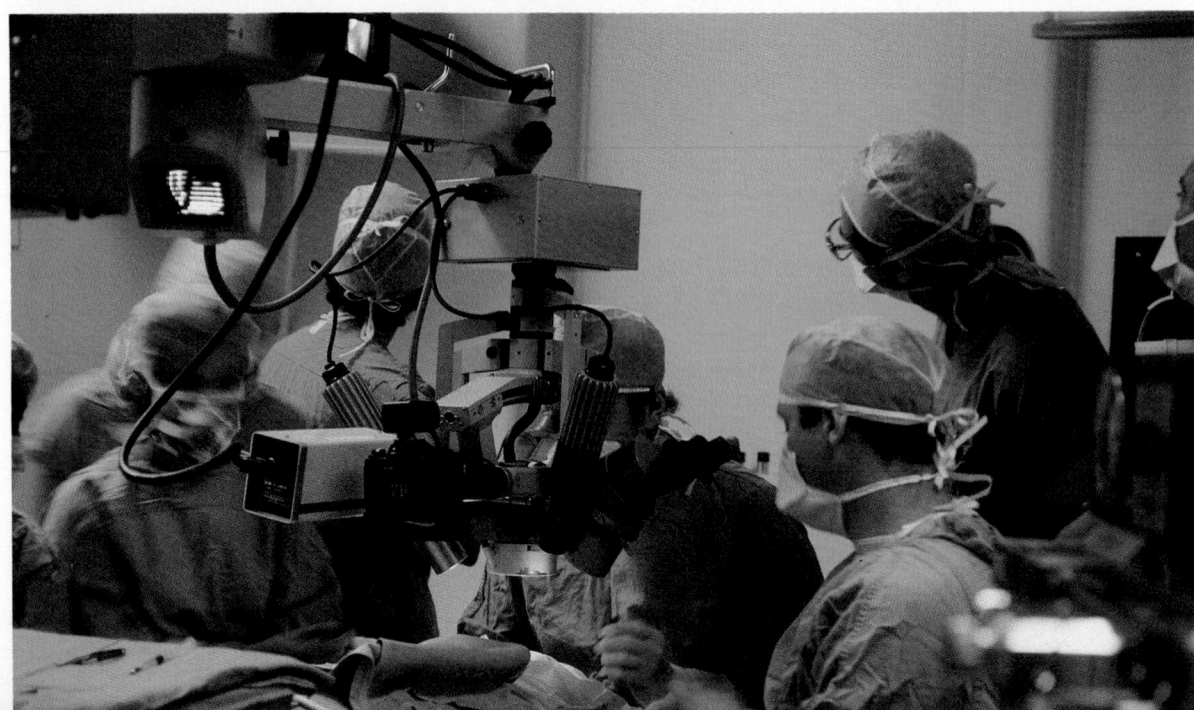

By the mid-1980's NASA's space shuttle program was averaging almost a dozen flights annually. As Robert Crippen, pilot of the first space shuttle flight, predicted in 1981, "We are really in the space business to stay."

By 1983 the costs had risen to $356 billion. The new advances have become too expensive for many of the people who need them desperately. In the slumping economy of the mid-1980's, many workers lost their jobs and their health insurance benefits. The needy families who use the Medicaid program and the elderly who used Medicare suffered as a result of federal budget cutting.

There are other types of concerns as well. Many scientists and nonscientists have worried that gene-splicing experimentation is dangerous and should be abandoned. Others would permit it to continue only under rigid supervision. In June 1980, however, the Supreme Court ruled that scientists could patent the new forms of life produced in their laboratories. In this particular case, patent rights were issued to the "inventor" of a newly developed strain of bacteria that eats crude oil.

The emerging computerized world. The computer has been the key to the new world that is emerging out of the amazing advances in science and technology. Scientists have continued to refine and improve computer designs and functions. A tiny silicon chip no larger than a small coin now outperforms the earliest room-sized computers. The largest computers can perform up to 800 million calculations a second and store as many as four million words. All of the stored data is instantly retrievable and can be communicated at the speed of light to any location on the earth or far into space.

Advances in design have allowed computers to be used in more and more areas. Computers guide robot welders on automobile assembly lines. In hospitals, computers are linked to X-ray machines. These CAT scanners, as they are called, provide detailed cross-sectional views of vital organs.

Today, people have more and more daily contact with computers. At the supermarket, computers "read" prices from labels on packages and add up the bill. In department stores

▲ Class activity: Have each student list as many specific uses of computers as possible; then compile the lists into one complete list.

967

computers check on credit card numbers and the amount a shopper may charge. Many banks have installed computerized teller machines that accept deposits and cash checks around the clock.

Computers have also found their way into homes. People use them to balance their budgets, figure their taxes, or play electronic games. With their computers connected to phone lines, people bank at home, check stock market figures, or get the latest news reports.

Computers are changing the job picture in the United States. From 1982 to 1995 the number of computer programmers is expected to grow by 75 percent. The number of computer service technicians is expected to increase by 97 percent. The possibility also exists that more office jobs will be done at home through computer hook-ups.

However, there are drawbacks to the increased use of computers. More robot welders and computer tellers mean fewer human welders and tellers. One expert estimates that some computer systems may eliminate as many as nine jobs for each one that remains. The question of job displacement and retraining for new jobs remains a serious one.

The spreading use of computers has created still other new problems. As banks and businesses increasingly have relied on computers for their transactions, computer crimes have mounted. A computer criminal is any person who electronically "breaks into" a computer system and instructs the computer to perform any transaction advantageous to the instructor or detrimental to the owner of the system.

The spreading use of computers has also meant that more information about individuals is being collected in computer memories. The increasing use of computers threatens the individual's right to privacy, especially if unauthorized people were able to gain access to such information.

Computer scientists agree that the computer is still in its infant stage of development. No one doubts that these "thinking machines" will continue to increase the efficiency of the human mind. How computers will be used in the future depends, finally, upon the values that men and women hold and choose to use in guiding their lives.

▲ **New demands on education.** A good education is essential for citizens trying to adapt to a society constantly being shaped by science and technology. The evidence is overwhelming that poorly educated, poorly trained men and women have little hope of earning an adequate living in an increasingly complex society. Even worse, inadequately educated citizens cannot help to solve the critical problems facing the nation and the world. Yet in the 1970's and 1980's, more people have been asking if schools in the United States are providing an adequate education.

There is strong evidence they are not. Standardized tests, administered to students across the nation, have registered steady declines from 1967 to 1982. Concern over the quality of public education became so great that President Reagan in 1981 named a National Commission on Excellence in Education to study the matter.

The commission's report, *The Nation at Risk,* which was issued in 1983, was shocking to many Americans. The report found and condemned "mediocrity in the classroom." It also warned that continued decline in the quality of education "threatens our future as a nation and a people." How did such a situation come about?

In the late 1950's strong federal efforts to improve the quality of education came in response to Soviet space achievements. The federal efforts first focused on the teaching of mathematics and the sciences. In the 1960's federal efforts spread to the humanities and the social sciences.

Money from the federal government and private foundations poured into experiments to improve the quality of education. Some efforts had positive results. The Head Start program, for example, gave disadvantaged preschoolers valuable learning experiences. Other projects, however, had less rewarding results. Some people have claimed that many projects got too far away from traditional teaching methods and did not demand of students performance standards that were high enough.

The schools also faced a variety of crises in these years. The 1960's was a time of overcrowding in the schools as the children of the postwar "baby boom" reached school age. During the 1970's the crowding eased, but the costs of classroom equipment, heating fuel, books, and other operating needs soared. One cost that many school districts managed to keep down was teacher salaries. As a result many qualified people left teaching for better-paying jobs in other fields.

▲ Discussion topic: Ask the students to list changes in education in recent years. Then ask how those changes reflect changes in society.

Changes in society also have had an impact on schools. Increasing numbers of families broke up as divorce rates climbed. The protests and permissiveness of the 1960's and 1970's found expression in a lack of respect for the authority of teachers. Racial tensions affected schools, as did the growing use of drugs by students. Conditions in many public schools were so bad that parents chose to enroll their children in private or parochial schools, even if this meant financial hardship.

By the 1980's many parents began demanding that schools go "back to basics." This meant increased discipline and tougher academic standards. The President's Commission had similar recommendations: more homework, longer school days, concentration on basic subjects. The Commission also favored increased pay and merit raises for teachers. It hoped that these steps would encourage good people to stay in education. Many states have also toughened their standards, some by increasing the number of credits required for a high school diploma. School districts have also cracked down on discipline problems.

In 1983 the standardized test scores rose for the first time in 16 years. In many concerned people, a cautious hope rose that the better test scores marked the beginning of a return to academic excellence.

Changing values. The changes that shook America's educational system are reflections of changes that have been affecting the whole of society from the 1960's through the 1980's. These changes are not confined to the United States. All the world's industrial nations and some of the developing ones have gone through similar times of unrest.

President Kennedy, during his time in office in the early 1960's, appealed strongly to the idealism of the American people, especially the young. In his Inaugural Address he called upon Americans to "ask what you can do for your country." Many Americans did, and found an outlet for their idealism by joining such organizations as the Peace Corps or such causes as the civil rights movement.

Kennedy's assassination was a blow to that idealism. Continuing involvement in Vietnam, a war which many people could not understand, was a second blow to idealism. A third blow was continuing poverty and discrimination despite the peaceful efforts of civil rights leaders and civil rights workers.

Resentment over Vietnam found expression in demonstrations and political activism that at times turned violent. Resentment over continuing racial injustices exploded in riots in many cities. The deaths of Robert Kennedy and Martin Luther King, Jr., also brought out resentment over a society that seemed to encourage violence.

The signs of unrest have been most apparent in the young. Many have adopted styles of dress, hair styles, and ways of living that set them apart from the "establishment." Some in the 1960's became "hippies," experimented with drugs, and joined communes. Others dedicated themselves to radical political action, attempting to revamp or to overthrow the existing political order.

During the 1970's the earlier, more violent protests died down. For one thing, the large majority of America's youth have stopped fighting against the "system." Instead, they have continued their education and their search for ways to earn a living. Also, young people have been granted a more important role in society. The Voting Rights Act of 1970 and the Twenty-sixth Amendment in 1971 have extended to 18-year-olds the right to vote.

But the unrest has continued, often in less visible ways than in the 1960's. Divorce rates have climbed. Growing numbers of single-parent families have taken their places alongside the traditional two-parent family groups. Some workers have turned their backs on the traditional business world and have sought out less financially rewarding but more personally satisfying jobs. Subjects rarely if ever discussed in private social gatherings as recently as the 1960's are now frankly considered in books, family magazines, motion pictures, and television programs.

Reaction to changes. By the late 1970's there were signs that a strong conservative reaction to the turmoil of earlier years was building. Many Americans felt that traditional goals and purposes were in danger of being lost. To many observers the strong Republican showing in the 1980 elections offered firm evidence that the nation had entered a more conservative time in its history.

The economy has brought other changes as well. For many people the major concerns of life are finding a job in a narrowing job market or making enough money to keep up with inflation. Where the 1960's had "hippies," the

1980's have "yuppies," young urban professionals concerned with their careers.

It remains unclear if the movement toward traditional values will remove the unrest of the two decades before the 1980's. For one thing, many of the changes that had been made are now "new" traditions. When two sets of traditions come into conflict, unrest often results.

Reexamining government's role. As Americans questioned their values and traditions in recent years, they also began to question the role of government in their lives.

As you have read, some founders of the nation were concerned that the federal government not have too much power. During the early 1800's debates on how powers should be divided between the federal and state levels of government were common. The Civil War seemed to settle the question of power, firmly establishing that the federal government had supreme authority.

Nevertheless, the federal government remained reluctant to assert authority in matters of daily life and business. For example, the first federal regulatory agency was not formed until 1887. Also, until the 1930's the federal government took no major role in trying to end the economic depressions into which the country plunged from time to time.

The Great Depression that started in 1929 led to a larger role for the federal government as state and local governments were powerless to relieve the widespread suffering that afflicted so many Americans. President Franklin Roosevelt's programs, such as Social Security, brought the federal government into daily life in an unprecedented way.

World War II and America's new role as world leader also encouraged the growth of the federal government. In the 1960's federal programs under Kennedy's New Frontier and Johnson's Great Society increased the size of government. Presidents Nixon and Ford promised to reduce the size and role of the federal government. In spite of their promises, public employment and federal spending increased.

More and more people began to question the role that the federal government was playing. Disenchantment with the federal government was heightened by the Watergate scandals and rising inflation and unemployment rates. In 1964 an opinion poll had asked Americans if they "trust the government in Washington to do what is right most of the time." At that time 62 percent of the people who were polled answered "yes." When the question was asked again in 1980, only 23 percent replied "yes."

Dissatisfaction with government showed up at the state level as well. In 1978 California voters approved Proposition 13, which required their state government to cut taxes and expenses. Since then 19 other states have passed similar measures.

During the election campaign of 1980 Ronald Reagan asked for the chance to reduce federal involvement in some aspects of people's lives. In his Inaugural Address he cautioned, "In this present crisis, government is not the solution to our problem; government is the problem." In his first messages to Congress, President Reagan called for sharply reduced federal programs in social welfare, education, research, and support of the arts. His calls received much early popular and Congressional support. Reagan also supported a constitutional amendment requiring that the federal government balance its budget. He believed that such an amendment would help slow the growth of government.

Nevertheless, how much the federal government's role can be reduced remains in question. The extent to which the federal government has been involved in daily life has not always been apparent. For example by 1980, ▲ government payments to individuals made up 28 percent of total personal income in the nation. Cutting back on this involvement would mean sacrifice and hardship for many citizens.

SECTION REVIEW

See underscored items, text pp. 966, 968 - 70.

Identify: *Columbia*, lasers, Head Start program, Twenty-sixth Amendment, Proposition 13

For answers to questions, see Answer Key, pp.A131-32.

1. **Organizing Ideas:** Describe some ways in which scientific research and technology have changed the daily lives of Americans.

2. **Summarizing Ideas: (a)** What problems did the educational system face during the 1960's and 1970's? **(b)** Describe some of the efforts to solve these problems.

3. **Analyzing Viewpoints:** What did President Reagan mean when he said, "In this present crisis, government is not the solution to our problem; government is the problem"?

4. **Determing Cause and Effect: (a)** Describe the changes in values in the 1970's and 1980's and **(b)** cite the reasons for each change.

▲   Discussion topic: The difficulty of reducing or eliminating government aid once it has been given.

Claude D. Pepper, the feisty congressman from Florida, is the oldest member of the United States Congress and a folk hero to the nation's senior citizens.

Pepper sponsored his first senior citizen legislation in 1929 when he was first elected to the Florida House of Representatives. He then served in the United States Senate from 1936 to 1951. In his memoirs, President Franklin D. Roosevelt described Pepper as "a model for the new kind of Southern political leader."

In 1963 he won election to the United States House of Representatives. Since 1977, when he became chairman and ranking member of the influential House Select Committee on Aging, Pepper has been an outspoken champion of the elderly. He has secured legislation in all areas of concern for the nation's senior citizens. Pepper has criticized the media for portraying senior citizens as "toothless, sexless, humorless, and witless. . . ." He has also attacked President Reagan's proposed cuts in social security benefits, lamenting their effects on the elderly and the needy.

The ageless Pepper, who frequently works a fifteen-hour day, has indicated that he will probably retire in the year 2000. He has, however, reserved the right to stay on the job.

2 American economic issues remain a source of continuing concern

See Teaching Suggestions in TMRG, p.TM231.

When President Reagan in his 1981 Inaugural Address said "in this crisis . . . government is the problem," the crisis he spoke of was an economic one. In both the 1980 and the 1984 Presidential campaigns, the economy was a major issue. Soaring prices and a growing national debt were only parts of the trouble. On economic fronts—productivity, growth, investment—the nation seemed to be slipping from its position as an industrial leader.

The roots of the problems. Many economists have traced the serious problems that affected the economy back to the mid-1960's. At that time the economy seemed healthy. The United States, however, was becoming more deeply involved in the Vietnam War. The federal government had spent heavily for this war with-

out increasing taxes. As money was pumped into the economy, the federal debt rose.

At the same time that the United States was waging the war in Vietnam, President Johnson declared a war on poverty. This war on poverty also pumped money into the economy, but it increased the debt as well.

The massive government spending helped fuel **inflation.** Inflation can be described simply as a significant rise in the cost of materials for agricultural and industrial production, labor, consumer goods, services, and credit. It can also be thought of as an overabundance of money in relation to the goods and services that money can buy.

Attempts to curb inflation. President Johnson at last called for a tax increase to cut the growing deficit and cool down the economy. The tax increase did not take effect until 1969, however, when Richard Nixon took office.

By then inflation was increasing at the rate of 4.7 percent a year. Americans were demanding that the President take action to halt inflation. President Nixon tried two methods of controlling inflation. First, he cut federal

971

spending for education, welfare, housing, urban renewal, and anti-pollution measures, reducing the budget by several billion dollars.

Second, Nixon encouraged the Federal Reserve Board and the nation's banks to increase interest rates sharply. The "tight money" policy, as it was called, was intended to make borrowing more expensive. This in turn would cut into the overabundance of money that allowed Americans to bid up the prices of goods and services.

Despite these measures, inflation continued at an alarming rate. Finally, in August 1971, Nixon announced a new economic program. Its main feature was a 90-day freeze on wages, prices, and rents. A Cost of Living Council was set up to develop guidelines for wages, prices, and profits after the freeze ended. Although both business and labor were unhappy with parts of the program, the rate of inflation did slow a little.

Encouraged by this development, Nixon eased the controls in January 1973, claiming that inflation was moderating and the economy was beginning to slow down. With restraints removed, prices began to soar. Nixon

again applied partial controls, which he removed in 1974. Once more inflation shot up. This time the rate was increased by new OPEC demands for higher oil prices.

Inflation and stagflation. When President Ford took office, the annual rate of inflation was 12 percent. Ford, like Nixon, was convinced that excessive government spending was a major cause of inflation. Ford tried to reduce government spending and slow down the economy. By 1975 the rate of inflation had dropped to 7 percent.

Ford's efforts, though, had unfortunate results. They brought about a nationwide slump in business, or recession, the worst since before World War II. During the winter of 1974–75, the nation's industrial output dropped, and millions of people lost their jobs. By the summer of 1975, more than 8 million men and women were unemployed.

A new word, **stagflation**, was used to describe the puzzling combination of a stagnant economy and a high rate of inflation. Traditional measures for aiding the economy were not effective with stagflation. Cuts in spending by the government to reduce inflation produced longer unemployment lines. Increased government spending and tax cuts helped stimulate employment, but they also increased the rate of inflation.

The recession did, finally, slow inflation. When President Carter took office in 1977, the inflation rate was 4.8 percent. However, the rate of unemployment remained high, about 7 percent. Carter tried to reduce this unemployment by putting more money into the economy. Federal spending was increased and federal taxes were cut. Such policies led to another rise in the inflation rate, and by late 1978 it had risen to 10 percent.

To combat inflation, Carter called for a program of voluntary wage and price controls. The federal guidelines asked workers to limit requests for wage increases to a maximum of 7 percent, including fringe benefits. Business, for its part, was asked to voluntarily limit price increases to a maximum of 5 percent.

Stronger measures, higher inflation. Carter's voluntary controls did not halt the rising cost of living. The increase in the cost of living was pushed along by OPEC's sharp boosts in the price of oil. By the spring of 1980, the rate of inflation had risen to more than 18 percent a

Consumer Price Index • 1970 - 1984

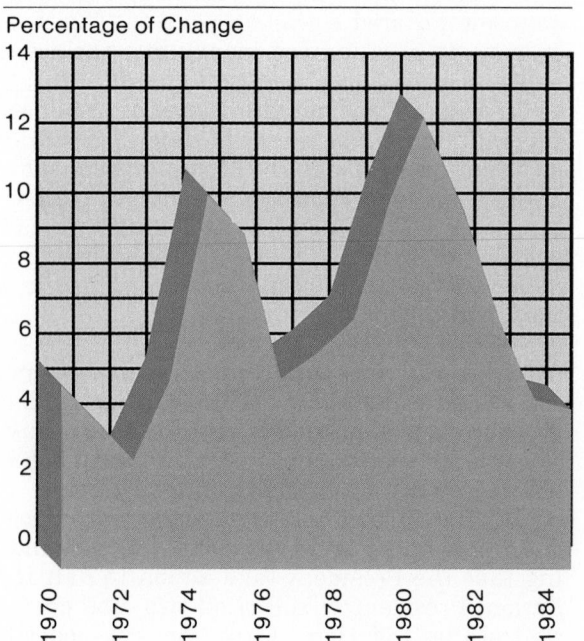

Percentage of Change

At this truck assembly plant, truck chassis begin their journey along the robot welding conveyor. Advanced technology has helped the American automobile industry remain competitive with those of foreign countries, but has reduced the number of jobs in the industry. Describe the effects of worldwide competition on the American automobile industry.

year. The value of the dollar shrank. In 1980 it took nearly $5 to buy what $1 had bought in 1940. The increases over just the last ten years were startling. In 1971 a gallon of gasoline cost about 37¢. By 1981 it cost about $1.27. In 1971 a rib roast sold for $1.18 a pound. By 1981 it was $3.69 a pound.

The nation's economy was in serious trouble, and the Carter administration redoubled its efforts to find a cure. The Federal Reserve Board tightened credit. Leading commercial banks raised the prime rate of interest on money borrowed to more than 20 percent. Carter also tried to cut federal spending. The anti-inflationary measures, however, had the undesirable side effect of increasing the nation's unemployment.

By 1980 the inflation crisis had become serious indeed. In the early years of the inflationary boom, incomes had kept ahead of costs. For example, from 1967 to 1973 the average real income of Americans, adjusting for inflation, rose 17.5 percent. But from 1974 to 1978 it rose only 5.5 percent. Starting in 1979 real income actually declined.

One economist put it this way: "The two-earner family has about peaked, average real weekly earnings are falling, and now you are going to have to put teenagers to work just to keep income stable."

The impact of the economic problems can be expressed another way. In 1972 the United States had the highest standard of living in the world. By 1980, it had slipped to fifth place.

Refer the students to the chart, Growth of Average Family Income, on page 1006. Ask the students what effects inflation would have on rising income.

With less real income, Americans were less ready to make major purchases, especially when they faced high interest rates on borrowed money as well. Thus industries vital to the nation's economy, such as the automobile and the housing industries, suffered. Because the inflation rate was usually higher than the rate of interest banks paid on savings accounts, people were also less willing or less able to save money.

Inflation and business. Inflation ate away at the welfare of businesses as well as that of individuals. People's unwillingness to make large purchases cut into business sales. The reduced rate of savings also meant that there was less money available to invest in business.

Inflation also made business leaders less willing to make necessary commitments in costly new equipment. Without such new equipment, the productivity of some key industries declined.

The results were striking. In the 1960's the rate of the nation's economic growth averaged 4.1 percent a year. In the 1970's it was only 2.9 percent. Likewise, the output of goods and services per worker, which had been growing at 1.9 percent a year from 1968 to 1973, dropped to 0.7 percent a year from 1973 to 1979.

World competition. The economic picture looked gloomier still when America's economic performance was compared with that of rival industrial nations. Japan and West Germany in particular had made amazing economic strides. They had invested heavily in new and efficient technology and were able to seize a sizable share of markets in other countries and even in the United States.

In 1962, United States-made aircraft commanded over 70 percent of worldwide sales. By 1979, the figure had shrunk to 58 percent. The records of automobile sales showed that the United States was losing ground to foreign competition. In 1960, almost 96 percent of all cars sold in this country were American-made. Twenty years later only 79 percent were produced in the United States.

Reagan's program. These were the economic challenges that Ronald Reagan faced when he took office in 1981. Constructing a strong new economic program became his major order of business.

Reagan's first priority was victory over inflation. In order to win this victory, the government needed to balance the budget—that is, reduce expenditures to match the amount of money available from revenue.

The Reagan administration called for a two-pronged attack on the problem. One prong was a sharp reduction in federal spending except for defense. The idea was to reduce expenses by cutting back on some programs, dropping others, and eliminating wasteful practices.

The second prong was a tax cut that called for across-the-board reductions in personal and corporate taxes. The purpose of these tax reductions was to encourage people and businesses to save and invest in the modernization of old plants and the construction of new ones. Investment would help to revitalize the economy. Revitalization would mean more goods and services, stabilized prices, and more jobs. With more workers on the job and more taxpayers, the government would be able to balance the budget. That was the broad outline of the President's plan.

In 1981, after heated debate, Congress enacted most of President Reagan's requests. There were tax cuts of 25 percent over three years for all Americans. Some business taxes were reduced as well. The federal budget was also slashed by $35 billion.

A slow start. Americans then waited to see what effect President Reagan's economic program would have. Would "Reaganomics" stabilize inflation and begin to improve the nation's economy?

As Reagan had promised, inflation rates began to drop. The reasons for the drop were not good, however. The nation's economy was slumping. People were not buying or investing. The stock market dropped, new car sales fell, and home building stalled.

In 1982 the inflation rate continued down, but the rate of unemployment soared. By the end of the year, more than 12 million Americans were out of work. More than 24,000 businesses had failed. One major indicator of economic conditions is the **gross national product** (GNP). This is the total value of all goods and services produced annually in the nation. In 1982, instead of growing, the GNP declined by 1.8 percent, the worst figure since 1946. The nation was clearly in a recession, and many feared it might be heading into a depression.

Turnaround. But December 1982 marked the low point. By 1985 economic conditions had gradually improved. Inflation rates remained low and unemployment dropped to around 8 percent. The GNP showed a very strong growth of 6.1 percent. Compared to 1982 the output of goods and services per worker increased by more than 12 percent.

The deficit. President Reagan, however, had not reached one of his major economic goals, a balanced budget. In fact, by 1985 the budget deficit was greater than ever. The deficit—how much more the government spends than it takes in—is expected to average, at the very least, $160 billion a year through the rest of the 1980's. Another estimate predicts it might be as high as $350 billion by the end of the 1980's.

Economists worry that the swelling budget deficit could undo the recovery. Since the government has not taken in enough money, it has had to borrow. If it borrows too much, the money available to businesses and individuals will have to be reduced. Interest rates will rise. Businesses will be reluctant to invest in new equipment, and people will hold back on major purchases. In short, there will be danger of a new recession or inflation.

President Reagan's political opponents insisted that taxes would have to be raised to reduce the deficit. In the campaign of 1984, though, Reagan held firm, promising no tax hikes.

SECTION REVIEW

See underscored items, text pp. 971 - 72, 974.
Identify: inflation, Cost of Living Council, stagflation, gross national product
For answers to questions, see Answer Key, p.A132.
1. **Evaluating Ideas:** How can government actions affect the rate of inflation?

2. **Determining Cause and Effect:** How did world competition affect the United States economy?

3. **Comparing Ideas: (a)** What event outside the United States had an effect on the economy during President Carter's time in office? **(b)** How did Carter's attempts to control the economy differ from Nixon's? **(c)** Describe President Reagan's program for improving the nation's economy.

4. **Analyzing Ideas:** How might the growing federal budget deficit be harmful to the nation's economy?

See Teaching Suggestions in TMRG, pp.TM231-32.
Many of the economic ups and downs you have just read about were directly related to energy—its scarcity or abundance.

Energy needs. Energy topped the list of critical resources. Without it American productivity would be drastically reduced. Sources of energy provided the essential power for American farming, lumbering, mining, manufacturing, transportation, communications, heating, cooking, lighting, air-conditioning, and countless other tasks.

The fossil fuels—coal, oil (petroleum), and natural gas—make up the major energy resources of the United States and the rest of the world. The world's dependence upon fossil fuels, however, is relatively new.

This cartoon satirizes the energy crisis of the early 1970's, when Arab oil price increases caused severe problems for the United States economy.

It is the Industrial Revolution, which began hardly more than 200 years ago, that brought the change. Only when industrialization began did people need to make heavy use of the fuels that had been buried in the earth for millions of years.

Moving toward crisis. The United States grew to be the world's largest industrial nation. It also became the world's largest producer, importer, and consumer of energy resources. Cheap fuel from the coal mines of the Appalachian region and the oil fields of Texas and Oklahoma had helped to build a way of life for many Americans.

From 1950 to 1970 American energy consumption doubled. By 1973 almost 47 percent of that energy came from oil. Big American cars cruised the highways, getting about 13 miles to a gallon of gasoline. With gasoline costing only about 39 cents a gallon, however, low mileage per gallon was no problem. Homes in the cooler winter climates were well heated, with thermostats set up into the 70's. Air conditioners roared away in summer, keeping homes nicely cooled when outside temperatures soared above the 80's. American industry also consumed vast amounts of energy. With fuel so cheap, factories and machinery were not always energy efficient.

In time the most accessible petroleum from America's fields began to run out. Oil was still available, but only in deeper pockets. It was now more expensive to bring petroleum and natural gas to the surface. An easier and cheaper answer seemed to be foreign oil, which was still plentiful and cheap. Early in 1973 a barrel of oil from the Middle East cost only $2.10. The United States began to rely more and more on imported oil for its energy needs.

End of an era. In 1960 many foreign oil producers had formed a **cartel**, or pool. The Organization of Petroleum Exporting Countries, or OPEC, as it was known, was designed to eliminate competition among members and to control the price of oil on the world market. At first price increases were small, but in 1973 they began to rise more rapidly.

OPEC had many Arab nations as members. In October 1973, angered by American support of Israel in the Yom Kippur War, OPEC halted all shipments of oil to the United States. When the embargo was lifted, the price of a barrel of oil had increased to almost $10.

Some Americans had suffered real hardships because of the embargo. All Americans paid higher prices for energy because of it. These price increases contributed to the inflation of the 1970's. But Americans still increased their use of foreign oil. By 1978 about 30 percent of the oil Americans used came from an OPEC nation.

Then came the Iranian revolution of 1978–79. All shipments of Iranian oil to the United States were cut off. Again lines formed at gas stations and again prices soared. By 1982 the price of oil had reached $34 a barrel.

Search for a policy. Many Americans felt that the events of the 1970's proved that the nation needed a national energy policy. After the first oil embargo, President Nixon had announced Project Independence. The goal of this project was to see the United States free of its reliance on foreign oil by the early 1980's.

A few steps were taken toward that goal. In 1977 Congress created the Cabinet-level Department of Energy. One of the major jobs of the new department was to conduct research and help coordinate efforts to develop solar energy and other alternative energy sources.

In 1978 President Carter, acting in spite of strong public opposition, announced that he was going to remove controls regulating the price of oil produced in the United States. The price of the deregulated oil and gasoline immediately began to rise to the levels charged by the OPEC countries. Consumers reacted to the higher prices by reducing their consumption of gasoline and oil, as Carter had hoped.

The following year President Carter presented a comprehensive energy program to Congress and to the American people. He proposed limiting petroleum imports to the 1977 levels, providing more aid for mass transit systems, and developing energy conservation measures. The heart of Carter's program was a plan for encouraging private industry to develop synthetic fuels and for the industrial and residential use of solar energy.

The Reagan administration brought a different approach to the energy problem. President Reagan favored some of Carter's moves. For example, he speeded up deregulation of domestic oil prices. Reagan argued that higher prices for domestic oil would encourage oil companies to search for and develop America's resources. This would, he believed, help free the nation of dependence on foreign oil.

The United States was late in establishing a systematic method for preserving its documents of enduring importance. During much of the nation's history, many significant documents were privately held, and some were lost. Few were available to scholars or to the public.

In the 1920's, several prominent scholars joined with federal agencies in urging Congress to correct this situation. In 1926 Congress appropriated funds for storing the nation's archival treasures. President Hoover laid the cornerstone of the National Archives on the Washington Mall in 1933. The building was designed in the neoclassical style by John Russell Pope.

The National Archives Act of 1934 directed the Archives to select, preserve, and make available the nation's most valuable documents to the government and the public. Since that time documents selected for inclusion in the Archives have been cleaned and stored in windowless stack areas, under carefully controlled conditions of temperature and humidity.

The nation's most treasured documents — the originals of the Declaration of Independence, the Constitution, and the Bill of Rights — are displayed in the great Exhibition Hall of the Archives. They are sealed in a bronze and glass case that can be lowered directly into an underground vault.

In other areas Reagan's policies differed from Carter's. Reagan spoke, at times, of eliminating the Department of Energy. He took no immediate steps to do so. Instead he played down the importance of that department. Also Reagan was not committed to synthetic and alternative fuels projects. He made heavy cuts in the budgets for these projects. Basically, President Reagan's actions reflected his belief that private citizens and businesses, not government, were the best hopes for a solution to the nation's energy problems.

Conservation measures. Private citizens, sometimes with the assistance or encouragement of the federal government, took action to solve the energy crisis.

For example, the federal government set standards requiring auto makers to produce more fuel-efficient cars. With gasoline costing $1.20 per gallon in 1983, many Americans bought smaller cars, most of which were fuel-efficient. Soon smaller cars accounted for 59 percent of all cars sold, and the average car was getting 26 miles per gallon of gasoline.

Americans tried to make their homes energy-efficient as well. They added insulation to walls and ceilings of their homes and weatherstripped doors and windows. They turned their thermostats down in winter. The appliances they bought in the 1980's were 50 percent more energy-efficient than the appliances of the 1970's. Approximately half a million homes were equipped with some form of solar heating.

Industry and agriculture also practiced energy conservation. New machinery for factories was more fuel-efficient. New production methods saved energy, too. The aluminum industry, for example, began to recycle cans. This practice saved up to 95 percent of the energy needed to make aluminum from raw ore.

There was another factor that led to energy conservation. The oil shortage and soaring prices had helped bring on the recession. But the recession then helped to lower the demand,

977

and with it, the price of oil. In the early 1980's approximately 30 percent of the nation's industrial capacity was idle. This greatly cut the demands for energy and oil.

The effects. The efforts of the federal government and private citizens had positive results for the nation's overall energy picture. The price of oil dropped to $27 a barrel and showed signs of going still lower. By 1983 the United States was importing 27 percent less oil from foreign sources than it had ten years before. Of this imported oil, OPEC nations supplied only about 7.5 percent. Overall use of oil dropped from 18.4 million barrels a day to 15.2 million.

The United States also increased its own production of oil. In addition the federal government stockpiled a reserve of almost 400 million barrels of oil in Texas and Louisiana for use in emergencies.

When the energy crisis was at its worst, doom and gloom estimates appeared. One predicted that the world's supply of petroleum might be exhausted by the year 2000, or even sooner. The effects of conservation efforts, however, surprised even the experts. Now, a more optimistic prediction states that oil supplies will last well into the 21st century. The outlooks for other sources of energy are just as good.

Natural gas. Natural gas, a combustible mixture of methane and other elements is usually found close to petroleum deposits. Predictions had been made that natural gas, too, would run out around the year 2000. New discoveries have changed this prediction. Deep wells, drilled to below 15,000 feet (4,500 meters) have hit vast, unexpected reserves of natural gas. If these resources are tapped, they will last well into the future.

Natural gas may even come to replace gasoline as a fuel in automobiles. Vehicles powered by natural gas are already in use in Italy and New Zealand. In the United States, many businesses have equipped their fleets of cars to run on natural gas.

Coal. During the 1970's coal provided about 18 percent of the energy consumed in the United States. It has been estimated since that all the world's coal reserves, of which 20 percent are in the United States, are large enough to meet the projected world energy demands for the next 200 to 300 years.

Important research is being done in the 1980's to discover new ways of using coal as a fuel. Experimental gassification plants are being built in which coal is processed into liquid fuel and gas.

There are, however, serious questions about the wisdom of using coal as a major source of energy. In the past the mining of coal had been enormously costly in terms of human life. Underground mining has been one of the world's most hazardous occupations. Miners live with the ever-present danger of accidents and the possibility of suffering from black lung disease. Surface or strip mining, while less costly in terms of human life and health, could damage the environment.

Increased use of coal as a fuel also has presented grave hazards to the environment. The effect of burning coal upon the world's climate is a matter of increasing concern. "Acid rain" ▲ produced by chemicals released into the air by burning coal has killed fish in many lakes and threatened both forests and farmlands.

Nuclear energy. Another energy source—nuclear power—also has posed major problems.

After World War II, nuclear fission—the splitting of atoms—seemed to promise a safe, cheap, clean, and unlimited source of power. Nuclear fission, however, failed to meet its early promise. Its failure has not been due entirely to technical problems, which have been, and continue to be, very difficult and complex. The failure has been due, in part, to environmentalists, who have insisted that nuclear plants meet strict safety standards. As nuclear knowledge has accumulated, awareness of the risks posed by nuclear radiation leaks has grown.

In 1979 nuclear risks were demonstrated in the nation's most serious nuclear accident. The accident occurred at Three Mile Island ● power plant, near Harrisburg, Pennsylvania. The plant's cooling system malfunctioned, threatening a dangerous meltdown of the nuclear reactor's core. Experts finally brought the reactor under control, but clean-up costs have risen into the millions. Despite efforts by environmentalists, Three Mile Island reopened on October 3, 1985, and is operating at 15 percent of its original capacity.

The near disaster heightened concern over the safety and cost of nuclear power. Public outcry grew for stricter safety regulations for nuclear plants.

▲   The United States and Canada are currently involved in cooperative projects to clean up the damage caused by acid rain.

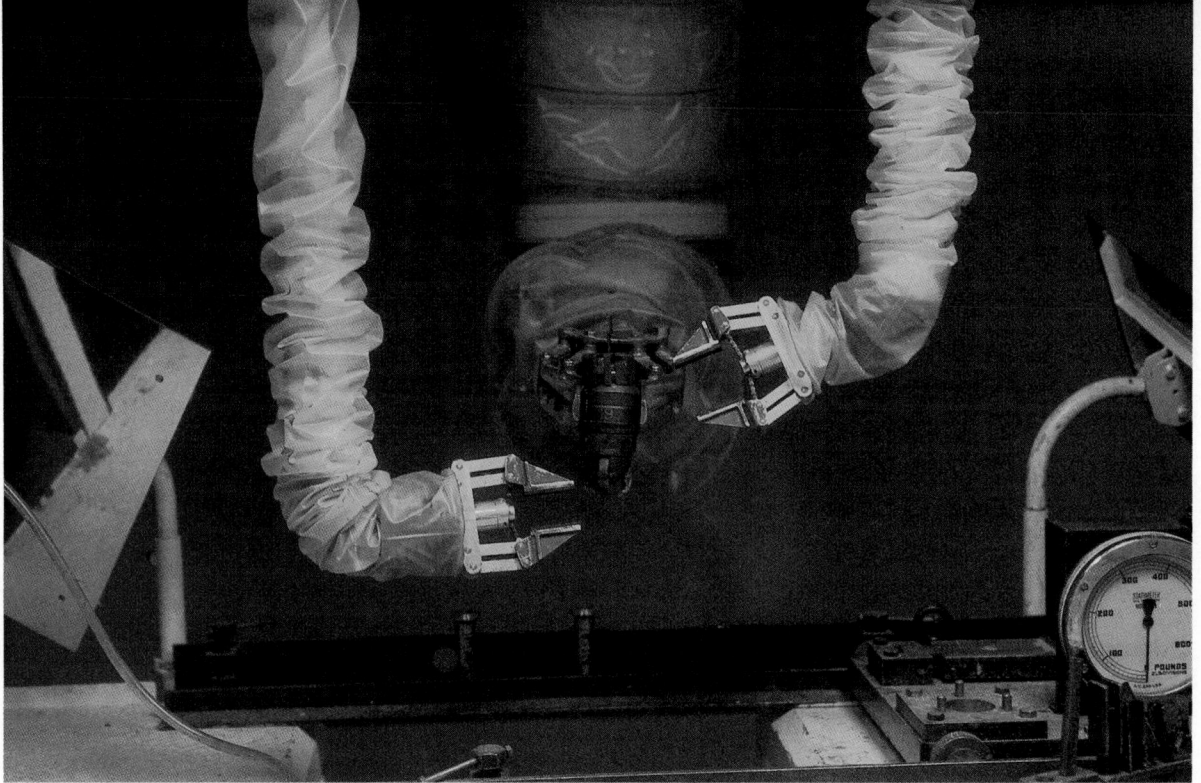

Modern technology is helping to make the use of nuclear power safer. This photo shows robotic hands working on a fuel cell at a nuclear power plant.

Other aspects of using nuclear power have troubled many people. How, they asked, is it possible, with our limited knowledge, to determine what impact nuclear plants will have on human beings and all other forms of life? How could an absolutely foolproof method be developed to seal, transport, and store the deadly waste of nuclear reactors?

Concerns over safety and skyrocketing construction costs have slowed the development of nuclear power plants. By the early 1980's there were 82 plants in operation and 48 under construction. However, no orders for new plants had been placed since 1978. Despite this fact, projections are that 20 percent of the electricity this nation will use in 1990 will be generated by nuclear power plants.

Fusion. Nuclear fusion held some hope as a safer source of atomic energy. In this process, light atoms of hydrogen are fused together to form a heavier element, releasing vast amounts of energy. Research into fusion power is continuing, but it is unlikely to bear results before the next century.

Energy alternatives. There are still other energy alternatives. One is the increased use of power generated by falling water—hydroelectricity. There are limits, however, to the amount of energy that can be secured from hydroelectric power. In fact, the output of energy from hydroelectric power is expected to fall by 1990.

Another energy option is geothermal energy. This is the power generated by the tapping of hot gases and steam in the depths of the earth. Several such plants are operating in Europe and the United States. However, geothermal energy does not appear likely to add much to the nation's energy resources in the near future.

The most promising possible energy source is the sun—the original source of all the earth's energy. Solar energy is inexhaustible. Scientists estimate that all of the United States' energy requirements for an entire year can be met by the amount of solar energy that falls on the surface of Lake Erie in a day. Efforts to harness solar energy have been increasingly successful in recent years. For example, solar batteries have been developed to supply electricity to spacecraft. Solar panels on homes can usually supply a house with heat and hot water. Energy credits on income taxes have help spur residential use of solar energy.

Discussion topic: Ask students to name problems with each type of energy alternative: hydroelectricity (requires large water supply), geothermal and tidal (both need research and development), solar (expensive, bulky), wind, (unpredictable).

979

Both Presidents Ford and Carter encouraged the development of solar energy devices. President Reagan, however, has appeared to have less interest in solar power as a potential energy source.

The outlook for energy. Much work remains to be done if alternatives to fossil fuels are to be developed. The conservation efforts of American citizens, however, mean that fossil fuel resources will last longer than people had guessed, allowing more time for energy research.

If the economic recovery of the 1980's continues, the odds are also good that energy savings from conservation will increase. With greater prosperity, consumers and businesses could invest in still more fuel-efficient vehicles and machines. It appears that the United States has become, and will remain, an energy-conscious society.

SECTION REVIEW

See underscored items, text pp. 975 - 76, 978 - 79.
Identify: fossil fuels, cartel, OPEC, Department of Energy, acid rain, Three Mile Island, fusion
For answers to questions, see Answer Key, p.A132.
1. **Sequencing Ideas:** What events lead to an energy crisis in the United States in the 1970's?

2. **Comparing Ideas:** Compare the energy programs of Presidents Carter and Reagan.

3. **Summarizing Ideas:** (a) What steps did American citizens and industry take to try to ease the energy crisis? (b) Name some of the alternative energy sources being used in the United States today. (c) What are the advantages and disadvantages of each?

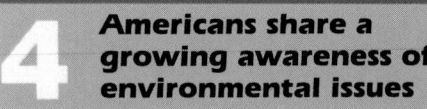

4 Americans share a growing awareness of environmental issues

See Teaching Suggestions in TMRG, pp.TM232-33.
Energy issues have been just a part of a broader subject—the environment. As Americans studied ways to manage energy resources, they also have explored ways to manage their environment.

Impacts on the environment. By the 1970's and 1980's it became clear that serious damage has been done to the most essential of all the natural resources—air, water, and the earth itself.

Clean air in many cities has been replaced by smog. Some 200 million tons of pollutants have poured into the air each day from motor vehicles, industries, homes, and power plants. Wastes pouring into the nation's rivers have turned many of them into virtual sewers. Growing shortages of fresh water in many areas of the country have led to strict regulations and sometimes to rationing.

The earth, as well as the air and water, has been deteriorating. Fertile land has been bulldozed to build highways, shopping malls, and housing developments. Irreplaceable farmland is vanishing at an estimated rate of 10,000 acres (4,000 hectares) every day.

The problem of wastes. The wastes produced by industrial societies have created problems for every form of life on the planet. Urban areas alone have generated tons of garbage and solid waste every day. Hazardous wastes from chemical plants, nuclear reactors, and other industries have polluted the air and accumulated in thousands of dumps across the countryside.

Finding proper ways to dispose of all the waste has been difficult. Much of it can be burned. Burning, however, releases pollutants and deadly fumes.

Burial has been another widely used method of disposal. Some wastes decompose safely or remain harmless underground. Other buried wastes might become deadly threats to the environment.

In the late 1970's and early 1980's, two events brought the issue of hazardous wastes into public awareness. Niagara Falls, New York, became the scene of one disaster. There homes had been constructed near an abandoned chemical waste dump known as Love Canal. In time, wastes seeped out of the dump and into the surrounding land and homes. Residents complained of strange illnesses, and a much higher than average number of children were born with birth defects.

In 1978 President Carter declared a state of emergency in the area. The state government finally agreed to move 800 families from the area and to purchase their homes.

The scene of the second incident was the tiny town of Times Beach, Missouri. At one time the streets of the town had been sprayed with waste oil to hold down dust. Ten years later it was discovered that the oil contained dioxin, a common chemical byproduct. Dioxin, however, is also one of the most deadly substances manufactured by humans. Attempts to clear the dioxin from the soil failed. The federal government then agreed to buy the land in the town and relocate the residents.

Managing resources. Many concerned citizens worry not just about pollutants added to the environment but also about resources removed from it. The oil shortages have raised the possibility that one day fuel might run out. Americans have begun to realize that other vital resources might also be limited.

Much of the productivity of the United States has come from resources within its own borders. At the beginning of the 1900's, the United States produced about 15 percent more raw materials than it consumed. By 1940, however, American industry had consumed more raw materials than the nation had produced. During the past 25 years the United States has become increasingly dependent upon the rest of the world for a large part of the materials it needs to maintain its industrial productivity.

Nevertheless, the nation still contains vast natural resources. The lands owned by the federal government itself contain 50 percent of the nation's coal, 80 percent of its shale oil, and 40 percent of its salable timber. Important deposits of copper, silver, asbestos, lead, beryllium, and other minerals are also found on these lands.

Some resources, such as timber, are renewable. Others, such as metals, can be recycled. Still others, such as coal, can be used only once, and then they are gone forever. Many Americans wonder what policy the nation should follow in using these precious resources.

A concerned awakening. By the mid-1960's one historian reminded Americans that "less than a century divides the era when America was looked upon as a Garden of Eden or savage wilderness. Frankly, no people have ever so quickly subdued their natural environment." For the most part, Americans accomplished this conquest with little thought to its effect on the environment.

To be sure, as early as the 1890's the policies of the federal government had begun to reflect the concerns of a few Americans about

Concern over environmental issues and a fear of nuclear energy has spurred protests and demonstrations. What are the main threats to the environment in the 1980's?

(pollution, loss of wilderness and arable land)

the need to conserve the nation's resources (see page 600). The early conservation movement, however, important as it was, had limited goals. The first conservationists were concerned mainly with regulating the use of particular resources—forests, wildlife, minerals, and the soil. A half century later, by the 1950's, more and more people were beginning to understand that the earth itself was being endangered by the waste and misuse of resources.

Major credit for arousing public concern probably belonged as much to Rachel Carson as to any other individual. In her bestselling book *Silent Spring,* published in 1962, she warned that "along with the possibility of the extinction of mankind by nuclear war, the central problem of our age has ... become the contamination of man's total environment." This warning received nationwide attention and began to influence the thinking of many government officials and private citizens.

Government action. The Kennedy and Johnson administrations responded to these warnings with new programs to safeguard the environment. Later, in 1970, during Nixon's first term, Congress created the Environmen-

The first "Earth Day" was celebrated in the spring of 1970. This was a national demonstration and symbolic clean-up to call attention to the serious problem of pollution. Earth Day is now celebrated every spring.

981

The newspaper editorial stated: "A few thousand words from her, and the world took a new direction." The "her" referred to by the editorial writer was Rachel Carson. The "new direction" was today's environmental movement.

DDT's first use as an insecticide took place during World War II when it was used successfully to kill insects around military installations. After the war DDT proved very effective in ridding American farms of insects that destroyed or damaged crops and livestock. DDT was also used effectively in tropical countries to destroy malaria-carrying mosquitoes. Many scientists hailed DDT as universally useful.

In 1962 Rachel Carson published *Silent Spring.* In the book she claimed that DDT was destroying much more than insect pests. Carson pointed out that the spraying of elm trees in Hanover, New Hampshire, resulted in a 70 percent drop in the robin population of the area. She showed the chain of events that took place when birds ate insects or food that had been sprayed with DDT. The eggs produced by the robins became so fragile that the baby robins were never properly matured and hatched.

The Carson book produced a storm of controversy between environmentally concerned groups and agricultural and chemical manufacturing groups. The farming and chemical groups were sure they would never have a destroyer of insect pests as efficient as DDT. Environmental groups, on the other hand, were equally sure of the longlasting and devastating side-effects of DDT.

Each group began to muster support. One report — that of President John F. Kennedy's Science Advisory Committee — was especially damaging to DDT's continued use. It pointed out the harm DDT did to field crops and to other plants. It showed the effect it had on other forms of animal life besides insects. It showed how DDT residues poisoned the soil, the water, and the atmosphere. It also hinted at the possibility of DDT causing cancer in humans who had ingested it into their bodies.

The publication of *Silent Spring* by Rachel Carson sparked a renewed interest in environmental concerns. It increased awareness about the close relationships that exist in nature. This increased awareness and concern eventually led to the banning of DDT by the administration of President Richard M. Nixon. That ban remains in effect today.

tal Protection Agency (EPA). In addition, state and local governments stepped up their environmental efforts.

By the mid-1970's an impressive body of federal, state, and local laws had been enacted. Laws regulated the use of pesticides, insecticides, and other potentially dangerous sprays. Species of wildlife threatened with extinction had been protected. Automobile makers had to provide pollution control devices on cars, trucks, and buses. Congress passed the Clean Air Act in 1970 and the Water Pollution Control Act in 1972. After the Love Canal incident, Congress also approved a $1.6 billion superfund for emergency cleanup of the nation's hazardous waste dumps.

Efforts had also been made to restore the natural beauty of the countryside by regulating junkyards and dumps. Federal and state governments set aside more land to preserve as wilderness or parks. Considerable progress had been made in the management and conservation of America's forests, soil, and water. A beginning had been made in conserving and recycling the nation's other natural resources as well.

A change in policy. Not all Americans have felt that increased action by the federal government is necessary. As economic conditions in the nation worsened in the late 1970's, many people called for easing of environmental regulations. Critics have argued that meeting strict clean air and clean water requirements would cost billions of dollars. They have claimed that foreign businesses that did not have to meet these standards could produce goods more cheaply and gain a larger share of the world market. Critics charged also that federal regulations have often been unclear and contradictory. These critics say that the cost of complying with such regulations should be weighed against the benefits they may produce. They further claim that the regulations should be enforced only if the benefits produced exceed the costs of compliance.

President Reagan has agreed with many of these points. He has proposed cutting back and simplifying environmental regulations. He also has criticized the focus of earlier administrations, claiming that their drive to acquire more land for parks and wilderness had led to the neglect of lands already in the system.

John S. Herrington was appointed Secretary of Energy in 1985. Support for the Department of Energy has diminished as memories of oil shortages in the 1970's fade.

Thus, Reagan had made deep cuts in the budgets of the Environmental Protection Agency and the Department of the Interior.

Reagan also has felt that the search for resources on federal lands should be encouraged. Such exploration would help cure the energy crisis and build up reserves of valuable minerals. Accordingly James Watt, then Secretary of the Interior, opened areas of the sea floor off the East and West coasts for oil exploration. Watt also leased large tracts of federal parks and wilderness to coal companies for mining.

Many groups condemned Reagan's environmental policies. The same groups pressured the President and Congress to maintain the environmental policies of previous administrations. James Watt resigned in October 1983. At that time Reagan firmly defended his environmental record. He softened his call, however, for changes in environmental policies.

Looking to the future. Environmental groups and President Reagan differed, often sharply, about environmental problems and actions needed to solve them. Many environmentalists believed that increased government involvement was needed. President Reagan and his supporters believed the task was one for private citizens and industry.

The United States has the resources at hand to solve environmental problems. It has the largest pool of scientists, engineers, and management experts of any industrial nation. During the twentieth century, Americans have been foremost in the movement into the scientific-technological world. Because they have often led the way, Americans have been among the first to meet the consequences of the reckless use of land and resources.

Urgent though the challenges of preserving the environment are, the American people have reason to move into the future with confidence. The same scientific genius and engineering talents that unknowingly created many of the as yet unsolved problems remain available to solve them.

SECTION REVIEW

See underscored items, text pp. 980 - 83.

Identify: Love Canal, dioxin, Rachel Carson, Environmental Protection Agency, James Watt

For answers to questions, see Answer Key, pp.A132-33.

1. **Analyzing Ideas: (a)** What are some ways of disposing of hazardous wastes? **(b)** What are some drawbacks to these methods?

2. **Synthesizing Ideas:** Describe actions the federal government took to eliminate problems in the environment.

3. **Comparing Ideas:** How did President Reagan's environmental policies differ from those of the Presidents who preceded him in office?

DEVELOPING HISTORY STUDY SKILLS

Relating Economics and History   Making Economic Decisions

In 1985 the United States government was spending nearly $1 trillion a year. Though that amount of money is tremendously large, Congress and the President must make crucial economic decisions when they prepare the annual budget. Money and resources are limited. Therefore, economic decisions often have far-reaching consequences. Citizens need to understand economic decision-making if they are to make worthwhile political and economic choices. They must also be familiar with the decision-making process so they can judge the actions of local, state, and national leaders.

You have already been introduced to the skill of evaluating decisions (Chapter 36, page 818). Review the steps listed on page 818 to refresh your memory.

How To Make Economic Decisions

To successfully make economic decisions, follow these guidelines.

1. **Define the issue.** The issue must be defined precisely enough to measure costs.
2. **List the alternatives.** Identify all possible courses of action.
3. **Compare the costs and benefits of each alternative.** Consider the cost-benefit ratio of each alternative. Be sure to consider long-range consequences.
4. **Evaluate each alternative.** Determine the option that will be most beneficial in relation to the costs.
5. **Make the decision.** After taking all factors into account, select the option that will best resolve the issue. Often making economic decisions is difficult. More information may be needed before a choice can be made.

Applying the Skill

In 1984 the United States spent more than $59 billion to purchase foreign oil. This figure accounted for more than 50 percent of the U.S. trade deficit. Some economists have suggested raising gasoline prices several cents to reduce gasoline consumption, thereby reducing the need

for foreign oil purchases. To make such a decision, an analysis of alternatives would take the following course of action.

- Analyze petroleum use. Determine if, in fact, the purchase of foreign oil is a problem of the magnitude indicated by trade statistics. If the problem is the tremendous expenditures for foreign oil, then these steps would follow.
- Consider alternatives to raising gasoline prices such as **(a)** incentives for increased U.S. oil production, **(b)** development of synthetic fuels at government expense, **(c)** federal laws requiring more fuel-efficient cars, and **(d)** limitations on petroleum imports to an established amount.
- Determine the benefits and costs of each alternative. If gasoline prices were raised, for example, people would spend more for gasoline and less on other goods and services. This could have a negative effect on the overall economy.
- Evaluate the benefit-cost ratio for each alternative. Limitations on petroleum imports might cause unemployment as refineries slowed down or closed. Also, less petroleum would be available for medicines and plastics. The money saved by limiting oil imports, however, could be used to spur other industries and the search for alternatives for petroleum-based products.

Practicing the Skill

Read Sections 2 and 3 of this chapter. Select an economic issue discussed on those pages of the textbook. Gather information about the issue from your textbook and other sources. Then on a separate sheet of paper, answer these questions.

1. What economic issue did you select?
2. What are the possible alternative solutions to the problem stated in question 1?
3. What are the benefit-cost relations of each of the alternatives?
4. Which solution appears to be the most beneficial? Why?

984   (Answers will vary.)

Since its foundation, the United States has grown from a rural society of small villages and towns to an urban society of large cities and suburbs. The economy of the United States has developed from a simple one based on self-sufficient farming to an infinitely more complex one based on the technology of an industrial society. The nation has emerged from relative isolation to a role of world leadership.

As the nation moves into the third century of its existence, a new generation of Americans faces new problems, new challenges, and new opportunities. The federal government and its budgets have grown greatly since the 1930's, and many citizens have been asking if such growth is necessary and helpful. The American economy, a marvel to people the world over, has seemed to falter in the face of continuing problems with inflation and increasing international competition. The American land, with its beauty and its wealth of natural resources, needs thoughtful care and management to insure that its treasures will be passed on to future generations.

The American people have solved many immense problems during the course of their nation's history. They need only the will and the commitment to meet the new challenges of the future.

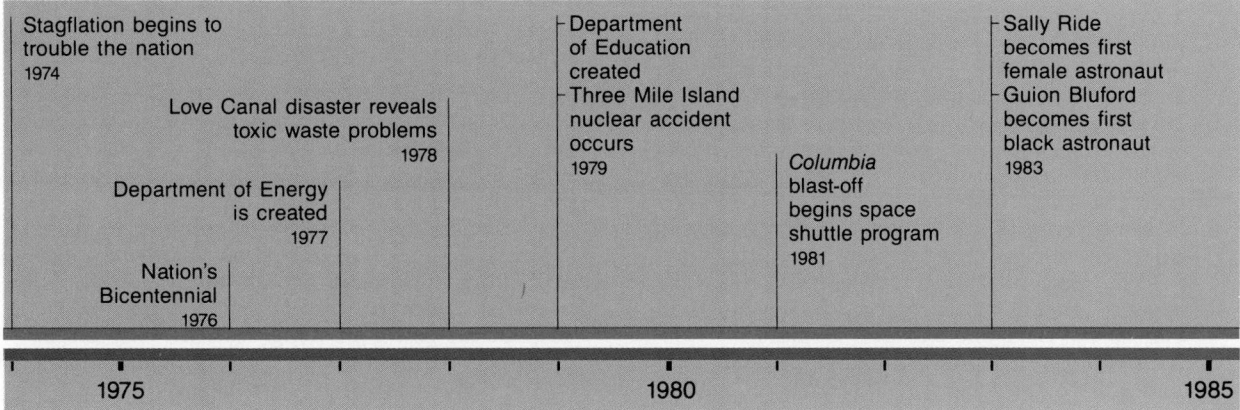

Stagflation begins to trouble the nation
1974

Love Canal disaster reveals toxic waste problems
1978

Department of Energy is created
1977

Nation's Bicentennial
1976

Department of Education created
Three Mile Island nuclear accident occurs
1979

Columbia blast-off begins space shuttle program
1981

Sally Ride becomes first female astronaut
Guion Bluford becomes first black astronaut
1983

1975   1980   1985

CHAPTER
43 REVIEW

Reviewing Important Terms

Decide whether each of the following sentences is true or false. If the sentence is false, replace the underlined term with the word or phrase that will make it true.

1. Lasers use <u>nuclear</u> energy for medical and scientific purposes.
2. The <u>energy crisis</u>, caused by an overdependence on <u>fossil fuels</u>, has spurred a search for alternative energy sources.
3. In the mid-1970's, <u>deflation</u>—a combination of a stagnant economy and a high rate of inflation—became a major economic problem.
4. In 1960, many oil producing nations formed a <u>cartel</u> to eliminate competition and to control the price of oil.
5. The massive government spending of the 1960's helped fuel <u>inflation</u>.
6. A <u>budget deficit</u> occurs whenever the federal government <u>spends</u> more money than it takes in during a fiscal year.

Practicing Critical Thinking Skills

1. **Analyzing Ideas.** How have computers changed Americans' way of life?
2. **Summarizing Ideas.** (a) Describe the economic problems facing the United States when Ronald Reagan became President. (b) What steps have been taken to solve each problem?
3. **Evaluating Ideas.** Should the United States try to solve its economic problems without regard for the economic situation in the rest of the world? Why or why not?
4. **Organizing Ideas.** (a) List the advantages and disadvantages of using each of the following as a major source of energy: oil, natural gas, coal, nuclear, solar. (b) Rank them according to your findings. (c) Write a paragraph in which you explain the reasons for your rankings.
5. **Interpreting Ideas.** (a) What are some causes of the environmental problems that the United States faces today? (b) How are Americans trying to solve these problems?
6. **Summarizing Ideas.** (a) What are the goals and objectives of the United States space programs? (b) The space program involves great risks and expense. Should the program be continued in view of the risks and expense? Explain.
7. **Analyzing Viewpoints.** Human history becomes more and more a race between education

and catastrophe. (a) What does this statement mean? (b) Do you agree? Explain.
8. **Relating Past to Present.** Pollution of the land and water and misuse of natural resources began with the first European settlers. (a) Explain this statement. (b) Do you agree? Explain.

Developing History Study Skills

Making Economic Decisions. Refer to the graph on text page 972 to answer the following questions.

1. What information does the graph show?
2. In what year was the Consumer Price Index the lowest? the highest?
3. By what percentage did the Consumer Price Index increase between 1972 and 1974? What does this measure indicate about the rate of inflation?
4. By what percentage did the Consumer Price Index decrease between 1980 and 1982? What does this measure indicate about the rate of inflation?
5. Between what years was the percentage of change in the Consumer Price Index the smallest? What does this small percentage of change indicate about the rate of inflation between those years?
6. Based on the data shown on the graph, when would consumers most likely have received the best value for the dollars they spent? Write a brief paragraph explaining the rationale behind your answer.

Relating Geography and History

During the 1970's cold weather and a scarcity of fossil fuels convinced many Americans to move to the Sunbelt. By studying the map on page 1005 and answering the questions below, you will better understand the causes and effects of this migration.

1. (a) How did the 1973 oil embargo affect energy prices? (b) What actions did Americans take to adapt to this situation?
2. Why did many Americans see a move to the Sunbelt as a solution to the oil shortage?
3. (a) In which states did the population increase by more than 25 percent between 1970 and 1980? (b) Which states had population decreases? (c) How has this migration changed the distribution of political power in Congress? (d) Why might the discovery of new energy sources be important to the states in the northern "Snowbelt"?

UNIT THIRTEEN
REVIEW

Discussing Ideas

1. Why might conflicts arise between the two goals of protecting the environment and decreasing United States dependence on foreign oil?
2. Did the United States assume more responsibility around the world during the 1960's, 1970's, and 1980's than it could meet? Give evidence to support your answer.
3. (a) What is the Third World? (b) How did its emergence affect the relationships between the United States and the Soviet Union?
4. Consider the New Deal, the Fair Deal, the New Frontier, and the Great Society. (a) How were these administrations similar? (b) How were they different?
5. Make a chart comparing blacks, Hispanics, Indians, and women in terms of (a) problems, (b) goals, (c) methods used to achieve goals, and (d) degree of success.
6. Of the Presidents since 1960, whom do you think has done the best job under the circumstances of the nation? Be sure to explain the standards by which you made your judgment.

Applying History Study Skills

Interpreting a News Story. The following news story was written by Peter Grier for the *Christian Science Monitor*. Read the news story and, answer the questions below.

> *Periodically, American satellites take pictures of a strange haze over the eastern Atlantic. The haze is not water vapor but dirt. . . .*
> *All over the globe, precious topsoil is blowing and washing away. Soil erosion now threatens the productivity of almost half the world's farmland, a just-released report by the Worldwatch Institute concludes.*
> *The report estimates that roughly 25 billion tons of the globe's topsoil is, in effect, disappearing each year. At that rate, the world will have 7 percent less topsoil in 1994 than it does today.*

(a) Review text page 938. Is this a standard news story, a feature, or a commentary? Explain. (b) What is the topic of the story? (c) What is the source of the writer's facts? (d) How does the story use statistics to support the main idea? (e) Does the story make you respond in any way to its content? Explain.

Making Connections

1. (a) Make a time line of major world events since 1960 involving the United States. (a) Which events have caused significant changes in United States foreign policy? Explain. (b) Make a time line of domestic events since 1960. Does there seem to be any connection between foreign and domestic affairs? Explain.
2. Listen to or read speeches by Dr. Martin Luther King, Jr. (a) Summarize briefly the main point of each speech. (b) Do you find the speeches persuasive? Why or why not?
3. Draw a political cartoon that might have appeared during the administration of each of the Presidents discussed in Unit Thirteen. Be sure to make clear the point of view of each cartoon.
4. Prepare a map of all or part of your municipality divided into its voting precincts. Indicate how each precinct included on your map voted in the 1980 and 1984 Presidential elections. (a) Find out why the voting results were the way they were. You might look into the number of voters registered in each party in each precinct or the ethnic or economic composition of the population of each precinct. (b) Make a generalization about the voting results in your municipality in these two elections based on your findings and the information in your textbook.

Reading in Depth

Borland, Hal, *When the Legends Die* (Boston: Houghton Mifflin). A novel about Tom Black Bull, a young Indian who tries to "find himself" after leaving the reservation.

Carpenter, M. Scott, et al., *We Seven* (New York: Simon and Schuster). Firsthand accounts of the early days of the American space program.

Carson, Rachel, *Silent Spring* (New York: Fawcett). The influential and moving warning about pesticides and the environment.

Grebler, Leo, et al., *The Mexican-American People: The Nation's Second Largest Minority* (New York: Free Press). Thorough study of Mexican-Americans in the southwestern United States.

Haley, Alex, *Roots* (New York: Dell). The story of the author's search for his own past—from Africa in the 1700's to the southern United States today.

REFERENCE
SECTION

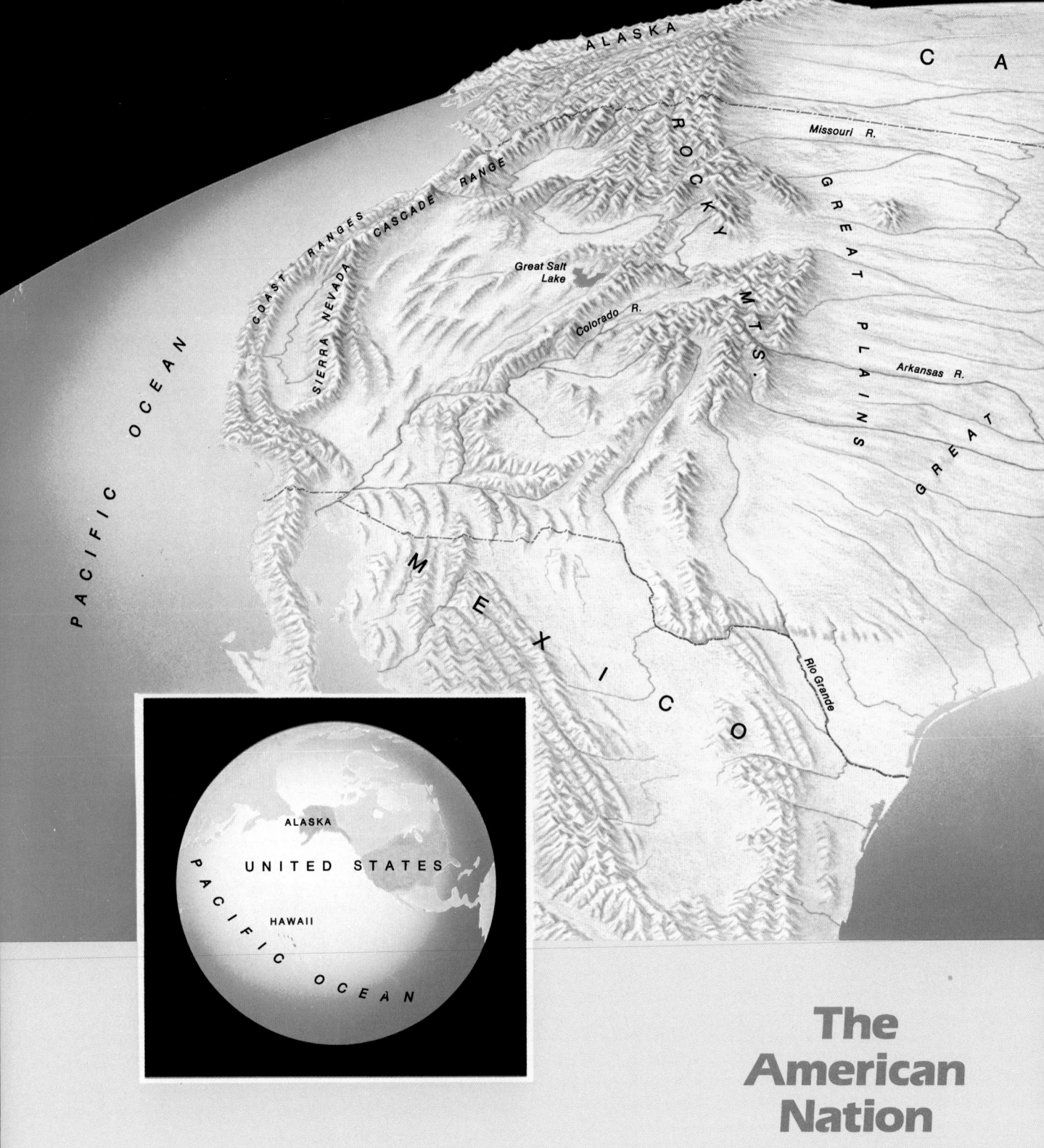

ALASKA

C A

Missouri R.

ROCKY

GREAT

Great Salt
Lake

Colorado R.

PLAINS

Arkansas R.

COAST RANGES

CASCADE RANGE

SIERRA NEVADA

MTS.

GREAT

PACIFIC OCEAN

M E X I C O

Rio Grande

ALASKA

UNITED STATES

PACIFIC

HAWAII

OCEAN

**The
American
Nation**

A vast land area and rich resources have helped the United States to grow into a powerful nation. The country began as 13 sparsely populated states. But within a few generations, American settlements extended from the Atlantic Coast to the Pacific Shore — and beyond. Soon vast new areas were added to the federal union as territories. Then as the territories became more populated, many more states were created, all of which were fully equal with the older ones.

The federal government and the many state and local governments were small at first. But as the country's population grew, so did the number of government employees. Federal, state, and local governments needed more employees and more money to meet their responsibilities in areas such as public welfare, education, and defense. To pay for the increased expenditures, governments increased taxes and added some new ones, such as income taxes and taxes for the social security fund. In recent years there have been many demands to reduce government taxes. There also have been demands for limiting government spending in many areas. You can become more informed about the issues raised in these demands by studying the graphs on the accompanying pages.

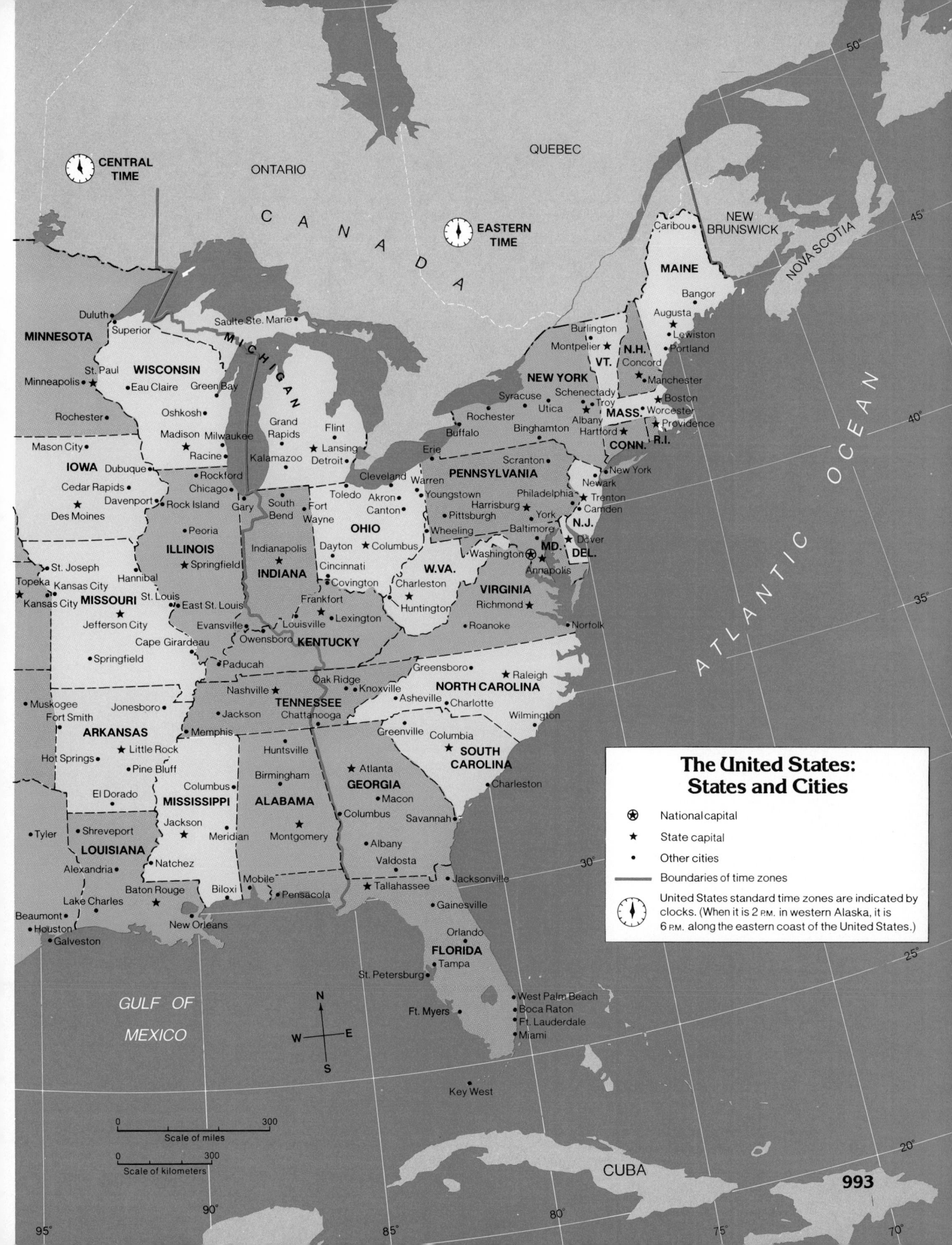

**The United States:
States and Cities**

⊛ National capital

★ State capital

• Other cities

━━━ Boundaries of time zones

🧭 United States standard time zones are indicated by clocks. (When it is 2 P.M. in western Alaska, it is 6 P.M. along the eastern coast of the United States.)

CENTRAL TIME

EASTERN TIME

QUEBEC

ONTARIO

CANADA

NEW BRUNSWICK

NOVA SCOTIA

ATLANTIC OCEAN

MAINE
• Caribou
Bangor •
Augusta ★
• Lewiston
Montpelier ★ N.H. • Portland
Burlington • VT. Concord ★
• Manchester

Duluth •
MINNESOTA
• Superior
Saulte Ste. Marie •
MICHIGAN
• St. Paul
WISCONSIN
Minneapolis • ★
• Eau Claire
• Green Bay
NEW YORK
Syracuse • • Utica Schenectady • Boston ★
Troy ★ MASS. • Worcester
Albany ★ Hartford ★ • Providence
• Rochester • Oshkosh
Grand Rapids
• Flint
Binghamton CONN. R.I.
Mason City •
Madison ★ Milwaukee
• Racine
• Kalamazoo
• Lansing
Buffalo •
• Rochester
Erie •
IOWA • Dubuque
• Rockford
Chicago •
PENNSYLVANIA
Scranton •
New York •
Cedar Rapids •
• Detroit
Cleveland • Warren •
Newark •
• Davenport
Rock Island •
Gary •
South Bend
Toledo • Akron •
Youngstown •
Philadelphia •
Trenton ★
Des Moines ★
• Peoria
Fort Wayne
Canton •
Pittsburgh •
Harrisburg ★
Camden •
York •
N.J.
ILLINOIS
OHIO
Dayton •
• Columbus
Wheeling •
Baltimore •
N.J.
St. Joseph •
Indianapolis ★
Cincinnati •
MD.
Dover ★
Topeka ★ Hannibal •
Springfield ★
INDIANA
• Covington
W.VA.
Washington ⊛
DEL.
Kansas City •
Kansas City
MISSOURI St. Louis •
East St. Louis •
Frankfort ★
Charleston •
Annapolis ★
Jefferson City ★
Evansville •
Louisville •
Lexington •
Huntington •
VIRGINIA
Richmond ★
Cape Girardeau •
Owensboro •
KENTUCKY
• Roanoke
• Norfolk
• Springfield
• Paducah
Greensboro •
★ Raleigh
Oak Ridge •
Knoxville •
NORTH CAROLINA
• Muskogee
Jonesboro •
Nashville ★
• Asheville
• Charlotte
Fort Smith
• Jackson
Chattanooga •
TENNESSEE
Greenville •
Wilmington •
ARKANSAS
• Memphis
Columbia ★
Hot Springs •
Little Rock ★
Huntsville •
SOUTH CAROLINA
• Pine Bluff
Birmingham •
★ Atlanta
• Charleston
El Dorado •
Columbus •
GEORGIA
MISSISSIPPI
ALABAMA
• Macon
• Tyler
• Shreveport
Jackson ★
Montgomery ★
• Columbus
Savannah •
LOUISIANA
Meridian •
• Albany
Alexandria •
Natchez •
Valdosta •
Lake Charles •
Mobile •
• Jacksonville
Beaumont •
Baton Rouge ★
Biloxi •
Tallahassee ★
• Houston
• Pensacola
• Gainesville
• Galveston
New Orleans •

GULF OF MEXICO

N
W E
S

Orlando •
FLORIDA
• Tampa
St. Petersburg •
• West Palm Beach
Ft. Myers •
• Boca Raton
• Ft. Lauderdale
• Miami

0 ─────── 300
Scale of miles

0 ─────── 300
Scale of kilometers

Key West •

CUBA

993

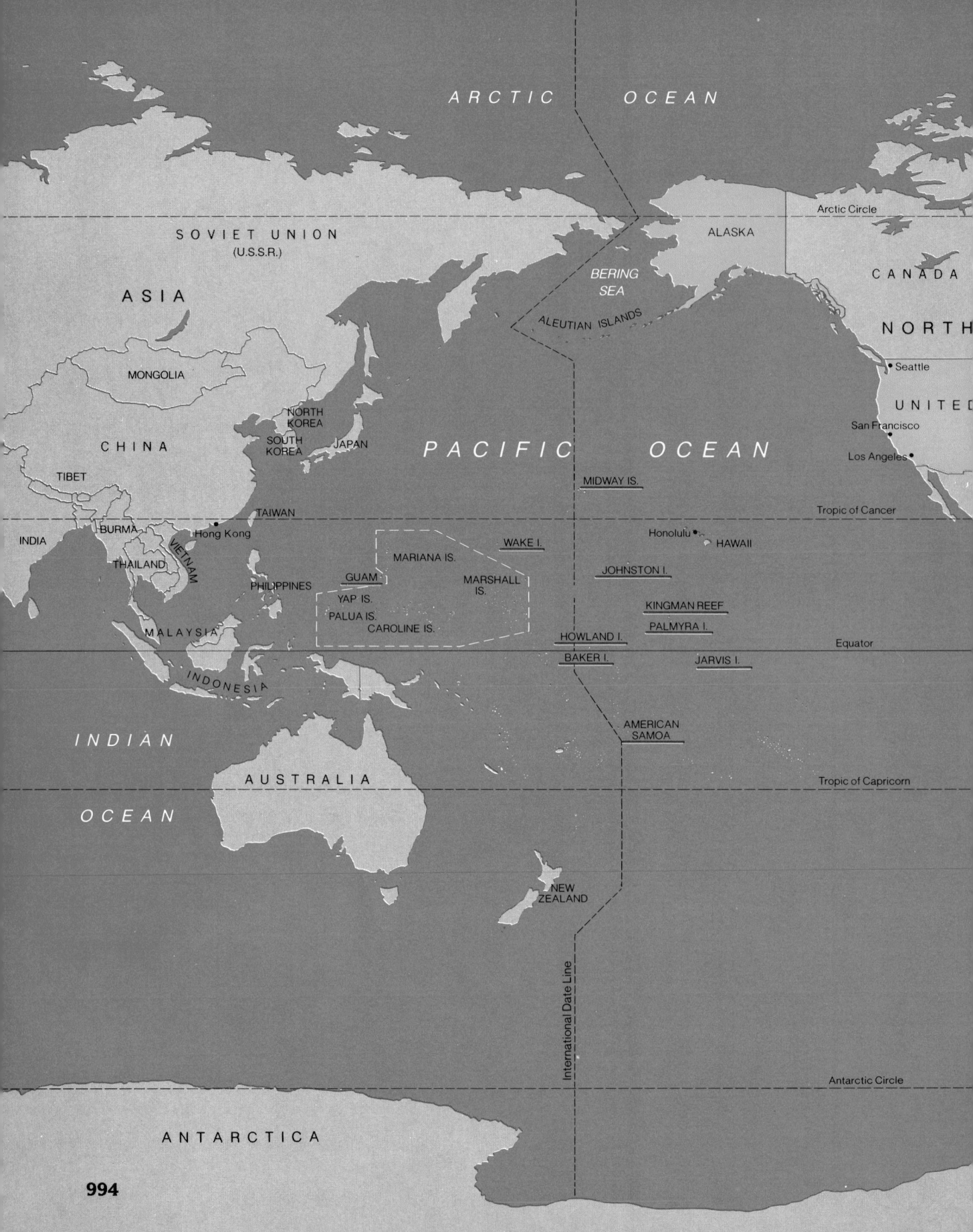

ARCTIC OCEAN

SOVIET UNION
(U.S.S.R.)

Arctic Circle

ALASKA

CANADA

ASIA

BERING
SEA

NORTH

MONGOLIA

ALEUTIAN ISLANDS

NORTH
KOREA

SOUTH
KOREA

JAPAN

PACIFIC OCEAN

Seattle

CHINA

UNITED

San Francisco

TIBET

TAIWAN

MIDWAY IS.

Los Angeles

Tropic of Cancer

INDIA

BURMA

Hong Kong

WAKE I.

Honolulu
HAWAII

THAILAND

MARIANA IS.

VIETNAM

GUAM

MARSHALL
IS.

JOHNSTON I.

PHILIPPINES

YAP IS.

PALUA IS.

CAROLINE IS.

KINGMAN REEF

PALMYRA I.

MALAYSIA

HOWLAND I.

Equator

BAKER I.

JARVIS I.

INDONESIA

INDIAN

AMERICAN
SAMOA

AUSTRALIA

Tropic of Capricorn

OCEAN

NEW
ZEALAND

International Date Line

Antarctic Circle

ANTARCTICA

994

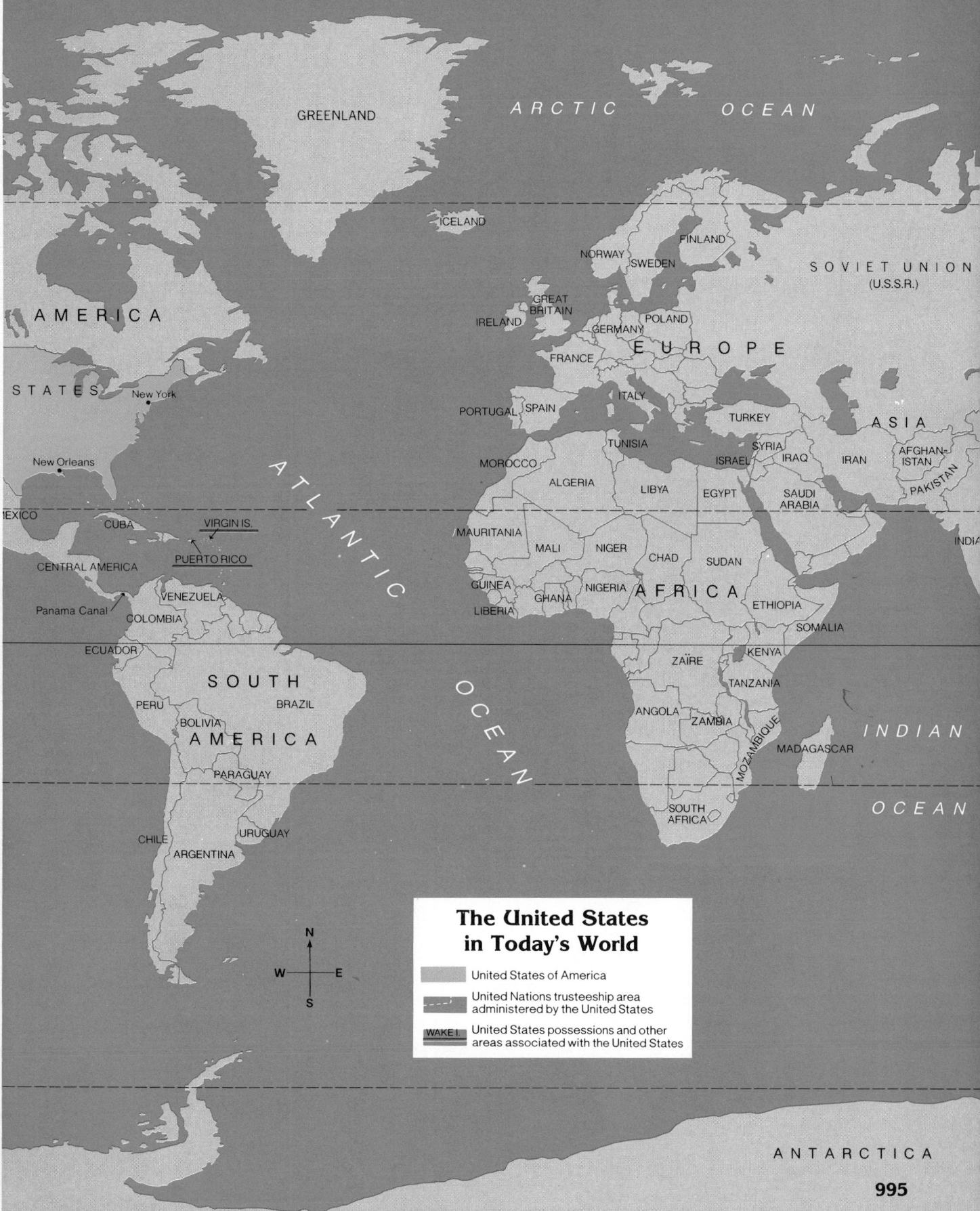

GREENLAND

ARCTIC   OCEAN

ICELAND

NORWAY   FINLAND
          SWEDEN
                              SOVIET UNION
                                   (U.S.S.R.)
IRELAND GREAT
          BRITAIN
A M E R I C A   GERMANY POLAND
          FRANCE   E U R O P E

S T A T E S
          New York   PORTUGAL SPAIN   ITALY   A S I A
                                             TURKEY
New Orleans   SYRIA
                              MOROCCO   ISRAEL IRAQ IRAN AFGHAN-
MEXICO   TUNISIA   ISTAN
          CUBA   VIRGIN IS.   ALGERIA LIBYA EGYPT SAUDI   PAKISTAN
                                                          ARABIA
          PUERTO RICO   INDIA
CENTRAL AMERICA   MAURITANIA
          VENEZUELA   MALI NIGER CHAD SUDAN
Panama Canal   COLOMBIA   GUINEA   A T L A N T I C
          ECUADOR   LIBERIA GHANA NIGERIA A F R I C A ETHIOPIA
                                                            SOMALIA
          PERU   S O U T H   BRAZIL   ZAÏRE KENYA
          BOLIVIA   TANZANIA   I N D I A N
                   A M E R I C A   ANGOLA ZAMBIA
          PARAGUAY   MOZAMBIQUE MADAGASCAR

CHILE   URUGUAY   SOUTH
          ARGENTINA   AFRICA   OCEAN

The United States
in Today's World

          United States of America

          United Nations trusteeship area
          administered by the United States

          WAKE I. United States possessions and other
                   areas associated with the United States

ATLANTIC OCEAN

PACIFIC OCEAN

ANTARCTICA

995

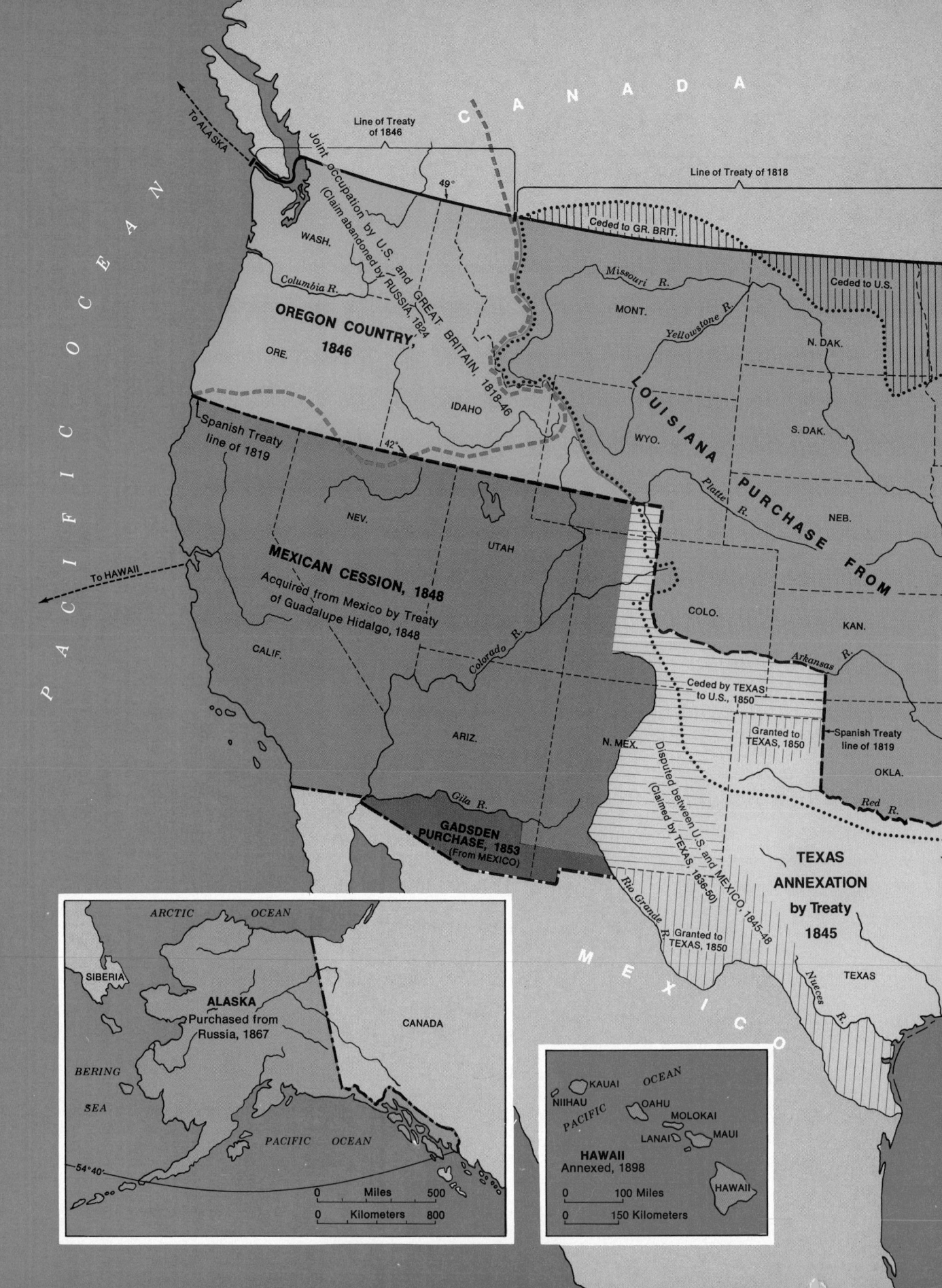

C A N A D A

Line of Treaty
of 1846

Line of Treaty of 1818

49°

To ALASKA

Joint occupation by U.S. and GREAT BRITAIN, 1818-46

(Claim abandoned by RUSSIA, 1824)

Ceded to GR. BRIT.

Ceded to U.S.

WASH.

Columbia R.

Missouri R.

MONT.

N. DAK.

Yellowstone R.

OREGON COUNTRY, 1846

ORE.

IDAHO

LOUISIANA PURCHASE FROM

S. DAK.

WYO.

Platte R.

NEB.

Spanish Treaty line of 1819

42°

NEV.

UTAH

COLO.

To HAWAII

MEXICAN CESSION, 1848
Acquired from Mexico by Treaty of Guadalupe Hidalgo, 1848

Colorado R.

KAN.

CALIF.

Arkansas R.

Ceded by TEXAS to U.S., 1850

Granted to TEXAS, 1850

Spanish Treaty line of 1819

ARIZ.

N. MEX.

Disputed between U.S. and MEXICO, 1845-48 (Claimed by TEXAS, 1836-50)

OKLA.

Gila R.

GADSDEN PURCHASE, 1853 (From MEXICO)

Red R.

TEXAS ANNEXATION by Treaty 1845

Rio Grande R.

Granted to TEXAS, 1850

M E X I C O

Nueces R.

TEXAS

PACIFIC OCEAN

ARCTIC OCEAN

SIBERIA

ALASKA
Purchased from Russia, 1867

CANADA

BERING SEA

PACIFIC OCEAN

54°40'

0   Miles   500

0   Kilometers   800

KAUAI

OCEAN

NIIHAU

PACIFIC

OAHU

MOLOKAI

LANAI

MAUI

HAWAII
Annexed, 1898

0   100 Miles

0   150 Kilometers

HAWAII

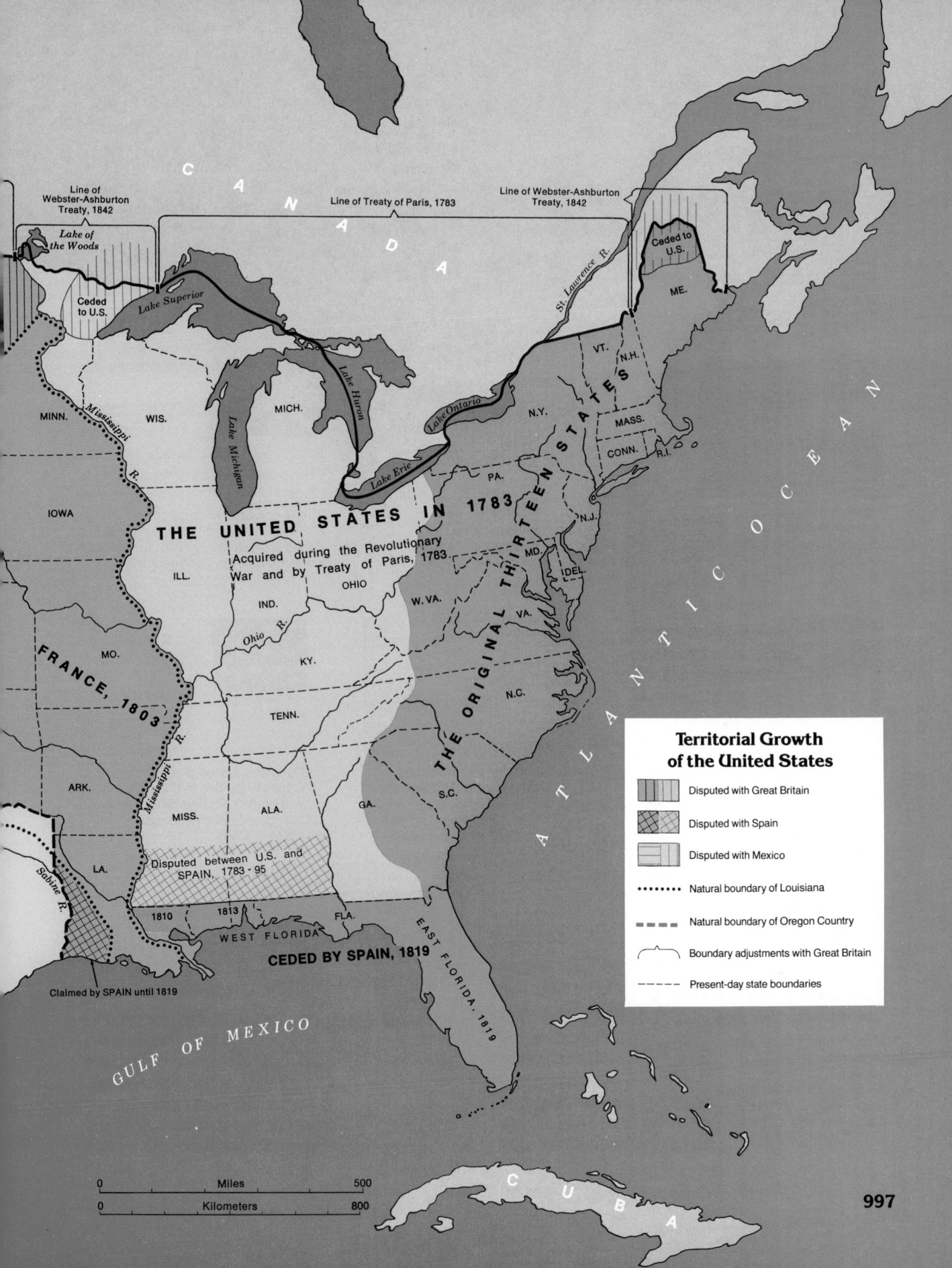

Territorial Growth of the United States

Line of Webster-Ashburton Treaty, 1842
Line of Treaty of Paris, 1783
Line of Webster-Ashburton Treaty, 1842

CANADA

Lake of the Woods
Ceded to U.S.
Lake Superior
Ceded to U.S.
ME.
St. Lawrence R.

Lake Michigan
Lake Huron
Lake Ontario
Lake Erie

VT.
N.H.
N.Y.
MASS.
CONN.
R.I.

MINN.
WIS.
MICH.
PA.
N.J.

IOWA

THE UNITED STATES IN 1783
Acquired during the Revolutionary War and by Treaty of Paris, 1783

ILL.
IND.
OHIO
W. VA.
MD.
DEL.
VA.

Mississippi R.
Ohio R.

MO.
KY.
N.C.

FRANCE, 1803

TENN.
S.C.

ARK.

MISS.
ALA.
GA.

THE ORIGINAL THIRTEEN STATES

Mississippi R.

Disputed between U.S. and SPAIN, 1783 - 95

LA.
Sabine R.
1810   1813   FLA.
WEST FLORIDA
EAST FLORIDA, 1819
CEDED BY SPAIN, 1819

Claimed by SPAIN until 1819

ATLANTIC OCEAN

GULF OF MEXICO

CUBA

Territorial Growth of the United States

▦	Disputed with Great Britain
▨	Disputed with Spain
▥	Disputed with Mexico
•••••	Natural boundary of Louisiana
– – –	Natural boundary of Oregon Country
⏜	Boundary adjustments with Great Britain
– – –	Present-day state boundaries

| 0 | Miles | 500 |
| 0 | Kilometers | 800 |

997

History of the American Flag

The American flag has always been a symbol of national unity. The 50 stars represent the 50 states. The 13 stripes represent the original 13 colonies.

Our flag was officially born on June 14, 1777, when the Continental Congress voted to adopt a national flag. It was to consist of 13 red and white stripes, with 13 stars on a blue field.

The flag has gone through many changes since then. Every time a new state enters the Union, a star is added. Ours is the only flag that changes as the nation grows. The present American flag (left) has been flying since 1960, after Hawaii became the 50th state.

During the Revolution many regiments fought under state or local flags. This flag probably flew at Breed's Hill.

The Navy Jack often flew on American ships during the Revolution. The rattlesnake was an early symbol of independence.

The Grand Union flag combined the flag of Great Britain and 13 stripes. It was first raised on January 1, 1776, to celebrate the forming of the Continental Army.

The first "Stars and Stripes" may have been the Bennington flag of August 1777. Its arrangement of 13 stars and stripes met the guidelines set by the Continental Congress that June.

Although there is no proof, legend has it that Philadelphia seamstress Betsy Ross made the nation's first flag. This is the flag she supposedly designed.

Congress added two stars and two stripes to the flag in 1795. During the War of 1812, Francis Scott Key wrote the "Star-Spangled Banner" in tribute to this flag.

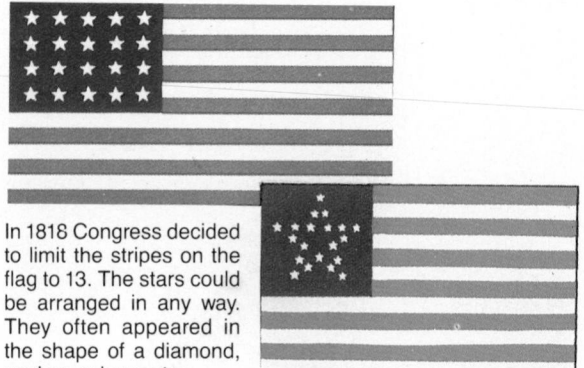

In 1818 Congress decided to limit the stripes on the flag to 13. The stars could be arranged in any way. They often appeared in the shape of a diamond, anchor, or large star.

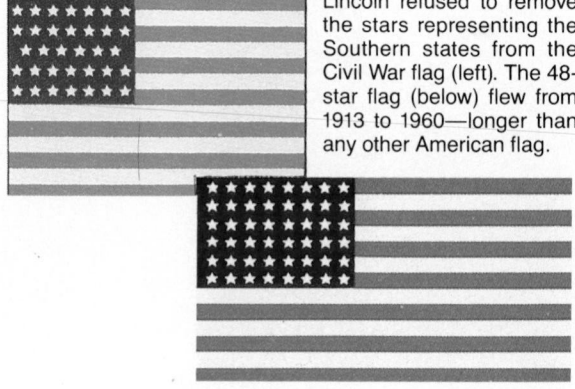

Lincoln refused to remove the stars representing the Southern states from the Civil War flag (left). The 48-star flag (below) flew from 1913 to 1960—longer than any other American flag.

STATES OF THE UNITED STATES

State	Date of Entry into Union	Area in Square Miles°	Population (1980 Census)	Capital City	Largest City (1980 Census)
Alabama	1819	51,609	3,890,061	Montgomery	Birmingham
Alaska	1959	586,400	400,481	Juneau	Anchorage
Arizona	1912	113,909	2,717,866	Phoenix	Phoenix
Arkansas	1836	53,104	2,285,513	Little Rock	Little Rock
California	1850	158,693	23,668,562	Sacramento	Los Angeles
Colorado	1876	104,247	2,888,834	Denver	Denver
Connecticut	1788	5,009	3,107,576	Hartford	Bridgeport
Delaware	1787	2,057	595,225	Dover	Wilmington
Florida	1845	58,560	9,739,992	Tallahassee	Jacksonville
Georgia	1788	58,876	5,464,265	Atlanta	Atlanta
Hawaii	1959	6,424	965,000	Honolulu	Honolulu
Idaho	1890	83,557	943,935	Boise	Boise
Illinois	1818	56,400	11,418,461	Springfield	Chicago
Indiana	1816	36,291	5,490,179	Indianapolis	Indianapolis
Iowa	1846	56,290	2,913,387	Des Moines	Des Moines
Kansas	1861	82,264	2,363,208	Topeka	Wichita
Kentucky	1792	40,395	3,661,433	Frankfort	Louisville
Louisiana	1812	48,523	4,203,972	Baton Rouge	New Orleans
Maine	1820	33,215	1,124,660	Augusta	Portland
Maryland	1788	10,577	4,216,446	Annapolis	Baltimore
Massachusetts	1788	8,257	5,737,037	Boston	Boston
Michigan	1837	58,216	9,258,344	Lansing	Detroit
Minnesota	1858	84,068	4,077,148	St. Paul	Minneapolis
Mississippi	1817	47,716	2,520,638	Jackson	Jackson
Missouri	1821	69,686	4,917,444	Jefferson City	St. Louis
Montana	1889	147,138	786,690	Helena	Billings
Nebraska	1867	77,227	1,570,006	Lincoln	Omaha
Nevada	1864	110,540	799,184	Carson City	Las Vegas
New Hampshire	1788	9,304	920,610	Concord	Manchester
New Jersey	1787	7,836	7,364,158	Trenton	Newark
New Mexico	1912	121,666	1,299,968	Sante Fe	Albuquerque
New York	1788	49,576	17,557,288	Albany	New York
North Carolina	1789	52,712	5,874,429	Raleigh	Charlotte
North Dakota	1889	70,665	652,695	Bismarck	Fargo
Ohio	1803	41,222	10,797,419	Columbus	Cleveland
Oklahoma	1907	69,919	3,025,266	Oklahoma City	Oklahoma City
Oregon	1859	96,981	2,632,663	Salem	Portland
Pennsylvania	1787	45,333	11,866,728	Harrisburg	Philadelphia
Rhode Island	1790	1,214	947,154	Providence	Providence
South Carolina	1788	31,055	3,121,820	Columbia	Columbia
South Dakota	1889	77,047	690,178	Pierre	Sioux Falls
Tennessee	1796	42,244	4,590,750	Nashville	Memphis
Texas	1845	267,339	14,228,383	Austin	Houston
Utah	1896	84,916	1,461,037	Salt Lake City	Salt Lake City
Vermont	1791	9,609	511,456	Montpelier	Burlington
Virginia	1788	40,815	5,346,279	Richmond	Norfolk
Washington	1889	68,192	4,130,163	Olympia	Seattle
West Virginia	1863	24,181	1,949,644	Charleston	Charleston
Wisconsin	1848	56,154	4,705,335	Madison	Milwaukee
Wyoming	1890	97,914	470,816	Cheyenne	Casper
District of Columbia		69	637,651		

Principal Territories, Possessions, and Dependencies	Area in Square Miles°	Population (1980 Census)	Capital City
Puerto Rico	3,435	3,196,520	San Juan
U.S. Virgin Islands	133	95,591	Charlotte Amalie
Guam	209	105,821	Agana
American Samoa	76	32,395	Pago Pago

°1 square mile = 2.59 square kilometers.

The American People

The people who settled America came from many lands. Indeed, all Americans were immigrants or the descendants of immigrants. The American Indians, the first Americans, for example, originally were hunting peoples who came to North America from Asia. Today the United States has a diverse population, composed of people with many national and racial backgrounds, religious beliefs, and regional loyalties. The following graphs and charts tell much about these Americans. One graph portrays which decades experienced the largest immigration to this country. Another graph shows which countries were the former homes of immigrants living in the United States in 1980. The following pages also provide information on how quickly the population of the country grew over the years and how specific regions, states, and cities have participated in this growth. In addition, this section of the Reference Section highlights certain trends that concern all Americans. There are graphs which show a rise in average life expectancy, a growth in family income, and an increase in educational enrollment. Graphs and charts, such as these shown here, are valuable tools for the study of the history of the United States. They support many of the themes stated in the textbook and provide a richer understanding of the American experience.

Immigration to the U. S. · 1821–1980

Millions of Immigrants

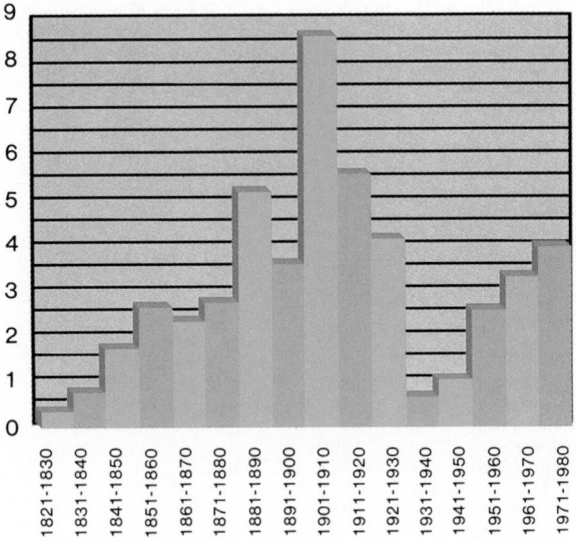

Source: *Statistical Abstract of the United States,* United States Immigration and Naturalization Service

Population Distribution · 1980

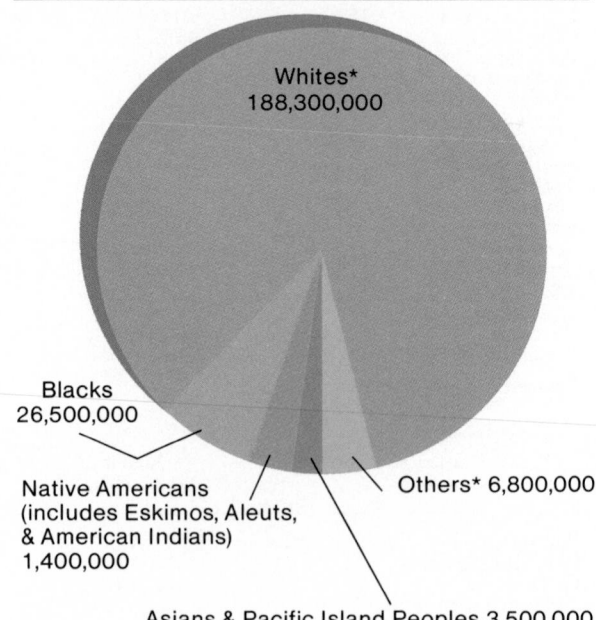

Whites*
188,300,000

Blacks
26,500,000

Native Americans
(includes Eskimos, Aleuts,
& American Indians)
1,400,000

Others* 6,800,000

Asians & Pacific Island Peoples 3,500,000

*In the 1980 census, 60 percent of Hispanic people were counted as "Whites" and forty percent as "Others."
Source: Bureau of the Census.

National Backgrounds of U.S. Immigrants • 1820–1980

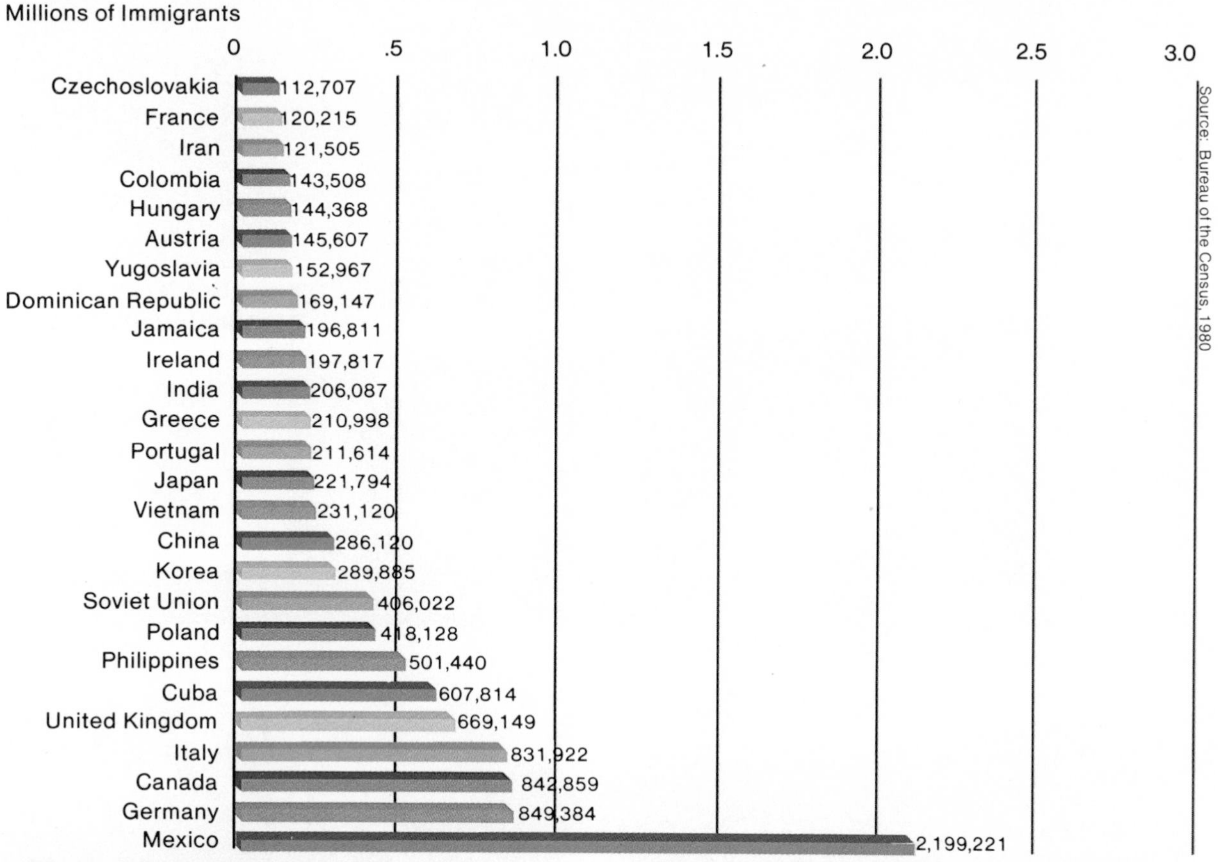

Millions of Immigrants

Source: Bureau of the Census, 1980

Country		Immigrants
Czechoslovakia		112,707
France		120,215
Iran		121,505
Colombia		143,508
Hungary		144,368
Austria		145,607
Yugoslavia		152,967
Dominican Republic		169,147
Jamaica		196,811
Ireland		197,817
India		206,087
Greece		210,998
Portugal		211,614
Japan		221,794
Vietnam		231,120
China		286,120
Korea		289,885
Soviet Union		406,022
Poland		418,128
Philippines		501,440
Cuba		607,814
United Kingdom		669,149
Italy		831,922
Canada		842,859
Germany		849,384
Mexico		2,199,221

Scale: 0, .5, 1.0, 1.5, 2.0, 2.5, 3.0

Population Distribution by Age Groups · 1980

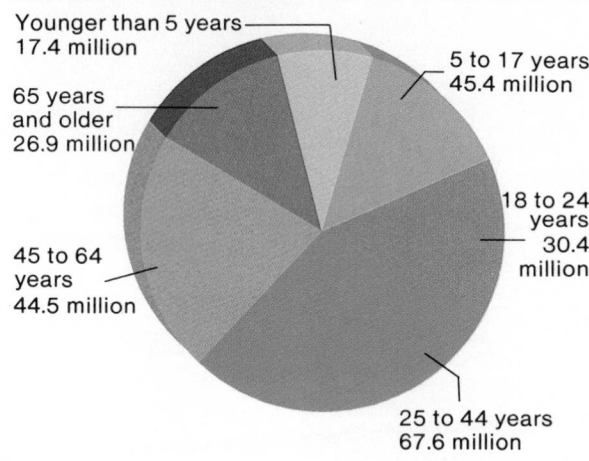

Younger than 5 years 17.4 million
5 to 17 years 45.4 million
65 years and older 26.9 million
18 to 24 years 30.4 million
45 to 64 years 44.5 million
25 to 44 years 67.6 million

Source: Bureau of the Census

Population Distribution by Church Affiliation · 1981

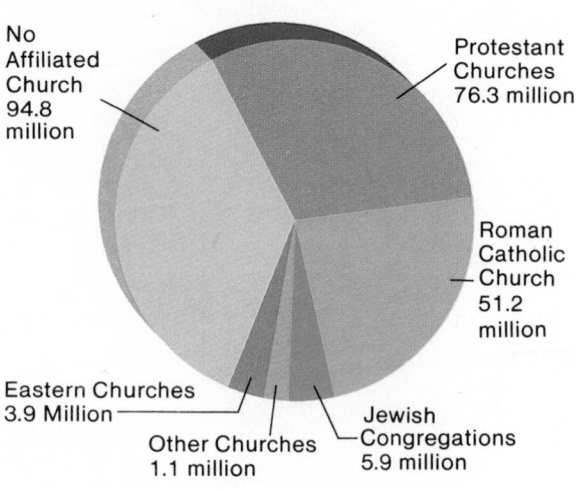

No Affiliated Church 94.8 million
Protestant Churches 76.3 million
Roman Catholic Church 51.2 million
Eastern Churches 3.9 Million
Other Churches 1.1 million
Jewish Congregations 5.9 million

Source: National Council of Churches

1001

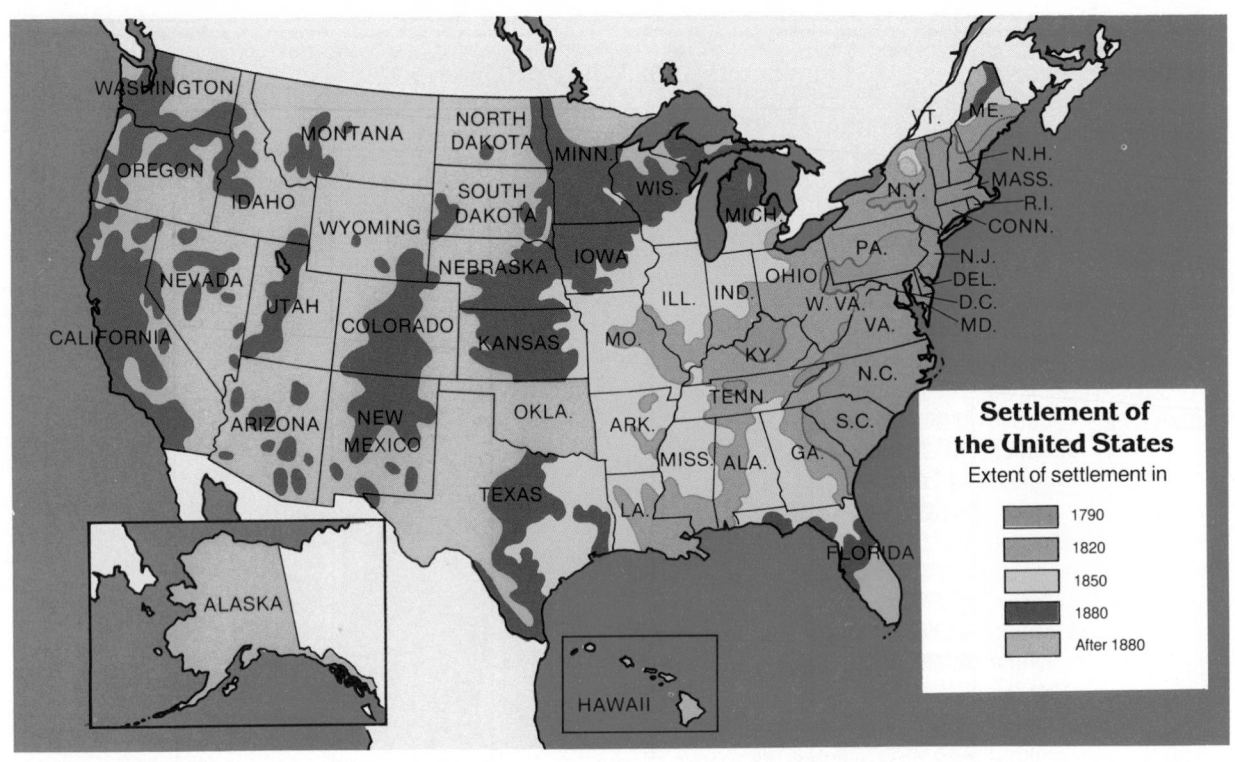

Settlement of the United States
Extent of settlement in
1790
1820
1850
1880
After 1880
WASHINGTON
OREGON
CALIFORNIA
NEVADA
IDAHO
MONTANA
WYOMING
UTAH
COLORADO
ARIZONA
NEW MEXICO
NORTH DAKOTA
SOUTH DAKOTA
NEBRASKA
KANSAS
OKLA.
TEXAS
MINN.
IOWA
MO.
ARK.
LA.
WIS.
ILL.
MICH.
IND.
OHIO
KY.
TENN.
MISS.
ALA.
GA.
FLORIDA
S.C.
N.C.
VA.
W. VA.
PA.
N.Y.
VT.
ME.
N.H.
MASS.
R.I.
CONN.
N.J.
DEL.
D.C.
MD.
ALASKA
HAWAII

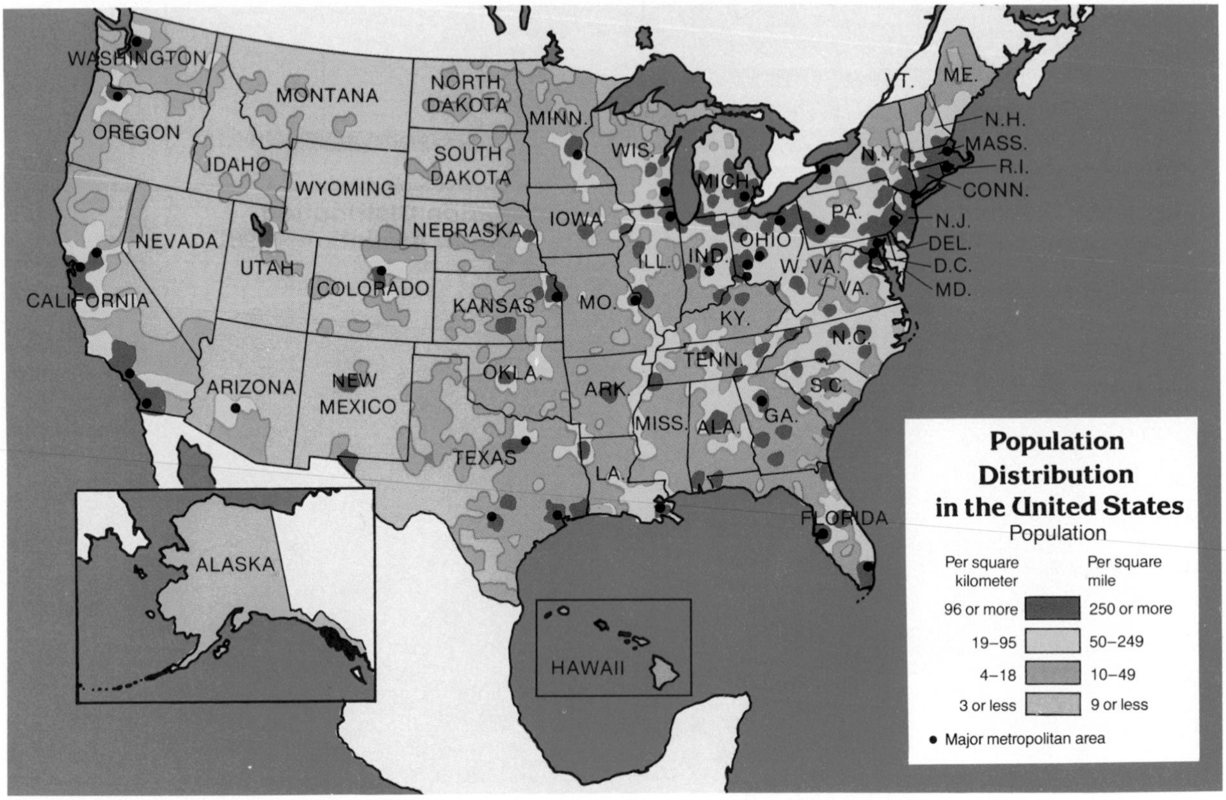

Population Distribution in the United States
Population
Per square kilometer
Per square mile
96 or more
250 or more
19–95
50–249
4–18
10–49
3 or less
9 or less
Major metropolitan area
WASHINGTON
OREGON
CALIFORNIA
NEVADA
IDAHO
MONTANA
WYOMING
UTAH
COLORADO
ARIZONA
NEW MEXICO
NORTH DAKOTA
SOUTH DAKOTA
NEBRASKA
KANSAS
OKLA.
TEXAS
MINN.
IOWA
MO.
ARK.
LA.
WIS.
ILL.
MICH.
IND.
OHIO
KY.
TENN.
MISS.
ALA.
GA.
FLORIDA
S.C.
N.C.
VA.
W. VA.
PA.
N.Y.
VT.
ME.
N.H.
MASS.
R.I.
CONN.
N.J.
DEL.
D.C.
MD.
ALASKA
HAWAII

Federal Receipts • 1900 - 1990

Billions of Dollars

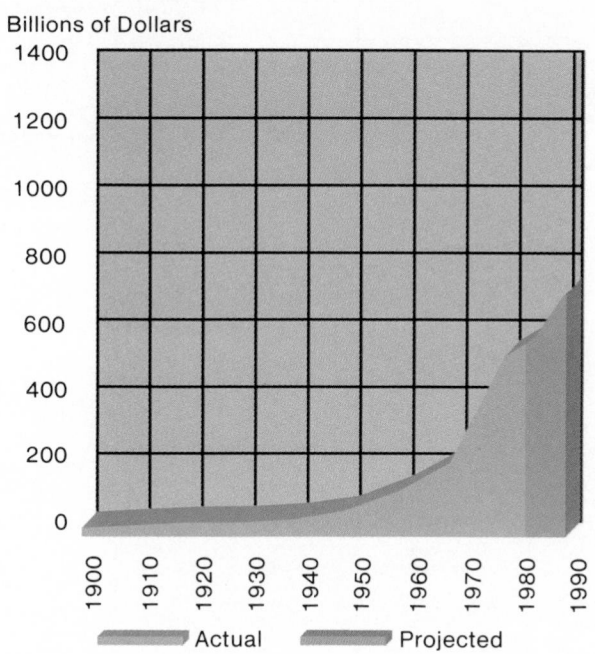

Actual ▬▬ Projected ▬▬

Federal Outlays • 1900 - 1990

Billions of Dollars

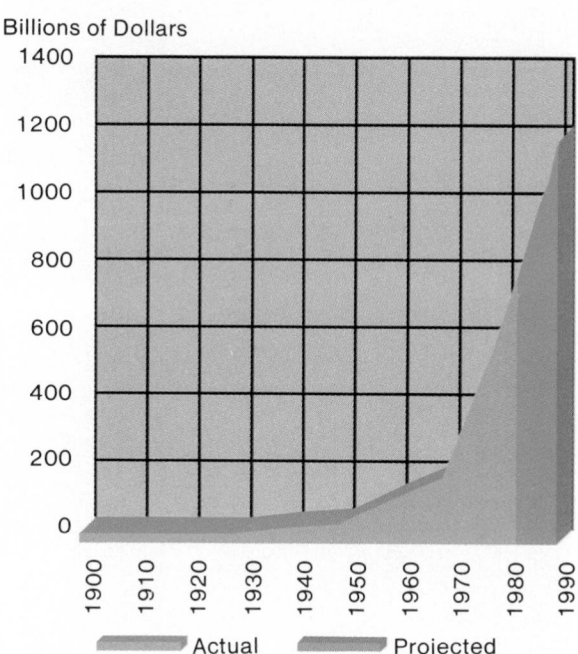

Actual ▬▬ Projected ▬▬

Distribution of Outlays • 1980

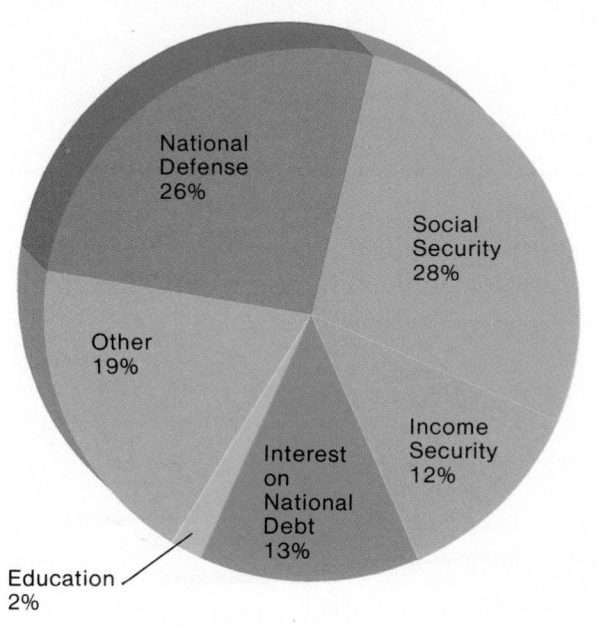

National Defense 26%
Social Security 28%
Other 19%
Income Security 12%
Interest on National Debt 13%
Education 2%

Government Employees • 1950 - 1990

Millions of Employees

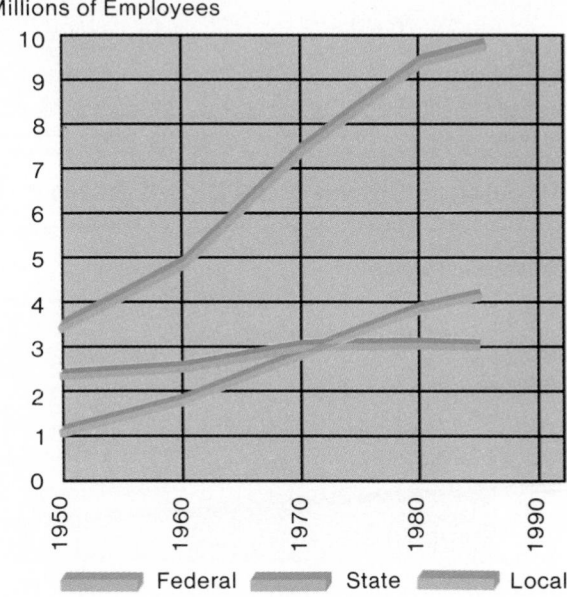

Federal ▬▬ State ▬▬ Local ▬▬

Population Growth of States and Their Largest Cities

State	Population at first census after entry	State population 1980	Representatives in Congress	Largest city in 1980	City population in 1890	City population in 1930	City population in 1980
1 Delaware	59,000	602,000	1	Wilmington	61,431	106,597	70,195
2 Pennsylvania	434,000	11,685,000	23	Philadelphia	1,046,964	1,950,961	1,688,210
3 New Jersey	184,000	7,438,000	14	Newark	181,830	442,337	329,248
4 Georgia	83,000	5,639,000	10	Atlanta	65,533	270,366	425,022
5 Connecticut	238,000	3,153,000	6	Bridgeport	48,866	146,716	142,546
6 Massachusetts	379,000	5,781,000	11	Boston	448,477	781,188	562,994
7 Maryland	320,000	4,265,000	8	Baltimore	434,439	804,874	786,775
8 South Carolina	249,000	3,203,000	6	Columbia	15,353	51,581	99,296
9 New Hampshire	142,000	951,000	2	Manchester	44,126	76,834	90,936
10 Virginia	692,000	5,491,000	10	Norfolk	34,871	129,710	266,979
11 New York	340,000	17,659,000	34	New York	2,507,414	6,930,446	7,071,030
12 North Carolina	394,000	6,019,000	11	Charlotte	11,557	82,675	314,447
13 Rhode Island	69,000	958,000	2	Providence	132,146	252,981	156,804
14 Vermont	154,000	516,000	1	Burlington	14,500	24,789	37,712
15 Kentucky	221,000	3,667,000	7	Louisville	161,129	307,745	298,451
16 Tennessee	106,000	4,651,000	9	Memphis	64,495	253,143	646,356
17 Ohio	231,000	10,791,000	21	Cleveland	261,353	900,429	573,822
18 Louisiana	153,000	4,362,000	8	New Orleans	242,039	458,762	557,482
19 Indiana	147,000	5,471,000	10	Indianapolis	105,436	364,161	700,807
20 Mississippi	75,000	2,551,000	5	Jackson	5,920	48,282	202,895
21 Illinois	55,000	11,448,000	22	Chicago	1,099,850	3,376,438	3,005,072
22 Alabama	128,000	3,943,000	7	Birmingham	26,178	259,678	284,413
23 Maine	298,000	1,133,000	2	Portland	36,425	70,810	61,572
24 Missouri	140,000	4,951,000	9	St. Louis	451,770	821,960	453,085
25 Arkansas	98,000	2,291,000	4	Little Rock	25,874	81,679	158,461
26 Michigan	212,000	9,109,000	18	Detroit	205,876	1,568,662	1,203,339
27 Florida	87,000	10,416,000	19	Jacksonville	17,201	129,549	540,896
28 Texas	213,000	14,280,000	27	Houston	27,557	292,352	1,594,086
29 Iowa	192,000	2,905,000	6	Des Moines	50,093	142,559	191,003
30 Wisconsin	305,000	4,765,000	9	Milwaukee	204,468	578,249	636,212
31 California	93,000	24,724,000	45	Los Angeles	50,395	1,238,048	2,966,763
32 Minnesota	172,000	4,133,000	8	Minneapolis	164,738	464,356	370,951
33 Oregon	52,000	2,649,000	5	Portland	46,385	301,815	366,383
34 Kansas	364,000	2,408,000	5	Wichita	23,853	111,110	279,272
35 West Virginia	442,000	1,948,000	4	Charleston	6,742	60,408	63,968
36 Nevada	42,000	881,000	2	Las Vegas	0	5,165	164,674
37 Nebraska	123,000	1,586,000	3	Omaha	148,514	214,006	311,681
38 Colorado	194,000	3,045,000	6	Denver	106,713	287,861	491,396
39 North Dakota	191,000	670,000	1	Fargo	5,664	28,619	61,308
40 South Dakota	349,000	691,000	1	Sioux Falls	7,205	33,362	81,343
41 Montana	143,000	801,000	2	Billings	836	16,380	66,798
42 Washington	357,000	4,245,000	8	Seattle	42,837	365,583	493,846
43 Idaho	89,000	965,000	2	Boise	2,311	21,544	102,451
44 Wyoming	63,000	502,000	1	Casper	544	16,619	51,016
45 Utah	277,000	1,554,000	3	Salt Lake City	44,843	140,267	163,033
46 Oklahoma	1,657,000	3,177,000	6	Oklahoma City	4,151	185,389	403,213
47 New Mexico	360,000	1,359,000	3	Albuquerque	3,785	26,570	331,767
48 Arizona	334,000	2,860,000	5	Phoenix	3,152	48,118	764,911
49 Alaska	229,000	3,943,000	1	Anchorage	0	2,500	173,017
50 Hawaii	642,000	994,000	2	Honolulu	22,907	138,445	365,048
District of Columbia	8,000 (1800)	631,000		Washington, D.C.	188,932	486,869	637,651

Population Growth in the United States • 1790-2020

Millions of People

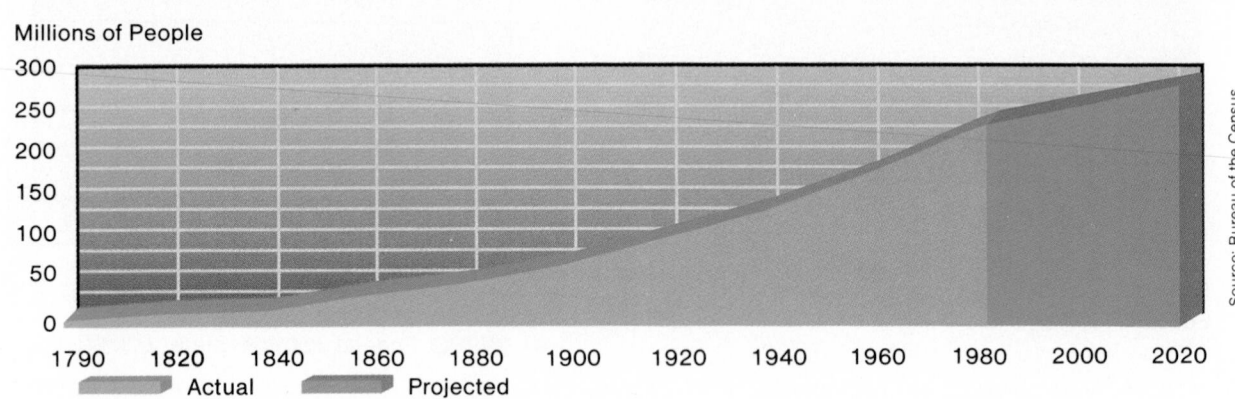

Actual   Projected

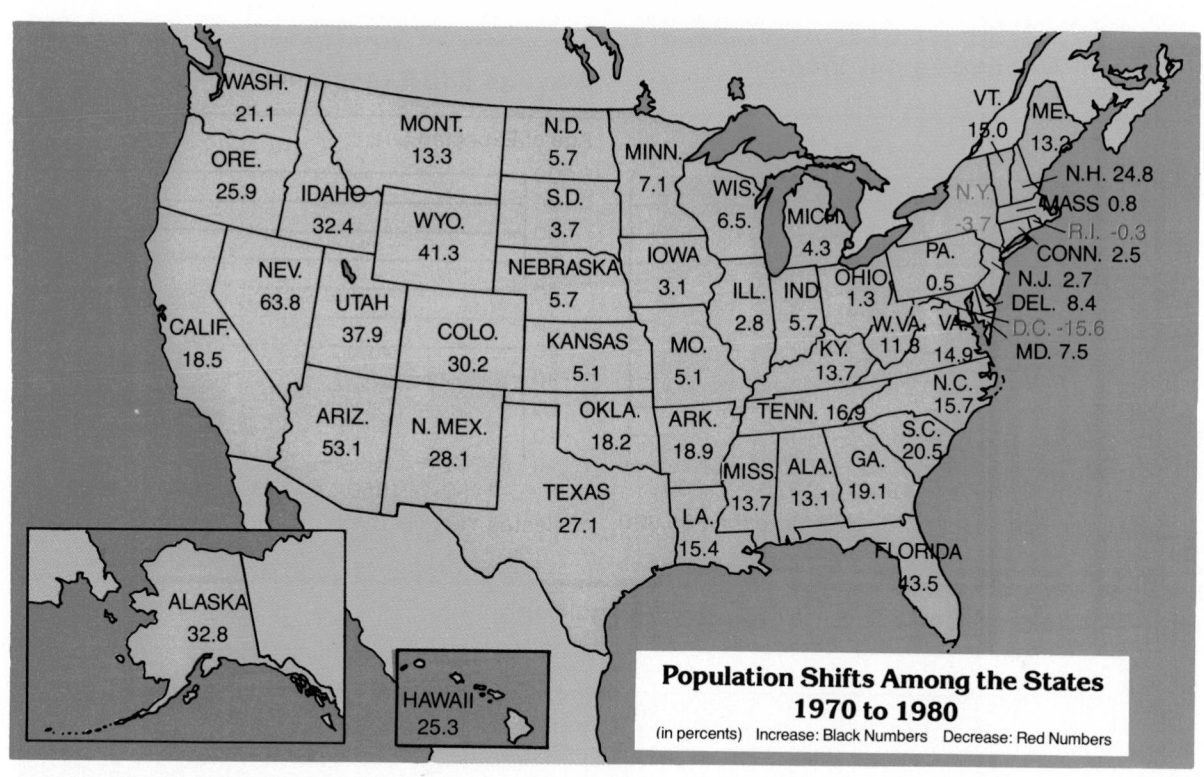

**Population Shifts Among the States
1970 to 1980**

(in percents)   Increase: Black Numbers   Decrease: Red Numbers

WASH. 21.1
ORE. 25.9
IDAHO 32.4
MONT. 13.3
N.D. 5.7
MINN. 7.1
VT. 15.0
ME. 13.3
N.H. 24.8
MASS 0.8
R.I. -0.3
CONN. 2.5
WYO. 41.3
S.D. 3.7
WIS. 6.5
MICH. 4.3
N.Y. -3.7
NEV. 63.8
UTAH 37.9
NEBRASKA 5.7
IOWA 3.1
ILL. 2.8
IND 5.7
OHIO 1.3
PA. 0.5
N.J. 2.7
DEL. 8.4
D.C. -15.6
MD. 7.5
CALIF. 18.5
COLO. 30.2
KANSAS 5.1
MO. 5.1
W.VA. 11.8
VA. 14.9
ARIZ. 53.1
N. MEX. 28.1
OKLA. 18.2
ARK. 18.9
TENN. 16.9
KY. 13.7
N.C. 15.7
S.C. 20.5
TEXAS 27.1
LA. 15.4
MISS. 13.7
ALA. 13.1
GA. 19.1
FLORIDA 43.5
ALASKA 32.8
HAWAII 25.3

Population Shifts – Urban, Suburban, Rural • 1950 - 1980

Census Year

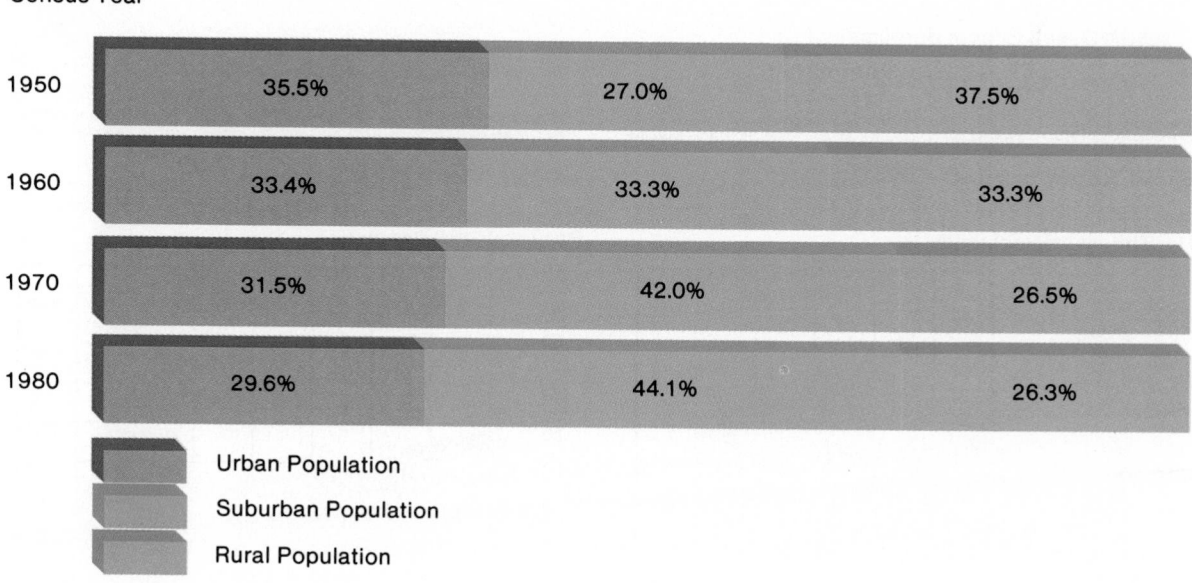

Census Year	Urban Population	Suburban Population	Rural Population
1950	35.5%	27.0%	37.5%
1960	33.4%	33.3%	33.3%
1970	31.5%	42.0%	26.5%
1980	29.6%	44.1%	26.3%

Urban Population
Suburban Population
Rural Population

Source: *Statistical Abstract of the United States*

Growth of Average Family Income 1940-1980

Percent of Population

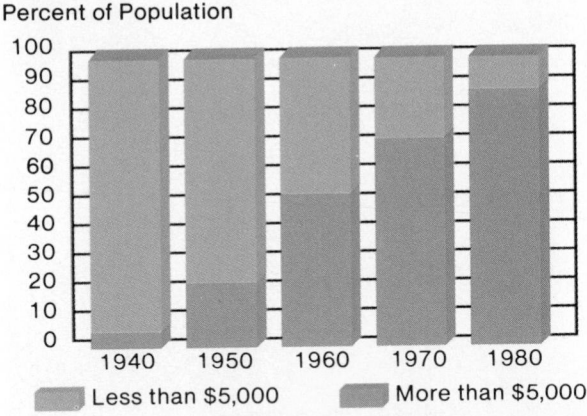

Less than $5,000   More than $5,000

Average Life Expectancy*

Age of Expected Life

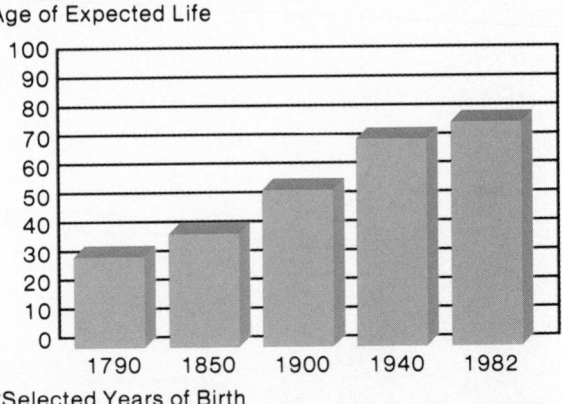

*Selected Years of Birth

High School and College Enrollment • 1910 - 1980

Millions of Students

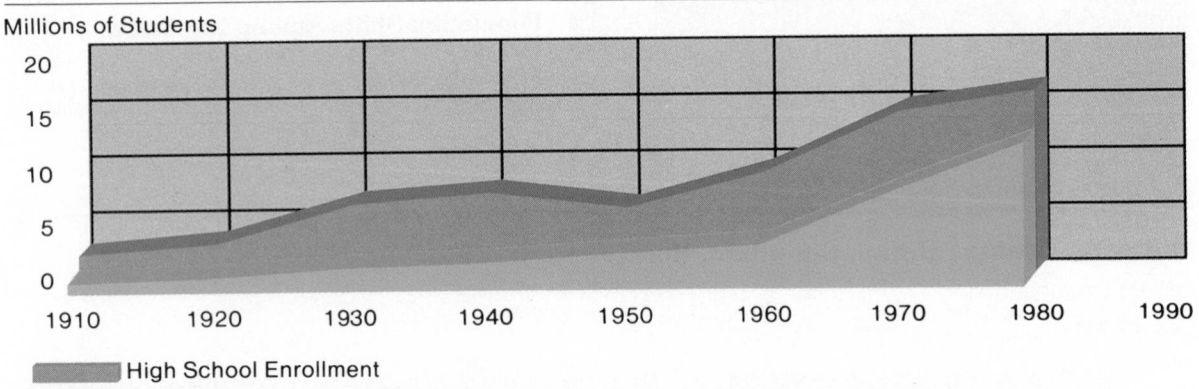

High School Enrollment

College Enrollment

Birth Rates • 1910 - 1980

Per Thousand Population

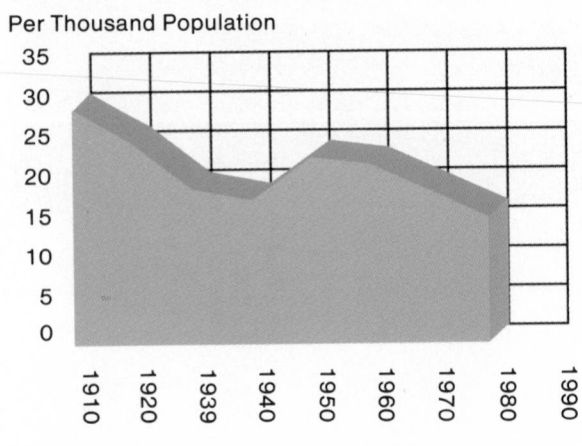

Death Rates • 1910 - 1980

Per Thousand Population

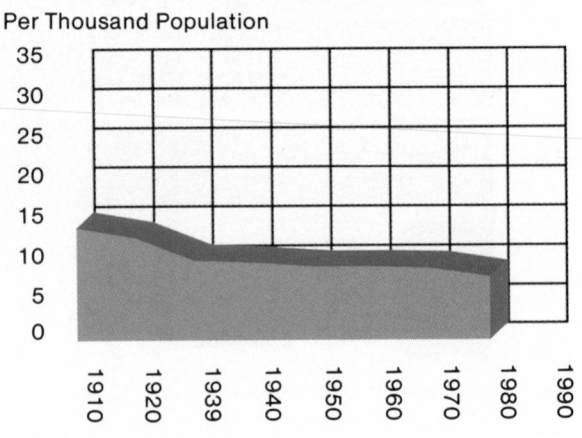

1006

The American Government

The framers of the United States Constitution, while drawing on political and historical experience, tempered their plan of government with two basic American values: freedom and democracy. American government is guided by those two values. Alexander Hamilton, writing soon after the Constitution was completed, wondered if good and responsive government could be established on such high principles. American government held the promise of being a good and responsive government, Hamilton claimed, but only time would tell how well it fulfilled that promise. This part of the Reference Section provides insight into American government. One chart illustrates the development of the American two-party political system. Another chart shows the changes in political party identification in the United States since 1968. The following pages also provide graphic illustrations of some unique features of American government. One chart lists the powers that are divided among the central and state governments in the federal system. The next chart identifies the three branches of the federal government and lists the departments under the jurisdiction of each branch. Another chart shows the separation of powers and the system of checks and balances established by the Constitution. This part of the Reference Section also highlights how government works. There are charts that show how the Constitution may be amended, how a bill becomes a law, and how the President is elected. The final chart provides information about the Presidents of the United States. These charts, together with the information on government in the textbook, will help you to evaluate how well American government has fulfilled its promise and lived up to the ideals of freedom and democracy.

Political Party Identification

Year	Democrats	Independents	Republicans
1968	53%	22%	25%
1970	46%	27%	27%
1972	43%	29%	28%
1974	44%	33%	23%
1976	48%	29%	23%
1978	46%	31%	23%
1980	45%	29%	26%
1982	45%	29%	26%
1984	42%	30%	28%

- ◼ Democrats
- ◻ Independents
- ◼ Republicans

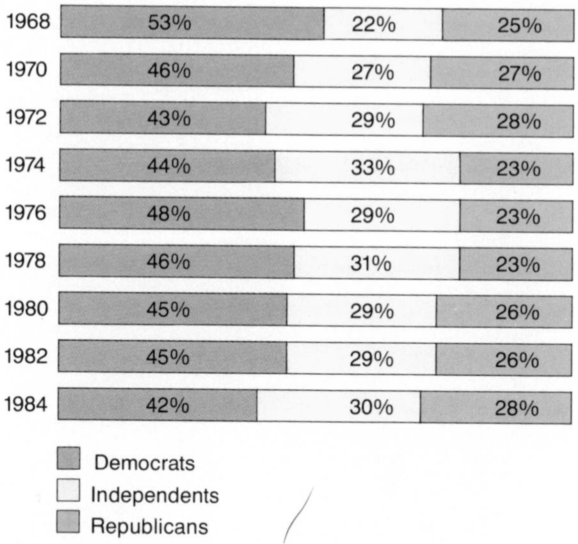

Source: The Gallop Poll

Development of the Two-Party System

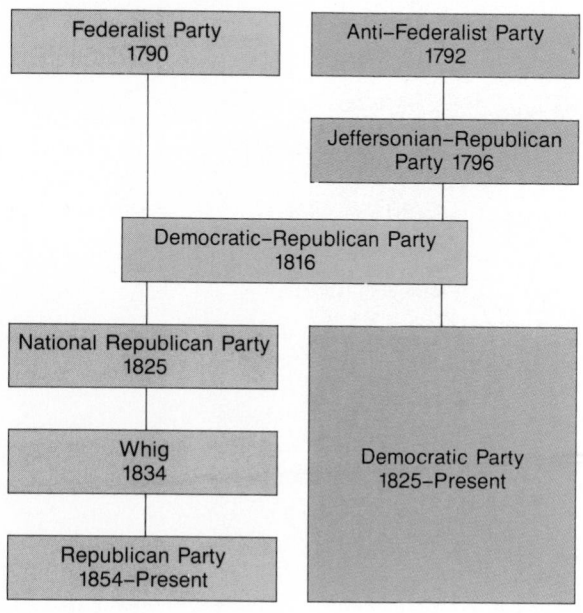

Federalist Party 1790

Anti–Federalist Party 1792

Jeffersonian–Republican Party 1796

Democratic–Republican Party 1816

National Republican Party 1825

Whig 1834

Republican Party 1854–Present

Democratic Party 1825–Present

1007

FEDERAL GOVERNMENT

Enumerated powers delegated to the Congress:

- to regulate interstate and foreign commerce
- to establish laws governing citizenship
- to coin money
- to control the postal system
- to regulate patents and copyrights
- to establish federal courts lower than the Supreme Court
- to declare war
- to establish and support the armed forces
- to pass all laws necessary and proper for carrying out the preceding powers

FEDERAL AND STATE GOVERNMENTS

Concurrent powers shared by the federal and state governments:

- to tax
- to borrow money
- to establish penal laws
- to charter banks
- to take property for public purposes by eminent domain

STATE GOVERNMENTS

Reserved powers retained by the state governments:

- to regulate suffrage for state elections
- to maintain a system of public education
- to establish marriage and divorce laws
- to establish laws governing corporations
- to establish traffic laws
- to regulate intrastate commerce
- Amendment 10 of the Constitution reserves to the state governments all powers not delegated to the federal government or prohibited by the Constitution.

PROHIBITED POWERS

Powers denied the federal government:

- to suspend the writ of *habeas corpus* except in cases of rebellion or invasion
- to levy taxes on exports
- to give preferential treatment in commerce or revenue to the ports of any state
- to draw money from the Treasury except by appropriation under a specific law
- to permit persons holding federal office to accept gifts from a foreign country without consent of Congress

Powers denied the federal and state governments:

- to pass bills of attainder
- to pass *ex post facto* laws
- to grant titles of nobility

Powers denied the state governments:

- to enter into treaties with other nations or with other states without the consent of Congress
- to coin money
- to impair obligations of contract
- to place a tax on imports or exports except to carry out their inspection laws
- to keep troops or ships in time of peace without consent of Congress

The Three Branches of the Federal Government

LEGISLATIVE BRANCH

HOUSE OF REPRESENTATIVES
Each state is represented in the House of Representatives based on population.

SENATE
Each state is represented in the Senate equally by two Senators.

Standing Committees of the House

Agriculture
Appropriations
Armed Services
Banking, Finance, and Urban Affairs
Budget
District of Columbia
Education and Labor
Foreign Affairs
Government Operations
House Administration
Interior and Insular Affairs
Interstate and Foreign Commerce

Judiciary
Merchant Marine and Fisheries
Post Office and Civil Service
Public Works and Transportation
Rules
Science and Technology
Small Business
Standards of Official Conduct
Veterans' Affairs
Ways and Means

Standing Committees of the Senate

Agriculture, Nutrition, and Forestry
Appropriations
Armed Services
Banking, Housing, and Urban Affairs
Budget
Commerce, Science, and Transportation
Energy and Natural Resources
Environment and Public Works

Finance
Foreign Relations
Governmental Affairs
Judiciary
Labor and Human Resources
Rules and Administration
Veterans' Affairs

EXECUTIVE BRANCH

Executive Departments

Department of State
Department of the Treasury
Department of Defense
Department of Justice
Department of the Interior
Department of Agriculture
Department of Commerce
Department of Labor
Department of Health and Human Services
Department of Education
Department of Housing and Urban Development
Department of Transportation
Department of Energy

The Executive Office

The White House
Office of Management and Budget
Council of Economic Advisers
Council on Environmental Quality
Domestic Policy Staff
National Security Council
Central Intelligence Agency
Office of Administration
Office of Science and Technology Policy
Office of the Special Representative for Trade

Independent Federal Agencies (Partial Listing)

ACTION
American Red Cross
Board of Governors of the Federal Reserve System
Environmental Protection Agency
Equal Employment Opportunity Commission
Farm Credit Administration
Federal Communications Commission

Federal Deposit Insurance Corporation
Federal Election Commission
Federal Mediation and Conciliation Service
Federal Trade Commission
General Services Administration
Interstate Commerce Commission

National Academy of Sciences
National Aeronautics and Space Administration
National Foundation on the Arts and Humanities
National Labor Relations Board
National Science Foundation
National Transportation Safety Board

Nuclear Regulatory Commission
Securities and Exchange Commission
Small Business Administration
Smithsonian Institution
Tennessee Valley Authority
United States Postal Service
Veterans Administration

JUDICIAL BRANCH

SUPREME COURT

Courts of Appeals

District Courts

Courts of the District of Columbia

Special Courts

Court of Claims
Court of Customs and Patent Appeals
Customs Court
Tax Court
Court of Military Appeals
Territorial Courts

System of Checks and Balances

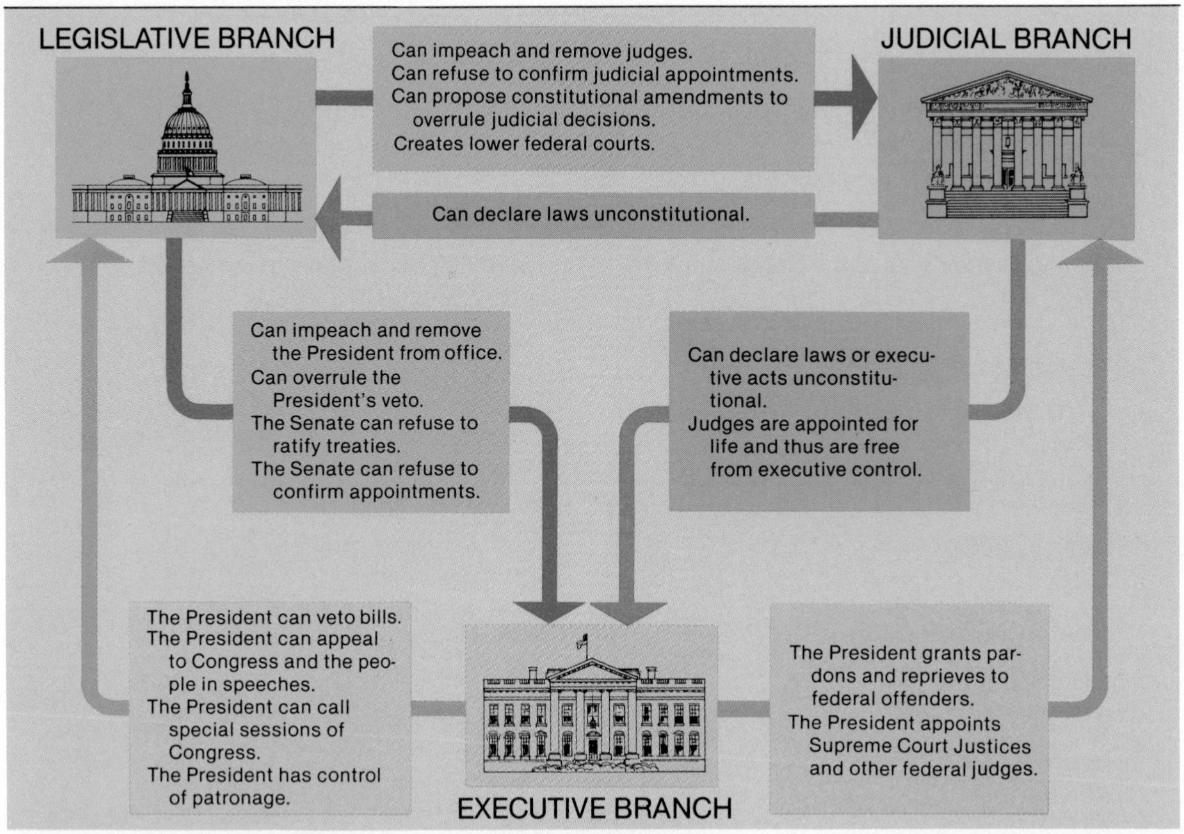

LEGISLATIVE BRANCH

Can impeach and remove judges.
Can refuse to confirm judicial appointments.
Can propose constitutional amendments to overrule judicial decisions.
Creates lower federal courts.

JUDICIAL BRANCH

Can declare laws unconstitutional.

Can impeach and remove the President from office.
Can overrule the President's veto.
The Senate can refuse to ratify treaties.
The Senate can refuse to confirm appointments.

Can declare laws or executive acts unconstitutional.
Judges are appointed for life and thus are free from executive control.

The President can veto bills.
The President can appeal to Congress and the people in speeches.
The President can call special sessions of Congress.
The President has control of patronage.

The President grants pardons and reprieves to federal offenders.
The President appoints Supreme Court Justices and other federal judges.

EXECUTIVE BRANCH

How the Constitution May Be Amended

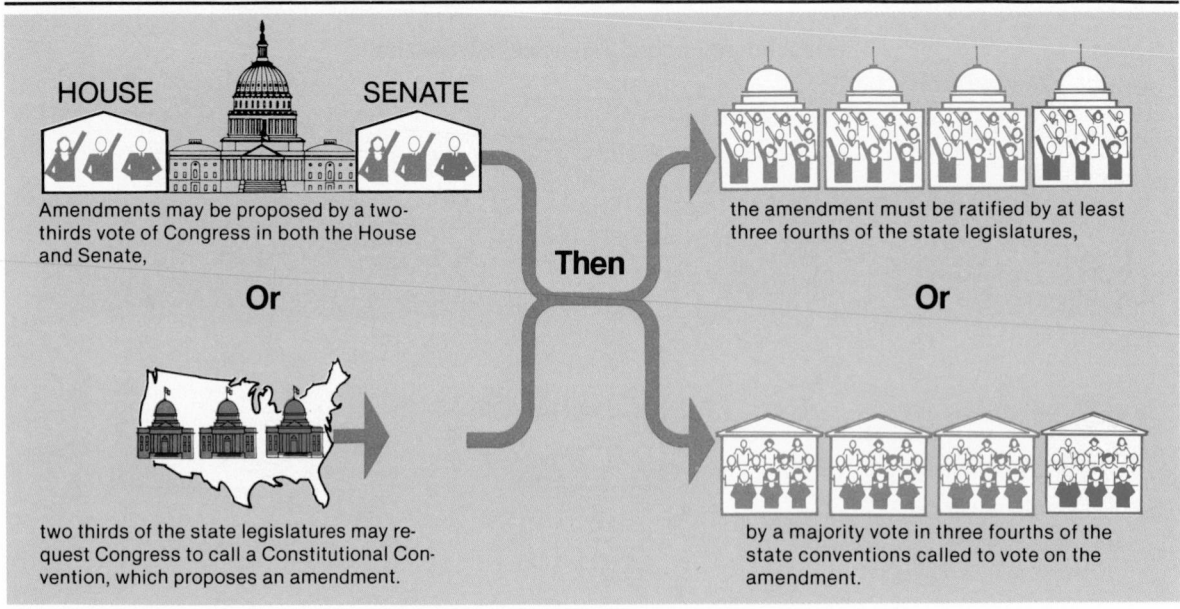

HOUSE   SENATE

Amendments may be proposed by a two-thirds vote of Congress in both the House and Senate,

Or

two thirds of the state legislatures may request Congress to call a Constitutional Convention, which proposes an amendment.

Then

the amendment must be ratified by at least three fourths of the state legislatures,

Or

by a majority vote in three fourths of the state conventions called to vote on the amendment.

How a Bill Becomes a Law

A typical bill begins when a group of citizens or private organizations, the President, or a group in Congress believes that a new law is needed. One or more members of Congress draft the bill and introduce it in the appropriate house—in this case the House of Representatives. Bills pertaining to the raising of money must originate in the House of Representatives; other bills may originate in the House or Senate.

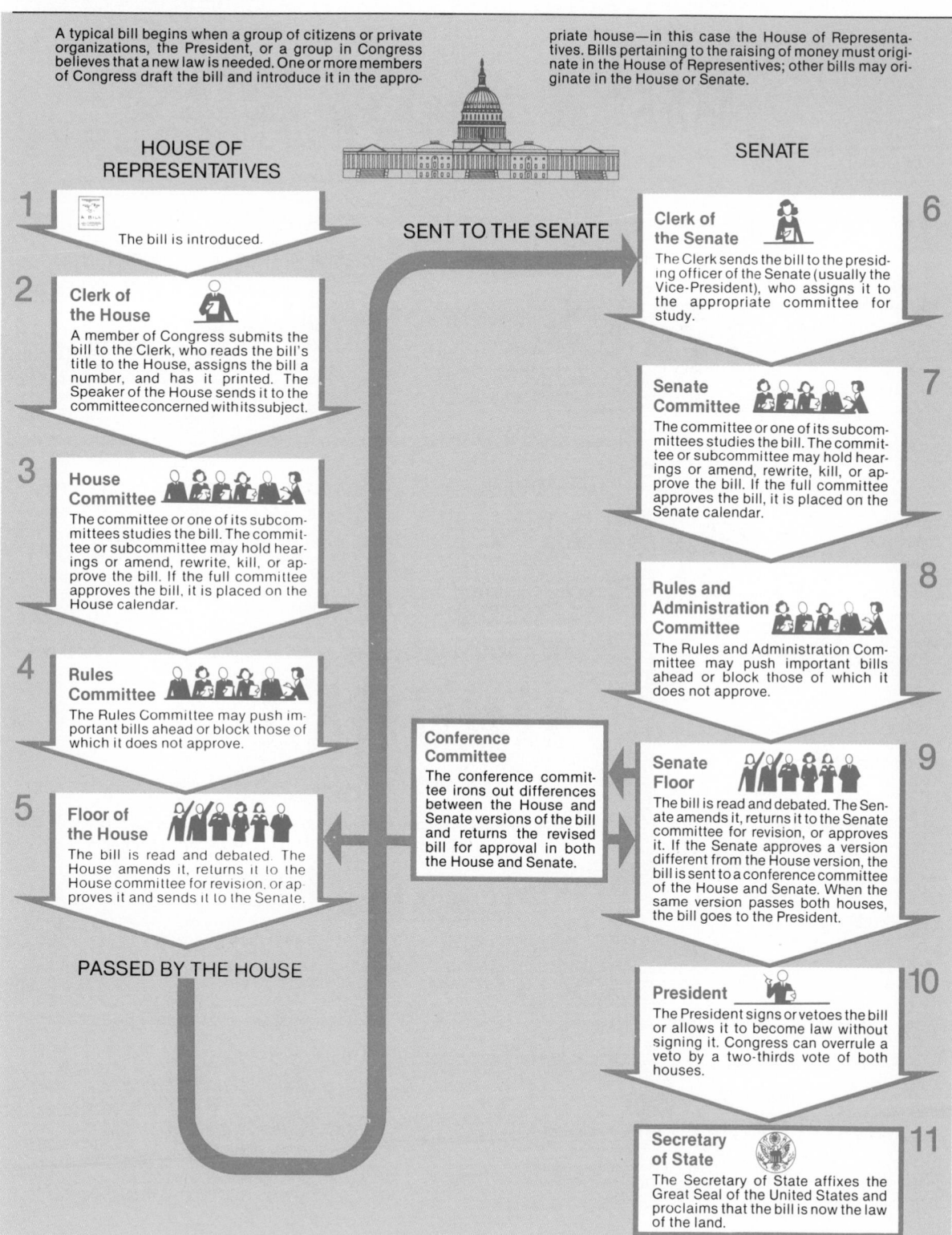

HOUSE OF REPRESENTATIVES

SENATE

SENT TO THE SENATE

1 The bill is introduced.

2 Clerk of the House
A member of Congress submits the bill to the Clerk, who reads the bill's title to the House, assigns the bill a number, and has it printed. The Speaker of the House sends it to the committee concerned with its subject.

3 House Committee
The committee or one of its subcommittees studies the bill. The committee or subcommittee may hold hearings or amend, rewrite, kill, or approve the bill. If the full committee approves the bill, it is placed on the House calendar.

4 Rules Committee
The Rules Committee may push important bills ahead or block those of which it does not approve.

5 Floor of the House
The bill is read and debated. The House amends it, returns it to the House committee for revision, or approves it and sends it to the Senate.

PASSED BY THE HOUSE

Conference Committee
The conference committee irons out differences between the House and Senate versions of the bill and returns the revised bill for approval in both the House and Senate.

6 Clerk of the Senate
The Clerk sends the bill to the presiding officer of the Senate (usually the Vice-President), who assigns it to the appropriate committee for study.

7 Senate Committee
The committee or one of its subcommittees studies the bill. The committee or subcommittee may hold hearings or amend, rewrite, kill, or approve the bill. If the full committee approves the bill, it is placed on the Senate calendar.

8 Rules and Administration Committee
The Rules and Administration Committee may push important bills ahead or block those of which it does not approve.

9 Senate Floor
The bill is read and debated. The Senate amends it, returns it to the Senate committee for revision, or approves it. If the Senate approves a version different from the House version, the bill is sent to a conference committee of the House and Senate. When the same version passes both houses, the bill goes to the President.

10 President
The President signs or vetoes the bill or allows it to become law without signing it. Congress can overrule a veto by a two-thirds vote of both houses.

11 Secretary of State
The Secretary of State affixes the Great Seal of the United States and proclaims that the bill is now the law of the land.

How a President Is Elected

TIME SEQUENCE			
WINTER AND SPRING OF ELECTION YEAR	STATE PRIMARIES 	STATE CAUCUSES 	STATE PARTY LEADERS 

In some states political parties hold primaries and caucuses to choose delegates to their national conventions. In other states party leaders choose these delegates.

SUMMER OF ELECTION YEAR

REPUBLICAN NATIONAL CONVENTION

The delegates to the Republican National Convention nominate candidates for President and Vice-President and adopt a platform on which they run.

DEMOCRATIC NATIONAL CONVENTION

The delegates to the Democratic National Convention nominate candidates for President and Vice-President and adopt a platform on which they run.

BEFORE ELECTION

STATE REPUBLICAN HEADQUARTERS

The Republican Party in each state chooses electors who promise to vote for the party's candidates for President and Vice-President. The number of electors chosen is equal to the number of the state's Senators and Representatives.

STATE DEMOCRATIC HEADQUARTERS

The Democratic Party in each state chooses electors who promise to vote for the party's candidates for President and Vice-President. The number of electors chosen is equal to the number of the state's Senators and Representatives.

ELECTION DAY (NOVEMBER)

In voting for a Presidential nominee, the voters actually vote for the electors of the nominee's party. This is the popular vote.

DECEMBER

IF PARTY WINS...

IF PARTY WINS...

In each state the electors of the party with the greatest popular vote assemble at the state capital. There they vote separately for Presidential and Vice-Presidential candidates, usually those of their own party. This is the electoral vote. Certified copies of the vote are sent to the President of the United States Senate.

JANUARY

The President of the Senate counts the electoral votes in the presence of both houses of Congress.

To be elected, a candidate must receive a majority of the electoral vote.

Presidents of the United States

	President	Years in Office	Party	Age Upon Taking Office	Vice President(s)
1	George Washington	1789–1797	Federalist	57	John Adams
2	John Adams	1797–1801	Federalist	61	Thomas Jefferson
3	Thomas Jefferson	1801–1809	Democratic-Republican	57	Aaron Burr George Clinton
4	James Madison	1809–1817	Democratic-Republican	57	George Clinton Elbridge Gerry
5	James Monroe	1817–1825	Democratic-Republican	58	Daniel D. Tompkins
6	John Quincy Adams	1825–1829	Democratic-Republican	57	John C. Calhoun
7	Andrew Jackson	1829–1837	Democrat	61	John C. Calhoun Martin Van Buren
8	Martin Van Buren	1837–1841	Democrat	54	Richard M. Johnson
9	William H. Harrison	1841–1841	Whig	68	John Tyler
10	John Tyler	1841–1845	Whig	51	—
11	James K. Polk	1845–1849	Democrat	49	George M. Dallas
12	Zachary Taylor	1849–1850	Whig	64	Millard Fillmore
13	Millard Fillmore	1850–1853	Whig	50	—
14	Franklin Pierce	1853–1857	Democrat	48	William R. King
15	James Buchanan	1857–1861	Democrat	65	John C. Breckinridge
16	Abraham Lincoln	1861–1865	Republican	52	Hannibal Hamlin Andrew Johnson
17	Andrew Johnson	1865–1869	Democrat	56	—
18	Ulysses S. Grant	1869–1877	Republican	46	Schuyler Colfax Henry Wilson
19	Rutherford B. Hayes	1877–1881	Republican	54	William A. Wheeler
20	James A. Garfield	1881–1881	Republican	49	Chester A. Arthur
21	Chester A. Arthur	1881–1885	Republican	50	—
22	Grover Cleveland	1885–1889	Democrat	47	Thomas A. Hendricks
23	Benjamin Harrison	1889–1893	Republican	55	Levi P. Morton
24	Grover Cleveland	1893–1897	Democrat	55	Adlai E. Stevenson
25	William McKinley	1897–1901	Republican	54	Garret A. Hobart Theodore Roosevelt
26	Theodore Roosevelt	1901–1909	Republican	42	Charles W. Fairbanks
27	William H. Taft	1909–1913	Republican	51	James S. Sherman
28	Woodrow Wilson	1913–1921	Democrat	56	Thomas R. Marshall
29	Warren G. Harding	1921–1923	Republican	55	Calvin Coolidge
30	Calvin Coolidge	1923–1929	Republican	51	Charles G. Dawes
31	Herbert Hoover	1929–1933	Republican	54	Charles Curtis
32	Franklin D. Roosevelt	1933–1945	Democrat	51	John N. Garner Henry A. Wallace Harry S Truman
33	Harry S Truman	1945–1953	Democrat	60	Alben Barkley
34	Dwight D. Eisenhower	1953–1961	Republican	62	Richard M. Nixon
35	John F. Kennedy	1961–1963	Democrat	43	Lyndon B. Johnson
36	Lyndon B. Johnson	1963–1969	Democrat	55	Hubert H. Humphrey
37	Richard M. Nixon	1969–1974	Republican	55	Spiro T. Agnew Gerald R. Ford
38	Gerald R. Ford	1974–1977	Republican	61	Nelson A. Rockefeller
39	Jimmy Carter	1977–1981	Democrat	52	Walter F. Mondale
40	Ronald Reagan	1981–	Republican	69	George Bush

Gross National Product • 1975 - 1984

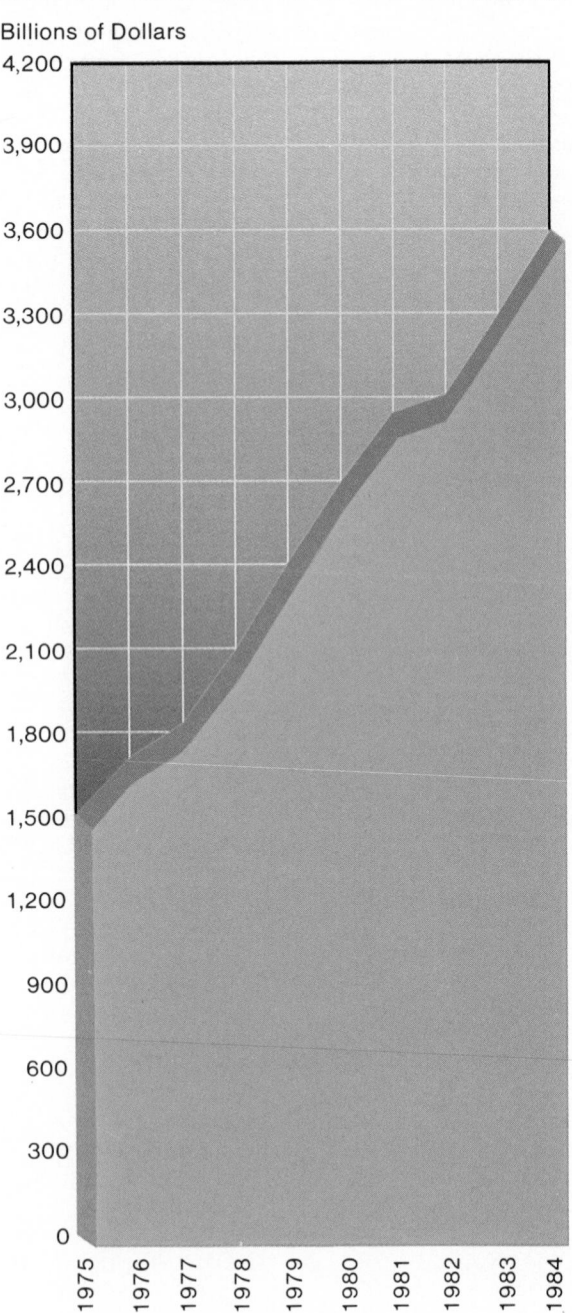

Billions of Dollars

4,200	
3,900	
3,600	
3,300	
3,000	
2,700	
2,400	
2,100	
1,800	
1,500	
1,200	
900	
600	
300	
0	

1975 1976 1977 1978 1979 1980 1981 1982 1983 1984

The American Economy

The United States, with its rich resources, advanced technology, and hardworking population, has experienced remarkable economic growth. There are many ways of measuring this growth. One is the Gross National Product (GNP), or the total value of all goods and services produced in the nation. This key measure of economic growth soared from $13.1 billion in 1890 to $3.7 trillion in 1984. Workers' productivity is another indicator of economic progress. For example, each farm worker produced nearly ten times as much food in 1980 as in 1900. The kind of work Americans perform has also changed, with a notable increase in service occupations and government Jobs. And the nation's economic growth has reflected advances in American know-how. From the years of hand tools to today's computer-operated machinery, each era has seen major improvements.

Major Advances in American Business and Industry

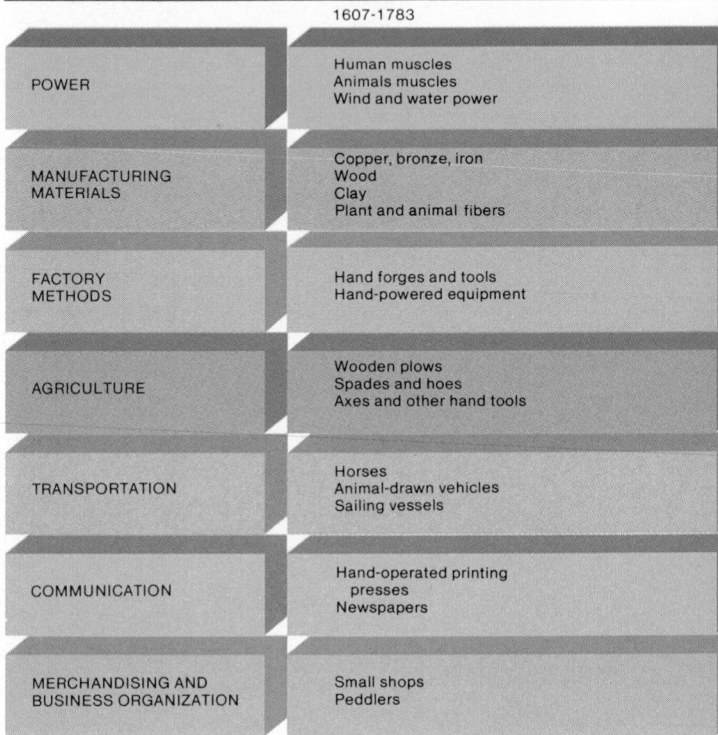

1607-1783

POWER	Human muscles Animals muscles Wind and water power
MANUFACTURING MATERIALS	Copper, bronze, iron Wood Clay Plant and animal fibers
FACTORY METHODS	Hand forges and tools Hand-powered equipment
AGRICULTURE	Wooden plows Spades and hoes Axes and other hand tools
TRANSPORTATION	Horses Animal-drawn vehicles Sailing vessels
COMMUNICATION	Hand-operated printing presses Newspapers
MERCHANDISING AND BUSINESS ORGANIZATION	Small shops Peddlers

Average Workweek • 1850 - 1980

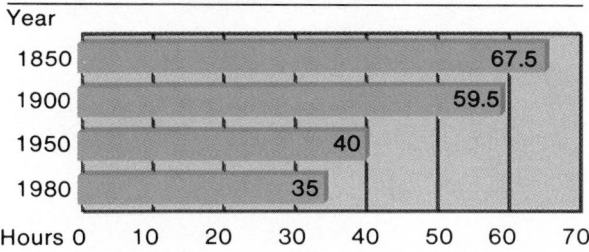

Year	Hours
1850	67.5
1900	59.5
1950	40
1980	35

Hours: 0 10 20 30 40 50 60 70

Source: *Statistical Abstract of The United States*

Output in Manufacturing • 1950 - 1980

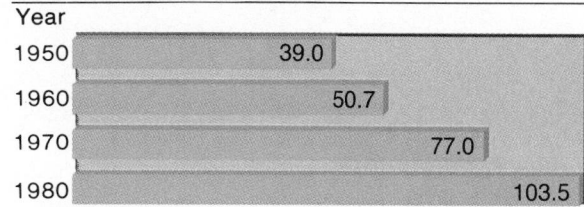

Year	
1950	39.0
1960	50.7
1970	77.0
1980	103.5

The index of output in manufacturing is a standard of measurement that indicates the increase or decrease of production by an average worker in an hour. Manufacturing production for 1970 = 100.
Source: *Monthly Labor Review*

Changes in Occupations • 1890 - 1980

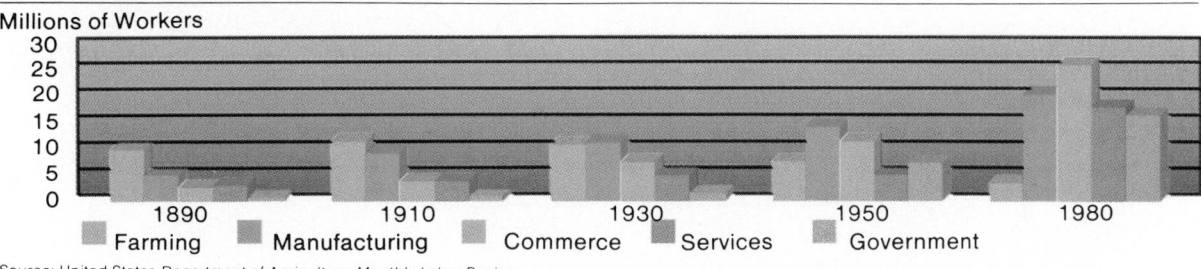

Millions of Workers
30 25 20 15 10 5 0

1890   1910   1930   1950   1980

■ Farming   ■ Manufacturing   ■ Commerce   ■ Services   ■ Government

Source: United States Department of Agriculture, *Monthly Labor Review*

1783 - 1850	1850 - 1900	1900 - 1920	1920 - Present
Steam Power	Electric Power Internal combustion engines		Atomic energy Solar energy Geothermal energy
Large-scale production of iron	Large-scale production of steel Development of combustion fuels: coal, oil, gas Development of light metals and alloys	Large-scale production of light metals and alloys Development of plastics and synthetics	Large-scale production of plastics and synthetics
Machinery powered by water and steam Interchangeable parts	Mass production, with centralized assembly of interchangeable parts	Conveyor-belt assembly line	Automation Computer-operated machinery
Iron and steel plows Cotton gin Mowing, threshing, and haying machines	McCormick reaper Barbed-wired fencing	Scientific agriculture	Large-scale mechanized agriculture Corporation farms
Canals Clipper ships Development of railroads and steamships	Large-scale steamship and railroads lines City trolleys, elevated trains	Automobiles, trucks, and buses Development of propeller-driven aircraft Subways	Space exploration Monorail trains Supersonic planes
Mechanized printing presses Telegraph Mass-circulation books and magazines	Transatlantic cable Telephones Phonographs Typewriters Cameras	Motion pictures Radios	Television Transistors Magnetic tapes Lasers Satellite transmissions
Individual-and family-owned factories and mills General stores	Chain stores Mail -order houses Growth of corporations Trusts	National advertising Holding companies	Shopping centers Conglomerate corporations Multinational corporations

CANADA

PACIFIC OCEAN

WASHINGTON

OREGON

IDAHO

MONTANA

NORTH DAKOTA

SOUTH DAKOTA

WYOMING

NEVADA

UTAH

COLORADO

NEBRASKA

CALIFORNIA

KANSAS

ARIZONA

NEW MEXICO

OKLAHOMA

TEXAS

MEXICO

ARCTIC OCEAN

SIBERIA

ALASKA

CANADA

BERING SEA

PACIFIC OCEAN

54°40'

0   Miles   500

0   Kilometers   800

KAUAI

NIIHAU

OAHU

OCEAN

MOLOKAI

PACIFIC

LANAI

MAUI

HAWAII

HAWAII

0   100 Miles

0   150 Kilometers

Agriculture in the United States

- General Farming
- Dairy
- Livestock and feed grains
- Wheat
- Cotton
- Tobacco and general farming
- Fruits, vegetables, and special products
- Livestock grazing
- No agricultural use

| 0 | | 400 miles |
| 0 | | 600 kilometers |

Average Size of Farms • 1860 - 1980

Years

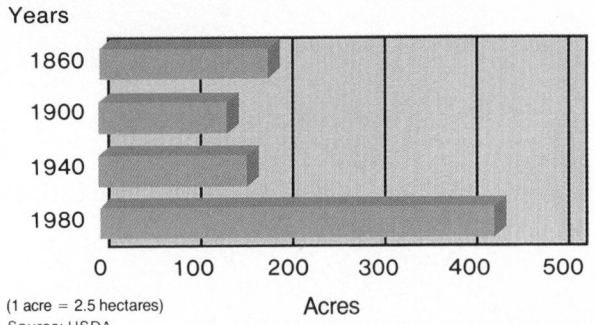

0   100   200   300   400   500

(1 acre = 2.5 hectares)
Acres

Source: USDA

People Fed by One Farm Worker 1900 - 1980

Years

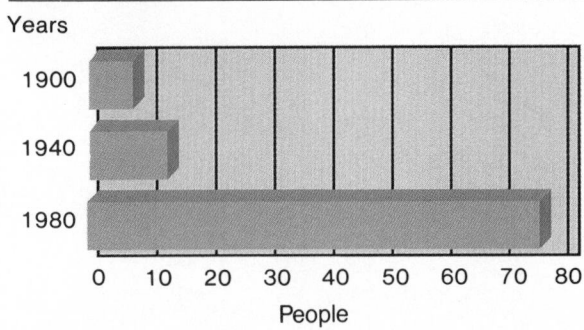

0   10   20   30   40   50   60   70   80

People

Source: USDA

Farm Acres Harvested and Farm Production • 1910 - 1980

Millions of Acres (1Acre = 2.5 hectares)

Production Index*

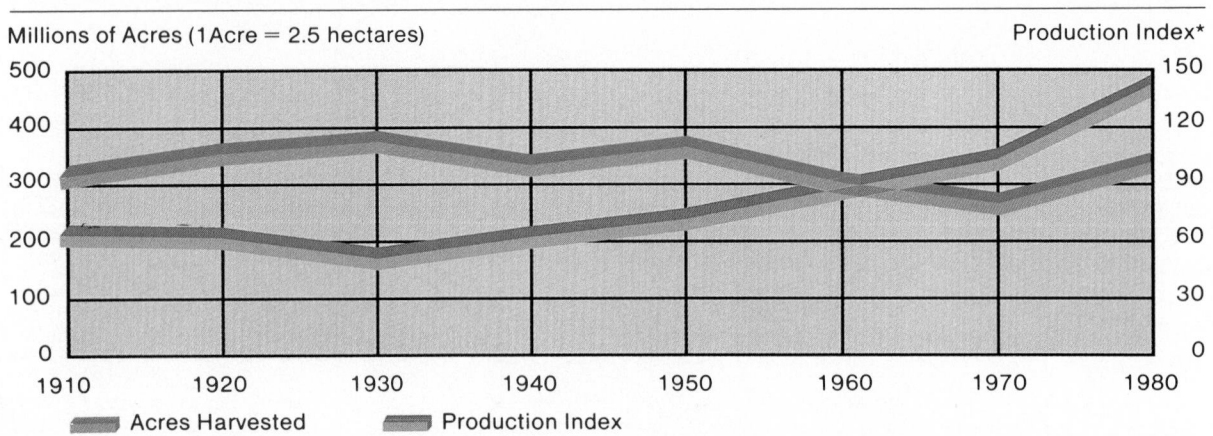

1910   1920   1930   1940   1950   1960   1970   1980

Acres Harvested   Production Index

*The production index measures the increase or decrease of total farm production, using 1967 farm production to equal 100.

United States Exports • 1880 - 1980

Percent of Total Exports

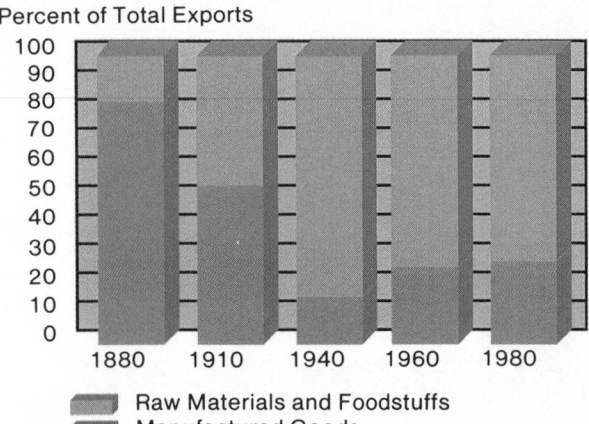

1880   1910   1940   1960   1980

Raw Materials and Foodstuffs
Manufactured Goods

United States Imports • 1880 - 1980

Percent of Total Imports

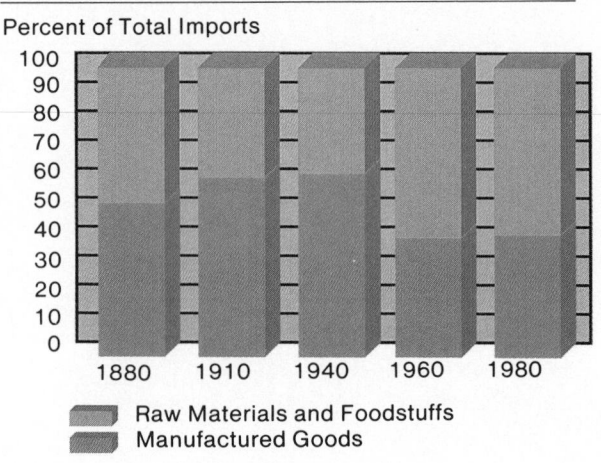

1880   1910   1940   1960   1980

Raw Materials and Foodstuffs
Manufactured Goods

The Rise and Fall of U.S. Tariffs

Cents Per Dollar of Dutiable Imports

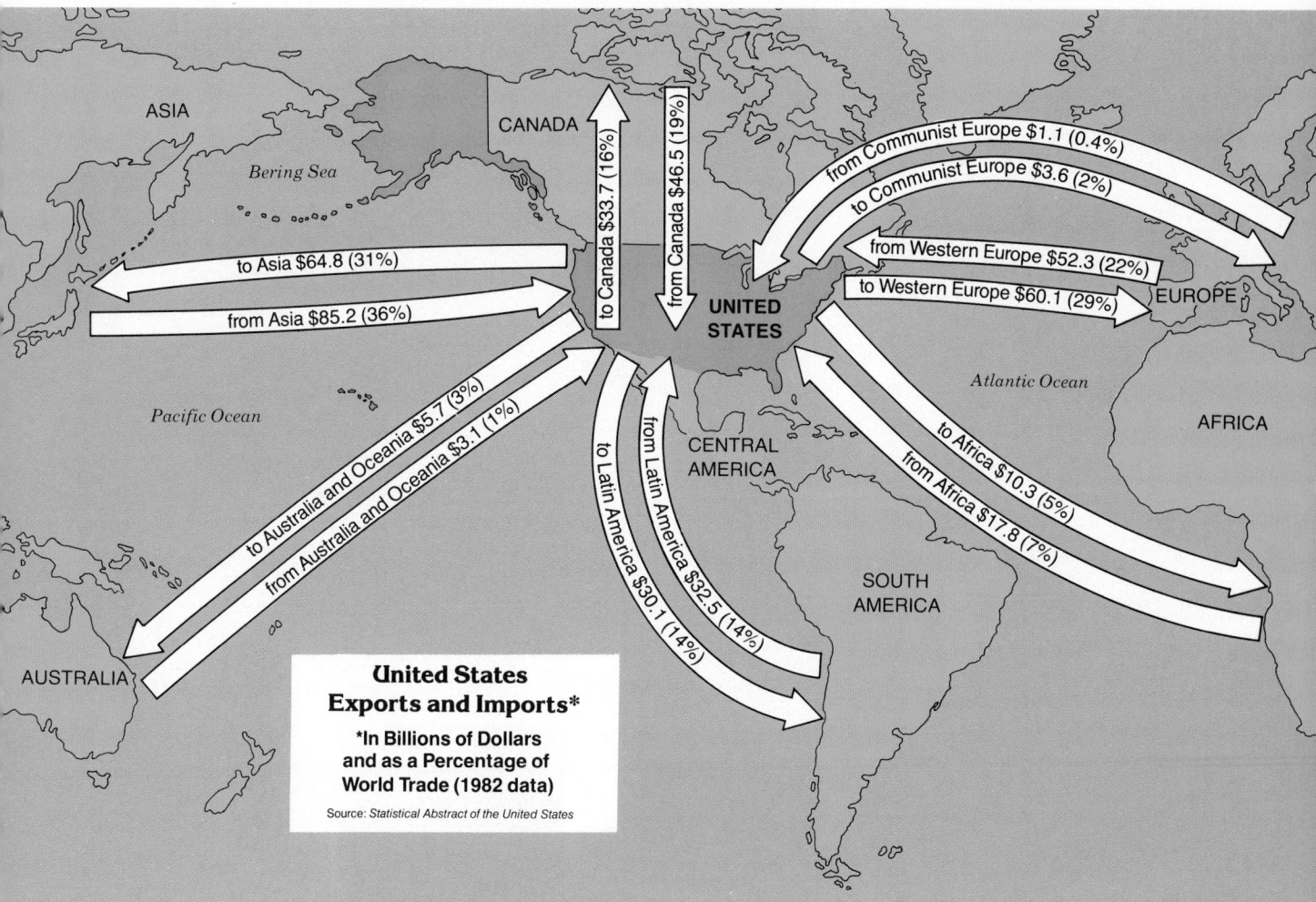

Graph showing tariff rates from 1789 to 1980, with labels:
Tariff of 1816, Tariff of Abominations, Tariff of 1832, Morrill Tariff, War and Postwar Tariffs, McKinley Tariff, Wilson-Gorman Tariff, Dingley Tariff, Payne–Aldrich Tariff, Hawley–Smoot Tariff, Reciprocal Trade Agreements, Fordney–McCumber Tariff, Underwood Tariff

Source: *Historical Statistics of The United States, Statistical Abstract of the United States*

to Canada $33.7 (16%)
from Canada $46.5 (19%)
from Communist Europe $1.1 (0.4%)
to Communist Europe $3.6 (2%)
from Western Europe $52.3 (22%)
to Western Europe $60.1 (29%)
to Asia $64.8 (31%)
from Asia $85.2 (36%)
to Australia and Oceania $5.7 (3%)
from Australia and Oceania $3.1 (1%)
to Latin America $30.1 (14%)
from Latin America $32.5 (14%)
to Africa $10.3 (5%)
from Africa $17.8 (7%)

United States Exports and Imports*

*In Billions of Dollars and as a Percentage of World Trade (1982 data)

Source: *Statistical Abstract of the United States*

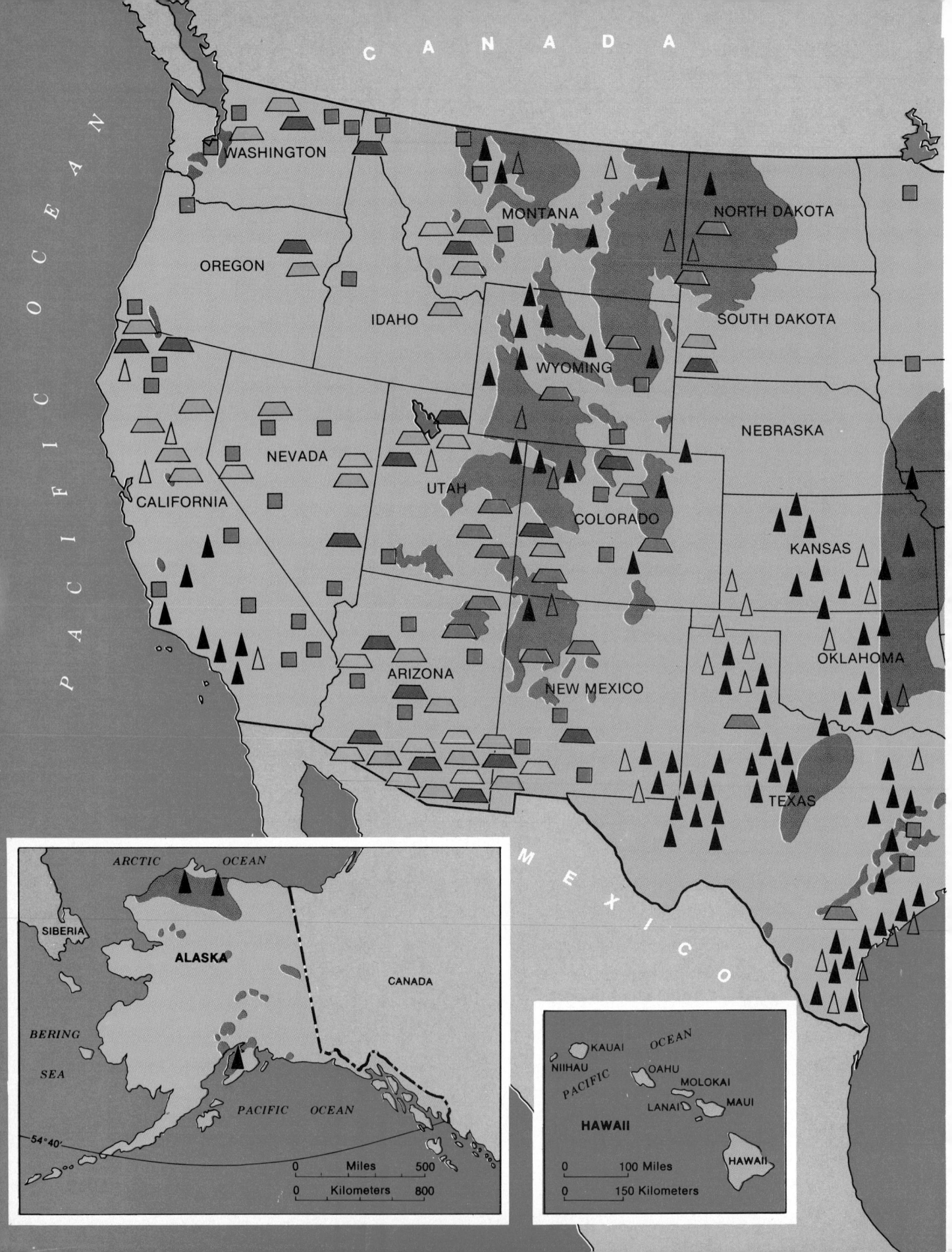

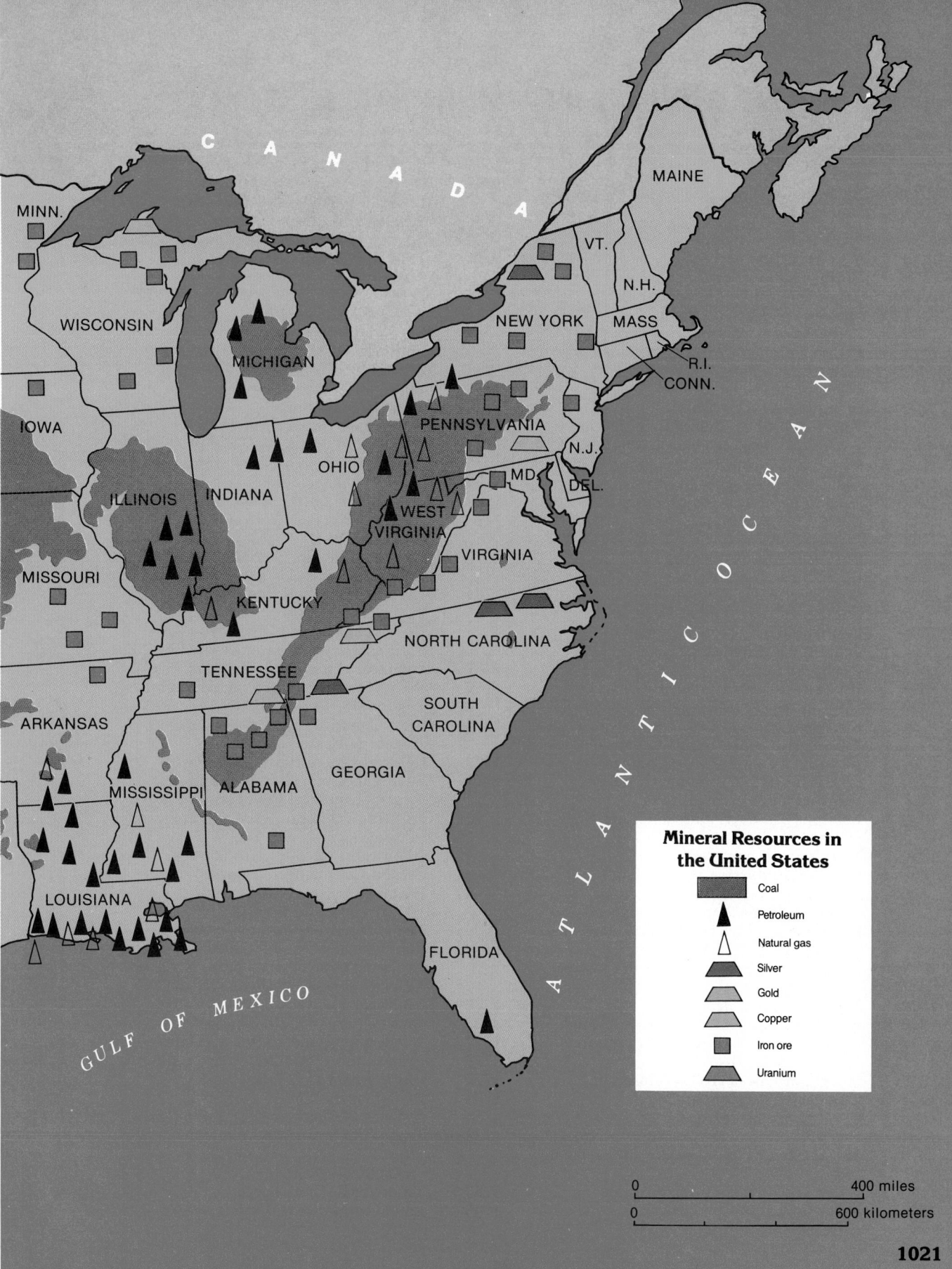

Mineral Resources in the United States

▬	Coal
▲	Petroleum
△	Natural gas
◢	Silver
◢	Gold
◢	Copper
▢	Iron ore
◢	Uranium

CANADA

MINN.
WISCONSIN
MICHIGAN
IOWA
ILLINOIS
INDIANA
OHIO
MISSOURI
KENTUCKY
WEST VIRGINIA
PENNSYLVANIA
VIRGINIA
NEW YORK
MAINE
VT.
N.H.
MASS
R.I.
CONN.
N.J.
DEL.
MD.
TENNESSEE
NORTH CAROLINA
SOUTH CAROLINA
ARKANSAS
MISSISSIPPI
ALABAMA
GEORGIA
LOUISIANA
FLORIDA

ATLANTIC OCEAN

GULF OF MEXICO

0	400 miles
0	600 kilometers

IMPORTANT EVENTS IN AMERICAN HISTORY

B.C.

30,000 Asian hunters begin to arrive in North America.

A.D.

200 Mayan culture develops.
1000 Vikings sail to North America.
1096 Crusades to Holy Land begin.
1271-95 Marco Polo visits the East.
1300 Aztec Empire expands.
1419 Prince Henry of Portugal establishes school for sailors.
1488 Dias reaches Cape of Good Hope.
1492 Columbus sails to America.
1493 Pope establishes Line of Demarcation.
1497-98 John Cabot explores North America.
1498 Da Gama reaches India.
1513 Balboa sights Pacific Ocean.
1519-22 Magellan's crew sails around world.
1521 Cortés conquers Aztec Empire.
1531 Pizarro lands in Peru.
1534 Cartier makes first voyage.
1541 De Soto reaches Mississippi River.
1565 St. Augustine is founded.
1587 English settlers land at Roanoke Island.
1588 English defeat Spanish Armada.
1607 Jamestown is founded.
1608 Quebec is founded.
1609 Hudson explores Hudson River.
1619 Virginia House of Burgesses first meets.
First women arrive at Jamestown.
First Africans arrive in English colonies.
1620 Pilgrims sign Mayflower Compact.
Pilgrims establish Plymouth Colony.
1624 Virginia becomes royal colony.
1630 Puritans establish Massachusetts Bay Colony.
1632 Maryland is chartered.
1634 First settlers arrive in Maryland.
1636 Harvard College is founded.
Roger Williams founds Providence.
1639 Fundamental Orders of Connecticut are drawn up.
First printing press in English colonies is set up.
1642 Montreal is founded.
1643 New England Confederation is formed.
1647 Massachusetts establishes first public schools in North America.
1649 Maryland Passes Act of Toleration.
1651-63 Navigation Acts are enforced.
1663 Carolina is chartered.
1664 England takes over New Amsterdam.
1673 Marquette and Joliet explore Mississippi River.
1676 Bacon leads rebellion in Virginia.
1679 New Hampshire is chartered.

1681 Pennsylvania is chartered.
1682 Quakers found Pennsylvania.
La Salle reaches Gulf of Mexico.
1685 Missions are established in Southwest.
1693 College of William and Mary is founded.
1701 Yale University is founded.
1718 New Orleans is founded.
1732 Franklin publishes first issue of *Poor Richard's Almanac.*
Georgia is chartered.
1733 English debtors settle in Georgia.
1735 Zenger trial is held.
1739 Whitefield's preaching begins to spread Great Awakening.
1750 Parliament passes Iron Act.
1754 French and Indian War begins.
Albany Plan of Union is proposed.
1755 Braddock defeated.
1759 British win Battle of Quebec.
1763 Treaty of Paris ends French and Indian War.
Pontiac's Rebellion breaks out.
Proclamation of 1763 is issued.
1764 Parliament passes Sugar Act.
1765 Parliament passes Stamp Act.
Parliament passes Quartering Act.
Stamp Act Congress meets in New York.
1767 Parliament passes Townshend Acts.
1769 Watt develops modern steam engine.
1770 Boston Massacre occurs.
1772 First Committee of Correspondence meets in Boston.
1773 Colonists stage Boston Tea Party.
1774 Parliament passes Intolerable Acts.
First Continental Congress meets.
1775 Fighting breaks out at Lexington and Concord.
Allen captures Fort Ticonderoga.
Second Continental Congress meets.
Battle of Bunker Hill is fought.
Wilderness Road is completed.
Boone leads settlers to Kentucky.
1776 *Common Sense* is published.
Declaration of Independence is signed.
Americans win Battle of Trenton.
1776 Americans win victory at Saratoga.
Howe occupies Philadelphia.
1777-78 Americans spend winter at Valley Forge.
1778 France and U.S. sign treaty of alliance.
1779 Clark recaptures Vincennes.
1781 British surrender at Yorktown.
Articles of Confederation are adopted.
1783 Treaty of Paris ends American Revolution; U.S. independence is recognized.
1784 Trade with China begins.
1785 Land Ordinance of 1785 is passed.

1786-87	Shays leads rebellion in Massachusetts.
1787	Northwest Ordinance is passed.
	Constitutional Convention meets.
1787-90	Gray sails *Columbia* around the world.
1788	U.S. Constitution is adopted.
	First settlers arrive in Northwest Territory.

George Washington
1732–99
Born in Virginia
No political party
President: 1789–97

1789	Congress creates Departments of State, Treasury, and War.
	Judiciary Act establishes Supreme Court.
	French Revolution begins.
1790	Slater builds cotton factory.
1791	Bill of Rights is added to Constitution.
	Vermont enters the Union.
	Bank of U.S. is chartered.
1792	Kentucky enters the Union.
1793	Neutrality Proclamation is issued.
	Whitney invents cotton gin.
1794	Whiskey Rebellion is crushed.
	Little Turtle is defeated at Fallen Timbers.
	Jay's Treaty is signed.
1796	Washington delivers Farewell Address.

John Adams
1735–1826
Born in Massachusetts
Federalist
President: 1797–1801

1797	XYZ Affair angers Americans.
1798	Eleventh Amendment is ratified.
	Alien and Sedition Acts are passed.
	Kentucky and Virginia Resolutions are passed.
1800	Prosser plans slave revolt.
1801	Marshall is appointed Chief Justice.

Thomas Jefferson
1743–1826
Born in Virginia
Democratic-Republican
President: 1801–09

1803	Ohio enters the Union.
	Louisiana Purchase is made.
1804	Twelfth Amendment is ratified.
	American warships bombard Tripoli.
1804-06	Lewis and Clark explore Louisiana Purchase.
1807	Embargo Act is passed.
	Fulton's steamboat *Clermont* voyages up Hudson River.

James Madison
1751–1836
Born in Virginia
Democratic-Republican
President: 1809–17

1809	Non-Intercourse Act is passed.
1811	Tecumseh is defeated at Tippecanoe.
1812	Louisiana enters the Union.
	War of 1812 begins.
1814	British burn Washington, D.C.
	Jackson defeats Creek at Battle of Horseshoe Bend.
	Hartford Convention meets.
	Lowell builds first modern textile mill.
	Treaty of Ghent is signed.
1815	Americans defeat British at Battle of New Orleans.
1816	Second Bank of the United States is chartered.
	Indiana enters the Union.

James Monroe
1758–1831
Born in Virginia
Democratic-Republican
President: 1817–25

1817-25	"Era of Good Feelings" occurs.
1817	Mississippi enters the Union.
	Rush-Bagot Agreement is signed.
	American Colonization Society is formed.
1818	Illinois enters the Union.
	Jackson invades Florida.
1819	Wood patents iron plow.
	McCulloch v. Maryland announced.
	Treaty gives Florida to the United States.
1820	Missouri Compromise is adopted.
	Maine enters the Union.
1821	Austin starts colony in Texas.
	Missouri enters the Union.
	First American public high school opens in Boston.
1822	Vesey plans slave revolt.
1823	Monroe Doctrine is proclaimed.

1023

John Quincy Adams

1767–1848
Born in Massachusetts
Democratic-Republican
President: 1825–29

1825   Erie Canal is completed.
1828   Tariff of Abominations is passed.

Andrew Jackson

1767–1845
Born in South Carolina
Democrat
President: 1829–37

1830   Webster and Hayne debate nullification.
        Cooper tests steam locomotive.
1831   McCormick builds mechanical reaper.
        Garrison publishes the *Liberator*.
        Turner leads slave revolt.
1832   Congress passes Tariff of 1832.
        Jackson vetoes Bank of U.S. charter.
        South Carolina adopts Ordinance of
          Nullification.
1833   Compromise tariff is passed.
        Oberlin College admits women.
1836   Texans are defeated at Alamo.
        Texas declares independence from
          Mexico.
        Arkansas enters the Union.

Martin Van Buren

1782–1862
Born in New York
Democrat
President 1837–41

1837   Michigan enters the Union.
        Panic of 1837 begins.
        Horace Mann begins school reform.
        Threshing machine is invented.
1838   Cherokee forced on Trail of Tears.

William Henry Harrison

1773–1841
Born in Virginia
Whig
President: Mar. 4–Apr. 4, 1841

1841   Harrison dies.

John Tyler

1790–1862
Born in Virginia
Whig
President: 1841–45

1842   Massachusetts Supreme Court declares
          labor unions legal.
        Webster-Ashburton Treaty is approved.
1844   Morse completes telegraph line.

James K. Polk

1795–1849
Born in North Carolina
Democrat
President: 1845–49

1845   U.S. annexes Texas by treaty.
        Florida enters the Union.
        Thoreau publishes *Walden*.
1846   Oregon boundary dispute is settled.
        Iowa enters the Union.
        Mexican War begins.
        California declares independence from
          Mexico.
        Wilmot Proviso is presented.
        Howe patents sewing machine.
1847   Mormons settle Utah.
1848   Mexican War ends; U.S. gains Mexican
          Cession.
        Seneca Falls Convention is held.
        Wisconsin enters the Union.

Zachary Taylor

1784–1850
Born in Virginia
Whig
President: 1849–50

1849   California gold rush begins.
1850   Taylor dies.

Millard Fillmore

1800–74
Born in New York
Whig
President: 1850–53

1850   Compromise of 1850 is adopted
        California enters the Union.

1850's	Bessemer steelmaking process is developed.
1851	Hawthorne publishes *House of Seven Gables*.
1852	National Road is completed. *Uncle Tom's Cabin* is published.

Franklin Pierce
1804–69
Born in New Hampshire
Democrat
President: 1853–57

1853	Gadsden Purchase is made. Perry arrives in Japan.
1854	Kansas-Nebraska Act is passed. Republican Party is formed.
1856	Clashes occur in "bleeding Kansas."

James Buchanan
1791–1868
Born in Pennsylvania
Democrat
President: 1857–61

1857	Dred Scott decision is handed down.
1858	Lincoln and Douglas debate issue of slavery. Overland Mail begins operations.
1859	Brown raids arsenal at Harpers Ferry. Drake strikes oil in Pennsylvania. Comstock Lode is discovered in Nevada. Oregon enters the Union.
1860	South Carolina secedes from the Union. Pony Express completes first run from Missouri to California.

Abraham Lincoln
1809–65
Born in Kentucky
Republican
President: 1861–65

1861	Confederate States of America is formed. Fort Sumter is attacked; Civil War begins. Lincoln orders blockade of South. Union forces are defeated at Bull Run.
1862	Battle of Antietam is fought. Morrill Act provides for agricultural colleges. Homestead Act is passed.

1863	Emancipation Proclamation is signed. Union forces capture Vicksburg. Confederates are defeated at Gettysburg. Union forces capture Chattanooga. West Virginia enters the Union.
1864	Grant is appointed Union commander. Sherman's army makes "March to the Sea." Sand Creek Massacre begins Cheyenne War. Nevada enters the Union.
1865	Freedmen's Bureau is created. Lee surrenders at Appomattox. Lincoln is assassinated.

Andrew Johnson
1808–75
Born in North Carolina
Democrat
President: 1865–69

1865	Reconstruction begins. Thirteenth Amendment abolishes slavery.
1865-86	Settlers and Indians on the plains clash.
1866	Transatlantic cable is completed. Congress passes Civil Rights Act. National Labor Union is founded.
1867	U.S. purchases Alaska. Nebraska enters the Union. Congressional plan of reconstruction is organized. Grange is organized as Patrons of Husbandry.
1868	Johnson is impeached and acquitted. Fourteenth Amendment guarantees civil rights to blacks. Cheyenne War Ends. U.S. and Sioux sign peace treaty.

Ulysses S. Grant
1822–85
Born in Ohio
Republican
President: 1869–77

1869	Transcontinental railroad is completed. Knights of Labor is founded.
1870	Fifteenth Amendment gives vote to blacks.
1870-71	Force Acts are passed.
1872	Amnesty Act is passed. Crédit Mobilier scandal is investigated.
1873	Depression begins. Steel plow is developed.
1874	Barbed wire is invented.

1875	Resumption Act is passed.
1876	Sioux defeat Custer at Little Bighorn.
	Colorado enters the Union.
	Philadelphia holds Centennial Exhibition.
	Presidential election is disputed.
	Bell demonstrates telephone.
1876-77	"Granger cases" are decided.
1877	House selects Hayes as President.

Rutherford B. Hayes
1822–93
Born in Ohio
Republican
President: 1877–81

1877	Reconstruction ends.
	Sioux are defeated.
1878	Congress passes Bland-Allison Act.
1879	Edison perfects electric light bulb.
1880-90	New immigration from eastern and southern Europe takes place.

James A. Garfield
1831–81
Born in Ohio
Republican
President: Mar. 4–Sept. 19, 1881

1881	Carver founds Tuskegee Institute.
	A Century of Dishonor is published.
	Garfield is assassinated.

Chester A. Arthur
1829–86
Born in Vermont
Republican
President: 1881–85

1882	Chinese Exclusion Act is passed.
	Rockefeller organizes Standard Oil Trust.
	First U.S. power plant is opened.
1883	Pendleton Act establishes civil service.
1884	Knights of Labor win Union Pacific Railroad strike.

Grover Cleveland
1837–1908
Born in New Jersey
Democrat
President: 1885–89

1886	Presidential Succession Act passes.
	Haymarket Riot occurs.
	A. F. of L. is founded.
1887	Interstate Commerce Commission is created.
	Hatch Act is passed.
	Dawes Act gives land to Indians.

Benjamin Harrison
1833–1901
Born in Ohio
Republican
President: 1889–93

1889	Oklahoma is opened for settlement.
	Washington, Montana, North Dakota, and South Dakota enter the Union.
	Addams opens Hull House.
	Department of Agriculture is created.
1890	Sherman Antitrust Act is passed.
	Wyoming and Idaho enter the Union.
	McKinley Tariff is passed.
	Sherman Silver Purchase Act passes.
1891	Populist Party is organized.
1892	Homestead Steel Strike occurs.

Grover Cleveland
1837–1908
Born in New Jersey
Democrat
President: 1893–97

1893	Silver Purchase Act is repealed.
	Chicago holds World's Fair.
1894	Wilson-Gorman Tariff passes.
	Pullman strike occurs.
1895	Marconi invents wireless telegraphy.
	Cubans revolt against Spain.
1896	Supreme Court upholds Jim Crow laws in *Plessy v. Ferguson*.
	Bryan is free silver candidate.
	Utah enters the Union.
	Gold is discovered in the Klondike.

William McKinley
1843–1901
Born in Ohio
Republican
President: 1897–1901

1897	Congress passes the Dingley Tariff.
1898	U.S. annexes Hawaii.
	Spanish-American War is fought; U.S.

gains Philippines, Guam, and Puerto Rico.

1899 First Hague Conference meets.

1899–1900 Open Door policy is proclaimed.

1900 International Ladies Garment Workers Union is founded.
Boxer Rebellion occurs.

1901 McKinley is assassinated.

Theodore Roosevelt
1858–1919
Born in New York
Republican
President: 1901–09

1901-02 Pan American Conference meets.

1902 Platt Amendment is adopted.
Newlands Act is passed.
Drago Doctrine is announced.
American forces withdraw from Cuba.

1903 Wright Brothers make first successful airplane flight.
Direct primary is adopted in Wisconsin.
Department of Commerce and Labor is created.
Congress passes Elkins Act.
U.S. acquires Canal Zone.

1904 Roosevelt Corollary is announced.
Shame of the Cities is published.

1905 Roosevelt negotiates Treaty of Portsmouth; receives Nobel Prize.

1906 U.S. sends troops to Cuba.
Pure Food and Drug Act is passed.
Congress passes Meat Inspection Act.
Burke Act modifies Dawes Act.

1907 Gentleman's Agreement is concluded with Japan.
Oklahoma enters the Union.
Second Hague Conference meets.

1908 White House holds Conservation Conference.
Court rules on Danbury Hatters.

William Howard Taft
1857–1930
Born in Ohio
Republican
President: 1909–13

1909 Congress passes the Payne-Aldrich Tariff.
Taft introduces "dollar diplomacy."
Ford develops Model T.
NAACP is founded.

1910 Congress passes the Mann-Elkins Act.

1911 Fire sweeps Triangle shirt factory.
Transcontinental plane flight occurs.

1912 Progressive Party is formed.
New Mexico enters the Union.
Arizona enters the Union.
Massachusetts passes first state minimum-wage law.

Woodrow Wilson
1856–1924
Born in Virginia
Democrat
President: 1913–21

1913 Sixteenth Amendment authorizes income tax.
Seventeenth Amendment provides for direct election of senators.
Congress passes the Underwood Tariff.
Federal Reserve Act is passed.

1914 World War I begins.
Wilson issues neutrality proclamation.
Panama Canal is opened.
Federal Trade Commission is created.
Clayton Antitrust Act is passed.

1915 German submarine sinks *Lusitania*.
Grandfather clauses are declared unconstitutional.

1916 Congress passes Jones Act.
U.S. sends troops into Mexico to capture Villa.

1917 Zimmermann telegram is intercepted.
U.S. enters World War I.
Smith-Hughes Act is passed.
Revolution breaks out in Russia.
U.S. purchases Virgin Islands.
Puerto Ricans are made U.S. citizens.

1918 World War I ends.
Wilson presents Fourteen Points.

1919 Treaty of Versailles is signed.
Prohibition begins with ratification of the Eighteenth Amendment.
"Palmer raids" take place.

1920 Senate rejects Versailles Treaty.
Nineteenth Amendment gives vote to women.
First U.S. radio station is started.

Warren G. Harding
1865–1923
Born in Ohio
Republican
President: 1921–23

1921 Law restricting immigration is passed.
Bureau of the Budget is set up.

	Veterans' Bureau is created.
1921-22	Washington Naval Conference meets.
1922	"Naval holiday" is declared.
	Mussolini seizes power in Italy.
	Fordney-McCumber Tariff is passed.
	Soviet Union is formed.
1923	Harding dies suddenly.

Calvin Coolidge

1872–1933
Born in Vermont
Republican
President: 1923–29

1924	Indians are made U.S. citizens.
	Teapot Dome scandal erupts.
	Congress passes Veterans' bonus bill.
1927	Lindbergh flies the Atlantic.
	Sacco and Vanzetti are executed.
	McNary-Haugen Bill is vetoed.
1928	Kellogg-Briand Pact condemns war.
	Roosevelt Corollary is renounced.

Herbert Hoover

1874–1964
Born in Iowa
Republican
President: 1929–33

1929	Stock market crash marks beginning of Great Depression.
1930	Public works programs begin.
	Congress passes Hawley-Smoot Tariff.
1931	Japan invades Manchuria.
1932	Reconstruction Finance Corporation is organized.
	Stimson Doctrine is announced.
1932-33	Federal Reserve powers are increased.

Franklin D. Roosevelt

1882–1945
Born in New York
Democrat
President: 1933–45

1933	Hitler comes to power in Germany.
	Twentieth Amendment is ratified.
	Roosevelt begins New Deal.
	Good Neighbor Policy is announced.
	CCC is created.
	AAA is passed.
	TVA is created.
	NIRA is passed.

	U.S. recognizes Soviet Union.
	Twenty-first Amendment repeals Prohibition.
1934	Securities and Exchange Commission is created.
	Platt Amendment is canceled.
	Reciprocal Trade Agreement Act is passed.
	Wheeler-Howard Act improves life of Indians.
1935	WPA is created.
	NIRA is ruled unconstitutional.
	Italy invades Ethiopia.
	Wagner Act is passed.
	Social Security Act is passed.
	Neutrality Act is passed.
	CIO is established.
1935-37	Neutrality Acts are passed.
1936	AAA is ruled unconstitutional.
	Germany invades the Rhineland.
1937	Japan invades central China.
1938	New AAA is passed.
	Munich Pact is signed.
	CIO separates from A. F. of L.
	Fair Labor Standards Act is passed.
	Food, Drug, and Cosmetic Act is passed.
1939	Germany invades Poland; World War II begins.
	Neutrality Act of 1937 is amended.
1940	France falls to Germany.
1941	Lend-Lease Act is passed.
	Germany invades Soviet Union.
	Atlantic Charter states Allied war aims.
	Japan attacks Pearl Harbor; U.S. enters World War II.
1942	Soviets stop Germans at Stalingrad.
	Corregidor surrenders to the Japanese.
	Marines invade Guadalcanal.
	Office of Price Administration is established.
1943	Allies stop Axis armies in North Africa and invade Italy.
	American forces advance in Pacific.
	Allied leaders meet in Cairo and Tehran.
1944	Allies land in France on D-Day.
1945	Big Three meet at Yalta.
	Roosevelt dies.

Harry S Truman

1884–1972
Born in Missouri
Democrat
President: 1945–53

1945	Germany surrenders.
	Atomic bombs are dropped on Japan; Japan surrenders.
	World War II ends.

United Nations is formed at San Francisco Conference.

Auto workers strike at General Motors.

1946 Steelworkers, coal miners, and railroad workers go on strike.

Philippines become independent.

1947 Truman Doctrine is announced.

Taft-Hartley Act is passed.

Congress passes Presidential Succession Act.

1948 Marshall Plan is enacted.

Berlin Airlift is begun.

1949 Point Four program is announced.

NATO is formed.

Soviet scientists successfully explode atomic bomb.

Communists gain control of China.

1950 Internal Security Act is passed.

Korean War begins.

1951 Twenty-second Amendment is ratified.

1952 U.S. tests hydrogen bomb.

Dwight D. Eisenhower

1890–1969
Born in Texas
Republican
President: 1953–61

1953 Department of Health, Education, and Welfare is created.

States get title to offshore oil.

Korean War ends.

1954 Supreme Court rules segregated schools unconstitutional.

West Germany is admitted to NATO.

1955 Warsaw Pact is created.

Blacks stage bus boycott in Montgomery.

1956 Hungarians revolt against Soviets.

Egypt seizes Suez Canal.

1957 Civil Rights Act is passed.

Soviet Union launches *Sputnik I*.

1958 United States launches first satellite into orbit.

Alaska enters the Union.

1958-59 Berlin crisis erupts.

1959 Castro comes to power in Cuba.

St. Lawrence Seaway is opened.

Hawaii enters the Union.

1960 Nation elects first Roman Catholic to the Presidency.

John F. Kennedy

1917–63
Born in Massachusetts
Democrat
President: 1961–63

1961 Alliance for Progress is established.

Peace Corps is established.

Bay of Pigs invasion fails.

Berlin Wall is built.

1962 First American orbits earth.

Cuban missile crisis almost leads to war.

U.S. sends first troops to Vietnam.

Trade Expansion Act is passed.

1963 U.S. and Soviet Union sign Limited Test Ban Treaty.

President Kennedy is assassinated.

Lyndon B. Johnson

1908–73
Born in Texas
Democrat
President: 1963–69

1964 Twenty-fourth Amendment bans use of poll tax.

Economic Opportunity Act is passed.

Civil Rights Act is passed.

Gulf of Tonkin Resolution is passed.

1965 Vietnam War escalates.

Voting Rights Act is passed.

Medicare is established.

Department of Housing and Urban Development created.

1966 National Organization for Women (NOW) is formed.

Department of Transportation is created.

1967 Twenty-fifth Amendment is ratified.

1968 Vietnam peace talks begin in Paris.

Dr. Martin Luther King, Jr., is assassinated.

Richard M. Nixon

1913–
Born in California
Republican
President: 1969–74

1969 American troops begin to withdraw from Vietnam.

American astronauts land on moon.

1970 U.S. invades Cambodia.

1971 Twenty-sixth Amendment lowers voting age to 18.

1972 Nixon visits China and Soviet Union.

1973 Vice President Agnew resigns; Nixon appoints Ford.

U.S. troops leave Vietnam.

OPEC announces oil embargo.

1974 Nixon resigns.

Gerald R. Ford

1913–
Born in Nebraska
Republican
President: 1974–77

1974   Ford pardons Nixon.
        Amnesty for draft evaders and military
          deserters announced.
1975   Americans and Soviets take part in joint
          space venture.
        Vietnam falls to Communists.
1976   The nation celebrates its Bicentennial.

James E. Carter, Jr.

1924–
Born in Georgia
Democrat
President: 1977–81

1977   Carter offers amnesty to draft evaders.
        Department of Energy is created.
1978   Senate ratifies new treaties with
          Panama.
1979   Accident occurs at Three Mile Island
          nuclear power plant.
        Camp David Accords are signed.
        Iranians seize Americans as hostages.
        Soviet Union invades Afghanistan.
1980   "Carter Doctrine" is announced.

U.S. protests Afghanistan invasion.
U.S. mission to free Iranian hostages
  fails.

Ronald W. Reagan

1911–
Born in Illinois
Republican
President: 1981–

1981   Iranians release American hostages.
        Reagan survives assassination attempt.
        Columbia completes first flight.
        Sandra Day O'Connor becomes first
          woman appointed to Supreme Court.
1983   U.S. Marines are sent to Lebanon.
1984   *Challenger* and *Discovery* continue
          space shuttle program.
        U.S. Marines leave Lebanon.
        Democrats nominate Geraldine Ferraro,
          first woman to be Vice-Presidential
          candidate of a major party.
        SALT talks resume
1985   Reagan begins second term.
        Space shuttle *Discovery* completes first
          secret military mission.
        Terrorists kidnap TWA passengers;
          hostages released 17 days later.
        Twenty-fifth Amendment is invoked
          while Reagan undergoes surgery.
        Space shuttle *Atlantis* makes
          first flight.
        U.S.–Soviet summit talks occur
          in Geneva, Switzerland.
1986   *Challenger* tragedy shocks the nation.

GLOSSARY

This glossary contains many of the terms you need to understand as you study American history. After each term, there is a brief definition or explanation of the meaning of the term as it is usually used in American history. The page number in parentheses after each definition refers to the page on which the term is boldfaced in the textbook.

The brief definitions in this glossary do not always provide all the information that you may need to know about these terms. Therefore, you may find it useful to turn to the page listed in parentheses to read more about any of the terms.

A

abolition Act of putting an end to a condition or institution, such as slavery. (page 153)

abolition society Group formed for the purpose of working toward a permanent end to slavery. (page 153)

academy Private school, usually for the secondary grades. (page 373)

adobe Sun-dried brick, often used by the Indians of the Southwest for building. (page 6)

affirmative action Program providing that preference be given to blacks and other minorities when they apply for jobs or schools. (page 950)

aggression Unprovoked attack on or invasion of another country. (page 782)

aggressor One responsible for an attack or invasion. (page 688)

alien Person who resides in a country of which he or she is not a citizen. (page 235)

alliance Organization of farmers formed for cooperative buying and political action (page 561); association of two or more nations joined together for mutual purposes and goals. (page 670)

almanac Book containing recipes, weather forecasts, advice on planting and harvesting, and other information. (page 88)

American dialect American version of the English language, with many words borrowed from other languages and newly invented words. (page 63)

Americanization Program of assimilating the Indians into the white American culture. (page 494)

American System Economic program before the Civil War that was to strengthen and unite the United States by a protective tariff, a national bank, and an efficient transportation system. (page 269)

amnesty Pardon before conviction for offenses committed against a government. (page 901)

anarchism Political belief that government is unnecessary. (page 545)

appeasement Attempt to satisfy the demands of an aggressor in order to maintain peace. (page 786)

arbitration Method of settling a dispute by seeking the judgment of an impartial person, whose decision all agree in advance to accept. (pages 539, 656)

armaments race Competition among countries to build up strength in military weapons; now called the **arms race.** (page 772)

armistice Truce; agreement to stop fighting. (page 684)

artisan Skilled worker. (page 59)

assembly line Method of manufacture in which the product passes along a moving belt while each worker performs one task in putting together the finished product. (pages 617, 739)

Australian ballot Ballot printed at public expense that lists all candidates and that is cast in secret. (page 594)

automation Use of machines in factories and plants to control the manufacture of products. (page 868)

Axis Powers Name given to Germany, Italy, and Japan during World War II.

B

baby boom Period from the late 1940's to the early 1960's when there was a great increase in the birth rate. (page 871)

balance-of-power system Arrangement by which strength is sufficiently divided among nations to prevent one nation or group of nations from becoming aggressive or dominant. (page 671)

balance of trade Difference between the value of goods sold to and bought from foreign nations. (page 103)

bank note Paper money. (page 226)

barrio Neighborhood where Spanish-speaking people live. (page 953)

belligerent Warring nation. (page 784)

bill of attainder Law that punishes a person by fine, imprisonment, or confiscation of property without a court trial. (page 179)

Bill of Rights List of individual freedoms guaranteed to every citizen by the government. (page 42)

bimetallism Monetary policy of furnishing security for the nation's currency with two metals—gold and silver. (page 563)

black code Set of laws passed by a southern state after the Civil War to control the conduct of the freed slaves and restrict their civil rights. (page 452)

black list List of workers considered undesirable by employers. Any person whose name appears on such a list is barred from employment in that industry. (page 542)

black power Term applied to the movement seeking the growth of black self-identity and racial pride through economic and political progress. (page 949)

blitzkrieg Term meaning lightning war, used to describe the speed of the German advance at the beginning of World War II. (page 790)

bloc Unified group of voters or nations. (page 394)

blockade Barrier set up around a port or region to prevent communication or trade. (page 252)

border state State which, on the outbreak of the Civil War, did not secede from the Union but which permitted slavery. Delaware, Maryland, Kentucky, and Missouri were the border states. (page 413)

bounty Payment made to encourage production of certain goods in the colonies (page 104) or to encourage enlistment in the army during the Civil War. (page 428)

bounty jumper Soldier who enlisted in the Union army for a financial reward, then deserted to reenlist under another name and collect another bounty. (page 428)

bracero Mexican who entered the United States under a 1942 treaty to work temporarily as a farm laborer. (page 808)

brinksmanship Policy stating that the United States must be prepared to go to the brink of war to keep the peace. (page 837)

bullion Unminted gold or silver. (page 560)

burgess Representative elected by the landowning voters of colonial Virginia. (page 24)

business combination Arrangement in which corporations in the same type of business join together to form a larger enterprise. (page 522)

business cycle Natural movement in the economy between periods of prosperity and periods of decline. (page 534)

C

cabinet A group consisting of the heads of the executive departments, called Secretaries, who advise the President. (page 224)

capital Property, equipment, and money used to produce goods or provide services. (page 266)

capitalism Economic system in which most businesses are privately owned and operated. (page 545)

capitalist Person who invests money in a business in order to make a profit. (page 266)

capital stock Money value of the outstanding shares of a joint-stock company. *See* joint-stock company. (page 227)

carpetbagger Northerner who moved to the South seeking economic and political opportunity. (page 457)

cartel Business arrangement in which companies form a pool to set prices and to limit competition. *See* pool. (page 976)

cash crop Product grown for the purpose of selling it to make a profit. (page 59)

caucus Private meeting of leaders of a political party to select candidates or set policies. (page 233)

cease-fire agreement Mutually acceptable decision to temporarily stop fighting. (page 925)

chain store Business establishment with branches in several cities. (page 520)

charter Document issued by a government granting certain rights, powers, or privileges to a person or group of people. (pages 23, 521)

Chautauqua movement Educational program begun in 1874 for summer visitors to Lake Chatauqua in upper New York State at which travel talks, state presentations, lectures, and religious services were given. (page 581)

cheap money policy Monetary program, included in the 1868 Democratic platform, calling for the issuing of more "greenbacks" to increase the money supply. Such a policy was seen as beneficial to the farmers and the poor. *See* hard money policy. (page 456)

checks and balances System whereby each branch of government checks or restrains the other branches. (page 177)

city manager form of government Organization of city government by which a city employs an appointed administrator to direct the government and the operations of the city. (page 595)

civilization Highly advanced culture. (page 4)

civil liberty Individual right that is protected by the Constitution against the power of government. (page 179)

civil rights Political, social, and economic rights of citizens, such as the right to vote and the right to equal treatment under the law. (page 452)

civil rights movement Organized effort by blacks and other minorities to secure the end of discrimination and the assurance of full equality in American society. (page 947)

civil service Jobs in federal, state, and local governments awarded on the basis of merit. (page 474)

clipper ship Fast, sleek sailing ship used by American merchants in the early 1800's. (page 314)

closed shop Workplace where only union members are hired; also called a union shop. *See* right-to-work law. (page 541)

cold war Term applied to the rivalry and ideological conflicts between the United States and the Soviet Union since World War II, in which confrontation stops short of direct military action. (page 825)

collective bargaining Process by which union officials and employers negotiate about wages, working conditions, and other aspects of employment. (page 319)

colony Land that is settled by a group of people from another country, but that comes under the control of that country. (page 17)

commercial farmer Agricultural worker who produces crops to sell for profit. (page 619)

commission form of government Organization of city government by which the power to run the city is placed in a council of several members. (page 595)

common law System of law based on custom, tradition, and precedents established by courts of law. (page 523)

communism Economic and social system in which the means of production are controlled by the state. (page 545)

compact theory Idea that the federal government was created by the states and acts as the agent of the states to carry out the powers that the states delegate to it. (page 236)

company town Community owned entirely by a business that employs all its residents. (page 533)

company union Labor association organized by employers rather than by the workers. (page 743)

compulsory military service Specified period of service in a nation's armed forces required by law. (page 256)

concentration Government policy of the 1850's that confined the Indians to certain limited areas of the western United States. In these areas the tribes were free to hunt and to carry on their own affairs. (page 490)

concentration camp World War II detention center set up by Nazis in which Jews, political prisoners, and other enemies of the Third Reich were tortured and killed. (page 812)

concurrent power Power that is shared by the federal government and the states. (page 177)

confederation League, or association, of states or nations established for a specific purpose. (pages 41, 155)

conquered provinces theory Idea, held by Representative Thaddeus Stevens, that the former Confederate states should be treated as nations defeated in war. (page 453)

conquistador Conqueror, especially

a Spanish soldier in the New World. (page 14)

conscription National selection of draftees for military service. (page 426)

consent of the governed Principle granting all adult males the right to vote, incorporated by Roger Williams into Rhode Island's original charter. (page 36)

conservation Preservation and protection of natural resources to prevent their exploitation and destruction. (page 601)

conservative *(adj)* Type of political outlook, often favoring a cautious, traditional approach; *(n)* person with a traditional and cautious political outlook. (page 125)

containment American foreign policy, begun during the Truman administration, under which the United States attempted to keep communism within its existing borders. (page 828)

contraband Name used to mean fugitive slave (page 424); war materials supplied to a warring nation by a neutral nation. (page 675)

convoy System of using warships to escort commercial vessels to their destination during World War II. (pages 681, 793)

cooling-off period Provision contained in the League of Nations Covenant requiring nations to wait for a time before engaging in combat. (page 687)

cooperative Association of farmers organized to bypass distributors by selling directly to urban markets and by purchasing machinery and necessities for farmers in large quantities. (page 557)

corporation Business organization in which three or more persons receive a charter from a state to organize a specific business. The corporation is legally an "artificial person." (page 521)

cost accounting Business practice of determining the cost of every item of production and marketing. (page 740)

cotton gin Machine that separated cotton seeds from fibers. (page 330)

county Unit of local government. (pages 95, 335)

county extension agent Employee hired through the 1914 Smith-Lever Act to provide information to farmers and their families on agriculture and home economics. (page 620)

coureur de bois Runner-of-the-woods, or French fur trader, who traveled in the wilderness and gathered furs for trading. (page 47)

craft union Labor organization made up of people who perform the same skilled job, such as carpenters or plumbers. (page 540)

Creole Person of Spanish descent born in the New World; the second highest social class in Spanish America. (page 17)

culture Way of life of a group of people, including all the characteristics and activities the group shares — language; religious practices; art; government; method of educating children; and ways of providing food, shelter, and clothing. (page 4)

culture area Region in which most of the people share the same culture. (page 6)

D

de facto segregation Segregation that is maintained by local residence patterns, not by any actual law. (page 948)

default To fail to pay a debt. (page 784)

deficit Amount by which spending exceeds income. (page 908)

deficit spending Governmental policy of spending more than is received in tax revenues. (page 733)

delegated power Power among those enumerated in the Constitution as belonging to the federal government. (page 176)

department store Business establishment that combines many specialty stores under one roof. (page 519)

depression Period of sharply decreased economic activity and high unemployment. (pages 161, 697)

détente Gradual relaxation and reduction of tensions between the United States and the Soviet Union. (page 928)

dictatorship Form of government in which one person or a small group of people completely controls the government and people of a nation. The leader of such a government is called a dictator. (page 782)

dime novel Publication costing ten cents and consisting of fictional stories of adventure or romance. (page 578)

diplomatic relations Regular conduct of international affairs between nations, including the exchange of diplomats and the carrying on of dialogues of mutual interest. (page 677)

direct primary Election in which registered members of a political party choose the party's candidates for office. (page 594)

direct relief Money, food, or jobs given by the government directly to needy people. (page 716)

direct tax Tax paid directly to the government. (page 110)

discrimination Unfair treatment of a person because of a racial, ethnic, religious, or other characteristic of that person. (page 446)

dividend Payment made to stockholders of a corporation from the firm's profits. (page 521)

divine right of kings Belief that the king was responsible only to God for his actions. (page 32)

division of labor Arrangement in manufacturing by which each worker specializes in a small part of a large job. (page 519)

dollar diplomacy Policy of the United States by which investment of money in Latin America in the early 1900's was encouraged. (page 658)

domino effect Term referring to the theory that if one nation in an area falls to communism, the others in that area will soon follow. (page 919)

dry farming Technique of deep plowing and careful cultivation to preserve soil moisture. (page 504)

due process of law Constitutional guarantee that government will not deprive a person of life, liberty, or property unfairly, arbitrarily, or without following standardized procedures. (page 454)

E

economic sanction Refusal to trade with a nation breaking an agreement. (page 687)

economy of abundance Term referring to an economic system that is capable of producing more goods and services that can be consumed by the public. (page 868)

efficiency engineering Methods, based on Frederick W. Taylor's studies, used to simplify and speed up each production stage along an assembly line. (page 617)

elastic clause Words in the Constitution that give Congress the power "to make all laws . . . necessary and proper" to carry out its delegated powers, beyond those laws directly authorized by the Constitution. (page 183)

elector Person selected by voters in each state to cast the official ballot electing the President and Vice President. (page 174)

emancipation Process of freeing from bondage. (page 375)

embargo Government order restricting trade. (page 252)

encomienda System of forced Indian labor. A Spanish settler received a land grant from the king, which included the labor of the Indians living on the land. The settler was trustee for the land and the Indians, and paid taxes to the king or the Church for the privilege of operating the land grant. (page 19)

energy crisis Scarcity of oil and soaring of gasoline prices, especially referring to the situation in the United States in 1973–74. (page 896)

enumerated goods Specific colonial products that could be sold only to Great Britain. (page 104)

equal protection of the law Constitutional guarantee that laws will be applied in an unbiased manner to all citizens, regardless of race, religion, sex, national origin, or other characteristic. (page 454)

established church Church, or religion recognized by law and supported by the state. Also called the official church. *See* separation of church and state. (page 83)

excise tax Tax imposed by the government of a country on goods manufactured, sold, or used within that country. (page 227)

executive power Constitutional authority granted to the President to enforce laws. (page 178)

executive privilege Exemption claimed by the executive branch of government from disclosure of information. (page 899)

export To sell a product outside a nation. (page 103)

ex post facto **law** Law that sets forth a penalty for committing an action that was not illegal at the time it took place. The passage of such laws is prohibited by the United States Constitution. (page 179)

extraterritoriality Policy permitting Americans in China, charged with violations of Chinese law, to be tried in American courts in China. (page 641)

F

factory system System under which goods are produced in a factory, rather than in the workers' homes. (page 265)

fascism System of government concentrating all political, economic, and cultural power in the hands of the state. (page 782)

favorite son Candidate whose name is placed in nomination on the first ballot by his or her state delegation as an honor. (page 285)

federal census Count taken every ten years, as required in the Constitution, of population characteristics such as family size, income, and occupation. (page 551)

federal government National government of the United States, headquartered in Washington, D.C. (page 174)

federalism System of government that divides power between the national, or federal, government and the state governments. (page 175)

federal union System in which states delegate some of their powers to the national government. (page 175)

financial capitalism Business situation in which whole industries are controlled by bankers, who invest money, influence business decisions, and share in the profits. *See* industrial capitalism. (page 527)

fiscal year Twelve-month period considered as a year for general accounting purposes. The fiscal year for the United States government begins each July 1. (page 702)

foreclosure Seizure of mortgaged property in order to collect a debt. (page 161)

franchise Right to vote. (page 174)

freedmen Term used to refer to former slaves—women and children as well as men. (page 452)

freedom of contract Right of workers and employers to decide on terms of employment. (page 621)

freedom of the seas Right of ships of a neutral nation to sail the oceans safely and freely. (page 252)

free public school Tax-supported institution for public education. (page 372)

free trade Exchange of goods between countries unhampered by regulations or protective tariffs. (page 606)

frontier Farthest edge of white settlement. (page 37)

frontiersman Pioneer—man, woman, or child—who chose not to settle down, but to roam the wilderness, matching wits and skills against Indians and nature. (page 65)

G

gang system Type of plantation labor in which groups of slaves were assigned to "drivers" who were also slaves. The gangs worked as long and as hard as the overseers or drivers saw fit. (page 338)

ghost town Abandoned mining community. (page 508)

gold reserves Amount of gold held by the federal government to back the currency in circulation. (page 563)

gold standard Until 1933, monetary policy of the United States that backed paper money with gold. (page 564)

government bond Certificate issued by a government in exchange for a loan of money. (page 225)

graduated income tax Method of taxation in which those with more income bear a heavier share of the government expenses. (page 606)

graft Acceptance of money or other rewards in exchange for political favors. (page 471)

grandfather clause Law eliminating a poll tax or literacy test for people whose fathers or grandfathers had voted in a certain year. (page 465)

greenback Paper money issued by the federal government during the Civil War. (pages 429, 559)

gross national product (GNP) Total money value of all goods and services produced in a nation annually. (pages 861, 974)

guerrilla Fighter, usually a rebel, who specializes in sudden, hit-and-run attacks against an established government. (page 139)

H

hard money policy Program calling for the reduction of the amount of money in circulation, making money harder to get and raising its value, also called sound money policy. *See* cheap money policy. (page 457)

hogan Navajo dwelling built of adobe and logs. (page 7)

holding company Business organization, chartered by a state, that holds a controlling interest in two or more corporations, without itself producing goods or services. (page 524)

Holocaust Term for the slaughter of millions of people, many of them Jews, at the hands of the Nazis in World War II. (page 812)

homestead Piece of land granted by the United States government to any individual who wished to settle a farm; usually 160 acres. (pages 430, 503)

hot line Direct telecommunication line between Washington and Moscow designed to prevent accidental nuclear war. (page 918)

human rights Term referring to the rights and privileges of all human beings. These rights are stated in the Declaration of Independence as life, liberty, and the pursuit of happiness. They are guaranteed and protected by the Bill of Rights. (page 930)

I

immigration Process of entering a country to take up residence. (page 535)

impeach To bring charges against a high government official, especially the President of the United States. (page 178) This process is known as **impeachment.** (page 455)

imperialism Policy of establishing colonies and building an empire. (page 631)

import To buy a product from another nation. (page 103)

import duty Tax on goods coming into a country. (page 105)

impress To take someone by force for public service. Great Britain took American sailors by force to serve in the British navy. (page 229) This action is called **impressment.** (page 252)

indenture Contract to work without wages for two to seven years in return for transportation to America. (page 32)

indentured servant Person who signed an indenture. (page 32)

Indian resettlement Policy of forcing Indian tribes to move west of the Mississippi river. (page 291)

indirect tax Tax included in the price paid by the purchaser of a product. (page 110)

individual proprietorship Type of business in which the owner invests all the money, makes all the decisions, and earns all the profits. (page 520)

industrial capitalism Business situation in which corporations are completely controlled by their industrial owners. These owners invest the money, make the business decisions, and collect the profits. *See* financial capitalism. (page 527)

industrial union Labor organization of all workers, skilled and unskilled, in a particular industry. (page 540)

inflation Economic term for a rise in prices. (pages 32, 896, 971)

initiative Procedure enabling voters in a state to introduce legislation for consideration by lawmakers. (page 594)

injunction Court order requiring or preventing a specific act. (page 544)

integration Policy ending the separation of groups; desegregation. (page 878)

interchangeable part Part of a tool or machine that can be replaced by another. (page 267)

interlocking directorate Business arrangement in which some or all of the directors of a company serve as the directors of several other companies. (page 524)

interstate commerce Trade between two or more states. (page 273)

interstate slave trade Shipment of slaves from the East to slave auction centers at Natchez and New Orleans where demand was high. (page 333)

isolationism Policy of noninvolvement in world affairs, especially war. (page 783)

J

Jim Crow laws Laws that enforced the separation of the races in railway cars, schools, and eventually in all public facilities. (page 466)

joint-stock company Trading organization that raised money by selling shares in the company to investors. (page 23)

journalism Profession of writing, editing, and reporting for newspapers and other media. (page 577)

judicial power Constitutional authority granted to the courts to interpret laws. (page 178)

judicial review Power of the Supreme Court to determine whether or not a law or treaty violates the Constitution. (page 184)

jurisdiction Right of control. (page 730)

justice of the peace County official appointed by the governor of a colony or state, who holds certain governmental powers. (pages 95, 335)

K

kitchen cabinet President Jackson's unofficial advisers. (page 290)

knowledge explosion Term indicating the rapid increase in the

amount of information available to the human race in recent years. (page 866)

L

labor movement Term referring to the process of organizing workers into unions for the purpose of stating and protecting their rights. (page 538)

land-grant college School established through enactment of the Morrill Act of 1862, whereby each state received land from the federal government to be sold to finance education in agriculture and mechanical arts. (page 431)

land speculator Person who buys land in order to resell it for a quick profit. (page 106)

legislative power Authority to make laws. (page 178)

legislature Lawmaking body of a government. (page 92)

liberal *(adj)* Type of political outlook often favoring moderate change and reform; *(n)* person seeking moderate change in society's political, social, and economic institutions. (page 621)

literacy test Determination of a person's ability to read and write as a requirement for voting. (page 465)

lobby *(n)* Pressure group that seeks to influence lawmakers; *(v)* to seek to influence lawmakers. (page 480)

local-color writer Author whose books are descriptive of small-town life. (page 578)

lockout Technique used by business owners to fight strikes by closing the factory. (page 543)

log cabin Basic structure of the forest areas, originally introduced by Swedish settlers. It usually had one room with a dirt floor, no windows, and a huge fireplace to hold a fire for light, warmth, and cooking. (page 65)

long drive Movement of cattle from Texas to rail centers in the North. (page 497)

long-haul shipment Term applied to cargo carried by railroads to cities served by more than one rail company. *See* short-haul shipment. (page 556)

longhorns Wild cattle of Texas. (page 497)

long house Iroquoian house in which several families, each with its own quarters, lived together. (page 75)

loose interpretation View that the national government should have powers that are implied by the

Constitution as well as those powers specifically named. (page 232)

Loyalist *See* Tory. (page 128)

M

mandate system Policy requiring sovereign nations to account for treatment of their colonies to the League of Nations. (page 686)

manifest destiny Term referring to the belief held by many Americans in the mid-1800's that it was the clear duty and fate of the United States to expand to the Pacific Ocean. (page 354)

martial law Rule by the military. (page 934)

mass circulation Term descriptive of a publication's widespread distribution. (page 577)

mass production Technique through which vast quantities of goods, all exactly alike, are manufactured quickly and cheaply. (pages 267, 519, 739)

massive retaliation Policy of demonstrating a willingness to destroy an aggressor nation with nuclear weapons if attacked. (page 837)

mediation Process of submitting a dispute to an impartial third party for recommended solutions. (page 668)

medium of exchange Something of value given for goods or services. (page 555)

mercantilism Policies used by a home country during the 1600's and 1700's to regulate the trade of its colonies in order to make the home country wealthy, powerful, and self-sufficient. (page 103)

merchant marine Nation's commercial fleet. (page 313)

merger Combination of two or more independent companies into one larger company. (page 740)

mestizo Person of Spanish and American Indian ancestry. (page 17)

Middle Passage Sea journey of African slaves to the New World, during which they were suffered inhuman treatment. (page 68)

midnight judge Jurist appointed in 1801 to ensure Federalist control of the judiciary. (page 238)

migrant worker Farmhand who moves from farm to farm to plant and harvest fruits and vegetables; often a Mexican-American. (page 952)

militia Civilians trained as soldiers. (page 50)

minimum wage Hourly pay rate established by government below which employers cannot ask employees to work. (page 621)

minority Part of the population constituting less than a half, differing from the majority and, therefore, often subjected to discriminatory treatment. (page 751)

minuteman Civilian citizen-soldier in the British colonies who was ready to fight at a minute's notice. (page 123)

monopoly Total control over a product, service, or trade in a particular region. (pages 11, 523)

moratorium Period of suspension, delay, or temporary halt in an activity. (page 769)

most-favored-nation clause Policy in which benefits of reciprocal trade agreements were extended to every nation having no discriminatory tariffs against the United States. (page 782)

muckraker Term used in the early 1900's to refer to a writer who exposed unfair practices in business and government. (page 593)

mulatto Person of mixed white and black ancestry. (page 18)

multilateral Many-sided. (page 787)

mutalista Self-aid society established by Mexican Americans to cooperatively solve their problems. (page 754)

N

national bank Banking system for the nation, proposed by Alexander Hamilton, consisting of a large central bank with branch banks in major United States cities. (page 226)

national debt Amount of money the federal government owes. (page 734)

nationalism Feelings of loyalty and pride toward one's nation. (pages 277, 669)

nationalization Term referring to the taking of control over an enterprise or resource by the national government. (page 839)

naturalized citizen Person born in one country who has become a citizen of another country. (page 235)

natural resources Air, land, forest, minerals, water, and energy resources of a nation. (page 600)

naval holiday Period during which no new warships are built. (page 772)

neutrality Policy of refusing to take sides in a war between other nations. (page 229)

Nisei Native-born Americans whose ancestors came from Japan. (page 808)

no-man's land Thin strip of ground between the trenches of opposing armies. (page 675)

nonaggression pact Agreement between nations to not attack or fight with each other. (page 787)

nonimportation agreement Written promise by a merchant not to import certain goods. (page 111)

normal school Educational institution established for the training of teachers. (page 372)

null and void State of being no longer in effect; without legal force. (page 236)

nullify To declare that a law is not in force and therefore need not be obeyed. (page 295)

O

one-crop agriculture System of farming that relies on a single crop to produce income. (page 461)

open-market economy Highly competitive economic system governed by supply and demand. (page 554)

open range Unfenced grasslands of the West, where livestock could graze at no expense to the owner. (page 498)

overseer Plantation supervisor who carried out the instructions of the owner. (page 59)

overspeculation Risky investments in land, commodities, or stocks, made in the hope of earning large profits. (page 271)

P

pacifist Person who believes that all wars are unjustified. (page 784)

pacify To bring peace. (page 635)

parity Equal status; government policy of guaranteeing farm prices based on a price set during a period of previous prosperity. (page 732)

partnership Type of business in which two or more people share the expenses, profits, and risks. (pages 313, 521)

patroon Person who received a huge grant of land in New Netherland, in exchange for bringing in 50 tenant farmers to work the land. (page 40)

pension grab Term for bills passed

in the 1880's on flimsy grounds by Congress, granting special pensions to Union veterans. (page 478)

peon Member of a class of landless laborers in Spanish America. (page 358)

pet bank Bank loyal to President Jackson's party in which federal funds were deposited. (page 294)

philanthropist Person who aids humanitarian causes, most often through financial support. (page 464)

picket line Parade of striking workers outside a place of business for the purpose of dissuading other workers from performing their jobs. (page 319)

pioneer Person who moves into unknown or unsettled territory. (page 64)

plantation Large farm that produces one or two cash crops as well as nearly all the food needed by the owner's family. (page 59)

planter Person who owned 20 slaves or more and planted at least one cash crop. A planter was a member of the smallest, but richest and most influential, group in the South. (page 334)

platform Statement of a political party's policies and programs. (page 299)

political machine Organization within a political party that controls elections by granting favors in exchange for votes or money. (page 473)

poll tax Fee required of all registered voters; used by some southern states between the 1890's and the passing of the 24th Amendment in 1964 to keep blacks from voting. (page 465)

pool (corporate) Business arrangement in which several corporations agree to divide all the business opportunities among themselves in an attempt to eliminate competition; ruled illegal in 1887. *See* cartel. (page 523)

popular sovereignty Right of the people in a territory to decide for themselves whether or not slavery should be permitted. (page 396)

precedent Model by which future actions are justified. (page 223)

presidio Fort established by the Spaniards. (page 17)

price controls Government method of fixing prices to avoid rapid inflation in times of severe shortages or national emergencies. (page 807)

privateer Merchant ship armed to attack enemy ships in time of war. (page 144)

profiteering Taking of unfair profits during a national crisis. (page 430)

progressive movement Organized effort begun in the early 1900's to correct abuses and injustices in United States life, to restore greater equality of economic opportunity, and to return government control to the people. (page 591)

prohibition Act of legally banning the manufacture, sale, and transportation of alcoholic beverages. (page 371)

proprietary colony English colony granted by the monarch to an individual or group. The owner of this type of colony was known as the **proprietor.** (page 42)

protective-reaction policy United States policy in the Vietnam War, adopted in 1969, of engaging the enemy only if attacked or directly threatened with attack. (page 924)

protective tariff Tax on imports, the main purpose of which is to protect a country's businesses from foreign competition. (pages 227, 480)

protectorate Term that refers to the status of a weaker nation whose affairs are supervised and partially controlled by a stronger nation. (page 651)

public domain Government-owned land. (page 430)

public education Education paid for with public funds; based on the idea that education of all the people is a public responsibility. (page 88)

public utility Business that performs such basic public services as supplying gas, water, electricity, and transportation. (page 591)

pump priming Term referring to a government's policy of stimulating the economy through a program of loans and federal spending. (page 716)

purse strings Control of financial resources. (page 96)

Q

quarantine President Kennedy's blockade of Cuba to prevent arrival of further Soviet shipments of offensive weapons. (page 917)

quota system Immigration policy established by the Emergency Quota Act of 1921 that limited to a specific percentage the number of people of a nationality who would be admitted to the United States each year. (page 767)

R

radical *(adj)* Type of political outlook, often calling for extreme action to bring about change (page 125); *(n)* person advocating extreme political views. (page 701)

ranch Large tract of fenced grazing land where a rancher raises cattle or other livestock. (page 499)

ratify To approve formally. (page 155)

rationing Policy of limiting the amount of certain goods that a person can buy; used during times of scarcity, war, or national emergency. (page 807)

real wages Salary measured in terms of actual purchasing power, or what the money will buy. (page 535)

rebate Partial refund of shipping charges given by railroad companies to large corporate customers in order to keep their business. (page 558)

rebellion of individuals theory Idea, held by Presidents Lincoln and Johnson, that the actions of specific persons were responsible for the Civil War. This being the case, the President could use his pardoning power to restore the states to the Union. (page 453)

recall Procedure enabling the voters to remove an elected official from office before that official's term has expired. (page 594)

recession Period of reduced economic activity, less severe than a depression. (page 728)

reciprocal trade agreement Agreement between nations to reduce tariffs on each other's goods. (page 782)

reclamation Process of restoring to use, as with making wasteland suitable for farming through irrigation. (page 600)

reconstruction Rebuilding; specifically the period after the Civil War, from 1865 to 1877, when the United States rebuilt the nation. (page 445)

referendum Procedure for referring bills to voters for approval or rejection. (page 594)

refugee Person fleeing danger or persecution or made homeless by war who finds residence outside his or her homeland. (page 925)

relocation Policy of assimilating the Indians into the dominant culture by encouraging them to move to the cities. (page 876)

reparations Payment for war damages made by a defeated country to the countries that have won the war. (pages 686, 769)

repartimiento Type of forced Indian labor in which a land grant recipient was given a specific number of Indians as laborers on a ranch, or in a factory, mine, or monastery. The Indians received a small wage and had to pay taxes to the Crown or the Church. (page 19)

republican form of government Government in which the supreme power rests with the voters, who elect representatives to operate the government for them. (page 170)

repudiate To refuse or reject, as the refusal to pay war debts. (page 446)

reservation Sharply defined tract of land set aside by the government for Indian resettlement. (page 491)

reserved power Power not granted to the federal government nor expressly forbidden to the states and therefore retained by the states or the people. (page 177)

revenue Income collected by a political unit. (page 109)

revenue sharing Policy of channeling federal funds to states and local communities to administer various public programs. (page 897)

revenue tariff Tax on imports, the purpose of which is to raise money for the government. (page 227)

right of deposit Right to unload riverboats at a port and to reload the products on oceangoing vessels. (page 230)

right-to-work law State law that prohibits closed or union shops. *See* closed shop, union shop. (page 849)

robber baron Term applied to early business leaders because of their selfishness, ruthless business methods, and exploitation of their workers. (page 527)

royal colony English colony in which the monarch appointed the governor and the colonists elected the members of the representative assembly. (page 25)

S

sachem Term for a chief among the Eastern Woodlands Indians. (page 74)

salary grab Term given to the 1873 vote by members of Congress to give themselves a 50 percent increase in salaries, retroactive for two years. (page 472)

salutary neglect Policy in 1600's

and early 1700's of deliberately failing to enforce mercantile laws. (page 106)

sand lotter Unemployed California worker. (page 536)

satellite nation Country that is dominated or strongly influenced by a more powerful country; especially a country of Eastern Europe dominated by the Soviet Union. (page 827)

scalawag Term applied to a southerner who cooperated with northerners during reconstruction. (page 458)

scorched-earth policy Technique used by a retreating army of destroying everything. (page 800)

search-and-destroy mission Military tactic in Vietnam War using air cover while ground forces destroyed Communist strongholds in the villages. (page 921)

secede Withdraw from an organization or governmental unit such as a country or a state. (page 407) This action is called **secession.** (page 236)

secondary boycott Support of a boycott by other unions and parties not directly involved in a dispute. (page 858)

section One-square-mile (2.6 square-kilometers) portion of land in a township. (page 157)

sectionalism Intense rivalry among regions before the Civil War. (page 265)

sedition Use of speeches to stir rebellion. (page 236)

segregate To keep separate or set apart from others. (page 85)

segregation Separation of racial groups in schools, housing, and other public places. (page 465)

selectman Town officer who administered the decisions adopted at the town meeting. (page 95)

self-determination Right of a country's people to decide that country's political future; one of President Wilson's Fourteen Points. (page 684)

self-governing colony English colony in which the people elected the governor as well as the members of the representative assembly. (page 34)

self-sufficient farmer Owner of a small farm that produces what is needed for the family and farm to survive. (page 618)

senatorial courtesy Custom that is part of the unwritten Constitution in which the President consults with the Senator (or Senators) in his party before appointing federal

officials from that Senator's home state. (page 185)

separate but equal Doctrine that required separate facilities for whites and blacks. (page 466)

separation of church and state Policy whereby there is no official government church, nor taxes imposed to support any one church, no church membership qualifications to vote, and freedom for all churches. (page 85)

separation of powers Principle that requires the division of the executive, legislative, and judicial powers into independent branches of government. (page 151)

settlement house Center for education and recreation, usually located in a poverty area of a major city. (page 575)

shaman Priest or priestess of an Eastern Woodlands Indian tribe. (page 75)

sharecropper Person who farms another person's land in exchange for a share of the crop. (page 461)

shareholder *See* stockholder. (page 521)

short-haul shipment Term applied to cargo carried by railroads to communities served by only one railroad. *See* long-haul shipment. (page 556)

sit-down strike Labor action in which workers occupy their factories until their demands are met, thereby preventing strikebreaking. (page 730)

sit-in Method of protest in which people sit down in a public place and resist being moved. Sit-ins were widely used by civil rights groups seeking to end segregation in the South. (page 947)

slave code Set of strict laws passed by a state to control the behavior of slaves. (page 70)

socialism Economic and political system in which workers, organized in unions, can vote themselves into power and by democratic means can reconstruct the economic and social foundations of society. (page 545)

social legislation Laws passed to improve conditions for wage earners. (page 620)

sod house Shelter built of bricklike chunks of soil. (page 504)

soil-bank program Agricultural program in which farmers were paid for withdrawing land from commercial cultivation. (page 857)

sovereign Existing independently; under no outside controlling government. (page 224)

specialty store Business establishment that sells a single line of goods, such as furniture, hardware, or shoes. (page 519)

specie Gold or silver coin. (page 299)

spiritual Religious song that combines Christian gospel hymns with African musical forms. (page 340)

spoils system Arrangement under which the political party that wins an election gives government jobs to its own party members. (page 289)

stagflation Term derived from a combination of the words *stagnant* and *inflation,* used to describe the situation that exists when business declines at the same time that prices rise. (page 972)

stalemate Battlefield situation in which neither side can advance or claim victory. (page 675)

staple crop Major agricultural product grown in large quantities, such as wheat or rice. (pages 329, 555)

states' rights All rights not specifically assigned to the federal government by the Constitution nor forbidden by it to the states. (page 294)

states' right theory View that state governments have the right to nullify a law passed by Congress. (page 236)

state suicide theory Idea, held by Senator Charles Sumner, that the Confederate states had ended their formal association with the Union when they seceded. Accordingly, the southern states were like any unorganized territory, and only Congress had the power to establish the terms of admission to the Union. (page 453)

stock Certificate of business ownership sold to raise capital for commercial operations. (page 521)

stockholder Person who invests money in a business through the purchase of stock. (page 521)

strict interpretation View that the national government should have only those powers specifically named in the Constitution. (page 232)

strike Refusal of laborers to work until their demands have been met. (pages 319, 539)

strikebreaker Nonunion worker hired to do the work of strikers. (pages 320, 543)

subsidy Money given by the government to a business or individual for a purpose that benefits the public as a whole. (pages 431, 719)

subsistence farm Agricultural unit on which farmers produce what is needed for survival. *See* self-sufficient farmer. (page 329)

suburb Residential area outside of a city. (page 872)

suffrage Right to vote. (pages 93, 435)

supply-side economics Fiscal program aimed at stimulating production and creating jobs. (page 907)

syndicate *(n)* Business organization that provides materials for publication in a number of newspapers at the same time; *(v)* to provide materials for publication in a number of newspapers at the same time. (page 577)

T

tallow White, specially treated, solid fat of cattle and sheep, used to make candles. (page 65)

tariff Tax on imports. (page 173)

task system Organization of a slave work unit so that each slave was assigned a particular job to do each day. A slave could stop working when the job was finished. (page 338)

technological unemployment Loss of jobs caused by the installation of new machines. (page 534)

tepee Cone-shaped tent of Plains Indians made of buffalo skin stretched over a frame of poles. (page 8)

telegraph Communications device, developed by Samuel F. B. Morse, for sending electronic transmissions over wire. (page 516)

temperance movement Organized activities of reformers who worked to end alcohol abuse. (page 370)

tenant farmer Person who rents land on which to farm. (pages 333, 461)

tenure of office Period during which an individual has the right to remain in office. (pages 333, 455)

termination Policy intended to transfer to the states all federal responsibilities for the Indians. (page 875)

territorial integrity Term applied to the protection of a nation's land from infringement by another nation. (page 657)

Third World Newly independent, non-aligned, and developing nations of Asia, Africa, and Latin America. (page 915)

tidewater river River that empties into the ocean where, at high tide, salt water reaches some distance upstream. (page 44)

title Written guarantee of ownership. (page 156)

toleration Policy allowing persons or groups to engage in practices of their choice, especially religious practices. (page 84)

toll road Road on which a fee is charged for use. (page 270)

Tory One who remained loyal to the British crown; also called a Loyalist. (page 128)

totalitarian Term applied to a dictatorship that exercises total control over a nation and suppresses individual freedom. (page 782)

town meeting Form of local government in which all citizens of a town meet together to discuss local issues and to vote directly on local laws. (page 95)

township Basic unit of land in the Old Northwest, measuring 36 square miles (93.6 square kilometers), which was subdivided and sold to settlers. (page 156)

transcontinental railroad Rail line, completed in 1869, that linked the Atlantic and Pacific seaboards, encouraging economic growth. (page 491)

treason Carefully defined act against the United States, such as attempting to overthrow the government, witnessed by two people or confessed to in open court; the Constitution protects the individual against unfair use of this charge. (page 179)

treaty port Chinese coastal city opened in the nineteenth century to trade by force or through negotiated agreements. (page 641)

trench warfare Military actions conducted from long lines of opposing ditches rather than across open battlefields. (page 675)

triangular trade Trade involving Africa, the West Indies, and the British colonies in America. Rum from the colonies was exchanged for slaves and gold in Africa; slaves were exchanged in the West Indies for molasses, sugar, and money; molasses and sugar were used in the colonies to make rum. (page 105)

tribute Money paid as an act of submission, to keep peace, or in exchange for protection. (page 250)

trunk line Major railroad route. (page 516)

trust Group of companies formed to regulate production, reduce costs, and eliminate competition. (pages 480, 523)

two-party system Political situation in which two major parties offer a choice between candidates and policies in elections. (page 233)

U

ultimatum Final statement of terms, the rejection of which may lead to the ending of diplomatic relations or to war. (page 634)

unalienable right Right that cannot be taken away, such as life, liberty, or the pursuit of happiness. (page 129)

unconstitutional Term applied to any action contrary to the provisions of the Constitution. (page 178)

unilateral One-sided. (page 787)

United Nations Name for the World War II Allies that was kept when they formed a permanent organization of countries in 1945. (page 801)

unwritten Constitution Government practices growing out of custom and tradition, not referred to in the Constitution but so firmly established that they are considered legitimate. (page 185)

urban Term referring to anything having to do with cities. (page 323)

urban center City with many factories, efficient transportation and communication systems, and a population greater that 2,500. (page 515)

urbanization Term referring to the transformation of rural areas into cities, and to the movement of people from the countryside to cities and industrial centers. (pages 571, 743)

urban renewal program In decaying cities, the replacement of old, dilapidated buildings with new ones. (page 871)

utopian community Community such as New Harmony or Brook Farm that attempted to attain ideal perfection by trying new social forms. (page 371)

V

vaquero Mexican cowhand; vaqueros invented most of the tools and clothing later used by American cowhands. (page 497)

veto To refuse to accept or approve. The President may veto a bill passed by Congress. (page 178)

viceroy Representative chosen by the monarch of Spain to govern the Spanish colonies in the Americas. (page 20)

vigilante Member of an unofficial, private police force. (page 507)

W

ward Status of the Indians on the reservations which made them dependent on the federal government for the necessities of life. (page 494)

Whig Name given to a colonial American Patriot. (page 128)

white flight Movement of the white middle class from the inner cities to the suburbs. (page 945)

white supremacy Social, economic, and cultural control of the black population by the white population. (page 70)

wickiup Circular Apache hut of brush that could be constructed in a few minutes. (page 7)

wildcat bank State bank that issued bank notes without having sufficient federal funds on deposit. (page 298)

women's rights movement Organized effort to gain equal rights for women. (page 368)

writ of assistance Court order in colonial America that allowed officials to enter and search any building at any time. (page 112)

writ of *habeas corpus* Court order that law enforcement officers show cause for the arrest and detention of a prisoner, designed to prevent unlawful arrest and imprisonment. (pages 179, 426, 460)

written constitution Official document setting forth a plan of government. (page 92)

Y

yellow-dog contract Written agreement through which employers force employees to promise not to join a labor union under penalty of firing. (page 542)

Z

zambo Person of American Indian and black ancestry. (page 18)

INDEX

II, 792; in 1800's, 274, *m275*
Colorado, 506, 594
Colorado Territory, 436, 506
Colored Alliance, 561
Columbia (space shuttle), 966, *p967*
Columbian Exposition (Chicago, 1893), 579–80
Columbia River, *m346, m348,* 349
Columbus, Christopher, 12, *m12*
Columbus, New Mexico, 239
Comanches (Indians), 7–8, 352, 354, 493, 506
commerce. See trade and commerce
Commerce and Labor, Department of, 598
Commercial Revolution, 11
Committee for Industrial Organization, 729–30
Committee on Public Information, 680
Committee to Reelect the President, 898
Committees of Correspondence, 115
Common Market, 889–90, 915, 916
communications: Mann-Elkins Act and, 603; in late 1800's, 515–16; in early 1900's, 616
communism, 545; cold war and, 827, 828; domestic, 850; Mc-Carthy and, *p856,* 860; "Red scare" (1920's) and, 701
company towns, *p532,* 532–33
Compiègne, France, *m683,* 684
Compromise of 1850, 397–99, *m400,* 402–03
computers, 867, 967, *p964*
Comstock Lode (Nevada), 507
Conant, James B., 946, 947
concentration camps: in Cuba, 633–35; in Germany, *f790,* 812; for Japanese Americans, *p807,* 808
Concord, Battle of, 123, 125, *m125*
Confederate States of America, 413–15; Emancipation Proclamation and, 423–24; foreign relations of, 433–34; formation of, 407; Fort Sumter taken by, *f408;* military campaigns of, *m418;* society and economy of, 426–28. See also Civil War; reconstruction; South
Confederation, 155; Constitutional Convention and, 169; as government, 159–63; land policy of, 156–59
Congo (Zaire), 916
Congregational Church, 35, 83
Congress, U.S.: blacks in, *f458,* 459, *p460;* Compromise of 1850 and, 397–98; under Construction, 159, 169; Constitution on, 178, 183–84, 189–97, 170–71; Great Compromise on, 170–71; impeachment of A. Johnson by, 456; Missouri Compromise and, 393, 394; post-Civil War corruption in, 471–73; reconstruction and 452–55, *p455,* 460; war powers of, 922, 925. *See also* Constitution; Continental Congress; House of Representatives; Senate
Congress of Industrial Organizations (CIO), 730, 859
Connecticut: colonial government of, 92, 151–52; as colony, 36–38; Constitution ratified by, 174; Fundamental Orders, *f92*

conquistadors, 14, 15–16
conscription. See draft
Conscription Act (1863), 428
conservation, 980–82; of energy, 978; T. Roosevelt and, 600–02; Taft and, 603
Constitution, U.S., 169–73, 175–77, 183–84, *p185;* Bill of Rights of, 179–80; compact theory of, 236; differences between Jefferson and Hamilton on, 232–33; electoral system in, 233–34, 238, 476; impeachment in, 456; ratification of, 173–75; separation of powers in, 177–78; taxation in, 481; text of and commentary on 189–218; war powers and, 935–36; Thirteenth Amendment to, 423–24, 435; Fourteenth Amendment to, 454, 455, 466, 574, 877; Fifteenth Amendment to, 457, 574; Sixteenth Amendment to, 603; Seventh Amendment to, 595; Eighteenth Amendment to, 680, 746; Nineteenth Amendment to, 594, 745; Twenty-first Amendment to, 747; Twenty-second Amendment to, 848; Twenty-third Amendment to, 889; Twenty-fourth Amendment to, 889; Twenty-fifth Amendment to, 899,900; Twenty-sixth Amendment to, 897, 968; Equal Rights Amendment to, 959
Constitution, bicentennial, 219, *p219*
Constitutional Convention, 169–73, *p176, p180*
Constitutional Union (Whig) **Party,** 406
constitutions: of colonial Connecticut, 92; of Confederate States of America, 407; of Kansas Territory, 401; of Missouri, 394; of reconstruction states, 448, 455, 459; of states, 151–53; of states, religion and, 374; of territories, 508
Continental Army, 134–42, *p143*
Continental Congress: First, *f117,* Second, on admission of new states, 157–59; borrowing by, 225; as government, 151–52, 155; independence declared at, 128; Laurens and, *p69;* money issued by, 159–60, *p163;* Revolutionary War and, 125, 126, 140–43, 145; on slavery, 152–53
Contract Labor Law (1864), 538, 539
Cook, James, 345
Coolidge, Calvin, 697, 698, *p770;* foreign policy of, 769–72; as President, 704–05
Cooper, James Fenimore, 279
Cooper, Peter, 312
cooperatives, agricultural, 558
Copperheads, 434, *p434*
Coral Sea, Battle of, 800
Corbin, Margaret, 143
Corinth, Mississippi, 418–419
corn, 227–28
Cornell, Ezra, 570
Cornwallis, Charles, 135, *p138,* 138–39
Coronado, Francisco Vásquez de, 16, *m16,* 35
corporations, 521–22; pools and trusts of, 523–24; workers in, in late 1800's, 533, 537. See *also* antitrust acts; business; industry, trusts

Cortés, Hernando, 15
Costa Rica, *m650,* 658
Cost of Living Council, 971
cotton: in pre-Civil War Southern economy, 329–34, *m330,* 336; Civil War and, 414–15; in post-Civil War South, 462–63; production, *c332;* slavery and, 374–75
cotton gin, *f71,* 375
Council of National Defense, 677
coureur de bois, 47, 48, 49
courts, *p237,* Constitution on, 178, 201–03. See *also* judicial branch; Supreme Court
Cousteau, Jacques, 980
cowboys, 497, *p497*
Cowpens, Battle of, *p138,* 138–139, *m140*
Cox, James M., 701
Coxey, Jacob, *f544*
Crandall, Prudence, 381
Crawford, William H., 285
Crazy Horse, 493
Crédit Mobilier, 471–72
Creeks (Indians), 9, 291–92, 505
Creoles, 17–18
"Crime of '73", 560
Crockett, Davy, 353
Cromwell, Oliver, 32
Crown Point, New York, 50–51, *m51,* 52, 125
Crusades, 10
Cruz, Juana Inés de la, *p18;*
Cuba, *m649;* Angola and, 930; Bay of Pigs invasion of, 916; captured by Britain, 51–53; missile crisis and, 917, *p917;* Nixon's policy toward, 927; Ostend Manifesto and, 399–400; Platt Amendment and, 781; in Spanish–American War, 633–36, *m636, p637,* 649; U.S. occupation of, 648–50; yellow fever in, *p653,* 653, *f654*
Cubans, 955, *p955*
Cuffe, Paul, 375
Cullen, Countee, 756
culture, 4; American development of, 277–79; of Indians, 3–10, *m6.* See *also* society
culture areas, 6, *m6*
Cumberland Road, 271, *m271*
Cummings, Kate, 436
currency. See money
Currency Act (Britain), 110
Cushing, Caleb, 641
Custer, George, *p492,* 493, 494
Czechoslovakia: creation of, *m683,* 686; in World War II, 763–65, *m786, m802,* post-World War II, 827, *m830*

D

Da Gama, Vasco, *m11,* 12
Dallas, Texas, 889–90
Dana, Charles A., 577
Danbury hatters' strike, 597
Dartmouth College v. Woodward (1819), 272–73
Daugherty, Harry M., 703
Davis, David, 476
Davis, Jefferson, 407, 426, *p435,* 448, 460
Davis, John W., 704
Davis, Joseph Emory, 334
Dawes, Charles G., 703
Dawes, William, Jr., 123, *m125*
Dawes Act (1887), 496, 753
Dean, John W., 899
death rates, *c1006*
Debs, Eugene V., 544–45, 605, 701
debts: Constitution on, 205–06, 212–13; of Revolutionary War,

225–26; under F. D. Roosevelt, 729, 733–34; for World War I, 703, 768–69, 784; for World War II, 805
Decatur, Stephen, 250–51, *f251*
Decisive Moments, *f22, f37, f71, f91, f129, f184, f231, f251, f292, f353, f368, f408, f420, f466, f490, f517, f592, f654, f686, f746, f811, f878, f982*
Declaration of Independence, *p127,* 128–33; state constitutions and, 151–52
Declaratory Act (Britain), 112
DDT, banning of, *f982*
Defense, Department of, 848
De Forest, Lee, 616
Deganawidah, 74, *f76*
Degas, Edgar, *p328*
De Gaulle, Charles, 791, 915
De Grasse, Marquis François, 139
Delaware: in Civil War, 413–14; colonial government of, 92; as colony, 42–44; Constitution ratified by, 174
Delaware River, 135, *m135, f172*
De Leon, Daniel, 545
De Léon, Juan Ponce, *m16,* 16
De Lôme, Enrique Dupuy, 634
Deloria, Vine, Jr., 956
democracy, 82–83; Bill of Rights for, 179–80; Declaration of Independence and, 129, A. Jackson on, 289; political, economic, and social, 284–85; post-Revolutionary, 154; in state constitutions, 151–52
Democratic Party: beginnings of, 285–86; blacks and, 753; in post-Civil War South, 464, 466; in election of 1836, 298; in election of 1844, 355, 395; in election of 1848, 396; in election of 1856, 393; in election of 1860, 403–05, 406; in election of 1864, 433–34, 435; in election of 1868, 456–57; in election of 1872, 474–75; in election of 1876, 475–76; in election of 1880, 477; in election of 1884, 478; in election of 1888, 479; in election of 1892, 480, 563; in election of 1896, 565; in election of 1900, 595; in election of 1908, 602–03; in election of 1912, 605; in election of 1916, 609; in election of 1920, 701; in election of 1924, 704; in election of 1928, 705; in election of 1932, 709–10; in election of 1936, 726, 728; in election of 1938, 733; in election of 1940, 734–35; in election of 1948, 849–50; in election of 1952, 853; in election of 1956, 858, *p858;* in election of 1960, 887; in election of 1964, 891; in election of 1968, 892–95; in election of 1972, 897; in election of 1974, 901; in election of 1976, 902; in election of 1980, 905, *p906;* in election of 1984, 908–09; Kansas dispute and, 401; reconstruction and, 446; Watergate burglary of, 898
Dempsey, John, 867
Denby, Edwin C., 701
Denmark, 659, *m683;* in World War II, 791, *m802, m812, m830*
department stores, 519
depressions, 161–62: of 1786, 161–62; of 1819, 271–72; of 1837, 298–99, *p298,* 321, of

ACKNOWLEDGMENTS *(Continued from page iv)*

Basic Books, Inc.: From *MORE WORK FOR MOTHER: The Ironies of Household Technology from the Open Hearth to the Microwave* (Titled: "Labor Saving Devices and Women") by Ruth Schwartz Cowan. © 1983 by Basic Books, Inc., Publishers. *Stanton Cook, as Executor of the Estate of Sherburne Cook:* From *The American Frontier* (Titled: "The Great Vacant Area" and "Reservation System in California") by Cummins & White. Copyright © 1968, 1972 by Benziger, Inc. *The Christian Science Monitor:* Adapted from "Better farming practices urged as world's topsoil washes away" by Peter Grier in *The Christian Science Monitor,* October 1, 1984. © 1984 by The Christian Science Publishing Society. All rights reserved. *The Colonial Williamsburg Foundation:* From "Training the Ruling Class" in *Seat of Empire: The Political Role of Eighteenth Century Williamsburg* by Carl Bridenbaugh. Copyright 1958 by Colonial Williamsburg, Incorporated. *Joan Daves:* From "I Have a Dream" by Martin Luther King, Jr. Copyright © 1963 by Martin Luther King, Jr. *Harcourt Brace Jovanovich, Inc.:* From *Middletown: A Study in American Culture* by Robert and Helen Lynd. Published by Harcourt Brace Jovanovich, Inc. From "The Raven on the Skyscraper" by Veronica and Paul King in *Impressions of America* by Ralph and Marian Brown. Published by Harcourt Brace Jovanovich, Inc. *Harper & Row, Publishers, Inc.:* "To Make a More Perfect Union" from *OUT OF OUR PAST: The Forces That Shaped Modern America,* Revised Edition by Carl N. Degler. Copyright © 1959, 1970 by Carl N. Degler. All rights reserved. Abridged excerpt from p. 448 in *THE AMERICAN NATION: A History of the United States Since 1865,* Vol. Two, Fifth Edition by John A. Garraty. Copyright © 1966, 1971, 1975, 1979, 1983 by John A. Garraty. From *The Big Change* by Frederick Lewis Allen. *D. C. Heath and Company:* "A Woman Assails Woman Suffrage" by Mrs. Gilbert E. Jones from pp. 618-620 in *The American Spirit,* Vol. 2, Fifth Edition. Copyright 1985 by D. C. Heath and Company. Published by D. C. Heath and Company. *Little, Brown and Company,* in association with the *Atlantic Monthly Press:* From *Origins of the American* by John C. Miller. Copyright 1943 by John C. Miller. *Marine Corps Association:* From "A Marine Sergeant Sees Pearl Harbor Bombed" by Roger Emmons in the *Marine Corps Gazette,* February 1944. *National Geographic Society:* "Passage of the Stamp Act" from *The Story of America.* Published by the National Geographic Society, 1984. *New York Teacher:* "Rules for Teachers 1872" from the oldest wooden schoolhouse in America, St. Augustine, FL in *New York Teacher,* the newspaper of the New York State United Teachers, AFT, AFL–CIO. *The New York Times Company:* From "Shultz Lists Gains for Mideast Peace from Hussein Visit" by Bernard Gwertzman in *The New York Times,* June 1, 1985. Copyright © 1985 by The New York Times Company. *W. W. Norton and Company, Inc.:* From *The Eisenhower Diaries* by Dwight D. Eisenhower, edited by Robert H. Ferrell. Published by W. W. Norton & Company, Inc. *Pantheon Books, a division of Random House, Inc.:* From "Peggy Terry and Her Mother, Mary Owsley" (Retitled: "Mary Owsley on the Depression") and from "Robin Langston" (Retitled: "Robin Langston on the Depression") in *Hard Times: An Oral History of the Great Depression* by Studs Terkel. Copyright © 1970 by Studs Terkel. *Michael Parenti:* From *The Anti-Communist Impulse* (Titled: "The Holy Crusade: Some Myths of Origin") by Michael Parenti. Published by Random House, 1969. *The Putnam Publishing Group:* From "The Incident on the Bus" by Rosa L. Parks in *My Soul is Rested* by Howell Raines. Copyright © 1977 by Howell Raines. *Random House, Inc.:* From *Special Envoy to Churchill and Stalin 1941-1946* by W. Averell Harriman and Elie Abel. Copyright ©1975 by W. Averell Harriman and Elie Abel. *University of Oklahoma Press:* From *Propaganda for War: The Campaign Against American Neutrality, 1914-1917* by H. C. Peterson. Copyright 1939 by the University of Oklahoma Press.

tion; 593, Culver Pictures; 596, Association for the Study of Afro-American Life and History, Inc.; 598, Library of Congress; 599, Library of Congress; 601, National Museum of American Art, Smithsonian Institution, loaned by U.S. Government Printing Office, National Park Service; 602, Harvard College Library; 604, Library of Congress; 607, The Bettmann Archive; 608, Schomberg Center for Black Culture, The New York Public Library, Astor, Lenox, and Tilden Foundations; 609, Library of Congress; 614, The Cleveland Museum of Art, Gift of Amelia Elizabeth White; 617, Historical Pictures Service; 618 (t), Edith Reichman/Monkmeyer Press Photo Service, (c) Lois Moulton, Click/Chicago, (b) © 1984 Dann P. Coffey/The Stock Broker; 619, UPI/Bettmann Newsphotos; 620, Culver Pictures; 621, Culver Pictures; 623 (l), Gabriel Maulin Studios, (r) Tom Tracy Photography.

UNIT NINE: 628–29, Chicago Historical Society; 630, The Granger Collection; 637, *St. Louis Post-Dispatch;* 638, Culver Pictures; 639, Culver Pictures; 642, The Granger Collection, (inset) HBJ Photo; Courtesy of Franklin D. Roosevelt Library; 648, The Granger Collection; 652, Culver Pictures; 653, Culver Pictures; 655, HBJ Library; 657, *New York Herald,* December 16, 1902, The New York Public Library; 658, S. Hormoth, (insert) U.S. Government Printing Office; 660, M. Farbman/© Time Inc., 1960; 666, Imperial War Museum; 670, Culver Pictures; 671, Library of Congress; 672 (t), Wally McNamee/Woodfin Camp & Associates, (b) J.A. Fernandez/Woodfin Camp & Associates; 673 (t) Michael Heron/Woodfin Camp & Associates, (bl) J.A. Fernandez/Woodfin Camp & Associates, (br) Marilyn Silverstone/Magnum Photos; 674, The Bettmann Archive; 676, Brown Brothers; 679, National Park Service from Picture Research, Washington, D.C.; 680, Collection of George J. Goodstadt; 682, The Bettmann Archive; 687, Imperial War Museum.

UNIT TEN: 694–95, Isaac Singer, *Employment Agency,* 1937, Collection of Whitney Museum of American Art, Acq. #37.44; 696, The Metropolitan Museum of Art, gift of Ettie Stettheimer, 1953; 698, UPI/Bettmann Newsphotos; 699, UPI/Bettmann Newsphotos; (inset) Culver Pictures; 700 (t), UPI/Bettmann Newsphotos, (b) Courtesy of the Whitney Museum of American Art; 702, The Granger Collection; 703, Brown Brothers; 704, New York Historical Society; 707, Brown Brothers; 710, Courtesy of Franklin D. Roosevelt Library; 714, *Street Scene,* by Victor Arnautoff, City and County of San Francisco Recreation and Park Department; 717, Culver Pictures; 719, The Art Institute of Chicago; 724, Photo by E. Irving Bloomstrann, From The New Britain Museum of American Art, John Butler Talbot Fund; 728, Library of Congress; 730, UPI/Bettmann Newsphotos; 734, Brown Brothers; 735, Wide World; 738, The Equitable, panel from mural *Contemporary America* by Thomas Hart Benton; 740, Memorial Art Gallery of the University of Rochester; 741, Hirz/Frederick Lewis; 742, The Granger Collection, (inset) HBJ photo; 745, Brown Brothers; 747, The Bettmann Archive; 749, Private Collection; 752, Terry Dintenfass, Inc.; 756, Whitney Museum of American Art; 758, The Bettmann Archive.

UNIT ELEVEN: 764–65, Bob Schwartz/Douglas Peebles Photography; 766, Library of Congress; 770, Photoworld/ FPG; 772, The Bettmann Archive; 773, Culver Pictures; 774, (l) Library of Congress, Bill Weems/Woodfin Camp & Associates; 778, Combat Art Section, U.S. Navy; 781, © Edward B. Marks Music Corp.; 783, Historical Pictures Service; 784, Culver Pictures; 788 (l), Robert H. Glaze/Artstreet, (r) Larry Dech/Tom Stack & Associates; 789, Willard Luce/Tom Stack & Associates; 790 (t), The Granger Collection, (b) National Archives; 791, Wide World; 792, The Bettmann Archive; 794, UPI/Bettmann Newsphotos; 798, Library of Congress; 801, UPI/Bettmann Newsphotos; 804, Library of Congress; 805, U.S. Marine Corps; 807, Brown Brothers; 809, The Bettmann Archive; 812, The Granger Collection; 814, The Bettmann Archive; 815, Charles Phelps Cushing.

UNIT TWELVE: 822–23, Cary Wolinsky/Stock, Boston; 824. United Nations; 831, UPI/Bettmann Newsphotos; 832, (l) Bohdan Hrynewych/Southern Light (r) J. P. Laffont/Sygma; 833, Wide World; 834, UPI/Bettmann Newsphotos; 836, UPI/Bettmann Newsphotos; 837, Wide World; 838, Wide World; 840, Burt Glinn/Magnum Photos; 841, National Air & Space Museum; 846, Library of Congress; 849, UPI/Bettmann Newsphotos; 853, Wayne Miller/Magnum Photos; 854, The Granger Collection; 855, Pictorial Parade; 856 (l) and (r), Drawing by John Fischetti, © by and permission of News America Syndicate; (c) Wide World Photos; 857, Wide World; 859, Erich Hartmann/Magnum; 860, Steve McCutcheon; 861, Porterfield–Clickering/Photo Researchers; 864, UPI/Bettmann Newsphotos; 866, Courtesy of Franklin D. Roosevelt Library; 867, Historical Pictures Service; 868, James Pickerell; 869, UPI/Bettmann Newsphotos; 870, George Hall/Woodfin Camp & Associates; 872, Photo Trends; 874, Lew Merrim/Monkmeyer Press Photo Service; 876, Katrina Thomas/Photo Researchers.

UNIT THIRTEEN: 884–85, Peter Arnold; 886, NASA; 891, Sybil Shackman/Monkmeyer Press Photo Service; 892, Shanks in *The Buffalo Evening News;* 894, Fred Ward/Black Star; 895, Liederman, *Long Island Press;* 896, John Aldridge and Sons/First Foto Bank, (inset) Lloyd Wolf/First Foto Bank; 900, Wally McNamee/Woodfin Camp & Associates; 901, Tiziou/Sygma; 903, UPI/Bettmann Newsphotos; 904, Andy Levin/Black Star; 905 (t), Eliz Resnick, DPI, (others) Tom Pantages; 906, Rick Friedman/Black Star; 907, Dennis Brack/Black Star; 908, Marc Pokempner/Black Star; 914, UPI/Bettmann Newsphotos; 917, Pictorial Parade; 920, Fred Ward/Black Star; 923, UPI/Bettmann Newsphotos; 924, © Hiroji Kubota/Magnum Photos; 926, Helmut Wimmer; 927, Tashi/Black Star; 931, Owen/Black Star; 932, Melloul/Sygma, Paris; 933, Rothco, *Albany Times Union;* 934, W. Laski/Black Star; 935, © J.L. Atlan/Sygma; 937, Arnold Saxe; 942, Mark Brett, Gamma/Liaison; 944, HBJ Photo; 945, Horizon Images/Monkmeyer, (inset) Yan Lukas/Art Resource; 946 (l), David S. Strickler/Monkmeyer Press Photo Service; (r) Andy Levin/Black Star; 947, Yoichi R. Okamoto/Photo Researchers; 948, Bob Adelman/Magnum Photos; 951, Wally McNamee/Woodfin Camp & Associates, (inset) Lawrence Fried/Magnum; 953, Herman J. Kokojan/Black Star; 955, UPI/Bettmann Newsphotos; 957, Dan Budnik/Woodfin Camp & Associates; 960, Supreme Court Historical Society; 961, Wally McNamee/Woodfin Camp & Associates, (inset) Larry Downing/Woodfin Camp & Associates; 964, TRW, Inc.; 966, Laimute Druskis/Taurus Photos; 967, NASA; 971, P.J. Heller/Write-On Ltd.; 973, James Pickerell; 975, Rothco, Pletcher/*Times-Picayune;* 977, RSA Robert Shafer/Folio, Inc., (inset) Bill Weems/Woodfin Camp & Associates; 979, © John Martmaras/Woodfin Camp & Associates; 981, Owen Franken/Stock, Boston; 983, U.S. Department of Energy.

FLAGS: 998 (tr); (c, all); (bl, upper); (br, lower), Granger Collection.

PRESIDENTS: 1012(tl) detail, painting by Gilbert Stuart, Metropolitan Museum of Art; 1023(br), Metropolitan Museum of Art; 1024 (second from br), Charles Phelps Cushing; 1025(bl), Bettmann Archive; 1027(br) Ewing Galloway; 1028(lc), Fabian Bachrach; 1028(bl), Franklin D. Roosevelt Library, Hyde Park, New York; 1028(br), Charles Phelps Cushing; 1029(tl), Chase News Photo; 1029(bl), Henry Grossman; 1029(tr), Fabian Bachrach; 1029(br), Official White House Photograph; 1030(tl), Courtesy of Gerald Ford's Office in Congress; 1030(bl), The White House; 1030(r), United Press International; all other photos, Library of Congress.

Challenges of the Future

(1984 to the present)

Discovery's successful 1988 launch

1061

1 Bush replaces Reagan as the nation's leader

See Teaching Suggestions in TMRG Supplements.

In 1988 Americans elected George Bush to lead them into the 1990's. The new President would follow Ronald Reagan, one of the nation's most popular Presidents. Despite domestic and foreign problems, the election of George Bush signaled a general satisfaction with Reagan's leadership.

During 1987 several Republican and Democratic candidates organized campaigns to run for the Presidency. They focused their attention on March 8, 1988. On that key date, nicknamed "Super Tuesday," the Republicans and Democrats would hold either primaries or caucuses in 18 states.

▲ **The Democratic candidates.** Several candidates sought the Democratic nomination, but there appeared to be no clear favorite. Governor Michael Dukakis of Massachusetts eventually emerged as the leading contender. His campaign focused on his successes as governor and on the Kennedy-Massachusetts connection. (The extremely popular President John Kennedy also was from Massachusetts.) Dukakis hoped that voters were ready for a change after eight years of Republican lead-

Reverend Jesse Jackson, the minister and political activist who sought the Democratic Presidential nomination in 1984, was again a candidate in 1988. Despite his eventual loss to Dukakis, Jackson remained an important force in the Democratic party.

ership by Reagan. On Super Tuesday Dukakis' well-organized campaign scored several victories, including wins in the key states of Texas and Florida. He was easily nominated at the Democratic Convention in Atlanta in July.

A major decision for Dukakis was his choice of a Vice-Presidential running mate. Many experts viewed the Reverend Jesse Jackson, whose support was critical to the Dukakis campaign, as the probable choice. Instead Dukakis chose Lloyd Bentsen, a powerful and experienced Senator from Texas. The selection of Bentsen gave the Democratic ticket balance. It teamed Dukakis, a governor from the Northeast, with a Vice-Presidential running mate from the Southwest who had experience in Congress. Dukakis supporters feared confrontations with Jackson supporters at the convention. But Dukakis and Bentsen were nominated. As the Democratic Convention ended, Dukakis held a 17 percent lead in the polls over George Bush, the Republican frontrunner.

The Republican candidates. Vice President George Bush seemed to be the logical choice for the Republican nomination for President. He had faithfully served as Reagan's Vice President for eight years and clearly wanted to be the next President. However, Bush had several challengers. One was Senator Robert Dole of Kansas, the Republican Party leader in the Senate. Another challenger was Pat Robertson, a lawyer, minister, executive, and television evangelist who hosted the "The 700 Club," a Christian television talk show. Jack Kemp, a conservative Representative from New York State and a former professional football star, was a third challenger.

The Republican candidates first tested their popularity with the voters in Iowa in June 1987. Senator Dole took first place, with Robertson finishing a surprising second and Bush a disappointing third. A week later, however, Bush won the New Hampshire primary. Then, on Super Tuesday, Bush crushed his opponents by winning in 16 of the 18 state elections. Bush based his campaign on his years of experience in government, his close relationship with Reagan, and a pledge of no new taxes. By the time the Republican Convention met in New Orleans in August, Bush had the nomination wrapped up.

Like Dukakis, Bush faced the task of choosing a running mate. Bush surprised nearly

Dukakis and Bush squared off in two televised debates. Neither substantially helped Dukakis' campaign.

everyone when he selected 41-year-old Senator Dan Quayle of Indiana. Bush thought by choosing Quayle he was giving the baby boomers one of their own—young, attractive, and aggressive. But Bush's selection of Quayle created problems for the campaign when Quayle had to answer charges that he used family influence to avoid military service in Vietnam.

On the final night of the convention, Bush stepped to the microphone to give his speech accepting the nomination for President. The speech was considered the best of Bush's career. He advocated a strong United States, said that a kinder, gentler America would be the goal of his Presidency, and added, "Read my lips. There will be no new taxes." This speech and the positive impression he made on the voters helped Bush gain a 7 percent lead over Dukakis in the polls within a few days after the convention.

The Presidential campaign. The campaign then moved into high gear. The contest between Bush and Dukakis was one in which both candidates mentioned issues but rarely gave specific proposals. Bush supported a Constitutional amendment to outlaw abortion and Dukakis opposed efforts to ban it. Dukakis opposed support for the contras, rebels seeking the overthrow of Nicaragua's government, and Bush favored such support. Bush supported the death penalty for certain crimes, and Dukakis opposed it. Dukakis proposed cuts in defense spending, and Bush supported spending at or near present levels. Bush opposed a tax increase, and Dukakis left open the possibility of an increase as a way to reduce the federal budget deficit.

Television had a major impact on the outcome of the election. Both candidates used tele-vision advertising. Bush's advertisements seemed to work best as his lead in the polls grew. Televised Presidential and Vice-Presidential debates also played a role. Although Dukakis rose slowly in the preference polls during the last weeks of the campaign, he could not overcome Bush's huge lead. ▲

Victory for Bush. Bush's victory was nearly a landslide. He won 54 percent of the popular vote and captured 426 electoral votes to Dukakis' 112. Bush had strong support in every geographic region of the country.

In spite of his huge victory, however, Bush was not able to help Republican candidates for the House and Senate ride to victory "on his coattails." The Democrats strengthened their majorities in the House and the Senate and President Bush had to begin working with a Democrat-controlled Congress. The difficulty of this situation was first seen in the confirmation defeat of John Tower, Bush's selection for Secretary of Defense. Despite this setback, Bush vowed to work with Congress to deal with the many critical issues that faced the nation.

SECTION REVIEW

See underscored items, text pp. 1062-63.

Identify: Super Tuesday, Jesse Jackson, Michael Dukakis, Lloyd Bentsen, George Bush, Dan Quayle, contra

For answers to questions, see TMRG Supplement.

1. **Organizing Ideas: (a)** What were the major issues of the 1988 election? **(b)** How did the candidates differ on each issue?

2. **Seeing Relationships:** How did television affect the election?

3. **Summarizing Ideas:** What were the results of the election?

▲ Bush became the first "sitting" Vice President since Martin Van Buren in 1836 to be elected President. His election also marked the first time since 1928 that Republicans had occupied the White House for three consecutive terms.

1063

See Teaching Suggestions in TMRG Supplement.

One of President Bush's first tasks was to develop a strategy to deal with the world's trouble spots. Many Americans applauded the growth of world democracy, such as the 1986 election of Corazon Aquino, which ended the rule of Philippine dictator Ferdinand Marcos. However, many trouble spots remained.

Relations with the Soviet Union. One positive development in foreign affairs was an improvement in relations with the Soviet Union. Reagan took a tough stand toward the Soviet Union during his first term (see pages 934–35). When the Soviets boycotted the 1984 Summer Olympics in Los Angeles, relations between the two superpowers sank to their lowest point since the early 1970's. However, in 1985 Mikhail Gorbachev became the leader of the Soviet Union.

Gorbachev ushered in a new era of Soviet leadership. He was energetic, young compared to previous Soviet leaders, and willing to make changes to improve Soviet life. And he soon proposed dramatic changes. Perhaps the most significant change was the new atmosphere of openness, called *glasnost* (GLAHS·nuhst), which seemed to promise more freedom for the Soviet people. In a practical application of *glasnost*, the Soviets released several political prisoners.

Equally dramatic was Gorbachev's plan of *perestroika* (per·uh·STROY·kuh), an effort to bolster and broaden the Soviet economy, dismiss ineffective officials, and restructure the government. Economically, Gorbachev advocated increasing foreign trade and decreasing military spending. The revenue from trade and the savings from reduced spending would be used for production incentives—unprecedented payments to workers for making quotas—and for building and modernizing factories.

But the most startling example of *perestroika* was the new election process set in motion in 1989. An election of representatives to the newly created Congress of People's Deputies, the supreme governing body, was held in March. It was the first election in Soviet history between competing candidates and the first by secret ballot. So revolutionary was the change that not only did famous dissident Andrei Sakharov speak to voters—an event unthinkable only three years earlier—but he was also nominated as a candidate.

Although Gorbachev's plans began changes at home, initial meetings between Reagan and Gorbachev produced little progress in ending the rivalry between the United States and the Soviet Union. Both remained hopeful, however, and the two leaders seemed to warm to each other. American and Soviet officials also held **disarmament talks** in attempts to reduce the number of weapons each nation had and to restrict future weapons development. Such talks resulted in the signing of the Intermediate Nuclear Forces (INF) Treaty in December 1987. This treaty called for the removal of

The results of the INF Treaty can be seen in this empty missile storage bunker in England. Before its removal according to treaty guidelines, a cruise missile with a nuclear warhead that was part of United States defenses in Western Europe rested in the bunker.

a number of nuclear weapons and for inspections to ensure that the guidelines would be followed.

Gorbachev visited the United Nations in December 1988. In a speech before the General Assembly, Gorbachev said, "The use of force no longer can or must be an instrument of foreign policy. . . . All of us, primarily the stronger of us, must exercise self-restraint and totally rule out any outward-oriented use of force. . . ." As if to demonstrate his sincerity, Gorbachev stepped up the withdrawal of Soviet ▲ troops from Afghanistan (see page 933). The withdrawal was completed early in 1989.

A massive earthquake in Armenia in the southern Soviet Union required Gorbachev's return home from New York and detailed discussions of the plan with President Reagan and then President-elect Bush and the American response to it had to be postponed.

In his speech at the U. N. Gorbachev delivered "a Christmas present for the world." His gift was a plan for reducing the Soviet military.

Events in Central America. The situation in Central America remained frustrating for Americans. Conflicts continued in El Salvador and Nicaragua, and new problems arose in Panama. Americans differed as to the method and level of involvement they wanted their government to take in these affairs.

In 1979, as you have read, Sandinista rebels overthrew the Nicaraguan government (see page 936). The Reagan administration accused the Sandinistas of aiding Communist guerrillas in El Salvador and asked Americans to support instead a group of Nicaraguan rebels in Honduras known as contras, whom he called "freedom fighters." Congress, however, repeatedly refused to vote financial support for the contras.

Therefore, some members of Reagan's administration sought other sources of funds for the contras. Some United States officials began secret negotiations with Iranian officials that resulted in selling weapons to Iran in exchange for the release of American hostages. Profits from these sales were used to finance the contras. News of these secret dealings, labeled the "Iran-contra Affair," reached the public in 1986. Later discoveries added charges that the CIA and other American agencies had assisted the contras in smuggling illegal drugs into the United States to raise more money. Investigations, resignations, dismissals, and indictments followed the revelations in what became a severe and far-reaching crisis for the Reagan administration. The trial of Lieutenant Colo-

nel Oliver North, a key figure in the scheme and the first to be prosecuted, began in January 1989.

On the other hand, Central America's efforts to solve its own problems brought hope. In 1987 the leaders of Guatemala, El Salvador, Honduras, Nicaragua, and Costa Rica signed a peace plan developed by Costa Rican President Oscar Arias Sanchez, earning Arias the Nobel Peace Prize. In February 1989, leaders of these same nations also agreed to plans to expel the contras from Honduras. Contra leader Adolfo Calero applauded the plan and claimed, "We are willing to return to Nicaragua as soon as we see that Ortega seriously begins to implement the commitments." Daniel Ortega, Nicaragua's president, sought a new beginning with the Bush administration as well. In February 1989 he asserted his willingness to discuss all American complaints in an attempt to "normalize all aspects of U.S.–Nicaraguan relations."

At the same time, Panamanians attempted to remove their corrupt leader, Manuel Noriega, but despite pressure from the United States, Noriega remained as leader of that troubled country. Also in 1989, rebel leaders in El Salvador offered a peace proposal and promised to abide by that country's election results. Alfredo Cristiani eventually won the election that was often interrupted by gunfire.

Conflicts in the Middle East. Affairs in the Middle East also remained troublesome. Iran and Iraq expanded their long war into the Persian Gulf by attacking oil tankers there. This

■ When Venezuela's government established austerity measures aimed at avoiding the economic problems experienced elsewhere in Latin America, riots broke out.

1065

United States military forces in the Persian Gulf responded to attacks on ships by bombing Iranian oil platforms and port facilities.

created a storm of protest from world leaders. Asserting the American belief in freedom of the seas and recognizing our reliance on Middle East oil, President Reagan ordered the United States Navy to patrol these international waters. In addition, oil tankers from many countries were "reflagged" under the American flag to discourage attack.

Two tragic developments highlighted minor skirmishes in the gulf. In May 1987 a missile from an Iraqi warplane hit an American ship, the *U.S.S. Stark,* leaving 37 sailors dead. ▲ In 1988 an American missile shot down an Iranian airliner mistaken for a military jet, killing more than 290 passengers. Finally in ■ August 1988, Iran and Iraq, with United Nations help, agreed to a cease-fire.

The problems between Palestinian refugees and Israel also attracted world attention. Bloody battles between Israeli troops and Palestinians occurred regularly in occupied areas (see page 958).

All this while, civil war raged in Lebanon, practically destroying the country and totally disrupting life (see page 936).

The shock of terrorism. In the last half of the 1980's, the world saw an upsurge in **terrorism,** or the use of violence on innocent people to achieve political goals promoted by the terrorists. Kidnapping was one important terrorist weapon. Beirut became the center of kidnapping and terrorist activity. Even the International Red Cross was forced to abandon Beirut when its office received terrorist threats.

Skyjacking and hijacking also were tools of terrorism. In 1984 the United States reacted to the use of these methods by passing a law making overseas skyjacking and hijacking a crime in the United States if Americans were the victims. Despite the law, in 1985 terrorists seized an American Trans World Airlines (TWA) jet after it left Athens and forced it to land in Beirut. For 17 days they controlled the jet at the airport before releasing their hostages. Of the 153 passengers who were held hostage, 104 were Americans. One American was killed. In 1985 terrorists seized an Italian cruise ship, the *Achille Lauro,* and killed an American passenger. American military jets intercepted the airplane carrying the hijackers to safety and forced it to land in Italian territory so that the terrorists could be charged and tried for their crimes.

When two Americans were killed in April 1986 by a bomb planted by Libyan terrorists in a West Berlin nightclub, the American government's frustration reached its peak. Because evidence pointed to Libyan involvement in many terrorist activities, President Reagan ordered United States jets to bomb targets along the Libyan coast. United States officials knew the bombing raid would not end terrorism. Nonetheless, the American public supported the decision.

The terrorism continued on December 21, 1988, when an American Pan Am jumbo jet exploded soon after takeoff from London, killing all on board. The wreckage fell on Lockerbie, Scotland, killing and injuring people on the ground as well. The suspected cause of the explosion: a terrorist bomb in a radio-cassette player in the baggage compartment. Evidence linked the explosion to Palestinian terrorists. However, in a speech before the U.N. General Assembly, Yasser Arafat, leader of the Palestine Liberation Organization (PLO), denied PLO involvement and publicly offered to help find the terrorists who were responsible.

To show the world that the United States was committed to fighting terrorism, in February 1989 United States officials brought the first terrorist to trial under the 1984 law. Fawaz Yunis, a Lebanese terrorist accused of two incidents of skyjacking in 1985, was captured and brought to the United States to face the charges. Yunis was convicted and sentenced to a long prison term. Many experts on terrorism, however, claimed terrorism would continue until world governments developed ways to deal with the problems that generate it.

South African apartheid. Trouble also plagued South Africa. Tormented by rebels seeking the independence of Namibia, South Africa agreed to leave Namibia in 1989 in return for Cuba's military withdrawal from neighboring Angola. This settlement relieved one major source of conflict for the South African government.

At home, however, the white-run government of South Africa faced growing demands from South African blacks and from many nations to end unjust racial policies. Many world governments, including the United States government, denounced South Africa's **apartheid** (uh·PAHR·tayt). This policy officially grouped people according to racial traits and severely limited the rights and privileges of nonwhites. The government frequently imprisoned South Africans who opposed apartheid. Despite the efforts of South African Bishop Desmond Tutu, who was awarded the 1985 Nobel Peace Prize, and other peacemakers both black and white, conflicts over apartheid grew. Over Reagan's veto Congress passed a **sanctions bill** that banned American investment in South Africa and the importation of South African products.

SECTION REVIEW

See underscored items, text pp. 1064–67.

Identify: Mikhail Gorbachev, *glasnost, perestroika,* disarmament talk, INF Treaty, Iran-contra Affair, *U.S.S. Stark,* terrorism, *Achille Lauro,* Yasser Arafat, apartheid, Desmond Tutu, sanction bill

For answers to questions, see TMRG Supplement.

1. **Interpreting Ideas: (a)** How did the relationship between the United States and the Soviet Union change since 1984? **(b)** Why did it change?

2. **Summarizing Ideas:** Explain the Iran-contra Affair.

3. **Seeing Relationships:** Why was the United States Navy present in the Persian Gulf?

4. **Organizing Ideas:** How did the United States government officially protest apartheid?

3 Americans reexamine their goals and values

For answers to questions, see TMRG Supplement.

The new President also faced many domestic concerns. Technology advanced at an ever-increasing speed. Economic and political problems and a series of scandals tested American values. And many of the social problems that had plagued the United States since the 1960's remained.

The Reagan years. As President Bush took office, many Americans paused to assess Ronald Reagan's eight years as President. Reagan had been enormously popular. Yet, although the economy and peace were stronger, the nation faced problems. Only 73 percent of the students who began high school completed it. Some states even began revoking the driver's licenses of dropouts in an effort to increase school attendance. People seeking affordable housing found prices pushed higher and higher by rising interest rates and building costs. The Reagan administration was criticized about its civil rights record (see page 950). And the sight of the homeless living on city streets became distressingly commonplace.

American technology. Americans continued to develop and use increasingly sophisticated computers and entertainment equipment. To prepare students for the future, many school systems began to require the teaching of **computer literacy,** or the ability to use computers. Televisions, stereo systems, and all other entertainment equipment changed greatly as technology advanced.

The space program. The United States space program suffered a severe setback in early 1986 when the space shuttle *Challenger* exploded shortly after liftoff. Faulty booster rocket design and lax launch procedures caused the tragedy. After nearly three years of equipment redesign and testing and the revision of launch guidelines, the shuttle *Discovery* successfully soared into late orbit in late September 1988 (see page 1061).

Scientists also sought data about the distant planets. A space probe named *Voyager II*

■ *Discovery* made a second successful liftoff on March 13, 1989 as the United States resumed its ambitious space program.

1067

The **Challenger** *crew of six astronauts and teacher Christa McAuliffe was killed in a fiery explosion 79 seconds after liftoff. Memorials have been dedicated to their bravery in Miami, Houston, and elsewhere around the country.*

hurtled toward the far reaches of the solar system, transmitting new data to Earth. By March 1989 *Voyager II* had passed Jupiter, Saturn, and Uranus and was expected to pass Neptune in August.

Other advances. Other technological breakthroughs also made the news. Surgeons refined the techniques for heart and other organ transplants with amazing success. Laser surgery allowed doctors to perform delicate operations on all parts of the human body.

Monumental advances were made in the field of **biotechnology,** or the commercial development of biological products. Research produced advances in medicine, agriculture, waste disposal, chemical manufacturing, food processing, and more. Scientists in laboratories reproduced human insulin, growth hormone, hepatitis B vaccine, and many other bioproducts. At the same time, however, activists warned of possible abuses and strongly protested experimentation on humans.

Scandals in government. The Iran-contra Affair was not the only incident that caused Americans to reexamine ethics in government. Over 100 people in Reagan's administration were accused of improper conduct. Two former White House aides were convicted in cases concerning illegal lobbying. Even Attorney General <u>Edwin Meese</u>, the nation's top law-enforcement official, was charged with wrong-

doing. Although investigations never resulted in indictments, officials on Meese's staff left in protest, and the Attorney General himself resigned in July 1988.

The federal deficit. Most economic experts evaluated Reagan's economic measures as a mixed success. Policies aimed at reducing inflation and unemployment succeeded. The inflation rate, which had soared to a shocking 13.5 percent in 1980, shrank to between 3 and 5 percent in the late 1980's. Unemployment reached 10 percent in 1982—its highest level since the Great Depression—but began a steady decline to about 6.5 percent by 1989.

Despite such successes, the economic news was generally negative. Although, overall unemployment had finally gone down, it remained high among minorities. In 1988 4.7 percent of the whites in the work force were unemployed, while 11.7 percent of the African Americans and 8.2 percent of the Hispanic Americans were jobless. Wages for minorities also fell below national averages.

The budget deficit also was a major source of concern, and attempts to balance the budget were unsuccessful. In 1988, for example, the government spent $163.3 billion dollars more than it collected in taxes. This economic situation alarmed many people. Others, however, pointed to strong growth despite the deficit as a sign that fear of the deficit was misplaced.

■ Other bioproducts help to strengthen the body's immune system, to inhibit high blood pressure, to dissolve blood clots, to hunt down and isolate viral infections, and to allow doctors to "see" inside the human body with unimaginable clarity.

The Crash of 1987. In October 1987 a record decline shook the stock market. Worries about the huge deficit, together with unfavorable United States trade balances and a loss of investor confidence, caused many stock prices to nosedive. This event is known as "the Crash of 1987." A series of stock market collapses that occurred around the world before the opening of the New York Stock Exchange at 9:30 AM EST on October 19 led to this crash, which was the most severe in the nation's history—a drop of 508 points in the Dow Jones Industrial Average. The plunge was greater than the Great Crash of 1929 that led to the Depression (see pages 705–10).

On paper, stock losses totaled almost $1 trillion. Even **blue-chip** companies such as McDonald's, American Express, and Westinghouse, whose stocks were considered solid investments, saw the value of their stock fall by over 40 percent. Financial reforms and government programs originally enacted after the Great Depression of 1929 promptly went into action, however, averting economic collapse.

The trade deficit. The unfavorable **balance of trade,** or the difference in the value of exports and imports, that helped trigger the Crash of 1987 was a familiar economic problem throughout the 1980's. Each year since the early 1970's American purchases of foreign goods had been greater than foreign sales of American products. This trend created an unfavorable balance of trade, or a **trade deficit** in which the nation imported more than it exported. Because people in the United States and the rest of the world were buying fewer American products and more foreign goods, American workers lost jobs and many industries struggled.

Although the government tried many tactics to improve the balance of trade, none worked well. President Reagan, an advocate of free trade, refused to recommend tariffs or other measures to restrict foreign competition.

Other economic troubles. Other disturbing economic news included discoveries of illegal **insider trading**—the use of confidential financial information by stockbrokers for personal gain—which resulted in convictions and fines for important brokers. Large brokerage firms such as E. F. Hutton and Drexel Burnham Lambert pleaded guilty to illegal activities and faced severe penalties. These events eroded

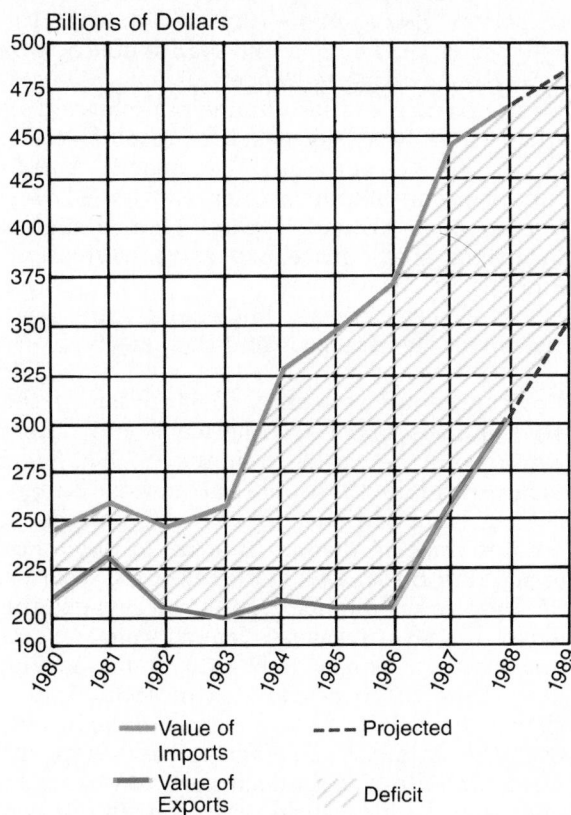

The Trade Deficit • 1980–1989

Billions of Dollars

Legend:
— Value of Imports
— Value of Exports
- - - Projected
/// Deficit

Source: *Statistical Abstract of the United States, 1989*

investor trust in stockbrokers. Many investors withdrew their money, and the number of new investors declined.

Mergers and **takeovers** of large corporations became commonplace. (A *merger* is a business arrangement in which two companies join together to do business. A *takeover* occurs when one company buys enough of another company's stock to control the company.) Such arrangements limit competition and place great financial power in the hands of a few very large corporations.

Problems also swept the banking industry. During the 1970's savings and loan associations (S&Ls) boomed as money from the sale of Texas oil poured in. Overbuilding by oil investors and loose lending policies, however, made the financial bases of many S&Ls shaky. When slumps hit the oil industry, many S&Ls went out of business. Although deposit insur-

For example, Kohlberg Kravits Roberts & Company, which already controlled Beatrice Foods, acquired RJR Nabisco, a food conglomerate with similar products.

1069

ance repaid most depositors, the public lost confidence in savings and loan associations and became wary of the entire banking industry. Despite the closings and government plans to bolster S&Ls, many experts felt that the collapse of the savings and loan industry was a disaster waiting to happen.

In addition to these financial problems, all Americans faced skyrocketing medical costs. Between 1965 and 1987 the amount Americans spent on health care soared from $42 billion to $500 billion. Experts blamed higher insurance costs, more expensive equipment, and the increasing age of the population for much of the increase. The rising costs especially troubled the poor and the elderly.

Environmental concerns. Destruction of the environment alarmed Americans and others throughout the world. In January 1989, *Time* magazine attracted people's attention by abandoning its traditional practice of honoring a notable man or woman in order to name our struggling Earth as its "Planet of the Year."

Despite the publicity, pollution ravaged the earth. In 1984 toxic gases leaked from a chemical plant in Bhopal (bo·PAHL), India, killing more than 3,300 people and in 1986 similar gases escaped in West Virginia. Beaches on both the Atlantic and Pacific coasts were littered with illegally dumped medical wastes. In 1988 an oil spill snaked down the Ohio River, endangering water supplies and wildlife. A massive spill in 1989 damaged Alaska's pristine environment. Acid rain continued to kill vegetation and pollute streams and lakes. And the hot, dry summer of 1988 served as an additional reminder of the fragile condition of the environment. The country suffered through a plague of wildfires, dry reservoirs, and failed crops.

Many people blamed these troublesome climate conditions on the **greenhouse effect.** Scientists theorized that this effect resulted when pollution in the atmosphere trapped heat energy, much as a greenhouse traps warmth. This energy then caused temperatures to rise. Other experts denied the existence of a greenhouse effect, pointing to studies that indicated that climates had remained basically unchanged for more than 100 years.

Scientists also became increasingly concerned that the delicate balance of gases in the atmosphere may be in jeopardy. Scientists feared that the level of carbon dioxide (CO_2) in the air, which had been increasing for 100 years because of industry's use of fossil fuels, would make the atmosphere hotter than usual. This extra heat would cause the earth's ice sheets to melt, resulting in floods in many parts of the world and changes in the world's weather patterns. Scientists also became alarmed about the level of another gas in the air—ozone (O_3). A thin ozone layer in the upper atmosphere protects the earth from the dangerous ultraviolet rays of the sun. Scientists suspected that emissions from supersonic airplanes and from certain manufactured products such as aerosol spray cans were damaging the ozone layer. In fact, they discovered a large hole in the ozone layer over Antarctica. In 1987 concern over this damage prompted 46 nations, including the United States, to sign an international agreement to take steps to preserve the ozone layer.

Environmental disasters even affected Antarctica. Many spectacular and unique species live in this icy world, and most were threatened by pollution and increased commercial fishing. These and other emergencies helped people realize that human activity was affecting the environment and perhaps even changing the earth's climate.

Chernobyl. A second major accident at a nuclear power plant provided another reason for environmental concern (see page 978). In 1986 human error resulted in a reactor meltdown at Chernobyl in the Soviet Union, causing radiation exposure that resulted in 31 deaths and possible injury between 6,000 and 24,000 others. The resulting explosions released a radioactive cloud that swept across Europe and the United States. The site was finally sealed in concrete, and a massive cleanup project was begun.

The Chernobyl accident reminded the world that using the atom's power involves risks. Experts in the United States inspected American nuclear power plants and plants manufacturing nuclear materials for weapons. The results of these inspections shocked the nation. Leaks had caused illnesses in employees and radioactive contamination of surrounding areas. Cleanup efforts began, but the problem of disposing of the deadly toxic wastes remained.

Disease, drugs, and violence. The spread of the disease Acquired Immune Deficiency Syndrome (AIDS), the use of illegal drugs, and widespread violence also troubled Americans.

Although AIDS first appeared in other parts of the world, between 1979 and 1989 it claimed the lives of about 44,000 Americans and was expected to claim millions of lives worldwide over the next few years. Studies indicated that AIDS was not inherited genetically. It was acquired through sexual contact with an infected partner or through the sharing of contaminated needles, usually associated with intravenous drug use. At the time there were no medicines to cure the disease or vaccines to prevent it. However, treatments were developed, and their effectiveness was monitored through long-range studies.

Besides adding to the spread of AIDS, the use of illegal drugs caused addictions that supported crime, destroyed lives, and strained society's resources. In the late 1980's, a new epidemic—crack cocaine—swept the nation. But although one in 18 seniors in 1988 admitted trying crack, the results of a nationwide survey of 16,000 seniors surprised and cheered Americans. According to the survey, drug use among high school students had dropped to its lowest level in 14 years.

Increasingly frequent and senseless outbreaks of violence also shocked Americans. Several incidents were highly publicized, including Patrick Purdy's attack with an assault rifle on a Stockton, California elementary school in January 1989 that left several students dead or injured. Such instances led people to question the effectiveness of existing gun control laws as well as the value and availability of services designed to help people who have become depressed or disoriented.

Other challenges. Other problems, such as scandals among religious leaders, world hunger, the plight of American farmers, seemingly unchecked immigration, and the question of civil rights also tested American confidence. Scandals involving leading religious figures Jim Bakker, Jimmy Swaggert, Pat Robertson, and Oral Roberts dealt blows to the revitalization of American religion. Despite these scandals, the number of churchgoers increased.

In addition, during the late 1980's a series of famines struck countries around the world. Hardest hit was Ethiopia, which received millions of dollars and tons of food and supplies from Americans. The Live Aid concert and others like it, in which popular music stars

SAY "NO" TO CRACK
AND OTHER DRUGS

Crack gained popularity because it was less expensive and easier to use than other illegal drugs. It also quickly addicted users. Many programs, both government-sponsored and private, aimed at stopping the spread of crack.

donated their talents and money, raised millions of dollars for the hungry.

In the United States the decline of farming was a problem. Most of the 2.2 million farms operating in the United States in 1989 were either very large farms managed by corporations or small farms tended by part-time farmers. The increasing costs of land, equipment, and supplies pushed more and more farmers into bankruptcy and forced them to find other jobs.

The steady waves of immigrants that poured into the United States also worried Americans. These new arrivals posed special problems for employers and social services and led many Americans to question immigration policies.

On a brighter note, women and minorities made significant advances despite the Reagan administration's conservative stand. During the late 1980's increasing numbers of women and minorities were elected to be mayors and councilmembers in several of America's largest cities. The selections of Ron Brown as National Committee Chairman of the Democratic Party and Bill White as the president of the

▲ Farm Aid concerts, modeled on the Live Aid concert, raised millions of dollars for American farmers and their families.

baseball's National League in early 1989—the first African Americans to lead those organizations—further highlighted the advances.

Responding to the challenges. The United States faced its challenges as it always had—by relying on the faith and hard work of its people.

The government played its part in a number of ways. Congress funded AIDS-related research and set up programs to combat illegal drug use. New legislation attacked economic problems. Congress passed the Balanced Budget and Emergency Control Act of 1985, ▲ known as the Gramm-Rudman-Hollings Act. This law required automatic across-the-board cuts in government spending when the deficit had gone beyond a target point. The plan's goal was to produce a balanced budget over time by forcing reductions in all programs. President Bush's proposal for the 1990 budget also aimed at reducing the deficit. If adopted, his proposal, which included reduced defense spending and increased welfare allotments, would cut the deficit by $71.1 billion.

Other legislation took aim at specific problems. Congress passed the Tax Reform Law of 1986, which wiped out many loopholes, or tax rules that gave specific groups tax breaks. Changes in Medicare benefits adopted in 1988 provided protection against catastrophic medical costs for the elderly. The Immigration Reform and Control Act of 1986 offered citizenship to about 2 million people living illegally in the United States and required employers to verify the citizenship of their workers.

In addition, in February 1989 Bush proposed an plan to bolster the sagging savings and loan industry. The plan included borrowing money through bond sales, reworking the depositor insurance fund, and appointing a regulatory agency to monitor policies.

SECTION REVIEW
See underscored items, text pp. 1067-72.

Identify: computer literacy, *Challenger, Discovery,* Edwin Meese, blue chip, insider trading, merger, takeover, Chernobyl, AIDS, crack cocaine, Gramm-Rudman-Hollings Act, Immigration Reform and Control Act of 1986
For answers to questions, see TMRG Supplement.
1. **Summarizing Ideas:** What were the major domestic concerns of Americans in the late 1980's?
2. **Evaluating Ideas:** Evaluate the governments response to a problem mentioned in this section.

4 United States population patterns continue to change

See Teaching Suggestions in TMRG Supplement.

The makeup of the American population continued to change. People from around the world still came to the United States seeking a better life. Life expectancy increased, so the proportion of older Americans rose. People still moved to urban areas. As the United States entered the 1990's, its population characteristics were significantly different than they had been just 20 years earlier.

Changing population patterns. In 1988 the nation's population topped 245 million and was expected to reach 260 million by the year 2000. The population growth rate, however, was relatively slow, despite a slight increase in the number of births during the 1980's, when the babies of the baby boom themselves became parents (see page 871).

Changes in population makeup. Changes in the makeup of the population continued. Whites remained the largest group, making up about 78 percent of the population, but minority groups experienced significant growth.

The fastest-growing groups were Asian Americans and Hispanic Americans. More than 4 million Asian Americans lived in the United States in 1989—about 2 percent of the population—and they accounted for nearly one half of all new immigrants. The 18 million Hispanics in the United States comprised more than 7 percent of the total population, and this number was steadily increasing. More than half of all Hispanic Americans were from Mexico. Puerto Ricans were the second-largest Hispanic group. About 2 million Puerto Ricans lived permanently in the United States, with the largest concentration in New York City. Cuban Americans were the third-largest Hispanic group and were concentrated in Florida. A steady stream of Hispanic immigrants also arrived from Nicaragua and other Central American countries.

The numbers of African Americans and Native Americans grew slightly in the 1980's. African Americans still made up about 12 percent of the nation's population, and Native Americans made up less than 1 percent.

■ Many Cuban Americans were political exiles who had fled from Cuba after Fidel Castro established a Communist regime there in 1959, and some hoped to return to Cuba eventually to reestablish a non-Communist system.

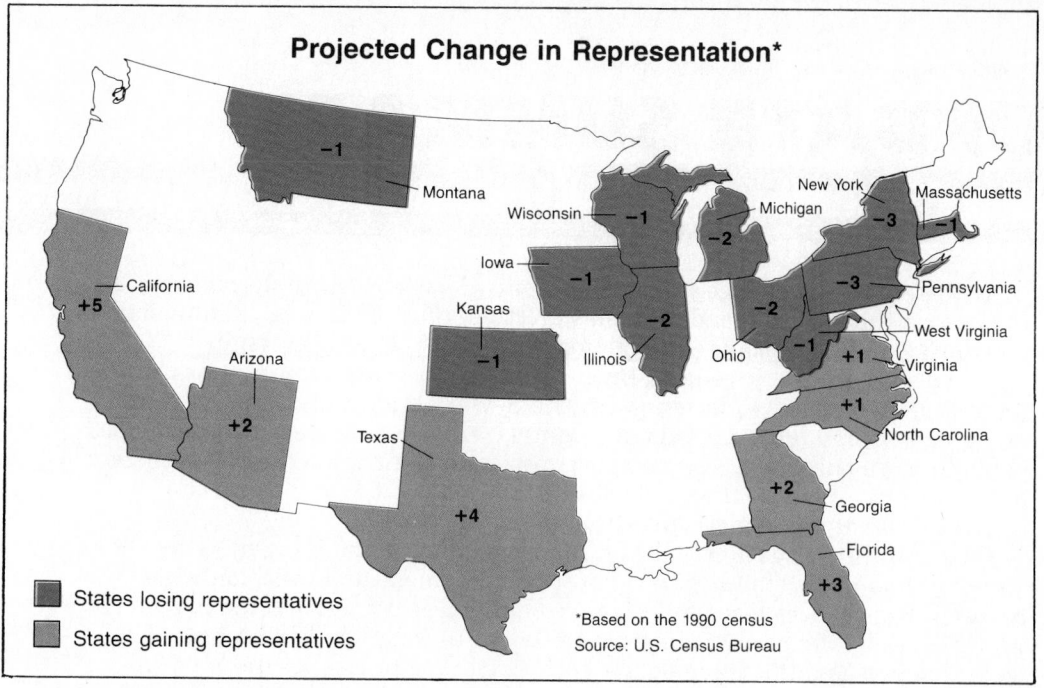

Projected Change in Representation*

States losing representatives
States gaining representatives

*Based on the 1990 census
Source: U.S. Census Bureau

Life expectancy and age distribution. Important trends in the areas of life expectancy and age distribution also continued. Improvements in health care and nutrition raised the average life expectancy of Americans to 75 years. This increase and the relatively slow birth rate changed the nation's **age distribution**, or the proportionate sizes of different age groups in the population. By the late 1980's older Americans were the fastest-growing part of the American population. This shift meant that more of the nation's resources than ever before were needed for the elderly.

Changing distribution. Change marked the distribution of people throughout the United States as well. This was due in part to the mobility of the American people.

Many Americans moved into urban areas. By 1989 only 23 percent of the population lived in rural areas, and only 5 percent actually lived on farms. The rest of the rural population lived in the open spaces of the countryside and commuted to jobs in cities and towns. The major attraction of cities and suburbs, as always, was job opportunities. The populations of some cities, especially those in the warmer southern and southwestern "Sunbelt" states, such as Orlando and Phoenix, more than doubled between 1970 and 1989. Rapid growth sent planners scurrying to map out new highway paths and to devise methods of providing services for the new arrivals.

Draw of the Sunbelt. The movement of people from the colder northern states to the Sunbelt continued (see page 944). Many were retired people who moved to enjoy the mild climate. Others were attracted by new job opportunities in expanding industries. These population shifts to the South and Southwest meant significant political and economic changes. Experts expected at least 18 Congressional seats to be reapportioned to Sunbelt states after the 1990 census.

Into the 1990's. Most citizens recognized the challenges facing their country. In his inaugural speech, President Bush called on the American values of "duty, sacrifice, commitment, and patriotism that finds its expression in taking part and pitching in" to help the United States handle the challenges. These values, he assured Americans, would allow them to deal with the problems the country would face in the future.

SECTION REVIEW

See underscored items, text pp. 1072-73.
Identify: age distribution, Sunbelt
See Teaching Suggestions in TMRG Supplement.
1. **Summarizing Ideas:** How has the population of the United States changed in the last 20 years?
2. **Determining Cause and Effect:** What political and economic changes do you foresee for the United States, based on the changing characteristics of its population?

■ For example, the number of people who were 65 years of age and older had increased from 4 percent of the population in 1900 to 12 percent in 1989, while the number of people under 18 had declined from 44 percent to 26.5 percent.

UPDATE SUMMARY

In 1988 Americans elected a new President. George Bush replaced Ronald Reagan as the nation's leader. Bush's election affirmed Reagan's immense popularity and Americans' satisfaction with his style of leadership.

In foreign affairs, President Bush dealt with a world moving toward unprecedented peace. Relations with the Soviet Union were improved, and Soviet troops had left Afghanistan. Central American leaders had developed plans to solve political and economic troubles in their countries. Nonetheless, problems remained. Conflicts raged in the Middle East, and terrorism increased, involving Americans throughout the world.

The domestic situation also had improved during the Reagan years. The economy had made steady gains, and unemployment and inflation were reduced. But leaders faced many other challenges. Minority unemployment was still high, and many young people failed to complete high school. The federal deficit and the trade deficit both continued to rise, as did medical expenses. Environmental disasters seemed more widespread than ever. And perhaps the greatest task facing America's leaders was regaining the faith of the people, which was lost because of scandals in government, business, and religion.

But as President Bush pointed out, Americans had successfully faced many challenges during the nation's history. With their typical determination, he said, they can face the challenges of the future.

▲ Reviewing Important Terms

Decide whether each of the following sentences is true or false. If the sentence is false, replace the underlined term with the word or phrase that will make it true.

1. Glasnost refers to an effort to bolster the economy and streamline the government of the Soviet Union.
2. Stockbrokers used blue chips to illegally make large sums of money in the stock market.
3. The United States disagreed with South Africa's policy of apartheid.
4. To protest apartheid, Congress passed a merger contract.
5. Birth rate is the term for the proportionate sizes of different age groups.
6. The trade deficit is the difference between the value of imports and the value of exports.
7. A discussion between the United States and the Soviet Union aimed at reducing the number of weapons is called a summit meeting.

Practicing Critical Thinking Skills

1. **Comparing Ideas.** How were the economic problems facing George Bush different from those that faced Reagan? How were they similar?

2. **Summarizing Ideas.** (a) What were the major events of the 1988 Presidential election? (b) What was Dukakis' strategy? Bush's?
3. **Organizing Ideas.** (a) List five major environmental concerns facing the world. (b) How did the accident at Chernobyl affect the United States?
4. **Determining Cause and Effect.** Explain the causes and results of the Crash of 1987.
5. **Analyzing Ideas.** What problems caused some Americans to lose confidence in their leadership?
6. **Evaluating Ideas.** Biotechnology produced many breakthroughs. In your opinion, should scientists continue to experiment with biological organisms? Why or why not?
7. **Synthesizing Ideas.** Review Unit 13. Which problems mentioned in this UPDATE were continuations of problems that the United States faced previously? Which problems were new?
8. **Interpreting Ideas.** How did government leaders respond to each of the major problems?
9. **Relating Past to Present.** How is the United States population different than it was 20 years ago?

Relating Geography and History

For the last 100 years, the United States has been a world leader. This has meant that America and Americans have been involved in events all over the world. To get a geographic sense of this world involvement, complete the following activities.

1. Visit your local or school library to research United States world trade. Make a list of the 10 countries to which the United States exports the greatest value of goods and the 10 countries from which it imports the most.
2. Research immigration to the United States in the 1980's, listing the 10 countries from which the most immigrants came during the decade.
3. Use your research to map United States world involvement by completing the following on an outline map of the world. (a) Draw an arrow from the United States to each of the countries to which the United States exports the most. (b) Draw an arrow to the United States from each of the countries from which the United States imports the most and from each of the countries that sends the most immigrants to the United States. (c) Color in blue all the countries or areas mentioned in this UPDATE in which the United States is involved.

GLOSSARY

This glossary contains many of the terms you need to understand as you study this UPDATE. After each term, there is a brief definition or explanation of the term as it is usually used in American history. The page number in parentheses after each definition refers to the page of this UPDATE on which the term is boldfaced.

The brief definitions in this glossary do not always provide all the information that you may need to know about these terms. Therefore, you may find it useful to turn to the page listed in parentheses to read more about the term.

A

age distribution Proportionate sizes of different age groups. (p. 1073)

apartheid Official policy of South Africa that divides the population into groups and determines rights and privileges based on racial characteristics. (p. 1067)

B

balance of trade Difference between the value of a country's imports and exports. (p. 1069)

biotechnology Business of developing commercial biological products. (p. 1068)

blue chip Company with a reputation as an excellent investment risk. (p. 1069)

C

computer literacy Ability to use a computer. (p. 1067)

D

disarmament talk Discussion aimed at reducing the number of weapons. (p. 1064)

G

glasnost Term referring to the spirit of openness brought to the Soviet Union by Mikhail Gorbachev. (p. 1064)

I

insider trading Illegal use of confidential stock and financial information for personal gain. (p. 1069)

M

merger Business arrangement in which two companies join together to do business. (p. 1069)

P

perestroika Effort to bolster the economy and streamline the government of the Soviet Union. (p. 1064)

S

sanctions bill Measure passed by Congress, usually involving trade, aimed at forcing a nation violating international law to stop its illegal actions. (p. 1067)

T

takeover Business situation in which one company buys enough of another company's stock to gain control of the company. (p. 1069)

trade deficit situation in which the value of a nation's imports is greater than the value of its exports. (p. 1069)

INDEX

This *Index* contains page references to the key people, places, and events mentioned in the UPDATE. The page number(s) after each entry refers to the page(s) of the UPDATE on which the term appears. Page numbers in *italics* that have *c, m,* or *p* written before them refer to charts, diagrams, or graphs *(c);* maps *(m);* or pictures *(p)*.

PICTURE CREDITS: Page 1061, Sygma Photos; 1062, J. L. Atlan/Sygma Photos; 1063, Ira Wyman/Sygma Photos; 1064, AP/Wide World Photos; 1065, Christopher Morris/Black Star; 1066, U.S. Navy Photo/Black Star; 1068, Mike Brown/Gamma-Liaison; 1071, U.S. Department of Education.